THE NAME IS FAMILIAR...

Who played Who in the movies

?

A Directory of Title Characters

Robert Anthony Nowlan • Gwendolyn Wright Nowlan

Neal-Schuman Publishers, Inc.

New York **London**

Published by Neal-Schuman Publishers, Inc.
100 Varick Street
New York, NY 10013

Printed and bound in the United States of America

Library of Congress Cataloging-in-Publication Data

Nowlan, Robert A.
    The name is familiar : who played who in the movies / Robert
Anthony Nowlan and Gwendolyn Wright Nowlan.
        p. cm.
    Includes bibliographical references and index.
    ISBN 1-55570-054-3
    1. Characters and characteristics in motion pictures—
Dictionaries. 2. Motion picture actors and actresses—Biography-
Dictionaries. I. Nowlan, Gwendolyn Wright, 1945-   . II. Title.
PN1995.9.C36N696   1993
791.43′028′0922—dc20
                                                                92-42877
                                                                CIP

For

Robert, Philip, Edward, Amy, Alexandra, Jennifer

Evan, Andrew

and

Annabel Lee

Contents

Acknowledgments

This book has been enhanced by the efforts of Claire Bennett, Thomas Clarie, Joanne Caruso, David Lester and Wenxian Zhang. We thank our families and friends for their understanding and encouragement. We also are grateful to Neal-Schuman Publishers for their work in preparing the book for publication. Finally, we wish to express our admiration for all the movie-makers—actors, writers, directors, producers, cinematographers, composers, editors, art directors, costumers, grips, best boys, extras—who contributed their efforts to the films featured in this book.

Introduction

In Romeo and Juliet, Shakespeare observes, "What's in a name? That which we call a rose, by any other name would smell as sweet." Perhaps so, but moviemakers have always known that the title of a film is an important factor in its box-office success. Potential viewers' first impression of a movie is its title. It alone may induce people to rush to a theater to see it or avoid it at all costs. SURF NAZIS MUST DIE may pull in adolescents, but it's likely to turn their parents off completely.

On the other hand, THE STORY OF THREE LOVES is sufficient warning for kids who don't want to sit through mushy romance and kissing scenes. The squeamish are given fair warning with THE TEXAS CHAINSAW MASSACRE, and audiences are automatically clued into the climax of GUNFIGHT AT THE OK CORRAL. Those of a literary bent knew what to expect from film adaptations of novels and plays such as DR. ZHIVAGO, THE GREAT GATSBY, WHO'S AFRAID OF VIRGINIA WOOLF? and CAT ON A HOT TIN ROOF.

Audiences were prepared to laugh when they bought tickets to I WAS A MALE WAR BRIDE, WHAT'S UP DOC?, BLOCKHEADS and MY FAVORITE WIFE. There were expectations of terpsichorean treats in DANCING LADY, BORN TO DANCE and FLASHDANCE. We knew old musical favorites were on tap in movie versions of Broadway hits such as THE KING AND I, GUYS AND DOLLS and OLIVER! Thrillers advertised themselves with titles such as NIGHT OF THE HUNTER, THE KILLERS and MURDER, MY SWEET.

Movie titles are frequently changed for foreign markets. This makes sense when the languages are different, of course, but also when two countries with a common language have different tastes, customs, and idioms. Or, the original title of a film may contain references unfamiliar outside the country of production. Following are some examples of films that have different titles in the United States and Great Britain.

Original American Title	*New British Title*
ABE LINCOLN IN ILLINOIS	SPIRIT OF THE PEOPLE
DAWN YANKEES	WHAT LOLA WANTS
THE FLIM FLAM MAN	ONE BORN EVERY MOMENT
A GIRL, A GUY AND A GOB	THE NAVY STEPS OUT
HALLELUJAH I'M A BUM	HALLELUJAH I'M A TRAMP
I MARRIED A COMMUNIST	THE WOMAN ON PIER 13
LADY OF BURLESQUE	STRIPTEASE LADY
SATAN NEVER SLEEPS	THE DEVIL NEVER SLEEPS
SWING SHIFT MAISIE	THE GIRL IN OVERALLS
WITCHFINDER GENERAL	THE CONQUEROR WORM

Original British Title	*New American Title*
THE CARD	THE PROMOTER
CARLETON BROWN OF THE F.O.	MAN IN A COCKED HAT
COSH BOY	THE SLASHER
DEAR OCTOPUS	THE RANDOLPH FAMILY
THE ELUSIVE PIMPERNEL	THE FIGHTING PIMPERNEL
FANNY BY GASLIGHT	MAN OF EVIL
FATHER BROWN	THE DETECTIVE
I LIVE IN GROSVENOR SQUARE	A YANK IN LONDON
THE IRON MAIDEN	THE SWINGIN' MAIDEN
THE RAKE'S PROGRESS	NOTORIOUS GENTLEMAN

Movies whose titles refer to a particular character or characters are the subject of this book. The book consists of three cross-referenced sections. The first section is an alphabetical listing of performers who have appeared in title roles, the films in which they had these roles, the names of their title characters, the year of production and the production company. Approximately 4,500 performers are included in this section.

The second section is an alphabetical listing of the title characters that lists the movie in which the character appeared, its year of production, the production company and a capsule description of the character. There are approximately 9,000 characters listed.

The third section is an alphabetical listing of the films whose title refers to a particular character or characters in the movie. Each entry in this section contains the year of release of the film, the studio or production company, the name of the title character and the performer who appeared in the role, the director and the other leading performers in the film. There are approximately 9,000 films included in the section. The earliest film included was released in 1910, the latest in the first half of 1992.

In deciding which films to include in this book, we have used the following criteria: the film must be *feature length*; it must be an *English language film*; and the *title must identify one or more characters in the movie* in some way. We have attempted to include all U.S. and British sound productions that meet these criteria, but certain silent films may have been omitted because their length is given in reels, not minutes of running time. Likewise, there may be a number of early Australian and Canadian films we have inadvertently missed.

We have not limited ourselves to movie titles that explicitly name a character. In addition to titles like DISRAELI, THE GUILT OF JANET AMES, MAD MAX and THE STORY OF TEMPLE DRAKE, readers will also find movies that *describe a character*, such as THE GUNFIGHTER, THE JAZZ SINGER, THE MAN WITH A STAR, and PLATINUM BLONDE. Also included are films whose titles are questions, the answers to which identify particular characters. Examples include WHOSE LIFE IS IT ANYWAY?, DO YOU LOVE ME? and WHAT DID YOU DO IN THE WAR, DADDY? We have also included films in which *pronouns suggest a character* or characters. These include YOU AND ME, MY BRILLIANT CAREER, ME AND MY GAL, and I'LL CRY TOMORROW. *Numbers in titles* can also refer to movie characters, as in THE DIRTY DOZEN, THE MAGNIFICENT SEVEN and FOUR DAUGHTERS. (We drew the line with ONE HUNDRED MEN AND A GIRL.)

Occasionally a movie title names the performers who appear in the film, as in ABBOTT AND COSTELLO MEET CAPTAIN KIDD and DEAR BRIGITTE. In the former we do not describe Abbott and Costello as title characters since they are not playing themselves. We do, however, describe Brigitte Bardot in the second film because she is playing herself. We could give many other explanations of why we choose not to include a particular movie or identify someone as a title character. Instead, let us simply say that we welcome readers' suggestions for inclusion of other films or title characters in a revised edition of this work.

Just for fun, following is a sampling of movie trivia questions that can be answered using this book. For readers who do not want to look up the answers, an answer key is provided at the end of the question section. In any case, we hope readers will find *The Name Is Familiar* useful for answering (or inventing) a wide variety of questions about who played who in the movies.

R.A.N.

G.W.N.

Trivia Quiz:
"The Name is Familiar . . ."

1. What is the alternate title of THE DEVIL AND DANIEL WEBSTER, which starred Walter Huston and Edward Arnold in the title roles?

2. Who starred in the NANCY DREW series of the 1930s?

3. What is the real name of THE COUNT OF MONTE CRISTO?

4. What is Marlene Dietrich's spy designation in the 1931 film DISHONORED?

5. In which film did Shirley Maclaine appear as a character named Charity Hope Valentine?

6. Which lovely actress made the sarong famous appearing as characters named Ulah, Tura and Aloma?

7. Who was the movies' first Tarzan and who played the ape man in 1935's THE NEW ADVENTURES OF TARZAN?

8. Who shot Liberty Valance? Give the name of the actor and his character.

9. Who besides Peter Sellers portrayed bumbling Inspector Jacques Clouseau, and what was the name of the film in which he appeared?

10. Name the twins who played the title characters in 1937's THE PRINCE AND THE PAUPER. Who played whom?

11. Who replaced Yul Brynner as Chris in the second sequel to THE MAGNIFICENT SEVEN?

12. Which pop singer portrayed Count Down in THE SON OF DRACULA (1974)?

13. When Paul Muni first escaped from the chain gang in I AM A FUGITIVE FROM A CHAIN GANG, he changed his name from James Allen to what?

14. What are Zero Mostel's and Gene Wilder's character names in the cult classic THE PRODUCERS, and what is the name of the show they produced, hoping it would be failure?

15. In which movie did George C. Scott believe himself to be Sherlock Holmes?

16. Who was THE THIRD MAN in the 1950 movie of the same name?

17. Name the two movies in which Glynis Johns portrayed a mermaid.

18. Name 20th Century Fox's answer to Shirley Temple who starred in such films as LITTLE MISS NOBODY, PEPPER and THE HOLY TERROR.

19. Name the title role played by Baby Peggy in a 1924 silent and by Guy Kibbee in 1936.

20. What is Klinton Spilsbury's movie claim to fame?

21. What movie role is shared by James Stewart and Audie Murphy?

22. Everyone knows that Frank Morgan appeared in the title role in THE WIZARD OF OZ. What was his character's name in the black-and-white segments?

23. Charlton Heston played the title role of BEN-HUR in 1959. Who had the same role in the 1925 silent production?

24. Which actor has jokingly been called the "inventor of the telephone" ever since appearing as Alexander Graham Bell in the 1939 biopic of the inventor?

25. Who originated the role of Judge Hardy in the first film of the Andy Hardy series, A FAMILY AFFAIR?

26. Margaret Sullavan appeared as Luisa Ginglebusher in THE GOOD FAIRY in 1935. Name the 1947 remake starring Deanna Durbin.

27. What last name did actress Barbara Hershey employ when she made BOXCAR BERTHA in 1972?

28. Name Greta Garbo's first talking role and her last film.

29. Which actress remembered Mama in I REMEMBER MAMA (1948)?

30. Name the troubled screenwriter played by John Turturro in the 1991 film of the same name.

31. Name the "Poverty Row" studio which produced a 1935 version of JANE EYRE starring Virginia Bruce.

32. What is the name of the mummy played by Lon Chaney, Jr., in three 1940s movies? Who played the same role in THE MUMMY'S HAND (1940)?

33. Name the two films in which Bette Davis played dual roles.

34. What is Mr. Deeds' first name in MR. DEEDS GOES TO TOWN?

35. Who most frequently played wise-cracking TORCHY BLANE? Name the other two actresses who also portrayed the hard-boiled reporter.

36. Name the first film in which Spencer Tracy and Katharine Hepburn appeared together.

37. Which jazz cornetist's life is the basis for Kirk Douglas' role in YOUNG MAN WITH A HORN?

38. Name the distinguished actor whose film roles included Benjamin Disraeli, Alexander Hamilton, Voltaire, Cardinal Richelieu and the Duke of Wellington.

39. Which actor did Paul Newman replace in the role of Rocky Graziano in SOMEBODY UP THERE LIKES ME (1956)?

40. What are the names of Dan Aykroyd's and John Belushi's characters in THE BLUES BROTHERS?

41. Name the film debut of Claude Rains. (Although his voice was heard throughout the movie, his face was seen only in the final scene.)

42. Onto whose body was dying bigot Ray Milland's head grafted in THE THING WITH TWO HEADS?

43. What is the name of Marilyn Monroe's character in GENTLEMAN PRE-FER BLONDES (1953), and who played the same role in the 1928 silent production?

44. Who played the three wives in A LETTER TO THREE WIVES?

45. Name the cult comedian and his 1983 film in which he portrayed a character named Dr. Michael Hfuhruhurr.

46. Which Oriental detective did Peter Lorre play in the late 1930s series?

47. Name the 1937 movie starring Wayne Morris playing Ward Guisenberry that was remade in 1962 starring Elvis Presley as Walter Gulick.

48. Name the movie and its nominal star that introduced the crazy antics of Dean Martin and Jerry Lewis to film audiences.

49. Name the role and the 1921 movie that is generally regarded to be the best of Richard Barthelmess' career. (In 1930, Richard Cromwell recreated the role, and it's also considered the high point of his career.)

50. Humphrey Bogart portrayed aging gangster Roy Earle in HIGH SIERRA in 1941. Name the 1955 remake and the actor who portrayed Earle.

51. Who starred in the title role in THE STORY OF WILL ROGERS?

52. What name is given to Johnny Sheffield in TARZAN FINDS A SON (1939)?

53. Name the silent-screen star whose roles include Rebecca Randall, Amarilly Jenkins, M'liss Smith and Tessibel Skinner.

54. Who had the title role in the 1929 production EVANGELINE, based on the poem by Henry Wadsworth Longfellow?

55. Name the "B" western star who appeared in several oaters as THE DURANGO KID.

56. Who played Thelma in THELMA AND LOUISE (1991)? Who played Louise?

57. Name the movie in which Fredric March portrayed The Grim Reaper.

58. Gloria Swanson starred in MALE AND FEMALE (1919). What is the name of the J.M. Barrie play on which it is based?

59. Name the three actresses who appeared as the show girls in LES GIRLS.

60. Name Dirk Bogarde's character in films such as DOCTOR IN THE HOUSE, DOCTOR AT SEA, and DOCTOR AT LARGE.

61. What is Ernest Borgnine's last name in MARTY?

62. Who appeared in the title role of THE THIN MAN?

63. What is Bob Hope's character Sylvester the Great's last name in THE PRINCESS AND THE PIRATE?

64. What is Henry Fonda's juror number in 12 ANGRY MEN?

65. In which movie did Edward G. Robinson play a character named Wong Low Get?

66. What is the title of the 1976 biopic of Woody Guthrie starring David Carradine?

67. Who received an Oscar nomination for her portrayal of RAMBLING ROSE?

68. Name the small town busybody played by Guy Kibbee in several second-feature comedies of the early '40s.

69. In which movie does Mae West proposition Cary Grant with the usually misquoted line: "Why don't you come up sometime and see me?"

70. In the film versions of GOODBYE MR. CHIPS (1939 & 1969), what is Mr. Chips' last name?

71. Who portrayed PETER PAN in the 1924 production of J.M. Barrie's classic?

72. Whom did Yul Brynner replace in the 1959 production of SOLOMON AND SHEBA?

73. What is the family name of the brother in SEVEN BRIDES FOR SEVEN BROTHERS (1954)?

74. Name the two actors who have portrayed Al Capp's cartoon character Li'l Abner in movies.

75. Name the movie in which William Holden, framed by crooked politicians, is helped by the ghost of Andrew Jackson to clear himself.

76. Who is the voice of toon character Roger Rabbit in WHO FRAMED ROGER RABBIT?

77. What is the nickname of child actor George Winslow, who played Henry Spofford III in GENTLEMEN PREFER BLONDES?

78. What is Maisie's last name in the films of the 40s starring Ann Sothern?

79. Name the movie in which Clifton Webb introduced the character of self-proclaimed genius Lynn Belvedere.

80. Name the nightclub entertainer portrayed by Frank Sinatra in the 1957 biopic THE JOKER IS WILD.

81. Name the last film in which Fred Astaire and Ginger Rogers appeared as dancing partners.

82. Who played Jane to Johnny Weissmuller's Tarzan, and what is Jane's last name in the series?

83. What is Virginia Mayo's burlesque name in SHE'S WORKING HER WAY THROUGH COLLEGE?

84. Priscilla, Rosemary and Lola Lane played three of the sisters in FOUR DAUGHTERS (1938), FOUR WIVES (1939) and FOUR MOTHERS (1941). Who played the fourth sister?

85. Which actor portrayed President Thomas Woodrow Wilson in the 1944 biopic WILSON?

86. Who is the secret identity of THE SCARLET PIMPERNEL?

87. Which speakeasy hostess was played by Betty Hutton in INCENDIARY BLONDE (1945)?

88. What is Clark Gable's line of work in THE HUCKSTERS?

89. Name the only movie in which the three Carradine brothers, David, Keith and Robert, have appeared together. What is the family name of their characters in the movie?

90. What is the name of Glenn Close's character in FATAL ATTRACTION?

91. Give Eddie Bracken's full name in HAIL THE CONQUERING HERO (1944).

92. Name the title of a 1984 movie starring Joseph Bottoms that is also the title of a completely different 1987 film starring Bruce Willis.

93. What role does Gary Busey play in 1984's THE BEAR?

94. Who are the two title performers to star in the only movie that Alfred Hitchcock filmed twice? What is the name of the movie?

95. Name the tall actress and one-time girlfriend of Dudley Moore who appeared in GOLDENGIRL in the 1979 film of that title.

96. Barbara Stanwyck's character in THE LADY EVE (1941) shares the same last name with Anne Baxter's character in ALL ABOUT EVE (1950). What is it?

97. In which Alfred Hitchcock film does Ingrid Bergman appear as Alicia Huberman?

98. Who was the Jackal's target in THE DAY OF THE JACKAL (1973)?

99. Name the character portrayed by Chief Thundercloud in 1939 and by Chuck Connors in 1962.

100. Name the Oscar-winning song by Sammy Cahn and Nicholas Brodsky sung by Mario Lanza and Kathryn Grayson in THE TOAST OF NEW ORLEANS.

101. Which actors portrayed THE SONS OF KATE ELDER in the 1965 western?

102. What is Steve McQueen's special skill in THE CINCINNATI KID (1965)?

103. Name the director of films such as DR. JEKYLL AND MR. HYDE (1932), BECKY SHARP (1935) and THE MARK OF ZORRO (1940)?

104. List the following five films of Jeannette MacDonald and Nelson Eddy in the order of their production from earliest to latest: I MARRIED AN ANGEL, NAUGHTY MARIETTA, SWEETHEARTS, ROSE MARIE, and THE GIRL OF THE GOLDEN WEST.

105. Who portrayed Matthew Broderick's disapproving sister in FERRIS BUELLER'S DAY OFF (1986)?

106. Name the film in which exotic beauty Maria Montez played twin sisters, good Tollea and evil Naja.

107. Which of the various actors who have portrayed Charlie Chan in the movies did it the most often?

108. Name the only sound film of silent-screen star Lon Chaney, Sr.

109. Which role and movie do Ronald Colman and Dirk Bogarde have in common?

110. In which movie does skinny little Maria Ouspenskaya portray an Amazon Queen?

111. Which actor has portrayed Robin Hood's follower Little John in three different movies in three different decades?

112. What is the common last name of Shirley Booth's character in THE MATCHMAKER (1958) and Dustin Hoffman's character in MARATHON MAN (1976)?

113. Name the Chicago White Sox baseball pitcher, portrayed by James Stewart in a 1949 biopic, who made a comeback after losing a leg in a hunting accident.

114. Who played the wife, doctor and nurse in WIFE, DOCTOR AND NURSE (1937)?

115. What was Gloria Holden's character's name in DRACULA'S DAUGHTER (1936)?

116. In which movie did Natalie Wood portray a character named Louise Hovick?

117. Who played the Spider Woman in SHERLOCK HOLMES AND THE SPIDER WOMAN (1944) and KISS OF THE SPIDER WOMAN (1985)?

118. Name the "Gentleman from Virginia" who starred in many westerns such as MAN IN THE SADDLE, THE MAN BEHIND THE GUN and BUCHANAN RIDES ALONE.

119. Who played Mama Lift in THROW MOMMA FROM THE TRAIN (1987)?

120. Which British actress, a member of a famous acting family, was brought to Hollywood to play the title role in ALICE IN WONDERLAND (1933), only to be replaced by Charlotte Henry?

121. What role originally played by Charles Laughton in ISLAND OF LOST SOULS (1932) did Burt Lancaster recreate in 1977?

122. Who plays Gruesome in DICK TRACY MEETS GRUESOME?

123. What is Leo Gorcey's character's nickname in the films in which he appears as Terence Mahoney?

124. Name the film in which Edmund Gwenn appears as an incompetent but successful counterfeiter.

125. Name the two real-life brothers who shared the role of the Falcon in the RKO series of the 1940s.

126. Alec Guinness and Stanley Holloway were the main members of THE LAVENDER HILL MOB (1951). Name their two cohorts.

127. In which film did Humphrey Bogart portray an executed murderer brought back to life, wearing makeup giving him an ashen face and short-cropped hair with a white streak in the middle?

128. Name the 1940 film in which Edward G. Robinson portrays a German scientist who develops a cure for venereal disease.

129. Who had a hit recording of the title song of the 1954 film ADVENTURES OF HAJII BABA?

130. Helen Gahagan, wife of actor Melvyn Douglas and a congresswoman defeated by a young Richard Nixon in a dirty tricks campaign, appeared in only one movie, playing the title role. Name the film.

131. What is Ann Carver's profession in the 1933 film ANN CARVER's PROFESSION starring Fay Wray?

132. What is the title of the 1957 biopic of silent screen star Lon Chaney starring James Cagney?

133. Which present-day superstar made his film debut as a 19-year-old in CRY BABY KILLER (1958)?

134. Victor McLaglen won an Academy Award for his portrayal of a doomed Irish informer in 1935's THE INFORMER. Name the Swedish actor who played the IRA betrayer in a 1929 version of the film.

135. Name the first master villain with whom a movie James Bond clashed and the actor who portrayed the evil one.

136. Which role did Christopher Lloyd play in the 1991 film THE ADDAMS FAMILY?

137. What is the last name of the characters played by Dolores Costello and Tim Holt in THE MAGNIFICENT AMBERSONS (1942)?

138. In which movie did Jimmy Durante play a character called Knobby Walsh?

139. Pat O'Brien portrayed Notre Dame football coach KNUTE ROCKNE— ALL AMERICAN (1940). Name the other real-life football coach Pat portrayed and the title of the 1943 movie.

140. What professional name did Arnold Schwarzenegger use when he made HERCULES IN NEW YORK (1970)?

141. Name the actor who not only portrayed Jesse James in one movie but Jesse's assassin Bob Ford in another film.

142. In which film did Barbara Stanwyck appear as an Aimee Semple MacPherson-like evangelist?

143. Who portrayed belly dancer Izora in LITTLE EGYPT (1951)?

144. Who was the first actor to appear as Dr. James Kildare in a movie?

145. What is the name of THE GREAT DICTATOR played by Charles Chaplin in the 1940 movie?

146. Name the five young stars of THE BREAKFAST CLUB (1985).

147. In which 1962 film did Laurence Harvey and Karl Boehm portray brothers?

148. Name the 1928 "lost generation" film starring Joan Crawford, Dorothy Sebastian and Anita Page.

149. What is Lupe Velez's character's name in the MEXICAN SPITFIRE series?

150. Name the U.S. president portrayed by Charles Heston in THE PRESIDENT'S LADY (1953) and the film in which he repeated the role.

ANSWERS

1. ALL THAT MONEY CAN BUY
2. Bonita Granville
3. Edmond Dantes
4. X-27
5. SWEET CHARITY (1969)
6. Dorothy Lamour
7. Elmo Lincoln in 1918; Herman Brix, later to be known as Bruce Bennett
8. John Wayne as Tom Doniphon
9. Alan Arkin; INSPECTOR CLOUSEAU (1968)
10. Bobby and Billy Mauch, the prince and pauper, respectively
11. Lee Van Cleef
12. Harry Nilsson
13. Allen James
14. Max Bialystock & Leo Bloom; SPRINGTIME FOR HITLER
15. THEY MIGHT BE GIANTS (1971)
16. Harry Lime, played by Orson Welles
17. MIRANDA (1949); MAD ABOUT MEN (1954)
18. Jane Withers
19. CAPTAIN JANUARY
20. He played the Lone Ranger in a very forgettable THE LEGEND OF THE LONE RANGER (1981)
21. Tom Destry Jr.
22. Professor Marvel
23. Ramon Novarro
24. Don Ameche
25. Lionel Barrymore
26. I'LL BE YOURS
27. Seagull
28. ANNA CHRISTIE (1930); TWO-FACED WOMAN (1941)
29. Barbara Bel Geddes
30. Barton Fink
31. Monogram
32. Kharis; Tom Tyler
33. A STOLEN LIFE (1946) and DEAD RINGER (1964)
34. Longfellow
35. Glenda Farrell; Lola Lane and Jane Wyman
36. WOMAN OF THE YEAR (1942)
37. Bix Beiderbecke
38. George Arliss
39. James Dean, who was killed in an automobile accident before filming began
40. Elwood and Joliet Jake
41. THE INVISIBLE MAN (1933)
42. Rosey Grier
43. Lorelei Lee; Ruth Taylor
44. Jeanne Crain, Linda Darnell, Ann Sothern
45. Steve Martin in THE MAN WITH TWO BRAINS (1983)
46. Mr. Moto
47. KID GALLAHAD
48. MY FRIEND IRMA (1949); Marie Wilson
49. David Kinemon; TOL'ABLE DAVID
50. I DIED A THOUSAND TIMES; Jack Palance
51. Will Rogers, Jr.
52. Boy
53. Mary Pickford
54. Dolores Del Rio
55. Charles Starrett
56. Geena Davis; Susan Sarandon
57. DEATH TAKES A HOLIDAY (1934)
58. THE ADMIRABLE CRICHTON
59. Mitzi Gaynor, Kay Kendall, Tania Elg
60. Simon Sparrow
61. Pilletti
62. Edward Ellis
63. Crosby
64. Eight
65. THE HATCHET MAN (1932)
66. BOUND FOR GLORY
67. Laura Dern (1991)
68. Scattergood Baines
69. SHE DONE HIM WRONG (1933)
70. Chipping
71. Betty Bronson
72. Tyrone Power who died during the filming
73. Pontipee
74. Granville Owens and Peter Palmer
75. THE REMARKABLE ANDREW (1942)
76. Charles Fleischer
77. "Foghorn"
78. Ravier
79. SITTING PRETTY (1948)
80. Joe E. Lewis
81. THE BARKLEYS OF BROADWAY (1949)
82. Maureen O'Sullivan; Parker
83. "Hot Garters Gertie"
84. Gale Page
85. Alexander Knox
86. Sir Percy Blakeney
87. Texas Guinan
88. Advertising account executive
89. THE LONG RIDERS (1980); Younger
90. Alex Forrest
91. Woodrow Lafayette Pershing Truesmith
92. BLIND DATE
93. Paul "Bear" Bryant
94. Leslie Banks and James Stewart in THE MAN WHO KNEW TOO MUCH (1934, 1956)
95. Susan Anton
96. Harrington
97. NOTORIOUS (1946)
98. Charles De Gaulle
99. Geronimo
100. "Be My Love"

101. John Wayne, Dean Martin, Earl Holliman, Michael Anderson, Jr.
102. Professional poker player
103. Rouben Mamoulian
104. NAUGHTY MARIETTA (1935), ROSE MARIE (1936), THE GIRL OF THE GOLDEN WEST (1938), SWEETHEARTS (1938), I MARRIED AN ANGEL (1942)
105. Jennifer Grey
106. COBRA WOMAN (1944)
107. Sidney Toler, 21 times
108. THE UNHOLY THREE (1930), a remake of his 1925 silent film
109. Sydney Carton in A TALE OF TWO CITIES (1935 and 1958)
110. TARZAN AND THE AMAZONS (1945)
111. Alan Hale; ROBIN HOOD (1922), THE ADVENTURES OF ROBIN HOOD (1938), ROGUES OF SHERWOOD FOREST (1950)
112. Levi
113. Monty Stratton
114. Loretta Young, Warner Baxter, Virginia Bruce
115. Countess Marya Zaleska
116. GYPSY (1962)
117. Gale Sondergaard and Sonia Braga
118. Randolph Scott
119. Anne Ramsey
120. Ida Lupino
121. Dr. Moreau
122. Boris Karloff
123. "Slip"
124. MISTER 880 (1950)
125. George Sanders and Tom Conway
126. Alfie Bass and Sid James
127. THE RETURN OF DR. X (1939)
128. DR. EHRLICH'S MAGIC BULLET
129. Nat "King" Cole
130. SHE (1935)
131. Attorney-at-law
132. MAN OF A THOUSAND FACES
133. Jack Nicholson
134. Lars Hansen
135. DR. NO. (1962); Joseph Wiseman
136. Uncle Fester
137. Minafer
138. PALOOKA (1933)
139. Frank Cavanaugh; THE IRON MAJOR
140. Arnold Strong
141. John Ireland
142. THE MIRACLE WOMAN (1931)
143. Rhonda Fleming
144. Joel McCrea in INTERNS CAN'T TAKE MONEY (1937)
145. Adenoid Hynkel
146. Emilio Estevez, Molly Ringwald, Anthony Michael Hall, Ally Sheedy, Judd Nelson
147. THE WONDERFUL WORLD OF THE BROTHERS GRIMM
148. OUR DANCING DAUGHTERS (1928)
149. Carmelita Lindsay
150. Andrew Jackson; THE BUCCANEER (1958)

I pray you

you (if any open this writing)

Make in your mouths the words that were our names.

Epistle To Be Left In The Earth
Archibald MacLeish

THE
PERFORMERS

A

ABBE, CHARLES
CAPPY RICKS (1921, Silent, Paramount)—Cappy Ricks

ABBOTT, BUD
BUCK PRIVATES (1941, Universal)—Slicker Smith
BUCK PRIVATES COME HOME (1947, Universal)—Slicker Smith

ABBOTT, JOHN
THE VAMPIRE'S GHOST (1945, Republic)—Webb Fallon

ABEL, WALTER
TWO IN THE DARK (1936, RKO)—The Man
RACKET BUSTERS (1938, Warners)—Hugh Allison

ACORD, ART
THE WESTERN ROVER (1927, Silent, Truart)—Art Hayes

ACOSTA, ENRIQUE
A MESSAGE TO GARCIA (1936, 20th Century Fox)—General Garcia

ACQUANETTA
CAPTIVE WILD WOMAN (1943, Universal)—Paula Dupree
JUNGLE WOMAN (1944, Universal)—Paula Dupree
TARZAN AND THE LEOPARD WOMAN (1946, RKO)—Lea

ADAMS, ABIGAIL
MARY LOU (1948, Columbia)—Mary Lou

ADAMS, BROOKE
A MAN, A WOMAN, AND A BANK (1979, Canada, Bennett)—Stacey

ADAMS, DONALD
THE MIKADO (1967, GB, Warners)—The Mikado

ADAMS, JANE
THE GIRL FROM SAN LORENZO (1950, United Artists)—Nora

ADAMS, JULIE
FOUR GIRLS IN TOWN (1956, Universal)—Kathy Conway

ADAMS, KIM
TED AND VENUS (1991, Double Helix)—Linda Turner

ADAMS, MAUD
OCTOPUSSY (1983, GB, MGM/United Artists)—Octopussy

ADAMS, NICK
YOUNG DILLINGER (1965, Allied Artists)—John Dillinger

ADAMS, ROBERT
KISENGA, MAN OF AFRICA (1952, GB, Two Cities)—Kisenga

ADAMS, TOM
THE SECOND BEST SECRET AGENT IN THE WORLD (1965, GB, Embassy)—Charles Vine

ADDAMS, DAWN
HOT MONEY GIRL (1962, GB, United Producers)—Hedi von Hartmann

ADLER, JAY
MY SIX CONVICTS (1952, Columbia)—Steve Kopac

ADLER, JUDY
UNDER AGE (1964, American International)—Linda Jenkins

AGNEW, BOBBY
THE COLLEGE HERO (1927, Silent, Columbia)—Bob Cantfield

AGUTTER, JENNY
THE RAILWAY CHILDREN (1971, GB, Universal)—Bobbie
AMY (1981, Buena Vista)—Amy

AHERNE, BRIAN
KING OF THE CASTLE (1925, Silent, GB, Stoll)—Colin O'Farrell
BELOVED ENEMY (1936, Goldwyn/United Artists)—Dennis Riordan
THE GREAT GARRICK (1937, Warners)—David Garrick
CAPTAIN FURY (1939, United Artists)—Captain Fury
MY SON, MY SON! (1940, United Artists)—William Essex
THE MAN WHO LOST HIMSELF (1941, Universal)—John Evans/ Malcolm Scott

AHERNE, PAT
VIRGINIA'S HUSBAND (1928, Silent, GB, Butchers)—Bill Hemingway

AIELLO, DANNY
THE CLOSER (1991, Ion Pictures)—Chester Grant
RUBY (1992, Triumph)—Jack Ruby

AIMEE, ANOUK
JUSTINE (1969, 20th Century Fox)—Justine

AINLEY, HENRY
THE PRINCE AND THE BEGGARMAID (1921, Silent, GB, Ideal)—Prince Olaf

AITKENS, MICHAEL
MOVING TARGETS (1987, Australia, Academy)—Riley

AJAYE, FRANKLYN
THE WRONG GUYS (1988, New World)—Franklyn

ALBERT, EDDIE
BROTHER RAT (1938, Warners)—Bing Edwards
AN ANGEL FROM TEXAS (1940, Warners)—Peter Coleman
BROTHER RAT AND A BABY (1940, Warners)—Bing Edwards
THE GREAT MR. NOBODY (1941, Warners)—Dreamy
THE DUDE GOES WEST (1948, Allied Artists)—Daniel Bone

ALBERT, EDWARD
GETTING EVEN (1986, American Dist. Group)—"Tag" Taggar

ALBERTSON, ARTHUR
THE ARGYLE CASE (1917, Warwick)—Bruce Argyle

ALBERTSON, FRANK
TRAVELLING HUSBANDS (1931, RKO)—Barry
FRAMED (1940, Universal)—Henry T. Parker
WHEN THE DALTONS RODE (1940, Universal)—Emmett Dalton

ALBERTSON, JACK
PICKUP ON 101 (1972, American International)—Obediah Bradley

ALDA, ALAN
PAPER LION (1968, United Artists)—George Plimpton
THE SEDUCTION OF JOE TYNAN (1979, Universal)—Joe Tynan
A NEW LIFE (1988, Paramount)—Steve Giardino

ALDA, ROBERT
TWO GALS AND A GUY (1951, United Artists)—Deke Oliver

ALDEN, GINGER
LADY GREY (1980, Maverick)—Lady Grey

ALDEN, MARY
THE POTTERS (1927, Silent, Paramount)—Ma Potter

ALDEN, NORMAN
ANDY (1965, Universal)—Andy

ALDON, LYNDA
MANKILLERS (1987, Action)—Rachel McKenna

ALDREDGE, TOM
THE TROUBLEMAKER (1964, Janus)—Jack Armstrong

ALEXANDER, BEN
PENROD AND SAM (1923, Silent, Associate First National)—
Penrod Schofield

ALEXANDER, JASON
I DON'T BUY KISSES ANYMORE (1992, Skouras)—Bernie
Fishbine

ALEXANDER, PETER
HOW TO SEDUCE A PLAYBOY (1968, Australia,
Intercontinental)—Peter Keller

ALEXANDER, ROSS
HERE COMES CARTER (1936, Warners)—Kent Carter

ALI, MUHAMMAD
THE GREATEST (1977, Columbia)—Muhammad Ali

ALLAN, ELIZABETH
THE SOLDIER AND THE LADY (1937, GB, RKO)—Nadia
THE GIRL WHO FORGOT (1939, GB, Butchers)—Leonora
Barradine

ALLAN, MARGUERITE
DAUGHTERS OF TODAY (1933, GB, United Artists)—Mavis
Sharpe

ALLAN, PAMELA
NOOSE FOR A LADY (1953, GB, Anglo-Amalgamated)—
Margaret Allan

ALLBRITTON, LOUISE
FIRED WIFE (1943, Universal)—Tig Callahan
HER PRIMITIVE MAN (1944, Universal)—Sheila Winthrop

ALLEN, ADRIANNE
THE WOMAN DECIDES (1932, GB, British International)—Lady
Pamela

ALLEN, GRACIE
MR. AND MRS. NORTH (1941, MGM)—Pamela North

ALLEN, IAN
IN THE DAYS OF ST. PATRICK (1920, Silent, GB, Janion)—St.
Patrick

ALLEN, JOSEPH JR.
MY SON, THE HERO (1943, Producers Releasing Corp.)—
Michael

ALLEN, JUDITH
YOUNG AND BEAUTIFUL (1934, Mascot)—June Dale

ALLEN, KAREN
A SMALL CIRCLE OF FRIENDS (1980, United Artists)—Jessica

ALLEN, REX
THE ARIZONA COWBOY (1950, Republic)—Rex Allen

ALLEN, STEVE
THE BENNY GOODMAN STORY (1956, Universal)—Benny
Goodman

ALLEN, WINIFRED
THE MAN HATER (1917, Silent, Triangle)—Phemie Sanders

ALLEN, WOODY
SLEEPER (1973, United Artists)—Miles Monroe
THE FRONT (1976, Columbia)—Howard Prince
ZELIG (1983, Orion)—Leonard Zelig
BROADWAY DANNY ROSE (1984, Orion)—Danny Rose

ALLENBY, FRANK
THE CRIME OF PETER FRAME (1938, GB, Fox British)—
Peter Frame

ALLEY, KIRSTIE
SIBLING RIVALRY (1990, Columbia)—Marjorie Turner

ALLGOOD, SARA
JUNO AND THE PAYCOCK (1930, GB, British International)—
Juno Boyle

ALLISON, MARY
THE WOMAN WHO FOOLED HERSELF (1922, Silent, Assocated
Exhibit)—Eva Lee
YOUTH FOR SALE (1924, Silent, Burr)—Molly Malloy

ALLISTER, CLAUDE
THREE LIVE GHOSTS (1929, United Artists)—Spoofy
THE MEDICINE MAN (1933, GB, Real Art)—Hon. Freddie
Wiltshire
THREE LIVE GHOSTS (1935, MGM)—Spoofy

ALLYSON, JUNE
TWO GIRLS AND A SAILOR (1944, MGM)—Patsy Deyo
THE SAILOR TAKES A WIFE (1946, MGM)—Mary
TWO GIRLS FROM BOSTON (1946, MGM)—Abigail Canford
Chandler
THE BRIDE GOES WILD (1948, MGM)—Martha Terryton
LITTLE WOMEN (1949, MGM)—Jo March
THE REFORMER AND THE REDHEAD (1950, MGM)—Kathleen
Maguire
TOO YOUNG TO KISS (1951, MGM)—Cynthia Potter
THE GIRL IN WHITE (1952, MGM)—Dr. Emily Barringer
WOMAN'S WORLD (1954, 20th Century Fox)—Katie
THE SHRIKE (1955, Universal)—Ann Downs
MY MAN GODFREY (1957, Universal)—Irene Bullock

ALOISI, JOHN
TOTO AND THE POACHERS (1958, GB, World Safari)—Toto

ALPAR, GITTA
THE LOVES OF MADAME DUBARRY (1938, GB, British Int.)—
Jeanne DuBarry

ALTAMURA, JOHN
THE TOXIC AVENGER PART II (1989, Troma)—The Toxic
Avenger

THE TOXIC AVENGER PART III, THE LAST TEMPTATION OF TOXIE (1989, Troma)—The Toxic Avenger

ALVARADO, TRINI
RICH KIDS (1979, United States)—Franny Phillips
AMERICAN FRIENDS (1991, MCEG/Virgin Vision)—Elinor Hartley

ALVIN, JOHN
THE SULLIVANS (1944, 20th Century Fox)—Matt Sullivan

ALVINA, ANICEE
FRIENDS (1971, GB, Paramount)—Michelle LaTour

ALZARDO, LYLE
DESTROYER (1988, Moviestore)—Ivan Poser

AMECHE, DON
THE STORY OF ALEXANDER GRAHAM BELL (1939, 20th Century Fox)—Alexander Graham Bell
FOUR SONS (1940, 20th Century Fox)—Chris Bernie
THAT'S MY MAN (1947, Republic)—Joe Grange
FOLKS (1992, 20th Century Fox)—Henry Aldrich

AMES, ADRIENNE
GIGOLETTE (1935, RKO)—Kay Parrish

AMES, GERALD
RUPERT OF HENTZAU (1915, GB, Jury)—Rupert
MR. JUSTICE RAFFLES (1921, GB, Silent, Hepworth)—A.J. Raffles

AMES, MICHAEL
I WAS FRAMED (1942, Warners)—Ken Marshall

AMES, ROBERT
RICH PEOPLE (1929, Pathe)—Noel Nevins

AMMAN, BETTY
DAUGHTERS OF TODAY (1933, GB, United Artists)—Joan Sharpe

AMPLAS, JOHN
MARTIN (1979, Libra)—Martin

ANDERS, LAURIE
THE MARSHAL'S DAUGHTER (1953, United Artists)—Laurie Dawson

ANDERS, MERRY
THE DALTON GIRLS (1957, United Artists)—Holly Dalton
FIVE BOLD WOMEN (1960, Citation)—The Missouri Lady
POLICE NURSE (1963, 20th Century Fox)—Joan Olson

ANDERSON, BRIDGETTE
SAVANNAH SMILES (1983, Gold Coast)—Savannah Driscoll

ANDERSON, ISA
NIGHT ANGEL (1990, Fries)—Lilith

ANDERSON, JAMES
HUNT THE MAN DOWN (1950, RKO)—Kincaid

ANDERSON, JOHN
THE LINCOLN CONSPIRACY (1977, Sunn Classic)—Abraham Lincoln

ANDERSON, JUDITH
LADY SCARFACE (1941, RKO)—Slade

ANDERSON, KEITH
ORPHANS (1987, Lorimar)—Phillip

ANDERSON, LOUIE
THE WRONG GUYS (1988, New World)—Louie

ANDERSON, MARY
BUBBLES (1920, Silent, Pioneer)—Bubbles Van Saynt

ANDERSON, MICHAEL JR.
THE SUNDOWNERS (1960, Warners)—Sean Carmody
THE SONS OF KATIE ELDER (1965, Paramount)—Bud Elder

ANDERSON, PAT
SUMMER SCHOOL TEACHERS (1977, New World)—Sally

ANDES, KEITH
DAMN CITIZEN (1958, Universal)—Col. Francis C. Grevemberg

ANDO, EIKO
THE BARBARIAN AND THE GEISHA (1958, 20th Century Fox)—Okichi

ANDOR, PAUL
ENEMY OF WOMEN (1944, Monogram)—Paul Joseph Goebbels

ANDRA, FERN
LOTUS LADY (1930, Audible/Greiver)—Tamarah

ANDRESS, URSULA
FOUR FOR TEXAS (1963, Warners)—Maxine Ritcher
SHE (1965, GB, MGM)—Ayesha

ANDREWS, DANA
BERLIN CORRESPONDENT (1942, 20th Century Fox)—Bill Roberts
TOWN TAMER (1965, Paramount)—Tom Rosser
JOHNNY RENO (1966, Paramount)—Johnny Reno

ANDREWS, JULIE
THE AMERICANIZATION OF EMILY (1964, MGM)—Emily Barham
MARY POPPINS (1964, Buena Vista)—Mary Poppins
THOROUGHLY MODERN MILLIE (1967, Universal)—Millie Dillmount
STAR! (1968, 20th Century Fox)—Gertrude Lawrence
DARLING LILI (1970, Paramount)—Lili Smith
VICTOR/VICTORIA (1982, MGM/United Artists)—Victor/Victoria

ANDREWS, LOIS
DIXIE DUGAN (1943, 20th Century Fox)—Dixie Dugan

ANGEL, HEATHER
SELF-MADE LADY (1932, GB, United Artists)—Sookey
THE HEADLINE GIRL (1935, Mascot)—Myrna Van Buren
HALF A SINNER (1940, Universal)—Anne Gladden

ANGELI, PIER
TERESA (1951, MGM)—Teresa

ANKERS, EVELYN
QUEEN OF BURLESQUE (1946, Producers Releasing Corp.)—Crystal McCoy
TEXAN MEETS CALAMITY JANE (1950, Columbia)—Calamity Jane

ANKRUM, MORRIS
SON OF ALI BABA (1952, Universal)—Ali Baba

ANNABELLA
THE BARONESS AND THE BUTLER (1938, 20th Century Fox)—
Baroness Katrina

ANNIS, FRANCESCA
THE EYES OF ANNIE JONES (1963, GB, 20th Century Fox)—
Annie Jones
THE PLEASURE GIRLS (1966, GB, Times)—Sally Feathers

ANN-MARGRET
KITTEN WITH A WHIP (1964, Universal)—Jody Dvorak
THE PLEASURE SEEKERS (1964, 20th Century Fox)—Fran
Hobson
THE SWINGER (1966, Paramount)—Kelly Olsson
THE TIGER AND THE PUSSYCAT (1967, Embassy)—Carolina

ANOUX, VICTORIA
THE TRUE STORY OF ESKIMO NELL (1975, Australia, Quest)—
Eskimo Nell

ANTHONY, SCOTT
SAVAGE MESSIAH (1972, GB, MGM)—Henri Gaudier-Brzeska

ANTON, SUSAN
GOLDENGIRL (1979, Avco Embassy)—Goldengirl

ANULKA
VAMPYRES, DAUGHTERS OF DRACULA (1977, GB, Cambist)—
Miriam

ARBUCKLE, MACKLYN
COUNTY CHAIRMAN (1914, Silent, Paramount)—Jim Hackler

ARBUCKLE, ROSCOE "FATTY"
BREWSTER'S MILLIONS (1921, Silent, Paramount)—Monte
Brewster
GASOLINE GUS (1921, Silent, Paramount)—Gasoline Gus

ARCHER, JOHN
A YANK IN INDO-CHINA (1952, Columbia)—Mulvancy

ARDEN, EDWIN
SIMON THE JESTER (1915, Silent, Gold Rooster)—
Simon de Gex

ARDEN, EVE
SHE COULDN'T SAY NO (1941, Warners)—Alice Hinsdale
OUR MISS BROOKS (1956, Warners)—Constance Brooks

ARDEN, ROBERT
THE DEPRAVED (1957, GB, United Artists)—Dave Dillon
THE CHILD AND THE KILLER (1959, GB, United Artists)—
Captain Joe Marsh

ARKIN, ALAN
INSPECTOR CLOUSEAU (1968, GB, United Artists)—Inspector
Jacques Clouseau
POPI (1969, United Artists)—Abraham Rodriguez
THE LAST OF THE RED HOT LOVERS (1972, Paramount)—
Barney Cashman
FREEBIE AND THE BEAN (1974, Warners)—Bean
RAFFERTY AND THE GOLD DUST TWINS (1975, Warners)—
Rafferty
THE IN-LAWS (1979, Warners)—Sheldon Kornpett

SIMON (1980, Warners)—Simon Mendelssohn
CHU CHU AND THE PHILLY FLASH (1981, 20th Century
Fox)—Flash
THE RETURN OF CAPTAIN INVINCIBLE (1983, Australia,
Keys)—Captain Invincible

ARKINS, ROBERT
THE COMMITMENTS (1991, GB, 20th Century Fox)—Jimmy
Rabbitte

ARLEN, RICHARD
THE MAN I LOVE (1929, Paramount)—Dum-Dum Brooks
THE SEA GOD (1930, Paramount)—Phillip "Pink" Barker
THE ALL-AMERICAN (1932, Universal)—Garry King
ACE OF ACES (1933, RKO)—Lt. Rex Thorne
THREE LIVE GHOSTS (1935, MGM)—Billy Foster
DAN MATTHEWS (1936, Columbia)—Dan Matthews
THE LEATHER-PUSHERS (1940, Universal)—Dick
THE MAN FROM MONTREAL (1940, Universal)—Clark Manning
THE LADY AND THE MONSTER (1944, Republic)—Patrick Cory
IDENTITY UNKNOWN (1945, Republic)—Johnny March
BUFFALO BILL RIDES AGAIN (1947, Screen Guild)—William
"Buffalo Bill" Cody

ARLISS, GEORGE
THE MAN WHO PLAYED GOD (1922, Silent, United Artists)—
John Arden
DISRAELI (1929, Warners)—Benjamin Disraeli
OLD ENGLISH (1930, Warners)—Sylvanus Heythorp
ALEXANDER HAMILTON (1931, Warners)—Alexander Hamilton
THE MILLIONAIRE (1931, Warners)—James Alden
THE MAN WHO PLAYED GOD (1932, Warners)—Montgomery
Royale
THE KING'S VACATION (1933, Warners)—King Philip
VOLTAIRE (1933, Warners)—Francois Marie Arouet Voltaire
THE WORKING MAN (1933, Warners)—John Reeves
THE HOUSE OF ROTHSCHILD (1934, 20th Century)—Mayer
Rothschild & Nathan Rothschild
THE LAST GENTLEMAN (1934, United Artists)—Cabot Barr
CARDINAL RICHELIEU (1935, Fox)—Cardinal Richelieu
THE IRON DUKE (1935, GB, Gaumont)—Duke of Wellington
MISTER HOBO (1936, GB, Gaumont)—Spike, The Guv'nor
DOCTOR SYN (1937, GB, Gaumont)—Dr. Syn
MAN OF AFFAIRS (1937, GB, Gaumont)—Lord Dunchester

ARMENDARIZ, PEDRO
THE THREE GODFATHERS (1948, MGM)—Pedro "Pete" Fuerte

ARMENDARIZ, PEDRO JR.
THE MAGNIFICENT SEVEN RIDE (1972, United Artists)—Pepe
Carral

ARMIDA
THE GIRL FROM MONTEREY (1943, Producers Releasing
Corp.)—Lita

ARMSTRONG, MABEL
MEG (1926, GB, Silent, Wardour)—Meg

ARMSTRONG, ROBERT
CELEBRITY (1928, Silent, Pathe)—Kid Regan
THE RACKETEER (1929, Pathe)—Mahlon Keane
EX-BAD BOY (1931, Universal)—Chester Binney
THE MYSTERY MAN (1935, Monogram)—Larry
THREE LEGIONNAIRES (1937, General)—Chuck

ARMSTRONG, TODD
JASON AND THE ARGONAUTS (1963, GB, Columbia)—Jason

ARNAUD, YVONNE
LADY IN DANGER (1934, GB, Gaumont)—Queen of Ardenberg
THE IMPROPER DUCHESS (1936, GB, GFD)—Duchess of Tann

ARNAZ, DESI JR.
BILLY TWO HATS (1973, GB, United Artists)—Billy Two Hats
MARCO (1973, Cinerama)—Marco Polo

ARNESS, JAMES
THE PEOPLE AGAINST O'HARA (1951, MGM)—Johnny O'Hara
THE THING (1951, RKO)—The Thing

ARNOLD, EDWARD
DIAMOND JIM (1935, Universal)—Diamond Jim Brady
MEET NERO WOLFE (1936, Columbia)—Nero Wolfe
SUTTER'S GOLD (1936, Universal)—John Sutter
JOHN MEADE'S WOMAN (1937, Paramount)—John Meade
THE TOAST OF NEW YORK (1937, RKO)—Jim Fisk
THE DEVIL AND DANIEL WEBSTER (1941, RKO)—Daniel Webster
UNHOLY PARTNERS (1941, MGM)—Merrill Lambert
THREE WISE FOOLS (1946, MGM)—Theodore Findley
MAN OF CONFLICT (1953, Atlas)—J.R. Compton

ARQUETTE, ROSANNA
BABY, IT'S YOU (1983, Paramount)—Jill
NOBODY'S FOOL (1986, Island)—Cassie
WENDY CRACKED A WALNUT (1990, Australia, Classic Films)—Wendy

ARTHUR, GEORGE K.
KIPPS (1921, Silent, GB, Stoll)—Arthur Kipps

ARTHUR, HENRY
ROAD DEMON (1938, 20th Century Fox)—Blake

ARTHUR, JEAN
HUSBAND HUNTERS (1927, Silent, Tiffany)—Letty Crane
THE EX-MRS. BRADFORD (1936, RKO)—Paula Bradford
IF YOU COULD ONLY COOK (1936, Columbia)—Joan Hawthorne
MORE THAN A SECRETARY (1936, Columbia)—Carol Baldwin
THE DEVIL AND MISS JONES (1941, RKO)—Mary Jones
A LADY TAKES A CHANCE (1943, RKO)—Mollie Truesdale
THE MORE THE MERRIER (1943, Columbia)—Connie Milligan

ASHER, JANE
HENRY VIII AND HIS SIX WIVES (1972, GB, EMI/MGM)—Jane Seymour

ASHLEY, ARTHUR
THE PRAISE AGENT (1919, Silent, World)—Jack Bartling

ASHLEY, JOHN
HIGH SCHOOL CAESAR (1960, Marathon/Filmgroup)—Mat Stevens

ASKEW, LUKE
THE MAGNIFICENT SEVEN RIDE (1972, United Artists)—Skinner

ASKEY, ARTHUR
CHARLEY'S BIG-HEARTED AUNT (1940, GB, Gainsborough)—Arthur Linden-Jones
KING ARTHUR WAS A GENTLEMAN (1942, GB, Gainsborough)—Arthur King
RAMSBOTTOM RIDES AGAIN (1956, GB, British Lion)—Bill Ramsbottom

ASKWITH, ROBIN
CONFESSIONS OF A WINDOW CLEANER (1974, GB, Columbia)—Timothy Lea
CONFESSIONS OF A POP PERFORMER (1975, GB, Columbia)—Timothy Lea
STAND UP VIRGIN SOLDIERS (1977, GB, Warners)—Brigg

ASNER, ED
O'HARA'S WIFE (1983, Davis-Panzer)—Bob O'Hara

ASSANTE, ARMAND
I, THE JURY (1982, 20th Century Fox)—Mike Hammer
BELIZAIRE THE CAJUN (1986, Skouras)—Belizaire Breaux
THE MAMBO KINGS (1992, Warner Brothers)—Cesar Castillo

ASTAIRE, FRED
SHALL WE DANCE (1937, RKO)—Pete "Petrov" Peters
THE STORY OF VERNON AND IRENE CASTLE (1939, RKO)—Vernon Castle
YOLANDA AND THE THIEF (1945, MGM)—Johnny Parkson Riggs
THE BARKLEY'S OF BROADWAY (1949, MGM)—Josh Barkley
DADDY LONG LEGS (1955, 20th Century Fox)—Jervis Pendleton
THE PLEASURE OF HIS COMPANY (1961, Paramount)—Biddeford "Pogo" Poole
FINIAN'S RAINBOW (1968, Warners)—Finian McLonergan

ASTHER, NILS
THE BITTER TEA OF GENERAL YEN (1933, Columbia)—General Yen
THE MAN IN THE HALF-MOON STREET (1944, Paramount)—Julian Karell
THAT MAN FROM TANGIER (1953, United Artists)—Henri

ASTIN, SEAN
STAYING TOGETHER (1989, Hemdale)—Duncan McDermott
TOY SOLDIERS (1991, Tri-Star)—Billy Tepper

ASTIN, STEVE
THE GOONIES (1985, Warners)—Mickey

ASTLEY, JOHN
JIMMY (1916, Silent, GB, Gaumont)—Jimmy St. Quinton

ASTOR, MARY
LADIES LOVE BRUTES (1930, Paramount)—Mimi Howell
RUNAWAY BRIDE (1930, RKO)—Mary
SMART WOMAN (1931, RKO)—Nancy Gibson
I AM A THIEF (1935, Warners)—Odette Mauclair
LADY FROM NOWHERE (1936, Columbia)—Polly
WOMAN AGAINST WOMAN (1938, MGM)—Cynthia Holland

ATKINS, DAVID
SQUIZZY TAYLOR (1984, Australia, Satori)—Squizzy Taylor

ATKINS, EILEEN
NELLY'S VERSION (1983, GB, Mithras)—Nelly

ATTENBOROUGH, RICHARD
THE OUTSIDER (1949, GB, Pilgrim/Variety)—Jack Read

FATHER'S DOING FINE (1952, GB, Marble Arch)—Dougall
THE MAN UPSTAIRS (1959, GB, British Lion)—Peter Watson

ATWILL, LIONEL
DOCTOR X (1932, Warners)—Doctor Xavier
THE MAD DOCTOR OF MARKET STREET (1942, Universal)—
Dr. Benson
THE STRANGE CASE OF DR. RX (1942, Universal)—Dr. Fish

AUBER, BRIGITTE
TO CATCH A THIEF (1955, Paramount)—Danielle Foussard

AUBERT, LEONORE
THE WIFE OF MONTE CRISTO (1946, Producers Releasing
Corp.)—Haydee, Countess of Monte Cristo

AULIN, EWA
CANDY (1968, Cinerama)—Candy

AUSTEN, LESLIE
A MAN AND A WOMAN (1917, Silent, Art Dramas)—James
Duncan

AUSTIN, JOE
HOME IS WHERE THE HART IS (1987, Canada, Atlantic)—Slim
"Paddy" Hart

AUSTIN, KAREN
LADIES CLUB (1986, New Line Cinema)—Joan Taylor

AUSTIN, PAMELA
THE PERILS OF PAULINE (1967, Universal)—Pauline

AUSTIN, VIVIAN
NIGHT CLUB GIRL (1944, Universal)—Eleanor

AUSTIN, WILLIAM
THREE MEN IN A BOAT (1933, GB, Associate British)—Harris

AVALON, FRANKIE
SERGEANT DEADHEAD (1965, American International)—
Sergeant Deadhead (Sgt. Donovan)

AYKROYD, DAN
THE BLUES BROTHERS (1980, Universal)—Elwood
NEIGHBORS (1981, Columbia)—Vic
DOCTOR DETROIT (1983, Universal)—Clifford Skirdlow
LOOSE CANNONS (1990, Tri-Star)—Ellis
TRADING PLACES (1983, Paramount)—Louis Winthrop III
GHOSTBUSTERS (1984, Columbia)—Dr. Raymond Stanz
GHOSTBUSTERS II (1989, Columbia)—Dr. Raymond Stanz

AYLMER, FELIX
MR. EMMANUEL (1945, GB, Ealing)—Mr. Emmanuel
GHOSTS OF BERKELEY SQUARE (1947, GB, Pathe)—Col.
Kelsoe

AYRES, AGNES
THE HEART RIDER (1923, Silent, Paramount)—Muriel Gray
HER MARKET VALUE (1925, Silent, Powell)—Nancy Dumont

AYRES, LEW
THE IRON MAN (1931, Universal)—Kid Mason
SILK HAT KID (1935, Fox)—Eddie Howard
THE LEATHERNECKS HAVE LANDED (1936, Republic)—
Woody Davis

KING OF THE NEWSBOYS (1938, Republic)—Jerry Flynn
YOUNG DR. KILDARE (1938, MGM)—Dr. James Kildare
CALLING DR. KILDARE (1939, MGM)—Dr. James Kildare
THE SECRET OF DR. KILDARE (1939, MGM)—Dr. James
Kildare
DR. KILDARE GOES HOME (1940, MGM)—Dr. James Kildare
DR. KILDARE'S CRISIS (1940, MGM)—Dr. James Kildare
DR. KILDARE'S STRANGEST CASE (1940, MGM)—Dr. James
Kildare
DR. KILDARE'S VICTORY (1941, MGM)—Dr. James Kildare
DR. KILDARE'S WEDDING DAY (1941, MGM)—Dr. James
Kildare
THE PEOPLE VS. DR. KILDARE (1941, MGM)—Dr. James
Kildare

B

BABY LEROY
MISS FANE'S BABY IS STOLEN (1934, Paramount)—
Michael Fane

BABY PEGGY
CAPTAIN JANUARY (1924, Silent, Principal)—Captain January

BABY SANDY
SANDY GETS HER MAN (1940, Universal)—Sandy
SANDY IS A LADY (1940, Universal)—Sandy

BACALL, LAUREN
WOMAN'S WORLD (1954, 20th Century Fox)—Elizabeth
DESIGNING WOMAN (1957, MGM)—Marilla Hagen

BACH, BARBARA
THE SPY WHO LOVED ME (1977, GB, United Artists)—Major
Anya Amasova

BACHELOR, STEPHANIE
THE UNDERCOVER WOMAN (1946, Republic)—Marcia Conroy

BACLANOVA, OLGA
DANGEROUS WOMAN (1929, Paramount)—Tania Gregory

BACON, KEVIN
FLATLINERS (1990, Columbia)—Labraccio
HE SAID, SHE SAID (1991, Paramount)—Dan Hansen

BAER, MAX
THE PRIZEFIGHTER AND THE LADY (1933, MGM)—Steve
Morgan

BAGGOT, KING
IVANHOE (1913, Silent, Imperator)—Ivanhoe

BAINTER, FAY
MOTHER CAREY'S CHICKENS (1938, RKO)—Mrs. Carey

THE LADY AND THE MOB (1939, Columbia)—Hattie Leonard
OUR NEIGHBORS—THE CARTERS (1939, Paramount)—Ellen
  Carter
YES, MY DARLING DAUGHTER (1939, Warners)—Ann Murray
MRS. WIGGS OF THE CABBAGE PATCH (1942, Paramount)—
  Mrs. Elvira Wiggs
THE WAR AGAINST MRS. HADLEY (1942, MGM)—Stella Hadley

BAIO, SCOTT
  BUGSY MALONE (1976, GB, Paramount)—Bugsy Malone

BAIRD, JIMMY
  THE SEVEN LITTLE FOYS (1955, Paramount)—Eddie Foy, Jr.

BAIRD, PETER
  HOWARD THE DUCK (1986, Universal)—Howard T. Duck

BAIRD, S.L.
  RATBOY (1986, Warners)—Ratboy

BAIRD, STEWART
  THE MOTH AND THE FLAME (1915, Silent, Paramount)—
  Edward Fletcher

BAKER, CARROLL
  BABY DOLL (1956, Warners)—Baby Doll
  HARLOW (1965, Paramount)—Jean Harlow
  SYLVIA (1965, Paramount)—Sylvia West

BAKER, DIANE
  TESS OF THE STORM COUNTRY (1961, 20th Century Fox)—
  Tess MacLean

BAKER, EVADNE
  SEVEN WOMEN FROM HELL (1961, 20th Century Fox)—Regan

BAKER, GEORGE
  A WOMAN FOR JOE (1955, GB, Rank)—Joe Harrao
  THE MOONRAKER (1958, GB, ABF-Pathe)—"The Moonraker,"
  Earl Anthony of Dawlish

BAKER, JOE DON
  WALKING TALL (1973, Cinerama)—Buford Pusser
  FRAMED (1975, Paramount)—Ron
  MITCHELL (1975, Allied Artists)—Mitchell

BAKER, KENNY
  MR. DODD TAKES THE AIR (1937, First National)—
  Claude Dodd

BAKER, REX "SNOWY"
  HIS LAST RACE (1923, Silent, Goldstone)—Dick Carleton

BAKER, SIR STANLEY
  HELL DRIVERS (1958, GB, Rank)

BAKEWELL, WILLIAM
  A MAN OF SENTIMENT (1933, First National)—John Russell

BALDWIN, ALEC
  THE MARRYING MAN (1991, Hollywood Pictures)—
  Charley Pearl

BALDWIN, ADAM
  MY BODYGUARD (1980, 20th Century Fox)—Lindemann

COHEN AND TATE (1989, Tri-Star)—Tate

BALDWIN, WILLIAM
  FLATLINERS (1990, Columbia)—Joe

BALE, CHRISTIAN
  NEWSIES (1992, Buena Vista/Disney)—Jack Kelly/Frances
  Sullivan

BALFOUR, BETTY
  SQUIBS (1921, GB, Silent,Jury)—Squibs Hopkins
  SQUIBS WINS THE CALCUTTA SWEEP (1922, GB, Silent,
    Jury)—Squibs Hopkins
  SQUIBS MP (1923, GB, Silent, Gaumont)—Squibs Hopkins
  SATAN'S SISTER (1925, Silent, GB, Woodfall)—Jude Tyler
  SQUIBS' HONEYMOON (1926, GB, Silent, Gaumont)—Squibs
    Hopkins (Lee)
  THE VAGABOND QUEEN (1931, GB, Wardour)—Sally
  SQUIBS (1935, GB, Gaumont)—Squibs Hopkins
  ELIZA COMES TO STAY (1936, GB, Twickenham)—Eliza
    Vandan

BALINT, ESTZER
  BAIL JUMPER (1990, Angelika)—Elaine

BALL, LUCILLE
  AFFAIRS OF ANNABEL (1938, RKO)—Annabel
  ANNABEL TAKES A TOUR (1938, RKO)—Annabel
  NEXT TIME I MARRY (1938, RKO)—Nancy Fleming
  PANAMA LADY (1939, RKO)—Lucy
  A GIRL, A GUY AND A GOB (1941, RKO)—Dot Duncan
  DUBARRY WAS A LADY (1943, MGM)—Mme. DuBarry
  LOVER COME BACK (1946, Universal)—Kay Williams
  TWO SMART PEOPLE (1946, MGM)—Ricki Woodner
  HER HUSBAND'S AFFAIRS (1947, Columbia)—Margaret Weldon
  MISS GRANT TAKES RICHMOND (1949, Columbia)—
    Ellen Grant
  THE FULLER BRUSH GIRL (1950, Columbia)—Sally Elliot
  MAME (1974, Warners)—Mame Dennis

BALLIN, MABEL
  JANE EYRE (1921, Silent, Hodkinson)—Jane Eyre
  BEAUTY AND THE BAD MAN (1925, Silent, Peninsula)—Cassie

BALSAM, MARTIN
  12 ANGRY MEN (1957, United Artists)—Juror No. 1
  THE GOODBYE PEOPLE (1984, Embassy)—Max Silverman

BALZARY, MICHAEL
  DUDES (1988, New Century-Vista)—Milo

BANCROFT, ANNE
  GIRL IN BLACK STOCKINGS (1957, United Artists)—
    Beth Dixon
  THE MIRACLE WORKER (1962, United Artists)—Annie Sullivan
  SEVEN WOMEN (1966, MGM)—Dr. D.R. Cartwright
  'NIGHT MOTHER (1986, Universal)—Thelma Cates

BANCROFT, GEORGE
  THE MIGHTY (1929, Paramount)—Blake Greeson
  THUNDERBOLT (1929, Paramount)—"Thunderbolt" Jim Lang
  THE WOLF OF WALL STREET (1929, Paramount)—Jim
    Bradford
  LADIES LOVE BRUTES (1930, Paramount)—Joe Forziati
  DERELICT (1930, Paramount)—Bill Rafferty

RICH MAN'S FOLLY (1931, Paramount)—Brock Trumbull
LADY AND GENT (1932, Paramount)—Slag Bailey
ELMER AND ELSIE (1934, Paramount)—Elmer Beebe
HELL-SHIP MORGAN (1936, Columbia)—Morgan
A DOCTOR'S DIARY (1937, Paramount)—Dr. Clem Driscoll
RACKETEERS IN EXILE (1937, Columbia)—William Waldo

BANDEROS, ANTONIO
THE MAMBO KINGS (1992, Warner Brothers)—Nestor Castillo

BANKHEAD, TALLULAH
THE CHEAT (1931, Paramount)—Elsa Carlyle
MY SIN (1931, Paramount)—Carlotta/"Ann Trevor"
TARNISHED LADY (1931, Paramount)—Nancy Courtney

BANKS, LESLIE
THE MAN WHO KNEW TOO MUCH (1935, GB, Gaumont)—Bob Lawrence
SANDERS OF THE RIVER (1935, GB, United Artists)—R.G. Sanders

BANKS, MONTY
ATTA BOY (1926, Silent, Pathe)—Monty Milde
THE COMPULSORY HUSBAND (1930, GB, British International)—Monty
SO YOU WON'T TALK (1935, GB, Warners)—Tony Cazari

BANKY, VILMA
THE WINNING OF BARBARA WORTH (1926, Silent, United Artists)—Barbara Worth
TWO LOVERS (1928, Silent, United Artists)—Donna Leonora de Vargas
A LADY TO LOVE (1930, MGM)—Lena Schultz

BANNEN, IAN
THE SAILOR FROM GIBRALTER (1967, GB, Lopert)—Alan

BANNERMAN, CELIA
BIDDY (1983, GB, Sands)—Biddy

BANNON, JIM
RIDE, RYDER, RIDE (1949, Eagle-Lion)—Red Ryder
THE COWBOY AND THE PRIZEFIGHTER (1950, Eagle-Lion)—Red Ryder
THE FIGHTING REDHEAD (1950, Eagle-Lion)—Red Ryder

BARA, THEDA
ROMEO AND JULIET (1916, Silent, Fox)—Juliet
THE DARLING OF PARIS (1917, Silent, Fox)—Esmeralda
THE TIGER WOMAN (1917, Silent, Fox)—Princess Petrovitch
WHEN A WOMAN SINS (1918, Silent, Fox)—Lillian Marchard/Poppea
KATHLEEN MAVOURNEEN (1919, Silent, World)—Kathleen Mavourneen
UNCHASTENED WOMAN (1925, Silent, Chadwick)—Caroline Knollys

BARBER, FRANCES
SAMMY AND ROSIE GET LAID (1987, GB, Cinecom)—Rosie Hobbs

BARBIER, GEORGE
MARRY THE BOSS' DAUGHTER (1941, 20th Century Fox)—J.W. Barrett

BARCLAY, JOHN
THE MIKADO (1939, GB, Universal)—The Mikado

BARDOT, BRIGITTE
DEAR BRIGITTE (1965, 20th Century Fox)—Brigitte Bardot

BARI, LYNN
MEET THE GIRLS (1938, 20th Century Fox)—Terry Wilson
FREE, BLONDE AND 21 (1940, 20th Century Fox)—Carol
MOON OVER HER SHOULDER (1941, 20th Century Fox)—Susan Rossiter

BARKER, JESS
GOOD LUCK MR. YATES (1943, Columbia)—Oliver Yates

BARKER, LEX
RETURN OF THE BADMEN (1948, RKO)—Emmett Dalton
TARZAN'S MAGIC FOUNTAIN (1949, RKO)—Tarzan
TARZAN AND THE SLAVE GIRL (1950, RKO)—Tarzan
TARZAN'S PERIL (1951, RKO)—Tarzan
TARZAN'S SAVAGE FURY (1952, RKO)—Tarzan
TARZAN AND THE SHE-DEVIL (1953, RKO)—Tarzan
THE MAN FROM BITTER RIDGE (1955, Universal)—Jeff Carr
THE DEERSLAYER (1957, 20th Century Fox)—The Deerslayer

BARKIN, ELLEN
SWITCH (1991, Warner Brothers)—Amanda Brooks

BARNES, BARRY K.
RETURN OF THE SCARLET PIMPERNEL (1938, GB, United Artists)—Sir Percy Blakeney
THIS MAN IN PARIS (1939, GB, Paramount)—Simon Drake
THIS MAN IS NEWS (1939, GB, Paramount)—Simon Drake
SPIES OF THE AIR (1940, GB, Associate British)—Jim Thurloe

BARNES, BINNIE
THE LADY IS WILLING (1934, GB, Columbia)—Helene Dupont
THE DIVORCE OF LADY X (1938, GB, London Films)—Lady Mere
WIFE, HUSBAND AND FRIEND (1939, 20th Century Fox)—Cecil Carver
THREE GIRLS ABOUT TOWN (1941, Columbia)—Faith Banner

BARNES, GLENN
THE GALAXY INVADER (1985, Moviecraft)—Alien

BARNES, T. ROY
ADAM AND EVA (1923, Silent, Paramount)—Adam Smith

BARR, PATRICK
THE CAVALIER OF THE STREETS (1937, GB, British & Dominions)—The Cavalier

BARR, ROSEANNE
SHE-DEVIL (1989, Orion)—Ruth Patchett
LOOK WHO'S TALKING TOO (1990, Tri-Star)—Voice of Julie

BARRAT, ROBERT H.
THE LAST OF THE MOHICANS (1936, UA)—Chingachgook
GRISSLY'S MILLIONS (1945, Republic)—Grissly Morgan

BARRAUD, GEORGE
THE RETURN OF RAFFLES (1932, GB, Markham)—A.J. Raffles

BARRESE, KATHERINE
JEZEBEL'S KISS (1990, Glickenhaus)—Jezebel

BARRETT, EDITH
LADIES IN RETIREMENT (1941, Columbia)—Louisa Creed

BARRETT, JUDITH
FLYING HOSTESS (1936, Universal)—Helen Brooks

BARRETT, WILSON
CONCERNING MR. MARTIN (1937, GB, Fox British)—Leo Martin

BARRIE, AMANDA
CARRY ON CLEO (1964, GB, Warners/Pathe)—Cleo

BARRIE, MONA
SUCH WOMEN ARE DANGEROUS (1934, Fox)—Wanda Paris
LADIES LOVE DANGER (1935, Fox)—Rita
MYSTERY WOMAN (1935, Fox)—Margaret Benoit

BARRIE, WENDY
THE MAN I WANT (1934, GB, British Lion)—Marion Round
GIVE HER A RING (1936, GB, British International)—Karen Swenson
A GIRL WITH IDEAS (1937, Universal)—Mary Morton
FOLLIES GIRL (1943, Producers Releasing Corp.)—Anne Merriday

BARRIER, EDGAR
SHERLOCK HOLMES AND THE VOICE OF TERROR (1942, Universal)—The Voice of Terror

BARRISCALE, BESSIE
BAWBS O' BLUE RIDGE (1916, Silent, Triangle)—Barbara "Bawbs" Colby
NOT MY SISTER (1916, Triangle)—Grace Tyler
HATER OF MEN (1917, Silent, Triangle)—Janice Salsbury

BARROWS, GEORGE
ROBOT MONSTER (1953, Three Dimensional Pictures)—Ro-Man

BARRY, COLIN
UNMAN, WITTERING AND ZIGO (1971, GB, Paramount)—Wittering

BARRY, DON "RED"
DAYS OF JESSE JAMES (1939, Republic)—Jesse James
THE MAN FROM THE RIO GRANDE (1943, Republic)—Lee Grant
WEST SIDE KID (1943, Republic)—Johnny April
CALIFORNIA JOE (1944, Republic)—Lt. Joe Weldon
MY BUDDY (1944, Republic)—Eddie Ballinger
SLIPPY MCGEE (1948, Republic)—Slippy McGee
THE CHICAGO KID (1945, Republic)—Joe Ferrill
I SHOT BILLY THE KID (1950, Lippert)—Billy the Kid

BARRY, JOAN
RICH AND STRANGE (1932, GB, British International)—Emily Hill
SALLY BISHOP (1932, GB, British Lion)—Sally Bishop
MRS. DANE'S DEFENCE (1933, GB, Paramount)—Mrs. Dane

BARRY, LEON
THE THREE MUSKETEERS, (1921, Silent, United Artists)—Athos

BARRY, NEILL
O.C. AND STIGGS (1987, MGM/United Artists)—Mark Stiggs

BARRY, RAYMOND
DADDY'S BOYS (1988, Concorde)—Daddy

BARRY, WESLEY
DINTY (1920, Silent, First National)—Dinty
PENROD (1922, Silent, Associated First National)—Penrod Schofield
THE COUNTRY KID (1923, Silent, Warners)—Ben Applegate
BATTLING BUNYON (1925, Silent, Crown)—Aiken "Battling" Bunyon
THE FIGHTING CUB (1925, Silent, Truart)—Thomas Patrick O'Toole

BARRYMORE, DREW
FIRESTARTER (1984, Universal)—Charlie McGee
IRRECONCILABLE DIFFERENCES (1984, Warners)—Casey Brodsky
GUNCRAZY (1992, Zeta Entertainment)—Anita Minteer
POISON IVY (1992, New Line)—Ivy

BARRYMORE, ETHEL
OUR MRS. MCCHESNEY (1918, Silent, Metro)—Emma McChesney
RASPUTIN AND THE EMPRESS (1932, MGM)—Empress Alexandra
KIND LADY (1951, MGM)—Mary Herries

BARRYMORE, JOHN
THE INCORRIGIBLE DUKANE (1915, Silent, Paramount)—James A. Dukane, Jr.
DR. JEKYLL AND MR. HYDE (1920, Silent, Paramount)—Dr. Jekyll & Mr. Hyde
SHERLOCK HOLMES (1922, Silent, Goldwyn)—Sherlock Holmes
BEAU BRUMMELL (1924, Silent, Warners)—George Bryan Brummell
DON JUAN (1926, Silent, Warners)—Don Juan
BELOVED ROGUE (1927, Silent, United Artists)—Francois Villon
GENERAL CRACK (1929, Warners)—General Crack
THE MAN FROM BLANKLEY'S (1930, Warners)—Lord Strathpeffer
THE MAD GENIUS (1931, Warners)—Ivan Tzarakov
SVENGALI (1931, Warners)—Svengali
ARSENE LUPIN (1932, MGM)—Duke of Charmerace (Arsene Lupin)
STATE'S ATTORNEY (1932, RKO)—Tom Cardigan
COUNSELLOR-AT-LAW (1933, Universal)—George Simon
TOPAZE (1933, RKO)—Auguste Topaze
LONG LOST FATHER (1934, RKO)—Carl Bellaire
THE GREAT MAN VOTES (1939, RKO)—Vance
THE GREAT PROFILE (1940, 20th Century Fox)—Evans Garrick

BARRYMORE, JOHN JR.
THE SUNDOWNERS (1950, Eagle-Lion)—Jeff Cloud

BARRYMORE, LIONEL
HIS FATHER'S SON (1917, Silent, Metro)—J. Dabney Barron
THE MASTER MIND (1920, Silent, First National)—Henry Allen
JIM THE PENMAN (1921, Silent, Associated First National)—James Ralston

11

BOOMERANG BILL (1922, Silent, Paramount)—Boomerang Bill
I AM THE MAN (1924, Silent, Chadwick)—James McQuade
THE IRON MAN (1925, Silent, Chadwick)—Philip Durban
GUILTY HANDS (1931, MGM)—Richard Grant
RASPUTIN AND THE EMPRESS (1932, MGM)—Rasputin
ONE MAN'S JOURNEY (1933, RKO)—Dr. Eli Watt
THE RETURN OF PETER GRIMM (1935, RKO)—Peter Grimm
CALLING DR. GILLESPIE (1942, MGM)—Dr. Leonard Gillespie
DR. GILLESPIE'S NEW ASSISTANT (1942, MGM)—Dr. Leonard Gillespie
DR. GILLESPIE'S CRIMINAL CASE (1943, MGM)—Dr. Leonard Gillespie
THREE MEN IN WHITE (1944, MGM)—Dr. Leonard Gillespie
THREE WISE FOOLS (1946, MGM)—Dr. Richard Gaunght

BARTHELMESS, RICHARD
I'LL GET HIM YET (1919, Silent, First National)—Scoop McCreedy
TOL'ABLE DAVID (1921, Silent, Associated First National)—David Kinemon
THE BOND BOY (1922, Silent, Associated First National)—Peter Newbolt
SONNY (1922, Silent, Associated First National)—Sonny
THE AMATEUR GENTLEMAN (1926, Silent, First National)—Barnabas Barty
RANSON'S FOLLY (1926, Silent, First National)—Lt. Ranson
THE WHITE BLACK SHEEP (1926, Silent, First National)—Robert Kincarin
SON OF THE GODS (1930, Warners)—Sam Lee
ALIAS THE DOCTOR (1932, First National)—Karl Muller
A MODERN HERO (1934, Warners)—Pierre Radler
SPY OF NAPOLEON (1939, GB, Syndicate)—Gerard de Lancy

BARTHOLOMEW, FREDDIE
DAVID COPPERFIELD (1935, MGM)—David Copperfield as a boy
THE DEVIL IS A SISSY (1936, MGM)—Claude
LITTLE LORD FAUNTLEROY (1936, United Artists)—Ceddie
KIDNAPPED (1938, 20th Century Fox)—David Balfour
LORD JEFF (1938, MGM)—Geoffrey Braemer
TWO BRIGHT BOYS (1939, Universal)—David Harrington
SWISS FAMILY ROBINSON (1940, RKO)—Jack Robinson

BARTLAM, DOROTHY
HER NIGHT OUT (1932, GB, Warners)—Kitty Vickery

BARTON, BUZZ
THE BANTAM COWBOY (1928, Silent, FBO)—David "Red" Hepner
THE FRECKLED RASCAL (1929, Silent, FBO/RKO)—Red Hepner

BARTON, JAMES
CAPTAIN HURRICANE (1935, RKO)—Zenas Henry

BARY, NEILL
JOEY (1985, GB, Satori)—Joey

BARYSHINIKOV, MIKHAIL
DANCERS (1987, Cannon)—Anton "Tony" Sergoyev

BASEHART, RICHARD
HE WALKED BY NIGHT (1948, Eagle-Lion)—Davis Morgan
THE BROTHERS KARAMAZOV (1958, MGM)—Ivan Karamazov
HITLER (1962, Allied Artists)—Adolf Hitler

BASINGER, KIM
BLIND DATE (1987, Tri-Star)—Nadia Gates
NADINE (1987, Tri-Star)—Nadine Hightower
MY STEPMOTHER IS AN ALIEN (1988, Weintraub)—Celeste Mills

BASQUETTE, LINA
THE GODLESS GIRL (1929, Pathe)—Judith Craig

BASS, ALFIE
THE LAVENDER HILL MOB (1951, GB, Ealing)—Shorty

BATEMAN, JASON
TEEN WOLF TOO (1987, Atlantic)—Todd Howard

BATES, ALAN
THE FIXER (1968, MGM)—Yakov Bok
BUTLEY (1974, GB, American Film Theatre)—Ben Butley
RETURN OF THE SOLDIER (1983, GB, 20th Century Fox)—Chris

BATES, BARBARA
JUNE BRIDE (1948, Warners)—Jeanne Brinker

BATES, RALPH
THE HORROR OF FRANKENSTEIN (1970, GB, Hammer/EMI)—Victor Frankenstein
DR. JEKYLL AND SISTER HYDE (1971, GB, Hammer)—Dr. Jekyll

BAUER, STEVEN
THIEF OF HEARTS (1985, Paramount)—Scott Muller

BAXTER, ALAN
MY SON IS A CRIMINAL (1939, Columbia)—Tim Halloran, Jr.
BAD MEN OF MISSOURI (1941, Warners)—Jesse James

BAXTER, ANNE
GUEST IN THE HOUSE (1944, United Artists)—Evelyn Heath
ALL ABOUT EVE (1950, 20th Century Fox)—Eve Harrington
MY WIFE'S BEST FRIEND (1952, 20th Century Fox)—Virginia Mason
THREE VIOLENT PEOPLE (1956, Paramount)—Lorna Hunter Saunders
THE LATE LIZ (1971, Gateway)—Liz Adams Hatch

BAXTER, BERYL
IDOL OF PARIS (1948, GB, Warners)—Theresa

BAXTER, FARNHAM
MEET THE DUKE (1949, GB, Associated British)—Duke Hogan

BAXTER, JANE
CONFIDENTIAL LADY (1939, GB, Warners)—Jill Trevor
DEATH OF AN ANGEL (1952, GB, Hammer)—Mary Welling

BAXTER, WARNER
HIS FORGOTTEN WIFE (1924, Silent, Film Booking)—Donald Allen/John Rolfe
THE GREAT GATSBY (1926, Paramount)—Jay Gatsby
THE COWARD (1927, Silent, R-C Pictures)—Clinton Philbrook
CRAIG'S WIFE (1928, Silent, Pathe)—Walter Craig
SUCH MEN ARE DANGEROUS (1930, Fox)—Ludwig Kranz
CISCO KID (1931, Fox)—Cisco Kid
DADDY LONG LEGS (1931, Fox)—Jervis Pendleton
DOCTORS' WIVES (1931, Fox)—Dr. Judson Penning

THE SQUAW MAN (1931, MGM)—Capt. James Wynnegate (Jim Carsten)

AMATEUR DADDY (1932, Fox)—Jim Gladden

SIX HOURS TO LIVE (1932, Fox)—Capt. Paul Onslow

KING OF BURLESQUE (1936, 20th Century Fox)—Kerry Bolton

THE PRISONER OF SHARK ISLAND (1936, 20th Century Fox)—Dr. Samuel A. Mudd

ROBIN HOOD OF EL DORADO (1936, MGM)—Joaquin Murrieta

WHITE HUNTER (1936, 20th Century Fox)—Capt. Clark Rutledge

WIFE, DOCTOR AND NURSE (1937, 20th Century Fox)—Dr. Judd Lewis

I'LL GIVE A MILLION (1938, 20th Century Fox)—Tony Newlander

RETURN OF THE CISCO KID (1939, 20th Century Fox)—Cisco Kid

WIFE, HUSBAND AND FRIEND (1939, 20th Century Fox)—Leonard Borland

ADAM HAD FOUR SONS (1941, Columbia)—Adam Stoddard

CRIME DOCTOR (1943, Columbia)—Dr. Robert Ordway

THE CRIME DOCTOR'S STRANGEST CASE (1943, Columbia)—Dr. Robert Ordway

THE CRIME DOCTOR'S CHALLENGE (1945, Columbia)—Dr. Robert Ordway

THE CRIME DOCTOR'S WARNING (1945, Columbia)—Dr. Robert Ordway

THE CRIME DOCTOR'S MAN HUNT (1946, Columbia)—Dr. Robert Ordway

THE CRIME DOCTOR'S GAMBLE (1947, Columbia)—Dr. Robert Ordway

THE GENTLEMAN FROM NOWHERE (1948, Columbia)—Earl Donovan

THE CRIME DOCTOR'S DIARY (1949, Columbia)—Dr. Robert Ordway

PRISON WARDEN (1949, Columbia)—Victor Burnell

BAYLEY, HILDA

MADAME LOUISE (1951, GB, Butchers)—Mme. Louise

BAYNE, BEVERLY

HER MARRIAGE VOW (1924, Silent, Warners)—Carol Hilton

BEAL, CINDY

SLAVE GIRLS FROM BEYOND INFINITY (1987, Titan/Urban Classics)—Tisa

BEAL, JOHN

THE LITTLE MINISTER (1934, RKO)—Gavin

LADDIE (1935, RKO)—Laddie Stanton

THE MAN WHO FOUND HIMSELF (1937, RKO)—Jim Stanton

KEY WITNESS (1947, Columbia)—Milton Higby

MESSENGER OF PEACE (1950, Astor)—Pastor Armin Ritter

MY SIX CONVICTS (1952, Columbia)—Doc

THE VAMPIRE (1957, United Artists)—Dr. Paul Beecher

BEALS, JENNIFER

THE BRIDE (1985, Columbia)—Eva

CINDERELLA (1985, Faerie Tale Theatre)—Cinderella

BEART, EMMANUELLE

DATE WITH AN ANGEL (1987, De Laurentiis)—Angel

BEATTIE, JIM

THE GREAT WHITE HOPE (1970, 20th Century Fox)—The Kid

BEATTY, NED

HEAR MY SONG (1991, GB, Miramax)—Josef Locke

BEATTY, ROBERT

GREEN FINGERS (1947, Anglo-American)—Thomas Stone

BEATTY, WARREN

DICK TRACY (1990, Buena Vista)—Dick Tracy

MICKEY ONE (1965, Columbia)—Mickey One

BONNIE AND CLYDE (1967, Warners)—Clyde Barrow

MCCABE AND MRS. MILLER (1971, Warners)—John McCabe

BUGSY (1991, Tri-Star)—Ben "Bugsy" Siegel

BEAUMONT, ENA

THE GIRL FROM DOWNING STREET (1918, GB, Silent, Butchers)—Peggy Marsden

PATRICIA BRENT, SPINSTER (1919, GB, Garrick)—Patricia Brent

BEBAN, GEORGE

THE ITALIAN (1915, Silent, New York Motion Picture)—The Italian

JULES OF THE STRONG HEART (1918, Silent, Paramount)—Jules Lemaire

ONE MORE AMERICAN (1918, Silent, Paramount)—Luigi Ricardo

THE LOVES OF RICARDO (1926, Silent, Beban)—Ricardo

BECKETT, SCOTTY

MICHAEL O'HALLORAN (1948, Monogram)—Michael O'Halloran

CORKY OF GASOLINE ALLEY (1951, Columbia)—Corky Wallett

BECKLEY, TONY

WHEN A STRANGER CALLS (1979, Columbia)—Curt Duncan

BECKWITH, REGINALD

MEN OF SHERWOOD FOREST (1957, GB, Hammer)—Friar Tuck

BEDELIA, BONNIE

LOVERS AND OTHER STRANGERS (1970, ABC/Cinerama)—Susan Henderson

THE STRANGE VENGEANCE OF ROSALIE (1972, 20th Century Fox)—Rosalie

HEART LIKE A WHEEL (1983, 20th Century Fox)—Shirley "Cha Cha" Muldowney

THE STRANGER (1987, Columbia)—Alice Kildee

BEDFORD, BARBARA

CINDERELLA OF THE HILLS (1921, Silent, Fox)—Norris Gradley

THE NOTORIOUS LADY (1927, Silent, First National)—Mary Marlowe

MARRY THE GIRL (1928, Silent, Sterling)—Elinor

BEDI, KABIR

SATAN'S MISTRESS (1982, Motion Picture Marketing)—The Spirit

BEE, MOLLY

GOING STEADY (1958, Columbia)—Julie Ann Turner

BEECROFT, DAVID

THE RAIN KILLER (1990, Concorde)—Dalton

BEERY, NOAH

HELLSHIP BRONSON (1928, Silent, Gotham)—Capt. Ira Bronson

PANAMINT'S BAD MAN (1938, 20th Century Fox)—Gorman

BEERY, NOAH JR.
STORMY (1935, Universal)—Stormy
THE DALTONS RIDE AGAIN (1945, Universal)—Ben Dalton

BEERY, WALLACE
CASEY AT THE BAT (1927, Silent, Paramount)—Casey
FIREMAN, SAVE MY CHILD (1927, Silent, Paramount)—Elmer
PARTNERS IN CRIME (1928, Silent, Paramount)—Mike Doolin
MIN AND BILL (1930, MGM)—Bill
THE CHAMP (1931, MGM)—Champ
HELL DIVERS (1932, MGM)—Windy
THE MIGHTY BARNUM (1934, United Artists)—Phineas T. Barnum
VIVA VILLA! (1934, MGM)—Pancho Villa
O'SHAUGHNESSY'S BOY (1935, MGM)—Windy O'Shaughnessy
OLD HUTCH (1936, MGM)—Hutch
THE GOOD OLD SOAK (1937, MGM)—Clem Hawley
BAD MAN OF BRIMSTONE (1938, MGM)—Trigger Bill
SERGEANT MADDEN (1939, MGM)—Shaun Madden
THE MAN FROM DAKOTA (1940, MGM)—Sgt. Barstow
THE BAD MAN (1941, MGM)—Pancho Lopez
BARNACLE BILL (1941, MGM)—Bill Johansen
BARBARY COAST GENT (1944, MGM)—Honest Plush Brannon
BAD BASCOMB (1946, MGM)—Zed Bascomb
THE MIGHTY MCGURK (1946, MGM)—Roy "Slag" McGurk
ALIAS A GENTLEMAN (1948, MGM)—Jim Breedin
BIG JACK (1949, MGM)—Big Jack Horner

BEGLEY, ED
12 ANGRY MEN (1957, United Artists)—Juror No. 10

BEGLEY, ED JR.
THE APPLEGATES (1990, Australia, Roadshow)—Dick Applegate

BEL GEDDES, BARBARA
I REMEMBER MAMA (1948, RKO)—Katrin
FIVE BRANDED WOMEN (1960, Paramount)—Marja

BELAFONTE, HARRY
THE ANGEL LEVINE (1970, United Artists)—Alexander Levine
BUCK AND THE PREACHER (1972, Columbia)—Preacher

BELL, CYNTHIA
THOSE REDHEADS FROM SEATTLE (1953, Paramount)—Connie Edmonds

BELL, JEANNE
TNT JACKSON (1975, New World)—TNT Jackson

BELL, KAY
THOSE REDHEADS FROM SEATTLE (1953, Paramount)—Neil Edmonds

BELL, REX
THE COWBOY KID (1928, Silent, Fox)—Jim Barrett
THE IDAHO KID (1937, Republic)—Idaho

BELL, ROBERT
THE GARBAGE PAIL KIDS (1987, Atlantic)—Foul Phil

BELL, TOM
THE SAILOR'S RETURN (1978, GB, Ospery)—William Targett

BELLAMY, FRANKLYN
THE BARTON MYSTERY (1932, GB, British & Dominions)—Gerald Barton

BELLAMY, MADGE
HIS FORGOTTEN WIFE (1924, Silent, Film Booking)—Suzanne Rolfe
BERTHA THE SEWING MACHINE GIRL (1926, Silent, Fox)—Bertha Sloan
SANDY (1926, Silent, Fox)—Sandy McNeil
LORNA DOONE (1927, Silent, Associated First National)—Lorna Doone
SILK LEGS (1927, Fox)—Ruth Stevens
THE TELEPHONE GIRL (1927, Silent, Lasky)—Kitty O'Brien
THE PLAY GIRL (1928, Silent, Fox)—Madge Norton
FUGITIVES (1929, Silent, Fox)—Alice Carroll
WHITE ZOMBIE (1932, United Artists)—Madeline Short

BELLAMY, RALPH
THIS MAN IS MINE (1934, RKO)—Jim Dunlap
THE HEALER (1935, Monogram)—The Doctor
MAN WHO LIVED TWICE (1936, Columbia)—James Blake/Slick Rawley
WILD BRIAN KENT (1936, 20th Century Fox)—Brian Kent
THE CRIME OF DR. HALLET (1938, Universal)—Dr. Paul Hallet
ELLERY QUEEN, MASTER DETECTIVE (1940, Columbia)—Ellery Queen
ELLERY QUEEN AND THE MURDER RING (1941, Columbia)—Ellery Queen
ELLERY QUEEN AND THE PERFECT CRIME (1941, Columbia)—Ellery Queen
ELLERY QUEEN'S PENTHOUSE MYSTERY (1941, Columbia)—Ellery Queen
THE GREAT IMPERSONATION (1942, Universal)—Baron von Ragenstein & Sir Edward Dominey

BELLER, KATHLEEN
TIME TRACKERS (1989, Concorde)—R.J.

BELMORE, ALICE
THE GIRL WHO TOOK THE WRONG TURN (1915, GB, Silent, British Empire)—Sophie Coventry

BELTRAN, ROBERT
EATING RAOUL (1982, 20th Century Fox)—Raoul
LATINO (1986, Cinecom)—Eddie Guerrero
KISS ME A KILLER (1991, Califilm)—Tony

BELUSHI, JAMES
THE PRINCIPAL (1987, Tri-Star)—Rick Latimer
REAL MEN (1987, MGM/United Artists)—Nick Pirandello
MR. DESTINY (1990, Buena Vista)—Larry Burrows
TAKING CARE OF BUSINESS (1990, Buena Vista)—Jimmy

BELUSHI, JOHN
OLD BOYFRIENDS (1979, Avco Embassy)—Eric Katz
THE BLUES BROTHERS (1980, Universal)—Joliet Jake
NEIGHBORS (1981, Columbia)—Earl Keese

BELZER, RICHARD
THE WRONG GUYS (1988, New World)—Belz

BENDIX, WILLIAM
ABROAD WITH TWO YANKS (1944, United Artists)—Biff Koraski

THE HAIRY APE (1944, United Artists)—Hank Smith
DON JUAN QUILLIGAN (1945, 20th Century Fox)—Patrick
Quilligan
THE BABE RUTH STORY (1948, Monogram/Allied Artists)—
George Herman "Babe" Ruth
THE LIFE OF RILEY (1949, Universal)—Chester A. Riley
KILL THE UMPIRE (1950, Columbia)—Bill Johnson

BENEDICT, BILLY
THREE KIDS AND A QUEEN (1935, Universal)—Flash

BENEDICT, RICHARD
OCEAN'S ELEVEN (1960, Warners)—"Curly" Steffens

BENING, ANNETTE
THE GRIFTERS (1990, Miramax)—Myra Langtry

BENJAMIN, RICHARD
THE MARRIAGE OF A YOUNG STOCKBROKER (1971, 20th
Century Fox)—William Arlen
PORTNOY'S COMPLAINT (1972, Warners)—Alexander Portnoy

BENNETT, ALMA
TWO MEN AND A MAID (1929, Tiffany)—Rose

BENNETT, BELLE
STELLA DALLAS (1925, Silent, United Artists)—Stella Dallas
RECKLESS LADY (1926, Silent, First National)—Mrs. Fleming
MOLLY AND ME (1929, Tiffany/Stahl)—Molly Wilson

BENNETT, BRUCE (HERMAN BRIX)
NEW ADVENTURES OF TARZAN (1935, Republic)—Tarzan
TARZAN AND THE GREEN GODDESS (1938, Principal)—Tarzan
THE OFFICER AND THE LADY (1941, Columbia)—Bob Conlon
UNDERGROUND AGENT (1942, Columbia)—Lee Graham
U-BOAT PRISONER (1944, Columbia)—Archie Gibbs
THE MAN I LOVE (1946, Warners)—Sam Thomas
THE YOUNGER BROTHERS (1949, Warners)—Jim Younger
DANIEL BOONE, TRAIL BLAZER (1957, Republic)—
Daniel Boone
FIEND OF DOPE ISLAND (1961, Essanjay)—Charlie Davis

BENNETT, CONSTANCE
RICH PEOPLE (1929, Pathe)—Connie Hayden
BORN TO LOVE (1931, RKO)—Doris Kendall
BOUGHT (1931, Warners)—Stephany Dale
LADY WITH A PAST (1932, RKO)—Venice Muir
TWO AGAINST THE WORLD (1932, Warners)—Dell Hamilton
OUTCAST LADY (1934, MGM)—Iris March
LADIES IN LOVE (1936, 20th Century Fox)—Yoli Haydn
MADAME SPY (1942, Universal)—Joan Bannister
SMART WOMAN (1948, Monogram-Allied Artists)—Paula
Rogers

BENNETT, ENID
THE LITTLE BROTHER (1917, Silent, Triangle)—Jerry Ross
KEEPING UP WITH LIZZIE (1921, Silent, Hodkinson)—Lizzie
Henshaw

BENNETT, JOAN
DOCTORS' WIVES (1931, Fox)—Nina Wyndham
CARELESS LADY (1932, Fox)—Sally Brown/Mrs. Illington
ME AND MY GAL (1932, Fox)—Helen Riley
SHE WANTED A MILLIONAIRE (1932, Fox)—Jane Miller

THE TRIAL OF VIVIENNE WARE (1932, Fox)—Vivienne Ware
WILD GIRL (1932, Fox)—Salomy Jane Clay
LITTLE WOMEN (1933, RKO)—Amy March
SHE COULDN'T TAKE IT (1935, Columbia)—Carol Van Dyke
BIG BROWN EYES (1936, Paramount)—Eve Fallon
TWO IN A CROWD (1936, Universal)—Julia Wayne
I MET MY LOVE AGAIN (1938, United Artists)—Julie
HOUSEKEEPER'S DAUGHTER (1939, United Artists)—Hilda
THE MAN I MARRY (1940, 20th Century Fox)—Carol Hoffman
SHE KNEW ALL THE ANSWERS (1941, Columbia)—Gloria
Winters
THE WIFE TAKES A FLYER (1942, Columbia)—Anita Woverman
THE WOMAN IN THE WINDOW (1945, RKO)—Alice Reed
THE MACOMBER AFFAIR (1947, United Artists)—Margaret
Macomber
NAVY WIFE (1956, Allied Artists)—Peg Blain

BENNETT, JOHN
THE BARBER OF STAMFORD HILL (1963, GB, British Lion)—
Mr. Figg

BENNETT, LINDA
THE SEVEN LITTLE FOYS (1955, Paramount)—Madeline Foy

BENNETT, MICKEY
THE DUMMY (1929, Paramount)—Barney

BENNETT, RICHARD
THE MAGNIFICENT AMBERSONS (1942, RKO)—Major
Amberson

BENNISON, LOUIS
OH, JOHNNY (1919, Silent, Goldwyn)—Johnny Burke

BENNY, JACK
THE MEDICINE MAN (1930, Tiffany)—Dr. John Harvey
MAN ABOUT TOWN (1939, Paramount)—Bob Temple
BUCK BENNY RIDES AGAIN (1940, Paramount)—Buck Benny
CHARLEY'S AUNT (1941, 20th Century Fox)—Babbs (Lord
Babberly)
THE MEANEST MAN IN THE WORLD (1943, 20th Century
Fox)—Richard Clark

BENSON, JODI
THE LITTLE MERMAID (1989, Buena Vista)—Voice of Ariel

BENSON, ROBBY
JORY (1972, Avco Embassy)—Jory
JEREMY (1973, United Artists)—Jeremy Jones
ODE TO BILLY JOE (1976, Warners)—Billy Joe McAllister
ONE ON ONE (1977, Warners)—Henry Steele
RUNNING BRAVE (1983, Canada, Buena Vista)—Billy Mills
HARRY AND SON (1984, Orion)—Howard
BEAUTY AND THE BEAST (1991, Animated, Buena Vista/
Disney)—Voice of the Beast

BENTLEY, JOHN
CALLING PAUL TEMPLE (1948, GB, Nettleford)—Paul Temple
PAUL TEMPLE'S TRIUMPH (1951, GB, Butchers)—Paul Temple
PAUL TEMPLE RETURNS (1952, GB, Butchers)—Paul Temple
SALUTE THE TOFF (1952, GB, Butchers)—Hon. Richard
Rollison

BERENGER, TOM
BUTCH AND SUNDANCE, THE EARLY DAYS (1979, 20th Century
Fox)—Butch Cassidy

15

DOGS OF WAR (1980, GB, United Artists)—Drew
PLATOON (1987, Orion)—Sgt. Barnes
SOMEONE TO WATCH OVER ME (1987, Columbia)—Mike Keegan
SHATTERED (1991, MGM/Pathe)—Dan Merrick

BERG, GERTRUDE
THE GOLDBERGS (1950, Paramount)—Molly Goldberg

BERGEN, CANDICE
THE GROUP (1966, United Artists)—Lakey Eastlake
T.R. BASKIN (1971, Paramount)—T.R. Baskin
RICH AND FAMOUS (1981, MGM/United Artists)—Merry Noel Blake

BERGEN, POLLY
KISSES FOR MY PRESIDENT (1964, Warners)—Leslie McCloud

BERGER, BERT
PEACE FOR A GUNFIGHTER (1967, Crown)—"The Preacher"

BERGIN, PATRICK
SLEEPING WITH THE ENEMY (1991, 20th Century Fox)—Martin

BERGMAN, INGRID
NOTORIOUS (1946, RKO)—Alicia Huberman
JOAN OF ARC (1948, RKO)—Joan of Arc
ANASTASIA (1956, 20th Century Fox)—Anastasia
FROM THE MIXED-UP FILES OF MRS. BASIL E. FRANKWEILER (1973, Cinema 3)—Mrs. Frankweiler

BERGMAN, SANDAHL
PROGRAMMED TO KILL (1987, Trans World)—Samira

BERGNER, ELIZABETH
CATHERINE THE GREAT (1934, GB, LMP/United Artists)—Catherine II
ESCAPE ME NEVER (1935, GB, United Artists)—Gemma Jones
STOLEN LIFE (1939, Paramount)—Sylvina & Martina Lawrence

BERLIN, JEANNIE
SHEILA LEVINE IS DEAD AND LIVING IN NEW YORK (1975, Paramount)—Sheila Levine

BERNARD, SUE
STRANGER IN HOLLYWOOD (1968, Roda/Emerson)—Woman

BERNHARDT, SARAH
QUEEN ELIZABETH (1912, Silent, Famous Players)—Elizabeth I

BEROVA, OLINKA
THE VENGEANCE OF SHE (1968, GB, Hammer-Seven Arts)—Carol/"She"

BEST, EDNA
MICHAEL AND MARY (1932, GB, Gainsborough)—Mary Rowe
SWISS FAMILY ROBINSON (1940, RKO)—Elizabeth Robinson

BEST, JAMES
SEVEN ANGRY MEN (1955, Allied Artists)—James Brown
MAN ON THE PROWL (1957, United Artists)—Doug Gerhardt

BESWICK, MARTINE
PREHISTORIC WOMEN (1967, GB, 20th Century Fox)—Queen Kari
DR. JEKYLL AND SISTER HYDE (1971, GB, Hammer)—Sister Hyde

THE HAPPY HOOKER GOES TO HOLLYWOOD (1980, Cannon)—Xaviera Hollander
THE OFFSPRING (1987, Conquest/TMS)—Katherine White

BEVAN, PAMELA
DARBY AND JOAN (1937, GB, MGM)—Darby Templeton

BEVAR, CAROL
WAITRESS (1982, Troma)—Jennifer

BEY, TURHAN
THE SPIRITUALIST (1948, Eagle-Lion)—Alexis
PRISONERS OF THE CASBAH (1953, Columbia)—Ahmed

BEYMER, RICHARD
ADVENTURES OF A YOUNG MAN (1962, 20th Century Fox)—Nick Adams

BICKFORD, CHARLES
HELL'S HEROES (1930, Universal)—Bob Sangster
A NOTORIOUS GENTLEMAN (1935, Universal)—Kirk Allen
PRIDE OF THE MARINES (1936, Columbia)—Steve Riley
GUILTY OF TREASON (1950, Eagle-Lion)—Cardinal Mindszenty

BIEHN, MICHAEL
THE FAN (1981, Paramount)—Douglas Breen
NAVY SEALS (1990, Orion)—Curran

BIJUERENDA, FREDERICK
MAN OF AFRICA (1956, GB, Eden)—Jonathan

BILLINGSLEY, PETER
THE DIRT BIKE KID (1985, Cinema Group)—Jack Simmons

BINNEY, CONSTANCE
THE CASE OF BECKY (1921, Silent, Realart)—Dorothy Stone/Becky
SUCH A LITTLE QUEEN (1921, Silent, Realart)—Ann Victoria of Gzbfernigambia
THE SLEEPWALKER (1922, Silent, Paramount)—Doris Dumond

BINNS, EDWARD
12 ANGRY MEN (1957, United Artists)—Juror No. 6

BIRD, NORMAN
THE SECRET PARTNER (1961, GB, MGM)—Ralph Beldon

BIRELL, TALA
SHE'S DANGEROUS (1937, Universal)—Stephanie Duval
JOSETTE (1938, 20th Century Fox)—Mme. Josette

BISHOP, JOEY
OCEAN'S ELEVEN (1960, Warners)—"Mushy" O'Conners

BISHOP, JULIE (JACQUELINE WELLS)
THE BOHEMIAN GIRL (1936, MGM)—Arline
PAID TO DANCE (1937, Columbia)—Joan Bradley
THE RANGER AND THE LADY (1940, Republic)—Jane
IDEA GIRL (1946, Universal)—Pat O'Rourke

BISSET, JACQUELINE
THE GRASSHOPPER (1970, National General)—Christine
RICH AND FAMOUS (1981, MGM/United Artists)—Liz Hamilton

BISSON, YANNICK
TOBY MCTEAGUE (1986, Canada, Spectrafilm)—Toby McTeague

BLACK, KAREN
LITTLE LAURA AND BIG JOHN (1973, Crown)—Laura

BLACKMAN, TOMMY
THE HALF PINT (1960, Sterling)—The Half Pint

BLACKWELL, CARYLE
THE MAN WHO COULD NOT LOSE (1914, Silent, Favorite)—
Champneys Carter
HIS BROTHER'S WIFE (1916, Silent, World)—Howard Barton
HIGH ROYAL HIGHNESS (1918, Silent, World)—Jack Christie
THE BELOVED VAGABOND (1923, Silent, GB, Astra-National)—
Gaston de Nerac

BLAIN, LUCITA
FIVE BOLD WOMEN (1960, Citation)—Maria the Knife

BLAINE, VIVIAN
DOLL FACE (1945, 20th Century Fox)—Doll Face
THREE LITTLE GIRLS IN BLUE (1946, 20th Century Fox)—Liz
GUYS AND DOLLS (1955, MGM)—Miss Adelaide

BLAIR, JANET
THREE GIRLS ABOUT TOWN (1941, Columbia)—Charity Banner
MY SISTER EILEEN (1942, Columbia)—Eileen Sherwood

BLAIR, LINDA
WILD HORSE HANK (1979, Canada, Film Consortium of
Canada)—Hank Bradford

BLAIR, LISA
THREE MEN AND A BABY (1987, Buena Vista)—Mary the Baby

BLAIR, MICHELLE
THREE MEN AND A BABY (1987, Buena Vista)—Mary the Baby

BLAISDELL, PAUL
IT CONQUERED THE WORLD (1956, American International)—
Visitor from Venus

BLAKE, JUDITH
WANTED: JANE TURNER (1936, RKO)—Jane Turner

BLAKE, ROBERT
MOKEY (1942, MGM)—Mokey Delano
TELL THEM WILLIE BOY IS HERE (1969, Universal)—
Willie Boy
CORKY (1972, MGM)—Corky

BLAKELY, COLIN
RED MONARCH (1983, GB, Enigma/Goldcrest)—Joseph Stalin

BLAKENEY, OLIVE
LEAVE IT TO BLANCHE (1934, GB, Warners)—Blanche
Wetherby

BLANCHAR, PIERRE
A ROYAL DIVORCE (1938, GB, Paramount)—Napoleon
Bonaparte

BLANCHARD, MARI
SHE DEVIL (1957, 20th Century Fox)—Kyra

BLANE, SALLY
MAYFAIR GIRL (1933, GB, Warners)—Brenda Mason

BLANKFIELD, MARK
JEKYLL AND HYDE. . .TOGETHER AGAIN (1982, Paramount)—
Dr. Jekyll & Mr. Hyde

FRANKENSTEIN GENERAL HOSPITAL (1988, New Star)—Dr.
Bob Frankenstein

BLEES, WILLIAM
FOUR JACKS AND A JILL (1941, RKO)—Eddie

BLINN, HOLBROOK
THE BAD MAN (1923, Silent, Associated First National)—
Pancho Lopez

BLONDELL, JOAN
MISS PINKERTON (1932, First National)—Miss Pinkerton
THREE ON A MATCH (1932, Warners)—Mary Keaton
BLONDIE JOHNSON (1933, Embassy)—Blondie Johnson
BROADWAY BAD (1933, Fox)—Tony Landers
THE GOLD DIGGERS OF 1933 (1933, Warners)—Carol King
DAMES (1934, Warners)—Mabel Anderson
HE WAS HER MAN (1934, Warners)—Rose Lawrence
KANSAS CITY PRINCESS (1934, Warners)—Rosy
SMARTY (1934, Warners)—Vicki Wallace Thorpe
MISS PACIFIC FLEET (1935, Warners)—Gloria Fay
THE TRAVELING SALESLADY (1935, First National)—Angela
Twitchell
GOLD DIGGERS OF 1937 (1936, Warners)—Norma Parry
STAGE STRUCK (1936, Warners)—Peggy Revere
THE KING AND THE CHORUS GIRL (1937, Warners)—Dorothy
STAND-IN (1937, United Artists)—Lester Plum
THERE'S ALWAYS A WOMAN (1938, Columbia)—Sally Reardon
GOOD GIRLS GO TO PARIS (1939, Columbia)—Jenny Swanson
TWO GIRLS ON BROADWAY (1940, MGM)—Molly Mahoney
LADY FOR A NIGHT (1941, Republic)—Jenny Blake
MODEL WIFE (1941, Universal)—Joan Keating Chambers
THREE GIRLS ABOUT TOWN (1941, Columbia)—Hope Banner

BLOOM, LINDSAY
SIX PACK ANNIE (1975, American International)—Annie

BLORE, ERIC
A GENTLEMAN'S GENTLEMAN (1939, GB, First National)—
Heppelwhite

BLOSSOM, ROBERTS
DERANGED (1974, Canada, American International)—
Ezra Cobb

BLUE, MONTE
THE BUSH LEAGUER (1927, Silent, Warners)—Buchanan
"Spec" White
ONE ROUND HOGAN (1927, Silent, Warners)—Robert
Emmett Hogan
THE STOKER (1932, Hoffman-Allied)—Dick

BLUNDELL, GRAEME
ALVIN PURPLE (1974, Australia, Roadshow)—Alvin Purple
ALVIN RIDES AGAIN (1974, Australia, Roadshow)—Alvin Purple
MELVIN, SON OF ALVIN (1984, Australia, Roadshow)—Alvin
Purple

BLUTEAU, LOTHAIRE
BLACK ROBE (1991, Canada/Australia, Goldwyn/Alliance/
Hoyts)—Father Laforgue

BLYTH, ANN
MR. PEABODY AND THE MERMAID (1948, Universal)—
Mermaid

ONCE MORE, MY DARLING (1949, Universal)—Marita Connell

I'LL NEVER FORGET YOU (1951, 20th Century Fox)—Helen Pettigrew

KATIE DID IT (1951, Universal)—Katherine Standish

SALLY AND SAINT ANNE (1952, Universal)—Sally O'Moyne

ROSE MARIE (1954, MGM)—Rose Marie Lemaitre

THE HELEN MORGAN STORY (1959, Warners)—Helen Morgan

BLYTHE, BETTY

QUEEN OF SHEBA (1921, Silent, Fox)—Queen of Sheba

HIS WIFE'S HUSBAND (1922, Silent, Pyramid)—Olympia Brewster

THE DARLING OF THE RICH (1923, Silent, B.B. Productions)—Charmion Winship

THE SPITFIRE (1924, Silent, Associated Exhibitors)—Jean Bronson

A WOMAN'S SECRET (1924, GB, Silent, Graham-Wilcox)—Dolores

BOARDMAN, ELEANOR

SHE GOES TO WAR (1929, United Artists)—Joan Morant

WOMEN LOVE ONCE (1931, Paramount)—Helen Fields

BOEHM, KARL

PEEPING TOM (1960, GB, Anglo-Amalgamated)—Mark Lewis

THE WONDERFUL WORLD OF THE BROTHERS GRIMM (1962, MGM)—Jacob Grimm

BOGARDE, DIRK

THE STRANGER IN BETWEEN (1952, GB, Universal)—Chris Lloyd

DOCTOR IN THE HOUSE (1954, GB, GFD)—Simon Sparrow

DOCTOR AT SEA (1955, GB, Rank)—Simon Sparrow

CAMPBELL'S KINGDOM (1957, GB, Rank)—Bruce Campbell

DOCTOR AT LARGE (1957, GB, Rank)—Simon Sparrow

THE SPANISH GARDENER (1957, GB, Rank)—Jose

DOCTOR IN DISTRESS (1963, GB, Rank)—Simon Sparrow

THE SERVANT (1964, GB, Springbok/Landau)—Hugo Barrett

AGENT 8 3/4 (1965, GB, Rank)—Nicholas Whistler

MCGUIRE, GO HOME! (1966, GB, Rank)—Major McGuire

SEBASTIAN (1968, GB, Paramount)—Sebastian

THE NIGHT PORTER (1974, Avco Embassy)—Max

BOGART, HUMPHREY

KING OF THE UNDERWORLD (1939, Warners)—Joe Gurney

THE RETURN OF DR. X (1939, Warners)—Marshall Quesne/Dr. Maurice Xavier

THEY DRIVE BY NIGHT (1940, Warners)—Paul Fabrini

THE BIG SHOT (1942, Warners)—Duke Berne

TOKYO JOE (1949, Columbia)—Joe Barrett

WE'RE NO ANGELS (1955, Paramount)—Joseph

BOHR, JOSE

ROGUE OF THE RIO GRANDE (1930, World-Wide)—El Malo

BOLAND, MARY

THE PRODIGAL WIFE (1918, Silent, Screencraft)—Marion Farnham

MAMA LOVES PAPA (1933, Paramount)—Jessie Todd

FOUR FRIGHTENED PEOPLE (1934, Paramount)—Mrs. Mardick

MAMA RUNS WILD (1938, Republic)—Alice Summers

BOLES, JOHN

CAPTAIN OF THE GUARD (1930, Universal)—Robert de Lisle

CRAIG'S WIFE (1936, Columbia)—Walter Craig

SHE MARRIED AN ARTIST (1938, Columbia)—Lee Thornwood

BOLGAR, BENJIE

THE LITTLEST HORSE THIEVES (1977, Buena Vista)—Tommy Sadler

BOLGER, RAY

FOUR JACKS AND A JILL (1941, RKO)—Nifty

WHERE'S CHARLEY (1952, GB, Warners)—Charley Wykeham

BOLOGNA, JOSEPH

MADE FOR EACH OTHER (1971, 20th Century Fox)—Gig "Giggy" Pinimba

BOLSTER, ANITA

THE TWO MRS. CARROLLS (1947, Warners)—Christine Carroll

BOND, DEREK

NICHOLAS NICKLEBY (1947, GB, Ealing)—Nicholas Nickleby

POET'S PUB (1949, GB, GFD)—Saturday Keith

BOND, LILLIAN

WHEN STRANGERS MARRY (1933, Columbia)—Marian Drake

BOND, TOMMY

FIVE LITTLE PEPPERS AND HOW THEY GREW (1939, Columbia)—Joey Pepper

FIVE LITTLE PEPPERS AT HOME (1940, Columbia)—Joey Pepper

FIVE LITTLE PEPPERS IN TROUBLE (1940, Columbia)—Joey Pepper

OUT WEST WITH THE PEPPERS (1940, Columbia)—Joey Pepper

BOND, WARD

WAGONMASTER (1950, RKO)—Elder Wiggs

THE HALLIDAY BRAND (1957, United Artists)—Big Dan Halliday

BONERZ, PETER

FUNNYMAN (1967, Korty)—Perry

BONNER, PRISCILLA

GIRLS WHO DARE (1929, Silent, Trinity)—Sally Casey

BOONE, PAT

COUNTRY BOY (1966, Ambassador)—Link Byrd, Jr.

BOONE, RICHARD

I BURY THE LIVING (1958, United Artists)—Robert Kraft

MADRON (1970, Four Star Excelsior)—Madron

BOOTH, CONNIE

AMERICAN FRIENDS (1991, GB, MCEG/Virgin Vision)—Caroline Hartley

BOOTH, JAMES

THE SECRET OF MY SUCCESS (1965, GB, MGM)—Arthur Tate

BOOTH, SHIRLEY

ABOUT MRS. LESLIE (1954, Paramount)—Mrs. Vivien Leslie

THE MATCHMAKER (1958, Paramount)—Dolly Levi

BORDEN, OLIVE

THE JOY GIRL (1927, Silent, Fox)—Jewel Courage

SINNERS IN LOVE (1928, FBO)—Ann Hardy

BORG, VEDA ANN
SHE'S IN THE ARMY (1942, Monogram)—Diane
ACCOMPLICE (1946, Producers Releasing Corp.)—Joyce
Bonniwell

BORGNINE, ERNEST
MARTY (1955, United Artists)—Marty Pilletti
THREE BRAVE MEN (1957, 20th Century Fox)—Bernie
Goldsmith
THE VIKINGS (1958, United Artists)—King Ragnar
MAN ON A STRING (1960, Columbia)—Boris Mitrov
MCHALE'S NAVY (1964, Universal)—Lt. Cmdr. Quinton McHale
THE WILD BUNCH (1969, Warners)—Dutch Engstrom

BORLAND, BARLOW
THE WITNESS VANISHES (1939, Universal)—Lucius Marplay

BORZAGE, FRANK
IMMEDIATE LEE (1916, Silent, Mutual)—Immediate Lee

BOS, JENNY
HENRY VIII AND HIS SIX WIVES (1972, GB, EMI/MGM)—Anne
Of Cleves

BOSCO, PHILIP
FLANAGAN (1985, United Films)—James Flanagan
SUSPECT (1987, Tri-Star)—Paul Gray
THE LUCKIEST MAN IN THE WORLD (1989, Second Effort)—
Sam Posner

BOSWORTH, HOBART
THE SEA WOLF (1913, Silent, Bosworth)—Wolf Larsen
THE BRUTE MASTER (1920, Silent, Pathe)—Bucko McAllister
THE MIRACLE WORKER (1932, Paramount)—The Patriarch

BOTTOMS, JOSEPH
BLIND DATE (1984, New Line)—Jonathan Ratcliffe
BORN TO RACE (1988, MGM-United Artists)—Al Pagura

BOTTOMS, SAM
HUNTER'S BLOOD (1987, Concorde)—David Rand

BOTTOMS, TIMOTHY
JOHNNY GOT HIS GUN (1971, Cinemation)—Joe Bonham
THE CRAZY WORLD OF JULIUS VROODER (1974, 20th Century
Fox)—Julius Vrooder

BOUCHER, PEGI
PRIVATE DUTY NURSES (1972, New World)—Lynn

BOUCHIER, CHILI (DOROTHY)
TO BE A LADY (1934, GB, British And Dominions)—Diane
Whitcombe
GYPSY (1937, First National)—Hassina

BOW, CLARA
LADIES OF THE MOB (1928, Silent, Paramount)—Yvonne
RED HAIR (1928, Silent, Paramount)—"Bubbles" McCoy
THE SATURDAY NIGHT KID (1929, Paramount)—Mayme
HER WEDDING NIGHT (1930, Paramount)—Norma Martin
TRUE TO THE NAVY (1930, Paramount)—Ruby Nolan
CALL HER SAVAGE (1932, Fox)—Nasa

BOWERS, JOHN
THE SKY PILOT (1921, Silent, Universal)—The Sky Pilot
THE BAREFOOT BOY (1923, Silent, Mission)—Dick Alden

BOWIE, DAVID
THE MAN WHO FELL TO EARTH (1976, GB, British Lion)—
Thomas Jerome Newton

BOWKER, JUDI
BROTHER SUN, SISTER MOON (1972, GB, Paramount/
Vic)—Clare

BOXLEITNER, BRUCE
TRON (1982, Buena Vista)—Tron

BOYD, DOROTHY
THE GIRL IN THE NIGHT (1931, GB, Wardour)—Cecile
VIRGINIA'S HUSBAND (1934, GB, Fox)—Virginia Trevor

BOYD, JANETTE
STRIPPER (1986, 20th Century Fox)—The Stripper

BOYD, SARAH
OLD ENOUGH (1984, Orion)—Lonnie Sloan

BOYD, WILLIAM
HER MAN O' WAR (1926, Silent, De Mille Pictures)—Jim
Sanderson
THE VOLGA BOATMAN (1926, Producers Distributing Corp.)—
Feodor
JIM THE CONQUEROR (1927, Silent, Metropolitan)—Jim
Burgess
THE COP (1928, Silent, Pathe)—Pete Smith
HIS FIRST COMMAND (1929, Pathe)—Terry Culver
THE LEATHERNECK (1929, Pathe)—Joseph Hanlon
OFFICER O'BRIEN (1930, Pathe)—Bill O'Brien
HOPALONG CASSIDY (1935, Paramount)—Hopalong Cassidy
FEDERAL AGENT (1936, Republic)—Bob
HOPALONG CASSIDY RETURNS (1936, Paramount)—Hopalong
Cassidy
HOPALONG RIDES AGAIN (1937, Paramount)—Hopalong
Cassidy
CASSIDY OF BAR 20 (1938, Paramount)—Hopalong Cassidy
SANTE FE MARSHALL (1940, Paramount)—Hopalong Cassidy
HOPPY SERVES A WRIT (1943, United Artists)—Hopalong
Cassidy
HOPPY'S HOLIDAY (1947, United Artists)—Hopalong Cassidy

BOYD, WILLIAM 'STAGE'
THE SPOILERS (1930, Paramount)—Alec McNamara

BOYER, CHARLES
CONFIDENTIAL AGENT (1945, Warners)—Denard

BOYLE, PETER
JOE (1970, Cannon)—Joe Curran
CRAZY JOE (1974, Columbia)—Joe Gallo
THE DREAM TEAM (1989, Universal)—Jack McDermott

BRACEWELL, EDITH
REBECCA THE JEWESS (1913, GB, Zenith/Big A)—Rebecca

BRACKEN, EDDIE
HAIL THE CONQUERING HERO (1944, Paramount)—Woodrow
Lafayette Pershing Truesmith

LADIES' MAN (1961, Paramount)—Henry Haskell

BRADEN, CHRISTOPHER
THE KID FROM CANADA (1957, GB, British Lion)—Andy Cameron

BRADLEY, GRACE
RED HEAD (1934, Monogram)—Dale Carter

BRADY, ALICE
THE BALLET GIRL (1916, Silent, World)—La Syrena/Jennie Raeburn
BETSY ROSS (1917, Silent, Peerless/World)—Betsy Ross
THE DANCER'S PERIL (1917, Silent, World)—Vasto/Lola
HER GREAT CHANCE (1918, Silent, Selznick)—Lola Gray
IN THE HOLLOW OF HER HAND (1919, Silent, Select)—Hetty Castelton
ANNA ASCENDS (1922, Silent, Paramount)—Anna Ayyob
SHOULD LADIES BEHAVE? (1933, MGM)—Laura Merrick
STAGE MOTHER (1933, MGM)—Kitty Lorraine
LADY TUBBS (1935, Universal)—Henrietta "Mom" Tubbs
MAMA STEPS OUT (1937, MGM)—Ada Cuppy

BRADY, BOB
OKAY BILL (1971, Four Star Excelsior)—Bill Thornberry

BRADY, SCOTT
THE LAW VS. BILLY THE KID (1954, Columbia)—Billy the Kid
GENTLEMEN MARRY BRUNETTES (1955, United Artists)—David Action
THE VANISHING AMERICAN (1955, Republic)—Blandy
THE STORM RIDER (1957, 20th Century Fox)—Jones
CAIN'S WAY (1969, MDA Associates)—Captain Cain

BRAGA, SONIA
KISS OF THE SPIDER WOMAN (1985, Island Alive)—Spider Woman

BRANAGH, KENNETH
HENRY V (1989, Great Britain, Goldwyn)—King Henry V

BRAND, NEVILLE
GUN BROTHERS (1956, United Artists)—Jubal

BRANDO, MARLON
THE MEN (1950, United Artists)—Ken Wilozek
VIVA ZAPATA! (1952, 20th Century Fox)—Emiliano Zapata
THE WILD ONE (1953, Columbia)—Johnny
GUYS AND DOLLS (1955, MGM)—Sky Masterson
THE YOUNG LIONS (1958, 20th Century Fox)—Christian Diestl
THE FUGITIVE KIND (1960, United Artists)—Val Xavier
THE UGLY AMERICAN (1963, Universal)—Harrison Carter MacWhite
THE GODFATHER (1972, Paramount)—Don Vito Corleone

BRANDON, ERIC
COLOSSUS: THE FORBIN PROJECT (1969, Universal)—Dr. Charles Forbin

BRANDON, HENRY
KILLER AT LARGE (1936, Columbia)—Mr. Zero
DRUMS OF FU MANCHU (1943, Republic)—Fu Manchu

BRASSELLE, KEITH
THE EDDIE CANTOR STORY (1953, Warners)—Eddie Cantor

THREE YOUNG TEXANS (1954, 20th Century Fox)—Tony Ballew

BRAUNER, ASHER
THE BOSS'S SON (1978, New American Cinema)—Bobby

BRAY, ROBERT
MY GUN IS QUICK (1957, United Artists)—Mike Hammer

BREAMER, SYLVIA
THE GIRL OF THE GOLDEN WEST (1923, Silent, Associated First National)—The Girl
HER TEMPORARY HUSBAND (1923, Silent, Associated First National)—Blanche Ingram

BREESE, EDMUND
THE SONG OF THE WAGE SLAVE (1915, Silent, Metro)—Ned Lane

BREL, JACQUES
JACQUES BREL IS ALIVE AND WELL AND LIVING IN PARIS (1979, Am. Film)—Jacques Brel

BREMER, LUCILLE
YOLANDA AND THE THIEF (1945, MGM)—Yolanda

BRENDEL, EL
MR. LEMON OF ORANGE (1931, Fox)—Mr. Lemon
OLSEN'S BIG MOMENT (1934, Fox)—Knute Olsen

BRENNAN, BRID
ANNE DEVLIN (1984, GB, Aeon Films)—Anne Devlin

BRENNAN, CLAIRE
SHE FREAK (1967, Sonney)—Jade Cochran

BRENNAN, WALTER
THREE GODFATHERS (1936, MGM)—Gus
AFFAIRS OF CAPPY RICKS (1937, Republic)—Cappy Ricks
GOD IS MY PARTNER (1957, 20th Century Fox)—Dr. Charles Grayson

BRENT, EVELYN
MY HUSBAND'S WIVES (1924, Silent, Fox)—Marie Wynn
ALIAS MARY FLYNN (1925, Silent, Film Bookings)—Mary Flynn
BROADWAY LADY (1925, Silent, R-C Pictures)—Rosalie Ryan
LADY ROBIN HOOD (1925, Silent, R-C Pictures)—Senorita Catalina/La Ortiga
THE IMPOSTER (1926, Silent, Gothic)—Judith Gilbert/Canada Nell
QUEEN OF DIAMONDS (1926, R-C Pictures)—Jeanette Durant
HIS TIGER LADY (1928, Silent, Paramount)—The Tiger Lady
PAGAN LADY (1931, Columbia)—Dot Hunter
DAUGHTER OF THE TONG (1939, Metropolitan)—The Illustrious One

BRENT, GEORGE
THE GO-GETTER (1937, Warners)—Bill Austin
RACKET BUSTERS (1938, Warners)—Denny Jordan
THE MAN WHO TALKED TOO MUCH (1940, Warners)—Stephen Forbes
'TIL WE MEET AGAIN (1940, Warners)—Dan Hardesty
THEY DARE NOT LOVE (1941, Columbia)—Prince Kurt von Rotenberg
SPECIAL AGENT (1949, Paramount)—Bill Bradford

BREON, EDMOND
THREE MEN IN A BOAT (1958, GB, Romulus/Valiant)—George

BRESSLAW, BERNARD
THE UGLY DUCKLING (1959, GB, Columbia)—Henry Jekyll/
Teddy Hyde

BREWER, TERESA
THOSE REDHEADS FROM SEATTLE (1953, Paramount)—Pat
Edmonds

BRIAN, MARY
HER FATHER SAID NO (1927, Silent, R-C Pictures)—Charlotte
Hamilton
THE MAN I LOVE (1929, Paramount)—Celia Fields
THE ROYAL FAMILY OF BROADWAY (1930, Paramount)—Gwen
Cavendish

BRICE, FANNY
MY MAN (1928, Warners)—Fannie Brand

BRIDGES, BEAU
THE LANDLORD (1970, United Artists)—Elgar Enders
ADAM'S WOMAN (1972, Australia, Warners)—Adam
THE WILD PAIR (1987, Trans World Entertainment)—Joe
Jennings
THE FABULOUS BAKER BROTHERS (1989, 20th Century Fox)—
Frank Baker

BRIDGES, JEFF
THE LAST AMERICAN HERO (1973, 20th Century Fox)—Elroy
Jackson, Jr.
THUNDERBOLT AND LIGHTFOOT (1974, United Artists)—
Lightfoot
CUTTER AND BONE (1981, United Artists)—Richard Bone
STARMAN (1984, Columbia)—Starman
TUCKER, THE MAN AND HIS DREAMS (1988, Paramount)—
Preston Tucker
THE FABULOUS BAKER BROTHERS (1989, 20th Century Fox)—
Jack Baker
SEE YOU IN THE MORNING (1989, Warners)—Larry Livingston

BRIDGES, LLOYD
SECRET SERVICE INVESTIGATOR (1948, Republic)—Steve
Mallory (Dan Redfern)
THE TALL TEXAN (1953, Lippert)—Ben Trask
THE WINTER PEOPLE (1989, Columbia)—William Wright

BRIGGS, JACK
FOUR JACKS AND A JILL (1941, RKO)—Nat

BRIMBLE, NICK
FRANKENSTEIN UNBOUND (1990, 20th Century Fox)—
Frankenstein's Monster

BRISSON, CARL
THE AMERICAN PRISONER (1929, GB, British International)—
Lt. Stark
THE MANXMAN (1929, GB, Silent, British International)—Pete
Quilliam
PRINCE OF ARCADIA (1933, GB, Woolf & Freedman)—
Prince Peter
TWO HEARTS IN WALTZ TIME (1934, GB, Gaumont)—Carl
Hoffman

BRITTON, BARBARA
TILL WE MEET AGAIN (1944, Paramount)—Sister Clothide
THE FABULOUS SUZANNE (1946, Republic)—Suzanne
BANDIT QUEEN (1950, GB, Lippert)—Lola
THE SPOILERS (1955, Universal)—Helen Chester

BRODERICK, HELEN
MEET THE MISSUS (1937, RKO)—Emma Foster

BRODERICK, MATTHEW
FERRIS BUELLER'S DAY OFF (1986, Orion)—Ferris Bueller
FAMILY BUSINESS (1989, Tri-Star)—Adam McMullen
THE FRESHMAN (1990, Tri-Star)—Clark Kellogg

BRODIE, STEVE
RETURN OF THE BADMEN (1948, RKO)—Cole Younger

BRODY, ESTELLE
KITTY (1929, GB, British International)—Kitty Greenwood
THE PLAYTHING (1929, GB, Wardour)—Joyce Bennett

BROGAN, HARRY
THE POACHER'S DAUGHTER (1960, GB, Show Corp. of
America)—Rabbit Hamil

BROLIN, JAMES
GABLE AND LOMBARD (1976, Universal)—Clark Gable

BROMFIELD, JOHN
CRIME AGAINST JOE (1956, United Artists)—Joe Manning

BROMILEY, DOROTHY
GIRLS OF PLEASURE ISLAND (1953, Paramount)—Gloria
Halyard

BROMLEY, SHEILA
REBELLIOUS DAUGHTERS (1938, Times)—Flo

BRONSON, BETTY
PETER PAN (1924, Silent, Paramount)—Peter Pan
A KISS FOR CINDERELLA (1926, Silent, Paramount)—
Cinderella

BRONSON, CHARLES
MACHINE GUN KELLY (1958, American International)—
Machine Gun Kelly
THE MAGNIFICENT SEVEN (1960, United Artists)—O'Reilly
THE DIRTY DOZEN (1967, GB, MGM)—Joseph Wladislaw
CHATO'S LAND (1972, United Artists)—Chato
THE MECHANIC (1972, United Artists)—Arthur Bishop
THE VALACHI PAPERS (1972, Columbia)—Joseph Valachi
MR. MAJESTYK (1974, United Artists)—Vince Majestyk
CHINO (1976, Universal)—Chino Valdez
ST. IVES (1976, Warners)—Raymond St. Ives
MURPHY'S LAW (1986, Cannon)—Jack Murphy

BROOK, CLIVE
THE HOME MAKER (1925, Silent, Universal)—Lester Knapp
THE RETURN OF SHERLOCK HOLMES (1929, Paramount)—
Sherlock Holmes
HUSBAND'S HOLIDAY (1931, Paramount)—George Boyd
THE LAWYER'S SECRET (1931, Paramount)—Drake Norris
THE MAN FROM YESTERDAY (1932, Paramount)—Capt.
Tony Clyde
SHERLOCK HOLMES (1932, Fox)—Sherlock Holmes
IF I WERE FREE (1933, RKO)—Gordon Evers

THE WARE CASE (1939, GB, Ealing)—Sir Hubert Ware
THE SHIPBUILDERS (1957, GB, Anglo-American)—
Leslie Pagan

BROOK, IRINA
THE GIRL IN THE PICTURE (1986, Goldwyn)—Mary

BROOK, LESLEY
PATRICIA GETS HER MAN (1937, GB, First National)—Patricia Fitzroy
SIDE STREET ANGEL (1937, GB, Warners)—Annie

BROOKE, HILARY
THE WOMAN IN GREEN (1945, Universal)—Lydia Marlow
CONFIDENCE GIRL (1952, United Artists)—Mary Webb

BROOKS, ALBERT
LOST IN AMERICA (1985, Warners)—David Howard
DEFENDING YOUR LIFE (1991, Warner Brothers)—Daniel Miller

BROOKS, LESLIE
NINE GIRLS (1944, Columbia)—Roberta Holloway
BLONDE ICE (1949, Film Classics)—Claire

BROOKS, LOUISE
THE CANARY MURDER CASE (1929, Paramount)—Margaret O'Dell

BROOKS, PHYLLIS
CITY GIRL (1938, 20th Century Fox)—Ellen Ward

BROPHY, KEVIN
THE LONG RIDERS (1980, United Artists)—John Younger

BROSNAN, PIERCE
TAFFIN (1988, MGM-United Artists)—Mark Taffin

BROUGH, MARY
A SISTER TO ASSIST'ER (1922, GB, Gaumont)—Mrs. Millie May
A SISTER TO ASSIST'ER (1927, GB, Gaumont)—Mrs. Millie May

BROWN, BRYAN
SWEET TALKER (1991, Australia, Seven Arts/New Line)—Harry Reynolds

BROWN, DARREN
CLARENCE AND ANGEL (1978, Gardner)—Clarence

BROWN, ERIC
THEY'RE PLAYING WITH FIRE (1984, New World)—Jay

BROWN, GIBRAN
MARVIN AND TIGE (1983, Major)—Tige Jackson

BROWN, JAMES
THE YOUNGER BROTHERS (1949, Warners)—Bob Younger

BROWN, JIM
THE DIRTY DOZEN (1967, GB, MGM)—Robert Jefferson
KENNER (1969, MGM)—Kenner
BLACK GUNN (1972, Columbia)—Gunn
SLAUGHTER (1972, American International)—Slaughter
I ESCAPED FROM DEVIL'S ISLAND (1973, United Artists)—Le Bras
SLAUGHTER'S BIG RIP-OFF (1973, American International)—Slaughter

BROWN, JOE E.
MOLLY AND ME (1929, Tiffany/Stahl)—Jim Wilson
LOCAL BOY MAKES GOOD (1931, First National)—John Miller
FIREMAN, SAVE MY CHILD (1932, Warners)—Joe Grant
THE TENDERFOOT (1932, Warners)—Peter Jones
ELMER THE GREAT (1933, Warners)—Elmer
SON OF A SAILOR (1933, First National)—Handsome Callahan
CIRCUS CLOWN (1934, First National)—Happy Howard
SIX-DAY BIKE RIDER (1934, First National)—Wilfred Simpson
A VERY HONORABLE GUY (1934, Warners)—Feet Samuels
ALIBI IKE (1935, Warners)—Frank X. Farrell
POLO JOE (1936, Warners)—Joe Bolton
THE GLADIATOR (1938, Columbia)—Hugo Kipp
SO YOU WON'T TALK (1940, Columbia)—Whiskers/Brute Hanson
SHUT MY BIG MOUTH (1942, Columbia)—Wellington Holmes
CHATTERBOX (1943, Republic)—Rex Vane
CASANOVA IN BURLESQUE (1944, Republic)—Joseph M. Kelly, Jr.

BROWN, JOHNNY MACK
BILLY THE KID (1930, MGM)—Billy Bonney
A LAWMAN IS BORN (1937, Republic)—Tom Mitchell
CHIP OF THE FLYING U (1940, Universal)—Chip Bennett
MAN FROM MONTANA (1941, Universal)—Bob Dawson
FIGHTING BILL FARGO (1942, Universal)—Bill Fargo
FLAME OF THE WEST (1945, Monogram)—John Poore
FRONTIER AGENT (1948, Monogram)—"Nevada" Jack McKensie

BROWN, NANCY
MAID OF THE MOUNTAINS (1932, GB, Wardour)—Teresa

BROWN, PAMELA
THE SECOND MRS. TANQUERAY (1952, GB, Associate British)—Paula Tanqueray

BROWN, THOMAS
HONEY, I SHRUNK THE KIDS (1989, Buena Vista)—Little Russ Thompson

BROWN, TOM
TOM BROWN OF CULVER (1932, Universal)—Tom Brown
TWO ALONE (1934, RKO)—Adam
FRECKLES (1935, RKO)—Freckles
I'D GIVE MY LIFE (1936, Paramount)—Nickie Elkins
OH JOHNNY, HOW YOU CAN LOVE (1940, Universal)—Johnny Sandham
THREE SONS O'GUNS (1941, Warners)—Eddie Patterson
DUKE OF CHICAGO (1949, Republic)—Jimmy Brody
I KILLED WILD BILL HICKOK (1956, Wheeler)—Wild Bill Hickok

BROWN, WALLY
ADVENTURES OF A ROOKIE (1943, RKO)—Jerry Miles
ROOKIES IN BURMA (1943, RKO)—Jerry Miles

BROWNE, CORAL
DREAMCHILD (1985, GB, Universal)—Alice Liddell Hargreaves

BROWNE, LESLIE
DANCERS (1987, Cannon)—Nadine

BROWNE, ROSCOE LEE
THE LIBERATION OF L.B. JONES (1970, Columbia)—L.B. Jones

BROWNING, RICOU
CREATURE FROM THE BLACK LAGOON (1954, Universal)—Gil Man
THE CREATURE WALKS AMONG US (1956, Universal)—The Creature

BRUCE, CAROL
THIS WOMAN IS MINE (1941, Universal)—Julie Morgan

BRUCE, DAVID
YOUNG DANIEL BOONE (1950, Monogram)—Daniel Boone

BRUCE, NIGEL
LORD CAMBER'S LADIES (1932, GB, British International)—Lord Camber

BRUCE, VIRGINIA
SKY BRIDE (1932, Paramount)—Ruth Dunning
JANE EYRE (1935, Monogram)—Jane Eyre
TIMES SQUARE LADY (1935, MGM)—Toni Bradley
BETWEEN TWO WOMEN (1937, MGM)—Patricia Sloan
WIFE, DOCTOR AND NURSE (1937, 20th Century Fox)—Steve
WOMAN AGAINST WOMAN (1937, MGM)—Maris Kent
WOMAN OF GLAMOUR (1937, Columbia)—Gloria Hudson
THERE'S THAT WOMAN AGAIN (1938, Columbia)—Sally Reardon
THE INVISIBLE WOMAN (1941, Universal)—Kitty Carroll

BRUNEL, BERNARD
CONDEMNED TO DEATH (1932, GB, Twickenham)—Tobias Lantern

BRYAN, JANE
GIRLS ON PROBATION (1938, Warners)—Connie Heath
THE SISTERS (1938, Warners)—Grace Elliott

BRYAN, WILLIAM
THE CONFESSIONS OF AMANS (1977, Bauer)—Amans

BRYAR, PAUL
SAINTLY SINNERS (1962, United Artists)—Duke

BRYNNER, YUL
THE KING AND I (1956, 20th Century Fox)—King of Siam
THE BROTHERS KARAMAZOV (1958, MGM)—Dimitri Karamazov
THE BUCCANEER (1958, Paramount)—Jean Lafite
SOLOMON AND SHEBA (1959, United Artists)—Solomon
THE MAGNIFICENT SEVEN (1960, United Artists)—Chris
KINGS OF THE SUN (1963, United Artists)—Black Eagle
INVITATION TO A GUNFIGHTER (1964, United Artists)—Jules Gaspard D'Estaing
THE DOUBLE MAN (1967, Warners)—Dan Slater/Kalmar
VILLA RIDES (1968, Paramount)—Pancho Villa
CATLOW (1971, MGM)—Catlow
THE ULTIMATE WARRIOR (1975, Warners)—Carson

BUCHANAN, JACK
THE AUDACIOUS MR. SQUIRE (1923, Silent, GB, British & Colonial)—Tom Squire
MAN OF MAYFAIR (1931, GB, Paramount)—Lord William
BREWSTER'S MILLIONS (1935, GB, British & Dominion)—Jack Brewster
THE AMAZING MR. FORREST (1943, GB, Producers Releasing)—John Forrest

BUCHHOLZ, HORST
THE MAGNIFICENT SEVEN (1960, United Artists)—Chico

BUCKINGHAM, YVONNE
THE CHRISTINE KEELER AFFAIR (1964, GB, Topaz)—Christine Keeler

BUETEL, JACK
THE OUTLAW (1943, RKO)—Billy the Kid
THE HALF-BREED (1952, RKO)—Charlie Wolf

BUFFALO BILL JR.
HARD HITTIN' HAMILTON (1924, Silent, Action)—Bill Hamilton
THE INTERFERIN' GENT (1927, Silent, Pathe)—Bill Stannard

BUGGY, NIALL
ZARDOZ (1974, GB, 20th Century Fox)—Zardoz

BUJOLD, GENEVIEVE
ISABEL (1968, Canada, Paramount)—Isabel
ANNE OF THE THOUSAND DAYS (1969, GB, Universal)—Anne Boleyn
THE TROJAN WOMEN (1971, Cinerama)—Cassandra
ALEX AND THE GYPSY (1976, 20th Century Fox)—Maritza
THE MODERNS (1988, Alive Films)—Libby Valentin

BUNDY, BROOKE
THE YOUNG RUNAWAYS (1968, MGM)—Shelley Allen

BUONO, VICTOR
THE STRANGLER (1964, Allied Artists)—Leo Kroll
BIG DADDY (1969, Syzygy/United)—A. Lincoln Beauregard

BURDON, ALBERT
OH BOY! (1938, GB, Associated British)—Percy Flower
JAILBIRDS (1939, GB, Butchers)—Bill Smith

BURKE, BILLIE
PEGGY (1916, Silent, Triangle)—Peggy Cameron
IN PURSUIT OF POLLY (1918, Silent, Paramount)—Polly Mardsen

BURKE, PAUL
ONCE YOU KISS A STRANGER (1969, Warners)—Jerry

BURKE, SIMON
SLATE, WYN & ME (1987, Australia, Ukiyo/Hemdale)—Wyn Jackson

BURKE, TOM
FATHER O'FLYNN (1938, Ireland, Butchers)—Father O'Flynn

BURNE, NANCY
NORAH O'NEALE (1934, GB, DuWorld)—Norah O'Neale

BURNETT, CAROL
PETE 'N' TILLIE (1972, Universal)—Tillie Schlaine
CHU CHU AND THE PHILLY FLASH (1981, 20th Century Fox)—Emily

BURNETT, DON
DAMON AND PYTHIAS (1962, MGM)—Pythias

BURNS, BOB
THE ARKANSAS TRAVELLER (1938, Paramount)—The Traveller
I'M FROM MISSOURI (1939, Paramount)—Sweeney Bliss
OUR LEADING CITIZEN (1939, Paramount)—Lem Schofield
ALIAS THE DEACON (1940, Universal)—Deke Caswell

BURNS, GEORGE
THE SUNSHINE BOYS (1975, United Artists)—Al Lewis
OH, GOD! (1977, Warners)—God
JUST YOU AND ME KID (1979, Columbia)—Bill
OH GOD, BOOK II (1980, Warners)—God
OH GOD! YOU DEVIL (1984, Warners)—God/Devil
18 AGAIN (1988, New World)—Jack Watson

BURR, RAYMOND
UNMASKED (1950, Republic)—Roger Lewis
PLEASE MURDER ME (1956, Distributors Corp.)—Craig Carlson

BURRELL, DAISY
JUST A GIRL (1916, Silent, GB, Samuelson)—Esmerelda

BURRUD, BILLY
THREE KIDS AND A QUEEN (1935, Universal)—Doc
THE COWBOY AND THE KID (1936, Universal)—Jimmy Thomas

BURSTYN, ELLEN
ALICE DOESN'T LIVE HERE ANYMORE (1975, Warners)—
Alice Hyatt

BURTON, JENNIFER
TRUCK STOP WOMEN (1974, LT Films)—Tina

BURTON, LANGHORNE
A MAN'S SHADOW (1920, GB, Silent, Butchers)—Peter
Beresford/Julian Grey

BURTON, RICHARD
MY COUSIN RACHEL (1952, 20th Century Fox)—Philip Ashley
PRINCE OF PLAYERS (1955, 20th Century Fox)—Edwin Booth
ALEXANDER THE GREAT (1956, Warners)—Alexander
the Great
THE V.I.P.S (1963, GB, MGM)—Paul Andros
BECKET (1964, GB, Paramount)—Thomas à Becket
HAMLET (1964, Electonovision/Warners)—Hamlet
THE SPY WHO CAME IN FROM THE COLD (1965, GB,
Paramount)—Alec Leamas
DOCTOR FAUSTUS (1967, GB, Columbia)—Dr. Faustus
VILLAIN (1971, GB, EMI-MGM)—Vic Dakin
BLUEBEARD (1972, Cinerama/Vulcano)—Baron von Sepper
HAMMERSMITH IS OUT (1972, Cinerama)—Hammersmith
EXORCIST II: THE HERETIC (1977, Warners)—Father Lamont
WAGNER (1983, GB, London Trust)—Richard Wagner

BURY, SEAN
FRIENDS (1971, GB, Paramount)—Paul Harrison

BUSBY, TOM
THE DIRTY DOZEN (1967, GB, MGM)—Milo Vladek

BUSCH, MAE
ONLY A SHOP GIRL (1922, Silent, C.B.C. Film Sales)—Josie
Jerome
CAMILLE OF THE BARBARY COAST (1925, Silent, Associated
Exhibit)—Camille Balishaw
HUSBAND HUNTERS (1927, Silent, Tiffany)—Marie Devere

BUSEY, GARY
THE BUDDY HOLLY STORY (1978, Columbia)—Buddy Holly
CARNY (1980, United Artists)—Frankie
THE BEAR (1984, Embassy)—Paul "Bear" Bryant
BULLETPROOF (1988, Cinetel-Virgin)—Frank 'Bulletproof'
McBain

BUSHELL, ANTHONY
THE REBEL SON (1939, GB, United Artists)—Andrew Boulba

BUSHMAN, FRANCIS X.
PENNINGTON'S CHOICE (1915, Silent, Metro)—Robert
Pennington
THE ADOPTED SON (1917, Silent, Metro)—Two-Gun Carter
FOUR SONS (1928, Silent, Fox)—Franz Bernie

BUSTER, RICKIE
BIG SHOTS (1987, 20th Century Fox)—Obie

BUTLER, LOIS
MICKEY (1948, Eagle Lion)—Mickey

BUTT, LAWSON
DANTE'S INFERNO (1924, Silent, Fox)—Alighieri Dante

BUTTERWORTH, CHARLES
BABY FACE HARRINGTON (1935, MGM)—Willie Harrington
THE SULTAN'S DAUGHTER (1943, Monogram)—Sultan

BUTTERWORTH, JOE
PENROD AND SAM (1923, Silent, Associate First National)—
Sam Williams

BUZZELL, EDDIE
LITTLE JOHNNY JONES (1930, Warners)—Johnny Jones

BYGRAVES, MAX
CHARLIE MOON (1956, GB, British Lion)—Charlie Moon

BYINGTON, SPRING
LOUISA (1950, Universal)—Louisa Norton
ACCORDING TO MRS. HOYLE (1951, Monogram)—Mrs. Hoyle

BYRD, RALPH
BROADWAY BIG SHOT (1942, Producers Releasing Corp.)—
Jimmy O'Brien
DUKE OF THE NAVY (1942, Producers Releasing Corp.)—
"Breeze" Duke
DICK TRACY MEETS GRUESOME (1947, RKO)—Dick Tracy
DICK TRACY'S DILEMMA (1947, RKO)—Dick Tracy

BYRNE, PATRICIA T.
NIGHT CALL NURSES (1974, New World)—Barbara

BYRON, ARTHUR
THE PRESIDENT VANISHES (1934, Paramount)—President
Stanley Craig

C

CAAN, JAMES
THE RAIN PEOPLE (1969, Warners)—Jimmie "Killer"
Kilgannon
RABBIT, RUN (1970, Warners)—Rabbit Angstrom
FREEBIE AND THE BEAN (1974, Warners)—Freebie
THE GAMBLER (1974, Paramount)—Axel

HARRY AND WALTER GO TO NEW YORK (1976, Columbia)—
Harry Dighby
COMES A HORSEMAN (1978, United Artists)—Frank
THIEF (1981, United Artists)—Frank

CABOT, BRUCE
MIDSHIPMAN JACK (1933, RKO)—Jack Austin
BAD GUY (1937, MGM)—Lucky Walden
MY SON IS GUILTY (1940, Columbia)—Ritzy Kerry
WILD BILL HICKOK RIDES (1942, Warners)—Wild Bill Hickok

CABOT, SUSAN
THE WASP WOMAN (1959, Allied Artists)—Janice Starling

CAESAR, ADOLPH
A SOLDIER'S STORY (1984, Columbia)—Sgt. Waters

CAGE, NICOLAS
THE BOY IN BLUE (1986, 20th Century Fox)—Ned Hanlan
MOONSTRUCK (1987, MGM/United Artists)—Ronny Cammareri
FIRE BIRDS (1990, Buena Vista)—Jack Preston
WILD AT HEART (1990, Goldwyn)—Sailor Ripley

CAGNEY, JAMES
THE PUBLIC ENEMY (1931, Warners)—Tom Powers
WINNER TAKE ALL (1932, Warners)—Jim Kane
LADY KILLER (1933, Warners)—Dan Quigley
THE MAYOR OF HELL (1933, Warners)—Patsy Gargan
PICTURE SNATCHER (1933, Warners)—Danny Kean
HE WAS HER MAN (1934, Warners)—Flicker Hayes
JIMMY THE GENT (1934, Warners)—Jimmy Corrigan
THE ST. LOUIS KID (1934, Warners)—Eddie Kennedy
DEVIL DOGS OF THE AIR (1935, Warners)—Tommy O'Toole
FRISCO KID (1935, Warners)—Bat Morgan
G-MAN (1935, Warners)—James "Brick" Davis
GREAT GUY (1936, Grand National)—Johnny Cave
EACH DAWN I DIE (1939, Warners)—Frank Ross
THE OKLAHOMA KID (1939, Warners)—Jim Kincaid
CAPTAINS OF THE CLOUDS (1942, Warners)—Brian MacLean
YANKEE DOODLE DANDY (1942, Warners)—George M. Cohan
JOHNNY COME LATELY (1943, United Artists)—Tom Richards
A LION IN THE STREETS (1953, Warners)—Hank Martin
TRIBUTE TO A BADMAN (1956, MGM)—Jeremy Rodock
MAN OF A THOUSAND FACES (1957, Universal)—Lon Chaney

CAIN, JANE
VANITY (1935, Columbia)—Vanity Faire

CAINE, MICHAEL
ALFIE (1966, GB, Paramount)—Alfie Elkins
GET CARTER (1971, MGM)—Jack Carter
X, Y & ZEE (1972, GB, Columbia)—Robert Blakely
PEEPER (1975, 20th Century Fox)—Tucker
DRESSED TO KILL (1980, Filmways)—Dr. Robert Elliott
THE JIGSAW MAN (1984, GB, United Film)—Sir Philip
Kimberly
THE HOLCROFT COVENANT (1985, Universal)—Noel Holcroft
THE WHISTLE BLOWER (1987, GB, Hemdale)—Frank Jones
DIRTY ROTTEN SCOUNDRELS (1988, Orion)—Lawrence
Jamison
WITHOUT A CLUE (1988, Orion)—Reginald Kincaid ('Sherlock
Holmes')

CALDWELL, ORVILLE
THE HARVESTER (1927, Silent, R-C Pictures)—David Langston

CALDWELL, SARAH
MRS. BROWN, YOU'VE GOT A LOVELY DAUGHTER (1968, GB,
MGM)—Judy Brown

CALEGORY, JADE
MAC AND ME (1988, Orion)—Eric Cruise

CALHERN, LOUIS
THE MAGNIFICENT YANKEE (1950, MGM)—Oliver Wendell
Holmes
JULIUS CAESAR (1953, MGM)—Julius Caesar

CALHOUN, ALICE
THE CHARMING DECEIVER (1921, Silent, Vitagraph)—Edith
Denton Marsden
THE ANGEL OF CROOKED STREET (1922, Silent, Vitagraph)—
Jennie Marsh
LITTLE WILDCAT (1922, Vitagraph)—Mag O' the Alley

CALHOUN, RORY
WAY OF A GAUCHO (1952, 20th Century Fox)—Martin
THE SPOILERS (1955, Universal)—Alex McNamara
DOMINO KID (1957, Columbia)—Domino
THE HIRED GUN (1957, MGM)—Gil McCord
UTAH BLAINE (1957, Columbia)—Utah Blaine
A FACE IN THE RAIN (1963, Embassy)—Rand
THE GUN HAWK (1963, Allied Artists)—Blaine Madden

CALL, JOHN
SANTA CLAUS CONQUERS THE MARTIANS (1964, Embassy)—
Santa Claus

CALLAN, MICHAEL
THE VICTORS (1963, Columbia)—Elridge
THE NEW INTERNS (1964, Columbia)—Dr. Alec Considine
THE MAGNIFICENT SEVEN RIDE (1972, United Artists)—Noah
Forbes

CALLARD, KAY
UNDERCOVER GIRL (1957, GB, Butchers)—Joan Foster
TOP FLOOR GIRL (1959, GB, Paramount)—Connie

CALLEIA, JOSEPH
MAN OF THE PEOPLE (1937, MGM)—Jack Moreno

CALTHROP, DONALD
NELSON (1918, GB, Silent, Apex)—Horatio Nelson

CALVERT, CATHERINE
THE CAREER OF KATHERINE BUSH (1919, Silent,
Paramount)—Katherine Bush

CALVERT, KEITH
SMILEY GETS A GUN (1959, GB, 20th Century Fox)—Smiley
Greevins

CALVERT, PHYLLIS
MADONNA OF THE SEVEN MOONS (1945, GB, Gainsborough)—
Maddalen Lambardi/Rosanna
THEY WERE SISTERS (1945, GB, Universal)—Lucy
MY OWN TRUE LOVE (1948, Paramount)—Joan Clews

CALVIN, HENRY
BABES IN TOYLAND (1961, Buena Vista)—Gonzorgo

CAMBRIDGE, GODFREY
WATERMELON MAN (1970, Columbia)—Jeff Gerber

CAMERON, KIRK
LIKE FATHER, LIKE SON (1987, Tri-Star)—Chris Hammond
LISTEN TO ME (1989, Columbia)—Tucker Muldowney

CAMERON, ROD
CAVALRY SCOUT (1951, Monogram)—Kirby Frye
RIDE THE MAN DOWN (1952, Republic)—Will Ballard
SPOILERS OF THE FOREST (1957, Republic)—Boyd Caldwell
THE MAN WHO DIED TWICE (1958, Republic)—Bill Brennon
REQUIEM FOR A GUNFIGHTER (1965, Embassy)—Dave
McCloud

CAMPBELL, BILL
THE ROCKETEER (1991, Buena Vista/Disney)—Cliff Secord

CAMPBELL, COLIN
THE LEATHER BOYS (1965, GB, Allied Artists)—Reggie

CAMPBELL, DOUGLAS
OEDIPUS REX (1957, Canada, Motion Pictures)—Oedipus

CAMPBELL, GLEN
NORWOOD (1970, Paramount)—Norwood Pratt

CAMPBELL, JOHN
THE SULLIVANS (1944, 20th Century Fox)—Frank Sullivan

CAMPBELL, NICHOLAS
KNIGHTS OF THE CITY (1986, New World)—Joey

CAMPBELL, PAUL
THE LUNATIC (1992, Triton)—Aloysius

CAMPBELL, WILLIAM
MAN IN THE VAULT (1956, RKO)—Tommy Dancer

CANDY, JOHN
ARMED AND DANGEROUS (1986, Columbia)—Frank Dooley
UNCLE BUCK (1989, Universal)—Uncle Buck Russell
WHO'S HARRY CRUMB? (1989, Tri-Star)—Harry Crumb
ONLY THE LONELY (1991, 20th Century Fox)—Danny Muldoon

CANNON, KATHY
PRIVATE DUTY NURSES (1972, New World)—Spring

CANNON, DYAN
BOB AND CAROL AND TED AND ALICE (1969,
Columbia)—Alice
DOCTORS' WIVES (1971, Columbia)—Lorrie Dellman

CANOVA, JUDY
SCATTERBRAIN (1940, Republic)—Judy Hull
SIS HOPKINS (1941, Republic)—Sis Hopkins
JOAN OF OZARK (1942, Republic)—Judy Hull
SLEEPYTIME GAL (1942, Republic)—Bessie Cobb
TRUE TO THE ARMY (1942, Paramount)—Daisy Hawkins
THE WAC FROM WALLA WALLA (1952, Republic)—Judy
UNTAMED HEIRESS (1954, Republic)—Judy

CANTINFLAS
PEPE (1960, Columbia)—Pepe

CANTOR, EDDIE
KID BOOTS (1926, Silent, Paramount)—Kid Boots
THE KID FROM SPAIN (1932, United Artists)—Eddie Williams
KID MILLIONS (1934, United Artists)—Eddie Wilson, Jr.
STRIKE ME PINK (1936, United Artists)—Eddie Pink
ALI BABA GOES TO TOWN (1937, 20th Century Fox)—Ali Baba

CANUTT, YAKIMA
THE HUMAN TORNADO (1925, Silent, R-C Pictures)—Jim
Marlow

CAPOBIANCO, CARMINE
PSYCHOS IN LOVE (1987, ICN Bleecker Infinity)—Joe
GALACTIC GIGOLO (1988, Urban Classics)—Eoj

CAPRI, AHNA
THE SPECIALIST (1975, Crown)—Londa

CAPRICE, JUNE
MODERN CINDERELLA (1917, Silent, Fox)—Joyce

CARA, IRENE
AARON LOVES ANGELA (1975, Columbia)—Angela

CARDI, PAT
AND NOW MIGUEL (1966, Universal)—Miguel

CARDOVA, MARK
CLARENCE AND ANGEL (1978, Gardner)—Angel

CARDWELL, JAMES
THE SULLIVANS (1944, 20th Century Fox)—George Sullivan

CAREW, ARTHUR
HIS WIFE'S HUSBAND (1922, Silent, Pyramid)—John Brainerd
DADDY (1923, Silent, First National)—Paul Savelli

CAREY, HARRY
THE MASTER CRACKSMAN (1914, Silent, Progressive)—
Gentleman Joe
A KNIGHT OF THE RANGE (1916, Silent, Artcraft)—
Cheyenne Harry
"IF ONLY" JIM (1921, Silent, Universal)—Jim Golden
TRADER HORN (1931, MGM)—Trader Horn
THE LAST OUTLAW (1936, RKO)—Dean Payton
MY SON IS GUILTY (1940, Columbia)—Tim Kerry
THE SHEPHERD OF THE HILLS (1941, Paramount)—Daniel
Howitt

CAREY, HARRY JR.
THE THREE GODFATHERS (1948, MGM)—William Kearney,
"The Abilene Kid"

CAREY, MACDONALD
DR. BROADWAY (1942, Paramount)—Dr. Timothy Kane
MY WIFE'S BEST FRIEND (1952, 20th Century Fox)—
George Mason
STRANGER AT MY DOOR (1956, Republic)—Hollis Jarret
MAN OR GUN (1958, Republic)—Maybe Smith

CAREY, PHIL
THE NEBRASKAN (1953, Columbia)—Wade Harper

CAREY, TIMOTHY
THE WORLD'S GREATEST SINNER (1962, Frenzy)—Clarence
Hilliard

CARIOU, LEN
ONE MAN (1979, Canada, National Film Board of Canada)—
Jason Brady

CARLISLE, MARY
SWEETHEART OF SIGMA CHI (1933, Monogram)—Vivian
GIRL O' MY DREAMS (1935, Monogram)—Gwen

CARLSON, KAREN
SHAME, SHAME, EVERYBODY KNOWS HER NAME (1969, J.E.R. Pictures)—Susan Barton
THE STUDENT NURSES (1970, New World)—Phred

CARLSON, RICHARD
WHITE CARGO (1942, MGM)—Langford
WHISPERING SMITH VERSUS SCOTLAND YARD (1952, GB, RKO)—Whispering Smith

CARLTON, CLAIRE
GIRL FROM HAVANA (1940, Republic)—Havana

CARLYLE, DAVID (ROBERT PAIGE)
MEET THE BOY FRIEND (1937, Republic)—Tony Page

CARMEN, JULIE
KISS ME A KILLER (1991, Califilm)—Teresa

CARMICHAEL, IAN
PRIVATE'S PROGRESS (1956, GB, British Lion)—Stanley Windrush
LUCKY JIM (1957, GB, Kingsley International)—Jim Dixon

CARNEY, ALAN
ROOKIES IN BURMA (1943, RKO)—Mike Strager

CARNEY, ART
HARRY AND TONTO (1974, 20th Century Fox)—Harry Coombs

CARNEY, GEORGE
A REAL BLOKE (1935, GB, Universal)—Bill
FATHER STEPS OUT (1937, Great Britain, RKO)—Joe Hardcastle

CARNINATI, TULLO
THREE SINNERS (1928, Silent, Paramount)—Raoul Stanislav

CAROL, CINDY
GIDGET GOES TO ROME (1963, Columbia)—Gidget (Francie Lawrence)

CAROL, SUE
GIRLS GONE WILD (1929, Silent, Fox)—Babs Holoworthy
DANCING SWEETIES (1930, Warners)—Molly O'Neill

CARON, LESLIE
LILI (1953, MGM)—Lili Daurier
GABY (1956, MGM)—Gaby
GIGI (1958, MGM)—Gigi
FANNY (1961, Warners)—Fanny

CARPENTER, FRANCIS
ALADDIN (1917, Silent, Fox)—Aladdin
JACK AND THE BEANSTALK (1917, Silent, Paramount)—Jack

CARPENTER, JOHN *See* **JOHN FORBES**

CARPENTER, PAUL
PAID TO KILL (1954, GB, Hammer)—Paul Kirby

CARR, ALEXANDER
IN HOLLYWOOD WITH POTASH AND PERLMUTTER (1924, Silent, Goldwyn)—Morris Perlmutter
PARTNERS AGAIN (1926, Silent, United Artists)—Morris Perlmutter

CARR, BETTY
SEVEN BRIDES FOR SEVEN BROTHERS (1954, MGM)—Sarah

CARRADINE, DAVID
THIEVES LIKE US (1974, United Artists)—Bowie
BOUND FOR GLORY (1976, United Artists)—Woody Guthrie
CANNONBALL (1976, New World)—Cannonball Buckman
FAST CHARLIE. . .THE MOONBEAM RIDER (1979, Universal)—Charlie Swattle
THE LONG RIDERS (1980, United Artists)—Cole Younger
THE WARRIOR AND THE SORCERESS (1984, New World)—Kain
SUNDOWN: THE VAMPIRE RETREAT (1990, Vestron)—Count Mardulak

CARRADINE, JOHN
HITLER'S MADMAN (1943, MGM)—Reinhard Heydrich
BLUEBEARD (1944, Producers Releasing Corp.)—Gaston
HOUSE OF DRACULA (1945, Universal)—Count Dracula
COSMIC MAN (1959, Allied Artists)—Cosmic Man
WIZARD OF MARS (1964, American General)—Wizard of Mars
BILLY THE KID VS. DRACULA (1966, Circle/EM)—Vampire Uncle

CARRADINE, KEITH
THE DUELLISTS (1977, GB, Paramount)—D'Hubert
THE LONG RIDERS (1980, United Artists)—Jim Younger
THE MODERNS (1988, Alive Films)—Nick Hart
THE BACHELOR (1991, Greycat Films)—Dr. Emil Grasler

CARRADINE, ROBERT
THE LONG RIDERS (1980, United Artists)—Bob Younger
REVENGE OF THE NERDS (1984, 20th Century Fox)—Lewis
REVENGE OF THE NERDS II (1987, 20th Century Fox)—Lewis

CARRILLO, LEO
MISTER ANTONIO (1929, Tiffany)—Antonio Camaradino
MEN ARE SUCH FOOLS (1933, RKO)—Tony Mello
THE GAY DESPERADO (1936, United Artists)—Pablo Braganza
THE GIRL AND THE GAMBLER (1939, RKO)—El Rayo

CARRINGTON, DEBBIE LEE
THE GARBAGE PAIL KIDS (1987, Atlantic)—Valerie Vomit

CARROLL, DEE
FIVE BOLD WOMEN (1960, Citation)—Crazy Hannah

CARROLL, DIAHANN
CLAUDINE (1974, 20th Century Fox)—Claudine

CARROLL, JOAN
OBLIGING YOUNG LADY (1941, RKO)—Bridget Potter

CARROLL, JOHN
HI GAUCHO (1936, RKO)—Lucio
I AM A CRIMINAL (1939, Monogram)—Brad McArthur
PIERRE OF THE PLAINS (1942, MGM)—Pierre

CARROLL, MADELEINE
I WAS A SPY (1934, GB, Gaumont)—Martha Cnockhaert
THE CASE AGAINST MRS. AMES (1936, Paramount)—Hope Ames
MY FAVORITE BLONDE (1942, Paramount)—Karen Bentley

CARROLL, NANCY
ABIE'S IRISH ROSE (1928, Part-Talkie, Paramount)—Rosemary Murphy
THE SHOPWORN ANGEL (1928, Paramount)—Daisy Heath
THE SIN SISTER (1929, Silent, Fox)—Pearl

SWEETIE (1929, Paramount)—Barbara Pell
THE NIGHT ANGEL (1931, Paramount)—Yula Martini
PERSONAL MAID (1931, Paramount)—Nora Ryan
CHILD OF MANHATTAN (1933, Columbia)—Madeleine McGonegal
I LOVE THAT MAN (1933, Paramount)—Grace Clark
WOMAN ACCUSED (1933, Paramount)—Glenda O'Brien
I'LL LOVE YOU ALWAYS (1935, Columbia)—Nora Clegg

CARRUTHERS, BEN
THE DIRTY DOZEN (1967, GB, MGM)—Glenn Gilpin

CARSON, JACK
TWO GUYS FROM TEXAS (1948, Warners)—Danny Foster
THE GOOD HUMOR MAN (1950, Columbia)—Biff Jones
THE GROOM WORE SPURS (1951, Universal)—Ben Castle

CARSON, TERENCE ("T.C.")
LIVIN' LARGE (1991, Goldwyn)—Dexter Jackson

CARTER, DONNIE
THE TWO LITTLE BEARS (1961, 20th Century Fox)—Timmy Davis

CARTER, HELENA BONHAM
LADY JANE (1986, GB, Paramount)—Lady Jane Grey

CARTER, LYNDA
BOBBIE JO AND THE OUTLAW (1976, American International)—Bobbie Jo James

CARTER, T.K.
HE'S MY GIRL (1987, Scotti)—Reggie/Regina

CARUSO, ENRICO
MY COUSIN (1918, Silent, Artcraft)—Mario Nanni/Cesare Carulli

CASEY, BERNIE
HIT MAN (1972, MGM)—Tyrone Tackett
MAURIE (1973, National General)—Maurice Stokes
DR. BLACK AND MR. HYDE (1976, Dimension)—Dr. Black/Mr. Hyde

CASEY, LARRY
THE GAY DECEIVERS (1969, Fanfare)—Elliot Crane

CASO, MARK
TEENAGE MUTANT NINJA TURTLES II: THE SECRET OF OOZE (1991, New Line)—Leonardo

CASSAVETES, JOHN
THE DIRTY DOZEN (1967, GB, MGM)—Victor Franko
HUSBANDS (1970, Columbia)—Gus
MIKEY AND NICKY (1976, Paramount)—Nicky
MARVIN AND TIGE (1983, Major)—Marvin Stewart

CASSEL, JEAN-PIERRE
THOSE MAGNIFICENT MEN IN THEIR FLYING MACHINES (1965, GB, 20th Century Fox)—Pierre Dubois

CASSEL, SEYMOUR
MINNIE AND MOSKOWITZ (1971, Universal)—Seymour Moskowitz

CASSON, ANN
DANCE PRETTY LADY (1932, GB, British Lion)—Jenny Pearl

CASTELTON, BARBARA
JUST SYLVIA (1918, Silent, World)—Sylvia

CASTILLO, GLORIA
REFORM SCHOOL GIRL (1957, American Int.)—Donna Price

CASTLE, PEGGY
HAREM GIRL (1952, Columbia)—Princess Shareen
THE OKLAHOMA WOMAN (1956, Sunset)—Marie "Oklahoma" Saunders
TWO-GUN LADY (1956, Associated Releasing)—Kate Masters

CATTRALL, KIM
MANNEQUIN (1987, 20th Century Fox)—Emmy

CAULFIELD, JOAN
DEAR RUTH (1947, Paramount)—Ruth Wilkins
THE SAINTED SISTERS (1948, Paramount)—Jane Stanton
DEAR WIFE (1949, Paramount)—Ruth Seacroft
THE PETTY GIRL (1950, Columbia)—Victoria Braymore
THE LADY SAYS NO (1951, United Artists)—Dorinda

CAVANAUGH, PAUL
CHAMPAGNE CHARLIE (1936, 20th Century Fox)—Charlie Courtland

CAVE, DES
PADDY (1970, Ireland, Allied Artists)—Paddy Maguire

CAVIN, R.A.
KINCAID, GAMBLER (1916, Silent, Universal)—Jim Kincaid

CAYTON, ELIZABETH
SLAVE GIRLS FROM BEYOND INFINITY (1987, Titan/Urban Classics)—Daria

CELLIER, FRANK
COLONEL BLOOD (1934, GB, MGM)—Colonel Blood

CHADWICK, CYRIL
THREE LIVE GHOSTS (1922, Silent, Paramount)—Spoofy

CHADWICK, HELENE
HER OWN FREE WILL (1924, Silent, Eastern Productions)—Nan Everard
CONFESSIONS OF A WIFE (1928, Silent, Excellent)—Marion Atwill

CHAFFEY, JOHN
THE OPTIMISTS (1973, GB, Paramount)—Mark

CHAKIRIS, GEORGE
KINGS OF THE SUN (1963, United Artists)—Balam

CHAMBERLAIN, RICHARD
THE THREE MUSKETEERS (1973, Panama)—Aramis
THE FOUR MUSKETEERS (1975, 20th Century Fox)—Aramis
THE COUNT OF MONTE CRISTO (1976, GB, ITC)—Edmond Dantes
ALLAN QUATERMAIN AND THE LOST CITY OF GOLD (1987, Cannon)—Allan Quatermain

CHAMPION, MARGE
GIVE A GIRL A BREAK (1953, MGM)—Madelyn Corlane

CHANCE, NAOMI
THE GAMBLER AND THE LADY (1952, GB, Hammer)—Lady Susan Willens

THE SAINT'S GIRL FRIDAY (1954, GB, RKO)—Lady
Carol Denby

CHANDLER, HELEN
SALVATION NELL (1931, Tiffany)—Nell Saunders
DANCE HALL HOSTESS (1933, Mayfair)—Texas Guinan

CHANDLER, JEFF
DEPORTED (1950, Universal)—Vic Smith
THE IRON MAN (1951, Universal)—Coke Mason
YANKEE BUCCANEER (1952, Universal)—Cmdr. David Porter
TAZA, SON OF COCHISE (1954, Universal)—Cochise
YANKEE PASHA (1954, Universal)—Jason
DRANGO (1957, United Artists)—Drango
MAN IN THE SHADOW (1957, Universal)—Sheriff Ben Sadler
A STORY OF DAVID (1960, GB, British Lion)—David
MERRILL'S MARAUDERS (1962, Warners)—Brig. Gen. Merrill

CHANDLER, JOHN
MAD DOG COLL (1961, Columbia)—Vincent Coll

CHANDLER, JOHN DAVID
THE YOUNG SAVAGES (1961, United Artists)—Arthur Reardon

CHANDLER, LANE
FIREBRAND JORDAN (1930, National Players)—Firebrand
Jordan

CHANEY, LON
ALL THE BROTHERS WERE VALIANT (1923, Silent, Metro)—
Mark Shore
THE HUNCHBACK OF NOTRE DAME (1923, Silent, Universal)—
Quasimodo
HE WHO GETS SLAPPED (1924, Silent, MGM)—"He Who Gets
Slapped"
PHANTOM OF THE OPERA (1925, Silent, Universal)—Erik, the
Phantom
THE UNHOLY THREE (1925, Silent, MGM)—Professor Echo
MR. WU (1927, Silent, MGM)—Mr. Wu
THE UNKNOWN (1927, Silent, MGM)—Alonzo
LAUGH, CLOWN, LAUGH (1928, Silent, MGM)—The Beppi
THE UNHOLY THREE (1930, MGM)—Prof. Echo

CHANEY, LON JR.
MAN MADE MONSTER (1941, Universal)—Dan McCormick
THE WOLF MAN (1941, Universal)—Larry Talbot
THE MUMMY'S TOMB (1942, Universal)—Kharis
CALLING DR. DEATH (1943, Universal)—Doctor Steele
FRANKENSTEIN MEETS THE WOLFMAN (1943, Universal)—
Lawrence Talbot/The Wolfman
SON OF DRACULA (1943, Universal)—Count Alucard
THE MUMMY'S CURSE (1944, Universal)—Kharis
THE MUMMY'S GHOST (1944, Universal)—Kharis
THE DALTONS RIDE AGAIN (1945, Universal)—Grat Dalton
BATTLE OF CHIEF PONTIAC (1952, Real Art)—Chief Pontiac
THE INDESTRUCTIBLE MAN (1956, Allied Artists)—The
Butcher

CHANG, SARI
CHINA GIRL (1987, Great American Vestron)—Tyan-Hwa

CHANNING, STOCKARD
DANDY, THE ALL AMERICAN GIRL (1976, MGM/United
Artists)—Dandy

THE APPLEGATES (1990, Australia, Roadshow)—Jane
Applegate

CHAPIN, BILLY
THE KID FROM LEFT FIELD (1952, 20th Century Fox)—Christy
Cooper

CHAPLIN, CHARLES
THE PILGRIM (1923, Silent, Associate First National)—The
Pilgrim
THE GREAT DICTATOR (1940, United Artists)—Adenoid Hynkel
MONSIEUR VERDOUX (1947, United Artists)—Henri Verdoux
A KING IN NEW YORK (1957, GB, Attica/Archway)—King
Shadhov

CHAPLIN, GERALDINE
REMEMBER MY NAME (1978, Columbia)—Emily

CHAPLIN, MILDRED HARRIS
POLLY OF THE STORM COUNTRY (1920, Silent, First
National)—Polly Hopkins

CHAPLIN, SYD
CHARLEY'S AUNT (1925, Silent, Christie)—Sir Fancourt
Babberley
THE MAN ON THE BOX (1925, Silent, Warners)—Bob
Warburton
THE BETTER 'OLE (1926, Silent, Warners)—Ole Bill
THE FORTUNE HUNTER (1927, Silent, Warners)—Nat Duncan

CHAPMAN, BEN
CREATURE FROM THE BLACK LAGOON (1954, Universal)—
Gil Man

CHAPMAN, EDWARD
JUNO AND THE PAYCOCK (1930, GB, British International)—
Capt. John "Paycock" Boyle

CHAPMAN, GRAHAM
MONTY PYTHON'S LIFE OF BRIAN (1979, GB, Warners)—Brian
YELLOWBEARD (1983, Orion)—Yellowbeard

CHAPMAN, JANET
LITTLE MISS THOROUGHBRED (1938, Warners)—Mary Ann

CHAPMAN, MARGUERITE
PARACHUTE NURSE (1942, Columbia)—Glenda White

CHAPMAN, SEAN
HELLRAISER (1987, GB, New World)—Frank Cotton

CHARBONNEAU, PATRICIA
CALL ME (1988, Vestron)—Anna

CHARISSE, CYD
THE HARVEY GIRLS (1946, MGM)—Deborah
PARTY GIRL (1958, MGM)—Vicki Gaye

CHARLES, DAVID
JULIA HAD TWO LOVERS (1990, South Gate)—Jack

CHARLESWORTH, DAVID
DEVIL DOLL (1964, GB, Galaworldfilm)—Hugo Novik

CHARLESWORTH, JOHN
JOHN OF THE FAIR (1962, GB, Continental)—John Claydon

CHASE, CHEVY
FLETCH (1985, Universal)—Fletch

THREE AMIGOS (1986, Orion)—Dusty Bottoms
FLETCH LIVES (1989, Universal)—Irwin Maurice 'Fletch' Fletcher
MEMOIRS OF AN INVISIBLE MAN (1992, Warner Brothers)—Nick Halloway

CHATTERTON, RUTH
MADAME X (1929, MGM)—Jacqueline
ANYBODY'S WOMAN (1930, Paramount)—Pansy Gray
THE LADY OF SCANDAL (1930, MGM)—Elsie
THE LAUGHING LADY (1930, Paramount)—Marjorie Lee
SARAH AND SON (1930, Paramount)—Sarah Storm
ONCE A LADY (1931, Paramount)—Anna Keremazoff
UNFAITHFUL (1931, Paramount)—Fay Kilkenny
FEMALE (1933, Warners)—Alison Drake
FRISCO JENNY (1933, Warners)—Frisco Jenny
LILLY TURNER (1933, Warners)—Lilly Turner
LADY OF SECRETS (1936, Columbia)—Celia Whittaker
A ROYAL DIVORCE (1938, GB, Paramount)—Josephine

CHEGWIN, KEITH
EGGHEAD'S ROBOT (1970, GB, Interfilm)—Egghead Wentworth

CHER
CHASTITY (1969, American International)—Chastity
MOONSTRUCK (1987, MGM/United Artists)—Loretta Castorini
THE WITCHES OF EASTWICK (1987, Warners)—Alexandra Medford

CHERRILL, VIRGINIA
GIRLS DEMAND EXCITEMENT (1931, Fox)—Joan Madison

CHESTNUT, MORRIS
BOYZ N THE HOOD (1991, Columbia/New Deal)—Ricky Baker

CHEVALIER, MAURICE
PLAYBOY OF PARIS (1930, Paramount)—Albert Loriflan
THE SMILING LIEUTENANT (1931, Paramount)—Niki
ONE HOUR WITH YOU (1932, Paramount)—Dr. Andre Bertier
THE BELOVED VAGABOND (1936, GB, Columbia)—Paragot

CHI, GRETA
LISETTE (1961, Medallion)—Lisette

CHIARI, WALTER
THOSE DARING YOUNG MEN IN THEIR JAUNTY JALOPIES (1969, GB/France/ Italy, Paramount)—Angelo Pincelli

CHIKLIS, MICHAEL
WIRED (1989, Taurus)—John Belushi

CHLUMSKY, ANNA
MY GIRL (1991, Columbia)—Vada Sultenfuss

CHONG, TOMMY
FAR OUT MAN (1990, New Line)—Far Out Man

CHRISTENSEN, STACY
THE VIRGIN QUEEN OF ST. FRANCIS HIGH (1987, Canada, Crown)—Diane

CHRISTIAN, LINDA
TARZAN AND THE MERMAIDS (1948, RKO)—Mara

CHRISTIAN, PAUL
THE THIEF OF VENICE (1952, 20th Century Fox)—Alfiere Lorenzo Contarini

CHRISTIANS, MADY
A WICKED WOMAN (1934, MGM)—Naomi Trice

CHRISTIE, JULIE
DARLING (1965, GB, Embassy)—Diana Scott
PETULIA (1968, Warners)—Petulia Danner
MCCABE AND MRS. MILLER (1971, Warners)—Constance Miller
MEMOIRS OF A SURVIVOR (1981, GB, EMI)—"D"

CHRISTOPHER, JORDAN
THE SIDELONG GLANCES OF A PIDGEON KICKER (1970, MGM)—Jonathan

CHRISTY, ANN
THE KID SISTER (1927, Silent, Columbia)—Mary Hall

CHURCHILL, BERTON
HALF A SINNER (1934, Universal)—Deacon

CHURCHILL, DIANA
JANE STEPS OUT (1938, GB, Associated British)—Jane Wilton

CHYLEK, EUGENIUSZ
JOHNNY ON THE RUN (1953, GB, International Realist)—Johnny

CIANNELLI, EDUARDO
THE CREEPER (1948, 20th Century Fox)—Dr. Van Glock

CILENTO, DIANE
A WOMAN FOR JOE (1955, GB, Rank)—Mary
THE ANGEL WHO PAWNED HER HARP (1956, GB, British Lion)—The Angel

CLAIRE, BERNICE
NO, NO NANETTE (1930, First National)—Nanette
TWO HEARTS IN HARMONY (1935, GB, British Int.)—Micky

CLAIRE, GERTRUDE
HIS MOTHER'S BOY (1918, Silent, Ince)—Mrs. Denton

CLAIRE, INA
THE ROYAL FAMILY OF BROADWAY (1930, Paramount)—Julia Cavendish

CLANTON, JIMMY
GO, JOHNNY, GO (1959, Hal Roach)—Johnny
TEENAGE MILLIONAIRE (1961, United Artists)—Bobby Chalmers

CLANTON, RONY
THE EDUCATION OF SONNY CARSON (1974, Paramount)—Sonny Carson

CLARE, MARY
NIGHT CLUB QUEEN (1934, GB, Universal)—Mary Brown
MRS. PYM OF SCOTLAND YARD (1939, GB, Grand National)—Mrs. Pym
THE THREE WEIRD SISTERS (1948, GB, Pathe)—Maude Morgan-Vaughn

CLARK, DANE
HER KIND OF MAN (1946, Warners)—Don Corwin
THE GAMBLER AND THE LADY (1952, GB, Hammer)—Jim Forster
TOUGHEST MAN ALIVE (1955, Allied Artists)—Lee
OUTLAW'S SON (1957, United Artists)—Nate Blaine

CLARK, DICK
THE YOUNG DOCTORS (1961, United Artists)—Dr. Alexander
KILLERS THREE (1968, American International)—Roger

CLARK, DONALD
FATHER'S LITTLE DIVIDEND (1951, MGM)—The Dividend

CLARK, JUDY
THE KID SISTER (1945, PRC)—Joan Hollingsworth
TWO BLONDES AND A REDHEAD (1947, Columbia)—
Vicki Adams

CLARK, LIDDY
KITTY AND THE BAGMAN (1983, Australia, Quartet)—Kitty
O'Rourke

CLARK, MARGUERITE
THE GOOSE GIRL (1915, Silent, Lasky)—Gretchen
THE PRINCE AND THE PAUPER (1915, Silent, Famous
Players)—Tom Canty/Edward, Prince of Wales
BAB'S DIARY (1917, Silent, Paramount)—Babs Archibald
LITTLE MISS HOOVER (1918, Paramount)—Nancy Craddock
PRUNELLA (1918, Silent, Paramount)—Prunella

CLARK, MARLENE
GANJA AND HESS (1973, Kelly-Jordan)—Ganja

CLARK, TAMMY
GIRL IN TROUBLE (1963, Vanguard)—Judy Collins

CLARKE, GEORGE
HERE'S GEORGE (1932, GB, Producers Distributors)—George
Muffitt

CLARKE, MAE
THE DANCERS (1930, Fox)—Maxine
THE GOOD BAD GIRL (1931, Columbia)—Marcia
IMPATIENT MAIDEN (1932, Universal)—Ruth Robbins
THREE WISE GIRLS (1932, Columbia)—Gladys Kane
PAROLE GIRL (1933, Columbia)—Sylvia Day

CLARKE, ROBERT
TALES OF ROBIN HOOD (1951, Lippert)—Robin Hood
THE HIDEOUS SUN DEMON (1959, Pacific International)—Dr.
Gilbert McKenna

CLARKSON, LANA
THE BARBARIAN QUEEN (1985, Cinema Group)—Amathea

CLARY, CHARLES
A CONNECTICUT YANKEE IN KING ARTHUR'S COURT (1921,
Silent, Fox)—King Arthur

CLAUSEN, CLAUS
THE DEVIL MAKES THREE (1952, MGM)—Heismann

CLAY, ANDREW DICE
THE ADVENTURES OF FORD FAIRLANE (1990, 20th Century
Fox)—Ford Fairlane

CLAY, NICHOLAS
THE DARWIN ADVENTURE (1972, GB, 20th Century Fox)—
Charles Darwin

CLAYBURGH, JILL
GABLE AND LOMBARD (1976, Universal)—Carol Lombard
AN UNMARRIED WOMAN (1978, 20th Century Fox)—Erica
STARTING OVER (1979, Paramount)—Marilyn Homberg

IT'S MY TURN (1980, Columbia)—Kate Gunzinger
I'M DANCING AS FAST AS I CAN (1982, Paramount)—Barbara
Gordon

CLAYTON, ETHEL
HIS BROTHER'S WIFE (1916, Silent, World)—Helen Barton
A LADY IN LOVE (1920, Silent, Paramount)—Barbara
THE SINS OF ROZANNE (1920, Silent, Paramount)—Rozanne
HER OWN MONEY (1922, Silent, Paramount)—Mildred Carr
IF I WERE QUEEN (1922, Silent, R-C Pictures)—Ruth Townley

CLAYWORTH, JUNE
STRANGE WIVES (1935, Universal)—Nadja

CLEMENSON, CHRISTIAN
DADDY'S BOYS (1988, Concorde)—Otis

CLEMENTS, STANLEY
SPOOK CHASERS (1957, Allied Artists)—Stanislaus "Duke"
Coreleski
SAINTLY SINNERS (1962, United Artists)—Slim

CLIFFORD, RUTH
A KENTUCKY CINDERELLA (1917, Silent, Bluebird)—A
Kentucky Cinderella
THE CABARET GIRL (1919, Silent, Universal/Bluebird)—
Ann Reid

CLIFFORD, WILLIAM
THE SECOND IN COMMAND (1915, Silent, Metro)—Major
Bingham

CLIFT, MONTGOMERY
THE YOUNG LIONS (1958, 20th Century Fox)—Noah Ackerman
THE MISFITS (1961, United Artists)—Pierce Howland
FREUD (1962, Universal)—Sigmund Freud
THE DEFECTOR (1966, Warners)—Prof. James Bower

CLIFTON, DORINDA
THE GIRL OF THE LIMBERLOST (1945, Columbia)—Elnora
Comstock

CLIVE, COLIN
FRANKENSTEIN (1931, Universal)—Dr. Henry Frankenstein
CHRISTOPHER STRONG (1933, RKO)—Christopher Strong
THE BRIDE OF FRANKENSTEIN (1935, Universal)—Dr. Henry
Frankenstein

CLOSE, GLENN
MAXIE (1985, Orion)—Maxie
FATAL ATTRACTION (1987, Paramount)—Alex Forrest
DANGEROUS LIAISONS (1988, Warners)—Marquis de Merteuil
IMMEDIATE FAMILY (1989, Columbia)—Linda Spector

CLUTE, CHESTER
MILLIONAIRES IN PRISON (1940, RKO)—Sidney Keats

COBB, IRVIN S.
EVERYBODY'S OLD MAN (1936, 20th Century Fox)—William
Franklin

COBB, LEE J.
THE MAN WHO CHEATED HIMSELF (1951, 20th Century Fox)—
Ed Cullen
12 ANGRY MEN (1957, United Artists)—Juror No. 3

COBURN, CHARLES
THE CAPTAIN IS A LADY (1940, MGM)—Capt. Abe Peabody
THE DEVIL AND MISS JONES (1941, RKO)—John P. Merrick
UNEXPECTED UNCLE (1941, RKO)—Seton Manley
THE MORE THE MERRIER (1943, Columbia)—Benjamin Dingle
MY KINGDOM FOR A COOK (1943, Columbia)—Rudyard Morley
COLONEL EFFINGHAM'S RAID (1945, 20th Century Fox)—Col. Effingham
B.F.'S DAUGHTER (1948, MGM)—B.F. Fulton
GENTLEMEN PREFER BLONDES (1953, 20th Century Fox)—Sir Francis Beekman
HOW TO MURDER A RICH UNCLE (1957, GB, Columbia)—Uncle George

COBURN, DAVID
BORN AMERICAN (1986, Cinema Group)—K.C.

COBURN, JAMES
THE MAGNIFICENT SEVEN (1960, United Artists)—Britt
OUR MAN FLINT (1966, 20th Century Fox)—Derek Flint
IN LIKE FLINT (1967, 20th Century Fox)—Derek Flint
THE PRESIDENT'S ANALYST (1967, Paramount)—Dr. Sidney Schaefer
DUFFY (1968, GB, Columbia)—Duffy
THE CAREY TREATMENT (1972, MGM)—Peter Carey
HARRY IN YOUR POCKET (1973, United Artists)—Harry
PAT GARRETT AND BILLY THE KID (1973, MGM)—Pat Garrett
THE LAST HARD MEN (1976, 20th Century Fox)—Zach Provo
LOVING COUPLES (1980, 20th Century Fox)—Walter
MR. PATMAN (1980, Canada, Film Consortium of Canada)—Mr. Patman

COCHRAN, STEVE
I, MOBSTER (1959, 20th Century Fox)—Joe Sante
THE DEADLY COMPANIONS (1961, Pathe-American)—Billy

CODY, BILL
DUGAN OF THE BAD LANDS (1931, Monogram)—Bill Dugan

CODY, LEW
OCCASIONALLY YOURS (1920, Silent, R-C Pictures)—Bruce Sands
RUPERT OF HENTZAU (1923, Silent, Selznick)—Rupert
HIS SECRETARY (1925, Silent, MGM)—David Colman
MAN AND MAID (1925, Silent, Metro-Goldwyn)—Sir Nicholas Thormonde
ADAM AND EVIL (1927, Silent, MGM)—Adam Trevelyan
A SINGLE MAN (1929, Silent, MGM)—Robin Worthington
THREE ROGUES (1930, Fox)—Ace Beaudry

COGHLAN, JUNIOR
LET 'ER GO GALLEGHER (1928, Silent, Pathe)—Gallegher
PENROD AND SAM (1931, First National)—Sam Williams

COHAN, GEORGE M.
THE PHANTOM PRESIDENT (1932, Paramount)—Doc Peter Varney

COHEN, JEFF
THE GOONIES (1985, Warners)—Chunk

COHEN, MITCHELL
THE TOXIC AVENGER (1985, Troma)—The Toxic Avenger

COLBERT, CLAUDETTE
THE LADY LIES (1929, Paramount)—Joyce Roamer
HIS WOMAN (1931, Paramount)—Sally Clark
SECRETS OF A SECRETARY (1931, Paramount)—Helen Blake
THE MISLEADING LADY (1932, Paramount)—Helen Steele
TORCH SINGER (1933, Paramount)—Sally Trent-Mimi Benton
CLEOPATRA (1934, Paramount)—Cleopatra
FOUR FRIGHTENED PEOPLE (1934, Paramount)—Judy Cavendish
THE BRIDE COMES HOME (1935, Paramount)—Jeanette Desmereau
THE GILDED LILY (1935, Paramount)—Lillian David
SHE MARRIED HER BOSS (1935, Columbia)—Julia Scott
I MET HIM IN PARIS (1937, Paramount)—Kay Denham
MAID OF SALEM (1937, Paramount)—Barbara Clarke
BLUEBEARD'S EIGHTH WIFE (1938, Paramount)—Nicole de Loiselle
ZAZA (1939, Paramount)—Zaza
GUEST WIFE (1945, United Artists)—Mary
THE EGG AND I (1947, Universal)—Betty MacDonald
BRIDE FOR SALE (1949, RKO)—Nora Shelly
TEXAS LADY (1955, RKO)—Prudence Webb

COLE, GEORGE
MY BROTHER'S KEEPER (1949, GB, Rank)—Willie Stannard
MR. POTTS GOES TO MOSCOW (1953, GB, Stratford)—George Potts

COLE, ROSALIE
THE CHILD (1977, Valiant International)—Rosalie

COLEMAN, GARY
JIMMY THE KID (1982, New World)—Jimmy

COLEMAN, NANCY
THE GAY SISTERS (1942, First National)—Susanna Gaylord
HER SISTER'S SECRET (1946, Producers Releasing Corp.)—Toni

COLEMAN, PETER
HANDY ANDY (1921, Silent, GB, Ideal)—Andy

COLGAN, MICHAEL
DONOVAN'S BRAIN (1953, United Artists)—Tom Donovan

COLICOS, JOHN
DOCTOR'S WIVES (1971, Columbia)—Mort Dellman

COLLET, CHRISTOPHER
FIRST BORN (1984, Paramount)—Jake

COLLIER, CONSTANCE
THE CODE OF MARCIA GRAY (1916, Silent, Paramount)—Marcia Gray
THE IMPOSSIBLE WOMAN (1919, Silent, GB, Ideal)—Mme. Kraska

COLLIER, LOIS
GIRL ON THE SPOT (1946, Universal)—Kathy Lorenz
MISS MINK OF 1949 (1949, 20th Century Fox)—Alice Forrester

COLLIER, WILLIAM, JR.
CARDIGAN (1922, Silent, American Releasing Corp.)—Michael Cardigan
THE RAINMAKER (1926, Silent, Paramount)—Bobby Robertson
TWO MEN AND A MAID (1929, Tiffany)—Jim Oxford
THE FIGHTING GENTLEMAN (1932, Monarch)—Jack Duncan

COLLINS, ALANA
NIGHT CALL NURSES (1974, New World)—Janis

COLLINS, ALEX B.
THE IMPOSTER (1915, Silent, World)—"Blink" Gregson

COLLINS, CHARLES
DANCING PIRATE (1936, RKO)—Jonathan Pride

COLLINS, COLLEEN
I, MAUREEN (1978, Canada, New Cinema)—Maureen

COLLINS, JOAN
THE ADVENTURES OF SADIE (1955, GB, 20th Century Fox)—
Sadie Patch
THE GIRL IN THE RED VELVET SWING (1955, 20th Century
Fox)—Evelyn Nesbitt Thaw
SEA WIFE (1957, GB, 20th Century Fox)—Sea Wife
ESTHER AND THE KING (1960, 20th Century Fox)—Esther

COLLINS, PAULINE
SHIRLEY VALENTINE (1989, Paramount)—Shirley Valentine-
Bradshaw

COLLINS, PHIL
BUSTER (1988, Tri-Star)—Buster Edwards

COLLINS, RAY
SPOILERS OF THE FOREST (1957, Republic)—Eric Warren

COLLINS, RUTH
NEW YORK'S FINEST (1988, Platinum)—Joy Sugarman
SEXPOT (1988, Platinum)—Ivy Barrington

COLLINS, STEPHEN
LOVING COUPLES (1980, 20th Century Fox)—Gregg

COLLINSON, MADELEINE
TWINS OF EVIL (1971, GB, Universal)—Frieda Gellhorn

COLLINSON, MARY
TWINS OF EVIL (1971, GB, Universal)—Maria Gellhorn

COLLYER, JUNE
THE THREE SISTERS (1930, Fox)—Elena

COLMAN, RONALD
HIS SUPREME MOMENT (1925, Silent, First National)—John
Douglas
BEAU GESTE (1926, Silent, Paramount)—Michael "Beau" Geste
TWO LOVERS (1928, Silent, United Artists)—Mark Van Rycke
BULLDOG DRUMMOND (1929, United Artists)—Bulldog
Drummond
RAFFLES (1930, United Artists)—A.J. Raffles
ARROWSMITH (1931, United Artists)—Dr. Martin Arrowsmith
THE MASQUERADER (1933, United Artists)—John Loder
BULLDOG DRUMMOND STRIKES BACK (1934, United Artists)—
Capt. Hugh Drummond
CLIVE OF INDIA (1935, Fox/United Artists)—Robert Clive
THE MAN WHO BROKE THE BANK AT MONTE CARLO (1935,
Fox)—Paul Gallard
UNDER TWO FLAGS (1936, 20th Century Fox)—Corporal Victor
THE PRISONER OF ZENDA (1937, United Artists)—King
Rudolf V
IF I WERE KING (1938, Paramount)—Francois Villon
LUCKY PARTNERS (1940, RKO)—David Grant
MY LIFE WITH CAROLINE (1941, RKO)—Anthony Mason

THE LATE GEORGE APLEY (1947, 20th Century Fox)—
George Apley

COLTRANE, ROBBIE
NUNS ON THE RUN (1990, GB, 20th Century Fox)—Sister
Inviolata (Charlie)
THE POPE MUST DIE (1991, GB, Palace/Miramax)—Father
David Albinzi

COMETHIERE, A.B.
BLACK KING (1932, Southland)—Charcoal Johnson

COMO, PERRY
IF I'M LUCKY (1946, 20th Century Fox)—Allen Clark

COMPSON, BETTY
COUNSEL FOR THE DEFENSE (1925, Silent, Associated
Exhibitors)—Katherine West
THE BELLE OF BROADWAY (1926, Silent, Columbia)—
Marie Duval
THE LADYBIRD (1927, Silent, First Division)—Diana Whyman
MASKED ANGEL (1928, GB, Silent, Chadwick)—Betty Carlisle
STREET GIRL (1929, RKO)—Frederika "Freddie" Joyzelle
WOMAN TO WOMAN (1929, Tiffany)—Lola
SHE GOT WHAT SHE WANTED (1930, Tiffany)—Mahyna

COMPTON, JOYCE
THE THREE SISTERS (1930, Fox)—Carlotta
SCARED TO DEATH (1947, Screen Guild)—Jane

COMPTON, JULIETTE
WOMAN TO WOMAN (1929, Tiffany)—Vesta

CONNELL, BETTY
SHE-DEVILS ON WHEELS (1968, Mayflower)—Queen

CONNELL, MAUREEN
KILL HER GENTLY (1958, GB, Columbia)—Kay Martin

CONNELLY, JENNIFER
SOME GIRLS (1989, MGM-United Artists)—Gabby

CONNERY, SEAN
SHALAKO (1968, GB, Cinerama)—Shalako
THE ANDERSON TAPES (1971, Columbia)—Anderson
THE MAN WHO WOULD BE KING (1975, GB, Allied Artists)—
Daniel Dravot
THE WIND AND THE LION (1975, MGM/United Artists)—Mulay
el Raisuli
THE NEXT MAN (1976, Allied Artists)—Khalif Abdul-Muhsen
ROBIN AND MARIAN (1976, GB, Columbia)—Robin Hood
THE UNTOUCHABLES (1987, Paramount)—James Malone
FAMILY BUSINESS (1989, Tri-Star)—Jessie McMullen
MEDICINE MAN (1992, Hollywood Pictures)—Dr. Robert
Campbell

CONNOLLY, WALTER
THE CAPTAIN HATES THE SEA (1934, Columbia)—Capt.
Helquist
FATHER BROWN, DETECTIVE (1935, Paramount)—
Father Brown
THE GREAT VICTOR HERBERT (1939, Paramount)—Victor
Herbert

CONNORS, CHUCK
GERONIMO (1962, United Artists)—Geronimo

THE MAD BOMBER (1973, Cinemation)—William Dorn

CONRAD, WILLIAM
THE KILLERS (1946, Universal)—Max

CONREID, HANS
THE 5,000 FINGERS OF DR. T (1953, Columbia)—Dr.
Terwilliker

CONSIDINE, JOHN
DOCTOR DEATH: SEEKER OF SOULS (1973, Cinerama)—
Dr. Death

CONTE, RICHARD
UNDER THE GUN (1951, Universal)—Bert Galvin
THE FIGHTER (1952, United Artists)—Filipe Rivera
THE BROTHERS RICO (1957, Columbia)—Eddie Rico
OCEAN'S ELEVEN (1960, Warners)—Anthony Bergdorf

CONTI, DIANE
TEENAGE GANG DEBS (1966, Jode/CID)—Terry

CONTI, TOM
MERRY CHRISTMAS MR. LAWRENCE (1983, GB, Universal)—
Col. John Lawrence

CONWAY, GARY
I WAS A TEENAGE FRANKENSTEIN (1958, American
International)—Teenage Monster
THE FARMER (1977, Columbia)—Kyle Martin

CONWAY, MORGAN
MILLIONAIRES IN PRISON (1940, RKO)—James Brent
DICK TRACY (1945, RKO)—Dick Tracy
DICK TRACY VS. CUEBALL (1946, RKO)—Dick Tracy

CONWAY, TIM
THE BILLION DOLLAR HOBO (1977, International Picture
Show)—Vernon Praiseworthy
THE PRIZE FIGHTER (1979, New World)—Bags
THE PRIVATE EYES (1980, New World)—Dr. Tart

CONWAY, TOM
THE FALCON'S BROTHER (1942, RKO)—Tom Lawrence
THE FALCON AND THE CO-EDS (1943, RKO)—Tom Lawrence
THE FALCON STRIKES BACK (1943, RKO)—Tom Lawrence
THE FALCON IN HOLLYWOOD (1944, RKO)—Tom Lawrence
THE FALCON IN MEXICO (1944, RKO)—Tom Lawrence
THE FALCON OUT WEST (1944, RKO)—Tom Lawrence
THE FALCON IN SAN FRANCISCO (1945, RKO)—Tom Lawrence
THE FALCON'S ADVENTURE (1946, RKO)—Tom Lawrence
THE FALCON'S ALIBI (1946, RKO)—Tom Lawrence
I CHEATED THE LAW (1949, 20th Century Fox)—John
Campbell
NORMAN CONQUEST (1953, GB, Lippert)—Norman Conquest
THE LAST MAN TO HANG (1956, GB, Columbia)—Sir Roderick
Strood

CONYNGHAM, FRED
BELOVED IMPOSTER (1936, GB, Radio)—George
THE MINSTREL BOY (1937, GB, Butchers)—Mike

COOGAN, JACKIE
THE KID (1921, Silent, Vitagraph)—The Kid
PECK'S BAD BOY (1921, Silent, Associate First National)—
Bill Peck

MY BOY (1922, Silent, Associate First National)—Jackie Blair
OLIVER TWIST (1922, Silent, Associate First National)—
Oliver Twist
A BOY OF FLANDERS (1924, Silent, MGM)—Nello
BUTTONS (1927, Silent, MGM)—Buttons
JOHNNY GET YOUR HAIR CUT (1927, Silent, MGM)—
Johnny O'Day
TOM SAWYER (1930, Paramount)—Jackie Coogan

COOGAN, KEITH
TOY SOLDIERS (1991, Tri-Star)—Snuffy Bradberry

COOGAN, ROBERT
SOOKY (1931, Paramount)—Sooky Wayne
HUMPHREY TAKES A CHANCE (1950, Monogram)—Humphrey
Pennyworth
JOE PALOOKA MEETS HUMPHREY (1950, Monogram)—
Humphrey Pennyworth

COOK, BILLY
TOM SAWYER, DETECTIVE (1939, Paramount)—Tom Sawyer

COOK, CLYDE
A SAILOR'S SWEETHEART (1927, Silent, Warners)—Sandy
MacTavish

COOK, LAWRENCE
THE SPOOK WHO SAT BY THE DOOR (1973, United Artists)—
Dan Freeman

COOK, MARIANNE
FOUR GIRLS IN TOWN (1956, Universal)—Ina Schiller

COOK, PETER
THOSE DARING YOUNG MEN IN THEIR JAUNTY JALOPIES
(1969, GB, Paramount)—Major Digby Dawlish
THE RISE AND RISE OF MICHAEL RIMMER (1970, GB,
Warners)—Michael Rimmer

COOK, RANDALL WILLIAM
I, MADMAN (1989, Trans World)—Malcolm Brand

COOKSON, GEORGINA
THE WOMAN WHO WOULDN'T DIE (1965, GB, Warners)—
Ellen Garth

COOKSON, PETER
SWINGTIME JOHNNY (1944, Universal)—Jonathan

COOPER, BEN
OUTLAW'S SON (1957, United Artists)—Jeff Blaine

COOPER, CAMI
THE APPLEGATES (1990, Roadshow)—Sally Applegate

COOPER, GARY
CHILDREN OF DIVORCE (1927, Silent, Paramount)—Ted
Larrabee
NEVADA (1927, Silent, Paramount)—Nevada
BEAU SABREUR (1928, Silent, Paramount)—Major Henri de
Beaujolais
THE VIRGINIAN (1929, Paramount)—The Virginian
A MAN FROM WYOMING (1930, Paramount)—Jim Baker
ONLY THE BRAVE (1930, Paramount)—Capt. James Braydon
THE TEXAN (1930, Paramount)—Enrique "Quico", The
Llano Kid

HIS WOMAN (1931, Paramount)—Capt. Sam Whalan
I TAKE THIS WOMAN (1931, Paramount)—Tom McNair
LIVES OF A BENGAL LANCER (1935, Paramount)—Lt. McGregor
PETER IBBETSON (1935, Paramount)—Peter Ibbetson
MR. DEEDS GOES TO TOWN (1936, Columbia)— Longfellow Deeds
THE PLAINSMAN (1937, Paramount)—Wild Bill Hickok
THE ADVENTURES OF MARCO POLO (1938, United Artists)— Marco Polo
BLUEBEARD'S EIGHTH WIFE (1938, Paramount)—Michael Brandon
THE COWBOY AND THE LADY (1938, United Artists)—Stretch
BEAU GESTE (1939, Paramount)—Beau Geste
THE WESTERNER (1940, United Artists)—Cole Hardin
MEET JOHN DOE (1941, Warners)—Long John Willoughby
SERGEANT YORK (1941, Warners)—Alvin C. York
THE PRIDE OF THE YANKEES (1942, RKO)—Lou Gehrig
CASANOVA BROWN (1944, RKO)—Casanova Brown
THE STORY OF DR. WASSELL (1944, Paramount)—Dr. Croyden M. Wassell
ALONG CAME JONES (1945, RKO)—Melody Jones
GOOD SAM (1948, RKO)—Sam Clayton
THE COURT MARTIAL OF BILLY MITCHELL (1955, Warners)— General Billy Mitchell
MAN OF THE WEST (1958, United Artists)—Link Jones
THEY CAME TO CORDURA (1959, Columbia)—Major Thomas Thorn

COOPER, GEORGE
SAILOR'S HOLIDAY (1929, Pathe)—Shorty

COOPER, JACKIE
SKIPPY (1931, Paramount)—Skippy Skinner
YOUNG DONOVAN'S KID (1931, RKO)—Midge Murray
FELLER NEEDS A FRIEND (1932, Cosmopolitan)—Eddie Randall
PECK'S BAD BOY (1934, Fox)—Bill Peck
DINKY (1935, Warners)—Dinky Daniels
O'SHAUGHNESSY'S BOY (1935, MGM)—Stubby O'Shaughnessy
TOUGH GUY (1936, MGM)—Freddie
BOY OF THE STREETS (1937, Monogram)—Chuck
GANGSTER'S BOY (1938, Monogram)—Larry Kelly
TWO BRIGHT BOYS (1939, Universal)—Roy O'Donnell
SEVENTEEN (1940, Paramount)—William Sylvanus Baxter
HER FIRST BEAU (1941, Columbia)—Chuck Harris
LIFE WITH HENRY (1941, Paramount)—Henry Aldrich
KILROY WAS HERE (1947, Monogram)—John J. Kilroy

COOPER, MIRIAM
THE INNOCENT SINNER (1917, Silent, Fox)—Mary Ellen Ellis
HER ACCIDENTAL HUSBAND (1923, Silent, Belasco)—Rena Goring

COOPER, RALPH
THE DUKE IS TOPS (1938, Million Dollar)—Duke Davis

COOPER, RICHARD
LORD RICHARD IN THE PANTRY (1930, GB, Warners)—Lord Richard Sandridge

COOPER, STUART
THE DIRTY DOZEN (1967, GB, MGM)—Roscoe Lever

COOTE, DAVID
TIM DRISCOLL'S DONKEY (1955, GB, British Lion)—Tim Driscoll

COOTE, ROBERT
THE THREE MUSKETEERS (1948, MGM)—Aramis

CORBETT, HARRY H.
COVER GIRL KILLER (1960, GB, Eros)—The Man
RATTLE OF A SIMPLE MAN (1964, GB, Associate British)— Percy Winthram
JOEY BOY (1965, GB, British Lion)—Joey Boy Thompson

CORBETT, JAMES J.
PRINCE OF AVENUE A (1920, Silent, Universal)—Barry O'Connor

CORBETT, JEFF
TALENT FOR THE GAME (1991, Paramount)—Sammy Bodeen

CORBIN, VIRGINIA LEE
FORGOTTEN WOMEN (1932, Monogram)—Sissy Salem

CORCORAN, KEVIN
TOBY TYLER (1960, Buena Vista)—Toby Tyler

CORD, ALEX
GRAYEAGLE (1977, American International)—Grayeagle

CORDA, MARIE
TESHA (1929, GB, Wardour)—Tesha

CORDAY, MARA
UNDERSEA GIRL (1957, Allied Artists)—Val Hudson

COREY, WENDELL
THE KILLER IS LOOSE (1956, United Artists)—Leon "Foggy" Poole

CORIO, ANN
SWAMP WOMAN (1941, Producers Releasing Corp.)—Annabelle
SARONG GIRL (1943, Monogram)—Dixie Barlow
THE SULTAN'S DAUGHTER (1943, Monogram)—Patra

CORNELIUS, JOE
TROG (1970, GB, Warners)—Trog

CORNWALL, ANNE
THE GOLD DIGGERS (1923, Silent, Warners)—Violet Dayne

CORRELL, CHARLES
AMOS 'N' ANDY (1930, Radio)—Amos Jones

CORRELL, MADY
MIDNIGHT MADONNA (1937, Paramount)—Kay Barrie

CORRIGAN, DOUGLAS
THE FLYING IRISHMAN (1939, RKO)—"Wrong Way" Corrigan

CORRIGAN, JAMES
PECK'S BAD BOY (1921, Silent, Associated First National)— Mr. Peck

CORRIGAN, JOE
STARCHASER: THE LEGEND OF ORIN (1985, Atlantic)—Orin

CORRIGAN, RAY "CRASH"
THE THREE MESQUITEERS (1936, Republic)—Tucson Smith
PALS OF THE SADDLE (1938, Republic)—Tucson Smith

IT! THE TERROR FROM BEYOND SPACE (1958, United Artists)—"It"

CORT, BUD
BREWSTER MCCLOUD (1970, MGM)—Brewster McCloud
HAROLD AND MAUDE (1971, Paramount)—Harold Chasen
WHY SHOOT THE TEACHER (1977, Canada, Ambasador)—Max Brown
THE SECRET DIARY OF SIGMUND FREUD (1984, 20th Century Fox)—Sigmund Freud
BRAIN DEAD (1990, Concorde)—Jack Halsey
TED AND VENUS (1991, Double Helix)—Ted Whitley

CORTESA, VALENTINA
SECRET PEOPLE (1952, GB, Ealing)—Maria Brentano

CORTEZ, RICARDO
HER MAN (1930, Pathe)—Johnnie
MEN OF CHANCE (1932, RKO)—Johnny Silk
BIG EXECUTIVE (1933, Paramount)—Victor Conway
POSTAL INSPECTOR (1936, Universal)—Bill Davis
THE CALIFORNIAN (1937, 20th Century Fox)—Ramon Escobar
TALK OF THE DEVIL (1937, GB, Gaumont)—Ray Allen

COSBY, BILL
HICKEY AND BOGGS (1972, United Artists)—Al Hickey
MAN AND BOY (1972, Jemmin/Levitt/Pickman)—Caleb Revers
MOTHER, JUGS & SPEED (1976, 20th Century Fox)—Mother
THE DEVIL AND MAX DEVLIN (1981, Buena Vista)—Barney Satin
LEONARD PART 6 (1987, Columbia)—Leonard
GHOST DAD (1990, Universal)—Elliot

COSTELLO, DOLORES
THE LITTLE IRISH GIRL (1926, Silent, Warners)—Dot Walker
THE COLLEGE WIDOW (1927, Silent, Warners)—Jane Witherspoon
THE GLAD RAG DOLL (1929, Warners)—Annabel Lea
MADONNA OF AVENUE A (1929, Warners)—Maria Morton
THE MAGNIFICENT AMBERSONS (1942, RKO)—Isabel Amberson Minafer

COSTELLO, LOU
BUCK PRIVATES (1941, Universal)—Herbie Brown
BUCK PRIVATES COME HOME (1947, Universal)—Herbie Brown
JACK AND THE BEANSTALK (1952, Warners)—Jack
DANCE WITH ME HENRY (1956, United Artists)—Lou Henry

COSTELLO, MAURICE
MR. BARNES OF NEW YORK (1914, Silent, Vitagraph)—Mr. Barnes
THE CROWN PRINCE'S DOUBLE (1916, Silent, Blue Ribbon)—Crown Prince Oscar & Barry Lawrence

COSTIGAN, GEORGE
RITA, SUE AND BOB TOO! (1987, GB, Orion)—Bob

COSTNER, KEVIN
AMERICAN FLYERS (1985, Warners)—Marcus
THE UNTOUCHABLES (1987, Paramount)—Eliot Ness
THE GUNRUNNER (1989, Canada, New World)—Ted Beaubien
DANCES WITH WOLVES (1990, Orion)—Lt. John Dunbar
ROBIN HOOD: PRINCE OF THIEVES (1991, Warner Brothers)—Robin of Locksley/Robin Hood

COTTEN, JOSEPH
I'LL BE SEEING YOU (1944, United Artists)—Zachary Morgan
WALK SOFTLY, STRANGER (1950, RKO)—Chris Hale
THE MAN WITH THE CLOAK (1951, MGM)—Dupin (Edgar Allan Poe)

COUDERC, PIERRE
THE PATCHWORK GIRL OF OZ (1914, Oz)—The Patchwork Girl

COUGHLIN, KEVIN
THE YOUNG RUNAWAYS (1968, MGM)—Dewey Norson
THE GAY DECEIVERS (1969, Fanfare)—Danny Devlin

COULTER, JACK
KEROUAC (1985, Daybreak)—Jack Kerouac

COURT, HAZEL
MODEL FOR MURDER (1960, GB, Cinema Associates)—Sally Meadows

COURTENAY, TOM
THE LONELINESS OF THE LONG DISTANCE RUNNER (1962, GB, Seven Arts)—Colin Smith
BILLY LIAR (1963, GB, Warners-Pathe)—Billy Fisher
PRIVATE POTTER (1963, MGM)—Pvt. Potter
OTLEY (1969, Columbia)—Gerald Arthur Otley
ONE DAY IN THE LIFE OF IVAN DENISOVICH (1971, Cinerama)—Ivan Denisovich
THE DRESSER (1983, Columbia)—Norman

COURTLAND, JEROME
THE BAREFOOT MAILMAN (1951, Columbia)—Steven Pierton

COURTNEIDGE, CICELY
AUNT SALLY (1933, GB, Gaumont)—Sally
ALONG CAME SALLY (1934, GB, Gaumont)—Sally Bird
THE WOMAN IN COMMAND (1934, GB, Gaumont)—Maisie Marvello
ME AND MARLBOROUGH (1935, GB, Gaumont)—Kit Rose
MISS TULIP STAYS THE NIGHT (1955, GB, Adelphi)—Millicent Tulip

COURTNEY, CHUCK
BILLY THE KID VS. DRACULA (1966, Circle/EM)—Billy the Kid

COURTNEY, JASON
THE FREEWAY MANIAC (1989, Cannon)—Arthur

COURTOT, MARGUERITE
JACQUELINE, OR BLAZING SADDLES (1923, Silent, Arrow)—Jacqueline Roland

COWARD, NOEL
THE SCOUNDREL (1935, Paramount)—Anthony Mallare

COYOTE, PETER
HEARTBREAKERS (1984, Orion)—Arthur Blue

CRABBE, LARRY "BUSTER"
KING OF THE JUNGLE (1933, Paramount)—Kaspa, the Lion Man
TARZAN THE FEARLESS (1933, Principal)—Tarzan
FLASH GORDON (1936, Universal)—Flash Gordon
NEVADA (1936, Paramount)—Nevada
BILLY THE KID WANTED (1941, Producers Releasing Corp.)—Billy the Kid

THE KID RIDES AGAIN (1943, Producers Releasing Corp.)—
Billy the Kid
THE CONTENDER (1944, Producers Releasing Corp.)—Gary
THE DRIFTER (1944, Producers Releasing Corp.)—Billy Carson/
Drifter Davis
FIGHTING BILL CARSON (1945, Producers Releasing Corp.)—
Bill Carson
GUN BROTHERS (1956, United Artists)—Chad

CRAIG, JAMES
DANGEROUS PARTNERS (1945, MGM)—Jeff Caighn
THE MAN FROM TEXAS (1948, Eagle-Lion)—El Paso Kid

CRAIG, MICHAEL
DOCTOR IN LOVE (1960, GB, Rank)—Dr. Richard Hare
THE IRISHMAN (1978, Australia, Greater Union)—Paddy Doolan

CRAIG, WENDY
JUST LIKE A WOMAN (1967, GB, Dormar/Monarch)—Scilla
Alexander

CRAIG, YVONNE
SEVEN WOMEN FROM HELL (1961, 20th Century Fox)—
Janet Cook

CRAIN, JEANNE
MARGIE (1946, 20th Century Fox)—Margie McDuff
APARTMENT FOR PEGGY (1948, 20th Century Fox)—Peggy
A LETTER TO THREE WIVES (1948, 20th Century Fox)—
Deborah Bishop
YOU WERE MEANT FOR ME (1948, 20th Century Fox)—Peggy
Mayhew
PINKY (1949, 20th Century Fox)—Pinky, Patricia Johnson
THE MODEL AND THE MARRIAGE BROKER (1951, 20th
Century Fox)—Kitty Bennett
TAKE CARE OF MY LITTLE GIRL (1951, 20th Century Fox)—
Liz Erickson
GENTLEMEN MARRY BRUNETTES (1955, United Artists)—
Connie

CRANE, BOB
SUPERDAD (1974, Buena Vista)—Charlie McCready

CRANE, RICHARD
JOHNNY COMES FLYING HOME (1946, 20th Century Fox)—
Johnny Martin

CRANE, WILLIAM H.
DAVID HARUM (1915, Silent, Famous Players)—David Harum
THREE WISE FOOLS (1923, Silent, Goldwyn)—Hon. James
Trumbull

CRAVEN, FRANK
OUR NEIGHBORS—THE CARTERS (1939, Paramount)—Doc
Carter
THE RICHEST MAN IN TOWN (1941, Columbia)—Abb Crothers

CRAVEN, JOHN
SOMEONE TO REMEMBER (1943, Republic)—Dan Freeman

CRAWFORD, ANNE
THEY WERE SISTERS (1945, GB, Universal)—Vera

CRAWFORD, BRODERICK
I CAN'T GIVE YOU ANYTHING BUT LOVE, BABY (1940,
Universal)—Sonny McGann

TEXAS RANGERS RIDE AGAIN (1940, Paramount)—Mace
Townsley
WHEN THE DALTONS RODE (1940, Universal)—Bob Dalton
BUTCH MINDS THE BABY (1942, Universal)—Aloysius
Grogan Butch
BAD MEN OF TOMBSTONE (1949, Monogram/Allied Artists)—
Morgan
THE PRIVATE FILES OF J. EDGAR HOOVER (1978, American
Int.)—J. Edgar Hoover

CRAWFORD, JOAN
THE TAXI DANCER (1927, Silent, MGM)—Joslyn Poe
OUR DANCING DAUGHTERS (1928, Silent, MGM)—Diana
Medford
OUR MODERN MAIDENS (1929, MGM)—Billie Brown
UNTAMED (1929, MGM)—Bingo
OUR BLUSHING BRIDES (1930, MGM)—Jerry Marsh
POSSESSED (1931, MGM)—Marian Martin
LETTY LYNTON (1932, MGM)—Letty Lynton
DANCING LADY (1933, MGM)—Janie Barlow
SADIE MCKEE (1934, MGM)—Sadie McKee
I LIVE MY LIFE (1935, MGM)—Kay
THE GORGEOUS HUSSY (1936, MGM)—Peggy O'Neal Eaton
THE BRIDE WORE RED (1937, MGM)—Anni
THE LAST OF MRS. CHEYNEY (1937, MGM)—Fay Cheyney
MANNEQUIN (1937, MGM)—Jessie Cassidy
THE WOMEN (1939, MGM)—Chrystal Allen
SUSAN AND GOD (1940, MGM)—Susan Trexel
WHEN LADIES MEET (1941, MGM)—Mary Howard
A WOMAN'S FACE (1941, MGM)—Anna Holm
THEY ALL KISSED THE BRIDE (1942, Columbia)—Margaret
J. Drew
MILDRED PIERCE (1945, Warners)—Mildred Pierce
DAISY KENYON (1947, 20th Century Fox)—Daisy Kenyon
POSSESSED (1947, Warners)—Louise Howell Graham
THE WOMAN ON THE BEACH (1947, RKO)—Peggy Butler
THE DAMNED DON'T CRY (1950, Warners)—Ethel Whitehead
(Lorna Hansen Forbes)
HARRIET CRAIG (1950, Columbia)—Harriet Craig
THIS WOMAN IS DANGEROUS (1952, Warners)—Beth Austin
FEMALE ON THE BEACH (1955, Universal)—Lynn Markham
QUEEN BEE (1955, Columbia)—Eva Phillips

CRAWFORD, JUNIA
THE GIRL IN THE PICTURE (1956, GB, Eros)—Pat Dryden

CRAWFORD, MICHAEL
HOW I WON THE WAR (1967, GB, United Artists)—Lt. Ernest
Goodbody
THE JOKERS (1967, GB, Universal)—Michael Tremayne
CONDORMAN (1981, Buena Vista)—Woody

CRAWFORD, WAYNE
JAKE SPEED (1986, New World)—Jake Speed

CRAWLEY, CONSTANCE
CHARLOTTE CORDAY (1914, Silent, Kennedy)—Charlotte
Corday

CREGAR, LAIRD
THE LODGER (1944, 20th Century Fox)—The Lodger

CRELEY, JACK
THE REINCARNATE (1971, Canada, Meridian)—Everet Julian

CRENNA, RICHARD
JOHN GOLDFARB, PLEASE COME HOME (1964, 20th Century Fox)—John Goldfarb
MAROONED (1969, Columbia)—Jim Pruett
A MAN CALLED NOON (1973, GB, National General)—Noon

CRIBBENS, BERNARD
DANGEROUS DAVIES—THE LAST DETECTIVE (1981, GB, ITC)—Dangerous Davies

CRISP, DONALD
THE COMMANDING OFFICER (1915, Silent, Paramount)—Colonel Archer

CROCKER, BARRY
ADVENTURES OF BARRY MCKENZIE (1972, Australia, Longford)—Barry McKenzie
BARRY MCKENZIE HOLDS HIS OWN (1975, Australia, Roadshow)—Barry McKenzie

CROMWELL, RICHARD
TOL'ABLE DAVID (1930, Columbia)—David Kinemon
THAT'S MY BOY (1932, Columbia)—Tommy
ENEMY AGENT (1940, Universal)—Jimmy Saunders
BABY FACE MORGAN (1942, Producers Releasing Corp.)—Baby Face Morgan

CRONIN, JOHN
THREE NUTS IN SEARCH OF A BOLT (1964, Harlequin)—Bruce Bernard

CROSBY, BING
DR. RHYTHM (1938, Paramount)—Dr. Remsen
THE STAR MAKER (1939, Paramount)—Larry Earl
WELCOME STRANGER (1947, Paramount)—Dr. Jim Pearson
A CONNECTICUT YANKEE IN KING ARTHUR'S COURT (1949, Paramount)—Hank Martin
MR. MUSIC (1950, Paramount)—Paul Merrick
HERE COMES THE GROOM (1951, Paramount)—Pete Garvey
MAN ON FIRE (1957, MGM)—Earl Carleton
ROBIN AND THE SEVEN HOODS (1964, Warners)—Allen A. Dale

CROSBY, BOB
THE SINGING SHERIFF (1944, Universal)—Bob Richards

CROSBY, CATHY LEE
COACH (1978, Crown)—Randy Rawlings

CROSMAN, HENRIETTE
THE ROYAL FAMILY OF BROADWAY (1930, Paramount)—Fanny Cavendish

CROSSE, RUPERT
THE REIVERS (1969, National General)—Ned McCaslin

CRUICKSHANK, ANDREW
THERE WAS A CROOKED MAN (1962, GB, United Artists)—McKillup

CRUISE, TOM
TOP GUN (1986, Paramount)—Maverick
BORN ON THE FOURTH OF JULY (1989, Universal)—Ron Kovic

CRYER, JON
DUDES (1987, New Century-Vista)—Grant

MORGAN STEWART'S COMING HOME (1987, New Century-Vista)—Morgan Stewart

CRYSTAL, ANITA
THE DEVIL'S SISTER (1966, Mustang Productions)—Rita Alvardo

CRYSTAL, BILLY
WHEN HARRY MET SALLY. . .(1989, Columbia)—Harry Burns
CITY SLICKERS (1991, Columbia)—Mitch Robbins

CUKA, FRANCES
HENRY VIII AND HIS SIX WIVES (1972, GB, EMI/MGM)—Katharine of Aragon

CULKIN, MACAULAY
HOME ALONE (1990, 20th Century Fox)—Kevin
MY GIRL (1991, Columbia)—Thomas J. Sennett

CULP, ROBERT
BOB AND CAROL AND TED AND ALICE (1969, Columbia)—Bob
HICKEY AND BOGGS (1972, United Artists)—Frank Boggs

CUMMINGS, CONSTANCE
STRANGERS ON A HONEYMOON (1937, GB, Gaumont)—October Jones

CUMMINGS, IRVING
THE INTERLOPER (1918, Silent, World)—Paul Whitney

CUMMINGS, ROBERT
THE PETTY GIRL (1950, Columbia)—George Petty

CUMMINS, PEGGY
GUN CRAZY (1949, United Artists)—Annie Laurie Starr
ALWAYS A BRIDE (1954, GB, General)—Clare Hemsley

CUMMINS, PETER
THE FIRM MAN (1975, Australia, Australian Film Institute)—Gerald Baxter

CUNEO, LESTER
THE MASKED AVENGER (1922, Silent, Doubleday)—Austin Patterson

CURTIS, ALAN
FOUR SONS (1940, 20th Century Fox)—Karl Bernie
THE DALTONS RIDE AGAIN (1945, Universal)—Emmett Dalton
PHILO VANCE'S GAMBLE (1947, Producers Releasing Corp.)—Philo Vance
PHILO VANCE'S SECRET MISSION (1947, Producers Releasing Corp.)—Philo Vance

CURTIS, JAMIE LEE
A FISH CALLED WANDA (1988, MGM)—Wanda Gershwitz

CURTIS, SCOTT
CAMERON'S CLOSET (1989, SVS)—Cameron Lansing

CURTIS, TONY
THE PRINCE WHO WAS A THIEF (1951, Universal)—Julna
NO ROOM FOR THE GROOM (1952, Universal)—Alvah Morrell
SON OF ALI BABA (1952, Universal)—Kashma Baba
THE ALL-AMERICAN (1953, Universal)—Nick Bonelli
HOUDINI (1953, Paramount)—Harry Houdini

JOHNNY DARK (1954, Universal)—Johnny Dark
MISTER CORY (1957, Universal)—Cory
THE DEFIANT ONES (1958, United Artists)—John "Joker" Jackson
THE GREAT IMPOSTER (1960, Universal)—Ferdinand Waldo Demara Jr.
THE OUTSIDER (1962, Universal)—Ira Hamilton Hayes
NOT WITH MY WIFE, YOU DON'T (1966, Warners)—Tom Ferris
THE BOSTON STRANGLER (1968, 20th Century Fox)—Albert DeSalvo
THOSE DARING YOUNG MEN IN THEIR JAUNTY JALOPIES (1969, GB, Paramount)—Chester Schofield
LEPKE (1975, Warners)—Louis "Lepke" Buchalter
WHERE IS PARSIFAL? (1984, GB, Young)—Parsifal Katenellbogen

CURWEN, PATRIC
THE RINGER (1932, GB, British Lion)—Dr. Lomond

CURZON, GEORGE
SEXTON BLAKE AND THE BEARDED DOCTOR (1935, GB, MGM)—Sexton Blake
SEXTON BLAKE AND THE MADEMOISELLE (1935, GB, MGM)—Sexton Blake
TWO HEARTS IN HARMONY (1935, GB, British Int.)—Lord Sheldon
SEXTON BLAKE AND THE HOODED TERROR (1938, GB, MGM)—Sexton Blake

CUSACK, CYRIL
SOLDIERS THREE (1951, MGM)—Pvt. Dennis Malloy

CUSACK, JOHN
BETTER OFF DEAD (1985, Warners)—Lane Myer
EIGHT MEN OUT (1988, Orion)—Buck Weaver
TAPEHEADS (1988, Avenue Pictures)—Ivan Alexcov
THE GRIFTERS (1990, Miramax)—Roy Dillon

CUSHING, PETER
THE CURSE OF FRANKENSTEIN (1957, GB, Hammer)—Baron Victor Frankenstein
THE REVENGE OF FRANKENSTEIN (1958, GB, Columbia)—Dr. Victor Stein
THE EVIL OF FRANKENSTEIN (1964, GB, Universal)—Baron Frankenstein
DR. TERROR'S HOUSE OF HORRORS (1965, GB, Amicus)—Dr. Schreck
DR. WHO AND THE DALEKS (1965, GB, Aaru)—Dr. Who
FRANKENSTEIN CREATED WOMAN (1965, GB, Hammer)—Baron Frankenstein
FRANKENSTEIN MUST BE DESTROYED (1969, GB, Hammer)—Baron Frankenstein
FRANKENSTEIN AND THE MONSTER FROM HELL (1974, GB, Hammer)—Baron Frankenstein

CUSTER, BOB
A MAN OF NERVE (1925, Silent, FBO)—Hackamore Henderson
THE DUDE COWBOY (1926, Silent, Independent)—Bob Ralston
THE FIGHTING BOOB (1926, Silent, R-C/FBO)—El Tigre
HAIR TRIGGER BAXTER (1926, Silent, Independent)—Baxter Brant
THE OKLAHOMA KID (1929, Silent, Syndicate Releasing)—The Kid

D

DAFOE, WILLEM
PLATOON (1987, Orion)—Sgt. Elias
THE LAST TEMPTATION OF CHRIST (1988, Universal)—Jesus Christ
LIGHT SLEEPER (1992, Seven Arts)—John Latour

DAGOVER, LIL
THE WOMAN FROM MONTE CARLO (1932, First National)—Lottie Corlaix

DAHL, ARLENE
MY WILD IRISH ROSE (1947, Warners)—Rose Donovan
THE DIAMOND QUEEN (1953, Warners)—Maya
WOMEN'S WORLD (1954, 20th Century Fox)—Carol
SHE PLAYED WITH FIRE (1957, GB, Columbia)—Sarah Moreton

DAILEY, DAN
YOU WERE MEANT FOR ME (1948, 20th Century Fox)—Chuck Arnold
MY BLUE HEAVEN (1950, 20th Century Fox)—Jack Moran
WHEN WILLIE COMES MARCHING HOME (1950, 20th Century Fox)—Bill Kluggs
CALL ME MISTER (1951, 20th Century Fox)—Shep Dooley
THE PRIDE OF ST. LOUIS (1952, 20th Century Fox)—Dizzy Dean
OH, MEN! OH, WOMEN! (1957, 20th Century Fox)—Arthur Turner
UNDERWATER WARRIOR (1958, MGM)—Cmdr. David Forest

DAILEY, IRENE
THE GRISSOM GANG (1971, Cinerama)—Ma Grissom

DAINTON, PATRICIA
WITNESS IN THE DARK (1959, GB, Rank)—Jane Pringle

DALE, CYNTHIA
HEAVENLY BODIES (1985, Universal)—Samantha

DALE, JENNIFER
SUZANNE (1980, Canada, Ambassador)—Suzanne McDonald
SEPARATE VACATIONS (1986, RSK Entertainment)—Sarah Moore

DALE, JIM
CARRY ON, DOCTOR (1969, GB, Rank)—Dr. James Nookey

D'ALGY, HELEN
THE COWBOY AND THE COUNTESS (1926, Silent, Fox)—Countess Justina

DALL, EVELYN
MISS LONDON LTD (1943, GB, GFD)—Terry Arden

DALTON, AUDREY
GIRLS OF PLEASURE ISLAND (1953, Paramount)—Hester Halyard

DALTON, DOROTHY
THE JUNGLE CHILD (1916, Silent, Triangle)—Ollante
FEMALE OF THE SPECIES (1917, Silent, Triangle)—Gloria Marley
THE HOMEBREAKER (1919, Silent, Paramount)—Mary Marsden

THE IDOL OF THE NORTH (1921, Silent, Paramount)—Colette Brissac
MORAN OF THE LADY LETTY (1922, Silent, Paramount)—Moran/Letty Sternersen
THE WOMAN WHO WALKED ALONE (1922, Silent, Paramount)—Iris Champneys

DALTON, TIMOTHY
THE DOCTOR AND THE DEVILS (1985, GB, 20th Century Fox)—Dr. Thomas Rock
LICENSE TO KILL (1989, MGM-United Artists)—James Bond
THE KING'S WHORE (1990, France/Austria/GB/Italy, J&M)—King Vittorio Amadeo

DALTREY, ROGER
LISZTOMANIA (1975, GB, Warners)—Franz Liszt
TOMMY (1975, GB, Columbia)—Tommy Walker
MCVICAR (1982, GB, Crown)—McVicar

D'AMBOISE, JACQUES
SEVEN BRIDES FOR SEVEN BROTHERS (1954, MGM)—Ephraim Pontabee

DAMEREL, DONNA
MYRT AND MARGE (1934, Universal)—Marge Spear

DAMITA, LILI
WOMAN BETWEEN (1931, RKO)—Mme. Julie
GOLDIE GETS ALONG (1933, RKO)—Goldie LaFarge

DAMON, MARK
YOUNG AND DANGEROUS (1957, 20th Century Fox)—Tommy Price
THE PARTY CRASHERS (1958, Paramount)—Twig Webster
BEAUTY AND THE BEAST (1963, United Artists)—Duke Eduardo

DAMPIER, CLAUDE
WANTED (1937, GB, Sound City)—Henry Oatfield

DANA, VIOLA
THE INNOCENCE OF RUTH (1916, Silent, Edison)—Ruth Travers
THE GIRL WITHOUT A SOUL (1917, Silent, Metro)—Priscilla Beaumont
DANGEROUS TO MEN (1920, Silent, Metro)—Eliza
HER FATAL MILLIONS (1923, Silent, Metro)—Mary Bishop
ALONG CAME RUTH (1924, Silent, MGM)—Ruth Ambrose
KOSHER KITTY KELLY (1926, Silent, R-C Pictures)—Kitty Kelly
NAUGHTY NANETTE (1927, Silent, R-C/FBO)—Nanette Pearson
SALVATION JANE (1927, Silent, R-C Pictures)—Salvation Jane

DANDRIDGE, DOROTHY
CARMEN JONES (1954, 20th Century Fox)—Carmen Jones
PORGY AND BESS (1959, Columbia)—Bess

DANEEL, SYLVIA
SEVEN WOMEN FROM HELL (1961, 20th Century Fox)—Ann Van Laer

D'ANGELO, BEVERLY
LONELY HEARTS (1991, Live Entertainment)—Alma

DANIELLE, SUZANNE
CARRY ON EMMANNUELLE (1978, GB, Hemdale)—Emmannuelle

DANIELS, BEBE
OH, LADY, LADY (1920, Silent, Realart)—May Barber
THE SPEED GIRL (1921, Silent, Paramount)—Betty Lee
NANCY FROM NOWHERE (1922, Silent, Paramount)—Nancy
NICE PEOPLE (1922, Silent, Paramount)—Theodora "Teddy" Gloucester
SINGED WINGS (1922, Silent, Paramount)—Bonita Della Guerda
SINNERS IN HEAVEN (1924, Silent, Paramount)—Barbara Stockley
MISS BLUEBEARD (1925, Silent, Paramount)—Colette Girard
THE CAMPUS FLIRT (1926, Silent, Paramount)—Patricia Mansfield
MISS BREWSTER'S MILLIONS (1926, Silent, Paramount)—Polly Brewster
SHE'S A SHEIK (1927, Paramount)—Zaida
THE FIFTY-FIFTY GIRL (1928, Silent, Paramount)—Kathleen O'Hara
RIO RITA (1929, RKO)—Rita Ferguson
ALIAS FRENCH GERTIE (1930, RKO)—Marie
DIXIANA (1930, RKO)—Dixiana
A SOUTHERN MAID (1933, GB, Wardour)—Dolores/Juanita
REGISTERED NURSE (1934, Warners)—Sylvia Benton
THE RETURN OF CAROL DEANE (1938, GB, Warners)—Carol Deane

DANIELY, LISA
LILLI MARLENE (1951, GB, RKO)—Lilli Marlene
THE WEDDING OF LILLI MARLENE (1953, GB, Monarch)—Lilli Marlene
TWO WIVES AT ONE WEDDING (1961, GB, Paramount)—Annette

DANNER, BLYTHE
LOVIN' MOLLY (1974, Columbia)—Molly
MAN, WOMAN AND CHILD (1983, Paramount)—Sheila Beckwith

DANNING, SYBIL
THEY'RE PLAYING WITH FIRE (1984, New World)—Diane
WARRIOR QUEEN (1987, Seymour Borde)—Berenice

DANO, ROYAL
TEACHERS (1984, MGM/United Artists)—Ditto

DANSON, TED
THREE MEN AND A BABY (1987, Buena Vista)—Jack Holden
COUSINS (1989, Paramnount)—Larry Kozinski
THREE MEN AND A LITTLE LADY (1990, Buena Vista)—Jack Holden

DANTE, MICHAEL
WINTERHAWK (1976, Howco Int.)—Chief Winterhawk

DANTINE, HELMUT
THE STRANGER FROM VENUS (1954, GB, Princess)—Stranger

DANTON, RAY
THE NIGHT RUNNER (1957, Universal)—Roy Turner
THE RISE AND FALL OF LEGS DIAMOND (1960, Warners)—Jack "Legs" Diamond

THE GEORGE RAFT STORY (1961, Allied Artists)—George Raft

DARCEL, DENISE
TARZAN AND THE SLAVE GIRL (1950, RKO)—Lola
FLAME OF CALCUTTA (1953, Columbia)—Suzanne Roget
SEVEN WOMEN FROM HELL (1961, 20th Century Fox)—
Claire Oudry

DARE, CARLA
CITIZEN SAINT (1947, State-Rights)—Mother Francis Cabrini

DARE, DOROTHY
GOLD DIGGERS OF 1935 (1935, Warners)—Arline Davis

DARIN, BOBBY
IF A MAN ANSWERS (1962, Universal)—Eugene Wright

DARLING, JEAN
JANE EYRE (1935, Monogram)—Young Jane Eyre

DARMOND, GRACE
THE BEAUTIFUL GAMBLER (1921, Silent, Universal)—Molly
Hanlon

DARNELL, LINDA
DAY-TIME WIFE (1939, 20th Century Fox)—Jane Norton
FOREVER AMBER (1947, 20th Century Fox)—Amber St. Clair
A LETTER TO THREE WIVES (1948, 20th Century Fox)—Lora
May Hollingsway
THE LADY PAYS OFF (1951, Universal)—Evelyn Warren

DARREN, JAMES
THE BROTHERS RICO (1957, Columbia)—Johnny Rico

DARRIEUX, DANIELLE
THE RAGE OF PARIS (1938, Universal)—Nicole de Cortillon

DARRO, FRANKIE
SO BIG (1924, Silent, First National)—Dirk Dejong as a boy
THE CIRCUS KID (1928, Film Booking Offices)—Buddy
LITTLE MEN (1935, Mascot)—Dan
THREE KIDS AND A QUEEN (1935, Universal)—Blackie
BORN TO FIGHT (1938, Commodore)—Baby Face
WANTED BY THE POLICE (1938, Monogram)—Danny

DARROW, JOHN
THE ARGYLE CASE (1929, Warners)—Bruce Argyle

DARWELL, JANE
PRIVATE NURSE (1941, 20th Century Fox)—Miss Adams
CAPTAIN TUGBOAT ANNIE (1945, Republic)—Tugboat Annie

DAVEN, DANIELLE
RABID GRANNIES (1989, Troma)—Elisabeth Remington

DAVENPORT, HARRY
GRANDPA GOES TO TOWN (1940, Republic)—Grandpa Higgins

DAVENPORT, NIGEL
STAND UP VIRGIN SOLDIERS (1977, GB, Warners)—Sgt.
Driscoll

DAVID, ELEANOR
SYLVIA (1985, MGM/United Artists)—Sylvia Henderson

DAVID, KEITH
PLATOON (1987, Orion)—King

DAVIDOVICH, LOLITA
BLAZE (1989, Buena Vista)—Blaze Starr

DAVIDSON, DORE
WELCOME STRANGER (1924, Silent, Producers Distributing
Corp.)—Isadore Solomon

DAVIDSON, MAX
THE RAG MAN (1925, Silent, Metro-Goldwyn)—Max Ginsberg

DAVIES, BETTY ANN
SHE KNEW WHAT SHE WANTED (1936, GB, Wardour)—Frankie

DAVIES, JOHN HOWARD
OLIVER TWIST (1951, GB, Rank)—Oliver Twist
TOM BROWN'S SCHOOL DAYS (1951, GB, United Artists)—
Tom Brown

DAVIES, MARION
CECILIA OF THE PINK ROSES (1918, Silent, Select)—Cecilia
Madden
GETTING MARY MARRIED (1919, Silent, Selznick)—Mary
ADAM AND EVA (1923, Silent, Paramount)—Eva King
JANICE MEREDITH (1924, Silent, Metro)—Janice Meredith
BEVERLY OF GRAUSTARK (1926, Silent, MGM)—Beverly
Calhoun
TILLIE THE TOILER (1927, Silent, MGM)—Tillie Jones
THE CARDBOARD LOVER (1928, Silent, MGM)—Sally
MARIANNE (1929, MGM)—Marianne
THE FLORODORA GIRL (1930, MGM)—Daisy
NOT SO DUMB (1930, MGM)—Dulcy
IT'S A WISE CHILD (1931, MGM)—Joyce
BLONDIE OF THE FOLLIES (1932, MGM)—Blondie McClune
POLLY OF THE CIRCUS (1932, MGM)—Polly Fisher
PEG O' MY HEART (1933, MGM)—Peg O'Connell
OPERATOR 13 (1934, MGM)—Gail Loveless/"Ann Clairbourne"
PAGE MISS GLORY (1935, Warners)—"Dawn" Glory/Loretta
Dalrymple
CAIN AND MABEL (1936, Warners)—Mabel O'Dare

DAVIS, BETTE
THREE ON A MATCH (1932, Warners)—Ruth Westcott
EX-LADY (1933, Warners)—Helen Bauer
FRONT PAGE WOMAN (1935, Warners)—Ellen Garfield
THE GIRL FROM TENTH AVENUE (1935, First National)—
Miriam Brady
DANGEROUS (1936, Warners)—Joyce Heath
SATAN MET A LADY (1936, Warners)—Valerie Purvis
IT'S LOVE I'M AFTER (1937, Warners)—Joyce Arden
MARKED WOMAN (1937, Warners)—Mary Dwight
THAT CERTAIN WOMAN (1937, Warners)—Mary Donnell
JEZEBEL (1938, Warners)—Julie Morrison
THE SISTERS (1938, Warners)—Louise Elliott
THE OLD MAID (1939, Warners)—Charlotte Lovell
THE PRIVATE LIVES OF ELIZABETH AND ESSEX (1939,
Warners)—Elizabeth I
THE BRIDE CAME C.O.D. (1941, Warners)—Joan Winfield
NOW, VOYAGER (1942, Warners)—Charlotte Vale
OLD ACQUAINTANCE (1943, Warners)—Kitty Marlowe
A STOLEN LIFE (1946, Warners)—Kate & Pat Bosworth
THE STAR (1953, 20th Century Fox)—Margaret Elliot
THE VIRGIN QUEEN (1955, 20th Century Fox)—Queen
Elizabeth I

WHAT EVER HAPPENED TO BABY JANE? (1962, Warners)—
Jane Hudson
DEAD RINGER (1964, Warners)—Margaret & Edith
HUSH. . .HUSH SWEET CHARLOTTE (1964, 20th Century Fox)—
Charlotte
THE NANNY (1965, GB, 20th Century Fox)—Nanny
BUNNY O'HARE (1971, American International)—Bunny O'Hare
WICKED STEPMOTHER (1989, MGM-United Artists)—Miranda

DAVIS, BRAD
A SMALL CIRCLE OF FRIENDS (1980, United Artists)—Leo
DaVinci

DAVIS, DANIEL (EDWARD D. WOOD, JR.)
GLEN OR GLENDA (1953, Paramount)—Glen/Glenda

DAVIS, GEENA
EARTH GIRLS ARE EASY (1989, Vestron)—Valerie Dale
THELMA AND LOUISE (1991, Pathe)—Thelma

DAVIS, JIM
THREE DESPERATE MEN (1951, Lippert)—Fred Denton
THE GAMBLER WORE A GUN (1961, United Artists)—Case
Silverthorn

DAVIS, JOAN
HOLD THAT CO-ED (1938, 20th Century Fox)—Lizzie
SALLY, IRENE AND MARY (1938, 20th Century Fox)—
Irene Keene
SHE GETS HER MAN (1945, Universal)—Jane "Pilky" Pilkington
SHE WROTE THE BOOK (1946, Universal)—Jane Featherstone
IF YOU KNEW SUSIE (1948, RKO)—Susie Parker
TRAVELLING SALESWOMAN (1950, Columbia)—Mabel King

DAVIS, JOHNNIE
MR. CHUMP (1938, Warners)—Bill Small

DAVIS, JUDY
MY BRILLIANT CAREER (1980, Australia, New South Wales)—
Sybylla Melvyn

DAVIS, LILLIAN HALL
THE HOTEL MOUSE (1923, Silent, GB, Jury)—Mauricette

DAVIS, LISA
THE DALTON GIRLS (1957, United Artists)—Rose Dalton

DAVIS, NATHAN
POLTERGEIST III (1988, MGM-United Artists)—Rev. Kane

DAVIS, OSSIE
SLAVES (1969, Continental)—Luke

DAVIS, OWEN JR.
BUNKER BEAN (1936, RKO)—Bunker Bean

DAVIS, ROGER
FLASH AND THE FIRECAT (1976, Sebastian)—Firecat

DAVIS, RUFE
THE TRAIL BLAZERS (1940, Republic)—Lullaby Joslin
PALS OF THE PECOS (1941, Republic)—Lullaby Joslin
SADDLEMATES (1941, Republic)—Lullaby Joslin
THE PHANTOM PLAINSMAN (1942, Republic)—Lullaby Joslin

DAVIS, SAMMY JR.
OCEAN'S ELEVEN (1960, Warners)—Josh Howard
ROBIN AND THE SEVEN HOODS (1964, Warners)—Will

A MAN CALLED ADAM (1966, Embassy)—Adam Johnson
SALT & PEPPER (1968, GB, United Artists)—Charles Salt

DAVIS, WARWICK
WILLOW (1988, MGM)—Willow Ufgood

DAVISON, BRUCE
WILLARD (1971, Cinerama)—Willard Stiles
LONGTIME COMPANION (1990, Goldwyn)—David

D'AVRIL, YOLA
THOSE THREE FRENCH GIRLS (1930, MGM)—Diane

DAW, MARJORIE
THE BUTTERFLY GIRL (1921, Silent, Playgoers)—Edith Folsom

DAWN, HAZEL
ONE OF OUR GIRLS (1914, Silent, Famous Players)—Miss
Shipley

DAWSON, BILLY
FATHER'S SON (1941, Warners)—Bill Emory

DAWSON, MARION
HIS WIFE'S MOTHER (1932, GB, British Int.)—Mrs. Trout

DAY, ALICE
PHYLLIS OF THE FOLLIES (1928, Silent, Universal)—Phyllis
Sherwood

DAY, DORIS
I'LL SEE YOU IN MY DREAMS (1951, Warners)—Grace
LeBoy Kahn
CALAMITY JANE (1953, Warners)—Calamity Jane Canary
LUCKY ME (1954, Warners)—Candy Williams
JULIE (1956, MGM)—Julie Benton
TEACHER'S PET (1958, Paramount)—Erica Stone
IT HAPPENED TO JANE (1959, Columbia)—Jane Osgood
LOVER COME BACK (1961, Universal)—Carol Templeton
THE BALLAD OF JOSIE (1968, Universal)—Josie Minick

DAY, FRANCES
TWO HEARTS IN WALTZ TIME (1934, GB, Gaumont)—
Helene Barry
THE GIRL FROM MAXIM'S (1936, GB, London Films)—"La
Mome"

DAY, JILL
ALL FOR MARY (1956, GB, Rank)—Mary

DAY, LARAINE
THE TRIAL OF MARY DUGAN (1941, MGM)—Mary Dugan
MY DEAR SECRETARY (1948, United Artists)—Stephanie
Gaylord

DAY-LEWIS, DANIEL
MY LEFT FOOT (1989, Great Britain, Miramax)—Christy Brown

DE CARLO, YVONNE
FRONTIER GAL (1945, Universal)—Lorena Dumont
SALOME, WHERE SHE DANCED (1945, Universal)—Salome
SLAVE GIRL (1947, Universal)—Francesca
SONG OF SCHEHERAZADE (1947, Universal)—Cara de Talavera
RIVER LADY (1948, Universal)—Sequin
CALAMITY JANE AND SAM BASS (1949, Universal)—
Calamity Jane

THE GAL WHO TOOK THE WEST (1949, Universal)—Lillian
Marlowe
BUCCANEER'S GIRL (1950, Universal)—Deborah McCoy
SCARLET ANGEL (1952, Universal)—Roxy McClanahan
FLAME OF THE ISLANDS (1955, Republic)—Rosalind Dee

DE CASALIS, JEANNE
CHARLEY'S BIG-HEARTED AUNT (1940, GB, Gainsborough)—
Aunt Lucy

DE CORDOBA, PEDRO
THE BANDOLERO (1924, Silent, MGM)—Dorando

DE CORDOVA, ARTURO
ADVENTURES OF CASANOVA (1948, Eagle-Lion)—Casanova

DE GRAF, JOSEPH
THE WILBY CONSPIRACY (1975, United Artists)—Wilby

DE GRASSE, SAM
IN THE PALACE OF THE KING (1923, Silent, Goldwyn)—King
Philip II

DE HAVEN, CARTER
THE COLLEGE ORPHAN (1915, Silent, Universal)—Jack
Bennett, Jr.

DE HAVEN, GLORIA
TWO GIRLS AND A SAILOR (1944, MGM)—Jean Deyo

DE HAVILLAND, OLIVIA
MY LOVER CAME BACK (1940, Warners)—Amelia Cullen
GOVERNMENT GIRL (1943, RKO)—Smokey
PRINCESS O'ROURKE (1943, Warners)—Princess Maria
O'Rourke
THE WELL-GROOMED BRIDE (1946, Paramount)—Margie
Dawson
THE HEIRESS (1949, Paramount)—Catherine Sloper
MY COUSIN RACHEL (1952, 20th Century Fox)—Rachel Ashley
THAT LADY (1955, 20th Century Fox)—Ana de Mendoza
THE AMBASSADOR'S DAUGHTER (1956, United Artists)—
Joan Fiske
LADY IN A CAGE (1964, Paramount)—Mrs. Hillyard

DE LA MOTTE, MARGUERITE
JUST LIKE A WOMAN (1923, Silent, Hodkinson)—Peggy Dean
THE GIRL WHO WOULDN'T WORK (1925, Silent, Schulberg)—
Mary Hale

DE LA PENA, GEORGE
NIJINSKY (1980, GB, Paramount)—Vaslav Nijinsky

DE LACEY, PHILLIPPE
THE ROYAL RIDER (1929, Silent, First National)—King
Michael XI
SARAH AND SON (1930, Paramount)—Bobby Storm Ashmore

DE LUISE, DOM
FATSO (1980, 20th Century Fox)—Dominick DiNapoli
MUNCHIE (1992, Concorde Pictures)—Voice of Munchie

DE MARNEY, DERRICK
THE SECOND MR. BUSH (1940, GB, Anglo-American)—Tony
MEET MR. CALLAGHAN (1954, GB, Pinnacle)—Slim Callaghan

DE MORNAY, REBECCA
THE SLUGGER'S WIFE (1985, Columbia)—Debby Palmer
AND GOD CREATED WOMAN (1988, Vestron)—Robin
DEALERS (1989, Great Britain, Rank)—Anna Schuman
THE HAND THAT ROCKS THE CRADLE (1992, Hollywood
Pictures)—Peyton Flanders

DE MOSS, DARCY
LIVING TO DIE (1990, PM)—Maggie

DE NIRO, ROBERT
THE GODFATHER, PART II (1974, Paramount)—Vito Corleone
THE LAST TYCOON (1976, Paramount)—Monroe Stahr
TAXI DRIVER (1976, Columbia)—Travis Bickle
THE DEER HUNTER (1978, Columbia/Warners)—Michael
RAGING BULL (1980, United Artists)—Jake LaMotta
KING OF COMEDY (1983, 20th Century Fox)—Rupert Pupkin
FALLING IN LOVE (1984, Paramount)—Frank Raftis
JACKKNIFE (1989, Cineplex/Odeon)—Joseph 'Megs' Megessey
WE'RE NO ANGELS (1989, Paramount)—Ned/Fr. Reilly
AWAKENINGS (1990, Columbia)—Leonard Lowe
GOODFELLAS (1990, Warners)—James Conway
STANLEY & IRIS (1990, MGM/UA)—Stanley
GUILTY BY SUSPICION (1991, Warner Brothers)—David Merrill

DE PUTTI, LYA
THE SCARLET LADY (1928, Silent, Columbia)—Lya

DE ROLF, PAUL
THE SEVEN LITTLE FOYS (1955, Paramount)—Richard Foy

DE ROUEN, REED
THE PLEASURE LOVERS (1964, GB, Butchers)—Eddie

DE SILVA, HOWARD
THREE HUSBANDS (1950, United Artists)—Dan McCabe

DE VARGAS, VALENTIN
THE FIREBRAND (1962, 20th Century Fox)—Joaquin Murieta

DE VITO, DANNY
WISE GUYS (1986, MGM/United Artists)—Harry Valentini
TIN MEN (1987, Buena Vista)—Ernest Tilley
TWINS (1988, Universal)—Vincent Benedict

DE WALT REYNOLDS, ADELINE
TUTTLES OF TAHITI (1942, RKO)—Mama Rusu Tuttle

DE WILDE, BRANDON
THE MISSOURI TRAVELLER (1958, Buena Vista)—Brian Turner
THOSE CALLOWAYS (1964, Buena Vista)—Bucky Calloway

DEACON, BRIAN
JESUS (1979, Warners)—Jesus

DEAK, MICHAEL S.
CELLER DWELLER (1988, Dove/Empire)—Celler Dweller

DEAN, JACK
TENNESSEE'S PARTNER (1916, Silent, Lasky)—Jack Hunter

DEAN, JAMES
REBEL WITHOUT A CAUSE (1955, Warners)—Jim

DEAN, LOREN
BILLY BATHGATE (1991, Buena Vista/Touchstone)—Billy
Bathgate

DEAN, MARGIA
SEVEN WOMEN FROM HELL (1961, 20th Century Fox)—Mara Shepherd

DEAN, PRISCILLA
THE STORM DAUGHTER (1924, Silent, Universal)—Kate Masterson
THE CRIMSON RUNNER (1925, Silent, Producers Distributing Corp.)—Bianca Schreber

DEE, FRANCES
LITTLE WOMEN (1933, RKO)—Meg March
HALF ANGEL (1936, 20th Century Fox)—Allison Lang
MEET THE STEWARTS (1942, Columbia)—Candace Goodwin Stewart

DEE, SANDRA
THE RELUCTANT DEBUTANTE (1958, MGM)—Jane Broadbent
GIDGET (1959, Columbia)—Francie Lawrence
ROMANOFF AND JULIET (1961, Universal)—Juliet Moulsworth
TAMMY, TELL ME TRUE (1961, Universal)—Tammy Tyree
TAKE HER, SHE'S MINE (1963, 20th Century Fox)—Mollie Michaelson
TAMMY AND THE DOCTOR (1963, Universal)—Tammy Tyree

DEKKER, ALBERT
DR. CYCLOPS (1940, Paramount)—Dr. Thorkell
THE PRETENDER (1947, Republic)—Kenneth Holden

DEL GADDO, RAMON
SWORD OF THE AVENGER (1948, Eagle Lion)—Roberto Bolagtas

DEL RIO, DOLORES
RAMONA (1928, Silent, United Artists)—Ramona
EVANGELINE (1929, United Artists)—Evangeline
THE BAD ONE (1930, United Artists)—Lita
BIRD OF PARADISE (1932, RKO)—Luana
GIRL OF THE RIO (1932, RKO)—Dolores
MADAME DU BARRY (1934, Warners)—Mme. Du Barry
I LIVE FOR LOVE (1935, Warners)—Donna Alvarez
ACCUSED (1936, GB, United Artists)—Gaby Seymour
THE WIDOW FROM MONTE CARLO (1936, Warners)—Inez

DELANEY, CHARLES
HOME JAMES (1928, Silent, Universal)—James Lacey

DELL, CLAUDIA
SWEET KITTY BELLAIRS (1930, Warners)—Kitty Bellairs

DELL, DOROTHY
WHARF ANGEL (1934, Paramount)—Toy

DELL, MYRNA
ROSE OF THE YUKON (1949, Republic)—Rose Flambeau

DELON, ALAIN
ONCE A THIEF (1965, MGM)—Eddie Pedak
SCORPIO (1973, United Artists)—Laurier

DELORA, JENNIFER
NEW YORK'S FINEST (1988, Platinum)—Loretta Michaels

DEMPSEY, PATRICK
IN THE MOOD (1987, Lorimar)—Ellsworth "Sonny" Wisecarver
LOVERBOY (1989, Tri-Star)—Randy Bodek
MOBSTERS (1991, Universal)—Meyer Lansky

DEMPSTER, CAROL
THE GIRL WHO STAYED AT HOME (1919, Silent, Paramount)—Atoline France
SALLY OF THE SAWDUST (1925, Silent, United Artists)—Sally
"THAT ROYLE GIRL" (1925, Silent, Parmount)—Joan Daisy Royle

DENBERG, SUSAN
FRANKENSTEIN CREATED WOMAN (1965, GB, Hammer)—Christina

DENEUVE, CATHERINE
APRIL FOOLS (1969, National General)—Catherine Gunther

DENISON, MICHAEL
MY BROTHER JONATHAN (1949, GB, Allied Artists)—Jonathan Dakers

DENNEHY, BRIAN
BELLY OF THE ARCHITECT (1987, GB, Hemdale)—Stourley Kracklite
THE LAST OF THE FINEST (1990, Orion)—Frank Daly

DENNING, RICHARD
ADAM HAD FOUR SONS (1941, Columbia)—Jack Stoddard
INSURANCE INVESTIGATOR (1951, Republic)—Tom Davison

DENNIS, SANDY
THE OUT-OF-TOWNERS (1970, Paramount)—Gwen Kellerman
THE THREE SISTERS (1977, Actor Studios Theatre)—Irina

DENNY, REGINALD
THE ABYSMAL BRUTE (1923, Silent, Universal)—Pat Glendon, Jr.
SKINNER'S DRESS SUIT (1926, Silent, Universal)—Skinner
WHAT HAPPENED TO JONES (1926, Silent, Universal)—Tom Jones
THE CHEERFUL FRAUD (1927, Silent, Universal)—Sir Michael Fairlie
HIS LUCKY DAY (1929, Part-Talkie, Universal)—Charles Blaydon
WHAT A MAN (1930, Sono-Art-Worldwide)—Wade Rawlins
THE IRON MASTER (1933, Allied Artists)—Steve Mason
DANCING MAN (1934, Pyramid)—Paul Drexell

DEPEW, JOSEPH
TIMOTHY'S QUEST (1922, Silent, American Releasing)—Timothy

DEPP, JOHNNY
CRY-BABY (1990, Universal)—Wade "Cry Baby" Walker
EDWARD SCISSORHANDS (1990, 20th Century Fox)—Edward Scissorhands

DEREK, JOHN
MASK OF THE AVENGER (1951, Columbia)—Capt. Renato Dimorna
SATURDAY'S HERO (1951, Columbia)—Steve Novak
PRINCE OF PIRATES (1953, Columbia)—Prince Roland
ADVENTURES OF HAJJI BABA (1954, 20th Century Fox)—Hajji Baba
THE OUTCAST (1954, Republic)—Jet Cosgrave
THE LEATHER SAINT (1956, Paramount)—Father Gil Allen

DERN, BRUCE
THE KING OF MARVIN GARDENS (1972, Columbia)—Jason
Staebler
HARRY TRACY—DESPERADO (1982, Canada, Guardian)—
Harry Tracy

DERN, LAURA
WILD AT HEART (1990, Goldwyn)—Lula Pace Fortune
RAMBLING ROSE (1991, Seven Arts/New Line)—Rose

DERR, RICHARD
THE INVISIBLE AVENGER (1958, Republic)—Lamont Cranston/
The Shadow

DESIANTE, PETER
HOWZER (1973, Universal)—Howard "Howzer" Carsell

DESMOND, WILLIAM
LIEUT. DANNY, U.S.A. (1916, Silent, Triangle)—Lt. Danny Ward
LAST OF THE INGRAHAMS (1917, Silent, Triangle)—Jules
Ingraham
AN HONEST MAN (1918, Silent, Triangle)—Benny Boggs
THE MEDDLER (1925, Silent, Universal)—Richard Gilmore

DESMONDE, JERRY
ALF'S BABY (1953, GB, Adelphi)—Alf Donkin

DESTI, LULI
SHE MARRIED AN ARTIST (1938, Columbia)—Toni Bonnet

DETMERS, MARUSCHKA
HANNA'S WAR (1988, Cannon)—Hanna Senesh

DEVANE, WILLIAM
YANKS (1979, Universal)—John

DEVEREAUX, JACK
THE MAN WHO MADE GOOD (1917, Silent, Triangle)—Tom
Burton

DEVIS, PAMELA
THE PERFECT WOMAN (1950, GB, Rank/Ealing)—Olga
the Robot

DEVORE, DOROTHY
THE PRAIRIE WIFE (1925, Silent, Metro-Goldwyn)—
Chaddie Green

DEVORSKA, JESS
JAKE THE PLUMBER (1927, Silent, R-C Pictures)—Jake

DEXTER, ANTHONY
VALENTINO (1951, Columbia)—Rudolph Valentino
THE BRIGAND (1952, Columbia)—Carlos DeLargo
CAPTAIN JOHN SMITH AND POCAHONTAS (1953, United
Artists)—Capt. John Smith
CAPTAIN KIDD AND THE SLAVE GIRL (1954, United Artists)—
Captain Kidd
THE PARSON AND THE OUTLAW (1957, Columbia)—Billy
the Kid

DEXTER, BRAD
THE MAGNIFICENT SEVEN (1960, United Artists)—Harry Luck

DEXTER, ELLIOTT
THE SQUAW MAN (1918, Silent, Paramount)—Capt. James
Wyngate

DIAMOND, GRACE
HER BIG ADVENTURE (1926, Silent, Kerman)—Betty Burton

DIAMOND, NEIL
THE JAZZ SINGER (1980, Associated Film/EMI)—Jess Robin

DICK, DOUGLAS
A YANK IN INDO-CHINA (1952, Columbia)—Clint Marshall

DICKINSON, ANGIE
THE SINS OF RACHEL CADE (1960, Warners)—Rachel Cade
JESSICA (1962, United Artists)—Jessica
BIG BAD MAMA (1974, Columbia)—Wilma McClathchie
CHARLIE CHAN AND THE CURSE OF THE DRAGON QUEEN
(1981, American Cinema) - Dragon Lady
BIG BAD MAMA II (1987, Concorde)—Wilma McClathchie

DICKSON, GLORIA
GOLD DIGGERS IN PARIS (1938, Warners)—Mona

DIETRICH, MARLENE
DISHONORED (1931, Paramount)—X-27
BLONDE VENUS (1932, Paramount)—Helen Faraday
THE SCARLET EMPRESS (1934, Paramount)—Sophia Frederica,
Catherine II
THE DEVIL IS A WOMAN (1935, Paramount)—Concha Perez
ANGEL (1937, Paramount)—Maria Barker
THE FLAME OF NEW ORLEANS (1941, Universal)—Claire
Ledeux
THE LADY IS WILLING (1942, Columbia)—Elizabeth Madden
WITNESS FOR THE PROSECUTION (1957, United Artists)—
Christine Helm Vole

DIFFRING, ANTON
THE MAN WHO COULD CHEAT DEATH (1959, GB, Hammer)—
Dr. Georges Bonner
ENTER INSPECTOR DUVAL (1961, GB, Columbia)—
Inspector Duval

DIGNAM, BASIL
SON OF A STRANGER (1957, GB, United Artists)—Dr. Delaney

DILLER, PHYLLIS
DID YOU HEAR THE ONE ABOUT THE TRAVELING
SALESLADY? (1968, Universal)—Agatha Knabehshu

DILLMAN, BRADFORD
FRANCIS OF ASSISI (1961, 20th Century Fox)—Francis
Bernardone
THE RESURRECTION OF ZACHARY WHEELER (1971, Gold Key/
Vidtronics)—Zachary Wheeler

DILLON, KEVIN
IMMEDIATE FAMILY (1989, Columbia)—Sam
WAR PARTY (1989, Tri-Star)—Skitty Harris
THE DOORS (1991, Tri-Star)—John Densmore

DILLON, MATT
TEX (1982, Buena Vista)—Tex McCormick
THE OUTSIDERS (1983, Warners)—Dallas Winston
FLAMINGO KID (1984, 20th Century Fox)—Jeffrey Willis
REBEL (1986, Vestron)—Rebel
DRUGSTORE COWBOY (1989, Avenue)—Bob
A KISS BEFORE DYING (1991, Universal)—Jonathan Corliss

DILLON, MELINDA
HARRY AND THE HENDERSONS (1987, Universal)—Nancy Henderson

DIN, AYUB KHAN
SAMMY AND ROSIE GET LAID (1987, GB, Cinecom)—Sammy

DISA
THE NOTORIOUS MRS. CARRICK (1924, GB, Silent, Stoll)—Mrs. Carrick

DISANTI, JOHN
EYES OF A STRANGER (1980, Warners)—Stanley Herbert

DIX, DOROTHY
THE FIRST MRS. FRASER (1932, GB, Sterling)—Janet Fraser

DIX, RICHARD
THE CHRISTIAN (1923, Silent, Goldwyn)—John Storm
TO THE LAST MAN (1923, Silent, Paramount)—Jean Isbell
SINNERS IN HEAVEN (1924, Silent, Paramount)—Alan Croft
THE QUARTERBACK (1926, Silent, Paramount)—Jack Stone
KNOCKOUT REILLY (1927, Silent, Paramount)—Dundee Reilly
THE LOVE DOCTOR (1929, Paramount)—Dr. Gerald Sumner
THE PUBLIC DEFENDER (1931, Fox)—Pike Winslow
YOUNG DONOVAN'S KID (1931, RKO)—Jim Donovan
THE GREAT JASPER (1933, RKO)—Jasper Horn
THE ARIZONIAN (1935, RKO)—Clay Talbot
SPECIAL INVESTIGATOR (1936, RKO)—Bill Fenwick
MAN OF CONQUEST (1939, Republic)—Sam Houston
MAN AGAINST THE SKY (1940, RKO)—Phil Mercedes
THE KANSAN (1943, United Artists)—John Bonniwell

DIXON, ADELE
WOMAN TO WOMAN (1946, GB, Anglo-American)—Sylvia Anson

DIXON, IVAN
NOTHING BUT A MAN (1964, Cinema V)—Duff Anderson

DIXON, RICHARD M.
RICHARD (1972, Aurora City Group)—Richard

DOBSON, TAMARA
CLEOPATRA JONES (1973, Warners)—Cleopatra Jones
CLEOPATRA JONES AND THE CASINO OF GOLD (1975, Warners)—Cleopatra Jones

DOCKSTADER, LEW
DAN (1914, All Star Features)—Dan

DODD, CLAIRE
THE WOMEN MEN MARRY (1937, MGM)—Claire Raeburn

DOGGETT, NORMA
SEVEN BRIDES FOR SEVEN BROTHERS (1954, MGM)—Martha

DOHERTY, SHANNEN
HEATHERS (1989, New World)—Heather Duke

DOLAN, YOLANDE
PENNY PRINCESS (1953, GB, Universal)—Lindy Smith

DOLENZ, AMI
SHE'S OUT OF CONTROL (1989, Columbia)—Katie Simpson

DOLMAN, RICHARD
LUCKY LOSER (1934, GB, Paramount)—Tom O'Grady

DOMBASLE, ARIELLE
THE BOSS' WIFE (1986, Tri-Star)—Louise

DOMERGUE, FAITH
SPIN A DARK WEB (1956, GB, Columbia)—Bella Francesi

DOMINGO, PLACIDO
OTELLO (1987, Cannon)—Otello

DONAHUE, MARY ELEANOR
THREE DARING DAUGHTERS (1948, MGM)—Alix Morgan

DONAHUE, TROY
PARRISH (1961, Warners)—Parrish McLean

DONALDSON, ARTHUR
THE CAPTAIN'S CAPTAIN (1919, Silent, Vitagraph)—Cap'n Abe

DONALDSON, TED
PERSONALITY KID (1946, Columbia)—Davey Roberts
THE DECISION OF CHRISTOPHER BLAKE (1948, Warners)—Christopher Blake

DONAT, ROBERT
THE COUNT OF MONTE CRISTO (1934, United Artists)—Edmond Dantes
THE GHOST GOES WEST (1936, United Artists)—Donald Glourie
KNIGHT WITHOUT ARMOUR (1937, GB, London Films)—Ainsley Fothergill
GOODBYE MR. CHIPS (1939, GB, MGM)—Charles Chipping
THE YOUNG MR. PITT (1942, GB, 20th Century Fox)—William Pitt
ADVENTURES OF TARTU (1943, GB, MGM)—Capt. Terence Stevenson

DONAT, SANDRA
THE SIN OF MONA KENT (1961, Mermaid/Astor)—Mona Kent

DONATH, LUDWIG
THE STRANGE DEATH OF ADOLF HITLER (1943, Universal)—Adolf Hitler

DONLAN, YOLANDE
MISS PILGRIM'S PROGRESS (1950, GB, Grand National)—Laramie Pilgrim

DONLEVY, BRIAN
BORN RECKLESS (1937, 20th Century Fox)—Bob "Hurry" Kane
SHARPSHOOTERS (1938, 20th Century Fox)—Steve Mitchell
THE GREAT MCGINTY (1940, Paramount)—Dan McGinty
WHEN THE DALTONS RODE (1940, Universal)—Grat Dalton
A GENTLEMAN AFTER DARK (1942, United Artists)—Harry Melton
TWO YANKS IN TRINIDAD (1942, Columbia)—Vince Barrows

DONNELL, JEFF
NINE GIRLS (1944, Columbia)—"Butch" Hendricks

DONNELLY, RUTH
PERSONAL MAID'S SERVICE (1935, Warners)—Lizzie

DONOVAN
THE PIED PIPER (1972, GB, Paramount)—Pied Piper

DOOLEY, PAUL
A PERFECT COUPLE (1979, 20th Century Fox)—Alex Theodopoulos

DOONAN, PATRIC
I'M A STRANGER (1952, GB, Corsair/Apex)—George Westcott

DORFF, STEPHEN
THE POWER OF ONE (1992, Warner Brothers)—P.K. at 18

DORN, DOLORES
TRUCK STOP WOMEN (1974, LT Films)—Trish

DORNE, SANDRA
MARILYN (1953, GB, Butchers)—Marilyn Saunders

DORO, MARIE
OLIVER TWIST (1916, Silent, Lasky)—Oliver Twist

DOROFF, SARAH ROWLAND
THREE FUGITIVES (1989, Buena Vista)—Meg Perry

DORS, DIANA
BLONDE SINNER (1956, GB, Allied Artists)—Mary Hilton
THE UNHOLY WIFE (1957, Universal)—Phyllis Hochen
I MARRIED A WOMAN (1958, RKO/Universal)—Janice Briggs

D'ORSAY, FIFI
THOSE THREE FRENCH GIRLS (1930, MGM)—Charmaine

DORSEY, JIMMY
THE FABULOUS DORSEYS (1947, United Artists)—Jimmy Dorsey

DORSEY, TOMMY
THE FABULOUS DORSEYS (1947, United Artists)—Tommy Dorsey

DOUGLAS, DONNA
FRANKIE AND JOHNNY (1966, United Artists)—Frankie

DOUGLAS, KIRK
MY DEAR SECRETARY (1948, United Artists)—Owen Waterbury
CHAMPION (1949, United Artists)—Midge Kelly
YOUNG MAN WITH A HORN (1950, Warners)—Rick Martin
DETECTIVE STORY (1951, Paramount)—Jim McLeod
THE JUGGLER (1953, Columbia)—Hans Muller
INDIAN FIGHTER (1955, United Artists)—Johnny Hawks
MAN WITHOUT A STAR (1955, Universal)—Dempsey Rae
THE RACERS (1955, 20th Century Fox)—Gino
TOP SECRET AFFAIR (1957, Warners)—Major General Melville Goodwin
THE VIKINGS (1958, United Artists)—Einar
THE DEVIL'S DISCIPLE (1959, United Artists)—Richard Dudgeon
SPARTACUS (1960, Universal)—Spartacus
STRANGERS WHEN WE MEET (1960, Columbia)—Larry Coe
LONELY ARE THE BRAVE (1962, Universal)—Jack Burns
SCALAWAG (1973, Paramount)—Peg
THE VILLAIN (1979, Columbia)—Cactus Jack
THE MAN FROM SNOWY RIVER (1983, Australia, 20th Century Fox)—Spur
TOUGH GUYS (1986, Touchstone)—Archie Long

DOUGLAS, LAWRENCE
KIDNAPPED (1971, GB, Omnibus/Am. Int.)—David Balfour

DOUGLAS, MELVYN
SHE MARRIED HER BOSS (1935, Columbia)—Richard Barclay
THE LONE WOLF RETURNS (1936, Columbia)—Michael Lanyard
I MET HIM IN PARIS (1937, Paramount)—George Potter
ARSENE LUPIN RETURNS (1938, MGM)—Arsene Lupin/Rene Farrand
AMAZING MR. WILLIAMS (1939, Columbia)—Kenny Williams
HE STAYED FOR BREAKFAST (1940, Columbia)—Paul Beloit
TOO MANY HUSBANDS (1940, Columbia)—Henry Lowndes
MY OWN TRUE LOVE (1948, Paramount)—Clive Heath
I NEVER SANG FOR MY FATHER (1970, Columbia)—Tom Garrison

DOUGLAS, MICHAEL
HAIL, HERO (1969, Cinema Center)—Carl Dixon
ADAM AT 6 A.M. (1970, National General)—Adam Gaines
FATAL ATTRACTION (1987, Paramount)—Dan Gallagher
THE WAR OF THE ROSES (1989, 20th Century Fox)—Oliver Rose

DOUGLAS, PAUL
LOVE THAT BRUTE (1950, 20th Century Fox)—Big Ed Hanley
THE GUY WHO CAME BACK (1951, 20th Century Fox)—Harry Joplin
JOE MACBETH (1955, Columbia)—Joe MacBeth

DOURIF, BRAD
THE HORSEPLAYER (1990, Relentless)—Bud

DOVE, BILLIE
YOUTH TO YOUTH (1922, Silent, Metro)—Eve Allinson
AMERICAN BEAUTY (1927, Silent, First National)—Millicent Howard
THE STOLEN BRIDE (1927, Silent, Gaumont)—Sari, Countess Thurzo
THE HEART OF A FOLLIES GIRL (1928, Silent, First National)—Teddy O'Day
HER PRIVATE LIFE (1929, First National/Warners)—Lady Helen Haden
THE PAINTED ANGEL (1929, Warners)—Mamie Hudler/Rodeo West
THE LADY WHO DARED (1931, First National)—Margaret Townsend

DOWLING, EDDIE
RAINBOW MAN (1929, Paramount)—Rainbow Ryan

DOWLING, JOSEPH J.
THE MIRACLE MAN (1919, Silent, Paramount)—The Patriarch

DOWNEY, MORTON
MOTHER'S BOY (1929, Pathe)—Tommy O'Day

DOWNEY, ROBERT
THE PICKUP ARTIST (1987, 20th Century Fox)—Jack Jericho

DOWNS, CATHY
MY DARLING CLEMENTINE (1946, 20th Century Fox)—Clementine

DOWNS, JOHNNY
ADAM HAD FOUR SONS (1941, Columbia)—David Stoddard
FRECKLES COMES HOME (1942, Monogram)—Freckles
WHAT A MAN! (1944, Monogram)—Henry Burrows

DRAKE, BETSY
THE SECOND WOMAN (1951, United Artists)—Ellen Foster

DRAKE, CAROL
WAITRESS (1982, Troma)—Andrea

DRAKE, CHARLIE
THE CRACKSMAN (1963, GB, Warners-Pathe)—Ernest Wright
MISTER TEN PERCENT (1967, GB, Associated British)—Percy
Pointer

DRAKE, FRANCES
LADIES SHOULD LISTEN (1934, Paramount)—Anna Mirelle

DRAKE, TOM
I'LL BE YOURS (1947, Universal)—George Prescott

DRESDELL, SONIA
THIS WAS A WOMAN (1949, GB, 20th Century Fox)—Sylvia
Russell

DRESSER, LOUISE
THE GOOSE WOMAN (1925, Silent, Universal)—Mary Holmes
(Marie de Nardi)
MOTHER KNOWS BEST (1928, Fox)—Ma Quail
STEPPING SISTERS (1932, Fox)—Mrs. Ramsey

DRESSLER, LIEUX
TRUCK STOP WOMEN (1974, LT Films)—Anna

DRESSLER, MARIE
TILLIE'S PUNCTURED ROMANCE (1914, Silent, Keystone)—
Tillie
TILLIE'S TOMATO SURPRISE (1915, Silent, Lubin)—Tillie
TILLIE WAKES UP (1917, Silent, World)—Tillie Tinklepaw
MIN AND BILL (1930, MGM)—Min Divot
EMMA (1932, MGM)—Emma Thatcher
TUGBOAT ANNIE (1933, MGM)—Annie Brennan

DREW, ELLEN
THE LADY'S FROM KENTUCKY (1939, Paramount)—Penelope
"Penny" Hollis
WOMEN WITHOUT NAMES (1940, Paramount)—Joyce King
THE MONSTER AND THE GIRL (1941, Paramount)—Susan
Webster
OUR WIFE (1941, Columbia)—Babe Marvin

DREYFUSS, LOUIS
DETECTIVE SCHOOL DROP OUTS (1986, Cannon)—Paul

DREYFUSS, RANDY
ELLIOT FAUMAN, Ph.D. (1990, Taurus)—Elliot Fauman

DREYFUSS, RICHARD
THE APPRENTICESHIP OF DUDDY KRAVITZ (1974, Canada,
Paramount)—Duddy Kravitz
WHOSE LIFE IS IT ANYWAY? (1981, MGM/United Artists)—
Ken Harrion
TIN MEN (1987, Buena Vista)—Bill "BB" Babowsky

DRISCOLL, BOBBY
WHEN I GROW UP (1951, Eagle Lion)—Josh Reed

DRISCOLL, MARTHA
BLONDE ALIBI (1946, Universal)—Marian Gale

DRISCOLL, PATRICIA
A WOMAN'S TEMPTATION (1959, GB, British Lion)—Betty

DRU, JOANNE
ABIE'S IRISH ROSE (1946, United Artists)—Rosemary Murphy

SHE WORE A YELLOW RIBBON (1949, RKO)—Olivia Dandridge

DU BREY, CLAIRE
MADAME SPY (1918, Silent, Butterfly)—Baroness Von Hulda

DUCHOVNY, DAVID
JULIA HAD TWO LOVERS (1990, South Gate)—Daniel

DU PONT, MISS (PATRICIA)
THE RAGE OF PARIS (1921, Silent, Universal)—Joan Coolidge
A WONDERFUL WIFE (1922, Silent, Universal)—Chum Lewin

DUDIKOFF, MICHAEL
PLATOON LEADER (1988, Cannon)—Lt. Jeff Knight

DUFF, HOWARD
CALAMITY JANE AND SAM BASS (1949, Universal)—Sam Bass
BLACKJACK KETCHUM, DESPERADO (1956, Columbia)—
Blackjack Ketchum

DUGAN, ED
FALLGUY (1962, International)—Sonny Martin

DUGGAN, ANDREW
THE CHAPMAN REPORT (1962, Warners)—Dr. Chapman

DUKAKIS, OLYMPIA
STEEL MAGNOLIAS (1989, Tri-Star)—Clariee Belcher
OVER THE HILL (1992, Australia, Greater Union)—Alma Harris

DUKE, PATTY
BILLIE (1965, United Artists)—Billie
ME, NATALIE (1968, National General)—Natalie Miller
YOU'LL LIKE MY MOTHER (1972, Universal)—Francesca
Kinsolving

DUKES, DAVID
MEN'S CLUB (1986, Paramount)—Philip

DULLEA, KEIR
DAVID AND LISA (1962, Continental)—David
THE FOX (1967, Warners)—Paul
PAPERBACK HERO (1973, Canada, Agincourt)—Rick

DUMBRILLE, DOUGLASS
PUBLIC MENACE (1935, Columbia)—Tonelli
THE MYSTERIOUS RIDER (1938, Paramount)—Ben Wade
THE THREE MUSKETEERS (1939, 20th Century Fox)—Athos
THE CATMAN OF PARIS (1946, Republic)—Henry Borchard

DUNA, STEFFI
INDISCRETIONS OF EVE (1932, GB, British Int.)—Eve
THE GIRL AND THE GAMBLER (1939, RKO)—Dolores

DUNAWAY, FAYE
BONNIE AND CLYDE (1967, Warners)—Bonnie Parker
PUZZLE OF A DOWNFALL CHILD (1970, Universal)—Lou
Andreas Sand
THE EYES OF LAURA MARS (1978, Columbia)—Laura Mars
MOMMIE DEAREST (1981, Paramount)—Joan Crawford
THE WICKED LADY (1983, GB, MGM/United Artists)—Lady
Barbara Skelton

DUNCAN, BUD
SNUFFY SMITH, YARD BIRD (1942, Monogram)—Snuffy Smith

DUNCAN, CARMEN
MOVING TARGETS (1987, Australia, Academy)—Eve

DUNCAN, JOHNNY
MILLION DOLLAR KID (1944, Monogram)—Roy Cortland

DUNCAN, MARY
CITY GIRL (1930, Fox)—Kate Tustine

DUNCAN, SANDY
STAR SPANGLED GIRL (1971, Paramount)—Amy Cooper

DUNCAN, WILLIAM
THE FARMER'S DAUGHTER (1940, Paramount)—Tom Bingham

DUNGAN, SEBASTIAN
MAN, WOMAN AND CHILD (1983, Paramount)—Jean-Claude Guerin

DUNN, JAMES
DANCE TEAM (1932, Fox)—Jimmy Mulligan
JIMMY AND SALLY (1933, Fox)—Jimmy O'Connor
SAILOR'S LUCK (1933, Fox)—Jimmy Harrigan
THE DARING YOUNG MAN (1935, Fox)—Don McLane
PRIDE OF THE NAVY (1939, Republic)—Speed Brennan
SON OF THE NAVY (1940, Monogram)—Malone

DUNNE, IRENE
THIRTEEN WOMEN (1932, RKO)—Laura Stanhope
ANN VICKERS (1933, RKO)—Ann Vickers
IF I WERE FREE (1933, RKO)—Sarah Cazenove
THE SECRET OF MADAME BLANCHE (1933, MGM)—Sally
THIS MAN IS MINE (1934, RKO)—Toni Dunlap
SWEET ADELINE (1935, Warners)—Adeline Schmidt
THEODORA GOES WILD (1936, Columbia)—Theodora Lynn
MY FAVORITE WIFE (1940, RKO)—Ellen Arden
LADY IN A JAM (1942, Universal)—Jane Palmer
ANNA AND THE KING OF SIAM (1946, 20th Century Fox)—
Anna Leonowens
I REMEMBER MAMA (1948, RKO)—Mama

DUNNOCK, MILDRED
SEVEN WOMEN (1966, MGM)—Jane Argent

DURAN, TOMMY
THE SEVEN LITTLE FOYS (1955, Paramount)—Irving Foy

DURBIN, DEANNA
100 MEN AND A GIRL (1937, Universal)—Patricia Cardwell
THREE SMART GIRLS (1937, Universal)—Penny Craig
MAD ABOUT MUSIC (1938, Universal)—Gloria Harkinson
THREE SMART GIRLS GROW UP (1939, Universal)—
Penny Craig
NICE GIRL? (1941, Universal)—Jane Dana
AMAZING MRS. HOLLIDAY (1943, Universal)—Ruth Kirke
HIS BUTLER'S SISTER (1943, Universal)—Ann Carter
LADY ON A TRAIN (1945, Universal)—Nikki Collins
I'LL BE YOURS (1947, Universal)—Louise Ginglebusher
FOR THE LOVE OF MARY (1948, Universal)—Mary Peppertree

DURHAM, STEVE
BORN AMERICAN (1986, Cinema Group)—Mitch

DURKIN, JAMES
HUCKLEBERRY FINN (1931, Paramount)—Huckleberry Finn

LITTLE MEN (1935, Mascot)—Franz

DUROCK, DICK
SWAMP THING (1982, Embassy)—Swamp Thing
THE RETURN OF THE SWAMP THING (1989, Miramax)—
Swamp Thing

DURYEA, DAN
BLACK BART (1948, Universal)—Charles E. Boles
JOHNNY STOOL PIDGEON (1949, Universal)—Johnny Evans
AL JENNINGS OF OKLAHOMA (1951, Columbia)—Al Jennings
SKY COMMAND (1953, Columbia)—Col. Ed Wyatt
THE BURGLAR (1956, Columbia)—Nat Harbin

DURYEA, GEORGE
THE DUDE WRANGLER (1930, Independent)—Tom Keene

DUTT, UTPAL
THE GURU (1969, 20th Century Fox)—Ustad Zafar Khan

DUVALL, ROBERT
THX 1138 (1971, Warners)—THX 1138
THE GREAT SANTINI (1979, Orion/Warners)—Bull Meechum

DUVALL, SHELLEY
THIEVES LIKE US (1974, United Artists)—Keechie
THREE WOMEN (1977, 20th Century Fox)—Millie Lammoreaux

DVORAK, ANN
THE STRANGE LOVE OF MOLLY LOUVAIN (1932, Warners)—
Molly Louvain
THREE ON A MATCH (1932, Warners)—Vivian Revere
HOUSEWIFE (1934, Warners)—Nan Wilson Reynolds
RACING LADY (1937, RKO)—Ruth Martin
CAFE HOSTESS (1940, Columbia)—Jo
GIRLS OF THE ROAD (1940, Columbia)—Kay Warren
FLAME OF THE BARBARY COAST (1945, Republic)—
Flaxen Tarry
THE BACHELOR'S DAUGHTERS (1946, United Artists)—Terry
I WAS AN AMERICAN SPY (1951, Monogram—Allied Artists)—
Claire Phillips

DWYER, LESLIE
MY WIFE'S LODGER (1952, GB, Adelphi)—Roger the Lodger

DWYER, RUTH
HIS MYSTERY GIRL (1923, Silent, Universal)—Gloria Bliss

DYALL, VALENTINE
VENGEANCE IS MINE (1948, GB, Eros)—Charles Heywood
DR. MORELLE—THE CASE OF THE MISSING HEIRESS (1949,
GB, Exclusive)—Dr. Morelle

DYE, JOHN
CAMPUS MAN (1987, RKO-Paramount)—Todd Barrett

DYLAN, BOB
RENALDO AND CLARA (1978, Lombard Street/Circuit)—
Renaldo

DYLAN, SARA
RENALDO AND CLARA (1978, Lombard Street/Circuit)—Clara

DZUNDZA, GEORGE
THE BUTCHER'S WIFE (1991, Paramount)—Leo

E

EARECKSON, JONI
JONI (1980, World Wide)—Joni Eareckson

EARLES, HARRY
THAT'S MY BABY (1926, Silent, Paramount)—The Baby

EAST, JEFF
HUCKLEBERRY FINN (1974, United Artists)—Huckleberry Finn

EASTWOOD, CLINT
COOGAN'S BLUFF (1968, Universal)—Coogan
KELLY'S HEROES (1970, MGM)—Kelly
THE BEGUILED (1971, Universal)—John McBurney
DIRTY HARRY (1971, Warners)—Harry Callahan
JOE KIDD (1972, Universal)—Joe Kidd
HIGH PLAINS DRIFTER (1973, Universal)—The Stranger
THUNDERBOLT AND LIGHTFOOT (1974, United Artists)—John "Thunderbolt" Doherty
THE ENFORCER (1976, Warners)—Harry Callahan
THE OUTLAW JOSEY WALES (1976, Warners)—Josey Wales
BRONCO BILLY (1980, Warners)—Bronco Billy
HONKYTONK MAN (1982, Warners)—Red Stovall
WHITE HUNTER, BLACK HEART (1990, Warners)—John Wilson

EATON, MARY
GLORIFYING THE AMERICAN GIRL (1930, Paramount)—Gloria Hughes

EATON, SHIRLEY
THE MILLION EYES OF SU-MURU (1967, GB, American International)—Su-Muru

ECCLES, HARRY
THE UNHOLY THREE (1925, Silent, MGM)—Tweedledee
THE UNHOLY THREE (1930, MGM)—Midget

ECCLES, TEDDY
MY SIDE OF THE MOUNTAIN (1969, Paramount)—Sam Gribley

EDDY, HELEN JEROME
KLONDIKE ANNIE (1936, Paramount)—Sister Annie Alden

EDDY, NELSON
SWEETHEARTS (1938, MGM)—Ernest Lane
THE CHOCOLATE SOLDIER (1941, MGM)—Karl Lang
I MARRIED AN ANGEL (1942, MGM)—Count Willie Palaffi

EDEN, ELANA
THE STORY OF RUTH (1960, 20th Century Fox)—Ruth

EDESON, ROBERT
THE CAVEMAN (1915, Silent, Vitagraph)—Haulick Smagg
A MAN'S PREROGATIVE (1915, Silent, Mutual)—Oliver Rand
DOCTOR'S SECRET (1929, Paramount)—Dr. Brodie

EDLIN, TUBBY
ALF'S BUTTON (1930, GB, Gaumont)—Alf Higgins

EDWARDS, ANTHONY
MR. NORTH (1988, Goldwyn)—Theophilus North

EDWARDS, ELAINE
THREE BLONDES IN HIS LIFE (1961, Cinema Assoc.)—Lois Collins

EDWARDS, HENRY
THE KINSMAN (1919, Silent, Hepworth)—Bert Gammage
AYLWIN (1920, Silent, GB, Hepworth)—Hal Aylwin
A TEMPORARY VAGABOND (1920, GB, Silent, Butchers)—Dick Derelict
THE FLAG LIEUTENANT (1926, GB, Silent, Astra)—Lt. Dicky Lascelles
FURTHER ADVENTURES OF THE FLAG LIEUTENANT (1927, Silent, GB, Neo-Art)—Lt. Dicky Lascelles
THE FLAG LIEUTENANT (1932, GB, Gaumont)—Lt. Dicky Lascelles
CAPTAIN'S ORDERS (1937, GB, Liberty Films)—Captain Trent

EDWARDS, JENNIFER
THE PERFECT MATCH (1987, Airtight)—Nancy Bryant

EDWARDS, JIMMY
THREE MEN IN A BOAT (1958, GB, Associate British)—Harris

EDWARDS, LANCE
PEACEMAKER (1990, Fries)—Townsend

EDWARDS, LUKE
THE WIZARD (1989, Universal)—Jimmy Woods

EDWARDS, PENNY
THE DALTON GIRLS (1957, United Artists)—Columbine Dalton

EDWARDS, VINCE
MR. UNIVERSE (1951, Eagle-Lion)—Tommy Tompkins
HIAWATHA (1952, Monogram)—Hiawatha
THE VICTORS (1963, Columbia)—Baker

EGAN, RICHARD
ESTHER AND THE KING (1960, 20th Century Fox)—King Ahasuerus

EGGERT, NICOLE
THE HAUNTING OF MORELLA (1990, Concorde)—Morella

EILERS, SALLY
BAD GIRL (1931, Fox)—Dorothy Haley
DANCE TEAM (1932, Fox)—Poppy Kirk
HAT CHECK GIRL (1932, Fox)—Gerry Marsh
SECOND HAND WIFE (1933, Fox)—Sandra Trumbell
SHE MADE HER BED (1934, Paramount)—Lura Gordon
ALIAS MARY DOW (1935, Universal)—Sally Gates
NURSE FROM BROOKLYN (1938, Universal)—Elizabeth Thomas
TARNISHED ANGEL (1938, RKO)—Connie Vinson
THEY MADE HER A SPY (1939, RKO)—Irene Eaton
A WAVE, A WAC AND A MARINE (1944, Monogram)—Margaret Ames

EISENBERG, AVNER
THE JEWEL OF THE NILE (1985, 20th Century Fox)—Holy Man/"Joe"

EKBERG, ANITA
VALERIE (1957, United Artists)—Valerie
FOUR FOR TEXAS (1963, Warners)—Elya Carlson

ELAN, JOAN
GIRLS OF PLEASURE ISLAND (1953, Paramount)—Violet Halyard

ELDREDGE, GEORGE
HIS BROTHER'S WIFE (1936, MGM)—Tom

ELDREDGE, JOHN
THE MURDER OF DR. HARRIGAN (1936, First National)—Dr. Harrigan

ELDRIDGE, CHARLES
HIS FATHER'S SON (1917, Silent, Metro)—Adam Barron

ELG, TANIA
LES GIRLS (1957, MGM)—Angele Ducros

ELLIOTT, ALICE
HIS DIVORCED WIFE (1919, Silent, Universal)—Nancy Haws

ELLIOTT, BIFF
I, THE JURY (1953, United Artists)—Mike Hammer

ELLIOTT, BILL
THE RETURN OF WILD BILL (1940, Columbia)—Wild Bill Saunders
KING OF DODGE CITY (1941, Columbia)—Wild Bill Elliott
THE RETURN OF DANIEL BOONE (1941, Columbia)—Dan Boone
THE SON OF DAVY CROCKETT (1941, Columbia)—Dave Crockett
CALLING WILD BILL ELLIOTT (1943, Republic)—Wild Bill Elliott
PLAINSMAN AND THE LADY (1946, Republic)—Sam Cotten
THE FABULOUS TEXAN (1947, Republic)—Jim McWade

ELLIOTT, FRANK
TAKE THE HEIR (1930, Big 4)—Lord Tweedham

ELLIOTT, SAM
MOLLY AND LAWLESS JOHN (1972, Producers Distriutors)—Johnny Lawler
LIFEGUARD (1976, Paramount)—Rick Carlson

ELLIOTT, STEPHEN
REPORT TO THE COMMISSIONER (1975, United Artists)—Police Commissioner

ELLIS, EDWARD
THE THIN MAN (1934, MGM)—Clyde Wyant
THE MAN IN BLUE (1937, Universal)—Martin Dunne
A MAN TO REMEMBER (1938, RKO)—Dr. John Abbott
MAIN STREET LAWYER (1939, Republic)—Link

ELLIS, MARY
FATAL LADY (1936, Paramount)—Marion Stuart/Maria Delasano/ Malevo

ELLIS, PATRICIA
THE CASE OF THE LUCKY LEGS (1935, First National)—Margie Clune
MELODY FOR TWO (1937, Warners)—Gale Starr
THE GAIETY GIRLS (1938, GB, United Artists)—Jeannette

ELLISON, JAMES
THEY MET IN ARGENTINA (1941, RKO)—Tim Kelly
ARMY SURGEON (1942, RKO)—Capt. James Mason
I WALKED WITH A ZOMBIE (1943, Columbia)—Wesley Rand
I KILLED GERONIMO (1950, Eagle Lion)—Capt. Jeff Packard
TEXAN MEETS CALAMITY JANE (1950, Columbia)—Gordon Hastings

ELSOM, ISOBEL
THE LAST WITNESS (1925, GB, Silent, Stoll)

ELTINGE, JULIAN
THE CLEVER MRS. CARFAX (1917, Silent, Paramount)—Temple Trask

ELVIDGE, JUNE
THE CRIMSON DOVE (1917, Silent, World)—Adrienne Durant
THE BEAUTIFUL MRS. REYNOLDS (1918, Silent, World)—Maria Reynolds
JOAN OF THE WOODS (1918, Silent, World)—Joan Travers
THE BLUFFER (1919, Silent, World)—Sybil

ELWES, CARY
HOT SHOTS (1991, 20th Century Fox)—Kent Gregory

ELY, RON
TARZAN'S DEADLY SILENCE (1970, National General)—Tarzan
TARZAN'S JUNGLE REBELLION (1970, National General)—Tarzan
DOC SAVAGE. . .THE MAN OF BRONZE (1975, Warners)—Doc Savage

EMERY, DICK
GET CHARLIE TULLY (1976, GB, Quintain)—Charlie Tully

ENGLISH, ALEX
AMAZING GRACE AND CHUCK (1987, Tri-Star)—Amazing Grace Smith

ENGLISH, MARLA
THE SHE-CREATURE (1956, American International)—Andrea
THREE BAD SISTERS (1956, United Artists)—Vicki
VOODOO WOMAN (1957, American International)—Marilyn Blanchard

ENGLUND, ROBERT
A NIGHTMARE ON ELM STREET 4: THE DREAM MASTER (1988, New Line)—Freddy Krueger
THE PHANTOM OF THE OPERA (1989, 21st Film)—The Phantom
FREDDY'S DEAD: THE FINAL NIGHTMARE (1991, New Line)—Freddy Krueger

ERIC, FRED
COLUMBUS (1923, Silent, Pathe)—Christopher Columbus

ERICKSON, LEE
THE SEVEN LITTLE FOYS (1955, Paramount)—Charley Foy

ERICSON, JOHN
THE RETURN OF JACK SLADE (1955, Allied Artists)—Jack Slade
PRETTY BOY FLOYD (1960, Continental)—Pretty Boy Floyd

ERIN, TAMI
THE NEW ADVENTURES OF PIPPI LONGSTOCKING (1988, Columbia)—Pippi Longstocking

ERNEST, GEORGE
FOUR SONS (1940, 20th Century Fox)—Fritz Bernie

ERROL, LEON
CLOTHES MAKE THE PIRATE (1925, Silent, First National)—Trem Tidd
FINN AND HADDIE (1931, Paramount)—Finley P. Haddock
MAMA LOVES PAPA (1945, RKO)—Wilbur Todd

ERWIN, STUART
PALOOKA (1934, United Artists)—Joe Palooka
ALL-AMERICAN CHUMP (1936, MGM)—Elmer
SMALL TOWN BOY (1937, Grand National)—Henry
MR. BOGGS STEPS OUT (1938, Grand National)—Oliver Boggs
PASSPORT HUSBAND (1938, 20th Century Fox)—Henry Cabot
WHEN THE DALTONS RODE (1940, Universal)—Ben Dalton
HE HIRED THE BOSS (1943, 20th Century Fox)—Hubert Wilkins
KILLER DILL (1947, Screen Guild)—Johnny Dill

ESTELITA
THE FABULOUS SENORITA (1952, Republic)—Estelita Rodriguez

ESTEVEZ, EMILIO
THE BREAKFAST CLUB (1985, Universal)—Andrew Clark
YOUNG GUNS (1988, 20th Century Fox)—Billy the Kid Bonney
MEN AT WORK (1990, Triumph)—James St. James
YOUNG GUNS II (1990, 20th Century Fox)—William H. Bonney

ESTEVEZ, JOE
SOULTAKER (1990, Action)—Soultaker

ESTRADA, ERIK
HOUR OF THE ASSASSIN (1987, Concorde)—Martin Fierro

EUBANK, SHARI
CHESTY ANDERSON, U.S. NAVY (1976, Atlas)—Chesty Anderson

EVANS, BARRY
ADVENTURES OF A TAXI DRIVER (1976, GB, Salon/Alpha)—Joe North

EVANS, CLIFFORD
HIS BROTHER'S KEEPER (1939, GB, Warners)—Jack Cornell
THE COURAGEOUS MR. PENN (1941, GB, British National)—William Penn
SUSPECTED PERSON (1943, GB, Producers Releasing Corp.)—Jim Raynor

EVANS, DALE
COWBOY AND THE SENORITA (1944, Republic)—Ysobel Martinez

EVANS, EDITH
QUEEN OF SPADES (1948, GB, Pathe)—Countess Ranevskaya
SOPHIE'S PLACE (1970, Warners)—Lady Sophie Fitzmore

EVANS, GENE
THE STEEL HELMET (1951, Lippert)—Sgt. Zack

EVANS, JOAN
ROSEANNA MCCOY (1949, RKO)—Roseanna McCoy

EVANS, MADGE
JAZZ BABIES (1932, Peerless)—Clarissa
FUGITIVE LOVERS (1934, MGM)—Letty Morris
ARMY GIRL (1938, Republic)—Julie Armstrong

EVANS, MAURICE
WHITE CARGO (1930, GB, Neo-Art)—Langford
THE GREAT GILBERT AND SULLIVAN (1953, GB, United Artists)—Arthur Sullivan
MACBETH (1963, Prominent)—Macbeth

EVANS, ROBERT
THE FIEND WHO WALKED THE WEST (1958, 20th Century Fox)—Felix Griffin

EVERETT, CHAD
JOHNNY TIGER (1966, Universal)—Johnny Tiger
FIRST TO FIGHT (1967, Warners)—Shanghai Jack Connell

EVERETT, RUPERT
DANCE WITH A STRANGER (1985, GB, Goldwyn)—David Blakely

EYER, RICHARD
THE INVISIBLE BOY (1957, MGM)—Timmie Merrinoe
JOHNNY ROCCO (1958, Allied Artists)—Johnny Rocco

EYTHE, WILLIAM
MR. RECKLESS (1948, Paramount)—Jeff Lundy
SPECIAL AGENT (1949, Paramount)—Johnny Douglas
CUSTOMS AGENT (1950, Columbia)—Bert Stewart

EYTON, BESSIE
THE SPOILERS (1914, Silent, Selig)—Helen Chester

EZIASHI, MAYNARD
MR. JOHNSON (1990, Avenue)—Mister Johnson

F

FABER, LESLIE
THE RINGER (1928, GB, Silent, Ideal)—Dr. Lomond

FABIAN (FORTE)
THE HOUND-DOG MAN (1959, 20th Century Fox)—Clint
A BULLET FOR PRETTY BOY (1970, American International)—Pretty Boy Floyd
LITTLE LAURA AND BIG JOHN (1973, Crown International)—John

FAHEY, JEFF
THE LAST OF THE FINEST (1990, Orion)—Ricky Rodriguez
THE LAWNMOWER MAN (1992, New Line)—Jobe Smith

FAHEY, MYRNA
THE HOUSE OF USHER (1960, American International)—Madeline Usher

FAIR, ELINOR
GOLD AND THE GIRL (1925, Silent, Fox)—Ann Donald

FAIRBANKS, DOUGLAS
THE GOOD BAD MAN (1916, Silent, Triangle)—"Passin' Through"
THE MATRIMANIAC (1916, Silent, Triangle)—Jimmy Conroy
REGGIE MIXES IN (1916, Triangle)—Reggie Morton
THE MAN FROM PAINTED POST (1917, Silent, Artcraft)—Fancy Jim Sherwood
A MODERN MUSKETEER (1917, Silent, Artcraft)—Ned Thacker
MR. FIX-IT (1918, Silent, Artcraft)—Mr. Fix-It

HIS MAJESTY, THE AMERICAN (1919, Silent, United Artists)—
William Brooks
THE KNICKERBOCKER BUCKAROO (1919, Silent, Artcraft)—
Teddy Drake
MARK OF ZORRO (1920, Silent, United Artists)—Don Diego
Vega/ Zorro
THE MOLLYCODDLE (1920, Silent, United Artists)—Richard
Marshall
THE NUT (1921, Silent, United Artists)—Charlie Jackson
ROBIN HOOD (1922, Silent, United Artists)—Robin Hood
STEPHEN STEPS OUT (1923, Silent, Paramount)—Stephen
Harlow, Jr.
THE THIEF OF BAGHDAD (1924, Silent, United Artists)—The
Thief of Baghdad
DON Q, SON OF ZORRO (1925, Silent, United Artists)—Don
Cesar de Vega/Zorro
THE BLACK PIRATE (1926, Silent, United Artists)—Michel
THE GAUCHO (1928, Silent, United Artists)—The Gaucho
MR. ROBINSON CRUSOE (1932, United Artists)—Steve Drewel

FAIRBANKS, DOUGLAS JR.
IT'S TOUGH TO BE FAMOUS (1932, First National/Warners)—
Scotty McClenahan
THE LIFE OF JIMMY DOLAN (1933, Warners)—Jimmy Dolan
PARACHUTE JUMPER (1933, Warners)—Bill Keller
THE PRIVATE LIFE OF DON JUAN (1934, United Artists)—
Don Juan
MAN OF THE MOMENT (1935, GB, Warners)—Tony
AMATEUR GENTLEMAN (1936, GB, United Artists)—
Barnabas Barty
WHEN THIEF MEETS THIEF (1937, GB, United Artists-Anglo)—
Ricky Moran
THE CORSICAN BROTHERS (1941, United Artists)—Mario/
Lucien
THE EXILE (1947, Universal)—Charles Stuart
SINBAD THE SAILOR (1947, RKO)—Sinbad
THE FIGHTING O'FLYNN (1949, Universal)—The O'Flynn
THE GREAT MANHUNT (1951, GB, Columbia)—Dr. John
Marlow
MR. DRAKE'S DUCK (1951, GB, United Artists)—Don Drake

FAIRBANKS, WILLIAM
PEACEFUL PETERS (1922, Silent, Arrow)—"Peaceful Peters"
THE BATTLING FOOL (1924, Silent, Perfection Pictures)—Mark
Jenkins
THE COWBOY AND THE FLAPPER (1924, Silent, Truart)—Dan
Patterson
THE FEARLESS LOVER (1925, Silent, Perfection)—Patrick
Michael Casey
THE HANDSOME BRUTE (1925, Silent, Columbia)—Larry O'Day
NEW CHAMPION (1925, Silent, Columbia)—Bob Nichols
SPEED MAD (1925, Silent, Columbia)—Bill Sanford

FAIRE, VIRGINIA BROWN
THE CHORUS KID (1928, Silent, Gotham)—Beatrice Brown

FALK, LISANNE
HEATHERS (1989, New World)—Heather McNamara

FALK, PETER
HUSBANDS (1970, Columbia)—Archie
MIKEY AND NICKY (1976, Paramount)—Mikey
THE CHEAP DETECTIVE (1979, Columbia)—Lou Peckinpaugh

THE IN-LAWS (1979, Warners)—Vince Ricardo

FALKENBURG, JINX
TWO LATINS FROM MANHATTAN (1941, Columbia)—Jinx Terry
LUCKY LEGS (1942, Columbia)—Gloria Carroll
SHE HAS WHAT IT TAKES (1943, Columbia)—Fay Weston
NICE GIRLS (1944, Columbia)—Jane Peters
TALK ABOUT A LADY (1946, Columbia)—Janie Clark

FALKNER, KEITH
THE SINGING COP (1938, GB, Warners)—Jack Richards

FARGAS, ANTONIO
CORNBREAD, EARL AND ME (1975, American International)—
One Eye

FARNSWORTH, RICHARD
THE GREY FOX (1983, Canada, United Artists)—Bill Miner

FARNUM, DUSTIN
THE SQUAW MAN (1914, Silent, Lasky)—Capt. James Wyngate
THE VIRGINIAN (1914, Silent, Lasky)—The Virginian
CAMEO KIRBY (1915, Paramount)—Cameo Kirby
CAPTAIN COURTESY (1915, Silent, Bosworth)—Captain
Courtesy
BEN BLAIR (1916, Silent, Paramount)—Ben Blair
THE PARSON OF PANAMINT (1916, Pallas)—Phillip Pharo
A MAN IN THE OPEN (1919, Silent, United Pictures)—
Sailor Jesse

FARNUM, WILLIAM
THE CONQUEROR (1917, Silent, Standard Pictures)—Sam
Houston
HIS GREATEST SACRIFICE (1921, Silent, Fox)—Richard Hall
THE DRIFTER (1932, State Rights)—The Drifter

FARR, DEREK
MAN ON THE RUN (1949, GB, Pathe)—Peter Burdon
THE MAN IN THE ROAD (1957, GB, Republic)—Ivan Mason

FARR, PATRICIA
ALL-AMERICAN SWEETHEART (1937, Columbia)—
Connie Adams
LADY BEHAVE (1937, Republic)—Clarice

FARRAR, DAVID
THE NIGHT INVADER (1943, GB, Warners)—Dick Marlow
MEET SEXTON BLAKE (1944, GB, British National)—
Sexton Blake
THE TROJAN BROTHERS (1946, GB, Anglo-American)—Sid
Nichols
MR. PERRIN AND MR. TRAILL (1948, GB, Ealing)—David Traill

FARRAR, GERALDINE
CARMEN (1915, Silent, Paramount)—Carmen
JOAN THE WOMAN (1916, Silent, Paramount)—Joan of Arc
RIDDLE: THE WOMAN (1920, Silent, Pathe)—Lilla

FARRAR, JANE
A SONG FOR MISS JULIE (1945, Republic)—Julie

FARRELL, BRIONI
THE STUDENT NURSES (1970, New World)—Lynn

FARRELL, CHARLES
LILIOM (1930, Fox)—Liliom

THE PRINCESS AND THE PLUMBER (1930, Fox)—Charlie
Peters
THE MAN WHO CAME BACK (1931, Fox)—Stephen Randolph

FARRELL, GLENDA
ADVENTUROUS BLONDE (1937, Warners)—Torchy Blane
GOLD DIGGERS OF 1937 (1937, Warners)—Genevieve Larkin
SMART BLONDE (1937, Warners)—Torchy Blane
TORCHY BLANE IN CHINATOWN (1938, Warners)—
Torchy Blane
TORCHY GETS HER MAN (1938, Warners)—Torchy Blane
TORCHY RUNS FOR MAYOR (1939, Warners)—Torchy Blane

FARRINGTON, ADELE
THE COUNTRY MOUSE (1914, Silent, Bosworth)—Addie
Balderson

FARROW, MIA
ROSEMARY'S BABY (1968, Paramount)—Rosemary Woodhouse
JOHN AND MARY (1969, 20th Century Fox)—Mary
THE HAUNTING OF JULIA (1981, GB/Canada,
Discovery)—Julia
HANNAH AND HER SISTERS (1986, Orion)—Hannah
ALICE (1990, Orion)—Alice

FAULKNER, GRAHAM
BROTHER SUN, SISTER MOON (1972, GB, Paramount/Vic)—
Francesco

FAVERSHAM, WILLIAM
THE SIN THAT WAS HIS (1920, Silent, Selznick)—Raymond
Chapelle

FAWCETT (-MAJORS), FARRAH
SOMEBODY KILLED HER HUSBAND (1978, Columbia)—
Jenny Moore
SUNBURN (1979, Paramount)—Ellie

FAY, FRANK
GOD'S GIFT TO WOMEN (1931, Warners)—Jacques Duryea
MEET THE MAYOR (1938, Times)—Spencer Brown

FAY, JIMMY
MILLION DOLLAR BABY (1935, Monogram)—Pat Sweeney

FAYE, ALICE
SHE LEARNED ABOUT SAILORS (1934, 20th Century Fox)—
Jean Legoi
SING, BABY, SING (1936, 20th Century Fox)—Joan Warren
YOU'RE A SWEETHEART (1937, Universal)—Betty Bradley
SALLY, IRENE AND MARY (1938, 20th Century Fox)—Sally Day
ROSE OF WASHINGTON SQUARE (1939, 20th Century Fox)—
Rose Sargent
LILLIAN RUSSELL (1940, 20th Century Fox)—Lillian Russell
FALLEN ANGEL (1945, 20th Century Fox)—June Mills

FAZENDA, LOUISE
A SAILOR'S SWEETHEART (1927, Silent, Warners)—
Cynthia Botts
TILLIE'S PUNCTURED ROMANCE (1928, Silent, Paramount)—
Tillie

FAZIO, RON
THE TOXIC AVENGER, PART II (1989, Troma)—The Toxic
Avenger

THE TOXIC AVENGER PART III: THE LAST TEMPTATION OF
TOXIE (1989, Troma) - The Toxic Avenger

FEARS, PEGGY
LOTTERY LOVER (1935, Fox)—Gaby Aimee

FELDMAN, COREY
THE GOONIES (1985, Warners)—Mouth

FELL, NORMAN
OCEAN'S ELEVEN (1960, Warners)—Peter Rheimer

FELLOWS, EDITH
THE LITTLE ADVENTURESS (1938, Columbia)—Pinky Horton
LITTLE MISS ROUGHNECK (1938, Columbia)—Foxine LaRue
FIVE LITTLE PEPPERS AND HOW THEY GREW (1939,
Columbia)—Polly Pepper
FIVE LITTLE PEPPERS AT HOME (1940, Columbia)—Polly
Pepper
FIVE LITTLE PEPPERS IN TROUBLE (1940, Columbia)—Polly
Pepper
OUT WEST WITH THE PEPPERS (1940, Columbia)—Polly
Pepper

FENNELLY, PARKER
THE KETTLE'S ON MACDONALD'S FARM (1957, Universal)—
Sledge Kettle

FENTON, SIMON
THE POWER OF ONE (1992, Warner Brothers)—P.K. at 12

FENWICK, IRENE
THE SENTIMENTAL LADY (1915, Silent, Kleine)—Amy Cary

FERDIN, PAMELYN
HAPPY BIRTHDAY, WANDA JUNE (1971, Columbia)—
Wanda June

FERGUSON, CASSON
ALIAS MARY BROWN (1918, Silent, Triangle)—Dick Browning
(alias Mary Brown)

FERGUSON, ELSIE
THE RISE OF JENNIE CUSHING (1917, Silent, Artcraft)—
Jennie Cushing
ROSE OF THE WORLD (1918, Silent, Artcraft)—Rosamund
English
HIS PARISIAN WIFE (1919, Silent, Artcraft)—Fauvette

FERGUSON, FRANK
TEXAS BAD MAN (1953, Allied Artists)—Gil

FERRADAY, LISA
FLAME OF STAMBOUL (1957, Columbia)—Lynette Garay

FERRARE, CRISTINA
MARY, MARY, BLOODY MARY (1975, Translor-Proa)—Mary

FERRER, JOSE
CYRANO DE BERGERAC (1950, United Artists)—Cyrano de
Bergerac
OLD EXPLORERS (1990, Taurus)—Warner Watney

FERRER, MEL
THE HANDS OF ORLAC (1964, Silent, Metro)—Nara Alexieff
EL GRECO (1966, 20th Century Fox)—El Greco

FERRI, ALESSANDRA
DANCERS (1987, Cannon)—Francesca

FERRIGNO, LOU
HERCULES II (1985, Cannon)—Hercules

FERRIS, BARBARA
A NICE GIRL LIKE ME (1969, GB, Avco Embassy)—Candida

FERRIS, IRENE
COVER GIRL (1985, New World)—Kit

FIEDLER, JOHN
12 ANGRY MEN (1957, United Artists)—Juror No. 2

FIELD, BETTY
SEVEN WOMEN (1966, MGM)—Florrie Pether

FIELD, SALLY
NORMA RAE (1979, 20th Century Fox)—Norma Rae
STEEL MAGNOLIAS (1989, Tri-Star)—M'Lynn Eatenton
NOT WITHOUT MY DAUGHTER (1991, MGM/Pathe)—Betty
Mahmoody

FIELD, SID
THE CARDBOARD CAVALIER (1949, GB, GFD)—Sidcup
Buttermeadow

FIELDING, ROMAINE
THE MAN WORTH WHILE (1921, Silent, Hillfield)—Don Ward

FIELDS, BENNY
MINSTREL MAN (1944, Producers Releasing Corp.)—Dixie Boy
Johnson

FIELDS, GRACIE
SALLY IN OUR ALLEY (1931, GB, RKO)—Sally Winch
QUEEN OF HEARTS (1936, GB, Associated Talking Pictures)—
Grace Perkins
SHIPYARD SALLY (1940, GB, 20th Century Fox)—Sally
Fitzgerald
MOLLY AND ME (1945, 20th Century Fox)—Molly

FIELDS, W.C.
SO'S YOUR OLD MAN (1926, Silent, Paramount)—Samuel
Bisbee
THE POTTERS (1927, Silent, Paramount)—Pa Potter
TILLIE AND GUS (1933, Paramount)—Augustus Q.
Winterbottom
THE MAN ON THE FLYING TRAPEZE (1937, United Artists)—
Ambrose Wolfinger
THE BANK DICK (1940, Universal)—Egbert Souse
MY LITTLE CHICKADEE (1940, Universal)—Cuthbert J. Twillie

FIGMAN, MAX
THE HOOSIER SCHOOLMASTER (1914, Silent, Alliance)—Ralph
Hartsook

FINCH, JON
MACBETH (1971, GB, Columbia)—Macbeth

FINCH, PETER
SIMON AND LAURA (1956, GB, Universal)—Simon Foster
WINDOM'S WAY (1958, GB, Rank)—Dr. Alec Windom
THE MAN WITH THE GREEN CARNATION (1960, GB,
Warwick)—Oscar Wilde
NO LOVE FOR JOHNNIE (1961, GB, Rank)—Johnnie Byrne

THE PUMPKIN EATER (1964, GB, Columbia)—Jake Armitage
THE NELSON AFFAIR (1973, GB, Universal)—Lord Horatio
Nelson

FINLAY, FRANK
THE THREE MUSKETEERS (1974, 20th Century Fox)—Porthos
THE FOUR MUSKETEERS (1975, 20th Century Fox)—Porthos

FINLEY, WILLIAM
PHANTOM OF THE PARADISE (1974, 20th Century Fox)—
Winslow the Phantom

FINNERAN, SIOBHAN
RITA, SUE AND BOB TOO! (1987, GB, Orion Classics)—Rita

FINNEY, ALBERT
TOM JONES (1963, GB, Woodfall/Lopert)—Tom Jones
TWO FOR THE ROAD (1967, GB, 20th Century Fox)—Mark
Wallace
CHARLIE BUBBLES (1968, GB, Regency/Universal)—Charlie
Bubbles
SCROOGE (1970, GB, National General)—Ebenezer Scrooge
GUMSHOE (1972, GB, Columbia)—Eddie Ginley

FIORENTINO, LINDA
THE MODERNS (1988, Alive Films)—Rachel Stone

FIRTH, COLIN
VALMONT (1989, Orion)—Vicomte de Valmont

FIRTH, PETER
ACES HIGH (1977, GB, Cine Artists/EMI)—Croft
JOSEPH ANDREWS (1977, GB, Paramount)—Joseph Andrews

FISCHER, MARGUERITE
THE GIRL FROM HIS TOWN (1915, Silent, American)—Sarah
Towney
MOLLY OF THE FOLLIES (1919, Silent, American)—Molly
Malone

FISHBURNE, LARRY
DEEP COVER (1992, New Line)—Russell Stevens, Jr./John
Q. Hull

FITZGERALD, BARRY
BROTH OF A BOY (1959, GB, British Lion)—Patrick Farrell

FITZGERALD, GERALDINE
THE GAY SISTERS (1942, First National)—Evelyn Gaylord
LADIES COURAGEOUS (1944, Universal)—Virgie Alford
THREE STRANGERS (1946, Warners)—Crystal

FIX, PAUL
THE NOTORIOUS MR. MONKS (1958, Republic)—
Benjamin Monks

FLANAGAN, BUD
ALF'S BUTTON AFLOAT (1938, GB, Gainsborough)—Alf Higgins

FLEA, *See* **MICHAEL BALZARY**

FLEISCHER, CHARLES
WHO FRAMED ROGER RABBIT? (1988, Buena Vista)—Voice of
Roger Rabbit

FLEMING, ERIC
SPELL OF THE HYPNOTIST (1956, Exploitation)—Dr. Hamilton

FLEMING, RHONDA

THE REDHEAD AND THE COWBOY (1950, Paramount)—
Candace Bronson
LITTLE EGYPT (1951, Universal)—Izora
SERPENT OF THE NILE (1953, Columbia)—Cleopatra
THOSE REDHEADS FROM SEATTLE (1953, Paramount)—Kathie
Edmonds

FLORANCE, SHEILA

A WOMAN'S TALE (1991, Australia, Beyond Films/Illumination
Films)—Martha

FLUGRATH, EDNA

THE PURSUIT OF PAMELA (1920, GB, Silent, Jury)—Pamela
Dodder
TRUE TILDA (1920, Silent, GB, Jury)—Tilda

FLYNN, ERIC

MR. BROWN COMES DOWN THE HILL (1966, GB,
Westminster)—Mr. Brown

FLYNN, ERROL

CAPTAIN BLOOD (1935, Warners)—Dr. Peter Blood
THE PERFECT SPECIMEN (1937, Warners)—Gerald
Beresford Wicks
THE ADVENTURES OF ROBIN HOOD (1938, Warners/First
National)—Robin Hood
THE PRIVATE LIVES OF ELIZABETH AND ESSEX (1939,
Warners)—Robert Devereux, Earl of Essex
THE SEA HAWK (1940, Warners)—Capt. Geoffrey Thorpe
GENTLEMAN JIM (1942, Warners)—James J. Corbett
THEY DIED WITH THEIR BOOTS ON (1942, Warners)—George
Armstrong Custer
ADVENTURES OF DON JUAN (1949, Warners)—Don Juan
ADVENTURES OF CAPTAIN FABIAN (1951, Republic)—Captain
Fabian
THE MASTER OF BALLANTRAE (1953, Warners)—James
Durrisdeer
KING'S RHAPSODY (1955, GB, United Artists)—King Richard of
Laurentia

FLYNN, MAURICE B. "LEFTY"

NO GUN MAN (1924, Silent, FBO)—Robert Jerome Vincent
HIGH AND HANDSOME (1925, Silent, R-C Pictures)—Joe
Hanrahan
THE COLLEGE BOOB (1926, Silent, Film Booking Offices)—
Aloysius Appleby

FOCH, NINA

NICE GIRLS (1944, Columbia)—Alice Blake
MY NAME IS JULIA ROSS (1945, Columbia)—Julia Ross

FONDA, HENRY

THE FARMER TAKES A WIFE (1935, 20th Century Fox)—Dan
Harrow
I DREAM TOO MUCH (1935, RKO)—Jonathan Street
SPENDTHRIFT (1936, Paramount)—Townsend Middleton
SLIM (1937, Warners)—Slim
I MET MY LOVE AGAIN (1938, United Artists)—Ives
YOUNG MR. LINCOLN (1939, 20th Century Fox)—Abraham
Lincoln
CHAD HANNA (1940, 20th Century Fox)—Chad Hanna
THE RETURN OF FRANK JAMES (1940, 20th Century Fox)—
Frank James (Ben Woodson)

YOU BELONG TO ME (1941, Columbia)—Peter Kirk
THE MAGNIFICENT DOPE (1942, 20th Century Fox)—Tad Page
THE MALE ANIMAL (1942, Warners)—Tommy Turner
MY DARLING CLEMENTINE (1946, 20th Century Fox)—
Wyatt Earp
THE FUGITIVE (1947, RKO)—The Fugitive
MISTER ROBERTS (1955, Warners)—Lt. (jg.) Doug Roberts
THE WRONG MAN (1956, Warners)—Christopher "Manny"
Balestrero
12 ANGRY MEN (1957, United Artists)—Juror No. 8
THE MAN WHO UNDERSTOOD WOMEN (1959, 20th Century
Fox)—Willie Bauche
SPENCER'S MOUNTAIN (1963, Warners)—Clay Spencer
THE ROUNDERS (1965, MGM)—Howdy Lewis
THERE WAS A CROOKED MAN (1970, Warners)—Woodward
Lopeman

FONDA, JANE

CAT BALLOU (1965, Columbia)—Katherine "Cat" Ballou
BARBARELLA (1968, France/Italy)—Barbarella
FUN WITH DICK AND JANE (1977, Columbia)—Jane Harper
STANLEY & IRIS (1990, MGM/UA)—Iris

FONDA, PETER

TAMMY AND THE DOCTOR (1963, Universal)—Dr. Mark
Cheswick
THE VICTORS (1963, Columbia)—Weaver
THE YOUNG LOVERS (1964, MGM)—Eddie Slocum
EASY RIDER (1969, Columbia)—Wyatt
THE HIRED HAND (1971, Universal)—Harry Collings
TWO PEOPLE (1973, Universal)—Evan Bonner
DIRTY MARY, CRAZY LARRY (1974, 20th Century Fox)—Larry

FONDACARO, PHIL

THE GARBAGE PAIL KIDS (1987, Atlantic Entertainment)—
Greaser Greg

FONTAINE, JOAN

A DAMSEL IN DISTRESS (1937, RKO)—Lady Alice
Marshmorton
MUSIC FOR MADAME (1937, RKO)—Jean Clemens
MAID'S NIGHT OUT (1938, RKO)—Sheila Harrison
THE CONSTANT NYMPH (1943, Warners)—Tessa Sanger
JANE EYRE (1944, 20th Century Fox)—Jane Eyre
AFFAIRS OF SUSAN (1945, Paramount)—Susan Darell
IVY (1947, Universal)—Ivy
LETTER FROM AN UNKNOWN WOMAN (1948, Universal)—Lisa
Berndie
BORN TO BE BAD (1950, RKO)—Christabel

FONTEYN, MARGOT

ROMEO AND JULIET (1966, GB, Embassy)—Juliet

FORAN, DICK

SHE LOVED A FIREMAN (1937, Warners)—Red Tyler
PRIVATE DETECTIVE (1939, Warners)—Jim Rickey
THE KID FROM KANSAS (1941, Universal)—Kansas

FORBES, JOHN See JOHN CARPENTER

FORBES, RALPH

THE AVENGER (1933, Monogram)—Norman Craig
THE HOUND OF THE BASKERVILLES (1939, 20th Century
Fox)—Sir Hugo Baskerville

FORBES-ROBERTSON, JOHNSTON
HAMLET (1913, Silent, GB, Gaumont)—Hamlet

FORD, CECIL
MEN OF IRELAND (1938, Ireland, Irish National)—Neal O'Moore

FORD, FRANCIS
WASHINGTON AT VALLEY FORGE (1914, Silent, Universal)—George Washington
THE HEART OF LINCOLN (1922, Silent, New Era)—Abraham Lincoln

FORD, GLENN
SO ENDS OUR NIGHT (1941, United Artists)—Ludwig Kern
THE ADVENTURES OF MARTIN EDEN (1942, Columbia)—Martin Eden
FLIGHT LIEUTENANT (1942, Columbia)—Danny Doyle
THE DESPERADOES (1943, Columbia)—Cheyenne Rogers
FRAMED (1947, Columbia)—Mike Lambert
THE MAN FROM COLORADO (1948, Columbia)—Col. Owen Devereaux
THE DOCTOR AND THE GIRL (1949, MGM)—Dr. Michael Corday
MR. SOFT TOUCH (1949, Columbia)—Joe Miracle
THE UNDERCOVER MAN (1949, Columbia)—Frank Warren
THE AMERICANO (1950, RKO)—Sam Dent
THE REDHEAD AND THE COWBOY (1950, Paramount)—Gil Kyle
YOUNG MAN WITH IDEAS (1952, MGM)—Maxwell Webster
THE MAN FROM THE ALAMO (1953, Universal)—John Stoud
THE VIOLENT MEN (1955, Columbia)—John Parrish
FASTEST GUN ALIVE (1956, MGM)—Brad Runyon
JUBAL (1956, Columbia)—Jubal Troop
IMITATION GENERAL (1958, MGM)—M/Sgt. Murphy Savage
THE SHEEPMAN (1958, MGM)—Jason Sweet
THE COURTSHIP OF EDDIE'S FATHER (1963, MGM)—Tom Corbett
THE ROUNDERS (1965, MGM)—Ben Jones
HEAVEN WITH A GUN (1969, MGM)—Jim Killian
SMITH (1969, Buena Vista)—Smith
SANTEE (1973, Crown International)—Santee

FORD, HARRISON
GOOD NIGHT, PAUL (1918, Silent, Selznick)—Paul Boudeaux
THE NERVOUS WRECK (1926, Silent, Producers Distributing Corp.)—Henry Williams

FORD, HARRISON
INDIANA JONES AND THE TEMPLE OF DOOM (1984, Paramount)—Indiana Jones
FRANTIC (1988, Warners)—Dr. Richard Walker
INDIANA JONES AND THE LAST CRUSADE (1989, Paramount)—Indiana Jones
PRESUMED INNOCENT (1990, Warners)—Rusty Sabich
REGARDING HENRY (1991, Paramount)—Henry Turner

FORD, WALLACE
MY WOMAN (1933, Columbia)—Chick Rollins
SWELL-HEAD (1935, Columbia)—Terry McCall

FORDE, EUGENIE
THE COURTESAN (1916, Silent, Mutual Masterpieces)—Mayda St. Maurice

FOREMAN, DEBORAH
VALLEY GIRL (1983, Atlantic)—Julie Richman
LUNATICS: A LOVE STORY (1991, Renaissance Pictures)—Nancy

FORMAN, DAVID
TEENAGE MUTANT NINJA TURTLES (1990, New Line)—Leonardo

FORMBY, GEORGE
I SEE ICE (1938, GB, Associated British)—George Bright
COME ON GEORGE (1939, GB, ATB/ABFD)—George
LET GEORGE DO IT (1940, GB, Ealing)—George
SOUTH AMERICAN GEORGE (1941, GB, Columbia)—George Butters
BELL-BOTTOM GEORGE (1943, GB, Columbia British)—George
HE STOOPS TO CONQUER (1944, GB, Playgoers/Columbia)—George Gribble
I DIDN'T DO IT (1945, GB, Columbia)—George Trotter
GEORGE IN CIVVY CLOTHES (1946, GB, Columbia)—George Harper

FORREST, ALLAN
PRINCE OF PILSEN (1926, Silent, Producers Distributing Corp.)—Frederick, Prince of Pilsen

FORREST, FREDERIC
HAMMETT (1982, Orion/Warners)—Dashiell Hammett

FORREST, MICHAEL
ATLAS (1960, Filmgroup)—Atlas

FORSAYTHE, MIMI
THREE RUSSIAN GIRLS (1943, United Artists)—Tamara

FORSTER, ROBERT
HARRY'S MACHINE (1986, Cannon)—Harry
PEACEMAKER (1990, Fries)—Yates

FORSYTHE, ELEANOR
PROSTITUTE (1980, GB, Kestrel)—Sandra

FORTIER, NICOLE
THE UNHOLY (1988, Vestron)—Demon

FOSS, KENELM
THE DOUBLE LIFE OF MR. ALFRED BURTON (1919, GB, Silent, Ideal)—Alfred Burton
THE JOYOUS ADVENTURES OF ARISTIDE PUJOL (1920, Silent, GB, Foss-Phillips)—Aristide Pujol

FOSTER, HELEN
SWEET SIXTEEN (1928, Silent, Rayart)—Cynthia Perry
LINDA (1929, Silent, Willis Kent)—Linda
SHOULD A GIRL MARRY? (1929, Rayart)—Alice Dunn

FOSTER, JODIE
NAPOLEON AND SAMANTHA (1972, Buena Vista)—Samantha
THE LITTLE GIRL WHO LIVES DOWN THE LANE (1977, Canada, Rank)—Rynn Jacobs
THE ACCUSED (1988, Paramount)—Sarah Tobias

FOSTER, NORMAN
YOUNG MAN OF MANHATTAN (1930, Paramount)—Toby McLean
PROFESSIONAL SWEETHEART (1933, RKO)—Jim Davey
HOOSIER SCHOOLMASTER (1935, Monogram)—Ralph Hartsook

I COVER CHINATOWN (1938, Banner)—Barton

FOSTER, PRESTON
THE MAN WHO DARED (1933, Fox)—Jan Novak
NORTHWEST MOUNTED POLICE (1940, Paramount)—Sgt. Jim Brett
ROGER TOUHY, GANGSTER (1944, 20th Century Fox)—Roger Touhy
STRANGE TRIANGLE (1946, 20th Century Fox)—Sam Crane
THREE DESPERATE MEN (1951, Lippert)—Tom Denton

FOSTER, RONALD
THE WALKING TARGET (1960, United Artists)—Nick Harbin

FOSTER, SUSANNA
FRISCO SAL (1945, Universal)—Sally

FOULK, ROBERT
HOLD THAT HYPNOTIST (1957, Allied Artists)—Dr. Noble

FOURCADE, CHRISTIAN
LITTLE BOY LOST (1953, Paramount)—Jean

FOWLEY, DOUGLAS
YANKEE FAKIR (1947, Republic)—Yankee Davis
THE BADGE OF MARSHAL BRENNAN (1957, Allied Artists)—Marshal Brennan

FOX, ANNE MARIE
RABID GRANNIES (1989, Troma)—Victoria Remington

FOX, EDWARD
THE DAY OF THE JACKAL (1973, GB, Universal)—The Jackal

FOX, JAMES
THOSE MAGNIFICENT MEN IN THEIR FLYING MACHINES (1965, GB, 20th Century Fox)—Richard Mays

FOX, MICHAEL J.
TEEN WOLF (1985, Atlantic)—Scott Howard
THE SECRET OF MY SUCCESS (1987, Universal)—Brantley Foster
DOC HOLLYWOOD (1991, Warner Brothers)—Ben Stone

FOX, SIDNEY
BAD SISTER (1931, Universal)—Marianne
NICE WOMAN (1932, Universal)—Bess Girard

FOY, EDDIE JR.
FOUR JACKS AND A JILL (1941, RKO)—Happy
YOKEL BOY (1942, Republic)—Joe Ruddy

FRANCE, C.V.
LORD EDGEWARE DIES (1934, GB, Realart/RKO)—Lord Edgeware

FRANCIOSA, ANTHONY
A MAN CALLED GANNON (1969, Universal)—Gannon

FRANCIS, ALEC B.
THREE WISE FOOLS (1923, Silent, Goldwyn)—Dr. Richard Gaunt
THE RETURN OF PETER GRIMM (1926, Silent, Fox)—Peter Grimm

FRANCIS, ANNE
SO YOUNG, SO BAD (1950, United Artists)—Loretta
LYDIA BAILEY (1952, 20th Century Fox)—Lydia Bailey

GIRL OF THE NIGHT (1960, Warners)—Bobbie

FRANCIS, KAY
GIRLS ABOUT TOWN (1931, Paramount)—Wanda Howard
FALSE MADONNA (1932, Paramount)—Tina
STRANGERS IN LOVE (1932, Paramount)—Diana Merrow
I LOVED A WOMAN (1933, First National/Warners)—Laura McDonald
MARY STEVENS, M.D. (1933, Warners)—Dr. Mary Stevens
DOCTOR MONICA (1934, Warners)—Dr. Monica Braden
I FOUND STELLA PARRISH (1935, First National/Warners)—Stella Parrish
THE WHITE ANGEL (1936, First National)—Florence Nightingale
FIRST LADY (1937, Warners)—Lucy Chase Wayne
MY BILL (1938, Warners)—Maggie Johnson
SECRETS OF AN ACTRESS (1938, Warners)—Ray Carter
WOMEN ARE LIKE THAT (1938, First National)—Claire Landin
WOMEN IN THE WIND (1939, Warners)—Janet Steele
PLAY GIRL (1940, RKO)—Grace Herbert
CHARLEY'S AUNT (1941, 20th Century Fox)—Donna Luia D'Alvadores
FOUR JILLS IN A JEEP (1944, 20th Century Fox)—Kay Francis

FRANCIS, OLIN
A KNIGHT OF THE WEST (1921, Silent, W.B.M. Photoplays)—Jack "Zip" Garvin

FRANCISCUS, JAMES
YOUNGBLOOD HAWKE (1964, Warners)—Youngblood Hawke
MAROONED (1969, Columbia)—Clayton Stone

FRANKLIN, DIANA
THE LAST AMERICAN VIRGIN (1982, Cannon)—Karen

FRANKLIN, JOHN
CHILDREN OF THE CORN (1984, New World)—Issac

FRANKLIN, PAMELA
THE INNOCENTS (1961, US/GB, 20th Century Fox)—Flora

FRANKS, CHLOE
THE LITTLEST HORSE THIEVES (1977, Buena Vista)—Alice Sandman

FRANVAL, JEAN
BLACK JACK (1979, GB, Kesterel)—Black Jack

FRANZ, ARTHUR
ABBOTT AND COSTELLO MEET THE INVISIBLE MAN (1951, Universal)—Tommy Nelson
THE SNIPER (1952, Columbia)—Eddie Miller
MONSTER OF THE CAMPUS (1958, Universal)—Dr. Donald Blake

FRANZ, EDUARD
THE FOUR SKULLS OF JONATHAN DRAKE (1959, United Artists)—Jonathan Drake

FRASER, BENTON
ENCINO MAN (1992, Hollywood Pictures)—Link

FRASER, JOHN
THE GOOD COMPANIONS (1957, GB, AB-Pathe)—Ingio Jolifant

FRASER, RONALD
THE MUSIC BOX KID (1960, United Artists)—Larry Shaw

FRAWLEY, WILLIAM
THREE MARRIED MEN (1936, Paramount)—Bill Mullins

FRAZEE, JANE
ROSIE THE RIVETER (1944, Republic)—Rosie Warren
SHE'S A SWEETHEART (1944, Columbia)—Maxine Lecour
CALENDAR GIRL (1947, Republic)—Patricia O'Neil

FRAZER, ROBERT
KEEPER OF THE BEES (1925, Silent, Film Booking Offices)—
James Lewis MacFarlane
WANTED—A COWARD (1927, Banne/Sterling)—Rupert
Garland

FREDERICK, HAL
TWO GENTLEMEN SHARING (1969, GB, American
International)—Andrew

FREDERICK, LYNNE
HENRY VIII AND HIS SIX WIVES (1972, GB, EMI/MGM)—
Catherine Howard

FREDERICK, PAULINE
BELLA DONNA (1915, Silent, Paramount)—Bella Donna
AUDREY (1916, Silent, Lasky/Paramount)—Audrey
THE MISTRESS OF SHENSTONE (1921, Silent, Robertson-
Cole)—Lady Myra Ingleby
HER HONOR THE GOVERNOR (1926, Silent, R-C Pictures)—
Adele Fenway
JOSSELYN'S WIFE (1926, Silent, Tiffany)—Lillian Josselyn
MUMSIE (1927, Silent, GB, Wilcox/W&F)—Mumsie

FREEBORN, DENISE
THE SEARCH FOR BRIDEY MURPHY (1956, Paramount)—
Bridey Murphy

FREEMAN, DEBORAH
MY CHAUFFEUR (1986, Crown)—Casey Meadows

FREEMAN, HELEN
THE PILGRIM LADY (1947, Republic)—Aunt Phoebe

FREEMAN, MONA
THAT BRENNAN GIRL (1946, Republic)—Ziggy Brennan
I WAS A SHOPLIFTER (1950, Universal)—Faye Burton
DEAR BRAT (1951, Paramount)—Miriam Wilkins

FREEMAN, MORGAN
DRIVING MISS DAISY (1989, Warners)—Hoke Colburn
LEAN ON ME (1989, Warners)—Joe Clark

FRENCH, HAROLD
I ADORE YOU (1933, GB, Warners/First National)—
Norman Young

FRIELS, COLIN
MALCOLM (1986, Australia, Vestron)—Malcolm
WEEKEND WITH KATE (1990, Australia, Emanuel)—
Richard Muir

FRIEND, PHILIP
BUCCANEER'S GIRL (1950, Universal)—Frederic Baptiste
THE HIGHWAYMAN (1951, Allied Artists/Monogram)—Jeremy

FROBE, GERT
GOLDFINGER (1964, GB, United Artists)—Goldfinger
THOSE MAGNIFICENT MEN IN THEIR FLYING MACHINES
(1965, GB, 20th Century Fox)—Col. Manfred von Holstein

FROMER, AIRION
BOY. . .A GIRL (1969, Jack Hanson)—The Girl

FRYE, KATHY
THREE RUSSIAN GIRLS (1943, United Artists)—Chijik

FUGARD, ATHOL
THE GUEST (1984, GB, RM Production)—Eugene Marais

FULLER, FRANCES
ELMER AND ELSIE (1934, Paramount)—Elsie Beebe

FULLER, LESLIE
POOR OLD BILL (1931, GB, Wardour)—Bill
HAWLEY'S OF HIGH STREET (1933, GB, British International)—
Bill Hawley
CAPTAIN BILL (1935, GB, Fuller Films)—Captain Bill
THE STOKER (1935, GB, Gaumont)—Bill
TWO SMART MEN (1940, GB, Anglo International)—Jimmy

FULLER, TORIA
THERE GOES THE BRIDE (1980, GB, Vanguard)—Judy
Westerby

FULLERTON, FIONA
ALICE'S ADVENTURES IN WONDERLAND (1972, GB, American
National)—Alice

FULTON, JIMMY
THE ADVENTUROUS SOUL (1927, Silent, Hi-Mark
Productions)—Dick Barlow
THE AIR MAIL PILOT (1928, Silent, Hi-Mark Productions)—
Jimmie Dean

FURNESS, BETTY
THEY WANTED TO MARRY (1937, RKO)—Sheila Hunter

FURST, STEPHEN
THE DREAM TEAM (1989, Universal)—Albert Ianuzzi

FURY, BILLY
I'VE GOTTA HORSE (1965, GB, Warners-Pathe)—Billy

FYFFE, WILL
KING OF HEARTS (1936, GB, Butchers)—Bill Saunders
WELL DONE, HENRY (1936, GB, Butchers)—Henry McNab
SEZ O'REILLY TO MACNAB (1938, GB, Gaumont/GFD)—
Malcolm MacNab
THE MYSTERIOUS MR. REEDER (1940, GB, Monogram)—J.G.
Reeder

G

GAAL, FRANCISKA
THE GIRL DOWNSTAIRS (1938, MGM)—Katerina Linz

GABIN, JEAN
THE IMPOSTER (1944, Universal)—Clement

GABLE, CLARK
HELL DIVERS (1932, MGM)—Steve
HOLD YOUR MAN (1933, MGM)—E. "Eddy" Huntington Hall
MEN IN WHITE (1934, MGM)—Dr. Ferguson
CAIN AND MABEL (1936, Warners)—Larry Cain
PARNELL (1937, MGM)—Charles Stewart Parnell
TEST PILOT (1938, MGM)—Jim Lane
THEY MET IN BOMBAY (1941, MGM)—Gerald Meldrick
SOMEWHERE I'LL FIND YOU (1942, MGM)—Jonathan Davis
THE HUCKSTERS (1947, MGM)—Victor Albee Norman
SOLDIER OF FORTUNE (1955, 20th Century Fox)—Hank Lee
THE TALL MEN (1955, 20th Century Fox)—Ben Allison
THE KING AND FOUR QUEENS (1956, United Artists)—
   Dan Kehoe
TEACHER'S PET (1958, Paramount)—Jim Gannon
THE MISFITS (1961, United Artists)—Gay Langland

GABOR, ZSA ZSA
THE GIRL IN THE KREMLIN (1957, Universal)—Greta Grisenko
QUEEN OF OUTER SPACE (1958, Allied Artists)—Talleah
PICTURE MOMMY DEAD (1966, Embassy)—Jessica Shelley

GADD, RENEE
WHERE'S SALLY (1936, GB, Warners)—Sally

GAEL, ANNA
THERESE AND ISABELLE (1968, Audubon Films)—Isabelle

GAHAGAN, HELEN
SHE (1935, RKO)—She

GAINS, COURTNEY
CHILDREN OF THE CORN (1984, New World)—Malachai

GALE, ED
HOWARD THE DUCK (1936, GB, Universal)—Howard T. Duck

GALE, MARGUERITE
HOW MOLLY MADE GOOD (1915, Silent, Kulee Features)—
   Molly Malone

GALE, RICHARD
WHO WAS MADDOX? (1964, Anglo Amalgamated)—Maddox

GALEN, HETTY
THE NIGHT THEY ROBBED BIG BERTHA'S (1975, Scotia
   American)—Big Bertha

GALLAGHER, PETER
SUMMER LOVES (1982, Orion)—Michael Papas

GALLAGHER, RICHARD "SKEETS"
ALEX THE GREAT (1928, Silent, FBO)—Alex

GALLIAN, KETTI
MARIE GALANTE (1934, Fox)—Marie Galante

GALLIER, ALEX
THE RUNAWAY (1964, GB, Columbia)—Andrian Peshkin

GAM, RITA
SAADIA (1953, MGM)—Saadia

GARBO, GRETA
FLESH AND THE DEVIL (1926, Silent, MGM)—Felicitas
   von Eltz
THE TEMPTRESS (1926, Silent, MGM)—Elena
THE DIVINE WOMAN (1928, Silent, MGM)—Marianne
A WOMAN OF AFFAIRS (1928, Silent, MGM)—Diana
THE MYSTERIOUS LADY (1929, Silent, MGM)—Tania
ANNA CHRISTIE (1930, MGM)—Anna Christie
MATA HARI (1931, MGM)—Mata Hari
SUSAN LENOX—HER FALL AND RISE (1931, MGM)—
   Susan Lenox
QUEEN CHRISTINA (1933, MGM)—Queen Christina
ANNA KARENINA (1935, MGM)—Anna Karenina
CAMILLE (1937, MGM)—Marguerite Gautier (Camille)
NINOTCHKA (1939, MGM)—Lena "Ninotchka" Yakushova
TWO-FACED WOMAN (1941, MGM)—Karin Borg Blake/
   Katherine Borg

GARCIA, ALLAN
MORGAN'S LAST RAID (1929, Silent, MGM)—Morgan

GARCIA, ANDY
THE UNTOUCHABLES (1987, Paramount)—George Stone

GARDINER, REGINALD
VIRGINIA'S HUSBAND (1928, GB, Silent, Butchers)—John
   Craddock

GARDNER, AVA
ONE TOUCH OF VENUS (1948, Universal)—Venus
MY FORBIDDEN PAST (1951, RKO)—Barbara Beaurevel
PANDORA AND THE FLYING DUTCHMAN (1951, GB, MGM)—
   Pandora Reynolds
THE NAKED MAJA (1959, United Artists)—Duchess of Alba
THE DEVIL'S WIDOW (1972, GB, British International)—
   Michaela

GARDNER, SHAYLE
ST. ELMO (1923, GB, Silent, Capital)—St. Elmo Murray

GARFIELD, ALLEN
TEACHERS (1984, MGM/United Artists)—Rosenberg

GARFIELD, JOHN
THEY MADE ME A CRIMINAL (1939, Warners)—Johnny
   Bradfield/"Jack Dorney"
SATURDAY'S CHILDREN (1940, Warners)—Rimes Rosson
THE FALLEN SPARROW (1943, RKO)—Kit
PRIDE OF THE MARINES (1945, Warners)—Al Schmid
UNDER MY SKIN (1950, 20th Century Fox)—Dan Butler
HE RAN ALL THE WAY (1951, United Artists)—Nick

GARGAN, WILLIAM
HEADLINE SHOOTER (1933, RKO)—Bill Allen
FOUR FRIGHTENED PEOPLE (1934, Paramount)—Stewart
   Corder
JOE AND ETHEL TURP CALL ON THE PRESIDENT (1939,
   MGM)—Joe Turp
A CLOSE CALL FOR ELLERY QUEEN (1942, Columbia)—
   Ellery Queen
A DESPERATE CHANCE FOR ELLERY QUEEN (1942,
   Columbia)—Ellery Queen
ENEMY AGENT MEETS ELLERY QUEEN (1942, Columbia)—
   Ellery Queen
HARRIGAN'S KID (1943, MGM)—Tom Harrigan

GARLAND, JUDY
BABES IN ARMS (1939, MGM)—Patsy Barton
LITTLE NELLIE KELLY (1940, MGM)—Nellie Kelly
BABES ON BROADWAY (1941, MGM)—Penny Morris
ZIEGFELD GIRL (1941, MGM)—Susan Gallagher
FOR ME AND MY GAL (1942, MGM)—Jo Hayden
PRESENTING LILY MARS (1943, MGM)—Lily Mars
THE HARVEY GIRLS (1946, MGM)—Susan Bradley
A STAR IS BORN (1954, Warners)—Esther Blodgett/Vicki Lester
I COULD GO ON SINGING (1963, United Artists)—Jenny Bowman

GARNER, JAMES
DARBY'S RANGERS (1958, Warners)—Major William Darby
CASH MCCALL (1960, Warners)—Cash McCall
THE WHEELER DEALERS (1963, MGM)—Henry Tyroon
A MAN COULD GET KILLED (1966, Universal)—William Beddoes
MISTER BUDDWING (1966, MGM)—Mister Buddwing
MARLOWE (1969, MGM)—Philip Marlowe
SUPPORT YOUR LOCAL SHERIFF (1969, United Artists)—Jason McCullough
A MAN CALLED SLEDGE (1971, Columbia)—Luther Sledge
SUPPORT YOUR LOCAL GUNFIGHTER (1971, United Artists)—Latigo Smith
THE CASTAWAY COWBOY (1974, Buena Vista/Disney)—Lincoln Costain
MURPHY'S ROMANCE (1985, Columbia)—Murphy Jones

GARNER, PEGGY ANN
JANE EYRE (1944, 20th Century Fox)—Jane Eyre
JUNIOR MISS (1945, 20th Century Fox)—Judy Graves

GARON, PAULINE
THE AVERAGE WOMAN (1924, Silent, C.C. Burr Pictures)—Sally Whipple
THE PAINTED FLAPPER (1924, Silent, Associate First National)—Arline Whitney
CHRISTINE OF THE BIG TOP (1926, Silent, Banner)—Christine
LADIES AT EASE (1927, Silent, First Division)—Polly

GARRETT, ANDI
I SAW WHAT YOU DID (1965, Universal)—Libby

GARRETT, BETTY
MY SISTER EILEEN (1955, Columbia)—Ruth Sherwood

GARRETT, MARTYN
THE BABY AND THE BATTLESHIP (1957, GB, British Lion)—The Baby

GARRICK, JOHN
SKY HAWK (1929, Fox)—Jack Bardell

GARSON, GREER
WHEN LADIES MEET (1941, MGM)—Claire Woodruff
MRS. MINIVER (1942, MGM)—Kay Miniver
MADAME CURIE (1943, MGM)—Marie Curie
MRS. PARKINGTON (1944, MGM)—Susie Parkington
DESIRE ME (1947, MGM)—Marise Aubert
JULIA MISBEHAVES (1948, MGM)—Julia Packett
THAT FORSYTE WOMAN (1949, MGM)—Irene Forsyte
THE MINIVER STORY (1950, GB, MGM)—Kay Miniver
THE LAW AND THE LADY (1951, MGM)—Jane Hoskins

HER TWELVE MEN (1954, MGM)—Jan Stewart
STRANGE LADY IN TOWN (1955, Warners)—Dr. Julia Winslow Garth

GASSMAN, VITTORIO
THE TIGER AND THE PUSSYCAT (1967, Embassy)—Francesco Vincenzini

GATES, RICK
SO LONG, BLUE BOY (1973, Maryon/Dakota)—Isaiah Jenkinson

GATESON, MARJORIE
JAZZ BABIES (1932, Peerless)—Ellie

GAVIN, JOHN
ROMANOFF AND JULIET (1961, Universal)—Igor Romanoff

GAYLE, MONICA
NEW GIRL IN TOWN (1977, New World)—Jamie

GAYNOR, JANET
SUNRISE—A SONG OF TWO HUMANS (1927, Silent, Fox)—The Wife
STREET ANGEL (1928, Fox)—Angela
CHRISTINA (1929, Fox)—Christina
MERELY MARY ANN (1931, Fox)—Mary Ann
TESS OF THE STORM COUNTRY (1932, Fox)—Tess Howland
PADDY, THE NEXT BEST THING (1933, Fox)—Paddy Adair
THE FARMER TAKES A WIFE (1935, 20th Century Fox)—Molly Larkins
LADIES IN LOVE (1936, 20th Century Fox)—Martha Kerenye
SMALL TOWN GIRL (1936, MGM)—Kay Brannan
A STAR IS BORN (1937, United Artists)—Esther Blodgett/Vicki Lester
THREE LOVES HAS NANCY (1938, MGM)—Nancy Briggs

GAYNOR, MITZI
GOLDEN GIRL (1951, 20th Century Fox)—Lotta Crabtree
THE "I DON'T CARE GIRL" (1952, 20th Century Fox)—Eva Tanguay
THREE YOUNG TEXANS (1954, 20th Century Fox)—Rusty Blair
LES GIRLS (1957, MGM)—Joy Henderson

GAYSON, EUNICE
LIGHT FINGERS (1957, GB, Archway)—Rose Levenham

GAZZARA, BEN
THE STRANGE ONE (1957, Columbia)—Jocko De Paris
THE YOUNG DOCTORS (1961, United Artists)—Dr. David Coleman
HUSBANDS (1970, Columbia)—Harry
CAPONE (1975, 20th Century Fox)—Alphonse "Al" Capone
SAINT JACK (1979, New World)—Jack Flowers

GEDLEY, PAMELA
CHERRY 2000 (1988, Orion)—Cherry 2000

GEDRICK, JASON
IRON EAGLE (1986, Tri-Star)—Doug

GEESON, JUDY
GOODBYE GEMINI (1977, MGM/Warners)—Jacki

GELDOF, BOB
NUMBER ONE (1984, GB, Stageform)—Harry "Flash" Gordon

GEMORA, CHARLIE
THE MONSTER AND THE GIRL (1941, Paramount)—The Ape

GENTRY, JIM
THE RAMRODDER (1969, Entertainment Ventures)—The
Ramrodder

GEORGE, GLADYS
VALIANT IS THE WORD FOR CARRIE (1936, Paramount)—
Carrie Snyder
MADAME X (1937, MGM)—Jacqueline Fleuriot

GEORGE, MURIEL
A SISTER TO ASSIST'ER (1938, GB, Columbia)—Mrs. May
A SISTER TO ASSIST'ER (1948, GB, Premier)—Gladys May

GEORGE, SUE
THE DALTON GIRLS (1957, United Artists)—Marigold Dalton

GEORGE, SUSAN
DIE SCREAMING, MARIANNE (1970, GB, London Screen)—
Marianne
LOLA (1971, GB, American International)—Lola "Twinky"
Londonderry
DIRTY MARY, CRAZY LARRY (1974, 20th Century Fox)—Mary

GERARD, CHARLES
THE HUN WITHIN (1918, Silent, Paramount)—Karl Wagner

GERARD, GIL
BUCK ROGERS IN THE 25TH CENTURY (1979, Universal)—
Buck Rogers

GERARD, TEDDIE
THE CAVE GIRL (1921, Silent, First National)—Margot

GERE, RICHARD
YANKS (1979, Universal)—Matt
AMERICAN GIGOLO (1980, Paramount)—Julian
AN OFFICER AND A GENTLEMAN (1982, Paramount)—
Zack Mayo
KING DAVID (1985, Paramount)—King David

GERRARD, GENE
LEAVE IT TO ME (1933, GB, British International)—
Sebastian Help

GERTZ, JAMI
DON'T TELL HER IT'S ME (1990, Hemdale)—Emily Pear
SIBLING RIVALRY (1990, Columbia)—Jeannine

GETTY, ESTELLE
STOP! OR MY MOTHER WILL SHOOT (1992, Universal)—Tutti
Bomowski

GIBB, CYNTHIA
MODERN GIRLS (1986, Atlantic)—Cece

GIBB, DON
JOCKS (1987, Crown)—Ripper

GIBSON, COLIN
JOHN AND JULIE (1957, GB, British Lion)—John Pritchett

GIBSON, HOOT
BLINKY (1923, Silent, Universal)—Geoffrey Arbuthnot
"Blinky" Islip

THE HURRICANE KID (1925, Silent, Universal)—The
Hurricane Kid
CHIP OF THE FLYING U (1926, Silent, Universal)—Chip
Bennett
A HERO ON HORSEBACK (1927, Silent, Universal)—Billy
Garford
THE RAWHIDE KID (1928, Silent, Universal)—Dennis O'Hara
KING OF THE RODEO (1929, Silent, Universal)—Montana Kid
THE LARIAT KID (1929, Silent, Universal)—Tom Richards
THE CONCENTRATIN' KID (1930, Universal)—Concentratin' Kid
THE GAY BUCKAROO (1932, Allied)—Clint Hale
SWIFTY (1936, Diversion)—Swifty
THE MARSHAL'S DAUGHTER (1953, United Artists)—Ben
Dawson

GIBSON, MEL
THE ROAD WARRIOR (1982, Australia, Warners)—Max
MAD MAX (1979, Australia, Filmways)—Max
TIM (1981, Australia, Pisces/Satori)—Tim Melville
MAD MAX BEYOND THUNDERDOME (1985, Australia,
Warners)—Max
LETHAL WEAPON (1987, Warners)—Martin Riggs
LETHAL WEAPON 2 (1989, Warners)—Martin Riggs
BIRD ON A WIRE (1990, Universal)—Rick Jarmin
HAMLET (1990, Warners)—Hamlet
LETHAL WEAPON 3 (1992, Warner Brothers)—Martin Riggs

GIBSON, SARAH
JANE EYRE (1971, GB, British Lion)—Jane Eyre

GIBSON, VIRGINIA
SEVEN BRIDES FOR SEVEN BROTHERS (1954, MGM)—Liza

GIBSON, WYNNE
THE CASE OF CLARA DEANE (1932, Paramount)—Clara Deane
LADY AND GENT (1932, Paramount)—Puff Rogers
THE STRANGE CASE OF CLARA DEANE (1932, Paramount)—
Clara Deane
AGGIE APPLEBY, MAKER OF MEN (1933, RKO)—Aggie
Appleby
HER BODYGUARD (1933, Paramount)—Margot Brienne
I GIVE MY LOVE (1934, Universal)—Judy Blair

GIELGUD, JOHN
THE GOOD COMPANIONS (1933, GB, Gaumont)—Inigo Jolifant
THE SECRET AGENT (1936, GB, Gaumont)—Edgar Brodie
(Richard Ashenden)
THE PRIME MINISTER (1941, GB, Warners)—Benjamin Disraeli
THE BARRETTS OF WIMPOLE STREET (1957, MGM)—Edward
Moulton Barrett
THE LOVED ONE (1965, MGM)—Sir Francis Hinsley
JULIUS CAESAR (1970, GB, Commonwealth)—Julius Caesar
PROSPERO'S BOOKS (1991, GB/Fr., Miramax)—Prospero

GIFFORD, FRANCES
HOLD THAT WOMAN (1940, Producers Releasing Corp.)—Mary
Mulvaney
SHE WENT TO THE RACES (1945, MGM)—Dr. Ann Wotters

GIFTOS, ELAINE
THE STUDENT NURSES (1970, New World)—Sharon

GIL, ARTURO
THE GARBAGE PAIL KIDS (1987, Atlantic Entertainment)—
Windy Winston

GILB, LESLEY
THE LADY DRACULA (1974, Media Cinema)—Lemora

GILBERT, JOHN
GLEAM O'DAWN (1922, Silent, Fox)—Gleam O'Dawn
THE LOVE GAMBLER (1922, Silent, Fox)—Dick Manners
ST. ELMO (1923, Silent, Fox)—St. Elmo Thornton
HIS HOUR (1924, Silent, Metro-Goldwyn)—Prince Gritzko
THE SNOB (1924, Silent, MGM)—Eugene Curry
BARDELYS THE MAGNIFICENT (1926, Silent, MGM)—Bardelys
FLESH AND THE DEVIL (1926, Silent, MGM)—Leo von Harden
HIS GLORIOUS NIGHT (1929, MGM)—Captain Kovacs
WAY FOR A SAILOR (1930, MGM)—Jack Berley
GENTLEMAN'S FATE (1931, MGM)—Jack Thomas

GILBERT, PAUL
THREE NUTS IN SEARCH OF A BOLT (1964, Harlequin)—
Joe Lynch

GILBEY, SHEELAGH
THE HAUNTING OF M (1979, Nu-Image)—Marianna

GILDEN, RICHARD
THE BLACK KLANSMAN (1966, US Films)—Jerry

GILL, BASIL
ADVENTURES OF DICK DOLAN (1917, Silent, GB, Broadwest)—
Dick Dolan
THE ADMIRABLE CRICHTON (1918, Silent, GB, Samuelson/
Jury)—Crichton
SHOULD A DOCTOR TELL? (1931, GB, British Lion)—Dr.
Bruce Smith
IMMORTAL GENTLEMAN (1935, GB, Equity Pictures)—William
Shakespeare

GILLIE, JEAN
TILLY OF BLOOMSBURY (1940, GB, RKO)—Tilly Welwyn

GILLINGWATER, CLAUDE
MY BOY (1922, Silent, Associate First National)—Captain Bill
THREE WISE FOOLS (1923, Silent, Goldwyn)—Theodore Findley

GILLIS, ANN
LITTLE ORPHAN ANNIE (1938, Paramount)—Little
Orphan Annie

GILMORE, DOUGLAS
HIS BUDDY'S WIFE (1925, Silent, Associated Exhibitors)—Bill
Mullaney

GILMORE, VIRGINIA
JENNIE (1941, 20th Century Fox)—Jennie
THAT OTHER WOMAN (1942, 20th Century Fox)—Emily

GINTY, ROBERT
THE EXTERMINATOR (1980, Interstar)—John Eastland
EXTERMINATOR 2 (1984, Cannon)—John Eastland

GIORDANO, DOMIZIANA
ZINA (1985, Film Forum)—Zina

GISH, DOROTHY
GRETCHEN, THE GREENHORN (1916, Silent, Triangle)—
Gretchen
THE LITTLE SCHOOL MA'AM (1916, Silent, Triangle)—Nan
BATTLING JANE (1918, Silent, Perfection Pictures)—
Battling Jane

I'LL GET HIM YET (1919, Silent, First National)—Suzy Faraday
Jones (Skinflint Jones)
NUGGET NELL (1919, Silent, Paramount)—Nugget Nell
LITTLE MISS REBELLION (1920, Silent, Paramount)—Grand
Duchess Marie
THE COUNTRY FLAPPER (1922, Silent, Producers Distributing
Corp.)—Jolanda
ORPHANS OF THE STORM (1922, Silent, United Artists)—
Louise Girard
NELL GWYNNE (1926, GB, Silent, First National)—Nell Gwynne
MADAME POMPADOUR (1927, GB, Paramount)—Mme.
Pompadour

GISH, LILLIAN
DAPHNE AND THE PIRATE (1916, Silent, Triangle)—Daphne
La Tour
AN INNOCENT MAGDALENE (1916, Silent, Triangle)—Dorothy
Raleigh
TRUE HEART SUSIE (1919, Silent, Artcraft)—Susie May
Trueheart
ORPHANS OF THE STORM (1922, Silent, United Artists)—
Henriette Girard
THE WHITE SISTER (1923, Silent, Metro)—Angela Chiaromonte
ROMOLA (1925, Silent, Metro-Goldwyn)—Romola
MISS SUSIE SLAGLE'S (1945, Paramount)—Susie Slagle
HAMBONE AND HILLIE (1984, New World)—Hillie

GLASS, GASTON
THE HERO (1923, Silent, Preferred Pictures)—Oswald Lane

GLASSER, PHILLIP
AN AMERICAN TAIL: FIEVEL GOES WEST (1991, Animated,
Universal)—Voice of Fievel Mousekewitz

GLAUM, LOUISE
I AM GUILTY (1921, Silent, Associated Producers)—Connie
MacNair

GLEASON, ADDA
RAMONA (1916, Silent, Clune)—Ramona

GLEASON, JACKIE
GIGOT (1962, 20th Century Fox)—Gigot
PAPA'S DELICATE CONDITION (1963, Paramount)—Jack
"Papa" Griffith
SOLDIER IN THE RAIN (1963, Allied Artists)—M/Sgt. Maxwell
Slaughter
SMOKEY AND THE BANDIT (1977, Universal)—Sheriff Buford
T. Justice
SMOKEY AND THE BANDIT II (1980, Universal)—Sheriff
Justice
SMOKEY AND THE BANDIT—PART 3 (1983, Universal)—
Sheriff Justice
NOTHING IN COMMON (1986, Tri-Star)—Max Basner

GLEASON, JAMES
THE SHANNONS OF BROADWAY (1929, Universal)—Mickey
Shannon
THE HIGGINS FAMILY (1938, Republic)—Joe Higgins
SHOULD HUSBANDS WORK? (1939, Republic)—Joe Higgins

GLEASON, LUCILLE WEBSTER
THE SHANNONS OF BROADWAY (1929, Universal)—Emma
Shannon
WOMAN UNAFRAID (1934, Goldsmith)—Officer Winthrop

THE HIGGINS FAMILY (1938, Republic)—Lillian Higgins

GLEASON, RUSSELL
A TENDERFOOT GOES WEST (1937, Hoffberg)—Pike
THE HIGGINS FAMILY (1938, Republic)—Stanley Higgins
UNDERCOVER AGENT (1939, Monogram)—Bill Trent

GLEDHILL, NICHOLAS
CAREFUL, HE MIGHT HEAR YOU (1984, Australia, 20th Century Fox)—P.S. "Bill"

GLEN, IAIN
FOOLS OF FORTUNE (1990, GB, Palace)—Willie Quinton

GLENN, SCOTT
VERNE MILLER (1988, Alive)—Verne Miller

GLENVILLE, PETER
HIS BROTHER'S KEEPER (1939, GB, Warners/First National)—Hicky Cornell

GLENVILLE, SHAUN
DR. O'DOWD (1940, GB, Warners)—Marius O'Dowd

GLOVER, JOHN
MEET THE HOLLOWHEADS (1989, Moviestore)—Henry Hollowhead

GLYNNE, ASHLEY
MR. H.C. ANDERSON (1950, GB, British Foundation)—Hans Christian Anderson

GOBBI, TITO
RIGOLETTO (1949, Minerva/Superfilm)—Rigoletto

GOBEL, GEORGE
I MARRIED A WOMAN (1958, RKO/Universal)—Marshall "Mickey" Briggs

GODDARD, PAULETTE
THE GHOST BREAKERS (1940, Paramount)—Mary Carter
THE LADY HAS PLANS (1942, Paramount)—Sidney Royce
I LOVE A SOLDIER (1944, Paramount)—Eva Morgan
KITTY (1945, Paramount)—Kitty
DIARY OF CHAMBERMAID (1946, United Artists)—Celestine
UNCONQUERED (1947, Paramount)—Abigail Martha "Abby" Hale
ANNA LUCASTA (1949, Columbia)—Anna Lucasta
BRIDE OF VENGEANCE (1949, Paramount)—Lucretia Borgia
SINS OF JEZEBEL (1953, Lippert)—Jezebel

GOFF, NORRIS
TWO WEEKS TO LIVE (1943, RKO)—Abner
PARTNERS IN TIME (1946, RKO)—Abner
LUM AND ABNER ABROAD (1956, Howco)—Abner

GOLAN, GILA
THREE ON A COUCH (1966, Columbia)—Anna Jacque

GOLCONDA, LIGIA
HER SACRIFICE (1931, GB, London Screenplays)—Margarita Darlow

GOLD, JIMMY
WISE GUYS (1937, GB, 20th Century Fox)

GOLDBERG, WHOOPI
BURGLAR (1987, Warners)—Bernice Rhodenbarr

FATAL BEAUTY (1987, MGM/United Artists)—Det. Rita Rizzoli
CLARA'S HEART (1988, Warners)—Clara Mayfield
SISTER ACT (1992, Touchstone)—Delores Von Cartier

GOLDBLUM, JEFF
MISTER FROST (1990, France/GB, Hugo/AAA/OMM)—Mr. Frost

GOLDEN, MICHAEL
THE MAN WITHOUT A BODY (1957, GB, Eros)—Nostradamus

GOLDEN, RICHARD
MEET MR. PENNY (1938, GB, British National)—Henry Penny

GOLDTHWAIT, BOBCAT
SHAKES THE CLOWN (1991, IRS Releasing)—Shakes the Clown

GOLINO, VALERIA
THE KING'S WHORE (1990, Fr./Austria/GB/Italy, J&M)—Jeanne de Luynes

GOMBELL, MINNA
STEPPING SISTERS (1932, Fox)—Rosie La Marr
WOMEN MUST DRESS (1935, Monogram)—Linda

GONZALES, CARL
THE LITTLE ONES (1965, GB, Columbia)—Jackie

GOODE, PETER B.
BROTHER RAT AND A BABY (1940, Warners)—"Commencement"

GOODING, CUBA, JR.
BOYZ N THE HOOD (1991, Columbia/New Deal)—Tre Styles
GLADIATOR (1992, Columbia)—Lincoln

GOODMAN, JOHN
KING RALPH (1991, Universal)—Ralph
THE BABE (1992, Universal)—George Herman "Babe" Ruth

GOODNER, CAROL
THE STUDENT'S ROMANCE (1936, GB, British International)—Veronika

GOODWIN, HAROLD
OLIVER TWIST, JR. (1921, Silent, Fox)—Oliver Twist Jr.

GORCEY, LEO
MR. WISE GUY (1942, Monogram)—Ethelbert "Muggs" McGinnis
MR. MUGGS STEPS OUT (1943, Monogram)—Ethelbert Aloysius "Muggs" McGinnis
MR. MUGGS RIDES AGAIN (1945, Monogram)—Ethelbert Aloysius "Muggs" McGinnis
SPOOK BUSTERS (1946, Monogram)—Terrence "Slip" Mahoney
HARD BOILED MAHONEY (1947, Monogram)—Slip Mahoney
NEWS HOUNDS (1947, Monogram)—Slip Mahoney
SPY CHASERS (1956, Allied Artists)—Terrence Aloysius "Slip" Mahoney

GORDON, BRUCE
DON X (1925, Silent, Steen/Goodman)—Don X/Frank Blair

GORDON, CHRISTINE
I WALKED WITH A ZOMBIE (1943, Columbia)—Jessica Holland

GORDON, HUNTLEY
HIS WIFE'S GOOD NAME (1916, Silent, Vitagraph)—Harry Weatherby
HIS WIFE'S HUSBAND (1922, Silent, Pyramid Pictures)—George Packard
BLUEBEARD'S 8TH WIFE (1923, Silent, Paramount)—John Brandon

GORDON, KITTY
THE BELOVED ADVENTURESS (1917, Silent, Peerless/World)—Juliette La Monde
ADELE (1919, Silent, United Artists)—Adele Bleneau

GORDON, LEO
QUANTRILL'S RAIDERS (1958, Allied Artists)—William Quantrill

GORDON, ROBERT
HUCK AND TOM (1918, Paramount)—Huck Finn

GORDON, RUTH
WHAT EVER HAPPENED TO AUNT ALICE? (1969, Palomar/Cinerama)—Mrs. Alice Dimmock
HAROLD AND MAUDE (1971, Paramount)—Maude

GORDON, VERA
THE COHENS AND THE KELLYS (1926, Silent, Universal)—Mrs. Cohen
THE COHENS AND THE KELLYS IN ATLANTIC CITY (1929, Universal)—Mrs. Cohen

GORING, MARIUS
MR. PERRIN AND MR. TRAILL (1948, GB, Ealing)—Vincent Perrin

GORTNER, MARJOE
BOBBIE JO AND THE OUTLAW (1976, American International)—Lyle Wheeler

GOSDEN, FREEMAN
AMOS 'N' ANDY (1930, Radio)—Amos Jones

GOSSETT, LOUIS JR.
ENEMY MINE (1985, 20th Century Fox)—The Drac

GOTT, BARBARA
A SISTER TO ASSIST'ER (1930, GB, Gaumont)—Mrs. May

GOUDAL, JETTA
HER MAN O'WAR (1926, Silent, De Mille Pictures)—Cherie Schultz

GOUGH, MICHAEL
SATAN'S SLAVE (1976, GB, Crown)—Alexander Yorke

GOULD, ELLIOTT
BOB AND CAROL AND TED AND ALICE (1969, Columbia)—Ted
I LOVE MY WIFE (1970, Universal)—Dr. Richard Burrows
S*P*Y*S (1974, 20th Century Fox)—Griff
HARRY AND WALTER GO TO NEW YORK (1976, Columbia)—Walter Hill
I WILL. . .I WILL. . .FOR NOW (1976, 20th Century Fox)—Les Bingham
THE SILENT PARTNER (1979, Canada, EMC Film Corp.)—Miles Cullen
THE LAST FLIGHT OF NOAH'S ARK (1980, Buena Vista)—Noah Dugan

THE DEVIL AND MAX DEVLIN (1981, Buena Vista)—Max Devlin
DEAD MEN DON'T DIE (1990, Trans Atlantic)—Barry

GOULDING, EDMUND
THREE LIVE GHOSTS (1922, Silent, Paramount)—Jimmy Grubbins

GOYA, MONA
THE LADY FROM THE SEA (1929, GB, British International)—Claire le Grange

GRABLE, BETTY
SWEET ROSIE O'GRADY (1943, 20th Century Fox)—Madeline Marlowe/Rosie O'Grady
PIN UP GIRL (1944, 20th Century Fox)—Lorry Jones
THE DOLLY SISTERS (1945, 20th Century Fox)—Jenny Dolly
MOTHER WORE TIGHTS (1947, 20th Century Fox)—Myrtle McKinley Burt
THE SHOCKING MISS PILGRIM (1947, 20th Century Fox)—Cynthia Pilgrim
THAT LADY IN ERMINE (1948, 20th Century Fox)—Francesca
THE BEAUTIFUL BLONDE FROM BASHFUL BEND (1949, 20th Century Fox)—Freddie
THE FARMER TAKES A WIFE (1953, 20th Century Fox)—Molly Larkins

GRAETZ, PAUL
MR. COHEN TAKES A WALK (1936, GB, Warners)—Jake Cohen

GRAHAM, GARY
THE LAST WARRIOR (1989, SVS)—Jim Kemp

GRAHAM, GERRIT
C.H.U.D.: BUD THE C.H.U.D. (1989, Vestron)—Bud the Chud

GRAHAM, JOHN
HILDUR AND THE MAGICIAN (1969, Canyon Cinema Cooperative)—The Magician

GRAHAM, MORLAND
OLD BILL AND SON (1940, GB, GFD)—Old Bill Busby

GRAHAM, WILLIAM
JUST WILLIAM'S LUCK (1948, GB, United Artists)—William Brown
WILLIAM COMES TO TOWN (1948, GB, United Artists)—William Brown

GRAHAME, GLORIA
PRISONERS OF THE CASBAH (1953, Columbia)—Princess Nadja

GRAHAME, MARGOT
I ADORE YOU (1933, GB, Warners/First National)—Margot Grahame
NIGHT WAITRESS (1936, RKO)—Helen Roberts
TWO IN THE DARK (1936, RKO)—Marie Smith

GRANGE, HAROLD "RED"
RACING ROMEO (1927, Silent, R-C Pictures)—Red Walden

GRANGE, RAY
RUDE BOY (1980, GB, Atlantic)—Ray

GRANGER, FARLEY
THEY LIVE BY NIGHT (1949, RKO)—Bowie

STRANGERS ON A TRAIN (1951, Warners)—Guy Haines

GRANGER, STEWART
WOMAN HATER (1949, GB, Rank)—Lord Terence Datchett
ADAM AND EVELYNE (1950, GB, Rank/Two Cities)—
Adam Black
SOLDIERS THREE (1951, MGM)—Pvt. Archibald Ackroyd
THE PRISONER OF ZENDA (1952, MGM)—King Rudolf V
SCARAMOUCHE (1952, MGM)—Scaramouche (Andre Moreau)
ALL THE BROTHERS WERE VALIANT (1953, MGM)—
Mark Shore
BEAU BRUMMELL (1954, MGM)—George Bryan "Beau"
Brummell
HARRY BLACK AND THE TIGER (1958, GB, 20th Century Fox)—
Harry Black

GRANT, BARRA
DAUGHTERS OF SATAN (1972, United Artists)—Chris
Robertson

GRANT, CARY
THE EAGLE AND THE HAWK (1933, Paramount)—Henry
Crocker
SHE DONE HIM WRONG (1933, Paramount)—Capt. Cummings
("The Hawk")
THE AMAZING QUEST OF ERNEST BLISS (1936, GB,
Klement)—Ernest Bliss
HIS GIRL FRIDAY (1940, Columbia)—Walter Burns
THE HOWARDS OF VIRGINIA (1940, Columbia)—Matt Howard
MY FAVORITE WIFE (1940, RKO)—Nick Arden
MR. LUCKY (1943, RKO)—Joe Adams
THE BACHELOR AND THE BOBBYSOXER (1947, RKO)—Dick
Nugent
MR. BLANDINGS BUILDS HIS DREAM HOUSE (1948, RKO)—
Jim Blandings
I WAS A MALE WAR BRIDE (1949, 20th Century Fox)—Capt.
Henri Richard
FATHER GOOSE (1964, Universal)—Walter Eckland

GRANT, DAVID
AMERICAN FLYERS (1985, Warners)—David

GRANT, RICHARD E.
WITHNAIL AND I (1987, GB, Cineplex Odeon)—Withnail

GRANVILLE, BONITA
BELOVED BRAT (1938, Warners)—Roberta
NANCY DREW—DETECTIVE (1938, Warners)—Nancy Drew
NANCY DREW AND THE HIDDEN STAIRCASE (1939, Warners)—
Nancy Drew
NANCY DREW—REPORTER (1939, Warners)—Nancy Drew
NANCY DREW, TROUBLE SHOOTER (1939, Warners)—
Nancy Drew
SENORITA FROM THE WEST (1945, Universal)—Jeannie Blake

GRAPEWIN, CHARLES
HERO FOR A DAY (1939, Universal)—Frank Higgins
I AM NOT AFRAID (1939, Warners)—Ulysses Porterfield

GRAVES, RALPH
THE SWELL-HEAD (1927, Silent, Columbia)—Lefty Malone
THE CHEER LEADER (1928, Silent, Gotham)—Jimmy Grant

GRAVET, FERNAND
THE KING AND THE CHORUS GIRL (1937, Warners)—Alfred

GRAVINA, CARLA
FIVE BRANDED WOMEN (1960, Paramount)—Mira

GRAY, BILLY
THE SEVEN LITTLE FOYS (1955, Paramount)—Brynie Foy

GRAY, CHARLES
THE NIGHT OF THE GENERALS (1967, GB, Columbia)—Gen.
von Seidlitz-Gabler

GRAY, COLLEEN
THE LEECH WOMAN (1960, Universal)—June Talbot

GRAY, DONALD
THE ATOMIC MAN (1955, Allied Artists)—Maitland

GRAY, DULCIE
THEY WERE SISTERS (1945, GB, Universal)—Charlotte
THERE WAS A YOUNG LADY (1953, GB, Butchers)—Elizabeth
Foster

GRAY, GILDA
ALOMA OF THE SOUTH SEAS (1926, Silent,
Paramount)—Aloma

GRAY, JANE
THE LITTLE GRAY LADY (1914, Silent, Famous Players)—
Anna Grey

GRAY, LAWRENCE
A FACE IN THE FOG (1936, Victory)—Peter Fortune

GRAY, LORNA
O, MY DARLING CLEMENTINE (1943, Republic)—Clementine

GRAY, MARGERY
HEIDI'S SONG (1982, Animated, Paramount)—Voice of Heidi

GRAY, SALLY
LADY IN DISTRESS (1942, GB, GFD)—Vivienne

GRAYSON, KATHRYN
ANDY HARDY'S PRIVATE SECRETARY (1941, MGM)—
Kathryn Land
RIO RITA (1942, MGM)—Rita Winslow
TWO SISTERS FROM BOSTON (1946, MGM)—Abigail Chandler
LOVELY TO LOOK AT (1952, MGM)—Stephanie
KISS ME KATE (1953, MGM)—Lilli Vanessi/Katherine

GREELEY, EVELYN
DIANE OF STAR HOLLOW (1921, Silent, Producers Security)—
Diane Orsini

GREEN, DANNY
THE LADYKILLERS (1956, GB, Ealing)—One-Round

GREEN, HARRY
THE KIBITZER (1929, Paramount)—Ike Lazarus

GREEN, HUGHIE
MEN OF THE SEA (1951, GB, Astor)—Jack Easy

GREEN, KERRI
THREE FOR THE ROAD (1987, New Century-Vista)—Robin
Kitteridge

GREEN, LARRY
THE GARBAGE PAIL KIDS (1987, Atlantic Entertainment)—
Nat Nerd

GREEN, MITZI
FINN AND HATTIE (1931, Paramount)—Mildred Haddock
LITTLE ORPHAN ANNIE (1932, RKO)—Little Orphan Annie

GREEN, NIGEL
LET'S KILL UNCLE (1966, Universal)—Major Harrison
GAWAIN AND THE GREEN KNIGHT (1973, GB, United Artists)—
Green Knight

GREENE, RICHARD
FOUR MEN AND A PRAYER (1938, 20th Century Fox)—
Geoff Leigh
THE HOUND OF THE BASKERVILLES (1939, 20th Century
Fox)—Sir Henry Baskerville
THE DESERT HAWK (1950, Universal)—Omar
THE BANDITS OF CORSICA (1953, Global/United Artists)—
Mario & Carlos Franchi
CAPTAIN SCARLETT (1953, United Artists)—Capt. Scarlett

GREENFIELD, ASHLEY
SOME GIRLS (1989, MGM-United Artists)—Simone

GREENSTREET, SIDNEY
THREE STRANGERS (1946, Warners)—Arbutney

GREENWOOD, CHARLOTTE
SO LONG LETTY (1929, Warners)—Letty Robbins
THE PERFECT SNOB (1941, 20th Century Fox)—Martha Mason

GREENWOOD, JOAN
A GIRL IN A MILLION (1946, GB, Oxford)—Gay Sultzman

GREER, JANE
THE COMPANY SHE KEEPS (1950, RKO)—Diane
YOU FOR ME (1952, MGM)—Katie McDermAd

GREGG, CHRISTINA
TWO WIVES AT ONE WEDDING (1961, GB, Paramount)—Janet
YOUNG, WILLING AND EAGER (1962, GB, Brenner)—
Carol Flynn

GREGORY, ANDRE
MY DINNER WITH ANDRE (1981, New Yorker)—Andre

GREGORY, JAMES
THE MANCHURIAN CANDIDATE (1962, United Artists)—
Senator John Iselin

GREGSON, JOHN
ROONEY (1958, GB, Rank)—James Ignatius Rooney
THE CAPTAIN'S TABLE (1960, GB, 20th Century Fox/Rank)—
Captain Ebbs

GREY, ANNE
SHE WAS ONLY A VILLAGE MAIDEN (1933, GB, MGM)—
Priscilla Protheroe

GREY, JANE
HER FIGHTING CHANCE (1917, Silent, Jacobs/Hall)—Marie

GREY, JOEL
MAN ON A SWING (1974, Paramount)—Franklin Wills

GREY, LORRAINE
SEXTON BLAKE AND THE MADEMOISELLE (1935, GB, MGM)—
Mlle. Roxanne

GREY, LYNDA
THE UNINVITED (1944, Paramount)—Ghost of Mary Meredith

GREY, MINNA
MRS. THOMPSON (1919, GB, Silent, Samuelson)—Mrs.
Thompson

GREY, NAN
THREE SMART GIRLS (1937, Universal)—Joan Craig
THREE SMART GIRLS GROW UP (1939, Universal)—Joan Craig
MARGIE (1940, Universal)—Margie
UNDER AGE (1941, Columbia)—Jane Baird

GREY, SHIRLEY
GIRL IN DANGER (1934, Columbia)—Gloria Gale
THE GIRL WHO CAME BACK (1935, First Division)—Gilda

GRIBBON, EDDIE
THREE ROGUES (1931, Fox)—Bronco Dawson

GRIECO, RICHARD
MOBSTERS (1991, Universal)—Bugsy Siegel

GRIER, PAM
COFFY (1971, American International)—Coffy
FOXY BROWN (1974, American International)—Foxy Brown
FRIDAY FOSTER (1975, American International)—Friday Foster
SHEBA BABY (1975, American International)—Sheba

GRIER, ROSEY
THE THING WITH TWO HEADS (1972, American
International)—Jack Moss

GRIFFEN, C. ELLIOTT
THE GIRL FROM HIS TOWN (1915, Silent, American)—Sarah
Towney

GRIFFIN, MICHAEL
SONNY BOY (1990, Triumph)—Sonny Boy

GRIFFITH, ANDY
A FACE IN THE CROWD (1957, Warners)—Lonesome Rhodes
ONIONHEAD (1958, Warners)—Al Woods

GRIFFITH, CORINNE
INTO HER KINGDOM (1926, Silent, First National)—Grand
Duchess Tatiana
SYNCOPATING SUE (1926, Silent, First National)—
Susan Adams
OUTCAST (1928, Silent, First National)—Miriam
PRISONERS (1929, Warners)—Tiza Riga
SATURDAY'S CHILDREN (1929, Warners)—Bobby Halvey
LILY CHRISTINE (1932, GB, Paramount British)—Lily Christine

GRIFFITH, GORDON
JUNGLE TRAIL OF THE SON OF TARZAN (1923, Silent,
National Films)—Jack, Son of Tarzan

GRIFFITH, MELANIE
WORKING GIRL (1988, 20th Century Fox)—Tess McGill
A STRANGER AMONG US (1992, Buena Vista)—Emily Eden

GRIFFITH, RAYMOND
A REGULAR FELLOW (1925, Silent, Paramount)—The Prince

GRIFFITHS, LINDA
LIANNA (1983, United Artists)—Lianna

GRODIN, CHARLES
THE HEARTBREAK KID (1972, 20th Century Fox)—Lenny
Cantrow

GROSS, AYRE
THE EXPERTS (1989, Paramount)—Wendell

GROSSMANN, MECHTHILD
SEDUCTION: THE CRUEL WOMAN (1989, First Run)—Wanda

GROSSMITH, GEORGE
GOD IS MY WITNESS (1931, Astor)—God

GROVES, FRED
THE LABOUR LEADER (1917, Silent, GB, British Actors)—John
Webster

GUARD, DOMINIC
THE GO-BETWEEN (1971, GB, MGM-EMI/Columbia)—Leo
Colston

GUEST, LANCE
THE LAST STARFIGHTER (1984, Universal)—Alex Rogan

GUINAN, TEXAS
QUEEN OF THE NIGHTCLUBS (1929, Warners)—Tex Malone

GUINNESS, ALEC
THE LAVENDER HILL MOB (1951, GB, Ealing)—Henry Holland
THE MAN IN THE WHITE SUIT (1952, GB, Rank)—Sidney
Stratton
THE PROMOTER (1952, GB, Universal)—Edward Henry "Denry"
Machin
THE CAPTAIN'S PARADISE (1953, GB, London Films)—Capt.
Henry St. James
THE DETECTIVE (1954, GB, Columbia)—Father Brown
THE PRISONER (1955, GB, Columbia)—The Prisoner
THE LADYKILLERS (1956, GB, Ealing)—Professor Marcus
THE SCAPEGOAT (1959, GB, MGM)—John Barrett
OUR MAN IN HAVANA (1960, GB, Columbia)—Jim Wormold
HITLER: THE LAST TEN DAYS (1973, GB, Paramount)—Adolf
Hitler

GUITTARD, LAURENCE
SOMEBODY KILLED HER HUSBAND (1978, Columbia)—
Preston Moore

GUIZAR, TITO
THE LLANO KID (1940, Paramount)—The Llano Kid

GULAGER, CLU
THE KILLERS (1964, Universal)—Lee
HUNTER'S BLOOD (1987, Concorde)—Mason Rand

GUNN, JUDY
BEAUTY AND THE BARGE (1937, GB, Twickenham/Wardour)—
Ethel Smedley

GURIE, SIGRID
THE FORGOTTEN WOMAN (1939, Universal)—Anne Kennedy

GUTTENBERG, STEVE
THREE MEN AND A BABY (1987, Buena Vista)—Michael
Kellam
DON'T TELL HER IT'S ME (1990, Hemdale)—Gus Kubieck
THREE MEN AND A LITTLE LADY (1990, Buena Vista)—
Michael Kellam

GUYSE, SHEILA
SEPIA CINDERELLA (1947, Herald)—Barbara

GWENN, EDMUND
THE BISHOP MISBEHAVES (1933, MGM)—Bishop
THE GOOD COMPANIONS (1933, GB, Gaumont)—Jess Oakroyd
SMITHY (1933, GB, Warners)—John Smith
THE ADMIRAL'S SECRET (1934, GB, Realart/RKO)—Admiral
Pitzporter
FATHER AND SON (1934, GB, Warners)—John Bolton
MISTER 880 (1950, 20th Century Fox)—Skipper Miller

GWILLIM, JACK
SENTENCED FOR LIFE (1960, GB, United Artists)—John
Richards

GWYNN, MICHAEL
THE DOCTOR'S DILEMMA (1958, GB, MGM)—Dr. Blenkenson

GWYNNE, FRED
MUNSTER, GO HOME (1966, Universal)—Herman Munster

H

HAAS, DOLLY
GIRLS WILL BE BOYS (1934, GB, Associated British)—Pat
Caverley

HAAS, LUKAS
WITNESS (1985, Paramount)—Samuel
THE WIZARD OF LONELINESS (1988, Skouras)—Wendall Olet
ALAN & NAOMI (1992, Triton)—Alan Silverman

HACKETT, JOAN
THE GROUP (1966, United Artists)—Dottie Renfrew

HACKMAN, GENE
MAROONED (1969, Columbia)—Buzz Lloyd
I NEVER SANG FOR MY FATHER (1970, Columbia)—Gene
Garrison
ZANDY'S BRIDE (1974, Warners)—Zandy Allan
BAT 21 (1988, Tri-Star)—Lt. Col. Iceal Hambleton
LOOSE CANNONS (1990, Tri-Star)—Mac

HADDON, DAYLE
CYBORG (1989, Cannon)—Pearl Prophet

HADLEY, REED
I SHOT JESSE JAMES (1949, Lippert)—Jesse James

HAGEN, ANNA
LYDIA (1964, Canada, Libra)—Lydia

HAGEN, ROSS
BAD CHARLESTON CHARLIE (1973, International Cinema)—
Charlie Jacobs

HAGERTY, JULIE
LOST IN AMERICA (1985, Warners)—Linda Howard

HAGGARD, STEPHEN
MOZART (1940, GB, ABF/Lopert)—Wolfgang Amadeus Mozart

HAGGERTY, DAN
THE LIFE AND TIMES OF GRIZZLY ADAMS (1974, Sunn Classics)—James Capen Adams

HAHN, PAULINE
TOO YOUNG TO LOVE (1960, GB, Rank)—Elizabeth Collins

HAIGH, KENNETH
EAGLE IN A CAGE (1971, National General)—Napoleon Bonaparte
MAN AT THE TOP (1973, GB, Anglo-EMI)—Joe Lampton

HAIM, COREY
LUCAS (1986, 20th Century Fox)—Lucas
THE LOST BOYS (1987, Warners)—Sam
LICENSE TO DRIVE (1988, 20th Century Fox)—Les

HAINES, WILLIAM
BROWN OF HARVARD (1926, Silent, MGM)—Tom Brown
SLIDE, KELLY, SLIDE (1927, Silent, MGM)—Jim Kelly
ALIAS JIMMY VALENTINE (1928, MGM)—Jimmy Valentine
THE DUKE STEPS OUT (1929, Silent, MGM)—Duke
A MAN'S MAN (1929, Silent, MGM)—Mel
JUST A GIGOLO (1931, MGM)—Lord Robert Brummell
THE NEW ADVENTURES OF GET-RICH-QUICK WALLINGFORD (1931, MGM)—J. Rufus Wallingford
A TAILOR MADE MAN (1931, MGM)—John Paul Burt

HALE, ALAN
SAILORS' HOLIDAY (1929, Pathe)—Adam Pike
WHEN THIEF MEETS THIEF (1937, GB, United Artists/Anglo)—Jim Dial/ Colonel Fane

HALE, ALAN JR.
SARGE GOES TO COLLEGE (1947, Monogram)—Sarge

HALE, BARBARA
LORNA DOONE (1951, Columbia)—Lorna Doone

HALE, GEORGIA
GYPSY OF THE NORTH (1928, Silent, Rayart)—Alice Culhane

HALE, MONTE
CALIFORNIA FIREBRAND (1948, Republic)—Monte Hale
RANGER OF THE CHEROKEE STRIP (1949, Republic)—Steve Howard

HALEY, JACK
HERE COMES THE GROOM (1934, Paramount)—Mike Scanlon
F MAN (1936, Paramount)—Johnny Dime
MISTER CINDERELLA (1936, MGM)—Joe Jenkins

HALL, ALEX
THE LEECH (1921, Silent, Pioneer)—Bill

HALL, ANTHONY MICHAEL
THE BREAKFAST CLUB (1985, Universal)—Brian Johnson
JOHNNY BE GOOD (1988, Orion)—Johnny Walker

HALL, ARCH JR.
THE SADIST (1963, Fairway-International)—Charley Tibbs

HALL, CYNTHIA
HIGH YELLOW (1965, Dinero/Thunder)—Cindy

HALL, ELLA
THE LOVE GIRL (1916, Silent, Bluebird)—Ambrosia
THE CHARMER (1917, Silent, Bluebird)—Ambrosia Lee

HALL, HUNTZ
SPOOK BUSTERS (1946, Monogram)—Sach
NEWS HOUNDS (1947, Monogram)—Sach
SPY CHASERS (1956, Allied Artists)—Horace Debussy "Sach" Jones
SPOOK CHASERS (1957, Allied Artists)—Horace Debussy "Sach" Jones

HALL, JAMES
FOUR SONS (1928, Silent, Fox)—Joseph Bernie
HELL'S ANGELS (1930, United Artists)—Roy Rutledge

HALL, JON
KIT CARSON (1940, United Artists)—Kit Carson
SAILOR'S LADY (1940, 20th Century Fox)—Danny Malone
INVISIBLE AGENT (1942, Universal)—Frank Raymond
TUTTLES OF TAHITI (1942, RKO)—Cheater Tuttle
WHITE SAVAGE (1943, Universal)—Kaloe
ALI BABA AND THE FORTY THIEVES (1944, Universal)—Ali Baba
INVISIBLE MAN'S REVENGE (1944, Universal)—Robert Griffin
THE MICHIGAN KID (1947, Universal)—Michigan Kid
THE PRINCE OF THIEVES (1948, Columbia)—Robin Hood
DEPUTY MARSHAL (1949, Lippert)—Ed Garry

HALL, KEVIN PETER
MONSTER IN THE CLOSET (1987, Troma)—The Monster
PREDATOR (1987, 20th Century Fox)—Predator
PREDATOR 2 (1990, 20th Century Fox)—Predator

HALL, LOIS
DAUGHTER OF THE JUNGLE (1949, Republic)—Ticoora

HALL, THURSTON
HE HIRED THE BOSS (1943, 20th Century Fox)—Mr. Bates

HALLIDAY, BRYANT
THE PROJECTED MAN (1967, GB, Universal)—Prof. Steiner

HALLIDAY, JOHN
CAPTAIN APPLEJACK (1931, Warners)—Captain Applejack

HALLIWELL, MILES
WINSTANLEY (1979, GB, British Film Institute)—Winstanley

HALLOR, EDITH
A MAN AND THE WOMAN (1917, Silent, Art Dramas)—Agnes van Suyden

HALOP, BILLY
LITTLE TOUGH GUY (1938, Universal)—Johnny Boylan
TOUGH AS THEY COME (1942, Universal)—Tommy Clark

HALSEY, BRETT
RETURN OF THE FLY (1959, 20th Century Fox)—Philippe Delambre
SPEED CRAZY (1959, Allied Artists)—Nick

HAMILTON, GEORGE
THE VICTORS (1963, Columbia)—Cpl. Trower
JACK OF DIAMONDS (1967, MGM)—Jeff Hill
EVEL KNIEVEL (1971, Fanfare)—Evel Knievel

ZORRO, THE GAY BLADE (1981, 20th Century Fox)—Don Diego Vega/ Bunny Wigglesworth-Zorro

HAMILTON, HALE
HIS BROTHER'S PLACE (1919, Silent, Metro)—Nelson Drake & Barrington Drake
JOHNNY ON THE SPOT (1919, Silent, Metro)—Johnny Rutledge

HAMILTON, JOHN
PHANTOM KILLER (1942, Monogram)—John G. Harrison

HAMILTON, LLOYD
HIS DARKER SELF (1924, Silent, G and H Pictures)—Claude Sappington

HAMILTON, MAHLON
DADDY LONG LEGS (1919, Silent, First National)—Jervis Pendelton

HAMILTON, NEIL
STRANGERS MAY KISS (1931, MGM)—Alan
TWO AGAINST THE WORLD (1932, Warners)—Dave Norton
MR. STRINGFELLOW SAYS NO (1937, GB, National Provincial)—Jeremy Stringfellow

HAMLIN, HARRY
KING OF THE MOUNTAIN (1981, Universal)—Steve

HAMMACK, WARREN
JOHNNY VIK (1973, Nauman)—Johnny Vik

HAMMERSTEIN, ELAINE
THE COUNTRY COUSIN (1919, Silent, Selznick)—Cousin Nancy
THE DAUGHTER PAYS (1920, Silent, Selznick)—Virginia Mynors
THE WAY OF A MAID (1921, Silent, Selznick)—Naida Castleton

HAMMOND, HARRIET
MAN AND MAID (1925, Silent, Metro-Goldwyn)—Alathea Bulteel

HAMMOND, KAY
BLITHE SPIRIT (1945, GB, Cineguild/Two Cities)—Elvira Condomine

HAMMOND, VIRGINIA
MISS CRUSOE (1919, Silent, World)—Dorothy Evans

HAMPTON, HOPE
THE GOLD DIGGERS (1923, Silent, Warners)—Jerry La Mar

HANCOCK, TONY
CALL ME GENIUS (1961, GB, Associated British Films)—Anthony Hancock
THE PUNCH AND JUDY MAN (1963, GB, Warner-Pathe)—Wally Pinner

HANDLEY, TOMMY
IT'S THAT MAN AGAIN (1943, GB, Gainsborough)—Mayor Handley

HANEY, BETTY JEAN
MARY JANE'S PA (1935, First National)—Mary Jane Preston

HANEY, DARYL
DADDY'S BOYS (1988, Concorde)—Jimmy

HANKS, TOM
BACHELOR PARTY (1984, 20th Century Fox)—Rick Grasso
THE MAN WITH ONE RED SHOE (1985, 20th Century Fox)—Richard
EVERY TIME WE SAY GOODBYE (1986, Tri-Star)—David
NOTHING IN COMMON (1986, Tri-Star)—David Basner
BIG (1988, 20th Century Fox)—Joshua Baskin
TURNER & HOOCH (1989, Buena Vista)—Scott Turner

HANNAFORD, DAVID
THE SECOND MATE (1950, GB, Associate British Films)—Bobby Tompkins

HANNAH, DARYL
SUMMER LOVERS (1982, Orion)—Cathy Featherest
RECKLESS (1984, MGM/United Artists)—Tracey Prescott
ROXANNE (1987, Columbia)—Roxanne Kowalski
HIGH SPIRITS (1988, Tri-Star)—Mary Plunkett
STEEL MAGNOLIAS (1989, Tri-Star)—Annelle Dupuy Desoto

HANN-BYRD, ADAM
LITTLE MAN TATE (1991, Orion)—Fred Tate

HANNEN, NICHOLAS
WHO KILLED JOHN SAVAGE? (1937, GB, Warners)—John Savage

HANNIGAN, ALYSON
MY STEPMOTHER IS AN ALIEN (1988, Weintraub)—Jessie Mills

HANSEN, JOHN
THE CHRISTINE JORGENSEN STORY (1970, United Artists)—Christine Jorgensen

HANSEN, JUANITA
THE POPPY GIRL'S HUSBAND (1919, Silent, Artcraft)—Polly

HANSON, LARS
CAPTAIN SALVATION (1927, Silent, MGM)—Anson Campbell
THE INFORMER (1929, GB, British International)—Gypo Nolan

HARBIN, SUZETTE
BOMBA AND THE JUNGLE GIRL (1952, Monogram)—The Jungle Girl, Boru

HARDERS, JANE
SHIRLEY THOMPSON VERSUS THE ALIENS (1968, Australia, Kolossal Films)—Shirley Thompson

HARDIE, RUSSELL
THE HARVESTER (1936, Republic)—David Langston

HARDING, ANN
GIRL OF THE GOLDEN WEST (1930, First National)—Minnie
HER PRIVATE AFFAIR (1930, Pathe)—Vera Kessler
WHEN LADIES MEET (1933, MGM)—Claire Woodruff
BIOGRAPHY OF A BACHELOR GIRL (1934, MGM)—Marion
GALLANT LADY (1934, United Artists)—Sally
THE LIFE OF VERGIE WINTERS (1934, RKO)—Vergie Winters
THE LADY CONSENTS (1936, RKO)—Anne Talbot

HARDING, JUNE
THE TROUBLE WITH ANGELS (1966, Columbia)—Rachel Devery

HARDING, LORRAINE
ANNABEL LEE (1921, Silent, Joam Film Sales)—Annabel Lee

HARDING, LYN
THE MAN WHO CHANGED HIS NAME (1934, GB, DuWorld)—
Selby Clive

HARDWICKE, CEDRIC
NELSON (1926, GB, Silent, British Instructional)—Horatio
Nelson
THE DREYFUS CASE (1931, GB, Columbia)—Alfred Dreyfus
THE KING OF PARTS (1934, GB, United Artists)—Max Till
STANLEY AND LIVINGSTON (1939, 20th Century Fox)—Dr.
David Livingston
A CONNECTICUT YANKEE IN KING ARTHUR'S COURT (1949,
Paramount)—King Arthur

HARDY, OLIVER
BABES IN TOYLAND (1934, MGM)—Oliver Dee
OUR RELATIONS (1936, MGM)—Oliver & Bert Hardy
THE FLYING DEUCES (1939, RKO)—Ollie
SAPS AT SEA (1940, United Artists)—Ollie
AIR RAID WARDENS (1943, MGM)—Ollie
THE DANCING MASTERS (1943, 20th Century Fox)—Ollie
JITTERBUGS (1944, 20th Century Fox)—Oliver Hardy

HARDY, SOPHIE
THREE HATS FOR LISA (1965, GB, Warners-Pathe)—
Lisa Milan

HARGREAVES, JOHN
DON'S PARTY (1976, Australia, Double Head Productions)—Don
MY FIRST WIFE (1985, Canada, Spectrafilm)—John

HARKER, GORDON
THE LAD (1935, GB, Twickenham)—Bill Shane
INSPECTOR HORNLEIGH (1939, GB, 20th Century Fox)—
Inspector Hornleigh
INSPECTOR HORNLEIGH ON VACATION (1939, GB, 20th
Century Fox)—Inspector Hornleigh
ONCE A CROOK (1941, GB, 20th Century Fox)—Charlie
Hopkins

HARLAN, KENNETH
I AM THE LAW (1922, Silent, Affiliated Distributors)—Robert
Fitzgerald
THE VIRGINIAN (1923, Silent, Premier)—The Virginian
RANGER OF THE BIG PINES (1925, Silent, Vitagraph)—Ross
Cavanaugh

HARLOW, JEAN
GOLDIE (1931, Fox)—Goldie
PLATINUM BLONDE (1931, Columbia)—Anne Schuyler
RED HEADED WOMAN (1932, MGM)—Lil Andrews
THREE WISE GIRLS (1932, Columbia)—Cassie Barnes
BOMBSHELL (1933, MGM)—Lola
THE GIRL FROM MISSOURI (1934, MGM)—Eadie
RECKLESS (1935, MGM)—Mona Leslie
SUZY (1936, MGM)—Suzy Trent
WIFE VERSUS SECRETARY (1936, MGM)—Helen "Whitey"
Wilson

HARMON, MARK
LET'S GET HARRY (1986, Tri-Star)—Harry Burke, Jr.
WORTH WINNING (1989, 20th Century Fox)—Taylor Worth

HARMON, TOM
HARMON OF MICHIGAN (1941, Columbia)—Tom Harmon

HARRIGAN, WILLIAM
HIS FAMILY TREE (1936, RKO)—Charles Murfree

HARRINGTON, LAURA
THE CITY GIRL (1984, Moon)—Anne

HARRIS, ED
WALKER (1987, Universal)—William Walker

HARRIS, JULIE
THE MEMBER OF THE WEDDING (1952, Columbia)—Frankie
Addams
THE POACHER'S DAUGHTER (1960, GB, Show Corp. of
America)—Sally Hamil

HARRIS, KAY
TILLIE THE TOILER (1941, Columbia)—Tillie the Toiler

HARRIS, MILDRED
THE SHOW GIRL (1927, Silent, Rayart)—Maizie Udell

HARRIS, RICHARD
CROMWELL (1970, GB, Columbia)—Oliver Cromwell
A MAN CALLED HORSE (1970, National General)—Lord John
Morgan
THE MAN IN THE WILDERNESS (1971, Warners)—
Zachary Bass
DEADLY TRACKERS (1973, Warners)—Kilpatrick
A RETURN OF A MAN CALLED HORSE (1976, United Artists)—
John Morgan
GULLIVER'S TRAVELS (1977, GB, Sunn Classics)—Lemuel
Gulliver
TRIUMPHS OF A MAN CALLED HORSE (1983, Redwing-
Transpacific)—John Morgan/"Man Called Horse"
MARTIN'S DAY (1985, MGM/United Artists)—Martin Steckert

HARRISON, ANDREW
THE LITTLEST HORSE THIEVES (1977, Buena Vista)—Dave
Sadler

HARRISON, GREGORY
JIM, THE WORLD'S GREATEST ATHLETE (1976, Universal)—
Jim Nolan

HARRISON, JIMMY
CHARLEY'S AUNT (1925, Silent, Cristie Film Co.)—Charley
Wykeham

HARRISON, KATHLEEN
HERE COMES THE HUGGETTS (1948, GB, Gainsborough)—
Ethel Huggett
MRS. GIBBONS' BOYS (1962, GB, British Lion)—Mrs. Gibbons

HARRISON, REX
THE GHOST AND MRS. MUIR (1942, 20th Century Fox)—The
Ghost of Capt. Daniel Gregg
A NOTORIOUS GENTLEMAN (1945, GB, Rank)—Vivian Kenway
THE FOXES OF HARROW (1947, 20th Century Fox)—
Stephen Fox
UNFAITHFULLY YOURS (1948, 20th Century Fox)—Sir Alfred
de Carter
THE CONSTANT HUSBAND (1955, GB, British Lion)—Charles
Hathaway
MY FAIR LADY (1964, Warners)—Prof. Henry Higgins
DOCTOR DOOLITTLE (1967, 20th Century Fox)—Dr. John
Doolittle

HARRY, DEBORAH
FOREVER, LULU (1987, Tri-Star)—Lulu

HART, DOLORES
LISA (1962, GB, 20th Century Fox)—Lisa Held

HART, MARIA
CATTLE QUEEN (1951, United Artists)—Queenie Hart

HART, NEAL
THE MAN FROM MONTANA (1917, Silent, Universal)—Duke
Farley
THE HEART OF A TEXAN (1922, Silent, Steiner)—King Calhoun

HART, SUSAN
GHOST IN THE INVISIBLE BIKINI (1966, American
International)—Ghost

HART, TEDDY
THREE MEN ON A HORSE (1936, Warners)—Frankie

HART, WILLIAM S.
THE CAPTIVE GOD (1916, Silent, Triangle)—Chiapa
THE PATRIOT (1916, Silent, Triangle)—Bob Wiley
TRUTHFUL TULLIVER (1917, Silent, Triangle)—"Truthful"
Tulliver
JOHN PETTICOATS (1919, Silent, Artcraft)—"Hardwood" John
Haynes
THE POPPY GIRL'S HUSBAND (1919, Silent, Artcraft)—Hairpin
Harry Dutton
O'MALLEY OF THE MOUNTED (1921, Silent, Paramount)—
O'Malley
SINGER JIM MCKEE (1924, Silent, Paramount)—"Singer"
Jim McKee

HARTCOURT, JAMES
HOBSON'S CHOICE (1931, GB, British International)—Hobson

HARTLEY, MARIETTE
O'HARA'S WIFE (1983, Davis-Panzer)—Harry O'Hara

HARTMAN, ELIZABETH
THE GROUP (1966, United Artists)—Priss Hartshorn

HARTNELL, WILLIAM
I'M AN EXPLOSIVE (1933, GB, Fox)—Edward Whimperly
CARRY ON SERGEANT (1959, GB, Anglo-Amalgamated)—Sgt.
Grimshaw
THE DESPERATE MAN (1959, GB, Allied Artists)—Smith

HARVEY, CLEM
OCEAN'S ELEVEN (1960, Warners)—Louis Jackson

HARVEY, LAURENCE
A KILLER WALKS (1952, GB, Grand National)—Ned
ROMEO AND JULIET (1954, GB, United Artists)—Romeo
I AM A CAMERA (1955, GB, Romulus-Remus)—Christopher
Isherwood
THREE MEN IN A BOAT (1958, GB, Romulus/Valiant)—George
THE WONDERFUL WORLD OF THE BROTHERS GRIMM (1962,
MGM)—Wilhelm Grimm
THE RUNNING MAN (1963, GB, Columbia)—Rex Black
A DANDY IN ASPIC (1968, GB, Columbia)—Alexander Eberlin

HARVEY, LEN
EXCUSE MY GLOVE (1936, GB, ABF)—Don Carter

HARVEY, LILLIAN
MY WEAKNESS (1933, Fox)—Looloo Blake

HARVEY, MICHAEL MARTIN
THE CASE OF CHARLES PEACE (1949, GB, Argyle/Monarch)—
Charles Peace

HASSE, O.E.
I CONFESS (1953, Warners)—Otto Keller

HASSO, SIGNE
DANGEROUS PARTNERS (1945, MGM)—Carola Ballister
STRANGE TRIANGLE (1946, 20th Century Fox)—
Francine Huber

HATCHER, MARY
VARIETY GIRL (1947, Paramount)—Catherine Brown

HATFIELD, HURD
THE PICTURE OF DORIAN GRAY (1945, MGM)—Dorian Gray

HATTON, RAYMOND
HIS BACK AGAINST THE WALL (1922, Silent, Goldwyn)—
Jeremy Dice
PARTNER'S IN CRIME (1928, Silent, Paramount)—"Scoop"
McGee, the Reporter
HELL'S HEROES (1930, Universal)—Barbwire Gibbons

HAUER, RUTGER
THE HITCHER (1986, Tri-Star)—John Ryder

HAUSER, WINGS
DEAD MAN WALKING (1988, Metropolis-Hit)—John Luger
THE CARPENTER (1989, Canada, Cinepix)—Ed

HAVER, JUNE
THE DOLLY SISTERS (1945, 20th Century Fox)—Rosie Dolly
THREE GIRLS IN BLUE (1946, 20th Century Fox)—Pam
OH, YOU BEAUTIFUL DOLL (1949, 20th Century Fox)—Doris
Breitenbach
THE DAUGHTER OF ROSIE O'GRADY (1950, Warners)—Patricia
O'Grady
THE GIRL NEXT DOOR (1953, 20th Century Fox)—Jeannie

HAVER, PHYLLIS
SAL OF SINGAPORE (1929, Pathe)—Sal
THE SHADY LADY (1929, Pathe)—Lola Mantell

HAVOC, JUNE
THE STORY OF MOLLY X (1949, Universal)—Molly X
LADY POSSESSED (1952, Republic)—Jean Wilson

HAWAKAWA, SESSUE
THE COURAGEOUS COWARD (1919, Silent, Haworth)—
Suki Iota
AN ARABIAN KNIGHT (1920, Silent, Haworth)—Ahmed

HAWKE, ETHAN
EXPLORERS (1985, Paramount)—Ben Crandall

HAWKES, CHESNEY
BUDDY'S SONG (1991, GB, Castle Premier)—Buddy

HAWKINS, JACK
GIDEON OF SCOTLAND YARD (1959, GB, Columbia)—Insp.
George Gideon
THE TWO-HEADED SPY (1959, GB, Columbia)—General Alex
Schottland

HAWLEY, WANDA
MISS HOBBS (1920, Silent, Realart)—Miss Hobbs
HER FACE VALUE (1921, Silent, Paramount)—Peggy Malone
THE OUTSIDE WOMAN (1921, Silent, Realart)—Dorothy Ralston

HAWN, GOLDIE
THERE'S A GIRL IN MY SOUP (1970, GB, Columbia)—Marion
THE GIRL FROM PETROVKA (1974, Universal)—Oktyabrina
THE DUCHESS AND THE DIRTWATER FOX (1976, 20th Century Fox)—Amanda Quaid
PRIVATE BENJAMIN (1980, Warners)—Judy Benjamin
BEST FRIENDS (1982, Warners)—Paula McCullen
OVERBOARD (1987, MGM/United Artists)—Joanna Stayton ("Annie Proffitt")
DECEIVED (1991, Buena Vista/Touchstone)—Adrienne
HOUSESITTER (1992, Universal)—Gwen

HAWTHORNE, DAVID
ROB ROY (1922, GB, Silent, Gaumont)—Rob Roy MacGregor
THE MATING OF MARCUS (1924, Silent, Stoll)—Marcus Netherby
THE PRESUMPTION OF STANLEY HAY, MP (1925, GB, Silent, Stoll)—Stanley Hay

HAWTHORNE, JOAN
THE BATTLEAXE (1962, GB, Danzinger)—Mrs. Page

HAWTREY, CHARLES
JAILBIRDS (1939, GB, Butchers)—Nick

HAY, ALEXANDRA
1,000 CONVICTS AND A WOMAN (1971, GB, American International)—Angela Thorne

HAY, NED
HIS WIFE'S MONEY (1920, Silent, Select)—Edward Uppington

HAY, WILL
DANDY DICK (1935, GB, British International)—Rev. Richard Jedd
OH, MR. PORTER (1937, GB, GFD)—William Porter
WINDBAG THE SAILOR (1937, GB, Gaumont)—Capt. Ben Cutlet
OLD BONES OF THE RIVER (1938, GB, GFD)—Prof. Benjamin Tibbetts
THE GOOSE STEPS OUT (1942, Ealing)—William Potts
MY LEARNED FRIEND (1943, GB, Ealing)—William Fitch

HAYDEN, RUSSELL
TWO IN A TAXI (1941, Columbia)—Jimmy Owens

HAYDEN, STERLING
JOHNNY GUITAR (1954, Republic)—Johnny Guitar
TOP GUN (1955, United Artists)—Rick Martin
THE IRON SHERIFF (1957, United Artists)—Sheriff Galt
KING OF THE GYPSIES (1978, Paramount)—King Zharko Stepanowicz

HAYDN, RICHARD
CHARLEY'S AUNT (1941, 20th Century Fox)—Charlie Wyckham
THE EMPEROR WALTZ (1948, Paramount)—Emperor Franz Josef

HAYE, HELEN
THE CASE OF THE FRIGHTENED LADY (1940, GB, British Lion)—Dowager Lady Lebanon

HAYES, ALLISON
ATTACK OF THE 50 FOOT WOMAN (1958, Allied Artists)—Nancy Archer

HAYES, HELEN
THE SIN OF MADELON CLAUDET (1931, MGM)—Madelon Claudet
THE SON-DAUGHTER (1932, MGM)—Lien Wha
THE WHITE SISTER (1933, MGM)—Angela Chiaromonte
WHAT EVERY WOMAN KNOWS (1934, MGM)—Maggie Wylie
VANESSA, HER LOVE STORY (1935, MGM)—Vanessa
MY SON JOHN (1952, Paramount)—Lucille Jefferson

HAYES, ISSAC
TRUCK TURNER (1974, American International)—Truck Turner

HAYES, JERRI
EMMA MAE (1976, Pro-International)—Emma Mae

HAYES, MAGGIE
GIRL IN THE WOODS (1958, Republic)—Belle Cory

HAYMES, BOB
SAILORS' HOLIDAY (1944, Columbia)—Bill Hayes

HAYMES, DICK
ST. BENNY THE DIP (1951, United Artists)—Benny

HAYTER, JAMES
THE PICKWICK PAPERS (1952, GB, Renown)—Samuel Pickwick

HAYWARD, CHARD
BROTHERS (1984, Australia, Areflex)—Adam Wild

HAYWARD, LOUIS
THE DUKE OF WEST POINT (1938, United Artists)—Steven Early
THE SAINT IN NEW YORK (1938, RKO)—Simon Templar
THE MAN IN THE IRON MASK (1939, United Artists)—Louis XIV/Philippe
MY SON! MY SON! (1940, United Artists)—Oliver Essex
SON OF MONTE CRISTO (1940, United Artists)—Count of Monte Cristo
THE RETURN OF MONTE CRISTO (1946, Columbia)—Edmund Dantes
THE PIRATES OF CAPRI (1949, Film Classics)—Capt. Sirocco
FORTUNES OF CAPTAIN BLOOD (1950, Columbia)—Capt. Peter Blood
THE LADY AND THE BANDIT (1951, Columbia)—Dick Turpin
THE SON OF DR. JEKYLL (1951, Columbia)—Edward Jekyll
CAPTAIN PIRATE (1952, Columbia)—Peter Blood
THE SAINT'S GIRL FRIDAY (1954, GB, RKO)—Simon Templar

HAYWARD, RICHARD
IRISH AND PROUD OF IT (1938, Ireland, Crusade)—Donogh O'Connor

HAYWARD, SUSAN
SMASH UP, THE STORY OF A WOMAN (1947, Universal)—Angie Evans
MY FOOLISH HEART (1949, RKO)—Eloise Winters
DAVID AND BATHSHEBA (1951, 20th Century Fox)—Bathsheba
WITH A SONG IN MY HEART (1952, 20th Century Fox)—Jane Froman
THE PRESIDENT'S LADY (1953, 20th Century Fox)—Rachel Donaldson Robards Jackson

WHITE WITCH DOCTOR (1953, 20th Century Fox)—Ellen
Burton
I'LL CRY TOMORROW (1955, MGM)—Lillian Roth
UNTAMED (1955, 20th Century Fox)—Katie O'Neill
TOP SECRET AFFAIR (1957, Warners)—Dottie Peale
I WANT TO LIVE! (1958, United Artists)—Barbara Graham
WOMAN OBSESSED (1959, 20th Century Fox)—Mary Sharron
ADA (1961, MGM)—Ada Gillis

HAYWORTH, RITA
WHO KILLED GAIL PRESTON? (1938, Columbia)—Gail Preston
THE LADY IN QUESTION (1940, Columbia)—Natalie Roguin
THE STRAWBERRY BLONDE (1941, Warners)—Virginia Brush
MY GAL SAL (1942, 20th Century Fox)—Sally Elliott
YOU WERE NEVER LOVELIER (1942, Columbia)—Maria Acuna
COVER GIRL (1944, Columbia)—Rusty Parker/Maribelle Hicks
GILDA (1946, Columbia)—Gilda Mundson
THE LADY FROM SHANGHAI (1948, Columbia)—Elsa Bannister
THE LOVES OF CARMEN (1948, Columbia)—Carmen Garcia
MISS SADIE THOMPSON (1953, Columbia)—Sadie Thompson
SALOME (1953, Columbia)—Salome
THEY CAME TO CORDURA (1959, Columbia)—Adelaide Geary

HAZELL, HY
CELIA (1949, GB, Exclusive)—Celia
THE LADY CRAVED EXCITEMENT (1950, GB, Hammer)—Pat

HEAD, MURRAY
GAWAIN AND THE GREEN KNIGHT (1973, GB, United Artists)—
Gawain

HEALEY, JAMES
STRANGERS (1990, Australia, Genesis)—Gary

HEARD, JOHN
CUTTER AND BONE (1981, United Artists)—Alex Cutter

HEARN, EDWARD
ONE OF THE BRAVEST (1925, Silent, Gotham/Lumis)—
Dan Kelly

HEARNE, RICHARD
THE TIME OF HIS LIFE (1955, GB, Renown)—Charles Pastry

HEATHERTON, JOEY
THE HAPPY HOOKER GOES TO WASHINGTON (1977, Cannon)—
Xaviera Hollander

HEDISON, AL
SON OF ROBIN HOOD (1959, GB, 20th Century Fox)—Jamie

HEDREN, TIPPI
MARNIE (1964, Universal)—Marnie Edgar

HEFFNER, KYLE T.
MUTANT ON THE BOUNTY (1989, Skouras)—Max

HEFLIN, MARTA
A PERFECT COUPLE (1979, 20th Century Fox)—Shella Shea

HEFLIN, VAN
SATURDAY'S HEROES (1937, RKO)—Val
TENNESSEE JOHNSON (1942, MGM)—Andrew Johnson
THE THREE MUSKETEERS (1948, MGM)—Athos
WEEKEND WITH FATHER (1951, Universal)—Brad Stubbs
GUNMAN'S WALK (1958, Columbia)—Lee Hackett

THE MAN ON THE OUTSIDE (1968, GB, Allied Artists)—Bill
MacLean

HELM, FAY
PHANTOM LADY (1944, Universal)—Ann Terry

HELMOND, KATHERINE
LADY IN WHITE (1988, New Century/Vista)—Amanda

HEMINGWAY, MARIEL
PERSONAL BEST (1982, Warners)—Chris Cahill
STAR 80 (1983, Warners)—Dorothy Stratton

HEMMINGS, DAVID
ALFRED THE GREAT (1969, GB, MGM)—Alfred the Great

HEMPEL, ANOUSKA
SWEET SUZY (1973, Signal)—Lady Susan
TIFFANY JONES (1976, Cineworld)—Tiffany Jones

HENDERSON, MARCIA
DEADLY DUO (1962, United Artists)—Sabena/Dara

HENDRICKS, BEN JR.
THE HEADLESS HORSEMAN (1922, Silent, Hodkinson Corp.)—
The Headless Horseman

HENDRIX, WANDA
MISS TATLOCK'S MILLIONS (1948, Paramount)—Nan Tatlock
THE ADMIRAL WAS A LADY (1950, United Artists)—Jean
Madison

HENIE, SONJA
ONE IN A MILLION (1936, 20th Century Fox)—Greta Muller
THE COUNTESS OF MONTE CRISTO (1948, 20th Century
Fox)—Karen

HENREID, PAUL
LAST OF THE BUCCANEERS (1950, Columbia)—Jean Laffite
THIEF OF DAMASCUS (1952, Columbia)—Abu Andar
PIRATES OF TRIPOLI (1955, Columbia)—Edri-Al-Gadrin

HENRY, CHARLOTTE
LENA RIVERS (1932, Tiffany)—Lena Rivers
ALICE IN WONDERLAND (1933, Paramount)—Alice

HENRY, LENNY
TRUE IDENTITY (1991, Buena Vista/Touchstone)—Miles Pope

HENRY, LEONARD
THE PUBLIC LIFE OF HENRY THE NINTH (1934, GB,
MGM)—Henry

HENRY, MIKE
TARZAN AND THE VALLEY OF GOLD (1966, American
International)—Tarzan
TARZAN AND THE GREAT RIVER (1967, Paramount)—Tarzan
TARZAN AND THE JUNGLE BOY (1968, Paramount)—Tarzan

HENRY, WILLIAM
FOUR MEN AND A PRAYER (1938, 20th Century Fox)—
Rodney Leigh
FEDERAL MAN (1950, Eagle Lion)—Sherrin

HENSON, ELIZABETH
THE GIRL WHO COULDN'T QUITE (1949, GB, Monarch)—Ruth

HENSON, LESLIE
OH DADDY! (1935, GB, Gaumont)—Lord Pye

HENSON, NICKY
THE BAWDY ADVENTURES OF TOM JONES (1976, GB, Universal)—Tom Jones

HEPBURN, AUDREY
SABRINA (1954, Paramount)—Sabrina Fairchild
FUNNY FACE (1957, Paramount)—Jo Stockton
THE NUN'S STORY (1959, Warners)—Sister Luke (Gabrielle Van Der Mal)
THE UNFORGIVEN (1960, United Artists)—Rachel Zachary
MY FAIR LADY (1964, Warners)—Eliza Doolittle
TWO FOR THE ROAD (1967, GB, 20th Century Fox)—Joanna Wallace
ROBIN AND MARIAN (1976, GB, Columbia)—Maid Marian

HEPBURN, DEE
GREGORY'S GIRL (1982, GB, Goldwyn)—Dorothy

HEPBURN, KATHARINE
LITTLE WOMEN (1933, RKO)—Jo March
SPITFIRE (1934, RKO)—Trigger Hicks
ALICE ADAMS (1935, RKO)—Alice Adams
MARY OF SCOTLAND (1936, RKO)—Mary Stuart
SYLVIA SCARLETT (1936, RKO)—Sylvia Scarlett
A WOMAN REBELS (1936, RKO)—Pamela Thistlewaite
KEEPER OF THE FLAME (1942, MGM)—Christine Forrest
WOMAN OF THE YEAR (1942, MGM)—Tess Harding
ADAM'S RIB (1949, MGM)—Amanda Bonner
PAT AND MIKE (1952, MGM)—Pat Pemberton
THE MADWOMAN OF CHAILLOT (1969, Warners)—Countess Aurelia
THE TROJAN WOMEN (1971, Cinerama)—Hecuba
THE ULTIMATE SOLUTION OF GRACE QUIGLEY (1984, MGM/United Artists)—Grace Quigley

HEPWORTH, RONNIE
DANNY BOY (1934, GB, Panther)—Danny

HERBERT, CHARLES
THE BOY AND THE PIRATES (1960, United Artists)—Jimmy Warren

HERBERT, HOLMES
HER LORD AND MASTER (1921, Silent, Vitagraph)—Viscount Canning
JOSSELYN'S WIFE (1926, Silent, Tiffany)—Thomas Josselyn
GENTLEMEN PREFER BLONDES (1928, Silent, Paramount)—Henry Spofford
THE TERROR (1928, Warners)—Goodman
THE CHARLATAN (1929, Universal)—Count Merlin/Peter Dwight

HERBERT, HUGH
THAT MAN'S HERE AGAIN (1937, Warners)—Thomas J. Jesse
MEET THE CHUMP (1941, Universal)—Hugh Mansfield

HERLIE, EILEEN
SHE DIDN'T SAY NO (1957, 20th Century Fox)—Bridget Monahan

HERMAN, PEE WEE (PAUL REUBENS)
PEE WEE'S BIG ADVENTURE (1985, Paramount)—Pee Wee Herman
BIG TOP PEE WEE (1988, Paramount)—Pee Wee Herman

HERNANDEZ, JUANO
INTRUDER IN THE DUST (1949, MGM)—Lucas Beauchamp

HERRMANN, EDWARD
HARRY'S WAR (1981, Taft International)—Harry

HERSHEY, BARBARA (SEAGULL)
THE BABY MAKER (1970, National General)—Tish Gray
BOXCAR BERTHA (1972, American International)—Bertha
HANNAH AND HER SISTERS (1986, Orion)—Lee
HOOSIERS (1986, Orion)—Myrna Fleener
SHY PEOPLE (1988, Cannon)—Ruth Sullivan

HERSHOLT, JEAN
THE OLD SOAK (1926, Silent, Universal)—Clement Hawley, Sr.
ALIAS THE DEACON (1928, Silent, Universal)—The Deacon
THE COUNTRY DOCTOR (1936, 20th Century Fox)—Dr. John Luke
MEET DR. CHRISTIAN (1939, RKO)—Dr. Paul Christian
THE COURAGEOUS DR. CHRISTIAN (1940, RKO)—Dr. Paul Christian
DR. CHRISTIAN MEETS THE WOMEN (1940, RKO)—Dr. Paul Christian

HERVEY, IRENE
THE GIRL SAID NO (1937, Grand National)—Pearl
LADY FIGHTS BACK (1937, Universal)—Heather McHale
FRISCO LIL (1942, Universal)—Lillian Grayson

HERVEY, LILLIAN
I AM SUZANNE (1934, Fox)—Suzanne

HESTON, CHARLTON
THE PRESIDENT'S LADY (1953, 20th Century Fox)—Andrew Jackson
THE SAVAGE (1953, Paramount)—Warbonnet/Jim Ahern
THE PRIVATE WAR OF MAJOR BENSON (1955, Universal)—Major Bernard Benson
THREE VIOLENT PEOPLE (1956, Paramount)—Colt Saunders
BEN-HUR (1959, Silent, MGM)—Judah Ben-Hur
EL CID (1961, Allied Artists)—Rodrigo Diaz de Bivar (El Cid)
MAJOR DUNDEE (1965, Columbia)—Major Amos Charles Dundee
PEER GYNT (1965, Willow/Brandon)—Peer Gynt
THE WAR LORD (1965, Universal)—Chrysagon
WILL PENNY (1968, Paramount)—Will Penny
NUMBER ONE (1969, United Artists)—Ron "Cat" Catlan
THE OMEGA MAN (1971, Warners)—Robert Nelville
ANTONY AND CLEOPATRA (1973, GB, Rank)—Antony
THE LAST HARD MEN (1976, 20th Century Fox)—Sam Burgade
THE MOUNTAIN MEN (1980, Columbia)—Bill Tyler

HEYWOOD, ANNE
THE DEPRAVED (1957, GB, United Artists)—Laura Wilton
I WANT WHAT I WANT (1972, GB, Cinerama)—Roy/Wendy
GOOD LUCK, MISS WYCKOFF (1979, Bel Air-Gradison)—Evelyn Wyckoff

HICKEY, WILLIAM
PRIZZI'S HONOR (1985, 20th Century Fox)—Don Corrado Prizzi

HICKS, RUSSELL
MR. WHAT'S HIS NAME (1935, GB, First National)—Alfred Henfield/Mons. Herbert Herbert
THE THREE MUSKETEERS (1939, 20th Century Fox)—Porthos

HICKS, (SIR) SEYMOUR
SCROOGE (1935, GB, Paramount)—Ebenezer Scrooge

HIERS, WALTER
MR. BILLINGS SPENDS HIS DIME (1923, Silent, Paramount)—
John Percival Billings

HIGBY, WILBUR
MY DAD (1922, Silent, R-C/Film Booking Office)—Barry O'Day

HIGGINS, ANTHONY
THE DRAUGHTMAN'S CONTRACT (1983, GB, United Artists)—
Mr. Nelville

HIGGINS, DAVID
HIS LAST DOLLAR (1914, Silent, Paramount)—Joe Braxton

HILL, HALLENE
THE SEARCH FOR BRIDEY MURPHY (1956, Paramount)—
Bridey Murphy at 66

HILL, LORNA
MY DARK LADY (1987, Film Gallery)—Lorna Dahomey

HILL, RICHARD
DEATHSTALKER (1984, New World)—Deathstalker

HILL, TERENCE
MR. BILLION (1977, 20th Century Fox)—Guido Falcone
SUPER FUZZ (1981, Avco Embassy)—Dave Speed

HILLARD, HARRY
ROMEO AND JULIET (1916, Silent, Fox)—Romeo

HILLER, WENDY
MAJOR BARBARA (1941, GB, Rank)—Major Barbara Undershaft
I KNOW WHERE I'M GOING (1947, GB, Archers)—Joan Webster
SONS AND LOVERS (1960, GB, 20th Century Fox)—Mrs. Morel

HILLIARD, HARRIET
HI, GOOD-LOOKIN' (1944, Universal)—Kelly Clark

HILLIE, VERNA
REBELLIOUS DAUGHTERS (1938, Times)—Babe

HILSOP, JOSEPH
THE LOVES OF ROBERT BURNS (1930, GB, British &
Dominions)—Robert Burns

HINDS, SAMUEL S.
THE SPOILERS (1942, Universal)—Judge Stillman

HINDWOOD, PETER
THE ROCKY HORROR PICTURE SHOW (1975, GB, 20th Century
Fox)—Rocky

HINDY, JOSEPH
LOVERS AND OTHER STRANGERS (1970, ABC/Cinerama)—
Richie Vecchio

HINES, JOHNNY
THE CUB (1915, Silent, World)—Steve Oldham
BURN 'EM UP BARNES (1921, Silent, Mastadon Films)—Burn
'Em Up Barnes
SURE FIRE FLINT (1922, Silent, Mastadon)—Sure Fire Flint
CONDUCTOR 1492 (1924, Silent, Warners)—Terry O'Toole
THE CRACKERJACK (1925, Silent, East Coast Films)—Tommy
Perkins

76

WHITE PANTS WILLIE (1927, Silent, First National)—Willie
Bascom
CHINATOWN CHARLIE (1928, Silent, First National)—Charlie

HINKLEY, TOMMY
THE HUMAN SHIELD (1992, Cannon)—Ben Matthews

HIRSCH, ELROY
CRAZYLEGS, ALL AMERICAN (1953, Republic)—Crazylegs
Hirsch
UNCHAINED (1955, Warners)—Steve Davitt

HIRSCH, JUDD
THE GOODBYE PEOPLE (1984, Embassy)—Arthur Korman

HOBART, ROSE
A LADY SURRENDERS (1930, Universal)—Isabel Beauvel
CONVENTION GIRL (1935, Flacon/FD)—Babe Lavall
PRISON GIRL (1942, Producers Releasing Corp.)—
Rosemary Walsh

HOBBS, HAYFORD
THE MANCHESTER MAN (1920, GB, Silent, Ideal)—Jabez Clegg

HOBSON, VALERIE
THE BRIDE OF FRANKENSTEIN (1935, Universal)—Elizabeth
Frankenstein
BLANCHE FURY (1948, GB, Universal)—Blanche Fury

HODDER, KANE
FRIDAY THE 13TH PART VIII—JASON TAKES MANHATTAN
(1989, Paramount)—Jason

HODGES, EDDIE
THE ADVENTURES OF HUCKLEBERRY FINN (1960, MGM)—
Huckleberry Finn

HODGES, JOY
PERSONAL SECRETARY (1938, Universal)—Gale Rogers

HODIAK, JOHN
SUNDAY DINNER FOR A SOLDIER (1944, 20th Century Fox)—
Eric Moore
TWO SMART PEOPLE (1946, MGM)—Ace Connors
THE ARNELO AFFAIR (1947, MGM)—Tony Arnelo
LOVE FROM A STRANGER (1947, Eagle Lion)—Manuel Cortez
CONQUEST OF COCHISE (1953, Columbia)—Cochise

HOEY, DENNIS
UNCIVILIZED (1937, Australia, Box Office Attractions)—Mara

HOEY, IRIS
HER REPUTATION (1931, GB, London Screenplays)—Sultitia
Sloane

HOFFMAN, BRIGIT
TIME TRACKERS (1989, Concorde)—Madeline

HOFFMAN, DUSTIN
THE GRADUATE (1967, Embassy Pictures)—Ben Braddock
JOHN AND MARY (1969, 20th Century Fox)—John
LITTLE BIG MAN (1970, National General)—Jack Crabb
LENNY (1974, United Artists)—Lenny Bruce
MARATHON MAN (1976, Paramount)—Babe Levy
KRAMER VS. KRAMER (1979, Columbia)—Ted Kramer
TOOTSIE (1982, Columbia)—Michael Dorsey-Dorothy Michaels
RAIN MAN (1988, United Artists)—Raymond Babbitt

FAMILY BUSINESS (1989, Tri-Star)—Vito McMullen
HOOK (1991, Tri-Star)—Captain Hook

HOGAN, BOSCO
A PORTRAIT OF THE ARTIST AS A YOUNG MAN (1979, Ireland, Mahler)—Stephen Dedalus

HOGAN, DICK
THREE SONS (1939, RKO)—Freddie Pardway

HOGAN, JACK
THE CAT BURGLAR (1961, United Artists)—Jack Coley

HOGAN, PAUL
"CROCODILE" DUNDEE (1986, Australia, Paramount)—Mick "Crocodile" Dundee
"CROCODILE" DUNDEE II (1988, Australia, Paramount)—Mick "Crocodile" Dundee
ALMOST AN ANGEL (1990, Paramount)—Terry Dean

HOLBROOK, HAL
THE KIDNAPPING OF THE PRESIDENT (1980, Canada, Crown International)—President Adam Scott

HOLDEN, FAY
OUT WEST WITH THE HARDY'S (1938, MGM)—Mrs. Hardy
LITTLE MISS BIG (1946, Universal)—Mary Jane Baxter

HOLDEN, GLORIA
DRACULA'S DAUGHTER (1936, Universal)—Countess Maria Zalenska

HOLDEN, WILLIAM
GOLDEN BOY (1939, Columbia)—Joe Bonaparte
MEET THE STEWARTS (1942, Columbia)—Michael Stewart
THE REMARKABLE ANDREW (1942, Paramount)—Andrew Long
FATHER IS A BACHELOR (1950, Columbia)—Johnny Rutledge
SUBMARINE COMMAND (1951, Paramount)—Cmdr. White
BOOTS MALONE (1952, Columbia)—Boots Malone
THE COUNTERFEIT TRAITOR (1962, Paramount)—Eric Erickson
ALVAREZ KELLY (1966, Columbia)—Alvarez Kelly
THE WILD BUNCH (1969, Warners)—Pike Bishop
WILD ROVERS (1971, MGM)—Frank Bodine
THE EARTHLING (1980, Filmways-Roadshow)—Patrick Foley

HOLLIDAY, JUDY
BORN YESTERDAY (1951, Columbia)—Billie Dawn
THE MARRYING KIND (1952, Columbia)—Florence Keefer
FULL OF LIFE (1956, Columbia)—Emily Rocco

HOLLOWAY, STANLEY
THE VICAR OF BRAY (1937, GB, Associate British Films)—The Vicar of Bray
THE LAVENDER HILL MOB (1951, GB, Ealing)—Pendlebury
MR. LORD SAYS NO (1952, GB, London Independent)—Henry Lord
MEET MR. LUCIFER (1953, GB, Ealing)—Sam Hollingsworth/Mr. Lucifer

HOLMES, HELEN
JUDITH OF THE CUMBERLANDS (1916, Silent, Signal)—Judith

HOLMES, MICHELLE
RITA, SUE AND BOB TOO! (1987, GB, Orion Classics)—Sue

HOLMES, PHILLIPS
THE DANCERS (1930, Fox)—Tony
MAN TO MAN (1931, Warners)—Michael Bolton
MEN MUST FIGHT (1933, MGM)—Bob Seward

HOLMES, STUART
HER HUSBAND'S TRADEMARK (1922, Silent, Paramount)—James Berkeley

HOLT, JACK
MAKING A MAN (1922, Silent, Paramount)—Horace Winsby
A GENTLEMAN OF LEISURE (1923, Silent, Paramount)—Robert Pitt
FATHER AND SON (1929, Columbia)—Frank Fields
MAKER OF MEN (1931, Columbia)—Dudley
MAN AGAINST WOMAN (1932, Columbia)—Johnny McCloud
MASTER OF MEN (1933, Columbia)—Buck Garrett
WHEN STRANGERS MARRY (1933, Columbia)—Steve Rand
THE WOMAN I STOLE (1933, Columbia)—Jim Bradler
THE WRECKER (1933, Columbia)—Chuck Regan
I'LL FIX IT (1934, Columbia)—Bill Grimes
AWAKENING OF JIM BURKE (1935, Columbia)—Jim Burke
CRASH DONOVAN (1936, Universal)—Crash Donovan
THE STRANGE CASE OF DR. MEADE (1939, Columbia)—Dr. Meade

HOLT, TIM
LADDIE (1940, RKO)—Laddie
THE FARGO KID (1941, RKO)—Fargo Kid
THE MAGNIFICENT AMBERSONS (1942, RKO)—George Amberson Minafer
THE ARIZONA RANGER (1948, RKO)—Bob Wade
INDIAN AGENT (1948, RKO)—Dave

HOLT, ULA
TARZAN AND THE GREEN GODDESS (1938, Principal)—Ula Vale

HOMEIER, SKIP
ARTHUR TAKES OVER (1948, 20th Century Fox)—Arthur Bixby
STRANGER AT MY DOOR (1956, Republic)—Clay Anderson

HOOKS, KEVIN
AARON LOVES ANGELA (1975, Columbia)—Aaron

HOOKS, ROBERT
TROUBLE MAN (1972, 20th Century Fox)—Mr. "T"

HOPE, BOB
THE GHOST BREAKERS (1940, Paramount)—Larry Lawrence
CAUGHT IN THE DRAFT (1941, Paramount)—Don Gilbert
MY FAVORITE BLONDE (1942, Paramount)—Larry Haines
THEY GOT ME COVERED (1943, RKO)—Robert Kittredge
THE PRINCESS AND THE PIRATE (1944, RKO)—"Sylvester the Great" Crosby
MONSIEUR BEAUCAIRE (1946, Paramount)—Mons. Beaucaire
MY FAVORITE BRUNETTE (1947, Paramount)—Ronnie Jackson
THE PALEFACE (1948, Paramount)—"Painless" Peter Potter
THE GREAT LOVER (1949, Paramount)—Freddie Hunter
SORROWFUL JONES (1949, Paramount)—Sorrowful Jones
FANCY PANTS (1950, Paramount)—Humphrey
THE LEMON DROP KID (1951, Paramount)—Lemon Drop Kid
MY FAVORITE SPY (1951, RKO)—Peanuts White
SON OF PALEFACE (1952, Paramount)—Junior Potter
CASANOVA'S BIG NIGHT (1954, Paramount)—Pippo Popolino

BEAU JAMES (1957, Paramount)—Jimmy Walker
ALIAS JESSE JAMES (1959, United Artists)—Milford Farnsworth
BACHELOR IN PARADISE (1961, MGM)—Adam J. Niles
CALL ME BWANA (1963, GB, Rank/United Artists)—Matt Merriwether
CRITIC'S CHOICE (1963, Warners)—Parker Ballantine
I'LL TAKE SWEDEN (1965, Columbia)—Bob Holcomb
THE PRIVATE NAVY OF SGT. O'FARRELL (1968, United Artists)—Master Sgt. Dan O'Farrell

HOPKINS, HAROLD
FANTASY MAN (1984, Australia, Centaur)—Nick Bailey

HOPKINS, MIRIAM
THE STORY OF TEMPLE DRAKE (1933, Paramount)—Temple Drake
THE RICHEST GIRL IN THE WORLD (1934, RKO)—Dorothy Hunter
BECKY SHARP (1935, Pioneer/RKO)—Becky Sharp
THESE THREE (1936, United Artists)—Martha Dobie
WISE GIRL (1937, RKO)—Susan Fletcher
WOMAN CHASES MAN (1937, United Artists)—Virginia Travis
THE WOMAN I LOVE (1937, RKO)—Mme. Helene Maury
LADY WITH RED HAIR (1940, Warners)—Mrs. Leslie Carter
OLD ACQUAINTANCE (1943, Warners)—Millie Drake

HOPKINS, RHONDA LEIGH
SUMMER SCHOOL TEACHERS (1977, New World)—Denise

HOPKIRK, GORDON
THE SKIPPER'S WOOING (1922, GB, Silent, Artistic)—The Skipper

HOPPER, DENNIS
KID BLUE (1973, 20th Century Fox)—Bickford Waner
MAD DOG MORGAN (1976, Australia, BEF)—Daniel Morgan
HOOSIERS (1986, Orion)—Shooter
RIDERS OF THE STORM (1988, Miramax)—Captain
PARIS TROUT (1991, Viacom Pictures)—Paris Trout

HOPPER, DEWOLF
CASEY AT THE BAT (1916, Silent, Triangle-Fine Arts)—Casey

HOPPER, VICTORIA
THE CONSTANT NYMPH (1933, GB, Gaumont/Fox)—Tess Sanger
LORNA DOONE (1935, GB, Associated British)—Lorna Doone

HOPSON, VIOLET
A MUNITION GIRL'S ROMANCE (1917, Silent, GB, Broadwest)—Jenny Jones
A DAUGHTER OF LOVE (1925, Silent, GB, Stoll)—Mary Tannerhill

HORAN, HILLARY
SATAN'S CHEERLEADERS (1977, World Amusements)—Chris

HORNE, DAVID
THE VILLAGE SQUIRE (1935, GB, British & Dominions)—Squire Hollis

HOROWITZ, ADAM
LOST ANGELS (1989, Orion)—Tim Doolan

HORTON, CLARA
NINETEEN AND PHYLLIS (1920, Silent, First National)—Phyllis Laurin

HORTON, EDWARD EVERETT
RUGGLES OF RED GAP (1923, Silent, Paramount)—Ruggles
THE AVIATOR (1929, Warners)—Robert Street
THE SAP (1929, Warners)—The Sap
ONCE A GENTLEMAN (1930, Art-World)—Oliver
HIS NIGHT OUT (1935, Universal)—Homer
THE MAN IN THE MIRROR (1936, GB, Wardour)—Jeremy Dike
NOBODY'S FOOL (1936, Universal)—Will Wright
BACHELOR DADDY (1942, Universal)—Joseph Smith

HOSKINS, BOB
HEART CONDITION (1990, New Line)—Jack Moony

HOUDINI, HARRY
THE MAN FROM BEYOND (1922, Silent, Houdini)—The Man From Beyond
HALDANE OF THE SECRET SERVICE (1923, Silent, Houdini Pictures)—Heath Haldane

HOUSTON, DONALD
THE SURGEON'S KNIFE (1957, GB, Grand National)—Dr. Alex Waring

HOUSTON, GEORGE
CAPTAIN CALAMITY (1936, Grand National)—Capt. Calamity
FRONTIER SCOUT (1939, Fine Arts)—Wild Bill Hickok

HOUSTON, GLYN
SOLO FOR SPARROW (1966, GB, Schoenfield)—Inspector Sparrow

HOVEY, TIM
TOY TIGER (1956, Universal)—Timmie Harkinson

HOWARD, ARLISS
PLAIN CLOTHES (1988, Paramount)—Nick Dunbar/'Nick Springsteen'

HOWARD, JOHN
BULLDOG DRUMMOND AT BAY (1937, GB, Wardour/Republic)—Hugh Drummond
BULLDOG DRUMMOND'S PERIL (1938, GB, Paramount)—Hugh Drummond
ARREST BULLDOG DRUMMOND (1939, GB, Paramount)—Capt. Hugh C. Drummond
TEXAS RANGERS RIDE AGAIN (1940, Paramount)—Jim Kingston
THE MAN WHO RETURNED TO LIFE (1942, Columbia)—David Jameson
THE UNDYING MONSTER (1942, 20th Century Fox)—Oliver Hammond

HOWARD, JOYCE
THEY MET IN THE DARK (1945, GB, Excelsior/English Films)—Laura Verity
WOMAN TO WOMAN (1946, GB, Anglo-American)—Nicolette Bonnet
MRS. FITZHERBERT (1950, GB, British National)—Maria Fitzherbert

HOWARD, LESLIE
BRITISH AGENT (1934, First National)—Stephen Locke

THE SCARLET PIMPERNEL (1935, GB, United Artists)—Sir
  Percy Blakeney
ROMEO AND JULIET (1936, MGM)—Romeo
PYGMALION (1938, GB, MGM)—Prof. Henry Higgins
PIMPERNEL SMITH (1942, GB, United Artists)—Prof.
  Horatio Smith

HOWARD, MARY
FOUR GIRLS IN WHITE (1939, MGM)—Mary Forbes

HOWARD, MILFORD W.
THE BISHOP OF THE OZARKS (1923, Silent, Cosmopolitan
  Films)—Roger Chapman

HOWARD, RONALD
MY BROTHER JONATHAN (1949, GB, Allied Artists)—Harold
  Dakers
MAN ACCUSED (1959, United Artists)—Bob Jensen

HOWARD, RONNIE
THE COURTSHIP OF EDDIE'S FATHER (1963, MGM)—Eddie
  Corbett

HOWARD, SYDNEY
THE MAYOR'S NEST (1932, GB, British & Dominions)—Joe
  Pilgrim
IT'S A COP (1934, GB, Britain & Dominions)—Constable
  Robert Spry
CHICK (1936, GB, United Artists)—Chick Beane
WHAT A MAN! (1937, GB, British Lion)—Samuel Pennyfeather

HOWARD, TREVOR
I BECAME A CRIMINAL (1947, Alliance/Warners)—Clem
  Morgan
OUTCAST OF THE ISLANDS (1952, GB, British Lion)—Peter
  Willens
SIR HENRY AT RAWLINSON END (1980, GB, Charisma)—Sir
  Henry Rawlinson
WINDWALKER (1980, Pacific International)—Windwalker

HOWARD, VANESSA
WHAT BECAME OF JACK AND JILL? (1972, GB, 20th Century
  Fox)—Jill

HOWE, MICHAEL
UNMAN, WITTERING AND ZIGO (1971, GB,
  Paramount)—Unman

HOWELL, C. THOMAS
THE OUTSIDERS (1983, Warners)—Ponyboy Curtis
SECRET ADMIRER (1985, Orion)—Michael Ryan
SOUL MAN (1986, New World)—Mark Watson
A TIGER'S TALE (1988, Atlantic)—Bubber Drumm

HOWERD, FRANKIE
CARRY ON DOCTOR (1968, GB, Rank)—Francis Bigger

HOWES, BOBBY
LORD BABS (1932, GB, Gainsborough)—Lord Basil "Babs"
  Drayford
THE TROJAN BROTHERS (1946, GB, Anglo-American)—Benny
  Castelli

HOWES, REED
THE CYCLONE RIDER (1924, Silent, Fox)—Richard Armstrong
BASHFUL BUCCANEER (1925, Silent, Rayart)—Jerry Logan

HOWES, SALLY ANN
THURSDAY'S CHILD (1943, GB, Pathe)—Fennis Wilson
STOP PRESS GIRL (1949, GB, GFD)—Jennifer Peters

HOWLAND, JOBYNA
STEPPING SISTERS (1932, Fox)—Lady Chetworth-Lynde

HOXIE, JACK
CYCLONE BLISS (1921, Silent, Unity Photoplays)—Jack Bliss
THE GALLOPING ACE (1924, Silent, Universal)—Jim Jordon
THE MAN FROM WYOMING (1924, Silent, Universal)—Ned
  Bannister

HOYAS, RODOLFO
VILLA! (1958, 20th Century Fox)—Pancho Villa

HUA, LI LI
CHINA DOLL (1958, United Artists)—Shu-Jen

HUDDLESTON, DAVID
THE KLANSMAN (1974, Paramount)—Mayor Hardy
SANTA CLAUS: THE MOVIE (1986, Tri-Star)—Santa Claus

HUDDLESTON, MICHAEL
FOUR FRIENDS (1981, Filmways)—David Levene

HUDSON, ERNIE
GHOSTBUSTERS (1984, Columbia)—Winston Zeddmore
GHOSTBUSTERS II (1989, Columbia)—Winston Zeddmore

HUDSON, ROCHELLE
THE SAVAGE GIRL (1932, Monarch)—The Goddess
SUCH WOMEN ARE DANGEROUS (1934, Fox)—Vernie Little
I'VE BEEN AROUND (1935, Universal)—Drue Waring
POPPY (1936, Paramount)—Poppy McGargle
CONVICTED WOMAN (1940, Columbia)—Betty Andrews
THE OFFICER AND THE LADY (1941, Columbia)—Bob Conlon

HUDSON, ROCK
TAZA, SON OF COCHISE (1954, Universal)—Taza
CAPTAIN LIGHTFOOT (1955, Universal)—Michael Martin
SEND ME NO FLOWERS (1964, Universal)—George Kimball
STRANGE BEDFELLOWS (1965, Universal)—Carter Harrison

HUFF, LOUISE
JACK AND JILL (1917, Silent, Paramount)—Mary Dwyer (Jill)

HUFF, MASTER JACK
ZANDER THE GREAT (1925, Silent, MGM)—Zander

HUGENY, SHARON
THE YOUNG LOVERS (1964, MGM)—Pam Burns

HUGH, SOTO JOE
THE KILLING OF A CHINESE BOOKIE (1976, Faces)—The
  Chinese Bookie

HUGHES, BARNARD
DA (1988, Filmdallas)—Da

HUGHES, CAROL
MARRY THE GIRL (1937, Warners)—Virginia Radway

HUGHES, GARETH
I CAN EXPLAIN (1922, Silent, Metro)—Jimmy Berry
LITTLE EVA ASCENDS (1922, Silent, Metro)—Roy St. George/
  Little Eva

HUGHES, KATHLEEN
THREE BAD SISTERS (1956, United Artists)—Valerie

HUGHES, LLOYD
RIP ROARING RILEY (1935, Puritan)—Rip Roaring Riley
KELLY OF THE SECRET SERVICE (1936, Victory/Principal)—
Ted Kelly

HUGHES, MARY BETH
THE COWBOY AND THE BLONDE (1941, 20th Century Fox)—
Crystal Wayne
TIMBER QUEEN (1944, Paramount)—Elaine

HUGHES, WENDY
MY FIRST WIFE (1985, Canada, Spectrafilm)—Helen

HULBERT, CLAUDE
HIS LORDSHIP REGRETS (1938, GB, Canterbury/RKO)—Lord
Cavender
MY LEARNED FRIEND (1943, GB, Ealing)—Claude Babbington

HULBERT, JACK
ALIAS BULLDOG DRUMMOND (1935, GB, Gaumont)—Jack
Pennington
JACK AHOY (1935, GB, Gaumont)—Jack Ponsonby
THE TWO OF US (1938, GB, Gaumont)—Jack Warrender

HULCE, TOM
AMADEUS (1984, Orion)—Wolfgang Amadeus Mozart
DOMENICK AND EUGENE (1988, Orion)—Domenick Luciano
PARENTHOOD (1989, Buena Vista)—Larry Buckman

HULETTE, GLADYS
MRS. SLACKER (1918, Silent, Pathe)—Susie Simpkins
A BOWERY CINDERELLA (1927, Silent, Excellent Pictures)—
Nora Denahy

HULL, DIANNE
ALOHA, BOBBY AND ROSE (1975, Columbia)—Rose

HULL, HENRY
THE HOOSIER SCHOOLMASTER (1924, Silent, Hodkinson
Corp.)—Ralph Hartsook
THE WEREWOLF OF LONDON (1935, Universal)—Dr. Glendon

HULL, JOSEPHINE
THE LADY FROM TEXAS (1951, Universal)—Miss Birdie

HULL, WARREN
HER HUSBAND'S SECRETARY (1937, First National/
Warners)—Bart
STAR REPORTER (1939, Monogram)—John

HULME, ANTHONY
SEND FOR PAUL TEMPLE (1946, GB, Butchers)—Paul Temple
THE MYSTERIOUS MR. NICHOLSON (1947, GB, Ambassador)—
Mr. Nicholson

HUME, BENITA
THE LADY OF THE LAKE (1928, GB, Silent, Gainsborough)—
Ellen Douglas
LORD CAMER'S LADIES (1932, GB, British International)—
Janet King
WOMAN WHO PLAY (1932, GB, Paramount British)—
Margaret Sones
WORST WOMAN IN PARIS (1933, Lasky/Fox)—Peggy Vane

HUNNICUTT, ARTHUR
THE KETTLES OF THE OZARKS (1956, Universal)—Sledge
Kettle

HUNT, MARSHA
GENTLE JULIA (1936, 20th Century Fox)—Julia Atwater
I'LL WAIT FOR YOU (1941, MGM)—Pauline Miller
THE AFFAIRS OF MARTHA (1942, MGM)—Martha Lindstrom
A LETTER FOR EVIE (1945, MGM)—Evie O'Connor
MARY RYAN, DETECTIVE (1949, Columbia)—Mary Ryan

HUNTER, GLENN
THE CRADLE BUSTER (1922, Silent, Patuwa Pictures)—
Benjamin Franklin Reed
SECOND FIDDLE (1923, Silent, Hodkinson)—Jim Bradley
MERTON OF THE MOVIES (1924, Silent, Paramount)—
Merton Gill
HIS BUDDY'S WIFE (1925, Silent, Associated Exhibitors)—
Jimmy McMorrow

HUNTER, HOLLY
MISS FIRECRACKER (1989, Corsair)—Carnelle Scott

HUNTER, IAN
HIS HOUSE IN ORDER (1928, GB, Ideal)—Hilary Jesson
THE PHYSICIAN (1928, GB, Silent, Gaumont)—Dr. Carey
LAZYBONES (1935, GB, RKO)—Sir Reginald Ford
THE MORALS OF MARCUS (1936, GB, Real Art)—Sir Marcus
Ordeyne

HUNTER, JACKIE
DON CHICAGO (1945, GB, British National)—Don Chicago

HUNTER, JEFFREY
SAILOR OF THE KING (1953, GB, 20th Century Fox)—
Andrew Brown
THREE YOUNG TEXANS (1954, 20th Century Fox)—Johnny Colt
SEVEN ANGRY MEN (1955, Allied Artists)—Owen Brown
THE SEARCHERS (1956, Warners)—Martin Pawley
GUN FOR A COWARD (1957, Universal)—Bless Keough
KEY WITNESS (1960, MGM)—Fred Morrow
KING OF KINGS (1961, MGM)—Jesus Christ
THE MAN FROM GALVESTON (1964, Warners)—Timothy
Higgins
THE CHRISTMAS KID (1968, Producers Releasing Corp.)—
Joe Novak

HUNTER, KIM
WHEN STRANGERS MARRY (1944, Monogram)—Millie Dean

HUNTER, NITA
SUSIE STEPS OUT (1946, United Artists)—Susie Russell

HUNTER, RONALD
THE ADVENTURE OF THE ACTION HUNTERS (1987, Bonner/
Troma)—Walter

HUNTER, ROSS
A GUY, A GAL AND A PAL (1945, Columbia)—Jimmy Jones

HUNTER, TAB
THE GIRL HE LEFT BEHIND (1956, Warners)—Andy Scheaffer

HURD, RUTH
RUBY (1971, Bartlett)—Ruby

HURT, JOHN
SINFUL DAVEY (1969, GB, United Artists)—Davey Haggart
LITTLE MALCOLM (1974, GB, Apple Films)—Malcolm Scrawdyke
THE ELEPHANT MAN (1980, GB, Paramount)—John Merrick
PARTNERS (1982, Paramount)—Kerwin
CHAMPIONS (1984, GB, EMB)—Bob Champion

HURT, MARY BETH
PARENTS (1988, Vestron)—Mom

HURT, WILLIAM
EYEWITNESS (1981, 20th Century Fox)—Daryll Deever
THE ACCIDENTAL TOURIST (1988, Warners)—Macon Leary
THE DOCTOR (1991, Buena Vista/Touchstone)—Dr. Jack MacKee

HUSSEY, OLIVIA
ROMEO AND JULIET (1968, GB/Italy, Paramount)—Juliet

HUSSEY, RUTH
RICH MAN, POOR GIRL (1938, MGM)—Joan Thayer
WOMAN OF THE NORTH COUNTRY (1952, Republic)—Christine Powell
THE LADY WANTS MINK (1953, Republic)—Nora Connors

HUSTON, ANJELICA
ENEMIES, A LOVE STORY (1989, 20th Century Fox)—Tamara
THE GRIFTERS (1990, Miramax)—Lilly Dillon
THE WITCHES (1990, Warners)—Grand High Witch
THE ADDAMS FAMILY (1991, Paramount)—Morticia Addams

HUSTON, JOHN
THE VISITOR (1980, International Picture Show)—Jersey Coloswitz

HUSTON, WALTER
GENTLEMEN OF THE PRESS (1929, Paramount)—Wickland Snell
ABRAHAM LINCOLN (1930, United Artists)—Abraham Lincoln
THE BAD MAN (1930, First National/Warners)—Pancho Lopez
THE RULING VOICE (1931, Warners)—Jack Bannister
DODSWORTH (1936, United Artists)—Sam Dodsworth
RHODES OF AFRICA (1936, GB, Gaumont)—Cecil Rhodes
THE DEVIL AND DANIEL WEBSTER (ALL THAT MONEY CAN BUY) (1941, RKO)—Mr. Scratch

HUTCHINSON, CHARLES
HITCH STIRS 'EM UP (1923, Silent, GB, Ideal)—Hurricane Hitch

HUTCHINSON, JOSEPHINE
I MARRIED A DOCTOR (1936, First National/Warners)—Carol Kennicott

HUTH, HAROLD
THE OUTSIDER (1933, GB, MGM)—Anton Ragatzy

HUTSON, VIRGINIA
WOMAN FROM HEADQUARTERS (1950, Republic)—Joyce

HUTTON, BETTY
INCENDIARY BLONDE (1945, Paramount)—Texas Guinan
DREAM GIRL (1947, Paramount)—Georgina Allerton
THE PERILS OF PAULINE (1947, Paramount)—Pearl White/ "Pauline"
ANNIE GET YOUR GUN (1950, MGM)—Annie Oakley
SOMEBODY LOVES ME (1952, Paramount)—Blossom Seeley

HUTTON, JIM
THE HORIZONTAL LIEUTENANT (1962, MGM)—2nd Lt. Merle Wye
HELLFIGHTERS (1968, Universal)—Greg Parker
PSYCHIC KILLER (1975, Avco Embassy)—Arnold

HUTTON, ROBERT
TOO YOUNG TO KNOW (1945, Warners)—Ira Enright
THE YOUNGER BROTHERS (1949, Warners)—Johnny Younger

HUTTON, TIMOTHY
ORDINARY PEOPLE (1980, Paramount)—Conrad Jarrett
DANIEL (1983, Paramount)—Daniel Isaacson
THE FALCON AND THE SNOWMAN (1985, Orion)— Christopher Boyce

HYAMS, LEILA
THE GIRL SAID NO (1930, MGM)—Mary Howe
PART TIME WIFE (1930, Fox)—Mrs. Murdock/Betty Rogers
SING SINNER, SING (1933, Majestic)—Lela Larson

HYLAND, PEGGY
PR   SIVE PEGGY (1917, Silent, Mayfair)—Peggy Patton
PEG OF THE PIRATES (1918, Silent, Fox)—Peg

HYSER, JOYCE
JUST ONE OF THE GUYS (1985, Columbia)—Terry

I

ICE CUBE
BOYZ N THE HOOD (1991, Columbia/New Deal)—Doughboy

IDLE, ERIC
NUNS ON THE RUN (1990, GB, 20th Century Fox)—Sister Euphemia (Brian Hope)

INESCOURT, FREIDA
WOMAN DOCTOR (1939, Republic)—Judith
A WOMAN IS THE JUDGE (1939, Columbia)—Mary Cabot

INGHAM, BARRIE
A CHALLENGE FOR ROBIN HOOD (1968, GB, 20th Century Fox)—Robin Hood

INGRAHAM, LLOYD
THE SPOILERS (1930, Paramount)—Judge Stillman

IRELAND, JILL
GIRLS OF THE LATIN QUARTER (1960, GB, New Realm)—Jill
SO EVIL SO YOUNG (1961, GB, United Artists)—Ann

IRELAND, JOHN
I SHOT JESSE JAMES (1949, Lippert)—Bob Ford
THE RETURN OF JESSE JAMES (1950, Lippert)—Jesse James
HURRICANE SMITH (1952, Paramount)—Hurricane Smith
GUNSLINGER (1956, Associated Releasing Corp.)—Cane Miro

I SAW WHAT YOU DID (1965, Universal)—Steve Marak

IRELAND, KATHY
ALIENS FROM L.A. (1988, Cannon)—Wanda Saknussemm

IRONS, JEREMY
DEAD RINGERS (1988, 20th Century Fox)—Beverly & Elliot Mantle
KAFKA (1991, Miramax)—Franz Kafka

IRVING, AMY
MICKI AND MAUDE (1984, Columbia)—Maude Salinger

IRVING, ELLIS
MEMBERS OF THE JURY (1937, GB, 20th Century Fox)—Walter Maitland

IRVING, ETHEL
CALL ME MAME (1933, GB, Warners)—Mame

IRVING, GEORGE
KING OF THE TURF (1926, Silent, Film Booking Offices)—Colonel Fairfax

IRWIN, MAY
MRS. BLACK IS BACK (1914, Silent, Famous Players)—Mrs. Black

ISHIHARA, YUJIRO
THOSE MAGNIFICENT MEN IN THEIR FLYING MACHINES (1965, GB, 20th Century Fox)—Yamamoto

IVANEK, ZELJKO
THE SENDER (1982, GB, Paramount)—The Sender

IVES, BURL
DAY OF THE OUTLAW (1959, United Artists)—Jack Bruhn
THE MCMASTERS (1970, Chevron)—Neal McMasters

IVEY, JUDITH
SISTER SISTER (88, New World)—Charlotte Bonnard

IVO, TOMMY
STEPCHILD (1947, Producers Releasing Corp.)—Jim Bullock

J

JACKSON, ANNE
SO YOUNG, SO BAD (1950, United Artists)—Jackie
THE SECRET LIFE OF AN AMERICAN WIFE (1968, 20th Century Fox)—Victoria Layton
FOLKS (1992, 20th Century Fox)—Mildred Aldrich

JACKSON, BARRY
MR. LOVE (1986, GB, Warners)—Donald Lovelace

JACKSON, GLENDA
WOMEN IN LOVE (1969, GB, United Artists)—Gundrun Brangwen
THE DEVIL IS A WOMAN (1975, GB, Fox British)—Sister Geraldine
HEDDA (1975, GB, Bowden)—Hedda Gabler
THE MAIDS (1975, GB, CineFilms)—Solange
THE ROMANTIC ENGLISHWOMAN (1975, GB, New World)—Elizabeth Fielding
THE INCREDIBLE SARAH (1976, GB, Readers Digest Prod.)—Sarah Bernhardt
THE CLASS OF MISS MACMICHAEL (1978, GB, Brut)—Conor MacMichael
STEVIE (1978, GB, First Artists)—Stevie Smith

JACKSON, LEONARD
SUPER SPOOK (1975, Leavitt-Pickman)—Super Spook

JACKSON, STONEY
JOCKS (1987, Crown)—Andy

JACOBI, DEREK
THE FOOL (1990, GB, Sands)—Sir John/Mr. Frederick

JACOBY, BOBBY
THE APPLEGATES (1990, Roadshow)—Johnny Applegate

JACOBY, SCOTT
RIVALS (1972, Avco Embassy)—Jaimie Sutton
BAXTER (1973, GB, National General)—Robert Baxter

JACQUES, HATTIE
CARRY ON NURSE (1959, GB, Anglo-Amalgamated)—Matron

JAFFE, SAM
GUNGA DIN (1939, RKO)—Gunga Din

JAGGER, DEAN
WANDERER OF THE WASTELAND (1935, Paramount)—Adam Larey
BRIGHAM YOUNG—FRONTIERSMAN (1940, 20th Century Fox)—Brigham Young
WHEN STRANGERS MARRY (1944, Monogram)—Paul Dean
A YANK IN LONDON (1946, GB, 20th Century Fox)—Sgt. John Patterson
C-MAN (1949, Film Classics)—Cliff Holden
THREE BRAVE MEN (1957, 20th Century Fox)—Rogers

JAGGER, MICK
NED KELLY (1970, GB, United Artists)—Ned Kelly

JAMES, JESSE JR.
JESSE JAMES AS THE OUTLAW (1921, Silent, Mesco)—Jesse James
JESSE JAMES UNDER THE BLACK FLAG (1921, Silent, Mesco)—Jesse James

JAMES, JOHN
SON OF BILLY THE KID (1949, Screen Guild)—Colt

JAMES, SIDNEY
THE MAN IN BLACK (1950, GB, Hammer)—Henry Clavering
THE LAVENDER HILL MOB (1958, MGM)—Lackery
CARRY ON CONSTABLE (1960, GB, Anglo-Amalgamated)—Sgt. Wilkins

CARRY ON CABBIE (1963, GB, Warners/Pathe)—Charlie
CARRY ON COWBOY (1966, GB, Warners/Pathe)—Rumpo Kid
CARRY ON HENRY VIII (1970, GB, Rank/AIP)—Henry VIII

JAMES, STEVE
STREET HUNTER (1990, 21st Century)—Logan Blade

JANIS, ELSIE
THE CAPRICES OF KITTY (1915, Silent, Bosworth)—Kitty
Bradley
MADCAP BETTY (1915, Silent, Bosworth)—Betty
WOMEN IN WAR (1940, Republic)—O'Neil

JANNEY, LEON
FATHER'S SON (1931, Warners)—Bill Emory
PENROD AND SAM (1931, First National)—Penrod Schofield

JANSON, HORST
CAPTAIN KRONOS: VAMPIRE HUNTER (1974, GB, Hammer/
Paramount)—Captain Kronos

JANSSEN, DAVID
KING OF THE ROARING TWENTIES (1961, Allied Artists)—
Arnold Rothstein
MACHO CALLAHAN (1970, Avco Embassy)—Diego "Macho"
Callahan

JANSSEN, EILENE
THE SEARCH FOR BRIDEY MURPHY (1956, Paramount)—
Bridey at 15

JARRATT, JOHN
THE GREAT MACARTHY (1975, Australia, Seven Keys)—
MacArthy

JASON, RICK
SIERRA BARON (1958, 20th Century Fox)—Miguel Delmonte

JASON, SYBIL
LITTLE BIG SHOT (1935, Warners)—Gloria Gibbs
THE CAPTAIN'S KID (1937, First National/Warners)—Abigail
Prentiss

JAYSTON, MICHAEL
NICHOLAS AND ALEXANDRA (1971, GB, Columbia)—Nicholas

JEAN, GLORIA
THE UNDER-PUP (1939, Universal)—Pip/Emma
EASY TO LOOK AT (1945, Universal)—Judy
I'LL REMEMBER APRIL (1945, Universal)—April
MANHATTAN ANGEL (1948, Columbia)—Gloria Cole
AN OLD-FASHIONED GIRL (1948, Eagle-Lion)—Polly Milton

JEANS, URSULA
THE WOMAN IN THE HALL (1949, GB, Rank)—Lorna Blake

JEFFERSON, THOMAS
RIP VAN WINKLE (1914, Silent, Rolfe/Alco)—Rip Van Winkle
RIP VAN WINKLE (1921, Silent, Lascelle/Hodkinson)—Rip Van
Winkle

JEFFRIES, HERB
CALYPSO JOE (1957, Allied Artists)—Calypso Joe

JENKINS, DANIEL H.
O.C. AND STIGGS (1987, MGM/United Artists)—Oliver
Cromwell "O.C." Ogilvie

JENKINS, JACKIE "BUTCH"
LITTLE MISTER JIM (1946, MGM)—Little Jim Tukker
MY BROTHER TALKS TO HORSES (1946, MGM)—Lewis
Penrose

JENNINGS, CLAUDIA
UNHOLY ROLLERS (1972, American International)—Karen
TRUCK STOP WOMEN (1974, LT Films)—Rose

JENNINGS, WAYLON
NASHVILLE REBEL (1966, American International)—
Arlin Grove

JENS, SALOME
TERROR FROM THE YEAR 5,000 (1958, American
International)—5,000 A.D. Woman
ANGEL BABY (1961, Allied Artists)—Angel Baby

JENSEN, EULAIE
MAN AND HIS WOMAN (1920, Silent, Pathe)—Clare Eaton
CHARLEY'S AUNT (1925, Silent, Cristie Film)—Donna Lucia
D'Alvadorez

JERGENS, ADELE
LADIES OF THE CHORUS (1948, Columbia)—May Martin
THE WOMAN FROM TANGIER (1948, Columbia)—Nylon

JERGER, BURR
GENERAL MASSACRE (1973, Jerger)—Gen. Massacre

JESSEL, GEORGE
PRIVATE IZZY MURPHY (1926, Silent, Warners)—Izzy Murphy
GINSBERG THE GREAT (1927, Silent, Warners)—Johnny
Ginsberg
SAILOR IZZY MURPHY (1927, Silent, Warners)—Izzy Murphy
LUCKY BOY (1929, Tiffany)—Georgie Jessel

JEWEL, ISABEL
SHE HAD TO CHOOSE (1934, Majestic)—Sally

JEWEL, JIMMY
ARTHUR'S HALLOWED GROUND (1986, GB, Cinecom)—Arthur

JILLETTE, PENN
PENN & TELLER GET KILLED (1989, Warners)—Penn

JILLSON, JOYCE
SUPERCHICK (1973, Crown)—Tara B. True (Superchick)

JOHANN, ZITA
SIN OF NORA MORAN (1933, Majestic)—Nora Moran

JOHN, ROSAMUND
SHE SHALL HAVE MURDER (1950, GB, Independent Film)—
Jane Hamish

JOHNES, ALEXANDRA
ZELLY AND ME (1988, Columbia)—Phoebe

JOHNS, ESME
I AM A GROUPIE (1970, GB, Eagle Films)—Sally

JOHNS, GLYNIS
THIS MAN IS MINE (1946, GB, Columbia British)—Millie
MIRANDA (1949, GB, Ealing)—Miranda
MAD ABOUT MEN (1954, GB, GFD)—Miranda
JOSEPHINE AND MEN (1955, GB, British Lion)—
Josephine Luton

JOHNSON, ARNOLD
PUTNEY SWOPE (1969, Cinema V Distributing)—Putney Swope

JOHNSON, BEN
THE WILD BUNCH (1969, Warners)—Tector Gorch

JOHNSON, CASEY
LITTLE MEN (1940, RKO)—Robby

JOHNSON, CHIC
THE GHOST CATCHERS (1944, Universal)—Chic

JOHNSON, DON
THE MAGIC GARDEN OF STANLEY SWEETHART (1970, MGM)—
Stanley Sweethart
A BOY AND HIS DOG (1975, LQJ Films)—Vic
HARLEY DAVIDSON AND THE MARLBORO MAN (1991, MGM)—
Marlboro

JOHNSON, EDWARD
TARZAN AND THE JUNGLE BOY (1968, Paramount)—Buhara

JOHNSON, KAY
MADAME SATAN (1930, MGM)—Angela Brooks
THE SPOILERS (1930, Paramount)—Helen Chester

JOHNSON, NOEL
REFORM GIRL (1933, Tower)—Lydia Johnson

JOHNSON, VAN
DR. GILLESPIE'S NEW ASSISTANT (1942, MGM)—Dr.
Randall Adams
THREE MEN IN WHITE (1944, MGM)—Dr. Randall Adams
TWO GIRLS AND A SAILOR (1944, MGM)—John Dyckman III
THREE GUYS NAMED MIKE (1951, MGM)—Michael Lawrence
MEN OF THE FIGHTING LADY (1954, MGM)—Lt. Howard
Thayer
KELLY AND ME (1957, Universal)—Len Carmody

JOHNSTON, MARGARET
PORTRAIT OF CLARE (1951, GB, Pathe)—Clare Hingston
THE PSYCOPATH (1966, GB, Paramount)—Mrs. Von Sturm

JOLSON, AL
THE JAZZ SINGER (1927, Part-Talkie, Warners)—Jack Robin
(Jakie Rabinowitz)
THE SINGING FOOL (1928, Warners)—Al
HALLELUJAH, I'M A BUM (1933, United Artists)—Bumper
WONDER BAR (1934, Warners)—Al Wonder
THE SINGING KID (1936, Warners)—Al Jackson

JONES, ALLAN
BOYS FROM SYRACUSE (1940, Mayfair/Universal)—Antipholus
of Syracuse
WHEN JOHNNY COMES MARCHING HOME (1943, Universal)—
Johnny Kovacs
YOU'RE A LUCKY FELLOW, MR, SMITH (1943, Universal)—
Tony Smith

JONES, CHARLES "BUCK"
THE ARIZONA ROMEO (1925, Silent, Fox)—Tom Long
THE COWBOY AND THE COUNTESS (1926, Silent, Fox)—Jerry
Whipple
A MAN FOUR-SQUARE (1926, Silent, Fox)—Craig Norton

WHITE EAGLE (1932, Columbia)—White Eagle
THE FIGHTING RANGER (1934, Columbia)—Jim
ROCKY RHODES (1934, Universal)—Rocky Rhodes
STONE OF SILVER CREEK (1935, Universal)—T. William Stone
THE COWBOY AND THE KID (1936, Universal)—Steve Davis
SUDDEN BILL DORN (1938, Universal)—Sudden Bill Dorn
UNMARRIED (1939, Paramount)—Slag Bailey

JONES, CHARLIE
BIG DAN (1923, Silent, Fox)—Dan O'Hara
CUPID'S FIREMAN (1923, Silent, Fox)—Andy McGee
LAZYBONES (1925, Silent, Fox)—Lazybones

JONES, CHRISTOPHER
CHUBASCO (1968, Warners)—Chubasco

JONES, DEAN
THE NEW INTERNS (1964, Columbia)—Dr. Lew Worship
TWO ON A GUILLOTINE (1965, Warners)—Val Henderson
THE SHAGGY D.A. (1976, Buena Vista)—Wilby Daniels

JONES, DUANE
GANJA AND HESS (1973, Kelly-Jordan)—Dr. Hess Green

JONES, GORDON
THEY WANTED TO MARRY (1937, RKO)—Jim Tyler

JONES, GRIFFITH
FACE BEHIND THE SCAR (1940, GB, Premier-Stafford)—
James Martin
THE SECRET FOUR (1940, GB, Ealing)—James Brodie

JONES, JAMES EARL
THE MAN (1972, Paramount)—Douglas Dilman

JONES, JENNIFER
THE SONG OF BERNADETTE (1943, 20th Century Fox)—
Bernadette Soubirous
CLUNY BROWN (1946, 20th Century Fox)—Cluny Brown
MADAME BOVARY (1949, MGM)—Emma Bovary
PORTRAIT OF JENNIE (1949, Selznick)—Jennie Appleton
CARRIE (1952, Paramount)—Carrie Meeber
RUBY GENTRY (1952, 20th Century Fox)—Ruby Gentry
INDISCRETION OF AN AMERICAN WIFE (1954, Columbia)—
Mary Forbes
GOOD MORNING, MISS DOVE (1955, 20th Century Fox)—
Miss Dove
THE BARRETTS OF WIMPOLE STREET (1957, MGM)—
Elizabeth Barrett

JONES, MARCIA MAE
TOMBOY (1940, Monogram)—Pat
NINE GIRLS (1944, Columbia)—Shirley Berke

JONES, SAM J.
FLASH GORDON (1980, Universal)—Flash Gordon
UNDER THE GUN (1989, Marquis)—Mike Braxton
DRIVING FORCE (1990, Australia, J&M)—Steve O'Neil

JONES, TOMMY LEE
THE RIVER RAT (1984, Paramount)—Billy
THE PACKAGE (1989, Orion)—Thomas Boyette

JORDAN, DOROTHY
SHIPMATES (1931, MGM)—Kit Corbin

JORDAN, RICHARD
OLD BOYFRIENDS (1979, Avco Embassy)—Jeff Turrin
MEN'S CLUB (1986, Paramount)—Kramer

JORY, VICTOR
THE DEVIL'S IN LOVE (1933, Fox)—Lt. Andre Morand
TOO TOUGH TO KILL (1935, Columbia)—John O'Hara
THE MAN WHO TURNED TO STONE (1957, Columbia)—Dr.
Murdock

JOURDAN, LOUIS
THE V.I.P.S (1963, GB, MGM)—Marc Champselle

JOY, LEATRICE
BUNTY PULLS THE STRINGS (1921, Silent, Goldwyn)—Bunty
Biggar
THE SILENT PARTNER (1923, Paramount)—Lisa Coburn
THE ANGEL OF BROADWAY (1927, Silent, Pathe Exchange)—
Babe Scott
NOBODY'S WIDOW (1927, Silent, Producers Distributing
Corp.)—Roxanna Smith
A MOST IMMORAL LADY (1929, First National)—Laura
Sargeant

JOYCE, ALICE
COUSIN KATE (1921, Silent, Vitagraph)—Kate Curtis
HER LORD AND MASTER (1921, Silent, Vitagraph)—Indiana
Stillwater
DANCING MOTHERS (1926, Silent, Paramount)—Ethel
Westcourt

JOYCE, BRENDA
PUBLIC DEB NO. 1 (1940, 20th Century Fox)—Penny Cooper
MARRY THE BOSS'S DAUGHTER (1941, 20th Century Fox)—
Frederika Barrett
PRIVATE NURSE (1941, 20th Century Fox)—Mary Malloy

JULIA, RAUL
THE PENITENT (1988, New Century/Vista)—Ramon
ROMERO (1989, Four Seasons)—Archbishop Oscar Romero
FRANKENSTEIN UNBOUND (1990, 20th Century Fox)—Dr.
Frankenstein
THE ADDAMS FAMILY (1991, Paramount)—Gomez Addams

JULIAN, RUPERT
BETTINA LOVED A SOLDIER (1916, Silent, Bluebird)—Jean
Reynaud
THE KAISER (1918, Silent, Renowned Pictures)—The Kaiser

JULIEN, MAX
THOMASINE AND BUSHROD (1974, Columbia)—Bushrod

JUMA
ODONGO (1956, GB, Columbia)—Odongo

JURGENS, CURT
THE ENEMY BELOW (1957, 20th Century Fox)—Von Stolberg
ME AND THE COLONEL (1958, Columbia)—Col. Prokoszny
I AIM AT THE STARS (1960, Columbia)—Wernher von Braun

JUSTICE, JAMES ROBERTSON
FATHER CAME TOO (1964, GB, Rank)—Sir Beverly Grant

JUSTIN, JOHN
THE MAN WHO LOVED REDHEADS (1955, London Films)—
Mark St. Neots

K

KAHN, MADELINE
FIRST FAMILY (1980, Warners)—Mrs. Link

KAITAN, ELIZABETH
ASSAULT OF THE KILLER BIMBOS (1988, Titan/
Empire)—LuLu

KAMAKAHI, PIA
STRIPPED TO KILL (1987, Concorde)—Eric

KANE, HELEN
DANGEROUS NAN MCGREW (1930, Paramount)—Nan McGrew

KANNER, ALEXIS
KINGS AND DESPERATE MEN (1984, GB, Blue Dolphin)—
Lucas Miller

KANTS, IVAR
BROTHERS (1984, Australia, Areflex)—Kevin Wild

KAPTURE, MITZI
ANGEL 3: THE FINAL CHAPTER (1988, New World)—
Angel/Molly

KARLOFF, BORIS
THE MASK OF FU MANCHU (1932, MGM)—Dr. Fu Manchu
THE MUMMY (1932, Universal)—Im-Ho-Tep
THE GHOUL (1934, Gaumont)—Prof. Morlant
THE MAN WHO LIVED AGAIN (1936, GB, Gaumont)—Dr.
Laurience
THE WALKING DEAD (1936, Warners)—John Ellman
MR. WONG, DETECTIVE (1938, Monogram)—James Lee Wong
THE MAN THEY COULD NOT HANG (1939, Columbia)—Dr.
Henryk Savaard
MR. WONG IN CHINATOWN (1939, Monogram)—James
Lee Wong
THE MYSTERY OF MR. WONG (1939, Monogram)—James
Lee Wong
THE MAN WITH NINE LIVES (1940, Columbia)—Dr. Leon
Kravaal
THE BODY SNATCHER (1945, RKO)—John Gray
DICK TRACY MEETS GRUESOME (1947, RKO)—Gruesome
COLONEL MARCH INVESTIGATES (1952, GB, Criterion)—
Col. March
ABBOTT AND COSTELLO MEET DR. JEKYLL AND MR. HYDE
(1954, Universal)—Dr. Henry Jekyll
FRANKENSTEIN 1970 (1958, Allied Artists)—Baron Victor von
Frankenstein
THE HAUNTED STRANGLER (1958, GB, Anglo-Amalgamated)—
James Rankin

KARNES, ROBERT
THREE HUSBANDS (1950, Warners)—Kenneth Whittaker

KARNS, ROSCOE
TROOPERS THREE (1930, Tiffany)—Bugs
THREE MARRIED MEN (1936, Paramount)—Peter Cary
CLARENCE (1937, Paramount)—Clarence Smith
MY SON, THE HERO (1943, Producers Releasing Corp)—
Big Time

KARRAS, ALEX
JACOB TWO-TWO MEETS THE HOODED FANG (1979, Canada, Gulkin)—The Hooded Fang

KASTNER, DAPHNA
JULIA HAD TWO LOVERS (1990, South Gate)—Julia

KATT, WILLIAM
BUTCH AND SUNDANCE, THE EARLY DAYS (1979, 20th Century Fox)—Sundance Kid
WHITE GHOST (1988, Gibraltar)—Steve Shepard

KAUFMAN, JOSEPH
JUD (1971, Duque Films)—Jud Carney

KAVANAUGH, SEAMUS
PROFESSOR TIM (1957, Ireland, RKO)—Professor Tim

KAYE, CAREN
MY TUTOR (1983, Crown International)—Terry

KAYE, DANNY
WONDER MAN (1945, RKO)—Buzzy Ballew/Edwin Dingle
THE KID FROM BROOKLYN (1946, Goldwyn/RKO)—Burleigh Sullivan
THE SECRET LIFE OF WALTER MITTY (1947, RKO)—Walter Mitty
THE INSPECTOR GENERAL (1949, Warners)—Georgi
HANS CHRISTIAN ANDERSEN (1952, RKO)—Hans Christian Andersen
THE COURT JESTER (1956, Paramount)—Hawkins
ME AND THE COLONEL (1958, Columbia)—S.I. Jacobowsky
MERRY ANDREW (1958, MGM)—Andrew Larabee
THE MAN FROM THE DINER'S CLUB (1963, Columbia)—Ernie Klenk

KAYE, NORMAN
MAN OF FLOWERS (1984, Australia, International Spectrafilm)—Charles Bremer

KAYE, STUBBY
THE COOL MIKADO (1963, GB, United Artists)—Judge Mikado

KEACH, JAMES
THE LONG RIDERS (1980, United Artists)—Jesse James

KEACH, STACY
THE TRAVELING EXECUTIONER (1970, MGM)—Jonas Candide
DOC (1971, United Artists)—Doc Holliday
THE NEW CENTURIONS (1972, Columbia)—Roy Fehler
LUTHER (1974, American Film Theatre)—Martin Luther
THE KILLER INSIDE ME (1976, Warners)—Lou Ford
THE LONG RIDERS (1980, United Artists)—Frank James
FALSE IDENTITY (1990, RKO)—Ben

KEANAN, STACI
LISA (1990, MGM/UA)—Lisa

KEANE, RAYMOND
THE LONE EAGLE (1927, Silent, Universal)—Lt. William Holmes

KEARNEY, STEVE
RIKKY AND PETE (1988, Australia, MGM/United Artists)—Pete

KEATON, BUSTER
THE SAPHEAD (1921, Silent, Metro)—Bertie Van Alstyne
THE NAVIGATOR (1924, Silent, MGM)—Rollo Treadway
SHERLOCK, JR. (1924, Silent, Metro)—Sherlock, Jr.
BATTLING BUTLER (1926, Silent, MGM)—Alfred Butler
THE CAMERAMAN (1928, Silent, MGM)—Luke Shannon (Buster)
STEAMBOAT BILL, JR. (1928, Silent, United Artists)—Steamboat Bill, Jr.
SPITE MARRIAGE (1929, MGM)—Elmer
PASSIONATE PLUMBER (1932, MGM)—Elmer Tuttle

KEATON, CAMILLE
I SPIT ON YOUR GRAVE (1983, Cinemagic)—Jennifer

KEATON, DIANE
ANNIE HALL (1977, United Artists)—Annie Hall
LOOKING FOR MR. GOODBAR (1977, Paramount)—Theresa Dunn
THE LITTLE DRUMMER GIRL (1984, Warners)—Charlie
MRS. SOFFEL (1984, MGM/United Artists)—Kate Soffel
THE GOOD MOTHER (1988, Touchstone)—Anna Dunlap

KEATON, MICHAEL
MR. MOM (1983, 20th Century Fox)—Jack
JOHNNY DANGEROUSLY (1984, 20th Century Fox)—Johnny Dangerously
BEETLEJUICE (1988, Warners)—Betelgeuse
CLEAN AND SOBER (1988, Warners)—Daryl Poynter
BATMAN (1989, Warners)—Batman/Bruce Wayne
THE DREAM TEAM (1989, Universal)—Billy Caulfield
ONE GOOD COP (1991, Hollywood Pictures)—Artie Lewis
BATMAN RETURNS (1992, Warner Brothers)—Batman/Bruce Wayne

KEATS, VIOLA
TOO MANY WIVES (1933, GB, Warners)—Sally
HER LAST AFFAIRE (1935, GB, Producers Distributors)—Lady Avril Weyre

KEEFE, CORNELIUS
MAN FROM HEADQUARTERS (1928, Silent, Rayart)—Yorke Norray
BROTHERS (1929, Silent, Rayart)—Tom Conroy

KEEL, HOWARD
CALLAWAY WENT THATAWAY (1951, MGM)—Smoky Callaway
THREE GUYS NAMED MIKE (1951, MGM)—Mike Jamison
KISS ME KATE (1953, MGM)—Fred Graham/Petruchio
SEVEN BRIDES FOR SEVEN BROTHERS (1954, MGM)—Adam Pontipee
THE BIG FISHERMAN (1959, Buena Vista)—Simon Peter
WACO (1966, Paramount)—Waco

KEELER, RUBY
GOLD DIGGERS OF 1933 (1933, Warners)—Polly Parker
DAMES (1934, Warners)—Barbara Hemingway
GO INTO YOUR DANCE (1935, Warners)—Dorothy Wayne
SHIPMATES FOREVER (1935, Warners)—June Blackburn
COLLEEN (1936, Warners)—Colleen Reiley
READY, WILLING AND ABLE (1937, Warners)—Jane Clarke
MOTHER CAREY'S CHICKENS (1938, RKO)—Kitty Carey
SWEETHEART OF THE CAMPUS (1941, Columbia)—Betty Blake

KEENAN, FRANK
THE DESPOILER (1915, Silent, Triangle)—Emir
JOE GRIMSBY'S BOY (1916, Silent, Ince)—Jim Grimsby

KEENE, GEORGE
A SOLDIER AND A MAN (1916, GB, Silent, British & Colonial)—
Harold Sinclair

KEENE, TOM
THE CHEYENNE KID (1933, RKO)—Cheyenne Kid

KEHOE, JACK
THE KILLERS (1984, Roth Film)—Harry

KEIL, MARGARET-ROSE
THAT KIND OF GIRL (1963, GB, Topaz-IA)—Eva

KEITEL, HARVEY
MOTHER, JUGS & SPEED (1976, 20th Century Fox)—Speed
THE DUELLISTS (1977, GB, Paramount)—Feraud
MEN'S CLUB (1986, Paramount)—Solly Berliner
THE TWO JAKES (1990, Paramount)—Jake Berman
BAD LIEUTENANT (1992, Odyssey)—LT

KEITH, BRIAN
FIVE AGAINST THE HOUSE (1955, Columbia)—Brick
THE DEADLY COMPANIONS (1961, Pathe-American)—
Yellowleg
THOSE CALLOWAYS (1964, Buena Vista)—Cam Calloway
SCANDALOUS JOHN (1971, Buena Vista)—John McCandless
THE WIND AND THE LION (1975, MGM/United Artists)—
Theodore Roosevelt

KEITH, DAVID
THE FURTHER ADVENTURES OF TENNESSEE BUCK (1988,
Trans World)—Buck Malone

KEITH, IAN
LIGHT FINGERS (1929, Columbia)—Light Fingers
BOURDOIR DIPLOMAT (1930, Universal)—Baron Valmi
PRINCE OF DIAMONDS (1930, Columbia)—Rupert Endon
THE DECEIVER (1931, Columbia)—Thorpe
THE PHANTOM OF PARIS (1931, MGM)—Marquis de Touchais

KELLAWAY, CECIL
THE GOOD FELLOWS (1943, Paramount)—Jim Hilton

KELLER, FRED A.
MY DARK LADY (1987, Film Gallery)—Sam Booth

KELLERMAN, SALLY
RAFFERTY AND THE GOLD DUST TWINS (1975, Warners)—
Mac Beachwood

KELLEY, SHEILA
SOME GIRLS (1989, MGM-United Artists)—Irenka

KELLINO, PAMELA
I MET A MURDERER (1939, GB, Grand National)—Jo

KELLOGG, BRUCE
DEERSLAYER (1943, Republic)—Deerslayer

KELLY, ED
RAILROADED (1947, Eagle Lion)—Steve Ryan

KELLY, GENE
FOR ME AND MY GAL (1942, MGM)—Harry Palmer
ON THE TOWN (1949, MGM)—Gabey
AN AMERICAN IN PARIS (1951, MGM)—Jerry Mulligan
SINGIN' IN THE RAIN (1952, MGM)—Don Lockwood

KELLY, GRACE
THE COUNTRY GIRL (1954, Paramount)—Georgie Elgin
THE SWAN (1956, MGM)—Princess Alexandra

KELLY, JIM
BLACK BELT JONES (1974, Warners)—Black Belt Jones

KELLY, MARTIN J.
FINNEGAN'S BALL (1927, Silent, First Division)—Finnegan

KELLY, NANCY
HE MARRIED HIS WIFE (1940, 20th Century Fox)—Valerie
Randall
SAILOR'S LADY (1940, 20th Century Fox)—Sally Gilroy
WOMAN WHO CAME BACK (1945, Republic)—Lorna Webster

KELLY, NORMAN
THREE LIVE GHOSTS (1922, Silent, Paramount)—Billy Foster

KELLY, PATSY
KELLY THE SECOND (1936, MGM)—Molly Kelly

KELLY, PAUL
THE SONG AND DANCE MAN (1936, 20th Century Fox)—Hap
Farrell
SPOILERS OF THE NORTH (1947, Republic)—Matt Garraway
DUFFY OF SAN QUENTIN (1954, Warners)—Warden Clinton
T. Duffy

KELLY, TOMMY
PECK'S BAD BOY WITH THE CIRCUS (1938, RKO)—Bill Peck
THE ADVENTURES OF TOM SAWYER (1939, Selznick
International)—Tom Sawyer

KELLY, WALTER C.
MCFADDEN'S FLATS (1935, Paramount)—Dan McFadden
THE VIRGINIA JUDGE (1935, Paramount)—Judge Davis

KEMP, GARY
THE KRAYS (1990, GB, Rank)—Ronald Kray

KEMP, JEREMY
FACE OF A STRANGER (1964, GB, Allied Artists)—Vince
Howard

KEMP, MARTIN
THE KRAYS (1990, GB, Rank)—Reginald Kray

KEMPER, CHARLES
AN ANGEL COMES TO BROADWAY (1945, Republic)—Phineas
Aloysius Higby

KEMPER, DENNIS
MY BROTHER'S WEDDING (1983, Burnett)—Wendell Monday

KENDALL, HENRY
RICH AND STRANGE (1932, GB, British International)—
Fred Hill
WATCH BEVERLY (1932, GB, Butchers)—Victor Beverly
COUNSEL'S OPINION (1933, GB, LFP/Paramount)—Logan
THE MAN OUTSIDE (1933, GB, RKO)—Harry Wainwright
THE MAN WHO WON (1933, GB, British International)—Sir
William Normand
GUEST OF HONOR (1934, GB, Warners)—Lord Strathpeffer
THE MAN I WANT (1934, GB, British Lion)—Peter Mason
THE SHADOW (1936, GB, United Artists)—Reggie Ogden, The
Shadow

KENDALL, KAY
SIMON AND LAURA (1956, GB, Universal)—Laura Foster
LES GIRLS (1957, MGM)—Lady Wren

KENNEDY, ARTHUR
BAD MEN OF MISSOURI (1941, First National/Warners)—Jim Younger
THE LUSTY MEN (1952, RKO)—Wes Merritt

KENNEDY, DOUGLAS
REVENUE AGENT (1950, Columbia)—Steve Adams

KENNEDY, EDGAR
THREE MEN ON A HORSE (1936, Warners)—Harry

KENNEDY, GEORGE
THE GOOD GUYS AND THE BAD GUYS (1969, Warners)—McKay

KENNEDY, LEON ISSAC
KNIGHTS OF THE CITY (1986, New World)—Troy

KENNEDY, MADGE
OUR LITTLE WIFE (1918, Silent, Goldwyn)—Dodo
A PERFECT LADY (1918, Silent, Goldwyn)—Lucille Le Jambon/Lucy Higgins

KENNEDY, SHEILA
ELLIE (1984, Film Ventures)—Ellie

KENNEY, JAMES
CIRCUS BOY (1947, GB, GFD)—Michael Scott
THE SLASHER (1953, GB, Lippert)—Roy Walsh
SON OF A STRANGER (1957, GB, United Artists)—Tom Adams

KENNEY, JUNE
TEENAGE DOLL (1957, Allied Artists)—Barbara

KENSIT, PATSY
ABSOLUTE BEGINNERS (1986, GB, Orion)—Suzette

KENT, BARBARA
GUARD THAT GIRL (1935, Columbia)—Jeanne

KENT, DOROTHEA
CARNIVAL QUEEN (1937, Universal)—Marion Prescott
SOME BLONDES ARE DANGEROUS (1937, Universal)—Rose Whitney

KENT, JEAN
THE GAY LADY (1949, GB, GFD)—Trottie True
GOOD TIME GIRL (1950, GB, Rank)—Gwen Rawlings
THE TAMING OF DOROTHY (1950, GB, Eagle-Lion)—Dorothy
THE RELUCTANT WIDOW (1951, GB, Fine Arts)—Elinor

KENT, ROBERT
CRIME OF DR. FORBES (1936, 20th Century Fox)—Dr. Michael Forbes
KING OF THE ROYAL MOUNTED (1936, 20th Century Fox)—Sgt. King

KENYON, DORIS
THE HALF-WAY GIRL (1925, Silent, First National)—Poppy La Rue
I WANT MY MAN (1925, Silent, First National)—Vida
IF I MARRY AGAIN (1925, Silent, First National)—Jocelyn Margot

THE BLONDE SAINT (1926, Silent, First National)—Ghirlaine Bellamy
LADIES AT PLAY (1926, Silent, First National)—Ann Harper

KERR, DEBORAH
THE ADVENTURESS (I SEE A DARK STRANGER) (1946, GB, General Films)—Birdie Quilty
THE KING AND I (1956, 20th Century Fox)—Anna Leonowens
THE SUNDOWNERS (1960, Warners)—Ida Carmody
PRUDENCE AND THE PILL (1968, GB, 20th Century Fox)—Prudence Hardcastle

KERRIGAN, J. WARREN
SAMSON (1914, Silent, Universal)—Samson
THE PRISONER OF THE PINES (1918, Silent, Paralta)—Hillaire Latour
THE JOYOUS LIAR (1919, Silent, Hodkinson/Pathe)—Burge Harlan
CAPTAIN BLOOD (1924, Silent, Vitagraph)—Peter Blood

KERRY, NORMAN
THE IRRESISTIBLE LOVER (1927, Silent, Universal)—J. Harrison Gray

KEVAN, JACK
THE MONSTER OF PIEDRAS BLANCAS (1959, Vanwick)—The Monster

KEYES, EVELYN
NINE GIRLS (1944, Columbia)—Mary O'Ryan
THE MATING OF MILLIE (1948, Columbia)—Millie McGonigle
MRS. MIKE (1949, United Artists)—Kathy O'Fallon

KEYLOUN, MARK
MIKE'S MURDER (1984, Warners)—Mike

KIBBEE, GUY
BABBITT (1934, First National/Warners)—George F. Babbitt
BIG HEARTED HERBERT (1934, Warners)—Herbert Kainess
MARY JANE'S PA (1935, First National)—Sam Preston
CAPTAIN JANUARY (1936, 20th Century Fox)—Capt. January
THE BIG SHOT (1937, RKO)—Mr. Simms
THE CAPTAIN'S KID (1937, First National/Warners)—Asa Plunkett
JIM HANVEY, DETECTIVE (1937, Republic)—Jim Hanvey
SCATTERGOD BAINES (1941, RKO)—Scattergood Baines
SCATTERGOOD MEETS BROADWAY (1941, RKO)—Scattergood Baines
SCATTERGOOD PULLS THE STRINGS (1941, RKO)—Scattergood Baines
SCATTERGOOD RIDES HIGH (1942, RKO)—Scattergood Baines
SCATTERGOOD SURVIVES A MURDER (1942, RKO)—Scattergood Baines

KIDD, RAE
UNASHAMED (1938, Cine-Grand)—Rae Lane

KIDDER, MARGOT
SISTERS (1973, American International)—Danielle Breton

KIEPURA, JAN
MY SONG FOR YOU (1935, GB, Gaumont)—Gatti

KIGER, ROBBY
CHILDREN OF THE CORN (1984, New World)—Job

KILBRIDE, PERCY
MA AND PA KETTLE (1949, Universal)—Pa Kettle
MA AND PA KETTLE GO TO TOWN (1950, Universal)—Pa Kettle
MA AND PA KETTLE BACK ON THE FARM (1951, Universal)—Pa Kettle
MA AND PA KETTLE AT THE FAIR (1952, Universal)—Pa Kettle
MA AND PA KETTLE ON VACATION (1953, Universal)—Pa Kettle
MA AND PA KETTLE AT HOME (1954, Universal)—Pa Kettle
MA AND PA KETTLE AT WAIKIKI (1955, Universal)—Pa Kettle

KILCULLEN, ROBERT
FINNEY (1969, Gold Coast)—Jim Finney

KILGAS, NANCY
SEVEN BRIDES FOR SEVEN BROTHERS (1954, MGM)—Alice

KILMER, VAL
REAL GENIUS (1985, Tri-Star)—Chris
THE DOORS (1991, Tri-Star)—Jim Morrison

KILMONIS, RUTA, *See* **RUTA LEE**

KIMBELL, ANNE
GIRLS AT SEA (1958, GB, Seven Arts)—Mary

KIMBROUGH, JOHN
LONE STAR RANGER (1942, 20th Century Fox)—Buck Duane
SUDDEN JIM (1942, 20th Century Fox)—Jim Majors

KIMMEL, ERIC
JOSHUA, THEN AND NOW (1985, Canada, 20th Century Fox)—Young Joshua Shapiro

KIMMELL, LESLIE
THE TALL TARGET (1951, MGM)—Abraham Lincoln

KING, ALAN
MEMORIES OF ME (1988, MGM/United Artists)—Abe Polin

KING, DENNIS
THE VAGABOND KING (1930, Paramount)—Francois Villon
THE DEVIL'S BROTHER (1933, MGM)—Fra Diavolo/Marquis de San Marco

KING, DIANA
THE SPELL OF AMY NUGENT (1945, GB, Pyramid)—Amy Nugent

KING, JOHN
THE THREE MUSKETEERS (1939, 20th Century Fox)—Aramis

KING, MOLLIE
HER MAJESTY (1922, Silent, Playgoers)—Rosalie Bowers

KING, MURRAY RAMSEY
KING, MURRAY (1969, Nowak/EYR)—King, Murray

KING, PERRY
THE POSSESSION OF JOEL DELANEY (1972, Paramount)—Joel Delaney
SWITCH (1991, Warner Brothers)—Steve Brooks

KING, WALTER WOOLF
MELODY FOR THREE (1941, RKO)—Antoine Pirelle

TODAY I HANG (1942, Producers Releasing Corp.)—Jim O'Brien
A YANK IN LIBYA (1942, Producers Releasing Corp.)—Mike Malone

KING, ZALMAN
SKI BUM (1971, Avco Embassy)—Johnny

KINGSLEY, BEN
GANDHI (1982, GB, Columbia)—Mahatma Gandhi
PASCALI'S ISLAND (1988, Avenue)—Basil Pascali

KINGSTON, NATALIE
HIS FIRST FLAME (1927, Silent, Sennett/Pathe Exchange)—Ethel Morgan

KINMONT, KATHLEEN
BRIDE OF THE RE-ANIMATOR (1991, Wildstreet Pictures)—The Bride

KINSKI, KLAUS
FITZCARRALDO (1982, New World)—Brian Sweeney Fitzgerald/Fitzcarraldo

KINSKI, NASTASSJA
TO THE DEVIL, A DAUGHTER (1976, GB, Hammer)—Catherine Beddows
TESS (1980, GB/France, Columbia)—Tess Durbeyfield
CAT PEOPLE (1982, Universal/RKO)—Irene Gallier
UNFAITHFULLY YOURS (1984, 20th Century Fox)—Daniella Eastman
MARIA'S LOVERS (1985, Cannon)—Maria Bosic

KIRBY, BRUNO
CITY SLICKERS (1991, Columbia)—Ed Furillo

KIRBY, JOYCE
THE COMPULSORY WIFE (1937, GB, Warners)—Bobby Carr

KIRK, TOMMY
THE SHAGGY DOG (1959, Buena Vista)—Wilby Daniels
THE MISADVENTURES OF MERLIN JONES (1964, Buena Vista)—Merlin Jones
THE MONKEY'S UNCLE (1965, Buena Vista)—Merlin Jones

KIRKHAM, KATHLEEN
THE INNOCENT CHEAT (1921, Silent, Arrow)—Mary Stanhope

KIRKLAND, SALLY
ANNA (1987, Magnus/Vestron)—Anna

KIRKWOOD, JAMES
BOB HAMPTON OF PLACER (1921, Silent, Associated First National)—Bob Hampton

KIRKWOOD, JOE JR.
JOE PALOOKA, CHAMP (1946, Monogram)—Joe Palooka
JOE PALOOKA IN WINNER TAKE ALL (1948, Monogram)—Joe Palooka
JOE PALOOKA IN THE BIG FIGHT (1949, Monogram)—Joe Palooka
JOE PALOOKA IN CONNECTICUT (1949, Monogram)—Joe Palooka
JOE PALOOKA IN THE SQUARED CIRCLE (1950, Monogram)—Joe Palooka

JOE PALOOKA MEETS HUMPHREY (1950, Monogram)—Joe
Palooka
JOE PALOOKA IN THE TRIPLE CROSS (1951, Monogram)—Joe
Palooka

KIRKWOOD, PAT
ONCE A SINNER (1952, GB, Argyle/Hoffberg)—Irene James

KISER, TERRY
WEEKEND AT BERNIE'S (1989, 20th Century Fox)—
Bernie Lomax

KITT, EARTHA
ANNA LUCASTA (1958, United Artists)—Anna Lucasta

KIVALINA
KIVALINA OF THE ICE LANDS (1925, Silent, B.C.R.
Productions)—Kivalina

KJELLIN, ALF
MY SIX CONVICTS (1952, Columbia)—Clem Randell

KLEIN, ROBERT
RIVALS (1972, Avco Embassy)—Peter Simon

KLEMPERER, WERNER
OPERATION EICHMANN (1961, Allied Artists)—Adolf Eichmann

KLINE, KEVIN
THE PIRATES OF PENZANCE (1983, Universal)—Pirate King
THE JANUARY MAN (1989, MGM-United Artists)—Nick Starkey
I LOVE YOU TO DEATH (1990, Tri-Star)—Joey Boca

KLUGMAN, JACK
12 ANGRY MEN (1957, United Artists)—Juror No. 5

KNAPP, EVALYN
AIR HOSTESS (1933, Columbia)—Kitty King
DANCE, GIRL, DANCE (1933, Invincible)—Sally
HIS PRIVATE SECRETARY (1933, Screencraft)—Marion Hall
LADIES CRAVE EXCITEMENT (1935, Mascot)—Wilma Howell

KNEPPER, ROB
WILD THING (1987, Atlantic)—Wild Thing

KNIEVEL, EVEL
VIVA KNIEVEL! (1977, Warners)—Evel Knievel

KNIGHT, CHRISTOPHER
STUDS LONIGAN (1960, United Artists)—Studs Lonigan

KNIGHT, ESMOND
THE BERMONDSEY KID (1933, GB, Warners/First National)—
Eddie Martin
FATHER AND SON (1934, GB, Warners)—Michael Bolton
STRAUSS' GREAT WALTZ (1934, GB, Gaumont)—Johann
"Shani" Strauss, Jr.

KNIGHT, FUZZY
LITTLE JOE, THE WRANGLER (1942, Universal)—Little
Joe Smith

KNIGHT, JAMES
THE KNAVE OF HEARTS (1919, Silent, GB, Harma)—Lord
Hillsdown

KNIGHT, JUNE
LADIES MUST LOVE (1933, Universal)—Jeannie

KNIGHT, MICHAEL E.
DATE WITH AN ANGEL (1987, De Laurentiis)—Jim Sanders

KNIGHT, SHIRLEY
THE GROUP (1966, United Artists)—Polly Andrews
THE RAIN PEOPLE (1969, Warners)—Natalie Ravenna

KNOTTS, DON
THE INCREDIBLE MR. LIMPET (1964, Warners)—Henry Limpet
THE GHOST AND MR. CHICKEN (1966, Universal)—
Luther Heggs
THE RELUCTANT ASTRONAUT (1967, Universal)—Roy Fleming
THE LOVE GOD? (1969, Universal)—Abner Audubon Peacock
THE PRIVATE EYES (1980, New World)—Inspector Winship

KNOWLES, PATRIC
THE STUDENT'S ROMANCE (1936, GB, British International)—
Max Brandt
THE PATIENT IN ROOM 18 (1938, Warners)—Lance O'Leary

KNOX, ALEXANDER
THE PHANTOM STRIKES (1939, GB, Monogram)—Dr. Lomond/
"The Ringer"
WILSON (1944, 20th Century Fox)—Thomas Woodrow Wilson
OVER 21 (1945, Columbia)—Max Wharton
THE JUDGE STEPS OUT (1949, RKO)—Judge Bailey
ONE JUST MAN (1955, GB, Pathe)—Judge Craig

KNOX, ELYSE
A WAVE, A WAC AND A MARINE (1944, Monogram)—Marian
SWEETHEART OF SIGMA CHI (1946, Monogram)—Betty Allen
LINDA BE GOOD (1947, Producers Releasing Corp.)—Linda
Prentiss
THERE'S A GIRL IN MY HEART (1949, Allied Artists)—Claire
Adamson

KOHLER, FRED
HELL'S HEROES (1930, Universal)—Wild Bill Kearney

KOMAI, TETSU
SECRETS OF WU SIN (1932, Invincible/Chesterfield)—Wu Sin

KONSTAM, PHYLLIS
TILLY OF BLOOMSBURY (1931, GB, Sterling)—Tilly Welwyn

KONSTRAM, ANNA
THEY DRIVE BY NIGHT (1938, GB, Warners)—Molly O'Neill

KORBUT, WILLIAM
ISSAC LITTLEFEATHERS (1984, Canada, Cinema Concepts/
London)—Issac Littlefeathers

KORSMO, CHARLIE
MEN DON'T LEAVE (1990, Warners)—Matt Macauley

KORTNER, FRITZ
ABDUL THE DAMNED (1935, GB, British International)—Abdul
Hamid II
THE CROUCHING BEAST (1936, RKO)—Ahmed Bey

KORVIN, CHARLES
ENTER ARSENE LUPIN (1944, Universal)—Arsene Lupin

THIS LOVE OF OURS (1945, Universal)—Michel Touzac

KORY, DAVID
DONDI (1961, Allied Artists)—Dondi

KOTERO, APOLLONIA
BLACK MAGIC WOMAN (1991, Trimark Pictures)—
Cassandra Perry

KRAUSE, BRIAN
SLEEPWALKER (1992, Columbia)—Charles Brady

KREUGER, KURT
MADEMOISELLE FIFI (1944, RKO)—Lt. von Eyrick

KRIGE, ALICE
SEE YOU IN THE MORNING (1989, Warners)—Beth Goodwin
SLEEPWALKER (1992, Columbia)—Mary Brady

KRIMS, MILTON
UNMASKED (1929, Artclass)—Prince Hamid

KRISTEL, SYLVIA
MATA HARI (1985, Cannon)—Mata Hari
DRACULA'S WIDOW (1988, DEG)—Vanessa

KRISTIEN, STANLEY
THE YOUNG SAVAGES (1961, United Artists)—Danny di Pace

KRISTOFFERSON, KRIS
CISCO PIKE (1971, Columbia)—Cisco Pike
PAT GARRETT AND BILLY THE KID (1973, MGM)—Billy the Kid
THE SAILOR WHO FELL FROM GRACE WITH THE SEA (1976, GB, Avco Embassy)—Jim Cameron

KROEGER, GARY
A MAN CALLED SARGE (1990, Cannon)—Sarge

KRUGER, HARDY
BACHELOR OF HEARTS (1958, GB, Rank)—Wolf Hauser
THE ONE THAT GOT AWAY (1958, GB, Rank)—Franz von Werra

KRUGER, OTTO
THE CRIME DOCTOR (1934, Radio Pictures)—Dan Gifford
SPRINGTIME FOR HENRY (1934, Fox)—Henry Dewlip
COUNSEL FOR CRIME (1937, Columbia)—William Mellon
HOUSEMASTER (1938, GB, Associated British)—Charles Donkin
DISBARRED (1939, Paramount)—Tyler Cradon
THE BIG BOSS (1941, Columbia)—Jim Maloney
EARL CARROLL'S VANITIES (1945, Republic)—Earl Carroll

KUHN, T.J.
RAISING ARIZONA (1987, 20th Century Fox)—Nathan Arizona Jr.

KUNOGH, NARLA
JEDDA, THE UNCIVILIZED (1956, Australia, Distributors Corp. of America) - Jedda

KUROWSKI, RON
THE CREATURE WASN'T NICE (1981, Creature Features)—The Creature

KWAN, NANCY
THE WORLD OF SUZIE WONG (1960, Paramount)—Suzie Wong

TAMAHINE (1964, GB, MGM)—Tamahine

L

LA MARR, BARBARA
HEART OF A SIREN (1925, Silent, First National)—Isabella Echevaria

LA PLANTE, LAURA
BUTTERFLY (1924, Silent, Universal)—Dora Collier
THE BEAUTIFUL CHEAT (1926, Silent, Universal)—Mary Callahan
HER BIG NIGHT (1926, Silent, Universal)—Frances Norcross/ Daphne Dix
MEET THE WIFE (1931, Columbia)—Gertrude Lennox
HER IMAGINARY LOVER (1933, GB, First National/ Warners)—Celia
THE CHURCH MOUSE (1934, GB, Warners)—Betty Miller
GIRL IN POSSESSION (1934, GB, First National)—Eve Chandler
WIDOW'S MIGHT (1934, GB, Warners)—Nancy Tweesdale

LA ROCQUE, ROD
THE COMING OF AMOS (1925, Silent, Cinema Corp. of America)—Amos Burden
CAPTAIN SWAGGER (1928, Silent, Pathe Exchange)—Captain Swagger (Hugh Drummond)
BEAU BANDIT (1930, RKO)—Montero
THE SHADOW STRIKES (1937, Grand National)—"The Shadow"

LA RUE, JACK
GENTLEMAN FROM DIXIE (1941, Monogram)—Thad Terrill
HARD GUY (1941, Producers Releasing Corp.)—Vic

LA RUE, LASH
CHEYENNE TAKES OVER (1947, Eagle-Lion)—Cheyenne
KING OF THE BULLWHIP (1950, Real Art)—Lash La Rue

LACTEEN, FRANK
HAWK OF THE HILLS (1929, Silent, Pathe Exchange)—The Hawk

LADD, ALAN
LUCKY JORDAN (1942, Paramount)—Lucky Jordan
THIS GUN FOR HIRE (1942, Paramount)—Philip Raven
SALTY O'ROURKE (1945, Paramount)—Salty O'Rourke
WHISPERING SMITH (1948, Paramount)—Luke "Whispering" Smith
THE GREAT GATSBY (1949, Paramount)—Jay Gatsby
CAPTAIN CAREY, U.S.A. (1950, Paramount)—Webster Carey
SHANE (1953, Paramount)—Shane
THE BLACK KNIGHT (1954, Columbia)—John, the Black Knight
PARATROOPER (1954, GB, Columbia)—Canada MacKendrick
THE MCCONNELL STORY (1955, Warners)—Joseph C. "Mac" McConnell
THE PROUD REBEL (1958, Buena Vista)—John Chandler
THE MAN IN THE NET (1959, United Artists)—John Hamilton
ONE FOOT IN HELL (1960, 20th Century Fox)—Mitch Barrett

LADD, DAVID
RAYMIE (1960, Allied Artists)—Raymie

LAFFAN, PATRICIA
DEVIL GIRL FROM MARS (1954, GB, British Lion)—Nyah

LAHTI, CHRISTINE
JUST BETWEEN FRIENDS (1986, Orion)—Sandy Dunlap

LAIRD, JENNY
THE GIRL ON THE CANAL (1947, GB, Ealing)—Mary Smith
EYE WITNESS (1950, GB, Warners)—Mary Baxter

LAKE, ALICE
SHOULD A WOMAN TELL? (1920, Silent, Metro)—Meta Maxon
THE INFAMOUS MISS REVELL (1921, Silent, Metro)—Julien Revell/ Paula Revell

LAKE, ARTHUR
HAROLD TEEN (1928, Silent, First National)—Harold Teen
SAILOR'S HOLIDAY (1944, Columbia)—Marble Head Tomkins
THE BIG SHOW-OFF (1945, Republic)—Sandy Elliott
BLONDIE'S HERO (1950, Columbia)—Dagwood Bumstead

LAKE, VERONICA
I MARRIED A WITCH (1942, Paramount/United Artists)—Jennifer
HOLD THAT BLONDE (1945, Paramount)—Sally Martin
THE SAINTED SISTERS (1948, Paramount)—Letty Stanton

LAMARR, HEDY
LADY OF THE TROPICS (1939, MGM)—Manon De Vargnes
I TAKE THIS WOMAN (1940, MGM)—Georgi Gragore
ZIEGFELD GIRL (1941, MGM)—Sandra Kolter
HER HIGHNESS AND THE BELLBOY (1945, MGM)—Princess Veronica
THE STRANGE WOMAN (1946, United Artists)—Jenny Hager
DISHONORED LADY (1947, United Artists)—Madeleine Damien
SAMSON AND DELILAH (1949, Paramount)—Delilah
A LADY WITHOUT A PASSPORT (1950, MGM)—Marianne Lorress
MY FAVORITE SPY (1951, RKO)—Lily Dalbray
THE FEMALE ANIMAL (1958, Universal)—Vanessa Windsor

LAMAS, LORENZO
NIGHT OF THE WARRIOR (1991, Trimark)—Miles Keane

LAMBERT, CHRISTOPHER
GREYSTOKE: THE LEGEND OF TARZAN (1984, Warners)—John Clayton/ Tarzan
HIGHLANDER (1986, 20th Century Fox)—Connor MacLeod
THE SICILIAN (1987, 20th Century Fox)—Salvatore Giuliano
WHY ME? (1990, Triumph)—Gus Cardinal

LAMONT, MOLLY
HIS WIFE'S MOTHER (1932, GB, British International)—Cynthia
LUCKY GIRL (1932, GB, Wardour)—Lady Moira Cavendish-Gascoyne

LAMOS, MARK
LONGTIME COMPANION (1990, Goldwyn/American Playhouse)—Sean

LAMOUR, DOROTHY
THE JUNGLE PRINCESS (1936, Paramount)—Ulah
HER JUNGLE LOVE (1938, Paramount)—Tura
ALOMA OF THE SOUTH SEAS (1941, Paramount)—Aloma
MY FAVORITE BRUNETTE (1947, Paramount)—Carlotta Montay
GIRL FROM MANHATTAN (1948, United Artists)—Carol Maynard
LULU BELLE (1948, Columbia)—Lulu Belle
THE LUCKY STIFF (1949, United Artists)—Anna Marie St. Claire

LAMPERT, ZOHRA
LET'S SCARE JESSICA TO DEATH (1971, Paramount)—Jessica

LANAGAN, GLENN
THE AMAZING COLOSSAL MAN (1957, American International)—Lt. Col. Glenn Manning

LANCASTER, ANN
THE RAILWAY CHILDREN (1971, GB, Universal)—Ruth

LANCASTER, BURT
ALL MY SONS (1948, Universal)—Chris Keller
I WALK ALONE (1948, Paramount)—Frankie Madison
JIM THORPE — ALL AMERICAN (1951, Warners)—Jim Thorpe
TEN TALL MEN (1951, Columbia)—Sgt. Mike Kincaid
THE CRIMSON PIRATE (1952, Warners)—Vallo
HIS MAJESTY O'KEEFE (1953, Warners)—Capt. David O'Keefe
APACHE (1954, United Artists)—Massai
THE KENTUCKIAN (1955, United Artists)—Big Eli
THE RAINMAKER (1956, Paramount)—Bill Starbuck
ELMER GANTRY (1960, United Artists)—Elmer Gantry
BIRDMAN OF ALCATRAZ (1962, United Artists)—Robert Stroud
THE PROFESSIONALS (1966, Columbia)—Bill Dolworth
THE SWIMMER (1968, Columbia)—Ned Merrill
LAWMAN (1971, United Artists)—Marshal Jered Maddox
VALDEZ IS COMING (1971, United Artists)—Bob Valdez
THE MIDNIGHT MAN (1974, Universal)—Jim Slade
MOSES (1976, GB/Italy, Avco Embassy)—Moses
THE ISLAND OF DR. MOREAU (1977, American International)—Dr. Moreau
TOUGH GUYS (1986, Touchstone)—Harry Doyle
ROCKY GIBRALTAR (1988, Columbia)—Levi Rockwell

LANCHESTER, ELSA
THE BRIDE OF FRANKENSTEIN (1935, Universal)—The Bride of the Monster
LADIES IN RETIREMENT (1941, Columbia)—Emily Creed

LANDAU, MARTIN
THE FALL OF THE HOUSE OF USHER (1980, Sunn Classics)—Roderick Usher

LANDER, DAVID
THE STRANGE CASE OF DR. MANNING (1958, GB, Republic)—Dr. Manning

LANDERS, JUDY
DR. ALIEN (1989, Phantom)—Ms. Xenobia

LANDI, ELISSA
THE WOMAN IN ROOM 13 (1932, Fox)—Laura Ramsey
THE WARRIOR'S HUSBAND (1933, Fox)—Antiope
SISTERS UNDER THE SKIN (1934, Columbia)—Blossom Bailey
ENTER MADAME (1935, Paramount)—Lisa Della Robbia

LANDIS, CAROLE
THE POWERS GIRL (1942, United Artists)—Kay Evans

FOUR JILLS IN A JEEP (1944, 20th Century Fox)—Carole
Landis

LANDIS, CULLEN
YOUTH TO YOUTH (1922, Silent, Metro)—Page Brookins
THE FIGHTING COWARD (1924, Silent, Paramount)—Tom
Rumford
JACK O'HEARTS (1926, Silent, Hartford Productions)—Jack
Farber

LANDIS, JOHN
SCHLOCK (1973, Gazotskie/Harris)—The Schlockthropus

LANDIS, NINA
RIKKY AND PETE (1988, Australia, MGM/United
Artists)—Rikky

LANDON, JUDY
PREHISTORIC WOMEN (1950, Eagle Lion)—Eras

LANDON, LAURENCE
YELLOW HAIR AND THE FORTRESS OF GOLD (1984, Crown)—
Yellow Hair

LANDON, MICHAEL
I WAS A TEENAGE WEREWOLF (1957, American
International)—Tony
THE LEGEND OF TOM DOOLEY (1959, Columbia)—Tom Dooley

LANDOR, ROSALYN
THE DEVIL'S BRIDE (1968, GB, Hammer)—Peggy de Richleau

LANDRY, KAREN
PATTI ROCKS (1988, FilmDallas)—Patti Rocks

LANDSBERG, DAVID
DETECTIVE SCHOOL DROP OUTS (1986, Orion)—Donald

LANE, ALLAN
THE DUKE COMES BACK (1937, Republic)—Duke

LANE, DIANE
TOUCHED BY LOVE (1980, Columbia)—Karen
CATTLE ANNIE AND LITTLE BRITCHES (1981, Universal)—
Jenny/Little Britches
LADY BEWARE (1987, International Video Entertainment)—
Katya Yarno

LANE, LOLA
THE GIRL FROM HAVANA (1929, Fox)—Joan Anders
PUBLIC STENOGRAPHER (1935, Screencraft/Marcy)—Ann
McNair
FOUR DAUGHTERS (1938, Warners)—Thea Lemp
TORCHY BLANE IN PANAMA (1938, Warners)—Torchy Blane
DAUGHTERS COURAGEOUS (1939, Warners)—Linda Masters
FOUR WIVES (1939, Warners)—Thea Lemp Crowley
FOUR MOTHERS (1941, Warners)—Thea Lemp Crowley
MISS V FROM MOSCOW (1942, Producers Releasing Corp.)—
Vera Marova

LANE, LUPINO
A FRIENDLY HUSBAND (1923, Silent, Fox)—Friend Husband
THE DEPUTY DRUMMER (1935, GB, Columbia)—
Adolphus Miggs

LANE, PRISCILLA
FOUR DAUGHTERS (1938, Warners)—Ann Lemp

DAUGHTERS COURAGEOUS (1939, Warners)—Buff Masters
FOUR WIVES (1939, Warners)—Ann Lemp Dietz
YES, MY DARLING DAUGHTER (1939, Warners)—Ellen Murray
FOUR MOTHERS (1941, Warners)—Ann Lemp Dietz
MILLION DOLLAR BABY (1941, Warners)—Pamela McAllister

LANE, ROSEMARY
FOUR DAUGHTERS (1938, Warners)—Kay Lemp
GOLD DIGGERS IN PARIS (1938, Warners)—Kay Morrow
DAUGHTERS COURAGEOUS (1939, Warners)—Tinka Masters
FOUR WIVES (1939, Warners)—Kay Lemp Forrest
FOUR MOTHERS (1941, Warners)—Kay Lemp Forrest

LANE, SARAH
I SAW WHAT YOU DID (1965, Universal)—Kit

LANE, VICKY
JUNGLE CAPTIVE (1945, Universal)—Paula the Ape Woman

LANG, ANTHONY
TONY DRAWS A HORSE (1951, GB, Rank)—Tony Fleming

LANG, JUNE
NANCY STEELE IS MISSING (1937, 20th Century Fox)—Nancy
Steele
MEET THE GIRLS (1938, 20th Century Fox)—Judy Davis
REDHEAD (1941, Monogram)—Dale Carter

LANG, MATHESON
THE WARE CASE (1917, Silent, GB, FBO)—Sir Hubert Ware
MR. WU (1919, Silent, GB, Stoll)—Mr. Wu
SLAVES OF DESTINY (1924, GB, Silent, Stoll)—Luke Charnock
THE QUALIFIED ADVENTURER (1925, GB, Silent, Stoll)—
Peter Duff
THE GREAT DEFENDER (1934, GB, Wardour)—Sir
Douglas Rolls
DRAKE THE PIRATE (1935, GB, Wardour)—Francis Drake
THE CARDINAL (1936, GB, Pathe)—Cardinal De Medici

LANG, PERRY
JOCKS (1987, Crown)—Jeff

LANGDON, HARRY
THE STRONG MAN (1926, Silent, First National)—Paul Bergot
HIS FIRST FLAME (1927, Silent, Sennett/Pathe Exchange)—
Harry Howells

LANGE, JESSICA
FRANCES (1982, Universal)—Frances Farmer

LANGELLA, FRANK
DRACULA (1979, Universal)—Count Dracula
MEN'S CLUB (1986, Paramount)—Harold Canterbury

LANGFORD, FRANCES
CAREER GIRL (1944, Producers Releasing Corp.)—Joan
THE BAMBOO BLONDE (1946, RKO)—Louise Anderson

LANGRICK, MARGARET
MY AMERICAN COUSIN (1986, Canada, Spectrafilm)—Sandy
Wilcox
HARRY AND THE HENDERSONS (1987, Universal)—Sarah
Henderson

LANSBURY, ANGELA
THE LADY VANISHES (1980, GB, Rank)—Miss Froy

LANSING, ROBERT
4D MAN (1959, Universal)—Scott Nelson

LANZA, MARIO
THE TOAST OF NEW ORLEANS (1950, MGM)—Pepe Abellard Duvalle
THE GREAT CARUSO (1951, MGM)—Enrico Caruso

LARRIMORE, FRANCINE
JOHN MEADE'S WOMAN (1937, Paramount)—Teddy Connor

LARSEN, KEITH
SON OF BELLE STARR (1953, Allied Artists)—The Kid
APACHE WARRIOR (1957, 20th Century Fox)—Apache Kid

LARSON, BOBBY
FIVE LITTLE PEPPERS AT HOME (1940, Columbia)—Davie Pepper
FIVE LITTLE PEPPERS IN TROUBLE (1940, Columbia)—Davie Pepper
OUT WEST WITH THE PEPPERS (1940, Columbia)—Davie Pepper

LATIMER, ROSS
THREE DESPERATE MEN (1951, Lippert)—Matt Denton

LATTANZI, MATT
MY TUTOR (1983, Crown International)—Bobby Chrystal

LAUCK, CHESTER
PARTNERS IN TIME (1946, RKO)—Lum
LUM AND ABNER ABROAD (1956, Howco)—Lum

LAUGHLIN, TOM
THE YOUNG SINNER (1957, United Screens)—Chris Wotan
BILLY JACK (1971, Warners)—Billy Jack
THE TRIAL OF BILLY JACK (1974, Taylor-Laughlin)—Billy Jack
THE MASTER GUN FIGHTER (1975, Taylor-Laughlin)—Finley
BILLY JACK GOES TO WASHINGTON (1977, Taylor-Laughlin)—Billy Jack

LAUGHTON, CHARLES
DEVIL AND THE DEEP (1932, Paramount)—Cmdr. Charles Sturm
THE PRIVATE LIFE OF HENRY VIII (1933, United Artists)—Henry VIII
THE BARRETTS OF WIMPOLE STREET (1934, MGM)—Edward Moulton Barrett
RUGGLES OF RED GAP (1935, Paramount)—Marmaduke Ruggles
REMBRANDT (1936, GB, United Artists)—Rembrandt van Rijn
THE BEACHCOMBER (1938, GB, Mayflower/Paramount)—Ginger Ted
THE HUNCHBACK OF NOTRE DAME (1939, RKO)—Quasimodo
THEY KNEW WHAT THEY WANTED (1940, RKO)—Tony
TUTTLES OF TAHITI (1942, RKO)—Jonas Tuttle
THE MAN FROM DOWN UNDER (1943, MGM)—Jocko Wilson
THIS LAND IS MINE (1943, RKO)—Arthur Lory
THE CANTERVILLE GHOST (1944, MGM)—The Canterville Ghost
THE SUSPECT (1944, Universal)—Philip
CAPTAIN KIDD (1945, United Artists)—Capt. William Kidd
ABBOTT AND COSTELLO MEET CAPTAIN KIDD (1952, Warners)—Captain Kidd

HOBSON'S CHOICE (1954, GB, British Lion)—Henry Horatio Hobson

LAURE, CAROL
THE SURROGATE (1984, Cinepix)—Anouk Van Derlin
MARIA CHAPDELAINE (1986, Canada, The Movie Store)—Maria Chapdelaine

LAUREL, STAN
BABES IN TOYLAND (1934, MGM)—Stanley Dum
OUR RELATIONS (1936, MGM)—Stan & Alfie Laurel
THE FLYING DEUCES (1939, RKO)—Stan
A CHUMP AT OXFORD (1940, United Artists)—Stan
SAPS AT SEA (1940, United Artists)—Stanley
AIR RAID WARDENS (1943, MGM)—Stan
THE DANCING MASTERS (1943, 20th Century Fox)—Stanley
JITTERBUGS (1943, 20th Century Fox)—Stan Laurel

LAURENT, AGNES
FRENCH MISTRESS (1960, GB, British Lion)—Madeleine Lefarge
MARY HAD A LITTLE (1961, GB, United Artists)—Mary Kirk

LAURIE, JANE
FOREIGN BODY (1986, GB, Orion)—Jo Masters

LAURIE, PIPER
RUBY (1977, Dimension)—Ruby Clarie

LAUTER, ED
THE MAGNIFICENT SEVEN RIDE (1972, United Artists)—Scott Elliott

LAW, JOHN PHILLIP
VON RICHTHOFEN AND BROWN (9170, United Artists)—Baron Manfred von Richthofen
THE GOLDEN VOYAGE OF SINBAD (1974, GB, Columbia)—Sinbad

LAWFORD, PETER
MY BROTHER TALKS TO HORSES (1946, MGM)—John S. Penrose
YOU FOR ME (1952, MGM)—Tony Brown
OCEAN'S ELEVEN (1960, Warners)—Jimmy Foster
SERGEANTS 3 (1962, United Artists)—Sgt. Larry Barrett
SALT & PEPPER (1968, GB, United Artists)—Christopher Pepper

LAWRENCE, GERTRUDE
LORD CAMBER'S LADIES (1932, GB, British International)—Shirley Neville
MIMI (1935, GB, Alliance)—Mimi

LAWRENCE, JOEY
OLIVER & COMPANY (1988, Buena Vista)—Voice of Oliver

LAWRENCE, MITTIE
NIGHT CALL NURSES (1974, New World)—Sandra

LAWSON, DENIS
LOCAL HERO (1983, GB, Warners)—Urquhart

LAWSON, WILFRID
PASTOR HALL (1940, GB, United Artists)—Pastor Frederick Hall
THE TERROR (1941, GB, Alliance)—Goodman

THE GREAT MR. HANDEL (1942, GB, GHW/Midfilm)—George
Frederick Handel

LAWTON, FRANK
YOUNG WOODLEY (1930, GB, British International)—Woodley
DAVID COPPERFIELD (1935, MGM)—David Copperfield
as a man
THE SECRET FOUR (1940, GB, Ealing)—Terry

LAYE, EVELYN
PRINCESS CHARMING (1935, GB, Gaumont)—Princess
Charming

LE, THUY THU
CASUALTIES OF WAR (1989, Columbia)—Oahn

LE BROCK, KELLY
THE WOMAN IN RED (1984, Orion)—Charlotte

LE MAT, PAUL
ALOHA, BOBBY AND ROSE (1975, Columbia)—Bobby
MELVIN AND HOWARD (1980, Universal)—Melvin Dummar
P.K. & THE KID (1987, Sunn Classics/Lorimar)—William
"Kid" Kane

LE MESURIER, JOHN
JACK THE RIPPER (1959, GB, Paramount)—Dr. Tranter
THE SANDWICH MAN (1966, GB, Rank)—The Sandwich Man

LE ROY, HAL
HAROLD TEEN (1934, Warners)—Harold Teen

LEACHMAN, CLORIS
CRAZY MAMA (1975, New World)—Melba

LEAKE, JIMMY
FIVE LITTLE PEPPERS AND HOW THEY GREW (1939,
Columbia)—Davie Pepper

LEASE, REX
CLANCY'S KOSHER WEDDING (1927, Silent, R-C Pictures)—
Tom Clancy
TROOPERS THREE (1930, Tiffany)—Eddie Haskins

LEBEDEFF, IVAN
THE GAY DIPLOMAT (1931, RKO)—Capt. Orloff

LEDERER, FRANCIS
MY AMERICAN WIFE (1936, Paramount)—Count Ferdinand von
und su Raidenach
THE LONE WOLF IN PARIS (1938, Columbia)—Michael
Lanyard
CONFESSIONS OF A NAZI SPY (1939, Warners)—Schneider
THE MAN I MARRIED (1940, 20th Century Fox)—Eric Hoffman
THE RETURN OF DRACULA (1958, United Artists)—Bellac

LEE, ANNA
MY LIFE WITH CAROLINE (1941, RKO)—Caroline Mason
G.I. WAR BRIDES (1946, Republic)—Linda Powell
SEVEN WOMEN (1966, MGM)—Mrs. Russell

LEE, ANNABELLE
COMMON LAW WIFE (1963, Texas Film Producers)—Linda

LEE, CHRISTOPHER
ALIAS JOHN PRESTON (1956, GB, British Lion)—John Preston
THE HORROR OF DRACULA (1958, GB, Hammer/Universal)—
Count Dracula

THE HOUND OF THE BASKERVILLES (1959, GB, Hammer)—Sir
Henry Baskerville
THE MUMMY (1959, GB, Hammer)—Kharis
THE PIRATES OF BLOOD RIVER (1962, GB, Hammer)—
LaRoche
THE FACE OF FU MANCHU (1965, GB, Seven Arts)—Fu
Manchu
DRACULA — PRINCE OF DARKNESS (1966, GB, Hammer)—
Count Dracula
RASPUTIN-THE MAD MONK (1966, GB, 20th Century Fox)—
Rasputin
THE BLOOD OF FU MANCHU (1968, GB, Udastex Films)—Fu
Manchu
THE CASTLE OF FU MANCHU (1968, GB, International
Cinema)—Fu Manchu
DRACULA HAS RISEN FROM HIS GRAVE (1968, GB, Hammer)—
Count Dracula
THE VENGEANCE OF FU MANCHU (1968, GB, Warners)—Fu
Manchu
THE SCARS OF DRACULA (1970, GB, Hammer-EMI)—Count
Dracula
TASTE THE BLOOD OF DRACULA (1970, GB, Hammer)—Count
Dracula
COUNT DRACULA (1971, GB, Filmer/Phoenix/Korona)—Count
Dracula
I, MONSTER (1971, GB, Amicus/Cannon)—Dr. Marlowe/
Mr. Blake
DRACULA A.D. 1972 (1972, GB, Hammer)—Count Dracula
THE MAN WITH THE GOLDEN GUN (1974, GB, United Artists)—
Scaramanga
THE KEEPER (1976, Canada, Lions Gate)—The Keeper
TO THE DEVIL, A DAUGHTER (1976, GB, Hammer)—Father
Michael Raynor
COUNT DRACULA AND HIS VAMPIRE BRIDE (1978, GB,
Hammer)—Dracula

LEE, DAVEY
SONNY BOY (1929, Warners)—Sonny Boy

LEE, GYPSY ROSE
BELLE OF THE YUKON (1944, RKO)—Belle DeValle

LEE, IDA
GRANDMOTHER'S HOUSE (1989, Omega)—Grandmother

LEE, LILA
THE ADORABLE CHEAT (1928, Silent, Chesterfield)—Marian
Dorsey
THE LITTLE WILD GIRL (1928, Silent, Trinity)—Marie Celeste
SECOND WIFE (1930, RKO)—Florence Wendell

LEE, MARY
THREE LITTLE SISTERS (1944, Republic)—Sue Scott

LEE, NORMA
WISE GIRLS (1930, MGM)—Kate Bence

LEE, SHARON
SECRETS OF A MODEL (1940, Continetal-Times)—Rita Wilson

LEHMANN, CARLA
TALK ABOUT JACQUELINE (1942, GB, MGM)—Jacqueline
Marlow

LEHR, ANNA
CIVILIZATION'S CHILD (1916, Silent, Triangle)—Berna

LEIBMAN, RON
THE SUPER COPS (1974, MGM/United Artists)—Dave Greenberg

LEIGH, BARBARA
THE STUDENT NURSES (1970, New World)—Priscilla

LEIGH, JANET
THE DOCTOR AND THE GIRL (1949, MGM)—Evelyn Heldon
LITTLE WOMEN (1949, MGM)—Meg March
CONFIDENTIAL CONNIE (1953, MGM)—Connie Bedloe
MY SISTER EILEEN (1955, Columbia)—Eileen Sherwood
JET PILOT (1957, RKO/Universal)—Anna

LEIGH, JENNIFER JASON
SISTER SISTER (1988, New World)—Lucy Bonnard

LEIGH, SUZANNA
THE PLEASURE GIRLS (1966, GB, Times Film)—Dee

LEIGH, VIVIEN
TWENTY-ONE DAYS TOGETHER (1940, GB, Columbia)—Wanda
THAT HAMILTON WOMAN (1941, United Artists)—Emma Hart Hamilton
CAESAR AND CLEOPATRA (1946, GB, Two Cities)—Cleopatra
ANNA KARENINA (1948, GB, Korda/British Lion)—Anna Karenina
THE ROMAN SPRING OF MRS. STONE (1961, Warners)—Karen Stone

LEIGH-HUNT, BARBARA
HENRY VIII AND HIS SIX WIVES (1972, GB, EMI/MGM)—Catherine Parr

LEIGHTON, MARGARET
SEVEN WOMEN (1966, MGM)—Agatha Andrews

LEIGHTON-PORTER, CHRISABEL
THE ADVENTURES OF JANE (1949, GB, New World)—Jane

LEMKOW, TUTTE
FIDDLER ON THE ROOF (1971, United Artists)—The Fiddler

LEMMON, CHRIS
WEEKEND WARRIORS (1986, The Movie Store)—Vince Tucker

LEMMON, JACK
COWBOY (1958, Columbia)—Frank Harris
GOOD NEIGHBOR SAM (1964, Columbia)—Sam Bissel
THE ODD COUPLE (1968, Paramount)—Felix Ungar
APRIL FOOLS (1969, Jaelm/National General)—Howard Brubaker
THE OUT-OF-TOWNERS (1970, Paramount)—George Kellerman
SAVE THE TIGER (1973, Paramount)—Harry Stoner
THE ENTERTAINER (1975, Seven Keys)—Archie Rice
THE PRISONER OF SECOND AVENUE (1975, Warners)—Mel
ALEX AND THE GYPSY (1976, 20th Century Fox)—Alexander Main
DAD (1989, Universal)—Jake Tremont

LEMON, GENEVIEVE
SWEETIE (1989, Australia, UGC)—Dawn 'Sweetie'

LENNIX, HARRY J.
THE FIVE HEARTBEATS (1991, 20th Century Fox)—Dresser

LENZ, KAY
BREEZY (1973, Universal)—Breezy

LEON
THE FIVE HEARTBEATS (1991, 20th Century Fox)—J.T.

LEONARD, JACK E.
THREE SAILORS AND A GIRL (1953, Warners)—Parky
FAT SPY (1966, Magna)—Irving/Herman

LEONARD, ROBERT SEAN
MY BEST FRIEND IS A VAMPIRE (1988, Kings Road)—Jeremy Capello

LEONELLI, ELISA
LULU (1978, Chase)—Lulu

LESLIE, GLADYS
MISS DULCIE FROM DIXIE (1919, Silent, Vitagraph)—Dulcie
SISTERS (1922, Silent, American Releasing)—Cherry Strickland

LESLIE, JOAN
TOO YOUNG TO KNOW (1945, Warners)—Sally Sawyer
CINDERELLA JONES (1946, Warners)—Judy Jones
JANIE GETS MARRIED (1946, Warners)—Janie Conway
THE SKIPPER SURPRISED HIS WIFE (1950, MGM)—Daphne Lattimer
FLIGHT NURSE (1953, Republic)—Lt. Polly Davis
THE WOMAN THEY ALMOST LYNCHED (1953, Republic)—Sally Maris

LESTER, BRUCE
THE FOOL AND THE PRINCESS (1948, GB, GFD)—Harry Granville

LESTER, BUDDY
OCEAN'S ELEVEN (1960, Warners)—Vincent Massler

LESTER, MARK
OLIVER! (1968, GB, Columbia)—Oliver Twist

LEVENE, SAM
THREE MEN ON A HORSE (1936, Warners)—Patsy

LEVIN, RACHEL
GABY—A TRUE STORY (1987, Tri-Star)—Gabriella "Gaby" Brimmer

LEVY, EUGENE
ARMED AND DANGEROUS (1986, Columbia)—Norman Kane

LEVY, JEREMY
RICH KIDS (1979, Allied Artists)—Jamie Harris

LEWIS, JERRY
SAILOR BEWARE (1951, Paramount)—Melvin Jones
THAT'S MY BOY (1951, Paramount)—"Junior" Jackson
JUMPING JACKS (1952, Paramount)—Hap Smith
THE STOOGE (1952, Paramount)—Ted Rogers
THE CADDY (1953, Paramount)—Joe Anthony
PARDNERS (1956, Paramount)—Wade Kingsley, Jr.
THE DELICATE DELINQUENT (1957, Paramount)—Sidney Pythias
THE SAD SACK (1957, Paramount)—Bixby

THE GEISHA BOY (1958, Paramount)—Gilbert Wooley
THE BELLBOY (1960, Paramount)—Stanley
CINDERFELLA (1960, Paramount)—Fella
THE ERRAND BOY (1961, Paramount)—Morty S. Tashman
THE LADIES' MAN (1961, Paramount)—Herbert H. Heebert
THE NUTTY PROFESSOR (1963, Paramount)—Prof. Julius Ferris Kelp
THE DISORDERLY ORDERLY (1964, Paramount)—Jerome Littlefield
THE PATSY (1964, Paramount)—Stanley Belt
THE BIG MOUTH (1967, Columbia)—Gerald Clamson

LEWIS, JOE
JAGUAR LIVES (1979, American International)—Jaguar

LEWIS, JULIETTE
MEET THE HOLLOWHEADS (1989, Moviestore)—Cindy Hollowhead

LEWIS, MITCHELL
JACQUES OF THE SILVER NORTH (1919, Silent, Select)—Jacques La Rouge

LEWIS, MONICA
AFFAIR WITH A STRANGER (1953, RKO)—Janet Boothe

LEWIS, RALPH
CASEY JONES (1927, Silent, Rayart)—Casey Jones
HELD BY THE LAW (1927, Silent, Universal)—George Travis

LEWIS, RICHARD
THE WRONG GUYS (1988, New World)—Rich

LEWIS, RONALD
STOP ME BEFORE I KILL (1961, GB, Columbia)—Alan Colby

LEWIS, TOMMY
THE CHANT OF JIMMIE BLACKSMITH (1980, Australia, Filmhouse Party Ltd.) - Jimmie Blacksmith

LHOEST, ANITA
CAPTIVE GIRL (1950, Columbia)—Joan

LICUDI, GABRIELLA
THE UNEARTHLY STRANGER (1964, GB, American International)—Julie Davidson

LIGHTNER, WINNIE
GOLD DIGGERS ON BROADWAY (1929, Warners)—Mabel
SHE COULDN'T SAY NO (1930, Warners)—Winnie Harper
GOLD DUST GERTIE (1931, Warners)—Gertie

LINAKER, KAY
GIRL FROM MANDALAY (1936, Republic)—Jeannie

LINCOLN, ABBEY
FOR LOVE OF IVY (1968, Palomar/Cinerama)—Ivy Moore

LINCOLN, ELMO
THE ROMANCE OF TARZAN (1918, Silent, First National)—Tarzan
TARZAN OF THE APES (1918, Silent, National Film)—Tarzan

LIND, CHARLES
ADAM HAD FOUR SONS (1941, Columbia)—Philip Stoddard

LIND, MYRTLE
NANCY COMES HOME (1918, Silent, Triangle)—Nancy Worthing

LINDEN, ERIC
GIRL LOVES BOY (1937, Grand National)—Robert Conrad
HERE'S FLASH CASEY (1937, Grand National)—Flash Casey

LINDEN, JENNIE
WOMEN IN LOVE (1969, GB, United Artists)—Ursula Brangwen

LINDER, LESLIE
MEN OF SHERWOOD FOREST (1957, GB, Hammer)—Little John (Little)

LINDSAY, MARGARET
THE LAW IN HER HANDS (1936, First National)—Mary Wentworth
PUBLIC ENEMY'S WIFE (1936, Warners)—Judith Maroc
THE SPOILERS (1942, Universal)—Helen Chester
NO PLACE FOR A LADY (1943, Columbia)—June Terry
HER SISTER'S SECRET (1946, Producers Releasing Corp.)—Renee

LINDSAY, ROBERT
BERT RIGBY, YOU'RE A FOOL (1989, Warners)—Bert Rigby

LINN-BAKER, MARK
MY FAVORITE YEAR (1982, MGM/United Artists)—Benjy Stone

LINOW, IVAN
THE UNHOLY THREE (1930, MGM)—Hercules

LIOTTA, RAY
DOMINICK AND EUGENE (1988, Orion)—Eugene Luciano
GOODFELLAS (1990, Warners)—Henry Hill

LIPMAN, NICOLA
MADELEINE IS (1971, Canada, Alliance)—Madeleine

LISI, VIRNA
NOT WITH MY WIFE, YOU DON'T (1966, Warners)—Julie Ferris

LISTER, MOIRA
WICKED WIFE (1955, GB, Allied Artists)—Babs Coates

LITEL, JOHN
FATHER'S SON (1941, Warners)—William Emory
MY BUDDY (1944, Republic)—Jim Connelly
THE GUILTY (1947, Monogram)—Alex Tremholt
THE DOLLAR BETTOR (1951, Real Art)—John Hewitt

LITHGOW, JOHN
HARRY AND THE HENDERSONS (1987, Universal)—George Henderson

LITTLE, ANN
NAN OF MUSIC MOUNTAIN (1917, Silent, Paramount)—Nan Morgan

LITTLE, MICHELLE
MY DEMON LOVER (1987, New Line Cinema)—Denny

LITTLE BILLY
THE TERROR OF TINY TOWN (1938, Columbia)—Haines

LIVELY, ROBYN
TEEN WITCH (1989, Trans World)—Louise

LIVESEY, ROGER
  COLONEL BLIMP (THE LIFE AND DEATH OF COLONEL
    BLIMP) (1945, GB, The Archers)—Clive Candy

LIVESEY, SAM
  HOUND OF THE BASKERVILLES (1939, 20th Century Fox)—Sir
    Hugo Baskerville

LIVINGSTON, MARGARET
  THE CHORUS LADY (1924, Silent, Regal)—Patricia O'Brien
  ACQUITTED (1929, Columbia)—Marian
  MORGAN'S MARUADERS (1929, Distinctive)—Capt. Lucy
    Morgan

LIVINGSTON, ROBERT
  BOLD CABALLERO (1936, Republic)—Zorro
  THE THREE MESQUITEERS (1936, Republic)—Stony Brooke
  THE TRAIL BLAZERS (1940, Republic)—Stony Brooke
  PALS OF THE PECOS (1941, Republic)—Stony Brooke
  SADDLEMATES (1941, Republic)—Stony Brooke

LLOSA, JUANITA
  DAUGHTER OF THE SUN GOD (1962, Condor)—Daughter of the
    Sun God

LLOYD, CHRISTOPHER
  THE DREAM TEAM (1989, Universal)—Henry Sikorsky
  THE ADDAMS FAMILY (1991, Paramount)—Uncle Fester
    Addams
  SUBURBAN COMMANDO (1991, New Line)—Charlie Wilcox

LLOYD, DORIS
  CHARLEY'S AUNT (1930, Columbia)—Donna D'Alvadoes
  SISTERS UNDER THE SKIN (1934, Columbia)—Elinor Yates

LLOYD, EMILY
  COOKIE (1989, Warners)—Carmella 'Cookie' Voltecki
  CHICAGO JOE AND THE SHOWGIRL (1990, GB, Palace)—
    Georgina Grayson

LLOYD, HAROLD
  A SAILOR-MADE MAN (1921, Silent, Pathe)—The Boy
  DOCTOR JACK (1922, Silent, Hal Roach)—Dr. Jack
  GRANDMA'S BOY (1922, Silent, Associated Exhibitors)—
    The Boy
  GIRL SHY (1924, Silent, Pathe)—Harold Meadows
  THE FRESHMAN (1925, Silent, Pathe Exchange)—Harold
    "Speedy" Lamb
  THE KID BROTHER (1927, Silent, Paramount)—Harold Hickey
  SPEEDY (1928, Silent, Paramount)—Harold "Speedy" Swift
  PROFESSOR BEWARE (1938, Paramount)—Prof. Dean Lambert

LLOYD, NORMAN
  SABOTEUR (1942, Universal)—Frank Fry

LO BIANCO, TONY
  BLOODBROTHERS (1978, Kings Road/Warners)—Tommy
    DeCoco

LOCKE, SONDRA
  THE SECOND COMING OF SUZANNE (1974, Barry)—Suzanne

LOCKHART, JUNE
  SHE-WOLF OF LONDON (1946, Universal)—Phyllis Allenby

LOCKWOOD, HAROLD
  BIG TREMAINE (1916, Silent, Metro)—John Tremaine, Jr.

LOCKWOOD, MARGARET
  THE GIRL IN THE NEWS (1941, GB, Fox British)—Anne
    Graham
  A GIRL MUST LIVE (1941, GB, Gainsborough)—Leslie James
  BEDELIA (1946, GB, General Films)—Bedelia
  THE WICKED LADY (1936, GB, Gainsborough)—Barbara Worth,
    Lady Skelton
  A LADY SURRENDERS (1947, GB, Gainsborough)—Lissa
    Campbell
  LAUGHING ANNIE (1954, GB, Republic)—Laughing Annie

LODEN, BARBARA
  WANDA (1971, Bardene International)—Wanda

LODER, JOHN
  MAXWELL ARCHER, MASTER DETECTIVE (1942, GB,
    Monogram)—Maxwell Archer
  THE BRIGHTON STRANGLER (1945, RKO)—Reginald

LODGE, JOHN
  BULLDOG DRUMMOND COMES BACK (1937, Paramount)—
    Bulldog Drummond

LOEB, PHILIP
  THE GOLDBERGS (1950, Paramount)—Jake Goldberg

LOFF, JEANETTE
  PARTY GIRL (1930, Tiffany)—Ellen Powell

LOGAN, JACQUELEINE
  SALOMY JANE (1923, Silent, Paramount)—Salomy Jane
  THE LEOPARD LADY (1928, Silent, Pathe)—Paula
  THE RIVER WOMAN (1928, Gotham/Lumas)—The Duchess
  THE BACHELOR GIRL (1929, Part-Talkie, Columbia)—Joyce

LOGAN, ROBERT
  MAN OUTSIDE (1988, Virgin Vision)—Jack Avery

LOLLOBRIGIDA, GINA
  SOLOMON AND SHEBA (1959, United Artists)—Magda, Queen
    of Sheba
  WOMAN OF STRAW (1964, GB, United Artists)—Maria
  STRANGE BEDFELLOWS (1965, Universal)—Toni Vincente
  BUONA SERA, MRS. CAMPBELL (1968, United Artists)—Mrs.
    Campbell

LOM, HERBERT
  THE PHANTOM OF THE OPERA (1962, GB, Universal)—Erik,
    the Phantom

LOMBARD, CAROLE
  I TAKE THIS WOMAN (1931, Paramount)—Kay Dowling
  SINNERS IN THE SUN (1932, Paramount)—Doris Blake
  NO MAN OF HER OWN (1933, Paramount)—Connie Randall
  WHITE WOMAN (1933, Paramount)—Judith Denning
  THE GAY BRIDE (1934, MGM)—Mary Magiz
  MY MAN GODFREY (1936, Universal)—Irene Bullock
  THE PRINCESS COMES ACROSS (1936, Paramount)—
    Princess Olga
  MADE FOR EACH OTHER (1939, United Artists)—Jane Mason
  THEY KNEW WHAT THEY WANTED (1940, RKO)—Amy

MR. AND MRS. SMITH (1941, RKO)—Ann Smith

LONE, JOHN
ICEMAN (1984, Universal)—Charlie
THE LAST EMPEROR (1987, Columbia)—Aisin-Gioro
"Henry" Pu Yi

LONG, LOTUS
LAST OF THE PAGANS (1936, MGM)—Lilleo
TOKYO ROSE (1945, Paramount)—Tokyo Rose

LONG, SHELLEY
IRRECONCILABLE DIFFERENCES (1984, Warners)—Lucy Van
Patten Brodsky
HELLO AGAIN (1987, Buena Vista)—Lucy Chadman

LONGDEN, JOHN
THE SILENCE OF DEAN MAITLAND (1934, Australia,
Cinesound)—Dean Maitland

LONGFELLOW, MALVINA
MARY LATIMER, NUN (1920, Silent, GB, Famous Pictures)—
Mary Latimer

LOOBY, ANNE
STRANGERS (1990, Australia, Genesis)—Anna

LOPEZ, TRINI
THE DIRTY DOZEN (1967, GB, MGM)—Pedro Jiminez

LORD, JACK
THE COUNTERFEIT KILLER (1969, Universal)—Don Owens

LORD, MARJORIE
THE STRANGE MRS. CRANE (1948, Eagle Lion)—Gina Crane

LORD, PAULINE
MRS. WIGGS OF THE CABBAGE PATCH (1934, Paramount)—
Mrs. Elvira Wiggs

LOREN, SOPHIA
THAT KIND OF WOMAN (1959, Paramount)—Kay
HELLER IN PINK TIGHTS (1960, Paramount)—Angela Rossini
THE MILLIONAIRESS (1960, GB, 20th Century Fox)—Epifania
Parerga
JUDITH (1965, Paramount)—Judith
A COUNTESS FROM HONG KONG (1967, GB, Rank)—Natasha
ANGELA (1977, Canada, Montreal Travel Co.)—Angela

LORRAINE, LOUISE
THE WILD GIRL (1925, Silent, Truart)—Pattie

LORRE, PETER
THANK YOU MR. MOTO (1937, 20th Century Fox)—Mr. Moto
THINK FAST MR. MOTO (1937, 20th Century Fox)—Mr. Moto
MR. MOTO TAKES A CHANCE (1938, 20th Century Fox)—
Mr. Moto
MR. MOTO TAKES A VACATION (1938, 20th Century Fox)—
Mr. Moto
MR. MOTO'S GAMBLE (1938, 20th Century Fox)—Mr. Moto
MYSTERIOUS MR. MOTO (1938, 20th Century Fox)—Mr. Moto
MR. MOTO IN DANGER ISLAND (1939, 20th Century Fox)—
Mr. Moto
MR. MOTO'S LAST WARNING (1939, 20th Century Fox)—
Mr. Moto

STRANGER ON THE THIRD FLOOR (1940, RKO)—Stranger
THE FACE BEHIND THE MASK (1941, Columbia)—Janos Szabo
THREE STRANGERS (1946, Warners)—Johnny West

LORCH, THEODORE
THE LAST OF THE MOHICANS (1920, Silent, AP)—
Chingachgook

LOTINGA, ERNIE
DR. JOSSER KC (1931, GB, Pathe)—Jimmy Josser
P.C. JOSSER (1931, GB, Gainsborough)—Jimmy Josser
JOSSER IN THE ARMY (1932, GB, British International)—
Jimmy Josser
JOSSER JOINS THE NAVY (1932, GB, British International)—
Jimmy Josser
JOSSER ON THE RIVER (1932, GB, British International)—
Jimmy Josser
JOSSER ON THE FARM (1934, GB, 20th Century Fox)—Jimmy
Josser

LOUIS, WILLARD
BABBITT (1924, Silent, Warners)—George F. Babbitt

LOUISE, ANITA
EVERYTHING'S ROSIE (1931, Radio Pictures)—Rosie
THE SISTERS (1938, Warners)—Helen Elliott
THE VILLAIN STILL PURSUED HER (1940, RKO)—Mary
TWO IN A TAXI (1941, Columbia)—Bonnie
NINE GIRLS (1944, Columbia)—Paula Canfield

LOUISE, TINA
THE STEPFORD WIVES (1975, Columbia)—Charmaine

LOVE, BESSIE
NINA, THE FLOWER GIRL (1917, Silent, Triangle)—Nina
HOW COULD YOU CAROLINE? (1918, Silent, Pathe)—Caroline
CAROLYN OF THE CORNERS (1919, Silent, Anderson-Brunton/
Pathe)—Carolyn
DESERTED AT THE ALTAR (1922, Silent, Goldwyn)—
Anna Moore
GENTLE JULIA (1923, Silent, Fox)—Julia Atwater
SALLY OF THE SCANDALS (1928, Silent, FBO)—Sally Rand

LOVE, MONTAGU
THE CROSS BEARER (1918, Silent, Metro)—Cardinal Mercier

LOVE, SUZANNA
THE DEVONSVILLE TERROR (1983, MPM/New West)—Jenny

LOVE, VICTOR
NATIVE SON (1986, Cinecom)—Bigger Thomas

LOVEJOY, FRANK
I WAS A COMMUNIST FOR THE F.B.I. (1951, Warners)—Matt
Cvetic
FINGER MAN (1955, Allied Artists)—Casey Martin
COLE YOUNGER, GUNFIGHTER (1958, Allied Artists)—Cole
Younger

LOVEJOY, HARRY
THE FARMER'S OTHER DAUGHTER (1965, United Producers)—
Horace Jefferson Brown

LOVELY, LOUISE
BETTINA LOVED A SOLDIER (1916, Silent, Bluebird)—Bettina

THE GIRL WHO WOULDN'T QUIT (1918, Silent, Universal)—
Joan Tracy

LOWE, ALICE
SHOULD A WIFE WORK? (1922, Silent, J.W. Film)—Nina Starr

LOWE, CHAD
APPRENTICE TO MURDER (1988, New World)—Billy Kelly

LOWE, EDMUND
SOUL MATES (1925, Silent, MGM)—Lord Tancred
BORN RECKLESS (1930, Fox)—Louis Beretti
ATTORNEY FOR THE DEFENSE (1932, Columbia)—Burton
CHANDU THE MAGICIAN (1932, Fox)—Chandu
HER BODYGUARD (1933, Paramount)—Casey McCarthy
I LOVE THAT MAN (1933, Paramount)—"Brains" Stanley
THE GREAT IMPERSONATION (1935, Universal)—Baron
Leopold Von Ragenstein/Sir Edward Dominey
KING SOLOMON OF BROADWAY (1935, Universal)—King
Solomon
MR. DYNAMITE (1935, Universal)—T.N. Thompson / "Mr.
Dynamite"
WOLF OF NEW YORK (1940, Republic)—Chris Faulkner
THE STRANGE MR. GREGORY (1945, Monogram)—Mr. Gregory

LOWE, ROB
YOUNGBLOOD (1986, MGM/United Artists)—Dean Youngblood
BAD INFLUENCE (1990, Triumph)—Alex

LOWELL, ROBERT
I ACCUSE MY PARENTS (1945, Producers Releasing Corp.)—
James Wilson

LOWERY, ROBERT
FOUR SONS (1940, 20th Century Fox)—Joseph Bernie
THEY MADE ME A KILLER (1946, Paramount)—Tom Durling
I SHOT BILLY THE KID (1950, Lippert)—Pat Garrett

LOY, MYRNA
THE GIRL FROM CHICAGO (1927, Silent, Warners)—Mary
Carlton
HARDBOILED ROSE (1929, Warners)—Rose Duhamel
THIRTEEN WOMEN (1932, RKO)—Ursula Georgi
THE PRIZEFIGHTER AND THE LADY (1933, MGM)—Belle
Morgan
WHEN LADIES MEET (1933, MGM)—Mary Howard
EVELYN PRENTICE (1934, MGM)—Evelyn Prentice
LIBELED LADY (1936, MGM)—Connie Allenbury
TO MARY WITH LOVE (1936, 20th Century Fox)—Mary Wallace
WIFE VERSUS SECRETARY (1936, MGM)—Linda Stanhope
I LOVE YOU AGAIN (1940, MGM)—Kay Wilson

LUCAN, ARTHUR
OLD MOTHER RILEY (1937, GB, Butchers)—Mrs. Riley
OLD MOTHER RILEY IN PARIS (1938, GB, Butchers)—
Mrs. Riley
OLD MOTHER RILEY JOINS UP (1939, GB, Anglo-American)—
Mrs. Riley
OLD MOTHER RILEY MP (1939, GB, Butchers)—Mrs. Riley
OLD MOTHER RILEY IN BUSINESS (1940, GB, Anglo-
American)—Mrs. Riley
OLD MOTHER RILEY IN SOCIETY (1940, GB, Anglo-
American)—Mrs. Riley

OLD MOTHER RILEY'S CIRCUS (1941, GB, Anglo-American)—
Mrs. Riley
OLD MOTHER RILEY'S GHOSTS (1941, GB, Anglo-American)—
Mrs. Riley
OLD MOTHER RILEY, DETECTIVE (1943, GB, Anglo-
American)—Mrs. Riley
OLD MOTHER RILEY OVERSEAS (1943, GB, Anglo-American)—
Mrs. Riley
OLD MOTHER RILEY AT HOME (1945, GB, Anglo-American)—
Mrs. Riley
OLD MOTHER RILEY, HEADMISTRESS (1950, GB, Renown)—
Mrs. Riley
OLD MOTHER RILEY'S JUNGLE TREASURE (1951, GB,
Renown)—Mrs. Riley
OLD MOTHER RILEY (1952, GB, Renown)—Mrs. Riley
MY SON, THE VAMPIRE (1963, GB, Renown)—Old Mother Riley

LUCAS, WILFRED
HELL-TO-PAY AUSTIN (1916, Silent, Triangle)—Hell-To-Pay
Austin
JIM BLUDSO (1917, Silent, Triangle)—Jim Bludso

LUCKING, WILLIAM
THE MAGNIFICENT SEVEN RIDE (1972, United Artists)—Walt
Drummond

LUEZ, LAURETTE
PREHISTORIC WOMEN (1950, Eagle Lion)—Tigri

LUGOSI, BELA
DRACULA (1931, Universal)—Count Dracula
THE APE MAN (1943, Monogram)—Dr. James Brewster
MYSTERIOUS MR. WONG (1935, Monogram)—Mr. Wong,
Mandarin
FRANKENSTEIN MEETS THE WOLF MAN (1943, Universal)—
The Monster
THE RETURN OF THE VAMPIRE (1944, Columbia)—
Armand Tesla
VOODOO MAN (1944, Monogram)—Dr. Richard Marlowe
MY SON THE VAMPIRE (1963, GB, Renown)—Baron Von
Housen

LUKAS, PAUL
THREE SINNERS (1928, Silent, Paramount)—Count Dietrich
Wallentin
THE BELOVED BACHELOR (1931, Paramount)—Michael Morda
STRICTLY DISHONORABLE (1931, Universal)—Count "Gus"
Di Ruva
AFFAIRS OF A GENTLEMAN (1934, Universal)—Gresham
THE THREE MUSKETEERS (1935, RKO)—Athos

LUKE, KEYE
THREE MEN IN WHITE (1944, MGM)—Dr. Lee Wong How

LUMLEY, JOANNA
COUNT DRACULA AND HIS VAMPIRE BRIDE (1978, GB,
Hammer)—Jessica

LUND, ANNALENA
FREE, WHITE AND 21 (1963, American International)—Greta
Mae Hansen

LUND, JOHN
BRONCO BUSTER (1952, Universal)—Tom Moody

LUNDE, CHRISTINE
MANKILLERS (1987, Action)—Maria Rosetti

LUNDGREN, DOLPH
RED SCORPION (1989, Shapiro Glickenhaus)—Lt. Nikolai
THE PUNISHER (1990, Castle Premier)—Frank Castle

LUNDIGAN, WILLIAM
SAILORS ON LEAVE (1941, Republic)—Chuck Stephens
I'D CLIMB THE HIGHEST MOUNTAIN (1951, 20th Century
Fox)—William Asbury Thompson

LUNT, ALFRED
THE GUARDSMAN (1931, MGM)—The Actor

LUPINO, DICKY
JUST WILLIAM (1939, GB, Associated British)—William Brown

LUPINO, IDA
HER FIRST AFFAIR (1932, GB, Sterling)—Anne
SMART GIRL (1935, Paramount)—Pat Reynolds
THE MAN I LOVE (1946, Warners)—Petey Brown
ESCAPE ME NEVER (1947, Warners)—Gemma Smith
WOMAN IN HIDING (1949, Universal)—Deborah Chandler Clark
BEWARE MY LOVELY (1952, RKO)—Mrs. Gordon

LUPINO, STANLEY
KING OF THE RITZ (1933, GB, British Lion)—Claude King

LUPTON, JOHN
THE CLOWN AND THE KID (1961, United Artists)—Peter
Stanton
JESSE JAMES MEETS FRANKENSTEIN'S DAUGHTER (1966,
Embassy)—Jesse James

LUTHER, ANNE
NEGLECTED WIVES (1920, Silent, Wisteria)—The Wife

LYDON, JIMMY
BOWERY BOY (1940, Republic)—Sock Dolan
LITTLE MEN (1940, RKO)—Dan
TOM BROWN'S SCHOOL DAYS (1940, RKO)—Tom Brown
HENRY ALDRICH FOR PRESIDENT (1941, Paramount)—Henry
Aldrich
HENRY ALDRICH, EDITOR (1942, Paramount)—Henry Aldrich
HENRY ALDRICH GETS GLAMOUR (1942, Paramount)—Henry
Aldrich
HENRY AND DIZZY (1942, Paramount)—Henry Aldrich
HENRY ALDRICH HAUNTS A HOUSE (1943, Paramount)—Henry
Aldrich
HENRY ALDRICH SWINGS IT (1943, Paramount)—Henry
Aldrich
HENRY ALDRICH, BOY SCOUT (1944, Paramount)—Henry
Aldrich
HENRY ALDRICH PLAYS CUPID (1944, Paramount)—Henry
Aldrich
HENRY ALDRICH'S LITTLE SECRET (1944, Paramount)—Henry
Aldrich
MY BEST GAL (1944, Republic)—Johnny McCloud

LYNCH, JOHN
CAL (1984, Ireland, Enigma/Warners)—Cal

LYND, MOIRA
THE PERFECT LADY (1931, GB, Wardour)—Anne Burnett

LYNLEY, CAROL
THE PLEASURE SEEKERS (1964, 20th Century Fox)—Maggie
Williams
HARLOW (1965, Electronovision/Magna)—Jean Harlow
ONCE YOU KISS A STRANGER (1969, Warners)—Diana

LYNN, DANI
THE CASE OF PATTY SMITH (1962, Handel)—Patty Smith

LYNN, DIANA
OUR HEARTS WERE YOUNG AND GAY (1944, Paramount)—
Emily Kimbrough
OUR HEARTS WERE GROWING UP (1946, Paramount)—Emily
Kimbrough
MY FRIEND IRMA (1949, Paramount)—Jane Stacey
MY FRIEND IRMA GOES WEST (1950, Paramount)—Jane
Stacey
PEGGY (1950, Universal)—Peggy Brookfield

LYNN, JANET
COOL IT, CAROL! (1970, GB, Miracle Films)—Carol Thatcher

LYNN, JEFFREY
MY LOVE CAME BACK (1940, Warners)—Tony Baldwin

LYNN, NINA
QUEEN OF THE WICKED (1916, GB, Silent, British Empire)—
Ligeah Dupont

LYNN, RALPH
JUST MY LUCK (1933, GB, British & Dominions)—David Blake

LYON, BEN
PAINTED PEOPLE (1924, Silent, Associated First National)—
Don Lane
HELL'S ANGELS (1930, United Artists)—Monte Rutledge
I COVER THE WATERFRONT (1933, United Artists)—Joseph
Miller
I SPY (1933, GB, British International)—Wally Sawyer

LYON, SUE
LOLITA (1962, MGM)—Lolita Haze
SEVEN WOMEN (1966, MGM)—Emma Clark

LYONS, H. AGAR
DR. SIN FANG (1937, GB, MGM)—Dr. Sin Fang

LYONS, ROBERT F.
THE TODD KILLINGS (1971, National General)—Skipper Todd

LYTELL, BERT
ALIAS LADYFINGERS (1921, Silent, Metro)—Robert Ashe
(Ladyfingers)
THE MAN WHO (1921, Silent, Metro)—Bedford Mills
SHERLOCK BROWN (1921, Silent, Metro)—William Brown
ALIAS THE LONE WOLF (1927, Silent, Columbia)—Michael
Lanyard
THE LONE WOLF'S DAUGHTER (1929, Columbia)—Michael
Lanyard
BROTHERS (1930, Columbia)—Bob Naughton/Eddie Connolly
LAST OF THE LONE WOLF (1930, Columbia)—Michael Lanyard

M

MABLEY, MOMS
AMAZING GRACE (1974, Paramount)—Grace

MACARTHUR, JAMES
THE YOUNG STRANGER (1957, Universal)—Hal Ditmar
THIRD MAN ON THE MOUNTAIN (1959, Buena Vista)—
Rudi Matt
KIDNAPPED (1960, Buena Vista)—David Balfour
SWISS FAMILY ROBINSON (1960, Buena Vista)—Fritz Robinson

MACCHIO, RALPH
THE OUTSIDERS (1983, Warners)—Johnny Cade
THE KARATE KID (1984, Columbia)—Daniel La Russo
THE KARATE KID, PART 2 (1986, Columbia)—Daniel La Russo
THE KARATE KID, PART III (1989, Columbia)—Daniel
La Russo

MACDERMOTT, MARC
RANSON'S FOLLY (1915, Silent, Edison)—Lt. Ranson

MACDONALD, FRANCIS
CARNATION KID (1929, Paramount)—Carnation Kid

MACDONALD, J. FARRELL
BRINGING UP FATHER (1928, Silent, MGM)—Jiggs
RILEY THE COP (1928, Silent, Fox)—James Riley

MACDONALD, JEANETTE
THE LOTTERY BRIDE (1930, United Artists)—Jenny Swanson
ANNABELLE'S AFFAIRS (1931, Fox)—Annabelle Leigh
ONE HOUR WITH YOU (1932, Paramount)—Colette Bertier
THE MERRY WIDOW (1934, MGM)—Sonia
NAUGHTY MARIETTA (1935, MGM)—Marietta Franini
ROSE MARIE (1936, MGM)—Marie de Flor
THE FIREFLY (1937, MGM)—Nina Maria Azara ("Mosca del
Fuego")
THE GIRL OF THE GOLDEN WEST (1938, MGM)—Mary
Robbins
SWEETHEARTS (1938, MGM)—Gwen Marlowe
I MARRIED AN ANGEL (1942, MGM)—Anna Zador/Brigitta

MACDONALD, KATHERINE
THE NOTORIOUS LISLE (1920, Silent, First National)—
Gaenor Lisle
THE BEAUTIFUL LIAR (1921, Silent, Preferred)—Helen Haynes
HER SOCIAL VALUE (1921, Associated First National)—
Mario Hoyte
THE INFIDEL (1922, Silent, Preferred Pictures)—Lola Daintry
THE SCARLET LILY (1923, Silent, Associated First National)—
Dora Mason

MACDONALD, WALLACE
HIS FOREIGN WIFE (1927, Silent, Pathe Exchange)—Johnny
Haines

MACGINNIS, NIALL
MARTIN LUTHER (1953, De Rochemont)—Martin Luther

MACGREGORY, N.
THE SPOILERS (1914, Silent, Selig)—Judge Stillman

MACK, HELEN
SECRETS OF A NURSE (1938, Universal)—Katherine
MacDonald

MACK, MARION
THE CARNIVAL GIRL (1926, Silent, Associated Exhibitors)—
Nanette

MACKAILL, DOROTHY
CHICKIE (1925, Silent, First National)—Chickie
JOANNA (1925, Silent, First National)—Joanna Manners
JUST ANOTHER BLONDE (1926, Silent, First National)—Jeanne
Cavanaugh
MAN CRAZY (1927, Silent, First National)—Clarissa Janeway
HIS CAPTIVE WOMAN (1929, First National/Warners)—Anna
Bergen
THE FLIRTING WIDOW (1930, Warners)—Celia
THE OFFICE WIFE (1930, Warners)—Anne Murdock
ONCE A SINNER (1931, Fox)—Diana Barry
SAFE IN HELL (1931, Warners)—Gilda Carlson
PICTURE BRIDES (1934, Allied Pictures)—Mame

MACKAY-PAYNE, BRONWYN
DAWN (1979, Australia, Aquataurus)—Dawn

MACKELLAR, HELEN
THE PAST OF MARY HOLMES (1933, RKO)—Mary Holmes
TWO AGAINST THE WORLD (1936, Warners)—Martha Carstairs
(Glory Penbrook)

MACKEN, WALTER
HOME IS THE HERO (1959, Ireland, British Lion)—Paddo
O'Reilly

MACKENZIE, ALASTAIR
DAVID COPPERFIELD (1970, GB, 20th Century Fox)—
Little David

MACLACHLAN, KYLE
THE DOORS (1991, Tri-Star)—Ray Manzarek

MACLAINE, IAN
THE BOY AND THE BRIDGE (1959, GB, Columbia)—
Tommy Doyle

MACLAINE, SHIRLEY
MY GEISHA (1962, Paramount)—Lucy Dell-Yoko Mori
TWO FOR THE SEESAW (1962, United Artists)—Gittel Mosca
IRMA LA DOUCE (1963, United Artists)—Irma La Douce
THE BLISS OF MRS. BLOSSOM (1968, GB, Paramount)—
Harriett Blossom
SWEET CHARITY (1969, Universal)—Charity Hope Valentine
TWO MULES FOR SISTER SARA (1970, Universal)—Sister Sara
DESPERATE CHARACTERS (1971, Paramount)—Sophie
LOVING COUPLES (1980, 20th Century Fox)—Evelyn
MADAME SOUSATZKA (1988, Cineplex Odeon)—Madame Irina
Sousatzka
STEEL MAGNOLIAS (1989, Tri-Star)—Ouiser Boudreaux

MACLANE, BARTON
MAN OF IRON (1935, Warners)—Chris Bennett
BIG TOWN CZAR (1939, Universal)—Phil Dailey
A GENTLE GANGSTER (1943, Republic)—Mike Hallit
MAN OF COURAGE (1943, Producers Releasing Corp.)—John
Wallace
THE UNDERDOG (1943, Producers Releasing Corp.)—John Tate

MACLEAN, DOUGLAS
CAPTAIN KIDD, JR (1919, Silent, Artcraft)—Jim Gleason
THE JAILBIRD (1920, Silent, Paramount)—Shakespeare Clancy
INTRODUCE ME (1925, Silent, Associated Exhibitors)—
   Jimmy Clark
THAT'S MY BABY (1926, Silent, Paramount)—Alan Boyd

MACMAHON, ALINE
GOLD DIGGERS OF 1933 (1933, Warners)—Trixie Lorraine
KIND LADY (1935, MGM)—Mary Herries

MACMURRAY, FRED
THE TEXAS RANGERS (1936, Paramount)—Jim Hawkins
MEN WITH WINGS (1938, Paramount)—Pat Falconer
TOO MANY HUSBANDS (1940, Columbia)—Bill Cardew
THE FOREST RANGERS (1942, Paramount)—Don Stuart
TAKE A LETTER DARLING (1942, Paramount)—Tom Verney
CAPTAIN EDDIE (1945, 20th Century Fox)—Edward
   Rickenbacker
PARDON MY PAST (1945, Columbia)—Eddie York
FATHER WAS A FULLBACK (1949, 20th Century Fox)—George
   Cooper
A MILLIONAIRE FOR CHRISTIE (1951, 20th Century Fox)—
   Peter Ulysses Lockwood
THE MOONLIGHTER (1953, Warners)—Wes Anderson
PUSHOVER (1954, Columbia)—Paul Sheridan
FACE OF A FUGITIVE (1959, Columbia)—Jim Larson/Ray
   Kincaid
THE ABSENT-MINDED PROFESSOR (1961, Walt Disney)—Prof.
   Ned Brainard
KISSES FOR MY PRESIDENT (1964, Warners)—Thad McCloud
FOLLOW ME, BOYS! (1966, Buena Vista)—Lemuel Siddons
THE HAPPIEST MILLIONAIRE (1967, Disney/Buena Vista)—
   Anthony J. Drexel Biddle
CHARLEY AND THE ANGEL (1973, Buena Vista)—Charley
   Appleby

MACNAUGHTON, ROBERT
I AM THE CHEESE (1983, Almi Productions)—Adam

MACRAE, GORDON
RETURN OF THE FRONTIERSMAN (1950, Warners)—Logan
   Barrett
THREE SAILORS AND A GIRL (1953, Warners)—Choir
   Boy Jones

MADISON, GUY
FIVE AGAINST THE HOUSE (1955, Columbia)—Al Mercer
THE HARD MAN (1957, Columbia)—Steve Burden

MADISON, LEIGH
THE PLEASURE LOVERS (1964, GB, Butchers)—Carol

MADISON, NOEL
SECRET AGENT OF JAPAN (1942, 20th Century Fox)—Saito

MADONNA
DESPERATELY SEEKING SUSAN (1985, Orion)—Susan
WHO'S THAT GIRL? (1987, Warners)—Nikki Finn

MADSEN, VIRGINIA
MODERN GIRLS (1986, Atlantic)—Kelly

MAGEE, PATRICK
PERSECUTION AND ASSASSINATION OF JEAN-PAUL MARAT
   AS PERFORMED BY THE INMATES OF THE ASYLUM OF
CHARENTON UNDER THE DIRECTION OF THE MARQUIS DE
   SADE (1967, GB, United Artists)—Marquis De Sade

MAGUIRE, GERARD
DEMONSTRATOR (1971, Australia, Columbia)—Steven Slater

MAHARIS, GEORGE
THE DESPERADOS (1969, Columbia)—Jacob Galt

MAHER, BILL
PIZZA MAN (1991, Megalomania)—Elmo Bunn

MAHL, HILDUR
HILDUR AND THE MAGICIAN (1969, Canyon Cinema
   Cooperative)—Hildur

MAHONEY, JOCK
I LIVED BEFORE (1956, Universal)—John Bolan
SLIM CARTER (1957, Universal)—Slim Carter
THE LAST OF THE FAST GUNS (1958, Universal)—Brad Ellison
THREE BLONDES IN HIS LIFE (1961, Cinema Associates)—
   Duke Wallace
TARZAN GOES TO INDIA (1962, MGM)—Tarzan
TARZAN'S THREE CHALLENGES (1963, MGM)—Tarzan

MAHONEY, WILL
SEZ O'REILLY TO MCNAB (1938, GB, Gaumont/GFD)—Timothy
   O'Reilly

MAIN, MARJORIE
TISH (1942, MGM)—Letitia Carberry
GENTLE ANNIE (1944, MGM)—Annie Goss
THE WISTFUL WIDOW OF WAGON GAP (1947, Universal)—
   Widow Hawkins
MA AND PA KETTLE (1949, Universal)—Ma Kettle
MA AND PA KETTLE GO TO TOWN (1950, Universal)—Ma
   Kettle
MRS. O'MALLEY AND MR. MALONE (1950, MGM)—Hattie
   O'Malley
MA AND PA KETTLE BACK ON THE FARM (1951, Universal)—
   Ma Kettle
MA AND PA KETTLE AT THE FAIR (1952, Universal)—Ma
   Kettle
MA AND PA KETTLE ON VACATION (1953, Universal)—Ma
   Kettle
MA AND PA KETTLE AT HOME (1954, Universal)—Ma Kettle
MA AND PA KETTLE AT WAIKIKI (1955, Universal)—Ma Kettle
THE KETTLES OF THE OZARKS (1956, Universal)—Ma Kettle
THE KETTLES ON MACDONALD'S FARM (1957, Universal)—Ma
   Kettle

MAITLAND, COLIN
THE DIRTY DOZEN (1967, GB, MGM)—Seth Sawyer

MAJER, RENATE
WAITRESS (1982, Troma)—Lindsey

MAJORS, LEE
THE NORSEMAN (1978, American International)—Thorvald
KEATON'S COP (1990, Cannon)—Mike Gable

MAKEHAM, ELIOT
MERELY MR. HAWKINS (1938, GB, RKO)—Alfred Hawkins

MAKEPEACE, CHRIS
MY BODYGUARD (1980, 20th Century Fox)—Clifford Peache

MALA
LAST OF THE PAGANS (1936, MGM)—Taro

MALCOLM, JOHN
WHERE HAS POOR MICKEY GONE? (1964, GB, Ledeck-Indigo)—Mick

MALINA, JUDITH
THE ADDAMS FAMILY (1991, Paramount)—Granny Addams

MALKOVICH, JOHN
MAKING MR. RIGHT (1987, Orion)—Ulysses
DANGEROUS LIAISONS (1988, Warners)—Vicomte de Valmont
OF MICE AND MEN (1992, MGM)—Lennie

MALO, GINA
THE TWO OF US (1938, GB, Gaumont)—Frances Wilson

MALONEY, LEO
THE APACHE RAIDER (1928, Silent, Pathe Exchange)—Apache Bob

MANCINI, AL
THE DIRTY DOZEN (1967, GB, MGM)—Tassos Bravos

MANCUSO, NICK
HEARTBREAKERS (1984, Orion)—Eli
DEATH OF AN ANGEL (1986, 20th Century Fox)—Father Angel

MANDEL, HOWIE
WALK LIKE A MAN (1987, MGM/United Artists)—Bobo Shand

MANDLOVA, ADINA
THE FOOL AND THE PRINCESS (1948, GB, GFD)—Moura

MANDYLOR, COSTAS
MOBSTERS (1991, Universal)—Frank Costello

MANGANO, SILVANO
FIVE BRANDED WOMEN (1960, Paramount)—Jovanka

MANN, PETER
THE SWORD OF ALI BABA (1965, Universal)—Ali Baba

MANNERING, CECIL
THE SINGLE MAN (1919, GB, Silent, Ideal)—Major Henry Worthington

MANNERS, DAVID
CROONER (1932, First National)—Teddy
MAN WANTED (1932, Warners)—Tom Sheridan
THE WARRIOR'S HUSBAND (1933, Fox)—Theseus
THE LUCK OF A SAILOR (1934, GB, Wardour)—Capt. Colin
THE MYSTERY OF EDWIN DROOD (1935, Universal)—Edwin Drood

MANOFF, DINAH
I OUGHT TO BE IN PICTURES (1982, 20th Century Fox)—Libby Tucker

MANON, GLORIA
THE WOMAN INSIDE (1981, 20th Century Fox)—Holly/Hollis

MANSFIELD, JAYNE
THE GIRL CAN'T HELP IT (1956, 20th Century Fox)—Jerri Jordan
IT TAKES A THIEF (1960, GB, Alliance)—Billy Lacrosse

MANTEE, PAUL
ROBINSON CRUSOE ON MARS (1964, Paramount)—Cmdr. Christopher "Kit" Draper
A MAN CALLED DAGGER (1967, MGM)—Dick Dagger

MANTELL, ROBERT B.
UNDER THE RED ROBE (1923, Silent, Cosmopolitan)—Cardinal Richelieu

MARA, ADELE
THE TIGER WOMAN (1945, Republic)—Sharon Winslow

MARCANO, JOSS
DELIVERY BOYS (1984, New World)—Max

MARCEAU, MARCEL
SHANKS (1974, Paramount)—Malcolm Shanks

MARCEL, NINO
THE HINDU (1953, GB, United Artists)—Gunga Ram

MARCH, DORIS
THE ETERNAL FEMININE (1931, GB, Paramount)—Yvonne de la Roche

MARCH, FREDRIC
THE ROYAL FAMILY OF BROADWAY (1930, Paramount)—Tony Cavendish
DR. JEKYLL AND MR. HYDE (1932, Paramount)—Dr. Henry Jekyll/Mr. Hyde
STRANGERS IN LOVE (1932, Paramount)—Buddy Frake
THE EAGLE AND THE HAWK (1933, Paramount)—Jerry Young
THE ADVENTURES OF CELLINI (1934, Fox/United Artists)—Benvenuto Cellini
ALL OF ME (1934, Paramount)—Don Ellis
DEATH TAKES A HOLIDAY (1934, Paramount)—Prince Sirki
ANTHONY ADVERSE (1936, Warners)—Anthony Adverse
THE BUCCANEER (1938, Paramount)—Jean Laffite
ONE FOOT IN HEAVEN (1941, Warners)—William Spence
SO ENDS OUR NIGHT (1941, United Artists)—Joseph Steiner
I MARRIED A WITCH (1942, Paramount/United Artists)—Wallace Wooley
THE ADVENTURES OF MARK TWAIN (1944, Warners)—Samuel Clemens/Mark Twain
CHRISTOPHER COLUMBUS (1949, GB, Rank/Universal)—Christopher Columbus
DEATH OF A SALESMAN (1952, Columbia)—Willy Loman
MAN ON A TIGHTROPE (1953, 20th Century Fox)—Karel Cernik

MARGETSON, ARTHUR
HIS GRACE GIVES NOTICE (1933, GB, Real Art/RKO)—George Barwick

MARGOLIN, JANET
DAVID AND LISA (1962, Continental)—Lisa

MARIANNA
GUERRILLA GIRL (1953, United Artists)—Zaira

MARIE, JEANNE
YOUNG NURSES IN LOVE (1989, Platinum)—Nurse Ellis

MARKEY, ENID
JIM GRIMSBY'S BOY (1916, Silent, Ince)—"Bill" Grimsby

MARKS, SHERRY
SATAN'S CHEERLEADERS (1977, World Amusements)—Sharon

MARIN, CHEECH
RUDE AWAKENING (1989, Orion)—Hesus

MARLEY, JOHN
BLADE (1973, Green/Pintoff)—Blade

MARLOWE, JO ANN
LITTLE IODINE (1946, United Artists)—Little Iodine

MARLOWE, KATHY
FIVE BOLD WOMEN (1960, Citation)—Faro Kitty

MARLOWE, SCOTT
LONNIE (1963, Dolphin/Futuramic)—Lonnie

MARLY, FLORENCE
QUEEN OF BLOOD (1966, American International)—"Queen of Blood"

MARMONT, PERCY
K — THE UNKNOWN (1924, Silent, Universal)—"K" Le Moyne
LORD JIM (1925, Silent, Paramount)—Lord Jim
HER IMAGINARY LOVER (1933, GB, First National/Warners)—Lord Michael Ware
DAVID LIVINGSTONE (1936, GB, MGM)—David Livingstone

MARS, KENNETH
DESPERATE CHARACTERS (1971, Paramount)—Otto

MARSH, GARRY
ASK BECCLES (1933, GB, British and Dominion)—Eustace Beccles
WHO KILLED FEN MARKHAM? (1937, GB, Ambassador)—Fen Markham

MARSH, JOAN
DARING DAUGHTERS (1933, Tower)—Betty Cummings

MARSH, MAE
MAGGIE (1916, Silent, Triangle)—Maggie
POLLY OF THE CIRCUS (1917, Silent, Goldwyn)—Polly
ALL WOMAN (1918, Silent, Goldwyn)—Susan Sweeney
LITTLE 'FRAID LADY (1920, Silent, R-C Pictures)—Cecilia
NOBODY'S KID (1921, Silent, R-C Pictures)—Mary Cary
PADDY, THE NEXT BEST THING (1923, GB, Graham/Wilcox)—Paddy Adair
THE MERRY WIDOW (1925, Silent, MGM)—Sally O'Hara

MARSH, MARIAN
BEAUTY AND THE BOSS (1932, Warners)—Susie Sachs
UNDER EIGHTEEN (1932, Warners)—Marge Evans
DARING DAUGHTERS (1933, Tower)—Terry Cummings
GIRL OF THE LIMBERLOST (1934, Monogram)—Elnora Comstock
UNKNOWN WOMAN (1935, Columbia)—Helen Griffith
PRISON NURSE (1938, Republic)—Judy

MARSH, YVONNE
THE LITTLE BALLERINA (1951, GB, Gaumont/British Lion)—Joan

MARSHAL, ALAN
TOM, DICK AND HARRY (1941, RKO)—Dick Hamilton

MARSHALL, BRENDA
ESPIONAGE AGENT (1939, Warners)—Brenda Ballard
MONEY AND THE WOMAN (1940, Warners)—Barbara Patterson
SINGAPORE WOMAN (1941, Warners)—Vicki Moore

MARSHALL, E.G.
12 ANGRY MEN (1957, United Artists)—Juror No. 4

MARSHALL, GREGORY
STEPCHILD (1947, Producers Releasing Corp.)—Tommy Bullock

MARSHALL, HERBERT
MICHAEL AND MARY (1932, GB, Gainsborough)—Michael Rowe
THE SOLITAIRE MAN (1933, MGM)—Oliver Lane
FOUR FRIGHTENED PEOPLE (1934, Paramount)—Arnold Ainger
IF YOU COULD ONLY COOK (1936, Columbia)—Jim Buchanan
TILL WE MEET AGAIN (1936, Paramount)—Alan Barclay

MARSHALL, JAMES
GLADIATOR (1992, Columbia)—Tommy Riley

MARSHALL, MERI D.
VALET GIRLS (1987, Lexyn/Empire)—Lucy

MARSHALL, TRUDY
LADIES OF WASHINGTON (1944, 20th Century Fox)—Carol

MARSHALL, TULLY
THE STRANGER (1924, Silent, Paramount)—The Stranger

MARSHALL, WILLIAM
BLACULA (1972, American International)—Blacula
SCREAM BLACULA SCREAM (1973, American International)—Manuwalde

MARSILLACH, CRISTINA
EVERY TIME WE SAY GOODBYE (1986, Tri-Star)—Sarah

MARSON, AILEEN
MY SONG FOR YOU (1935, GB, Gaumont)—Mary Newberg

MARTIN, ALLEN JR.
JOHNNY HOLIDAY (1949, United Artists)—Johnny Holiday

MARTIN, DEAN
JUMPING JACKS (1952, Paramount)—Chick Allen
PARDNERS (1956, Paramount)—Slim Mosely, Jr.
THE YOUNG LIONS (1958, 20th Century Fox)—Michael Whiteacre
OCEAN'S ELEVEN (1960, Warners)—Sam Harmon
SERGEANTS 3 (1962, United Artists)—Sgt. Chip Deal
FOUR FOR TEXAS (1963, Warners)—Joe Jarrett
ROBIN AND THE SEVEN HOODS (1964, Warners)—Little John
THE SONS OF KATE ELDER (1965, Paramount)—Tom Elder
MISTER RICCO (1975, MGM/United Artists)—Joe Ricco

MARTIN, DINO JR.
BOY. . .A GIRL (1969, Henson)—The Boy

MARTIN, DEWEY
TENNESSEE CHAMP (1954, MGM)—Daniel Norson

MARTIN, PAMELA SUE
THE LADY IN RED (1979, New World)—Polly Franklin

MARTIN, RICHARD
ADVENTURES OF DON COYOTE (1947, Comet/United Artists)—
Don Coyote

MARTIN, ROSS
THE COLOSSUS OF NEW YORK (1970, Paramount)—The
Colossus' Brain

MARTIN, STEVE
THE JERK (1979, Universal)—Navin Johnson
THE MAN WITH TWO BRAINS (1983, Warners)—Dr. Michael
Hfuhruhurr
ALL OF ME (1984, Universal)—Roger Cobb
THE LONELY GUY (1984, Universal)—Larry Hubbard
THREE AMIGOS (1986, Orion)—Lucky Day
DIRTY ROTTEN SCOUNDRELS (1988, Orion)—Freddy Benson
PARENTHOOD (1989, Buena Vista)—Gil Buckman
MY BLUE HEAVEN (1990, Warners)—Vinnie
FATHER OF THE BRIDE (1991, Buena Vista/Touchstone)—
George Banks

MARTIN, TONY
WINNER TAKE ALL (1939, 20th Century Fox)—Steve Bishop
QUINCANNON, FRONTIER SCOUT (1956, United Artists)—Linus
Quincannon

MARTIN, VIVIAN
THE LITTLE MADEMOISELLE (1915, Silent, World)—The
French Girl
LITTLE MISS BROWN (1915, Silent, World)—Betty Brown
A KISS FOR SUSIE (1917, Silent, Paramount)—Susie Nolan
MOLLY ENTANGLED (1917, Silent, Paramount)—Molly Shawn
HIS OFFICIAL FIANCE (1919, Silent, Paramount)—
Monica Trant
THE HOME TOWN GIRL (1919, Silent, Paramount)—Nell
Fanshawe
JANE GOES A'WOOING (1919, Paramount)—Jane Neill
LITTLE COMRADE (1919, Silent, Paramount)—Genevieve
Hubbard

MARTINELLI, ELSA
FOUR GIRLS IN TOWN (1956, Universal)—Maria Antonelli
STOWAWAY GIRL (1957, GB, Paramount)—Manuela Hunt

MARTINEZ, CHICO
THE VISITORS (1972, United Artists)—Tony Rodriguez

MARTINEZ, JOAQUIN
ULZANA'S RAID (1972, Universal)—Ulzana

MARTINEZ, VELIA
THE DEVIL'S SISTERS (1966, Mustang)—Carmen Alvardo

MARTINS, DANNY
THE HOSTAGE (1966, Heartland/Crown)—Davey Cleaves

MARVIN, LEE
THE MAN WHO SHOT LIBERTY VALANCE (1962, Paramount)—
Liberty Valance
THE KILLERS (1964, Universal)—Charlie
THE PROFESSIONALS (1966, Columbia)—Henry Rico Farden
SERGEANT RYKER (1968, Universal)—Sgt. Paul Ryker
MONTE WALSH (1970, National General)—Monte Walsh
EMPEROR OF THE NORTH POLE (1973, 20th Century
Fox)—A No. 1
THE SPIKES GANG (1974, United Artists)—Harry Spikes

MASON, GLADYS
THE VEILED WOMAN (1917, Silent, GB, British Empire)—
Coralie Travers

MASON, JAMES
PRISON BREAKER (1936, GB, Columbia)—Bunny Barnes
I MET A MURDERER (1939, GB, Grand National)—Mark
Warrow
THE MAN IN GREY (1943, GB, Gaumont)—Marquis of Rohan
THEY MET IN THE DARK (1945, GB, Excelsior/English Films)—
Cmdr. Richard Heritage
ODD MAN OUT (1947, GB, GFD)—Johnny McQueen
MAN OF EVIL (1948, GB, Gainsborough)—Lord Manderstroke
THE DESERT FOX (1951, 20th Century Fox)—Erwin Rommel
PANDORA AND THE FLYING DUTCHMAN (1951, GB, MGM)—
Hendrick van der Zee
THE MAN BETWEEN (1953, GB, United Artists)—Ivo Kern

MASON, MARSHA
THE GOODBYE GIRL (1977, MGM/Warner)—Paula McFadden
ONLY WHEN I LAUGH (1981, Columbia)—Georgia

MASON, SHIRLEY
QUEENIE (1921, Silent, 20th Century Fox)—Queenie Gurkin
WING TOY (1921, Silent, Fox)—Wing Toy
JACKIE (1921, Silent, Fox)—Jackie
LITTLE MISS SMILES (1922, Silent, Fox)—Ruth Aaronson
THE NEW TEACHER (1922, Silent, Fox)—Constance Bailey
THE RAGGED HEIRESS (1922, Silent, Fox)—Lucia Moreton
CURLYTOP (1924, Silent, Fox)—Curlytop
MY HUSBAND'S WIVES (1924, Silent, Fox)—Vale Harvey
SALLY IN OUR ALLEY (1927, Silent, Columbia)—Sally Williams
STRANDED (1927, Silent, Sterling)—Sally Simpson
ANNE AGAINST THE WORLD (1929, Silent, Rayart)—Anne

MASSEY, ILONA
INTERNATIONAL LADY (1941, United Artists)—Carla Nillson
FRANKENSTEIN MEETS THE WOLF MAN (1943, Universal)—
Baroness Elsa Frankenstein

MASSEY, RAYMOND
UNDER THE RED ROBE (1937, GB, 20th Century Fox)—
Cardinal Richelieu
ABE LINCOLN IN ILLINOIS (1940, RKO)—Abraham Lincoln
SEVEN ANGRY MEN (1955, Allied Artists)—John Brown

MASTEN, LOIS
NECROMANCER (1989, Bonaire/Spectrum)—Lisa

MASTERSON, MARY STUART
IMMEDIATE FAMILY (1989, Columbia)—Lucy Moore

MASTRANTONIO, MARY ELIZABETH
FOOLS OF FORTUNE (1990, GB, Palace)—Marianne

MASTROIANNI, MARCELLO
LEO THE LAST (1970, GB, United Artists)—Leo

MATHERS, JAMES
DR. JEKYLL'S DUNGEON OF DEATH (1982, New American)—
Dr. Jekyll

MATHESON, TIM
DREAMER (1979, 20th Century Fox)—Dreamer

MATHEWS, KERWIN
THE SEVENTH VOYAGE OF SINBAD (1958, Columbia)—Captain
Sinbad
THE THREE WORLDS OF GULLIVER (1960, GB, Columbia)—Dr.
Lemuel Gulliver
JACK THE GIANT KILLER (1962, United Artists)—Jack

MATHIAS, BOB
THE BOB MATHIAS STORY (1954, Allied Artists)—Bob Mathias

MATTHAU, WALTER
GANGSTER STORY (1959, States Rights)—Jack Martin
A GUIDE FOR THE MARRIED MAN (1967, 20th Century Fox)—
Paul Manning
THE ODD COUPLE (1968, Paramount)—Oscar Madison
KOTCH (1971, ABC-Cinerama)—Joseph P. Kotcher
PETE 'N' TILLIE (1972, Universal)—Pete Seltzer
CHARLEY VARRICK (1973, Universal)—Charley Varrick
THE LAUGHING POLICEMAN (1973, 20th Century Fox)—Jake
Martin
THE SUNSHINE BOYS (1975, United Artists)—Willy Clark
THE SURVIVORS (1983, Columbia)—Sonny Palusco

MATTHEWS, A.E.
CARRY ON ADMIRAL (1957, GB, Renown)—Admiral Godfrey

MATTHEWS, CHRISTOPHER
COME BACK PETER (1971, GB, Donwin)—Peter

MATTHEWS, JESSIE
THE MIDSHIPMAID (1932, GB, Gaumont)—Celia Newbiggin
THE GOOD COMPANIONS (1933, GB, Gaumont)—Susie Dean
THERE GOES THE BRIDE (1933, GB, Gaumont)—Annette
Marquand
FIRST A GIRL (1935, GB, Gaumont)—Elizabeth

MATTHEWS, KERWIN
FIVE AGAINST THE HOUSE (1955, Columbia)—Ronnie

MATTHEWS, LESTER
THE MELODY MAKER (1933, GB, Warners)—Tony Borrodaile

MATTOX, MATT
SEVEN BRIDES FOR SEVEN BROTHERS (1954, MGM)—Caleb
Pontipee

MATURE, VICTOR
CAPTAIN CAUTION (1940, United Artists)—Dan Marvin
MY GAL SAL (1942, 20th Century Fox)—Paul Dreiser
SAMSON AND DELILAH (1949, Paramount)—Samson
DEMETRIUS AND THE GLADIATORS (1954, 20th Century Fox)—
Demetrius
CHIEF CRAZY HORSE (1955, Universal)—Crazy Horse
THE SHARKFIGHTERS (1956, United Artists)—Lt. Cmdr. Ben
Staves
ZARAK (1956, GB, Columbia)—Zarak Khan
THE BANDIT OF ZHOBE (1959, Columbia)—Kasin Khan
HANNIBAL (1960, United Artists)—Hannibal
EVERY LITTLE CROOK AND NANNY (1972, MGM)—Carmine
Ganucci

MAUCH, BILLY
PENROD AND SAM (1937, Warners)—Penrod Schofield
THE PRINCE AND THE PAUPER (1937, Warners)—Tom Canty
PENROD AND HIS TWIN BROTHER (1938, Warners)—Penrod
Schofield

PENROD'S DOUBLE TROUBLE (1938, Warners)—Penrod
Schofield

MAUCH, BOBBY
THE PRINCE AND THE PAUPER (1937, Warners)—Prince
Edward
PENROD AND HIS TWIN BROTHER (1938, Warners)—Danny
PENROD'S DOUBLE TROUBLE (1938, Warners)—Danny

MAUDE, ARTHUR
HEAD OF THE FAMILY (1933, GB, First National/Warners)—
Eddie, the Plumber

MAUDE, CHARLES
THE HOUSE OF TEMPERLEY (1913, Silent, GB, Jury)—Capt.
Jack Temperley

MAUDE, CYRIL
GRUMPY (1930, Paramount)—Grumpy Bullivant

MAUDE, JOAN
THE TEMPTRESS (1926, Silent, MGM)—Lady Clifford

MAXWELL, LOIS
TWILIGHT WOMEN (1953, GB, Lippert)—Christine Ralston
WOMAN IN HIDING (1953, GB, Hammer)—Thelma Tasman

MAY, DORIS
GAY AND DEVILISH (1922, Silent, Robertson-Cole)—Franchon
Browne

MAYALL, RIK
DROP DEAD FRED (1991, New Line)—Drop Dead Fred

MAYEHOFF, EDDIE
THAT'S MY BOY (1951, Paramount)—"Jarring Jack" Jackson

MAYER, CHIP
SURVIVOR (1988, Vestron)—Survivor

MAYFAIR, MITZI
FOUR JILLS IN A JEEP (1944, 20th Century Fox)—Mitzi
Mayfair

MAYNARD, KEN
SENOR AMERICANO (1929, Universal)—Michael Banning
THE WAGON MASTER (1929, Universal)—The Rambler
KING OF THE ARENA (1933, Universal)—Firebrand Kenton
THE FUGITIVE SHERIFF (1936, Columbia)—Ken Marshall
HEIR TO TROUBLE (1936, Columbia)—Ken Armstrong
WHIRLWIND HORSEMAN (1938, Grand National)—Ken Morton
PHANTOM RANCHER (1940, Colony)—Mitchell

MAYNARD, KERMIT
FIGHTING TEXAN (1937, Ambassador)—Burke

MAYO, FRANK
DR. JIM (1921, Silent, Universal)—Dr. Jim Keene

MAYO, RAYMOND
THE KILLERS (1984, Roth Film)—Bill

MAYO, VIRGINIA
THE PRINCESS AND THE PIRATE (1944, RKO)—Princess
Margaret
SMART GIRLS DON'T TALK (1948, Warners)—Linda Vickers
FLAXY MARTIN (1949, Warners)—Flaxy Martin
THE GIRL FROM JONES BEACH (1949, Warners)—Ruth Wilson

SHE'S WORKING HER WAY THROUGH COLLEGE (1952, Warners)—Angela Gardner ("Hot Garters Gertie")
SHE'S BACK ON BROADWAY (1953, Warners)—Catherine Terris
SOUTH SEA WOMAN (1953, Warners)—Ginger Martin
PEARL OF THE SOUTH PACIFIC (1955, RKO)—Rita Delaine

MAYRON, MELANIE
STICKY FINGERS (1988, Spectrafilm)—Lolly

MCALLISTER, PAUL
HIS BROTHER'S WIFE (1916, Silent, World)—Richard Barton
NOAH'S ARK (1928, Warners)—Noah

MCAVOY, MAY
A HOMESPUN VAMP (1922, Silent, Paramount)—Meg Mackenzie
HER REPUTATION (1923, Silent, Associated First National)—Jacqueline Lanier
ONLY 38 (1923, Silent, Paramount)—Lucy Stanley
LADY WINDERMERE'S FAN (1925, Warners)—Lady Windermere
IF I WERE SINGLE (1927, Silent, Warners)—May Howard
SLIGHTLY USED (1927, Silent, Warners)—Cynthia Martin

MCBAIN, DIANE
CLAUDELLE INGLISH (1961, Warners)—Claudelle Inglish

MCBAN, MICKEY
FATHER AND SON (1929, Columbia)—Jimmy Fields

MCCALLA, IRISH
FIVE BOLD WOMEN (1960, Citation)—Big Pearl

MCCALLIN, CLEMENT
THE ROSSITER CASE (1950, GB, Hammer)—Peter Rossiter

MCCALLISTER, LON
BOY FROM INDIANA (1950, Ventura/Eagle-Lion)—Lon Decker
A YANK IN KOREA (1951, Columbia)—Andy Smith

MCCALLUM, DAVID
SOL MADRID (1968, MGM)—Sol Madrid

MCCANN, CHUCK
THE PROJECTIONIST (1970, Maglan/Maron)—Projectionist

MCCANN, DAN
KENNY AND CO. (1976, 20th Century Fox)—Kenny

MCCARTHY, SHEILA
I'VE HEARD THE MERMAIDS SINGING (1987, Canada, Miramax)—Polly Vandersma

MCCLANATHAN, MICHAEL
THE SKY PIRATE (1970, Filmmakers Dist. Center)—Joe

MCCLELLAND, FERGUS
A BOY TEN FEET TALL (1965, GB, Paramount)—Sammy Hartland

MCCLEMENTS, CATHERINE
WEEKEND WITH KATE (1990, Australia, Emanuel)—Kate Muir

MCCLORY, SEAN
I COVER THE UNDERWORLD (1955, Republic)—John O'Hara

MCCLURE, DOUG
KING'S PIRATE (1967, Universal)—Lt. Brian Fleming

MCCLURE, GREG
THE GREAT JOHN L. (1945, United Artists)—John L. Sullivan

MCCLURE, MARC
THE PERFECT MATCH (1987, Airtight)—Tim Wainwright

MCCORMACK, JOHN
SONG O' MY HEART (1930, Fox)—Sean O'Callaghan

MCCORMACK, PATTY
THE BAD SEED (1956, Warners)—Rhoda
KATHY O' (1958, Universal)—Kathy O'Rourke
THE YOUNG RUNAWAYS (1968, United Artists)—Deanie Donford

MCCOWEN, ALEC
TRAVELS WITH MY AUNT (1972, GB, MGM)—Henry Pulling

MCCOY, TIM
THE ADVENTURER (1928, Silent, MGM)—Jim McClellan
THE DESERT RIDER (1929, Silent, MGM)—Jed Tyler
THE FIGHTING FOOL (1932, Columbia)—Tim Collins
THE MAN FROM GUN TOWN (1936, Puritan)—Tim Hanlon
THE TRAITOR (1936, Puritan)—Tim Vallance
THE WESTERNER (1936, Columbia)—Tim Addison
FIGHTING RENEGADE (1939, Victory)—Lighting Bill Carson/El Puma
FRONTIER CRUSADER (1940, Producers Releasing Corp.)—Trigger Tim Rand
THE TEXAS MARSHAL (1941, Producers Releasing Corp.)—Tim Rand

MCCRACKEN, MICHAEL SHAWN
THE KINDRED (1987, F-M Entertainment)—Anthony

MCCRARY, DARIUS
BIG SHOTS (1987, 20th Century Fox)—Jeremy "Scam" Henderson

MCCREA, JOEL
KEPT HUSBANDS (1931, RKO)—Dick
THESE THREE (1936, United Artists)—Dr. Joseph Cardin
TWO IN A CROWD (1936, Universal)—Larry Stevens
INTERNES CAN'T TAKE MONEY (1937, Paramount)—Jimmie Kildare
WOMAN CHASES MAN (1937, United Artists)—Kenneth Nolan
FOREIGN CORRESPONDENT (1940, United Artists)—Johnny Jones/Huntley Haverstock
HE MARRIED HIS WIFE (1940, 20th Century Fox)—T.H. Randall
SULLIVAN'S TRAVELS (1941, Paramount)—John L. Sullivan
THE GREAT MAN'S LADY (1942, Paramount)—Ethan Hoyt
THE VIRGINIAN (1946, Paramount)—The Virginian
RAMROD (1947, United Artists)—Dave Nash
THE OUTRIDERS (1950, MGM)—Will Owen
SADDLE TRAMP (1950, Universal)—Chuck Connor
THE LONE HAND (1953, Universal)—Zachary Hallock
STRANGER ON HORSEBACK (1955, United Artists)—Rick Thorne
THE FIRST TEXAN (1956, Allied Artists)—Sam Houston
THE OKLAHOMAN (1957, Allied Artists)—Dr. John Brighton
THE TALL STRANGER (1957, Allied Artists)—Ned Bannon
TROOPER HOOK (1957, United Artists)—Sgt. Hook

MCDERMOTT, HUGH
THIS MAN IS MINE (1946, GB, Columbia British)—Bill
McKenzie
JOHNNY ON THE SPOT (1954, GB, New Realm)—Johnny
Breakes

MCDONALD, FRANCIS
I LOVE YOU ALONE (1918, Silent, Triangle)—Jules Mardon
CAPTAIN FLY-BY-NIGHT (1922, Silent, R-C Pictures)—
Captain Fly-By-Night

MCDONALD, GRACE
HAT CHECK HONEY (1932, Fox)—Gerry Marsh

MCDONALD, KENNETH
DYNAMITE DAN (1924, Silent, Sunset)—Dan
HE WHO LAUGHS LAST (1925, Silent, Barsky Corp.)—Jimmy
Taylor

MCDONALD, MARIE
GETTING GERTIE'S GARTER (1945, United Artists)—Gertie

MCDOWALL, RODDY
SON OF FURY (1942, 20th Century Fox)—Benjamin Blake
as a boy
MY FRIEND FLICKA (1943, 20th Century Fox)—Ken
McLaughlin
KIDNAPPED (1948, Monogram)—David Balfour
THE ADVENTURES OF BULLWHIP GRIFFIN (1967, Disney/
Buena Vista)—Bullwhip Griffin

MCDOWELL, MALCOLM
O LUCKY MAN! (1973, GB, Warners)—Mick Travis
ROYAL FLASH (1975, GB, 20th Century Fox)—Harry Flashman
ACES HIGH (1977, GB, Cine Artists/EMI)—Gresham
DISTURBED (1990, Live)—Dr. Russell
SCHWEITZER (1990, Concorde)—Albert Schweitzer

MCENERY, JOHN
BARTLEBY (1970, GB, Pantheon/British Lion)—Bartleby

MCENERY, PETER
THE FIGHTING PRINCE OF DONEGAL (1966, GB, Buena
Vista)—Hugh O'Donnell
THE ADVENTURES OF GERARD (1970, GB, Nigel/United
Artists)—Col. Etienne Gerard
ENTERTAINING MR. SLOANE (1970, GB, Warner Pathe)—Mr.
Sloane

MCEVOY, ANNEMARIE
CHILDREN OF THE CORN (1984, New World)—Sarah

MCFARLAND, SPANKY
GENERAL SPANKY (1937, MGM)—Spanky

MCFARLANE, HAMISH
THE NAVIGATOR (1989, Australia, Circle)—Griffin

MCGANN, PAUL
WITHNAIL AND I (1987, GB, Cineplex Odeon)—Marwood-"I"
DEALERS (1989, Great Britain, Rank)—Daniel Pascoe

MCGAVIN, DARREN
BULLET FOR A BADMAN (1964, Universal)—Sam Ward

MCGEE, VONETTA
MELINDA (1972, MGM)—Melinda

THOMASINE AND BUSHROD (1974, Columbia)—Thomasine

MCGILL, MOYNA
MIRIAM ROZELLA (1924, GB, Silent, ASTRA-N)—Miriam
Rozella

MCGILLIS, KELLY
THE WINTER PEOPLE (1989, Columbia)—Collie Wright

MCGINLEY, ROBERT
SHREDDER ORPHEUS (1990, Image Network)—Orpheus

MCGOOHAN, PATRICK
HELL DRIVERS (1958, GB, Rank)—Red
TWO LIVING, ONE DEAD (1964, GB, Emerson)—Berger
DR. SYN, ALIAS THE SCARECROW (1975, Disney)—Dr. Syn
KINGS AND DESPERATE MEN (1984, GB, Blue Dolphin)—John
Kingsley

MCGOVERN, ELIZABETH
SHE'S HAVING A BABY (1988, Paramount)—Kristy Briggs

MCGRAIL, WALTER
SPECIAL AGENT K-7 (1937, Syndicate Releasing Co.)—Lanny

MCGRAW, CHARLES
THE KILLERS (1946, Universal)—Al

MCGREEVEY, MIKE
THE CLOWN AND THE KID (1961, United Artists)—Shawn

MCGREGOR, MALCOLM
ALL THE BROTHERS WERE VALIANT (1923, Silent, Metro)—
Joel Shore
THE HAPPY WARRIOR (1927, Silent, Vitagraph)—Ralph

MCGUIRE, DEREK
THE HERO (1982, GB, Maya)—Dermid

MCGUIRE, DOROTHY
CLAUDIA (1943, 20th Century Fox)—Claudia Naughton
CLAUDIA AND DAVID (1946, 20th Century Fox)—Claudia
Naughton
SWISS FAMILY ROBINSON (1960, Buena Vista)—Mother
Robinson

MCHUGH, CHARLES
FINNEGAN'S BALL (1927, Silent, First Division)—Danny
Finnegan

MCHUGH, FRANK
HE COULDN'T SAY NO (1938, Warners)—Lambert Hunkins

MCKAY, GARDNER
I SAILED TO TAHITI WITH AN ALL GIRL CREW (1969,
World)—Gardner

MCKAY, JOHN
THE REJUVENATOR (1988, SVS)—Dr. Gregory Ashton

MCKAY, WANDA
JUNGLE GODDESS (1948, Lippert/Screen Guild)—Greta
Vanderhorn

MCKEAN, MICHAEL
YOUNG DOCTORS IN LOVE (1982, 20th Century Fox)—Dr.
Simon August

MCKEE, KATHERINE
QUADROON (1972, Presidio)—Coral

MCKEE, RAYMOND
THE LAMPLIGHTER (1921, Silent, Fox)—Willie Sullivan

MCKELLEN, IAN
PRIEST OF LOVE (1981, GB, Filmsway)—D.H. Lawrence

MCKENNA, SIOBHAN
DAUGHTER OF DARKNESS (1948, GB, Paramount)—Emily Beaudine

MCKENNA, VIRGINIA
CARVE HER NAME WITH PRIDE (1958, GB, Rank)—Violette Szabo

MCKENZIE, FAY
SIERRA SUE (1941, Republic)—Sue Larrabee

MCKERN, LEO
A JOLLY BAD FELLOW (1964, GB, British Lion)—Prof. Bowles-Ottery
RYAN'S DAUGHTER (1970, GB, MGM)—Tom Ryan
TRAVELLING NORTH (1988, Australia, View)—Frank

MCKIM, ROBERT
A CERTAIN RICH MAN (1921, Silent, Great Authors Pictures)—John Barclay

MCKNIGHT, DAVID
J.D.'S REVENGE (1976, American International)—J.D. Walker

MCLAGLEN, VICTOR
THE BELOVED BRUTE (1924, Silent, Vitagraph)—Charles Hinges
THE GAY CORINTHIAN (1924, Silent, GB, Butchers)—Squire Hardcastle
A GIRL IN EVERY PORT (1928, Silent, Fox)—Spike Madden
CAPTAIN LASH (1929, Silent, Fox)—Captain Lash
STRONG BOY (1929, Silent, Fox)—Strong Boy
A DEVIL WITH WOMEN (1930, Fox)—Jerry Maxton
THE UNHOLY THREE (1930, MGM)—Hercules
THREE ROGUES (1931, Fox)—Bull Stanley
THE GAY CABALLERO (1932, Fox)—Don Bob Harkness
DICK TURPIN (1933, GB, Gaumont)—Dick Turpin
THE INFORMER (1935, RKO)—Gypo Nolan
THE MAGNIFICENT BRUTE (1936, Universal)—Big Steve Andrews
PROFESSIONAL SOLDIER (1936, 20th Century Fox)—Michael Donovan
THE BIG GUY (1939, Universal)—Warden Whitlock
EX-CHAMP (1939, Universal)—Gunner Grey

MCLEAN, DIRK
THE INCUBUS (1982, Canada, Film Ventures)—Incubus

MCLEOD, CATHERINE
THAT'S MY MAN (1947, Republic)—Ronnie Grange
MY WIFE'S BEST FRIEND (1952, 20th Century Fox)—Jane Richards

MCNAUGHTON, CHARLES
THREE LIVE GHOSTS (1929, United Artists)—Jimmie Grubbins
THREE LIVE GHOSTS (1935, MGM)—Jimmie Grubbins

MCNAUGHTON, GUS
THE STRANGE ADVENTURES OF MR. SMITH (1937, GB, RKO)—Will Smith

MCNICHOL, KRISTY
LITTLE DARLINGS (1980, Paramount)—Angel
JUST THE WAY YOU ARE (1984, MGM/United Artists)—Susan Berlanger
DREAM LOVER (1986, MGM/United Artists)—Kathy Gardner

MCNICHOL, PETER
DRAGONSLAYER (1981, Disney/Paramount)—Galen

MCPHAIL, ADDIE
THE THREE SISTERS (1930, Fox)—Antonia

MCQUEEN, STEVE
THE MAGNIFICENT SEVEN (1960, United Artists)—Vin
THE WAR LOVER (1962, Columbia)—Buzz Rickson
LOVE WITH THE PROPER STRANGER (1963, Paramount)—Rocky Papasano
THE CINCINNATI KID (1965, MGM)—Cincinnati Kid
NEVADA SMITH (1966, Paramount)—Nevada Smith / Max Brand
BULLITT (1968, Warners)—Bullitt
THE THOMAS CROWN AFFAIR (1968, United Artists)—Thomas Crown
THE REIVERS (1969, National General)—Boon Hoggenbeck
JUNIOR BONNER (1972, Cinerama)—Junior Bonner
PAPILLON (1973, United Artists)—Henri Charriere, Papillon
AN ENEMY OF THE PEOPLE (1978, Warners)—Dr. Thomas Stockmann
THE HUNTER (1980, Paramount)—Papa Thorsen
TOM HORN (1980, Warners)—Tom Horn

MCQUEENEY, ROBERT
THE WORLD WAS HIS JURY (1958, Columbia)—Capt. Jerry Barrett

MCSHANE, IAN
YESTERDAY'S HERO (1979, GB, EMI)—Rod Turner

MCWADE, EDWARD
THE CASE OF THE STUTTERING BISHOP (1937, First National/Warners)—Bishop Mallory

MCWADE, ROBERT
CAPPY RICKS RETURNS (1935, Republic)—Cappy Ricks

MEADOWS, JOYCE
THE GIRL IN LOVER'S LANE (1960, Filmgroup)—Carrie

MEATLOAF
ROADIE (1980, United Artists)—Travis W. Redfish

MEDINA, PATRICIA
KISS THE BRIDE GOODBYE (1944, GB, Butchers)—Joan Dodd
THE LADY AND THE BANDIT (1951, Columbia)—Joyce Greene
LADY IN THE IRON MASK (1952, 20th Century Fox)—Princess Anne/ Princess Louise
SIREN OF BAGDAD (1953, Columbia)—Zendi
THE BUCKSKIN LADY (1957, United Artists)—Angela Medley

MEDWIN, MICHAEL
THE TECKMAN MYSTERY (1955, GB, Associated Artists)—Martin Teckman

MEEHAN, JACK
THE COURAGEOUS COWARD (1924, Silent, Sable)—
Jimmy Reed

MEEK, DONALD
THREE LEGIONNAIRES (1937, General)—U.S. Grant

MEEKER, GEORGE
FOUR SONS (1928, Silent, Fox)—Andres Bernie
A GUY, A GAL AND A PAL (1945, Columbia)—Granville
Breckenridge

MEFFRE, ARMAND
HERE COMES SANTA CLAUS (1984, New World)—Santa Claus

MEGOWAN, DON
THE CREATURE WALKS AMONG US (1956, Universal)—The
Creature

MEHAFFEY, BLANCHE
THE PRINCESS FROM HOBOKEN (1927, Silent, Tiffany)—Sheila
O'Toole

MEIGHAN, THOMAS
MALE AND FEMALE (1919, Silent, Paramount)—Crichton
A PRINCE THERE WAS (1921, Silent, Paramount)—Charles
Edward Martin
THE BACHELOR DADDY (1922, Silent, Paramount)—Richard
Chester
THE MAN WHO SAW TOMORROW (1922, Silent, Paramount)—
Burke Hammond
OUR LEADING CITIZEN (1922, Silent, Paramount)—Thomas
Bentley
THE ALASKAN (1924, Silent, Paramount)—Alan Holt
THE CONFIDENCE MAN (1924, Silent, Paramount)—Dan
Corvan
THE CANADIAN (1926, Silent, Paramount)—Frank Taylor
PECK'S BAD BOY (1934, Fox)—Dad Peck

MEILLON, JOHN
THE PICTURE SHOW MAN (1980, Australia, Limelight)—Pop

MELTON, JAMES
MELODY FOR TWO (1937, Warners)—Tod Weaver

MENGATTI, JOHN
KNIGHTS OF THE CITY (1986, New World)—Mookie

MENJOU, ADOLPHE
THE KING ON MAIN STREET (1925, Silent, Paramount)—Serge
IV, King of Molvania
THE GRAND DUCHESS AND THE WAITER (1926, Paramount)—
Albert Durant
A SOCIETY CELEBRITY (1926, Silent, Paramount)—Max Haber
SORROWS OF SATAN (1926, Silent, Paramount)—Prince Lucio
de Rimanez
HIS PRIVATE LIFE (1928, Silent, Paramount)—Georges St.
Germain
HIS TIGER LADY (1928, Silent, Paramount)—Henri
THE GREAT LOVER (1931, MGM)—Jean Paurel
BACHELOR'S AFFAIRS (1932, Fox)—Andrew Hoyt
KING OF THE TURF (1939, United Artists)—Jim Mason
THE BACHELOR'S DAUGHTERS (1946, United Artists)—
Mr. Moody
THE HUCKSTERS (1947, MGM)—Mr. Kimberly

MERCER, BERYL
MOTHER'S BOY (1929, Pathe)—Ma O'Day

MERCOURI, MELINA
THE GYPSY AND THE GENTLEMAN (1958, GB, Rank)—Belle
PHAEDRA (1962, Lopert)—Phaedra

MEREDITH, BURGESS
THERE GOES THE GROOM (1937, RKO)—Dick Matthews
TOM, DICK AND HARRY (1941, RKO)—Harry
JOE BUTTERFLY (1957, Universal)—Joe Butterfly
KING LEAR (1988, US/France, Cannon)—Don Learo

MEREDITH, JUDY
SUMMER LOVE (1958, Universal)—Joan Wright

MERESEREAU, VIOLET
THE HONOR OF MARY BLAKE (1916, Silent, Bluebird)—
Mary Blake
THE BOY GIRL (1917, Silent, Bluebird)—"Jack" Channing

MERIN, EDA REISS
DON'T TELL MOM THE BABYSITTER'S DEAD (1991, Warner
Brothers)—Lil Sturak

MERIVALE, JOHN
THE LIST OF ADRIAN MESSENGER (1963, Universal)—Adrian
Messenger

MERKEL, UNA
DON'T TELL THE WIFE (1937, RKO)—Nancy Dorset
FOUR GIRLS IN WHITE (1939, MGM)—Gerie Robbins

MERMAN, ETHEL
CALL ME MADAM (1953, 20th Century Fox)—Mrs. Sally Adams

MERRALL, MARY
THE THREE WEIRD SISTERS (1948, GB, Pathe)—Isobel
Morgan-Vaughn

MERRICK, LYNN
NINE GIRLS (1944, Columbia)—Eve Sharon
BLONDE FROM BROOKLYN (1945, Columbia)—Susan Parker
A GUY, A GAL AND A PAL (1945, Columbia)—Helen Carter

MERRILL, FRANK
BATTLING MASON (1924, Silent, Hercules)—Mason
THE HOLLYWOOD REPORTER (1926, Silent, Hercules)—Billy
Hudson

MERRILL, GARY
PHONE CALL FROM A STRANGER (1952, 20th Century Fox)—
David Trask

METHOT, MAYO
NIGHT CLUB LADY (1932, Columbia)—Lola Carewe
WOMAN IN PRISON (1938, Columbia)—Daisy Saunders

METTE, NANCY
MEET THE HOLLOWHEADS (1989, Moviestore)—Miriam
Hollowhead

METZLER, JIM
FOUR FRIENDS (1981, Filmways)—Tom Donaldson

MEYRINK, MICHELLE
NICE GIRLS DON'T EXPLODE (1987, New World)—April

MICHAEL, GERTRUDE
THE NOTORIOUS SOPHIE LANG (1934, Paramount)—
Sophie Lang
THE RETURN OF SOPHIE LANG (1936, Paramount)—
Sophie Lang
SECOND WIFE (1936, RKO)—Virginia Howard
SOPHIE LANG GOES WEST (1937, Paramount)—Sophie Lang
JUST LIKE A WOMAN (1939, GB, Alliance)—Ann Heston

MICHAELS, BEVERLY
THE GIRL ON THE BRIDGE (1951, 20th Century Fox)—Clara
PICKUP (1951, Columbia)—Betty
WICKED WOMAN (1953, United Artists)—Billie Nash
BLONDE BAIT (1956, Associated Film Dist. Corp.)—
Angela Booth

MICHELENA, BEATRIX
SALOMY JANE (1914, Silent, California Motion Picture)—
Salomy Jane

MICHELL, KEITH
THE GYPSY AND THE GENTLEMAN (1958, GB, Rank)—Sir Paul
Deverill
HENRY VIII AND HIS SIX WIVES (1972, GB, EMI/MGM)—
Henry VIII

MIDDLETON, CHARLES
STRANGLER OF THE SWAMP (1945, Producers Releasing
Corp.)—The Strangler

MIDDLETON, GUY
THE HARASSED HERO (1954, GB, AP-Pathe)—Murray Selwyn

MIDDLETON, JAMES W.
THE SHEPHERD OF THE HILLS (1964, Macco/Howco)—Daniel
Howitt

MIDDLETON, RAY
HURRICANE SMITH (1942, Republic)—Hurricane Smith

MIDLER, BETTE
THE ROSE (1979, 20th Century Fox)—Rose
STELLA (1990, Buena Vista)—Stella Claire Dallas

MILES, LILLIAN
MAN AGAINST WOMAN (1932, Columbia)—Lola Parker

MILES, SARAH
RYAN'S DAUGHTER (1970, GB, MGM)—Rosy Ryan
LADY CAROLINE LAMB (1972, GB, United Artists)—Lady
Caroline Lamb
THE MAN WHO LOVED CAT DANCING (1973, MGM)—
Catherine Crocker

MILES, VERA
FIVE BRANDED WOMEN (1960, Paramount)—Daniza
THOSE CALLOWAYS (1964, Buena Vista)—Liddy Calloway
MOLLY AND LAWLESS JOHN (1972, Producers Distributing
Corp.)—Molly Parker

MILJAN, JOHN
I ACCUSE MY PARENTS (1945, Producers Releasing Corp.)—
Dan Wilson

MILLAIS-SCOTT, IMOGEN
SALOME'S LAST DANCE (1988, Vestron)—Salome/Rose

MILLAND, RAY
BULLDOG DRUMMOND ESCAPES (1937, Paramount)—Captain
Drummond
HER JUNGLE LOVE (1938, Paramount)—Bob Mitchell
MEN WITH WINGS (1938, Paramount)—Scott Barnes
DOCTOR TAKES A WIFE (1940, Columbia)—Dr. Timothy
Sterling
THE MAJOR AND THE MINOR (1942, Paramount)—Major Kirby
TILL WE MEET AGAIN (1944, Paramount)—John
SO EVIL MY LOVE (1948, GB, Paramount)—Mark Bellis
ALIAS NICK BEAL (1949, Paramount)—Nick Beal
THE THIEF (1952, United Artists)—Allan Fields
A MAN ALONE (1955, Republic)—Wes Steele
THREE BRAVE MEN (1957, 20th Century Fox)—Joe Di Marco
THE SAFECRACKER (1958, GB, MGM)—Colley Dawson
"X" — THE MAN WITH X-RAY EYES (1963, American
International)—D. James Xavier
HOSTILE WITNESS (1968, GB, United Artists)—Simon Crawford
THE THING WITH TWO HEADS (1972, American
International)—Dr. Maxwell Kirshner

MILLER, ANN
REVEILLE WITH BEVERLY (1943, Columbia)—Beverly Ross
EADIE WAS A LADY (1945, Columbia)—Eadie Allen/
Edithea Alden
EVE KNEW HER APPLES (1945, Columbia)—Eve Porter

MILLER, CARL
TRAVELLING HUSBANDS (1931, RKO)—Ben

MILLER, COLLEEN
PLAYGIRL (1954, Universal)—Phyllis Matthews

MILLER, DENNY
TARZAN, THE APE MAN (1959, MGM)—Tarzan

MILLER, HUGH
THE PUPPET MAN (1921, GB, FBO)—Alcide le Beau

MILLER, MANDY
DANCE LITTLE LADY (1954, GB, Renown)—Jill Gordon
CHILD IN THE HOUSE (1956, GB, Eros)—Elizabeth Lorimer

MILLER, MARILYN
SALLY (1929, Warners)—Sally
SUNNY (1930, First National)—Sunny

MILLER, MAX
EDUCATED EVANS (1936, GB, Warners/First National)—Evans
THANK EVANS (1938, GB, Warners)—Evans

MILLER, PATSY RUTH
THE GIRL ON THE STAIRS (1924, Silent, Producers Distributing
Corp.)—Dora Sinclair
HER HUSBAND'S SECRET (1925, Silent, First National)—Judy
Brewster
ROSE OF THE WORLD (1925, Silent, Warners)—Rose Kirby
OH, WHAT A NURSE! (1926, Silent, Warners)—June Harrison
WHAT EVERY GIRL SHOULD KNOW (1927, Silent, Warners)—
Mary Sullivan
BEAUTIFUL BUT DUMB (1928, Silent, Tiffany-Stahl)—
Janet Brady
THE FALL OF EVE (1929, Columbia)—Eve Grant

MILLIAN, ANDRA
STACY'S KNIGHTS (1983, Crown)—Stacy

MILLIGAN, SPIKE
POSTMAN'S KNOCK (1962, GB, MGM)—Harold Petts
THE GREAT MCGONAGALL (1975, GB, Scotia American)—
William McGonagall

MILLS, HAYLEY
POLLYANNA (1960, Warners)—Pollyanna
GYPSY GIRL (1966, GB, Rank)—Brydie White
THE TROUBLE WITH ANGELS (1966, Columbia)—Mary Clancy
TAKE A GIRL LIKE YOU (1970, GB, Columbia)—Jenny Bunn

MILLS, JOHN
OLD BILL AND SON (1940, GB, GFD)—Young Bill Busby
THE OCTOBER MAN (1948, GB, Eagle-Lion)—Jim Ackland
THE HISTORY OF MR. POLLY (1949, GB, Rank)—Alfred Polly
SCOTT OF THE ANTARTIC (1949, GB, Ealing)—Capt. Robert
Falcon Scott
THE GENTLE GUNMAN (1952, GB, Ealing)—Terence Sullivan
MR. DENNING DRIVES NORTH (1953, GB, London Films)—Tom
Denning
SWISS FAMILY ROBINSON (1960, Buena Vista)—Father
Robinson
THE SINGER NOT THE SONG (1961, GB, Rank/Warners)—
Father Keogh
THE VALIANT (1962, GB, United Artists)—Capt. Morgan

MILLS, JULIET
NURSE ON WHEELS (1964, GB, Anglo Amalgamated)—
Joanna Jones

MILLS, SHIRLEY
NINE GIRLS (1944, Columbia)—"Tennessee" Collingwood

MILNER, MARTIN
THE PRIVATE LIVES OF ADAM AND EVE (1961, Universal)—
Ad Simms/Adam
SULLIVAN'S EMPIRE (1967, Universal)—John Sullivan, Jr.

MILOS, MILOS
INCUBUS (1966, Daystar)—Incubus

MILTON, BILLY
THREE MEN IN A BOAT (1933, GB, Associate British
Films)—Jimmy
KING OF THE CASTLE (1936, GB, GFD)—Monty King

MILTON, GERALD
THE BEAST OF BUDAPEST (1958, Allied Artists)—Zagon

MIMIEUX, YVETTE
THREE IN THE ATTIC (1968, American International)—Tobey
Clinton

MINEO, SAL
DINO (1957, Allied Artists)—Dino
THE GENE KRUPA STORY (1959, Columbia)—Gene Krupa

MINNELLI, LIZA
THE STERILE CUCKOO (1969, Paramount)—Pookie
TELL ME THAT YOU LOVE ME, JUNIE MOON (1970,
Paramount)—Junie Moon

MINTER, MARY MILES
DIMPLES (1916, Silent, Metro)—Dimples
ANNE OF GREEN GABLES (1919, Silent, Realart)—Anne
Shirley

JENNY BE GOOD (1920, Silent, Realart)—Jenny Riano
JUDY OF ROGUES' HARBOR (1920, Silent, Realart)—Judy
NURSE MARJORIE (1920, Silent, Realart)—Nurse Marjorie
DON'T CALL ME LITTLE GIRL (1921, Silent, Realart)—Jerry
HER WINNING WAY (1921, Silent, Paramount)—Ann Annington
THE LITTLE CLOWN (1921, Realart)—Pat
THE COWBOY AND THE LADY (1922, Silent, Paramount)—
Jessica Weston
THE HEART SPECIALIST (1922, Silent, Paramount)—Rosalie
Beckwith
TILLIE (1922, Silent, Paramount)—Tillie Getz

MIRAND, EVAN
MY BEST FRIEND IS A VAMPIRE (1988, Kings Road)—Ralph

MITCHELL, CAMERON
THE TALL MEN (1955, 20th Century Fox)—Clint Allison
THE UNSTOPPABLE MAN (1961, GB, Argo/Sutton)—James
Kennedy

MITCHELL, CHUCK
PORKY'S (1982, 20th Century Fox)—Porky
PORKY'S REVENGE (1985, 20th Century Fox)—Porky

MITCHELL, GRANT
MAN TO MAN (1931, Warners)—Barber John Bolton
PECK'S BAD BOY WITH THE CIRCUS (1938, RKO)—Mr. Peck
THE HEADLEYS AT HOME (1939, Standard)—Ernest Headley
FATHER IS A PRINCE (1940, Warners)—Herbert Bower

MITCHELL, HOWARD M.
THE TRAFFIC COP (1916, Silent, Thanhouser)—Casey of
Traffic "C"

MITCHELL, JAMES
THE PEACEMAKER (1956, United Artists)—Terrall Butler

MITCHELL, MILLARD
MY SIX CONVICTS (1952, Columbia)—James Connie

MITCHELL, SASHA
SPIKE OF BENSONHURST (1988, Filmdallas)—Spike Fumo

MITCHELL, THOMAS
SWISS FAMILY ROBINSON (1940, RKO)—William Robinson
THE IMMORTAL SERGEANT (1943, 20th Century Fox)—
Sgt. Kelly

MITCHELL, YVONNE
WOMAN IN A DRESSING GOWN (1957, GB, Warners)—Amy
Preston

MITCHUM, JIM
THE VICTORS (1963, Columbia)—Grogan

MITCHUM, ROBERT
NEVADA (1944, RKO)—Jim "Nevada" Lacy
RACHEL AND THE STRANGER (1948, RKO)—Jim Fairways
HIS KIND OF WOMAN (1951, RKO)—Dan Milner
THE LUSTY MEN (1952, RKO)—Jeff McCloud
MAN WITH THE GUN (1955, United Artists)—Clint Tolinger
THE NIGHT OF THE HUNTER (1955, United Artists)—Preacher
Harry Powell
NOT AS A STRANGER (1955, United Artists)—Lucas Marsh
HEAVEN KNOWS MR. ALLISON (1957, 20th Century Fox)—Mr.
Allison

THE SUNDOWNERS (1960, Warners)—Paddy Carmody
THE LAST TIME I SAW ARCHIE (1961, United Artists)—
  Archie Hall
TWO FOR THE SEESAW (1962, United Artists)—Jerry Ryan
MAN IN THE MIDDLE (1964, 20th Century Fox)—Lt. Col.
  Barney Adams
MISTER MOSES (1965, United Artists)—Joe Moses
THE GOOD GUYS AND THE BAD GUYS (1969, Warners)—Flagg
THE AMBASSADOR (1985, Cannon)—Ambassador Peter Hacker

MIX, TOM
DICK TURPIN (1925, Silent, Fox)—Dick Turpin
THE YANKEE SENOR (1926, Silent, Fox)—Paul Wharton
THE CIRCUS ACE (1927, Silent, Fox)—Tom Terry
A HORSEMAN OF THE PLAINS (1928, Silent, Fox)—Tom Swift
KING COWBOY (1928, Silent, FBO)—Tex Rogers
DESTRY RIDES AGAIN (1932, Universal)—Tom Destry Jr.
MY PAL, THE KING (1932, Universal)—Tom Reed

MOBLEY, MARY ANN
GET YOURSELF A COLLEGE GIRL (1964, MGM)—Terry
THREE ON A COUCH (1966, Columbia)—Susan Manning

MOBLEY, ROGER
BOY WHO CAUGHT A CROOK (1961, United Artists)—The Kid

MODINE, MATTHEW
BIRDY (1984, Tri-Star)—Birdy
ORPHANS (1987, Lorimar)—Treat

MOEDE, TITUS
RAT PFINK AND BOO BOO (1966, Morgan/Craddock)—
  Boo Boo

MOFFETT, SHARYN
CHILD OF DIVORCE (1946, RKO)—Bobby

MOHR, GERALD
THE NOTORIOUS LONE WOLF (1946, Columbia)—Michael
  Lanyard
LONE WOLF IN LONDON (1947, Columbia)—Michael Lanyard
THE LONE WOLF IN MEXICO (1947, Columbia)—Michael
  Lanyard

MOLLISON, CLIFFORD
MISTER CINDERS (1934, GB, Wardour)—Jim Lancaster

MOLLISON, HENRY
WHAT THE BUTLER SAW (1950, Hammer)—Bembridge

MONG, WILLIAM V.
THE HOPPER (1918, Silent, Triangle)—The Hopper
THE CLOWN (1927, Silent, Columbia)—Albert Wells

MONKHOUSE, BOB
DENTIST IN THE CHAIR (1960, GB, Renown)—David Cookson

MONKMAN, PHYLLIS
HER HERITAGE (1919, Silent, GB, Ward's)—Lady Mary Strode

MONROE, MARILYN
LADIES OF THE CHORUS (1948, Columbia)—Peggy Martin
GENTLEMEN PREFER BLONDES (1953, 20th Century Fox)—
  Lorelei Lee

THE PRINCE AND THE SHOWGIRL (1957, GB, Warners)—Elsie
  Marina
THE MISFITS (1961, United Artists)—Roslyn Taber

MONROE, VAUGHN
TOUGHEST MAN IN ARIZONA (1952, Republic)—Matt Landry

MONTALBAN, RICARDO
MY MAN AND I (1952, MGM)—Chu Chu Ramirez
LATIN LOVERS (1953, MGM)—Roberto Santos
STAR TREK II: THE WRATH OF KHAN (1982,
  Paramount)—Khan

MONTAND, YVES
MY GEISHA (1962, Paramount)—Paul Robaix

MONTEZ, MARIA
THE MYSTERY OF MARIE ROGET (1942, Universal)—
  Marie Roget
COBRA WOMAN (1944, Universal)—Tollea/Naja
GYPSY WILDCAT (1944, Universal)—Carla
SIREN OF ATLANTIS (1948, United Artists)—Queen Antinea

MONTEZ, MARIO
LUPE (1967, Film-Makers Cooperative)—Lupe Velez

MONTGOMERY, GEORGE
THE COWBOY AND THE BLONDE (1941, 20th Century Fox)—
  Lank Garrett
LAST OF THE DUANES (1941, 20th Century Fox)—Buck Duane
TEN GENTLEMAN FROM WEST POINT (1942, 20th Century
  Fox)—Dawson
DAVY CROCKETT, INDIAN SCOUT (1950, United Artists)—Davy
  Crockett
THE TEXAS RANGERS (1951, Columbia)—Johnny Carver
THE PATHFINDER (1952, Columbia)—Pathfinder
JACK MCCALL, DESPERADO (1953, Columbia)—Jack McCall
THE LONE GUN (1954, United Artists)—Cruz
MASTERSON OF KANSAS (1954, Columbia)—Bat Masterson
MAN FROM GOD'S COUNTRY (1958, Allied Artists)—Dan
  Beattie

MONTGOMERY, ROBERT
THEIR OWN DESIRE (1929, MGM)—Jack
THREE LIVE GHOSTS (1929, United Artists)—William Foster
THE MAN IN POSSESSION (1931, MGM)—Raymond Dabney
PRIVATE LIVES (1931, MGM)—Elyot Chase
SHIPMATES (1931, MGM)—Jonesy
FUGITIVE LOVERS (1934, MGM)—Paul Porter
PICADILLY JIM (1936, MGM)—Jim Crocker
TROUBLE FOR TRUE (1936, MGM)—Prince Florizel
THE EARL OF CHICAGO (1940, MGM)—Silky Kilmount
MR. AND MRS. SMITH (1941, RKO)—David Smith

MONTY, HAL
SKIMPY IN THE NAVY (1949, GB, Advance/Adelphi)—Skimpy
  Carter

MOON, GEORGE
ME AND MY PAL (1939, GB, Pathe)—Hal Thomson

MOORE, ALICE
WOMAN AGAINST THE WORLD (1938, Columbia)—Anna
  Masters

MOORE, ALVY
FIVE AGAINST THE HOUSE (1955, Columbia)—Roy

MOORE, CANDY
TOMBOY AND THE CHAMP (1961, Universal)—Tommy Jo

MOORE, CHRISTINE
ALEXA (1989, Platinum)—Alexa Avery

MOORE, CLAYTON
BUFFALO BILL IN TOMAHAWK TERRITORY (1952, United Artists)—Buffalo Bill Cody
THE LONE RANGER (1955, Warners)—The Lone Ranger
THE LONE RANGER AND THE LOST CITY OF GOLD (1958, United Artists)—The Lone Ranger

MOORE, CLEO
ONE GIRL'S CONFESSION (1953, Columbia)—Mary Adams
THE OTHER WOMAN (1954, 20th Century Fox)—Sherry

MOORE, COLLEEN
THE WALL FLOWER (1922, Silent, Goldwyn)—Idalene Nobbin
THE HUNTRESS (1923, Silent, Associated First National)—Bela
PAINTED PEOPLE (1924, Silent, Associated First National)—Ellie Byrne
SALLY (1925, Silent, First National)—Sally
IRENE (1926, Silent, First National)—Irene O'Dare
TWINKLETOES (1926, Silent, First National)—Twinkletoes
HER WILD OAT (1927, Silent, First National)—Mary Brown
OH, KAY (1928, First National)—Lady Kay Rutfield
SMILING IRISH EYES (1929, Warners)—Kathleen O'Connor

MOORE, DEMI
THE BUTCHER'S WIFE (1991, Paramount)—Marina

MOORE, DICKIE
SO BIG (1932, Warners)—Dirk Dejong
OLIVER TWIST (1933, Monogram)—Oliver Twist
LITTLE MEN (1935, Mascot)—Demi
TIMOTHY'S QUEST (1936, Paramount)—Timothy
MY BILL (1938, Warners)—Bill Colbrook

MOORE, DUDLEY
ARTHUR (1981, Orion/Warners)—Arthur Bach
LOVESICK (1983, Warners)—Saul Benjamin
UNFAITHFULLY YOURS (1984, 20th Century Fox)—Claude Eastman
LIKE FATHER, LIKE SON (1987, Tri-Star)—Dr. Jack Hammond
ARTHUR ON THE ROCKS (1988, Warners)—Arthur Bach
CRAZY PEOPLE (1990, Paramount)—Emory Leeson

MOORE, GRACE
A LADY'S MORALS (1930, MGM)—Jenny Lind
I'LL TAKE ROMANCE (1937, Columbia)—Elsa Terry

MOORE, KENNETH
THE COMEDY MAN (1964, GB, British Lion)—Chick Byrd

MOORE, KIERON
A MAN ABOUT THE HOUSE (1947, GB, British Lion)—Salvatore
TEN TALL MEN (1951, Columbia)—Cpl. Pierre Molier
DR. BLOOD'S COFFIN (1961, United Artists)—Dr. Peter Blood

MOORE, MARY TYLER
ORDINARY PEOPLE (1980, Paramount)—Beth Jarrett

JUST BETWEEN FRIENDS (1986, Orion)—Holly Davis

MOORE, MATT
HIS MAJESTY, BUNKER BEAN (1925, Silent, Warners)—Bunker Bean
HOW BAXTER BUTTED IN (1925, Silent, Warners)—Henry Baxter
THE CAVEMAN (1926, Silent, Warners)—Mike Smagg
HIS JAZZ BRIDE (1926, Silents, Warners)—Dick Gregory

MOORE, NORMA
UNWED MOTHER (1958, Allied Artists)—Betty Miller

MOORE, OWEN
HER TEMPORARY HUSBAND (1923, Silent, Associated First National)—Thomas Burton

MOORE, PAULINE
THREE BLIND MICE (1938, 20th Century Fox)—Elizabeth Charters

MOORE, ROGER
THE MAN WHO HAUNTED HIMSELF (1970, GB, Associated British)—Harold Pelham
THE SPY WHO LOVED ME (1977, GB, United Artists)—James Bond
FFOLKES (1980, GB, Universal)—ffolkes

MOORE, TIM
BOY! WHAT A GIRL (1947, Herald)—Bumpsie, the Girl

MOORE, TOM
THE CINDERELLA MAN (1917, Silent, Goldwyn)—Anthony Quintard
BROWN OF HARVARD (1918, Silent, Selig)—Tom Brown
GO WEST, YOUNG MAN (1919, Silent, Goldwyn)—Dick Latham
THE COWBOY AND THE LADY (1922, Silent, Paramount)—Teddy North
BIG BROTHERS (1923, Silent, Paramount)—Jimmy Donovan
ANYBODY HERE SEEN KELLY? (1928, Silent, Universal)—Pat Kelly
HIS LAST HAUL (1928, Silent, FBO)—Joe Hammond

MOORE, UNITY
JO THE CROSSING SWEEPER (1918, Silent, GB, Barker)—Jo

MOORE, VICTOR
THE CLOWN (1916, Silent, Paramount)—Riffle

MOORMAN, ELIZABETH
ELIZA'S HOROSCOPE (1975, Canada, O-Zali)—Eliza

MORALES, ESAI
BAD BOYS (1983, EMI/Universal)—Paco

MORALES, MARK
DISORDERLIES (1987, Warners)—Markie

MORAN, FRANK
THE RETURN OF THE APE MAN (1944, Monogram)—Ape Monster

MORAN, JACKIE
MICHAEL O'HALLORAN (1937, Republic)—Michael O'Halloran
BAREFOOT BOY (1938, Monogram)—Billy Whittaker

MORAN, PEGGY
I CANT' GIVE YOU ANYTHING BUT LOVE, BABY (1940, Universal)—Linda Carroll

MORAN, PERCY
JACK, SAM AND PETE (1919, Silent, GB, Pollock-Daring)—Jack

MORAN, POLLY
TWO WISE MAIDS (1937, Republic)—Prudence Matthews

MORANIS, RICK
HONEY, I SHRUNK THE KIDS (1989, Buena Vista)—Wayne Szalinski
PARENTHOOD (1989, Buena Vista)—Nathan

MORE, KENNETH
THE ADMIRABLE CRICHTON (1957, GB, Columbia)—Bill Crichton
THE SHERIFF OF FRACTURED JAW (1958, GB, 20th Century Fox)—Jonathan Tibbs
MAN IN THE MOON (1961, GB, TransLux)—William Blood

MOREAU, JEANNE
FIVE BRANDED WOMEN (1960, Paramount)—Ljuba
GREAT CATHERINE (1968, GB, Warners)—Catherine the Great of Russia

MORECAMBE, ERIC
THE MAGNIFICENT TWO (1967, Rank)—Eric

MORELL, ANDRE
THEY CAN'T HANG ME (1955, GB, British Lion)—Robert Pitt

MORENO, ANTONIO
ALADDIN FROM BROADWAY (1917, Silent, Vitagraph)—Jack Stanton
CAPTAIN OF THE HORSE TROOP (1917, Silent, Vitagraph)—Capt. George Curtis
MY AMERICAN WIFE (1923, Paramount)—Manuel La Tassa
HER HUSBAND'S SECRET (1925, Silent, First National)—Elliott Owen

MORENO, RITA
SO YOUNG, SO BAD (1950, United Artists)—Dolores

MOREY, HARRY
THE KING OF DIAMONDS (1918, Silent, Vitagraph)—Oliver Bennett

MORGAN, DENNIS
BAD MEN OF MISSOURI (1941, First National/Warners)—Cole Younger
CAPTAINS OF THE CLOUDS (1942, Warners)—Johnny Dutton
GOD IS MY CO-PILOT (1945, Warners)—Col. Robert L. Scott
MY WILD IRISH ROSE (1947, Warners)—Chauncey Olcott
TWO GUYS FROM TEXAS (1948, Warners)—Steve Carroll
PERFECT STRANGERS (1950, Warners)—David Campbell

MORGAN, FRANK
THE PERFECT GENTLEMAN (1935, MGM)—Major Chatteris
THE WIZARD OF OZ (1939, MGM)—The Wizard of Oz (Professor Marvel)
HENRY GOES ARIZONA (1939, MGM)—Henry Conroy
THE GHOST COMES HOME (1940, MGM)—Vern Adams
THE VANISHING VIRGINIAN (1941, MGM)—Robert Yancey
STRANGER IN TOWN (1943, MGM)—John Josephus Grant

MORGAN, HELEN
FRANKIE AND JOHNNY (1936, Republic)—Frankie

MORGAN, HENRY "HARRY"
MY SIX CONVICTS (1952, Columbia)—Dawson
CHARLEY AND THE ANGEL (1973, Buena Vista)—The Angel

MORGAN, JOAN
LADY NOGGS-PEERESS (1929, GB, Silent, Butchers)—Lady Noggs

MORGAN, MICHELLE
JOAN OF PARIS (1942, RKO)—Joan

MORGAN, RALPH
NIGHT MONSTER (1942, Universal)—Kurt Ingston

MORIARTY, CATHY
NEIGHBORS (1981, Columbia)—Ramona

MORIARTY, MICHAEL
Q (1982, United Film Distribution)—Jimmy Quinn

MORISON, PATRICIA
DANGER WOMAN (1946, Universal)—Eve Ruppert
DRESSED TO KILL (1946, Universal)—Hilda Courtney
TARZAN AND THE HUNTRESS (1947, RKO)—Tanya

MORLEY, COLEEN
THE DESERT FLOWER (1925, Silent, First National)—Maggie Fortune

MORLEY, KAREN
THE GIRL FROM SCOTLAND YARD (1937, Paramount)—Viola Beech

MORLEY, ROBERT
GHOSTS OF BERKELEY SQUARE (1947, GB, Pathe)—Gen. Burlap
THE GREAT GILBERT AND SULLIVAN (1953, GB, United Artists)—W.S. Gilbert
OSCAR WILDE (1960, GB, Vantage/Four City)—Oscar Wilde

MORRIS, CAROL
BORN TO BE LOVED (1959, Universal)—Dorothy

MORRIS, CHESTER
THE BAT WHISPERS (1930, United Artists)—Detective Anderson
THE CASE OF SERGEANT GRISCHA (1930, RKO)—Sgt. Grischa
COCK OF THE AIR (1932, Hughes/United Artists)—Lt. Roger Craig
SINNERS IN THE SUN (1932, Paramount)—Jimmie Martin
KING FOR A NIGHT (1933, Universal)—Bud Williams
SOCIETY DOCTOR (1935, MGM)—Dr. Morgan
PUBLIC HERO NO. 1 (1935, MGM)—Jeff Crane
FRANKIE AND JOHNNY (1936, Republic)—Johnny
THEY MET IN A TAXI (1936, Columbia)—Jimmy
THREE GODFATHERS (1936, MGM)—Bob
I PROMISE TO PAY (1937, Columbia)—Eddie Lang

CONFESSIONS OF BOSTON BLACKIE (1941, Columbia)—
Boston Blackie
MEET BOSTON BLACKIE (1941, Columbia)—Boston Blackie
ALIAS BOSTON BLACKIE (1942, Columbia)—Boston Blackie
BOSTON BLACKIE GOES TO HOLLYWOOD (1942, Columbia)—
Boston Blackie
I LIVE ON DANGER (1942, Paramount)—Jeff Morrell
AERIAL GUNNER (1943, Paramount)—Foxy Pattis
AFTER MIDNIGHT WITH BOSTON BLACKIE (1943, Columbia)—
Boston Blackie
GAMBLER'S CHOICE (1944, Paramount)—Ross Hadley
BOSTON BLACKIE BOOKED ON SUSPICION (1945, Columbia)—
Boston Blackie
BOSTON BLACKIE'S RENDEZVOUS (1945, Columbia)—Boston
Blackie
BOSTON BLACKIE AND THE LAW (1946, Columbia)—Boston
Blackie
A CLOSE CALL FOR BOSTON BLACKIE (1946, Columbia)—
Boston Blackie
TRAPPED BY BOSTON BLACKIE (1948, Columbia)—Boston
Blackie
BOSTON BLACKIE'S CHINESE VENTURE (1949, Columbia)—
Boston Blackie

MORRIS, GARRETT
THE CENSUS TAKER (1984, Argentum/Borde)—Harvey McGraw

MORRIS, GLENN
TARZAN'S REVENGE (1938, 20th Century Fox)—Tarzan

MORRIS, MARIANNE
VAMPYRES, DAUGHTERS OF DRACULA (1977, GB,
Cambist)—Fran

MORRIS, WAYNE
THE KID COMES BACK (1937, Warners)—Rush Conway
KID GALLAHAD (1937, Warners)—Kid Gallahad / Ward
Guisenberry
BROTHER RAT (1938, Warners)—Billy Randolph
THE KID FROM KOKOMO (1939, Warners)—Homer Baston
BROTHER RAT AND A BABY (1940, Warners)—Billy Randolph
THE QUARTERBACK (1940, Paramount)—Bill Jones
BAD MEN OF MISSOURI (1941, First National/Warners)—Bob
Younger
THREE SONS O'GUNS (1941, Warners)—Charley Patterson
THE YOUNGER BROTHERS (1949, Warners)—Cole Younger
THE DESPERADO (1954, Allied Artists)—Sam Garrett

MORROW, VIC
PORTRAIT OF A MONSTER (1961, Warners)—"Dutch Schultz"
(Arthur Flegenheimer)

MORSE, HELEN
CADDIE (1976, Australia, Atlantic)—Caddie

MORSE, ROBERT
OH DAD, POOD DAD, MAMA'S HUNG YOU IN THE CLOSET
AND I'M FEELIN' SO SAD (1967, Paramount)—Jonathan
Rosepettle

MORSE, WILLIAM A.
THE SHOOTING OF DAN MCGREW (1915, Silent, Metro)—Dan
McGrew

MORTON, CHARLES
FOUR SONS (1928, Silent, Fox)—Johann Bernie

MORTON, DEAN
THE DAKOTA KID (1951, Republic)—Dakota Kid

MORTON, JOE
THE BROTHER FROM ANOTHER PLANET (1984, A-Train
Films)—The Brother

MOSLEY, ROGER E.
LEADBELLY (1976, Paramount)—Huddie Leadbetter

MOSTEL, ZERO
THE PRODUCERS (1967, Embassy)—Max Bialystock
ONCE UPON A SCOUNDREL (1973, Carlyle)—Carlos del Refugio
MASTERMIND (1977, Goldstone)—Inspector Hoku

MOUNT, PEGGY
LADIES WHO DO (1964, GB, Continental Distributing)—
Mrs. Cragg

MOVITA
ROSE OF THE RIO GRANDE (1938, Monogram)—Rosita
THE GIRL FROM RIO (1939, Monogram)—Marquita

MOWBRAY, ALAN
THE VILLAIN STILL PURSUED HER (1940, RKO)—Cribbs
THE DEVIL WITH HITLER (1942, United Artists)—The Devil
THE MAD MARTINDALES (1942, 20th Century Fox)—Hugo
Martindale
ABBOTT AND COSTELLO MEET THE KILLER, BORIS KARLOFF
(1949, Universal)—Melton

MOWER, JACK
KIT CARSON OVER THE GREAT DIVIDE (1925, Silent, Sunset)—
Kit Carson

MOXEY, HUGH
MEET SIMON CHERRY (1949, GB, Hammer)—Rev. Simon
Cherry

MUDIE, LEONARD
THE MYSTERY OF MR. X (1934, MGM)—Mr. X

MUELLER, MAUREEN
ENID IS SLEEPING (1990, Vestron)—Enid

MUIR, DAVID
DR. HACKENSTEIN (1988, Vista Street)—Dr. Elliot Hackenstein

MUIR, JEAN
DESIRABLE (1934, Warners)—Lois Johnson
HER HUSBAND'S SECRETARY (1937, First National/
Warners)—Carol

MULHALL, JACK
THE BUTTER AND EGG MAN (1928, Silent, First National)—
Peter Jones
THE FALL GUY (1930, RKO)—Johnny Quinlan

MULLANE, DONNA
THE OPTIMISTS (1973, GB, Paramount)—Liz

MULLEN, BARBARA
GIRL IN DISTRESS (1941, GB, GFD)—Jeannie McLean

MULLEN, PATTY
FRANKENHOOKER (1990, Glickenhaus)—Elizabeth

MULLER, RENATE
THE OFFICE GIRL (1932, GB, RKO)—Susie Surster

MULLIGAN, RICHARD
S.O.B. (1981, Paramount)—Felix Farmer
TEACHERS (1984, MGM/United Artists)—Herbert

MULRONEY, DERMOT
YOUNG GUNS (1988, 20th Century Fox)—"Dirty Steve"
Stephens
STAYING TOGETHER (1989, Hemdale)—Kit McDermott
BRIGHT ANGEL (1990, Hemdale)—George Russell

MUNI, PAUL
SCARFACE (1932, United Artists)—Tony Camonte
I AM A FUGITIVE FROM A CHAIN GANG (1932, Warners)—
James Allen / Allen James
HI, NELLIE (1934, Warners)—Sam Bradshaw (Nellie Nelson)
DR. SOCRATES (1935, Warners)—Dr. Caldwell
THE STORY OF LOUIS PASTEUR (1936, Warners)—Louis
Pasteur
THE LIFE OF EMILE ZOLA (1937, Warners)—Emile Zola
THE WOMAN I LOVE (1937, RKO)—Lt. Claude Maury
JUAREZ (1939, Warners)—Benito Juarez
THE LAST ANGRY MAN (1959, Columbia)—Dr. Sam Ableman

MUNSEL, PATRICE
MELBA (1953, GB, United Artists)—Nellie Melba

MUNSHIN, JULES
ON THE TOWN (1949, MGM)—Ozzie

MUNSON, ONA
HOT HEIRESS (1931, First National/Warners)—Juliette Hunter
LADY FROM LOUISIANA (1941, Republic)—Julie Mirbeau

MURPHY, AUDIE
BAD BOY (1949, Allied Artists/Monogram)—Danny Leister
THE KID FRM TEXAS (1950, Universal)—Billy the Kid
THE CIMARRON KID (1951, Universal)—Cimarron Kid
DESTRY (1954, Universal)—Tom Destry Jr.
WORLD IN MY CORNER (1956, Universal)—Tommy Shea
THE QUIET AMERICAN (1958, United Artists)—The American
THE QUICK GUN (1964, Columbia)—Clint Cooper
THE TEXICAN (1966, Columbia)—Jess Carlin

MURPHY, EDDIE
TRADING PLACES (1983, Paramount)—Billy Ray Valentine
BEVERLY HILLS COP (1984, Paramount)—Axel Foley
BEVERLY HILLS COP II (1987, Paramount)—Axel Foley
COMING TO AMERICA (1988, Paramout)—Prince Akeem

MURPHY, EDNA
NOBODY'S BRIDE (1923, Silent, Universal)—Doris Standish
HIS BUDDY'S WIFE (1925, Silent, Associated Exhibitors)—Mary
Mullaney

MURPHY, GEORGE
I'LL LOVE YOU ALWAYS (1935, Columbia)—Carl Brent
A GIRL. A GUY AND A GOB (1941, RKO)—Coffee Cup
TOM, DICK AND HARRY (1941, RKO)—Tom

THE MAYOR OF 44TH STREET (1942, RKO)—Joe Jonathan

MURPHY, JOHNNY
THE COMMITMENTS (1991, GB, 20th Century Fox)—Joey "The
Lips" Fagan

MURPHY, ROSEMARY
YOU'LL LIKE MY MOTHER (1972, Universal)—Mrs. Kinsolving

MURPHY, SEAN
THE ADVENTURE OF THE ACTION HUNTERS (1987, Bonner/
Troma)—Betty

MURPHY, TIMOTHY PATRICK
SAM'S SON (1984, Invictus)—Gene Orowitz

MURRAY, BILL
GHOSTBUSTERS (1984, Columbia)—Dr. Peter Venkman
SCROOGED (1988, Paramount)—Frank Cross
GHOSTBUSTERS II (1989, Columbia)—Dr. Peter Venkman
WHAT ABOUT BOB? (1991, Buena Vista/Touchstone)—
Bob Wiley

MURRAY, CHARLES
THE WIZARD OF OZ (1922, Silent, Universal)—The
Wizard of Oz
THE COHENS AND THE KELLYS (1926, Silent, Universal)—
Patrick Kelly
FLYING ROMEOS (1928, Silent, First National)—Cohan
THE HEAD MAN (1928, Silent, First National)—Watts
CLANCY IN WALL STREET (1930, Aristocrat)—Michael Clancy

MURRAY, DON
THE HOODLUM PRIEST (1961, United Artists)—Rev. Charles
Dismas Clark
ONE MAN'S WAY (1964, United Artists)—Norman Vincent Peale
KID RODELO (1966, Paramount)—Kid Rodelo
THE PLAINSMAN (1966, Universal)—Wild Bill Hickok
DEADLY HERO (1976, Avco Embassy)—Ed Lacy

MURRAY, J. HAROLD
CAMEO KIRBY (1930, Fox)—Cameo Kirby

MURRAY, MAE
THE BIG SISTER (1916, Silent, Paramount)—Betty Norton
THE PLOW GIRL (1916, Silent, Lasky)—Margot
THE GILDED LILY (1921, Silent, Paramount)—Lillian Drake
BROADWAY ROSE (1922, Silent, Tiffany)—Rosalie Lawrence
THE FRENCH DOLL (1923, Silent, Tiffany/Metro)—Georgine
Mazulier
CIRCE THE ENCHANTRESS (1924, Silent, MGM)—Circe /
Cecilie Brunne

MURRAY, STEPHEN
MASTER SPY (1964, GB, Allied Artists)—Boris Turganev

MYERS, CARMEL
THE GIRL IN THE DARK (1918, Silent, Bluebird)—Lois Fox
THE GIRL FROM RIO (1927, Silent, Gotham)—Lola

MYERS, HARRY
A CONNECTICUT YANKEE IN KING ARTHUR'S COURT (1921,
Silent, Fox)—Martin Cavendish

MYERS, MIKE
WAYNE'S WORLD (1992, Paramount)—Wayne Campbell

MYLES, MEG
SATAN IN HIGH HEELS (1962, Vega/Cosmic)—Stacey Kane

N

NACE, ANTHONY
A SON COMES HOME (1936, Paramount)—Brennan Grady

NADER, GEORGE
MAN AFRAID (1957, Universal)—Rev. David Collins

NAGEL, ANNA
SHOULD A GIRL MARRY? (1939, Monogram)—Margaret

NAGEL, CONRAD
THE MICHIGAN KID (1928, Silent, Universal)—Jimmy Cowan
KID GLOVES (1929, Warners)—Kid Gloves
THE MAN CALLED BACK (1932, Tiffany)—Dr. David Yorke

NAISH, J. CARROLL
KING OF ALCATRAZ (1938, Paramount)—Steve Murkill
UNDERCOVER DOCTOR (1939, Paramount)—Dr. Bartley Morgan
THE MONSTER MAKER (1944, Producers Releasing Corp.)—Dr. Igor Markoff
SITTING BULL (1954, United Artists)—Chief Sitting Bull
BLOOD OF FRANKENSTEIN (1970, Independent-International)—Frankenstein

NAISMITH, LAURENCE
THE AMAZING MR. BLUNDEN (1973, GB, Hemisphere)—Mr. Blunden

NAMARA, MARGUERITE
CARMEN (1931, GB, BIP/Wardour)—Carmen

NAMATH, JOE
C.C. AND COMPANY (1971, Avco Embassy)—C.C. Ryder
THE LAST REBEL (1971, Columbia)—Burnside Hollis

NANCE, JOHN
ERASERHEAD (1978, AFI/Libra)—Henry Spencer

NAUGHTON, CHARLIE
WISE GUYS (1937, GB, 20th Century Fox)—Charlie

NAUGHTON, DAVID
AN AMERICAN WEREWOLF IN LONDON (1981, Universal)—David Kessler
SEPARATE VACATIONS (1986, RSK Entertainment)—Richard Moore

NAYLOR, TONEY
THE GARBAGE MAN (1963, Cinema Distributors of America)—Garbage Man

NAZIMOVA, ALLA
CAMILLE (1921, Silent, Metro)—Camille
SALOME (1922, Silent, Allied Productions)—Salome
MY SON (1925, Silent, First National)—Ana Silva

NEAGLE, ANNA
THE LITTLE DAMOZEL (1933, GB, British & Dominions)—Julie Alardy
NELL GWYN (1935, GB, United Artists)—Nell Gwyn
THE RUNAWAY QUEEN (1935, GB, United Artists)—Queen Nadina
PEG OF OLD DRURY (1936, GB, Paramount)—Peg Woffington
VICTORIA THE GREAT (1937, GB, RKO)—Queen Victoria
GIRL IN THE STREET (1938, GB, Gaumont)—Jacqueline
NURSE EDITH CAVELL (1939, RKO)—Edith Cavell
IRENE (1940, RKO)—Irene O'Dare
NO, NO NANETTE (1940, RKO)—Nanette
SUNNY (1941, RKO)—Sunny Sullivan
WINGS AND THE WOMAN (1942, GB, RKO)—Amy Johnson
ELIZABETH OF LADYMEAD (1949, GB, British Lion)—Beth/Elizabeth/Betty/Liz
THE LADY WITH A LAMP (1951, GB, British Lion)—Florence Nightingale
ODETTE (1951, GB, United Artists)—Odette
THE LADY IS A SQUARE (1959, GB, Pathe ABF)—Frances Baring

NEAL, PATRICIA
JOHN LOVES MARY (1949, Warners)—Mary McKinley
AN UNREMARKABLE LIFE (1989, SVS)—Frances McEllany

NEAL, SIRI
THE CHILDREN (1990, GB/West Germany, Isolde/Film Four)—Judith

NEAL, TOM
MIRACLE KID (1942, Producers Releasing Corp.)—Jimmy
THERE'S SOMETHING ABOUT A SOLDIER (1943, Columbia)—Wally Williams
FIRST YANK IN TOKYO (1945, RKO)—Major Ross

NEDELL, BERNARD
THE MAN FROM CHICAGO (1931, GB, British International)—Nick Dugan
THE LIVE WIRE (1937, GB, British Lion)—James Cody

NEELEY, TED
JESUS CHRIST, SUPERSTAR (1973, Universal)—Jesus Christ

NEESON, LIAM
SUSPECT (1987, Tri-Star)—Carl Wayne Anderson
HIGH SPIRITS (1988, Tri-Star)—Martin Brogan
NEXT OF KIN (1989, Warners)—Briar Gates
THE BIG MAN (1990, GB, Miramax)—Danny Scoular
DARKMAN (1990, Universal)—Darkman
UNDER SUSPICION (1991, GB, Columbia/Rank)—Tony Aaron

NEGRI, POLA
BELLA DONNA (1923, Silent, Paramount)—Bella Donna
THE CHEAT (1923, Silent, Paramount)—Carmelita de Cordoba
THE CHARMER (1925, Silent, Paramount)—Mariposa
GOOD AND NAUGHTY (1926, Silent, Paramount)—Germaine Morris
THE WOMAN ON TRIAL (1927, Silent, Paramount)—Julie
THREE SINNERS (1928, Silent, Paramount)—Baroness Gerda Wallentin
THE WOMAN HE SCORNED (1930, GB, Warners)—Louise
A WOMAN COMMANDS (1932, RKO)—Mme. Maria Draga

NEIL, CHRISTOPHER
ADVENTURES OF A PRIVATE EYE (1977, GB, Salon/Alpha)—
Bob West

NEIL, HILDEGARD
ANTONY AND CLEOPATRA (1973, GB, Rank)—Cleopatra

NEILL, JAMES
THE WARRENS OF VIRGINIA (1915, Silent, Lasky)—General
Warren

NELLIGAN, KATE
ELENI (1985, Warners)—Eleni

NELSON, BARRY
A YANK ON THE BURMA ROAD (1942, MGM)—Joe Tracey
THE MAN WITH MY FACE (1951, United Artists)—Chick
Graham/Albert Rand

NELSON, CRAIG T.
THE OSTERMAN WEEKEND (1983, 20th Century Fox)—Bernard
Osterman

NELSON, DAVID
HERE COMES THE NELSONS (1952, Universal)—David

NELSON, ED
THE DEVIL'S PARTNER (1958, Huron)—Nick/Pete

NELSON, FRANCES
ONE OF MANY (1917, Silent, Metro)—Shirley Bryson

NELSON, GENE
THREE SAILORS AND A GIRL (1953, Warners)—Twitch

NELSON, HARRIET
HERE COMES THE NELSONS (1952, Universal)—Harriet

NELSON, JOHN ALLEN
HUNK (1987, Crown International)—Hunk Golden
DEATHSTALKER AND THE WARRIORS FROM HELL (1989,
Concorde)—Deathstalker

NELSON, JUDD
THE BREAKFAST CLUB (1985, Universal)—John Bender
RELENTLESS (1989, New Line)—Buck Taylor

NELSON, LORI
HOT ROD GIRL (1956, American International)—Lisa

NELSON, OZZIE
HERE COME THE NELSONS (1952, Universal)—Ozzie

NELSON, RICKY
HERE COMES THE NELSONS (1952, Universal)—Ricky

NELSON, WILLIE
BARBAROSA (1982, Universal)—Barbarosa
SONGWRITER (1984, Tri-Star)—Doc Jenkins
RED HEADED STRANGER (1987, Alive)—Rev. Julian Shay

NEPHEW, NEIL
THE YOUNG SAVAGES (1961, United Artists)—Anthony Aposta

NERO, FRANCO
THE VIRGIN AND THE GYPSY (1970, GB, Chevron)—Gypsy
DEAF SMITH AND JOHNNY EARS (1971, MGM)—Johnny Ears
ENTER THE NINJA (1982, Cannon)—Cole

NESBIT, EVELYN
I WANT TO FORGET (1918, Silent, Fox)—Varda Deering
THE HIDDEN WOMAN (1922, Silent, American Releasing Co.)—
Ann Wesley

NETTLETON, LOIS
MAIL ORDER BRIDE (1964, MGM)—Annie Boley

NEVILLE, JOHN
THE ADVENTURES OF BARON MUNCHAUSEN (1989,
Columbia)—Baron Munchausen

NEWHART, BOB
FIRST FAMILY (1980, Warners)—President Manfred Link

NEWILL, JAMES
RENFREW OF THE ROYAL MOUNTED (1937, Grand National)—
Renfrew

NEWLEY, ANTHONY
IDOL ON PARADE (1959, GB, Columbia)—Jeep Jackson
THE SMALL WORLD OF SAMMY LEE (1963, GB, British Lion)—
Sammy Lee
MR. QUILP (1975, GB, Avco Embassy)—Daniel Quilp

NEWMAN, BARRY
THE LAWYER (1969, Paramount)—Tony Petrocelli

NEWMAN, NANETTE
THE STEPFORD WIVES (1975, Columbia)—Carol

NEWMAN, PAUL
SOMEBODY UP THERE LIKES ME (1956, MGM)—Rocky
Graziano (Barbella)
THE LEFT-HANDED GUN (1958, Warners)—Billy Bonney
THE YOUNG PHILADELPHIANS (1959, Warners)—Tony
Lawrence
THE HUSTLER (1961, 20th Century Fox)—"Fast" Eddie Felson
HUD (1963, Paramount)—Hud Bannon
HARPER (1966, Warners)—Lew Harper
COOL HAND LUKE (1967, Warners)—Luke
HOMBRE (1967, 20th Century Fox)—John Russell
THE SECRET WAR OF HARRY FRIGG (1968, Universal)—
Harry Frigg
BUTCH CASSIDY AND THE SUNDANCE KID (1969, 20th Century
Fox)—Butch Cassidy
THE LIFE AND TIMES OF JUDGE ROY BEAN (1972, National
General)—Judge Roy Bean
THE MACKINTOSH MAN (1973, GB, Warners)—Rearden
BUFFALO BILL AND THE INDIANS (1976, United Artists)—
Buffalo Bill Cody
HARRY AND SON (1984, Orion)—Harry
MR. & MRS. BRIDGE (1990, Miramax)—Walter Bridge

NEWMAR, JULIE
SEVEN BRIDES FOR SEVEN BROTHERS (1954, MGM)—Dorcas

NEWTON, ROBERT
HATTER'S CASTLE (1948, GB, Paramount)—James Brodie
SOLDIERS THREE (1951, MGM)—Pvt. Jock Sykes
BLACKBEARD THE PIRATE (1952, RKO)—Blackbeard
LONG JOHN SILVER (1954, Australia, Dist. Corp of America)—
Long John Silver
THE BEACHCOMBER (1955, GB, MacQuitty/United Artists)—
Ginger Ted

NEWTON, WAYNE
80 STEPS TO JONAH (1969, Warners)—Mark Jonah Winters

NEWTON-JOHN, OLIVIA
TWO OF A KIND (1983, 20th Century Fox)—Debbie

NICHOLAS, PAUL
WHAT BECAME OF JACK AND JILL? (1972, GB, 20th Century Fox)—Johnny/ Jack

NICHOLS, BARBARA
THE KING AND FOUR QUEENS (1956, United Artists)—Birdie

NICHOLS, RICHARD
LITTLE MEN (1940, RKO)—Teddy

NICHOLSON, JACK
THE CRY BABY KILLER (1958, Allied Artists)—Jimmy
ONE FLEW OVER THE CUCKOO'S NEST (1975, United Artists)—Randle Patrick McMurphy
THE TWO JAKES (1990, Paramount)—Jake Gittes

NICOL, ALEX
CHAMP FOR A DAY (1953, Republic)—George Wilson
STRANGER IN TOWN (1957, GB, Eros)—John Madison

NICOLS, ROSEMARY
THE PLEASURE GIRLS (1966, GB, Times)—Marion

NIELSEN, BRIGITTE
RED SONJA (1985, MGM/United Artists)—Red Sonja

NIELSEN, LESLIE
TAMMY AND THE BACHELOR (1957, Universal)—Peter Brent

NIELSON, JOHN
HONKY (1971, Getty-Fromkess-Stonehenge)—Wayne "Honky" Divine

NIGH, WILLIAM
HIS GREAT TRIUMPH (1916, Silent, Metro)—"Buttsy" Gallagher

NILSSON, ANNA Q.
ADAM'S RIB (1923, Silent, Paramount)—Mrs. Michael Ramsey
INEZ FROM HOLLYWOOD (1924, Silent, First National)—Inez Laranetta
MISS NOBODY (1926, Silent, First National)—Barbara Brown

NILSSON, HARRY
THE SON OF DRACULA (1974, GB, Cinemation/Apple)—Count Down

NIMOY, LEONARD
KID MONK BARONI (1952, Real Art)—Paul "Monk" Baroni
STAR TREK III: THE SEARCH FOR SPOCK (1984, Paramount)—Mr. Spock

NISSEN, GRETA
SECRET AGENT (1933, GB, British International)—Marchesa Marcella
HIRED WIFE (1934, Pinnacle)—Vivian Mathews

NIVEN, DAVID
FOUR MEN AND A PRAYER (1938, 20th Century Fox)—Christopher Leigh
RAFFLES (1939, United Artists)—A.J. Raffles
THE PERFECT MARRIAGE (1946, Paramount)—Dale Williams
THE BISHOP'S WIFE (1947, RKO)—Bishop Henry Brougham
BONNIE PRINCE CHARLIE (1948, GB, British Lion)—Prince Charles
THE FIGHTING PIMPERNEL (1950, GB, British Lion)—Sir Percy Blakeney
MY MAN GODFREY (1957, Universal)—Godfrey
THE BEST OF ENEMIES (1962, Columbia)—Major Richardson
THE EXTRAORDINARY SEAMAN (1969, MGM)—Lt. Cmdr. Finchhaven
OLD DRACULA (1975, GB, American International)—Count Dracula
PAPER TIGER (1975, GB, MacLean)—Walter Bradbury

NIXON, MARIAN
EX-FLAME (1931, Tiffany)—Lady Catherine Austin
REBECCA OF SUNNYBROOK FARM (1932, Fox)—Rebecca
FACE IN THE SKY (1933, Fox)—Madge

NOAH, TIM
DAREDREAMER (1990, Lensman)—Winston

NOEL, SID (NOEL RIDEAU)
THE WACKY WORLD OF DR. MORGUS (1962, Calogne-Sevin)—Dr. Morgus

NOLAN, DORIS
THE MAN I MARRY (1936, Universal)—Rena Allen

NOLAN, LLOYD
CHARTER PILOT (1940, 20th Century Fox)—King Morgan
THE MAN WHO WOULDN'T TALK (1940, 20th Century Fox)—Joe Monday
MICHAEL SHAYNE, PRIVATE DETECTIVE (1940, 20th Century Fox)—Michael Shayne
MR. DYNAMITE (1941, Universal)—Tommy N. Thornton

NOLAN, MARY
SHANGHAI LADY (1929, Universal)—Cassie Cook

NOLTE, NICK
UNDER FIRE (1983, Orion)—Russell Price
TEACHERS (1984, MGM/United Artists)—Alex
DOWN AND OUT IN BEVERLY HILLS (1986, Touchstone)—Jerry Baskin
FAREWELL TO THE KING (1989, Orion)—Learoyd
THREE FUGITIVES (1989, Beuna Vista)—Daniel Lucas
THE PRINCE OF TIDES (1991, Columbia)—Tom Wingo

NOONAN, TOMMY
GENTLEMEN PREFER BLONDES (1953, 20th Century Fox)—Gus Esmond
THREE NUTS IN SEARCH OF A BOLT (1964, Harlequin)—Tommy

NORMAND, MABEL
JOAN OF PLATTSBURG (1918, Silent, Goldwyn)—Joan
PECK'S BAD GIRL (1918, Silent, Goldwyn)—Minnie Peck
THE JINX (1919, Silent, Goldwyn)—Jinx
MICKEY (1919, Silent, Sennett)—Mickey
THE PEST (1919, Silent, Goldwyn)—Jiggs
MOLLY O' (1921, Silent, Paramount)—Molly O'
WHAT HAPPENED TO ROSA? (1921, Silent, Goldwyn)—Mayme Ladd
SUZANNA (1922, Silent, Allied)—Suzanna

NORRIS, CHUCK
GOOD GUYS WEAR BLACK (1978, Mar Vista)—John T. Booker

LONE WOLF MCQUADE (1983, Orion)—J.J. McQuade
BRADDOCK: MISSING IN ACTION III (1988, Cannon)—Col.
James Braddock
HERO AND THE TERROR (1988, Cannon)—Herrara 'Hero'
O'Brien
THE HITMAN (1991, Cannon)—Garret/Grogan

NORRIS, MIKE
BORN AMERICAN (1986, Cinema Group)—Savoy

NORRIS, RICHARD
ABIE'S IRISH ROSE (1946, United Artists)—Abie Levy

NORTH, NEIL
THE WINSLOW BOY (1950, GB, Eagle-Lion)—Ronnie Winslow

NORTH, SHEREE
THE LIEUTENANT WORE SKIRTS (1956, 20th Century Fox)—
Katy Whitcomb

NORTON, KEN
MANDINGO (1975, Paramount)—Mede
DRUM (1976, United Artists)—Drum

NOURI, MICHAEL
THE IMAGEMAKER (1986, Castle Hill)—Roger Blackwell

NOVA, HEDDA
THE SPITFIRE OF SEVILLE (1919, Silent, Universal)—
Carmelita

NOVA, LOU
THE COWBOY AND THE PRIZEFIGHTER (1950, Eagle-
Lion)—Bull

NOVAK, JANE
ISOBEL (1920, Silent, Davis)—Isobel Deane
COLLEEN OF THE PINES (1922, Silent, Film Booking Offices)—
Joan Cameron
THELMA (1922, Silent, Film Booking Office of America)—
Thelma Guildmar

NOVAK, KIM
FIVE AGAINST THE HOUSE (1955, Columbia)—Kay Greylek
JEANNE EAGELS (1957, Columbia)—Jeanne Eagels
STRANGERS WHEN WE MEET (1960, Columbia)—Maggie Gault
THE NOTORIOUS LANDLADY (1962, Columbia)—Carlye
Hardwicke
THE AMOROUS ADVENTURES OF MOLL FLANDERS (1965,
Paramount)—Moll Flanders
THE LEGEND OF LYLAH CLARE (1968, MGM)—Lylah Clare/
Elsa Brinkmann

NOVARA, MEDEA
THE MAD EMPRESS (1940, Warners)—Empress Carlotta

NOVARRO, RAMON
SCARAMOUCHE (1923, Silent, Metro)—Scaramouche (Andre-
Louis Moreau)
THE ARAB (1924, Silent, MGM)—Jamil Abdullah Azam
BEN-HUR (1925, Silent, MGM)—Ben-Hur
A CERTAIN YOUNG MAN (1928, Silent, MGM)—Lord Gerald
Brinsley
THE PAGAN (1929, MGM)—Henry Shoesmith Jr.
SON OF INDIA (1931, MGM)—Karim
THE BARBARIAN (1933, MGM)—Jamil

LAUGHING BOY (1934, MGM)—Laughing Boy
THE SHEIK STEPS OUT (1937, Republic)—Ahmed Ben Nesib

NOVELLO, IVOR
THE MAN WITHOUT DESIRE (1923, Silent, GB, Atlas Biocraft)—
Count Vittorio Donaldo
THE RAT (1925, GB, Silent, Gainsborough)—"The Rat", Pierre
Boucheron
THE LODGER (1926, Silent, GB, Gainsborough)—The Lodger/
Jonathan Drew
THE RETURN OF THE RAT (1929, GB, Gainsborough)—Pierre
"The Rat" Boucheron
THE LODGER (1932, GB, Twickenham)—The Lodger

NUGENT, ELLIOTT
VIRTUOUS HUSBAND (1931, Universal)—Daniel Curtis

NUREYEV, RUDOLF
ROMEO AND JULIET (1966, GB, Embassy)—Romeo
VALENTINO (1977, GB, United Artists)—Rudolph Valentino

NUTTER, MAYF
HUNTER'S BLOOD (1987, Concorde)—Ralph Coleman

NUYEN, FRANCE
A GIRL NAMED TAMIKO (1962, Paramount)—Tamiko

OAKIE, JACK
THE SAP FROM SYRACUSE (1930, Paramount)—Littleton
Looney
THE SOCIAL LION (1930, Paramount)—Marco Perkins
THE GANG BUSTER (1931, Paramount)—Charlie
"Cyclone" Case
SAILOR BE GOOD (1933, RKO)—Kelsey Jones
SITTING PRETTY (1933, Paramount)—Chick Parker
THE TEXAS RANGERS (1936, Paramount)—Wahoo Jones
SUPER SLEUTH (1937, RKO)—Willard "Bill" Martin
THE MERRY MONAHANS (1944, Universal)—Pete Monahan

OAKMAN, WHEELER
THE NE'ER-DO-WELL (1916, Silent, Selig)—Kirk Anthony
THE HALF BREED (1922, Silent, Associated First National)—
Delmar Spavinaw
SLIPPY MCGEE (1923, Silent, Associate First National)—
Slippy McGee

OATES, WARREN
THE WILD BUNCH (1969, Warners)—Lyle Gorch
CHANDLER (1971, MGM)—Chandler
DILLINGER (1973, American International)—John Dillinger

OBERON, MERLE
BELOVED ENEMY (1936, Goldwyn/United Artists)—Helen
Drummond
THESE THREE (1936, United Artists)—Karen Wright
THE COWBOY AND THE LADY (1938, Goldwyn/United Artists)—
Mary Smith

'TIL WE MEET AGAIN (1940, Warners)—Joan Ames
LYDIA (1941, United Artists)—Lydia MacMillan
THIS LOVE OF OURS (1945, Universal)—Karin Touzac

O'BRIEN, CLAY
ONE LITTLE INDIAN (1973, Buena Vista)—Mark
MACKINTOSH & T.J. (1975, Penland)—T.J.

O'BRIEN, DAVID
THE MAN WHO WALKED ALONE (1945, Producers Releasing
Corp.)—Cpl. Marion Scott

O'BRIEN, EDMOND
A GIRL, A GUY AND A GOB (1941, RKO)—Stephen Herrick
D.O.A. (1950, United Artists)—Frank Bigelow
TWO OF A KIND (1951, Columbia)—Lefty Farrell
THE BIGAMIST (1953, Filmakers)—Harry Graham
MAN IN THE DARK (1953, Columbia)—Steve Rawley/
James Blake
THE THIRD VOICE (1960, 20th Century Fox)—The Voice

O'BRIEN, EUGENE
THE PERFECT LOVER (1919, Silent, Selznick)—Brian Lazar
CHIVALROUS CHARLIE (1921, Silent, Selznick)—Charles Riley
CHANNING OF THE NORTHWEST (1922, Silent, Selznick)—
Channing
JOHN SMITH (1922, Silent, Selznick)—John Smith

O'BRIEN, GEORGE
THE ROUGHNECK (1924, Silent, Fox)—Jerry Delaney
SUNRISE — A SONG OF TWO HUMANS (1927, Silent, Fox)—
The Man
LAST OF THE DUANES (1930, Fox)—Buck Duane
THE LONE STAR RANGER (1930, Fox)—Buck Duane
A HOLY TERROR (1931, 20th Century Fox)—Tony Hard
THE DUDE RANGER (1934, Fox)—Ernest Selby
FRONTIER MARSHAL (1934, Fox)—Michael Wyatt
COWBOY MILLIONAIRE (1935, Fox)—Bob Walker
HARD ROCK HARRIGAN (1935, Fox)—"Hard Rock" Harrigan
WHEN A MAN'S A MAN (1935, Fox)—Larry Knight
WHISPERING SMITH SPEAKS (1935, Fox)—Whispering Smith
DANIEL BOONE (1936, RKO)—Daniel Boone
O'MALLEY OF THE MOUNTED (1936, 20th Century Fox)—
O'Malley
HOLLYWOOD COWBOY (1937, RKO)—Jeffrey Carson
PARK AVENUE LOGGER (1937, RKO)—Grant Curran
THE FIGHTING GRINGO (1939, RKO)—Wade Barton
THE MARSHAL OF MESA CITY (1939, RKO)—Mason

O'BRIEN, MARGARET
JOURNEY FOR MARGARET (1942, MGM)—Margaret
LOST ANGEL (1944, MGM)—Alpha
TENTH AVENUE ANGEL (1948, MGM)—Flavia Mills
LITTLE WOMEN (1949, MGM)—Beth March
HER FIRST ROMANCE (1951, Columbia)—Betty Foster

O'BRIEN, PAT
COLLEGE COACH (1933, Warners)—Coach Gore
I SELL ANYTHING (1934, First National/Warners)—Spot Cash
Cutler
THE PERSONALITY KID (1934, Warners)—Ritzy McCarthy
DEVIL DOGS OF THE AIR (1935, Warners)—Lt. William
Brannigan

I MARRIED A DOCTOR (1936, First National/Warners)—Dr.
William Kennicott
THE GREAT O'MALLEY (1937, Warners)—James Aloysius
O'Malley
KNUTE ROCKNE — ALL AMERICAN (1940, Warners)—Knute
Rockne
TWO YANKS IN TRINIDAD (1942, Columbia)—Tim Reardon
HIS BUTLER'S SISTER (1943, Universal)—Martin Carter
THE IRON MAJOR (1943, RKO)—Frank Cavanaugh
MAN ALIVE (1945, RKO)—Speed
FIGHTING FATHER DUNNE (1948, RKO)—Father Dunne
CRIMINAL LAWYER (1951, Columbia)—James Regan

O'BRIEN, VIRGINIA
THE HARVEY GIRLS (1946, MGM)—Alma

O'CONNELL, EDDIE
ABSOLUTE BEGINNERS (1986, GB, Orion)—Colin

O'CONNOR, DONALD
MR. BIG (1943, Universal)—Donald
TOP MAN (1943, Universal)—Don Warren
THE MERRY MONAHANS (1944, Universal)—Jimmy Monahan
PATRICK THE GREAT (1945, Universal)—Pat Donahue Jr.
THE MILKMAN (1950, Universal)—Roger Bradley
I LOVE MELVIN (1953, MGM)—Melvin Hooper
THE BUSTER KEATON STORY (1957, Paramount)—Buster
Keaton

O'CONNOR, GLYNNIS
THOSE LIPS, THOSE EYES (1980, United Artists)—Ramona
MELANIE (1982, Canada, Embassy)—Melanie Daniel

O'CONOR, HUGH
MY LEFT FOOT (1989, GB, Miramax)—Young Christy Brown

O'DAY, MOLLY
SISTERS (1930, Columbia)—Molly Shannon

O'DEA, JIMMY
JIMMY BOY (1935, GB, Universal)—Jimmy
DARBY O'GILL AND THE LITTLE PEOPLE (1959, Buena
Vista)—King Brian

O'DELL, BRYAN
YOUNGBLOOD (1978, American International)—Youngblood

ODETTE, MARY
JOHN HERRIOT'S WIFE (1920, Silent, GB, Anglo-Hollandia)—
Camillia Herriot

O'DONNELL, CATHY
THEY LIVE BY NIGHT (1949, RKO)—Keechie

O'DONNELL, CHRIS
MEN DON'T LEAVE (1990, Warners)—Chris Macauley

O'DRISCOLL, MARTHA
MIDNIGHT ANGEL (1941, Paramount)—Mary
HI BEAUTIFUL (1944, Universal)—Patty Callahan
HER LUCKY NIGHT (1945, Universal)—Connie

OFFERMAN, GEORGE JR.
THE SULLIVANS (1944, 20th Century Fox)—Joe Sullivan

O'GRADY, MONTY
SPARROWS (1926, Silent, United Artists)—Splutters

O'HALLORAN, JACK
FAREWELL, MY LOVELY (1975, Avco Embassy)—Moose Malloy

O'HARA, MAUREEN
DANCE, GIRL, DANCE (1940, RKO)—Judy
THEY MET IN ARGENTINA (1941, RKO)—Lolita
THE FOXES OF HARROW (1947, 20th Century Fox)—Odalie D'Arceneaux Fox
AFFAIRS OF ADELAIDE (1949, 20th Century Fox)—Adelaide Culver
A WOMAN'S SECRET (1949, RKO)—Marian Washburn
THE REDHEAD FROM WYOMING (1953, Universal)—Kate Maxwell
LADY GODIVA (1955, Universal) -Lady Godiva
THE DEADLY COMPANIONS (1961, Pathe-American)—Kit

O'HARA, PAIGE
BEAUTY AND THE BEAST (1991, Animated, Buena Vista/Disney)—Voice of Belle

O'HERLIHY, DAN
THE ADVENTURES OF ROBINSON CRUSOE (1954, United Artists)—Robinson Crusoe
THE CABINET OF CALIGARI (1962, 20th Century Fox)—Caligari

O'KEEFE, DENNIS
THE CHASER (1938, MGM)—Thomas Z. Brandon
BURN 'EM UP O'CONNOR (1939, MGM)—Jerry O'Connor
THE KID FROM TEXAS (1939, MGM)—William Quincy Malone
UNEXPECTED FATHER (1939, Universal)—Jimmy Hanley
MR. DISTRICT ATTORNEY (1941, Republic)—P. Cadwalder Jones
WEEKEND FOR THREE (1941, RKO)—Jim Craig
ABROAD WITH TWO YANKS (1944, United Artists)—Jeff Reardon
BREWSTER'S MILLIONS (1945, United Artists)—Monty Brewster
MR. DISTRICT ATTORNEY (1946, Columbia)—Steve Bennett
T-MEN (1947, Eagle-Lion)—Dennis O'Brien
THE EAGLE AND THE HAWK (1950, Paramount)—Whitney Randolph

O'KEEFE, MICHAEL
FINDERS KEEPERS (1984, CBS/Warners)—Michael Rangeloff
THE SLUGGER'S WIFE (1985, Columbia)—Darryl Palmer
THE WHOOPEE BOYS (1986, Paramount)—Jake

O'KEEFE, MILES
TARZAN, THE APE MAN (1981, MGM/United Artists)—Tarzan
THE DRIFTER (1988, Concorde)—Trey
THE LONE RUNNER (1988, Trans World)—Garrett

O'KEEFE, PAUL
THE DAYDREAMER (1966, Embassy)—Hans Christian Anderson

OLAND, WARNER
WHAT HAPPENED TO FATHER (1927, Silent, Warners)—W. Bradberry
THE MYSTERIOUS DR. FU MANCHU (1929, Paramount)—Dr. Fu Manchu
THE RETURN OF DR. FU MANCHU (1930, Paramount)—Dr. Fu Manchu
CHARLIE CHAN CARRIES ON (1931, Fox)—Charlie Chan
CHARLIE CHAN'S CHANCE (1932, Fox)—Charlie Chan
CHARLIE CHAN'S GREATEST CASE (1933, Fox)—Charlie Chan
CHARLIE CHAN IN LONDON (1934, Fox)—Charlie Chan
CHARLIE CHAN'S COURAGE (1934, Fox)—Charlie Chan
CHARLIE CHAN IN EGYPT (1935, 20th Century Fox)—Charlie Chan
CHARLIE CHAN IN PARIS (1935, 20th Century Fox)—Charlie Chan
CHARLIE CHAN IN SHANGHAI (1935, 20th Century Fox)—Charlie Chan
CHARLIE CHAN AT THE CIRCUS (1936, 20th Century Fox)—Charlie Chan
CHARLIE CHAN AT THE OPERA (1936, 20th Century Fox)—Charlie Chan
CHARLIE CHAN AT THE RACETRACK (1936, 20th Century Fox)—Charlie Chan
CHARLIE CHAN'S SECRET (1936, 20th Century Fox)—Charlie Chan
CHARLIE CHAN AT MONTE CARLO (1937, 20th Century Fox)—Charlie Chan
CHARLIE CHAN AT THE OLYMPICS (1937, 20th Century Fox)—Charlie Chan
CHARLIE CHAN ON BROADWAY (1937, 20th Century Fox)—Charlie Chan

OLDLAND, LILLIAN
VIRGINIA'S HUSBAND (1928, GB, Silent, Butchers)—Virginia Trevor

OLDMAN, GARY
SID & NANCY (1986, GB, Goldwyn)—Sid Vicious
ROSENCRANTZ AND GUILDENSTERN ARE DEAD (1990, Cinecom)—Rosencrantz

OLIN, LENA
ENEMIES, A LOVE STORY (1989, 20th Century Fox)—Masha

OLIVER, BARRET
D.A.R.Y.L. (1985, Paramount)—Daryl

OLIVER, EDNA MAY
FANNY FOLEY HERSELF (1931, RKO)—Fanny Foley
LADIES OF THE JURY (1932, RKO)—Mrs. Crane

OLIVER, MICHAEL
PROBLEM CHILD (1990, Universal)—Junior Healy
PROBLEM CHILD 2 (1991, Universal)—Junior Healy

OLIVER, SUSAN
THE GREEN-EYED BLONDE (1957, Warners)—Greeneyes

OLIVERI, ROBERT
HONEY, I SHRUNK THE KIDS (1989, Buena Vista)—Nick Szalinski

OLIVIER, LAURENCE
TWENTY-ONE DAYS TOGETHER (1940, GB, Columbia)—Larry Durrant
HENRY V (1946, GB, Two Cities/United Artists)—King Henry V
HAMLET (1948, GB, Rank)—Hamlet
RICHARD III (1956, GB, Lopert)—Richard of Gloucester
THE PRINCE AND THE SHOWGIRL (1957, GB, Warners)—Charles, Prince Regent
THE ENTERTAINER (1960, GB, British Lion)—Archie Rice
OTHELLO (1965, Warners)—Othello

OLMOS, EDWARD JAMES
THE BALLAD OF GREGORIO CORTEZ (1983, Embassy)—
Gregorio Cortez
AMERICAN ME (1992, Universal)—Santana

OLMSTEAD, GERTRUDE
SWEET ADELINE (1926, Silent, Chadwick)—Adeline
THE LONE WOLF'S DAUGHTER (1929, Columbia)—Helen
Fairchild
THE TIME, THE PLACE AND THE GIRL (1929, Warners)—
Mae Ellis

O'LOINGSIGH, PADRAG
THE COURIER (1988, Vestron)—The Courier

OLSEN, MORONI
THE THREE MUSKETEERS (1935, RKO)—Porthos

OLSEN, OLE
THE GHOST CATCHERS (1944, Universal)—Ole

OLSON, JACK
TIME WALKER (1982, New World)—Ankh Venaris, Mummy

O'MAHONEY, JOCK
THE KANGAROO KID (1950, Australia, Allied Australian)—Tex
Kinnane

O'MALLEY, PAT
THE FIGHTING AMERICAN (1924, Silent, Universal)—Bill
Pendleton

O'NEAL, GRIFFIN
THE ESCAPE ARTIST (1982, Orion-Warners)—Danny Masters
HADLEY'S REBELLION (1984, East India/ADI)—Hadley
Hickman

O'NEAL, RON
SUPERFLY (1972, Warners)—Youngblood Priest
SUPERFLY T.N.T. (1973, Paramount)—Youngblood Priest

O'NEAL, RYAN
WILD ROVERS (1971, MGM)—Ross Bodine
WHAT'S UP DOC? (1972, Warners)—Prof. Howard Bannister
THE THIEF WHO CAME TO DINNER (1973, Warners)—Webster
BARRY LYNDON (1975, GB, Hawk-Peregrine)—Barry Lyndon
THE DRIVER (1978, 20th Century Fox)—The Driver
OLIVER'S STORY (1978, Paramount)—Oliver Barrett IV
PARTNERS (1982, Paramount)—Benson
IRRECONCILABLE DIFFERENCES (1984, Warners)—Albert
Brodsky
TOUGH GUYS DON'T DANCE (1987, Cannon)—Tim Madden

O'NEAL, TATUM
LITTLE DARLINGS (1980, Paramount)—Ferris

O'NEIL, NANCE
THE IRON WOMAN (1916, Silent, Metro)—Sarah Maitland

O'NEIL, SALLY
MIKE (1926, Silent, MGM)—Mike
BECKY (1927, Silent, MGM)—Rebecca O'Brien McCloskey
HARDBOILED (1929, Silent, FBO)—Teena Johnson
KATHLEEN MAVOURNEEN (1930, Tiffany)—Kathleen
Mavoureen
SISTERS (1930, Columbia)—Sally Malone
THE BRAT (1931, Fox)—The Brat

THE MOTH (1934, Showmen's Pictures)—Diana Wyman
KATHLEEN (1938, Ireland, Hoffberg)—Kathleen O'Moore

O'NEILL, AMY
HONEY, I SHRUNK THE KIDS (1989, Buena Vista)—Amy
Szalinski

O'NEILL, ED
DUTCH (1991, 20th Century Fox)—Dutch

O'NEILL, EDWARD
THE KING'S DAUGHTER (1916, Silent, GB, Jury)—The King

O'NEILL, HENRY
TWO AGAINST THE WORLD (1936, Warners)—Jim Carstairs

ONTKEAN, MICHAEL
WILLIE AND PHIL (1980, 20th Century Fox)—Willie Kaufman

ONYX, NARDA
JESSE JAMES MEETS FRANKENSTEIN'S DAUGHTER (1966,
Embassy)—Maria Frankenstein

OPPER, DAN
ANDROID (1982, New World)—Max 404

O'QUINN, TERRY
THE STEPFATHER (1987, New Century-Vista)—Jerry Blake
STEPFATHER 2: MAKE ROOM FOR DADDY (1989, ITC)—Dr.
Gene Clifford

ORBISON, ROY
THE FASTEST GUITAR ALIVE (1967, MGM)—Johnny

ORESTE (KIRKOP)
THE VAGABOND KING (1956, Paramount)—Francois Villon

ORLANDI, FELICE
THE PUSHER (1960, United Artists)—The Pusher

ORMAN, ROSCOE
WILLIE DYNAMITE (1973, Universal)—Willie Dynamite

ORR, WILLIAM T.
THREE SONS O'GUNS (1941, Warners)—Kenneth Patterson

OSBORNE, BABY MARIE
A LITTLE PATRIOT (1917, Silent, Pathe)—The Little Patriot
CUPID BY PROXY (1918, Silent, Pathe)—Marie Stewart
DOLLY'S VACATION (1918, Silent, Pathe)—Dolly McKenzie

OSBORNE, VIVIENNE
I ACCUSE MY PARENTS (1945, Producers Releasing Corp.)—
Mrs. Wilson

OSCAR, HENRY
THE CASE OF GABRIEL PERRY (1935, GB, British Lion)—
Gabriel Perry
SEXTON BLAKE AND THE BEARDED DOCTOR (1935, GB,
MGM)—Dr. Gibbs

O'SHEA, MICHAEL
JACK LONDON (1943, United Artists)—Jack London
MAN FROM FRISCO (1944, Republic)—Matt Braddock
DISC JOCKEY (1951, Allied Artists)—Mike Richards

O'SHEA, MILO
THE PLAYBOYS (1992, US/Ireland, Goldwyn)—Freddie

OSTRICHE, MURIEL
A DAUGHTER OF THE SEA (1915, Silent, World)—The Girl

O'SULLIVAN, BRIAN
MEN OF IRELAND (1938, Ireland, Irish National)—Liam

O'SULLIVAN, MAUREEN
THE PRINCESS AND THE PLUMBER (1930, Fox)—Princess
Louise
TARZAN AND HIS MATE (1934, MGM)—Jane Parker
WOMAN WANTED (1935, MGM)—Ann
BETWEEN TWO WOMEN (1937, MGM)—Claire Donahue
MY DEAR MISS ALDRICH (1937, MGM)—Martha Aldrich

O'SULLIVAN, RICHARD
DANGEROUS EXILE (1958, GB, Rank)—Louis VVII
THE WEBSTER BOY (1962, GB, Regal)—Jimmy Webster

O'TOOLE, ANNETTE
ONE ON ONE (1977, Warners)—Janet Hays

O'TOOLE, PETER
LAWRENCE OF ARABIA (1962, GB, Columbia)—T.E. Lawrence
LORD JIM (1965, GB, Columbia)—Lord Jim
THE NIGHT OF THE GENERALS (1967, GB, Columbia)—
General Tanz
THE LION IN WINTER (1968, GB, Avco Embassy)—King
Henry II
GOODBYE MR. CHIPS (1969, APJAC/MGM)—Arthur Chipping
MURPHY'S WAR (1971, GB, Paramount)—Murphy
MAN OF LA MANCHA (1972, United Artists)—Don Quixote
THE RULING CLASS (1972, GB, Avco Embassy)—Jack, 14th
Earl of Gurney
CREATOR (1985, Universal)—Harry

OUSPENSKAYA, MARIA
TARZAN AND THE AMAZONS (1945, RKO)—Amazon Queen

OVERMAN, LYNNE
THREE MARRIED MEN (1936, Paramount)—Jeff Mullins

OWEN, BILL
NOT SO DUSTY (1956, GB, Eros)—Dusty

OWEN, GRANVILLE
LI'L ABNER (1940, RKO) -Li'l Abner Yokum

OWEN, SEENA
THE WOMAN GOD CHANGED (1921, Silent, Paramount)—Anna
Janssen
SISTERS (1922, Silent, American Releasing)—Alix Strickland
THE HUNTED WOMAN (1925, Silent, Fox)—Joanne Grey

OWENS, PATRICIA
SEVEN WOMEN FROM HELL (1961, 20th Century Fox)—Grace
Ingram

OWENSBY, EARL
SEABO (1978, E.O. Corp.)—Seabo

OXENBOULD, BEN
FATTY FINN (1980, Australia, Children's Films)—Fatty Finn

OXLEY, DAVID
THE HOUND OF THE BASKERVILLES (1959, GB, Hammer)—Sir
Hugo Baskerville

P

PACE, JUDY
THREE IN THE ATTIC (1968, American International)—Eulice

PACINO, AL
SERPICO (1973, Paramount)—Frank Serpico
THE GODFATHER, PART II (1974, Paramount)—Michael
Corleone
BOBBY DEERFIELD (1977, Columbia)—Bobby Deerfield
AUTHOR! AUTHOR! (1982, 20th Century Fox)—Ivan Travalian
SCARFACE (1983, Universal)—Tony Montana
THE GODFATHER PART III (1990, Paramount)—Michael
Corleone
FRANKIE AND JOHNNY (1991, Paramount)—Johnny

PADDEN, SARAH
MIDNIGHT LADY (1932, Chesterfield)—Nita St. George

PADDOCK, CHARLES
THE OLYMPIC HERO (1928, Silent, Zakaro-Supreme)—Charlie
Patterson

PADILLA, MANUEL
THE YOUNG AND THE BRAVE (1963, MGM)—Han

PAGE, ANITA
OUR DANCING DAUGHTERS (1928, Silent, MGM)—Ann
OUR MODERN MAIDENS (1929, MGM)—Kentucky
OUR BLUSHING BRIDES (1930, MGM)—Connie
WAR NURSE (1930, MGM)—Joy
JUNGLE BRIDE (1933, Monogram)—Doris Evans

PAGE, BRADLEY
THE CARTER CASE (1947, Republic)—Elliott Carter

PAGE, DOROTHY
THE SINGING COWGIRL (1939, Grand National)—Dorothy
Hendrick

PAGE, GALE
DAUGHTERS COURAGEOUS (1939, Warners)—Cora Masters
FOUR DAUGHTERS (1938, Warners)—Emma Lemp
FOUR WIVES (1939, Warners)—Emma Lemp
FOUR MOTHERS (1940, Warners)—Emma Lemp Talbot

PAGE, GERALDINE
THE THREE SISTERS (1977, Actor Studios Theatre)—Olga

PAGET, DEBRA
BIRD OF PARADISE (1951, 20th Century Fox)—Kalua
PRINCESS OF THE NILE (1954, 20th Century Fox)—Princess
Shalimar

PAIGE, JANIS
HER KIND OF MAN (1946, Warners)—Georgia King
FUGITIVE LADY (1951, Republic)—Barbara Clementi
TWO GALS AND A GUY (1951, United Artists)—Della Oliver &
Sylvia Latour

PAIGE, ROBERT
MEET THE BOY FRIEND (1937, Republic)—Tony Page
COWBOY IN MANHATTAN (1943, Universal)—Bob
HER PRIMITIVE MAN (1944, Universal)—Pete Matthews

PAINE, HEIDI
NEW YORK'S FINEST (1988, Platinum)—Carley Pointer

PAIS, JOCH
TEENAGE MUTANT NINJA TURTLES (1990, New Line)—
Raphael

PALANCE, JACK
MAN IN THE ATTIC (1953, 20th Century Fox)—Slade
I DIED A THOUSAND TIMES (1955, Warners)—Roy Earle
THE LONELY MAN (1957, Paramount)—Jacob Wade
THE DESPERADOS (1969, Columbia)—Parson Josiah Galt
ONE MAN JURY (1978, Cal-Am Artists)—Wade

PALIN, MICHAEL
THE MISSIONARY (1982, Columbia)—Rev. Charles Fortesque

PALLETTE, EUGENE
THE THREE MUSKETEERS (1921, Silent, United Artists)—
Aramis

PALMER, LILLI
MY GIRL TISA (1948, Warners)—Tisa Kepes

PALMER, PETER
LI'L ABNER (1959, Paramount)—Li'l Abner Yokum

PANTOLINO, JOE
THE LAST OF THE FINEST (1990, Orion)—Wayne Gross

PANTSARI, BUDDY
TRADER HORNEE (1970, Entertainment Ventures)—Hamilton
Hornee

PANZER, PAUL
THE ANCIENT MARINER (1925, Silent, Fox)—The Mariner

PAPAS, IRENE
THE TROJAN WOMEN (1971, Cinerama)—Helen

PARE, MICHAEL
EDDIE AND THE CRUISERS (1983, Aurora)—Eddie Wilson
EDDIE AND THE CRUISERS II; EDDIE LIVES (1989, Aurora)—
Eddie Wilson/ Joe West

PARKER, CECIL
CAPTAIN BOYCOTT (1947, GB, GFD)—Captain Boycott
THE AMAZING MR. BEECHAM (1949, GB, Two Cities)—
Benjamin Beecham
DEAR MR. PROHACK (1949, GB, GFD)—Arthur Prohack
THE LADYKILLERS (1956, GB, Ealing)—The Mayor

PARKER, CECILIA
GIRL LOVES BOY (1937, Grand National)—Dorothy McCarthy
SWEETHEART OF THE NAVY (1937, Grand National)—Joan
JUDGE HARDY'S CHILDREN (1938, MGM)—Marian Hardy
OUT WEST WITH THE HARDY'S (1938, MGM)—Marian Hardy
GAMBLING DAUGHTERS (1941, Producers Releasing Corp.)—
Diana Cameron

PARKER, COREY
HOW I GOT INTO COLLEGE (1989, 20th Century Fox)—Marlon
Browne

PARKER, EDWIN
ABBOTT AND COSTELLO MEET DR. JEKYLL AND MR. HYDE
(1953, Universal)—Mr. Hyde

ABBOTT AND COSTELLO MEET THE MUMMY (1955,
Universal)—Kharis

PARKER, ELEANOR
THE WOMAN IN WHITE (1948, Warners)—Anne Catherick
CAGED (1950, Warners)—Marie Allen
A MILLIONAIRE FOR CHRISTY (1951, 20th Century Fox)—
Christy Sloane
THE KING AND FOUR QUEENS (1956, United Artists)—Sabina
LIZZIE (1957, MGM)—Elizabeth Richmond

PARKER, FESS
DAVY CROCKETT, KING OF THE WILD FRONTIER (1955,
Disney) -Davy Crockett
DAVY CROCKETT AND THE RIVER PIRATES (1956, Disney)—
Davy Crockett

PARKER, JAMESON
A SMALL CIRCLE OF FRIENDS (1980, United Artists)—Nick
Baxter

PARKER, JEAN
LITTLE WOMEN (1933, RKO)—Beth March
TWO ALONE (1934, RKO)—Mazie
PRINCESS O'HARA (1935, Universal)—Princess O'Hara
SHE MARRIED A COP (1939, Republic)—Linda
GIRL FROM ALASKA (1942, Republic)—Mary "Pete" McCoy
ADVENTURES OF KITTY O'DAY (1944, Monogram)—Kitty O'Day
DETECTIVE KITTY O'DAY (1944, Monogram)—Kitty O'Day
LADY IN THE DEATH HOUSE (1944, Producers Releasing
Corp.)—Mary

PARKER, MARY
THE HOSTAGE (1956, GB, Fairbanks-Westridge/Eros)—Rosa
Gonzuelo

PARKER, SARAH JESSICA
GIRLS JUST WANT TO HAVE FUN (1985, New World)—
Janey Glenn

PARKER, WILLARD
THE GREAT JESSE JAMES RAID (1953, Lippert)—Jesse James
LONE TEXAN (1959, 20th Century Fox)—Clint Bannister

PARKINS, BARBARA
PUPPET ON A CHAIN (1971, GB, FBO)—Maggie
CHRISTINA (1974, Canada, New World)—Christina

PARKS, LARRY
THE JOLSON STORY (1946, Columbia)—Al Jolson
THE SWORDSMAN (1947, Columbia)—Alexander MacArden
JOLSON SINGS AGAIN (1949, Columbia)—Al Jolson

PARKS, MICHAEL
BUS RILEY'S BACK IN TOWN (1965, Universal)—Bus Riley
THE RETURN OF JOSEY WALES (1987, Multi-Tacar)—
Josey Wales

PARRISH, HELEN
THREE SMART GIRLS GROW UP (1939, Universal)—Kay Craig

PARRISH, LESLIE
THREE ON A COUCH (1966, Columbia)—Mary Lou Mauve

PARTON, DOLLY
STEEL MAGNOLIAS (1989, Tri-Star)—Truvy Jones

PATACHON, PAT
ALF'S CARPET (1929, GB, British International)—Alf Higgins

PATCH, WALLY
TWO SMART MEN (1940, GB, Anglo International)—Wally
NOT SO DUSTY (1956, GB, Eros)—Dusty Gray

PATRIC, JASON
THE LOST BOYS (1987, Warners)—Michael

PATRICK, BUTCH
THE TWO LITTLE BEARS (1961, 20th Century Fox)—Billy Davis

PATRICK, DOROTHY
THE BLONDE BANDIT (1950, Republic)—Gloria Dell

PATRICK, GAIL
WOMAN IN BONDAGE (1943, Monogram)—Margot Bracken
UP IN MABEL'S ROOM (1944, United Artists)—Mabel Essington

PATRICK, LEE
THE NURSE'S SECRET (1941, Warners)—Ruth Adams

PATRICK, NIGEL
THE PASSIONATE SENTRY (1952, GB, Fine Arts)—Miles
    Cornwell
THE MAN INSIDE (1958, GB, Columbia)—Sam Carter

PATTERSON, ELIZABETH
JAZZ BABIES (1932, Peerless)—Babs
WHO KILLED AUNT MAGGIE? (1940, Republic)—Aunt Maggie
    Ambler

PAUL, DAVID
DOUBLE TROUBLE (1992, MPCA)—David

PAUL, PETER
DOUBLE TROUBLE (1992, MPCA)—Peter

PAUL, STUART
EMANON (1987, Paul Ent.)—Emanon

PAULL, MORGAN
DIRTY O'NEIL (1974, American International)—Jimmy O'Neil

PAVAROTTI, LUCIANO
YES, GIORGIO (1982, MGM/United Artists)—Giorgio Fini

PAVITT, ERIC
MY FRIEND THE KING (1931, GB, Fox)—King Ludwig

PAVLOVA, ANNA
DUMB GIRL OF PORTICI (1916, Silent, Universal)—Fenella

PAVLOW, MURIEL
EYEWITNESS (1956, GB, Rank)—Lucy Church

PAYNE, HETTIE
PAULA (1915, GB, Silent, Holnfirth/Initial)—Paula

PAYNE, JOHN
KID NIGHTINGALE (1939, Warners)—Steve Nelson
KING OF THE LUMBERJACKS (1940, Warners)—Slim
CAPTAIN CHINA (1949, Paramount)—Captain China
THE EAGLE AND THE HAWK (1950, Paramount)—Todd
    Croyden
THE VANQUISHED (1953, Paramount)—Rock Grayson
TENNESSEE'S PARTNER (1955, RKO)—Tennessee
THE BOSS (1956, United Artists)—Matt Brady

PAYNE, LAURENCE
THE COURT MARTIAL OF MAJOR KELLER (1961, GB,
    Danzinger)—Major Keller

PAYTON, BARBARA
BAD BLONDE (1953, GB, Lippert)—Lorna Vecchi

PAXTON, BILL
THE LAST OF THE FINEST (1990, Orion)—Howard
    (Hojo) Jones

PEARCE, AL
HERE COMES ELMER (1943, Republic)—Elmer Blurt/Al
    Pearce

PEACOCK, KIM
MY LORD THE CHAUFFEUR (1927, GB, Silent, British
    Classics)—Philip Parr

PEARL, JACK
MEET THE BARON (1933, MGM)—The Baron

PEARSON, JESSE
BYE BYE BIRDIE (1963, Columbia)—Conrad Birdie

PEARSON, LLOYD
SCHWEIK'S NEW ADVENTURES (1943, GB, Eden/Coronet)—
    Schweik

PEARSON, VIRGINIA
IMPOSSIBLE CATHERINE (1919, Silent, Pearson Photoplays)—
    Catherine Kimberly

PEARY, HAROLD
THE GREAT GILDERSLEEVE (1942, RKO)—Throckmorton P.
    Gildersleeve
GILDERSLEEVE ON BROADWAY (1943, RKO)—Throckmorton
    P. Gildersleeve
GILDERSLEEVE'S BAD DAY (1943, RKO)—Throckmorton P.
    Gildersleeve
GILDERSLEEVE'S GHOST (1944, RKO)—Throckmorton P.
    Gildersleeve

PECK, CHARLES
FIVE LITTLE PEPPERS AND HOW THEY GREW (1939,
    Columbia)—Ben Pepper
FIVE LITTLE PEPPERS AT HOME (1940, Columbia)—Ben
    Pepper
FIVE LITTLE PEPPERS IN TROUBLE (1940, Columbia)—Ben
    Pepper
OUT WEST WITH THE PEPPERS (1940, Columbia)—Ben Pepper

PECK, GREGORY
SPELLBOUND (1945, United Artists)—John J.B. Ballantine
THE GREAT SINNER (1949, MGM)—Feodor Dostoyevsky
THE GUNFIGHTER (1950, 20th Century Fox)—Johnny Ringo
CAPTAIN HORATIO HORNBLOWER (1951, GB, Warners)—
    Horatio Hornblower
DAVID AND BATHSHEBA (1951, 20th Century Fox)—King David
THE WORLD IN HIS ARMS (1952, Universal)—Jonathan Clark
MAN WITH A MILLION (1954, GB, United Artists)—
    Jerry Adams
NIGHT PEOPLE (1954, 20th Century Fox)—Col. Van Dyke
THE MAN IN THE GREY FLANNEL SUIT (1956, 20th Century
    Fox)—Tom Rath

BELOVED INFIDEL (1959, 20th Century Fox)—F. Scott
Fitzgerald
CAPTAIN NEWMAN M.D. (1963, Universal)—Capt. Josiah
Newman
MACKENNA'S GOLD (1969, Columbia)—MacKenna
I WALK THE LINE (1970, Columbia)—Sheriff Henry Tawes
MACARTHUR (1977, Universal)—Gen. Douglas MacArthur
OLD GRINGO (1989, Columbia)—Ambrose Bierce

PELIKAN, LISA
JENNIFER (1978, American International)—Jennifer Baylor

PELLETIER, ANDREA
MARIE-ANN (1978, Canada, Canadian Film Production)—
Marie-Ann

PENDLETON, NAT
TOP SERGEANT MULLIGAN (1941, Monogram)—Sgt. Mulligan

PENN, CLIFFORD
FALL GUY (1947, Monogram)—Tom Cochrane

PENN, SEAN
BAD BOYS (1983, EMI/Universal)—Mick
THE FALCON AND THE SNOWMAN (1985, Orion)—Daulton Lee
WE'RE NO ANGELS (1989, Paramount)—Jim/Fr. Brown
STATE OF GRACE (1990, Orion)—Terry

PENNEBAKER, JUDY
THE FARMER'S OTHER DAUGHTER (1965, United Producers)—
June Brown

PENNELL, LARRY
SEVEN ANGRY MEN (1955, Allied Artists)—Oliver Brown

PENNER, JOE
I'M FROM THE CITY (1938, RKO)—Pete
MR. DOODLE KICKS OFF (1938, RKO)—Doodle Bugs
BOYS FROM SYRACUSE (1940, Mayfair/Universal)—Dromio of
Syracuse
MILLIONAIRE PLAYBOY (1940, RKO)—Joe Zany

PENNINGTON, ANN
THE RAINBOW PRINCESS (1916, Silent, Famous Players)—
Hope Daingerfield
MAD DANCER (1925, Silent, Janus)—Mimi
GOLD DIGGERS ON BROADWAY (1929, Warners)—Ann Collins

PENROSE, PETER
SORRELL AND SON (1934, GB, United Artists)—Kit Sorrell

PEPPARD, GEORGE
THE VICTORS (1963, Columbia)—Cpl. Chase
P.J. (1968, Universal)—P.J. Detweiler
THE EXECUTIONER (1970, GB, Columbia)—John Shay
NEWMAN'S LAW (1974, Universal)—Vince Newman

PERCY, EILEEN
MAID OF THE WEST (1921, Silent, Universal)—Betty
THE FLIRT (1922, Silent, Universal)—Cora Madison

PERKINS, ANTHONY
PSYCHO (1960, Paramount)—Norman Bates
THE FOOL KILLER (1965, Allied Artists)—Milo Bogardus
PSYCHO II (1983, Universal)—Norman Bates
PSYCHO III (1986, Universal)—Norman Bates

PERKINS, ELIZABETH
HE SAID, SHE SAID (1991, Paramount)—Lorie Bryer

PERKINS, GILBERT
TEENAGE MONSTER (1958, Marquette-Howco)—Charles
Cannon

PERKINS, MILLIE
THE DIARY OF ANNE FRANK (1959, 20th Century Fox)—
Anne Frank

PERKINS, VALENTINE
PRISONERS IN PETTICOATS (1950, Republic)—Joan Grey

PERREAU, JANINE
THREE FOR BEDROOM C (1952, Warners)—Barbara Haven

PERRIN, JACK
THE KNOCKOUT KID (1927, Silent, Paramount)—Jack Lanning

PERRINE, VALERIE
W.C. FIELDS AND ME (1976, Universal)—Carlotta Monti

PERRINS, LESLIE
EXPERT'S OPINION (1935, GB, Paramount)—Richard Steele
THE SHADOW OF MIKE EMERALD (1935, GB, Radio)—Mike
Emerald
THE SILENT PASSENGER (1935, GB, Associate British Films)—
Maurice Windermere

PERROTT, WILLIAM
SON OF BILLY THE KID (1949, Screen Guild)—Billy the Kid

PERRY, JOAN
COUNTERFEIT LADY (1937, Columbia)—Phyllis

PERSSON, ESSY
THERESE AND ISABELLE (1968, Audubon Films)—Therese

PESCI, JOE
GOODFELLAS (1990, Warners)—Tommy DeVito
THE SUPER (1991, 20th Century Fox)—Louie Kritski
MY COUSIN VINNY (1992, 20th Century Fox)—Vinny Gambini

PETERS, HOUSE
HELD TO ANSWER (1923, Silent, Metro)—John Hampstead
RAFFLES, THE AMATEUR CRACKSMAN (1925, Universal)—A.J.
Raffles

PETERS, JEAN
ANNE OF THE INDIES (1951, 20th Century Fox)—Anne
WAIT 'TIL THE SUN SHINES NELLIE (1952, 20th Century
Fox)—Nellie Halper
VICKI (1953, 20th Century Fox)—Vicki Lynn

PETERS, NOEL
THE INVISIBLE MANIAC (1990, Smoking Gun Pictures)—Kevin
Dornwinkle

PETERS, PAGE
THE WARRENS OF VIRGINIA (1915, Silent, Lasky)—Arthur
Warren

PETERSON, AMANDA
CAN'T BUY ME LOVE (1987, Buena Vista)—Cindy Mancini

PETERSON, CASSANDRA
ELVIRA: MISTRESS OF THE DARK (1988, New World)—Elvira

PETERSON, COLIN
SMILEY (1957, GB, 20th Century Fox)—Smiley Greevins

PETERSON, DOROTHY
MOTHERS CRY (1930, First National)—Mary K. Williams

PETERSON, NAN
LOUISIANA HUSSEY (1960, Bon Are/Howco)—Nina Duprez

PETERSON, STEWART
PONY EXPRESS RIDER (1976, Doty-Drayton)—Jimmy

PETERSON, WILLIAM
MANHUNTER (1986, De Laurentiis)—Will Graham

PETTET, JOANNA
THE GROUP (1966, United Artists)—Kay Strong

PFEIFFER, MICHELLE
LADYHAWKE (1985, Warners/20th Century Fox)—Isabeau
THE WITCHES OF EASTWICK (1987, Warners)—Sukie
Ridgemont
DANGEROUS LIAISONS (1988, Warners)—Madame de Tourvel
MARRIED TO THE MOB (1988, Orion)—Angela DeMarco
FRANKIE AND JOHNNY (1991, Paramount)—Frankie

PHILBIN, JOHN
SHY PEOPLE (1988, Cannon)—Tommy Sullivan

PHILBIN, MARY
ROSE OF PARIS (1924, Silent, Universal)—Mitsi
STELLA MARIS (1925, Silent, Universal)—Stella Maris

PHILLIPS, DOROTHY
HURRICANE'S GAL (1922, Silent, Associated First
National)—Lola
SLANDER THE WOMAN (1923, Silent, Associated First
National)—Yvonne Desmarest

PHILLIPS, GUY
SATAN'S SISTER (1925, Silent, GB, Woodfall)—Satan Tyler

PHILLIPS, LOU DIAMOND
YOUNG GUNS (1988, 20th Century Fox)—Chavez Y Chavez
RENEGADES (1989, Universal)—Hank
YOUNG GUNS II (1990, 20th Century Fox)—Chavez Y Chavez

PHILLIPS, MACKENZIE
RAFFERTY AND THE GOLD DUST TWINS (1975, Warners)—
Frisbee

PHILLIPS, ROBIN
DECLINE AND FALL. . .OF A BIRD WATCHER (1969, GB, Fox)—
Paul Pennyfeather
TWO GENTLEMEN SHARING (1969, GB, American
International)—Roddy
DAVID COPPERFIELD (1970, GB, 20th Century Fox)—David
Copperfield

PHILLIPS, LESLIE
THE MAN WHO LIKED FUNERALS (1959, GB, Rank)—
Simon Hurd
DOCTOR IN TROUBLE (1970, GB, Rank)—Dr. Burke

PHOENIX, RIVER
EXPLORERS (1985, Paramount)—Wolfgang Muller

LITTLE NIKITA (1988, Columbia)—Jeff Grant
A NIGHT IN THE LIFE OF JIMMY REARDON (1988, 20th
Century Fox)—Jimmy Reardon
RUNNING ON EMPTY (1988, Warners)—Danny Pope
INDIANA JONES AND THE LAST CRUSADE (1989,
Paramount)—Young Indy Jones

PICERNI, PAUL
THE BROTHERS RICO (1957, Columbia)—Gino Rico

PICHON, ANNE
FAREWELL TO CINDERELLA (1937, GB, RKO)—Margaret

PICKERING, SARAH
LITTLE DORRIT (1988, GB, Cannon)—Little Dorrit

PICKFORD, JACK
JACK AND JILL (1917, Silent, Paramount)—Jack Ranney
HIS MAJESTY, BUNKER BEAN (1918, Silent, Paramount)—
Bunker Bean
HUCK AND TOM (1918, Paramount)—Tom Sawyer
GARRISON'S FINISH (1923, Silent, Allied Producers)—Billy
Garrison
THE HILL BILLY (1924, Silent, Allied Producers)—Jed McCoy
MY SON (1925, Silent, First National)—Tony Silva

PICKFORD, MARY
SUCH A LITTLE QUEEN (1914, Silent, Famous Players)—
Queen Anna Victoria
TESS OF THE STORM COUNTRY (1914, Silent, Famous
Players) -Tess
CINDERELLA (1915, Silent, Famous Players)—Cinderella
LITTLE PAL (1915, Silent, Famous Players)—"Little Pal"
MADAME BUTTERFLY (1915, Silent, Famous Players)—Cho-
Cho-San
MISTRESS NELL (1915, Silent, Famous Players)—Mistress Nell
RAGS (1915, Silent, Famous Players)—"Rags"/Alice McCloud
HULDA FROM HOLLAND (1916, Silent, Artcraft)—Hulda
POOR LITTLE RICH GIRL (1917, Silent, Artcraft)—Gwendolyn
REBECCA OF SUNNYBROOK FARM (1917, Silent, Artcraft)—
Rebecca Randall
AMARILLY OF CLOTHESLINE ALLEY (1918, Silent, Artscraft)—
Amarilly Jenkins
HOW COULD YOU JEAN? (1918, Silent, Artcraft) -Jean Mackaye
JOHANNA ENLISTS (1918, Silent, Artcraft)—Johanna
Renssaller
M'LISS (1918, Silent, Artcraft)—M'liss Smith
STELLA MARIS (1918, Silent, Artcraft)—Stella Maris
THE HOODLUM (1919, Silent, First National)—Amy Burke
POLLYANNA (1920, Silent, United Artists)—Pollyanna
LITTLE LORD FAUNTLEROY (1921, Silent, United Artists)—
Cedric
TESS OF THE STORM COUNTRY (1922, Silent, United Artists)—
Tessibel Skinner
ROSITA (1923, Silent, United Artists)—Rosita
LITTLE ANNIE ROONEY (1925, Silent, United Artists)—Annie
Rooney
SPARROWS (1926, Silent, United Artists)—Mama Mollie
MY BEST GIRL (1927, Silent, United Artists)—Maggie Johnson
COQUETTE (1929, United Artists)—Norma Besant
THE TAMING OF THE SHREW (1929, United Artists)—
Katherine
KIKI (1931, United Artists)—Kiki

PIDGEON, WALTER
MY DEAR MISS ALDRICH (1937, MGM)—Ken Morley
NICK CARTER, MASTER DETECTIVE (1939, MGM)—Nick Carter
SOCIETY LAWYER (1939, MGM)—Christopher Durant
THE MINIVER STORY (1950, GB, MGM)—Clem Miniver
CALLING BULLDOG DRUMMOND (1951, GB, MGM)—Hugh Drummond
THE UNKNOWN MAN (1951, MGM)—Dwight Bradley Mason

PILBEAM, NOVA
LITTLE FRIEND (1934, GB, Gaumont)—Felicity Hughes
LADY JANE GREY (1936, GB, Gaumont)—Lady Jane Grey
YOUNG AND INNOCENT (1938, GB, Gaumont)—Erica Burgoyne

PINCHOT, BRONSON
BLAME IT ON THE BELLBOY (1992, GB/US, Buena Vista)—Bellboy

PINSENT, GORDON
THE ROWDYMAN (1973, Canada, Crowley)—Will Cole

PINZA, EZIO
MR. IMPERIUM (1951, MGM)—Mr. Imperium
STRICTLY DISHONORABLE (1951, MGM)—Augustino Caraffa

PISCOPO, JOE
WISE GUYS (1986, MGM/United Artists)—Moe Dickstein

PITT, ARCHIE
BARNACLE BILL (1935, GB, City/Butchers)—Bill Harris

PITT, BRAD
JOHNNY SUEDE (1991, Vega/Balthazar)—Johnny Suede

PITT, INGRID
THE VAMPIRE LOVERS (1970, GB, Hammer)—Marcilla Karnstein
COUNTESS DRACULA (1972, GB, Hammer)—Countess Elizabeth Nadasdy

PITTMAN, TOM
HIGH SCHOOL BIG SHOT (1959, Filmgroup-Sparta)—Marv

PITTS, ZASU
PATSY (1921, Silent, Truart)—Patsy
HER FIRST MATE (1933, Universal)—Mary Horner
THEY JUST WANT TO GET MARRIED (1933, Universal)—Molly Hull
LOVE BIRDS (1934, Universal)—Araminta Tootle
THEIR BIG MOMENT (1934, RKO)—Tillie Whim
AFFAIR OF SUSAN (1935, Universal)—Susan Todd
SHE GETS HER MAN (1935, Universal)—Esmerelda
WANTED (1937, GB, Sound City)—Winnie Oatfield

PLATT, MARC
SEVEN BRIDES FOR SEVEN BROTHERS (1954, MGM)—Daniel Pontabee

PLATT, OLIVER
FLATLINERS (1990, Columbia)—Steckle

PLEASANCE, DONALD
DR. CRIPPEN (1963, GB, Pathe)—Dr. Hawley Harvey Crippen
THE GUEST (1963, GB, Janus)—Davis
THE NIGHT OF THE GENERALS (1967, GB, Columbia)—Gen. Kahlenberger

PLIMPTON, MARTHA
SAMANTHA (1991, Planet)—Samantha

PLOWRIGHT, JOAN
THREE SISTERS (1974, GB, British Lion)—Masha

PLUMMER, AMANDA
CATTLE ANNIE AND LITTLE BRITCHES (1981, Universal)—Cattle Annie

PLUMMER, CHRISTOPHER
THE HIGH COMMISSIONER (1968, US/GB, Rank/Cinerama)—Sir James Quentin
OEDIPUS THE KING (1968, GB, Universal)—Oedipus
ACES HIGH (1977, GB, Cine Artists/EMI)—Sinclair
THE BOSS' WIFE (1986, Tri-Star)—Roalvang

POHLMANN, ERIC
THE MAN WHO COULDN'T TALK (1964, GB, Falcon-Taurus)—The Consul

POITIER, SIDNEY
THE DEFIANT ONES (1958, United Artists)—Noah Cullen
PORGY AND BESS (1959, Columbia)—Porgy
GUESS WHO'S COMING TO DINNER? (1967, Columbia)—John Prentice
TO SIR, WITH LOVE (1967, GB, Columbia)—Mark Thackeray
THE LOST MAN (1969, Universal)—Jason Higgs
THEY CALL ME MR. TIBBS (1970, United Artists)—Virgil Tibbs
BROTHER JOHN (1971, Columbia)—John Kane
BUCK AND THE PREACHER (1972, Columbia)—Buck

POLLARD, MICHAEL J.
LITTLE FAUSS AND BIG HALSY (1970, Paramount)—Little Fauss
DIRTY LITTLE BILLY (1972, Columbia)—Billy Bonney

PONS, LILY
THAT GIRL FROM PARIS (1937, RKO)—Nikki Martin

PORIZKOVA, PAULINA
HER ALIBI (1989, Warners)—Nina Ionescu

PORTER, ALISON
CURLY SUE (1991, Warner Brothers)—Curly Sue Dancer

PORTER, BETH
THE NAKED WITCH (1964, Mishkin)—Beth

PORTER, JEAN
BETTY CO-ED (1946, Columbia)—Joanne Leeds
TWO BLONDES AND A REDHEAD (1947, Columbia)—Catherine Abbott
G.I. JANE (1951, Lippert)—Jan

PORTER, ROBIE
THREE (1969, GB, United Artists)—Bert

PORTER, VALERIE
THREE BLONDES IN HIS LIFE (1961, Cinema Associates)—Martha Carr

PORTMAN, ERIC
SQUADRON LEADER X (1943, RKO)—Erich Kohler
WANTED FOR MURDER (1946, GB, 20th Century Fox)—Victor Colebrooke
DEAR MURDERER (1947, GB, Gainsborough)—Lee Warren

HIS EXCELLENCY (1952, GB, Ealing)—George Harrison
THE SPIDER AND THE FLY (1952, GB, GFD)—Fernand
 Maubert
THE GOOD COMPANIONS (1957, GB, AB-Pathe)—Jess Oakroyd

POST, WILLIAM JR.
MR. AMD MRS. NORTH (1941, MGM)—Gerald P. North

POTTER, MARTIN
GOODBYE GEMINI (1970, GB, Cinerama)—Julian

POULTON, MABEL
A DAUGHTER IN REVOLT (1927, Silent, GB, Allied Artists)—
 Aimee Scroope
NOT QUITE A LADY (1928, GB, Silent, Wardour)—Ethel
 Borridge

POWELL, ALISA
SATAN'S CHEERLEADERS (1977, World Amusements)—Debbie

POWELL, DAVID
HIS PARISIAN WIFE (1919, Silent, Artcraft)—Martin Wesley

POWELL, DICK
BROADWAY GONDOLIER (1935, Warners)—Richard Purcell
SHIPMATES FOREVER (1935, Warners)—Richard John
 Melville III
THE SINGING MARINE (1937, Warners)—Robert Brent
COWBOY FROM BROOKLYN (1938, Warners)—Elly Jordan
JOHNNY O'CLOCK (1947, Columbia)—Johnny O'Clock
MRS. MIKE (1949, United Artists)—Sgt. Mike Flannigan
THE REFORMER AND THE REDHEAD (1950, MGM)—Andrew
 Rockton Hale

POWELL, EDDIE
THE MUMMY'S SHROUD (1967, GB, Hammer)—Mummy

POWELL, ELEANOR
BORN TO DANCE (1936, MGM)—Nora Paige
ROSALIE (1937, MGM)—Rosalie Romanikoff
LADY BE GOOD (1941, MGM)—Marilyn Marsh

POWELL, JANE
A DATE WITH JUDY (1948, MGM)—Judy Foster
THREE DARING DAUGHTERS (1948, MGM)—Tess Morgan
NANCY GOES TO RIO (1950, MGM)—Nancy Barklay
RICH, YOUNG AND PRETTY (1951, MGM)—Elizabeth Rogers
SMALL TOWN GIRL (1953, MGM)—Cindy Kimbell
THREE SAILORS AND A GIRL (1953, Warners)—Penny Watson
ATHENA (1954, MGM)—Athena Mulvain
SEVEN BRIDES FOR SEVEN BROTHERS (1954, MGM)—Milly
THE GIRL MOST LIKELY (1957, RKO/Universal)—Dodie

POWELL, ROBERT
MAHLER (1974, GB, Mayfair)—Gustave Mahler
HARLEQUIN (1980, Australia, Hemdale/New Image)—
 Gregory Wolfe

POWELL, SANDY
LEAVE IT TO ME (1937, GB, British Lion)—Sandy
I'VE GOT A HORSE (1938, GB, British Lion)—Sandy

POWELL, WILLIAM
FOR THE DEFENSE (1930, Paramount)—William Foster
LADIES' MAN (1931, Paramount)—Jamie Darricott
MAN OF THE WORLD (1931, Paramount)—Michael Trevor

LAWYER MAN (1933, Warners)—Anton Adam
PRIVATE DETECTIVE 62 (1933, Warners)—Donald Free
AFTER THE THIN MAN (1936, MGM)—Nick Charles
THE GREAT ZIEGFELD (1936, MGM)—Florenz Ziegfeld
MY MAN GODFREY (1936, Universal)—Godfrey Parke
THE BARONESS AND THE BUTLER (1938, 20th Century Fox)—
 Johann Porok
ANOTHER THIN MAN (1939, MGM)—Nick Charles
I LOVE YOU AGAIN (1940, MGM)—Larry Wilson/George Carey
SHADOW OF THE THIN MAN (1941, MGM)—Nick Charles
THE THIN MAN GOES HOME (1944, MGM)—Nick Charles
ZIEGFELD FOLLIES (1945, MGM)—Florenz Ziegfeld
THE HOODLUM SAINT (1946, MGM)—Terry Ellerton O'Neill
LIFE WITH FATHER (1947, Warners)—Clarence Day
THE SENATOR WAS INDISCREET (1947, Universal)—Senator
 Melvin G. Ashton
SONG OF THE THIN MAN (1947, MGM)—Nick Charles
MR. PEABODY AND THE MERMAID (1948, Universal)—Mr.
 Peabody

POWER, HARTLEY
YES, MR. BROWN (1933, GB, British and Dominions)—
 Mr. Brown

POWER, TYRONE
ALEXANDER'S RAGTIME BAND (1938, 20th Century Fox)—
 Roger Grant
JESSE JAMES (1939, 20th Century Fox)—Jesse James
JOHNNY APOLLO (1940, 20th Century Fox)—Bob Cain (Johnny
 Apollo)
THE MARK OF ZORRO (1940, 20th Century Fox)—Don
 Diego Vega
A YANK IN THE R.A.F. (1941, 20th Century Fox)—Tim Baker
SON OF FURY (1942, 20th Century Fox)—Benjamin Blake
CAPTAIN FROM CASTILE (1947, 20th Century Fox)—Pedro de
 Vargas
PRINCE OF FOXES (1949, 20th Century Fox)—Andrea Corsini
AN AMERICAN GUERRILLA IN THE PHILIPPINES (1950, 20th
 Century Fox)—Ensign Chuck Palmer
I'LL NEVER FORGET YOU (1951, 20th Century Fox)—Peter
 Standish
DIPLOMATIC COURIER (1952, 20th Century Fox)—Mike Kells
PONY SOLDIER (1952, 20th Century Fox)—Duncan MacDonald
KING OF THE KHYBER RIFLES (1953, 20th Century Fox)—
 Capt. Alan King
THE MISSISSIPPI GAMBLER (1953, Universal)—Mark Fallon
THE EDDY DUCHIN STORY (1956, Columbia)—Eddy Duchin

POWER, TYRONE SR.
JOHN NEEDHAM'S DOUBLE (1916, Silent, Bluebird)—John
 Needham & Joseph Norbury

POWERS, MALA
ROSE OF CIMARRON (1952, 20th Century Fox)—Rose of
 Cimarron

POWERS, MARIE
THE MEDIUM (1951, Transfilm)—Mme. Flora

POWERS, STEFANIE
DIE, DIE, MY DARLING (1965, GB, Hammer)—Pat Carroll

POWERS, TOM
THE PHANTOM SPEAKS (1945, Republic)—Harvey Bogardus

POWNEY, CLARE
THE GIRL (1987, GB, Lux/Shapiro)—Pat Carlson

PREISSER, JUNE
SWEATER GIRL (1942, Paramount)—Susan Lawrence
TWO BLONDES AND A REDHEAD (1947, Columbia)—Patti Calhoun

PRENTICE, JORDAN
HOWARD THE DUCK (1986, Universal)—Howard T. Duck

PRENTISS, PAULA
THE STEPFORD WIVES (1975, Columbia)—Bobby

PRESLEY, ELVIS
KID GALAHAD (1962, United Artists)—Kid Galahad/Walter Gulick
KISSIN' COUSINS (1964, MGM)—Josh Morgan & Jodie Tatum
ROUSTABOUT (1964, Paramount)—Charlie Rogers
FRANKIE AND JOHNNY (1966, United Artists)—Johnny
STAY AWAY, JOE (1968, MGM)—Joe Lightcloud
CHARRO (1969, National General)—Jess Wade

PRESSON, JASON
THE STONE BOY (1984, 20th Century Fox)—Arnold Hillerman
EXPLORERS (1985, Paramount)—Darren Woods

PRESTON, BILLY
SGT. PEPPER'S LONELY HEARTS CLUB BAND (1978, Universal)—Sgt. Pepper

PRESTON, KELLY
SPELLBINDER (1988, MGM/United Artists)—Miranda Reed

PRESTON, MIKE
METALSTORM: THE DESTRUCTION OF JARED-SYN (1983, Universal)—Jared-Syn

PRESTON, ROBERT
NORTHWEST MOUNTED POLICE (1940, Paramount)—Constable McDuff
THE SUNDOWNERS (1950, Eagle Lion)—"Kid Witchita" Cloud
THE MUSIC MAN (1962, Warners)—Harold Hill

PREVOST, MARIE
NOBODY'S FOOL (1921, Silent, Universal)—Polly Gordon
HER NIGHT OF NIGHTS (1922, Silent, Universal)—Molly May Malone
ALMOST A LADY (1926, Silent, Producers Distributing Corp.)—Marcia Blake
HIS JAZZ BRIDE (1926, Silent, Warners)—Gloria Gregory
MAN BAIT (1926, Silent, Producers Distributing Corp.)—Madge Dreyer
THE NIGHT BRIDE (1927, Silent, Producers Distributing Corp.)—Cynthia Stockton
BLONDE FOR A NIGHT (1928, Silent, Pathe Exchange)—Marie
THREE WISE GIRLS (1932, Columbia)—Dot

PRICE, ALAN
ALFIE DARLING (1975, GB, Signal/EMI)—Alfie

PRICE, DENNIS
THE BAD LORD BYRON (1949, GB, Triton/GFD)—Lord Byron
BACHELOR IN PARIS (1953, GB, Lippert)—Matthew Ibbetson
VICTIM (1961, GB, Pathe)—Calloway
WATCH IT SAILOR (1961, GB, Hammer)—Lt. Cmdr. Hardcastle
THE AMOROUS MR. PRAWN (1964, GB, British Lion)—Mr. Prawn

PRICE, KATE
THE COHENS AND THE KELLYS (1926, Silent, Universal)—Mrs. Kelly
THE COHENS AND THE KELLYS IN ATLANTIC CITY (1929, Universal)—Mrs. Kelly

PRICE, NANCY
THE THREE WEIRD SISTERS (1948, GB, Pathe)—Gertrude Morgan-Vaughn

PRICE, VINCENT
THE INVISIBLE MAN RETURNS (1940, Universal)—Geoffrey Ratcliffe
THE BARON OF ARIZONA (1950, Lippert)—James Addison Reavis
CASANOVA'S BIG NIGHT (1954, Paramount)—Casanova
THE MAD MAGICIAN (1954, Columbia)—Gallico
THE BAT (1959, Allied Artists)—Dr. Malcolm Wells
THE HOUSE OF USHER (1960, American International)—Roderick Usher
MASTER OF THE WORLD (1961, American International)—Robur
CONFESSIONS OF AN OPIUM EATER (1962, Allied Artists)—DeQuincey
DIARY OF A MADMAN (1963, United Artists)—Simon Cordier
THE LAST MAN ON EARTH (1964, American International)—Robert Morgan
DR. GOLDFOOT AND THE BIKINI MACHINE (1965, American International)—Dr. Goldfoot
DR. GOLDFOOT AND THE GIRL BOMBS (1966, American International)—Dr. Goldfoot
THE ABOMINABLE DR. PHIBES (1971, American International)—Dr. Anton Phibes
DOCTOR PHIBES RISES AGAIN (1972, GB, American International)—Dr. Anton Phibes

PRIESS, WOLFGANG
RAID ON ROMMEL (1971, Universal)—General Erwin Rommel

PRINE, ANDREW
SIMON, KING OF WITCHES (1971, Fanfare)—Simon

PRINGLE, AILEEN
ONE YEAR TO LIVE (1925, Silent, First National)—Elsie Duchanier
SOUL MATES (1925, Silent, MGM)—Velma Markrute
THE WILDERNESS WOMAN (1926, Silent, First National)—Juneau MacLean/ Junie

PROCHOW, JURGEN
THE MAN INSIDE (1990, New Line)—Gunther Wallraff

PROUTY, JED
EDUCATING FATHER (1936, 20th Century Fox)—John Jones

PROVINE, DOROTHY
THE BONNIE PARKER STORY (1958, American International)—Bonnie Parker
THE THIRTY FOOT BRIDE OF CANDY ROCK (1959, Columbia)—Emmy Lou Raven

PROWSE, DAVE
FRANKENSTEIN AND THE MONSTER (1974, GB, Hammer)—
The Monster

PRUSSING, LOUISE
HIS WIFE'S MONEY (1920, Silent, Select)—Laura Uppington

PRYCE, JONATHAN
THE PLOUGHMAN'S LUNCH (1984, GB, Goldwyn)—James
Penfield

PRYOR, RICHARD
THE WIZ (1978, Universal)—The Wiz
STIR CRAZY (1980, Columbia)—Harry Monroe
SOME KIND OF HERO (1982, Paramount)—Eddie Keller
THE TOY (1982, Columbia)—Jack Brown
BREWSTER'S MILLIONS (1985, Universal)—Montgomery
Brewster
JO JO DANCER YOUR LIFE IS CALLING (1986, Columbia)—Jo
Jo Dancer
SEE NO EVIL, HEAR NO EVIL (1989, Tri-Star)—Wally Karew

PURCELL, DICK
KING OF HOCKEY (1936, Warners)—Gabby Dugan

PURDEE, NATHAN
THE RETURN OF SUPERFLY (1990, Triton)—Youngblood Priest

PURDOM, EDMOND
THE EGYPTIAN (1954, 20th Century Fox)—Sinuhe
THE STUDENT PRINCE (1954, MGM)—Prince Karl
THE KING'S THIEF (1955, MGM)—Michael Dermott
THE PRODIGAL (1955, MGM)—Micah

PURNELL, LOUISE
THREE SISTERS (1974, GB, British Lion)—Irina

PURVIANCE, EDNA
A WOMAN OF PARIS (1923, Silent, United Artists)—Marie
St. Clair

PYLE, DENVER
GUARDIAN OF THE WILDERNESS (1977, Sunn Classics)—
Galen Clark

Q

QUAID, DENNIS
THE LONG RIDERS (1980, United Artists)—Ed Miller
TOUGH AGAIN (1983, 20th Century Fox)—Art Long
ENEMY MINE (1985, 20th Century Fox)—Davidge
D.O.A. (1988, Touchstone)—Dexter Cornell
EVERYBODY'S ALL AMERICAN (1988, Warners)—Gavin "Grey
Ghost" Grey

QUAID, RANDY
THE LONG RIDERS (1980, United Artists)—Clell Miller
PARENTS (1988, Vestron)—Dad

QUAN, KE HUY
GOONIES (1985, Warners)—Data

QUARRY, ROBERT
COUNT YORGA, VAMPIRE (1970, American International)—
Count Yorga
THE RETURN OF COUNT YORGA (1971, American
International)—Count Yorga
THE DEATHMASTER (1972, American International)—Khorda

QUAYLE, ANTHONY
THE MAN WHO WOULDN'T TALK (1958, GB, British Lion)—Dr.
Frank Smith

QUIGLEY, CHARLES
SPECIAL INSPECTOR (1939, Syndicate Releasing Co.)—
Tom Evans

QUILL, TIM
STAYING TOGETHER (1989, Hemdale)—Brian McDermott

QUILLAN, EDDIE
THE SOPHOMORE (1929, Pathe)—Joe Collins
THE BIG SHOT (1931, RKO-Pathe)—Ray
GENTLEMAN FROM LOUISIANA (1936, Republic)—Tod Mason
HERE COMES KELLY (1943, Monogram)—Jimmy Kelly

QUINN, AIDAN
CRUSOE (1989, Island)—Robinson Crusoe
THE PLAYBOYS (1992, US/Ireland, Goldwyn)—Tom

QUINN, AILEEN
ANNIE (1982, Columbia)—Annie

QUINN, ANTHONY
THE MAGNIFICENT MATADOR (1955, 20th Century Fox)—Luis
Santos
MAN FROM DEL RIO (1956, United Artists)—Dave Robles
THE SAVAGE INNOCENTS (1960, GB, Paramount)—Inuk
REQUIEM FOR A HEAVYWEIGHT (1962, Columbia)—Mountain
Rivera
ZORBA THE GREEK (1964, 20th Century Fox)—Alexis Zorba
DEAF SMITH AND JOHNNY EARS (1971, MGM)—Erastus
"Deaf" Smith
THE GREEK TYCOON (1978, Universal)—Theo Tomasis

QUINN, FRANCESCO
PLATOON (1987, Orion)—Rhah

QUINN, PAT
ALICE'S RESTAURANT (1969, United Artists)—Alice

R

RADFORD, BASIL
THE GALLOPING MAJOR (1951, GB, Independent Film Dist.)—
Major Arthur Hill

RADNER, GILDA
FIRST FAMILY (1980, Warners)—Gloria Link

HAUNTED HONEYMOON (1986, Orion)—Vickie Pearle Abbot

RAEBURN, FRANCES
SWING OUT, SISTER (1945, Universal)—Donna

RAFFERTY, CHIPS
THE OVERLANDERS (1946, GB/Australia, Ealing)—Dan McAlpine
KING OF THE CORAL SEAS (1956, Australia, Allied Artists)—Ted King

RAFT, GEORGE
UNDER-COVER MAN (1932, Paramount)—Nick Darrow
YOU AND ME (1938, Paramount)—Joe Dennis
I STOLE A MILLION (1939, Universal)—Joe Laurik (Harris)
THEY DRIVE BY NIGHT (1940, Warners)—Joe Fabrini
JOHNNY ANGEL (1945, RKO)—Johnny Angel
MR. ACE (1946, United Artists)—Eddie Ace
JOHNNY ALLEGRO (1949, Columbia)—Johnny Allegro
LUCKY NICK CAIN (1951, 20th Century Fox)—Nick Cain
LOAN SHARK (1952, Lippert)—Joe Gargan
THE MAN FROM CAIRO (1953, Lippert)—Mike Canelli
A BULLET FOR JOEY (1955, United Artists)—Joe Victor

RAGLAN, JAMES
THE FLYING DOCTOR (1936, Australia, GFD)—Dr. John Vaughn

RAILSBACK, STEVE
THE VISITORS (1972, United Artists)—Mike Nickerson
THE STUNT MAN (1980, 20th Century Fox)—Cameron

RAIMI, THEODORE
LUNATICS: A LOVE STORY (1991, Renaissance Pictures)—Hank

RAINER, LUISE
THE TOY WIFE (1938, MGM)—Gilberta Brigard

RAINES, ELLA
THE SECOND FACE (1950, Eagle Lion)—Phyllis Holmes

RAINS, CLAUDE
THE INVISIBLE MAN (1933, Universal)—Jack Griffin
THE CLAIRVOYANT (1935, GB, Gainsborough)—Maximus
THE MAN WHO RECLAIMED HIS HEAD (1935, Universal)—Paul Verin
HERE COMES MR. JORDAN (1941, Columbia)—Mr. Jordan
PHANTOM OF THE OPERA (1943, Universal)—Enrique Claudin
MR. SKEFFINGTON (1944, Warners)—Job Skeffington
CAESAR AND CLEOPATRA (1946, GB, Two Cities)—Julius Caesar
THE UNSUSPECTED (1947, Warners)—Alexander Grandison

RALL, TOMMY
SEVEN BRIDES FOR SEVEN BROTHERS (1954, MGM)—Frank Pontabee

RALSTON, ESTHER
THE AMERICAN VENUS (1926, Silent, Paramount)—Mary Gray
CHILDREN OF DIVORCE (1927, Silent, Paramount)—Jean Waddington
HALF A BRIDE (1928, Paramount)—Patience Winslow
THE CASE OF LENA SMITH (1929, Silent, Paramount)—Lena Smith
LONELY WIVES (1931, RKO-Pathe)—Mrs. Smith

RALSTON, VERA HRUBA
THE LADY AND THE MONSTER (1944, Republic)—Janice Farell
PLAINSMAN AND THE LADY (1946, Republic)—Ann Arnesen
ANGEL ON THE AMAZON (1948, Republic)—Christine Ridgeway
I JANE DOE (1948, Republic)—Annette Dubois alias Jane Doe
BELLE LE GRAND (1951, Republic)—Belle Le Grand

RAMBEAU, MARJORIE
TUGBOAT ANNIE SAILS AGAIN (1940, Warners)—Tugboat Annie

RAMER, HENRY
RENO AND THE DOC (1984, Canada, New World)—Hugo "Doc" Billings

RAMIS, HAROLD
GHOSTBUSTERS (1984, Columbia)—Dr. Egon Spengler
GHOSTBUSTERS II (1989, Columbia)—Dr. Egon Spengler

RAMPLING, CHARLOTTE
THREE (1969, GB, United Artists)—Marty
HENRY VIII AND HIS SIX WIVES (1972, GB, EMI/MGM)—Anne Boleyn
FAREWELL, MY LOVELY (1975, Avco Embassy)—Mrs. Velma Grayle

RAMSEY, ANNE
THROW MOMMA FROM THE TRAIN (1987, Orion)—Momma Lift

RANDALL, ANN
STACEY (1973, New World)—Stacey Hansen

RANDALL, BRAD
WHO SHOT PATAKANGO? (1990, Patakango Ltd.)—Patakango

RANDALL, JACK
THE CHEYENNE KID (1940, Monogram)—The Cheyenne Kid
THE KID FROM SANTE FE (1940, Monogram)—Sante Fe

RANDALL, STEPHANIE
PREHISTORIC WOMEN (1967, GB, 20th Century Fox)—Amyak

RANDALL, TONY
WILL SUCCESS SPOIL ROCK HUNTER (1957, 20th Century Fox)—Rock Hunter
SEVEN FACES OF DR. LAO (1964, MGM)—Dr. Lao/Merlin the Magician/Pan/ The Abominable Snowman/Medusa/The Great Serpent/Appolonius of Tyana

RANDELL, RON
SMITHY (1946, Australia, Columbia)—Sir Charles Kingsford-Smith
THE LONE WOLF AND HIS LADY (1949, Columbia)—Michael Lanyard
THE MOST DANGEROUS MAN ALIVE (1961, Columbia)—Eddie Candell

RANDOLPH, WINDSOR TAYLOR
AMAZONS (1987, MGM/United Artists)—Dyala

RANKIN, ARTHUR
BROTHERS (1929, Silent, Rayart)—Bob Conroy

RASCHE, DAVID
MASTERS OF MENACE (1990, New Line)—Buddy

RATCLIFFE, E.J.
IN THE PALACE OF THE KING (1915, Silent, Select)—King
Philip II

RATHBONE, BASIL
LOVE FROM A STRANGER (1937, GB, United Artists)—Gerald
Lovell
THE ADVENTURES OF SHERLOCK HOLMES (1939, 20th
Century Fox)—Sherlock Holmes
SON OF FRANKENSTEIN (1939, Universal)—Baron Wolf von
Frankenstein
THE MAD DOCTOR (1941, Paramount)—Dr. George Sebastian
SHERLOCK HOLMES AND THE SECRET WEAPON (1942,
Universal)—Sherlock Holmes
SHERLOCK HOLMES AND THE VOICE OF TERROR (1942,
Universal)—Sherlock Holmes
SHERLOCK HOLMES FACES DEATH (1943, Universal)—
Sherlock Holmes
SHERLOCK HOLMES IN WASHINGTON (1943, Universal)—
Sherlock Holmes
SHERLOCK HOLMES AND THE SPIDER WOMAN (1944,
Universal)—Sherlock Holmes

RATOFF, GREGORY
ABDULLA'S HAREM (1956, GB, Sonofilms)—Abdulla

RAUM, WARREN
ROBBY (1968, Bluewood)—Robby

RAVEL, SANDRA
THOSE THREE FRENCH GIRLS (1930, MGM)—Madelon

RAWLINSON, HERBERT
MAN AND HIS WOMAN (1920, Silent, Pathe)—Dr. John
Worthing
THE MILLIONAIRE (1921, Silent, Universal)—Jack Norman
THE SCRAPPER (1922, Universal)—Malloy
HIS MYSTERY GIRL (1923, Silent, Universal)—Kerry Reynolds
RAILROADED (1923, Silent, Universal)—Richard Ragland
JACK O' CLUBS (1924, Silent, Universal)—John Francis Foley

RAY, ADELE
THE MOTH AND THE FLAME (1915, Silent, Paramount)—
Marion Walton

RAY, ALDO
THE MARRYING KIND (1952, Columbia)—Florence Keefer
WE'RE NO ANGELS (1955, Paramount)—Albert
JOHNNY NOBODY (1965, GB, Viceroy-Medallion)—Johnny
Nobody

RAY, ANDREW
THE MUDLARK (1950, GB, 20th Century Fox)—Wheeler, the
Mudlark

RAY, CHARLES
THE HONORABLE ALGY (1916, Silent, Triangle)—The
Honorable Algy
THE PINCH HITTER (1917, Silent, Triangle)—Joel Parker
THE HIRED HAND (1918, Silent, Paramount)—Ezry Hollins
HIS OWN HOME TOWN (1918, Silent, Ince)—Jimmy Duncan
HIS MOTHER'S BOY (1918, Silent, Ince)—Matthew Denton
BILL HENRY (1919, Silent, Paramount)—Bill Henry Jenkins
ALARM CLOCK ANDY (1920, Silent, Paramount)—Andrew Gray

HOMER COMES HOME (1920, Silent, Triangle)—Homer
Cavender
NINETEEN AND PHYLLIS (1920, Silent, First National)—
Andrew Jackson Cavanaugh
AN OLD FASHIONED BOY (1920, Silent, Paramount)—David
Warrington
ALIAS JULIUS CAESAR (1922, Silent, Associated First
National)—Billy Barnes
THE BARNSTORMER (1922, Silent, Associated First National)—
Joel "Utility" Matthews
A TAILOR MADE MAN (1922, Silent, United Artists)—John
Paul Burt

RAY, RENE
JENIFER HALE (1937, GB, 20th Century Fox)—Jenifer Hale
TWILIGHT WOMEN (1953, GB, Lippert)—Vivianne Bruce

RAY, TED
CARRY ON TEACHER (1962, GB, Anglo-Amalgamated)—
William Wakefield

RAYE, MARTHA
HIDEAWAY GIRL (1937, Paramount)—Helen Flint
THE FARMER'S DAUGHTER (1940, Paramount)—Patience
Bingham
FOUR JILLS IN A JEEP (1944, 20th Century Fox)—
Martha Raye

RAYMOND, GARY
THE PLAYBOY OF THE WESTERN WORLD (1963, Ireland,
Janus-Lion)—Christy Mahon

RAYMOND, GENE
BEHOLD MY WIFE (1935, Paramount)—Michael Carter

RAYMOND, HELEN
THE ABLEMINDED LADY (1922, Silent, Pacific Films)—
Widow McGee

RAYMOND, RUTH
A WOMAN OBSESSED (1989, Platinum)—Arline Bellings

REA, STEPHEN
DANNY BOY (1984, Ireland, Triumph)—Danny

READ, BARBARA
THREE SMART GIRLS (1937, Universal)—Kay Craig

READICK, BOBBY
HARRIGAN'S KID (1943, MGM)—Benny McNeil

REAGAN, RONALD
BROTHER RAT (1938, Warners)—Dan Crawford
BROTHER RAT AND A BABY (1940, Warners)—Dan Crawford
JOHN LOVES MARY (1949, Warners)—John Lawrence
PRISONER OF WAR (1954, MGM)—Web Sloane
TENNESSEE'S PARTNER (1955, RKO)—Cowpoke

REATE, J.L.
THE GOLDEN CHILD (1986, Paramount)—The Golden Child

REBAR, ALEX
THE INCREDIBLE MELTING MAN (1978, American
International)—The Melting Man

REDD, MARY-ROBIN
THE GROUP (1966, United Artists)—Pokey Prothero

REDFORD, ROBERT
BUTCH CASSIDY AND THE SUNDANCE KID (1969, 20th Century Fox)—Sundance Kid
DOWNHILL RACER (1969, Paramount)—Davis Chappellet
LITTLE FAUSS AND BIG HALSY (1970, Paramount)—Big Halsy
THE CANDIDATE (1972, Warners)—Bill McKay
JEREMIAH JOHNSON (1972, Warners)—Jeremiah Johnson
THE GREAT GATSBY (1974, Paramount)—Jay Gatsby
THE GREAT WALDO PEPPER (1975, Universal)—Waldo Pepper
THE ELECTRIC HORSEMAN (1979, Columbia/Universal)—Sonny Steele
BRUBAKER (1980, 20th Century Fox)—Brubaker
THE NATURAL (1984, Tri-Star)—Roy Hobbs
LEGAL EAGLES (1986, Universal)—Tom Logan

REDGRAVE, LYNN
GEORGY GIRL (1966, GB, Columbia)—Georgy
EVERY LITTLE CROOK AND NANNY (1972, MGM)—Miss Poole
THE HAPPY HOOKER (1976, Cannon)—Xaviera Hollander

REDGRAVE, MICHAEL
KIPPS (1941, GB, 20th Century Fox)—Arthur Kipps
THE SMUGGLERS (1948, GB, Eagle-Lion)—Richard Carylon
UNCLE VANYA (1977, GB, British Home Entertainment)—Uncle Vanya

REDGRAVE, VANESSA
ISADORA (1968, GB, Universal)—Isadora Duncan
MARY, QUEEN OF SCOTS (1971, GB, Universal)—Mary Stuart
THE TROJAN WOMEN (1971, Cinerama)—Andromache
JULIA (1977, 20th Century Fox)—Julia
AGATHA (1979, GB, Sweetwal/Warners)—Agatha Christie
THE BOSTONIANS (1984, Merchant Ivory/Almi)—Olive Chancellor

REED, ALAN JR.
GOING STEADY (1958, Columbia)—Calvin Potter

REED, DAVID
TALES OF A SALESMAN (1965, Rossmore)—Herman

REED, DONNA
FAITHFUL IN MY FASHION (1946, MGM)—Jean Kendrick

REED, JERRY
W.W. AND THE DIXIE DANCEKINGS (1975, 20th Century Fox)—Wayne
SMOKEY AND THE BANDIT—PART 3 (1983, Universal)—Bandit

REED, LYDIA
THE SEVEN LITTLE FOYS (1955, Paramount)—Mary Foy

REED, MAXWELL
THE DARK MAN (1951, GB, GFD)—The Dark Man

REED, OLIVER
THE GIRL GETTERS (1966, GB, American International)—Tinker
THE JOKERS (1967, GB, Universal)—David Tremayne
HANNIBAL BROOKS (1969, GB, United Artists)—Hannibal Brooks
THE THREE MUSKETEERS (1974, 20th Century Fox)—Athos
THE FOUR MUSKETEERS (1975, 20th Century Fox)—Athos
DR. HECKYL AND MR. HYPE (1980, Cannon)—Dr. Heckyl/Mr. Hype

REED, PAMELA
THE GOODBYE PEOPLE (1984, Embassy)—Nancie Scot

REED, PENELOPE
AMAZONS (1987, MGM/United Artists)—Tashi

REED, PHILIP
THE LAST OF THE MOHICANS (1936, United Artists)—Uncas
WEEKEND FOR THREE (1941, RKO)—Randy Bloodworth
I COVER BIG TOWN (1947, Paramount)—Steve Wilson

REED, SUSAN
GLAMOUR GIRL (1947, Columbia)—Jennia Higgins

REEVE, CHRISTOPHER
SUPERMAN (1978, Warners)—Superman (Clark Kent)
SUPERMAN II (1980, Warners)—Superman (Clark Kent)
MONSIGNOR (1982, 20th Century Fox)—Monsignor Flaherty
SUPERMAN III (1983, Warners)—Superman (Clark Kent)
THE BOSTONIANS (1984, Merchant Ivory/Almi)—Basil Ransom
THE AVIATOR (1985, MGM/United Artists)—Edgar Anscombe
SUPERMAN IV: THE QUEST FOR PEACE (1987, Warners)—Superman (Clark Kent)

REEVES, GEORGE
SUPERMAN AND THE MOLE MEN (1951, Lippert)—Superman (Clark Kent)

REEVES, JIM
KIMBERLEY JIM (1965, South Africa, Embassy)—Jim Madison

REEVES, KEANU
THE PRINCE OF PENNSYLVANIA (1988, New Line)—Rupert Marshetta
BILL & TED'S EXCELLENT ADVENTURE (1989, Orion)—Ted 'Theodore' Logan
BILL & TED'S BOGUS JOURNEY (1991, Orion)—Theodore "Ted" Logan

REEVES, SASKIA
ANTONIA AND JANE (1991, GB, Miramax)—Antonia McGill

REGAN, PHIL
LAUGHING IRISH EYES (1936, Republic)—Danno O'Keefe
SHE MARRIED A COP (1939, Republic)—Jimmy

REGGIANI, SERGE
SECRET PEOPLE (1952, GB, Ealing)—Louis

REICHERT, KITTENS
SO'S YOUR OLD MAN (1926, Silent, Paramount)—Alice Bisbee

REID, CARL BENTON
THE SPOILERS (1955, Universal)—Judge Stillman

REID, WALLACE
THE HOSTAGE (1917, Silent, Paramount)—Lt. Ivo Kemper
ALIAS MIKE MORAN (1919, Silent, Paramount)—Larry Young
HAWTHORNE OF THE U.S.A. (1919, Paramount)—Anthony Hamilton Hawthorne
THE AFFAIRS OF ANATOL (1921, Silent, Paramount)—Anatol De Witt Spencer
CLARENCE (1922, Silent, Paramount)—Clarence Smith
THE DICTATOR (1922, Silent, Paramount)—Brock Travers
THE WOMAN'S CHAMPION (1922, Paramount)—William Burroughs

REINHOLD, JUDGE
RUTHLESS PEOPLE (1986, Buena Vista)—Ken Kessler
VICE VERSA (1988, Columbia)—Marshall Seymour

REINKING, ANN
MICKI AND MAUDE (1984, Columbia)—Micki Salinger

REMBERG, ERIKA
CANDIDATE FOR MURDER (1966, GB, Schoenfield Films)—
Helene Edwards

REMSEN, BERT
DADDY'S DYIN' . . . WHO'S GOT THE WILL (1990, MGM/
UA)—Daddy

RENALDO, DUNCAN
THE CISCO KID RETURNS (1945, Monogram)—Cisco Kid
THE DARING CABALLERO (1949, United Artists)—Cisco Kid
THE GAY AMIGO (1949, United Artists)—Cisco Kid

RENDEL, ROBERT
TWICE BRANDED (1936, GB, RKO)—Charles Hamilton

RENN, ADRIANNE
THE WIFE OF GENERAL LING (1938, GB, Gaumont)—Tai

RENNIE, JAMES
PARTY HUSBAND (1931, Warners)—Jay Hogarth

RETTIG, TOMMY
SO BIG (1953, Warners)—Dirk DeJong

REVIER, DOROTHY
BROADWAY MADONNA (1922, Silent, Quality Films)—Vivian
Collins
THE COWBOY AND THE FLAPPER (1924, Silent, Truart)—Alice
Allison
WANDERING GIRLS (1927, Silent, Columbia)—Peggy Marston
THE SQUEALER (1930, Columbia)—Margaret Hart
ANYBODY'S BLONDE (1931, Action)—Janet
WIDOW IN SCARLET (1932, Mayfair)—Baroness Orsani

REVUELTAS, ROSAURA
SALT OF THE EARTH (1954, Independent Productions)—
Esperanza Quintero

REYNA, MAURICE
THE BOY WHO STOLE A MILLION (1960, GB, British-
Lion)—Paco

REYNOLDS, BURT
SAM WHISKEY (1969, United Artists)—Sam Whiskey
THE MAN WHO LOVED CAT DANCING (1973, MGM)—Jay
Grobart
SHAMUS (1973, Columbia)—Shamus McCoy
W.W. AND THE DIXIE DANCEKINGS (1976, Universal)—W.W.
Bright
GATOR (1976, United Artists)—Gator McKlusky
SMOKEY AND THE BANDIT (1977, Universal)—Bandit
HOOPER (1978, Warners)—Sonny Hooper
STARTING OVER (1979, Paramount)—Phil Potter
SMOKEY AND THE BANDIT II (1980, Universal)—Bandit
BEST FRIENDS (1982, Warners)—Richard Babson
SHARKY'S MACHINE (1982, Warners)—Sharky
THE MAN WHO LOVED WOMEN (1983, Columbia)—David

SMOKEY AND THE BANDIT — PART 3 (1983, Universal)—The
Real Bandit
STROKER ACE (1983, Universal/Warners)—Stroker Ace
STICK (1985, Universal)—Stick
MALONE (1987, Orion)—Richard Malone
RENT-A-COP (1988, Kings Road)—Church
ALL DOGS GO TO HEAVEN (1989, animated, United Artists)—
Voice of Charley

REYNOLDS, DEBBIE
GIVE A GIRL A BREAK (1953, MGM)—Suzy Doolittle
I LOVE MELVIN (1953, MGM)—Judy LeRoy
SUSAN SLEPT HERE (1954, RKO)—Susan
TAMMY AND THE BACHELOR (1957, Universal)—Tammy Tyree
MARY, MARY (1963, Warners)—Mary McKellaway
GOODBYE CHARLIE (1964, 20th Century Fox)—Charlie Sorel
THE UNSINKABLE MOLLY BROWN (1964, MGM)—Molly Brown
THE SINGING NUN (1966, MGM)—Sister Ann
CHARLOTTE'S WEB (1973, Animated, Paramount)—Voice of
Charlotte

REYNOLDS, JOYCE
JANIE (1944, Warners)—Janie Conway
WALLFLOWER (1948, Warners)—Jackie Linnett

REYNOLDS, MARJORIE
REBELLIOUS DAUGHTERS (1938, Times)—Claire

REYNOLDS, PETER
SMART ALEC (1951, GB, Grand National)—Alec Albion

REYNOLDS, VERA
CORPORAL KATE (1926, Silent, Producers Dist. Corp.)—Kate

RHYS, PAUL
VINCENT AND THEO (1990, GB/France, Hemdale)—Theo
van Gogh

RIALSON, CANDICE
SUMMER SCHOOL TEACHERS (1977, New World)—Conklin T

RIANO, RENO
JIGGS AND MAGGIE IN SOCIETY (1948, Monogram)—Maggie
JIGGS AND MAGGIE OUT WEST (1950, Monogram)—Maggie

RICCI, CHRISTINA
THE ADDAMS FAMILY (1991, Paramount)—Wednesday Addams

RICE, FLORENCE
FUGITIVE LADY (1934, Columbia)—Ann Duncan
FOUR GIRLS IN WHITE (1939, MGM)—Norma Page
THE BLONDE FROM SINGAPORE (1941, Columbia)—Mary
Brooks

RICH, IRENE
YESTERDAY'S WIFE (1923, Silent, Columbia)—Megan Daye
BEHOLD THIS WOMAN (1924, Silent, Vitagraph)—Louise
Maurel
A LOST LADY (1924, Silent, Warners)—Marian Forrester
THE SILVER SLAVE (1927, Silent, Warners)—Bernice Randall
CRAIG'S WIFE (1928, Silent, Pathe Exchange)—Harriet Craig
NED MCCOBB'S DAUGHTER (1929, Silent, Pathe)—Carrie
McCobb
THEY HAD TO SEE PARIS (1929, Fox)—Mrs. Peters
QUEEN OF THE YUKON (1940, Monogram)—Sadie

RICHARDS, ADDISON
LONE COWBOY (1934, Paramount)—Dobe Jones

RICHARDS, JEFF
SEVEN BRIDES FOR SEVEN BROTHERS (1954, MGM)—
Benjamin Pontabee

RICHARDS, PAUL
KISS DADDY GOOD NIGHT (1987, Beast of Eden)—William B.
Tilden

RICHARDSON, IAN
PERSECUTION AND ASSASSINATION OF JEAN-PAUL MARAT
AS PERFORMED BY THE INMATES OF THE ASYLUM OF
CHARENTON UNDER THE DIRECTION OF THE MARQUIS DE
SADE (1967, GB, United Artists)—Jean-Paul Marat

RICHARDSON, JACK
MAN ABOVE THE LAW (1918, Silent, Triangle)—Duce Chalmers

RICHARDSON, MIRANDA
DANCE WITH A STRANGER (1985, GB, Goldwyn)—Ruth Ellis

RICHARDSON, NATASHA
PATTY HEARST (1988, Atlantic)—Patty Hearst
THE HANDMAID'S TALE (1990, Cinecom)—Kate

RICHARDSON, RALPH
THE RETURN OF BULLDOG DRUMMOND (1934, GB, British
International)—Hugh Drummond
THE FUGITIVE (1940, GB, Universal)—Will Kobling

RICHMAN, CHARLES
THE MAN FROM HOME (1914, Silent, Lasky)—Daniel
Vorhees Pike
THE IDLER (1915, Silent, Box Office Attractions)—Mark Cross

RICHMAN, MARK
AGENT FOR H.A.R.M. (1966, Universal)—Adam Chance

RICHMOND, KANE
THE SHADOW STRIKES RETURNS (1946, Monogram)—Lamont
Cranston

RICHMOND, WARNER
JAN OF THE BIG SNOWS (1922, Silent, American Releasing
Corp.)—Jan Allaire
THE APACHE (1928, Silent, Columbia)—Gaston Laroux

RIGBY, EDWARD
MR. SMITH CARRIES ON (1937, GB, British & Dominions)—
Mr. Smith
SALUTE JOHN CITIZEN (1945, Paramount)—Mr. Bunting

RINGWALD, MOLLY
SIXTEEN CANDLES (1984, Universal)—Samatha "Sam" Baker
THE BREAKFAST CLUB (1985, Universal)—Claire Standish
PRETTY IN PINK (1986, Paramount)—Andie
P.K. & THE KID (1987, Sunn Classics/Lorimar)—Paula
Kathleen "P.K." Bayette
BETSY'S WEDDING (1990, Touchstone)—Betsy Hopper

RISDON, ELISABETH
THE PRINCESS OF HAPPY CHANCE (1916, GB, Silent, Jury)—
Princess Felicia
MAMA LOVES PAPA (1945, RKO)—Jessie Todd

RITCH, STEVEN
THE WEREWOLF (1956, Columbia)—Duncan March

RITTER, JOHN
HERO AT LARGE (1980, MGM)—Steve Nichols
REAL MEN (1987, MGM/United Artists)—Nick Pirandello

RITTER, TEX
SING, COWBOY, SING (1937, Grand National)—Tex Archer
COWBOY FROM SUNDOWN (1940, Monogram)—Tex Rokett

RITTER, THELMA
THE MODEL AND THE MARRIAGE BROKER (1951, 20th
Century Fox)—Mae Swazey

THE RITZ BROTHERS
THE THREE MUSKETEERS (1939, 20th Century Fox)—The
Three Lackeys

RIVERO, GEORGE
FIST FIGHTER (1989, Taurus)—C.J. Thunderbird

ROBARDS, JASON JR.
THE BALLAD OF CABLE HOGUE (1970, Warners)—
Cable Hogue
MR. SYCAMORE (1975, Capricorn)—John Gwilt
MELVIN AND HOWARD (1980, Universal)—Howard Hughes
MAX DUGAN RETURNS (1983, 20th Century Fox)—Max Dugan
PARENTHOOD (1989, Universal)—Frank Buckman

ROBBINS, MARTY
BALLAD OF A GUNFIGHTER (1964, Ward/Parade)—Marty
Robbins

ROBBINS, TIM
TAPEHEADS (1988, Avenue)—Josh Tager
ERIK THE VIKING (1989, Orion)—Erik
JACOB'S LADDER (1990, Tri-Star)—Jacob Singer
BOB ROBERTS (1992, Paramount/Miramax)—Bob Roberts
THE PLAYER (1992, Fine Line/Avenue)—Griffin Mill

ROBERTS, ARTHUR
NOT OF THIS EARTH (1988, Concorde)—The Alien

ROBERTS, BEVERLY
GOD'S COUNTRY AND THE WOMAN (1937, Warners)—Jo
Barton
HER HUSBAND'S SECRETARY (1937, First National/
Warners)—Diane

ROBERTS, DES
GUESS WHAT HAPPENED TO COUNT DRACULA (1970, Merrick
International)—Count Dracula

ROBERTS, EDITH
HER FIVE-FOOT HIGHNESS (1920, Silent, Universal)—Eileen
WHITE YOUTH (1920, Silent, Universal)—Aline Ann Belame
THE JAZZ GIRL (1926, Silent, Motion Picture Guild)—
Janet Marsh

ROBERTS, ERIC
THE POPE OF GREENWICH VILLAGE (1984, MGM/United
Artists)—Paulie
THE COCA-COLA KID (1986, Cinecom)—Becker
BEST OF THE BEST (1989, Taurus)—Alex Grady
RUDE AWAKENING (1989, Orion)—Fred

ROBERTS, JULIA
STEEL MAGNOLIAS (1989, Tri-Star)—Shelby Eatenton
Latcherie
FLATLINERS (1990, Columbia)—Rachel
PRETTY WOMAN (1990, Buena Vista)—Vivian Ward
SLEEPING WITH THE ENEMY (1991, 20th Century Fox)—
Sara/Laura

ROBERTS, LYNNE
GIRLS OF THE BIG HOUSE (1945, Republic)—Jeanne Crail
SIOUX CITY SUE (1946, Republic)—Sue Warner
THAT'S MY GAL (1947, Republic)—Natalie Adams

ROBERTS, TANYA
SHEENA (1984, Columbia)—Sheena

ROBERTS, THEODORE
THE CIRCUS MAN (1914, Silent, Lasky)—Thomas Braddock
NED MCCOBB'S DAUGHTER (1929, Silent, Pathe)—Ned
McCobb

ROBERTSHAW, JERROLD
DON QUIXOTE (1923, GB, Silent, Stoll)—Don Quixote

ROBERTSON, CLIFF
CHARLY (1968, Selmur)—Charly Gordon
TOO LATE THE HERO (1970, Cinerama)—Lt. Lawson
ACE ELI AND RODGER OF THE SKY (1973, 20th Century
Fox)—Eli
J.W. COOP (1976, American International)—J.W. Coop

ROBERTSON, DALE
RETURN OF THE TEXAN (1952, 20th Century Fox)—Sam
Crockett
THE FARMER TAKES A WIFE (1953, 20th Century Fox)—Molly
Larkins
THE GAMBLER FROM NATCHEZ (1954, 20th Century Fox)—
Vance Colby
SON OF SINBAD (1955, RKO)—Sinbad

ROBERTSON, GUY
KING KELLY OF THE U.S.A. (1934, Monogram)—Kelly

ROBERTSON, WILLARD
MY SON IS A CRIMINAL (1939, Columbia)—Tim Halloran Sr.

ROBESON, PAUL
THE EMPEROR JONES (1933, United Artists)—Brutus Jones
BIG FELLA (1937, GB, Lion-Beaconsfield)—Joe

ROBEY, GEORGE
THE PREHISTORIC MAN (1924, GB, Silent, Stoll)—He-of-the-
Beetle-Brow

ROBILLARD, ELIZABETH
A DAY IN THE LIFE OF JOE EGG (1972, GB, Columbia)—Jo

ROBINSON, BILLY
THE WRESTLER (1974, Entertainment Ventures)—Billy Taylor

ROBINSON, DARREN
DISORDERLIES (1987, Warners)—Buffy

ROBINSON, EDWARD G.
LITTLE CAESAR (1931, Warners)—Cesare Enrico Bandello
(Rico- Little Caesar)

THE HATCHET MAN (1932, First National/Warners)—Wong
Low Get
SILVER DOLLAR (1932, First National)—Yates "Silver Dollar"
Martin
THE LITTLE GIANT (1933, Warners)—James Francis "Bugs"
Ahearn
THE MAN WITH TWO FACES (1934, Warners)—Damon Wells
THE LAST GANGSTER (1937, MGM)—Joe Krozac
THE AMAZING DR. CLITTERHOUSE (1938, Warners)—Dr.
Clitterhouse
I AM THE LAW (1938, Columbia)—John Lindsay
BROTHER ORCHID (1940, First National/Warners)—Little
John Sarto
A DISPATCH FROM REUTERS (1940, Warners)—Julius Reuter
DR. EHRLICH'S MAGIC BULLET (1940, Warners)—Dr. Paul
Ehrlich
THE SEA WOLF (1941, Warners)—Wolf Larsen
UNHOLY PARTNERS (1941, MGM)—Bruce Corey
MR. WINKLE GOES TO WAR (1944, Columbia)—Wilbert George
Winkle
ALL MY SONS (1948, Universal)—Joe Keller
THE VIOLENT MEN (1955, Columbia)—Lew Wilkinson

ROBINSON, JACKIE
THE JACKIE ROBINSON STORY (1950, Eagle Lion)—Jackie
Robinson

ROBINSON, RUTH
THE SEARCH FOR BRIDEY MURPHY (1956, Paramount)—
Bridey Murphy at 4

ROBSON, FLORA
SEVEN WOMEN (1966, MGM)—Miss Binns

ROBSON, MAY
THE SHE-WOLF (1931, Universal)—Harriet Breen
LADY FOR A DAY (1933, Columbia)—Apple Annie
LADY BY CHOICE (1934, Columbia)—Patsy Patterson
GRAND OLD GIRL (1935, RKO)—Laura Bayles
THREE KIDS AND A QUEEN (1935, Universal)—Mary Jane
Baxter
WOMAN IN DISTRESS (1937, Columbia)—Phoebe Tuttle
GRANNY GET YOUR GUN (1940, First National)—Minerva
Hatton

ROC, PATRICIA
THE FARMER'S WIFE (1941, GB, Pathe)—Sibley Sweetland
THE PERFECT WOMAN (1950, GB, Rank/Ealing)—Penelope
Belmond

ROCHE, DOMINIC
MY WIFE'S LODGER (1952, GB, Adelphi)—Willie Higginbotham

ROCHE, JOHN
THE DONOVAN AFFAIR (1929, Columbia)—Jack Donovan

ROCK, CHARLES
BEAU BROCADE (1916, GB, Artistic)—Sir Humphrey Challoner

RODGERS, JIMMIE
LITTLE SHEPHERD OF KINGDOM COME (1961, 20th Century
Fox)—Chad

RODRIGUEZ, ESTELITA
BELLE OF OLD MEXICO (1950, Republic)—Rosita

HAVANA ROSE (1951, Republic)—Estelita DeMarco

RODRIGUEZ, PAUL
THE WHOOPEE BOYS (1986, Paramount)—Barney

ROEBUCK, DANIEL
DUDES (1987, New Century-Vista)—Biscuit

ROGERS, CHARLES "BUDDY"
MY BEST GIRL (1927, Silent, United Artists)—Joe Grant
ABIE'S IRISH ROSE (1928, Part-Talkie, Paramount)—Abie Levy
WEEKEND MILLIONAIRE (1937, GB, Gaumont)—Pierre
THE PARSON AND THE OUTLAW (1957, Columbia)—Rev.
  Jericho Jones

ROGERS, GINGER
THE GAY DIVORCEE (1934, RKO)—Mimi Glossop
SHALL WE DANCE (1937, RKO)—Linda Keene
VIVACIOUS LADY (1938, RKO)—Frances Brent
BACHELOR MOTHER (1939, RKO)—Polly Parrish
FIFTH AVENUE GIRL (1939, RKO)—Mary Grey
THE STORY OF VERNON AND IRENE CASTLE (1939, RKO)—
  Irene Castle
KITTY FOYLE (1940, RKO)—Kitty Foyle
LUCKY PARTNERS (1940, RKO)—Jean Newton
THE MAJOR AND THE MINOR (1942, Paramount)—Susan
  Applegate
ROXIE HART (1942, 20th Century Fox)—Roxie Hart
I'LL BE SEEING YOU (1944, United Artists)—Mary Marshall
LADY IN THE DARK (1944, Paramount)—Liza Elliott
MAGNIFICENT DOLL (1946, Universal)—Dolly Payne Madison
THE BARKLEY'S OF BROADWAY (1949, MGM)—Dinah Barkley
PERFECT STRANGERS (1950, Warners)—Terry Scott
FOREVER FEMALE (1953, Paramount)—Beatrice Page
BEAUTIFUL STRANGER (TWIST OF FATE) (1954, GB, British
  Lion)—"Johnny" Victor
THE FIRST TRAVELING SALESLADY (1956, RKO)—Rose Gillray
OH, MEN! OH, WOMEN! (1957, 20th Century Fox)—Mildred
  Turner

ROGERS, MIMI
SOMEONE TO WATCH OVER ME (1987, Columbia)—Claire
  Gregory

ROGERS, ROY
THE ARIZONA KID (1939, Republic)—Roy Rogers
CARSON CITY KID (1940, Republic)—Carson City Kid
THE RANGER AND THE LADY (1940, Republic)—Capt. Colt
YOUNG BILL HICKOK (1940, Republic)—Bill Hickok
YOUNG BUFFALO BILL (1940, Republic)—Bill Cody
JESSE JAMES AT BAY (1941, Republic)—Jesse James
KING OF THE COWBOYS (1943, Republic)—Roy Rogers
COWBOY AND THE SENORITA (1944, Republic)—Roy Rogers
MACKINTOSH & T.J. (1975, Penland)—Mackintosh

ROGERS, WILL
JUBILO (1919, Silent, Goldwyn)—Jubilo
DOUBLING FOR ROMEO (1921, Silent, Goldwyn)—Sam/Romeo
THEY HAD TO SEE PARIS (1929, Fox)—Pike Peters
LIGHTNIN' (1930, Fox)—"Lightnin'" Bill Jones
AMBASSADOR BILL (1931, Fox)—Bill Harper
A CONNECTICUT YANKEE (1931, Fox)—Hank Martin
DR. BULL (1933, Fox)—Dr. Bull

MISTER SKITCH (1933, Fox)—Mr. Skitch
DAVID HARUM (1934, Fox)—David Harum
HANDY ANDY (1934, Fox)—Andrew Yates
JUDGE PRIEST (1934, Fox)—Judge William "Billy" Priest
THE COUNTY CHAIRMAN (1935, Fox)—Jim Hackler
DOUBTING THOMAS (1935, 20th Century Fox)—Thomas Brown

ROGERS, WILL JR.
THE STORY OF WILL ROGERS (1952, Warners)—Will Rogers
THE BOY FROM OKLAHOMA (1954, Warners)—Tom Brewster

ROLAND, GILBERT
MEN OF THE NORTH (1930, MGM)—Louis LeBey
KING OF THE BANDITS (1948, Monogram)—Cisco Kid
TEN TALL MEN (1951, Columbia)—Cpl. Luis Delgado
MY SIX CONVICTS (1952, Columbia)—Punch Rinero

ROLF, TUTTA
DRESSED TO THRILL (1935, Fox)—Colette Dubois/Nadia
  Petrova

ROLFE, GUY
THE SPIDER AND THE FLY (1952, GB, GFD)—Philippe de
  Ledocq
MR. SARDONICUS (1953, 20th Century Fox)—Sardonicus

ROLFING, TOM
HE KNOWS YOU'RE ALONE (1980, MGM-United Artists)—The
  Killer

ROMAN, LETICIA
FANNY HILL: MEMOIRS OF A WOMAN OF PLEASURE (1965,
  Favorite Films)—Fanny Hill

ROMAN, RUTH
BELLE STARR'S DAUGHTER (1947, Alson/20th Century Fox)—
  Rose of Cimarron

ROME, STEWART
THE PRODIGAL SON (1923, GB, Silent, Stoll)—Magnus
  Stephenson
THE MAN WHO CHANGED HIS NAME (1928, Silent, British
  Lion)—Selby Clive

ROMEN, RACHEL
THE DESERT RAVEN (1965, Allied Artists)—Raven

ROMEN, SUSAN
WEEKEND WITH THE BABYSITTER (1970, Dundee/Crown)—
  Candy Wilson

ROMERO, CESAR
PUBLIC ENEMY'S WIFE (1936, Warners)—Gene Maroc
THE CISCO KID AND THE LADY (1939, 20th Century Fox)—
  Cisco Kid
THE GAY CABALLERO (1940, 20th Century Fox)—Cisco Kid
LUCKY CISCO KID (1940, 20th Century Fox)—Cisco Kid
VIVA CISCO KID (1940, 20th Century Fox)—Cisco Kid
TALL, DARK AND HANDSOME (1941, 20th Century Fox)—Shep
  Morrison
A GENTLEMAN AT HEART (1942, 20th Century Fox)—Tony
  Miller
ONCE A THIEF (1950, United Artists)—Mitch

ROMERO, NED
THE TALISMAN (1966, Gillman)—The Indian

RONAY, EDINA
PREHISTORIC WOMEN (1967, GB, 20th Century Fox)—Saria

RONSON, ADELE
HER UNBORN CHILD (1930, Windsor Picture Plays)—Dorothy Kennedy

ROOKER, MICHAEL
EIGHT MEN OUT (1988, Orion)—Chick Gandil
HENRY: PORTRAIT OF A SERIAL KILLER (1989, Maljack)—Henry

ROONEY, MICKEY
MY PAL, THE KING (1932, Universal)—King Charles V
HOOSIER SCHOOLBOY (1937, Monogram)—Shockey
BABES IN ARMS (1939, MGM)—Mickey Moran
HUCKLEBERRY FINN (1939, MGM)—Huckleberry Finn
JUDGE HARDY'S CHILDREN (1938, MGM)—Andy Hardy
LOVE FINDS ANDY HARDY (1938, MGM)—Andy Hardy
OUT WEST WITH THE HARDY'S (1938, MGM)—Andy Hardy
ANDY HARDY GETS SPRING FEVER (1939, MGM)—Andy Hardy
JUDGE HARDY AND SON (1939, MGM)—Andy Hardy
ANDY HARDY MEETS THE DEBUTANTE (1940, MGM)—Andy Hardy
YOUNG TOM EDISON (1940, MGM)—Tom Edison
ANDY HARDY'S PRIVATE SECRETARY (1941, MGM)—Andy Hardy
BABES ON BROADWAY (1941, MGM)—Tommy Williams
LIFE BEGINS FOR ANDY HARDY (1941, MGM)—Andy Hardy
MEN OF BOY'S TOWN (1941, MGM)—Whitey Marsh
ANDY HARDY'S DOUBLE LIFE (1942, MGM)—Andy Hardy
THE COURTSHIP OF ANDY HARDY (1942, MGM)—Andy Hardy
A YANK AT ETON (1942, MGM)—Timothy Dennis
GIRL-CRAZY (1943, MGM)—Danny Churchill Jr.
ANDY HARDY'S BLONDE TROUBLE (1944, MGM)—Andy Hardy
LOVE LAUGHS AT ANDY HARDY (1946, MGM)—Andy Hardy
KILLER MCCOY (1947, MGM)—Tommy McCoy
THE BIG WHEEL (1949, United Artists)—Billy Coy
THE FIREBALL (1950, 20th Century Fox)—Johnny Casar
HE'S A COCKEYED WONDER (1950, Columbia)—Freddie Frisby
MY BROTHER, THE OUTLAW (1951, Eagle-Lion)—Denny O'More
THE ATOMIC MAN (1955, Allied Artists)—Blix Waterberry
BABY FACE NELSON (1957, United Artists)—Baby Face Nelson
ANDY HARDY COMES HOME (1958, MGM)—Andy Hardy
THE BIG OPERATOR (1959, MGM)—Little Joe Braun

ROOSEVELT, BUDDY
CYCLONE JONES (1923, Silent, Fox)—Cyclone Jones
WHALLOPING WALLACE (1924, Silent, Artclass)—Buddy Wallace
THE BANDIT BUSTER (1926, Silent, Action)—Buddy Miller

ROSAY, FRANCOISE
JOHNNY FRENCHMAN (1946, GB, Ealing)—Lanec Florrie

ROSE, GEORGE
TRACK THE MAN DOWN (1956, GB, Republic)—Rick Lambert

ROSE, TIM
HOWARD THE DUCK (1986, Universal)—Howard T. Duck

ROSENBERG, STEPHEN
JACOB TWO-TWO MEETS THE HOODED FANG (1979, Canada, Gulkin)—Jacob Two-Two

ROSENBLOOM, "SLAPSIE" MAXIE
SKIPALONG ROSENBLOOM (1951, United Artists)—Skipalong Rosenbloom

ROSENTHAL, SHEILA
NOT WITHOUT MY DAUGHTER (1991, MGM/Pathe)—Mahtob Mahmoody

ROSMER, MILTON
BELPHEGOR THE MOUNTEBANK (1921, Silent, GB, Ideal)—Belphegor

ROSS, CHARLES J.
THE SENATOR (1915, Silent, Equitable)—Senator Rivers

ROSS, DIANA
LADY SINGS THE BLUES (1972, Paramount)—Billie Holiday
MAHOGANY (1975, Paramount)—Tracy/Mahogany

ROSS, JANET
THE KING'S DAUGHTER (1916, Silent, GB, Jury)—Helene

ROSS, KATHARINE
THE STEPFORD WIVES (1975, Columbia)—Joanna

ROSSELLINI, ISABELLA
ZELLY AND ME (1988, Columbia)—Zelly (Mademoiselle)
COUSINS (1989, Paramount)—Maria Hardy

ROSSITTO, SUE
THE GARBAGE PAIL KIDS (1987, Atlantic Entertainment)—Messie Tessie

ROTH, TIM
ROSENCRANTZ AND GUILDENSTERN ARE DEAD (1990, Cinecom)—Guildenstern
VINCENT AND THEO (1990, GB/France, Hemdale)—Vincent van Gogh

ROTHROCK, CYNTHIA
CHINA O'BRIEN (1991, Imperial/Golden Harvest)—China O'Brien

ROUNDTREE, RICHARD
SHAFT (1971, MGM)—John Shaft
SHAFT'S BIG SCORE (1972, MGM)—John Shaft
SHAFT IN AFRICA (1973, MGM)—John Shaft
MAN FRIDAY (1975, GB, Avco Embassy)—Friday

ROUNSEVILLE, ROBERT
THE TALES OF HOFFMAN (1951, GB, Lopert)—Hoffman

ROURKE, MICKEY
ANGEL HEART (1987, Tri-Star)—Harry Angel
BARFLY (1987, Cannon)—Henry Chinaski
JOHNNY HANDSOME (1989, Tri-Star)—John Sedley
HOMEBOY (1989, 20th Century Fox)—Johnny Walker
HARLEY DAVIDSON AND THE MARLBORO MAN (1991, MGM)—Harley Davidson

ROUSSE, DOLORES
NO MOTHER TO GUIDE HER (1923, Silent, Fox)—Kathleen Pearson

ROWE, GREG
STORM BOY (1976, Australia, South Australian Film)—Storm Boy

ROWE, MISTY
GOODBYE NORMA JEAN (1976, Filmways)—Norma Jean Baker

ROWE, NICHOLAS
YOUNG SHERLOCK HOLMES (1985, GB, Paramount)—Sherlock Holmes

ROWLANDS, GENA
MINNIE AND MOSCOWITZ (1971, Universal)—Minnie Moore
A WOMAN UNDER THE INFLUENCE (1974, International)—Mabel Longhetti
GLORIA (1980, Columbia)—Gloria Swenson
ANOTHER WOMAN (1988, Orion)—Marion

ROY, HARRY
RHYTHM RACKETEER (1937, GB, British International)—Harry Grand/Nap Connors

ROYSTON, GERALD
LITTLE LORD FAUNTLEROY (1914, GB, Silent, Kinematograph)—Cedric Erroll

RUBENS, ALMA
I LOVE YOU (1918, Silent, Triangle)—Felice
THE REJECTED WOMAN (1924, Silent, Cosmopolitan)—Diame Du Prez
THE GILDED BUTTERFLY (1926, Silent, Fox)—Linda Haverhill
THE HEART OF SALOME (1927, Silent, Fox)—Helene

RUBIN, MICHAEL
I WAS A TEENAGE ZOMBIE (1987, Horizon)—Dan Wake

RUBINSTEIN, JOHN
ZACHARIAH (1971, ABC Pictures)—Zachariah
IN SEARCH OF HISTORIC JESUS (1980, Sunn Classics)—Jesus Christ

RUCK, ALAN
THREE FOR THE ROAD (1987, New Century-Vista)—Tommy "T.S."

RUDOY, JOSHUA
HARRY AND THE HENDERSONS (1987, Universal)—Ernie Henderson

RUGGLES, CHARLIE
CHARLEY'S AUNT (1930, Columbia)—Lord Babberly
MAMA LOVES PAPA (1933, Paramount)—Wilbur Todd
HIS EXCITING NIGHT (1938, Universal)—Tripp
FRIENDLY ENEMIES (1942, United Artists)—Henry Block
THE LOVEABLE CHEAT (1949, Film Classics)—Claude Mercadet

RULE, JANICE
THREE WOMEN (1977, 20th Century Fox)—Willie Hart

RUSH, BARBARA
THE YOUNG PHILADELPHIANS (1959, Warners)—Joan Dickinson

RUSHTON, JARED
HONEY, I SHRUNK THE KIDS (1989, Buena Vista)—Ron Thompson
A CRY IN THE WILD (1990, Concorde)—Brian

RUSSELL, BETSY
AVENGING ANGEL (1985, New World)—Angel/Molly

TOMBOY (1985, Crown International)—Tommy Boyd

RUSSELL, BRYAN
EMIL AND THE DETECTIVES (1964, Buena Vista)—Emil

RUSSELL, GAIL
OUR HEARTS WERE YOUNG AND GAY (1944, Paramount)—Cornelia Otis Skinner
THE BACHELOR'S DAUGHTERS (1946, United Artists)—Eileen
OUR HEARTS WERE GROWING UP (1946, Paramount)—Cornelia Otis Skinner
ANGEL AND THE BADMAN (1947, Republic)—Prudence Worth

RUSSELL, JANE
YOUNG WIDOW (1946, United Artists)—Joan Kenwood
HIS KIND OF WOMAN (1951, RKO)—Lenore Brent
MONTANA BELLE (1952, RKO)—Belle Starr
GENTLEMEN MARRY BRUNETTES (1955, United Artists)—Bonnie
THE REVOLT OF MAMIE STOVER (1956. 20th Century Fox)—Mamie Stover

RUSSELL, KURT
NOW YOU SEE HIM, NOW YOU DON'T (1972, Buena Vista)—Dexter Riley
THE STRONGEST MAN IN THE WORLD (1975, Buena Vista)—Dexter Riley
TANGO AND CASH (1989, Warners)—Gabe Cash

RUSSELL, MARA
THE TRIAL OF MADAME X (1948, GB, EPC British)—Jacqueline

RUSSELL, ROSALIND
CRAIG'S WIFE (1936, Columbia)—Harriet Craig
TROUBLE FOR TRUE (1936, MGM)—Miss Vandeleur (Princess Branda)
THE WOMEN (1939, MGM)—Sylvia Fowler
HIS GIRL FRIDAY (1940, Columbia)—Hildy Johnson
THEY MET IN BOMBAY (1941, MGM)—Anya Von Duren
MY SISTER EILEEN (1942, Columbia)—Ruth Sherwood
WHAT A WOMAN! (1943, Columbia)—Carol Ainsley
SHE WOULDN'T SAY YES (1945, Columbia)—Susan Lane
SISTER KENNY (1946, RKO)—Elizabeth Kenny
THE GUILT OF JANET AMES (1947, Columbia)—Janet Ames
MOURNING BECOMES ELECTRA (1947, RKO)—Lavinia Mannon
A WOMAN OF DISTINCTION (1950, Columbia)—Susan Middlecott
NEVER WAVE AT A WAC (1952, RKO)—Jo McBain
AUNTIE MAME (1958, Warners)—Mame Dennis
A MAJORITY OF ONE (1961, Warners)—Mrs. Jacoby
OH DAD, POOR DAD, MAMA'S HUNG YOU IN THE CLOSET AND I'M FEELIN' SO SAD (1967, Paramount)—Mme. Rosepettle
ROSIE (1967, Universal)—Rosie Lord
MRS. POLLIFAX — SPY (1971, United Artists)—Mrs. Emily Pollifax

RUSSELL, THERESA
BLACK WIDOW (1987, 20th Century Fox)—Catharine
WHORE (1991, Trimark)—Liz

RUSSELL, WILLIAM
HOBBS IN A HURRY (1918, Silent, Pathe)—J. Warren Hobbs Jr.
HIGH GEAR JEFFREY (1921, Silent, American Film)—Jeffrey Claiborne

ALIAS THE NIGHT WIND (1923, Silent, Fox)—Bing Howard
THE HEAD OF THE FAMILY (1928, Silent, Gotham)—Eddie, The Plumber

RUSSO, J. DUKE
THE DON IS DEAD (1973, Universal)—Don Aggimio Bernardo

RUTH, BABE
BABE COMES HOME (1927, Silent, First National)—Babe Dugan

RUTHERFORD, ANN
WATERFRONT LADY (1935, Mascot-Republic)—Joan O'Brien
FOUR GIRLS IN WHITE (1939, MGM)—Patricia Page
ORCHESTRA WIVES (1942, 20th Century Fox)—Connie Abbott

RUTHERFORD, MARGARET
MISS ROBIN HOOD (1952, GB, Union)—Miss Honey
AUNT CLARA (1954, GB, British Lion)—Clara Hilton
MURDER, SHE SAID (1961, GB, MGM)—Miss Jane Marple
THE V.I.P.S (1963, GB, MGM)—Duchess of Brighton

RYAN, EDWARD
THE SULLIVANS (1944, 20th Century Fox)—Al Sullivan

RYAN, JACQUELINE
JACQUELINE (1956, GB, Rank)—Jacqueline McNeil

RYAN, KATHLEEN
ESTHER WATERS (1948, GB, Rank/GFD)—Esther Waters

RYAN, KELLY
THE OUTLAW'S DAUGHTER (1954, 20th Century Fox)—Kate

RYAN, MEG
WHEN HARRY MET SALLY. . . (1989, Columbia)—Sally Albright

RYAN, MITCHELL
GLORY BOY (1971, Cinerama)—Sgt. Martin Flood
THE WINTER PEOPLE (1989, Columbia)—Drury Campbell

RYAN, PEGGY
THE MERRY MONAHANS (1944, Universal)—Patsy Monahan

RYAN, RICHARD
DAVID AND JONATHAN (1920, Silent, GB, General)—Jonathan Hawksley

RYAN, ROBERT
RETURN OF THE BADMEN (1948, RKO)—Sundance Kid
THE SET-UP (1949, RKO)—Bill "Stoker" Thompson
THE TALL MEN (1955, 20th Century Fox)—Nathan Stark
THE PROFESSIONALS (1966, Columbia)—Hans Ehrengard
CAPTAIN NEMO AND THE UNDERWATER CITY (1969, GB, MGM)—Captain Nemo

RYAN, SHELIA
LADIES OF WASHINGTON (1944, 20th Century Fox)—Jerry

RYAN, TOMMY
TENTH AVENUE KID (1938, Republic)—Tommy
MICKEY, THE KID (1939, Republic)—Mickey
ORPHANS OF THE STREET (1939, Republic)—Tommy

RYDER, ALFRED
T-MEN (1947, Eagle-Lion)—Tony Genaro

S

SABU
ELEPHANT BOY (1937, GB, United Artists)—Toomai
THE THIEF OF BAGHDAD (1940, GB, London Films)—Abu

SACCHI, ROBERT
THE MAN WITH BOGART'S FACE (1980, 20th Century Fox)—Sam Marlow

SACHS, LEONARD
JOHN WESLEY (1954, GB, Commission of Methodist Church)—John Wesley

SACHS, MARTIN
SLATE, WYN & ME (1987, Australia, Ukiyo/Hemdale)—Slate Jackson

SAGER, RAY
THE WIZARD OF GORE (1970, Mayflower)—Montag the Magnificent

SALE, CHARLES "CHIC"
HIS NIBS (1921, Silent, Exceptional Pictures)—Theodore Bender
STAR WITNESS (1931, Warners)—Grandad Summerville
THE EXPERT (1932, Warners)—Grandpa Minick

SALENGER, MEREDITH
THE JOURNEY OF NATTY GANN (1985, Buena Vista)—Natty Gann

SALISBURY, MONROE
HIS DIVORCED WIFE (1919, Silent, Universal)—Ash Whipple
THE BARBARIAN (1921, Silent, Pioneer)—Eric Straive

SALMI, ALBERT
THE BROTHERS KARAMAZOV (1958, MGM)—Smerdyakov

SAMPSON, TIM
WAR PARTY (1989, Tri-Star)—Warren Cutfoot

SAMPSON, WILL
FISH HAWK (1981, Canada, Avco Embassy)—Fish Hawk

SANCHEZ, JAIME
THE WILD BUNCH (1969, Warners)—Angel

SANDERS, GEORGE
LANCER SPY (1937, 20th Century Fox)—Lt. Michael Bruce
FOUR MEN AND A PRAYER (1938, 20th Century Fox)—Wyatt Leigh
THE SAINT IN LONDON (1939, GB, RKO)—Simon Templar
THE SAINT STRIKES BACK (1939, RKO)—Simon Templar
THE OUTSIDER (1940, GB, Associated British Films)—Anton Ragatzy
THE SAINT TAKES OVER (1940, RKO)—Simon Templar
THE SAINT'S DOUBLE TROUBLE (1940, RKO)—Simon Templar & Duke Piato
A DATE WITH THE FALCON (1941, RKO)—Gay Lawrence, the Falcon
THE GAY FALCON (1941, RKO)—Gay Lawrence, the Falcon
THE SAINT IN PALM SPRINGS (1941, RKO)—Simon Templar
THE FALCON TAKES OVER (1942, RKO)—Gay Lawrence
THE FALCON'S BROTHER (1942, RKO)—Gay Lawrence

THE PRIVATE LIFE OF BEL AMI (1947, United Artists)—
Georges Duroy
KING RICHARD AND THE CRUSADERS (1954, Warners)—King
Richard III
DEATH OF A SCOUNDREL (1956, RKO)—Clementi Sabourin
BLUEBEARD'S TEN HONEYMOONS (1960, Allied Artists)—
Landru

SANDS, ANITA
DIARY OF A HIGH SCHOOL BRIDE (1959, American
International)—Judy

SANDS, DICK
PHANTOM FROM SPACE (1953, United Artists)—Phantom

SANDS, JOHN
ALADDIN AND HIS LAMP (1952, Monogram)—Aladdin

SANDS, LESLIE
THE RAGMAN'S DAUGHTER (1974, GB, Penelope-Harpoon)—
Mr. Randall, the Ragman

SANDS, TOMMY
SING, BOY, SING (1958, 20th Century Fox)—Virgil Walker

SANTSCHI, TOM
THE SPOILERS (1914, Silent, Selig)—Alec McNamara
PRIDE OF THE FORCE (1925, Silent, Rayart)—Officer Moore

SARANDON, CHRIS
THE SENTINEL (1977, Universal)—Michael Lerman
THE RESURRECTED (1992, Scotti Bros.)—Charles Dexter Ward/
Joseph Curween

SARANDON, SUSAN
LOVING COUPLES (1980, 20th Century Fox)—Stephanie
THE WITCHES OF EASTWICK (1987, Warners)—Jane Spofford
THELMA AND LOUISE (1991, Pathe)—Louise

SARGENT, LEWIS
HUCKLEBERRY FINN (1920, Silent, Paramount)—
Huckleberry Finn

SARRAZIN, MICHAEL
IN SEARCH OF GREGORY (1970, GB/Italy, Universal)—Gregory
THE REINCARNATION OF PETER PROUD (1975, American
International)—Peter Proud
FOR PETE'S SAKE (1977, Columbia)—Pete

SAUNDERS, LINDA
MARA OF THE WILDERNESS (1966, Allied Artists)—Mara Wade

SAVAGE, ANN
KLONDIKE KATE (1944, Columbia)—Kathleen O'Day

SAVAGE, FRED
VICE VERSA (1988, Columbia)—Charlie Seymour

SAVAGE, JOHN
THE AMATEUR (1982, 20th Century Fox)—Heller

SAVALAS, TELLY
THE DIRTY DOZEN (1967, GB, MGM)—Archer Maggott

SAWYER, JOE
YANKS AHOY (1943, United Artists)—Sgt. Ames

SAXON, JOHN
SUMMER LOVE (1958, Universal)—Jim Daley

SAXON, MARIE
THE BROADWAY HOOFER (1929, Columbia)—Adele

SAXON, VIN
RAT PFINK AND BOO BOO (1966, Morgan/Craddock)—
Rat Pfink

SAYLOR, SYD
THE THREE MESQUITEERS (1936, Republic)—Lullaby Joslin

SCALA, GIA
FOUR GIRLS IN TOWN (1956, Universal)—Vicki Dauray

SCAMMELL, DAVID
REVENGE OF THE RADIOACTIVE REPORTER (1990, Canada,
Pryceless)—Mike R. Wave

SCARDINO, DON
HOMER (1970, Palomar/National General)—Homer Edwards

SCARWID, DIANA
LADIES CLUB (1986, New Line Cinema)—Lucy Bricker

SCHEFF, FRITZI
PRETTY MRS. SMITH (1915, Silent, Paramount)—
Drucilla Smith

SCHEIDER, ROY
52 PICK-UP (1986, Cannon)—Harry Mitchell
MEN'S CLUB (1986, Paramount)—Cavanaugh
COHEN AND TATE (1989, Tri-Star)—Cohen

SCHELL, MAXIMILIAN
THE MAN IN THE GLASS BOOTH (1975, American Film
Theatre)—Arthur Goldman

SCHENCK, JOSEPH T.
THEY LEARNED ABOUT WOMEN (1930, MGM)—Jack

SCHILDKRAUT, JOSEPH
THE HEART THIEF (1927, Silent, Metropolitan)—Paul Kurt
MISSISSIPPI GAMBLER (1929, Universal)—Jack Morgan
COCK O' THE WALK (1930, Sono-Art-World-Wide)—Carlos

SCHILDKRAUT, RUDOLPH
THE COUNTRY DOCTOR (1927, Silent, Pathe Exchange)—Dr.
Amos Rinker

SCHMIDT, JOSEPH
A STAR FELL FROM HEAVEN (1936, GB, Wardour)—Josef

SCHNEIDER, JOHN
EDDIE MACON'S RUN (1983, Universal)—Eddie Macon

SCHNEIDER, ROMY
MY LOVER, MY SON (1970, GB, MGM)—Francesca Anderson

SCHOELEN, JILL
RICH GIRL (1991, Studio Three/Film West)—Courtney Wells

SCHOFIELD, JOHNNIE
SAM SMALL LEAVES TOWN (1937, GB, British Screen
Service)—Sam Small

SCHRAGE, LISA
HELLO MARY LOU, PROM NIGHT II (1987, Canada, Simcom/
Norstar)—Mary Lou Maloney

SCHWARTZ, MAURICE
TEVYA (1939, Jewish Historical Society)—Tevya

SCHWARZENEGGER, ARNOLD (ARNOLD STRONG)
HERCULES IN NEW YORK (1970, RAF/United Artists)—
Hercules
CONAN THE BARBARIAN (1982, Universal)—Conan
CONAN THE DESTROYER (1984, Universal)—Conan
THE TERMINATOR (1984, Orion)—Terminator
COMMANDO (1985, 20th Century Fox)—John Matrix
THE RUNNING MAN (1987, Tri-Star)—Ben "Butcher of
Bakersfield" Richards
TWINS (1988, Universal)—Julius Benedict
KINDERGARTEN COP (1990, Universal)—Kimble
TOTAL RECALL (1990, Tri-Star)—Quaid/Hauser
TERMINATOR 2: JUDGMENT DAY (1991, Tri-Star)—Terminator

SCOFIELD, PAUL
A MAN FOR ALL SEASONS (1966, GB, Columbia)—Sir
Thomas More
KING LEAR (1971, GB/Denmark, Filmways)—King Lear

SCOTT, CAMPBELL
DYING YOUNG (1991, 20th Century Fox)—Victor Geddes

SCOTT, GEORGE C.
NOT WITH MY WIFE, YOU DON'T (1966, Warners)—Tank
Martin
THE FLIM-FLAM MAN (1967, 20th Century Fox)—
Mordecai Jones
PATTON (1970, 20th Century Fox)—General George S. Patton
THEY MIGHT BE GIANTS (1971, Universal)—Justin Plafair/
"Sherlock Holmes"
THE NEW CENTURIONS (1972, Columbia)—Sgt. Kilvinsky

SCOTT, GORDON
TARZAN'S HIDDEN JUNGLE (1955, RKO)—Tarzan
TARZAN AND THE LOST SAFARI (1957, GB, MGM)—Tarzan
TARZAN'S FIGHT FOR LIFE (1958, MGM)—Tarzan
TARZAN'S GREATEST ADVENTURE (1959, GB, Paramount)—
Tarzan
TARZAN THE MAGNIFICENT (1960, GB, Paramount)—Tarzan

SCOTT, JANETTE
NO PLACE FOR JENNIFER (1950, GB, Pathe)—Jennifer
THE GOOD COMPANIONS (1957, GB, AB-Pathe)—Susie Dean
HAPPY IS THE BRIDE (1958, GB, Panthar/Kassler)—
Janet Boyd
HIS AND HERS (1961, GB, Sabre/Eros)—Fran Blake
PARANOIAC (1963, GB, Universal)—Eleanor Ashby

SCOTT, LIZABETH
YOU CAME ALONG (1945, Paramount)—Ivy Hotchkiss
TWO OF A KIND (1951, Columbia)—Brandy Kirby
STOLEN FACE (1952, GB, Hammer/Lippert)—Alice Brent/Lilly

SCOTT, MABEL JULIENNE
BEHOLD MY WIFE (1920, Silent, Paramount)—Lali (Armour)

SCOTT, MARGARETTA
A WOMAN POSSESSED (1958, GB, United Artists)—Katherine
Winthrop

SCOTT, MARTHA
THE HOWARDS OF VIRGINIA (1940, Columbia)—Jane Peyton
Howard
CHEERS FOR MISS BISHOP (1941, United Artists)—Ella Bishop
THEY DARE NOT LOVE (1941, Columbia)—Marta Keller

SCOTT, RANDOLPH
MAN OF THE FOREST (1933, Paramount)—Brett Dale
THE TEXANS (1938, Paramount)—Kirk Jordan
FRONTIER MARSHAL (1939, 20th Century Fox)—Wyatt Earp
THE SPOILERS (1942, Universal)—Alexander McNamara
THE DESPERADOES (1943, Columbia)—Steve Upton
THE GUNFIGHTERS (1947, Columbia)—Brazos Kane
THE DOOLINS OF OKLAHOMA (1949, Columbia)—Bill Doolin
FIGHTING MAN OF THE PLAINS (1949, 20th Century Fox)—
Jim Dancer
THE NEVADAN (1950, Columbia)—Andrew Barkley
MAN IN THE SADDLE (1951, Columbia)—Owen Merritt
SUGARFOOT (1951, Warners)—Sugarfoot
THE MAN BEHIND THE GUN (1952, Warners)—Major Callicut
THE STRANGER WORE A GUN (1953, Columbia)—Jeff Travis
THE BOUNTY HUNTER (1954, Warners)—Jim Kipp
RIDING SHOTGUN (1954, Warners)—Larry Delong
TALL MAN RIDING (1955, Warners)—Larry Madden
THE TALL T (1957, Columbia)—Pat Brennan
BUCHANAN RIDES ALONE (1958, Columbia)—Buchanan

SCOTT, ZACHARY
THE MASK OF DIMITRIOS (1944, Warners)—Dimitrios
THE SOUTHERNER (1945, United Artists)—Sam Tucker
RUTHLESS (1948, Eagle Lion)—Horace Vendig
GUILTY BYSTANDER (1950, Film Classics)—Max Thursday
VIOLENT STRANGER (1957, GB, Anglo Amalgamated)—John
Sullivan

SCOTT-TAYLOR, JONATHAN
DAMIEN-OMEN II (1978, 20th Century Fox)—Damien Thorn

SEAGAL, STEVEN
ABOVE THE LAW (1988, Warners)—Nico Toscani
HARD TO KILL (1990, Warners)—Mason Storm
MARKED FOR DEATH (1990, 20th Century Fox)—Hatcher
OUT FOR JUSTICE (1991, Warner Brothers)—Gino Felino

SEAGROVE, JENNY
THE GUARDIAN (1990, Universal)—Camilla

SEAGULL, BARBARA, *see* **BARBARA HERSHEY**

SEALEY, SCOTT
THE BOY WHO CRIED WEREWOLF (1973, Universal)—Richie
Bridgeston

SEARS, HEATHER
THE STORY OF ESTHER COSTELLO (1957, GB, Columbia)—
Esther Costello

SEATON, ARTHUR
THE HOWARD CASE (1936, GB, Universal)—Howard

SEBASTIAN, DOROTHY
SPITE MARRIAGE (1929, MGM)—Trilby Drew
LADIES MUST PLAY (1930, Columbia)—Norma
OUR BLUSHING BRIDES (1930, MGM)—Franky

SEBERG, JEAN
SAINT JOAN (1957, United Artists)—Joan of Arc
LILITH (1964, Columbia)—Lilith Arthur

SECOMBE, HARRY
DAVY (1958, GB, Ealing)—Davy

SEDGWICK, JOSIE
THE OUTLAW'S DAUGHTER (1925, Silent, Universal)—
Flora Dale

SEESE, DOROTHY ANN
FIVE LITTLE PEPPERS AND HOW THEY GREW (1939,
Columbia)—Phronsie Pepper
FIVE LITTLE PEPPERS AT HOME (1940, Columbia)—Phronsie
Pepper
FIVE LITTLE PEPPERS IN TROUBLE (1940, Columbia)—
Phronsie Pepper
OUT WEST WITH THE PEPPERS (1940, Columbia)—Phronsie
Pepper

SEGAL, GEORGE
THE YOUNG DOCTORS (1961, United Artists)—Dr. Howard
THE NEW INTERNS (1964, Columbia)—Dr. Tony Parelli
KING RAT (1965, Columbia)—Cpl. King
THE QUILLER MEMORANDUM (1966, GB, 20th Century Fox)—
Quiller
THE OWL AND THE PUSSYCAT (1970, Columbia)—Felix
BLUME IN LOVE (1973, Samuel Bronston)—Blume
THE TERMINAL MAN (1974, Warners)—Harry Benson
THE DUCHESS AND THE DIRTWATER FOX (1976, 20th Century
Fox)—Charlie Malloy
FUN WITH DICK AND JANE (1977, Columbia)—Dick Harper
THE LAST MARRIED COUPLE IN AMERICA (1980, Universal)—
Jeff Thompson

SEGAL, VIVIENNE
BRIDE OF THE REGIMENT (1930, First National)—Countess
Anna-Marie

SELBY, DAVID
THE SUPER COPS (1974, MGM/United Artists)—Bob Hantz

SELLECK, TOM
LASSITER (1984, Warners)—Lassiter
THREE MEN AND A BABY (1987, Buena Vista)—Peter Mitchell
HER ALIBI (1989, Warners)—Phil Blackwood
AN INNOCENT MAN (1989, Buena Vista)—Jimmie Rainwood
QUIGLEY DOWN UNDER (1990, MGM/UA)—Matthew Quigley
THREE MEN AND A LITTLE LADY (1990, Buena Vista)—Peter
Mitchell

SELLERS, ALAN
IT! (1967, GB, Warners)—The Golem

SELLERS, PETER
THE LADYKILLERS (1956, GB, Ealing)—Harry
I LIKE MONEY (1962, GB, 20th Century Fox)—Mr. Topaze
DR. STRANGELOVE: OR HOW I LEARNED TO STOP WORRYING
AND LOVE THE BOMB (1964, Columbia)—Dr. Strangelove
THE WORLD OF HENRY ORIENT (1964, United Artists)—Henry
Orient
AFTER THE FOX (1966, United Artists)—Aldo Vannuci
THE BOBO (1967, GB, Warners)—Juan Bautista
HOFFMAN (1970, GB, Associated British Films)—Benjamin
Hoffman
THE OPTIMISTS (1973, GB, Paramount)—Sam
THE PRISONER OF ZENDA (1979, Universal)—Rudolph
THE FIENDISH PLOT OF FU MANCHU (1980, Orion)—Fu
Manchu

SELTEN, MORTON
HIS MAJESTY AND CO. (1935, GB, Fox)—King of Poldavia

SELWYN, EDGAR
PIERRE OF THE PLAINS (1914, Silent, All Star)—Pierre

SEMON, LARRY
SPUDS (1927, Silent, Pathe Exchange)—"Spuds"

SERIOUS, YAHOO
YOUNG EINSTEIN (1989, Australia, Warners)—Albert Einstein

SERRANO, VINCENT
A MODERN MONTE CRISTO (1917, Silent, Thanhouser)—Dr.
Emerson

SESSIONS, ALMIRA
MY KINGDOM FOR A COOK (1943, Columbia)—Hattie

SETON, BRUCE
IF I WERE BOSS (1933, GB, Columbia)—Steve
FIFTY-SHILLING BOXER (1937, GB, RKO)—Jack Foster
FABIAN OF SCOTLAND YARD (1954, GB, Beauchamp/Eros)—
Supt. Fabian

SEURAT, PILAR
SEVEN WOMEN (1961, 20th Century Fox)—Mai-Lu Ferguson

SEYMOUR, CLARINE
THE IDOL DANCER (1920, Silent, First National)—Mary

SHAKMAN, MATT
MEET THE HOLLOWHEADS (1989, Moviestore)—Billy
Hollowhead

SHANDEL, PIA
THE VISITOR (1973, Canada, Highwood)—Becca

SHANE, SARA
THE KING AND FOUR QUEENS (1956, United Artists)—Oralie
THREE BAD SISTERS (1956, United Artists)—Lorna

SHANKS, DONALD
HALLOWEEN 5: THE REVENGE OF MICHAEL MYERS (1989,
Galaxy)—Michael Myers

SHANLEY, BILLY
THE SILENT WITNESS (1962, Emerson)—Danny

SHANNON, HARRY
THE FARMER'S DAUGHTER (1947, RKO)—Mr. Holstrom

SHANNON, PEGGY
PAINTED WOMAN (1932, Fox)—Kiddo
SOCIETY GIRL (1932, Fox)—Judy Gelett

SHAPS, CYRIL
RETURN OF A STRANGER (1962, GB, Danzinger)—Homer Trent

SHARIF, OMAR
DOCTOR ZHIVAGO (1965, MGM)—Yuri Zhivago
GENGHIS KHAN (1965, Columbia)—Temulin-Genghis Khan
CHE! (1969, 20th Century Fox)—Che Guevara
THE RAINBOW THIEF (1990, Burrill)—Dima

SHARKEY, RAY
THE IDOLMAKER (1980, United Artists)—Vincent Vacarri
WILL AND PHIL (1980, 20th Century Fox)—Phil D'Amico

SHARPE, ALBERT
DARBY O'GILL AND THE LITTLE PEOPLE (1959, Disney/Buena Vista)—Darby O'Gill

SHATNER, WILLIAM
THE BROTHERS KARAMAZOV (1958, MGM)—Alexey Karamazov
THE INTRUDER (1962, Pathe-America)—Adam Cramer

SHAW, BUD
BYE-BYE BUDDY (1929, Part-Talkie, Trinity Pictures)—Buddy O'Brien

SHAW, JULIAN
REVENGE OF BILLY THE KID (1992, GB, Montage)—
Billy T. Kid

SHAW, MARTIN
THE HOUND OF THE BASKERVILLES (1983, GB, Mapelton)—
Sir Henry Baskerville

SHAW, ROBERT
ADAM HAD FOUR SONS (1941, Columbia)—Chris

SHAW, ROBERT
THE LUCK OF GINGER COFFEY (1964, Continental Distributing)—Ginger Coffey
CUSTER OF THE WEST (1968, Cinerama)—General George A. Custer
THE HIRELING (1973, GB, World/Columbia)—Leadbetter

SHAW, WINI
BROADWAY HOSTESS (1935, Warners)—Winnie Wharton

SHAWLEE, JOAN
PREHISTORIC WOMEN (1950, Eagle Lion)—Lotee

SHAWN, DICK
THE WIZARD OF BAGHDAD (1960, 20th Century Fox)—Genii-Ali Mahmud

SHAWN, WALLACE
MY DINNER WITH ANDRE (1981, New Yorker)—Wally

SHAYNE, ROBERT
THE NEANDERTHAL MAN (1953, United Artists)—Dr. Cliff Groves

SHEA, ERIC
ACE ELI AND RODGER OF THE SKY (1973, 20th Century Fox)—Eric Shea

SHEA, JOHN
MISSING (1982, Universal)—Charles Horman

SHEARER, MOIRA
THE MAN WHO LOVED REDHEADS (1955, London Films)—Sylvia/Daphne/Olga/ Colette

SHEARER, NORMA
HER SECRETARY (1925, Silent, MGM)—Ruth Lawrence
LADY OF THE NIGHT (1925, Silent, MGM)—Florence
THE ACTRESS (1928, Silent, MGM)—Rose Trelawney
A LADY OF CHANCE (1928, MGM)—Dolly
THE LAST OF MRS. CHEYNEY (1929, MGM)—Mrs. Fay Cheyney
THEIR OWN DESIRE (1929, MGM)—Lally Marlett
THE TRIAL OF MARY DUGAN (1929, MGM)—Mary Dugan
THE DIVORCEE (1930, MGM)—Jerry
A FREE SOUL (1931, MGM)—Jan Ashe

PRIVATE LIVES (1931, MGM)—Amanda Chase Payne
STRANGERS MAY KISS (1931, MGM)—Lisbeth Corbin
THE BARRETTS OF WIMPOLE STREET (1934, MGM)—
Elizabeth Barrett
ROMEO AND JULIET (1936, MGM)—Juliet
MARIE ANTOINETTE (1938, MGM)—Marie Antoinette
IDIOT'S DELIGHT (1939, MGM)—Irene Fellara
THE WOMEN (1939, MGM)—Mary Haines
HER CARDBOARD LOVER (1942, MGM)—Consuelo Croyden

SHEEDY, ALLY
THE BREAKFAST CLUB (1985, Universal)—Allison Reynolds
MAID TO ORDER (1987, New Century-Vista)—Jessie Montgomery
ONLY THE LONELY (1991, 20th Century Fox)—Theresa Luna

SHEEN, CHARLIE
PLATOON (1987, Orion)—Chris
THREE FOR THE ROAD (1987, New Century-Vista)—Paul Tracy
EIGHT MEN OUT (1988, Orion)—Hap Felsch
YOUNG GUNS (1988, 20th Century Fox)—Dick Brewer
MEN AT WORK (1990, Triumph)—Carl Taylor
NAVY SEALS (1990, Orion)—Hawkins
THE ROOKIE (1990, Warners)—David Ackerman
HOT SHOTS (1991, 20th Century Fox)—Topper Harley

SHEEN, MARTIN
MAN, WOMAN AND CHILD (1983, Paramount)—Bob Beckwith

SHEFFIELD, JOHNNY
TARZAN FINDS A SON (1939, MGM)—Boy
LITTLE ORVIE (1940, RKO)—Orvie Stone
BOMBA ON PANTHER ISLAND (1949, Monogram)—Bomba
BOMBA THE JUNGLE BOY (1949, Monogram)—Bomba
BOMBA AND THE HIDDEN CITY (1950, Monogram)—Bomba
BOMBA AND THE JUNGLE GIRL (1952, Monogram)—Bomba
LORD OF THE JUNGLE (1955, Allied Artists)—Bomba

SHELDON, GENE
BABES IN TOYLAND (1961, Buena Vista)—Roderigo

SHELLEY, BARBARA
CAT GIRL (1957, American International)—Leonora

SHELTON, DEBORAH
PERFECT VICTIM (1988, Vertigo)—Liz Winters

SHENTALL, SUSAN
ROMEO AND JULIET (1954, GB, United Artists)—Juliet

SHEPARD, JEWEL
HOLLYWOOD HOT TUBS 2: EDUCATING CRYSTAL (1990, Alimar)—Crystal

SHEPARD, SAM
RAGGEDY MAN (1981, Universal)—Bailey
FOOL FOR LOVE (1985, Cannon)—Eddie

SHEPHERD, CYBILL
DAISY MILLER (1974, Paramount)—Annie P. "Daisy" Miller

SHEPHERD, ELIZABETH
THE TOMB OF LIGEIA (1965, GB, American International)—
Lady Ligeia Fell

SHEPPARD, DELIA
WITCHCRAFT PART II: THE TEMPTRESS (1990, Vista Street)—Dolores

SHEPPARD, PAULA
ALICE, SWEET ALICE (1978, Allied Artists)—Alice

SHEPPERD, JOHN, *See* **SHEPPERD STRUDWICK**

SHER, ANTONY
SHADEY (1987, GB, Film Four/Skouras)—Oliver Shadey

SHERIDAN, ANN
THE FOOTLOOSE HEIRESS (1937, Warners)—Kay Allyn
SHE LOVES A FIREMAN (1937, Warners)—Margie Shannon
JUKE GIRL (1942, Warners)—Lola Mears
THE DOUGHGIRLS (1944, Warners)—Edna
NORA PRENTISS (1947, Warners)—Nora Prentiss
THE UNFAITHFUL (1947, Warners)—Chris Hunter
STELLA (1950, 20th Century Fox)—Stella
WOMAN ON THE RUN (1950, Universal)—Eleanor Johnson

SHERIDAN, DINAH
THE STORY OF SHIRLEY YORKE (1948, GB, Butchers)—Shirley Yorke

SHERIDAN, NICOLLETTE
THE SURE THING (1985, Embassy)—The Sure Thing

SHERMAN, KERRY
SATAN'S CHEERLEADERS (1977, World Amusements)—Patti

SHERMAN, LOWELL
HE KNEW WOMEN (1930, RKO)—Geoffrey Clarke

SHERWOOD, GALE
BLONDE SAVAGE (1947, Ensign/Eagle-Lion)—Meelah

SHIELDS, BROOKE
PRETTY BABY (1978, Paramount)—Violet
JUST YOU AND ME, KID (1979, Columbia)—Kate
WANDA NEVADA (1979, United Artists)—Wanda Nevada

SHILLING, MARION
WISE GIRLS (1930, MGM)—Ruth Bence
FORGOTTEN WOMEN (1932, Monogram)—Patricia Young

SHIMKUS, JOANNA
THE VIRGIN AND THE GYPSY (1970, GB, Chevron)—Yvette

SHIRLEY, ALEISA
SWEET SIXTEEN (1983, Century International)—Melissa

SHIRLEY, ANNE
ANNE OF GREEN GABLES (1934, RKO)—Anne Shirley
CHATTERBOX (1936, RKO)—Jenny Yates
MAKE WAY FOR A LADY (1936, RKO)—June Drew
M'LISS (1936, RKO)—M'liss Smith
MOTHER CAREY'S CHICKENS (1938, RKO)—Nancy Carey
ANNE OF WINDY POPLARS (1940, RKO)—Anne Shirley
SATURDAY'S CHILDREN (1940, Warners)—Anne Shirley
FOUR JACKS AND A JILL (1941, RKO)—Nina
WEST POINT WIDOW (1941, Paramount)—Nancy Hull
LADY BODYGUARD (1942, Paramount)—A.C. Baker

SHOR, DAN
DADDY'S BOYS (1988, Concorde)—Hawk

SHORT, GERTRUDE
LADIES AT EASE (1927, Silent, First Division)—Gert

SHORT, MARTIN
THE THREE AMIGOS (1986, Orion)—Ned Nederlander
THREE FUGITIVES (1989, Buena Vista)—Ned Perry

SHORTER, KEN
STONE (1974, Australia, BEF Australia)—Stone

SHOTTER, CONSTANCE
FOR THE LOVE OF MIKE (1933, GB, BIP/Wardour)—Mike

SHOTTER, WINIFRED
MARRY THE GIRL (1935, GB, British Lion)—Doris Chattaway

SHOTWELL, MARIE
ONE WOMAN TO ANOTHER (1927, Silent, Paramount)—Mrs. Gray

SHRINER, WIL
TIME TRACKERS (1989, Concorde)—Charles

SHUE, ELISABETH
ADVENTURES IN BABYSITTING (1987, Buena Vista)—Chris Parker

SHUFORD, ANDY
FELLER NEEDS A FRIEND (1932, Cosmopolitan)—Froggie

SIDNEY, GEORGE
IN HOLLYWOOD WITH POTASH AND PERLMUTTER (1924, Silent, Goldwyn)—Abe Potash
THE COHENS AND THE KELLYS (1926, Silent, Universal)—Jacob Cohen
PARTNERS AGAIN (1926, Silent, United Artists)—Abe Potash
THE AUCTIONEER (1927, Silent, Fox)—Simon Levi
FLYING ROMEOS (1928, Silent, First National)—Cohen
THE COHENS AND THE KELLYS IN ATLANTIC CITY (1929, Universal)—Jacob Cohen

SIDNEY, SYLVIA
LADIES OF THE BIG HOUSE (1932, Paramount)—Kathleen Storm
MADAME BUTTERFLY (1932, Paramount)—Cho-Cho San
JENNIE GERHARDT (1933, Paramount)—Jennie Gerhardt
PICK-UP (1933, Paramount)—Mary Richards
GOOD DAME (1934, Paramount)—Lillie Taylor
THIRTY-DAY PRINCESS (1934, Paramount)—Nancy Lane
BEHOLD MY WIFE (1935, Paramount)—Tonita Stormcloud
MARY BURNS, FUGITIVE (1935, Paramount)—Mary Burns
YOU AND ME (1938, Paramount)—Helen Dennis

SIEGMANN, GEORGE
THE THREE MUSKETEERS (1921, Silent, United Artists)—Porthos

SIEMASZKO, CASEY
YOUNG GUNS (1988, 20th Century Fox)—Charley Bowdre

SIERCHIO, TOM
DELIVERY BOYS (1984, New World)—Joey

SIKKING, JAMES B.
THE MAGNIFICENT SEVEN RIDE (1972, United Artists)—Hayes

SILAS, EVERETT
MY BROTHER'S WEDDING (1938, Burnett)—Pierce Monday

SILLS, MILTON
BEHOLD MY WIFE (1920, Silent, Paramount)—Frank Armour
LEGALLY DEAD (1923, Silent, Universal)—Will Campbell
I WANT MY MAN (1925, Silent, First National)—Gulian Eyre
THE SILENT LOVER (1926, Silent, First National)—Count
Pierre Tornai
HARD-BOILED HAGGERTY (1927, Silent, First National)—
Hard-Boiled Haggerty
THE BARKER (1928, Part-Talkie, First National/Warners)—
Nifty Miller
THE HAWK'S NEST (1928, Silent, First National)—The Hawk/
John Finchley
HIS CAPTIVE WOMAN (1929, First National/Warners)—Officer
McCarthy
THE SEA WOLF (1930, Fox)—Wolf Larsen

SILVA, HENRY
OCEAN'S ELEVEN (1960, Warners)—Roger Corneal
JOHNNY COOL (1963, United Artists)—Johnny Cool/Giordano
THE RETURN OF MR. MOTO (1965, GB, 20th Century Fox)—
Mr. Moto

SILVA, TRINIDAD
JOCKS (1987, Crown)—Chito

SILVER, RON
ENEMIES, A LOVE STORY (1989, 20th Century Fox)—Herman

SILVERHEELS, JAY
BRAVE WARRIOR (1952, Columbia)—Chief Tecumseh

SILVERS, PHIL
TOP BANANA (1954, United Artists)—Jerry Biffle

SIM, ALASTAIR
SCROOGE (1951, GB, Renown)—Ebenezer Scrooge
AN INSPECTOR CALLS (1954, GB, British Lion)—
Inspector Poole

SIMMONS, GENE
WANTED: DEAD OR ALIVE (1987, New World)—Malak
Al Rahim

SIMMONS, JEAN
ADAM AND EVELYNE (1950, GB, Rank/Two Cities)—Evelyne
Wallace
THE ACTRESS (1953, MGM)—Ruth Gordon Jones
ANGEL FACE (1953, RKO)—Diane Tremayne
YOUNG BESS (1953, MGM)—Elizabeth I
GUYS AND DOLLS (1955, MGM)—Sarah Brown
HILDA CRANE (1956, 20th Century Fox)—Hilda Crane
DOMINIQUE (1978, GB, Subotsky)—Dominique Ballard
DESIREE (1954, 20th Century Fox)—Desiree Clary
SHE COULDN'T SAY NO (1954, RKO)—Corby Lane

SIMMS, GINNY
SHADY LADY (1945, Universal)—Lee Appleby

SIMON, SIMONE
CAT PEOPLE (1942, RKO)—Irena Dubrovna
THE CURSE OF THE CAT PEOPLE (1944, RKO)—Irena

SIMPSON, PEGGY
DARBY AND JOAN (1937, GB, MGM)—Joan Templeton

SINATRA, FRANK
THE KISSING BANDIT (1948, MGM)—Ricardo
ON THE TOWN (1949, MGM)—Chip
MEET DANNY WILSON (1952, Universal)—Danny Wilson
GUYS AND DOLLS (1955, MGM)—Nathan Detroit
THE MAN WITH THE GOLDEN ARM (1955, United Artists)—
Frankie Machine
JOHNNY CONCHO (1956, United Artists)—Johnny Concho
THE JOKER IS WILD (1957, Paramount)—Joe E. Lewis
PAL JOEY (1957, Columbia)—Joey Evans
OCEAN'S ELEVEN (1960, Warners)—Danny Ocean
SERGEANTS 3 (1962, United Artists)—1st Sgt. Mike Merry
FOUR FOR TEXAS (1963, Warners)—Zack Thomas
ROBIN AND THE SEVEN HOODS (1964, Warners)—Robbo
VON RYAN'S EXPRESS (1965, 20th Century Fox)—Col. Joseph
L. Ryan
THE NAKED RUNNER (1967, GB, Warners)—Sam Laker
TONY ROME (1967, 20th Century Fox)—Tony Rome
THE DETECTIVE (1968, 20th Century Fox)—Joe Leland
DIRTY DINGUS MAGEE (1970, MGM)—Dingus Magee

SINCLAIR, GORDON JOHN
GREGORY'S GIRL (1982, GB, Goldwyn)—Gregory

SINCLAIR, HUGH
STRANGERS ON A HONEYMOON (1937, GB, Gaumont)—Quigley
THE SECRET FOUR (1940, GB, Ealing)—Humphrey Mansfield
THE SAINT'S VACATION (1941, GB, RKO)—Simon Templar
THE SAINT MEETS THE TIGER (1943, GB, RKO/Republic)—
Simon Templar

SINGER, MARC
IF YOU COULD SEE WHAT I HEAR (1982, Cypress Grove)—Tom
Sullivan
THE BEASTMASTER (1982, MGM/United Artists)—Dar
BEASTMASTER 2: THROUGH THE PORTALS OF TIME (1991,
New Line)—Dar

SINGLETON, PENNY
BLONDIE (1938, Columbia)—Blondie
BLONDIE BRINGS UP BABY (1939, Columbia)—Blondie
BLONDIE MEETS THE BOSS (1939, Columbia)—Blondie
BLONDIE TAKES A VACATION (1939, Columbia)—Blondie
BLONDIE HAS SERVANT TROUBLE (1940, Columbia)—Blondie
BLONDIE ON A BUDGET (1940, Columbia)—Blondie
BLONDIE PLAYS CUPID (1940, Columbia)—Blondie
BLONDIE GOES LATIN (1941, Columbia)—Blondie
BLONDIE GOES TO COLLEGE (1941, Columbia)—Blondie
BLONDIE IN SOCIETY (1941, Columbia)—Blondie
GO WEST, YOUNG LADY (1941, Columbia)—Belinda Pendergast
BLONDIE FOR VICTORY (1942, Columbia)—Blondie
BLONDIE'S BLESSED EVENT (1942, Columbia)—Blondie
LEAVE IT TO BLONDIE (1945, Columbia)—Blondie
BLONDIE KNOWS BEST (1946, Columbia)—Blondie
BLONDIE'S LUCKY DAY (1946, Columbia)—Blondie
LIFE WITH BLONDIE (1946, Columbia)—Blondie
BLONDIE IN THE DOUGH (1947, Columbia)—Blondie
BLONDIE'S ANNIVERSARY (1947, Columbia)—Blondie
BLONDIE'S BIG MOMENT (1947, Columbia)—Blondie
BLONDIE'S HOLIDAY (1947, Columbia)—Blondie
BLONDIE'S REWARD (1948, Columbia)—Blondie
BLONDIE'S SECRET (1948, Columbia)—Blondie
BLONDIE HITS THE JACKPOT (1949, Columbia)—Blondie

BEWARE OF BLONDIE (1950, Columbia)—Blondie
BLONDIE'S HERO (1950, Columbia)—Blondie

SINISE, GARY
OF MICE AND MEN (1992, MGM)—George

SISTI, MICHELAN
TEENAGE MUTANT NINJA TURTLES (1990, New Line)—
Michelangelo
TEENAGE MUTANT NINJA TURTLES II: THE SECRET OF OOZE
(1991, New Line)—Michelangelo

SKELLY, HAL
MEN ARE LIKE THAT (1930, Paramount)—Aubrey Piper

SKELTON, RED
I DOOD IT (1943, MGM)—Joseph Rivington Reynolds
THE SHOW-OFF (1946, MGM)—Aubrey Piper
MERTON OF THE MOVIES (1947, MGM)—Merton Gill
FULLER BRUSH MAN (1948, Columbia)—Red Jones
A SOUTHERN YANKEE (1948, MGM)—Aubrey Filmore
THE YELLOW CAB MAN (1950, MGM)—Augustus "Red" Pirdy
EXCUSE MY DUST (1951, MGM)—Joe Belden
THE CLOWN (1953, MGM)—Dodo Delwyn
HALF A HERO (1953, MGM)—Ben Dobson
PUBLIC PIDGEON NO. 1 (1957, RKO/Universal)—Rusty Morgan

SKILLAN, GEORGE
THE MERCHANT OF VENICE (1916, GB, Silent, Broadwest)—
Antonio

SKINNER, ANITA
SOLE SURVIVOR (1984, Grand National)—Denise Watson

SKIPWORTH, ALISON
MADAME RACKETEER (1932, Paramount)—"Countess von
Claudwig"/Martha Hicks
TILLIE AND GUS (1933, Paramount)—Tillie Winterbootom
HITCH HIKE LADY (1936, Republic)—Mrs. Amelia Blake
TWO WISE MAIDS (1937, Republic)—Agatha Stanton

SKYE, IONE
THE RACHEL PAPERS (1989, United Artists)—Rachel
Seth-Smith

SLATER, CHRISTIAN
YOUNG GUNS II (1990, 20th Century Fox)—Arkansas Dave
Rudabaugh
MOBSTERS (1991, Universal)—Lucky Luciano
KUFFS (1992, Universal)—George Kuffs

SLATER, HELEN
SUPERGIRL (1984, Tri-Star)—Supergirl/Linda Lee
THE LEGEND OF BILLIE JOE (1985, Tri-Star)—Billie Jean
RUTHLESS PEOPLE (1986, Buena Vista)—Sandy Kessler
STICKY FINGERS (1988, Spectrafilm)—Hattie

SLATER, JOHN
JOHNNY, YOU'RE WANTED (1956, GB, Anglo-Amalgamated)—
Johnny

SLAUGHTER, TOD
CRIMES OF STEPHEN HAWKE (1936, GB, MGM)—
Stephen Hawke
THE TICKET OF LEAVE MAN (1937, GB, MGM)—Tiger Dalton

THE DEMON BARBER OF FLEET STREET (1939, GB, MGM)—
Sweeney Todd
THE GREED OF THE WILLIAM HART (1948, GB, Butchers)—
William Hart
KING OF THE UNDERWORLD (1952, GB, Bushey)—
Terence Riley

SLEAP, STEVE
HOWARD THE DUCK (1986, Universal)—Howard T. Duck

SLEZAK, WALTER
THE PIRATE (1948, MGM)—Macoco, "Mack the Black"
DR. COPPELIUS (1968, Gala)—Dr. Coppelius
THE MYSTERIOUS HOUSE OF DR. C (1976, Bronston)—Dr.
Coppelius

SLOANE, EVERETT
THE ENFORCER (1951, Warners)—Albert Mendoza

SLOANE, OLIVE
MY WIFE'S LODGER (1952, GB, Adelphi)—Maggie
Higginbotham

SMART, J. SCOTT
THE FAT MAN (1951, Universal)—Brad Runyon

SMITH, ALEXIS
THE DOUGHGIRLS (1944, Warners)—Nan
UNDERCOVER GIRL (1950, Universal)—Christine Miller / "Sal
Willis"

SMITH, BUBBA
THE WILD PAIR (1987, Trans World Entertainment)—Benny
Avalon

SMITH, C. AUBREY
JOHN GLAYDE'S HONOR (1915, Silent, Gold Rooster)—John
Glayde
JAFFERY (1916, Silent, Frohaman Amusement Co.)—Jaffery
BACHELOR FATHER (1931, MGM)—Sir Basil Winterton

SMITH, CHARLES
HENRY AND DIZZY (1942, Paramount)—Dizzy Stevens

SMITH, CHARLES MARTIN
THE UNTOUCHABLES (1987, Paramount)—Oscar Wallace

SMITH, JOHN
SEVEN ANGRY MEN (1955, Allied Artists)—Frederick Brown

SMITH, KIM
THE LITTLE ONES (1965, GB, Columbia)—Ted

SMITH, LEWIS
THE HEAVENLY KID (1985, Orion)—Bobby

SMITH, MADELEINE
THE VAMPIRE LOVERS (1970, GB, Hammer)—Emma Morton

SMITH, MAGGIE
THE PRIME OF MISS JEAN BRODIE (1969, GB, 20th Century
Fox)—Jean Brodie
TRAVELS WITH MY AUNT (1972, GB, MGM)—Aunt Augusta
LILY IN LOVE (1985, New Line Cinema)—Lily Wynn
THE LONELY PASSION OF JUDITH HEARNE (1987, GB,
Island)—Judith Hearne

SMITH, REX
THE PIRATES OF PENZANCE (1983, Universal)—Frederic

SMITH, SALLY
IN TROUBLE WITH EVE (1964, GB, Mancunian)—Eve

SMITH, WILLIAM
RUN, ANGEL, RUN (1969, Fanfare)—Angel

SNODGRESS, CARRIE
DIARY OF A MAD HOUSEWIFE (1970, Universal)—Tina Balser

SNYDER, NANCY
THE KIRLIAN WITNESS (1978, Sampson and Cranor)—Rilla

SNYDER, SUZANNE
PRETTYKILL (1987, Dax Avant/Spectrafilm)—Francie

SOCAS, MARIA
THE WARRIOR AND THE SORCERESS (1984, New World)—Naja

SOLARI, RUDY
THE BOSS' SON (1978, New American Cinema)—Joseph

SOMMER, ELKE
DEADLIER THAN THE MALE (1967, GB, Universal)—Irma Eckman
THE WICKED DREAMS OF PAULA SCHULTZ (1968, United Artists)—Paul Schultz

SONDERGAARD, GALE
ENEMY AGENT MEETS ELLERY QUEEN (1942, Columbia)—Mrs. Van Dorn
SHERLOCK HOLMES AND THE SPIDER WOMAN (1944, Universal)—Andrea Spedding
THE SPIDER WOMAN STRIKES BACK (1946, Universal)—Zenobia Dollard

SONJIN
CHINA SLAVER (1929, Silent, Trinity Pictures)—The Cobra

SONKER, HANS
PATRICIA GETS HER MAN (1937, GB, First National)—Count Stephan D'Orlet

SONORA
THE NOTORIOUS CLEOPATRA (1970, Boxoffice International)—Cleopatra

SONT, GERRY
MELVIN, SON OF ALVIN (1984, Australia, Roadshow)—Melvin Simpson

SORDI, ALBERTO
THE BEST OF ENEMIES (1962, Columbia)—Captain Blasi
THOSE MAGNIFICENT MEN IN THEIR FLYING MACHINES (1965, GB, 20th Century Fox)—Count Emilio Ponticelli

SORIERO, JIM
DELIVERY BOYS (1984, New World)—Conrad

SORVINO, PAUL
BLOODBROTHERS (1978, Kings Road/Warners)—Chubby DeCoco

SOTHERN, ANN
THE HELL CAT (1934, Columbia)—Geraldine Graham
MY AMERICAN WIFE (1936, Paramount)—Mary Cantillon
SMARTEST GIRL IN TOWN (1936, RKO)—Francis Cooke
SHE'S GOT EVERYTHING (1938, RKO)—Carol Rogers
JOE AND ETHEL TURP CALL ON THE PRESIDENT (1939, MGM)—Ethel Turp
MAISIE (1939, MGM)—Maisie Ravier
CONGO MAISIE (1940, MGM)—Maisie Ravier
DULCY (1940, MGM)—Dulcy Ward
GO RUSH MAISIE (1940, MGM)—Maisie Ravier
MAISIE WAS A LADY (1941, MGM)—Maisie Ravier
RINGSIDE MAISIE (1941, MGM)—Maisie Ravier
MAISIE GETS HER MAN (1942, MGM)—Maisie Ravier
PANAMA HATTIE (1942, MGM)—Hattie Maloney
SWING SHIFT MAISIE (1943, MGM)—Maisie Ravier
THREE HEARTS FOR JULIA (1943, MGM)—Julia Seabrook
MAISIE GOES TO RENO (1944, MGM)—Maisie Ravier
UP GOES MAISIE (1946, MGM)—Maisie Ravier
UNDERCOVER MAISIE (1947, MGM)—Maisie Ravier
A LETTER TO THREE WIVES (1948, 20th Century Fox)—Rita Phipps

SPACE, ARTHUR
THE VANISHING WESTERNER (1950, Republic)—John Fast

SPACEK, SISSY
CARRIE (1976, United Artists)—Carrie White
THREE WOMEN (1977, 20th Century Fox)—Pinky Rose
COAL MINER'S DAUGHTER (1980, Universal)—Loretta Lynn
MARIE (1985, MGM/United Artists)—Marie Ragghianti

SPADER, JAMES
JACK'S BACK (1988, Palisades)—John Werford

SPEED, CAROL
ABBY (1974, American International)—Abby Williams

SPELL, GEORGE
MAN AND BOY (1972, Jemmin/Levitt/Pickman)—Billy Revers

SPELSON, PETER
THE PSYCHOTRONIC MAN (1980, International Harmony)—Rocky Foscoe

SPENSER, JEREMY
DEVIL ON HORSEBACK (1954, GB, British Lion)—Moppy Parfitt

SPILSBURY, KLINTON
THE LEGEND OF THE LONE RANGER (1981, Universal)—The Lone Ranger/ John Reid

SPINELL, JOE
MANIAC (1980, Magnum)—Frank Zito

ST. JOHN, BETTA
DREAM WIFE (1953, MGM)—Tarji

ST. JOHN, HOWARD
COUNTERSPY MEETS SCOTLAND YARD (1950, Columbia)—David Harding
DAVID HARDING, COUNTERSPY (1950, Columbia)—David Harding

ST. JOHN, JILL
SUMMER LOVE (1958, Universal)—Erica Landis

ST. POLIS, JOHN
MELODY MAN (1930, Columbia)—Earl von Kemper

STACK, ROBERT
MY BROTHER, THE OUTLAW (1951, Eagle-Lion)—Patrick O'More
THE TARNISHED ANGELS (1957, Universal)—Roger Shumann
JOHN PAUL JONES (1959, Warners)—John Paul Jones

STACKER, STEVEN
BOBBIKINS (1959, GB, 20th Century Fox)—Bobbikins

STAFF, HARRY WALKER
SCRATCH HARRY (1969, Cannon)—Harry

STALLONE, SYLVESTER
ROCKY (1976, United Artists)—Rocky Balboa
ROCKY II (1979, United Artists)—Rocky Balboa
ROCKY III (1982, MGM/United Artists)—Rocky Balboa
RAMBO: FIRST BLOOD PART II (1985, Tri-Star)—Rambo
ROCKY IV (1985, MGM/United Artists)—Rocky Balboa
COBRA (1986, Warners)—Marion Cobretti
RAMBO III (1988, Tri-Star)—John Rambo
TANGO AND CASH (1989, Warners)—Ray Tango
ROCKY V (1990, MGM/UA)—Rocky Balboa
STOP! OR MY MOTHER WILL SHOOT (1992, Universal)—Joe Bomowski

STALMASTER, HAL
JOHNNY TREMAIN (1957, Buena Vista)—Johnny Tremain

STAMP, TERENCE
BILLY BUDD (1962, United Artists)—Billy Budd
THE COLLECTOR (1965, Columbia)—Freddie Clegg
BLUE (1968, Paramount)—Blue
THE MIND OF MR. SOAMES (1970, GB, Columbia)—John Soames

STANDING, WYNDHAM
THE MARRIAGE OF WILLIAM ASHE (1921, Silent, Metro)—William Ashe
THE INNER MAN (1922, Silent, Playgoers)—Thurlow Michael Barclay Jr.

STANDISH, SCHUYLER
MELODY FOR THREE (1941, RKO)—Billy Stanley

STANLEY, FORREST
HIS OFFICIAL FIANCEE (1919, Silent, Paramount)—William Waters
HER ACCIDENTAL HUSBAND (1923, Silent, Belasco)—Gordon Gray
BEAUTY AND THE BAD MAN (1925, Silent, Peninsula Studios)—Madoc Bill

STANLEY, KIM
THE GODDESS (1958, Columbia)—Emily Ann Faulkner

STANMORE, FRANK
MR. NOBODY (1927, GB, Silent, Fox)—Mr. Nobody

STANNARD, DON
DICK BARTON—SPECIAL AGENT (1949, GB, Hammer)—Dick Barton
DICK BARTON STRIKES BACK (1949, GB, Exclusive)—Dick Barton
DICK BARTON AT BAY (1950, GB, Hammer)—Dick Barton

STANTON, HARRY DEAN
REPO MAN (1984, Universal)—Bud

STANTON, JOHN
KITTY AND THE BAGMAN (1983, Australia, Quartet)—Bagman

STANTON, PAUL
SO'S YOUR UNCLE (1943, Universal)—John L. Curtis

STANTON, ROBERT
THREE SONS (1939, RKO)—Bert Pardway

STANWYCK, BARBARA
MEXICALI ROSE (1929, Columbia)—Mexicali Rose
LADIES OF LEISURE (1930, Columbia)—Kay Arnold
THE MIRACLE WOMAN (1931, Columbia)—Florence "Faith" Fallon
NIGHT NURSE (1931, Warners)—Lora Hart
BABY FACE (1933, Warners)—Lily "Baby Face" Powers
LADIES THEY TALK ABOUT (1933, Warners)—Nan Taylor
GAMBLING LADY (1934, First National)—Lady Lee
A LOST LADY (1934, Warners)—Marian Ormsby
ANNIE OAKLEY (1935, RKO)—Annie Oakley
THE SECRET BRIDE (1935, Warners)—Ruth Vincent
THE WOMAN IN RED (1935, Warners)—Shelby Barrett
THE BRIDE WALKS OUT (1936, RKO)—Carolyn Martin
HIS BROTHER'S WIFE (1936, MGM)—Rita Wilson
STELLA DALLAS (1937, United Artists)—Stella Martin Dallas
THE MAD MISS MANTON (1938, RKO)—Melsa Manton
THE LADY EVE (1941, Paramount)—Jean Harrington/Eve
YOU BELONG TO ME (1941, Columbia)—Helen Hunt
THE GAY SISTERS (1942, First National)—Fiona Gaylord
THE GREAT MAN'S LADY (1942, Paramount)—Hannah Sempler
LADY OF BURLESQUE (1943, United Artists)—Dixie Daisy
THE BRIDE WORE BOOTS (1946, Paramount)—Sally Warren
MY REPUTATION (1946, Warners)—Jessica Drummond
THE STRANGE LOVE OF MARTHA IVERS (1946, Paramount)—Martha Ivers
THE TWO MRS. CARROLLS (1947, Warners)—Sally Morton Carroll
B.F.'S DAUGHTER (1948, MGM)—Polly Fulton
THE LADY GAMBLES (1949, Universal)—Joan Boothe
THE FILE ON THELMA JORDAN (1950, Paramount)—Thelma Jordan
NO MAN OF HER OWN (1950, Paramount)—Helen Ferguson
TO PLEASE A LADY (1950, MGM)—Reina Forbes
CATTLE QUEEN OF MONTANA (1954, RKO)—Sierra Nevada Jones
WITNESS TO MURDER (1954, GB, Rank)—Cheryl Draper
THE MAVERICK QUEEN (1956, Republic)—Kit Banion
THE NIGHT WALKER (1964, Universal)—Irene Trent

STAPLETON, JOAN
THE DEVIL'S MISTRESS (1968, Holiday Films)—Liah

STARK, KOO
EMILY (1976, GB, Emily)—Emily

STARKE, PAULINE
INNOCENT'S PROGRESS (1918, Silent, Mutual)—Tessa Fayne
SALVATION NELL (1921, Silent, Associate First National)—Nell Sanders

STARR, RINGO
CAVEMAN (1981, United Artists)—Atouk

STARR, SALLY
FOR THE LOVE O' LIL (1930, Columbia)—Lil

STARRETT, CHARLES
GALLANT DEFENDER (1935, Columbia)—Johnny Flagg
THE COWBOY STAR (1936, Columbia)—Spencer Yorke
ONE MAN JUSTICE (1937, Columbia)—Larry Clarke
TWO-FISTED SHERIFF (1937, Columbia)—Dick Houston
THE MAN FROM SUNDOWN (1939, Columbia)—Larry Whalen
THE DURANGO KID (1940, Columbia)—Bill Lowery/
Durango Kid
THE MEDICO OF PAINTED SPRINGS (1941, Columbia)—Dr.
Steven Monroe
COWBOY IN THE CLOUDS (1943, Columbia)—Steve Kendall
THE FIGHTING BUCKAROO (1943, Columbia)—Steve Harrison
THE KID FROM AMARILLO (1951, Columbia)—The
Durango Kid
THE KID FROM BROKEN GUN (1952, Columbia)—The Durango
Kid/Steve Reynolds

STAUTON, IMELDA
ANTONIA AND JANE (1991, GB, Miramax)—Jane Hartman

STEEL, PIPPA
THE VAMPIRE LOVERS (1970, GB, Hammer)—Laura Spielsdorf

STEELE, BOB
THE BANDIT'S SON (1927, Silent, FBO)—Bob McCall
CAPTAIN CARELESS (1928, Silent, FBO)—Bob Gordon
MAN IN THE ROUGH (1928, Silent, FBO)—Bruce Sherwood
THE AMAZING VAGABOND (1929, RKO)—Jimmy Hobbs
SON OF OKLAHOMA (1932, World Wide)—Dan Clayton
THE GUN RANGER (1937, Republic)—Don Larsen
LIGHTNIN' CRANDALL (1937, Republic)—Bob Crandall
SUNDOWN SAUNDERS (1937, Supreme)—Sundown Saunders
COLORADO KID (1938, Republic)—Colorado Kid
THE TRAIL BLAZERS (1940, Republic)—Tucson Smith
PALS OF THE PECOS (1941, Republic)—Tuscon Smith
SADDLEMATES (1941, Republic)—Tuscon Smith
THE PHANTOM PLAINSMEN (1942, Republic)—Tuscon Smith
THE NAVAJO KID (1946, Producers Releasing Corp.)—
Navajo Kid
SIX MAN GUN (1946, Producers Releasing Corp.)—Bob Storm

STEELE, MARY
GIRLS AT SEA (1958, GB, Seven Arts)—Jill

STEELE, TOMMY
THE DUKE WORE JEANS (1958, GB, Anglo Amalgamated)—
Tony Whitecliffe/ Tommy Hudson
TOMMY THE TOREADOR (1960, GB, Warners-Pathe)—Tommy
Tomkins
THE DREAM MAKER (1963, GB, British Lion)—Billy Bowles
WHERE'S JACK (1969, GB, Paramount)—Jack Sheppard

STEENBURGEN, MARY
PARENTHOOD (1989, Universal)—Karen Buckman

STEIGER, ROD
AL CAPONE (1959, Allied Artists)—Al Capone
THE PAWNBROKER (1965, Allied Artists)—Sol Nazerman
THE SERGEANT (1968, Warners)—Master Sgt. Albert Callan
THE ILLUSTRATED MAN (1969, Warners)—Carl
HENNESSY (1975, GB, American International)—Hennessy
W.C. FIELDS AND ME (1976, Universal)—W.C. Fields

STEIN, MARGARET SOPHIE
ENEMIES, A LOVE STORY (1989, 20th Century Fox)—Yadwiga

STEN, ANNA
NANA (1934, United Artists)—Nana
THREE RUSSIAN GIRLS (1943, United Artists)—Natasha
THE NUN AND THE SERGEANT (1962, United Artists)—
The Nun

STENSGAARD, YUTTE
LUST FOR A VAMPIRE (1971, GB, Hammer)—Mircalla/
Carmilla

STEPHEN, SUSAN
WHITE HUNTRESS (1957, American International)—Ruth
Meecham

STEPHENS, MARTIN
THE WITNESS (1959, GB, Anglo Amalgamated)—Peter Brindon

STEPHENS, MARVIN
RIDE, KELLY, RIDE (1941, 20th Century Fox)—Corn Cob Kelly

STEPHENS, ROBERT
THE PRIVATE LIFE OF SHERLOCK HOLMES (1970, GB, United
Artists)—Sherlock Holmes

STEPHENSON, HENRY
GUILTY AS HELL (1932, Paramount)—Dr. Tindall

STEPHENSON, JAMES
WANTED BY SCOTLAND YARD (1939, GB, Pathe/Monogram)—
"Fingers"
CALLING PHILO VANCE (1940, Warners)—Philo Vance

STEPHENSON, ROSS
I'M GOING TO GET YOU. . .ELLIOT BOY (1971, Canada,
Columbia)—Elliot Markson

STEPPLING, JOHN
HER FATHER SAID NO (1927, Silent, R-C Pictures)—John
Hamilton

STERLING, EDYTHE
NANCY'S BIRTHRIGHT (1916, Silent, Mutual)—Nancy Levine
THE GIRL WHO DARED (1920, Silent, Republic)—Barbara
Hampton

STERLING, FORD
GENTLEMEN PREFER BLONDES (1928, Silent, Paramount)—
Gus Eisman

STERLING, ROBERT
I'LL WAIT FOR YOU (1941, MGM)—"Lucky" Wilson
THE SUNDOWNERS (1950, Eagle Lion)—Tom Cloud

STERN, DANIEL
CITY SLICKERS (1991, Columbia)—Phil Berquist

STERN, TOM
CLAY PIGEON (1971, Tracon/MGM)—Joe Ryan

STEVENS, BRINKE
SLAVE GIRLS FROM BEYOND INFINITY (1987, Titan/Urban
Classics)—Shela

STEVENS, CONNIE
SUSAN SLADE (1961, Warners)—Susan Slade
TWO ON A GUILLOTINE (1965, Warners)—Melinda Duquesne

SCORCHY (1976, American International)—Sgt. Jackie Parker

STEVENS, CRAIG
GUNN (1967, Paramount)—Peter Gunn

STEVENS, EMILY
KILDARE OF STORM (1918, Silent, Metro)—Mrs. Kildare

STEVENS, MARK
JACK SLADE (1953, Allied Artists)—Jack Slade
THE MAN IN THE WATER (1963, Crown International)—
Capt. James

STEVENS, MARTIN
THE INNOCENTS (1961, U.S./GB, 20th Century Fox)—Miles

STEVENS, ONSLOW
I CAN'T ESCAPE (1934, Syndicate Releasing Corp.)—Steve
Nichols/ Cummings
THE THREE MUSKETEERS (1935, RKO)—Aramis

STEVENS, SHADOE
TRAXX (1988, DEG)—Traxx

STEVENS, STELLA
LAS VEGAS LADY (1976, Crown.International)—Lucky

STEVENS, WARREN
ACCUSED OF MURDER (1974, Republic)—Stan

STEVENSON, AL
MISTER BROWN (1972, Andrieux)—George Brown

STEVENSON, VENETIA
THE SERGEANT WAS A LADY (1961, Universal)—Sgt. Judy
Fraser

STEWART, ALEXANDRA
WAITING FOR CAROLINE (1969, Canada, National Film
Board)—Caroline

STEWART, ANITA
HER MAD BARGAIN (1921, Silent, Associated First National)—
Alice Lambert
NAME THE WOMAN (1928, Silent, Columbia)—Florence

STEWART, APRIL
VALET GIRLS (1987, Lexyn/Empire)—Rosalind

STEWART, FREDDIE
HIGH SCHOOL HERO (1946, Monogram)—Freddie

STEWART, HAMILTON
THE HANGING JUDGE (1918, Silent, GB, Hepworth)—Sir John
Veasey

STEWART, JAMES
NEXT TIME WE LOVE (1936, Universal)—Christopher Tyler
DESTRY RIDES AGAIN (1939, Universal)—Tom Destry Jr.
MADE FOR EACH OTHER (1939, United Artists)—
Johnny Mason
MR. SMITH GOES TO WASHINGTON (1939, Columbia)—
Jefferson Smith
THE STRATTON STORY (1949, MGM)—Monty Stratton
CARBINE WILLIAMS (1952, MGM)—Marsh Williams
THE GLENN MILLER STORY (1953, Universal)—Glenn Miller
THE MAN FROM LARAMIE (1955, Columbia)—Will Lockhart

THE MAN WHO KNEW TOO MUCH (1956, Paramount)—Dr. Ben
McKenna
TWO RODE TOGETHER (1961, Columbia)—Guthrie McCabe
MR. HOBBS TAKES A VACATION (1962, 20th Century Fox)—
Roger Hobbs

STEWART, LUCILLE LEE
HIS WIFE'S GOOD NAME (1916, Silent, Vitagraph)—Mary Ellen
Weatherby

STEWART, ROY
ONE SHOT ROSS (1917, Silent, Triangle)—One Shot Ross
KEITH OF THE BORDER (1918, Silent, Triangle)—Jack Keith
BUFFALO BILL ON THE U.P. TRAIL (1926, Silent, Sunset)—
Buffalo Bill Cody

STEWART, SOPHIE
MARIGOLD (1938, GB, Associated British Films)—Marigold
Sellar

STICH, PAT
THE LONERS (1972, Fanfare)—Julio

STIMSON, SARA
LITTLE MISS MARKER (1980, Universal)—The Kid/Miss
Marker

STOCKFIELD, BETTY
WOMAN IN CHAINS (1932, GB, RKO)—Grace Marwood
ANNE ONE HUNDRED (1933, GB, British & Dominions/
Paramount)—Anne Briston

STOCKWELL, DEAN
THE BOY WITH GREEN HAIR (1949, RKO)—Peter
KIM (1950, MGM)—Kim
SONS AND LOVERS (1960, GB, 20th Century Fox)—Paul Morel
THE LONERS (1972, Fanfare)—Stein
WEREWOLF OF WASHINGTON (1973, Milico/Diplomat)—Jack
Whittier

STOCKWELL, GUY
BEAU GESTE (1966, Universal)—Beau Geste

STOCKWELL, JOHN
MY SCIENCE PROJECT (1985, Buena Vista)—Michael Harlan

STOLTZ, ERIC
MASK (1985, Universal)—Rocky Dennis

STONE, FRED
JOHNNY GET YOUR GUN (1919, Silent, Paramount)—Johnny
Wiggins
THE FARMER IN THE DELL (1936, RKO)—Pa Boyer

STONE, GEORGE E.
THE BIG BRAIN (1933, RKO)—Max Werner

STONE, LEWIS
THE PRISONER OF ZENDA (1922, Silent, Metro)—King Rudolf
THE PATRIOT (1928, Paramount)—Count Pahlen
THREE GODFATHERS (1936, MGM)—Doc
THE MAN WHO CRIED WOLF (1937, Universal)—Lawrence
Fontaine
JUDGE HARDY'S CHILDREN (1938, MGM)—Judge Hardy
OUT WEST WITH THE HARDY'S (1938, MGM)—Judge Hardy
JOE AND ETHEL TURP CALL ON THE PRESIDENT (1939,
MGM)—The President

JUDGE HARDY AND SON (1939, MGM)—Judge Hardy
THREE WISE FOOLS (1946, MGM)—Judge Thomas Trumbull

STONE, LEWIS R.
BEAU REVEL (1921, Silent, Paramount)—Lawrence
"Beau" Revel
FATHER'S SON (1931, Warners)—William Emory

STONE, MILBURN
THE JUDGE (1949, Emerald)—Martin Strang

STONEHOUSE, RUTH
THE SLIM PRINCESS (1915, Silent, Essanay)—The Slim
Princess

STOREY, EDITH
ON HER WEDDING NIGHT (1915, Silent, Vitagraph)—Helen
Carter

STORM, GALE
GAMBLING DAUGHTERS (1941, Producers Releasing Corp.)—
Lillian
NEARLY EIGHTEEN (1943, Monogram)—Jane
SUNBONNET SUE (1945, Monogram)—Sue Casey

STRADER, SCOTT
JOCKS (1987, Crown)—The Kid

STRANG, DEBORAH
RAMBLIN' GAL (1991, Aquarius)—Ruby

STRANGE, GLENN
THE MAD MONSTER (1942, Producers Releasing Corp.)—Petro
ABBOTT AND COSTELLO MEET FRANKENSTEIN (1948,
Universal)—Frankenstein's Monster

STRASBERG, SUSAN
STAGE STRUCK (1958, RKO/Buena Vista)—Eva Lovelace

STRASSMAN, MARCIA
HONEY, I SHRUNK THE KIDS (1989, Buena Vista)—Diane
Szalinski

STRATAS, TERESA
LA TRAVIATA (1982, Universal)—Violette Valery

STRATHAIRN, DAVID
EIGHT MEN OUT (1988, Orion)—Ed Cicotte

STRATTON, DOROTHY R.
GALAXINA (1980, Crown International)—Galaxina

STRAUSS, PETER
SOLDIER BLUE (1970, Avco Embassy)—Pvt. Honus Gant
SPACEHUNTER: ADVENTURES IN THE FORBIDDEN ZONE
(1983, Columbia)—Wolff

STREEP, MERYL
KRAMER VS. KRAMER (1979, Columbia)—Joanna Kramer
THE FRENCH LIEUTENANT'S WOMAN (1981, United
Artists)—Sarah
SOPHIE'S CHOICE (1982, Universal)—Sophie Zwaistowska
SILKWOOD (1983, 20th Century Fox)—Karen Silkwood
FALLING IN LOVE (1984, Paramount)—Molly Gilmore

STREISAND, BARBRA
FUNNY GIRL (1968, Columbia)—Fanny Brice
HELLO, DOLLY! (1969, 20th Century Fox)—Dolly Levi

THE OWL AND THE PUSSYCAT (1970, Columbia)—Doris
FUNNY LADY (1975, Columbia)—Fanny Brice
A STAR IS BORN (1976, Warners)—Esther Hoffman
YENTL (1983, MGM/United Artists)—Yentl

STRICKLYN, RAY
YOUNG JESSE JAMES (1960, 20th Century Fox)—Jesse James

STRODE, WOODY
SERGEANT RUTLEDGE (1960, Warners)—1st Sgt. Braxton
Rutledge
THE PROFESSIONALS (1966, Columbia)—Jacob Sharp

STRONG, ANDREW
THE COMMITMENTS (1991, GB, 20th Century Fox)—Deco Cuffe

STROUD, DON
VON RICHTHOFEN AND BROWN (1970, United Artists)—
Roy Brown
MURPH THE SURF (1974, Caruth C. Byrd)—Jack Murphy

STROUD, PAULINE
ALF'S BABY (1953, GB, Adelphi)—Pamela Weston
LADY GODIVA RIDES AGAIN (1955, GB, London/Carroll)—
Marjorie Clark

STROUSE, NICHOLAS
DOIN' TIME ON PLANET EARTH (1989, Cannon)—Ryan
Richmond

STRUDWICK, SHEPPERD (JOHN SHEPPERD)
THE LOVES OF EDGAR ALLAN POE (1942, 20th Century Fox)—
Edgar Allan Poe
STRANGE TRIANGLE (1946, 20th Century Fox)—Earl Huber
THREE HUSBANDS (1950, United Artists)—Arthur Evans

STUART, BINKIE
LITTLE MISS SOMEBODY (1937, GB, Butchers)—Binkie Sladen
LITTLE DOLLY DAYDREAM (1938, GB, Butchers)—Dolly
ROSE OF TRALEE (1938, Ireland, Butchers)—Rose O'Malley
LITTLE MISS MOLLY (1940, Alliance)—Molly Martin

STUART, GLORIA
GIRL IN 419 (1933, Paramount)—Mary Dolan
THE LOST CAPTIVE (1934, Universal)—Alice Trask
GOLD DIGGERS OF 1935 (1935, Warners)—Amy Prentiss
THE GIRL ON THE FRONT PAGE (1936, Universal)—Joan
Langford
GIRL OVERBOARD (1937, Universal)—Mary Chesbrooke
THE LADY ESCAPES (1937, 20th Century Fox)—Linda Ryan
THE LADY OBJECTS (1938, Columbia)—Ann Adams

STUART, JOHN
HOUND OF THE BASKERVILLES (1932, GB, Gainsborough)—Sir
Henry Baskerville
MEN OF STEEL (1932, GB, United Artists)—James "Iron" Harg
ENEMY OF THE POLICE (1933, GB, Warners/First National)—
John Meakin
THE HOUSE OF TRENT (1933, GB, Ensign)—Dr. Trent &
John Trent
MR. QUINCEY OF MONTE CARLO (1933, GB, Warners)—Mr.
Quincey
ONCE A THIEF (1935, GB, Paramount British)—Roger
Drummond
THE ELDER BROTHER (1937, GB, Paramount)—Ronald Bellairs
CAPTAIN MOONLIGHT (1940, GB, Olympia)—Captain Moonlight

STUART, NICK
HIGH SCHOOL HERO (1927, Silent, Fox)—Pete Greer
FIGHTING PLAYBOY (1937, Northern Films)—Don

STUART, NORMAN
ARNOLD (1973, Cinerama)—Arnold

STURZ, LISA
HOWARD THE DUCK (1986, Universal)—Howard T. Duck

STYLES, EDWIN
THE FIVE POUND MAN (1937, GB, Fox British)—Richard Fordyce

SULLAVAN, MARGARET
THE GOOD FAIRY (1935, Universal)—Luisa "Lu" Ginglebusher
NEXT TIME WE LOVE (1936, Universal)—Cicely Tyler
SHOPWORN ANGEL (1938, MGM)—Daisy Heath
SO ENDS OUR NIGHT (1941, United Artists)—Ruth Holland
NO SAD SONGS FOR ME (1950, Columbia)—Mary Scott

SULLIVAN, BARRY
THE GANGSTER (1947, Allied Artists)—Shubunka
BAD MEN OF TOMBSTONE (1949, Monogram/Allied Artists)—Tom
THE OUTRIDERS (1950, MGM)—Jesse Wallace
THREE GUYS NAMED MIKE (1951, MGM)—Mike Tracy
WOLF LARSEN (1958, Allied Artists)—Wolf Larsen

SULLIVAN, BILLY
THE GALLANT FOOL (1926, Silent, Rayart)—Billy Banner
ONE PUNCH O'DAY (1926, Silent, Rayart)—Jimmy O'Day
SPEED CHANCE (1926, Silent, Rayart)—Billy Meeks
SPEED COP (1926, Silent, Rayart)—The Speed Cop

SULLIVAN, FRANCIS L.
THE SECRET FOUR (1940, GB, Ealing)—Leon Poiccard

SUMMERVILLE, SLIM
TROOPERS THREE (1930, Tiffany)—Sunny
UNEXPECTED FATHER (1932, Universal)—Jasper Jones
HER FIRST MATE (1933, Universal)—John Horner
THEY JUST HAD TO GET MARRIED (1933, Universal)—Sam Sutton
LOVE BIRDS (1934, Universal)—Henry Whipple
THEIR BIG MOMENT (1934, RKO)—Bill

SUMPTER, DONALD
THE BLACK PANTHER (1977, GB, Impics Prod.)—Donald Neilson

SURATT, VALESKA
THE IMMIGRANT (1915, Silent, Lasky)—Masha
THE NEW YORK PEACOCK (1917, Silent, Fox)—Zena

SUTHERLAND, DONALD
THE DIRTY DOZEN (1967, GB, MGM)—Vernon Pinkley
ALEX IN WONDERLAND (1970, MGM)—Alex
KLUTE (1971, Warners)—John Klute
S*P*Y*S (1974, 20th Century Fox)—Brulard
A MAN, A WOMAN AND A BANK (1979, Canada, Bennett Films)—Reese
ORDINARY PEOPLE (1980, Paramount)—Calvin Jarrett
THE TROUBLE WITH SPIES (1987, Brigade/DEG)—Appleton Porter

SUTHERLAND, KIEFER
THE BAY BOY (1985, Orion)—Donald Campbell
YOUNG GUNS (1988, 20th Century Fox)—Doc Scurlock
RENEGADES (1989, Universal)—Buster McHenry
CHICAGO JOE AND THE SHOWGIRL (1990, GB, Palace)—Rick Allen
FLATLINERS (1990, Columbia)—Nelson
YOUNG GUNS II (1990, 20th Century Fox)—Doc Sourlock

SUTTON, DUDLEY
THE LEATHER BOYS (1965, GB, Allied Artists)—Pete

SUTTON, JOHN
TEN GENTLEMEN FROM WEST POINT (1942, 20th Century Fox)—Howard Shelton

SUZMAN, JANET
NICHOLAS AND ALEXANDRA (1971, GB, Columbia)—Alexandra

SVENSON, BO
WALKING TALL, PART II (1975, American International)—Buford Pusser

SWAIN, MACK
THE COHENS AND THE KELLYS IN ATLANTIC CITY (1929, Universal)—Patrick Kelly

SWANSON, GLORIA
MALE AND FEMALE (1919, Silent, Paramount)—Lady Mary Lasenby
HER GILDED CAGE (1922, Silent, Paramount)—Suzanne Ornoff
HER HUSBAND'S TRADEMARK (1922, Silent, Paramount)—Lois Miller
THE IMPOSSIBLE MRS. BELLEW (1922, Silent, Paramount)—Betty Bellew
BLUEBEARD'S 8TH WIFE (1923, Silent, Paramount)—Mona de Briac
MY AMERICAN WIFE (1923, Silent, Paramount)—Natalie Chester
HER LOVE STORY (1924, Silent, Paramount)—Princess Marie
THE UNTAMED LADY (1926, Silent Paramount)—St. Calir Van Tassel
QUEEN KELLY (1929, Silent, United Artists)—Queen Kelly
SADIE THOMPSON (1928, Silent, United Artists)—Sadie Thompson
THE TRESPASSER (1929, United Artists)—Marion Donnell
WHAT A WIDOW (1930, United Artists)—Tamarind Brooks
FATHER TAKES A WIFE (1941, RKO)—Leslie Collier
THREE FOR BEDROOM C (1952, Warners)—Ann Haven

SWANSON, KRISTY
MANNEQUIN ON THE RUN (1991, 20th Century Fox)—Jessie

SWARTHOUT, GLADYS
ROSE OF THE RANCHO (1936, Paramount)—Rosita Castro

SWAYZE, DON
SHY PEOPLE (1988, Cannon)—Mark Sullivan

SWAYZE, PATRICK
TIGER WARSAW (1988, Sony)—Chuck "Tiger" Warsaw
NEXT OF KIN (1989, Warners)—Truman Gates
GHOST (1990, Paramount)—Sam Wheat

SWEANEY, DEBRA
THEY CALL ME MACHO WOMAN (1990, Troma Team)—Susan

SWEENEY, D.B.
EIGHT MEN OUT (1988, Orion)—Shoeless Joe Jackson

SWEENEY, JOSEPH
12 ANGRY MEN (1957, United Artists)—Juror No. 9

SWEET, BLANCHE
JUDITH OF BETHULIA (1914, Silent, Biograph)—Judith of Bethulia
THE WARREN'S OF VIRGINIA (1915, Silent, Lasky)—Agatha Warren
THE DUPE (1916, Silent, Lasky)—Ethel Hale
ANNA CHRISTIE (1923, Silent, Associated First National)—Anna Christie
TESS OF THE D'UBERVILLES (1924, Silent, Metro-Goldwyn)—Tess
SINGED (1927, Silent, Fox)—Dolly Wall

SWIFT, SUSAN
AUDREY ROSE (1977, United Artists)—Ivy Templeton

SWINBURNE, NORA
HER STRANGE DESIRE (1931, GB, British International)—Lady Diana Bromford
TOO MANY WIVES (1933, GB, Warners)—Hilary Wildeley

SWOFFORD, KEN
HUNTER'S BLOOD (1987, Concorde)—Al Coleman

SYDNEY, BASIL
THE FARMER'S WIFE (1941, GB, Pathe)—Samuel Sweetland

SYMS, SYLVIA
TEENAGE BAD GIRL (1959, GB, Everest/DCA)—Janet Carr

T

TAAFE, ALICE
NOT MY SISTER (1916, Silent, Triangle)—Ruth Tyler

TABLER, DEMPSEY
JUNGLE TRAIL OF THE SON OF TARZAN (1923, Silent, National Films)—Tarzan

TALBOT, LYLE
THREE LEGIONNAIRES (1937, General)—Jimmy

TALBOTT, GLORIA
DAUGHTER OF DR. JEKYLL (1957, Allied Artists)—Janet Smith
TAMING SUTTON'S GAL (1957, Republic)—Lou Sutton
I MARRIED A MONSTER FROM OUTER SPACE (1958, Paramount)—Marge Farrell

TALLIER, NADINE
GIRLS AT SEA (1958, GB, Seven Arts)—Antoinette

TALMADGE, CONSTANCE
ROMANCE AND ARABELLA (1919, Silent, Selznick)—Arabella Cadenhouse
WOMAN'S PLACE (1921, Silent, Associated First National)—Josephine Gerson
HER NIGHT OF ROMANCE (1924, Silent, First National)—Dorothy Adams
HER SISTER FROM PARIS (1925, Silent, First National)—Helen Weyringer /Lola

TALMADGE, NORMA
MARTHA'S VINDICATION (1916, Silent, Triangle)—Martha
THE SOCIAL SECRETARY (1916, Silent, Triangle)—Mayme
WAY OF A WOMAN (1919, Silent, Selznick)—Nancy Lee
THE ONLY WOMAN (1924, Silent, First National)—Helen Brinsley
KIKI (1926, Silent, First National)—Kiki
CAMILLE (1927, Silent, First National)—Marguerite Gautier (Camille)
DUBARRY, WOMAN OF PASSION (1930, United Artists)—Jeanette Vaubernier /Mme. DuBarry

TALMADGE, RICHARD
THE UNKNOWN (1921, Silent, Goldstone)—The Unknown
THE CUB REPORTER (1922, Silent, Oldstone)—Dick Harvey
SPEED KING (1923, Silent, Goldstone)—Jimmy Martin
JIMMIE'S MILLIONS (1925, Silent, Film Booking Offices)—Jimmie Wicherly
THE CAVALIER (1928, Tiffany/Stahl)—El Caballero

TALMAN, WILLIAM
THE HITCH-HIKER (1953, RKO)—Emmett Meyers

TAMBLYN, RUSS
THE KID FROM CLEVELAND (1949, Republic)—Johnny Barrows
SEVEN BRIDES FOR SEVEN BROTHERS (1954, MGM)—Gideon Pontabee
TOM THUMB (1958, GB, MGM)—Tom Thumb
SATAN'S SADIST (1969, Independent-International)—Anchor

TAMIROFF, AKIM
THE GENERAL DIED AT DAWN (1936, Paramount)—General Yang
THE GREAT GAMBINI (1937, Paramount)—Gambini
KING OF GAMBLERS (1937, Paramount)—Steve Kalkas
DANGEROUS TO KNOW (1938, Paramount)—Stephen Recka
KING OF CHINATOWN (1939, Paramount)—Frank Baturin
THE MAGNIFICENT FRAUD (1939, Paramount)—Jules LaCroix/ President Alvarado

TANDY, JESSICA
A WOMAN'S VENGEANCE (1947, Universal)—Janet Spence
DRIVING MISS DAISY (1989, Warners)—Miss Daisy Werthan

TANI, YOKO
THE SAVAGE INNOCENTS (1960, GB, Paramount)—Asiak

TANNER, TONY
STOP THE WORLD — I WANT TO GET OFF (1966, GB, Warners)—Littlechap

TARKINGTON, ROCKNE
BLACK SAMSON (1974, Warners)—Samson

TASHMAN, LILYAN
THE WOMAN WHO DID NOT CARE (1927, Silent, Lumis)—Iris Carroll
GIRLS ABOUT TOWN (1931, Paramount)—Marie Bailey

TASKER, HAROLD
JULIUS CAESAR (1952, Avon/Brandon)—Julius Caesar

TAUBER, CHAIM
MOTEL, THE OPERATOR (1940, Cinema Film)—Motel

TAYLOR, ALMA
IRIS (1915, GB, Silent, Ideal)—Iris
THE AMERICAN HEIRESS (1917, Silent, GB, Hepworth)—Bessie

TAYLOR, DON
LOVE SLAVES OF THE AMAZONS (1957, Universal)—Dr. Peter Masters
MEN OF SHERWOOD FOREST (1957, GB, Hammer)—Robin Hood

TAYLOR, ELIZABETH
CYNTHIA (1947, MGM)—Cynthia Bishop
LITTLE WOMEN (1949, MGM)—Amy March
FATHER OF THE BRIDE (1950, MGM)—Kay Banks
THE GIRL WHO HAD EVERYTHING (1953, MGM)—Jean Latimer
CAT ON A HOT TIN ROOF (1958, MGM)—Maggie Pollitt
CLEOPATRA (1963, 20th Century Fox)—Cleopatra
THE V.I.P.S (1963, GB, MGM)—Frances Andros
THE TAMING OF THE SHREW (1967, Columbia)—Katarina
X, Y & ZEE (1972, GB, Columbia)—Zee Blakeley

TAYLOR, ESTELLE
THE WHIP WOMAN (1928, Silent, First National)—Sari

TAYLOR, JOAN
APACHE WOMAN (1955, Golden State)—Anne Libeau
GIRLS IN PRISON (1956, American International)—Anne Carson

TAYLOR, JOYCE
BEAUTY AND THE BEAST (1963, United Artists)—Lady Althea

TAYLOR, KENT
THE MYSTERIOUS RIDER (1933, Paramount)—Wade Benton
MY MARRIAGE (1936, 20th Century Fox)—John DeWitt Tyler III
THREE SONS (1939, RKO)—Gene Pardway
I'M STILL ALIVE (1940, RKO)—Steve Bonnett
SUED FOR LIBEL (1940, RKO)—Steve
MISSISSIPPI GAMBLER (1942, Universal)—Johnny Forbes
THE DALTONS RIDE AGAIN (1945, Universal)—Bob Dalton
FEDERAL AGENT AT LARGE (1950, Republic)—Matt Reedy

TAYLOR, NOAH
THE YEAR MY VOICE BROKE (1988, Avenue)—Danny

TAYLOR, RENEE
MADE FOR EACH OTHER (1971, 20th Century Fox)—Pandora "Panda" Gold

TAYLOR, ROBERT
HIS BROTHER'S WIFE (1936, MGM)—Chris
THREE COMRADES (1938, MGM)—Erich Lohkamp
A YANK AT OXFORD (1938, MGM)—Lee Sheridan
BILLY THE KID (1941, MGM)—Billy Bonney
HER CARDBOARD LOVER (1942, MGM)—Terry Trindale
JOHNNY EAGER (1942, MGM)—Johnny Eager
CONSPIRATOR (1949, GB, MGM)—Major Michael Curragh
IVANHOE (1952, GB, MGM)—Ivanhoe
ALL THE BROTHERS WERE VALIANT (1953, MGM)—Joel Shore
ROGUE COP (1954, MGM)—Christopher Kelvaney
QUENTIN DURWARD (1955, MGM)—Quentin Durward
THE ADVENTURES OF QUENTIN DURWARD (1956, GB, MGM British)—Quentin Durward
THE LAW AND JAKE WADE (1958, MGM)—Jake Wade
THE HANGMAN (1959, Paramount)—Mackenzie Bovard
CATTLE KING (1963, MGM)—Sam Brassfield

TAYLOR, ROD
THE V.I.P.S (1963, GB, MGM)—Les Mangan
YOUNG CASSIDY (1965, MGM)—John Cassidy
THE LIQUIDATOR (1966, GB, MGM)—Boysie Oakes
CHUKA (1967, Paramount)—Chuka
THE MAN WHO HAD POWER OVER WOMEN (1970, GB, Avco Embassy)—Peter Reaney
TRADER HORN (1973, MGM)—Trader Horn

TAYLOR, RUTH
GENTLEMEN PREFER BLONDES (1928, Silent, Paramount)—Lorelei Lee
THE COLLEGE COQUETTE (1929, Columbia)—Betty Forrester

TAYLOR, WILLIAM
DIARY OF A BACHELOR (1964, American International)—Skip O'Hara

TCHERINA, LUDMILLA
OH ROSALINDA (1956, GB, Pathe)—Rosalinda

TEARLE, CONWAY
THE FIGHTER (1921, Silent, Selznick)—Caleb Conover
THE REFEREE (1922, Silent, Selznick)—John McArdle
SMOKE BELLEW (1929, Silent, First Division)—Kit "Smoke" Bellew

TELLEGEN, LOU
THE OUTSIDER (1926, Silent, Fox)—Anton Ragatzy

TELLER
PENN AND TELLER GET KILLED (1989, Warners)—Teller

TEMPLE, SHIRLEY
THE RED-HAIRED ALIBI (1932, Tower)—Gloria
BABY, TAKE A BOW (1934, Fox)—Shirley
LITTLE MISS MARKER (1934, Paramount)—Miss Marker
CURLY TOP (1935, Fox)—Elizabeth Blair
THE LITTLE COLONEL (1935, Fox)—Lloyd Sherman
THE LITTLEST REBEL (1935, Fox)—Virginia Houston Cary
OUR LITTLE GIRL (1935, Fox)—Molly Middleton
DIMPLES (1936, 20th Century Fox)—Sylvia Dolores Appleby (Dimples)
POOR LITTLE RICH GIRL (1936, 20th Century Fox)—Barbara Barry
STOWAWAY (1936, 20th Century Fox)—Ching-Ching
HEIDI (1937, 20th Century Fox)—Heidi
WEE WILLIE WINKLE (1937, 20th Century Fox)—Priscilla Williams
LITTLE MISS BROADWAY (1938, 20th Century Fox)—Betsy Brown
REBECCA OF SUNNYBROOK FARM (1938, 20th Century Fox)—Rebecca Winstead
THE LITTLE PRINCESS (1939, 20th Century Fox)—Sara Crewe

SUSANNAH OF THE MOUNTIES (1939, 20th Century Fox)—
Susannah Sheldon
KATHLEEN (1941, MGM)—Kathleen Davis
MISS ANNIE ROONEY (1942, United Artists)—Annie Rooney
THE BACHELOR AND THE BOBBYSOXER (1947, RKO)—Susan
Turner
THAT HAGEN GIRL (1947, Warners)—Mary Hagen
A KISS FOR CORLISS (1949, United Artists)—Corliss Archer

TENDETER, KAY
THE FALL OF THE HOUSE OF USHER (1952, GB, Vigilant)—
Lord Roderick Usher

TENNANT, VICTORIA
THE RAGMAN'S DAUGHTER (1974, GB, Penelope-Harpoon)—
Doris Randall

TERHUNE, MAX
PALS OF THE SADDLE (1938, Republic)—Lullaby Joslin

TERLECKY, JOHN
DEATHSTALKER II (1988, Concorde)—Deathstalker

TERRY, ALICE
CONFESSIONS OF A QUEEN (1925, Silent, MGM)—Queen
Frederika

TERRY, DON
FUGITIVES (1929, Silent, Fox)—Dick Starr

TERRY, HARRY
THE FACE AT THE WINDOW (1939, GB, British Lion)—
The Face

TERRY, HAZEL
MISSING, BELIEVED MARRIED (1937, GB, British &
Dominions)—Hermione Blakiston

TERRY, JOHN
HAWK THE SLAYER (1980, GB, Chips/ITC)—Hawk

TERRY, PHILLIP
THE MONSTER AND THE GIRL (1941, Paramount)—Scott
Webster

TERRY, RUTH
PISTOL PACKIN' MAMA (1943, Republic)—Vicki Norris-Sally
Benson
THREE LITTLE SISTERS (1944, Republic)—Hallie Scott

TERRY-THOMAS
MAN IN A COCKED HAT (1960, GB, Boulting Bros.)—Cardogen
de Vere Carlton-Browne
HIS AND HERS (1961, GB, Sabre/Eros)—Reggie Blake
THOSE MAGNIFICENT MEN IN THEIR FLYING MACHINES
(1965, GB, 20th Century Fox)—Sir Percival Ware-Armitage
THOSE DARING YOUNG MEN IN THEIR JAUNTY JALOPIES
(1969, GB/France/ Italy, Paramount)—Sir Cuthbert Ware-
Armitage

TERRY, WILLIAM
JOHNNY DOESN'T LIVE HERE ANYMORE (1944, Monogram)—
Johnny Moore

TESSIER, JACK
JACK TAR (1915, Silent, GB, Barker)—Lt. Jack Atherley

THAYER, TINA
SECRETS OF A CO-ED (1942, Producers Releasing Corp.)—
Brenda Reynolds

THAXTER, PHYLLIS
BEWITCHED (1945, MGM)—Joan Arlis Ellis

THELEN, JODI
FOUR FRIENDS (1981, Filmways)—Georgia Miles

THIBEAULT, DEBI
PSYCHOS IN LOVE (1987, ICN Bleeker Infinity)—Kate

THOMAS, DANNY
I'LL SEE YOU IN MY DREAMS (1951, Warners)—Gus Kahn
THE JAZZ SINGER (1953, Warners)—Jerry Golding

THOMAS, FRANK
WEDNESDAY'S CHILD (1934, RKO)—Bobby Phillips

THOMAS, HEATHER
RED BLOODED AMERICAN GIRL (1990, Canada, SC
Entertainment)—Paula

THOMAS, MARLO
JENNY (1969, ABC-Palomar)—Jenny Marsh

THOMAS, OLIVE
INDISCREET CORRINE (1917, Silent, Triangle)—Corrine
Chilvere
THE FLAPPER (1920, Silent, Selznick)—Ginger King

THOMAS, RACHEL
HAZEL'S PEOPLE (1978, A People's Place)—Hazel

THOMERSON, TIM
THE WRONG GUYS (1988, New World)—Tim

THOMPSON, CINDY ANN
CAVEGIRL (1986, Crown International)—Eba

THOMPSON, DUANE
HUSBAND HUNTERS (1927, Silent, Tiffany)—Helen Gray
HER SUMMER HERO (1928, Silent, FBO Pictures)—Joan
Stanton

THOMPSON, EMMA
DEAD AGAIN (1991, Paramount)—Grace

THOMPSON, FRED
GALLOPING GALLAGHER (1924, Silent, Monogram)—Bill
Gallagher
DON MIKE (1927, Silent, FBO)—Don Miguel Arguello

THOMPSON, JACK
PETERSEN (1974, Australia, Avco Embassy)—Tony "Jock"
Petersen
SCOBIE MALONE (1975, Australia, Kingcroft/Cemp-Regent)—
Scobie Malone

THOMPSON, KENNETH
BELLAMY TRIAL (1929, Part-Talkie, MGM)—Stephen Bellamy

THOMPSON, KEVIN
THE GARBAGE PAIL KIDS (1987, Atlantic Entertainment)—
Ali Gator
SPACED INVADERS (1990, Buena Vista)—Blaznee

THOMPSON, MARSHALL
MY SIX CONVICTS (1952, Columbia)—Blivens Scott
A YANK IN VIET-NAM (1964, Allied Artists)—Major Benson

THOMPSON, PETER
A YANK IN ERMINE (1955, GB, Monarch)—Joe Turner

THOMPSON, ROBERT
PATRICK (1979, Australia, Filmways)—Patrick

THOMSETT, SALLY
THE RAILWAY CHILDREN (1971, GB, Universal)—Phyllis

THOMSON, BEATRIX
THE CROWN VS STEVENS (1936, Warners)—Doris Stevens

THOMSON, FRED
JESSE JAMES (1927, Silent, Paramount)—Jesse James
KIT CARSON (1928, Silent, Paramount)—Kit Carson

THORNTON, EDITH
ON PROBATION (1924, Silent, Steiner)—Mary Forrest

THORNTON, SIGRID
SLATE, WYN & ME (1987, Australia, Ukiyo/Hemdale)—Blanche McBride

THRETT, MAGGIE
THREE IN THE ATTIC (1968, American International)—Jan

THUNDERCLOUD, CHIEF
GERONIMO (1939, Paramount)—Geronimo
I KILLED GERONIMO (1950, Eagle-Lion)—Geronimo

THURMAN, MARY
THE SIN OF MARTHA QUEED (1921, Silent, Associated Exhibitors)—Martha Queed

THURMAN, UMA
KISS DADDY GOOD NIGHT (1987, Beast of Eden)—Laura
HENRY AND JUNE (1990, Universal)—June Miller

THYSSEN, GRETA
THREE BLONDES IN HIS LIFE (1961, Cinema Associates)—Helen Fortner

TIBBETT, LAWRENCE
THE PRODIGAL (1931, MGM)—Jeffry Farraday

TIERNEY, GENE
BELLE STARR (1941, 20th Century Fox)—Belle Starr
CHINA GIRL (1942, 20th Century Fox)—Miss Young
THE GHOST AND MRS. MUIR (1942, 20th Century Fox)—Lucy Muir
LAURA (1944, 20th Century Fox)—Laura Hunt
LEAVE HER TO HEAVEN (1946, 20th Century Fox)—Ellen Berent

TIERNEY, LAWRENCE
DILLINGER (1945, Monogram)—John Dillinger
BORN TO KILL (1947, RKO)—Sam
THE DEVIL THUMBS A RIDE (1947, RKO)—Steve
BODYGUARD (1948, RKO)—Mike Carter

TIFFIN, PAMELA
THE PLEASURE SEEKERS (1964, 20th Fox)—Susie Higgins

TILDEN, LEIF
TEENAGE MUTANT NINJA TURTLES (1990, New Line)—Donatello
TEENAGE MUTANT NINJA TURTLES 2: THE SECRET OF OOZE (1991, New Line)—Donatello

TILLER, NADJA
PORTRAIT OF A SINNER (1961, GB, Renown)—Ila Hansen
LULU (1962, Australia, Gloria)—Lulu

TILLEY, VESTA
THE GIRL WHO LOVES A SOLDIER (1916, GB, Silent, Moss)—Vesta Beaumont

TILLY, MEG
AGNES OF GOD (1985, Columbia)—Sister Agnes
THE GIRL IN THE SWING (1989, GB/US, J&M)—Karin Foster

TOBIAS, OLIVER
THE STUD (1979, GB, Trans-American)—Tony Blake

TOBIN, GENEVIEVE
EASY TO LOVE (1934, Warners)—Carol
UNCERTAIN LADY (1934, Universal)—Doris
KATE PLUS TEN (1938, GB, GFD)—Kate Westhanger

TODD, ANN
THE WATER GYPSIES (1932, GB, RKO)—Jane Bell
SO EVIL MY LOVE (1948, GB, Paramount)—Olivia Harwood
ONE WOMAN'S STORY (1949, GB, GFD/Universal)—Mary Justin
MADELEINE (1950, GB, Rank)—Madeleine Smith

TODD, ANN E.
THREE DARING DAUGHTERS (1948, MGM)—Ilka Morgan

TODD, RICHARD
THE STORY OF ROBIN HOOD (1952, GB, Disney/RKO)—Robin Hood
ROB ROY, THE HIGHLAND ROGUE (1954, GB, Disney/RKO)—Rob Roy MacGregor
THE MAN CALLED PETER (1955, 20th Century Fox)—Peter Marshall
SANDERS (1963, GB, Hallam/Planet)—Inspector Harry Sanders

TODD, THELMA
VAMPING VENUS (1928, Silent, First National)—Venus
CHEATING BLONDES (1933, Equitable)—Anne Merrick

TOLER, SIDNEY
CHARLIE CHAN IN HONOLULU (1938, 20th Century Fox)—Charlie Chan
CHARLIE CHAN AT TREASURE ISLAND (1939, 20th Century Fox)—Charlie Chan
CHARLIE CHAN IN RENO (1939, 20th Century Fox)—Charlie Chan
CHARLIE CHAN IN THE CITY OF DARKNESS (1939, 20th Century Fox)—Charlie Chan
CHARLIE CHAN AT THE WAX MUSEUM (1940, 20th Century Fox)—Charlie Chan
CHARLIE CHAN IN PANAMA (1940, 20th Century Fox)—Charlie Chan
CHARLIE CHAN'S MURDER CRUISE (1940, 20th Century Fox)—Charlie Chan
CHARLIE CHAN IN RIO (1941, 20th Century Fox)—Charlie Chan

CHARLIE CHAN IN BLACK MAGIC (1944, Monogram)—
Charlie Chan
CHARLIE CHAN IN THE SECRET SERVICE (1944, Monogram)—
Charlie Chan

TOMEI, CONCETTA
DON'T TELL MOM THE BABYSITTER'S DEAD (1991, Warner
Brothers)—Mrs. Crandall

TOMLIN, LILY
THE INCREDIBLE SHRINKING WOMAN (1981, Universal)—Pat
Kramer
ALL OF ME (1984, Universal)—Edwina Cutwater

TOMLIN, PINKY
SWING IT PROFESSOR (1937, Ambassador)—Prof. Artemis
Roberts

TOMLINSON, DAVID
SO LONG AT THE FAIR (1951, GB, Rank)—Johnny Barton
THREE MEN IN A BOAT (1958, GB, Romulus/Valiant)—J

TONE, FRANCHOT
GENTLEMEN ARE BORN (1934, First National)—Bob Bailey
THE KING STEPS OUT (1936, Columbia)—Emperor Franz Josef
THEY GAVE HIM A GUN (1937, MGM)—Jimmy David
THREE COMRADES (1938, MGM)—Otto Koster
THIS WOMAN IS MINE (1941, Universal)—Robert Stevens
THE WIFE TAKES A FLYER (1942, Columbia)—Christopher
Reynolds
HIS BROTHER'S SISTER (1943, Universal)—Charles Gerard
PILOT NO. 5 (1943, MGM)—George Braynor Collins
HER HUSBAND'S AFFAIRS (1947, Columbia)—William Weldon
I LOVE TROUBLE (1947, Columbia)—Stuart Bailey
THE MAN ON THE EIFFEL TOWER (1949, RKO)—Radek

TOOMEY, REGIS
STATE TROOPER (1933, Columbia)—Michael Ralph

TOPOL
GALILEO (1975, GB, American Film Theatre)—Galileo Galilei

TORA, LIA
THE VEILED WOMAN (1929, Fox)—Nanon

TORN, RIP
A STRANGER IS WAITING (1982, MGM/United Artists)—Artie
Taggart

TOTTER, AUDREY
FBI GIRL (1951, Lippert)—Shirley Wayne

TOWNE, ROSELLA
ADVENTURES OF JANE ARDEN (1939, Warners)—Jane Arden

TOWNSEND, ANNA
GRANDMA'S BOY (1922, Silent, Associated Exhibitors)—
Grandma

TOWNSEND, GENEVIEVE
A GIRL OF LONDON (1925, GB, Silent, Stoll)—Lil

TOWNSEND, ROBERT
THE FIVE HEARTBEATS (1991, 20th Century Fox)—Duck

TRACEY, RAY
JOE PANTHER (1976, Artists Creation)—Joe Panther

TRACY, ARTHUR
THE STREET SINGER (1937, GB, Wardour)—Richard King

TRACY, JOHN
THE DRIFTER (1966, Surfilms)—Alan

TRACY, LEE
THE NIGHT MAYOR (1932, Columbia)—Bobby Kingston
PRIVATE JONES (1933, Universal)—Bill Jones
I'LL TELL THE WORLD (1934, Universal)—Stanley Brown
THE LEMON DROP KID (1934, Paramount)—Wally Brooks
CRIMINAL LAWYER (1937, RKO)—Brandon
FIXER DUGAN (1939, RKO)—Charlie Dugan
THE SPELLBINDER (1939, RKO)—Jed Marlowe
I'LL TELL THE WORLD (1945, Universal)—Gabriel Patton

TRACY, SPENCER
ME AND MY GAL (1932, Fox)—Dan Dolan
A MAN'S CASTLE (1933, Columbia)—Bill
THE SHOW-OFF (1934, MGM)—Aubrey Piper
MURDER MAN (1935, MGM)—Steve Gray
CAPTAINS COURAGEOUS (1937, MGM)—Manuel
STANLEY AND LIVINGSTONE (1939, 20th Century Fox)—Henry
M. Stanley
EDISON, THE MAN (1940, MGM)—Thomas Alva Edison
I TAKE THIS WOMAN (1940, MGM)—Karl Decker
DR. JEKYL AND MR. HYDE (1941, MGM)—Dr. Harry Jekyl/
Mr. Hyde
CASS TIMBERLANE (1947, MGM)—Cass Timberlane
ADAM'S RIB (1949, MGM)—Adam Bonner
EDWARD, MY SON (1949, MGM)—Arnold Boult
FATHER OF THE BRIDE (1950, MGM)—Stanley Banks
FATHER'S LITTLE DIVIDEND (1951, MGM)—Stanley Banks
PAT AND MIKE (1952, MGM)—Mike Conovan
THE OLD MAN AND THE SEA (1958, Warners)—The Old Man

TRACY, WILLIAM
YANKS AHOY (1943, United Artists)—Sgt. Doubleday
MR. WALKIE TALKIE (1952, Lippert)—Sgt. Doubleday

TRAIN, JACK
COLONEL BOGEY (1948, GB, GFD)—Voice of Uncle James (Col.
Bogey)

TRAVERS, BERNIE
DIRTYMOUTH (1970, Superior)—Lenny Bruce

TRAVERS, BILL
WEE GEORDIE (1956, GB, British & Dominions)—Geordie
MacTaggart
TWO LIVING, ONE DEAD (1964, GB, Emerson)—Anderson

TRAVERS, LINDEN
NO ORCHIDS FOR MISS BLANDISH (1948, GB, Renown)—Miss
Blandish

TRAVERS, SUSAN
THE SNAKE WOMAN (1961, GB, United Artists)—Atheris
Adderson

TRAVIS, DOUGLAS
TWO (1975, Colmar)—Steven

TRAVIS, JUNE
CIRCUS GIRL (1937, Republic)—Kay Rogers

TRAVOLTA, JOEY
HUNTER'S BLOOD (1987, Concorde)—Marty Adler

TRAVOLTA, JOHN
URBAN COWBOY (1980, Paramount)—Bud
TWO OF A KIND (1983, 20th Century Fox)—Zack
THE EXPERTS (1989, Paramount)—Travis

TREACHER, ARTHUR
THANK YOU, JEEVES (1936, 20th Century Fox)—Jeeves
STEP LIVELY, JEEVES (1937, 20th Century Fox)—Jeeves

TRENT, ANTHONY
THE TOMCAT (1968, GB, Tigon-Global)—Tom

TRENT, JOHN
STUNT PILOT (1939, Monogram)—Tailspin Tommy

TREVARTHEN, NOEL
ESCORT FOR HIRE (1960, GB, MGM)—Steve

TREVELYAN, HILDA
WHAT EVERY WOMAN KNOWS (1917, GB, Silent, Lucoque)—Maggie Wylie

TREVOR, CLAIRE
JIMMY AND SALLY (1933, Fox)—Sally Johnson
HOLD THAT GIRL (1934, Fox)—Tony Bellamy
ELINOR NORTON (1935, Fox)—Elinor Norton
CAREER WOMAN (1936, 20th Century Fox)—Carroll Aiken
MY MARRIAGE (1936, 20th Century Fox)—Carol Barton
NAVY WIFE (1936, 20th Century Fox)—Vicky Blake
BIG TOWN GIRL (1937, 20th Century Fox)—Fay Loring
THE WOMAN OF THE TOWN (1943, United Artists)—Dora Hand
THE BACHELOR'S DAUGHTERS (1946, United Artists)—Cynthia

TREVOR, HUGH
HER SUMMER HERO (1928, Silent, FBO Pictures)—Kenneth Holmes

TRIMINGHAM, ERNEST A.
JACK, SAM AND PETE (1919, Silent, GB, Pollock-Daring)—Pete

TRINDER, TOMMY
CHAMPAGNE CHARLIE (1944, GB, Ealing)—George Leybourne

TROOBNICK, GENE
HARVEY MIDDLEMAN, FIREMAN (1965, Columbia)—Harvey Middleman

TROUM, KENN
TEENAGE MUTANT NINJA TURTLES II: THE SECRET OF OOZE (1991, New Line)—Raphael

TRYON, GLENN
A HERO FOR A NIGHT (1927, Silent, Universal)—Hiram Hastings
THE GATE CRASHER (1928, Silent, Universal)—Dick Henshaw
THE KID'S CLEVER (1929, Universal)—Bugs Raymond
SKINNER STEPS OUT (1929, Universal)—William Henry Skiner

TRYON, TOM
THREE VIOLENT PEOPLE (1956, Paramount)—Cinch Saunders
I MARRIED A MONSTER FROM OUTER SPACE (1958, Paramount)—Bill Farrell
MOON PILOT (1962, Buena Vista)—Capt. Richmond Talbot

THE CARDINAL (1963, Columbia)—Stephen Fermoyle

TUBB, BARRY
VALENTINO RETURNS (1989, Skouras)—Wayne Gibbs

TUCKER, FORREST
THE LAST BANDIT (1949, Republic)—Jim Plummer
THE QUIET GUN (1957, 20th Century Fox)—Carl

TUCKER, RICHARD
THE BENSON MURDER CASE (1930, Paramount)—Anthony Benson

TUFTS, SONNY
I LOVE A SOLDIER (1944, Paramount)—Dan Gilgore
SWELL GUY (1946, Universal)—Jim Duncan

TURNER, FLORENCE
A WELSH SINGER (1915, GB, Silent, Butchers)—Mifanwy

TURNER, FRED
THE JACK KNIFE MAN (1920, Silent, First National)—Peter Lane

TURNER, GEORGE
THE BIG STRONG MAN (1922, Silent, GB, Quality Plays)—George Herrick
HENRY STEPS OUT (1940, GB, American International)—Henry Smith

TURNER, KATHLEEN
PEGGY SUE GOT MARRIED (1986, Tri-Star)—Peggy Sue Kelcher Bodell
JULIA AND JULIA (1988, Cinecom)—Julia
THE WAR OF THE ROSES (1989, 20th Century Fox)—Barbara Rose
V.I. WARSHAWSKI (1991, Hollywood Pictures)—V.I. Warshawski

TURNER, LANA
DANCING CO-ED (1939, MGM)—Patty Marlow
THESE GLAMOUR GIRLS (1939, MGM)—Jane Thomas
TWO GIRLS ON BROADWAY (1940, MGM)—Pat Mahoney
ZIEGFELD GIRL (1941, MGM)—Shelia Regan
SOMEWHERE I'LL FIND YOU (1942, MGM)—Paula Lane
A LIFE OF HER OWN (1950, MGM)—Lily Brannel James
THE MERRY WIDOW (1952, MGM)—Crystal Radek
LATIN LOVERS (1953, MGM)—Nora Taylor
DIANE (1955, MGM)—Diane de Poitiers
THE LADY TAKES A FLYER (1958, Universal)—Maggie Colby
MADAME X (1966, Universal)—Holly Parker

TURNER, TIERRE
CORNBREAD, EARL AND ME (1975, American International)—Earl

TURPIN, BEN
SMALL TOWN HERO (1921, Silent, Associate Producers)—Sam Smith

TURTURRO, JOHN
MEN OF RESPECT (1990, Central City)—Mike Battaglia
BARTON FINK (1991, 20th Century Fox)—Barton Fink
MAC (1992, Tennenbaum/Goodman)—Niccolo "Mac" Vitelli

TUSHINGHAM, RITA
GIRL WITH GREEN EYES (1964, GB, Lopert)—Kate Brady

THE HOUSEKEEPER (1987, Canada, Castlehill-Kodiak)—
Eunice Parchamn

TUTTLE, LURENE
MA BARKER'S KILLER BROOD (1960, Filmservice)—Ma Barker

TWELVETREES, HELEN
HER MAN (1930, Pathe)—Frankie
MILLIE (1931, RKO)—Millie
A WOMAN OF EXPERIENCE (1931, RKO)—Elsa
PANAMA FLO (1932, RKO)—Flo Bennett
UNASHAMED (1932, MGM)—Joan Ogden
YOUNG BRIDE (1932, RKO)—Allie Smith
MY WOMAN (1933, Columbia)—Connie Riley
SHE WAS A LADY (1934, Fox)—Sheila Vane
UNMARRIED (1939, Paramount)—Pat Rogers

TYLER, GRANT
DANNY BOY (1941, GB, Butchers)—Danny

TYLER, TOM
THE COWBOY MUSKETEER (1925, Silent, R-C Pictures)—Tom
Latigo
THE COWBOY COP (1926, Silent, R-C Pictures)—Jerry McGill
TOM AND HIS PALS (1926, Silent, R-C Pictures)—Tom Duffy
THE SONORA KID (1927, Silent, FBO)—Tom MacReady
THE AVENGING RIDER (1928, Silent, FBO Pictures)—Tom
Larkin
THE DESERT PIRATE (1928, Silent, FBO)—Tom Corrigan
CHEYENNE RIDES AGAIN (1937, Victory)—Cheyenne
THE MUMMY'S HAND (1940, Universal)—Kharis
THE PHANTOM PLAINSMAN (1942, Republic)—Stony Brooke

U

UDVARNOKY, MARTIN
THE OTHER (1972, 20th Century Fox)—Holland Perry

UGGAMS, LESLIE
BLACK GIRL (1972, Cinerama)—Netta

ULLMAN, TRACEY
I LOVE YOU TO DEATH (1990, Tri-Star)—Rosalie Boca

ULLMAN, LIV
POPE JOAN (1972, GB, Columbia)—Joan
ZANDY'S BRIDE (1974, Warners)—Hannah Lund

ULRIC, LEONORE
SOUTH SEA ROSE (1929, Fox)—Rosalie Dumay

ULRICH, LEONORE
KILMENY (1915, Silent, Paramount)—Kilmeny

UNDERWOOD, JAY
THE BOY WHO COULD FLY (1986, Lorimar)—Eric

THE INVISIBLE KID (1988, Columbia)—Grover Dunn
THE GUMSHOE KID (1990, Skouras)—Jeff Sherman

URICH, ROBERT
THE ICE PIRATES (1984, MGM/United Artists)—Jason

USTINOV, PETER
PRIVATE ANGELO (1949, GB, Pathe)—Pvt. Angelo
WE'RE NO ANGELS (1955, Paramount)—Jules
BLACKBEARD'S GHOST (1968, Buena Vista)—Capt. Blackbeard
VIVA MAX! (1969, Commonwealth United)—Gen. Maximilian
Rodrigues de Santos
CHARLIE CHAN AND THE CURSE OF THE DRAGON QUEEN
(1981, American Cinema) - Charlie Chan

V

VACARRO, BRENDA
I LOVE MY WIFE (1970, Universal)—Judy Burrows

VAIL, MYRTLE
MYRT AND MARGE (1934, Universal)—Myrt Minter

VALE, VIRGINIA
BLONDE COMET (1941, Producers Releasing Corp.)—
Beverly Blake

VALENTINE, SCOTT
MY DEMON LOVER (1987, New Line Cinema)—Kaz

VALENTINO, RUDOLPH
THE SHEIK (1921, Silent, Paramount)—Sheik Ahmed Ben
Hassan
A SAINTED DEVIL (1924, Silent, Paramount)—Don Alonzo
Castro
MONSIEUR BEAUCAIRE (1924, Silent, Paramount)—Mons.
Beaucaire
SON OF THE SHEIK (1926, Silent, United Artists)—Ahmed/
The Sheik

VALLEE, RUDY
VAGABOND LOVER (1929, RKO)—Rudy Bronson

VALLI, ALIDA
THE PARADINE CASE (1947, United Artists)—Maddalena, Anna
Paradine

VALLI, VIRGINIA
LADIES MUST DRESS (1927, Silent, Fox)—Eve

VALLIN, RICK
SMART GUY (1943, Monogram)—Johnny
LAST OF THE REDMEN (1947, Columbia)—Uncas

VAN, BOBBY
THE AFFAIRS OF DOBIE GILLIS (1953, MGM)—Dobie Gillis

VAN, GUS
THEY LEARNED ABOUT WOMEN (1930, MGM)—Jerry

VAN BUREN, MABEL
THE GIRL OF THE GOLDEN WEST (1915, Silent, Lasky)—
The Girl
SHOULD A WIFE FORGIVE? (1915, Silent, World)—Mary
Holmes
THE WARRENS OF VIRGINIA (1915, Silent, Lasky)—Mrs.
Warren

VAN CLEEF, LEE
CAPTAIN APACHE (1971, GB, Scotia International)—Captain
Apache
THE MAGNIFICENT SEVEN RIDE (1972, United Artists)—Chris

VAN DAMME, JEAN-CLAUDE
KICKBOXER (1989, Kings Road/Pathe)—Kurt Sloane
DOUBLE IMPACT (1991, Columbia)—Chad/Alex

VAN DOREN, MAMIE
THE PRIVATE LIVES OF ADAM AND EVE (1961, Universal)—
Evie Simms/Eve
THREE NUTS IN SEARCH OF A BOLT (1964, Harlequin)—Saxie
Symbol

VAN DREELEN, JOHN
THE ENEMY GENERAL (1960, Columbia)—General Burger

VAN DYKE, CONNIE
W.W. AND THE DIXIE DANCEKINGS (1975, 20th Century
Fox)—Dixie

VAN DYKE, DICK
LT. ROBIN CRUSOE, U.S.N. (1966, Buena Vista)—Lt. Robin
Crusoe
FITZWILLY (1967, United Artists)—Fitzwilliam
THE COMIC (1969, Columbia)—Billy Bright
SOME KIND OF NUT (1969, United Artists)—Fred Amidon
THE RUNNER STUMBLES (1979, 20th Century Fox)—Father
Rivard

VAN EYCK, PETER
THE DEVIL'S AGENT (1962, GB, British Lion)—George Droste

VAN EYSSEN, JOHN
MEN OF SHERWOOD FOREST (1957, GB, Hammer)—Will
Scarlett

VANILLA ICE
COOL AS ICE (1991, Universal)—Johnny

VAN LOAN, PHILIP
JESUS OF NAZARETH (1928, Silent, Ideal)—Jesus Christ

VAN VOREEN, MONIQUE
TARZAN AND THE SHE-DEVIL (1953, RKO)—Lyra

VARCONI, VICTOR
CAPTAIN THUNDER (1931, Warners)—Capt. Thunder

VARNEY, JIM
ERNEST GOES TO CAMP (1987, Buena Vista)—Ernest P.
Worrell
ERNEST SAVES CHRISTMAS (1988, Touchstone)—Ernest P.
Worrell

ERNEST GOES TO JAIL (1990, Buena Vista)—Ernest P. Worrell
ERNEST SCARED STUPID (1991, Touchstone)—Ernest P.
Worrell

VARSI, DIANE
KILLERS THREE (1968, American International)—Carol Ward

VAUGHN, ALBERTA
THE ADORABLE DECEIVER (1926, Silent, Film Booking
Offices)—Princess Sylvia

VAUGHN, KATHLEEN
THE PRINCE AND THE BEGGARMAID (1921, GB, Silent,
Ideal)—Princess Monika

VAUGHN, PETER
TWO LIVING, ONE DEAD (1964, GB, Emerson)—John Kester
HAMMERHEAD (1968, Columbia)—Hammerhead

VAUGHN, ROBERT
TEENAGE CAVEMAN (1958, American International)—The Boy
THE MAGNIFICENT SEVEN (1960, United Artists)—Lee

VAWTER, RON
KING BLANK (1983, Metafilms)—King Blank

VEIDT, CONRAD
THE MAN WHO LAUGHS (1927, Silent, Universal)—Gwynplaine
THE WANDERING JEW (1935, GB, Gaumont)—The
Wandering Jew
KING OF THE DAMNED (1936, GB, Gaumont)—Convict 83
NAZI AGENT (1942, MGM)—Otto Becker

VELASQUEZ, ANDRES
THE LITTLEST OUTLAW (1955, Buena Vista)—Pablito

VELEZ, LUPE
LADY OF THE PAVEMENTS (1929, United Artists)—Nanon
del Rayon
TIGER ROSE (1930, Warners)—Rose
THE GIRL FROM MEXICO (1939, RKO)—Carmelita
MEXICAN SPITFIRE (1939, RKO)—Carmelita Lindsay
MEXICAN SPITFIRE OUT WEST (1940, RKO)—Carmelita
Lindsay
HONOLULU LU (1941, Columbia)—Consuelo Cordoba
MEXICAN SPITFIRE'S BABY (1941, RKO)—Carmelita Lindsay
SIX LESSONS FROM MADAME LA ZONGA (1941, Universal)—
Madame La Zonga
MEXICAN SPITFIRE AT SEA (1942, RKO)—Carmelita Lindsay
MEXICAN SPITFIRE SEES A GHOST (1942, RKO)—Carmelita
Lindsay
MEXICAN SPITFIRE'S ELEPHANT (1942, RKO)—Carmelita
Lindsay
LADIES' DAY (1943, RKO)—Pepita
MEXICAN SPITFIRE'S BLESSED EVENT (1943, RKO)—
Carmelita Lindsay
REDHEAD FROM MANHATTAN (1954, Columbia)—Rita
Manners

VENABLE, EVELYN
FEMALE FUGITIVE (1938, Monogram)—Peggy Mallory
VAGABOND LADY (1935, MGM)—Josephine Spiggins
THE HEADLEY'S AT HOME (1939, Standard)—Pamela Headley

VENABLE, SARAH
TWO (1975, Colmar)—Ellen

VERA-ELLEN
THREE LITTLE GIRLS IN BLUE (1946, 20th Century Fox)—Myra
THE BELLE OF NEW YORK (1952, MGM)—Angela Bonfils

VERDUGO, ELENA
PANAMA SAL (1957, Republic)—Sal Reagan

VERNO, JERRY
MY FRIEND THE KING (1931, GB, Fox)—Jim
HIS LORDSHIP (1932, GB, United Artists)—Bert Gibbs
HIS WIFE'S MOTHER (1932, GB, British International)—Henry

VERNON, GLENN
DING DONG WILLIAMS (1946, RKO)—Ding Dong Williams

VERNON, JOHN
I'M GONNA GET YOU SUCKA (1988, MGM-United Artists)—Mr. Big

VICKERS, MARTHA
THE TIME, THE PLACE AND THE GIRL (1946, Warners)—Victoria Cassel
DAUGHTER OF THE WEST (1949, Film Classics)—Lolita Moreno

VICTOR, CHARLES
THE FRIGHTENED MAN (1952, GB, Tempean)—Mr. Roselli
THE EMBEZZLER (1954, GB, GFD)—Henry Paulson

VICTOR, HENRY
THE PICTURE OF DORIAN GRAY (1916, GB, Silent, Neptune)—Dorian Gray
JOHN HERIOT'S WIFE (1920, Silent, GB, Anglo-Hollandia)—John Heriot

VIDOR, FLORENCE
HAIL THE WOMEN (1921, Silent, Associated Producers)—Judith Beresford
ALICE ADAMS (1923, Silent, Associated Exhibitors)—Alice Adams
CHRISTINE OF THE HUNGRY HEART (1924, Silent, First National)—Christine Madison
THE GRAND DUCHESS AND THE WAITER (1926, Paramount)—Grand Duchess Zenia
ONE WOMAN TO ANOTHER (1927, Silent, Paramount)—Rita Farrell
THE MAGNIFICENT FLIRT (1928, Silent, Paramount)—Mme. Florence Laverne

VIGODA, ABE
KEATON'S COP (1990, Cannon)—Louie Keaton

VIHARO, ROBERT
HAPPY BIRTHDAY, GEMINI (1980, United Artists)—Nick Geminiani

VILLARD, TOM
THE TROUBLE WITH DICK (1987, Frolix)—Dick Kendred

VINCE, PRUITT TAYLOR
SHY PEOPLE (1988, Cannon)—Paul Sullivan

VINCENT, ALEX
CHILD'S PLAY (1988, United Artists)—Andy Barclay

VINCENT, JAN-MICHAEL
THE WORLD'S GREATEST ATHLETE (1973, Buena Vista)—Nanu
BABY BLUE MARINE (1976, Columbia)—Marion Hedgepth

VINCENT, JUNE
THE LONE WOLF AND HIS LADY (1949, Columbia)—Grace Duffy

VINCENTE, ROY
THE MONSTER OF HIGHGATE PONDS (1961, GB, Halas & Batchelor)—The Monster

VINTAS, GUSTAV
SILENT ASSASSINS (1988, Panache-Forum)—Kendrick
VAMPIRE AT MIDNIGHT (1988, Skouras)—Victor Radhoff

VITTI, MONICA
MODESTY BLAISE (1966, GB, 20th Century Fox)—Modesty Blaise

VOGEL, MITCH
THE REIVERS (1969, National General)—Lucius McCaslin

VOIGHT, JON
FEARLESS FRANK (1967, American International)—Frank/False Frank
MIDNIGHT COWBOY (1969, United Artists)—Joe Buck
THE ALL-AMERICAN BOY (1973, Warners)—Vic Bealer
CONRACK (1974, 20th Century Fox)—Pat Conroy
THE CHAMP (1979, United Artists/MGM—Billy

VOLPE, FRED
THE ADVENTURES OF MR. PICKWICK (1921, Silent, GB, Bentley)—Samuel Pickwick

VON DOHLEN, LENNY
BILLY GALVIN (1986, Vestron)—Billy Galvin

VON RUE, GRETA
HIS FOREIGN WIFE (1927, Silent, Pathe)—Hilda Schultzenbach

VON SCHELLENDORF, HEINRICH
RAWHEAD REX (1987, GB, Alpine-Paradise-Green Man)—Rawhead Rex

VON STROHEIM, ERIC
THE GREAT GABBO (1929, Art World Wide)—Great Gabbo
THE CRIME OF DR. CRESPI (1936, Republic)—Dr. Crespi
THE MASK OF DILJON (1946, Producers Releasing Corp.)—Diljon

VON SYDOW, MAX
THE EXORCIST (1973, Warners)—Father Merrin
FATHER (1990, Australia, Barron)—Joe Mueller

VON TWARDOWSKI, HANS
HANGMEN ALSO DIE (1943, United Artists)—Reinhard Heydrich

VOSKOVEC, GEORGE
12 ANGRY MEN (1957, United Artists)—Juror No. 11
UNCLE VANYA (1958, Continental)—Ivan Petrovich "Uncle Vanya" Voinitsky

VOSPER, FRANK
SPY OF NAPOLEON (1939, GB, Syndicate)—Louis Napoleon II

W

WAGNER, CHRISTIE
SHE-DEVILS ON WHEELS (1968, Mayflower)—Karen

WAGNER, LINDSAY
TWO PEOPLE (1973, Universal)—Deirdre McCluskey

WAGNER, ROBERT
PRINCE VALIANT (1954, 20th Century Fox) -Prince Valiant
THE TRUE STORY OF JESSE JAMES (1957, 20th Century Fox)—Jesse James
BANNING (1967, Universal)—Banning

WAHL, KEN
THE SOLDIER (1982, Embassy)—The Soldier

WAITE, GENEVIEVE
JOANNA (1968, GB, 20th Century Fox)—Joanna

WAKEFIELD, DUGGIE
SPY FOR A DAY (1939, GB, Paramount)—Sam Gates

WAKEFIELD, HUGH
THE FORTUNATE FOOL (1933, GB, Associated British)—Jim Falconer

WAKEFIELD, OLIVER
THERE WAS A YOUNG MAN (1937, GB, Fox British)—George Peabody

WALBROOK, ANTON
THE SOLDIER AND THE LADY (1937, GB, RKO)—Michael Strogoff
THE RAT (1938, GB, RKO)—Jean Boucheron, "The Rat"

WALBURN, RAYMOND
HENRY THE RAINMAKER (1949, Monogram)—Henry Latham
LEAVE IT TO HENRY (1949, Monogram)—Henry Latham
FATHER MAKES GOOD (1950, Monogram)—Henry Latham
FATHER'S WILD GAME (1950, Monogram)—Henry Latham
FATHER TAKES THE AIR (1951, Monogram)—Henry Latham

WALES, WALLY
THE FIGHTING CHEAT (1926, Silent, Action/Artclass)—Tom Rumford

WALKEN, CHRISTOPHER
DOGS OF WAR (1980, GB, United Artists)—Shannon
KING OF NEW YORK (1990, Ital/U.S., Reteitalia/Scena)—Frank White
MCBAIN (1991, Shapiro Glickenhaus Ent.)—McBain

WALKER, CHERYL
THREE LITTLE SISTERS (1944, Republic)—Lily Scott

WALKER, CLINT
YELLOWSTONE KELLY (1959, Warners)—Yellowstone Kelly
THE DIRTY DOZEN (1967, GB, MGM)—Samson Posey
MORE DEAD THAN ALIVE (1968, United Artists)—"Killer" Cain
BAKER'S HAWK (1976, Doty-Dayton)—Dan Baker

WALKER, HELEN
MY TRUE STORY (1951, Columbia)—Ann Martin

WALKER, JOHNNIE
MY DAD (1922, Silent, R-C/Film Booking Offices)—Tom O'Day
THE MAILMAN (1923, Silent, Film Booking Offices)—Johnnie Morley
THE SWELLHEAD (1930, Tiffany)—Bill "Cyclone" Hickey

WALKER, JUNE
WAR NURSE (1930, MGM)—Babs

WALKER, KATHRYN
NEIGHBORS (1981, Columbia)—Enid Keese

WALKER, KIM
HEATHERS (1989, New World)—Heather Chandler

WALKER, LILLIAN
THE KID (1916, Silent, Vitagraph)—The Kid

WALKER, ROBERT
SEE HERE, PRIVATE HARGROVE (1944, MGM)—Pvt. Marion Hargrove
HER HIGHNESS AND THE BELLBOY (1945, MGM)—Jimmy Dobson
WHAT NEXT, CORPORAL HARGROVE? (1945, MGM)—Cpl. Marion Hargrove
THE SAILOR TAKES A WIFE (1946, MGM)—John
THE SKIPPER SURPRISED HIS WIFE (1950, MGM)—Cmdr. William Lattimer
STRANGERS ON A TRAIN (1951, Warners)—Bruno Anthony
MY SON JOHN (1952, Paramount)—John Jefferson

WALKER, ROBERT, JR.
ENSIGN PULVER (1964, Warners)—Ensign Pulver
KILLERS THREE (1968, American International)—Johnny Ward
YOUNG BILLY YOUNG (1969, United Artists)—Billy Young
THE SPECTRE OF EDGAR ALLAN POE (1974, Cinerama)—Edgar Allan Poe

WALKER, SYD
OLD BILL THROUGH THE AGES (1924, Silent, GB, Ideal) - Old Bill

WALKER, TIPPY
JENNIFER ON MY MIND (1971, United Artists)—Jenny

WALLACE, COLEY
THE JOE LOUIS STORY (1953, United Artists)—Joe Louis

WALLACH, ELI
THE VICTORS (1963, Columbia)—Sgt. Craig
THE TIGER MAKES OUT (1967, Columbia)—Ben Harris
SAM'S SON (1984, Invictus)—Sam Orowitz

WALLEY, DEBORAH
GIDGET GOES HAWAIIAN (1961, Columbia)—Gidget (Francie Lawrence)

WALLS, TOM
LEAVE IT TO SMITH (1934, GB, Gaumont)—Smith
MEET AND MARLBOROUGH (1935, GB, Gaumont)—Duke of Marlborough
OLD IRON (1938, GB, British Lion)—Sir Henry Woodstock
THE MASTER OF BANKDAM (1947, GB, GFD)—Simeon Crowther, Sr.

WALSH, DERMOT
UNDERCOVER AGENT (1935, GB, Lippert)—Manning

THE STRAW MAN (1953, GB, United Artists)—Mal Farris

WALSH, GEORGE
THE MEDIATOR (1916, Silent, Fox)—Lish Henley
JACK SPURLOCK, PRODIGAL (1918, Silent, Fox)—Jack Spurlock
SLAVE OF DESIRE (1923, Silent, Goldwyn)—Ralph Valentin
THE COUNT OF LUXEMBOURG (1926, Silent, Chadwick)—Rene Duval
HIS RISE TO FAME (1927, Silent, Excellent Pictures)—Jerry Drake

WALSH, KAY
THE DEVIL'S OWN (1967, GB, Hammer)—Stephanie Bax

WALTER, JESSICA
THE GROUP (1966, United Artists)—Libby MacAusland

WALTERS, JULIE
EDUCATING RITA (1983, Columbia)—Rita
SHE'LL BE WEARING PINK PAJAMAS (1986, Film Forum)—Fran
PERSONAL SERVICES (1987, GB, Zenith/UIP-Vestron)

WALTHALL, HENRY B.
HIS ROBE OF HONOR (1918, Silent, Paralta)—Julian Randolph
HUMDRUM BROWN (1918, Silent, Essanay)—Humdrum Brown
THE BOWERY BISHOP (1924, Silent, Selznick)—Norman Strong

WALTON, GLADYS
THE ROWDY (1921, Silent, Universal)—Kit Purcell
THE LAVENDER BATH LADY (1922, Silent, Universal)—Mamie Conroy
SECOND HAND ROSE (1922, Silent, Universal)—Rose O'Grady
THE NEAR LADY (1923, Silent, Universal)—Nora Schultz

WANNAMAKER, SAM
MY GIRL TISA (1948, Warners)—Mark Denek

WARBURTON, PATRICK
MASTER OF DRAGONARD (1990, Cannon)—Richard Abdee

WARD, FANNIE
THE CHEAT (1915, Silent, Paramount)—Edith Hardy
THE MARRIAGE OF KITTY (1915, Silent, Metro)—Katherine Silverton
TENNESSEE'S PARTNER (1916, Silent, Lasky)—Tennessee
THE CRYSTAL GAZER (1917, Silent, Paramount)—Norma Dugan
A JAPANESE NIGHTINGALE (1918, Silent, Pathe)—Yuki

WARD, FRED
TIMERIDER (1983, Jensen-Farley)—Lyle Swann
REMO WILLIAMS: THE ADVENTURE BEGINS. . . (1985, Orion)—Remo Williams
HENRY AND JUNE (1990, Universal)—Henry Miller

WARD, PENELOPE
HER MAN GILBEY (1949, GB, Universal)—Joan Heseltine

WARD, POLLY
ANNIE LAURIE (1927, Silent, MGM)—Annie Laurie

WARD, RACHEL
THE GOOD WIFE (1987, Australia, Atlantic)—Marge Hills

WARD, ROBIN
DR. FRANKENSTEIN ON CAMPUS (1970, Canada, Agincourt-Glen Warren)—Viktor Frankenstein

WARD, SIMON
YOUNG WINSTON (1972, GB, Columbia)—Winston Churchill
ACES HIGH (1977, GB, Cine Artists)—Crawford
THE CHOSEN (1978, GB/Italy, AIP)—Angel Caine

WARDE, FREDERICK
HINTON'S DOUBLE (1917, Silent, Thanhouser)—Joshua Stephens/John Evart Hinton

WARDEN, JACK
12 ANGRY MEN (1957, United Artists)—Juror No. 7
PASSED AWAY (1992, Hollywood Pictures)—Jack Scanlan

WARE, HELEN
ONE NIGHT AT SUSIE'S (1930, Warners) -Susie

WARNER, DAVID
MORGAN! (1966, GB, Cinema V)—Morgan Delt

WARNER, H. B.
THE MAN WHO TURNED WHITE (1919, Silent, Superior)—Capt. Rand/Ali Zaman
WHISPERING SMITH (1926, Silent, Producers Releasing Corp.)—Luke "Whispering" Smith
THE KING OF KINGS (1927, Silent, DeMille Pictures)—Jesus Christ
THE CRUSADER (1932, Majestic)—Phillip Brandon
SORRELL AND SON (1934, GB, United Artists)—Capt. Stephen Sorrell

WARNER, JACK
HERE COME THE HUGGETTS (1948, GB, Gainsborough)—Joe Huggett
MY BROTHER'S KEEPER (1949, GB, Rank)—George Martin

WARNER, STEVEN
THE LITTLE PRINCE (1974, GB, Paramount)—The Little Prince

WARREN, ALYN
THE COURTSHIP OF MILES STANDISH (1923, Silent, Associated Exhibitors) - Miles Standish

WARREN, BRUCE
MOTHER AND SON (1931, Monogram)—Son

WARREN, GARY
THE RAILWAY CHILDREN (1971, GB, Universal)—Peter

WARREN, GLORIA
CINDERELLA SWINGS IT (1942, RKO)—Betty Palmer

WARREN, JAMES
WANDERER OF THE WASTELAND (1945, RKO)—Adam Larey
THREE FOR BEDROOM C (1952, Warners)—Oli J. Thrumm

WARREN, LESLEY ANN
PICKUP ON 101 (1972, American International)—Nickie

WARREN, MICHAEL
NORMAN. . .IS THAT YOU? (1976, MGM/United Artists)—Norman Chambers

WARRENDER, HAROLD
IVORY HUNTER (1952, GB, Ealing)—Mannering

WARWICK, DIONNE
SLAVES (1969, Continental)—Cassy

WARWICK, JOHN
PASSENGER TO LONDON (1937, GB, Fox British)—Frank Drayton
BAD BOY (1938, GB, Radius)—Nick Bryan
JOHN HALIFAX — GENTLEMAN (1938, GB, MGM)—John Halifax

WARWICK, ROBERT
ALL MAN (1916, Silent, Peerless/World)—Jim Blake
THE MAN WHO FORGOT (1917, Silent, World)—John Smith
JACK STRAW (1920, Silent, Paramount)—Archduke Sebastian (Jack Straw)
THE RETURN OF JIMMY VALENTINE (1936, Republic)—"Jimmy Valentine" Davis
GANGSTER'S BOY (1938, Monogram)—Tim "Knuckles" Kelly

WASHBOURNE, MONA
MRS. BROWN, YOU'VE GOT A LOVELY DAUGHTER (1968, GB, MGM)—Mrs. Brown

WASHBURN, BRYANT
SKINNER'S DRESS SUIT (1917, Silent, Universal)—William Henry Skinner
AN AMATEUR DEVIL (1921, Silent, Paramount)—Carver Endicott
MY HUSBAND'S WIVES (1924, Silent, Fox)—William Harvey
SKINNER'S BIG IDEA (1928, Silent, FBO)—William Henry Skinner

WASHINGTON, DENZEL
THE MIGHTY QUINN (1989, MGM-United Artists)—Xavier Quinn

WASSON, CRAIG
THE OUTSIDER (1980, Paramount)—Michael Flaherty
FOUR FRIENDS (1981, Filmways)—Danilo Prozor
MEN'S CLUB (1986, Paramount)—Paul

WATERMAN, DENNIS
MY LOVER, MY SON (1970, GB, MGM)—James Anderson

WATERMAN, FELICITY
LENA'S HOLIDAY (1991, Prism/Crown)—Lena Jung

WATERS, DORIS
GERT AND DAISY'S WEEKEND (1941, GB, Butchers)—Daisy
GERT AND DAISY CLEAN UP (1942, GB, Butchers)—Daisy

WATERS, ELSIE
GERT AND DAISY'S WEEKEND (1941, GB, Butchers)—Gert
GERT AND DAISY CLEAN UP (1942, GB, Butchers)—Gert

WATERSTON, SAM
THREE (1969, GB, United Artists)—Taylor
SWEET WILLIAM (1980, GB, World Northal)

WATFORD, GWENDOLINE
THE FALL OF THE HOUSE OF USHER (1952, GB, Vigilant)—Lady Usher

WATKINS, GARY
DESERT WARRIOR (1985, Cinema Group)—Trace

WATKINS, LINDA
GOOD SPORT (1931, Fox)—Marilyn Parker
SOB SISTER (1931, Fox)—Jane Ray

WATSON, BOBBY (BOBS)
THE DEVIL WITH HITLER (1942, United Artists)—Adolf Hitler
HITLER—DEAD OR ALIVE (1942, Charles House)—Adolf Hitler
THAT NAZTY NUISANCE (1943, United Artists)—Adolf Hitler
THE HITLER GANG (1944, Paramount)—Adolf Hitler

WATSON, DEBBIE
TAMMY AND THE MILLIONAIRE (1967, Universal)

WATSON, HARRY
PENROD AND SAM (1937, Warners)—Sam Williams

WATTS, JEANNE
THREE SISTERS (1974, GB, British Lion)—Olga

WATTS, SAL
SOLOMON KING (1974, Sal-Wa-Stage Struck)—Solomon King

WAYANS, KEENAN IVORY
I'M GONNA GET YOU SUCKA (1988, MGM-United Artists)—Jack Spade

WAYNE, DAVID
M (1951, Columbia)—Martin Harrow

WAYNE, JOHN
MEN ARE LIKE THAT (1931, Columbia)—Lt. Bob Benton
HIS PRIVATE SECRETARY (1933, Screencraft)—Dick Wallace
THE MAN FROM MONTEREY (1933, Warners)—Capt. John Holmes
THE LUCKY TEXAN (1934, Monogram)—Jerry Mason
RANDY RIDES ALONE (1934, Monogram)—Randy Bowers
THE STAR PACKER (1934, Monogram)—John Travers
DAWN RIDER (1935, Lone Star)—John Mason
KING OF THE PECOS (1936, Republic)—John Clayburn
I COVER THE WAR (1937, Universal)—Bob Adams
IDOL OF THE CROWDS (1937, Universal)—Johnny Hanson
PALS OF THE SADDLE (1938, Republic)—Stony Brooke
A MAN BETRAYED (1941, Republic)—Lynn Hollister
TALL IN THE SADDLE (1944, RKO)—Rocklin
ANGEL AND THE BADMAN (1947, Republic)—Quirt Evans
THE THREE GODFATHERS (1948, MGM)—Robert Marmaduke Hightower
THE FIGHTING KENTUCKIAN (1949, Republic)—John Breen
BIG JIM MCLAIN (1952, Warners)—Jim McLain
THE QUIET MAN (1952, Republic)—Sean Thornton
HONDO (1953, Warners)—Hondo Lane
THE CONQUEROR (1956, RKO)—Temujin
THE SEARCHERS (1956, Warners)—Ethan Edwards
THE BARBARIAN AND THE GEISHA (1958, 20th Century Fox)—Townsend Harris
THE MAN WHO SHOT LIBERTY VALANCE (1962, Paramount)—Tom Doniphon
DONOVAN'S REEF (1963, Paramount)—Guns Donovan
MCLINTOCK! (1963, United Artists)—George Washington McLintock
THE SONS OF KATIE ELDER (1965, Paramount)—John Elder
HELLFIGHTERS (1968, Universal)—Chanc Buckman
CHISUM (1970, Warners)—John Chisum
BIG JAKE (1971, National General)—Jacob McCandles

CAHILL, UNITED STATES MARSHAL (1973, Warners)—J.D. Cahill
MCQ (1974, Warners)—Det. Lt. Lon McQ
BRANNIGAN (1975, GB, United Artists)—Jim Brannigan
ROOSTER COGBURN (1975, Universal)—Rooster Cogburn
THE SHOOTIST (1976, Paramount)—John Bernard Books

WAYNE, PATRICK
SINBAD AND THE EYE OF THE TIGER (1977, Columbia)—Sinbad

WEATHERS, CARL
ACTION JACKSON (1988, Lorimar)—Action Jackson
HURRICANE SMITH (1992, Australia, Warner Brothers/Greater Union)—Billy Smith

WEAVER, DENNIS
SEVEN ANGRY MEN (1955, Allied Artists)—John Brown Jr.

WEAVER, LEON
ARKANSAS JUDGE (1941, Republic)—Abner

WEAVER, MARJORIE
SALLY, IRENE AND MARY (1938, 20th Century Fox)—Mary Stevens
THREE BLIND MICE (1938, 20th Century Fox)—Moira Charters
THE CISCO KID AND THE LADY (1939, 20th Century Fox)—Julie Lawson
THE MAD MARTINDALES (1942, 20th Century Fox)—Evelyn Martindale

WEAVING, HUGO
THE RIGHT HAND MAN (1987, Australia, New World)—Ned Devine

WEBB, CHLOE
SID & NANCY (1986, GB, Goldwyn)—Nancy Sungen

WEBB, CLIFTON
SITTING PRETTY (1948, 20th Century Fox)—Lynn Belvedere
MR. BELVEDERE GOES TO COLLEGE (1949, 20th Century Fox)—Lynn Belvedere
MR. BELVEDERE RINGS THE BELL (1951, 20th Century Fox)—Lynn Belvedere
MR. SCOUTMASTER (1953, 20th Century Fox)—Robert Jordan
THE REMARKABLE MR. PENNYPACKER (1959, 20th Century Fox)—Pa Pennypacker

WEBB, DICK
BARNABY (1919, Silent, Barker)—Barnaby

WEBB, GEOFFREY
DAVID AND JONATHAN (1920, Silent, GB, General)—David Mortlake

WEBB, JACK
PETE KELLY'S BLUES (1955, Warners)—Pete Kelly
THE D.I. (1957, Warners)—T/Sgt. Jim Moore
THE LAST TIME I SAW ARCHIE (1961, United Artists)—Bill Bowers

WEBBER, DIANE
THE MERMAIDS OF TIBURON (1962, Aquarez-Pacifica)—Mermaid Queen

WEBBER, ROBERT
12 ANGRY MEN (1957, United Artists)—Juror No. 12

THE NUN AND THE SERGEANT (1962, United Artists)—Sgt. McGrath

WEBSTER, BEN
THE HOUSE OF TEMPERLEY (1913, Silent, GB, Jury)—Sir Charles Temperley
THE GAY LORD QUEX (1917, GB, Silent, Ideal)—Lord Quex

WEBSTER, MARY
EIGHTEEN AND ANXIOUS (1957, Republic)—Judy

WEIDLER, VIRGINIA
GIRL OF THE OZARKS (1936, Paramount)—Edie Moseley
BAD LITTLE ANGEL (1939, MGM)—Patsy

WEISMAN, ROBIN
THREE MEN AND A LITTLE LADY (1990, Buena Vista)—Mary

WEISSMULLER, JOHNNY
TARZAN, THE APE MAN (1932, MGM)—Tarzan
TARZAN AND HIS MATE (1934, MGM)—Tarzan
TARZAN ESCAPES (1936, MGM)—Tarzan
TARZAN FINDS A SON (1939, MGM)—Tarzan
TARZAN'S SECRET TREASURE (1941, MGM)—Tarzan
TARZAN'S NEW YORK ADVENTURE (1942, MGM)—Tarzan
TARZAN'S DESERT MYSTERY (1943, RKO)—Tarzan
TARZAN TRIUMPHS (1943, RKO)—Tarzan
TARZAN AND THE AMAZONS (1945, RKO)—Tarzan
TARZAN AND THE LEOPARD WOMAN (1946, RKO)—Tarzan
TARZAN AND THE HUNTRESS (1947, RKO)—Tarzan
JUNGLE JIM (1948, Columbia)—Jungle Jim
TARZAN AND THE MERMAIDS (1948, RKO)—Tarzan
JUNGLE JIM IN THE FORBIDDEN LAND (1952, Columbia)—Jungle Jim

WELCH, JAMES
THE NEW CLOWN (1916, GB, Silent, Ideal)—Lord Cyril Garston

WELCH, RAQUEL
FATHOM (1967, 20th Century Fox)—Fathom Harvill
HANNIE CALDER (1971, GB, Paramount)—Hannie Calder
KANSAS CITY BOMBER (1972, MGM)—Diane "K.C." Carr
MOTHER, JUGS AND SPEED (1976, 20th Century Fox)—Jugs

WELD, TUESDAY
PRETTY POISON (1968, 20th Century Fox)—Sue Ann Stepanek

WELFORD, NANCY
GOLD DIGGERS ON BROADWAY (1929, Warners)—Jerry
JAZZ CINDERELLA (1930, Chesterfield)—Patricia Murray

WELLER, PETER
THE ADVENTURES OF BUCKAROO BANZAI: ACROSS THE 8TH DIMENSION (1984, 20th Century Fox)—Buckaroo Banzai
ROBOCOP (1987, Orion)—Alex J. Murphy/Robocop
ROBOCOP 2 (1990, Orion)—Robocop

WELLES, ORSON
CITIZEN KANE (1941, Mercury/RKO)—Charles Foster Kane
THE STRANGER (1946, RKO)—Prof. Charles Rankin/Franz Kindler
MACBETH (1948, Republic)—Macbeth
THE THIRD MAN (1950, GB, London Films)—Harry Lime
OTHELLO (1955, United Artists)—Othello
MR. ARKADIN (1962, GB, Talbot-Cari)—Gregory Arkadin
THE V.I.P.S (1963, GB, MGM)—Max Buda

WELLS, JACQUELINE *See* **JULIE BISHOP**

WELLS, MARY
HOWARD THE DUCK (1986, Universal)—Howard T. Duck

WELLS, TICO
THE FIVE HEARTBEATS (1991, 20th Century Fox)—Choirboy

WELSH, KEN
RENO AND THE DOC (1984, Canada, New World)—Reginald "Reno" Coltchinsky

WESSEL, DICK
DICK TRACY VS. CUEBALL (1946, RKO)—Cueball

WEST, ADAM
BATMAN (1966, 20th Century Fox)—Batman (Bruce Wayne)

WEST, MAE
I'M NO ANGEL (1933, RKO)—Tira
SHE DONE HIM WRONG (1933, Paramount)—Lady Lou
BELLE OF THE NINETIES (1934, Paramount)—Ruby Carter
MY LITTLE CHICKADEE (1940, Universal)—Flower Belle Lee

WEST, MARTIN
FRECKLES (1960, 20th Century Fox)—Freckles

WESTLEY, HELEN
ROBERTA (1935, RKO)—Roberta

WESTOVER, WINIFRED
ANNE OF LITTLE SMOKY (1921, Silent, Playgoers)—Anne Brockton
LUMMOX (1930, United Artists)—Bertha Oberg

WETHERELL, M.A.
LIVINGSTONE (1925, GB, Silent, Butchers)—David Livingstone
ROBINSON CRUSOE (1927, GB, Silent, Epic)—Robinson Crusoe

WHALEN, MICHAEL
THE MAN I MARRY (1936, Universal)—Ken Durkin

WHATLEY, FRANK
THE DOORS (1991, Tri-Star)—Robby Krieger

WHEATON, WIL
TOY SOLDIERS (1991, Tri-Star)—Joey Trotta

WHEELER, BERT
COCKEYED CAVALIERS (1934, RKO)—Bert
THE NITWITS (1935, RKO)—Johnnie
THE RAINMAKERS (1935, Radio Pictures)—Billy

WHITAKER, CHRISTINE
ASSAULT OF THE KILLER BIMBOS (1988, Empire)—Peaches

WHITAKER, FOREST
PLATOON (1987, Orion)—Big Harold
BIRD (1988, Warners)—Charlie "Yardbird" Parker

WHITAKER, JOHNNIE
NAPOLEON AND SAMANTHA (1972, Buena Vista)—Napoleon Wilson
TOM SAWYER (1973, United Artists)—Tom Sawyer

WHITE, ALICE
LINGERIE (1928, Silent, Tiffany)—Angele Ree / "Lingerie"
SHOW GIRL (1928, Warners)—Dixie Dugan
NAUGHTY BABY (1929, Silent, First National)—Rosie McGill
THE GIRL FROM WOOLWORTH'S (1929, First National)—Pat King
SHOW GIRL IN HOLLYWOOD (1930, Warners)—Dixie Dugan
SWEET MAMA (1930, First National)—Goldie
THE WIDOW FROM CHICAGO (1930, First National)—Polly Henderson
THE NAUGHTY FLIRT (1931, Warners)—Kay Elliott

WHITE, CAROL
LINDA (1960, GB, Independent Artists)—Linda
POOR COW (1968, GB, National General)—Joy
DULCIMA (1971, GB, EMI)—Dulcima Gaskain

WHITE, CHRISSIE
LILY OF THE ALLEY (1923, GB, Hepworth)—Lily

WHITE, DEAN
RETURN OF THE BADMEN (1948, RKO)—Billy the Kid

WHITE, J. FISHER
THE MAN WHO MADE DIAMONDS (1937, GB, Warners)—Prof. Calthrop

WHITELAW, BILLIE
THE KRAYS (1990, GB, Rank)—Violet Kray

WHITELEY, JON
THE LITTLEST KIDNAPPERS (1954, GB, United Artists)—Harry

WHITEMAN, PAUL
THE KING OF JAZZ (1930, Universal)—Paul Whiteman

WHITESIDE, WALKER
THE BELGIAN (1917, Silent, Olcott)—Victor Morenne

WHITING, LEONARD
ROMEO AND JULIET (1968, GB/Italy, Paramount)—Romeo

WHITMAN, ALFRED
CAVANAUGH OF THE RANGERS (1918, Silent, Vitagraph)—Ross Cavanaugh

WHITMAN, STUART
JOHNNY TROUBLE (1957, Warners)—Johnny
THOSE MAGNIFICENT MEN IN THEIR FLYING MACHINES (1965, GB, 20th Century Fox)—Orvil Newton

WHITMAN, WALT
THE TAR HEEL WARRIOR (1917, Silent, Triangle)—Col. Dabney Mills

WHITMORE, JAMES
MRS. O'MALLEY AND MR. MALONE (1950, MGM)—John J. Malone
THE OUTRIDERS (1950, MGM)—Clint Priest
FACE OF FIRE (1959, Allied Artists)—Monk Johnson
BLACK LIKE ME (1964, Continental)—John Finley Horton
OLD EXPLORERS (1990, Taurus)—Leinen Roth

WHITTY, DAME MAY
THE LADY VANISHES (1938, GB, Gaumont)—Miss Froy

WIDDOES, KATHLEEN
THE GROUP (1966, United Artists)—Helena Davison

WIDMAN, JOHN
MY AMERICAN COUSIN (1986, Canada, Spectrafilm)—Butch Walker

WIDMARK, RICHARD
SLATTERY'S HURRICANE (1949, 20th Century Fox)—Will
Slattery
THE FROGMAN (1951, 20th Century Fox)—Lt. Cmdr. John
Lawrence
MY PAL GUS (1952, 20th Century Fox)—Dave Jennings
TWO RODE TOGETHER (1961, Columbia)—Lt. Jim Gary
MADIGAN (1968, Universal)—Det. Daniel Madigan
DEATH OF A GUNFIGHTER (1969, Universal)—Marshal
Frank Patch

WIECK, DOROTHEA
MISS FANE'S BABY IS STOLEN (1934, Paramount)—
Madeline Fane

WIEST, DIANNE
HANNAH AND HER SISTERS (1986, Orion)—Holly
PARENTHOOD (1989, Universal)—Helen

WILBUR, CRANE
THE LOVE LIAR (1916, Silent, Centaur)—David McCare

WILBUR, GEORGE
HALLOWEEN IV: THE RETURN OF MICHAEL MYERS (1988,
Galaxy)—Michael Myers

WILBY, JAMES
MAURICE (1987, GB, Cinecom)—Maurice Hall

WILCOX, CLAIRE
FORTY POUNDS OF TROUBLE (1962, Universal)—Penny Piper

WILD, LOIS
CARYL OF THE MOUNTAINS (1936, Marcy/Reliable)—
Caryl Foray

WILDE, CORNELL
THE BANDIT OF SHERWOOD FOREST (1946, Columbia)—
Robert of Nottingham
OMAR KHAYYAM (1957, Paramount)—Omar Khayyam
SWORD OF LANCELOT (1963, GB, Universal)—Lancelot
THE NAKED PREY (1966, Paramount)—The Man

WILDE, LEE
TWICE BLESSED (1945, MGM)—Terry Turner

WILDE, LYNN
TWICE BLESSED (1945, MGM)—Stephanie Hale

WILDE, SONYA
I PASSED FOR WHITE (1960, Allied Artists)—Bernice Lee/Lila
Brownell

WILDER, GENE
THE PRODUCERS (1967, Embassy)—Leo Bloom
QUACKSER FORTUNE HAS A COUSIN IN THE BRONX (1970,
UMC)—Quackser Fortune
WILLIE WONKA AND THE CHOCOLATE FACTORY (1971,
Paramount)—Willie Wonka
YOUNG FRANKENSTEIN (1974, 20th Century Fox)—Dr.
Frederick Frankenstein
THE ADVENTURES OF SHERLOCK HOLMES' SMARTER
BROTHER (1975, GB, 20th Century Fox)—Sigerson Holmes
THE WORLD'S GREATEST LOVER (1977, 20th Century Fox)—
Rudy Valentine
THE FRISCO KID (1979, Warners)—Avram Belinsky

STIR CRAZY (1980, Columbia)—Skip Donahue
HAUNTED HONEYMOON (1986, Orion)—Larry Abbot
SEE NO EVIL, HEAR NO EVIL (1989, Tri-Star)—Dave Lyons
ANOTHER YOU (1991, Tri-Star)—George/Abe Fielding

WILDING, MICHAEL
THE COURTNEY AFFAIR (1947, GB, British Lion)—Sir Edward
Courtney
HER MAN GIBLEY (1949, GB, Universal)—Tom Gibley
THE MAN IN THE DINGHY (1951, GB, Snader)—Nicholas
Foster
TRENT'S LAST CASE (1953, GB, British Lion)—Philip Trent

WILKES, DONNA
ANGEL (1984, New World)—Angel/Molly

WILKES, JEAN
THE KING AND FOUR QUEENS (1956, United Artists)—Ruby

WILKES, KEITH
CORNBREAD, EARL AND ME (1975, American International)—
Cornbread

WILLEY, EDDIE
JACK, SAM AND PETE (1919, Silent, GB, Pollock-
Daring)—Sam

WILLIAM, WARREN
BEAUTY AND THE BEAST (1932, Warners)—Baron von Ullrich
THE MATCH KING (1932, First National)—Paul Kroll
THE MOUTHPIECE (1932, Warners)—Vincent Day
THE MIND READER (1933, First National)—Chandra Chandler
SATAN MET A LADY (1936, Warners)—Ted Shayne
TIMES SQUARE PLAYBOY (1936, Warners)—Vic Arnold
THE LONE WOLF SPY HUNT (1939, Columbia)—Michael
Lanyard
THE LONE WOLF KEEPS A DATE (1940, Columbia)—Michael
Lanyard
THE LONE WOLF MEETS A LADY (1940, Columbia)—Michael
Lanyard
THE LONE WOLF STRIKES (1940, Columbia)—Michael Lanyard
THE LONE WOLF TAKES A CHANCE (1941, Columbia)—
Michael Lanyard
SECRETS OF THE LONE WOLF (1941, Columbia)—Michael
Lanyard

WILLIAMS, BILL
THE CLAY PIDGEON (1949, RKO)—Jim Fletcher
ROOKIE FIREMAN (1950, Columbia)—Joe Blake

WILLIAMS, BILLY DEE
BINGO LONG TRAVELING ALL STARS AND MOTOR KINGS
(1976, Motown/Pan Arts)—Bingo Long
SCOTT JOPLIN (1977, Universal)—Scott Joplin

WILLIAMS, BRANSBY
ADAM BEDE (1918, Silent, GB, International Exclusives)—
Adam Bede

WILLIAMS, CLARA
THE CRIMINAL (1916, Silent, Triangle)—Naneta

WILLIAMS, EMYLN
THEY DRIVE BY NIGHT (1938, GB, Warners)—Shorty Matthews
I ACCUSE (1958, GB, MGM)—Emile Zola

WILLIAMS, ESTHER
BATHING BEAUTY (1944, MGM)—Caroline Brooks
NEPTUNE'S DAUGHTER (1949, MGM)—Eve Barrett
THE DUCHESS OF IDAHO (1950, MGM)—Christine Riverton Duncan
MILLION DOLLARD MERMAID (1952, MGM)—Annette Kellerman
DANGEROUS WHEN WET (1953, MGM)—Katy
EASY TO LOVE (1953, MGM)—Julie Hallerton
JUPITER'S DAUGHTER (1955, MGM)—Amytis

WILLIAMS, GRANT
THE INCREDIBLE SHRINKING MAN (1957, Universal)— Scott Carey

WILLIAMS, GUINN "BIG BOY"
THE JACK RIDER (1921, Silent, Aywon)—Frank Stevens
THE FRESHIE (1922, Silent, Herbst/Di Lorenzo)—Charles Taylor
CYCLONE JONES (1923, Silent, Aywon)—Cyclone Jones
THE COWBOY KING (1928, Silent, Fox)—Jim Barrett
MY MAN (1928, Warners)—Joe Halsey

WILLIAMS, GUY
CAPTAIN SINBAD (1953, MGM)—Captain Sinbad
SEVEN ANGRY MEN (1955, Allied Artists)—Salmon Brown
THE SIGN OF ZORRO (1960, Buena Vista)—Zorro (Don Diego)
DAMON AND PYTHIAS (1962, MGM)—Damon

WILLIAMS, HUGH
CHARLEY'S AUNT (1930, Columbia)—Charley Wykeham
SORRELL AND SON (1934, GB, United Artists)—Kit Sorrell
LIEUTENANT DARING, RN (1935, GB, Butchers)—Lt. Bob Daring
HIS LORDSHIP GOES TO PRESS (1939, GB, RKO)—Lord Bill Wilmer
AN IDEAL HUSBAND (1948, GB, British Lion)—Sir Robert Chiltern

WILLIAMS, JOBETH
AMERICAN DREAMER (1984, Warners)—Cathy Palmer

WILLIAMS, JOHN
EMIL (1938, GB, Gaumont)—Emil Blake

WILLIAMS, JOYCE
PRIVATE DUTY NURSES (1972, New World)—Lola

WILLIAMS, KENNETH
THE HOUND OF THE BASKERVILLES (1980, GB, Hemdale)— Sir Henry Baskerville

WILLIAMS, KIMBERLY
FATHER OF THE BRIDE (1991, Buena Vista/Touchstone)— Annie Banks

WILLIAMS, RICHARD
HEART OF A CHILD (1958, GB, Rank)—Karl Spell
THE CHILD AND THE KILLER (1959, GB, United Artists)— Tommy Martin

WILLIAMS, ROBIN
POPEYE (1980, Paramount)—Popeye
THE WORLD ACCORDING TO GARP (1982, Warners)—T.S. Garp
THE SURVIVORS (1983, Columbia)—Donald Quinelle
CADILLAC MAN (1990, Orion)—Joey O'Brien

THE FISHER KING (1991, Tri-Star)—Parry

WILLIAMS, TREAT
PRINCE OF THE CITY (1981, Warners)—Daniel Ciello
THE PURSUIT OF D.B. COOPER (1981, Universal)—Meade (D.B. Cooper)
MEN'S CLUB (1986, Paramount)—Terry

WILLIAMSON, FRED
HAMMER (1972, United Artists)—B.J. Hammer
THE LEGEND OF NIGGER CHARLEY (1972, Paramount)— Nigger Charley
BLACK CAESAR (1973, American International)—Tommy Gibbs
THE SOUL OF NIGGER CHARLEY (1973, Paramount)—Nigger Charley
THAT MAN BOLT (1973, Universal)—Jefferson Bolt
BOSS NIGGER (1974, Boss/Dimension)—Boss Nigger
JOSHUA (1976, Lone Star)—Joshua
MEET JOHNNY BARROWS (1976, Atlas)—Johnny Barrows

WILLIAMSON, NICOL
HAMLET (1969, GB, Woodfall-Filmways)—Hamlet
THE EXORCIST III (1990, 20th Century Fox)—Father Morning

WILLIS, BRUCE
BLIND DATE (1987, Tri-Star)—Walter Davis
DIE HARD (1988, 20th Century Fox)—John McClane
LOOK WHO'S TALKING (1989, Tri-Star)—Voice of Mikey
DIE HARD 2 (1990, 20th Century Fox)—John McClane
HUDSON HAWKE (1991, Tri-Star)—Hudson Hawke
THE LAST BOY SCOUT (1991, Warner Brothers)—Joe Hallenbeck

WILLIS, DAVE
ME AND MY PAL (1939, GB, Pathe)—Dave Craig

WILLS, ANEKE
THE PLEASURE GIRLS (1966, GB, Times)—Angela

WILLS, BREMER
WHAT HAPPENED TO HARKNESS (1934, GB, Warners)— Bernard Harkness

WILMER, DOUGLAS
THE ADVENTURES OF SHERLOCK HOLMES' SMARTER BROTHER (1976, 20th Century Fox)—Sherlock Holmes

WILSON, AL
THE AIR HAWK (1924, Silent, Film Booking Offices)—Al Parker
"SKY-HIGH" SAUNDERS (1927, Silent, Universal)—"Sky-High" Saunders
THE SKY SKIDDER (1929, Silent, Universal)—Al Simpkins

WILSON, LEWIS
SAILORS' HOLIDAY (1944, Columbia)—Iron Man Collins

WILSON, LOIS
WHAT EVERY WOMAN KNOWS (1934, MGM)—Maggie Wylie

WILSON, MARGERY
BRIDE OF HATE (1916, Silent, Triangle/Kay-Bee)—Mercedes Mendoza

WILSON, MARIE
SWEEPSTAKES WINNER (1939, Warners)—Jenny Jones
MY FRIEND IRMA (1949, Paramount)—Irma Peterson

MY FRIEND IRMA GOES WEST (1950, Paramount)—Irma Peterson

WILSON, SCOTT
THE GRISSOM GANG (1971, Cinerama)—Slim Grissom

WIMBLEY, DAMON
DISORDERLIES (1987, Warners)—Kool Rock

WIMMER, BRIAN
LATE FOR DINNER (1991, Columbia)—Willie Husband

WINDSOR, CLAIRE
NELLIE, THE BEAUTIFUL CLOAK MODEL (1924, Silent, Cosmopolitan)—Nellie
JUST A WOMAN (1925, Silent, First National)—June Holton

WINDSOR, MARIE
DAKOTA LIL (1950, 20th Century Fox)—Dakota Lil

WINFIELD, PAUL
GORDON'S WAR (1973, 20th Century Fox)—Gordon

WINFRIED, WINNA
LITTLE MISS NOBODY (1933, GB, Warners)—Karen Bergen
NAUGHTY CINDERELLA (1933, GB, Warners)—Brita Rasmusson

WINGER, DEBRA
LEGAL EAGLES (1986, Universal)—Laura Kelly
BETRAYED (1988, MGM/United Artists)—Catherine Weaver

WINKLER, HENRY
THE ONE AND ONLY (1978, Paramount)—Andy Schmidt

WINNINGER, CHARLES
FRIENDLY ENEMIES (1942, United Artists)—Karl Pfeiffer

WINSLOW, GEORGE "FOGHORN"
MY PAL GUS (1952, 20th Century Fox)—Gus Jennings
GENTLEMEN PREFER BLONDES (1953, 20th Century Fox)—Henry Spofford III

WINTER, ALEX
BILL & TED'S EXCELLENT ADVENTURE (1989, Orion)—Bill S. Preston
BILL & TED'S BOGUS JOURNEY (1991, Orion)—Bill S. Preston

WINTER, VINCENT
THE LITTLE KIDNAPPERS (1954, GB, United Artists)—Davy

WINTERS, D.D.
TANYA'S ISLAND (1981, Canada, Int. Film Exchange)—Tanya

WINTERS, JONATHAN
OH DAD, POOR DAD, MAMA'S HUNG YOU IN THE CLOSET AND I'M FEELIN' SO SAD (1967, Paramount)—Dad Rosepettle

WINTERS, SHELLEY
FRENCHIE (1950, Universal)—Frenchie Fontaine
SOUTH SEA SINNER (1950, Universal)—Coral
MY MAN AND I (1952, MGM)—Nancy
BLOODY MAMA (1970, American International)—Kate "Ma" Barker
WHAT'S THE MATTER WITH HELEN? (1971, United Artists)—Helen Hill
WHO SLEW AUNTIE ROO? (1971, American International)—Rosie Forrest

WIRTH, BILLY
WAR PARTY (1989, Tri-Star)—Sonny Crowkiller

WISDOM, NORMAN
MAN OF THE MOMENT (1955, GB, Group)—Norman
JUST MY LUCK (1957, GB, Rank)—Norman
THE SQUARE PEG (1958, GB, Rank)—Norman Pitkin
THE EARLY BIRD (1965, GB, Rank)—Norman Pitkin

WISE, ERNIE
THE MAGNIFICENT TWO (1967, Rank)—Ernie

WISEMAN, JOSEPH
DR. NO (1962, GB, United Artists)—Dr. No

WITCHER, GUY
THE POWER OF ONE (1992, Warner Brothers)—P.K. at 7

WITHERS, GOOGIE
THE LOVES OF JOANNA GODDEN (1947, GB, Ealing)—Joanna Godden
THE NICKEL QUEEN (1971, Australia, Woomera)—Meg Blake

WITHERS, GRANT
SATURDAY'S CHILDREN (1940, Warners)—Jim O'Neill
DANCING SWEETIES (1930, Warners)—Bill Cleaver

WITHERS, JANE
GINGER (1935, Fox)—Ginger
PADDY O'DAY (1935, Fox)—Paddy O'Day
LITTLE MISS NOBODY (1936, 20th Century Fox)—Judy Devlin
PEPPER (1936, 20th Century Fox)—Pepper Jolly
CHECKERS (1937, 20th Century Fox)—Checkers
THE HOLY TERROR (1937. 20th Century Fox)—Corky Wallace
ARIZONA WILDCAT (1938, 20th Century Fox)—Mary Jane Patterson
GIRL FROM AVENUE A (1940, 20th Century Fox)—Jane
HER FIRST BEAU (1941, Columbia)—Penny Wood
SMALL TOWN DEB (1941, 20th Century Fox)—Patricia Randell
A VERY YOUNG LADY (1941, 20th Century Fox)—Kitty Russell
THE MAD MARTINDALES (1942, 20th Century Fox)—Kathy Martindale
MY BEST GAL (1944, Republic)—Kitty O'Hara
AFFAIRS OF GERALDINE (1946, Republic)—Geraldine Cooper

WOLF, HILLARY
BIG GIRLS DON'T CRY . . . THEY GET EVEN (1992, New Line)—Laura

WOLFIT, DONALD
THE RINGER (1953, GB, London/Regent)—Dr. Lomond
SVENGALI (1955, GB, MGM)—Svengali

WONG, ANNA MAY
DAUGHTER OF THE DRAGON (1931, Paramount)—Ling Moy
DAUGHTER OF SHANGHAI (1937, Paramount)—Lan Ying Lin
LADY FROM CHUNKING (1943, Producers Releasing Corp.)—Kwan Mei

WONTER, ARTHUR
A GENTLEMAN OF PARIS (1931, GB, Gaumont)—Judge Le Fevre
SHERLOCK HOLMES' FATAL HOUR (1931, GB, First Division)—Sherlock Holmes
THE TRIUMPH OF SHERLOCK HOLMES (1935, GB, Real Art)—Sherlock Holmes

WOOD, HELEN
GIVE A GIRL A BREAK (1953, MGM)—Joanna Moss

WOOD, LANA
SATAN'S MISTRESS (1982, Motion Picture Marketing)—Lisa

WOOD, NATALIE
THE GIRL HE LEFT BEHIND (1956, Warners)—Susan Daniels
MARJORIE MORNINGSTAR (1958, Warners)—Marjorie Morgenstern
GYPSY (1962, Warners)—Louise Hovick (Gypsy Rose Lee)
SEX AND THE SINGLE GIRL (1964, Warners)—Dr. Helen Brown
INSIDE DAISY CLOVER (1965)—Warners)—Daisy Clover
PENELOPE (1966, MGM)—Penelope Elcott
THIS PROPERTY IS CONDEMNED (1966, Paramount)—Alva Starr
BOB AND CAROL AND TED AND ALICE (1969, Columbia)—Carol
THE LAST MARRIED COUPLE IN AMERICA (1980, Universal)—Mari Thompson

WOOD, PEGGY
HOUSEKEEPER'S DAUGHTER (1939, United Artists)—Olga

WOODBURY, JOAN
TWO LATINS FROM MANHATTAN (1941, Columbia)—Lois Morgan

WOODMAN, PARDOE
THE MYSTERY OF MR. BERNARD BROWN (1921, Silent, GB, Stoll)—Bernard Brown

WOODRUFF, JAMES
PUMPKINHEAD (1988, MGM-United Artists)—Pumpkinhead

WOODS, DONALD
ONCE A DOCTOR (1937, Warners)—Steven Brace
TALENT SCOUT (1937, Warners)—Steve Stewart
I WAS A PRISONER ON DEVIL'S ISLAND (1941, Columbia)—Joel Grant
SO'S YOUR UNCLE (1943, Universal)—Steve Curtis
TAMMY AND THE MILLIONAIRE (1967, Universal)—John Brent

WOODS, ILENE
CINDERELLA (1950, Animated Disney/RKO)—Cinderella's Voice

WOODS, JAMES
JOSHUA, THEN AND NOW (1985, Canada, 20th Century Fox)—Joshua Shapiro
COP (1987, Atlantic)—Lloyd Hopkins
TRUE BELIEVER (1989, Columbia)—Ernie Dodd
IMMEDIATE FAMILY (1989, Columbia)—Michael Spector

WOODWARD, EDWARD
THE WICKER MAN (1974, GB, British Lion)—Sgt. Neil Howie
CALLAN (1975, GB, Cinema National)—Callan
BREAKER MORANT (1980, Australia, New World)—Lt. Harry Morant

WOODWARD, JOANNE
THREE FACES OF EVE (1957, 20th Century Fox)—Eve
THE STRIPPER (1963, 20th Century Fox)—Lila Green
A BIG HAND FOR THE LITTLE LADY (1966, Warners)—Mary
RACHEL, RACHEL (1968, Warners)—Rachel Cameron
THEY MIGHT BE GIANTS (1971, Universal)—Dr. Mildred Watson
MR. & MRS. BRIDGE (1990, Miramax)—India Bridge

WOOLLEY, MONTY
THE MAN WHO CAME TO DINNER (1942, Warners)—Sheridan Whiteside
THE PIED PIPER (1942, 20th Century Fox)—Howard
MOLLY AND ME (1945, 20th Century Fox)—Graham

WOOLSEY, ROBERT
COCKEYED CAVALIERS (1934, RKO)—Bob
THE NITWITS (1935, RKO)—Newton
THE RAINMAKERS (1935, Radio Pictures)—Roscoe

WOOLF, ED
THE COLOSSUS OF NEW YORK (1970, Paramount)—The Colossus

WORKMAN, JIMMY
THE ADDAMS FAMILY (1991, Paramount)—Pugsley Addams

WRAY, FAY
ANN CARVER'S PROFESSION (1933, Columbia)—Ann Carver
THE WOMAN I STOLE (1933, Columbia)—Vida Corew
THE COUNTESS OF MONTE CARLO (1934, Universal)—Janet
MADAME SPY (1934, Universal)—Maria Franck/B-24
WOMAN IN THE DARK (1934, RKO)—Louise Lorimer
ROAMING LADY (1936, Columbia)—Joyce
THEY MET IN A TAXI (1936, Columbia)—Mary
MELODY FOR THREE (1941, RKO)—Mary Stanley

WRAY, JOHN
THE CZAR OF BROADWAY (1930, Universal)—Mort Bradley

WRIGHT, HAIDEE
AUNT RACHEL (1920, Silent, GB, Samuelson/Granger)—Aunt Rachel

WRIGHT, MARIE
SILVER TOP (1938, GB, Paramount)—Mrs. Deeping

WRIGHT, MICHAEL
THE FIVE HEARTBEATS (1991, 20th Century Fox)—Eddie

WRIGHT, RICHARD
NATIVE SON (1951, Classic)—Bigger Thomas

WRIGHT, ROBIN
THE PRINCESS BRIDE (1987, 20th Century Fox)—Buttercup

WRIGHT, TERESA
THE IMPERFECT LADY (1947, Paramount)—Millicent Hopkins

WRIGHT, WILLIAM
PHILO VANCE RETURNS (1947, Producers Releasing Corp.)—Philo Vance

WYATT, JANE
THE LUCKIEST GIRL IN THE WORLD (1936, Universal)—Pat Duncan
GIRL FROM GOD'S COUNTRY (1940, Republic)—Anne Webster
WEEKEND FOR THREE (1941, RKO)—Ellen Craig
THE BACHELOR'S DAUGHTERS (1946, United Artists)—Marta

WYMAN, JANE
TORCHY PLAYS WITH FIRE (1939, Warners)—Torchy Blane

THE DOUGHGIRLS (1944, Warners)—Vivian
THE LADY TAKES A SAILOR (1949, Warners)—Jennifer Smith
LUCY GALLANT (1955, Paramount)—Lucy Gallant

WYNN, ED
THE CHIEF (1933, MGM)—Henry Summers

WYNN, GEORGE
THE FLAG LIEUTENANT (1919, GB, Silent, Jury)—Lt. Dicky Lascelles

WYNN, MAY
THE WHITE SQUAW (1956, Columbia)—Ectay-O-Wahnee

WYNNE, GILBERT
CLEGG (1969, GB, Tigon)—Harry Clegg

WYNTER, DANA
FRAULEIN (1958, 20th Century Fox)—Erika Angermann

Y

YAMA, CONRAD
THE CHAIRMAN (1969, 20th Century Fox)—The Chairman

YAMAGUCHI, SHIRLEY
JAPANESE WAR BRIDE (1952, 20th Century Fox)—Tae Shimizu

YARNALL, CELESTE
EVE (1968, GB, Commonwealth)—Eve

YORK, MICHAEL
THE STRANGE AFFAIR (1968, GB, Paramount)—Peter Strange
ENGLAND MADE ME (1973, GB, Cine Globe)—Anthony Farrant
THE FOUR MUSKETEERS (1975, 20th Century Fox)—D'Artagnan
LOGAN'S RUN (1976, MGM/United States)—Logan
THE LAST REMAKE OF BEAU GESTE (1977, Universal)—Beau Geste

YORK, SUSANNAH
JANE EYRE (1971, GB, British Lion)—Jane Eyre
X, Y & ZEE (1972, GB, Columbia)—Stella
THE MAIDS (1975, GB, CineFilms)—Claire
ELIZA FRASER (1976, Australia, Hexagon)—Eliza Fraser

YORKE, AUGUSTUS
THE TAILOR OF BOND STREET (1916, GB, Silent, Gerrard)—Marcovitch Einstein

YORKE, EDITH
MOTHERS-IN-LAW (1923, Silent, Preferred)—"Mom" Wingate

YOUNG, ALAN
AARON SLICK FROM PUNKIN CRICK (1952, Paramount)—Aaron Slick

ANDROCLES AND THE LION (1952, RKO)—Androcles
GENTLEMEN MARRY BRUNETTES (1955, United Artists)—Charles Biddle

YOUNG, BURT
UNCLE JOE SHANNON (1978, United Artists)—Joe Shannon

YOUNG, CLARA KIMBALL
LOLA (1914, Silent, World)—Lola
TRILBY (1915, Silent, World)—Trilby
CAMILLE (1916, Silent, World)—Camille
THE FORBIDDEN WOMAN (1920, Silent, Equity)—Diane Sorel
THE HANDS OF NARA (1922, Silent, Metro)—Nara Alexieff
CORDELIA THE MAGNIFICENT (1923, Silent, Metro)—Cordelia Marlow
MOTHER AND SON (1931, Monogram)—Mother

YOUNG, GIG
THE THREE MUSKETEERS (1948, MGM)—Porthos

YOUNG, LORETTA
THE GIRL IN THE GLASS CAGE (1929, First National)—Gladys Cosgrove
BIG BUSINESS GIRL (1931, Warners)—Claire McIntyre
TOO YOUNG TO MARRY (1931, Warners)—Elaine Bumpstead
PLAY GIRL (1932, Warners)—Buster
MIDNIGHT MARY (1933, MGM)—Mary Martin
SHE HAD TO SAY YES (1933, Warners)—Florence Denny
BORN TO BE BAD (1934, Fox/United Artists)—Letty Strong
LADIES IN LOVE (1936, 20th Century Fox)—Susie Schmidt
RAMONA (1936, 20th Century Fox)—Ramona
WIFE, DOCTOR AND NURSE (1937, 20th Century Fox)—Ina Lewis
THREE BLIND MICE (1938, 20th Century Fox)—Pamela Charters
WIFE, HUSBAND AND FRIEND (1939, 20th Century Fox)—Doris Blair Borland
DOCTOR TAKES A WIFE (1940, Columbia)—June Cameron
LADY FROM CHEYENNE (1941, Universal)—Annie
LADIES COURAGEOUS (1944, Universal)—Roberta Harper
THE PERFECT MARRIAGE (1946, Paramount)—Maggie Williams
THE BISHOP'S WIFE (1947, RKO)—Julia Brougham
THE FARMER'S DAUGHTER (1947, RKO)—Katrin Holstrom
RACHEL AND THE STRANGER (1948, RKO)—Rachel
ACCUSED (1949, Paramount)—Wilma Tuttle
MOTHER IS A FRESHMAN (1949, 20th Century Fox)—Abigail "Abby" Fortitude Abbott
HALF ANGEL (1951, 20th Century Fox)—Nora
PAULA (1952, Columbia)—Paula Rogers

YOUNG, ROBERT
SWORN ENEMY (1936, MGM)—"Hank" Sherman
RICH MAN, POOR GIRL (1938, MGM)—Bill Harrison
THREE COMRADES (1938, MGM)—Gottfried Lenz
H.M. PULHAM, ESQ. (1941, MGM)—Harry Pulham
MARRIED BACHELOR (1941, MGM)—Randolf Haven
JOE SMITH, ALL-AMERICAN (1942, MGM)—Joe Smith
CLAUDIA AND DAVID (1946, 20th Century Fox)—David Naughton
THEY WON'T BELIEVE ME (1947, RKO)—Larry Ballentine

YOUNG, ROLAND
HIS DOUBLE LIFE (1933, Paramount)—Priam Farrel

THE MAN WHO COULD WORK MIRACLES (1937, GB, United Artists)—George McWhirter Fotheringay
TOPPER (1937, MGM)—Cosmo Topper
TOPPER TAKES A TRIP (1939, United Artists)—Cosmo Topper
TOPPER RETURNS (1941, United Artists)—Cosmo Topper

YOUNG, SEAN
YOUNG DOCTORS IN LOVE (1982, 20th Century Fox)—Dr. Stephanie Brody
A KISS BEFORE DYING (1991, Universal)—Dory Carlsson

YOUNG, TONY
HE RIDES TALL (1964, Universal)—Marshal Morg Rocklin
TAGGART (1964, Universal)—Kent Taggart

YOUNGMAN, HENNY
A WAVE, A WAC AND A MARINE (1944, Monogram)—Henny

YOUNGS, JIM
HOT SHOT (1987, Arista)—Jimmy Kristidis

YULE, JOE
BRINGING UP FATHER (1946, Monogram)—Jiggs
JIGGS AND MAGGIE IN SOCIETY (1948, Monogram)—Jiggs
JIGGS AND MAGGIE OUT WEST (1950, Monogram)—Jiggs

YUNE, JOHNNY
THEY CALL ME BRUCE (1982, Film Ventures)—Bruce Won
THEY STILL CALL ME BRUCE (1987, Ji-Hee-Pandra/ Shapiro)—Bruce Won

YURKA, BLANCHE
QUEEN OF THE MOB (1940, Paramount)—Ma Webster

Z

ZADORA, PIA
THE LONELY LADY (1983, Universal)—Jerilee

ZAGAREA, ANITA
QUEEN OF HEARTS (1989, GB, Cinecom)—Rosa

ZAOURI, VANESSA
ALAN & NAOMI (1992, Triton)—Naomi Kirschenbaum

Z'DAR, ROBERT
THE NIGHT STALKER (1987, Chrystie-Striker/Almi)—Sommers
MANIAC COP (1988, Shapiro Glickenhaus)—Matt Cordell
MANIAC COP 2 (1990, Movie House Sales)—Matt Cordell

ZETTERLING, MAI
FRIEDA (1947, GB, Rank)—Frieda Dawson
THE GIRL IN THE PAINTING (1948, GB, Universal)—Hildegarde
NAUGHTY ARLETTE (1951, GB, United Artists)—Arlette
ONLY TWO CAN PLAY (1962, GB, Columbia)—Elizabeth Gruffydd-Williams

ZIEN, CHIP
HOWARD THE DUCK (1986, Universal)—Howard T. Duck

ZOE, NINA
GARBO TALKS (1984, MGM/United Artists)—Greta Garbo

ZORINA, VERA
ON YOUR TOES (1939, Warners)—Vera
I WAS AN ADVENTURESS (1940, 20th Century Fox)—Countess Tanya Vronsky

ZUCCO, GEORGE
DR. RENAULT'S SECRET (1942, 20th Century Fox)—Dr. Renault
THE MAD GHOUL (1943, Universal)—Dr. Alfred Morris
WHO KILLED "DOC" ROBBIN? (1945, United Artists)—Doc Robbin

ZUEHLKE, JOSHUA
AMAZING GRACE AND CHUCK (1987, Tri-Star)—Chuck Murdock

THE
TITLE
CHARACTERS

A

A NO. 1
EMPEROR OF THE NORTH POLE (1973, 20th Century Fox)—Thirties hobo **Lee Marvin** finally fights back against sadistic train guard Ernest Borgnine after the latter throws fellow "bo" Keith Carradine from the moving train to his death.

AARON
AARON LOVES ANGELA (1975, Columbia)—In a variation on the Romeo and Juliet theme, **Kevin Hooks** is a New York ghetto black in love with Puerto Rican Irene Cara.

AARONSON, RUTH
LITTLE MISS SMILES (1922, Silent, Fox)—The Aaronson family lives in a New York tenement and suffers many hardships but their cheerful young daughter **Shirley Mason** marries a doctor.

ABBOT, LARRY & VICKIE PEARLE
HAUNTED HONEYMOON (1986, Orion)—Radio star **Gene Wilder** takes his new bride **Gilda Radner** to meet his family in a spooky old house presided over by Dom DeLuise, playing Wilder's wealthy old aunt. Whatever happened to Wilder as a talented funny man?

ABBOTT, ABIGAIL "ABBY" FORTITUDE
MOTHER IS A FRESHMAN (1949, 20th Century Fox)—**Loretta Young** enrolls in college along with her daughter. Both fall for professor Van Johnson.

ABBOTT, CATHERINE
TWO BLONDES AND A REDHEAD (1947, Columbia)—**Jean Porter** is a college student who goes AWOL. to appear as a chorus girl in a Broadway show. When the show closes, she invites two of her chorine friends to her society home with predictable results.

ABBOTT, CONNIE
ORCHESTRA WIVES (1942, 20th Century Fox)—Small-town girl **Ann Rutherford** marries a trumpet player of a travelling band. She finds that marriage and one-night stands don't make for sweet music.

ABBOTT, DR. JOHN
A MAN TO REMEMBER (1938, RKO)—In this touching film, **Edward Ellis** portrays a country doctor filled with the milk of human kindness, sensitivity, understanding and community concern.

ABDEE, RICHARD
MASTER OF DRAGONARD HILL (1990, Cannon)—Set in St. Kitts, this trashy story begins after a slave revolt led by **Patrick Warburton**. Now happily married to blonde Kimberly Sissons, they live at their inherited plantation, Dragonard Hill. Sex, sadism and slavery get the place jumping in no time.

ABDUL-MUHSEN, KHALIF
THE NEXT MAN (1976, Allied Artists)—Saudi Arabian Minister of State **Sean Connery** is the target of a female assassin at the United Nations.

ABDULLA
ABDULLA'S HAREM (1956, GB, Sonofilms)—**Gregory Ratoff** gives a hammy performance as a King Farouk-like character who loses his kingdom while unsuccessfully pursuing English model Kay Kendall.

ABELMAN, DR. SAM
THE LAST ANGRY MAN (1959, Columbia)—TV producer David Wayne plans a documentary featuring **Paul Muni**, a Jewish doctor who works in a Brooklyn slum. Wayne believes Muni is a dedicated, humane man of medicine. Things go awry when he learns Muni detests the people he treats.

"THE ABILENE KID" *See* WILLIAM KEARNEY

ABNER
ARKANSAS JUDGE (1941, Republic)—Using homespun common sense Arkansas Judge **Leon Weaver** sets things straight when an innocent scrubwoman is accused of stealing a widow's savings.

ABNER
TWO WEEKS TO LIVE (1943, RKO); PARTNERS IN TIME (1946, RKO); LUM AND ABNER ABROAD (1956, HOWCO)—LUM AND ABNER was a popular radio show for many years. The down-home humor didn't transfer well to the silver screen. In the first film, **Norris Goff** as Abner believes he has only a short time to live, but as is usual for him, he's mistaken. In the second film, Goff and partner **Chester Lauck** as Lum take a trip. This latter feature is actually three short TV shows linked together by a narration.

ABOMINABLE SNOWMAN, THE
SEVEN FACES OF DR. LAO (1964, MGM)—The Abominable Snowman is one of the disguises that elderly Chinaman **Tony Randall** assumes to combat land-grabbing villain Arthur O'Connell.

ABU
THE THIEF OF BAGHDAD (1940, GB, London Films)—In the kind of film they don't make any more, **Sabu** is a young thief in Baghdad who teams up with a deposed Caliph John Justin to help him win back his throne and lovely June Duprez from evil wizard Conrad Veidt. In the process, he temporarily is changed into a mongrel dog, outwits a huge genie, steals a sacred jewel from a temple and rides a flying carpet to save his friend from being beheaded.

ACE, EDDIE
MR. ACE (1946, UA)—Political boss **George Raft** almost manipulates the electorate into choosing congresswoman Sylvia Sidney as governor, but she grows disgusted with the dirty business.

ACE, STROKER
STROKER ACE (1983, Universal/Warner Brothers)—**Burt Reynolds** doesn't carry off his "good ole boy" routine with his usual charm in this uninteresting story of a race car driver and his buxom girlfriend Loni Anderson.

ACKERMAN, DAVID
THE ROOKIE (1990, Warner Brothers)—In this entry in the buddy picture sub-genre, rich kid **Charlie Sheen** works out his hostility toward his parents by becoming a cop. His partner is Dirty Harry-like Clint Eastwood. When the latter is taken hostage by a stolen-car gang, Sheen must grow up quickly.

ACKERMAN, NOAH
THE YOUNG LIONS (1958, 20th Century Fox)—**Montgomery Clift**, a Jewish GI during WWII, experiences the weariness and lack of understanding of what is happening, an experience which is the common lot of foot soldiers moving from one battle to the next.

ACKLAND, JIM
THE OCTOBER MAN (1948, GB, Eagle-Lion)—While staying at a small hotel, a head wound causes **John Mills** to fall into a state of depression and to be suspected of a murder.

ACKROYD, PVT. ARCHIBALD

SOLDIERS THREE (1951, MGM)—In this un-official remake of GUNGA DIN, we assume that **Stewart Granger** is repeating the Cary Grant role.

ACTION, DAVID

GENTLEMEN MARRY BRUNETTES (1955, UA)—**Scott Brady** is one of the "gentlemen" who showgirls Jane Russell and Jeanne Crain size up as rich catches while husband hunting in Paris.

ACTOR, THE

THE GUARDSMAN (1931, MGM)—Suspecting his actress wife, Lynn Fontanne, of being unfaithful, **Alfred Lunt** disguises himself as an officer and makes love to her. When he confronts her, she insists she knew who he was all along. But did she?

ACUNA, MARIA

YOU WERE NEVER LOVELIER (1948, 20th Century Fox)—Argentinean hotel magnate Adolphe Menjou attempts to interest his beautiful daughter **Rita Hayworth** in romance by inventing an imaginary admirer who she believes to be American band leader Fred Astaire. Astaire never had a lovelier dancing partner nor a more talented one.

ADAIR, PADDY

PADDY, THE NEXT BEST THING (1923, GB, Graham/Wilcox); (1933, Fox)—**Mae Marsh** and **Janet Gaynor** took turns portraying the Irish tomboy in New York who wins the love of a man who at first doesn't see her as a romantic possibility.

ADAM

ADAM'S WOMAN (1972, Australia, Warner Brothers)—**Beau Bridges**, an American sailor, wrongly convicted and sentenced to an 1840 Australian penal colony is allowed to marry a prisoner and begin a settlement in the outback. Their settlement flourishes as other married prisoners join them.

ADAM

I AM THE CHEESE (1983, Almi Productions)—Teenager **Robert McNaughton**, who has witnessed his parents' death, tries to sort out reality from fantasy while under psychiatric care.

ADAM *See* AD SIMMS

ADAM

TWO ALONE (1934, RKO)—When **Tom Brown** gets his farm girlfriend pregnant, their troubles multiply, and there's no one to help or understand.

ADAM, ANTON

LAWYER MAN (1933, Warner Brothers)—Successful lawyer **William Powell** is accused of blackmail by a political boss who can't control Powell, but our hero is proven innocent.

ADAMS, ALICE

ALICE ADAMS (1923, Silent, Associated Exhibitors); (1935, RKO)—Dissatisfied with her family's modest means, **Florence Vidor** sets her cap for wealthy Arthur Russell. She leads him to believe that her family is well-off. At a dinner in her home, he learns the truth and leaves her. In the 1935 remake, **Katharine Hepburn** wins her young man, Fred MacMurray, despite her deceit.

ADAMS, ANN

THE LADY OBJECTS (1938, Columbia)—After college **Gloria Stuart** marries her sweetheart and prospers in a law career, while her husband finds it hard to establish himself as an architect. The marriage is on the rocks until he is implicated in a murder and she defends him in court.

ADAMS, LT. COL. BARNEY

MAN IN THE MIDDLE (1964, 20th Century Fox)—In WWII India, American Lieutenant Keenan Wynn is accused of a murder. His defense attorney **Robert Mitchum** is ordered to lose the case to smooth over problems between American and British troops.

ADAMS, BOB

I COVER THE WAR (1937, Universal)—Newsreel cameraman **John Wayne** goes to Samari to cover a rebel uprising.

ADAMS, CONNIE

ALL AMERICAN SWEETHEART (1937, Columbia)—Co-ed **Patricia Farr** gets caught up in an attempt by racketeers to control a college rowing team.

ADAMS, DOROTHY

HER NIGHT OF ROMANCE (1924, Silent, First National)—Heiress **Constance Talmadge** disguises herself while traveling in Europe and falls in love with an impoverished nobleman, posing as a doctor.

ADAMS, JAMES CAPEN

THE LIFE AND TIMES OF GRIZZLY ADAMS (1974, Sunn Classic)—Mountain man **Dan Haggerty** finds peace and happiness in the wilderness with a bear. To each his own, we presume.

ADAMS, JERRY

MAN WITH A MILLION (1954, GB, UA)—To settle a bet, two wealthy men give pauper **Gregory Peck** a million pound note and set him loose in London.

ADAMS, JOE

MR. LUCKY (1943, RKO)—During WWII, gambler **Cary Grant** intends to use a group of women running a "Bundles for Britain" charity to set up a gambling ship, but Laraine Day and his own patriotism get to him before the end of the film.

ADAMS, MARY

ONE GIRL'S CONFESSION (1953, Columbia)—**Cleo Moore** steals from her guardian, hides the loot and makes the best of her prison sentence, knowing the money will be waiting for her when she is released.

ADAMS, MISS

PRIVATE NURSE (1941, 20th Century Fox)—The title just about says it all. The film tells of the work of **Jane Darwell** whose patients include the 10-year old son of a mobster.

ADAMS, NATALIE

THAT'S MY GAL (1947, Republic)—When some investors in a disastrous musical review die, their executor, **Lynne Roberts**, steps in and ensures the show is a smash. This ruins the plans of swindlers who would have benefited by a failure. Do you suppose this is where Mel Brooks got the idea for THE PRODUCERS?

ADAMS, NICK

ADVENTURES OF A YOUNG MAN (1962, 20th Century Fox)—**Richard Beymer** gives a wooden performance as a young Ernest Hemingway, setting out from rural Michigan for New York and the fame that awaits him.

ADAMS, DR. RANDALL

DR. GILLESPIE'S NEW ASSISTANT (1942, MGM); THREE MEN IN WHITE (1944, MGM)—when Lew Ayres was dropped from the successful Dr. Kildare series after declaring himself a conscientious objector to serving as a soldier in the war, MGM needed a romantic lead to replace him. Handsome, charming **Van Johnson** filled the bill nicely. By the 1944 film, Johnson is firmly established as the brash young medical assistant who inevitably clashes with old crusty Lionel Barrymore as Dr. Gillespie.

ADAMS, RUTH
THE NURSE'S SECRET (1941, Warner Brothers)—**Lee Patrick** is a nurse sent to care for an elderly wealthy woman in a large country home. When a murder is committed she assists a cop in solving the case.

ADAMS, MRS. SALLY
CALL ME MADAM (1953, 20th Century Fox)—Washington hostess **Ethel Merman** is named ambassador to a small European country where she falls in love with its foreign minister, George Sanders. Her best song is "You're Just in Love" with Donald O'Connor.

ADAMS, STEVE
REVENUE AGENT (1950, Columbia)—In this unimportant quickie for the second (or third) houses, **Douglas Kennedy** is a Treasury agent foiling a plot to sneak a million dollars in gold dust out of the country.

ADAMS, SUSAN
SYNCOPATING SUE (1926, Silent, First National)—**Corrine Griffith**, hired to play a piano in a music shop, has ambitions to become a stage star. She gets her chance when a producer comes on to her and her sister.

ADAMS, TOM
SON OF A STRANGER (1957, GB, UA)—**James Kenney** assaults elderly women and steals their purses for a living. He hates his dying mother, but dreams of his unknown father. After murdering one of his victims, he learns that his father is a local doctor. In their meeting the physician is accidently shot, and Kenney is hanged for the deed.

ADAMS, VERN
THE GHOST COMES HOME (1940, MGM)—When **Frank Morgan** returns home after a two-month absence, he finds his family members have prospered, living on his insurance benefits, and have mixed-feelings about seeing him again.

ADAMS, VICKI
TWO BLONDES AND A REDHEAD (1947, Columbia)—**Judy Clark** is one of two chorines invited to visit the home of a society girl after the show all three were in folded. The society men are much taken by Clark and her friend.

ADAMSON, CLAIRE
THERE'S A GIRL IN MY HEART (1949, Allied Artists)—Lew Bowman tries to swindle young widow **Elyse Knox** out of a valuable piece of land but falls in love with her instead.

ADDAMS, FRANKIE
THE MEMBER OF THE WEDDING (1952, Columbia)—**Julie Harris** repeats her Broadway role of a 12 year old girl who is catapulted into adolescence, experiencing such events as her brother's wedding, running away from home, a near sexual encounter with a drunken soldier and the death of her young cousin, Brandon De Wilde.

ADDAMS, MORTICIA, GOMEZ, UNCLE FESTER, GRANNY, WEDNESDAY & PUGSLEY
THE ADDAMS FAMILY (1991, Paramount)—Looking properly funereal in her long black gown, **Angelica Huston** drives **Raul Julia** mad with desire. **Christopher Lloyd** starts out as a fraud, but he's a real member of the weird family by the end. **Christina Ricci** and **Jimmy Workman** are very good as the strange children. They have the best scene staging a bloody excerpt from *Hamlet* for a school talent show. The assembled parents are aghast; the adult Addams are very proud.

ADDERSON, ATHERIS
THE SNAKE WOMAN (1961, GB, UA)—In the 19th century moors, **Susan Travers** kills her victims by turning herself into a deadly cobra.

ADDISON, TIM
THE WESTERNER (1936, Columbia)—Rodeo cowboy **Tim McCoy** buys a ranch and finds he must deal with rustlers and an accusation of murder against him.

ADELAIDE, MISS
GUYS AND DOLLS (1955, MGM)—**Vivian Blaine**, re-creating her Broadway role in the Frank Loesser musical, is the best thing in the movie. She is a brassy but beautiful nightclub entertainer who has been waiting for years for her gambler fiance Frank Sinatra to marry her. Blaine's best number is "Adelaide's Lament."

ADELE
THE BROADWAY HOOFER (1929, Columbia)—**Marie Saxon**, proud of her great legs, joins a burlesque line just for the fun of it. She becomes the partner in a specialty number with a man who she comes to love and later saves when he freezes in his Broadway debut.

ADELINE *See* ADELINE SCHMIDT

ADJUTANT
TWO MEN AND A MAID (1929, Tiffany)—**Eddie Gribbon**, the cruel adjutant of a French Foreign Legion Fort, mellows enough to allow William Collier, Jr. to escape and return to his wife after Gribbon's mistress, Alma Bennett, dies trying to help Collier get away.

ADLER, MARTY
HUNTER'S BLOOD (1987, Concorde)—**Joey Travolta**, a city lout, joins four others for some deer hunting in the wilds of Arkansas. In this film, reminiscent of DELIVERANCE, they run afoul of local rednecks.

ADVERSE, ANTHONY
ANTHONY ADVERSE (1936, Warner Brothers)—Ambitious young illegitimate **Fredric March** is embittered when through a misunderstanding his wife Olivia de Havilland leaves him to pursue her singing career. March travels the world over and has many adventures before encountering de Havilland again, now the toast of Paris as an opera star and mistress of Napoleon Bonaparte. She gives him custody of their son, of whose existence March was unaware, and father and son set sail for America and a new life.

AGNES, SISTER
AGNES OF GOD (1985, Columbia)—Did naive, unworldly **Meg Tilly** murder her child at birth—and who is the father? The movie doesn't satisfactorily answer these questions.

AHASUERUS, KING
ESTHER AND THE KING (1960, 20th Century Fox)—Persian king **Richard Egan** finds Jewish maiden Joan Collins, whom he selects to replace his murdered wife, is a great help in fending off his enemies.

AHEARN, JAMES FRANCIS "BUGS"
THE LITTLE GIANT (1933, Warner Brothers)—At the end of Prohibition, beer baron **Edward G. Robinson** attempts to go straight and crash society. It was Robinson's first comedy role, and he was quite up to the challenge.

AHERN, JIM See WARBONNET

AHMED
AN ARABIAN KNIGHT (1920, Silent, Haworth)—A young woman is convinced that Egyptian donkey boy **Sessue Hawakawa** was her lover in an earlier incarnation. He has to deal with the here and the now, when a Pasha kidnaps the girl.

AHMED
PRISONERS OF THE CASBAH (1953, Columbia)—**Turhan Bey**, never much of an actor, doesn't even appear to be trying in this third-rate Eastern about a princess and her lover, Bey, who take refuge from the Grand Vizar in the Casbah.

AHMED See THE SHIEK

AIKEN, CARROLL
CAREER WOMAN (1936, 20th Century Fox)—Recent law school graduate **Claire Trevor** returns to her home town, where with the help of a flamboyant city lawyer, she defends friend Isabel Jewell against the charge of killing her father.

AIMEE, GABY
LOTTERY LOVER (1935, Fox)—Sailors in Paris for a spree draw lots for a date with Folies Bergere dancer **Peggy Fears**. Shy Lew Ayres is the winner.

AINGER, ARNOLD
FOUR FRIGHTENED PEOPLE (1934, Paramount)—In this so-so Cecil B. De Mille studio-bound production, **Herbert Marshall** is one of four survivors of a shipwreck who must make a long journey through a dangerous jungle.

AINSLEY, CAROL
WHAT A WOMAN! (1943, Columbia)—Literary agent **Rosalind Russell** must find the male lead for the Hollywood production of a book she's just sold to the movies. She chooses the author, strongman Willard Parker.

AKEEM, PRINCE
COMING TO AMERICA (1988, Paramount)—**Eddie Murphy** is a black African prince who travels to New York to find a fun wife. The beautiful bride chosen for him by his parents is too dutiful for his tastes. With his aide-de-camp Arsenio Hall, he escapes the responsibility of his royal duties in Queens, where he meets sexy Shari Hedley, the daughter of a fast food restaurant owner. Murphy and Hall also appear in minor cameo roles.

AL
THE KILLERS (1946, Universal)—Charles McGraw plays one of the killers sent to wipe out an unprotesting Burt Lancaster in this first of three films based on Ernest Hemingway's short story.

AL
THE SINGING FOOL (1928, Warner Brothers)—Entertainer **Al Jolson's** career hits the skids when his young son dies. Only the hardest of the hard-hearted won't shed a tear when Jolson sings "Sonny Boy."

ALADDIN
ALADDIN (1917, Silent, Fox); ALADDIN AND HIS LAMP (1952, Monogram)—In the 1917 version of the familiar story of Aladdin and his wonderful lamp, **Francis Carpenter** and other children play all the parts. In 1952, pickpocket **John Sands** comes into possession of the lamp and uses it to win the Caliph's daughter and defeat an evil prince.

ALAN
THE DRIFTER (1966, Surfilms)—**John Tracy**, alienated from his concert pianist father, travels the country, moving from one meaningless affair to the next.

ALAN
THE SAILOR FROM GIBRALTAR (1967, GB, Lopert)—While on holiday, clerk **Ian Bannen** abandons his mistress to take up with a rich French woman. He becomes the elusive sailor whom she has been seeking.

ALAN
STRANGERS MAY KISS (1931, MGM)—Norma Shearer has an undying love for newspaper reporter **Neil Hamilton,** who is too busy following stories all over the world to pay much attention to her. Finally, when she is about to marry Robert Montgomery, who has always loved her, Hamilton is ready to tie the knot himself, that is, until he discovers that she has had a series of lovers.

ALARDY, JULIE
THE LITTLE DAMOZEL (1933, GB, British & Dominions)—In **Anna Neagle's** first major role, she portrays a singer who a gambler is paid to marry, but it's more than a fair bet that he'll come to love her.

ALBERT
WE'RE NO ANGELS (1955, Paramount)—**Aldo Ray,** on Devil's Island for murdering his uncle, is one of three escaped convicts who bring Christmas cheer to a storekeeper, his wife, and daughter before they return to the prison compound.

ALBINIZI, FATHER DAVID
THE POPE MUST DIE (1991, GB, Palace/Miramax)—Because of a clerical error, Priest **Robbie Coltrane,** who doubles as an automobile mechanic and a rock musician in a rural Italian community, is elected Pope. Just as Christ chased the money-lenders from the temple, Coltrane boots the mob from the Vatican.

ALBION, ALEC
SMART ALEC (1951, GB, Grand National)—**Peter Reynolds** tells the police commissioner that he has a premonition that his rich uncle will be killed. Reynolds then kills his uncle using a boreless gun and an ice bullet, but a twist of fate brings him to justice.

ALBRIGHT, SALLY
WHEN HARRY MET SALLY . . . (1989, Columbia)—Over a ten-year period, **Meg Ryan** and Billy Crystal maintain a platonic friendship, but things change when he is shocked by his divorce and her long-time lover dumps her. Guess we'll have to join all the other reviewers who take note of Ryan's faking an orgasm in a crowded restaurant as a high point of this adult comedy.

ALDEN, EDITHEA *See* EADIE ALLEN

ALDEN, DICK
THE BAREFOOT BOY (1923, Silent, Mission Film Co.); (1938, Monogram)—In the silent film, **John Bowers** is mistreated by his stepfather and is wrongly accused of setting fire to the schoolhouse. The 12 year old runs away, vowing revenge. Years later, he returns, rich and intent on closing down the mill, but his childhood sweetheart changes his mind. **Jackie Moran** has a different name, Billy Whittaker, in the remake.

ALDEN, JAMES
THE MILLIONAIRE (1931, Warner Brothers)—**George Arliss** is a Henry Ford-like industrialist, forced to retire but who can't stand being idle. So he poses as a poor man and goes partners with a young man in a gasoline station.

ALDEN, SISTER ANNIE
KLONDIKE ANNIE (1936, Paramount)—**Helen Jerome Eddy** is the real Alaskan missionary whom torch singer, on the run, Mae West impersonates.

ALDRICH, HENRY
HENRY ALDRICH FOR PRESIDENT (1941, Paramount); LIFE WITH HENRY (1941, PARAMOUNT); HENRY ALDRICH, EDITOR (1942, Paramount); HENRY ALDRICH GETS GLAMOUR (1942, Paramount); HENRY AND DIZZY (1942, Paramount); HENRY ALDRICH HAUNTS A HOUSE (1943, Paramount); HENRY ALDRICH SWINGS IT (1943, Paramount); HENRY ALDRICH, BOY SCOUT (1944, Paramount); HENRY ALDRICH PLAYS CUPID (1944, Paramount); HENRY ALDRICH'S LITTLE SECRET (1944, Paramount)—**Jimmy Lydon** played the awkward small-town youngster who always seems to be in some kind of innocent trouble. The titles of the films just about say it all about the plots.

ALDRICH, HENRY & MILDRED
FOLKS (1992, 20th Century Fox)—Elderly **Don Ameche** is senile; his wife **Anne Jackson** is ill. She asks her children Tom Selleck and Christine Ebersole to kill them for their insurance money. Sounds like a laugh riot, doesn't it?

ALDRICH, MARTHA
MY DEAR MISS ALDRICH (1937, MGM)—**Maureen O'Sullivan**, the beautiful new owner of a newspaper, is in constant disagreement with editor Walter Pidgeon about how it should be run.

ALEX
ALEX IN WONDERLAND—(1970, MGM)—**Donald Sutherland** is director Paul Mazursky's alter ego in this story of a movie maker who must come up with a new smash after his very successful film debut.

ALEX
ALEX THE GREAT (1928, Silent, FBO)—Vermont Yankee simpleton **Richard "Skeets" Gallagher** travels to the city where he finds a wonderful job and an heiress willing to marry him.

ALEX
BAD INFLUENCE (1990, Triumph)—Devilish **Rob Lowe** provides dull yuppie investment broker James Spader with excitement, but before long babyfaced psycho Lowe dictates all aspects of Spader's romantic and professional life. Lowe even videotapes Spader having sex, a little bow we suppose to Spader's film "sex, lies and videotape" and Lowe's own troubles with videotaping his sexual conquests in real life.

ALEX
TEACHERS (1984, MGM/UA)—**Nick Nolte** is the dedicated teacher who takes time out from bedding down reporter JoBeth Williams and fighting administrators Judd Hirsch and Lee Grant to help straighten out troubled student Ralph Macchio.

ALEXANDER, DR.
THE YOUNG DOCTORS (1961, UA)—His performance in this standard medical movie may be what sent **Dick Clark** hustling back to hosting American Bandstand.

ALEXANDER, SCILLA
JUST LIKE A WOMAN (1967, GB, Dormar/Monarch)—**Wendy Craig** is a TV director's wife who leaves him to find a better station in life for herself.

ALEXANDER THE GREAT
ALEXANDER THE GREAT (1956, UA)—After succeeding his father Fredric March as King of Macedonia, **Richard Burton** cuts the Gordian knot and conquers all the known world before dying at the age of 32.

ALEXANDRA, EMPRESS
RASPUTIN AND THE EMPRESS (1932, MGM); NICHOLAS AND ALEXANDRA (1971, GB, Columbia)—First **Ethel Barrymore** and then **Janet Suzman** appear as the last Czarina of Russia who comes under the destructive influence of the mad monk Rasputin.

ALEXANDRA, PRINCESS
THE SWAN (1956, MGM)—Despite growing romantic feelings for her tutor Louis Jourdan, Hungarian princess **Grace Kelly** is being groomed as a bride for the crown prince Alec Guinness.

ALEXCOV, IVAN
TAPEHEADS (1988, DEG-Avenue)—After being fired as security guards **John Cusack** and his pal Tim Robbins try their hands in video productions. Their motto is "You Do What You Gotta, So You Can Do What You Wanna."

ALEXIEFF, NARA
THE HANDS OF NARA (1922, Silent, Metro)—**Clara Kimball Young**, a Russian refugee from the Bolshevik Revolution, comes to New York, sponsored by a society woman. Young proves to have healing powers in her hands, and many men fall in love with her.

ALEXIS
THE SPIRITUALIST (1948, Eagle Lion)—In a knockdown of the previous year's NIGHTMARE ALLEY, **Turhan Bey** creates some realistic ghosts to fleece rich clients.

ALFIE, *See* ALFIE ELKINS

ALFORD, VIRGIE
LADIES COURAGEOUS (1944, Universal)—**Geraldine Fitzgerald**, a member of the WAFS (Women's Auxiliary Flying Squad), almost shoots down the program when she carelessly cracks up a plane.

ALFRED
THE KING AND THE CHORUS GIRL (1937, Warner Brothers)—A visiting king-to-be, **Fernand Gravet**, falls for a New York chorus girl, Joan Blondell.

ALFRED THE GREAT

ALFRED THE GREAT (1969, GB, MGM)—In this foul-mouthed tedious, historical drama, **David Hemmings** unites the Brits to defeat the invading Danes.

ALI BABA

ALI BABA GOES TO TOWN (1937, 20th Century Fox); ALI BABA AND THE FORTY THIEVES (1944, Universal); SON OF ALI BABA (1952, UNIVERSAL); THE SWORD OF ALI BABA (1965, Universal)—While working as an extra in an Arabian Nights movie, **Eddie Cantor** dreams he is back in old Bagdad where he becomes a Franklin D. Roosevelt-like chief minister to the sultan. In the 1944 fantasy, **Jon Hall**, with the help of the forty thieves who have raised him, regains his throne from evil Kurt Katch who had murdered Hall's father. In the bargain, Jon wins the hand of lovely Maria Montez. In the 1952 inevitable "Son of . . ." film, **Morris Ankrum** plays the aging Ali Baba. The 1965 movie starring **Peter Mann** as the leader of the forty thieves lifted a great deal of footage from the 1944 film.

ALI GATOR

THE GARBAGE PAIL KIDS (1987, Atlantic Entertainment)—In one of the most tasteless movies aimed at a kid audience, **Kevin Thompson** is one of seven disgusting rip-offs of the Cabbage Patch Kids. His specialty is eating human toes and at that he's the most acceptable of the bunch.

ALI, MUHAMMAD

THE GREATEST (1977, Columbia)—**Muhammad Ali** plays himself in this less than fascinating biopic of the heavyweight boxing champion.

ALICE

ALICE (1990, Orion)—Pampered but underappreciated housewife **Mia Farrow** feels she's missing something in life, but she's not sure what. An encounter with unorthodox herbalist-acupuncturist Keye Luke unlocks her secret self and leads her on adventures not found through the looking glass or down a rabbit's hole.

ALICE

ALICE IN WONDERLAND (1933, Paramount); ALICE'S ADVENTURES IN WONDERLAND (1972, GB, American National)—Ida Lupino was brought from England to play Lewis Carroll's young heroine, but the studio heads changed their minds and miscast **Charlotte Henry** as the young girl who encounters a wide assortment of strange characters after falling down a rabbit hole. In 1972, the call of "Off with their heads" should be made against the makers of the tedious musical starring **Fiona Fullerton**, who makes Charlotte Henry look good.

ALICE

ALICE, SWEET ALICE (1978, Allied Artists)—In this bucket of gore, **Paula Sheppard** is suspected of being the killer of young Brooke Shields in the latter's film debut.

ALICE

ALICE'S RESTAURANT (1969, UA)—**Pat Quinn** operates a counter-culture restaurant at the time of the Vietnam war which is celebrated in Arlo Guthrie's hit song "Alice's Restaurant Massacre."

ALICE

BOB AND CAROL AND TED AND ALICE (1969, Columbia)—**Dyan Cannon**, her husband Elliott Gould, and their friends Natalie Wood and Robert Culp toy with the idea of mate swapping but don't carry through. If made in today's movie climate, the four would have started the movie in bed together.

ALICE

SEVEN BRIDES FOR SEVEN BROTHERS (1954, MGM)—**Nancy Kilgas** is the bride kidnapped by Tommy Rall, in this wonderful dance musical.

ALIEN

THE GALAXY INVADER (1985, Moviecraft Entertainment)—**Glenn Barnes**, an alien explorer, crash lands his spacecraft in a backwoods area of the U.S.

ALIEN, THE

NOT OF THIS EARTH (1988, Concorde)—Alien **Arthur Roberts** is visiting Earth. He needs frequent blood transfusions, and takes them any way he can get them.

ALLAIRE, JAN

JAN OF THE BIG SNOWS (1922, Silent, American Releasing Corp.)—**Warner Richmond**, an inexperienced young man, becomes infatuated with the wife of the owner of a northern trading post and vows to protect her from all others when her husband disappears on a trapping mission.

ALLAN, MARGARET

NOOSE FOR A LADY (1953, GB, Anglo-Amalgamated)—A private eye proves his convicted cousin **Pamela Allan** didn't poison her blackmailer husband.

ALLAN, ZANDY

ZANDY'S BRIDE (1974, Warner Brothers)—**Gene Hackman** is a pioneer who sends for a mail-order bride, Liv Ullmann. Amazing the things you can get from Montgomery Ward.

ALLEGRO, JOHNNY

JOHNNY ALLEGRO (1949, Columbia)—Ex-gangster George Raft helps the FBI get a counterfeiter so Raft can marry the man's wife. The plot is reminiscent of GILDA even to having George Macready in a similar role.

ALLEN, BETTY

SWEETHEART OF SIGMA CHI (1946, Monogram)—**Elyse Knox** plots to snag the college's rowing champ, but the two must deal with local hoods who wish to fix a boat race.

ALLEN, BILL

HEADLINE SHOOTER (1933, RKO)—Newsreel photographer **William Gargan** spends more time on his job than with the woman who loves him. During a flood the two decide to pull their oars in the same direction as man and wife.

ALLEN, CHICK

JUMPING JACKS (1952, Paramount)—Nightclub performer **Dean Martin** and his partner Jerry Lewis join the paratroopers with predictable results.

ALLEN, CHRYSTAL

THE WOMEN (1939, MGM)—In this marvelous, bitchy film based on Clare Booth's hit play, **Joan Crawford**, one of 135 women and no men who make up the cast, is a chorus girl who steals Norma Shearer's husband but is not exactly faithful to the never seen man. After deciding she has divorced in haste, Shearer goes after her man and gets him back from Crawford.

ALLEN, DONALD *See* JOHN ROLFE

ALLEN, EADIE/EDITHEA ALDEN
EADIE WAS A LADY (1945, Columbia)—During the day **Ann Miller** is Edithea Alden, a student at a prim and proper school. At night she is Eadie, the top attraction in a hot burlesque show.

ALLEN, FATHER GIL
THE LEATHER SAINT (1956, Paramount)—Catholic priest **John Derek** becomes a prize fighter to raise funds for his parish hospital.

ALLEN, HENRY
THE MASTER MIND (1920, Silent, First National)—**Lionel Barrymore** plans to avenge the execution of his innocent brother by ruining the presiding judge whose mistake cost the man his life.

ALLEN, JAMES
I AM A FUGITIVE FROM A CHAIN GANG (1932, Warner Brothers)—**Paul Muni** gives a powerful performance as an innocent man sentenced to a cruel southern chain gang. He escapes, changes his name to Allen James and becomes a prominent Chicago citizen. Glenda Farrell blackmails him into marrying her, and when Muni falls in love with Helen Vinson, Farrell blows the whistle on him and he is returned to the chain gang. The next time he escapes, he becomes a thief to survive.

ALLEN, KIRK
A NOTORIOUS GENTLEMAN (1935, Universal)—**Charles Bickford** plans a murder so as to incriminate the victim's fiancee.

ALLEN, MARIE
CAGED (1950, Warner Brothers)—Naive, sweet, young **Eleanor Parker** is innocently involved in a robbery in which a man is killed by her husband. She is convicted as an accomplice and sent to a tough women's prison where she is so brutalized that she becomes a hardened, bitter woman who accepts the offer of a crooked lawyer—her freedom if she will become a prostitute.

ALLEN, RAY
TALK OF THE DEVIL (1937, GB, Gaumont)—In a dreary film, **Ricardo Cortez** impersonates a business magnate and involves him in a crooked deal. The man kills himself in disgrace.

ALLEN, RENA
THE MAN I MARRY (1936, Universal)—**Doris Nolan**, who runs a play-reading agency, falls in love with playwright Michael Whalen. With the help of her uncle, a Broadway producer, she gets her lover's work staged. Initially, Whalen isn't happy to discover he didn't make it totally on his own.

ALLEN, REX
THE ARIZONA COWBOY (1950, Republic)—Movie cowboys such as **Rex Allen** often played themselves in their movies, possibly because their names were on their saddle and other pieces of equipment. In the first of 31 films featuring singing cowboy Allen, he's trying to prove his father innocent of a crime.

ALLEN, RICK
CHICAGO JOE AND THE SHOWGIRL (1990, GB, Palace)—Obsessed with fantasies of gangsters and their molls, **Kiefer Sutherland** is easily led astray by Emily Lloyd, who has her own unhealthy need for criminal kicks. Neither Lloyd nor Sutherland bring much to their parts.

ALLEN, SHELLY
THE YOUNG RUNAWAYS (1968, MGM)—**Brooke Bundy** runs away from home to Chicago where she finds herself involved with dope dealing, prostitution and poverty. She decides home isn't so bad after all.

ALLENBURY, CONNIE
LIBELED LADY (1936, MGM)—When **Myrna Loy** sues newspaperman Spencer Tracy for libeling her in his paper, Tracy talks his pal William Powell into compromising Loy, so the suit will be thrown out of court.

ALLENBY, PHYLLIS
SHE-WOLF OF LONDON (1946, Universal)—**June Lockhart** believes she is the family werewolf in this almost laughable horror film.

ALLERTON, GEORGINA
DREAM GIRL (1947, Paramount)—**Betty Hutton** is sort of a female Walter Mitty, who finds one of her daydreams coming true and causing her a lot of trouble.

ALLISON, ALICE
THE COWBOY AND THE FLAPPER (1924, Silent, Truart)—Wild twenties girl **Dorothy Revier** is taken captive by a bunch of outlaws and is rescued by a marshal who infiltrates the kidnap gang.

ALLISON, BEN & CLINT
THE TALL MEN (1955, 20th Century Fox)—Brothers **Clark Gable** and **Cameron Mitchell**, late of the Confederate Army, sign on with Robert Ryan's cattle drive. They fight each other and Indians and vie for the attention of Jane Russell.

ALLISON, EVE
YOUTH TO YOUTH (1922, Silent, Metro)—**Billie Dove**, a Broadway star, runs away when it is rumored that she's the mistress of producer Wallace Beery. She joins a traveling show and falls in love with a farm boy so impressed with her act that he writes old friend Beery to catch her act.

ALLISON, HUGH
RACKET BUSTERS (1938, Warner Brothers)—**Walter Abel** and George Brent are special prosecutors after a gangster intent on building a trucking empire.

ALLISON, MR.
HEAVEN KNOWS, MR. ALLISON (1957, 20th Century Fox)—Marine **Robert Mitchum** and nun Deborah Kerr are marooned on a Pacific island during WWII. They put aside their initial antagonism towards each other to outwit the Japanese.

ALLYN, KAY
THE FOOTLOOSE HEIRESS (1937, Warner Brothers)—Society girl **Ann Sheridan** must marry before midnight of her eighteenth birthday to win a bet. A man well below her station in life fills her need for husband material.

ALMA
THE HARVEY GIRLS (1946, MGM)—Deadpan **Virginia O'Brien**, one of the Harvey restaurant waitresses in a western railroad town, delights audiences with her rendition of "The Wild, Wild West."

ALMA
LONELY HEARTS (1991, Live Entertainment)—Shortly after emerging as a slimmed-down and attractive woman, **Beverly D'Angelo** is given the rush by smoothie Eric Roberts. After she makes a small

investment in one of his real estate deals, Roberts disappears. D'Angelo tracks him down and in order to remain part of his life, she becomes his accomplice in fleecing wealthy, lonely ladies.

ALOMA

ALOMA OF THE SOUTH SEAS (1926, Silent, Paramount); (1941, Paramount)—Beautiful Paradise Island dancer **Gilda Gray** is confused about her feelings toward her native lover and an American who is trying to forget his true love. Everything is straightened out after a great storm. In the remake, Jon Hall, who has been away to school for 15 years returns to his island adamant against marrying the girl picked to be his wife when both were children. He runs into **Dorothy Lamour** and falls in love with her. Of course, she is his intended, but they must survive a volcanic eruption before they can tie the knot.

ALONZO

THE UNKNOWN (1927, Silent, MGM)—**Lon Chaney**, a fugitive from the law, joins a circus posing as a man with no arms, who nevertheless has a trick shooting and knife throwing act. His assistant is Joan Crawford who doesn't like to be "pawed" by men, which makes Chaney think she's attracted to him. Chaney later kills the circus manager, and Crawford gets enough of a glimpse of the murderer to note that he has a double thumb. Chaney arranges to have both his arms amputated in part because he feels this will enable him to win Joan and so she will never be able to identify him. Seems she fancies the strongman so Chaney tries to kill his rival but is killed instead.

ALOYSIUS

THE LUNATIC (1992, Triton)—Innocent black lad **Paul Campbell** talks to animals and plants and everyone believes he's a lunatic. Visiting German photographer Julie T. Wallace makes Campbell her love slave, soon extending it to a menage a trois by inviting butcher Carl Bradshaw into their bed.

ALPHA

LOST ANGEL (1944, MGM)—Reporter James Craig adopts **Margaret O'Brien**, a precocious child being raised as a genius by scientists. She learns some of the simple joys of childhood in her new home.

ALTHEA, LADY

BEAUTY AND THE BEAST (1963, UA)—In this rip-off of the Jean Cocteau 1947 classic, Beauty **Joyce Taylor** appears to be having trouble keeping a straight face.

ALUCARD, COUNT *See* DRACULA

ALVARDO, CARMEN & RITA

THE DEVIL'S SISTERS (1966, Mustang)—**Velia Martinez & Anita Crystal** run a white slavery ring in Tijuana. They enjoy stripping and tying their new girls with barbed wire.

ALVARDO, GENERAL *See* JULES LACROIX

ALVARES, DONNA

I LIVE FOR LOVE (1935, Warner Brothers)—**Dolores Del Rio** is a socialite who has visions of making it in show business.

AMADEO, KING VITTORIO

THE KING'S WHORE (1990, Fr./Austria/GB/Italy, J&M) -Italian King **Timothy Dalton** falls madly in love with Valeria Golino, his chamberlain's wife. At first she resists his lust for her, but eventually the pressure to become his lover proves too great. She accepts the arrangement but demands a whore's payment. Despite his obsession with her, he is never able to have her love.

AMANDA

LADY IN WHITE (1988, New Century-Vista)—When she discovered her daughter's lifeless body on the rocks below their cliffside house, **Katharine Helmond** committed suicide. Many years later her ghost and that of her daughter are still haunting the rocky seaside cliffs, seeking each other.

AMANS

THE CONFESSIONS OF AMANS (1977, Bauer International)—**William Bryan** is a wandering philosophy student who falls in love with the wife of a lord whom he has been hired to tutor.

AMASOVA, MAJOR ANYA

THE SPY WHO LOVED ME (1977, GB, UA)—James Bond, as portrayed by Roger Moore, teams up with beautiful Russian spy **Barbara Bach** to thwart megalomaniac Curt Jurgens.

AMATHEA

THE BARBARIAN QUEEN (1985, Concorde/Cinema Group)—In a sword and sorcery story, **Lana Clarkston** is a warrior seeking revenge for the atrocities suffered by her tribe.

AMAZON QUEEN

TARZAN AND THE AMAZONS (1945, RKO)—The film doesn't explain what little old wrinkled **Maria Ouspenskaya** is doing as the queen of a tribe of tall voluptuous warriors—or where they all came from originally, since there are no males in evidence.

AMBERSON, MAJOR

THE MAGNIFICENT AMBERSONS (1942, RKO)—**Richard Bennett**, father of Joan and Constance, appears as the patriarch of Booth Tarkington's Indiana family of wealth and privilege. When he dies, his family discovers that the family fortune has been squandered.

AMBERSON (MINIFER), GEORGE AND ISABEL *See* MINIFER

AMBLER, AUNT MAGGIE

WHO KILLED AUNT MAGGIE? (1940, Republic)—**Elizabeth Patterson** will become a corpse, but she'll have plenty of company in this fairly good mystery, considering the studio.

AMBROSE, RUTH

ALONG CAME RUTH (1924, Silent, MGM)—Discouraged interior director **Viola Dane** deserts the big city for Action, Maine, where she makes a success of a general store and finds a likely lad for a husband.

AMBROSIA

THE LOVE GIRL (1916, Silent, Bluebird)—**Ella Hall** is a little orphaned country girl who moves to the city to live with relatives. She is given little affection until she rescues her cousin from kidnappers.

AMERICAN, THE

THE QUIET AMERICAN (1957, 20th Century Fox)—**Audie Murphy**, an American in Saigon, saves a journalist who has been duped into betraying the United States to the communists.

AMES, HOPE

THE CASE AGAINST MRS. AMES (1936, Paramount)—It seems that **Madeleine Carroll** is constantly on trial, first for the murder of her husband, then for the custody of her son.

AMES, JANET
THE GUILT OF JANET AMES (1947, Columbia)—When her husband is killed in the war, paralyzed **Rosalind Russell** seeks the cause hoping to discover if his sacrifice was worthwhile.

AMES, JOAN
'TIL WE MEET AGAIN (1940, Warner Brothers)—In the ultimate soap opera, dying **Merle Oberon** falls in love with George Brent, who is being taken back to the U.S. to be executed. They fall in love on the ocean liner carrying them from Hong Kong and keep their fates from each other—promising to meet again—but it's not to be in this life.

AMES, MARGARET
A WAVE, A WAC AND A MARINE (1944, Monogram)—Broadway talent agent Henny Youngman signs **Sally Eilers** and Elyse Knox for the cast of the Broadway show, but they're the wrong girls. No problem, they have the talent.

AMES, SGT.
YANKS AHOY (1943, Allied Artists)—**Joe Sawyer** and William Tracy are a couple of dim-witted American Army sergeants whose antics get them into a lot of trouble, but all is forgiven when they capture a Japanese mini-sub.

AMIDON, FRED
SOME KIND OF NUT (1969, UA)—**Dick Van Dyke** is a bank clerk who grows a beard and is thought to be flouting authority.

AMY
AMY (1981, Buena Vista)—In 1913, **Jenny Agutter** leaves her domineering husband to teach in a school for the deaf and blind. Besides helping her students, she learns to be independent and self-reliant.

AMY
THEY KNEW WHAT THEY WANTED (1940, RKO)—Waitress **Carole Lombard** carries on a correspondence with an Italian Californian vineyard owner and agrees to marry him. The bridegroom to be, Charles Laughton, sent her the picture of his handsome foreman, William Gargan, claiming it is his photo. Although Lombard has an affair with Gargan, she goes through with her marriage to Laughton.

AMYAK
PREHISTORIC WOMEN (1967, GB, 20th Century Fox)—**Stephanie Randall** is one of a tribe of prehistoric women hunters. Why is it the women look so modernly sexy, and the men look like little more than animals? Silly question!

AMYTIS
JUPITER'S DARLING (1955, MGM)—Temptress **Esther Williams** tries to prevent Hannibal from sacking Rome by taking his mind off war. The sheer lunacy of this movie must be seen to be believed—and then it won't be believed.

ANASTASIA
ANASTASIA (1956, 20th Century Fox)—When White Russian General Yul Brynner finds a destitute suicidal amnesiac, **Ingrid Bergman**, he is struck by how much she looks like the youngest daughter of the last Czar of Russia. Ingrid is groomed to play the role and almost carries it off.

ANCHOR
SATAN'S SADIST (1969, Independent-International)—**Russ Tamblyn** and his gang of motorcycle punks spend their time raping and killing college girls and drinking LSD in their coffee. Well, what ya goin' to do, man?

ANDAR, ABU
THIEF OF DAMASCUS (1952, Columbia)—With the help of Aladdin, Sinbad and Scheherazade, General **Paul Henreid** deposes the wicked ruler of Damascus. To cut costs, the producer intersperses scenes from JOAN OF ARC, which makes for an unusual costume mix.

ANDERS, JOAN
THE GIRL FROM HAVANA (1929, Fox)—In an early talkie, **Lola Lane** is a detective who solves an ingenious jewel heist, which takes place when the store is full of customers and employees.

ANDERSON
THE ANDERSON TAPES (1971, Columbia)—Habitual criminal **Sean Connery**, just out of prison, plans to pull off a big caper in a posh New York apartment house. He's unaware that he is being taped by several law-enforcement agencies. He's gunned down during the break-in.

ANDERSON
TWO LIVING, ONE DEAD (1964, GB, Emerson)—**Bill Travers**, Patrick McGoohan and another postal employee are interrupted by robbers. Travers is seriously wounded, the other man is killed, and McGoohan gives the robbers what they want. Later Travers is treated as a hero, McGoohan as a coward, but it turns out that Travers was an inside man on the robbery.

ANDERSON, CARL WAYNE
SUSPECT (1987, Tri-Star)—**Liam Neeson** is a helpless, homeless and speechless vet accused of murdering a woman. But public defender Cher, with the help of juror Dennis Quaid, who makes his own investigation of both the case and Cher, is able to show that the judge, John Mahoney, is the real murderer.

ANDERSON, CHESTY
CHESTY ANDERSON, U.S. NAVY (1976, Atlas)—This film contains all the familiar tasteless, giggly, adolescent jokes ever made about spectacularly well-endowed young women—in this case **Shari Eubank**.

ANDERSON, CLAY
STRANGER AT MY DOOR (1956, Republic)—**Skip Homeier**, a young gunman, takes refuge in the home of preacher Macdonald Carey who tries to reform him.

ANDERSON, DETECTIVE
THE BAT WHISPERS (1930, UA)—It's naughty to give away the identity of the maniac murderer of this picture but the thrust of our book demands that we tell you that it's ugh! aah! ooo! **Chester Morris**.

ANDERSON, DUFF
NOTHING BUT A MAN (1964, Cinema V)—Black worker **Ivan Dixon** comes to realize that his family should not be made to suffer because of his frustrations over racial inequalities.

ANDERSON, FRANCESCA & JAMES
MY LOVER, MY SON (1970, GB, MGM)—When her lover is killed, unhappily married **Romy Schneider** turns her attentions to her son **Dennis Waterman**. The two develop a most unhealthy relationship. When her husband objects, Schneider kills him and Waterman, believing he killed his father, takes the blame.

ANDERSON, HANS CHRISTIAN
MR. H.C. ANDERSON (1950, GB, British Found.) HANS CHRISTIAN ANDERSON (1952, RKO); THE DAYDREAMER (1966, Embassy)—The 1950 biopic features some animated presentations of the storyteller's tales and oddly enough "Ali Baba and the Forty Thieves." In 1952 **Danny Kaye** is effective as the famed Danish author of fairy tales. He sings a few decent Frank Loesser numbers and falls in love with a married ballerina. In the 1966 film **Paul O'Keefe** is the story teller who at 13 meets animated versions of many of the characters he will write of later.

ANDERSON, LOUISE
THE BAMBOO BLONDE (1946, RKO)—**Frances Langford** shares the title name with a B-29 christened for her by the pilot. The plane becomes the scourge of the Japanese, sinking battleships and shooting down scores of Zeros.

ANDERSON, MABEL
DAMES (1934, Warner Brothers)—Doing what she did best at this point in her career, **Joan Blondell** is a wise-cracking, gold-digging chorus girl. The movie's plot deals with the problems of putting on a Broadway show and is barely enough to get from one marvelous Busby Berkeley production number to the next.

ANDERSON, WES
THE MOONLIGHTER (1953, Warner Brothers)—**Fred MacMurray** is accused of herding cows during the day and rustling them at night. A lynch mob gets the wrong man, and Fred becomes an avenging angel for the poor unfortunate victim.

ANDIE
PRETTY IN PINK (1986, Paramount)—When **Molly Ringwald**, one of the "have-nots" at her high school, is invited out by one of the "haves," she learns how cruel his friends can be.

ANDRE
MY DINNER WITH ANDRE (1981, New Yorker)—In an unusual movie **Andre Gregory** sups with Wallace Shawn and over a two hour period the former shares his philosophies and uncommon life-experiences with the latter.

ANDREA
THE SHE-CREATURE (1956, American International)—**Marla English** is hypnotized by the Great Lombardi bringing out her former self, a prehistoric sea-monster bent on killing.

ANDREA
WAITRESS (1982, Troma)—**Carol Drake** is an actress working as a waitress while waiting to get her break in show business. Doesn't everyone?

ANDREW
TWO GENTLEMEN SHARING (1969, GB, American International)—**Hal Frederick** is a Black Jamaican lawyer sharing a London flat with a white advertising executive. Their interracial friendship is not shared by others in their lives.

ANDREWS, AGATHA
SEVEN WOMEN (1966, MGM)—**Margaret Leighton** is one of the staff at a thirties Chinese mission which is overrun by bandits.

ANDREWS, BETTY
CONVICTED WOMAN (1940, Columbia)—In this routine women's prison picture, **Rochelle Hudson** is the obligatory framed inmate.

ANDREWS, JOSEPH
JOSEPH ANDREWS (1977, GB, Paramount)—**Peter Firth** is a naive eighteenth century footman in a story of many hidden identities. The film demonstrates that making a movie from a work of Henry Fielding, author of "Tom Jones," does not guarantee an exciting and amusing picture.

ANDREWS, LIL
RED HEADED WOMAN (1932, MGM)—When shopgirl **Jean Harlow** marries her boss, she finds that she isn't accepted by his society friends.

ANDREWS, POLLY
THE GROUP (1966, UA)—**Shirley Knight**, one of eight friends and graduates of Smith College during the depression, works for a hospital and has an affair with a married man who won't divorce his wife. Knight ends up with a psychiatrist as her love.

ANDREWS, BIG STEVE
THE MAGNIFICENT BRUTE (1936, Universal)—Steel furnace boss **Victor McLaglen** becomes one-third of a romantic triangle with Binnie Barnes and William Hall. He rescues a child from being boiled alive when the boy falls into a crucible into which molten steel is about to be poured.

ANDROCLES
ANDROCLES AND THE LION (1952, RKO)—**Alan Young's** kindness of removing a thorn from a lion's paw is repaid later in the Roman arena in this lively production of the droll George Bernard Shaw play.

ANDROMACHE
THE TROJAN WOMEN (1971, Cinerama)—**Vanessa Redgrave** is one of four Trojan women lamenting their fate after the fall of Troy to Greece in this production of the Euripedes play.

ANDROS, FRANCES & PAUL
THE V.I.P.S (1963, GB, MGM)—Bored **Elizabeth Taylor** is running away from her husband **Richard Burton** with Louis Jourdan. When her plane is delayed, despondent and suicidal Burton arrives at the airport, hoping to change her mind.

ANDY
ANDY (1965, Universal)—In a touching story, **Norman Alden** portrays a middle-aged mentally retarded man who lives with dignity in a New York slum neighborhood.

ANDY
HANDY ANDY (1921, Silent, GB, Ideal)—Nineteenth century Irish stable boy **Peter Coleman** takes the identity of his cousin in order to foil a kidnapping and is almost forced to marry his sister.

ANDY
JOCKS (1987, Crown)—**Stoney Jackson**, an effeminate black, is one member of a college tennis team that the school's president has ordered the athletic director to win a championship with—or else.

ANGEL
ANGEL (1984, New World); AVENGING ANGEL (1985, New World); ANGEL 3: THE FINAL CHAPTER (1988, New World)—During the day **Donna Wilkes** is Molly, a 15-year-old high school honor student. At night she's a spike-heeled, mini-skirted Hollywood Strip hooker, who goes gunning for a psychotic killer of prostitutes. In the sequel, Wilkes is replaced by **Betsy Russell** who, looking more the part of a street-walker, returns to her old haunts to track down the killer of a police detective who had helped her get off the

streets. In the final chapter, Angel/Molly, now played by **Mitzi Kapture** is still concerned for the street people, and discovers that she has a kid sister who is mixed up in the porno video racket.

ANGEL

CLARENCE AND ANGEL (1978, Gardner)—New York street smart kid **Mark Cardova** befriends shy Darren Brown, just arrived from South Carolina, and teaches the illiterate how to read.

ANGEL

DATE WITH AN ANGEL (1987, De Laurentiis)—Heavenly messenger **Emmanuelle Beart**, on a mission to pick up Michael E. Knight, collides with a communications satellite, breaks a wing and falls into Knight's swimming pool. His fiancee is not thrilled by the new "woman" in Knight's life.

ANGEL

LITTLE DARLINGS (1980, Paramount)—**Kristy McNichol** and Tatum O'Neal compete to see which one will be the first to lose her virginity. Kristy wins but it seems like losing.

ANGEL

RUN, ANGEL, RUN (1969, Fanfare)—**William Smith** quits a motorcycle gang after selling a biker exposure story to a magazine. He settles down on a sheep ranch with his girlfriend, but his former buddies show up seeking revenge.

ANGEL

THE WILD BUNCH (1969, Warner Brothers)—**Jaime Sanchez** is a Mexican member of an outlaw gang that moves south of the border to put distance between them and a pursuing posse. Sanchez is brutalized by a Mexican general, but belatedly the rest of the Wild Bunch decide to come to his aid.

ANGEL BABY

ANGEL BABY (1961, Allied Artists)—Mute **Salome Jens** has her speech restored by a faith healer who then exploits her.

ANGEL, FATHER

DEATH OF AN ANGEL (1986, 20th Century Fox)—**Nick Mancuso** is a charismatic Mexican religious zealot who helps Episcopalian priest Bonnie Bedelia refind her faith.

ANGEL, HARRY

ANGEL HEART (1987, Tri-Star)—In a film not for the squeamish, fifties private eye **Mickey Rourke** is hired by devilish Robert De Niro to locate a man who must repay a debt. During the investigation, bodies pile up as a result of horrible voodoo deaths. In the end Rourke discovers that he's the murderer and missing debtor.

ANGEL, JOHNNY

JOHNNY ANGEL (1945, RKO)—There are many interesting plot twists in this mystery, which has seaman **George Raft** solving his father's murder.

ANGEL, THE

THE ANGEL WHO PAWNED HER HARP (1956, GB, British Lion)—Real angel **Diane Cilento** arrives on a goodwill visit to seamy Islington and helps a pawnbroker and his friends.

ANGEL, THE

CHARLEY AND THE ANGEL (1973, Buena Vista/Disney)—**Harry Morgan**, an impatient angel, comes to take thirties sporting goods storekeeper Fred MacMurray to his reward. But Fred escapes death three times playing for time to be better to his family, which he has long ignored.

ANGELA

AARON LOVES ANGELA (1975, Columbia)—In a contemporary New York ghetto, **Irene Cara's** love for Kevin Hooks exists side by side with pimps, prostitutes and drug pushers.

ANGELA

ANGELA (1977, Canada, Montreal Travel Co.)—When prostitute **Sophia Loren** has a baby, she quits turning tricks and becomes a waitress in Montreal. When her man returns from Vietnam, he doesn't believe the baby is his and throws her out. Years later, she is killed, unwittingly making love to her son.

ANGELA

THE PLEASURE GIRLS (1966, GB, Times Film)—**Anneke Wills** is one of four girls sharing a London flat having trouble with their boyfriends at a time when jumping into bed with a member of the opposite sex in a movie still required a decision.

ANGELA

STREET ANGEL (1928, Fox)—Unwilling prostitute **Janet Gaynor** becomes a star of the circus.

ANGELO, PVT.

PRIVATE ANGELO (1949, GB, ABF-Pathe)—**Peter Ustinov** is an Italian soldier who hates war and runs from his army, the Germans and the invading Allied troops.

ANGERMANN, ERIKA

FRAULEIN (1958, 20th Century Fox)—In Berlin just after the end of WWII, many German girls turned to prostitution to survive. **Dana Wynter**, daughter of a renowned professor, didn't but is believed to have. She has some problems with the Communists but things get better when she is rescued by a serviceman whom she helped escape from the Nazis during the war.

ANGSTROM, RABBIT

RABBIT, RUN (1970, Warner Brothers)—**James Caan** abandons his pregnant wife to be with a prostitute. The John Updike story doesn't make for a good movie.

ANN

OUR DANCING DAUGHTERS (1928, Silent, MGM)—Hard-drinking blonde **Anita Page** is pushed into marriage to a millionaire's son, but conveniently falls down stairs and kills herself so that Joan Crawford can get the young man.

ANN

SO EVIL SO YOUNG (1961, GB, UA)—Framed **Jill Ireland** escapes from a reformatory to prove that she is not a robber.

ANN

WOMAN WANTED (1935, MGM)—**Maureen O'Sullivan**, fleeing a murder charge, is taken in by lawyer Joel McCrea who proves her innocent.

ANN, SISTER

THE SINGING NUN (1966, MGM)—In this awful musical, **Debbie Reynolds** appears as a nun who moves out of the convent to share her music with the world. Get thee back to a nunnery!

ANNA

ANNA (1987, Magnus/Vestron)—Former Andy Warhol actress **Sally Kirkland** earned an Oscar nomination in this All About Eve-like story. Sally is Bette Davis to supermodel Paulina Porizkova's Anne Baxter.

ANNA

CALL ME (1988, Vestron)—When **Patricia Charbonneau** receives a late night call from a heavy breather, the ding-a-ling believes it's her boyfriend playing games and agrees to meet him at a local bar. After she arrives, she not only witnesses a brutal murder, but finds herself an unwilling participant in the crime.

ANNA

JET PILOT (1957, RKO/Universal)—Do you believe **Janet Leigh** as a Russian jet pilot who falls for American pilot Clark Gable? Neither did audiences in 1957.

ANNA

STRANGERS (1990, Australia, Genesis)—Think of a mish-mash mixture of STRANGERS ON A TRAIN and FATAL ATTRACTION and you have an idea of this minor entry. Mentally unstable **Anne Looby** has a hot and heavy affair with James Healey, whom she meets on a plane. She is playing for real and his rejection of her leads to several deaths, including Healey's grasping wife Mary Regan.

ANNA

TRUCK STOP WOMEN (1974, LT Women)—**Lieux Dressler** is the ring leader of a gang of prostitutes and robbers operating out of a Southwestern truck stop. She has trouble with the local Mafia which want a piece of the action.

ANNA VICTORIA OF GZBFERNIGAMBIA

SUCH A LITTLE QUEEN (1914, Silent, Famous Players); (1921, Silent, Realart)—**Mary Pickford and Constance Binney** portray the queen of a mythical European country who flees to the U.S. when revolution breaks out. There, she receives the attention of a wealthy young man until her intended, the King of Hetland, comes for her.

ANNABEL

AFFAIRS OF ANNABEL (1938, RKO); ANNABEL TAKES A TOUR (1938, RKO) -When her movie career takes a downward spin, **Lucille Ball's** zany press agent Jack Oakie comes up with a stunt that gets her kidnapped by gangsters who force her to participate in a crime. In the sequel, while on promotional tour, Ball is romantically linked with a famous song writer. She falls for her press agent's puffery and the song writer, only to discover he's already married.

ANNABELLA

SWAMP WOMAN (1941, Producers Releasing Corp.)—**Ann Corio** is a saloon singer who returns to her Florida hometown and finds her old boyfriend engaged to her niece. Ann wants him back and will stop at nothing to get her way.

ANNA-MARIE, COUNTESS

BRIDE OF THE REGIMENT (1930, First National)—When the Austrians invade the castle of **Vivienne Segal's** husband, an Italian count, the conquering commander offers to spare her husband's life if she will sleep with him. Her virtue remains intact when the commander in a drunken stupor dreams she gives herself to him. Satisfied, he releases her husband. Must have been a quite convincing succubus.

ANNE

ANNE AGAINST THE WORLD (1929, Silent, Rayart)—Musical comedy star **Shirley Mason** marries a wealthy man but is still pursued by a producer. Her husband tests her fidelity by acting penniless. Mason leaves him to return to her former life but true love wins out.

ANNE

ANNE OF THE INDIES (1951, 20th Century Fox)—**Jean Peters** is a swashbuckling pirate captain who dallies with French officer Louis Jourdan before engaging in a sea battle with Blackbeard.

ANNE

THE CITY GIRL (1984, Moon)—The film examines the life and loves of **Laura Harrington**, a young woman trying to make it as a photographer.

ANNE

HER FIRST AFFAIRE (1932, GB, Sterling)—Infatuated **Ida Lupino** wishes to have an affair with a married author of sensational novels.

ANNE OF CLEVES

HENRY VIII AND HIS SIX WIVES (1972, GB, EMI/MGM)—**Jenny Bos's** marriage to Henry as his fourth consort is a political arrangement with the German Lutherans. Henry has been said to have found her "no better than a Flanders mare." The marriage was later annulled by Parliament.

ANNE, PRINCESS

THE LADY IN THE IRON MASK (1952, 20th Century Fox)—Take the story of THE MAN IN THE IRON MASK, substitute **Patricia Medina** for Louis Hayward and you have the idea of this film. Medina plays twin sisters: Princess Anne, who is replaced on her throne by Princess Louise.

ANNETTE

TWO WIVES AT ONE WEDDING (1961, GB, Paramount)—**Lisa Daniely** attempts to blackmail Gordon Jackson shortly after he marries socialite Christine Gregg. Daniely claims that the two were married years earlier in France.

ANNI

THE BRIDE WORE RED (1937, MGM)—A whimsical count arranges for chorus girl **Joan Crawford** to spend two weeks at a swank Tyrol resort where she is pursued by two rich men, Robert Young and Franchot Tone.

ANNIE

ANNIE (1982, Columbia)—Except for the singing of the song "Tomorrow" by cute little **Aileen Quinn** as the redheaded comic strip moppet, this musical mishmash is disappointing.

ANNIE

LADY FROM CHEYENNE (1941, Universal)—**Loretta Young** is a feminist schoolteacher in 1880 Wyoming fighting for women's rights.

ANNIE

SIDE STREET ANGEL (1937, GB, Warner Brothers)—**Lesley Brook** helps run a hotel for "reformed" crooks. A wealthy young man arrives claiming to be a gentleman thief after being jilted by his society girlfriend. Naturally, he falls for Brook.

ANNIE

SIX PACK ANNIE (1975, American International)—Well-endowed **Lindsay Bloom** arrives in Miami to work as a prostitute in order to raise money to save her mother's diner. You don't find many kids like that anymore.

ANNINGTON, ANN

HER WINNING WAY (1921, Silent, Paramount)—**Mary Miles Minter**, a book reporter for a major newspaper, is assigned to interview an author who doesn't give interviews. She resorts to posing as his maid and is responsible for the breakup of his engagement to a woman chosen by his mother.

ANSCOMBE, EDGAR
THE AVIATOR (1985, MGM/UA)—**Christopher Reeve** is a pilot who flies the mail. He is forced to take Rosanna Arquette along as a passenger and isn't pleased. After some harrowing adventures, she grows on him.

ANSON, SYLVIA
WOMAN TO WOMAN (1946, GB, Anglo-American)—**Adele Dixon** refuses to give a divorce to her husband who has had an affair with a dancer with a heart condition—resulting in a child.

ANTHONY
THE KINDRED (1987, F-M Entertainment)—**Michael Shawn McCracken** is a hideous hybrid creature cloned from a cell sample of David Allen Brooks' blood in this second-rate horror film wasting Kim Hunter and Rod Steiger.

ANTHONY, JOE
THE CADDY (1953, Paramount)—**Jerry Lewis** is the caddy-manager of pro golfer Dean Martin in a comedy not up to par.

ANTHONY, KIRK
THE NE'ER DO WELL (1916, Silent, Pathe)—**Wheeler Oakman**, a shiftless playboy is thrown unconscious and penniless aboard a ship bound for Panama, where he is wrongly accused of murder.

ANTINEA, QUEEN
SIREN OF ATLANTIS (1948, UA)—Two explorers find the lost continent of Atlantis and fall in love with its queen, **Maria Montez.**

ANTIOPE
THE WARRIOR'S HUSBAND (1933, Fox)—**Elissa Landi** is the sister of the Amazon Queen of Pontus in 800 B.C. where all the men are pansies. When The Greeks led by David Manners invade Pontus, the Amazons discover what real men are like and take Greek husbands whom they gladly acknowledge as their masters.

ANTIPHOLUS OF SYRACUSE
BOYS FROM SYRACUSE (1940, Mayfair/Universal)—In a musical comedy adaptation of William Shakespeare's "A Comedy of Errors," **Allan Jones** and his twin brother are separated at birth. Jones' twin goes on to become emperor, conquers Syracuse and decrees that all Syracusians must die, thus dooming his own father and brother.

ANTOINETTE
GIRLS AT SEA (1958, GB, Seven Arts)—**Nadine Tallier** is one of three beautiful girls who attended a party aboard a ship and aren't able to leave before it is ordered on maneuvers.

ANTONELLI, MARIA
FOUR GIRLS IN TOWN (1956, Universal)—**Elsa Martinelli** is Italy's representative when girls from various countries are chosen for Hollywood screen tests.

ANTONIA
THE THREE SISTERS (1930, Fox)—**Addie McPhail** is one of three sisters who discover the money they are sending their mother back in the old country is being pocketed by another.

ANTONIO
THE MERCHANT OF VENICE (1918, GB, Silent, Broadwest)—**Matheson Lang,** as Shylock, wants his 'pound of flesh' from merchant **George Skillan** in an early version of Shakespeare's immortal play.

ANTONY
ANTONY AND CLEOPATRA (1973, GB, Rank)—**Charlton Heston** directed himself in this sluggish telling of the love story of the Roman general and the Queen of the Nile. The director needed a better actor, and the actor required a more knowing director.

ANTONY, BRUNO
STRANGERS ON A TRAIN (1951, Warner Brothers)—Wishing to have his father dead, **Robert Walker** proposes to Farley Granger that they trade murders. Granger doesn't take Walker seriously until the latter kills Granger's promiscuous wife and insists Granger carry out his part of the bargain.

APACHE BOB
THE APACHE RAIDER (1928, Silent, Pathe Exchange)—Regarded as a bandit, **Leo Maloney** steals his cattle from a rancher who has obtained his herd illegally—thus showing that two wrongs make a right.

APACHE KID
APACHE WARRIOR (1957, 20th Century Fox)—In a far too familiar story, **Keith Larsen** leads the redskins on the war path when his brother is killed.

APE, THE
THE MONSTER AND THE GIRL (1941, Paramount)—When **Phillip Terry** is framed for murder, scientist George Zucco gets permission to implant the former's brain in an ape after Terry is executed. The ape goes on a rampage, killing those who had framed Terry.

APE MONSTER, THE
THE RETURN OF THE APE MAN (1944, Monogram)—Yeah, he or it is back, this time represented by **Frank Moran**, and his disposition hasn't improved.

APLEY, GEORGE
THE LATE GEORGE APLEY (1947, 20th Century Fox)—In this entertaining examination of the family life of Boston blueblood **Ronald Colman**, nothing much happens.

APOSTO, ANTHONY
THE YOUNG SAVAGES (1961, UA)—When three gang members brutally kill a blind member of another gang, **Neil Nephew** is one of three arrested for murder. Assistant District Attorney. Burt Lancaster discovers that Nephew is retarded and not responsible. The latter is sent to a mental institution.

APPLE ANNIE
LADY FOR A DAY (1933, Columbia)—New York gamblers and racketeers arrange for a poor old apple seller **May Robson** to pass for a rich woman when her daughter comes to introduce her mother to her wealthy South American fiance.

APPLEBY, AGGIE
AGGIE APPLEBY, MAKER OF MEN (1933, RKO)—**Wynne Gibson**, loved by two men, toughens up a society lad and tames a rough-neck.

APPLEBY, ALOYSIUS
THE COLLEGE BOOB (1926, Silent, Fox)—**Lefty Flynn** is off to college with the intention of passing up playing sports, despite his considerable ability. He finds he has to fight a jealous senior and join the football team to get respect.

APPLEBY, CHARLEY

CHARLEY AND THE ANGEL (1973, Buena Vista)—**Fred MacMurray** is too busy with his depression era business to have time for his family. Angel Harry Morgan visits Fred to tell him his life is over. Fred begs successfully for time to amend his ways.

APPLEBY, LEE

SHADY LADY (1945, Universal)—**Ginny Simms** assists elderly cardshark Charles Coburn catch others of his profession for the District Attorney.

APPLEBY, SYLVIA DOLORES

DIMPLES (1936, 20th Century Fox)—In the Bowery of pre-Civil War New York, **Shirley Temple** is hard-pressed to save her destitute reprobate of a grandfather, Frank Morgan.

APPLEGATE, BEN

THE COUNTRY KID (1923, Silent, Warner Brothers)—The eldest of three orphans, **Wesley Barry** runs the farm on which they live. An uncle, eager to get the farm, charges that Barry is incompetent to run the farm and look after his younger brothers, but a kindly judge disagrees and a neighboring couple adopts all three.

APPLEGATE, DICK, JANE, SALLY & JOHNNY

THE APPLEGATES (1990, Australia, Roadshow)—A family of giant Brazilian cockroaches assume the form of a typical American family who look like **Ed Begley, Jr.**, **Stockard Channing**, **Cami Cooper** and **Bobby Jacoby**. In this satire, the cockroaches learn about humans from the primer *Fun with Dick and Jane*.

APPLEGATE, SUSAN

THE MAJOR AND THE MINOR (1942, Paramount)—In order to travel for half fare on a train, **Ginger Rogers** poses as a twelve year old. She is aided by Ray Milland, head of a boy's military school, who is taken in by her disguise—but romance is the end result.

APPLETON, JENNIE

PORTRAIT OF JENNIE (1949, Selznick)—Each time unsuccessful artist Joseph Cotten comes across **Jennifer Jones** in Central Park, she appears older. Finally when she appears to him as a young woman, he falls in love with her and paints her portrait, which becomes his masterpiece. He learns that she died many years earlier and there is nothing he can do to change the fact, though he tries.

APOLLO, JOHNNY

JOHNNY APOLLO (1940, 20th Century Fox)—Real name Bob Cain, wealthy **Tyrone Power** resentful of his father's dishonest dealings becomes a crook himself.

APPOLLONIUS OF TYANA

SEVEN FACES OF DR. LAO (1964, MGM)—Appollonius is one more of the disguises assumed by elderly Chinaman magician **Tony Randall** when he brings his traveling show to a terrorized western desert town.

APRIL

I'LL REMEMBER APRIL (1945, Universal)—**Gloria Jean**, daughter of a once rich man, becomes a radio singer and gets mixed up in a murder.

APRIL

NICE GIRLS DON'T EXPLODE (1987, New World)—**Michelle Meyrink's** mother Barbara Harris tries to make it appear that her daughter causes fires and explosions, but her boyfriend sets things straight. You have to be desperate to watch this.

APRIL, JOHNNY

WEST SIDE KID (1943, Republic)—**Donald "Red" Barry** is a gangster hired to kill a newspaper publisher for a $25 fee. Barry learns that the publisher is arranging his own death to get out of an unhappy family situation. Rather than complete his contract, Barry decides to put things right in the publisher's life.

ARAMIS

THE THREE MUSKETEERS (1921, Silent, UA); (1935, RKO); ((1939, 20th Century Fox); (1948, MGM); (1974, 20th Century Fox); THE FOUR MUSKETEERS (1975, 20th Century Fox)—**Eugene Pallette, Onslow Stevens, John King, Robert Coote and Richard Chamberlain** each appeared in the Alexandre Dumas story of three musketeers of the queen and a new recruit, D'Artagnan, who save the honor of the queen who Cardinal Richelieu is intent on discrediting in the King's eyes. With the exception of Chamberlain who appeared in the role in the last two films mentioned above, the role of Aramis seemed that of comedy relief. In the 1974 and 1975 movies, Frank Finlay as Porthos handled this chore although all four friends took their living and killing lightly.

ARBUTNEY

THREE STRANGERS (1946, Warner Brothers)—**Sidney Greenstreet**, Peter Lorre and Geraldine Fitzgerald are an unusual trio who find themselves sharing a winning sweepstakes ticket. Sidney and Peter's criminal activities make collecting rather difficult.

ARCHER, COLONEL

THE COMMANDING OFFICER (1915, Silent, Paramount)—When he is left to raise the two children of his deceased sister, **Donald Crisp** marries the daughter of a retired officer to have someone take care of the children. The couple don't get along, and she is paid court by a series of suitors, one of whom is killed, with suspicion pointing to Crisp as the culprit.

ARCHER, CORLISS

A KISS FOR CORLISS (1949, UA)—In her final film, **Shirley Temple** develops a crush on middle-aged roue David Niven and convinces all that he reciprocates her interest.

ARCHER, MAXWELL

MAXWELL ARCHER, MASTER DETECTIVE (1942, GB, Monogram)—Private detective **John Loder's** solution of a mysterious crime doesn't sit well with the lads at Scotland Yard.

ARCHER, NANCY

ATTACK OF THE 50 FOOT WOMAN (1958, Allied Artists)—An atomic blast causes **Allison Hayes** to experience exceptional growth. Before being blown away with a riot gun, she squeezes the life out of her unfaithful husband.

ARCHER, TEX

SING, COWBOY, SING (1937, Grand National)—**Tex Ritter** leads a wagon train of supplies headed west which is attacked by a gang that want the cargo themselves.

ARCHIBALD, BABS

BAB'S DIARY (1917, Silent, Paramount)—While home from boarding school for the holidays, **Marguerite Clark** makes up an imaginary fiance, but a man of that name shows up to complicate her life.

ARCHIE

HUSBANDS (1970, Columbia)—When a close friend suddenly dies, **Peter Falk**, John Cassavetes and Ben Gazarra go on a spree, ending up in London where they have a brief fling with three willing women.

ARDEN, ELLEN & NICK

MY FAVORITE WIFE (1940, RKO)—After having had his long missing wife **Irene Dunne** declared legally dead, **Cary Grant** marries Gail Patrick and sets off on his honeymoon. Dunne shows up to throw a damper on the celebration. Seems she's spent the last seven years alone on a deserted island with Randolph Scott.

ARDEN, JANE

ADVENTURES OF JANE ARDEN (1939, Warner Brothers)—**Roselle Towne**, an investigative reporter, outwits a gang of jewel smugglers.

ARDEN, JOHN *See* MONTGOMERY ROYALE

ARDEN, JOYCE

IT'S LOVE I'M AFTER (1937, Warner Brothers/First National)—**Bette Davis**, co-star and fiancee of matinee idol Leslie Howard, explodes when he becomes involved with Olivia de Havilland.

ARDEN, TERRY

MISS LONDON LTD. (1943, GB, GFD)—**Evelyn Dall**, daughter of an American owner of an escort agency in London during WWII, teams up with Arthur Askey to scare up more customers.

ARGEN, JANE

SEVEN WOMEN (1966, MGM)—In director John Ford's last feature film, **Mildred Dunnock** gives her usual strong character performance as one of seven female missionaries who, in 1935, are running a Chinese mission that is threatened by the troops of a brutal war lord.

ARGUELLO, DON MIGUEL

DON MIKE (1927, Silent, FBO)—California aristocrat **Richard Thompson** fights to keep his land and wins the love of beautiful Ruth Cliffoer. Never heard of her, did you say?

ARGYLE, BRUCE

THE ARGYLE CASE (1917, Warwick); (1929, Warner Brothers)—When **Arthur Albertson**, the head of the Argyle family, is murdered in a house full of secret agents and secret panels, a detective must sort things out. In 1929, **John Darrow** fills the bill as the corpse.

ARIEL

THE LITTLE MERMAID (1989, Disney/Buena Vista)—**Jodi Benson** supplies the voice of the little mermaid who trades her voice to Ursula the Sea Witch (voice of Pat Carroll) for a human body, so she may be with a prince with whom she has fallen in love, after saving him from a shipwreck.

ARIZONA, NATHAN JR.

RAISING ARIZONA (1987, 20th Century Fox)—When ex-con Nicolas Cage and his ex-cop wife Holly Hunter discover they can't have children of their own, they kidnap **T.K. Kuhn**, a quintuplet recently born into a local wealthy family.

ARKADIN, GREGORY

MR. ARKADIN (1962, GB, Talbot-Cari)—Director Orson Welles presents actor **Orson Welles** as one of the world's richest and most ruthless men. He ultimately takes his own life by jumping out of a plane.

ARLEN, WILLIAM

THE MARRIAGE OF A YOUNG STOCKBROKER (1971, 20th Century Fox)—Bored with his wife and his marriage, **Richard Benjamin** experiments with voyeurism and extra-marital affairs.

ARLETTE

NAUGHTY ARLETTE (1951, GB, UA)—Art teacher **Mai Zetterling** falls in love with her daughter's French classmate. Is it really necessary, in 1951, to point out that the love object is male?

ARLINE

THE BOHEMIAN GIRL (1936, MGM)—**Jacqueline Wells** (later to call herself Julie Bishop), the child of a nobleman, is stolen by gypsies who raise her as one of their own.

ARMITAGE, JAKE

THE PUMPKIN EATER (1964, GB, Columbia)—**Peter Finch**, third husband of mother of eight Anne Bancroft, has a series of affairs which once again threatens Bancroft's marital status. At least we know she believes in marriage and families.

ARMOUR, FRANK & LALI

BEHOLD MY WIFE (1920, Silent, Paramount)—When his family conspires with his fiancee for her to marry another, **Milton Sills** spites them by wedding Canadian half-breed **Mabel Julienne Scott**. She proves her mettle, winning the love and respect of her in-laws as well as that of her husband.

ARMSTRONG, JACK

THE TROUBLEMAKER (1964, Janus)—Chicken farmer **Tom Aldredge** comes to New York to open a coffee house and is shocked by all the corrupt city officials with their hands out. He eventually takes all of them on, up to and including a crooked police commissioner.

ARMSTRONG, JULIE

ARMY GIRL (1938, Republic)—Army brat **Madge Evans** is the daughter of the post commander at the time the cavalry is changing from horses to tanks.

ARMSTRONG, KEN

HEIR TO TROUBLE (1936, Columbia)—**Ken Maynard** inherits a mine and a baby when his friend dies. A varmint who wants the mine tries to implicate Ken in his friend's death, but with the help of his remarkable horse Tarzan, he's able to prove his innocence.

ARMSTRONG, RICHARD

THE CYCLONE RIDER (1924, Silent, Fox)—**Reed Howes** invents a carburetor that will make his car a sure winner in a road race, but he has to lose to avert being killed by a mobster.

ARNELO, TONY

THE ARNELO AFFAIR (1947, MGM)—Evil but slick Chicago nightclub owner **John Hodiak** takes advantage of the infatuation of a married woman to serve his own needs in a murder case.

ARNESEN, ANN

THE PLAINSMAN AND THE LADY (1946, Republic)—**Vera Ralston** is the lovely prize won by Wild Bill Elliott when he settles the problems of the Pony Express.

ARNOLD

ARNOLD (1973, Cinerama)—Dead man **Norman Stuart** toys with his heirs through a series of cassette recordings. The result is murder.

ARNOLD

PSYCHIC KILLER (1975, Avco Embassy)—Deranged **Jim Hutton** acquires psychic powers which he uses to take revenge on those who wronged him.

ARNOLD, CHUCK

YOU WERE MEANT FOR ME (1948, 20th Century Fox)—Band leader **Dan Dailey** sweeps small town girl Jeanne Crain off her feet. They marry before either knows much about each other. This is just one of hundreds of movies in which a couple meant for each other marry for the wrong reason and must discover they unconsciously did the right thing.

ARNOLD, KAY

LADIES OF LEISURE (1930, Columbia)—In this early Frank Capra film, gold digger **Barbara Stanwyck** develops a conscience and gives up the rich fiance she has snared. Can you guess what happens next?

ARNOLD, VIC

TIMES SQUARE PLAYBOY (1936, Warner Brothers)—When wealthy **Warren William** falls for a girl half his age, he is warned by an old friend that she may be a gold digger. Hurt by the accusation, she breaks things off with William which convinces both William and his friend of her sincere love.

ARROWSMITH, DR. MARTIN

ARROWSMITH (1931, UA)—After his wife and inspiration is killed by bubonic plague, idealistic physician **Ronald Colman** spends his life in the West Indies searching for a cure.

ARTHUR

ARTHUR'S HALLOWED GROUND (1986, GB, Cinecom)—**Jimmy Jewel**, the caretaker of a cricket field, battles with his superiors over what is to be done with his favorite place.

ARTHUR

THE FREEWAY MANIAC (1989, Cannon Group)—After escaping from a maximum-security asylum, parent-killer **Jason Courtney** looks for more people to kill.

ARTHUR, KING

A CONNECTICUT YANKEE IN KING ARTHUR'S COURT (1921, Silent, Fox); (1949, Paramount)—**Charles Clary** portrays the British monarch of Round Table fame who is visited by time traveler Harry Myers who arrives from nineteenth century Connecticut. In the 1949 remake, **Cedric Hardwicke** portrays the king as an aging man with a constant cold.

ARTHUR, LILITH

LILITH (1964, Columbia)—**Jean Seberg**, a nymphomaniac patient at a mental hospital, has an affair with her therapist, Warren Beatty, but two-times him with a woman, Anne Meacham.

ASHBY, ELEANOR

PARANOIAC (1963, GB, Universal)—**Janette Scott**, a young heiress, is saved from a suicide try by a young man claiming to be her deceased brother.

ASHE, JAN

A FREE SOUL (1931, MGM)—An unconventional lawyer defends a gangster against a murder charge and is dismayed to find that his free-spirited daughter **Norma Shearer** has fallen in love with the mobster.

ASHE, ROBERT

ALIAS LADYFINGERS (1921, Silent, Metro)—Orphan **Bert Lytell**, raised by a safecracker to become an infamous thief known as Ladyfingers, is discovered to be the heir to a vast estate.

ASHE, WILLIAM

THE MARRIAGE OF WILLIAM ASHE (1921, Silent, Metro)—**Wyndham Standing**, Britain's Secretary of House Affairs, marries a French convent-trained girl who shocks London with her caricatures of Parliamentary members and her semi-nude appearance at a gala.

ASHENDEN, RICHARD *See* EDGAR BRODIE

ASHLEY, PHILIP & RACHEL

MY COUSIN RACHEL (1952, 20th Century Fox)—When his foster father dies unexpectedly in Italy, **Richard Burton** suspects that the deceased's mysterious new wife **Olivia de Havilland** had something to do with it. But when she arrives at her late husband's Cornish home, a romance blooms between the two.

ASHMORE, BOBBY STORM

SARAH AND SON (1930, Paramount)—Widow Ruth Chatterton seeks to locate **Philippe de Lacey**, her son taken from her by her husband when the child was a baby. Chatterton, who made a living suffering through mother-sacrifice, is quite good.

ASHTON, DR. GREGORY

THE REJUVENATOR (1988, Jewel/SVS)—Scientist **John McKay** has discovered a serum which reverses the aging process. Former movie queen is eager to be a guinea pig. It works—but there are nasty side effects.

ASHTON, SENATOR MELVILE

THE SENATOR WAS INDISCREET (1947, Universal)—Foolish senator **William Powell**, with ambitions of becoming president, hires a press agent to push his cause, but entries from his diary prove embarrassing.

ASIAK

THE SAVAGE INNOCENTS (1960, GB, MGM)—When her husband Anthony Quinn accidently kills a mountie, Eskimo wife **Yoko Tani** flees north with her man.

ATHERLEY, LT. JACK

JACK TAR (1915, Silent, GB, Barker)—Fetched to Smyrna by an admiral's daughter, naval officer **Jack Tessier**, masquerading as a Turk, saves the consulate from a German spy.

ATHOS

THE THREE MUSKETEERS (1921, Silent, UA); (1935, RKO); (1939, 20th Century Fox); (1948, MGM); (1974, 20th Century Fox); THE FOUR MUSKETEERS (1975, 20th Century Fox)—**Leon Barry, Paul Lukas, Douglass Dumbrille, Van Heflin and Oliver Reed** each impersonate the king's musketeer once married to the infamous Milady De Winter. Athos ultimately orders her execution by beheading.

ATLAS

ATLAS (1960, Filmgroup)—Greek god **Michael Forrest** battles another strong man for the favors of a lovely earthling.

ATOUK
CAVEMAN (1981, UA)—Ex-Beatle **Ringo Starr** is a caveman in one zillion B.C. who forms his own tribe of outcasts and invents "Rock 'n' Roll."

ATWATER, JULIA
GENTLE JULIA (1923, Silent, Fox); (1936, 20th Century Fox) - **Bessie Love**, a pretty girl from a small town, becomes infatuated with an older man and follows him to Chicago where she discovers he has a wife. She hurries home to the boy who has always loved her. In the remake, **Marsha Hunt** is saved from making a fool of herself with a cad by her younger sister, Jane Withers.

ATWELL, MARION
CONFESSIONS OF A WIFE (1928, Silent, Excellent Pictures)—Compulsive gambler **Helene Chadwick** is blackmailed by her creditors into helping them gain entrance to a fancy ball where they plan to rob the guests. She informs the police, saves the day, confesses her weakness to her family and is forgiven.

AUBERT, MARISE
DESIRE ME (1947, MGM)—Just when **Greer Garson** finds a new love, Richard Hart, who brings her word of her husband Robert Mitchum's death in an escape attempt from a prison camp, Mitchum shows up. Hart and Mitchum struggle near a cliff, and the former falls to his death. Garson requires psychiatric help to get over her guilt for being unfaithful to Mitchum.

AUDREY
AUDREY (1916, Silent, Lasky/Paramount)—In a type of role which made Mary Pickford America's Sweetheart, **Pauline Frederick** portrays a hoyden dressed in rags who is transformed into a beauty and marries a nobleman.

AUGUST, DR. SIMON
YOUNG DOCTORS IN LOVE (1982, UA)—In this hit or miss spoof of hospital movies, **Michael McKean** is a fledgling surgeon afraid of surgery but who must pick up the scalpel to save his love Sean Young's life.

AUGUSTA, AUNT
TRAVELS WITH MY AUNT (1972, GB, MGM)—Eccentric **Maggie Smith** takes her straight-laced bank accountant nephew Alec McCowen on a wild trip all over Europe in this enjoyable adaptation of the Graham Greene novel.

AURELIA, COUNTESS
THE MADWOMAN OF CHAILLOT (1969, Warner Brothers)—In a peculiar and unsuccessful allegory, **Katharine Hepburn** is an eccentric woman with eccentric friends who lives in a beautiful world that no longer exists -if it ever did.

AUSTIN, BETH
THIS WOMAN IS DANGEROUS (1952, Warner Brothers)—Hard-as-nails gangster **Joan Crawford** goes all gooey for her surgeon after he restores her sight in an eye operation.

AUSTIN, BILL
THE GO-GETTER (1937, Warner Brothers)—Despite having lost a leg, navy veteran **George Brent** is determined to become a success.

AUSTIN, HELL-TO-PAY
HELL-TO-PAY AUSTIN (1916, Silent, Triangle)—**Wilfred Lucas** is a hard-drinking, two-fisted fighting man who becomes a decent Christian with the help of Bessie Love, daughter of a minister who died of alcoholism.

AUSTIN, JACK
MIDSHIPMAN JACK (1933, RKO)—**Bruce Cabot**, newly arrived at the Naval Academy, has some trouble adjusting but soon learns the ropes and becomes a model for the men of later classes.

AUSTIN, LADY CATHERINE
EX-FLAME (1931, Tiffany)—In what was described as a modernized version of "East Lynne," **Marian Nixon** is sent into exile when her closest male friend dies of heart disease while visiting Nixon, creating a scandal that rocks all of England.

AVALON, BENNY
THE WILD PAIR (1987, Trans World Entertainment)—**Bubba Smith** is a cop who works with ghetto kids. He is reluctantly teamed with FBI agent Beau Bridges to put away drug dealer Raymond St. Jacques. They are not happy working together but as often is the case in these mixed movie racial teams, they come to respect each other.

AVERY, ALEXA
ALEXA (1989, Platinum-B)—Being a prostitute has been lucrative for luscious **Christina Moore**, but it hasn't made her happy. Beware! Voyeurs will be disappointed.

AVERY, JACK
MAN OUTSIDE (1988, Virgin Vision)—Lawyer **Robert Logan** drives his Porsche into the Arkansas backwoods and becomes a hermit. Anthropology professor Kathleen Quinlan becomes intrigued in finding out why.

AXEL
THE GAMBLER (1974, Paramount)—College professor **James Caan** is a compulsive gambler with a will to lose, although he insists he's always just about to make a big killing.

AYESHA *See* **SHE WHO MUST BE OBEYED**

AYLWIN, HAL
ALYWIN (1920 Silent, GB, Hepworth)—**Henry Edwards'** stepmother disapproves of his love for a girl who goes mad when her drunken father dies in a landslide.

AYYOB, ANNA
ANNA ASCENDS (1922, Silent, Paramount)—Syrian immigrant **Alice Brady** believes that she has killed her boss, the head of a gem smuggling operation. She assumes another identity and becomes a best-selling author, but years later confesses her part in the man's "death," only to discover he's very much alive.

AZAM, JAMIL ABDULLAH
THE ARAB (1924, Silent, MGM)—After being disowned by his father because he made a desert raid at the time of the feast of Ramadan, **Ramon Novarro** becomes a guide in a Turkish city and foils the plans of its governor to massacre the Christians. When his father dies, he returns to become the chief of his Bedouin people, leaving behind the American girl with whom he has fallen in love.

AZARA, NINA MARIA
THE FIREFLY (1937, MGM)—Known as "Mosca del Fuego" **Jeanette MacDonald** is a Spanish dancer who also is a spy during the

Napoleonic Wars. It's in this movie that Allan Jones sings "Donkey Serenade" to MacDonald, a song forever after associated with him.

B

B-24, *See* MARIA FRANCK

BABBERLEY, SIR FANCOURT
CHARLEY'S AUNT (1925, Silent, Cristie); (1930, Columbia); (1941, 20th Century Fox)—When two Oxford students invite two young ladies to visit them for a weekend, the aunt of a third Oxford student is to chaperon. When she is delayed, the gentleman played at various times by **Syd Chaplin, Charlie Ruggles** and **Jack Benny** impersonates his aunt and then the fun begins.

BABBINGTON, CLAUDE
MY LEARNED FRIEND (1943, GB, Ealing)—**Claude Hulbert** is chased across the face of Big Ben by crazed Mervyn Johns who has been killing everyone he considers to be responsible for his prison term for forgery.

BABBITT, GEORGE S.
BABBITT (1924, Silent, Warner Brothers); (1934, First National/ Warner Brothers)—**Willard Louis** and **Guy Kibbee** each are impressive as the middle-aged prosperous Zenith Real Estate Man who begins an affair with a young woman for whom he plans to leave his wife. The pleas of his son change his mind, and he returns to his forgiving spouse.

BABBITT, RAYMOND
RAIN MAN (1988, UA)—When selfish con man Tom Cruise discovers that he has an older brother who has been left all of their father's three million dollar estate, he conspires to get his hands on the money by taking custody of his brother. Sibling **Dustin Hoffman**, in an Oscar winning performance of rare sensitivity and credibility, is an autistic savant with a remarkable memory, which Cruise exploits to win a fortune at the blackjack tables in Las Vegas. By the end of the film the brothers have been able to reach each other, if only modestly, before Cruise agrees that Hoffman should be returned to the hospital where he feels most safe.

BABE
REBELLIOUS DAUGHTERS (1938, Times)—**Verna Hillie** is one of three mistreated daughters who escape to the city where they are easy pickings for unscrupulous men.

BABOWSKY, BILL "BB"
TIN MEN (1987, Buena Vista)—In Baltimore in the fifties, **Richard Dreyfuss** is an aluminum siding salesman-con man who gets into a feud with another "tin man," Danny De Vito. Trying to get even with his adversary, Dreyfuss seduces De Vito's wife Barbara Hershey. This is just fine with De Vito who wants to get rid of her anyway. In the end, both men lose their licenses, but there are hints they may team up to sell Volkswagen Bugs.

BABS
JAZZ BABIES (1932, Peerless)—**Elizabeth Patterson** is a showgirl in a Chicago nightclub. A prude attempts to close down what he considers a lewd show. Patterson and friends arrange to put on a special show for his benefit. It's a version of "Midsummer Night's Dream." He's so impressed with the production that he takes it to Broadway, where it folds in one night. Patterson gives up show business and marries a grain dealer from Evanston.

BABS
WAR NURSE (1930, MGM)—**June Walker** is one of a group of WWI army nurses stationed in France who care for the wounded between romantic interludes with pilots.

BABSON, RICHARD
BEST FRIENDS (1982, Warner Brothers)—**Burt Reynolds** and Goldie Hawn are two writers whose professional collaboration is put under a strain when they marry each other.

BABY, THE
THAT'S MY BABY (1926, Silent, Paramount)—Midget **Harry Earles** appears as a baby left on the doorstep of bachelor Douglas MacLean, who has sworn off women for life after being jilted at the altar.

BABY, THE
THE BABY AND THE BATTLESHIP (1957, GB, British Lion)—Two sailors on leave get stuck with baby **Martyn Garrett** whom they must conceal on their battleship.

BABY DOLL
BABY DOLL (1956, Warner Brothers)—**Carroll Baker** is the child-wife of a witless older cotton mill owner. She is seduced by a revenge seeking business rival of her husband. Censors had a field day with this movie of physical and moral decadence. Baker popularized a new sleeping apparel for women, "baby doll" nighties.

BABY FACE
BORN TO FIGHT (1938, Commodore)—**Frankie Darro** is an up and coming boxer whose trainer hides him from gamblers.

BACH, ARTHUR
ARTHUR (1981, Orion/Warner Brothers); ARTHUR ON THE ROCKS (1988, Warner Brothers)—**Dudley Moore**, a rich, childish, insulting, useless, alcoholic hedonist, is threatened with the loss of his inheritance unless he marries a society girl chosen for him by his family. He falls in love with kookie waitress Liza Minnelli. He's willing to give up his fortune for her but isn't required to do so. What's the message? There is none. The first film was a large hit, probably because of the work of John Gielgud, but even a cameo appearance by the great actor as a ghost in the second wasn't enough to save it from bombing. Perhaps audiences no longer find drunks funny. In the sequel, after seven years of marriage to Liza, Dudley is being blackmailed by the father of the girl he dumped for Minnelli to terminate his marriage. No one seems to care.

BAGMAN
KITTY AND THE BAGMAN (1983, Australia, Quartet)—**John Stanton**, a crooked cop, helps Liddy Clark become queen of the Sidney underworld in the twenties.

BAGS
THE PRIZEFIGHTER (1979, New World)—**Tim Conway** is a goofy 1930s boxer managed by Don Knotts. These two funny TV comedians just can't seem to make it on the big screen.

BAILEY
RAGGEDY MAN (1981, Universal)—Mysterious stranger **Sam Shepard** protects divorcee Sissy Spacek and her two young children in a small Texas Gulf town during WWII.

BAILEY, BLOSSOM

SISTERS UNDER THE SKIN (1934, Columbia)—**Elissa Landi**, mistress to elderly Frank Morgan, leaves him for bohemian composer Joseph Schildkraut.

BAILEY, BOB

GENTLEMEN ARE BORN (1934, First National)—**Franchot Tone** and three other recent college graduates try to make ends meet for themselves and their families during the Depression.

BAILEY, CONSTANCE

THE NEW TEACHER (1922, Silent, Fox)—Society girl **Shirley Mason** refuses to marry her young man because she wishes to do something meaningful with her life. Her answer is to become a teacher in the slums of New York's Lower East Side. Talk about culture shock!

BAILEY, JUDGE

THE JUDGE STEPS OUT (1949, RKO)—**Alexander Knox**, fed up with the nagging of his wife and daughter, disappears from his home to become a cook in a California restaurant. Knox sorts things out with sympathetic Ann Sothern, before returning to his Boston home.

BAILEY, LYDIA

LYDIA BAILEY (1952, 20th Century Fox)—In 1802, wayward heiress **Anne Francis** supports Napoleon's attempt to take over Haiti, but has her mind changed by the treachery of the French, their mistreatment of the blacks and handsome Boston lawyer Dale Robertson.

BAILEY, MARIE

GIRLS ABOUT TOWN (1931, Paramount)—**Lilyan Tashman** and Kay Francis are gold digging roommates supported in a luxurious apartment by a businessman. They'd give it all up in a moment for true love.

BAILEY, NICK

FANTASY MAN (1984, Australia, Centaur)—**Harold Hopkins**, a disenchanted office worker, is bored with his job and his wife, and she's bored with him. He fantasizes about a woman who owns a snack bar, and she considers an affair with an old flame, but nothing happens. Boring!!!

BAILEY, SLAG

LADY AND GENT (1932, Paramount)—**George Bancroft**, a washed-up boxer, takes care of an orphan with the help of his gal, club owner Wynne Gibson.

BAILEY, SLAG

UNMARRIED (1939, Paramount)—Ex-boxer **Buck Jones** who wants nothing to do with marriage, thank you, raises orphan Donald O'Connor by himself.

BAILEY, STUART

I LOVE TROUBLE (1947, Columbia)—Smart-alecky private detective **Franchot Tone** romances Janet Blair while searching for her missing sister-in-law.

BAINES, SCATTERGOOD

SCATTERGOOD BAINES (1941, RKO): SCATTERGOOD MEETS BROADWAY (1941, RKO); SCATTERGOOD PULLS THE STRINGS (1941, RKO); SCATTERGOOD RIDES HIGH (1942, RKO); SCATTERGOOD SURVIVES A MURDER (1942, RKO)—**Guy Kibbee** portrays a likeable, small town busybody in this modest second feature comedy series.

BAIRD, JANE

UNDER AGE (1941, Columbia)—Just released from a detention center, **Nan Grey** is forced by mobsters to lure wealthy men to tourist resorts where crooked gamblers separate them from their money.

BAKER

THE VICTORS (1963, Columbia)—**Vince Edwards** is a member of a squad of foot soldiers in Europe during WWII. To illustrate the grim uncertainty of war, Edwards disappears from the film about 20 minutes after it starts and is never referred to again. Audiences don't know if he has been killed, wounded, sent home or what.

BAKER, A.C.

LADY BODYGUARD (1942, Paramount)—When advertising agent **Anne Shirley** accidently gives away a $1 million life insurance policy rather than a $1,000 one to test pilot Eddie Albert, it's up to her to see that he has no accidents.

BAKER, DAN

BAKER'S HAWK (1976, Doty-Dayton)—**Clint Walker** comes to the aid of an old man whom vigilantes are trying to drive from his land.

BAKER, FRANK

THE FABULOUS BAKER BOYS (1989, 20th Century Fox)—**Beau Bridges** and his real-life brother Jeff appear as cocktail lounge pianists, who decide that their act needs some spicing up. Lovely Michelle Pfeiffer is plenty peppery.

BAKER, JACK

THE FABULOUS BAKER BOYS (1989, 20th Century Fox)—**Jeff Bridges** is the sibling who benefits the most when sexy Michelle Pfeiffer joins his cocktail piano act with his brother Beau.

BAKER, JIM

A MAN FROM WYOMING (1930, Paramount)—**Gary Cooper**, a captain in the Army Engineer Corp during WWI, marries AWOL ambulance driver June Collyer whom he had been sent to arrest.

BAKER, NORMA JEAN

GOODBYE NORMA JEAN (1976, Filmways)—**Misty Rowe** plays Marilyn Monroe when she was still just Norma Jean Baker, seemingly willing to endure any sexual indignity to see her dream of Hollywood fame be fulfilled.

BAKER, RICKY

BOYZ N THE HOOD (1991, Columbia/New Deal)—When he becomes a father while still in high school, **Morris Chestnut** gives up his dream of a football scholarship, and decides to join the army.

BAKER, SAMANTHA "SAM"

SIXTEEN CANDLES (1984, Universal)—The family of **Molly Ringwald** are so involved with the wedding preparations of her older sister that they forget her sixteenth birthday. Not to worry, the hunk she's been dreaming about takes a special interest in her.

BAKER, TIM

A YANK IN THE R.A.F. (1941, 20th Century Fox)—Cocky American **Tyrone Power** joins the Royal Air Force to impress singer Betty Grable and after some initial adjustment problems becomes part of the team.

BALAM

KINGS OF THE SUN (1963, UA)—**George Chakiris**, king of the Mayans, leads his people to the coast where the Indians led by Yul Brynner make the newcomers feel unwelcome. Later the two chiefs become friends and unite to fight a common enemy. Miss this one and read a nice copy of the National Geographic.

BALBOA, ROCKY

ROCKY (1976, UA); ROCKY II (1979, UA); ROCKY III (1982, MGM/UA); ROCKY IV (1985, MGM/UA); ROCKY V (1990, MGM;UA)—Five foot seven muscular **Sylvester Stallone** makes audiences believe in his Cinderella story of a club boxer who gets to face the champ. Before the series is over he's won the title, taken many a bloody beating and taken apart Russian fighting machine Dolph Lundgren, who kills ex-champ Carl Weathers in an exhibition match. The series is uplifting as the none-too-bright but dedicated fighter in and out of the ring makes his dreams come true by pure grit and determination. In the last film, Stallone is again bankrupted by mismanagement of his money, has a strained relationship with his son Sage Stallone and suffers from brain damage from too many beatings. But game guy that he is, this doesn't prevent him from engaging in a bare-knuckled street brawl.

BALDERSON, ADDIE

THE COUNTRY MOUSE (1914, Silent, Bosworth)—**Adele Farrington**, the plain wife of a newly elected California legislator, doesn't fit into his new society, but like Cinderella, breaks out of her shell and becomes a million-dollar beauty.

BALDWIN, CAROL

MORE THAN A SECRETARY (1936, Columbia)—Plain-looking **Jean Arthur** (hard to imagine) competes with glamorous Dorothea Kent for her boss George Brent, who runs a health magazine.

BALDWIN, TONY

MY LOVE CAME BACK (1940, Warner Brothers)—**Jeffrey Lynn** dearly loves violin student Olivia de Havilland, but he would like an explanation as to why his rich boss Charles Winninger is paying her tuition to a music academy.

BALESTERO, CHRISTOPHER "MANNY"

THE WRONG MAN (1956, Warner Brothers)—**Henry Fonda** stars in the true story of a musician who, through a chain of circumstantial evidence and mistaken identity is arrested and almost convicted of a crime he did not commit.

BALFOUR, DAVID

KIDNAPPED (1938, 20th Century Fox); (1948, Monogram); (1960, Buena Vista); (1971, GB, Omnibus/American International)—**Freddie Bartholomew, Roddy McDowall, James MacArthur** and **Lawrence Douglas** each star as Robert Louis Stevenson's young hero, who is sold as a slave by his wicked uncle and rescued by an outlaw.

BALISHAW, CAMILLE

CAMILLE OF THE BARBARY COAST (1925, Silent, Assoc. Exhibitors)—Barbary Coast denizen **Mae Busch** takes in Owen Moore, a former convict, rehabilitates, and falls in love with him. She is ready to give him up when Moore's father who had disowned him wants his son back but not Busch. The old man relents when Busch's lover refuses to leave her.

BALLANTINE, JOHN "J.B."

SPELLBOUND (1945, UA)—When **Gregory Peck** shows up to become the new head of a mental institution it soon becomes clear that he's an imposter who may have killed the man he's impersonating. Ingrid Bergman, a psychiatrist at the institution, falls in love

with amnesiac Peck and probes his mind and dreams to discover whether he's a murderer. The dream scenes in this Alfred Hitchcock winner were designed by Salvador Dali.

BALLARD, BRENDA

ESPIONAGE AGENT (1939, Warner Brothers)—American spy **Brenda Marshall** falls in love with American diplomat Joel McCrea in Europe just prior to the beginning of WWI. Together they steal evidence of Nazi espionage in the U.S.

BALLARD, DOMINIQUE

DOMINIQUE (1978, GB, Subotsky)—In an attempt to get his hand on his wife **Jean Simmons'** money, Cliff Robertson tries to drive her crazy. She kills herself and is buried, but then the haunting begins. It's an unappealing ripoff of the DIABOLIQUE story.

BALLARD, WILL

RIDE THE MAN DOWN (1952, Republic)—Ranch foreman **Rod Cameron** has his hands full with both rustlers and land-grabbers, but he holds together the outfit for his deceased boss's daughter.

BALLENTINE, LARRY

THEY WON'T BELIEVE ME (1947, RKO)—In flashbacks **Robert Young**, cast against type, is shown to be a loathsome broker who drives his wife to suicide by his affairs. He is on trial for the murder of Susan Hayward, one of his mistresses. Just as the jury returns to announce its verdict, Young loses his cool, tries to escape and is shot down by the police. Then we learn the jury's ironic verdict—not guilty.

BALLENTINE, PARKER

CRITIC'S CHOICE (1963, Warner Brothers)—Theater critic **Bob Hope's** marriage almost ends when he candidly reviews a play written by his wife Lucille Ball. The magic between the two comedians seen in FANCY PANTS and THE FACTS OF LIFE is missing.

BALLEW, BUZZY

WONDER MAN (1945, RKO)—**Danny Kaye**, a zany nightclub super-star, engaged to dancer Vera-Ellen, has evidence to give against mobster Steve Cochran. The latter has Kaye knocked-off and dumped in a lagoon in Brooklyn's Prospect Park. Kaye's ghost invades the body of his twin brother (also Kaye), from whom he has been separated since childhood, forcing his meek and quiet sibling to solve his murder.

BALLEW, TONY

THREE YOUNG TEXANS (1954, 20th Century Fox)—Miscast in a Western, **Keefe Brasselle**, ranch hand Jeffery Hunter and rancher's daughter Mitzi Gaynor (who's also very much in the wrong genre) rob a train with the idea of giving the loot back later. Things don't work out as they planned.

BALLINGER, EDDIE

MY BUDDY (1944, Republic)—WWI hero **Donald Barry** can't find work and drifts into the life of a gangster. After serving a prison sentence for a crime he didn't commit, he's killed in a shootout after killing a man. He leaves a note with a priest asking that his story be told so it might not happen to another.

BALLISTER, CAROLA

DANGEROUS PARTNERS (1945, MGM)—**Signe Hasso** and James Craig discover a fortune in a downed plane—but will they live to enjoy it?

BALLOU, KATHERINE "CAT"
CAT BALLOU (1965, Columbia)—When her father is killed by agents working for a railroad tycoon who wants the deceased's land, **Jane Fonda** teams up with drunken ex-gun fighter Lee Marvin, an outlaw with a small price on his head Michael Callan, phony preacher Dwayne Hickman, and Indian Tom Nardini, to take revenge by becoming train robbers. It almost gets her hanged.

BALSER, TINA
DIARY OF A MAD HOUSEWIFE (1970, Universal)—**Carrie Snodgress's** husband Richard Benjamin treats her with a condescending and belittling attitude, which just about makes her crazy.

BANDELO, CESARE ENRICO "RICO-LITTLE CAESAR"
LITTLE CAESAR (1931, Warner Brothers)—Edward G. Robinson gives a career making performance as a mobster, somewhat modeled on Al Capone, who moves from a two-bit hood to a gang leader until his death in a hail of bullets and his last words, "Mother of Mercy, is this the end of Rico?"

BANDIT
SMOKEY AND THE BANDIT (1977, Universal); SMOKEY AND THE BANDIT II (1980, UNIVERSAL); SMOKEY AND THE BANDIT PART 3 (1983, Universal)—Georgia bootlegger **Burt Reynolds** picks up runaway bride Sally Fields and the chase with her irate father-in-law-to-be sheriff Jackie Gleason in hot pursuit is on. If you enjoy squealing tires, cars jumping over creeks and demolition derbies, these films are for you. The sequels are just more of the same. Reynolds only makes a cameo appearance in the 1983 picture, letting **Jerry Reed** play the heavy-footed bandit.

BANION, KIT
THE MAVERICK QUEEN (1956, Republic)—**Barbara Stanwyck**, a Southern girl, moves west after the Civil War and opens a hotel-saloon with her partners, the leaders of the Wild Bunch gang.

BANKS, ANNIE
FATHER OF THE BRIDE (1991, Buena Vista/Touchstone)—**Kimberly Williams**, a 19-year-old actress in her first film role, gets to play an older woman of 21. When she tells parents Steve Martin and Diane Keaton that she's engaged, the fun begins—well, for everyone except Martin, who must pay the bills.

BANKS, GEORGE
FATHER OF THE BRIDE (1991, Buena Vista/Touchstone)—In the 1950 version of this movie, Spencer Tracy's name was Stanley T. Banks. As was Tracy with Elizabeth Taylor, **Steve Martin** is stunned when his beloved daughter Kimberly Williams announces that she's engaged. Martin goes a little nuts, but he's entitled: the cost of the wedding and reception is a fortune.

BANKS, STANLEY & KAY
FATHER OF THE BRIDE (1950, MGM); FATHER'S LITTLE DIVIDEND (1951, MGM)—**Spencer Tracy** discovers how a wedding can disrupt a family when daughter **Elizabeth Taylor** announces her engagement. In the sequel, Tracy doesn't hit it off with his grandson Donald Clark.

BANNER, BILLY
THE GALLANT FOOL (1926, Silent, Realart)—**Billy Sullivan**, the son of a millionaire, impersonates a prince in order to collect a debt owed his father.

BANNER, HOPE, FAITH & CHARITY
THREE GIRLS ABOUT A TOWN (1941, Columbia)—**Joan Blondell, Binnie Barnes,** and **Janet Blair** are sisters who discover what appears to be a corpse in their hotel room.

BANNING
BANNING (1967, Universal)—**Robert Wagner** is a golf-pro at a plush country club where servicing the female members is part of the job. In hock to a gambler, Wagner has to find a way to put his golf skills to work to come up with a lot of money.

BANNING, MICHAEL
SENOR AMERICANO (1929, Universal)—**Ken Maynard** cleans up a section of California, chasing out the criminal element so the region can be annexed by the United States.

BANNISTER, CLINT
LONE TEXAN (1959, 20th Century Fox)—**Willard Parker** is regarded as a turncoat in his Texas town for having fought on the Union side. He redeems himself by opposing his brother who uses the town as the center of his outlaw activities.

BANNISTER, ELSA
THE LADY FROM SHANGHAI (1948, Columbia)—By the time this movie was finished, so was the marriage of **Rita Hayworth** and director/co-star Orson Welles. His ambivalence about her comes through in the story of a mysterious woman, Hayworth, and her crippled husband Everett Sloane who have a shoot-out in the Hall of Mirrors of an amusement park.

BANNISTER, PROF. HOWARD
WHAT'S UP DOC? (1972, Warner Brothers)—**Ryan O'Neal** is an absent-minded musicologist, one of two being considered for a prize by a wealthy eccentric. He's being looked over along with his whining fiancee Madeleine Kahn by the wealthy donor of the prize, but Khan is pushed out of the picture by wacko Barbra Streisand, who for some reason wants the nerdy O'Neal.

BANNISTER, JACK
THE RULING VOICE (1931, Warner Brothers)—**Walter Huston,** the boss of an extortion ring, almost is able to retire and reform when his daughter repudiates him and he's gunned down by a trusted henchman.

BANNISTER, JOAN
MADAME SPY (1942, Universal)—**Constance Bennett** and her new reporter husband Don Porter travel through war-torn Europe on their honeymoon. When they return, Porter is shocked that she makes contact with several Nazi espionage agents, but it's OK, she's really an American agent.

BANNISTER, NED
THE MAN FROM WYOMING (1924, Silent, Universal)—**Jack Hoxie,** a sheepman, is accused of murder by a cattle rancher who wants Hoxie's land.

BANNON, HUD
HUD (1963, Paramount)—Hell-raising, modern-day rancher **Paul Newman** lives with a nephew who idolizes him and his father who despises him. Newman doesn't seem to have any redeeming qualities. He tries to rape Patricia Neal, the family housekeeper, and sheds no tears when his father Melvyn Douglas dies or his nephew Brandon De Mille abandons the old homestead in disgust.

BANNON, NED
THE TALL STRANGER (1957, Allied Artists)—Drifter **Joel McCrea** helps save a wagon train from cattle barons who don't want homesteaders in their country.

BANZAI, BUCKEROO
THE ADVENTURES OF BUCKEROO BANZAI: ACROSS THE 8TH DIMENSION (1984, 20th Century Fox)—**Peter Weller** is a neurosurgeon and physicist who grows weary of science and becomes a rock star and super hero.

BAPTISTE, FREDERIC
BUCCANEER'S GIRL (1950, Universal)—Freebooter **Phillip Friend** discovers a lovely stowaway Yvonne de Carlo aboard his ship. Instead of making her walk the plank, he sends her to school in New Orleans where she becomes a refined lady and with the Robin Hood-like Friend stands up to local tyrant, Robert Douglas.

BARBARA
A LADY IN LOVE (1920, Silent, Paramount)—Convent girl **Ethel Clayton** marries a man and then discovers he already has a wife and child. Horrors! What will she do?

BARBARA
NIGHT CALL NURSES (1974, New World)—In a drive-in soft porn special, **Patricia T. Byrne** is an angel of mercy who tends to all of the needs of her male patients.

BARBARA
SEPIA CINDERELLA (1947, Herald)—When black songwriter Billy Daniels becomes a success, he briefly forgets his sweetheart **Sheila Guyse** but soon tires of society women and hurries back to her.

BARBARA
TEENAGE DOLL (1957, Allied Artists)—High school sweetie **June Kenney** doesn't want to spend her evenings doing homework so she hangs out with punks on the streets. Get a job!

BARBAROSA
BARBAROSA (1982, Universal)—Country and Western singer **Willie Nelson**, an amicable bandit, avoids assassination attempts by his wife's relatives prompted by a feud.

BARBELLA, ROCKY *See* ROCKY GRAZIANO

BARBER, MAY
OH, LADY, LADY (1920, Silent, Goldwyn)—Actress **Bebe Daniels** and press agent Harrison Ford conspire to break up the romance of a young couple.

BARCLAY, ALAN
TILL WE MEET AGAIN (1936, Paramount)—English actor **Herbert Marshall** and ex-lover German actress Gertrude Michael discover that they are spies for opposite sides in WWI.

BARCLAY, ANDY
CHILD'S PLAY (1988, UA)—**Alex Vincent** knows who—or what—is responsible for a bizarre series of murders, but no one except his mother will believe him.

BARCLAY, JOHN
A CERTAIN RICH MAN (1921, Silent, Great Authors Pictures)—**Robert McKim**, the head of a wheat company in a small town, ruthlessly crushes his rival. He gets his comeuppance when the death of his wife makes him believe he's being punished for his behavior.

BARCLAY, RICHARD
SHE MARRIED HER BOSS (1935, Columbia)—**Melvyn Douglas** marries his secretary but then takes her for granted until she takes appropriate action. Misfiles his clothes, perhaps.

BARCLAY, THURLOW MICHAEL, JR.
THE INNER MAN (1922, Silent, Playgoers)—Faint-hearted mathematics teacher **Wyndham Standing** is sent to Kentucky by his father to check on a mine owned by his family. Somehow the trip brings out the best in him. He saves the mine from crooks and wins the girl he loves. Mathematicians always show their stuff when called upon.

BARDELL, JACK
SKY HAWK (1929, Fox)—When rich young **John Garrick's** plane crashes, he is paralyzed from the waist down but manages to recover and fly once again when a German Zeppelin attacks London.

BARDELYS
BARDELYS THE MAGNIFICENT (1926, Silent, MGM)—**John Gilbert** wagers his estate that he can win the hand of aristocrat Eleanor Boardman within three months. He wins the bet but he is almost executed for treason in the process.

BARDOT, BRIGITTE
DEAR BRIGITTE (1965, 20th Century Fox)—Billy Mumy, the scientific and mathematically precocious young son of American professor James Stewart, also has some advanced interest in **Brigitte Bardot** with whom he corresponds. When the family travels to France, they meet the famous sex kitten appearing as herself.

BARING, FRANCES
THE LADY IS A SQUARE (1959, GB, Pathe ABF)—**Anna Neagle** is a classical music performer, fresh out of funds to finance her concerts since her husband passed on. Pop musician Frankie Vaughan, who has a thing for Neagle's daughters, provides the necessary bread, though initially Neagle is not taken with his talent or music.

BARKER, KATE "MA"
MA BARKER'S KILLER BROOD (1960, Filmservice); Bloody MAMA (1970, American International)—In the 1960 film, **Lurene Tuttle** is the matriarchal leader of a band of brutal bank robbers. On a sicker scale, **Shelley Winters** and her kill-crazy sons terrorize the populace as they rob and murder during the 1930s. Ma has plenty of "love" for her boys.

BARKER, MARIA
ANGEL (1937, Paramount)—While on a vacation without her husband Herbert Marshall, **Marlene Dietrich** falls in love with Melvyn Douglas.

BARKER, PHILIP "PINK"
THE SEA GOD (1930, Paramount)—When diver **Richard Arlen's** underwater air line is cut, he merely walks from the sea and the natives believe him to be a "sea god."

BARKIN, JERRY
DOWN AND OUT IN BEVERLY HILLS (1986, Touchstone)—Homeless **Nick Nolte** wanders on to the estate of wealthy Richard Dreyfuss and walks into the pool. He is rescued by Dreyfuss and made at home as an honored guest. Nolte changes the lives of all the members of the family—perhaps even for the better.

BARKLAY, NANCY
NANCY GOES TO RIO (1950, MGM)—**Jane Powell** and her actress mother Ann Sothern are competitors for the same part and the same man. Powell gets the part, Sothern gets the man. Seems fair.

BARKLEY, ANDREW
THE NEVADAN (1950, Columbia)—Marshal **Randolph Scott** recovers stolen gold and captures the robbers in an undistinguished Western.

BARKLEY, JOSH & DINAH
THE BARKLEYS OF BROADWAY (1949, MGM)—**Fred Astaire** and **Ginger Rogers** are a highly successful dancing team when she leaves him to appear on the dramatic stage. The pair are reunited before the fade-out. The magic of the 1930s dancing couple isn't there anymore. They didn't want to work together again, and it shows.

BARLOW, DICK
THE ADVENTUROUS SOUL (1927, Silent, Hi-Mark)—When a man arranges to have his worthless son shanghaied aboard one of his ships, the press crew gets **Jimmy Fulton**, the sweetheart of the intended young man's sister, instead. Fulton makes good under the brother's name but his love straightens out who is whom.

BARLOW, DIXIE
SARONG GIRL (1943, Monogram)—Stripper **Ann Corio** is cast as an exotic dancer, out on bail after police close her show in which she was showing too much.

BARLOW, JANIE
DANCING LADY (1933, MGM)—In a fairly routine backstage romance, **Joan Crawford** is foisted on show director Clark Gable by wealthy backer Franchot Tone whom Joan has promised to marry if she's not successful. She is and wins the love of an initially unimpressed Gable.

BARNABY
BARNABY (1919, Silent, Barker)—**Dick Webb** is a dashing young squire who has a series of adventures and finds love.

BARNES, BILLY
ALIAS JULIUS CAESAR (1922, Silent, Associated First National)—Friends of **Charles Ray** lock him in the shower and take away all his clothes. He escapes wearing only the shower curtain. The police pick him up and, believing him crazy, put him in jail, from which he escapes with a jewel thief. The two go to a party at which Ray gets the blame for the thief's work.

BARNES, BUNNY
PRISON BREAKER (1936, GB, Columbia)—British secret service agent **James Mason** is sent to prison when he accidently kills one of the henchmen of an international thief, whom Mason is trying to prevent from stealing a treaty. Mason escapes and carries out his assignment with the help of the crook's daughter.

BARNES, BURN 'EM UP
BURN 'EM UP BARNES (1921, Silent, Mastodon)—**Johnny Hines**, a millionaire's speed-mad son, is disowned by his father. Hines goes on the bum until meeting a girl who needs his help.

BARNES, CASSIE
THREE WISE GIRLS (1932, Columbia)—**Jean Harlow** moves from a small town to New York and with the help of more experienced Mae Clarke and Marie Prevost becomes a model. Harlow falls for a scoundrel who turns out to be married. He promises to get a divorce but Harlow shows him the door.

BARNES, MR.
MR. BARNES OF NEW YORK (1914, Silent, Vitagraph)—**Maurice Costello**, an American business man, has numerous thrilling adventures abroad, including being present during the bombardment of an Egyptian city.

BARNES, SCOTT
MEN WITH WINGS (1938, Paramount)—When Fred MacMurray loses his life fighting for the Chinese, long-time friend and fellow pilot **Ray Milland** moves in to console MacMurray's widow, Louise Campbell, whom he has always loved.

BARNES, SGT.
PLATOON (1987, Orion)—The war in Vietnam has deranged and brutalized **Tom Berenger**. He orders the inhabitants of a village killed and when Willem DaFoe threatens to bring him up on charges, Berenger sees to it that he doesn't get the opportunity.

BARNEY
THE DUMMY (1929, Paramount)—Detective agency office boy **Mickey Bennett** pretends to be deaf and dumb in order to help catch kidnappers but almost loses his life when his deception is discovered when he mumbles in his sleep.

BARNEY
THE WHOOPEE BOYS (1986, Paramount)—Obnoxious misfit **Paul Rodriguez** and partner Michael O'Keefe save a school for needy children, while trying to break into Palm Beach society.

BARNHAM, EMILY
THE AMERICANIZATION OF EMILY (1964, MGM)—**Julie Andrews** is an English girl in love with American naval officer James Garner who a crazy admiral decides should be the first American casualty in the invasion at Normandy. Andrews was desperately trying to shed her sugar and spice image.

BARNUM, P.T.
THE MIGHTY BARNUM (1934, UA)—**Wallace Beery** seems right at home in the role of the great showman who gave the world fascinating freaks and fakes to gawk at, but the production values aren't as good as they should have been.

BARON, THE
MEET THE BARON (1933, MGM)—Radio comedian **Jack Pearl** is a fake baron mistaken for the real thing. The plot's not the thing in this comedy also featuring Jimmy Durante, Zasu Pitts, and an early appearance of the Three Stooges, although they weren't yet called that.

BARONI, PAUL "MONK"
KID MONK BARONI (1952, Real Art)—A bowery priest attempts to reform street kid **Leonard Nimoy** by teaching him how to box. There's a long road Nimoy must travel before he shows himself worthy of the priest's faith.

BARR, CABOT
THE LAST GENTLEMAN (1934, UA)—**George Arliss**, an eccentric wealthy gentleman, reaches from the grave to continue his control of his family, having had himself filmed reading his will.

BARRADINE, LEONORA
THE GIRL WHO FORGOT (1939, GB, Butchers)—**Elizabeth Allan** forgets her mother and is almost taken by a scoundrel after her trust fund. Forget it.

BARRETT, ELIZABETH & EDWARD MOULTON
THE BARRETTS OF WIMPOLE STREET (1934, MGM); (1957, MGM)—**Norma Shearer** and **Charles Laughton** play the sickly British poet and her tyrannical father who has an almost incestuous love for her. He certainly is not willing to give her up to Robert Browning without struggle. There are other Barrett siblings living at Wimpole Street but Shearer and Laughton dominate. **Jennifer Jones** and **John Gielgud's** interpretation of the same roles in 1957 are not nearly as memorable.

BARRETT, EVE
NEPTUNE'S DAUGHTER (1949, MGM)—**Esther Williams** heads up a swimsuit company and is romanced by polo-playing Ricardo Montalban. The two join Red Skelton and Betty Garrett to sing a hot version of "Baby It's Cold Outside."

BARRETT, HUGO
THE SERVANT (1964, GB, Springbok/Landau)—Manservant **Dirk Bogarde**, with the help of his sexy "sister" Sarah Miles, gradually switches roles with his rich ineffectual master, James Fox.

BARRETT, CAPT. JERRY
THE WORLD WAS HIS JURY (1958, Columbia)—**Robert McQueeney**, a ship captain, is accused of criminal negligence in a sea disaster.

BARRETT, JIM
THE COWBOY KID (1922, Silent, Aywon Film Corp.)—Cowboy **Rex Bell** becomes involved with the daughter of a banker whose establishment is regularly robbed.

BARRETT, JOE
TOKYO JOE (1949, Columbia)—After WWII **Humphrey Bogart** returns to Tokyo to reclaim his wife and fortune but runs afoul of both Sessue Hayakawa and Alexander Knox.

BARRETT, JOHN
THE SCAPEGOAT (1959, GB, MGM)—Shy Bachelor **Alec Guinness**, in Paris on holiday, is persuaded to assume the identity of a look-alike nobleman, who is planning a murder.

BARRETT, FREDERIKA & J.W.
MARRY THE BOSS'S DAUGHTER (1941, 20th Century Fox)—It just goes to show what a good deed can do for a guy. Naive Bruce Edwards arrives in New York and returns a lost dog to **Brenda Joyce**, who is so pleased that she convinces her father **George Barbier** to give Edwards a job and eventually her.

BARRETT, SGT. LARRY
SERGEANTS 3 (1962, UA)—In a rip-off of GUNGA DIN set in the American West, **Peter Lawford** has the Douglas Fairbanks role with Sammy Davis Jr. debasing himself as the dim Gunga Din-like character.

BARRETT, LOGAN
RETURN OF THE FRONTIERSMAN (1950, Warner Brothers)—**Gordon MacRae**, in a non-singing role, proves that the sheriff's son is being framed for murder.

BARRETT, MITCH
ONE FOOT IN HELL (1960, 20th Century Fox)—**Alan Ladd** hates everyone in an Arizona town because they didn't help him save his dying wife. He joins forces with a motley crew of villains to take his revenge but one of his cohorts, Don Murray, develops a conscience and kills psychopath Ladd before he can complete his plan.

BARRETT, OLIVER IV
OLIVER'S STORY (1978, Paramount)—It's been several years since **Ryan O'Neal** lost his wife Ali McGraw to a strange illness, and Candice Bergen seems just the woman to make him live again.

BARRETT, SHELBY
THE WOMAN IN RED (1935, Warner Brothers)—Professional horsewoman **Barbara Stanwyck** marries society man Gene Raymond but later her marriage is threatened when she's accused of having an affair with John Eldredge.

BARRETT, TODD
CAMPUS MAN (1987, RKO/Paramount)—Arizona State student **John Dye** can't make tuition costs until he comes up with the bright idea of producing a calendar featuring his hunk of a roommate.

BARRIE, KAY
MIDNIGHT MADONNA (1937, Paramount)—**Mady Correll** and her ex-husband Warren William fight over custody of their daughter. He's a gambler who had deserted his family and is only interested now because the child has inherited a lot of money from her grandfather. Correll is found to be an unfit mother because she's an entertainer, but she eventually gets her daughter back.

BARRINGER, DR. EMILY
THE GIRL IN WHITE (1952, MGM)—**June Allyson** struggles valiantly to obtain a medical education in 1902.

BARRINGTON, IVY
SEXPOT (1988, Platinum)—**Ruth Collins** portrays a manipulative eight-time widow, who marries old men and then kills them—no not with sex.

BARRON, J. DABNEY & ADAM
HIS FATHER'S SON (1917, Silent, Metro)—Wealthy **Lionel Barrymore** throws out his playboy son **Charles Eldridge** with the prediction that the young man will be on skid row within the month. Instead Eldridge reforms, finds a good paying job and marries a girl who has half ownership in a jewel which Barrymore had been coveting.

BARROW, CLYDE
BONNIE AND CLYDE (1967, Warner Brothers)—The way **Warren Beatty** played him, Barrow had no trouble with robbing and killing, but he didn't function very well in bed with his partner Bonnie Parker (Faye Dunaway).

BARROWS, JOHNNY
THE KID FROM CLEVELAND (1949, Republic)—Juvenile delinquent **Russ Tamblyn** is straightened out with help from the Cleveland Indians baseball team.

BARROWS, JOHNNY
MEAN JOHNNY BARROWS (1976, Atlas)—**Fred Williamson** was a mean pro football player (some say dirty), and he seemed meant for roles such as this Vietnam vet who has been dishonorably discharged for striking an officer. He takes sides in a Mafia gang war, single-handedly wiping out most of the soldiers of one crime family.

BARROWS, VINCE
TWO YANKS IN TRINIDAD (1942, Columbia)—Hoods **Brian Donlevy** and Pat O'Brien join the army to employ their dubious talents for fighting against the enemy.

BARRY

DEAD MEN DON'T DIE (1990, Trans Atlantic)—When news anchor **Elliot Gould** stumbles across a drug deal in progress, he's murdered. His body is discovered by rival anchor Melissa Anderson, who is more interested in his story than his death. Voodoo cleaning lady Mabel King brings him back to life, but he's not exactly normal.

BARRY

TRAVELING HUSBANDS (1931, RKO)—Young salesman **Frank Albertson** is flat broke and having no luck with the mercenary daughter of a client at a sales conference.

BARRY, BARBARA

POOR LITTLE RICH GIRL (1936, 20th Century Fox)—**Shirley Temple**, the daughter of a wealthy widowed soap manufacturer, is set on her own when the train she is taking to boarding school has an accident. She teams up with song-and-dance team Alice Faye and Jack Haley, who put her in their act. The trio gets a job on a radio show sponsored by a competitor of her father. It gets her reunited with her widowed papa who has never had much time for Shirley.

BARRY, DIANA

ONCE A SINNER (1931, Fox)—**Dorothy MacKaill** and her inventor husband Joel McCrea move to the city where he overhears a conversation which implies MacKaill once was a "kept" woman. That just about sinks the marriage.

BARRY, HELENE

TWO HEARTS IN WALTZ TIME (1934, GB, Gaumont)—Viennese composer Carl Brisson falls in love with **Frances Day** without realizing that she is the star of the opera company which is to perform his newest composition.

BARSTOW, SGT.

THE MAN FROM DAKOTA (1940, MGM)—Union soldier **Wallace Beery** escapes from a Confederate prison and makes his way back to his lines with the help of Russian emigre Dolores Del Rio. She is in possession of a strategic map which she took from a Reb officer whom she killed.

BART

HER HUSBAND'S SECRETARY (1937, First National)—**Warren Hull** must feel like the rope in a tug of war as his wife and his secretary fight over who shall have him.

BART, JOHN PAUL

A TAILOR MADE MAN (1922, Silent, UA); (1931, MGM)—**Charles Ray** and **William Haines** are both amusing as a pants-presser who borrows an expensive suit, crashes a society party and lands a labor-relations job with a shipping company. Even when he is exposed and reduced to his former position, he proves his worth when he fights his way through a gang of agitators and prevents a strike.

BARTLEBY

BARTLEBY (1970, GB, Pantheon/British Lion)—Clerk **John McEnery** slowly withdraws from life as he refuses or is unable to adjust to his surroundings.

BARTLING, JACK

THE PRAISE AGENT (1919, Silent, World)—Publicist **Arthur Ashley** is in love with the daughter of a an anti-suffragette U.S. Senator, who is married to one of the leaders of the votes for women movement.

BARTON

I COVER CHINATOWN (1938, Banner Films)—Bus driver **Norman Foster's** sightseeing route is Chinatown. In the course of his work, he gets mixed up with some jewel thieves.

BARTON, CAROL

MY MARRIAGE (1936, 20th Century Fox)—**Claire Trevor's** father is murdered by gangsters, and the brother of the society man she's about to marry is inadvertently involved. Trevor's mother-in-law-to-be changes her tune as to whether Claire is suitable for her son when she learns about her other son's activities.

BARTON, DICK

DICK BARTON—SPECIAL AGENT (1948, GB, Hammer); DICK BARTON STRIKES BACK (1949, GB, Exclusive); DICK BARTON AT BAY (1950, GB, Hammer)—Private detective **Don Stannard** deals, respectively, with smugglers and foreign agents intent on destroying England with germ bombs in reservoirs, foreign agents beaming atomic rays at the populace and an anarchist with a death ray.

BARTON, GERALD

THE BARTON MYSTERY (1932, GB, British & Dominions)—When **Franklyn Bellamy** is murdered during a seance, the fake medium admits she killed the victim, a black-mailer, in self-defense.

BARTON, HOWARD, HELEN & RICHARD

HIS BROTHER'S WIFE (1916, Silent, World) -**Carlyle Blackwell, Ethel Clayton** and **Paul McAllister** are the triangle of the title. Blackwell covets his brother's wife, and she's a bit interested herself.

BARTON, JO

GOD'S COUNTRY AND THE WOMAN (1937, Warner Brothers)—**Beverly Roberts** runs a logging camp and falls for George Brent, the brother of a rival, who has just arrived from Paris.

BARTON, JOHNNY

SO LONG AT THE FAIR (1951, GB, Rank)—When Jean Simmons and her brother **David Tomlinson** arrive in Paris for the 1889 World's Exposition, he disappears, and everyone denies he ever existed. With the help of artist Dirk Bogarde, she gets to the bottom of Tomlinson's disappearance.

BARTON, PATSY

BABES IN ARMS (1939, MGM)—**Judy Garland** and Mickey Rooney do everything except sweep out the theatre in this Rodgers and Hart, Busby Berkley choreographed musical about the teen sons and daughters of retired vaudevillians who put on a Broadway show.

BARTON, SUSAN

SHAME, SHAME, EVERYBODY KNOWS HER NAME (1969, J.E.R. Pictures)—**Karen Carlson**, a naive midwesterner, moves to New York and when her romances with men don't pan out, she moves in with a lesbian lover.

BARTON, WADE

THE FIGHTING GRINGO (1939, RKO)—**George O'Brien** leads a band of do-gooders looking for trouble who find it with a Mexican rancher falsely accused of murder. O'Brien clears the man and wins the rancher's daughter.

BARTY, BARNABAS

THE AMATEUR GENTLEMAN (1926, Silent, First National); (1936, GB, UA)—**Richard Barthelmess** in 1926 and **Douglas Fairbanks, Jr.** in 1936 are men with prizefighting backgrounds who inherit fortunes and pass themselves off as gentlemen in London.

BARWICK, GEORGE

HIS GRACE GIVES NOTICE (1933, GB, Real Art/RKO)—**Arthur Margetson**, a mere butler, is in love with his employer's daughter. She'll have nothing to do with him of course. Margetson learns that he has inherited a dukedom but doesn't tell the object of his affections until after he has rescued her from a gangster and married her.

BASCOMB, WILLIE

WHITE PANTS WILLIE (1927, Silent, First National)—Inventor **Johnny Hines** and his laundryman George Kuwa bluff their way into a fancy ball at a hotel where a wealthy society girl that he admires is staying. Not only does he get the girl but her father helps him sell his automobile invention.

BASCOMB, ZEB

BAD BASCOMB (1946, MGM)—Sentimental bank robber **Wallace Beery** develops a fatherly affection for a little orphan girl, helps some Mormon settlers and gives up his outlaw ways.

BASKERVILLE, SIR HENRY & SIR HUGO

THE HOUND OF THE BASKERVILLES (1932, GB, Gainsborough); (1939, 20th Century Fox); (1959, GB, Hammer); (1980, GB, Hemdale); (1983, GB, Mapleton)—**John Stuart, Richard Greene, Christopher Lee, Kenneth Williams** and **Martin Shaw** each appeared as the English Lord who must be protected by Sherlock Holmes from a curse placed on the family at the time of their cruel ancestor Sir Hugo, played by **Sam Livesey, Ralph Forbes** and **David Oxley** in the first three movies. The despicable cad did not appear in the last two productions.

BASKIN, JOSHUA

BIG (1988, 20th Century Fox)—**Tom Hanks** is superb in his Oscar-nominated performance as a 35-year old man with the mind of a 13-year old boy. No, he's not mentally retarded. He's what happened to young David Moscow when he wished to become "big." When David's mother won't believe that Hanks is her son, he heads for New York where the wide-eyed, guileless boy-man gets a job with a toy company and attracts the attention of Elizabeth Perkins, who is interested in him sexually. Hanks is still at the stage of hitting girls who interest him. Hanks is flawless as he shows his emotions from the point of view of the child in him.

BASKIN, T.R.

T.R. BASKIN (1971, Paramount)—Small-town girl **Candice Bergen** moves to Chicago where she has many meaningless relationships with men. It's a tale of loneliness and lack of communication.

BASNER, DAVID & MAX

NOTHING IN COMMON (1986, Tri-Star)—**Tom Hanks** and Jackie Gleason are father and son who, as the title suggests, have nothing in common, but when Hanks' mother Eva Marie Saint leaves Gleason, the two reluctantly try to get to know each other. It is Gleason's last movie appearance.

BASS, SAM

CALAMITY JANE AND SAM BASS (1949, Universal)—**Howard Duff** is a Westerner forced into a life of crime after killing a man. His romantic interests are Yvonne de Carlo as Calamity Jane and good girl Dorothy Hart.

BASS, ZACHARY

MAN IN THE WILDERNESS (1971, Warner Brothers)—In a very violent film, **Richard Harris** who has been abandoned in the wilderness fights for survival and revenge.

BASTON, HOMER

THE KID FROM KOKOMO (1939, Warner Brothers)—**Wayne Morris** is punch happy even before he enters the ring, and things don't get better for him after putting on the gloves. He even thinks Whistler's painting is of his (Morris') mother.

BATES, MR.

HE HIRED THE BOSS (1943, 20th Century Fox)—When Stuart Erwin's investments make him enough money to buy the concern for which he works, he fires **Thurston Hall**, his boss who wouldn't give him a $10 raise so he could marry his girl. Shortly thereafter he hires him back—and thus the title.

BATES, NORMAN

PSYCHO (1960, Paramount); PSYCHO II (1983, Universal); PSYCHO III (1986, Universal)—**Anthony Perkins** has a terrible mother-fixation complex, going so far as mummifying her and speaking with himself in her voice. When he shows interest in runaway Janet Leigh, he dresses as his mother and brutally slaughters her while she's taking a shower. The first remake has Perkins released from the insane asylum years later apparently cured, but some murders reminiscent of those he committed put this in doubt. The third is more of the same, saved only by the fact that Perkins has always been one of the best actors portraying psychopaths.

BATHGATE, BILLY

BILLY BATHGATE (1991, Buena Vista/Touchstone)—Flunky **Loren Dean** witnesses Dustin Hoffman, as Dutch Schultz, taking his once-valued top enforcer Bruce Willis for a late-night boat ride that will include a pair of cement shoes and a one-way swim. Dean earns a place in Hoffman's gang, but is in danger when he is seduced by Willis's mistress Nicole Kidman, whom Hoffman fancies for himself.

BATHSHEBA

DAVID AND BATHSHEBA (1951, 20th Century Fox)—When David (Gregory Peck) spies **Susan Hayward** at her bath, he knows he must have her. He goes so far as to order her husband on a suicide mission. This gets him Hayward, but the God of Israel is not happy. Hayward is almost invited to be the guest of honor at a stone-throwing party.

BATMAN

BATMAN (1966, 20th Century Fox); BATMAN (1989, Warner Brothers); BATMAN RETURNS (1992, Warner Brothers)—Wooden **Adam West** is millionaire Bruce Wayne, whose secret identity is caped and hooded crime fighter Batman. With his ward Dick Grayson (Burt Ward) as Boy Wonder Robin, the Caped Crusader fights super criminals, such as the Joker, the Penguin, the Riddler, and Catwoman. The 1989 film was one of the all time box-office hits, not so much because of **Michael Keaton** as a Robin-less Batman, but for the performance of Jack Nicholson as the Joker. Batman's new foes are Danny DeVito as the Penguin, who, seeking some respect, decides to run for mayor of Gotham City, 'purr'fect Michelle Pfeiffer as Catwoman, as sexy a villain as you'd ever want to meet, and Christopher Walken, as industrial tycoon Max Schreck, whose specialty is ripping off the city.

BATTAGLIA, MIKE

MEN OF RESPECT (1990, Central City)—The first mobster film based on Shakespeare's *Macbeth* was JOE MACBETH, filmed in 1955, starring Paul Douglas and Ruth Roman. In this version, **John Turturro** is the ambitious hood, urged to eliminate Don Rod Steiger and take over his rackets by Katherine Borowitz.

BATTLING JANE

BATTLING JANE (1918, Silent, Paramount)—**Dorothy Gish** assumes the care and raising of a baby, when the tot's mother dies. When the child wins a perfect baby contest, the father shows up trying to collect the prize money, but Gish proves too much for him.

BATURIN, FRANK

KING OF CHINATOWN (1939, Paramount)—**Akim Tamiroff**, the big boss of illegal activities in Chinatown, finds himself in a gang war with former underlings Anthony Quinn and J. Carroll Naish. Before he dies, he gives physician Anna May Wong, who treated him, $50,000 for Chinese war relief.

BAUCHE, WILLIE

THE MAN WHO UNDERSTOOD WOMEN (1959, 20th Century Fox)—**Henry Fonda** is a movie-making genius, but he has no idea how to make his wife Leslie Caron happy.

BAUER, HELEN

EX-LADY (1933, Warner Brothers)—Artist **Bette Davis** holds outrageous views on love and marriage until she falls in love and then she becomes more conventional.

BAUTISTA, JUAN

THE BOBO (1967, GB, Warner Brothers)—**Peter Sellers**, a poor unsuccessful matador, is offered a singing contract if he can seduce local unattainable beauty Britt Ekland within three days. He does but she dumps a dye on him that turns him blue.

BAX, STEPHANIE

THE DEVIL'S OWN (1967, GB, Hammer)—Private school headmistress Joan Fontaine discovers that journalist **Kay Walsh**, who controls the community through witch-craft, plans to sacrifice student Ingrid Brett in a voodoo ceremony.

BAXTER, GERALD

THE FIRM MAN (1975, Australia, Australian Film Institute) -**Peter Cummins** works for an organization referred to as "The Firm." His wife has an affair with an old friend, and Cummins has visions. What does it all mean? Who knows? Who cares?

BAXTER, HENRY

HOW BAXTER BUTTED IN (1925, Silent, Warner Brothers)—**Matt Moore**, a shy clerk in the circulation department of a big city newspaper, dreams of doing heroic deeds. He falls in love with a pretty stenographer and proves his bravery in taking care of his family responsibilities and saving children in a fire. He's recognized as a hero and wins his girl.

BAXTER, MARY

EYE WITNESS (1950, GB, Warner Brothers)—**Jenny Laird** is the missing eye witness to a murder, whom American lawyer Robert Montgomery must find to defend a friend accused of the crime.

BAXTER, MARY JANE

LITTLE MISS BIG (1946, Universal)—**Fay Holden** is committed to a mental institution by her nephew because she plans to leave her money to her dog rather than him. She escapes and takes refuge in a poor barber's home. After proving she's not looney, she takes care of the barber and his family.

BAXTER, NICK

A SMALL CIRCLE OF FRIENDS (1980, UA)—The producers take a nostalgic look backward on the happy times of protest during the sixties when a menage a trois made college almost bearable for **Jameson Parker** and his friends.

BAXTER, ROBERT

BAXTER (1973, GB, National General)—**Scott Jacoby**, a youth with a speech defect, endures the emotional stress of the breakup of his parents' marriage.

BAXTER, WILLIAM SYLVANUS

SEVENTEEN (1940, Paramount)—In an adaptation of the Booth Tarkington story, **Jackie Cooper** is an adolescent experiencing growing pains. Pretty tame stuff.

BAYETTE, PAULA KATHLEEN "P.K."

P.K. & THE KID (1987, SUNN Classics/ Lorimar)—This film was made before **Molly Ringwald** became a star. It was taken off the shelf and released in an attempt to capitalize on her new found popularity. She's a 15-year-old runaway trying to escape the mistreatment of her brutish father. She teams up with a none-too-bright arm-wrestler.

BAYLES, LAURA

GRAND OLD GIRL (1935, RKO)—**May Robson**, a teacher for 38 years, is forced to retire because she has been making trouble for a local gambler who has been corrupting her students.

BAYLOR, JENNIFER

JENNIFER (1978, American International)—**Lisa Pelikan** is a high school student who gets no respect but ala CARRIE she takes her revenge.

BEACHWOOD, MAC

RAFFERTY AND THE GOLD DUST TWINS (1975, Warner Brothers)—**Sally Kellerman** and MacKenzie Phillips kidnap driving instructor Alan Arkin, forcing him at gunpoint to drive them from Los Angeles to Arizona. Before the trip is over, they become fast friends.

BEAL, NICK

ALIAS NICK BEAL (1949, Paramount)—**Ray Milland** appears to honest politician Thomas Mitchell who'd give his soul to put some crooks out of business. Milland makes it possible for Mitchell to illegally get his hands on some books, which give him his wish. Hero Mitchell is nominated for governor and with some help from Milland, which always requires Mitchell to compromise his principals, he wins the election. Mitchell comes to his senses and is able to sever his connections with Milland and save his soul.

BEALER, VIC

THE ALL-AMERICAN BOY (1973, Warner Brothers)—**Jon Voight** is a boxer with hopes of winning an Olympic medal.

BEAN

FREEBIE AND THE BEAN (1974, Warner Brothers)—Single-minded San Francisco cops **Alan Arkin** and James Caan almost do more damage to the city than service as they try to get the goods on a numbers racket mobster.

BEAN, BUNKER

HIS MAJESTY, BUNKER BEAN (1918, Silent, Paramount); (1925, Silent, Warner Brothers); BUNKER BEAN (1936, RKO) The title character, played respectively by **Jack Pickford, Matt Moore** and **Owen Davis, Jr.**, is told by a fortune teller that he is the reincarnation of both Napoleon Bonaparte and an Egyptian pharaoh. This heady news changes the meek clerk into an aggressive man who wins the hand of his boss' daughter.

BEAN, JUDGE ROY
LIFE AND TIMES OF JUDGE ROY BEAN (1972, National General) - **Paul Newman**, the self-appointed "Law, West of the Pecos," hangs all offenders and confiscates their possessions. He has a life-long infatuation for actress Lily Langtry whom he has never seen.

BEANE, CHICK
CHICK (1936, GB, UA)—College porter **Sydney Howard** inherits an earldom and must defend his estate against con men who pretend to have struck oil on the grounds.

BEAST, THE
BEAUTY AND THE BEAST (1991, Animated, Buena Vista/Disney)—Few would have thought of **Robby Benson** for the voice of the beast, but he delivers a booming bass when he's trying to be scary and changes to an appealing boyish timbre when being kind and loving. It's time for Benson to dump the "Robby."

BEATTIE, DAN
MAN FROM GOD'S COUNTRY (1958, Allied Artists)—Fast on the draw sheriff **George Montgomery** is asked to resign because his gun's the only one still being fired. He has to move on and find a town to clean up that's not quite so peaceful.

BEAUBIEN, TED
THE GUNRUNNER (1989, Canada, New World)—Made years earlier, this feeble action film was released in 1989 to cash-in on **Kevin Costner's** star status. No doubt the star would just as soon forget this plotless bore.

BEAUCAIRE, MONS.
MONSIEUR BEAUCAIRE (1924, Silent, Paramount); (1946, Paramount)—**Rudolph Valentino** plays the dual role of a duke who must escape from France during the reign of Louis XV and the dashing barber whom he poses as. In 1946, **Bob Hope** portrays a dumb barber who has to pose as a duke, known as a master swordsman and lover.

BEAUCHAMP, LUCAS
INTRUDER IN THE DUST (1949, MGM)—In one of the most powerful movies about racial prejudice ever made, marvelous black actor **Juano Hernandez** is arrested for the murder of a white man. A mob of local citizens want to lynch him, but with the help of a young white boy Claude Jarman, Jr. and an old lady Elizabeth Patterson, the sheriff Will Geer is able to prove that the dignified, proud black man is innocent and apprehend the real killer.

BEAUDINE, EMILY
DAUGHTER OF DARKNESS (1948, GB, Paramount)—Irish servant girl **Siobhan McKenna** certainly attracts men, but her intentions are deadly.

BEAUDRY, ACE
THREE ROGUES (1931, Fox)—Card shark **Lew Cody** competes with bank robber Victor McLaglen and rustler Eddie Gribbon for the hand of Fay Wray because she has a map which tells the location of a gold mine.

BEAUMONT, PRISCILLA
THE GIRL WITHOUT A SOUL (1917, Silent, Metro)—**Viola Dane** portrays twin sisters. Priscilla steals church funds, and her sister's boyfriend is blamed.

BEAUMONT, VESTA
THE GIRL WHO LOVES A SOLDIER (1916, GB, Silent, Moss) Nurse **Vesta Tilley** disguises herself as a man to be near her wounded fiance during WWI.

BEAUREGARD, A. LINCOLN
BIG DADDY (1969, Syzygy/United)—**Victor Buono** has to fight off a rival for his moronic swamp girl in the Florida Everglades. If you wonder why you never heard of the picture before, it's probably because you didn't frequent drive-in movies.

BEAUREVEL, BARBARA
MY FORBIDDEN PAST (1951, RKO)—**Ava Gardner**, a girl with a shady past, comes into some money but finds it can't buy her the love of physician Robert Mitchum.

BEAUVEL, ISABEL
A LADY SURRENDERS (1930, Universal)—It takes an attempted suicide by her husband Conrad Nagel to get **Rose Hobart** to agree to a divorce so he can marry Genevieve Tobin.

BECCA
THE VISITOR (1973, Canada, Highwood)—Student **Pia Shandel** rents a house for 5 weeks to do research and finds it comes complete with a ghost with whom she falls in love.

BECCLES, EUSTACE
ASK BECCLES (1933, GB, British and Dominions)—**Garry Marsh** steals a priceless jewel but returns it when an innocent man is arrested for the crime.

BECKER
THE COCA-COLA KID (1986, Cinecom)—Trouble-shooting Coke executive **Eric Roberts** is sent to Australia to win the soda market from a hard-nosed businessman with his own soft drink.

BECKER, OTTO
NAZI AGENT (1942, MGM)—Freedom-loving **Conrad Veidt** takes the place of his Nazi brother and breaks up a spy ring.

BECKET, THOMAS
BECKET (1964, GB, Paramount)—**Richard Burton**, wenching friend of King Henry II (Peter O'Toole), is first made Chancellor of England and then Archbishop of Canterbury by his friend and monarch. Burton takes the latter job seriously and opposes the king's plans for the church and is murdered in his own cathedral by some of the king's barons.

BECKWITH, BOB & SHEILA
MAN, WOMAN AND CHILD (1983, Paramount)—**Martin Sheen** and **Blythe Danner's** wedded bliss is shattered when his illegitimate son, whose existence Sheen was unaware of, comes to live with them after his mother's death.

BECKWITH, ROSALIE
THE HEART SPECIALIST (1922, Silent, Paramount)—Reporter **Mary Miles Minter** is mistaken for a distant relative of war hero Allan Forrest and co-heir to his estate. She is able to prevent Forrest's doctor and sister from poisoning him to get his money and ends up with the grateful lad.

BEDDOES, CATHERINE
TO THE DEVIL, A DAUGHTER (1976, GB, Hammer)—**Nastassja Kinski** is being set up by defrocked priest Christopher Lee to be the central role in a satanic rite.

BEDDOES, WILLIAM
A MAN COULD GET KILLED (1966, Universal)—**James Garner**, an American businessman in Lisbon, is mistaken for a British secret agent who has recovered some stolen industrial diamonds. The crooks want back what Garner does not have.

BEDE, ADAM
ADAM BEDE (1918, Silent, GB, International Exclusives)—Squire's son **Bransby Williams** saves a farmer's niece from being found guilty of murdering an illegitimate baby.

BEDELIA
BEDELIA (1946, GB, General Films)—**Margaret Lockwood** is a greedy woman who has poisoned three husbands for their money and is about to do in number four when an investigator intercedes.

BEDLOE, CONNIE
CONFIDENTIAL CONNIE (1953, MGM)—**Janet Leigh** and her college professor husband Van Johnson have a tough time making ends meet because he is estranged from his cattle baron father. When the latter learns that he's to become a grandfather, he arranges with a local butcher to give Leigh and Johnson special prices on meat. Soon everyone expects these prices.

BEEBE, ELMER & ELSIE
ELMER AND ELSIE (1934, Paramount)—**Frances Fuller** has grand plans for meek and retiring husband **George Bancroft**, but he would prefer to fade into the background.

BEECH, VIOLA
THE GIRL FROM SCOTLAND YARD (1937, Paramount)—**Karen Morley**, a detective, investigates the cause of a series of explosions.

BEECHAM, BENJAMIN
THE AMAZING MR. BEECHAM (1949, GB, Two Cities)—Butler **Cecil Parker** stands for Parliament against his employer's son.

BEECHER, DR. PAUL
THE VAMPIRE (1957, UA)—When researcher **John Beal** injects himself with bat serum, he becomes a vampire.

BEEKMAN, SIR FRANCIS
GENTLEMEN PREFER BLONDES (1928, Silent, Paramount; (1953, 20th Century Fox)—**Mack Swain** and **Charles Coburn** each appear as wealthy older men on a transatlantic cruise who are delighted to be taken by gold digger Lorelei Lee.

BELA
THE HUNTRESS (1923, Silent, Associated First National)—White girl **Colleen Moore** has been raised by American Indians as one of their own. She falls in love with prospector Lloyd Hughes and runs away when faced with being forced to marry an Indian brave instead of her love.

BELAME, ALINE ANN
WHITE YOUTH (1920, Silent, Universal)—Louisiana orphan **Edith Roberts** is forced by her grand-father to marry one of his elderly friends. Lucky for her a Yankee shows up and takes her away before the ceremony.

BELCHER, CLARIEE
STEEL MAGNOLIAS (1989, Tri-Star)—**Olympia Dukakis** has most of the best lines in this melodrama with humor, featuring the talk of six southern women at a beauty parlor.

BELDEN, JOE
EXCUSE MY DUST (1951, MGM)—**Red Skelton**, the inventor of an automobile, is in love with the daughter of the local livery stable owner. For some reason Red and Dad just don't get along.

BELDON, RALPH
THE SECRET PARTNER (1961, GB, MGM)—Blackmailing dentist **Norman Bird** is forced by a mysterious stranger to rob a businessman.

BELINSKY, AVRAM
THE FRISCO KID (1979, Warner Brothers)—While rabbi **Gene Wilder** is on his way to San Francisco, he teams up with a Western outlaw. Well, it seemed like a good idea.

BELL, ALEXANDER GRAHAM
THE STORY OF ALEXANDER GRAHAM BELL (1939, 20th Century Fox)—For years the joke was that **Don Ameche** invented the telephone after he appeared in this appealing biopic as the man who did.

BELL, JUNE
THE WATER GYPSIES (1932, GB, RKO)—**Ann Todd** is one of two girls whose life on a Thames River barge is examined in this naive movie.

BELLA DONNA
BELLA DONNA (1915, Silent, Paramount); (1923, Silent, Paramount)—In 1915, **Pauline Frederick**, an adventurer who uses men for her own purposes and pleasures, has the tables turned on her by an Egyptian. In 1923, **Pola Negri** proves to be a worthy successor to Frederick in the role of the man-tamer.

BELLAC
THE RETURN OF DRACULA (1958, UA)—**Francis Lederer** is Dracula and he returns. What else do you want to know?

BELLAIRE, CARL
LONG LOST FATHER (1934, RKO)—**John Barrymore**, the manager of a London night club, is confronted with the new singer, his daughter whom he had abandoned years earlier. She wants nothing to do with him but when she makes some wrong choices of companions, his paternal instinct takes over.

BELLAIRS, KITTY
SWEET KITTY BELLAIRS (1930, Warner Brothers)—**Claudia Dell** lives in the days of stagecoaches in England and finds romance at a seaside resort. Sweet but dull.

BELLAIRS, RONALD
THE ELDER BROTHER (1937, GB, Paramount)—**John Stuart**, recently engaged, confesses to the murder of a married woman with whom his brother was having an affair.

BELLAMY, GHIRLAINE
THE BLONDE SAINT (1926, Silent, First National)—**Doris Kenyon's** puritanical ideals win her the title, until she is all but kidnapped by a man who rushes her off to an Italian isle where he declares his love. During a cholera outbreak, she confesses she loves him also.

BELLAMY, STEPHEN
BELLAMY TRIAL (1929, Part-Talkie, MGM)—**Kenneth Thompson** and a beautiful Leatrice Joy are on trial for the murder of his

cheating wife when a mysterious witness comes forward and clears them.

BELLAMY, TONY

HOLD THAT GIRL (1934, Fox)—To get a story, reporter **Claire Trevor** joins a fan dance troupe. When the cops raid the show, she's arrested along with the others. In the court, she's forced to demonstrate the dance for the judge and spectators.

BELLBOY, THE

BLAME IT ON THE BELLBOY (1992, GB/US, Buena Vista)—The inability of Venetian bellboy **Bronson Pinchot** to pronounce three similarly sounding names results in Dudley Moore, Bryan Brown and Richard Griffiths being given messages meant for one or the other of them. There are few laughs in this mistaken-identity farce.

BELLE

BEAUTY AND THE BEAST (1991, Animated, Buena Vista/Disney)—Beautifully voiced by **Paige O'Hara**, Beauty is a brainy young woman kidnapped by the Beast. Her initial aversion turns to an appreciation for his inner beauty and sensitivity.

BELLE

THE GYPSY AND THE GENTLEMAN (1958, GB, Rank)—**Melina Mercouri** is a tempestuous gypsy who marries a penniless aristocrat.

BELLEW, BETTY

THE IMPOSSIBLE MRS. BELLEW (1922, Silent, Paramount)—When her husband returns home from an evening with his mistress, he finds his wife **Gloria Swanson** in the presence of a male neighbor. Even though nothing has been going on between the two, the husband shoots the man, is arrested and tried for the crime. Gloria keeps her silence, and the jury frees the husband who in their opinion merely exercised the unwritten law. Swanson, however, is disgraced, and loses her husband. She flees to Europe, where she becomes part of an early day jet set. Talk about double standards.

BELLEW, KIT "SMOKE"

SMOKE BELLEW (1929, Silent, First Division)—Trying to escape his past, **Conway Tearle** moves to Alaska and falls in love with a prospector's daughter. The three strike it rich.

BELLINGS, ARLINE

A WOMAN OBSESSED (1989, Platinum)—Wealthy, high-strung New York dilettante **Ruth Raymond** reveals to lawyer Gregory Patrick that she is his mother and that the portrait of him, hanging in a gallery, is actually that of his father. There will be more revelations in this family reunion.

BELLIS, MARK

SO EVIL MY LOVE (1948, GB, Paramount)—Scoundrel **Ray Milland** is a caddish artist who entices a missionary's widow, Ann Todd, into framing Geraldine Fitzgerald of a murder.

BELMOND, PENELOPE

THE PERFECT WOMAN (1950, GB, Rank/Ealing)—**Patricia Roc** exchanges places with her uncle's robot woman when he hires an escort to show his creation around town.

BELOIT, PAUL

HE STAYED FOR BREAKFAST (1940, Columbia)—Parisian communist **Melvyn Douglas** takes a shot at a capitalist and is pursued by the police. To give them the slip, he ducks into Loretta Young's apartment. Young who is the ex-wife of the man Douglas tried to kill shows him some advantages of capitalism.

BELPHEGOR

BELPHEGOR THE MOUNTEBANK (1921, Silent, GB, Ideal)—In Ruritania, rogue **Milton Rosmer** poses as a count he killed and weds a princess, but an heir to the throne steals their child.

BELT, STANLEY

THE PATSY (1964, Paramount)—**Jerry Lewis** is a bellboy who is being groomed by Hollywood executives to replace a dead comedian.

BELUSHI, JOHN

WIRED (1989, Taurus)—**Michael Chiklis** struggles valiantly in this weird and uninteresting biopic of the late Saturday Night Life comedian, but is defeated by the screenplay and Larry Peerce's direction.

BELVEDERE, LYNN

SITTING PRETTY (1948, 20th Century Fox); MR. BELVEDERE GOES TO COLLEGE (1949, 20th Century Fox); MR. BELVEDERE RINGS THE BELL (1951, 20th Century Fox)—**Clifton Webb**, a self-proclaimed genius, accepts the job of live-in baby-sitter for the three unruly kids of Robert Young and Maureen O'Hara in order to get material for a book he's writing. He trains everyone in the family to do things his way. In the first sequel, Webb, who had never bothered with formal education, has need for a college education. He gets his diploma within a year. In the final film, Webb moves into an old folks home to test his theories on aging.

BELZ

THE WRONG GUYS (1988, New World)—**Richard Belzer** is one of several stand-up comedians, who fall on their faces, in this dumb piece about grown-up (it says here) members of a Cub Scout troop holding a reunion.

BEMBRIDGE

WHAT THE BUTLER SAW (1950, Hammer)—When the earl for whom he works retires from a post as governor of a tropical island, butler **Henry Mollison** returns with his employer to England but takes along an island princess as his bride.

BEN

FALSE IDENTITY (1990, RKO)—Presumed dead, **Stacy Keach** returns to his home town after 17 years. He's trying to determine his real identity, which he lost when a murder attempt left him disfigured and with a metal plate in his head.

BEN

TRAVELLING HUSBANDS (1931, RKO)—Raunchy star salesman **Carl Miller** lustily pursues Constance Cummings at a sales conference.

BENCE, KATE & RUTH

WISE GIRLS (1930, MGM)—**Norma Lee** marries plumber Elliott Nugent to make her real love jealous. It works! Nugent has the marriage annulled and marries Lee's sister **Marion Shilling**.

BENDER, JOHN

THE BREAKFAST CLUB (1985, Universal)—**Judd Nelson**, a greaser-like teenager, joins four other high schoolers in an all-day Saturday detention. He seems incorrigible, but naturally he has a sensitive side, which nice girl Molly Ringwald brings out.

BENDER, THEODORE

HIS NIBS (1921, Silent, Exceptional Pictures)—**Charles "Chic" Sale**, the owner and operator of an old-fashioned movie house, informs his patrons that he has snipped out all the titles of the movie they are about to see. But not to worry, he plans to give a running commentary about the action.

BENEDICT, JULIUS & VINCENT

TWINS (1988, Universal)—The comical premise of this movie is that former Mr. Universe **Arnold Schwarzenegger** and pint-size **Danny De Vito** are twins (fraternal, of course), the result of a genetic experiment that went haywire. The boys, separated at birth, are reunited 35 years later. The two are as opposite as can be. Schwarzenegger, reared on a desert island, is pure of spirit, mind and body. De Vito is totally corrupt, having been kicked out of an orphanage at age 14 for getting a nun into trouble. Unfortunately, after getting past the description of the "twins," only De Vito is funny, and the effort of carrying a huge load like Arnold seems too much for the delightfully entertaining little man.

BEN-HUR, JUDAH

BEN-HUR (1925, Silent, MGM); (1959, MGM)—**Ramon Novarro** in 1925 and **Charlton Heston** in 1959 appear as the Jewish aristocrat who at the time of Christ is betrayed by a Roman who was his childhood friend. Sentenced to the galleys for life, he is rewarded with his freedom when he saves the Roman officer in charge of the slave ships. Later he takes revenge on his former friend in a chariot race in the Roman coliseum. Epics? Yes! Best Picture of the Year? No way!

BENJAMIN, JUDY

PRIVATE BENJAMIN (1980, Warner Brothers)—When her new husband dies while they are making love, disconsolate, wealthy and aimless **Goldie Hawn** is talked into joining the army. It's not the way she was led to believe, and her run-ins with officer Eileen Brennan are classical. She eventually finds herself, becomes a good soldier and starts a new romance.

BENJAMIN, SAUL

LOVESICK (1983, Warner Brothers)—Psychiatrist **Dudley Moore**, who has talks with the ghost of Sigmund Freud, falls hopelessly in love with his patient Elizabeth McGovern. The little man is reaching, but he doesn't quite touch us.

BENNETT, CHIP

CHIP OF THE FLYING U (1926, Silent, Universal); (1940, Universal) —**Hoot Gibson** falls in love with the physician sister of the rancher for whom he works. In order to be near her, he fakes an injury. The two fall in love, but when she discovers his deception she sends him away. He sweeps her up and carries her off to the preacher. In the remake, **Johnny Mack Brown**, foreman of a ranch, is suspected of a series of holdups. He exposes the real outlaws.

BENNETT, CHRIS

MAN OF IRON (1935, Warner Brothers)—Factory worker **Barton MacLane** advances to the position of vice-president of his company, but at the expense of losing his friends.

BENNETT, FLO

PANAMA FLO (1932, RKO)—**Helen Twelvetrees**, a showgirl on the run from the police takes a job as a housekeeper for businessman Charles Bickford. When her gangster boyfriend Robert Armstrong shows up and makes trouble, she shoots him, but the fatal bullet is fired by Bickford.

BENNETT, JACK JR.

THE COLLEGE ORPHAN (1915, Silent, Universal)—When shy college student **Carter De Haven** is expelled through the efforts of

another lad, his father disowns him until he redeems himself by choosing the proper girl to be his bride.

BENNETT, JOYCE

THE PLAYTHING (1929, GB, Wardour)—**Estelle Brody**, a wild beautiful sophisticate, is unimpressed with the efforts of a dull Scotsman to impress her.

BENNETT, KITTY

THE MODEL AND THE MARRIAGE BROKER (1951, 20th Century Fox) -When Thelma Ritter discovers that **Jeanne Crain** is having an affair with a married man, she decides to find a more suitable match for the young girl.

BENNETT, OLIVER

THE KING OF DIAMONDS (1918, Silent, Vitagraph)—**Harry Morey's** doctor wants him out of the way so he can have a clear path to Morey's wife. The medic inoculates Morey with leprosy, but our hero survives.

BENNETT, STEVE

MR. DISTRICT ATTORNEY (1946, Columbia)—**Dennis O'Keefe** appeared in a 1941 film with the same title, but his character's name was P. Caldweller Jones. In this version of the popular radio show, O'Keefe is an assistant D.A. who falls for a no-good girl who kills two men and has similar plans for O'Keefe.

BENNY

ST. BENNY THE DIP (1951, UA)—**Dick Haymes** is a gambler who escapes the police by dressing as a priest and then is called upon to live up to his collar.

BENNY, BUCK

BUCK BENNY RIDES AGAIN (1940, Paramount)—When **Jack Benny** boasts of his cowboy skills on his radio show, a friend invites him to visit his dude ranch where Jack makes a fool of himself.

BENOIT, MARGARET

MYSTERY WOMAN (1935, Fox)—**Mona Barrie** must find a document which will clear her husband of a crime that has caused him to be sent to Devil's Island.

BENSON

PARTNERS (1982, Paramount)—**Ryan O'Neal** teams up with gay cop John Hurt to go undercover in San Francisco to solve the murder of a homosexual.

BENSON, ANTHONY

THE BENSON MURDER CASE (1930, Paramount)—Notorious womanizer and wealthy stockbroker **Richard Tucker** is shot to death in his country estate, and it's up to Philo Vance (William Powell) to solve the case.

BENSON, MAJOR BERNARD

THE PRIVATE WAR OF MAJOR BENSON (1955, Universal)—Stern disciplinarian **Charlton Heston** gets in trouble with his military superiors by shooting off his mouth to reporters. As punishment his new assignment is at a military school run by nuns. His cadets run in age from 6 to 15. Well naturally he tries to treat the kids like his former troops and of course they rebel. It takes a while, but the two sides adjust to each other and Heston is reassigned to a command of real soldiers whom he treats more humanely.

BENSON, DR.

THE MAD DOCTOR OF MARKET STREET (1942, Universal)— **Lionel Atwill** puts people into suspended animation and later revives them as one of his bogus curing methods. One day he makes a mistake and can't bring his victim back. He escapes to an island where his tricks make him king.

BENSON, FREDDY
DIRTY ROTTEN SCOUNDRELS (1988, Orion)—**Steve Martin** has the Marlon Brando role in this remake of the 1964 comedy, BEDTIME STORY. Martin is a small-time American con-man who arrives in the resort areas of the south of France, which sophisticated con-man Michael Caine considers his private domain. The two flim-flam men make a bet: the first to swindle 50 thousand dollars from a woman gets to keep it and the territory.

BENSON, HARRY
THE TERMINAL MAN (1974, Warner Brothers)—Scientist **George Segal's** brain is hooked up to a computer which changes him into a homicidal maniac.

BENSON, MAJOR
A YANK IN VIET NAM (1941, 20th Century Fox)—Marine **Marshall Thompson** is in Saigon to help the South Vietnamese. So that's when the first advisors were assigned to Nam.

BENSON, SALLY See **VICKI NORRIS**

BENTLEY, KAREN
MY FAVORITE BLONDE (1942, Paramount)—**Madeline Carroll**, a beautiful British agent, is forced to seek help from bungling vaudevillian Bob Hope to get away from Nazi spies.

BENTLEY, THOMAS
OUR LEADING CITIZEN (1922, Silent, Paramount)—Small town lawyer **Thomas Meighan** goes off to war, comes home a hero and is persuaded to run for congress. He wins despite refusing to cooperate with a political machine.

BENTON, LT. BOB
MEN ARE LIKE THAT (1931, Columbia)—West Point grad **John Wayne** finds that his commanding officer at the Arizona Army Post to which he's assigned is married to his former lady friend, Laura La Plante.

BENTON, JULIE
JULIE (1956, MGM)—**Doris Day** discovers that hubby Louis Jourdan killed his first wife and has similar plans for her. If that wasn't enough, she's forced to land a plane when Jourdan kills the pilot and co-pilot before being killed himself.

BENTON, MIMI See **SALLY TRENT**

BENTON, SYLVIA
REGISTERED NURSE (1934, Warner Brothers)—When her husband becomes insane, nurse **Bebe Daniels** is pursued by two surgeons. It's a ridiculous melodrama but no worse than some of the TV hospital stories of a few decades later.

BENTON, WADE
THE MYSTERIOUS RIDER (1933, Paramount)—Cowboy **Kent Taylor** defeats Irving Pichel who has been cheating homesteaders and wins pretty Gail Patrick in the bargain.

BEPPI, THE
LAUGH, CLOWN, LAUGH (1928, Silent, MGM)—**Lon Chaney**, a circus clown, makes audiences laugh while his own heart is breaking when he discovers that his ward whom he loves prefers

another man. He commits suicide as part of his act to free her to marry the man of her choice.

BERENICE
WARRIOR QUEEN (1987, Seymour Borde)—**Sybil Danning**, the mistress of the Roman emperor, goes to Pompeii for a holiday, attends a slave auction and takes interest in a girl bought by the largest local brothel. It's just another softcore sex exploitation film.

BERENT, ELLEN
LEAVE HER TO HEAVEN (1946, 20th Century Fox)—**Gene Tierney** will allow nothing to stand in her way of getting Cornel Wilde, even to allowing his crippled brother drown. Her selfishness causes so much heartache to so many that ultimately she commits suicide.

BERESFORD, JUDITH
HAIL THE WOMAN (1921, Silent, Associated Producers)—**Florence Vidor** stands up to her father when he arranges to buy off the father of a girl made pregnant by his son. The result is that both girls are thrown out. The pregnant woman goes to New York to have her baby. Vidor discovers that her brother, a cringing coward studying for the ministry, is actually married to the girl but afraid to speak up. Vidor goes to New York and retrieves the baby after its mother dies and brings it home on the very day her brother is to be ordained. He confesses his sin and acknowledges his son.

BERESFORD, PETER
A MAN'S SHADOW (1920, GB, Silent, Butchers)—**Langhorne Burton**, the look-alike of a bum, uses the resemblance to his advantage so he may kill a Jewish money lender, but his mistress betrays him.

BERETTI, LOUIS
BORN RECKLESS (1930, Fox)—Offered the choice of prison or serving in WWI, gangster **Edmund Lowe** chooses the military. He becomes a hero. After the war he reverts to his criminal ways but reforms when he falls in love with a society woman.

BERGDORF, ANTHONY
OCEAN'S ELEVEN (1960, Warner Brothers)—**Richard Conte** is forced to deliver one of the all-time stupid lines "Is it the big casino?" when a doctor informs him that his condition is fatal. Other than that, all he has to do is use his electrical skills to help some old war buddies rob five Las Vegas casinos at the same time before expiring. His colleagues give him one hell of an expensive send-off.

BERGEN, ANNA
HIS CAPTIVE WOMAN (1929, First National/Warner Brothers)—In one of the strangest courtroom movies on record, gold digger **Dorothy MacKaill** is on trial for the murder of the man who had kept her for years. When it looks like she's sure to be convicted, a police officer testifies what a good woman she was when the two of them had been shipwrecked on a desert isle years before. That's good enough for the judge who sentences her to return to the island with the cop.

BERGEN, KAREN
LITTLE MISS NOBODY (1933, GB, Warner Brothers)—**Winna Winifried** lives in an orphanage and is as sweet and moral as can be. When she discovers that a lawyer who is looking to adopt a little girl is actually her father, she exchanges papers with another girl who she believes is more in need of adoption, but her deception is discovered and she's reunited with her real father.

BERGER

TWO LIVING, ONE DEAD (1964, GB, Emerson)—When masked robbers break in on three post office clerks, one is killed, a second is seriously wounded and the third, **Patrick McGoohan**, cooperates with the robbers who get away with lots of cash. This leads to McGoohan being accused of cowardice, or worse, being the inside man on the job.

BERGOT, PAUL

THE STRONG MAN (1926, Silent, First National)—**Harry Langdon**, a Belgian soldier in WWI, falls in love with American pen pal Priscilla Bonner. After the war, Langdon goes to the U.S. to search for his love. He finds that she is blind and her father is not thrilled with Langdon, but he changes his tune when our hero breaks up the gang of bootleggers who have terrorized the town.

BERKE, SHIRLEY

NINE GIRLS (1944, Columbia)—**Marcia Mae Jones** is one of a group of smart-alecky sorority sisters, each a suspect, when the nastiest of them, Anita Louise, is murdered.

BERKELEY, JAMES

HER HUSBAND'S TRADEMARK (1922, Silent, Paramount)—**Stuart Holmes'** ambition is to become rich. He wins the hand of Gloria Swanson from his rival Richard Wayne. Years later, although not rich, Holmes dresses his wife in luxurious clothes, the trademark of his prosperity. Wayne comes back into the picture, and the three are soon in Mexico where Swanson realizes she's still in love with Wayne. Holmes is conveniently killed by bandits.

BERLANGER, SUSAN

JUST THE WAY YOU ARE (1984, MGM/UA)—Flautist **Kristy McNichol** overcomes a childhood disease that forces her to wear a leg brace and is able to function just like "ordinary" people.

BERLINER, SOLLY

MEN'S CLUB (1986, Paramount)—**Harvey Keitel** is one of seven men who start an encounter group. Pretty boring.

BERMAN, JAKE

THE TWO JAKES (1990, Paramount)—When **Harvey Keitel** hires private investigator Jack Nicholson to discover if his wife Meg Tilly is being unfaithful, it seems like routine work for Nicholson. But after Keitel kills Tilly's lover, who just happens to be his partner, and the audiotape of the lovers in bed turns up the name of Katherine Mulwray, killed in CHINATOWN (74), Nicholson finds himself mixed up in another case of sex, murder, deceit and misuse of a precious resource—this time oil.

BERNA

CIVILIZATION'S CHILD (1916, Silent, Triangle)—**Anne Lehr**, a Russian Jew, is raised by her father ignorant of the world. When he dies, she discovers how terrible it is to be a Russian Jew and so emigrates to the U.S. where things aren't much better.

BERNARDO, DON AGGIMIO

THE DON IS DEAD (1973, Universal)—**J. Duke Russo** is the Mafioso leader who doesn't survive the battle between two crime families.

BERNARDONE, FRANCIS

FRANCIS OF ASSISI (1961, 20th Century Fox)—**Bradford Dillman** portrays the wealthy young man who founds a religious order whose members take a vow of poverty. Franciscans are more flesh and blood people than they appear in this dreary biopic.

BERNDIE, LISA

LETTER FROM AN UNKNOWN WOMAN (1948, Universal)—From childhood **Joan Fontaine** has loved self-centered musician Louis Jourdan, who does not notice her. When grown, they meet and have a wonderfully romantic night together. He is to go away on a concert tour but promises to return to her. He promptly forgets her, but she is left with a tangible token of their love: a child. Fontaine marries an officer, but years later encounters Jourdan again, who does not recognize her. They share love again, but as before he forgets about her as soon as they are parted. She writes him a letter telling him of their child who has died. She also is dying. Finally, Jourdan remembers her, just as he is about to go to his death in a duel with her husband. Fontaine is incredibly good.

BERNE, DUKE

THE BIG SHOT (1942, Warner Brothers)—**Humphrey Bogart** not only inherits a fortune from his big-city uncle but the dead man's gang of crooks as well.

BERNHARDT, SARAH

THE INCREDIBLE SARAH (1976, GB, Readers Digest)—Flamboyant actress **Glenda Jackson** portrays the legendary French actress up to the age of 35.

BERNIE BROTHERS

FOUR SONS (1928, Silent, Fox); (1940, 20th Century Fox); 1928: Joseph—**James Hall**; Johann—**Charles Morton**; Franz—**Francis X. Bushman**; Andres—**George Meeker**; 1940: Chris—**Don Ameche**; Karl—**Alan Curtis**; Fritz—**George Ernest**; Joseph—**Robert Lowery** The war changes from 1928 to 1940, but the story of how a Czech family is divided by mixed localities is predictable sentimentality.

BERQUIST, PHIL

CITY SLICKERS (1991, Columbia)—Having broken up with his dominating wife and losing his job with her father's company in the bargain, **Daniel Stern** goes West to try his hand as a modern-day cowpuncher. He returns with more confidence and Helen Slater.

BERRY, JIMMY

I CAN EXPLAIN (1922, Silent, Metro)—**Gareth Hughes**, the junior partner in a business firm, innocently becomes involved with his partner's wife, which leads to his fiancee cancelling their engagement and his partner challenging him to a duel in South America.

BERT

THREE (1969, GB, UA)—**Robie Porter** and his pal Sam Waterston travel around Europe in a battered car, meeting many women, but both develop an interest in Charlotte Rampling. To protect their friendship they pledge to keep their relationship with Rampling platonic, but neither can resist the willing girl.

BERT & BOB

COCKEYED CAVALIERS (1934, RKO)—**Bert Wheeler** and partner **Robert Woolsey** were a minor comedy team of the thirties, popular in the sticks. This time the two are in sixteenth century England where they are mistaken for the king's physicians.

BERTHA

BOXCAR BERTHA (1972, American International)—When her father dies during the Depression, **Barbara (Hershey) Seagull** hits the road, teams up with a union organizer and helps him rob trains.

BERTIER, DR. ANDRE & COLETTE

ONE HOUR WITH YOU (1932, Paramount)—**Maurice Chevalier** and **Jeanette MacDonald** are a married couple. Chevalier is a physician with a roving eye that settles on MacDonald's best friend Genevieve Tobin, who won't let friendship get in the way of an affair. Her husband Roland Young has Tobin followed by a detective and threatens to divorce her and name Chevalier correspondent. Chevalier confesses to MacDonald, who rushes into the arms of Charlie Ruggles who had been waiting for just such an opportunity. After gaining her revenge on her gander, MacDonald gets Chevalier to agree that the two will no longer stray from their marriage bed. It's all delightfully naughty as are the songs, especially "Three Times A Day."

BESANT, NORMA

COQUETTE (1929, UA)—In her first talkie, **Mary Pickford** is a flirtatious southern flapper who falls in love with a man her father hates so much that he shoots and kills him, then takes his own life, leaving little Mary all alone in the world.

BESS

ADAM'S WOMAN (1972, Australia, Warner Brothers)—In 1840 Australia, **Jane Merrow** is a convict who marries fellow-convict Beau Bridges and helps him found a settlement in the outback.

BESS

PORGY AND BESS (1959, Columbia)—**Dorothy Dandridge** and Sidney Poitier are the leads in the American operetta set in "Catfish Row" of Charleston. Dandridge is a floozy adored by crippled Poitier. She's hooked on heroin supplied by "Sportin' Life" (Sammy Davis, Jr.) and is the woman of tough stevedore Crown (Brock Peters). While the latter is in hiding after killing a man in a crap game, Poitier takes in Dandridge and they fall in love. When Peters comes back looking for his woman, Poitier kills him. Sidney is forced to go into hiding and while he's gone, Dandridge agrees to go to New York with Davis. Poitier returns and follows her to the big city. Although Dandridge was a fine singer, her range was not enough for the Gershwin songs so her singing was dubbed by Adele Addison.

BESSIE

THE AMERICAN HEIRESS (1917, Silent, GB, Hepworth)—**Alma Taylor**, a maid posing as an heiress, is kidnapped by thieves and rescued by the butler.

BETELGEUSE

BEETLEJUICE (1988, Warner Brothers)—When young married ghosts Alec Baldwin and Geena Davis find they are not very effective in haunting their big old Connecticut home, now owned by some despicable yuppies, they hire **Michael Keaton**, a renegade demon, who advertises his services on ghostly TV, to scare the devil out of the new inhabitants. The film isn't very scary, nor is it very funny.

BETH

THE NAKED WITCH (1964, Mishkin)—When witchcraft researcher Robert Burgos digs up 200 year old witch **Beth Porter**, she jumps out of her coffin and once again terrorizes the area.

BETH

ORDINARY PEOPLE (1980, Paramount)—Icy **Mary Tyler Moore** is the mother of Timothy Hutton, a teenager filled with remorse and guilt because he was unable to save his brother from drowning in a boating accident. Her marriage and family is crumbling, and there is nothing she seems capable of doing about it.

BETH/ELIZABETH/BETTY/LIZ

ELIZABETH OF LADYMEAD (1949, GB, British Lion)—**Anna Neagle** appears in four roles as the much changed wives of husbands home from wars in 1854, 1903, 1919 and 1946.

BETTINA

BETTINA LOVED A SOLDIER (1916, Silent, Bluebird)—**Louise Lovely** has had 35 marriage proposals, but each of her suitors cared more for her fortune than her. Along comes a soldier so poor that he leaves her because of her wealth. For Lovely, this is proof of his love for her.

BETTY

THE ADVENTURE OF THE ACTION HUNTERS (1987, Bonner/Troma)—**Sean Murphy** and boyfriend Ronald Hunter hear the dying pleas of an old sailor for help as he is killed by gangsters. Murphy and Hunter join the search for a million dollars in loot the deceased has hidden.

BETTY

MADCAP BETTY (1915, Silent, Bosworth)—Convent-reared **Elsie Janis** dreams of several romantic adventures and upon awakening, decides to marry her fiance immediately.

BETTY

MAID OF THE WEST (1921, Silent, Universal)—Wealthy Texan **Eileen Percy** is sent to New York to forget the pilot she loves. But he shows up to retrieve her pearl necklace stolen by crooks.

BETTY

PICKUP (1951, Columbia)—**Beverly Michaels** is a floozy picked up by middle-aged widower Hugo Haas, who tells her he has a large savings account. She marries him for his money and is soon planning his murder with her lover.

BETTY

A WOMAN'S TEMPTATION (1959, GB, British Lion)—When struggling widow **Patricia Driscoll** finds some stolen money, she hides it to be used for her son's education. The crooks come for the loot and are defeated by a friend of Driscoll. She turns the money over to the police and is rewarded.

BEVERLY, VICTOR

WATCH BEVERLY (1932, GB, Butchers)—Diplomat **Henry Kendall** is outraged to learn that a British businessman has agreed to pay a dictator a large sum of money for oil drilling rights. Kendall disguises himself as the dictator and collects the bribe which he turns over to the British government.

BEY, AHMED

THE CROUCHING BEAST (1936, RKO)—During WWI Turkish spy **Fritz Kortner** is after an American newspaperwoman in Turkey covering the war.

BIALYSTOCK, MAX

THE PRODUCERS (1967, Embassy)—**Zero Mostel** is outstanding as a producer of Broadway shows which are backed by funds he romances out of elderly ladies. When accountant Gene Wilder casually suggests that a dishonest person could make a lot of money if he got a lot of investors to back a show that was sure to fail, Mostel rises to the challenge. He and Wilder produce a musical called "Springtime for Hitler" which praises the dictator. Believing it will be a sure bust, Mostel sells several thousand percent shares in the show to his little old ladies —but surprise! It's a smash hit, and the two go to prison.

BICKLE, TRAVIS

TAXI DRIVER (1976, Columbia)—Vietnam veteran and loner **Robert De Niro** is considerably strange. He drives a cab in some of the meanest streets in New York but becomes some kind of hero when he blows away the perverts who are pimping 12 year old prostitute Jodie Foster.

BIDDLE, ANTHONY J. DREXEL

THE HAPPIEST MILLIONAIRE (1967, Buena Vista) **Fred MacMurray** found a new career with the Walt Disney Studio, appearing as carefree eccentrics as in this silly musical in which he's a millionaire who raises alligators.

BIDDLE, CHARLES

GENTLEMEN MARRY BRUNETTES (1955, UA)—**Alan Young** is one of the wimpy but wealthy men who look good to Jane Russell and Jeanne Crain when they are in Paris checking out the millionaires.

BIDDY

BIDDY (1983, GB, Sands)—Audiences are treated to the ho-hum life of an English nanny **Celia Bannerman** from her middle-age on.

BIERCE, AMBROSE

OLD GRINGO (1989, Columbia)—**Gregory Peck** portrays the American short story writer, who disappeared in Mexico in 1913. According to this latest failed attempt to resurrect the Western, he died happily in the arms of an aging, but still smashing Jane Fonda.

BIFFLE, JERRY

TOP BANANA (1954, UA)—**Phil Silvers** is what else?—a TV comedian in this revue based on his, and others' old burlesque routines.

BIG BERTHA

THE NIGHT THEY RAIDED BIG BERTHA'S (1975, Scotia American)—**Hetty Galen** runs a massage parlor. On the night of the title, her establishment is invaded by a bungling burglar.

BIG ELI

THE KENTUCKIAN (1955, UA)—**Burt Lancaster** sets out with his son from his home in Kentucky looking for a better life. On the way he gets involved in a feud and is beaten with a horsewhip by a brutal Walter Matthau in the latter's first movie.

BIG HALSY

LITTLE FAUSS AND BIG HALSY (1970, Paramount)—Loudmouth **Robert Redford** teams with drunken and slow-witted motorcycle racer Michael J. Pollard. They follow the circuit with Redford as racer and Pollard as mechanic. They both fall for Lauren Hutton. Any bets on whom she prefers?

BIG HAROLD

PLATOON (1987, Orion)—**Forest Whittaker** is a member of a platoon in Vietnam whose experiences represent those of the many men who fought and died in the jungles of the country often without a good idea of what they were meant to accomplish.

BIG, MR.

I'M GONNA GET YOU SUCKA (1988, MGM-UA)—**John Vernon** is the ruthless gold-chain pusher on whom writer-director Keenan Ivory Wayans vows vengeance after his brother dies from wearing too many heavy gold chains. It is a funny parody of the black-oriented exploitation films.

BIG PEARL

FIVE BOLD WOMEN (1960, Citation)—**Irish McCalla** is one of five female murderers being brought across Texas to prison by U.S. Marshal Jeff Morrow. She doesn't survive the trip.

BIG TIME

MY SON, THE HERO (1943, PRC)—**Roscoe Karns** has written his war correspondent son elaborate tales of what a big success he is in aiding the war effort back home. He has to put his money where his mouth is when his son comes for a visit.

BIGELOW, FRANK

D.O.A. (1950, UA)—**Edmond O'Brien** has been fed a slow acting poison to which there is no antidote. Before he dies, he intends to find out why and who's responsible.

BIGGAR, BUNTY

BUNTY PULLS THE STRINGS (1921, Silent, Goldwyn)—**Leatrice Joy** controls her stern church elder and two brothers in a small Scottish village by subtle diplomacy. She needs all her skills when one of the brothers robs a bank and wishes to return the loot.

BIGGER, FRANCIS

CARRY ON DOCTOR (1968, GB, Rank)—**Frankie Howerd** is a medical quack who treats a reluctant patient in a hospital staffed by incompetents.

BILL

JUST YOU AND ME, KID (1979, Columbia)—Ex-vaudevillian **George Burns** discovers naked Brooke Shields in the trunk of his car. Seems she's a runaway who has run afoul of a drug dealer. George, ever the gallant gentleman, shelters her.

BILL

THE KILLERS (1984, Roth Film)—Robber **Raymond Mayo** teams with a former insurance man to break into a Beverly Hills mansion, where they kill the owner and his wife for no apparent reason.

BILL

THE LEECH (1921, Silent, Pioneer)—**Alex Hall** experienced a minor leg wound during WWI. He sits around feeling sorry for himself and depending on others to take care of him. His brother, who lost his leg in battle, has learned to live with his loss and found a job. Hall finally wises up after a dream.

BILL

A MAN'S CASTLE (1933, Columbia)—During the Depression, **Spencer Tracy**, a rough and tumble man, lives in a shantytown. He takes in starving Loretta Young, and she turns their hovel into a home. Tracy meets showgirl Glenda Farrell who offers him a better life. Although tempted, he decides to move on with Young and look for a brighter future elsewhere when she informs him she's carrying his child.

BILL

MIN AND BILL (1930, MGM)—**Wallace Beery** and Marie Dressler are a loveable old couple, he's a fisherman and she's the owner of a run-down waterfront hotel. Beery dotes on Dorothy Jordan, a young girl he has looked after since her mother deserted her years earlier. The authorities want to get Jordan out of her squalid living conditions. Beery and Dressler fight to prevent this, but their troubles aren't over as Jordan's greedy blackmailing mother shows up when she finds that Jordan has snagged herself a wealthy fellow.

BILL

POOR OLD BILL (1931, GB, Wardour)—When **Leslie Fuller** comes home from the war, he is accompanied by a fellow who feels he has a right to stay with Fuller since he saved Fuller's life during the war. Try as he may, Fuller can't get rid of the intruder until another ex-soldier shows up and convinces them that it was he who saved Fuller's life. The unwanted guest leaves, and the new one moves in because after all he's saved Fuller's life, hadn't he?

BILL

A REAL BLOKE (1935, GB, Universal)—When **George Carney** loses his job, he keeps the news from his family until after his daughter's wedding. His depression is deepened when his son-in-law suffers a tragic accident. The only thing that saves his sanity is the birth of his grandson which somehow gives him hope for the future.

BILL

THE STOKER (1935, GB, Gaumont)—Railroad stoker **Leslie Fuller** befriends a young apprentice who just happens to be the son of the railroad company's chairman. Fuller puts the young man wise to the plans of a gold digger.

BILL

THEIR BIG MOMENT (1934, RKO)—**Slim Summerville** and Zasu Pitts are phony mind readers who solve a mystery in a supposedly haunted house.

BILLIE

BILLIE (1965, UA)—Teenage tomboy **Patty Duke** has troubles with males because she's better at sports than they are.

BILLIE JEAN

THE LEGEND OF BILLIE JEAN (1985, Tri-Star)—**Helen Slater** and her brother are implicated in a shooting and unjustly accused of other crimes. They run from the police and become folk heroes in Texas.

BILLINGS, HUGO "DOC"

RENO AND THE DOC (1984, Canada, New World)—Former con man **Henry Ramer** runs into middle age mountain man Ken Walsh and encourages the man to enter a professional skiing competition which he wins.

BILLINGS, JOHN PERCIVAL

MR. BILLINGS SPENDS HIS DIME (1923, Silent, Paramount)—**Walter Hiers** becomes so infatuated with the girl pictured on his cigar band that he journeys to the South American country where her father is the President, puts down a revolution and wins the grateful girl.

BILLY *See* **CHAMP**

BILLY

THE DEADLY COMPANIONS (1961, Pathe-American)—**Steve Cochran**, a trigger-happy gunman, joins three other losers in robbing a bank, and then they must try to survive a trip through Indian country and their growing animosity towards each other.

BILLY

I'VE GOTTA HORSE (1965, GB, Warner Brothers-Pathe)—Pop singer Billy Fury is irresponsible. When he buys a racehorse, he spends so much time at the track he almost forgets about his show's opening night.

BILLY

THE RAINMAKERS (1935, Radio Pictures)—**Bert Wheeler** and partner Robert Woolsey arrive in the California farm area with a rain-making machine which they claim will end a drought.

BILLY

THE RIVER RAT (1984, Paramount)—**Tommy Lee Jones** has been in prison for 13 years when he returns to his Cajun home to meet his daughter for the first time.

BILLY JACK

BILLY JACK (1971, Warner Brothers); THE TRIAL OF BILLY JACK (1974, Taylor-Laughlin); BILLY JACK GOES TO WASHINGTON (1977, Taylor-Laughlin)—**Tom Laughlin** is a half-breed Vietnam veteran who roams the Arizona desert protecting wildlife and runaway teenagers from a racist community. In the first sequel, this keeper of the peace through the use of violence participates in a massacre. The final film is a poor rip-off of MR. SMITH GOES TO WASHINGTON. Even though Frank Capra, Jr. is its producer, it's still an affront to a great movie and the marvelous populist director.

BILLY T. KID

REVENGE OF BILLY THE KID (1992, GB, Montage)—Set on a fictional island, the movie starts with drunken farmer Michael Balfour bedding the family goat. The result is a monster, half-human, half-goat **Julian Shaw**. Fearing his secret will out, Balfour wraps Shaw in a sack and throws him in a river. Shaw survives and returns to graze on the locals.

BILLY THE KID

BILLY THE KID (1930, MGM)—**John Mack Brown**; BILLY THE KID (1941, MGM)—**Robert Taylor**; BILLY THE KID WANTED (1941, PRC)—**Buster Crabbe**; THE KID RIDES AGAIN (1943, PRC)—**Buster Crabbe**; THE OUTLAW (1943, RKO)—**Jack Buetel**; RETURN OF THE BADMEN (1948, RKO)—**Dean White**; SON OF BILLY THE KID (1949, Screen Guild)—**William Perrott**; I SHOT BILLY THE KID (1950, Lippert)—**Don Barry**; THE KID FROM TEXAS (1950, Universal)—**Audie Murphy**; THE PARSON AND THE OUTLAW (1957, Columbia)—**Anthony Dexter**; THE LAW VS. BILLY THE KID (1954, Columbia)—**Scott Brady**; THE LEFT-HANDED GUN (1958, Warner Brothers)—**Paul Newman**; BILLY THE KID VS. DRACULA (1966, Circle/EM)—**Chuck Courtney**; DIRTY LITTLE BILLY (1972, Columbia)—**Michael J. Pollard**; PAT GARRETT AND BILLY THE KID (1973, MGM)—**Kris Kristofferson**; YOUNG GUNS (1988, 20th Century Fox)—**Emilio Estevez**; YOUNG GUNS II (1990, 20th Century Fox)—Western outlaw William Bonney, known as Billy the Kid, was a half-witted gunman said to have killed 21 men, the same as the number of years he lived. He was shot down by Pat Garrett, a bounty hunter and former friend. Bonney has been portrayed many times and in many ways on the screen. He has been brutal, victimized, misunderstood, occasionally on the side of the law, just about to go straight, and even once engaged to a girl whose uncle is a vampire, but never accurately until Michael J. Pollard was assigned the role in 1972. In the 1988 film and its sequel, Estevez gives Billy a humorous side. The films are fairly enjoyable, but seem unlikely to rescue the dying western genre.

BILLY TWO HATS

BILLY TWO HATS (1973, GB, UA)—**Desi Arnaz, Jr.** is a half-breed who maintains a friendship with Gregory Peck, an old Scottish outlaw, until the latter's death.

BINGHAM, LES

I WILL . . . I WILL . . . FOR NOW (1976, 20th Century Fox)—**Elliott Gould** divorces his wife Diane Keaton and then the two try to learn the things about each other that they should have discovered before marriage and divorce.

BINGHAM, MAJOR
THE SECOND IN COMMAND (1915, Silent, Metro)—**William Clifford** and Francis X. Bushman are British officers fighting in the Boer War who love the same girl. During the heat of battle, Clifford admits he gained an advantage with the girl using unfair tactics and if they both survive, he'll bow out of the triangle.

BINGHAM, PATIENCE & TOM
THE FARMER'S DAUGHTER (1940, Paramount)—**Martha Raye**, the stage struck daughter of farmer **William Duncan**, tries to get noticed by a Broadway company rehearsing a musical nearby the old homestead.

BINGO
UNTAMED (1929, MGM)—Oil heiress **Joan Crawford**, raised in the tropics, falls in love with a poor man Robert Montgomery.

BINNEY, CHESTER
EX-BAD BOY (1931, Universal)—Fresh from the farm **Robert Armstrong** tries to pass himself off as a sharpie with a tainted past in order to win Jean Arthur.

BINNS, MISS
SEVEN WOMEN (1966, MGM)—**Flora Robson** brings cholera sufferers to a U.S. mission in China being overrun by a Mongol war lord.

BIRD, SALLY
ALONG CAME SALLY (1934, GB, Gaumont)—In this musical, **Cicely Courtneidge** is a stage-struck woman who poses as a French star and saves an American night club owner from gangsters.

BIRDIE
THE KING AND FOUR QUEENS (1956, UA)—**Barbara Nichols** is one of Jo Van Fleet's sexually frustrated daughters-in-law, living with their pistol packing mother-in-law in an almost deserted Western town. When Clark Gable, who is on the run from the law, rides into town, Nichols and the other can almost be seen licking their chops. However the real attraction is $100,000 hidden by one of the girl's husbands somewhere in the town.

BIRDIE, CONRAD
BYE BYE BIRDIE (1963, Columbia)—**Jesse Pearson**, an Elvis Presley-like rock star, is drafted into the army. It is arranged for him to give a symbolic farewell kiss to all of his adoring female fans on the Ed Sullivan Show by kissing Sweet Apple, Iowa teenager Ann-Margret. His singing and hip-shaking has a devastating effect on all the females in the small town.

BIRDIE, MISS
THE LADY FROM TEXAS (1951, Universal)—Kindly old **Josephine Hull** is victimized by Craig Stevens when he purchases her ranch for much less than it's worth. She fights Stevens in a court battle where he tries to prove her crazy, but justice triumphs.

BIRDY
BIRDY (1984, Tri-Star)—**Matthew Modine** from South Philadelphia is a strange young man who wishes to become a bird so he can fly away from all his troubles.

BISBEE, SAMUEL & ALICE
SO'S YOUR OLD MAN (1926, Silent, Paramount)—Boozing inventor **W.C. Fields** just about ruins his daughter **Kittens Reichert's** chances of marrying her wealthy young man but redeems himself when he sells his invention of a shatterproof automobile glass. A lot of marvelously funny things happen before this is accomplished.

BISCUIT
DUDES (1987, New Century-Vista)—Punker **Daniel Roebuck**, who sports a bleached blond Mohawk, and two friends leave New York headed for Los Angeles. Along the way they encounter bikers who kill one of their number. Roebuck and the other survivor take revenge.

BISHOP
THE BISHOP MISBEHAVES (1933, MGM)—Bishop **Edmund Gwenn** leaves his miter behind and becomes a detective long enough to investigate the theft of an inventor's plans.

BISHOP, ARTHUR
THE MECHANIC (1972, UA)—A mechanic in this film is a hired assassin, and **Charles Bronson** takes pride in his work. He even has an apprentice in the person of Jan-Michael Vincent. It's reassuring that the old skills aren't lost as the generations pass.

BISHOP, CYNTHIA
CYNTHIA (1947, MGM)—It's the story about lovely teenager **Elizabeth Taylor's** first date and first kiss.

BISHOP, DEBORAH
A LETTER TO THREE WIVES (1948, 20th Century Fox)—**Jeanne Crain** is one of three women who receive a letter from a female acquaintance claiming she's running off with one of their husbands. As each recalls her life with her man to see if she is the one, Crain remembers how her husband Jeffrey Lynn claims he has never forgotten the woman in question. At the end of the film it looks like Crain is the loser in this marital lottery, but not so.

BISHOP, ELLA
CHEERS FOR MISS BISHOP (1941, UA)—Fifty years of schoolteacher **Martha Scott's** life is shown in flashback. Her life has been made difficult by two frustrating romances, which made her concentrate on her students.

BISHOP, MARY
HER FATAL MILLIONS (1923, Silent, Metro)—**Viola Dana** works as a salesgirl in a jewelry store. She borrows some of the merchandise to convince a former sweetheart that she's a rich man's wife.

BISHOP, PIKE
THE WILD BUNCH (1969, Warner Brothers)—**William Holden** leads a gang of aging Western outlaws, seeking somewhere to practice their trade while being hunted by a posse led by an ex-gang member, Robert Ryan. They move into Mexico and become involved with various revolutionary groups. It's a violent and bloody masterpiece.

BISHOP, SALLY
SALLY BISHOP (1932, GB, British Lion)—Typist **Joan Barry**, the mistress of a wealthy industrialist, is thrown out after three years in favor of a socialite.

BISHOP, STEVE
WINNER TAKE ALL (1939, 20th Century Fox)—When **Tony Martin** wins a benefit boxing match, mobsters set up a series of fights for him. He wins without knowing his opponents all took dives. When his head gets too big, a female sportswriter romantically interested in him arranges a match for him in which he's beaten to a pulp. With friends like her . . . .

BISSEL, SAM

GOOD NEIGHBOR SAM (1964, Columbia)—Advertising man **Jack Lemmon** has the trust of puritanical client Edward G. Robinson, who insists that his account be handled by a good family man. Lemmon almost blows it when Robinson comes to believe that Romy Schneider is his wife and not Dorothy Provine. Schneider on the other hand needs Lemmon to pose as her husband or face losing millions of inheritance money if it's discovered she's divorced.

BIXBY

THE SAD SACK (1957, Paramount)—**Jerry Lewis** appears as the army loser created by cartoonist George Baker.

BIXBY, ARTHUR

ARTHUR TAKES OVER (1948, 20th Century Fox)—When his father arranges for his sister to marry a rich man, **Skip Homeier** comes up with a scheme to save her as she is already secretly married.

BLACK, ADAM

ADAM AND EVELYNE (1950, GB, Rank/Two Cities)—**Stewart Granger**, a gambler, takes responsibility for a homeless girl, who believes him to be her father. He isn't, and they become romantically involved.

BLACK, DR./MR. HYDE

DR. BLACK AND MR. HYDE (1976, Dimension)—**Bernie Casey** stars in this black exploitation film with its Dr. Jekyll and Mr. Hyde story.

BLACK EAGLE

KINGS OF THE SUN (1963, UA)—**Yul Brynner**, an Indian chief, gives his life protecting that of George Chakaris, king of the Mayans.

BLACK, HARRY

HARRY BLACK AND THE TIGER (1958, GB, 20th Century Fox)—One-legged hunter **Stewart Granger** stalks a man-eating tiger in India. His task is complicated by the arrival of the man whose cowardice was the cause of Granger losing his leg.

BLACK, HARRY

TARGET: HARRY (1980, Corman/ABC)—In a rehash of THE MALTESE FALCON story, **Vic Morrow** has the role that corresponds to Humphrey Bogart's Sam Spade and "corresponds" is the kindest word that can be used to describe it.

BLACK JACK

BLACK JACK (1979, GB, Kestrel/National)—**Jean Franval**, an eighteenth century Frenchman, hires a lad Stephen Hirst to speak for him after he has miraculously escaped from a hanging.

BLACK, MRS.

MRS. BLACK IS BACK (1914, Silent, Famous Players)—Claiming to be 29, **May Irwin** lies about her age when she marries a professor, but then her fully grown son shows up.

BLACK, REX

THE RUNNING MAN (1963, GB, Columbia)—**Laurence Harvey** fakes his death so his wife Lee Remick can collect his insurance, but investigator Alan Bates isn't fooled.

BLACKBEARD

BLACKBEARD THE PIRATE (1952, RKO); BLACKBEARD'S GHOST (1968, Buena Vista)—**Robert Newton** is the rascally seventeenth century pirate who meets a terrible end, buried up to his neck in the sand facing the sea as the tide comes in. **Peter Ustinov** appears as the pirate's ghost who returns to help the old ladies who own a hotel he loved.

BLACKBURN, JUNE

SHIPMATES FOREVER (1935, Warner Brothers)—**Ruby Keeler** is a major reason why admiral's son Dick Powell disappoints his father by choosing a song and dance career rather than one with the navy.

BLACKIE

THREE KIDS AND A QUEEN (1935, Universal)—**Frankie Darro** is one of three poor youngsters who kidnap rich old lady May Robson. To their dismay, she's happy and doesn't wish to be ransomed.

BLACKSMITH, JIMMIE

THE CHANT OF JIMMIE BLACKSMITH (1980, Australia, Filmhouse)—Non-professional actor **Tommy Lewis** appears as an aborigine educated by a minister. Although he learns the tenets of Christianity, he's left to live in the squalor of native villages where he is badly treated by whites. He goes on a murderous rampage, flees to the outback, pursued by whites who kill him.

BLACKWELL, ROGER

THE IMAGEMAKER (1986, Castle Hill)—**Michael Nouri**, an ex-media advisor to the President, has an audio tape that could prove damaging to the chief executive, and people are dying to get their hands on it.

BLACKWOOD, PHIL

HER ALIBI (1989, Warner Brothers)—Successful writer **Tom Selleck** experiences writer-block until he provides beautiful murder-suspect Paulina Porizkova with an alibi. Will she repay the favor by killing him, so he can't change his story?

BLACULA

BLACULA (1972, American International); SCREAM, BLACULA, SCREAM (1973, American International)—In 1815 Transylvania, African prince **William Marshall** becomes a victim of Dracula. One hundred fifty years later his body is shipped to the U.S. where he's revived and follows his master's way of surviving. The sequel is just more of the same.

BLADE

BLADE (1973, Green/Pintoff)—Middle-aged detective **John Marley** sets to work solving the murder of the daughter of an old enemy, now a powerful politician.

BLADE, LOGAN

STREET HUNTER (1990, 21st Century)—Dressed in a slicker, boots and a wide-brimmed hat, **Steve James** and his Doberman partner ply his trade as bounty hunter in modern New York City.

BLAIN, PEG

NAVY WIFE (1956, Allied Artists)—**Joan Bennett** learns about Oriental customs when she visits her navy commander husband in Japan.

BLAINE, NATE & JEFF

OUTLAW'S SON (1957, UA)—Former outlaw **Dane Clark**, who deserted his son **Ben Cooper** when the latter was a child, shows up to prevent the boy from following in his footsteps.

BLAINE, UTAH

UTAH BLAINE (1957, Columbia)—In a familiar story, cowpoke **Rory Calhoun** fights off land grabbers.

BLAIR, BEN
BEN BLAIR (1916, Silent, Paramount)—Westerner **Dustin Farnum's** girl is taken back east by her mother where a stylish wedding is arranged for her. Farnum reads of it and shows up before the ceremonies, giving the girl 20 minutes to pack her things and return west with him. She resists for 19 minutes.

BLAIR, DON
THE GIRL FROM HIS TOWN (1915, Silent, American)—**C. Elliott Griffen**, a callow youth, loves a girl who worked at a soda fountain before going on the stage as a singer. He almost marries a British gold digger, but as fate would have it, his former sweetheart arrives in town and the two are reunited.

BLAIR, ELIZABETH
CURLY TOP (1935, Fox)—**Shirley Temple** is found in an orphanage by millionaire John Boles who falls for her older sister, Rochelle Hudson. Boles sets up both girls in the lap of luxury in New York. Don't worry. It's not like it sounds. Boles and Hudson will marry and take care of little Shirley.

BLAIR, FRANK
DON X (1925, Silent, Steen Goodman)—**Bruce Gordon**, the head of the Cattleman's Protective Association, poses as Don X, a wealthy Mexican beef buyer in order to catch some rustlers.

BLAIR, JACKIE
MY BOY (1922, Silent, Associated First National)—When his mother dies on the trip across the ocean, immigrant **Jackie Coogan** escapes from Ellis Island and takes up with a sickly old ex-sea captain Claude Gillingwater. Later Coogan's wealthy American grandmother takes him in and provides a new home for the old man.

BLAIR, JUDY
I GIVE MY LOVE (1934, Universal)—**Wynne Gibson**, who gave up her son when she went to prison for murdering her husband, becomes her artist son's model when she gets out without him realizing who she is.

BLAIR, RUSTY
THREE YOUNG TEXANS (1954, 20th Century Fox)—**Mitzi Gaynor** looks out of place in this Western clinker as a rancher's daughter who teams up with two cowpokes to rob a train.

BLAISE, MODESTY
MODESTY BLAISE (1966, GB, 20th Century Fox)—Comic strip super-agent Modesty Blaise is impersonated by **Monica Vitti** in a case of stolen diamonds and a sadistic master criminal.

BLAKE
ROAD DEMON (1938, 20th Century Fox)—Truck driver **Henry Arthur** helps out an Indianapolis 500 Race driver, Thomas Beck, saving him from the crooks who had killed the lad's racing father years earlier.

BLAKE, ALICE
NINE GIRLS (1944, Columbia)—Did sensitive and high-strung **Nina Foch** kill sorority sister Anita Louise? After all, Louise was blackmailing Foch.

BLAKE, MRS. AMELIA
HITCH HIKE LADY (1936, Republic)—**Alison Skipworth**, an elderly British housekeeper, having put some money by, comes to America to visit her son whom she believes is prospering. In fact, he's in San Quentin. Not having enough money to travel in style across country to her son, she hitchhikes, teaming up with four others who are aware of the truth about her son but keep it from her.

BLAKE, BENJAMIN
SON OF FURY (1942, 20th Century Fox)—**Roddy McDowall**, the illegitimate son of a nobleman, grows up to become **Tyrone Power** who sails the seven seas before returning to claim his rightful inheritance.

BLAKE, BETTY
SWEETHEART OF THE CAMPUS (1941, Columbia)—After three years away from the cameras, **Ruby Keeler** returns as a college girl who dances with Ozzie Nelson's band. She should have remained in retirement.

BLAKE, BEVERLY
BLONDE COMET (1941, Producers Releasing Corp.)—Racing driver **Virginia Vale** is trying to win enough money to save her father's failing tire business.

BLAKE, BUDDY
CYCLONE BUDDY (1924, Silent, Approved Pictures)—Unjustly accused of murder, **Buddy Roosevelt** escapes from court and rounds up the outlaw gang of raiders who have been attempting to drive his employer from his ranch.

BLAKE, CHRISTOPHER
THE DECISION OF CHRISTOPHER BLAKE (1948, Warner Brothers)—Twelve year old **Ted Donaldson** is successful in reuniting his divorcing parents.

BLAKE, DAVID
JUST MY LUCK (1933, GB, British & Dominions)—Middle-aged music teacher **Ralph Lynn** attempts to overcome his supreme shyness by taking a self-help course. It seems to help in this nothing film.

BLAKE, DR. DONALD
MONSTER ON THE CAMPUS (1958, Universal)—**Arthur Franz** is a college professor studying a prehistoric fish found in Madagascar. When some slime from the fish gets into his tobacco, it turns him into a Neanderthal man with an axe who lays waste to the college campus. Wonder where we can get some of that slime?

BLAKE, DORIS
SINNERS IN THE SUN (1932, Paramount)—**Carole Lombard**, part of a triangle involving two men, finally decides money isn't everything. But it is something.

BLAKE, EMIL
EMIL (1938, GB, Gaumont)—In this movie, also known as EMIL AND THE DETECTIVES, young **John Williams** is given drugged candy by George Hayes who then proceeds to steal the boy's money. Williams enlists some children to track down the thief.

BLAKE, HELEN
SECRETS OF A SECRETARY (1931, Paramount)—**Claudette Colbert's** ex-husband Herbert Marshall is blackmailing her new boss. File it away.

BLAKE, JAMES (SLICK RAWLEY)
THE MAN WHO LIVED TWICE (1936, Columbia); MAN IN THE DARK (1953, Columbia)—**Ralph Bellamy**, a scarred murderer,

takes refuge in a hospital where a doctor performs an operation that not only alters his face but also his personality. He becomes a new man, but his past resurfaces. He is convicted of the earlier murder but is pardoned by the governor. **Edmond O'Brien** repeats the role in the 1953 remake.

BLAKE, JEANNIE
SENORITA FROM THE WEST (1945, Universal)—**Bonita Granville** runs away to become a singer and falls for Allan Jones who dubs the voice of a radio crooner.

BLAKE, JENNY
LADY FOR A NIGHT (1941, Republic)—**Joan Blondell** runs a casino on a Mississippi river boat. When wealthy Ray Middleton loses a bundle, she offers to return it to him if he'll marry her so she can be part of society. He agrees but his family is not pleased. Middleton's aunt tries to poison Blondell, but Middleton drinks the potion. Blondell is charged with his murder but is proven innocent. Blondell returns to her river boat and old boyfriend John Wayne.

BLAKE, JERRY
THE STEPFATHER (1987, New Century-Vista)—When marriage and family life don't work out according to plan for **Terry O'Quinn**, he merely changes his identity, kills his family and moves on to a new one. He finally meets his match with new wife Shelley Hack and stepdaughter Jill Schoelen, but it's a close call for the innocent.

BLAKE, JIM
ALL MAN (1916, Silent, Peerless/World)—In a Western photographed in New Jersey but meant to be located in Montana, **Robert Warwick** is a cowboy hero.

BLAKE, JOE
ROOKIE FIREMAN (1950, Columbia)—Hope there were a lot of firemen interested in seeing this slow-action B movie. **Bill Williams** as what else—a rookie fireman.

BLAKE, KAREN BORG
TWO-FACED WOMAN (1941, MGM)—In her last film **Greta Garbo** is a ski instructor who fears she may lose her husband Melvyn Douglas to Constance Bennett. To keep him in the family she goes after him, impersonating her more vivacious imaginary twin, Katherine Borg.

BLAKE, LOOLOO
MY WEAKNESS (1933, Fox)—Hotel clerk **Lillian Harvey** is madly in love with sophisticated Lew Ayres, but can't get a tumble from the man of her dreams. Her friends take two weeks and completely transform her into a new woman —one who gets her man.

BLAKE, LORNA
THE WOMAN IN THE HALL (1949, GB, Rank)—When well-intentioned **Ursula Jeans** takes to begging, she becomes a bad influence on her daughter.

BLAKE, MARCIA
ALMOST A LADY (1926, Silent, Producers Dist. Co.)—**Marie Prevost**, a clothes model for the fashionable boutique of Monsieur Henri, becomes embroiled with a social climbing woman and the latter's flirty husband.

BLAKE, MARY
THE HONOR OF MARY BLAKE (1916, Silent, Triangle)—**Violet Mereserau**, a young actress with a repertoire company, marries a

middle-aged manager of a Broadway show who promises to make her a star. When they arrive back at his apartment after the wedding ceremony, they are greeted by the man's wife who he had deserted years before. Mereserau beats a hasty retreat to the repertoire company.

BLAKE, MEG
THE NICKEL QUEEN (1971, Australia)—**Googie Withers** runs a pub in the Australian hinterlands. She gets a taste of the good life when nickel deposits are found on her land.

BLAKE, MERRY NOEL
RICH AND FAMOUS (1981, MGM/UA)—**Candice Bergen** and Jacqueline Bisset star in this remake of OLD ACQUAINTANCE filmed in 1943 with Bette Davis and Miriam Hopkins. The two are writers, Bisset a favorite of the critics but not the public and Bergen the author of runaway trashy best-sellers.

BLAKE, MR. *See* **DR. MARLOWE**

BLAKE, REGGIE & FRAN
HIS AND HERS (1961, GB, Sabre/Eros)—Author **Terry-Thomas** gets lost in the deserts of North Africa and lives with the Bedouin tribes for a long time. By the time he is rescued, he has adopted Bedouin customs and expects his wife **Janette Scott** to do the same, but she'll have none of it and divides the house into two halves —his and hers.

BLAKE, SEXTON
SEXTON BLAKE AND THE BEARDED DOCTOR (1935, GB, MGM); SEXTON BLAKE AND THE MADEMOISELLE (1935, GB, MGM); SEXTON BLAKE AND THE HOODED TERROR (1938, GB, MGM); MEET SEXTON BLAKE (1944, GB, British National)—British detective **George Cuzon** is a poor substitute for Sherlock Holmes in the cheaply made 1930s movies. Things didn't improve much in 1944 with **David Farrar** as the detective with the job of locating a ring and some photographs taken from the body of a man killed in an air raid. The items are important for discerning a new formula for materials to make airplanes.

BLAKE, TONY
THE STUD (1979, GB, Trans-American)—**Oliver Tobias** manages the nightclub owned by Joan Collins' husband. To keep his job, he has to keep Collins satisfied in the sack.

BLAKE, VICKY
NAVY WIFE (1936, 20th Century Fox)—Having seen the bad effects of divorce up close **Claire Trevor** is wary of love and marriage, but a widowed doctor and his crippled daughter change her mind.

BLAKELY, ZEE & ROBERT
X, Y & ZEE (1972, GB, Columbia)—**Elizabeth Taylor** and **Michael Caine** are a married couple who each maintain a sexual relationship with Susannah York. The presentation is as tasteless as director Brian G. Hutton can make it.

BLAKELY, DAVID
DANCE WITH A STRANGER (1985, GB, Goldwyn)—This film tells the true story of a mother, Ruth Ellis, who shoots and kills her lover (**Rupert Everett**) and becomes the last woman in England to be hanged.

BLAKENEY, SIR PERCY
THE SCARLET PIMPERNEL (1934, GB, London Films); THE RETURN OF THE SCARLET PIMPERNEL (1938, Great Britain, UA); THE FIGHTING PIMPERNEL (1950, GB, British Lion)—**Leslie**

Howard is superb as the "demmed elusive Pimpernel" who rescues French aristocrats from the guillotine while posing as a foppish effeminate British Lord. Neither **Barry K. Barnes** in a sequel of sorts or **David Niven** in the 1950 remake does as much for the role.

BLAKISTON, HERMIONE

MISSING, BELIEVED MARRIED (1937, GB, British & Dominions)—Heiress **Hazel Terry** flees her wedding when she discovers her bridegroom is a fortune hunter. She suffers a head wound and loses her memory. She's rescued by a couple of street vendors.

BLANCHARD, MARILYN

VOODOO WOMAN (1957, American International)—A deranged scientist turns his wife **Marla English** into a zombie.

BLANDINGS, JIM

MR. BLANDINGS BUILDS HIS DREAM HOUSE (1948, RKO)—**Cary Grant** and his wife Myrna Loy buy an old house in Connecticut and find they must rebuild it from scratch at an unbelievable expense (unbelievable for them at the time and so little by today's standards). It's an enjoyable comedy with Melvyn Douglas as family best friend who still has a thing for Loy.

BLANDISH, MISS

NO ORCHIDS FOR MISS BLANDISH (1948, GB, Renown)—Sadistic gangster Jack La Rue kills wealthy **Linden Travers'** fiance and kidnaps her. When the police close in and kill La Rue, Travers leaps from a window to her death clasping an orchid to her breast. Symbolic perhaps, but senseless for sure.

BLANDY

THE VANISHING AMERICAN (1955, Republic)—**Scott Brady** comes to the aid of Navajos to fight off white land grabbers.

BLANE, TORCHY

ADVENTUROUS BLONDE (1937, Warner Brothers); SMART BLONDE (1937, Warner Brothers); TORCHY BLAINE IN CHINATOWN (1938, Warner Brothers); TORCHY GETS HER MAN (1938, Warner Brothers); TORCHY RUNS FOR MAYOR (1939, Warner Brothers)—**Glenda Farrell**; TORCHY BLAINE IN PANAMA (1938, Warner Brothers)—**Lola Lane**; TORCHY PLAYS WITH DYNAMITE (1939, Warner Brothers)—**Jane Wyman**—Farrell had the longest run as the hard-boiled reporter, who always is several steps ahead of her tough but dumb police inspector boy-friend Barton MacLane. Lane and Wyman were merely pale imitators of the fiery Farrell.

BLANK, KING

KING BLANK (1983, Metafilms)—There's not much to this movie which details the arguments of **Ron Vawter** and his wife in their room and a sleazy bar.

BLASI, CAPTAIN

THE BEST OF ENEMIES (1962, Columbia)—**Alberto Sordi** is an Italian officer who comes to respect and be respected by British officer David Niven, as the two commanders and their men put aside their WWII fight to get across an African desert together.

BLAYDON, CHARLES

HIS LUCKY DAY (1929, Part-Talkie, Universal)—Real estate agent **Reginald Denny** rents the place next to that of the father of his fiancee to gangsters.

BLAZNEE

SPACED INVADERS (1990, Buena Vista)—**Kevin Thompson** is the only actor to supply both his body and voice for one of the five misdirected aliens who find themselves in the United States Midwest. The one-liners and sight-gags are a mixed bag.

BLENEAU, ADELE

ADELE (1919, Silent, UA)—World War I nurse **Kitty Gordon** is offered her lover's life by the Germans if she will spy for them. She turns the tables on them and saves her man.

BLENKENSON, DR.

THE DOCTOR'S DILEMMA (1958, GB, MGM)—Leslie Caron attempts to convince **Michael Gwynn** to treat the TB of her immoral artist husband.

BLISS, ERNEST

THE AMAZING QUEST OF ERNEST BLISS (1936, GB, Klement)—Millionaire **Cary Grant** wagers that he can live independently of his fortune for a year. Big deal! Most of us do so for all our lives.

BLISS, GLORIA

HIS MYSTERY GIRL (1923, Silent, Universal)—Herbert Rawlinson is tricked by friends into believing that he is helping **Ruth Dwyer**, a damsel in distress. After an adventure involving stolen jewelry, he marries her.

BLISS, JACK

CYCLONE BLISS (1921, Silent, Unity Photoplays)—Quiet and fair minded **Jack Hoxie** traces his missing father to an outlaw hide-out called Hell's Hole and takes on the lot of them single-handedly.

BLISS, SWEENEY

I'M FROM MISSOURI (1939, Paramount)—Missouri mule breeder **Bob Burns** takes his prize animal to a livestock show to impress a representative of the British army with his mules.

BLOCK, HENRY

FRIENDLY ENEMIES (1942, UA)—**Charlie Ruggles** is a German immigrant completely loyal to his new home in the United States. He has many arguments with his friend Charles Winninger who is sympathetic to the Nazi cause. Ruggles and circumstances win Winninger over as he discovers the worst about the Nazis.

BLODGETT, ESTHER

A STAR IS BORN (1937, UA); (1954, Warner Brothers) (1976, Warner Brothers)—**Janet Gaynor** is trying to break into the movies. She does so with the help of alcoholic and fading actor Fredric March. As her star ascends, his plummets, and he commits suicide rather than be a burden to her. The 1954 version is more of the same, except that **Judy Garland**, naturally becomes a musical star whose career outshines that of drunken husband James Mason, In 1976, **Barbra Streisand**, starting out as Esther Hoffman, becomes a pop singing star while lover Kris Kristofferson hits the skids.

BLONDIE

BLONDIE (1938, Columbia); BLONDIE BRINGS UP BABY (1939, Columbia); BLONDIE MEETS THE BOSS (1939, Columbia); BLONDIE TAKES A VACATION (1939, Columbia); BLONDIE HAS SERVANT PROBLEMS (1940, Columbia); BLONDIE ON A BUDGET (1940, Columbia); BLONDIE PLAYS CUPID (1940, Columbia); BLONDIE GOES LATIN (1941, Columbia); BLONDIE GOES TO COLLEGE (1941, Columbia); BLONDIE IN SOCIETY (1941, Columbia); BLONDIE FOR VICTORY (1942, Columbia); BLONDIE GOES TO COLLEGE (1942, Columbia); BLONDIE'S BLESSED EVENT (1942, Columbia); LEAVE IT TO BLONDIE (1945, Columbia); BLONDIE KNOWS BEST

(1946, Columbia); BLONDIE'S LUCKY DAY (1946, Columbia); LIFE WITH BLONDIE (1946, Columbia); BLONDIE IN THE DOUGH (1947, Columbia); BLONDIE'S ANNIVERSARY (1947, Columbia); BLONDIE'S BIG MOMENT (1947, Columbia); BLONDIE'S LUCKY DAY (1947, Columbia); BLONDIE'S REWARD (1948, Columbia); BLONDIE HITS THE JACKPOT (1949, Columbia); BLONDIE'S BIG DEAL (1949, Columbia); BLONDIE'S SECRET (1949, Columbia); BEWARE OF BLONDIE (1950, Columbia); BLONDIE'S HERO (1950, Columbia)—**Penny Singleton** portrays the comic strip wife and mother who although no great brain is a lot smarter than her husband Dagwood, played throughout the years by **Arthur Lake**, and all the other regulars in the series.

BLOOD, COLONEL
COLONEL BLOOD (1934, GB, MGM)—When Irish rebel **Frank Cellier** is captured as he tries to steal the crown jewels, he so charms King Charles II that the monarch frees him.

BLOOD, DR. PETER
CAPTAIN BLOOD (1924, Silent, Vitagraph); (1935, Warner Brothers); FORTUNES OF CAPTAIN BLOOD (1950, Columbia); CAPTAIN PIRATE (1952, Columbia)—**J. Warren Kerrigan** and **Errol Flynn** star as an Irish surgeon sentenced to slavery in Jamaica for giving medical attention to rebels who plotted to kill James I of England. With other prisoners, he escapes, becomes a pirate and when a new monarch takes over, becomes governor of Jamaica. The 1935 film made a star of Flynn. In the 1950 film, **Louis Hayward** escapes from his pursuers by taking over their ship. In 1952 Hayward, the now retired physician-buccaneer, is forced to run up the skull and crossbones once again when a scoundrel uses the name of Peter Blood in making his pirate raids.

BLOOD, DR. PETER
DR. BLOOD'S COFFIN (1961, UA)—**Kieron Moore**, a surgeon barred from practicing medicine, goes into the Frankenstein business.

BLOOD, WILLIAM
MAN IN THE MOON (1961, GB, TransLux)—**Kenneth More**, the ultimate average man used as a human guinea pig for scientific research, is chosen to be the first astronaut.

BLOODWORTH, RANDY
WEEKEND FOR THREE (1941, RKO)—Obnoxious **Philip Reed** visits newlyweds Dennis O'Keefe and Jane Wyatt. At first Wyatt uses Reed to make O'Keefe jealous but when their guest refuses to leave, she plots with O'Keefe to get rid of him.

BLOOM, LEO
THE PRODUCERS (1967, Embassy)—Insecure accountant **Gene Wilder** innocently suggests a way to make money by putting on a Broadway show which is doomed to fail. His partner is Zero Mostel. They choose the worst play, the worst director and the worst star. It's a smash hit. Where did they go right?

BLOSSOM, HARRIETT
THE BLISS OF MRS. BLOSSOM (1968, GB, Paramount)—**Shirley MacLaine**, the wife of a bra manufacturer, keeps her lover hidden in the attic of her home.

BLUDSOE, JIM
JIM BLUDSOE (1917, Silent, Triangle)—**Wilfrid Lucas** and his wife part because she's a southerner who is angry that he's joined the Union Army. While he's fighting, she elopes with a river boat

gambler who later dumps her. Jim learns of his wife's plight and takes her back. Bedfellows make strange politics.

BLUE
BLUE (1968, Paramount)—**Terence Stamp**, the adopted son of a Mexican bandit, rescues a girl and her father and lives with them for two years. At the end of this time his foster father comes a-calling with the result being a great deal of bloodshed.

BLUE, ARTHUR
HEARTBREAKERS (1984, Orion)—**Peter Coyote** and his childhood friend Nick Mancuso find their friendship severely tested as they compete to get ahead in the world.

BLUME
BLUME IN LOVE (1973, Bronston)—**George Segal's** wife Susan Anspach divorces him when she finds him in bed with his secretary. For a while, he enjoys his renewed sexual freedom but soon wants Anspach back. By this time, she's moved in with Kris Kristofferson. But Segal's up to the competition.

BLUNDEN, MR.
THE AMAZING MR. BLUNDEN (1973, GB, Hemisphere)—In 1918, **Laurence Naismith** offers a homeless widow and her two children work in his mansion. Here they meet two ghost children and discover that Naismith is also a ghost.

BLURT, ELMER
HERE COMES ELMER (1943, Republic)—**Al Pearce** recreates his radio character, door-to-door salesman Elmer Blurt who, after knocking at a door, usually says "Nobody home, I hope, I hope."

BOB
BOB AND CAROL AND TED AND ALICE (1969, Columbia)—**Robert Culp** has an open marriage with wife Natalie Wood, but is it open enough to withstand mate-swappping with their good friends, Dyan Cannon and Elliott Gould?

BOB See BERT & BOB

BOB
COWBOY IN MANHATTAN (1943, Universal)—Cowboy songwriter **Robert Paige** poses as a millionaire to impress the female singer of a musical group.

BOB
DRUGSTORE COWBOY (1989, Avenue)—In one of the better movies of a year of good movies, **Matt Dillon** is superb as the leader of a bedraggled group of addicts who feed their needs by robbing drugstores. It's a darkly funny and realistic look at drug addiction.

BOB
FEDERAL AGENT (1936, Republic)—**William Boyd** is a federal agent pursuing spies who have killed his best friend and who are trying to steal a new explosive.

BOB
RITA, SUE AND BOB TOO! (1987, GB, Orion)—**George Costigan** initiates two hefty teenage baby sitters to sex, and when his wife leaves him, they move in with him for more advanced lessons.

BOB
THREE GODFATHERS (1936, MGM)—**Chester Morris** and two other outlaws fleeing in the desert come across a dying woman who

has just given birth. They risk their lives and freedom to get the child to safety. The film was made on two other occasions by director John Ford, as a silent called MARKED MEN in 1919 and again as THREE GODFATHERS in 1948, the latter with John Wayne, Pedro Armendariz and Harry Carey, Jr.

BOBBIE

GIRL OF THE NIGHT (1960, Warner Brothers)—Prostitute **Anne Francis** considers her reasons for choosing the life of a hooker while in psychoanalysis.

BOBBIE

THE RAILWAY CHILDREN (1971, GB, Universal)—**Jenny Agutter** is one of the children of Dinah Sheridan, wife of a British Foreign Service Officer, who has been unjustly sent to prison on a charge of treason. Sheridan gets Agutter and the others to make a game of their reduced circumstances. They play at being "poor." Spending most of their time playing among trains, they meet a wealthy man who helps clear their father.

BOBBIKINS

BOBBIKINS (1959, GB, 20th Century Fox)—**Steven Stacker** is a talking baby who passes on stock tips from the British Chancellor of the Exchequer to his struggling father.

BOBBY

ALOHA, BOBBY AND ROSE (1975, Columbia)—Mechanic **Paul LeMat** innocently becomes involved in a crime and must flee Los Angeles with his girlfriend, hightailing it for the Mexican border.

BOBBY

THE BOSS' SON (1978, New American Cinema)—**Asher Brauner** wants to live a life different from the one his father, who is in the carpet business, has planned for him. But it is mom who really get upset when he defies his father.

BOBBY

CHILD OF DIVORCE (1946, RKO)—**Sharyn Moffett** sadly watches as her parents divorce. She is shuffled from house to house, ultimately being sent to a boarding school.

BOBBY

THE HEAVENLY KID (1985, Orion)—**Lewis Smith**, who died in a "chicken" car race, is sent back to earth to help teenager Jason Gedrick, who needs a lot of help.

BOBBY

THE STEPFORD WIVES (1975, Columbia)—**Paula Prentiss** shares Katharine Ross' conviction that Stepford is a dismally boring place filled with strange acting wives who seem only to live to accommodate their husband's every whim. Ultimately, the men behind this unusual behavior change Prentiss into another of these mindless women.

BOCA, ROSALIE & JOEY

I LOVE YOU TO DEATH (1990, Tri Star)—In a mild black comedy, **Tracey Ullman** is encouraged by her mother Joan Plowright to hire druggies William Hurt and Keanu Reeves to assassinate her husband Kevin Kline, who has been unfaithful—over and over again.

BODEK, RANDY

LOVERBOY (1989, Tri-Star)—College sophomore **Patrick Dempsey** earns tuition money by delivering pizzas. His best and most generous customers are lonely lovely older women looking for a lot more than pepperoni.

BODELL, PEGGY SUE KELCHER

PEGGY SUE GOT MARRIED (1986, Tri-Star)—**Kathleen Turner** is considering divorcing her husband Nicolas Cage. While attending a high school reunion, she passes out and awakens as a teenager back in her parent's home. This time she's not so sure she'll marry high school sweetheart Cage. She plays the field a bit, before waking up once again to reassess her decision about divorce.

BODINE, ROSS

WILD ROVERS (1971, MGM)—Old cowhand **William Holden** teams up with young cowboy Ryan O'Neal to rob a bank so they can live in style. It's supposed to be a western comedy, isn't it? Perhaps it's about gay caballeros.

BOGARDUS, HARVEY

THE PHANTOM SPEAKS (1945, Republic)—Executed murderer **Tom Powers** revives and assumes the identity of a mild-mannered scientist. In this guise, he continues his heinous crimes. A reporter figures out what's going on.

BOGARDUS, MILO

THE FOOL KILLER (1965, Allied Artists)—**Anthony Perkins** becomes the "fool killer" that orphan Edward Albert has been told about. Perkins once again is a convincing psycho.

BOGEY, COL. See UNCLE JAMES

BOGGS, BENNY

AN HONEST MAN (1918, Silent, Triangle)—Good-natured young tramp **William Desmond** is turned down when he tries to enlist because he's intoxicated. He takes a job working for an old farmer. When the latter has a heart attack, he asks Desmond to deliver a bundle to the farmer's runaway daughter, noting that Desmond can be trusted because he's an honest man. Desmond finally finds the girl, delivers the bundle which contains her inheritance, falls in love with her and at last is allowed to enlist in the army.

BOGGS, FRANK

HICKEY AND BOGGS (1972, UA)—**Robert Culp** and Bill Cosby try to cash in on their TV "I Spy" popularity, appearing as private eyes who are on the trail of a missing girl and some $400,000 stolen from a bank. The film has been described as a modern film noir.

BOGGS, OLIVER

MR. BOGGS STEPS OUT (1938, Grand National)—**Stuart Erwin** invests the money he wins for having the best guess of how many beans are in a barrel by buying a barrel factory. Try to stave off your boredom.

BOK, YAKOV

THE FIXER (1968, MGM)—**Alan Bates**, a Jew in Russia, denies his heritage, but he still becomes a scapegoat and is unjustly imprisoned until his case attracts international interest.

BOLAGTAS, ROBERTO

SWORD OF THE AVENGER (1948, Eagle-Lion)—**Ramon Del Gado**, a Spanish sailor imprisoned by the Philippine government in the 1800s, escapes by tunnelling and takes his revenge.

BOLAN, JOHN

I'VE LIVED BEFORE (1956, Universal)—Pilot **Jock Mahoney** begins to believe that he's the reincarnation of a flyer killed in WWI.

BOLES, CHARLES E.

BLACK BART (1948, Universal)—**Dan Duryea**, a former outlaw, now a respectable California rancher, occasionally pulls a robbery disguised as Black Bart just to relive the good old days. This leads to his death in a rain of bullets but not before a visiting Lola Montez falls for him.

BOLEY, ANNIE
MAIL ORDER BRIDE (1964, MGM)—Buddy Ebsen tries his best to find a groom for his guardian, wild westerner **Lois Nettleton.**

BOLEYN, ANNE
ANNE OF THE THOUSAND DAYS (1969, GB, Universal); HENRY VIII AND HIS SIX WIVES (1972, GB, EMI/MGM)—**Genevieve Bujold** portrays Anne Boleyn, Henry VIII's second wife who is beheaded on a trumped up charge of infidelity when she cannot produce a male heir. She does however give England and the world, Elizabeth I. **Charlotte Rampling** is impressive in her portrayal of the unfortunate Boleyn in the second entry.

BOLT, JEFFERSON
THAT MAN BOLT (1973, Universal)—**Fred Williamson** is a black diplomatic courier and expert in Kung Fu. He needs to be.

BOLTON, BARBER JOHN & MICHAEL
MAN TO MAN (1931, Warner Brothers)—**Phillips Holmes** is shocked to learn that his father **Grant Mitchell** is in prison for murder. When Mitchell gets out, Holmes won't have anything to do with him until the father bails his son out of his financial difficulties.

BOLTON, JOE
POLO JOE (1936, Warner Brothers)—**Joe E. Brown,** who is afraid of horses, claims to be a polo star to impress Carol Hughes, and then is forced to prove it.

BOLTON, JOHN & MICHAEL
FATHER AND SON (1934, GB, Warner Brothers)—Bank clerk **Esmond Knight** takes the blame for a theft which he believes his father **Edmund Gwenn,** an ex-convict, committed.

BOLTON, KERRY
KING OF BURLESQUE (1936, 20th Century Fox)—In a big-time musical, **Warner Baxter** is a vaudeville impresario who risks everything on a Broadway show, which fails and sends him back to burlesque.

BOMBA
BOMBA ON PANTHER ISLAND (1949, Monogram); BOMBA THE JUNGLE BOY (1949, Monogram); BOMBA AND THE HIDDEN CITY (1950, Monogram); BOMBA AND THE JUNGLE GIRL (1952, Monogram); LORD OF THE JUNGLE (1955, Allied Artists)—When **Johnny Sheffield** grew too old to play Boy in the TARZAN movies, he remained in the jungle as a teenager who, like Tarzan, was raised by the inhabitants of the jungle after his parents were killed.

BOMOSKI, JOE & TUTTI
STOP! OR MY MOTHER WILL SHOOT (1992, Universal)—Cop **Sylvester Stallone** is embarrassed by the visit of his hyper-meddlesome mother **Estelle Getty.** Things get worse when Getty is a key witness in a drive-by shooting and becomes her son's pistol-packing mama and partner in fighting crime.

BONAPARTE, NAPOLEON *See* NAPOLEON

BONAPARTE, JOE
GOLDEN BOY (1939, Columbia)—**William Holden** got his big movie break when Barbara Stanwyck picked him to star opposite her in

the story of a poor lad, torn between his love for the violin and a career as a prizefighter.

BOND, JAMES
THE SPY WHO LOVED ME (1977, GB, UA); LICENSE TO KILL (1989, MGM-UA)—Droll **Roger Moore,** as James Bond, teams with Russian spy Barbara Bach to track down and defeat megalomaniac shipping magnate Curt Jurgens who has an undersea missile base. In the 1989 film, **Timothy Dalton** lends his dark good looks to 'double-o, seven.' With a little help from lovelies Carey Lowell and Talisa Soto he puts Columbian drug dealer Robert Davi out of business.

BONE, DANIEL
THE DUDE GOES WEST (1948, Allied Artists)—Eastern gunsmith **Eddie Albert** heads west because he believes he will have more business. On the way he undergoes numerous disasters but does meet and fall in love with Gale Storm. He ultimately shows he not only can fix guns but can use them too as he faces bad guys out to steal Storm's gold mine.

BONE, RICHARD
CUTTER AND BONE (1981, UA)—Handsome **Jeff Bridges,** a man of no convictions, has an affair with the wife of crippled Vietnam veteran John Heard. All three become involved in the murder of a young woman.

BONELLI, NICK
THE ALL-AMERICAN (1952, Universal)—When his parents are killed, college football star **Tony Curtis** loses interest in playing games.

BONFILS, ANGELA
THE BELLE OF NEW YORK (1952, MGM)—**Vera-Ellen,** a Bowery social worker during the gay nineties, is pursued by playboy Fred Astaire, who is even willing to take a job to impress her.

BONHAM, JOE
JOHNNY GOT HIS GUN (1971, Cinemation)—The story by Dalton Trumbo of a WWI soldier who has had all his limbs amputated, and is deaf, dumb and blind was not great drama in prose form. It is even less so in a movie starring **Timothy Bottoms** as the unfortunate doughboy. It's an anti-war movie, but it's so horrifying that one shrinks from the message rather than embracing it.

BONNARD, CHARLOTTE & LUCY
SISTER SISTER (1988, New World)—**Judith Ivey** and her sister **Jennifer Jason Leigh** live together in a southern gothic horror of an old plantation house. One is loony, but it takes the arrival of Eric Stoltz to raise some sexual tension to identify which one.

BONNER, ADAM & AMANDA
ADAM'S RIB (1949, MGM)—**Spencer Tracy** and **Katharine Hepburn** are married lawyers who find themselves on opposite sides in a court case. Tracy is prosecuting Judy Holliday, charged with trying to kill her husband Tom Ewell and his mistress Jean Hagen, and Hepburn is defending. Kate's courtroom ploys, which win an acquittal for her client, almost sink her own marriage.

BONNER, EVAN
TWO PEOPLE (1973, Universal)—Expatriate **Peter Fonda** becomes involved with fashion model Lindsay Wagner on a train from Marrakech to Casablanca.

BONNER, DR. GEORGES
THE MAN WHO COULD CHEAT DEATH (1959, GB, Hammer) Surgeon **Anton Diffring** appears to be in his mid-thirties, but he's actually over 100, having been kept alive and young through gland transplants from unwilling donors.

BONNER, JUNIOR
JUNIOR BONNER (1972, Cinerama)—**Steve McQueen**, a tired rodeo champion, goes home to visit his separated parents, Robert Preston and Ida Lupino, and his entrepreneur brother Joe Don Baker. The movie is a slice-of-life drama.

BONNET, NICOLETTE
WOMAN TO WOMAN (1946, GB, Anglo-American)—**Joyce Howard**, a French ballerina, has a son by married, shell-shocked officer Douglass Montgomery. Later she gives up her son to her lover's wife Adele Dixon, who can't have children.

BONNET, TONI
SHE MARRIED AN ARTIST (1938, Columbia)—**Luli Deste** is jealous of all the pretty models who sit for her artist husband John Boles.

BONNETT, STEVE
I'M STILL ALIVE (1940, RKO)—When one of his colleagues is killed, stuntman **Kent Taylor** and his wife, actress Linda Hayes, almost split over his line of work.

BONNEY, BILLY *See* **BILLY THE KID**

BONNIE
GENTLEMAN MARRY BRUNETTES (1955, UA)—**Jane Russell** and her sister Jeanne Crain are in Paris where they learn that their mother and aunt (Jane and Jeanne, again) were quite the toast of the City of Lights in the twenties.

BONNIE
TWO IN A TAXI (1941, Columbia)—**Anita Louise** is the girlfriend of taxi driver Russell Hayden who will do just about anything to get enough money so they can marry. But everything goes wrong.

BONNIWELL, JOHN
THE KANSAN (1943, UA)—While on his way to Oregon, **Richard Dix** stops a bank robbery in a Kansas town and is given the job of Marshal. His main problems from then on are with a banker who's trying to take over the town.

BONNIWELL, JOYCE
ACCOMPLICE (1946, Producers Releasing Corp.)—**Veda Ann Borg** is the ex-flame of private detective Richard Arlen, whom she hires to locate her missing husband.

BOO BOO
RAT PFINK AND BOO BOO (1966, Morgan/Craddock)—**Titus Moede**, a gardener, and his rock 'n' roll singing friend put on costumes something like those of Batman and Robin and become superheroes.

BOOKER, JOHN T.
GOOD GUYS WEAR BLACK (1978, Mar Vista)—Vietnam vet **Chuck Norris** is led to believe that members of his old unit were betrayed by the CIA. He's obsessed with learning the truth.

BOOKS, JOHN BERNARD
THE SHOOTIST (1976, Paramount)—Aging gunman **John Wayne** learns that he's dying of cancer. Rather than go out quietly, he challenges the most ruthless gunmen around and dies in a shoot-out.

BOOMERANG BILL
BOOMERANG BILL (1922, Silent, Paramount)—**Lionel Barrymore** is an ex-holdup man who loses everything, including the woman he loves, when he is sent to prison. When he gets out, he's reduced to selling shoestrings. Nice rehabilitation job!

BOONE, DANIEL
DANIEL BOONE (1936, RKO); THE RETURN OF DANIEL BOONE (1941, Columbia); YOUNG DANIEL BOONE (1950, Monogram); DANIEL BOONE, TRAIL BLAZER (1957, Republic)-In the 1936 film, **George O'Brien** leads settlers from North Carolina to the wilds of Kentucky where they are attacked by Indians led by a renegade. When the Indians are put to rout, O'Brien and his friends find so-called civilized people are worse as Virginia aristocrats claim the land they have built up. In the fourth film, **Bruce Bennett** appears in the same role with basically the same story. The 1941 movie has **Bill Elliott** as Dan Boone, grandson of the legendary frontiersman. Elliott has to deal with land grabbers just as did grand daddy. The 1950 film examines the early years of the frontiersman, with **David Bruce** in the title role.

BOOTH, ANGELA
BLONDE BAIT (1956, GB, Associated Film Dist. Co.)—In an attempt to find a missing murderer, Scotland Yard allows the suspect's girlfriend, **Beverly Michaels**, to escape from prison, hoping she will lead them to him.

BOOTH, EDWIN
PRINCE OF PLAYERS (1955, 20th Century Fox)—**Richard Burton** portrays the stage actor, once proclaimed the world's best, but now mostly remembered because his brother John Wilkes Booth, played by John Derek, assassinated Abraham Lincoln.

BOOTH, SAM
MY DARK LADY (1987, Film Gallery)—**Fred A. Keller**, a Shakespearean actor, is on the lam after being caught shoplifting while dressed as Santa Claus. He takes refuge in a boarding house run by black woman Lora Hill. Keller helps Hill increase her business to the point where she can send her son to an exclusive boarding school.

BOOTHE, JANET
AFFAIR WITH A STRANGER (1953, RKO)—**Monica Lewis'** affair with married playwright Victor Mature makes the papers but his wife, Jean Simmons, takes him back.

BOOTHE, JEAN
THE LADY GAMBLES (1949, Universal)—Bored housewife **Barbara Stanwyck** becomes addicted to gambling which leads to a beating and an attempted suicide.

BORCHARD, HENRY
THE CATMAN OF PARIS (1946, Republic)—Stupid detectives take no notice of clues that will lead them to **Douglass Dumbrille** as a homicidal maniac and concentrate on trailing an innocent man.

BORG, KATHERINE *See* **BLAKE, KAREN BORG**

BORGIA, LUCRETIA
BRIDE OF VENGEANCE (1949, Paramount)—**Paulette Goddard** plots the death of all members of an aristocratic clan that she holds responsible for the murder of her beloved husband.

BORLAND, DORIS BLAIR & LEONARD

WIFE, HUSBAND & FRIEND (1939, 20th Century Fox)—**Loretta Young** has visions of herself as a professional singer. Binnie Barnes, who is a singer, convinces Young's husband **Warner Baxter** that he has the musical talent and gets him a job singing. He's just as untalented as Young. Both give up their show business ambitions.

BORRIDGE, ETHEL

NOT QUITE A LADY (1928, GB, Silent, Wardour)—**Mabel Poulton's** plan for discouraging a working class girl from marrying her aristocratic son is to bore the poor thing to death at a deliberately dull house party.

BORRODAILE, TONY

THE MELODY MAKER (1933, GB, Warner Brothers)—**Lester Matthews** steals the sonata written by Joan Marion and turns it into a musical comedy. She is not immediately pleased.

BORU, THE JUNGLE GIRL

BOMBA AND THE JUNGLE GIRL (1952, Monogram)—About the same time that Bomba (Johnny Sheffield) discovers the skeletons of his parents, he also discovers the opposite sex in the person of **Suzette Harbin**

BOSIC, MARIA

MARIA'S LOVERS (1985, Cannon)—Fantasizing about being married to **Nastassja Kinski** is what kept John Heard going as he survived the torture of his Japanese captors in WWI. When he actually marries her, he can't perform sexually, because she reminds him of the suffering he endured. He finds sexual relief with the town tramp, and Maria takes up with a traveling singer, Keith Carradine.

BOSS NIGGER

BOSS NIGGER (1974, Boss/Dimension)—**Fred Williamson**, a black bounty hunter in the old West, terrorizes a town where a man he's seeking is hiding.

BOSTON BLACKIE

CONFESSIONS OF BOSTON BLACKIE (1941, Columbia); MEET BOSTON BLACKIE (1941, Columbia); ALIAS BOSTON BLACKIE (1942, Columbia); BOSTON BLACKIE GOES TO HOLLYWOOD (1942, Columbia); A CLOSE CALL FOR BOSTON BLACKIE (1946, Columbia); AFTER MIDNIGHT WITH BOSTON BLACKIE (1943, Columbia); BOSTON BLACKIE BOOKED ON SUSPICION (1945, Columbia); BOSTON BLACKIE'S RENDEZVOUS (1945, Columbia); BOSTON BLACKIE AND THE LAW (1946, Columbia) TRAPPED BY BOSTON BLACKIE (1948, Columbia); BOSTON BLACKIE'S CHINESE VENTURE (1949, Columbia)—**Chester Morris** stars as a former thief, now on the right side of the law, but still not completely trusted by the police. The titles of the movies give the gist of the Boston Blackie cases.

BOSWORTH, KATE & PAT

A STOLEN LIFE (1946, Warner Brothers)—**Bette Davis** appears as twins who are quite different in disposition. The unprincipled Bette assumes her sweet dead sister's identity to marry Glenn Ford. He eventually catches on.

BOTTOMS, DUSTY

THREE AMIGOS (1986, Orion)—**Chevy Chase**, Steve Martin and Martin Short are discharged movie cowboy heros who arrive in a Mexican town under the false expectation that they are to be honored for their movie work. The peasants, believing the three are real heroes, want them to rid the town of violent bandits.

BOTTS, CYNTHIA

A SAILOR'S SWEETHEART (1927, Silent, Warner Brothers)—When spinster **Louise Fazenda** inherits a fortune, she's off to Hawaii in search of a husband. Her first choice is a bigamist, but she has better luck with a sailor.

BOUCHERON, PIERRE "THE RAT"

THE RAT (1925, GB, Silent, Gainsborough); THE RETURN OF THE RAT (1929, GB, Gainsborough); (1938, GB, RKO)—**Ivor Novello** appears as an Apache in the first two films based on his play. He kills a man who forces himself on his beloved Mae Marsh, but she takes the blame. In the sequel, Novello retires from crime to marry his sweetheart, but the marriage doesn't work out and he's back in his old line of work before long. In the 1938 film, **Anton Walbrook** is an honorable jewel thief who takes the blame when the daughter of an imprisoned friend whom he's raising kills a man trying to abduct her.

BOUDEAUX, PAUL

GOOD NIGHT, PAUL (1918, Silent, Selznick)—Married Constance Talmadge poses as **Harrison Ford's** wife so the latter's uncle will come through with a promised $50,000 when Ford marries.

BOUDREAUX, OUISER

STEEL MAGNOLIAS (1989, Tri-Star)—Old maid **Shirley MacLaine** will be the first to admit that she's been in a bad mood for about forty years. For all of her fussing with her character, she nevertheless, delights audiences with her acting.

BOULBA, ANDREW

THE REBEL SON (1939, GB, UA)—**Anthony Bushell** opposes his Cossack father when the latter leads an attack on Poland in the sixteenth century. Both father and son are killed in the war. The same story was told in TARAS BULBA in 1962 with Yul Brynner and Tony Curtis as father and son.

BOULT, ARNOLD

EDWARD, MY SON (1949, MGM)—Tyrannical businessman **Spencer Tracy** cares only for his son, never seen in the film. He spoils the boy to such a point it's no wonder he grows up to be a rotter. When Tracy's wife tries to protest, she's promptly put in her place. She turns to drink, which eventually kills her. Tracy's son abandons his mistress when he discovers she is pregnant, then the scoundrel is killed in a plane crash. Tracy is sent to prison for torching his own business. When he gets out, he seeks his grandson but he is never allowed to see the boy.

BOVARD, MACKENZIE

THE HANGMAN (1959, Paramount)—Deputy Marshal **Robert Taylor**, who always gets his man, rides into a town to arrest Jack Lord for a crime committed years earlier. Lord has reformed and is among the town's leading citizens, and they don't want Taylor to take him to his punishment. Taylor, hard to convince of the possibility of a man changing so completely, finally relents and leaves the town without his prey.

BOVARY, EMMA

MADAME BOVARY (1949, MGM)—**Jennifer Jones**, Gustave Flaubert's passionate heroine, finds herself married to dull Van Heflin so she has an affair with Louis Jourdan and commits suicide when it doesn't work out.

BOWDEEN, SAMMY

TALENT FOR THE GAME (1991, Paramount)—California Angels baseball scout **Edward James Olmos** wins a front office job when he signs rifle-armed pitching phenomenon Jeff Corbett. Olmos loses the job when he stands up for the boy against an oil owner who forces the kid to start immediately in the big leagues.

BOWDRE, CHARLEY

YOUNG GUNS (1988, 20th Century Fox)—The real Bowdre, played in this western by **Casey Siemaszko**, was several years older than Billy the Kid, but somewhat in awe of the young gunman, always ready to follow his hero into some dangerous and dishonest business. He apparently wasn't very bright, for the Kid sacrificed his admirer to save himself.

BOWER, HERBERT

FATHER IS A PRINCE (1935, Paramount)—Penny-pincher **Grant Mitchell's** cheap ways almost destroy his family.

BOWER, PROF. JAMES

THE DEFECTOR (1966, Warner Brothers)—In his last film, **Montgomery Cliff** is an American physicist who becomes involved with spies in East Germany. He is fed some drugs that give him a bad trip, which is shared by the audience. The tragedy is to see a once outstanding actor who, through his own excesses, is reduced to appearing in such trash.

BOWERS, BILL

THE LAST TIME I SAW ARCHIE (1961, UA)—**Jack Webb** directed this service comedy about the friendship of pilot Webb and con man Robert Mitchum, the former who becomes a Hollywood screenwriter and the latter a top studio executive.

BOWERS, RANDY

RANDY RIDES ALONE (1934, Monogram)—Singing cowboy **John Wayne** investigates a series of express office robberies and murders. Gene Autry and Roy Rogers had nothing to fear from the Duke in the singing area.

BOWERS, ROSALIE

HER MAJESTY (1922, Silent, Playgoers)—**Mollie King** plays identical orphaned twins, one who is raised by a poor farm family and Rosalie who is raised by a wealthy family, which causes her to become a snob. Because of a mix-up, Rosalie almost steals her sister's beau.

BOWLES, BILLY

THE DREAM MAKER (1963, GB, British Lion)—Orphan **Tommy Steele** raises money for the institution in which he was raised by putting on a musical review.

BOWLES-OTTERY, PROF.

A JOLLY BAD FELLOW (1964, GB, British Lion)—**Leo McKern** discovers a serum which causes hysterics followed by death. The poison leaves no trace, and he uses it to kill his imagined enemies. Unfortunately for him, he remembers too late that a cigarette he has just lit contains the poison.

BOWIE

THEY LIVE BY NIGHT (1949, RKO); THIEVES LIKE US (1974, UA)—In the 1930s, **Farley Granger** and girl-friend Cathy O'Donnell pull off some robberies and become Bonnie and Clyde-like fugitives. Their doom is almost preordained. In the 1974 remake, **David Carradine** is a small-town hood who briefly teams up with Shelley Duvall for a crime spree until he's gunned down in a hail of bullets.

BOWMAN, JENNY

I COULD GO ON SINGING (1963, UA)—In her last film, **Judy Garland** is an American singing star in London, where she looks up a former lover, Dirk Bogarde. She had his child, which he adopted, and now Garland wants to claim her son.

BOY

TARZAN FINDS A SON (1939, MGM)—Tarzan (Johnny Weissmuller) and Jane (Maureen O'Sullivan) didn't have any children that we know about in the Tarzan series (fertility problems, we suppose), but they did adopt young **Johnny Sheffield** who, like Tarzan, was left to fend for himself in the jungle when his parents were killed. Sheffield was just like a son to Weissmuller in real life, and the two continued to appear together in the series when Maureen O'Sullivan begged out.

BOY, THE

BOY . . . A GIRL (1969, Hanson)—Fifteen year old **Dino Martin, Jr.** and Arion Fromer experiment with love and sex.

BOY, THE

GRANDMA'S BOY (1922, Silent, Associated Exhibitors)—**Harold Lloyd's** grandma helps her cowardly grandson develop courage by telling him a story about how years earlier the lad's timid grandfather became a hero.

BOY, THE

A SAILOR-MADE MAN (1921, Silent, Pathe)—**Harold Lloyd**, an unambitious, wealthy young man, is told by the father of his sweetheart that there will be no wedding bells until Lloyd amounts to something. Lloyd joins the navy and proves his worth when he rescues his girl from a villainous maharajah who has captured her yacht.

BOY, THE

TEENAGE CAVEMAN (1958, American International)—**Robert Vaughn** probably would like to forget his appearance as a prehistoric adolescent.

BOYCE, CHRISTOPHER

THE FALCON AND THE SNOWMAN (1985, Orion)—**Timothy Hutton** and his childhood friend Sean Penn decide to sell United States secrets to the Russians. The film, based on a true case, doesn't really clarify their motives.

BOYCOTT, CAPTAIN

CAPTAIN BOYCOTT (1947, GB, GFD)—**Cecil Parker** appears as the English rent-collector who gives his name to the practice of refusing to buy or deal with another as a kind of protest.

BOYD, ALAN

THAT'S MY BABY (1926, Silent, Paramount)—When his bride doesn't show up for his wedding, **Douglas MacLean** swears off women and almost immediately falls madly in love with the daughter of a business competitor.

BOYD, GEORGE

HUSBAND'S HOLIDAY (1931, Paramount)—**Clive Brook's** wife, Vivienne Osborne, is the patient type. She ignores his long-running affair with Juliette Compton, even when Clive moves in with his paramour. She's certain the affair will run its course, and he'll come home to her and his children. He does when his mistress, frustrated that she will never be his wife, commits suicide. There's a moral here someplace, we suppose.

BOYD, TOMMY

TOMBOY (1985, Crown International)—**Betsy Russell** is a whiz with mechanical things and can take a motor apart and put it back together again so it will really hum. She's also into racing, and when a handsome racing hunk (Jerry Dinome) comes onto the scene, she keeps taking off her shirt so he will have no doubts that she's female.

BOYER, PA
THE FARMER IN THE DELL (1936, RKO)—Pushy stage mother, Esther Dale insists that her family leave the farm and move to Hollywood so daughter Jean Parker can become a star, but it's father **Fred Stone** who is discovered.

BOYETTE, THOMAS
THE PACKAGE (1989, Orion)—**Tommy Lee Jones** is a U.S. soldier, being escorted back from a summit meeting in Germany to the U.S. by sergeant Gene Hackman. But both the assignment and Jones are not what they seem to be.

BOYLAN, JOHNNY
LITTLE TOUGH GUY (1938, Universal)—New york slum kid **Billy Halop** gets mixed-up with a gang and is sent to a brutal reform school.

BOYLE, JUNO & CAPT. JOHN "PAYCOCK"
JUNO AND THE PAYCOCK (1930, GB, British International)—**Sara Allgood** and **Edward Chapman** head up a lower class family expecting to inherit a fortune, which never comes. The movie was director Alfred Hitchcock's second sound film, following MURDER (1930).

BRACE, STEVEN
ONCE A DOCTOR (1937, Warner Brothers)—**Donald Woods** and his foster brother Gordon Oliver hope to follow in the footsteps of Oliver's father, a noted surgeon. They both love the same woman, Jean Muir. Woods is thrown out of medical school when he's blamed for the death of a patient, thus alienating him from his foster father. Later Oliver confesses that he was responsible for the death, and Woods is taken back into the medical community and wins Muir.

BRACKEN, MARGOT
WOMAN IN BONDAGE (1943, Monogram)—**Gail Patrick** suffers at the hands of the Nazis when they occupy her European town.

BRADBERRY, SNUFFY
TOY SOLDIERS (1991, Tri-Star)—When a band of terrorists invades a rich kids' school to force the release of a South American drug king, **Keith Coogan** is one of the youngsters who use practical jokes to thwart the bad guys.

BRADBERRY, W.
WHAT HAPPENED TO FATHER (1927, Silent, Warner Brothers)—Henpecked Egyptologist **Warner Oland** writes a musical comedy and finally stands up to his overbearing wife, Vera Lewis, preventing her from breaking up their daughter's romance.

BRADBURY, WALTER
PAPER TIGER (1975, GB, MacLean)—**David Niven**, the English tutor to the son of a Japanese ambassador, regales the boy with tales of his heroics during the war. When Niven and the boy are kidnapped, the youngster expects Niven to rise to the occasion. Despite the fact his stories were all lies, he does.

BRADDOCK, BEN
THE GRADUATE (1967, Embassy Pictures)—Recent college graduate **Dustin Hoffman** is seduced by Anne Bancroft, the wife of a business associate of his father. She's in the affair strictly for the sex. After a while this wears a bit thin for Hoffman. He's coerced into taking out Bancroft's daughter, Katharine Ross, much to the displeasure of Bancroft. He falls in love with Ross, who learns of her mother's affair with Hoffman and flees back to college. Hoffman follows, intent on winning her promise to marry him. She vacillates but accepts the proposal of a BMOC. She is rescued at the church by Hoffman, and the two ride off into the sunset on a bus. The movie meant a lot to the generation who were the age of the principals at the time of its release, but we're not sure they could say what it meant.

BRADDOCK, COL. JAMES
BRADDOCK: MISSING IN ACTION III (1988, Cannon)—**Chuck Norris** is back in Vietnam for the third time. Single-handedly he revenges the American defeat and rescues a bunch of Amerasian children in the process.

BRADDOCK, MATT
MAN FROM FRISCO (1944, Republic)—**Michael O'Shea** is a ship builder who discovers a new, cheaper way to make ships.

BRADDOCK, THOMAS
THE CIRCUS MAN (1914, Silent, Lasky)—Circus owner **Theodore Roberts** rises above his problems and finds happiness in his life.

BRADEN, DR. MONICA
DOCTOR MONICA (1934, Warner Brothers)—**Kay Francis** is an obstetrician who delivers the baby of a woman who has been having an affair with Francis' husband, Warren William. When the woman commits suicide, Francis takes the child to raise but never lets William discover that the child is his.

BRADFIELD, JOHNNY
THEY MADE ME A CRIMINAL (1939, Warner Brothers)—Thinking he has killed an opponent, boxer **John Garfield** goes on the run, hiding out on a western farm where he helps Gloria Dickson and her aunt May Robson make something out of some city juvenile delinquents, the Dead End kids.

BRADFORD, BILL
SPECIAL AGENT (1935, Warner Brothers)—Popular newsman **George Brent** romances Bette Davis who keeps the books for mobster Ricardo Cortez. Brent's working with the government which hopes to put Cortez away on the charge of tax evasion. Davis falls in love with Brent and agrees to help him. Cortez has her kidnapped so she can't testify against him, but Brent rescues her.

BRADFORD, HANK
WILD HORSE HANK (1979, Canada, Film Consortium of Canada) - College student **Linda Blair** attempts to prevent wild horses from being used for dog food.

BRADFORD, JIM
THE WOLF OF WALL STREET (1929, Paramount)—In a role usually considered his best, **George Bancroft** is a market manipulator who gets even with his competitor Paul Lukas and his unfaithful wife Ogla Baclanova by ruining them in the stock market while at the same time making a fortune for his maid's boyfriend.

BRADFORD, PAULA
THE EX-MRS. BRADFORD (1936, RKO)—**Jean Arthur** gets her ex-husband William Powell involved in solving a murder. For all her talent, Arthur doesn't work as well with Powell in this kind of thing as does Myrna Loy.

BRADLER, JIM
THE WOMAN I STOLE (1933, Columbia)—Hero **Jack Holt** seems intent on ruining his best friend and stealing the man's wife, but it's

all part of his plot to subvert the plans of a villainous desert bandit to take over their company.

BRADLEY, BETTY
YOU'RE A SWEETHEART (1937, Universal)—**Alice Faye** is the star of a big Broadway musical show which is saved by a publicity stunt thought up by George Murphy.

BRADLEY, JIM
SECOND FIDDLE (1923, Silent, Hodkinson)—Trying to prove that he's as good as his brother, **Glenn Hunter** holds a killer at bay with a pistol, but faints when he learns that the gun was empty. This earns him more taunts from his cruel brother. He gets another go at the murderer when the latter escapes from prison.

BRADLEY, JOAN
PAID TO DANCE (1937, Columbia)—Ten-cents-a-dance girl **Jacqueline Wells (Julie Bishop)** and others of her profession are exploited by gangsters. She's rescued by a detective who breaks up the criminal ring.

BRADLEY, KITTY
THE CAPRICES OF KITTY (1915, Silent, Bosworth)—School girl **Elsie Janis** falls in love with Courtenay Foote, the young man who comes to her rescue when her auto breaks down. Her guardian explains that the conditions of her inheritance require her not to see her fiance for six months, unless she's willing to forsake her legacy. Janis makes the most of the half-year.

BRADLEY, MORT
THE CZAR OF BROADWAY (1930, Universal)—New York political boss **John Wray** controls not only the most popular nightclub but also most of the press, but the managing editor of the Times, John Harron, is determined to expose Wray's crooked dealings.

BRADLEY, OBEDIAH
PICKUP ON 101 (1972, American International)—**Jack Albertson**, a lovable hobo, teams-up with hitchhiker Lesley Ann Warren. They are picked up by out-of-work singer Martin Sheen. Dying of a heart attack, Albertson's last request is that he be buried on a farm he once owned. The present owner won't allow it so Sheen and Warren have Albertson cremated and spread his ashes on the land.

BRADLEY, ROGER
THE MILKMAN (1950, Universal)—Milkmen **Donald O'Connor** and Jimmy Durante get involved with gangsters in this modest comedy.

BRADLEY, SUSAN
THE HARVEY GIRLS (1946, MGM)—When mail-order bride **Judy Garland** arrives in a small New Mexico town, she finds her intended is the town drunk. Stranded, she takes a job as a waitress for the Fred Harvey chain of restaurants and finds herself being pursued by saloon keeper John Hodiak and a judge, Preston Foster. The fine musical numbers include Johnny Mercer and Fred Warren's Academy Award winning "On the Atchinson, Topeka and the Sante Fe."

BRADLEY, TONI
TIMES SQUARE LADY (1935, MGM)—**Virginia Bruce**, the daughter of a Broadway hustler, is being cheated by her father's lawyer. One of the crooked attorney's junior partners helps her out.

BRADSHAW, SAM
HI, NELLIE! (1934, Warner Brothers)—Newspaper editor **Paul Muni** loses a fight with his publisher and is demoted to writing the lonely hearts column, supposedly authored by a woman named Nellie Nelson. Despite some bouts with hard drink, Muni works at the new assignment and makes the column a huge success. When he solves a major crime in the guise of Nellie, he wins back his former job.

BRADY, DIAMOND JIM
DIAMOND JIM (1935, Universal)—**Edward Arnold** is enjoyable in this amusing biopic of the 1890s New York millionaire with a passion for Lillian Russell and food—lots of food.

BRADY, JANET
BEAUTIFUL BUT DUMB (1928, Silent, Tiffany-Stahl)—**Patsy Ruth Miller** is a stenographer who decides she wishes to marry her boss. She changes her simpering personality to that of a flapper, and gets the job done.

BRADY, JASON
ONE MAN (1979, Canada, National Film Board of Canada)—When TV newsman **Len Cariou** investigates a story of a factory's pollution of a slum area, he is harassed by the company and his bosses who don't wish to offend big business.

BRADY, KATE
GIRL WITH GREEN EYES (1964, GB, Lopert)—Fresh from the country, **Rita Tushingham** arrives in Dublin, where she moves in with Peter Finch, a much older divorced writer. The relationship lasts through the summer but ends when they discover that other than passion, they have nothing in common.

BRADY, MATT
THE BOSS (1956, UA)—After WWI **John Payne** finds his niche as a corrupt political boss in a small town and soon controls an entire state.

BRADY, MIRIAM
THE GIRL FROM TENTH AVENUE (1935, First National)—While in an alcoholic stupor, lawyer Ian Hunter marries **Bette Davis** but thinks better of it when he learns his ex-fiancee Katharine Alexander wants him back. Bette will have something to say about that.

BRAEMER, GEOFFREY
LORD JEFF (1938, MGM)—When well-brought-up **Freddie Bartholomew** gets into trouble, he is sent to a naval school where he will get more supervision.

BRAGANZA, PABLO
THE GAY DESPERADO (1936, UA)—**Leo Carrillo**, a Mexican bandit who patterns himself after American movie gangsters, kidnaps opera star Nino Martini and heiress Ida Lupino.

BRAINARD, PROF. NED
THE ABSENT MINDED PROFESSOR (1961, Disney)—Professor **Fred MacMurray** invents flying flubber which, when applied to the soles of the sneakers of the college basketball players, allows them to soar over their opponents and win some games for a change. Michael "Air" Jordan flies without flubber.

BRAINERD, JOHN
HIS WIFE'S HUSBAND (1922, Silent, Pyramid)—**Arthur Carewe** marries Betty Blythe but is only interested in her physically. She runs away and later marries Huntley Gordon. Carewe shows up to make trouble, but it seems he was married when he tried to marry Blythe.

BRAND, FANNY
MY MAN (1928, Warner Brothers)—In a primitive musical, **Fanny Brice** is a plain Jewish girl who falls for a shiftless man. Her rendition of the title song is heart-wrenching.

BRAND, LETITIA
THE LAST WITNESS (1925, GB, Silent, Stoll)—**Isobel Elsom** is on trial for the murder of her Member of Parliament lover. She is being prosecuted by the King's Counsel who just happens to be her husband.

BRAND, MALCOLM
I, MADMAN (1989, Trans World)—**Randall William Cook** is the author of a book called I, Madman. Murders that follow his book precisely, begin to occur. Is our hero a fictional maniac come to life?

BRAND, MAX *See* NEVADA SMITH

BRANDON
CRIMINAL LAWYER (1937, RKO)—District Attorney **Lee Tracy** owes his success to underworld influences. He ultimately turns on his mobster friends and reforms.

BRANDON, MICHAEL
BLUEBEARD'S EIGHTH WIFE (1923, Silent, Paramount); (1938, Paramount)—**Huntley Gordon** in 1923 and **Gary Cooper** in 1938 have had seven previous wives when the daughter of an impoverished Frenchman marries him, intending to teach him that he can't trade in wives like so many discarded automobiles.

BRANDON, PHILLIP
THE CRUSADER (1932, Majestic)—Crusading D.A. **H.B. Warner** tries to get his innocent sister acquitted of a murder charge.

BRANDON, THOMAS Z.
THE CHASER (1938, MGM)—Ambulance chasing lawyer **Dennis O'Keefe** falls for Ann Morriss, hired by a company from which he has won a large number of cases. Her assignment is to get the goods on him, so he'll be disbarred.

BRANDT, MAX
THE STUDENT'S ROMANCE (1936, GB, British International)—In Heidelberg in 1825, down-on-his-luck songwriter student **Patric Knowles** is helped out by Carol Goodner, who loves him madly. He, however, falls for Grete Natzler, but when it turns out that she is pledged to another, Knowles returns to Goodner.

BRANGWEN, GUNDRUN & URSULA
WOMEN IN LOVE (1969, GB, UA)—**Glenda Jackson** and **Jennie Linden**, two young women from the British Midlands, have their first sexual experiences with Oliver Reed and Alan Bates. Jackson won an Academy Award for her performance in the film based on the novel by D. H. Lawrence.

BRANNAN, KAY
SMALL TOWN GIRL (1936, MGM)—New England girl **Janet Gaynor** meets doctor Robert Taylor when he stops to ask her directions to a football game. He invites her along and after an evening of drunken festivities, the two wake up the next morning to find themselves wed. Even though he's engaged to Binnie Barnes and she has an understanding with James Stewart, they decide to try to make the marriage work.

BRANNIGAN, JIM
BRANNIGAN (1975, GB, UA)—**John Wayne** is an Irish-American cop sent from Chicago to pick up a gangster in London. Talk about the proverbial bull in a China shop.

BRANNIGAN, LT. WILLIAM
DEVIL DOGS OF THE AIR (1935, Warner Brothers)—**Pat O'Brien**, a member of the Marine Flying Corps, goes by the book. He has a rough time getting brash flyer James Cagney even to look at the book.

BRANNON, HONEST PLUSH
BARBARY COAST GENT (1944, MGM)—When **Wallace Beery** is run out of the Barbary Coast in the 1880s, he heads for a Gold Rush in Nevada where he becomes a Robin Hood-like thief.

BRANT, BAXTER
HAIR TRIGGER BAXTER (1926, Silent, Independent Pictures)—**Bob Custer** saves his girl from the clutches of a rustler, who had been weeding out the herd of the girl's father's ranch.

BRASSFIELD, SAM
CATTLE KING (1963, MGM)—**Robert Taylor**, a well-to-do rancher, becomes embroiled in a range war with rival Robert Middleton, who is out to prevent fences and barbed wire being used in Wyoming in 1883.

BRAT, THE
THE BRAT (1931, Fox)—**Sally O'Neil**, a cockney waif, is taken in by a wealthy land owner Alan Dinehart. Her candid comments are not appreciated in her new society.

BRAUN, LITTLE JOE
THE BIG OPERATOR (1959, MGM)—**Mickey Rooney**, the racketeering head of a labor union, goes berserk when he's investigated by a U.S. Senate panel.

BRAVOS, TASSOS
THE DIRTY DOZEN (1967, GB, MGM)—**Al Mancini**, one of twelve imprisoned criminal American GI's, is given the opportunity to have his sentence reviewed if he survives a suicide attack on a chateau behind enemy lines where a large number of German officers are enjoying R & R. He's given a clear record, posthumously.

BRAXTON, JOE
HIS LAST DOLLAR (1914, Silent, Paramount)—Fleeced of his fortune in New York, westerner **David Higgins** bounces back when he wins a big race.

BRAXTON, MIKE
UNDER THE GUN (1989, Marquis)—St. Louis cop **Sam Jones** receives a terrified last phone call from his brother in L.A. The young man is crushed and killed in a phone booth by a truck. Jones hurries to L.A. and finds himself 'under the gun' in tracking down his brother's killers.

BRAYDON, CAPT. JAMES
ONLY THE BRAVE (1930, Paramount)—Union officer **Gary Cooper** volunteers to spy when his fiancee jilts him. He goes behind enemy lines and turns up in the mansion of Mary Brian. The two fall in love, but it takes the arrival of the cavalry at the last moment to save him from a Confederate firing squad.

BRAYMORE, VICTORIA
THE PETTY GIRL (1950, Columbia)—When calendar artist Robert Cummings sees **Joan Caulfield** on the beach in a bathing suit, he's

determined to get her to pose for him. Caulfield's a prim college professor, and his insistence gets her fired. He goes back to New York, and she follows to get even. They marry. Guess that'll teach him.

BREAKES, JOHNNY
JOHNNY ON THE SPOT (1954, GB, New Realm)—**Hugh McDermott** is released from prison intent on clearing his name of the crime for which he was sentenced.

BREAUX, BELIZAIRE
BELIZAIRE THE CAJUN (1986, Skouras)—The film takes a look at the Cajuns living in Louisiana in 1859, with particular attention to **Armand Assante**. Let the good times roll!

BRECKENRIDGE, GRANVILLE
A GUY, A GAL AND A PAL (1945, Columbia)—Although romantically involved with both civilian **George Meeker** and marine Jimmy Jones, Lynn Merrick decides she likes the look of a uniform.

BREEDIN, JIM
ALIAS A GENTLEMAN (1948, MGM)—Ex-con **Wallace Beery** searches for his daughter and tries to go straight.

BREEN, DOUGLAS
THE FAN (1981, Paramount)—**Michael Biehn** is infatuated with actress Lauren Bacall. He's also a dangerous psychopath who will kill anyone he thinks is keeping him from his beloved, including Bacall herself.

BREEN, HARRIET
THE SHE WOLF (1931, Universal)—**May Robson** is a ruthless Wall Street businesswoman out to destroy her deceased husband's business adversary whom she truly hates.

BREEN, JOHN
THE FIGHTING KENTUCKIAN (1949, Republic)—In one of his poorer roles, **John Wayne** is an 1810 frontiersman who leads his men against land-grabbers. The film is notable for featuring Oliver Hardy as Wayne's sidekick with no Stan Laurel in sight.

BREEZY
BREEZY (1973, Universal)—Young hippy **Kay Lenz's** love affair with 50-year old William Holden rejuvenates him. Beats the hell out of vitamins.

BREITENBACH DORIS
OH, YOU BEAUTIFUL DOLL (1949, 20th Century Fox)—The star of this film is S.Z. "Cuddles" Sakall who portrays songwriter Fred Fisher (real name, Breitenbach), the composer of "Peg O' My Heart" and "Chicago." **June Haver** plays his singer-dancer daughter.

BREL, JACQUES
JACQUES BREL IS ALIVE AND WELL AND LIVING IN PARIS (1979, American Film)—There is no plot in this musical review featuring the songs of Belgian balladeer **Jacques Brel**

BREMER, CHARLES
MAN OF FLOWERS (1984, Australia, International Spectrafilm)—Eccentric old **Norman Kaye** collects art and flowers, and watches women undress. He is an observer of life rather than a participant because of his strict upbringing.

BRENNAN, ANNIE
TUGBOAT ANNIE (1933, MGM); TUGBOAT ANNIE SAILS AGAIN (1940, Warner Brothers)—Loveable old comedian **Marie Dressler**, the skipper of the tugboat Narcissus, is married to ne'er-do-well boozer Wallace Beery. They smooth out the problems in the love life of Robert Young and Maureen O'Sullivan. In 1940 **Marjorie Rambeau** takes over in a dismal story in which Ronald Reagan saves her tugboat job.

BRENNAN, MARSHAL
THE BADGE OF MARSHAL BRENNAN (1957, Allied Artists)—Cowboy **Douglas Fowley** takes the badge of a dying marshal. It has a mystical effect on him, forcing him to face the bad guys and clean up a lawless town.

BRENNAN, PAT
THE TALL T (1957, Columbia)—**Randolph Scott**, an Arizona rancher, is taken hostage by three stagecoach robbers. He outwits them.

BRENNAN, SPEED
PRIDE OF THE NAVY (1939, Republic)—Kicked out of the Naval Academy because of rowdy behavior, **James Dunn** becomes a speed boat designer and is hired by the Navy to build a small torpedo boat.

BRENNAN, ZIGGY
THAT BRENNAN GIRL (1946, Republic)—Young mother **Mona Freeman** neglects her baby so she can have a good time. Shame, shame, everybody knows your name.

BRENNON, BILL
THE MAN WHO DIED TWICE (1958, Republic)—Ex-skater Vera Ralston's husband **Rod Cameron** is burned to death —or is he? It was Ralston's last movie. She was never better —or worse. She never could act. Cameron isn't exactly Laurence Olivier, either.

BRENT, ALICE
STOLEN FACE (1952, GB, Hammer/Lippert)—Plastic surgeon Paul Henreid loves and loses concert pianist **Lizabeth Scott**. So he gives an ex-prison inmate his beloved's face, but he can't keep her. Eventually the real Scott returns to Henreid.

BRENT, CARL
I'LL LOVE YOU ALWAYS (1935, Columbia)—The marriage of engineer **George Murphy** and his actress wife Nancy Carroll is on the rocks. She finds herself pregnant but doesn't tell him. Murphy steals some money, is arrested and sent to prison, but keeps it a secret from Carroll by telling her he'll be in Russia on business. Not that anyone really cares, but this ridiculous tale ends with his pardon and his first sight of his son.

BRENT, FRANCES
VIVACIOUS LADY (1938, RKO)—When nightclub singer **Ginger Rogers** marries college botany professor James Stewart, she doesn't hit it off with his parents.

BRENT, JAMES
MILLIONAIRES IN PRISON (1940, RKO)—Millionaire stock broker **Morgan Conway** is sent to prison for his part in a phony stock deal. The pen is run like a country club, but Conway proves his worth by volunteering to be a guinea pig in some Malta fever research.

BRENT, JOHN
TAMMY AND THE MILLIONAIRE (1967, Universal)—**Donald Woods**, a young millionaire, hires Tammy (Debbie Watson) as a secretary with romance the result.

BRENT, LENORE

HIS KIND OF WOMAN (1951, RKO)—The kind of woman **Jane Russell** is is voluptuous and promiscuous, qualities that sleepy-eyed gambler Robert Mitchum likes in a woman. Fortunately for him, she's also loyal when her man is in danger —which understates Mitchum's predicament. He's to exchange faces and identities with mobster Raymond Burr, who will then be able to return to the U.S., while Mitchum will be dead. Russell leads an odd assortment of rescuers who raid Burr's stronghold and save Mitchum.

BRENT, PATRICIA

PATRICIA BRENT, SPINSTER (1919, GB, Garrick)—Spinster **Ena Beaumont** has the last laugh when she cons a man into posing as her fiance.

BRENT, PETER

TAMMY AND THE BACHELOR (1957, Universal)—Backwoods tomboy Debbie Reynolds falls for stranded pilot **Leslie Nielsen**.

BRENT, ROBERT

THE SINGING MARINE (1937, Warner Brothers)—Marine **Dick Powell** becomes an overnight sensation when he wins a radio contest as a singer. His head swells with his success, costing him his buddies and girl. He finally wises up.

BRENT, SUSAN

HAT CHECK HONEY (1944, Universal)—Hat check girl **Grace MacDonald** helps her boyfriend, Richard Davis, get a job as a singer with a band, and then he almost forgets her.

BRENTANO, MARIA

SECRET PEOPLE (1952, GB, Ealing)—**Valentina Cortesa** and her sister Audrey Hepburn are forced to flee to London in 1930 after their father is murdered by an evil European ruler. Seven years later, Cortesa is reunited with the boy she left behind, and the two plot to kill the ruler with a time bomb but kill an innocent bystander instead.

BRETON, DANIELLE

SISTERS (1973, American International)—When **Margot Kidder**, a homicidal maniac, commits a murder she is observed by reporter Jennifer Salt, who reports the crime to the police. They don't believe her because Kidder and her accomplice have cleaned up the murder site. Salt pushes the investigation herself and discovers that Kidder is a Siamese twin, separated from her sibling at birth.

BRETT, SGT. JIM

NORTHWEST MOUNTED POLICE (1940, Paramount)—**Preston Foster**, a no-nonsense Mountie, competes with Texas Ranger Gary Cooper for beautiful nurse Madeleine Carroll and the rights to George Bancroft, a bad one wanted in two countries. Foster gets Carroll and Cooper gets Bancroft. It's not a fair exchange.

BREWER, DICK

YOUNG GUNS (1988, 20th Century Fox)—**Charlie Sheen** is given an elaborate death scene in this non-historical story of the Regulator gang, led by a young Billy the Kid, played by Sheen's brother Emilio Estevez.

BREWSTER, DR. JAMES

THE APE MAN (1943, Monogram)—**Bela Lugosi** injects himself with a serum that turns him into an ape monster.

BREWSTER, JUDY

HER HUSBAND'S SECRET (1925, Silent, First National)—**Patsy Ruth Miller**, the daughter of a wealthy banker, brings home Antonio Moreno, introducing him as her fiance. Her father discovers that Moreno is guilty of a fraudulent investment promotion. Moreno tries to commit suicide but survives. The banker takes Moreno into the business when Miller reveals that they have been married for three months and are expecting a baby.

BREWSTER, MONTE (MONTY)

BREWSTER'S MILLIONS (1921, Silent, Paramount) (1935, GB, British & Dominions); (1945, UA); (1985, Universal); MISS BREWSTER'S MILLIONS (1926, Silent, Paramount)—The premise of this oft-filmed story is quite simple. Monte Brewster (in the 1935 production, he was Jack Brewster) will receive a number of million dollars if he can spend a million (or more) dollars in a stated period of time without letting anyone know what he's doing or why and at the end have nothing to show for it. Over the years the amount to be inherited, the amount to be spent and the time period have been changed, but whether Brewster is played by **Roscoe "Fatty" Arbuckle**, **Jack Buchanan**, **Dennis O'Keefe** or **Richard Pryor**, he has his hands full with things complicated by those who want him to fail and his friends who are trying to help him keep some of his money. In 1926, the sex of Brewster was changed with **Bebe Daniels** as Polly Brewster facing the same predicament.

BREWSTER, OLYMPIA

HIS WIFE'S HUSBAND (1922, Silent, Pyramid)—**Betty Blythe** marries a lecherous man who treats her as a sexual plaything. She feigns suicide and disappears. Years later her first husband finds her, now married to a successful lawyer who has just been elected mayor. The first hubby tries to blackmail the second, but she proves that her first marriage was invalid.

BREWSTER, POLLY *See* **MONTE BREWSTER**

BREWSTER, TOM

THE BOY FROM OKLAHOMA (1954, Warner Brothers)—Lawyer **Will Rogers, Jr.** drifts into a town ruled over by tyrant Anthony Caruso. Rogers is made sheriff and rounds up all the bad guys, using only his lariat and his faith in the Lord.

BRIAN

A CRY IN THE WILD (1990, Concorde)—Thirteen-year-old **Jared Rushton** is stranded in an isolated, heavily wooded area in Canada after crash landing the plane he is traveling in when the pilot suffers a fatal heart attack. The story details his efforts to survive.

BRIAN

MONTY PYTHON'S LIFE OF BRIAN (1979, GB, Warner Brothers)—As a baby, **Graham Chapman** is mistaken for the Messiah by three wise men who find him born in a manger. In a tasteless farce, which also is lacking in humor, Chapman's life parallels that of Christ even to the point of crucifixion.

BRIAN, KING

DARBY O'GILL AND THE LITTLE PEOPLE (1959, Buena Vista)—**Jimmy O'Dea** is the King of Leprechauns in Ireland. He is made so drunk by Irish caretaker Albert Sharpe that he grants his drinking companion three wishes and then promptly tricks him into wasting two of them.

BRICE, FANNY

FUNNY GIRL (1968, Columbia); FUNNY LADY (1975, Columbia)—**Barbra Streisand** is excellent as Fanny Brice in the film version of her Broadway hit. Seven years later, the magic seems gone from the role and her performance.

BRICK

FIVE AGAINST THE HOUSE (1955, Columbia)—**Brian Keith** is one of five college students who plot to rob casinos in Las Vegas as an experiment, planning to return the money after the heist, but war vet Keith decides he wants to keep the loot.

BRICKER, LUCY

LADIES CLUB (1986, New Line Cinema)—**Diana Scarwid**, a rape victim, joins with others who have experienced the same brutal indignity to take their revenge on rapists.

BRIDE, THE

BRIDE OF RE-ANIMATOR (1991, Wildstreet Pictures)—**Kathleen Kinmont** is a stitched-together monster with a see-through torso created by crazy scientist Jeffrey Combs.

BRIDE OF FRANKENSTEIN'S MONSTER

THE BRIDE OF FRANKENSTEIN (1935, Universal)—When Baron Frankenstein decides that a wife is what is needed to soften his monster's personality, he goes back into the laboratory to whip up a bride. The result is **Elsa Lanchester**, who is not pleased with her prospective mate.

BRIDGE, WALTER & INDIA

MR. & MRS. BRIDGE (1990, Miramax)—**Paul Newman** and **Joanne Woodward** are excellent as a stuffy Kansas City attorney and his unfulfilled wife. The film, produced by Ismail Merchant and directed by James Ivory, is intelligently scripted by their frequent collaborator, Ruth Prawer Jhabvala, adapted from two Evan S. Connell novels, *Mrs. Bridge* (1959) and *Mr. Bridge* (1969).

BRIDGESTON, RICHIE

THE BOY WHO CRIED WEREWOLF (1973, Universal)—**Scott Sealey**, upset by his parent's divorce, tries to get them back together again, but after his father is bitten by a werewolf, becoming one himself, the possibilities seem remote.

BRIENNE, MARGOT

HER BODYGUARD (1933, Paramount)—Bodyguard Edmund Lowe, with ambitions of becoming an actor, is hired by a wealthy man to protect his girlfriend actress, **Wynne Gibson**. The two are a big help to each other.

BRIGAND, GILBERTA

THE TOY WIFE (1938, MGM)—Flirtatious **Luise Rainer** causes much jealousy and tragedy in Louisiana in the early 19th century.

BRIGG

STAND UP VIRGIN SOLDIERS (1977, GB, Warner Brothers)—**Robin Askwith** is one of several young British recruits stationed in Singapore who are working overtime to eliminate their virginal status.

BRIGGS, KRISTY

SHE'S HAVING A BABY (1988, Paramount)—In a movie that might be subtitled, "Can This Marriage Be Saved?" **Elizabeth McGovern** is a 50s housewife, sexless and boring, married to dismal and dumb Kevin Bacon, who can't stand her or anything else in his life. Many couples mistakenly believe that a baby will make a bad marriage better. This sour ball should be spit out.

BRIGGS, MARSHALL "MICKEY" & JANICE

I MARRIED A WOMAN (1958, RKO/ Universal)—Advertising man **George Gobel** marries **Diana Dors**, the winner of a beauty contest sponsored by a beer company. Gobel has trouble keeping Dors and his job.

BRIGGS, NANCY

THREE LOVES HAS NANCY (1938, MGM)—When **Janet Gaynor** is stood up by her bridegroom, she decides to play the field for a while before coming up with a new husband candidate.

BRIGHT, BILLY

THE COMIC (1969, Columbia)—**Dick Van Dyke** is quite appealing as the pathetic silent screen comic whose career and life is ruined by his womanizing and drinking problems.

BRIGHT, GEORGE

I SEE ICE (1938, GB, Associated British)—**George Formby**, the prop man for an ice show, becomes a newspaper photographer when he invents a new camera.

BRIGHT, W.W.

W.W. AND THE DIXIE DANCEKINGS (1975, 20th Century Fox)—Stick-up man **Burt Reynolds** teams up with a country and western group with ambitions of making it to the Grand Old Opry. Reynolds finances them by robbing service stations.

BRIGHTON, DR. JOHN

THE OKLAHOMAN (1957, Allied Artists)—While on the way to California, physician **Joel McCrea's** wife dies in child birth. He decides to settle down in the Oklahoma town where she's buried. He runs afoul of cattle barons when he treats an Indian whose land they wish to steal.

BRIGITTA *See* ANNA ZADOR

BRIMMER, GABRIELLA "GABY"

GABY —A TRUE STORY (1987, Tri-Star)—**Rachel Levin** gives a memorable performance in the true story of a woman whose body is almost completely paralyzed by cerebral palsy but whose mind soars with hope and plans.

BRINDON, PETER

THE WITNESS (1959, GB, Anglo-Amalgamated)—**Martin Stephens** suffers many taunts from his classmates because his father is in prison. The 10 year old witnessed a crime of which his father is suspected. The police use young Stephens as bait to catch the real criminals, and he is re-united with his father.

BRINKER, JEANNE

JUNE BRIDE (1948, Warner Brothers)—When a magazine plans to cover a typical middle-American wedding, the editor and reporters move into the home of the bride-to-be **Barbara Bates** and change everything to suit what they believe their readers will want. Foreign correspondent Robert Montgomery is assigned to the wedding coverage by editor Bette Davis, hoping to get him to resign. Instead he discovers that the bride is in love with the bridegroom's brother, and he encourages the two to elope.

BRINKMAN, ELSA *See* LYLAH CLARE

BRINSLEY, LORD GERALD

A CERTAIN YOUNG MAN (1928, Silent, MGM)—**Ramon Novarro** is an English lord who prefers married women. While hiding from some outraged husband, he encounters a girl and is in love with a single woman for the first time in his life.

BRINSLEY, HELEN

THE ONLY WOMAN (1924, Silent, First National)—A ruthless millionaire blackmails **Norma Talmadge** into marrying his drunken son Eugene O'Brien, in the hope she will straighten him out. She does and decides she really loves her reformed husband.

BRISSAC, COLETTE

THE IDOL OF THE NORTH (1921, Silent, Paramount)—Dance hall girl **Dorothy Dalton** marries engineer Edwin August while he's drunk. Later, his gold-digging ex-girlfriend Marguerite Marsh tries to steal him back, so little Dorothy protects her investment with her shootin' iron.

BRISTON, ANNE

ANNE ONE HUNDRED (1933, GB, British & Dominions)—**Betty Stockfield** inherits a soap factory and outwits an unscrupulous rival.

BRITT

THE MAGNIFICENT SEVEN (1960, UA)—**James Coburn** is one of the gunmen hired by Mexican villagers to protect them from a gang of bandits. Coburn is equally adept with a knife or a gun, but his skill can't save his life.

BROADBENT, JANE

THE RELUCTANT DEBUTANTE (1958, MGM)—**Sandra Dee's** father Rex Harrison and his new wife Kay Kendall want her to make her society debut in London, but British boys bore her. She's ga-ga for American musician John Saxon, who has an undeserved bad reputation when it comes to girls.

BROCKTON, ANNE

ANNE OF LITTLE SMOKY (1921, Silent, Playgoers)—**Winifred Westover** and her family claim the Little Smoky region as their own and resist when the government turns it into a forest and game preserve. Westover is loved by a forest ranger whose job puts him into conflict with Westover's family.

BRODIE, DR.

DOCTOR'S SECRET (1929, Paramount)—Physician **Robert Edeson** comes to the aid of an automobile accident victim. The doctor is unable to save the man, who was running away with married Ruth Chatterton. Edeson proceeds to a cocktail party and tells his host and the other guests about the incident without realizing his host's wife is the unlucky lady. She arrives late and her husband accuses her of being the central character in the doctor's story, but both deny it.

BRODIE, EDGAR

THE SECRET AGENT (1936, GB, Gaumont)—War hero **John Gielgud** reads in the paper of his death and funeral. The explanation is that he has been given the assignment of assassinating an enemy agent in Switzerland, and no one knows what he looks like. Gielgud is accompanied on his mission by Madeleine Carroll, posing as his wife. Gielgud kills an innocent man, and it is only as he is taking a train home that he realizes the real enemy agent is charming, helpful American Robert Young.

BRODIE, JAMES

HATTER'S CASTLE (1948, GB, Paramount)—**Robert Newton**, a tyrannical Scottish hat maker, lives with his wife and daughter who are terrorized by him and his violent temper. His wife dies of cancer. His daughter is believed killed in a train wreck. His son commits suicide when he is found cheating on a scholarship exam. Add to this that his business is bankrupt and his mistress has left him. Is it any wonder that he goes mad and burns down his huge mansion, which he calls Hatter's Castle.

BRODIE, JAMES

THE SECRET FOUR (1940, GB, Ealing)—**Griffith Jones** is one of three Britishers who avenge the death of a friend killed by traitors and in the process foil an attempt to block the Suez Canal.

BRODIE, JEAN

THE PRIME OF MISS JEAN BRODIE (1969, 20th Century Fox)—**Maggie Smith** won an Oscar for her portrayal of the slightly mad teacher in an upscale girl's private school. She inspires her students, but she attempts to completely dominate them and control what they think. She competes with one girl for the love of a fellow teacher and is responsible for sending another to her death in Spain when Smith convinces her to go and fight on the fascists' side during the Civil War. Smith is ultimately fired and never understands why or how she has failed her charges.

BRODSKY, ALBERT, LUCY VAN PATTEN & CASEY

IRRECONCILABLE DIFFERENCES (1984, Warner Brothers)—When her parents **Ryan O'Neal** and **Shelley Long** become too successful and too busy to have time for each other or her, their daughter **Drew Barrymore** sues them for divorce.

BRODY, CHARLES & MARY

SLEEPWALKERS (1992, Columbia)—**Brian Krause** and his mom **Alice Krige** are incestuous monsters called sleepwalkers. They survive by draining the life force from virginal girls.

BRODY, JIMMY

DUKE OF CHICAGO (1949, Republic)—Ex-boxer **Tom Brown**, now in the publishing business, is forced to come out of retirement to save his company.

BRODY, DR. STEPHANIE

YOUNG DOCTORS IN LOVE (1982, 20th Century Fox)—Intern **Sean Young** has a rare ailment which will claim her life unless she has a special operation that only her lover and fellow intern has the skill to perform. But he's afraid to attempt surgery. Despite this diagnosis, the film is a comedy with a mish-mash of medical jokes and jokers.

BROGAN, MARTIN

HIGH SPIRITS (1988, Tri-Star)—For 300 years ghosts **Liam Neeson** and Daryl Hannah repeat the events of their wedding night. He stabs her to death when she refuses to consummate their marriage. One night American tourist Steve Guttenberg wanders in on this apparition, falls immediately for Hannah and prevents the stabbing. This interruption puts both spirits into a tizzy. Briefly Neeson takes up with Guttenberg's wife Beverly D'Angelo.

BROMFORD, LADY DIANA

HER STRANGE DESIRE (1931, GB, British Int.)—Married to a lord, Lady **Nora Swinburne** tries to seduce chauffeur Laurence Olivier, and when he refuses she has him charged with an assault, of which he is acquitted.

BRONCO BILLY

BRONCO BILLY (1980, Warner Brothers)—**Clint Eastwood** is the owner and main attraction of a small traveling wild west show. He has trouble keeping partners in his knife throwing act until spoiled runaway heiress Sondra Locke shows up.

BRONSON, CANDACE

THE REDHEAD AND THE COWBOY (1950, Paramount)—**Rhonda Fleming** is a Confederate sympathizer who carries a message to irregular rebel troops about a shipment of Union gold. Her companions on her journey are cowboy Glenn Ford, who needs her as a witness to clear him of a murder charge, and Union undercover officer Edmond O'Brien.

BRONSON, CAPT. IRA
HELLSHIP BRONSON (1928, Silent, Gotham)—When sailor **Noah Beery** believes his wife is unfaithful, he leaves her, taking their son with him. Years later he gives his life to save his son, the girl the lad loves and his mother, who Beery discovers was guiltless.

BRONSON, JEAN
THE SPITFIRE (1924, Silent, Associated Exhibitors)—**Betty Blythe** dumps her fiance Elliott Dexter, when he innocently allows a show girl to spend the night in his apartment. Blythe becomes an actress and takes back Dexter when he saves her from the clutches of lecherous producer Lowell Sherman.

BRONSON, RUDY
VAGABOND LOVER (1929, RKO)—In his movie debut, **Rudy Vallee** portrays a small town hick who learns to play a saxaphone through a mail order course, proclaims himself the "Saxaphone King" and gets good notices.

BROOKE, STONY
THE THREE MESQUITEERS (1936, Republic); PALS OF THE SADDLE (1938, Republic); THE TRAIL BLAZERS (1940, Republic); PALS OF THE PECOS (1941, Republic); SADDLEMATES (1941, Republic); THE PHANTOM PLAINSMEN (1942, Republic) - **Robert Livingston**, then **John Wayne**, **Livingston** again and finally **Tom Tyler** appeared as Stony Brooke, one of three modern-day cowboys who have many exciting adventures in the west. The stories are all about the same with the Three Mesquiteers displaying exceptional courage as they bring wrong-doers to justice.

BROOKFIELD, PEGGY
PEGGY (1950, Universal)—**Diana Lynn** is secretly married to an Ohio State football player Rock Hudson, whom her retiring professor father Charles Coburn despises. Unable to bring herself to tell her father of her marriage, she moves to Pasadena with Coburn, where she is elected Rose Bowl Queen. Surprise, surprise, the Big Ten representative in the Rose Bowl is none other that Hudson's Ohio State team.

BROOKINS, PAGE
YOUTH TO YOUTH (1922, Silent, Metro)—Penniless **Cullen Landis** falls in love with Broadway star Billie Dove who has changed her identity when it was falsely reported that she was the mistress of producer Noah Beery. Landis is so impressed with Dove's talent that he asks old friend Beery to come to see her.

BROOKS, AMANDA & STEVE
SWITCH (1991, Warner Brothers)—Ladykiller **Perry King** is murdered by three ladies he's used and abused. Sent to Purgatory, he's given a chance to escape a fiery fate by returning to Earth to find one woman who likes him. The only hitch: he returns as sexy blonde Ellen Barkin, who discovers what it's like to be a sex object.

BROOKS, ANGELA
MADAME SATAN (1930, MGM)—When socialite **Kay Johnson** finds her husband looking elsewhere for romance and excitement, she disguises herself as a femme fatale and wins him back.

BROOKS, CAROLINE
BATHING BEAUTY (1944, MGM)—College swimming instructor **Esther Williams** is loved by goofy songwriter Red Skelton. That's about all the plot necessary to set up some stunning swimming sequences.

BROOKS, CONSTANCE
OUR MISS BROOKS (1956, Warner Brothers)—The popular radio and TV high school English teacher created by **Eve Arden** is still pursuing her shy biology teacher friend, here played by Robert Rockwell. She makes him jealous by tutoring a boy whose father, Don Porter, shows interest in Arden.

BROOKS, DUM-DUM
THE MAN I LOVE (1929, Paramount)—Small-town boxer **Richard Arlen** gets his chance against the champ in a New York bout.

BROOKS, HANNIBAL
HANNIBAL BROOKS (1969, GB, UA)—**Oliver Reed** and Michael J. Pollard escape from a German POW camp into Switzerland riding an elephant.

BROOKS, HELEN
FLYING HOSTESS (1936, Universal)—**Judith Barrett** is probably the first film stewardess forced to land an airplane after the pilot has been put out of commission, but she isn't the last.

BROOKS, MARY
THE BLONDE FROM SINGAPORE (1941, Columbia)—Adventurer **Florence Rice** is unaware that a couple of flyboys are smuggling pearls into the country, hidden in her belongings.

BROOKS, TAMARIND
WHAT A WIDOW (1930, UA)—Widow **Gloria Swanson** finds herself left very well off when her elderly husband dies. She goes on a world-wide shopping spree before finding another man to marry. When things get tough, the tough go shopping.

BROOKS, WALLY
THE LEMON DROP KID (1934, Paramount); (1951, Paramount)—**Lee Tracy** and **Bob Hope** each appear as the Damon Runyan character fond of lemon drops. Both are race track touts, but the story lines differ. In the first, Tracy robs a bank to pay for a specialist for his wife who has a possibly terminal illness. He's caught and she dies. While in prison, his son is being cared for by friends. In 1951, Hope gets in trouble with gambling gangster Lloyd Nolan to whom he has given a bad tip which costs Nolan a bundle of money. He expects Hope to make good his loss. Hope tries to raise the money by running a Christmas scam involving some old "dames."

BROOKS, WILLIAM
HIS MAJESTY, THE AMERICAN (1919, Silent, UA)—In his first film for the company he helped form, **Douglas Fairbanks** discovers that he's in line for a European throne. When he visits the country, he's forced to deal with some conspirators intent on taking over the kingdom.

BROTHER, THE
THE BROTHER FROM ANOTHER PLANET (1984, A-Train)—**Joe Morton**, an alien slave, escapes from his native planet and arrives in New York's Harlem where he's pursued by space bounty hunters.

BROUGHAM, BISHOP HENRY & JULIA
THE BISHOP'S WIFE (1947, RKO)—Episcopalian Bishop **David Niven** is having trouble building a cathedral. When he prays for help, angel Cary Grant is sent, but as far as Niven is concerned, Grant is paying more attention to Niven's lovely wife **Loretta Young**

than to working the miracle that seems necessary. But God works in strange ways.

BROWN, ANDREW

SAILOR OF THE KING (1953, GB, 20th Century Fox)—**Jeffrey Hunter** is the product of a one-night stand between his mother and naval officer Michael Rennie at the time of WWI. During WWII, Hunter is the only survivor when his ship is sunk by the Germans. He comes ashore on a deserted island, where he keeps a German cruiser pinned down until British ships arrive and sink it. The commander of the British fleet is none other than Rennie, although neither is aware of their relationship.

BROWN, ANDY

AMOS 'N' ANDY (1930, Radio)—**Charles Correll** and partner Freeman Gosden appear in their popular radio roles as a loutish, loafing, ladies' man Andy and hard working cab driver Amos. Their humor, once so popular in this country that movie theaters scheduled their showings around the broadcast of the radio show, now is mostly considered embarrassing and racist.

BROWN, BARBARA

MISS NOBODY (1926, Silent, First National)—**Anna Q. Nilsson**, left penniless in California when her father dies in New York, disguises herself as a boy in order to ride the rails back to the Big Apple. She falls in love with Walter Pidgeon, who is not fooled by her disguise. He turns out to be a famous writer who has gone on the bum to get ideas for books.

BROWN, BEATRICE

THE CHORUS KID (1928, Silent, Gotham)—Former chorus girl **Virginia Brown Faire** inherits a fortune and returns to school run by a Thelma Hill whose rich father, Bryant Washburn, Faire would like to catch and does.

BROWN, BERNARD

THE MYSTERY OF BERNARD BROWN (1921, Silent, GB, Stoll)—British novelist **Pardoe Woodman** must prove himself innocent of murdering the fiance of a squire's daughter.

BROWN, BETSY

LITTLE MISS BROADWAY (1938, 20th Century Fox)—**Shirley Temple** is adopted by the owner of a hotel for vaudeville entertainers. There's not much plot, but the film gives her the opportunity to strut her stuff with the likes of George Murphy, Jimmy Durante, Edna May Oliver, Jane Darwell, El Brendel, Donald Meek and Claude Gillingwater.

BROWN, BETTY

LITTLE MISS BROWN (1915, Silent, World)—**Vivian Martin** has a number of comical marital mixups with the guests and employees at a Hartford, Connecticut hotel where she is staying.

BROWN, BILLIE

OUR MODERN MAIDENS (1929, MGM)—**Joan Crawford** and her fiance Douglas Fairbanks, Jr. both fall in love with others before their wedding and then almost make the mistake of going through with the marriage.

BROWN, CASANOVA

CASANOVA BROWN (1944, RKO)—**Gary Cooper** is about to marry Anita Louise when he learns that Teresa Wright whom he married and divorced in haste is pregnant. When the child is born he kidnaps it, but in trying to raise the baby he realizes the child needs a mother —but which woman?

BROWN, CATHERINE

VARIETY GIRL (1947, Paramount)—**Mary Hatcher** is the living embodiment of the abandoned child found in a Pittsburgh theater by John Harris, who with his friends started Variety Clubs to provide help for young theatrical hopefuls, down on their luck. The barest of plots provides the setting for this musical extravaganza, which employed all of the studio's performers.

BROWN, CHRISTY

MY LEFT FOOT (1989, GB, Miramax)—In one of the finest and most moving movies of the eighties, **Daniel Day-Lewis** stuns with his performance as Irish-born author and artist Christy Brown who, although crippled from birth with a severe case of cerebral palsy, is able to carve out a place in life using only his brilliant mind and his left foot. Day-Lewis' performance is memorable, but no more so than that of Hugh O'Connor who plays Christy as a boy. This is no three-handkerchief tearjerker, but a celebration of a remarkable life. There are tears, of course, but tears of joy.

BROWN, CLUNY

CLUNY BROWN (1946, 20th Century Fox)—**Jennifer Jones**, a plumber's niece, enters the service and falls in love with a Czech refugee, Charles Boyer.

BROWN, FATHER

FATHER BROWN, DETECTIVE (1935, Paramount); THE DETECTIVE (1954, GB, Columbia)—**Walter Connolly** and **Alec Guinness** appear as the Catholic priest who is able to recover a sacred cross from a French thief, who is a master of disguise. More important to the cleric is he's able to get the thief to reform.

BROWN, FOXY

FOXY BROWN (1974, American International)—Violence abounds in this story of black nurse **Pam Grier** out to avenge the murder of her lover by drug pushers.

BROWN, GEORGE

MISTER BROWN (1972, Andrieux)—In an all black cast, **Al Stevenson** moves from Louisiana to Los Angeles hoping for a better life. Although he opens a bakery, he can't make it work and is forced to take a job as a garbage collector.

BROWN, HERBIE

BUCK PRIVATES (1941, Universal); BUCK PRIVATES COME HOME (1947, Universal)—**Lou Costello** and his partner Bud Abbott join the army and accidently become heroes. In the sequel, Lou smuggles a little French girl into the U.S. after WWII.

BROWN, DR. HELEN

SEX AND THE SINGLE GIRL (1964, Warner Brothers)—Only the title is preserved from Helen Gurley Brown's best selling non-fiction book. **Natalie Wood** is a naive young virginal psychologist who runs "The International Institute of Advanced Marital and Pre-Marital Studies." Tony Curtis is a reporter who plans to write an expose' of the organization for a scandal magazine but falls in love with Wood instead.

BROWN, HUMDRUM

HUMDRUM BROWN (1918, Silent, Essanay)—Bank teller **Henry B. Walthall** has been engaged for five years to librarian Mary Charleson. They cannot marry because he must support his sister, who is married to an alcoholic brute. The latter sticks-up the bank with the compliance of the bank president, forcing it to fail and costing Walthall his job. He eventually brings the guilty to justice and this reward is enough to care for his sister's family, which allows him to finally marry his sweetheart.

BROWN, JACK

THE TOY (1982, Columbia)—Jackie Gleason is a business man too busy to have any time for his son, but he will buy the boy anything he wants. The child chooses **Richard Pryor** for his new toy and Gleason arranges for it.

BROWN, JOHN, OWEN, OLIVER, FREDERICK, JASON, JOHN, JR. & SALMON

SEVEN ANGRY MEN (1955, Allied Artists)—**Raymond Massey, Jeffrey Hunter, Larry Pennell, John Smith, James Best, Dennis Weaver** and **Guy Williams**. In his second appearance as the fanatic abolitionist (his first was SANTE FE TRAIL in 1940), Massey portrays the domineering man who not only sacrifices his own life but those of his six sons in his bloody struggle to free slaves.

BROWN, JUNE & HORACE JEFFERSON

THE FARMER'S OTHER DAUGHTER (1965, United Producers Releasing Corporation)—In this country comedy, farmer **Harry Lovejoy** lives with his daughter **Judy Pennebaker**, who falls in love with bathing suit salesman Bill Michael, who gets all the local belles to wear his products in a beauty pageant. When the suits disintegrate, Pennebaker has to save Michael from being lynched.

BROWN, MARY

HER WILD OAT (1927, Silent, First National)—**Colleen Moore** attempts to enter an exclusive summer society resort, but this lunch wagon operator is snubbed by the other guests until she disguises herself as a duchess.

BROWN, MARY

NIGHT CLUB QUEEN (1934, GB, Universal)—When lawyer Lewis Casson is paralyzed in an accident, his wife **Mary Clare** supports him by opening a nightclub. When her partner is killed, she's accused of murder and Casson defends her in court.

BROWN, MAX

WHY SHOOT THE TEACHER (1977, Canada, Ambassador)—**Bud Cort** is sent to teach in a one-room school house in a small Saskatchewan town during the Depression. The kids are uncooperative and there's no money to pay his salary. He finds some solace with lonely Samantha Eggar, mother of three of his students.

BROWN, MOLLY

THE UNSINKABLE MOLLY BROWN (1964, MGM)—Modeled on a real character's life, **Debbie Reynolds** is a poor tomboy who marries Harve Presnell, who shortly thereafter strikes it rich. Unable to break into Denver society, Reynolds makes several crossings to Europe to get some culture. On one return trip, she is a survivor of the Titanic sinking, the origin of the moniker in the title. The songs and dances in the musical are not memorable, the best being "I'm Not Down, Yet."

BROWN, MR.

MR. BROWN COMES DOWN THE HILL (1966, GB, Westminster)—**Eric Flynn**, a mysterious preacher, helps a few people before he becomes a martyr to his beliefs.

BROWN, MR.

YES, MR. BROWN (1933, GB, British & Dominions)—**Hartley Power** is Jack Buchanan's boss. Buchanan hopes Power's visit means he will be made a partner. When Buchanan's wife, Margot Grahame, walks out on him, Buchanan recruits his secretary Elsie Randolph to pose as his spouse. Power falls for Randolph, but everything works out in the end.

BROWN, MRS. & JUDY

MRS. BROWN, YOU'VE GOT A LOVELY DAUGHTER (1968, GB, MGM)—The movie is based on the hit song by Herman's Hermits. **Mona Washbourne** is Mrs. Brown and **Sarah Caldwell** is her lovely daughter.

BROWN, PETEY

THE MAN I LOVE (1946, Warner Brothers)—In order to save her brother and sister, **Ida Lupino** takes up with mobster and nightclub owner Robert Alda.

BROWN, ROY

VON RICHTOFEN AND BROWN (1970, UA)—**Don Stroud** is a Canadian pilot fighting on the British side in WWI. He finally shoots down the notorious Red Baron.

BROWN, SALLY

CARELESS LADY (1932, Fox)—Country ugly duckling **Joan Bennett** is transformed into a radiant beauty when she becomes a New York model. She meets John Boles when a speakeasy is raided. She moves to Paris and on a whim pretends she is Boles' wife, calling herself Mrs. Illington. He pursues her, but she tells their friends the marriage is over. A reel later, everything is straightened out.

BROWN, SARAH

GUYS AND DOLLS (1955, MGM)—**Jean Simmons** is a Salvation Army-like lass whom gambler Marlon Brando bets he can get to accompany him to Havana for a weekend. She does, but he falls in love with her and gallantly announces he's lost his wager.

BROWN, SPENCER

MEET THE MAYOR (1938, Times)—**Frank Fay**, an elevator operator in a small town hotel, finds himself running for mayor.

BROWN, STANLEY

I'LL TELL THE WORLD (1934, Universal)—Station manager **Lee Tracy** must come up with some new ways to attract audiences for his failing radio station.

BROWN, THOMAS

DOUBTING THOMAS (1935, 20th Century Fox)—**Will Rogers** makes a fool of himself in a small-town society amateur show, but his comments on the other acts are fun.

BROWN, TOM

BROWN OF HARVARD (1918, Silent, Selig);—(1926, Silent, MGM) - **Tom Moore** in 1918 and **William Haines** in 1926 portrayed the handsome college Don Juan who arrives at Harvard and has a hard time adjusting until he proves his athletic prowess.

BROWN, TOM

TOM BROWN OF CULVER (1932, Universal)—**Tom Brown** gave his name to his character in this movie about an unruly kid becoming an outstanding cadet at a military academy despite discovering that the father he thought had died a hero in WWI was a coward and is alive.

BROWN, TOM

TOM BROWN'S SCHOOLDAYS (1940, RKO); (1951, GB, UA)—**Jimmy Lydon** and **John Howard Davies** each appear as the English boy who must leave his comfortable home to attend a school filled with unruly hooligans. He becomes a man almost in spite of himself and the conditions.

BROWN, TONY

YOU FOR ME (1952, MGM)—**Peter Lawford**, a suave young millionaire playboy, is admitted to the hospital which he supports with his contributions. Nurse Jane Greer is persuaded to play-up to him to keep the donations coming in, even though she's in love with a doctor.

BROWN, WILLIAM

JUST WILLIAM (1939, GB, Associated British); JUST WILLIAM'S LUCK (1948, GB, UA)—**Dicky Lupino** and **William Graham** appear as the mischievous leader of a British boy's gang in films based on stories which had their peak popularity in the forties.

BROWN, WILLIAM

SHERLOCK BROWN (1921, Silent, Metro)—**Bert Lytell** is a bumbling fool who takes a mail order course in crime detection and foils a plot to steal a secret formula.

BROWN, WILLIAM

WILLIAM COMES TO TOWN (1948, GB, UA)—Youngster **William Graham** and his friends invade the Prime Minister's home demanding shorter school days and larger allowances.

BROWNE, FRANCHON

GAY AND DEVILISH (1934, MGM)—In order to save her father's business, **Doris May** agrees to marry a wealthy elderly man. Before the wedding, she meets and falls in love with the man's nephew. From here, you can write the ending.

BROWNE, MARLON

HOW I GOT INTO COLLEGE (1989, 20th Century Fox)—The film falls short of dealing with an important problem, the trauma many high school students and their parents experience when they believe that getting into that one special college is a make-or-break proposition, as far as one's future is concerned. Instead the filmmakers play it for cheap laughs as they follow **Corey Parker's** attempts to win admission to the institution of his choice.

BROWNING, DICK

ALIAS MARY BROWN (1918, Silent, Triangle)—Burglar **Casson Ferguson** disguises himself as a woman but only steals from those who drove his parents to an early grave.

BROWNWELL, LILA *See* **BERNICE LEE**

BRUBAKER

BRUBAKER (1980, 20th Century Fox)—Before taking over as the new warden of a southern prison farm, **Robert Redford** has himself incarcerated for a month so he can learn about the place. He sees inhumanity and brutality at every corner but can't get anyone to care enough to change things.

BRUBAKER, HOWARD

APRIL FOOLS (1969, Jalem/National General)—**Jack Lemmon**, an unhappy New York married man, runs away to Paris with Catherine Deneuve, an equally unhappy married woman.

BRUCE, BERNARD

THREE NUTS IN SEARCH OF A BOLT (1964, Harlequin)—**John Cronin** is one of the three "nuts" whose trauma is acted out by Tommy Noonan for a TV psychiatrist. A nutcracker should be used on this trash.

BRUCE, LENNY

DIRTYMOUTH (1970, Superior); LENNY (1974, UA)—**Bernie Travers** and **Dustin Hoffman** each appear as the comedian whose routines,

considered so offensive at the time that he was constantly arrested, would now be viewed as models of restraint. Dirty mouth comedians of today owe him a lot. That's progress, we suppose.

BRUCE, LT. MICHAEL

LANCER SPY (1937, 20th Century Fox)—When a German spy is captured, the British replace him with their own agent, **George Sanders**, the man's exact double.

BRUCE, VIVIANNE

TWILIGHT WOMAN (1953, GB, Lippert)—**Rene Ray**, the pregnant mistress of a condemned killer, checks into a boarding house unaware that the proprietor runs a black market baby adoption racket.

BRUHN, JACK

DAY OF THE OUTLAW (1959, UA)—**Burl Ives**, the leader of a gang of army renegades, plans to rape the women and kill the men of a western town, until they are confronted by Robert Ryan.

BRULAND

S*P*Y*S (1974, 20th Century Fox)—Trying to recreate the magic of the teaming of **Donald Sutherland** and Elliot Gould in M*A*S*H, 20th Century Fox has the duo portraying bungling U.S. agents who incur the wrath of both the CIA and the KGB.

BRUMMELL, GEORGE BRYAN

BEAU BRUMMELL (1924, Silent, Warner Brothers); (1954, MGM)—**John Barrymore** and **Stewart Granger** both were dashing as the British taste-maker and friend of the Prince of Wales whose arrogance and insolence lost him both the love of his life and the friendship of the future king.

BRUMMELL, LORD ROBERT

JUST A GIGOLO (1931, MGM)—In order to put off possible gold diggers, English Lord **William Haines** poses as a gigolo.

BRUNNE, CECILIE *See* **CIRCE**

BRUSH, VIRGINIA

THE STRAWBERRY BLONDE (1941, Warner Brothers)—Turn-of-the-century **Rita Hayworth** chooses wheeler-dealer Jack Carson over dentist James Cagney. Years later, Cagney finally realizes how shallow Hayworth is and how fortunate he is to have married Olivia de Havilland.

BRYAN, NICK

BAD BOY (1938, GB, Radius)—Ex-con **John Warwick**, trying to reform, rescues his sister from the clutches of his old crime boss.

BRYANT, NANCY

THE PERFECT MATCH (1987, Airfight)—**Jennifer Edwards** is a shy thirtyish college student who answers an ad placed by thirtyish insecure loner Mark McClure. On their first date, they lie about their backgrounds and almost end things right then, but the relationship picks up as they learn more about each other.

BRYANT, PAUL "BEAR"

THE BEAR (1984, Embassy)—**Gary Busey** stars in this admiring biopic of the popular college football coach.

BRYER, LORIE

HE SAID, SHE SAID (1991, Paramount)—In flashback, **Elizabeth Perkins** gives her version of her romance with co-worker Kevin

Bacon. Her version differs markedly from his. Neither version makes for an interesting movie.

BRYSON, SHIRLEY
ONE OF MANY (1917, Silent, Metro)—**Frances Nelson** barters herself to a millionaire for the funds to pay for her mother's operation. When he's had his way with her, he throws her out. She becomes a nightclub dancer, nurses a drunk back to health, marries him and then discovers he's the son of the man who ruined her. The coincidences in movies are something else.

BRZESKA *See* **HENRI GAUDIER**

BUBBLES, CHARLIE
CHARLIE BUBBLES (1968, GB, Regency/Universal)—Successful English writer **Albert Finney** is dissatisfied with his life and returns to his home in the North Country hoping to rekindle something. He discovers as Thomas Wolfe says: "You can't go home again."

BUCHALTER, LOUIS "LEPKE"
LEPKE (1975, Warner Brothers)—**Tony Curtis** portrays the small-time crook who founds Murder Incorporated, a murder-for-pay service.

BUCHANAN
BUCHANAN RIDES ALONE (1958, Columbia)—**Randolph Scott** is thrown into jail in a border town but is set free when he turns the most influential members of the community against each other.

BUCHANAN, JIM
IF YOU COULD ONLY COOK (1936, Columbia)—Automotive engineer **Herbert Marshall** is convinced to pose with Jean Arthur as a butler-cook team in a mobster's mansion.

BUCK
BUCK AND THE PREACHER (1972, Columbia)—Black wagon master **Sidney Poitier** teams with a black con-man preacher to outwit nightriders chasing escaped slaves.

BUCK, JOE
MIDNIGHT COWBOY (1969, UA)—**Jon Voight** comes to New York from Texas with plans of making his fortune by selling his services as a stud to rich women. Instead, he spends a cruel cold winter trying to help tubercular con-man Dustin Hoffman.

BUCKMAN, CANNONBALL
CANNONBALL (1976, New World)—**David Carradine** enters the Trans-American Grand Prix cross country race with a top prize of $100,000. If crashing cars and automobile pile-ups are your thing, the movie is bound to please.

BUCKMAN, CHANCE
HELLFIGHTERS (1968, Universal)—**John Wayne** heads a crew of daring men who travel throughout the world putting out oil fires. The story is based on the life of real oil fire fighter Red Adair.

BUCKMAN, FRANK, GIL, KAREN & LARRY
PARENTHOOD (1989, Universal)—This film explores the problems of being a parent as experienced by **Jason Robards**, his first son **Steve Martin**, the latter's wife **Mary Steenburgen** and his worthless second son **Tom Hulce**.

BUDDWING, MISTER
MISTER BUDDWING (1966, MGM)—When **James Garner** wakes up in Central Park, he has no idea who he is. The movie is a tale of what he finds out about himself. He's not a very interesting fellow.

BUD
THE HORSEPLAYER (1990, Relentless)—Emotionally fragile horseplayer **Brad Dourif** is used by callous painter M.K. Harris and his girlfriend Sammi Davis. It is revealed that Dourif is a paroled killer, who had been abused by his painter father. Uh, oh.

BUD
REPO MAN (1984, Universal)—**Harry Dean Stanton** has the highly unpopular and dangerous job of repossessing automobiles from deadbeats who can't or won't pay their debts.

BUD
URBAN COWBOY (1980, Paramount)—Texas farm boy **John Travolta** moves to Houston to work at an oil refinery. He spends his nights at a honky-tonk nightclub whose biggest attraction is a bucking mechanical bull on which the patrons test their bravery. He meets, marries and deserts Debra Winger, the best thing in this mindless movie.

BUD THE CHUD
C.H.U.D. II: BUD THE C.H.U.D. (1989, Vestron)—C.H.U.D. stands for Cannibalistic Humanoid Underground Dwellers. These creatures live in sewers in New York, coming up at night to munch on U.A.G.D.'s (Unsuspecting Above Ground Dwellers). In the 1984 original, all of the C.H.U.D.s, save one were destroyed. Well, this Bud's for all those dozen or so people who yearned for a sequel.

BUDA, MAX
THE VIPS (1963, GB, MGM)—**Orson Welles** is a movie director who never spends enough time in any country long enough to owe taxes. A delayed departure of a plane from London will cost him a fortune unless he can come up with another way to beat the tax man.

BUDD, BILLY
BILLY BUDD (1962, UA)—**Terence Stamp**, a naive innocent seaman, is sadistically treated by Robert Ryan, the master of arms of his ship. When Stamp accidently kills his tormentor, Captain Peter Ustinov reluctantly hangs the boy for his unpremeditated crime.

BUDDY
BUDDY'S SONG (1991, GB, Castle Premier)—Aging rocker Roger Daltrey turns away from petty crime to guide the burgeoning musical career of his son **Chesney Hawks**. The youngster has been named after Buddy Holly.

BUDDY
THE CIRCUS KID (1928, FBO)—**Frankie Darro**, an orphan and natural acrobat, runs away to join the circus. He learns about life observing a romantic triangle that ends in tragedy.

BUDDY
MASTERS OF MENACE (1990, New Line)—In a spoof of biker films, gang leader **David Rasche** and his group of hairy undesirables hit the road to take the body of a biker (James Belushi in a cameo) home for burial after he has been killed in an accident.

BUELLER, FERRIS
FERRIS BUELLER'S DAY OFF (1986, Orion)—No one in this teenage exploitation picture is very appealing, least of all **Matthew Broderick**, a high school gold brick who easily bamboozles his parents, teachers, girl and best friend when he decides to skip school.

BUFFY
DISORDERLIES (1987, Warner Brothers)—**Darren Robinson** is one of the large orderlies in an unfunny movie. He and two other

hefty bags are hired to care for ailing, elderly Ralph Bellamy, whose relatives hope will die due to incompetent care. Instead he gets better.

BUGS
TROOPERS THREE (1930, Tiffany)—**Roscoe Karns**, Rex Lease and Slim Summerville join the army when they lose their vaudeville jobs with predictable comedy results.

BUHARA
TARZAN AND THE JUNGLE BOY (1968, Paramount)—**Edward Johnson** is a jungle boy rescued by modern Tarzan, Mike Henry.

BULL
THE COWBOY AND THE PRIZEFIGHTER (1950, Eagle Lion)—Journeyman prizefighter **Lou Nova** portrays a crooked boxer who together with his equally dishonest manager is exposed by Red Ryder.

BULL, DR.
DR. BULL (1933, Fox)—What **Will Rogers** doesn't know about medicine would fill volumes but what he knows about people serves his career well.

BULLITT
BULLITT (1968, Warner Brothers)—San Francisco police detective **Steve McQueen** conceals the death of an underworld witness in his care so McQueen can find the killers himself.

BULLIVANT, GRUMPY
GRUMPY (1930, Paramount)—Elderly **Cyril Maude** completely controls all the members of his family and he's not very pleasant about it.

BULLOCK, IRENE
MY MAN GODFREY (1936, Universal); (1957, Universal)—**Carole Lombard** and **June Allyson** each play the younger daughter of a wacky wealthy family who find a "forgotten man" during a scavenger hunt and set him up as the family butler. The girls then proceed to fall in love with the poor unfortunate who turns out to be richer than they are.

BULLOCK, JIM & TOMMY
STEPCHILD (1947, PRC)—When **Tommy Ivo** and **Gregory Marshall** are mistreated by their father's new wife, dear old dad beats a hasty retreat back to their mother.

BULTEEL, ALATHEA
MAN AND MAID (1925, Silent, Metro-Goldwyn)—**Harriet Hammond**, a member of the British Red Cross, saves the life of an officer during WWI. After the war, she finds herself working as his secretary. She's in love with him, but it takes a while for him to reach the same point.

BUMPER
HALLELUJAH, I'M A BUM (1933, UA)—**Al Jolson**, a happy New York tramp, rescues Madge Evans, the mistress of the mayor, when she attempts suicide by jumping in a lake. The experience causes her to lose her memory, and she falls in love with Jolson. He decides to get a job and be worthy of the girl. The mayor who has been a long time friend of Al tells the reformed bum how much he needs Evans. So Jolson brings the mayor and Evans together, and the shock causes her to regain her memory but now with no recollection of her love for Jolson. Al takes it rather well and returns to being a hobo. An unusual feature of the film is that the dialogue is done in rhyming couplets.

BUMSIE, THE GIRL
BOY! WHAT A GIRL (1947, Herald)—In this all-black musical, female impersonator **Tim Moore** helps two shoestring producers raise the money to put on a show.

BUMSTEAD, BLONDIE & DAGWOOD *See* BLONDIE

BUMSTEAD, ELAINE
TOO YOUNG TO MARRY (1931, Warner Brothers)—**Loretta Young** is the only one in her family to take her henpecked father's side. He repays the favor when he gets up the nerve to assert himself with his wife and insist that Young be allowed to marry her poor beau.

BUNN, ELMO
PIZZA MAN (1991, Megalomania)—Cynical pizza deliveryman **Bill Maher** gets dragged into a political conspiracy while trying to collect for a large sausage and anchovy pizza.

BUNN, JENNY
TAKE A GIRL LIKE YOU (1970, GB, Columbia)—Oliver Reed very much wishes to bed naive teacher **Hayley Mills** but gets nowhere with her until she's convinced of his sincerity. Even then she goes to bed with his friend Noel Harrison first. Mills tells Reed she wants him to pursue her with more vigor.

BUNTING, MR.
SALUTE JOHN CITIZEN (1942, GB, British National)—During WWII, elderly clerk **Edward Rigby** must convince his pacifist son that everyone must do their duty. The German Blitz of London is the clincher.

BUNYON, AIKEN "BATTLING"
BATTLING BUNYON (1925, Silent, Crown)—Mechanic **Wesley Barry** needs $1,000 to buy a partnership in a garage and raises it by fighting the lightweight boxing champ.

BURDEN, AMOS
THE COMING OF AMOS (1925, Silent, Cinema Corp. of America)—Australian sheep rancher **Rod La Rocque** fulfills a promise made to his dying mother to visit an uncle who lives on the Riviera. There he attracts Russian princess Jetta Goudal, married to a scoundrel.

BURDEN, STEVE
THE HARD MAN (1957, Columbia)—Texas Ranger **Guy Madison** quits when he develops a reputation for only bringing back dead outlaws. He takes a job as a deputy sheriff and finds himself in the middle of a range war. He's encouraged to kill rancher Lorne Greene by the latter's wife, Valerie French.

BURDON, PETER
MAN ON THE RUN (1949, GB, Pathe)—Army deserter **Derek Farr** innocently becomes involved in a jewel heist.

BURGADE, SAM
THE LAST HARD MEN (1976, 20th Century Fox)—**Charlton Heston**, an ex-lawman, is responsible for sending James Coburn to prison and the latter's wife's death. Coburn escapes, seeking revenge. He kidnaps Heston's daughter, threatening to rape her. This stirs Heston from his retirement.

BURGER, GENERAL
THE ENEMY GENERAL (1960, Columbia)—American officer Van Johnson takes revenge on a German general **John Van Dreelen** who has killed Johnson's girlfriend.

BURGESS, JIM

JIM THE CONQUEROR (1927, Silent, Metropolitan)—**William Boyd** sees pretty Elinor Fair in Rome and New York, but it's not until he gets back home in the West that he discovers she's the daughter of a local ranch owner. She's not much interested in him until he proves his worth in a cattle war.

BURGOYNE, ERICA

YOUNG AND INNOCENT (1938, GB, Gaumont)—Eighteen year old **Nova Pilbeam**, daughter of a police inspector, helps the young man, Derrick de Marney, her father believes has strangled an actress. Pilbeam's faith is proven well-founded in this charming Alfred Hitchcock picture.

BURKE

THE FIGHTING TROOPER (1935, Ambassador)—**Kermit Maynard** makes his first sound movie in the story of a new Mountie who goes undercover to catch the man who killed one of his fellow Mounties.

BURKE, AMY

THE HOODLUM (1919, Silent, First National)—Slum girl **Mary Pickford** falls for a man accused of murder. She gets him off, and he discovers that his heroine is in fact the spoiled granddaughter of a millionaire.

BURKE, DR.

DOCTOR IN TROUBLE (1970, GB, Rank)—**Leslie Phillips** is no Dirk Bogarde, and this is no DOCTOR IN THE HOUSE. Our medical hero finds himself a stowaway on an ocean liner.

BURKE, HARRY, JR.

LET'S GET HARRY (1986, Tri-Star)—**Mark Harmon** is an American in Columbia overseeing the construction of a new pumping station. He is kidnapped by terrorists and when the U.S. government refuses to negotiate with the kidnappers, some of his friends back home hire a mercenary to lead them in a rescue mission. This stinker didn't have a long run in the theaters.

BURKE, JIM

AWAKENING OF JIM BURKE (1935, Columbia)—Tough construction worker **Jack Holt** takes his son's violin from him because he doesn't want a sissy for a son. But the lad (Jimmie Butler) returns to his musical studies after developing his muscles working with Holt.

BURKE, JOHNNY

OH, JOHNNY (1919, Silent, Goldwyn)—Westerner **Louis Bennison** must go east to save his mine. While there, he becomes society's darling.

BURLAP, GENERAL

GHOSTS OF BERKELEY SQUARE (1947, GB, Pathe)—Two British ghosts, **Robert Morley** and Felix Aylmer, are doomed to spend eternity in a London house unless royalty pays a visit.

BURNELL, VICTOR

PRISON WARDEN (1949, Columbia)—Public health officer **Warner Baxter** accepts the post of warden at a prison greatly in need of reform. Among his problems is that his wife Anna Lee helps her ex-lover Harlan Warde break out of the joint.

BURNETT, ANNE

THE PERFECT LADY (1931, GB, Wardour)—When her fiance dumps her for a gold digging French actress, **Moira Lynd** pretends to be a maid and gets a job with her rival. She not only breaks up the romance but finds a more deserving man for herself.

BURNS, HARRY

WHEN HARRY MET SALLY . . . (1989, Columbia)—**Billy Crystal** maintains it is impossible for men and women to be just friends, because men wish to make every woman they meet. Still, he maintains an on-again, off-again friendship with Meg Ryan. But after his divorce and her being dumped by her long-time significant other, sex rears its head. After a time of being unable to make any commitment, Crystal finds staying an entire night with Ryan beats the singles scene and so they are married.

BURNS, JACK

LONELY ARE THE BRAVE (1962, Universal)—Aging cowboy **Kirk Douglas** finds the West has changed and no longer has a place for his kind of rebel. He escapes jail and is tracked by a posse using jeeps and helicopters. He's killed by a truck on a highway when his horse is spooked by the traffic while trying to cross the road.

BURNS, MARY

MARY BURNS, FUGITIVE (1935, Paramount)—**Sylvia Sidney**, the innocent girlfriend of a gangster, is convicted of a crime through circumstantial evidence. Sent to prison, she eventually escapes and meets a new lover, Melvyn Douglas, who hides her until she is cleared of any wrong doing.

BURNS, PAM

THE YOUNG LOVERS (1964, MGM)—Teacher **Sharon Hugeny** is pregnant due to an affair with student Peter Fonda. She decides to have an abortion but can't go through with it. Fonda belatedly decides he must do right by her.

BURNS, ROBERT

THE LOVES OF ROBERT BURNS (1930, GB, British & Dominions)—Operatic tenor **Joseph Hilsop** portrays the Scottish writer in a fictitious and not very interesting account of his life.

BURNS, WALTER

HIS GIRL FRIDAY (1940, Columbia)—Newspaper editor **Cary Grant** tricks his ex-wife and star reporter Rosalind Russell to delay her marriage to Ralph Bellamy and cover one last case—an execution. The movie is a fast-paced, laugh-a-minute black comedy remake of THE FRONT PAGE.

BURROUGHS, WILLIAM

THE WORLD'S CHAMPION (1922, Paramount)—**Wallace Reid** is given a beating by an English lord when he tries to rise above his station and romance a noblewoman. Reid stows away on a ship bound for the U.S. where he becomes the middleweight boxing champion. He returns to England as a celebrity, gives the Lord a pasting and wins the noblewoman.

BURROWS, HENRY

WHAT A MAN! (1944, Monogram)—Clerk **Johnny Downs** has an unexpected visitor to his apartment, fugitive Wanda MacKay who feigns illness to prolong her stay until she reckons it's safe to be seen on the street again. Doesn't bother Downs in the least. He marries her.

BURROWS, LARRY

MR. DESTINY (1990, Buena Vista)—In a sappy clone of IT'S A WONDERFUL LIFE, **James Belushi** is shown the errors of his ways by guardian angel Michael Caine.

BURROWS, DR. RICHARD & JUDY

I LOVE MY WIFE (1970, Universal)—**Elliott Gould** is a successful doctor who throughout his marriage to **Brenda Vaccaro** has many affairs with other women. None of them apparently move him or teach him anything in this mindless sex comedy.

BURT, MYRTLE MCKINLEY

MOTHER WORE TIGHTS (1947, 20th Century Fox)—Turn-of-the-century vaudevillian **Betty Grable** teams up with her husband Dan Dailey. She takes time off to have two daughters. When the girls are old enough, they are sent to an exclusive boarding school, and Grable goes back to the stage. The oldest daughter Mona Freeman is ashamed of how her parents make their living. She learns some humility and an appreciation for Mom and Dad before the picture finishes.

BURTON

ATTORNEY FOR THE DEFENSE (1932, Columbia)—More concerned with his own career than justice, prosecutor **Edmund Lowe** secures the conviction of an innocent man. His conscience bothers him, and he repays his debt by serving as the defense attorney for the convicted man's son in a later murder trial.

BURTON, ALFRED

THE DOUBLE LIFE OF MR. ALFRED BURTON (1919, Silent, GB, Ideal)—Cockney **Kenelm Foss** eats from the tree of life and becomes a poet.

BURTON, BETTY

HER BIG ADVENTURE (1926, Silent, Kerman)—**Grace Diamond**, the beautiful secretary of a wealthy man, receives a $1000 bonus which she decides to spend posing as a countess. She stays at a hotel where Herbert Rawlinson, the son of her employer, who is on the outs with his father is working as a bellboy. The two deceitful people fall in love and then sort things out.

BURTON, ELLEN

WHITE WITCH DOCTOR (1953, 20th Century Fox)—In the Belgian Congo in 1907, missionary nurse **Susan Hayward** hires Robert Mitchum and Walter Slezak to guide her to a feared tribe. Mitchum and Slezak are interested because there are reports of gold in the region. When Mitchum and Hayward fall in love, he has to kill Slezak.

BURTON, FAYE

I WAS A SHOPLIFTER (1950, Universal)—Shoplifter **Mona Freeman** is compelled by a crime syndicate to join their gang of thieves.

BURTON, THOMAS

HER TEMPORARY HUSBAND (1923, Silent, Associated First National)—Sylvia Breamer must marry quickly to receive an inheritance. She chooses a decrepit old invalid not long for this world as her "temporary" husband, but handsome young **Owen Moore** disguises himself as the bridegroom, hoping to share in the inheritance. When Breamer discovers the deception, she decides to make Moore her permanent husband.

BURTON, TOM

THE MAN WHO MADE GOOD (1917, Silent, Triangle)—**Jack Devereaux**, a boy from the country, succeeds because he has true grit.

BUSBY, OLD BILL & YOUNG BILL

OLD BILL AND SON (1940, GB, GFD)—WWI doughboy **Morland Graham** follows his son **John Mills** to France during WWII by joining the Pioneer Corps when no other military branch will take him because of his age.

BUSH, KATHERINE

THE CAREER OF KATHERINE BUSH (1919, Silent, Paramount)—Bored Typist **Catherine Calvert** is not altogether virginal and it shows.

BUSHROD

THOMASINE AND BUSHROD (1974, Columbia)—**Max Julien** and Vonetta McKee form a black Bonnie and Clyde-like outlaw team in Texas in 1911 in a black exploitation-comedy.

BUSTER

PLAY GIRL (1932, Warner Brothers)—Naive **Loretta Young** falls in love and marries a gambler Norman Foster, whose obsession leads them to ruin. Pregnant Young makes a pitiful sight in this Depression melodrama.

BUTCH, ALOYSIUS GROGAN

BUTCH MINDS THE BABY (1942, Universal)—Ex-safecracker **Broderick Crawford** takes a job as a janitor and prevents Virginia Bruce from committing suicide. He then becomes the protector of the girl and her baby.

BUTCHER, THE

THE INDESTRUCTIBLE MAN (1956, Allied Artists)—**Lon Chaney, Jr.**, executed in the gas chamber for a series of murders, is brought back to life and he's looking for revenge.

BUTLER, ALFRED

BATTLING BUTLER (1926, Silent, MGM)—Wealthy **Buster Keaton** falls in love with Sally O'Neil, whose family is unimpressed with his money but take to him when he claims to be a boxer. He later is put to the test. He takes a non-comical beating before triumphing over his brutish adversary.

BUTLER, DAN

UNDER MY SKIN (1950, 20th Century Fox)—**John Garfield**, a crooked jockey, travels through Europe with his young son, looking for work. He's killed after a race for double-crossing a gambler by winning the race.

BUTLER, PEGGY

THE WOMAN ON THE BEACH (1947, RKO)—**Joan Bennett** meets married Robert Ryan on the beach. As he falls in love with her, he learns more of her past. She was something of a gold digger and is responsible for her artist husband's blindness. Ultimately Ryan sees no future with Bennett and returns to his wife.

BUTLER, TERRALL

THE PEACEMAKER (1956, UA)—Former gunslinger turned preacher **James Mitchell** must bring peace to his warring flock of ranchers and farmers.

BUTLEY, BEN

BUTLEY (1974, GB, American Film Theatre)—**Alan Bates**, an English lecturer at a British University College, has personal problems and homosexual affairs.

BUTTERCUP

THE PRINCESS BRIDE (1987, 20th Century Fox)—In a comical fairy tale, **Robin Wright** finds, loses and re-finds true love, but before she can settle down with him she has to survive a plot by an evil prince to use her death as an excuse to declare war on a neighboring country.

BUTTERFLY, JOE
JOE BUTTERFLY (1957, Universal)—**Burgess Meredith** portrays a Japanese native who helps Audie Murphy publish a magazine for American troops occupying Japan just after WWII. It's somewhat like THE TEAHOUSE OF THE AUGUST MOON but not nearly as enjoyable, although Meredith is very good.

BUTTERMEADOW, SIDCUP
THE CARDBOARD CAVALIER (1949, GB, GFD)—In a seventeenth century slapstick comedy, **Sid Field** is a bumbling peasant innocently involved in a plot to kill William Cromwell.

BUTTERS, GEORGE
SOUTH AMERICAN GEORGE (1941, GB, Columbia)—As a favor to his double, **George Formby** poses as a noted South American tenor, so the opera star can both honor his contract and pursue a romance at the same time.

BUTTONS
BUTTONS (1927, Silent, MGM)—Street urchin **Jackie Coogan** is hired as a page boy on a transatlantic ocean liner. He gets in trouble when he tries to persuade the captain that the latter's fiancee is cheating on him.

BYRD, CHICK
THE COMEDY MAN (1964, GB, British Lion)—Middle-aged actor **Kenneth More** becomes wealthy doing television commercials but gives it up to return to the stage in an effort to regain his professional pride.

BYRD, LINK, JR.
COUNTRY BOY (1966, Ambassador)—In a country-western musical, **Pat Boone**, a service station attendant, gets his chance as a singer in Nashville, but is overcome by stage fright. He goes on to be a rock star, performing in an Abraham Lincoln costume, "Ain't That a Shame."

BYRNE, ELLIE
PAINTED PEOPLE (1924, Silent, Associated First National)—**Colleen Moore** and Ben Lyon fulfill their dreams, she to become an actress, he a writer, before discovering their love for each other.

BYRNE, JOHNNIE
NO LOVE FOR JOHNNIE (1961, GB, Rank)—**Peter Finch**, a member of the House of Commons, finds his political career hurt by his relationships with women.

BYRON, LORD
THE BAD LORD BYRON (1949, GB, Triton/GFD)—While dying in Greece, **Dennis Price** dreams that a heavenly court of inquiry has been convened to determine his fate after death.

C

CABALLERO, EL
THE CAVALIER (1928, Tiffany/Stahl)—Masked rider **Richard Talmadge** saves Spanish girl Barbara Bedford from marrying a wealthy man she doesn't love. While in Talmadge's custody and on the run from her father, the two fall in love.

CABOT, HENRY
PASSPORT HUSBAND (1938, 20th Century Fox)—**Stuart Erwin**, a bus boy working in a South American night club, gets involved with a gun moll, which lands him in hot water with her gangster friends.

CABOT, MARY
A WOMAN IS THE JUDGE (1939, Columbia)—**Frieda Inescourt** is the judge in a case in which her long lost daughter is accused of murder. She switches to the other side and successfully defends her child.

CABRINI, MOTHER FRANCES
CITIZEN SAINT (1947, State-Rights)—**Carla Dare** portrays the first American citizen to be named a saint of the Catholic Church. However, she was born in Italy.

CACTUS JACK
THE VILLAIN (1979, Columbia)—In this "live-action cartoon" **Kirk Douglas**, a mean-spirited but incompetent villain, tries to steal money, but is constantly foiled in ways reminiscent of Wile E. Coyote of the Roadrunner cartoons.

CADDIE
CADDIE (1976, Australia)—Sydney barmaid **Helen Morse** is deserted by her husband, leaving her to raise two children by herself during the Depression. Her name is derived from Cadillac, given to her by a pub regular who admires her high performance.

CADE, JOHNNY
THE OUTSIDERS (1983, Warner Brothers)—**Ralph Macchio** is one of a group of kids from the wrong side of the tracks, growing up in Oklahoma in the sixties. The film is based on the popular novel by S.E. Hinton which sold over four million copies.

CADE, RACHEL
THE SINS OF RACHEL CADE (1960, Warner Brothers)—**Angie Dickinson** is an American missionary nurse in the Belgian Congo. Her sins are falling in love with a downed pilot and having his baby out of wedlock.

CADENHOUSE, ARABELLA
ROMANCE AND ARABELLA (1919, Silent, Selznick)—**Constance Talmadge** is the young widow of a stodgy old man. This time around she's looking for romance and takes up with four swains before choosing the most conservative of this bunch for her new husband.

CAESAR, JULIUS
CAESAR AND CLEOPATRA (1946, GB, Two Cities)—JULIUS CAESAR (1950, Avon/Brandon); (1953, MGM); (1970, GB, American International)—In the 1946 film, **Claude Rains** is an aging, wise Caesar. Vivien Leigh appears as a childlike Cleopatra in the George Bernard Shaw story. She fears Rains but expects him to awaken her sexuality like a god. Rains informs her that he's not the one she's looking for, but that soon she will meet Mark Antony. **Harold Tasker, Louis Calhern** and **John Gielgud** appeared as the conqueror in the Shakespearean telling of his death at the hands of Brutus, Cassius and others. Charlton Heston is Mark Antony both in the 1950 and the 1970 films. The 1950 film was an unofficial debut for Heston in pictures. Marlon Brando is Antony in the 1953 picture with Gielgud prepping as Cassius.

CAHILL, CHRIS
PERSONAL BEST (1982, Warner Brothers)—While preparing for the 1980 Olympics, runner **Mariel Hemingway** trains and then has an affair with Patrice Donnelly. Later she takes Scott Glenn to bed.

243

CAHILL, J.D.

CAHILL, UNITED STATES MARSHAL (1973, Warner Brothers)—U.S. Marshal **John Wayne** is shocked to find his own two sons involved in a bank robbery due to his parental neglect. Wayne amends his child-rearing ways and captures the real villain.

CAIGHN, JEFF

DANGEROUS PARTNERS (1945, MGM)—Shady **James Craig** and sexy Signe Hasso break up a spy ring headed by Edmund Gwenn.

CAIN, BOB

JOHNNY APOLLO (1940, 20th Century Fox)—College boy **Tyrone Power** changes his name to Johnny Apollo and becomes a crook after his father Edward Arnold is jailed for embezzlement. Power winds up in the same prison as his father.

CAIN, CAPT.

CAIN'S WAY (1969, M.D.A. Associates)—**Scott Brady's** family has been slaughtered by a gang of Confederate renegades. He tracks them down and cuts off their heads for trophies. They make great pieces for the mantle.

CAIN, "KILLER"

MORE DEAD THAN ALIVE (1968, UA)—After spending nearly 20 years in Yuma Prison, **Clint Walker** is released and goes to great lengths to keep from returning to the life that got him sent to prison.

CAIN, LARRY

CAIN AND MABEL (1936, Warner Brothers)—Heavyweight boxer **Clark Gable** is romantically linked with musical comedy star Marion Davies as a publicity stunt, but when they meet, there are sparks of a real romance.

CAIN, NICK

LUCKY NICK CAIN (1951, 20th Century Fox)—**George Raft** finds himself accused of murder when he gets mixed up with a counterfeiting ring.

CAINE, ANGEL

THE CHOSEN (1978, GB/Italy, AIP)—**Simon Ward** is the anti-Christ who plans to destroy the world by setting off a chain of nuclear explosions. His father Kirk Douglas must stop him.

CAL

CAL (1984, Ireland)—Northern Ireland youth **John Lynch** finds it's not so easy to quit the IRA when he grows weary of the violence.

CALAMITY JANE

CALAMITY JANE AND SAM BASS (1949, Universal); THE TEXAN MEETS CALAMITY JANE (1950, Columbia); CALAMITY JANE (1953, Warner Brothers)—Wicked **Yvonne De Carlo** steals Howard Duff from good girl Dorothy Hart in the 1949 film. Lovely scream queen **Evelyn Ankers** fights for ownership of a saloon and gets help from Texas lawyer James Ellison in the 1950 picture. In 1953, **Doris Day** sings the Academy Award winning "Secret Love" and other songs as she portrays the frontierswoman, scout and stage coach driver—a spicy, sweet and cute gal in buckskin.

CALDWELL, BOYD

SPOILERS OF THE FOREST (1957, Republic)—**Rod Cameron** is a lumberman who falls in love with Vera Ralston. She owns 64,000 acres of prime timberland. My Vera, you look lovely with all those trees in the background.

CALDWELL, DR.

DR. SOCRATES (1935, Warner Brothers)—Strictly by accident small town doctor **Paul Muni** becomes physician for a gang of crooks.

CALHOUN, BEVERLY

BEVERLY OF GRANSTARK (1926, Silent, MGM)—**Marion Davies** impersonates her young cousin who is to be crowned king, but is in danger of being killed before the coronation.

CALHOUN, KING

THE HEART OF A TEXAN (1922, Silent, Steiner)—**Neal Hart**, son of an old Texas ranching family, helps a widow hold her land, on which her scheming ex-foreman has designs.

CALHOUN, PATTI

TWO BLONDES AND A REDHEAD (1947, Columbia)—Chorus girl **June Preisser** is invited into the swell home of a socialite after a show the two have been in closes. Cute Preisser fits in by not fitting in.

CALIGARI

THE CABINET OF CALIGARI (1962, 20th Century Fox)—**Dan O'Herlihy** offers Glynis Johns the hospitality of his creepy old house. He subjects her to torture and humiliations, but she awakens to find it all was a dream.

CALLAGHAN, SLIM

MEET MR. CALLAGHAN (1954, GB, Pinnacle)—Detective **Derrick de Marney** initially suspects that the heir who hired him did in her benefactor, but by shrewd reasoning discovers that it was her fiance who put away the old man.

CALLAHAN, DIEGO "MACHO"

MACHO CALLAHAN (1970, Avco Embassy)—Killer **David Janssen** escapes from a Confederate prison and goes after those responsible for his being there. It's a routine western with all the usual cliches.

CALLAHAN, HANDSOME

SON OF A SAILOR (1933, First National)—**Joe E. Brown** is a sailor who wants nothing to do with battles. Despite this he accidently exposes an espionage ring and wins a promotion when he hooks up with the admiral's daughter.

CALLAHAN, HARRY

DIRTY HARRY (1971, Warner Brothers); THE ENFORCER (1976, Malpaso/Warner Brothers)—Avenging angel San Francisco police detective **Clint Eastwood** is determined to bring in psychopathic killer Andy Robinson, even if he has to give up his badge to do so. It's difficult for Eastwood to keep in mind that the child killer is entitled to his constitutional rights. In the 1976 film, Clint's back taking on all the dirty jobs they can throw his way, including a female partner played by Tyne Daly. He discovers she's not bad for a "girl."

CALLAHAN, MARY

THE BEAUTIFUL CHEAT (1926, Silent, Universal)—Beautiful shop girl **Laura La Plante** is taken to Europe by a press agent and brought back as Maritza Chernovska, a Russian actress who owns the crown jewels.

CALLAHAN, PATTY

HI BEAUTIFUL (1944, Universal)—Shortly after real estate agent **Martha O'Driscoll** allows homeless GI Noah Beery, Jr. to move into a model home, they win the "Happiest GI Couple" contest, even though they aren't married.

CALLAHAN, TIG

FIRED WIFE (1943, Universal)—In order to keep her radio job, **Louise Albritton** must keep her marriage to Robert Paige a secret. This makes him an inviting target for Diana Barrymore.

CALLAN

CALLAN (1975, Cinema National)—British spy **Edward Woodward** is demoted for being too caring and is given the assignment of assassinating a German businessman.

CALLAN, MASTER SGT. ALBERT

THE SERGEANT (1968, Warner Brothers)—Tough army sergeant **Rod Steiger**, stationed at a dreary army base during the fifties, finally acknowledges his homosexual leanings.

CALLAWAY, SMOKY

CALLAWAY WENT THATAWAY (1951, MGM)—**Howard Keel** plays both an old time B Western movie star who is making millions from his oaters on television and the young look-alike who is hired to make public appearances for the aging, fat, alcoholic and mean-spirited actor.

CALLICUT, MAJOR

THE MAN BEHIND THE GUN (1952, Warner Brothers)—**Randolph Scott** goes undercover to foil those who would keep California from joining the Union.

CALLOWAY

VICTIM (1961, GB, Pathe)—**Dennis Price** is one of several British homosexuals who are being blackmailed until Queen's counsel Dirk Bogarde, who although married has homosexual tendencies, risks his career to put an end to their hold on Price.

CALLOWAY, CAM, LIDDY & BUCKY

THOSE CALLOWAYS (1964, Buena Vista)—**Brian Keith**, a Maine trapper, his wife **Vera Miles** and son **Brandon De Wilde** come to the rescue of wild geese endangered by hunters.

CALTHROP, PROF.

THE MAN WHO MADE DIAMONDS (1937, GB, Warner Brothers)—When **J. Fisher White** comes up with a formula for manufacturing diamonds, he's murdered by his assistant. The professor's daughter almost meets the same fate before justice is done.

CALVIN

ORDINARY PEOPLE (1980, Paramount)—**Donald Sutherland**, his wife and son are ordinary people who are forced to come to grips with the repressed tragedy of the death of another son.

CALYPSO JOE

CALYPSO JOE (1957, Allied Artists)—**Herb Jeffries** has little to do with the minuscule plot of this film. He's in it only to sing seven calypso numbers.

CAMARADINO, ANTONIO

MISTER ANTONIO (1929, Tiffany)—Organ grinder **Leo Carillo** falls in love with Virginia Valli, the daughter of a crooked mayor. The politician tries to convince Carillo that the girl has no interest in him, but she straps herself to his donkey and begs him to take her with him.

CAMBER, LORD

LORD CAMBER'S LADIES (1932, GB, British International)—Nobleman **Nigel Bruce** is involved with too many women and tries murder to deal with the situation.

CAMERON

THE STUNT MAN (1980, 20th Century Fox)—Veteran **Steve Railsback**, a fugitive, is shielded from the police by megalomaniacal movie director Peter O'Toole who convinces Railsback to replace a stunt man who has been killed. Railsback finds the movie business is not really glamorous and that O'Toole is willing to sacrifice his stunt man's life to get the shots he wants.

CAMERON, ANDY

THE KID FROM CANADA (1957, GB, British Lion)—Ten-year-old **Christopher Braden**, living in Scotland, doesn't impress the locals with his bragging about his horseman accomplishments back in Canada until he demonstrates his skills while rescuing an endangered shepherd.

CAMERON, DIANA

GAMBLING DAUGHTERS (1941, PRC)—Wealthy **Cecilia Parker** and her sister Gale Storm become involved with gamblers and are implicated in a murder.

CAMERON, JIM

THE SAILOR WHO FELL FROM GRACE WITH THE SEA (1976, GB, Avco Embassy)—**Kris Kristofferson** is castrated by a precocious boy who resents the sailor's affair with his mother.

CAMERON, JOAN

COLLEEN OF THE PINES (1922, Silent, FBO)—When her sister elopes with a trapper and returns with his child, **Jane Novak** pretends the child is hers to protect her sister from the wrath of their father. A mountie whom Novak loves believes her sister has killed the trapper, but all ends well.

CAMERON, JUNE

THE DOCTOR TAKES A WIFE (1940, Columbia)—Young doctor Ray Milland is forced to pretend that he is married to socialite **Loretta Young**

CAMERON, PEGGY

PEGGY (1916, Silent, Triangle)—In her screen debut **Billie Burke** is a free-spirited New York socialite who is whisked away to Scotland where she is to live with a puritanical guardian.

CAMERON, RACHEL

RACHEL, RACHEL (1968, Warner Brothers)—Middle-aged spinster schoolteacher **Joanne Woodward** believes romance has passed her by until an old friend re-enters her life. Woodward's husband Paul Newman makes his directorial debut with the film.

CAMILLA

THE GUARDIAN (1990, Universal)—When a young yuppie couple hires **Jenny Seagrove** to be their baby's nanny, audiences know just by looking at her that it's a mistake. Indeed it is; she worships a nearby tree, and her tree loves baby food.

CAMILLE

CAMILLE (1916, Silent, World); (1921, Silent, Metro); (1927, Silent, First National); (1937, MGM)—**Clara Kimball Young, Nazimova, Norma Talmadge** and **Greta Garbo** each appeared as Marguerite Gautier known as Dame aux Camelias in the Dumas story of a coquette, the kept woman of rich men, who falls in love with a young man unaware of her past history. She gives him up rather than ruin his career but when she contracts tuberculosis she dies in his arms.

CAMMARERI, RONNY

MOONSTRUCK (1987, MGM/UA)—**Nicolas Cage** is the weakest link in this delightful romantic comedy. He is the angry baker who falls in love with his brother's fiancee, Cher. She catches his passion and their problem is how to break the news to her fiance when he returns from a trip to Italy to see his ailing mother.

CAMONTE, TONY
SCARFACE (1932, UA)—**Paul Muni** is delightfully mean and nasty in this gripping drama, loosely based on the life of Chicago's Al Capone. Muni stars as a scarfaced gunman who seizes control of the mob from his mentor and rules the South Side of Chicago with guns and violence. He also seemingly has an incestuous yearning for his sister Ann Dvorak.

CAMPBELL, ANSON
CAPTAIN SALVATION (1927, Silent, MGM)—Recently graduated from a theological seminary, **Lars Hanson** comes to the defense of a fallen woman but his efforts are rejected by the puritanical villagers of his New England coastal town. He leaves on a prison ship and finds the pitiful girl who he convinces never to revert to her former life. When the captain makes advances, she kills herself rather than submit. Hanson battles the captain, takes over the ship, converts the convicts and sails home to marry his sweetheart.

CAMPBELL, BRUCE
CAMPBELL'S KINGDOM (1957, GB, Rank)—**Dirk Bogarde** inherits a valley which his grandfather believed contained oil. Bogarde has to fight off the efforts of an unscrupulous contractor to flood the valley to power a hyrdo-electric dam.

CAMPBELL, MRS. CARLA
BUONA SERA, MRS. CAMPBELL (1968, UA)—Italian **Gina Lollobrigida** has conned money from three ex-GIs, each of whom believes he fathered her child during WWII. All three show up with their wives in Italy for a reunion, expecting to see their love child.

CAMPBELL, DAVID
PERFECT STRANGERS (1950, Warner Brothers)—Jurors of a murder case **Dennis Morgan** and Ginger Rogers fall in love.

CAMPBELL, DONALD
THE BAY BOY (1985, Orion)—**Kiefer Sutherland** stars in a very unremarkable portrait of the coming of age of a teen in rural Canada in the thirites.

CAMPBELL, DRURY
THE WINTER PEOPLE (1989, Columbia)—**Mitchell Ryan** is the stern patriarch of an Appalachian family during the Depression. When his son is killed, and the guilt seems to lie at the door-steps of Kelly McGillis, her family, and her new lover Kurt Russell, Ryan demands revenge. To prevent bloodshed, McGillis presents Ryan with her baby and the news that the dead man is the child's father. Ultimately, Ryan returns the baby to the heartbroken McGillis.

CAMPBELL, JOHN
I CHEATED THE LAW (1949, 20th Century Fox)—Attorney **Tom Conway** wins an acquittal on a murder charge for guilty mobster Steve Brodie. He then cleverly traps Brodie into confessing to his crimes.

CAMPBELL, LISSA
A LADY SURRENDERS (1944, GB, Gainsborough)—Dying concert pianist **Margaret Lockwood** falls in love with pilot Stewart Granger who is losing his sight. The film is also called LOVE STORY.

CAMPBELL, DR. ROBERT
MEDICINE MAN (1992, Hollywood Pictures)—**Sean Connery** believes he's isolated a cure for cancer in a strain of wildflowers that grow only 100 feet up in the towering tropical trees near his jungle outpost. Research scientist Lorraine Bracco arrives and when they are not arguing, they struggle to replicate Connery's results before civilization arrives and destroys the jungle and the cancer cure.

CAMPBELL, WAYNE
WAYNE'S WORLD (1992, Paramount)—**Mike Myers'** performance as a heavy metal teen fronting a cable access TV show in Aurora, Illinois with his zany sidekick Dana Carvey will appeal to everyone -Not!

CAMPBELL, WILL
LEGALLY DEAD (1923, Silent, Universal)—Writer **Milton Sills** believes that most executed cons are innocent. He breaks up a robbery in which a cop is killed, but he's arrested for the crime, sentenced to death, hanged and declared legally dead. But when he is proven innocent, a doctor brings him back to life.

CANADA NELL *See* JUDITH GILBERT

CANDELL, EDDIE
THE MOST DANGEROUS MAN ALIVE (1961, Columbia)—When escaped convict **Ron Randell** is caught in a chemical explosion he is transformed into an "iron man" which makes him impervious to harm as he seeks revenge on his enemies. Well, he does rust a bit.

CANDIDA
A NICE GIRL LIKE ME (1969, GB, Avco Embassy)—**Barbara Ferris** needs to learn about birth control as she becomes pregnant by two different men (need we say not at the same time). Her parents attempt to force her to marry her stuffy cousin, but she settles on Harry Andrews, her father's caretaker.

CANDIDE, JONAS
THE TRAVELLING EXECUTIONER (1970, MGM)—In this period piece black comedy, **Stacy Keach** travels around the country with his own electric chair, offering a service formerly handled by hangmen. He falls in love with one of his prospective clients, which leads him to be forcefully invited to sit in his own malfunctioning death chair.

CANDY
CANDY (1968, Italy/France, Cinerama)—**Ewa Aulin** is the incredibly naive and innocent young sex-pot lusted after by an alcoholic poet, a Mexican gardener, a bizarre guru, a hunchback and even her own father and uncle.

CANDY, CLIVE
COLONEL BLIMP (1945, GB, The Archers)—The film details the life and romances of stuffy British officer **Roger Livesey** from his days as a dashing young lieutenant in the Boer Wars of 1902 to 1943 when he tries to be of some use at old age during the London Blitz. Deborah Kerr plays the three loves of his life, none of whom he succeeds in winning.

CANELLI, MIKE
THE MAN FROM CAIRO (1953, Lippert)—In a corny crime story **George Raft** is in Algeria where he's mistaken for the man who French Intelligence has engaged to locate $100 million in gold, which was hidden in the desert during the WWII.

CANFIELD, PAULA
NINE GIRLS (1944, Columbia)—Mean and manipulative sorority girl **Anita Louise** is murdered and at least eight of her sorority sisters have motives for killing her.

CANNING, VISCOUNT

HER LORD AND MASTER (1921, Silent, Vitagraph)—**Holmes Herbert** marries Alice Joyce, the spoiled daughter of an American railroad magnate and takes her to his home in England where they clash over their different notions of social propriety.

CANNON, CHARLES

TEENAGE MONSTER (1958, Marquette-Howco)—**Gilbert Perkins**, hit by a meteor, is turned into a hairy monster who goes on a murderous rage, abetted by his protective mother. Come on, Ma, kids have to go out on their own sometime.

CANTERBURY, HAROLD

MEN'S CLUB (1986, Paramount)—In a movie that didn't have much of a shelf life, **Frank Langella** is one of seven men who start an encounter group. The film was in and out of theaters so fast that most people had to catch it on cable TV.

CANTERVILLE GHOST

THE CANTERVILLE GHOST (1944, MGM)—Ghost **Charles Laughton** is forced to walk the passageways of his castle until one of his descendants proves himself a hero to make up for Laughton's cowardice 300 years earlier.

CANTFIELD, BOB

THE COLLEGE HERO (1927, Silent, Columbia)—College freshman **Bobby Agnew** becomes a football star but suffers an injury caused by his roommate who cares for Pauline Garon, the same girl as does Agnew. Despite the injury, he scores the winning touchdown in the big game.

CANTILLON, MARY

MY AMERICAN WIFE (1936, Paramount)—**Ann Sothern** is introduced to a handsome count Francis Lederer by her eccentric aunt. At first Sothern's retired cowboy father doesn't cotton to Lederer, but changes his mind when he discovers the nobleman is an outstanding horseman.

CANTOR, EDDIE

THE EDDIE CANTOR STORY (1953, Warner Brothers)—Warner Brothers hoped that this film starring **Keefe Brasselle** as "Old Saucer Eyes" would be as big a success as was THE JOLSON STORY. It was not.

CANTROW, LENNY

THE HEARTBREAK KID (1972, 20th Century Fox)—While in Florida on his honeymoon with Jeannie Berlin, **Charles Grodin** falls in love with Cybill Shepherd. He is determined to divorce his wife and win the approval of Shepherd and her father to marry her. Surprisingly he is successful.

CANTY, TOM

THE PRINCE AND THE PAUPER (1915, Silent, Famous Players) (1937, Warner Brothers)—**Marguerite Clark** and **Billy Mauch** star as the London ragamuffin who is the exact double of Prince Edward, son of Henry VIII. The two boys exchange places, with Canty almost crowned king and the real prince being brutalized by Canty's criminal father. In the silent movie, Clark also played the prince while in 1937, Mauch's twin brother Bobby played the royal double.

CAPELLO, JEREMY

MY BEST FRIEND IS A VAMPIRE (1988, Kings Road)—When teenage delivery boy **Robert Sean Leonard** drops some groceries off at the house of sexy vampire Cecilia Peck, she seduces him. He departs with fangs and a taste for blood. It's more a comedy than a horror flick.

CAP'N ABE

THE CAPTAIN'S CAPTAIN (1919, Silent, Vitagraph)—**Arthur Donaldson** is a captain who has never been to sea. He runs a store in a fisherman's village. In order to impress his customers, he invents a brother who is a pirate. He is ultimately forced to disappear and show up as his brother.

CAPONE, AL

AL CAPONE (1959, Allied Artists); CAPONE (1975, 20th Century Fox)—**Rod Steiger** rises from being a henchman for gang leader Big Jim Colosimo, whom he murders, to become the head of Chicago's South Side mob. **Ben Gazzara** also portrays the celebrity gangster, whose troubles with Chicago's North Side gangs lead to war in the streets. Capone is sent to prison for income tax evasion and on his release dies a crazy man, a result of untreated syphilis.

CAPTAIN

RIDERS OF THE STORM (1988, Miramax)—In a film originally entitled THE AMERICAN WAY, **Dennis Hopper** is the leader of a group of wacked-out Vietnam veterans, pledged to preventing the American government from conning the public into another Vietnam.

CAPTAIN APACHE

CAPTAIN APACHE (1971, GB, Scotia International)—Indian Union officer **Lee Van Cleef** is assigned the investigation of the murder of an Indian commissioner. He discovers a plot to start an Indian war by having President Grant assassinated by men disguised as Indians.

CAPTAIN APPLEJACK

CAPTAIN APPLEJACK (1931, Warner Brothers)—Meek **John Halliday** finds the needed courage when his home is invaded by robbers after his buried treasure.

CAPTAIN BILL

CAPTAIN BILL (1935, GB, Fuller)—**Leslie Fuller** is a bargeman who helps teacher Judy Kelly escape from a gang of rumrunners chasing her.

CAPTAIN BILL

MY BOY (1922, Silent, Associated First National)—Impoverished old sea captain **Claude Gillingwater** takes in immigrant boy Jackie Coogan, whose mother died on the ocean trip from Europe, forcing him to escape from Ellis Island and risk being sent back home.

CAPTAIN CALAMITY

CAPTAIN CALAMITY (1936, Grand National)—When South Seas denizen **George Houston** invents a phony fortune, every cutthroat in the region is after it, but he beats them all.

CAPTAIN CHINA

CAPTAIN CHINA (1949, Paramount)—**John Payne** loses his command when he piles his ship up on reefs while in his cups over losing his girlfriend. He's able to clear himself of responsibility.

CAPTAIN COURTESY

CAPTAIN COURTESY (1915, Silent, Bosworth)—In California in 1840, American **Dustin Farnum's** parents are killed by Mexicans, so he takes the name of Captain Courtesy and robs and harasses Mexicans at every opportunity. It's not part of the "Good Neighbor" policy.

CAPTAIN FLY-BY-NIGHT

CAPTAIN FLY-BY-NIGHT (1922, Silent, R-C Pictures)—Notorious highwayman **Francis McDonald** escapes pursuing soldiers by posing as a victim of his robbery, Captain Fly-By-Night, but is exposed by a government agent doing the same thing.

CARAFFA, AUGUSTINO

STRICTLY DISHONORABLE (1951, MGM)—When Janet Leigh falls in love with opera star and lady's man **Ezio Pinza**, they find themselves in a compromising position and he marries her to protect her reputation.

CARBERRY, LETITIA

TISH (1942, MGM)—Old maids **Marjorie Main**, Zasu Pitts and Aline MacMahon adopt an orphan with comical results—well, not as comical as the studio had hoped.

CARDEN, BILL

TOO MANY HUSBANDS (1940, Columbia)—**Fred MacMurray**, supposedly drowned, shows up after his wife has remarried. The familiar plot was rehashed in 1955 in THREE FOR THE SHOW.

CARDIGAN, MICHAEL

CARDIGAN (1922, Silent, American Releasing Corp.)—Two years before the American Revolution, **William Collier, Jr.**, an unwilling subject of King George III, falls in love with the English governor's ward, Silver Heels (Betty Carpenter), and joins the Minutemen to fight the British at Lexington and Concord.

CARDIGAN, TOM

STATE'S ATTORNEY (1932, RKO)—This film is worth seeing for **John Barrymore's** performance as an ambitious and flamboyant lawyer but not for the story.

CARDIN, DR. JOSEPH

THESE THREE (1936, UA)—When Lillian Hellman was forced to revise her play, "The Children's Hour," eliminating the lesbian angle, she substituted an accusation of heterosexual misbehavior involving two schoolmistresses Merle Oberon and Miriam Hopkins, and **Joel McCrea** made by a malicious schoolgirl, brilliantly played by Bonita Granville.

CARDINAL, GUS

WHY ME? (1990, Triumph)—In a frantic caper comedy, French star **Christopher Lambert** is a charming con man and expert safecracker. He steals a cursed ruby, which makes him the target of police, the Turkish government and nutty American terrorists.

CARDWELL, PATRICIA

100 MEN AND A GIRL (1937, Universal)—**Deanna Durbin** comes up with a keen idea during the Depression. She convinces conductor Leopold Stokowski to form an orchestra of unemployed musicians like her father Adolphe Menjou. Incidentally, she is the featured soloist.

CAREWE, LOLA

NIGHT CLUB LADY (1932, Columbia)—**Mayo Methot**, Humphrey Bogart's battling mate during their marriage, is a night club hostess who is murdered.

CAREY, DR.

THE PHYSICIAN (1928, GB, Silent, Gaumont)—Temperance lecturer **Ian Hunter** is really a secret drinker and to his fiancee's shock, has a bastard son. Physician, heal thy self.

CAREY, GEORGE See LARRY WILSON

CAREY, MRS., NANCY & KITTY

MOTHER CAREY'S CHICKENS (1938, RKO)—**Fay Bainter, Anne Shirley** and **Ruby Keeler** portray a widow and her two daughters who struggle to keep their home through great adversities.

CAREY, PETER

THE CAREY TREATMENT (1972, MGM)—Pathologist **James Coburn** goes to Boston where he uses his skills to prove that fellow doctor, James Hong, is innocent of an abortion-manslaughter death. He also finds the real butcher.

CAREY, SCOTT

THE INCREDIBLE SHRINKING MAN (1957, Universal)—After coming in contact with a mysterious fog, **Grant Williams** discovers he is shrinking. The special effects are excellent.

CAREY, WEBSTER

CAPTAIN CAREY U.S.A. (1950, Paramount)—Other than giving the world Nat King Cole's song "Mona Lisa," this film with **Alan Ladd** as a former O.S.S. officer tracking down a war time traitor has little to recommend it.

CARL

THE ILLUSTRATED MAN (1969, Warner Brothers)—In this Ray Bradbury story, each of the tattoos which almost completely cover **Rod Steiger's** body tells a strange futuristic story of violence and death. Otherworld witch Clare Bloom exchanges sexual favors with Steiger for the right to cover his body with the tattoos.

CARL

THE QUIET GUN (1957, 20th Century Fox)—Sheriff **Forrest Tucker** must deal with land grabbers in this routine western. He defies his town by arresting an entire lynch mob.

CARLA

GYPSY WILDCAT (1944, Universal)—**Maria Montez**, the best-looking, no-talent actress to grace the silver screen, gives her usual low-notch performance as a Transylvanian gypsy who is really a countess.

CARLETON, DICK

HIS LAST RACE (1923, Silent, Goldstone)—When his suit is rejected, **Rex "Snowy" Baker** seeks solace in the woods where he starts a health resort. Years later his former sweetheart shows up, now a widow with a sickly child. Baker enters a horse race to win the money so he can marry her. After numerous complications he wins the race and her hand.

CARLETON, EARL

MAN ON FIRE (1957, MGM)—When **Bing Crosby's** wife divorces him, he won't turn over custody of their son as required by the court.

CARLIN, JESS

THE TEXICAN (1966, Columbia)—Ex-lawman **Audie Murphy** returns from exile to a Texas frontier town, ruled by Broderick Crawford, to avenge the death of his brother.

CARLISLE, BETTY

MASKED ANGEL (1928, GB, Silent, Chadwick)—Night club hostess **Betty Compson** flees from an un-justified charge of murder, taking refuge in a hospital where she falls in love with a blind soldier whom she nurses back to health.

CARLOS

COCK O' THE WALK (1930, Sono-Art/World-Wide)—Whether the title is an apt description of **Joseph Schildkraut**, who preys on lonely wives of wealthy men, or not is questionable.

CARLOTTA

THE THREE SISTERS (1930, Fox)—**Joyce Compton** is one of three girls who discover that the money they have been sending to their mother in Italy finds its way into the hands of another. They go back to the old country to put things right.

CARLOTTA, EMPRESS

THE MAD EMPRESS (1940, Warner Brothers)—**Medea Novara** portrays Maximilian's empress in Mexico. According to this film, the royal pair are innocent dupes of Napoleon III. They believed the Mexican people welcomed their rule.

CARLSON, CRAIG

PLEASE MURDER ME (1956, Distributors Corp. of America)—Lawyer **Raymond Burr** (no, not Perry Mason), defends Angela Lansbury, accused of murder, at a great cost to himself.

CARLSON, GILDA

SAFE IN HELL (1931, Warner Brothers)—Tough call girl **Dorothy Mackaill** believes she's killed one of her tricks after a fight which led to a fire. She escapes to an island where all the seedy-looking male characters put the make on her. The guy she thought she killed shows up, and this time she gets the job done.

CARLSON, PAT

THE GIRL (1987, GB, Lux/Shapiro)—**Clare Powney** portrays a fourteen-year-old Lolita type who seduces respected lawyer Franco Nero. He takes her away to an island where they do nothing but make love all day, all night, inside and outside. When a blackmailer threatens their bliss, Powney calmly kills him. She later will dispatch Nero as well. That's the trouble with kids nowadays—moody!

CARLSON, RICK

LIFEGUARD (1976, Paramount)—**Sam Elliott** is surprisingly enjoyable in this modest picture about an aging lifeguard who wonders if he shouldn't seek a new way of making a living.

CARLSSON, DORY

A KISS BEFORE DYING (1991, Universal)—**Sean Young**, the daughter of industrial magnate Max Von Sydow, meets Matt Dillon at college. When she announces that she's pregnant, he gives her a kiss and shoves her off the top of a building.

CARLTON, MARY

THE GIRL FROM CHICAGO (1927, Silent, Warner Brothers)—Southern **Myrna Loy** arrives in New York to clear her brother of murder, by passing herself off as a gun moll from Chicago. It works but it's a near thing for her, her brother and an undercover cop.

CARLTON-BROWNE, CARDOGEN DE VERE

MAN IN A COCKED HAT (1960, GB, Boulting Bros.)—When the British re-discover the island of Gallardia, which had been forgotten for 50 years, bumbling Foreign Service officer **Terry-Thomas** is put in charge.

CARLYLE, ELSA

THE CHEAT (1931, Paramount)—**Tallulah Bankhead** falls into the clutches of a fake Indian prince. When she attempts to repay the money she owes him, he makes it clear that he wishes a more personal payment. When she refuses, he brands her a cheat with the family crest. She shoots him. Her husband arrives in time to take the rap, but is acquitted when in the courtroom she reveals the brand on her shoulder.

CARLYON, RICHARD

THE SMUGGLERS (1948, GB, Eagle-Lion)—Early in the nineteenth century, cruel smuggler chief **Michael Redgrave** takes in orphan Richard Attenborough. The latter repays his mean mentor by refusing to name Redgrave when he gives evidence against the smugglers at their trial.

CARMELITA

THE GIRL FROM MEXICO (1939, RKO)—In the first of a series of movies in which **Lupe Velez** would be billed as the "Mexican Spitfire," she is a south-of-the-border entertainer hired to star on a radio show. She's a smash acting as a sexy stereotype, a fiery Mexican woman.

CARMELITA

THE SPITFIRE OF SEVILLE (1919, Silent, Universal)—Mexican girl **Hedda Nova** plays havoc with the lives of several young men before settling on one.

CARMEN

CARMEN (1915, Silent, Paramount); (1931, GB, BIP/Wardour)—**Geraldine Farrar** and **Marguerite Namara** star as the totally amoral girl willing to sell herself to the highest bidder. She so captivates soldier Don Juan (Wallace Reid) that he kills her when he finds he can't have her all to himself.

CARMILLA *See* **MIRCALLA**

CARMODY, IDA, PADDY & SEAN

THE SUNDOWNERS (1960, Warner Brothers)—Irish rovers, **Deborah Kerr, Robert Mitchum** and **Michael Anderson, Jr.** travel the Australia outback, taking whatever work comes their way. Despite having very little, they share what they have with whomever they meet and seem reasonably happy.

CARMODY, LEN

KELLY AND ME (1957, Universal)—Struggling song-and-dance man **Van Johnson** gains success when his German shepherd, Kelly, becomes a silent screen star.

CARNATION KID

CARNATION KID (1929, Paramount)—Hit man **Frances McDonald** is sent by a vice lord to murder an honest district attorney. On the way to the job, McDonald is recognized because of his ever present carnation. He forces salesman Douglas MacLean to exchange clothes with him and naturally MacLean is mistaken for the killer.

CARNEY, JUD

JUD (1971, Duque/Maron)—This story of the difficult adjustments facing Vietnam veteran **Joseph Kaufmann** when he returns home is no THE BEST YEARS OF OUR LIVES.

CAROL

BOB AND CAROL AND TED AND ALICE (1969, Columbia)—**Natalie Wood** and hubby Robert Culp, pot-smoking believers in open marriage, try to introduce their way of life to their more conservative friends Elliot Gould and Dyan Cannon.

CAROL

EASY TO LOVE (1953, MGM)—Except for the spectacular Cypress Gardens water ballets, this forgettable musical starring **Esther**

Williams can easily be skipped. As Williams once observed, all they ever changed for her movies were her suits and the water.

CAROL
FREE, BLONDE AND 21 (1940, 20th Century Fox)—Dedicated artist **Lynn Bari**, a resident of a New York hotel for women, winds up marrying a millionaire.

CAROL
HER HUSBAND'S SECRETARY (1937, First National/Warner Brothers)—**Jean Muir** feels her husband Warren Hull pays more attention to his secretary Beverly Roberts than to her. The film lasts sixty-one minutes, but the story is only enough for about ten.

CAROL
LADIES OF WASHINGTON (1944, 20th Century Fox)—Government girl **Trudy Marshall** lives in a Washington apartment house occupied by other women like herself. In a city in which the odds of women to men is about six-to-one, she finds herself a doctor to take her away from it all.

CAROL
THE PLEASURE LOVERS (1964, GB, Butchers)—Nightwatchman's daughter **Leigh Madison** is abducted by Reed De Rouen, the American mastermind of an English bank robbery. Her presence at their hide-out causes considerable tension among De Rouen's unstable accomplices. De Rouen comes to feel affection for Madison and ultimately sacrifices his life to save hers.

CAROL
THE STEPFORD WIVES (1975, Columbia)—**Nanette Newman** seems a perfect wife, totally devoted to her husband and children—so newcomer to Stepford, Connecticut, Katharine Ross knows something must be seriously wrong with her. Perfect wives and in Connecticut yet—there's something rotten here, that's for sure.

CAROL
THE VENGEANCE OF SHE (1968, GB, Hammer-Seven Arts)—**Olinka Berova** is possessed by the spirit of long-dead Queen Ayesha, "She who must be obeyed." Perhaps Berova could use an exorcist.

CAROL
WOMAN'S WORLD (1954, 20th Century Fox)—Ambitious and manipulative **Arlene Dahl** believes that her sexual flirtations with her husband Van Heflin's superiors have advanced his career, but it's only when Heflin dumps her that the president of his company appoints Van to be the new general manager.

CAROLINA
THE TIGER AND THE PUSSYCAT (1967, Embassy)—In a modest sex-comedy, promiscuous American **Ann-Margret** has a wild affair with middle-aged Italian Vittorio Gassman and ages him.

CAROLINE
HOW COULD YOU CAROLINE? (1918, Silent, Pathe)—**Bessie Love**, looking for a soul-mate, first settles on a rough-neck chauffeur with taking ways. She finally returns to her childhood sweetheart, but causes a bit of trouble at his bachelor's party where she poses as the evening's entertainment.

CAROLINE
WAITING FOR CAROLINE (1969, Canada, National Film Board)—**Alexandra Stewart** is fought over by several men but her heart belongs to daddy.

CAROLYN
CAROLYN OF THE CORNERS (1919, Silent, Pathe)—**Bessie Love** is an orphaned child who together with her dog brings happiness wherever she goes, and she gets around quite a bit for such a young tyke.

CARR, BOBBY
THE COMPULSORY WIFE (1937, GB, Warner Brothers)—**Joyce Kirby** is forced to spend the night with Henry Kendall in a remote cottage when their clothes are stolen.

CARR, DIANE "K.C."
KANSAS CITY BOMBER (1972, MGM)—**Raquel Welch** is the new kid in town, well on her way to replacing Helen Kallianotes as the roller derby queen. The movie is to drama as roller derby is to sport.

CARR, JANET
TEENAGE BAD GIRL (1959, GB, Everest/DCA)—British teenager **Sylvia Sims** drifts into life on the seamy side.

CARR, JEFF
THE MAN FROM BITTER RIDGE (1955, Universal)—In an extremely dated plot of cattleman versus homesteaders **Lex Barker** does not distinguish himself.

CARR, MARTHA
THREE BLONDES IN HIS LIFE (1961, Cinema Associates)—**Valerie Porter** is one of the women in the life of a recently deceased insurance investigator. Did she help get him that way?

CARR, MILDRED
HER OWN MONEY (1922, Silent, Paramount)—**Ethel Clayton**, a capable businesswoman, marries an extravagant and dictatorial real estate broker. When he goes into debt, Clayton has to find a way to help him without harming his fragile pride.

CARRAL, PEPE
THE MAGNIFICENT SEVEN RIDE (1972, UA)—**Pedro Armendariz, Jr.**, the son of the marvelous Mexican actor, is one of five tough convicts who team up with Lee Van Cleef (who has replaced Yul Brynner as Chris), and newspaper reporter Michael Callan to track down bandits who have kidnapped a group of widowed women.

CARRIE
THE GIRL IN LOVER'S LANE (1960, Filmgroup)—When small town girl **Joyce Meadows** is murdered in lover's lane, itinerant Brett Halsey is suspected of the crime, but the killer turns out to be half-witted Jack Elam.

CARROLL, ALICE
FUGITIVES (1929, Silent, Fox)—Nightclub singer **Madge Bellamy** is accused of murdering her boss. She is sent to prison by young D.A. Don Terry, who then turns around, helps her escape and proves her innocence.

CARROLL, EARL
EARL CARROLL'S VANITIES (1945, Republic)—Broadway entrepreneur **Otto Kruger** puts on a slightly naughty extravaganza starring Ruritanian princess Constance Moore.

CARROLL, GLORIA
LUCKY LEGS (1942, Columbia)—At the risk of being labeled sexists, we note that **Jinx Falkenberg's** legs are the only thing this stupid, would-be comedy about an embezzler's will has to stand on.

CARROLL, IRIS

THE WOMAN WHO DID NOT CARE (1927, Silent, Lumis)—**Lillyan Tashman** hates men, having suffered all her life at their hands. She decides to turn the tables on them and make them suffer, wanting her and not being able to have her. This goes on until she finds the right man, a misogynist sea captain.

CARROLL, KITTY

THE INVISIBLE WOMAN (1941, Universal)—After crazy professor John Barrymore discovers the secret of invisibility, model **Virginia Bruce** uses it to take revenge on her slave-driving ex-boss.

CARROLL, LINDA

I CAN'T GIVE YOU ANYTHING BUT LOVE, BABY (1940, Universal) - Gangster Broderick Crawford kidnaps composer Johnny Downs to help him write a song he hopes will help him win back his girl **Peggy Moran**.

CARROLL, PAT

DIE, DIE MY DARLING (1965, GB, Hammer)—**Stefanie Powers** visits Tallulah Bankhead (in her last movie), the deranged mother of the man whom she was planning to marry before his death. Mom holds Powers captive, insisting that she remain a virgin until re-united in death with her intended. Ma doesn't plan for there to be a long separation.

CARROLL, SALLY MORTON & CHRISTINE

THE TWO MRS. CARROLLS (1947, Warner Brothers)—Psychotic artist Humphrey Bogart, terribly miscast, likes to paint his wives as the Angel of Death and then murder them with poisoned milk. **Anita Bolster** meets such a fate with **Barbara Stanwyck** next on Bogie's list. He even has a model in mind for his next portrait.

CARROLL, STEVE

TWO GUYS FROM TEXAS (1948, Warner Brothers)—**Dennis Morgan** and vaudeville partner Jack Carson are on the lam, chased by some big city crooks in Texas. Morgan and Carson made a nice predictable team.

CARSELL, HOWARD "HOWZER"

HOWZER (1973, Universal)—Twelve-year-old **Peter Deisante** and his fourteen year-old friend Melissa Stocking run away from home intent on making it to Los Angeles. It's a routine and familiar teenage road picture.

CARSON

THE ULTIMATE WARRIOR (1975, Warner Brothers) -In New York in 2012, gangster Max Von Sydow rules the Big Apple with **Yul Brynner** the only one strong enough to oppose him in an ecologically poisoned city.

CARSON, ANNE

GIRLS IN PRISON (1956, American International)—**Joan Taylor** is wrongly sent to prison, but other female cons believe that she knows the whereabouts of stolen loot, and they intend to get the location from her.

CARSON, BILL

FIGHTING BILL CARSON (1945, PRC)—**Buster Crabbe** uses a female member of a gang of stagecoach bandits as bait to catch her accomplices.

CARSON, BILLY

THE DRIFTER (1944, PRC)—**Buster Crabbe** is a western bank robber who tries to convince people he's sort of a Robin Hood.

CARSON CITY KID

CARSON CITY KID (1940, Republic)—**Roy Rogers** is a gunslinger chasing the man who killed his brother. Now, there's a novel plot for a Western.

CARSON, ELYA

FOUR FOR TEXAS (1963, Warner Brothers)—Whether **Anita Ekberg** ever had any acting ability will not be discovered in this poor excuse for a Western in which her mammary talents and those of Ursula Andress are exploited. The film features Frank Sinatra and Dean Martin as friendly enemies intent on controlling the gambling in Galveston of the 1870s.

CARSON, JEFFREY

HOLLYWOOD COWBOY (1937, RKO)—Vacationing movie cowboy George O'Brien takes on some city gangsters who have moved west and threaten ranchers.

CARSON, KIT

KIT CARSON (1928, Silent, Paramount); (1940, UA); KIT CARSON OVER THE GREAT DIVIDE (1925, Silent, Sunset)—**Fred Thomson, Jon Hall** and **Jack Mower** each appeared as the fabled scout who guides John C. Fremont, his troops and a caravan of covered wagons across the plains and mountains to California. Carson has also been portrayed by **Johnny Mack Brown** in FIGHTING WITH KIT CARSON (1933), **Sammy McKim** in THE PAINTED STALLION (1938) and **Wild Bill Elliott** in OVERLAND WITH KIT CARSON (1939).

CARSON, LIGHTING BILL

FIGHTING RENEGADE (1939, Victory)—**Tim McCoy**, wrongly accused of having killed the leader of an expedition to Indian burial grounds in Mexico, disguises himself as a notorious bandit El Puma and clears himself.

CARSON, SONNY

THE EDUCATION OF SONNY CARSON (1974, Paramount)—**Rony Clanton** appears as a rebellious black youth in the fifties and sixties in Brooklyn. It's not exactly "The Education of Henry Adams," but it is based on Carson's autobiography.

CARSTAIRS, MARTHA & JIM

TWO AGAINST THE WORLD (1936, Warner Brothers)—In a remake of FIVE STAR FINAL, a yellow rag newspaper drudges up a twenty-year-old murder case which causes the suicide of **Helen MacKellar** and **Henry O'Neill**, two people involved in the long forgotten crime.

CARSTEN, JIM *See* CAPT. JAMES WYNNEGATE

CARTER, ANN & MARTIN

HIS BUTLER'S SISTER (1943, Universal)—**Deanna Durbin** moves to New York to stay with her half-brother **Pat O'Brien** while seeking a musical career. She falls for her brother's employer Franchot Tone.

CARTER, CHAMPNEYS

THE MAN WHO COULD NOT LOSE (1914, Silent, Favorite Players)—**Carlyle Blackwell** sees a horse race in his dream. When he awakes, he bets everything he has on the horse he dreamed won—and what do you know—it wins.

CARTER, DALE

RED HEAD (1934, Monogram); (1941, Monogram)—**Grace Bradley** and **June Lang** appear as an artist's model who innocently gets involved in an accidental death because of her looks.

CARTER, DON

EXCUSE MY GLOVE (1936, GB, ABF)—Boxer **Len Harvey** appears as a shy glass collector whose boxing ability is noticed by a sharp promoter. Harvey becomes a champ.

CARTER, ELLEN & DOC

OUR NEIGHBORS, THE CARTERS (1939, Paramount)—**Fay Bainter** and **Frank Craven** are so poor that they give serious consideration to the offer of their wealthy neighbor to adopt one of their children.

CARTER, ELLIOTT

THE CARTER CASE (1947, Republic)—**Bradley Page**, publisher of a fashion magazine, is murdered, and it's up to the D.A. and a female reporter to find his killer.

CARTER, HELEN

A GUY, A GAL AND A PAL (1945, Columbia)—Needing a seat on a train, **Lynn Merrick** induces Ross Hunter to pretend to be her husband. Yeah, we don't see the relation either.

CARTER, HELEN

ON HER WEDDING NIGHT (1915, Silent, Vitagraph)—**Edith Storey** is talking on the phone to her groom on their wedding day when he is shot and killed. The best man decides to devote his life to taking care of her. Ultimately, they will marry.

CARTER, JACK

GET CARTER (1971, MGM)—Small-time British hood **Michael Caine** searches the underworld for those responsible for his brother's death.

CARTER, JOE

THE MORE THE MERRIER (1943, Columbia)—In a lovely romantic comedy, the wartime housing shortage in Washington finds Jean Arthur renting part of her apartment to elderly Charles Coburn, who turns around and rents half of his half to **Joel McCrea**. Coburn then proceeds to play Cupid for the young couple.

CARTER, KENT

HERE COMES CARTER (1936, First National/Warner Brothers)—Angry because he was fired as a press agent, **Ross Alexander** takes his revenge on the actor who had him fired by announcing over the radio that the actor's brother is a gangster. This results in the actor being blackballed.

CARTER, MRS. LESLIE

LADY WITH RED HAIR (1940, Warner Brothers)—**Miriam Hopkins** stars in this mildly interesting biopic of the noted stage actress and her association with impresario David Belasco played by Claude Rains.

CARTER, MARY

THE GHOST BREAKERS (1940, Paramount)—**Paulette Goddard** inherits a West Indian castle and with Bob Hope as her protector, fights crooks, ghosts and zombies to locate a hidden treasure.

CARTER, MICHAEL

BEHOLD MY WIFE (1935, Paramount)—When his family scuttles his plans to marry a stenographer, **Gene Raymond** heads west, where to spite his family, he marries and brings home an Indian bride, Sylvia Sidney. He learns to love her and so does his family when she takes the blame for a shooting by his sister.

CARTER, MIKE

BODYGUARD (1948, RKO)—Ex-cop **Lawrence Tierney** is hired by a widow to protect her from black-mailers. He gets hung with a murder rap for his troubles.

CARTER, NICK

NICK CARTER, MASTER DETECTIVE (1939, MGM)—**Walter Pidgeon** uncovers a spy ring at a plane factory in this dull mystery.

CARTER, RAY

SECRETS OF AN ACTRESS (1938, Warner Brothers)—Actress **Kay Francis** falls for one of the backers of her show, George Brent, who neglects to tell her that he's already married, although separated from his wife. In movies, these little complications all seem to work their way out by the last reel.

CARTER, RUBY

BELLE OF THE NINETIES (1934, Paramount)—Yukon saloon keeper **Mae West** loves two men (at least), one of whom is a crook.

CARTER, SAM

THE MAN INSIDE (1958, GB, Columbia)—Bookkeeper **Nigel Patrick** steals a priceless diamond and is chased across Europe by an assortment of people who want it.

CARTER, SKIMPY

SKIMPY IN THE NAVY (1949, GB, Advance/Adelphi)—Soldier **Hal Monty** and his buddies leave the army in order to join the navy and help a friend look for buried treasure.

CARTER, SLIM

SLIM CARTER (1957, Universal)—Cowboy singer **Jock Mahoney** is turned into a western star by a beautiful publicist Julie Adams, but it causes an increase in the size of Mahoney's Stetson.

CARTER, TWO-GUN

THE ADOPTED SON (1917, Silent, Metro)—**Francis X. Bushman** is drawn into the feud between two Kentucky families, the Conovers and the McLanes, when a Conover boy is killed during a truce and Bushman is asked to take his place by the dead boy's sister. He does, but things get tense when it's discovered he's really a McLane.

CARTWRIGHT, DR. D. R.

SEVEN WOMEN (1966, MGM)—In Mongolia in 1935, physician **Anne Bancroft** joins a mission staff headed by inflexible Margaret Leighton. When the mission is invaded by war-lord Mike Mazurki, Bancroft uses her body to exercise sexual power over the invader and save the women of the mission. This film about women was a strange final directorial effort for John Ford.

CARULLI, CESARE *See* **MARIO NANNI**

CARUSO, ENRICO

THE GREAT CARUSO (1951, MGM)—**Mario Lanza** portrays the famous Italian tenor in a rather dull biopic.

CARVER, ANN

ANN CARVER'S PROFESSION (1933, Columbia)—Scream queen **Fay Wray** is a lawyer's lawyer, equally at home with civil, corporate and criminal cases. Jurists and other attorneys are in awe of this female counsellor. Her wimpy architect husband, Gene Raymond, feels and is inadequate. He becomes a nightclub singer and takes up with a shady lady. When the latter drinks herself to death, Raymond is accused of her murder. Wray comes to his rescue and gets him acquitted in court.

CARVER, CECIL

WIFE, HUSBAND AND FRIEND (1939, 20th Century Fox)—Professional singer **Binnie Barnes** encourages her friend's husband to attempt a singing career, just as his wife is doing. Neither husband Warner Baxter or wife Loretta Young have any real talent.

CARVER, JOHNNY

THE TEXAS RANGERS (1951, Columbia)—Texas Ranger **George Montgomery** is pitted against notorious outlaw Sam Bass, played by William Bishop.

CARY, AMY

THE SENTIMENTAL LADY (1915, Silent, Kleine)—**Irene Fenwick** has all of her money in utility stocks in a company which her fiance's crooked father is trying to ruin. A young attorney for the small stockholders saves the day and wins Fenwick.

CARY, MARY

NOBODY'S KID (1921, Silent, R-C Pictures)—**Mae Marsh** endures cruel treatment in an orphanage until she discovers that she is a member of an aristocratic British family.

CARY, PETER

THREE MARRIED MEN (1936, Paramount)—**Roscoe Karns** is victimized by the two married brothers of his intended, Mary Brian.

CARY, VIRGINIA HOUSTON

THE LITTLEST REBEL (1935, Fox)—Sweet little southern girl **Shirley Temple** persuades President Lincoln to release her Confederate officer father John Boles from a union prison. Temple is a delight dancing with Bill "Bojangles" Robinson.

CASANOVA

ADVENTURES OF CASANOVA (1948, Eagle-Lion); CASANOVA'S BIG NIGHT (1954, Paramount) —In the poverty row production of 1948, the great lover, played by **Arturo de Cordova**, is a Sicilian Robin Hood who thwarts the plans of a treacherous Austrian envoy. In the 1954 film, **Bob Hope** is mistaken for the romantic swordsman played by Vincent Price. Hope tries to live up or down to the lady's man reputation with predictable comical expectations.

CASAR, JOHNNY

THE FIREBALL (1950, 20th Century Fox)—**Mickey Rooney**, an orphaned juvenile delinquent, spends all his energy on becoming a roller-skating champ.

CASE, CHARLES "CYCLONE"

THE GANG BUSTER (1931, Paramount)—Small town schnook **Jack Oakie** accidently thwarts a gang of big city crooks.

CASEY

CASEY AT THE BAT (1916, Silent, Triangle-Fine Arts); (1927, Silent, Paramount)—Filmmakers can make a movie from just about anything as these pictures starring **De Wolf Hopper** and **Wallace Beery** as the mighty Casey, who brought no joy to Mudville because he "struck out," bear out.

CASEY, FLASH

HERE'S FLASH CASEY (1937, Grand National)—Photographer **Eric Linden** sets a goal of having the world's largest news photo agency within two years. It doesn't seem likely.

CASEY OF TRAFFIC "C"

THE TRAFFIC COP (1916, Silent, Thanhouser) Traffic cop **Howard M. Mitchell** saves the fortune of a bank president's ward and wins the girl.

CASEY, PATRICK MICHAEL

THE FEARLESS LOVER (1925, Silent, Perfection)—Young policeman **William Fairbanks** is forced to arrest his girlfriend's brother. When he learns that the boy was forced into a life of crime by a gangster, Fairbanks goes after the real villain and secures his future brother-in-law's release.

CASEY, SALLY

GIRLS WHO DARE (1929, Silent, Trinity)—A wealthy young man convinces his objecting father to allow him to marry chorus girl **Priscilla Bonner**. The clincher is that the old man is messing around with the hostess at the club where Bonner works.

CASEY, SUE

SUNBONNET SUE (1945, Monogram)—During the Gay nineties **Gale Storm** sings in her father's Bowery saloon and is discovered by a society swell.

CASH, GABE

TANGO AND CASH (1989, Warner Brothers)—**Kurt Russell** is a slovenly top LA cop who competes with sophisticated detective Sylvester Stallone for the big busts. They are teamed up to combat drug dealer Jack Palance, and are framed for murder before they can get their act together. It's got it's amusing moments, but Russell looks hideous in drag.

CASHMAN, BARNEY

LAST OF THE RED HOT LOVERS (1972, Paramount)—Middle-aged **Alan Arkin's** attempts at having an extra-marital affair provide comical complications. It's not Neal Simon at his best.

CASSANDRA

THE TROJAN WOMEN (1971, Cinerama)—**Genevieve Bujold** is one of four fine actors who appear in this lifeless production of the Euripides play. The others are Katharine Hepburn, Irene Papas and Vanessa Redgrave.

CASSEL, VICTORIA

THE TIME, THE PLACE AND THE GIRL (1946, Warner Brothers) - **Martha Vickers** stars with Dennis Morgan, Jack Carson and Janis Paige in this routine "putting on a show" musical comedy.

CASSIDY, BUTCH

BUTCH CASSIDY AND THE SUNDANCE KID (1969, 20th Century Fox); BUTCH AND SUNDANCE, THE EARLY DAYS (1979, 20th Century Fox)—**Paul Newman** played the part of the infamous western badman for laughs in a marvelously entertaining farce. Unfortunately **Tom Berenger** in the prequel was forced to play things fairly straight as the picture explored the exploits of "the Hole-in-the-Wall gang."

CASSIDY, HOPALONG

HOPALONG CASSIDY (1935, Paramount); HOPALONG CASSIDY RETURNS (1936, Paramount); HOPALONG RIDES AGAIN (1937, Paramount); CASSIDY OF BAR 20 (1938, Paramount); SANTE FE MARSHAL (1940, PARAMOUNT); HOPPY SERVES A WRIT (1943, UA); HOPPY'S HOLIDAY (1947, UA)—Hopalong Cassidy, a gentleman cowboy who wore black, is the creation of Clarence E. Mulford. **William Boyd** made sixty-six films as Hoppy. He wisely bought the rights to them, edited them for TV and made a fortune, becoming a folk hero at the same time.

CASSIDY, JESSIE

MANNEQUIN (1937, MGM)—**Joan Crawford** marries two-bit con artist Alan Curtis. At their wedding dinner, they are toasted by shipping magnate Spencer Tracy who is sitting at an adjoining table. There's a spark between Crawford and Tracy, which later ignites into a passionate flame when Joan leaves her husband to become a model and meets Spence again. This is the only film the two ever made together.

CASSIDY, YOUNG
YOUNG CASSIDY (1965, MGM)—**Rod Taylor** stars in a romanticized version of the young adulthood of Irish poet Sean O'Casey.

CASSIE
BEAUTY AND THE BAD MAN (1925, Silent, Peninsula)—**Mabel Ballin**, who has a beautiful voice, is sent abroad to study singing by western gambler Russell Simpson. She returns, becomes an opera star and marries Simpson after her husband is conveniently disposed of.

CASSIE
NOBODY'S FOOL (1986, Island Pictures)—Waitress **Rosanna Arquette** becomes an outcast in her small southwestern town when she becomes an unwed mother. She begins to find herself through an encounter with Eric Roberts who's just passing through.

CASSY
SLAVES (1969, Continental)—Pop singer **Dionne Warwick** isn't too bad (or very good, for that matter) starring as 1850 Kentucky plantation owner Stephen Boyd's mistress and slave. She is helped to escape by Ossie Davis at the cost of his life.

CASTELLI, BENNY
THE TROJAN BROTHERS (1946, GB, Anglo-American)—**Bobby Howes** is one part of a vaudevillian horse, the part that switches flies with its tail.

CASTELTON, HETTY
IN THE HOLLOW OF HER HAND (1919, Silent, Select)—**Alice Brady** kills a man, whom she believed was unmarried, when he lures her to a roadhouse and attacks her. She attempts to commit suicide but is prevented from doing so by the deceased's wife who takes Brady into her home and cares for her. Later when the widow is accused of the murder of her husband, Brady confesses what happened and is found to have been justified in killing the man as she defended her honor.

CASTILLO, CESAR & NESTOR
THE MAMBO KINGS (1992, Warner Brothers)—**Armand Assante** and **Antonio Banderos** are Cuban immigrant musicians. They have an up and down career, peaking with an appearance on the 'I Love Lucy' show.

CASTLE, BEN
THE GROOM WORE SPURS (1951, Universal)—Attorney Ginger Rogers marries and divorces cowboy-actor **Jack Carson**, but comes to his defense when he needs a lawyer.

CASTLE, FRANK
THE PUNISHER (1990, Castle Premier)—Even before the film begins, Marvel Comics character **Dolph Lundgren** has killed over a hundred people and is shooting for two hundred, employing as many means of slaughter as he can think of.

CASTLE, VERNON & IRENE
THE STORY OF VERNON AND IRENE CASTLE (1939, RKO)—**Fred Astaire** and **Ginger Rogers** star in this rambling musical biopic of a husband and wife team who began their career dancing in Paris and became world famous entertainers until he is killed in WWI.

CASTLETON, NAIDA
THE WAY OF A MAID (1921, Silent, Selznick)—Wealthy **Elaine Hammerstein** attends a costume party dressed as a maid, which she is later taken for by a rich manufacturer. She goes along with his misapprehension, but later her family loses its money, and she finds herself working for the man's family as a maid for real. Things work out for her as you might suspect.

CASTORINI, LORETTA
MOONSTRUCK (1987, MGM/UA)—**Cher** wins an Academy Award for her excellent performance as a young widow who finally gets Danny Aiello to propose. When he must hurry to Italy to be with his dying mother, Cher is left with the task of healing the breach between Aiello and his estranged brother Nicolas Cage. Cher certainly knows how to smooth things over with Cage. Passion overcomes them and they soon find themselves in bed and incidentally in love. The extra large moon in Little Italy made them do it.

CASTRO, DON ALONZO
A SAINTED DEVIL (1924, Silent, Paramount)—Argentinean aristocrat **Rudolph Valentino's** bride Helen D'Algy is kidnapped on their wedding night. He is led to believe that she went willingly with her abductor. This makes him a hater of all women, but later he discovers that D'Algy was true to him and they live happily ever after—we suppose.

CASTRO, ROSITA
ROSE OF THE RANCHO (1936, Paramount)—Bandit **Gladys Swarthout** is pursued by dull government agent John Boles, for whom she proves no match.

CASWELL, DEKE
ALIAS THE DEACON (1940, Universal)—Card sharp **Bob Burns** poses as a preacher in this modest "B" comedy.

CATALINA, SENORITA
LADY ROBIN HOOD (1925, Silent, R-C Pictures)—**Evelyn Brent**, the ward of a Spanish aristocrat, fed-up with the injustice of an evil governor, disguises herself as a bandit to champion the cause of the peasants. She rids the province of the corrupt official and wins the love of American mine owner Robert Ellis.

CATES, THELMA
'NIGHT MOTHER (1986, Universal)—**Anne Bancroft** spends the night trying to talk her unhappy daughter Sissy Spacek out of her plan to take her own life. It's a fine play, but doesn't seem suitable for a movie.

CATHERICK, ANNE
THE WOMAN IN WHITE (1948, Warner Brothers)—**Eleanor Parker**, an emotionally tormented heiress, is saved from villains by new tutor Gig Young in this gothic thriller based on the work of Wilkie Collins.

CATHERINE
BLACK WIDOW (1987, 20th Century Fox)—**Theresa Russell** marries extremely wealthy men, sees to it that she is named in their will and then murders them. Debra Winger is the investigator who attempts to put an end to Russell's naughty ways. Russell seems more interested in Winger than is in her best interest.

CATHERINE II
CATHERINE THE GREAT (1934, GB, LMP/UA): THE SCARLET EMPRESS (1934, Paramount); GREAT CATHERINE (1968, GB,

Warner Brothers)—**Elizabeth Bergner's** portrayal of the frightened German princess, who became the ruler of Russia on the death of her husband Douglas Fairbanks, Jr. was over-shadowed by that of **Marlene Dietrich** in THE SCARLET EMPRESS, released the same year. In 1968, **Jeanne Moreau** is regally beautiful but unimpressive as the Russian Empress.

CATLAN, RON "CAT"
NUMBER ONE (1969, UA)—**Charlton Heston** is the aging quarterback for the New Orleans professional football team. That must be the reason the "Whodats" were losers for so many years.

CATLOW
CATLOW (1971, MGM)—**Yul Brynner**, intent on stealing $2 million in gold from a Yankee prison, has to deal with tough lawman Richard Crenna, mean villain Leonard Nimoy and the Mexican army.

CATTLE ANNIE
CATTLE ANNIE AND LITTLE BRITCHES (1981, Universal)—Inspired by the Ned Buntline dime novels, **Amanda Plummer** and Diane Lane join up with a gang of western outlaws, headed by Burt Lancaster. There are some good moments in this comedy-western but more would have been appreciated.

CAULDER, HANNIE
HANNIE CAULDER (1971, GB, Paramount)—**Raquel Welch** is a fetching gunslinger out to avenge herself on three outlaws who raped her and killed her husband.

CAULFIELD, BILLY
THE DREAM TEAM (1989, Universal)—**Michael Keaton** has a serious attitude problem in this story of four mental patients, who find themselves on their own in New York city, after their doctor-chaperon is put into a hospital with a coma, after suffering a beating from two crooked cops.

CAVALIER, THE
THE CAVALIER OF THE STREETS (1937, GB, British & Dominions)-Blackmailer **Patrick Barr** nobly confesses to murdering his partner in order to save a barrister's wife accused of the crime.

CAVANAUGH
MEN'S CLUB (1986, Paramount)—**Roy Scheider** is a member of a men's encounter group in a talky film that didn't encounter many paying theater patrons.

CAVANAUGH, ANDREW JACKSON
NINETEEN AND PHYLLIS (1920, Silent, First National)—Poor country boy **Charles Ray** wins the hand of Clara Horton, a judge's granddaughter, beating the time of the son of the wealthiest family in the region.

CAVANAUGH, FRANK
THE IRON MAJOR (1943, RKO)—**Pat O'Brien** returns to the football field, portraying the legendary coach of Dartmouth, Boston College and Fordham. Pat came out of WWI a major with belief in three things—"love of God, love of country and love of family." If that sounds like the basis for a sloppy sentimental film—you're right.

CAVANAUGH, JEANNE
JUST ANOTHER BLONDE (1926, Silent, First National)—**Dorothy MacKaill** loves the brother of her girlfriend's beau but he disapproves of all women, except his mother. He changes his mind.

CAVANAUGH, ROSS
CAVANAUGH OF THE RANGERS (1918, Silent, Vitagraph); RANGER OF THE BIG PINES (1925, Silent, Vitagraph)—Texas ranger **Alfred Whitman** is required to see that the laws limiting the number of sheep allowed to graze on the range are enforced. This puts him in the middle of a war between sheepmen and cattlemen. In 1925, **Kenneth Harlan** assumed the role of the gallant Texas Ranger.

CAVE, JOHNNY
GREAT GUY (1936, Grand National)—Ex-boxer **James Cagney** fights racketeers who are cheating the public when he takes a job with the Bureau of Weights and Measures. Cagney was sparring with his home studio Warner Brothers by making this cheap production with poverty row studio Grand National.

CAVELL, EDITH
NURSE EDITH CAVELL (1939, RKO)—**Anna Neagle** stars as the WWI British nurse executed by the Germans as a spy. It's moderately interesting.

CAVENDER, HOMER
HOMER COMES HOME (1920, Silent, Triangle)—In one of his typical roles, **Charles Ray** is a country boob who returns from the city to his hometown, becomes a financial success and wins the village belle.

CAVENDER, LORD
HIS LORDSHIP REGRETS (1938, GB, RKO)—Financially embarrassed nobleman **Claude Hulbert** woos heiress, Gina Malo, but falls for Winifred Shotter. Malo proves to be a gold-digging phony while true love Shotter turns out to be a real heiress.

CAVENDISH, JUDY
FOUR FRIGHTENED PEOPLE (1934, Paramount)—**Claudette Colbert** is one of four survivors of a bubonic plague outbreak aboard a ship. They escape in a lifeboat and then must make a perilous trek through a dangerous jungle.

CAVENDISH, JULIA, TONY, GWEN & FANNY
THE ROYAL FAMILY OF BROADWAY (1930, Paramount)—**Ina Claire**, **Fredric March**, **Mary Brian** and **Henrietta Crosman** lampoon the Barrymores in this funny comedy based on a stage play by George S. Kaufman and Edna Ferber. Ethel Barrymore, it has been said, was not amused.

CAVENDISH, MARTIN
A CONNECTICUT YANKEE IN KING ARTHUR'S COURT (1921, Silent, Fox)—In later film productions of the Mark Twain story, the Connecticut Yankee is called Hank Martin. In this silent version, nineteenth century blacksmith **Harry Myers** finds himself back in the court of King Arthur when he awakens from a blow to the head. He puts his Yankee know-how to good use.

CAVENDISH-GASCOYNE, LADY MOIRA
LUCKY GIRL (1932, GB, Wardour)—**Molly Lamont**, the daughter of a duke, has to clear up the mess when the Ruritanian king Gene Gerrard, whom she has come to love, is taken for a jewel thief while traveling incognito.

CAVERLEY, PAT
GIRLS WILL BE BOYS (1934, GB, Associated British)—**Dolly Haas** poses as a duke's grandson to get into the old man's all-male estate. The old man thinks his grandson is too skinny and puts "him" on a

strict exercise program under the supervision of the duke's steward Esmond Knight. The latter discovers Dolly's secret when he has to rescue her from drowning when she goes swimming in the nude.

CAZARI, TONY
SO YOU WON'T TALK (1935, GB, Warner Brothers)—In order to inherit a fortune, **Monty Banks** must not talk or write for 30 days.

CAZENOVE, SARAH
IF I WERE FREE (1933, RKO)—Unhappily married **Irene Dunne** attempts to find happiness with unhappily married Clive Brook. Audiences also were unhappy.

CECE
MODERN GIRLS (1986, Atlantic)—Do miss this stinker about **Cynthia Gibb** and two of her girlfriends who make the rounds of L.A. punk spots one night and early morning.

CECILE
THE GIRL IN THE NIGHT (1931, GB, Wardour)—**Dorothy Boyd** and Henry Edwards take shelter from a storm in a house they believe to be abandoned, but it's the hideout of assorted crooks.

CECILIA
LITTLE 'FRAID LADY (1920, Silent, R-C Pictures)—Heart sick over a failed romance, artist **Mae Marsh** leaves the city and finds true love in a near wilderness.

CELESTE, MARIE
THE LITTLE WILD GIRL (1928, Silent, Trinity)—**Lila Lee** is discovered in the North Woods where her father is killed in a forest fire and her fiance is lost, believed dead. She becomes a Broadway star, but returns home when she is implicated in a murder. There is a happy ending when she is reunited with her intended who has inherited a fortune.

CELESTINE
DIARY OF A CHAMBERMAID (1946, UA)—**Paulette Goddard** gives one of her best performances as the servant girl who drives the men of three houses to wild behavior out of desire for her.

CELIA
CELIA (1949, GB, Exclusive)—**Hy Hazell** poses as her own aunt to expose her step-uncle as a poisoner.

CELIA
THE FLIRTING WIDOW (1930, Warner Brothers); HER IMAGINARY LOVER (1933, GB, First National/Warner Brothers)—**Dorothy Mackaill** and **Laura La Plante** each portray the woman who invents a fiance to fend off an excess of suitors. But it turns out there really is a Lord by the name chosen by our heroine. When he shows up (Basil Rathbone and Percy Marmont, respectively), he's initially annoyed at having his good name used in such a shameful way, but ultimately falls in love with his "fiancee."

CELLAR DWELLER
CELLAR DWELLER (1988, Dove/Empire)—When Deborah Mullowney attempts to create a comic book based on a 1951 cartoonist's horror stories, she gives form to the beast of the stories, in the person, or thing, of **Michael S. Deak**.

CELLINI, BENVENUTO
THE AFFAIRS OF CELLINI (1934, Fox/UA)—Sixteenth century rake **Fredric March**, a talented artist and duelist, would rather

pursue a pretty face than a career as an artist or writer, but he does it all.

CERNIK, KAREL
MAN ON A TIGHTROPE (1953, 20th Century Fox)—Czech travelling circus owner **Fredric March** plans to get his entire troupe across the Iron Curtain border to freedom.

CHAD
GUN BROTHERS (1956, UA)—In one of his last feature roles **Buster Crabbe**, a former cavalryman, discovers that his rancher brother Neville Brand is the leader of a gang of outlaws terrorizing the region. By the end of the film, Brand has joined Crabbe to put an end to all of the lawlessness.

CHAD
LITTLE SHEPHERD OF KINGDOM COME (1961, 20th Century Fox)—Southern farm boy **Jimmie Rogers** fights for the Union during the Civil War, an allegiance which doesn't sit well with the locals when he returns to his home after the war.

CHAD & ALEX
DOUBLE IMPACT (1991, Columbia)—There's no use trying to separate the roles of 'Muscles from Brussels' **Jean-Claude Van Damme** in this martial arts knockoff of *The Corsican Brothers*. Van Damme makes no effort to distinguish one twin from the other.

CHADMAN, LUCY
HELLO AGAIN (1987, Buena Vista)—**Shelley Long** dies but is brought back to life by her witchy sister. This causes some problems for her stuffy husband who has remarried. Long finds comfort with an understanding doctor.

CHAIRMAN, THE
THE CHAIRMAN (1969, 20th Century Fox)—**Conrad Yama** portrays China's Mao Tse Tung in this mild adventure yarn concerning the attempts of U.S. spy Gregory Peck to pick up conversations of the Chair-man with other Chinese leaders through a miniature transmitter implanted in his skull.

CHALLONER, SIR HUMPHREY
BEAU BROCADE (1916, GB, Silent, Artistic)—**Charles Rock**, a cashiered officer and card sharp turned highwayman, proves a lord, posing as an apprentice, was framed of a crime by his cousin.

CHALMERS, BOBBY
TEENAGE MILLIONAIRE (1961, UA)—**Jimmy Clanton** inherits a fortune and becomes a rock 'n' roll star.

CHALMERS, DUCE
MAN ABOVE THE LAW (1918, Silent, Triangle)—**Jack Richardson**, a fugitive from justice, heads west and operates a saloon catering to Indians and Mexicans. He has a child with a squaw and finally comes to realize the harm his whiskey is doing, closes his establishment, marries his squaw and starts a new life with his family.

CHAMBERS, JOAN KEATING
MODEL WIFE (1941, Universal)—Fashion model **Joan Blondell** marries Dick Powell, but he can't tell his boss for fear of losing his job. She becomes pregnant, and it looks like their secret will come out.

CHAMBERS, NORMAN
NORMAN ... IS THAT YOU? (1976, MGM/UA)—Former UCLA basketball star and teammate of Kareem Jabbar, **Michael Warren**

stars in this unattractive comedy about parents discovering their son is gay.

CHAMP

THE CHAMP (1931, MGM)—**Wallace Beery** won an Academy Award for his performance in this maudlin picture about a washed-up boxer and his young son Jackie Cooper who still thinks of his Dad as champ. Beery's ex-wife wants custody of Cooper, believing she and her new husband can provide the lad a more appropriate life. Before this can occur Beery has to die so Cooper can really turn on his famous water works.

CHAMPION, BOB

CHAMPIONS (1984, GB, EMB)—**John Hurt**, a leading British jockey, overcomes cancer and a leg injury to his horse to win the Grand National.

CHAMPNEYS, IRIS

THE WOMAN WHO WALKED ALONE (1922, Silent, Paramount)—English noblewoman **Dorothy Dalton** is wrongly accused of adultery by the husband she was forced to marry when she attempted to retrieve compromising love letters written by her sister.

CHAMPSELLE, MARC

THE V.I.P.S (1963, GB, MGM)—Married Elizabeth Taylor is running away from her husband Richard Burton with charming gigolo **Louis Jourdan**, but their plane is delayed and hubby shows up at the airport to plead his case. Taylor is only using Jourdan to get Burton to pay attention to her.

CHAN, CHARLIE

CHARLIE CHAN CARRIES ON (1931, Fox); CHARLIE CHAN'S CHANCE (1932, Fox); CHARLIE CHAN'S GREATEST CASE (1933, Fox); CHARLIE CHAN'S COURAGE (1934, Fox); CHARLIE CHAN IN LONDON (1934, Fox); CHARLIE CHAN IN EGYPT (1935, 20th Century Fox); CHARLIE CHAN IN PARIS (1935, 20th Century Fox); CHARLIE CHAN IN SHANGHAI (1935, 20th Century Fox); CHARLIE CHAN AT THE CIRCUS (1936, 20th Century Fox); CHARLIE CHAN AT THE OPERA (1936, 20th Century Fox); CHARLIE CHAN AT THE RACE TRACK (1936, 20th Century Fox); CHARLIE CHAN'S SECRET (1936, 20th Century Fox); CHARLIE CHAN AT MONTE CARLO (1937, 20th Century Fox); CHARLIE CHAN AT THE OLYMPICS (1937, 20th Century Fox); CHARLIE CHAN ON BROADWAY (1937, 20th Century Fox)—**Warner Oland** CHARLIE CHAN IN HONOLULU (1938, 20th Century Fox); CHARLIE CHAN IN RENO (1939, 20th Century Fox); CHARLIE CHAN ON TREASURE ISLAND (1939, 20th Century Fox); CHARLIE CHAN IN PANAMA (1940, 20th Century Fox); CHARLIE CHAN'S MURDER CRUISE (1940, 20th Century Fox); CHARLIE CHAN AT THE WAX MUSEUM (1940, 20th Century Fox); CHARLIE CHAN IN RIO (1941, 20th Century Fox); CHARLIE CHAN IN BLACK MAGIC (1944, Monogram); CHARLIE CHAN IN THE SECRET SERVICE (1944, Monogram)—**Sidney Toler** CHARLIE CHAN AND THE CURSE OF THE DRAGON LADY (1980, UA)—**Peter Ustinov** The Honolulu oriental detective, created by Earl Derr Biggers, first appeared in a silent serial with George Kuwa as the polite private eye with the large family. Kuwa was followed by Kamiyama Sojin and E.L. Park, who each portrayed him once in a silent film. With talkies, Swedish character actor **Warner Oland** supplied quaint aphorisms as he instructed his sons and solved murders in sixteen enjoyable films. With Oland's death, chubby **Sidney Toler** played the role for laughs in twenty-two films. He was followed by Roland Winters in six films, which did not include Chan's name in the title. Chan has been played on TV by J. Carrol

Naish and Ross Martin. In 1972, **Keye Luke** who was Charlie's number two son to Toler's Chan, provided the voice of Chan in a cartoon series. Finally (perhaps, not) **Peter Ustinov** brought his talents to a ragged 1980 production which is an insulting parody to those who still appreciate the work of Oland and Toler.

CHANCE, ADAM

AGENT FOR H.A.R.M. (1966, Universal)—In a spoof of the James Bond movies, **Mark Richman** must prevent Russian agents from abducting a prominent scientist. He's about a .007.

CHANCELLOR, OLIVE

THE BOSTONIANS (1984, Merchant Ivory/Almi)—**Vanessa Redgrave** is Henry James' feminist heroine of the 1870s, a fanatic reformer who competes with her southern cousin Christopher Reeve for the affection of feminist orator Madeleine Potter.

CHANDLER

CHANDLER (1971, MGM)—Alcoholic ex-private eye **Warren Oates** has his share of troubles when he agrees to keep track of a government witness.

CHANDLER, ABIGAIL & MARTHA CANFORD

TWO SISTERS FROM BOSTON (1946, MGM)—**Kathryn Grayson** has aspirations of singing at the Met, but first must make a living along with her sister **June Allyson** at a turn-of-the century Bowery saloon run by Jimmy Durante.

CHANDLER, CHANDRA

THE MIND READER (1933, First National)—When phony mind reader **Warren William** tries to go straight to please his wife Constance Cummings, he ends up in jail.

CHANDLER, EVE

GIRL IN POSSESSION (1934, GB, First National)—**Laura La Plante** arrives in England to discover that her expected inheritance isn't worth much, and most of her possessions including a stately manor and grounds are now owned by a lord.

CHANDLER, HEATHER

HEATHERS (1989, New World)—**Kim Walker** is the witchy leader of the most exclusive cliche at Westerburg High in Sherwood, Ohio. She's also the first to be murdered by Winona Ryder and Christian Slater, who make her death appear to be a suicide. It's an unusually fascinating black comedy.

CHANDLER, JOHN

THE PROUD REBEL (1958, Buena Vista)—After the Civil War, Southerner **Alan Ladd** wanders through the Northern states seeking someone to cure his psychologically mute son, played by Ladd's own son, David. The boy finds his voice when it is needed to save his father.

CHANDU

CHANDU THE MAGICIAN (1932, Fox)—Spiritualist **Edmund Lowe** battles madman Bela Lugosi who has perfected a death ray which could destroy the world.

CHANEY, LON

MAN OF A THOUSAND FACES (1957, Universal)—**James Cagney** is excellent in this rather bleak production of the troubled personal life of the great silent screen star who becomes alienated from his son Roger Smith over his treatment of his first wife Dorothy Malone. With the help of his second wife Jane Greer, they are reconciled before he dies.

CHANNING
CHANNING OF THE NORTHWEST (1922, Silent, Selznick)—London gentleman **Eugene O'Brien** falls in love with a dancer, but she breaks off their engagement when she learns that he has been disinherited. He moves to Canada where he becomes a Mountie who gets his man—and his woman.

CHANNING, "JACK"
THE BOY GIRL (1917, Silent, Bluebird)—**Violet Mesereau**, raised by her father as a boy, finds her tomboy ways cause her maiden aunts great consternation when they take her in after the death of her father. But she proves to have the best qualities of both sexes.

CHAPDELAINE, MARIA
MARIA CHAPDELAINE (1986, Canada, The Movie Store)—Convent-educated **Carol Laure** is loved by a fugitive, a trapper and her child-hood sweetheart in Canada in 1912. Nothing much happens.

CHAPELLE, RAYMOND
THE SIN THAT WAS HIS (1920, Silent, Selznick)—Gambler **William Faversham**, who once studied for the priesthood, takes the blame when a woman shoots her son by accident.

CHAPMAN, DR.
THE CHAPMAN REPORT (1962, Warner Brothers)—Kinsey-like sex researcher **Andrew Duggan's** study of female sexual behavior sparks more than a little excitement in a high-class American suburb.

CHAPMAN, ROGER
THE BISHOP OF THE OZARKS (1923, Silent, Cosmopolitan)—Escaped convict **Milford W. Howard** assumes the identity and duties of an Ozark preacher, even to the point of becoming chaplin at the state penitentiary.

CHAPPELLET, DAVIS
DOWNHILL RACER (1969, Paramount)—**Robert Redford** is something of a ski bum. He wins a place on the American national team competing in Europe. If one is not fond of snow and skiing, there's nothing to it.

CHARLES
TIME TRACKERS (1989, Concorde)—**Wil Shriner** is one of three scientists of 2033 who chase after a madman, who has stolen a time machine, and headed for the past.

CHARLES V, KING
MY PAL, THE KING (1932, Universal)—Very young **Mickey Rooney** walks out on a cabinet meeting of his country and ends up with Tom Mix, who runs a visiting Wild West show. Mix and others in the show must rescue Rooney from an evil minister planning to do away with the pint-sized king. It's good fun.

CHARLES, NICK
AFTER THE THIN MAN (1936, MGM); ANOTHER THIN MAN (1939, MGM); SHADOW OF THE THIN MAN (1941, MGM); THE THIN MAN GOES HOME (1944, MGM); SONG OF THE THIN MAN (1947, MGM);—As noted elsewhere, Edward Ellis, the murder victim in THE THIN MAN is the title character in the first film featuring **William Powell** and Myrna Loy as Nick and Nora Charles. The success of that film led to a series of five additional "Thin Man" films with the title now referring to Powell. The interesting thing about AFTER THE THIN MAN is that Nick and Nora must solve three murders, and Jimmy Stewart is the culprit. In ANOTHER THIN MAN, the title refers to Nick and Nora's baby. In SHADOW OF THE THIN MAN, the Charles' solve a racetrack crime. After a three year lay off, the Charles are back in 1944 in an inferior murder mystery. In the last film in the series, the Charles track down a murderer in jazz circles.

CHARLES, PRINCE
BONNIE PRINCE CHARLES (1948, GB, British Lion)—**David Niven**, the last hope of the Stuarts, returns to England in 1745 to retake the British throne but is eventually forced to flee to France again.

CHARLES, PRINCE REGENT
THE PRINCE AND THE SHOWGIRL (1957, GB, Warner Brothers)—**Laurence Olivier** portrays a lecherous Prince Regent who plots to win his country's throne from his teenage son. Old pro Olivier was not amused by the delaying practices of his co-star, Marilyn Monroe.

CHARLIE
ALL DOGS GO TO HEAVEN (1989, animated, UA)—**Burt Reynolds** is the voice of a mangy canine convict, who escapes from the pen. When he tries to muscle back into the gambling business he ran with Vic Tayback, the latter has him rubbed out. Perhaps thinking he's a cat, our four-legged hero returns to earth to seek revenge.

CHARLIE
CARRY ON CABBY (1963, GB, Warner Brothers/Pathe)—**Sid James** owns a fleet of taxis, which make him wealthy, but his wife Hattie Jacques feels he spends too much time at work. To teach him a lesson, she invests in a rival cab company that employs sexy female drivers in revealing uniforms. It nearly wipes out James' business.

CHARLIE
CHINATOWN CHARLIE (1928, Silent, First National)—China-town tour guide **Johnny Hines** protects one of his female passengers from a gang trying to steal her ring, which is believed to have supernatural powers.

CHARLIE
ICEMAN (1984, Universal)—An arctic exploration team discover the body of a prehistoric man, **John Lone**, frozen for 40,000 years. To everyone's surprise, he thaws out and revives. Now what to do with him is the question.

CHARLIE
THE KILLERS (1964, Universal)—Hit men **Lee Marvin** and Clu Gulager are ordered to kill John Cassavetes, a teacher at a school for the blind. When Cassavetes makes no effort to resist his death, the killers are determined to find the reason.

CHARLIE
THE LITTLE DRUMMER GIRL (1984, Warner Brothers)—Actress **Diane Keaton** is recruited by an Israeli general to help trap a Palestinian terrorist. She agrees even though she holds sympathies for the Arab cause.

CHARLIE
WISE GUYS (1937, GB, 20th Century Fox)—**Charlie Naughton** and his friend Jimmy Gold try to win big at the races so they can buy their uncle's loan company.

CHARLOTTE
CHARLOTTE'S WEB (1973, Animated, Paramount)—**Debbie Reynolds** provides the voice of E.B. White's spider who makes it her

life's work to prevent her friend, Wilbur the pig, from becoming a ham sandwich.

CHARLOTTE
HUSH . . . HUSH SWEET CHARLOTTE (1964, 20th Century Fox)—When she was a young woman, **Bette Davis'** fiance was killed and dismembered. Davis always suspected that her father was the murderer. She fears that the proposed demolition of her house for a new highway will reveal some of her fiance's missing parts and prove her father to be the mad killer. She invites her cousin Olivia de Havilland to her home to help fight the highway commission. Instead de Havilland and family doctor Joseph Cotten conspire to drive Davis mad so they can get her money.

CHARLOTTE
THE WISE SISTERS (1945, GB, Universal)—In a movie which examines the three very different marriages of a trio of English sisters, **Dulcie Gray** marries cruel monster James Mason who drives her to alcoholism. Finally in desperation, she commits suicide.

CHARLOTTE
THE WOMAN IN RED (1984, Orion)—Beautiful and sexy **Kelly Le Brock** captivates married Gene Wilder when he observes the scrumptious model gyrating seductively above an air grate in a garage as air billows up her full red skirt a la Marilyn Monroe in THE SEVEN YEAR ITCH. Le Brock is receptive to an affair, but circumstances keep postponing the consummation. In the end Wilder is forced to vacate Kelly's bed and hide out on the ledge many floors above the street when her husband comes home unexpectedly. The best thing in the movie is Stevie Wonder's song "I Just Called to Say I Love You."

CHARMAINE
THE STEPFORD WIVES (1975, Columbia)—**Tina Louise** has a healthy contempt for her hard-working husband and is delighted when Katharine Ross and Paula Prentiss invite her to join a consciousness raising woman's group. But before long, she changes and becomes like so many other wives in Stepford, Connecticut: totally devoted to their husbands, wishing only to satisfy every chauvinistic fantasy they can imagine.

CHARMAINE
THOSE THREE FRENCH GIRLS (1930, MGM)—**Fifi D'Orsay**, Yola d'Avril and Sandra Ravel look cute in this minor musical but don't have much to do.

CHARNOCK, LUKE
SLAVES OF DESTINY (1924, GB, Silent, Stoll)—Englishman **Matheson Lang**, sold into slavery in Africa, eventually wins his freedom and the woman he loves when her mean husband is killed by a blind beggar.

CHARRIERE, HENRI
PAPILLON (1973, Allied Artists)—**Steve McQueen** is "Papillon" or "butterfly," who makes numerous escapes from Devil's Island, but is brought back time after time. The film is based on a true account of the life of Charriere in the hellish French colonial prison.

CHARTERS, PAMELA, MOIRA & ELIZABETH
THREE BLIND MICE (1938, 20th Century Fox)—**Loretta Young, Marjorie Weaver** and **Pauline Moore** are three girls from Kansas in the big city hoping to trap rich husbands. They are partially successful.

CHASE, CPL.
THE VICTORS (1963, Columbia)—In this linear story of an infantry squad in Europe towards the end of WWII, **George Peppard** takes time out from battles and killings to take a bath in a tub, with Melina Mercouri passing out the soap and towels.

CHASE, ELYOT
PRIVATE LIVES (1931, MGM)—Next door to **Robert Montgomery's** honeymoon suite is his ex-wife Norma Shearer also on her second honeymoon. It's not very long until Shearer looks a lot better to Montgomery than his new wife Una Merkel, and she's feeling the same about her new spouse, Reginald Denny.

CHASEN, HAROLD
HAROLD AND MAUDE (1971, Paramount)—Weird young **Bud Cort**, obsessed with death, has an affair with eighty-year-old Ruth Gordon. This black comedy, frequently hilarious, often flat, has become a cult classic.

CHASTITY
CHASTITY (1969, American International)—**Cher** is chaste but her road adventures threaten her standing.

CHATO
CHATO'S LAND (1972, UA)—Embittered Apache **Charles Bronson** kills a sheriff and is chased across the west by a posse which he ultimately destroys.

CHATTAWAY, DORIS
MARRY THE GIRL (1935, GB, British Lion)—**Winifred Shotter's** mother forces her to sue wealthy Sonnie Hale for breach of promise after he becomes engaged to another. You just know mother knows best, and Shotter ends up with Hale.

CHATTERIS, MAJOR
THE PERFECT GENTLEMAN (1935, MGM)—Retired officer **Frank Morgan** helps actress Cicely Courtneidge make a comeback. What was meant to be a showcase for British variety star Courtneidge in the U.S. didn't make it.

CHAVEZ Y CHAVEZ
YOUNG GUNS (1988, 20th Century Fox); YOUNG GUNS II (1990, 20th Century Fox)—Following up his success as Richie Valens in LA BAMBA, **Lou Diamond Phillips** seems to be having a good time as a young gunslinger and outlaw who teams up with Billy the Kid and his Regulator gang, originally deputized to help fight crime, but which couldn't tell the good guys from the bad. In the sequel, Phillips and the other members of the Western Brat Pack are on the run from sheriff Pat Garrett.

CHECKERS
CHECKERS (1937, 20th Century Fox)—**Jane Withers**, niece of a race horse owner, brings him success at the track.

CHERRY, REV. SIMON
MEET SIMON CHERRY (1949, GB, Hammer)—Anglican minister and amateur detective **Hugh Moxey** helps clear a girl of a murder charge.

CHERRY 2000
CHERRY 2000 (1988, Orion)—Filmed in 1985, the film was given a straight to video release in 1988. Set in the year 2017, it seems the only safe sex is to be had with robots. Yuppie-like David Andrews short-circuits his sexual toy **Pamela Gridley** and then is forced to

turn to a live female, Melanie Griffith. Oh, that's the reason the film was finally released.

CHESBROOKE, MARY
GIRL OVERBOARD (1937, Universal)—Beautiful **Gloria Stuart** is suspected of murder aboard a ship.

CHESTER, HELEN
THE SPOILERS (1914, Silent, Selig);(1930, Paramount); (1942, Universal); (1955, Universal)—**Bessie Eyton, Kay Johnson, Margaret Lindsay** and **Barbara Britton** each appear as the seemingly innocent niece of a crooked judge. In reality, she is very much in on the scam run by her uncle and a con man intent on stealing the claims of miners in an Alaskan boom town. These proper appearing ladies are the bad-good girls contrasted respectively with Kathlyn Williams, Betty Compson, Marlene Dietrich and Anne Baxter as Cherry Malotte, the good-bad girl.

CHESTER, NATALIE
MY AMERICAN WIFE (1923, Silent, Paramount)—**Gloria Swanson**, from Kentucky, finds love and romance with Argentinian Antonio Moreno, who fights a duel for her honor.

CHESTER, RICHARD
THE BACHELOR DADDY (1922, Silent, Paramount)—Mineowner **Thomas Meighan** needs a mother for his foreman's five children when the latter is killed. His fiancee breaks off the engagement when he makes it clear he plans to have a ready-made family. His secretary, who has long loved Meighan, steps in and solves his problem.

CHESWICK, DR. MARK
TAMMY AND THE DOCTOR (1963, Universal)—**Peter Fonda** provides the romance for Tammy, played by Sandra Dee, when the backwoods girl becomes a nurse's aide.

CHETWORTH-LYNDE, LADY
STEPPING SISTERS (1932, Fox)—**Jobyna Howland**, Louise Dresser and Minna Gombell, all proper society ladies, start drinking and reminiscing about their days in burlesque while attending a gala, the result of which was supposed to be very funny—but it wasn't.

CHEYENNE
CHEYENNE RIDES AGAIN (1937, Victory)—**Tom Tyler** is hired by the cattleman's association to infiltrate a gang of rustlers.

CHEYENNE
CHEYENNE TAKES OVER (1947, Eagle-Lion)—**Lash LaRue** puts things right when the heir to a ranch is killed and the only witness is afraid to talk.

CHEYENNE HARRY
A KNIGHT OF THE RANGE (1916, Silent, Universal)—**Harry Carey** takes the blame for a stagecoach holdup to protect the fiance of the woman he loves. His good deed doesn't go unrewarded.

CHEYENNE KID
THE CHEYENNE KID (1933, RKO); (1940, Monogram)—**Tom Keene** and **Jack Randall** each appear as a cowboy mistaken for a murdering outlaw. He's thrown into jail, escapes and captures the real killer.

CHEYNEY, FAY
THE LAST OF MRS. CHEYNEY (1929, MGM); (1937, MGM)—**Norma Shearer** and **Joan Crawford** appear as an adventurer intent on stealing her hostess' pearl necklace. When she falls in love with a society man also spending the weekend at her intended victim's country home, she doesn't wish to go through with the theft, but her accomplice convinces her to do so. She's caught in the act and leaves her punishment up to the guests, but she gets off and gets her man because she has something on everyone present.

CHIAPA
THE CAPTIVE GOD (1916, Silent, Triangle)—A Spanish boy, washed ashore somewhere off Mexico, is raised by peaceful cliff dwellers. When he becomes a man, **William S. Hart**, he is made a chief of the tribe. When his people are attacked by the Aztecs, Hart proves to be a mighty warrior, but he's captured and is to be offered as a sacrifice to the sun god. But through the intercession of Aztec King Montezuma's daughter Enid Markey, he is spared.

CHIAROMONTE, ANGELA
THE WHITE SISTER (1923, Silent, Metro); (1933, MGM)—**Lillian Gish** and **Helen Hayes** play an Italian aristocrat cheated out of her inheritance by her nasty sister. She is in love with an officer (Ronald Colman in the silent, Clark Gable in the talkie). When he is reported killed in battle, she enters a convent. Her lover comes back, begging her to leave her order and come to him, but having taken her final vows, she refuses. Her love is killed trying to save villagers after an eruption by Vesuvius.

CHIC
THE GHOST CATCHERS (1944, Universal)—**Chic Johnson** and his partner Ole Olsen get tangled up with a southern colonel and his beautiful daughter in a spooky old mansion.

CHICKIE
CHICKIE (1925, Silent, First National)—Stenographer **Dorothy Mackaill** submits to a young law clerk at a millionaire's party. Afterwards, the millionaire takes an interest in her and proposes marriage, but is repulsed by her when she reveals she no longer is a virgin. She learns she is pregnant but can't locate the father. The latter shows up after the child is born, ready to do the "decent thing."

CHICO
THE MAGNIFICENT SEVEN (1960, UA)—German actor **Horst Buchholz** portrays a farm boy with ambitions of becoming a gunslinger. He's allowed to join six others who are hired to defend a Mexican farm village from bandits led by Eli Wallach. When all the smoke has cleared, Horst stays in the village with a pretty senorita.

CHIJIK
THREE RUSSIAN GIRLS (1943, UA)—**Kathy Frye** is one of three Russian nurses who tend to injured Americans in WWII after a plane crash. The purpose of the picture was to show the U.S. how wonderful were our Russian allies, but at the time of the House Un-American Activities Committee in the fifties, such films were looked upon as giving aid and comfort to the "godless" communists.

CHILTERN, SIR ROBERT
AN IDEAL HUSBAND (1948, GB, British Lion)—Member of Parliament **Hugh Williams** is being blackmailed by adventurer Paulette Goddard to promote a phony canal scheme.

CHILVERE, CORRINE
INDISCREET CORRINE (1917, Silent, Triangle)—**Olive Thomas** attempts to create a shady "past" for herself, first by becoming engaged to a phony South America millionaire and then by taking up with any fellow who could help her develop a wicked reputation.

CHINASKI, HENRY
BARFLY (1987, Cannon)—**Mickey Rourke** gives a winning perform-ance as a hard-drinking, fist-fighting barfly who revels in his existence. The character is meant to be the young Charles Bukowski, a cult novelist/poet who describes the Los Angeles lowlife which includes him.

CHINESE BOOKIE, THE
THE KILLING OF A CHINESE BOOKIE (1976, Faces)—Sunset Strip nightclub owner Ben Gazzara is in hock to local loan sharks who offer to forgive his debt if he will kill Chinese Bookie **Soto Joe Hugh**. Gazzara does but makes such a mess of it that he's ordered hit as well.

CHINGACHGOOK
THE LAST OF THE MOHICANS (1920, Silent, AP); (1936, UA)—**Theodore Lorch** played the role in the silent film and **Robert Barrat** in the remake. When the vicious Huron Magua kills Chingachgook's son Uncas, Chingachgook becomes the last of the Mohicans.

CHING-CHING
STOWAWAY (1936, 20th Century Fox)—**Shirley Temple**, the ward of murdered missionaries, hides in the trunk of Robert Young's car which is being loaded on an ocean liner headed for the U.S. Young and his new bride Alice Faye adopt Temple. When the couple consider divorcing, Temple turns on the charm and keeps them together.

CHIP
ON THE TOWN (1949, MGM)—Skinny sailor **Frank Sinatra** is no match for amorous taxi driver Betty Garrett when Frank, Gene Kelly and Jules Muschin spend a 24-hour leave in New York.

CHIPPING, CHARLES (ARTHUR)
GOODBYE MR. CHIPS (1939, GB, MGM); (1969, APJAC/MGM)—**Robert Donat** is superb as the shy British school-master who as a novice teacher became a strict disciplinarian. His aloofness made him unpopular with his young charges until he meets and falls in love with Greer Garson who brings out his humanity. She dies in childbirth losing the child, but her influence stays with him throughout his long life, making him the most beloved teacher of several generations of "his boys." In the musical remake, Peter O'Toole (his first name being given as Arthur), is excellent but the film as a whole is disappointing, and the Leslie Bricusse songs seem to serve no purpose.

CHISUM, JOHN
CHISUM (1970, Warner Brothers)—New Mexico cattle baron **John Wayne** has his problems with greedy rival Forrest Tucker in this action-adventure film based on the Lincoln County range war of the early 1880s.

CHITO
JOCKS (1987, Crown)—**Trinidad Silva**, a babbling praying Mexi-can, is one member of a weird assortment of tennis players whom coach Richard Roundtree has been ordered to turn into champs or lose his job. The ending of this waste-of-time film is as predictable as tomorrow's sunrise.

CHO-CHO-SAN
MADAME BUTTERFLY (1915, Silent, Famous Players); (1932, Para-mount)—Even without the Puccini music, these pictures about the Japanese girl who has a son, sired by an American naval officer, and commits suicide when he comes back years later with a wife to pick up the boy, are guaranteed to bring tears to the eyes, as **Mary Pickford** and **Sylvia Sidney** suffer so effectively.

CHOIRBOY
THE FIVE HEARTBEATS (1991, 20th Century Fox)—**Tico Wells** is a member of a fictional 1965 rhythm and blues group.

CHRIS
HIS BROTHER'S WIFE (1936, MGM)—Young scientist **Robert Taylor** is helped out by his brother John Eldredge on the condition that he disappear. This allows Eldredge to marry Taylor's fiancee Barbara Stanwyck, who believes she has been deserted.

CHRIS
THE MAGNIFICENT SEVEN (1960, UA); THE RETURN OF THE SEVEN (1966, UA); THE MAGNIFICENT SEVEN RIDE (1972, UA)—**Yul Brynner** is very effective as the gunslinger who puts together a team of hired guns to "swat some flies" in a Mexican village just south of the border. He yearns for peace but he only knows killing. He and the other six kill forty bandits, losing only four of their own number. Brynner appeared in the same role in an inferior sequel, RETURN OF THE SEVEN in 1966. For the final go at Japan's THE SEVEN SAMURAI, **Lee Van Cleef** stands in for Brynner, but it's just a routine shoot 'em up.

CHRIS
PLATOON (1987, Orion)—Audiences see what **Charlie Sheen** sees when the former college student joins a combat platoon in Vietnam. One feels like they are having their noses rubbed into the dirt, sweat and blood of a war not totally understood by those involved.

CHRIS
REAL GENIUS (1985, Tri-Star)—Science prodigy **Val Kilmer** leads a revolt against his egomaniacal mentor William Atherton, who is using the talents of Kilmer and other genius kids to build a laser weapon for the CIA.

CHRIS
RETURN OF THE SOLDIER (1983, GB, 20th Century Fox)—**Alan Bates**, a shell-shocked WWI British army officer, has had all his post-adolescent memory blocked out. He has no feeling for his wife Julie Christie, but wishes to rekindle a romance with a teenage farm girl, now grown into drab, married woman Glenda Jackson.

CHRIS
SATAN'S CHEERLEADERS (1977, World Amusements)—**Hillary Horan** is one of the stuck-up cheerleaders whom janitor Jack Kruschen, a member of a satanic cult, plans to make brides of the devil. This is an obnoxious piece of junk—far below even the trash usually reserved for drive-in theater passion pits of the period.

CHRISTABEL
BORN TO BE BAD (1950, RKO)—Ambitious **Joan Fontaine** marries millionaire Zachary Scott but continues her affair with moody novelist Robert Ryan. She ultimately dumps both men to go on to new conquests.

CHRISTIAN, DR. PAUL
MEET DR. CHRISTIAN (1939, RKO); THE COURAGEOUS DR. CHRISTIAN (1940, RKO); DR. CHRISTIAN MEETS THE WOMEN (1940, RKO)—Humanitarian **Jean Hersholt** portrays the saintly doctor who solves everybody's problem more through folksy good

sense than remarkable medical talents. Still, in 1940, he leads a crusade against a spinal meningitis epidemic. In the third film, he exposes a quack's diet scam.

CHRISTIE, AGATHA
AGATHA (1979, GB, Warner Brothers)—The film concentrates on the 1926 disappearance of the famed British mystery writer, as played by **Vanessa Redgrave**. When she showed up again, she claimed to have had amnesia and could remember nothing. Miss Marple would never have bought that.

CHRISTIE, ANNA
ANNA CHRISTIE (1923, Silent, Associated First National); (1930, MGM)—**Blanche Sweet** and **Greta Garbo** appear as a waterfront prostitute, abandoned by her seaman father as a child, but who catches up with him, moving in with him as his boozy mistress. She leaves this happy home to seek a new life with a young sailor. Neither movie is outstanding, but the second is remembered as Garbo's first talkie, with her first line being: "Give me a whiskey, and don't be stingy."

CHRISTIE, JACK
HIS ROYAL HIGHNESS (1918, Silent, World)—**Carlyle Blackwell** and his college roommate go to Europe, where the latter is the heir to the throne of Wallanga. When the heir is hurt in a fight with an Apache in Paris, Blackwell takes his place, showing "his" country some American know-how. He falls in love with a princess before relinquishing the throne to his roommate.

CHRISTINA
CHRISTINA (1929, Fox)—**Janet Gaynor**, daughter of a Dutch toy maker, falls in love with the shill for a seedy carnival.

CHRISTINA
CHRISTINA (1974, Canada, New World)—**Barbara Parkins** offers Peter Haskell $25,000 to marry her, in name only. Just as he's falling in love with her, she disappears. Trying to find her, he discovers the conspiracy behind the offer.

CHRISTINA
FRANKENSTEIN CREATED WOMAN (1965, GB, Hammer)—Peter Cushing as Frankenstein revives dead **Susan Denberg** with the soul of her deceased lover. The two merged as one go on a murderous rampage.

CHRISTINA, QUEEN
QUEEN CHRISTINA (1933, MGM)—**Greta Garbo** is exquisite as the seventeenth century Swedish queen who gives up her throne for Spanish lover John Gilbert, who is killed. Garbo's haunting face at the end of the picture is said to be the result of the instructions of director Rouben Mamoulian to think of absolutely nothing.

CHRISTINE
CHRISTINE OF THE BIG TOP (1926, Silent, Banner)—Orphan **Pauline Garon**, daughter of circus performers, falls in love with young surgeon Cullen Landis, who has lost his nerve. He has joined the circus as a physician and vet. Eventually Landis must perform extraordinary surgery on Garon when she is seriously injured in a trapeze accident.

CHRISTINE
THE GRASSHOPPER (1970, National General Pictures)—Canadian **Jacqueline Bisset** tries to make it as a Las Vegas showgirl, but when this doesn't prove to be a stepping stone to show business stardom, she becomes a call girl.

CHRISTINE, LILY
LILY CHRISTINE (1932, GB, Paramount British)—In her final film appearance, silent screen star **Corrine Griffith** is a stranded married woman forced to spend the night with Colin Clive. Even though nothing amiss happens, her husband Jack Trevor sues for divorce and Griffith attempts suicide.

CHRYSAGON
THE WAR LORD (1965, Universal)—Eleventh century feudal knight **Charlton Heston** evokes the law that allows him to deflower the brides of his vassals on their wedding nights. He is selective in exercising his right.

CHRYSTAL, BOBBY
MY TUTOR (1983, Crown International)—**Matt Lattanzi** gets what any horny failing high school boy could ever want, a luscious older female live-in tutor Caren Kaye, who enjoys taking nude midnight swims in the pool. Categorize this one under Male Fantasy #-23109.

CHUBASCO
CHUBASCO (1968, Warner Brothers)—Rather than be thrown into jail, **Christopher Jones** joins the San Diego tuna fleet. He falls in love with Susan Strasberg, the daughter of Portuguese fisherman Richard Egan, who doesn't approve of the match until Jones proves his worth.

CHUCK
BOY OF THE STREETS (1937, Monogram)—Slum boy **Jackie Cooper** gets mixed up with racketeers.

CHUCK
THE THREE LEGIONNAIRES (1937, General)—**Robert Armstrong** and his buddy Lyle Talbot are not legionnaires. They are American soldiers in Russia who get into a lot of trouble with their personal crusade against the communist government.

CHUKA
CHUKA (1967, Paramount)—Wandering gunfighter **Rod Taylor** meanders into a remote cavalry fort the night before it is besieged by a horde of Arapahos. For most of the film, nothing much happens and when the action begins, it isn't worth the wait.

CHUNK
THE GOONIES (1985, Warner Brothers)—Whenever one films the story of the adventures of a bunch of kids, one has to be overweight and always thinking of food. **Jeff Cohen** fills this role in this hit-and-miss yarn of the adventures of underprivileged kids who find a treasure map. Look for Anne Ramsey, nominated for an Academy Award for her performance in THROW MAMA FROM THE TRAIN, warming up in this one.

CHURCH
RENT-A-COP (1988, Kings Row)—**Burt Reynolds**, a former cop, busted to being a security guard in a department store, and sharp-tongued, heart of gold, hooker Liza Minnelli exchange insults in this run-of-the-mill comedy thriller. To be reinstated on the force he has to solve a blown million dollar drug bust and save Liza from the baddies. Reynolds can no longer assume that the public will accept him in anything just by being charming.

CHURCH, LUCY
EYEWITNESS (1956, GB, Rank)—**Muriel Parlow** is run over by a bus after witnessing a robbery. The gangsters invade her hospital to kill her but are constantly foiled.

CHURCHILL, DANNY, JR.

GIRL CRAZY (1943, MGM)—**Mickey Rooney** teams for the eighth time with Judy Garland in this George and Ira Gershwin musical about love at a desert college. The George and Ira Gershwin songs including "I Got Rhythm," "Embraceable You," "Fascinating Rhythm," "Bidin' My Time" and "But Not For Me" made wonderful numbers for the pint-sized whizzes.

CHURCHILL, WINSTON

YOUNG WINSTON (1972, GB, Columbia)—**Simon Ward** gives a pretty good account of himself, portraying the great British statesman. When he was a young man, he had several harrowing adventures as a journalist and a soldier in South Africa. The film ends with Churchill's first election to Parliament.

CICOTTE, ED

EIGHT MEN OUT (1988, Orion)—In this story of the eight Chicago White Sox ballplayers who were barred for life from the game for throwing the 1919 World Series to the Cincinnati Reds, **David Strathairn** appears as the 14-year-veteran pitcher, earning only $5,500 from miserly owner Charles Comiskey, even though he had won 29 games during the year. Cicotte was denied a $10,000 bonus because as "The Old Roman" said "29 is not 30," meaning 30 wins. Disgruntled Cicotte accepted the gambler's offer and served up sweet pitches to the Reds' players who hit long drives, many of which were caught by his outfielders with circus catches. They insisted if Cicotte was going to throw the game, he had to do it by himself.

CID, EL

EL CID (1961, Allied Artists)—**Charlton Heston** appears as Rodrigo Diaz de Bivar, known as El Cid, the Spanish soldier and epic hero who drove the Moors from Spain.

CIELLO, DANIEL

PRINCE OF THE CITY (1981, Warner Brothers)—New York vice cop **Treat Williams** is induced to blow the whistle on his crooked fellow officers.

CIMARRON KID

THE CIMARRON KID (1951, Universal)—**Audie Murphy** is an ex-member of the Dalton gang, and they want him back. Don't ask us why.

CINCINNATI KID

THE CINCINNATI KID (1965, MGM)—In an attempt to do for poker what THE HUSTLER did for pool, **Steve McQueen** is a young player out to take champ Edward G. Robinson in a not so friendly game in New Orleans. Others in the big game have their own agenda, and McQueen has two queens away from the table, Ann-Margret and Tuesday Weld.

CINDERELLA

CINDERELLA (1915, Silent, Famous Players); A KISS FOR CINDERELLA (1926, Silent); (1950, Animated, Disney/ RKO); (1985, Faerie Tale Theatre)—**Mary Pickford** gives a winning performance as the put-upon youngster who makes a big hit at the prince's ball with the help of a fairy godmother. **Betty Bronson** followed in the role in 1926. In the 1950 animated version of the fairy tale, **Ilene Woods** provides the voice of Cinderella. In 1985, **Jennifer Beals** is a particularly beautiful Cinderella.

CINDY

HIGH YELLOW (1965, Dinero/Thunder)—Seventeen year old black servant **Cynthia Hall** is light enough to pass for white, but after observing the white folks for whom she works and their messed up lives, she develops some black pride.

CIRCE

CIRCE THE ENCHANTRESS (1924, Silent, MGM)—**Mae Murray** portrays both the enchantress of ancient times who turns men into swine by magic and a modern counterpart who does it with liquor. How does that Ogden Nash rhyme go? "Magic is Tragic, but Liquor is Quicker." No, we guess that's "Candy is Dandy."

CISCO KID

CISCO KID (1931, Fox); THE CISCO KID AND THE LADY (1939, 20th Century Fox); RETURN OF THE CISCO KID (1939, 20th Century Fox); THE GAY CABALLERO (1940, 20th Century Fox); LUCKY CISCO KID (1940, 20th Century Fox); VIVA CISCO KID (1940, 20th Century Fox); THE CISCO KID RETURNS (1945, Monogram); KING OF THE BANDITS (1948, Monogram); THE DARING CABALLERO (1949, UA); THE GAY AMIGO (1949, UA)—**Warner Baxter** in the 30s, **Cesar Romero** taking over late in 1939 and continuing into the early 1940s, and **Duncan Renaldo** in the mid to late 1940s (replaced by **Gilbert Roland** in 1948) each appeared as O. Henry's ruthless Mexican bandit, but generally he is portrayed as a dashing western Robin Hood usually accompanied by a fat side-kick Pancho, along for comic relief—but the characterization can't be too amusing to Mexicans.

CLAIBORNE, JEFFREY

HIGH GEAR JEFFREY (1921, Silent, American Film)—Wealthy **William Russell** rescues a girl from the advances of a chauffeur and accepts a job in her mother's taxi company. He has to expose some gangsters threatening the company before winning the girl.

"CLAIRBOURNE, ANN" *See* GAIL LOVELASS

CLAIRE

BLONDE ICE (1949, Film Classics)—Socialite **Leslie Brooks** kills her husbands and lovers because she enjoys reading about the scandals in the newspapers. It takes police psychologist David Leonard to trick her into making a confession before the crazed woman accidently kills herself, fleeing the police.

CLAIRE

BROTHER SUN, SISTER MOON (1972, GB, Paramount/Vic)—**Judi Bowker** is one of the followers of a hip Francis of Assisi. She forsakes everything she had been taught to appreciate by her wealthy family in order to join a flower child-like commune. The songs by folk-singer Donovan are not memorable.

CLAIRE

THE MAIDS (1975, GB, Cine Films)—Paris maids **Susannah York** and Glenda Jackson plot a sado-masochistic ritual murder of their employer but don't carry it out.

CLAIRE

REBELLIOUS DAUGHTERS (1938, Times)—Unable to get any loving attention at home, small town girl **Marjorie Reynolds** heads for the big city where she attracts a lot of attention—all the wrong kind until the right man comes along to protect her.

CLAIRE, RUBY

RUBY (1977, Dimension)—Drive-in theater owner **Piper Laurie** had been the lover of a gangster killed many years earlier. Somehow his spirit enters the body of their deaf-mute daughter and now he has the means to get some revenge.

CLAMSON, GERALD

THE BIG MOUTH (1967, Columbia)—In a role which is reminiscent of the Edward G. Robinson film THE WHOLE TOWN'S TALKING, **Jerry Lewis** is a meek bank clerk who finds he's the exact double of a dying mobster. See the Robinson film.

CLANCY, MARY

THE TROUBLE WITH ANGELS (1966, Columbia)—New student **Hayley Mills** is one of the ringleaders of a group of girls who make their all-female school chaotic for Mother Superior Rosalind Russell. Mills proves she's really a good egg and decides she wants to become a nun.

CLANCY, MICHAEL

CLANCY IN WALL STREET (1930, Aristocrat)—When **Charles Murray** has a windfall in the stock market, he deserts his partner and their plumbing business to test the waters of high finance some more. When he's wiped out on Black Friday, his ex-partner forgives him and takes Murray back into the business.

CLANCY, SHAKESPEARE

THE JAILBIRD (1920, Silent, Paramount)—Crook **Douglas MacLean** escapes from prison, inherits a small town newspaper, becomes involved in an oil swindle which turns out to be a gusher, and reforms.

CLANCY, TOM

CLANCY'S KOSHER WEDDING (1927, Silent, R-C Pictures)—**Rex Lease** loves Leah Cohen played by Ann Brody, but her family prefers that she marry a Jewish prize fighter. The latter and Lease fight at a picnic with the agreement that the winner gets the girl. Lease wins.

CLARA

THE GIRL ON THE BRIDGE (1951, 20th Century Fox)—**Beverly Michaels** is no actress, and she gets no help from co-star and director Hugo Haas, a movie maker who consistently made poor movies. He's a watchmaker married to Michaels, who drives him to suicide. This movie could drive movie lovers to the brink of suicide.

CLARA

RENALDO AND CLARA (1978, Lombard Street Circuit)—**Sara Dylan** is the wife of songwriter singer Bob Dylan. She doesn't have his talent for acting, and he has none.

CLARE, LYLAH

THE LEGEND OF LYLAH CLARE (1968, MGM)—Insane movie director Peter Finch finds a girl, **Kim Novak**, who is a double for his former star creation who died mysteriously. Sounds like Kim is repeating her VERTIGO role.

CLARENCE

CLARENCE AND ANGEL (1978, Gardner)—**Darren Brown**, a shy illiterate kid from South Carolina, is taught to read by a sharp New York street kid, kung-fu mad Mark Cardova.

CLARICE

LADY BEHAVE (1937, Republic)—Having had a bit too much to drink, **Patricia Farr** forgets that she already has a husband and marries a millionaire. It takes her sister Sally Eilers to bail her out of the mess.

CLARISSA

JAZZ BABIES (1932, Peerless)—**Madge Evans** works as a dancer-singer in a naughty Chicago nightspot where the girls wear as little as the law will allow. The club is in danger of being closed by a bluenose so the "entertainers" put on a private showing of "Mid-summer Night's Dream" to prove that the place is a legit club with lots of culture. When this doesn't work, Evans marries a grain dealer and settles down in Evanston.

CLARK, ALLEN

IF I'M LUCKY (1946, 20th Century Fox)—**Perry Como** goes into politics in this dreadful remake of the studio's THANKS FOR A MILLION. Como's singing can't save this turkey.

CLARK, ANDREW

THE BREAKFAST CLUB (1985, Universal)—**Emilio Estevez** is a jock, in a Saturday detention with four other high school students. He and the others appear to learn more from each other than they do from their parents and teachers, a sad commentary on modern times.

CLARK, DEBORAH CHANDLER

WOMAN IN HIDING (1953, GB, Hammer)—After escaping her husband's attempts to kill her, **Ida Lupino** goes into hiding until enough evidence is rounded up to put him away. The film is short on suspense.

CLARK, REV. CHARLES DISMAS S.J.

THE HOODLUM PRIEST (1961, UA)—Jesuit priest and teacher **Don Murray** tries to help criminals, especially condemned killer Keir Dullea. It's a depressing story which fails to impress on a dramatic level.

CLARK, EMMA

SEVEN WOMEN (1966, MGM)—**Sue Lyon** is an aide to Margaret Leighton, the no-nonsense head of an American religious mission in Mongolia in 1935. Leighton appears to have "unnatural" designs on her pretty assistant.

CLARK, GALEN

GUARDIAN OF THE WILDERNESS (1977, Sunn Classics)—Suffering from black lung disease, ex-miner **Denver Pyle** settles in the Sequoia Forest of Yosemite. He persuades President Abraham Lincoln to sign a bill which would save the forest from lumber companies.

CLARK, GRACE

I LOVE THAT MAN (1933, Paramount)—**Nancy Carroll** is determined to get her con-man boyfriend Edmund Lowe on the straight and narrow path. It's too late. Two thugs shoot him, but he marries Carroll just before expiring.

CLARK, JANIE

TALK ABOUT A LADY (1946, Columbia)—Country girl **Jinx Falkenberg** inherits a lot of money and a nightclub. Trudy Marshall who works at the club feels she had earned the inheritance. That's it for dramatic conflict in this feeble musical.

CLARK, JIMMY

INTRODUCE ME (1925, Silent, Associated Exhibitors)—**Douglas MacLean** allows a girl he's trying to impress to believe that he is a famous mountain climber. When the real climber shows up at the Alps, he's happy to go along with the joke. Now MacLean is scared to death of heights. Get the picture? Now write the rest of the screenplay.

CLARK, JOE

LEAN ON ME (1989, Warner Brothers)—**Morgan Freeman** is excellent as the Paterson, New Jersey high school principal who cleaned up his school, kicked out the druggies, and enforced a dictatorial discipline on faculty and students alike. Whether improved education resulted from his questionable means is not clear.

CLARK, JONATHAN
THE WORLD IN HIS ARMS (1952, Universal)—**Gregory Peck**, a tough sea captain, falls in love with beautiful Russian countess Ann Blyth.

CLARK, KELLY
HI, GOOD LOOKIN' (1944, Universal)—Singer **Harriet Hillard** arrives from the Midwest and becomes a smash vocalist on Hollywood radio.

CLARK, MARJORIE
LADY GODIVA RIDES AGAIN (1955, GB, London/Carroll)—Beauty contest winner **Pauline Stroud** discovers that the world of glamour has a seamy side.

CLARK, RICHARD
THE MEANEST MAN IN THE WORLD (1943, 20th Century Fox)—Soft-hearted unsuccessful lawyer **Jack Benny** makes it big when he turns nasty and mean.

CLARK, SALLY
HIS WOMAN (1931, Paramount)—When the captain of a tramp steamer, Gary Cooper, is left with an abandoned baby, he taps runaway tramp **Claudette Colbert** to be the child's seagoing mother.

CLARK, TOMMY
TOUGH AS THEY COME (1942, Universal)—**Billy Halop** is the leader of the Little Tough Guys, one of many spin-offs of former Dead End Kids members. He and his friends uncover the illegal activities of the finance company for which they are working.

CLARK, WILLY
THE SUNSHINE BOYS (1975, UA)—**Walter Matthau** is excellent as a crusty old vaudevillian who has never forgiven George Burns, his partner of forty or more years for retiring and splitting up the act. The two are to be reunited one more time on a TV special about the history of comedy. When Burns and Matthau are brought together, their love-hate relationship is off and running once again. While filming their famous doctor's sketch, things which annoyed Matthau for all the years erupt, causing him to blow the sketch and suffer a heart attack. As he recovers from this, it's clear that he has lost none of his sarcasm or irascible behavior.

CLARKE, BARBARA
MAID OF SALEM (1937, Paramount)—**Claudette Colbert** almost goes up in smoke when she is accused of being a witch in colonial America, but she is saved at the last moment by Fred MacMurray.

CLARKE, GEOFFREY
HE KNEW WOMEN (1930, RKO)—Novelist **Lowell Sherman** dumps loving Frances Dade for a wealthy widow upon whom he leeches until someone better comes along for her.

CLARKE, JANE
READY, WILLING AND ABLE (1937, Warner Brothers)—**Ruby Keeler**, a cutie of very limited talents, is mistakenly signed as the lead in a Broadway show by the writers. The backers wanted them to sign British actress Winifred Shaw. The film is touched with tragedy as co-star Ross Alexander committed suicide before it was released.

CLARKE, LARRY
ONE MAN JUSTICE (1937, Columbia)—For many young movie fans and many not so young, **Charles Starrett** was the best thing ever seen in a western. In this one, he's the exact double of a man believed long dead. In fact he is the man, having had a bout of amnesia. He cleans up a town and reclaims his wife and ranch, which he had forgotten.

CLARY, DESIREE
DESIREE (1954, 20th Century Fox)—**Jean Simmons**, a fictitious French girl, continuously turns up in Napoleon Bonaparte's life whenever anything of historical interest is about to happen. But Napoleon, played by Marlon Brando, never quite gets to loving her—although he does use her.

CLAUDE
THE DEVIL IS A SISSY (1936, Metro)—When his parents announce that they are divorcing, **Freddie Bartholomew** takes up with a bad crowd.

CLAUDET, MADELON
THE SIN OF MADELON CLAUDET (1931, MGM)—**Helen Hayes** won an Oscar for her fine performance in her film debut in this weeper about a mother separated from her illegitimate child.

CLAUDIN, ENRIQUE (ERIK)
PHANTOM OF THE OPERA (1925, Silent, Universal); (1943, Universal); (1962, GB, Universal)—**Lon Chaney, Sr., Claude Rains** and **Hebert Lom** each portrayed the musician driven mad when he is disfigured by having acid thrown into his face. He takes refuge in the sewers under the Paris Opera House from where he undertakes to advance the career of a young female singer whom he loves, even to the point of killing her rivals. Finally he kidnaps her and takes her to his subterranean home, where in the best scene in each picture, she unmasks him, revealing his horrible face.

CLAUDINE
CLAUDINE (1974, 20th Century Fox)—Mother of six, **Diahann Carroll** tries to hold her family together in an environment where cheating is the rule and is usually rewarded. She falls for garbage man James Earl Jones, but he runs away from any long-term commitment, but her children get him to change his mind.

CLAVERING, HENRY
THE MAN IN BLACK (1950, GB, Hammer)—**Sidney James** fakes his own death and thwarts his shrewish wife's plans to drive his daughter mad so she will not inherit any of her father's money.

CLAY, SALOMY JANE
WILD GIRL (1932, Fox)—**Joan Bennett** is not so much wild as she is a tomboy in this story set in the Sierras after the Civil War. She falls in love with and runs off to the high country with Charles Farrell after he kills the varmint who seduced his sister.

CLAYBURN, JOHN
KING OF THE PECOS (1936, Republic)—When lawyer **John Wayne's** efforts to avenge the death of his parents can't be accomplished within the law, he employs gun justice.

CLAYDON, JOHN
JOHN OF THE FAIR (1962, GB, Continental)—In a story set in eighteenth century England, fourteen-year-old **John Charlesworth** is an assistant in a carnival medicine show when it is discovered that he is the heir to a title. This leads to him being kidnapped by an evil uncle. His carny friends come to his rescue.

CLAYTON, DAN

SON OF OKLAHOMA (1932, World Wide)—**Bob Steele** who appeared in more movies than he or anyone else can count stars in this one as the man a boy becomes after being separated from his parents. The three are ultimately reunited into a happy family once again.

CLAYTON, JOHN *See* TARZAN

CLAYTON, SAM

GOOD SAM (1948, RKO)—Guileless small town businessman **Gary Cooper** is charitable to a fault—literally. Just ask his harassed wife, Ann Sheridan.

CLEAVER, BILL

DANCING SWEETIES (1930, Warner Brothers)—**Grant Withers** meets Sue Carol during a dance contest and proposes that they team up both on and off the dance floor. Later, when she can't measure up to his dance expectations, he briefly deserts her, but in the end they dance off into the sunset.

CLEAVES, DAVEY

THE HOSTAGE (1966, Heartland/Crown)—Six-year-old **Danny Martin** is trapped in a moving van which contains his family's belongings and is being driven by two murderers. When they discover the boy, he senses that they are going to kill him and he flees, with them in hot pursuit.

CLEGG, FREDDIE

THE COLLECTOR (1965, Columbia)—Mousy clerk **Terence Stamp's** only interest is collecting butterflies. He falls in love with Samantha Eggar but when she repulses him, he kidnaps her and keeps her in a well-appointed cellar. He doesn't lay a hand on her, merely observing her as he does his butterflies.

CLEGG, HARRY

CLEGG (1969, GB, Tigon)—Detective **Gilbert Wynne** investigates a series of murders committed by a crazed prostitute.

CLEGG, JABEZ

THE MANCHESTER MAN (1920, GB, Silent, Ideal)—In 1800 Lancaster, clerk **Hayford Hobbs** loves Aileen Bagot, the daughter of a wealthy merchant, but she runs away with a criminal.

CLEGG, NORA

I'LL LOVE YOU ALWAYS (1935, Columbia)—**Nancy Carroll** doesn't tell her husband George Murphy that she is pregnant. When he's sent to prison for stealing, he has her believing he's away in Russia on business.

CLEMENS, JEAN

MUSIC FOR MADAME (1937, RKO)—**Joan Fontaine** is the romantic interest of opera star Nino Martini. His efforts to make it big in Hollywood are threatened when he becomes the unwitting front for some crooks. The film doesn't give Fontaine much opportunity to show her acting talents.

CLEMENS, SAMUEL

THE ADVENTURES OF MARK TWAIN (1944, Warner Brothers)—**Fredric March** is convincing in his portrayal of the great American humorist, but Hal Holbrook he's not.

CLEMENT

THE IMPOSTER (1944, Universal)—Saved from the guillotine by a Nazi air raid, **Jean Gabin** joins the French resistance movement and becomes a hero.

CLEMENTI, BARBARA

FUGITIVE LADY (1951, Republic)—When **Janis Paige's** husband Eduardo Ciannelli falls to his death, insurance investigator Tony Centa suspects foul play. Sure enough, Paige did the dirty deed.

CLEMENTINE

MY DARLING CLEMENTINE (1946, 20th Century Fox)—**Cathy Downs** is the nice sensible girl to whom Henry Fonda as Wyatt Earp pays court in this black and white western masterpiece. He sure does think her name is pretty.

CLEMENTINE

O, MY DARLING CLEMENTINE (1943, Republic)—**Lorna Gray** helps road musician Roy Acuff put on a show in Dixie.

CLEO

CARRY ON CLEO (1964, GB, Warner Brothers/Pathe)—**Amanda Barrie** stars in this lame parody of Elizabeth Taylor's CLEOPATRA. It contains the usual slapstick and silly sex jokes.

CLEOPATRA

CLEOPATRA (1934, Paramount); (1963, 20th Century Fox); CAESAR AND CLEOPATRA (1946, GB, Two Cities); SERPENT OF THE NILE (1953, Columbia); THE NOTORIOUS CLEOPATRA (1970, Box Office Int.); ANTONY AND CLEOPATRA (1973, GB, Rank)—**Claudette Colbert, Elizabeth Taylor, Vivien Leigh, Rhonda Fleming, Sonora** and **Hildegard Neil** gamely tried to bring to life the Queen of the Nile, but with the exception of Leigh who had George Bernard Shaw in her corner, the ladies sunk along with their barges.

CLEWS, JOAN

MY OWN TRUE LOVE (1948, Paramount)—Widower Melvyn Douglas, trying to adjust after WWII, falls in love with **Phyllis Calvert**, a woman young enough to be his daughter. It's one way to reclaim your youth, but it also may be hazardous to one's health.

CLIFFORD, DR. GENE

STEPFATHER 2: MAKE ROOM FOR DADDY (1989, Milli-meter) - You just can't keep a good man down, especially if his movie made a lot of money. When last seen, the stepfather, portrayed by **Terry O'Quinn** was fatally shot and stabbed, but he's back as a predatory patriarch, raising body counts wherever he goes.

CLIFFORD, LADY

THE TEMPTRESS (1949, GB, Ambassador)—**Joan Maude** promises a physician working on a polio cure half of her inheritance if he will murder her husband. He does but the money goes to her son. Physician, Cure Thyself!

CLINT

THE HOUND DOG MAN (1959, 20th Century Fox)—Rock 'n' roll sensation, sixteen-year-old **Fabian** (Forte) is surprisingly good as one of two 1912 teenagers who waste their whole summer instead of tending to their farm chores—and for them it doesn't get any better than that.

CLINTON, TOBEY

THREE IN THE ATTIC (1968, American International)—When campus Don Juan, Christopher Jones refuses to tie himself down to the girl he loves, **Yvette Mimieux**, and instead shacks up with two hippies (one black, one Jewish), the three girls unite and keep Jones prisoner in an attic where they take turns having sex with him, until physically exhausted he agrees to be faithful to one of them—Mimieux.

CLITTERHOUSE, DR.
THE AMAZING DR. CLITTERHOUSE (1938, Warner Brothers)—Criminologist **Edward G. Robinson** joins a mob to further his research and discovers he enjoys the life of a criminal.

CLIVE, ROBERT
CLIVE OF INDIA (1935, Fox/UA)—**Ronald Colman** portrays the great British empire builder who felt India was best ruled as a British colony—the white man's burden, don't you know.

CLIVE, SELBY
THE MAN WHO CHANGED HIS NAME (1928, Silent, GB, British Lion); (1934, GB, DuWorld)—**Stewart Rains** and **Lyn Harding** appear as a man who shortens his name, which is the same as that of a wife-murderer. His new wife begins to believe he is the latter and is plotting to kill her.

CLOTHIDE, SISTER
TILL WE MEET AGAIN (1944, Paramount)—Young French novice nun **Barbara Britton** leaves the convent to pose as the wife of downed American pilot Ray Milland, helping him escape from the Nazis.

CLOUD, "KID WICHITA," TOM & JEFF
THE SUNDOWNERS (1950, Eagle Lion)—**Robert Preston, Robert Sterling** and **John Barrymore, Jr.** are brothers. The eldest, Preston, a desperado, is idolized by the youngest, Barrymore, who wants to grow up to be just like his sibling. Preston conveniently kills the husband loved by brother Sterling. As was customary at this time in Preston's career, he doesn't survive.

CLOUSEAU, JACQUES
INSPECTOR CLOUSEAU (1968, GB, UA)—It's **Alan Arkin**, not Peter Sellers, playing the incompetent French policeman in the weakest film in the series (we choose not to acknowledge TRAIL OF THE PINK PANTHER, a poorly put together set of out-takes from early films in the series, released after Sellers' death). Arkin is called to London to help investigate the Great Train Robbery.

CLOVER, DAISY
INSIDE DAISY CLOVER (1965, Warner Brothers)—In the 1930s adolescent **Natalie Wood** sends a recording of her singing voice to Hollywood. She is quickly whisked to the coast where she becomes a star, but makes a mess of her personal life.

CLUNE, MARGIE
THE CASE OF THE LUCKY LEGS (1935, First National/ Warner Brothers)—**Patricia Ellis** is the owner of the gams mentioned in the title. She's suspected of murdering the promoter of the "Lucky Legs" contest but she's defended by Perry Mason—'nuff said.

CLYDE, CAPT. TONY
THE MAN FROM YESTERDAY (1932, Paramount)—**Clive Brook** marries Claudette Colbert during a WWI Paris air raid. He's reported killed in action but she refuses to marry the doctor, Charles Boyer, whom she loves, until Brook returns, sees how things are and goes off to die.

CNOCKHAERT, MARTHA
I WAS A SPY (1934, GB, Gaumont)—**Madeleine Carroll** appears in the true story of a Belgian nurse who becomes a spy during WWI. She is spared her co-spy Herbert Marshall's fate, a German firing squad, when the Allies rescue her.

COATES, BABS
WICKED WIFE (1955, GB, Allied Artists)—**Moira Lister** is the title character, but she doesn't seem too wicked. She's an alcoholic accidently killed by her horse-owner husband, Nigel Patrick.

COBB, BESSIE
SLEEPYTIME GAL (1942, Republic)—The comedy of **Judy Canova** takes some getting used to. Her exaggerated speech and confused and confusing use of vocabulary is not everybody's cup of white lightning. In this forgettable picture, Canova is mistaken for a nightclub singer on a mob's hit list.

COBB, EZRA
DERANGED (1974, Canada, American International)—**Roberts Blossom** appears as a middle-aged psychotic farmer who kills women and then stuffs and preserves them as trophies. The film is based on Wisconsin farmer Ed Gein, who murdered and skinned dozens of women in the 1950s. You have to be hard-up for something to do to view this nauseating movie.

COBB, ROGER
ALL OF ME (1984, Universal)—**Steve Martin** finds himself possessed by the soul of recently deceased wealthy Lily Tomlin when her plan to have her spirit transferred to another woman goes awry.

COBRA, THE
CHINA SLAVER (1929, Silent, Trinity)—**Sonjin** is the Chinese boss of an island which serves as a base for narcotics traffic and white slavery.

COBRETTI, MARION
COBRA (1986, Warner Brothers)—**Sylvester Stallone** is a "good" cop. Everyone else is bad. There's a lot of action but no story to speak of.

COBURN, LISA
THE SILENT PARTNER (1923, Paramount)—Thrifty **Leatrice Joy** saves all the money and luxuries her stockbroker husband lavishes on her and is thus able to bail him out when he's bullish in a bear market.

COCHISE
CONQUEST OF COCHISE (1953, Columbia); TAZA, SON OF COCHISE (1954, Universal)—**John Hodiak** takes over from Jeff Chandler in the role of the great Apache leader (Chandler won a Best Supporting Actor nomination for his role of Cochise in BROKEN ARROW) and makes Chandler look like quite an actor by comparison. In 1954, Chandler briefly reprises the role, but it's Rock Hudson's picture.

COCHRAN, JADE
SHE FREAK (1967, Sonney)—This is an uncredited ripoff of Tod Browning's FREAKS. **Claire Brennen**, married to the owner of a freak show, is having an affair with Lee Raymond who runs the ferris wheel. Midget Felix Silla squeals on her to her husband, a fight ensues and Raymond kills Brennan's husband. Now the owner of the show, Brennan plans to punish Silla, but the freaks band together and make Claire a new attraction in her own show.

COCHRANE, TOM
FALL GUY (1947, Monogram)—Poor **Clifford Penn** can't remember anything about a night on which it would appear he murdered a woman. But if he was guilty, it wouldn't be much of a movie, would it?

CODY, BUFFALO BILL
BUFFALO BILL ON THE U.P. TRAIL (1926, Silent, Sunset) -Roy Stewart; YOUNG BUFFALO BILL (1940, REPUBLIC)—Roy Rogers; BUFFALO BILL (1944, 20th Century Fox)—Joel McCrea; BUFFALO BILL RIDES AGAIN (1947, Screen Guild)—Richard Arlen; BUFFALO BILL IN TOMAHAWK TERRITORY (1952, UA)—Clayton Moore; BUFFALO BILL AND THE INDIANS (1976, UA)—Paul Newman—William F. Cody is a fine example of what can happen if one has a good P.R. man. His exploits, what there were of them, were exaggerated in dime novels which captured the imagination of folks in the East. A good businessman, Cody exploited his legend and headed up Wild West shows which made him a fortune. The plots of the movies above generally deal with the legend, not the man.

CODY, JAMES
THE LIVE WIRE (1937, GB, British Lion)—Bernard Nedell is an American con man in England. He saves an embezzler from committing suicide, takes the man's place and in six months with a little book-juggling puts everything hunky-dory once again.

COE, LARRY
STRANGERS WHEN WE MEET (1960, Columbia)—In a none too attractive soap opera, married architect Kirk Douglas has an affair with a married neighbor Kim Novak. Oh, how these sinners suffer mental torment for their transgressions.

COFFEE CUP
A GIRL, A GUY AND A GOB (1941, RKO)—When obnoxious George Murphy dumps secretary Lucille Ball, she ends up in the arms of sailor Edmond O'Brien.

COFFEY, GINGER
THE LUCK OF GINGER COFFEY (1964, Continental Distributing) - Robert Shaw is an Irish immigrant in Canada with an attitude problem. His efforts to better himself and provide for his family often go awry.

COFFY
COFFY (1971, American International)—The title refers to the color of tough street girl Pam Grier, who becomes a one-woman avenging machine when her younger sister becomes permanently spaced-out on heroin.

COGBURN, ROOSTER
ROOSTER COGBURN (1975, Universal)—John Wayne got the last word with Kim Darby in TRUE GRIT in which his portrayal of an aging, fat, one-eyed Marshal working out of Fort Smith, Kansas won him a popular Academy Award. In the sequel, he wasn't as fortunate playing opposite Katharine Hepburn, a bible-thumping missionary.

COHAN
FLYING ROMEOS (1928, Silent, First National)—Charles Murray is George Sidney's rival for manicurist Fritzi Ridgeway. When they discover she's just wild for flyers, they sign up for lessons, leading to some dangerous but funny stunts.

COHAN, GEORGE M.
YANKEE DOODLE DANDY (1942, Warner Brothers)—James Cagney is just plain marvelous in the role of the singer, dancer, composer, playwright, producer, etc., George M. Cohan. There might as well be no one else in the show, the way Cagney dominated the proceedings. Cohan, who died in 1942, surely must have approved.

COHEN
FLYING ROMEOS (1928, Silent, First National)—Barber George Sidney would like to beat his partner Charles Murray's time with manicurist Fritzi Ridgeway, a nut about flyers. Their adventures in the sky include being mistaken for hot-shot stunt pilots. By the time they get down to earth, Ridgeway has married another aviator.

COHEN
COHEN AND TATE (1989, Tri-Star)—Mob hitman Roy Scheider has worked alone for thirty years. He hates it that he must now work with a young hot-head Alec Baldwin. A kidnapped nine-year-old son of the victims of the two killers uses this antagonism to his advantage, as the three travel from the site of the murders to Houston, and the mob leaders.

COHEN, JACOB & MRS.
THE COHENS AND THE KELLYS (1926, Silent, Universal); THE COHENS AND KELLYS IN ATLANTIC CITY (1929, Universal)—George Sidney and Vera Gordon are the Jewish half of the two family comedy team whose friendly rivalry gave audiences plenty of laughs. The Cohens and the Kellys also battled in Paris, Scotland, Africa, Hollywood and Trouble.

COHEN, JAKE
MR. COHEN TAKES A WALK (1936, GB, Warner Brothers)—Paul Graetz creates a successful business from his humble beginnings as a peddler. His son takes over the business and makes Graetz feel unnecessary. When his wife dies, he takes to wandering, but when he learns that all his workers have gone on strike, he retakes control of his company and returns to old management practices.

COLBROOK, MARY & BILL
MY BILL (1938, Warner Brothers)—Kay Francis is the widowed mother of four, all ungrateful for her efforts, save the youngest, Dickie Moore, who rewards his mother when he is left a fortune by a neighbor to whom he endeared himself.

COLBURN, HOKE
DRIVING MISS DAISY (1989, Warner Brothers)—Some critics found fault with the movie, because they believed Morgan Freeman, as an aging black chauffeur for a wealthy Jewish matron over a period of 25 years, represented black-white relations the way whites wished they were. This criticism of a superb film is ridiculous. Hopefully there is room in movie stories for black characters who do not rage like those in a Spike Lee film. At no time was the dignity of Freeman's character compromised by his relationship with Jessica Tandy's Miss Daisy, who came to recognize that he was her best friend.

COLBY, ALAN
STOP ME BEFORE I KILL (1961, GB, Columbia)—Ronald Lewis is hurt in an accident just before his honeymoon with Diane Cilento. He finds himself having strange urges to strangle his wife every time they make love. He discovers that his psychiatrist and his wife are a bit too friendly, but the doctor almost convinces him that his suspicions are all in his mind.

COLBY, BARBARA "BAWBS"
BAWBS O' BLUE RIDGE (1916, Silent, Triangle)—Bessie Barriscale lives in a mountain community with her spinster aunt. Author Arthur Shirley moves into the region, and the two fall in love.

COLBY, MAGGIE
THE LADY TAKES A FLYER (1958, Universal)—Lana Turner stars in the true story of a husband and wife airplane ferrying service. Her

husband, Jeff Chandler, saves her life and their marriage when he talks her and her plane down when she finds herself lost in a thick fog.

COLBY, VANCE
THE GAMBLER FROM NATCHEZ (1954, 20th Century Fox)—Like a western Count of Monte Cristo, **Dale Robertson** returns to New Orleans and avenges his father's murder, disposing of the culprits one by one.

COLE
ENTER THE NINJA (1982, Cannon)—**Franco Nero** is a practitioner of an ancient oriental martial art of killing. Being killed in a stylized fashion doesn't make it easier to take.

COLE, GLORIA
MANHATTAN ANGEL (1948, Columbia)—**Gloria Jean** fights the plans to build a factory on the sight of a community youth center on the Lower East Side of New York.

COLE, WILL
THE ROWDYMAN (1973, Canada, Crowley)—**Gordon Pinsent** is a drunken skirt chaser who causes the death of his childhood friend.

COLEBROOKE, VICTOR
WANTED FOR MURDER (1946, GB, 20th Century Fox)—Obsessed by the fact that his father was a Victorian hangman, **Eric Portman** adopts the unhealthy hobby of strangling women.

COLEMAN, AL & RALPH
HUNTER'S BLOOD (1987, Concorde)—**Ken Swofford** and **Mayf Nutter** are among the city hunters who encounter some murderous hill-billies when they enter a woods for rest and relaxation.

COLEMAN, DAVID
HIS SECRETARY (1925, Silent, MGM)—When **Lew Cody** jokes that he wouldn't kiss his plain looking secretary Norma Shearer for $1000, she transforms herself into a beauty and charges him $1000 for a kiss.

COLEMAN, DR. DAVID
THE YOUNG DOCTORS (1961, UA)—**Ben Gazarra** is the new young doctor on the beat in the pathology department of a major hospital. He clashes with his senior Fredric March, but the two men come to respect each other before March retires and turns the department over to Gazarra.

COLEMAN, PETER
AN ANGEL FROM TEXAS (1940, Warner Brothers)—In another film based on George S. Kaufman's play "The Butter and Egg Man," **Eddie Albert** is a country hick who comes to the city with money which he's conned into investing in a flop show.

COLETTE
THE MAN WHO LOVED REDHEADS (1955, London Films)—**Moira Shearer**, as a French mannequin, makes one of her four appearances as a redheaded lover of wealthy Englishman John Justin, who has a thing for carrot-tops.

COLEY, JACK
THE CAT BURGLAR (1961, UA)—When burglar **Jack Hogan** steals a briefcase containing secret documents, he finds himself the target of spies for a foreign power.

COLIN
ABSOLUTE BEGINNERS (1986, GB, Orion)—**Eddie O'Connell** is one of the teenagers in this British musical set in 1958 about—what else—misunderstood teens.

COLIN, CAPT.
THE LUCK OF A SAILOR (1934, GB, Wardour)—**David Manners** lucks out and wins commoner Greta Nissen when the subjects of her husband, a king, plead with her to give up her husband so he can marry an heiress. Too bad, real people can't settle their romantic problems in 66 minutes.

COLL, VINCENT
MAD DOG COLL (1961, Columbia)—In another of the many movies based on the exploits of criminals with catchy nicknames, **John Chandler** portrays one of the bloodiest killers of the twenties. This is not among the better pictures in this sub-genre.

COLLIER, DORA
BUTTERFLY (1924, Silent, Universal)—Selfish **Laura La Plante** flits from man to man, even to the sweetheart of her older sister Ruth Clifford, who has made every sacrifice for La Plante.

COLLIER, LESLIE
FATHER TAKES A WIFE (1941, RKO)—**Gloria Swanson** makes one of her numerous comebacks as a reluctantly retired actress who marries widower Adolphe Menjou.

COLLINGS, HARRY
THE HIRED HAND (1971, Universal)—During the 1880s in New Mexico, drifter **Peter Fonda** decides to return to the wife he had abandoned many years earlier.

COLLINS, ANN
GOLD DIGGERS OF BROADWAY (1929, Warner Brothers)—In the first talkie Gold Diggers movie, **Ann Pennington** is one of three chorus girls who are nice to men who are nice to them. The sheep they fleece are all willing lambs.

COLLINS, REV. DAVID
MAN AFRAID (1957, Universal)—**George Nader** and his family are threatened by Eduard Franz, the psychopathic father of a teenage burglar, whom preacher Nader killed when the former broke into Nader's home.

COLLINS, ELIZABETH
TOO YOUNG TO LOVE (1960, GB, Rank)—New York kid **Paulene Hahn's** life is seen in flashbacks including an affair with a sailor which leads to an abortion and her arrest for prostitution.

COLLINS, GEORGE BRAYNOR
PILOT NO. 5 (1943, MGM)—While **Franchot Tone** is off flying a suicide mission, his pilot buddies discuss his life, which we see in flashbacks.

COLLINS, IRON MAN
SAILOR'S HOLIDAY (1944, Columbia)—Sailor **Lewis Wilson** is in Hollywood with his buddy Arthur Lake who dreams of getting a kiss from Rita Hayworth. A lot of guys had that dream.

COLLINS, JOE
THE SOPHOMORE (1929, Pathe)—**Eddie Quillan** stars in another of the many movies about some college boob who accidently wins the big game and the campus sweetie.

COLLINS, JUDY
GIRL IN TROUBLE (1963, Vanguard)—Deciding to taste a bit of life before settling down to marriage, **Tammy Clark** hits the road as a hitchhiker. She's picked up by a creep who attacks her. She beats him with a rock and believes she has killed him. She turns up on Bourbon Street in New Orleans where she becomes a hooker. Her fiance shows up and takes her away from her sinful life.

COLLINS, LOIS
THREE BLONDES IN HIS LIFE (1961, Cinema Associates)—**Elaine Edwards** is one of the three blondes whom private eye Jock Mahoney encounters while trying to solve his friend's murder.

COLLINS, NIKKI
LADY ON A TRAIN (1945, Universal)—With the help of mystery writer David Bruce, **Deanna Durbin** tracks down the culprit in a murder which she witnesses from her train compartment.

COLLINS, TIM
THE FIGHTING FOOL (1932, Columbia)—**Tim McCoy** alternates his time chasing a bandit known as "The Shadow" and courting Marceline Day. He gets both, the former being his own brother.

COLLINS, VIVIAN
BROADWAY MADONNA (1922, Silent, Quality Film)—Cabaret dancer **Dorothy Revier** is forced by her husband to encourage the attentions of a wealthy man so the latter's father may be blackmailed.

COLLINSWOOD, "TENNESSEE"
NINE GIRLS (1944, Columbia)—**Shirley Mills** is one of the many sorority sisters who had a motive for killing nasty blackmailer Anita Louise.

COLORADO KID
COLORADO KID (1938, Republic)—When wanderer **Bob Steele** is accused of murder, a friend helps him break out of prison so he can clear himself.

COLOSSUS, THE & THE COLOSSUS' BRAIN
THE COLOSSUS OF NEW YORK (1970 Pyramid)—The brain of recently deceased brilliant scientist **Ross Martin** is transplanted into a twelve foot robot by Martin's demented brother. The robot played by **Ed Woolf** is homicidal.

COLOSWITZ, JERSEY
THE VISITOR (1980, International Picture Show)—Rather than appear in this ripoff of THE OMEN about the efforts of members of an occult group to produce a demonic child, **John Huston** should have written a passable script for it and directed it.

COLSTON, LEO
THE GO-BETWEEN (1971, GB, MGM/EMI/Columbia)—During Edwardian times, twelve-year-old **Dominic Guard** carries love letters from farmer Alan Bates to his friend's sister Julie Christie.

COLT
SON OF BILLY THE KID (1949, Screen Guild)—In a typical "Son of" B movie, **John James**, probably illegitimate, shows he has no better sense than his gunfighting father.

COLT, CAPT.
THE RANGER AND THE LADY (1940, Republic)—Texas Ranger **Roy Rogers** is forced to collect taxes from Jacqueline Wells' wagon train. Rogers also has to keep his eyes on Henry Brandon, an assistant to Sam Houston, who is trying to acquire power while his boss is away in Washington.

COLT, JOHNNY
THREE YOUNG TEXANS (1954, 20th Century Fox)—**Jeffrey Hunter** robs a train so that his father can't be blackmailed into doing it. He's aided by Mitzi Gaynor and Keefe Brasselle.

COLUMBUS, CHRISTOPHER
COLUMBUS (1923, Silent, Pathe Exchange); CHRISTOPHER CO-LUMBUS (1949, GB, Rank/ Universal)—**Fred Eric** and **Fredric March** both appear in routine stories of how Columbus raised the money he needed to sail west to find a new route to India. Thanks a lot, Isabella.

"COMMENCEMENT"
BROTHER RAT AND A BABY (1940, Warner Brothers)—**Peter B. Goode** is the baby born to ex-military cadet Eddie Albert and his wife Jane Bryan. The kid is a better actor that the adults, including Ronald Reagan, Jane Wyman, Wayne Morris and Priscilla Lane.

COMPTON, J.R.
MAN OF CONFLICT (1953, Atlas)—**Edward Arnold** and his son John Agar don't agree on business methods. So what else is new?

COMSTOCK, ELNORA
GIRL OF THE LIMBERLOST (1934, Monogram); (1945, Columbia)—**Marian Marsh** and **Dorinda Clifton** appeared in the two sound versions of the Gene Stratton Porter story of a mother who despises her child because her pregnancy led to the death of her husband, when she couldn't save him from bayou quicksand because of her condition. The mother won't even bother sending Marsh or Clifton to school until she has a change of heart upon learning her husband had carried on with other women.

CONAN
CONAN THE BARBARIAN (1982, Universal); CONAN THE DE-STROYER (1984, Universal)—**Arnold Schwarzenegger**, muscles and dull looks, is rather appealing in these sword and sorcery stories, which despite being complete rubbish are kind of fun.

CONCENTRATIN' KID
THE CONCENTRATIN' KID (1930, Universal)—Cowboy **Hoot Gibson** is in love with a radio singer Kathryn Crawford, whom he has never seen. He bets he can win her and when he rescues her from rustlers, he collects his wager.

CONCHO, JOHNNY
JOHNNY CONCHO (1956, RKO)—Folks put up with the bullying of **Frank Sinatra** because his brother is a feared gunfighter. When the latter is killed, Frank has to come to terms with his cowardice.

CONDOMINE, ELVIRA
BLITHE SPIRIT (1945, GB, Cineguild/Two Cities)—**Kay Hammond** is delightful as the deceased first wife of writer Rex Harrison. Her spirit is conjured up during a seance. She plots to kill Harrison, so he can join her, but her plans go awry when Harrison's second wife Constance Cummings is the victim, and joins Hammond as a spook pestering Harrison. We just love listening to Hammond's plummy voice.

CONKLIN, T.
SUMMER SCHOOL TEACHERS (1977, New World)—Physical Edu-cation teacher **Candice Rialson** coaches the girl's football team at a

California high school. She is suspended when she steals the financial books of a crooked coach.

CONLON, BOB
THE OFFICER AND THE LADY (1941, Columbia)—Patrolman **Bruce Bennett** foils a jewel robbery and rescues his girlfriend Rochelle Hunter and her father from an escaped convict.

CONNELL, MARITA
ONCE MORE, MY DARLING (1949, Universal)—**Ann Blyth** elopes with ex-movie star Robert Montgomery after they recover jewelry stolen by Nazis.

CONNELL, SHANGHAI JACK
FIRST TO FIGHT (1967, Warner Brothers)—In WWII, one-time hero **Chad Everett** briefly loses his nerve on the battlefield.

CONNELLY, JIM
MY BUDDY (1944, Republic)—**John Litel** portrays a priest who recounts the life and crimes of WWI vet Donald Barry, who came home from war unable to find any work. So he turned to crime, which led to his death.

CONNIE
GENTLEMEN MARRY BRUNETTES (1955, UA)—By the time **Jeanne Crain** decided to shake her innocent appeal for that of a sexy lady, she had become the mother of a brood of children, which in Crain's case seemed only to have improved her shape. She and Jane Russell are two American shop girls seeking rich husbands in Paris where they discover their aunts were notorious party girls years earlier. Crain and Russell appear as their aunts in flashbacks.

CONNIE
HER LUCKY NIGHT (1945, Universal)—**Martha O'Driscoll** believes a fortune teller and comes up with a wild scheme to capture her dream man.

CONNIE
OUR BLUSHING BRIDES (1930, MGM)—**Anita Page** and room-mates Joan Crawford and Dorothy Sebastian are out to snag rich husbands during the Roaring Twenties.

CONNIE
TOP FLOOR GIRL (1959, GB, Paramount)—It appears that clerk **Kay Callard** will do anything to make it to the top including marrying the son of her richest client, even though she loves another man.

CONNIE, JAMES
MY SIX CONVICTS (1952, Columbia)—**Millard Mitchell** is a convicted safecracker who convinces five others to act on prison psychologist John Beal's offer to help them. Later Mitchell is called on to use his talents to open an accidently locked bank vault, for which he is given a 24-hour furlough from prison.

CONNOLLY, EDDIE *See* **BOB NAUGHTON**

CONNOR, CHUCK
SADDLE TRAMP (1950, Universal)—Peaceful stranger **Joel McCrea** arrives in the middle of a range war to look after a dead friend's kids and finds he has to strap on some guns and make some varmints real "peaceful."

CONNOR, TEDDY
JOHN MEADE'S WOMAN (1937, Paramount)—Country girl **Francine Larrimore** marries lumber baron Edward Arnold. When he cheats local farmers out of their land, she leads a revolt against her husband.

CONNORS, ACE
TWO SMART PEOPLE (1946, MGM)—Con-man **John Hodiak** romances lady crook Lucille Ball in New Orleans.

CONNORS, NAP *See* **HARRY GRAND**

CONNORS, NORA
THE LADY WANTS MINK (1953, Republic)—When her husband can't afford to buy her a mink coat, **Ruth Hussey** tries to raise minks so she can make her own coat. This was supposed to lead to some comical situations.

CONOVAN, MIKE
PAT AND MIKE (1952, MGM)—**Spencer Tracy** is a sports promoter who attempts to make a champion of Physical Education instructor Katharine Hepburn. Tracy discovers that Hepburn becomes rattled whenever her criticizing fiance is around, so Tracy replaces him as Kate's romantic interest.

CONOVER, CALEB
THE FIGHTER (1921, Silent, Selznick)—**Conway Tearle**, a self-made man, takes the blame when it is reported that his ward's father was a crook. The ward, Winifred Westover, turns on Tearle but when she learns of his sacrifice, she marries him.

CONQUEST, NORMAN
NORMAN CONQUEST (1953, GB, Lippert)—Private detective **Tom Conway** is drugged by femme fatale Eva Bartok and set up for a murder charge.

CONRAD
DELIVERY BOYS (1984, New World)—Pizza delivery boy **Jim Soriero** is one of a troupe of break dancers intent on winning a dance contest.

CONRAD
ORDINARY PEOPLE (1980, Paramount)—**Timothy Hutton** suffers because he survived, and his brother did not. He feels he must be at least partially to blame for his brother's death by drowning because he couldn't save him. Hutton's parents, Donald Sutherland and Mary Tyler Moore, are too busy coming to grips with their one son's death to save the other.

CONRAD, ROBERT
GIRL LOVES BOY (1937, Grand National)—**Eric Linden** is loved by Cecilia Parker, but he is briefly dazzled by a gold digger.

CONROY, HENRY
HENRY GOES TO ARIZONA (1939, MGM)—Vaudevillian **Frank Morgan** inherits a ranch in Arizona after his half-brother is murdered. Not very happy with the acquisition, Morgan changes from coward to hero when he thwarts a crooked banker.

CONROY, JIMMY
THE MATRIMANIAC (1916, Silent, Triangle)—**Douglas Fairbanks** uses every possible mode of transportation to rush to the side of his sweetheart Constance Talmadge from whom he has been separated by her disapproving father.

CONROY, MAMIE
THE LAVENDER BATH LADY (1922, Silent, Universal)—**Gladys Walton** saves millionaire Charlotte Pierce from being kidnapped,

which gets her invited into the latter's home as a member of the family.

CONROY, MARCIA

THE UNDERCOVER WOMAN (1946, Republic)—**Stephanie Bachelor** is a private investigator hired to trail a husband thought to be having an affair. When her prey is murdered, she has something more to investigate.

CONROY, PAT

CONRACK (1974, 20th Century Fox)—In a true story, **Jon Voight** is a teacher who goes to a small island off the coast of South Carolina where black children have been deprived of an education. His unique and unusual methods of teaching help the kids, many of whom are illiterate and retarded. He runs into trouble with traditional hard-line educational bureaucrats who remove him from his post. The title is the way the children mispronounce Voight's name.

CONROY, TOM & BOB

BROTHERS (1929, Silent, Rayart)—**Cornelius Keefe** and **Arthur Rankin** are brothers separated in childhood. Keefe, the elder, drifts into crime and later, without recognizing Rankin as his brother, tries to involve him in a con game. When he discovers who Rankin is, Keefe takes the blame for a crime of which Rankin is accused, but the latter is able to get them both off.

CONSIDINE, DR. ALEC

THE NEW INTERNS (1964, Columbia)—**Michael Callan** is one of the new young doctors in this cliche-filled hospital drama in which the physicians seem more in need of treatment than do their patients.

CONSUL, THE

THE MAN WHO COULDN'T WALK (1964, GB, Falcon-Taurus)—Even though confined to a wheelchair, **Eric Pohlman** heads a gang of jewel thieves. By the end of the film, he no longer needs the wheelchair—or anything else.

CONTARINI, ALFIERE LORENZO

THE THIEF OF VENICE (1952, 20th Century Fox)—In Venice in the Middle Ages, naval officer **Paul Christian** turns to thievery to get enough money to stand up to a despot.

CONVICT 83

KING OF THE DAMMED (1936, GB, Gaumont)—**Conrad Veidt** leads a revolt of the convicts on an island prison against a cruel commandant.

CONWAY, JAMES

GOODFELLAS (1990, Warner Brothers)—Playing an Irish hood, **Robert De Niro** can never become a 'made man' in the Mafia. He's betrayed by his long-time friend and colleague Ray Liotta, who testifies against him, resulting in a long prison term for De Niro. This exceptional movie could only have been made better if there was more of De Niro in it.

CONWAY, JANIE

JANIE (1944, Warner Brothers); JANIE GETS MARRIED (1946, Warner Brothers)—In the first film, precocious teenager **Joyce Reynolds** runs off in search of romance with a soldier stationed at a nearby army base. In the sequel, Janie, now played by **Joan Leslie**, has wed her soldier, is out of the army, and finds that marriage has its ups and downs.

CONWAY, KATHY

FOUR GIRLS IN TOWN (1956, Universal)—**Julie Adams** is the American entry in an international competition for the title role in a movie.

CONWAY, RUSH

THE KID COMES BACK (1937, Warner Brothers)—**Wayne Morris** finds he must meet his mentor Barton MacLane in the ring. The elder fighter knocks Morris out but it's all one big happy family when Morris marries MacLane's sister.

CONWAY, VICTOR

BIG EXECUTIVE (1933, Paramount)—**Ricardo Cortez** has his problems in the business world and is forced into bankruptcy by the grandfather of his sweetheart.

COOGAN

COOGAN'S BLUFF (1968, Universal)—Arizona deputy sheriff **Clint Eastwood** takes an escaped killer back to New York, loses him and then uses western methods to re-capture him.

COOK, CASSIE

SHANGHAI LADY (1929, Universal)—**Mary Nolan**, a former prostitute, loses her job in an opium den and falls for an ex-con. Each believes the other is a nice respectable person.

COOK, JANET

SEVEN WOMEN FROM HELL (1961, 20th Century Fox)—**Yvonne Craig** is one of the female prisoners in a Japanese POW camp in WWII New Guinea. Seven of them, including Craig, escape but they don't all survive.

COOKE, FRANCIS

SMARTEST GIRL IN TOWN (1936, RKO)—Model **Ann Sothern**, searching for a rich husband, barely notices Gene Raymond, a millionaire posing as a model so he can be near her.

COOKSON, DAVID

DENTIST IN THE CHAIR (1960, GB, Renown)—Dental student **Bob Monkhouse** innocently acquires thousands of dollars worth of dental equipment, which he must dispose of before he is arrested by the police.

COOL, JOHNNY

JOHNNY COOL (1963, UA)—**Henry Silva**, a Sicilian thug named Johnny Giordano, is to be the instrument of death for an exiled Mafia leader seeking revenge against former associates. Cool, Silva is not; he seems more like he's in a trance.

COOLIDGE, JOAN

THE RAGE OF PARIS (1921, Silent, Universal)—**Miss (Patrice) Du Pont** makes her film debut as a young woman who runs away from the abusive husband she was forced to marry and becomes the dancing rage of Paris.

COOMBS, HARRY

HARRY AND TONTO (1974, 20th Century Fox)—**Art Carney** won an Oscar for his touching performance as an aging man, unwanted by his grown children, who journeys across the country with his cat, Tonto.

COOP, J.W.

J.W. COOP (1971, Columbia)—Just out of prison after ten years, rodeo rider **Cliff Robertson** goes after the national championship of the Rodeo Cowboys Association.

COOPER, AMY
STAR SPANGLED GIRL (1971, Paramount)—Cute girl-next-door **Sandy Duncan** falls in with campus radicals.

COOPER, CHRISTY
THE KID FROM LEFT FIELD (1953, GB, British Lion)—Bat boy **Billy Chapin** passes on some tips which breaks a major league team out of its prolonged slump. He's rewarded by being named the team's manager. When it's discovered that Chapin was merely passing on the advice of his father Dan Dailey, an ex-major leaguer reduced to selling peanuts in the stands, Dailey is made manager.

COOPER, CLINT
THE QUICK GUN (1964, Columbia)—Drifter **Audie Murphy** helps a young sheriff defend his town from marauding outlaws after Murphy returns home to claim his father's farm.

COOPER, D.B. *See* MEADE

COOPER, GEORGE
FATHER WAS A FULLBACK (1949, 20th Century Fox)—**Fred MacMurray's** failure as a football coach is almost matched by his chaotic family life.

COOPER, GERALDINE
AFFAIRS OF GERALDINE (1946, Republic)—**Jane Withers** inherits a fortune but her life is complicated by her brothers who attempt to dredge up a husband for her to fulfill a death bed promise to their mother.

COOPER, PENNY
PUBLIC DEB NO. 1 (1940, 20th Century Fox)—Beautiful debutante **Brenda Joyce** portrays a beautiful debutante. What did you expect—acting?

COPPELIUS, DR.
DR. COPPELIUS (1968, Gala); THE MYSTERIOUS HOUSE OF DR. C. (1976, Bronston)—**Walter Slezak** creates a beautiful dancing robot to be his companion. He fails to implant a soul in the robot and finds he's still lonely. Eight years later, Slezak is back in his laboratory, but the horror of the original has been toned down and the sequel deals with the adventures of the dolls locked in the doctor's house.

COPPERFIELD, DAVID
DAVID COPPERFIELD (1935, MGM); (1970, GB, 20th Century Fox)—**Freddie Bartholomew** and **Frank Lawton** are the young and adult David, respectively, in a film in which MGM taught the world something about bringing a Dickens' classic winningly to the screen. Lawton even looked like what one would expect Bartholomew to grow up to be. The 1970 production with **Alastair MacKenzie** and **Robin Phillips** in the child and adult roles, respectively, doesn't have the charm of the thirties effort.

CORAL
QUADROON (1972, Presidio)—In 1835, New Orleans whore **Katherine McKee** falls in love with a northern white man who teaches her to read. That's a no-no.

CORAL
SOUTH SEA SINNER (1950, Universal)—Cabaret singer **Shelley Winters** is the female side of what is supposed to be a seamy exotic island triangle involving easy-going MacDonald Carey and possessive cafe owner Luther Adler. Better take a nap.

CORBETT, JAMES J.
GENTLEMAN JIM (1942, Warner Brothers)—This film would be absolutely nothing except for the brash charm of **Errol Flynn** as the Irishman who took the heavyweight championship from John L. Sullivan by being a boxer rather than a brawler.

CORBETT, TOM & EDDIE
THE COURTSHIP OF EDDIE'S FATHER (1963, MGM)—Widower **Glenn Ford's** young son **Ronnie Howard** makes a concentrated effort to find a wife for Ford and mother for himself. After going through candidates including Stella Stevens and Dina Merrill, father and son agree on Shirley Jones.

CORBIN, KIT
SHIPMATES (1931, MGM)—**Dorothy Jordan** portrays the admiral's daughter in this tale of a young sailor Robert Montgomery who must compete with petty officer Ernest Torrence for her.

CORBIN, LISBETH
STRANGERS MAY KISS (1931, MGM)—**Norma Shearer** is obsessed with her love for newspaperman Neil Hamilton, who doesn't seem to share her intensity of feelings. Even though she takes other lovers while Hamilton is away on assignments, she can't get him out of her mind. Just about when she's prepared to marry longtime suitor Robert Montgomery, Hamilton shows up ready to settle down with her.

CORDAY, CHARLOTTE
CHARLOTTE CORDAY (1914, Silent, Kennedy)—Marat orders the execution of the lover of Charlotte Corday (**Constance Crawley**). He offers to spare the young man's life if she will . . . well you know. She tells him to tear up the death warrant and then stabs Marat to death. Danton finds the order to release her lover and sets the man free but Crawley goes to the guillotine.

CORDAY, DR. MICHAEL
THE DOCTOR AND THE GIRL (1949, MGM)—**Glenn Ford** is a brilliant doctor who gives up his lucrative practice to marry Janet Leigh and tend to the sick in a poor working district.

CORDELL, MATT
MANIAC COP (1988, Shapiro Glickenhaus); MANIAC COP II (1990, Movie House Sales)—Troublesome cop **Robert Z'dar** is framed on a trumped-up murder charge. After arriving at prison, he is brutally attacked by knife-wielding inmates. A sympathetic prison doctor declares him dead, and allows Z'dar's girlfriend to take away his zombie-like body. Later, he revives and goes on a killing spree. In the sequel, Z'dar is resurrected to become a disfigured supernatural killer stalking the streets of New York.

CORDER, STEWART
FOUR FRIGHTENED PEOPLE (1934, Paramount)—Newsman **William Gargan** joins geography teacher Claudette Colbert, chemist Herbert Marshall and the wife of a British official, Mary Boland, in escaping from a coastal steamer in a lifeboat, when bubonic plague breaks out aboard. When they reach land, they must journey through dangerous jungles to reach the Malayan mainland.

CORDIER, SIMON
DIARY OF A MADMAN (1963, UA)—**Vincent Price** tries to justify his murdering ways to a magistrate by claiming he's possessed by an evil spirit.

CORDOBA, CONSUELO
HONOLULU LU (1941, Columbia)—**Lupe Velez** becomes a beauty queen in Hawaii. The fiery one is up to her usual antics.

CORELESKI, STANISLAUS "DUKE"
SPOOK CHASERS (1957, Allied Artists)—**Stanley Clements** leads the Bowery Boys in this romp through a haunted house.

COREW, VIDA
THE WOMAN I STOLE (1933, Columbia)—**Fay Wray** is a faithless wife, whom Jack Holt steals from his best friend. But it was only a sham on Holt's part to thwart some desert bandits, and when that's completed he walks away from Wray.

COREY, BRUCE
UNHOLY PARTNERS (1941, MGM)—During Prohibition, honest newspaperman **Edward G. Robinson** falls into the control of racketeer Edward Arnold. Some Faustian overtones, it would seem.

CORKY
CORKY (1972, MGM)—Selfish, arrogant southern loser **Robert Blake's** greatest love is a cherry red automobile. When he accuses his long-suffering wife of infidelity, he gets into trouble with the police and during a frantic search his precious car is nearly destroyed.

CORLAIX, LOTTIE
THE WOMAN FROM MONTE CRISTO (1932, First National)—**Lil Dagover** must reveal her adulterous affair with a handsome young naval lieutenant in order to save her husband from a court-martial charge of dereliction of duty in the sinking of his ship.

CORLANE, MADELYN
GIVE A GIRL A BREAK (1953, MGM)—Cute **Marge Champion** competes with Debbie Reynolds and Helen Wood for a part in a big Broadway musical. The decision will be made by the director, a guy named Gower Champion. Any bets on who gets the job?

CORLEONE, DON VITO & MICHAEL
THE GODFATHER (1972, Paramount); THE GODFATHER PART II (1974, Paramount); THE GODFATHER PART III (1990, Paramount)—**Marlon Brando** plays the older Don Vito Corleone in this motion picture two-part masterpiece of Francis Ford Coppola and Mario Puzo. Brando won a well-deserved Oscar for his performance as a man who made offers which could not be refused. **Robert De Niro** won the Oscar for his performance as the young Vito in the sequel and, as outstanding as he was, it's a shame that **Al Pacino** as Michael Corleone, Don Vito's son and successor as godfather, did not get similar recognition for his simply superb performance. In the third film, **Pacino** is back as Michael, hoping to atone for his past sins and become a legitimate businessman serving the Catholic Church. Of course, it will require many killings and attempts to corrupt willing church officials to accomplish his ends. The film is a disappointment in comparison with the previous two masterpieces in the series; in fact, it is disappointing without making the comparison.

CORLISS, JONATHAN
A KISS BEFORE DYING (1991, Universal)—In an inferior remake of the 1956 thriller, **Matt Dillon** becomes involved with wealthy Sean Young at college. When he learns that she's pregnant, he pushes her off a roof of a building. A short time later, he pursues and marries Young's twin.

CORNBREAD
CORNBREAD, EARL AND ME (1975, American International)—NBA pro basketball player **Keith Wilkes** is a high school basketball star, idolized by the people in the ghetto where he lives. He is mistakenly slain by two police officers who claim he was involved with a crime and had a gun when he was shot.

CORNEAL, ROGER
OCEAN'S ELEVEN (1960, Warner Brothers)—**Henry Silva** rounds up Frank Sinatra's former army squadron so they can rob five Las Vegas casinos at one time. His almost moronic grin makes it seem that he's having a grand time.

CORNELL, DEXTER
D.O.A. (1988, Touchstone)—**Dennis Quaid** stars in this remake of a 1949 picture of the same name. He's a cynical English professor, who has been poisoned with a slow-acting toxin, and has less than 48 hours to solve his own murder. He does so with the help of student Meg Ryan, who doesn't have him as a lover for very long. It's a disappointing film with no style to call its own.

CORNELL, JACK & HICKY
HIS BROTHER'S KEEPER (1939, GB, Warner Brothers)—**Clifford Evans** and **Peter Glenville** are brothers who both have affairs with Tamara Desni, which leads to tragedy for all three.

CORNWELL, MILES
THE PASSIONATE SENTRY (1952, GB, Fine Arts)—Madcap Peggy Cummins falls in love with **Nigel Patrick**, a sentry at Buckingham Palace.

CORRIGAN, JIMMY
JIMMY THE GENT (1934, Warner Brothers)—Crooked business-man **James Cagney** is so taken with Bette Davis he's even willing to go straight—well, to all appearances, anyway.

CORRIGAN, TOM
THE DESERT PIRATE (1928, Silent, FBO)—Sheriff **Tom Tyler** adopts Frankie Darro, clears the father of his sweetheart and takes apart a saloon filled with bad'uns.

CORRIGAN, "WRONG WAY"
THE FLYING IRISHMAN (1939, RKO)—This film tells the true story of **Douglas "Wrong Way" Corrigan** who, when denied permission to fly across the ocean, filed a flight plan for crossing the country from the east to the west, but ended up in Ireland instead.

CORSINI, ANDREA
PRINCE OF FOXES (1949, 20th Century Fox)—**Tyrone Power** eventually will turn against his friend and mentor Cesare Borgia played by Orson Welles.

CORTEZ, GREGORIO
THE BALLAD OF GREGORIO CORTEZ (1983, Embassy)—In San Antonio in 1901, **Edward James Olmos** is arrested due to mistaken identity. He accidently kills a sheriff and takes off with a posse of Texas rangers in pursuit. He eventually turns himself in when he learns his family is being held hostage. He's nearly lynched but at his trial he's cleared of all charges against him.

CORTEZ, MANUEL
LOVE FROM A STRANGER (1947, Eagle-Lion)—Sweep-stakes winner Sylvia Sidney comes to suspect that the husband she barely knows, **John Hodiak**, is a killer.

CORTLAND, ROY
MILLION DOLLAR KID (1944, Monogram)—**Johnny Duncan**, a rich man's kid, teams with a bunch of punks to harass the East Side Kids. When his brother is killed in the war, he changes sides.

CORVAN, DAN
THE CONFIDENCE MAN (1924, Silent, Paramount)—Con-man **Thomas Meighan** sells phony oil stock to people in Florida, but he's put on the straight and narrow path by an old lady and a trusting young woman.

CORWIN, DON
HER KIND OF MAN (1946, Warner Brothers)—Janis Paige turns to gossip columnist **Dane Clark** after being wooed by big time gambler Zachary Scott. It's a typical Warner's B movie, fast and forgettable.

CORY
MISTER CORY (1957, Universal)—Chicago slum kid **Tony Curtis** grows up to be a big-shot gambler.

CORY, BELLE
GIRL IN THE WOODS (1958, Republic)—Married to lumberjack Forrest Tucker, **Maggie Hayes** finds her man and herself in the middle of a feud, which results in him being wrongly accused of a robbery.

CORY, PATRICK
THE LADY AND THE MONSTER (1944, Republic)—In the first screen version of DONOVAN'S BRAIN, **Richard Arlen** is a scientist who finds himself controlled by an evil living bodiless brain.

COSGRAVE, JET
THE OUTCAST (1954, Republic)—**John Derek** returns to Colorado to fight his evil uncle over ownership of his late father's ranch.

COSGROVE, GLADYS
THE GIRL IN THE GLASS CAGE (1929, First National)—Among her problems, movie theater cashier **Loretta Young** is loved by a gangster, and her uncle steals the theater's receipts for which she is responsible.

COSMIC MAN
THE COSMIC MAN (1959, Allied Artists)—**John Carradine** who has black skin and casts a white shadow, comes to earth in a large sphere bringing a message of peace and nuclear sanity, but earthlings don't wish to hear it. It's a none-too-intriguing rip-off of THE DAY THE EARTH STOOD STILL (1951).

COSTAIN, LINCOLN
THE CASTAWAY COWBOY (1974, Buena Vista)—**James Garner** saves the day for a Hawaiian potato farmer who is being harassed by the mean fellow who holds the mortgage.

COSTELLO, ESTHER
THE STORY OF ESTHER COSTELLO (1957, GB, Columbia)—Blind, deaf, mute Irish girl, **Heather Sears** is adopted by American socialite Joan Crawford. Sears' plight becomes an international concern.

COSTELLO, FRANK
MOBSTERS (1991, Universal)—**Costa Mandylor's** role is so ill-defined the movie could have gotten along with just a trio of young mobsters.

COTTCHINSKY, REGINALD "RENO"
RENO AND THE DOC (1984, Canada, New World)—Mountain man **Ken Welsh** befriends former con man Henry Ramer. They discover they are telepathic. Ramer convinces Welsh to enter a skiing competition, which he wins. Exciting, eh?

COTTEN, SAM
PLAINSMAN AND THE LADY (1946, Republic)—**William Elliott** steps in for John Wayne in this corny Western about the establishing of the Pony Express. The Duke had made two movies before with Vera Ralston, the untalented wife of Republic's chief Herbert Yates, and enough was enough.

COTTON, FRANK
HELLRAISER (1987, GB, New World)—In what has been billed as a new direction in science fiction, **Sean Chapman** purchases a mysterious Chinese puzzle box. When he opens it, he discovers that he has entered hell. The film and its 1989 sequel are short on drama but the special effects are excellent.

COUNT OF MONTE CRISTO
SON OF MONTE CRISTO (1940, UA)—**Louis Hayward** doesn't portray Edmond Dantes this time. He's that worthy's son, and he has his own problems with scoundrels and beautiful Joan Bennett.

COURAGE, JEWEL
THE JOY GIRL (1927, Silent, Fox)—**Olive Borden** rejects the chauffeur she loves to marry a millionaire and then discovers the two men had exchanged identities. Gotcha!

COURIER, THE
THE COURIER (1988, Vestron)—**Padrag O'Loingsigh** is a messenger in this story, set in Dublin, for Gabriel Byrne, the king of dope peddlers. O'Loingsigh meets his expected fate by being shot on a fire escape and falling to his death on the pavement below.

COURTLAND, CHARLIE
CHAMPAGNE CHARLIE (1936, 20th Century Fox)—Suave gambler **Paul Cavanaugh** plans to marry wealthy Helen Wood so she can pay off his debts but murder intervenes.

COURTNEY, SIR EDWARD
THE COURTNEY AFFAIR (1947, GB, British Lion)—When aristocrat **Michael Wilding** marries his mother's Irish maid Anna Neagle, they are ostracized. When she can take it no longer, she leaves him and returns to Ireland to have their baby. They are re-united years later when he runs into her, now a WWI entertainer.

COURTNEY, HILDA
DRESSED TO KILL (1946, Universal)—In the last of the Sherlock Holmes series starring Basil Rathbone, **Patricia Morison** is the villain in a story of an attempt to recover stolen Bank of England engraving plates which have been hidden in music boxes.

COURTNEY, NANCY
TARNISHED LADY (1931, Paramount)—**Tallulah Bankhead** marries Clive Brook for his money but discovers almost too late that she actually loves him.

COVENTRY, SOPHIE
THE GIRL WHO TOOK THE WRONG TURNING (1915, GB, Silent, British Empire)—**Alice Belmore** is led into a life of vice by her brother-in-law.

COWAN, JIMMY

THE MICHIGAN KID (1928, Silent, Universal)—**Conrad Nagel** is one of two North Woods men who compete for Renee Adoree and fight a raging forest fire.

COWPOKE

TENNESSEE'S PARTNER (1955, RKO)—When cowboy **Ronald Reagan** takes gambler John Payne's side in a dispute, he finds himself charged along with Payne for the murder of an old prospector.

COY, BILLY

THE BIG WHEEL (1949, UA)—**Mickey Rooney**, the son of a racing driver, follows in his father's tire tracks, but the consequences make it appear he should have left the car in the garage.

CRABB, JACK

LITTLE BIG MAN (1970, National General)—**Dustin Hoffman** stars as a 121-year-old veteran of the Indian wars who aimlessly reminisces about his life as an adopted son of the Cheyenne, a mule-skinner, a gun fighter and a scout for Custer, who survives Little Big Horn. There may be a message in this modestly interesting western, but we're not sure what it is.

CRABTREE, LOTTA

GOLDEN GIRL (1951, 20th Century Fox)—**Mitzi Gaynor** is as good as she would get in this western biopic of a showgirl who becomes a musical star after the Civil War.

CRACK, GENERAL

GENERAL CRACK (1929, Warner Brothers)—This swashbuckler about the adventures of an eighteenth century brigand prince was John Barrymore's first talking picture.

CRADDOCK, JOHN

VIRGINIA'S HUSBAND (1934, GB, Fox)—**Reginald Gardiner** is pressed into service to pose as the husband of man-hating feminist Dorothy Boyd when the latter's rich aunt shows up.

CRADDOCK, NANCY

LITTLE MISS HOOVER (1918, Paramount)—**Marguerite Clark** and Eugene O'Brien's love story is interspersed with the propaganda message of encouraging farmers to be more productive for the war effort.

CRADON, TYLER

DISBARRED (1939, Paramount)—Disbarred attorney **Otto Kruger** becomes a crime czar. He is done in by lawyer Gail Patrick.

CRAGG, MRS.

LADIES WHO DO (1964, GB, Continental Distributing)—Cleaning lady **Peggy Mount** finds information in the waste paper baskets which she empties that enables her and her friends to make a killing in the stock market.

CRAIG, DAVID

ME AND MY PAL (1939, GB, Pathe)—**Dave Willis** and his pal George Moon are conned into helping a crook fleece an insurance company. They believe they are working with the police.

CRAIG, HARRIET & WALTER

CRAIG'S WIFE (1928, Silent, Pathe Exchange); (1936, Columbia); HARRIET CRAIG (1950, Columbia)—**Irene Rich** and **Warner Baxter** in 1928 and **Rosalind Russell** and **John Boles** in 1936 portrayed a wife, who loves her meticulously kept house more than her husband, who comes in a distant second in her affections. **Joan Crawford** picked up the dust cloth in 1950 with Wendell Corey as her husband not even mentioned in the title. The guys finally get wise and leave Harriet to her real love, but their departure doesn't even cause a ripple in Harriet's well-appointed home.

CRAIG, JIM & ELLEN

WEEKEND FOR THREE (1941, RKO)—Married couple **Dennis O'Keefe and Jane Wyatt** find themselves with a house guest, Philip Reed, whom they can't stand and can't get rid of.

CRAIG, JUDGE

ONE JUST MAN (1955, GB, Pathe)—Judge **Alexander Knox** takes it upon himself to deal with law breakers.

CRAIG, JUDITH

THE GODLESS GIRL (1929, Pathe)—**Lina Basquette** is the leader of a high-school organization known as the Atheist Society. In a brawl with a religious group headed by George Duryea, a girl is killed and Basquette and Duryea land in a reformatory. They briefly escape the brutalities but are re-captured. Now in love with Duryea, Basquette becomes an early born-again Christian.

CRAIG, NORMAN

THE AVENGER (1933, Monogram)—Former District Attorney **Ralph Forbes**, just out of prison, sets out to get those who framed him.

CRAIG, PENNY, JOAN & KAY

THREE SMART GIRLS (1937, Universal); THREE SMART GIRLS GROW UP (1939, Universal)—**Deanna Durbin, Nan Grey** and **Barbara Read/Helen Parrish** save their father from gold digger Binnie Barnes in the first film and help each other find boyfriends in the sequel.

CRAIG, LT. ROGER

COCK OF THE AIR (1932, Hughes/UA)—A romance is arranged by WWI allies France and the U.S. between charming air ace **Chester Morris** and temperamental actress Billie Dove. After a rough start, it takes.

CRAIG, SGT.

THE VICTORS (1963, Columbia)—**Eli Wallach** heads an army squad in Europe during the last part of WWII. Having survived through many battles, he finally gets hit, having most of his face blown away. Wallach's performance is the most powerful of the various members of the squad, but that is to be expected. He's an actor, and the others like George Peppard, George Hamilton and Vince Edwards were just learning their craft.

CRAIG, PRESIDENT STANLEY

THE PRESIDENT VANISHES (1934, Paramount)—**Arthur Byron**, the President of the U.S., agrees to drop out of sight for a few days, pretending to be kidnapped in order to keep the country out of a European war.

CRAIL, JEANNE

GIRLS OF THE BIG HOUSE (1945, Republic)—In another of the many "women in prison" movies, **Lynne Roberts** is the obligatory innocent wrongly imprisoned. There, she learns how cruel some women can be before being sprung by her lawyer.

CRAMER, ADAM

THE INTRUDER (1962, Pathe-America)—Mild-mannered **William Shatner** arrives in a southern town and stirs up racial trouble.

CRANDALL, BEN
EXPLORERS (1985, Paramount)—In a comedy sci-fi that is not for everyone, three lads, **Ethan Hawke**, River Phoenix and Jason Presson journey through outer space, meeting some very surprising aliens. Come to think of it, the boys are the aliens.

CRANDALL, BOB
LIGHTNIN' CRANDALL (1937, Republic)—Gunfighter **Bob Steele** seeks a quieter life but doesn't find it in Arizona where he becomes involved in a feud among cattle ranchers.

CRANDALL, MRS.
DON'T TELL MOM THE BABYSITTER'S DEAD (1991, Warner Brothers)—Ditzy **Concetta Tomei** leaves her five kids with a seemingly sweet little old lady babysitter and goes on vacation. The babysitter dies, and the kids plot to keep the news from mom so she won't come home.

CRANE, ELLIOT
THE GAY DECEIVERS (1969, Fanfare)—**Larry Casey** and Kevin Coughlin avoid the draft by pretending they are homosexuals. They have to keep up the deception to fool a suspicious recruiting officer.

CRANE, GINA
THE STRANGE MRS. CRANE (1948, Eagle-Lion)—**Marjorie Lord**, the wife of a gubernatorial candidate, is accused of killing her former con-man partner.

CRANE, HILDA
HILDA CRANE (1956, 20th Century Fox)—**Jean Simmons** can't seem to live with or without men. She has lived with several men and is now married for the third time without having high hopes that it will last. Men! Can't live without them. Can't shoot them.

CRANE, JEFF
PUBLIC HERO NO. 1 (1935, MGM)—G-man **Chester Morris** goes undercover to get the goods on the notorious Purple Gang.

CRANE, LETTY
HUSBAND HUNTERS (1927, Silent, Tiffany)—Small-town innocent **Jean Arthur** moves in with two experienced chorus girls who teach the younger woman about men. She wises up after an unhappy relationship with a cad and settles down with a dependable man.

CRANE, MRS.
LADIES OF THE JURY (1932, RKO)—**Edna May Oliver** is the only hold-out in a 11-1 vote for conviction of a woman of killing her husband. Oliver shows 'em.

CRANE, SAM
STRANGE TRIANGLE (1946, 20th Century Fox)—**Preston Foster** becomes involved in an embezzlement because of his interest in married seductress Signe Hasso.

CRANSTON, LAMONT (THE SHADOW)
THE SHADOW RETURNS (1946, Monogram); THE INVISIBLE AVENGER (1958, Republic)—**Kane Richmond** and **Richard Derr** appear as radio's super detective who "knows what evil lurks in the hearts of men" and can cloud men's minds so he seems invisible. In the 1946 film, he shows up the police and solves the case of jewels stolen from a grave. The 1958 story deals with the murder of a New Orleans jazz man.

CRAWFORD
ACES HIGH (1977, GB, Cine Artists/EMI)—Young WWI pilot **Simon Ward** is helped by an older flyer Christopher Plummer, when Ward develops a case of frayed nerves.

CRAWFORD, DAN
BROTHER RAT (1938, Warner Brothers); BROTHER RAT AND A BABY (1940, Warner Brothers)—Easygoing Virginia Military Academy cadet **Ronald Reagan** is always willing to go along with the plans of his buddy Wayne Morris. This willingness inevitably gets them and Eddie Albert into trouble. The sequel is just more of the same after graduation.

CRAWFORD, JOAN
MOMMIE DEAREST (1981, Paramount)—**Faye Dunaway** has the looks of Crawford down pat but she doesn't project the strength of the actress in this hatchet piece based on the book by Crawford's adopted daughter.

CRAWFORD, SIMON
HOSTILE WITNESS (1968, GB, UA)—Barrister **Ray Milland** suffers a nervous break-down after the death of his daughter and is charged with murder.

CRAZY HANNAH
FIVE BOLD WOMEN (1960, Citation)—**Dee Carroll** is one of five women being escorted to a western prison by marshal Jeff Morrow. During the journey, they're attacked both by Indians and a gang of outlaws.

CRAZY HORSE
CHIEF CRAZY HORSE (1955, Universal)—**Victor Mature** isn't too bad as the Sioux chief whose friendship with cavalry major John Lund erodes, leading to a climactic battle between the red men and the whites.

CREATURE, THE
THE CREATURE WALKS AMONG US (1956, Universal)—**Don Megowan (Ricou Browning** in water sequences), the badly burned Creature from the Black Lagoon, is captured and taken to the estate of a man who believes his wife has been unfaithful. This was the final of the Black Lagoon Creature movies.

CREATURE, THE
THE CREATURE WASN'T NICE (1981, Creature Features)—When a spaceship makes a stop at an unexplored planet, it picks up a clump of matter which becomes a mad monster, played by **Ron Kurowski**.

CREED, EMILY & LOUISA
LADIES IN RETIREMENT (1941, Columbia)—**Elsa Lanchester** and **Edith Barrett** are the two mentally disturbed sisters of housekeeper Ida Lupino. Ida kills her mistress rather than see them sent to a mental institution.

CRESPI, DR.
THE CRIME OF DR. CRESPI (1936, Republic)—**Erich von Stroheim** drugs a rival into a state of suspended animation and has him buried alive. Stroheim gets paid back in kind.

CREWE, SARA
THE LITTLE PRINCESS (1939, 20th Century Fox)—**Shirley Temple** is left in a harsh Victorian boarding school while her father Ian Hunter goes to fight in the Boer War. Despite news that he has been killed, little Shirley keeps up her spirits as she searches military hospitals for him. She finds him and the sight of his daughter cures Hunter's amnesia.

CRIBBS

THE VILLAIN STILL PURSUED HER (1940, RKO)—In this traditional temperance melodrama, villain **Alan Mowbray** leads hero Richard Cromwell into using strong spirits so Mowbray can win the hand—or something—of the fair heroine, Anita Louise. Boo! Hiss!

CRICHTON, BILL

THE ADMIRABLE CRICHTON (1918, Silent, GB, Samuelson/ Jury); (1957, GB, Columbia); MALE AND FEMALE (1919, Silent, Paramount)—**Basil Gill**, **Kenneth More** and **Thomas Meighan** appear as J.M. Barrie's manservant who has the know-how to assume a leadership role when the family for whom he works and their various boating guests are shipwrecked on a desert island.

CRIPPEN, DR. HAWLEY HARVEY

DR. CRIPPEN (1963, GB, Pathe)—Shy doctor **Donald Pleasance** murders his wife and elopes with working girl Samantha Eggar in this film based on a real Edwardian murder case. The eye and ear specialist was hanged and his lover found innocent.

CROCKER, CATHERINE

THE MAN WHO LOVED CAT DANCING (1973, MGM)—Discontented wife **Sarah Miles** runs away from her stuffy husband George Hamilton and takes up with a gang of outlaws led by Burt Reynolds. Her husband and a posse are in hot pursuit.

CROCKER, HENRY

THE EAGLE AND THE HAWK (1933, Paramount)—In a film very much like THE DAWN PATROL, **Cary Grant** is a WWI British flyer who clashes with Fredric March, the leader of the squadron. March is sick of war and the dying of young men. Grant still sees the battle as glorious.

CROCKER, JIM

PICADILLY JIM (1936, MGM)—Cartoonist **Robert Montgomery** helps his bumbling father Frank Morgan marry by making the bride's stuffy parents look ridiculous.

CROCKETT, DAVE

THE SON OF DAVE CROCKETT (1941, Columbia)—**Bill Elliott** is sent to Texas by President Grant to convince the residents to vote to join the Union. Not everyone wants to hear Elliott's arguments.

CROCKETT, DAVY

DAVID CROCKETT, INDIAN SCOUT (1950, UA); DAVY CROCKETT, KING OF THE WILD FRONTIER (1955, Disney); DAVY CROCKETT AND THE RIVER PIRATES (1956, Disney)—**George Montgomery** appears as the legendary frontiersman in 1950, but it was with **Fess Parker** that Crockett and his coonskin cap became a national craze. "Killed him a ba'r when he was only three."

CROCKETT, SAM

RETURN OF THE TEXAN (1952, 20th Century Fox)—**Dale Robertson**, a widower with two sons, returns to his old Texas homestead and finds himself in a fight with wealthy landowner Richard Boone.

CROFT

ACES HIGH (1977, GB, Cine Artists/EMI)—**Peter Firth** is a young WWI British airman who loses his virginity shortly before losing his life in the skies.

CROFT, ALAN

SINNERS IN HEAVEN (1924, Silent, Paramount)—Pilot **Richard Dix** and his passenger Bebe Daniels crash land on an island where they are at first taken for gods by the natives. When Dix carelessly cuts himself while shaving (gods have to look their best, you know), the worship ceremonies end, but Daniels and Dix still look good to their hosts, who prove to be cannibals. Our intrepid duo are saved from being the main course in an island luau when a rescue plane arrives during the cocktail hour.

CROMWELL, OLIVER

CROMWELL (1970, GB, Columbia)—**Richard Harris** makes a dour Cromwell, leader of the Roundheads, who abolished the monarchy in England and sent King Charles I to the executioner's block. He could have just as well bored the king to death.

CROSBY, "SYLVESTER THE GREAT"

THE PRINCESS AND THE PIRATE (1944, RKO)—**Bob Hope** saves Virginia Mayo from pirate captain Victor McLaglen and dishonest island governor Walter Slezak. Hope's last name is of course an in-joke.

CROSS, FRANK

SCROOGED (1988, Paramount)—The trouble with **Bill Murray**, as a scrooge-like ratings-man program chief of a TV network, is that he's so much better as a man who makes everyone's life miserable than as a born-again believer in the power of love and the importance of old-fashioned family values. Murray is a very droll fellow, but not once he gives up being mean and uncaring. He looks like he's about to break out in a grin, saying don't take me seriously. Re-run Alastair Sim's SCROOGE once more.

CROSS, MARK

THE IDLER (1915, Silent, Box Office Attractions)—Wealthy young Englishman **Charles Richman** secretly marries an actress who milks him until he won't pay blackmail any longer. She exposes their marriage and his parents pack him off to America, leaving behind the girl he really loves. In the U.S., he changes his nature and eventually returns home to the right girl for him.

CROTHERS, ABB

THE RICHEST MAN IN TOWN (1941, Columbia)—**Frank Craven's** constant feud with Edgar Buchanan is interrupted long enough for them to deal with a con-man.

CROWKILLER, SONNY

WAR PARTY (1989, Tri-Star)—When a deranged white man, dressed as a soldier, uses real bullets in an reenactment of a massacre of Indians, he kills a Native American. **Billy Wirth** and four friends retaliate for the murder.

CROWLEY, THEA LEMP *See* THEA LEMP

CROWN, THOMAS

THE THOMAS CROWN AFFAIR (1968, UA)—Bored, wealthy **Steve McQueen** masterminds a bank robbery and then plays cat and mouse games with the beautiful insurance investigator Faye Dunaway who is trying to get the goods on him.

CROWTHER, SIMEON, SR.

THE MASTER OF BANKDAM (1947, GB, GFD)—**Tom Walls**, the owner of a Yorkshire wool mill, dies before he can write his son Stephen Murray out of his will. The latter indirectly caused the death of his brother and rival Dennis Price. The struggle for control continues into the next generation of Crowthers.

CROYDEN, CONSUELO

HER CARDBOARD LOVER (1942, MGM)—**Norma Shearer** ends her film career with this shoddy piece in which she is a flirtatious divorcee who hires Robert Taylor to pose as her lover in order to make her ex-husband and suitor George Sanders jealous. With Taylor in the picture, do you really think Sanders will get Shearer?

CROYDEN, TODD
THE EAGLE AND THE HAWK (1950, Paramount)—U.S. government agent **John Payne** tracks down Dennis O'Keefe who is supplying arms to Mexican rebels led by Juarez. The two work together to prevent a planned invasion of Texas by French troops.

CRUISE, ERIC
MAC AND ME (1988, Orion)—In a clear E.T. rip-off, wheelchair bound **Jade Calegory** befriends a Mysterious Alien Creature, separated from his family.

CRUMB, HARRY
WHO'S HARRY CRUMB? (1989, Tri-Star)—**John Candy** portrays an inept private detective, brought in on a kidnapping case, with the expectation that he will bungle it. He does, but he also solves the case.

CRUSOE, LT. ROBIN
LT. ROBIN CRUSOE (1966, Buena Vista)—U.S. navy pilot **Dick Van Dyke** is forced to parachute onto a Pacific island where he gets tangled up with a local women's lib movement. The movie could have used a boost from Henny Youngman and Rose Marie.

CRUSOE, ROBINSON
ROBINSON CRUSOE (1927, GB, Silent, Epic); THE ADVENTURES OF ROBINSON CRUSOE (1954, UA); CRUSOE (1989, Island)—**M.A. Wetherell** stars as the shipwrecked man in the silent version. It was re-released in 1932 with a soundtrack. In 1954, **Dan O'Herlihy** was nominated for an Academy Award for his strong portrayal of Daniel Defoe's seventeenth century mariner, shipwrecked on a tropical island, otherwise uninhabited until the late arrival of Friday. The 1989 version updates and transplants the story to the nineteenth century and a place somewhere off West Africa. **Aidan Quinn**, as the lonely voyager, stars in a film without any Friday, but filled with an attempt to make an anti-racist message.

CRUZ
THE LONE GUN (1954, UA)—Heroic marshal **George Montgomery** must face up to the bad guys all by himself. Well so did Gary Cooper in HIGH NOON (1952).

CRYSTAL
HOLLYWOOD HOT TUBS 2: EDUCATING CRYSTAL (1990, Alimar)—In this comic book sequel to Chuck Vincent's 1984 sexual exploitation film, valley girl **Jewel Shepard** fights attempts by evil Bart Braverman to take over her mother's hot tub/health spa outfit.

CRYSTAL
THREE STRANGERS (1946, Warner Brothers)—**Geraldine Fitzgerald**, Sydney Greenstreet and Peter Lorre are three desperate characters who share a winning sweepstakes ticket. It's quite enjoyable but wasn't a box-office success because it didn't have a bankable big name star in it.

CUEBALL
DICK TRACY VS CUEBALL (1946, RKO)—**Dick Wessel**, looking grotesque in his bald wig, is on a murdering rampage, strangling fellow gang-members who have double-crossed him. He gets his, when his foot is caught in a train switcher, just as a fast freight bears down on him. Cueball in all the pockets!

CUFFE, DECO
THE COMMITMENTS (1991, GB, 20th Century Fox)—Vulgar 16-year-old **Andrew Strong** is the lead singer of a Dublin soul group. His driving whiskey voice is worth hearing.

CULHANE, ALICE
GYPSY OF THE NORTH (1928, Silent, Rayart)—**Georgia Hale** made a career playing Alaskan dance hall girls. She was much better in Charles Chaplin's THE GOLD RUSH.

CULLEN, AMELIA
MY LOVE CAME BACK (1940, Warner Brothers)—**Olivia de Havilland**, an aspiring violinist attending a music academy, is also interested in finding a husband. Jeffrey Lynn seems a likely candidate but everyone suspects the worst when it's discovered that music company owner Charles Winninger is paying de Havilland's tuition.

CULLEN, ED
THE MAN WHO CHEATED HIMSELF (1951, 20th Century Fox)—Homicide detective **Lee J. Cobb** covers up for his lover Jane Wyatt when she kills her husband.

CULLEN, MILES
THE SILENT PARTNER (1979, Canada, EMC Film Corp.)—Bank teller **Elliott Gould** outsmarts sadistic bank robber Christopher Plummer. Gould learns of the planned heist ahead of time and pulls a switch, keeping the loot for himself.

CULLEN, NOAH
THE DEFIANT ONES (1958, UA)—Black prisoner **Sidney Poitier** is chained to redneck Tony Curtis. An accident to the car taking them to prison gives them the opportunity to escape. Their mutual hatred turns to an understanding that they need each other. What could have been a phony brotherhood message is quite effective due to the convincing work of Poitier and Curtis.

CULVER, ADELAIDE
AFFAIRS OF ADELAIDE (1949, 20th Century Fox)—**Maureen O'Hara**, a member of a wealthy family, marries two poverty-stricken and failed men, both played by Dana Andrews, the first an artist and the second a lawyer.

CULVER, TERRY
HIS FIRST COMMAND (1929, Pathe)—In his pre-Hopalong Cassidy days, **William Boyd** is a newly commissioned army officer with his first command. His smart-ass ways might attract the ladies, but the army would have sacked him in a moment.

CUMMINGS *See* STEVE NICHOLS

CUMMINGS, CAPT. ("THE HAWK")
SHE DONE HIM WRONG (1933, Paramount)—**Cary Grant** poses as a Salvation Army officer so he can get the goods on Gay Nineties saloon keeper Mae West. You can just imagine the look West gives Grant as she sizes him up.

CUMMINGS, TERRY & BETTY
DARING DAUGHTERS (1933, Tower)—Cold-hearted gold-digger **Marian Marsh** protects her younger sister **Joan Marsh** (the two actresses are not related), just in town from the country, from city cads, but finds she needs help when one of her gentlemen steals money from her.

CUPPY, ADA
MAMA STEPS OUT (1937, MGM)—**Alice Brady** tests the waters of the smart crowd at the Riviera and finds it not to her liking.

CURIE, MARIE

MADAME CURIE (1943, MGM)—**Greer Garson** portrays the scientist who discovers radium. Ever faithful Walter Pidgeon portrays her colleague and husband Pierre. It's a rather dull biopic but done in the usual high style of MGM.

CURLYTOP

CURLYTOP (1924, Silent, Fox)—Millionaire Wallace MacDonald discovers **Shirley Mason** and her sister Diana Miller in an orphanage. He falls for Miller and sets both up in luxury in New York. The story would be remade in 1935 with Shirley Temple in the title role.

CURRAGH, MAJOR MICHAEL

CONSPIRATOR (1949, GB, MGM)—**Robert Taylor**, a British Army Officer in the employ of the Russians, marries naive American Elizabeth Taylor, who begs him to give up his life as spy and traitor. His Russian superiors order him to kill his wife. He can't bring himself to do so and rather than wait to be eliminated, he commits suicide.

CURRAN

NAVY SEALS (1990, Orion)—**Michael Biehn** is a member of a team of Navy commandos who make quick work of Middle Eastern terrorists in besieged Beirut.

CURRAN, GRANT

PARK AVENUE LOGGER (1937, RKO)—**George O'Brien's** wealthy father thinks he needs to become more of a man. O'Brien is sent to a lumber camp where he becomes a top wrestler, exposes some crooks and wins the love of a pretty girl.

CURRAN, JOE

JOE (1970, Cannon)—Bigot **Peter Boyle** befriends Dennis Patrick, who has just killed his daughter's drug addicted boyfriend. Despite the difference in their backgrounds, they find common ground in their hatred of hippies.

CURRY, EUGENE

THE SNOB (1924, Silent, MGM)—Schoolteacher **John Gilbert**, anxious to make a place for himself in society, marries Norma Shearer but continues an affair with Phyllis Haver, who he believes can feed his ambition. What Gilbert doesn't know is that Shearer is an heiress.

CURTIS, CAPT. GEORGE

CAPTAIN OF THE GRAY HORSE TROOP (1917, Silent, Vitagraph)—Army officer **Antonio Moreno** is sympathetic to the American Indians, whose land is being legally stolen by ranchers pulling strings and greasing palms in Washington.

CURTIS, DANIEL

VIRTUOUS HUSBAND (1931, Universal)—Wealthy young **Elliott Nugent** lets the books and letters of his deceased mother guide his life when he marries.

CURTIS, KATE

COUSIN KATE (1921, Silent, Vitagraph)—Novelist **Alice Joyce's** views on love are considered unconventional by her family, but she's called in to mend romantic fences between her cousin and a nature lover. She meets the latter without knowing his identity and the two fall in love. It's OK, the cousin prefers another man anyway.

CURTIS, PONYBOY

THE OUTSIDERS (1983, Warner Brothers)—Gang warfare sixties style in Tulsa, Oklahoma is seen through the eyes of C. **Thomas Howell**, a boy who likes poetry and GONE WITH THE WIND.

CURTIS, STEVE & JOHN L.

SO'S YOUR UNCLE (1943, Universal)—**Donald Woods** impersonates his uncle **Paul Stanton** in this musical comedy and finds himself wooed by his girlfriend's aunt.

CUSHING, JENNIE

THE RISE OF JENNIE CUSHING (1917, Silent, Artcraft)—Slum girl **Elsie Ferguson** becomes the common law wife of an artist Elliott Dexter after years in a reformatory. When her past is revealed, she runs away to spare him embarrassment, but he brings her back and this time they get married.

CUSTER, GENERAL GEORGE A.

THEY DIED WITH THEIR BOOTS ON (1942, Warner Brothers); CUSTER OF THE WEST (1968, Cinerama)—The 1942 film romanticizes the life of the Civil War's youngest general, even to the point of having **Errol Flynn** knowingly and willingly going to death with his Third Cavalry so that his dying deposition can be used against the unscrupulous men who are trying to steal Indian land. But my, are the film and its star entertaining. **Robert Shaw** offers a fine performance as the glory-mad officer who speaks with forked-tongue to the red man and gets his comeuppance at the Little Big Horn.

CUTFOOT, WARREN

WAR PARTY (1989, Tri-Star)—**Tim Sampson**, son of the late Will Sampson, is one of the Native American lads who seeks revenge for the killing of an Indian at a reenactment of a bloody battle, which took place 100 years earlier.

CUTLER, SPOT CASH

I SELL ANYTHING (1934, First National/Warner Brothers) - Auctioneer **Pat O'Brien** is hired by Claire Dodd to sell her boyfriend's antiques, but she pulls a fast one, substituting fakes for the real things.

CUTLET, CAPT. BEN

WINDBAG THE SAILOR (1937, GB, Gaumont)—Seaman **Will Hay** has many tall tales to tell. He's able to foil the attempts of his ship's crew to scuttle the vessel for the insurance money.

CUTTER, ALEX

CUTTER AND BONE (1981, UA)—Vulgar crippled Vietnam veteran **John Heard** and pretty boy Jeff Bridges, who's having an affair with Heard's wife, combine to play detective when Heard sees a man he thinks may be a murderer. The film is also known as CUTTER'S WAY.

CUTWATER, EDWINA

ALL OF ME (1984, Universal)—**Lily Tomlin** is a crotchety millionaire whose soul and spirit find their way into the body of idealistic lawyer Steve Martin. She certainly interferes with his sex life.

CVETIC, MATT

I WAS A COMMUNIST FOR THE FBI (1951, Warner Brothers)—This film made during the great "red" scare of the fifties stars **Frank Lovejoy** as an FBI agent who goes undercover to join the Communist party (which wasn't outlawed, by the way). The time came when there were more FBI agents in the Communist party than anyone else. In the same period, only three FBI agents were assigned to investigate organized crime. Hoover had his priorities, you know.

CYNTHIA

THE BACHELOR'S DAUGHTER (1946, UA)—**Claire Trevor** is one of four department store sales girls who persuade floorwalker Adolphe

Menjou, a bachelor, to act as their father, so they can appear as a wealthy Long Island family and perhaps catch some rich husbands.

CYNTHIA

HIS WIFE'S MOTHER (1932, GB, British International)—**Molly Lamont** catches her son-in-law Jerry Verno with a show girl. He tries to convince her that he's his own double.

D

"D"

MEMOIRS OF A SURVIVOR (1981, GB, EMI)—In this sci-fi film, **Julie Christie**, a survivor of a nuclear holocaust, lives in a decayed society with teenager Leonie Mellinger.

DA

DA (1988, Filmdallas)—DA is a one-man show with characters. The movie, like the play it's based on, is all **Barnard Hughes**. He is majestic as the Irish father Martin Sheen has come home to bury in the small village of Dalkey. As Sheen goes through the chores of settling the end of his father's life, Hughes' presence constantly interrupts, imposing his views on anything and everything. Sheen's letting-go of his lifelong love-hate relationship with a garrulous man who humiliated and outraged him allows him to take note of his Da's love, companionship and good humor—memories of a father well worth having.

DA VINCI, LEO

A SMALL CIRCLE OF FRIENDS (1980, UA)—**Brad Davis** is one of a group of Harvard students living in turmoil during the radical sixties. The memories are dim and dim-witted.

DABNEY, RAYMOND

THE MAN IN POSSESSION (1931, MGM)—**Robert Montgomery** poses as a butler to help Irene Purcell. The two fall in love. Not much here.

DAD

PARENTS (1988, Vestron)—**Randy Quaid** and his wife Mary Beth Hurt don't believe their son, who has trouble distinguishing nightmares from reality, until the boy reveals his parents' strange eating habits.

DADDY

DADDY'S BOYS (1988, Concorde)—During the Depression, tough old **Raymond J. Barry** and his three morose or retarded sons are looking for a woman—good or bad—to take care of them.

DADDY

DADDY'S DYIN' . . . WHO'S GOT THE WILL? (1990, MGM/UA)—Dotty old daddy **Bert Remsen's** days are numbered, but he can't remember where he's hidden his will. A slew of squabbling family members attempt to settle old scores around the old man's death bed.

DAGGER, DICK

A MAN CALLED DAGGER (1967, MGM)—**Paul Mantee** stars in another of the many films trying to cash in on the success of the James Bond movies. He's a secret agent with a lot of neat gadgets

which he uses in his pursuit of a former Nazi concentration camp commandant.

DAHOMEY, LORNA

MY DARK LADY (1987, Film Gallery)—Black **Lorna Hill** runs a boarding house where failed Shakespearean actor Fred A. Keller takes refuge after being caught shop-lifting while wearing a Santa Claus suit. Keller takes an interest in Hill's son, trying to get him into a good private school, but they experience some prejudicial resistance on the part of the headmaster.

DAILEY, PHIL

BIG TOWN CZAR (1939, Universal)—**Barton Maclane's** plans to take over the illegal activities of a city lead to him being framed for murder and his kid brother getting killed in a shoot-out.

DAINGERFIELD, HOPE

THE RAINBOW PRINCESS (1916, Silent, Famous Players)—Circus star **Ann Pennington** is tricked by the owner of the show into posing as the long-lost granddaughter of a millionaire.

DAINTRY, LOLA

THE INFIDEL (1922, Silent, Preferred)—**Katherine MacDonald**, posing as a castaway, is taken to a South Seas island by industrialist Joseph Dowling, where she accepts the hospitality of missionary Robert Ellis. The trio have quite a bit of trouble with the locals, until marines arrive to quell the uprising.

DAISY

THE FLORODORA GIRL (1930, MGM)—In the early 1900s, Florodora girl **Marion Davies** falls for a caring millionaire.

DAISY

GERT AND DAISY'S WEEKEND (1941, GB, Butchers); GERT AND DAISY CLEAN UP (1942, GB, Butchers)—**Doris Waters** and her sister Elsie Waters are Cockney waitresses whose brand of silly humor appeals to some in the British Isles, but they are almost not understandable to others.

DAISY, DIXIE

LADY OF BURLESQUE (1943, UA)—In this adaptation of Gypsy Rose Lee's "G-String Murders," **Barbara Stanwyck** is a burlesque queen who may be the next victim of a maniac who strangles strippers with their own G-strings. The thrills aren't much, but Barbara looks at home in her role.

DAKERS, JONATHAN & HAROLD

MY BROTHER JONATHAN (1949, GB, Allied Artists) -**Michael Dennison** and **Ronald Howard** are brothers who love the same woman, Beatrice Campbell. Dennison, the elder, loses her to Howard, but before the two can marry, Howard is killed in WWI, leaving Campbell with an illegitimate child. Dennison marries her, but loses her in childbirth and is faced with raising his brother's child.

DAKIN, VIC

VILLAIN (1971, GB, EMI-MGM)—Sadistic homosexual thief **Richard Burton** is loved only by his "mum," Cathleen Nesbitt. Take out the four-letter words and there is very little dialogue.

DAKOTA KID

THE DAKOTA KID (1951, Republic)—A villainous saloonkeeper brings in killer **Dean Morton** to dispose of sheriff James Bell, so he can have his way in running a western town. He's thwarted by two kids, Michael Chapin and Eilene Janssen, who learn the gunman's identity in time to tip off Bell.

DAKOTA LIL

DAKOTA LIL (1950, 20th Century Fox)—Forger **Marie Windsor** helps government agent George Montgomery infiltrate a gang of western counterfeiters.

DALBRAY, LILY

MY FAVORITE SPY (1951, RKO)—**Hedy Lamarr** is the former lover of a famous spy played by Bob Hope. Hope also appears as a cowardly burlesque comic who is the spy's exact double. It's been said that Lamarr stole the show, so Hope demanded the picture be recut to make him look the better of the two.

DALE, ALLEN A.

ROBIN AND SEVEN HOODS (1964, Warner Brothers)—**Bing Crosby** looks seedy in this low-comedy of Frank Sinatra's Rat Pack buddies doing a Robin Hood-like story of Chicago thirties mobsters. Crosby runs an orphanage which Sinatra gifts with the $50,000 Barbara Rush gives Ole Blue Eyes to discover who rubbed out her father. Bing informs the papers of Sinatra's generosity, making him a reluctant hero.

DALE, BRETT

MAN OF THE FOREST (1933, Paramount)—Woodsman **Randolph Scott** learns that Wallace Beery and Barton Maclane are planning to kidnap Verna Hillie, the niece of rancher Harry Carey, so he carries her off first and falls in love with her.

DALE, FLORA

THE OUTLAW'S DAUGHTER (1925, Silent, Universal)—**Josie Sedgwick** saves the life of Edward Hearne, the miner who cared for her after she was shot.

DALE, JUNE

YOUNG AND BEAUTIFUL (1934, Mascot)—Public relations man William Haines decides to show his girl **Judith Allen** how much he thinks of her by making her a movie star. She'd prefer candy and flowers, and romantic evenings.

DALE, STEPHANY

BOUGHT (1931, Warner Brothers)—Slum girl **Constance Bennett** looks to improve her lot by snaring a rich man. Later, no longer pure, but a lot wiser, she returns to her struggling boyfriend, Ben Lyon.

DALE, VALERIE

EARTH GIRLS ARE EASY (1989, Vestron)—Three furry, pastel-colored space aliens crash their UFO in zany manicurist **Geena Davis'** pool. When shaved, Mr. Blue turns out to be Davis' real-life husband Jeff Goldblum, who wins her heart.

DALEY, JIM

SUMMER LOVE (1958, Universal)—**John Saxon** heads up a musical combo which gets its first professional gig at a co-ed summer camp. He has several female "groupies" to choose from, including Molly Bee and Jill St. John.

DALLAS, STELLA

STELLA DALLAS (1925, Silent, UA); (1937, UA); STELLA (1990, Buena Vista)—**Belle Bennett**, **Barbara Stanwyck** and **Bette Midler** each portray the uncouth woman who loses her rich lover and eventually gives up her daughter to him and his new wife, because they can give the young woman a better life. Watching the mother stand outside in the rain as her daughter is married inside her ex-lover's home causes one to choke back a few tears.

DALRYMPLE, LORETTA *See* "DAWN" GLORY

DALTON

THE RAIN KILLER (1990, Concorde)—**David Beecroft** appears as a LA serial killer who only works on rainy nights. When the weather is wet, he stalks the streets for wealthy, attractive women to slash and slaughter.

DALTON, HOLLY, ROSE, COLUMBINE & MARIGOLD

THE DALTON GIRLS (1957, UA)—In a lame western, bad girls **Merry Anders, Lisa Davis, Penny Edwards** and **Sue George** give up studying outlawery with the help of lawman John Russell.

DALTON, GRAT, BOB, BEN & EMMETT

WHEN THE DALTONS RODE (1940, Universal); THE DALTONS RIDE AGAIN (1945, Universal); RETURN OF THE BADMEN (1948, RKO) -**Brian Donlevy, Broderick Crawford, Stuart Erwin** and **Frank Albertson** impersonated the infamous Dalton brothers in a fine 1940 movie. The excitement was still present when **Lon Chaney, Jr., Kent Taylor, Noah Beery, Jr.** and **Alan Curtis** assumed the roles. In 1948, only Emmett played by **Lex Barker** was featured in an all-star array of western outlaws.

DALTON, TIGER

THE TICKET OF LEAVE MAN (1937, GB, MGM)—**Tod Slaughter** heads an organization meant to help ex-cons—help them become a part of a crime syndicate, that is.

D'ALVADOREZ, DONNA LUCIA

CHARLEY'S AUNT (1925, Silent, Cristie Film Co.); (1930, Columbia); (1941, 20th Century Fox)—**Eulalie Jensen, Doris Lloyd** and **Kay Francis** are effective in varying degrees as the Oxford student's aunt whose late arrival to act as chaperon for visiting young ladies forces one of the undergraduates to impersonate the aunt.

DALY, FRANK

THE LAST OF THE FINEST (1990, Orion)—**Brian Dennehy** heads up a team of dedicated cops who stumble onto a bunch of corrupt police officials and feds while working on a drug bust.

D'AMICO, PHIL

WILLIE AND PHIL (1980, 20th Century Fox)—**Ray Sharkey** and friend Michael Ontkean share Margot Kidder in this attempt by director Paul Mazursky to film his version of JULES ET JIM.

DAMIEN, MADELEINE

DISHONORED LADY (1947, UA)—**Hedy Lamarr's** shady past leads her to be accused of murdering a former lover, rich jeweler John Loder, but is saved by her new love, scientist Dennis O'Keefe.

DAMON

DAMON AND PYTHIAS (1962, MGM)—**Guy Williams** and **Don Burnett** portray the legendary friends from Sicily of 400 B.C. If you know the legend, the movie can safely be missed.

DAN

DAN (1914, All Star Feature)—The foremost minstrel man of his day, **Lew Dockstader** appears in black face as a faithful servant who saves his master's son, a Confederate officer, from a Union firing squad by sneaking in the prison and disguising the condemned as a "darkie" with the help of some charcoal.

DAN

DYNAMITE DAN (1924, Silent, Sunset)—**Kenneth McDonald** knocks out the heavyweight champion when the latter annoys his girlfriend. McDonald turns pro, and the fight ends with him meeting the champ once more, this time in the ring and defeating him.

DAN

LITTLE MEN (1935, Mascot); (1940, RKO)—**Frankie Darro** and **Jimmy Lydon** portray an orphan who becomes involved with three amiable swindlers in these free adaptations of Louisa Mae Alcott's novel.

DANCER, CURLY SUE

CURLY SUE (1991, Warner Brothers)—Con man James Belushi and his adopted daughter **Alison Porter** work a scam on corporate attorney Kelly Lynch. Porter is no Tatum O'Neal in this predictable, ho-hum comedy.

DANA, JANE

NICE GIRL? (1941, Universal)—Teenager **Deanna Durbin** carries on a flirtation with the representative of a New York scientific foundation, Franchot Tone, who's visiting her father.

DANCER, JIM

FIGHTING MAN OF THE PLAINS (1949, 20th Century Fox)—Gunman turned lawman **Randolph Scott** cleans up a town with the help of Jesse James, played by Dale Robertson.

DANCER, JO JO

JO JO DANCER, YOUR LIFE IS CALLING (1986, Columbia)—**Richard Pryor** appears in a semi-autobiographical film and while some of the events are poignantly detailed, too much is left out to make it great comedy or drama.

DANCER, TOMMY

MAN IN THE VAULT (1956, RKO)—Locksmith **William Campbell** is forced to help gangsters by making keys that will unlock a bank's safety deposit boxes.

DANDRIDGE, OLIVIA

SHE WORE A YELLOW RIBBON (1949, RKO)—**Joanne Dru** looks smashing in this western and so say two young shavetails, John Agar and Harry Carey, Jr. and a veteran widower cavalry officer, John Wayne.

DANDY

DANDY, THE ALL AMERICAN GIRL (1976, MGM/UA)—**Stockard Channing**, convicted many times of car theft, desperately wishes to legitimately own a Dino Ferrari. In Great Britain, the film was released as SWEET REVENGE.

DANE, MRS.

MRS. DANE'S DEFENCE (1933, GB, Paramount)—**Joan Barry** flees scandal in Monte Carlo by moving to England where she assumes the identity of a deceased cousin.

DANGEROUSLY, JOHNNY

JOHNNY DANGEROUSLY (1984, 20th Century Fox)—In a spoof of thirties gangster movies, **Michael Keaton** and Joe Piscopo are rival mob bosses. Jimmy Cagney in THE PUBLIC ENEMY was funnier.

DANIEL

JULIA HAS TWO LOVERS (1990, South Gate)—When **David Duchovny** mistakenly gets Daphna Kastner on the phone, they so like each

other's phone voices that they spend the morning getting acquainted, mostly concentrating on their sex lives. Ultimately they connect in person to make love, giving the film a little romantic triangle, the third side being Kastner's live-in lover David Charles.

DANIEL

THE KARATE KID (1984, Columbia); THE KARATE KID, PART 2 (1986, Columbia)—Likeable kid **Ralph Macchio** is beset by bullies until Noriyuki "Pat" Morita teaches him karate and self-confidence. In the sequel, Macchio accompanies Morita to Japan where both encounter dangerous enemies and romance. By the third film in the series, Daniel had acquired a last name. So for THE KARATE KID, PART III, see LA RUSSO, DANIEL.

DANIEL, MELANIE

MELANIE (1982, Canada, Embassy)—Illiterate Arkansas woman **Glynnis O'Connor** loses custody of her son to his father. She follows the boy and his father to California and becomes involved both with lawyer Paul Sorvino and has-been rock star Burton Cummings (formerly with the Guess Who).

DANIELS, DINKY

DINKY (1935, Warner Brothers)—Military school cadet **Jackie Cooper's** mother Mary Astor is framed for a crime she didn't commit and sent to prison, causing Master Cooper considerable trauma.

DANIELS, SUSAN

THE GIRL HE LEFT BEHIND (1956, Warner Brothers)—**Natalie Wood** is the girl back home, whom spoiled draftee Tab Hunter wants to get back to so badly he's willing to take a dishonorable discharge.

DANIELS, WILBY

THE SHAGGY DOG (1959, Buena Vista); THE SHAGGY D.A. (1976, Buena Vista)—Young **Tommy Kirk** turns into a big shaggy dog (which neither seems to surprise nor bother his father Fred MacMurray) and catches some crooks. By the sequel, Kirk has grown up to become lawyer **Dean Jones** who uses a magic ring to become a talking dog and expose political corruption.

DANIZA

FIVE BRANDED WOMEN (1960, Paramount)—**Vera Miles** is one of five girls who have their heads shaved for taking German lovers during WWII, but they redeem themselves by joining the Yugoslavian underground.

DANNER, PETULIA

PETULIA (1968, Warner Brothers)—Physician George C. Scott falls for kooky **Julie Christie** who has troubles with her father Joseph Cotten, who controls her, and her husband Richard Chamberlain, who beats her.

DANNY

DANNY BOY (1934, GB, Panther); (1941, GB, Butchers)—**Ronnie Hepworth** and **Grant Tyler** portray the boy, left behind to be a street entertainer with his father when his mother leaves them to pursue her own musical career.

DANNY

DANNY BOY (1984, Ireland, Triumph)—Saxophonist **Stephen Rea** is a witness to a double homicide. He decides to take his own revenge for the murders.

DANNY

PENROD AND HIS TWIN BROTHER (1938, Warner Brothers); PENROD'S DOUBLE TROUBLE (1938, Warner Brothers)—Warner

Brothers must have felt it only fair to create a role in the Penrod series for its young star Billy Mauch's twin bother **Bobby Mauch**. The result is a double dose of mischief.

DANNY

THE SILENT WITNESS (1962, Emerson)—Newsboy **Billy Shanley** witnesses a murder while delivering papers and is chased into an amusement park where the climactic scene takes place at the top of a roller coaster.

DANNY

WANTED BY THE POLICE (1938, Monogram)—Good kid **Frankie Darro** falls in with the wrong crowd, a bunch of young car thieves. His sister's boyfriend Robert Kent, a cop, straightens him out.

DANNY

THE YEAR MY VOICE BROKE (1988, Australia, Avenue)—Young **Noah Taylor's** first impulses of sexual desire are directed toward 16-year-old Leone Carmen, whose emergence into womanhood leaves little time for her confused younger friend and his puppy lust.

DANTE, ALIGHIERI

DANTE'S INFERNO (1924, Silent, Fox)—**Lawson Butt** portrays the author of the Inferno in this story of how a ruthless businessman dreams of the Inferno and upon awakening mends his ways.

DANTES, EDMOND

THE COUNT OF MONTE CRISTO (1934, UA); THE RETURN OF MONTE CRISTO (1946, Columbia); THE COUNT OF MONTE CRISTO (1975, GB, ITC)—As far as most movie fans of sufficient age are concerned, **Robert Donat** is Edmond Dantes, the Count of Monte Cristo. Unjustly imprisoned for life, Dantes escapes after many years and finds a hidden fortune, which makes him the richest man in the world. He returns to Paris to take revenge on the three villains responsible for his suffering. **Richard Chamberlain** and **Louis Hayward's** interpretations of the role are merely adequate compared to that of Donat.

DAPHNE

THE MAN WHO LOVED REDHEADS (1955, GB, London Films)—In this role, one of four she plays in the movie, **Moira Shearer** is a cockney girl, the second of four redheads whom John Justin loves in his life, although he is married to a brunette all the time.

DAR

THE BEASTMASTER (1982, MGM/UA)—In this sword and sorcery fantasy, **Marc Singer's** remarkable ability to communicate with animals serves him well in his fight against evil Rip Torn. No, he's not a young, muscular Dr. Doolittle.

DARA *See* SABENA

DARBY, MAJOR WILLIAM

DARBY'S RANGERS (1958, Warner Brothers)—**James Garner** oversees the training of a crack group of commandos to be sent into action in North Africa and Sicily.

DARELL, SUSAN

AFFAIRS OF SUSAN (1945, Paramount)—Walter Abel meets three men who have been romantically involved with his fiancee **Joan Fontaine** and discovers each remember her quite differently, and none of their descriptions of her matches his.

DARIA

SLAVE GIRLS FROM BEYOND INFINITY (1987, Titan/Urban Classics)—**Elizabeth Cayton** is involved in a hunt to the death like that found in THE MOST DANGEROUS GAME. Only this time, the action takes place on a distant planet. We think it's meant to be a spoof—either that or it's just poorly directed and acted—or perhaps both.

DARING, LT. BOB

LIEUTENANT DARING RN (1935, GB, Butchers)—**Hugh Williams** rescues his girl from Chinese pirates and at the same time clears himself of charges of stealing important secret documents.

DARK, JOHNNY

JOHNNY DARK (1954, Universal)—**Tony Curtis** designs and races cars for an automobile manufacturer. He steals his newest design and enters the Canada-to-Mexico cross-country race which naturally he wins.

DARK MAN, THE

THE DARK MAN (1951, GB, GFD)—Mysterious murderer **Maxwell Reed** haunts a seaside resort hotel.

DARKMAN

DARKMAN (1990, Universal)—After an experiment goes wrong, horribly disfigured, bandaged **Liam Neeson**, energized with super powers, stalks the night seeking revenge.

DARLOW, MARGARITA

HER SACRIFICE (1926, Silent, Sanford)—**Ligia Golconda** refuses to marry the man she loves because of the shame she feels for having once been seduced by a scoundrel. Her man persists.

DARRICOTT, JAMIE

LADIES' MAN (1931, Paramount)—**William Powell** is a professional escort of rich women who need a good-looking man to squire them around town. His problems begin when he falls in love with Carole Lombard, the daughter of his best client.

DARROW, NICK

UNDER-COVER MAN (1932, Paramount)—**George Raft** avenges his father's death by going undercover for the FBI and breaking up a bond-stealing gang.

D'ARTAGNAN

THE FOUR MUSKETEERS (1975, 20th Century Fox)—**Michael York**, a young man from Gascony, came to Paris in the prequel to this movie (THE THREE MUSKETEERS) to follow in the footsteps of his father and become a musketeer. He succeeds and now with friends Athos, Aramis and Porthos does battle with Milady de Winter and Rochefort, agents of Cardinal Richelieu.

DARWIN, CHARLES

THE DARWIN ADVENTURE (1972, GB, 20th Century Fox)—**Nicholas Clay** portrays the scientist who developed the theory of evolution while serving as ship's naturalist on the Beagle during its voyages in the 1830s.

DARYL

D.A.R.Y.L. (1985, Paramount)—When Mary Beth Hurt and Michael McKean adopt **Barret Oliver**, he seems too good to be true, and he is.

"DATA"

THE GOONIES (1985, Warner Brothers)—**Ke Huy Quan** is one of a group of housing project kids who find a treasure map and a treasure ship. They have all the adventure kids could ever want to fill one Saturday afternoon.

DATCHETT, LORD TERENCE
WOMAN HATER (1949, GB, Rank)—**Stewart Granger** uses a clever ploy to disprove a film star's claim that she hates men and wishes to be alone.

DAUGHTER OF THE SUN GOD
DAUGHTER OF THE SUN GOD (1962, Condor)—When explorers, archaeologists and criminals arrive at a lost Incan city, they encounter **Juanita Llosa** and her people, who are not thrilled by the arrival of unwanted visitors.

DAURAY, VICKI
FOUR GIRLS IN TOWN (1956, Universal)—Italian **Gia Scala** is one of four international beauties brought to Hollywood to compete for the lead in a movie.

DAURIER, LILI
LILI (1953, MGM)—**Leslie Caron** is a charming pleasure as a naive 16-year-old French girl who becomes a part of a puppet act run by a bitter cripple Mel Ferrer. The puppets are so real to her that her simple conversations with them enchant audiences. Caron is infatuated with magician Jean Pierre Aumont, who she doesn't know is married to his assistant Zsa Zsa Gabor. It takes a while but Caron finally connects the cruel Ferrer with the sensitive man who puts such love and understanding in the mouth of his puppets.

DAVE
INDIAN AGENT (1948, RKO)—**Tim Holt** steps in on the side of the red men, when crooked speculators attempt to divert supplies for the Indians to their own use.

DAVEY, JIM
PROFESSIONAL SWEETHEART (1933, RKO)—Kentucky hick **Norman Foster** is hired to be a professional sweetheart for radio's "Purity Girl" Ginger Rogers, in order to protect her image. It's 99 and 44/100 pure that the two fall in love.

DAVID
AMERICAN FLYERS (1985, Warner Brothers)—**David Grant** and his brother Kevin Costner make herculean efforts to train for and win their toughest bicycle race. One of the brothers is dying. Rent the video to find out which one.

DAVID
DAVID AND LISA (1962, Continental)—In a beautiful and touching film, **Keir Dullea** is a mentally disturbed youngster who finds friendship and more with Janet Margolin, a girl who can't stand to be touched.

DAVID
EVERY TIME WE SAY GOODBYE (1986, Tri-Star)—American flyer **Tom Hanks** falls in love with Sephardic Jew Cristina Marsillach in WWII Jerusalem.

DAVID
LONGTIME COMPANION (1990, Goldwyn)—**Bruce Davison** gives a stunning performance as the conscience of a group of gay men coming to terms with AIDS and the impending deaths of their lovers, friends, and ultimately themselves.

DAVID
THE MAN WHO LOVED WOMEN (1983, Columbia)—This remake of a French film directed in 1977 by Francois Truffaut has **Burt Reynolds** as an incurable womanizer—and a very successful one at that. He barely meets a woman before she's plotting how to get him in her bed. Well, it's not much of a chore. As a comedy, the film isn't very funny. If it's meant to be more than a soft-core male fantasy, it failed.

DAVID, JIMMY
THEY GAVE HIM A GUN (1937, MGM)—WWI veteran **Franchot Tone** has been hardened by battle and despite the efforts of his friend Spencer Tracy, he turns to crime and goes down in a hail of bullets.

DAVID, KING
DAVID AND BATHSHEBA (1957, 20th Century Fox); A STORY OF DAVID (1960, GB, British Lion); KING DAVID (1985, Paramount)—When the king of the Hebrews **Gregory Peck** spies beautiful Susan Hayward at her bath across the courtyard from the king's palace, he is determined that she will be his. To ensure this, he sends her husband off on a suicide mission. The couple marry, and a baby arrives a little too quickly for those counting months. Led by the priests, the people demand that Hayward be stoned to death as an adulteress which they reason will satisfy God and cause him to end the drought that Israel has been experiencing since Peck and Hayward's wedding. Peck saves the day by writing the 23rd Psalm, the rains come and he and Hayward swear to spend the rest of their lives doing God's work. In the second feature, **Jeff Chandler** bores audiences with his weak portrayal of the legendary Hebrew king. In 1985, **Richard Gere** portrays the young David who defeats the giant Goliath and goes on to an uneasy reign as king. It's a flop.

DAVID, LILLIAN
THE GILDED LILY (1935, Paramount)—Stenographer **Claudette Colbert**, enjoys a seemingly platonic relationship, sitting on a park bench talking about everything with reporter Fred MacMurray. When she is given a rush by British peer Ray Milland, Colbert decides to buy American.

DAVIDGE
ENEMY MINE (1985, 20th Century Fox)—In this outer space version of THE DEFIANT ONES, American astronaut **Dennis Quaid** and his enemy, Lou Gossett, Jr., an alien hermaphroditic lizard, are forced to work together to survive.

DAVIDSON, HARLEY
HARLEY DAVIDSON AND THE MARLBORO MAN (1991, MGM)—In an attempt to help a friend in the wild, wild west of 1996 Burbank, **Mickey Rourke** and his good-buddy Don Johnson rob a bank and get all their friends killed.

DAVIDSON, JULIE
THE UNEARTHLY STRANGER (1964, GB, American Int.)—Scientists, working on a time-space formula, discover that the wife of one of them, **Gabrielle Licudi**, is an alien trying to steal the secret.

DAVIES, DANGEROUS
DANGEROUS DAVIES, THE LAST DETECTIVE (1981, GB, ITC)—Detective **Bernard Cribbens** doggedly tracks down the murderer of a long dead teenage girl, though his methods are hopelessly out-of-date.

DAVIS
THE GUEST (1963, GB, Janus)—Tramp **Donald Pleasance** is invited to stay in a house owned by brothers Alan Bates and Robert Shaw. The rest of the movie is a verbal sparring match over the visitor by the brothers. The meaning of the film is lost on many,

including your authors. The movie has also been called THE CARETAKER.

DAVIS, ARLENE
GOLD DIGGERS OF 1935, (1935, Warner Brothers)—**Dorothy Dare**, one of the employees of a New England summer resort, lives none-too-well on the tips of the guests. What she needs is a wealthy "friend."

DAVIS, BILL
POSTAL INSPECTOR (1936, Universal)—Postal inspector **Ricardo Cortez** must deal with the plans of a crook to rob a mail shipment.

DAVIS, BILLY & TIMMY
THE TWO LITTLE BEARS (1961, 20th Century Fox)—Eddie Albert discovers that his two children, **Butch Patrick** and **Donnie Carter** turn into little bears at night. Kids do the darndest things.

DAVIS, CHARLIE
FIEND ON DOPE ISLAND (1961, Essanjay)—**Bruce Bennett** builds a empire on a Caribbean island, based on black market activities in arms and drugs. He gets his just deserts by the fade-out.

DAVIS, DRIFTER
THE DRIFTER (1944, PRC)—**Buster Crabbe** leads two lives, one as a bank robber, and the other as a Western Robin Hood.

DAVIS, DUKE
THE DUKE IS THE TOPS (1938, Million Dollar)—In an all-black musical, **Ralph Cooper** and Lena Horne are a producer-performer team. They break up their partnership when she gets a chance on Broadway. Her show is a flop until Cooper comes along and sets it right, making the team a smash.

DAVIS, HOLLY
JUST BETWEEN FRIENDS (1986, Orion)—**Mary Tyler Moore** discovers that her new friend Christine Lahti was her deceased husband's mistress. Soap opera stuff and not very good soap opera.

DAVIS, JAMES "BRICK"
G-MEN (1935, Warner Brothers)—To counter the claims that **James Cagney** was glorifying gangsters in his movie appearances, the little cock-of-the-walk appears as a lawyer, who becomes a government agent when his best friend is killed. He soon suspects that another old friend is behind the killing.

DAVIS, "JIMMY VALENTINE"
THE RETURN OF JIMMY VALENTINE (1936, Republic)—A newspaper looking for a circulation gimmick offers a reward for anyone, who can come up with the whereabouts of an aging safecracker. **Robert Warwick**, who has assumed a new name and has retired, doesn't want to be found. Warwick had played a young Jimmy Valentine in a 1920 film.

DAVIS, JONATHAN
SOMEWHERE I'LL FIND YOU (1942, MGM)—**Clark Gable** portrays a war correspondent romancing fellow journalist Lana Turner. It was the last movie he made before joining the U.S. Air Corps.

DAVIS, JUDGE
THE VIRGINIA JUDGE (1935, Paramount)—Grace Kelly's uncle **Walter C. Kelly** wrote and starred in this routine small-town tale of a kindly judge, who tries to get a youngster back on the straight and narrow. Kelly rode this old horse many years on the vaudeville stage before making the film version.

DAVIS, JUDY
MEET THE GIRLS (1938, 20th Century Fox)—**June Lang** and her friend Lynn Bari lose their jobs as entertainers in Honolulu. They stow away on an ocean liner headed for San Francisco. This leads them to being mixed up with jewel thieves before making it safely home.

DAVIS, KATHLEEN
KATHLEEN (1941, MGM)—Grown up now, poor little rich girl **Shirley Temple** finds a new wife, Laraine Day, for her widower father, Herbert Marshall.

DAVIS, LT. POLLY
FLIGHT NURSE (1953, Republic)—**Joan Leslie** is an Air Force nurse at the front lines during the Korean War.

DAVIS, STEVE
THE COWBOY AND THE KID (1936, Universal)—Cowboy **Buck Jones** befriends Billy Burrud when the boy's father is killed.

DAVIS, WALTER
BLIND DATE (1987, Tri-Star)—While one always takes his chances with a blind date, **Bruce Willis** is initially pleased with beautiful Kim Basinger. When her ex-lover shows up, Willis' troubles are just beginning. Despite losing his job, his car and almost his mind, he's hooked on Basinger.

DAVIS, WOODY
THE LEATHERNECKS HAVE LANDED (1936, Republic)—**Lew Ayres**, a marine stationed in China, is thrown out of the corps after a buddy is killed in a barroom brawl. Ayres gets involved with gunrunners but comes out on the right side before the end of the picture.

DAVIS, YANKEE
YANKEE FAKIR (1947, Republic)—Insurance salesman **Douglas Fowley** moves west, and falls in love with a sheriff's daughter. When the lawman is killed, Fowley takes it on himself to find the murderer.

DAVISON, HELENA
THE GROUP (1966, UA)—**Kathleen Widdoes** is the wealthiest of eight young friends who graduate from college in the midst of the Great Depression. She would like to teach, but her parents don't want their daughter to work for a living, so she spends her life collecting art work.

DAVISON, TOM
INSURANCE INVESTIGATOR (1951, Republic)—**Richard Denning** discovers a "double indemnity" accidental death racket, and almost falls victim to it.

DAVITT, STEVE
UNCHAINED (1955, Warner Brothers)—The best thing about this average prison story, starring professional football star **Elroy Hirsch**, is the song "Unchained Melody," which has been beautifully recorded by the likes of Roy Hamilton, Joe Williams, and the Righteous Brothers.

DAVY
DAVY (1958, GB, Ealing)—Music Hall entertainer **Harry Secombe** is given the opportunity to audition at Covent Garden.

DAVY
THE LITTLE KIDNAPPERS (1954, GB, UA)—In a charming little gem, **Vincent Winter** and Jon Whiteley are two orphaned Nova

Scotian children, who are not allowed a pet by their grandparents, who are raising them. They steal a baby to have something to love. The two youngsters appear so natural, that we hate to leave them after all things are put right.

DAWLISH, MAJOR DIGBY

THOSE DARING YOUNG MEN IN THEIR JAUNTY JALOPIES (1969, GB/France/Italy, Paramount)—**Peter Cook** is an Englishman competing in a 1920s 1500 mile motor rally to Monte Carlo.

DAWN (FRASER)

DAWN (1979, Australia, Aquatamus)—**Browyn Mackay-Payne** appears as controversial Australian swimming star Dawn Fraser, whose behavior at the Olympics caused her to be censured in newspapers all over the world. She was ultimately banned from Olympic competition for ten years, which in effect was a life-time ban.

DAWN (SWEETIE)

SWEETIE (1989, Australia, Arenafilm)—Fat and sassy **Genevieve Lemon** gobbles up life while her sister Karen Colston, a control freak, is a paranoid bundle of nerves. Violently spoiled, Lemon rules the roost until she's killed in a fall. It's a domestic slapstick tragedy.

DAWN, BILLIE

BORN YESTERDAY (1951, Columbia)—**Judy Holliday** is the unedu-cated, but not stupid mistress, of crooked loud-mouthed business-man Broderick Crawford. Crawford hires writer William Holden to give Holliday some class. Holden not only teaches her what to talk about, but also what to think about. Judy and her tutor develop tender feelings for each other, and Holliday outsmarts the wheeling-and-dealing junk dealer Crawford.

DAWSON

MY SIX CONVICTS (1952, Columbia)—**Harry Morgan** is a callous killer, who would do just about anything and anybody to escape from the pen. He's one of six cons who enter into group therapy with the new prison psychologist. Morgan thinks the Doc will make a swell shield in an escape attempt.

DAWSON

TEN GENTLEMEN FROM WEST POINT (1942, 20th Century Fox)—In the early 1800s, backwoodsman **George Montgomery** is one of the first recruits to the new military academy at West Point.

DAWSON, BOB

MAN FROM MONTANA (1941, Universal)—Sheriff **Johnny Mack Brown** finds himself between a rock and a hard place in an inevitable conflict between cattlemen and homesteaders.

DAWSON, BRONCO

THREE ROGUES (1931, Fox)—Rustler **Eddie Gribbon** and two other rogues figure that Fay Wray would make an awful good wife. Her main appeal is she has a map that tells the location of a gold mine. And some women think perfume, cosmetics and fancy clothes attract men.

DAWSON, COLLEY

THE SAFECRACKER (1958, GB, MGM)—Safecracker **Ray Milland** is released from prison to help commandos in a WWII raid.

DAWSON, LAURIE & BEN

THE MARSHAL'S DAUGHTER (1953, UA)—**Laurie Anders** and **Hoot Gibson** are the title characters in what is meant to be a comedy western, starring Ken Murray. Anders likes the "wide open spaces."

DAWSON, MARGIE

THE WELL-GROOMED BRIDE (1946, Paramount)—Naval officer Ray Milland searches war-time San Francisco for a magnum of champagne with which to launch a ship. **Olivia De Havilland** has the only bottle.

DAY, CLARENCE

LIFE WITH FATHER (1947, Warner Brothers)—**William Powell** is the tyrannical head of a family of carrot-tops in New York of the 1880s. His major conflict with his wife Irene Dunne is over his refusal to be baptized. To satisfy Powell and Dunne, their names above the title had to be alternated in different prints so both would receive top billing.

DAY, LUCKY

THREE AMIGOS (1986, Orion)—**Steve Martin** is one of three movie cowboy heroes, who are taken for the real thing by Mexican villagers and the bandits who are harassing them.

DAY, SALLY

SALLY, IRENE AND MARY (1938, 20th Century Fox)—**Alice Faye** gets top billing in this simple-minded musical comedy about three girls trying to make it in show business.

DAY, SYLVIA

PAROLE GIRL (1933, Columbia)—After being paroled, **Mae Clarke** visits Ralph Bellamy, the store manager who she helped con, causing her to be sent to prison. She wishes to make amends, and the two fall in love.

DAY, VINCENT

THE MOUTHPIECE (1932, Warner Brothers)—When Assistant District Attorney **Warren William** discovers that he has sent an innocent man to the electric chair, he quits his post, takes to drink, and hires himself out to mobsters. He later double-crosses his gangster employers to save the life of the brother of a woman he has come to love. He is machine-gunned to death in the street while reading a newspaper.

DAYE, MEGAN

YESTERDAY'S WIFE (1923, Silent, Columbia)—**Irene Rich,** happily married to Lewis Dayton, divorces him after a minor squabble. He remarries but his new wife is killed in a boating action. It looks like Rich and Dayton are back in business.

DAYNE, VIOLET

THE GOLD DIGGERS (1923, Silent, Warner Brothers)—Showgirl **Anne Cornwall's** best friend Hope Hampton pretends to be a vamp, so Cornwall will look good by comparison. They hope to convince a wealthy man to allow his nephew to marry Cornwall.

DE BEAUJOLAIS, MAJOR HENRI

BEAU SABREUR (1928, Silent, Paramount)—Legionnaire **Gary Cooper** rescues Evelyn Brent, a journalist he has come to love, and personally disposes of traitor William Powell at a desert oasis.

DE BERGERAC, CYRANO

CYRANO DE BERGERAC (1950, UA)—**Jose Ferrer** won an Acade-my Award for his portrayal of the 17th century poet-swordsman, who helps an officer win the love of the girl they both adore. Ferrer believes he has no chance of winning her for himself because of his prodigious nose. It's only as he is dying that he confesses his love to her.

DE BIVAR, RODRIGO DIAZ *See* EL CID

DE BRIAC, MONA
BLUEBEARD'S 8TH WIFE (1923, Silent, Paramount)—**Gloria Swanson**, daughter of an impoverished French man, marries a millionaire. She discovers that he has been previously married seven times, throwing out wives like old clothes. Clothes-horse Swanson is determined to teach him a lesson.

DE CARTER, SIR ALFRED & DAPHNE
UNFAITHFULLY YOURS (1948, 20th Century Fox)—Orchestra conductor **Rex Harrison** believes his wife **Linda Darnell** is unfaithful. While conducting a concert, he considers three different plans for dealing with her infidelity. The film was remade in 1983 with Dudley Moore and Nastassja Kinski.

DE COCO, CHUBBY & TOMMY
BLOODBROTHERS (1978, Kings Road/Warner Brothers) -**Paul Sorvino** and **Tony Lo Bianco** are Italian working stiff brothers who don't know what to make of the decision of the latter's son, Richard Gere, to work with disturbed children, rather than follow the family tradition of becoming construction workers.

DE CORDOBA, CARMELITA
THE CHEAT (1923, Silent, Paramount)—South American beauty **Pola Negri** elopes with a New York broker. She falls in the clutches of a fake Indian prince. When she attempts to repay him what she owes him, he demands her body. She refuses and he brands her as a cheat with the family crest. She shoots him. Her husband arrives in time to take the blame, but is acquitted when in the courtroom, she lowers the neck of her dress to show the brand on her shoulder.

DE CORTILLON, NICOLE
THE RAGE OF PARIS (1938, Universal)—**Danielle Darrieux's** plans to nail a millionaire-husband is financed by a former actress and a headwaiter, Helen Broderick and Mischa Auer.

DE FLOR, MARIE
ROSE MARIE (1936, MGM)—**Jeannette MacDonald** is an opera star touring Canada when her brother James Stewart is jailed for robbing a bank. He escapes, killing a Mountie in the process. MacDonald is determined to find him, but so is Mountie Nelson Eddy. The two meet, fall in love, sing some Rudolf Friml songs, separate, and he follows her to Stewart's hiding place to get his man. MacDonald and Eddy split, but are brought together again when she finds she can no longer sing. "Will you answer trueeee . . . ?"

DE GEX, SIMON
SIMON THE JESTER (1915, Silent, Gold Rooster)—**Edwin Arden**, an aristocratic member of Parliament, learns he has only a few months to live. This changes him considerably. He has many unusual experiences and gives away all his money. Then he has a life-saving operation, and marries a music hall entertainer. Always get a second opinion.

DE LA ROCHE, YVONNE
THE ETERNAL FEMININE (1931, GB, Paramount)—Actress **Doris March** gives up her career when she marries, but when her husband is injured in an accident, she goes back to work in order to earn enough to care for him.

DE LANCY, GERARD
SPY OF NAPOLEON (1939, GB, Syndicate)—Nobleman **Richard Barthelmess** is spared execution, for his part in an assassination plot against Louis Napoleon, when he marries the latter's illegitimate daughter. He also becomes an undercover agent for the emperor.

DE LARGO, CARLOS
THE BRIGAND (1952, Columbia)—Fugitive **Anthony Dexter** poses as his double, a king, until the monarch can recover from a wound. Yeah, it does sound like THE PRISONER OF ZENDA.

DE LEDOCQ, PHILIPPE
THE SPIDER AND THE FLY (1952, GB, GFD)—Parisian safecracker **Guy Rolfe** constantly outwits Eric Portman, an Inspector of the Surete. During WWI Rolfe's talents are used in support of the war effort.

DE LISLE, ROBERT
CAPTAIN OF THE GUARD (1930, Universal)—**John Boles** portrays the composer of the French National Anthem, "La Marseillaise."

DE LOISELLE, NICOLE
BLUEBEARD'S 8TH WIFE (1938, Paramount)—In this remake of the 1923 film starring Gloria Swanson, it is Claudette Colbert's turn to teach many-times married millionaire Gary Cooper something about trifling with a girl's affections.

DE LUYNES, JEANNE
THE KING'S WHORE (1990, Fr./Austria/GB/Italy, J&H)—Seventeenth-century Italian noblewoman **Valeria Golino** is happily in love with her husband. Her problems begin when the king, Timothy Dalton, decides he must have her as his own. At first she resists the monarch, but after being urged to give herself to him by everyone at court, the clergy and even her husband, she agrees to become not the king's mistress but his whore. She insists she be paid a whore's fee, jewelry and art.

DE MARCO, ANGELA
MARRIED TO THE MOB (1988, Orion)—When **Michelle Pfeiffer's** hit-man husband Alec Baldwin is wasted by the mob, she decides that she has had enough and moves to Manhattan's Lower East Side to begin a new life. What she doesn't know is that both the FBI and the "family" are keeping tabs on her. To further complicate her life, she falls in love with G-man Matthew Modine and must fend off the advances of married mob-boss Dean Stockwell.

DE MARCO, ESTELITA
HAVANA ROSE (1951, Republic)—**Estelita Rodriguez** continuously messes up her ambassador father's efforts to secure a large loan for their country.

DE MEDICI, CARDINAL
THE CARDINAL (1936, GB, Pathe)—In 15th century Rome, Cardinal **Matheson Lang** is morally torn. The information that will clear his brother of murder was revealed in the confessional, the seal of which he cannot break.

DE MENDOZA, ANA
THAT LADY (1955, GB, 20th Century Fox)—Based on fact, this tepid historical romance stars **Olivia de Havilland** as a beautiful princess of Spain in 1580. She wears a patch over her right eye, having lost it fighting a duel over the king's honor. This lovely widow falls in love with Gilbert Roland, one of the king's ministers, thus incurring the displeasure of the monarch.

DE MERTEUIL, MARQUISE
DANGEROUS LIAISONS (1988, Warner Brothers)—**Glenn Close** devotes herself to sexual liaisons, not so much for pleasure, but for

power over her lovers. She agrees to spend one night with an equally decadent John Malkovich if he is successful in his quest to persuade a faithful and highly moral young wife to give herself to him completely. Close was nominated for, but denied, an Academy Award for her rich portrayal of a woman who offers her lovers cruelty rather than passion.

DE NARDI, MARIE *See* MARY HOLMES

DE NERAC, GASTON
THE BELOVED VAGABOND (1923, Silent, GB, Astra-National) -At the turn of the century, jilted French artist **Caryle Blackwell** becomes a vagabond, and falls in love with an orphan girl.

DE PACE, DANNY
THE YOUNG SAVAGES (1961, UA)—Juvenile delinquent **Stanley Kristien** may or may not have been responsible for the murder of a rival gang member. Assistant District Attorney Burt Lancaster seeks the truth.

DE PARIS, JOCKO
THE STRANGE ONE (1957, Columbia)—In his screen debut, **Ben Gazzara**, a sadistic cadet at a southern military college, has a strange hold over various undergraduates.

DE POITIERS, DIANE
DIANE (1955, MGM)—In the 16th century, French whore **Lana Turner** is befriended by Francis the First, who employs her to teach his son, Roger Moore. Turner teaches Moore quite a bit and even though he must marry Catherine de Medici when he takes the throne as King Henry II, his mistress Turner holds first place in his heart.

DE QUINCEY
CONFESSIONS OF AN OPIUM EATER (1962, Allied Artists)—Early 1800s thrill seeker **Vincent Price** involves himself in San Francisco Tong wars, helping runaway slave girls escape the violence.

DE RIMANEZ, PRINCE LUCIO
SORROWS OF SATAN (1926, Silent, Paramount)—In a Faustian-like story, devil **Adolphe Menjou** appears in the form of a count to writer Ricardo Cortez, who has cursed God for his lack of success. Menjou is defeated by Carol Dempster's love for Cortez and her firm believe in the goodness of God. It was Dempster's last film.

DE RICHELEAU, PEGGY
THE DEVIL'S BRIDE (1968, GB, Hammer)—**Rosalyn Landor** is kidnapped to become a sacrifice to the Angel of Death, who shows up to claim his bride, but is driven off by nobleman Christopher Lee.

DE SADE, MARQUIS
MARAT-SADE (1967, GB, UA)—**Patrick Magee** organizes the inmates of an insane asylum against his one intellectual rival, Ian Richardson. In the end the inmates go berserk.

DE SALVO, ALBERT
THE BOSTON STRANGLER (1968, 20th Century Fox)—**Tony Curtis** gives one of his better performances as the laborer murderer who terrorized Boston in the mid-sixties.

DE SAN MARCO, MARQUIS *See* FRA DIAVOLO

DE SOTO, ANNELLE DUPUY
STEEL MAGNOLIAS (1989, Tri-Star)—Beautician **Daryl Hannah** is dumb but sincere. It's hard to believe that behind those ridiculous glasses and stilted speech is the glamorous Hannah. She is dumped by one husband, finds another, but not before first finding Jesus.

DE TALAVERA, CARA
SONG OF SCHEHERAZADE (1947, Universal)—**Yvonne De Carlo** portrays the beautiful dancer, who in 1865 Morocco inspired Russian naval cadet Rimsky-Korsakoff, played by Jean Pierre Aumont, to compose his greatest music.

DE TOURVEL, MADAME
DANGEROUS LIAISONS (1988, Warner Brothers)—Beautiful **Michelle Pfeiffer** almost runs away with the acting honors with her portrayal of a faithful wife, who is no match for the cruel seducer John Malkovich. He must have her on his terms. This means not merely physical surrender, but loving him, fully aware of how much she has forsaken her convictions. Her love for him, and his abandonment of her when he's finished with her causes her to die of heartbreak and shame. Pfeiffer was nominated for an Academy Award but lost to Geena Davis of THE ACCIDENTAL TOURIST.

DE VALLE, BELLE
BELLE OF THE YUKON (1944, RKO)—**Gypsy Rose Lee**, a dance-hall singer in a Yukon saloon run by a former con-man, has fled North to escape the law.

DE VALMONT, VICOMTE
DANGEROUS LIAISONS (1988, Warner Brothers); VALMONT (1989, Orion)—Leering, mannered **John Malkovich** is remarkable as the swindling seducer who shares with Glenn Close the view that the purpose of an affair is to control one's partner and cause them to suffer. He casually beds convent-reared virgin Uma Thurman as a favor to Close, who seeks revenge on a former lover who has chosen the young woman as his fiancee because he will only marry a virgin. Malkovich has set as his main target the virtuous young wife Michelle Pfeiffer. His struggle to control her, body and soul, leads to both their deaths. **Colin Firth** has the misfortune to appear in the same role a year later. No matter how good his performance as the count, few ventured into theaters to see a repeat of a story from the previous year.

DE VARGAS, DONNA LENORA
TWO LOVERS (1928, Silent, UA)—**Vilma Banky** and Ronald Colman make the last of their movie teamings in this story of the struggle of the Flemish people to overthrow their Spanish oppressors.

DE VARGAS, PEDRO
CAPTAIN FROM CASTILE (1947, 20th Century Fox)—Spanish nobleman **Tyrone Power's** family runs afoul of the Inquisition. While in prison Power believes that he has killed his family's oppressor, John Sutton, after getting the latter to deny God. Power escapes to the new world, joining the forces of Hernando Cortez, played by Cesar Romero. Sutton has survived, and arrives in the Americas to carry on the infamous work of the Inquisition. Someone does the job right this time, and Power is accused of Sutton's murder. He is saved from death when an Indian who has been abused by Sutton confesses to the assassination.

DE VARGNES, MANON
LADY OF THE TROPICS (1939, MGM)—Beautiful Indochinese half-caste **Hedy Lamarr** inspires American Robert Taylor to jump ship to be with her. The problem is he can't find any work. She can't get a passport to leave the country with Taylor unless she will sleep with wealthy Eurasian Joseph Schildkraut. She doesn't, but Taylor thinks

she has. He wants to kill Schildkraut. She beats him to it, but also kills herself.

DE VEGA, DON CESAR

DON Q, SON OF ZORRO (1925, Silent, Warner Brothers)—In a sequel to THE MARK OF ZORRO, which also starred **Douglas Fairbanks**, Zorro's son is sent to Spain by his father. While there, Fairbanks charms the court but is forced to pull a fake suicide to smoke out the real culprits when he is accused of murder.

DE VITO, TOMMY

GOODFELLAS (1990, Warner Brothers)—**Joe Pesci** gives what many see as the definitive interpretation of the unusual psychology of a Mafia mobster. He's a good friend and fun to be with, but without warning he becomes a brutal madman who kills with relish and a rage that is chilling to watch. For all his violence, his own death comes as a quiet coup de grace. Pesci's performance is so good he not only deserves his Oscar for best supporting actor, but should be given a whole slew of statuettes.

DEACON, THE

ALIAS THE DEACON (1928, Silent, Universal); HALF A SINNER (1934, Universal)—**Jean Hersholt** and **Berton Churchill** appear as a professional gambler and cardsharp who, posing as a hillbilly deacon, teams up with a young hobo and a girl posing as a boy. The deacon recognizes the girl as the daughter he deserted when she was a child. He uses his skills with cards to set up the young man, then hits the road, content that his daughter will be well-cared for.

DEADHEAD, SGT. O.K.

SERGEANT DEADHEAD (1965, American, Int.)—**Frankie Avalon**, really Sgt. Donovan, is sent into space with a chimp. The experience changes Avalon's personality, making him a woman-chaser, who disrupts the missile base with his monkey-shines.

DEAL, SGT. CHIP

SERGEANTS 3 (1962, UA)—**Dean Martin** has the Cary Grant role in the unacknowledged western version of GUNGA DIN. It's just another excuse for Frank Sinatra and his friends to make some money while having some fun making a silly movie.

DEAN, DIZZY

THE PRIDE OF ST. LOUIS (1952, 20th Century Fox)—**Dan Dailey** portrays the uneducated and unconventional baseball pitcher, who had his best years with the Gas House Gang of the Old St. Louis Cardinals. He still had enough left when traded to the Chicago Cubs to add a few more heroic chapters to his sports legend.

DEAN, JIMMIE

THE AIR MAIL PILOT (1928, Silent, Hi-Mark Productions)—Young air mail pilot **James F. Fulton** is denied seeing his girl on orders of her father. The older man relents when Fulton foils crooks who rob the mail.

DEAN, PAUL & MILLIE

WHEN STRANGERS MARRY (1944, Monogram)—After **Dean Jagger** and **Kim Hunter** marry, she comes to suspect that he may be a murderer, and she may be his next victim.

DEAN, PEGGY

JUST LIKE A WOMAN (1923, Silent, Hodkinson)—**Marguerite De La Motte** leaves a boarding school to live with her aunts, who do not approve of her, because her mother had been an actress. De La Motte acts as prim and proper as required until she sheds the act to win Ralph Graves.

DEAN, SUSIE

THE GOOD COMPANIONS (1933, GB, Gaumont); (1957, GB, AB-Pathe)—**Jessie Matthews** and **Janette Scott** appear as the star of a struggling concert party, that is saved by the efforts and support of a lonely spinster.

DEAN, TERRY

ALMOST AN ANGEL (1990, Paramount)—In a vanity project, **Paul Hogan** abandons his success as Crocodile Dundee to make a nothing comedy. He plays an electronics expert, just released from prison who becomes a remarkable humanitarian.

DEANE, CAROL

THE RETURN OF CAROL DEANE (1938, GB, Warner Brothers)—**Bebe Daniels** appears in this film of sacrificing mother love. She spends 15 years in prison for accidently killing an artist, and she doesn't want her son to have anything to do with her. When he's grown, she saves him from being taken by gamblers and then disappears again.

DEANE, CLARA

THE STRANGE CASE OF CLARA DEANE (1932, Paramount)—In this tearjerker, **Wynne Gibson** receives a long prison sentence for a crime she didn't commit. She's forced to place her daughter with foster parents and then loses track of the girl. When she gets out of prison she finds her daughter grown, with no knowledge of her real mother and engaged to a wealthy man. What would you do if you were Gibson?

DEANE, ISOBEL

ISOBEL (1920, Silent, Davis)—**Jane Novak** and her husband Edward J. Pell escape to an Eskimo village after killing a whaler captain who tried to rape her. They are tracked by Mountie House Peters who falls in love with Novak and she with him. Pell has the good grace to get killed so the lovers can be together.

DEATH, DR.

DOCTOR DEATH, SEEKER OF SOULS (1973, Cinerama)—A thousand years ago, **John Considine** learned the secret of immortality. It consists of transferring his soul to a new body every now and then. Moe Howard of the Three Stooges makes his final screen appearance in an all too brief sequence.

DEATHSTALKER

THE DEATHSTALKER (1984, New World); DEATHSTALKER II (1988, Concorde); DEATHSTALKER AND THE WARRIORS FROM HELL (1989, Concorde)—In another of the many too many sword and fantasy films, muscular **Richard Hill** is invincible as long as he has the Sword of Justice. In the sequel he is replaced by **John Terlecky**, a muscular lad who frolics with topless women and poorly made-up creatures. Next comes **John Allen Nelson** who continues the inconsequential quest of an all-muscle, no-brain retard.

DEBBIE

SATAN'S CHEERLEADERS (1977, World Amusements)—**Alisa Powell** is one of a group of high school cheerleaders who falls in with a Satanic cult in this made for drive-in passion pits.

DEBBIE

TWO OF A KIND (1983, 20th Century Fox)—**Olivia Newton-John** and John Travolta try to recapture some of their magic together in GREASE. It's a strange and unnecessary film about angels trying to get God to change his mind about nuking the human race once and for all.

DEBORAH

THE HARVEY GIRLS (1946, MGM)—Lovely dancer **Cyd Charisse** is one of the railroad waitresses in this delightful Western musical.

DECKER, KARL

I TAKE THIS WOMAN (1940, MGM)—Doctor **Spencer Tracy** marries beautiful European Hedy Lamarr, whom he has saved from a suicide attempt. He finds to his sorrow that he doesn't love her. Tracy didn't love this movie either. He was being used in an attempt to find something Lamarr could do, other than look smashing. There were no discoveries made in this feeble melodrama.

DECKER, LON

BOY FROM INDIANA (1950, Ventura/Eagle Lion)—**Lon McCallister** lands a job as a jockey, unaware that the horse's owner has been using drugs to make the animal run faster.

DEDALUS, STEPHEN

A PORTRAIT OF THE ARTIST AS A YOUNG MAN (1979, Ireland, Mahler)—**Bosco Hogan** stars in this essentially unsuccessful attempt to film James Joyce's autobiographical novel about the coming of age of an Irish youth.

DEE

THE PLEASURE GIRLS (1966, GB, Times Film)—**Suzanne Leigh** is one of four girls who lives together with her brother in a rooming house in London while they wait discovery and fame as models.

DEE, ROSALIND

FLAME OF THE ISLANDS (1955, Republic)—**Yvonne De Carlo** uses some ill-gotten funds to open a gambling club in the Bahamas. She has to fight off the mob, which wants a piece of the action.

DEEDS, LONGFELLOW

MR. DEEDS GOES TO TOWN (1936, Columbia)—When Vermont hick **Gary Cooper** inherits his uncle's vast fortune, he moves to New York and finds himself on every sucker list in town. Everyone wants some of his dough. Reporter Jean Arthur worms her way into his confidence and takes advantage of him to get scoops. Despite this, she rallies around him when he's forced to defend his sanity for deciding to give away his money, which has not brought him happiness. Cooper is just about perfect as Frank Capra's populist hero.

DEEPING, MRS.

SILVER TOP (1938, GB, Paramount)—Sweet old **Marie Wright** is beset by all sorts of crooks when she inherits a small fortune.

DEERFIELD, BOBBY

BOBBY DEERFIELD (1977, Columbia)—Top-flight auto race driver **Al Pacino** finds it lonely at the top. His affair with mysterious Marthe Keller, whom he meets at a hospital while visiting an injured driver, doesn't help much.

DEERING, VARDA

I WANT TO FORGET (1918, Silent, Fox)—**Evelyn Nesbit**, "The Girl in the Red Velvet Swing" of the Stanford White-Harry K. Thaw murder case, plays a vamp in this melodrama meant to take advantage of her notoriety.

DEERSLAYER

DEERSLAYER (1943, Republic); (1957, 20th Century Fox)—**Bruce Kellogg** and **Lex Barker** each portray James Fenimore Cooper's hero, who as a boy was adopted by the Mohicans and raised to become the foremost woodsman in the new world. Despite his upbringing, he's forever taking the side of the whites against the red men, even when their cause seems just.

DEEVER, DARYLL

EYEWITNESS (1981, 20th Century Fox)—Janitor **William Hurt** is obsessed with TV newscaster Sigourney Weaver. He meets her when she interviews him about a murder which took place in his building. He leads her to believe that he knows something about the murder, which he does not. The ploy works, as she goes to bed with him, but an unwanted bonus is that the murderer marks Hurt and Weaver for extinction.

DEJONG, DIRK

SO BIG (1924, Silent, First National); (1932, Warner Brothers); (1953, Warner Brothers)—In these productions of Edna Ferber's novel, **Frankie Darro, Dickie Moore** and **Tommy Rettig** each appear as the son of a schoolteacher and an illiterate farmer. The boy is spoiled by his mother after the death of his father, and grows up to cause his mother much heartache.

DEL RAYON, NANON

LADY OF THE PAVEMENTS (1929, UA)—**Lupe Velez** is a cabaret singer, whom a Prussian count marries on the rebound after his fiancee proves unfaithful. Then he discovers he actually loves Lupe.

DEL REFUGIO, CARLOS

ONCE UPON A SCOUNDREL (1973, Carlyle)—**Zero Mostel** portrays a wealthy Mexican, who gets his rival for Priscilla Garcia out of the way by framing him for a theft. Garcia has to convince Mostel that her true love is dead in order to get him released from prison.

DELAMBRE, PHILIPPE

RETURN OF THE FLY (1959, 20th Century Fox)—**Brett Halsey** portrays the son of the scientist who had such bad luck with matter transformation. Halsey continues his father's experiments, and sure enough suffers the same fate as dear old dad, becoming part man, part fly. In 1986, THE FLY was remade and in 1989, the sequel was remade.

DELANEY, DR.

SON OF A STRANGER (1957, GB, UA)—**Basil Dignam**, a small town doctor, is accidently killed by his vicious slum son James Kenney, whom he hasn't seen for years. Kenney is hanged for the crime.

DELANEY, JERRY

THE ROUGHNECK (1924, Silent, Fox)—When he believes he has killed a man in a boxing match, **George O'Brien** escapes to a South Seas island. There he's reunited with his long-lost mother and saves Billie Dove from a cad by giving the scoundrel a sound beating.

DELANEY, JOEL

THE POSSESSION OF JOEL DELANEY (1972, Paramount)—**Perry King** is possessed by the spirit of a dead Puerto Rican friend (fiend) who used to chop off the heads of girls. Sister Shirley MacLaine can't help King and nothing can help this totally moronic movie.

DELANIE, RITA

PEARL OF THE SOUTH PACIFIC (1955, RKO)—**Virginia Mayo**, looking good in a sarong, is on a small Pacific Island with two thieves, Dennis Morgan and David Farrar, planning to steal a treasure of black pearls. The natives and an octopus have other ideas.

DELANO, MOKEY

MOKEY (1942, MGM)—**Bobby Blake** has problems dealing with his new stepmother. The film is a so-so "B" show-case of new talent, including Dan Dailey and Donna Reed. Blake, as Mickey Gubitosi, worked in the "Our Gang" comedies.

DELASANO, MARIA *See* MARION STUART

DELGADO, CPL. LUIS
TEN TALL MEN (1951, Columbia)—**Gilbert Roland** is one of the French Foreign Legionnaires let out of the brig in order to protect a city from an invasion of the Riffs.

DELILAH
SAMSON AND DELILAH (1949, Paramount)—Philistine **Hedy Lamarr** discovers the secret of Samson's (Victor Mature) strength and gives him a haircut. Lamarr dies with everyone else when Hebrew stong man Mature, now blinded, sufficiently regains his strength to pull down a temple in which his enemies are partying.

DELL, GLORIA
THE BLONDE BANDIT (1950, Republic)—Sweet, young **Dorothy Patrick** goes west to marry a man she discovers is already a bigamist. She becomes involved with a bookie and participates in a hold-up with him. She turns states evidence on her lover but promises to wait for him.

DELL, LUCY
MY GEISHA (1962, Paramount)—Movie actress **Shirley MacLaine's** husband Yves Montand produces all her movies. Looking to do something a bit different, he goes to Japan to produce a version of "Madame Butterfly," planning to use some unknown Japanese girl in the lead. Maclaine hurries to Japan, poses as a Geisha girl and wins the part without Montand recognizing her.

DELLA GUERDA, BONITA
SINGED WINGS (1922, Silent, Paramount)—Impoverished Spanish aristocrat **Bebe Daniels** is reduced to dancing in a San Francisco cabaret. On top of this she must deal with a family curse, which says she will be killed by a jester after declaring her love for a handsome prince.

DELLMAN, LORRIE & MORT
DOCTOR'S WIVES (1971, Columbia)—**Dyan Cannon** appears for eight minutes in this film, but gets top billing, probably because she has slept with all the colleagues of her cuckolded doctor husband **John Colicos.**

DELMONTE, MIGUEL
SIERRA BARON (1958, 20th Century Fox)—**Rick Jason** appears in another of the many westerns depicting a land-grabbing cattle baron who gets his just deserts.

DELONG, LARRY
RIDING SHOTGUN (1954, Warner Brothers)—**Randolph Scott** is mistaken for a notorious outlaw. To clear his name, he has to wipe out the bandit's whole gang.

DELT, MORGAN
MORGAN! (1966, GB, Cinema V)—**David Warner** is quite wonderful as a half-mad, English communist artist with a gorilla fixation. He is determined to win back his ex-wife, Vanessa Redgrave, who has divorced him and remarried.

DELWYN, DODO
THE CLOWN (1953, MGM)—In a variation on THE CHAMP, **Red Skelton**, a former vaudeville star, now an alcoholic, is taken care of by his adoring son Tim Considine. He's offered his own TV show. Things are looking up, but Red dies moments after the successful first show.

DEMARA, FERDINAND WALDO, JR.
THE GREAT IMPOSTER (1960, Universal)—In a movie based on a real person, uneducated **Tony Curtis** poses as a college professor, a penologist, a Trappist monk, and a Canadian Naval surgeon who successfully performs operations aboard a ship.

DEMETRIUS
DEMETRIUS AND THE GLADIATORS (1954, 20th Century Fox)—After being converted to Christianity in THE ROBE, when he was forced to attend the crucifixion of Christ, **Victor Mature** loses his faith long enough in the sequel to become a gladiator and romp around with Susan Hayward, appearing as Messalina. When his main squeeze, Debra Paget, is brought out of the coma she fell into after being assaulted by other gladiators, he's born again.

DEMI
LITTLE MEN (1935, Mascot)—**Dickie Moore** is one of several Hollywood kids hired to appear in this adaptation of Louisa Mae Alcott's novel. Unfortunately it wasn't of the calibre of LITTLE WOMEN.

DEMON
THE UNHOLY (1988, Vestron)—Gorgeous naked redheaded succubus **Nicole Fortier** seduces priests before dispatching them to hell. It takes all the strength he can muster for Father Ben Cross to rebuke her. This ticks her off, so she transforms herself into a giant monster, and slobbers all over the reverend.

DENAHY, NORA
A BOWERY CINDERELLA (1927, Silent, Excellent Pictures)—**Gladys Hulette** works as a designer of women's clothes. She is compromised by a millionaire theatrical backer, but is eventually reconciled with her true love.

DENARD
CONFIDENTIAL AGENT (1945, Warner Brothers)—Spanish loyalist **Charles Boyer** has run-ins with fascist villains while in England.

DENBY, LADY CAROL
THE SAINT'S GIRL FRIDAY (1954, GB, RKO)—**Naomi Chance** is the next intended victim of murdering gamblers, but Louis Hayward, the Saint, saves her.

DENEK, MARK
MY GIRL TISA (1948, Warner Brothers)—Lawyer **Sam Wanamaker** helps immigrant Lilli Palmer achieve her goal of getting her father to America, but it takes the help of Theodore Roosevelt to do the trick.

DENHAM, KAY
I MET HIM IN PARIS (1937, Paramount)—**Claudette Colbert** dumps boring fiance Lee Bowman and runs off to Paris where she takes up with playwright Melvyn Douglas and secretly-married playboy Robert Young. The three go to Switzerland, where after some slapstick, Colbert ends up with the right man.

DENISE
SUMMER SCHOOL TEACHERS (1977, New World)—Chemistry teacher **Rhonda Leigh Hopkins** becomes romantically involved with a high school teacher mixed up in a stolen car ring.

DENISOVICH, IVAN

ONE DAY IN THE LIFE OF IVAN DENISOVICH (1971, Cinerama) - **Tom Courtenay** gives a memorable performance as a prisoner in a Siberian labor camp in the 1950s. The film is based on Alexander Solzhenitzyn's novel.

DENNING, JUDITH

WHITE WOMAN (1933, Paramount)—**Carole Lombard** is saved from deportation when she marries Charles Laughton, the cruel overseer of a Malaysian rubber plantation. Her life with Laughton is pretty tough until Kent Taylor shows up. The two escape a native uprising which takes Laughton's life.

DENNING, TOM

MR. DENNING DRIVES NORTH (1953, GB, London Films)—**John Mills** accidently kills an international thief whom he's trying to bribe to leave his daughter alone. Mills loses the body and he spends the rest of the movie searching for it so he can cover up his daughter's lover's death.

DENNIS, HELEN & JOE

YOU AND ME (1938, Paramount)—**Sylvia Sidney** and **George Raft** are two ex-cons working at a department story. They wed even though her parole conditions require her to have permission to marry. Raft distraught that their wedding is illegal, organizes a gang to rob the store. Sidney calculates the take for each member of the gang and proves to them that it doesn't pay to risk a jail sentence.

DENNIS, MAME

AUNTIE MAME (1958, Warner Brothers): MAME (1974, Warner Brothers)—**Rosalind Russell** is a delight as the eccentric aunt who raises her 12-year-old nephew on whatever fad is current, but does a pretty good job of it, nevertheless. The musical remake suffers from the fact that **Lucille Ball** is a bit too long in the tooth for the role and it shows.

DENNIS, ROCKY

MASK (1985, Universal)—Teenager **Eric Stoltz** is afflicted with a disfiguring disease, but it doesn't stop him from finding success in school or attempting to get his mother Cher to kick her drug habit.

DENNIS, TIMOTHY

A YANK AT EATON (1942, MGM)—**Mickey Rooney** stars with prissy Freddie Bartholomew in A YANK AT OXFORD for short people.

DENNY

MY DREAM LOVER (1987, New Line Cinema)—**Michelle Little** is the girl who turns Scott Valentine into a real monster whenever he gets close to making love to her.

DENNY, FLORENCE

SHE HAD TO SAY YES (1933, Warner Brothers)—Secretary **Loretta Young** entertains prospective buyers by showing them the town. Her fiance Regis Toomey questions this means of making a living, so she dumps him. That's OK. Lyle Talbot is a better catch anyway.

DENSMORE, JOHN

THE DOORS (1991, Tri-Star)—**Kevin Dillon** portrays one of the rock musicians whose group is named for Aldous Huxley's *The Doors of Perception.*

DENT, SAM

THE AMERICANO (1955, RKO)—Texas cowboy **Glenn Ford** is in Brazil fighting banditos on a Brahma bull raising ranch.

DENTON, MATTHEW & MRS.

HIS MOTHER'S BOY (1918, Silent, Ince)—**Charles Ray** is a real mother's boy. Ma, **Gertrude Claire**, pets and cares for him like he is an infant. Ray doesn't assert his manhood until the girl he loves (no, not mom) is in danger.

DENTON, TOM, FRED & MATT

THREE DESPERATE MEN (1951, Lippert)—**Preston Foster, Jim Davis** and **Ross Latimer** are brothers, who go on a rampage of robbery and murder after they break Davis out of jail for a crime he didn't commit.

DERELICT, DICK

A TEMPORARY VAGABOND (1920, GB, Silent, Butchers)—Mean squire **Henry Edwards** imposes on everyone in the village where he settles down to write a novel.

DERMID

HERO (1982, GB, Maya)—In this sword and fantasy film, **Derek McGuire** joins a Hero clan after surviving assassination attempts. He sleeps with an old woman and wakes up to find her changed into a beautiful young girl. He escapes an enemy in a boat hurled into a whirlpool. The dialogue is spoken entirely in Gaelic.

DERMOTT, MICHAEL

THE KING'S THIEF (1955, MGM)—In order to expose corrupt and evil duke David Niven to the king, George Sanders, **Edmund Purdom** attempts to steal the crown jewels.

DESMAREST, YVONNE

SLANDER THE WOMAN (1923, Silent, Associated First National)—**Dorothy Phillips**, wrongly accused in a murder case, escapes to the north woods, followed by the judge who tried her case, who now realizes he treated her badly. They fall in love.

DESMEREAU, JEANETTE

THE BRIDE COMES HOME (1935, Paramount)—Penniless socialite **Claudette Colbert** takes a job with a magazine. She falls in love with its editor, Fred MacMurray. They plan to marry, but when she tries to make slight improvements in him, MacMurray blows up. On the rebound, Colbert quickly agrees to marry writer Robert Young but MacMurray stops their elopement and substitutes himself for the would-be groom.

D'ESTAING, JULES GASPARD

INVITATION TO A GUNFIGHTER (1964, UA)—**Yul Brynner** is a polite gunslinger. He gives lessons on how to properly pronounce his name before killing his victims. He has been hired by crooked Pat Hingle to keep the farmers he's cheated in their place. When Brynner becomes a problem, Hingle inveigles one of the farmers, George Segal, to face the gunman.

DESTRY, TOM JR.

DESTRY RIDES AGAIN (1932, Universal); (1939, Universal); DESTRY (1954, Universal)—**Tom Mix, James Stewart** and **Audie Murphy** each played Max Brand's mild-mannered lawman, who unlike his father tries to use his mind rather than his guns to deal with problems. Sweet reason just doesn't work and he has to strap on his six guns to clean up the corruption in Bottleneck. The 1939 version with James Stewart is justifiably considered a western classic. The other two do not disappoint.

DETROIT, NATHAN

GUYS AND DOLLS (1955, MGM)—**Frank Sinatra** hardly gets to sing in this Damon Runyan based musical. Sinatra is looking for a place to hold a floating crap game, and unsuccessfully puts off his long-time fiancee Vivian Blaine, who insists on a wedding.

DETWEILER, P.J.

P.J. (1968, Universal)—Private eye **George Peppard** takes the assignment of being a bodyguard for wealthy Raymond Burr's mistress, Gayle Hunnicutt. While her body is well worth guarding, things are not all peaches and cream for Peppard.

DEVERE, MARIE

HUSBAND HUNTERS (1927, Silent, Tiffany)—**Mae Busch** instructs small town innocent Jean Arthur on how to snare men who buzz around showgirls like them.

DEVEREAUX, COL. OWEN

THE MAN FROM COLORADO (1948, Columbia)—The Civil War has made a psychopath of Army officer **Glenn Ford**, but this doesn't prevent him from being made a Federal judge.

DEVEREAUX, ROBERT (EARL OF ESSEX)

THE PRIVATE LIVES OF ELIZABETH AND ESSEX (1939, Warner Brothers)—**Errol Flynn** is loved by Bette Davis, who appears as Elizabeth I of England, but this doesn't stop her from having his head chopped off when he tries to usurp her throne.

DEVERITT, SIR PAUL

THE GYPSY AND THE GENTLEMAN (1958, GB, Rank)—About to marry a woman he doesn't care for, wealthy nobleman **Keith Mitchell** takes up with gypsy Melina Mercouri. They marry and Mercouri discovers that her new husband is deeply in debt, which doesn't sit well with her.

DEVERY, RACHEL

THE TROUBLE WITH ANGELS (1966, Columbia)—**June Harding** and Hayley Mills are hell-raisers at a convent school, but not really bad kids, just mischievous brats.

DEVIL, THE

THE DEVIL WITH HITLER (1942, UA)—In this farce, devil **Alan Mowbray** arrives in Germany to insist that Hitler must perform one good deed before he goes to hell.

DEVINE, NED

THE RIGHT HAND MAN (1987, Australia, New World)—**Hugo Weaving** is the carriage driver, companion to wealthy diabetic Rupert Everett, who has only one arm—the left one. The latter persuades Weaving to impregnate the woman Everett loves so he will have an heir. No caustic comments are required at this point.

DEVLIN, ANNE

ANNE DEVLIN (1984, GB, Aeon Films)—**Brid Brennan** portrays a real-life Irish girl who took part in an abortive revolution in the early 19th century, spending many years in prison.

DEVLIN, DANNY

THE GAY DECEIVERS (1969, Fanfare)—**Kevin Coughlin** and Larry Casey avoid the draft by pretending to be homo-sexual lovers. The recruiting officer doesn't believe them. When he begins to shadow them, they must really act as gay lovers.

DEVLIN, JUDY

LITTLE MISS NOBODY (1936, 20th Century Fox)—Orphan **Jane Withers** discovers that she is the long lost daughter of lawyer Ralph Morgan, who has been seeking her everywhere. In a gesture of kindness she changes papers with another girl so the poor unfortu-

nate will be adopted, but she is discovered and reunited with her father.

DEVLIN, MAX

THE DEVIL AND MAX DEVLIN (1981, Buena Vista)—**Elliot Gould** is a mediocre Faust in this not-up-to-date story of a man, who makes a pact with the devil.

DEWLIP, HENRY

SPRINGTIME FOR HENRY (1934, Fox)—**Otto Kruger** almost gives up his married lover for his dependable secretary, but comes to his senses in time.

DEYO, PATSY & JEAN

TWO GIRLS AND A SAILOR (1944, MGM)—**June Allyson** and **Gloria De Haven** run a serviceman's canteen unaware that it's being bankrolled by bashful millionaire sailor, Van Johnson.

D'HUBERT

THE DUELLISTS (1977, GB, Paramount)—**Keith Carradine** is one of two Hussar officers who in the early 1800s challenge each other to a series of duels. After 16 years, they call a truce.

DI MARCO, JOE

THREE BRAVE MEN (1957, 20th Century Fox)—**Ray Milland** is the lawyer who gets Naval security employee Ernest Borgnine re-employed with back pay, when it's proved he was fired for Communist affiliations, which amounted to subscribing to a Communist publication and joining a Communist study-group.

DI NAPOLI, DOMINICK

FATSO (1980, 20th Century Fox)—Obese **Dom DeLuise** and over-weight Anne Bancroft meet at Chubby Checkers, a sort of Alcoholic's Anonymous for weight watchers.

DI RUVA, COUNT "GUS"

STRICTLY DISHONORABLE (1931, Universal)—**Paul Lukas**, a philanderer/singer, announces to engaged Southern beauty Sidney Fox that his intentions are "strictly dishonorable."

DIAL, JIM

WHEN THIEF MEETS THIEF (1937, GB, UA/Anglo)—**Alan Hale**, ex-crooked partner of cat burglar Douglas Fairbanks, is killed in a battle with Fairbanks, but the evidence seems to suggest that Valerie Hobson, loved by Fairbanks and engaged to Hale did the dirty deed.

DIAMOND, JACK "LEGS"

THE RISE AND FALL OF LEGS DIAMOND (1960, Warner Brothers)—**Ray Danton** is at his best portraying the almost legendary New York mobster, whose stay at the top of the rackets is challenged successfully by the Mafia after Prohibition. Ruined, he is shot to death in his hotel bedroom.

DIANA

ONCE YOU KISS A STRANGER (1969, Warner Brothers)—Psychotic **Carol Lynley** seduces golf pro Paul Burke. She proposes to kill Burke's main competitor if he will kill her psychiatrist, who rightly wants to put her away. It's a poor remake of Alfred Hitchcock's STRANGERS ON A TRAIN.

DIANA

A WOMAN OF AFFAIRS (1928, Silent, MGM)—**Greta Garbo** has a number of affairs and marries a thief. When she learns of his profession, he commits suicide. Garbo has never gotten over John Gilbert, whom she was prevented from marrying. Distraught, she deliberately drives her car into the tree where Gilbert first declared his love for her.

DIANE

THE COMPANY SHE KEEPS (1950, RKO)—**Jane Greer** has just completed a five-year stretch for passing a bad check. She makes a play for the boyfriend of her parole officer, and an old acquaintance gets her into the kind of trouble which could send her back to prison.

DIANE

HER HUSBAND'S SECRETARY (1937, First National)—Secretary **Beverly Roberts** battles wife Jean Muir for Warren Hull.

DIANE

SHE'S IN THE ARMY (1942, Monogram)—Singer **Veda Ann Borg** joins the U.S. Army Ambulance Corps and falls in love with officer Lyle Talbot.

DIANE

THEY'RE PLAYING WITH FIRE (1984, New World)—Professor **Sybil Danning** seduces one of her students, Eric Brown, to get him to help her and her husband kill the latter's mother and grandmother in order to collect a large inheritance.

DIANE

THOSE THREE FRENCH GIRLS (1930, MGM)—**Yola D'Avril** looks cute in this minor musical with more episodes about three girls in the countryside than plot.

DIANE

THE VIRGIN QUEEN OF ST. FRANCES HIGH (1987, Canada, Crown Int.)—**Stacy Christensen** is just an innocent girl but a boy has bet a loudmouth that he can change her designation and bed her.

DICE, JEREMY

HIS BACK AGAINST THE WALL (1922, Silent, Goldwyn)—**Raymond Hatton** proves cowardly when a bully gets fresh with his girl. He loses the girl and his job as a finisher in a New York tailor shop. He goes West and accidently becomes a hero. The next time a bully threatens his new girl he stands up to the man.

DICK

KEPT HUSBANDS (1931, RKO)—Steel worker **Joel McCrea** marries rich Dorothy Mackaill, but he doesn't like living on her money. There could be worse problems.

DICK

THE LEATHER-PUSHERS (1940, Universal)—Boxer **Richard Arlen's** contract is raffled off and won by sportswriter Astrid Allwyn, who has been giving him a bad time in her column.

DICK

THE STOKER (1932, Hoffman-Allied)—After his wife goes through all of his money, **Monte Blue** ends up working in a ship's boiler room. He moves on to other more glamorous work.

DICKINSON, JOAN

THE YOUNG PHILADELPHIANS (1959, Warner Brothers)—**Barbara Rush**, the daughter of a prominent Philadelphia lawyer, is loved by Paul Newman, a bastard both literally and figuratively. Her father offers Newman a job in his law office if he will stay away from Rush. Newman accepts and Rush marries another, but the romance isn't over until it's over.

DICKSTEIN, MOE

WISE GUYS (1986, MGM/UA)—**Joe Piscopo** and Danny DeVito are two small time New York hoods who double-cross their boss and are given a contract on each other, even though they are the closest of friends. They come out of the funny mess smelling like roses.

DIESTL, CHRISTIAN

THE YOUNG LIONS (1958, 20th Century Fox)—**Marlon Brando**, a former ski instructor, becomes an officer with the Afrika Corps. As the war wears on he becomes more and more disenchanted with the Nazis. He is shot dead trying to surrender to two Americans who didn't understand his intentions.

DIETZ, ANN LEMP *See* **ANN LEMP**

DIGHBY, HARRY

HARRY AND WALTER GO TO NEW YORK (1976, Columbia)—**James Caan** and Elliott Gould are out-of-work 1890s vaudeville entertainers, who get hooked up with master criminal Michael Caine and a plan for a major bank robbery.

DIKE, JEREMY

THE MAN IN THE MIRROR (1936, GB, Wardour)—The title character is meek businessman **Edward Everett Horton's** alter ego, who takes over for his timid reflection in the mirror and proves he has the courage his other self lacks.

DILJON

THE MASK OF DILJON (1946, PRC)—Illusionist **Erich von Stroheim** loses his head and goes on a murderous rampage, and then he really loses his head.

DILL, JOHNNY

KILLER DILL (1947, Screen Guild)—Timid salesman **Stuart Erwin** finds himself in serious trouble when he's mistaken for a killer, who has just rubbed out a rival mobster.

DILLINGER, JOHN

DILLINGER (1945, Monogram); (1973, American International); YOUNG DILLINGER (1965, Allied Artists)—**Lawrence Tierney** is excellent in this hard-hitting tale of the life and death of the notorious bank robber and killer. Unfortunately, Tierney has spent the rest of his life trying to prove he is as tough as his role. **Warren Oates** repeated the role in a violent and sometimes comical story of Dillinger's last year of life, before being gunned down in 1934 as he left a Chicago movie theater with the infamous lady in red. The 1965 movie purported to show how young **Nick Adams** turned to a life of crime, which would lead to his body being riddled by bullets from FBI guns.

DILLMOUNT, MILLIE

THOROUGHLY MODERN MILLIE (1967, Universal)—**Julie Andrews** is a gold-digging secretary during the Roaring Twenties, who falls for her handsome boss, John Gavin. The movie is worth seeing for one of the rare movie appearances of Bea Lillie, as a white slaver.

DILLON, DAVE

THE DEPRAVED (1957, GB, UA)—American officer **Robert Arden** helps Anne Heywood kill her husband.

DILLON, LILLY & ROY

THE GRIFTERS (1990, Miramax)—When she was 14, hard-hearted **Anjelica Huston** gave birth to a child who grows up to be **John Cusack**. The relationship between the two is not exactly typical mother and son. She has ignored him all his life, and he has developed a hate for her, tinged with a bit of the old Oedipus complex. She recognizes this when she needs his ill-gotten money so that she can escape from her mobster boss Pat Hingle, who has ordered her killed after Cusack's manipulative girlfriend Annette Bening informs him that Huston has been stealing from him.

DILMAN, DOUGLAS

THE MAN (1972, Paramount)—President Pro Tem of the Senate **James Earl Jones** becomes the first Black President of the U.S. when the president and the Speaker of the House are killed in a plane crash and the Vice President is in a hospital with a stroke. Jones has to fight to get the respect the job deserves, even from his daughter Janet MacLachlan.

DIMA

THE RAINBOW THIEF (1990, Burrill)—**Omar Sharif** is the servant of reclusive eccentric Peter O'Toole. Sharif follows his master when O'Toole retreats to the sewers of some unnamed European city to make his home and scavenges for food for the pair on the streets by the harbor. Later, Sharif must rescue O'Toole, who is trapped in the sewers by a flood.

DIME, JOHNNY

F MAN (1936, Paramount)—Soda-jerk **Jack Haley** wants to become a G-man. The agency makes him an F-man (Fountain-man) and he captures a crook with a water pistol.

DIMITRIOS

THE MASK OF DIMITRIOS (1944, Warner Brothers)—The tremendous acting promise shown by **Zachary Scott** in this tale of a deceased arch-criminal, who practiced "murder, treason and betrayal," seldom surfaced in his subsequent films. In this film noir, surrounded by some superb character actors, including Peter Lorre, Sydney Greenstreet, George Tobias, Victor Francen, Steven Geray, Florence Bates, Eduardo Ciannelli and Kurt Katch, Scott in his screen debut is masterful.

DIMMOCK, MRS. ALICE

WHAT EVER HAPPENED TO AUNT ALICE? (1969, Palomar/Cinerama)—**Ruth Gordon** is killed and buried among the trees by Geraldine Page, the genteel widow for whom Gordon worked as a housekeeper. That's the answer to the title question. Page loses many housekeepers that way, but always manages to keep their savings.

DIMORNA, CAPT. RICARDO

MASK OF THE AVENGER (1951, Columbia)—**John Derek** is a soldier just home from the Austrian-Italian war of 1848. His father has been killed by a traitor and Derek swears revenge.

DIMPLES

DIMPLES (1916, Silent, Metro)—Unknown to her, **Mary Miles Minter's** miserly father has stuffed her doll with a large sum of money. It comes in handy when she discovers it just in time to help her young man when he's caught in a market margin squeeze.

DIMPLES *See* DOLORES APPLEBY

DINGLE, BENJAMIN

THE MORE THE MERRIER (1943, Columbia)—**Charles Coburn** was a superb comic talent. Nowhere was this more evident than in this wonderful film about a WWII Washington housing shortage. Coburn cons single girl Jean Arthur into subletting part of her small apartment to him. He decides that Arthur needs some male companionship. To that end, he sublets half of his sublet to Air

Force mechanic Joel McCrea, and then plays the most delightful Cupid for the young couple. When people say they don't make movies like they use to, this is one they mean.

DINGLE, EDWIN *See* BUZZY BALLEW

DINO

DINO (1957, Allied Artists)—Just out of prison, **Sal Mineo** is treated so kindly by social worker Brian Keith that when his younger brother takes to crime, Mineo hurries the lad to Keith and both brothers get their lives straightened out.

DINTY

DINTY (1920, Silent, First National)—Orphan newsboy **Wesley Barry** rescues the daughter of a judge from members of a San Francisco tong and is rewarded by being adopted by the jurist.

DISRAELI, BENJAMIN

DISRAELI (1929, Warner Brothers); THE PRIME MINISTER (1941, GB, Warner Brothers)—**George Arliss** won one of the first Academy Awards for his endearing portrayal of the witty, gallant, genial ally and Prime Minister of Queen Victoria. The film takes many liberties with the facts, but set the standard for screen biopics that would endure for a long time. The 1941 film had a modest budget, but **John Gielgud** gives a notable performance.

DITMAR, HAL

THE YOUNG STRANGER (1957, Universal)—Neglected 16-year-old **James MacArthur** gets into trouble. That's about the extent of it.

DITTO

TEACHERS (1984, MGM/UA) High school teacher **Royal Dano's** methods of instruction are so predictable: students pick up a work sheet from his desk, which is behind them at the back of the room. They complete it and put it back on his desk at the end of the class. Meanwhile, teacher Dano either reads a paper or dozes. One day none of his classes note that he has quietly died during the first period. Funny, it's not funny.

DIVIDEND, THE

FATHER'S LITTLE DIVIDEND (1951, MGM)—**Donald Clark** is the baby son of Elizabeth Taylor and Don Taylor and the grandson of Spencer Tracy and Joan Bennett in this so-so sequel to the delightful FATHER OF THE BRIDE.

DIVINE, WAYNE "HONKY"

HONKY (1971, Getty-Fromkers-Stonehenge)—**John Nielson** is a young white man who develops a relationship with rich black girl Brenda Sykes. The families don't approve, but for the lovers the worst is yet to come. In a climatic scene, Nielson suffers a brutal beating by whites who proceed to rape Sykes.

DIVOT, MIN

MIN AND BILL (1930, MGM)—Sixtyish **Marie Dressler** and fiftyish Wallace Beery made an unlikely but wonderful romantic duo in this story of Dressler, the owner of a cheap California waterfront hotel, and Beery, a local fisherman she loves. The two unite to fight the plans of authorities to take Dressler's daughter from her and place her in a more healthy and decent atmosphere.

DIX, DAPHNE *See* FRANCES NORCROSS

DIXIANA

DIXIANA (1930, RKO)—In New Orleans of the 1840s, **Bebe Daniels** is a circus performer, who has a tough time convincing a wealthy southerner that she is worthy to marry the grand dame's son, Everett Marshall.

DIXIE

W.W. AND THE DIXIE DANCEKINGS (1975, 20th Century Fox)—**Connie Van Dyke** is the girl singer with a country group which wants to appear on the Grand Ole Opry. They are assisted by bandit Burt Reynolds.

DIXON, BETH

GIRL IN BLACK STOCKINGS (1957, UA)—Psychotic killer **Anne Bancroft** mutilates girls whom she feels are competition for her romantic interest.

DIXON, CARL

HAIL, HERO (1969, NGP)—**Michael Douglas** surprises his parents by announcing that he's dropping out of school to enlist in the army. He had been arrested for failing to register for the draft. He still is anti-war, but plans to go to Vietnam and "love the enemy." Douglas makes his screen debut in this film, which had some meaning at the time, but now just seems weird.

DIXON, JIM

LUCKY JIM (1957, GB, Kingsley International)—**Ian Carmichael** gives a fine comical performance as a junior History lecturer at an English University, who has a series of very funny misadventures one weekend.

DOBIE, MARTHA

THESE THREE (1936, UA)—**Miriam Hopkins** and Merle Oberon open a school for wealthy girls. They make friends with young doctor Joel McCrea. Mean-spirited and malicious young Bonita Granville tells her grandmother that the three are up to some sexual shenanigans. It almost ruins the lives of all three. This is a film version of Lillian Hellman's "The Children's Hour" with accusations of a lesbian relationship between the two women being replaced with a more acceptable heterosexual scandal. The story was refilmed in 1961 under it's original name and with the lesbian relationship being used.

DOBSON, BEN

HALF A HERO (1953, MGM)—Henpecked **Red Skelton** lives in a suburban housing development, but would rather be back in the city. He is given the assignment of writing an article about how awful life in suburbia is, but in doing so changes his mind about it.

DOBSON, JIMMY

HER HIGHNESS AND THE BELLBOY (1945, MGM)—Bellboy **Robert Walker** mistakenly believes that visiting princess Hedy Lamarr is romantically interested in him. We can understand how that beautiful blank look might be misinterpreted.

DOC

MY SIX CONVICTS (1952, Columbia)—New prison psychologist **John Beal** forms group therapy sessions for six cons, not all of whom wish to use it to better understand their problems and anti-social behavior.

DOC

THREE GODFATHERS (1936, MGM)—**Lewis Stone**, one of three bandits making their escape across the desert after robbing the New Jerusalem bank, comes across a dying woman and her newborn baby. The three risk their lives to bring the child to safety.

DOC

THREE KIDS AND A QUEEN (1935, Universal)—Six-year-old Master **Billy Burrud** is quite cute in this enjoyable film, in which three kids "kidnap" elderly recluse May Robson. She goes along with the scheme to collect $50,000 from her greedy family.

DOCTOR, THE

THE HEALER (1935, Monogram)—Physician **Ralph Bellamy** forgets his ideals to become a success, but little crippled Mickey Rooney steers him back on the right path.

DODD, CLAUDE

MR. DODD TAKES THE AIR (1937, First National)—After **Kenny Baker** becomes a radio singing star, his girlfriend Jane Wyman saves his invention, which revitalizes old radio sets, from being stolen.

DODD, EDDIE

TRUE BELIEVER (1989, Columbia)—During the 1960s and 1970s, **James Woods** was a crusading Civil Rights lawyer. In the 1980s, he's defending drug traffickers and is one of their best customers. When idealistic Robert Downey, Jr. arrives to clerk for Woods, the latter puts the former back on the track of helping needy people.

DODD, JOAN

KISS THE BRIDE GOODBYE (1944, GB, Butchers)—**Patricia Medina's** true love returns from war to discover that she has given into her mother's urging to marry her wealthy boss. True love will be served.

DODDER, PAMELA

THE PURSUIT OF PAMELA (1920, GB, Silent, Jury)—**Edna Flugrath**, an heiress in China, runs away from her husband. She marries her lover after her servant injects the unwanted spouse with a rare disease. You're lucky when you can find good help.

DODIE

THE GIRL MOST LIKELY (1957, RKO/Universal)—Somehow **Jane Powell** becomes engaged to three men and can't make up her mind which one to marry. It's a remake of TOM, DICK AND HARRY.

DODO

OUR LITTLE WIFE (1918, Silent, Goldwyn)—When she returns from her European honeymoon, **Madge Kennedy** has more suitors than before she left.

DODSWORTH, SAM

DODSWORTH (1936, UA)—Manufacturer **Walter Huston** agrees to sell his business and travel with his self-indulgent wife, Ruth Chatterton. She's obsessed with old age. As the two travel through the world, she takes up with an assortment of gigolos and penniless aristocrats. During an ocean voyage to Europe, Huston meets attractive and understanding widow Mary Astor. When Chatterton asks for a divorce, so she may marry a baron, Huston seeks out Astor. The movie concludes with what appears to be a new beginning for them. Huston has found an answer to his dilemma, expressed by: Love has got to stop someplace short of suicide.

DOHERTY, JOHN "THUNDERBOLT"

THUNDERBOLT AND LIGHTFOOT (1974, UA)—After escaping from prison, bank robber **Clint Eastwood** disguises himself as a preacher, and teams up with drifter Jeff Bridges. Eastwood is pained to discover that a new building stands on the spot where he buried his loot.

DOLAN, DAN

ME AND MY GAL (1932, Fox)—Policeman **Spencer Tracy's** beat is the waterfront area of downtown New York. He spends quite a bit of time at a hash house where waitress Joan Bennett is the best dish. Before the two can wed, Tracy must save Bennett's younger sister from a no-good crook with whom she has become infatuated.

DOLAN, DICK

ADVENTURES OF DICK DOLAN (1917, Silent, GB, Broadwest)— Tramp **Basil Gill** reforms and saves a soldier's wife from a gambler.

DOLAN, JIMMY

THE LIFE OF JIMMY DOLAN (1933, Warner Brothers)—Boxer **Douglas Fairbanks, Jr.** accidently kills a reporter. He is able to make his escape when he is believed killed in an automobile accident. He hides out at a home for crippled children. When money is needed to pay off the mortgage on the home, Fairbanks goes back into the ring to get it, at the risk of his own freedom.

DOLAN, MARY

GIRL IN 419 (1933, Paramount)—**Gloria Stuart**, the badly beaten girlfriend of a slain big-time gambler, is treated by womanizing doctor James Dunn, who falls in love with her. Stuart's problems aren't over, as the killer of her former boyfriend plans to finish the job on her.

DOLAN, SOCK

BOWERY BOY (1940, Republic)—Juvenile delinquent **Jimmy Lydon** gets into trouble with mobsters during an epidemic in the Bowery, caused by tainted food.

DOLL FACE

DOLL FACE (1945, 20th Century Fox)—In a back-stage musical, lovely stripper **Vivian Blaine** moves into the legitimate theater. Her co-star is Perry Como, whose film career was shortened when he told Darryl Zanuck what he thought of him.

DOLLARD, ZENOBIA

THE SPIDER WOMAN STRIKES BACK (1946, Universal)—Evil scientist **Gale Sondergaard** pretends to be blind, so she can entice pretty young women to become her nurse-companions. Once in her employ, Sondergaard and her grotesque servant Rondo Hatton drain the blood of the girls. Sondergaard uses the blood in experiments with plants and insects.

DOLLY

A LADY OF CHANCE (1928, MGM)—**Norma Shearer** lures men to her room, where her partner Lowell Sherman breaks in on them, acting the part of the outraged husband—but one who can be bought off. The team breaks up when Shearer falls in love with inventor Johnny Mack Brown. Sherman returns, blackmailing Norma into helping him cheat Brown out of his formula for a new concrete mix. Rather than betray her lover, Shearer turns herself in. She is sent to jail, but Brown arranges for a parole.

DOLLY

LITTLE DOLLY DAYDREAM (1938, GB, Butchers)—**Binkie Stuart** is taken from her loving mother, and put into the custody of a wicked aunt. Binkie escapes, takes up with organ grinder Talbot O'Farrell, helps capture a gang of crooks, and is allowed to rejoin her mother.

DOLLY, JENNY AND ROSIE

THE DOLLY SISTERS (1945, 20th Century Fox)—Fox didn't allow the fact that the vaudeville Dolly sisters were brunettes to interfere in casting its two reigning blond stars **Betty Grable** and **June Haver** in the roles. Audiences didn't mind that the film was just one more in a series of enjoyable but fluffy musical biopics, which had little to do with the lives of the artists portrayed.

DOLORES

GIRL OF THE RIO (1932, RKO); THE GIRL AND THE GAMBLER (1939, RKO) -**Dolores Del Rio** and **Steffi Duna** take turns in the role of the dance-hall senorita, who spends most of her time trying to brush-off the unwanted attentions of a persistent caballero, played both times by Leo Carrillo. He has wagered that he can get her to accompany him to his hideout, but she's angry with him for what he's done to her lover.

DOLORES

SO YOUNG, SO BAD (1950, UA)—**Rita Moreno** is one of the inmates at a woman's penitentiary who testify that the enlightened prison reforms introduced by Paul Henreid really work.

DOLORES

A WOMAN'S SECRET (1924, GB, Silent, Graham-Wilcox)—Beautiful dancer **Betty Blythe** is accused when her lover Herbert Langley kills the nobleman who tried to ruin her. Gypsies save her from life in prison.

DOLORES

WITCHCRAFT PART II: THE TEMPTRESS (1990, Vista Street)—In this sequel to a 1988 direct-to-video flick, **Delia Sheppard** (who was doubtless seen by more people in ROCKY V) is a temptress with plans for transforming young innocent Charles Solomon into a supreme warlock with powers to take over the world.

DOLWORTH, BILL

THE PROFESSIONALS (1966, Columbia)—Explosives expert **Burt Lancaster** is one of four western mercenaries hired by wealthy Ralph Bellamy to rescue his beautiful young wife from Mexican bandit-revolutionary Jack Palance, who has kidnapped her. They discover she wasn't kidnapped and wants to stay with her lover. By that time a lot of Mexicans have been killed.

DOMINEY, SIR EVERARD (EDWARD) *See* BARON LEOPOLD VON RAGENSTEIN

DOMINO

DOMINO KID (1957, Columbia)—Texan **Rory Calhoun** is looking for vengeance. He gets it. Isn't that nice?

DON

DON'S PARTY (1976, Australia, Double Head Productions)—**John Hargreaves** hosts a party for some friends to watch the election results on the telly. The more they drink, the more they reveal themselves, and the truth is not very attractive.

DON

FIGHTING PLAYBOY (1937, Northern Films)—After **Nick Stuart** squanders his fortune, he goes to the Canadian North woods, makes a new fortune, and wins a bride.

DON CHICAGO

DON CHICAGO (1945, GB, British National)—American gangster **Jackie Hunter's** plans to steal the crown jewels is thwarted by a bobby.

DON COYOTE

ADVENTURES OF DON COYOTE (1947, Comet/UA)—Mexican ranch hand **Richard Martin** defends Frances Rafferty, the attractive owner of the ranch, from the takeover attempts of some villains.

DON DIEGO *See* **ZORRO**

DON JUAN

DON JUAN (1926, Silent, Warner Brothers); THE PRIVATE LIFE OF DON JUAN (1934, UA); ADVENTURES OF DON JUAN (1949, Warner Brothers)—As played by **John Barrymore**, the great lover and swordsman Don Juan outwits the Borgias, so he may have the one woman he really wants. The film was the first to use the Vitaphone sound technique, but only employed music and sound effects, leaving dialogue to THE JAZZ SINGER, which appeared the next year. In his last film, **Douglas Fairbanks, Sr.** portrays a middle-aged Don Juan, who must come out of retirement when an imposter masquerades as him, but no one will believe that Fairbanks is the great lover. **Errol Flynn's** career was in sharp decline when he portrayed his tongue-in-cheek swashbuckler. The excitement just isn't there.

DON QUIXOTE

DON QUIXOTE (1923, GB, Silent, Stoll); MAN OF LA MANCHA (1972, UA)—**Jerrold Robertshaw** and **Peter O'Toole** were the movies' notion of Miguel Cervantes' crazy knight errant, who tilted with windmills, and mistook a tavern wench for his lady Dulcina. The musical version, based on the hugely successful Broadway show, is marred, because the voices of non-singers O'Toole, Sophia Loren and James Coco were not dubbed.

DON X

DON X (1925, Silent, Steen/Goodman)—Cattleman **Bruce Gordon** poses as a Mexican beef buyer in order to bring a rustling rancher to justice.

DONAHUE, CLAIRE

BETWEEN TWO WOMEN (1937, MGM)—Nurse **Maureen O'Sullivan** is married to a no-good, and is loved by doctor Franchot Tone. The latter marries Virginia Bruce on the rebound. His wife doesn't care for the hours he devotes to medicine. When O'Sullivan's husband conveniently dies in the hospital because Tone was out entertaining Bruce, rather than taking care of his patient, Tone quits Bruce and hurries to O'Sullivan.

DONAHUE, PAT, JR.

PATRICK THE GREAT (1945, Universal)—**Donald O'Connor** and his father Donald Cook are competing for the same role in a Broadway show. It ruins their relationship.

DONAHUE, SKIP

STIR CRAZY (1980, Columbia)—New York losers **Gene Wilder** and Richard Pryor are wrongly sent to prison for 120 years for a bank robbery. In the pen, they spoof all the prison cliches without adding anything new.

DONALD

DETECTIVE SCHOOL DROPOUTS (1986, Cannon)—**David Landsberg** and his partner are inept would-be detectives, who somehow outwit an organized crime gang. The little man is occasionally funny, but not often enough.

DONALD

MR. BIG (1943, Universal)—**Donald O'Connor** and other teens turn a dramatic school's annual show into a song-and-dance musical.

DONALD, ANN

GOLD AND THE GIRL (1925, Silent, Fox)—When undercover agent Buck Jones infiltrates a gang of outlaws, he falls in love with **Elinor Fair**, the niece of the gang's boss.

DONALDO, COUNT VITTORIO

THE MAN WITHOUT DESIRE (1923, GB, Silent, Atlas Biocraft)—In 1723 Venice, **Ivor Novello** finds a way to suspend life. He is reunited with his lover, Nina Vanna, 200 years later.

DONALDSON, TOM

FOUR FRIENDS (1981, Filmways)—This disappointing story of the friendship of **Jim Metzler** with two guys and a gal through the 60s and 70s tries to show too much and doesn't show enough.

DONATELLO

TEENAGE MUTANT NINJA TURTLES (1990, New Line); TEENAGE MUTANT NINJA TURTLES II: THE SECRET OF OOZE (1991, New Line)—**Leif Tilden** is, of course, unrecognizable as one of the four super hero turtles, supposedly mutilated by radioactive goop. It's also difficult for those not familiar with the cartoon characters to keep straight which is which. In the sequel, **Tilden** and his three green super hero buddies return to find their archenemy Shredder.

DONDI

DONDI (1961, Allied Artists)—Portraying the little comic strip war orphan who is brought to the U.S. as a combination male Little Orphan Annie, Shirley Temple and Pollyanna doesn't work, because **David Kory** is not appealing, and the story is less so.

DONFORD, DEANIE

THE YOUNG RUNAWAYS (1968, MGM)—**Patty McCormack** and two friends run away to see what the Windy City has to offer. For them, it offers misery, suffering, and pain. The three are happy to be able to go home again.

DONIPHON, TOM

THE MAN WHO SHOT LIBERTY VALANCE (1962, Paramount)—**John Wayne** shoots cruel gunfighter-highwayman Lee Marvin, but lets tenderfoot lawyer James Stewart take the credit. The latter gets Wayne's girl Vera Miles and a distinguished political career. The Duke dies almost penniless and forgotten.

DONKIN, ALF

ALF'S BABY (1953, GB. Adelphi)—**Jerry Desmond** is one of three bachelor brothers who adopt a baby who later—as grown-up Pauline Stroud—falls for a crooked garage man.

DONKIN, CHARLES

HOUSEMASTER (1938, GB, Associated British)—**Otto Kruger** is a kindly housemaster in a British public (which means, private) school. The new headmaster believes that Kruger's understanding handling of the boys in his charge is proof that he's mollycoddling them. Attempts to fire Kruger backfire, with the headmaster getting his walking papers.

DONNA

SWING OUT SISTER (1945, Universal)—Her parents believe that **Frances Raeburn** is studying classical music in preparation for a concert career. Actually, the socialite is singing in a nightclub.

DONNELL, MARION

THE TRESPASSER (1929, UA); THAT CERTAIN WOMAN (1937, Warner Brothers)—Silent star **Gloria Swanson** talks and even sings in this tearjerker. She's a young mother dumped by her husband, when his father uses his riches to lure his weakling son from his responsibilities. Swanson makes it on her own, even inheriting half a million dollars from a lawyer for whom she worked. **Bette Davis** shows up in the 1937 remake, although her character's first name is Mary.

DONOVAN, CRASH

CRASH DONOVAN (1936, Universal)—Former carnival stunt driver **Jack Holt** is now a California motorcycle cop.

DONOVAN, EARL

THE GENTLEMAN FROM NOWHERE (1948, Columbia)—Boxer **Warner Baxter** is presumed dead when he disappears following a chemical plant explosion. Baxter has to clean up his problems in the past to have a future.

DONOVAN, GUNS

DONOVAN'S REEF (1963, Paramount)—In a slapstick film, **John Wayne** and Lee Marvin are constantly slugging each other and anyone else who gets too close. The plot? We don't believe there is one.

DONOVAN, JIMMY (JIM)

BIG BROTHER (1923, Silent, Paramount); YOUNG DONOVAN'S KID (1931, RKO)—**Tom Moore** and **Richard Dix** star as a mobster, given custody of the young brother of a gangster killed in a police raid. Rather than risk losing the kid, of whom he has become quite fond, the mobster reforms.

DONOVAN, MICHAEL

PROFESSIONAL SOLDIER (1936, 20th Century Fox)—**Victor McLaglen** and some cohorts are hired to kidnap Freddie Bartholomew, the boy prince of a mythical kingdom. He carries out the assignment, but later he thwarts the usurpers and helps put Freddie back on his throne.

DONOVAN, ROSE

MY WILD IRISH ROSE (1947, Warner Brothers)—**Arlene Dahl** is glamorous as the inspiration for Irish tenor Chauncey Olcott (played by Dennis Morgan), but she is little more than decoration in this minor musical.

DONOVAN, SGT. *See* **O.K. DEADHEAD**

DONOVAN, TOM

DONOVAN'S BRAIN (1953, UA)—When **Michael Colgan** dies in scientist Lew Ayres' laboratory, the latter hooks up the deceased's brain to a machine, keeping it alive. Gradually, the evil Colgan's brain takes possession of Ayres. It's a pretty fine sci-fi movie, neither hurt nor helped by the presence of ex-first lady Nancy Davis.

DOODLE BUGS

MR. DOODLE KICKS OFF (1938, RKO)—**Joe Penner**, the son of a wealthy merchant, is urged by his father to become a sports star. Daddy offers a lot of money to a college if his son is put on the football team. The coach finds something Penner can do for the team.

DOOLAN, PADDY

THE IRISHMAN (1978, Australia, Greater Union)—Irish teamster **Michael Craig** resists the changes that autos and trucks are bringing to Australia of the 1920s. He hates to see the passing of horse-drawn lorries.

DOOLEY, SHEP

CALL ME MISTER (1951, 20th Century Fox)—Separated from wife Betty Grable and wanting her back, **Dan Dailey** forges a document which allows him to stay in Korea to direct a camp show in which she's starring.

DOOLEY, TOM

THE LEGEND OF TOM DOOLEY (1959, Columbia)—**Michael Landon** portrays the condemned killer made famous in the Kingston Trio's version of the Civil War folk song.

DOOLAN, TIM

LOST ANGELS (1989, Orion)—Pampered Los Angeles brat **Adam Horowitz** has become too much for his uncaring parents to handle. They send him to an Arizona institute for troubled teens. In flashbacks, we learn of the events leading to his institutionalization.

DOOLIN, BILL

THE DOOLINS OF OKLAHOMA (1949, Columbia)—Misunderstood, former outlaw **Randolph Scott** would like to go straight, but members of his former gang have other ideas. There's not much in this film that has anything to do with the life of the real 1890s Oklahoma bandit.

DOOLIN, MIKE

PARTNERS IN CRIME (1928, Silent, Paramount)—Dumb private eye **Wallace Beery** teams with wise-cracking reporter Raymond Hatton to solve a murder.

DOOLITTLE, ELIZA

MY FAIR LADY (1964, Warner Brothers)—**Audrey Hepburn's** appearance as Eliza, the Cockney flower girl, taught to speak proper English by elocutionist Henry Higgins (portrayed by Rex Harrison, who originated the role on Broadway) was challenged by those who imagined that only the original Eliza, Julie Andrews, could handle the role. Whether Julie would have done a better job in the movie is moot. What is more to the point, Hepburn's performance, while charming, didn't match that of Wendy Hiller in the non-musical version PYGMALION (1938). Hepburn was lovely, but lacked the rough edge that poverty would have given her, and which Hiller provided so beautifully, making her transformation into a woman who could be mistaken for a duchess all the more remarkable.

DOOLITTLE, DR. JOHN

DOCTOR DOOLITTLE (1967, 20th Century Fox)—This foolish-told tale, of **Rex Harrison** learning to speak the language of animals, is one of the all-time box office failures. Harrison appears to be trying to reprise his Henry Higgins role, with the livestock as his Eliza Doolittles.

DOOLITTLE, SUZY

GIVE A GIRL A BREAK (1953, MGM)—**Debbie Reynolds** is one of three would-be Broadway stars competing for the lead role in a new production when the star walks out.

DOONE, LORNA

LORNA DOONE (1927, Silent, Associated First National); (1935, GB, Associated British); (1951, Columbia)—The role of the 1600s English girl, who as a child is kidnapped from her royal parents by the Doones, a family of rascally criminals, is played as an adult in the three films, respectively by **Madge Bellamy**, **Victoria Hopper**, and **Barbara Hale**.

DORANDO THE BANDOLERO

THE BANDOLERO (1924, Silent, MGM)—Spanish officer **Pedro de Cordoba** becomes a notorious bandit when his wife is abducted by his commanding officer. He takes revenge by kidnapping the latter's son.

DORCAS

SEVEN BRIDES FOR SEVEN BROTHERS (1954, MGM)—Eighteen-year-old **Julie Newmar** is the voluptuous girl kidnapped to be the bride for mountain man Jeff Richards. The latter, in today's parlance, might be described as a "hunk," but because of his limited ability to express emotion, a hunk of what, we're not sure. Newmar went on to appear in numerous Broadway shows and as Catwoman on TV's "Batman."

DORINDA

THE LADY SAYS NO (1951, UA)—**Joan Caulfield** has just written a book uncomplimentary to men. Ultimately, photographer David Niven gets her to rethink her position.

DORIS

THE OWL AND THE PUSSYCAT (1970, Columbia)—**Barbra Streisand** moves in with timid book salesman and would be writer George Segal, when his complaining gets her thrown out of her room next to his. Ultimately, his landlord kicks him out as well, and these two most unlikely personalities fall in love.

DORIS

UNCERTAIN LADY (1934, Universal)—Lovely, wacky **Genevieve Tobin** has a series of amusing misadventures with Edward Everett Horton.

D'ORLET, COUNT STEPHAN

PATRICIA GETS HER MAN (1937, GB, First National)—Philandering count **Hans Sonker** falls in love with Lesley Brook, while he's supposed to be helping her snare a movie star.

DORN, SUDDEN BILL

SUDDEN BILL DORN (1938, Universal)—**Buck Jones** lives up to his name in dealing with the new bad guys in town, who show up when gold is discovered.

DORN, WILLIAM

THE MAD BOMBER (1973, Cinemation)—Dangerous madman **Chuck Connors** blows up schools and hospitals. Cop Vince Edwards must catch him.

DORNWINKLE, KEVIN

THE INVISIBLE MANIAC (1990, Smoking Gun)—Cruelly treated by his mother as a child, as an adult **Noel Peters** has a serious Peeping Tom problem. He develops an invisibility ray, which advances his avocation, but turns him into a crazy killer. Claude Rains did it better in THE INVISIBLE MAN (33).

DOROTHY

BORN TO BE LOVED (1959, Universal)—Nearsighted seamstress **Carol Morris'** romance with music student Dick Kallman is encouraged by the young man's teacher, Hugo Haas. Morris was Miss Universe of 1957. Her talent was not acting.

DOROTHY

THE KING AND THE CHORUS GIRL (1937, Warner Brothers)—Deposed monarch Fernand Gravet falls in love with **Joan Blondell**, a chorus girl at the Folies Bergere.

DOROTHY

GREGORY'S GIRL (1982, GB, Goldwyn)—**Dee Hepburn** is the newest player on a school's winless soccer team. She's also the best player, which only adds to the problems of Gordon John Sinclair, her gangling clumsy teammate who idolizes her. It's a pleasure to enjoy a film in which teens are not all portrayed as sex-crazed boys and sex-pot girls. Hepburn, Sinclair and others are a delight.

DOROTHY

THE TAMING OF DOROTHY (1950, GB, Eagle-Lion)—**Jean Kent** is the shrewish wife of a mild-mannered Italian Robert Beatty, who just happens to look like a gangster (also Beatty). The latter changes places with his double and puts Kent in her place. When her husband returns, he uses the mannerisms of the gangster to keep her.

DORSET, NANCY

DON'T TELL THE WIFE (1937, RKO)—**Una Merkel** is kept in the dark about the swindle her husband Lynne Overman and just-out-of-prison con man Thurston Hall are trying to pull.

DORSEY, MARION

THE ADORABLE CHEAT (1928, Silent, Chesterfield)—**Lila Lee**, the daughter of a wealthy manufacturer, falls in love with her father's shipping clerk Cornelius Keefe. Unknown to anyone, she takes a job as her lover's assistant using an assumed name.

DORSEY, MICHAEL

TOOTSIE (1982, Columbia)—Unable to find any work as an actor, **Dustin Hoffman** disguises himself as a woman and gets a leading part on a soap opera. Its star, Jessica Lange, is a woman he hasn't been able to get to first base with. The latter takes Hoffman as a woman into her confidence and Lange's father develops a crush on the phony dame. It's all good fun, with Hoffman very good in his female role.

DORSEY, TOMMY & JIMMY

THE FABULOUS DORSEYS (1947, UA)—**Tommy** and **Jimmy Dorsey** portray themselves in this show-biz biopic which is only good when featuring their music.

DOSTOYEVSKY, FEODOR

THE GREAT SINNER (1949, MGM)—Gambling mania just about ruins **Gregory Peck** in this un-convincing melodrama.

DOT

THREE WISE GIRLS (1932, Columbia)—**Marie Prevost**, Jean Harlow and Mae Clarke are three girls in New York, who learn that it's no picnic trying to make a living while keeping the wolves at bay. Prevost comes out all right, falling in love with a likeable chauffeur, Andy Devine.

DOUBLEDAY, SGT.

YANKS AHOY (1943, UA); MR. WALKIE TALKIE (1952, Lippert) - **William Tracy** and Joe Sawyer appeared in a series of minor comedies, which saw them as rather stupid soldiers who fought each other as much as the enemy. Tracy is a constant talker which almost drives Sawyer batty.

DOUG

IRON EAGLE (1986, Tri-Star)—**Jason Gedrick** steals a plane and goes beyond the Iron Curtain to rescue his father whom the U.S. has all but written off.

DOUGALL

FATHER'S DOING FINE (1952, GB, Marble Arch)—**Richard Attenborough** is the nervous husband of Diane Hart, the pregnant daughter of eccentric widow Heather Thatcher, who has three more equally daffy daughters. This madcap farce is based on the British stage hit "Little Lambs Eat Ivy," which would have made a better title.

DOUGHBOY

BOYZ N THE HOOD (1991, Universal)—**Ice Cube** has a foul mouth, a pistol and no ambition—a deadly combination in an LA slum.

DOUGLAS, ELLEN

THE LADY OF THE LAKE (1928, GB, Silent, Gainsborough)—Exiled **Benita Hume** saves king Percy Marmont from bandits in this production based on the poem by Sir Walter Scott.

DOUGLAS, JOHN

HIS SUPREME MOMENT (1925, Silent, First National)—Mining engineer **Ronald Colman** attends the theater with Kathleen Myers and immediately falls in love with the star of the show, Blanche Sweet. He proposes marriage and she proposes that they live together for a year as brother and sister before they marry. He agrees but the arrangement doesn't work and he goes back to Myers who's interested in a more conventional relationship.

DOUGLAS, JOHNNY

SPECIAL AGENT (1949, Paramount)—Railroad special agent **William Eythe** solves the robbery of a payroll from a train in which the engineer is killed.

DOVE, MISS

GOOD MORNING MISS DOVE (1955, 20th Century Fox)—**Jennifer Jones** reminisces in old age of her life as a teacher and the students she influenced.

DOWLING, KAY

I TAKE THIS WOMAN (1931, Paramount)—Wacky socialite **Carole Lombard** falls in love with cowboy Gary Cooper, agreeing to share his ramshackle house with him.

DOWN, COUNT

SON OF DRACULA (1974, GB, Cinemation/Apple)—Pop singer **Harry Nilsson** is the son of the vampire count in a "Rock 'n' Roll" comedy-horror film, featuring performers Ringo Starr, Peter Frampton, Keith Moon and John Bonham. "Can't Live, If Living Is Without You"—you're blood that is.

DOWNS, ANN

THE SHRIKE (1955, Universal)—In her most dramatic role, **June Allyson** is a vicious woman, who manipulates husband Jose Ferrer to such a point that he has a complete mental breakdown. But the film is weakened by giving Allyson redeeming qualities that she didn't have in the play. The producers also add an unbelievable happy ending.

DOYLE, DANNY

FLIGHT LIEUTENANT (1942, Columbia)—**Glenn Ford** is the son of pilot Pat O'Brien, whose plane crashed in a jungle, killing the co-pilot, with no trace of Pat. As a grown man, Ford falls for Evelyn Keyes, the co-pilot's daughter. O'Brien shows up to save Ford, replacing him in testing an experimental plane which crashes, killing O'Brien.

DOYLE, HARRY

TOUGH GUYS (1986, Touchstone)—**Burt Lancaster** and Kirk Douglas are elderly criminals released from prison after thirty years and told not to associate with each other or they will be in violation of their parole. They discover how badly the elderly are often treated in society and to prove they are still alive, hijack a train.

DOYLE, TOMMY

THE BOY ON THE BRIDGE (1959, GB, Columbia)—When **Ian MacLaine** sees his father arrested after a street brawl, he believes his dad has killed someone. Maclaine runs away and takes up residence in London's Tower Bridge.

DRAC, THE

ENEMY MINE (1985, 20th Century Fox)—**Louis Gossett Jr.** is an alien with a lizard's skin and face who must learn to cooperate with his enemy, American astronaut Dennis Quaid, if the two are to survive in space.

DRACULA, COUNT

DRACULA (1931, Universal); (1958, GB, Hammer); (1979, GB, Universal)—**Bela Lugosi, Christopher Lee** and **Frank Langella**; DRACULA AD 1972 (1972, GB, Hammer); DRACULA HAS RISEN FROM THE GRAVE (1968, GB, Hammer); DRACULA, PRINCE OF DARKNESS (1965, Hammer); COUNT DRACULA AND HIS VAMPIRE BRIDE (1978, GB, Hammer); THE HOUSE OF DRACULA (1958, GB, Hammer/Universal); THE SCARS OF DRACULA (1970, GB, Hammer-EMI); TASTE THE BLOOD OF DRACULA (1970, GB, Hammer) —**Christopher Lee**; GUESS WHAT HAPPENED TO COUNT DRACULA (1970, Merrick International)—**Des Roberts**; HOUSE OF DRACULA (1945, Universal)—**John Carradine** OLD DRACULA (1975, GB, American Int.)—**David Niven**

While Christopher Lee has appeared as Count Dracula the most times, for most people the role will always belong to Bela Lugosi who so ominously informs Dwight Frye as Renfield, "I never drink . . . wine!" Audiences have been ever fascinated with the bloodsucking count who can assume the form of a bat or a wolf but cannot survive sunlight. A stake in the heart does him no good, either.

DRAGA, MME. MARIE

A WOMAN COMMANDS (1932, RKO)—In her first talking picture, sultry vamp **Pola Negri** marries a king who is soon assassinated. She maintains an affair with an officer whom she nearly brings to ruin by her demands for costly gifts. This would be Negri's last U.S. picture until a cameo role in a piece of 1943 fluff, HI DIDDLE DIDDLE.

DRAGON LADY

CHARLIE CHAN AND THE CURSE OF THE DRAGON LADY (1981, American Cinema)—**Angie Dickinson** is Charlie Chan's beautiful nemesis in this dreadful and tasteless entry in the long series of Charlie Chan movies. Peter Ustinov sinks (stinks?) as the Oriental detective.

DRAKE, ALISON

FEMALE (1933, Warner Brothers)—**Ruth Chatterton**, the head of an auto factory, is a "manizer" in the evenings, but is all business during the day, that is until George Brent comes along, and she goes all "female" over him. She even makes him co-boss of her company. Rubbish!

DRAKE, BUDDY & ARTHUR

STRANGERS IN LOVE (1932, Paramount)—**Fredric March** plays twin brothers, one good, one bad. The bad arranges to have the good disinherited. Seeking help from his brother, the good March's request for financial aid causes the bad March to die of a stroke. Good March impersonates his brother, getting the latter's fortune and the love of the deceased's secretary Kay Francis.

DRAKE, DON
MR. DRAKE'S DUCK (1951, GB, UA)—Gentleman farmer **Douglas Fairbanks, Jr.'s** duck lays a uranium egg which gets both into the middle of an international disagreement.

DRAKE, FRANCIS
DRAKE THE PIRATE (1935, GB, Wardour)—**Matheson Lang** portrays the first circumnavigator of the globe.

DRAKE, JERRY
HIS RISE TO FAME (1927, Silent, Excellent)—**George Walsh**, a ne'er-do-well, is ordered beaten-up by a crooked fight promoter when Walsh comes on to dancer Peggy Shaw at a cabaret. Walsh rethinks his life, goes to a gym, becomes a skilled fighter, and goes back to the cabaret to demonstrate what he's learned.

DRAKE, JONATHAN
THE FOUR SKULLS OF JONATHAN DRAKE (1959, UA)—**Eduard Franz** is the latest member of the Drake family to be threatened by a 200-year-old curse which has Jivaro Indians seeking Drake's head to shrink.

DRAKE, LILLIAN
THE GILDED LILY (1921, Silent, Paramount)—Cafe hostess **Mae Murray** chooses country boy Jason Robards Sr. for her husband over playboy Lowell Sherman, but returns to the latter when Robards proves to be a hopeless alcoholic.

DRAKE, MARION
WHEN STRANGERS MARRY (1933, Columbia)—**Lillian Bond** is a spoiled rich kid, whose marriage to Jack Holt complicates his efforts to build a railway at the straits of Malay.

DRAKE, MILLIE
OLD ACQUAINTANCE (1943, Warner Brothers)—**Miriam Hopkins** is beautifully bitchy in this story of two writers, the other being Bette Davis. The two compete and spar throughout their lives. Hopkins and Davis did not get along on the set either.

DRAKE, NELSON & BARRINGTON
HIS BROTHER'S PLACE (1919, Silent, Metro)—**Hale Hamilton** portrays twin brothers: one, Nelson, becomes a pepless clergyman; the other, Barrington, an energetic broker. When Nelson is about to lose his pastorate because of his shortcomings, Barrington steps in to shake things up. The deception doesn't fool Nelson's fiancee, but she does fall in love with Barrington.

DRAKE, SIMON
THIS MAN IS NEWS (1939, GB, Paramount); THIS MAN IN PARIS (1939, GB, Paramount)—**Barry K. Barnes** is Britain's answer to Nick Charles with Valerie Hobson filling Nora Charles' high heels. In the first, the pair wisecrack their way to the solution of an underworld murder. In the sequel, the constantly arguing couple are in Paris, where they solve a crime involving forgery and murder.

DRAKE, TEDDY
THE KNICKERBOCKER BUCKAROO (1919, Silent, Artcraft)—Eastern playboy **Douglas Fairbanks** follows Horace Greeley's advice. In the West, he saves Marjorie Daw and her fortune from outlaws.

DRAKE, TEMPLE
THE STORY OF TEMPLE DRAKE (1933, Paramount)—**Miriam Hopkins** stars as a hedonistic daughter of a prominent Southern judge, during Prohibition. She is kidnapped by hooch-running hoodlum Jack La Rue, who rapes her and carries her off to the big city, where he installs her as the star of his fancy house of prostitution. Hopkins finds she enjoys all of this decadence, but she does eventually have a falling-out with La Rue and kills him with his own gun. The movie, based on William Faulkner's "Sanctuary," has the dubious distinction of being the film that inspired the creation of the Roman Catholic Legion of Decency.

DRANGO
DRANGO (1957, UA)—Carpetbaggers send Union Army officer **Jeff Chandler** to restore peace in a town which the soldiers in his command had plundered during the Civil War.

DRAPER, CHERYL
WITNESS TO MURDER (1954, UA)—**Barbara Stanwyck** awakes one night and sees a murder being committed as she looks out her window. She calls the police, but by the time they have arrived, the murderer, George Sanders, has hidden the body and the cops think she must have been dreaming. Sanders who discovers her name knows she wasn't. He tries to drive her mad and when this doesn't work he plans to murder her, making it appear she took her own life.

DRAPER, CMDR. CHRISTOPHER "KIT"
ROBINSON CRUSOE OF MARS (1964, Paramount) -Astronaut **Paul Mantee** must abandon his space ship after it is hit by a meteor. He lands on the surface of Mars where he lives up to the title of the film.

DRAVOT, DANIEL
THE MAN WHO WOULD BE KING (1975, GB, Allied Artists)—**Sean Connery** and Michael Caine are British sergeants seeking their fortunes in a remote region of India in the 1880s. Circumstances cause the natives to believe that Connery is the son of a long gone god whose coming had been foretold. When Connery is proven to be a mere mortal, his life is forfeited.

DRAYFORD, LORD BASIL "BABS"
LORD BABS (1932, GB, Gainsborough)—Ship's steward **Bobby Howes** inherits an earldom, which he's not sure he wants.

DRAYTON, FRANK
PASSENGER TO LONDON (1937, GB, Fox British)—**John Warwick** saves the British empire by preventing secret documents from falling into the hands of foreign agents. Sort of a British Ollie North, we suppose. Wonder if he had a shredder?

DREAMER
DREAMER (1979, 20th Century Fox)—**Tim Matheson** would like to do for bowling what Sylvester Stallone did for boxing in this story of a small town kegler who becomes the national champ. He doesn't succeed.

DREAMY
THE GREAT MR. NOBODY (1941, Warner Brothers)—Bungling newspaper classified advertisement salesman **Eddie Albert** has his creative promotional ideas stolen by others, but he finally gets things straightened out and wins the girl he's been dreaming of, Joan Leslie.

DREISER, PAUL
MY GAL SAL (1942, 20th Century Fox)—**Victor Mature**, using the name Paul Dresser, is the song-writing brother of author Theodore

Dreiser who wrote the story on which this movie is based. Mature's inspiration for the title song is Sally Elliott, played by Rita Hayworth.

DRESSER

THE FIVE HEARTBEATS (1991, 20th Century Fox)—**Harry J. Lennix** is smooth and self-possessed in his role as a member of a black 60s singing group.

DREW

DOGS OF WAR (1980, GB, UA)—**Tom Berenger** is one of the soldiers of fortune recruited by mercenary Christopher Walken to overthrow the government in a West African country.

DREW, JONATHAN *See* THE LODGER

DREW, JUNE

MAKE WAY FOR A LADY (1936, RKO)—**Anne Shirley** is on the lookout for a new wife for her widower father Herbert Marshall. Her choice is Margot Grahame, but Marshall makes his own selection, Gertrude Michael.

DREW, MARGARET J.

THEY ALL KISSED THE BRIDE (1942, Columbia)—**Joan Crawford** stepped in for Carole Lombard in this movie when the latter was killed in an airplane crash. Crawford portrays a tough-as-nails trucking magnate who finds romance with Melvyn Douglas, a crusading newspaper reporter. It's a genuinely funny movie.

DREW, NANCY

NANCY DREW—DETECTIVE (1938, Warner Brothers); NANCY DREW AND THE HIDDEN STAIRCASE (1939, Warner Brothers); NANCY DREW-REPORTER (1939, Warner Brothers); NANCY DREW, TROUBLE SHOOTER (1939, Warner Brothers)—**Bonita Granville** starred as the Carolyn Keene created youthful amateur sleuth. The pictures aren't memorable, but they provided some enjoyable escapism at the time they were released, before TV shows of similiar quality kept audiences at home on their couches.

DREW, TRILBY

SPITE MARRIAGE (1929, Silent, MGM)—Stage actress **Dorothy Sebastian** is loved by pants presser Buster Keaton. When she's jilted, she marries Keaton out of spite. There are the to-be-expected complications before Sebastian discovers that she's married the right man.

DREWELL, STEVE

MR. ROBINSON CRUSOE (1932, UA)—Wealthy hunter **Douglas Fairbanks, Jr.** takes up residence on a deserted island, and in no time has built and furnished a shelter that resembles a Park Avenue penthouse. To make things complete, Saturday shows up. (Saturday is Maria Alba.) Home, Sweet, Home.

DREXELL, PAUL

DANCING MAN (1934, Pyramid)—Gigolo **Reginald Denny** romances both a woman and her daughter. When the older woman is found murdered, he's suspected.

DREYER, MADGE

MAN BAIT (1926, Silent, PDC)—Shopgirl **Marie Prevost** is fired for slugging a customer who made a pass. Her next job is as a taxi-dancer. She becomes the fiancee of the son of her former employer. Her in-laws-to-be snub her, but everything works our alright as she falls for her fiance's brother.

DREYFUS, ALFRED

DREYFUS (1931, GB, Columbia)—**Cedric Hardwicke**, the only Jew on the French general staff, is framed for treason and is sent to Devil's Island. His case becomes an international cause celebre, championed by the writer Emile Zola. The latter with the help of Georges Clemenceau, who will later become the Premier of France during WWI, discover the duplicity that finally, after years of imprisonment, vindicates Hardwicke. In THE LIFE OF EMILE ZOLA, starring Paul Muni as the writer, Joseph Schildkraut won an Academy Award for his portrayal of Dreyfus. In 1958 Jose Ferrer appeared as Dreyfus in I ACCUSE.

DRIFTER, THE

THE DRIFTER (1932, State Rights)—Itinerant lumberjack **William Farnum** drifts into the middle of a war between two lumber barons.

DRISCOLL, DR. CLEM

A DOCTOR'S DIARY (1937, Paramount)—**George Bancroft** relates the story of militant doctor John Trent, impatient with red tape which he believes holds up his research on spinal meningitis. Trent, who accuses others of malpractice, is not above using unethical practices himself.

DRISCOLL, SAVANNAH

SAVANNAH SMILES (1983, Gold Coast)—Little **Bridgette Anderson** runs away from home because her parents don't pay enough attention to her. The little darling is picked up by a pair of escaped cons, who plan to hold her for ransom, but she so charms them, they see she gets home without a charge.

DRISCOLL, SGT.

STAND UP VIRGIN SOLDIERS (1977, GB, Syndicate)—British soldier **Nigel Davenport**, stationed in Singapore, is more interested in losing his virginity than in finding communists.

DRISCOLL, TIM

TIM DRISCOLL'S DONKEY (1955, GB, British Lion)—When Irish lad **David Coote's** pet donkey is sold by mistake, he's off to England to track down the animal.

DRIVER, THE

THE DRIVER (1978, 20th Century Fox)—**Ryan O'Neal** drives the get-away car for a gang of crooks. He's very, very good at what he does, but police detective Bruce Dern is determined to put him away.

DROMIO OF SYRACUSE

BOYS FROM SYRACUSE (1940, Universal)—**Joe Penner** appears as twin slaves, one who serves a twin separated from his brother at birth, and has gone on to be Emperor and conqueror of Syracuse, and as Dromio, the slave of the twin who remained in Syracuse and who now faces execution by the decree of his brother that all native Syracusan males must die.

DROOD, EDWIN

THE MYSTERY OF EDWIN DROOD (1935, Universal)—Claude Rains strangles **David Manners**, his rival for Heather Angel, and then tries to shift the blame to Douglass Montgomery.

DROP DEAD FRED

DROP DEAD FRED (1991, New Line)—After splitting with her husband, Phoebe Cates returns to live with her dominating mother Marsha Mason. Cates discovers a music box that contains her long-forgotten imaginary friend, played by **Rik Mayall**. He tells her he's been released to wreak havoc until she's having fun again.

DROSTE, GEORGE

THE DEVIL'S AGENT (1962, GB, British Lion)—Vienna wine merchant **Peter Van Eyck** offers his services to a U.S. intelligence agency tracking Soviet spies.

DRUM

DRUM (1976, UA)—In the sequel to MANDINGO, **Ken Norton**, who starred as the slave Mede in the previous picture, now appears as his grandson. It is a story about a slave breeder and the sex he and his teenage daughter have with their slaves. It's trash.

DRUMM, BUBBER

A TIGER'S TALE (1988, Atlantic)—Nineteen-year-old **C. Thomas Howell** spends his time with bratty sex-starved Kelly Preston, but gets his real sexual education from the latter's mom, Ann-Margret.

DRUMMOND, HELEN

BELOVED ENEMY (1936, Goldwyn/UA)—During the "Troubles" in Ireland, British **Merle Oberon**, formerly the fiancee of a British English officer, falls in love with Irish revolutionary Brian Aherne.

DRUMMOND, CAPT. HUGH

BULLDOG DRUMMOND (1922, GB, Silent, Astra); (1929, UA)— **Carlyle Blackwell** and **Ronald Colman**; BULLDOG DRUMMOND STRIKES BACK (1934, UA)—**Ronald Colman** THE RETURN OF BULLDOG DRUMMOND (1934, GB, Wardour)—**Ralph Richardson**; BULLDOG DRUMMOND AT BAY (1937, GB, Wardour)—**John Lodge**; BULLDOG DRUMMOND ESCAPES (1937, Paramount)— **Ray Milland**; BULLDOG DRUMMOND COMES BACK (1937, Paramount); BULLDOG DRUMMOND'S REVENGE (1938, Paramount); BULLDOG DRUMMOND'S PERIL (1938, Paramount); BULLDOG DRUMMOND IN AFRICA (1938, Paramount); ARREST BULLDOG DRUMMOND (1939, Paramount); BULLDOG DRUMMOND'S SECRET POLICE (1939, Paramount); BULLDOG DRUMMOND'S BRIDE (1939, Paramount);—**John Howard**; BULLDOG SEES IT THROUGH (1939, GB, ABPC)—**Jack Buchanan**; BULLDOG DRUMMOND AT BAY (1947, PRC); BULLDOG DRUMMOND STRIKES BACK (1947, PRC)—**Ron Randell**; CALLING BULLDOG DRUMMOND (1951, MGM)—**Walter Pidgeon**—'Sapper' (Hector McNeil) created debonair ex-war hero Drummond, who is pretty much a Fascist, enjoying taking vengeance on the villains he encounters in the exploits he seeks, so as not to be bored.

DRUMMOND, HUGH See CAPTAIN SWAGGER

DRUMMOND, JESSICA

MY REPUTATION (1946, Warner Brothers)—Society woman **Barbara Stanwyck** scandalizes her friends when she falls for womanizer George Brent after her husband dies.

DRUMMOND, ROGER

ONCE A THIEF (1935, GB, Paramount British)—Chemist **John Stuart** "borrows" some money from a purse, and is sent to prison when it's discovered that a piece of valuable jewelry is missing from the bag.

DRUMMOND, WALT

THE MAGNIFICENT SEVEN RIDE (1972, UA)—**William Lucking** is one of five convicts who team with Lee Van Cleef and Michael Callan to protect some widows from Mexican bandits. It's a shame that studios don't realize there's nothing left for a second sequel to an outstanding original movie.

DRYDEN, PAT

THE GIRL IN THE PICTURE (1956, GB, Eros)—Reporter Donald Houston searches for **Junia Crawford**, a girl in a photograph and the only one who knows the identity of a killer.

DU BARRY, MME.

DU BARRY WAS A LADY (1943, MGM); DU BARRY, WOMAN OF PASSION (1930, UA); THE LOVES OF MADAME DU BARRY (1938, GB, British Int.); MADAME DU BARRY (1934, Warner Brothers)— When Red Skelton is given a Mickey Finn, he awakens in the court of France's Louis XV where **Lucille Ball** is Mme. Du Barry. The Cole Porter musical is fun but no great shakes. **Norma Talmadge** played the role of Du Barry straight in a rather dull account of the love affair between Louis XV (William Farnum) and his mistress. The British production and the Warner Brothers film are unimpressive movies starring **Gitta Alpar** and **Dolores Del Rio**, respectively, in the title role.

DU PREZ, DIANE

THE REJECTED WOMAN (1924, Silent, Cosmopolitian)—Northwest girl **Alma Reubens** falls in love with socialite Conrad Nagel, when his plane crash-lands in her backyard. She follows him back to New York, but is a thing of ridicule because of her clothes and ways of acting. These can be changed.

DU TOUCHAIS, MARQUIS

THE PHANTOM OF PARIS (1931, MGM)—Magician John Gilbert is wrongly accused of murdering Leila Hyams's father. Confused, she marries **Ian Keith**, her other suitor and the actual killer.

DUANE, BUCK

LAST OF THE DUANES (1930, Fox); (1941, 20th Century Fox) THE LONE STAR RANGER (1930, Fox); (1942, 20th Century Fox)— **George O'Brien, George Montgomery** and **John Kimborough** all appear as the gunman, accused of murder who must clear himself. It was a tired old tale when Zane Grey wrote it and repeated filming didn't take the ache out of the old bones.

DUBOIS, ANNETTE (aka JANE DOE)

I, JANE DOE (1948, Republic)—French girl **Vera Ralston** is on trail for murder. How she came to this point is told in flashbacks, but its not very interesting.

DUBOIS, COLETTE

DRESSED TO THRILL (1935, Fox)—**Tutta Rolf** appears as a Russian singer and her look-alike dressmaker. In neither role is Rolf worth seeing.

DUBROVNA, IRENA

CAT PEOPLE (1942, RKO)—**Simone Simon** is convinced that if she makes love to her new husband Kent Smith she will change into a panther and go on a murderous rampage. (What's the matter with the old "I have a headache" excuse?). Everyone believes she's wacko but the psychiatrist who treats her is killed by a large cat.

DUCHANIER, ELSIE

ONE YEAR TO LIVE (1925, Silent, First National)—**Aileen Pringle**, the maid of a French dancing star, is told she has only one year to live. She agrees to go to bed with a theatrical producer if he can make her a star while she's still around to enjoy it. He does, but she doesn't because an admirer saves her and proves her diagnosis was in error. Welcher!

DUCHESS, THE
THE RIVER WOMAN (1928, Gotham/Lumas)—**Jacqueline Logan** is the object of affection of both Lionel Barrymore and Charles Delaney. Seeing that the other two are really in love, Barrymore sacrifices his life to save theirs when the mighty Mississippi overflows its boundaries into their community.

DUCHESS OF ALBA
THE NAKED MAJA (1959, UA)—**Ava Gardner** posed both with and without clothes for her lover, painter Francisco Goya, played by Tony Franciosa in this passionless biopic.

DUCHESS OF BRIGHTON
THE V.I.P.S (1963, GB, MGM)—Dotty **Margaret Rutherford** is the best thing in this overly long soap opera about an assortment of very important passengers stranded in an airport when the London fog grounds all flights. Rutherford fears flying and is delighted when film director Orson Welles pays her to use her estate in his next film, thus making her trip to the U.S. to raise cash to pay her taxes unnecessary. Rutherford won an Oscar as Best Supporting Actress.

DUCHESS OF TANN
THE IMPROPER DUCHESS (1936, GB, GFD)—**Yvonne Arnaud** is a duchess in Washington trying to negotiate a loan.

DUCHIN, EDDY
THE EDDY DUCHIN STORY (1956, Columbia)—**Tyrone Power** portrays the New York cafe society pianist, now known for being the father of Peter Duchin, who followed in his father's footsteps. The movie is a tearjerker, as Power loses his first wife giving birth to their son, whom he blames for her death. After being reconciled with his son and marrying a new wife, Power learns that he's dying of leukemia. The piano playing of Carmen Cavallero is special.

DUCK
THE FIVE HEARTBEATS (1991, 20th Century Fox)—**Robert Townsend** is the leader of a 60s black singing group. Townsend is also the film's executive producer, director and co-sreenwriter with Keenan Ivory Wayans.

DUCK, HOWARD T.
HOWARD THE DUCK (1986, Universal)—**Ed Gale/Chip Zien/Tim Rose/Steve Sleap/Peter Baird/Mary Wells/ Lisa Sturz/Jordan Prentice** all contribute to the presentation of an alien duck who falls to earth and saves the planet from life forms planning an invasion. The special effects are excellent but that's not enough to get most people to shell out the price of a ticket to this turkey—that is, duck.

DUCROS, ANGELE
LES GIRLS (1957, MGM)—**Tania Elg**, now married to a French industrialist, sues her former partner in a show business act, Kay Kendall, when the latter writes her candid autobiography in which she relates that Elg attempted to seduce the male star of their act, Gene Kelly, and when that didn't work, attempted suicide. That's not how Elg remembers it. Everyone, including Mitzi Gaynor, the fourth member of the act, has a different recollection of the romantic entanglements.

DUDGEON, RICHARD
THE DEVIL'S DISCIPLE (1959, UA)—During the American Revolutionary War, scoundrel **Kirk Douglas** allows the British to believe he is a rebel minister they are seeking and as a result is sentenced to be hanged by Laurence Olivier as "Gentleman Johnny" Burgoyne.

The George Bernard Shaw farce is enjoyable if one isn't looking for too much.

DUDLEY
MAKER OF MEN (1931, Columbia)—**Jack Holt** is a football coach of a losing team. When his son's mistakes cost the team a victory, the boy enrolls in a rival college and scores the winning touchdown in a game against his father's team. Talk about rats jumping ship.

DUFF, PETER
THE QUALIFIED ADVENTURER (1925, GB, Silent, Stoll)—Author **Matheson Lang** puts down a mutiny on a ship in the South Seas with the help of the Chinese cook who turns out to be a Manchurian prince.

DUFFY
DUFFY (1968, GB, Columbia)—Aging hippie **James Coburn** is recruited by two sons of wealthy James Mason to help them swindle a large amount of money from their mean-spirited father.

DUFFY, WARDEN CLINTON T.
DUFFY OF SAN QUENTIN (1954, Warner Brothers)—New warden of San Quentin, **Paul Kelly** has plans to rehabilitate the prisoners, no matter how hard and brutal they may be. He seems to have some success, particularly with tough con, Louis Hayward.

DUFFY, GRACE
THE LONE WOLF AND HIS LADY (1949, Columbia)—**June Vincent** really has very little to do or say in this, till now, last of the Lone Wolf series, with Ron Randell playing the former jewel thief, now a reporter, who gets in trouble when he's to cover the exhibition of a famous diamond and it disappears.

DUFFY, TOM
TOM AND HIS PALS (1926, Silent, R-C Pictures)—**Tom Tyler** allows a movie company to use his ranch for location shooting, but he isn't willing to allow the leading man to move in on his girlfriend, even though he's infatuated with the female lead.

DUGAN, BABE
BABE COMES HOME (1927, Silent, First National)—**Babe Ruth** may have been the greatest ball player to put on cleats, but as this clinker about a baseball player whose wife insists he give up the dirty habit of chewing tobacco proves, he's not much of an actor.

DUGAN, BILL
DUGAN OF THE BAD LANDS (1931, Monogram)—Saddle tramp **Bill Cody** helps an assaulted sheriff track down the crooked deputy who turned on his lawman boss.

DUGAN, CHARLIE
FIXER DUGAN (1939, RKO)—**Lee Tracy** arbitrates problems between the circus for which he works and anyone, such as the law, who has differences of opinion with the circus or its people.

DUGAN, DIXIE
DIXIE DUGAN (1943, 20th Century Fox)—**Lois Andrews** appears as the comic strip working girl who wishes to be treated as an equal at her job, but is given menial work by her chauvinistic boss. She's shows him a thing or two.

DUGAN, DIXIE
SHOW GIRL (1928, Warner Brothers); SHOW GIRL IN HOLLYWOOD (1930, Warner Brothers)—**Alice White** is helped to realize her ambition to be a show business star by a cub reporter. In the sequel,

she takes her show on the road to Hollywood, where she becomes a smash on the silver screen.

DUGAN, GABBY

KING OF HOCKEY (1936, Warner Brothers)—**Dick Purcell** is a hockey player blinded when injured by a teammate. He's bitter, but his girlfriend raises the money for an operation that restores his sight and the dumb hockey puck goes back on the ice and leads his team to the championship. He doesn't look much like Wayne Gretsky.

DUGAN, MARY

THE TRIAL OF MARY DUGAN (1929, MGM); (1941, MGM)—**Norma Shearer** and **Laraine Day** portray a girl accused of killing her boyfriend. Her brother, a new lawyer doesn't think much of the way that her defense lawyer is handling the case and takes over. He will eventually not only prove her innocence but show the real culprit to be her first lawyer who was planning to see that she was convicted.

DUGAN, MAX

MAX DUGAN RETURNS (1983, 20th Century Fox)—**Jason Robards Jr.**, who hasn't earned his money legitimately, shows up after a long absence to shower his single parent daughter Marsha Mason and his grandson with gifts in lieu of love, but that flows three ways before the film ends, with Robards hitting the road again, just ahead of a cop, Donald Sutherland, who's been courting Mason.

DUGAN, NICK

THE MAN FROM CHICAGO (1931, GB, British Int.)—American gangster **Bernard Nedell** gets away with murder in England, including the elimination of a Scotland Yard Inspector, until he's run over by a car driven by his girlfriend—well, perhaps not such a great friend.

DUGAN, NOAH

THE LAST FLIGHT OF NOAH'S ARK (1980, Buena Vista)—Grouchy pilot **Elliott Gould** reluctantly flies an orphanage worker, a cargo of animals, and two stowaway squalling kids across the Pacific. They crash land onto an island where two Japanese soldiers who don't know WWII is over are still on duty. It's another one of the cute Disney movies. We hate cute Disney movies.

DUGAN, NORMA

THE CRYSTAL GAZER (1917, Silent, Paramount)—**Fannie Ward** is one of two sisters raised by different families when their mother died. She has been raised by a hypnotist who has made her into a famous medium. Her sister was raised by a wealthy society family and the plot thickens when their paths cross again.

DUHAMEL, ROSE

HARDBOILED ROSE (1929, Warner Brothers)—**Myrna Loy** is a refined Southern girl, forced to work in a gambling house to pay off her suicide father's debts.

DUKANE, JAMES A. JR.

THE INCORRIGIBLE DUKANE (1915, Silent, Paramount)—**John Barrymore** undercovers a plot to skim some profits from the construction of a dam by using shoddy materials. He foils the plot of course.

DUKE, "BREEZE"

DUKE OF THE NAVY (1942, PRC)—Sailor **Ralph Byrd** is mistaken for the son of a wealthy woman and prevents her from being milked by a con man.

DUKE

THE DUKE STEPS OUT (1929, Silent, MGM)—Wealthy **William Haines** becomes a professional boxer to show his father that he can make it on her own.

DUKE

SAINTLY SINNERS (1962, UA)—**Paul Bryar** and Stanley Clements borrow an ex-con's car to use in a bank robbery. Before they can recover their loot from the spare tire of the car it is repossessed and sold to a priest, who later is accused of the bank robbery. The boys, good Catholics, no doubt, 'fess up.

DUKE, HEATHER

HEATHERS (1989, New World)—When Kim Walker, the leader of the most exclusive high school clique, apparently commits suicide, **Shannen Doherty** steps into the former's high-heel spikes and proves to be a greater witch than the first.

DUKE OF CHARMERACE *See* **ARSENE LUPIN**

DULCIE

MISS DULCIE FROM DIXIE (1919, Silent, Vitagraph)—**Gladys Leslie** is a Southern belle who goes north to put an end to the feud between her father and uncle.

DULCY

NOT SO DUMB (1930, MGM)—**Marion Davies** has a habit of doing the wrong things at the wrong times, but at a dinner party given to impress her fiance's important investors, she does right for a change, but that's not how it seems at first.

DUM, STANLEY & DEE, OLIVER

BABES IN TOYLAND (1934, MGM)—**Stan Laurel** and **Oliver Hardy** become the unsung heroes of Toyland when they save the home of the old woman in a shoe and prevent Little Bo-Peep from being forced to marry evil old Barnaby.

DUMAY, ROSALIE

SOUTH SEA ROSE (1929, Fox)—**Leonore Ulric** is a French girl living in the South Seas, whom sea captain Charles Bickford believes to be just right for him. But when they get back to New England, her free-spirited life style shocks the locals.

DUMMAR, MELVIN

MELVIN AND HOWARD (1980, Universal)—Factory worker **Paul Le Mat** picks up an old man in the Nevada desert who claims to be Howard Hughes.

DUMOND, DORIS

THE SLEEPWALKER (1922, Silent, Paramount)—**Constance Binney's** sleepwalking almost gets her arrested for being a jewel thief, but in such a state she also rescues a baby before it can fall off a building's ledge.

DUMONT, LORENA

FRONTIER GAL (1945, Universal)—Cowboy Rod Cameron peacefully arrives in town and is forced at gun point to marry saloon owner **Yvonne De Carlo**

DUMONT, NANCY

HER MARKET VALUE (1925, Silent, Powell)—**Agnes Ayres's** husband loses his fortune in the stock market and commits suicide, leaving Ayres to three wealthy friends "in trust." The three help her financially but all seem to wish to own the stock exclusively.

DUNBAR, LT. JOHN

DANCES WITH WOLVES (1990, Orion)—In his directorial debut, **Kevin Costner** comes up a winner with his long production featuring a Union officer who after the Civil War opts to be sent to a deserted outpost at the farthest reaches of the frontier, which he wishes to see before it disappears. At first his only living companions are his horse and a curious wolf. He makes contact with the Sioux and discovers that theirs is a rich culture. He also finds love with a white woman, Mary McDonnell, who has been raised by the Indians since she was captured in a raid as a child. Costner won an Oscar for his directorial debut, and the film was named Best Picture.

DUNBAR, NICK (NICK SPRINGSTEEN)

PLAIN CLOTHES (1988, Paramount)—Young cop **Arliss Howard** goes undercover as a student in a high school to solve the murder of a teacher.

DUNCAN, ANN

FUGITIVE LADY (1934, Columbia)—**Florence Rice** elopes with a jewel thief, but she doesn't know his occupation. When he goes on the lam she is sentenced to prison for his crime. During a wreck of a train taking her to prison, she is mixed up with the fiancee of a rich man and the two fall in love.

DUNCAN, CHRISTINE RIVERTON

THE DUCHESS OF IDAHO (1950, MGM)—**Esther Williams** is a swim star, who takes the unusual approach of bringing her friend Paula Raymond together with the man she adores, playboy John Lund, by making a play for Lund herself. Williams' boyfriend, Van Johnson, doesn't understand the ploy either.

DUNCAN, CURT

WHEN A STRANGER CALLS (1979, Columbia)—**Tony Beckley** is a maniac, who terrorizes a babysitter by threatening to murder the children in her charge. It's a good old fashion scary horror show— for the first 20 minutes; after that it's routine stuff.

DUNCAN, DOT

A GIRL, A GUY AND A GOB (1941, RKO)—**Lucille Ball**, who thinks she loves George Murphy, is loved by shy country boy Edmond O'Brien. When Murphy dumps her, O'Brien begins to look better.

DUNCAN, ISADORA

ISADORA (1968, GB, Universal)—**Vanessa Redgrave** was nominated for an Oscar for her portrayal of unconventional dancer Isadora Duncan, whose life style shocked the world.

DUNCAN, JACK

THE FIGHTING GENTLEMAN (1932, Monarch)—**William Allen, Jr.**, a mechanic with ambitions of becoming a boxer, is knocked out in the first round of his first fight, but after some intense training he reverses the outcome in a rematch.

DUNCAN, JAMES

A MAN AND THE WOMAN (1917, Silent, Art Drama)—**Leslie Austen** is a poor young man, who is induced to marry wealthy Edith Hallor in order to give her child a legitimate birth. He grows to love his wife and child, but it takes her a bit longer to realize that she feels the same.

DUNCAN, JIM

SWELL GUY (1946, Universal)—Amicable actor **Sonny Tufts** portrays a man who is not the great guy that the townsfolk believe him to be. Just ask his brother, his sister-in-law and the maid.

DUNCAN, JIMMY

HIS OWN HOME TOWN (1918, Silent, Ince)—**Charles Ray** leaves his home town to make his way in the world. The first attempt isn't very successful, and when he comes home, he's driven out of town by crooked politicians. He writes a successful play under an assumed name, goes home and kicks out the scoundrels.

DUNCAN, NAT

THE FORTUNE HUNTER (1927, Silent, Warner Brothers)—**Syd Chaplin** is an impoverished spendthrift, who tries to reverse his condition in a small town.

DUNCAN, PAT

THE LUCKIEST GIRL IN THE WORLD (1936, Universal)—**Jane Wyatt**, a wealthy socialite, must live on $150 for a month to prove to her father that she can stand being married to a poor man.

DUNCHESTER, LORD

MAN OF AFFAIRS (1937, GB, Gaumont)—**George Arliss** appears in the dual roles of the Foreign Secretary of Great Britain and his brother, a detective. The two solve a kidnapping plot and a mysterious murder.

DUNDEE, MAJOR AMOS CHARLES

MAJOR DUNDEE (1965, Columbia)—Discredited Union officer and martinet **Charlton Heston** leads an expedition of Confederate prisoners, Union deserters and convicted felons after a tribe of renegade Apaches who have kidnapped some white children.

DUNDEE, MICK "CROCODILE"

"CROCODILE" DUNDEE (1986, Australia, Paramount); "CROCODILE" DUNDEE II (1988, Australia, Paramount)—**Paul Hogan** is a charming, unaffected crocodile poacher who takes American reporter Linda Kozlowski on a tour of the Outback and she in turn introduces him to the canyons of Manhattan. The sequel isn't as enjoyable but Hogan still is disarming as he rescues Kozlowski from Columbian drug smugglers.

DUNLAP, ANNA

THE GOOD MOTHER (1988, Touchstone)—One is so aware of how well **Diane Keaton** is acting in this story of a divorced mother, that it's only on later reflection that one notes how phony and illogical the story is. Keaton loses custody of her small daughter, because she allows the child to sleep in her bed while she's making love to writer Liam Neeson. It's a film in which all the bad things which happen could be avoided or managed so as not to separate Keaton from her daughter. One leaves the movie very dissatisfied.

DUNLAP, SANDY

JUST BETWEEN FRIENDS (1986, Orion)—**Christine Lahti** was having an affair with her new friend Mary Tyler Moore's husband at the time of his death from a heart attack.

DUNLAP, TONI & JIM

THIS MAN IS MINE (1934, RKO)—**Irene Dunne** and **Ralph Bellamy** are happily married until her sister decides to destroy the marriage to get Bellamy for herself. Dunne's not about to let this happen. This film is the exception to the rule that Bellamy never gets the girl.

DUNN, ALICE

SHOULD A GIRL MARRY? (1929, Realart)—**Helen Foster** kills a cad who has wronged her alcoholic sister. She's acquitted but has to listen to a lecture from a stern judge about how naughty she's been.

DUNN, GROVER

THE INVISIBLE KID (1988, Columbia)—Nerd **Jay Underwood** comes up with a magic powder which makes him invisible. With invisibility comes the confidence to win the pretty girl next door, who couldn't see him at all when he was visible. The movie gathers together most of the bad features of the teen exploitation comedy films and dumps them together in one yecchy mess.

DUNN, THERESA

LOOKING FOR MR. GOODBAR (1977, Paramount)—**Diane Keaton**, a teacher of deaf children, and daughter of a tyrannical Catholic father, seeks affection in one night stands with men whom she meets in bars. One kills her.

DUNNE, FATHER

FIGHTING FATHER DUNNE (1948, RKO)—**Pat O'Brien** is a priest in the early 1900s, who tries to help poor unfortunate boys in St. Louis, including one who gets religion just before he's executed for a murder.

DUNNE, MARTIN

THE MAN IN BLUE (1937, Universal)—Cop **Edward Ellis** adopts the young son of a thief he killed during a robbery.

DUNNING, RUTH

SKY BRIDE (1932, Paramount)—**Virginia Bruce** is the romantic interest of ex-pilot Richard Arlen; the only one who can save a youngster who stows away in a plane to test a homemade parachute.

DUPIN

THE MAN WITH A CLOAK (1951, MGM)—In 1848 New York, mysterious stranger **Joseph Cotten**, who turns out to be Edgar Allan Poe, helps young French girl Leslie Caron keep her inheritance from her Uncle, which the old man's housekeeper Barbara Stanwyck and butler Joe De Santis are trying to get for themselves.

DUPONT, HELENE

THE LADY IS WILLING (1934, GB, Columbia)—**Binnie Barnes** is kidnapped by detective Leslie Howard, hired by three businessmen, who wish to prevent Barnes from signing papers, which will allow her husband Cedric Hardwicke to sell his property. Barnes falls in love with her abductor.

DUPONT, LIGEAH

QUEEN OF THE WICKED (1916, GB, Silent, British, Empire)—Ex-dancer **Nina Lynn** drugs and strangles her husband, cleans out his safe, and frames a nobleman of the crime. Wicked? Nah, just high-strung.

DUPREE, PAULA

CAPTIVE WILD WOMAN (1943, Universal); JUNGLE WOMAN (1944, Universal)—Mad scientist John Carradine turns a wild ape into a half-ape, half-woman creature, played by **Acquanetta**. The creature falls for Milburn Stone but becomes enraged when he spurns "her" for Evelyn Ankers. In the sequel, the alluring but violent jungle woman is back and is killed by scientist J. Carroll Naish who is cleared of murder when the corpse turns into that of an ape.

DUPREZ, NINA

LOUISIANA HUSSY (1960, Howco)—Evil Cajan **Nan Peterson** just about ruins the life of everyone she meets.

DUQUENSE, MELINDA

TWO ON A GUILLOTINE (1965, Warner Brothers)—**Connie Stevens** is saved from the fate of her mother, having her head chopped off during a magic act, by the daring-do of reporter Dean Jones, who

agrees to stay with her in her father's eerie mansion for seven nights, so she can claim her inheritance.

DURALLE, PEPE ABELLAND

THE TOAST OF NEW ORLEANS (1950, MGM)—**Mario Lanza** is a rough-and-ready fisherman with a great voice. Impresario David Niven wants to team him with opera diva Kathryn Grayson, who initially is put off by Lanza (in real life she never got over the feeling). They lend their voices to several classical pieces and the Oscar-nominated "Be My Love" written for the movie by Sammy Cahn and Nicholas Brodszky.

DURANGO KID *See* **BILL LOWERY**

DURANGO KID, THE

THE KID FROM AMARILLO (1951, Columbia); THE KID FROM BROKEN GUN (1952, Columbia)—**Charles Starrett** is also known as Steve Reynolds in these two limp westerns with predictable heroics by Starrett.

DURANT, ADRIENNE

THE CRIMSON DOVE (1917, Silent, World)—**June Elvidge** is a woman with a past who cleans up her act in the present so she'll have a future with a minister she has come to love.

DURANT, ALBERT

THE GRAND DUCHESS AND THE WAITER (1926, Paramount)—In order to meet a Grand Duchess, played by Florence Vidor, French millionaire **Adolphe Menjou** enters service in her household and the two fall in love.

DURANT, CHRISTOPHER

SOCIETY LAWYER (1939, MGM)—Successful lawyer **Walter Pidgeon** is embarrassed by the gratitude of a racketeer he helped.

DURANT, JEANETTE

QUEEN O' DIAMONDS (1926, R-C Pictures)—Chorus girl **Evelyn Brent** poses as a Broadway actress whom she greatly resembles.

DURBAN, PHILIP

THE IRON MAN (1925, Silent, Chadwick)—Mildred Harris weds millionaire **Lionel Barrymore** on the rebound, when she is jilted by a prince her father tried to buy for her. Harris learns to love Barrymore.

DURBEYFIELD, TESS

TESS OF THE D'UBERVILLES (1924, Silent, Metro-Goldwyn); TESS (1980, Gb/France, Columbia)—**Blanche Sweet** and **Nastassja Kinski** appear as Thomas Hardy's tragic heroine who is executed for the murder of the man who ruined her.

DURKIN, KEN

THE MAN I MARRY (1936, Universal)—Wealthy **Michael Whalen** decides to write a novel to prove to his overbearing mother that he can make it on his own.

DURLING, TOM

THEY MADE ME A KILLER (1946, Paramount)—Escaped con **Robert Lowery** is helped by the sister of a man he supposedly killed in a holdup to prove he was framed.

DURNOY, ELSA

TILL WE MEET AGAIN (1936, Paramount)—**Gertrude Michael** is a German actress, who in 1914, meets and falls in love with English actor Herbert Marshall. With WWI they find themselves at odds, spying for their countries. They opt to seek a separate peace, fleeing to Holland, where they marry.

DUROY, GEORGES
THE PRIVATE AFFAIRS OF BEL AMI (1947, UA)—**George Sanders** is in his element as Guy de Maupassant's cynical journalist, who climbs the ladder of fame by stepping heavily on the ruined lives of his friends.

DURRANT, LARRY
TWENTY-ONE DAYS TOGETHER (1937, GB, Columbia)—**Laurence Olivier** accidently kills a man. When a crazy old eccentric is accused of the crime, Olivier and his love Vivian Leigh try to squeeze a lifetime into 21 days before Olivier will confess and clear the innocent man, preventing him from being brought to trial. As fate would have it, the accused man dies of heart failure, and Olivier need say nothing. The cruelty of allowing an innocent man to experience suffering and fear during his last days is not made an issue in the movie. But we suppose as he was not of the upper class, he wasn't supposed to have any feelings.

DURRISDEER, JAMES
THE MASTER OF BALLANTRAE (1953, Warner Brothers)—**Errol Flynn's** last film for Warner Brothers has him as the heir to a Scottish title, who joins a rebellion against the British in 1745. The rebels are easily defeated so Flynn takes off for the West Indies where he amasses a fortune. When he returns to Scotland, he discovers his brother has assumed his title and is engaged to Flynn's longtime sweetheart. Flynn allows his brother to keep the title but not the woman.

DURWARD, QUENTIN
THE ADVENTURES OF QUENTIN DURWARD (1956, GB, MGM British)—In 1465, a Lord's nephew, **Robert Taylor,** saves the duke's ward, Kay Kendall, from a political kidnapping.

DURYEA, JACQUES
GOD'S GIFT TO WOMEN (1931, Warner Brothers)—**Frank Fay** is very popular with the ladies, a curse which he gladly suffers until Laura La Plante comes along. She wants nothing to do with him, and through her father has a doctor tell Fay that her kiss would kill him. When he kisses her anyway, she decides that she means more to him than life and agrees to marry him.

DUTCH
DUTCH (1991, 20th Century Fox)—Salt of the earth **Ed O'Neill** volunteers to pick up his girlfriend's snotty kid, Ethan Randall, at an elite boarding school and bring him home for Thanksgiving. A la *Captains Courageous*, O'Neill teaches the angry boy some important lessons on the road.

DUTTON, HAIRPIN HARRY
THE POPPY GIRL'S HUSBAND (1919, Silent, Artcraft)—**William S. Hart,** in a non-western role, is paroled from prison only to discover that his wife has divorced him and married the detective who framed him. He would like to take revenge but when he meets his son, without revealing that he's the boy's father, he develops a loving relationship with the lad. He learns that his ex-wife and the detective are about to set him up once more. Enraged, he plans to disfigure his ex-wife, but is stopped by the crying of his son. He takes the boy with him, heading west to find a new life.

DUTTON, JOHNNY
CAPTAINS OF THE CLOUDS (1942, Warner Brothers)—**Dennis Morgan** turns out to be James Cagney's flight instructor when the two bush pilots join the Royal Canadian Air Corps at the outbreak of WWII. Cagney can't deal with the discipline, especially when it comes from Morgan who Jimmy feels doesn't know as much about flying as he does.

DUVAL, INSPECTOR
ENTER INSPECTOR DUVAL (1964, GB, Columbia)—**Anton Diffring**, a French police inspector, helps Scotland Yard in the case of a socialite murdered during a jewel robbery.

DUVAL, RENE
THE COUNT OF LUXEMBOURG (1926, Silent, Chadwick)—When a Duke is prevented from marrying Helen Lee Worthing because she has no title, he arranges for a quick proxy marriage of her to the impoverished Count of Luxemborg, **George Walsh**. Before the Duke can arrange for a divorce, Worthing and Walsh meet and fall in love.

DUVAL, MARIE
THE BELLE OF BROADWAY (1926, Silent, Columbia)—**Betty Compson**, once the toast of the Paris theatre world, is now a rejuvenated actress.

DUVAL, STEPHANIE
SHE'S DANGEROUS (1937, Universal)—Beautiful jewel thief **Tala Birell** is actually a detective investigating bond thieves.

DVORAK, JODY
KITTEN WITH A WHIP (1964, Universal)—Reform school runaway **Ann-Margret** takes refuge in the home of a politician whose wife is away.

DWYER, MARY (JILL)
JACK AND JILL (1917, Silent, Paramount)—**Louise Huff** is the Bowery sweetheart of boxer Jack Pickford, who flees west after killing a man in the ring.

DWIGHT, MARY
MARKED WOMAN (1937, Warner Brothers)—Nightclub girl **Bette Davis** is persuaded to testify against an underworld boss and when he gets off, she's in deep trouble.

DWIGHT, PETER
THE CHARLATAN (1929, Universal)—Circus clown **Holmes Herbert** poses as a mystic to deceive his ex-wife, who deserted him 15 years earlier for a rich man, taking their baby with her. Herbert is accused of her murder, but things aren't as they seem.

DYALA
AMAZONS (1987, MGM/UA)—In this dreadful sword and fantasy film, **Windsor Taylor Randolph**, one of many bosomy warriors, saves her Amazon city from the villains with the help of a magical sword and a magical horse. The women in the film bare their bodies at every opportunity, but their acting is so bad, audiences yearn for Arnold Schwarzenegger.

DYCKMAN, JOHN III
TWO GIRLS AND A SAILOR (1944, MGM)—**Van Johnson** is a shy millionaire sailor attracted to sisters June Allyson and Gloria De Haven. In this wartime musical, many real-life entertainers are doing their bit for service men in a club run by the sisters and anonymously financed by Johnson. The performers include Jimmy Durante, Leon Horne, Harry James & his Orchestra, Jose Iturbi, Gracie Allen, and dead-pan singer Virginia O'Brien.

DYKE, JAMES

THE VALIANT (1929, Fox)—Drifter **Paul Muni** murders a man and is sentenced to die in the electric chair. Hoping to spare his family he denies his identity but his mother and sister learn of his predicament and come a-running.

DYNAMITE, MR. (T.H. THOMPSON)

MR. DYNAMITE (1935, Universal)—Gambler **Edmund Lowe** hires a detective to investigate a murder in his casino.

DYNAMITE, WILLIE

WILLIE DYNAMITE (1973, Universal)—**Roscoe Orman** is a black pimp in New York City. His reign is brief.

E

EADIE

THE GIRL FROM MISSOURI (1934, MGM)—**Jean Harlow** is encouraged to "go all the way" with various men, even by her innkeeper father, who feels it will be good for business. Harlow takes off for the big city and even when she becomes a show girl, she's determined to save herself until wedding vows are said over her and some preferably rich man. She falls in love with Franchot Tone, who proposes she become his mistress. She almost gives in, but when his father interferes in his love life, Tone decides to marry the girl.

EAGELS, JEANNE

JEANNE EAGELS (1957, Columbia)—**Kim Novak** portrays the side-show girl who became a Broadway star but dies from drug addiction. It's a somber, none-too-interesting biopic.

EAGER, JOHNNY

JOHNNY EAGER (1942, MGM)—Big time hoodlum **Robert Taylor**, a man of few redeeming qualities, makes a play for society girl Lana Turner. Van Heflin as a drunken friend of Taylor won an Oscar for his Greek chorus-like role.

EARECKSON, JONI

JONI (1980, World Wide)—**Joni Eareckson** plays herself in the story of a woman who becomes a quadriplegic after a diving accident. She overcomes her to-be-expected depression, finding solace in religion.

EARL

CORNBREAD, EARL AND ME (1975, American International)—**Tierre Turner** is a friend of ghetto athletic star Keith Wilkes. The latter is gunned down by a policeman who wrongly believes he's involved in a crime.

EARL, LARRY

THE STAR MAKER (1939, Paramount)—Songwriter **Bing Crosby** makes it big organizing kid shows. The character is based on Gus Edwards.

EARLE, ROY

I DIED A THOUSAND TIMES (1955, Warner Brothers)—**Jack Palance** stars in this inferior remake of HIGH SIERRA, which had Humphrey Bogart as Roy Earle. Aging ex-con Palance plans one last big job, but everything goes wrong. Palance is hunted down and killed like an animal, but audiences have seen something of another side of the "mad-dog" killer.

EARLEY, STEVEN

THE DUKE OF WEST POINT (1938, UA)—**Louis Hayward's** mouth gets him into trouble at West Point until he proves he knows his place.

EARP, WYATT

FRONTIER MARSHAL (1939, 20th Century Fox); MY DARLING CLEMENTINE (1946, 20th Century Fox)—**Randolph Scott** and **Henry Fonda** are among the many actors to give their interpretations of the western marshall. Surely, Fonda, in John Ford's moody black-and-white masterpiece, is the most enjoyable, if not the most accurate depiction.

EARS, JOHNNY

DEAF SMITH AND JOHNNY EARS (1971, MGM)—**Franco Nero** teams with deaf mute Anthony Quinn in Texas in this eminently forgettable spaghetti western.

EASTLAKE, LAKEY

THE GROUP (1966, UA)—**Candice Bergen** is the lesbian member of a group of young women who graduated together from college during the Depression. Their lives for the next twenty years are followed in this interesting production of the best-selling novel by Mary McCarthy.

EASTLAND, JOHN

THE EXTERMINATOR (1980, Interstar); EXTERMINATOR 2 (1984, Cannon)—Extremely sick Vietnam vet **Robert Ginty** gets his kicks gruesomely killing street criminals. He and the cop out to stop him are ultimately eliminated by the CIA. This cheap and disgusting rip-off of DEATH WISH did well enough at the box office to spawn a sequel, which is equally gross.

EASTMAN, CLAUDE & DANIELLA

UNFAITHFULLY YOURS (1984, 20th Century Fox)—Orchestra conductor **Dudley Moore** wrongly believes that his wife **Natassja Kinski** is having an affair with guest artist Armand Assante. While conducting, Moore plots his revenge which works beautifully in his imagination, but not when implemented.

EASY, JACK

MEN OF THE SEA (1951, GB, Astor)—In the 18th century, **Hughie Green** enlists in the British navy, and among his exploits is rescuing beautiful Margaret Lockwood from pirates.

EATENTON, M'LYNN

STEEL MAGNOLIAS (1989, Tri-Star)—**Sally Field** is a remarkable actress. Just when one is convinced she can't be taken for a serious actress, she shows her mettle, portraying everyone's notion of a loving, devoted mother, as she stands by her dying daughter Julia Robert's bed and later her grave, where her anger and grief are as real as anyone could ever expect from an actress.

EATON, CLARE

MAN AND HIS WOMAN (1920, Silent, Pathe)—Nurse **Eulalie Jensen** saves Herbert Rawlinson, the physician she loves, from his addiction to alcohol and drugs.

EATON, IRENE

THEY MADE HER A SPY (1939, RKO)—**Sally Eilers** joins the U.S. Army Intelligence Corps to avenge her brother's death.

EATON, PEGGY O'NEAL
THE GORGEOUS HUSSY (1936, MGM)—Recalling how badly so-called good people had treated his wife, Lionel Barrymore, appearing as President Andrew Jackson, champions **Joan Crawford**, the wife of one of his cabinet members, against the other cabinet members and their wives who consider Crawford, daughter of an innkeeper, little more than trash.

EBA
CAVEGIRL (1986, Crown International)—Daniel Roebuck gets sent back to prehistoric times, and finds tasty morsel **Cindy Ann Thompson** more than willing to learn about 20th century sex methods. It's demeaning to all sexes and cave people.

EBERLIN, ALEXANDER
A DANDY IN ASPIC (1968, GB, Columbia)—Double agent **Laurence Harvey** is ordered to kill himself. We can't say if the fact that Harvey took over direction of the film when Anthony Mann died is responsible for this being such a lousy film but we're sure it's a contributing factor. Another is Harvey's acting.

EBBS, CAPTAIN
THE CAPTAIN'S TABLE (1960, GB, 20th Century Fox/Rank)—**John Gregson** must learn manners when he is transferred from skippering a cargo ship to a luxury liner.

ECHEVARIA, ISABELLA
HEART OF A SIREN (1925, Silent, First National)—**Barbara La Marr**, whose beauty Louis B. Mayer would remember when it was necessary to come up with a new name for Hedwig Keisler who became Hedy Lamarr, plays a woman who has a long list of rejected admirers. She develops an interest in Briton Conway Teale, who seems indifferent to her charms. Taking this as a challenge, she sets out to captivate him. By the time she succeeds, she must admit she's in love with him, also.

ECHO, PROFESSOR
THE UNHOLY THREE (1925, Silent, MGM); (1930, MGM)—The 1930 production is the only talkie ever made by star character actor **Lon Chaney, Sr.** He is a ventriloquist who teams with a dwarf and a strong man to carry out various crimes which lead to murder.

ECKLAND, WALTER
FATHER GOOSE (1964, Universal)—In WWII, beach bum **Cary Grant** is forced to manage a strategic watching station on a South Sea Island and look after teacher Leslie Caron and her seven female students.

ECKMAN, IRMA
DEADLIER THAN THE MALE (1967, GB, Universal)—In a Bulldog Drummond story modelled on a James Bond movie, **Elke Sommer** is one of the leaders of a group of female assassins.

ECTAY-O-WAHNEE
THE WHITE SQUAW (1956, Columbia)—**May Wynn** was Donna Lee Hickey until she took her character's name in THE CAINE MUTINY. Her modest film career wasn't helped much by this boring tale of a rancher resisting the government's plan to give his land back to the Indians.

ED
THE CARPENTER (1989, Canada, Capstone)—In a movie that doesn't make it clear which sequences are real and which imagined, **Wings Hauser** is a carpenter, who may be a ghost, who may have murdered a man who tried to rape Lynne Adams, who may have made love to Adams, who . . . .

EDDIE
EDDIE AND THE CRUISERS (1983, Aurora)—1960s rock star **Michael Pare** mysteriously disappears and is presumed dead, although his body has never been found. Years later, the missing tapes of his groups session will be valuable to whomever has them. In 1989 there was a sequel in which we learned Eddie's last name to be Wilson, but he is using the assumed name of Joe West. For more on this see, WILSON, EDDIE.

EDDIE
THE FIVE HEARTBEATS (1991, 20th Century Fox)—**Michael Wright**, the lead singer of a 60s rhythm and blues group, succumbs to drug abuse.

EDDIE
FOOL FOR LOVE (1985, Cannon)—**Sam Shepard** stars with Kim Basinger in his vague play about the self-destructive love of two people who can't seem to break the bond holding them together.

EDDIE
FOUR JACKS AND A JILL (1941, RKO)—**William Blees** is one of four struggling musicians who help Anne Shirley with her singing career.

EDDIE
THE PLEASURE LOVERS (1964, GB, Butchers)—American **Reed De Rouen** and three others pull off a bank robbery in England. They are forced to take Leigh Madison as a hostage. She causes trouble among the four. De Rouen becomes her protector as a sort of affection grows between the two even though De Rouen raped her.

EDDIE THE PLUMBER
THE HEAD OF THE FAMILY (1928, Silent, Gotham)—Plumber **William Russell** is put in charge of a horribly behaving family while the head of the house escapes to a spa. On his return he finds that Russell has straightened out his family.

EDEN, EMILY
A STRANGER AMONG US (1992, Hollywood Pictures)—Tough-talking, short-skirt-wearing, WASPy cop **Melanie Griffith** investigates a murder in New York's cloistered Hasidic community. She goes undercover by moving in with the Brooklyn group's rabbi, Lee Richardson, to search for the killer. She develops a yen for Hasidic Jew Eric Thal. She can't understand why he won't just jump into bed with her.

EDEN, MARTIN
THE ADVENTURES OF MARTIN EDEN (1942, Columbia)—**Glenn Ford** appears in this terribly routine tale of the hardships of life at sea for an aspiring writer, no doubt modeling on the story's author, Jack London. This one should have been buried at sea.

EDGAR, MARNIE
MARNIE (1964, Universal)—**Tippi Hedren's** stealing from her various employers is due to some hidden childhood trauma. Sean Connery marries the reluctant women and treats her frigidity with rape, before discovering what messed up her life so badly.

EDGEWARE, LORD
LORD EDGEWARE DIES (1934, GB, Realart/RKO)—Aging, wealthy aristocrat **C.V. France's** murder is solved by Agatha Christie's Inspector Hercule Poirot, played by Austin Trevor.

EDISON, THOMAS ALVA

EDISON THE MAN (1940, MGM); YOUNG TOM EDISON (1940, MGM)—**Spencer Tracy** and **Mickey Rooney** present us the life of the "Wizard of Menlo Park," both man and boy in two fairly interesting biopics, with the second being more fictional than the first.

EDITH *See* MARGARET

EDMONDS, KATHIE, PAT, NEIL & CONNIE

THOSE REDHEADS FROM SEATTLE (1953, Paramount)—**Rhonda Fleming, Teresa Brewer** and **Kay** and **Cynthia Bell** are all pretty carrot tops in a story which requires little more of them. Their mother, Agnes Moorehead, takes them with her to the Yukon during the gold rush. They're just what the prospectors have been missing.

EDNA

THE DOUGHGIRLS (1944, Warner Brothers)—**Ann Sheridan** is one of a group of men-hungry women living in a hotel for women in overcrowed WWII Washington. The risque humor of the play on which the film is based, is unfortunately toned down for the silver screen.

EDRI-AL-GADRIN

PIRATES OF TRIPOLI (1955, Columbia)—**Paul Henreid** rescues oriental princess Patricia Medina in this combination swashbuckler—Arabian Nights fantasy.

EDWARD, PRINCE OF WALES

THE PRINCE AND THE PAUPER (1915, Silent, Famous Players); (1937, Warner Brothers)—**Marguerite Clark** and **Bobby Mauch** portray the son of Henry VIII. The young prince exchanges places with a London street urchin, his exact double, putting both in danger of losing their lives at the hands of scoundrels, both high and low born.

EDWARDS, BING

BROTHER RAT (1938, Warner Brothers); BROTHER RAT AND A BABY (1940, Warner Brothers)—Seen after all the intervening years **Eddie Albert's** performance as the secretly married and father-to-be cadet at a military school is still the best thing in this brisk but badly dated comedy. The sequel finds Albert and his friends graduated, but not any brighter as they conspire to get Eddie a coaching job with their alma mater.

EDWARDS, BUSTER

BUSTER (1988, GB, Tri-Star)—Rock star **Phil Collins** portrays a small-time London crook in 1963. He calls himself "Lucky" because he's only spent two weeks in jail during his long career.

EDWARDS, ETHAN

THE SEARCHERS (1956, Warner Brothers)—**John Wayne** and half-breed Jeffrey Hunter search five years for Wayne's niece Natalie Wood, kidnapped when Indians slaughtered Wayne's brother's family, raping and mutilating Wood's older sister. When asked if he wants to give up the search, Wayne in characteristic fashion, grunts "That'll be the day." Hunter figures out that the Duke intends to kill the poor "spoiled" Wood when he finds her. Hunter is along to prevent the murder of his "sister." When Wayne does catch up with the Indians who have Wood, he dispatches them, but gently takes Natalie in his arms and carries her home. This John Ford directed classic might have been a western masterpiece if the director knew how to handle comedy relief characters and situations. Only delightful Hank Worden as a crazy old coot doesn't seem a caricature.

EDWARDS, HELENE

CANDIDATE FOR MURDER (1966, GB, Schoenfeld)—When **Erika Remberg's** husband Michael Gough believes her unfaithful, he imports German hit man Hans Borsody to kill her. The gunman decides she's innocent and won't fulfill the contract. Don't you just hate it when workmen don't do what their paid for.

EDWARDS, HOMER

HOMER (1970, Palomar/National General)—**Don Scardino** is a poor misunderstood sixties rock group leader. He opposes the Vietnam War, likes sex and dope and that's about the extent of what he stands for. The sound track featuring various rock groups is the best part of this loser.

EFFINGHAM, COL.

COLONEL EFFINGHAM'S RAID (1945, 20th Century Fox)—When his town's most famous landmark is threatened with destruction, retired Colonel **Charles Coburn** dons his uniform once more and leads the charge against the would-be violaters of history.

EHRENGARD, HANS

THE PROFESSIONALS (1966, Columbia)—**Robert Ryan's** concern for horses (greater than his concern for human life in this violent western) almost gets him and his three companions killed before they can get started in rescuing Ralph Bellamy's wife, kidnapped by a Mexican bandit-revolutionary.

EHRLICH, DR. PAUL

DR. EHRLICH'S MAGIC BULLET (1940, Warner Brothers)—**Edward G. Robinson** is excellent in this absorbing and well-done biopic of the German scientist who developed a cure for venereal disease. It's amazing the film was made, considering the subject and the time.

EICHMANN, ADOLF

OPERATION EICHMANN (1961, Allied Artists)—**Werner Klemeper,** Colonel Klink on TV's Hogan's Hero, is a far different kind of Nazi in this portrayal of a man who managed the extermination of six million Jews during WWII.

EILEEN

THE BACHELOR'S DAUGHTERS (1946, UA)—**Gail Russell** is one of four salesgirls who persuade floorwalker Adolphe Menjou to act as their father so they can snare rich husbands.

EILEEN

HER FIVE-FOOT HIGHNESS (1920, Silent, Universal)—**Edith Roberts** is forced to expose a chorus girl posing as her to claim her rightful inheritance to an English title. However, she gives it up and since it's leap year proposes to her shy cowboy sweetheart, and returns to the American west.

EINAR

THE VIKINGS (1958, UA)—**Kirk Douglas** is a brutal viking chieftan, who finds he can't bring himself to kill his half-brother Tony Curtis when the Vikings invade England and Curtis stands between him and the princess, Janet Leigh, whom they both want. Before Douglas discovered that Curtis was the result of a one-night rape between his father and an English noblewoman, he had acted so cruelly and uncaring about human life, that one finds it hard to believe he'd have any trouble slaughtering any number of relatives.

EINSTEIN, ALBERT

YOUNG EINSTEIN (1989, Australia, Warner Brothers)—We've been told that this farce starring writer-director **Yahoo Serious** as Albert

313

Einstein was a huge hit Down Under. We guess something got lost in the translation.

EINSTEIN, MARCOVITCH
THE TAILOR OF BOND STREET (1916, GB, Silent, Gerrard)—**Augustus Yorke** is a Jew who denies his background, changes his name and ignores his father in order to become a success. He is reconciled with his father as the latter lays dying.

EISMAN (ESMOND), GUS
GENTLEMEN PREFER BLONDES (1928, Silent, Paramount) (1953, 20th Century Fox)—First **Ford Sterling** and then **Tommy Noonan** portrayed the poor sap whose wealthy daddy doesn't approve of his relationship with gold digger Loreli Lee. How she behaves on an ocean voyage to France without him will determine their future together.

EL GRECO
EL GRECO (1966, 20th Century Fox)—**Mel Ferrer** portrays the painter from Crete who became famous in Spain and barely escaped being burned at the stake during the Inquisition.

EL PASO KID
THE MAN FROM TEXAS (1948, Eagle-Lion)—Bank robber **James Craig** proves he's not all bad by helping a poor widow.

EL TIGRE
THE FIGHTING BOOB (1926, Silent, R-C/FBO)—**Bob Custer** takes the place of a gassed army buddy and helps a rancher fight a gang trying to steal his land.

ELAINE
BAIL JUMPER (1990, Angelika)—A series of natural disasters, including several tornados, an earthquake, a meteorite crash, an invasion by grasshoppers, a tidal wave and a total eclipse of the sun, helps bail jumper **Eszter Balint** and her petty thief boyfriend B.J. Spalding stay one step ahead of the law.

ELAINE
TIMBER QUEEN (1944, Paramount)—Widow **Mary Beth Hughes** is aided by one of her husband's war buddies, Richard Arlen, in fighting the crooks trying to put her sawmill out of business.

ELCOT, PENELOPE
PENELOPE (1966, MGM)—**Natalie Wood** disguises herself as a little old lady and robs her husband's company in an attempt to get his attention. She confesses her crime to loony psychiatrist Dick Shawn who's in love with her. He tries to help her replace the stolen money. T'aint funny.

ELDER, JOHN, TOM, BUD & MATT
THE SONS OF KATE ELDER (1965, Paramount)—**John Wayne, Dean Martin, Michael Anderson, Jr.** and **Earl Holliman** are four brothers out to find the rascals who killed their father and swindled their mother. Only the eldest and the youngest survive the gun-play.

ELEANOR
NIGHT CLUB GIRL (1944, Universal)—**Vivian Austin** and her brother take their act to Hollywood, where they are given an audition at a nightclub. In this musical comedy, neither the music nor the comedy is much.

ELENA
THE TEMPTRESS (1926, Silent, MGM)—Immoral **Greta Garbo** drives men to ruin, disgrace, murder and suicide. Although this second American film of Garbo is no great shakes, it established her as a star.

ELENA
THE THREE SISTERS (1930, Fox)—**June Collyer** is one of three sisters who have moved to America from Italy. They learn that the money they had been sending to their mother in the old country has been going to a third party. They go back home and straighten out the problem.

ELENI
ELENI (1985, Warner Brothers)—Greek mother **Kate Nelligan** gives her life to save her children from the communist factions in her village.

ELGIN, GEORGIE
THE COUNTRY GIRL (1954, Paramount)—**Grace Kelly** won an Oscar for her sensitive portrayal of the wife of alcoholic has-been Bing Crosby, trying a show business comeback through the efforts of producer William Holden. Kelly and Holden's constant bickering leads to other more tender feelings.

ELI
ACE ELI AND RODGER OF THE SKY (1973, 20th Century Fox)—**Cliff Robertson**, a barnstorming former WWI pilot, gives flying shows in Kansas with his young son in tow. The boy's presence doesn't effect Robertson's luck with early day groupies.

ELIAS, SGT.
PLATOON (1987, Orion)—**Willem Dafoe** is the sensitive Vietnam sergeant whose confrontation with a murdering sergeant played by Tom Berenger leads to his own death.

ELINOR
MARRY THE GIRL (1928, Silent, Sterling)—**Barbara Bedford** is passed off as the widow of a millionaire's son by the old man's crooked servants. The problem is the son's not dead and on his return foils the plot but falls in love with his "wife."

ELINOR
THE RELUCTANT WIDOW (1951, GB, Fine Arts)—Governess **Jean Kent** marries a British Lord who soon thereafter goes to his maker, leaving her his vast estate. Kent discovers some of the people working for her are spies for Napoleon, searching for some papers which detail Wellington's plans. She finds them first and delivers them where they belong.

ELIZA
DANGEROUS TO MEN (1920, Silent, Metro)—When her father dies **Viola Dana** is removed from boarding school and sent to live with a guardian. She imagines the latter will be some old man so she dresses as a tomboy, hoping she will be sent back to school. To her delight, her guardian is handsome young bachelor Milton Sills with whom she immediately falls in love. He of course treats her as a child—until he learns better.

ELIZA
ELIZA'S HOROSCOPE (1975, Canada, O-Zali)—**Elizabeth Moorman** is told by a fortune teller that she will marry a rich man. She decides she had better help fate along.

ELIZABETH
FIRST A GIRL (1935, GB, Gaumont)—Lovely **Jessie Matthews** gets a job impersonating a female impersonator who has a case of

laryngitis. She's a smash and tours Europe, masquerading as a male entertainer in drag. The story was used in 1982 in VICTOR/ VICTORIA, starring Julie Andrews.

ELIZABETH

FRANKENHOOKER (1990, Glickenhaus)—There is little left of **Patty Mullen** after a run-in with a remote-control lawn mower, but her boyfriend James Lorinz has an idea. He offers high-powered crack to a room filled with Times Square streetwalkers. When they literally explode, he collects the various parts he needs to reconstruct Mullen. There's one little problem, though: the new Mullen wants to turn tricks. Her clients suffer a variety of gruesome, gory deaths.

ELIZABETH

WOMAN'S WORLD (1954, 20th Century Fox)—When Clifton Webb calls three men and their wives to New York so he may choose which will be his company's new general manager, intelligent and strong-willed **Lauren Bacall** hopes her hard-working hubby, Fred MacMurray, will be passed over, because she feels the total commitment he will have to make to the job will jeopardize their marriage.

ELIZABETH I, QUEEN

QUEEN ELIZABETH (1912, Silent, Famous Players); THE PRIVATE LIFE OF ELIZABETH AND ESSEX (1939, Warner Brothers); YOUNG BESS (1953, MGM); THE VIRGIN QUEEN (1955, 20th Century Fox)—**Sarah Bernhardt, Bette Davis** and **Jean Simmons** each portrayed the great British Queen, daughter of Henry VIII and Anne Boleyn. Davis did it twice in 1939 and 1955. Each movie concentrated on one of her supposed romances, the first with Lord Essex whom she had beheaded and the second with Sir Walter Raleigh, who much later would also lose his head. Simmons plays the queen-to-be before she advances to the throne.

ELKINS, ALFIE

ALFIE (1966, GB, Paramount); ALFIE DARLING (1975, GB, Signal/ EMI)—Amoral **Michael Caine** beds anything in skirts, even if he's only modestly attracted to the woman. He's unable to develop any feeling for his conquests and always acts in a completely selfish manner. Audiences in the amoral 1960s ate it up, being strangely drawn to the Cockney anti-hero. By 1975, few cared to follow the sexual dalliances of lorry driver **Alan Price**, who meets a girl who is his female counterpart in the "find them, feel them, f..k them, forget them" school of romance.

ELKINS, NICKIE

I'D GIVE MY LIFE (1936, Paramount)—Delinquent **Tom Brown** won't allow his convict father Robert Gleckler to ruin governor Guy Standing by revealing that Brown is the illegitimate son of Standing's wife Janet Beecher.

ELLEN

TWO (1975, Colmar)—**Sarah Venable** is kidnapped by Vietnam vet Douglas Travis, who has escaped from an army hospital. He takes her to a remote cabin in the mountains. He agrees to release her if she will spend two days with her. What choice does she have?

ELLIE

ELLIE (1984, Film Ventures)—**Sheila Kennedy** is the voluptuous daughter of Shelley Winter's most recently deceased husband. Seems Winters marries elderly men and then with the help of her three lunatic sons makes sure they have a fatal accident. Kennedy proves she can also cause accidents.

ELLIE

JAZZ BABIES (1932, Peerless)—**Marjorie Gateson**, Madge Evans and Elizabeth Patterson work in a naughty nightclub. To prevent a bluenose from closing the club, they put on a production of "A Midsummer's Night Dream." Gateson kidnaps a girl who plans to upset their plans, using a hearse to whisk her away.

ELLIE

SUNBURN (1979, Paramount)—Model **Farah Fawcett (-Majors)** is hired to investigate cases of murder, suicide and blackmail. Why hire a model? Well, we guess because she looks good and needs the work.

ELLIOT

GHOST DAD (1990, Universal)—**Bill Cosby** should restrict his activities to television and commercials, where he shines. In this silly ghost story, Cosby is dead, but just refuses to leave his earthly existence. Patrick Swayze he ain't.

ELLIOT, MARGARET

THE STAR (1953, 20th Century Fox)—One-time Oscar winner **Bette Davis** has fallen on hard times and finds all the people who were there with their hand out when she was on top, don't want to know her now. Then former actor Sterling Hayden who has loved her for years gets up the courage to let her know how he feels.

ELLIOTT, KAY

THE NAUGHTY FLIRT (1931, Warner Brothers)—Heiress **Alice White** is a selfish pain, who breaks up with her fiance Paul Page when he tells her off. She takes up with stock market loser Douglas Gilmore, who's only interested in her money. At the altar, White finally realizes that she really loves Page.

ELLIOTT, LIZA

LADY IN THE DARK (1944, Paramount)—Successful fashion magazine editor **Ginger Rogers** is torn between three men, which causes her to have some wild fantasy dreams which she relates to her shrink. The film was Rogers first appearance in a color movie. It tries to be too many things, but still is enjoyable.

ELLIOTT, LOUISE, HELEN & GRACE

THE SISTERS (1938, Warner Brothers)—**Bette Davis, Anita Louise** and **Jane Bryan** are sisters whose turn-of-the-century romances and marriages are explored in a film where the performances are better than the story and production.

ELLIOTT, DR. ROBERT

DRESSED TO KILL (1980, Filmways)—Suave, schizoid psychiatrist **Michael Caine** treats wealthy women with oversexed egos. Dressed in drag, he's his own most disturbed patient, the razor-wielding killer of Angie Dickinson.

ELLIOTT, SALLY

THE FULLER BRUSH GIRL (1950, Columbia)—Door-to-door saleswoman **Lucille Ball** gets involved in a murder, forcing her to flee from the cops with her boyfriend Eddie Albert.

ELLIOTT, SALLY

MY GAL SAL (1942, 20th Century Fox)—Turn-of-the-century Broadway star **Rita Hayworth** inspires song writer Paul Dresser, played by Victor Mature.

ELLIOTT, SANDY

THE BIG SHOW-OFF (1945, Republic)—**Arthur Lake** did play roles other than Dagwood Bumstead. Here he's a honky-tonk piano player, humbled in a wrestling match when he pretends to be a famous grappler to impress a girl.

ELLIOTT, SCOTT
THE MAGNIFICENT SEVEN RIDE (1972, UA)—**Ed Lauter**, a tough convict teams up with gunslinger Chris, this time played by Lee Van Cleef, and five others to once more journey south of the border to rout Mexican bandits who have captured some widows.

ELLIOTT, WILD BILL
CALLING WILD BILL ELLIOTT (1943, Republic)—With the help of Gabby Hayes, cowboy star **Bill Elliott** puts away a crooked governor.

ELLIS
LOOSE CANNONS (1990, Tri-Star)—In this loser, sick cop **Dan Aykroyd** lapses into multiple personalities. Some are funny, but this derivative comedy-adventure-cop-buddy film is a failure in each genre.

ELLIS, DON
ALL OF ME (1934, Paramount)—The love life of engineering professor **Fredric March** and his wealthy student-mistress Miriam Hopkins is enhanced by the example of thief George Raft and his pregnant girlfriend Helen Mack, who commit suicide rather than be separated. It's a strange film.

ELLIS, JOAN ARLIN
BEWITCHED (1945, MGM)—On the eve of the execution of schizophrenic killer **Phyllis Thaxter**, psychiatrist Edmund Gwenn discovers another personality possessing her who is the real murderer.

ELLIS, MAE
THE TIME, THE PLACE AND THE GIRL (1929, Warner Brothers)—**Gertrude Olmstead** saves Grant Withers from being the fall guy in his boss's plan to have the good-looking Withers sell worthless bonds to flirtatious females.

ELLIS, MARY ELLEN
THE INNOCENT SINNER (1917, Silent, Fox)—**Miriam Cooper** is a virtuous country girl, seduced by a city cad.

ELLIS, NURSE
YOUNG NURSES IN LOVE (1989, Platinum)—This unofficial sequel to YOUNG DOCTORS IN LOVE stars **Jeanne Marie** as a Soviet agent posing as an American nurse. She infiltrates a hospital in order to break into its world famous sperm bank, which stores the frozen issue of the likes of Einstein and FDR.

ELLIS, RUTH
DANCE WITH A STRANGER (1985, GB, Goldwyn)—**Miranda Richardson** portrays the last woman to be executed in Britain. She falls in love with a ne'er-do-well by whom she becomes pregnant. She kills him because of his physical and emotional abuse.

ELLISON, BRAD
THE LAST OF THE FAST GUNS (1958, Universal)—Gunslinger **Jock Mahoney** is hired to find Eduard Franz who disappeared into Mexico years earlier.

ELLMAN, JOHN
THE WALKING DEAD (1936, Warner Brothers)—Former convict **Boris Karloff** is framed for the murder of the judge who sent him to prison. He's executed for the crime but his innocence is established

30 seconds thereafter. A scientist revives Karloff but he appears more zombie than alive. He scares to death those responsible for his execution, all save two who run their car into a power line and are electrocuted after killing Karloff a second time.

ELMER
ALL-AMERICAN CHUMP (1936, MGM)—Country boy **Stuart Erwin** proves to be a mathematical genius, exploited by gangsters. You couldn't get a giggle out of this movie if the theater was filled with laughing gas.

ELMER
ELMER THE GREAT (1933, Warner Brothers/First National)—Baseball star **Joe E. Brown** foils crooked gamblers as he leads the Cubs to a World Series victory over the Yankees. As a life-time Cub fan, the male half of your author team appreciates this fantasy.

ELMER
FIREMAN, SAVE MY CHILD (1927, Silent, Paramount)—**Wallace Beery** and his partner Raymond Hatton are fireman who provide plenty of slapstick humor in this entertaining comedy.

ELMER
SPITE MARRIAGE (1929, Silent, MGM)—In his last silent film, **Buster Keaton** falls in love with stage actress Dorothy Sebastian, who marries him out of spite when she's jilted by her leading man. Before the film is over, Sebastian will discover she married the right man.

ELRIDGE
THE VICTORS (1963, Columbia)—**Michael Callan** is one of the foot-soldiers whose war-time experiences are detailed in Carl Foreman's powerful anti-war film. Foreman's message comes through strongly despite the fact the studio cut it extensively to give it stronger box-office appeal.

ELSA
A WOMAN OF EXPERIENCE (1931, RKO)—Shady lady **Helen Twelvetrees** is recruited by Austrian Intelligence to seduce Lew Cody, suspected of being a German spy. She does so even though she is in love with a young naval officer.

ELSIE
THE LADY OF SCANDAL (1930, MGM)—Stage star **Ruth Chatterton** has a brief affair with her fiance Ralph Forbes' cousin Basil Rathbone before leaving both men and returning to her career.

ELVIRA
ELVIRA: MISTRESS OF THE DARK (1988, New World)—**Cassandra Peterson** is the busty hostess of various TV horror shows shown around the country. She jokes about the lousy movies and her protruding mammary glands. Things are pretty much the same in her film debut.

EMANON
EMANON (1987, Paul Entertainers)—Wino **Stuart Paul**, who helps the downtrodden, is christened Emanon, no-name spelled backwards, by a wealthy fatherless boy. Could this be Christ come back to earth? He does suffer a kind of crucifixion and sparks an argument among religions as to whose God he is.

EMERALD, MIKE
THE SHADOW OF MIKE EMERALD (1935, GB, Radio Pictures)—**Leslie Perrins** has ruined a group of fanciers and they want to take revenge.

EMIL

EMIL AND THE DETECTIVES (1964, Buena Vista)—When young **Bryan Russell** is robbed by pickpocket Heinz Schubert, while travelling by train to visit his grandmother in Berlin, Russell enlists the aid of a group of kids to help him catch the culprit. This is the sixth movie version of Erich Kastner's novel.

EMILY

CHU CHU AND THE PHILLY FLASH (1981, 20th Century Fox)—**Carole Burnett** is a failed entertainer reduced to picking up pennies as a one-person street band. She teams up with a drunken ex-pitcher, Alan Arkin, when they both spot a briefcase in the street which proves a break for both.

EMILY

EMILY (1976, GB, Emily)—**Koo Stark**, perhaps best remembered as the soft-porn star who was England's "Randy Andy's" companion for a time, removes her clothes at every opportunity in this film about her sexual coming of age in a 1928 finishing school.

EMILY

REMEMBER MY NAME (1978, Columbia)—**Geraldine Chaplin**, the ex-wife of Anthony Perkins, who is now married to Berry Berenson, is out of prison after serving a term for murder. Chaplin tries to win Perkins back and eliminate Berenson.

EMILY

THAT OTHER WOMAN (1942, 20th Century Fox)—**Virginia Gilmore** will stop at nothing to win the love of her boss James Ellison, but none of her efforts make for an entertaining movie.

EMIR

THE DESPOILER (1915, Silent, Triangle)—**Frank Keenan** has his way with a colonel's daughter Enid Markey, when she courageously agrees to give herself to him in order to spare other women from mass rape by Keenan's men. She takes revenge on Keenan, killing him with his own revolver. The colonel has the killer of his second in command brought to him and kills her with his pistol before lifting her veil and seeing she's his daughter.

EMMA MAE

EMMA MAE (1976, Pro-International)—Poor naive country black girl **Jerri Hayes** moves to the city and falls in love with a gang leader who robs and abandons her. By the end of the movie, she's a tough independent street girl.

EMMANNUELLE

CARRY ON EMMANNUELLE (1978, GB, Hemdale)—In a parody of the soft-porn Emmannuelle series, **Suzanee Danielle**, the wife of a French Ambassador, sleeps with just about everyone in London.

EMMANUEL, MR.

MR. EMMANUEL (1945, GB, Ealing)—In 1936, elderly Jew **Felix Aylmer** goes to Germany in search of the mother of an orphan boy and is imprisoned and tortured by the Gestapo.

EMERSON, DR.

A MODERN MONTE CRISTO (1917, Silent, Thanhouser)—**Vincent Serrano**, ruined by Thomas A. Curran, disappears for years and upon his return is fabulously wealthy. He is now ready to have his revenge.

EMONY

MANNEQUIN (1987, 20th Century Fox)—Department store mannequin **Kim Cattrall** comes to life and helps window designer Andrew McCarthy come up with some winning ideas. She comes to life but the movie never does.

EMORY, BILL & WILLIAM

FATHER'S SON (1931, Warner Brothers); (1941, Warner Brothers)—**Leon Janney** and **Lewis Stone**; **Billy Dawson** and **John Litel** are Booth Tarkington's troublesome boy and his long-suffering father in typically weak family stories from Warner Brothers.

ENDERS, ELGAR

THE LANDLORD (1970, UA)—**Beau Bridges**, a rich young white man, buys a tenement in Brooklyn where he learns to live with his militant and angry black neighbors. It's a devastatingly funny satire.

ENDICOTT, CARVER

AN AMATEUR DEVIL (1921, Silent, Paramount)—Rich bore **Bryant Washburn** is given the choice of getting with it or getting out by his girlfriend who wants a more regular fellow.

ENDON, RUPERT

PRINCE OF DIAMONDS (1930, Columbia)—Diamond merchant **Ian Keith** falls in love with Aileen Pringle, a girl with expensive tastes.

ENGLISH, ROSAMUND

ROSE OF THE WORLD (1918, Silent, Artcraft)—**Elsie Ferguson's** husband is reported killed in India. She marries the governor of the province and returns with him to England. While rereading her first husbands letters, she realizes how much she still loves him. She asks her Indian maid to pray to the eastern gods to bring her husband's spirit to her. They do better than that. Husband number one shows up, having survived the battle.

ENGSTROM, DUTCH

THE WILD BUNCH (1969, Warner Brothers)—**Ernest Borgnine** is William Holden's number two man in a group of aging outlaws, pursued by a posse, led by former colleague Robert Ryan. They ride into Mexico where they become involved with a violent revolutionary general.

ENID

ENID IS SLEEPING (1990, Vestron)—In a macabre comedy, Elizabeth Perkins accidently kills her sister **Maureen Mueller** when she finds her sibling in bed with Perkins' husband Judge Reinhold. The rest of the film deals with attempts to get rid of Mueller's body.

ENRIGHT, IRA

TOO YOUNG TO KNOW (1945, Warner Brothers)—Teenagers **Robert Hutton** and Joan Leslie marry before he goes off to battle. After three years fighting the Japanese he learns that his wife has left him and given away their son, whom he didn't even know they had. He gets a chance to go home and straighten things out.

EOJ

GALACTIC GIGOLO (1988, Urban Classics)—**Carmine Capobianco** portrays a piece of broccoli from the planet Crowak, all of whose inhabitants are vegetables. He wins a TV game show contest. His prize is a two-week trip to the planet Earth, staying in Prospect, Connecticut, home of the horniest humans in the world. He arrives looking like Elvis Presley and has great luck with Prospect females with lines such as: "Hi, I'm Eoj from the planet Crowak, and I'm here to partake in sexual relations with Earth women."

ERAS

PREHISTORIC WOMEN (1950, Eagle-Lion)—**Judy Landors** is one of a clan of leopard-skinned dressed women who capture men to ensure the continuation of their race. Wonder what happened to their fathers and brothers?

ERIC

THE BOY WHO COULD FLY (1986, Lorimar)—After the death of his parents in a plane crash, **Jay Underwood** becomes autistic and develops the ability to fly.

ERIC

STRIPPED TO KILL (1987, Concorde)—**Pia Kamakaki** poses as a female stripper and murders other strippers. He is "exposed" by undercover police officer Kay Lenz who has joined the bump and grind corps.

ERIC & ERNIE

THE MAGNIFICENT TWO (1967, GB, Rank)—**Eric Morecombe** and **Ernie Wise** are two zany British salesmen in South America at the time of a revolution.

ERICA

AN UNMARRIED WOMAN (1978, 20th Century Fox)—When her husband of many years leaves her for a younger woman, **Jill Clayburgh** learns the rules of courtship have changed since she was last single, but they are not easier to deal with. She meets some real creeps who wish to use her; uses one creep for her own sexual needs; and finds romance with a married artist, Alan Bates.

ERICKSON, ERIC

THE COUNTERFEIT TRAITOR (1962, Paramount)—**William Holden**, an oil importer born in the U.S. but now a naturalized Swede, is recruited by the British to spy for them during his numerous trips to Nazi Germany. The exciting espionage picture drags at times.

ERICKSON, LIZ

TAKE CARE OF MY LITTLE GIRL (1951, 20th Century Fox)—**Jeanne Crain** desperately wishes to be accepted by her mother's prestigious college sorority until she learns what a phony elitist system it really is.

ERIK

ERIK THE VIKING (1989, Orion)—Viking **Tim Robbins** is tired of raping and pillaging. Looking for a way to bring peace to his world, he's put on a quest to find the Horn of Resounding.

ERROLL, CEDRIC

LITTLE LORD FAUNTLEROY (1914, GB, Silent, Kinemato-graph); (1921, Silent, UA); (1936, UA)—**Gerald Resptor, Mary Pickford** and **Freddie Bartholomew** each portray the prissy Brooklyn boy who is an heir to a British fortune. He must go to England and win over his grandfather who hates all things American. The lad's relationship with his mother, whom he calls "dearest," seems unnatural and has been known to turn stomachs.

ESCOBAR, RAMON

THE CALIFORNIAN (1937, 20th Century Fox)—Happy-go-lucky Latin bandit **Ricardo Cortez** sides with the poor California peons who are losing their land to rich land-grabbers.

ESKIMO NELL

THE TRUE STORY OF ESKIMO NELL (1975, Australia, Quest/ Filmways)—**Victoria Anoux** is the Alaskan love of Max Gillies, a peeping tom who calls himself Dead-Eye-Dick. He and Serge Lazareff, called Mexico Pete, have some delightfully fun adventures on their way to see Anoux.

ESMERELDA

THE DARLING OF PARIS (1917, Silent, Fox)—**Theda Bara** stars as the gypsy girl in this version of Victor Hugo's "The Hunchback of Notre Dame."

ESMERELDA

JUST A GIRL (1916, Silent, GB, Samuelson)—**Daisy Burrell** is an Australian heiress who rejects an impoverished lord to marry a miner (no, not a minor).

ESMERELDA

SHE GETS HER MAN (1935, Universal)—Dumb waitress **Zasu Pitts** is made a national heroine by a press agent when she accidentally prevents a bank robbery.

ESSEX, WILLIAM & OLIVER

MY SON, MY SON! (1940, UA)—Newly rich **Brian Aherne** spoils his son **Scotty Beckett** who grows into rotter **Louis Hayward**, a totally ungrateful man.

ESSINGTON, MABEL

UP IN MABEL'S ROOM (1944, UA)—Newlywed Dennis O'Keefe innocently gets mixed up with **Gail Patrick**, the fiancee of his business partner, and new wife Marjorie Reynolds doesn't understand.

ESTHER

ESTHER AND THE KING (1960, 20th Century Fox)—Jewish **Joan Collins** marries Persian king Richard Egan in order to get him to cease his oppression of her people.

EULICE

THREE IN THE ATTIC (1968, American International)—Swinging black hippie **Judy Pace**, along with campus cuties Yvette Mimieux and Maggie Thrett, hold college Casanova Christopher Jones prisoner in an attic where he's forced to make love to them until he agrees to remain faithful to one. It's a harsh punishment and not for the squeamish.

EUPHEMIA, SISTER (BRIAN HOPE)

NUNS ON THE RUN (1990, GB, 20th Century Fox)—Monty Python alumnus **Eric Idle** and Robbie Coltrane are minor British crooks. In an attempt to escape their life and mobster colleagues, they don the habits of nuns and take refuge in a convent school for girls. Also at the school is Camille Coduri, a woman Idle has fallen in love with. It works!

EVA

THE BRIDE (1985, Columbia)—Frankenstein, played by rock star Sting, finally gets things right when he produces **Jennifer Beals** as a prospective bride for his gross, dim-witted monster.

EVA

THAT KIND OF GIRL (1963, GB, Topaz-IA)—Infected Austrian tart **Margaret-Rose Keil** spreads venereal disease through a British community.

EVANGELINE

EVANGELINE (1929, UA)—**Dolores Del Rio**, who once claimed she would never make a talking picture, isn't required to say anything in this production based on Henry Wadsworth Longfellow's poem about exiled Arcadians settling in the Louisiana bayous.

EVANS

EDUCATED EVANS (1936, GB, Warner Brothers/First National)—**Max Miller**, in his usual role as a comical race track tout, becomes wealthy betting on the wrong horse.

EVANS

THANK EVANS (1938, GB, Warner Brothers)—Race track tout **Max Miller** helps a down-on-his-luck lord being fleeced by a crooked trainer.

EVANS, ANGIE

SMASH UP, THE STORY OF A WOMAN (1947, Universal)—**Susan Hayward**, a famous nightclub singer, becomes an alcoholic after her husband Lee Bowman, a struggling composer, makes it big and has little time for her.

EVANS, ARTHUR

THREE HUSBANDS (1950, UA)—**Shepperd Strudwick** is one of three men who receive letters from a recently deceased bachelor, claiming to have had affairs with their wives. It's the male side of A LETTER TO THREE WIVES.

EVANS, DORIS

JUNGLE BRIDE (1953, Monogram)—**Anita Page** and Charles Starrett are free to marry after being cleared of the charge of murder when Page's brother is proven to be the guilty party. The action mostly takes place in a jungle after the ship on which Page and Starrett are travelling is wrecked—that's how Monogram comes up with the title.

EVANS, DOROTHY

MISS CRUSOE (1919, Silent, World)—**Virginia Hammond** and her friend are vacationing on an island in Chesapeake Bay, where they encounter Rod La Rocque whom they believe to be an escaped convict but who is really a famous detective who wins Miss Hammond.

EVANS, JOEY

PAL JOEY (1957, Columbia)—Heel **Frank Sinatra** has a way with the ladies. He's a brash entertainer in a cheap San Francisco joint who cons his way into being a kept man of rich Rita Hayworth, a one-time stripper. She's buying him a club all his own as long as he's good, but with Kim Novak around, he blows his chance. The Rodgers and Hart songs are great and "Ole Blue Eyes" is in good voice.

EVANS, JOHN

THE MAN WHO LOST HIMSELF (1941, Universal)—Planter **Brian Aherne** assumes the identity of a drunken millionaire who has been killed.

EVANS, JOHNNY

JOHNNY STOOL PIDGEON (1949, Universal)—Treasury agent Howard Duff springs con **Dan Duryea** from prison so he can help track down a narcotics gang.

EVANS, KAY

THE POWERS GIRL (1942, UA)—Model **Carole Landis** is one-third of a triangle which includes her sister, Anne Shirley, and camera-man George Murphy.

EVANS, MARGE

UNDER EIGHTEEN (1932, Warner Brothers)—**Marian March** is saved from the clutches of a lecherous theatrical producer by grocery clerk Regis Toomey.

EVANS, QUIRT

ANGEL AND THE BADMAN (1947, Republic)—Gunfighter **John Wayne** hides out with the Quakers and is reformed by the love of pacifist Gail Russell. The latter's love affair with Wayne in real life contributed to her problems with alcohol, leading to an early death.

EVANS, TOM

SPECIAL INSPECTOR (1939, Syndicate)—Treasury agent **Charles Quigley** is out to stop a gang of murdering fur truck hijackers.

EVE

EVE (1968, GB, Commonwealth)—**Celeste Yarnale** saves American pilot Robert Walker Jr. when he crashes his plane in the Amazon jungles. She's worshipped as a goddess by the local natives. Her meeting with Walker causes her nothing but trouble.

EVE *See* EVIE SIMMS

EVE

IN TROUBLE WITH EVE (1964, GB, Mancunian)—**Sally Smith** and the local police inspector create scandal in a small British town when he's caught with her and his pants are down.

EVE

INDISCRETIONS OF EVE (1932, GB, British International)—**Steffi Duna**, a model in a mannequin shop, is pursued by a wealthy aristocrat Fred Conyngham, until she catches him.

EVE

LADIES MUST DRESS (1927, Silent, Fox)—Stenographer **Virginia Valli** wins her fellow when she takes her friend's advice and dresses with more pizzazz. "Why Miss Valli—you're beautiful without your glasses."

EVE *See* JEAN HARRINGTON

EVE

MOVING TARGETS (1987, Australia, Academy)—**Carmen Duncan** is a former German terrorist, living in Sydney, Australia with her daughter. She has a bank account filled with loot from various robberies. An IRA killer and ex-lover arrives, wanting some of the money to help him elude a hit man hired by his former colleagues for blowing an assignment. The rest of the movie is one big chase.

EVE

THE THREE FACES OF EVE (1957, 20th Century Fox)—**Joanne Woodward** won an Academy Award for her stunning performance as a woman with three distinct personalities, each fighting to be dominant. Woodward gives three different performances, each outstanding.

EVELYN

LOVING COUPLES (1980, 20th Century Fox)—**Shirley MacLaine** and her doctor husband James Coburn each take younger lovers: she, hunk Stephen Collins, and he, sexy sweet Susan Sarandon. The youngsters prove too much for MacLaine and Coburn who decide each other is just about their speed.

EVERARD, NAN

HER OWN FREE WILL (1924, Silent, Eastern Productions)—**Helene Chadwick** marries a wealthy admirer, rather than her true love to help her impoverished father.

EVERS, GORDON

IF I WERE FREE (1933, RKO)—Attorney **Clive Brook** and antique dealer Irene Dunne both are in failing marriages. They meet by chance and fall in love. His wife has no intention of giving him a divorce and her missing husband returns looking to try again. Can these marriages be dissolved?

EYRE, GULIAN

I WANT MY MAN (1925, Silent, First National)—American soldier **Milton Sills**, blinded in WWI, marries nurse Doris Kenyon and remains in France at the end of the hostilities. Later his sight is restored by an operation, only to find Kenyon has left him to get a divorce, because she feels he only needed her when he could not see. Both will see the light.

EYRE, JANE

JANE EYRE (1921, Silent, Hodkinson); (1935, Monogram); (1944, 20th Century Fox); (1971, GB, British Lion)—**Mabel Ballin, Virginia Bruce; Joan Fontaine** and **Susannah York** each have appeared as Charlotte Bronte's heroine who takes a job as governess with brooding Edward Rochester with whom she falls in love. Their wedding is interrupted by a man announcing that Rochester has a living mad wife whom he keeps locked up in the manor. Apparently not securely, because after Jane runs away, the demented one gets loose and burns down the mansion, blinding Rochester and killing herself. The good news is that he's now free to marry Jane. **Jean Darling, Peggy Ann Garner** and **Sarah Gibson** appeared as the young orphan Jane in the three sound productions.

F

FABIAN, CAPT.

ADVENTURES OF CAPTAIN FABIAN (1951, Republic)—Sea captain **Errol Flynn** falls in love with servant girl Micheline Presle, who uses Flynn to move into rich households. Flynn is blamed when a spineless dandy, Vincent Price, whom Presle marries, kills his uncle for money. It's sad to see Flynn's fortunes as an actor had fallen so far that he could get himself trapped in this stinker.

FABIAN, SUPT.

FABIAN OF THE YARD (1954, GB, Beauchamp/Eros)—**Bruce Seton** of Scotland Yard solves three cases: a murder by strangulation, a blackmail plot, and a bomb threat by IRA terrorists.

FABRINI, JOE AND PAUL

THEY DRIVE BY NIGHT (1940, Warner Brothers)—**George Raft** and **Humphrey Bogart** are truck driving brothers. Bogart is killed in an accident, and Raft gets mixed up in a murder when he turns his attention from Ann Sheridan to married Ida Lupino.

FACE, THE

THE FACE AT THE WINDOW (1939, GB, British Lion)—Deformed **Harry Terry** and his brother Tod Slaughter terrorize Paris as a cover for a planned bank robbery.

FAGAN, JOEY 'THE LIPS'

THE COMMITMENTS (1991, GB, 20th Century Fox)—**Johnny Murphy** plays the messianic 45-year-old trumpeter with the "Saviors of Soul" Dublin musical group. He claims to have toured with great American soul performers.

FAIRCHILD, HELEN

THE LONE WOLF'S DAUGHTER (1929, Columbia)—**Gertrude Olmstead** is Michael Lanyard's adopted American daughter. While visiting her, the Lone Wolf (played her by Bert Lytell) stops a jewel robbery and captures two men wanted by Scotland Yard.

FAIRCHILD, SABRINA

SABRINA (1954, Paramount)—**Audrey Hepburn**, the daughter of the chauffeur of a wealthy family, has always had a crush on the youngest son, playboy William Holden. She goes to study in Paris, and when she returns, all grown up, he's also interested, but she ends up with older brother Humphrey Bogart. The match just doesn't figure.

FAIRE, VANITY

VANITY (1935, Columbia)—Egotistical actress **Jane Cain** fakes her own death so she can enjoy the sorrow of her adoring fans.

FAIRFAX, COL.

KING OF THE TURF (1926, Silent, FBO)—Horse breeder **George Irving** is framed by his business partner. He's sent to prison, where he must serve his full term because his partner died before he could sign a confession exonerating Irving. When Irving gets out, he and some friends clear his name and win the coveted gold cup in a horse race as well.

FAIRLANE, FORD

THE ADVENTURES OF FORD FAIRLANE (1990, 20th Century Fox)—For those outraged by what passes for jokes from comedian **Andrew Dice Clay**, this is a movie on which they definitely should pass. It's Clay at his vulgar and obnoxious worst, with a private-eye story just thin enough to allow him to fling his verbal abuse in all directions.

FAIRLIE, SIR MICHAEL

THE CHEERFUL FRAUD (1927, Silent, Universal)—After being snubbed by Gertrude Olmstead, a social secretary to a prominent family, **Reginald Denny** poses as a servant in the home to be near her. Denny in turn is impersonated by an international thief, but after a series of comical mix-ups, Denny captures the thief and Olmstead.

FAIRWAYS, JIM

RACHEL AND THE STRANGER (1948, RKO)—Pioneer farmer William Holden treats bondswoman Loretta Young, whom he married to give his son a mother, like a slave, Then stranger **Robert Mitchum** arrives and arouses first Holden's jealousy and finally his love for Young.

FALCONE, GUIDO

MR. BILLION (1977, 20th Century Fox)—Italian auto mechanic **Terence Hill** has inherited his uncle's estate, but must take claim of it in San Francisco within 20 days, something that Jackie Gleason, the executor of the estate, hopes to prevent.

FALCONER, JIM

THE FORTUNATE FOOL (1933, GB, Associate British) -Ex-boxer **Hugh Wakefield** falls in love with impoverished Joan Wyndham. Wakefield's fiancee Elizabeth Jenns frames Wyndham for a crime, but writer Jack Raine sets things straight.

FALCONER, PAT

MEN WITH WINGS (1938, Paramount)—**Fred MacMurray** and Ray Milland are civil aviation pioneers who fall out over Louise Campbell. The love story gets in the way of the air spectacle.

FALLON, EVE

BIG BROWN EYES (1936, Paramount)—Wisecracking manicurist **Joan Bennett** and her cop boyfriend Cary Grant catch a jewel thief.

FALLON, FLORENCE "FAITH"

THE MIRACLE WOMAN (1931, Columbia)—Phony evangelist **Barbara Stanwyck** becomes an out-and-out con-artist and trickster in this splendid production, inspired by the life of 1920s evangelist Aimee Semple Macpherson.

FALLON, MARK

THE MISSISSIPPI GAMBLER (1953, Universal)—**Tyrone Power**, son of a New York fencing master, has nothing but trouble with a proud New Orleans family. The son, John Baier, hates him because Ty has gallantly refused to kill him in a duel. Daughter Piper Laurie despises Power because he's socially beneath her and she loves him. She finally gets her emotions squared away, leaving New Orleans with Power to start a new life. (Eight to five it won't last.)

FALLON, WEBB

THE VAMPIRE'S GHOST (1945, Republic)—**John Abbott** is a 400-year-old zombie-vampire who runs the underworld on the west coast of Africa. He must wander the earth forever because of a curse put on him in 1588. By the end of the film, he reluctantly finds his rest.

FANE, MADELINE AND MICHAEL

MISS FANE'S BABY IS STOLEN (1934, Paramount)—The kidnapping of the Lindbergh baby made this movie a natural. **Dorothy Wieck** is a famous movie star whose child **Baby Le Roy** is kidnapped from his lavish Beverly Hills home. Unlike the Lindbergh case, the movie has a happy ending.

FANG, DR. SIN

DR. SIN FANG (1937, GB, MGM)—**H. Agar Lyons** is an evil Chinese villain, who plans to steal a secret formula for curing cancer.

FANNY

FANNY (1961, Warner Brothers)—Young Marseilles girl, **Leslie Caron**, finds herself alone and pregnant when her lover Horst Buchholz runs off to sea. She accepts a marriage proposal from aged Maurice Chevalier, who is delighted to have a son. Later, Buchholz returns for Caron and his son, but she tells him that Chevalier has been a real father to the boy; and although she still loves Buchholz, she will not leave the man who has treated her so well.

FANSHAWE, NELL

THE HOME TOWN GIRL (1919, Silent, Paramount)—Small-town belle **Vivian Martin** has many suitors, but her weakness is for a soda fountain clerk, Ralph Graves, for whom she throws over the local banker's son. When Graves gets in with the wrong crowd, he goes to the city to make his fortune, misusing his employer's funds. Martin comes to his rescue.

FAR OUT MAN

FAR OUT MAN (1990, New Line)—**Tommy Chong** employs most of his family in this far-from-anything, headed-for-video romp. He is a burned-out hippie, searching for his ex-girlfriend and their son.

FARADAY, HELEN

BLONDE VENUS (1932, Paramount)—When German cafe singer **Marlene Dietrich** marries American research chemist Herbert Marshall, she retires to raise a family. When Marshall is exposed to radium and needs an expensive operation to save his life, she takes up with playboy Cary Grant to get the money. Marshall is not grateful and divorces her. She goes through a period of degradation as a prostitute before returning to her singing once more and becoming the rage of Paris. Grant arranges for a reconciliation for her with Marshall and her son.

FARBER, JACK

JACK O'HEARTS (1926, Silent, Hartford Productions)-Young minister **Cullen Landis** is unjustly sent to prison. He never loses faith and ultimately his name is cleared.

FARDEN, HENRY RICO

THE PROFESSIONALS (1966, Columbia)—**Lee Marvin** leads a group of four mercenaries hired to rescue Ralph Bellamy's young wife (Claudia Cardinale) from the camp of Mexican bandit/revolutionary Jack Palance. She doesn't want to be rescued and leave the man she really loves, which poses a dilemma for Marvin and his colleagues. After killing dozens of Palance's followers in the process of fleeing with Cardinale, they allow Palance to take her with him, while Bellamy helplessly looks on.

FARELL, JANICE

THE LADY AND THE MONSTER (1944, Republic)—In an early version of DONOVAN'S BRAIN, scientist Erich von Stroheim keeps alive the brain of a mortally wounded financier. The brain dominates von Stroheim's assistant, Richard Arlen, much to the horror of his love, **Vera Hruba Ralston**. The film was the first non-musical role for Ralston, the soon-to-be wife of studio chief Herbert Yates.

FARGO, BILL

FIGHTING BILL FARGO—(1942, Universal)—Just out of prison, **Johnny Mack Brown** plans to restart his father's newspaper. He gets involved with the sheriff's election and is able to help kick out the crooks.

FARGO KID

THE FARGO KID (1941, RKO)—When **Tim Holt** is mistaken for a notorious gunslinger, he takes advantage of it to help put an end to the crooked dealings of a town's mining bosses.

FARLEY, DUKE

THE MAN FROM MONTANA (1917, Silent, Universal)— **Neal Hart** clears himself of transporting a woman across state lines for immoral purposes, and then takes on the outlaws who stole his mine.

FARMER, FELIX

S.O.B. (1981, Paramount)—Hollywood director **Richard Mulligan** goes off the deep end when his latest epic starring his wife, Julie Andrews, is a flop. He decides to remake it as a pornographic picture in which Andrews exposes her breasts. The things Andrews has to do to shed her Mary Poppins image.

FARMER, FRANCES

FRANCES (1982, Universal)—**Jessica Lange** is superb in her portrayal of the rebellious, beautiful movie actress of the late 1930s and 1940s, who paid a huge price for trying to be independent. Her mother, played by Kim Stanley, and the Hollywood establishment conspired to tame this willful woman. She drinks to excess, has auto accidents, curses the police. As a result, she is institutionalized, where she is brutalized and repeatedly raped. She ultimately submits to a brain operation that takes the life out of her. Lange looks very much like her subject, and her performance earned her an Academy Award nomination. Nevertheless, it's a depressing film.

FARNHAM, MARION

THE PRODIGAL WIFE (1918, Silent, Screencraft)—When her lover deserts her and she is wrongly informed that her daughter has died, **Mary Boland** leaves her neglected husband and child to turn to prostitution. Later, Boland encounters her daughter and tells her her miserable life story to prevent the girl from making the same mistakes.

FARNSWORTH, MILFORD

ALIAS JESSE JAMES (1959, UA)—**Bob Hope** accidently sells an insurance policy to outlaw Jesse James. He is ordered to ensure that his client has no fatal accidents.

FARO, KITTY

FIVE BOLD WOMEN (1951, Citation)—**Kathy Marlowe** is one of five women being escorted to prison by marshall Jeff Morrow. They are attacked by Indians and then by a gang of outlaws led by the husband of one of the women.

FARRADAY, JEFFREY

THE PRODIGAL (1931, MGM)—**Lawrence Tibbett**, the son of a prominent Southern plantation owner, takes to the road, riding the rails as a hobo. After a few years as a tramp, he returns home and finds himself falling for his brother's wife. The star is a better singer than actor. The best song is "Without A Song" by Vincent Youmans, Edward Eliscu and Billy Rose.

FARRAND, RENE *See* ARSENE LUPIN

FARRANT, ANTHONY

ENGLAND MADE ME (1973, GB, Cine Globe)—In 1935, Englishman **Michael York** passes through Nazi Germany on his way home from the Far East and becomes involved with decadent financier Peter Finch.

FARREL, PRIAM

HIS DOUBLE LIFE (1933, Paramount)—English artist **Roland Young's** death is mistakenly reported. His valet is buried in his place and Young is able to attend his own funeral at Westminster Abbey. Later, when he begins to paint again, the art world is thrown into a dither. He's accused of faking the paintings of a dead artist. He eventually is able to prove that he's still alive. The story was filmed again in 1943 as *Holy Matrimony* starring Monty Woolley.

FARRELL, BILL & MARGE

I MARRIED A MONSTER FROM OUTER SPACE (1958, Paramount)—Just before **Tom Tryon** and **Gloria Talbot** are married, his body is invaded by an alien from a planet where females have become extinct. To maintain their race, the aliens must have children with Earth women. Talbot slowly catches on that not only is her husband an alien, but so are many of the other men in her town.

FARRELL, FRANK X.

ALIBI IKE (1935, Warner Brothers)—Baseball player **Joe E. Brown** has trouble with curves, both on and off the diamond.

FARRELL, HAP

THE SONG AND DANCE MAN (1936, 20th Century Fox)—Song-and-dance man **Paul Kelly** has a heart of gold, as well as a drinking and gambling problem. He does his best to ensure that his partner Claire Trevor is provided with whatever she needs, including a different man.

FARRELL, LEFTY

TWO OF A KIND 1951, Columbia)—Carnival showman **Edmond O'Brien** poses as the son of a wealthy couple, who has been missing since he was two. His co-conspirators in the swindle are Lizabeth Scott and Alexander Knox. The masquerade doesn't take in the wealthy man, so Knox feels he must be eliminated. Murder is too much for O'Brien and Scott.

FARRELL, PATRICK

BROTH OF A BOY (1959, GB, British Lion)—The 110th birthday of mean, old poacher **Barry Fitzgerald** is being celebrated by his village and covered by television.

FARRELL, RITA

ONE WOMAN TO ANOTHER (1927, Silent, Paramount)—**Florence Vidor** and her intended Theodore Von Eltz encounter a passel of problems getting to the altar. When she's quarantined with some children, vamp Hedda Hopper is given a shot at Von Eltz. Vidor handles her competition in grand fashion.

FARRIS, MAL

THE STRAW MAN (1953, GB, UA)—When detective **Dermot Walsh** tries to kill insurance investigator Clifford Evans, Walsh is killed by his employer, Lana Morris. Evans does not let the fact that Morris saved his life prevent him from doing his job. He goes on to prove that Morris killed her husband and his mistress, and was planning to set Walsh up to take the fall.

FAST, JOHN

THE VANISHING WESTERNER (1950, Republic)—When sheriff **Arthur Space** disappears, cowboy Monte Hale is accused of murdering the missing man. Space returns to town disguised as his English nobleman brother and stirs up the town so much they almost lynch Hale.

FAULKNER, CHRIS

WOLF OF NEW YORK (1940, Republic)—Criminal lawyer **Edmund Lowe** loses his first case, and the only innocent man he's ever defended is executed. This causes Lowe to become a champion of justice. He becomes district attorney, now prosecuting the criminals he'd earlier gotten off.

FAULKNER, EMILY ANN

THE GODDESS (1958, Columbia)—With no offense directed at **Kim Stanley's** attractiveness, she seems an odd choice for the lead in this film a clef of Marilyn Monroe. Small-town fast girl Stanley moves from bed to bed as she becomes a Hollywood sex symbol. This gives her no satisfaction, nor do any of her romances.

FAUMAN, ELLIOT

ELLIOT FAUMAN, PH.D. (1990, Taurus)—While researching a paper on prostitutes, psychology professor **Randy Dreyfuss** falls in love with actress Jean Kasem, whom he mistakes for a hooker. If that's what he wants, she's willing to go along with it.

FAUSTUS, DR.

DOCTOR FAUSTUS (1967, GB, Columbia)—**Richard Burton** and wife Elizabeth Taylor are over-matched in their attempt to film Christopher Marlowe's version of the selling of Faustus' soul to Mephistopheles. Burton's direction is uninspired, and Taylor as Helen of Troy is not quite as good as when she portrayed Cleopatra.

FAUVETTE

HIS PARISIAN WIFE (1919, Silent, Artcraft)—In Paris, young writer **Elsie Ferguson** meets and marries American lawyer David Powell. He takes his tempermental wife to the New England home of his staid parents, who do not approve of their daughter-in-law's ideas. Powell sides with his parents, which leads to a divorce.

Ferguson becomes a famous writer, but not a financially successful one. Her ex bails her out and they are reunited.

FAY, GLORIA

MISS PACIFIC FLEET (1935, Warner Brothers)—**Joan Blondell** and Glenda Farrell are stranded show girls trying to make their way back to New York. They come up with a scheme to have the sailors hold a beauty contest, which Blondell wins.

FAYNE, TESSA

INNOCENT'S PROGRESS (1918, Silent, Mutual)—**Pauline Starke**, an orphan residing with her aunt in a small village, is employed at the local candy store. Here she meets a traveling actor, who fills her head with notions of joining him on the New York stage. But when she seeks him out in the big city, she discovers that he's struggling to survive with a wife and family. A rich, ailing man saves her from an assault and takes her into his home. With her help, he recovers and marries her.

FEATHEREST, CATHY

SUMMER LOVERS (1982, Orion)—One summer, **Daryl Hannah** is a part of a menage a trois on a Greek island. Her partners are rich kid Peter Gallagher and archeologist Valerie Quenessen.

FEATHERS, SALLY

THE PLEASURE GIRLS (1966, GB, Times Film)—**Francesca Annis** moves into a house with three other girls and the brother of one. She's in London, hoping to become a famous model. The romances of all the girls seem more trouble than they're worth. Annis takes up with a photographer who misreads her and tries to force her into bed. She seeks comfort from the brother, but finds him in the arms of a male lover. Somehow it's hard to really care about anyone in this movie.

FEATHERSTONE, JANE

SHE WROTE THE BOOK (1946, Universal)—After suffering a blow to the head, plain-looking teacher **Joan Davis** comes to, believing that she's a famous author with a wild sex life.

FEHLER, ROY

THE NEW CENTURIONS (1972, Columbia)—Old cop George C. Scott teaches new cop **Stacy Keach** a few important lessons, but not how to survive.

FELICIA, PRINCESS

THE PRINCESS OF HAPPY CHANCE (1916, GB, Silent, Jury)—**Elizabeth Risdon** escapes a forced marriage in her mythical country by exchanging places with her exact double.

FELICE

I LOVE YOU (1918, Silent, Triangle)—Young millionaire Francis McDonald falls in love with Italian peasant girl **Alma Rubens**, when he sees her portrait, painted by artist Wheeler Oakman. Through the artist, he finds and marries her, but Oakman tries to seduce Rubens. For a while it looks as if the marriage is ruined, but everyone gets what they deserve.

FELINO, GINO

OUT FOR JUSTICE (1991, Warner Brothers)—Pony-tailed Italian cop **Steven Seagal** pursues vicious drugged-out killer William Forsythe, who has gunned down Seagal's partner in front of his wife and kids.

FELIX

THE OWL AND THE PUSSYCAT (1970, Columbia)—Bookstore salesman and would-be author **George Segal** gets hooked up with prostitute Barbra Streisand. Despite the fact that they are almost complete opposites, they fall in love.

FELL, LADY LIGEIA

THE TOMB OF LIGEIA (1965, GB, American International)—Dear old Vincent Price preserves the body of his first wife, **Elizabeth Shepherd**, and resorts to necrophilia upon occasion. He takes a new wife, who looks exactly like the first. The new bride is in for a difficult time.

FELLA

CINDERFELLA (1960, Paramount)—In a take-off on the Cinderella story, **Jerry Lewis** is loony but not very funny. Ed Wynn as his fairy godfather has his moments.

FELLARA, IRENE

IDIOT'S DELIGHT (1939, MGM)—At the outbreak of WWII, **Norma Shearer**, posing as a Russian countess, runs into an old flame, hoofer Clark Gable, in a hotel on the Swiss border. Gable and Shearer are not Lunt and Fontaine and succeed only in looking silly: she with a horrible blonde wig, and he trying to dance with an all-girl troupe.

FELSCH, HAP

EIGHT MEN OUT (1988, Orion)—**Charlie Sheen** is a good-natured, foolish Chicago White Sox player who, along with several teammates, is banned from baseball for life for throwing the 1919 World Series. Baseball players aren't much brighter today—but they sure are paid better. To get them to throw a game would require the gamblers to negotiate with the players' agents.

FELSON, "FAST EDDIE"

THE HUSTLER (1961, 20th Century Fox)—**Paul Newman** won an Oscar for the sequel to this movie, *The Color of Money*. He should have won it for this one. He's a pool hustler who comes to the big city to take on Minnesota Fats, played by Jackie Gleason. In the first match, he lacks the character to win, but after teaming up with crippled Piper Laurie and despicable promoter George C. Scott, he develops the inner strength to take the fat man.

FENELLA

DUMB GIRL OF PORTICI (1916, Silent, Universal)—**Anna Pavlova**, the foremost ballerina of her time, stars in this tedious film production of the Daniel Francois Esprit opera, *Masaniello*. A bit of trivia: Boris Karloff made his film debut as an extra in this movie.

FENWAY, ADELE

HER HONOR THE GOVERNOR (1926, Silent, R-C Pictures)—Governor **Pauline Frederick** is threatened by a political boss when she won't play ball on a water power bill. He intends to release information that her husband wasn't divorced from his first wife when he married Frederick. The political boss is killed, and Frederick's son is arrested for the murder, but is ultimately cleared.

FENWICK, BILL

SPECIAL INVESTIGATOR (1936, RKO)—Criminal lawyer **Richard Dix** joins the Justice Department and becomes a special agent after his FBI agent brother is killed by the mobsters Dix has been defending.

FEODOR

THE VOLGA BOATMAN (1926, PDC)—Russian serf **William Boyd** wins the love of a Russian princess when he saves her from the wrath of some vengeful Reds.

FERAUD

THE DUELLISTS (1977, GB, Paramount)—**Harvey Keitel** and Keith Carradine are officers in Napoleon's army who carry on a longstanding feud. It's an eccentric but basically enjoyable production of the Joseph Conrad story.

FERGUSON, DR.

MEN IN WHITE (1934, MGM)—Socialite Myrna Loy resents the time her ambitious boyfriend **Clark Gable** gives to his profession. both change their views of his responsibility when he can do nothing to save the life of his ex-girlfriend, Elizabeth Allen, who develops peritonitis after aborting Gable's child.

FERGUSON, HELEN

NO MAN OF HER OWN (1950, Paramount)—Pregnant **Barbara Stanwyck** is believed to be the surviving wife of a wealthy couple's son, after both the son and his new wife are killed in a train crash. Everything is going well, until the arrival of the father of Stanwyck's child, who seeks to cut himself in on the deal.

FERGUSON, MAI-LU

SEVEN WOMEN FROM HELL (1961, 20th Century Fox) **Pilar Seurat** is one of the seven women who escape from a Japanese prison camp in new Guinea in WWII. It's a trite, predictable film.

FERGUSON, RITA

RIO RITA (1929, RKO)—In this early sound film, the romance of **Bebe Daniels** and Texas ranger John Boles is threatened by the possibility that her brother is the notorious bandit Boles is pursuing. The stars of the film are meant to be comedians Bert Wheeler and Robert Woolsey, who had starred in the stage production.

FERMOYLE, STEPHEN

THE CARDINAL (1963, Columbia)—In this tedious film, **Tom Tryon** portrays an Irish Catholic priest who moves up the church's hierarchy step by step and by the film's end is made cardinal. His experiences as a priest include fighting the Klan in the South and ending a romance with Romy Schneider, which sees him break his vows.

FERRILL, JOE

THE CHICAGO KID (1945, Republic)—**Donald Barry**, a good lad, goes bad as he seeks revenge on the man whose testimony sent his father to prison.

FERRIS

LITTLE DARLINGS (1980, Paramount)—**Tatum O'Neal** and Kristy McNichol have a wager as to whom will be the first to shuck her virginity. Perhaps such a story line could've been handled in an amusing way that wouldn't be offensive, but those responsible for this horrid attempt at comedy don't have the skill.

FERRIS, TOM & JULIE

NOT WITH MY WIFE, YOU DON'T (1966, Warner Brothers)—**Tony Curtis** beats out fellow Air Forcer officer George C. Scott in the romance sweepstakes for **Virni Lisi** by convincing her that Scott didn't survive his last mission. Years later, Curtis and Lisi are married, Curtis is a gofer for a general and hot-shot Scott shows up again still interested in Lisi.

FFOLKES

FFOLKES (1980, GB, Universal)—Eccentric counter-terrorist **Roger Moore** is hired by the British government, when Tony Perkins and a team of terrorists threaten to blow up two North Sea oil rigs unless they are paid a large ransom.

FIDDLER

FIDDLER ON THE ROOF (1971, UA)—**Tutte Lemkow** plays his fiddle from the roof and at the wedding of Tevye's daughter.

FIELDING, ELIZABETH

THE ROMANTIC ENGLISHWOMAN (1975, GB, New World)—Discontented **Glenda Jackson**, on holiday at Baden Baden, falls in love with drug-smuggler Helmut Berger, while her husband, Michael Caine is at home writing a novel with the same theme.

FIELDS, ALAN

THE THIEF (1952, UA)—Nuclear physicist **Ray Milland** says not a word in this film as he flees the FBI, which believes he is a spy.

FIELDS, CELIA

THE MAN I LOVE (1929, Paramount)—**Mary Brian** is the wife of small-town boxer Richard Arlen. When he batters the champ in an exhibition match, he then gets a real chance for the title. Why, it's just like Rocky.

FIELDS, FRANK & JIMMY

FATHER AND SON (1929, Columbia)—Widower **Jack Holt's** gift of a phonograph recorder to his 10-year-old son, **Mickey McBan**, will ultimately be used to prove that neither father nor son killed a shady countess.

FIELDS, HELEN

WOMEN LOVE ONCE (1931, Paramount)—**Eleanor Boardman** is most understanding of her husband Paul Lukas' desire to live a bohemian life as an artist. He is finally shocked back into his senses with the death of their daughter in an automobile accident.

FIELDS, W.C.

W.C. FIELDS AND ME (1976, Universal)—**Rod Steiger** is unpleasant as the alcoholic comedian in this biopic, which is based on the memoirs of Fields' longtime mistress Carlotta Monti. The movie is something Fields never was as a performer—boring!

FIERRO, MARTIN

HOUR OF THE ASSASSIN (1987, Concorde)—**Erik Estrada** is hired by right-wing generals to assassinate a newly elected democratic leader of a South American country.

FIGG, MR.

THE BARBER OF STAMFORD HILL (1963, GB, British Lion) -**John Bennett** is a lonely Jewish barber, whose social life consists of Friday night chess games with a dim-witted friend. One day, he decides to change his life by proposing marriage to a widow with two children, but she scares him off and he returns to his chess game.

FILMORE, AUBREY

A SOUTHERN YANKEE (1948, MGM)—**Red Skelton**, a bell-boy in a St. Louis hotel during the Civil War, becomes a Union spy, posing as the infamous Confederate agent, "The Gray Spider," who has been captured by the Yanks. It's not Skelton at his best, but there is some fun.

FINCHHAVEN, LT. CMDR.

THE EXTRAORDINARY SEAMAN (1969, MGM)—During WWII, four stranded sailors are washed ashore, where they find a British gunboat, commanded by **David Niven**, the ghost of a man who drowned 30 years earlier. This film sank out of sight before many saw it.

FINCHLEY, JOHN *See* **THE HAWK**

FINDLEY, THEODORE
THREE WISE FOOLS (1923, Silent, Goldwyn); (1946, MGM)—**Claude Gillingwater** and **Edward Arnold** each appear as one of three crusty old gentlemen who adopt an orphan, who proceeds to soften them. Eleanor Boardman and Margaret O'Brien portray the orphan in the films.

"FINGERS"
WANTED BY SCOTLAND YARD (1939, GB, Pathe/Monogram)—Suave thief **James Stephenson** is obsessed with taking revenge on the man who drove his former lover to suicide.

FINI, GIORGI
YES, GIORGIO (1982, MGM/UA)—Close your eyes and listen to tenor **Luciano Pavarotti** sing, but miss his acting in this predictable star vehicle about an international opera star and the throat specialist (Kathryn Harrold) with whom he falls in love.

FINK, BARTON
BARTON FINK (1991, 20th Century Fox)—Serious New York dramatist **John Turturro** succumbs to a lucrative offer to write for a 1941 Hollywood studio. He suffers severe writer's block. A shocking murder occurs half-way through the movie, throwing the film off into an unexpected direction.

FINLEY
THE MASTER GUN FIGHTER (1975, Taylor-Laughlin)—**Tom Laughlin** gives another of his pretentious performances as a mysterious avenger of wrongs committed during the California gold rush.

FINN, FATTY
FATTY FINN (1980, Australia, Children's Films)—**Ben Oxenbould** portrays the comic strip character, who finds himself in the middle of a street gang war in Sydney during the Depression.

FINN, HUCKLEBERRY
HUCK AND TOM (1918, Paramount); HUCKLEBERRY FINN (1931, Paramount); (1939, MGM); (1974, UA); THE ADVENTURES OF HUCKLEBERRY FINN (1960, MGM)—**Robert Gordon, Lewis Sargent, James Durkin, Mickey Rooney, Jeff East** and **Eddie Hodges** each starred as Mark Twain's irrepressible juvenile revel, who runs away with escaped slave Jim on a raft on the mighty Mississippi. When Huck disappears, Jim is taken into custody and is accused of killing the boy. Huck arrives just in time to prevent Jim from being lynched. Of the various portrayals, Rooney's beats out Durkin's by a narrow margin for the best.

FINN, NIKKI
WHO'S THAT GIRL (1987, Warner Brothers)—Pop-singing idol **Madonna**, a petty thief, is being released from prison as the film opens. She has spent four years in jail after wrongly being convicted of killing her boyfriend. She's out to find the man who set her up. This requires finding a safety deposit box whose key she has, but location she doesn't know. She is unwillingly aided in her quest by an engaged preppie, Griffin Dunne.

FINNEGAN
FINNEGAN'S WAKE (1965, Expanding Cinema)—**Martin J. Kelly** views his own death and his wake, where many hard-drinking friends and foes come to say their farewells. It's an ambitious production of James Joyce's last work.

FINNEGAN, DANNY
FINNEGAN'S BALL (1927, Silent, First Division) -**Charles McHugh** snubs his old friends, the Flannigans, when he believes he has inherited a fortune. This proves a hardship for his son and the Flannigans' daughter, who plan to marry. The inheritance proves to be bogus, and the Flannigans forgive the Finnegans in time for the wedding.

FINNEY, JIM
FINNEY (1969, Gold Coach)—Former Chicago Bear football player **Robert Kilcullen** finds no one interested in his paintings. He gets no understanding from his singer wife Joan Sundstrom, who's too busy with her successful career to be concerned with his problems of adjusting to life after football.

FIRECAT
FLASH AND THE FIRECAT (1976, Sebastian)—The producers of this movie seem to be trying for a version of BONNIE AND CLYDE. Outlaws **Roger Davis** and Tricia Sembera use dune buggies rather than sedans in their robberies.

FISH, DR.
THE STRANGE CASE OF DR. RX (1942, Universal)—Mysterious **Lionel Atwill** plays judge, jury and executioner as he murders guilty felons who are gotten off by brilliant lawyer Samuel S. Hinds.

FISH HAWK
FISH HAWK (1981, Canada, Avco Embassy)—Alcoholic Indian **Will Sampson** attempts to beat his addiction for the benefit of a youngster who thinks he's a great guy.

FISHBINE, BERNIE
I DON'T BUY KISSES ANYMORE (1992, Skouras)—When lonely, chubby **Jason Alexander** meets ambitious aerobics nut Nia Peeples, he falls in love. She puts him off, so he joins a gym, gives up his nightly routine of buying a sack of candy kisses and batters away at his excess pounds. Peeples makes Alexander the focus of her graduate thesis, a psychological study of the obese male. This complicates things, but true love triumphs.

FISHER, BILLY
BILLY LIAR (1963, GB, Vic Films/Warner Brothers/Pathe)—Dreamer **Tom Courtenay** works for a funeral director. He's a pathological liar, who fibs just for the fun of it. He's involved with three women, but prefers his fantasy world to all of them.

FISHER, POLLY
POLLY OF THE CIRCUS (1932, MGM)—Trapeze artist **Marion Davies** falls for minister Clark Gable. The romance threatens Gable's career, as his parishioner and his bishop do not approve of the match. Gable rightfully seems uncomfortable in a role for which he is miscast.

FISK, JIM
THE TOAST OF NEW YORK (1937, RKO)—Nineteenth-century medicine showman **Edward Arnold** becomes a notorious Wall Street financier.

FISKE, JOAN
THE AMBASSADOR'S DAUGHTER (1956, UA)—**Olivia De Havilland**, daughter of the American Ambassador to France, decides to investigate the claim of an American senator that U.S. forces in Paris are in mortal danger.

FITCH, WILLIAM

MY LEARNED FRIEND (1943, GB, Ealing)—In his final film, shady lawyer **Will Hay** is the last on a list of intended murder victims of a madman, who is taking revenge on all those responsible for his conviction.

FITZGERALD, BRIAN SWEENEY/FITZCARRALDO

FITZCARRALDO (1982, New World Pictures)—In turn-of-the-century Peru, eccentric Irishman **Klaus Kinski** succeeds against all odds in building an opera house in the jungle.

FITZGERALD, F. SCOTT

BELOVED INFIDEL (1959, 20th Century Fox)—**Gregory Peck** portrays the troubled writer in this story of his love affair with Sheila Graham, played by Deborah Kerr. The former British chorus girl, turned gossip columnist, can't cure his alcoholism.

FITZGERALD, ROBERT

I AM THE LAW (1922, Silent, Affiliated Distributors)—Royal Mounted Policeman **Kenneth Harlan** rescues Alice Lake from the clutches of a dance hall owner. She falls for Harlan's brother Gaston Glass, a mountie who's having an affair with the wife of another officer. When this latter officer is killed, Harlan takes the blame, believing he's dying and this brother is the guilty party. Harlan is almost lynched before the truth comes out and Lake sees Harlan in a new light.

FITZGERALD, SALLY

SHIPYARD SALLY (1940, GB, 20th Century Fox)—**Gracie Fields**, who manages her father's pub next to the shipyards, rallies the workers to march on London when the shipyards are closed.

FITZHERBERT, MARIA

MRS. FITZHERBERT (1950, GB, British National)—In 1783, the Prince of Wales, played by Peter Graves, falls in love with a Catholic widow, **Joyce Howard**. When he threatens suicide, Howard agrees to a secret marriage. Rumors spread about the marriage, but Graves insists to his mother, the Queen, that he's not married. Howard runs away, and Graves, like a good boy, marries a nice Protestant princess.

FITZMORE, LADY SOPHIE

SOPHIE'S PLACE (1970, Warner Brothers)—**Edith Evans** unwittingly welcomes two kindly crooks, Telly Savalas and Warren Oakes, into her stately mansion. She treats them so well, they give up their plans to steal all her belongings.

FITZROY, PATRICIA

PATRICIA GETS HER MAN (1937, GB, First National)—While vacationing in the South of France, **Lesley Brook** enlists the help of philandering nobleman Hans Sonker to snare film star Edwin Styles. Instead, Sonker lets Brook find out what a stinker Styles is, winning the fair lady for himself.

FITZWILLIAM

FITZWILLY (1967, UA)—In order to keep his employer Edith Evans living in the style to which she is accustomed, butler **Dick Van Dyke** organizes the household staff into a crime syndicate.

5,000 A.D. WOMAN

TERROR FROM THE YEAR 5,000 (1958, American International)—Alien **Salome Jens** is transported back to 1958 in a time machine, so she may bring a man back with her to the future to restart a human race not contaminated by radioactivity. What a line to get a guy into bed!

FIX-IT, MR.

MR. FIX-IT (1918, Silent, Artcraft)—**Douglas Fairbanks** takes the place of his U.S. roommate, when the latter is called home from studies in England to marry a wealthy girl he hasn't seen since childhood.

FLAGG

THE GOOD GUYS AND THE BAD GUYS (1969, Warner Brothers)—Aging sheriff **Robert Mitchum** and old-time train robber George Kennedy are baited by a bunch of young punks into one last showdown.

FLAGG, JOHNNY

GALLANT DEFENDER (1935, Columbia)—In the first of his many Westerns for Columbia, **Charles Starrett** is unjustly accused of murder. He proves his innocence while helping the homesteaders in their battle with cattlemen.

FLAHERTY, MICHAEL

THE OUTSIDER (1980, Paramount)—American **Craig Wasson**, inspired by his grandfather's stories of fighting the British, goes to Ireland to join the IRA, and finds they will only trust him with paper shuffling.

FLAHERTY, MONSIGNOR

MONSIGNOR (1987, 20th Century Fox)—We're not sure what calling priest **Christopher Reeve** is supposed to have heard. He goes about the business of putting the Vatican's financial affairs in order after WWII by involving the Holy See with the mafia. On a personal note, he takes young nun Genevieve Bujold as his mistress. We are not shocked by such goings on by a man of the cloth, but we are shocked that a movie with such juicy items could be so utterly boring.

FLAMBEAU, ROSE

ROSE OF THE YUKON (1949, Republic) **Myrna Dell** is a singer in an Alaskan saloon in this ho-hum story of the reappearance of supposedly dead Army captain William Wright. Dell is caught in the middle between Wright and Major Steve Brodie, who's supposed to bring Wright in to face a murder charge.

FLANAGAN, JAMES

FLANAGAN (1985, United Film)—Cab driver **Philip Bosco** dreams of parking his hack for good and becoming a Shakespearian actor.

FLANDERS, MOLL

THE AMOROUS ADVENTURES OF MOLL FLANDERS (1965, Paramount)—**Kim Novak** stars in this dog with fleas about an ambitious servant girl, who repeatedly sacrifices her virtue to a succession of rich gentlemen, but gives her heart to highwayman Richard Johnson.

FLANDERS, PEYTON

THE HAND THAT ROCKS THE CRADLE (1992, Hollywood Pictures)—In an incredibly contrived story, **Rebecca De Mornay** blames Annabella Sciorra for the suicide of her doctor husband and her miscarriage. De Mornay talks her way into Sciorra's home as a nanny for a new baby. People would be more careful choosing a trash collector than were Sciorra and her husband, Matt McCoy. De Mornay sets about ruining Sciorra's marriage, stealing her husband and baby and tossing in a murder for good measure.

FLANNIGAN, SGT. MIKE

MRS. MIKE (1949, UA)—At the turn of the century, Canadian Mountie **Dick Powell** takes his Boston-born bride Evelyn Keyes to live in the rugged Northwest Woods.

FLASH

CHU CHU AND THE PHILLY FLASH (1981, 20th Century Fox)—**Alan Arkin**, an ex-relief pitcher for the Philadelphia Phillies, has spent the last 20 years on a perpetual drunk. He and street entertainer Carol Burnett find a briefcase filled with government secrets, which changes their lives.

FLASH

FLASH AND THE FIRECAT (1976, Warner Brothers)—**Tricia Sembera** and Roger Davis look for one big score as they ride around like latter-day Bonnie and Clydes in dune buggies.

FLASH

THREE KIDS AND A QUEEN (1935, Universal)—**Billy Benedict** is one of three young Hell's Kitchen kids who take in May Robson, the world's wealthiest woman, when her horse is spooked and she's thrown from her carriage. They hold her for ransom, and she goes along with the scheme because she knows her relatives are trying to have her committed to an insane asylum.

FLASHMAN, HARRY

ROYAL FLASH (1975, GB, 20th Century Fox)—**Malcolm McDowell** is the grown-up bullying braggart of Thomas Hughes' novel, *Tom Brown's School Days*. He may wed a duchess. The romp is intended to be hilariously funny. It isn't!

FLEENER, MYRNA

HOOSIERS (1986, Orion)—**Barbara Hershey**, a teacher in her Indiana hometown high school, develops a romantic attachment to the new basketball coach, Gene Hackman.

FLEGENHEIMER, ARTHUR *See* "DUTCH SCHULTZ"

FLEMING, LT. BRIAN

KING'S PIRATE (1967, Universal)—In 1700, British naval officer **Doug McClure** masquerades as a pirate to put an end to the activity of buccaneers operating out of Madagascar.

FLEMING, MRS.

RECKLESS LADY (1926, Silent, First National)—**Belle Bennett** is forced into an affair with Russian aristocrat Lowell Sherman in order to cover her gambling debts. When her husband, James Kirkwood, divorces her for her infidelity, Bennett takes her daughter Lois Moran with her to Monte Carlo, where Sherman puts a move on Moran. Bennett loses everything gambling to raise enough money to escape with her daughter. She confesses her wasted life to Moran and is about to commit suicide when Kirkwood arrives and puts everything right.

FLEMING, NANCY

NEXT TIME I MARRY (1938, RKO)—**Lucille Ball** will inherit $20 million if she marries a "real American." Even though she's engaged to a foreigner, she weds ditch digger James Ellison, planning to divorce him as soon as she gets the money. But as things always happen in movies like this, she ultimately falls in love with her American husband.

FLEMING, ROY

THE RELUCTANT ASTRONAUT (1967, Universal)—**Don Knotts** has an exaggerated fear of heights, but through a strange series of events becomes an astronaut. The film reminds one somewhat of Eddie Bracken and HAIL THE CONQUERING HERO, but it's not as funny.

FLEMING, TONY

TONY DRAWS A HORSE (1951, GB, Rank)—When eight-year-old **Anthony Lang** draws an anatomically correct picture of a horse on his doctor father's consulting room door, Dad wants to smack him, while psychiatrist Mom wants to encourage his creativity. The row almost ruins the marriage.

FLETCH

FLETCH (1985, Universal); FLETCH LIVES (1989, Universal) - Smart-alecky newspaper reporter **Chevy Chase** uncovers a drug ring operated by corrupt police chief Joe Don Baker and wealthy businessman Tim Matheson, when the latter hires Chase to murder him. Chase assumes several outrageous and transparent identities, which no one in the cast seems to get wise to. In the equally silly 1989 sequel, we learn that Chase's character's full name is Irwin Maurice "Fletch" Fletcher.

FLETCHER, EDWARD

THE MOTH AND THE FLAME (1915, Silent, Paramount)—**Stewart Baird** is the scoundrel who seduced and deserted poor innocent Adele Ray. She gets her revenge by breaking up his wedding, telling all assembled how he done her wrong.

FLETCHER, JIM

THE CLAY PIGEON (1949, RKO)—Regaining consciousness after months in a coma in a naval hospital, **Bill Williams** discovers that he's to be court-martialed on charges of treason and causing the death of a friend in a Japanese prison camp. He's able to prove he was framed and find the real culprit.

FLETCHER, SUSAN

WISE GIRL (1937, RKO)—Heiress **Miriam Hopkins** poses as a poor Greenwich Village artist in an attempt to convince her destitute brother-in-law, Ray Milland, to allow her to adopt her deceased sister's two kids.

FLEURIOT, JACQUELINE *See* JACQUELINE

FLINT, DEREK

OUR MAN FLINT (1966, 20th Century Fox); IN LIKE FLINT (1967, 20th Century Fox)—**James Coburn** portrays a thinking man's James Bond in these spoofs of the genre. Everyone plays things straight, but nothing is taken seriously. It's hard to successfully spoof a spoof.

FLINT, HELEN

HIDEAWAY GIRL (1937, Paramount)—**Martha Raye** marries phony count Monroe Owsley, who pawns other people's jewelry.

FLINT, SURE FIRE

SURE FIRE FLINT (1922, Silent, Mastadon)—WWI vet **Johnny Hines** has a tough time keeping a job until he saves Doris Kenyon, the daughter of one of his bosses, from a safe in which a villain has locked her.

FLO

REBELLIOUS DAUGHTERS (1938, Times)—Mistreated **Sheila Browley** leaves her family home and moves to the big city, where she is used by cads until she finds a man willing to take care of the poor simpleton.

FLOOD, SGT. MARTIN

GLORY BOY (1971, Cinerama)—**Mitchell Ryan** is a psychopathic killer/police sergeant. He's just the kind of guy who will appeal to the jingoistic and macho-man father (Arthur Kennedy) of returning Vietnam vet Michael Moriarty.

FLORA

THE INNOCENTS (1961, US/GB, 20th Century Fox)—New governess Deborah Kerr begins to suspect that her charges, angelic little **Pamela Franklin** and her adorable brother Martin Stephens are possessed by the spirits of evil dead servants.

FLORA, MME.

THE MEDIUM (1951, Transfilm)—In this filmed version of the Gian-Carlo Menotti opera, fake medium **Marie Powers** feels a genuine manifestation, shoots at it and kills her assistant, a mute.

FLORENCE

LADY OF THE NIGHT (1925, Silent, MGM)—**Norma Shearer** plays the dual roles of Florence, the daughter of wealthy parents, and Molly, a slum girl, both of whom are after the same man, Malcolm McGregor. Florence gets the prize.

FLORENCE

NAME THE WOMAN (1928, Silent, Columbia)—Gaston Glass is acquitted during his murder trial when a mysterious masked woman admits she was with him at the time of the crime. Played by **Anita Stewart,** the compromised woman is the wife of the prosecuting attorney.

FLORIZEL, PRINCE

TROUBLE FOR TRUE (1936, MGM)—Prince **Robert Montgomery** must escape a gang of killers, who are intent on preventing him from assuming the throne and marrying his beloved.

FLORRIE, LANEC

JOHNNY FRENCHMAN (1946, GB, Ealing)—French poacher **Francoise Rosay's** problems with Cromwell fishermen are resolved when romance blossoms across the English Channel.

FLOWER, PERCY

OH BOY! (1938, GB, Associated British Films)—Scientist **Albert Burdon** takes a potion that turns him into a child. While in this state, he overhears a plot to steal the crown jewels. When he reverts to his normal state, he is able to stop the crooks.

FLOWERS, JACK

SAINT JACK (1979, New World)—American wanderer **Ben Gazzara** finds his niche in life as a pimp in Singapore.

FLOYD, PRETTY BOY

PRETTY BOY FLOYD (1960, Continental); A BULLET FOR PRETTY BOY (1970, American International)—Neither movie about the life of criminal Floyd is other than the routine, "how I led a life of crime" junk. **John Ericson** and **Fabian Forte**, respectively, appear as the handsome outlaw.

FLYNN, CAROL

YOUNG, WILLING AND EAGER (1962, GB, Brenner)—**Christina Gregg**, a 17-year-old runaway, hitchhikes to Soho in London, where she gets a job as a waitress. She marries singer Jess Conrad when she finds herself pregnant with his child. Intent on emigrating to Canada, they burglarize her boss' home, killing him in the process. Wounded in the robbery, Conrad bleeds to death as the couple flees from the police.

FLYNN, JERRY

KING OF THE NEWSBOYS (1938, Republic)—**Lew Ayres** loses his girl, Helen Mack, to mobster Victor Varconi. Ayres compensates by becoming a big wheel in the newspaper trucking business. He moves into a penthouse and makes another try for Mack. He wins her but loses his penthouse.

FLYNN, MARY

ALIAS MARY FLYNN (1925, Silent, FBO)—Thief **Evelyn Brent** takes refuge from her former associates in the car of William V. Mong. He gives her a fresh start, and his son, Malcolm McGregor, an assistant D.A., falls in love with her. To save her benefactor from a blackmailer, Brent must revert to her old ways for one last time.

FOLEY, AXEL

BEVERLY HILLS COP (1984, Paramount); BEVERLY HILLS COP II (1987, Paramount)—**Eddie Murphy** is a foul-mouthed, jive-talking, Detroit police detective who becomes involved with crime in the rarefied air of Beverly Hills, California. He teams with an Abbott and Costello like pair of local cops, who are of minor help to him, as he tracks down the killer of his friend and puts an end to a cocaine-smuggling scheme. In the sequel, he continues to use his questionable police tactics of entrapment, chicanery and illegal behavior to solve something called the alphabet murders. Laughing at Murphy's antics in the two movies, especially the second, is almost embarrassing, since everything he does is in such bad taste.

FOLEY, FANNY

FANNY FOLEY HERSELF (1931, RKO)—Vaudeville performer **Edna May Oliver** tries to prevent her wealthy father-in-law from taking her two daughters from her. The producers couldn't seem to decide whether the movie was a comedy or a drama. Audiences decided it was neither.

FOLEY, JOHN FRANCIS

JACK O' CLUBS (1924, Silent, Universal)—Cop **Herbert Rawlison** loses his nerve, when he believes he has shot his sweetheart Ruth Dwyer. When, later, he learns the shot was actually fired by a gangster, Rawlison cleans up his area of the city.

FOLEY, PATRICK

THE EARTHLING (1980, Filmways-Roadshow)—**William Holden** has returned to his native Australia, dying of cancer. He spends his remaining days teaching orphan Ricky Schroder what he knows about surviving.

FOLSOM, EDITH

THE BUTTERFLY GIRL (1921, Silent, Playgoers)—Young and wealthy **Marjorie Daw's** greatest ambition is to have a dozen or more admirers worshiping her. She does all she can to achieve her goal, not caring whom she hurts. Then she finds how it feels when the shoe is on the other foot.

FONTAINE, FRENCHIE

FRENCHIE (1950, Universal)—Gambler **Shelley Winters** leaves New Orleans for the Western town of Bottleneck, where she opens a saloon and plans to avenge her father's death.

FONTAINE, LAWRENCE

THE MAN WHO CRIED WOLF (1937, Universal)—Actor **Lewis Stone** constantly confesses to crimes he didn't commit, thinking the police won't believe him when he confesses to a murder he did do.

FORAY, CARYL
CARYL OF THE MOUNTAINS (1936, Marcy/Reliable)—**Lois Wild** provides the romantic interest for Mountie Francis X. Bushman, but the star of the movie is his dog Rin Tin Tin Jr.

FORBES, JOHNNY
MISSISSIPPI GAMBLER (1942, Universal)—New York reporter **Kent Taylor**, a witness to a murder at a race track, trails the killer to a small Mississippi town.

FORBES, LORNA HAUSER See **ETHEL WHITEHEAD**

FORBES, MARY
FOUR GIRLS IN WHITE (1939, MGM)—**Mary Howard** is one of four nurses in training, whose career and romances are examined in this routine hospital movie.

FORBES, MARY
INDISCRETION OF AN AMERICAN WIFE (1954, Columbia)—American housewife **Jennifer Jones** and her Italian lover Montgomery Clift have a final go at love-making in an empty railroad car, but are interrupted and arrested, charged with lewd behavior. The police commissioner changes his mind, drops the charges and sends the couple on their separate ways. Nothing to it.

FORBES, DR. MICHAEL
CRIME OF DR. FORBES (1936, 20th Century Fox)—**Robert Kent's** older colleague, suffering from a debilitating illness, begs Kent to give him an overdose of opium to end his suffering. Kent falls in love with the sick physician's young wife and when the man dies of an overdose, Kent is accused of his murder.

FORBES, NOAH
THE MAGNIFICENT SEVEN RIDE (1972, UA)—Eastern newspaper reporter **Michael Callan** joins with Chris, now played by Lee Van Cleef, and five convicts to rescue some widowed white women from Mexican bandits. With films like this, one tends to wish sequels banned.

FORBES, REGINA
TO PLEASE A LADY (1950, MGM)—Midget racing car driver Clark Gable falls for reporter **Barbara Stanwyck**, who has been hounding him in her column.

FORBES, STEPHEN
THE MAN WHO TALKED TOO MUCH (1940, Warner Brothers)—When lawyer **George Brent** is betrayed by his idealistic younger brother William Lundigan, he frames the latter on a murder charge, and then proceeds to save him from the electric chair by getting the real killer to confess.

FORBIN, DR. CHARLES
COLOSSUS: THE FORBIN PROJECT (1969, Universal)—**Eric Brandon** must find a way to disarm his creation, a massive computer, when the monster becomes power hungry with plans of ruling the world. The film is better than it sounds.

FORD, BOB
I SHOT JESSE JAMES (1949, Lippert)—**John Ireland** shoots and kills his one-time friend Reed Hadley, hoping to win a pardon for himself, so he can marry his girl and settle down. But in the back, Ireland, now really!

FORD, LOU
THE KILLER INSIDE ME (1976, Warner Brothers)—Deputy sheriff **Stacy Keach** has periods of brutal and violent behavior when he experiences childhood flashbacks.

FORD, SIR REGINALD
LAZYBONES (1935, GB, RKO)—**Ian Hunter** is a ne'er-do-well baronet who has lost his money. He hopes to recoup his fortune by marrying a wealthy American, Claire Luce, but she proves to be as penniless as he.

FORDYCE, RICHARD
THE FIVE POUND MAN (1937, GB, Fox British)—Ex-con **Edwin Styles** seeks those who framed him on a counterfeiting charge. At a charity auction his services as a butler are bought with what proves to be a phony five-pound note. Styles is able to confront the wealthy man heading the counterfeiting ring. The latter commits suicide rather than go to jail.

FOREST, CMDR. DAVID
UNDERWATER WARRIOR (1958, MGM)—Naval reserve commander **Dan Dailey** trains U.S. frogmen in this dull documentary-like film.

FOREST, ROSIE
WHO SLEW AUNTIE ROO? (1971, American International)—Madwoman **Shelley Winters** menaces two orphan children in this crude adaptation of Hansel and Gretel.

FORREST, ALEX
FATAL ATTRACTION (1987, Paramount)—Married New York lawyer Michael Douglas has what he takes to be a wild one week-end affair with book editor **Glenn Close**. She has other ideas. She claims to be pregnant and wants Douglas to leave his wife and child for her. She tries suicide, sabotaging his car, par-boiling the pet rabbit of his daughter, kidnapping the daughter and, when all else fails, attempting to kill Douglas' wife in her own bathroom. It takes the joint efforts of both Douglas and his wife Anne Archer to put Close away for good. The moral for men seems to be: "If you stray, you will pay." There are many similarities between this movie and the 1971 PLAY MISTY FOR ME, starring Clint Eastwood and Jessica Walter.

FORREST, CHRISTINE
KEEPER OF THE FLAME (1942, MGM)—Reporter Spencer Tracy digs into the sinister background of **Katharine Hepburn's** dead hero husband, discovering his fascist leanings.

FORREST, JOHN
THE AMAZING MR. FORREST (1943, GB, PRC)—Jewel thief **Jack Buchanan** has a falling out with his gang.

FORREST, KAY LEMP See **KAY LEMP**

FORREST, MARY
ON PROBATION (1924, Silent, Steiner)—When she's arrested for speeding, flapper **Edith Thornton** finds she has no friends, but a kindly judge puts her on probation and introduces her to his son, Robert Ellis, whom she marries. If you suspect there must be more to the movie than that, you're wrong.

FORRESTER, ALICE
MISS MINK OF 1949 (1949, 20th Century Fox)—**Lois Collier** wins a mink coat in a contest. Trying to live up to the extravagance of such

a possession puts a major strain on her marriage to Jimmy Lydon, a man of very modest resources.

FORRESTER, BETTY
THE COLLEGE COQUETTE (1929, Columbia)—College tramp **Ruth Taylor** fixes up innocent freshman Jobyna Ralston with cad William Collier, Jr., who ruins the girl and then walks out on her. Taylor's not what's generally considered a good Big Sister.

FORRESTER, MARIAN
A LOST LADY (1924, Silent, Warner Brothers)—**Irene Rich** moves from one wealthy elderly husband to the next.

FORSTER, JIM
THE GAMBLER AND THE LADY (1952, GB, Hammer)—Casino owner **Dane Clark** tries to break into British upper class society by ditching his singer girlfriend Kathleen Byron for aristocratic Naomi Chance. Clark better watch out for the woman scorned.

FORSYTE, IRENE
THAT FORSYTE WOMAN (1949, MGM)—**Greer Garson**, the wife of Edwardian man of property Errol Flynn, falls in love with Robert Young, the fiance of her niece Janet Leigh. Garson's grand, Flynn is flat and the bottom line is boredom.

FORTESCUE, REV. CHARLES
THE MISSIONARY (1982, Columbia)—In the East End of London in 1906, former African missionary **Michael Palin** sets up a Mission for Fallen Women. The fallen women and some quasi-chaste ones keep falling into Palin's bed.

FORTNER, HELEN
THREE BLONDES IN HIS LIFE (1961, Cinema Associates)—**Greta Thyssen** is one of three blondes who help and distract private eye Jock Mahoney as he investigates a friend's murder.

FORTUNE, LULA PACE
WILD AT HEART (1990, Goldwyn)—Raped at 13, **Laura Dern** witnessed the murder of her father, arranged by her witchy mother Diane Ladd and her mobster lover. It's little wonder that Dern grows up to be totally screwed up and takes up with Nicolas Cage, who is equally bizarre. But since the behavior of just about everyone else is so weird, Dern and Cage seem almost normal by comparison.

FORTUNE, MAGGIE
THE DESERT FLOWER (1925, Silent, First National)—**Colleen Moore** resists the lecherous advances of her stepfather, while raising her baby sister and reforming her alcoholic boyfriend.

FORTUNE, PETER
A FACE IN THE FOG (1936, Victory)—Playwright **Laurence Grey** disguises himself as a hunchback, then kills members of the cast of a play. Oh what the heck, every author's wanted to do that to those who ruin his or her creation.

FORTUNE, QUACKSTER
QUACKSTER FORTUNE HAS A COUSIN IN THE BRONX (1970, UMC)—**Gene Wilder** makes a living in Dublin by following horses through the streets and picking up their droppings, which he then sells as fertilizer. He has an affair with an American, Margot Kidder, studying at Trinity College. When a new law is passed banning horses on the streets of Dublin, Wilder's means of making a living is over. He receives a small inheritance from a cousin who dies in the Bronx. With these funds, he buys a bus and starts a sightseeing service for tourists. The movie was made at a time when Wilder was still a very droll entertainer.

FORZIATI, JOE
LADIES LOVE BRUTES (1930, Paramount)—**George Bancroft**, a crude, wealthy building contractor falls in love with society woman Mary Astor, estranged from her husband Fredric March. Despite the title, Astor doesn't love Bancroft.

FOSCOE, ROCKY
THE PSYCHOTRONIC MAN (1980, International Harmony)—Barber **Peter Spelson** can cause people to commit suicide or induce their instant death merely by looking at his victim and blinking.

FOSTER, BETTY
HER FIRST ROMANCE (1951, Columbia)—**Margaret O'Brien**, growing up now, causes her parents a lot of trouble when she tries to help Allen Martin, Jr., the boy on whom she has a tremendous crush.

FOSTER, BILLY (WILLIAM)
THREE LIVE GHOSTS (1922, Silent, Paramount); (1929, UA); (1935, MGM)—**Norman Kelly**, **Robert Montgomery** and **Richard Arlen** each portray one of three soldiers who return from WWI to find the war department has reported them dead, and it never makes a mistake—or admits to one.

FOSTER, BRANTLEY
THE SECRET OF MY SUCCESS (1987, Universal)—**Michael J. Fox** is moving up the corporate latter by sleeping with his boss' wife, Margaret Whitton. Helen Slater, the girl he really loves, has gotten a leg up, so to speak, by sleeping with the boss, Richard Jordon. The bedroom arrangements will be straightened out before the end of this less-than-funny film.

FOSTER, DANNY
TWO GUYS FROM TEXAS (1948, Warner Brothers)—**Jack Carson** and Dennis Morgan are vaudevillians on the run from crooks. That's about the extent of the plot.

FOSTER, ELIZABETH
THERE WAS A YOUNG LADY (1953, GB, Butchers)—**Dulcie Gray**, secretary to a diamond merchant, is kidnapped by thieves who want to steal her boss' stock. She helps to organize the gang but gets a message to her boss who comes to her rescue.

FOSTER, ELLEN
THE SECOND WOMAN (1951, UA)—**Betsy Drake** helps architect Robert Young, who seems psychotic, discover that he's a victim of the revenge plot of a madman. Just because you think someone's out to get you, it doesn't mean you're paranoid.

FOSTER, EMMA
MEET THE MISSUS (1937, RKO)—**Helen Broderick** so dominates her meek husband Victor Moore, that he has been turned into a househusband, while she spends her time clipping newspaper coupons and entering contests. He beats her in a housewife contest.

FOSTER, FRIDAY
FRIDAY FOSTER (1975, American International)—Newspaper photographer **Pam Grier** stumbles across a plot to kill black politicians.

FOSTER, JACK
FIFTY-SHILLING BOXER (1937, GB, RKO)—Circus performer **Bruce Seaton** dreams of becoming a boxer. He gets his chance, sort of, when he's cast as a boxer in a movie.

FOSTER, JIMMY
OCEAN'S ELEVEN (1960, Warner Brothers)—It's Cesar Romero, a mobster and the latest husband of Ilka Chase—who plays **Peter Lawford's** mother—who figures out that Lawford, Frank Sinatra, Dean Martin and others are behind the New Year's eve robbery of five Las Vegas casinos.

FOSTER, JOAN
UNDERCOVER GIRL (1957, GB, Butchers)—Nightclub girl **Kay Callard** helps the brother of a murdered reporter bust up a drug ring.

FOSTER, JUDY
A DATE WITH JUDY (1948, MGM)—**Jane Powell** and Elizabeth Taylor are two pretty teens competing for Robert Stack in this piece of fluff. Carmen Miranda steals the show.

FOSTER, KARIN
THE GIRL IN THE SWING (1989, GB, Panorama/J&M)—In a confusing film, **Meg Tilly** is a German secretary, with some unusual phobias, such as churches, whose marriage to reserved British art dealer Rupert Frazer is most mysterious.

FOSTER, NICHOLAS
THE MAN IN THE DINGHY (1951, GB, Snader)—**Michael Wilding** stows away on a yacht bound for Norway. His unwilling hosts can't seem to get rid of him, because he's in love with their cook.

FOSTER, SIMON & LAURA
SIMON AND LAURA (1956, GB, Universal)—**Peter Finch** and **Kay Kendall**, actors who play a married couple on TV, are wed in real life and hate each other, but can't separate because they are too successful.

FOSTER, WILLIAM
FOR THE DEFENSE (1930, Paramount)—**William Powell** portrays a brilliant lawyer, who is sent to Sing Sing for jury tampering. It's an interesting film based on the career of William Fallon, a major criminal lawyer of the 1910s and 1920s.

FOTHERGILL, AINSLEY
KNIGHT WITHOUT ARMOUR (1937, GB, London Films)—During the Russian Revolution, British translator **Robert Donat** helps widowed countess Marlene Dietrich escape to safety. As usual the performance of Donat is first class. So is the performance of Dietrich—which is not so usual. It's a first-rate romantic thriller.

FOTHERINGAY, GEORGE MCWHISTER
THE MAN WHO COULD WORK MIRACLES (1937, GB, UA)—**Roland Young** a London clerk, finds that the gods have given him the power to work miracles. By not taking his gift seriously enough, he almost causes the end of the world.

FOUL PHIL
THE GARBAGE PAIL KIDS (1987, Atlantic Entertainment)—**Robert Bell** is another of the midgets in grotesque costumes who gross out everyone in the audience over 12 in this inane film based on a mistake made by the Topps Bubble Gum Company.

FOUSSARD, DANIELLE
TO CATCH A THIEF (1955, Paramount)—**Brigitte Auber**, a cute French girl, emulates Cary Grant's modus operandi as a cat burglar on the Riviera.

FOWLER, SYLVIA
THE WOMEN (1939, MGM)—**Rosalind Russell** is the "friend" of Norma Shearer who lets her pal know that her husband is dallying with Joan Crawford. This sends Shearer off to get a divorce, closely followed by Russell, when her husband leaves her for a younger woman. Russell changes friends and becomes a close chum of Crawford who by now has married Shearer's ex. Russell must be something of a jinx, because Shearer steals her ex back from Crawford. This delightfully bitchy work by Claire Boothe has a cast of 135 women and no men.

FOX, LOIS
THE GIRL IN THE DARK (1918, Silent, Bluebird)—**Carmel Myers** and Ashton Dearholt outwit Chinatown villains who are after a green seal ring.

FOX, STEPHEN ODALIE D'ARCENEAUYX
THE FOXES OF HARROW (1947, 20th Century Fox)—Rascally gambler **Rex Harrison** becomes a rich New Orleans landowner. He marries fiery Southern aristocrat Maureen O'Hara. Their union is anything but tranquil. This adaptation of the best-selling Frank Yerby novel might have been better if Tyrone Power hadn't turned down the leading role, but he'd play a similar part in MISSISSIPPI GAMBLER in 1953.

FOY, BRYNIE, CHARLEY, RICHARD, MARY, MADELEINE, EDDIE JR. & IRVING
THE SEVEN LITTLE FOYS (1955, Paramount)—**Billy Gray, Lee Erickson, Paul De Rolf, Lydia Reed, Linda Bennett, Jimmy Baird** and **Tommy Duran** are the seven children of vaudevillian Eddie Foy, played by Bob Hope. Dad incorporates the youngsters into his act when their mother dies.

FOYLE, KITTY
KITTY FOYLE (1940, RKO)—**Ginger Rogers** won an Oscar for her portrayal of a working girl who marries into a wealthy family, but doesn't find happiness there.

FRA DIAVOLO
THE DEVIL'S BROTHER (1933, MGM)—In this Laurel & Hardy comedy, the boys are misfit servants to bandit **Dennis King**. The latter poses as a wealthy marquis in order to learn where the wealthy women he courts hide their jewels.

FRAME, PETER
THE CRIME OF PETER FRAME (1938, GB, Fox British)—Chemist **Frank Allenby**, disfigured in a lab accident, takes drastic measures when he suspects his wife of having an affair with a playwright.

FRAN
SHE'LL BE WEARING PINK PAJAMAS (1986, Film Forum)—**Julie Walters** changes her life by signing up for an outdoor survival session. She gains not only self-confidence but self-knowledge.

FRAN
VAMPYRES, DAUGHTERS OF DRACULA (1977, GB, Cambist)—**Marianne Morris** and Anulka are a pair of undead lovers who spend

the day making love in a double coffin and the nights draining blood from campers on the grounds of their castle.

FRANCE, ATOLINE
THE GIRL WHO STAYED AT HOME (1919, Silent, Paramount)—**Carol Dempster** is a girl left behind by two brothers who go off to fight in WWI.

FRANCESCA
DANCERS (1987, Cannon)—World famous dancer Mikhail Baryshnikov dallies with innocent young ballerina **Alessandra Ferri**.

FRANCESCA
SLAVE GIRL (1947, Universal)—Beautiful slave girl **Yvonne De Carlo** assists American George Brent rescue ten kidnapped seamen from Tripoli pirates.

FRANCESCA
THAT LADY IN ERMINE (1948, 20th Century Fox)—Director Ernst Lubitsch died during the filming of this minor musical and Otto Preminger finished. **Betty Grable** finds her ancestors in a mythical country, stepping out of their portraits to help repel invaders.

FRANCESCO
BROTHER SUN, SISTER MOON (1972, GB, Paramount/Vic Films)—When **Graham Faulkner** returns from the crusades, he becomes Francis of Assisi and establishes an order of monks who strive to help their fellow man. The movie portrays Francis as an early flower-child.

FRANCESI, BELLA
SPIN A DARK WEB (1956, GB, Columbia)—**Faith Domergue**, sister of a powerful London mobster, seduces her lover Lee Patterson into a life of crime.

FRANCHI, MARIO & CARLOS
THE BANDITS OF CORSICA (1953, Global/UA)—**Richard Greene** portrays both Siamese twins, separated at birth and sent to live with two different families. As adults, the two band together to overthrow a tyrant.

FRANCIE
PRETTYKILL (1987, Dax Avant/Spectrafilm)—**Suzanne Snyder** is a schizophrenic prostitute in this inept thriller.

FRANCIS, KAY
FOUR JILLS IN A JEEP (1944, 20th Century Fox)—**Kay Francis** manages to always look marvelous as she and three other Hollywood actresses travel overseas to entertain WWII servicemen.

FRANCK, MARIA
MADAME SPY (1934, Universal)—Russian spy **Fay Wray** keeps he eyes on her new husband Nils Asther, who is a WWI Austrian agent.

"FRANINI, MARIETTA"
NAUGHTY MARIETTA (1935, MGM)—French princess **Jeanette MacDonald** flees to America and falls in love with Indian scout Nelson Eddy. If you like a simple operetta with good music, this Victor Herbert work featuring songs such as: "Italian Street Song," "Tramp, Tramp, Tramp," "I'm Falling in Love with Someone" and "Ah, Sweet Mystery of Life" won't disappoint.

FRANK
COMES A HORSEMAN (1978, UA)—Returning from WWII service, **James Caan** throws in with rancher Jane Fonda in fighting her former lover, Jason Robards, who plans to carve out an empire for himself which will include her land.

FRANK
THIEF (1981, UA)—Being a professional thief is no guarantee of happiness seems to be the message of this film starring **James Caan**

FRANK/FALSE FRANK
FEARLESS FRANK (1967, American International)—**Jon Voight**, a country rube in Chicago, is shot by mobsters. He comes to and discovers that he has super powers—or is that his replica, "False Frank?"

FRANK
TRAVELLING NORTH (1988, Australia, View Pictures)—Crusty 70-year-old retired engineer induces much younger Julie Blake to accompany him when he leaves Melbourne for a seaside cottage in Northern Australia. Their life there is not tranquil.

FRANK, ANNE
THE DIARY OF ANNE FRANK (1959, 20th Century Fox)—**Millie Perkins** is unexceptional as the young diarist who lives with her family for two years in a factory attic, hiding from the Nazis, only to be discovered and sent to concentration camps where all die, save the father.

FRANKENSTEIN
BLOOD OF FRANKENSTEIN (1970, Ind.-International)—**J. Carroll Naish** is a wheelchair bound curator of a horror museum with some real monsters around him.

FRANKENSTEIN, DR.
FRANKENSTEIN UNBOUND (1990, 20th Century Fox)—Mad 21st-century scientist John Hurt develops a laser that accidently transports him back to Switzerland in 1817. There he meets **Raul Julia**, Mary Wollstonecraft (Godwin) Shelley's obsessed scientist. Hurt wars with Julia and the latter's rampaging monster, played by Nick Brimble, but he also identifies with them.

FRANKENSTEIN, DR. BOB
FRANKENSTEIN GENERAL HOSPITAL (1988, New Star)—**Mark Blankfield** is the great-great grandson of the legendary Baron von Frankenstein. Although he has changed his name to Frankenheimer, Blankfield is secretly working on creating a perfect human being. This wretched comedy-horror film gives the sub-genre a bad name.

FRANKENSTEIN, ELIZABETH
THE BRIDE OF FRANKENSTEIN (1935, Universal)—**Valerie Hobson** is the wife of Colin Clive, who plays Dr. Frankenstein, the creator of a monster and a female mate, Elsa Lanchester, whom he hopes will pacify murdering hulk Boris Karloff.

FRANKENSTEIN, BARONESS ELSA
FRANKENSTEIN MEETS THE WOLF MAN (1943, Universal)—Lawrence Talbot (Lon Chaney) seeks out Dr. Frankenstein whom he hopes can cure his problems of becoming a wolf man. The good doctor is dead, but his lovely daughter, **Ilona Massey**, would like to help.

FRANKENSTEIN, DR. FREDERICK
YOUNG FRANKENSTEIN (1974, 20th Century Fox)—In this Mel Brooks spoof, **Gene Wilder** is a 20th Century descendant of Baron

Frankenstein. He continues the latter's work and comes up with a sensitive monster, Peter Boyle. The film is fun if you can stand some of the most horrible puns the writers can come up with.

FRANKENSTEIN, DR. HENRY
FRANKENSTEIN (1931, Universal)—**Colin Clive** started everything as he gave his creation life. Clive, a strange one in real life, seemed as maniacal as his monster was ruthless. Clive would return to the role in THE BRIDE OF FRANKENSTEIN (1935).

FRANKENSTEIN, MARIA
JESSE JAMES MEETS FRANKENSTEIN'S DAUGHTER (1966, Embassy)—Actually **Naida Onyx** is the Baron's granddaughter. She transplants the brain from the original monster into the body of an outlaw, turning him into a mindless killer whom even Jesse James, played by John Lupton, doesn't want to mess with.

FRANKENSTEIN, BARON VICTOR
THE CURSE OF FRANKENSTEIN (1957, GB, Hammer); THE EVIL OF FRANKENSTEIN (1964, GB, Hammer/Universal); FRANKENSTEIN CREATED WOMAN (1965, GB, Hammer); FRANKENSTEIN MUST BE DESTROYED (1969, GB, Hammer); FRANKENSTEIN AND THE MONSTER FROM HELL (1974, GB, Hammer); FRANKENSTEIN 1970 (1958, Allied Artists); DR. FRANKENSTEIN ON CAMPUS (1970, Canada, Agincourt-Glen);THE HORROR OF FRANKENSTEIN (1970, GB, Hammer/EMI)—**Peter Cushing** made a decent living appearing as the infamous scientist in the various Hammer features. **Boris Karloff** who in 1931 was deliberately not given credit for appearing as Frankenstein's monster, takes a turn as a 20th Century Count Frankenstein, who opens up his castle to TV-film makers to raise money for his experiments. In 1970, **Robin Ward** is the count, now working for a Canadian University, using computers to assist his research in electronic brain control. **Ralph Bates** subs for Cushing in the 1970 Hammer film.

FRANKENSTEIN, BARON WOLF
SON OF FRANKENSTEIN (1939, Universal)—**Basil Rathbone** is excellent as the son of the creator of the monster. He revives his father's creation in the most stylish of the Universal Frankenstein movies. Lionel Atwill as the one-arm police inspector is superb.

FRANKENSTEIN'S MONSTER
ABBOTT AND COSTELLO MEET FRANKENSTEIN (1948, Universal)—**Glenn Strange**, who later would show up as the bartender in TV's Gunsmoke, puts on the Frankenstein's Monster make-up and scares the daylights out of Lou Costello.

FRANKIE
CARNY (1980, UA)—**Gary Busey** is the carnival "Bozo" who sits above a water tank and taunts customers to buy a chance to dunk him by hitting a target with a baseball. He's a man with much pent-up hostility until he takes in runaway Jodie Foster.

FRANKIE
FRANKIE AND JOHNNY (1936, Republic); (1966, UA)—**Helen Morgan** and **Donna Douglas** are about as different as two actresses could be, yet both portray the woman whose man did her wrong. Morgan was among the very best blues singers of her time, and Douglas was the sexy, cuddly member of TV's Beverly Hillbillies.

FRANKIE
HER MAN (1930, Pathe)—**Helen Twelvetrees** is the number one girlfriend of Ricardo Cortez, a French pimp, who enjoys stabbing men in the back, when they get too rough with his girls. Twelvetrees enjoys picking the pockets of her sailor "johns" but she meets her match with one, Phillips Holmes, who takes her away from her decadent world.

FRANKIE
SHE KNEW WHAT SHE WANTED (1936, GB, Wardour)—**Betty Ann Davies** is an obnoxious anti-social girl whose tantrums help her get the man she wants. What kind of a lesson is that?

FRANKIE
THREE MEN ON A HORSE (1936, Warner Brothers)—**Teddy Hart** is one of three gamblers who take advantage of the ability of Frank McHugh, a writer of greeting cards, to pick the winners of horse races. The film, based on a Broadway hit, is quite funny.

FRANKLIN, POLLY
THE LADY IN RED (1979, New World)—Whore **Pamela Sue Martin**, John Dillinger's lover, unwittingly sets him up to be gunned down in a hail of FBI bullets outside a Chicago movie theater. She takes up the robbing ways of Dillinger and meets a violent end.

FRANKLIN, WILLIAM
EVERYBODY'S OLD MAN (1936, 20th Century Fox)—When he learns of the death of his competitor and former partner, **Irvin S. Cobb** takes a year off to help the deceased's family.

FRANKLYN
THE WRONG GUYS (1988, New World)—Advice-dispensing radio personality joins four of his old buddies in a reunion of their Cub Scout Den.

FRANKO, VICTOR
THE DIRTY DOZEN (1967, GB, MGM)—**John Cassavetes** is one of twelve condemned soldier-prisoners, chosen for a suicidal mission behind German lines during WWII. He looks maniacal and acts sneaky and mean, a man who always looks out for number one. Nevertheless he dies almost valiantly.

FRANKWEILER, MRS.
FROM THE MIXED-UP FILES ON MRS. BASIL E. FRANKWEILER (1973, CINEMA 5)—Art collector **Ingrid Bergman**, a woman in her seventies, befriends a couple of kids, Sally Prager and Johnny Doran, who spend a week hiding out in New York's Metropolitan Museum of Art.

FRANKY
OUR BLUSHING BRIDES (1930, MGM)—Department store model **Dorothy Sebastian**, an innocent from a small town, gets in trouble with the law, when she hooks up with the wrong kind of guys.

FRANZ
LITTLE MEN (1935, Mascot)—**Junior Durkin** is one of many of Hollywood's juveniles thrown into this sequel to LITTLE WOMEN. Professor Bhaer (Ralph Morgan) operates a boy's school with his wife Jo March (Erin O'Brien-Moore). The film is not in the same class with the 1933 gem staring Katharine Hepburn.

FRANZ JOSEF, EMPEROR
THE KING STEPS OUT (1936, Columbia); THE EMPEROR WALTZ (1948, Paramount)—Grace Moore saves her younger sister Freida Inescourt from an unwanted royal marriage with **Franchot Tone** by

winning him herself. In the 1948 film, **Richard Hayden** appears as the Emperor, whom crack American salesman Bing Crosby is trying to interest in a new invention, the phonograph.

FRASER, ELIZA
ELIZA FRASER (1976, Australia, Hexagon)—**Susannah York** and Noel Ferrier are shipwrecked off the coast of Australia. They are held captive by aborigines for a time before being rescued.

FRASER, JANET
THE FIRST MRS. FRASER (1932, GB, Sterling)—**Dorothy Dix**, the first wife of Henry Ainley, gets the goods on the infidelities of his second, Joan Barry, whom he divorces to return to Dix.

FRASER, SGT. JUDY
THE SERGEANT WAS A LADY (1961, Universal)—**Venetia Stevenson** is the sergeant of a WAC detachment on a remote Pacific Isle. Due to a clerical error a man is assigned to her unit.

FRECKLES
FRECKLES (1935, RKO); (1960, 20th Century Fox); FRECKLES COMES HOME (1942, Monogram)—**Tom Brown, Martin West and Johnny Downs** each appear in sound versions of Gene Stratton Porter's novel about a clever orphan who takes a job in a lumber camp as a watchman and wins the love of a pretty schoolteacher. In the 1942 sequel, our hero is fresh from college. He rids his home town of some gangsters and wins the heart of the daughter of the owner of the bank. Freckles is fickle, it would seem.

FRED
RUDE AWAKENING (1989, Orion)—**Eric Roberts and Cheech Marin**, two sixties hippies who dropped out 20 years ago, reappear in New York. They are confounded by the 1980 yuppies.

FREDDIE
THE BEAUTIFUL BLONDE FROM BASHFUL BEND (1949, 20th Century Fox)—Writer-director Preston Sturges' last Hollywood movie lacked his usual comic genius. Saloon entertainer **Betty Grable** accidently shoots a judge in the bottom. She flees to another western town, where she's mistaken for the new schoolmarm.

FREDDIE
HIGH SCHOOL HERO (1946, Monogram)—**Freddie Stewart** finally rallies his undermanned and undertalented high school football team to victory over some underserving brutes. Pass on this one or better yet, punt!

FREDDIE
THE PLAYBOYS (1992, US/Ireland, Goldwyn)—**Milo O'Shea** is grand as a traveling actor who shows his versatility by giving an impromptu version of *Gone with the Wind* after catching the original in a local cinema.

FREDDIE
TOUGH GUY (1936, MGM)—**Jackie Cooper** runs away with his dog Rin Tin Tin because his father hates the animal. He must have been the only person in the world who felt that way.

FREDERIC
THE PIRATES OF PENZANCE (1983, Universal)—**Rex Smith** has been raised by pirates, but decides on his 21st birthday to go straight and find love and comfort with lovely Mabel, played by Linda Ronstadt, one of the many daughters of Major-General George Rose. The pirate chief, Kevin Kline, has other plans. The Gilbert and Sullivan music is great, but the production isn't anything special.

FREDERICK *See* PRINCE OF PILSEN

FREDERIKA, QUEEN
CONFESSIONS OF A QUEEN (1925, Silent, MGM)—**Alice Terry** becomes the queen of a small mythical country. Her husband Lewis Stone is indifferent to her, preferring his various mistresses. He changes his ideas about Terry when his people overthrow him, and he's forced to go into exile with his wife.

FREE, DONALD
PRIVATE DETECTIVE 62 (1933, Warner Brothers)—**William Powell** goes undercover in Paris to get the goods on Margaret Lindsay, but can't turn her in because he falls in love with her.

FREEBIE
FREEBIE AND THE BEAN (1974, Warner Brothers)—San Francisco cop **James Caan** and his partner Alan Arkin nearly destroy the city by the bay trying to link a mobster with the numbers racket.

FREEMAN, DAN
SOMEONE TO REMEMBER (1943, Republic)—**John Craven** shares the same name as the long lost son of sweet old Mabel Paige, who deludes herself into believing the student is her grandson. She dies a peaceful death, never learning that her son had died long ago and Craven is not her grandson.

FREEMAN, DAN
THE SPOOK WHO SAT BY THE DOOR (1973, UA)—**Laurence Cook**, a token black CIA agent, uses his knowledge to organize gangs of teenage guerillas to plague the white communities.

FRENCH GIRL, THE
THE LITTLE MADEMOISELLE (1915, Silent, World)—When she is separated from her guardians while visiting the U.S., cute French girl **Vivian Martin** is befriended by Arthur Ashley, the disinherited son of a millionaire. It's a mighty small world as Ashley is the driver of a racing car manufactured by the very man Martin's guardians were on the way to meet.

FREUD, SIGMUND
FREUD (1962, Universal); THE SECRET DIARY OF SIGMUND FREUD (1984, 20th Century Fox)—**Montgomery Clift** is earnest in his portrayal of the father of modern psychiatry, but the film is not as interesting as one would expect, considering the subject. However, compared with the feeble comedy attempt to show Dr. Freud's early life, with **Bud Cort** in the leading role, it's great entertainment.

FRIAR TUCK
MEN OF SHERWOOD FOREST (1957, GB, Hammer)—**Reginald Beckwith** portrays the well-fed chaplain and swordsmen with Robin Hood's merry band of outlaws.

FRIDAY
MAN FRIDAY (1975, GB, Avco Embassy)—**Richard Roundtree** appears as the intelligent native who joins Robinson Crusoe (Peter O'Toole) on a deserted island in another telling of the Daniel Defoe story.

FRIEND HUSBAND

A FRIENDLY HUSBAND (1923, Silent, Fox)—**Lupino Lane** and his family are taking a vacation by trailer. The film is filled with sight gags and crazy stunts, but it didn't endear British music hall star Lane to American audiences.

FRIGG, HARRY

THE SECRET WAR OF HARRY FRIGG (1968, Universal)—When four Allied generals are unable to agree on any plan for escaping from their Italian captures during WWII, the army briefly makes escape expert, private **Paul Newman**, a higher ranked general sent in to get them out.

FRISBEE

RAFFERTY AND THE GOLD DUST TWINS (1975, Warner Brothers)—**Mackenzie Phillips** is one of two female vagrants who force Alan Arkin at gunpoint to drive them to New Orleans. The threesome have a series of adventures in this moderately interesting "road" movie.

FRISBY, FREDDIE

HE'S A COCKEYED WONDER (1950, Columbia)—**Mickey Rooney**, a blundering magician, finds it very difficult to get on the right side of his girl's father. He finally proves himself by thwarting some crooks.

FRISCO JENNY

FRISCO JENNY (1933, Warner Brothers)—**Ruth Chatterton**, the madame of a popular San Francisco bordello, is a leader of the city's underworld. Her illegitimate son, whom she gave away as a child to a wealthy family, has become the district attorney, pledged to clean up the city. When one of Chatterton's lieutenants decides that the D.A. must be eliminated, she kills her colleague and is sent to the gallows for the crime, without her son ever knowing he has won the conviction which condemned his own mother.

FROGGIE

FELLER NEEDS A FRIEND (1932, Cosmopolitan)—**Andy Shuford** is the bullying cousin of crippled, friendless Jackie Cooper.

FROMAN, JANE

WITH A SONG IN MY HEART (1952, 20th Century Fox)—**Susan Hayward** is top notch in this biopic of singer Jane Froman, crippled in a plane crash, but who eventually makes a comeback. Froman supplied her singing voice.

FROST, MR.

MISTER FROST (1990, Fr./GB, Hugo/AAA/OMM)—Seemingly mild-mannered English country gentleman **Jeff Goldblum** casually confesses to the torture murders of 24 men, whom he then buried on his property. All the world's shrinks want and get a shot at understanding Goldblum's motivation.

FROY, MISS

THE LADY VANISHES (1938, GB, Gaumont); (1980, GB, Rank)—**Dame May Whitty** is priceless as the British spy, whose very existence on a train is denied by many passengers for various reasons, causing Margaret Lockwood's sanity to be questioned. **Angela Lansbury** wasn't the worst thing in the remake of the Alfred Hitchcock classic, but that's only because her co-stars Cybill Shepherd and Elliott Gould were even more horribly miscast.

FRY, FRANK

SABOTEUR (1942, Universal)—**Norman Lloyd** is the real saboteur in this exciting Hitchcock movie. He meets his end atop the Statue of Liberty in a struggle with Robert Cummings, who had been framed for Lloyd's activities.

FRYE, KIRBY

CAVALRY SCOUT (1951, Monogram)—Army Scout **Rod Cameron** tries to break up a ring of gun smugglers, who are selling firearms to the Indians. He sure wants to stop the red men from getting their hands on a Gatling gun.

FU MANCHU

THE MYSTERIOUS DR. FU MANCHU (1929, Paramount); THE RETURN OF DR. FU MANCHU (1930, Paramount); THE MASK OF FU MANCHU (1932, MGM); DRUM OF FU MANCHU (1943, Republic); THE FACE OF FU MANCHU (1965, GB, Seven Arts); THE BLOOD OF FU MANCHU (1968, GB, Udastex Films); THE CASTLE OF FU MANCHU (1968, GB, International Cinema); THE VENGEANCE OF FU MANCHU (1968, GB, Warner Brothers); THE FIENDISH PLOT OF DR. FU MANCHU (1980, Orion)—**Warner Oland, Boris Karloff, Henry Brandon, Christopher Lee** and Peter Sellers each appeared at least once as the evil Oriental master criminal, created by Sax Rohmer. The movies have a certain decadent appeal, particularly when The Yellow Menace's daughter, played by someone like Myrna Loy, gets the hots by sexually torturing some captured male Caucasian. Christopher Lee's great height seemed to suit Fu Manchu. Peter Sellers once again proved that when he's hot, he's hot, and when he's not, he's not. As Fu Manchu, he's ice cold.

FUERTE, PEDRO "PETE"

THE THREE GODFATHERS (1948, MGM)—**Pedro Armendariz** is one of the three outlaws who risk their lives and freedom to get a new born baby to safety after the child's mother dies in the desert.

FUGITVE, THE

THE FUGITIVE (1947, RKO)—Saintly priest **Henry Fonda** is hunted as a criminal in a country where religion and the clergy have been outlawed. Despite his ever present fears of being caught, he continues his under-ground ministry. He is finally trapped and martyred. Fonda is excellent in the central role and the work of Dolores Del Rio and Pedro Armendariz is outstanding.

FULTON, POLLY & B.F.

B.F.'S DAUGHTER (1948, MGM)—**Barbara Stanwyck** secures her penniless liberal professor husband Van Heflin's rise to prominence without letting on that she's the daughter of millionaire **Charles Coburn**.

FUMO, SPIKE

SPIKE OF BENSONHURST (1988, Filmdallas)—In this satire on the deterioration of traditional values among small time hustlers and minor Mafia soldiers, **Sasha Mitchell** is a would-be prizefighter who wins or loses on cue from gamblers. He falls in and out of favor with Mafia chief Ernest Borgnine through the latter's bubble-headed but beautiful daughter.

FURILLO, ED

CITY SLICKERS (1991, Columbia)—**Bruno Kirby** takes time off from his constant pursuit of ever-younger women to go on a modern cattle drive with two of his New York City buddies, Billy Crystal and Daniel Stern. Kirby shares a bitter but beautifully rendered memory of his best and worst day.

FURY, BLANCHE

BLANCHE FURY (1948, GB, Universal)—Governess **Valerie Hobson** marries a wealthy heir, then plots to kill him with the assistance of her lover Stewart Granger. The story is based on the Rush murder case of the 1800s.

FURY, CAPTAIN

CAPTAIN FURY (1939, UA)—**Brian Aherne** is an Irish freedom fighter sent to a penal colony in Australia. He and a handful of other prisoners escape from the harsh treatment of evil George Zucco and becomes a sort of bush country Robin Hood, as he champions the cause of the small farmers against land grabbers. It's a young boy's dream of an action-adventure film with good performances from Aherne, John Carradine and Victor McLaglen.

G

GABBO, GREAT

THE GREAT GABBO (1929, Art World Wide)—Ventriloquist **Erich von Stroheim's** personality becomes dominated by that of his dummy.

GABBY

SOME GIRLS (1989, MGM-UA)—When his college sweetheart **Jennifer Connelly** announces that she no longer loves him, go-with-the-flow Patrick Dempsey looks for sack time with her beautiful, teasing sisters.

GABEY

ON THE TOWN (1949, MGM)—**Gene Kelly** is one of three sailors on a 24-hour leave in New York City. He falls in love with "Miss Turnstile," Vera-Ellen. He finds her, loses her and wins her before the leave is over. Kelly gives an exuberant, vital performance in one of the all-time favorite Hollywood musicals.

GABLE, CLARK

GABLE AND LOMBARD (1976, Universal)—**James Brolin** is a dud, appearing as the King, in this story of the romance and marriage of Gable and Carole Lombard, played by Jill Clayburgh. The only thing Brolin and Gable have in common is a mustache and big ears.

GABLE, MIKE

KEATON'S COP (1990, Cannon)—One-time six-million-dollar man **Lee Majors** is a cop who joins forces with mobster Abe Vigoda to discover who has ordered a hit of Vigoda. The trail leads to well-preserved former pin-up June Wilkinson, named Big Mama for obvious reasons.

GABLER, HEDDA

HEDDA (1975, GB, Bowden)—**Glenda Jackson** stars in a production of the Henrik Ibsen play, centered around a selfish, pregnant woman, bored and hating the idea of carrying her husband's child. She takes revenge on a former lover, but her scheme leads to her own suicide.

GABY

GABY (1956, MGM)—In this flabby remake of WATERLOO BRIDGE, **Leslie Caron** is a ballerina, whose WWII romance with soldier John Kerr ends tragically.

GAINES, ADAM

ADAM AT 6 A.M. (1970, Solar/National General)—**Michael Douglas**, a hip college professor, begins to question his life. He travels to Missouri to locate some real people, but they are as much a disappointment to him as all others.

GALANTE, MARIE

MARIE GALANTE (1934, Fox)—While stranded in the Panama Canal Zone, French girl **Ketti Gallian** finds herself mixed up in a plot to blow up the Canal.

GALAXINA

GALAXINA (1980, Crown International)—The late Playmate of the year, **Dorothy R. Stratton**, murdered by her husband, appears in this piece of trash as a female robot assigned to a police squad car. She is exploited by all kinds of men.

GALE, GLORIA

GIRL IN DANGER (1934, Columbia)—Thrill-seeking society girl **Shirley Grey** helps a jewel thief by hiding a valuable emerald in her luxurious apartment. Inspector Trent, played by Ralph Bellamy, is on the case.

GALE, MARIAN

BLONDE ALIBI (1946, Universal)—**Martha Driscoll** sets out to prove that her commercial pilot, boyfriend Tom Neal, is innocent of murdering his rival for Driscoll.

GALEN

DRAGONSLAYER (1981, Disney/Paramount)—In this sword-and-sorcery fantasy, sorcerer's apprentice **Peter MacNichol** is to use his master's magic amulet to slay a dragon, but finds he may not be up to the task.

GALILEI, GALILEO

GALILEO (1975, GB, American Film Theatre)—**Topol** portrays the 17th century Italian astronomer and mathematician, branded a heretic for his theories.

GALLAGHER, BILL

GALLOPING GALLAGHER (1924, Silent, Monogram)—Wanderer **Fred Thompson** moseys into a western town, is made its sheriff, and saves minister Hazel Keener from a gang of outlaws. Thompson's horse Silver King seemed a better actor than most in this routine western.

GALLAGHER, "BUTTSY"

HIS GREAT TRIUMPH (1916, Silent, Metro)—Mental defective **William Nigh** has been raised in the slums. He has been browbeaten by everyone, to the point he's afraid of his shadow. But with one great exhibition of courage, he changes everything.

GALLAGHER, DAN

FATAL ATTRACTION (1987, Paramount)—**Michael Douglas** almost accidently falls into a weekend affair with wildly seductive Glenn Close, but then finds he can't get rid of her. Worse yet, it appears she's a loony and a dangerous one, who threatens not only him, but his wife and child as well. Many wives pointed to Douglas's situation as a warning to their husbands in case they felt like trying a one-night stand.

GALLAGHER, SUSAN

ZIEGFELD GIRL (1941, MGM)—The professional and romantic problems of new Ziegfeld girls **Judy Garland**, Lana Turner and Hedy

Lamarr serve to provide a minimal plot for this all-star musical review.

GALLANT, LUCY
LUCY GALLANT (1955, Paramount)—Dressmaker **Jane Wyman** becomes a successful businesswoman, running a chain of fashion stores, but has less luck in her private love life.

GALLARD, PAUL
THE MAN WHO BROKE THE BANK AT MONTE CARLO (1935, Fox)—Russian emigre **Ronald Colman** becomes a taxi driver in France, wins a fortune at the roulette tables, loses it all, and happily returns to driving his cab.

GALLEGHER
LET 'ER GO GALLEGHER (1928, Silent, Pathe)—Newsboy **Junior Coghlan** is a witness to a murder committed by a well-known gangster. Coghlan tips-off reporter friend Harrison Ford. Coghlan and Ford ultimately bring the murderer to justice.

GALLICO
THE MAD MAGICIAN (1954, Columbia)—Deranged magician **Vincent Price** murders anyone who stands in his way of making it to the big time in his profession. Price is hokey but as always an enjoyable ham.

GALLIER, IRENE
CAT PEOPLE (1982, Universal/RKO)—**Natassja Kinski** appears in this remake of the lovely 1942 Val Lewton thriller. Kinski resists an incestuous relationship with her brother. Each time after sex, her kind turn into dangerous felines who must kill before becoming human again. If you can, forget this one and see the 1942 movie.

GALLO, JOE
CRAZY JOE (1974, Columbia)—**Peter Boyle** stars in this biopic of the New York Mafia hood who briefly operates independently of the mob families, but meets a violent end.

GALT, PARSON JOSIAH & JACOB
THE DESPERADOS (1969, Columbia)—**Jack Palance** and **George Maharis** are the fanatical leaders of a gang of violent outlaws terrorizing the west after the Civil War.

GALT, SHERIFF
THE IRON SHERIFF (1957, UA)—Lawman **Sterling Hayden's** son is accused of murder and its up to his Pa to prove his innocence. After this movie, Hayden felt compelled to flee movies for awhile and sail away on his boat.

GALVIN, BERT
UNDER THE GUN (1951, Universal)—Ruthless racketeer **Richard Conte**, convicted of murder, becomes a prison trustee when an inmate he persuaded to attempt to escape is killed.

GALVIN, BILLY
BILLY GALVIN (1986, Vestron)—**Lenny Von Dohlen** and his daddy are at odds over the type of work the young man will seek. Von Dohlen wants to don a hard hat like his old man and work in the construction trade. His father has something better in mind for his son. The youngster may be right.

GAMBINI, VINNY
MY COUSIN VINNY (1992, 20th Century Fox)—When Brooklyn college student Ralph Macchio and his pal Mitchell Whitfield are mistakenly nabbed for murder in a small Alabama town, he calls in his cousin **Joe Pesci**, a lawyer who's never tried a case. Pesci arrives in town with his mouthy, beautiful girlfriend, Maria Tomei, who just about steals the film.

GAMMAGE, BERT
THE KINSMAN (1919, Silent, Hepworth)—**Henry Edwards** appears both as an Australian gentlemen and his commoner London cousin. The latter, believing the former has drowned, impersonates his relative in a manner that disgusts the gentleman's family and friends.

GANDHI, MAHATMA
GANDHI (1982, GB, Columbia)—**Ben Kingsley** won an Oscar for his performance as the great Indian leader pacifist and martyr. The picture won six other Academy Awards, including Best Picture and Best Director for Richard Attenborough, but as is the case with most epics, there are too many people and too many incidents to really get a handle on the character of the saintly man.

GANDIER, HENRI
SAVAGE MESSIAH (1972, GB, MGM)—**Scott Antony** stars in this biopic of the sculptor who died during WWI at the age of 24. It concentrates on his platonic affair with Sophie Brezeska (Dorothy Tutin), a Polish woman twenty years older than he.

GANDIL, CHICK
EIGHT MEN OUT (1988, Orion)—While the other seven Chicago White Sox players banned from baseball for life for throwing the 1919 World Series were just naive country boys, who couldn't resist the temptation to make some real money after playing for penny-pinching owner Charles Comiskey, **Michael Rooker** was the team troublemaker. He did the gambler's bidding in recruiting his teammates.

GANJA
GANJA AND HESS (1973, Kelly-Jordan)—**Marlene Clark** is the bride of a black vampire Duane Jones, who yearns to return to his African roots.

GANN, NATTY
THE JOURNEY OF NATTY GANN (1985, Buena Vista)—Fourteen-year-old **Meredith Salenger** rides the rails during the Great Depression in search of her missing father. Her journey takes her from Chicago to Seattle. It's a fine movie that most of the family can and will enjoy.

GANNON
A MAN CALLED GANNON (1969, Universal)—Drifter **Tony Franciosa** takes young cowpoke Michael Sarrazin under his wing, but they end up on opposite sides in a range war.

GANNON, JIM
TEACHER'S PET (1958, Paramount)—Newspaper editor **Clark Gable** has no use for journalism schools until he meets Professor Doris Day, whose class he joins to show her up, but instead stays to fall in love.

GANT, PVT. HONUS
SOLDIER BLUE (1970, Avco Embassy)—When a paymaster's detachment of the U.S. cavalry is ambushed by Indians, only **Peter Strauss** and Candice Bergen survive to make the trek through the desert back to safety.

GANTRY, ELMER
ELMER GANTRY (1960, UA)—**Burt Lancaster** won an Academy Award for his ringing portrayal of a con-man who joins an evangelist's band. The only difference between him and Sister

Falconer, played by Jean Simmons, is that he knows he's a phony. It's not that he has no faith, it's merely that his interest in Simmons is more physical that spiritual. He is all but ruined by a former sweetheart, now a prostitute, Shirley Jones, who releases fake photos of him making love to her. Lancaster is ideal for the likeable flim-flam man.

GANUCCI, CARMINE
EVERY LITTLE CROOK AND NANNY (1972, MGM)—Mafia Don **Victor Mature** has trouble with his son's nanny Lynn Redgrave, who kidnaps the boy.

GARAY, LYNETTE
FLAME OF STAMBOUL (1957, Columbia)—Dancer **Lisa Ferraday** is used by villain George Zucco to distract a high-ranking Egyptian official, who is carrying the Suez defense plans.

GARBAGE MAN
THE GARBAGE MAN (1963, Cinema Dist. of America)—Garbage man **Toney Naylor** rides a small cart pulled by a talking horse, who has no use for modern sanitation methods.

GARBO, GRETA
GARBO TALKS (1984, MGM/UA)—**Nina Zoe** is the legendary actress who wishes to be left alone. Her role is small. She is mostly seen walking away. Ron Silver desperately tries to fulfill his dying mother Anne Bancroft's last wish to meet her idol, Greta Garbo.

GARCIA, CARMEN
THE LOVES OF CARMEN (1948, Columbia)—**Rita Hayworth** appears in a series of exotic costumes, but the drama based on a story by Merimee is much ado about nothing.

GARCIA, GENERAL
A MESSAGE TO GARCIA (1936, 20th Century Fox)—During the Spanish-American war, Cuban girl Barbara Stanwyck helps American agent John Boles to get through to rebel leader **Enrique Acosta** with a diplomatic message.

GARDNER
I SAILED TO TAHITI WITH AN ALL GIRL CREW (1969, World)—Male chauvinist **Gardner McKay** bets he can win a race to Tahiti using mere women as his crew. The film used to make this movie is perfect for stink bombs.

GARDNER, ANGELA ("HOT GARTERS GERTIE")
SHE'S WORKING HER WAY THROUGH COLLEGE (1952, Warner Brothers)—Burlesque queen **Virginia Mayo** goes to College and teaches English Professor Ronald Reagan things he didn't learn in Graduate School.

GARDNER, KATHY
DREAM LOVER (1986, MGM/UA)—**Kristy McNichol** takes the psychological cure after an assault and the treatment is more threatening than her original trauma.

GARFIELD, ELLEN
FRONT PAGE WOMAN (1935, Warner Brothers)—**Bette Davis** and George Brent are rival reporters who try to scoop each other. He's a mean chauvinist, not above dirty tricks to make Davis look bad, but she fools him. He has to acknowledge that she's not just a woman, she's a newspaper "man."

GARFORD, BILLY
A HERO ON HORSEBACK (1927, Silent, Universal)—**Hoot Gibson**, a happy-go-lucky cowboy, loses most of the $500 loaned to him by a rancher on gambling. Gibson hires himself out to an old prospector and falls in love with the man's daughter. Gibson must also survive an accusation that he's a bank robber before he gets his financial problems straightened away.

GARGAN, JOE
LOAN SHARK (1952, Lippert)—**George Raft** is entangled with the loan shark racket in a tire factory. He works his way into the gang, and a shoot-out smashes the ring that is emptying the pockets of the workers and that killed his brother.

GARGAN, PATSY
THE MAYOR OF HELL (1933, Warner Brothers)—Racketeer **James Cagney's** life is changed when he is made superintendent of a reform school. The Dead End Kids give Cagney all he can handle.

GARLAND, RUPERT
WANTED—A COWARD (1927, Silent, Banne/Sterling)—Adventurer **Robert Frazer** claims that all men, himself included, are actually cowards. Then he goes out to prove himself a hero.

GARP, T.S.
THE WORLD ACCORDING TO GARP (1982, Warner Brothers)—**Robin Williams**, the product of his nurse mother Glenn Close impregnating herself by an insane dying airman, grows up to be a writer, but always in the shadow of his remarkable mother. It's difficult to say if the movie or the novel by John Irving on which it's based has any point.

GARRAWAY, MATT
SPOILERS OF THE NORTH (1947, Republic)—Evil fisherman **Paul Kelly** attempts to hook Evelyn Ankers, hoping she will loan him the money to start a cannery. After this is accomplished, he dumps her and turns the charm on Adrian Booth to help him hire illegal Indian laborers for the cannery. He'd be on top of the world if his charm worked with men as well as women.

GARRETT
THE LONE RUNNER (1988, Trans World)—Rugged loner **Miles O'Keefe** rides a horse through the Moroccan desert, carrying a cross-bow which fires explosive arrows. He must rescue a European heiress and a sackful of priceless diamonds.

GARRETT/GROGAN
THE HITMAN (1991, Cannon)—Undercover cop **Chuck Norris** tries to get the goods on Seattle gangster Al Waxman and his Vancouver counterpart Marcel Sabourin. To solidify his cover, Norris happily kills Waxman's enemies in cold blood.

GARRETT, BUCK
MASTER OF MEN (1933, Columbia)—Financier **Jack Holt** is ruined by his wife on the eve of the Great Stock Market Crash, because he doesn't pay enough attention to her. They face poverty together, happily.

GARRETT, LANK
THE COWBOY AND THE BLONDE (1941, 20th Century Fox)—Cowboy actor **George Montgomery** tames shrewish actress Mary Beth Hughes.

GARRETT, PAT
I SHOT BILLY THE KID (1950, Lippert); PAT GARRETT AND BILLY THE KID (1973, MGM)—**Robert Lowery** and **James Coburn** each were former friends of the mercurial young killer Billy the Kid, but

are forced to gun down the fast gun. The "B" movie actually is preferable to the violent, bloody Sam Peckinpah film. The first looks like how things might have been, the second how the director fantasizes his message.

GARRETT, SAM
THE DESPERADO (1954, Allied Artists)—Veteran gun-fighter **Wayne Morris** comes to the aid of James Lydon when the latter is framed for the murder of carpetbagger Nestor Paiva.

GARRICK, DAVID
THE GREAT GARRICK (1937, Warner Brothers)—**Brian Aherne** portrays the great egotistical actor. Members of the Comedie Francaise perpetrate a hoax to try to teach him a lesson, but the plan doesn't have the desired effect on the pompous thespian.

GARRICK, EVANS
THE GREAT PROFILE (1940, 20th Century Fox)—It's rather sad watching dissipated downsliding actor **John Barrymore** in this self-parody of the disgraceful shenanigans of a failed, conceited actor.

GARRISON, BILLY
GARRISON'S FINISH (1923, Silent, Allied Producers)—Jockey **Jack Pickford** loses a big race because he was doped by a gambler. The authorities believe he threw the race, and he is suspended. He makes it back to racing by the end of the movie, winning the Kentucky Derby for a horsewoman, Madge Bellamy, who nursed him back to health after he was injured in a barroom brawl.

GARRISON, GENE & TOM
I NEVER SANG FOR MY FATHER (1970, Columbia)—After his mother's death, middle-aged widower **Gene Hackman** is stuck with his grouchy old father **Melvyn Douglas**, who tries to prevent Hackman from remarrying.

GARRY, ED
DEPUTY MARSHAL (1949, Lippert)—**Jon Hall** not only captures the bank robbers he's been trailing, but he also prevents land grabbers from stealing Frances Langford's land. He also steals Langford's heart.

GARSTON, LORD CYRIL
THE NEW CLOWN (1916, GB, Silent, Ideal)—**James Welch** believes that he is responsible for a man's death, so he joins a travelling circus as a clown.

GARTH, ELLEN
THE WOMAN WHO WOULDN'T DIE (1965, GB, Warner Brothers)—**Georgina Clarkson** makes everyone's life unbearable, causing her husband Gary Merrill to decide to do away with her, but it's not an easy task.

GARTH, DR. JULIUS WINSLOW
STRANGE LADY IN TOWN (1955, Warner Brothers)—**Greer Garson** stars as a female doctor practicing in 1880 Sante Fe. It's a quaint western star vehicle.

GARVEY, PETE
HERE COMES THE GROOM (1951, Paramount)—Journalist **Bing Crosby** adopts war orphans Jacques Gencel and Beverly Washburn. To keep them in the U.S., he must marry within five days. He chooses former girl-friend Jane Wyman to be the lucky bride, but she's engaged to Franchot Tone, a man with 40 million dollars. No sweat! Crosby wins Wyman from Tone singing the Oscar winning "In the Cool, Cool, Cool of the Evening" by Johnny Mercer and Hoagy Carmichael.

GARVIN, JACK "ZIP"
A KNIGHT OF THE WEST (1921, Silent, W.B.M. Photo-plays)—Extremely bashful cowboy **Olin Francis** doesn't have the nerve to confess his love for the daughter of a neighboring rancher. When he rescues her from rustlers, she does all the talking.

GARY
THE CONTENDER (1944, PRC)—Truckdriver **Buster Crabbe** turns to boxing to keep his son in an expensive military academy, but hits the skids because of booze and a gold-digging blonde. He finds his old friends, old girl, and his son's old school are the best.

GARY
STRANGERS (1990, Australia, Genesis)—When **James Healey** hooks up with wild Anne Looby on a plane, they have a steamy tryst in a hotel room. He treats it as just a one-night stand. A la FATAL ATTRACTION, Looby has a more permanent relationship in mind, and she's willing to kill to get her way.

GARY, LT. JIM
TWO RODE TOGETHER (1961, Columbia)—Cavalry officer **Richard Widmark** and Texas lawman James Stewart team up to find a tribe of Comanches, bartering with them for some long-time-held-captive white women.

GASKAIN, DULCIMA
DULCIMA (1971, GB, EMI)—Farmer's daughter **Carol White** reluctantly goes to live with lecherous old miser John Mills.

GASOLINE GUS
GASOLINE GUS (1921, Silent, Paramount)—**Roscoe "Fatty" Arbuckle** makes a fortune with a fake oil well. Because of the infamous "Arbuckle-Virginia Rappe" case, this film has never been shown in the U.S., even though Arbuckle was cleared of the young woman's death.

GASSKO, RICK
BACHELOR PARTY (1984, 20th Century Fox)—**Tom Hanks** is not exactly George Grizzard's notion of a husband for his daughter Tawny Kitaen. Hanks' bachelor party thrown by his friends almost sinks the marriage before the ceremony.

GASTON
BLUEBEARD (1944, PRC)—**John Carradine** portrays a Parisian strangler of young women.

GATES, BRIAR AND TRUMAN
NEXT OF KIN (1989, Warner Brothers)—When Chicago mobster Adam Baldwin kills their brother, Kentucky farmer **Liam Neeson** and Chicago cop **Patrick Swayze** have different ideas on how to deal with the killing.

GATES, NADIA
BLIND DATE (1987, Tri-Star)—Beautiful **Kim Basinger** is Bruce Willis' blind date. The only problem—he doesn't know the effect of alcohol on the luscious blonde. Before the date is over he learns. In addition he loses his job, wrecks his car, is arrested and naturally is in love. It's a dumb premise and isn't presented very well.

GATES, SALLY
ALIAS MARY DOW (1935, Universal)—Taxi-dancer **Sally Eilers** is persuaded to pose as a girl who had been kidnapped eighteen years earlier.

GATES, SAM

SPY FOR A DAY (1939, GB, Paramount)—Farm hand **Duggie Wakefield** is discovered to be the exact double of a spy in this modest British comedy.

GATSBY, JAY

THE GREAT GATSBY (1926, Paramount); (1949, Paramount); (1974, Paramount)—**Warner Baxter, Alan Ladd** and **Robert Redford** each appear as the ex-army officer who becomes very wealthy under strange circumstances, in order to be worthy of a married southern belle he has always loved. The best production of the F. Scott Fitzgerald production would seem to be the Ladd version.

GATTI

MY SONG FOR YOU (1935, GB, Gaumont)—Grand opera star **Jan Krepura** takes an interest in the career of a young Aileen Marson, and falls in love for her.

GAUCHO, THE

THE GAUCHO (1928, Silent, UA)—Outlaw **Douglas Fairbanks** mocks God and tries to seduce Geraine Greear, the Girl of the Shrine, but is unable to go through with it because of her innocence. Such goings-on shocked Fairbanks' fans.

GAULT, MAGGIE

STRANGERS WHEN WE MEET (1960, Columbia)—Married **Kim Novak** has an affair with Kirk Douglas, a married architect. Everyone suffers, but not nearly as much as the audience.

GAUNT, DR. RICHARD

THREE WISE FOOLS (1923, Silent, Goldwyn): (1946, MGM) -**Alec B. Francis** and **Lionel Barrymore** star as the medical member of the trio of three crotchety old men whose lives are enhanced by a charming orphan. Barrymore is supposed to have observed that in medieval times, his co-star Margaret O'Brien would have been burned as a witch.

GAUTIER, MARGUERITE

CAMILLE (1927, Silent, First National); (1937, MGM)—**Norma Talmadge** and **Greta Garbo** each star as Alexandre Dumas dying courtesan, who falls for a naive young man who loves her, and dies radiantly in his arms. It's all so, sob, sob, beautifully sad.

GAVIN

THE LITTLE MINISTER (1934, RKO)—In 1840 Scotland, new minister **John Beal** falls unsuitably in love with gypsy girl Katharine Hepburn. It's OK, she's really the wayward daughter of a local nobleman.

GAWAIN

GAWAIN AND THE GREEN KNIGHT (1973, GB, UA)—**Murray Head** accepts the challenge of the Green Knight to take his best shot at chopping off his head, with the condition that afterwards The Green Knight gets his turn. Head chops off the Green Knight's head but the decapitated body picks up his head and makes an appointment with Head to take his swing. Heady stuff!

GAYE, VICKI

PARTY GIRL (1958, MGM)—During the Roaring Twenties in Chicago, crippled married criminal lawyer Robert Taylor wins party-girl **Cyd Charisse** away from an Al Capone-like mobster, Lee J. Cobb.

GAYLORD, FIONA, EVELYN, SUSANNA

THE GAY SISTERS (1942, First National)—Three aristocratic sisters, **Barbara Stanwyck, Geraldine Fitzgerald** and **Nancy Cole-** man refuse to sell their mansion to make way for urban development.

GAYLORD, STEPHANIE

MY DEAR SECRETARY (1948, UA)—**Laraine Day** takes a job as secretary to disorganized writer Kirk Douglas, but she's the one who writes a best-selling book.

GEARY, ADELAIDE

THEY CAME TO CORDURA (1959, Columbia)—Fugitive **Rita Hayworth** adds a little spice to the band of heroes in the campaign against Pancho Villa, led by disgraced army major Gary Cooper across the desert toward a military assembly point in Cordura. The seven travelers have trouble with bandits, weather and each other.

GEDDES, VICTOR

DYING YOUNG (1991, 20th Century Fox)—**Campbell Scott** is an immensely wealthy young man who has been battling leukemia for 10 years. He hires Julia Roberts as a nurse to help him through the bouts of violent illness caused by chemotherapy treatments. When they take a beach house together, they fall in love.

GEHRIG, LOU

THE PRIDE OF THE YANKEES (1942, RKO)—**Gary Cooper** is excellent in what is probably the best baseball biopic, playing the legendary Iron Man of the New York Yankees. He set a record for consecutive games played, with only his fatal disease amytrophic lateral sclerosis, often referred to as "Lou Gehrig's disease" getting him out of the line-up.

GELETT, JUDY

SOCIETY GIRL (1932, Fox)—Society girl **Peggy Shannon** falls in love with prizefighter James Dunn in this weak drama.

GELLHORN, FRIEDA & MARIA

TWINS OF EVIL (1971, GB, Universal)—Identical Austrian twins **Madeleine & Mary Collinson** come under the spell of count Damien Thomas who heads up a vampire cult.

GEMINIANI, NICK

HAPPY BIRTHDAY, GEMINI (1980, UA)—**Robert Viharo** has a sexual identity crisis in this disappointing adaptation of Albert Innuarto's long running Broadway play "Gemini."

GENARO, TONY

T-MEN (1947, Eagle-Lion)—**Alfred Ryder** and Dennis O'Keefe are undercover Treasury men after a gang of counterfeiters. Ryder's wife accidently blows his cover and he's killed while O'Keefe stands by helplessly. Before he dies, Ryder is able to tip his partner off to the location of a key that sinks the gang.

GENTLEMAN JOE

THE MASTER CRACKSMAN (1914, Silent, Progressive Motion Pictures)—Safecracker **Harry Carey** saves an innocent lad from being executed by solving the case.

GENTRY, RUBY

RUBY GENTRY (1952, 20th Century Fox)—Tempestuous Carolina swamp girl **Jennifer Jones** has a love-hate relationship with local aristocrat Charlton Heston. She takes her revenge on him when he decides to marry a blue-blooded young woman.

GEORGE

COME ON GEORGE (1939, GB, ATP/ABFD); LET GEORGE DO IT (1940, GB, Ealing); BELL-BOTTOM GEORGE (1943, GB, Columbia British)—These are a few of the comedy star vehicles for **George**

Formby who definitely is an acquired taste, but who had many British fans.

GEORGE
BELOVED IMPOSTER (1936, GB, Stafford/Radio)—Would-be star **Fred Conyngham** believes he has murdered a beautiful singer, a girl who rejected his advances.

GEORGE
OF MICE AND MEN (1939, MGM); (1992, MGM)—In these movie versions of the classic John Steinbeck novel, **Burgess Meredith** and **Gary Sinise** (who also directed the later film) play the taciturn friend of childlike Lennie who, after Lennie accidentally kills a woman, feels he must kill his friend.

GEORGE
THREE MEN IN A BOAT (1933, GB, Associate British Films); (1958, GB, Romulus/Valiant)—**Edmond Breon** and **Laurence Harvey** each appear as one of three men who have some misadventures during an 1890s boating holiday on the Thames.

GEORGE/ABE FIELDING
ANOTHER YOU (1991, Tri-Star)—Pathological liar **Gene Wilder** is released from a mental institution in the custody of Hollywood street hustler Richard Pryor, performing court-mandated public service. Stephen Land and Mercedes Ruehl maneuver gullible Wilder into impersonating a missing heir.

GEORGE, UNCLE
HOW TO MURDER A RICH UNCLE (1957, GB, Columbia)—Impoverished nobleman Nigel Patrick decides to murder his rich uncle **Charles Coburn**.

GEORGI, URSULA
THIRTEEN WOMEN (1932, RKO)—Half-caste **Myrna Loy** systematically murders women who as college girls snubbed Loy years earlier.

GEORGI
THE INSPECTOR GENERAL (1949, Warner Brothers)—Medicine show stooge **Danny Kaye** is mistaken for the Inspector General by the corrupt officials of a small village.

GEORGIA
ONLY WHEN I LAUGH (1981, Columbia)—This supposed comedy by Neil Simon about alcoholic actress **Martha Mason**, trying to rebuild her life and her relationship with her teenage daughter Kristy McNichol is more tearful than funny.

GEORGY
GEORGY GIRL (1966, GB, Columbia)—Unattractive, overweight **Lynn Redgrave** takes some vicarious pleasure in preparing for the illegitimate birth of her selfish roommate Charlotte Rampling's baby with the baby's father Alan Bates. Redgrave is crushed when Rampling has an abortion. Lynn finally gives in to the urgings of her father's middle-aged employer, lecherous James Mason, and marries him—one of his two proposals.

GERARD, CHARLES
HIS BUTLER'S SISTER (1943, Universal)—Deanna Durbin goes to New York to visit her half-brother Pat O'Brien, butler to Franchot Tone. She finds romance with the latter as well as a singing career.

GERARD, COL. ETIENNE
THE ADVENTURES OF GERARD (1970, GB, Nigel Films/UA) - Napoleon Hussar **Peter McEnery** becomes a double-spy and wins beautiful Claudia Cardinale in this dreadful historical spoof.

GERARD, HENRIETTA & LAURIE
ORPHANS OF THE STORM (1922, Silent, Griffith/UA)—**Lillian and Dorothy Gish** are sisters caught up in the French Revolution of 1789. Dorothy is blinded by a plague, which takes the lives of their parents. Lillian takes Dorothy to Paris in hopes of finding a doctor who can cure her. The girls are separated when Lillian is abducted by a villainous nobleman and Dorothy is taken in by a cripple. Both girls are in desperate peril for their lives and their virtues, but manage to hang on to both, find true love and get Dorothy's sight back. It's an exciting film, with the Gishes superb.

GERALDINE, SISTER
THE DEVIL IS A WOMAN (1975, GB, Fox British)—**Glenda Jackson** heads a religious hostel where she casts spells over the permanent guests. Exorcise this bomb from your viewing plans.

GERBER, JEFF
WATERMELON MAN (1970, Columbia)—A bigoted insurance man wakes up one morning to find he has become black man **Godfrey Cambridge**. The latter gets even for the thousands of minstrel shows by appearing in white-face before turning back.

GERHARDT, DOUG
MAN ON THE PROWL (1957, UA)—**James Best** killed the last girl who wasn't taken in by his charm. Now he's on the prowl for married mother of two, Mala Powers, whom he tries to trick or coerce into coming to him.

GERHARDT, JENNIE
JENNIE GERHARDT (1933, Paramount)—Unmarried mother **Sylvia Sidney** suffers exceedingly for her sin, but gets the man she loves by the end of the film.

GERONIMO
GERONIMO (1939, Paramount); (1962, UA); I KILLED GERONIMO (1950, Eagle-Lion)—**Chief Thundercloud** has the title role in both the 1939 and 1950 films, but he's not treated as a sympathetic character. The 1939 movie was advertised as brutal attacks on white settlers by savages. In 1962, **Chuck Connors** and his remaining braves seek peace in 1883, but are betrayed by white men.

GERSHWITZ, WANDA
A FISH CALLED WANDA (1988, MGM)—The movie contains a fish called Wanda, but it's named after **Jamie Lee Curtis**, one of four misfits who rob a London jeweler and spend the rest of the film double-crossing each other. When the leader of the gang, Tom Georgeson, is arrested without revealing where he's hidden the loot, Curtis and her lover Kevin Kline (who won the Best Supporting Actor Oscar) work on their boss' barrister John Cleese to get the information they need. It's a very funny film, with Curtis, as usual, looking just wonderful.

GERSON, JOSEPHINE
WOMAN'S PLACE (1921, Silent, First National)—**Constance Talmadge** runs for political office against her fiance, Kenneth Harlan. He wins, but appoints women to the most important posts, while Talmadge decides to forswear politics for marriage. We guess it's like one of our college professors put it. She noted "Most of the girls in my class went to college to get a husband. I got a Ph.D."

GERT

GERT AND DAISY'S WEEKEND (1941, GB, Butchers); GERT AND DAISY CLEAN UP (1942, GB, Butchers)—**Elsie Waters** and her sister **Doris** portray two cockney girls in charge of some rowdy child evacuees in the first film. In the second feature, they are cafe workers, who constantly get themselves fired.

GERT

LADIES AT EASE (1927, Silent, First Division)—**Gertrude Short** and Pauline Garon are underwear models, who steal the boyfriends of two show business sisters. They lose their job, lock up the sisters, and as a lark go on the stage in their place. They are so bad, they have the audience rolling in the aisles with laughter and are rewarded with a long-running contract.

GERTIE

GETTING GERTIE'S GARTER (1945, UA)—Dennis O'Keefe tries all kinds of ploys to recover an incriminating garter from **Marie "The Body" McDonald**.

GERTIE

GOLD DUST GERTIE (1931, Warner Brothers)—Tough divorcee **Winnie Lightner** attempts to sponge off her former husbands.

GESTE, MICHAEL "BEAU"

BEAU GESTE (1926, Silent, Paramount); (1939, Paramount); (1966, Universal); THE LAST REMAKE OF BEAU GESTE (1977, Universal)—**Ronald Colman** and **Gary Cooper** both are wonderful as the eldest of the three Geste brothers who run off to join the French Foreign Legion and find themselves under the command of "the cruelest beast and the bravest soldier," their sergeant. Beau dies in an attack on a desert outpost by Bedouin tribes. His brother John kills the sergeant who was desecrating Beau's body, and his other brother gives him the Viking funeral he always wanted, using the fort as his pyre and the sergeant as the dog placed at his feet. **Guy Stockwell** and **Michael York** just can't match up to the earlier performances. Stockwell plays it straight, but York is in a spoof with Marty Feldman.

GETZ, TILLIE

TILLIE (1922, Silent, Paramount)—**Mary Miles Minter** is kept as a virtual slave by her Pennsylvania Dutch father, who keeps from her the news that she will inherit a fortune if she becomes a Mennonite. Mary attempts suicide but is rescued by young Allan Forrest, who not only sees that she gets what she has coming but marries her as well.

GHOST, THE

GHOST IN THE INVISIBLE BIKINI (1966, American International)—Don't get your hopes up, lechers; **Susan Hart** is sometimes an invisible ghost wearing a bikini, but not a visible lovely wearing an invisible bikini. Nevertheless, this mindless beach party picture has plenty of obligatory fanny shots of various beach bunnies.

GIARDINO, STEVE

A NEW LIFE (1988, Paramount)—If you buy the premise of writer-director **Alan Alda**, the cause of the break-up of actor Alan Alda's 26-year marriage is wife Ann-Margret. This time he's going to choose a mate more carefully. Is lovely Veronica Hamel the answer? To find out, one must sit through a lot of sincere talk as actor Alda changes from an angry, selfish bore to an aware, helpful bore.

GIBBONS, BARBWIRE

HELL'S HEROES (1930, Universal)—**Raymond Hatton** stars with Charles Bickford and Fred Kohler in this version of the often-filmed THE THREE GODFATHERS. The three outlaws give their lives to see that a newborn baby, put in their care by his dying mother in the desert, reaches safety.

GIBBONS, MRS.

MRS. GIBBONS' BOYS (1962, GB, British Lion)—Widow **Kathleen Harrison** plans to make a respectable marriage for the sake of her three convict sons. Look sharp, dearie, the lads will be home on parole any minute now.

GIBBS, ARCHIE

U-BOAT PRISONER (1944, Columbia)—**Bruce Bennett** poses as a spy so he can sabotage a Nazi submarine from the inside. Easier that way, we suppose.

GIBBS, BERT

HIS LORDSHIP (1932, GB, Westminister/UA)—British plumber **Jerry Verno** becomes a lord and poses as the fiance of a Russian movie star.

GIBBS, DR.

SEXTON BLAKE AND THE BEARDED DOCTOR (1935, GB, MGM)—Murderer **Henry Oscar** plots to defraud an insurance company but he didn't count on Sexton Blake, played by George Curzon, entering the case.

GIBBS, GLORIA

LITTLE BIG SHOT (1935, Warner Brothers)—When gangster's child **Sybil Jason** is orphaned, she is cared for by two con men. Warner Brothers' answer to Shirley Temple wasn't bad, she just wasn't good enough to compete with little Curly Top.

GIBBS, TOMMY

BLACK CAESAR (1973, American International)—**Fred Williamson** stars as a black gangster in a film based on Edward G. Robinson's LITTLE CAESAR.

GIBBS, WAYNE

VALENTINO RETURNS (1989, Skouras)—Frustrated 1950s teen **Barry Tubb** hopes his purchase of a flamingo pink Cadillac will enhance his romance with Jenny Wright.

GIBLEY, TOM

HER MAN GIBLEY (1949, GB, Universal)—**Michael Wilding** is one of four people whose romantic escapades in Geneva are put on parade. What did Elizabeth Taylor see in this guy?

GIBSON, NANCY

SMART WOMAN (1931, RKO)—When **Mary Astor** returns from a trip abroad, she finds her husband Robert Ames has found a new love. Determined to win Ames back, she enlists the aid of John Halliday to make Ames jealous, but then she thinks she's fallen in love with Halliday.

GIDEON, INSP. GEORGE

GIDEON OF SCOTLAND YARD (1959, GB, Columbia)—Audiences follow the adventures of Scotland Yard inspector **Jack Hawkins** during one eventful day.

GIDGET *See* **FRANCIE LAWRENCE**

GIFFORD, DAN

CRIME DOCTOR (1934, Radio Pictures)—Criminologist **Otto Kruger** employs his expertise to take revenge against his wife's lover.

GIGI

GIGI (1958, MGM)—**Leslie Caron** is being raised by her aunt and grandma to follow their line of work as a courtesan. She is found to be a delightful child by bored wealthy Parisian Louis Jourdan. When he finds that she has grown into a beautiful desirable young woman, he first proposes an arrangement, but amends this to ask her to become his wife. Caron is delightful and the Lerner and Loewe music is magical. The most appealing performances from an outstanding cast are given by Maurice Chevalier and Hermione Gingold, who are especially charming and touching in their duet "I Remember It Well."

GIGOT

GIGOT (1962, 20th Century Fox)—The mute caretaker of a Montmartre boarding house, **Jackie Gleason** cares for a sick prostitute and her child. Gleason is as appealing here as in his "Poor Soul" character on TV.

GIL

TEXAS BADMAN (1953, Allied Artists)—Texas sheriff Wayne Morris must bring in his own father, desperado **Frank Ferguson**.

GIL MAN

CREATURE FROM THE BLACK LAGOON (1954, Universal)—Scientists come across a fearful creature, half man, half fish, played by **Ben Chapman (Ricou Browning** in water sequences) up the Amazon river.

GILBERT, DON

CAUGHT IN THE DRAFT (1941, Paramount)—Film star **Bob Hope** is drafted into the army. He takes his manager Lynne Overman and chauffeur Eddie Bracken with him. At this time, Hope was still a very funny man, not yet reduced to the caricature of a stupid braggart, which he later would don like a pair of baggy pants for a series of so-so movies and some real dogs.

GILBERT, JUDITH

THE IMPOSTER (1926, Silent, Gothic)—**Evelyn Brent** tries to save her brother from scandal when he steals a family jewel to pay a gambler. She determines to recover the gem, by posing as a girl of the streets, called Canada Nell. After a series of maneuvers she is able to accomplish her purpose.

GILBERT, W.S.

THE GREAT GILBERT AND SULLIVAN (1953, GB, UA)—**Robert Morley** portrays librettist William Gilbert, brought together in 1875 with composer Arthur Sullivan under the auspices of Rupert D'Orly Carte to become the leading exponents of light operetta. Later, Sullivan is convinced to turn his hand to more serious music (a dreadful, snobbish description which must be used, lacking a better one). Many scenes from the most famous works of the pair are included in this quite decent biopic.

GILDA

THE GIRL WHO CAME BACK (1935, First Division)—Former gunmoll **Shirley Grey**, who has gone straight since moving to California, pulls off a jewelry heist for some poorly motivated reason and double-crosses her associates.

GILDERSLEEVE, THROCKMORTON P.

THE GREAT GILDERSLEEVE (1942, RKO); GILDERSLEEVE ON BROADWAY (1943, RKO); GILDERSLEEVE'S BAD DAY (1943, RKO); GILDERSLEEVE'S GHOST (1944, RKO)—**Harold Peary** had played a water commissioner on a popular radio comedy program. These hour films had enough comedy material for 15 minutes and seemed to last forever. Gildersleeve should have stayed on radio.

GILGORE, DAN

I LOVE A SOLDIER (1944, Paramount)—Mr. Nice Guy **Sonny Tufts** is a lonely soldier who changes Paulette Goddard's mind about the risk of war-time marriages.

GILL, MERTON

MERTON OF THE MOVIES (1924, Silent, Paramount); (1947, MGM) -**Glenn Hunter** and **Red Skelton** star in George S. Kaufman's story of a sappy comic who makes it big in the early days of filmmaking.

GILLESPIE, DR. LEONARD

CALLING DR. GILLESPIE (1942, MGM); DR. GILLESPIE'S NEW ASSISTANT (1942, MGM); DR. GILLESPIE'S CRIMINAL CASE (1943, MGM); THREE MEN IN WHITE (1944, MGM)—When Lew Ayres announced that he was a conscientious objector, his character of Dr. Kildare was dropped from the highly successful series and **Lionel Barrymore** became the star. In the first film he's working with a Dutch psychiatrist on a case of homicidal mania. In the second film, Van Johnson comes aboard as the young doctor who will clash with his senior colleague. In the third, Barrymore tries unsuccessfully to get a psychopathic killer transferred to a mental hospital. In the last movie, Keye Luke vies with Van Johnson for the position of Barrymore's second-in-command.

GILLIS, ADA

ADA (1961, MGM)—Call girl **Susan Hayward** marries politician Dean Martin, becoming his closest confidante. They survive the damage to his career as governor when her sordid past is revealed.

GILLIS, DOBIE

THE AFFAIRS OF DOBIE GILLIS (1953, MGM)—**Bobby Van** portrays Max Schulman's accident-prone college student, but he's no Dwayne Hickman, who picked up the role on TV in 1959.

GILLRAY, ROSE

THE FIRST TRAVELING SALESLADY (1956, RKO)—**Ginger Rogers** sets out with loony Carol Channing to sell barbed-wire in the old west. For cattlemen, travelling women salesmen is shocking enough—but barbed wire?

GILMORE, MOLLY

FALLING IN LOVE (1984, Paramount)—**Meryl Streep** and Robert De Niro are railroad commuters who fall in love as they travel back and forth each day from Westchester to New York City. The two married people have an affair against their better judgment. It doesn't work as well as BRIEF ENCOUNTER.

GILMORE, RICHARD

THE MEDDLER (1925, Silent, Universal)—**William Desmond**, a Wall Street broker, becomes a highwayman in the West after being jilted by his fiancee. He's known as "The Meddler," always returning everything he steals, except some worthless memento. He falls in love with one of his victims, marries her and settles down to a new life in the west.

GILPIN, GLENN

THE DIRTY DOZEN (1967, GB, MGM)—**Ben Carruthers** is one of the lesser-lights among the GI-prisoners, who are given the chance to clear their records by taking part in an almost suicide raid behind enemy lines. He pays for his crimes by dying in the line of duty.

GILROY, SALLY

SAILOR'S LADY (1940, 20th Century Fox)—**Nancy Kelly** adopts a 10-month-old baby when the child's parents are killed. This comes as a surprise to her navy fiance Jon Hall when he returns from sea. To make matters worse, the tyke is accidently left aboard Hall's ship as it sails off for war maneuvers.

GINGER

GINGER (1935, Fox)—**Jane Withers**, a Shirley Temple clone, is an orphan, who has the expected miseries, but ensures a happy ending by her good sense.

GINGER TED

THE BEACHCOMBER (1938, GB, Mayflower/Paramount); (1955, GB, MacQuitty/UA)—**Charles Laughton** and **Robert Newton** appear in the story of an alcoholic ne'er-do-well in the Dutch East Indies who gives up his romancing of the native girls after an adventure with a female missionary. The Laughton film was released in Great Britain as VESSEL OF WRATH with Newton playing the sensible governor in that version.

GINGLEBUSHER, LUISA "LU"

THE GOOD FAIRY (1935, Universal); I'LL BE YOURS (1947, Universal)—**Margaret Sullavan** and **Deanna Durbin** each portray a naive girl who ensnares three rich men and helps out a struggling lawyer whose name she picks from the phone book. The first production of the Ferenc Molnar story is sparkling, mostly because of Sullavan. The remake did little for Durbin's sagging career.

GINLEY, EDDIE

GUMSHOE (1972, GB, Columbia)—Liverpool bingo caller **Albert Finney** dreams of becoming a Humphrey Bogart like private eye, and finds himself in the middle of a murder case.

GINO

THE RACERS (1955, 20th Century Fox)—**Kirk Douglas** stars in a contrived and boring look at the world of international road racers.

GINSBERG, JOHNNY

GINSBERG THE GREAT (1927, Silent, Warner Brothers)—Would-be carnival magician **George Jessel** saves a theatrical producer's jewels from being stolen. In what proved to be a poor career move, Jessel turned down the starring role in the first talkie THE JAZZ SINGER to appear in this nothing.

GINSBERG, MAX

THE RAG MAN (1925, Silent, Metro-Goldwyn)—Kindly Jewish junk dealer **Max Davidson** takes in Irish orphan Jackie Coogan after the orphanage burns down. The two become New York's most successful antique dealers.

GIRARD, BESS

NICE WOMAN (1932, Universal)—**Sidney Fox's** mother tries to convince her that it's just as easy to love a rich man as a poor one.

GIRARD, COLETTE

MISS BLUEBEARD (1925, Silent, Paramount)—French actress **Bebe Daniels** is mistakenly married by an intoxicated French mayor to Kenneth MacKenzie, posing as his best friend Robert Frazer. After the wedding they are separated and Daniels takes the train to Paris to be with her husband, who of course is Frazer. The latter immediately falls in love with Daniels, but she holds out for the man—not the name—she married.

GIRL, THE

BOY . . . A GIRL (1969, Jack Hanson)—Fifteen-year-old **Airion Fromer** discovers love and sex with like-aged Dino Martin, Jr. but takes a post-graduate course with Kerwin Mathews, a man twice her age, before returning to Martin.

GIRL, THE

A DAUGHTER OF THE SEA (1915, Silent, World)—**Muriel Ostriche**, a poor girl from a fishing village, saves a wealthy woman from drowning. She is rewarded by being taken into the rich woman's home, where Ostriche falls for her benefactor's son, but must prove herself worthy to marry into the family by taking blame for a murder done by her lover's sister.

GIRL, THE

THE GIRL OF THE GOLDEN WEST (1915, Silent, Lasky); (1923, Silent, Associated First National)—**Mabel Van Buren** and **Sylvia Breamer** portray a decent girl who loves a notorious outlaw and saves him because of it.

GITTES, JAKE

THE TWO JAKES (1990, Paramount)—**Jack Nicholson** is back as private investigator Jake Gittes. The film is set 11 years after the end of CHINATOWN (74). He's still making a good living spying on unfaithful wives. This time he's trying to get the goods on Meg Tilly for her husband Harvey Keitel. Keitel seems to be committing a crime of passion when he kills Tilly's lover, but there's more here than meets the eye.

GIULIANO, SALVATORE

THE SICILIAN (1987, 20th Century Fox)—**Christopher Lambert** portrays a Sicilian bandit who steals from the Mafia leaders to give to the poor peasants. He is betrayed by his second-in-command. Give this one the kiss of death.

GLADDEN, ANNE

HALF A SINNER (1940, Universal)—Looking for adventure **Heather Angel** steals a car, but gets more than she bargained for when she discovers the body of a dead gangster in the back seat.

GLADDEN, JIM

AMATEUR DADDY (1932, Fox)—**Warner Baxter** makes a promise to a dying construction worker buddy, and finds himself raising the deceased's four kids.

GLAYDE, JOHN

JOHN GLAYDE'S HONOR (1915, Silent, Gold Rooster)—**C. Aubrey Smith** loses his wife to an artist because he's too busy becoming a success to have any time for her.

GLEASON, JIM

CAPTAIN KIDD, JR. (1919, Silent, Artcraft)—**Douglas MacLean's** grandfather leaves him a treasure map, advising him that a fortune will be his if he will but look for it. Old gramps has actually played a hoax on his grandson.

GLEN/GLENDA

GLEN OR GLENDA? (1953, Paramount)—**Daniel Davis (Edward D. Wood, Jr.)** "stars?" in this abomination about a transvestite who finds it difficult to explain to his fiancee why he wants to wear her clothes. We still haven't figured out Bela Lugosi's purpose in this film, which has also been called I CHANGED MY SEX, I LED TWO LIVES, and HE OR SHE. Apparently the producers don't know the difference between a transvestite and a transsexual.

GLENDON, DR.

THE WEREWOLF OF LONDON (1935, Universal)—London physician **Henry Hull** is bitten by a werewolf while in Tibet. Back in London he goes on a murdering rampage when the moon is full.

GLENDON, PAT JR.

THE ABYSMAL BRUTE (1923, Silent, Universal)—Professional prizefighter **Reginald Denny** falls in love with a San Francisco socialite, but keeps his occupation concealed until he wins her love.

GLENN

FIGHTING TEXAN (1937, Ambassador)—**Kermit Maynard** and a partner buy a ranch. When his partner is murdered, Maynard is suspected of the crime. He has to track down the real culprit.

GLENN, JANEY

GIRLS JUST WANT TO HAVE FUN (1985, New World)—Teenage dancer **Sarah Jessica Parker** tries to land a job with a local dance video show, but comes up against the rules of her strict father and the disapproval of the nuns at her Catholic school.

GLORIA

THE RED-HAIRED ALIBI (1932, Tower)—In her first screen appearance, **Shirley Temple** is able to prevent her daddy Theodore von Eltz from being sent to jail by Merna Kennedy. But Shirley is wrong about her daddy; he really is up to no good.

GLORY, "DAWN"

PAGE MISS GLORY (1935, Warner Brothers)—Con-man Pat O'Brien wins a beauty contest with a composite photograph of a woman and then has to come up with a girl that looks exactly like the picture. **Marion Davies** fills the bill.

GLOSSOP, MIMI

THE GAY DIVORCEE (1934, RKO)—The producers were forced to change the name of the Broadway hit from "The Gay Divorce" to "The Gay Divorcee" on the theory that a divorcee might be gay, but not a divorce or at least it shouldn't be. **Ginger Rogers** seeking a divorce, mistakes author Fred Astaire for a professional corespondent hired to be found with her in a Brighton hotel. Rogers and Astaire danced marvelously to the Academy Award winning "The Continental" by Con Conrad and Herb Magidson.

GLOUCESTER, THEODORA "TEDDY"

NICE PEOPLE (1922, Silent, Paramount)—Flapper **Bebe Daniels** changes her ways after being rescued from scandal by Wallace Reid, when she spends the night with Conrad Nagel, who had too much to drink. She marries Reid and becomes most respectful.

GLOURIE, DONALD

THE GHOST GOES WEST (1936, UA)—When millionaire **Robert Donat** buys his ancestral Scottish castle and transports it stone by stone to America, its ghost, also played by Donat, goes along as well.

GOD

GOD IS MY WITNESS (1931, Astor); OH, GOD! (1977, Warner Brothers); OH GOD! BOOK II (1980, Warner Brothers); OH GOD! YOU DEVIL (1984, Warner Brothers)—Playing God for laughs is a risky business for an actor, because as the *Satanic Verses* episode demonstrates, some people are outraged by any disrespect they perceive. In 1931, two Damon Runyan characters make a deal with **George Grossmith** who they believe to be God, to amend their ways and only do good things. But Grossmith turns out to be merely a harmless old nut. In the three later pictures **George Burns** is a home-spun Jewish God and in the final, he even becomes the devil in a strange Faustian comedy.

GODDEN, JOANNA

THE LOVES OF JOANNA GODDEN (1947, GB, Ealing)—Romney Marsh turn-of-the-century female farmer **Googie Withers** is pursued by three suitors.

GODDESS, THE

THE SAVAGE GIRL (1932, Monarch)—Innocent white girl **Rochelle Hudson**, garbed in a brief leopard skin outfit, has been raised by African natives as a goddess. Things get a bit hot when two hunters arrive and fight over her.

GODFREY

MY MAN GODFREY (1936, Universal); (1957, Universal)—**William Powell** and **David Niven** portray "forgotten men" whom a daffy daughter of a loony wealthy family brings home as a piece for a scavenger hunt. Powell and Niven are established as the family's butler and bring a little order to their employer's nutty lives. Daughter Carole Lombard in the original and June Allyson in the remake, naturally fall in love with their servant, who turns out to have more money than they do. The first film is delightfully screwy, the remake is a waste.

GODFREY, ADMIRAL

CARRY ON ADMIRAL (1957, GB, Renown)—**A.E. Matthews** has a lesser role in this naval entry into the "Carry on" series. Two friends exchange identities after a drinking bout, with a press relations executive taking command of a Royal Navy ship.

GODIVA, LADY

LADY GODIVA (1955, Universal)—**Maureen O'Hara** covers things up rather effectively with her long hair, when she takes her famous nude ride through the streets of Coventry.

GOEBBELS, PAUL JOSEPH

ENEMY OF WOMEN (1944, Monogram)—**Paul Andor** gives a weak performance as the Nazi propaganda minister, who according to this picture spent most of his time trying to ruin the life of actress Claudia Drake, who rejected him when he was a struggling young playwright.

GOLD, PANDORA "PANDA"

MADE FOR EACH OTHER (1971, RF)—**Renee Taylor** and her real-life husband Joseph Bologna wrote and starred in this enjoyable comedy about two New Yorkers with inferiority complexes. If our experiences with the Big Apple are any indication, they must be the only ones with this problem.

GOLDBERG, MOLLY & JAKE

THE GOLDBERGS (1950, Paramount)—**Gertrude Berg** and **Philip Loeb** star in this warm and touching episode in the lives of the popular Jewish radio and television family.

GOLDEN CHILD, THE

THE GOLDEN CHILD (1986, Paramount)—"Perfect child" **J.L. Reate** is abducted by villains despite his magical powers and according to prophecy only Eddie Murphy can rescue him. It's Murphy at his worse and he's better than anyone else in this bomb.

GOLDEN, HUNK

HUNK (1987, Crown International)—Nerdish social misfit **John Allen Nelson** sells his soul to devil James Coco for a sexy masculine body, which he thinks will get him all the girls.

GOLDEN, JIM

"IF ONLY" JIM (1921, Silent, Universal)—Itinerant gold miner **Harry Carey** finds an abandoned baby and becomes a responsible person, working his claim into a bonanza.

GOLDENGIRL

GOLDENGIRL (1979, Avco Embassy)—Beautiful **Susan Anton** is the result, when scientist Curt Jurgens subjects his daughter to dangerous drugs (steroids?) which transform her into an abnormally tall Olympian track star. The results prove tragic in the end.

GOLDFARB, JOHN

JOHN GOLDFARB, PLEASE COME HOME (1964, 20th Century Fox)—The University of Notre Dame tried to prohibit this film from being released because it showed the Notre Dame football team getting drunk and messing around with harem cuties. The university should have left the job to the critics and the few people who went to see this junky piece about a none-too-bright American spy pilot **Richard Crenna**, forced to prepare a football team made up of the subjects of Middle Eastern potentate for a game with the Fighting Irish.

GOLDFINGER

GOLDFINGER (1964, GB, UA)—In one of the most enjoyable James Bond movies, **Gert Frobe**, a man with an obsession for gold, plots to rob Fort Knox. He's assisted by Harold Sakata, an Oriental gentleman called "Oddjob" who wears a deadly hat, and lesbian pilot Pussy Galore, played by Honor Blackman.

GOLDFOOT, DR.

DR. GOLDFOOT AND THE BIKINI MACHINE (1965, American International); DR. GOLDFOOT AND THE GIRL BOMBS (1966, American International)—**Vincent Price** manufactures lovely female robots, programmed to lure rich men into their clutches. In the sequel, Price teams up with Red China to cause problems between the U.S. and the USSR.

GOLDIE

GOLDIE (1931, Fox)—When gold-digger **Jean Harlow** succumbs to Spencer Tracy, who puts a tattoo on all the women he has, Warren Hymer knows that his buddy Tracy was right when he warned him that Harlow wasn't really interested in him.

GOLDIE

SWEET MAMA (1930, First National)—**Alice White** gets her sweetheart David Manners to go straight by seeing that his mob buddies are, one by one, sent to jail.

GOLDING, JERRY

THE JAZZ SINGER (1953, Warner Brothers)—**Danny Thomas** brings his own interpretation of the story of a son of a cantor, who is alienated from his father when he chooses show business over following in his father's footsteps. It's schmaltzy but has Miss Peggy Lee in top singing form.

GOLDMAN, ARTHUR

THE MAN IN THE GLASS BOOTH (1975, American Film Theatre) - **Maximilian Schell** portrays a glib Jewish industrialist being tried as a Nazi war criminal.

GOLDSMITH, BERNIE

THREE BRAVE MEN (1957, 20th Century Fox)—Civilian employee in the U.S. Navy **Ernest Borgnine** is suspended as a security risk. It takes a lawsuit brought by his attorney Ray Milland and the good offices of government official Dean Jagger to get him reinstated.

GOLEM, THE

IT! (1967, GB, Warner Brothers)—**Alan Sellers** portrays the famed Golem of Czechoslovakia, which comes into the possession of unbalanced Roddy McDowall, who telepathically controls the creature, causing it to kill several people and destroy London Bridge. Officials decide to drop an atomic bomb on the creature, but while the explosion takes care of Roddy, Sellers escapes by walking off into the sea. So far, no one has taken advantage of the survival to bring it back in another movie.

GONZORGO

BABES IN TOYLAND (1961, Buena Vista)—**Henry Calvin**, who has made a few bucks impersonating Oliver Hardy, reprises the great comedian's role in this sticky sweet remake of the 1934 movie.

GONZUELO, ROSA

THE HOSTAGE (1956, GB, Fairbanks-Westridge/Eros)—**Mary Parker**, the daughter of a South American president, is abducted by terrorists in London, who promise to kill her if a revolutionary is executed as ordered by her father.

GOODBODY, LT. ERNEST

HOW I WON THE WAR (1967, GB, UA)—During WWII doltish officer **Michael Crawford** survives many tribulations including the grisly deaths of his comrades. It's a black comedy with very few yuks.

GOODMAN

THE TERROR (1928, Warner Brothers); (1941, GB, Alliance)—**Holmes Herbert** and **Wilfrid Lawson** appear as a mysterious killer, lurking in the cellars of a country house. The 1928 film was the first without any subtitles, even the credits were spoken—but not very well, according to critics.

GOODMAN, BENNY

THE BENNY GOODMAN STORY (1956, Universal)—**Steve Allen** stars in a routine musical biopic. His subject comes from the obligatory poor, but supportive family. He suffers through many disappointments until his music catches on, about the time beaming Donna Reed comes into his life, and from then on he's a smash. For those who love "Swing," the Benny Goodman music is great.

GOODWIN, BETH

SEE YOU IN THE MORNING (1989, Warner Brothers)—Potential world class photographer **Alice Krige** subordinates her career to her role as the wife of concert pianist David Dukes and their two children. But when Dukes dies, she finds a new relationship with divorced psychiatrist Jeff Bridges.

GOODWIN, MAJOR GENERAL MELVILLE

TOP SECRET AFFAIR (1957, Warner Brothers) -Newspaper publisher Susan Hayward's plans to discredit military diplomat **Kirk Douglas** are scuttled when she falls in love with him.

GORCH, LYLE & TECTOR

THE WILD BUNCH (1969, Warner Brothers)—**Warren Oates** and **Ben Johnson** are brothers, who seriously question their leader William Holden's judgment when they discover that a bank robbery that they pulled—resulting in the massacre of innocent people as well as the loss of several members of the outlaw gang—netted them bags filled with washers. To add to their upset, they realize they are being chased by a bloodthirsty posse led by a former colleague of Holden. Still they follow him into Mexico and an eventual confrontation with a ruthless army general.

GORDON

GORDON'S WAR (1973, 20th Century Fox)—Returning Vietnam vet **Paul Winfield** declares war on Harlem drug bosses when he discovers his wife has died from an overdose.

GORDON, BARBARA

I'M DANCING AS FAST AS I CAN (1982, Paramount)—**Jill Clayburgh**, a successful TV documentary maker, is falling apart because of her dependency on valium.

GORDON, BOB

CAPTAIN CARELESS (1928, Silent, FBO)—**Bob Steele** rushes to the rescue of his sweetheart, shipwrecked on a cannibal-infested island.

GORDON, CHARLY

CHARLY (1968, Selmur)—**Cliff Robertson** won an Academy Award for his portrayal of a mentally retarded man, who becomes a genius due to new surgical methods, but then learns that the effects are not permanent and that he will revert to his earlier mental state.

GORDON, FLASH

FLASH GORDON (1936, Universal); (1980, Universal)—The space hero of the 25th Century was the comic strip creation of Alex Raymond. For most fans of movie serials, **Larry "Buster" Crabbe** is the definitive Flash Gordon, with his wild and wooly clashes with Ming the Merciless, played evilly by Charles Middleton. **Sam J. Jones** came along more that 40 years later in a campy satire of the original. Camp means: "We know, we're making a nonsensical piece of trash, but look how much we're spending to do it."

GORDON, HARRY "FLASH"

NUMBER ONE (1984, GB, Stageform)—**Bob Geldof**, the lead singer for the Boomtown Rats, known for his fund-raising efforts for the hungry, plays a small-time pool shark who's convinced to compete in professional snooker matches. Gamblers would like him to throw the match.

GORDON, JILL

DANCE LITTLE LADY (1954, GB, Renown)—Talented dancer **Mandy Miller**, the young daughter of crippled former dancer Mai Zetterling, is the center of a struggle between her mother and her father Terence Morgan, who deserted his wife and child for another dancing meal-ticket when Zetterling was injured. Now he wants to take his child prodigy daughter to Hollywood. Instead, he ends up sacrificing his life for the child.

GORDON, LAURA

SHE MADE HER BED (1934, Paramount)—**Sally Eilers**, married to cheating fairgrounds' owner Robert Armstrong, is in love with Richard Arlen. Armstrong is nicely gotten out of the way by a man-eating carnival tiger, who almost gets the couple's baby, saved only because Eilers puts the child in an ice box before she runs from her home. You think the plot is ridiculous? We have barely touched the absurdity of this film.

GORDON, MRS.

BEWARE, MY LOVELY (1952, RKO)—Widow **Ida Lupino** hires mental defective Robert Ryan as a handyman without knowing he's escaped from an institution. He holds her captive, threatening to rape and kill her—but being mentally defective, he forgets.

GORDON, POLLY

NOBODY'S FOOL (1921, Silent, Universal)—**Marie Prevost**, who at the start of the film is quite unattractive, changes into a beauty after inheriting a fortune. She also wins the love of an author, who has written that women are unnecessary. Unnecessary for what?

GORE, COACH

COLLEGE COACH (1933, Warner Brothers)—Tough football coach **Pat O'Brien** discovers the best player on campus is timid chemistry student, Dick Powell.

GORING, RENA

HER ACCIDENTAL HUSBAND (1923, Silent, Belasco)—**Miriam Cooper** and her fisherman father rescue wealthy young Forrest Stanley at sea at the cost of her father's life. Cooper insists, and Stanley agrees that he should marry her and carry on at her father's trade. As usually happens in these movie marriages that begin for the wrong reason, the couple is deeply in love by the fade-out.

GORMAN

PANAMINT'S BAD MAN (1938, 20th Century Fox)—**Noah Beery Sr.** is a mean bad man—you can just tell the way he twitches his moustache. He gets his.

GOSS, ANNIE

GENTLE ANNIE (1944, MGM)—Rancher **Marjorie Main** moonlights with an occasional bank robbery to augment her income. She finds it hard to understand that the Marshal doesn't approve.

GRACE

AMAZING GRACE (1974, Paramount)—This comedy with **Moms Mabley** as an elderly busy-body, who brings discomfort to some corrupt Baltimore politicians, doesn't get enough out of its star or the veteran black performers, Slappy White, Butterfly McQueen and Stepin Fetchit.

GRACE

DEAD AGAIN (1991, Paramount)—Is amnesiac **Emma Thompson** the reincarnation of a concert pianist killed by her composer husband in 1940? Is private detective Kenneth Branagh, who is trying to help her discover her identity, the reincarnation of the executed husband? Is present-day Branagh fated to kill the present-day Thompson? We'll never tell.

GRADLEY, NORRIS

CINDERELLA OF THE HILLS (1921, Silent, Fox)—When her parents divorce, **Barbara Bedford** stays with her father, hoping for a reconciliation, but he marries again, and Bedford is snubbed and mistreated by her stepmother. When the new wife proves unfaithful, Bedford is able to get her parents together again.

GRADY, ALEX

BEST OF THE BEST (1989, Taurus)—**Eric Roberts** is a quiet, thoughtful member of a U.S. karate team. He should have re-thought appearing in this bland film.

GRADY, BRENNAN

A SON COMES HOME (1936, Paramount)—**Anthony Nace** is the long missing son of tough San Francisco Chowder House owner Mary Boland. Drifter Donald Woods, on the lam for a murder he tried to prevent, impersonates the missing son. When he sees the picture of his "father," Woods realizes that the true son committed the murder he viewed. Nace shows up and is butchered by police bullets after clearing up his parentage.

GRAGORE, GEORGI

I TAKE THIS WOMAN (1940, MGM)—It's only after Spencer Tracy marries beautiful European **Hedy Lamarr** and brings her home that

347

he discovers that he doesn't love her. She's one of those women who seems less attractive the more you know her.

GRAHAM

MOLLY AND ME (1945, 20th Century Fox)—Crotchety old **Monty Woolley** hires Gracie Fields as his housekeeper, and she tames the old curmudgeon.

GRAHAM, ANNE

THE GIRL IN THE NEWS (1941, GB, Fox British)—Nurse **Margaret Lockwood** is framed for the murder of her employer.

GRAHAM, BARBARA

I WANT TO LIVE! (1958, UA)—**Susan Hayward** won an Academy Award for her portrayal of the real-life prostitute who went to the gas chamber, even though there is considerable doubt that she was guilty of murder. Movies with such themes are difficult to describe as enjoyable. They should, however, be thoughtful and thought-provoking. For those opposed to capital punishment, Hayward's portrayal will seem heart-breaking. For those who consider the death penalty a deterrent, she will be seen as a pitiful woman who gets what she deserves.

GRAHAM, CHUCK

THE MAN WITH MY FACE (1951, UA)—**Barry Nelson** discovers that he has an exact double, who is slowly replacing him both at home and at his office. It reaches a point where Nelson is declared to be the imposter. It's an intriguing story which reads better than it looks.

GRAHAM, FRED

KISS ME KATE (1953, MGM)—Musical comedy producer and star **Howard Keel** cons his estranged wife Kathryn Grayson into appearing opposite him in a musical version of "The Taming of the Shrew." By the end of the show within a show, the shrew has been tamed and Keel and Grayson are reunited.

GRAHAM, GERALDINE

THE HELL CAT (1934, Columbia)—**Ann Sothern** and tough reporter Robert Armstrong battle each other when they combine to break-up a gang of smugglers of Chinese aliens into the U.S., using her father's yacht without his knowledge.

GRAHAM, HARRY

THE BIGAMIST (1953, Filmakers)—Travelling salesman **Edmond O'Brien** has two wives. The only thing interesting about this production is that it features two of producer Collier Young's wives (sequentially, of course), Joan Fontaine and Ida Lupino.

GRAHAM, LEE

UNDERGROUND AGENT (1942, Columbia)—Government agent **Bruce Bennett** invents a word scrambler which prevents Axis spies from eavesdropping at a defense plant.

GRAHAM, LOUISE HOWELL

POSSESSED (1947, Warner Brothers)—**Joan Crawford** goes nuts when she can't get the man she loves, Van Heflin. Others pay for her displeasure. It's sort of an early FATAL ATTRACTION.

GRAHAM, WILL

MANHUNTER (1986, De Laurentiis)—In order to track down serial murderers, FBI agent **William Peterson** puts himself in their psychotic state of mind in order to predict their next moves.

GRAHAME, MARGOT

I ADORE YOU (1933, GB, Warner Brothers)—Because of his love for actress **Margot Grahame**, Harold French buys the failing movie studio for which she works.

GRAND, HARRY

RHYTHM RACKETEER (1937, GB, British International)—While traveling by ocean liner to London, Chicago mobster **Harry Roy** discovers that the ship's band-leader is his exact double. Roy steals some jewels and lays the blame on the musician.

GRAND HIGH WITCH

THE WITCHES (1990, Warner Brothers)—Nine-year-old Jason Fraser learns of a witch's plot to feed doctored chocolate to all British children, which will turn them all into mice. He's captured, and the leader of the witches, **Anjelica Huston**, forces him to drink the potion. Can a mouse save all the children? Are you kidding? The story is by Jim Henson.

GRANDISON, ALEXANDER

THE UNSUSPECTED (1947, Warner Brothers)—Radio star **Claude Rains** is the host of a show on which he relates murder stories. He also commits murders, believing he has come up with a fool-proof scheme to allow him to get away with his crimes.

GRANDMA

GRANDMA'S BOY (1922, Silent, Associate Exhibitors)—Grand-mother **Anna Townsend** comforts her cowardly small-town grand-son Harold Lloyd. She tells him a story of how his equally fearful grandfather had become invincible when an old hag gave him a magical charm. Townsend passes the charm onto Lloyd which endows him with so much valor, he captures a dangerous killer all by himself. The amulet he carried is merely a handle from one of the old lady's umbrellas.

GRANDMOTHER

GRANDMOTHER'S HOUSE (1989, Omega)—After their father dies, teenager Kim Valentine and her little brother, Eric Foster, move in with their grandparents, **Ida Lee** and Len Lesser. Some strange things seem to be going on at grandmother's house.

GRANGE, JOE & RONNIE

THAT'S MY MAN (1947, Republic)—**Don Ameche** and **Catherine McLeod's** marriage is wrecked by his gambling, bringing him to financial ruin; but a noble horse, Gallant Man, wins the big race and saves their bacon.

GRANT

DUDES (1987, New Century-Vista)—**Jon Cryer**, one of a group of punks from New York traveling across country, has a run-in with a gang of Wyoming rednecks. There are no heroes.

GRANT, SIR BEVERLY

FATHER CAME TOO (1964, GB, Rank)—Newlyweds Sally Smith and Stanley Baker are forced to live with her overbearing actor-manager father, **James Robertson Justice.**

GRANT, CHESTER

THE CLOSER (1991, Ion Pictures)—Overbearing real estate broker **Danny Aiello** invites his two leading salesmen Michael Pare and Joseph Cortese to share Thanksgiving dinner with him, so that he can judge which one should be his successor.

GRANT, DAVID

LUCKY PARTNERS (1940, RKO)—Strangers **Ronald Colman** and Ginger Rogers share a sweepstake ticket, agreeing to go away together if they win. Guess what? They do and they are able to convince her fiance Jack Carson not to object to their holiday together. What a schnook!

GRANT, ELLEN
MISS GRANT TAKES RICHMOND (1949, Columbia)—Crooked bookie William Holden gets daffy **Lucille Ball** to be a front for an illegal real estate deal.

GRANT, EVE
THE FALL OF EVE (1929, Columbia)—Trying to close a deal with a client, a businessman takes the man to a fancy nightclub, inviting **Patsy Ruth Miller** to soften the man up. When the client's wife insists on tagging along, Miller is introduced as the businessman's wife, but the man's real wife drops into the club and comedy is at hand.

GRANT, JEFF
LITTLE NIKITA (1988, Columbia)—FBI agent Sidney Poitier informs young **River Phoenix** that his very American parents are K.G.B. "sleepers," Russian agents who have been waiting for over 20 years to get the word from the U.S.S.R. that their time to act has come. Well, they've received the word. Poitier was away from the front of the camera for a long time. Maybe he should have waited a bit longer for something more worthy of his talents.

GRANT, JIMMY
THE CHEERLEADER (1928, Silent, Gotham)—Cheerleader **Ralph Graves** finally gets his chance to play for his college's football team and stars in the victory.

GRANT, JOE
FIREMAN, SAVE MY CHILD (1932, Warner Brothers)—Fireman **Joe E. Brown** is more interested in baseball than putting out fires, but becomes a hero, nevertheless.

GRANT, JOE
MY BEST GIRL (1927, Silent, UA)—**Charles Rogers**, who would become co-star Mary Pickford's third husband, is the son of Mary's boss at the five-and-dime store where the plucky salesgirl works to earn enough to care for her family.

GRANT, JOEL
I WAS A PRISONER ON DEVIL'S ISLAND (1941, Columbia)—**Donald Woods** is sentenced to Devil's Island for killing the captain of the freighter on which he was first mate. He falls for Sally Eilers, the wife of Eduardo Ciannelli, the prison's doctor, who is selling medicine meant for prisoners on the island's black market. After getting nary a thank you for braving a storm to get medicine for sick prisoners, Woods escapes the island with Eilers.

GRANT, JOHN JOSEPHUS
A STRANGER IN TOWN (1943, MGM)—While on a fishing vacation in a small town, Supreme Court Justice **Frank Morgan** helps an honest young lawyer fight the corruption of the mayor and his cronies.

GRANT, LEE
THE MAN FROM THE RIO GRANDE (1943, Republic)—**Don "Red" Barry** saves the inheritance of 8-year old ice skating star Twinkle Watts that a scheming outlaw is trying to steal.

GRANT, RICHARD
GUILTY HANDS (1931, MGM)—District Attorney **Lionel Barrymore's** attempt to frame a girl for a murder he's committed goes awry when rigor mortis makes the gun in the hand of the victim go off and kill Barrymore.

GRANT, ROGER
ALEXANDER'S RAGTIME BAND (1938, 20th Century Fox)—**Tyrone Power** stars in this lovely sentimental story of two songwriters, Power and Don Ameche, who vie for the affections of musical comedy star Alice Faye in the period from 1911 to 1939. The film is really only an excuse to feature 26 of Irving Berlin's biggest hit songs.

GRANT, U.S.
THREE LEGIONNAIRES (1937, General)—**Donald Meek** calls himself General Grant to confuse the Bolsheviks as he helps two American Army buddies in Russia lead a bungling crusade against the government. Nobody belongs to the French Foreign Legion.

GRANVILLE, HARRY
THE FOOL AND THE PRINCESS (1948, GB, GFD)—**Bruce Lester** returns home to his wife after WWII, but can't forget Adina Manlova, who claimed to be a Russian princess. Lester leaves his wife to find Manlova, but discovering she's not what she claims, he hurries back to his wife.

GRAVES, JUDY
JUNIOR MISS (1945, 20th Century Fox)—Teenage matchmaker **Peggy Ann Garner** meddles in her family's affairs in this lively adaptation of the Broadway hit.

GRAY, ANDREW
ALARM CLOCK ANDY (1920, Silent, Paramount)—**Charles Ray** is a bashful stuttering clerk, who must overcome his shyness to win his boss' daughter.

GRAY, DORIAN
THE PICTURE OF DORIAN GRAY (1916, GB, Silent, Neptune); (1945, MGM)—**Henry Victor** and **Hurd Hatfield** appear as Oscar Wilde's classic libertine who maintains his eternally young and handsome appearance over years while a portrait that he keeps of himself in an attic shows the excesses of his lifestyle. Hatfield, a hand-some actor, who looked too much like Tyrone Power, never had a role to match this one. As excellent as he was, George Sanders was given the best lines.

GRAY, DUSTY
NOT SO DUSTY (1936, GB, RKO); (1956, GB, Eros)—**Wally Patch** and **Bill Owen** each appear as one of two British garbage men, who come across a rare and valuable book, which was inadvertently discarded. One version of this comedy probably was all that was needed.

GRAY, GORDON
HER ACCIDENTAL HUSBAND (1923, Silent, Belasco)—**Forrest Stanley** marries the daughter of the fisherman who rescued him from a boating accident, giving his life in the effort. The girl believes Stanley owes it to her and the memory of her father to take up the life of a fisherman. Stanley does but when this doesn't work out, he takes his new wife to the home of his wealthy parents where she's as out of place as a pork chop in the catch of the day. All works out well, we're happy to report.

GRAY, HELEN
HUSBAND HUNTERS (1927, Silent, Tiffany)—**Duane Thompson** and Mae Busch are a couple of wisecracking chorus girls who take

small town innocent Jean Arthur under their wings, advising her how to deal with men.

GRAY, J. HARRISON
THE IRRESISTIBLE LOVER (1927, Silent, Universal)—**Norman Kerry**, an insatiably romantic playboy, has too many women in his life, until one takes control of things.

GRAY, JOANNA
THE HUNTED WOMAN (1925, Silent, Fox)—**Seena Owen** is in the Alaskan gold fields seeking her missing husband. This unworthy shows up after she has fallen in love with an author, and is being pursued by some questionable other types, who are after her and her husband's gold mine. All excess baggage is disposed of by the fade-out, allowing Owen to live happily ever after with her writer.

GRAY, JOHN
THE BODY SNATCHER (1945, RKO)—**Boris Karloff** supplies cadavers for tormented scientist Henry Daniell's experiments. When fresh bodies are in short supply, Karloff finds it convenient to provide his own subjects.

GRAY, LOLA
HER GREAT CHANCE (1918, Silent, Selznick)—Salesgirl **Alice Brady** dates millionaire's son David Powell, but won't marry until he develops his own means of earning a living, independent of his father.

GRAY, MARCIA
THE CODE OF MARCIA GRAY (1916, Silent, Paramount)—Based on a true story, **Constance Collier** strives to come up with bail money for her husband Henry DeVere, who's manipulation of funds has caused his bank to fail. Their society friends turn their backs on her. Collier pawns her jewelry, but Forrest Stanley, a lawyer who loved her, posts DeVere's bond and redeems her jewelry. DeVere, now out of prison, proposes fleeing to South America, but Collier won't accompany him. Before hubby can leave the country, one of his ruined creditors kills him, allowing Collier and Stanley to find happiness together.

GRAY, MARY
THE AMERICAN VENUS (1926, Silent, Paramount)—**Esther Ralston** wins a beauty contest. It's an exploitation film, based on the charge that the previous year's Miss America contest had been fixed.

GRAY, MRS.
ONE WOMAN TO ANOTHER (1927, Silent, Paramount)—**Marie Shotwell** tries to take advantage of the fact that Florence Vidor, the fiancee of Theodore Von Eltz, has been quarantined with some children who have the measles, in order to vamp him for herself.

GRAY, MURIEL
THE HEART RAIDER (1923, Silent, Paramount)—**Agnes Ayres** chases down the man of her dreams by any and all means, which are almost too much for her poor father.

GRAY, PANSY
ANYBODY'S WOMAN (1930, Paramount)—**Ruth Chatterton**, so good being so bad, is a chorus girl who marries a drunken lawyer and reforms him.

GRAY, STEVE
THE MURDER MAN (1935, MGM)—Hard-drinking Reporter **Spencer Tracy**, who specializes in covering homicides, commits a murder and shifts the blame to another.

GRAY, TISH
THE BABY MAKER (1970, National General)—Free-thinking **Barbara Hershey** agrees to have a baby for a childless couple.

GRAYEAGLE
GRAYEAGLE (1977, American International)—In a flawed adaptation of the flawed classic THE SEARCHERS, Ben Johnson relentlessly tracks down Indian **Alex Cord** who has kidnapped his daughter.

GRAYLE, MRS. VELMA
FAREWELL, MY LOVELY (1975, Avco Embassy)—**Charlotte Rampling** is Velma, whom private eye Philip Marlowe, played by sleepy-eyed Robert Mitchum, promises to find for ex-convict Jack O'Halloran in this exciting remake of MURDER, MY SWEET.

GRAYSON, DR. CHARLES
GOD IS MY PARTNER (1957, 20th Century Fox)—When retired surgeon **Walter Brennan** begins donating his money to religious causes, his family attempts to have him declared incompetent.

GRAYSON, GEORGINA
CHICAGO JOE AND THE SHOWGIRL (1990, GB, Palace)—In a "Bonnie and Clyde" action film based on a sensational 1944 British murder case, showgirl **Emily Lloyd** teams up with thrill-seeking American G.I. Kiefer Sutherland on a six-day crime spree of theft and murder.

GRAYSON, LILLIAN
FRISCO LIL (1942, Universal)—In order to clear her father of murder, law student **Irene Hervey** sets out to find the real killer.

GRAYSON, ROCK
THE VANQUISHED (1953, Paramount)—Returning from the Civil War, former Confederate officer **John Payne** finds his home town in the hands of corrupt officials.

GRAZIANO, ROCKY
SOMEBODY UP THERE LIKES ME (1956, MGM)—**Paul Newman** moved into the role of the former middleweight boxing champion after James Dean was killed in an automobile accident. His charming mugging in the highly sentimental biopic may have saved Newman's career after his disastrous debut in THE SILVER CHALICE.

GREASER GREG
THE GARBAGE PAIL KIDS (1987, Atlantic Entertainment)—**Phil Fondacara** is a midget portraying a hoodish punk in this putrid movie inspired by some gross bubble gum cards from Topps satirizing The Cabbage Patch Kids. To give you an idea of how bad the movie is, it stars Anthony Newley.

GREAT SERPENT, THE
SEVEN FACES OF DR. LAO (1964, MGM)—**Tony Randall** puts on yet another face in this story of a mysterious Chinese magician, who arrives in a small western community at the last part of the 19th century and causes some good things to happen.

GREAVINS, SMILEY
SMILEY (1957, GB, 20th Century Fox); SMILEY GETS A GUN (1959, GB, 20th Century Fox)—**Colin Petersen** and **Keith Calvert**, respectively, appear as a lad, who in the first film gets involved with drug smugglers as he tries to earn a bicycle. In the sequel, he's a bit older and now is trying to prove he has a right to own a gun.

GREEN, CHADDIE

THE PRAIRIE WIFE (1925, Silent, Metro-Goldwyn)—Impoverished society woman **Dorothy Devore** marries Herbert Rawlinson and moves west with him after returning from Europe. It's a new kind of life on the prairie, but Devore proves she belongs.

GREEN, DR. HESS

GANJA AND HESS (1973, Kelly-Jordan)—Black present-day vampire **Duane Jones** yearns to return to Africa with his new wife Marlene Clark.

GREEN KNIGHT

GAWAIN AND THE GREEN KNIGHT (1973, GB, UA)—**Nigel Green** arrives at the court of King Arthur and offers any knight the right to try to chop off his head, with the proviso that he gets the second swing. Murray Head as Gawain accepts the challenge, whacks off Green's head and then is astonished as Green picks up his head and discusses when he gets to do the honors for Head.

GREEN, LILA

THE STRIPPER (1963, 20th Century Fox)—Aging beauty queen **Joanne Woodward**, with a somewhat tarnished reputation, returns to her Kansas hometown and has an affair with an old friend's 19-year-old son, Richard Beymer. He tries to dissuade her from taking a job as a stripper.

GREENBERG, DAVE

THE SUPER COPS (1974, MGM/UA)—**Ron Leibman** and his partner David Selby, nicknamed Batman and Robin for their unorthodox police methods are suspended for breaking too many rules but that hardly slows down their fight against crime.

GREENE, JOYCE

THE LADY AND THE BANDIT (1951, Columbia)—**Patricia Medina** is the love of British highwayman Dick Turpin, played by Louis Hayward. It's a harmless rewriting of history.

GREENEYES

THE GREEN-EYED BLONDE (1957, Warner Brothers)—Lusty **Susan Oliver** is a rebellious teenager who rebels her way into homicide and her own end.

GREENWOOD, KITTY

KITTY (1929, GB, British International)—Just before pilot John Stuart heads off to war, he marries **Estelle Brody**. His jealous mother breaks them up by writing her son that his wife is cheating on him. Stuart cracks up a plane and comes home a cripple. Will he walk again? Will he get wise to is mother? Will he and Brody get together again? What do you think?

GREER, PETE

HIGH SCHOOL HERO (1927, Silent, Fox)—**Nick Stuart** is what the title suggests in this adolescent triangle plot involving Stuart, his life-long rival John Darrow and new classmate Sally Phipps.

GREESON, BLAKE

THE MIGHTY (1929, Paramount)—Gangster **George Bancroft** goes to WWI, rising to the rank of major. After the war, he visits a family to tell them of the death of their son in his arms. He falls in love with the deceased's sister and decides to settle down with her, rather than return to the rackets.

GREGG

LOVING COUPLES (1980, 20th Century Fox)—**Stephen Collins** is picked by medical doctor Shirley Maclaine for a lover when her surgeon husband hasn't enough time for her. Collins' girlfriend, Susan Sarandon, takes up with MacLaine's husband James Coburn. Collins doesn't have it in him to be faithful. He's a real estate agent pulled into bed by Sally Kellerman while he's showing her a home. Their love-making is almost interrupted by the arrival home of the house's owner.

GREGG, CAPT. DANIEL (GHOST)

THE GHOST AND MRS. MUIR (1942, 20th Century Fox)—**Rex Harrison** portrays the ghost of a gruff, bad-tempered sea captain into whose English seaside cottage widow Gene Tierney and her two children move. She falls in love with the ghost, never re-marries, and when she dies of old age, her youthful spirit leaves her body and goes off arm and arm with Harrison.

GREGORY

GREGORY'S GIRL (1982, GB, Goldwyn)—In a lovely if sometimes hard to understand comedy because of the Scottish accents, **Gordon St. Clair** is an awkward kid who has just experienced a growth spurt of five inches. He moves like a drunken stork and has to be the worst player on his school's winless soccer team. He falls in love with the team's newest member and best player, a girl named Dorothy, played winningly by Dee Hepburn.

GREGORY

IN SEARCH OF GREGORY (1970, GB/Italy, Universal)—**Michael Sarrazin** is and isn't Gregory. Let us explain. Julie Christie goes to her father's wedding in Geneva on the promise that she will be introduced to a remarkable young man named Gregory. He doesn't show, so Christie fantasizes about him, imagining he's the handsome athlete Michael Sarrazin whose photo she saw at the airport. She runs into Sarrazin, goes to bed with him and finds him, shall we say, wanting. She leaves Geneva, without knowing the man in the phone booth next to her, whose face we don't see, is the mysterious Gregory trying to reach her.

GREGORY, CLAIRE

SOMEONE TO WATCH OVER ME (1987, Columbia)—Married cop Tom Berenger falls in love with **Mimi Rogers**, a witness he's guarding.

GREGORY, GLORIA & DICK

HIS JAZZ BRIDE (1926, Silent, Warner Brothers)—Married **Marie Prevost**, looking for some fun, leaves her strait-laced husband **Matt Moore** for a jazzy time on a pleasure cruise. The ship starts to sink and Moore is off in a speedboat to rescue his wayward bride, almost arriving too late. Prevost now has a better appreciation of old "stick-in-the-mud" Moore.

GREGORY, KENT

HOT SHOTS (1991, 20th Century Fox)—**Cary Elwes** is a self-absorbed pilot competing with Charlie Sheen for the title of hottest hot dog in the sky.

GREGORY, MR.

THE STRANGE MR. GREGORY (1945, Monogram)—Magician **Edmund Lowe** will go to any length to win married Jean Rogers in this poverty-row special.

GREGORY, TANIA

DANGEROUS WOMAN (1929, Paramount)—Evil Russian-born **Olga Baclanova** uses jungle magic to seduce young men disposing of them after she's had her way with them. When his brother falls victim to his wife, Clive Brook puts poison in Olga's orange juice, killing her. He is saved from paying for his crime when his assistant puts a poison snake next to her body and gets rid of the poisoned orange juice. Remember "a day without orange juice is like a day without sunshine."

GREGSON, "BLINK"

THE IMPOSTER (1915, Silent, World)—**Alex B. Francis** doubles as "Blink" and his brother Bert who take turns impersonating their late father, also played by Francis. They right the wrongs their father caused in his business deals.

GRESHAM

ACES HIGH (1977, GB, Cine Artists/EMI)—**Malcolm McDowell** leads the men of the crack 76th Squadron WWI flying circus, despite being deeply frightened, by being astonishingly brave, helped along by whiskey.

GRESHAM

AFFAIRS OF A GENTLEMAN (1934, Universal)—In this dandy old-fashioned suspenseful drama, novelist **Paul Lukas** is found dead with a note saying no one is to be blamed for his death, but the police have other ideas, and look into his many affairs with married women which he wrote about in his books.

GRETCHEN

THE GOOSE GIRL (1915, Silent, Lasky)—Goose tender **Marguerite Clark** is the legitimate princess of her mythical European country, having been kidnapped as an infant from her castle, and replaced by the chancellor's daughter. Clarke will collect her prince-charming before it's all over.

GRETCHEN

GRETCHEN, THE GREENHORN (1916, Silent, Triangle)—**Dorothy Gish**, the daughter of an old Dutch engraver, moves with her father to New York, where she falls in love with an Italian-American. Counterfeiters kidnap her father to force him to make their plates, but he's rescued by some Irish-American kids. It's a melting-pot story.

GREVEMBERG, COL. FRANCIS C.

DAMN CITIZEN (1958, Universal)—**Keith Andes** attempts to clean up the corruption in the Louisiana state police force.

GREY, ANNA

THE LITTLE GRAY LADY (1914, Silent, Famous Players)—**Jane Gray** is the country sweetheart of a farm boy who has given into the temptations of the big city. She rescues him from his sinful life, forgives him and takes him back to God's country.

GREY, GAVIN "GREY GHOST"

EVEYBODY'S ALL-AMERICAN (1988, Warner Brothers) -**Dennis Quaid** comes through with his best work as the Louisiana All-American football player of the 1950s, who marries campus queen Jessica Lange and for the next 25 years grows older without growing up. He's fearful of all change and if his crew-cut remains, even he notices that his body has deserted him, his wife is not as adoring, and very few people wish to hear him once more give the blow-by-blow accounts of his triumphs back in college.

GREY, GUNNER

EX-CHAMP (1939, Universal)—Former boxer **Victor McLaglen** goes back into the ring to help erase his son's gambling debts.

GREY, JOAN

PRISONERS IN PETTICOATS (1950, Republic)—**Valentine Perkins**, who plays piano in a nightclub, becomes involved with the under-

world, and goes to jail rather than reveal her true identity, the daughter of a respected professor.

GREY, JULIAN

A MAN'S SHADOW (1920, GB, Silent, Butchers)—**Langhorne Burton**, down on his luck, murders a Jewish money lender, and is betrayed by his former lover.

GREY, LADY

LADY GREY (1980, Maverick)—Elvis Presley's last girlfriend **Ginger Alden** appears as a country singer, hoping to become a star. No way!

GREY, LADY JANE

LADY JANE GREY (1936, GB, Gaumont); LADY JANE (1986, GB, Paramount)—**Nova Pilbeam** and **Helena Bonham Carter** each portray the 16-year-old noblewoman who was put on the British throne for just nine days after the death of Henry's VIII's only male heir, Edward. The pitiful girl and her young husband are beheaded.

GREY, MARY

FIFTH AVENUE GIRL (1939, RKO)—Unemployed **Ginger Rogers** is persuaded by a millionaire to pose as a gold digger and annoy his greedy family.

GREYLEK, KAY

FIVE AGAINST THE HOUSE (1955, Columbia)—**Kim Novak** looks sexy as the only female among the five college students who plan to rob Las Vegas casinos. Kids nowadays have no ambition. On break, all they do is go to Florida for beer, sex and sun.

GRIBBLE, GEORGE

HE SNOOPS TO CONQUER (1944, GB, Columbia)—Handyman **George Formby** exposes a corrupt village council.

GRIBLEY, SAM

MY SIDE OF THE MOUNTAIN (1969, Paramount)—Thirteen-year-old **Teddy Eccles** runs away from home to get closer to nature.

GRIFF

S*P*Y*S (1974, 20th Century Fox)—CIA agents **Elliott Gould** and Donald Sutherland are deemed expendable by their superiors.

GRIFFIN

THE NAVIGATOR (1989, Australia, Arenafilm)—In 1348 Cumbria, New Zealand, psychic young **Hamish McFarlane** dreams of a way to save his village from the advancing black plague. He and four others find the means to transport themselves to the present time to do the trick.

GRIFFIN, BULLWHIP

THE ADVENTURES OF BULLWHIP GRIFFIN (1967, Buena Vista) - During the 1849 California gold rush, Bostonian butler **Roddy McDowell** learns how to take care of himself with the help of a bullwhip.

GRIFFIN, FELIX

THE FIEND WHO WALKED THE WEST (1958, 20th Century Fox)— In this western remake of KISS OF DEATH, sadistic killer **Robert Evans**, released from prison, terrorizes the west.

GRIFFIN, JACK

THE INVISIBLE MAN (1933, Universal)—**Claude Rains** is not seen in this movie until he's dying. Scientist Rains learns the secret of invisibility, but it turns him into a murdering madman. The film began Rains' long and distinguished movie career.

GRIFFIN, ROBERT
INVISIBLE MAN'S REVENGE (1944, Universal)—In a film of the Invisible Man series which need not have been made, **Jon Hall**, made invisible by a doctor so he may obtain an estate, kills the doctor when the latter refuses to make Hall visible again.

GRIFFITH, HELEN
UNKNOWN WOMAN (1935, Columbia)—Attorney Richard Cromwell falls in love with federal agent **Marian Marsh**, who is on the trail of a criminal and some stolen bonds.

GRIFFITH, JACK "PAPA"
PAPA'S DELICATE CONDITION (1963, Paramount)—**Jackie Gleason** drinks. And when he drinks, he's likely to buy anything, such as a pharmacy so he'll have access to alcohol during Prohibition or perhaps a circus for his daughter. His wife Glynis Johns has just about all she can take, and leaves him, but he convinces her to return to him.

GRIMES, BILL
I'LL FIX IT (1934, Columbia)—**Jack Holt** runs a small town by hook or by crook. He gets in trouble when he fires the high school principal Mona Barrie, because she won't help him get his younger brother on a sports team. He also has some trouble with a crooked real estate deal, but is saved by the lies of the principal, who has come to love Holt.

GRIMM, PETER
THE RETURN OF PETER GRIMM (1926, Silent, Fox); (1935, RKO)—**Alec B. Francis** and **Lionel Barrymore** portray a girl's guardian, who swears to him on his death bed that she will honor his wish that she marry his nephew. When the old man expires, the girl discovers her intended has fathered another woman's child. The old man rises from the grave, enters his nephew's mind and turns him into a decent person, worthy to marry the girl.

GRIMM, WILHELM & JACOB
THE WONDERFUL WORLD OF THE BROTHERS GRIMM (1962, MGM)—**Laurence Harvey** and **Karl Boehm** portray the famous German fairy tale writers in a film in which three of their stories "The Dancing Princess," "The Cobbler and the Elves" and "The Singing Bone" are dramatized.

GRIMSBY, JIM & "BILL"
JIM GRIMSBY'S BOY (1916, Silent, Ince)—**Frank Keenan** and **Enid Markey** portray a mountain man and the daughter whom he has raised as a boy. Calling Markey "Bill" and dressing her in male clothes doesn't fool Mother Nature, nor a handsome young sheriff.

GRIMSHAW, SGT.
CARRY ON SERGEANT (1959, GB, Anglo-Amalgamated)—**William Hartnell**, a British training sergeant, desperately wishes to win the Best Troop Award before retirement. His last group of trainees consists of the greatest screw-ups any army has ever seen, but they help him achieve his dream.

GRISCHA, SGT.
THE CASE OF SERGEANT GRISCHA (1930, RKO)—**Chester Morris**, a WWI Russian POW in Germany, escapes and is given shelter by Betty Compson. He makes it back to Russia and is recaptured by the Germans. Because he is carrying the identity tag of a dead Russian spy, he is executed.

GRISENKO, GRETA
THE GIRL IN THE KREMLIN (1957, Universal)—Former OSS man Lex Barker joins forces with an anti-communist group to locate beautiful **Zsa Zsa Gabor**.

GRISSOM, SLIM & MA
THE GRISSOM GANG (1971, Cinerama)—**Scott Wilson** and **Irene Dailey** star in this remake of NO ORCHIDS FOR MISS BLANDISH as son and mother, part of a gang of grotesques who kidnap heiress Kim Darby. Wilson falls for Darby.

GRITZKO, PRINCE
HIS HOUR (1924, Silent, Metro-Goldwyn)—**John Gilbert** is a Russian prince with a reputation as quite an accomplished lover. Englishwoman Aileen Pringle is attracted to him, but attempts to remain aloof rather than become another notch on his bed's headboard. One night during a storm, she's forced to take refuge in his lodge. She faints and when she awakens, she finds her clothes in disarray. Believing that Gilbert has taken her virtue, she strangely consents to marry him but discovers she's really in love with him, and he with her.

GROBART, JAY
THE MAN WHO LOVED CAT DANCING (1973, MGM)—**Burt Reynolds**, one of a gang of train robbers who kidnap runaway wife Sarah Miles, falls in love with her.

GROGAN
THE VICTORS (1963, Columbia)—**Jim Mitchum** has one of those unimportant roles as just another dogface in the infantry platoon, whose progress is traced during WWII as they move forward in Europe.

GROSS, WAYNE
THE LAST OF THE FINEST (1990, Orion)—**Joe Pantoliano** is one of a group of dedicated LAPD cops suspended for being overly zealous in fighting drug traffickers.

GROVE, ARLIN
NASHVILLE REBEL (1966, American International)—**Waylon Jennings**, an ex-GI, becomes a country singing sensation which is of course precisely what Jennings is. Other country artists heard from include: Tex Ritter, Sonny James, Faron Young, Loretta Lynn, Porter Waggoner, and the Wilburn Brothers.

GROVES, DR. CLIFF
THE NEANDERTHAL MAN (1953, UA)—Scientist **Robert Shayne** experiments with a new serum, using himself as a guinea pig. The result is that he becomes the title character.

GRUBBINS, JIMMY
THREE LIVE GHOSTS (1922, Silent, Paramount); (1929, UA); (1935, MGM)—**Edmund Goulding** in the first and **Charles McNaughton** in the last two films are one of three doughboys who return from WWI to find that they have been declared legally dead.

GRUESOME
DICK TRACY MEETS GRUESOME (1947, RKO)—**Boris Karloff** carries off his crimes by temporarily freezing everyone stiff with a mysterious gas. Ralph Byrd as Dick Tracy must and does bring Karloff to justice.

GUERIN, JEAN-CLAUDE
MAN, WOMAN AND CHILD (1983, Paramount)—**Sebastian Dugan** is Martin Sheen's son from a youthful fling. His arrival strains Sheen's marriage to Blythe Danner.

GUERRERO, EDDIE

LATINO (1986, Cinecom International)—Chicano Green Beret **Robert Beltran** is in Nicaragua, "advising" the U.S. backed contras against the Sandinistas. The makers of the movie make no effort to explore the causes of the conflict. It's simply the contras wear black hats, the Sandinistas wear white. Were it only so simple.

GUEVARA, CHE

CHE! (1969, 20th Century Fox)—**Omar Sharif** is dreadful as the travelling revolutionary, but he has competition for worst actor of the year from Jack Palance, playing Fidel Castro.

GUILDMAR, THELMA

THELMA (1922, Silent, FBO)—Norwegian **Jane Novak** marries English aristocrat Vernon Steel, moving to London with him. His friends do their best to break up the marriage, with Novak hurrying back to her homeland after they make her believe he has been unfaithful. Steel follows her and convinces her it isn't true.

GUINAN, TEXAS

DANCE HALL HOSTESS (1933, Mayfair); INCENDIARY BLONDE (1945, Paramount)—**Helen Chandler** and **Betty Hutton** each appear as the 1920s nightclub queen who delighted her customers by calling them suckers, which they were.

GUISENBERRY, WARD See KID GALAHAD

GUITAR, JOHNNY

JOHNNY GUITAR (1954, Republic)—Hard-boiled drifter **Sterling Hayden** moseys into the building feud between tough saloon keeper Joan Crawford and ruthless, brutal cattle baroness Mercedes McCambridge. The film is a most atypical western, directed by Nicholas Ray. It's flawed, but still a most outstanding entry in the western genre.

GUILICK, WALTER See KID GALAHAD

GULLIVER, LEMUEL

THE THREE WORLDS OF GULLIVER (1960, GB, Columbia); GULLIVER'S TRAVELS (1977, GB, Sunn Classics)—**Kerwin Mathews** and **Richard Harris** each appear as Jonathan Swift's hero who has adventures in Lilliput. Neither film does the classic justice. In the second film, the Lilliputians are toons.

GUNGA DIN

GUNGA DIN (1939, RKO)—**Sam Jaffe** portrays the Indian water bearer who wishes to become a soldier like his British masters Victor McLaglen, Cary Grant and Douglas Fairbanks. With quiet dignity he gives his life to save the troops.

GUNN

BLACK GUNN (1972, Columbia)—Black nightclub owner **Jim Brown** seeks revenge when his brother is killed.

GUNN, PETER

GUNN (1967, Paramount)—**Craig Stevens** repeats his very successful TV private eye, but as is usually the case it doesn't transfer to the big screen successfully. Where, for instance, is luscious Lola Albright?

GUNTHER, CATHERINE

THE APRIL FOOLS (1969, Jaelm/National General)—Unhappily married **Catherine Deneuve** runs away to Paris with married American businessman Jack Lemmon. The film was meant as a salute to the screwball romantic comedies of the 1930s. Mostly, it's a waste of the talent of the leads, to say nothing of that of Myrna Loy and Charles Boyer.

GUNZINGER, KATE

IT'S MY TURN (1980, Columbia)—Mathematics professor **Jill Clayburgh** decides to seize life by the throat when she falls in love with ex-major league baseball player Michael Douglas, the son of her father's new wife.

GURKIN, QUEENIE

QUEENIE (1921, Silent, 20th Century Fox)—**Shirley Mason** becomes a domestic in a wealthy man's home and ultimately marries a rich young poet.

GURNEY, JOE

KING OF THE UNDERWORLD (1939, Warner Brothers)—Title character **Humphrey Bogart** becomes involved with lady doctor Kay Francis. The patient (i.e. this movie) died.

GUS

HUSBANDS (1970, Columbia)—**John Cassavetes** is one of three married men, shocked by the death of a friend, who get drunk and impulsively fly to London for a weekend of dissipation.

GUS

THREE GODFATHERS (1936, MGM)—**Walter Brennan** is one of three outlaws who pledge to a dying woman in a desert to get her newborn baby to safety.

GUTHRIE, WOODY

BOUND FOR GLORY (1976, UA)—**David Carradine** stars in this fair-to-middlin' biopic of Arlo Guthrie's pappy, who gave the country some great folk music as he travelled from the Texas Dust Bowl to California in 1936. The photographer and musical director both won an Academy Award.

GUV'NOR, THE See FRANCIS ROTHSCHILD

GWEN

GIRL O' MY DREAMS (1935, Monogram)—**Mary Carlisle** is the sweet co-ed, who inspires the dreams of a college newspaper editor, the school's most popular boy and a track star.

GWEN

HOUSESITTER (1992, Universal)—**Goldie Hawn** is a zany woman who passes herself off as Steve Martin's wife after a one night stand. Her performance won't bring back screwball comedy. The movie is only mildly amusing, and the laughs are far too predictable.

GWENDOLYN

POOR LITTLE RICH GIRL (1917, Silent, Artcraft)—This is the first film in which America's Sweetheart **Mary Pickford** portrayed a child. She was 20 and her character was 11, the poor little rich girl of the title. She would continue to play children into her 30s because her fans demanded it.

GWILT, JOHN

MR. SYCAMORE (1975, Capricorn)—Timid mailman **Jason Robards Jr.**, with a nagging wife and a crush on a librarian, decides to escape his problems by becoming a tree.

GWYN, NELL

NELL GWYN (1935, GB, UA); NELL GWYNNE (1926, GB, Silent, First National)—**Anna Neagle** and **Dorothy Gish** each starred as the London street orange-seller who became Charles II's favorite mistress.

GWYNPLAINE
THE MAN WHO LAUGHS (1927, Silent, Universal)—**Conrad Veidt** has his expression permanently changed into a smile by surgery on the order of his father's rival King James II. He becomes a freak and clown with a traveling show, and finds happiness with a blind girl who can't see his grotesque grin.

GYNT, PEER
PEER GYNT (1965, Willow/Brandon)—This silent film was made in 1941 at Northwestern University, when its star **Charlton Heston** was 16 years old. It was released in 1965 to take advantage of his new stardom. Heston is a world adventurer, who steals sacred robes and is faithful to his love for a maiden.

GYPSY
THE VIRGIN AND THE GYPSY (1970, GB, Chevron)—Libidinous gypsy **Franco Nero** lifts the Victorian restrictions placed on virgin Joanna Shimkus. She sheds them enthusiastically.

H

HABER, MAX
A SOCIAL CELEBRITY (1926, Silent, Paramount)—**Adolphe Menjou** is a small-time woman's hair stylist, who follows his manicurist Louise Brooks to New York. He finds the going tough in the Big Apple. But when he's persuaded by one of his clients to pose as a French nobleman, he becomes all the rage. The bubble bursts, however, and he and Brooks return to their small town.

HACKENSTEIN, DR. ELLIOT
DR. HACKENSTEIN (1988, Vista)—In this horror spoof, mad doctor **David Muir** borrows body parts from three attractive but unwilling donors, intending to bring his wife back to life.

HACKER, PETER
THE AMBASSADOR (1985, Cannon)—**Robert Mitchum**, the controversial American ambassador to Israel, gets nothing but criticism for his attempts to solve the Palestinian problem.

HACKETT, LEE
GUNMAN'S WALK (1958, Columbia)—Tough rancher **Van Heflin** tries to raise his two sons, Tab Hunter and James Darren, to be decent citizens, but one follows too closely in his father's footsteps.

HADDOCK, FINLEY P. & MILDRED
FINN AND HATTIE (1931, Paramount)—Naive newly rich **Leon Errol** takes his family to Europe, where his daughter **Mitzi Green** comically mistreats her English cousin, but saves her father from being taken in by a con-man and a vamp.

HADEN, LADY HELEN
HER PRIVATE LIFE (1929, First National/Warner Brothers)—**Billie Dove**, the wife of a vulgar, self-made millionaire Montagu Love, goes through a messy divorce after taking an interest in gambler Walter Pidgeon.

HADLEY, ROSS
GAMBLER'S CHOICE (1944, Paramount)—Three childhood friends grow up: one, **Chester Morris**, to become a gambler; another, a policeman who must go after his buddy; and the third, a singer who cares for both of the men.

HADLEY, STELLA
THE WAR AGAINST MRS. HADLEY (1942, MGM)—Washington matron **Fay Bainter** attempts to ignore WWII and maintain her precious social life. She learns.

HAGEN, DUKE
MEET THE DUKE (1949, GB, Associate British)—**Farham Baxter**, a boxer from Brooklyn, inherits a dukedom, but discovers his servants are crooks searching for treasure.

HAGEN, MARY
THAT HAGEN GIRL (1947, Warner Brothers)—In her first grown-up role, **Shirley Temple** is an illegitimate girl, whose life is made miserable by malicious gossips, who suspect lawyer and war hero Ronald Reagan is her father. No, he's her romantic interest. Reagan rightly didn't wish to do this stinker.

HAGER, JENNY
THE STRANGE WOMAN (1946, UA)—In the early 19th century in Bangor, Maine, **Hedy Lamarr** marries elderly lumber baron Gene Lockhart; fools around with her step-son Louis Hayward, whose father she gets to kill; dumps Hayward for George Sanders; and is killed herself when she tries to run down Sanders and a nice girl he's with. Despite all this the picture's not very interesting.

HAGGART, DAVID
SINFUL DAVEY (1969, GB, UA)—**John Hurt** stars in the true story of an 1821 army deserter, who turns highwayman in Scotland.

HAGGERTY, HARD-BOILED
HARD-BOILED HAGGERTY (1927, Silent, First National)—American WWI air ace **Milton Sills** falls in love with a girl, who appears to have a notorious reputation, but not to worry, that's her sister.

HAINES
THE TERROR OF TINY TOWN (1938, Columbia)—**Little Billy** is the villain in this Western, which takes itself quite seriously, except that the cast consists of nothing but midgets. Little Billy attempts to start a range war but is thwarted by Billy Curtis, whose reward is the lovely Yvonne Moray. It's a hoot!

HAINES, GUY
STRANGERS ON A TRAIN (1951, Warner Brothers)—Tennis star **Farley Granger** is traveling to see a U.S. senator's daughter, Ruth Roman, after an unsuccessful attempt to convince his estranged and promiscuous wife to give him a divorce. On the train, he encounters Robert Walker, who explains his idea for the perfect crime. Two people who have no connection to each other exchange murders. When they part, Granger thinks nothing more of the conversation, but crazy Walker believes they have a deal, and proceeds to kill Granger's wife, and expects Granger to keep his part of the bargain by killing Walker's father.

HAINES, JOHNNY
HIS FOREIGN WIFE (1927, Silent, Pathe Exchange)—When doughboy **Wallace MacDonald** brings home a German wife after WWI, he

finds that his family hold her personally responsible, as a symbol of her nation, for the death of MacDonald's brother in the conflict.

HAINES, LARRY
MY FAVORITE BLONDE (1942, Paramount)—Burlesque comedian **Bob Hope**, who plays straight man for a trained penguin, finds himself in deep water when he reluctantly agrees to help beautiful British spy, Madeleine Carroll.

HAINES, MARY
THE WOMEN (1939, MGM)—In the bitchiest classic motion picture of all time, **Norma Shearer** leads a cast of 135 females and no men. She is a married woman who learns from a "dear friend" that her husband is fooling around with shop girl Joan Crawford. Impulsively, she goes to Reno and gets a divorce. Crawford marries her ex, but after a while Shearer decides she wants her man back and sharpens her claws for a good cat fight with Joan.

HAJJI BABA
ADVENTURES OF HAJJI BABA (1954, 20th Century Fox)—In this lightweight Arabian Nights piece, barber **John Derek** saves a princess from marrying a rogue, and claims her for himself. Nat "King" Cole had a pretty good hit with the title song.

HALDANE, HEATH
HALDANE OF THE SECRET SERVICE (1923, Silent, Houdini)—Escape artist **Harry Houdini** stars as a man who traces the murderer of his detective father to the feet of the father of the girl he loves.

HALE, ABIGAIL MARTHA "ABBY"
UNCONQUERED (1947, Paramount)—Bond slave **Paulette Goddard** is bought by Gary Cooper to annoy villain Howard Da Silva. Cooper sets her free, but Da Silva claims her as his property. Goddard and Cooper are reunited at Fort Pitt, where Da Silva has the Indians on the war-path against the unwanted 18th century colonial settlers.

HALE, ANDREW ROCKTON
THE REFORMER AND THE REDHEAD (1950, MGM)—**Dick Powell**, a small town reform candidate for mayor, dumps his crooked mentor and wins the election with the help of June Allyson, the daughter of the zoo superintendent.

HALE, CLINT
THE GAY BUCKAROO (1932, Allied)—Rancher **Hoot Gibson** is given a lot of trouble by his rival, bad guy gambler Roy D'Arcy, for the hand of Merna Kennedy.

HALE, CHRIS
WALK SOFTLY STRANGER (1950, RKO)—While on the lam from the police, **Joseph Cotten** falls for crippled Alida Valli, who promises to wait for him if he gives himself up.

HALE, ETHEL
THE DUPE (1916, Silent, Lasky)—**Blanche Sweet** is hired by a wealthy woman to help her get rid of her husband, as she's become interested in a playboy. But it's Sweet who ends up with the reformed playboy.

HALE, JENNIFER
JENNIFER HALE (1937, GB, 20th Century Fox)—An architect is able to prove that chorus girl **Rene Ray** didn't kill her producer.

HALE, MARY
THE GIRL WHO WOULDN'T WORK (1920, Silent, Schulberg)—**Marguerite De La Motte's** flirting with playboy-philanderer Lionel

Barrymore results in her father accidentally shooting Barrymore's former mistress. Barrymore bankrupts himself paying De La Motte's father's legal fees to get him acquitted of the crime.

HALE, MONTE
CALIFORNIA FIREBRAND (1948, Republic)—In a story resembling SUPPORT YOUR LOCAL GUNFIGHTER, drifter **Monte Hale** agrees to protect a mining town from a gang of outlaws by pretending to be a notorious gunslinger.

HALE, STEPHANIE
TWICE BLESSED (1945, MGM)—**Lynn Wilde** and her twin sister, one living with their mother and one with their father, have different last names. They conspire to get their divorced parents together again by exchanging identities.

HALEY, DOROTHY
BAD GIRL (1931, Fox)—**Sally Eilers** meets James Dunn at Coney Island, spends the night with him and finds herself pregnant. Dunn does the honorable thing and marries Eilers, even though he must give up his dream of owning his own radio store. Things are tough for the young couple, but that doesn't make the movie any more interesting.

HALF PINT, THE
THE HALF PINT (1960, Sterling)—Six-year old **Tommy Blackman** is chasing a chimp who is chasing a tramp. The police are chasing everyone.

HALIFAX, JOHN
JOHN HALIFAX—GENTLEMAN (1938, GB, MGM)—In 1790, apprentice **John Warwick** inherits a mill and marries a lord's disowned ward.

HALL, ANNIE
ANNIE HALL (1977, UA)—**Diane Keaton** is a delight as the kookie WASPish girlfriend of Jewish comedian Woody Allen. The story parallels the one-time relationship between Allen and Keaton.

HALL, ARCHIE
THE LAST TIME I SAW ARCHIE (1961, UA)—Con-man **Robert Mitchum** is a member of a group of college grads snagged for Civilian Pilot Training at an air base near Denver. It's supposed to be a comedy, but producer-director-co-star Jack Webb didn't provide enough laughs.

HALL, E. "EDDY" HUNTINGTON
HOLD YOUR MAN (1933, MGM)—Selfish con-man **Clark Gable** allows his good-natured blonde girlfriend Jean Harlow to go to prison for a crime he committed, but ultimately turns himself in so she will be released.

HALL, PASTOR FREDERICK
PASTOR HALL (1940, GB, UA)—In Germany in 1940, brave pastor **Wilfrid Lawson** denounces the Nazis and is executed.

HALL, MARY
THE KID SISTER (1927, Silent, Columbia)—**Ann Christy** moves to the city to be with her virtuous sister, chorus girl Marguerite De La Motte. When Christy is arrested at a notorious roadhouse while protecting her honor, De La Motte is forced to offer hers to raise the money to get her sister out of jail.

HALL, MAURICE

MAURICE (1987, GB, Cinecom)—Set in England of 1910, **James Wilby** is a young man who must come to terms with his homosexuality.

HALL, RICHARD

HIS GREATEST SACRIFICE (1921, Silent, Fox)—**William Farnum**, a successful writer, kills his opera singer wife's lover and is sentenced to life imprisonment. He is released 20 years later, at which time he seeks out his daughter, sees that she's happy and begs to be sent back to prison, but his daughter insists on his living with her.

HALLENBECK, JOE

THE LAST BOY SCOUT (1991, Warner Brothers)—Former Secret Service agent **Bruce Willis'** devotion to justice is what lost him the job and forces him to work as a private eye. He's hired to protect Halle Berry, the girlfriend of former pro quarterback Damon Wayans, banned from the game for gambling. When Berry is killed, Willis and Wayans team up to find out what's going on.

HALLERTON, JULIE

EASY TO LOVE (1953, MGM)—Swimsuit model **Esther Williams** yearns for her boss Van Johnson, who doesn't notice her until Tony Martin comes into the picture. Williams is yummy-looking in her Cypress Garden watercade spectaculars.

HALLIDAY, BIG DAN

THE HALLIDAY BRAND (1957, UA)—**Ward Bond**, rancher and sheriff of a small community, allows a crowd to lynch the half-breed who is in love with his daughter, thus alienating him from his eldest son Joseph Cotten.

HALLIT, MIKE

A GENTLE GANGSTER (1943, Republic)—Gangster **Barton Maclane** gives up his criminal ways and settles down. Twenty years later, mobster Jack La Rue threatens to disrupt his peaceful life. With the help of some other reformed mobsters, he chases his former colleague out of town.

HALLOCK, ZACHARY

THE LONE HAND (1953, Universal)—Widower-rancher **Joel McCrea**, who has just taken a new bride, finds himself mixed-up with a gang of outlaws.

HALLORAN, TIM SR. & JR.

MY SON IS A CRIMINAL (1939, Columbia)—To his great shame, retired policeman **Willard Robertson** finds that his son **Alan Baxter**, who he hoped would follow in his footsteps, has chosen the wrong side of the law. Coming out of retirement, Robertson kills his son in a shootout.

HALLOWAY, NICK

MEMOIRS OF AN INVISIBLE MAN (1992, Warner Brothers)—Stock analyst **Chevy Chase** is turned invisible by a freak accident. He is chased by ruthless government agent Sam Neill, who wants Chase to use his gift working for the CIA. Chase is assisted by Daryl Hannah, who became involved with him just before his fateful optical mishap.

HALPER, NELLIE

WAIT 'TIL THE SUN SHINES NELLIE (1952, 20th Century Fox) - **Jean Peters** doesn't share her husband barber David Wayne's love of their small town. She yearns for the excitement of the big city. She deserts him for a lover, but both are killed in a railroad accident. Wayne raises his two kids and has a lot of other heartaches, but as an honored old man in his community he dotes on his granddaughter Nellie, also played by Peters.

HALSEY, JACK

BRAIN DEAD (1990, Concorde)—**Bud Cort** plays a cracked-up mathematician. He is operated on by neurologist Bill Pullman, who is hoping to unlock a secret formula from Cort's crazed mind.

HALSEY, JOE

MY MAN (1928, Part-Talkie, Warner Brothers)—Before becoming a Broadway star, Fanny Brice has an unhappy love affair with **Guinn "Big Boy" Williams**. When she reaches the top, she sings the title song which Williams inspired.

HALVEY, BOBBY

SATURDAY'S CHILDREN (1929, Warner Brothers); (1940, Warner Brothers)—**Corinne Griffith** and **Anne Shirley** portray the girl who tricks a man with travelling on his mind into marriage. Wedded bliss it's not.

HALYARD, VIOLET, HESTER & GLORIA

THE GIRLS OF PLEASURE ISLAND (1953, Paramount)—**Joan Elan, Audrey Dalton** and **Dorothy Bromsley** are three pretty English girls living in 1945 with their father on a small Pacific island when 1500 U.S. marines land. With odds like that one might expect some excitement. One would be disappointed.

HAMBLETON, LT. COL. ICEAL

BAT 21 (1988, Tri-Star)—**Gene Hackman** portrays a 53-year-old Air Force strategist shot down over Korea during a routine reconnaissance mission. The air force goes to great efforts to rescue this decent but worried man. The film's title is Hackman's radio code name, which he uses as he keeps in contact with "Bird Dog," played by Danny Glover, a pilot trying to locate Hackman. Hackman is more realistic than the gung-ho Rambo types usually found in war movies these days.

HAMID, ABDUL II

ABDUL THE DAMNED (1935, GB, British International)—**Fritz Kortner** stars in this account of the last years of the rule of the Turkish Sultan in the early 1900s. Kortner employs assassination to thwart efforts to establish democratic government in his country but this leads to his eventual downfall.

HAMID, PRINCE

UNMASKED (1929, Artclass)—Mystic **Milton Krims** hypnotizes a girl into poisoning the wife of a man from whom he's trying to bilk money.

HAMIL, SALLY & RABBIT

THE POACHER'S DAUGHTER (1960, GB, Show Corp. of America)—**Julie Harry**, daughter of Irish poacher **Harry Brogan**, tames a wild young man who has inherited a nearby farm.

HAMILTON, ALEXANDER

ALEXANDER HAMILTON (1931, Warner Brothers)—**George Arliss'** political career is threatened as a result of his affair with a married woman. It's a fine biopic of America's 18th century financier.

HAMILTON, BILL

HARD HITTIN' HAMILTON (1924, Silent, Action)—**Buffalo Bill Jr.** (real name, Jay Wilsey), the new owner of the Lazy-B ranch, has a run-in with his foreman, foiling the latter's attempts to foreclose on a woman rancher. He must prove himself innocent of a murder charge.

HAMILTON, CHARLES

TWICE BRANDED (1936, GB, RKO)—Upon his release from prison, having been framed for fraud, father **Robert Rendel** is forced to pose as his family's uncle.

HAMILTON, CHARLOTTE & JOHN

HER FATHER SAID NO (1927, Silent, R-C Pictures)—**Mary Brian** elopes with ex-boxer Danny O'Shea, despite her father **John Steppling's** objections.

HAMILTON, DELL

TWO AGAINST THE WORLD (1932, Warner Brothers)—Society woman **Constance Bennett** takes the blame for a murder committed by her good-for-nothing brother. She is defended in court by Neil Hamilton, a young lawyer she loves.

HAMILTON, DICK

TOM, DICK AND HARRY (1941, RKO)—**Alan Marshal** almost wins Ginger Rogers over his two rivals, but he fails her litmus test—no bells ring.

HAMILTON, DR.

SPELL OF THE HYPNOTIST (1956, Exploitation)—**Eric Fleming**, a psychiatrist, treats Nancy Malone, who, under hypnosis, insists she is the Austrian Crown Prince's lover, who died with him in a suicide pact at Mayerling some 70 years earlier.

HAMILTON, EMMA HART

THAT HAMILTON WOMAN (1941, UA)—Married **Vivien Leigh** has a scandalous affair with British naval hero Lord Nelson, played by her then-lover and husband-to-be Laurence Olivier.

HAMILTON, JOHN

THE MAN IN THE NET (1959, UA)—When artist **Alan Ladd** is accused of murdering his wife, he flees, and is aided by children.

HAMILTON, LIZ

RICH AND FAMOUS (1981, MGM/UA)—**Jacqueline Bisset** stars in this boring sexed-up remake of OLD ACQUAINTANCES. She is one of two authors who have been in competition most of their lives.

HAMISH, JANE

SHE SHALL HAVE MURDER (1950, GB, Independent Film)—Law clerk **Rosamund John**, hoping to become a writer of thrillers, solves the murder of an eccentric old lady.

HAMLET

HAMLET (1913, Silent, GB, Gaumont); (1948, GB, Rank); (1964, Electronovision/Warner Brothers); (1969, GB, Woodfall-Film-ways); (1990, Warner Brothers)—**Johnston Forbes-Robertson, Laurence Olivier, Richard Burton, Nicol Williamson** and **Mel Gibson** each gave it their all as Shakespeare's melancholy Dane. Olivier won an Academy Award for his performance.

HAMMER, B.J.

HAMMER (1972, UA)—Black boxer **Fred Williamson** takes on the syndicate in this violent movie.

HAMMER, MIKE

I, THE JURY (1953, UA); (1982, 20th Century Fox); MY GUN IS QUICK (1957, UA)—**Biff Elliot, Armand Assante** and **Robert Bray** each star as Mickey Spillane's avenging angel and private eye, in what once were considered shocking stories of sex and violence.

HAMMERHEAD

HAMMERHEAD (1968, Columbia)—James Bond clone **Peter Vaughan** is a secret agent chasing a master criminal.

HAMMERSMITH

HAMMERSMITH IS OUT (1972, Cinerama)—In an updating of the Faustian legend, homicidal mental patient **Richard Burton** escapes with the help of a male nurse, and becomes the most influential person in the country.

HAMMETT, DASHIELL

HAMMETT (1982, Orion/Warner Brothers)—It's San Francisco, 1928; mystery writer **Frederic Forrest** finds himself involved with murder, kidnapping, blackmail, and prostitution when he agrees to search for a missing Chinese girl.

HAMMOND, BURKE

THE MAN WHO SAW TOMORROW (1922, Silent, Paramount)—**Thomas Meighan**, who can't make up his mind as to which of two women he should marry, is put into a hypnotic trance in which he is able to see the future he would share with each.

HAMMOND, DR. JACK & CHRIS

LIKE FATHER, LIKE SON (1987, Tri-Star) -In one of a slew of movies featuring age transformations, father and son **Dudley Moore** and **Kirk Cameron** switch identities after drinking a Bloody Mary drink containing an old Indian concoction. This example of the sub-sub genre fails miserably on just about every count.

HAMMOND, JOE

HIS LAST HAUL (1928, Silent, FBO)—**Tom Moore** joins the Salvation Army, declaring that he has forsaken his life of crime, but a few days later, disguised as Santa Claus, he's up to his old tricks and soon finds himself behind iron bars.

HAMMOND, OLIVER

THE UNDYING MONSTER (1942, 20th Century Fox)—Old family member **John Howard**, a werewolf, is discovered to be the one murdering members of his English family.

HAMPSTEAD, JOHN

HELD TO ANSWER (1923, Silent, Metro)—**House Peters**, an actor turned minister, is accused of theft by his jealous sweetheart. The real culprit is the brother of the reverend's current fiancee.

HAMPTON, BARBARA

THE GIRL WHO DARED (1920, Silent, Republic)—Female sheriff **Edythe Sterling** brings a crooked lawman and a gang of Mexican bandits to justice.

HAMPTON, BOB

BOB HAMPTON OF PLACER (1921, Silent, Associated First National)—**James Kirkwood**, an officer wrongly sent to prison for murder, becomes a notorious gambler and gunslinger when he's released. His name is cleared after his death with Custer at Little Big Horn.

HAN

THE YOUNG AND THE BRAVE (1963, MGM)—Korean lad **Manuel Padilla** loses his parents while helping American POWs escape from their captors.

HANCOCK, ANTHONY

CALL ME GENIUS (1961, GB, Associate British)—**Tony Hancock**, an artist of little talent, passes off the paintings of another as his, and soon is all the rage in the art world.

HAND, DORA
THE WOMAN OF THE TOWN (1943, UA)—**Claire Trevor** is the dance-hall love of Bat Masterson, played by Albert Dekker. When she's shot down in Dodge City by Barry Sullivan, Dekker gets mad.

HANDEL, GEORGE FREDERICK
THE GREAT MR. HANDEL (1942, GB, GFD)—**Wilfrid Lawson** stars in this decent tale of how the great composer wrote the Messiah.

HANDLEY, MAYOR
IT'S THAT MAN AGAIN (1943, GB, Gainsborough)—**Tommy Handley**, the mayor of Foaming-at-the-Mouth, puts on a show to raise money to refurbish a bombed-out theatre.

HANK
RENEGADES (1989, Universal)—**Lou Diamond Phillips** does his best to look stoical in his role as an American Indian who has vowed to avenge the death of his brother.

HANLAN, NED
THE BOY IN BLUE (1986, 20th Century Fox)—**Nicolas Cage** stars in this biopic of the Canadian lad who was the best rower in international sculling for ten years during the 19th century.

HANLEY, BIG ED
LOVE THAT BRUTE (1950, 20th Century Fox)—Supposedly ruthless Chicago gang leader **Paul Douglas** rubs out his enemies, but actually the soft-hearted mobster keeps them in comfort and luxury, locked in his cellar.

HANLEY, JIMMY
UNEXPECTED FATHER (1939, Universal)—After his former dancing partner dies, **Dennis O'Keefe** adopts her child rather than see the baby sent to an orphanage.

HANLON, JOSEPH
THE LEATHERNECK (1929, Pathe)—**William Boyd** is a marine accused of desertion and murder. The Russian woman whom he married during WWI arrives to save him during his court martial.

HANLON, MOLLY
THE BEAUTIFUL GAMBLER (1921, Silent, Universal)—**Grace Darmond's** lover kills her brutal gambler husband—or did he? It's a confused and confusing picture.

HANLON, TIM
THE MAN FROM GUN TOWN (1936, Puritan)—**Tim McCoy** comes to the rescue of rancher Ruth McArthur, accused of the murder of her brother.

HANNAH
HANNAH AND HER SISTERS (1986, Orion)—**Mia Farrow** is the heart and soul of a large extended family, which consists of her warring parents, her two sisters, her husband, her ex-husband and various lovers. It's Woody Allen at his best as writer-director.

HANNIBAL
HANNIBAL (1960, Warner Brothers)—Beefcake king **Victor Mature** stars as the general who crosses the Alps with elephants, but has quite a bit of trouble with a Roman senator's daughter.

HANRAHAN, JOE
HIGH AND HANDSOME (1925, Silent, R-C Pictures)—Cop **Maurice B. "Lefty" Flynn** turns to boxing after being suspended from the force for refusing a boxing promotor's bribe to keep his mouth shut about a badly constructed balcony in an arena.

HANSEN, DAN
HE SAID, SHE SAID (1991, Paramount)—In flashback, **Kevin Bacon** gives his version of his romance with co-worker Elizabeth Perkins. His version differs markedly from hers. Neither version makes for an interesting movie.

HANSEN, GRETA MAE
FREE, WHITE AND 21 (1963, American International)—White, Swedish **Annalena Lund** comes to Texas to take part in the Freedom Rides of the sixties. A black motel owner is accused of raping her.

HANSEN, ILA
PORTRAIT OF A SINNER (1961, GB, Renown)—Archeologist Tony Britton dumps a newspaper publishing heiress for German nymphomaniac **Nadja Tilley**.

HANSEN, JOHNNY
IDOL OF THE CROWDS (1937, Universal)—Hockey star **John Wayne** is offered a bribe to throw a game.

HANSEN, STACEY
STACEY (1973, New World)—Former Playmate **Anne Randall** is a super sexy private eye, working on a murder and blackmail case involving a Moonie-like religious cult.

HANSEN, WOLF
BACHELOR OF HEARTS (1958, GB, Rank)—**Hardy Kruger** stars in this episodic comedy about the adventures of a German exchange student at Cambridge.

HANTZ, BOB
THE SUPER COPS (1974, MGM/UA)—**David Selby** and his partner Ron Leibman use unorthodox police methods in dealing with drug dealers in the black Bedford-Stuyvesant area of Brooklyn.

HANVEY, JIM
JIM HANVEY, DETECTIVE (1937, Republic)—Insurance company detective **Guy Kibbee** investigates the theft of a valuable emerald.

HAPPY
FOUR JACKS AND A JILL (1941, RKO)—**Eddie Foy, Jr.** provides a bit of comedy in this story of four musicians who must replace their singer, when the incumbent is convinced to retire by her mobster boyfriend.

HARBIN, NAT
THE BURGLAR (1956, Columbia)—**Dan Duryea** and his gang steal a jewelled necklace from a mansion. A crooked cop kidnaps Duryea's sister Jayne Mansfield, holding her for the ransom of the necklace. Duryea brings the jewels but is killed anyway.

HARBIN, NICK
THE WALKING TARGET (1960, UA)—Ex-convict **Ronald Foster** is convinced to turn over the loot of a payroll robbery by the widow of his former accomplice.

HARD, TONY
A HOLY TERROR (1931, Fox)—Polo-playing Easterner **George O'Brien** flies his plane west to investigate the murder of his father. He crashes his plane into the bathroom of Sally Eilers, and what should a girl do after such an introduction? She falls in love with O'Brien. This doesn't sit well with her ranch foreman sweetheart, Humphrey Bogart. O'Brien accuses James Kirkwood of killing his father and discovers that Kirkwood is his real father. The deceased is the scoundrel who stole Kirkwood's wife and son years earlier.

HARDCASTLE, JOE

FATHER STEPS OUT (1937, GB, RKO)—Cheese manufacturer **George Carney** is saved from society swindlers by his chauffeur.

HARDCASTLE, LT. CMDR.

WATCH IT SAILOR! (1961, GB, Hammer)—Naval officer **Dennis Price** has mother-in-law problems, and is hit with a paternity suit on the eve of his wedding.

HARDCASTLE, PRUDENCE

PRUDENCE AND THE PILL (1968, GB, 20th Century Fox) -**Deborah Kerr's** teenage daughter swipes her mother's birth control pills and replaces them with aspirin. Expect a rise in the birth rate.

HARDCASTLE, SQUIRE

THE GAY CORINTHIAN (1924, GB, Silent, Butchers)—Boxer **Victor McLaglen** saves lady Betty Faire, who has joined a band of gypsies when she learns that she is the subject of a wager.

HARDESTY, DAN

'TIL WE MEET AGAIN (1941, RKO)—In a remake of ONE WAY PASSAGE (1932), condemned **George Brent**, being taken to his execution on an ocean liner from Hong Kong to San Francisco, meets and falls in love with Merle Oberon, who is dying of a rare malady. They keep their fates from each other. Carol Burnett did a wonderful spoof of this story on her TV show.

HARDIN, COLE

THE WESTERNER (1940, UA)—Drifter **Gary Cooper**, accused of being a horse thief, is saved from hanging in Judge Roy Bean's court, because he convinces "The Law West of Pecos," beautifully played by Walter Brennan, that he can get the judge an introduction to actress Lily Langtry.

HARDING, TESS

WOMAN OF THE YEAR (1942, MGM)—In their first film together, **Katharine Hepburn** and Spencer Tracy, a famous political columnist and a gruff sportswriter, respectively, marry but run into domestic squabbles, because she puts her career ahead of wifely duties. In a not very feminist finale, she promises to do better in order to keep her man.

HARDWICKE, CARLYE

THE NOTORIOUS LANDLADY (1962, Columbia)—**Kim Novak** rents a London apartment to American diplomat Jack Lemmon. He is used by Scotland Yard to keep an eye on her because she's suspected of murdering her husband. Lemmon finds it hard to believe that anyone who looks like Novak can be a murderer, no matter how much the evidence seems to suggest it.

HARDY, ANDY

JUDGE HARDY'S CHILDREN (1938, MGM); LOVE FINDS ANDY HARDY (1938, MGM); OUT WEST WITH THE HARDY'S (1938, MGM); ANDY HARDY GETS SPRING FEVER (1939, MGM); JUDGE HARDY AND SON (1939, MGM) ANDY HARDY MEETS THE DEBUTANTE (1940, MGM); ANDY HARDY'S PRIVATE SECRETARY (1941, MGM); LIFE BEGINS FOR ANDY HARDY (1941, MGM); ANDY HARDY'S DOUBLE LIFE (1942, MGM); ANDY HARDY'S BLONDE TROUBLE (1942, MGM); LOVE LAUGHS AT ANDY HARDY (1946, MGM); ANDY HARDY COMES HOME (1958, MGM)—**Mickey Rooney** was awarded a special honorary Academy Award in 1938 "for bringing to the screen the spirit and personification of youth" and "for setting a high standard of ability and achievement." The Academy was taking note of his role of Andy Hardy, which he first played in a 1937 film called A FAMILY AFFAIR, with Lionel

Barrymore in the role of his father. In subsequent films of the long running series, Lewis Stone starred as the wise and always understanding Judge Hardy, who gave the idealized All American teenager wise counsel, which Andy was smart enough to take. The films introduced a lot of short starlets who picked up a bit of experience working with the young ball of fire before getting on with their careers. Andy Hardy treated these young ladies with more respect than did the swinging Mickey Rooney.

HARDY, ANN

SINNERS IN LOVE (1928, Silent, FBO)—**Olive Borden** moves to New York to work in a gambling house. When she finds the roulette wheels are fixed, she quits, much to the distress of gambler Huntley Gordon, who loves her. Borden's former lover gets her mixed up with New York's biggest cad. Borden shoots this louse when he tries to have his way with her. She's found innocent of the crime, and settles down to married life with Gordon, who has pledged to amend his ways.

HARDY, JUDGE

JUDGE HARDY'S CHILDREN (1938, MGM); OUT WEST WITH THE HARDYS (1938, MGM); JUDGE HARDY AND SON (1939, MGM)—**Lewis Stone**, who by the time of the Hardy series had had a long and distinguished career, seemed the perfect father to a headstrong but basically good kid, Andy Hardy. In each of the films, the time came when Andy is in over his head, due to some scheme or another. He dutifully takes himself into his father's study for a serious talk, which always did a world of good.

HARDY, MARIA

COUSINS (1989, Paramount)—When her husband William Peterson begins an affair with Sean Young, **Isabella Rossellini** and cuckolded husband Ted Danson comfort each other. This leads to love in this remake of the 1986 French film COUSINE, which won the Oscar for Best Foreign Language Film.

HARDY, MARIAN

JUDGE HARDY'S CHILDREN (1938, MGM); OUT WEST WITH THE HARDYS (1938, MGM)—**Cecilia Parker** played Mickey Rooney's older sister in the series. As Rooney's role became more dominant, hers became less significant. She loved her brother and he loved her, but for the most part her role was merely supportive.

HARDY, MAYOR

THE KLANSMAN (1974, Paramount)—Alabama sheriff Lee Marvin confronts the local Ku Klux Klan, led by **David Huddleston**.

HARDY, MRS.

OUT WEST WITH THE HARDYS (1938, MGM)—**Fay Holden** is the mother of the Hardy family. If Lewis Stone is its head, she is its heart.

HARDY, OLIVER

OUR RELATIONS (1936, MGM); JITTERBUGS (1943, 20th Century Fox)—In OUR RELATIONS, **Oliver Hardy** not only appeared as his usual blustering self but also his long lost twin brother Bert. In the 1943 film, Hardy and Stan Laurel help a nightclub singer fend off mobsters.

HARE, DR. RICHARD

DOCTOR IN LOVE (1960, GB, Rank)—**Michael Craig** replaces Dirk Bogarde as one of two hospital doctors, who take over a country practice. They still must contend with Sir Lancelot Spratt, delightfully played by James Robertson Justice.

HARGREAVES, ALICE LIDDELL

DREAMCHILD (1985, GB, Universal)—**Coral Browne** portrays the woman, who as a girl was Lewis Carroll's model for his Alice in Wonderland. She's now in her 80s, and has come to the United States for the centenary of the author's birth. She's not certain she understands what all the fuss is about.

HARGROVE, PVT. MARION

SEE HERE, PRIVATE HARGROVE (1944, MGM); WHAT NEXT, CORPORAL HARGROVE? (1945, MGM)—**Robert Walker**, an A-number-one screw-up, has a series of comical misadventures when he joins the Army in WWII. By the sequel, he's been promoted, and is having a romance with a French mademoiselle. You'd hardly know a war was on.

HARKINSON, GLORIA

MAD ABOUT MUSIC (1938, Universal)—**Deanna Durbin** has bragged so much to her classmates at a Swiss girl's school about her non-existent father that she has to produce him, and gets charming Herbert Marshall to accept the role.

HARKINSON, TIMMIE

TOY TIGER (1956, Universal)—**Tim Hovey** stars in this flat remake of MAD ABOUT MUSIC. He adopts his widowed mother Laraine Day's business associate Jeff Chandler as his father.

HARKNESS, BERNARD

WHAT HAPPENED TO HARKNESS? (1934, GB, Warner Brothers)—In this comedy, the village policeman investigates the apparent death of miser **Bremer Wills**.

HARKNESS, DON BOB

THE GAY CABALLERO (1932, Fox)—Friendly old **Victor McLaglen** is the mysterious outlaw El Coyote, who really isn't a bad guy after all.

HARLAN, BINGE

THE JOYOUS LIAR (1919, Silent, Hodkinson/Pathe)—Artist **J. Warren Kerrigan** enters a house and finds a girl being held captive by two thugs. She escapes while he takes a knock on the noggin. When the police arrive, they arrest Kerrigan, who is released into the custody of the girl's father, a famous criminologist. Kerrigan accepts the sentence gladly so he can be near the girl, whom he eventually wins.

HARLAN, MICHAEL

MY SCIENCE PROJECT (1985, Buena Vista)—**John Stockwell** stars in this tasteless comedy about high school students who find a gadget which causes time and space warps.

HARLEY, TOPPER

HOT SHOTS (1991, 20th Century Fox)—In a none-too-funny spoof of "Top Gun," **Charlie Sheen** is a maverick navy pilot. Valeria Golino plays his Kelly McGillis.

HARLOW, JEAN

HARLOW (1965, Electronovision/Magna); (1965, Paramount)—Neither **Carol Lynley** nor **Carroll Baker** is convincing in her portrayal of the blonde bombshell. Somehow lost in both productions is that Harlow was not only a sex symbol, but a rather talented comedian and a tough lady who had some miserably bad luck in her romances. The films did attempt to portray what a troublesome harridan was Harlow's mother, and what a totally loathsome leech was her step-father.

HARLOW, STEPHEN, JR.

STEPHEN STEPS OUT (1923, Silent, Paramount)—In his screen debut, 13-year-old **Douglas Fairbanks, Jr.** is a student, who flunks a course in Turkish history. His father sends the lad to Turkey, where he becomes expert on his subject, and even saves the Sultan's son from kidnappers.

HARMON, SAM

OCEAN'S ELEVEN (1960, Warner Brothers)—**Dean Martin** is Frank Sinatra's number one lieutenant in the robbery of five Las Vegas casinos on New Year's Eve.

HARMON, TOM

HARMON OF MICHIGAN (1941, Columbia)—All-American **Tom Harmon** portrays All-American Tom Harmon without making a fool of himself. He may not have been Mark Harmon, his son, but he was at least as good an actor as his late son-in-law Ricky Nelson.

HARPER, ANN

LADIES AT PLAY (1926, Silent, First National)—**Doris Kenyon** has exactly three days to marry in order to earn a $6 million inheritance.

HARPER, BILL

AMBASSADOR BILL (1931, Fox)—Oklahoma cattle man **Will Rogers** is appointed U.S. ambassador to a European country ruled by a regent.

HARPER, DICK & JANE

FUN WITH DICK AND JANE (1977, Columbia)—When aerospace engineer **George Segal** loses his job and can't find any work at comparable pay, he and wife **Jane Fonda** turn to a life of crime. Things works out when they steal from Segal's former boss who had been stealing from the government.

HARPER, GEORGE

GEORGE IN CIVVY STREET (1946, GB, Columbia)—Ex-soldier **George Formby** returns to run his country pub and foils his crooked rival.

HARPER, LEW

HARPER (1966, Warner Brothers)—Wealthy Lauren Bacall has lost her husband and doesn't know where to find him—and she's not all that sure she cares. L.A. Philip Marlowe-like private eye **Paul Newman** stumbles on the solution to the missing spouse and assorted murders by dealing with the likes of Shelley Winters, Julie Harris and Pamela Tiffin.

HARPER, ROBERTA

LADIES COURAGEOUS (1944, Universal)—**Loretta Young** is one of the female pilots who ferried military planes from base to base during WWII.

HARPER, WADE

THE NEBRASKAN (1953, Columbia)—Army scout **Phil Carey** proves the innocence of an Indian accused of killing a Sioux chief. Even 3D doesn't help this hopeless Western.

HARPER, WINNIE

SHE COULDN'T SAY NO (1930, Warner Brothers)—Cabaret singer **Winnie Lightner** becomes a show business success with the help of gangster Chester Morris.

HARRAS, JOE

A WOMAN FOR JOE (1955, GB, Rank)—Fair owner **George Baker** has a falling out with his star attraction, midget Jimmy Karoubi, because they both fall for the new attraction, singer Diane Cilento.

HARRIGAN, DR.

THE MURDER OF DR. HARRIGAN (1936, First National)—When physician **John Eldredge** is murdered, a whole surgery of doctors, nurses and patients are suspected of the crime.

HARRIGAN, "HARD ROCK"

HARD ROCK HARRIGAN (1935, Fox)—**George O'Brien**, foreman of a gang of laborers building a tunnel, has several run-ins with his assistant. Still, when the latter is trapped in a cave-in, O'Brien risks his life to save him.

HARRIGAN, JIMMY

SAILOR'S LUCK (1933, Fox)—By accident, sailor **James Dunn** finds himself with unemployed Sally Eilers like an albatross around his neck. He gets into several scrapes because of her, but ends up marrying her.

HARRIGAN, TOM

HARRIGAN'S KID (1943, MGM)—Unsportsmanlike ex-jockey **William Gargan** teaches youngster Bobby Readick about racing and cheating. That they both eventually reform is no big surprise.

HARRINGTON, DAVID

TWO BRIGHT BOYS (1939, Universal)—**Freddie Bartholomew** and his father Melville Cooper prevent a swindler from stealing a valuable piece of Texas property from his American friend, Jackie Cooper.

HARRINGTON, JEAN

THE LADY EVE (1941, Paramount)—**Barbara Stanwyck** gives one of her best performances as a seductive cardsharp, who tries to fleece millionaire simpleton Henry Fonda aboard an ocean liner. When the poor fish slips from her hook, she poses as a different woman and gives it another go, this time landing him, as her husband.

HARRINGTON, EVE

ALL ABOUT EVE (1950, 20th Century Fox)—Beneath her timid, helpful and idolizing exterior, **Anne Baxter** is a ruthless, ambitious, would-be stage actress, who wants everything aging first lady of the stage Bette Davis has, including her fiance, her roles, her playwright, her director, etc. Baxter at last gets the roles and is a huge success. She does lose the friendship of a few people who have been kind to her, but this seems a small price for fame. Hollywood's code, which hates to see a villain go unpunished, causes the producers to introduce a girl who would just love to be useful to Baxter, who Anne doesn't recognize as a reincarnation of herself.

HARRINGTON, WILLIE

BABY FACE HARRINGTON (1935, MGM)—Timid bank clerk **Charles Butterworth** is mistakenly identified as America's most wanted killer. This mobster spoof miscast Butterworth and he wasn't enough of a star to make it a winner at the box office.

HARRION, KEN

WHOSE LIFE IS IT ANYWAY? (1981, MGM/UA)—**Richard Dreyfuss** gives a strong performance as a witty sculptor, paralyzed after an automobile accident. He fights to be allowed to die.

HARRIS

THREE MEN IN A BOAT (1933, GB, Associated First National); (1958, GB, Romulus/Valiant)—**William Austin** and **Jimmy Edwards** are each one-third of a trio of Englishmen traveling along the Thames by boat, getting into trouble all along the way. Too bad, neither version is very amusing.

HARRIS, ALMA

OVER THE HILL (1992, Australia, Greater Union)—Sixty-year-old widow **Olympia Dukakis** leaves Bar Harbor, Maine for a new life in the Australian outback.

HARRIS, BEN

THE TIGER MAKES OUT (1967, Columbia)—Middle-aged New York City mailman **Eli Wallach** has had enough of society's mistreatment of him. Among other attempts at revenge on an uncaring city, he kidnaps married Anne Jackson, who rather enjoys the experience, because she shares his sense of frustration.

HARRIS, BILL

BARNACLE BILL (1935, GB, City/Butchers)—Widower **Archie Pitt** makes every sacrifice for his young daughter, even leaving the sea to be with her. When she is grown and breaks down social barriers to marry a wealthy young man, he returns to sailoring.

HARRIS, CHUCK

HER FIRST BEAU (1941, Columbia)—Jane Withers finds her childhood sweetheart **Jackie Cooper** is taking her for granted. Neither Withers nor Cooper appeared comfortable with their near-adult roles.

HARRIS, JAMIE

RICH KIDS (1979, UA)—**Jeremy Levy** and Trini Alvarado are going through puberty at the same time their parents' marriages are breaking up—and it's hard to say which hurts most.

HARRIS, SKITTY

WAR PARTY (1989, Tri-Star)—A hundred years after the massacre of Blackfoot Indians by whites, **Kevin Dillon** and a group of other Native Americans decide to get even when a drunken actor appearing in a reenactment of the tragedy pumps live ammunition into the Indians.

HARRIS, TOWNSEND

THE BARBARIAN AND THE GEISHA (1958, 20th Century Fox)—**John Wayne**, laughably miscast as America's first U.S. Consul-General to Japan, overcomes his reluctant hosts' opposition to opening trade between the two countries. Now listen up, papa-san.

HARRISON, BILL

RICH MAN, POOR GIRL (1936, MGM)—Neither family is quite prepared to handle the announcement of wealthy **Robert Young's** decision to marry poor Ruth Hussey.

HARRISON, CARTER

STRANGE BEDFELLOWS (1965, Universal)—Oil executive **Rock Hudson** doesn't know what trouble is, until he decides to divorce his fiery Italian wife Gina Lollobrigida.

HARRISON, GEORGE

HIS EXCELLENCY (1952, GB, Ealing)—Former longshoreman labor leader **Eric Portman** is appointed governor of a British island colony. His blunt manner upsets people, but he wins them over when his experience enables him to put down a riot before it can get started.

HARRISON, JOHN G.

PHANTOM KILLER (1942, Monogram)—**John Hamilton** stars in this modest "B" thriller about a clever killer with a near perfect alibi.

HARRISON, JUNE
OH, WHAT A NURSE! (1926, Silent, Warner Brothers)—Wealthy young **Patsy Ruth Miller** is prevented from marrying a fortune hunter by newspaper reporter Syd Chaplin, impersonating a female lovelorn columnist.

HARRISON, MAJOR
LET'S KILL UNCLE (1966, Universal)—When Pat Cardi discovers that his uncle, **Nigel Green**, is trying to murder him for a $5 million dollar inheritance, Cardi decides to do unto the older man before he can do unto him.

HARRISON, PAUL
FRIENDS (1971, GB, Paramount)—French teenagers **Sean Bury** and Anicee Alvina run away from their unloving parents to set up housekeeping together on a deserted beach. After they have a baby, their parents come to get them, promising to be better. There's nothing here worth thinking about, because there's nothing here.

HARRISON, SHEILA
MAID'S NIGHT OUT (1938, RKO)—Millionaire's son Allan Lane becomes a milkman for a month to win a bet from his father. He encounters **Joan Fontaine**, whom he mistakes for a maid. Moderately funny.

HARRISON, STEVE
THE FIGHTING BUCKAROO (1943, Columbia)—**Charles Starrett** rides into a western town to clear his friend of charges of being the head of a gang of rustlers.

HARROW, DAN
THE FARMER TAKES A WIFE (1935, 20th Century Fox); (1953, 20th Century Fox)—In his screen debut, **Henry Fonda** portrays a young 1800s farmer who works on the Erie Canal so he can make enough money to buy some land and settle down with Janet Gaynor. **Dale Robertson** repeats the role in 1953, but the story is now a technicolor musical starring Betty Grable.

HARROW, MARTIN
M (1951, Columbia)—**David Wayne** is no Peter Lorre in this tale of a murderer of children, caught by the city's criminal profession because his crimes are bringing police heat on all their illegal activities.

HARRY
HARRY AND SON (1984, Orion)—Construction worker and widower **Paul Newman** can't get anywhere with his artistically inclined son, Robby Benson. Bridging the generation gaps never gets any easier.

HARRY
HARRY AND THE HENDERSONS (1987, Universal)—**Kevin Peter Hall** portrays Bigfoot, who accidently runs into a sensitive, caring family, which only wants to protect him from the curious and dangerous.

HARRY
HARRY IN YOUR POCKET (1973, UA)—The film spends too little time on the subject of pickpocketing as practiced by **James Coburn**, Michael Sarrazin and old gentleman thief, Walter Pidgeon, and too much on their chasing around the country.

HARRY
HARRY'S MACHINE (1986, Cannon)—**Robert Forster** stars in and directs this comedy about a down-and-out detective who is forced to take his runaway niece with him on his investigations. The film is also known as HOLLYWOOD HARRY.

HARRY
HARRY'S WAR (1981, Taft International)—Taxpayer **Edward Herrmann** takes on the IRS, which made a mistake on his return. He loses just about everything in his war. The Internal Revenue Service is never a laughing matter.

HARRY
HUSBANDS (1970, Columbia)—**Ben Gazarra** is one of three men who realize their mortality when a friend of theirs dies. After the funeral, the three try to escape the thought of their own end by impulsively flying to London for a weekend of dissipation.

HARRY
THE KILLERS (1984, Roth)—Former insurance man **Jack Kehoe** helps a small-time thief burglarize a mansion. Murder and rape follow.

HARRY
THE LADY KILLERS (1956, GB, Ealing)—**Peter Sellers** is a member of a gang of robbers, who feel they must eliminate their old landlady Katie Johnson, who is onto them, but they knock each other off instead.

HARRY
THE LITTLE KIDNAPPERS (1954, GB, UA)—**Jon Whiteley** and Vincent Winter won special Academy Awards for their charming portrayal of orphaned Nova Scotia kids, circa 1900, who "adopt" an abandoned baby when their grandfather won't allow them to have a pet. More natural acting by children, one is not likely to see.

HARRY
SCRATCH HARRY (1969, Cannon)—While his bisexual wife is away, **Harry Walker Staff** lives it up. When she returns she jumps into bed with one of Staff's girlfriends. The latter kills herself after the experience. This leads to Staff and his wife killing each other. Staff's guardian angel scratches his name off his list. Let us know if you figure out what it is supposed to mean.

HARRY
THREE MEN ON A HORSE (1936, Warner Brothers)—**Edgar Kennedy** is one of three gamblers who benefit from the ability of a timid Brooklyn greetings card writer to pick racehorse winners.

HARRY
TOM, DICK AND HARRY (1941, RKO)—**Burgess Meredith** wins out over Alan Marshal and George Murphy for Ginger Rogers because his kisses ring her bell.

HART, LORA
NIGHT NURSE (1931, Warner Brothers)—Nurse **Barbara Stanwyck** uncovers a plot by other members of the household against her patient's children.

HART, MARGARET
THE SQUEALER (1930, Columbia)—After escaping prison to take care of the squealer who got him sent up for killing his rival, bootlegger Jack Holt discovers that his wife **Dorothy Revier** turned him in to save him from a worse fate from a rival gang. Holt deliberately walks into a police trap and is killed.

HART, NICK
THE MODERNS (1988, Alive Films)—This film appears to be a tribute to the spirit of Paris during the 1920s. Artist **Keith Carradine** is paid more for his forgeries than his original creations. Carradine

and his friends are part of the Lost Generation, but for many the movie is just plain lost.

HART, QUEENIE
CATTLE QUEEN (1951, UA)—**Maria Hart** is handy cracking a whip in this terrible oater, aka QUEEN OF THE WEST.

HART, ROXIE
ROXIE HART (1942, 20th Century Fox)—Just to bask in the limelight of the publicity, twenties showgirl **Ginger Rogers** confesses to a murder she didn't commit. Sharp, crooked lawyer Adolphe Menjou gets her off. The movie's dedication reads: "To all the beautiful women in the world, who have shot their husbands full of holes out of pique."

HART, SLIM "PAPPY"
HOME IS WHERE THE HART IS (1987, Canada, Atlantic)—Two 73-year-old British twin brothers come home to visit their senile 103-year-old "pappy," **Joe Austin**, only to find him and his new bride missing. They discover that he's been kidnapped by a roller derby queen nurse, who has killed his bride. She plans to marry Austin for his money. Heard enough? All right, behave or we'll tell you more.

HART, WILLIAM
THE GREED OF WILLIAM HART (1948, GB, Butchers)—**Tod Slaughter** and Henry Oscar star in this account of the careers and deaths of 19th Century Edinburgh grave robbers, Burke and Hare.

HART, WILLIE
THREE WOMEN (1977, 20th Century Fox)—Embittered artist **Janice Rule** never speaks, instead she puts her thoughts in her murals. She is pregnant and married to a cheating ex-stuntman, Robert Fortier. The film examines her relationship and involvement with Sissy Spacek, a new member of the staff of an old-age home, and her crush on attendant Shelley Duvall. Mighty strange!

HARTLAND, SAMMY
A BOY TEN FEET TALL (1965, GB, Paramount)—In 1956 Africa, 10-year-old orphan **Fergus McClelland** travels from Port Said to Durban, encountering a blind peddler, a diamond smuggler, and other interesting, but not necessarily solid citizens. In Great Britain the film is entitled SAMMY GOING SOUTH.

HARTLEY, CAROLINE & ELINOR
AMERICAN FRIENDS (1991, MCEG/Virgin Vision)—In the 1860s, Oxford classics don Michael Palin takes a walking vacation in Switzerland where he meets Americans **Connie Booth** and **Trini Alvarado**. The girls later show up at Oxford looking for romance and soon become involved in campus politics.

HARTMAN, JANE
ANTONIA AND JANE (1991, GB, Miramax)—**Imelda Stauton** tells her therapist she feels a failure because her boyfriend can only get aroused when he reads to him from Iris Murdoch.

HARTSHORN, PRISS
THE GROUP (1966, UA)—After graduation from college in the thirties, **Elizabeth Hartman** wishes to work for Franklin D. Roosevelt's program; but when it is chopped by Congress, she marries a pediatrician, and has two stillbirths before delivering a healthy baby.

HARTSOOK, RALPH
THE HOOSIER SCHOOLTEACHER (1914, Silent, Alliance); (1924, Silent, Hodkinson); (1935, Monogram)—**Max Figman, Henry Hull** and **Norman Foster** each portray the Indiana schoolmaster, who successfully defends himself against a charge of robbery and marries a 20-year-old servant girl.

HARVEY, DR. JOHN
THE MEDICINE MAN (1930, Tiffany)—Traveling con-man **Jack Benny** uses and deserts women as he moves from town to town. When he meets waif Betty Bronson, abused by her cruel father, Benny undergoes a complete change of behavior, all for the better—it says here.

HARVEY, VALE & WILLIAM
MY HUSBAND'S WIVES (1924, Silent, Fox)—**Shirley Mason** invites an old school chum to visit, unaware that the lady was once married to her husband **Bryant Washburn**.

HARVILL, FATHOM
FATHOM (1967, 20th Century Fox)—**Raquel Welch** is a gorgeous sky-diving spy in a totally silly and unnecessary romp.

HARWOOD, OLIVE
SO EVIL MY LOVE (1948, GB, Paramount)—In this Victorian melodrama, missionary's widow **Ann Todd** is enticed into a life of crime and decadence by a scoundrelly artist, Ray Milland.

HASKELL, HENRY
LADIES' MAN (1947, Paramount)—**Eddie Bracken** is way past his comical prime as an accident-prone houseboy in a hotel for aspiring actresses.

HASKINS, EDDIE
TROOPERS THREE (1930, Tiffany)—Romantic lead **Rex Lease** is overshadowed by the actions of Roscoe Karns and Slim Summerville in this story of three army recruits. At least Lease gets the girl, Dorothy Gulliver.

HASSAN, SHEIK AHMED BEN
THE SHEIK (1921, Silent, Paramount)—**Rudolph Valentino** starred in the film production of E. M. Hull's best seller. Rudy, a desert chieftain, takes English heiress Agnes Ayres to his oasis tent for a night of love and passion. Millions of flappers, housewives and spinsters wished they could have been in her place. The literary merits of the movie are about nil, but there is little doubt that no actor before, and perhaps none since, has enthralled more females with his intense passionate sneers than Valentino.

HASSINA
GYPSY (1937, First National)—Aging playboy Roland Young marries gypsy **Chili Boucher**, but returns her to her lover when he finds he can't make her happy.

HASTINGS, HIRAM
A HERO FOR A NIGHT (1927, Silent, Universal)—Taxi driver **Glenn Tryon** builds his own airplane, which he hopes to enter in a big race. Somehow he ends up crashing it in Russia after a flight across the ocean with pretty Patsy Ruth Miller.

HATCH, LIZ ADAMS
THE LATE LIZ (1971, Gateway)—When **Anne Baxter** gets religion, she kicks out ole demon rum. The movie is enough to drive one to drink.

HATCHER
MARKED FOR DEATH (1990, 20th Century Fox)—Drug Enforcement Agency troubleshooter **Steven Seagal** uses his martial arts

ability to deal violently with a gang of Jamaican drug dealers who have marked him and his family for death.

HATTIE
MY KINGDOM FOR A COOK (1943, Columbia)—While on a lecture tour in the United States, gourmet Charles Coburn steals his hostess' cook, **Almira Sessions**.

HATTIE
STICKY FINGERS (1988, Spectrafilm)—Musician **Helen Slater** goes on a spending spree with $900,000 of drug-dealers' money. This gets her in trouble both with the cops and the thugs, who want the dough back.

HATTON, MINERVA
GRANNY GET YOUR GUN (1940, First National)—When her granddaughter is accused of murder, **May Robson** becomes sheriff, and brings in the real culprit.

HAVANA
GIRL FROM HAVANA (1940, Republic)—**Claire Carlton** appears in this story about problems in South American oil fields. The film is a reworking of ROUGH RIDERS' ROUNDUP, which was a slight adaptation of FORGED PASSPORT, which had its origins in THE LEATHERNECKS HAVE LANDED, all four movies being filmed and released by Republic, a studio which strongly believed in getting the most it could from a screenplay.

HAVEN, ANN & BARBARA
THREE FOR BEDROOM C (1952, Warner Brothers)—**Gloria Swanson** had made a triumphant movie comeback in SUNSET BOULEVARD, then she went and ruined things by appearing in this inept piece of nothing about film actress Swanson and her bratty daughter **Janine Perreau** taking a train compartment reserved for Harvard professor James Warren.

HAVEN, RANDOLF
MARRIED BACHELOR (1941, MGM)—Single author **Robert Young**, an authority on how to be a happy spouse, is called on by Ruth Hussey to defend his expertise.

HAVERHILL, LINDA
THE GILDED BUTTERFLY (1926, silent, Fox)—In a most improbable story, fortune hunter **Alma Rubens** returns from Monte Carlo, broke and in love with handsome Bert Lytell. She owes quite a bit of money to a friend of her father, who will forgive the debt in return for her sexual favors. She chooses to try to collect from an insurance company after burning her clothes. She's caught. On the way to the police station, the patrol car in which she's riding is involved in an accident, and a woman is killed. A kindly policeman allows Rubens to change identities with the deceased and escape.

HAVERSTOCK, HUNTLEY *See* JOHNNY JONES

HAWK
DADDY'S BOYS (1988, Concorde)—**Dan Shor** is one of three retarded louts, looking for a woman—any woman willing to play mother to them and their psycho daddy.

HAWK, THE
HAWK OF THE HILLS (1929, Silent, Pathe Exchange)—**Frank Lacteen**, the half-breed leader of a gang of Indian and renegade whites which preys on prospectors, is finally brought to justice by Walter Miller, a federal agent who infiltrates the gang.

HAWK
HAWK THE SLAYER (1980, GB, Chips/ITC)—In this medieval fantasy **John Terry**, the slain ruler's son, uses a magic sword to defeat his evil brother.

HAWK, THE
THE HAWK'S NEST (1928, Silent, First National)—**Milton Sills**, the owner of a Chinatown cafe, sets out to find the murderer of one of his employees. He has plastic surgery on his disfigured face so he can masquerade as a Chicago gangster.

HAWKE, HUDSON
HUDSON HAWKE (1991, Tri-Star)—Just released from prison, cat burglar **Bruce Willis** is drawn into a plot to steal a bunch of Leonardo da Vinci artifacts. It's a stupid, scatological film; the spectacular flop of that year.

HAWKE, YOUNGBLOOD
YOUNGBLOOD HAWKE (1964, Warner Brothers)—**James Franciscus** stars in this sappy production of Herman Wouk's sappy novel about a former Kentucky truck driver. He is spoiled by success after becoming a best selling novelist in New York City.

HAWKINS
THE COURT JESTER (1956, Paramount)—Lowly valet **Danny Kaye** becomes the leader of a peasant rebellion to restore the rightful heir to the throne of England.

HAWKINS
NAVY SEALS (1990, Orion)—Imagine **Charlie Sheen** as Tom Cruise and action taking place under the sea rather than in the skies a la TOP GUN and you have the idea of this film.

HAWKINS, ALFRED
MERELY MR. HAWKINS (1938, GB, RKO)—**Eliot Markham**, who rightly deserves his position as president of the Henpecked Husband's League, wins a new standing in his home when he's able to prove that his wife is innocently involved in a fraudulent bond scheme, and that his daughter doesn't want to marry the man her mother has picked out for her.

HAWKINS, DAISY
TRUE TO THE ARMY (1942, Paramount)—**Judy Canova**, on the lam from a bunch of gangsters, takes refuge at an Army base. The supposed humor deals with her trying to keep her gender a secret.

HAWKINS, JIM
THE TEXAS RANGERS (1936, Paramount)—**Fred MacMurray** and his buddy Jack Oakie give up their cowboy wandering to join the Texas Rangers. Later, they must go after another old pal Lloyd Nolan, who's on the opposite side of the law. The film was remade in 1949 as THE STREETS OF LAREDO.

HAWKINS, WIDOW
THE WISTFUL WIDOW OF WAGON GAP (1947, Universal)—**Marjorie Main** is a delight as a western widow with a slew of children. It's believed that Lou Costello killed her husband so he's responsible for her and her brood. Anyone who kills him will inherit his responsibility. With this threat as a weapon, Costello is made sheriff, and pulls Main's name out like a six-gun when anyone threatens to stand up to him. When it's learned that the widow may be rich, many men are eager to become her new protector, putting Costello's life in danger.

HAWKS, JOHNNY

THE INDIAN FIGHTER (1955, UA)—**Kirk Douglas** is an old Indian fighter, whenever he can find an old Indian to fight. No, we mean, he protects a wagon train from the Sioux.

HAWLEY, BILL

HAWLEY'S OF HIGH STREET (1933, GB, British International)—Draper **Leslie Fuller** and Moore Marriott are bitter rivals for a local council election. They use every dirty, underhanded trick they can think of to undermine the other's campaign, including a battle with two meat joints. The election ends in a tie.

HAWLEY, CLEM

THE OLD SOAK (1926, Silent, Universal); THE GOOD OLD SOAK (1937, MGM)—**Jean Hersholt** and **Wallace Beery** star as a small town drunk who outwits a teetotaler banker, guilty of stealing some valuable stock certificates.

HAWS, NANCY

HIS DIVORCED WIFE (1919, Silent, Universal)—**Alice Elliot** stars in this old-fashioned melodrama set in the southern hills. She's the town belle won by the village blacksmith. He must survive an accusation of murdering one of his rivals for her hand. Thinking him guilty, Elliot divorces him.

HAWTHORNE, ANTHONY HAMILTON

HAWTHORNE OF THE U.S.A. (1919, Silent, Paramount)—American **Wallace Reid** makes a killing at Monte Carlo, visits a small European country, falls for its ruler's daughter, and using his Yankee ingenuity saves the country from a communist take over.

HAWTHORNE, JOAN

IF YOU COULD ONLY COOK (1936, Columbia)—Poor girl **Jean Arthur** and millionaire Herbert Marshall take domestic jobs as a cook and butler in this thin comedy.

HAY, STANLEY

THE PRESUMPTION OF STANLEY HAY, MP (1925, GB, Silent, Stoll)—Member of Parliament **David Hawthorne** marries the princess of a small mythical country, and saves her from abduction.

HAYDEE, COUNTESS OF MONTE CRISTO

THE WIFE OF MONTE CRISTO (1946, PRC)—**Leonore Aubert** picks up the sword and dons tight-fitting masculine clothes which only enhance her shapely figure, rather than disguise it. She confounds the prefect of police, John Loder, who is pursuing her husband, the Count of Monte Cristo, played in a rare heroic role by Martin Kosleck.

HAYDEN, CONNIE

RICH PEOPLE (1929, Pathe)—Bored heiress **Constance Bennett** almost goes through with a marriage to wealthy Robert Ames, but leaves him at the altar to run to her true love, insurance salesman Regis Toomey.

HAYDEN, JO

FOR ME AND MY GAL (1942, MGM)—**Judy Garland** stars with newcomer Gene Kelly in this delightful, nostalgic look at pre-WWI vaudeville life.

HAYDEN, JOHN

I LOVED A WOMAN (1933, First National/Warner Brothers)—**Edward G. Robinson** loves Kay Francis, but his social-climbing wife Genevieve Tobin won't be a sport and give him a divorce, so the couple must have a back street affair. Francis becomes a successful singer, and Robinson a powerful Chicago meat packer, but disaster awaits them.

HAYDN, YOLI

LADIES IN LOVE (1936, 20th Century Fox)—**Constance Bennett** catches herself a businessman in this amusing comedy about three Budapest working girls. They pool their resources to rent an expensive apartment so as to attract wealthy suitors.

HAYES

THE MAGNIFICENT SEVEN RIDE (1972, UA)—Who asked the seven to ride again? Convict **James B. Sikking** joins Lee Van Cleef and five others to protect a small Mexican town from bandit Rudolfo Acosta, whose gang has already killed the male inhabitants and raped the women. Closing the barn door after the horse has escaped, we suppose.

HAYES, ART

THE WESTERN ROVER (1927, Silent, Truart)—Circus performer **Art Acord** takes a job working on a ranch after the show folds, and saves the cattle from being rustled.

HAYES, BILL

SAILOR'S HOLIDAY (1944, Columbia)—**Bob Haymes** and two other merchant marine buddies have a fun time touring Columbia Studios, where they meet a trio of cuties.

HAYES, FLICKER

HE WAS HER MAN (1934, Warner Brothers)—Ex-con, safecracker **James Cagney** is one third of a romantic triangle involving San Francisco prostitute Joan Blondell and her fisherman fiance, Victor Jory.

HAYES, IRA HAMILTON

THE OUTSIDER (1962, Universal)—Indian **Tony Curtis**, one of the participants in the famous flag raising on Iwo Jima during WWII, can't cope with his hero status in a white society.

HAYNES, "HARDWOOD" JOHN

JOHN PETTICOATS (1919, Silent, Artcraft)—Lumberjack **William S. Hart** inherits a ten-story department store in New Orleans. He installs himself as a detective with only his head saleslady knowing he's the owner. He wins the prettiest New Orleans belle even though his Northwest woods ways are not right for selling ladies petticoats.

HAYNES, HELEN

THE BEAUTIFUL LIAR (1921, Silent, Preferred)—Office girl **Katherine MacDonald** steps in at a benefit for a star whom she greatly resembles, when the latter refuses to go on. MacDonald wins the heart of a rich customer of her firm, whom she has loved from afar.

HAYS, JANET

ONE ON ONE (1977, Warner Brothers)—No **Annette O'Toole** doesn't go up against basketball phenom Robby Benson in a game of "Horse." She's his true blue girlfriend, who's there when he discovers sports isn't everything.

HAZE, LOLITA

LOLITA (1962, MGM)—**Sue Lyon** plays the young teen for whom James Mason develops an unnatural passion, even to the point of marrying her gross mother, Shelley Winters, to be near her. When Winters is conveniently killed, running in front of an automobile when she learns of Mason's true feelings, Lyon and Mason become lovers. In the book by Vladimir Nabokov, Lolita was even younger without a nymphet's body, but the producers were afraid that would be considered too dirty for the screen.

HAZEL

HAZEL'S PEOPLE (1978, A People's Place)—**Rachel Thomas** is one of the Pennsylvania Mennonites New York hippy Graham Beckel is touched by in this dull predictable film. It's not worth a look.

"HE-OF-THE-BEETLE-BROW"

THE PREHISTORIC MAN (1924, GB, Silent, Stoll)—In a weird comedy, caveman **George Robey** elopes in a stolen car, saving his bride from kidnappers.

"HE WHO GETS SLAPPED"

HE WHO GETS SLAPPED (1924, Silent, MGM)—In one of his most outstanding roles, **Lon Chaney, Sr.** is a scientist, whose domestic and professional humiliations drive him to become a masochistic circus clown. Learning that Tully Marshall, the father of bareback rider Norma Shearer, whom Chaney loves, plans to marry her to Marc MacDermott, the man who stole both Lon's wife and invention, Chaney releases a lion which kills both Marshall and MacDermott, but not before he is fatally stabbed. As Chaney staggers and stumbles around the circus ring, dying, the audience believing it's part of his act, roars with laughter. The film was the first for the newly formed MGM studio.

HEADLESS HORSEMAN, THE

THE HEADLESS HORSEMAN (1922, Silent, Hodkinson)—**Ben Hendricks, Jr.** as "Brom" Bones scares away his competition for lovely Katrina Van Tassel (Lois Meridith), the lanky new schoolteacher, Ichabod Crane (Will Rogers), by masquerading as the legendary "headless horseman."

HEADLEY, PAMELA & ERNEST

THE HEADLEYS AT HOME (1939, Standard)—Ambitious **Evelyn Venable** orders her henpecked husband, **Grant Mitchell**, to invite a prominent banker he doesn't know to dinner. Mitchell invites an actor instead and then discovers that his guest is a bank robber.

HEALEY, JUNIOR

PROBLEM CHILD (1990, Universal); PROBLEM CHILD 2 (1991, Universal)—If the character played by **Michael Oliver** was featured in the hit movie HOME ALONE, the few people who would have seen the film would sympathize with his parents for deserting him and would root for the villains to do him in. Oliver's character is an absolutely unlikable little brat. When he is adopted by yuppie couple John Ritter and Amy Yasbeck, the nuns who run the orphanage cheer as he leaves. In the sequel, John Ritter and Oliver move to a new town where the youngster fears reverting to his unhealthy habits of the original film will cause him to lose his adopted dad to some divorcees.

HEARNE, JUDITH

THE LONELY PASSION OF JUDITH HEARNE (1987, GB, Island)—In 1950s Ireland, plain spinster **Maggie Smith**, who has been sheltered from the carnal world by her looks and her religion, meets American Irishman Bob Hoskins, who brings out her dormant personality.

HEARST, PATTY

PATTY HEARST (1988, Atlantic)—**Natasha Richardson**, daughter of Vanessa Redgrave and Tony Richardson, is excellent in her portrayal of the kidnapped, brainwashed heiress, who helped her captives rob banks and served a prison sentence for her crime.

HEATH, CLIVE

MY OWN TRUE LOVE (1948, Paramount)—Widower **Melvyn Douglas** is about to remarry, when his son Philip Friend returns home from a Japanese POW camp, minus a leg, with his Malayan wife and child. Friend misinterprets his father's fiancee Phyllis Calvert's compassion as love.

HEATH, CONNIE

GIRLS ON PROBATION (1938, Warner Brothers)—Witless young **Jane Bryan** runs with the wrong crowd, and finds herself serving a prison term before she's completely rehabilitated.

HEATH, DAISY

THE SHOPWORN ANGEL (1928, Paramount); (1938, MGM)—**Nancy Carroll** and **Margaret Sullavan** star as the actress, who is amused by the love of an ingenuous young soldier while continuing her affair with a rich man. When the doughboy must embark for the war, she finally realizes how much the innocent young man means to her. It's a lovely bittersweet romance with both actresses very good in the part, as are Gary Cooper and James Stewart as the sincere soldier.

HEATH, EVELYN

GUEST IN THE HOUSE (1944, UA)—**Anne Baxter** practiced deceit and scheming long before her appearance in ALL ABOUT EVE. In this movie, she's invited into the home of artist Ralph Bellamy and his wife Ruth Warrick. She repays their kindness by driving away his model, setting his daughter against him, exploiting the love for her of his brother and making a play for Bellamy himself.

HECKYL, DR./MR. HYPE

DR. HECKYL AND MR. HYPE (1980, Cannon)—Ugly podiatrist **Oliver Reed** is transformed into a handsome murderer.

HECUBA

THE TROJAN WOMEN (1971, Cinerama)—In what appears to be "too many fine actresses spoil Euripides," **Katharine Hepburn** and her co-stars Vanessa Redgrave, Irene Papas and Genevieve Bujold, need more than a Greek chorus to rouse this flat production of the laments of the women of Troy after their men are beaten in battle.

HEDGEPETH, MARION

BABY BLUE MARINE (1976, Columbia)—**Jon-Michael Vincent**, a marine drop-out during WWII, poses as a hero by assuming the identity of a real gyrene. The film is a dramatic version of Preston Sturges' HAIL THE CONQUERING HERO, a filming decision of questionable wisdom. For those who like such things, it's possible to catch a glimpse of another wooden actor, Richard Gere, in a small role.

HEEBERT, HERBERT H.

THE LADIES' MAN (1961, Paramount)—Woman-hating, dim-witted houseboy **Jerry Lewis** works at a Hollywood hotel for girls, run by Metropolitan Opera star Helen Traubel. Amazingly, one of the guests falls in love with him, proving there's hope for everyone.

HEGGS, LUTHER

THE GHOST AND MR. CHICKEN (1966, Universal)—Playing his usual incompetent role, **Don Knotts**, a newspaper typesetter, gets into some trouble with a ghost when he tries to become a real reporter.

HEIDI

HEIDI (1937, 20th Century Fox); HEIDI'S STORY (1982, Animated, Paramount)—Orphan **Shirley Temple** melts the cold heart of her bitter grandfather Jean Hersholt, who has not spoken a word since his son ran away with a girl years before. In the 1982 animated version of the Johanna Spyri story, **Margery Grey** provides the voice of the darling little girl.

HEIMSLEY, CLARE
ALWAYS A BRIDE (1954, GB, General)—In Monte Carlo treasury agent Terence Morgan loves a con-man's daughter, **Peggy Cummins**.

HELD, LISA
LISA (1962, GB, 20th Century Fox)—In 1946, Dutch inspector Stephen Boyd smuggles Jewish girl **Dolores Hart** from Holland to Palestine by way of Tangier. In Great Britain, the movie is titled THE INSPECTOR.

HELDON, EVELYN
THE DOCTOR AND THE GIRL (1949, MGM)—**Janet Leigh** is the attractive romantic interest of dedicated doctor Glenn Ford. He renounces specialization to treat the poor.

HELEN
MY FIRST WIFE (1985, Canada, Spectrafilm)—**Wendy Hughes'** husband John Hargreaves literally goes crazy when she leaves him after ten years of marriage.

HELEN
PARENTHOOD (1989, Universal)—**Dianne Wiest** tries to make the best of a tough job, raising two teens alone. Her promiscuous daughter Martha Plimpton marries aimless Keanu Reeves, while her son Leaf Phoenix collects pornography. It's a good thing she has a sense of humor.

HELEN
THE TROJAN WOMEN (1971, Cinerama)—**Irene Papas** stars with Katharine Hepburn, Vanessa Redgrave and Genevieve Bujold in this faithful but flat Greek-American production of Euripides play about the plight of the Women of Troy after their men are defeated by the Greeks.

HELENE
THE HEART OF SALOME (1927, Silent, Fox)—**Alma Rubens**, like Salome of the Bible, offers herself to her employer if he will take the life of her former lover. She gloats when the latter is manacled and imprisoned in a dungeon, but has a change of heart, saves him and effects a reconciliation.

HELENE
THE KING'S DAUGHTER (1916, Silent, GB, Jury)—**Janet Ross**, an assassin's daughter, learns she is the King's bastard and dies to save his life.

HELLER
THE AMATEUR (1982, 20th Century Fox)—When CIA computer technologist **John Savage** tracks down the terrorists who seized the American Consulate in Munich and killed his girlfriend, he finds himself hunted—by the CIA.

HELP, SEBASTIAN
LEAVE IT TO ME (1933, GB, British International)—**Gene Gerrard** poses as poet in order to steal a lady's valuable necklace, and save it from thieves.

HELQUIST, CAPT.
THE CAPTAIN HATES THE SEA (1934, Columbia)—**Walter Connolly** stars as a bored, disgruntled captain of an ocean liner. It's a kind of comical GRAND HOTEL at sea. This is the last film ever made by silent screen star John Gilbert.

HEMINGWAY, BILL
VIRGINIA'S HUSBAND (1928, GB, Silent, Butchers); (1934, GB, Fox)—Lillian Oldland hires ex-officer **Pat Aherne** to pose as her husband to deceive rich relatives. In 1934, Reginald Gardiner had the role of the phony husband, but he was called John Craddock.

HENDERSON, GEORGE, NANCY, SARAH & ERNIE
HARRY AND THE HENDERSONS (1987, Universal)—**John Lithgow, Melinda Dillon, Margaret Langrick** and **Joshua Ruday** are the Henderson family. While on a trip into the woods they encounter a Bigfoot-like creature, whom they take home with them believing it dead. It revives, and becomes a member of the family.

HENDERSON, HACKAMORE
A MAN OF NERVE (1925, Silent, FBO)—**Bob Custer** falls in love with Jean Arthur, the owner of a woman's hat store. He's framed for rustling, but with the help of Arthur, escapes from a lynch mob and tracks down the real villain.

HENDERSON, JEREMY "SCAM"
BIG SHOTS (1987, 20th Century Fox)—**Darius McCrary**, a young black boy, and Ricky Busker an inexperienced white boy who recently lost his father, strike up a friendship, getting involved with dead bodies and hired killers.

HENDERSON, JOY
LES GIRLS (1957, MGM)—**Mitzi Gaynor**, Kay Kendall, and Tania Elg are leggy show girls who team with Gene Kelly in a show business act. Years after the act disbands, Kendall writes a memoir which Elg feels obligated to challenge in court. Audiences are treated to four different versions of who loved Kelly. Whatever the truth of the past, Gaynor has him now.

HENDERSON, POLLY
THE WIDOW FROM CHICAGO (1930, First National)—**Alice White** is determined to have her revenge on Edward G. Robinson, a cop who killed her brother.

HENDERSON, SUSAN
LOVERS AND OTHER STRANGERS (1970, ABC/Cinerma)—**Bonnie Bedelia** and Michael Brandon, who have been living together for over a year, are about to be married. During the weekend of the wedding, and especially at their reception, audiences savor the failures and triumphs in the marriages of members of their two families. It's a delightful movie, guaranteed to bring a few tears of joy to the eyes. Special kudos go to Richard Castellano and Bea Arthur as Brandon's parents, and to Robert Dishy and Marian Hailey, members of the bridal party who struggle to establish a relationship of some sort.

HENDERSON, SYLVIA
SYLVIA (1985, MGM/UA)—In the 1940s **Eleanor David** is a New Zealand educator, who develops innovative reading methods for Maori children, despite the opposition of the educational establishment.

HENDERSON, VAL
TWO ON A GUILLOTINE (1965, Warner Brothers)—**Dean Jones** stars in this inept thriller with Connie Stevens. She must spend a night in a haunted house to receive an inheritance from her late father Cesar Romero. Jones volunteers to stay with her. Silly boy!

HENDRICK, DOROTHY
THE SINGING COWGIRL (1939, Grand National)—With the help of David O'Brien, cowgirl **Dorothy Page** saves a boy from a neighbor-

ing ranch from a gang of outlaws, who have invaded his home and killed his parents while looking for gold. The idea of a female heroine in a Western series just didn't turn audiences on in the thirties.

HENDRICKS, "BUTCH"
NINE GIRLS (1944, Columbia)—**Jeff Donnell** is one of the wise-cracking sorority girls suspected of murdering their nasty housemate, Anita Louise.

HENFIELD, ALFRED/M. HERBERT
MR. WHAT'S HIS NAME (1935, GB, First National)—**Seymour Hicks**, a married millionaire, weds a beautician while suffering from amnesia.

HENLEY, LISH
THE MEDIATOR (1916, Silent, Fox)—When decent **George Walsh** beats a drunk in a fight, he then discovers his victim is a family-man down on his luck. Walsh straightens out the man and his problems and ends up with the reformed drunk's daughter as his wife.

HENNESSY
HENNESSY (1975, GB, American International)—Bitter over the death of his family in the Belfast troubles, IRA member **Rod Steiger** travels to London to blow up Parliament.

HENRI
HIS TIGER LADY (1928, Silent, Paramount)—**Adolphe Menjou** is an extra in a Paris Folies revue. His job is to sit astride an elephant in a rajah's costume. He falls in love with regular customer Evelyn Brent, a haughty duchess. Wearing his costume he meets her and wins her love, when he shows tremendous courage in a tiger cage. He then confesses his sham, admitting that the tiger whose cage he entered was dead. The next day she proves her love for him by joining his show as a member of the chorus line.

HENRI
THAT MAN FROM TANGIER (1953, UA)—Impoverished Spanish count **Nils Asther** is persuaded to pose as the husband of spoiled rich American, Nancy Coleman.

HENRY
HENRY: PORTRAIT OF A SERIAL KILLER (1989, Maljack)—In a frightening and very disturbing film, **Michael Rooker** portrays a low-lifer who constantly changes the way he kills his victims, in order to throw off the police.

HENRY
HIS WIFE'S MOTHER (1932, GB, British International)—**Jerry Verno** poses as his double to fool his mother-in-law, when she encounters him with a woman other than her daughter.

HENRY
THE PUBLIC LIFE OF HENRY THE NINTH (1934, GB, MGM)—Unemployed street entertainer **Leonard Henry** gets a job at the Henry VIII pub, becoming a star singer, called Henry the Ninth by his fans.

HENRY
SMALL TOWN BOY (1937, Grand National)—After finding a $1,000 bill, **Stuart Erwin** changes from a shy small town boy to a ruthless businessman.

HENRY
A WAVE, A WAC AND A MARINE (1944, Monogram)—**Henny Youngman** stars in this disastrous comedy produced by Lou Costello and his father. The sound is so bad, it's hard to make sense of Youngman's rapid fire jokes. Some wags who have seen the script claim that's a plus.

HENRY II
THE LION IN WINTER (1968, GB, Avco-Embassy)—In 1138 at Christmastime, **Peter O'Toole** royally battles with his banished queen, Katharine Hepburn, as Eleanor of Aquitaine. The main bone of contention is which of his sons will be O'Toole's successor. O'Toole was nominated for an Academy Award, but it was Hepburn who walked off with an Oscar.

HENRY V
HENRY V (1946, GB, Two Cities/UA); (1989, GB, BBC-Goldwyn)—**Laurence Olivier** and **Kenneth Branagh** are both superb in all of their roles in the production of this Shakespearean masterpiece: producer, screenwriter, director and star. Both films are triumphs of filmmaking.

HENRY VIII
THE PRIVATE LIFE OF HENRY VIII (1933, UA); CARRY ON HENRY VIII (1970, GB, Rank/AIP); HENRY VIII AND HIS SIX WIVES (1972, GB, EMI/MGM)—**Charles Laughton, Sid James** and **Keith Michell** each star as the British monarch, who broke with Rome over his need to be rid of his first wife, who could not bear him an heir. Laughton is superb in a classic film. James is amusing in a spoof and Michell is quite regal in what is essentially a TV miniseries released in theaters.

HENRY, ZENAS
CAPTAIN HURRICANE (1935, RKO)—Old salt **James Barton**, who just wants to retire and enjoy his Cape Cod home, is forced to return to the sea to earn enough money to prevent foreclosure on his home.

HENSHAW, DICK
THE GATE CRASHER (1928, Silent, Universal)—Poster-hanger **Glenn Tryon** is involved in an auto accident with Broadway actress Patsy Ruth Miller. When he later reads in the newspaper that her jewels have been stolen, he travels to New York to retrieve them for her. Not only does he do just that, he also wins her love.

HENSHAW, LIZZIE
KEEPING UP WITH LIZZIE (1921, Silent, Hodkinson)—**Enid Bennett** and Edward Hearn are separated by their business rival fathers. She's sent to finishing school. Later she returns from Europe with a fortune-hunting no-count count, whom Hearn exposes as a phony, and finally the young lovers are permitted a life together.

HEPELWHITE
A GENTLEMAN'S GENTLEMAN (1939, GB, First National)—In Switzerland, valet **Eric Blore** blackmails his master over a supposed poisoning.

HEPNER, DAVID "RED"
THE BANTAM COWBOY (1928, Silent, FBO); THE FRECKLED RASCAL (1929, Silent, FBO/RKO)—**Buzz Barton** starred in a series of these westerns as a kid cowboy. They're not good enough to criticize or bad enough to recommend.

HERBERT
TEACHERS (1984, MGM/UA)—**Richard Mulligan**, having just escaped from a mental hospital, is mistaken for a substitute history teacher in a high school. Of course he proves to be the most

interesting and successful member of the staff. You don't have to be crazy to be a good teacher, but of course it helps.

HERBERT, GRACE

PLAY GIRL (1940, MGM)—Aging gold-digger **Kay Francis** chooses to pass on her knowledge of how to squeeze money from men to young Mildred Coles. The latter is a quick study and soon is rolling in dough which she's gotten from a series of sugar-daddies. Coles shocks her teacher when she falls in love with James Ellison and plans to marry him. The blow is softened somewhat when it's revealed that Ellison is a Texas multi-millionaire.

HERBERT, STANLEY

EYES OF A STRANGER (1980, Warner Brothers)—**John D. Santi**, a psychopathic killer, is tracked down by Lauren Tewes, who played Julie on TV's The Love Boat. We guess the little screen series didn't have enough blood, guts and sexual molestation for her.

HERBERT, VICTOR

THE GREAT VICTOR HERBERT (1939, Paramount)—**Walter Connolly** portrays the famous composer in a story which intersperses the music of Herbert with Connolly acting as a middle-age cupid for a young couple.

HERCULES

HERCULES IN NEW YORK (1970, RAF/UA)—See **Arnold Strong (Schwarzenegger)** before he learned to act, in a silly story of Hercules set down in modern Manhattan, where he becomes a professional wrestler.

HERCULES

HERCULES (1983, Cannon); HERCULES II (1985, Cannon)—**Lou Ferrigno**, the former green-bodied muscular man on TV's The Incredible Hulk, performs heroic acts of strength, like attempting to act in special-effects-laden films which might be considered too elementary for pre-schoolers.

HERCULES

THE UNHOLY THREE (1925, Silent, MGM); (1930, MGM)—**Victor McLaglen** and **Ivan Linow** each portray the strong man member of a gang of circus-trained crooks led by Lon Chaney, Sr.

HERELTINE, JOAN

HER MAN GIBLEY (1949, GB, Two-Cities/Universal)—In a film released as ENGLISH WITHOUT TEARS, **Penelope Ward** goes to Switzerland to plead the case of migratory birds, and falls in love with her aunt's butler, Michael Wilding, whom she has taken along. He becomes worthy of her during the war when he becomes an officer and a gentleman.

HERIOT, CAMILLA & JOHN

JOHN HERIOT'S WIFE (1920, Silent, GB, Anglo-Hollandia)—A moneylender cancels Anna Bosilova's debts when she wrestles financial secrets from **Mary Odette**, wife of minister **Henry Victor**.

HERITAGE, CMDR. RICHARD

THEY MET IN THE DARK (1945, GB, Excelsior)—Court-martialled commander **James Mason** unmasks spies posing as theatrical agents.

HERMAN

ENEMIES, A LOVE STORY (1989, 20th Century Fox)—Almost innocently, Holocaust survivor **Ron Silver** finds himself with three wives, one in each of three burroughs of New York.

HERMAN

TALES OF A SALESMAN (1965, Rossmore)—Traveling salesman **David Reed** is assisted in increasing sales by a ghost. The film also features several nearly naked women trying to arouse our hero.

HERMAN, PEE WEE

PEE WEE'S BIG ADVENTURE (1985, Paramount); (1988, Paramount)—**Pee Wee Herman** either will make one giggle with glee or gag with disgust. The unhealthy-looking creature, who doesn't fit very well in the real world, finds he likes girls in this episodic comedy set in a circus.

HERRICK, GEORGE

THE BIG STRONG MAN (1922, Silent, GB, Quality Plays)—Plumber **George Turner** poses as an artist to force a publisher to pay his bill.

HERRICK, STEPHEN

A GIRL, A GUY AND A GOB (1941, RKO)—Wealthy snob **Edmond O'Brien** vies with boisterous gob George Murphy for stenographer Lucille Ball.

HERRIES, MARY

KIND LADY (1935, MGM); (1951, MGM)—**Aline MacMahon** and **Ethel Barrymore** portray the invalid lady whose home is invaded by a con-man and his criminal friends.

HESTON, ANN

JUST LIKE A WOMAN (1939, GB, Alliance)—Jeweller's agent John Lodge, seeking black pearls, saves rival **Gertrude Michael** from crooks.

HESUS

RUDE AWAKENING (1989, Orion)—Sixties hippie dropout **Cheech Marin** and his buddy Eric Roberts have spent the last twenty years living in the jungles of South America. When in 1989, they return to New York, they experience the movie's title.

HEWITT, JOHN

TWO DOLLAR BETTOR (1951, Real Art)—**John Litel's** betting just for fun gets out of hand, and before long he's a gambling addict. It ruins his life and then ends it.

HEYDRICH, REINHARD

HANGMEN ALSO DIE (1943, UA); HITLER'S MADMAN (1943, MGM)—**Hans von Twardowski** and **John Carradine** are frightening in the title role. Each portrays the notorious Prague's Gestapo head, whose assassination resulted in the Nazis wiping out all the residences of the small Czech village of Lidice.

HEYTHORP, SYLVANUS

OLD ENGLISH (1930, Warner Brothers)—So he may arrange for the financial security of his grandchildren, **George Arliss** makes some illegal arrangements, involving his prearranged death.

HEYWOOD, CHARLES

VENGEANCE IS MINE (1948, GB, Eros)—Told he has but six months to live, **Valentine Dyall** hires a man to kill him, intending to frame the man responsible for his recent, unjustified imprisonment. When he's later told that the diagnosis was incorrect, he searches in vain for his assassin-to-be, who has died.

HFUHRUHURR, DR. MICHAEL

THE MAN WITH TWO BRAINS (1983, Warner Brothers) -Scientist **Steve Martin** is trapped in a loveless marriage to Kathleen Turner. He gradually falls in love with a patient (the voice of Sissy Spacek).

The only trouble is that all that's left of her is her brain. Martin becomes anxious to find a new body for the brain. Any ideas?

HIAWATHA

HIAWATHA (1952, Monogram)—**Vince Edwards** stars as Henry Wadsworth's Ojibway (Chippewa) Indian brave, who falls in love with and marries the fair Minnehaha, played by Yvette Dugay.

HICKEY, BILL "CYCLONE"

THE SWELLHEAD (1930, Tiffany)—**Johnny Walker's** boxing career hits the skids when he feels he no longer needs his manager James Gleason. He wises up and brings Gleason back. Sort of reminds one of Mike Tyson, doesn't it?

HICKMAN, HADLEY

HADLEY'S REBELLION (1984, East India Co./AOI)—Teenage wrestler **Griffin O'Neal** has problems. Well, who doesn't? Quit your belly-aching.

HICKOK, WILD BILL

THE PLAINSMAN (1937, Paramount); (1966, Universal); FRONTIER SCOUT (1939, Fine Arts); YOUNG BILL HICKOK (1940, Republic); KING OF DODGE CITY (1941, Columbia); WILD BILL HICKOK RIDES (1942, Warner Brothers); I KILLED WILD BILL HICKOK (1956, Wheeler)—**Gary Cooper, Don Murray, George Houston, Roy Rogers, Bill Elliott, Bruce Cabot** and **Tom Brown** each appear as the American frontiersman and gunfighter, with Cooper's interpretation being the most satisfying. Hickok was shot in the back by Jack McCall while playing poker. His hand, aces and eights, has ever since been called "a deadman's hand."

HICKORY, HAROLD

THE KID BROTHER (1927, Silent, Paramount)—Meek **Harold Lloyd**, the son of a western sheriff, who tries to raise his sons to be he-men, finally rises to the occasion and defeats the meanest man in town.

HICKS, TRIGGER

SPITFIRE (1934, RKO)—Hot-tempered Ozark mountain girl **Katharine Hepburn** is driven from her community, when she shares her belief that the sick can be cured and the dead risen through the power of prayer.

HIGBY, MILTON

KEY WITNESS (1947, Columbia)—Inventor **John Beal** must pose as a hobo after he is implicated in his girlfriend's murder.

HIGBY, PHINEAS ALOYSIUS

AN ANGEL COMES TO BROOKLYN (1945, Republic)—Guardian angel **Charles Kemper** comes to earth to help a group of kids put on a Broadway show.

HIGGINBOTHAM, WILLIE & MAGGIE

MY WIFE'S LODGER (1952, GB, Adelphi)—**Dominic Roche** returns home after six years of overseas duty with the army to find his wife **Olive Sloane** has taken a firmly installed lodger. Roche learns the unwanted intruder in his home is a crook, and kicks him out.

HIGGINS, ALF

ALF'S CARPET (1929, GB, British International); ALF'S BUTTON (1930, GB, Gaumont); ALF'S BUTTON AFLOAT (1938, GB, Gainsborough)—**Patachon, Tubby Edlin** and **Bud Flanagan** each have some luck with magic. In the first, Patachon is a bus driver who finds a magic carpet and saves a girl's father from a caliph. In the second, soldier Edlin is cleaning a button on his uniform when a

genie appears. The same thing happens to Flanagan in the final film. In both cases the button once was part of Aladdin's lamp.

HIGGINS, FRANK

HERO FOR A DAY (1939, Universal)—When night watchman **Charley Grapewin** is mistaken for a wealthy college alumnus, his family and friends rally around to help him carry off the masquerade for one day.

HIGGINS, GRANDPA

GRANDPA GOES TO TOWN (1940, Republic)—**Harry Davenport** discovers gold in the ghost town, that his wife Lucille Gleason bought from a crooked real estate dealer, using up just about all of their life savings.

HIGGINS, PROF. HENRY

PYGMALION (1938, GB, MGM); MY FAIR LADY (1964, Warner Brothers)—**Leslie Howard** and **Rex Harrison** star as George Bernard Shaw's elocution professor, who teaches a Cockney flower girl to speak so well, she's mistaken for a duchess.

HIGGINS, JENNIE

GLAMOUR GIRL (1947, Columbia)—Small-town girl **Susan Reed**, a zither-playing whiz, takes the big city by storm.

HIGGINS, JOE, LILLIAN & STANELY

THE HIGGINS FAMILY (1939, Warner Brothers)—**James, Lucille** and **Russell Gleason** are a once happy family, which finds itself in divorce court when James Gleason becomes bored after 25 years of marriage, and Lucille develops aspirations to become a radio star. Son Russell helps them come to their senses.

HIGGINS, JOE

SHOULD HUSBANDS WORK? (1939, Republic)—**James Gleason** stars with wife Lucille and son Russell in yet another of the Higgins family movies. He's about to get a promotion until Lucille lets out a business secret about a proposed merger.

HIGGINS, SUSIE

THE PLEASURE SEEKERS (1964, 20th Century Fox)—In a THREE COINS IN THE FOUNTAIN -like story, art student **Pamela Tiffin** and two other American girls, Carol Lynley and Ann-Margret are in Madrid looking for husbands. Tiffin walks off with nobleman Tony Franciosa.

HIGGINS, TIMOTHY

THE MAN FROM GALVESTON (1964, Warner Brothers)—Clever western lawyer **Jeffrey Hunter** proves his mettle in the courtroom when he solves a murder almost like he was Perry Mason.

HIGGS, JASON

THE LOST MAN (1969, Universal)—When former Army lieutenant **Sidney Poitier** comes home, he becomes involved in the civil rights movement.

HIGHTOWER, NADINE

NADINE (1987, Tri-Star)—When dumb hairdresser **Kim Basinger** finds herself mixed up in mayhem and murder, she seeks the help of her ex-husband Jeff Bridges, not exactly an Einstein himself.

HIGHTOWER, ROBERT MARMADUKE

THE THREE GODFATHERS (1948, MGM)—**John Wayne** and his two bank-robbing side-kicks Pedro Armendariz and Harry Carey, Jr., come across a dying woman in an Arizona desert, and promise to get her newborn baby to safety. The Duke finally staggers into New Jerusalem, Arizona, on Christmas Eve, with the baby in his arms.

HILDA
HOUSEKEEPER'S DAUGHTER (1939, UA)—Tough dame **Joan Bennett** helps a wealthy college professor, Ray Milland, solve the murder of a showgirl in this zany, broad comedy thriller.

HILDEGARDE
THE GIRL IN THE PAINTING (1948, GB, Gainsborough)—In Germany after WWII, major Guy Rolfe searches displaced persons' camps for a girl in a painting, amnesiac **Mai Zettering**. The film is called PORTRAIT FROM LIFE in Great Britain.

HILDUR
HILDUR AND THE MAGICIAN (1969, Canyon Cinema Corp.)—**Hildur Mahl** sets out to rescue a princess who has been kidnapped by an evil gnome in this charming fairy tale.

HILL, MAJOR ARTHUR
THE GALLOPING MAJOR (1951, GB, Independent Film Distributors)—**Basil Radford**, a pet show owner, heads up a syndicate which buys a horse which wins the Grand National.

HILL, FANNY
FANNY HILL: MEMOIRS OF A WOMAN OF PLEASURE (1965, Favorite Films)—**Letita Roman** stars as the 18th century woman of pleasure in this tacky spoof of an the 200-year-old piece of literary pornography.

HILL, FRED & EMILY
RICH AND STRANGE (1932, GB, British International)—Clerk **Henry Kendall** and wife **Joan Barry** take a world cruise after being left a legacy, with both becoming involved in flirtations.

HILL, HAROLD
THE MUSIC MAN (1962, Warner Brothers)—**Robert Preston** recreates his triumphant Broadway role as a con-man salesman. He arrives in a small Iowa town to sell unwanted musical instruments and uniforms for a boys' band. His blarney is so good, he takes in just about everyone, except Marian the Librarian, played by Shirley Jones. But she finally falls in love with the marvelous phony.

HILL, HELEN
WHAT'S THE MATTER WITH HELEN? (1971, UA)—Dance teachers **Shelley Winters** and Debbie Reynolds run a thirties school for would-be-Shirley Temples in Hollywood. Winters begins to hallucinate, killing elocution teacher Michael MacLiammoir. It's OK, she inherited her murderous behavior from her son, who with Reynolds' son are Leopold-and-Loeb-like killers.

HILL, HENRY
GOODFELLAS (1990, Warner Brothers)—The film is based on the real-life story of former Mafia hood Henry Hill who joined the mob while still a teen. In the film he grows up to be **Ray Liotta**, who tries to cut a bigger slice of an illegal pie than he's entitled to. Ultimately, he testifies against his former friends and at the time of the film's release was in the Federal Witness Protection program.

HILL, JEFF
JACK OF DIAMONDS (1967, MGM)—Cat burglar **George Hamilton** steals the jewelry of Carroll Baker, Zsa Zsa Gabor and Lilli Palmer. The sun-tan kid is no competition for Cary Grant.

HILL, WALTER
HARRY AND WALTER GO TO NEW YORK (1976, Columbia)—When 1890s vaudevillians **Elliott Gould** and James Caan can't get anywhere is show business, they try their hands as safecrackers in the Big Apple.

HILLERMAN, ARNOLD
THE STONE BOY (1984, 20th Century Fox)—After country boy **Jason Presson** accidentally shoots and kills his brother, whom he adores, he begins to withdraw from reality.

HILLIARD, CLARENCE
THE WORLD'S GREATEST SINNER (1962, Frenzy)—Refusing to believe in the existence of a supreme being, insurance salesman **Timothy Carey** proclaims himself to be God, and with guitar in hand gathers followers and receives financial support from a wealthy old woman. A miracle ends his divinity.

HILLIE
HAMBONE AND HILLIE (1984, New World)—When her dog and constant companion Hambone is accidentally set loose from his travel cage, while boarding a flight home from New York to Los Angeles, dear old **Lillian Gish** begins a dangerous 3,000 mile trek across the country looking for her friend.

HILLS, MARGE
THE GOOD WIFE (1987, Australia, Atlantic)—Married **Rachel Ward** is made to pay for her sins of sexual obsession for the new man in town, Sam Neill, by being forced to humble herself before her husband.

HILLSDOWN, LORD
THE KNAVE OF HEARTS (1919, Silent, GB, Harma)—Lord **James Knight** and the niece of a discharged worker, are tricked into marrying, but it's all right, they learn to love each other.

HILTON, CAROL
HER MARRIAGE VOW (1924, Silent, Warner Brothers)—Neglected by her hard-working husband Monte Blue, **Beverly Bayne** attends a neighbor's party and as he watches from their apartment, it sure looks to Blue that Bayne is offering a lot of encouragement to a former suitor who's attending the party.

HILTON, CLARA
AUNT CLARA (1954, GB, British Lion)—Pious old **Margaret Rutherford** inherits racing greyhounds, a pub and a brothel. Hope her good fortune is not wasted.

HILTON, JIM
THE GOOD FELLOWS (1943, Paramount)—**Cecil Kellaway** spends more time at his fraternal lodge meetings than with his business or family.

HILTON, MARY
BLONDE SINNER (1956, GB. Allied Artists)—Condemned prisoner **Diana Dors** recalls why she shot her pianist lover's new mistress. The film is titled YIELD TO THE NIGHT in Great Britain.

HILYARD, MRS.
LADY IN A CAGE (1964, Paramount)—Rich widow **Olivia De Havilland** becomes trapped in the elevator in her unoccupied home. She is taunted and menaced by three intruders, James Caan, Ann Sothern and Jeff Corey, who hold a regular orgy of robbery and vandalism.

HINGES, CHARLES
THE BELOVED BRUTE (1924, Silent, Vitagraph)—**Victor McLaglen's** father predicts on his death bed that Vic will always be a fighter without a soul, and will someday be beaten by his long-lost brother. Dear old Dad is almost right.

HINGSTON, CLARE

PORTRAIT OF CLARE (1951, GB, Pathe)—In the early 1900s, **Margaret Johnston** makes three marriages: to a dull solicitor, a rich man and at last a barrister.

HINSDALE, ALICE

SHE COULDN'T SAY NO (1941, Warner Brothers)—**Eve Arden** and her lawyer fiance find themselves on opposite sides of a breach of promise suit, involving 80-year-old Clem Bevans and the woman he's been dating for 15 years, Vera Lewis.

HINSLEY, SIR FRANCIS

THE LOVED ONE (1965, MGM)—When British actor **John Gielgud** finds that Hollywood no longer wants him for its movies, he hangs himself. Then his only living relative, Robert Morse, learns about California's death industry. It's a very unusual and frequently hilarious black comedy.

HINTON, JOHN EVART

HINTON'S DOUBLE (1917, Silent, Thanhouser)—**Frederick Warde** portrays a businessman and the double he gets to serve a prison term for him. Warde as Hinton will eventually show some redeeming qualities.

HITLER, ADOLF

HITLER—DEAD OR ALIVE (1943, Charles House); THAT NATZY NUISANCE (1943, UA); THE HITLER GANG (1944, Paramount); THE STRANGE DEATH OF ADOLF HITLER (1943, Universal); HITLER (1962, Allied Artists); HITLER—THE LAST TEN DAYS (1973, GB, Paramount)—**Bobs Watson, Ludwig Donath, Richard Basehart** and **Alec Guinness** all portrayed Hitler, but Bobs Watson almost made a career of the role. Despite the fact that Watson was supposed to be a ridiculous figure, he came off better than the others who seemed unable to get under the skin of their subject.

HOBBS, J. WARREN, JR.

HOBBS IN A HURRY (1918, Silent, Pathe)—**William Russell** sells what he thinks is a worthless mine to an Englishman. When he learns it is valuable, he tries to buy it back. The Englishman's twin brother sells the mine to Russell and his brother sells it to the father of Russell's fiancee. It turns out the mine really is worthless. Hobbs didn't hurry enough and neither did the movie according to critics of the time.

HOBBS, JIMMY

AMAZING VAGABOND (1929, Silent, RKO)—Rich man's son **Bob Steele** is sent west to a lumber camp to become a man. He does just that, defeating a crook and winning a girl, besides.

HOBBS, MISS

MISS HOBBS (1920, Silent, Realart)—Man-hater **Wanda Hawley** persuades two of her friends to leave their men, but they all change their tunes after Harrison Ford comes along and makes Hawley appreciate the difference in the two sexes.

HOBBS, ROGER

MR. HOBBS TAKES A VACATION (1962, 20th Century Fox)—**James Stewart** makes the mistake of taking a vacation with his entire family at a run-down beach cottage. Nothing works, including the relationships between his two married daughters and their husbands.

HOBBS, ROSIE

SAMMY AND ROSIE GET LAID (1987, GB, Cinecom)—**Frances Barber** and her husband Shashi Kapoor's sexually liberated life is too much for Shashi's father, an arrogant Middle Eastern politician, who has fled his country, and come to live with them in London.

HOBBS, ROY

THE NATURAL (1984, Tri-Star)—Nineteen-year-old **Robert Redford** appears on his way to becoming a great major league pitcher. But on the way to the stadium, he meets and dallies with Barbara Hershey, who shoots him. Fifteen years later, Redford shows up at the clubhouse of the New York Knights, and reluctantly is given a chance by the team's manager. Redford now seems to be the greatest hitter the game has seen. His team starts winning and looks to be in danger of winning the pennant, something its owner doesn't want, because he's got money on the other outcome. The owner sends femme fatale Kim Basinger to distract him, but Redford becomes reunited with Glenn Close, his sweetheart of long ago, and in a display of great courage, strength and determination, hits a pennant winning home run while poisoned and bleeding from his old gun wound.

HOBSON, FRAN

THE PLEASURE SEEKERS (1964, 20th Century Fox)—**Ann-Margret**, Carol Lynley and Pamela Tiffin are American girls in Madrid, seeking husbands. Singer-dancer Ann-Margret makes her mother proud by catching a young Spanish doctor, Andre Lawrence.

HOBSON, HENRY HORATIO

HOBSON'S CHOICE (1931, GB, British International); (1954, GB, British Lion)—**James Hartcourt** and **Charles Laughton** each portray a tyrannical Lancashire bootmaker, who refuses to give dowries for his three daughters, because he doesn't wish to lose them as slave labor. One, Brenda de Banzie, marries her father's downtrodden but talented apprentice, setting him up in competition with the old miser, nearly ruining him, until he agrees to make his son-in-law a full partner.

HOCHEN, PHYLLIS

THE UNHOLY WIFE (1957, Universal)—Married to an older vineyard owner, **Diane Dors** plots to murder her husband but kills a friend by mistake and is sent to prison for the accidental death of her mother-in-law.

HOFFMAN, BENJAMIN

HOFFMAN (1970, GB, Associate British)—Middle-aged **Peter Sellers** blackmails teenager Sinead Cusack into spending a weekend with him.

HOFFMAN, CARL

TWO HEARTS IN WALTZ TIME (1934, GB, Gaumont)—In Vienna composer **Carl Brisson** falls in love with Frances Day without knowing she is to star in his operetta.

HOFFMAN, CAROL & ERIC

THE MAN I MARRIED (1940, 20th Century Fox)—American **Joan Bennett** marries German **Francis Lederer** in 1938, and discovers that he's becoming a Nazi. She tries to leave Germany with their son, and is aided by her father-in-law, who informs his son that his mother was Jewish.

HOFFMAN, ESTHER

A STAR IS BORN (1976, Warner Brothers)—In the fourth version of the show business story, **Barbra Streisand's** meteoric rise as a new pop singing star parallels the decline of the career of her mentor and lover Kris Kristofferson.

HOFFMANN

TALES OF HOFFMANN (1951, GB, Lopert)—In love with ballerina Moira Shearer, poet **Robert Rounseville** recalls three loves: a life size doll, Shearer, he believed to be real; a courtesan, Ludmilla Tcherina, who stole his soul; and Ann Ayars, a girl forbidden to sing, who dies when she does so.

HOGAN, ROBERT EMMETT

ONE-ROUND HOGAN (1927, Silent, Warner Brothers)—**Monte Blue**, the son of a former boxer (played by one time heavyweight champion, James J. Jeffries), wins the big bout and the girl Leila Hyams, who had always opposed his involvement in the sport.

HOGARTH, JAY

PARTY HUSBAND (1931, Warner Brothers)—When **James Rennie** and his wife Dorothy Mackaill practice what years later would be called an "open marriage," they soon discover they have no marriage. His wise old mother Mary Doran shows them the way back to a happy union.

HOGGENBECK, BOON

THE REIVERS (1969, National General)—In 1905 Mississippi, **Steve McQueen**, Rupert Crosse and young Mitch Vogel are adventurers who set off in a stolen car looking for fun and excitement.

HOGUE, CABLE

THE BALLAD OF CABLE HOGUE (1970, Warner Brothers)—Left to die by his partners, gold prospector **Jason Robards Jr.** finds water in the desert. He turns his water hole into a profitable business as a way station for stagecoaches. Robards is ineffective in his attempts to take revenge, and dies trying to be a hero.

HOKU, INSPECTOR

MASTERMIND (1977, Goldstone)—**Zero Mostel** appears in a spoof of the Charlie Chan movies, but Sidney Toler who replaced Warner Oland in the roles years earlier had already turned the series into an enjoyable spoof. Give Mostel some credit, however—parts of the movie are good fun.

HOLCOMB, BOB

I'LL TAKE SWEDEN (1965, UA)—With his days as a popular movie comedian long passed, **Bob Hope** continued to appear in unimaginative and unfunny films such as this one. He's an oil executive, who gets himself transferred to Sweden so he can separate his nubile daughter Tuesday Weld from her motorcycling bum of a boyfriend, Frankie Avalon. Hope discovers the latter is preferable to the no-good playboy she takes up with in Stockholm.

HOLCROFT, NOEL

THE HOLCROFT COVENANT (1985, Universal)—**Michael Caine** unravels a plot to use the money hidden by three Nazi officers in the closing days of WWII to establish an international terrorist network. It is to send the world into anarchy, out of which will arise a "Fourth Reich."

HOLDEN, CLIFF

C-MAN (1949, Film Classics)—Customs agent **Dean Jagger** trails a gang of jewel smugglers from Paris to New York.

HOLDEN, JACK

THREE MEN AND A BABY (1987, Buena Vista); THREE MEN AND A LITTLE LADY (1990, Buena Vista)—**Ted Danson** is away from the luxurious apartment he shares with two other bachelors, Tom Selleck and Steve Guttenberg, when one of his lovers leaves a baby for him to care for. He and his roommates must not only deal with formulas and dirty diapers, but drug dealers as well. The film is the American version of the 1985 French film THREE MEN AND A CRADLE. In the sequel, actor Danson has not matured, but his daughter has. He tries to insert some of the good-natured mischief found in his television "Cheers" character.

HOLDEN, KENNETH

THE PRETENDER (1947, Republic)—**Albert Dekker** hires a hitman to kill the fiance of Catherine Craig, whom he wishes to marry. He tells the hired gun that the picture of his intended victim will appear in the newspaper. Dekker ends up marrying Craig, however, and the paper carries a picture of the bride and groom, leading the hit man to believe that Dekker wants himself wiped out.

HOLIDAY, BILLIE

LADY SINGS THE BLUES (1972, Paramount)—**Diana Ross** makes an impressive film debut as "Lady Day," the black blues singer whose life and career is ruined by drugs.

HOLIDAY, JOHNNY

JOHNNY HOLIDAY (1949, UA)—Wayward **Allen Martin Jr.** is sent to a model reform school where he comes under the bad influence of older delinquent Stanley Clements. However, Martin is rehabilitated, through the efforts of kindly supervisor William Bendix, but the latter has to take a bullet from Clements to get the job done.

HOLLAND, CYNTHIA

WOMAN AGAINST WOMAN (1938, MGM)—When patient Herbert Marshall gets no relief from his ex-wife **Mary Astor** and his new bride Virginia Bruce, who are constantly fighting over him and bedeviling the poor man, he finally puts his foot down.

HOLLAND, HENRY

THE LAVENDER HILL MOB (1951, GB, Ealing)—Timid bank clerk **Alec Guinness** has planned a perfect robbery for 20 years. With the help of Stanley Holloway, Sid James and Alfie Bass, he steals a million pounds in gold bars, melts them down into gold statuettes of the Eiffel Tower and smuggles them out of the country. Things start to unravel when six of the statuettes are accidentally sold to English schoolgirls visiting Paris. The film is one of Ealing's comedy masterpieces and Guinness is a dream.

HOLLAND, JESSICA

I WALKED WITH A ZOMBIE (1943, Columbia)—When nurse Frances Dee arrives in the West Indies to care for Tom Conway's wife **Christine Gordon**, she tries to instill some life in the pale silent blonde by taking her to a voodoo ceremony but Gordon's been there before.

HOLLAND, RUTH

SO ENDS OUR NIGHT (1941, UA)—Jewish **Margaret Sullavan** flees the Nazi regime in Germany with Aryan Fredric March, opposed to Hitler, and half-Ayran, half-Jewish Glenn Ford. They must move from country to country as the Nazis continue their march through Europe. They finally make it to Switzerland, where Sullavan and Ford marry.

HOLLANDER, XAVIERA

THE HAPPY HOOKER (1976, Cannon); THE HAPPY HOOKER GOES TO WASHINGTON (1977, Cannon); THE HAPPY HOOKER GOES TO HOLLYWOOD (1980, Cannon)—**Lynn Redgrave, Joey Heatherton** and **Martine Bestwick** each appear as the Dutch girl, who takes to a career in prostitution, finds she enjoys the life and becomes an Andy Warhol-like celebrity and sex advisor.

HOLLIDAY, JOHN "DOC"

DOC (1971, UA)—Many actors including Victor Mature in MY DARLING CLEMENTINE, Kirk Douglas in GUNFIGHT AT THE OK CORRAL and Jason Robards, Jr. in THE HOUR OF THE GUN have appeared as the consumptive dentist turned western gambler and gunfighter, but only **Stacy Keach** appeared in a movie named for him.

HOLLINS, EZRY

THE HIRED HAND (1918, Silent, Paramount)—**Charles Ray** never scored any higher than with this sentimental, but moving story of a lonely farmhand, who must endure quite a bit of heartache before being reunited with his country sweetheart.

HOLLINGSWAY, LORA MAY

A LETTER TO THREE WIVES (1948, 20th Century Fox)—**Linda Darnell**, a girl from the wrong side of the tracks, marries wealthy businessman Paul Douglas. Their marriage isn't peaceful, but still she hopes she's not the wife whose husband has been stolen by a woman (never seen), who announces she has done exactly that in letters to three wives.

HOLLINGSWORTH, JOAN

THE KID SISTER (1945, PRC)—**Judy Clark** decides she is grown-up, and so sets her sights on her older sister's fiance. In her pursuit of the unwilling love object, she gets hooked-up with a burglar, and is mistaken for his moll. She eventually settles for her intended target's younger brother.

HOLLINSWORTH, SAM

MEET MR. LUCIFER (1953, GB, Ealing)—**Stanley Holloway** appears both as a TV star and as the devil who wants Sam to use TV to make people miserable. But Sam's efforts backfire. The film of course is not true to real life. We all know that TV makes many people miserable.

HOLLIS, BURNSIDE

THE LAST REBEL (1971, Columbia)—Broadway **Joe Namath** whose alma mater is the University of Alabama, is a Confederate soldier, who raises havoc in a small Mississippi town after the Civil War. Did you really do that Joe? What a hell of a guy.

HOLLIS, PENELOPE "PENNY"

THE LADY'S FROM KENTUCKY (1939, Paramount)—A horse owner's daughter, **Ellen Drew**, has a falling-out with her bookie boyfriend George Raft, when he enters the horse in a big race. But when the animal wins, they are reunited.

HOLLIS, SQUIRE

THE VILLAGE SQUIRE (1935, GB, British & Dominions)—Pompous squire **David Horne** insists that his village put on a production of Macbeth. The show is saved by a visiting film star, trying to have an anonymous holiday, who ends up falling in love with Horne's daughter.

HOLLISTER, LYNN

A MAN BETRAYED (1941, Republic)—Small-town lawyer **John Wayne** moves to the city to investigate the death of a friend. He stays to lead a crusade against a crooked political boss, even though he's fallen in love with the man's daughter, Frances Dee.

HOLLOWAY, ROBERTA

NINE GIRLS (1944, Columbia)—**Leslie Brooks** is one of the suspects in the murder of mean-spirited Anita Louise, when a bunch of sorority girls go to a lodge for a weekend.

HOLLOWHEAD, BILLY, BUD, CINDY, HENRY AND MIRIAM

MEET THE HOLLOWHEADS (1989, Moviestore)—**Matt Shakman, Lightfield Lewis,** and **Juliette Lewis** are the detestable children of **John Glover** and **Nancy Mette.** This lunatic family live in a nauseating future world, where dear old dad is transformed from a meek meter reader into a ferocious defender of his family and home.

HOLLY

HANNAH AND HER SISTERS (1986, Orion)—**Dianne Wiest** ends up with her sister Mia Farrow's former husband, hypochondriac Woody Allen in this agreeable family farce.

HOLLY, BUDDY

THE BUDDY HOLLY STORY (1978, Columbia)—**Gary Busey** is very convincing as the fifties rock 'n' roll star who died at a very early age in a plane crash, which also took the lives of The Big Bopper (J.P. Richardson) and Ritchie Valens.

HOLLY/HOLLIS

THE WOMAN INSIDE (1981, 20th Century Fox)—Vietnam veteran **Gloria Manon** has a sex change operation. The only reason to take note of this movie is to say goodbye to trouper Joan Blondell in her final screen appearance as her/his aunt.

HOLM, ANNA

A WOMAN'S FACE (1941, MGM)—Scarred and embittered **Joan Crawford** turns to a life of crime, but experiences a re-birth when plastic surgeon Melvyn Douglas turns her into a beauty.

HOLMES, CAPT. JOHN

THE MAN FROM MONTEREY (1933, Warner Brothers)—U.S. Army Captain **John Wayne** goes to Monterey to prevent Mexican land-holders from being swindled by crooks.

HOLMES, KENNETH

HER SUMMER HERO (1928, Silent, FBO)—College champion swimmer and summer lifeguard **Hugh Trevor** saves Duane Thompson from drowning. The two have a summer romance, but in the fall, she turns to his biggest competitor. The winner of the big college swimming race wins her. Guess who?

HOLMES, MARY

THE GOOSE WOMAN (1925, Silent, Universal); THE PAST OF MARY HOLMES (1933, RKO)—International opera star **Louise Dresser** (Helen McKellar in 1933) gives birth to an illegitimate child, causing her to lose her following at the height of her career. She turns to guzzling gin, and tending geese to make her living. Embittered, she brings up her son without any show of affection. When as a man (Jack Pickford and Eric Linden, respectively), he falls in love with a local actress, his mother almost gets him convicted of murder, when she sees the chance to once again see her name on the front pages of newspapers.

HOLMES, MARY

SHOULD A WIFE FORGIVE? (1915, Silent, World)—When vamp Lillian Lorraine lures her husband Henry King away, **Mabel Van Buren** is faced with the burning question of the title. He wants to come home, after the temptress is shot to death, during a struggle involving King and the millionaire who has been keeping her.

HOLMES, OLIVER WENDELL

THE MAGNIFICENT YANKEE (1950, MGM)—**Louis Calhern** does a nice job as Supreme Court Chief Justice, Oliver Wendell Holmes, showing the latter part of his life and career.

HOLMES, PHYLLIS

THE SECOND FACE (1950, Eagle-Lion)—Grotesquely disfigured dress-designer **Ella Raines** comes out of a plastic surgery operation looking like, well, Ella Raines—and that's not bad.

HOLMES, SHERLOCK

SHERLOCK HOLMES (1927, Silent, Goldwyn); (1932, Fox); THE RETURN OF SHERLOCK HOLMES (1929, Paramount); SHERLOCK HOLMES' FATAL HOUR (1931, GB, First Division); THE TRIUMPH OF SHERLOCK HOLMES (1935, GB, Real Art); THE ADVENTURES OF SHERLOCK HOLMES (1939, 20th Century Fox); SHERLOCK HOLMES AND THE SECRET WEAPON (1942, Universal); SHERLOCK HOLMES AND THE VOICE OF TERROR (1942, Universal); SHERLOCK HOLMES FACES DEATH (1943, Universal); SHERLOCK HOLMES IN WASHINGTON (1943, Universal); SHERLOCK HOLMES AND THE SPIDER WOMAN (1944, Universal); THE PRIVATE LIFE OF SHERLOCK HOLMES (1970, GB, UA); THE ADVENTURES OF SHERLOCK HOLMES' SMARTER BROTHER (1975, GB, 20th Century Fox); YOUNG SHERLOCK HOLMES (1985, GB, Paramount)— **John Barrymore, Clive Brook, Arthur Wonter, Basil Rathbone, Douglas Wilmer** and **Nicholas Rowe** each portrayed Arthur Conan Doyle's brilliant deductive sleuth, who together with his friend and companion Dr. Watson, solved numerous baffling crimes committed by worthy opponents, most particularly Professor Moriarty. Rathbone had the longest run as the pipe-smoking, violin-playing detective, and for many will always be the image provoked by the mere mention of Sherlock Holmes. Similarly, Nigel Bruce will surely come to mind when thinking of Dr. John Watson.

HOLMES, SIGERSON

THE ADVENTURES OF SHERLOCK HOLMES' SMARTER BROTHER (1975, GB, 20th Century Fox)—Arthur Conan Doyle did gift Sherlock Holmes with a brother Sigerson, here played in a spoofing fashion by **Gene Wilder**. He falls in love with dance-hall damsel-in-distress Madeline Kahn. Wilder doesn't make Sigerson appear brighter than his more famous brother, just more egotistical.

HOLMES, WELLINGTON

SHUT MY BIG MOUTH (1942, Columbia)—In a western spoof, **Joe E. Brown** is an eastern dude, made a western sheriff. He outwits the villain Victor Jory. Brown plays a good part of the picture in drag, and although not as funny as Milton Berle, he has some hilarious moments.

HOLMES, LT. WILLIAM

THE LONE EAGLE (1927, Silent, Universal)—**Raymond Keane** overcomes his initial cowardice as a member of WWI's Royal Flying Corps to shoot down a great German ace.

HOLOWORTHY, BABS

GIRLS GONE WILD (1929, Silent, Fox)—**Sue Carol** breaks with her boyfriend Nick Stuart, when she discovers that it was his father, a motorcycle cop, who refused her bribe and hauled her into court when he caught her speeding. She has renewed appreciation both for Stuart and his father when they save her from gangsters taking her for a "ride."

HOLSTROM, KATRIN & MR.

THE FARMER'S DAUGHTER (1947, RKO)—**Loretta Young** is very appealing as the Swedish farm girl, who takes a job as a maid in the home of congressman Joseph Cotten. She eventually enters politics herself, wins the election, Cotten, and an Academy Award. **Harry Shannon** is her farmer father.

HOLT, ALAN

THE ALASKAN (1924, Silent, Paramount)—**Thomas Meighan** uses both his fists and a Senate Investigating Committee to fight off robber barons, trying to take the over the land and enterprises of long-time Alaskan settlers. Too bad someone like Meighan wasn't around to prevent Exxon from spilling its product in the waters of Prince William Sound.

HOLY MAN (JOE)

THE JEWEL OF THE NILE (1985, 20th Century Fox)—**Avner Eisenberg** is the precious "jewel" that evil potentate Spiros Focas must have to ensure his rule in this so-so sequel to ROMANCING THE STONE. Holy man Eisenberg is rescued by Michael Douglas and Kathleen Turner, and delivered to the rebels who rally around him to bring down Focas.

HOMBERG, MARILYN

STARTING OVER (1979, Paramount)—**Jill Clayburgh** and Burt Reynolds, two lonely, recently divorced people, tentatively begin an affair, which shows signs of being permanent, until Reynolds' ex-wife, beautiful Candice Bergen, comes back into his life. It's not long before Reynolds recalls what broke up their marriage and he runs back to Clayburgh hoping they can make a go of things.

HOMER

HIS NIGHT OUT (1935, Universal)—Told by a quack doctor that he has only three months to live, timid purchasing agent **Edward Everett Horton** gets involved in a robbery and is kidnapped by the gang responsible.

HONEY, MISS

MISS ROBIN HOOD (1952, GB, Union)—**Margaret Rutherford** inveigles Richard Hearne, a writer of adventure stories for girls, to help her recover a secret formula for whiskey stolen from her forbearers.

HONORABLE ALGY, THE

THE HONORABLE ALGY (1916, Silent, Triangle)—**Charles Ray**, the younger son of a noble family that has fallen on hard times, is sent to America to find a wealthy bride. On the trip over, he recovers the diamonds of an American girl. His reward is enough to tide his family over and he's allowed to marry his British sweetheart.

HOODED FANG, THE

JACOB TWO-TWO MEETS THE HOODED FANG (1979, Canada, Gulkin)—Nasty kid-hater **Alex Karras** plays guard to Stephen Rosenberg, when the boy fantasizes that he has been sentenced to prison for insulting adults. Karras turns out to be a pussy cat, mad only because kids find him cute. Strangely, opponents of this former Detroit Lions professional ball player, who looked across the line at him, never called him cute.

HOOK, CAPTAIN

HOOK (1991, Tri-Star)—Seeking revenge on his enemy Peter Pan, grown to be workaholic lawyer Robin Williams, **Dustin Hoffman** kidnaps Williams' children and gives the no-longer-believing Williams three days to prepare for a fight to the death.

HOOK, SGT.

TROOPER HOOK (1957, UA)—When Barbara Stanwyck's husband refuses to take her and her half-breed son back after she is rescued from the Indian who forced her to be his wife, he conveniently dies. **Joel McCrea**, who escorted her home, and is apparently more tolerant of these things, rides off with Barbara and her son.

HOOPER, MELVIN
I LOVE MELVIN (1953, MGM)—Photographer's assistant **Donald O'Connor** falls in love with well-born chorus girl Debbie Reynolds.

HOOPER, SONNY
HOOPER (1978, Warner Brothers)—Aging stunt man **Burt Reynolds**, pushed by a young rival, Jan-Vincent Michael, decides to go for one last sensational stunt before packing it in.

HOPPER, BETSY
BETSY'S WEDDING (1990, Touchstone)—Alan Alda got the idea for this film after his real daughter's wedding. We hope it was more interesting than the one of his reel daughter **Molly Ringwald**. The guest list is a disaster.

HOW, DR. LEE WONG
THREE MEN IN WHITE (1944, MGM)—**Keye Luke**, Van Johnson and Lionel Barrymore are the three medical men of the title. Barrymore, confined to a wheelchair must choose a new assistant. He gives each a case to deal with. How they handle it and themselves will determine who gets the job. It's not Luke.

HOWARD
HARRY AND SON (1984, Orion)—Artistic young **Robby Benson** and his working-man widower father can't seem to find any common ground, particularly after Dad, Paul Newman, loses his job and self-respect. Benson has played the role too often.

HOWARD
THE HOWARD CASE (1936, GB, Universal)—Lawyer **Arthur Seaton** kills his cousin, who looks exactly like him, to cover up the fact that he's gambled his firm's money speculating on gold shares. He tries to shift the blame onto his partner, but the police aren't fooled.

HOWARD
THE PIED PIPER (1942, 20th Century Fox)—While vacationing in France, elderly Englishman **Monty Woolley** is caught up in the invasion by the Germans. Although claiming to hate children, he agrees to get a couple safely to England and on the way home, picks up several more of various nationalities. It's a charming story with irascible Woolley quite wonderful.

HOWARD, BING
ALIAS THE NIGHT WIND (1923, Silent, Fox)—Daredevil, athletic **William Russell** must clear himself of charges of theft.

HOWARD, CATHERINE
HENRY VIII AND HIS SIX WIVES (1972, GB, EMI/MGM)—**Lynne Frederick** is Henry's fifth wife. Like Anne Boleyn she is sent to the block for the crime of infidelity.

HOWARD, DAVID & LINDA
LOST IN AMERICA (1985, Warner Brothers)—**Albert Brooks** and **Julie Hagerty** are a married couple who give up everything for the freedom of exploring the country. The result for the couple is lots of pain and for the audience plenty of laughs.

HOWARD, DR.
THE YOUNG DOCTORS (1961, UA)—**George Segal** made his screen debut in this over-wrought soap opera, combining all the cliches of the Kildare/Gillespie series as well as the numerous TV medical shows. Segal does nothing special, except supply a new face.

HOWARD, EDDIE
SILK HAT KID (1935, Fox)—Shady nightclub dealer **Lew Ayres** contributes money to help run a settlement house for wayward kids. His motive is to impress Mae Clarke who works at the house. Problems arise when Ayres' bodyguard also falls for Clarke.

HOWARD, JOSH
OCEAN'S ELEVEN (1960, Warner Brothers)—**Sammy Davis, Jr.** does a little singing and shuffling as he helps Frank Sinatra and other members of a former combat outfit rob five Las Vegas casinos one New Year's Eve.

HOWARD, MARY
WHEN LADIES MEET (1941, MGM)—Novelist **Joan Crawford** falls in love with her married publisher Herbert Marshall. Robert Taylor, who loves Crawford, arranges for her to meet and become friends with Marshall's wife Greer Garson, without either knowing what they have in common. When Crawford discovers that her new friend is her lover's wife, she leaves Marshall and walks into the arms of Taylor. She could've done worse.

HOWARD, MATT & JANE PEYTON
THE HOWARDS OF VIRGINIA (1940, Columbia)—Virginia surveyor **Cary Grant** marries aristocratic **Martha Scott**, becomes involved in politics, and joins the Colonial army at the breakout of the Revolutionary War.

HOWARD, MAY
IF I WERE SINGLE (1927, Silent, Warner Brothers)—**May McAvoy** and Conrad Nagel are happily married, but after he has a flirtation with one of her old school chums, McAvoy does the same with a music teacher. The four become stranded together in a car in the middle of nowhere, which gives McAvoy and Nagel a chance to get things back to the status quo.

HOWARD, MILLICENT
AMERICAN BEAUTY (1927, Silent, First National)—**Billie Dove** chooses love over money in this simple tale of true love triumphant.

HOWARD, SCOTT
TEEN WOLF (1985, Atlantic)—Young heartthrob **Michael J. Fox** discovers he can change into a werewolf. Rather than tear victims apart, the Fox who becomes a wolf uses his ability to lead his high school basketball team to a championship.

HOWARD, STEVE
RANGER OF THE CHEROKEE STRIP (1949, Republic)—Texas ranger **Monte Hale**, with the help of Douglas Kennedy, the Cherokee Indian he's suppose to bring in, foils the plans of cattlemen trying to squeeze the Indians off the land awarded to them by the government.

HOWARD, TODD
TEEN WOLF TOO (1987, Atlantic)—As poor as was TEEN WOLF, nothing could prepare audiences for the sequel starring **Jason Bateman** as the original teen wolf's cousin. He also bays at the moon.

HOWARD, VINCE
FACE OF A STRANGER (1964, GB, Allied Artists)—Ex-con **Jeremy Kemp** poses as his cell mate in order to fool the latter's blind wife Rosemary Leach into revealing where her husband's hidden loot is.

HOWARD, VIRGINIA
SECOND WIFE (1936, RKO)—Walter Abel is faced with the monumental decision of going abroad to be with his seriously ill 10-year-old son or stay at home with his new wife **Gertrude Michael** who is expecting her first child. Audiences had no such trouble in making a decision. They walked out in large numbers.

HOWARD, WANDA

GIRLS ABOUT TOWN (1931, Paramount)—**Kay Francis** is described as a "party girl," but as she rents her favors to wealthy visiting businessmen by the hour, day or weekend, she shouldn't be so coy about her profession and what she's called.

HOWE, MARY

THE GIRL SAID NO (1930, MGM)—**Leila Hyams** has a tough time discouraging William Haines. She turns him down in favor of Francis X. Bushman, but Haines won't take no for an answer and goes to ridiculous measures to try to change her mind, including kidnapping her bound and gagged from the altar on her wedding day.

HOWELL, MIMI

LADIES LOVE BRUTES (1930, Paramount)—**Mary Astor** doesn't immediately love wealthy but crude building contractor George Bancroft. But with a little polishing, this diamond in the rough looks better and better to the divorced socialite.

HOWELL, WILMA

LADIES CRAVE EXCITEMENT (1935, Mascot)—**Evalyn Knapp** and Norman Foster are rival news photographers, who fall in love after meeting so often at news events. This movie could use some excitement.

HOWELLS, HARRY

HIS FIRST FLAME (1927, Silent, Sennett/Pathe Exchange)—Returning home from college, **Harry Langdon** becomes engaged to Ruth Hiatt, who is only interested in his money. Her sister Natalie Kingston really loves Langdon. She sets her house afire so he'll rescue her. The house flame ignites one between Langdon and Kingston and they marry.

HOWIE, SGT. NEIL

THE WICKER MAN (1974, GB, British Lion)—Policeman **Edward Woodward** investigates the disappearance of a child on a pagan Scottish island.

HOWITT, DANIEL

THE SHEPHERD OF THE HILLS (1941, Paramount)—When **Harry Carey** returns to the Ozark hills, his son John Wayne, who has never seen his father, vows to kill Carey, because he believes that the latter deserted his mother, causing her early death. That's not quite the story, Duke.

HOWLAND, PERCE

THE MISFITS (1961, UA)—Broken, bronco-buster **Montgomery Clift** teams-up with Clark Gable and Eli Wallach to catch wild mustangs for dog food. All three become involved with divorcee Marilyn Monroe who is disgusted and outraged by their plans.

HOWLAND, TESS

TESS OF THE STORM COUNTRY (1932, Fox)—Fiery sea-captain's daughter **Janet Gaynor** is a squatter, along with her father Dudley Digges, on the land of Claude Gillingwater. She must endure seeing her home go up in flames, her father wrongly convicted of arson, the loss of her beau, Charles Farrell, son of Gillingwater, and the rumor that she is about to have an illegitimate child, before everything is satisfactorily straightened out, and she's able to marry Farrell.

HOYLE, MRS.

ACCORDING TO MRS. HOYLE (1951, Monogram)—Retired schoolteacher **Spring Byington** finds her boardinghouse taken over by a gang of mobsters. One turns out to be her long lost son.

HOYT, ANDREW

BACHELOR'S AFFAIRS (1932, Fox)—**Adolphe Menjou**, trapped in a marriage of convenience with ding-a-ling Joan Marsh, tries to put some life in his life by having an affair. It almost ends his life.

HOYT, ETHAN

THE GREAT MAN'S LADY (1942, Paramount)—**Joel McCrea** is encouraged and inspired by his wife Barbara Stanwyck to strike it rich in the West by finding oil.

HOYTE, MARION

HER SOCIAL VALUE (1921, Silent, Associated First National) - Salesgirl **Katharine MacDonald** falls in love with and marries architect Roy Stewart, which just about ruins his career. Not wishing to destroy him, she makes it appear that she has left him for another man, but they will be reunited.

HUBBARD, GENEVIEVE

LITTLE COMRADE (1919, Silent, Paramount)—**Vivian Martin's** sister and mother convince the irresponsible girl that she should join the war effort. She becomes a farmette and wins the heart of a young farmer.

HUBBARD, LARRY

THE LONELY GUY (1984, Universal)—Greeting card writer **Steve Martin** becomes a lonely guy, when he comes home and finds his live-in-lover in bed with a younger guy. The film is only for real Steve Martin aficionados.

HUBER, FRANCINE & EARL

STRANGE TRIANGLE (1946, 20th Century Fox)—Worthless **Signe Hasso's** extravagances have driven her husband **John Shepperd (Shepperd Strudwick)** to gamble with bank funds. Hasso helps him out somewhat by spending a few days with bank supervisor Preston Foster, who has been called in to investigate missing funds.

HUBERMAN, ALICIA

NOTORIOUS (1946, RKO)—**Ingrid Bergman**, the daughter of a convicted Nazi spy, atones for his sins by helping to expose a group of Nazi plotters in South America. She goes so far as to marry one of the leaders, Claude Rains, even though she's in love with her American contact Cary Grant. Rains discovers Bergman's plot and attempts to kill her by gradual poisoning. Just in the nick of time Grant comes to the rescue and carries her off.

HUDLER, MAMIE

THE PAINTED ANGEL (1929, Warner Brothers)—The plot which follows the rise of New Orleans singer **Billie Dove** to queen of the New York night clubs is just thick enough to get to Dove's various musical numbers.

HUDSON, BILLY

THE HOLLYWOOD REPORTER (1926, Silent, Hercules Film)—Reporter **Frank Merrill** will be given permission to marry his editor's daughter, if he can come up with some dirt on a political boss, who has threatened to reveal that the editor once served time in prison. Merrill not only comes up with the dirt, but also is able to show that his boss was framed of the crime which landed him in jail.

HUDSON, GLORIA

WOMEN OF GLAMOUR (1937, Columbia)—Loved by both gold-digger **Virginia Bruce** and socialite Leona Maricle, Melvyn Douglas chooses the former.

HUDSON, JANE
WHATEVER HAPPENED TO BABY JANE? (1962, Warner Brothers)—Former child star **Bette Davis** tries to drive her crippled sister, former movie queen Joan Crawford, mad. As good as it was, we would have preferred to witness the real life battles of the two legendary stars on the set.

HUDSON, VAL
UNDERSEA GIRL (1957, Allied Artists)—**Mara Corday** is one of many, searching for loot located at the bottom of the ocean.

HUGGETT, JOE & ETHEL
HERE COME THE HUGGETTS (1948, GB, Gainsborough)—**Jack Warner** and **Kathleen Harrison's** well-ordered lives are severely tested by the seven day stay of their glamorous blonde niece Diana Dors.

HUGHES, FELICITY
LITTLE FRIEND (1934, GB, Gaumont)—**Nova Pilbeam** is excellent as the young daughter of a divorcing couple. In the court she tries to shield her mother against charges of adultery brought by her father. It all proves too much for her. Her attempted suicide brings the warring parents back together.

HUGHES, GLORIA
GLORIFYING THE AMERICAN GIRL (1930, Paramount)—**Mary Eaton** impersonates the show girl, who becomes a star in a film, which was basically a spectacular revue, with stars and show-girls from Broadway's Ziegfeld's Follies.

HUGHES, HOWARD
MELVIN AND HOWARD (1980, Universal)—**Jason Robards, Jr.** appears as Howard Hughes, who leaves a fortune to perennial loser Paul Le Mat. Le Mat claims to have picked up Hughes, whom he believed to be no more than an inebriated drunk on a Nevada highway, and driven him to Las Vegas. Although Le Mat never collects a cent, he does achieve Andy Warhol celebrity status.

HULDA
HULDA FROM HOLLAND (1916, Silent, Artcraft)—When her parents die, little Dutch girl, **Mary Pickford**, the eldest child, becomes the mother for her three younger brothers. A bachelor uncle in Pennsylvania sends for them, but because of an automobile accident is unable to meet them, and the four are stranded in New York. It takes some of the usual Hollywood coincidences, but everything works out all right by the fade-out.

HULL, JUDY
SCATTERBRAIN (1940, Republic); JOAN OF OZARK (1942, Republic) -Hillbilly comedienne **Judy Canova** was the queen of Republic studios. Her yodelling, corn-fed humor, and buck teeth enlivened these modest programmers. In the first, Judy is an Ozark girl, mistakenly "discovered" by a Hollywood film producer to be made a new star. In the second, Canova gets tangled-up with a German spy when she bags a Nazi carrier pidgeon while hunting quail.

HULL, MOLLY
THEY JUST HAD TO GET MARRIED (1933, Universal)—When their rich employer leaves all his money to servants **Zasu Pitts** and Slim Summerville, they marry because now they can afford to.

HULL, NANCY
WEST POINT WIDOW (1941, Paramount)—Young mother **Anne Shirley** has had her marriage to West Point cadet and football star Richard Denning annulled to protect his career, as the Academy bans cadet marriages. She plans to remarry him when he graduates. When that time comes, he has other interests, but Shirley has intern Richard Carlson to fall back on.

HUMPHREY
FANCY PANTS (1950, Paramount)—Clumsy actor **Bob Hope** is mistaken for an English butler and brought to the wild West by the newly rich mother of Lucille Ball. Out West, Hope is taken for a nobleman, and lives down to the part. The film is a remake of RUGGLES OF RED GAP with Hope almost as good as Charles Laughton, who starred in the earlier film.

HUNKINS, LAMBERT
HE COULDN'T SAY NO (1938, Warner Brothers)—Timid advertising clerk **Frank McHugh** finally gets the girl of his choice, rather than the one being foisted upon him by mother Cora Witherspoon, with some help from a statue called "Courage."

HUNT, HELEN
YOU BELONG TO ME (1941, Columbia)—Physician **Barbara Stanwyck's** husband Henry Fonda is wary of her male patients. Neither Miss Stanwyck nor Fonda would point to this one with pride.

HUNT, LAURA
LAURA (1944, 20th Century Fox)—At the beginning of the movie it appears that lovely **Gene Tierney** has been murdered. The police detective, Dana Andrews, assigned to the case, falls in love with her portrait. When it turns out that she's not really dead, he continues the love. Tierney's life is still in danger, and Andrews must determine who had killed a model believing her to be Tierney, and prevent the assailant from striking again.

HUNT, MANUELA
STOWAWAY GIRL (1957, GB, Paramount)—Both drunkard captain Trevor Howard and brutish engineer Pedro Armendariz fall for South American stowaway **Elsa Martinelli**. In Great Britain, the film was released as MANUELA.

HUNTER, CHRIS
THE UNFAITHFUL (1947, Warner Brothers)—Married **Ann Sheridan** deeply regrets having been unfaithful to her husband while he was away at war. Now that he's back, she finds herself mixed-up in a murder case, the victim being her onetime lover.

HUNTER, DOROTHY
THE RICHEST GIRL IN THE WORLD (1934, RKO)—In order to determine if men would be interested in her for herself alone, wealthy **Miriam Hopkins** switches places with her secretary Fay Wray. Joel McCrea is the main love interest.

HUNTER, DOT
PAGAN LADY (1931, Columbia)—"Pagan Lady" **Evelyn Brent** leads astray Conrad Nagel, the nephew of an evangelist, in this cheap imitation of RAIN.

HUNTER, FREDDIE
THE GREAT LOVER (1949, Paramount)—Boy-scout leader **Bob Hope** becomes involved with beautiful duchess Rhonda Fleming and murderer Roland Young, while taking his troop to Europe aboard an ocean liner.

HUNTER, JACK
TENNESSEE'S PARTNER (1916, Silent, Lasky)—**Jack Dean** places a little girl in a convent school to honor the request of her father before he died of a gunshot wound, inflicted by Charles Clary, the man who had run off with the deceased's wife. Years later, the girl

has grown to become Fannie Ward. She goes west to find Dean whom she believes is her father. Instead she's abducted by Clary, who decides to make her his bride. Dean rescues Ward and strings up Clary. He then rides off into the sunset with Ward—and you know what that means.

HUNTER, JULIETTE
HOT HEIRESS (1931, First National/Warner Brothers)—Socialite **Ona Munson** attempts to pass off riveter Ben Lyon as an architect in this lousy musical with unsingable songs by Richard Rodgers and Lorenz Hart.

HUNTER, ROCK
WILL SUCCESS SPOIL ROCK HUNTER (1957, 20th Century Fox)—In danger of losing a lipstick manufacturer as an account, advertising account executive **Tony Randall** induces Hollywood movie queen Jayne Mansfield to become identified with the product. His association with Mansfield makes Randall a celebrity, but it's too much for him, so he retires to a chicken farm.

HUNTER, SHEILA
THEY WANTED TO GET MARRIED (1937, RKO)—Debutante **Betty Furness** falls in love with working slob, news photographer Gordon Jones, but must overcome the objections to their marriage by her blue-blooded rich father.

HURD, SIMON
THE MAN WHO LIKED FUNERALS (1959, GB, Rank)—Printer **Leslie Phillips** forges memoirs of deceased celebrities in order to blackmail their relatives, and raise money to save a Boys' Club.

HURRICANE HUTCH
HUTCH STIRS 'EM UP (1923, Silent, GB, Ideal)—Cowboy **Charles Hutchinson** saves a village girl from a mad squire's torture chamber.

HURRICANE KID, THE
THE HURRICANE KID (1925, Silent, Universal)—Cowboy **Hoot Gibson** gets the best of a rival, tames a wild horse, wins a big race, and a girl.

HUSBAND, WILLIE
LATE FOR DINNER (1991, Columbia)—In 1962, **Brian Wimmer** and his brother-in-law are shot in an altercation. A doctor gives them heavy doses of cryonics, which puts them in a deep freeze for 23 years. When they revive, still youthful-looking Wimmer seeks out his fiftyish wife Marcia Gay Harden and his now adult daughter, Colleen Flynn, who never knew him.

HUTCH
OLD HUTCH (1936, MGM)—When good-for-nothing **Wallace Beery** finds a fortune, he can't spend it, because everyone knows he hasn't held a job in years.

HUTTON, JUNE
JUST A WOMAN (1925, Silent, First National)—When **Claire Windsor** and her husband Conway Tearle become rich, because of an invention of roomer Percy Marmont, Tearle starts seeing an old girlfriend. He files divorce actions against Windsor, accusing her of having an affair. But he comes to his senses and takes back Windsor.

HYATT, ALICE
ALICE DOESN'T LIVE HERE ANYMORE (1975, Warner Brothers)—Widow **Ellen Burstyn** and her young son hit the road for Monterey

and a hoped-for singing career. She finds she has to take a job as a waitress in Mel's Cafe.

HYDE, MR. *See* DR. BLACK

HYDE, MR. *See* DR. JEKYLL

HYDE, SISTER
DR. JEKYLL AND SISTER HYDE (1971, GB, Hammer)—Good Dr. Jekyll, played by Ralph Bates, becomes the evil and very beautiful Sister Hyde, played by **Martine Beswick**.

HYDE, TEDDY
THE UGLY DUCKLING (1959, GB, Columbia)—**Bernard Bresslaw** a descendant of Dr. Jekyll, discovers his ancestor's formula for transforming personalities. He becomes Teddy Hyde, a fearless, suave criminal. Back as Jekyll, he rounds up Hyde's gang. As a comedy, it's frightening. As a thriller, it's comical.

HYNKEL, ADENOID
THE GREAT DICTATOR (1940, UA)—**Charles Chaplin** gives his comical interpretation of Adolf Hitler, with Jack Oakie impersonating a Mussolini-like character. Chaplin about ruins the fine satire with a six-minute curtain call in which he preaches to his audience.

I

I
WITHNAIL AND I (1987, GB, Cineplex Odeon)—**Paul Marwood**, who is left unnamed in the film, is a handsome, bespectacled out-of-work actor living in 1969 with another actor: eccentric self-absorbed, gaunt, sarcastic and dissipated Richard E. Grant, also unemployed. Their decision to take a vacation in the country proves disastrous.

IANUZZI, ALBERT
THE DREAM TEAM (1989, Universal)—Of the four mental patients, who find themselves stranded in New York after their doctor-chaperon is sent to a hospital in a coma, **Stephen Furst** seems the least in tune with reality. He only speaks in baseball cliches, which only rarely have anything to do with the situation at hand.

IBBETSON, MATTHEW
BACHELOR IN PARIS (1953, GB, Lippert)—**Dennis Price** is an English businessman with a dominant mother. He is loved by French star Anne Vernon, who is engaged to loony count Mischa Auer.

IBBETSON, PETER
PETER IBBETSON (1935, Paramount)—London architect **Gary Cooper** accidentally kills his childhood sweetheart Ann Harding's husband. He spends the rest of his life in a dungeon, but is reunited with his love in his dreams and after death.

IDAHO
THE IDAHO KID (1937, Republic)—**Rex Ball** tries to make peace with his father, who has disowned him.

ILLINGTON, MRS. *See* **SALLY BROWN**

THE ILLUSTRIOUS ONE
DAUGHTER OF THE TONG (1939, Metropolitan)—**Evelyn Brent** is an Oriental head of a gang of smugglers.

IM-HO-TEP
THE MUMMY (1932, Universal)—Egyptian high priest **Boris Karloff** is buried alive with a dead princess. Thirty-five hundred years later he is revived when his tomb is desecrated by archaeologists. He takes his revenge using the identity of Ardeth Bey.

IMPERIUM, MR.
MR. IMPERIUM (1951, MGM)—Prince **Ezio Pinza** falls in love with night club singer Lana Turner. When he moves up to king, she's out of the picture.

INCUBUS
INCUBUS (1966, Daystar)—Incubus **Milos Milos** frustrates a witch out to win good man William Shatner. The movie's dialogue is spoken in Esperanto, the international language, which didn't enhance the film's chances. Let's sleep through it.

INCUBUS
THE INCUBUS (1982, Canada, Film Ventures)—**Dirk McLean** is an incubus who causes doctor John Cassavetes to have disturbing dreams about sex crimes. But are they dreams?

INDIAN, THE
THE TALISMAN (1966, Gillman)—**Ned Romero** and his braves wipe out a wagon train, but he can't bring himself to kill the last survivor, Linda Hawkins, so he becomes her protector. She falls in love with him, but when she gets the chance, returns to whites who brutally rape her. She returns to Romero, who vows revenge, with slow death to be their fate.

INEZ
THE WIDOW FROM MONTE CARLO (1936, Warner Brothers)—Widowed duchess **Dolores Del Rio** is pursued by suave suitor Warren William.

INGLEBY, LADY MYRA
THE MISTRESS OF SHENSTONE (1921, Silent, Robertson -Cole)—Englishwoman **Pauline Frederick** escapes to Cornwall to mourn the accidental death of her husband during WWI.

INGLISH, CLAUDELLE
CLAUDELLE INGLISH (1961, Warner Brothers)—Farm girl **Diane McBain** defies her mother when she refuses to marry a well-to-do landowner, preferring instead a dirt-farmer.

INGRAHAM, JULES
LAST OF THE INGRAHAMS (1917, Silent, Associated First National)—**William Desmond**, the last remaining member of a New England puritan family, is slowly killing himself with alcohol. A woman, scorned by everyone, helps him reclaim himself and they marry suggesting that the last of the Ingrahams hasn't been seen yet.

INGRAM, BLANCHE
HER TEMPORARY HUSBAND (1923, Silent, Associated First National)—**Sylvia Breamer** needs a husband in a hurry, so she may inherit her aunt's fortune. She picks out an old man, but is tricked into marrying a young man.

INGRAM, GRACE
SEVEN WOMEN FROM HELL (1961, 20th Century Fox)—**Patricia Owens** and six other women escape from a Japanese prison camp in New Guinea. They are forced to kill a wealthy planter, who had planned to return them to the Japanese.

INGSTON, KURT
NIGHT MONSTER (1942, Universal)—**Ralph Morgan** has had both his legs amputated, and the responsible doctors are being killed one by one. Is Morgan behind the killings? Do bees buzz?

INUK
THE SAVAGE INNOCENTS (1960, GB, Paramount)—Eskimo **Anthony Quinn** goes to a trading post to swap skins. Later he kills a man who refuses Quinn's offer of his wife, part of Eskimo courtesy for visitors. He and his wife become fugitives, but don't understand why.

INVINCIBLE, CAPT.
THE RETURN OF CAPTAIN INVINCIBLE (1983, Australia, Keys)—**Alan Arkin**, an ex-super hero, must come out of retirement to take on evil Christopher Lee.

INVIOLATA, SISTER (CHARLIE)
NUNS ON THE RUN (1990, 20th Century Fox)—Petty British criminals **Robbie Coltrane** and Eric Idle dress in convent drag to escape members of their gang who don't want them to quit the rackets. Lapsed Catholic Coltrane does his hilarious best to instruct Protestant Idle on how to act as a nun.

IODINE, LITTLE
LITTLE IODINE (1946, UA)—**Jo Ann Marlowe** stars as the cartoon strip little girl, who gives her folks a hard time.

IONESCU, NINA
HER ALIBI (1989, Warner Brothers)—Ex-model **Paulina Porizkova** is certainly a beauty, but would anyone other than writer Tom Selleck give her an alibi when she's accused of murder—especially when it seems she's trying to kill him?

IOTA, SUKI
THE COURAGEOUS COWARD (1919, Silent, Haworth)—Japanese-American **Sessue Hayakawa** yearns for a girl with old fashioned Japanese values. He finds one but while he's off at school, she becomes a singer, develops American habits and even picks up a Caucasian admirer.

IRENKA
SOME GIRLS (1989, MGM-UA)—Fetching beauty **Sheila Kelley** provides quite a distraction for Patrick Dempsey, when he visits her sister, his college sweetheart, Jennifer Connelly, and her family in Quebec City during Christmas holiday.

IRENA
THE CURSE OF THE CAT PEOPLE (1944, RKO)—The film is not a true sequel to CAT PEOPLE although **Simone Simon** stars in both. This time she is the ghost of a Kent Smith's first wife. She appears to Kent's little girl.

IRINA
THREE SISTERS (1974, GB, British Lion); (1977, Actor Studios Theatre)—Louise Parnell and Sandy Dennis play one of the sisters in the Anton Chekhov play about a very unhappy 19th century Russian family.

IRIS
IRIS (1915, Silent, GB, Ideal)—When wealthy widow **Alma Taylor** is forbidden to marry, she takes a lover.

IRIS
STANLEY AND IRIS (1990, MGM/UA)—Beleaguered working-class widow **Jane Fonda** has enough problems. She really doesn't need to get involved with illiterate loner Robert De Niro, but she does. Few in the audiences cared.

IRVING (HERMAN)
FAT SPY (1966, Magus)—**Jack E. Leonard**, Phyllis Diller and Jordan Christopher seek the fountain of youth in Florida. Instead they find a bunch of pop-singers and Jayne Mansfield.

ISABEAU
LADYHAWKE (1985, Warner Brothers/20th Century Fox)—In this medieval fantasy, an evil bishop has put a spell over the lovers **Michelle Pfeiffer** and Rutger Hauer. During the day she is a hawk, and at night when she reverts to a woman, he becomes a wolf.

ISABEL
ISABEL (1968, Canada, Paramount)—With the help of a fisherman, **Genevieve Bujold** overcomes the trauma of the death of her parents and brother, and an attack by a group of drunks.

ISABELLE
THERESE AND ISABELLE (1968, Audobon Films)—**Anna Gael** and Essy Persson are two French schoolgirls who have a torrid affair.

ISBELL, JEAN
TO THE LAST MAN (1923, Silent, Paramount)—**Richard Dix** is a member of a cattle ranching family, while Lois Wilson belongs to a family of sheepherders. A feud erupts, leaving only Dix and Wilson alive.

ISELIN, SENATOR JOHN
THE MANCHURIAN CANDIDATE (1962, UA)—During the Korean War, Laurence Harvey is brainwashed while a POW. He returns to the U.S. as a sleeping bomb to be awakened by his contact, who turns out to be his mother Angela Lansbury, the wife of U.S. senator **James Gregory**, who is being nominated as a vice-presidential candidate. Harvey is to assassinate the presidential candidate so Gregory can pick up the mantle and do the communists' bidding.

ISHERWOOD, CHRISTOPHER
I AM A CAMERA (1955, GB, Romulus-Remus)—**Laurence Harvey**, an English writer in Berlin in the 30s, takes note of the rise of the Nazi party. He has a romance with a deliberately decadent cabaret performer Julie Harris.

ISLIP, GEOFFREY ARBUTHNOT "BLINKY"
BLINKY (1923, Silent, Universal) Bespectacled **Hoot Gibson** gets no respect from his fellow cavalrymen because his only previous military experience was as a boy scout. But he uses that experience to rescue the commander's daughter from kidnappers.

ISSAC
CHILDREN OF THE CORN (1984, New World)—**John Franklin** and his other juvenile cultists have taken over an Iowa town in this filming of a Stephen King short story.

ISSACSON, DANIEL
DANIEL (1983, Paramount)—In a fictionalized story based on the Rosenberg spy case, **Timothy Hutton** plays the son of executed spies. He muses about his parents guilt or innocence and learns to adjust to this glitch in his past.

"IT"
IT! THE TERROR FROM BEYOND SPACE (1958, UA)—**Ray "Crash" Corrigan** is an alien stowaway aboard a space ship returning to earth.

THE ITALIAN (BEPPO DONNETTI)
THE ITALIAN (1915, Silent, New York Motion Picture)—**George Beban**, a young gondolier, loves Clara Williams, but her father won't give his consent to their marriage, until Beban proves he can provide for a family. Beban immigrates to America and within a year is able to send for Clara, but their troubles are just beginning.

IVANHOE
IVANHOE (1915, Silent, Imperator); (1952, GB, MGM)—**King Baggot** and **Robert Taylor** portray the Saxon knight who works to save the throne for King Richard, held captive on his way back from the Crusades.

IVERS, MARTHA
THE STRANGE LOVE OF MARTHA IVERS (1946, Paramount)—As a teenager **Barbara Stanwyck** got away with the murder of her wealthy aunt. Years later Van Heflin, who knows the truth, arrives back in town leading Barbara and her weakling husband Kirk Douglas to suspect the worst. The two use various means to get rid of Heflin but end up doing away with themselves instead.

IVES
I MET MY LOVE AGAIN (1938, UA)—Vermont College professor **Henry Fonda's** life is thrown in an uproar when his ex-lover Joan Bennett, who left him and eloped ten years earlier, comes back home as a widow.

IVY
IVY (1947, Universal)—In Edwardian England, innocent looking **Joan Fontaine** is a poisoner who gets her just desserts.

IVY
POISON IVY (1992, New Line)—Sexy 17-year-old **Drew Barrymore** befriends bookish Sara Gilbert. Before long, Barrymore is living with and dominating Gilbert's family. She makes it with Gilbert's recovering-alcoholic dad Tom Skerritt, while mom Diane Ladd is passed out in bed next to them.

IZORA
LITTLE EGYPT (1951, Universal)—American **Rhonda Fleming** poses as a dancer from Egypt and makes the belly-dance the naughty sensation of Chicago's World Fair.

J

J (Jimmy)
THREE MEN IN A BOAT (1933, GB, Associate British Films); (1958, GB, Romulus/Valiant)—**Billy Milton** in 1933 and **David Tomlinson**

in 1958 find adventure and romance during a boating holiday with two friends on the Thames.

J.T.
THE FIVE HEARTBEATS (1991, 20th Century Fox)—**Leon** is a member of a 60s soul group in a musical-comedy-drama with an unexpected twist.

JACK, DR.
DOCTOR JACK (1922, Silent)—**Harold Lloyd** prescribes sunshine, good cheer and common sense for many of his patients. He decides the proper treatment for an invalid girl is excitement, which he supplies, dressing and acting like an escaped lunatic. It works.

JACK
JACK AND THE BEANSTALK (1917, Silent, Fox); (1952, Warner Brothers)-**Francis Carpenter** appears in a kiddy version of the fairy tale and **Lou Costello** is his usual nitwit self in his interpretation of the giant killer.

JACK
JACK, SAM AND PETE (1919, Silent, GB, Pollock-Daring)—**Percy Moran** and two other cowboys rescue a kidnapped child from a gang of jewel thieves.

JACK
JACK THE GIANT KILLER (1962, UA)—**Kerwin Mathews** fights giants, monsters, and an evil magician on the way to rescuing a grateful princess.

JACK
JULIA HAS TWO LOVERS (1990, South Gate)—When **David Charles** asks his live-in lover Daphna Kastner to marry him, she angers him by putting him off. She angers him more by taking up with David Duchovny, who enters their life when he misdials her phone number.

JACK
JUNGLE TRAIL OF THE SON OF TARZAN (1923, Silent, National Films)—Now living in England as Lord Greystoke, Tarzan and his wife Jane are protected from an old enemy by their son **Gordon Griffith**.

JACK
MR. MOM (1983, 20th Century Fox)—When he loses his job, **Michael Keaton** stays home, minding the house and three kids, while his wife Teri Garr goes to work for an advertising agency. Everything is predictable but amusingly presented.

JACK, 14TH EARL OF GURNEY
THE RULING CLASS (1972, GB, Avco Embassy)—**Peter O'Toole**, a paranoid schizophrenic who believes he's God, inherits an earldom.

JACK
THEIR OWN DESIRE (1929, MGM)—When Belle Bennett discovers that her father is having an affair, she takes her mother away to a resort where Bennett meets and falls in love with **Robert Montgomery**. Wouldn't you just know it, his mother is the mistress of her father.

JACK
THEY LEARNED ABOUT WOMEN (1930, MGM)—After the season, baseball star **Joseph T. Schenck** and his teammate become successes in vaudeville as singers. They both fall in love with the same girl, but it's another woman, a vamp, who breaks them up.

JACKAL, THE
THE DAY OF THE JACKAL (1973, GB, Universal)—Assassin **Edward Fox** is hired to murder General Charles De Gaulle. He doesn't succeed you know—and that's one of the reasons the film isn't as suspenseful as it should have been.

JACKI
GOODBYE GEMINI (1970, GB, Cinerama)—**Judy Geeson** and her twin Martin Potter become involved with blackmail, homosexuality and murder.

JACKIE
JACKIE (1921, Silent, Fox)—**Shirley Mason** is a Russian waif in New York with a talent for dancing. She dances in the street for pennies, while a crippled boy plays an accordion. A wealthy young man struck with her talent and beauty pays for an operation for the boy, makes a star of Mason and marries her.

JACKIE
THE LITTLE ONES (1965, GB, Columbia)—**Carl Gonzales** and Kim Smith run away to Liverpool, when their parents are cruel to them.

JACKIE
SO YOUNG, SO BAD (1950, UA)—In her movie debut, **Anne Jackson** is one of several juvenile delinquent girls abused by a sadistic matron, and treated with kindness by psychiatrist Paul Henreid.

JACKSON, ACTION
ACTION JACKSON (1988, Lorimar)—Detroit cop, **Carl Weathers**, slow to anger, is out to get a power mad automobile executive, whose henchmen are killing the leaders of the automobile union. The picture has all the action and violence anyone could hope for and Vanity to give men someone to think about in case they get bored.

JACKSON, AL
THE SINGING KID (1936, Warner Brothers)—Either **Al Jolson** was losing his touch or audiences were becoming more demanding, because this star vehicle wasn't very successful. Jolson is a Broadway star, who heads for a rest in the country, when he loses his voice. He gets it back as well as a new love, and returns to the stage in triumph.

JACKSON, ANDREW & RACHEL DONALDSON ROBARDS
THE PRESIDENT'S LADY (1953, 20th Century Fox)—The film deals with the heartache experienced by **Charlton Heston** and **Susan Hayward** when it is found that their marriage is not legal because her first husband had not divorced her as he had claimed. She dies before she can go to Washington with Heston as the new President.

JACKSON, CHARLIE
THE NUT (1921, Silent, UA)—Before **Douglas Fairbanks** found his niche in costume adventure pictures, he appeared in contemporary life comedies such as this. He's a wealthy young man, who is more hinderance than help to Marguerite De La Motte, a sociologist with some new ideas about how to turn slum kids into decent citizens.

JACKSON, DEXTER
LIVIN' LARGE (1991, Goldwyn)—Young Atlanta homeboy **T.C Carson** accidently wins a chance to appear as a TV news reporter. Ratings-mad Blanche Baker re-molds him, but he finds that success in the white-man's world requires him to sell his friends and his soul.

JACKSON, ELROY JR.

THE LAST AMERICAN HERO (1973, 20th Century Fox)—**Jeff Bridges**, son of a jailed North Carolina moonshiner, takes to racing to raise money to get his father out of prison. He becomes a very successful stock car racer, complete with a wealthy promoter and groupie girlfriend.

JACKSON, JEEP

IDOL ON PARADE (1959, GB, Columbia)—When singer **Anthony Newley** is drafted, his agent arranges to smuggle him out of camp so he can still give concerts.

JACKSON, JOHN "JOKER"

THE DEFIANT ONES (1958, UA)—When racist **Tony Curtis** and black Sidney Poitier escape from a truck taking them to prison, still chained together, they must learn some tolerance. It's not just that they develop respect and concern for each other, the brotherhood message is handled intelligently and dramatically.

JACKSON, JUNIOR & "JARRING JACK"

THAT'S MY BOY (1951, Paramount)—**Jerry Lewis** is not all his football loving father **Eddie Mayehoff** could want in a son, but with the help of Lewis' athletic college roommate Dean Martin, Jerry makes Dad proud.

JACKSON, LOUIS

OCEAN'S ELEVEN (1960, Warner Brothers)—**Clem Harvey** has one of the more minor roles as one of twelve army buddies who plot to rob five of Las Vegas' casinos on New Year's Eve.

JACKSON, RONNIE

MY FAVORITE BRUNETTE (1947, Paramount)—Baby photographer **Bob Hope**, mistaken for a tough private eye, finds himself involved with beautiful Dorothy Lamour and a gang of villains, who frame him for murder.

JACKSON, SHOELESS JOE

EIGHT MEN OUT (1988, Orion)—"Say it ain't so, Joe" is the mournful plea of a young fan of the Chicago White Sox outfielder, who may have been the greatest hitter the game ever knew. Played by **D.B. Sweeney**, he's just one of the eight banned from baseball for life for throwing the 1919 World Series.

JACKSON, TIGE

MARVIN AND TIGE (1983, Major)—**Gibran Brown** is an aimless eleven year old who tries to kill himself. He's taken in by loser John Cassavetes.

JACKSON, TNT

TNT JACKSON (1975, New World)—Ex-Playmate **Jeanne Bell**, a voluptuous karate expert, is searching for her brother. Guys into pain will just love her.

JACKSON, WYN & SLATE

SLATE, WYN AND ME (1987, Australia, Hemdale)—**Simon Burke** and **Martin Sachs**, two hell-raising Australian brothers, rob a bank, and shoot a policeman. They throw Sigrid Thornton, a witness to their crime, into the trunk of their car, and make their flight to the Outback. She makes the most of her predicament.

JACOB TWO-TWO

JACOB TWO-TWO MEETS THE HOODED FANG (1979, Canada, Gulkin) -Youngster **Stephen Rosenberg** fantasizes that he has been sentenced for two years, two months, two weeks, two days, two hours and two minutes to a dungeon guarded by the Hooded Fang for insulting some adults.

JACOBOWSKY, S.I.

ME AND THE COLONEL (1958, Columbia)—Jewish **Danny Kaye** and an anti-semitic Polish Colonel must work together during a WWII crisis.

JACOBS, CHARLIE

BAD CHARLESTON CHARLIE (1973, International Cinema)—Dumb coal miner **Ross Hagen** becomes a dumb gangster during the 1920s.

JACOBS, RYNN

THE LITTLE GIRL WHO LIVES DOWN THE LANE (1977, Canada, Rank)—Child molester Martin Sheen menaces little **Jodie Foster**.

JACOBY, MRS.

A MAJORITY OF ONE (1961, Warner Brothers)—Widowed, Jewish, Brooklyn mother **Rosalind Russell** has an unlikely romance with a widowed Japanese diplomat in Tokyo. Neither the casting of Russell nor Alec Guinness as the Japanese diplomat was exactly inspired.

JACQUE, ANNA

THREE ON A COUCH (1966, Columbia)—**Gila Golan** is one of psychiatrist Janet Leigh's man-hating patients, who simply can't be left behind, while Leigh and her artist fiance Jerry Lewis go to Paris for a honeymoon. To deal with Golan's problem, Lewis disguises himself and becomes her boyfriend, thus solving her problems and one-third of his.

JACQUELINE

GIRL IN THE STREET (1938, GB, Gaumont)—In this film called LONDON MELODY in Great Britain, **Anna Neagle** is a street performer taken in by a diplomat Tulio Carminati, who pays for her dancing lessons. He takes the blame for the failure of his colleague, whom he believes Neagle loves. She realizes she loves Carminati and follows him when he leaves the country.

JACQUELINE (Fleuriot)

MADAME X (1929, MGM); (1937, MGM); THE TRIAL OF MADAME X (1948, GB, EPC British); (1966, Universal)—**Ruth Chatterton, Gladys George, Mara Russell** and **Lana Turner** each starred in a version of Frenchman Alexandre Bisson's tearjerking story of a married woman whose affair with a diplomat leads her into a life of degradation, ending when she is defended against a murder charge by the son she had lost when he was a child. He never knows who she is. In the 1966 film, Turner's character is named Holly Parker.

JAFFERY

JAFFERY (1916, Silent, Frohman Amusement Corp.)—When an author dies he leaves a manuscript for a novel with C. **Aubrey Smith**, who uses this as an opportunity to make something of himself and win the girl he has long loved.

JAGUAR

JAGUAR LIVES (1979, American International)—**Joe Lewis** is another karate expert fighting drug cartels.

JAKE

FIRST BORN (1984, Paramount)—Teenage **Christopher Collet** must cope with his divorced mother's dangerous affair with a real lout, who moves in and takes over.

JAKE

JAKE THE PLUMBER (1927, Silent, R-C Pictures)—**Jess Devorska** is an apprentice to an Irish plumber. He must support his widowed mother, and hopes to marry Sharon Lynn and earn enough to support her entire family. Due to a series of strange circumstances, he rides a horse to victory in a big race, which leads to the fulfillment of his dreams.

JAKE

THE WHOOPEE BOYS (1986, Paramount)—**Michael O'Keefe** and his buddy try to break into Palm Beach society. He's a crude stinker.

JAMES, ALLEN *See* **JAMES ALLEN**

JAMES, BOBBIE JO

BOBBIE JO AND THE OUTLAW (1976, American International) - Carhop **Lynda Carter**, looking for some excitement, teams up with Marjoe Gortner and his gang to do a little robbing and killing.

JAMES, CAPT.

THE MAN IN THE WATER (1963, Crown Int.)—**Mark Stevens**, a charter boat captain out of Key West, Florida, smuggles a group of Cuban refugees into the U.S., and loses his license.

JAMES, FRANK

THE RETURN OF FRANK JAMES (1940, 20th Century Fox); THE LONG RIDERS (1980, UA)—**Henry Fonda** had played Frank James in JESSE JAMES, which starred Tyrone Power in the title role. In the sequel, he continues his outlaw ways, while seeking to avenge his brother's death at the hands of the Ford Brothers. The producers of the 1980 movie thought it would be novel to have real life brothers play the various outlaw brothers, who participated in the Great Northfield, Minnesota bank hold-up. **Stacy Keach** and his brother James Keach were the notorious James brothers, Frank and Jesse, respectively.

JAMES, IRENE

ONCE A SINNER (1952, GB, Argyle/Hoffberg)—Adventurer **Pat Kirkwood** lures a bank clerk from his fiancee, and marries him. She later leaves him for a former lover, but he follows her, and becomes involved in a murder. Kirkwood kills herself to keep him out of the case.

JAMES, JESSE

JESSE JAMES AS THE OUTLAW (1921, Silent, Mesco); JESSE JAMES UNDER THE BLACK FLAG (1921, Silent, Mesco)—**Jesse James, Jr.**; JESSE JAMES (1927, Silent, Paramount)—**Fred Thompson**, (1939, 20th Century Fox)—**Tyrone Power**; DAYS OF JESSE JAMES (1939, Republic)—**Donald Barry**; BAD MEN OF MISSOURI (1941, Warner Brothers)—**Alan Baxter**; JESSE JAMES AT BAY (1941, Republic)—**Roy Rogers**; I SHOT JESSE JAMES (1949, Lippert)—**Reed Hadley**; THE GREAT JESSE JAMES RAID (1953, Lippert)—**Willard Parker**; THE TRUE STORY OF JESSE JAMES (1957, 20th Century Fox)—**Robert Wagner**; YOUNG JESSE JAMES (1960, 20th Century Fox)—**Ray Stricklyn**; JESSE JAMES MEETS FRANKENSTEIN'S DAUGHTER (1966, Embassy)—**John Lupton**; THE LONG RIDERS (1980, UA)—**James Keach**—As with many legendary western characters, the real story of Jesse James probably still hasn't been told, but a lot of fine action has been generated in trying to tell the tale of the bank and train robber, who was shot in the back by one of his own men, Bob Ford. And as Carl Sandburg put it, "the dirty little coward, shot Mr. Howard and now poor Jesse is in his grave."

JAMES, LESLIE

A GIRL MUST LIVE (1939, GB, Gainsborough)—**Margaret Lockwood** runs away from a Swiss finishing school, and saves an earl from a blackmailing scheme.

JAMES, LILY BRANNEL

A LIFE OF HER OWN (1950, MGM)—**Lana Turner** is a New York model who rises to the top of her profession, but her love life is anything but successful.

JAMES, UNCLE *See* **COL. BOGEY**

JAMESON, DAVID

THE MAN WHO RETURNED TO LIFE (1942, Columbia)—**John Howard** picks up his family, leaving a southern town for California without telling anyone. Later he reads that a man is about to be hanged for his murder. He returns in time to save the man.

JAMIE

NEW GIRL IN TOWN (1977, New World)—**Monica Gayle** is willing to do anything to achieve her goal of becoming a country and western singing star.

JAMIE

SON OF ROBIN HOOD (1959, GB, 20th Century Fox)—When he returns from the Crusades, **Al Hedison** finds England in danger of being taken over by David Farrar. Al takes the identity of the son of Robin Hood to oppose the usurper.

JAMIL

THE BARBARIAN (1933, MGM)—**Ramon Novarro**, a Bedouin leader temporarily on the outs with his father, has a brief affair with American Myrna Loy in Cairo.

JAMISON, MIKE

THREE GUYS NAMED MIKE (1951, MGM)—You probably guessed that **Howard Keel** is one of three guys named Mike, who are out to win stewardess Jane Wyman.

JAMISON, LAWRENCE

DIRTY ROTTEN SCOUNDRELS (1988, Orion)—Suave conman **Michael Caine** specializes in separating wealthy women from their money. He's challenged by American conman Steve Martin for Caine's turf in the south of France. A contest is arranged to determine who's the best flim-flam man.

JAN

G.I. JANE (1951, Lippert)—Army inductee Tom Neal dreams about a romance with WAC **Jean Porter** before it happens for real.

JAN

THREE IN THE ATTIC (1968, American Int.)—**Maggie Thrett** is one of three girls, who takes revenge on a Romeo, who was bedding all three at the same time. They lock him in an attic so they may all use him at their leisure. We know some guys who would welcome such torture.

JANE

THE ADVENTURES OF JANE (1949, GB, New World/Keystone)—**Christabel Leighton-Porter** always seems to be losing her clothes. She's duped into smuggling jewels into England by a crook.

JANE

GIRL FROM AVENUE A (1940, 20th Century Fox)—At the turn of the century, street waif **Jane Withers** is taken into the home of a wealthy eccentric, whose son she inspires to write a play.

JANE

NEARLY EIGHTEEN (1943, Monogram)—**Gale Storm** has the talent to be a singer, but as she's not yet eighteen she can't work in nightclubs. She decides to enter a music academy for more training while waiting for her 18th birthday but now she's too old. She opts for acting younger rather than older than she really is, and has an affair with one of her teachers.

JANE

THE RANGER AND THE LADY (1940, Republic)—**Jacqueline Wells (Julie Bishop)**, runs a wagon train, and has an on-again, off-again relationship with Texas Ranger Roy Rogers.

JANE

SCARED TO DEATH (1947, Screen Guild)—In this film told in flashbacks, **Joyce Compton** is a corpse who tells the audience how she got that way.

JANET

ANYBODY'S BLONDE (1931, Action)—Lonelyhearts columnist **Dorothy Revier** takes a job as a dancer in a nightclub to find her boxer brother's murderer.

JANET

THE COUNTESS OF MONTE CRISTO (1934, Universal)—**Fay Wray**, who has a bit part in a film, borrows the star's wardrobe. With friend Nancy Kelly, posing as her maid, she passes herself off as a countess.

JANET

TWO WIVES AT ONE WEDDING (1961, GB, Paramount)—When physician Gordon Jackson marries socialite **Christine Gregg**, Frenchwoman Lisa Daniely shows up after the ceremony claiming to be married to Jackson.

JANEWAY, CLARISSA

MAN CRAZY (1927, Silent, First National)—Daughter of a prominent New England family, **Dorothy Mackaill** prefers a truck driver to the scion of a wealthy family her grandmother has in mind for her. When her truckdriver sweetheart is hijacked by gangsters, she helps him return the favor.

JANIS

NIGHT CALL NURSES (1974, New World)—**Alana Collins** is one of three nurses working the night shift in a psychiatric clinic, which is a hot bed of sex and violence.

JANSSEN, ANNA

THE WOMAN GOD CHANGED (1921, Silent, Paramount)—After spending most of the picture being wild and wicked, **Seena Owen** is regenerated.

JANUARY, CAPTAIN

CAPTAIN JANUARY (1924, Silent, Principal); (1936, 20th Century Fox)—In 1924, Captain January is the name given to the little girl played by **Baby Peggy** rescued from the sea by a kindly old lighthouse keeper. He attempts to raise the child as his own. In 1936, the name is reserved for **Guy Kibbee**, the lighthouse keeper, and Shirley Temple is the child he rescues.

JARED-SYN

METALSTORM: THE DESTRUCTION OF JARED-SYN (1983, Universal) Set sometime in the future, megalomaniac **Mike Preston** is intent on ruling the world. A hunter is sent to deny him his desire.

JARMIN, RICK

BIRD ON A WIRE (1990, Universal)—Those who went to this movie to view **Mel Gibson** and Goldie Hawn got all it had to offer. The story about federal witness Gibson being chased by murdering drug runners isn't exciting, and the attempts at humor are old hat.

JARRET, HOLLIS

STRANGER AT MY DOOR (1956, Republic)—Western preacher **MacDonald Carey** tries to reform outlaw Skip Homeier.

JARRETT, JOE

FOUR FOR TEXAS (1963, Warner Brothers)—**Dean Martin** portrays his usual good-natured lecher role as a con-man battling rival Frank Sinatra for control of a Texas town.

JASON

FRIDAY THE 13TH PART VIII—JASON TAKES MANHATTAN (1989, Paramount)—The ski-masked killing maniac, played by **Kane Holder**, is back up to his old tricks, aboard a ship full of high school seniors, bound for a class trip to Manhattan.

JASON

THE ICE PIRATES (1984, MGM/UA)—At some point in the future, water becomes the most valuable commodity. **Robert Urich** plots to get himself some.

JASON

JASON AND THE ARGONAUTS (1963, GB, Columbia)—**Todd Armstrong** has many adventures as he searches for the Golden Fleece. Some of the special effects are very clever.

JASON

YANKEE PASHA (1954, Universal)—**Jeff Chandler** follows Rhonda Fleming to Marseilles, where he learns she's been kidnapped by Barbary pirates. He's off in a flash to rescue his lady love.

JAY

THEY'RE PLAYING WITH FIRE (1984, New World)—English professor **Eric Brown** enlists the help of a student to kill his mother for his inheritance.

JEAN

LITTLE BOY LOST (1953, Paramount)—In this overly sentimental tearjerker, **Christian Fourcade** may be the son that American reporter Bing Crosby has never seen. His wife was killed in an air raid in France during the war, and what happened to the boy Bing doesn't know. Bing discovers Christian at an orphanage and adopts him, even when he realizes the boy is not his.

JEANNE

GUARD THAT GIRL (1935, Columbia)—Detective Robert Allen is looking into a bow and arrow murder attempt on the life of heiress **Barbara Kent** . Robin Hood, perhaps?

JEANNETTE

THE GAIETY GIRLS (1938, GB, UA)—In a very predictable, mistaken identity story, Parisian chorus girl **Patricia Ellis** pretends to be having an affair with a millionaire banker to keep the show's backers at bay. When the millionaire hears of her claim, he poses as a reporter to get to know her and falls for her for real.

JEANNIE

GIRL FROM MANDALAY (1936, Republic)—Nightclub entertainer **Kay Linaker** marries Englishman Conrad Nagel in Mandalay, after his fiancee gives him the brush. She's not well-received by others in his social set until she shows what she's made of during an epidemic.

JEANNIE

THE GIRL NEXT DOOR (1953, 20th Century Fox)—Broadway star **June Haver** moves next door to cartoonist Dan Dailey. His young son, Billy Gray, objects to the romance which grows between them.

JEANNIE

LADIES MUST LOVE (1933, Universal)—When four young girls find the going tough, they sign a contract agreeing to split everything they earn four ways. Then **June Knight** gets a job in a nightclub and meets a rich young man who showers her with expensive gifts. Guess how much Knight thinks of that contract now?

JEANNINE

SIBLING RIVALRY (1990, Columbia)—In this amusing black comedy, slow-witted **Jami Gertz** and her older sister Kirstie Alley aren't the only set of siblings, but they are representative.

JEDD, REV. RICHARD

DANDY DICK (1935, GB, British Int.)—When village vicar **Will Hay** tries to raise money for a steeple for his church, he's accused of trying to fix horse races.

JEDDA

JEDDA, THE UNCIVILIZED (1956, Australia, Distributors Corp. of America)—Aborigine **Narla Knough**, brought up by kindly white farmers, runs off to the wilds, when she falls in love with a tribesman.

JEEVES

THANK YOU JEEVES (1936, 20th Century Fox); STEP LIVELY, JEEVES (1937, 20th Century Fox)—**Arthur Treacher** is excellent as P.G. Wodehouse's disdainful butler. In the first film, he helps his employer David Niven bring secret-stealing spies to justice. In the second, Treacher is tricked into believing that he's the heir to the fortune of Sir Francis Drake.

JEFF

JOCKS (1987, Crown)—**Perry Lang**, a puritanical rich kid, is on a college tennis team even though he's afraid of being hit by the ball. He, and a few other misfit athletes, are what a coach must work with to build a championship team, or lose his job.

JEFFERSON, LUCILLE & JOHN

MY SON JOHN (1952, Paramount)—**Helen Hayes** dotes on her son **Robert Walker** until the good Catholic woman discovers her son is a godless communist.

JEFFERSON, ROBERT

THE DIRTY DOZEN (1967, GB, MGM)—Ex-professional football player **Jim Brown's** broken-field running ability almost gets him through a suicide mission at a French chateau, filled by high-ranking German officers, but like eleven other of the condemned G.I. convicts, he never returns to receive his pardon.

JEKYLL, EDWARD

THE SON OF DR. JEKYLL (1951, Columbia)—The movie doesn't explain how the highly moral Dr. Jekyll, unmarried at the time he and his alter-ego Mr. Hyde lost his life, had a son. It's just the usual ploy of retelling basically the same horror story set in the next generation. **Louis Hayward** appears as the title character.

JEKYLL, DR. HENRY

DR. JEKYLL AND MR. HYDE (1920, Silent, Paramount); (1932, Paramount); (1941, MGM)—**John Barrymore, Fredric March, Spencer Tracy**; ABBOTT AND COSTELLO MEET DR. JEKYLL AND MR. HYDE (1952, Warner Brothers)—**Boris Karloff**; THE UGLY DUCKLING (1959, GB, Columbia)—**Bernard Brassland**; DR. JE-KYLL AND SISTER HYDE (1971, Hammer)—**Ralph Bates**; DR. JEKYLL'S DUNGEON OF DEATH (1982, New American)—**James Mathers**; JEKYLL AND HYDE . . . TOGETHER AGAIN (1982, Para-mount)—**Mark Blankfield**; As can be seen, many efforts have been made to bring to the screen the conflict of good and evil within the soul of man, which Robert Louis Stevenson's character was able to separate into two persons. Unfortunately, the evil side destroys the good.

JENKINS, AMARILLY

AMARILLY OF CLOTHESLINE ALLEY (1918, Silent, Artcraft)—**Mary Pickford** is the sweetheart of a section on the east side of New York known as "Clothesline Alley." She briefly becomes involved with a society swell, but soon learns that they are not meant for each other.

JENKINS, BILL HENRY

BILL HENRY (1919, Silent, Paramount)—**Charles Ray** made a comfortable living playing true-hearted country bumpkins, as in this rural comedy.

JENKINS, DOC

SONGWRITER (1984, Tri-Star)—To no one's surprise country and western singer **Willie Nelson** becomes a smash country and western singer in this ho-hum movie.

JENKINS, JOE

MISTER CINDERELLA (1936, MGM)—In this silly slapstick film, **Jack Haley** is a barber posing as a millionaire.

JENKINS, LINDA

UNDER AGE (1964, American Int.)—**Judy Adler's** mother is charged with rape for encouraging sexual activity between the 14-year-old girl and her Mexican boyfriend.

JENKINS, MARK

THE BATTLING FOOL (1924, Silent, Perfection)—**William Fair-banks**, a minister's son, gets the idea of becoming a professional boxer, when he is able to protect a girl from a gang of ruffians. He goes on to become a champ.

JENKINSON, ISIAH

SO LONG, BLUE BOY (1973, Maryon/Dakota)—Gay sculptor **Rick Gates** has an affair with a professor, until the latter is accidently killed. Then Gates takes up with one of his models, but this one decides he prefers women.

JENNIE

JENNIE (1941, 20th Century Fox)—When **Virginia Gilmore** marries into the family of set-in-his-ways, household tyrant Ludwig Stossel, she organizes a strike by the family members.

JENNIFER

I MARRIED A WITCH (1942, Paramount/UA)—**Veronica Lake** is very fetching as a 17th century witch, reincarnated as a 1942 vamp, out to take revenge on the man who had her condemned and burned. She ruins the career and life of the fellow's ancestor, ambitious politician Fredric March.

JENNIFER

I SPIT ON YOUR GRAVE (1983, Cinemagic)—Having been repeat-edly raped by a gang of men at a resort, **Camille Keaton** goes on a murderous rampage, taking revenge against her attackers.

JENNIFER

NO PLACE FOR JENNIFER (1950, GB, Pathe)—Twelve-year-old **Janette Scott** runs away when her parents divorce.

JENNIFER

WAITRESS (1982, Troma)—Busty blonde **Carol Bever** is one of three young women working as waitresses in a New York restaurant. Their lives and loves are depicted in this comedy.

JENNINGS, AL

AL JENNINGS OF OKLAHOMA (1951, Columbia)—Oklahoma brothers **Dan Duryea** and Dick Foran turn to a life of crime after their home is attacked by renegade Union soldiers. This biopic has little to do with the life of the brutal Oklahoma outlaw Al Jennings.

JENNINGS, DAVE & GUS

MY PAL GUS (1952, 20th Century Fox)—Wealthy divorced **Richard Widmark** falls in love and marries Joanne Dru, his son **George "Foghorn" Winslow's** teacher. Widmark's former wife shows up and demands a lot of money, or she'll get the courts to force him to give up their son. Realizing how much the boy means to him, Widmark pays up.

JENNINGS, JOE

THE WILD PAIR (1987, Trans World Entertainment)—FBI agent **Beau Bridges** teams with ghetto cop Bubba Smith to get the goods on a drug king-pin.

JENNY (LITTLE BRITCHES)

CATTLE ANNIE AND LITTLE BRITCHES (1981, Hemdale/UATC)—**Diane Lane** and her friend Amanda Plummer head west to join up with what's left of the Dalton gang. The girls get them to pull a few more jobs.

JENNY

THE DEVONSVILLE TERROR (1983, MPM/New West)—The new teacher in the town of Devonsville, **Suzanne Love**, finds herself dealing with the curse of a witch of 300 years ago.

JENNY

JENNIFER ON MY MIND (1971, UA)—Bored WASP **Tippy Walker** takes up with aimless Jewish Michael Brandon. He introduces her to the drug world which ultimately results with her death.

JENSON, BOB

MAN ACCUSED (1959, UA)—**Ronald Howard**, engaged to a baronet's daughter, is framed for murder.

JEREMY

THE HIGHWAYMAN (1957, Allied Artists/Monogram)—Nobleman **Philip Friend** masquerades as a highwayman in 1760s England in order to help his oppressed people.

JERICHO, JACK

THE PICKUP ARTIST (1987, 20th Century Fox)—**Robert Downey**, a womanizer who practices pickup lines in front of a mirror, meets his match in Molly Ringwald—or does he?

JERILEE

THE LONELY LADY (1983, KGA Industries)—**Pia Zadora's** husband financed this film about the trials and tribulations of a young woman working toward her goal of becoming a film star. Unfortunately for Pia, art doesn't imitate life.

JEROME, JOSIE

ONLY A SHOP GIRL (1922, Silent, C.B.C. Film)—**Mae Busch** is accused of the murder of a department store owner, but is cleared when her sister makes a death bed confession to the crime.

JERRY

THE BLACK KLANSMAN (1966, US Films)—Light-skinned black man **Richard Gildern** is outraged when he learns that his daughter has been killed in a Klan burning of a southern church. He is able to join the Klan chapter responsible and seek his own particular revenge.

JERRY

THE DIVORCEE (1930, MGM)—**Norma Shearer** marries newspaperman Chester Morris, but at the time of their third anniversary she learns that he's having an affair. She turns to her husband's best friend for comfort. Soon they obtain a divorce and go their separate ways, but eventually are reconciled.

JERRY

DON'T CALL ME LITTLE GIRL (1921, Silent, Realart)—When **Mary Miles Minter** gets a look at her aunt's fiance, she decides he's just the lad for her. At the wedding Minter gets her aunt to marry the best man, the one she loved all along, and Mary gets the groom.

JERRY

GOLD DIGGERS ON BROADWAY (1929, Warner Brothers)—**Nancy Welford** is one of three showgirl roommates who look for sugar daddies—and have no trouble finding them.

JERRY

LADIES OF WASHINGTON (1944, 20th Century Fox)—Embittered by an unhappy love affair, government girl **Sheila Ryan** takes up with a man, who turns out to be an enemy agent.

JERRY

ONCE YOU KISS A STRANGER (1969, Warner Brothers)—In a reworking of STRANGERS ON A TRAIN, psychotic Carol Lynley kills pro golfer **Paul Burke's** arch rival and expects Burke to follow through on his part of the bargain, by killing her psychiatrist who correctly believes that Lynley should be put away.

JERRY

THEY LEARNED ABOUT WOMEN (1930, MGM)—After playing in the World Series, **Gus Van** and his baseball buddy Joseph T. Schenck become a singing team in Vaudeville. Their partnership is brought to an end by women. They do get back to the World Series the next year, however.

JESSE, SAILOR

A MAN IN THE OPEN (1919, Silent, United Pictures)—**Dustin Farnum** starts out as a sailor, but changes careers and becomes a cowboy, before joining the Texas Rangers in this western thriller.

JESSE, THOMAS S.

THAT MAN'S HERE AGAIN (1937, Warner Brothers)—Inebriated **Hugh Herbert** plays cupid for an elevator operator and a chambermaid.

JESSEL, GEORGIE

LUCKY BOY (1929, Tiffany)—**George Jessel**, a Jewish jeweler's son from the Bronx, breaks into show business by renting his own theater and selling tickets to friends and neighbors. He ultimately gets his wish and becomes a Broadway star, winning the hand of the neighborhood girl he's always loved.

JESSICA

COUNT DRACULA AND HIS VAMPIRE BRIDE (1978, GB, Hammer)—**Joanna Lumley** is the helpmate of the vampire count, played by Christopher Lee, who is now in modern London, developing a new strain of bubonic plague with which to kill everyone on Earth. One neck at a time is just too slow.

JESSICA

JESSICA (1962, UA)—Sexy American midwife **Angie Dickinson's** arrival in a small Sicilian village delights the men but upsets the jealous women. They decide if there are no more babies, then Dickinson will move on.

JESSICA

LET'S SCARE JESSICA TO DEATH (1971, Paramount)—**Zohra Lampert** is taking a rest in the country to recover from a nervous breakdown, but it appears that supernatural forces don't want her to get well.

JESSICA

A SMALL CIRCLE OF FRIENDS (1980, UA)—Sixties Harvard student **Karen Allen** joins her friends Brad Davis and Jameson Parker in a menage-a-trois. They seem to be so compatible on the things they protest—but things don't work out as planned.

JESSIE

MANNEQUIN ON THE MOVE (1991, 20th Century Fox)—A thousand years ago, Bavarian peasant girl **Kristy Swanson** was hexed to prevent her marriage to a prince. She was turned into a statue that finds its way to a Philadelphia department store window. When William Ragsdale removes a necklace from the statue, Swanson returns to life.

JESSON, HILARY

HIS HOUSE IN ORDER (1928, GB, Ideal)—**Ian Hunter** reveres the memory of his first wife, until he learns their son is not his.

JESUS

THE KING OF KINGS (1927, Silent, DeMille); (1961, MGM)—**H.B. Warner** and **Jeffrey Hunter**; JESUS OF NAZARETH (1928, Silent, Ideal)—**Philip Van Loan**; JESUS CHRIST, SUPERSTAR (1973, Universal)—**Ted Neeley**; JESUS (1979, Warner Brothers)—**Brian Deacon**; IN SEARCH OF HISTORIC JESUS (1980, Sunn Classics)—**John Rubenstein**; THE LAST TEMPTATION OF CHRIST (1988, Universal)—**Willem Dafoe**—Appearing as Jesus Christ can be quite a strain on an actor. With such strong and disparate feelings about Jesus among the public, the impersonator is bound to disappoint, upset and even enrage a majority of viewers. Poor Jeffrey Hunter got stuck with the tag "I was a teenage Jesus" as a result of his performance. Ted Neeley in the rock opera was seen as some kind of wimp, and Willem Dafoe was hated by millions, who refused to see his picture but felt compelled to condemn it, as they heard it concentrated too much on Jesus as a sexual man.

JEZEBEL

JEZEBEL'S KISS (1990, Glickenhaus)—If the idea of this film is that buxom **Katherine Barrese** wishes to take revenge against the men who killed her beloved grandfather when she was eight, why does she have sex with each of them? Could it be the real intention is to show as much of her flesh as possible?

JEZEBEL

SINS OF JEZEBEL (1953, Lippert)—Poor, beautiful **Paulette Goddard** deserved better than being miscast in this dreadful costume piece about the Biblical princess, who worships the god Baal and marries the king of Israel, causing him no end of trouble with the one true God.

JIGGS

BRINGING UP FATHER (1928, Silent, MGM)—**J. Farrell MacDonald**; (1946, Monogram); JIGGS AND MAGGIE IN SOCIETY (1948, Monogram); JIGGS AND MAGGIE OUT WEST (1950, Monogram) —**Joe Yule**—These films, based on the comic strip character created by George McManus, are not very funny, and they weren't much when first released.

JIGGS

THE PEST (1919, Silent, Goldwyn)—At birth **Mabel Normand** and another baby were mixed up. Years later, Normand is able to save her real father, a millionaire from the misery being caused him by his supposed child.

JILL

GIRLS AT SEA (1958, GB, Seven Arts)—**Mary Steele** is one of three girls stranded on board HMS Scotia after an engagement party. When admiral Michael Hordern decides to go to sea with the ship, the captain and crew do their best to hide the girls.

JILL

GIRLS OF LATIN QUARTER (1960, GB, New Realm)—**Jill Ireland** is one of the girls working at a nightclub visited by a timid heir.

JILL

WHAT BECAME OF JACK AND JILL? (1972, GB, 20th Century Fox)—**Vanessa Howard** and her boyfriend attempt to scare to death his grandmother to hurry up his inheritance.

JIM

THE FIGHTING RANGER (1934, Columbia)—**Buck Jones** tracks down the killer of his brother in Mexico. A lot of lead goes a-flying.

JIM

MY FRIEND THE KING (1931, GB, Fox)—Cabdriver **Jerry Verno** poses as a pretty, young countess in order to rescue a young Ruritanian prince from revolutionaries.

JIM

REBEL WITHOUT A CAUSE (1955, Warner Brothers)—Few actors made a bigger impression with just three films (his other screen exposure was little more than as an extra), than did **James Dean**, whose remarkable performance in EAST OF EDEN as the cool loner was followed in his second film as an alienated teenager who couldn't refuse a challenge. He was dead at 24 before his last film GIANT was released, but his legend survives.

JIM/FR. BROWN

WE'RE NO ANGELS (1989, Paramount)—Set near the Canadian border at the time of the Depression, this film, loosely based on the 1955 film of the same name, stars **Sean Penn** and Robert De Niro as two escaped convicts, who somehow are mistaken for priests at a shrine.

JIMINEZ, PEDRO

THE DIRTY DOZEN (1967, GB, MGM)—It's too bad **Trini Lopez** wasn't given a few songs to sing, because he sure had little to do in this action-adventure, other than await his death during a suicide mission of condemned G.I.s.

JIMMY

THE CRY BABY KILLER (1958, Allied Artists)—In his first movie role, 21-year-old **Jack Nicholson** shoots up two hoods, and then holes up in the rest room of a drive-in theater with three hostages.

JIMMY

DADDY'S BOYS (1988, Concorde)—Morose **Daryl Haney** and whore Laura Burkett find that robbing and killing is a sexual turn-on.

JIMMY

JIMMY BOY (1935, GB, Universal)—**Jimmy O'Dea**, an elevator operator in a London Hotel, thwarts a ring of spies.

JIMMY

JIMMY THE KID (1982, New World)—When **Gary Coleman**, the brilliant son of wealthy parents, is kidnapped, his bungling abductors teach him how to enjoy being a kid.

JIMMY

MIRACLE KID (1942, Producers Releasing Corp.)—**Tom Neal** is pushed into the boxing ring and it almost costs him the girl he loves.

JIMMY

PONY EXPRESS RIDER (1976, Doty-Drayton)—In order to avenge the death of his father, **Stewart Petersen** joins the Pony Express.

JIMMY

SHE MARRIED A COP (1939, Republic)—Irish singer **Phil Regan** appears as an Irish cop with a pleasant voice, who is hired to be the voice of a cartoon character "Paddy the Pig." He sees himself as a bit too good for such a role.

JIMMY

THEY MET IN A TAXI (1936, Columbia)—When Fay Wray accidently takes the valuable pearls of a society woman, she takes refuge in the cab of **Chester Morris**, which leads to a romance.

JIMMY

THREE LEGIONNAIRES (1937, General)—**Lyle Talbot** is one of two American Army buddies in Russia, who have a lot of trouble with the Soviets.

JIMMY

TAKING CARE OF BUSINESS (1990, Buena Vista)—Soon to be paroled convict **James Belushi** takes an early furlough in order to see the Chicago Cubs in a World Series game. (Who wouldn't?) He finds the filofax of compulsive businessman Charles Grodin. He assumes Grodin's identity and lives the good life, complete with willing bed partner Loryn Locklin, the sexy daughter of Grodin's boss.

JIMMY *See* J

JIMMY

TWO SMART MEN (1940, GB, Anglo Int.)—**Leslie Fuller** and his partner in an unsuccessful casting agency act as butler and cook for a friend's social climbing sister with all the to-be-expected results.

JIMMY

WISE GUYS (1937, GB, 20th Century Fox)—**Jimmy Gold** and his pal Charlie Naughton try to win enough money at the races to buy a loan company, but they are outsmarted by a couple of crooks.

JINX

THE JINX (1919, Silent, Goldwyn)—**Mabel Normand** does odd jobs around a circus, such as manicuring an elephant's toenails. Everything goes wrong for the poor girl, but things change when the show's wild man proves his love for her.

JILL

BABY, IT'S YOU (1983, Paramount)—Up-and-coming screen personality **Rosanna Arquette's** high school romance has to be put on hold when she goes away to college.

JO

CAFE HOSTESS (1940, Columbia)—**Ann Dvorak** is the mistress of the murdering rat who runs the cafe where she works for the underworld.

JO

A DAY IN THE DEATH OF JOE EGG (1972, GB, Columbia)—**Elizabeth Robillard** portrays a spastic child, whom schoolteacher father Alan Bates tries to kill.

JO

I MET A MURDERER (1939, GB, Grand National)—Author **Pamela Kellino** gives shelter and more than a little comfort to fugitive farmer James Mason, who has killed his shrewish wife.

JO

JO, THE CROSSING SWEEPER (1918, Silent, GB, Barker)—**Unity Moore** dies of grief when she is accused of murdering an attorney, who revealed the existence of a child from a former marriage.

JOAN

CAPTIVE GIRL (1950, Columbia)—Blonde jungle goddess **Anita Lhoest** is rescued by Jungle Jim from the clutches of a mad medicine man.

JOAN

CAREER GIRL (1944, Producers Releasing Corp.)—**Frances Langford** is in New York from Kansas City to become a star and despite the usual setbacks she's signed to appear in a Broadway show.

JOAN

JOAN OF PARIS (1942, RKO)—**Michelle Morgan** and Paul Henreid make their U.S. film debut in this story of Parisian barmaid Morgan, who sacrifices her life to help Free French forces flyer Henreid escape from the Gestapo.

JOAN

JOAN OF PLATTSBURG (1918, Silent, Goldwyn)—Orphan **Mabel Normand** is given a copy of the life of Joan of Arc. This inspires the patriotic little girl to serve her country. She does so, when she overhears some spies, whom she reports to the authorities.

JOAN

THE LITTLE BALLERINA (1951, GB, Gaumont/British Lion)—**Yvonne Marsh** is a poor girl, who realizes her dream of becoming a ballerina.

JOAN

POPE JOAN (1972, GB, Columbia)—Raped German **Liv Ullman** poses as a monk, and is ultimately nominated Pope.

JOAN

SWEETHEART OF THE NAVY (1937, Grand National)—**Cecilia Parker**, a singer in a waterfront dive, is helped out of a jam by a group of sailors.

JOAN OF ARC

JOAN THE WOMAN (1916, Silent, Paramount) ; JOAN OF ARC (1948, RKO); SAINT JOAN (1957, UA)—**Geraldine Farrar, Ingrid**

Bergman and **Jean Seberg** each struggled with the demanding role of the Maid of Orleans, who makes the Dauphin King of France, but is betrayed and burned at the stake as a heretic with Church officials doing the dirty work for her enemies. Perhaps the most memorable performance as Joan was French Actress Falconetti in her only film, 1928's THE PASSION OF JOAN OF ARC. Ingrid Bergman was nominated for an Academy Award for her portrayal, but many critics found her performance less than laudable. Seberg could be forgiven if her portrayal was less than superb, she was a complete unknown with no previous experience when director Otto Preminger cast her for the part.

JOANNA

JOANNA (1968, GB, 20th Century Fox)—Amoral London art student **Genevieve Waite** has many affairs, some real, some imagined.

JOANNA

THE STEPFORD WIVES (1975, Columbia)—Would-be liberated woman **Katharine Ross** reluctantly accompanies her husband and kids to the suburb of Stepford. There she finds the women to be totally devoted to their husbands' every whim. She comes to believe that the women are high tech robots and she's soon to be replaced in a similar way.

JOB

CHILDREN OF THE CORN (1984, New World)—**Robby Kiger** is one of a group of juvenile cultists with sacrificial murder on their minds.

JOE

BIG FELLA (1937, GB, Lion-Beaconsfield)—Indolent **Paul Robeson**, known all over Marseilles for his fine singing voice, is hired to find a kidnapped boy. He does, but the boy, who actually has run away, threatens to name Robeson as his kidnapper if he forces him to go home.

JOE

FLATLINERS (1990, Columbia)—Experiencing death and returning seems like a good way to make medical history, but as usually happens in movies in which scientific types meddle in what "should be left to God," there's a down side. Just ask **William Baldwin**.

JOE

PSYCHOS IN LOVE (1987, ICN Bleeker Infinity)—**Carmine Capobianco** despises grapes. He also has problems with women. When his dates find him a bit strange, he kills them. He finally finds the perfect girl for him, Debi Thibeault, who's just as warped and murderous as he is.

JOE

THE SKY PIRATE (1970, Filmmakers)—**Michael McClanthan** hijacks a plane to Cuba, and the audience doesn't know why—by the time they do, they don't care.

JOEY

DELIVERY BOYS (1984, New World)—**Tom Sierchio** is one of three pizza delivery boys, who wish to win a breakdance contest prize of $10,000.

JOEY

JOEY (1985, GB, Satori)—The best thing about this movie with **Neill Barry** as a rock musician, whose father once was a producer of hit records but now is an alcoholic gas station attendant, is the appearances of groups like Silhouettes, Elegants, The Limelights and The Teenagers.

JOEY

KNIGHTS OF THE CITY (1986, New World)—**Nicholas Campbell** is one of the members of Miami street gangs, which fight each other over turf.

JOHANSEN, BILL

BARNACLE BILL (1941, MGM)—Old sailor **Wallace Beery** tries to resist Marjorie Main's plans to marry him.

JOHN

JOHN AND MARY (1969, 20th Century Fox)—**Dustin Hoffman** and Mia Farrow meet in a bar. They don't exchange names, but do spend the night making love. They are reluctant to become involved because of past romantic disappointments. Perhaps they should limit their sex to masturbation. You know what Woody Allen says about it.

JOHN

LITTLE LAURA AND BIG JOHN (1973, Crown Int.)—Former Rock 'n' Roll star **Fabian Forte** makes his film comeback in this comedy BONNIE AND CLYDE-like movie.

JOHN

MY FIRST WIFE (1985, Canada, Spectrafilm)—When his wife of ten years leaves him, **John Hardgreaves** literally goes crazy.

JOHN

THE SAILOR TAKES A WIFE (1946, MGM)—June Allyson marries sailor **Robert Walker**, believing he's a naval hero. Once he's discharged, the glamour wears off, and the couple have a tough time making adjustments to civilian life.

JOHN

STAR REPORTER (1939, Monogram)—When **Warren Hull** inherits a newspaper from his father, who has been murdered by gangsters, he uses it as a weapon to fight crime.

JOHN

TILL WE MEET AGAIN (1944, Paramount)—Pilot **Ray Milland**, shot down over occupied France, is helped in his escape by Barbara Britton, a novice nun posing as his wife.

JOHN

YANKS (1979, Universal)—American officer **William Devane** has a wartime romance in England with married British woman Vanessa Redgrave.

JOHN, SIR/MR. FREDERICK

THE FOOL (1990, GB, Sands)—In a wordy film, 1857 theater critic **Derek Jacobi** engineers a financial scam to show up the monied classes, starts to take himself too seriously and becomes what he hates most.

JOHN, THE BLACK KNIGHT

THE BLACK KNIGHT (1954, Columbia)—Small in stature, **Alan Ladd** doesn't quite live up to expectations of how a knight championing the cause of King Arthur should look. Still, his height probably would have been about right for the time the movie is supposed to take place.

JOHNNIE

THE NITWITS (1935, RKO)—**Bert Wheeler** and Robert Woolsey aren't everybody's cup of tea. Wheeler did have the good sense to have young Betty Grable cast as his girlfriend in this comedy mystery about a blackmailer.

JOHNNY

COOL AS ICE (1991, Universal)—Rapper **Vanilla Ice** and his three motorcycle buddies ride into a small town where he falls for straightlaced beauty Kristin Minter. Her parents' cover, after 20 years in the Witness Protection Program, has just been blown.

JOHNNY

THE FASTEST GUITAR ALIVE (1967, MGM)—The late great **Roy Orbison** is a Confederate spy, who steals a Union shipment of gold. After the war he is viewed as a criminal. Orbison employs, would you believe, a shotgun guitar or is it a guitar shotgun?

JOHNNY

FRANKIE & JOHNNY (1991, Paramount)—Sensitive former con **Al Pacino** takes a job as a short-order cook in a coffee shop where Michelle Pfeiffer works as a waitress. The pair begin a satisfying sexual relationship, but Pacino wants more. Pfeiffer resists, but Pacino proves love is possible for them.

JOHNNY

GO, JOHNNY, GO (1959, Hal Roach)—Orphan **Jimmy Clanton** is taken in by rock 'n' roll disk jockey Alan Freed, who makes a singing star of the lad.

JOHNNY

HER MAN (1930, Pathe)—**Ricardo Cortez**; FRANKIE AND JOHNNY (1936, Republic); (1966, UA)— **Chester Morris** and **Elvis Presley**—Hollywood squeezed just about everything it could from the old saloon song about Frankie and her man Johnny, who did her wrong. In the song Frankie shoots Johnny dead, but you could hardly believe Hollywood would let that happen to someone like Elvis Presley.

JOHNNY

JOHNNY ON THE RUN (1953, GB, International Realist)—Polish orphan **Eugeniuse Chylek** runs away from his cruel foster-mother, and unwittingly becomes the accomplice of thieves. He takes refuge in a Scottish village where he is befriended by the children of an international village.

JOHNNY

JOHNNY TROUBLE (1957, Warner Brothers)—Widowed invalid Ethel Barrymore only lives for the day when her son, who walked out on her and her husband 27 years earlier, will return to her. When the apartment building she lives in is sold to a college as a boy's dormitory, she is allowed to stay. She becomes convinced that one of the freshmen, **Stuart Whitman**, always in trouble, is her grandson. He isn't, but it doesn't matter.

JOHNNY

JOHNNY, YOU'RE WANTED (1958, GB, Anglo-Amalgamated)—Truck driver **John Slater** is implicated, when a hitchhiker to whom he has given a lift is found murdered.

JOHNNY

THE RETURN OF JESSE JAMES (1950, Lippert)—The title is not accurate or this entry would be with the rest of the films about the Missouri badman. **John Ireland** greatly resembles the late Jesse James, a fact the surviving members of the James gang exploit.

JOHNNY

SKI BUM (1971, Avco Embassy)—Ski bum **Zalman King** works at a ski lodge, and has an affair with married Charlotte Rampling. That's about it.

JOHNNY

SMART GUY (1943, Monogram)—In order to look like a good citizen just before being tried on manslaughter charges, **Rick Vallin** adopts a poor newsboy. This leads to a change for the better in his character.

JOHNNY

THE WILD ONE (1953, Columbia)—**Marlon Brando**, a leather jacket motorcycle punk, and two gangs of Hells Angels-like bikers terrorize a small town, until the state police come to the rescue.

JOHNNY-JACK

WHAT BECAME OF JACK AND JILL? (1972, GB, 20th Century Fox)—Having told his grandmother that young people have a plan to eliminate people who reach a certain age, it's no wonder that Mona Washbourne grows suspicious of her grandson **Paul Nicholas's** plans, and writes him out of her will.

JOHNSON, MR.

MR. JOHNSON (1990, Avenue)—Nigerian actor **Maynard Eziashi** is a young African obsessed with things British. He tries as much as possible to model himself on his white British boss, dull and lifeless bureaucrat Pierce Brosnan.

JOHNSON, ADAM

A MAN CALLED ADAM (1966, Embassy)—Jazz musician **Sammy Davis, Jr.** considers himself responsible for a car accident in which his family is killed. He uses the rest of the film to search for some meaning to life.

JOHNSON, AMY

WINGS AND THE WOMAN (1942, GB, RKO)—**Anna Neagle** appears as Britain's pioneering woman aviator, whose marriage to daredevil pilot Jim Mollison (Robert Newton) had plenty of turbulence.

JOHNSON, ANDREW

TENNESSEE JOHNSON (1942, MGM)—**Van Heflin** portrays the uneducated politician from Tennessee who ascends to the presidency on the death of Abraham Lincoln and is impeached.

JOHNSON, BILL

KILL THE UMPIRE (1950, Columbia)—**William Bendix**, a fanatic baseball enthusiast, goes to an umpire school, so he can get paid for being part of what he loves most. But he discovers fans don't always agree with his calls.

JOHNSON, BLONDIE

BLONDIE JOHNSON (1933, Embassy)—**Joan Blondell** is forced to become a hooker after her mother dies. She becomes gun moll to gangster Chester Morris, and ends up in prison.

JOHNSON, BRIAN

THE BREAKFAST CLUB (1985, Universal)—**Anthony Michael Hall** is the grind and nerdy member of a Saturday morning high school detention class. It comes out that he tried to kill himself when he didn't get his usual "A."

JOHNSON, CHARCOAL

BLACK KING (1932, Southland)—**A.B. Comethiere** is a black con man who leads a bogus back-to-Africa movement in order to fleece his followers.

JOHNSON, DIXIE BOY

MINSTREL MAN (1944, Producers Releasing Corp.)—Minstrel singer **Benny Fields** gives his baby daughter up for adoption, when his wife dies bringing the child into the world. When the girl is grown she becomes a singer, and is joined on stage by her long lost father to sing a song he wrote.

JOHNSON, ELEANOR

WOMAN ON THE RUN (1950, Universal)—When **Ann Sheridan's** husband witnesses a gangland slaying, he runs away rather than get involved. Ann goes looking for him when she learns he's suffering from a heart disease. She's not the only one interested in finding her husband.

JOHNSON, HILDY

HIS GIRL FRIDAY (1940, Columbia)—Ace reporter **Rosalind Russell** is giving up her career to marry steady but dull Ralph Bellamy. Her editor and former husband Cary Grant doesn't want to lose her. He talks her into covering an execution of a supposed cop killer. The man escapes and Russell helps prove that he's innocent before setting out with Bellamy.

JOHNSON, JEREMIAH

JEREMIAH JOHNSON (1972, Warner Brothers)—Mexican War veteran **Robert Redford** opts for a life of solitude as a mountain man. He finds that the life is a constant struggle against hostile Indians and the elements.

JOHNSON, LOIS

DESIRABLE (1934, Warner Brothers)—**Jean Muir's** vain, selfish actress mother Verree Teasdale has kept her daughter in a boarding school, rather than let anyone find she has a grown daughter. The cat's out of the bag when Muir shows up to visit mom in New York.

JOHNSON, LYDIA

REFORM GIRL (1933, Tower)—Fresh out of prison, **Noel Johnson** seems intent on returning, as she slips back into a criminal life, this time trying to frame a politician.

JOHNSON, MAGGIE

MY BEST GIRL (1927, Silent, UA)—**Mary Pickford** is the 18-year-old good member of a no-account family. She falls in love with the new clerk at the five-and-ten where she works. He turns out to be the boss's son.

JOHNSON, MONK

FACE OF FIRE (1959, Allied Artists)—While saving a boy from a burning building, **James Whitmore** is horribly burned and disfigured. This results in him being mistreated by his neighbors, turning him into a murderer.

JOHNSON, NAVIN

THE JERK (1979, Universal)—**Steve Martin** sort of grows on you. For many, the first impression of him in this film is that he's indeed a jerk and the movie is bubble-gum comedy. On reflection, one is forced to admit that his portrayal of a man who leaves his family (all black, by the way) to seek fame, fortune and love has some truly amusing moments—more hits than misses.

JOHNSON, PATRICIA "PINKY"

PINKY (1949, 20th Century Fox)—Light-complexioned Negro **Jeanne Crain** returns south after becoming a nurse in the North, because of her love for a white doctor. Crain cares for Ethel Barrymore, who employs Jeanne's grandmother Ethel Waters as a washerwoman. When Barrymore dies, Crain is left some money which is contested in court by the old lady's relatives.

JOHNSON, SALLY

JIMMY AND SALLY (1933, Fox)—**Claire Trevor** helps publicity man Jimmy O'Connor break away from the mobsters, for whom he had been working.

JOHNSON, TEENA

HARDBOILED (1929, Silent, FBO)—Follies showgirl **Sally O'Neill** marries the playboy son of an oil millionaire. She refuses a $100,000 payoff to give the younger man a divorce. As a result her husband is disowned by his father. Later when O'Neill proves she wasn't just a gold-digger, there is a reconciliation all around.

JOLANDA

THE COUNTRY FLAPPER (1922, Silent, Producers Dist. Co.)—Country girl **Dorothy Gish** blackmails the father of her beau to agree to their marriage, by threatening to reveal that the good churchman is a moonshiner.

JOLIET JAKE

THE BLUES BROTHERS (1980, Universal)—Just out of prison, **John Belushi** joins his brother Dan Aykroyd in trying to raise money for a nun who once taught them. In the process, they nearly destroy Chicago.

JOLIFANT, INIGO

THE GOOD COMPANIONS (1933, GB, Gaumont); (1957, GB, AB-Pathe)—**John Gielgud** and **John Fraser** appear as the disillusioned music teacher who, with a middle-aged spinster and a joiner, sponsors a failing concert party. Due to a lot of hard work by its young leading lady, it becomes a success.

JOLLY, PEPPER

PEPPER (1936, 20th Century Fox)—Little Miss Fixit **Jane Withers** improves both the health and disposition of ailing, crotchety millionaire Irvin S. Cobb.

JOLSON, AL

THE JOLSON STORY (1946, Columbia); JOLSON SINGS AGAIN (1949, Columbia)—**Larry Parks** had this one excellent role before his career was ruined by the House Un-American Activities Committee. He was the perfect body through which Al Jolson's marvelous voice passed.

JONATHAN

MAN OF AFRICA (1956, GB, Eden)—Life among pygmies of Uganda is explored in this documentary-style film with **Frederick Bijuerenda** as the title character.

JONATHAN

THE SIDELONG GLANCES OF A PIDGEON KICKER (1970, MGM)—With a title like this, how good does the movie have to be? That depends on one's toleration for another movie about alienation, strange behavior, and casual sex. **Jordan Christopher** does actually kick Central Park pigeons, but only to express his frustration about himself and the world in which he lives. That's about as mean as cow-tipping.

JONATHAN

SWINGTIME JOHNNY (1944, Universal)—The Andrews Sisters help **Peter Cookson** keep his munitions factory safe from saboteurs.

JONATHAN, JOE

THE MAYOR OF 44TH STREET (1942, RKO)—**George Murphy** takes over a dance band booking agency once run by a crook. After making it a successful business, he finds that the former owner, fresh from prison, wants it back.

JONES
THE STORM RIDER (1957, 20th Century Fox)—Former gunman **Scott Brady** is hired by a group of small ranchers to defend them against a big rancher, who plans to steal their land.

JONES, AMOS
AMOS 'N' ANDY (1930, Radio)—**Freeman Gosden** in black face recreates one of his famous radio roles as the gentle owner of the Fresh-Air Taxi Company.

JONES, ANNIE
THE EYES OF ANNIE JONES (1963, GB, 20th Century Fox)—Orphan **Francesca Annis'** extra-sensory perception reveals that the murderer of a mill-owner is her brother's hired man.

JONES, BEN
THE ROUNDERS (1965, MGM)—**Glenn Ford** and his partner Henry Fonda are a pair of ancient and aimless cowboys, who travel around Arizona, hoping to make enough money to open a bar and stay in one place. It doesn't seem likely because of their fondness for loose women and booze. They don't have exactly the kind of success they hoped for, when they take ownership of a horse they hope to race.

JONES, BIFF
THE GOOD HUMOR MAN (1950, Columbia)—Ice cream truck driver **Jack Carson** is seduced by Jean Wallace into taking part in a payroll robbery. It's an enjoyable slapstick comedy.

JONES, BILL
PRIVATE JONES (1933, Universal)—American **Lee Tracy** is drafted and finds himself in the French trenches.

JONES, BILL
THE QUARTERBACK (1940, Paramount)—Shy college lad **Wayne Morris** becomes a hero when his athletic twin replaces him and leads the football team to victory.

JONES, BLACK BELT
BLACK BELT JONES (1974, Warner Brothers)—Exit Bruce Lee, enter **Jim Kelly**, in the slash and chop world of movies. Not that the story matters much in this action-packed violent picture, but Kelly is out for revenge against the mobsters who killed his girl's father, an owner of a Karate school, where Kelly plies his trade.

JONES, BRUTUS
THE EMPEROR JONES (1933, UA)—The great black actor-singer **Paul Robeson** portrays a sleeping car porter, who kills a man in a craps game. He is convicted of murder, and sent to a chain gang from which he escapes. He moves on to a Caribbean island where he sets himself up as a despotic ruler.

JONES, CARMEN
CARMEN JONES (1954, 20th Century Fox)—**Dorothy Dandridge** is the tempestuous Carmen in this all-black version of the Bizet opera. The songs have new words to reflect the fact that the story takes place in the U.S. Harry Belafonte is the black soldier, Joe, who deserts his good girl fiancee from back home for bad, bad Dandridge.

JONES, CASEY
CASEY JONES (1927, Silent, Rayart)—**Ralph Lewis** plays the legendary railroad engineer, made famous in song.

JONES, CHOIR BOY
THREE SAILORS AND A GIRL (1953, Warner Brothers)—**Gordon MacRae** is joined by two gob friends and pretty Jane Powell in a musical remake of the often-filmed THE BUTTER AND EGG MAN.

JONES, CLEOPATRA
CLEOPATRA JONES (1973, Warner Brothers); CLEOPATRA JONES AND THE CASINO OF GOLD (1975, Warner Brothers)—Statuesque **Tamara Jones**, a black U.S. government agent, uses her karate training in her fight against drug pushers. In the sequel she's on the trail of Stella Stevens, the leader of an international narcotics ring.

JONES, CYCLONE
CYCLONE JONES (1923, Silent, Aywon Film)—**Guinn "Big Boy" Williams** falls in love with the daughter of a sheep farmer. She rejects his courting, until he saves her from a runaway horse, and her father from the fury of the local cattle ranchers.

JONES, DOBE
LONE COWBOY (1934, Paramount)—Little Jackie Cooper lives with **Addison Richards** on his ranch, after the latter's wife runs off with Richards' foreman. Later, in a wild gun fight the foreman is killed and Cooper, Richards and his wife are reunited.

JONES, FRANK
THE WHISTLE BLOWER (1987, GB, Hemsdale)—When his son is killed by British intelligence operatives, because he had been overheard stating that he hated how the leaks in the British Intelligence listening center where he works have been "plugged" (i.e. killed), **Michael Caine** agrees to tell what he knows to a liberal journalist. The latter is also killed and now Caine is really mad, and is determined to blow the whistle on British operatives.

JONES, GEMMA
ESCAPE ME NEVER (1935, GB, UA)—**Elizabeth Bergner**, stranded in Vienna with a baby, weds a composer who loves his brother's fiancee.

JONES, HORACE DEBUSSY "SACH"
SPOOK BUSTERS (1946, Monogram); SPY CHASERS (1956, Allied Artists); SPOOK CHASERS (1957, Allied Artists)—**Huntz Hall**, one of the original Dead End Kids, made a career of playing a comical schnook, usually but not always a foil for Leo Gorcey. The films in this entry are not great comedies but if one is in the mood for a certain kind of stupid silliness, here would be the place to look.

JONES, HOWARD (HOJO)
THE LAST OF THE FINEST (1990, Orion)—**Bill Paxton** is one of a group of cops who band together to fight a scheme by the feds to trade drugs for arms to supply Central American contras.

JONES, INDIANA
INDIANA JONES AND THE TEMPLE OF DOOM (1984, Paramount); INDIANA JONES AND THE LAST CRUSADE (1989, Paramount)—In the further adventures of American archaeologist **Harrison Ford**, Steven Spielberg and George Lucas give us a prequel of sorts. The events of the first film take place in 1935 in India prior to the action in RAIDERS OF THE LOST ARK. There were some complaints that where the constant action of the latter film was merely frightening, a great deal in the second movie is downright gross and offensive. The 1989 film surely couldn't disappoint fans of RAIDERS OF THE LOST ARK, as it's packed with adventure and surprises, and as an added bonus has Sean Connery as Indy Jones' father. There's even a sort of prologue to the movie, with River Phoenix as a teenage Indy.

JONES, JASPER

UNEXPECTED FATHER (1932, Universal)—**Slim Summerville** loses his fiancee when he takes in an orphan to care for. Fortunately, nursemaid Zasu Pitts is ready to step in and help Summerville with the child.

JONES, JENNY

A MUNITION GIRL'S ROMANCE (1917, Silent, GB, Broadwest)—**Violet Hopson**, working in a munitions plant, helps a weapons designer save his plans from a spy.

JONES, JENNY

SWEEPSTAKES WINNER (1939, Warner Brothers)—Beautiful but dumb **Marie Wilson** gives $1,000 to a bookie, who loses it but compensates her by giving her a winning ticket in the Irish Sweepstakes.

JONES, JEREMY

JEREMY (1973, UA)—**Robby Benson** is a rather goofy teenager who plays both the cello and basketball. He falls madly in love with a new girl in school. If one doesn't expect too much, there are some charming moments in this adolescent romancer.

JONES, (REV.) JERICHO

THE PARSON AND THE OUTLAW (1957, Columbia)—When local preacher **Charles "Buddy" Rogers** is killed by a band of outlaws, his friend Billy the Kid, who had retired, straps on his guns and goes looking for revenge.

JONES, JIMMY

A GUY, A GAL AND A PAL (1945, Columbia)—Marine **Ross Hunter** wins Lynn Merrick from his civilian friend George Meeker because she likes men in uniforms.

JONES, JOANNA

NURSE ON WHEELS (1964, GB, Anglo-Amalgamated)—**Juliet Mills**, a visiting nurse engaged to a farmer, objects to his plans to evict some tenants.

JONES, JOHN

EDUCATING FATHER (1936, 20th Century Fox)—**Jed Prouty** wishes his son to be a druggist like he is, and not a pilot, but changes his mind when his son is able to fly his dad home from a fishing trip in time to save his store's lease.

JONES, JOHN PAUL

JOHN PAUL JONES (1969, Warner Brothers)—**Robert Stack** is adequate in this not very exciting yarn about the famous American naval captain of the Revolutionary War, who later serves Catherine the Great of Russia.

JONES, JOHNNY (HUNTLEY HAVERSTOCK)

FOREIGN CORRESPONDENT (1940, UA)—In 1938, American journalist **Joel McCrea** witnesses an assassination of a Dutch statesman in Amsterdam. McCrea and other reporters investigate the murder. In the process, he is almost pushed off the top of Westminster Abbey, finds some secrets at a Windmill whose blades are turning the wrong way, survives a plane crash, falls in love with the daughter of the author of a peace plan, exposes this man as a fifth columnist and gives a flag raising speech to America, urging the U.S. to join the fight against the Nazis.

JONES, JUDY

CINDERELLA JONES (1946, Warner Brothers)—**Joan Leslie** stands to inherit ten million dollars (and this was when that was a lot of money) if she marries a man of unusual intellect by a certain date.

Isn't it wonderful that in Robert Alda she finds the smarty she needs, and falls in love with him as well?

JONES, KELSEY

SAILOR BE GOOD (1933, RKO)—Comedian **Jack Oakie** is a Navy boxing champ, who falls for dance hall girl Vivienne Osborne. She's had more gobs than Oakie has had ports of call.

JONES, L.B.

THE LIBERATION OF L.B. JONES (1970, Columbia)—Wealthy black southern funeral director **Roscoe Lee Browne** plans to divorce his wife because she has had an affair with a white policeman. Things come to a head when Browne is shot and castrated by the policeman and his buddy.

JONES, LORRY

PIN UP GIRL (1944, 20th Century Fox)—During WWII, **Betty Grable** was the favorite pin-up of GIs all over the world. So why not take advantage of the fact and make a movie about how a pretty girl can attain such a lofty distinction?

JONES, "LIGHTNIN'" BILL

LIGHTNIN' (1930, Fox)—**Will Rogers**, who is partial to liquor, does odd jobs around a hotel run by his wife and their adopted daughter. Schemers who know that the railroad is to pass through the sight of the hotel convince Rogers' wife to sell her place, but the sale requires Rogers approval, which he won't give, and for once he's proven correct.

JONES, LINK

MAN OF THE WEST (1958, UA)—Twenty years earlier **Gary Cooper** gave up his outlaw ways, but now it looks as if he'll have to study violence once again when he and Julie London find themselves in the camp of the very gang he left, now run by Cooper's near crazy and sadistic uncle, Lee J. Cobb.

JONES, LITTLE JOHNNY

LITTLE JOHNNY JONES (1930, Warner Brothers)—**Eddie Buzzell**, standing in for George M. Cohan, is an American jockey who wins the English Derby aboard the horse Yankee Doodle Dandy.

JONES, MARY

THE DEVIL AND MISS JONES (1941, RKO)—When the world's richest man, Charles Coburn, takes a lowly job in one of his department stores to learn why his employees are always complaining, he learns more than he bargained for from sincere salesgirl **Jean Arthur**, who befriends the old skinflint not knowing who he is.

JONES, MELODY

ALONG CAME JONES (1945, RKO)—For once **Gary Cooper** doesn't play a bigger than life western hero. Instead he's a cowboy who can't hit the side of a barn with a gun. He runs into Loretta Young who is being chased by nasty villain, Dan Duryea, for whom Cooper is mistaken.

JONES, MELVIN

SAILOR BEWARE (1951, Paramount)—**Jerry Lewis** and partner Dean Martin are on a submarine cruise to Honolulu. Their antics are beginning to wear thin.

JONES, MERLIN

THE MISADVENTURES OF MERLIN JONES (1964, Buena Vista); THE MONKEY'S UNCLE (1965, Buena Vista)—Genius college student **Tommy Kirk** invents a machine that allows him to read minds, but it's a mixed blessing. In the sequel, he performs study-while-you-sleep experiments on a monkey. Neither film is as funny as a barrel full of monkeys.

JONES, MORDECAI
THE FLIM FLAM MAN (1967, 20th Century Fox)—**George C. Scott** is a grand ham as an aging southern con artist who teams up with AWOL soldier Michael Sarrazin to fleece the deserving.

JONES, MURPHY
MURPHY'S ROMANCE (1985, Columbia)—Small town pharmacist and widower James Garner has a romance with divorcee Sally Field. Their love is complicated by his reluctance to become too involved with anyone, including her child, and her ex-husband who shows up hoping to rekindle the old flame.

JONES, OCTOBER
STRANGERS ON A HONEYMOON (1937, GB, Gaumont)—**Constance Cummings** marries Hugh Sinclair, a titled man posing as a tramp, who prevents her land from being stolen.

JONES, P. CADWALLER
MR. DISTRICT ATTORNEY (1941, Republic)—**Dennis O'Keefe**, fresh out of law school and working for the District Attorney's office, is assigned to locate a former politician, who had disappeared years earlier after taking a large bribe.

JONES, PETER
THE BUTTER AND EGG MAN (1928, Silent, First National); THE TENDERFOOT (1932, Warner Brothers)—The difference between these two film versions of the George S. Kaufman play, besides sound, is that the silent is more faithful to the story of hick **Jack Mulhall**, who comes to the big city with a bankroll, which he uses to finance a turkey of a revue. In 1932, the story is tailored to the special comedy talents of **Joe E. Brown**, a cowboy, who backs a Broadway show starring Ginger Rogers.

JONES, RED
FULLER BRUSH MAN (1948, Columbia)—The great clown **Red Skelton** scores high comical marks as a door-to-door brush salesman, who becomes involved in a murder.

JONES, RUTH GORDON
THE ACTRESS (1953, MGM)—Based on the memories of actress Ruth Gordon, **Jean Simmons** is the young daughter of retired seaman Spencer Tracy. She wants to become an actress, while he has plans for her to become a physical education teacher. The crusty old gent proves his love for his daughter.

JONES, SIERRA NEVADA
CATTLE QUEEN OF MONTANA (1954, RKO)—With the help of Ronald Reagan, **Barbara Stanwyck** fights like the devil against a gang of land-grabbers.

JONES, SORROWFUL
SORROWFUL JONES (1949, Paramount)—In this remake of Shirley Temple's 1934 hit LITTLE MISS MARKER, **Bob Hope** is a bookie, who gets stuck with a gambler's little girl, when the father is killed after leaving the child as his marker for a bet.

JONES, SUZY FARRAGUT (SKINFLINT JONES)
I'LL GET HIM YET (1919, Silent, First National)—Great screen comedian **Dorothy Gish**, the daughter of a millionaire, has her heart set on marrying reporter Richard Barthelmess. He doesn't wish to be thought a fortune hunter. Gish swears never to take any money from her father but doesn't tell Barthelmess that she's worth $5 million herself.

JONES, TIFFANY
TIFFANY JONES (1976, Cineworld)—**Anouska Hempel** is a super sexy agent who finds her life in constant peril, as she attempts to safeguard some valuable secrets.

JONES, TILLIE
TILLIE THE TOILER (1927, Silent, MGM); (1941, Columbia)—**Marion Davies** and **Kay Harris** portray the beautiful but dumb office girl created for the King Syndicate comics by Russ Westover.

JONES, TOM
TOM JONES (1963, GB, Woodfall Lopert); THE BAWDY ADVENTURES OF TOM JONES (1976, GB, Universal)—**Albert Finney** is delightful as the bastard raised by a squire in England. He discovers how wonderful women can be—the more the merrier. He also finds love with Susannah York, whose father enjoys drinking and wenching with Finney but doesn't see him as a son-in-law because of his lowly birth status. In the 1976 film, the film makers tried to spice up the story with **Nicky Hansen** as Jones, but it made for an inferior presentation of the Henry Fielding story.

JONES, TOM
WHAT HAPPENED TO JONES (1926, Silent, Universal)—First of all, **Reginald Denny**, on the eve of his wedding, attends a poker game raided by the police. He escapes into a Turkish bath, which he leaves disguised as a woman. Still trying to throw off the trailing police, Denny dresses up as a bishop, but then the real bishop shows up to officiate at Denny's wedding. Ultimately, Denny marries his fiancee, but in the back of a speeding car rather than in a church.

JONES, TRUVY
STEEL MAGNOLIAS (1989, Tri-Star)—**Dolly Parton** runs a beauty parlor, where most of the action involving six southern women takes place. She supports a rather useless husband, Sam Shepard.

JONES, WAHOO
THE TEXAS RANGERS (1936, Paramount)—**Jack Oakie** and his buddy Fred MacMurray join the Texas Rangers, while another friend Lloyd Nolan becomes a notorious outlaw. It falls to Oakie and MacMurray to bring in Nolan.

JONESY
SHIPMATES (1931, MGM)—Sailor **Robert Montgomery** gets himself appointed to the Naval Academy in order to be suitable husband material for an admiral's daughter.

JOPLIN, HARRY
THE GUY WHO CAME BACK (1951, 20th Century Fox)—Pro football player **Paul Douglas** can't accept the fact that his playing days are over. He leaves his wife, Joan Bennett, to take up with Linda Darnell. When a manpower shortage caused by the war gives him a chance to make a comeback, he finally realizes he's only fooling himself.

JOPLIN, SCOTT
SCOTT JOPLIN (1977, Universal)—**Billy Dee Williams** is pleasant enough as the turn-of-the-century black composer of ragtime tunes.

JORDAN, DENNY
RACKET BUSTERS (1938, Warner Brothers)—Trucker **George Brent** won't play ball with gangster Humphrey Bogart, who runs a protection racket in the New York trucking industry.

JORDAN, ELLY
COWBOY FROM BROOKLYN (1938, Warner Brothers)—Drifter **Dick Powell** takes a job on a ranch, where he is discovered by talent scout Pat O'Brien. In a flash he becomes a radio star.

JORDAN, FIREBRAND
FIREBRAND JORDAN (1930, National Players)—In this silly song-filled horse opera, **Lane Chandler** is assigned to help the sheriff find a gang of counterfeiters.

JORDAN, JERRI
THE GIRL CAN'T HELP IT (1956, 20th Century Fox)—**Jayne Mansfield's** gangster boyfriend hires agent Tom Ewell to make her a star, but all she wants to be is a housewife, and that's what she becomes, when she falls in love with Ewell.

JORDAN, JIM
THE GALLOPING ACE (1924, Silent, Universal)—**Jack Hoxie** stars in this routine horse opera, complete with lots of riding and shooting.

JORDAN, KIRK
THE TEXANS (1938, Paramount)—While not involved in the struggle between farmers and cattlemen, the rise of the Ku Klux Klan, and other problems in Texas after the Civil War, **Randolph Scott** competes with Robert Cummings for the love of Joan Bennett.

JORDAN, LUCKY
LUCKY JORDAN (1942, Paramount)—In his first top, solo-billed starring role, **Alan Ladd** is a selfish con-man, with an aversion to serving his country. but he becomes a hero, outwitting a Nazi spy ring.

JORDAN, MR.
HERE COMES MR. JORDAN (1941, Columbia)—**Claude Rains** is the heavenly bureaucrat who must find boxer Robert Montgomery a new body when his old one becomes unavailable due to an error by one of Rains' agents.

JORDAN, ROBERT
MR. SCOUTMASTER (1953, 20th Century Fox)—Writer **Clifton Webb** becomes a scoutmaster to gather material for a book. Not particularly fond of children, he has some heavy conflicts with his boys before both sides learn a thing or two about pulling together.

JORDAN, THELMA
THE FILE ON THELMA JORDAN (1950, Paramount)—**Barbara Stanwyck** is a heartless murderer, but District Attorney Wendell Corey is so smitten with her, he deliberately loses the case and ruins his career. She's not the type to show any gratitude but she doesn't get away scot-free.

JORGENSEN, CHRISTINE
THE CHRISTINE JORGENSEN STORY (1970, UA)—**John Hansen** appears as ex-G.I. George Jorgensen who undergoes one of the first sex-change operations.

JORY
JORY (1972, Avco Embassy)—With a little help from his friends **Robby Benson** is induced to give up gunslinging for ranching.

JOSE
THE SPANISH GARDENER (1957, GB, Rank)—**Dirk Bogarde** is a gardener working for British diplomat Michael Hordern. Dirk befriends the diplomat's son, annoying the father, who has Bogarde arrested for a theft. When Bogarde escapes and is shot, he's found by the boy, who pleads for his friend, making his father see the error of his ways.

JOSEF
A STAR FELL FROM HEAVEN (1936, GB, Wardour)—Tiny tenor **Joseph Schmidt's** voice is used, when a temperamental star of a film loses his voice. When the hoax is exposed, Schmidt becomes a star.

JOSEPH
THE BOSS'S SON (1978, New American Cinema)—**Rudy Solari** and his secret-drinker wife would like their son to go into his carpet business, but the boy has other plans.

JOSEPH
WE'RE NO ANGELS (1955, Paramount)—Forger **Humphrey Bogart**, a convict on Devil's Island, uses his skill to make it appear that a storekeeper is successful when he's visited by his tyrannical employer and relative. Bogart is aided in bringing Christmas cheer to the storekeeper's family by Aldo Ray, Peter Ustinov and a little friend who makes certain that the despicable relative Basil Rathbone will cause no further trouble.

JOSEPHINE
A ROYAL DIVORCE (1938, GB, Paramount)—Napoleon Bonaparte (Pierre Blanchar) marries widow **Ruth Chatterton**, whom he later divorces because she cannot give him an heir.

JOSETTE, MLLE.
JOSETTE (1938, 20th Century Fox)—Gold digger **Tala Birell** marries an elderly man and in a mistaken identity story, both of his sons fall in love with her.

JOSHUA
JOSHUA (1976, Lone Star)—**Fred Williamson** wrote the script for this mishmash of a movie, set in the West just after the Civil War, so let him explain what it's all about.

JOSLIN, LULLABY
THE THREE MESQUITEERS (1936, Republic); PALS OF THE SADDLE (1938, Republic); THE TRAIL BLAZERS (1940, Republic); PALS OF THE PECOS (1941, Republic); SADDLEMATES (1941, REPUBLIC); THE PHANTOM PLAINSMEN (1942, Republic)—**Syd Saylor** in 1936, **Max Terhune** in 1938 and **Rufe Davis** in the later pictures supply the comedy relief for the enjoyable western stories of three cowboy friends, who like France's Three Musketeers are gallant protectors of those in need of their help.

JOSSELYN, LILLIAN & THOMAS
JOSSELYN'S WIFE (1926, Silent, Tiffany)—**Pauline Frederick** and **Holmes Herbert** have been married six months, when they are visited by her former lover and his wife. This leads to some vexing problems for the newlyweds.

JOSSER, JIMMY
DR. JOSSER KC (1931, GB, Pathe); P.C. JOSSER (1931, GB, Gainsborough); JOSSER IN THE ARMY (1932, GB, British Int.); JOSSER JOINS THE NAVY (1932, GB, British Int.); JOSSER ON THE RIVER (1932, GB, British Int.); JOSSER ON THE FARM (1934, GB, 20th Century Fox)—British comedian **Ernie Lotinga's** films did not depend much on plot. If he was doctor, lawyer, Indian chief, soldier, sailor or what not, he's always the same and definitely (at the time) an acquired taste.

JOVANKA

FIVE BRANDED WOMEN (1960, Paramount)—**Silvano Mangano** is one of five Yugoslavian girls whose heads are shaved for having taken German lovers. Disgraced, they redeem themselves by becoming partisans who fight the invaders.

JOY

POOR COW (1968, GB, National General)—Thief's wife **Carol White** lives in squalor. She and her baby move in with her criminal husband's buddy while her old man is in prison.

JOY

WAR NURSE (1930, MGM)-Pampered, convent-trained **Anita Page** volunteers for nursing duty with the Red Cross in France at the outbreak of WWI. Despite an initial tough adjustment period, Page, along with her fellow volunteers, provides much needed medical attention.

JOYCE

THE BACHELOR GIRL (1929, Part-Talkie, Columbia)—**Jacqueline Logan**, a beautiful and efficient secretary, is in love with the shiftless office boy, William Collier, Jr. When he's fired, she gets him another job, but he pushes his work off on her, and she's so competent it seems he's doing well, but he starts believing it himself, and is fired. Years later when he's on a continuing downward spiral, and she's a successful businesswoman, they meet again, and their old love is revived. He pledges to make himself worthy of her.

JOYCE

IT'S A WISE CHILD (1931, MGM)—When **Marion Davies** claims to be pregnant, the possibilities for the father seem to be three-fold, but the little scamp isn't telling the truth.

JOYCE

MODERN CINDERELLA (1917, Silent, Fox)—Teenager **June Caprice** has a crush on her older sister's beau. On the night of a big dance, she puts on makeup and a beautiful dress, and wins the attention of the man of her choice. She runs away from the dance losing a slipper—and, oh, you know the rest of the story.

JOYCE

ROAMING LADY (1936, Columbia)—**Fay Wray** stows away on Ralph Bellamy's plane bound for China. The two are captured by revolutionaries and Bellamy has to agree to fly for the rebels to save their lives.

JOYCE

WOMAN FROM HEADQUARTERS (1950, Republic)—Pretty **Virginia Hutson** is a city cop, who successfully keeps crime out of the neighborhood to which she is assigned.

JOYZELLE, FREDERIKA "FREDDIE"

STREET GIRL (1929, RKO)—In the first official RKO production, **Betty Compson**, a violinist, who works with a quartet of jazz musicians, falls in love with the pianist. Her love life is complicated by the attentions of a Balkan prince.

JUANITA

A SOUTHERN MAID (1933, GB, Wardour)—In this modest musical, **Bebe Daniels** has the dual role of two women who at 20-year intervals reject the same man.

JUAREZ, BENITO

JUAREZ (1939, Warner Brothers)—In a distinguished performance, **Paul Muni** is the Indian President of Mexico, intent on seeing his country become a democracy, free of French influence and Napoleon III's hand-picked emperor for the country, Maximillian. As is usual with Muni he blends his personality with that of the character he's creating, with the result he seems to become his role.

JUBAL

GUN BROTHERS (1956, UA)—We don't know if **Neville Brand's** mother liked his brother Buster Crabbe best, but the two just don't seem to get along, and even come close to having a showdown when they are forced to team together against an attack of western outlaws.

JUBILO

JUBILO (1919, Silent, Goldwyn)—If **Will Rogers'** reputation had to rest on this film, he would have been promptly forgotten, according to the reviews at the time. It is a not so tender love story.

JUDITH

THE CHILDREN (1990, GB/West Germany, Isolde/Film Four)—On a voyage home from Brazil to Europe, middle-aged mining engineer Ben Kingsley meets a group of seven children. Rather than hurry to his life-long love Kim Novak, who lives in an Alpine village, Kingsley tarries in Venice to be near the children, who hold some kind of fascination for him. When he ultimately leaves, the children follow. From then on, Kingsley is torn between Novak, who proves demanding, and the guileless, budding eldest child **Siri Neal**.

JUDITH

JUDITH (1965, Paramount)—Austrian **Sophia Loren** is enlisted by Israeli freedom fighter Peter Finch to track down her war-criminal Nazi husband, now based in Syria.

JUDITH

WOMAN DOCTOR (1939, Republic)—In an anti-feminist movie, physician **Frieda Inescourt** is treated like a scoundrel for practicing her craft rather than staying home and taking care of her husband and daughter.

JUDITH OF BETHULIA

JUDITH OF BETHULIA (1914, Silent, Biograph)—In his final film for Biograph, director D.W. Griffith presents **Blanche Sweet** as a wealthy, lonely, young widow whose fortress city lies in the path of the Assyrians, who are marching on Jerusalem. She goes to the Assyrian leader, vamps him silly, and when he's dead drunk, she cuts off his head which she hangs from the city's wall, causing the enemy to panic and retreat in disorder.

JUDITH OF THE CUMBERLANDS

JUDITH OF THE CUMBERLANDS (1916, Silent, Signal)—**Helen Holmes** is a member of one of two feuding mountain families. The war ends when one of their number is almost lynched.

JUDY

DANCE, GIRL, DANCE (1940, RKO)—**Maureen O'Hara** and Lucille Ball played dancers with surprisingly modern views on the relation between men and women.

JUDY

DIARY OF A HIGH SCHOOL BRIDE (1959, American International)—**Anita Sands** is a seventeen-year-old high school student in this look at the difficulties faced in teen marriages.

JUDY

EASY TO LOOK AT (1945, Universal)—The story of a young costume designer, who becomes a success in New York by stealing the ideas of others, is just enough to fill in around the edges of the songs of its star **Gloria Jean**.

JUDY
EIGHTEEN AND ANXIOUS (1957, Universal)—Eighteen-year-old **Mary Webster** is anxious because she's pregnant and unwed. That's enough to make one anxious.

JUDY
JUDY OF ROGUES' HARBOR (1920, Silent, Realart)—**Mary Miles Minter** is one of a group of orphans who escapes the cruelty of a man posing as their grandfather.

JUDY
PRISON NURSE (1938, Republic)—Yes, **Marian Marsh** is a prison nurse. For Republic, at the time, that's enough of a plot to make a movie.

JUDY
UNTAMED HEIRESS (1954, Republic)—An old prospector who once loved **Judy Canova's** opera singer mother hires private investigators to find his lost love, but she's dead and Canova's all he's going to get.

JUDY
THE WAC FROM WALLA WALLA (1952, Republic)—Hillbilly comedian **Judy Canova** comes from a long line of Army men. Not to let down the family tradition, she enlists in the WACs.

JUGS
MOTHER, SPEED AND JUGS (1976, 20th Century Fox)—Neither feminists nor **Raquel Welch** are very happy with the name given to her character in this story of three paramedics, working in a big city.

JULES
WE'RE NO ANGELS (1955, Paramount)—**Peter Ustinov** is a delight as one of the three Devil's Island convicts who escape and mean to rob a storekeeper, but instead stay around and straighten out the problems of the man's family.

JULIA
THE HAUNTING OF JULIA (1981, GB/Canada, Discovery)—After the death of her daughter, **Mia Farrow** blames herself. She and her husband, Keir Dullea, take up residence in an old house, and strange things begin happening.

JULIA
JULIA (1977, 20th Century Fox)—**Vanessa Redgrave**, the daughter of a wealthy family, rejects her position in society to become a social activist in the 1930s. She fights the Nazis in Germany with no thought of her own well-being.

JULIA
JULIA AND JULIA (1988, Cinecom)—Unfortunate **Kathleen Turner** loses her husband in an automobile accident on their wedding day. A few years later she's living and working in silent sorrow in Trieste. One night she comes home to find her hubby hasn't died and that she lives with him and their small son. From then she drifts back and forth from one life to the other, without knowing which is real.

JULIA
JULIA HAS TWO LOVERS (1990, South Gate)—When **Daphna Kastner's** live-in lover of two years David Charles asks her to marry

him, she stalls, afraid of a permanent relationship. Answering the phone, she finds herself drawn to wrong number David Duchovny. They spend the morning together talking to each other on portable phones and ultimately become lovers.

JULIAN
AMERICAN GIGOLO (1980, Paramount)—Heartthrob **Richard Gere** is a prostitute who caters only to wealthy women. When one of his clients is found dead, he discovers he's been set up as the fall guy for the murder.

JULIAN
GOODBYE GEMINI (1970, GB, Cinerama)—**Martin Potter** has an incestuous relationship with his twin Judy Geeson. When another man shows an interest in Geeson, Potter gets him drunk and takes him to a homosexual orgy. Then he induces Geeson to help him kill the man.

JULIAN, EVERETT
THE REINCARNATE (1971, Canada, Meridian)—**Jack Creley**, a dying lawyer and member of an ancient cult, must find a virgin to sacrifice in order to preserve his age-old spirit.

JULIE
I MET MY LOVE AGAIN (1938, UA)—Although engaged to small-town lad Henry Fonda, **Joan Bennett** elopes in Europe with a playboy. Ten years later she returns home a widow, and after some to-be-expected complications wins back Fonda, now a college professor.

JULIE
JOHN AND JULIE (1957, GB, British Lion)—Six-year-olds **Lesley Dudley** and Colin Gibson walk to London to see a coronation.

JULIE
LOOK WHO'S TALKING TOO (1990, Tri-Star)—If you don't appreciate or understand the appeal of Roseanne Barr (and we confess to be among this number), the use of her voice in this unappealing sequel to the 1989 hit will grate not delight. She plays the new baby sister of little Mikey (whose voice, as in the original film, is supplied by Bruce Willis)—and the two use baby talk that would make parents blush.

JULIE
A SONG FOR MISS JULIE (1945, Republic)—**Jane Farrar** is the last surviving relative of a southern gentleman of the 1850s, whose story is to be the basis for a Broadway show.

JULIE
THE WOMAN ON TRIAL (1927, Silent, Paramount)—**Pola Negri** is on trial for murder. The man she killed was hired by her ex-husband to get Negri into a compromising position, so he can prove she's not fit to raise their son. Negri is acquitted to cheers from the audience.

JULIE, MME.
WOMAN BETWEEN (1931, RKO)—Beautiful French modiste **Lili Damita** marries a widower against the wishes of the man's son. But soon bored Damita and the son are drawn together in a more realistic love.

JULIET
ROMEO AND JULIET (1916, Silent, Fox); (1936, MGM); (1954, GB, UA); (1966, GB, Embassy); (1968, GB/Italy, Paramount)—**Theda Bara, Norma Shearer, Susan Shentall, Margot Fonteyn** and

Olivia Hussey each played the star-crossed lover of Romeo. The films are a mixed bag, with supporting players more impressive than the stars. Only Hussey was the age of Shakespeare's teenage heroine.

JULIO
THE LONERS (1972, Fanfare)—**Pat Stich** is a rebellious teenage hitchhiker, running away from his miserable mother. He's picked up along with a retarded teen by a half-breed. They go on a robbery spree across the country.

JULNA
THE PRINCE WHO WAS A THIEF (1951, Universal)—In thirteenth century Tangiers, **Tony Curtis** is a prince, who has been denied his birthright by usurpers, and is reduced to being a thief. With the help of his foster father Everett Sloane and sexy little Piper Laurie he puts things right.

JUNG, LENA
LENA'S HOLIDAY (1991, Prism/Crown)—When East German tourist **Felicity Waterman** arrives in LA, her bags are switched at the airport with those of a woman who is murdered.

JUNGLE JIM
JUNGLE JIM (1948, Columbia); JUNGLE JIM IN THE FORBIDDEN LAND (1952, Columbia)—When **Johnny Weissmuller's** middle got too big to make a convincing Lord of the Jungle, he turned in Tarzan's loin cloth for a shirt and shorts, but stayed in the jungle as a sort of Great White Hunter.

JUNIE See JUNEAU MACLEAN

JUNIOR See JUNIOR HEALEY

JURORS
12 ANGRY MEN (1957, UA)—**1. Martin Balsam, 2. John Fiedler, 3. Lee J. Cobb, 4. E.G. Marshall, 5. Jack Klugman, 6. Edward Binns, 7. Jack Warden, 8. Henry Fonda, 9. Joseph Sweeney, 10. Ed Begley, 11. George Voskovec, 12. Robert Webber**—In a superb drama, the twelve members of a jury are about to convict a boy of murdering his father when Henry Fonda starts picking at each piece of evidence that has convinced each juror of the youngster's guilt. In the end the jury votes for acquittal.

JUSTICE, SHERIFF BUFORD T.
SMOKEY AND THE BANDIT (1977, Universal); SMOKEY AND THE BANDIT II (1980, Universal); SMOKEY AND THE BANDIT—PART 3 (1983, Universal)—**Jackie Gleason** portrays a redneck southern sheriff, always several car lengths behind his fast-moving prey Burt Reynolds in these eternal chase movies.

JUSTIN, MARY
ONE WOMAN'S STORY (1949, GB, GFD/Universal)—In this film entitled THE PASSIONATE FRIENDS in Great Britain, lovely **Ann Todd**, married to a considerably older man, runs into an ex-lover and realizes the flame still burns.

JUSTINA, COUNTESS
THE COWBOY AND THE COUNTESS (1926, Silent, Fox)—Belgravian countess **Helen D'Algy** is touring the American West. When her automobile has an accident, she is aided by cowboy Buck Jones, and the rest is, as they say, history.

JUSTINE
JUSTINE (1969, 20th Century Fox)—**Anouk Aimee** is married to wealthy Coptic Christian John Vernon, but is also loved by others,

including the British Consular officer in Egypt. She becomes involved in a plot to sell arms to the Jewish underground in Palestine.

K

K.C.
BORN AMERICAN (1986, Cinema Group)—**David Coburn** is one of three American high school boys who cross over into Russia while on vacation. They land in a Russian prison, where the guards play chess on a giant board with live pieces and, when taken, they are not just merely removed from the board.

KAFKA, FRANZ
KAFKA (1991, Miramax)—Writer **Jeremy Irons** is drawn into a maze of intrigue, murder and anarchy in this muddled crime melodrama.

KAHLENBERGER, GENERAL
THE NIGHT OF THE GENERALS (1967, GB, Columbia)—**Donald Pleasance** is one of three German generals suspected of being the brutal murderer of whores in Paris during WWII.

KAIN
THE WARRIOR AND THE SORCERESS (1984, New World)—In an inferior Sword and Sorcery film (some might claim all such films are inferior), **David Carradine** is a Clint Eastwood-like "Dark Warrior," who gets paid for encouraging two families to destroy each other over control of a desert well, separating their houses.

KAINESS, HERBERT
BIG HEARTED HERBERT (1934, Warner Brothers)—**Guy Kibbee** is a stingy old grouch whose family teaches him a lesson, changing him somewhat for the better.

KAISER, THE
THE KAISER (1919, Silent, Renowned Pictures)—The sub-title of this anti-German film is BEAST OF BERLIN, which ought to give you some notion of how **Rupert Julian** played the German ruler, who plunged the world into war. He gets considerable pleasure out of people's suffering, especially women and children.

KALMAR (DAN SLATER)
THE DOUBLE MAN (1967, Warner Brothers)—**Yul Brynner** plays both a CIA agent and his double. Telling them apart becomes a real problem for the CIA.

KALOE
WHITE SAVAGE (1943, Universal)—Shark hunter **Jon Hall** gets permission from Maria Montez, the beautiful ruler of a South Pacific Island to fish in her waters. He hooks her.

KANE, BOB "HURRY"
BORN RECKLESS (1937, 20th Century Fox)—Auto racer **Brian Donlevy** takes a job as a cabdriver with a company, being leaned on by gangster Barton MacLane. Donlevy finds evidence to put an end to MacLane's interference.

KANE, BRAZOS

GUNFIGHTERS (1947, Columbia)—Although gunfighter **Randolph Scott** has a hankering to retire, he finds himself caught up in a range war.

KANE, CHARLES FOSTER

CITIZEN KANE (1941, RKO)—In what many consider the greatest film ever made, young genius **Orson Welles** portrays a William Randolph Hearst-like financial giant. His story is told disjointedly, but effectively, through the remembrances of various people, who loved and hated him. The camera angles and the telling sequences are perhaps now familiar devices, but they were mostly new when employed by Welles in a project which was almost totally his to develop.

KANE, GLADYS

THREE WISE GIRLS (1932, Columbia)—**Mae Clarke** shows small-town soda-jerk Jean Harlow how to succeed as a model in New York.

KANE, JIM

WINNER TAKES ALL (1932, Warner Brothers)—Egotistical boxer **James Cagney** dumps his sweetheart for a society woman, and lives to regret the decision.

KANE, JOHN

BROTHER JOHN (1971, Columbia)—When **Sidney Poitier** arrives in his hometown for the funeral of his sister, he is mistaken for a labor agitator, but in reality he's a messenger from heaven.

KANE, NORMAN

ARMED AND DANGEROUS (1986, Columbia)—Former lawyer **Eugene Levy** goes into partnership with fired cop John Candy as security guards. They discover that their boss is using the company as a front for an embezzling plot.

KANE, REV.

POLTERGEIST III (1988, MGM-UA)—**Nathan Davis** appears in the mirror and beckons Heather O'Rourke "into the light" in the third film of this series.

KANE, STACEY

SATAN IN HIGH HEELS (1962, Vega/Cosmic)—With a title like this you know enough to prepare the stuffing because it's a big turkey. Sleazy stripper **Meg Myles** deserts her junkie husband, whom she later persuades to kill one of her two lovers.

KANE, DR. TIMOTHY

DR. BROADWAY (1942, Paramount)—Physician **MacDonald Carey** is forced to play detective when he becomes the stooge in a murder case.

KANE, WILLIAM "KID"

P.K. & THE KID (1987, Sunn Classics/Lorimar)—Lifetime loser **Paul Le Mat's** one dream is to win an arm-wrestling championship. He picks up fifteen-year-old runaway Molly Ringwald whose degenerate father is hot on her trail. Le Mat realizes his dream and is in time to interrupt a savage beating Ringwald is receiving from her father.

KANSAS

THE KID FROM KANSAS (1941, Universal)—**Dick Foran** is mixed-up in a murder on a banana plantation.

KARAMAZOV, DMITRI, IVAN & ALEXEY

THE BROTHERS KARAMAZOV (1958, MGM)—**Yul Brynner, Richard Basehart** and **William Shatner** are the three legitimate sons of degenerate Lee J. Cobb. Brynner is an always in debt army officer, who loves Maria Schell. She considers Cobb's offer of money to become his mistress. Basehart, the intellectual of the trio and an observer of life rather than a participant, loves Claire Bloom, who feels an obligation to marry Brynner. Shatner is an ascetic whose love for everyone is hard to believe—or take.

KARELL, JULIAN

THE MAN IN THE HALF-MOON STREET (1944, Paramount)—Young-appearing **Nils Asther** is actually ancient. He is kept young and vibrant through a series of glandular transplants from unfortunate victims.

KAREN

THE COUNTESS OF MONTE CARLO (1948, Universal)—Looking for romance, **Sonja Henie** poses as a rich woman and checks into a swanky hotel. It was to be Henie's last film and her worst.

KAREN

THE LAST AMERICAN VIRGIN (1982, Cannon)—In this teenage sex exploitation film, one cannot but hope and pray that the young people portrayed are in no way typical of today's horny adolescents. **Diana Franklin** may or may not still have her virginity, but she has lost about everything else, especially her dignity, by appearing as the wet dream of three buddies in search of sexual kicks.

KAREN

SHE-DEVILS ON WHEELS (1968, Mayflower)—**Christine Wagner**, a member of a violent female motorcycle gang, battles other gangs with chains. She chooses her male lovers from stud lines.

KAREN

TOUCHED BY LOVE (1980, Columbia)—With the loving help of nurse Deborah Raffin, cerebral palsy victim **Diane Lane** becomes a functioning teenager.

KAREN

UNHOLY ROLLERS (1972, American International)—Former Playmate of the Year **Claudia Jennings** maneuvers around on roller skates in this predictable leer at the Roller Derby circuit.

KARENINA, ANNA

ANNA KARENINA (1935, MGM); (1948, GB, Korda/British Lion)—First **Greta Garbo** and then **Vivien Leigh** play the wife of a Russian civil servant who falls in love with a Czarist officer. Her husband resolves to divorce her, taking their son from her. When her lover leaves Moscow alone, she thinks she's lost him and throws herself under a train.

KAREW, WALLY

SEE NO EVIL, HEAR NO EVIL (1989, Tri-Star)—Blind **Richard Pryor** is thrown together with deaf Gene Wilder, when they are witnesses, of sorts, to a murder. Joan Severance is the most beautiful murderer we've seen in a long time.

KARI, QUEEN

PREHISTORIC WOMEN (1967, GB, 20th Century Fox)—**Martine Beswick**, the queen of a tribe of Amazons in Africa, chooses hunter Michael Latimer to satisfy her lust.

KARIM

SON OF INDIA (1931, MGM)—Left an orphan when his merchant father is killed by robbers, Indian **Ramon Novarro** makes his way to Bombay, where he is befriended by a white man, but when he falls in love with white girl Madge Evans, he's reminded who he is and who he is not.

KARL, PRINCE

THE STUDENT PRINCE (1954, MGM)—When **Mario Lanza** became too chubby for the role, **Edmund Purdom** was brought in to provide the body for the young prince, who goes to the University at Heidelberg and falls in love with a beer hall waitress. But the romance cannot be, as he is called home to assume the throne when his father dies. The Sigmund Romberg songs are great, and Lanza is in fine voice.

KARNSTEIN, MARCILLA

THE VAMPIRE LOVERS (1970, GB, Hammer)—**Ingrid Pitt** is an ageless vampire who seduces her female victims before draining them of their blood.

KASHMA BABA

SON OF ALI BABA (1952, Universal)—Back in old Bagdad, **Tony Curtis** is the adopted son of Ali Baba—but Curtis is really a prince of a fellow, who with the help of cute little Piper Laurie thwarts the plans of the evil Caliph Victor Jory. Sound like the plot of other Curtis movies of the time? It is.

KASPA, THE LION MAN

KING OF THE JUNGLE (1933, Paramount)—When Paramount saw how popular MGM's first Tarzan feature with Johnny Weissmuller was, it hired it's own Olympian swimming champ **Buster Crabbe**. He was given a loin cloth, assorted animal friends and starred as a Jungle dweller, captured with some lions by a circus owner, and brought to the U.S. as an attraction.

KATE

CORPORAL KATE (1926, Silent, Producers Dist. Corp.)—Brooklyn manicurist **Vera Reynolds** and her friend form a song-and-dance team to entertain the troops at the French front during WWI. They both fall in love with the same man. Vera loses an arm during a German assault, and her friend is killed.

KATE

THE HANDMAID'S TALE (1990 Cinecom)—In an unnamed country in the future, **Natasha Richardson** portrays a young mother and widow who is kidnapped to serve as a breeder for state security chief Robert Duvall and his wife Faye Dunaway, who has been left barren by pervasive environmental contamination.

KATE

JUST YOU AND ME KID (1979, Columbia)—Beautiful **Brooke Shields'** lack of acting ability is made all too evident working with old pro George Burns, who hides the runaway girl from drug dealers.

KATE

THE OUTLAW'S DAUGHTER (1954, 20th Century Fox)—**Kelly Ryan** teams up with a gang of outlaws when she is led to believe that the marshal killed her father.

KATE

PSYCHOS IN LOVE (1987, ICN Bleeker Infinity)—Psycho Carmine Capobianco, a balding, overweight bar owner dates pretty girls, and when things go wrong, he kills them. He finds his soul mate in the person of **Debi Thibeault** who kills her dates if she doesn't like their conversation. They move in together and double their fun.

KATHERINE (KATHARINA)

THE TAMING OF THE SHREW (1929, UA); (1967, Columbia) — **Mary Pickford's** shrewish behavior makes it look like both she and her younger sister will remain unwed. Their wealthy, merchant father won't allow the marriage of the younger girl until Pickford is

wed. Along comes Douglas Fairbanks as Petruchio and tames the shrew. In 1967, **Elizabeth Taylor** is the man-hating Katherina, who meets her match in Richard Burton.

KATHARINE (Catherine) OF ARAGON

HENRY VIII AND HIS SIX WIVES (1972, GB, EMS/MGM)—Suppose **Frances Cuka** had produced an heir for Henry VIII (Keith Michell). Would that have meant the other five ladies would never have become his queen?

KATHERINE *See* LILY VANESSI

KATIE

WOMAN'S WORLD (1954, 20th Century Fox)—**June Allyson's** husband Cornell Wilde is one of three executives being considered for the position of general manager of Clifton Webb's company. Webb is as interested in the wives as the men. Allyson hopes hubby doesn't get the job. He doesn't.

KATRIN

I REMEMBER MAMA (1948, RKO)—**Barbara Bel Geddes** narrates and co-stars with Irene Dunne as Mama in this quaint remembrance of a girl growing up in a Norwegian family in San Francisco—but mostly, she remembers Mama.

KATRINA, BARONESS

THE BARONESS AND THE BUTLER (1938, 20th Century Fox)—**Annabella** is the daughter of the prime minister of Hungary. The prime minister's butler William Powell is elected to parliament and becomes leader of the opposition. Annabella thinks, "What cheek," but finally comes to love Powell.

KATY

DANGEROUS WHEN WET (1953, MGM)—**Esther Williams** wins fame, fortune and Fernando (Lamas, that is) for swimming the English Channel.

KATZ, ERIC

OLD BOYFRIENDS (1979, Avco Embassy)—**John Belushi** is one of the men whom Talia Shire wishes to make pay for their mistreatment of her in the past.

KATZENELLBOGEN, PARSIFAL

WHERE IS PARSIFAL? (1984, GB, Young)—**Tony Curtis** is an inventor seeking someone to finance a skywriting process.

KAUFMAN, WILLIE

WILLIE AND PHIL (1980, 20th Century Fox)—Jewish photographer **Michael Ontkean** and his friend, teacher Ray Sharkey of New York's Greenwich Village, both fall in love with an earthy girl from Kentucky, Margot Kidder. She's willing to work out an arrangement to accommodate everyone.

KAY

I LIVE MY LIFE (1935, MGM)—When flighty society girl **Joan Crawford** falls in love with deadly-serious archeologist Brian Aherne, she finds it difficult to live down to his quiet life.

KAY

THAT KIND OF WOMAN (1959, Paramount)—Sophisticated **Sophia Loren**, engaged to millionaire George Sanders, finds true love with young naive soldier Tab Hunter. Yeah, we don't believe it either.

KAZ

MY DEMON LOVER (1987, New Line Cinema)—Poor **Scott Valentine** has a big problem. He's a derelict, who literally becomes some kind of a beast anytime he's sexually aroused. He attaches himself to a young woman who turns him on but also causes him to grow horns, body hair, and fangs.

KEAN, DANNY
PICTURE SNATCHER (1933, Warner Brothers)—Callous photographer **James Cagney** goes after shocking pictures such as a woman being executed in the electric chair.

KEANE, DR. JIM
DR. JIM (1921, Silent, Universal)—Great surgeon **Frank Mayo** loves his wife, but she resents the time he spends on his practice. When he suffers a nervous breakdown, they take a cruise aboard a ship on which she is the only woman. She is attracted to the beastly captain. During a storm Mayo must save his rival's life, and this brings his wife to her senses.

KEANE, MAHLON
THE RACKETEER (1929, Pathe)—Racketeer **Robert Armstrong** takes interest in a married woman who is having an affair with a down-and-out violinist. His interest and unusual noble gesture costs him his life.

KEANE, MILES
NIGHT OF THE WARRIOR (1991, Trimark)—**Lorenzo Lamas** is a martial-arts kickboxer who wants to retire. Anthony Geary tries to blackmail Lamas into continuing his career. Geary beats up Lamas' mother (real and screen) Arlene Dahl, and kidnaps his girlfriend Kathleen Kinmont. This makes Lamas angry.

KEARNEY, WILD BILL
HELL'S HEROES (1930, Universal): THE THREE GODFATHERS (1948, MGM)—**Fred Kohler** and two of his companions rob a bank and flee into the desert, where they come across a dying woman, who has just given birth to a baby. She pleads with them to be the child's godfathers, and take the baby to his father in New Jerusalem. They do, but at the cost of their lives. In 1948, **Harry Carey, Jr.,** plays essentially the same role.

KEATON, BUSTER
THE BUSTER KEATON STORY (1957, Paramount)—**Donald O'Connor's** performance as the great silent movie comedian, whose drinking problems ruined his career, is nothing special.

KEATON, LOUIE
KEATON'S COP (1990, Cannon)—Crusty mobster **Abe Vigoda** teams up with cop Lee Majors to determine who put out a hit on Vigoda and killed Don Rickles instead.

KEATON, MARY
THREE ON A MATCH (1932, Warner Brothers)—Showgirl **Joan Blondell** meets Bette Davis and Ann Dvorak for lunch. The three grew up together in a slum neighborhood and haven't seen each other for 12 years.

KEATS, SIDNEY
MILLIONAIRE PRISON (1940, RKO)—**Chester Clute** is one of the wealthy white collar criminals serving time in an almost country club-like pen. The humanitarian warden believes in letting his "guests" continue the pursuit of their interests.

KEECHIE
THEY LIVE BY NIGHT (1949, RKO); THIEVES LIKE US (1974, UA)-**Cathy O'Donnell** and Farley Granger play doomed lovers in a story of youngsters, who fall into a life of crime almost accidentally with their end seeming almost pre-ordained. In the 1974 remake,

Shelley Duvall falls in love with young hood Keith Carradine, a member of a gang of bank robbers, specializing in small towns. She is prevented from saving her lover as he is riddled by police bullets. Duvall and Carradine don't seem to be quite the victims of their destiny to the extent of O'Donnell and Granger.

KEEFER, FLORENCE & CHET
THE MARRYING KIND (1952, Columbia)—In a rather charming and heartwarming story, **Judy Holiday** and **Aldo Ray** change their mind about divorce after recalling their bittersweet years together.

KEEGAN, MIKE
SOMEONE TO WATCH OVER ME (1987, Columbia)—Detective **Tom Berenger** is given the 8 p.m. to 4 a.m. shift of watching Mimi Rogers, a witness to a murder. Even though he's happily married, the two begin an affair. It nearly causes the death of Berenger's wife and child.

KEELER, CHRISTINE
THE CHRISTINE KEELER AFFAIR (1964, GB, Topaz)—In this quickie exploitation movie, audiences are presented with one version of how model-prostitute **Yvonne Buckingham** became involved with Russian spies and British cabinet officers. A superior movie on the subject, SCANDAL, was released in 1989, with Joanne Whalley-Kilmer as Christine Keeler, John Hurt as Dr. Stephen Ward and Ian McKellen as Britain's Minister of War, John Profumo.

KEENE, IRENE
SALLY, IRENE AND MARY (1938, 20th Century Fox)—Manicurist **Joan Davis** hopes to become a Broadway star. With her friends Alice Faye and Marjorie Weaver, she starts a successful supper club on a broken-down old ferry. Davis provides most of the humor from the female side.

KEENE, LINDA
SHALL WE DANCE (1937, RKO)—Revue star **Ginger Rogers** and renowned ballet dancer Fred Astaire team up in a familiar story of boy meets girl, boy loses girl, boy wins girl. Rogers and Astaire sang more than they danced and that's a shame. They did one dance routine on roller skates.

KEENE, TOM
THE DUDE WRANGLER (1930, Independent)—Totally under the domination of his aunt, **George Duryea** spends his time designing embroidery patterns. Determined to make good, he buys a ranch in Wyoming, arriving dressed in full cowboy regalia, but at first he's a complete bust. Something in the western air makes a man of him. He defeats a villian and wins a girl.

KEEPER, THE
THE KEEPER (1976, Canada, Lions Gate)—Crippled superintendent of an asylum **Christopher Lee** plots to kill the heirs to his residents' fortunes.

KEESE, EARL & ENID
NEIGHBORS (1981, Columbia)—**John Belushi** and his wife **Kathryn Walker** are suburban homeowners whose peaceful existence is placed in turmoil when wacky Dan Aykroyd and his equally nutty wife Cathy Moriarty move in next door.

KEHOE, DAN
THE KING AND FOUR QUEENS (1956, UA)—On the run from the law, **Clark Gable** arrives in an almost abandoned western town to find Jo Van Fleet and her four daughters-in-law searching for a

large amount of money, hidden there by one of Jo's sons. Gable figures he can share in the loot and the four beauties as well.

KEITH, JACK
KEITH OF THE BORDER (1918, Silent, Triangle)—Texas Ranger **Roy Stewart** works the area near a great southwest desert. He tracks down some murdering varmints, who have kidnapped a girl waiting in a small town for the arrival of her father. Stewart gets his man and his woman.

KEITH, SATURDAY
POET'S PUB (1949, GB, GFD)—Poet **Derek Bond** becomes the manager of a country inn, and foils crooks after a priceless antique.

KELLAM, MICHAEL
THREE MEN AND A BABY (1987, Buena Vista); THREE MEN AND A LITTLE LADY (1990, Buena Vista)—**Steve Guttenberg**, Tom Selleck and Ted Danson are three successful swinging bachelors, who share a plush New York apartment. Their tranquil life is greatly changed by the arrival of a beautiful female, the baby daughter of Ted Danson, dropped off by the child's mother. If this wasn't enough of a problem, the three are innocently drawn into troubles with drug smugglers. The film is based on the French film of a year earlier, THREE MEN AND A CRADLE. In both the original and the sequel, Guttenberg is like a third wheel on a motorcycle, definitely an afterthought when it comes to handing out lines or direction.

KELLER, BILL
PARACHUTE JUMPER (1933, Warner Brothers)—Ex-WWI pilot **Douglas Fairbanks, Jr.** is employed by a mobster to fly drugs into the States from Canada.

KELLER, EDDIE
SOME KIND OF HERO (1982, Paramount)—After serving six years as a prisoner of war in Vietnam, **Richard Pryor** comes home to find his wife has found another man. The army believes he's some kind of collaborator for having signed statements demanded by the Viet Cong to save his buddy's life. He takes up with high-priced call-girl Margot Kidder, and steals a lot of money which he uses long enough to set himself up, and then returns it.

KELLER, JOE & CHRIS
ALL MY SONS (1948, Universal)—Small town munitions manufacturer **Edward G. Robinson's** partner has just died in prison, where he was sent for shipping defective parts to the Army Air Force during WWII. Robinson's son **Burt Lancaster**, back from the service, unhappily comes to the conclusion that it was his father, not Robinson's partner, who was the guilty party.

KELLER, MAJOR
THE COURT MARTIAL OF MAJOR KELLER (1961, GB, Danzinger)—At his court martial, **Laurence Payne** proves he shot his commanding officer for deserting to the enemy.

KELLER, MARTA
THEY DARE NOT LOVE (1941, Columbia)—Austrian **Martha Scott** and George Brent fall in love as they attempt to flee the Nazis. Noble Brent offers to exchange himself to save the lives of seven hostages held by the Germans, one being Scott's fiance.

KELLER, OTTO
I CONFESS (1953, Warner Brothers)—**O.E. Hasse** confesses to Canadian priest Montgomery Clift that he killed a man. Bound by the seal of the confessional, Clift is not able to reveal what Hasse has told him, even when circumstantial evidence seems enough to convict and hang Clift for the crime.

KELLER, PETER
HOW TO SEDUCE A PLAYBOY (1968, Australia, Intercontinental)—When a computer malfunctions, **Peter Alexander** is chosen "Playboy of the Year" by a men's magazine which then parades him all over the world with a series of gorgeous women.

KELLERMAN, ANNETTE
MILLION DOLLAR MERMAID (1952, MGM)—**Esther Williams** portrays the shocking 1910-1920 swimming champion whose one-piece bathing suits were considered scandalous, when she wore them in public. The film didn't mention Kellerman's appearing nude in some movie scenes that she made.

KELLERMAN, GEORGE & GWEN
THE OUT-OF-TOWNERS (1970, Paramount)—**Jack Lemmon** and **Sandy Dennis** travel from Ohio to the Big Apple so Lemmon may be interviewed for a big promotion. Literally everything goes wrong as the pair suffer loss of baggage, no hotel reservations, being robbed and forced to sleep in Central Park. They decide to stay in Ohio.

KELLOGG, CLARK
THE FRESHMAN (1990, Tri-Star)—In an amusing spoof, college student **Matthew Broderick** gets involved with a loony Mafia family, headed by Marlon Brando in a delightful parody of his role as the don in THE GODFATHER.

KELLS, MIKE
DIPLOMATIC COURIER (1952, 20th Century Fox)—U.S. agent **Tyrone Power** is in Trieste to retrieve secret papers stolen from a murdered fellow agent. This is easier said than done, what with murder attempts and a romance with Russian spy Patricia Neal.

KELLY
KELLY'S HEROES (1970, MGM)—**Clint Eastwood** leads a group of American GIs who, while behind German lines in WWII, rob a bank.

KELLY
KING KELLY OF THE USA (1934, Monogram)—In a boring musical, while on a transatlantic cruise, **Guy Robertson** falls in love with a princess.

KELLY
MODERN GIRLS (1986, Atlantic)—If your mentality runs to pre-teenage and your glands a bit older, you might enjoy this comedy. **Virginia Madsen** and two girlfriends hang out at Los Angeles rock clubs.

KELLY, ALVAREZ
ALVAREZ KELLY (1966, Columbia)—Mexican-American cattleman **William Holden** sells his herd to the Union army during the Civil War, and then is kidnapped by Confederate forces, who force him to help them steal the cattle from the Yanks.

KELLY, BILLY
APPRENTICE TO MURDER (1988, New World)—**Chad Lowe**, who no doubt got this role because he's a blond version of his older brother, Rob, assists country doctor Donald Sutherland in a deal with a mysterious neighbor, who begins to show signs of demonic power.

KELLY, CORN COB
RIDE, KELLY, RIDE (1941, 20th Century Fox)—Jockey **Marvin Stephens** outwits gamblers, who try to get him to throw a race.

KELLY, DAN

ONE OF THE BRAVEST (1925, Silent, Gotham/Lumis)—While **Edward Hearn** proves his bravery saving a tailor and his daughter from hoodlums, he has a deathly fear of fires. This is unfortunate because his father is Captain of an engine company, and expects his son to follow the family tradition and become a fireman. Naturally, he proves his mettle by rushing into a burning building to save the occupants which include his father and a swindler.

KELLY, JACK/FRANCIS SULLIVAN

NEWSIES (1992, Buena Vista/Disney)—In an old-fashioned musical, **Christian Bale** leads the 1899 New York news boys strike against publisher Joseph Pulitzer, played by Robert Duvall.

KELLY, JIM

SLIDE, KELLY, SLIDE (1927, Silent, MGM)—**William Haines** is the star pitcher for the New York Yankees, but as his fame grows so does his hat size and soon his egotism hurts the team's chances of winning the World Series. Haines comes through for the crippled team mascot, hitting a home run and winning the last game of the Series for the Yanks.

KELLY, JIMMY

HERE COMES KELLY (1943, Monogram)—Minor movie comedian **Eddie Quillan** is a constant failure, always in trouble, until his girl gets him a job as a process server and he becomes a hero.

KELLY, JOSEPH M. JR.

CASANOVA IN BURLESQUE (1944, Republic)—In the summers, **Joe E. Brown** is a burlesque clown, and during the winters, he's a Shakespearean professor at a small college. He is blackmailed by June Havoc into playing the leading role in "The Taming of the Shrew."

KELLY, KITTY

KOSHER KITTY KELLY (1926, Silent, R-C Pictures)—**Viola Dane** and her poor Irish family find their lives wrapped up in those of their poor Jewish neighbors. Dane loves the son of the Jewish family, but trouble erupts between the families. In the end the young lovers are reunited.

KELLY, LARRY & TIM

GANGSTER'S BOY (1938, Monogram)—High school kid **Jackie Cooper** works hard to take away the stigma of being the son of ex-con **Robert Warwick**.

KELLY, LAURA

LEGAL EAGLES (1986, Universal)—It isn't so much that **Debra Winger** doesn't wish to defend Daryl Hannah on a murder charge, but she'd prefer that her co-counselor in the case, Robert Redford, would stop sleeping with Hannah, at least in ways that make the nightly news.

KELLY, GEORGE "MACHINE GUN"

MACHINE GUN KELLY (1958, American International)—**Charles Bronson** is a vicious hood, who prefers to use tommy guns in his work. He rises to the top in his profession as one of the ten most wanted public enemies.

KELLY, MIDGE

CHAMPION (1949, UA)—Ruthless boxer **Kirk Douglas** alienates his family and friends, leaves his wife for a nightclub singer, but soon dumps her for yet another dame. He's a bad one all right, but does he deserve to go mad and die after his last fight to pay for his sins?

KELLY, MOLLY

KELLY THE SECOND (1936, MGM)—Comedian **Patsy Kelly** is the manager of punch-drunk fighter Guinn "Big Boy" Williams, whom she guides to a championship.

KELLY, NED

NED KELLY (1970, GB, UA)—Rolling Stones lead singer **Mick Jagger** proves he's not much of an actor in his portrayal of the 19th century Australian bandit.

KELLY, NELLIE

LITTLE NELLIE KELLY (1940, MGM)—**Judy Garland** portrays both the title character, a girl who tries to end the feud between her father and her maternal grandfather, and her own mother, who dies in childbirth.

KELLY, PAT

ANYBODY HERE SEEN KELLY? (1928, Silent, Universal)—When doughboy **Tom Moore** goes home to New York after WWI, French girl Bessie Love follows him. She finds him directing traffic at 42nd and Broadway. The loving couple have troubles with a customs official, but marry in time to insure that Love can stay in the country.

KELLY, PATRICK & MRS.

THE COHENS AND THE KELLYS (1926, Silent, Universal); THE COHENS AND THE KELLYS IN ATLANTIC CITY (1929, Universal)—The adventures of an Irish cop and a Jewish shop owner and their families are filled with stereotypes, with some of the antics considered tasteless today, but audiences at the time loved these comedies. The Cohens and Kellys also made it to Africa, Scotland and Paris with **J. Farrell MacDonald** as Mr. Kelly in Gay Paree.—**Charles Murray** originated the role of Patrick Kelly. **Mack Swain** took over for the Atlantic City caper. **Kate Price** was Mrs. Kelly in all the features.

KELLY, PETE

PETE KELLY'S BLUES (1955, Warner Brothers)—During Prohibition days, coronet player **Jack Webb** leads a small combo, but runs afoul of gangster Edmond O'Brien. Webb's drummer Martin Milner is killed, when the kid attempts to defy the mobster's orders. When he's not blowing his horn, Webb is being chased by wealthy flapper Janet Leigh.

KELLY, QUEEN

QUEEN KELLY (1929, Silent, UA)—This 11-reel Erich von Stroheim-directed film was cut to 9-reels by its star **Gloria Swanson**, but it was not released in the United States until the 1980s. In the film, a Ruritanian prince scheduled to marry his cousin, the queen, spies Swanson and is totally infatuated. He kidnaps her and takes her to his chateau. The queen arrives and drives poor Swanson out with a lash. Gloria throws herself in a river and drowns. At least that's the European version. Another ending has Swanson surviving, going to German East Africa, where her brothel-operating aunt forces her to marry a degenerate, drunken cripple. After her husband dies, Swanson's prince comes for her. The queen has been assassinated, the prince is king and he makes Swanson his queen.

KELLY, SGT.

THE IMMORTAL SERGEANT (1943, 20th Century Fox)—**Thomas Mitchell**, a tough inspirational British army sergeant, is lost with his platoon in the deserts of North Africa during WWII. When he dies, his spirit helps corporal Henry Fonda find the strength of character to lead the survivors back to their lines.

KELLY, TED

KELLY OF THE SECRET SERVICE (1936, Victory/Principal)—It is agent **Lloyd Hughes'** assignment to recover the missing plans for a guided missile installation.

KELLY, TIM

THEY MET IN ARGENTINA (1941, RKO)—This stinker couldn't have helped the U.S.'s "Good Neighbor" policy, and it did nothing for the career of **James Ellison** as an amorous young man not interested in love and marriage. He falls into the clutches of Maureen O'Hara, used to getting what she wants.

KELLY, YELLOWSTONE

YELLOWSTONE KELLY (1959, Warner Brothers)—Fur-trapper **Clint Walker** finds trouble both with Indians and the U.S. Cavalry.

KELP, PROF. JULIUS FERRIS

THE NUTTY PROFESSOR (1963, Paramount)—In a sort of comedy Dr. Jekyll and Mr. Hyde, **Jerry Lewis** is a shy chemistry professor who develops a potion which turns him into a swinging ladies' man.

KELSOE, COL.

GHOSTS OF BERKELEY SQUARE (1947, GB, Pathe)—**Felix Aylmer** is the head of St. Michael's school for boys. During WWII it has been evacuated to an old Scottish castle, whose caretaker tells him that when the pipes play, the head of the school will die. The pipes play, and Aylmer follows the tradition as does his successor. The next head solves the mystery.

KELVANEY, CHRISTOPHER

ROGUE COP (1954, MGM)—**Robert Taylor**, from a long line of cops, is in the pocket of mobster George Raft. But the worm turns when Raft does in Taylor's younger brother, a cop who won't be bought.

KEMP, JIM

THE LAST WARRIOR (1989, GB, SVS)—**Gary Graham** is the sole American soldier posted on an obscure South Pacific island during the final days of WWII. Before long, he finds himself and beautiful Maria Holvoe being tracked by three imperial Japanese marines.

KEMPER, LT. IVO

THE HOSTAGE (1917, Silent, Paramount)—A Lowlander commander is forced to give his son **Wallace Reid** as a hostage to the Highlanders. Reid's father has instructed his son to violate the truce at the appropriate moment, but this is made difficult for him, when he is treated with such kindness by his Highlander host, and he falls in love with his captor's daughter.

KENDALL, DORIS

BORN TO LOVE (1931, RKO)—During WWI, American nurse **Constance Bennett** meets and falls in love with pilot Joel McCrea. He goes off to battle, is shot down, and is presumed dead. Bennett has his baby, and marries another officer to give the child a dad. Then McCrea shows up.

KENDALL, STEVE

COWBOY IN THE CLOUDS (1943, Columbia)—**Charles Starrett** is a member of the Civilian Air Patrol, which is threatened by cattlemen, who consider the whole idea a stupid waste of money. Starrett demonstrates its value when he rescues a rancher's daughter from a forest fire.

KENDRED, DICK

THE TROUBLE WITH DICK (1987, Frolix)—Writer **Tom Villard**, a once successful producer of literary science fiction, has writer's

block. He moves into a boarding house, has a couple of affairs at the same time, which so drains him he has no energy to write even things that will be rejected. Well at least he's keeping busy.

KENDRICK

SILENT ASSASSINS (1988, Panache-Forum)—Ex-CIA agent **Gustav Vintas** kidnaps a research scientist, who holds half the formula for a deadly new biological formula. Vintas and his partners have become professional assassins.

KENDRICK, JEAN

FAITHFUL IN MY FASHION (1946, MGM)—This comedy, starring **Donna Reed**, has a department store setting. Salesgirl Reed's romance with soldier Tom Drake is being helped or hindered, depending on your point of view, by her co-workers.

KENNER

KENNER (1969, MGM)—American seaman **Jim Brown** is in Bombay tracking down the drug smuggler, who killed his best friend.

KENNEDY, ANNE

THE FORGOTTEN WOMAN (1939, Universal)—Forced to assist gangsters in a robbery, **Sigrid Gurie** is arrested as an accessory.

KENNEDY, DOROTHY

HER UNBORN CHILD (1930, Windsor)—**Adele Ronson** is in love with Paul Clare, completely under the domination of Doris Rankin. The latter poses as his aunt, but is really his mother. He's not too shy to get Ronson pregnant, but is afraid to get married. Ronson considers an abortion before her lover finally gets up the nerve to marry her.

KENNEDY, EDDIE

THE ST. LOUIS KID (1934, Warner Brothers)—Truck driver **James Cagney** finds himself in the middle of a milk war between truckers and dairy farmers.

KENNEDY, JAMES

THE UNSTOPPABLE MAN (1961, GB, Argo/Sutton)—American industrialist **Cameron Mitchell** rescues his kidnapped son without any help from the police.

KENNICOTT, DR. WILLIAM & CAROL

I MARRIED A DOCTOR (1936, First National/Warner Brothers)—Small-town doctor **Pat O'Brien** marries idealistic city girl **Josephine Hutchinson** in this version of Sinclair Lewis' Main Street with a happy ending.

KENNY

KENNY AND CO. (1976, 20th Century Fox)—Teenage **Dan McCann** survives adolescent growing pains. The presentation is nicely done.

KENNY, ELIZABETH

SISTER KENNY (1946, RKO)—As played by **Rosalind Russell**, Elizabeth Kenny, the nurse who achieved fame for her treatment of infantile paralysis, must have been at least a saint. It would have been better to portray her as the caring human she really was.

KENT, BRIAN

WILD BRIAN KENT (1936, 20th Century Fox)—**Ralph Bellamy** is a wealthy cad, who finally learns some responsibility, when he helps a Kansas girl and her aunt prevent a crooked real estate broker from stealing their ranch.

KENT, CLARK *See* SUPERMAN

KENT, MARIS
WOMAN AGAINST WOMAN (1938, MGM)—Herbert Marshall's wife number two, **Virginia Bruce**, battles with wife number one, Mary Astor, for his love.

KENT, MONA
THE SIN OF MONA KENT (1961, Mermaid/Astor)—In a not very interesting melodrama, audiences are treated to the rise and fall of Broadway star **Sandra Donat**.

KENTON, FIREBRAND
KING OF THE ARENA (1933, Universal)—Back in the days when you could tell the good guys from the bad ones in Westerns, **Ken Maynard** wears a white chapeau in this shoot 'em up set in a circus.

KENTUCKY
OUR MODERN MAIDENS (1929, MGM)—Joan Crawford's marriage to Douglas Fairbanks, Jr. is in jeopardy when she discovers he's having an affair with **Anita Page**.

KENWAY, VIVIAN
A NOTORIOUS GENTLEMAN (1945, GB, Rank)—Known as THE RAKE'S PROGRESS in Great Britain, this is the story of rotter **Rex Harrison**, who is sent down from Oxford. Given a job on his father's office, he seduces his best friend's wife, then swindles another woman, whom he marries for her money then drives to suicide when he has an affair with his father's secretary.

KENWOOD, JOAN
YOUNG WIDOW (1946, UA)—**Jane Russell**, well known to the public due to the publicity for the unreleased THE OUTLAW, actually made her movie debut in this film about a young widow trying to forget her husband, who was killed in the war.

KENYON, DAISY
DAISY KENYON (1947, 20th Century Fox)—Commercial artist **Joan Crawford** is engaged in an affair with married attorney Dana Andrews. This is going nowhere, so Crawford is happy when she meets nice single Henry Fonda, whom she marries. Later Andrews divorces his wife and tries to induce Crawford to do likewise with Fonda. She is sorely tempted.

KENYON, WALLY
THE FIGHTING CHEAT (1926, Silent, Action/Artclass)—**Wally Wales** comes across an outlaw left for dead by his companions and promises the man—who believes he's dying—to take some money to his mother. Wales does and falls in love with the bandit's sister. Later the bandit, who survived, saves the young lovers from an ambush.

KEOUGH, BLESS
GUN FOR A COWARD (1957, Universal)—**Jeffrey Hunter**, the younger brother of rancher Fred MacMurray, is regarded as a coward because he hates violence. Circumstances will force him to strap on a shootin' iron.

KEOUGH, FATHER
THE SINGER NOT THE SONG (1961, GB, Rank/Warner Brothers)—A Mexican bandit, Dirk Bogarde, alphabetically kills villagers to spite the priest, **John Mills**, who loves a landowner's daughter.

KEPES, TISA
MY GIRL TISA (1948, Warner Brothers)—In New York in the 1890s, immigrant girl **Lilli Palmer** is threatened with deportation, until Theodore Roosevelt intercedes in her behalf.

KEREMAZOFF, ANNA
ONCE A LADY (1931, Paramount)—**Ruth Chatterton**, who was almost typecast in such roles, deserts her husband and daughter, letting them think her dead. Twenty years later she reenters their lives.

KERENYE, MARTHA
LADIES IN LOVE (1936, 20th Century Fox)—Budapest working girl **Janet Gaynor** and two of her friends, Loretta Young and Constance Bennett, pool their resources in order to afford an expensive apartment. They hope it will help them catch rich husbands. Gaynor accidently takes the poison Young planned for herself when a romance with a nobleman doesn't pan out. This brings a doctor, whom Gaynor has always loved, back into her life.

KERN, IVO
THE MAN BETWEEN (1953, GB, UA)—**James Mason** is a racketeer operating in divided Berlin.

KERN, LUDWIG
SO ENDS OUR NIGHT (1941, UA)—**Glenn Ford**, whose mother is Jewish, joins Jew Margaret Sullavan and Aryan Fredric March in trying to escape the Nazis. Ford and Sullavan make it to Switzerland, where they marry.

KEROUAC, JACK
KEROUAC (1985, Daybreak)—In this semi-documentary, **Jack Coulter** acts out some of the episodes in the life of the chronicler of the "beat" generation.

KERRY, TIM & RITZY
MY SON IS GUILTY (1940, Columbia)—Hell's Kitchen cop **Harry Carey** tries to help his son **Bruce Cabot**, who has just been released from prison, but the lad is no good. Cabot kills a cop during a crime, and is killed by his father in a shootout.

KERWIN
PARTNERS (1982, Paramount)—Homosexual cop **John Hurt** teams with straight cop Ryan O'Neal to act as gay lovers, so they can go undercover in San Francisco to solve a murder case.

KESSLER, DAVID
AN AMERICAN WEREWOLF IN LONDON (1981, Universal)—There are no limits to facial and hand hair growth for **David Naughton**. His transformation to a werewolf is complete in this comedy-horror pic.

KESSLER, KEN & SANDY
RUTHLESS PEOPLE (1986, Buena Vista)—**Judge Reinhold** and **Helen Slater**, a shy and harmless married couple, kidnap Danny DeVito's wife Bette Midler, because DeVito had stolen Slater's dress design ideas and made a fortune. They figure the ransom will about cover what they lost, but DeVito, glad to be rid of Midler, won't pay the ransom.

KESSLER, VERA
HER PRIVATE AFFAIR (1930, Pathe)—While **Ann Harding** and her judge husband were briefly separated, she wrote some incriminating letters to Lawford Davidson, who later blackmails her. She accidently kills her tormentor when he puts a move on her. Davidson's butler is charged with the murder, but is acquitted.

KESTER, JOHN
TWO LIVING, ONE DEAD (1964, GB, Emerson)—When three post office clerks are robbed by masked gunmen, **Peter Vaughan** is the one who is killed, another is seriously wounded and the remaining clerk is considered a coward for giving the gunmen what they wanted.

KETCHUM, BLACKJACK
BLACKJACK KETCHUM, DESPERADO (1956, Columbia)—Retired gunfighter **Howard Duff** is called upon to tame a wild town.

KETTLE, MA, PA & SLEDGE
MA AND PA KETTLE (1949, Universal); MA AND PA KETTLE GO TO TOWN (1950, Universal) MA AND PA KETTLE AT THE FAIR (1952, Universal); MA AND PA KETTLE ON VACATION (1953, Universal) MA AND PA KETTLE AT HOME (1954, Universal); MA AND PA KETTLE AT WAIKIKI (1955, Universal); THE KETTLES ON OLD MACDONALD'S FARM (1957, Universal); THE KETTLES OF THE OZARKS (1956, Universal)—**Marjorie Main** and **Percy Kilbride** made their first appearance as Ma and Pa Kettle in THE EGG AND I in support of Claudette Colbert and Fred MacMurray. Audiences were so delighted with the hard working Ma, the always loafing Pa and their brood of kids, that Universal brought them back for six more films. When Percy Kilbride could no longer work, Main went on for two more films, first with **Parker Fennelly** and then **Arthur Hunicutt** as two male relatives with Pa Kettle's ideas about avoiding exertion.

KEVIN
HOME ALONE (1990, 20th Century Fox)—In the hectic rush to get his large extended family to the airport for a holiday in Paris, **Macauley Culkin** is accidently left behind. Culkin is endangered by a team of dopey burglars who are systematically cleaning out all the homes in the neighborhood. They prove no match for the resourceful eight-year-old.

KHAN
STAR TREK II: THE WRATH OF KHAN (1982, Paramount)—When the star ship Enterprise's sister ship Reliant lands on a planet ruled by **Ricardo Montalban**, he's delighted. Seems that Capt. Kirk had marooned him there years before, and he's raring for revenge.

KHAN, ELI
HEARTBREAKERS (1984, Orion)—Businessman **Nick Mancuso** and his longtime friend Peter Coyote, now in their middle 30s, are as about as different as two men can be. Mancuso is a Jewish heir to a garment district business, who avoids women, while Coyote is a wild artist into whips and chains with his many female conquests. The two men briefly share a menage a trois with Carole Laure, but then compete for her exclusively.

KHAN, GENGHIS *See* TEMULIN

KHAN, GRACE LEBOY & GUS
I'LL SEE YOU IN MY DREAMS (1951, Warner Brothers)—Perky **Doris Day** is the ever-loyal wife of Tin Pan Alley songwriter **Danny Thomas** in a pleasant if not particularly accurate biopic.

KHAN, KASIN
THE BANDIT OF ZHOBE (1959, Columbia)—**Victor Mature** is an Indian bandit annoying the British.

KHAN, USTAD ZAFAR
THE GURU (1969, 20th Century Fox)—English pop singer Michael York goes to India to learn enlightenment from Guru **Utpal Dutt**.

York is not earnest enough to benefit from the teachings of the master but he does find love with wandering hippie Rita Tushingham.

KHAN, ZARAK
ZARAK (1956, GB, Columbia)—**Victor Mature** and his band of outlaws at India's Northwest Frontier are captured by British officer Michael Wilding and his men. Mature escapes, but later gives his life to save his enemy. It's silly escapism.

KHARIS
THE MUMMY'S HAND (1940, Universal); THE MUMMY'S TOMB (1942, Universal); THE MUMMY'S CURSE (1944, Universal); THE MUMMY'S GHOST (1944, Universal); ABBOTT AND COSTELLO MEET THE MUMMY (1955, Universal); THE MUMMY (1959, GB, Hammer)—In 1940, **Tom Tyler** made a frightening figure as the murderous mummy, kept alive for over 3000 years by a secret elixir so he can protect the tomb of a dead princess from desecraters. In 1942, **Lon Chaney, Jr.** was kept alive by tanna leaves, which must have contained a love potion as well, since he develops tender feelings for Elyse Knox. Chaney is back in 1944 with two more goes as the well-wrapped one with murder on his mind. In 1955, Abbott and Costello were menaced by stuntman **Edwin Parker** as the protector of the tomb. Hammer studios gave audiences a hammy **Christopher Lee** in 1959 in a story much the same as the earlier ones.

KHAYYAM, OMAR
OMAR KHAYYAM (1957, Paramount)—**Cornel Wilde** is corny as the 11th century Persian astronomer and poet.

KID, THE
BOY WHO CAUGHT A CROOK (1961, UA)—With the help of an old tramp, Don Beddoe, **Roger Mobley** and his dog track down a crook.

KID, THE
THE GREAT WHITE HOPE (1970, 20th Century Fox)—If this is the story of the black heavyweight champion Jack Johnson, then **Jim Beattie** must be white Jess Willard, who knocked out Johnson in a bout in Havana in the 26th round.

KID, THE
JOCKS (1987, Crown)—**Scott Strader** is a delinquent stud and star of a college tennis team, made up of an assortment of misfits. The coach has been ordered to whip them into champions or else.

KID, THE
THE KID (1916, Silent, Vitagraph)—Born out of wedlock, **Lillian Walker** has been raised by a newspaperman. On her 19th birthday, she learns of her origins and gets a job with her protector's paper. Her first assignment is to cover a price-fixing story involving—who else?—her father.

KID, THE
THE KID (1921, Silent, Associated First National)—Look at the close-ups of little **Jackie Coogan** and you will see the eyes of a great actor. He is an abandoned child adopted by tenement tramp Charlie Chaplin. Five years later, his mother, now a successful singer reunited with her husband, wants the child back. Prepare to shed tears.

KID, THE *See* MISS MARKER

KID, THE
THE OKLAHOMA KID (1929, Silent, Syndicate Releasing Co.)—While delivering his boss's cattle from Oklahoma to New Mexico,

Bob Custer is beaten and impersonated by a member of a gang of swindlers. It takes a map tattooed on Custer's arm to expose the deception.

KID, THE

SON OF BELLE STARR (1953, Allied Artists)—When your mother is the infamous Belle Starr, there seems to be no other line of work for **Keith Larson** to enter except being an outlaw.

KID BOOTS

KID BOOTS (1926, Silent, Paramount)—**Eddie Cantor** is the buddy and caddy-master to professional golfer Lawrence Gray. The latter has inherited a fortune, and would like to unload the wife he is tricked into marrying. Cantor saves the day, much like Puss 'n' Boots.

KID GALAHAD

KID GALAHAD (1937, Warner Brothers); (Ward Gussenberry); (1962, UA) (Walter Gulick)—**Wayne Morris** and **Elvis Presley** portray a boxer who wins a championship, but almost loses his girl. Presley sings between rounds to keep up his spirits.

KID GLOVES

KID GLOVES (1929, Warner Brothers)—Bootlegger **Conrad Nagel** is forced by her fiance to marry Lois Wilson when he discovers them in an innocent but incriminating situation. Later the fiance, a bootlegger, realizing that Wilson was not two-timing him, wants her back and decides to kill Nagel. The latter survives and so does the marriage.

KID RODELO

KID RODELO (1966, Paramount)—Drifter **Don Murray** competes with a gang of killers for a cache of gold.

KIDD, JOE

JOE KIDD (1972, Universal)—Loner **Clint Eastwood** is hired by rancher Robert Duvall to lead a band of gunmen against Spanish-American John Saxon, who is trying to have the original Spanish land grants honored to benefit his people. Eastwood soon switches sides in the confrontation.

KIDD, CAPT. WILLIAM

CAPTAIN KIDD (1945, UA); ABBOTT AND COSTELLO MEET CAPTAIN KIDD (1952, Warner Brothers); CAPTAIN KIDD AND THE SLAVE GIRL (1954, UA)—**Charles Laughton** provides a hammy performance as the bloodthirsty pirate, later hanged for his crimes, but it was only a warm-up for his absurd recreation of the role in the Abbott and Costello film. **Anthony Dexter** is more dashing than Laughton but the 1954 movie is nothing to get excited about.

KIDDO

PAINTED WOMAN (1932, Fox)—Singapore nightclub singer **Peggy Shannon** accidently becomes involved in a murder, and has to beat it out of town. She is marooned on a small island where she meets Spencer Tracy and falls in love. They marry despite her lurid background and are happy until an old flame shows up determined to take up where he left off.

KIKI

KIKI (1926, Silent, First National); (1931, UA)—First **Norma Talmadge** and then **Mary Pickford** star as the Parisian gamine who becomes a chorus girl, fights constantly with the show's star, but gets the advantage when she steals the star's lover, the manager of the show.

KILDARE, DR. JAMES

INTERNS CAN'T TAKE MONEY (1937, Paramount); YOUNG DR. KILDARE (1938, MGM); CALLING DR. KILDARE (1939, MGM); THE SECRET OF DR. KILDARE (1939, MGM); DR. KILDARE GOES HOME (1940, MGM); DR. KILDARE'S CRISIS (1940, MGM) DR. KILDARE'S STRANGEST CASE (1940, MGM); DR. KILDARE'S VICTORY (1941, MGM); DR. KILDARE'S WEDDING DAY (1941, MGM); THE PEOPLE VS. DR. KILDARE (1941, MGM)—The answer to the trivia question "Who originated the movie role of Max Brand's medical character Dr. Kildare?" is **Joel McCrea** in the 1937 Paramount film. It has nothing to do with the series starring **Lew Ayres**. In it, McCrea helps gangster's widow Barbara Stanwyck recover her missing child. From then on MGM took over, presenting soft-spoken Ayres as the sensitive and dedicated young physician who works under the direction of grouchy old Dr. Gillespie (Lionel Barrymore). Ayres was written out of the series when the star of ALL QUIET ON THE WESTERN FRONT declared himself a conscientious objector during WWII. Ayres did serve during the war but as a non-combatant.

KILDARE, MRS.

KILDARE OF THE STORM (1918, Silent, Metro)—**Emily Stevens** is stuck in an unhappy marriage of convenience. She falls in love with a doctor who is sent to prison for murder when her husband is killed. Later a servant confesses to the crime and Stevens and the doctor are free to marry.

KILDEE, ALICE

THE STRANGER (1987, Columbia)—**Bonnie Bedelia** witnesses a brutal murder, is shot at, and totally loses her memory. She is treated by a psychiatrist who helps her remember something more than a murder of an unknown victim by some unidentified murderers.

KILGANNON, JIMMIE "KILLER"

THE RAIN PEOPLE (1969, Warner Brothers)—Brain damaged, handsome hitchhiker **James Caan** is picked up by pregnant Shirley Knight. She has deserted her Long Island home and husband and is heading west. Knight has the seduction of Caan in mind, but there are many obstacles.

KILKERRY, FAY

UNFAITHFUL (1931, Paramount)—In another of her many weepers, **Ruth Chatterton** sacrifices her reputation to save that of her sister-in-law.

KILLER, THE

HE KNOWS YOU'RE ALONE (1980, MGM/UA)—**Tom Rolfing**, a knife-wielding maniac, turns a wedding into a bloodbath.

KILLIAN, JIM

HEAVEN WITH A GUN (1969, MGM)—Gunfighter-turned-preacher **Glenn Ford** tries to make peace between warring sheepmen and cattlemen.

KILMENY

KILMENY (1915, Silent, Paramount)—When she was a child, the gypsies stole **Leonore Ulrich**. When she is grown she runs away from them but is rejected by all other societies and returns to the only family she ever knew.

KILMOUNT, SULKY

THE EARL OF CHICAGO (1940, MGM)—American gangster **Robert Montgomery** inherits a British title, kills a former criminal colleague, is tried in the House of Lords, and is hanged for the crime.

KILPATRICK
DEADLY TRACKERS (1973, Warner Brothers)—When sheriff **Richard Harris's** family is brutally murdered by bank robbers, he's on their trail to give them similar treatment in this gory Western.

KILROY, JOHN J.
KILROY WAS HERE (1947, Monogram)—**Jackie Cooper** is the Kilroy of the famous WWII slogan "Kilroy Was Here." He's now in college and things are not going so well for him. He's always in and out of trouble.

KILVINSKY, SGT.
THE NEW CENTURIONS (1972, Columbia)—Old street cop **George C. Scott** teaches his new young partner Stacy Keach how to get along, but he has no lessons for himself and shortly after retiring from the force, kills himself.

KIM
KIM (1950, MGM)—**Dean Stockwell** appears as Rudyard Kipling's boy hero, a school-hating son of an English envoy, who disguises himself as a native boy, so he can have some adventures—and so he does.

KIMBALL, GEORGE
SEND ME NO FLOWERS (1964, Universal)—Mistakenly believing his days are numbered, **Rock Hudson** feels he must find a replacement husband for his wife Doris Day. She completely misunderstands his efforts.

KIMBELL, CINDY
SMALL TOWN GIRL (1953, MGM)—**Jane Powell** stars in the remake of the 1936 movie of the same name (starring Janet Gaynor). She's a judge's daughter, who falls in love with millionaire Farley Granger, who is given 30 days in the slammer for speeding through her small community. The plot is just enough to allow for a number of Busby Berkeley-staged musical numbers performed by Miss Powell, Ann Miller and Bobby Van.

KIMBERLY, CATHERINE
IMPOSSIBLE CATHERINE (1919, Silent, Pearson)—In a modern version of "The Taming of the Shrew," **Virginia Pearson** is the impossible daughter of a millionaire. She changes nicely when she meets a man who drags her off to a lumber camp where he forces her "to act like a woman."

KIMBERLY, MR.
THE HUCKSTERS (1947, MGM)—**Adolphe Menjou** is the head of an advertising agency. He's caught in the middle between his disgusting client Sydney Greenstreet and his best idea man, Clark Gable, just back from WWII.

KIMBERLY, SIR PHILIP
THE JIGSAW MAN (1984, GB, United Film)—Former British secret service agent **Michael Caine**, who had his face reconstructed after defecting to the Soviets, is back in England for one last mission—but for whom is he working?

KIMBLE
KINDERGARTEN COP (1990, Universal)—It must be in **Arnold Schwarzenegger's** contract that he will alternate his brutal killing-machine persona with that of a comical, muscle-bound klutz. There are few laughs in this film about a cop who goes undercover in a kindergarten to put away a murderous drug dealer. Don't be misinformed; this film is not for the kiddies. There's too much violence for that but in comparison to TOTAL RECALL, it's a comedy.

KIMBROUGH, EMILY
OUR HEARTS WERE YOUNG AND GAY (1944, Paramount); OUR HEARTS WERE GROWING UP (1946, Paramount)—**Diana Lynn** and her friend Gail Russell, appearing as actress Cornelia Otis Skinner, displayed much youthful exuberance in this charming memoir. The sequel didn't have the same magic and bombed at the box offices.

KINCAID
HUNT THE MAN DOWN (1950, RKO)—Penniless **James Anderson**, accused of a murder, is brought to trial 12 years after the crime occurred. Public defender Gig Young is able to clear him.

KINCAID, JIM
THE OKLAHOMA KID (1939, Warner Brothers)—Good-bad-guy **James Cagney** is out to avenge the lynching of his father in a not-to-be-taken-too-seriously Western in which Humphrey Bogart portrays the bad-bad-guy. Cagney even sings a Spanish version of "Rockabye Baby."

KINCAID, SGT. MIKE
TEN TALL MEN (1951, Columbia)—In a Foreign Legion spoof, **Burt Lancaster** and nine other assorted refugees from the world provide the expected heroics in defending France's African possessions against natives, who understandably resent their presence.

KINCAID, RAY *See* JIM LARSON

KINCAID, REGINALD (SHERLOCK HOLMES)
WITHOUT A CLUE (1988, Orion)—In a dull mystery spoof, Dr. Watson, played by Ben Kingsley, is the deductive genius, while dumb actor **Michael Caine** has been hired to impersonate Kingsley's creation.

KITCARIN, ROBERT
THE WHITE BLACK SHEEP (1926, Silent, First National)—When **Richard Barthelmess** assumes responsibility for a theft of which his fiancee is guilty, his father disowns him. Barthelmess joins the British forces in Palestine. He goes undercover in a desert chief's camp and learns of plans to attack the British which he reveals to his father, the British commander of the area. This and his former fiancee's confession lead to a reconciliation between father and son.

KINDLER, FRANZ *See* PROFESSOR CHARLES RANKIN

KINEMON, DAVID
TOL'ABLE DAVID (1921, Silent, Associated First National); (1930, Columbia)—**Richard Barthelmess** and **Richard Cromwell** each found the role of the Virginia mountain youngster, who overcomes a reputation as a coward by facing the three fugitives who crippled his brother, to be among the high points of his career.

KING
PLATOON (1987, Orion)—**Keith David** is one of the lesser grunts in this spectacular presentation of how it was to be a combat soldier in Vietnam.

KING, THE
THE KING'S DAUGHTER (1916, Silent, GB, Jury)—An assassin's daughter gives her life to save her king, **Edward O'Neill**, when she discovers she is really his illegitimate daughter.

KING, CAPT. ALAN

KING OF THE KHYBER RIFLES (1953, 20th Century Fox)—Half-caste **Tyrone Power**, a captain in the Khyber Rifles in India in the 1850s, is not considered acceptable as a prospective bridegroom for Terry Moore by her father Michael Rennie, Power's commanding officer. However, his bravery in battle changes Rennie's mind.

KING, ARTHUR

KING ARTHUR WAS A GENTLEMAN (1942, GB, Gainsborough)—Obsessed with the King Arthur legend, army recruit **Arthur Askey** is given a sword by his friends which he imagines to be Excalibur. It gives him courage when sent to the front, where he becomes a hero.

KING, CAROL

GOLD DIGGERS OF 1933 (1933, Warner Brothers)—In this delightful escapist musical, showgirl **Joan Blondell** snatches off Warren William, the older brother of wealthy Dick Powell, when the former arrives in New York to save Powell from the clutches of dancer Ruby Keeler.

KING, CLAUDE

KING OF THE RITZ (1933, GB, British Lion)—**Stanley Lupino**, the head porter at the Ritz hotel, wins the love of a rich widow, but ends up with the maid who loves him.

KING, CPL.

KING RAT (1965, Columbia)—Japanese prisoner of war **George Segal** survives because he's a sharp trader. This doesn't sit too well with some of his fellow prisoners.

KING, DAISY

THE GIRL FROM WOOLWORTH'S (1929, First National)—**Alice White** doesn't tell the man who recovers her purse from a subway train that she's merely a singing clerk at the five and ten store, and he doesn't admit that he's just a subway guard. Instead they claim more glamorous jobs. This causes expected problems for the young couple, but all is cleared up before the final clinch.

KING, EVA

ADAM AND EVA (1923, Silent, Paramount)—**Marion Davies** is the extravagant daughter of a wealthy man. He is fed up with her various parasitic suitors. He puts employee T. Roy Barnes in charge of his business and family and goes to South America. Barnes announces that the business is bankrupt. Davies rises to the challenge and inspires her family to move to a farm where all work hard, and she falls in love with Barnes.

KING, GARRY

THE ALL-AMERICAN (1932, Universal)—Football hero **Richard Arlen's** head grows too big for his helmet in this cliche-filled sports film.

KING, GEORGIA

HER KIND OF MAN (1946, Warner Brothers)—Singer **Janis Paige** is one leg (a very nice one, in fact) of a triangle involving Prohibition mobster Zachary Scott and newspaper columnist Dane Clark.

KING, GINGER

THE FLAPPER (1920, Silent, Selznick)—Strictly raised school girl **Olive Thomas** kicks up her heels, getting into a lot of innocent trouble.

KING, JANET

LORD CAMBER'S LADIES (1932, GB, British Int.)—When Nigel Bruce's wife, a former vaudeville star, dies **Benita Hume**, whom Bruce had once loved, is suspected of poisoning her, but she's cleared.

KING, JOYCE

WOMEN WITHOUT NAMES (1940, Paramount)—Innocent **Ellen Drew** and her new husband are convicted of murder. She is sent to prison but finds an eyewitness there who saves her man from the gallows.

KING, KITTY

AIR HOSTESS (1933, Columbia)—Well it only goes to show there's a potential movie in everyone's life, even air hostess (stewardess) **Evalyn Knapp**, who flies out of Albuquerque.

KING, MABEL

TRAVELING SALESWOMAN (1950, Columbia)—**Joan Davis** and her fiance Andy Devine try to find something funny about selling soap.

KING, MONTY

KING OF THE CASTLE (1936, GB, GFD)—**Billy Milton**, the heir to a title, is assisted in proving his claim to the inheritance by butler Claude Dampier.

KING, MURRAY

KING, MURRAY (1969, Amran Nowak/EYR)—In what is billed as a "fictional documentary," **Murray Ramsey King** is an obnoxious salesman spending a weekend in Las Vegas. It is a very strange and not very interesting piece, no matter what you call it.

KING OF POLDAVIA

HIS MAJESTY AND CO. (1935, GB, Fox)—King of Poldavia **Morton Selten** and his family take up exile in London, where his daughter falls in love with a struggling singer.

KING OF SIAM, THE

THE KING AND I (1956, 20th Century Fox)—**Yul Brynner** magnificently recreates his stage triumph in this rather long musical. The King of Siam is given advice on how to bring his country into the modern world by Deborah Kerr, the English schoolmistress he employs to teach his many children.

KING, RICHARD

THE STREET SINGER (1937, GB, Wardour)—**Arthur Tracy**, ever after known as "The Street Singer" with theme song "Marta," is a musical comedy star who becomes fed up with the life. He becomes a busker who sings in the street.

KING, SGT.

KING OF THE ROYAL MOUNTED (1936, 20th Century Fox)—Comic strip mountie hero Sgt. King is portrayed by **Robert Kent** in a story about a girl, her gold mine and a crooked lawyer who is trying to steal it from her.

KING, SOLOMON

SOLOMON KING (1974, Sal-Wa-Stage Struck)—In another below-par black exploitation film, **Sal Watts** avenges the death of a princess and ex-lover when he organizes a commando raid against an Arab sheikdom.

KING, TED

KING OF THE CORAL SEA (1956, Australia, Allied Artists)—**Chips Rafferty** deals with smugglers trying to sneak illegal oriental aliens into Australia.

KINGSFORD-SMITH, SIR CHARLES
SMITHY (1946, Australia, Columbia)—**Ron Randell** stars in this biopic of the Australian air hero.

KINGSLEY, JOHN
KINGS AND DESPERATE MEN (1984, GB, Blue Dolphin)—When a political extremist takes over a radio station at gunpoint, talk show host **Patrick McGoohan** stages a call-in trial on the points that upset the terrorist.

KINGSLEY, WADE, JR.
PARDNERS (1956, Paramount)—**Jerry Lewis** and Dean Martin make fun of classic western cliches in this remake of RHYTHM ON THE RANGE (1936).

KINSOLVING, MRS. & FRANCESCA
YOU'LL LIKE MY MOTHER (1972, Universal)—**Rosemary Murphy** is the mother-in-law **Patty Duke** has never met. When her husband is killed in Vietnam, Duke decides to visit his family and it's a weird and dangerous one indeed.

KINGSTON, BOBBY
THE NIGHT MAYOR (1932, Columbia)—**Lee Tracy** portrays a Jimmy Walker-like mayor of New York who prefers nightclubs, race tracks and showgirls to city hall.

KINGSTON, JIM
TEXAS RANGERS RIDE AGAIN (1940, Paramount)—In a contemporary western, Texas ranger **John Howard** saves May Robson's ranch from rustlers.

KINKAID, JIM
KINKAID, GAMBLER (1916, Silent, Universal)—**R.A. Cavin**, a gambler accused of a major theft, is so smitten by the female detective sent to get him that he allows her to transport him back across the border from Mexico to the U.S.

KIPP, HUGO
THE GLADIATOR (1938, Columbia)—When college student **Joe E. Brown** is given a serum developed by a professor, he develops amazing strength, making him a football hero. Unfortunately, the effects begin to wear off just as he begins a wrestling match with a champ.

KIPP, JIM
THE BOUNTY HUNTER (1954, Warner Brothers)—Bounty hunter **Randolph Scott's** specialty is bringing in train robbers.

KIPPS, ARTHUR
KIPPS (1921, Silent, GB, Stoll); (1941, GB, 20th Century Fox)—First **George K. Arthur** and then **Michael Redgrave** star as the draper's assistant who comes into a fortune and chooses to marry his childhood sweetheart rather than an impoverished society girl.

KIRBY, BRANDY
TWO OF A KIND (1951, Columbia)—**Lizabeth Scott** and Alexander Knox scheme to swindle a couple who will pay anything to get back their long missing son. They arrange to have carnival showman Edmond O'Brien pose as the missing son, but the con artists split when Scott falls for O'Brien.

KIRBY, CAMEO
CAMEO KIRBY (1915, Silent, Paramount); (1930, Fox)—In 1915, **Dustin Farnum** played Booth Tarkington's hero, a decent river boat gambler of the mid 1800s, who rescues a pretty girl from hooligans and her father from dishonest gamblers out to get his plantation. It

was slow-moving drivel then and things didn't improve with the advent of sound and **J. Harold Murray** in the title role.

KIRBY, MAJOR
THE MAJOR AND THE MINOR (1942, Paramount)—**Ray Milland**, the commander of a boy's military school, befriends a 12-year-old girl riding a train. Turns out she's adult Ginger Rogers trying to travel for half fare. The two to-be-lovers get the age problem straightened out eventually, but did Milland's character have a Lolita complex?

KIRBY, PAUL
PAID TO KILL (1954, GB, Hammer)—**Paul Carpenter** is blackmailed by failed financier Dane Clark to kill him within five days so Clark's wife can collect his insurance.

KIRBY, ROSE
ROSE OF THE WORLD (1925, Silent, Warner Brothers)—**Patsy Ruth Miller** is loved by wealthy Allan Forrest, but because of the difference in their social status, he doesn't marry her. She ends up with a rotten husband and Forrest is caught by a vamp. Both spouses expire conveniently and Miller is reunited with Forrest.

KIRK, MARY
MARY HAD A LITTLE (1961, GB, UA)—A producer wagers that he can hypnotize **Agnes Laurent** into having a perfect baby—whatever that is.

KIRK, PETER
YOU BELONG TO ME (1941, Columbia)—Millionaire playboy **Henry Fonda** marries Barbara Stanwyck, a physician, but becomes increasingly jealous of her male patients.

KIRK, POPPY
DANCE TEAM (1932, Fox)—**Sally Eilers** and James Dunn are ballroom dancers who make it big as a team. But they split, due to some misunderstandings about the attentions paid to Eilers by a rich man.

KIRKE, RUTH
AMAZING MRS. HOLLIDAY (1943, Universal)—**Deanna Durbin**, an American school teacher in China, smuggles nine Chinese orphans back to the states, but it's not an easy mission.

KIRSCHENBAUM, NAOMI
ALAN AND NAOMI (1992, Triton)—Fourteen-year-old **Vanessa Zaouri** is virtually catatonic. She was traumatized when the Nazis killed her father. Lukas Haas patiently tries to break her out of her trance.

KIRSHNER, DR. MAXWELL
THE THING WITH TWO HEADS (1972, American Int.)—Racist brain surgeon **Ray Milland** is dying of cancer. He arranges to have his head transplanted onto the body of a healthy convict volunteer. Surprise! His donor body belongs to black Roosevelt Grier.

KISENGA
KISENGA, MAN OF AFRICA (1952, GB, Two Cities)—African composer **Robert Adams** is a hit in Europe but returns home to oppose a witch doctor making trouble for his tribe.

KIT
COVERGIRL (1985, New World)—Don't wait around to see **Irene Ferris** as a model who has a meteoric rise in her field. The success and the heartache are totally predictable.

KIT

THE DEADLY COMPANIONS (1961, Pathe-American)—When gunslinger Brian Keith accidently kills dance-hall girl **Maureen O'Hara's** son, he tries to make amends by escorting her through Indian and outlaw territory in the desert.

KIT

THE FALLEN SPARROW (1943, RKO)—Spanish Civil War veteran **John Garfield** comes home to the U.S. after two years of torture as a prisoner of the Fascists. In New York, Nazis use beautiful Maureen O'Hara to drug him and use psychological tricks to make him divulge secrets that he wouldn't tell while in Spain.

KIT

I SAW WHAT YOU DID (1965, Universal)—**Sarah Lane** is one of two girls who think it would be just peachy keen to call someone at random and speak the film's title. One who receives their call is John Ireland. He has just killed his wife and he recognizes his callers.

KITTERIDGE, ROBIN

THREE FOR THE ROAD (1987, New Century/Vista)—Senator's daughter **Kerri Green** is being driven to a southern psychiatric clinic by the senator's most junior aide, Charlie Sheen, and his friend. Her father wants the troublesome child, whom he regularly abuses, out of the way during a political campaign. The aide and his friend come to treat the girl with kindness and understanding.

KITTREDGE, ROBERT

THEY GOT ME COVERED (1943, RKO)—Moscow news agency correspondent **Bob Hope** is so busy enjoying himself that he doesn't get the news that Hitler has invaded Russia and he doesn't report it either. Fired and in disgrace back in the states, Hope attempts to win back his job by getting the goods on some Nazi agents.

KITTY

KITTY (1945, Paramount)—Lovely **Paulette Goddard** is transformed from a London guttersnipe into a duchess by 18th century fop Ray Milland, who hopes to cash in when she marries well.

KIVALINA

KIVALINA OF THE ICE LANDS (1925, Silent, B.C.R. Productions)—**Kivalina** is the bride-to-be of the great Eskimo hunter Aguvaluk. He must first bring in the hides of 40 seals to pay his father's debts. He must also bring in the hide of a silver fox as interest on the debts.

KLENK, ERNIE

THE MAN FROM THE DINER'S CLUB (1963, Columbia)—Diner's Club clerk **Danny Kaye** inadvertently issues a card to gangster Telly Savalas. So what, you might ask? It's just a ploy to bring together schnook Kaye, in one of his least interesting movies, and Savalas, who plans to use Kaye for his own devious purposes.

KLUGGS, BILL

WHEN WILLIE COMES MARCHING HOME (1950, 20th Century Fox)—When eager **Dan Dailey** is the first in his town to enlist at the outbreak of WWII, he's hoping to see lots of action. Instead, because of his skills he is assigned to his hometown air base as a gunnery instructor. One night a gunner takes ill and Dailey replaces him on an overseas mission. Dailey is forced to bail out over France. He meets a beautiful resistance fighter who takes him to the site of Nazi rocket emplacements. Dailey gets back to America and makes a report on what he has learned, which proves vital to the war effort.

But Dailey is sworn to secrecy and can tell no one about his experience and as far as the people of his home town are concerned, he's never been away.

KLUTE, JOHN

KLUTE (1971, Warner Brothers)—Small-town cop **Donald Sutherland** is on leave in New York, seeking an explanation as to what happened to a friend who has disappeared. His major lead in the case is model-prostitute Jane Fonda. Laconic Sutherland underplays the role superbly.

KNABEHSHU, AGATHA

DID YOU HEAR THE ONE ABOUT THE TRAVELING SALESLADY? (1968, Universal)—Traveling saleslady **Phyllis Diller** arrives in a small Missouri town in 1890 selling pianolas. It's meant to be a comedy.

KNAPP, LESTER

THE HOME MAKER (1925, Silent, Universal)—This domestic drama is an unfunny MR. MOM. When **Clive Brook** is fired, he attempts suicide but only cripples himself. His wife is forced to find a job and from his wheelchair, he runs the house and minds the children. The arrangement works so well that when he regains the use of his legs, they keep things the way they are.

KNIEVEL, EVEL

EVEL KNIEVEL (1971, Fanfare); VIVA KNIEVEL! (1977, Warner Brothers)—Apparently not impressed by the performance of **George Hamilton** who portrayed him in the 1971 film biopic, in 1977 stuntman **Evel Knievel** attempts a stunt he's not equipped to handle—acting.

KNIGHT, LT. JEFF

PLATOON LEADER (1988, Cannon)—**Michael Dudikoff** is a young lieutenant just in from the States. He's stationed at a small Vietnam firebase. At first his inexperience makes him the butt of the jokes of his battle-hardened troops, but with the help of a sergeant, he proves his worth.

KNIGHT, LARRY

WHEN A MAN'S A MAN (1935, Fox)—Down and out **George O'Brien** heads west and a hoped for brighter future. He gets his break when he divines a well site during a drought.

KNOLLYS, CAROLINE

UNCHASTENED WOMAN (1925, Silent, Chadwick)—Just as she's about to announce that she's pregnant, **Theda Bara** finds her husband in the arms of his secretary. Without telling him that he's to become a father, she runs off to Europe where she becomes the toast of the continent. Her husband makes an unannounced visit, looking for evidence against her in divorce proceedings but instead is introduced to his son. The two reconcile.

KOBLING, WILL

THE FUGITIVE (1940, GB, Universal)—When barber **Ralph Richardson** commits a petty crime, he finds himself involved in murder and blackmail.

KOHLER, ERICH

SQUADRON LEADER X (1943, RKO)—Nazi pilot **Eric Portman** is in WWII London, tracked both by the British and his treacherous comrades, who wish to eliminate him. He is aided by Ann Dvorak, a young girl of German extraction, who finds herself in the position of betraying her country or being sent to prison.

KOLTER, SANDRA

ZIEGFELD GIRL (1941, MGM)—In this all-star musical, **Hedy Lamarr**, Judy Garland and Lana Turner find their lives changed when they are recruited to be Ziegfeld girls.

KOOL ROCK

DISORDERLIES (1987, Warner Brothers)—**Damon Wimbley** is one of three obese black rap singers who call themselves "The Fat Boys." Wealthy old Ralph Bellamy is put in their care by his nephew who hopes their ineptness will result in the old man kicking the bucket so the nephew can inherit his fortune.

KOPAC, STEVE

MY SIX CONVICTS (1952, Columbia)—Embezzler **Jay Adler** joins a convict encounter group headed by psychologist John Beal in this prison comedy.

KORASKI, BIFF

ABROAD WITH TWO YANKS (1944, UA)—The title is a cheap pun. The two soldiers are **William Bendix** and Dennis O'Keefe—the broad is Helen Walker, whom they both meet and fall for in Australia. If you're in a silly mood, this might do.

KORDA

THE DEATHMASTER (1972, American International)—Vampire **Robert Quarry's** coffin washes up on the coast of Southern California, where he becomes a murdering guru to a band of hippies.

KORMAN, ARTHUR

THE GOODBYE PEOPLE (1984, Embassy)—**Judd Hirsch** and Pamela Reed help Martin Balsam realize his long-time dream of rebuilding his Coney Island hot-dog stand.

KORNPETT, SHELDON

THE IN-LAWS (1979, Warner Brothers)—Dentist **Alan Arkin** and nutzy CIA agent Peter Falk have some dangerous adventures in a banana republic in the days just before their children are to marry. They survive and are much richer for the experience.

KOSTER, OTTO

THREE COMRADES (1938, MGM)—German WWI veterans **Franchot Tone**, Robert Taylor and Robert Young find things tough after the armistice. They all share a love for dying Margaret Sullavan.

KOTCHER, JOSEPH P.

KOTCH (1971, ABC Cinerama)—Appearances to the contrary, **Walter Matthau** is not ready to be put out to pasture as his children seem to believe.

KOVACS, CAPTAIN

HIS GLORIOUS NIGHT (1929, MGM)—Cavalry officer **John Gilbert** has an affair with a princess, Catherine Dale Owen. Her mother convinces the girl that she cannot maintain a relationship with a peasant's son. However, in an attempt to recover some of the letters of the princess, the royal parent learns Gilbert's price: Owen must spend the night with him. The lovers are allowed to reconcile.

KOVACS, JOHNNY

WHEN JOHNNY COMES MARCHING HOME (1943, Universal)—While on leave, soldier **Allan Jones** visits his old boarding house, and revives a romance with beautiful Gloria Jean. The plot is just enough to get to the patriotic musical numbers.

KOVIC, RON

BORN ON THE FOURTH OF JULY (1989, Universal)—**Tom Cruise** gives a strong performance as gung-ho American teen, who enlists in the marines and is sent to Vietnam. Seeing women and children killed, accidently shooting one of his own men, and having his spinal column severed, take their toll on his convictions. On his return home, paralyzed from mid-chest on down, he slowly becomes an anti-Vietnam demonstrator, so much so that he is ultimately invited to address the Democratic National Convention. It's a true story.

KOWALSKI, ROXANNE

ROXANNE (1987, Columbia)—In a modern-day adaptation of the Cyrano de Bergerac story by Rostand, **Daryl Hannah** is the lovely object of affection of long-nosed fireman Steve Martin. He conceals his love and reluctantly helps a crude stud bed his beloved. But as Martin wrote the screenplay, he gets Hannah in the end.

KOZINSKI, LARRY

COUSINS (1989, Paramount)—When his wife Sean Young starts an affair with William Petersen, **Ted Danson** and the cheated wife Isabella Rossellini take comfort from each other.

KRACKKLITE, STOURLEY

BELLY OF THE ARCHITECT (1987, GB, Hemdale)—Architect **Brian Dennehy**, in Rome working on a project, begins to suspect that his young wife and an Italian architect are poisoning him.

KRAFT, ROBERT

I BURY THE LIVING (1958, UA)—**Richard Boone**, who sells cemetery plots, accidentally discovers that placing a pin on a map of the cemetery in a person's plot causes that person's death. Guess what happens when he pulls out pins.

KRAMER

MEN'S CLUB (1986, Paramount)—**Richard Jordan** forms an encounter group for seven of his male friends in his home. Too bad he bothered.

KRAMER, PAT

THE INCREDIBLE SHRINKING WOMAN (1981, Universal)—In a contemporary remake of THE INCREDIBLE SHRINKING MAN (1957), **Lily Tomlin** finds herself shrinking in size when she spills a new perfume sample given to her by her marketing husband. The special effects are quite good.

KRAMER, TED & JOANNA

KRAMER VS. KRAMER (1979, Columbia)—When his wife **Meryl Streep** leaves him to find herself, busy executive **Dustin Hoffman** is left to be both father and mother to their son, Justin Henry. Just when he's getting good at it (at the cost of his job), Streep decides she wants the boy. A court awards Justin to his mother, but seeing how unhappy the decision makes everyone, Streep relents and allows the lad to stay with Hoffman.

KRANZ, LUDWIG

SUCH MEN ARE DANGEROUS (1930, Fox)—Disfigured **Warner Baxter** takes as a wife a woman who is marrying him only for financial reasons. She makes it clear that his appearance is abhorrent to her. He leaves for Europe making it appear that he has committed suicide. There he has an operation which gives him a handsome face. He returns with plans to take revenge on his wife, but when she falls in love with him, he forgives her.

KRASKA, MME.

THE IMPOSSIBLE WOMAN (1919, Silent, GB, Ideal)—Eccentric **Constance Collier** and her poetry-writing gentleman friend cause a lot of trouble for her ward, when the girl marries a lawyer.

KRAVAAL, DR. LEON

THE MAN WITH NINE LIVES (1940, Columbia)—**Boris Karloff's** cancer cure attempt is to freeze his patients in a Canadian ice cave. He is treated to his own cure and after thawing out has a run-in with mounties who object to his plans to freeze the healthy.

KRAVITZ, DUDDY

THE APPRENTICESHIP OF DUDDY KRAVITZ (1974, Canada, Paramount—The year is 1948 and young Canadian Jewish schemer **Richard Dreyfuss** will do just about anything to raise the money to buy a plot of land he fancies.

KRAY, VIOLET, RONALD & REGINALD

THE KRAYS (1990, GB, Rank)—**Billie Whitelaw** is the smothering, subtly encouraging mother of **Gary** and **Martin Kemp**, who are two warped and violent British twin-brother gangsters. The story is based on real-life sociopaths in London in the 1950s and 1960s.

KRIEGER, ROBBY

THE DOORS (1991, Tri-Star)—**Frank Whaley's** role is purely supportive to that of Val Kilmer's Jim Morrison, a pretentious poet and would-be filmmaker who helped light everyone's fire.

KRISTIDIS, JIMMY

HOT SHOT (1987, Arista)—Wealthy **Jim Younger** becomes a professional soccer player, but his hot-dogging doesn't sit well with his teammates. Younger heads to Brazil where he becomes the protege of soccer immortal Pele. When he returns to his team, he shows that he can fit in to a team concept of play.

KROLL, PAUL

THE MATCH KING (1932, First National)—**Warren William** portrays a Ivar Krueger-like character, the man who made a fortune in the ordinary match business, by borrowing money, then borrowing more to pay back the initial loan, then borrowing more to pay off the second, and so forth. This pyramid of matches of course came tumbling down on him and his investors.

KROLL, LEO

THE STRANGLER (1964, Allied Artists)—Overweight lab technician **Victor Buono** enjoys killing the nurses who attend his possessive mother.

KRONOS, CAPTAIN

CAPTAIN KRONOS: VAMPIRE HUNTER (1974, GB, Hammer)—With the help of a hunchback and a pretty girl, **Horst Janson** seeks out and destroys vampires. Some are damn difficult to kill.

KROZAC, JOE

THE LAST GANGSTER (1937, MGM)—Former big-time mobster **Edward G. Robinson**, now way past his prime, is released from prison after serving a long term. He finds the world a lot different and he no longer has any power or family.

KRUEGER, FREDDIE

A NIGHTMARE ON ELM STREET 4: THE DREAM MASTER (1988, New Line)—Dream Warriors Rodney Eastman, Ken Sagoes and Tuesday Knight suddenly are plagued by dreams of the supposedly dead and buried **Robert Englund**.

KRUPA, GENE

THE GENE KRUPA STORY (1959, Columbia)—**Sal Mineo**, not one of the most healthy-looking actors, makes big band drummer Gene Krupa seem to be on one long bad trip.

KUBIEK, GUS

DON'T TELL HER IT'S ME (1990, Hemdale)—It takes a sensitive touch to film a story in which a central character is suffering from some disease or disorder. Screenwriter Sarah Bird and director Malcolm Mowbray don't have it. **Steve Guttenberg** is all but unrecognizable because of the chemotherapy treatment he's undergone for Hodgkin's disease. Not too surprisingly, the object of his desire, Jami Gertz, is not turned on by either his appearance or his attitude. Guttenberg's sister Shelly Long volunteers for the job of transforming her brother into a Mel Gibson-like stud. It's meant to be a comedy, but it's grotesque.

KUFFS, GEORGE

KUFFS (1992, Universal)—Ne'er-do-well high school dropout **Christian Slater** becomes a cop to avenge the death of his brother Bruce Boxleitner. It's standard stuff with few laughs.

KULKAS, STEVE

KING OF THE GAMBLERS (1937, Paramount)—A-Number One villian **Akim Tamiroff**, a slot machine Czar, is put out of business by investigative reporter Lloyd Nolan.

KURT, PAUL

THE HEART THIEF (1927, Silent, Metropolitan)—Embittered by war, **Joseph Schildkraut** wastes his life gambling. He falls in love with a woman, but she is disgusted with his life style. He later has an opportunity to show some redeeming qualities and win her love.

KYLE, GIL

THE REDHEAD AND THE COWBOY (1950, Paramount)—Cowpoke **Glenn Ford** is mistaken for a Confederate agent by Rhonda Fleming, who is carrying Civil War secrets.

KYRA

SHE DEVIL (1957, 20th Century Fox)—Dying of tuberculosis, **Mari Blanchard** agrees to take a new serum never tried before. It not only cures her and makes her strong, it also makes her a killer.

L

LA CROIX, JULES

THE MAGNIFICENT FRAUD (1939, Paramount)—Actor **Akim Tamiroff** accepts a most dangerous role, posing as a dictator who has been assassinated.

LA DOUCE, IRMA

IRMA LA DOUCE (1963, UA)—Paris street-walker **Shirley MacLaine** is won by former police officer Jack Lemmon in a fight with her pimp. Lemmon falls in love with her, deciding he wishes to keep her for himself. He disguises himself as a rich man, who insists on being her only customer. This deception is almost the death of him.

LA FARGE, GOLDIE

GOLDIE GETS ALONG (1933, RKO)—**Lili Damita** deserts her New Jersey sweetheart to head for Hollywood. Along the way she becomes involved in a phony beauty contest.

LA MAR, JERRY

THE GOLD DIGGERS (1923, Silent, Warner Brothers)—**Hope Hampton** is not a gold digger and neither is her friend Anne Cornwall. However, Hampton poses as one to vamp the uncle of Cornwall's love, because the elder man has claimed that all chorus girls are gold diggers. Hampton plans to make Cornwall look good by comparison. Of course Hampton and the uncle fall in love.

LA MARR, ROSIE

STEPPING SISTERS (1932, Fox)—**Minna Gombell** and two friends, all former burlesque queens, set a society party on its ear.

LA MONDE, JULIETTE

THE BELOVED ADVENTURESS (1917, Silent, Peerless)—Actress **Kitty Gordon** has been thrown out by her parents for being less than pure. When they die, Gordon vows to prevent her younger sister from making the same mistakes that she has. She is as good as her word, even to the point of shooting her own lover who has designs on the younger girl.

LA MOTTA, JAKE

RAGING BULL (1980, UA)—**Robert De Niro** put on a great deal of weight to accurately portray the out-of-shape boxer La Motta. De Niro won an Oscar for his remarkably fine performance.

LA ORTEGA *See* SENORITA CATALINA

LA ROCHE

THE PIRATES OF BLOOD RIVER (1962, GB, Hammer)—**Christopher Lee**, dressed all in black and wearing an eye patch, forces Kerwin Matthews to guide him and his band of cutthroats to a Huguenot settlement in the Caribbean in order to steal a solid gold relic.

LA ROUGE, JACQUES

JACQUES OF THE SILVER NORTH (1919, Silent, Select)—One reviewer bemoaning what this film might have been, claimed that the producers "by a series of masterly moves, pulled defeat right out of the jaws of victory." French Canadian **Mitchell Lewis** will do just about anything for the girl he loves and since she's always getting into trouble, he's kept fairly busy.

LA RUE, FOXINE

LITTLE MISS ROUGHNECK (1938, Columbia)—Would-be Hollywood child star **Edith Fellows's** career is almost ruined before it starts by her obnoxious stage mother.

LA RUE, LASH

KING OF THE BULLWHIP (1950, Real Art)—**Lash La Rue** makes use of his talent with a bullwhip, posing as a bandit in order to solve a gold-bullion robbery.

LA RUE, POPPY

THE HALF-WAY GIRL (1925, Silent, First National)—**Doris Kenyon**, the hostess in a Singapore dive, gives shelter to Lloyd Hughes, the son of the Superintendent of Police. Hughes accidently killed a man while drunk. The two fall in love and she helps him plan an escape on a steamer. Hughes's father mistakes Kenyon for a prostitute and sends her to the red light district from which she escapes in time to catch up with her lover before his steamer sails.

LA RUSSO, DANIEL

THE KARATE KID, PART III (1989, Columbia)—In the first two films in this series, **Ralph Macchio's** last name wasn't used. Now since he's 29, still playing a sixteen-year-old, the producers must

have thought it was time to re-christen him. He's still learning to kick and shout from loveable old Pat Morita.

LA TASSA, MANUEL

MY AMERICAN WIFE (1923, Silent, Paramount)—Because of a horse race, Argentinian playboy **Antonio Moreno** meets and falls in love with Kentuckian Gloria Swanson. She marries him and convinces him that it is his duty to participate in his government.

LA TOUR, DAPHNE

DAPHNE AND THE PIRATE (1916, Silent, Triangle)—**Lillian Gish** is forcibly removed from France, and transported to Louisiana where women are scarce. When the shipload of women is attacked by pirates, Gish mans a cannon and blows the buccaneers away.

LA TOUR, JOHN

LIGHT SLEEPER (1992, Seven Arts)—**Willem Dafoe** works as a delivery boy for cocaine dealer Susan Sarandon. The latter, seeing the handwriting on the wall, plans to get out of the trade. Dafoe lives alone in an ascetic apartment, constantly writing in his diary. When his former lover Dana Delany overdoses, Dafoe gets a gun.

LA TOUR, MICHELLE

FRIENDS (1971, GB, Paramount)—Orphaned French girl **Anicee Alvina** and a neglected English boy, Sean Bury, make a world of their own at a secluded seashore, learning of life and love. Then his parents show up to take the babies who have had a baby home.

LA ZONGA, MADAME

SIX LESSONS FROM MADAME LA ZONGA (1941, Universal)—Noisy, loud-mouthed **Lupe Velez** causes quite a sensation on a ship headed to Havana.

LABRACCIO

FLATLINERS (1990, Columbia)—Medical student **Kevin Bacon** and four of his classmates experience death and return, but find that the door has not been completely closed behind them.

LACROSSE, BILLY

IT TAKES A THIEF (1960, GB, Alliance)—Can you see **Jayne Mansfield** as the leader of a gang of British crooks? The producers of this movie apparently could.

LACEY, JAMES

HOME JAMES (1928, Silent, Universal)—**Charles Delaney**, son of a department store owner, is mistaken by store clerk Laura La Plante for a chauffeur. He allows her to continue in her misconception, even to the point of taking her to his father's mansion and acting as if she were the mistress of the house.

LACKERY

THE LAVENDER HILL MOB (1951, GB, Ealing)—**Sid James** is one of the two lesser members of the gang headed by Alec Guinness and Stanley Holloway, planning and executing a heist of gold from the bank, where meek little Guinness has worked for many years.

LACY, ED

DEADLY HERO (1976, Avco Embassy)—Righteous cop **Don Murray** kills a black man attacking a woman. Could it be that his motive was due to discrimination?

LACY, JIM "NEVADA"

NEVADA (1944, RKO)—**Robert Mitchum** recreates a 1927 Gary Cooper role as a criminal cowboy who tries to go straight.

LADD, MAYME

WHAT HAPPENED TO ROSA? (1921, Silent, Goldwyn)—Shopgirl **Mabel Normand** is told by a fortune teller that she is the reincarnation of a noble Spanish lady. In a Cinderella-like story, she attends a masquerade party on a ship dressed as a highborn Spanish maiden and falls for doctor Hugh Thompson. Rather than reveal her identity, Normand discards her clothing and swims ashore. Thompson thinks she's drowned, but he later discovers her again (wearing her Spanish costume) and proposes.

LADDIE

LADDIE (1940, RKO)—Indiana farmer **Tim Holt** and English girl Virginia Gilmore are brought together by the latter's little sister Joan Carroll.

LADY LOU

SHE DONE HIM WRONG (1933, Paramount)—Shady lady **Mae West** runs a Bowery saloon during the Gay Nineties. She's attracted to Salvation Army laddie Cary Grant, unaware that he's an undercover agent sent to get the goods on her. She propositions Grant with her often misquoted line: "Why don't you come up sometime and see me? I'm home every night."

LADYFINGERS *See* ROBERT ASHE

LAFARGE, MADELEINE

A FRENCH MISTRESS (1960, GB, British Lion)—Public school headmaster Cecil Parker suspects that French teacher **Agnes Laurent**, loved by his son, is his own illegitimate daughter.

LAFITTE, JEAN

THE BUCCANEER (1938, Paramount); (1958, Paramount); LAST OF THE BUCCANEERS (1950, Columbia)—**Fredric March** and **Yul Brynner** appear as the notorious pirate who refuses to attack American ships from his Louisiana bayou headquarters. He even comes to the aid of General Andrew Jackson in the defense of New Orleans in a battle that takes place after the war is over. **Paul Henreid** played the role in a routine swashbuckler which didn't do much for Henreid or Lafitte.

LAKER, SAM

THE NAKED RUNNER (1967, GB, Warner Brothers)—American businessman **Frank Sinatra** is induced by the kidnapping of his son to assassinate a British spy who has defected to the Russians.

LAMB, LADY CAROLINE

LADY CAROLINE LAMB (1972, GB, UA)—**Sarah Miles** is the wife of a member of Parliament, whose affair with Lord Byron causes her downfall.

LAMB, HAROLD "SPEEDY"

THE FRESHMAN (1925, Silent, Pathe Exchange)—College student **Harold Lloyd**, the butt of the jokes of his classmates, becomes a campus hero when he wins the big game. It also earns him the girl of his dreams. The film is one of Lloyd's best.

LAMBARDI, MADDALEN

MADONNA OF THE SEVEN MOONS (1945, GB, Gainsborough) When **Phyllis Calvert** was a child she was raped. Later, as a prim wife, the experience causes her to run away to become the mistress of a gypsy thief, Stewart Granger.

LAMBERT, ALICE

HER MAD BARGAIN (1921, Silent, Associated First National) - Despairing model **Anita Stewart** attempts suicide, but is convinced by a sculptor to put off killing herself for a while. Instead he will insure her for $35,000 (a portion of which she will get at once) and then at the end of six months she will accidentally kill herself. Love saves her from her mad bargain.

LAMBERT, PROF. DEAN

PROFESSOR BEWARE (1938, Paramount)—In a film which had too many writers, **Harold Lloyd** plays a professor of archeology who believes he is the reincarnation of an ancient Egyptian. Only in the last 20 minutes do we see vintage Lloyd.

LAMBERT, MERRILL

UNHOLY PARTNERS (1941, MGM)—During Prohibition, underworld king **Edward Arnold** corrupts crusading newspaper editor Edward G. Robinson.

LAMBERT, MIKE

FRAMED (1947, Columbia)—When innocent **Glenn Ford** is arrested for a robbery, it gives the real thief a chance to escape.

LAMBERT, RICK

TRACK THE MAN DOWN (1956, GB, Republic)—**George Rose** double-crosses his accomplices in a robbery at a race track. The case carrying the loot gets misplaced but a reporter tracks it and Rose down.

LAMMOREAUX, MILLIE

THREE WOMEN (1977, 20th Century Fox)—**Shelley Duvall**, an attendant in an old folks home, finds that new female staff member Sissy Spacek has a crush on her.

LAMONT, FATHER

EXORCIST II: THE HERETIC (1977, Warner Brothers)—In the sequel to THE EXORCIST, it's **Richard Burton's** turn to take a crack at the demon still possessing Linda Blair.

LAMPTON, JOE

MAN AT THE TOP (1973, GB, Anglo EMI)—**Kenneth Haigh**, who starred in the British TV spin-off of ROOM AT THE TOP, makes one yearn for Laurence Harvey, which is quite a feat.

LANCASTER, JIM

MISTER CINDERS (1934, GB, Wardour)—**Clifford Mollison** is a male Cinderella who works as a virtual servant in the home of his better-off relatives. Of course, they have two worthless sons. The princess in the plot is the daughter of an American oil baron. She and Mollison get together.

LANCE, NANCY

THIRTY-DAY PRINCESS (1934, Paramount)—When a princess visiting the United States becomes ill, **Sylvia Sidney** becomes her substitute, and finds romance with Cary Grant.

LANCELOT

SWORD OF LANCELOT (1963, GB, Universal)—**Cornel Wilde** gives a surprisingly fine performance as the knight who loved and was loved by both King Arthur, played by Brian Aherne, and Guinevere, played by Wilde's wife Jean Wallace.

LAND, KATHRYN

ANDY HARDY'S PRIVATE SECRETARY (1941, MGM)—MGM gave many of its young starlets experience by putting them in Andy Hardy movies. **Kathryn Grayson** got the same treatment and the usual rush by star Mickey Rooney but she refused to date the pint-size stud.

LANDERS, TONY

BROADWAY BAD (1933, Fox)—When she is divorced by her jerk of a husband, who wrongly suspects her of unfaithfulness, **Joan Blondell** claims that her son was fathered by another man, so she can keep him with her. That'll fix the SOB.

LANDIN, CLAIRE

WOMEN ARE LIKE THAT (1938, First National)—**Kay Francis's** attempts to rescue hubby Pat O'Brien's failing business is viewed as meddling and almost ends their marriage. Men are frequently touchy like that.

LANDIS, CAROLE

FOUR JILLS IN A JEEP (1944, 20th Century Fox)—**Carole Landis** plays herself in this story about the wartime adventures of four glamorous movie stars entertaining servicemen in England and North Africa. Dick Haymes makes his movie debut as a singing soldier.

LANDIS, ERICA

SUMMER LOVE (1958, Universal)—Musical combo leader John Saxon has romances with both **Jill St. John** and Molly Bee, when his group gets a gig at a co-ed summer camp.

LANDRU

BLUEBEARD'S TEN HONEYMOONS (1960, Allied Artists)—**George Sanders** appears as the French wife-murderer, Landru. It's no pun to note that the action is repetitive.

LANDRY, MATT

TOUGHEST MAN IN ARIZONA (1952, Republic)—Singing bandleader **Vaughn Monroe** ("Ghost Riders in the Sky") is a marshal trailing the man who sold guns to the Indians, which they used in a massacre.

LANE, CORBY

SHE COULDN'T SAY NO (1954, RKO)—Wealthy **Jean Simmons** has returned to a small Arkansas town where her life was saved by the inhabitants, who paid for an operation when she was a child. Her attempts to repay them for their kindness almost destroy the community.

LANE, DON

PAINTED PEOPLE (1924, Silent, Associated First National)—**Ben Lyon** and Colleen Moore grew up together in a shabby factory town. They each dream of marrying well, but after becoming successes they realize that they love each other.

LANE, ERNEST

SWEETHEARTS (1938, MGM)—**Nelson Eddy** and Jeanette MacDonald appear as a temperamental theatre couple in the Victor Herbert operetta, spiced by the acid wit of writer Dorothy Parker and her husband Alan Campbell.

LANE, HONDO

HONDO (1953, Warner Brothers)—Former Cavalry dispatch rider and gunslinger **John Wayne** defends lonely Geraldine Page and her young son from Apache raids in the Southwest in 1874. The Duke likes how baking powder makes Page smell.

LANE, JIM

TEST PILOT (1938, MGM)—Test pilot **Clark Gable** is forced to land on a Kansas farm where he falls in love with Myrna Loy. The marriage gets off to a shaky start because she finds it difficult to adjust to his lifestyle.

LANE, NED

THE SONG OF THE WAGE SLAVE (1915, Silent, Metro)—**Edmund Breeze** is a working stiff, who marries pregnant Helen Martin, when the father, Fraunie Fraunholz, is forbidden by his mill owner father from marrying the girl. When finally Fraunholz takes over from his deceased father, he wants Martin and his child. Breeze steps aside, but leads a union fight against the mill owner. When Breeze sacrifices his life to save Fraunholz in a bombing of the mill, the owner meets the workers' demands.

LANE, OLIVER

THE SOLITAIRE MAN (1933, MGM)—The confrontation between double-crossing crooks, one of whom is **Herbert Marshall**, takes place in the cabin of a Paris to London airplane.

LANE, PAULA

SOMEWHERE I'LL FIND YOU (1942, MGM)—**Lana Turner** is one third of a romantic triangle involving brothers Clark Gable and Robert Sterling. The production of the movie was interrupted by the air-crash death of Gable's wife Carole Lombard.

LANE, PETER

THE JACK KNIFE MAN (1920, Silent, First National)—Old recluse **Fred Turner** raises a little boy on his houseboat after the youngster's mother dies.

LANE, RAE

UNASHAMED (1938, Cine-Grand)—Smitten with her chronically ill boss, **Rae Kidd** convinces him to take a cure in a remote nature camp. He agrees and finds Kidd there when he arrives. She's in the buff as is everyone else because its a nudist camp. Well, the boss finally notices Kidd.

LANE, SUSAN

SHE WOULDN'T SAY YES (1945, Columbia)—Psychiatrist **Rosalind Russell** becomes involved with one of her patients. Shrink from this one.

LANG, ALLISON

HALF ANGEL (1936, 20th Century Fox)—After being acquitted of charges of poisoning her father, **Frances Dee** is later arrested again when her benefactor dies of poisoning.

LANG, EDDIE

I PROMISE TO PAY (1937, Columbia)—Honest family man **Chester Morris** is taken in by loan sharks.

LANG, KARL

THE CHOCOLATE SOLDIER (1941, MGM)—**Nelson Eddy** and Rise Stevens are married actors. They are the toast of Vienna. He's jealous of all the men who pay her court. To test her loyalty he poses as a Russian count who attempts to seduce her. She sees through his disguise, but pretends to be acceptable to his advances. Later she confesses she knew it was him all along, but will he ever be sure?

LANE, OSWALD

THE HERO (1923, Silent, Preferred)—**Gaston Glass** trades on his reputation as a war hero in his home town. He shows his gratitude to his brother who has taken him in by making love to his sibling's maid and is working on his brother's wife when he steals some money entrusted to his brother. On his way out of town he notices a fire in a school, saves several children and dies but not before directing that the money be returned to his brother.

LANG, SOPHIE

THE NOTORIOUS SOPHIE LANG (1934, Paramount); THE RETURN OF SOPHIE LANG (1936, Paramount); SOPHIE LANG GOES WEST (1937, Paramount)—Notorious jewel thief **Gertrude Michael** always manages to elude the traps set for her by police in these three second features.

LANG, "THUNDERBOLT" JIM

THUNDERBOLT (1929, Paramount)—From his death cell in Sing Sing, **George Bancroft** frames Richard Arlen, his rival for Fay Wray, for a robbery. The younger man is put in a cell next to Bancroft, who plots to kill Arlen on the night of his execution.

LANGFORD

WHITE CARGO (1930, GB, Neo-Art); (1942, MGM)—**Maurice Evans** and **Richard Carlson** each portray the British rubber planter in Africa, who marries and is ruined by the seductive and wicked native girl Tondelayo.

LANGFORD, JOAN

THE GIRL ON THE FRONT PAGE (1936, Universal)—**Gloria Stuart**, heiress to a powerful newspaper, takes a job with it under an assumed name and helps the editor crack a blackmail racket.

LANGLAND, GAY

THE MISFITS (1961, UA)—In his final film appearance **Clark Gable**, an aging modern day cowboy, joins Montgomery Clift and Eli Wallach in capturing wild horses, which they plan to sell to dog food makers. Marilyn Monroe opposes their plans and they turn the four-legged "misfits" loose. Some believe that Gable's exertion in the film contributed to his fatal heart attack.

LANGSTON, DAVID

THE HARVESTER (1927, Silent, R-C Pictures); (1936, Republic)—Dim-witted farmer David Langston played first by **Orville Caldwell** and then **Russell Hardie** is Ma's choice for her dopey daughter. May they be dull ever after.

LANGTRY, MYRA

THE GRIFTERS (1990, Miramax)—**Annette Bening** is a sexy piece of baggage in this film with no heroes. She appreciates the value of her sexual attractiveness to men and is more than willing to barter her body for whatever she wants. One thing she wants is to have small-time con man John Cusack become her new partner in the grand scam. Cusack's mother Anjelica Huston, a roving race track bag woman, stands in her way. Someone must be eliminated.

LANIER, JACQUELINE

HER REPUTATION (1923, Silent, Associated First National)—When her guardian is killed by an unsuccessful suitor for her hand, **May McAvoy** is blamed for the man's death. She runs away to escape the notoriety and joins a troupe of dancers. Everything works out in the end, and she inherits her guardian's fortune.

LANNING, JACK

THE KNOCKOUT KID (1927, Silent, Paramount)—When the son of a millionaire, **Jack Perrin**, wins a prizefight, his father, who does not approve of boxing, disinherits him. Perrin goes west, where he is almost lynched when suspected of being a rustler. He avoids the advances of an amorous widow and falls in love with the latter's niece.

LANNY

SPECIAL AGENT K-7 (1937, Syndicate Releasing Co.)—FBI agent **Walter McGrail** is called into a murder case and finds the main suspect to be the boyfriend of a female friend. What would J. Edgar do?

LANSING, CAMERON

CAMERON'S CLOSET (1989, SVS)—Ten-year-old **Scott Curtis** lives with his parapsychologist father. After the latter dies, Curtis is sent to live with his mother and her live-in lover. Things aren't going well, and they get worse when a demon is found in Curtis' closet.

LANSKY, MEYER

MOBSTERS (1991, Universal)—**Patrick Dempsey** tries very hard to be a tough mobster, but he looks like a little boy play-acting.

LANTERN, TOBIAS

CONDEMNED TO DEATH (1932, GB, Twickenham)—**Bernard Brunel** is sentenced to death by judge Arthur Wonter. Three years after his death by hanging, murders similar to those committed by Brunel occur. It's discovered that the judge has committed the murders, having been hypnotized by Brunel's spirit.

LANYARD, MICHAEL

ALIAS THE LONE WOLF (1927, Silent, Columbia); THE LONE WOLF'S DAUGHTER (1929, Columbia); LAST OF THE LONE WOLF (1930, Columbia)—**Bert Lytell**; THE LONE WOLF IN PARIS (1938, Columbia)—**Francis Lederer**; THE LONE WOLF RETURNS (1936, Columbia); THE LONE WOLF SPY HUNT (1939, Columbia); THE LONE WOLF KEEPS A DATE (1940, Columbia); THE LONE WOLF MEETS A LADY (1940, Columbia); THE LONE WOLF STRIKES (1940, Columbia); THE LONE WOLF TAKES A CHANCE (1941, Columbia); SECRETS OF THE LONE WOLF (1941, Columbia)—**Warren William**; THE NOTORIOUS LONE WOLF (1946, Columbia); THE LONE WOLF IN LONDON (1947, Columbia); THE LONE WOLF IN MEXICO (1947, Columbia)—**Gerald Mohr**; THE LONE WOLF AND HIS LADY (1949, Columbia)—**Ron Randell**—Columbia would return time after time to the exploits of Louis Joseph Vance's jewel thief extraordinaire. Even though the debonair cracksman had retired, the police refuse to believe it and when a crime is committed which seems to fit his M.O., he has to track down the culprits himself.

LAO, DR.

SEVEN FACES OF DR. LAO (1964, MGM)—**Tony Randall** is the proprietor of a magical circus who changes the lives of the inhabitants of a small western town.

LARABEE, ANDREW

MERRY ANDREW (1958, MGM)—In a film not up to his usual standards, **Danny Kaye** is a professor who briefly joins a circus and falls in love with Pier Angeli.

LARANETTA, INEZ

INEZ FROM HOLLYWOOD (1924, Silent, First National)—Movie vamp **Anna Q. Nilsson**, believed to be "The Worst Woman in Hollywood," tries to shield her sister from the impulses of men. The one man she does respect, she gives up to ensure her sister's happiness.

LAREY, ADAM

WANDERER OF THE WASTELAND (1930, Paramount); (1935, Paramount)—**Jack Holt** and **Dean Jagger** each star as a young mining engineer who shoots his brother in a quarrel, and wounds the sheriff while escaping from town. He later will return to atone for his crimes and is allowed to marry his girl.

LARKIN, GENEVIEVE

GOLD DIGGERS OF 1937 (1936, Warner Brothers)—**Glenda Farrell** and Victor Moore provide the comedy in this musical story of insurance salesman Dick Powell who becomes the producer of a Broadway show.

LARKIN, TOM

THE AVENGING RIDER (1928, Silent, FBO)—When the owner of the ranch where he is foreman is murdered, **Tom Tyler** and the deceased's niece share the estate. They take an immediate dislike to each other, but Tyler has bigger problems when he is accused of having murdered his benefactor. He clears himself, finds the real culprit and then goes to work improving his relationship with his partner.

LARKINS, MOLLY

THE FARMER TAKES A WIFE (1935, 20th Century Fox); (1953, 20th Century Fox)—**Janet Gaynor** and **Betty Grable** each star as the girlfriend of a tough Erie Canal captain who hires a young farmer as a seaman. Romance develops between the girl and the farmer, with her finally agreeing with him that living ashore is the preferable life. The 1953 version is a pleasant but not memorable musical.

LAROUX, GASTON

THE APACHE (1928, Silent, Columbia)—When a police official is mysteriously killed, Apache **Warner Richmond** is suspected because the official was trying to seduce Margaret Livingston, Richmond's lover and partner. But the culprit proves to be Livingston's former partner in a knife-throwing act.

LARRABEE, SUE

SIERRA SUE (1941, Republic)—In this Gene Autry western **Fay McKenzie** is the romantic interest for the singing cowboy, who's brought in to investigate the death of a rancher's cattle.

LARRABEE, TED

CHILDREN OF DIVORCE (1927, Silent, Paramount)—Before becoming a star, ladies' man **Gary Cooper** appeared in a mixed bag of pictures including this forgettable one as a member of the social set who after a wild party is tricked into marrying a flapper.

LARRY

DIRTY MARY, CRAZY LARRY (1974, 20th Century Fox)—**Peter Fonda** and his buddy Adam Roarke extort $150,000 from a supermarket manager with which they purchase a souped-up racing car, but find parolee Susan George goes along with the car.

LARRY

THE MYSTERY MAN (1935, Monogram)—When Chicago reporter **Robert Armstrong** is given a bonus for solving a mystery, he celebrates so much that he wakes up broke in St. Louis. He has to solve another mystery to get the funds to return to the Windy City.

LARSEN, WOLF

THE SEA WOLF (1913, Silent, Bosworth); (1930, Fox); (1941, Warner Brothers); WOLF LARSEN (1958, Allied Artists)—**Hobart Bosworth, Milton Sills, Edward G. Robinson** and **Barry Sullivan** each appeared as the absolute master of a sea schooner, a mystic and philosopher, who rules his men with an iron hand. When a ferry going from San Francisco to Oakland collides with a steamer, Wolf Larsen picks up survivors Maud Brewster and Humphrey Van Weyden, whom he treats as prisoners. He decides to marry Brewster but at the ceremony, the crew mutinies, Larsen is stricken with blindness and is lost when his ship goes down in flames. In 1941, a new role was introduced to provide a young love interest for Maud

(Ida Lupino) in the person of seaman John Garfield. Each of the film versions of the Jack London story is effectively done.

LARSON, DON

THE GUN RANGER (1937, Republic)—Perhaps the producers of the Dirty Harry movies saw this film about Texas Ranger **Bob Steele** who throws down his badge when the law lets a murderer go free and goes after the killer on his own.

LARSON, JIM

FACE OF A FUGITIVE (1959, Columbia)—**Fred MacMurray** is forced to start over in a new western town when he's falsely accused of a murder, but he can't shake his past.

LARSON, LELA

SING SINNER, SING (1933, Majestic)—Torch singer **Leslie Hyams** (who can't and doesn't sing) has trouble with her jealous millionaire husband.

LASCELLES, LT. DICKY

THE FLAG LIEUTENANT (1919, GB, Silent, Jury); (1926, GB, Silent, Astra); (1932, GB, Gaumont); FURTHER ADVENTURES OF THE FLAG LIEUTENANT (1927, GB, Silent, Neo-Art) -**George Wynn** in the first two pictures and **Henry Edwards** in the others star as the lieutenant who is branded a coward after saving a beleaguered fort and giving the credit to an amnesiac major. Edwards also stars in a silent sequel in which he escapes from spies and regains stolen plans.

LASENBY, LADY MARY

MALE AND FEMALE (1919, Silent, Paramount)—Cecil B. De Mille was not satisfied with the title of Sir James Barrie's play "The Admirable Crichton" and chose one that sounded a bit more racy. It's still the same story, however, of English butler Thomas Meighan who proves to be superior to aristocrats when his employer, his family and some of their friends are shipwrecked on a deserted island. His employer's daughter **Gloria Swanson** falls in love with her servant, at least until they are rescued.

LASH, CAPTAIN

CAPTAIN LASH (1929, Silent, Fox)—**Victor McLaglen** is the boss of the black gang of an ocean liner. He becomes involved with a classy female passenger, who tries to use McLaglen to smuggle some diamonds she and her confederates have stolen from a jewel collector, but McLaglen proves too smart for them.

LASSITER

LASSITER (1984, Warner Brothers)—Jewel thief **Tom Selleck** is recruited by the FBI to steal jewels for them.

LATCHERIE, SHELBY EATENTON

STEEL MAGNOLIAS (1989, Tri-Star)—In an Academy Award-nominated performance, Julia Roberts marries and, despite warnings about her diabetic condition, has a baby.

LATHAM, DICK

GO WEST, YOUNG MAN (1919, Silent, Goldwyn)—When shiftless **Tom Moore** is all but thrown out of his home by his millionaire father, he goes west and makes something of himself, even to the point of being elected sheriff.

LATHAM, HENRY

HENRY THE RAINMAKER (1949, Monogram); LEAVE IT TO HENRY (1949, Monogram); FATHER MAKES GOOD; (1950, Monogram); FATHER'S WILD GAME (1950, Monogram); FATHER TAKES THE AIR (1951, Monogram)—**Raymond Walburn**, who reminds one of

Esquire magazine's racy elderly gentleman logo, is Mister Average Citizen. His efforts to put things right in his home or community are near disasters, before working out.

LATIGO, TOM
THE COWBOY MUSKETEER (1925, Silent, R-C Pictures)—**Tom Tyler** poses as a notorious thug to help Frances Dare locate a missing map to her late father's gold mine, which some no-good skunk is also trying to find.

LATIMER, JEAN
THE GIRL WHO HAD EVERYTHING (1953, MGM)—**Elizabeth Taylor**, daughter of a famous criminal lawyer, almost is brought to ruin by her infatuation with one of her father's unsavory clients, Fernando Lamas.

LATIMER, MARY
MARY LATIMER, NUN (1920, Silent, GB, Famous Pictures)—When a Peer's son, married to slum girl **Malvina Longfellow**, deserts his wife, she becomes London's most famous music hall singer.

LATIMER, RICK
THE PRINCIPAL (1987, Tri-Star)—**James Belushi** is appointed principal of an unmanageable high school. With the help of security officer Lou Gossett, he finds ways to manage it. Most schools shown in movies nowadays are either populated by violent anti-social druggies or horny adolescents for whom studies can't compete with getting high or sex. In either case there's little education taking place. An exception is STAND AND DELIVER (1988), with Oscar nominee Edward James Olmos as a successful Hispanic calculus teacher.

LATTIMER, CMDR. WILLIAM & DAPHNE
THE SKIPPER SURPRISED HIS WIFE (1950, MGM)—Ex-sea captain **Robert Walker** attempts to run his home like he did his ship, which does not please wife **Joan Leslie**.

LATOUR, HILLAIRE
THE PRISONER OF THE PINES (1918, Silent, Paralta)—**J. William Kerrigan** seems to be a slow learner. He leaves his wife and child to work in a lumber camp to earn money for them. After a year, he's on his way home to his family but is relieved of his poke by a whore in a saloon. He goes back in the woods for another year and on his way home loses all his money to the very same girl. The next year, he's ready for her and almost strangles her to death until she returns everything she has stolen from him. Then he goes home to his wife and child.

LATOUR, SYLVIA
TWO GALS AND A GUY (1951, UA)—**Janis Paige**, the female partner of a married TV star team, leaves the show in order to take care of adopted twins. Yep, it sounds exciting to us also.

LAUGHING ANNIE
LAUGHING ANNIE (1954, GB, Republic)—It's rather embarrassing for singer **Margaret Lockwood** but she has laughing fits. This is certainly not a comedy. Her lover, an ex-boxer has lost the use of his hands. The two drift aimlessly through Japanese waterfront dives in the 1890s. It's based on Joseph Conrad's "Between the Tides."

LAUGHING BOY
LAUGHING BOY (1934, MGM)—Fortunately few people saw **Ramon Novarro** make a fool of himself as a Navajo brave, who marries outcast Lupe Velez.

LAURA
BIG GIRLS DON'T CRY . . . THEY GET EVEN (1992, New Line)—Neglected by her parents, **Hilary Wolf** flees to the woods with her stepbrother Dan Futterman to avoid taking a family trip to Hawaii. The pursuit of the runaways by their extended family gives the members the opportunity to resolve their respective problems.

LAURA
KISS DADDY GOOD NIGHT (1987, Beast of Eden)—In a film which can't decide which genre it's trying to join, amoral **Uma Thurman** rolls drunks and is the obsession of an older neighbor.

LAURA
LITTLE LAURA AND BIG JOHN (1973, Crown International)—**Karen Black** and boyfriend Fabian are outlaws on the lam from the cops. It's standard stuff, with the stars something of an odd couple.

LAUREL, STAN
OUR RELATIONS (1936, MGM); JITTERBUGS (1943, 20th Century Fox)—**Stan Laurel** and Oliver Hardy appeared together in many shorts and feature length films. These two were not among their best. In the first, the boys get mixed up with their long lost twins. In the second, the comic legends donned the garb of the 1940s, including a zoot suit for Ollie and a dress for Stan as they dealt with some crooks.

LAURIE, ANNIE
ANNIE LAURIE (1927, Silent, MGM)—The English governor's daughter **Polly Ward** finds herself in the middle of the feud between the MacDonald and Campbell clans when a MacDonald begins courting her. Even so, she prefers one of the Campbells.

LAURIER
SCORPIO (1973, UA)—Hit man **Alain Delon** is hired by the CIA to eliminate one of their own, aging agent Burt Lancaster. He successfully carries out the mission, but in a sort of domino effect, he's also assassinated.

LAURIENCE, DR.
THE MAN WHO LIVED AGAIN (1936, GB, Gaumont)—When **Boris Karloff** discovers that the assistant he loves is in love with another, Karloff merely uses his brain-transfer machine and transfers his brain into the younger man's body. Things go wrong.

LAURIK, JOE
I STOLE A MILLION (1939, Universal)—After escaping from prison, **George Raft** meets Claire Trevor and attempts to go straight, but his past catches up with him.

LAURIN, PHYLLIS
NINETEEN AND PHYLLIS (1920, Silent, First National)—**Clara Horton**, the granddaughter of a southern judge, is the prize a poor boy wins when he beats out the son of the wealthiest family in the area.

LAVALL, BABE
CONVENTION GIRL (1935, Flacon/FD)—**Rose Hobart**, a cabaret hostess with the proverbial heart of gold, finds herself in trouble when she helps a travelling salesman, greatly annoying her gangster boyfriend.

LAVERNE, MME. FLORENCE
THE MAGNIFICENT FLIRT (1928, Silent, Paramount)—When a count tries to discourage a romance between his nephew and **Florence Vidor's** daughter, mama tricks the count into marrying

421

her and giving his blessing to the marriage of the younger couple as well.

LAWLER, JOHNNY

MOLLY AND LAWLESS JOHN (1972, Producers Distributing Corp.)—Outlaw **Sam Elliott** appeals to Vera Miles maternal instincts and so the sheriff's wife helps him escape from jail, going with him. When he strays, she kills him and returns home claiming that he had kidnapped her. Don't mess with mama.

LAWRENCE, BARBARA

THE CROWN PRINCE'S DOUBLE (1916, Silent, Blue Ribbon) - Crown Prince **Maurice Costello** is deposed before he is to marry a neighboring princess. He goes to the United States where he falls in love and marries. When his homeland decides they want him back, he sends a double in his place.

LAWRENCE, BOB

THE MAN WHO KNEW TOO MUCH (1935, GB, Gaumont)—**Leslie Banks** and his wife Edna Best are vacationing in Switzerland, when they learn of an assassination plot from a dying Frenchman. To prevent them from telling what they know, the murderers kidnap the couple's daughter. From then on it's a matter of locating the child before the assassination can be carried out. Director Alfred Hitchcock remade the movie in 1956 with James Stewart and Doris Day.

LAWRENCE, D.H.

PRIEST OF LOVE (1981, GB, Filmways)—**Ian McKellen** stars in the biopic of the controversial author of "Lady Chatterley's Lover," "Sons and Lovers" and "Women in Love."

LAWRENCE, FRANCIE

GIDGET (1959, Columbia); GIDGET GOES HAWAIIAN (1961, Columbia); GIDGET GOES TO ROME (1963, Columbia)—**Sandra Dee** introduced the plucky teenager, who finds romance when she becomes a sort of mascot for a group of college boy surfers. **Deborah Walley** and **Cindy Carol** followed in pictures of diminishing interest to the public.

LAWRENCE, GAY, THE FALCON

A DATE WITH THE FALCON (1941, RKO); THE GAY FALCON (1941, RKO); THE FALCON TAKES OVER (1942, RKO); THE FALCON'S BROTHER (1942, RKO) —When Leslie Charteris wanted more money for the rights to his creation of Simon Templar, The Saint, RKO moved **George Sanders** from one debonair amateur sleuth to a new one, Gay Lawrence, The Falcon. Charteris screamed bloody murder, but to no avail, that the new character really was The Saint with a name change.

LAWRENCE, GERTRUDE

STAR! (1968, 20th Century Fox)—**Julie Andrews** appears as musical star Gertrude Lawrence in a flawed and unsuccessful film, which attempts to balance the star's successes on stage with her romantic failures off.

LAWRENCE, COL. JOHN

MERRY CHRISTMAS MR. LAWRENCE (1983, GB, Universal)—**Tom Conti** is a British prisoner of war in a Japanese POW camp in Java in 1942. He strikes up a strange relationship with the commandant, Ryuichi Sakamoto.

LAWRENCE, LT. CMDR. JOHN

THE FROGMAN (1951, 20th Century Fox)—**Richard Widmark** is the commander of a squad of underwater demolition divers. Typical-ly in such movies his men consider him a martinet until he risks his own life and proves to them that much discipline is required in their line of work.

LAWRENCE, JOHN

JOHN LOVES MARY (1949, Warner Brothers)—American GI **Ronald Reagan** agrees to a marriage of convenience with English girl Virginia Field. It doesn't sit well with his fiancee back home, Patricia Neal.

LAWRENCE, LARRY

THE GHOST BREAKERS (1940, Paramount)—**Bob Hope** is Paulette Goddard's champion when she inherits a spooky Cuban mansion. Hope is in top form as he throws out some really funny wisecracks to cover up his fear.

LAWRENCE, MICHAEL

THREE GUYS NAMED MIKE (1950, MGM)—**Van Johnson** is one of three guys with the same first name (oh, you caught that?) competing for stewardess Jane Wyman.

LAWRENCE, ROSALIE

BROADWAY ROSE (1922, Silent, Tiffany)—Broadway dancing star **Mae Murray** falls in love with a wealthy young man. His parents don't consider her a suitable wife for their son. When he informs her that he doesn't consider her worth losing his inheritance, she goes home to her childhood sweetheart.

LAWRENCE, ROSE

HE WAS HER MAN (1934, Warner Brothers)—Former prostitute **Joan Blondell** takes up with safe-cracker James Cagney, when he's released from prison. It was the seventh and last time that Blondell and Cagney appeared together.

LAWRENCE, RUTH

HIS SECRETARY (1925, Silent, MGM)—**Norma Shearer**, a severely dressed stenographer, secretly is in love with her concern's junior partner. She overhears him saying he wouldn't kiss her for $1,000 dollars. She goes to a beauty parlor and emerges a ravishing beauty. Before she admits she loves the man she makes him pay her $1,000 for a kiss.

LAWRENCE, SUSAN

SWEATER GIRL (1942, Paramount)—Apple-cheeked **June Preisser** nicely handles the detective work in this college campus mystery, noted for two hit songs by Frank Loesser, "I Don't Want to Walk Without You" and "I Said No."

LAWRENCE, SYLVINA & MARTINA

A STOLEN LIFE (1939, Paramount)-**Elizabeth Bergner** plays identical twins with quite different personalities. The nasty one takes her sibling's identity and husband, when the sweet sister is killed in an accident. Bette Davis would recreate the roles in 1946.

LAWRENCE, T.E.

LAWRENCE OF ARABIA (1962, GB, Columbia)—**Peter O'Toole** is a stunner as the complex British hero of the Arab cause against the Turks at the time of WWI. His sensitivity erodes to cruelty in one spectacular scene. Although the movie doesn't give us much insight in the man, O'Toole's performance is so brilliant, the supporting cast so outstanding and the photography so awesome, that we hardly care.

LAWRENCE, TOM, THE FALCON

THE FALCON'S BROTHER (1942, RKO); THE FALCON AND THE CO-EDS (1943, RKO); THE FALCON STRIKES BACK (1943, RKO);

THE FALCON IN HOLLYWOOD (1944, RKO); THE FALCON IN MEXICO (1944, RKO); THE FALCON OUT WEST (1944, RKO); THE FALCON IN SAN FRANCISCO (1945, RKO); THE FALCON'S ADVENTURE (1946, RKO); THE FALCON'S ALIBI (1946, RKO)—When George Sanders grew tired of his B roles as the Robin Hood-like trouble shooter, he arranged for his real-life brother **Tom Conway** to take over and the latter was quite good in some better-than-average mysteries.

LAWRENCE, TONY
THE YOUNG PHILADELPHIANS (1959, Warner Brothers)—Ambitious lawyer **Paul Newman** works harder at making it with the snobbish Philadelphia blue bloods than at the law in this pretentious soap opera.

LAWSON, LT.
TOO LATE THE HERO (1970, Cinerama)—American officer **Cliff Robertson** leads a British combat patrol, whose mission is to wipe out a Japanese communication site. He and his men are chased through the jungle by the Japanese, who broadcast messages via loudspeakers that their lives will be spared only if they surrender.

LAWSON, JULIE
THE CISCO KID AND THE LADY (1939, 20th Century Fox)—**Marjorie Weaver** is the Cisco Kid's love interest in the first of 20th Century Fox's films starring Cesar Romero as the Mexican bandit.

LAYTON, VICTORIA
THE SECRET LIFE OF AN AMERICAN WIFE (1968, 20th Century Fox)—To prove her desirability, an insecure press agent's wife **Anne Jackson** decides to seduce famous movie star Walter Matthau.

LAZAR, BRIAN
THE PERFECT LOVER (1919, Silent, Selznick)—When artist **Eugene O'Brien** was single he was the darling of New York society ladies and his work much in demand. When he marries his childhood sweetheart, the ladies cool to him and his work.

LAZARUS, IKE
THE KIBITZER (1929, Paramount)—**Harry Green** kibitzes nightly when his friends gather for pinochle in his tobacco shop. He also kibitzes about his daughter's romances, but does guarantee that when she marries it's to the right boy and that he has a future.

LAZYBONES
LAZYBONES (1925, Silent, Fox)—**Charles Jones** is a loveable but shiftless character who takes in the illegitimate child of his sweetheart's sister. This prevents their marriage and years later Jones has notions of marrying his guardian but steps aside when he discovers she loves another. It looks like he may finally get together with his old flame.

LE BEAU, ALCIDE
THE PUPPET MAN (1921, GB, FBO)—Horribly disfigured **Hugh Miller** becomes a puppeteer with a circus. He does his best to discourage the affection a young girl has for him.

LE BEY, LOUIS
MEN OF THE NORTH (1930, MGM)—French Canadian **Gilbert Roland** is accused of stealing gold from a mine, but eludes capture. He meets and falls in love with the mineowner's daughter, rescues the mineowner from a snowslide, saves a Mountie's life, and is vindicated—all in the time it takes to say "Sacre Bleu."

LE BRAS
I ESCAPED FROM DEVIL'S ISLAND (1973, UA)—This film starring **Jim Brown**, who did what the title said he did, was released a month or so before PAPILLON, but the head start didn't help this potboiler much at the box office.

LE FEVRE, JUDGE
A GENTLEMAN OF PARIS (1931, GB, Gaumont)—Respected Paris judge **Arthur Wonter** is actually a philanderer. He witnesses a crime in a place he shouldn't be. In time, he must try the case in which the accused is a former mistress. The jury finds her guilty but he confesses his knowledge of the crime, which ruins his career. Despite all the coincidences, it's good drama.

LE GRAND, BELLE
BELLE LE GRAND (1951, Republic)—In the early days of San Francisco, gambler **Vera Ralston** joins forces with the owner of a silver mine to fight off a gang of villains.

LE GRANGE, CLAIRE
THE LADY FROM THE SEA (1929, GB, British International)—When **Mona Goya** is rescued from a shipwreck she tries to steal her rescuer from his fiancee.

LE JAMBON, LUCILLE
A PERFECT LADY (1918, Silent, Goldwyn)—Burlesque queen **Madge Kennedy** works to put her sister through school. When the sheriff closes the show, Kennedy opens an ice cream parlor, but a deacon wishes to run the "sinner" out of town. He shuts up when a picture is produced of the deacon holding a chorus girl on his lap.

LE MOYNE, "K"
K—THE UNKNOWN (1924, Silent, Universal)—Mysterious lodger **Percy Marmont** saves the life of a shooting victim and is forced to reveal that he is a famous surgeon.

LE ROY, JUDY
I LOVE MELVIN (1953, MGM)—Donald O'Connor gets somewhere with **Debbie Reynolds** when he cons her into believing he can get her picture on the cover of LOOK magazine.

LEA
TARZAN AND THE LEOPARD WOMAN (1946, RKO)—**Acquanetta** appears as the sexy high priestess of a leopard cult. Johnny Weissmuller as Tarzan has his hands full with this worthy female adversary.

LEA, ANNABEL
THE GLAD RAG DOLL (1929, Warner Brothers)—**Dolores Costello**, the star of a Broadway show, is fired because Ralph Graves does not want his brother to become involved with her. He considers her not good enough for their family. Seeking revenge Costello discovers that all of Graves' relatives have naughty little secrets.

LEA, TIMOTHY
CONFESSIONS OF A POP PERFORMER (1975, GB, Columbia); CONFESSIONS OF A WINDOW CLEANER (1974, GB, Columbia)—**Robin Askwith**, an accident-prone city bumpkin, promotes a first-rate pop group which briefly makes it to the big time. In the prequel he's cleaning up in another way. He peers in on various women in different stages of undress.

LEADBETTER
THE HIRELING (1973, GB, World/Columbia)—After chauffeur **Robert Shaw** helps an unbalanced Lady, Sarah Miles, with her depression, he mistakenly believes she's interested in him.

LEAMAS, ALEC

THE SPY WHO CAME IN FROM THE COLD (1965, GB, Paramount)—British intelligence officer **Richard Burton**, in charge of espionage in Germany, is sent home when another agent is killed at the Berlin Wall. Burton's new assignment is to eliminate the head of the East German spy organization. Unfortunately for Burton, his superiors are not quite on the level with him.

LEAR, KING

KING LEAR (1971, GB/Denmark, Filmways)—Photographed in Denmark, **Paul Scofield** is an admirable Lear, but the production of Shakespeare's most demanding play is not for everyone.

LEARO, DON

KING LEAR (1988, U.S./France,Cannon)—This adaptation of "King Lear" from a script by Norman Mailer is directed by Jean-Luc Godard. **Burgess Meredith** is a Mafioso Lear, with Molly Ringwald as Cordelia. It's a weird production.

LEAROYD

FAREWELL TO THE KING (1989, Orion)—WWII American army deserter **Nick Nolte** has become the king of a tribe of Dayak headhunters in Borneo. He contracts to lead his tribe against the Japanese, but he is betrayed by his American contact.

LEARY, MACON

THE ACCIDENTAL TOURIST (1988, Warner Brothers)—Mild-mannered travel writer **William Hurt's** young son has died and his wife Kathleen Turner leaves him. He finds a new life with eccentric but appealing Geena Davis and her son. What makes the movie special is the odd behavior of Hurt's siblings Amy Wright, David Ogden Stiers and Ed Begley, Jr.

LEBANON, DOWAGER LADY

THE CASE OF THE FRIGHTENED LADY (1940, GB, British Lion)—**Helen Haye** fears that others will discover that her son has inherited the murderous tendencies of the family.

LECOUR, MAXINE

SHE'S A SWEETHEART (1944, Columbia)—Singer **Jane Frazee** hooks soldier Larry Parks in this modest musical comedy. Character actress Jane Darwell, who converts her large home into a boarding house for soldiers on leave, is the real star.

LEDBETTER, HUDDIE

LEADBELLY (1976, Paramount)—**Robert E. Mosley** stars in a typical biopic, tracing the ups and mostly downs of the legendary black folk-singer.

LEDUX, CLAIRE

THE FLAME OF NEW ORLEANS (1941, Universal)—Posing as a countess with plans of hooking a wealthy New Orleans banker, adventurer **Marlene Dietrich** instead falls for young seaman Bruce Cabot.

LEE

HANNAH AND HER SISTERS (1986, Orion)—**Barbara Hershey** doesn't know what to say when her brother-in-law Michael Caine tells her he loves her and wants to make love to her. She says yes and later goodbye in this superb examination of a New York family held together by Rock of Gibralter Mia Farrow as Caine's wife.

LEE

THE KILLERS (1964, Universal)—**Clu Gulager** and Lee Marvin are hit men surprised when their target, a teacher in the school for the blind, puts up no effort to prevent his death.

LEE

THE MAGNIFICENT SEVEN (1960, UA)—**Robert Vaughn**, a gunfighter who has lost his nerve, is one of seven gunslingers hired by a Mexican village to protect them from bandits. He goes out with guns blazing—we assume cured.

LEE

TOUGHEST MAN ALIVE (1955, Allied Artists)—John Garfield clone **Dane Clark** is a U.S. agent posing as a gunrunner in order to break up a smuggling ring.

LEE, AMBROSIA

THE CHARMER (1917, Silent, Bluebird)—**Ella Hall** is a child star in a story meant to entertain kids. It's essentially a series of fairy tales.

LEE, ANNABEL

ANNABEL LEE (1921, Silent, Joam Film Society)—Inspired by the Edgar Allan Poe poem, wealthy Colonel Lee doesn't approve of his daughter's choice for a husband, a young fisherman. **Lorraine Harding** as the daughter waits for her love, even when he is long gone, shipwrecked on a desert island. He finally hails a passing ship and returns to Harding.

LEE, BERNICE

I PASSED FOR WHITE (1960, Allied Artists)—**Sonja Wilde's** attempts to pass for white are disastrous to the black girl.

LEE, BETTY

THE SPEED GIRL (1921, Silent, Paramount)—Movie star **Bebe Daniels** does all her own dangerous stunts. But the most dangerous is sorting out which of two men she will marry.

LEE, DAULTON

THE FALCON AND THE SNOWMAN (1985, Orion)—Druggie **Sean Penn** and his friend Timothy Hutton become spies, selling American secrets to the KGB. It's a true story but doesn't really explain why these American boys would betray their country.

LEE, EVA

THE WOMAN WHO FOOLED HERSELF (1922, Silent, Associate Exhibitors)—New York showgirl **Mary Allison** is hired to go to South America and vamp Robert Ellis, so that her employers can get an option on his grandfather's land. She wins the lad over, but falls for him as well. Surprise!

LEE, FLOWER BELLE

MY LITTLE CHICKADEE (1940, Universal)—In her only film appearance with W.C. Fields, **Mae West** fakes a marriage to the card-cheating con man, when she is run out of one western town while searching for her mysterious masked lover.

LEE, HANK

SOLDIER OF FORTUNE (1955, 20th Century Fox)—**Clark Gable** is hired by Susan Hayward to locate her photographer husband who disappeared in Red China. By the time the missing man is found, Hayward is in love with Gable.

LEE, IMMEDIATE

IMMEDIATE LEE (1916, Silent, Mutual)—Don't you just love the clever title? **Frank Borzage** wrote, directed and starred in this western in which he gets a brazen dance hall "siren" to give up her sinful life and seek a new one with him.

LEE, LADY

GAMBLING LADY (1934, First National)—Despite the fact that her gambler father committed suicide because he couldn't pay his debts, **Barbara Stanwyck** can't resist the gaming tables. There she finds handsome Joel McCrea.

LEE, LINDA *See* **SUPERGIRL**

LEE, LORELEI

GENTLEMEN PREFER BLONDES (1928, Silent, Paramount); (1953, 20th Century Fox)—**Ruth Taylor** and **Marilyn Monroe** each appear as one half of a team of show-biz beauties diamond mining the wealthy men on an ocean liner headed for Paris. It's doubtful that anyone will remember Ruth Taylor in the role, as Marilyn Monroe seemed such a perfect gold-digging Lorelei.

LEE, MARJORIE

THE LAUGHING LADY (1930, Paramount)—**Ruth Chatterton** is rescued from drowning by a lifeguard, while her husband is away on a business trip. She's grateful but not as much as the lifeguard believes when he enters her hotel room that evening. Guess what other hotel guests believe when they see him leaving her room?

LEE, MARY

PICTURE BRIDES (1934, Allied Artists)—**Dorothy Libaire** is the less attractive of two mail order brides sent for by two American fugitives digging for diamonds in Brazil. Her husband is so disappointed that he shoots a native just to blow off steam.

LEE, NANCY

WAY OF A WOMAN (1919, Silent, Selznick)—**Norma Talmadge**, an impoverished southern girl, marries a millionaire rather than the man she loves, so she can take care of the old folks at home. Course, he's an old buzzard and when he kicks off and leaves her his money, she's free to win back the man she really loves, only slightly soiled as they said in those days.

LEE, SAM

SON OF THE GODS (1930, Warner Brothers)—Raised by a wealthy Chinese merchant whom he believes is his father, **Richard Barthelmess** has learned to handle the sting of prejudice. He falls for an American girl, when both are visiting the Riviera. Things look good until he tells her that he is Chinese. She proceeds to beat him with her riding crop, a sure sign she's displeased. Barthelmess returns home in time to be with his dying father, who isn't his father. He was born to some good old white folks. When she hears of this the girl comes running and he forgives her for her playfulness. Maybe he's into S & M.

LEE, SAMMY

THE SMALL WORLD OF SAMMY LEE (1963, GB, British Lion)—**Anthony Newley** is the M.C. at a sleazy Soho striptease joint. He has just five hours to raise the money he owes a bookie or face a brutal beating. The five hours are a test of just how low he will fall to avoid the beating.

LEEDS, JOANNE

BETTY CO-ED (1946, Columbia)—Carnival singer **Jean Porter** is accepted in a sorority and reforms the snobbish attitudes of the sisters. That'll be the day.

LEESON, EMORY

CRAZY PEOPLE (1990, Paramount)—Just before shooting began on this picture, John Malkovich was replaced by **Dudley Moore**. No doubt a great deal more than the height of the central character changed. Moore portrays a burnt-out advertising man, whose honest approach to promoting products gets him sent to a sanitarium, where he is befriended by a lovely group of zanies. When his series of honesty ads begins to pay off, Moore's tyrannical boss and the other high-powered promoters can't cut the mustard in coming up with new ones, so Moore must be sent for.

LEGOI, JEAN

SHE LEARNED ABOUT SAILORS (1934, Fox)—In Shanghai, **Alice Faye** makes a marriage of convenience with sailor Lew Ayres so they both can go home to the U.S., but there they aren't so sure they want an annulment.

LEIGH, ANNABELLE

ANNABELLE'S AFFAIRS (1931, Fox)—When her husband disappears, **Jeanette MacDonald** takes a job as a cook in her rival's home. Then her husband shows up.

LEIGH, GEOFF, WYATT, CHRISTOPHER & RODNEY

FOUR MEN AND A PRAYER (1938, (20th Century Fox)—The four sons of unjustly cashiered British Army officer C. Aubrey Smith, **Richard Greene**, **George Sanders**, **David Niven** and **William Henry** attempt to avenge their father's death and clear his name, even though it takes them all over the world looking for clues.

LEISTER, DANNY

BAD BOY (1949, Allied Artists/Monogram)—**Audie Murphy** is sent to prison for armed robbery, where experts discover that his antisocial behavior is caused by his mistaken belief that he is responsible for his mother's death.

LELAND, JOE

THE DETECTIVE (1968, 20th Century Fox)—New York homicide cop **Frank Sinatra** is disillusioned because he helped send an innocent man to the chair, and he finds that his department is almost totally corrupt.

LEMAIRE, JULES

JULES OF THE STRONG HEART (1918, Silent, Paramount)—French Canadian lumberjack **George Beban** cares for the motherless child of a friend, and saves the lumber camp owner's daughter, who has befriended him.

LEMAITRE, ROSE MARIE

ROSE MARIE (1954, MGM)—**Ann Blyth** is the girl loved both by mountie Howard Keel and French Canadian trapper Fernando Lamas in this blah version of the Rudolf Friml operetta.

LEMON DROP KID, THE

THE LEMON DROP KID (1951, Paramount)—Racetrack tout **Bob Hope** gives gangster Lloyd Nolan some bad tips and has to come up with $10,000 or take the consequences. Hope is willing to con anyone to avoid his fate, but accidentally does the right thing.

LEMON, MR.

MR. LEMON OF ORANGE (1931, Fox)—In this comedy **El Brendel** looks exactly like a notorious gangster, but the police pursue the wrong man.

LEMORE

THE LADY DRACULA (1974, Media Cinema)—During the 1920s, female vampire **Lesley Gilb**, living in a Georgia woods, preys on children.

425

LEMP, ANNA, THEA, KAY & EMMA

FOUR DAUGHTERS (1938, Warner Brothers); FOUR WIVES (1939, Warner Brothers); FOUR MOTHERS (1941, Warner Brothers)—John Garfield was a sensation in the first film about four attractive small town girls, **Priscilla Lane, Lola Lane, Rosemary Lane** and **Gale Page**, but the script killed him off and the two self-explanatory titled sequels certainly missed him.

LENNIE

OF MICE AND MEN (1939, UA); (1992, MGM)—Lon Chaney, Jr. sensitively portrays Lennie in the 1939 clsasic. **John Malkovich** with his slightly crossed eyes, thinning hair and slow reactions gives a fine interpretation of the incredibly strong simpleton who accidently kills a woman and as a result is killed by his friend Gary Sinise.

LENNOX, GERTRUDE

MEET THE WIFE (1931, Columbia)—**Laura La Plante** finds herself in one of the many pictures in which a husband, believed dead, shows up just about the time that his wife remarries.

LENOX, SUSAN

SUSAN LENOX—HER FALL AND RISE (1931, MGM)—Farmer's daughter **Greta Garbo**, after a brief affair with construction worker Clark Gable, leaves him to become the mistress of a wealthy politician. Later she returns to Gable and goes with him to South America.

LENZ, GOTTFRIED

THREE COMRADES (1938, MGM)—**Robert Young** is one of three German friends who love the same dying girl, Margaret Sullavan, during the hard times of the twenties. It's an enjoyable tearjerker with Sullavan dying beautifully. Young, who is fatally wounded in a street riot, doesn't have such a tranquil end.

LEO

THE BUTCHER'S WIFE (1991, Paramount)—New York butcher **George Dzundza** can hardly believe his good luck when country beauty Demi Moore announces she wants to marry him. Back in New York, he discovers there are certain disadvantages to being married to a clairvoyant.

LEO

LEO THE LAST (1970, GB, UA)—Bird-watcher **Marcello Mastroianni**, the last in the line of a deposed European monarchy, arrives in London to stay at his family's mansion, which is now in the middle of a black ghetto. At first, he is unmoved by the problems of his neighbors, but when he finally comes to the rescue of a black girl, whom a pimp wishes to lead into a life as a prostitute, Mastroianni burns his own mansion as a gesture of solidarity with those around him.

LEONARD

LEONARD PART 6 (1987, Columbia)—In one of the most disappointing films of the year, **Bill Cosby** proved to be just one more actor who will do anything for a buck. He's a secret agent brought out of retirement to battle a madwoman bent on world domination.

LEONARD, HATTIE

THE LADY AND THE MOB (1939, Columbia)—Grand dame **Fay Bainter** puts together a mob in this comedy-gangster movie.

LEONARDO

TEENAGE MUTANT NINJA TURTLES (1990, New Line); TEENAGE MUTANT NINJA TURTLES II: THE SECRET OF OOZE (1991, New Line)—**David Forman** is one of the quartet of mutated turtles who live in the sewers of New York. They take on the challenge posed by the Foot Clan, a group of rotten teens trained in martial arts who are terrorizing the streets of New York City. In the sequel, **Mark Caso** replaces David Forman, as the quartet seeks the secret of their origins.

LEONORA

CAT GIRL (1957, American International)—A family curse turns **Barbara Shelley** into a killer leopard. There's nothing much to it and it's not very scary.

LEONOWENS, ANNA

ANNA AND THE KING OF SIAM (1946, 20th Century Fox)—THE KING AND I (1956, 20th Century Fox)—**Irene Dunne** and **Deborah Kerr** appear as the British schoolteacher who is hired by the King of Siam to teach his numerous children. She also is able to give the King, played respectively by Rex Harrison and Yul Brynner, a bit of good English advice on how to run his country. Will the white man's burden never end?

LERMAN, MICHAEL

THE SENTINEL (1977, Universal)—**Chris Sarandon** is in line to act as a guardian at the Gate to Hell located in a Brooklyn brownstone. It's another of those films with cameo roles by over-the-hill former stars such as Jose Ferrer, Ava Gardner and Arthur Kennedy.

LES

LICENSE TO DRIVE (1988, 20th Century Fox)—When sixteen-year-old **Corey Haim** fails his driver's test, he lets on that he's passed. He also takes his grandfather's classic car without permission in order to have a 'hot' date with Heather Graham. No sixteen-year-old should be allowed to drive.

LESLIE, MONA

RECKLESS (1935, MGM)—In a story almost too close to her own tragic marriage to Paul Bern to bear, **Jean Harlow** is a musical star whose marriage to an irresponsible alcoholic leads to scandal with his suicide.

LESLIE, MRS. VIVIEN

ABOUT MRS. LESLIE (1954, Paramount)—**Shirley Booth** reminisces about her life as the mistress of airplane manufacturer Robert Ryan, about whom she knows very little. He's dead now, and she pretends she is his widow.

LESTER, VICKI See **ESTHER BLODGETT**

LEVENE, DAVID

FOUR FRIENDS (1981, Filmways)—**Michael Huddleston** is one of four friends who live through the turmoils of the 1960s. Director Arthur Penn's attempts to honestly explain the times but seems to have very little to say.

LEVENHAM, ROSE

LIGHT FINGERS (1957, GB, Archway)—**Eunice Gayson's** mean husband thinks his junk-buying wife is a shoplifter suffering from kleptomania.

LEVER, ROSCOE

THE DIRTY DOZEN (1967, GB, MGM)—**Stuart Cooper** is one of the twelve convicted GIs—murderers, rapists and thieves—who are offered the chance of earning pardons if they will join a suicide mission into Nazi-occupied France to blow up a chateau filled with high-ranking German officers. Cooper wins his pardon, but isn't around to hear about it.

LEVI, BABE

MARATHON MAN (1976, Paramount)—Marathon runner **Dustin Hoffman** becomes involved in a plot by Laurence Olivier, a murderous Dr. Mengele-like Nazi fugitive, who has plans for a Fourth Reich.

LEVI, DOLLY

THE MATCHMAKER (1958, Paramount); HELLO, DOLLY! (1969, 20th Century Fox)—**Shirley Booth** and **Barbra Streisand** appear as the Yonkers matchmaker who has plans to set herself up with a prosperous feed merchant. Booth is a doll. Streisand, in the musical version, is a dud.

LEVI, SIMON

THE AUCTIONEER (1927, Silent, Fox)—Jewish immigrant **George Sidney** adopts the child of a woman who dies at sea. He works hard in his new country and builds up a successful pawnbroking-auctioneering business. An evil broker causes him to lose everything, and he finds himself once again a street peddler. He ultimately gets his money back and sees his adopted daughter make a good marriage.

LEVINE, ALEXANDER

THE ANGEL LEVINE (1970, UA)—Jewish tailor Zero Mostel suffers like Job, until he encounters **Harry Belafonte**, who claims to be a Jewish angel, who must perform a miracle before 24 hours pass to be confirmed as an angel. Mostel is skeptical and the time frame passes without Mostel benefiting from the angel's visit.

LEVINE, NANCY

NANCY'S BIRTHRIGHT (1916, Silent, Mutual)—**Edythe Sterling** is badly treated by her cruel father after the death of her mother. Later she discovers that she is the descendant of a very wealthy family. Happens every day.

LEVINE, SHEILA

SHEILA LEVINE IS DEAD AND LIVING IN NEW YORK (1975, Paramount)—Suburban **Jeannie Berlin** picks up and takes her neuroses with her to Manhattan where she hopes to find a career and a husband. It was meant to be a comedy, but we barely smiled.

LEVY, ABIE

ABIE'S IRISH ROSE (1928, Part-Talkie, Paramount); (1946, UA) - **Charles Rogers** and **Richard Norris** appear as the Jewish lad who meets and marries Roman Catholic Rosemary Murphy (played respectively by Nancy Carroll and Joanne Dru) in an Episcopal church. To please their prejudiced families, they undergo additional marriages by a rabbi and a priest. This doesn't help, but the birth of twins does.

LEWIN, CHUM

A WONDERFUL WIFE (1922, Silent, Universal)—**Miss Du Pont**, bored when she accompanies her husband to an island off the coast of Africa, vamps the commissioner, hoping to get a better position for her hubby. The latter doesn't appreciate the help. The commissioner sends her husband on a dangerous jungle expedition to get rid of him, but Miss Du Pont loves her husband. She forces the commissioner at gun point to lead a search party for her man.

LEWIS

REVENGE OF THE NERDS (1984, 20th Century Fox); REVENGE OF THE NERDS II: NERDS IN PARADISE (1987, 20th Century Fox)—There are many nerds in these two movies: Anthony Edwards, Tim Busfield, Andrew Cassese, Curtis Armstrong, Larry B. Scott, Brian Tochi, etc., but **Robert Carradine** is their leader. As defined in these movies, a nerd is a hard-studying grind with few social graces who is always being put down by the college campus party animals, athletes and attractive girls. Despite this, the nerds come out on top in both movies, and weird looking Carradine gets a knockout of a girl both times.

LEWIS, AL

THE SUNSHINE BOYS (1975, UA)—After replacing his old friend Jack Benny, who had died before filming could begin, **George Burns** won an Oscar for his portrayal of an aging member of a vaudeville comedy team who reluctantly agrees to appear one more time with his ex-partner Walter Matthau. The latter has never forgiven Burns for retiring.

LEWIS, ARTIE

ONE GOOD COP (1991, Hollywood Pictures)—When his partner Anthony La Paglia is killed attempting to save a woman's life, decent cop **Michael Keaton** and his fashion designer wife struggle with the authorities over custody of his partner's three orphaned little girls.

LEWIS, HOWDY

THE ROUNDERS (1965, MGM)—**Henry Fonda** and Glenn Ford are a pair of aging cowboys, hired by a cheap rancher to break a string of wild horses. They find their hands full with one particularily mean animal.

LEWIS, INA & DR. JUDD

WIFE, DOCTOR AND NURSE (1937, 20th Century Fox)—Society girl **Loretta Young** marries Park Avenue doctor **Warner Baxter** and discovers that his nurse Virginia Bruce is also in love with him. She insists that her husband dismiss Bruce. He does, but his work suffers so much that Young decides he needs his nurse also and arranges for her to return to work.

LEWIS, JOE E.

THE JOKER IS WILD (1957, Paramount)—When young singer **Frank Sinatra** defies Chicago mobsters, they slash his vocal chords, turning him into an alcoholic nightclub comedian. Sinatra sings some nice tunes, even though Joe E. Lewis never sounded so good.

LEWIS, MARK

PEEPING TOM (1960, GB, Anglo-Amalgamated)—Sickie photographer **Karl Boehm** kills models with physical imperfections with a spiked tripod while filming them. He also films the police investigations of the murders, and finally his own suicide.

LEWIS, ROGER

UNMASKED (1950, Republic)—Scandal sheet editor **Raymond Burr** seems to have gotten away with murdering his mistress, when the latter's husband, who is suspected of the crime, commits suicide.

LEYBOURNE, GEORGE

CHAMPAGNE CHARLIE (1944, GB, Ealing)—**Tommy Trinder** is a small-time comedian going nowhere, until he changes his name and then he's off to stardom.

LIAH

THE DEVIL'S MISTRESS (1968, Holiday Films)—When four cowboys escaping from the law in the 1870s come across an isolated cabin, they murder the frontiersman they find there and rape his bewitching half-caste mistress **Joan Stapleton**. They make the mistake of taking her with them and she mysteriously causes the death of the four, one by one, and returns to her resurrected lover.

LIAM

MEN OF IRELAND (1938, Ireland, Irish National)—**Brian O'Sullivan** is a fisherman of the Blasket Islands. He is the rival of a visiting medical student for a comely local lass. O'Sullivan drowns despite the efforts of his rival to save him, but not before giving his blessing to the match of the other two parts of this Irish triangle.

LIANNA

LIANNA (1983, UA)—Unhappy professor's wife and mother of two, **Linda Griffiths** finds happiness in a lesbian relationship with one of her husband's colleagues.

LIBBY

I SAW WHAT YOU DID (1965, Universal)—Teenager **Andi Garrett** and her friend randomly dial phone numbers and declare "I saw what you did." John Ireland receives such a call just after the murder of his wife (uxoricide to the erudite). He thinks he recognizes the girls, and boy are they in trouble.

LIBEAU, ANNIE

APACHE WOMAN (1955, Golden State)—Lloyd Bridges, investigating a series of robberies of supposedly peaceful Apaches, falls for half-breed **Joan Taylor**.

LIFT, MOMMA

THROW MOMMA FROM THE TRAIN (1987, Orion)—Danny De Vito wants to trade murders with his college writing teacher Billy Crystal, ala STRANGERS ON A TRAIN. De Vito will murder Crystal's ex-wife Kate Mulgrew and Crystal is to do away with De Vito's nasty, demanding mama, **Anne Ramsey**.

LIGHT FINGERS

LIGHT FINGERS (1929, Columbia)—**Ian Keith**, a brilliant crook, finds that amateurs are interfering with his trade, when he infiltrates a home intent on stealing the jewels. This causes him to go straight.

LIGHTCLOUD, JOE

STAY AWAY, JOE (1968, MGM)—Half-caste Navajo **Elvis Presley** rides in rodeos, chases girls, sings a few putrid songs and generally makes a fool of himself.

LIGHTFOOT

THUNDERBOLT AND LIGHTFOOT (1974, UA)—**Jeff Bridges** was nominated for an Oscar for his performance as a young drifter, who teams up with Vietnam vet Clint Eastwood to pull a big armed robbery.

LIL

FOR THE LOVE O' LIL (1930, Columbia)—**Sally Starr** is the prize sought both by a wealthy socialite and a poor girl-shy fellow. She makes her preference known, when she fakes a drowning and gets the poor boy to propose while they are in the water.

LIL

A GIRL OF LONDON (1925, Silent, GB, Stoll)—Runaway heiress **Genevieve Townsend**, being chased by crooks, poses as an Irish girl wanted by the police.

LILIOM

LILIOM (1930, Fox)—Budapest carousel barker **Charles Farrell** falls for servant girl Rose Hobart, whom he marries. Not a good provider, Farrell decides he better get going when he discovers that Hobart is pregnant. His means of raising funds is a robbery in which he is killed. He's given another chance in heaven, but his return to earth only proves that he hasn't learned anything or improved.

LILITH

NIGHT ANGEL (1990, Fries)—Loosely based on the legend of a she-devil who steals the souls of men, this film features **Isa Anderson** as a primordial creature who takes on the appearance of a beautiful woman so she may create evil by using her powers of seduction.

LILLA

RIDDLE: THE WOMAN (1920, Silent, Pathe)—**Geraldine Farrar** encourages and then spurns the man who is trying to seduce her. It's how she does it that makes it worth seeing.

LILLEO

LAST OF THE PAGANS (1936, MGM)—**Lotus Long** and Mala, as the lovers are the only professional actors in this film about life on Tahiti.

LILLIAN

GAMBLING DAUGHTERS (1941, PRC)—**Gale Storm** and her sister are rich young women who become involved with gamblers and murder.

LILLY *See* ALICE BRENT

LILY

LILY OF THE ALLEY (1923, GB, Hepworth)—Coffee stall keeper's wife **Chrissie White** dreams he is blinded and dies in a fire.

LIME, HARRY

THE THIRD MAN (1950, GB, London Films)—When author Joseph Cotten arrives in post-war Vienna, he is informed that his friend **Orson Welles** has been killed in an accident. Trying to find out more about the death and the lack of a body, Cotten investigates and discovers that Welles is a horrible Black Market trafficker in drugs and medicine, and that he is very much alive. Cotten and British officer Trevor Howard trap Welles in the sewers below the streets, where this time he is killed for real. The haunting theme of the movie, played on a zither by Anton Karas, became a worldwide hit.

LIMPET, HENRY

THE INCREDIBLE MR. LIMPET (1964, Warner Brothers)—In 1940, fish-lover **Don Knotts** falls from a dock at Coney Island and is transformed into a dolphin. During WWII, animated Knotts-dolphin becomes a hero by tracking German U-boats.

LIN, LAN YING

DAUGHTER OF SHANGHAI (1937, Paramount)—Detective **Anna May Wong** helps solve a murder case associated with the smuggling of illegal aliens into the USA.

LINCOLN

GLADIATOR (1992, Columbia)—Ailing black fighter **Cuba Gooding, Jr.** is forced by ruthless white businessman Brian Dennehy to fight his white pal James Marshall. The two buddies refuse to beat each other's brains out for a bloodthirsty crowd.

LINCOLN, ABRAHAM

THE HEART OF LINCOLN (1922, Silent, New Era); ABRAHAM LINCOLN (1930, UA); ABE LINCOLN IN ILLINOIS (1940, RKO); THE TALL TARGET (1951, MGM) THE LINCOLN CONSPIRACY (1977, Sunn Classics); YOUNG MR. LINCOLN (1939, 20th Century Fox)—**Francis Ford, Walter Huston, Raymond Massey, Leslie Kimmell, John Anderson** and **Henry Fonda** all portrayed Abraham Lincoln at various stages in his life and career. It's generally agreed that Raymond Massey and Henry Fonda gave the most agreeable portrayals and that Walter Huston made The Great Emancipator seem a bore.

LIND, JENNY

A LADY'S MORALS (1930, MGM)—**Gracie Moore** stars in this fictionalized version of the life of "The Swedish Nightingale." Most of the picture is spent on an on again, off again romance with musician Reginald Denny, who is going blind. He once had helped her find the means to restore her voice when she lost it.

LINDA

COMMON LAW WIFE (1963, Texas Film Producers)—**Annabelle Lee** is the common law wife of a southern redneck. She finds her hold on her man threatened by a sensuous newcomer after the man's money. This rival and her moonshiner lover kill Lee's "husband" with poisoned whiskey. Lee takes revenge before committing suicide by drinking the whiskey. Stupid!

LINDA

LINDA (1929, Silent, Willis Kent)—**Helen Foster** is forced by her brutish father to marry a man she doesn't love, an aging lumberjack. Her husband is an understanding man, who tries to make her life better. He is even understanding when she falls in love with a doctor, but she stays with her ailing husband until he dies.

LINDA

LINDA (1960, GB, Independent Artists)—Jealous teenager **Carol White** joins a tough gang's fight with a rival bunch of juvenile misfits at a church social.

LINDA

SHE MARRIED A COP (1939, Republic)—**Jean Parker** discovers a singing cop, Phil Regan. He thinks she's going to make him a star. Instead, she's got him a job of dubbing for an Irish pig in a cartoon feature. They marry, but when he finds out the purpose of his voice, he leaves her. But like MacArthur, he will return.

LINDA

WOMEN MUST DRESS (1935, Monogram)—**Minna Gombell** leaves her philandering husband, taking their daughter with her. The two women play around for awhile, until they discover the life isn't all it's cracked up to be. They return to husband and father, with all vowing to be on their best behavior, henceforth.

LINDEN-JONES, ARTHUR

CHARLEY'S BIG-HEARTED AUNT (1940, GB, Gainsborough) - Although not called Charley, **Arthur Askey** does his impersonation of a classmate's aunt in order to provide a chaperon for a couple of refined young ladies visiting Oxford.

LINDERMANN

MY BODYGUARD (1980, 20th Century Fox)—King-sized high school loner **Adam Baldwin** is hired by pint-sized Chris Makepeace to protect him from the protection racket run by bully Matt Dillon.

LINDSAY, CARMELITA

MEXICAN SPITFIRE (1939, RKO); MEXICAN SPITFIRE OUT WEST (1940, RKO); MEXICAN SPITFIRE'S BABY (1941, RKO); MEXICAN SPITFIRE AT SEA (1942, RKO); MEXICAN SPITFIRE SEES A GHOST (1942, RKO); MEXICAN SPITFIRE'S ELEPHANT (1942, RKO); MEXICAN SPITFIRE'S BLESSED EVENT (1943, RKO)—Starting with THE GIRL FROM MEXICO, **Lupe Velez** appeared in eight "B" movies as the wife of a businessman named Lindsay (Donald Woods), but her real co-star was Leon Errol, as her husband's accident prone uncle. The plots were of little importance,

just an excuse for sexy Lupe to act like a hot tamale and Errol to be a rubber-legged ass.

LINDSAY, JOHN

I AM THE LAW (1938, Columbia)—College law professor **Edward G. Robinson** takes the job of special prosecutor to help clean up the rackets in New York City. The film tells a story that was old hat at the time it was released, but Robinson handles the role with authority. He even dances.

LINDSEY

WAITRESS (1982, Troma)—**Renata Majer** is one of three beautiful waitresses in a crazy restaurant, where everything wild that can happen does.

LINDSTROM, MARTHA

THE AFFAIRS OF MARTHA (1942, MGM)—Family maid **Marsha Hunt** secretly marries the son of her employer and writes a book about her life. This throws her town into a turmoil since no one knows whose maid has written the book.

"LINGERIE" *See* ANGELE REE

LINK

ENCINO MAN (1992, Hollywood Pictures)—Sean Astin uncovers Cro-Magnon man **Brendon Fraser** while digging a back yard swimming pool. Fraser revives when the block of ice that entombs him melts. Astin and his friend Pauly Shore try to pass off Fraser as a transfer student to Encino High.

LINK

MAIN STREET LAWYER (1939, Republic)—Small town lawyer **Edward Ellis** deliberately loses the case of his gangster client, because of the latter's involvement with Ellis' adopted daughter.

LINK, PRESIDENT MANFRED, GLORIA & MRS.

FIRST FAMILY (1980, Warner Brothers)—**Bob Newhart, Gilda Radner** and **Madeleine Kahn** are not very funny in this satire of life in the White House for one President and his family.

LINNETT, JACKIE

WALLFLOWER (1948, Warner Brothers)—It is the simple tale of two sisters, **Joyce Reynolds** and Janis Paige, both after the same man, Robert Hutton.

LINZ, KATERINA

THE GIRL DOWNSTAIRS (1938, MGM)—Servant girl **Franciska Gaal** wins her employer Rita Johnson's fiance Franchot Tone despite her naivete. It was the last of three Hollywood movies for the beauty from Budapest.

LISA

DAVID AND LISA (1962, Continental)—Fifteen-year-old **Janet Margolin** as Liza talks only in rhyme and as Muriel is totally mute. She develops a relationship with a boy so emotionally disturbed that he can't stand to be touched. These two ill children help each other to better health.

LISA

HOT ROD GIRL (1956, American International)—**Lori Nelson** is the sex interest in this drive-in special about teenagers and their hot rod cars, which they race in and sometimes die in.

LISA

LISA (1990, MGM/UA)—Fourteen-year-old **Staci Keanan** sets up herself and her mother Cheryl Ladd as victims when she makes provocative phone calls to a stranger, D.W. Moffett. He just happens to be "The Candlelight Killer," who breaks into women's apartments and sets out candles and glasses of wine before strangling them. Moral: Don't make crank phone calls.

LISA
NECROMANCER (1989, Spectrum)—When sweet coed Elizabeth Kaitan is raped by three low-lifes who blackmail her into not telling her story to the police, she seeks the help of necromancer **Lois Masten**, who knows how to deal with the creeps.

LISA
SATAN'S MISTRESS (1982, Motion Picture Marketing)—Bored, wealthy housewife **Lana Wood** spends most of the movie half-naked making love to an unseen spirit. It's not a pretty sight.

LISETTE
LISETTE (1961, Medallion)—Florida newspaper editor John Agar sponsors an Indochina orphan who turns out to be beautiful Eurasian woman **Greta Chi**. Agar has an affair with her, but finds her to be generally bad news for anyone who gets involved with her.

LISLE, GAENOR
THE NOTORIOUS MISS LISLE (1920, Silent, First National)—**Katherine MacDonald**, billed as "America's Beauty," appears as a woman wrongly accused of being a corespondent in a sensational London divorce case.

LISZT, FRANZ
LISZTOMANIA (1975, GB, Warner Brothers)—Director Ken Russell depicts **Roger Daltrey** as Liszt, the first pop star. We wish he hadn't.

LITA
THE BAD ONE (1930, UA)—**Dolores Del Rio**, a Spanish dancer in a Marseilles cafe, gets an American sailor to jump ship to be with her. He has to fight off a Swede for her hand, but he kills the fellow and then refuses to see Del Rio, because he believes she deceived him. She goes to great extremes to get to him, even becoming engaged to a brutal prison guard.

LITA
THE GIRL FROM MONTEREY (1943, PRC)—**Armida** is the manager and sister of a boxer. She tries to convince him not to fight the man she loves.

LITTLE BRITCHES *See* **JENNY**

LITTLE CAESAR *See* **CESARE ENRICO BANDELLO**

LITTLE (AMY) DORRIT
LITTLE DORRIT (1988, Cannon)—The six-hour adaptation of the Charles Dickens story concerns itself with the curious love story of middle-aged Arthur Clennam (Derek Jacobi), brought up by a religious zealot mother, and the much younger, pure Little Dorrit, played by **Sarah Pickering**. The film contains some very rich performances by some of Britain's finest character actors, notably Oscar-nominated Alec Guinness.

LITTLE EVA *See* **ROY ST. GEORGE**

LITTLE FAUSS
LITTLE FAUSS AND BIG HALSY (1970, Paramount)—**Michael J. Pollard** is motorcycle racer Robert Redford's mechanic, as the two travel the country winning races and women.

LITTLE JOHN (LITTLE)
MEN OF SHERWOOD FOREST (1957, GB, Hammer)—**Leslie Linder** portrays one of Robin Hood's most loyal and "biggest" followers.

LITTLE JOHN
ROBIN AND THE SEVEN HOODS (1964, Warner Brothers)—**Dean Martin** is second-in-command to 1920s Chicago mobster Frank Sinatra in another Rat Pack romp that audiences could have done without.

LITTLE ORPHAN ANNIE
LITTLE ORPHAN ANNIE (1932, RKO); (1938, Paramount); ANNIE (1982, Columbia)—**Mitzi Green**, **Ann Gillis** and **Aileen Quinn** each appear as the red-headed moppet, who with her dog Sandy has numerous adventures. Billionaire Daddy Warbucks shows up in the nick of time to save her when things look worse. Oh, yes, comic strip favorites Punjab and The Asp are around also. The 1982 musical, directed by John Huston with Albert Finney as Daddy Warbucks, is an interesting failure.

"LITTLE PAL"
LITTLE PAL (1915, Silent, Famous Players)—**Mary Pickford** loves the prospector whom she stays with, but the man is already married. When his wife shows up pleading with her husband to return to civilization, Pickford "nobly" steals enough gold ore to send them on their way and then commits suicide.

LITTLE PATRIOT, THE
A LITTLE PATRIOT (1917, Silent, Pathe)—**Baby Marie Osborne** and her friends thwart the plans of a German spy to blow up a torpedo and its inventor, whom she then discovers is her grandfather, who disinherited her mother when she married against his wishes.

LITTLE PRINCE, THE
THE LITTLE PRINCE (1974, GB, Paramount)—**Steven Warner** is a little alien prince from Asteroid B-612. He visits the earth in this musical production of the Antoine de Saint-Exupery fable.

LITTLE, VERNIE
SUCH WOMEN ARE DANGEROUS (1934, Fox)—When man about town Warner Baxter is wrongly accused of murder, women, whom he has discarded, such as **Rochelle Hudson**, are happy to help put him away.

LITTLECHAP
STOP THE WORLD—I WANT TO GET OFF (1966, GB, Warner Brothers)—Clown **Tony Tanner** creates a character, Littlechap, who has a driving ambition to become a success. Through marriage to the boss's daughter he gets his first break, and goes on from there to one success and mistress after another.

LITTLEFEATHERS, ISSAC
ISSAC LITTLEFEATHERS (1984, Canada, Cinema Concept)—**William Korbut**, the half-breed son of a hockey-player and an Indian woman, is taken in by a Jewish storekeeper, who wants to raise the boy in his religion. Korbut finds all the cultures confusing and is always getting into trouble, until he's reunited with his real father.

LITTLEFIELD, JEROME
THE DISORDERLY ORDERLY (1964, Paramount)—**Jerry Lewis** becomes a hospital orderly, hoping to become a physician like his father. His problem is that he's a victim of "neurotic identification empathy," which means he suffers the pains of his patients. After a

lot of nonsense, Lewis overcomes his neurosis and enrolls in medical school.

LIVINGSTON, LARRY

SEE YOU IN THE MORNING (1989, Warner Brothers)—After divorcing his successful television model wife Farrah Fawcett, psychiatrist **Jeff Bridges** takes up with widow Alice Krige.

LIVINGSTONE, DAVID

LIVINGSTONE (1925, GB, Silent, Butchers); DAVID LIVINGSTONE (1936, GB, MGM); STANLEY AND LIVINGSTONE —**M.A. Wetherell, Percy Marmont** and **Cedric Hardwicke** each appear as the medical missionary who drops out of sight in Africa for years, until newspaperman Henry Stanley finds him and says, "Dr. Livingstone, I presume."

LIZ

THE OPTIMISTS (1973, GB, Paramount)—**Donna Mullane** is one of two children befriended by a busker (street entertainer), Peter Sellers, who helps them get a dog.

LIZ

THREE LITTLE GIRLS IN BLUE (1946, 20th Century Fox)—In Atlantic City in 1905, three young women, **Vivian Blaine**, June Haver and Vera-Ellen are out to grab off rich husbands along the Boardwalk.

LIZ

WHORE (1991, Trimark)—Addressing the camera directly, **Theresa Russell** offers a running commentary on her career as a vulgar prostitute, working the streets of Los Angeles.

LIZA

SEVEN BRIDES FOR SEVEN BROTHERS (1954, MGM)—**Virginia Gibson** is the girl for Ephraim Pontabee (Jacques d'Amboise) in the best western musical ever produced. He and his brothers are mountain men, who kidnap the beauties of their choice and spend a chaste winter together on their snowbound ranch. They are happy to oblige the girls' shotgun-toting fathers, who insist that there be a series of quick weddings with the arrival of a thaw.

LIZZIE

HOLD THAT CO-ED (1938, 20th Century Fox)—**Joan Davis** is one of the co-eds at a university, which politician John Barrymore, in his last good role, visits to drum up votes.

LIZZIE

PERSONAL MAID'S SERVICE (1935, Warner Brothers)—**Ruth Donnelly** is a sort of early Hazel as a maid, who also solves everybody's problems.

LJUBA

FIVE BRANDED WOMEN (1960, Paramount)—**Jeanne Moreau** is one of five Yugoslav girls, who had affairs with German soldiers. As punishment they have their heads shaved. They take their revenge by joining the Partisans and killing Germans.

LLANO KID, THE

THE LLANO KID (1940, Paramount)—Western bandit **Tito Guizar's** past catches up with him when he poses as a long lost heir.

LLOYD, BUZZ

MAROONED (1969, Columbia)—After five months in space, the space ship carrying pilot **Gene Hackman**, scientist James Franciscus and mission commander Richard Crenna malfunctions on reentry leaving the astronauts no way to return to earth. As Mission Control works for ways to rescue the men, whose oxygen supply is running out, Hackman loses his nerve and is at least in part responsible for Crenna's death, when the latter commits sacrificial suicide.

LLOYD, CHRIS

THE STRANGER IN BETWEEN (1952, GB, Universal)—Six-year-old Jon Whitely accidentally sets his home on fire. He runs away—right into the arms of murderer **Dirk Bogarde**, who uses the child as a hostage.

LOCKE, STEPHEN

BRITISH AGENT (1934, First National)—During the early days of the Russian Revolution, **Leslie Howard** is the British Consul-General. He falls in love with Lenin's secretary even though politically they are poles apart.

LOCKHART, WILL

THE MAN FROM LARAMIE (1955, Columbia)—**James Stewart** rides from Laramie, Wyoming to New Mexico, tracking down the man who sold automatic rifles to the Apaches. This led to the death of Stewart's cavalry officer younger brother.

LOCKWOOD, DON

SINGIN' IN THE RAIN (1952, MGM)—Silent screen star **Gene Kelly** is able to make the adjustment to sound, but his co-star Jean Hagen has a horrible voice to match her horrible disposition. The solution to save an already filmed movie is to have Debbie Reynolds dub Hagen's voice. Kelly falls in love with Reynolds and demonstrates the strange things love will make one do, when in a famous sequence he dances in the rain. The film is one of the two or three best Hollywood musicals ever made. You can look it up.

LOCKWOOD, PETER ULYSSES

A MILLIONAIRE FOR CHRISTY (1951, 20th Century Fox)—When radio entertainer **Fred MacMurray** inherits a fortune, secretary Eleanor Parker decides she's going to marry him, even though he's already engaged.

LODER, JOHN

THE MASQUERADER (1933, UA)—**Ronald Colman**, as Loder, is the journalist look-alike cousin of Sir John Chilcotte, also played by Colman. The nasty Member of Parliament takes himself off to a clinic to dry out while his cousin impersonates him. The latter does such a good job that the M.P.'s career is enhanced and his wife feels their romance has been rekindled.

LODGER, THE

THE LODGER (1926, Silent, GB, Gainsborough); (1932, GB, Twickenham); (1944, 20th Century Fox)—**Ivor Novello** appeared in the two British versions of the story of a man, who rents a room in the home of an old couple in 19th century London. Slowly, his landlady comes to suspect that he's Jack the Ripper. The poor man is almost torn apart by a mob before his innocence is determined. In the 1944 movie with **Laird Cregar**, the lodger this time really is Jack The Ripper. Laird is marvelous.

LOGAN

COUNSEL'S OPINION (1933, GB, LFP/Paramount)—Widow Binnie Barnes impersonates the cheating wife of a lord in order to win the affections of lawyer **Henry Kendall**.

LOGAN

LOGAN'S RUN (1976, MGM/UA)—In a futuristic society, anyone reaching the age of 30 is put to death. **Michael York's** job is to chase down any of those who run rather than meet their fate joyfully.

431

When it's York's turn, he runs and discovers a community of people long past thirty. Someone should have marked this stinker "30" before it was released.

LOGAN, JERRY
BASHFUL BUCCANEER (1925, Silent, Rayart)—**Reed Howes** writes lurid stories about sailors and the sea even though he has never been on a ship in his life. He goes in search of pirate treasure, but has to deal with a mutiny instead.

LOGAN, THEODORE "TED"
BILL & TED'S EXCELLENT ADVENTURE (1989, Orion); BILL AND TED'S BOGUS JOURNEY (1991, Orion)—The instructions given to **Keanu Reeves** and his co-star Alex Winter must have been: "Give the worst interpretation of the worst teenagers of all time." Give them "A" for their effort. The two nincompoops learn some superficial history by going into the past. In the sequel, Reeves and his buddy Winter battle two evil robot versions of themselves.

LOGAN, TOM
LEGAL EAGLES (1986, Universal)—**Robert Redford** and Debra Winger find themselves teaming up to defend Darryl Hannah on a murder charge. Winger is interested in Redford, and she does wish that he would stay out of their client's bed, especially when their affair makes the news.

LOHKAMP, ERICH
THREE COMRADES (1938, MGM)—In this film based on Erich Remarque's novel about post-WWI Germany, **Robert Taylor** is one of three close friends, all of whom love Margaret Sullavan, who is dying of tuberculosis. She weds Taylor, though their time together is short.

LOLA
BANDIT QUEEN (1950, GB, Lippert)—When **Barbara Britton** returns to California, she arrives in time to see her parents killed. She becomes a female Zorro to avenge their deaths.

LOLA
BOMBSHELL (1933, MGM)—Sexpot movie star **Jean Harlow** wants to be known for finer things, but is thwarted by her P.R. man, who wishes to keep her image just as it is.

LOLA *See* VASTO

LOLA
THE GIRL FROM RIO (1927, Silent, Gotham)—**Carmel Myers** is a beautiful cafe dancer in Rio de Janeiro, pursued by three men, her dancing partner, a coffee grower and an American. It's the last she loves and marries, but not before a lot of problems are dealt with.

LOLA *See* HELEN WEYRINGER

LOLA
HURRICANE'S GAL (1922, Silent, Associated First National)—**Dorothy Phillips** has inherited her father's smuggling business. She makes the mistake of falling for a government agent trying to close down her enterprise.

LOLA
LOLA (1914, Silent, World)—When **Clara Kimball Young** is killed in an accident, her scientist father uses his invention, which brings people back to life. It works but it changes her personality from a sweet girl to an immoral sex-craving woman. Oh, a modern girl.

LOLA
PRIVATE DUTY NURSES (1972, New World)—In Roger Corman's second "Nurses" movie, beautiful Florence Nightingales like **Joyce Williams** spend more time in water beds than in caring for patients.

LOLA
TARZAN AND THE SLAVE GIRL (1950, RKO)—Tarzan, played by Lex Barker, and Jane, by Vanessa Brown, get involved with slave girl **Denise Darcel** of the lost tribe of Lionians.

LOLA
WOMAN TO WOMAN (1929, Tiffany)—French ballerina **Betty Compson** has a brief affair with an English officer during WWI. He goes off to the front, where it is reported he has been killed. She is left pregnant. Her lover has survived, though he loses his memory (well at least of her). He goes home and marries another. Years later, Compson meets her lover again, and lets him know that he has fathered a son. This is doubly bittersweet because his wife cannot have children. Compson, who knows she is dying, gives their son to his father to raise.

LOLITA
THEY MET IN ARGENTINA (1941, RKO)—**Maureen O'Hara**, an Irish senorita, used to having her way, wants James Ellison, who doesn't want to fall in love. The musical score arguably contains the worst songs ever written by Rodgers and Hart.

LOLLY
STICKY FINGERS (1988, Spectrafilm)—Cello player **Melanie Mayron** and violinist Helen Slater are not making enough money even to pay their rent. They get their hands on a suitcase containing a million dollars in drug money. Well, that solves one problem, but causes many more.

LOMAN, WILLY
DEATH OF A SALESMAN (1952, Columbia)—**Fredric March** is impressive as Arthur Miller's travelling salesman, whose dreams for himself and his sons seem never to be achieved. The fault lies not in the stars but in themselves.

LOMAX, BERNIE
WEEKEND AT BERNIE'S (1989, 20th Century Fox)—In a one-joke movie, obnoxious CEO **Terry Kiser** is having a weekend extravaganza at his beach house. He invites two of his junior accountants who have discovered a series of fraudulent insurance claims in Kiser's books. A mobster has the crooked insurance president killed, but his accountants try to see that he still enjoys his party.

LOMBARD, CAROLE
GABLE AND LOMBARD (1976, Universal)—**Jill Clayburgh** is a fairly talented actress, but she has little to work with in this terrible biopic about the romance and marriage of Clark Gable and Carole Lombard, which ended when the latter's plane crashed, while she was on a USO tour at the beginning of WWII.

LOMOND, DR.
THE RINGER (1928, GB, Silent, Ideal); (1932, GB, British Lion); (1953, GB, London/Regent); THE PHANTOM STRIKES (1939, GB, Monogram) -**Leslie Faber, Patric Curwen, Donald Wolfit** and **Alexander Knox** each provided their interpretations of author Edgar Wallace's criminal master of disguise. For those who enjoy movie boo boos, a character in the 1932 film warns "The Ringer has been seen in Deptford." The thing is that no one knows what the Ringer looks like.

LONDA

THE SPECIALIST (1975, Crown)—**Ahna Capri** was a macho hit woman long before Kathleen Turner of PRIZZI'S HONOR began making movies.

LONDON, JACK

JACK LONDON (1943, UA)—**Michael O'Shea**, a pleasant enough personality, was never a great shakes as an actor. At least in this biopic—of the author of numerous adventure yarns—he meets Virginia Mayo, whom he married.

LONDONDERRY, LOLA "TWINKY"

LOLA (1971, GB, American International)—A middle-aged porno writer weds sixteen-year-old nymphet **Susan George** and takes her to New York. The film was released as TWINKY in Great Britain.

LONE RANGER, THE

THE LONE RANGER (1955, Warner Brothers); THE LONE RANGER AND THE LOST CITY OF GOLD (1958, UA); THE LEGEND OF THE LONE RANGER (1981, Universal)—For most people of a certain age group, **Clayton Moore** will always be The Lone Ranger and Jay Silverheels, Tonto. For almost everyone, the name **Klinton Spilsbury** will not be remembered for anything, but trivia masters will insist he played The Lone Ranger in 1981 and lost.

LONIGAN, STUDS

STUDS LONIGAN (1960, UA)—James T. Farrell wasn't happy with this production of his trilogy of novels written in the 1930s. To make things worse, Studs, a macho Irish-American pool-hall bum played by **Christopher Knight**, survives and does the right thing by his pregnant girlfriend.

LONG, ANDREW

THE REMARKABLE ANDREW (1942, Paramount)—When small-town clerk **William Holden** is framed by crooked politicians, he is helped by the ghost of Andrew Jackson, played by Brian Donlevy, and other historical characters dedicated to the truth.

LONG, ARCHIE

TOUGH GUYS (1986, Touchstone)—Train robbers **Kirk Douglas** and Burt Lancaster are released after thirty years in prison. They find they have no place in society, so they go back to what they know best, robbing trains.

LONG, ART

TOUGH ENOUGH (1983, 20th Century Fox)—When country and western singer-composer **Dennis Quaid** can't earn enough to give his wife and baby any kind of life, he turns to prizefighting. Now, there's a sensible career move.

LONG, BINGO

BINGO LONG TRAVELLING ALL-STARS AND MOTOR KINGS (1976, Motown)—**Billy Dee Williams** forms an independent Black baseball team, and goes on a barnstorming tour across the country during the 1940s.

LONG, TOM

THE ARIZONA ROMEO (1925, Silent, Fox)—Rancher **Buck Jones** falls for a manicurist but when he thinks she wishes to marry an easterner, he helps her, changing his and her mind only when he discovers she's only marrying the other man to spite her father.

LONGHETTI, MABEL

A WOMAN UNDER THE INFLUENCE (1974, International)—Lower-middle-class housewife **Gena Rowlands** searches for her identity.

LONGSTOCKING, PIPPI

THE NEW ADVENTURES OF PIPPI LONGSTOCKING (1988, Columbia)—Previous Pippi movies were made in Sweden in the 1970s and dubbed in English. In this one, **Tami Erin** as Pippi loses her father during a shipwreck in the South Seas, and winds up in a small coastal town. She settles into a deserted house with a pet horse and monkey, and takes every advantage of being parentless.

LONNIE

LONNIE (1963, Dolphin/Futuramic)—Loser **Scott Marlowe's** luck is all bad. He rents his car to a revolutionary who uses it in a jewel robbery. His childhood sweetheart has turned to prostitution, and he's kidnapped by crooks escaping in a boat.

LOONEY, LITTLETON

THE SAP FROM SYRACUSE (1930, Paramount)—Handyman **Jack Oakie** uses a modest inheritance to take an ocean voyage to Europe. He is mistakenly believed to be a wealthy mining expert, and is pursued by gold diggers. At the same time, he tries to court a female mine owner, who is the target of crooks. The sap outsmarts everyone and even comes up with a great mining idea.

LOPERMAN, WOODWARD

THERE WAS A CROOKED MAN (1970, Warner Brothers)—Western warden **Henry Fonda** trails escaped convict Kirk Douglas. When the latter is killed by a rattlesnake, while retrieving $500,000 which he had hidden, Fonda grabs the loot and hits out for Mexico.

LOPEZ, PANCHO

THE BAD MAN (1923, Silent, Associated First National); (1930, First National/Warner Brothers); (1941, MGM)—**Holbrook Blinn**, **Walter Huston** and **Wallace Beery** each star as the swaggering Mexican bandit, who lives life to the fullest, rewarding his friends and taking revenge on his enemies.

LORD, HENRY

MR. LORD SAYS NO (1952, GB, London Independent)—Nothing will induce Cockney grocer **Stanley Holloway** to give up his shop in order to make way for the building of the Festival of Britain exhibition.

LORD JIM

LORD JIM (1925, Silent, Paramount); (1965, GB, Columbia)—Having abandoned his ship in a storm, with the result that many of his passengers are killed, first officer **Percy Marmont** (in 1925 and **Peter O'Toole** in the remake), seeks personal redemption as he travels through the Orient. He becomes a hero to Patusan natives, when he leads a revolt against an oppressive warlord, but is forced to sacrifice his own life to appease the chief when the latter's son is killed.

LORD, ROSIE

ROSIE! (1967, Universal)—**Rosalind Russell's** daughters, eager to get their hands on her money, attempt to have her declared incompetent, but the widow's granddaughter and an old lawyer, who loves her, comes to her rescue.

LORENZ, KATHY

GIRL ON THE SPOT (1946, Universal)—**Lois Collier** is in trouble because she witnessed a murder, and the killer has plans for her.

LORETTA

SO YOUNG, SO BAD (1950, UA)—**Anne Francis** is one of several juvenile delinquent types who is exploited in this cliche-filled film about an authoritarian girls reform school with only kindly psychiatrist Paul Henreid trying to help the girls.

LORIFLAN, ALBERT
PLAYBOY OF PARIS (1930, Paramount)—Waiter **Maurice Chevalier** is loved by Frances Dee, daughter of a Parisian cafe owner. The latter plans to marry his daughter to a wealthy man, until he learns that Chevalier has come into a large inheritance, making him the rage of the City of Lights.

LORIMER, ELIZABETH
CHILD IN THE HOUSE (1956, GB, Eros)—When her mother becomes ill and her father hides out from the police, twelve-year-old **Mandy Miller** goes to stay with her fussy aunt and uncle.

LORIMER, LOUISE
WOMAN IN THE DARK (1934, RKO)—In this lesser Dashiell Hammett effort, **Fay Wray** and her former lover, villain Melvyn Douglas, make Ralph Bellamy's attempt to go straight after he gets out of prison all the more difficult.

LORING, FAY
BIG TOWN GIRL (1937, 20th Century Fox)—**Claire Trevor** is a radio singer masquerading as a French countess to evade her escaped convict husband.

LORNA
THREE BAD SISTERS (1956, UA)—**Sara Shane's** older sister Kathleen Hughes has already disfigured and driven another sister to suicide in order to get all of their father's estate. Now she's out to rid herself of the last of her sibling competition.

LORRAINE, KITTY
STAGE MOTHER (1933, MGM)—This "B" movie shot in a couple of weeks on a sound stage casts **Alice Brady** in the all-too-familiar role of a pushy stage mother, working for her daughter Maureen O'Sullivan's career.

LORRAINE, TRIXIE
GOLD DIGGERS OF 1933 (1933, Warner Brothers)—**Aline MacMahon**, the eldest of three chorus girls looking for work or wealthy men, picks off well-to-do lawyer Guy Kibbee.

LORRESS, MARIANNE
A LADY WITHOUT A PASSPORT (1950, MGM)—Refugee **Hedy Lamarr** is a one of a group of aliens slated to be smuggled from Cuba to the United States. Wouldn't you know that she falls for the undercover agent who's out to catch the smugglers.

LORY, ARTHUR
THIS LAND IS MINE (1943, RKO)—Set in an unnamed country in occupied Europe, **Charles Laughton** is featured as a fearful teacher who develops some backbone and stands up for his country, by making an impassioned speech about liberty in a court when he's on trial for a murder he did not commit.

LOTEE
PREHISTORIC WOMEN (1959, Eagle-Lion)—**Joan Shawlee** is one of the beauties in animal-skins, who capture men for their pleasure, and have some fun with a dragon and a hairy giant.

LOUIE
THE WRONG GUYS (1988, New World)—Teddy bear **Louie Anderson** invites the former members of his Cub Scout troop to a reunion. It's not as funny as it sounds.

LOUIS
THE LADYKILLERS (1956, GB, Ealing)—In this British black comedy, **Herbert Lom** is one of a group of criminals who pull a heist. When their ancient landlady gets wind of it, they decide one of them must kill her, but they bump each other off instead.

LOUIS
SECRET PEOPLE (1952, GB, Ealing)—**Serge Reggiani** and two female exiles plot the assassination of the tyrants who have taken over their country.

LOUIS XIV
THE MAN IN THE IRON MASK (1939, UA)—**Louis Hayward** has the dual roles of the French king who keeps his twin brother imprisoned, wearing an iron mask and the twin. The evil king gets his chance to wear the horrible mask before he goes to his death.

LOUIS XVII
DANGEROUS EXILE (1958, GB, Rank)—An English girl helps a French duke save the Dauphin of France, **Richard O'Sullivan**, from the agents of the Republic.

LOUIS, JOE
THE JOE LOUIS STORY (1953, UA)—**Coley Wallace** is a good choice to play the "Brown Bomber" in a story long on schmaltz and short on facts.

LOUISE
THE BOSS' WIFE (1986, Tri-Star)—The Boss' wife **Arielle Dombarle** is out to seduce an ambitious young stockbroker.

LOUISE
TEEN WITCH (1989, Trans World)—Unpopular teen **Robin Lively** has a serious crush on football star Dan Gathier, but the hunk already has a gorgeous girlfriend. When Livley discovers that she is a witch, her prospects improve.

LOUISE
THELMA AND LOUISE (1991, Pathe)—When a denizen of a roadside bar tries to rape her friend Geena Davis, **Susan Sarandon** shoots and kills him. The women are then on the run, pursued by Arkansas cop Harvey Keitel. Even though there's no chance they'll get away scot free, they have a wonderful run until the climactic scene.

LOUISE
THE WOMAN HE SCORNED (1930, GB, Warner Brothers)—Lighthouse keeper's wife **Pola Negri** shelters her fugitive lover. The film was made as a silent in 1929 with sound added in 1930.

LOUISE, MME.
MADAME LOUISE (1951, GB, Butchers)—**Hilda Bayley** loses her fashionable Mayfair dress shop to a bookmaker, who immediately proceeds to update the operation. In the end, Bayley regains her salon.

LOUISE, PRINCESS
THE PRINCESS AND THE PLUMBER (1930, Fox)—**Maureen O'Sullivan** is the daughter of an impoverished prince. He wants her to marry the man of his choice, but she has her way and marries Charles Farrell, the head of a large plumbing concern, who had been hired to fix the prince's castle's pipes.

LOUVAIN, MOLLY
THE STRANGE LOVE OF MOLLY LOUVAIN (1932, Warner Brothers) -**Ann Dvorak** has a brief affair with a man, and is left with a

baby to care for. Not to fret, she's attracts men despite her less than perfect past and the excess baggage of a kid.

LOVELACE, DONALD
MR. LOVE (1986, GB, Warner Brothers)—Everyone thinks that gardener **Barry Jackson**, in a loveless marriage for thirty years, is a joke, but who are all those women who show up grief-stricken at his funeral?

LOVELACE, EVA
STAGE STRUCK (1958, RKO/Buena Vista)—**Susan Strasberg** stars in this remake of MORNING GLORY. She is a small-town girl with stars in her eyes. Many men help her advance her career in the theater and when she becomes a star, she no longer needs any of them.

LOVELESS, GAIL
OPERATOR 13 (1934, MGM)—During the Civil War, northern spy **Marion Davies** is ordered to eliminate southern officer Gary Cooper, but of course they fall in love.

LOVELL, CHARLOTTE
THE OLD MAID (1939, Warner Brothers)—To ensure her daughter's happiness when her lover dies, unwed mother **Bette Davis** allows her cousin Miriam Hopkins to bring up the unsuspecting girl as her own. She believes that Davis is just her fussy old maiden aunt. Considering what it is, it's very good. Audiences should see the play performed at Edith Wharton's home, The Mount, outside of Lennox, Massachusetts.

LOVELL, GERALD
LOVE FROM A STRANGER (1937, GB, UA)—After coming into a fortune, Ann Harding quarrels with her fiance and marries **Basil Rathbone**, a man she hardly knows. She soon suspects that he is a man who marries and then murders rich women. She turns the tables on him, scaring him to death.

LOWE, LEONARD
AWAKENINGS (1990, Columbia)—Based on an actual case, this sympathetic production is the story of shy neurologist Robin Williams, who in 1966 uses a new drug L-DOPA to treat a group of patients rendered almost motionless by encephalitis in the 1920s. He first "awakens" **Robert De Niro**, who is brilliant in the role. Watching De Niro make his first struggling steps towards his mother Ruth Nelson, who has cared for him for 30 years, is heart-rending. The effect of the drug is temporary, unfortunately, and at the end of the film they have returned to their statuelike trances, having shown that there are cognizant, feeling people inside those pitiful bodies.

LOWERY, BILL
THE DURANGO KID (1940, Columbia)—**Charles Starrett** is a gun-fanning western Robin Hood who helps homesteaders hold off rustlers.

LOWNDES, HENRY
TOO MANY HUSBANDS (1940, Columbia)—**Melvyn Douglas** marries Jean Arthur, but then her first husband Fred MacMurray, believed dead, shows up.

LT
BAD LIEUTENANT (1992, Odyssey)—Foul-mouthed, corrupt, drug- and alcohol-abusing, in-debt gambler, lapsed Catholic cop **Harvey Keitel** is assigned the cases of a raped nun and a series of random murders.

LU ANA
BIRD OF PARADISE (1932, RKO)—Lovely **Dolores Del Rio**, whose accent hurt her in talkies, was more than adequate as a South Seas beauty whose idyllic love affair with sailor Ray Milland is ended when she must perform her duties as a princess and jump into a smoldering volcano to please the gods and protect her people.

LUCAS
LUCAS (1986, 20th Century Fox)—Pint-sized **Corey Haim** develops a major crush on an older woman of sixteen. He's willing to do anything to win her, including risking his life on the football team. Fortunately for him, lovely young Winona Ryder is waiting for him to notice her.

LUCAS, DANIEL
THREE FUGITIVES (1989, Buena Vista)—Just out of prison, **Nick Nolte** becomes involved with nervous little Martin Short and his little daughter when the former robs a bank. The police believe Nolte is the thief.

LUCASTA, ANNA
ANNA LUCASTA (1949, Columbia); (1958, UA)—At first ANNA LUCASTA was an all-black Broadway play. When it was first brought to the screen all the roles were for whites with **Paulette Goddard** as a waterfront prostitute, who opts for a new life. In 1958, producers went back to the all-black version with sexy **Eartha Kitt** in the title role. It wasn't much, no matter what color the actors.

LUCIANO, DOMINICK & EUGENE
DOMINICK AND EUGENE (1988, Orion)—**Tom Hulce** and **Ray Liotta** are fraternal twins living together in Pittsburgh. Kind-hearted, mentally handicapped Hulce works as a garbage collector, putting Liotta through medical school. When Liotta begins seeing fellow med student Jamie Lee Curtis, he considers leaving home to study with her at Stanford. Hulce realizes his comfortable world is falling apart.

LUCIANO, LUCKY
MOBSTERS (1991, Universal)—Still working on his Jack Nicholson imitation, **Christian Slater** is the leader of a group of twentysomething hoods, who upset the older dons of crime.

LUCIEN *See* **MARIO**

LUCIFER, MR.
MEET MR. LUCIFER (1953, GB, Ealing)—Devil **Stanley Holloway** recruits a pantomime comic to make TV a curse.

LUCIO
HI GAUCHO! (1936, RKO)—Spanish gent **John Carroll** saves Steffi Duna from bandit Rod La Rocque, but nothing could save this dreadful musical.

LUCK, HARRY
THE MAGNIFICENT SEVEN (1960, UA)—**Brad Dexter** is a gunslinger who agrees to join six others to defend a Mexican village from bandits. He believes there must be a fortune of some kind involved. When he's fatally wounded, Yul Brynner allows him to die happy by telling him he was right all along. The seven were really after a fortune in gold.

LUCKY
LAS VEGAS LADY (1976, Crown International)—**Stella Stevens** would like to leave her seamy past behind her, but she becomes involved in an amusement park heist.

LUCY

PANAMA LADY (1939, RKO)—Cabaret dancer **Lucille Ball** is almost shanghaied to a wilderness camp of an oil prospector. She is followed by her gun-running ex-boyfriend. The triangle becomes a quadrangle with Steffi Duna as a jealous native girl before things are sorted out as to whom belongs to whom and who cares.

LUCY

THEY WERE SISTERS (1945, GB, Universal)—In a none-too-interesting potboiler, **Phyllis Calvert** loses her daughter, sees one sister become something of a tramp, and her other sister marry a sadistic beast, causing her to commit suicide.

LUCY

VALET GIRLS (1987, Lexyn/Empire)—Aspiring singer **Meri D. Marshall** works for a car parking service in Los Angeles. She and her sexy female friends are hired to work at a swanky party held each weekend at the posh estate of a talent agent, but parking cars is only part of their expected duties. It's a typical teen sex comedy, filled with adolescent giggles about "dirty" things.

LUCY, AUNT

CHARLEY'S BIG-HEARTED AUNT (1940, GB, Gainsborough)—**Jeanne de Casalis** is the aunt whose delay in arriving at Oxford to chaperon two visiting young ladies, forces Arthur Askey to impersonate her.

LUDWIG, KING

MY FRIEND THE KING (1931, GB, Fox)—Taxi driver Jerry Verno masquerades as a demure countess in order to rescue a Ruritanian prince, **Eric Pavitt**, from revolutionaries.

LUGER, JOHN

DEAD MAN WALKING (1988, Metropolis-Hit)—The film is set in 2004, after a plague has wiped out half the earth's population. Those infected with the disease are called zero people, representing their chances of survival. One, **Wings Hauser**, is induced to enter the plague zone to rescue the kidnapped daughter of an industrialist.

LUKE

COOL HAND LUKE (1967, Warner Brothers)—**Paul Newman** is sent to a country prison farm for cutting the heads off parking meters while drunk. He wins the respect of the yard's bully Arthur Kennedy. Newman escapes several times, but is brought back and made to wear chains. He is given the treatment from the guards and just when he seems to have been broken, he escapes one more time, but this time he's not brought back alive.

LUKE

SLAVES (1969, Continental)—**Ozzie Davis** is a slave owned by Stephen Boyd. Davis tries to help Boyd's slave-mistress and an infant escape, but is beaten to death for his efforts. His death emboldens the other slaves who help fulfill Davis' plan.

LUKE, DR. JOHN

THE COUNTRY DOCTOR (1936, 20th Century Fox)—In a fictionalized account of the birth of Canada's Dionne quintuplets, **Jean Hersholt** portrays the doctor who delivered them.

LUKE, SISTER

THE NUN'S STORY (1959, Warner Brothers)—In the Congo, Belgian nun **Audrey Hepburn** experiences a spiritual tug-of-war as to whether she has the necessary self-discipline and calling to remain in her order. Adding to her confusion are the views of an attractive atheist doctor, Peter Finch. She ultimately decides she is unsuited to the life and "jumps over the wall."

LULU

ASSAULT OF THE KILLER BIMBOS (1988, Titan/Empire)—Ding-a-ling waitress **Elizabeth Kaitan** and two other cheap women must clear themselves of a murder charge.

LULU

FOREVER, LULU (1987, Tri-Star)—Singing star **Deborah Harry** gets top billing but appears only briefly in this knockoff of DESPERATELY SEEKING SUSAN.

LULU

LULU (1962, Australia, Gloria); (1978, Chase)—**Nadja Tiller** and **Elisa Leonelli** each star in remakes of Pabst's PANDORA'S BOX. Lulu becomes the mistress of a doctor when she is only 14. He transforms her into a worldly woman, and marries her to a wealthy man, who dies of a heart attack after catching her in bed with an artist. She marries the latter, but he commits suicide. She marries the doctor but kills him. She ends up in London as a prostitute and becomes one of Jack the Ripper's victims. We still prefer Louise Brooks, one of the most striking-looking women ever to appear in the movies.

LULU BELLE

LULU BELLE (1948, Columbia)—Around the turn of the century, **Dorothy Lamour** is a saloon singer, who marries an attorney, but goes through a string of lovers as she moves on to become a Broadway star.

LUM

PARTNERS IN TIME (1946, RKO); LUM AND ABNER ABROAD (1956, Howco)—Radio stars **Chester Lauck** and Norris Goff appear as young Lum and Abner in the 1946 film. Audiences are let in on how they met and formed the "Jot-Em-Down" store in Pine Ridge Arkansas. The 1956 film was just three of their TV shows stitched together and certainly not up to their radio level of home-spun humor.

LUNA, THERESA

ONLY THE LONELY (1991, 20th Century Fox)—Shy, lonely **Ally Sheedy** is a cosmetician in her father's funeral parlor. She falls for lonely Irish cop John Candy—but their romance is threatened by Maureen O'Hara, Candy's Archie Bunker-like mother, who has bullied her son all his life.

LUND, HANNAH

ZANDY'S BRIDE (1974, Warner Brothers)—**Liv Ullmann** is the beautiful mail-order bride who mellows gruff California rancher Gene Hackman who sent for her.

LUNDY, JEFF

MR. RECKLESS (1948, Paramount)—Oil driller **William Eythe** and his roughneck friends find all bets are off when a pretty girl, Barbara Britton, comes into the picture.

LUPIN, ARSENE

ARSENE LUPIN (1932, MGM); ARSENE LUPIN RETURNS (1938, MGM); ENTER ARSENE LUPIN (1944, Universal)—**John Barrymore, Melvyn Douglas** and **Charles Korvin** each star as the infamous super-burglar, resentfully pursued by a detective who thinks he knows the identity of his adversary. In the sequel, he's out to steal a $250,000 gem.

LUTHER, MARTIN

MARTIN LUTHER (1953, De Rochemont); LUTHER (1974, American Film Theatre)—**Niall MacGinnis** is quite good in his portrayal of the world's first Protestant, his career and doubts. In 1974, **Stacy Keach** starred in the John Osborne production about the German cleric, who changed the course of history when he led the Protestant Revolution of the 16th century.

LUTON, JOSEPHINE

JOSEPHINE AND MEN (1955, GB, British Lion)—**Glynis Johns** throws out her husband to marry a struggling writer, but when her first husband becomes involved in a scandal, she returns to him. When he's cleared, she returns to the writer. It seems she'll be with whomever needs mothering at the time.

LYA

THE SCARLET LADY (1928, Silent, Columbia)—Russian revolutionary **Lya De Putti**, hiding from Cossacks, seeks refuge in the estate of Prince Nicholas. Nicholas falls in love with her but learning she is a Red, will have no more to do with her. She returns to the people, and when the Reds take over, Nicholas disguises himself as a servant, but De Putti does not give him away. They flee the country together as love conquers political loyalties.

LYDIA

LYDIA (1964, Canada, Libra)—Americans **Anna Hagen** and Gordon Pinsent meet and fall in love on a Greek Isle, where he has gone to contemplate his terminal illness.

LYNCH, JOE

THREE NUTS IN SEARCH OF A BOLT (1964, Harlequin)—**Paul Gilbert** is one of three "nuts" who can't afford to go to an expensive psychiatrist. They hire an actor to act out their problems and thus have three treatments for the price of one.

LYNDON, BARRY

BARRY LYNDON (1975, GB, Hawk-Peregrine)—**Ryan O'Neal** stars as Thackeray's 18th-century Irish gentleman of fortune, who allows his success to go to his head. The film's background scenes are so beautifully photographed, it's a shame they allowed those actors to get in the way up front.

LYNN

THE STUDENT NURSES (1970, New World)—**Brioni Farrell** is one of four beautiful student nurses, who seem to have learned more about sex and aberrations than medicine. The film's success caused the production of many others in similiar veins.

LYNN, LORETTA

COAL MINER'S DAUGHTER (1980, Universal)—**Sissy Spacek** won an Academy Award for her portrayal of the country and western star who married at 13 and went on to become a Grand Old Opry favorite.

LYNN

PRIVATE DUTY NURSES (1972, New World)—Nurse **Pegi Boucher** becomes involved with a married doctor, and a heroin-addicted drug dealer in this medical mishmash.

LYNN, THOEDORE

THEODORA GOES WILD (1936, Columbia)—**Irene Dunne** successfully moves from weepies to screwball comedy as a small town librarian, who writes a sensational best-selling novel about the goings on in small towns. It's fiction but nobody will believe her.

LYNN, VICKI

VICKI (1953, 20th Century Fox)—**Jean Peters** stars in a remake of I WAKE UP SCREAMING. She's a waitress, who is groomed to become a top model by a slick publicist, but she's murdered. Her sister joins forces with the publicist to find Peters' murderer.

LYNTON, LETTY

LETTY LYNTON (1932, MGM)—Socialite **Joan Crawford's** shipboard romance with a respected Long Island man is jeopardized by the arrival of her blackmailing ex-lover.

LYONS, DAVE

SEE NO EVIL, HEAR NO EVIL (1989, Tri-Star)—**Gene Wilder** becomes Richard Pryor's eyes and the latter becomes Wilder's ears as the deaf and blind partners work to solve a murder and save their lives.

LYRA

TARZAN AND THE SHE-DEVIL (1953, RKO)—Seductive **Monique Van Vooren** has Lex Barker, as Tarzan, whipped when he interferes with her plans and those of her ivory-stealing partners.

MABEL

GOLD DIGGERS ON BROADWAY (1929, Warner Brothers)—**Winnie Lightner** is one of three Broadway cuties on the look-out for sugar daddies in the now all too familiar story.

MAC

LOOSE CANNONS (1990, Tri-Star)— **Gene Hackman** makes many movies, too many. He should have passed on this one. Gruff policeman Hackman is teamed with Dan Ackroyd, reactivated too quickly from a nervous breakdown. LETHAL WEAPON this ain't.

MACANSLAND, LIBBY

THE GROUP (1966, UA)—**Jessica Walter** is one of the eight graduates of Vassar's class of 1933, whose lives are chronicled for the next 20 years.

MACARDEN, ALEXANDER

THE SWORDSMAN (1947, Columbia)—**Larry Parks**, such a smash in THE JOLSON STORY, proved difficult to cast. His appearance as an 18th century Scot, who ends a feud so he can marry the girl of his choice didn't do much for his career. Worse things awaited him, including the HUAC.

MACARTHUR, DOUGLAS

MACARTHUR (1977, Universal)—During WWII, homes all over the U.S. had colored pictures cut out of newspapers of Franklin Delano Roosevelt and Douglas MacArthur pinned up on their walls. **Gregory Peck** gives a rather fine performance as the famous general in a film that crowded in much of the events of his life from his command in the Philippines at Corregidor at the start of the war, through his "Old soldiers never die speech" in Congress, after being fired by President Truman during the Korean War.

MACARTHY
THE GREAT MACARTHY (1975, Australia , Seven Keys)—**John Jarratt**, a great soccer player from the outback, finds being a star is a great life as long as it lasts, but it doesn't last.

MACAULEY, CHRIS & MATT
MEN DON'T LEAVE (1990, Warner Brothers)—While it's not an absolute that the men of the title are Jessica Lange's two sons **Chris O'Donnell** and **Charlie Korsmo**, it's these two who stand by their widowed mother when she takes to her bed in an almost catatonic state. The boys have contributed to her stress. Sixteen-year-old O'Donnell is, well, 16, and besides, he begins an affair with older woman Joan Cusack. Younger son Korsmo hides his grief over his father by turning to petty thievery, trying to get some money for his mom.

MACBETH
MACBETH (1948, Republic); (1963, Paramount); (1971, GB, Columbia)—**Orson Welles, Maurice Evans** and **Jon Finch** each appeared as Shakespeare's thane, who helps the prophecy of three witches along by killing his king and the children of a friend. As king, he can only stand by helplessly when his co-conspirator wife goes mad. Macbeth is eventually defeated by Macduff, not born of woman.

MACBETH, JOE
JOE MACBETH (1955, Columbia)—In a modern variation on the Macbeth story, mobster **Paul Douglas** is encouraged by his wife Ruth Roman to eliminate his boss and take over the gang.

MACDONALD, BETTY
THE EGG AND I (1947, Universal)—City couple **Claudette Colbert** and Fred MacMurray move to the Pacific Northwest to embark on a new life as chicken farmers. They are the nominal stars of this movie, but Marjorie Main and Percy Kilbride as Ma and Pa Kettle steal the show.

MACDONALD, DUNCAN
PONY SOLDIER (1952, 20th Century Fox)—Mountie **Tyrone Power** sets off after a tribe of hostile Creek Indians in 1876. They have illegally crossed the border into the U.S. to hunt buffalo.

MACDONALD, KATHERINE
SECRETS OF A NURSE (1938, Universal)—Nurse **Helen Mack** keeps faith with her ex-boxer boyfriend Dick Foran when he is framed for murder.

MACFARLANE, JAMES LEWIS
KEEPER OF THE BEES (1925, Silent, FBO)—**Robert Frazer** believes he has only a year to live because of wounds he received in WWI. He inherits half-interest in an apiary, and marries a girl about to drown herself because she is to have a child born out of wedlock. His wife disappears after the ceremony but he gets her back as well as his health.

MACGREGOR, ROB ROY
ROB ROY (1922, GB, Silent, Gaumont); ROB ROY, THE HIGHLAND ROGUE (1954, GB, Disney/RKO)—**David Hawthorne** and **Richard Todd** both appear as the Scottish rebel, who is quite a thorn in the side of the English in 1715.

MACHINE, FRANKIE
THE MAN WITH THE GOLDEN ARM (1955, UA)—Chicago junkie card dealer and jazz drummer **Frank Sinatra** is married to seem-ingly crippled Eleanor Parker. She would prefer he remained dependent on drugs. He's in love with Kim Novak who helps him go "cold turkey."

MACHIN, EDWARD HENRY "DENRY"
THE PROMOTER (1952, GB, Universal)—Called THE CARD in Great Britain, this film stars **Alec Guinness** as the youngest mayor of Bursley. He is pursued with varying amounts of ardor by a countess, a gold digger and a sweet local thing. Care to guess whom he chooses?

MACKAYE, JEAN
HOW COULD YOU JEAN? (1918, Silent, Artcraft)—When wealthy **Mary Pickford** loses her fortune, she must take work as a cook. No sweat, a banker's son falls in love with her.

MACKEE, DR. JACK
THE DOCTOR (1991, Buena Vista/Touchstone)—Surgeon **William Hurt** believes a physician should maintain an emotional distance from his patients. When he learns he has throat cancer, he discovers how it feels to be at the mercy of indifferent medical personnel, who treat patients like inconvenient objects.

MACKENDRICK, CANADA
PARATROOPER (1954, GB, Columbia)—Canadian **Alan Ladd** refuses a commission with the paratroops, because he believes he's responsible for the death of a friend. The film is called THE RED BERET in England.

MACKENNA
MACKENNA'S GOLD (1969, Columbia)—Sheriff **Gregory Peck** has a map that purports to locate The Lost Dutchman Mine. This draws an odd assortment of bandits, prospectors, Indians and other gold-hungry westerners like flies to a dead carcass.

MACKENZIE, MEG
A HOMESPUN VAMP (1922, Silent, Paramount)—Country orphan **May McAvoy** lives with her two cruel uncles, who plan to marry her to a blacksmith. When she takes in an injured writer while they are away, they insist he marry her. To protect her honor he goes along with the wedding, planning to get an annulment later, but by the time the papers are ready, he has fallen in love with her.

MACKINTOSH
MACKINTOSH & T.J. (1975, Penland)—**Roy Rogers** plays a hard-working cowboy who takes on the role of Big Brother to a drifter's teenage son.

MACLEAN, BILL
THE MAN OUTSIDE (1968, GB, Allied Artists)—Ex-CIA agent **Van Heflin** is framed for murder by Russians, but saves himself and a kidnapped girl.

MACLEAN, BRIAN
CAPTAINS OF THE CLOUDS (1942, Warner Brothers)—Canadian bush pilot **James Cagney** joins the WWII Royal Canadian Air Force, but because he won't accept discipline, he is washed out. He later proves his mettle while shuttling American bombers to England.

MACLEAN, JUNEAU
THE WILDERNESS WOMAN (1926, Silent, First National)—**Aileen Pringle** is the daughter of an Alaskan miner, who has made a million. When they move to New York, the pair are the targets of various con-men, but they aren't as dumb as they appear.

MACLEAN, TESS

TESS OF THE STORM COUNTRY (1961, 20th Century Fox)—Scottish lass **Diane Baker** arrives in the Pennsylvania Dutch country to find her intended husband deceased. She finds happiness with Mennonite lad Jack Ging. The two join the fight to stop a chemical plant from polluting the streams.

MACLEOD, CONNOR

HIGHLANDER (1986, 20th Century Fox)—**Christopher Lambert**, a 16th century Scot, is chosen to be one of a small group of immortals who will fight each other throughout the centuries, with the last to survive gaining a valuable power. The final battle takes place atop a skyscraper in modern-day Manhattan.

MACMICHAEL, CONOR

THE CLASS OF MISS MACMICHAEL (1978, GB, Brut)—**Glenda Jackson** has about equal amounts of trouble with the headmaster of her school as she does with the obnoxious social misfits she's trying to teach. It touches on the same topics as BLACKBOARD JUNGLE and TO SIR WITH LOVE, but lacks direction.

MACMILLAN, LYDIA

LYDIA (1941, UA)—**Merle Oberon** has had romantic experiences with four men, but when the one she really cares for goes away to sea and doesn't return, she devotes her life caring for blind children. In old age she meets her one true love once again, but he doesn't remember her.

MACNAIR, CONNIE

I AM GUILTY (1921, Silent, Associate Producers)—**Louise Glaum** is implicated in the murder of a friend of her husband, because she's caught with a revolver in her hand, standing over his dead body. Despite this, it's proven that the deceased's wife did him in.

MACOCO, "MACK THE KNIFE"

THE PIRATE (1948, MGM)—Judy Garland dreams of an infamous Caribbean pirate, with whom she feels she can find excitement and romance. She's unaware that the corrupt mayor of her West Indian village, whom she is being forced to marry, **Walter Slezak**, is in fact the buccaneer and no bargain.

MACOMBER, MARGARET

THE MACOMBER AFFAIR (1947, UA)—Married to weakling Robert Preston, **Joan Bennett** puts the make on manly great game hunter Gregory Peck while the three are on safari in Kenya. She shoots hubby dead while trying to protect him from a stampeding buffalo—or was she?

MACON, EDDIE

EDDIE MACON'S RUN (1983, Universal)—**John Schneider**, of TV's Dukes of Hazzard "fame," makes his screen debut as an escaped con, being pursued by tough lawman Kirk Douglas.

MACREADY, TOM

THE SONORA KID (1927, Silent, FBO)—**Tom Tyler** has to rescue his boss's daughter from a phony kidnapping plot before he's allowed to marry her.

MACTAGGART, GEORDIE

WEE GEORDIE (1956, GB, British & Dominions)—A frail Scot lad takes to exercising and grows to be **Bill Travers**, who wins the gold medal in the hammer throw at the Melbourne Olympics.

MACTAVISH, SANDY

A SAILOR'S SWEETHEART (1927, Silent, Warner Brothers)—Sailor **Clyde Cook** falls overboard with Louise Fazenda when she struggles with her new husband, whom she has just discovered is a bigamist. Cook and Fazenda have some wild adventures before deciding that they are right for each other.

MACWHITE, HARRISON CARTER

THE UGLY AMERICAN (1963, Universal)—**Marlon Brando**, the newly appointed U.S. Ambassador to a Southeast Asian country, discovers an old friend heads up the anti-American, pro-communist native faction.

MADDEN, BLAINE

THE GUN HAWK (1963, Allied Artists)—Dying gunman **Rory Calhoun** goads young gunslinger Rod Lauren to finish him off in the only way that makes sense to Calhoun—in a shoot-out.

MADDEN, CECILIA

CECILIA OF THE PINK ROSES (1918, Silent, Select)—**Marion Davies** learned well from her dying mother, but her brother becomes careless and gets in with the wrong kind of people, even falling for the old "Oh my God. It's my husband!" con. Davies brings him back home and back to church.

MADDEN, ELIZABETH

THE LADY IS WILLING (1942, Columbia)—When musical-comedy star **Marlene Dietrich** finds an abandoned baby, she convinces pediatrician Fred MacMurray to make a marriage of convenience with her to give the child a home.

MADDEN, LARRY

TALL MAN RIDING (1955, Warner Brothers)—**Randolph Scott** returns to his home to find his town completely controlled by cheating gambler Robert Barrat. To complicate matters, Scott is in love with the latter's daughter, Dorothy Malone.

MADDEN, SHAUN

SERGEANT MADDEN (1939, MGM)—**Wallace Beery** is a good cop. Unfortunately for him, his son Alan Curtis is a bad cop.

MADDEN, SPIKE

A GIRL IN EVERY PORT (1928, Silent, Fox)—**Victor McLaglen** convinces his sailor friend Robert Armstrong to be true to the sailor's credo of "a girl in every port," and not settle down with French tart Louise Brooks (who would tempt most men).

MADDEN, TIM

TOUGH GUYS DON'T DANCE (1987, Cannon)—**Ryan O'Neal** isn't so tough in this mishmash written and directed by Norman Mailer. O'Neal portrays a man who may have committed a murder, but can't remember.

MADDOX

WHO WAS MADDOX? (1964, GB, Anglo-Amalgamated)—Police superintendent Bernard Lee exposes the blackmailer behind the murder of **Richard Gale**, chairman of a publishing house.

MADDOX, MARSHAL JERED

LAWMAN (1971, UA)—Marshal **Burt Lancaster** rides into town with the warrants for seven men, all employees and friends of the region's most powerful rancher Lee J. Cobb, who at first tries to solve things peaceful like—but when that cuts no ice with Lancaster, the blood flows, while almost bemused sheriff Robert Ryan looks on.

MADELEINE

MADELEINE IS (1971, Canada, Alliance)—Messed-up **Nicola Lipman** finally dumps her Marxist lover for a more conventional businessman, who hasn't quite got it altogether either.

MADELINE
TIME TRACKERS (1989, Concorde)—When evil Lee Bergere steals a time machine's computer chip, which allows him to escape into the past, weapons expert **Brigit Hoffman** joins with two scientists to track him.

MADELON
THOSE THREE FRENCH GIRLS (1930, MGM)—**Sandra Ravel** is one of three French models, who together with an English nobleman trying to help them, are thrown into jail after a misunderstanding with their landlord. All escape and make it to the nobleman's estate where he chooses among them for his own.

MADGE
FACE IN THE SKY (1933, Fox)—Sign painter Spencer Tracy uses the sweet face of his beloved **Marian Nixon** to get to the top in his business.

MADIGAN, DET. DANIEL
MADIGAN (1968, Universal)—**Richard Widmark** is one of a breed of tough movie cops who is willing to bend the law to get his man, even though his equally tough superior, Henry Fonda, is always on his case.

MADISON, CHRISTINE
CHRISTINE OF THE HUNGRY HEART (1924, Silent, First National)—Desiring more out of life, **Florence Vidor** divorces her drunkard husband and marries a doctor by whom she has a son. Later her husband neglects her and she finds comfort elsewhere. After some bad times, all is forgiven.

MADISON, CORA
THE FLIRT (1922, Silent, Universal)—**Eileen Perry** is a small-town flirt in this moderately amusing comedy.

MADISON, DOLLY PAYNE
MAGNIFICENT DOLL (1946, Universal)—Eighteenth century widow **Ginger Rogers** is courted by many men. Among them are Burgess Meredith as James Madison, whom she marries and David Niven as Aaron Burr, whom she never forgets.

MADISON, FRANKIE
I WALK ALONE (1948, Paramount)—Just out of prison, **Burt Lancaster** is looking for revenge and his pay-off from his ex-gang boss, Kirk Douglas. These two have a fine shoot-out in a darkened room.

MADISON, JEAN
THE ADMIRAL WAS A LADY (1950, UA)—**Wanda Hendrix** is really just an ex-Wave who joins up with four ex-airmen looking to avoid work.

MADISON, JIM
KIMBERLEY JIM (1965, South Africa, Embassy)—**Jim Reeves** is one of two gamblers, who win a diamond mine in a fixed poker game. Did we forget to tell you, it's a musical?

MADISON, JOAN
GIRLS DEMAND EXCITEMENT (1931, Fox)—**Virginia Cherrill** appears in a film we suppose is the GIRLS JUST WANT TO HAVE FUN of it's day, but society wasn't quite as broad minded in 1931 as in 1985.

MADISON, JOHN
STRANGER IN TOWN (1957, GB, Eros)—Reporter **Alex Nicol** probes the mysterious shooting death of a an American composer living in a small English village. He finds that the composer was actually a blackmailer, and many people had reasons to wish him dead.

MADISON, OSCAR
THE ODD COUPLE (1968, Paramount)—**Walter Matthau** is much nastier and menacing than Jack Klugman in this Neil Simon comedy about two divorced men of extremely differently lifestyles, temperament and interests, trying to share a New York apartment.

MADOC, BILL
BEAUTY AND THE BAD MAN (1925, Silent, Peninsula)—**Forrest Stanley** is a western outlaw so impressed with the singing of Mabel Ballin that he gives her the $10,000 he has just won in a poker game so she can go to Europe to study voice. She becomes an opera star and Stanley spends some time in jail for a killing, but they eventually marry.

MADRID, SOL
SOL MADRID (1968, MGM)—In reality, Junkie **David McCallum** is a drug squad undercover agent seeking the source of the Mafia's heroin supply. We thought everybody knew that. Preventing them from smuggling it into the country is the problem.

MADRON
MADRON (1970, Four Star Excelsior)—Gunslinger **Richard Boone** and nun Leslie Caron have survived a wagon train massacre but must elude Apaches to reach safety.

MAG O' THE ALLEY
LITTLE WILDCAT (1922, Vitagraph)—Poor **Alice Calhoun** is released from jail into the custody of Herbert Fortier, who wishes to prove to Judge Ramsey Wallace that such girls can be reformed. The judge is doubtful, but the reclamation is so successful Wallace eventually marries Calhoun.

MAGDA, QUEEN OF SHEBA
SOLOMON AND SHEBA (1959, UA)—**Gina Lollobrigida**, as Sheba, had to get used to a new Solomon, Yul Brynner, after Tyrone Power died of a heart attack during the filming. The film was a critical failure, but a box office success possibly because of the scanty outfits wore by Lollobrigida.

MAGEE, DINGUS
DIRTY DINGUS MAGEE (1970, MGM)—In a movie "old blue eyes" may wish to forget, **Frank Sinatra** is a thieving 1880 cowboy in New Mexico, who is always in trouble with the law, the Indians and especially women.

MAGGIE
JIGGS AND MAGGIE IN SOCIETY (1948, Monogram); JIGGS AND MAGGIE OUT WEST (1950, Monogram)—**Reno Riano** plays the social climbing shrewish wife of recently wealthy Irish working man Jiggs (Joe Yule). All he wants is peace, and some corned-beef and cabbage.

MAGGIE
THE LITTLE LIAR (1916, Silent, Triangle)—Slum girl **Mae Marsh's** imagination gets her in all kinds of trouble.

MAGGIE

LIVING TO DIE (1990, PM)—When hooker **Darcy DeMoss** dies of an overdose, she doesn't let this prevent her from reappearing and taking up with ex-cop Wings Hauser in a failed attempt at film noir.

MAGGIE

PUPPET ON A CHAIN (1971, GB, Cinerama)—Interpol agent Sven-Bertil Taube and his assistant **Barbara Parkins** unmask an inspector as a heroin smuggler.

MAGGOTT, ARCHER

THE DIRTY DOZEN (1964, Warner Brothers)—Maniacal, condemned killer **Telly Savalas** reverts to form, almost ruining the mission he and eleven other GI cons have been sent behind German lines to carry out. He attacks and kills a German girl at a French Chateau used for R&R by top German officers during WWII.

MAGICIAN, THE

HILDUR AND THE MAGICIAN (1969, Canyon)—**John Graham** is a bumbling magician, who provides the narration for this fantasy about a princess kidnapped by an evil gnome. The kids like it.

MAGIZ, MARY

THE GAY BRIDE (1934, MGM)—Gold digger **Carole Lombard** finds romance with gangsters a bit too dangerous, so settles for an office boy, Chester Morris.

MAGUIRE, KATHLEEN

THE REFORMER AND THE REDHEAD (1950, MGM)—Zoo-keeper's daughter **June Allyson** likes large pets, and the reform candidate for mayor, Dick Powell.

MAGUIRE, PADDY

PADDY (1970, Ireland, Allied Artists)—**Des Cave** attempts to keep active sexually while maintaining a normal home life.

MAHMOODY, BETTY & MAHTOB

NOT WITHOUT MY DAUGHTER (1991, MGM/Pathe)—In a true story, **Sally Field** reluctantly agrees to accompany her Iranian husband Alfred Molina back to Teheran for a visit. At the end of two weeks, Molina tells her that they are to remain in Iran permanently. After two years of suffering in a country where women have no rights, Field makes contact with an underground of Iranians who help Field and her four-year-old daughter **Sheila Rosenthal** escape over the mountains into Turkey.

MAHMUD, ALI -GENII

THE WIZARD OF BAGHDAD (1960, 20th Century Fox)—**Dick Shawn** is a bust as genie's go, but he still tries to help a young prince and princess against a wicked usurping sultan.

MAHLER, GUSTAV

MAHLER (1974, GB, Mayfair)—**Robert Powell** stars in a routine biopic of the German symphonic composer.

MAHOGANY

MAHOGANY (1975, Paramount)—Top fashion designer **Diana Ross's** love for black Billy Dee Williams is complicated by sleazy white photographer Anthony Perkins.

MAHON, CHRISTY

THE PLAYBOY OF THE WESTERN WORLD (1963, Ireland, Janus-Lion)—Braggart Irishman **Gary Raymond** entertains villagers with his tales of how he did in his old dad in this stagy production of J.M. Synge's classic.

MAHONE, MOLLY MAY

HER NIGHT OF NIGHTS (1922, Silent, Universal)—Model **Marie Prevost** is nearly compromised by her boss's son, but she hangs in there, and marries her shipping clerk boyfriend.

MAHONEY, PAT & MOLLY

TWO GIRLS ON BROADWAY (1940, MGM)—**Lana Turner** and **Joan Blondell** are a vaudeville sisters act, which breaks up when song-and-dance man George Murphy goes for one of them. Guess which one.

MAHONEY, SLIP

HARD BOILED MAHONEY (1947, Monogram); NEWS HOUNDS (1947, Monogram); SPY CHASERS (1956, Allied Artists)—**Leo Gorcey** leads the Bowery boys in a series of comedy films. In the first, Gorcey and buddy Huntz Hall are mistaken for detectives. In the second they find themselves seeking scoops, and in the third they foil some spies.

MAHYNA

SHE GOT WHAT SHE WANTED (1930, Tiffany)—Russian peasant girl **Betty Compson** wants "the soul of love," but marries a writer. When the two move to New York, she has plenty of attention from other men, and is sorely tempted, but ultimately sees that her husband Gaston Glass is whom she wants.

MAIN, ALEXANDER

ALEX AND THE GYPSY (1976, 20th Century Fox)—Bail bondsman **Jack Lemmon** has an affair with a wild young gypsy, Genevieve Bujold, when she is charged with murder.

MAITLAND

THE ATOMIC MAN (1955, Allied Artists)—**Donald Gray**, who has suffered an overdose of radiation, now has a mind which works seven seconds ahead. He always knows the immediate future.

MAITLAND, DEAN

THE SILENCE OF DEAN MAITLAND (1934, Australia, Cinesound) - Minister **John Longden** molests the town tease, getting the girl pregnant. When he has an argument with her father, the latter is accidentally killed, but the local doctor is blamed for the crime and sent to prison. Twenty years later the doctor is released, intent on killing the minister, now a dean. Longden finally confesses his crime to his congregation from the pulpit and collapses, suffering a fatal heart attack.

MAITLAND, SARAH

THE IRON WOMAN (1916, Silent, Metro)—**Nance O'Neal** appears in a jumbled picture about a woman with a great spirit.

MAITLAND, WALTER

MEMBER OF THE JURY (1937, GB, 20th Century Fox)—**Ellis Irving** is a juror in the trial of his rich employer, who has been so kind to him. He refuses to vote for conviction and then through a painstaking examination of the evidence, he is delighted to find the man really innocent of the charge of murder.

MAJESTYK, VINCE

MR. MAJESTYK (1974, UA)—California watermelon farmer **Charles Bronson** fights exploiters of Chicano farm laborers, while on the look out for a hit man gunning for him.

MAJORS, JIM

SUNDOWN JIM (1942, 20th Century Fox)—U.S. Marshal **John Kimbrough** moves into a mountain town to rid it of its feuding elements.

MALACHAI

CHILDREN OF THE CORN (1984, New World)—In this production of a Stephen King horror novel, **Courtney Gains** is one of the children who has been mesmerized by a young minister into slaughtering all adults.

MALAH AL RAHIM

WANTED: DEAD OR ALIVE (1987, New World)—The grandson of the bounty hunter, played by Steve McQueen on the western TV series, is CIA agent Rutger Hauer, pursuing terroist **Gene Simmons**.

MALCOLM

MALCOLM (1986, Australia, Vestron)—Mechanical genius **Colin Friels**, slow-witted in all other ways, finds himself taking up a life of crime in this very strange comedy.

MALEVO *See* MARION STUART

MALLARE, ANTHONY

THE SCOUNDREL (1935, Paramount)—**Noel Coward** makes his adult film debut as a deceased author who returns to life to search for true love.

MALLORY, BISHOP

THE CASE OF THE STUTTERING BISHOP (1937, First National/ Warner Brothers)—**Edward McWade** has the rather minor title role in this Perry Mason story, starring Donald Woods. Mason attempts to establish whether a young woman really is the grand-daughter of a millionaire.

MALLORY, CHARLIE

THE DUCHESS AND THE DIRTWATER FOX (1976, 20th Century Fox)—Gambler **George Segal** and dance-hall girl Goldie Hawn are attracted to each other, but mostly they bicker through their encounters with travelling Mormons, a western Jewish wedding, and outlaws.

MALLORY, MARY

PRIVATE NURSE (1941, 20th Century Fox)—Nurse **Brenda Joyce** and her older colleague Jane Darwell attend to the 10-year-old daughter of ex-mobster Sheldon Leonard.

MALLORY, PEGGY

FEMALE FUGITIVE (1938, Monogram)—**Evelyn Venable** looks very pretty as she tries to help her no-good truck-hijacker husband, Craig Reynolds. She falls in love with artist Reed Hadley. Reynolds will be conveniently killed.

MALLORY, STEVE

SECRET SERVICE INVESTIGATOR (1948, Republic)—Ex-GI **Lloyd Bridges** is taken in by a counterfeiter posing as a Treasury agent. Bridges wises up and calls in a T-Man who looks just like him to clean up the gang.

MALLOY

THE SCRAPPER (1922, Silent, Universal)—Handsome Irishman **Herbert Rawlinson** is put in charge of the construction of a skyscraper. He falls for the boss's daughter, and beats the pants off of a big man trying to sabotage the project.

MALLOY, PVT. DENNIS

SOLDIERS THREE (1951, MGM)—In this GUNGA DIN-like film, shy a Gunga Din, **Cyril Cusack**, Robert Newton and Stewart Granger provide lots of horseplay in India. The critics hated it but audiences ate it up.

MALLOY, MOLLY

YOUTH FOR SALE (1924, Silent, Burr)—**Mary Allison** is blinded by her first drink of bootleg hootch. She is helped through her ordeal by her best friend.

MALLOY, MOOSE

FAREWELL, MY LOVELY (1975, Avco Embassy)—**Jack O'Halloran** hires Robert Mitchum, as private eye Philip Marlowe, to find the girlfriend he lost track of while he was in prison. Mike Mazurki played the role in 1945's MURDER MY SWEET.

MALO, EL

THE ROGUE OF THE RIO GRANDE (1930, World-Wide)—Mexican bandit **Jose Bohr** enjoys making those trying to capture him look foolish.

MALONE

SON OF THE NAVY (1940, Monogram)—Sailor **James Dunn** has no thoughts of raising a family, but he hadn't counted on orphan Martin Spelman, who tags Dunn to be his dad.

MALONE, BOOTS

BOOTS MALONE (1952, Columbia)—Corrupt jockey's agent **William Holden** trains a rich man's son to be a jockey, and then tells the youngster he has to throw a race or be killed by gamblers.

MALONE, BUCK

THE FURTHER ADVENTURES OF TENNESSEE BUCK (1988, Trans World)—Drunken big-game hunter **David Keith** is bailed out of jail by nerd Brant Van Hoffman, who wants Keith to take him and beauty queen Kathy Shower to a jungle island to shoot a white tiger. Writing the rest of the script should be child's play.

MALONE, BUGSY

BUGSY MALONE (1976, GB, Paramount)—**Scott Baio** has the title role in this typical "roaring twenties" gangster film, filled with mobsters, tough molls, speakeasies and shoot-outs. The only difference is that all roles are played by 12 or 13-year-old kids, the most notable of whom were Jodie Foster as a seductive singer and John Cassisi as the Big Man of the rackets.

MALONE, DANNY

SAILOR'S LADY (1940, 20th Century Fox)—Sailor **Jon Hall** promises to marry Nancy Kelly when he returns from the sea, but things are complicated when she's left in charge of a one-year-old orphan, who is accidentally left on board a battleship, only to be discovered during a mock battle.

MALONE, JAMES

THE UNTOUCHABLES (1987, Paramount)—**Sean Connery** won an Academy Award for his portrayal of an honest Irish Chicago cop, who helps Eliot Ness, played by Kevin Costner, get Al Capone on charges of income tax evasion.

MALONE, JOHN J.

MRS. O'MALLEY AND MR. MALONE (1950, MGM)—Shyster lawyer **James Whitmore** teams in this comedy thriller with widow Marjorie

Main, in what was meant to be a series, but it didn't garner enough interest to rate even a sequel.

MALONE, LEFTY
THE SWELL-HEAD (1927, Silent, Columbia)—**Ralph Graves** becomes a boxer in order to get money for his crippled mother's operation. His success, based on setups he doesn't know about, gives him a considerable swelled-head. When the promoters put him in a fight with a real opponent, he nearly gets his fat head handed to him.

MALONE, MIKE
A YANK IN LIBYA (1942, PRC)—American correspondent **Walter Woolf King** uncovers a Nazi plot in Libya.

MALONE, MOLLY
HOW MOLLY MADE GOOD (1915, Silent, Kulee Features)—Irish immigrant **Marguerite Gale** gets a job with a newspaper. Her assignment is to interview celebrities such as Cyril Scott, May Robson, Julia Dean, Henry Kolker and Henrietta Crosman. Well, at the time they were celebrities.

MALONE, MOLLY
MOLLY OF THE FOLLIES (1919, Silent, American)—Side-show dancer **Margarita Fischer** must compete with her own mother for acrobat Jack Mower.

MALONE, PEGGY
HER FACE VALUE (1921, Silent, Paramount)—In this romantic drama, **Wanda Hawley** is a movie star, who must choose between her wealthy admirer and her poor husband.

MALONE, RICHARD
MALONE (1987, Orion)—Ex-CIA hit man **Burt Reynolds** accidentally finds himself in a small Oregon town, where he has to come out of retirement to take on the murderous henchmen of ruthless millionaire Cliff Robertson.

MALONE, SALLY
SISTERS (1930, Columbia)—New York fashion model **Sally O'Neil** is saved from making a fool of herself with a Chicago gangster by small-town hick Russell Gleason and O'Neil's sister Molly O'Day.

MALONE, SCOBIE
SCOBIE MALONE (1975, Australia, Kingsport/Regent)—Australian private detective **Jack Thompson** looks into the death of a blackmailer of both a cabinet member and a gang boss.

MALONE, TEX
QUEEN OF THE NIGHTCLUBS (1929, Warner Brothers)—**Texas Guinan's** greeting to the customers of her nightclub was "Hello, suckers!" and they loved it. In this film she's essentially playing herself, with a little plot line thrown in for spice.

MALONE, WILLIAM QUINCY
THE KID FROM TEXAS (1939, MGM)—The most unusual thing about this fun "B" western is a polo game between the cowboys and the Indians. **Dennis O'Keefe** stars and he's always likeable, if not always good.

MALONEY, HATTIE
PANAMA HATTIE (1942, MGM)—**Ann Sothern** stands-in for Ethel Merman, who had starred in the Broadway version of this Cole Porter musical, and the transformation was not a success. Sothern is a Panama nightclub singer. The high-point of the lousy film is the marvelous Lena Horne singing "Just One of Those Things."

MALONEY, JIM
THE BIG BOSS (1941, Columbia)—**Otto Kruger** and John Litel are brothers, separated as children, who as adults find themselves on opposite sides in politics.

MALONEY, MARY LOU
HELLO MARY LOU, PROM NIGHT II (1987, Canada, Simcom/Norstar)—**Lisa Scrage** returns from the grave to take revenge on her killers, who now run the school she attended.

MAMA
I REMEMBER MAMA (1948, RKO)—**Irene Dunne** delighted audiences as the heart and soul of a turn-of-the-century San Francisco Norwegian family, as remembered years later by her adoring daughter. Dunne was charming in a magical little masterpiece.

MAMA MOLLIE
SPARROWS (1926, Silent, UA)—**Mary Pickford** is the oldest of ten abandoned children working on a baby farm run by cruel Gustav von Seyffertitz in an alligator-infested Louisiana swamp. She leads the kids through the swamp to safety. The villain sinks to his death, while chasing after them.

MAME
CALL ME MAME (1933, GB, Warner Brothers)—**Ethel Irving** arrives from Mexico just as her hard-drinking son is about to inherit a title and estate.

MAME
PICTURE BRIDES (1934, Allied Pictures)—**Dorothy Mackaill** is the better-looking one of two girls who arrive in Brazil to answer an advertisement for wives by American miners, Regis Toomey and Alan Hale.

MAN, THE
COVER GIRL KILLER (1960, GB, Eros)—A pinup magazine publisher and a model help police trap a maniac, **Harry H. Corbett**, who is as the title says, killing cover girls, or at least would-be cover girls.

MAN, THE
THE NAKED PREY (1966, Paramount)—**Cornel Wilde** is the writer, producer, director and star of this action film about a white hunter in Africa, who is stripped and told he can save himself from death, the fate natives inflicted on his less athletic-looking companions, if he can outrun a group of warriors who will pursue him, both day and night, through the wilderness.

MAN, THE
SUNRISE—A SONG OF TWO HUMANS (1927, Silent, Fox)—In a beautiful silent film, **George O'Brien** is a young farmer married to Janet Gaynor. He is tempted by Margaret Livingston, a city woman, who persuades him to murder his wife, sell the farm and run away with her. Sensing what is on his mind, Gaynor is in a panic as she and her husband ride into the city on a trolley. He on the other hand is filled with contrition, and the two renew their wedding vows in a church. They have a wonderful day together but on the way home a storm overtakes them and he gives her rushes to protect her while he swims ashore. His wife is lost. He hurries to the city to kill

Livingston, but just as he is about to strangle the Jezebel, word comes that his wife has been found alive. At her bedside, he watches the sunrise.

MAN, THE

TWO IN THE DARK (1936, RKO)—Amnesiac **Walter Abel** is worried that he may have murdered a theatrical producer, but can't remember it.

MAN CALLED HORSE *See* LORD JOHN MORGAN

MAN FROM BEYOND, THE

THE MAN FROM BEYOND (1922, Silent, Houdini)—**Harry Houdini** is found frozen in a body of ice. On being revived, Houdini seems strange to his rescuers, until it's discovered that he had been frozen over 100 years earlier.

MANCINI, CINDY

CAN'T BUY ME LOVE (1987, Buena Vista)—Teen Patrick Dempsey gives beautiful senior **Amanda Peterson** $1000 of his hard-earned money to pretend she's his girlfriend.

MANDERSTOKE, LORD

MAN OF EVIL (1948, GB, Gainsborough)—This film is called FANNY BY GASLIGHT in Great Britain, which would have made Phyllis Calvert the title character. She is the illegitimate daughter of a cabinet minister, whom she goes to live with after her foster father is killed by evil **James Mason**. When Calvert's father's wife, Mason's mistress, threatens a scandal over the girl, the minister commits suicide. Stewart Granger, secretary to the deceased, kills Mason in a duel over Calvert.

MANGAN, LES

THE V.I.P.S (1963, GB, MGM)—Australian entrepreneur **Rod Taylor** is concerned that the fog that has forced the cancellation of his flight from London to New York will prevent him from securing financing to fight off a hostile takeover of one of his companies. His devoted secretary Maggie Smith, who secretly loves him, finds a solution.

MANLEY, SETON

UNEXPECTED UNCLE (1941, RKO)—**Charles Coburn** forsakes his riches to preach the gospel of happiness and honesty. We hope that these are not incompatible with a few bucks.

MANNERING

IVORY HUNTER (1952, GB, Ealing)—Called WHERE NO VULTURES FLY in England, this film has **Harold Warrender** as an ivory poacher, whom African game warden Anthony Steel must catch.

MANNERS, DICK

THE LOVE GAMBLER (1922, Silent, Fox)—**John Gilbert** bets he can tame a wild horse, and kiss the daughter of his boss merely by whistling a certain tune. Apparently he's a hell of a whistler.

MANNERS, JOANNA

JOANNA (1925, Silent, First National)—**Dorothy Mackaill** inherits a million dollars, and takes up with a fast-living crowd. Later, she discovers that her "inheritance" is a fake and she was set up so a bet about her chastity could be checked.

MANNERS, RITA

REDHEAD FROM MANHATTAN (1954, Columbia)—**Lupe Velez** appears in dual roles: the star of a Broadway show, and her twin sister who takes her place when she becomes pregnant.

MANNING

UNDERCOVER AGENT (1935, GB, Lippert)—**Dermot Walsh** is the title character in the film, called COUNTERSPY in Great Britain. He's an auditor who discovers a spy ring, using a nursing home as a front.

MANNING, DR.

THE STRANGE CASE OF DR. MANNING (1958, GB, Republic)—When **David Lander** is kidnapped, his wife hires a detective who calls the police in on the case. This makes it difficult for her to deliver the ransom. She does, but Lander is found dead. The film is called MORNING CALL in England.

MANNING, CLARK

THE MAN FROM MONTREAL (1940, Universal)—**Richard Arlen**, a trapper arrested for carrying stolen pelts, escapes, and sets out to catch the real crooks.

MANNING, LT. COL. GLENN

THE AMAZING COLOSSAL MAN (1957, American International)—**Glenn Langan** walks into a desert explosion of a plutonium bomb. His body is burned by the radiation, but heals overnight and starts growing. There not being many women of his enormous size, he's more that a bit put out, going on a rampage in Las Vegas, tearing the city apart. He's finally destroyed by the army at the Hoover Dam.

MANNING, JOE

CRIME AGAINST JOE (1956, UA)—When young artist **John Bromfield** goes on a binge, he wakes up the next day to find himself accused of murdering a girl he had met the night before.

MANNING, PAUL

A GUIDE FOR THE MARRIED MAN (1967, 20th Century Fox)—Despite being married to luscious Inger Stevens, **Walter Matthau** sees the world filled with willing sexy girls and he wants some. He is given a training course in how to and how not to have an affair by his more experienced friend Robert Morse.

MANNING, SUSAN

THREE ON A COUCH (1966, Columbia)—**Mary Ann Mobley** is one of psychiatrist Janet Leigh's patients, whom she believes she can't leave to go to Paris with her fiance Jerry Lewis on a honeymoon. Lewis disguises himself and cures all of the patients himself.

MANNON, LAVINA

MOURNING BECOMES ELECTRA (1947, RKO)—In this adaptation of the Eugene O'Neill play, based on the Greek tragedy cycle *The Oresteia*, Civil War general Raymond Massey is killed by his wife Katina Paxinou. Michael Redgrave portrays their son, who is inflamed with desires for revenge by his sister **Rosalind Russell**. This film is an excellent example to use if one wishes to illustrate the meaning of "too stagy a movie." Factoring in inflation, it's one of the all-time greatest money losers.

MANSFIELD, HUGH

MEET THE CHUMP (1941, Universal)—**Hugh Herbert** has frittered away a $10 million dollar trust fund, set up for his nephew. As the time comes for the young man to take charge of his fortune, his trustee uncle Herbert contemplates suicide, but then comes up with the idea of having his nephew declared incompetent.

MANSFIELD, HUMPHREY

THE SECRET FOUR (1940, GB, Ealing)—**Hugh Sinclair** and two other members of The Four Just Men, who oppose all foreign plotters against England, avenge the murder of one of their members, as they foil a plot to block the Suez Canal.

MANSFIELD, PATRICIA
THE CAMPUS FLIRT (1926, Silent, Paramount)—In a familiar story with the sexes changed, heiress **Bebe Daniels** finds she's not popular at college. She takes up with a wild crowd, but proves her worth when she becomes a star athlete.

MANTELL, LOLA
THE SHADY LADY (1929, Pathe)—Innocent **Phyllis Haver**, circumstantially involved in a murder case in New York, flees to Havana, where she becomes known by the title of the film.

MANTLE, BEVERLY & ELLIOT
DEAD RINGERS (1988, 20th Century Fox)—Had this psychological thriller been released late in 1988, **Jeremy Irons** might have been nominated for two Academy Awards for his brilliant performance as identical twin gynecologists, drug addicts who trade women. Their odd behavior surfaces when Genevieve Bujold falls in love with one of them. Despite the marvelous acting, it's difficult to say one enjoys the film.

MANTON, MELISSA
THE MAD MISS MANTON (1938, RKO)—Madcap socialite **Barbara Stanwyck** teams with newspaperman Henry Fonda to solve murders. They have quite an admirable success record.

MANUEL
CAPTAINS COURAGEOUS (1937, MGM)—Portugese fisherman **Spencer Tracy** gives spoiled rich boy Freddie Bartholomew some needed lessons on sharing and helping, when the lad is rescued by the fishing boats after falling overboard from an ocean liner. Tracy won an Academy Award for his touching performance.

MANUWALDE
SCREAM BLACULA, SCREAM (1973, American International)—**William Marshall** is called Manuwalde in this sequel to BLACULA. He is pitted against voodoo princess Pam Grier in an unintentionally laughable production.

MANZAREK, RAY
THE DOORS (1991, Tri-Star)—Together with Val Kilmer, Kevin Dillon and Frank Whaley, **Kyle MacLachlan** is a member of one of the most popular rock groups of all time.

MARA
TARZAN AND THE MERMAIDS (1948, RKO)—Native girl **Linda Christian** is helped by Tarzan to rid her island people of an evil god who resides in a pyramid.

MARA
UNCIVILIZED (1937, Australia, Box Office Attractions)—**Dennis Hoey**, who would become better known as Inspector LaStrade in the Basil Rathbone Sherlock Holmes series, appears here as a Tarzan-like white man among the Australian aborigines.

MARAIS, EUGENE
THE GUEST (1984, GB, RM Productions)—**Athol Fugard** stars in this biopic of the South African poet and naturalist, as he tries to kick his morphine habit.

MARAK, STEVE
I SAW WHAT YOU DID (1965, Universal)—Two teenage girls randomly dial the phone and say "I saw what you did and I know who

you are." One of their calls is answered by **John Ireland**, who has just murdered his wife and he thinks he recognizes his callers.

MARAT, JEAN-PAUL
MARAT-SADE (1966, GB, UA)—**Ian Richardson** portrays Marat in the filmed play whose full title tells the plot: THE PERSECUTION AND ASSASSINATION OF JEAN-MARIE MARAT AS PERFORMED BY THE INMATES OF THE ASYLUM OF CHARENTON UNDER THE DIRECTION OF THE MARQUIS DE SADE.

MARCELLA, MARCHESA
SECRET AGENT (1933, GB, British International)—**Greta Nissen** is an Italian spy, a fact that Austrian officer Carl Ludwig Diehl discovers only after he's fallen in love with her.

MARCH, COL.
COLONEL MARCH INVESTIGATES (1952, GB, Criterion)—**Boris Karloff** is an eye-patched Scotland Yard Inspector. He heads up the Department of Queer Complaints. We see him deal with some of these.

MARCH, DUNCAN
THE WEREWOLF (1956, Columbia)—Discontented family man **Steven Ritch** is accidentally turned into a werewolf by a scientist's serum. Now he has something to do at night.

MARCH, IRIS
OUTCAST LADY (1934, MGM)—In this remake of A WOMAN OF AFFAIRS (1929), **Constance Bennett** has the Greta Garbo role of a reckless, aristocratic Englishwoman. When her husband, revealed as a thief, commits suicide, she strives to pay back what he stole.

MARCH, JERRY
OUR BLUSHING BRIDES (1930, MGM)—Department store model **Joan Crawford** holds off the advances of her boss's son, Robert Montgomery, until he proposes a more honorable relationship than the one he had been trying to sell her.

MARCH, JO, AMY, BETH & MEG
LITTLE WOMEN (1933, RKO); (1949, MGM)—**Katharine Hepburn, Joan Bennett, Jean Parker** and **Frances Dee** starred in the 1933 version of Louisa May Alcott's story of four sisters growing up in Concord, Massachusetts at the time of the Civil War; **June Allyson, Elizabeth Taylor, Margaret O'Brien** and **Janet Leigh** picked up the roles in 1949. The 1933 film with headstrong writer-to-be Hepburn, flighty Bennett who steals Hepburn's beau, doomed Parker and Dee, whose planned marriage threatens the family unity, is considered to be among the best things Hollywood ever did. The 1949 remake can't match the original, but as a slice of Americana, albeit a very sentimental one, it doesn't disappoint.

MARCH, JOHNNY
IDENTITY UNKNOWN (1945, Republic)—WWII soldier **Richard Arlen** returns home with no memory of his earlier life.

MARCHARD, LILLIAN
WHEN A WOMAN SINS (1918, Silent, Fox)—Nurse **Theda Bara** causes a young man to blow out his brains before she is regenerated by an Episcopal priest, whom she marries.

MARCHMORTON, LADY ALICE
A DAMSEL IN DISTRESS (1937, RKO)—**Joan Fontaine** was a change from Ginger Rogers for Fred Astaire, but not only could she not dance, at this point in her career, her acting wasn't up to par. She gets away with it up to a point because she's supposed to be an

aristocratic British heiress, pursued by breezy American musical comedy composer, Astaire.

MARCIA

THE GOOD BAD GIRL (1931, Columbia)—**Mae Clarke** dumps her gangster boyfriend for a wealthy man, who knows nothing of her sordid past. After the wedding and a baby, the old friend breaks out of prison, looking for trouble.

MARCUS

AMERICAN FLYERS (1985, Warner Brothers)—**Kevin Costner**, a professor of sports medicine at the University of Wisconsin, fears his younger brother may have inherited the problem that killed their father. The two men enter a bicycle race called the "Hell of the West." They win before the fatal condition strikes.

MARCUS, PROFESSOR

THE LADYKILLERS (1956, GB, Ealing)—**Alec Guinness** is the leader of a "chamber ensemble," actually robbers, who carry off a big job. Their landlady Katie Johnson discovers the loot but no one will believe her. Guinness and his cohorts plot to kill her, but instead bump each other off, one by one.

MARDICK, MRS.

FOUR FRIGHTENED PEOPLE (1934, Paramount)—**Mary Boland** is one of four people who escape from an epidemic of bubonic plague on their ship, only to find they must face the terrors of a Malayan jungle if they are to reach safety.

MARDON, JULES

I LOVE YOU (1918, Silent, Triangle)—Millionaire **Francis McDonald** first falls in love with a girl in a painting and then the girl Alma Reubens herself. They marry but the artist who painted the portrait almost ruins things for the couple.

MARDULAK, COUNT

SUNDOWN: THE VAMPIRE RETREAT (1990, Vestron)—This vampire comedy-western features **David Carradine**, a vampire who runs a clinic to cure others like him of the nasty habit of bloodsucking. His main adversary, vampire John Ireland, wants to go back to preying on straight humans.

MARGARET

FAREWELL TO CINDERELLA (1937, GB, RKO)—**Anne Pichon** is the drudge of a family, visited by an uncle from Australia, whom they believe is rich. Her sisters make a play for the visitor, who really is poor, but he does help get Pichon together with an artist she loves.

MARGARET

JOURNEY FOR MARGARET (1942, MGM)—In her strange pointed hat, **Margaret O'Brien** is a London blitz orphan, adopted by American reporter Robert Young and his wife Laraine Day. O'Brien as a child is a far better actress than most older ladies of the screen, and in this heart-tugger, she's just about perfect.

MARGARET

SHOULD A GIRL MARRY? (1939, Monogram)—In 1939, what do you think the answer has to be? **Anna Nagel** is the romantic interest of an honest surgeon. He is being set up by two crooked sawbones.

MARGARET & EDITH

DEAD RINGER (1964, Warner Brothers)—For the second time in her career (the other being A STOLEN LIFE in 1946), **Bette Davis** portrays twins, one of whom assumes the identity of the other after the first's death. In this film, poor bitter Davis murders wealthy widow Davis.

MARGARET, PRINCESS

THE PRINCESS AND THE PIRATE (1944, RKO)—Beautiful princess **Virginia Mayo**, along with cowardly actor Bob Hope, are captured by pirates. They escape, and make it to a West Indian island, whose governor, Walter Slezak, has a yen for the shapely Mayo.

MARGIE

MARGIE (1940, Universal)—**Nan Grey** will go to any extreme to help her husband become a successful songwriter.

MARGO

MODERN GIRLS (1986, Atlantic)—**Daphne Zuniga** and two female friends have a wild night in L.A. rock clubs. The film is funny if you're notion of humor is sexual and on the intellectual level of Hee Haw.

MARGOT

THE CAVE GIRL (1921, Silent, First National)—**Teddie Gerard** keeps house for her guardian, a professor who wishes to revert to the natural way of living. That's fine for him, but she's the one who has to scrounge for food in the winter. Of course while foraging she comes across the man she will love.

MARGOT

THE PLOW GIRL (1916, Silent, Lasky)—**Mae Murray** is passed off as the long lost granddaughter of an aristocrat, whose son and daughter-in-law were killed in South America. Turns out, as things do in movies where coincidence is a major plot angle, that she really is.

MARGOT, JOCELYN

IF I MARRY AGAIN (1925, Silent, First National)—**Doris Kenyon**, the daughter os a San Francisco madam, marries a socialite, much to the chagrin of his father. Dad punishes the couple by sending his son to manage a plantation in the tropics. Four years later, Kenyon's husband dies and she swears that their son will have every privilege he has coming to him. When she stops short of blackmailing and socially embarrassing the old man by re-opening her mother's bordello, grandpa comes around.

MARIA

WOMAN OF STRAW (1964, GB, UA)—Italian nurse **Gina Lollobrigida** and Sean Connery, the nephew of wealthy Ralph Richardson, hatch a plot to get the old cripple's money. The plan is to get Richardson to marry Lollobrigida, change his will and then conveniently die.

MARIAN

ACQUITTED (1929, Columbia)—**Margaret Livingston**, serving a term in a prison, falls in love with a physician serving a life sentence for a murder, of which she believes him innocent. When she gets out, she sets about proving it.

MARIAN

A WAVE, A WAC AND A MARINE (1944, Monogram)—**Elyse Knox** was one of several pretty girls in this showcase for comedian Henny Youngman, playing a fast-talking gangster.

MARIAN, MAID

ROBIN AND MARIAN (1976, GB, Columbia)—In a dull film, **Audrey Hepburn** portrays Maid Marian, reunited with Robin Hood, many years after their romance. Love blossomed at the time he helped save the throne of England for Richard the Lion Heart. Looking up old boyfriends isn't such a good idea, even in the twelfth century.

MARIANNE

BAD SISTER (1931, Universal)—Small-town bubble-head **Sidney Fox** falls for a con man. She helps him swindle her father and other town's folk. It is Fox's screen debut, but the film is better remembered for being Bette Davis' first film, as Fox's level-headed sibling.

MARIANNE

DIE SCREAMING, MARIANNE (1970, GB, London Screen)—**Susan George**, a judge's illegitimate daughter, is the instrument in a blackmailer's scheme.

MARIANNE

THE DIVINE WOMAN (1928, Silent, MGM)—French peasant **Greta Garbo** travels to Paris where she becomes the mistress of a former lover of her mother, when he promises to make her a star of the stage.

MARIANNE

FOOLS OF FORTUNE (1990, GB, Palace)—Lovely **Mary Elizabeth Mastrantonio** comforts Iain Glaen, her childhood playmate, at the time of the Irish war of Independence. The result of the comforting is a child, but by this time the introspective and withdrawn Glen has disappeared, still reeling from the massacre of his family and destruction of his grand rural home by the British when he was a child.

MARIANNE

THE HAUNTING OF M (1979, Nu-Image)—Old spinster **Sheelagh Gilbey** is haunted by a young ghost.

MARIANNE

MARIANNE (1929, MGM)—**Marion Davies** enters the talkie sweepstakes as a French girl, who on occasion poses as a male Army officer. Of course, there were songs, now best forgotten.

MARIE

ALIAS FRENCH GERTIE (1930, RKO)—**Bebe Daniels** and her soon-to-be real-life husband Ben Lyon are a pair of safecrackers, both after the same loot. After they discover each other to be real jewels, Daniels wants Lyon to go straight, but he keeps falling back into bad habits.

MARIE

BLONDE FOR A NIGHT (1928, Silent, Pathe Exchange)—After an argument with her husband, **Marie Prevost** dons a blonde wig and attracts the attention of one of her husband's biggest customers. He recommends the ravishing blonde to Prevost's husband. Deciding to test her husband's fidelity, she leads him on, but he remains faithful to his wife.

MARIE

HER FIGHTING CHANCE (1917, Silent, R-C Pictures)—Religious **Jane Grey** is willing to give herself to a brute to save her husband from being hanged.

MARIE, GRAND DUCHESS

LITTLE MISS REBELLION (1920, Silent, Paramount)—In this comedy, **Dorothy Gish** is a royal exile visiting New York.

MARIE, PRINCESS

HER LOVE STORY (1924, Silent, Paramount)—**Gloria Swanson**, princess of a fictional Balkan state, falls in love with Ian Keith, the Captain of the King's Guard, but her father has arranged a marriage for her with the king of a neighboring country. The lovers are wed by a gypsy, but her father doesn't think that makes it legal. He changes his mind when a child arrives.

MARIE THE KNIFE

FIVE BOLD WOMEN (1960, Citation)—**Lucita Blain** is a murderer, being taken to prison across Texas by a US Marshal. Getting there is not half the fun.

MARIE-ANN

MARIE-ANN (1978, Canada, Canadian Film Production)—**Andrea Pelletier** allows herself to be adopted by an Indian tribe to satisfy her husband, who has an Indian mistress, and doesn't want Pelletier around. It's either that or be sent back to the farm from whence she came.

MARIE ANTOINETTE

MARIE ANTOINETTE (1938, MGM)—**Norma Shearer's** husband, Irving Thalberg, planned for her to make this and perhaps one or two more prestigious films before retiring, but he died two years earlier, and for reasons best known to Shearer, not all of her final pictures would have pleased the MGM genius. In this extravagant production, Shearer, one of the great clothes horses of Hollywood history, was in her glory, what with all of the beautiful gowns she was able to wear as the French queen who ended her day taking a ride in a tumbrel and losing her head at the guillotine.

MARINA

THE BUTCHER'S WIFE (1991, Paramount)—When country clairvoyant **Demi Moore** moves to New York with her butcher husband, George Dzundza, her visions start to touch all those whom she meets. This is not met with cheers by local psychologist Jeff Daniels, whose patients need him far less once they have the benefit of Moore's stargazing.

MARINA, ELSIE

THE PRINCE AND THE SHOWGIRL (1957, GB, Warner Brothers)—In London at the time of the coronation of George V, American showgirl **Marilyn Monroe** becomes romantically involved with Laurence Olivier, the Prince Regent of Carpathia, although she keeps slipping out of his seduction traps.

MARINER, THE

THE ANCIENT MARINER (1925, Silent, Fox)—**Paul Panzer**, best known for his villain roles in The Perils of Pauline serials, appears as Samuel Taylor Coleridge's mariner in this story within a story film, consisting of a modern sequence in which an old sailor relates the tale, and the Ancient Mariner sequence itself.

MARIO/LUCIEN

THE CORSICAN BROTHERS (1941, UA)—**Douglas Fairbanks, Jr.** plays the two Siamese twins separated at birth who feel each other's pain and suffering. As adults they unite to fight against the tyrant who had murdered their parents, and is terrorizing their land and the people of Corsica.

MARION

ANOTHER WOMAN (1988, Orion)—**Gena Rowlands** gives another of her stellar performances in this Woody Allen directed movie. College professor Rowlands takes an apartment next door to the office of a psychologist and becomes obsessed with the life of one of his patients.

MARION

BIOGRAPHY OF A BACHELOR GIRL (1934, MGM)—Painter **Ann Harding** causes quite a stir when she publishes her steamy memoirs.

MARION

THE PLEASURE GIRLS (1966, GB, Times Films)—The movie details the romances and problems of several models, including **Rosemary Nicol**, who share a house.

MARION

THERE'S A GIRL IN MY SOUP (1970, GB, Columbia)—British TV personality Peter Sellers has an affair with young kookie American, **Goldie Hawn**

MARIPOSA

THE CHARMER (1925, Silent, Paramount)—Dancer **Pola Negri** becomes involved with both a millionaire and his chauffeur.

MARIS, SALLY

THE WOMAN THEY ALMOST LYNCHED (1953, Republic)—Fresh from the East, **Joan Leslie** inherits a saloon frequented by Charles Quantrill. She opposes the Confederate raider, even to the point of slapping on a gun belt and confronting his woman. She's taken into custody, suspected of being a northern spy and almost swings from a tree limb.

MARIS, STELLA

STELLA MARIS (1918, Silent, Artcraft); (1925, Silent, Universal)—**Mary Pickford** and **Mary Philbin** each play the crippled young aristocratic woman, loved by a man whose wife is killed by an orphan, so the two can be together. Realizing that Stella loves yet another man, the newly made widower steps out of the picture so Stella can be with her real lover. Confusing? You bet!

MARITZA

ALEX AND THE GYPSY (1976, 20th Century Fox)—Bitter bailsman Jack Lemmon bails out gypsy **Genevieve Bujold** for assaulting her loutish lover. He takes her home with him, and keeps her virtually a prisoner as they argue and make love. He at last allows her to escape, even though he knows it will ruin him.

MARJA

FIVE BRANDED WOMEN (1960, Paramount)—Disgraced for consorting with the Germans, **Barbara Bel Geddes** and four other Yugoslavian girls have their heads shaved. They take out their anger on the Nazis by joining the underground.

MARJORIE, NURSE

NURSE MARJORIE (1920, Silent, Realart)—Aristocratic nurse **Mary Miles Minter** marries a leader of England's Labor party, much to the consternation of her family.

MARK

ONE LITTLE INDIAN (1973, Buena Vista)—Plucky runaway Indian boy **Clay O'Brien**, together with drifter James Garner and sensible Vera Miles, make a western family who grieve the loss of their camel.

MARK

THE OPTIMISTS (1973, GB, Paramount)—**John Chaffey** and another slum youngster, Donna Mullane, are taken in by London street busker (entertainer) Peter Sellers.

MARKER, MISS

LITTLE MISS MARKER (1934, Paramount); (1980, Universal)—**Shirley Temple** and **Sara Stimson** each star as a cute little girl, left with a grumpy bachelor gambler as security for a bet by her father, who promptly gets himself killed. The rest of the movie deals with how the moppet softens the gambler's hard, hard heart.

MARKHAM, LYNN

FEMALE ON THE BEACH (1955, Universal)—Shortly after she marries Jeff Chandler, whom she doesn't know very well, **Joan Crawford** begins to suspect that he plans to kill her.

MARKIE

DISORDERLIES (1987, Warner Brothers)—**Mark Morales** is one of a rap group, The Fat Boys, who save millionaire Ralph Bellamy from being done in for his money by his nephew.

MARKOFF, DR. IGOR

THE MONSTER MAKER (1944, PRC)—When the girl of his dreams spurns him, **J. Carrol Naish** takes revenge by injecting her father with germs, which turn him into a monster.

MARKRUTE, VELMA

SOUL MATES (1925, Silent, MGM)—Voluptuous **Aileen Pringle** holds off lustful Lord Edmund Lowe until he pays off her mortgage, held by her evil uncle.

MARKSON, ELLIOTT

I'M GOING TO GET YOU . . . ELLIOTT BOY (1971, Canada, Columbia)—**Ross Stephenson** is sent to prison, where he becomes a "wife" to a fellow inmate. When he gets out, he goes back to his girlfriend, but when she gets greedy, he kills her. Even if well done, this story wouldn't be much—and it's not well done.

MARKUM, FEN

WHO KILLED FEN MARKUM? (1937, GB, Ambassador)—Nun Mary Glynne proves actress June Rowland and her fiance Anthony Bushell didn't kill producer **Garry Marsh**.

MARLBORO

HARLEY DAVIDSON AND THE MARLBORO MAN (1991, MGM)—Dressed in rodeo garb and affecting a phony-sounding drawl, **Don Johnson** is one of two inept rebels who try to help a friend who's about to lose their old hangout, the Rock 'n' Roll Bar & Grill to a bank planning to foreclose on the mortgage.

MARLBOROUGH, DUKE OF

ME AND MARLBOROUGH (1935, GB, Gaumont)—In 1709 Kit Ross, played by Cicely Courtneidge, disguises herself as a man and joins the ranks of the Duke of Marlborough, **Tom Wells**, to prove her husband is innocent of spying.

MARLENE, LILLI

LILLI MARLENE (1951, GB, RKO); THE WEDDING OF LILLI MARLENE (1953, GB, Monarch)-French girl **Lisa Daniely**, whose song "Lilli Marlene" is loved by Allies and Germans alike, is kidnapped by the Nazis and forced to make broadcasts for them. She is rescued by the British. In the sequel, she attempts to become a success in show business before she marries her broadcaster lover.

MARLETT, LALLY

THEIR OWN DESIRE (1929, MGM)—**Norma Shearer** is having an affair with Robert Montgomery. Guess what? Her mother is having an affair with his father.

MARLEY, GLORIA

FEMALE OF THE SPECIES (1917, Silent, Triangle)—**Dorothy Dalton** is thrown over by Howard Hickman for Enid Markey, whom he marries. Later Dalton and Hickman meet on a train which has an accident. Hickman loses his memory, and Dalton convinces him they are married. What a laugh they all have, when he finds out differently.

MARLOW, DICK

THE NIGHT INVADER (1943, GB, Warner Brothers)—British agent **David Farrar** is helped by pro-British baroness Sybilla Binder to get a secret document out of Nazi occupied Holland.

MARLOW, JACQUELINE

TALK ABOUT JACQUELINE (1942, GB, MGM)—Notorious playgirl **Carla Lehmann** marries physician Hugh Williams, and is afraid he will find out about her past.

MARLOW, JED

THE SPELLBINDER (1939, RKO)—Shyster **Lee Tracy** gets his comeuppance, because he defends clients he knows are guilty. Who's suppose to defend them, we'd like to know.

MARLOW, JIM

THE HUMAN TORNADO (1925, Silent, R-C Pictures)—**Yakima Canutt**, one of the great all-time stunt men and dear friend of John Wayne, has a starring role as a man wrongly accused of stealing a mining company's strongbox. The villain of the piece turns out to be Canutt's brother, who has been cheating Canutt out of his rightful piece of the mining company.

MARLOW, LYDIA

THE WOMAN IN GREEN (1945, Universal)—**Hillary Brooke** teams with Dr. Moriarty to use hypnotism to combat Sherlock Holmes, in a case of murdered women found with their little fingers missing.

MARLOW, PATTY

DANCING CO-ED (1939, MGM)—More great movies were released in 1939 than any other year. This one with **Lana Turner** wasn't one of them. But at 19, in a story no more complicated than the title, she was well worth a look.

MARLOW, SAM

THE MAN WITH BOGART'S FACE (1980, 20th Century Fox)—**Robert Sacchi** has his face surgically altered so that he will look like Humphrey Bogart. He then opens a detective agency. Appears he's confusing Bogie with one or more of his movie characters. Look for the original is our recommendation.

MARLOWE, CORDELIA

CORDELIA THE MAGNIFICENT (1923, Silent, Metro)—Society girl **Clara Kimball Young** gets hooked up with a crooked lawyer, who comes up with a blackmail scheme when her family fortune disappears.

MARLOWE, DR.

I, MONSTER (1971, GB, Amicus/Cannon)—In a Dr. Jekyll and Mr. Hyde story, scientist **Christopher Lee's** experiments turn him into a sadistic monster.

MARLOWE, DR. JOHN

THE GREAT MANHUNT (1951, GB, Columbia)—Surgeon **Douglas Fairbanks, Jr.** is forced to treat a dying dictator. When the latter breathes his last, his followers pursue Fairbanks, intent on killing him, so he can't reveal the death of his patient.

MARLOWE, GWEN

SWEETHEARTS (1938, MGM)—**Jeannette MacDonald** and husband Nelson Eddy are long past being sweethearts. Instead, this temperamental theater couple are usually fighting, but they're too successful to break up.

MARLOWE, KITTY

OLD ACQUAINTANCE (1943, Warner Brothers)—Writers **Bette Davis** and Miriam Hopkins engage in a bitchy twenty year personal and professional feud.

MARLOWE, LILLIAN

THE GAL WHO TOOK THE WEST (1949, Universal)—**Yvonne De Carlo** is the reason for a long-standing feud between westerners Scott Brady and John Russell.

MARLOWE, MADELINE

SWEET ROSIE O'GRADY (1943, 20th Century Fox)—Turn-of-the-century Brooklyn singer and dancer **Betty Grable** goes to London to snare a duke, but her lowly origins are exposed by Police Gazette reporter Robert Young who wants her for himself.

MARLOWE, MARY

THE NOTORIOUS LADY (1927, Silent, First National)—**Barbara Bedford's** husband Lewis Stone kills a man he suspects she's having an affair with. She lies about her involvement with the deceased to save her husband. He heads off to Africa. Shortly word comes that he has been killed.

MARLOWE, PHILIP

MARLOWE (1969, MGM)—**James Garner** should have stuck to *Maverick*. In this one, he gets stuck with a poor story about the Raymond Chandler private eye, and nothing—not dope, sex or violence—could bring it up to the class of THE BIG SLEEP or MURDER, MY SWEET.

MARLOWE, DR. RICHARD

VOODOO MAN (1944, Monogram)—**Bela Lugosi** kidnaps girls, hoping to find one whose mind is worthy of being transferred into the body of his wife, who is in a permanent trance. The operations turn the donors into zombies and do no noticeable good for Lugosi's wife.

MAROC, JUDITH & GENE

PUBLIC ENEMY'S WIFE (1936, Warner Brothers)—**Margaret Lindsay** has spent three years in prison for a crime she didn't commit. She divorces her husband **Cesar Romero**, who is serving a life term and despite his threats of what he'll do if she ever dumps him for another man, she becomes engaged to playboy Dick Foran.

MARPLAY, LUCIUS

THE WITNESS VANISHES (1939, Universal)—When newspaper owner Edmund Lowe takes on some murderers, they arrange to have him committed to an asylum. He escapes and seeks witness **Barlow Borland** who can prove he knows what he's talking about.

MAROVA, VERA

MISS V FROM MOSCOW (1942, PRC)—**Lola Lane** portrays a Soviet agent in Paris, who confounds the Nazis and helps a downed American pilot escape.

MARPLE, MISS JANE

MURDER SHE SAID (1961, GB, MGM)—**Margaret Rutherford**, a great comical talent in her seventieth year, portrays Agatha Christie's amateur detective most delightfully, solving a cunning murder case.

MARQUAND, ANNETTE

THERE GOES THE BRIDE (1933, GB, Gaumont)—**Jessie Matthews** flees an arranged marriage, and is taken for another man's fiancee.

MARQUIS OF ROHAN
THE MAN IN GREY (1943, GB, Gaumont)—**James Mason** flogs his lover Margaret Lockwood to death after she causes the death of his unloved wife, her longtime friend.

MARQUITA
THE GIRL FROM RIO (1939, Monogram)—**Movita**, better known for her topless role as Clark Gable's island lover in MUTINY ON THE BOUNTY, is a singer in a New York nightclub and is spying on the owner, who may be the real culprit in a crime for which her brother has been framed.

MARS, LAURA
THE EYES OF LAURA MARS (1978, Columbia)—High fashion photographer **Faye Dunaway** has visions of horrible deaths of the models she photographs. Her visions come true.

MARS, LILY
PRESENTING LILY MARS (1943, MGM)—Stage-struck small-town girl **Judy Garland** falls in love with Van Heflin, a New York producer who makes her a star.

MARSDEN, EDITH DENTON
THE CHARMING DECEIVER (1921, Silent, Vitagraph)—**Alice Calhoun** is the daughter of a woman who had been disowned by her wealthy father. The now lonely old man brings her into his home, and tries to play cupid for her and a neighbor. What he doesn't know is that Calhoun is already married to a louse serving a jail term for forgery.

MARSDEN, MARY
THE HOMEBREAKER (1919, Silent, Paramount)—Travelling saleswoman **Dorothy Falton** and the head of her company conspire to teach Douglas MacLean, the man she loves and the boss's son, some lessons in responsibility.

MARSDEN, PEGGY
THE GIRL FROM DOWNING STREET (1918, GB, Silent, Butchers) - Spy **Ena Beaumont** steals the plans of the Hindenburg Line, and is pursued by a German spy who is really British.

MARSDEN, POLLY
IN PURSUIT OF POLLY (1918, Silent, Paramount)—**Billie Burke**, daughter of a wealthy man, is besieged with suitors. She accepts the proposals of marriage from three of them.

MARSH, GERRY
HAT CHECK GIRL (1932, Fox)—**Sally Eilers** works in the title occupation at a nightclub frequented by gangsters. She falls in love with Purnell Pratt, a millionaire playboy, who is accused of murder.

MARSH, JANET
THE JAZZ GIRL (1926, Silent, Motion Picture Guild)—Amateur detective **Edith Roberts** helps a reporter she loves clean up a gang of rum runners.

MARSH, JENNY
THE ANGEL OF CROOKED STREET (1922, Silent, Vitagraph)—**Alice Calhoun**, working as a maid because her family has hit hard times, is accused of theft and is sent to reform school. There she studies taking revenge when she gets out.

MARSH, JENNY
JENNY (1969, ABC-Palomar)—Filmmaker Alan Alda marries pregnant **Marlo Thomas** to avoid the draft.

MARSH, CAPT. JOE
THE CHILD AND THE KILLER (1959, GB, UA)—U.S. Army deserter **Robert Arden** forces a seven-year-old widow's son to help him.

MARSH, LUCAS
NOT AS A STRANGER (1955, UA)—In a drama that moves about as fast as **Robert Mitchum's** expression changes, our sleepy looking hero is an ambitious medical student, who marries chief surgical nurse Olivia de Havilland, so she can support him while he finishes his training. Once in practice, he has an affair with bored, wealthy Gloria Grahame. The movie is a prescription for insomnia.

MARSH, MARILYN
LADY BE GOOD (1941, MGM)—**Eleanor Powell** is smashing in the Busby Berkeley staged musical production of "Fascinating Rhythm." The plot? Be satisfied with a good musical number.

MARSH, WHITEY
MEN OF BOYS TOWN (1941, MGM)—**Mickey Rooney** is back at Father Flanagan's Boys Town where the Mick helps a new kid with reasons to be sour to see the light.

MARSHALL, CLINT
A YANK IN INDOCHINA (1952, Columbia)—American pilot **Douglas Dick** becomes involved in guerrilla warfare.

MARSHALL, KEN
THE FUGITIVE SHERIFF (1936, Columbia)—**Ken Maynard** is elected sheriff, but the outlaws who backed his opponent have their own way of demanding a recount.

MARSHALL, KEN
I WAS FRAMED (1942, Warner Brothers)—Taking a page from EACH DAWN I DIE, **Michael Ames**, a reporter trying to get the goods on dishonest politicians, is framed and sent to jail. He escapes to seek revenge.

MARSHALL, MARY
I'LL BE SEEING YOU (1944, UA)—**Ginger Rogers**, a prisoner on parole, meets shell-shocked ex-soldier Joseph Cotten on a train at Christmas. She invites him to spend the holidays with her on her aunt and uncle's farm. There they fall in love and deal with the crises of their individual problems. The title song by Irving Kahal and Sammy Fain has become a classic.

MARSHALL, PETER
A MAN CALLED PETER (1955, 20th Century Fox)—Scottish minister **Richard Todd** becomes the pastor of the Church of Presidents in Washington and chaplain to the Senate. It's a respectful but not preachy movie, based on the recollections of the clergyman's wife.

MARSHALL, RICHARD
THE MOLLYCODDLE (1920, Silent, UA)—**Douglas Fairbanks** overcomes his reputation as a pampered playboy weakling, when he rescues heroine Ruth Renick from villain Wallace Beery in a rousing climatic battle.

MARSHETTA, RUPERT
THE PRINCE OF PENNSYLVANIA (1988, New Line)—**Keanu Reeves** is the rebellious teenage son of a coal miner. The latter sells his stocks and real estate, so that neither his unfaithful wife, nor son will receive anything. Reeves devises a plan to kidnap his father and get his inheritance.

MARSTON, PEGGY
WANDERING GIRLS (1927, Silent, Columbia)—**Dorothy Revier** runs away from home because her father doesn't understand her. She becomes involved with some crooks and finds herself facing a charge of stealing jewels.

MARTA
THE BACHELOR'S DAUGHTERS (1946, UA)—**Jane Wyatt** and three other department store salesgirls persuade unmarried floor-walker Adolphe Menjou to pose as their father, so they can attract wealthy young men. Wyatt picks off the store owner's son.

MARTHA
MARTHA'S VINDICATION (1916, Silent, Triangle)—**Norma Talmadge** takes the heat and pretends the illegitimate child of her friend is hers. Later, the truth comes out and she marries the steadfast young man who never doubted her.

MARTHA
SEVEN BRIDES FOR SEVEN BROTHERS (1954, MGM)—**Norma Doggett** is one of six girls kidnapped by the Oregon ranching Pontipee boys, inspired by their other brother Howard Keel who has just taken a bride and tells his siblings about the Sabine (Sobbin') Women. His bride Jane Powell and the town folks are not amused, but everything works out in the Spring.

MARTHA
A WOMAN'S TALE (1991, Australia, Beyond Films/Illumination Films)—Terminally ill, **Sheila Florance** is nevertheless fiercely determined to hold on to her independence. She lives alone in a small apartment with her cat, her canary and her memories. Her only friend is a nurse who visits her every day.

MARTIN
MARTIN (1979, Libra)—Teenager **John Amplas** thinks he's a Vampire. A late-night radio talk show makes him a local celebrity.

MARTIN
SLEEPING WITH THE ENEMY (1991, 20th Century Fox)—**Patrick Bergin**, an overbearing control freak, subjects his wife Julia Roberts to so much abuse she fakes her suicide and assumes a new identity. When Bergin catches on, he finds and terrorizes her.

MARTIN
WAY OF A GAUCHO (1952, 20th Century Fox)—Argentinian gaucho **Rory Calhoun** resists the inroads of civilization by organizing an outlaw band to fight the advance of the railroad. But Calhoun eventually comes around, accepting changes in the Pampas, and settles down with Gene Tierney.

MARTIN, ANN
MY TRUE STORY (1951, Columbia)—Convicted jewel thief **Helen Walker** is paroled through the efforts of a mob boss, who wants to use her talent in a caper he's planned. She'd like to go straight, if you don't mind. He does, so she has to find a way to foil his plans.

MARTIN, CAROLYN
THE BRIDE WALKS OUT (1936, RKO)—Bride **Barbara Stanwyck** has champagne tastes, and a husband who offers her beer. She splits and takes up with a millionaire, but love wins out over security.

MARTIN, CASEY
FINGER MAN (1955, Allied Artists)—Ex-con **Frank Lovejoy** is given the choice of helping the FBI nab a syndicate head, or go back

in the joint himself. Lovejoy opts for the right side of the law. Good thinking, Frank!

MARTIN, CHARLES EDWARD
A PRINCE THERE WAS (1921, Silent, Paramount)—Millionaire **Thomas Meighan** passes himself off as an assistant editor in order to get closer to aspiring writer Mildred Harris, whom he loves.

MARTIN, CYNTHIA
SLIGHTLY USED (1927, Silent, Warner Brothers)—To get around her father's insistence that her two younger sisters cannot marry until she has, **May McAvoy** invents a husband for herself, whom she calls Major Smith. When the fictitious individual shows up, the fun begins.

MARTIN, EDDIE
THE BERMONDSEY KID (1933, GB, Warner Brothers/First National)—Boxing English newsboy **Esmond Knight** is forced to fight a sick friend for the championship.

MARTIN, FLAXY
FLAXY MARTIN (1949, Warner Brothers)—Honest lawyer Zachary Scott confesses to a murder to protect his avaricious lover, **Virginia Mayo**.

MARTIN, GEORGE
MY BROTHER'S KEEPER (1949, GB, Rank)—Hardened con **Jack Warner**, handcuffed to an innocent youth, escapes, kills a man, and is blown up in a mine-field, trying to get away from the police.

MARTIN, GINGER
SOUTH SEA WOMAN (1953, Warner Brothers)—Out-of-work showgirl **Virginia Mayo** teams up with two high-spirited A.W.O.L. marines, Burt Lancaster and Chuck Connors, in the Pacific Islands in the early days of WWII.

MARTIN, HANK
A CONNECTICUT YANKEE (1931, Fox); A CONNECTICUT YANKEE IN KING ARTHUR'S COURT (1949, Paramount)—**Will Rogers** and **Bing Crosby** each appear as Mark Twain's hero from 19th century Connecticut, who finds himself transformed back to the court of King Arthur where he applies Yankee know-how to win the title Sir Boss.

MARTIN, HANK
A LION IN THE STREETS (1953, Warner Brothers)—**James Cagney** does right by his role as a back-country southern peddler who rises to become governor of the state, but is destroyed by his own ruthlessness and corruption. It was compared unfavorably with ALL THE KING'S MEN and the Academy Award-winning performance of Broderick Crawford four years earlier in a similar Huey Long-like story.

MARTIN, JACK
GANGSTER STORY (1959, States Rights)—**Walter Matthau** directed and starred in this simple film about a girl trying to reform her criminal boyfriend.

MARTIN, JAKE
THE LAUGHING POLICEMAN (1973, 20th Century Fox)—**Walter Matthau** is assigned to investigate the slaughter of a number of bus passengers including a fellow policeman. He and his partner Bruce Dern discover the cop was killed because he was on the trail of a closet gay into violent sex.

451

MARTIN, JAMES

FACE BEHIND THE SCAR (1940, GB, Premier-Stafford)—In this film released in Great Britain in 1937 as RETURN OF THE STRANGER, **Griffith Jones** is a disfigured man who returns from exile to find his fiancee has married another.

MARTIN, JIMMIE

SINNERS IN THE SUN (1932, Paramount)—**Chester Morris** and his lover Carole Lombard split to see how life is with the rich set, but this doesn't make them happy so they get back together again.

MARTIN, JIMMY

SPEED KING (1923, Silent, Goldstone)—Motorcycle racer **Richard Talmadge** is in the kingdom of Mandavia for a competition, when he is tricked into masquerading as the king. A villain wishes to use Talmadge to help him usurp the throne. Talmadge falls in love with a princess, and on discovering the real purpose of his impersonation, sees that justice is done.

MARTIN, JOHNNY

JOHNNY DOESN'T LIVE HERE ANYMORE (1944, Monogram)—**William Terry** is the fellow who has passed out many keys to the apartment of war worker Simone Simon. She has more male company than she can handle.

MARTIN, KAY

KILL HER GENTLY (1958, GB, Columbia)—**Maureen Connell's** husband hires escaped convicts to kill her for having him certified as insane. Seems a perfectly normal response.

MARTIN, KYLE

THE FARMER (1977, Columbia)—After WWII, vet **Gary Conway** tries to keep his Georgia farm going, but gets tangled up with the Syndicate.

MARTIN, LEO

CONCERNING MR. MARTIN (1937, GB, Fox British)—Gentleman thief **Wilson Barrett** frames a club owner who swindled a girl.

MARTIN, MARIAN

POSSESSED (1931, MGM)—**Joan Crawford** starred in two movies with this title. In this film, she is a factory girl who moves to New York, and becomes the secret mistress of a married lawyer, so as not to ruin his political ambitions.

MARTIN, MARY

MIDNIGHT MARY (1933, MGM)—Lovely **Loretta Young** is an underworld moll on trial for murder.

MARTIN, MAY & PEGGY

LADIES OF THE CHORUS (1948, Columbia)—**Adele Jergens** and **Marilyn Monroe** are mother and daughter burlesque show girls. When Monroe, in her second film, falls for a socialite, Jergens puts her foot down, because it reminds her too much of a similar unhappy experience, which she had when she was her daughter's age.

MARTIN, MICHAEL

CAPTAIN LIGHTFOOT (1955, Universal)—Irish rebel **Rock Hudson** leads a 19th century revolt against the British.

MARTIN, MOLLY

LITTLE MISS MOLLY (1940, Alliance)—Five-year-old orphan **Binkie Stuart** is mistreated by her aunt, but she knows the secret of her father's will, which she eventually uses to help her and her older sister Maureen O'Hara.

MARTIN, NIKKI

THAT GIRL FROM PARIS (1937, RKO)—This was the biggest hit of **Lily Pons'** movie career, which should tell you something about her movie career. Pons becomes a singer with a pop band after refusing a marriage of convenience. Coming from France, she has a few problems about illegal entry in the U.S., but it's no big deal.

MARTIN, NORMA

HER WEDDING NIGHT (1930, Paramount)—Movie star **Clara Bow** marries songwriter Ralph Forbes on the Riviera, after a series of mistaken identity crises are resolved.

MARTIN, RICK

TOP GUN (1955, UA)—**Sterling Hayden** bails out a western town, using his talent with guns, but then is ostracized because he's a gunslinger.

MARTIN, RICK

YOUNG MAN WITH A HORN (1950, Warner Brothers)—**Kirk Douglas** plays a Bix Beiderbecke-like jazz coronet player, who, unlike his inspiration, survives his problems with alcoholism and marriage to the wrong woman.

MARTIN, RUTH

RACING LADY (1937, RKO)—Horsewoman **Ann Dvorak** is hired by Smith Ballew (one of the all-time worst actors in movies, but fortunately very briefly so) to train a thoroughbred he's purchased. The horse showed more camera talent than did Ballew.

MARTIN, SALLY

HOLD THAT BLONDE (1945, Paramount)—Kleptomaniac millionaire Eddie Bracken falls for a seductive jewel thief, **Veronica Lake**.

MARTIN, SONNY

FALLGUY (1962, International Films)—When teenager **Ed Dugan** reports a gangland killing of a mob boss, the police chief, who is in the employ of the murderers, tries to frame Dugan for the killing.

MARTIN, TANK

NOT WITH MY WIFE YOU DON'T (1966, Warner Brothers)—Air Force officers **George C. Scott** and Tony Curtis both make a play for beautiful Virna Lisi. When she has trouble choosing between them, Curtis tricks her into believing Scott has been killed in a mission, and she marries Tony. Years later dashing Scott shows up again and still looks good to Lisi who is now bored with Curtis.

MARTIN, TOMMY

THE CHILD AND THE KILLER (1959, GB, UA)—An American Army officer, on the run from a murder charge, forces seven-year-old **Richard Williams** to lead him to safety in the wilderness.

MARTIN, WILLARD "BILL"

SUPER SLEUTH (1937, RKO)—**Jack Oakie** portrays a silly-ass movie detective. He is so stupid he believes that he's as clever at detection as is the Sherlock he plays, who has writers doing his thinking for him. With nothing going for him, of course he solves a real crime.

MARTIN, YATES "SILVER DOLLAR"

SILVER DOLLAR (1932, First National)—Kansas farmer **Edward G. Robinson** strikes it rich in the Colorado silver mines, and helps turn Denver into a thriving town, but ends up broke.

MARTINDALES, KATHY, EVELYN & HUGO

THE MAD MARTINDALES (1942, 20th Century Fox)—Child star **Jane Withers** makes her last screen appearance in this nothing, which sees her trying to save her wacky father, **Alan Mowbray**, from his own stupid schemes. In the process Jane only annoys her snooty sister, **Marjorie Weaver**.

MARTINEZ, YSOBEL

THE COWBOY AND THE SENORITA (1944, Republic)—**Dale Evans** appears in her first film with husband-to-be Roy Rogers, as a girl with a gold mine, which a villain tries to seize—but Rogers prevents it.

MARTINI, YULA

THE NIGHT ANGEL (1931, Paramount)—In a movie which did nothing for **Nancy Carroll's** career, she's the daughter of a Prague madame. Carroll falls in love with her mother's lawyer when the brothel-keeper is sent to prison. It's a good thing, because Carroll needs an attorney when she accidentally kills the bordello's bouncer, who was always making passes at her.

MARTINSON, DELLA

THE STREET IS MY BEAT (1966, Harmer/Emerson)—**Sharry Marshall** is happy to escape her mother when she receives an offer of marriage. Her mother is happy to give permission for the marriage of her teenage daughter because her prospective son-in-law gives her $200. Marshall soon finds the deal is too good to be true when her husband sets her up in his house of prostitution.

MARTY

THREE (1968, GB, UA)—Two young men on a motoring holiday on the continent meet **Charlotte Rampling** and pledge that their relationship with her will remain platonic. That's easier said than done.

MARV

HIGH SCHOOL BIG SHOT (1959, Filmgroup Sparta)—**Tom Pittman** has a high I.Q. where studies are concerned, but is an idiot in dealing with girls. When one he's been particularly good to double-crosses him, death to many follows.

MARVELLO, MAISIE

THE WOMAN IN COMMAND (1934, GB, Gaumont)—Released as SOLDIERS OF THE KING in Great Britain, this film is the story of the problems a lieutenant has in winning permission to marry music hall star **Cicely Courtneidge**.

MARWOOD, GRACE

WOMAN IN CHAINS (1932, GB, RKO)—**Betty Stockfield** is loved by Owen Nares, the doctor treating her cruel husband, Allan Jeayes. The latter is killed by a vengeful servant.

MARVIN, BABE

OUR WIFE (1941, Columbia)—**Ellen Drew** is composer Melvyn Douglas's ex-wife. In this comedy, he is torn between returning to her, or making a new life with lady scientist Ruth Hussey. It's a comedy which may make one smile rather than laugh.

MARVIN, DAN

CAPTAIN CAUTION (1940, UA)—In 1812, **Victor Mature** is wrongly suspected of cowardice, when actually he acted prudently. He proves what he's made of in a sea battle with the British.

MARY

ALL FOR MARY (1956, GB, Rank)—While on a skiing holiday in Switzerland two Englishmen both fall for the innkeeper's daughter, **Jill Day**. Both come down with chickenpox, and are nursed by an old nanny who sees to it that the right one wins the Day.

MARY

A BIG HAND FOR THE LITTLE LADY (1966, Warner Brothers)—**Joanne Woodward** is forced to take over her husband's poker hand in the biggest game ever held in Texas, after he appears to suffer a heart attack. Very little is what it appears to be in this enjoyable production.

MARY

GETTING MARY MARRIED (1919, Silent, Selznick)—**Marion Davies**, the stepdaughter of a millionaire, is named his heir, but she must live with his brother's family after his death. The will also provides that if Davies marries, the money goes to the brother. Naturally, the brother makes Davies life so miserable, she accepts a marriage proposal. The laugh is that her husband is wealthier than her step-father, and after all debts have been paid, step-dad's fortune is worth less than $2.

MARY

THE GIRL IN THE PICTURE (1986, Goldwyn)—Photographer Gordon John Sinclair goes to great lengths to break up with his live-in girlfriend **Irinia Brook**. When she's gone, he decides he wants her back.

MARY

GIRLS AT SEA (1958, GB, Seven Arts)—**Anne Kimbell** is one of the girls who didn't depart a party aboard a ship soon enough, and now must be hidden from the admiral.

MARY

GUEST WIFE (1945, UA)—To help out foreign correspondent Don Ameche, who must produce a wife or be fired, married **Claudette Colbert** poses as his spouse. She's later accused of living with a married man—her real husband.

MARY

THE IDOL DANCER (1920, Silent, First National)—A minister's adopted native daughter **Clarine Seymour** helps regenerate a drunken American beachcomber on an island where the natives are restless.

MARY

JOHN AND MARY (1969, 20th Century Fox)—**Mia Farrow** meets Dustin Hoffman in a bar. They spend the night together without exchanging names. The next morning they try to decide if they want the affair to continue. The emptiness of the relationship is appalling.

MARY

LADY IN THE DEATH HOUSE (1944, PRC)—Innocent **Jean Parker** is on the death row of a prison. Will kindly Psychologist Lionel Atwill be able to save her?

MARY

MARY, MARY, BLOODY MARY (1975, Translor-Proa)—Lesbian vampire **Cristina Ferrare** stabs her lovers in the neck and drinks their blood.

MARY

MIDNIGHT ANGEL (1941, Paramount)—Robert Preston, the inventor of an anti-aircraft weapon, has been framed for murder and sentenced to death. **Martha O'Driscoll** helps find the enemy agents behind his predicament when he escapes during a city-wide blackout.

MARY

DIRTY MARY, CRAZY HARRY (1974, 20th Century Fox)—Parolee **Susan George** insists on trailing along with race-car driver Peter Fonda and his buddy after they find her in an expensive car they hope to race. There's nobody in this movie to take home to mom for dinner.

MARY

RUNAWAY BRIDE (1930, RKO)—**Mary Astor** and Lloyd Hughes marry. That's the last thing that makes any sense in this dreadful movie about honeymooners who make only mistakes.

MARY

THE SAILOR TAKES A WIFE (1946, MGM)—**June Allyson** marries sailor Robert Walker and they're cute ever after. It's worthy of being forgotten.

MARY

THEY MET IN A TAXI (1936, Columbia)—**Fay Wray** is accused of stealing a pearl necklace from a society woman's home where Wray had been modeling a wedding dress. The necklace got caught on the underside of the dress without Wray knowing it. She escapes her accusers, and finds sanctuary in a cab driven by Chester Morris. A romance blossoms and all ends well.

MARY

THREE MEN AND A BABY (1987, Buena Vista); THREE MEN AND A LITTLE LADY (1990, Buena Vista)—**Lisa** and **Michelle Blair** alternate as the baby left by her mother with three swinging bachelors. They are also rather busy with some drug dealers, who believe the boys have something they want. In the sequel, the baby has grown to be five-year-old **Robin Weisman**. When the child goes to school, tongues wag about her and her mother's living arrangements with the three bachelors. Nancy Travis, the mother, decides she should move out and marry for Mary's sake.

MARY

THE VILLAIN STILL PURSUED HER (1940, RKO)—The title of this experiment is the best thing about it. The studio decided to make an old-fashioned melodrama with a hissable villain and a sweet young thing—**Anita Louise**, who looked good tied to railroad tracks, or meeting any equally dastardly end.

MARY

THE WOMAN FOR JOE (1955, GB, Rank)—Midget George Baker loves singer **Diane Cilento** who loves the fairground owner.

MARY ANN

LITTLE MISS THOROUGHBRED (1938, Warner Brothers)—Brought up by nuns in an orphanage, **Janet Chapman** is, nevertheless, convinced that she has a father somewhere and sets out to find him. What she finds is gambler John Litel, who eventually adopts the little dear.

MARY ANN

MERELY MARY ANN (1931, Fox)—In a Cinderella story, cleaning woman **Janet Gaynor** falls in love with gentleman boarder, Charles Farrell. It amounts to nothing but it once again teams "America's Sweethearts."

MARY LOU

MARY LOU (1948, Columbia)—**Abigail Adams** has been a popular singer with a band but is leaving. Joan Barton and Glenda Farrell fight over which one will be the new "Mary Lou."

MASHA

ENEMIES, A LOVE STORY (1989, 20th Century Fox)—**Lena Olin** continues a charming tradition of imported Swedish actresses becoming worldwide stars. She portrays Ron Silver's mistress, but when she insists, he marries her, even though the Holocaust survivor already has two wives in New York City. In the end, Olin commits suicide.

MASHA

THE IMMIGRANT (1915, Silent, Lasky)—Russian **Valeska Suratt** is raped by a construction company owner. She agrees to marry her attacker (don't ask us why, maybe she believes she's getting even—having him marry "spoiled goods"), but she falls in love with a mining engineer. Her nasty husband is so angry, he blows up a dam, killing himself and freeing Suratt to marry the engineer.

MASHA

THREE SISTERS (1974, GB, British Lion); (1977, Actors Studio Theater)—In 1900 **Joan Plowright** and **Kim Stanley** each appear as one of three orphaned Russian sisters, whose life and loves are explored in these productions of the Anton Chekhov play.

MASON

BATTLING MASON (1924, Silent, Hercules)—While running for office in New York City, **Frank Merrill** agrees not to engage in any fisticuffs. He's given plenty of provocation, but keeps his pledge and is branded a coward. When some brutes attack his girlfriend, all bets are off and he knocks out the bunch and still wins the election.

MASON

THE MARSHAL OF MESA CITY (1939, RKO)—Former marshal **George O'Brien** is forced into service to rid a community of a band of outlaws.

MASON, ANTHONY & CAROLINE

MY LIFE WITH CAROLINE (1941, RKO)—Suave (what else?) publisher **Ronald Colman** must constantly chase after his wife **Anna Lee** or lose her to the likes of Reginald Gardiner or Gilbert Roland. Sure!

MASON, BRENDA

MAYFAIR GIRL (1933, GB, Warner Brothers)—American **Sally Blane** is framed for killing a cad while she was drunk. John Stuart, a lawyer who loves her but doesn't approve of the crowd she's fallen in with, comes to her rescue.

MASON, COKE

THE IRON MAN (1951, Universal)—Ex-coal miner turned boxer **Jeff Chandler** is hated because he's a killer in the ring.

MASON, DORA

THE SCARLET LILY (1923, Silent, Associated First National)—Homeless, broke and without a job, **Katherine MacDonald** accepts the offer of a married man to use his apartment and care for her dying sister during the month he's away. He comes home early and soon after so does his wife. The wife slaps him with a divorce suit naming MacDonald as corespondent.

MASON, DWIGHT BRADLEY

THE UNKNOWN MAN (1951, MGM)—**Walter Pidgeon** is a murder trial lawyer who gets his client off, discovers he's actually guilty and makes sure justice prevails. Is this what's taught at Harvard Law School?

MASON, IVAN

THE MAN IN THE ROAD (1957, GB, Republic)—Amnesiac scientist **Derek Farr** is saved from spies running the nursing home where he's confined by novelist Ella Raines.

MASON, CAPT. JAMES

ARMY SURGEON (1942, RKO)—During WWII, military doctor **James Ellison** is one-third of a romantic triangle involving brave nurse, Jane Wyatt, and dashing flyer, Kent Taylor.

MASON, JANE & JOHNNY

MADE FOR EACH OTHER (1939, UA)—**Carole Lombard**, from Boston, marries struggling New York lawyer **James Stewart**, and finds they must take in his meddling mother. They can barely afford to hire a maid so you know that they are financially strapped. Can this marriage survive?

MASON, JERRY

THE LUCKY TEXAN (1934, Monogram)—This movie is more notable for the debut of George "Gabby" Hayes as a comical sidekick than for easterner **John Wayne** in the West fighting claim jumpers.

MASON, JIM

KING OF THE TURF (1939, UA)—**Adolphe Menjou** isn't dressed to the "T's" in this story of a once famous stable owner who has fallen on hard times, but with the help of boy jockey Roger Daniel and a colt they buy, he makes a comeback.

MASON, JOHN

DAWN RIDER (1935, Lone Star)—**John Wayne** hunts the killer of his father, the occupation and preoccupation of one in every two cowboys in Hollywood B westerns.

MASON, KID

THE IRON MAN (1931, Universal)—Boxer **Lew Ayres** is torn between listening to his manager Robert Armstrong or capricious girlfriend Jean Harlow. Since Harlow is only in Ayres corner when he's on the upswing, it's not much of a fight.

MASON, MARTHA

THE PERFECT SNOB (1941, 20th Century Fox)—**Charlotte Greenwood** teaches her daughter to seek wealth when she marries, while her father (who apparently missed somewhere along the line) recommends she seek love.

MASON, PETER

THE MAN I WANT (1934, GB, British Lion)—**Henry Kendall** recovers a knight's stolen jewels in this comedy.

MASON, STEVE

THE IRON MASTER (1933, Allied Artists)—Mill worker **Reginald Denny** is chosen to manage his deceased boss's estate. This doesn't sit well with the dead man's son and daughter who try to ruin him.

MASON, TOD

GENTLEMAN FROM LOUISIANA (1936, Republic)—Jockey **Eddie Quillan** has trouble with crooked gamblers.

MASON, VIRGINIA & GEORGE

MY WIFE'S BEST FRIEND (1952, 20th Century Fox) -**Anne Baxter's** husband **MacDonald Carey** admits to her that he's had an affair with her best friend. She imagines the revenge she would take had she been anyone of a number of historical women, such as Joan of Arc, Cleopatra, etc.

MASSACRE, GENERAL

GENERAL MASSACRE (1973, Burr Jerger)—General **Burr Jerger** is awaiting trial for killing innocent civilians in Vietnam.

MASSAI

APACHE (1954, UA)—Apache brave **Burt Lancaster** time and time again escapes from the white man, but each time is recaptured. He learns from a Cherokee about planting corn and living off the land. He picks up his love Jean Peters, and heads for a new life when the Cavalry arrive. Lancaster wanted an ending of the Indian being senselessly shot just as he was adopting the ways of peace, but the studio insisted on a happy ending, thereby just about ruining the dramatic effect of the film.

MASSLER, VINCENT

OCEAN'S ELEVEN (1960, Warner Brothers)—**Buddy Lester** is another of Frank Sinatra's war-time cronies, who participates in robbing five Las Vegas casinos at precisely midnight on New Years Eve.

MASTERS, ANNA

WOMAN AGAINST THE WORLD (1938, Columbia)—Widow **Alice Moore** has her child taken from her by her aunt, whom Moore accidentally kills. She's convicted of murder and sent to prison, but a lawyer gets her paroled and then her troubles begin.

MASTERS, BUFF, TRINKA, LINDA & CORA

DAUGHTERS COURAGEOUS (1939, Warner Brothers)—**Priscilla, Rosemary** and **Lola Lane**, and **Gale Page**; and John Garfield were such a hit together in FOUR DAUGHTERS (1938) that the studio had to come up with this film to bring them together again, (Garfield's character had been killed in FOUR DAUGHTERS). This time, Priscilla Lane is sweet on Garfield, who like their long absent father Claude Rains, who shows up just when their mother is remarrying, has traveling feet, and is not a dependable catch for a husband.

MASTERS, DANNY

THE ESCAPE ARTIST (1982, Orion-Warner Brothers)—**Griffin O'Neal** is a young magician exploited by adults.

MASTERS, JO

FOREIGN BODY (1986, GB, Orion)—Itinerant Indian **Victor Banerjee** poses as a doctor in London and finds he has more sack mates than he can handle.

MASTERS, KATE

TWO-GUN LADY (1956, Associated Releasing Company)—This film demonstrates that it's not just the men who go gunning for the dirty rats that did in their relatives. This time its **Peggy Castle** loaded for bear in her determination to do in the rats who killed her parents.

MASTERS, DR. PETER

LOVE SLAVES OF THE AMAZONS (1957, Universal)—**Don Taylor** is one of the men captured by a tribe of female warriors, who have stud service plans for their captives.

MASTERSON, BAT

MASTERSON OF KANSAS (1954, Columbia)—**George Montgomery** teams up with the Earps and Doc Holliday to prevent an Indian war in Kansas.

MASTERSON, KATE

THE STORM DAUGHTER (1924, Silent, Universal)—**Priscilla Dean**, a forgiving woman, tames the bestial skipper who violently tried to seduce her.

MASTERSON, SKY
GUYS AND DOLLS (1955, MGM)—New York gambler **Marlon Brando** is tricked into betting that he can get Salvation Army girl Jean Simmons to go away to Havana for the weekend with him. He succeeds, but to save her reputation, says he lost the bet.

MATA HARI
MATA HARI (1931, MGM); (1985, Cannon)—**Greta Garbo** and **Sylvia Kristel** each appear as the WWI German spy, who poses as a dancer in France, and is sent before a firing squad when her cover is blown.

MATHEWS, DICK
THERE GOES THE GROOM (1937, RKO)—**Burgess Meredith** has just returned from Alaska where he made a gold strike. He smells like fresh fish to a wacky family with financial problems, but with eligible daughters.

MATHEWS, VIVIAN
HIRED WIFE (1934, Pinnacle)—The arranged marriage of **Greta Nissen** and Weldon Heyburn is to end after a year. That's all the time he needs to be wed to collect an inheritance dependent upon him being married. Nissen has other plans.

MATHIAS, BOB
THE BOB MATHIAS STORY (1954, Allied Artists)—**Bob Mathias** appears as himself in this satisfactory account of the triumphs of the two-time Olympic decathlon winner.

MATRIX, JOHN
COMMANDO (1985, 20th Century Fox)—**Arnold Schwarzenegger** is a mean and strong "mother," who goes on a rampage when his 11-year-old daughter is kidnapped by a South American dictator. This guy could settle the problems in Nicaragua all by himself.

MATRON
CARRY ON NURSE (1959, GB, Anglo-Amalgamated)—**Hattie Jacques**, as the matron, is the only nurse in a crazy hospital who is not young, voluptuous, and ready for just about anything. She and all the other loonies in this film, staff and patients alike, made this "Carry On" entry a surprisingly big hit in the United States.

MATT
YANKS (1979, Universal)—Lonely GI cook **Richard Gere**, stationed in England during WWII, seeks out the company of Lisa Eichhorn, a British girl who is also lonely. Her parents don't approve of the friendship, rather resenting the Americans for all they have and the way they are making it with the British girls, while the British boys are off dying in the war.

MATT, RUDI
THIRD MAN ON THE MOUNTAIN (1959, Buena Vista)—In 1865, Swiss dishwasher **James MacArthur** dreams of climbing the local mountain. He gets his chance when he befriends a distinguished mountaineer Michael Rennie.

MATTHEWS, BEN
THE HUMAN SHIELD (1992, Cannon)—Diabetic **Tommy Hinkley** is taken hostage by a ruthless power-mad Iraqi general Steve Inwood, a Saddam Hussein clone. Former US Marine and CIA agent Michael Dudikoff comes to the rescue of his brother. Ho hum.

MATTHEWS, DAN
DAN MATTHEWS (1936, Columbia)—Militant minister **Richard Arlen** is trying to rid his locale of the decadence which is leading the young people straight to hell.

MATTHEWS, JOEL "UTILITY"
THE BARNSTORMER (1922, Silent, Associated First National)—**Charles Ray**, son of a wealthy farmer, seeks a career on the stage. His first chance in show business is a none too glamorous job with a travelling troupe of players. He never makes it in show biz, but he does win the hand of the female lead.

MATTHEWS, PETE
HER PRIMITIVE MAN (1944, Universal)—Louise Allbritton sets out to prove that writer **Robert Paige's** notions of savages is pure fiction by going into the jungle in search of a primitive man. She finds one who turns out to be Paige in disguise.

MATTHEWS, PHYLLIS
PLAYGIRL (1954, Universal)—Beautiful small-town girl, **Colleen Miller**, finds romance with both a playboy and a murderer.

MATTHEWS, PRUDENCE
TWO WISE MAIDS (1937, Republic)—**Polly Moran** teams with Alison Skipworth in this family story about the efforts to dismiss an elderly schoolteacher.

MATTHEWS, SHORTY
THEY DRIVE BY NIGHT (1938, GB, Warner Brothers)—Truck driver Allyn Jeayes and Anna Konstam help **Emlyn Williams**, fresh out of prison and a fugitive, capture a silk-stocking strangler.

MAUBERT, FERNAND
THE SPIDER AND THE FLY (1952, GB, GFD)—In France in 1914, Police Inspector **Eric Portman** knows that Guy Rolfe is a brilliant safecracker, but he can't pin anything on him. With the outbreak of war, Portman, now in Intelligence, persuades Rolfe to undertake a dangerous mission, the theft of papers from the Germans.

MAUCLAIR, ODETTE
I AM A THIEF (1935, Warner Brothers)—**Mary Astor** is one of several people out to get the Karenia diamonds carried by Ricardo Cortez, a passenger on the Paris to Istanbul express.

MAUDE
HAROLD AND MAUDE (1971, Paramount)—Eighty-year-old **Ruth Gordon** has an affair with twenty-year-old Bud Cort. He is obsessed with death and dying in this cult favorite.

MAUREEN
I, MAUREEN (1978, Canada, New Cinema)—When **Colleen Collins** has a premonition, she picks up and leaves her husband and child to become a person of her own.

MAUREL, LOUISE
BEHOLD THIS WOMAN (1924, Silent, Vitagraph)—Screen star **Irene Rich** is loved by a cattleman who isn't pleased when she seems to have a relationship with a rich idler.

MAURICETTE
THE HOTEL MOUSE (1923, Silent, GB, Jury)—Thief **Lillian Hall Davis** helps an American recoup his gambling losses and letters from a blackmailer.

MAURY, LT. CLAUDE & MME HELENE
THE WOMAN I LOVE (1937, RKO)—**Paul Muni** and **Miriam Hopkins** are two-thirds of a romantic triangle with Louis Hayward forming the hypotenuse. It all takes place during WWI in a French flying squadron.

MAUVE, MARY LOU
THREE ON A COUCH (1966, Columbia)—**Leslie Parrish** is one of the patients of psychiatrist Janet Leigh, whom a disguised Jerry Lewis must romance to get her over her hang-ups and the need for Leigh to postpone marriage and a honeymoon with Lewis.

MAVERICK
TOP GUN (1985, UA)—**Tom Cruise** is an obnoxiously cocky cadet at an elite naval aviation training school. He is convinced he can outfly any one in the air. His on the ground romance with lovely Kelly McGillis just isn't believable. She's too smart to be taken in by the likes of this stud.

MAVOUREEN, KATHLEEN
KATHLEEN MAVOUREEN (1919, Silent, World); (1930, Tiffany)—**Theda Bara** and **Sally O'Neil** portray an Irish immigrant sought as a bride by a good honest plumber and a wealthy gentleman who may have killed a few people. You know how hard it is to get a plumber?

MAX
DELIVERY BOYS (1984, New World)—**Joss Marcano** is one of a group of Pizza delivery boys who hope to win the $10,000 prize in a breakdance contest.

MAX
THE KILLERS (1946, Universal)—In the first of two filmings of the Hemingway short story, **William Conrad** plays one of the hired killers who are surprised to find that their victim, Burt Lancaster, has been expecting them and puts up no fight to save his life.

MAX
MUTANT ON THE BOUNTY (1989, Skouras)—With a great title like that, you don't expect a good story too, do you? **Kyle T. Heffner**, the title character, has been traveling through space as a beam of a particle of light for 23 years before being intercepted by the crew of the spaceship Bounty.

MAX
THE NIGHT PORTER (1974, Avco Embassy)—If you like sordid sado-masochistic films with no redeeming social values, this voyeur's delight featuring **Dirk Bogarde** as an ex-Nazi and Charlotte Rampling as the girl he used sexually in a concentration camp is just for you. For others, it may make you sick.

MAX, MAD
MAD MAX (1979, Australia, Filmways), THE ROAD WARRIOR (1982, Kennedy Miller/Warner Brothers); MAD MAX BEYOND THUNDERDOME (1985, Australia, Warner Brothers)—Sometime in the future after most of the world has been destroyed by wars, **Mel Gibson** tries to survive as one of the last of the good guys. In the first film, Gibson is an ex-cop in a high-speed chase after the motorcycle crazies who have killed his wife and child. In the sequel, loner Gibson reluctantly helps a small oil-producing community in their battle with the crazed bad guys after the fuel. In the final film, Gibson has a battle to the death in the Thunderdome arena, is exiled to the desert by the Queen of Bartertown, Tina Turner, and is looked on as some expected savior by a tribe of wild children.

MAX 404
ANDROID (1982, New World)—Scientist Klaus Kinski's robot assistant **Dan Opper** discovers he's to be replaced by a bosomy female android and so rebels.

MAXIE
MAXIE (1985, Orion)—**Glenn Close** portrays both a married woman and the spirit of a long dead flapper who invades the modern girl's body. The ghost has her way with her host's husband, and pursues the film career her death denied her.

MAXIMUS
THE CLAIRVOYANT (1935, GB, Gainsborough)—Fake mind reader **Claude Rains** starts to make predictions which come true, including a tunnel disaster.

MAXINE
THE DANCERS (1930, Fox)—**Mae Clarke**, a dancer in a Canadian saloon, falls in love with new arrival Phillips Holmes, but he's true to his childhood sweetheart, Lois Moran, even though she goes through men like they were going to be hard to find. Clarke picks up her love after Moran confesses all and kills herself.

MAXON, META
SHOULD A WOMAN TELL? (1920, Silent, Metro)—**Alice Lake** has been raped. Just before her marriage she sends a note to her fiance, detailing the assault, but he never receives it. They marry and when she foolishly brings the subject of the assault up, he's outraged and leaves her. She marries the man who ruined her, but her first hubby comes back, beats the lout to death, and the two live happily ever after. We believe the answer to the question of the title is NO!

MAXTON, JERRY
A DEVIL WITH WOMEN (1930, Fox)—**Victor McLaglen** and a very young Humphrey Bogart, in his first film, are rivals for the love of Luana Alcaniz, when the tough soldier of fortune and rich playboy aren't busy tracking down a Central American bandit.

MAXWELL, KATE
THE REDHEAD FROM WYOMING (1953, Universal)—Ranch and saloon owner **Maureen O'Hara** has no idea that she's fronting for a gang of rustlers.

MAY, MRS, MILLIE (GLADYS)
A SISTER TO ASSIST'ER (1922, GB, Gaumont); (1927, GB, Gaumont)—**May Brough**; (1930, Gaumont)—**Barbara Gott**; (1938, GB, Columbia); (1948, GB, Premier)—**Muriel George**—In a comedy which sure tickled the English, each of the three actresses appeared as a poor old woman, posing as a nonexistent rich twin to fool a mean landlady, who wants to throw the old gal out on the street.

MAYA
THE DIAMOND QUEEN (1953, Warner Brothers)—In the 17th century, **Arlene Dahl** is the Queen of Nepal, where jeweller Fernando Lamas has journeyed to seek a blue diamond for the crown of Louis XIV of France. Hokum!

MAYFAIR, MITZI
FOUR JILLS IN A JEEP (1944, 20th Century Fox)—**Mitzi Mayfair** is one of four USO actresses who play themselves in a story detailing their entertainment of the boys. Never smudged their makeup either.

MAYFIELD, CLARA
CLARA'S HEART (1988, Warner Brothers)—Jamaican maid **Whoopi Goldberg** experiences quite a bit of hostility from young master Neil Patrick Harris, when she enters employment in a wealthy household that has recently lost Harris' baby sister. Goldberg and Harris grow closer as his parents steadily grow apart.

MAYHEW, PEGGY

YOU WERE MEANT FOR ME (1948, 20th Century Fox)—**Jeanne Crain** is married to band leader Dan Dailey. They travel through the Midwest trying to get a break, but the Great Depression puts an end to the dream of Broadway. Crain goes home, and Dailey takes off by himself, establishes himself, and sends for his wife.

MAYME

THE SATURDAY NIGHT KID (1929, Paramount)—Redhead "It Girl" **Clara Bow** and her sister Jean Arthur are naughty department store sales girls after the same man. Jean Harlow has a bit role in the movie.

MAYME

THE SOCIAL SECRETARY (1916, Silent, Triangle)—**Norma Talmadge** is the social secretary for a wealthy woman. She straightens out a great deal more that her employer's mail.

MAYNARD, CAROL

GIRL FROM MANHATTAN (1948, UA)—**Dorothy Lamour** returns to her old hometown from New York in time to expose an unscrupulous financier. He plans to destroy her uncle's boardinghouse to put up a church. How low can you get?

MAYO, RICHARD

THOSE MAGNIFICENT MEN IN THEIR FLYING MACHINES (1965, 20th Century Fox)—**James Fox** provides Sarah Miles with excitement on motorcycles and early day airplanes, but when it comes to offering her excitement in the romance area, the well-to-do British gentleman is over-matched by itinerant American flyer Stuart Whitman.

MAYO, ZACK

AN OFFICER AND A GENTLEMAN (1982, Paramount)—**Richard Gere** survives the rigors of relentless training at a Naval Officer Candidate Training School, and especially the demands and taunts of drill instructor Louis Gossett Jr. He also survives the sack time with local girl Debra Winger, looking for a ticket out of her going nowhere life.

MAYOR, THE

THE LADYKILLERS (1956, GB, Ealing)—**Cecil Parker** is one of a gang of thieves who pull off a robbery, and feel they must dispose of their sweet old landlady, when she catches on to their criminal activities. But this is easier said than done.

MAZIE

TWO ALONE (1934, RKO)—Orphan **Jean Parker** falls for Tom Brown, a runaway from a reform school. They are enslaved by a dirty old man, but Parker's real father shows up and sees that she and Brown are properly hitched.

MAZULER, GEORGINE

THE FRENCH DOLL (1923, Silent, Tiffany)—Her parents force **Mae Murray** to sell fake antiques and then herself as the intended wife of a rich Palm Beach playboy. The latter finally discovers that Murray is a real treasure.

MCALLISTER, BILLY JOE

ODE TO BILLY JOE (1976, Warner Brothers)—The film, based on the popular song, explains why adolescent Billy Joe McAllister, sensitively played by **Robby Benson**, chooses to end his life by jumping off the Tallahatchie Bridge.

MCALLISTER, BUCK

THE BRUTE MASTER (1920, Silent, Pathe)—**Hobart Bosworth** is the brutal skipper of a South Sea schooner on which Anna Q. Nilsson is sailing. He tries to get her in his bunk but she resists him. On an island, Bosworth must rescue Nilsson from natives who plan to do unto her what sailors did to a native girl. Bosworth is tamed by Nilsson and they fall into a clinch by the fade-out.

MCALLISTER, PAMELA

MILLION DOLLAR BABY (1941, Warner Brothers)—**Priscilla Lane** is prepared to give up her million dollar inheritance to get back her boyfriend. We can see how all that money could be an impediment to romance.

MCALPINE, DAN

THE OVERLANDERS (1946, GB/Australia, Ealing)—In 1942, **Chips Rafferty** and other Australian drovers herd cattle 1600 miles to escape a Japanese threat.

MCBAIN, FRANK "BULLETPROOF"

BULLETPROOF (1988, Cinetel-Virgin)—Over the years, 37 bullets have been removed from the body of individualistic LA cop **Gary Busey**. In this movie, he gets his chance to dodge some more bullets with his name on them.

MCBAIN, JO

NEVER WAVE AT A WAC (1952, RKO)—Washington socialite **Rosalind Russell** joins the WACs so she can be reunited with boyfriend William Ching, who is stationed in Paris. Her ex-husband Paul Douglas makes the most of her enlistment.

MCBRIDE, BLANCHE

SLATE, WYN & ME (1987, Australia, Ukiyo/Hemsdale) **Sigrid Thornton** is kidnapped by two brothers because he witnessed them robbing a bank and killing a cop.

MCBURNEY, JOHN

THE BEGUILED (1971, Universal)—Wounded Union soldier **Clint Eastwood** takes refuge at a southern girls school. He turns up the sexual temperature of students and teachers alike, particularly headmistress Geraldine Page, who prevents him from leaving by amputating his leg.

MCCABE, DAN

THREE HUSBANDS (1950, UA)—In this weak copy of A LETTER TO THREE WIVES, **Howard Da Silva** is one of three husbands who find their marriages in shambles after they each receive a posthumous letter from a recently deceased bachelor, claiming to have had an affair with their wives. It was all a bad joke.

MCCABE, GUTHRIE

TWO RODE TOGETHER (1961, Columbia)—Texas Marshal **James Stewart** doesn't cotton to the army ways when he is required to help a Cavalry officer, Richard Widmark, lead a wagon train on a mission to rescue white captives of the Comanches.

MCCABE, JOHN

MCCABE AND MRS. MILLER (1971, Warner Brothers)—Two-bit western gambler **Warren Beatty** and prostitute Julie Christie open a bordello in half-built, mud-strewn mining-town Presbyterian Church around the turn of the century. The operation is so successful, the big mining outfits want to be cut into the deal—something Beatty foolishly refuses.

MCCALL, BOB

THE BANDIT'S SON (1927, Silent, FBO)—**Bob Steele** saves his father, an ex-gunslinger, from being lynched for a crime he didn't commit, and captures the real culprit.

MCCALL, CASH

CASH MCCALL (1960, Warner Brothers)—Finagling financial genius **James Garner's** activities almost sink his romance with Natalie Wood.

MCCALL, JACK

JACK MCCALL, DESPERADO (1953, Columbia)—At the time of the Civil War, **George Montgomery** tracks the man who had him framed as a spy.

MCCALL, TERRY

SWELL-HEAD (1935, Columbia)—Egomaniac baseball player **Wallace Ford** finally sees the light when a high, inside fast one plunks him on the cranium.

MCCANDLES, JACOB

BIG JAKE (1971, National General)—When his grandson, whom he has never seen, is kidnapped, **John Wayne** and two of his sons pursue the abductors, and engage them in a bloody shootout. Everyone seems to be surprised to see that Wayne's character is still alive. When they comment that they thought he was dead, he replies menacingly, "Not by a long shot."

MCCANDLES, JOHN

SCANDALOUS JOHN (1971, Buena Vista)—In a flawed attempt to transfer the Don Quixote story to the American West, **Brian Keith** is a rancher threatened with bankruptcy. He sets off with Alfonso Arau to sell his one undernourished cow at market in hopes of paying his mortgage.

MCCARDLE, JOHN

THE REFEREE (1922, Silent, Selznick)—Former boxer **Conway Tearle**, forced into retirement by an auto accident, becomes a referee. He stops a fight in progress when he realizes it has been fixed.

MCCARE, DAVID

THE LOVE LIAR (1916, Silent, Centaur)—**Crane Wilbur** can have any girl he wants, but he does not want them for long. He finally feels the other side of the coin when he falls for a cabaret singer who can have any man she wants. She also has a short attention span.

MCARTHUR, BRAD

I AM A CRIMINAL (1939, Monogram)—**John Carroll**, a Clark Gable pretender, plays a shady gambler reformed by a young boy.

MCCARTHY, CASEY

HER BODYGUARD (1933, Paramount)—When a millionaire hires **Edmund Lowe** to keep rival admirers away from Broadway beauty Wynne Gibson, she falls for her bodyguard.

MCCARTHY, DOROTHY

GIRL LOVES BOY (1937, Great National)—In a placid period piece **Cecilia Parker** loves Eric Linden.

MCCARTHY, OFFICE

HIS CAPTIVE WOMAN (1929, First National/Warner Brothers)—Police officer **Milton Sills** is sent to a South Sea island to arrest dancer Dorothy Mackaill who had killed her sugar daddy. On the way back to trial, their ship is wrecked with Sills and Mackaill stranded on a deserted island. When they are rescued, Sills convinces the judge at her trial to sentence Mackaill to his custody back on the island.

MCCARTHY, RITZY

THE PERSONALITY KID (1934, Warner Brothers)—Boxer **Pat O'Brien** almost lets his career ruin his marriage. When his wife announces they are to have a baby, O'Brien shapes up.

MCCASLIN, LUCIUS & NED

THE REIVERS (1969, National General)—In 1905, Mississippi boy **Mitch Vogel**, black **Rupert Crosse** and Steve McQueen "borrow" a car, and drive on to numerous experiences before reaching Memphis.

MCCHESNEY, EMMA

OUR MRS. MCCHESNEY (1918, Silent, Metro)—Department store buyer **Ethel Barrymore** comes up with a new dress style. She brings her irresponsible son into the business, and sends the chorus girl he married to finishing school. All turns out well, with Barrymore marrying her boss after her new creation is a smash.

MCCLANE, JOHN

DIE HARD (1988, 20th Century Fox); DIE HARD 2 (1990, 20th Century Fox)—On Christmas Eve in Los Angeles, New York cop **Bruce Willis** is visiting his estranged wife Bonnie Bedelia at the Japanese conglomerate for which she works. Terrorists strike, taking over the Christmas party, and for the next 12 hours, Willis seems to be the only one who knows what to do. L.A. cops and the FBI only complicate his efforts to end the siege. The film is violent and silly, but exciting to watch. The sequel is set in an airport at Christmas. Willis singlehandedly makes the skies friendly again, once more rescuing his wife Bedelia, who like Willis always seems to be in the wrong place at the right time.

MCCLATCHIE, WILMA

BIG BAD MAMA (1974, Columbia); BIG BAD MAMA II (1987, Concorde)—To escape their 1930s poverty existence in Texas, tough **Angie Dickinson** and her daughters turn to bank robberies. The sequel is just more of the same and has no excuse for being made.

MCCLELLAN, JIM

THE ADVENTURER (1928, Silent, MGM)—**Tim McCoy** is in the middle of a South American revolution. Dorothy Sebastian makes it tolerable.

MCCLENAHAN, SCOTTY

IT'S TOUGH TO BE FAMOUS (1932, First National/ Warner Brothers)—When naval officer **Douglas Fairbanks, Jr.** risks his life to save the crew of a damaged submarine, he becomes an instant celebrity, something he's not quite ready for.

MCCLOSKEY, REBECCA O'BRIEN

BECKY (1927, Silent, MGM)—New York sales-girl **Sally O'Neil** gets a chance to be in a Broadway show. This leads her to an involvement with a playboy who ultimately rejects her.

MCCLOUD, ALICE/"RAGS"

RAGS (1915, Silent, Famous Players)—**Mary Pickford** plays both a mother and the daughter she gives life as she dies in childbirth. The daughter becomes a tom-boy, who despite the squalor in which she lives, finds things to be happy about. Among these is a handsome engineer, whom she finally wins after many problems caused by her drunken father.

MCCLOUD, BREWSTER
BREWSTER MCCLOUD (1970, MGM)—**Bud Cort** builds mechanical wings which he uses to fly with, while committing several murders.

MCCLOUD, DAVE
REQUIEM FOR A GUNFIGHTER (1965, Embassy)—**Rod Cameron** impersonates a judge at a trial to ensure justice is done—well, maybe not exactly justice.

MCCLOUD, JEFF
THE LUSTY MEN (1952, RKO)—Ex-rodeo rider **Robert Mitchum** is tired and would like to settle down. He is induced to help Arthur Kennedy get started as a rodeo performer, in part because of his interest in Kennedy's wife Susan Hayward, who like him, wants security and domesticity, not the aimless, uncertain life of a cowboy.

MCCLOUD, JOHNNY
MAN AGAINST WOMAN (1932, Columbia)—Detective **Jack Holt** is tricked into delivering a crook to the latter's former associates. They then announce they plan to bump off both of them.

MCCLOUD, JOHNNY
MY BEST GAL (1944, Republic)—Young composer **Jimmy Lydon** is helped to achieve his dream of having a Broadway show by drugstore assistant Jane Withers, who finds a backer for him.

MCCLUNE, BLONDIE
BLONDIE OF THE FOLLIES (1932, MGM)—New York show girl **Marion Davies** competes with another Follies cutie Billie Dove for Robert Montgomery. Davies and Jimmy Durante do a take-off of Greta Garbo and John Barrymore in GRAND HOTEL.

MCCLUSKEY, DEIRDRE
TWO PEOPLE (1973, Universal)—Fashion model **Lindsay Wagner** meets and falls for expatriate Peter Fonda on a train from Marrakech to Casablanca.

MCCOBB, CARRIE & NED
NED MCCOBB'S DAUGHTER (1929, Silent, Pathe)—**Irene Rich** runs a restaurant in part of a large house owned by her father **Theodore Roberts**, captain of a local ferry. Rich's husband Robert Armstrong steals from her customers so he can buy gifts for a waitress. But Armstrong does protect his wife and children from his rat of a brother.

MCCONNELL, JOSEPH C. JR.
THE MCCONNELL STORY (1955, Warner Brothers)—**Alan Ladd** stars in the story of the late brave airman, who became America's first triple jet ace in Korea.

MCCORD, GIL
THE HIRED GUN (1957, MGM)—Bounty hunter **Rory Calhoun** is sent to bring in escaped murderer Anne Francis. When he catches up with her, he thinks, "Can this be the body of a killer?" and tracks down the real culprit.

MCCORMICK, DAN
MAN MADE MONSTER (1941, Universal)—**Lon Chaney Jr.** is billed as "Dynamo Dan, the Electric Man" with a circus because he can absorb electricity. Chaney falls into the hands of mad doctor Lionel Atwill, who turns him into a zombie-like killer. Chaney survives the electric chair and goes out after his mentor Atwill. Good thing he wasn't in California—execution is by lethal gas there.

MCCORMICK, TEX
TEX (1982, Buena Vista)—It's a poignant story of the coming of age of youngster **Matt Dillon**, without parental guidance, in a small Texas town.

MCCOY, "BUBBLES"
RED HAIR (1928, Silent, Paramount)—Gold-digging manicurist **Clara Bow** snags wealthy Lane Chandler, who keeps her in expensive clothes and jewels. When she is snubbed by his society friends at their engagement party, she throws a tantrum, strips to her undies and dives into the swimming pool. The judges awarded her a 5.5 as the entry was a little off.

MCCOY, CRYSTAL
QUEEN OF BURLESQUE (1946, PRC)—**Evelyn Ankers** gets involved in a murder case which takes place backstage at a Burlesque house where she works.

MCCOY, DEBORAH
BUCCANEER'S GIRL (1950, Universal)—New Orleans singer **Yvonne de Carlo** learns the identity of a pirate, which she refuses to reveal to the authorities, as she has fallen in love with the buccaneer, Phillip Friend.

MCCOY, JED
THE HILL BILLY (1924, Silent, Allied Productions)—**Jack Pickford's** father is killed by Frank Leigh, who then marries Jack's mother. Pickford loves the killer's niece, Lucille Ricksen. The latter is forced to marry Leigh's. son. When the son is killed, Pickford is accused of the crime. He's acquitted and goes looking for his father's killer. Pickford and Leigh engage in a rousing fight aboard a raft headed downstream towards violent rapids. Ricksen loses an uncle, but she won't be a widow for long.

MCCOY, MARY "PETE"
GIRL FROM ALASKA (1942, Republic)—**Jean Parker**, the daughter of a prospector, who hit it rich in the Alaskan gold rush, is menaced by villain Jerome Cowan. He wishes to rob her father of his gold and she of her virtue. She's saved by Ray Middleton, who is fleeing authorities under the mistaken notion that he has killed a lawman.

MCCOY, ROSEANNA
ROSEANNA MCCOY (1949, RKO)—**Joan Evans** and Farley Granger are the Juliet and Romeo-like lovers in this story of the feud of the Hatfields and the McCoys.

MCCOY, SHAMUS
SHAMUS (1973, Columbia)—Private eye **Burt Reynolds** is hired to recover some stolen diamonds. He takes his lumps as he competes with Dyan Cannon and others also interested in the "ice."

MCCOY, TOMMY
KILLER MCCOY (1947, MGM)—Boxer **Mickey Rooney** has problems both in the ring and with his alcoholic father, James Dunn.

MCCLANAHAN, ROXY
SCARLET ANGEL (1952, Universal)—When saloon girl **Yvonne De Carlo** befriends the dying widow of a Union soldier, she poses as the dead woman so as to be taken in by the husband's rich San Francisco family. She will later choose love, in the person of Rock Hudson, over wealth.

MCCLOUD, THAD & LESLIE
KISSES FOR MY PRESIDENT (1964, Warner Brothers)—**Fred MacMurray** becomes the first "First Gentleman" when his wife

Polly Bergen is elected the first woman President of the U.S. Every situation that a typical sophomore could think up is employed in this light-weight comedy.

MCCREADY, CHARLIE
SUPERDAD (1974, Buena Vista)—Middle-aged **Bob Crane** attempts to bridge the generation gap by competing with his daughter's fiance in various activities. Superstinker!

MCCREEDY, SCOOP
I'LL GET HIM YET (1919, Silent, First National)—Reporter **Richard Barthelmess** won't marry Dorothy Gish, daughter of a millionaire, because he doesn't wish to be seen as a fortune hunter. Gish pledges not to touch a penny of her father's money, but doesn't tell Barthelmess that she's worth $5 million in her own right.

MCCULLEN, PAULA
BEST FRIENDS (1982, Warner Brothers)—When successful screenwriters **Goldie Hawn** and partner Burt Reynolds decide to marry, it kills their working relationship.

MCCULLOUGH, JASON
SUPPORT YOUR LOCAL SHERIFF (1969, UA)—In this lovely western spoof, **James Garner** is an unheroic stranger, hired as a sheriff in a town harassed by Walter Brennan and his loutish sons. Garner refuses to play things according to the "Code of the West," but he gets the job done.

MCDERMAD, KATIE
YOU FOR ME (1952, MGM)—**Jane Greer** is the object of affection of both millionaire Peter Lawford and poor old boy, Gig Young.

MCDERMOTT, BRIAN, DUNCAN AND KIT
STAYING TOGETHER (1989, Hemdale)—Ranging in age from 17 to 20, **Tim Quill**, **Sean Astin** and **Dermot Mulroney** expect to inherit the family's fried chicken business one day. Their father, who never liked chicken, unexpectedly sells the business, and the effect of this on the lives of the three boys—individually and collectively—is the subject of the remainder of the movie.

MCDERMOTT, JACK
THE DREAM TEAM (1989, Universal)—Mental patient **Jack Boyle** sees himself as a Christ figure. Along with three others, with varying personality problems, he must learn to cope in New York City when his doctor-chaperon is hospitalized in a coma.

MCDONALD, LAURA
I LOVED A WOMAN (1933, First National/Warner Brothers)—**Kay Francis**, a successful singer, has a long-running back street affair with Chicago meat packer Edward G. Robinson, whose wife won't give him a divorce.

MCDONALD, SUZANNE
SUZANNE (1980, Canada, Ambassador)—**Jennifer Dale** is torn between a desire to experience adventure and a need for peace.

MCDUFF, CONSTABLE
NORTHWEST MOUNTED POLICE (1940, Paramount)—**Robert Preston** pays more attention to half-breed Paulette Goddard than to his duties as a Mountie and it costs him his life, but Texas Ranger Gary Cooper saves his reputation.

MCDUFF, MARGIE
MARGIE (1946, 20th Century Fox)—In this charming period piece, **Jeannie Crain** is a 1928 Ohio high school student who wishes she was more popular with boys like her friend. Despite or perhaps because she's always losing her bloomers, she draws the attention of her handsome French teacher, Glenn Langan.

MCELLANY, FRANCES
AN UNREMARKABLE LIFE (1989, SVS)—Retired sinister schoolteacher **Patricia Neal** is fussed over by her sister Shelley Winters as if Neal were a child. The interdependent relationship is threatened when romance belatedly enters Neal's life.

MCFADDEN, DAN
MCFADDEN'S FLATS (1935, Paramount)—**Walter C. Kelly** and Andy Clyde alternate as best friends and worst enemies, until their children fall in love.

MCFADDEN, PAULA
THE GOODBYE GIRL (1977, MGM/Warner Brothers)—**Marsha Mason** discovers that her live-in lover has skipped the country and subletted the apartment he shared with Mason and her daughter to actor Richard Dreyfuss. Dreyfuss, Mason and the daughter share the flat in a state of uneasy peace, but love rears its ugly head and the laughs cease.

MCGANN, SONNY
I CAN'T GIVE YOU ANYTHING BUT LOVE, BABY (1940, Universal) - Gangster **Broderick Crawford** kidnaps songwriter Johnny Downs to provide the music for the lyrics he's written. Crawford hopes it will bring back his sweetheart.

MCGARGLE, POPPY
POPPY (1936, Paramount)—W.C. Fields tries to palm off his daughter **Rochelle Hudson** as an heiress. Turns out she really is, and isn't Fields' daughter.

MCGEE, ANDY
CUPID'S FIREMAN (1923, Silent, Fox)—Against his mother's wishes, **Charles Jones** becomes a fireman, rescues a beautiful woman from a blazing house, and marries her when she becomes a widow.

MCGEE, CHARLEY
FIRESTARTER (1984, Universal)—In this film based on a novel by Stephen King, cute little **Drew Barrymore** is able to will fires to start. It's quite a weapon and the government agency responsible, through drugs given to Barrymore's parents when they were graduate students, wants to examine her and then dispose of her.

MCGEE, SLIPPY
SLIPPY MCGEE (1923, Silent, Associated First National) (1948, Republic)—**Wheeler Oakman** and **Donald Barry** portray a safecracker who loses his leg while escaping from the police. He's nursed back to health by a girl, whom a villain is trying to blackmail into marrying him. The safecracker pulls one last job and destroys the incriminating evidence against the girl.

MCGEE, "SCOOP"
PARTNERS IN CRIME (1928, Silent, Paramount)—**Raymond Hatton**, as a wise-cracking reporter, and Wallace Beery, as a half-witted private eye, satirize underworld movies in a simple story in which they out-fumble the cops and catch the crooks.

MCGEE, WIDOW
THE ABLEMINDED LADY (1922, Silent, Pacific)—**Helen Raymond** is a thrice-married widow with her sights set on number four, ranch hand Henry B. Walthall, a confirmed bachelor.

MCGILL, ANTONIA

ANTONIA AND JANE (1991, GB, Miramax)—**Saskia Reeves** and her childhood chum Imelda Stauton alternate telling their stories to the same therapist. Reeves is happily married to Stauton's former boyfriend.

MCGILL, JERRY

THE COWBOY COP (1926, Silent, R-C Pictures)—Arizona cowboy **Tom Tyler** joins the mounted police after being robbed in Los Angeles. He finds himself up against society jewel thieves.

MCGILL, ROSIE

NAUGHTY BABY (1929, Silent, First National)—Hat check girl **Alice White** would really like to find a wealthy man to marry. She already has three admirers who don't quite meet her demands, but they're willing to help her any way they can.

MCGILL, TESS

WORKING GIRL (1988, 20th Century Fox)—Tippi Hedren's daughter **Melanie Griffith** tells Harrison Ford that she has a head for business and a body for sin. She demonstrates a bit of both talents in this story, in which she plays nasty Sigourney Weaver's secretary, who takes the opportunity to show what she knows about business while her boss is recovering from a skiing accident. Griffith and her friend Joan Cusack are so appealing in their Oscar-nominated roles that when they outsmart Weaver in her equally outstanding Oscar-nominated performance, one tends to cheer.

MCGINNIS, ETHELBERT ALOYSIUS "MUGGS"

MR. WISE GUY (1942, Monogram); MR. MUGGS STEPS OUT (1943, Monogram; MR. MUGGS RIDES AGAIN (1945, Monogram)—**Leo Gorcey** is the star of these East Side Kids movies. The films are played a bit more straight than the later comedies featuring Gorcey and Huntz Hall. For instance in the first, the boys must break out of reform school to save the older brother of one of them from execution for a murder he didn't commit.

MCGINTY, DAN

THE GREAT MCGINTY (1940, Paramount)—Hobo **Brian Donlevy** learns the political ropes so well, he's elected mayor and is well on his way to becoming governor when he ruins everything by doing something honest, forcing him to leave the country.

MCGONAGALL, WILLIAM

THE GREAT MCGONAGALL (1975, GB, Scotia American) In a crazy comedy, Scots weaver/poet **Spike Milligan** saves his beloved Queen Victoria (Peter Sellers—yes, Peter Sellers) from assassination.

MCGONGEAL, MADELEINE

CHILD OF MANHATTAN (1933, Columbia)—Dance hall hostess **Nancy Carroll** is made pregnant by millionaire John Boles. She loses the baby after they marry. She runs away to get a divorce so she can marry Charles Jones, but for some strange reason Boles comes after her and takes her back home. Sixteen-year-old Betty Grable has a small role as a dancer.

MCGONIGLE, MILLIE

THE MATING OF MILLIE (1948, Columbia)—Glenn Ford tries to help **Evelyn Keyes** find a husband, so she can adopt a child, but falls in love with her himself.

MCGRATH, SGT.

THE NUN AND THE SERGEANT (1962, UA)—**Robert Webber** is a sergeant, leading a group of stockade soldiers on a dangerous mission in Korea. They are assisted by a nun and a group of Korean schoolgirls.

MCGRAW, HARVEY

THE CENSUS TAKER (1984, Argentum/Borde)—Saturday Night Live alumnus **Garrett Morris** goes nowhere with this film. He's an obnoxious census taker, who so annoys one couple that they shoot him dead and then must find some place to hide his body.

MCGREGOR, LT.

LIVES OF A BENGAL LANCER (1935, Paramount)—When a cowardly second lieutenant, son of the commanding officer, arrives at the Northwest border in India in the 19th century, veteran officer **Gary Cooper** feels sorry for the lad. It costs Cooper his life, although he wins a medal posthumously, and is given a hero's funeral. Jolly, good show!

MCGREW, DAN

THE SHOOTING OF DAN MCGREW (1915, Silent, Metro)—**William A. Morse** gets shot by the piano player. The latter escapes across the frozen tundra with the girl named Lou.

MCGREW, NAN

DANGEROUS NAN MCGREW (1930, Paramount)—Sharpshooter **Helen Kane** headlines a medicine show in northern Canada.

MCGUIRE, MAJOR

MCGUIRE GO HOME! (1966, GB, Rank)—While seeking guerilla leader George Chakris in Cyprus in 1957, British Intelligence officer **Dirk Bogarde** falls in love with American archeologist Susan Strasberg.

MCGURK, ROY "SLAG"

THE MIGHTY MCGURK (1946, MGM)—In the Bowery of the early 1900s, punchy boxer **Wallace Beery** is idolized by young Dean Stockwell. Sounds like THE CHAMP doesn't it? If so, its a knockoff, not a knockdown.

MCHALE, HEATHER

LADY FIGHTS BACK (1937, Universal)—Nature lover **Irene Hervey** finds herself in conflict with Kent Taylor, an engineer in charge of building a dam. The obvious line here would be beneath us.

MCHALE, LT. CMDR. QUINTON

MCHALE'S NAVY (1964, Universal)—**Ernest Borgnine** had the good sense to absent himself from the sequel of this take-off of his TV situation-comedy, MCHALE'S ARMY JOINS THE AIR FORCE. He should have stayed away from the first as well.

MCHENRY, BUSTER

RENEGADES (1989, Universal)—Undercover cop **Kiefer Sutherland** becomes involved in a diamond robbery, that goes bad, because of the sadism of its criminal mastermind, Rob Knepper.

MCINTYRE, CLAIRE

BIG BUSINESS GIRL (1931, Warner Brothers/First National)—**Loretta Young** climbs the business ladder from stenographer to advertising copy editor while all the time encouraging the career of her jealous husband, band leader Frank Albertson.

MCKAY, BILL

THE CANDIDATE (1972, Warner Brothers)—Young liberal **Robert Redford** runs for the U.S. Senate against a popular incumbent. Redford is packaged by a group of savvy political pros led by Joe Boyle. Expecting to lose, Redford asks in the last line of the movie,

"What do we do now?" after pulling off an upset and winning the seat.

MCKAY

THE GOOD GUYS AND THE BAD GUYS (1969, Warner Brothers)—Over-the-hill train robber **George Kennedy** teams up with aging sheriff Robert Mitchum to stop an outlaw gang from robbing a train.

MCKEE, SADIE

SADIE MCKEE (1934, MGM)—Former maid **Joan Crawford** becomes a New York nightclub star with a little help from the men in her life: her former employer, a playboy, and an alcoholic millionaire.

MCKEE, "SINGER JIM"

SINGER JIM MCKEE (1924, Silent, Paramount)—Failed gold-miner **William S. Hart** raises his partner's daughter after the man is killed trying to rob a stagecoach. Hart tries to support his young charge by becoming a bandit. After serving a prison term, Hart and his ward, Phyllis Haver, realize they are in love.

MCKELLAWAY, MARY

MARY, MARY (1963, Warner Brothers)—This production of the stage hit has **Debbie Reynolds** as the nagging ex-wife of Barry Nelson, who is about to marry again. The small cast talks a great deal about love and sex but they don't have much to say that is amusing or new.

MCKENNA, DR. BEN

THE MAN WHO KNEW TOO MUCH (1956, Paramount)—In the only remake of a film of Alfred Hitchcock's career, **James Stewart** and his wife Doris Day innocently become involved in an assassination plot. To keep them from telling what they know, which isn't much, their son is kidnapped. This one has the dreadful Oscar winning song "Que Sera Sera," screeched by Doris Day as Stewart's wife.

MCKENNA, DR. GILBERT

THE HIDEOUS SUN DEMON (1959, Pacific International) -After **Robert Clarke** is exposed to radiation, every sun ray turns him into a scaly lizard monster with a bad disposition. We thought lizards liked sun.

MCKENNA, RACHEL

MANKILLERS (1987, Action)—**Lynde Aldon** is one of a dozen women recruited and trained by the CIA to wipe out a renegade agent, who's living south of the border.

MCKENZIE, BARRY

ADVENTURES OF BARRY MCKENZIE (1972, Australia, Langford); BARRY MCKENZIE HOLDS HIS OWN (1975, Australia, Roadshow)—These films, based on a comic strip, have Melbournian **Barry Crocker**, not especially fond of the British, stranded in England. The sequel is just more of the same. The humor of the pieces is probably not everyone's can of beer.

MCKENZIE, BILL

THIS MAN IS MINE (1946, GB, Columbia British)—Visiting Canadian soldier **Hugh McDermott** is pursued by both a family's daughter, Nova Pilbeam, and her ex-maid Glynnis Johns, now serving in uniform herself.

MCKENZIE, DOLLY

DOLLY'S VACATION (1918, Silent, Pathe)—With the help of some well-trained animals, **Baby Marie Osborne** and her little friends turn her uncle's farm into a madhouse.

MCKENZIE, "NEVADA" JACK

FRONTIER AGENT (1948, Monogram)—Government agent **Johnny Mack Brown** leaps into the saddle of his faithful steed and rides after the bad guys.

MCKILLUP

THERE WAS A CROOKED MAN (1962, GB, UA)—Crooked mayor **Andrew Cruickshank**'s schemes are thwarted by Norman Wisdom, an ex-safecracker and his gang posing as members of the U.S. Army.

MCKINLEY, MARY

JOHN LOVES MARY (1949, Warner Brothers)—**Patricia Neal** finds it difficult to be understanding when her fiance, army sergeant Ronald Reagan, marries an English woman to get her into the U.S. for a buddy.

MCKLUSKY, GATOR

GATOR (1976, UA)—Good Ole Boy **Burt Reynolds**, a moonshiner, is forced by the revenue agents to get the goods on an old buddy—now a corrupt southern political boss.

MCLAIN, JIM

BIG JIM MCLAIN (1952, Warner Brothers)—Wouldn't you know **John Wayne** would take the role of a special agent for the House Un-American Activities Committee (HUAC) and look heroic smashing an evil communist ring in Hawaii.

MCLANE, DON

THE DARING YOUNG MAN (1935, Fox)—**James Dunn** postpones his wedding to fellow reporter Mae Clarke to do an under-cover prison story. Some have been so unkind to liken marriage to a prison sentence. We don't hold to this view.

MCLAUGHLIN, KEN

MY FRIEND FLICKA (1943, 20th Century Fox)—When **Roddy McDowall**'s father finally agrees that the lad can have a pet colt, he's not happy with his son's choice. The horse, which McDowall calls Flicka, is from a mare that had shown madness. Flicka appears to have inherited some of the mother's wildness, but McDowall's patience is rewarded and Flicka grows into a magnificent animal. It's what used to be called a heart-warming movie.

MCLEAN, JEANNIE

GIRL IN DISTRESS (1941, GB, GFD)—Scottish lass **Barbara Mullen** inherits a small amount of money, which she decides to use to treat herself to a vacation in Vienna. While there, she is mistaken for a rich girl by a gigolo, but leaves with washing-machine salesman Michael Redgrave. The film was released as JEANNIE in Great Britain.

MCLEAN, PARRISH

PARRISH (1961, Warner Brothers)—**Troy Donahue** has good looks, but it doesn't compensate for his lack of acting ability in this story of a young Connecticut Valley tobacco grower trying to be accepted in snobbish society.

MCLEAN, TOBY

YOUNG MAN OF MANHATTAN (1930, Paramount)—Sports writer **Norman Foster** is married to movie columnist Claudette Colbert (at the time they were married in real life). Everything is ducky until Ginger Rogers, in her feature-film debut, comes along and gums up the wedded bliss.

MCLEOD, JIM

DETECTIVE STORY (1951, Paramount)—Police detective **Kirk Douglas** can't or won't distinguish between a major crime and a minor one. He also is unforgiving of anyone who ever made a mistake. This includes the wife he adores, who long before she met him became pregnant by a petty crook and had an abortion at the hands of a butcher, whom Douglas despises. Douglas is just too pure for this world, so its arranged that he leave it.

MCLINTOCK, GEORGE WASHINGTON

MCLINTOCK! (1963, UA)—In a Western version of *The Taming of the Shrew*, **John Wayne** is frustrated by the attitude of his estranged wife, and isn't altogether pleased by the effect on their daughter. In the ending, which is as male chauvinistic as has been filmed, Wayne trails wife Maureen O'Hara all over town with the promise that he's going to give her a good spanking. To the cheers of the towns folks, he does, and it seems to tame her. There's an outdated message here.

MCLONERGAN, FINIAN

FINIAN'S RAINBOW (1968, Warner Brothers)—**Fred Astaire's** feet were still willing, and he insisted that he be shown dancing in full-body shots to prove he hadn't lost his touch, but Fred was defeated by the handling of this 1947 Broadway musical. Perhaps it should have been made 20 years earlier. Astaire has stolen leprechaun Tommy Steele's gold, and the latter wants it back.

MCMASTERS, NEAL

THE MCMASTERS (1970, Chevron)—This film was released with alternate endings. Neither were anything to cheer about. After the Civil War, black union officer Brock Peters returns to the ranch of his former master, **Burl Ives**. Peters is ultimately made co-owner of the property.

MCMORROW, JIMMY

HIS BUDDY'S WIFE (1925, Silent, Associated Exhibitors)—**Glenn Hunter** and Douglas Gilmore become close friends during the fighting in WWI France. Gilmore asks Hunter to look after his family if anything happens to him. Gilmore does not come back from a patrol and Hunter goes to Gilmore's farm to take care of his buddy's wife, Edna Murphy. The two plan to marry, but Gilmore shows up and Hunter walks out of their lives.

MCMULLEN, ADAM, JESSE AND VITO

FAMILY BUSINESS (1989, Tri-Star)—**Matthew Broderick** leaves graduate school to enlist his thieving grandfather **Sean Connery** in a heist he'd like to pull. Eventually, the young man's father, **Dustin Hoffman**, a one-time crook gone straight, is brought in on the caper.

MCMURPHY, RANDLE PATRICK

ONE FLEW OVER THE CUCKOO'S NEST (1975, UA)—This film was the first to win all five top Oscars (film, director, actor, actress, screenplay) since IT HAPPENED ONE NIGHT. **Jack Nicholson** is a brilliant anti-hero. He fights the system with gusto while confined to a mental hospital. His main human adversary is head nurse Louise Fletcher, who will not allow any deviation from the rules. We know the type.

MCNAB, HENRY

WELL DONE, HENRY (1936, GB, Butchers)—Henpecked **Will Fyffe** outwits a crooked financier, and helps his daughter elope.

MCNAB, MALCOLM

SEZ O'REILLY TO MCNAB (1938, GB, Gaumont/GFD)—Scots businessman **Will Fyffe** and an Irish broker promote diet pills.

MCNAIR, ANN

PUBLIC STENOGRAPHER (1935, Screencraft/Marcy)—You might not believe that the story of a public stenographer, played by **Lola Lane**, would make much of a movie. You would be right. Lane's not Joan Crawford in GRAND HOTEL, you know.

MCNAIR, TOM

I TAKE THIS WOMAN (1931, Paramount)—Cowboy **Gary Cooper** and wild heiress Carole Lombard marry before they find out if they are in love. They are in the process of getting a divorce when they realize what they feel for each other.

MCNAMARA, ALEC

THE SPOILERS (1914, Silent, Selig); (1930, Paramount); (1942, Universal); (1955, Universal)—**Thomas Santschi, William "Stage" Boyd, Randolph Scott** and **Rory Calhoun** each play a claim jumper who does things within the law in Alaska during the great Gold Rush. This character has a spectacular fistfight with the hero and in each picture it's the highlight of the film and among the best ever seen in the movies.

MCNAMARA, HEATHER

HEATHERS (1989, New World)—Cheerleader **Lisanne Falk** is the least dominating of the three Heathers who form the most exclusive clique at Sherwood, Ohio's Westerburg High. Ultimately, she becomes a victim of the mean snobbery and abuse she visited on others.

MCNEIL, BENNY

HARRIGAN'S KID (1943, MGM)—Top jockey **Bobby Readick** is the title character in a familiar and not well presented race track yarn.

MCNEIL, JACQUELINE

JACQUELINE (1956, GB, Rank)—In Ireland, **Jacqueline Ryan**, the daughter of a drunkard ship-builder, helps her dad find farm work.

MCNEIL, SANDY

SANDY (1926, Silent, Fox)—Flapper **Madge Bellamy** reluctantly marries the man her father has chosen for her. The man is cruel and causes the death of their child. Bellamy leaves him, becoming involved with two other men. One, Harrison Ford, shoots her and kills himself. The other, Leslie Fenton, is tried for the murder of Ford, but is acquitted when Bellamy recovers in time to tell what really happened.

MCQ, DET. LT. LON

MCQ (1974, Warner Brothers)—Seattle police detective **John Wayne** seeks the killer of his police buddy. He finds the villain to be someone he thought he knew better.

MCQUADE, J.J.

LONE WOLF MCQUADE (1983, Orion)—Martial arts expert **Chuck Norris** appears as a modern Texas Ranger. He takes on a band of mercenaries.

MCQUADE, JAMES

I AM THE MAN (1924, Silent, Chadwick)—Major city political boss **Lionel Barrymore** blackmails Seena Owen into marrying him, even though she loves the district attorney. You know what they say about ill-gotten gains.

MCQUEEN, JOHNNY

ODD MAN OUT (1947, GB, GFD)—**James Mason** is very impressive as a wounded IRA leader, hunted down by the police. He's a Christ-like figure, helped and betrayed as he hurries towards his death, aided by Kathleen Ryan, who chooses to die with him.

MCTEAGUE, TOBY

TOBY MCTEAGUE (1986, Canada, Spectrafilm)—**Yannick Bisson** races husky dog teams in this standard film.

MCVICAR

MCVICAR (1982, GB, Crown International)—**Roger Daltrey**, England's Public Enemy Number One, escapes from prison. He should never have left the WHO.

MCWADE, JIM

THE FABULOUS TEXAN (1947, Republic)—Returning to Texas after the Civil War, Confederate officer **William Elliott** finds things ruled by despotic Albert Dekker who killed Elliott's father. With the help of old friend John Carroll, now a bank robber, Wild Bill leads a crusade against Dekker.

MEADE

THE PURSUIT OF D.B. COOPER (1981, Universal)—The hijacker of a plane, who parachuted out of the plane in 1971 with a $200,000 ransom, never to be heard of again, has been made into a good ole boy folk hero, something akin to Burt Reynolds in SMOKEY AND THE BANDIT. **Treat Williams** handles the role well enough, but hijacking a plane just isn't a hilarious comedy idea.

MEADE, DR.

STRANGE CASE OF DR. MEADE (1939, Columbia)—New York physician **Jack Holt** clashes with southern medico Paul Everton, who wishes to treat an epidemic with herbs and old-fashioned methods.

MEADE, JOHN

JOHN MEADE'S WOMAN (1937, Paramount)—Business tycoon **Edward Arnold** is rejected by the woman he loves. He marries Francine Larrimore on the rebound. He's soon sorry, as she sides with the farmers he's trying to cheat out of their land.

MEADOWS, CASEY

MY CHAUFFEUR (1986, Orion)—**Deborah Freeman** is an aggressive, slightly kooky girl who upsets the male drivers, when she becomes the first female hired as a chauffeur for a limousine service. Some of her clients also mistake the extent of her services.

MEADOWS, HAROLD

GIRL SHY (1924, Silent, Pathe)—Shy, stuttering tailor's apprentice **Harold Lloyd** writes a book called "The Secrets of Making Love," which involves him with any number of vamps, flappers and nice girls.

MEADOWS, SALLY

MODEL FOR MURDER (1960, GB, Cinema Associates)—The Stabbing of fashion model **Hazel Court** is blamed on American merchant marine officer Keith Andres by jewel smugglers.

MEAKIN, JOHN

ENEMY OF THE POLICE (1933, GB, Warner Brothers)—A reform guild's secretary, **John Stuart**, is mistaken for a criminal and is given psychological treatment.

MEARS, LOLA

JUKE GIRL (1942, Warner Brothers)—**Ann Sheridan** tried hard to save this inferior melodrama about itinerant Florida crop-pickers

caught in the middle of a marketing war, but others involved didn't seem to care.

MEDE

MANDINGO (1975, Paramount)—Handsome young black slave **Ken Norton** arouses all the sexual passion that the master's white daughter-in-law Susan George can muster. Her husband is regularly bedding a black female slave, so George may have believed he was racially tolerant. Nope, he has a mean double standard in him.

MEDFORD, ALEXANDRA

THE WITCHES OF EASTWICK (1987, Warner Brothers)—**Cher** is one of the three witches (read unconventional women) in a small hamlet who, unknown to themselves, have sent for self-proclaimed "horny little devil" Jack Nicholson. He provides them with sex and fathers a child by each.

MEDFORD, "DANGEROUS" DIANA

OUR DANCING DAUGHTERS (1928, Silent, MGM)—Twenties flapper **Joan Crawford** loses her wealthy boyfriend John Mack Brown to gold digger Anita Page, but gets him back when her drunken rival falls to her death. This is the film that made Crawford a major star.

MEDLEY, ANGELA

THE BUCKSKIN LADY (1957, UA)—**Patricia Medina**, the girlfriend of western bank robber Gerald Mohr, takes an interest in young doctor Richard Denning.

MEDUSA

SEVEN FACES OF DR. LAO (1964, MGM)—Medusa is just one the of the seven disguises **Tony Randall** assumes as a Chinese showman, who sets up a magic show in a western town, and changes the lives of the locals.

MEEBER, CARRIE

CARRIE (1952, Paramount)—Small-town girl **Jennifer Jones** arrives in Chicago with plans to be an actress. She is aided by assorted lovers (including restaurant manager Laurence Olivier) who are ruined because of her. The film is based on Theodore Dreiser's "Sister Carrie."

MEECHAM, BULL

THE GREAT SANTINI (1979, Orion/Warner Brothers)—**Robert Duvall** is the unpredictable head of an unstable family in a film which owes its reputation to Duvall's superb performance.

MEECHAM, RUTH

WHITE HUNTRESS (1957, American International)—**Susan Stephen**, the daughter of the leader of some settlers traveling through African jungles, is admired by the party's two guides, Robert Urquhart and John Bentley. Villain Alan Tarlton wishes to divert them to search for gold.

MEEKS, BILLY

SPEED CRAZED (1926, Silent, Rayart)—**Billy Sullivan** is forced to drive the get-away car used in a holdup. He's captured and sentenced to jail. He escapes from prison and eventually wins a car race, and sees to it that the crooked gambler who got him into trouble in the first place is arrested and his name cleared.

MEELAH

BLONDE SAVAGE (1947, Eagle Lion)—White jungle princess **Gale Sherwood** lives among African natives. She is revealed to be the long-lost daughter of an explorer.

MEG

MEG (1926, GB, Silent, Wardour)—Runaway **Mabel Armitage** nurses her sister's fiance Noel Greenwood, a mine owner's son, back to health. Bye, bye, sister.

MEGERSEY, JOSEPH "MEGS"

JACKNIFE (1989, Cineplex Odeon)—**Robert De Niro** received the title nickname back in Vietnam because of his fondness for wrecking vehicles. Romance blossoms for the still angry veteran when he visits buddy Ed Harris, who lives with his sister Kathy Baker.

MEI, KWAN

LADY FROM CHUNGKING (1943, PRC)—Chinese patriot **Anna May Wong** has trouble with enemy general Harold Huber, and competes with White Russian Mae Clarke for downed Flying Tiger pilot Rick Vallin.

MEL

A MAN'S MAN (1929, Silent, MGM)—Soda-jerk **William Haines** wins the love of aspiring actress Josephine Dunn.

MEL

THE PRISONER OF SECOND AVENUE (1975, Warner Brothers)—When middle-aged New Yorker **Jack Lemmon** loses his job, he also loses his sense of well-being and nearly suffers a complete breakdown, but is helped to come back by his loving wife, Anne Bancroft. The hard-edge of the humor in this Neil Simon piece makes it difficult to like.

MELBA

CRAZY MAMA (1975, New World)—When widow **Cloris Leachman** loses her beauty parlor she turns to crime, leading a gang which includes her pregnant daughter and the girl's boyfriend.

MELBA, NELLIE

MELBA (1953, GB, UA)—American soprano **Patrice Munsel** impersonates Australian-born prima donna Nellie Melba, but we can see right through her shallow portrayal. She approximates her subject only when she sings. This movie makes a good case for hiring an actress whose singing voice is dubbed.

MELDRICK, GERALD

THEY MET IN BOMBAY (1941, MGM)—Jewel thief **Clark Gable** falls in love with female jewel thief Rosalind Russell in India. He becomes a hero fighting the Japanese during WWII. Gable and Russell will get together again.

MELINDA

MELINDA (1972, MGM)—In a typical black-exploitation movie, Calvin Lockhart stars as a black disc jockey who goes after the killers of his girlfriend **Vonetta McGee**.

MELISSA

SWEET SIXTEEN (1983, Century International)—It's a predictable and not very mysterious story of the murders of the classmates of **Aleisa Shirley** just as she is about to turn sixteen. Do not confuse with SIXTEEN CANDLES, starring Molly Ringwald.

MELLO, TONY

MEN ARE SUCH FOOLS (1933, RKO)—**Leo Carrillo** is an unlucky Italian, who brings his German bride to America and finds her sleeping around. He beats her up, and is sent to prison. He's paroled and finds his wife has committed suicide. Carrillo kills her lover and is put back in prison for life, where he loses his memory.

MELLON, WILLIAM

COUNSEL FOR CRIME (1937, Columbia)—**Otto Kruger** plays a ruthless lawyer in the employ of the mobs.

MELTING MAN, THE

THE INCREDIBLE MELTING MAN (1978, American International)—On his return from orbiting Saturn, astronaut **Alex Rebar**, a goofy skeleton oozing blood, has murder on his mind.

MELTON

ABBOTT AND COSTELLO MEET THE KILLER, BORIS KARLOFF (1949, Universal)—Boris Karloff isn't the killer of a famous criminal lawyer at a swanky resort hotel. **Alan Mowbray** is. But you can never go by the title of an Abbott and Costello movie. In ABBOTT AND COSTELLO GO TO MARS, the boys actually landed on Venus.

MELTON, HARRY

A GENTLEMAN AFTER DARK (1942, UA)—**Brian Donlevy**, a jewel thief and a murderer, gives himself up to his boyhood friend, Preston Foster, now a cop, on the condition that Foster will raise Donlevy's daughter and keep the child away from her no-good mother, Miriam Hopkins. Years later Hopkins plans to ruin her daughter's chance for happiness in marrying a wealthy man, so Donlevy escapes from prison and indirectly causes Hopkins' death.

MELVILLE, RICHARD JOHN III

SHIPMATES FOREVER (1935, Warner Brothers)—**Dick Powell**, the son of an admiral, would rather sing than sail, but with the good advice of Ruby Keeler, he finds he can do both.

MELVILLE, TIM

TIM (1981, Australia, Pisces/Satori)—A romance develops between handsome, mentally retarded young **Mel Gibson** and Piper Laurie, a businesswoman in her mid-forties.

MELVYN, SYBYLLA

MY BRILLIANT CAREER (1980, Australia, New South Wales)—**Judy Davis's** parents despair at her refusal to accept her lot in life, that of drudgery and convention. She insists on having her independence.

MENDELSSOHN, SIMON

SIMON (1980, Warner Brothers)—**Alan Arkin** is brainwashed into believing he's an alien from outer space.

MENDOZA, ALBERT

THE ENFORCER (1957, Warner Brothers)—**Everett Sloane** is the founder of MURDER INCORPORATED. District attorney Humphrey Bogart has just overnight to find some evidence to convict Sloane after his chief witness falls to his death, or be forced to let the murder-for-hire boss go free. It's a fine suspenseful movie.

MENDOZA, MERCEDES

BRIDE OF HATE (1916, Silent, Triangle/Kay Bee)—**Margery Wilson** is the instrument of revenge a southern doctor uses against the seducer of his grand-niece. The cad marries Wilson and then is told by the doctor that "You have married a nigger!" Only when the man has gone to wrack and ruin through drink. and lies dying from a gunshot wound, does the doctor reveal that Wilson is really white, half-Spanish to be exact.

MERCADET, CLAUDE

THE LOVABLE CHEAT (1949, Film Classics)—French con-man **Charles Ruggles** is trying to raise money to arrange a good marriage for his daughter.

MERCEDES, PHIL

MEN AGAINST THE SKY (1940, RKO)—Over-the-hill and discredited flyer **Richard Dix** tries to bring happiness to his sister Wendy Barrie and the man she loves, Kent Taylor, by allowing her to take credit for his design for a new plane.

MERCER, AL

FIVE AGAINST THE HOUSE (1955, Columbia)—**Guy Madison** is the brains of five college students who plan to rob the casinos in Las Vegas to prove it can be done and then return the money, but one of their members has other plans.

MERCIER, CARDINAL

THE CROSS BEARER (1918, Silent, Metro)—At the time of WWI, Belgian cardinal **Montagu Love** defies the Germans by ordering them to stay off the property of the Church or face its curse.

MERE, LADY

THE DIVORCE OF LADY X (1938, GB, London Films)—Barrister Laurence Olivier is to sue unfaithful wife **Binnie Barnes** for divorce on behalf of his client. But Lord Larry believes that the wife is Merle Oberon, the woman he allowed to stay in his hotel room one fateful night.

MEREDITH, JANICE

JANICE MEREDITH (1924, Silent, Metro)—**Marion Davies** and Harrison Ford's love story is set at the time of the American Revolutionary War. The film is filled with many familiar historical occurrences and individuals.

MEREDITH, MARY (THE GHOST)

THE UNINVITED (1944, Paramount)—**Lynda Grey** doesn't have a speaking role in this marvelously frightening ghost story, but her eerie menacing presence is felt by all throughout the film.

MERLIN, COUNT

THE CHARLATAN (1929, Universal)—Fifteen years earlier, circus clown **Holmes Herbert's** wife ran off with a rich man, taking their daughter with her. Now Herbert poses as an Indian seer who discovers his ex is about to dump her second husband for another lover. When she is killed, Herbert is the prime suspect.

MERLIN THE MAGICIAN

SEVEN FACES OF DR. LAO (1964, MGM)—**Tony Randall** takes the form of Merlin in his Chinese magic show when it visits a small western town.

MERMAID

MR. PEABODY AND THE MERMAID (1948, Universal)—**Ann Blyth**, an early Darryl Hannah, is a mermaid hooked by fifty-year-old William Powell while he is in the West Indies. Her existence is cause for questioning Powell's sanity. Powell falls in love with Blyth (she doesn't appear to have Hannah's ability to become all woman on occasion, so the relationship would appear platonic), but she eventually goes back from whence she came and Powell goes back to his wife.

MERMAID QUEEN

THE MERMAIDS OF TIBURON (1962, Aquarez-Pacifica)—**Diane Webber**, the former Marguerite Empey when she was baring all for Playboy magazine, was added to the more sexually explicit release of this silly underseas adventure about mermaids, thought to be the protectors of a fortune in rare pearls.

MERRICK, ANNE

CHEATING BLONDES (1933, Equitable)—**Thelma Todd** is the only blonde and she's not so much a cheat as she is a tease. When she turns down a marriage proposal of a reporter—bad sport that he is—he tries to pin a murder rap on her.

MERRICK, DAN

SHATTERED (1991, MGM/Pathe)—Plagued by violent memories of his life before he was in a devastating car crash that disfigured him and wiped out his memory of his wife, Greta Scacchi, **Tom Berenger** hires private detective Bob Hoskins to help him sort things out.

MERRICK, JOHN

THE ELEPHANT MAN (1980, GB, Paramount)—**John Hurt** is superb as the hideously deformed Victorian man who, after suffering as a freak for most of his life, is a hit in London society.

MERRICK, JOHN P.

THE DEVIL AND MISS JONES (1941, RKO)—**Charles Coburn**, a delightful old cupid, brings together Jean Arthur and Joel McCrea in an apartment they share in crowded Washington. The film was remade in 1966 in WALK, DON'T RUN. But Cary Grant in his film farewell can't match the charm of Coburn.

MERRICK, LAURA

SHOULD LADIES BEHAVE? (1933, MGM)—**Alice Brady** is one of three women, each infatuated with the same man, Conway Tearle, and willing to go to great extremes to get him.

MERRICK, PAUL

MR. MUSIC (1950, Paramount)—Broadway songwriter **Bing Crosby** doesn't write any songs worthy of the voice of singer Crosby in this tame story of a man who would rather play golf than finish a show he's supposed to be writing.

MERRIDAY, ANNE

FOLLIES GIRL (1943, PRC)—Army private Gordon Oliver falls in love with dress designer **Wendy Barrie**. His father puts on a ritzy burlesque show and everyone swings.

MERRILL, BRIG. GEN.

MERRILL'S MARAUDERS (1962, Warner Brothers)—**Jeff Chandler** leads a group of volunteers on a dangerous mission in Burma in 1942. The film demonstrates that war is not glamorous.

MERRILL, DAVID

GUILTY BY SUSPICION (1991, Warner Brothers)—Promising movie director **Robert De Niro** refuses to cooperate with the House Un-American Committee, becomes a hostile witness and is blackballed.

MERRILL, NED

THE SWIMMER (1968, Columbia)—In a strange and not quite successful movie, middle-aged **Burt Lancaster** decides to swim home from a party via the swimming pools of all of his suburban neighbors. Each pool evokes different memories.

MERRIMAN, TOBY

THE DERELICT (1937, GB, Independent Film Distributors)—Old tramp **Malcolm Morley** sells his drawings in order to pay for an operation for a widow's crippled son.

MERRIN, FATHER

THE EXORCIST (1973, Warner Brothers)—**Max Von Sydow** is called in to cast out the demon which has taken up residence in the body of little girl Linda Blair. The film's reputation will not survive the passage of time.

MERRINOE, TIMMIE

THE INVISIBLE BOY (1957, MGM)—**Richard Eyer's** scientist father lets him play with Robby the Robot. Robby makes the boy invisible, which is fun but leads to some problems.

MERRITT, OWEN

MAN IN THE SADDLE (1951, Columbia)—**Randolph Scott** is excellent as the Westerner who reluctantly does battle with gunfighter John Russell, sent to kill him, and then Alexander Knox, the man who sent Russell.

MERRITT, WES

THE LUSTY MEN (1952, RKO)—**Arthur Kennedy,** married to Susan Hayward, has the notion he'd like the life of a cowboy and rodeo rider. He gets weary cowboy Robert Mitchum to instruct him in the highlights of both. The lessons don't take too well as Kennedy doesn't make it as a rodeo star, and Mitchum is killed in the rodeo ring.

MERRIWETHER, MATT

CALL ME BWANA (1963, GB, Rank/UA)—**Bob Hope** makes another one of his embarrassing film appearances in this stinker about a phony author of exploration books, sent by the U.S. government to recover a space capsule lost in an African jungle.

MERROW, DIANA

STRANGERS IN LOVE (1932, Paramount)—**Kay Francis** is the secretary of bad twin Fredric March, who has forged his father's will to disinherit good twin Fredric March. When the bad twin has a heart attack, the good twin takes his place, fooling everyone including Miss Francis with whom he falls in love.

MERRY, FIRST SGT. MIKE

SERGEANTS 3 (1962, MGM)—In a lousy westernization of GUNGA DIN, **Frank Sinatra** stands in for Victor McLaglen—and is that a laugh. The film has some comical moments but is not worth staying up past ten o'clock to see on television.

MESSENGER, ADRIAN

THE LIST OF ADRIAN MESSENGER (1963, Universal)—**John Merivale** is a young Englishman who asks an old friend to check to see what has become of a group of men on a list he has. Merivale then is one of many killed when the plane he is travelling in is blown out of the air by a bomb. His friend, George C. Scott, discovers that those on the list are dead. He must then solve the mystery of what they have to do with his friend and why everyone on the list has been killed. Kirk Douglas shows up to provide the answers.

MESSY TESSIE

THE GARBAGE PAIL KIDS (1987, Atlantic)—**Sue Rossitto's** contribution to making adults in the audience sick is politely put as a nasty case of nasal drip. Pre-teens, who begged to see this movie, no doubt enjoy being grossed out. This junk comes from bubble-gum cards parodying the Cabbage Patch Kids? Topps should be ashamed of themselves.

MEXICALI ROSE

MEXICALI ROSE (1929, Columbia)—**Barbara Stanwyck's** man-crazy behavior gets her kicked out of town, and eventually leads to her murder.

MICAH

THE PRODIGAL (1955, MGM)—**Edmund Purdom** appears in this biblical trash as the rich man's son who squanders his inheritance, but is taken in by his father after he has suffered and learned some humility. His homecoming isn't welcomed by his hard-working brother or the fatted-calf.

MICHAEL

THE DEER HUNTER (1978, Columbia/Warner Brothers)—**Robert De Niro** is a Pennsylvania steel worker who does hunt deer, which he insists must be taken with a single shot. He and two friends join the army, are sent to Vietnam, are captured by the enemy, tortured by being forced to play a version of Russian roulette, and finally escape, with only De Niro coming home "whole" in any real sense.

MICHAEL

THE LOST BOYS (1987, Warner Brothers)—A new family in a California town discovers the local juvenile delinquents like **Jason Patric,** on top of everything else, are vampires.

MICHAEL

MY SON, THE HERO (1943, PRC)—War correspondent **Joseph Allen Jr.** comes home to find that his father Roscoe Karns has been doing his bit for the war effort.

MICHAEL XI, KING

THE ROYAL RIDER (1929, Silent, First National)—**Phillipe De Lacey,** the king of Alvania, is so impressed by the performers in Ken Maynard's Wild West Show that he hires them to be his palace guards.

MICHAELA

THE DEVIL'S WIDOW (1972, GB, British International)—Roddy McDowall directed this horror movie, and he should be sent back to the Planet of the Apes. In it, **Ava Gardner** is an older woman who uses witchcraft to keep her the center of young jet-setters.

MICHAELS, DOROTHY See MICHAEL DORSEY

MICHAELS, LORETTA

NEW YORK'S FINEST (1988, Platinum)—**Jennifer Delora** and two other Queens hookers are tired of being hassled by the vice squad. They take lessons on being ladies from a transvestite.

MICHAELSON, MOLLIE

TAKE HER, SHE'S MINE (1963, 20th Century Fox)—**Sandra Dee's** father James Stewart tries to protect her from college beatniks and a French artist whom he doesn't trust as far as he can throw. Of course, it's a losing battle.

MICHEL

THE BLACK PIRATE (1926, Silent, UA)—In the first full-length two-tone Technicolor movie, **Douglas Fairbanks** climbs to the top of a ship's mast and then descends to the deck by piercing the sail with his sword, ripping the canvas as he goes down. The movie is worth seeing for this scene alone. As for the story, Fairbanks is an aristocrat who becomes a pirate to avenge his father's death.

MICHELANGELO

TEENAGE MUTANT NINJA TURTLES (1990, New Line); TEENAGE MUTANT NINJA TURTLES II: THE SECRET OF OOZE (1991, New Line)—Is **Michelan Sisti** the teenage turtle who casually tosses around words like "bodacious," "awesome" and "gnarly"? Well it's one of the four. If you've seen one teenage mutant ninja turtle, you've seen 'em all. In the sequel, **Sisti** and his three mean reptilian superheroes learn of their origins from their giant rat master Splinter (voice of Kevin Clark).

MICHIGAN KID

THE MICHIGAN KID (1947, Universal)—**Jon Hall** is one of an assortment of characters searching for a treasure which has been stolen from a stagecoach.

MICK

BAD BOYS (1983, EMI/Universal)—**Sean Penn** and Esai Morales are Chicago gang members sworn to kill each other in prison.

MICK

WHERE HAS POOR MICKEY GONE? (1964, GB, Ledecl-Indigo)—An Italian carnival magician Warren Mitchell, persecuted by hooligan **John Malcolm** and two of his buddies, makes them all three disappear.

MICKEY

THE GOONIES (1985, Warner Brothers)—**Sean Austin** and his friends in a housing development, scheduled for elimination, discover a treasure ship underground. The production is hit-and-miss but it has some enjoyable parts, even if the story is unevenly developed and the acting is hammy.

MICKEY

MICKEY (1919, Silent, Sennett)—**Mabel Normand** is very funny as a western girl sent east, and forced to work as a maid.

MICKEY

MICKEY (1948, Eagle Lion)—Teenager **Lois Butler** plays matchmaker for her widower father.

MICKEY

MICKEY, THE KID (1939, Republic)—**Tommy Ryan** lives in the slums with his criminal father, Bruce Cabot. When the latter kills a bank teller in a hold-up, he takes Ryan with him on the run, hijacking a bus full of school kids. Cabot will be killed doing one good thing, and Ryan becomes a hero by saving the kids from freezing to death when the bus gets stuck in a snowdrift.

MICKEY

TWO HEARTS IN HARMONY (1935, GB, British International)—Cabaret singer **Bernice Claire** marries Lord George Curzon, after being made his son's nanny.

MICKEY ONE

MICKEY ONE (1960, Columbia)—Nightclub comedian **Warren Beatty** searches for some meaning to his life, but he seems hopelessly lost.

MIDDLECOTT, SUSAN

A WOMAN OF DISTINCTION (1950, Columbia)—Scandal revolves around a visiting professor Ray Milland and it trickles over into the life of Dean **Rosalind Russell**.

MIDDLEMAN, HARVEY

HARVEY MIDDLEMAN, FIREMAN (1965, Columbia)—Mild-mannered fireman **Gene Troobnick** exhibits some of the characteristics of Walter Mitty.

MIDDLETON, MOLLY

OUR LITTLE GIRL (1935, Fox)—**Shirley Temple** stars in this overly-sentimental piece as a doctor's daughter who brings her parents back together.

MIDDLETON, TOWNSEND

SPENDTHRIFT (1936, Paramount)—Polo-playing millionaire playboy **Henry Fonda** spends all of his money. Now what is he to do? Just remember in Hollywood, anything is possible.

MIDGET

THE UNHOLY THREE (1930, MGM)—**Harry Eccles** is a midget who poses as a baby, working scams with his carnival friends, Lon Chaney as a carnival ventriloquist and strong man Ivan Linow. In the silent version in 1925, Eccles played the same role but was called Tweedledee.

MIFAWNY

A WELCH SINGER (1915, GB, Silent, Butchers)—Shepherdess **Florence Turner** becomes an opera star.

MIGGS, ADOLPHUS

THE DEPUTY DRUMMER (1935, GB, Columbia)—Poor composer **Lupino Lane**, posing as a lord, attends a house-party given by a lady, where he catches jewel thieves.

MIGUEL

. . . AND NOW MIGUEL (1966, Universal)—Young **Pat Cardi** waits impatiently for the day when he can accompany his shepherd father into the mountains and tend their flock of sheep.

MIKADO, THE

THE MIKADO (1939, GB, Universal); (1967, GB, Warner Brothers)—**John Barclay** appears in the title role in this version of the Gilbert and Sullivan operetta. **Donald Adams** takes over in the 1967 production. G&S fans will appreciate "Three Little Maids," "Tit-Willow, Tit-Willow," "The Flowers That Bloom in the Spring, Tra La" and "A Wandering Minstrel."

MIKADO, JUDGE

THE COOL MIKADO (1963, GB, UA)—While in Tokyo, Kevin Scott, the soldier son of American judge **Stubby Kaye**, is kidnapped by the gangster fiance of Jill Mai Meredith, the girl Scott loves.

MIKE

FOR THE LOVE OF MIKE (1933, GB, BIP/Wardour)—Heiress **Constance Shotter** asks her guardian's secretary to steal back her power of attorney.

MIKE

MIKE (1926, Silent, MGM)—**Sally O'Neil** lives in a converted freight car with her railroad worker father, and loves telegrapher William Hianes.

MIKE

MIKE'S MURDER (1984, Warner Brothers)—When small-time L.A. drug dealer and part-time tennis pro **Mark Keyloun** is killed, his one-night-stand girlfriend Debra Winger tries to find out why. She's the only one who cares, and that includes the audience.

MIKE

THE MINSTREL BOY (1937, GB, Butchers)—Irish band leader **Fred Conyngham** marries a socialite despite the fact she suspects he loves the singer with his band.

MIKEY

MIKEY AND NICKY (1976, Paramount)—Elaine May directed this story of **Peter Falk** and John Cassavetes, two small-time criminals who have been friends since childhood.

MIKEY
LOOK WHO'S TALKING (1989, Tri-Star)—In a movie that may start a trend, **Bruce Willis** is the voice of unmarried Kirstie Alley's baby. The little bastard would like to find a husband for mommy and a daddy for himself. Would you believe John Travolta?

MILAN, LISA
THREE HATS FOR LISA (1965, GB, Warner Brothers-Pathe)—A dock worker and a taxi driver help Italian film star **Sophie Hardy** steal a bowler, a busby and a policeman's helmet to add to her collection of head-wear.

MILDE, MONTY
ATTA BOY! (1926, Silent, Pathe Exchange)—Comedian **Monty Banks** is a tiny man who takes his life in his hands doing a series of dangerous stunts which makes for some very funny moments.

MILES
THE INNOCENTS (1961, US/GB, 20th Century Fox)—In this classic chiller, based on Henry James "The Turn if the Screw," **Martin Stephens** and his sister Pamela Franklin seem to be possessed by former servants, now dead.

MILES, GEORGIA
FOUR FRIENDS (1981, Filmways)—**Jodi Thelan** is a free-thinking young woman, loved by young immigrant Craig Wasson and two of his friends during the 1960s and 1970s.

MILES, JERRY
ADVENTURES OF A ROOKIE (1943, RKO); ROOKIES IN BURMA (1943, RKO)—**Wally Brown** and his movie partner Alan Carney are a pair of nitwit army recruits, who run afoul of all army regulations. The duo has learned nothing by the time they are stationed in Burma. If anything they are even more scatterbrained.

MILL, GRIFFIN
THE PLAYER (1992, First Line/Avenue)—Hot-shot studio executive **Tim Robbins** receives a series of threatening postcards from a disgruntled screenwriter. Unnerved, Robbins tracks down the man he suspects of sending the cards and accidently kills him in a fight. The postcards keep coming, but in this satire of the Hollywood power structure, Robbins discovers he can live with having killed an innocent man. He becomes a hypocrite and is rewarded with more power in the movie industry. The film is filled with cameo appearances by dozens of film stars.

MILLER, ANNE P. "DAISY"
DAISY MILLER (1974, Paramount)—**Cybill Shepherd** appears as Henry James' 1878 American girl, touring the continent. She falls in love with Barry Brown and dies of malaria.

MILLER, BETTY
THE CHURCH MOUSE (1934, GB, Warner Brothers)—Efficient and straight-laced secretary **Laura La Plante** changes her dowdy looks, becomes an irresistible beauty and wins her banker employer, Ian Hunter.

MILLER, BETTY
UNWED MOTHER (1958, Allied Artists)—**Norma Moore** appears in a movie whose title tells all there is to know. The film doesn't have any new insights in the problem of a girl "in trouble."

MILLER, BUDDY
THE BANDIT BUSTER (1926, Silent, Action)—**Buddy Roosevelt** tracks down a kidnapped millionaire, rescuing him in time to complete a deal that makes both of them rich.

MILLER, CHRISTINE ("SAL WILLIS")
UNDERCOVER GIRL (1950, Universal)—New York policewoman **Alexis Smith** goes undercover to investigate her father's death, and uncovers a drug ring.

MILLER, CONSTANCE
MCCABE AND MRS. MILLER (1971, Warner Brothers)—Prostitute **Julie Christie** teams with small-time gambler Warren Beatty to provide the things that miners in a western boom town most want after a hard day's dig. The big mining interests want to cut themselves in when the enterprise becomes a huge success.

MILLER, DANIEL
DEFENDING YOUR LIFE (1991, Warner Brothers)—After crashing his new BMW into a bus, **Albert Brooks** dies and arrives at Judgment City, where the recently deceased have their lives reviewed in order to determine their next destination. He falls for Meryl Streep, but it doesn't look like they're going to go to the same place.

MILLER, ED & CLELL
THE LONG RIDERS (1980, UA)—**Dennis** and **Randy Quaid** are among the real life brothers who team up in this western story of outlaw brothers, attempting to rob the banks of Northfield, Minnesota. They receive a welcome they aren't expecting.

MILLER, EDDIE
THE SNIPER (1952, Columbia)—In a fine "B" picture, mentally deranged **Arthur Franz** can't stop himself from shooting women.

MILLER, GLENN
THE GLENN MILLER STORY (1953, Universal)—**James Stewart** sort of looks like Glenn Miller in this biopic in which the best things are the authentic Glenn Miller music.

MILLER, HANS
THE JUGGLER (1953, Columbia)—German-Jew juggler **Kirk Douglas**, has survived the Nazi concentration camps, which took the lives of his wife and children. He tries to adjust to a new life in Israel.

MILLER, HENRY & JUNE
HENRY AND JUNE (1990, Universal)—The title of the film and the title of the book upon which it is based is misleading . It should be called HENRY AND ANAIS, since it is the story of the secret passionate love affair of writers Henry Miller and Anais Nin in Paris in 1931-32. **Fred Ward** is splendid as the hedonist writer whose work would still be considered obscene by many. Marie de Madeiros is excellent as the insatiable Nin. **Uma Thurman** is Miller's wife, who also shares de Medeiros' bed, but is not so understanding when she learns Ward is doing the same.

MILLER, JANE
SHE WANTED A MILLIONAIRE (1932, Fox)—**Joan Bennett** gets what she wanted, millionaire James Kirkwood, but his extreme jealously and bouts of insanity make his money look less attractive. When he's killed after trying to do in Bennett, she goes back to old sweetheart Spencer Tracy, less financially well-off but much more amicable.

MILLER, JOHN
LOCAL BOY MAKES GOOD (1931, First National)—To impress a girl at another college, botanist **Joe E. Brown** claims to be a great athlete. Then he must live up to the boast.

MILLER, JOSEPH

I COVER THE WATERFRONT (1933, UA)—Reporter **Ben Lyon's** beat is the waterfront. He falls in love with Claudette Colbert, the daughter of the smuggler whose activities he's trying to expose.

MILLER, LOIS

HER HUSBAND'S TRADEMARK (1922, Silent, Paramount)—**Gloria Swanson's** husband Stuart Holmes likes to have his wife dress well, even when he doesn't have the where-for-all to buy her things. When she attracts the attention of wealthy Richard Wayne, Holmes hopes to benefit from the infatuation.

MILLER, LUCAS

KINGS AND DESPERATE MEN (1984, GB, Blue Dolphin)—Political extremist **Alexis Kannen** takes over a radio station at gun point. A talk show host holds a "call-in trial."

MILLER, NATALIE

ME, NATALIE (1969, National General)—**Patty Duke** gives a fine performance as an unattractive N.Y.C. girl trying to discover who she is.

MILLER, NIFTY

THE BARKER (1928, Part-Talkie, First National/Warner Brothers)—Sound was added after the completion of this story of tent-show barker **Milton Sills**, and the addition almost ruined the film.

MILLER, PAULINE

I'LL WAIT FOR YOU (1941, MGM)—**Marsha Hunt** is the farmer's daughter, who makes New York racketeer Robert Sterling like the country air when he's forced to flee the cops of the big city. The title is what Hunt promises to do for Sterling when he decides to go straight and pay his debt to society.

MILLER, SKIPPER

MISTER 880 (1950, 20th Century Fox)—**Edmund Gwenn** is a lovable old incompetent counterfeiter. His five dollar bills look like they were made by a child, but still he is able to pass them for years, before being caught by a sympathetic treasury agent, Burt Lancaster.

MILLER, TONY

A GENTLEMAN AT HEART (1942, 20th Century Fox)—Bookie **Cesar Romero** falls in love with Carole Landis, the manager of an art shop. She introduces him to the finer things, causing him to give up taking bets on nags and to enter the art world where he discovers there are as many chiselers and crooks as there are in gambling.

MILLER VERNE

VERNE MILLER (1988, Alive)—**Scott Glenn** appears as a real-life midwestern gangster of the twenties. It's terrible.

MILLIE

MILLIE (1931, RKO)—**Helen Twelvetrees**, who has had her share of unsuccessful love affairs, guns down one of her former lovers who's now sniffing around her daughter.

MILLIE

THIS MAN IS MINE (1946, GB, Columbia British)—**Glynis Johns** is the daughter of a crazy family, in whose home Canadian soldier Hugh McDermott is billeted over a Christmas holiday. She goes for him, but so do others.

MILLIGAN, CONNIE

THE MORE THE MERRIER (1943, Columbia)—**Jean Arthur** finds herself sharing the rent of a hard-to-find apartment in crowded pre-WWII Washington with old smoothy Charles Coburn, who turns around and rents half of his half to handsome Joel McCrea. With a boost from Coburn, romance blooms in this sparkling comedy.

MILLS, BEDFORD

THE MAN WHO (1921, Silent, Metro)—Bank clerk **Bert Lytell** can get nowhere with a socialite until he proves himself a man of the world. Deciding that shoes are too expensive, he leads a crusade to do without shoes, becoming a national curiosity. He finds a girl who likes him despite the fact that her father is the president of a shoe company.

MILLS, BILLY

RUNNING BRAVE (1983, Canada, Buena Vista)—**Robby Benson** stars in the true story of a South Dakota Sioux Indian who becomes the only American in Olympic history to win the gold medal in the 10,000 meter run (at the 1964 Tokyo Olympics).

MILLS, CELESTE & JESSIE

MY STEPMOTHER IS AN ALIEN (1988, Weintraub)—Widower Dan Aykroyd marries alien, **Kim Basinger**. His 11-year old daughter **Alyson Hannigan** is perturbed when she discovers that her new mother is from a different galaxy.

MILLS, COL. DABNEY

THE TAR HEEL WARRIOR (1917, Silent, Triangle)—**Walt Whitman**, a gentleman of the old South, loses his plantation, loses $5,000 entrusted to him by his granddaughter's stockbroker husband, and loses his will to live.

MILLS, FLAVIA

TENTH AVENUE ANGEL (1948, MGM)—Loveable **Margaret O'Brien**, living in a New York tenement, tries to improve the conditions of her neighbors.

MILLS, JUNE

FALLEN ANGEL (1945, 20th Century Fox)—**Alice Faye** retired from films after this dramatic role as a wealthy woman who is part of a romantic triangle with a press agent and a sultry waitress, who is murdered.

MILLY

SEVEN BRIDES FOR SEVEN BROTHERS (1954, MGM)—When mountain man Howard Keel goes to town one day looking for a bride, he feels that cute little **Jane Powell** is just the gal for him. Sensing something which passes for love at first sight, she agrees. What he didn't tell her was that she must share her home with Keels's six loutish brothers. When the latter, encouraged by Keel, kidnap brides for themselves, Powell sends her husband off for a long lonely winter. The arrival of spring and her baby puts things right for all concerned.

MILNER, DAN

HIS KIND OF WOMAN (1951, RKO)—The sparks flew between **Robert Mitchum** and co-star Jane Russell in this story of gambler Mitchum being set up to be the fall-guy in an attempt to smuggle a Lucky Luciano-like mobster back into the U.S.

MILO

DUDES (1987, New Century-Vista)—**Flea (Michael Balzary)** and his punk rock buddies are not well-received when they tour in redneck country in the South.

MILTON, POLLY

AN OLD-FASHIONED GIRL (1948, Eagle Lion)—**Gloria Jean** is an independent music teacher intent on making it on her own, rather than come under the dominance of her wealthy relatives.

MIMI

THE MAD DANCER (1925, Silent, Janus)—**Ann Pennington** poses nude for a sculptor, and her sacrifice for art haunts her for years to come.

MIMI

MIMI (1935, GB, Alliance)—In this version of *La Boheme*, in 1850 poor French girl **Gertrude Lawrence** helps a playwright to succeed before she dies.

MINAFER, ISABEL AMBERSON & GEORGE AMBERSON

THE MAGNIFICENT AMBERSONS (1942, RKO)—In what Orson Welles considered to be a film ruined by the studio's cutting, **Dolores Costello** is the daughter of the head of a once proud Indiana family. Years earlier, she had turned down Joseph Cotten as a husband, as he didn't appear to have enough ambition. Years later, Cotten, now a success in the automobile business, returns with his daughter Anne Baxter, still interested in widow Costello. Her son, **Tim Holt**, a spoiled prig who believes he and his family deserve the special place they have in society, does all in his power to deny his mother happiness with Cotten, even though he's smitten with Baxter. He gets his comeuppance when he discovers the family fortune has vanished, much to the delight of most of the locals. We don't know what the film might have been if produced exactly as Welles wanted, but we do know a film masterpiece when we see one.

MINDSZENTY, CARDINAL

GUILTY OF TREASON (1950, Eagle Lion)—**Charles Bickford** is splendid in his recreation of the Hungarian Cardinal brought to trial by the Communists on the charge of treason.

MINER, BILL

THE GREY FOX (1983, Canada, UA)—**Richard Farnsworth**, an old-time train robber, is released from prison after many years. At his time in life, how is he going to learn a new trade? Farnsworth is a delight.

MINICK, GRANDPA

THE EXPERT (1932, Warner Brothers)—This film depended more on the personality of **Charles "Chic" Sale** than it did on Edna Ferber's story of an elderly man who moves in with his son who lives in Chicago.

MINICK, JOSIE

THE BALLAD OF JOSIE (1968, Universal)—In 1890, Wyoming widow **Doris Day** turns a run-down farm into a sheep ranch, and even as cute as she is, cattlemen are not pleased.

MINIVER, KAY & CLEM

MRS. MINIVER (1942, MGM); THE MINIVER STORY (1950, GB, MGM)—**Greer Garson** wasn't the first choice for the role of Kay Miniver. Norma Shearer and Ann Harding who had more clout than Garson with the studio turned down the role because they didn't want audiences to think of them as women old enough to have a grown son as did the noble English woman. With her husband, played by **Walter Pidgeon**, Garson dealt with war with courage and dignity on what should have been the home-front, but death and destruction comes to their village. Revisionist movie historians and critics would have us believe that this beautiful movie is merely sentimental propaganda, but for those old enough or sensitive enough this picture marvelously shows how a family dealt with pain and hardship and still had enough hope to go on. The sequel is another thing altogether, being merely a boring attempt to cash in on the success of the earlier picture. In it Garson is dying and that was also the fate of the movie.

MINNIE

GIRL OF THE GOLDEN WEST (1930, First National)—**Ann Harding** plays poker with a sheriff who loves her to determine if she and her highwayman lover will keep their freedom.

MINTEER, ANITA

GUNCRAZY (1992, Zeta Entertainment)—Sixteen-year-old class tramp **Drew Barrymore** corresponds with convict James Le Gros. When he writes, "I always dreamed of a girl who likes guns," Barrymore learns to shoot. She even kills her mom's boyfriend, Joe Dallesandro when he tries to end their sexual relationship. When Le Gros gets out of prison, he's a born-again Christian. They try to live the straight life but gun lust gets to them and they start a killing spree.

MIRA

FIVE BRANDED WOMEN (1960, Paramount)—**Carla Gravina** is one of five Yugoslavian girls who have their hair sheared for consorting with the Germans. They redeem themselves in the underground.

MIRACLE, JOE

MR. SOFT TOUCH (1949, Columbia)—Ex-GI **Glenn Ford** has a romance with a social worker, Evelyn Keyes, and a run-in with a nightclub-owning gangster.

MIRANDA

MIRANDA (1949, GB, Ealing); MAD ABOUT MEN (1954, GB, FBO)—Married Doctor Griffith Jones is trapped by a mermaid, **Glynis Johns**. She threatens to keep him in her cave unless he shows her the sights of London. He puts her in a wheelchair with a blanket over her fish parts and complies. She picks up a school of male admirers. In the sequel, Johns is back as mermaid Miranda and a young woman who at least facially is Miranda's double. Thus the picture has all the usual aspects of mistaken identity plots as well as keeping a secret about Johns' tail.

MIRANDA

WICKED STEPMOTHER (1989, MGM-UA)—In her final film, **Bette Davis** is a sorceress. Her character disappears about halfway through the film, replaced by Barbara Carrera, claiming to be Davis' daughter.

MIRBEAU, JULIE

LADY FROM LOUISIANA (1941, Republic)—In old Mississippi, **Ona Munson**, the daughter of a man who runs a lottery, falls in love with John Wayne, only to discover that he's a lawyer charged with putting an end to her father's illegal business.

MIRCALLA

LUST FOR A VAMPIRE (1971, Hammer)—**Yvette Stensgaard** is a lesbian vampire plying her trade at a girls' boarding school. She does have time for vamping a couple of men.

MIRELLE, ANNA

LADIES SHOULD LISTEN (1934, Paramount)—Switchboard operator **Frances Drake** is secretly in love with a young man about town, Cary Grant.

MIRIAM

OUTCAST (1928, Silent, First National)—**Corinne Griffith** jilts her lover for a wealthy man, regrets her decision, tries to go back to the first fellow, is talked out of it by the man's new romantic interest, and returns once again to her husband.

MIRIAM

VAMPYRES, DAUGHTERS OF DRACULA (1977, GB, Cambist)—**Anulka** is a bisexual vampire. She lures men to the castle she shares with her vampire sister-lover Marianne Moore for blood and sex orgies.

MIRO, CANE

THE GUNSLINGER (1956, Associated Releasing Corp.)—**John Ireland** sort of gets lost in the shuffle in this western which features two women, Beverly Garland and Allison Hayes, taking each other on, ankle deep in mud in a western war.

MISSOURI LADY, THE

FIVE BOLD WOMEN (1960, Citation)—**Merry Anders** is one of five female murderers being transported across Texas to prison by U.S. Marshal Jeff Morrow. He and Anders are romantically interested in each other but she doesn't survive the trip, what with its Indian attacks and the hardships.

MITCH

BORN AMERICAN (1986, Cinema Group)—**Steve Durham** is one of three young Americans vacationing in Finland. When they accidently cross the border into the U.S.S.R., they discover the Cold War isn't over.

MITCH

ONCE A THIEF (1950, UA)—Con-man **Cesar Romero** relieves shoplifter June Havoc of all her savings and then turns her over to the police. When she gets out of prison, she gets even and Romero is accidentally killed.

MITCHELL

MITCHELL (1975, Allied Artists)—**Joe Don Baker** is a tough city cop who hates drug dealers.

MITCHELL

PHANTOM RANCHER (1940, Colony)—**Ken Maynard** tries to undo the harm his late uncle had done local farmers by donning a mask and going around to the farms of his uncle's victims, leaving them with enough money to pay their mortgages.

MITCHELL, BOB

HER JUNGLE LOVE (1938, Paramount)—**Ray Milland** and Dorothy Lamour, so successful in JUNGLE PRINCESS, were brought together again in a romance between handsome visitor Milland and sarong-wrapped island girl, Lamour.

MITCHELL, GEN. BILLY

THE COURT MARTIAL OF BILLY MITCHELL (1955, Warner Brothers)—Air force advocate **Gary Cooper** prophesied not only the importance of bombers in future wars but also the attack of the Japanese on Pearl Harbor many years before it happened. His reward is to be court-martialed for defying his superiors.

MITCHELL, HARRY

52 PICK-UP (1986, Cannon)—**Roy Scheider** is picked by a gang as a likely blackmail victim. They have him seduced by a beautiful girl and when he refuses to buckle under to their threats of exposing his infidelity to his wife, Ann-Margret, they kill the girl with his gun to have something else to hold over his head.

MITCHELL, PETER

THREE MEN AND A BABY (1987, Buena Vista); THREE MEN AND A LITTLE LADY (1990, Buena Vista)—**Tom Selleck** is one of three successful bachelors who find their lives complicated by a baby left at their door by the ex-lover of one of their members, Ted Danson. In the sequel, confirmed bachelor Selleck has fallen in love with the now five-year-old's mother Nancy Travis but hasn't admitted it to himself or her. Travis accepts a proposal of marriage and plans to move to England. This moves Selleck to action, and together with Danson and Guttenberg, he's off to England to claim Travis for himself.

MITCHELL, STEVE

SHARPSHOOTERS (1938, 20th Century Fox)—**Brian Donlevy** is a newsreel cameraman who gets shots of the assassination of the king of a mythical country, and discovers a plot to also kill the crown prince.

MITCHELL, TOM

A LAWMAN IS BORN (1937, Republic)—**Johnny Mack Brown**, once an up-and-coming actor in dramas, spent most of his later career in westerns such as this one in which he foils land grabbers.

MITROV, BORIS

MAN ON A STRING (1960, Columbia)—Russian-born Hollywood producer **Ernest Borgnine** is forced by the Russians to work as a spy because of his family in the old country, but he becomes a double-agent.

MITSI

THE ROSE OF PARIS (1924, Silent, Universal)—Orphan **Mary Philbin** leaves the convent where she was raised to go to Paris where she is cheated out of her inheritance, and falls in love with a Marquis who puts things right.

MITTY, WALTER

THE SECRET LIFE OF WALTER MITTY (1947, RKO)—**Danny Kaye** is at his best as a mama's boy who constantly daydreams of his acts of derring-do, always admired by the same beautiful blonde. Then his dreams come true as the real-life girl, Virginia Mayo, needs his help with murderous spies.

MOLIER, CPL. PIERRE

TEN TALL MEN (1951, Columbia)—In this tongue in cheek farce, **Kieron Moore** is one of nine jailed French Foreign Legionnaires who volunteer to follow sergeant Burt Lancaster in defending a city from an attack by Riff bandits.

MOLLY *See* **ANGEL**

MOLLY

LOVIN' MOLLY (1974, Columbia)—**Blythe Danner** is excellent as the lifelong love of two Texas friends.

MOLLY

MOLLY AND ME (1945, 20th Century Fox)—**Gracie Fields** leads a group of out-of-work English entertainers, who take domestic positions in the home of grumpy old Monty Woolley and change his life.

MOLLY O'

MOLLY O' (1921, Silent, Associated First National)—**Mabel Normand**, the daughter of an Irish laborer, falls in love with a prominent physician on seeing his picture in a newspaper. Sure . . . and doesn't she ultimately win him.

MOM
PARENTS (1988, Vestron)—**Mary Beth Hurt's** son may or may not have an overactive imagination, but his parents are a bit strange themselves.

"MOME, LA"
THE GIRL FROM MAXIM'S (1936, GB, London Films)—Married doctor Leslie Henson is forced to pass off Parisian singer **Frances Day** as his wife.

MONA
GOLD DIGGERS IN PARIS (1938, Warner Brothers)—The Gold Diggers formula had just about petered out when **Gloria Dickson** joined some other pretty young women in Paris looking for rich husbands.

MONAHAN, JIMMY, PATSY & PETE
THE MERRY MONAHANS (1944, Universal)—**Donald O'Connor** and **Peggy Ryan** are the two grown children of vaudevillian **Jack Oakie** who, twenty years after being tricked into an unhappy marriage, meets his former sweetheart, Rosemary De Camp, who has a grown daughter, Ann Blyth.

MONAHAN, BRIDGET
SHE DIDN'T SAY NO (1962, GB, Warner Brothers)—**Eileen Herlie** is a widow with five children by five different men. Her neighbors in a small village wish she'd move away.

MONDAY, JOE
THE MAN WHO WOULDN'T TALK (1940, 20th Century Fox)—**Lloyd Nolan** is involved in a crime and accidentally kills the witness who could clear him. He resigns himself to death, changing his name so his family won't be hurt, but the police are not interested in a martyr victim, and seek out the truth which eventually sets Nolan free.

MONDAY, PIERCE & WENDELL
MY BROTHER'S WEDDING (1983, Burnett)—Angry Watts resident **Everett Silas** must choose between going to his best friend's funeral or attending the wedding of his brother **Dennis Kemper**, whom Silas resents.

MONIKA, PRINCESS
THE PRINCE AND THE BEGGERMAID (1921, GB, Silent, Ideal) - **Kathleen Vaughn** poses as a beggar to escape marrying a king's hunch-backed brother.

MONKS, BENJAMIN
THE NOTORIOUS MR. MONKS (1958, Republic)—**Paul Fix** is a murdering hitchhiker.

MONROE, HARRY
STIR CRAZY (1980, Columbia)—New Yorkers **Richard Pryor** and Gene Wilder, on their way to California, are wrongly convicted of bank robbery and are thrown into the pen. They have some comical moments as they consider making a break-out.

MONROE, MILES
SLEEPER (1973, UA)—**Woody Allen** is accidentally frozen and wakes up 200 years later in a fascist state where all the work is done by robots. Secret police brainwash or totally eliminate anyone who

chooses to have an independent thought. It's not among Allen's best work.

MONROE, DR. STEVEN
THE MEDICO OF PAINTED SPRINGS (1941, Columbia)—In this first of a trio of films in which **Charles Starrett** played Dr. Monroe, he examines recruits for Teddy Roosevelt's Rough Riders and straightens out troubles between cattlemen and sheepmen.

MONSTER, THE
FRANKENSTEIN AND THE MONSTER FROM HELL (1974, GB, Hammer)—**Dave Prowse**, who later becomes STAR WARS' Darth Vader, is Frankenstein's creation, a hairy ape-like creature put together with parts from inmates of an insane asylum.

MONSTER, THE
FRANKENSTEIN MEETS THE WOLF MAN (1943, Universal)—**Bela Lugosi** takes over Boris Karloff's role as Baron Frankenstein's spare-parts creation. He has his problems with Lon Chaney's wolf man in this first of the all-star monster movies.

MONSTER, THE
MONSTER IN THE CLOSET (1987, Troma)—In this spoof-tribute to the sci-fi flicks of the 1950s, **Kevin Peter Hall** is a monster who pops out of closets and kills people.

MONSTER, THE
THE MONSTER OF HIGHGATE PONDS (1961, GB, Halas & Batchelor) - Children hatch a Malayan monster, **Roy Vincente**, and save it from circus showmen.

MONSTER, THE
THE MONSTER OF PIEDRAS BLANCAS (1959, Vanwick)—**Jack Kevan** portrays the monster which lives in a cave near a lighthouse. He has horns, claws and a hellish face. He enjoys ripping the heads off of people. Kevan also is the producer of the film.

MONTAG THE MAGNIFICENT
THE WIZARD OF GORE (1970, Mayflower)—**Ray Sager** is a magician who asks for female volunteers from the audience. He saws a woman in half and drives a stake through the head of another. His assistants leave the theater whole, but later experience horrible deaths.

MONTANA KID
KING OF THE RODEO (1929, Silent, Universal)—The title refers to **Hoot Gibson** who is the star of the rodeo circuit.

MONTANA, TONY
SCARFACE (1983, Universal)—**Al Pacino** appears in an up-to-date version of the Paul Muni classic gangster film. The setting this time is Miami and Pacino is a Cuban refugee who moves up the crime ladder, changing from bootlegging to drug-dealing. The film is excessively violent and long.

MONTAY, CARLOTTA
MY FAVORITE BRUNETTE (1947, Paramount)—**Dorothy Lamour** mistakes baby photographer Bob Hope for a private eye. The mistake almost gets Hope fried in the electric chair, but Dotty comes to his rescue in the nick of time.

MONTERO
BEAU BANDIT (1930, RKO)—**Rod La Rocque**, a Mexican bandit with a soft streak, takes time out from robbing a bank and escaping from a posse to help a pretty girl from falling into the clutches of a skinflint banker.

MONTGOMERY, JESSIE
MAID TO ORDER (1987, New Century-Vista)—Rich self-centered **Ally Sheedy** loses her identity and is forced to take employment as a maid with a strange Malibu couple.

MONTI, CARLOTTA
W.C. FIELDS AND ME (1976, Universal)—**Valerie Perrine** portrays W.C. Fields' longtime mistress in this boring biopic of the great comedian (who was it seems not a great human being), based on the book by Monti.

MONTY
THE COMPULSORY HUSBAND (1930, GB, British International)—Engaged **Monty Banks** shelters a runaway girl and pretends to be her husband.

MOODY, MR.
THE BACHELOR'S DAUGHTERS (1946, UA)—Four salesgirls persuade bachelor floorwalker **Adolphe Menjou** to pretend to be their father to in enhance their chances of catching wealthy husbands.

MOODY, TOM
BRONCO BUSTER (1952, Universal)—**John Lund** is one of two rodeo riders in competition for the championship and Joyce Holden.

MOOKIE
KNIGHTS OF THE CITY (1986, New World)—**John Mengatti** is a member of a Miami street gang in a fight with another gang over turf.

MOON, CHARLIE
CHARLIE MOON (1956, GB, British Lion)—Ex-circus star **Max Bygraves** finds life on the legitimate stage shallow and returns to the tents and sawdust.

MOON, JUNIE
TELL ME THAT YOU LOVE ME, JUNIE MOON (1970, Paramount)—This film deals with the relationships of facially disfigured **Liza Minnelli**, homosexual Robert Moore, and epileptic Ken Howard.

MOONY, JACK
HEART CONDITION (1990, New Line)—Racist vice cop **Bob Hopkins** is given the heart of black lawyer Denzel Washington, who has stolen Hopkins' girlfriend, hooker Chloe Webb. The dead Washington becomes a constant unwanted companion, only seen by Hopkins. Washington won't leave until Hopkins solves who killed him.

MOONLIGHT, CAPT.
CAPTAIN MOONLIGHT (1940, GB, Olympia)—Title character **John Stuart** is an 1815 highwayman, who just disappears in this film about a country girl forced to marry a gambler.

"MOONRAKER, THE" (EARL ANTHONY OF DAWLISH)
THE MOONRAKER (1958, GB, ABF-Pathe)—**George Baker**, a noble highwayman, helps the king's son escape the Roundheads of Cromwell and find safety in France.

MOORE, ANNA
DESERTED AT THE ALTAR (1922, Silent, Goldwyn)—**Bessie Love's** wedding is ruined by her dishonest guardian when he arranges for a woman carrying a baby to arrive at the church and claim Love's groom to be the child's father. The truth comes out but not before the unfortunate groom is almost lynched by an angry mob.

MOORE, ERIC
SUNDAY DINNER FOR A SOLDIER (1944, 20th Century Fox)—**John Hodiak** is the serviceman invited to have Sunday dinner with a poor Florida houseboat family consisting of grandfather Charles Winninger and four children, the eldest of whom, Anne Baxter, he falls in love with.

MOORE, IVY
FOR LOVE OF IVY (1968, Palomar/Cinerama)—When black maid **Abbey Lincoln** announces she's quitting, the wealthy family for whom she works tries to find a boyfriend for her so she'll stay.

MOORE, T/SGT. JIM
THE D.I. (1957, Warner Brothers)—**Jack Webb** appears as a Joe Friday-like marine drill instructor, tough as nails and unrelenting in his demands on the new recruits, particularly one mama's boy, Don Dubbins, to whom he really puts the screws.

MOORE, JENNY & PRESTON
SOMEBODY KILLED HER HUSBAND (1978, Columbia)—Read our lips. Somebody killed **Farah Fawcett-Majors's** husband **Laurence Guittard**. Maybe the producers should have called in Kate Jackson and Jacklyn Smith to help out with this bomb.

MOORE, JOHNNY
JOHNNY DOESN'T LIVE HERE ANYMORE (1944, Monogram)—**William Terry** has gone away but left behind keys to his old apartment with various men, who discover war worker Simone Simon living there now.

MOORE, LUCY
IMMEDIATE FAMILY (1989, Columbia)—Glenn Close and husband James Woods want a baby, but Close can't conceive. They arrange to adopt the baby of unwed mother **Mary Stuart Masterson**, but when she gives birth, Masterson changes her mind.

MOORE, MINNIE
MINNIE AND MOSKOWITZ (1971, Universal)—Director-actor John Cassavetes wrote the screenplay and directed this examination of an unhappy couple, starring his wife **Gena Rowlands** and Seymour Cassel.

MOORE, OFFICER
PRIDE OF THE FORCE (1925, Silent, Rayart)—**Tom Santschi**, a good cop, is passed over for promotion, until he breaks up a bank robbery.

MOORE, RICHARD & SARAH
SEPARATE VACATIONS (1986, RSK Entertainment)—**David Naughton** talks wife **Jennifer Dale** into separate vacations. He's off to Mexico looking for some casual sex. She's at a ski resort with the kids and a babysitter, but she has more opportunities than he does.

MOORE, VICKI
SINGAPORE WOMAN (1941, Warner Brothers)—In a remake of DANGEROUS, **Brenda Marshall** seems to be a jinx for herself and any man who becomes involved with her.

MORAN (LETTY STERNSEN)
MORAN OF THE LADY LETTY—(1922, silent, Paramount)—**Dorothy Dalton** disguises herself as a man when her ship, the Lady Letty, catches fire and sinks. She is rescued by brutal sea captain Walter

Long. Her champion is Rudolph Valentino who had been shanghaied by Long.

MORAN, JACK

MY BLUE HEAVEN (1950, 20th Century Fox)—**Don Dailey** and wife Betty Grable are radio entertainers who find it impossible to adopt a child because of their occupations. They resort to devious means to get a child, but have it taken away from them. Relax, there's a happy ending.

MORAN, MICKEY

BABES IN ARMS (1939, MGM)—**Mickey Rooney**, Judy Garland and other sons and daughters of retired vaudevillians put on a really big show. Rooney and Garland are spectacular, singing and dancing to songs such as "Where or When," "The Lady Is a Tramp," "I Cried For You," "You Are My Lucky Star" and the title number, all by Richard Rodgers and Lorenz Hart.

MORAN, NORA

SIN OF NORA MORAN (1933, Majestic)—Former circus girl **Zita Johann** faces the electric chair as she takes the blame when her lover, the governor, kills the circus boss.

MORAND, LT. ANDRE

THE DEVIL'S IN LOVE (1933, Fox)—**Victor Jory**, a doctor falsely accused of murder, must prove his innocence.

MORANT, LT. HARRY

BREAKER MORANT (1980, Australia, New World)—In 1901 South Africa, three Australian soldiers are put on trial for killing Boer prisoners. **Edward Woodward** and Bryan Brown go before a firing squad.

MORANT, JOAN

SHE GOES TO WAR (1929, UA)—**Eleanor Boardman** has an unsympathetic role as a socialite, who goes to France during WWI in search of glory, and learns from a lieutenant that social position means nothing, especially during war.

MORDA, MICHAEL

THE BELOVED BACHELOR (1931, Paramount)—Philanderer **Paul Lukas** adopts a child, who when grown to be Dorothy Jordan falls in love with him and puts an end to his womanizing.

MORE, SIR THOMAS

A MAN FOR ALL SEASONS (1966, GB, Columbia)—It is a pleasure for the ear just to listen to **Paul Scofield** in his Oscar winning performance as the Chancellor of England. He breaks with Henry VIII (Robert Shaw) over the latter's decision to divorce his wife and marry Anne Boleyn. Despite all his best lawyer maneuvers, Scofield puts his faith ahead of his king and goes to the executioner's block.

MOREAU, ANDRE-LOUIS *See* SCARAMOUCHE

MOREAU, DR.

THE ISLAND OF DR. MOREAU (1977, American International)—**Burt Lancaster** portrays the mad island doctor who has created a breed of half-man, half-beast "humanimals." Burt's work isn't as frightening as was Charles Laughton's in the original production, released in 1933 as ISLAND OF LOST SOULS.

MOREL, PAUL & MRS.

SONS AND LOVERS (1960, GB, 20th Century Fox)—The affection that son **Dean Stockwell** has for his mother **Wendy Hiller** is played down in this admirable production of the D.H. Lawrence story. Stockwell's desire to become an artist offends his rough miner-father Trevor Howard, but he finds support from his gentle mother.

MORELLA

THE HAUNTING OF MORELLA (1990, Concorde)—In this softcore porn version of an Edgar Allan Poe horror story, **Nicole Eggert** is crucified by a crowd of witch-haters. She vows to return and get revenge—and don't you know she does.

MORELLE, DR.

DR. MORELLE—THE CASE OF THE MISSING HEIRESS (1949, GB, Exclusive)—Detective **Valentine Dyall** solves the cremation murder of a secretary's sister.

MORENNE, VICTOR

THE BELGIAN (1917, Silent, Olcott)—Belgian fisherman **Walter Whiteside** has a talent for sculpturing. He goes off to Paris to establish himself. On his return, he finds that his sweetheart has taken up with a German spy.

MORENO, JACK

MAN OF THE PEOPLE (1937, MGM)—In his only starring role top-notch character actor **Joseph Calleia** is an Italian immigrant who studies to be a lawyer at night school, but finds he can't get anywhere without working for corrupt politicians.

MORENO, LOLITA

DAUGHTER OF THE WEST (1949, Film Classics)—Convent-educated Indian girl **Martha Vickers** rediscovers her roots on a Navajo reservation in the 1880s. She and educated Indian Philip Reed ban together to stop the Indian agent from stealing valuable mineral rights that belong to the tribe.

MORETON, LUCIA

THE RAGGED HEIRESS (1922, Silent, Fox)—**Shirley Mason** tries hard to make the most of this hard-to-believe story of a maid posing as an heiress, who really is the heiress.

MORETON, SARAH

SHE PLAYED WITH FIRE (1957, GB, Columbia)—Insurance investigator Jack Hawkins becomes involved with arsonist **Arlene Dahl**.

MORGAN

BAD MEN OF TOMBSTONE (1949, Monogram)—**Broderick Crawford**, the leader of a gang of western outlaws, leads them to their deaths on the streets of Tombstone. What kind of leader-ship is that?

MORGAN

HELL-SHIP MORGAN (1936, Columbia)—Sea Captain **George Bancroft** gives up his life during a hurricane, so that his wife Ann Sothern can be with Victor Jory, the man she really loves.

MORGAN

MORGAN'S LAST RAID (1929, Silent, MGM)—**Allan Garcia** leads a band of Confederate raiders in this Civil War tale. Tim McCoy is branded a coward because he refuses to fight against his native state of Tennessee.

MORGAN, BABY FACE

BABY FACE MORGAN (1942, PRC)—Country rube **Richard Cromwell** poses as a tough mobster.

MORGAN, DR. BARTLEY
UNDERCOVER DOCTOR (1939, Paramount)—Saw-bones **J. Carrol Naish** patches up wounded criminals, until put out of business by G-men.

MORGAN, BAT
FRISCO KID (1935, Warner Brothers)—Tough sailor **James Cagney** becomes a power on San Francisco's wild and unlawful Barbary Coast. He's almost lynched by vigilantes out to clean up the town, but is saved by a girl from Nob Hill.

MORGAN, BELLE & STEVE
THE PRIZEFIGHTER AND THE LADY (1933, MGM)—Just so there can be no misunderstanding, **Myrna Loy** is the lady and **Max Baer** is the boxer in this predictable story of a prizefighter and a big-time gambler mobster's moll.

MORGAN, CAPT.
THE VALIANT (1962, GB, UA)—The Valiant is the name of a WWII battleship in Alexandria Harbor, but it also applies to its captain **John Mills** who must find where two Italian frog-men have laid a time-fuse before it blows up the ship. It's an enjoyable piece of suspense.

MORGAN, CLEM
I BECAME A CRIMINAL (1947, GB, Alliance/Warner Brothers)—Titled THEY MADE ME A FUGITIVE in Great Britain, this film has **Trevor Howard** as a framed crook who breaks jail to take revenge on Soho dope dealers who put him there.

MORGAN, DANIEL
MAD DOG MORGAN (1976, Australia Motion Picture Co./BEF)—**Dennis Hopper** portrays a legendary Australian outlaw of the 1800s.

MORGAN, DAVIS
HE WALKED BY NIGHT (1948, Eagle Lion)—**Richard Basehart** is a killer hunted by the police. The semi-documentary presentation helps to make this a fine suspenseful film.

MORGAN, DR.
SOCIETY DOCTOR (1935, MGM)—**Chester Morris's** medical views are considered too radical for his hospital so he goes into private practice, but later returns to the hospital, wounded by a criminal, to supervise his own operation, under spinal anaesthetic.

MORGAN, ETHEL
HIS FIRST FLAME (1927, Silent, Sennett/Pathe Exchange)—**Natalie Kingston** sets her house on fire to catch the attention of her sister's fiance, a fireman. It might have been cheaper to buy tickets to the Fireman's Ball.

MORGAN, EVE
I LOVE A SOLDIER (1944, Paramount)—WWII shipyard welder **Paulette Goddard**, despite a reputation for being un-attainable, falls for Sonny Tufts, a married GI on leave.

MORGAN, GRISSLY
GRISSLY'S MILLIONS (1945, Republic)—**Robert H. Barrat's** greedy relatives are anxiously awaiting him to kick-off, but murder is an unexpected guest in his home.

MORGAN, HELEN
THE HELEN MORGAN STORY (1959, Warner Brothers)—**Ann Blyth** retired after completing this biopic of the great 1920s-1930s torch singer. Gogi Grant dubbed the singing for Blyth who clearly had no understanding of the woman she was playing, or how to project Morgan's qualities, which made her torch songs so filled with feeling and meaning.

MORGAN, JACK
MISSISSIPPI GAMBLER (1929, Universal)—Riverboat gambler **Joseph Schildkraut** cheats the father of the girl he loves, but later redeems himself.

MORGAN, LORD JOHN
A MAN CALLED HORSE (1970, National General Pictures) THE RETURN OF A MAN CALLED HORSE (1976, UA), TRIUMPH OF A MAN CALLED HORSE (1982, CFI)—One picture with **Richard Harris** as the English Lord captured by the Sioux is enough. Three is excessive. At least he had the good grace only to make a cameo appearance in the third. Harris proves he is a man, winning the respect of his captors by enduring the grisly Sun Vow Initiation ceremony in which he is suspended in midair from ropes inserted in his chest.

MORGAN, JOSH
KISSIN' COUSINS (1964, MGM)—**Elvis Presley** is an Air Force officer assigned to talk a hillbilly moonshiner into allowing the government to build a missile base on the site of the still. Presley discovers that the man's nephew, also played by Presley is his cousin and exact double.

MORGAN, JULIE
THIS WOMAN IS MINE (1941, Universal)—**Carol Bruce** stows away on a dangerous fur-trading expedition and is wooed by the captain and two-crew members.

MORGAN, KING
CHARTER PILOT (1940, 20th Century Fox)—Ace pilot **Lloyd Nolan** marries radio broadcaster Lynn Bari, promising her he'll take a safe desk job. But his love of flying adventures makes it a difficult promise to keep.

MORGAN, LOIS
TWO LATINS FROM MANHATTAN (1941, Columbia)—When a Manhattan nightclub imports two entertainers from Havana, the club's public relations woman gets her two roommates, **Joan Woodbury** and Jinx Falkenberg to substitute for them. They're a smash.

MORGAN, CAPT. LUCY
MORGAN'S MARAUDERS (1929, Distinctive)—In this spoof of swashbuckling pirate films, all the buccaneers are female, led by **Margaret Livingstone**.

MORGAN, NAN
NAN OF MUSIC MOUNTAIN (1917, Silent, Paramount)—**Ann Little's** family has been harboring a desperado, whom stage-line manager Wallace Reid is after. Reid gets both the outlaw and Little.

MORGAN, RICKY
WHEN THIEF MEETS THIEF (1937, GB, UA-Anglo) London cat burglar **Douglas Fairbanks, Jr.** is reformed by a good woman, Valerie Hobson, the fiancee of Alan Hale, who once was Fairbanks' partner-in-crime.

MORGAN, ROBERT
THE LAST MAN ON EARTH (1964, American International)—**Vincent Price** spends his lonely time burning dead bodies and

driving stakes through the hearts of ghouls who happen by. It's dirty work, but someone has to do it—and who better than dear old Vincent.

MORGAN, RUSTY
PUBLIC PIDGEON NO. 1 (1957, RKO/Universal)—Lunchroom counterman **Red Skelton** is conned by a gang of crooks into believing that he has been made a G-man.

MORGAN, TESS, ALEX & ILKA
THREE DARING DAUGHTERS (1948, MGM)—**Jane Powell, Mary Eleanor Donahue** and **Anne E. Todd** are sisters, dismayed to learn that their mother, Jeanette MacDonald, plans to remarry.

MORGAN, ZACHARY
I'LL BE SEEING YOU (1944, UA)—Shell-shocked soldier **Joseph Cotten** finds romance with prisoner-on-a-furlough Ginger Rogers during the Christmas holidays. Love cures his problems and he promises to wait for Rogers to finish her sentence.

MORGAN-VAUGHN, GERTRUDE, MAUDE & ISOBEL
THE THREE WEIRD SISTERS (1948, GB, Pathe)—**Nancy Price, Mary Clare** and **Mary Merrall** are crippled sisters plotting to kill their half-brother and his secretary.

MORGENSTERN, MARJORIE
MARJORIE MORNINGSTAR (1958, Warner Brothers)—**Natalie Wood** is a Jewish girl who has ambitions to become a Broadway star. She falls for Gene Kelly, the producer of a summer theatrical show at a resort. He's reached the limit of his show business talent, but doesn't know it. Wood also will find that she hasn't got star quality or the spark to make it to the top.

MORGUS, DR.
THE WACKY WORLD OF DR. MORGUS (1962, Calogne-Sevin)—**Sid Noel (Noel Rideau)** is a mad scientist who invents a machine that will break down a person's molecular structure and then revive it. The machine falls into the wrong hands. Anybody's hands would be the wrong hands.

MORI, YOKO *See* **LUCY DELL**

MORLANT, PROF.
THE GHOUL (1934, GB, Gaumont)—Egyptologist professor **Boris Karloff** dies and is buried with a jewel called the Eternal Light in his hand. He had claimed that he would return from the grave to take revenge if the jewel is stolen. It is and he does.

MORLEY, JOHNNIE
THE MAILMAN (1923, Silent, FBA)—Postman **Johnnie Walker** is framed for stealing bonds and murdering a mail ship's officer.

MORLEY, KEN
MY DEAR MISS ALDRICH (1937, MGM)—Newspaper editor **Walter Pidgeon** and his glamorous new publisher, Maureen O'Sullivan, don't see eye-to-eye on anything. Just wait.

MORLEY, RUDYARD
MY KINGDOM FOR A COOK (1943, Columbia)—British author **Charles Coburn** on tour in the U.S., steals his hostess' cook.

MORNING, FATHER
THE EXORCIST III (1990, 20th Century Fox)—While **Nicol Williamson** appears as the title character, his role is minor in the story of weary

police detective George C. Scott investigating a series of murders by someone operating in behalf of the devil.

MORRELL, ALVAH
NO ROOM FOR THE GROOM (1952, Universal)—When soldier **Tony Curtis** returns to his home, he discovers that 17 of his bride's relatives have moved in with them.

MORRELL, JEFF
I LIVE ON DANGER (1942, Paramount)—Radio reporter **Chester Morris** stumbles onto a murder plot.

MORRIS, DR. ALFRED
THE MAD GHOUL (1943, Universal)—Mad scientist **George Zucco** turns nice-guy David Bruce into one of the living-dead who robs fresh graves and kills to get new hearts.

MORRIS, GERMAINE
GOOD AND NAUGHTY (1926, Silent, Paramount)—**Pola Negri** changes from an ugly duckling into a smashing swan during a cruise on a yacht. Sea air is so good for you.

MORRIS, LETTY
FUGITIVE LOVERS (1934, MGM)—Convict George Montgomery escapes on a transcontinental bus and falls in love with passenger **Madge Evans**.

MORRIS, PENNY
BABES ON BROADWAY (1941, MGM)—Young **Judy Garland** can't win a part on Broadway so she, her boy-friend Mickey Rooney, and their other aspiring young actor friends decide to produce their own Broadway show.

MORRISON, JIM
THE DOORS (1991, Tri-Star)—The film concentrates on the short life of rock legend Jim Morrison, portrayed by **Val Kilmer**. The rock idol is a charismatic drunk and drug abuser, obsessed with death.

MORRISON, JULIE
JEZEBEL (1938, Warner Brothers)—Scandalous New Orleans belle **Bette Davis** loses her fiance Henry Fonda in the 1850s by going too far in trying to make him jealous. She proves her good qualities as she nurses the victims of a yellow fever plague. Davis was hoping this film would convince David O. Selznick that she could play Scarlett O'Hara.

MORRISON, SHEP
TALL, DARK AND HANDSOME (1941, 20th Century Fox)—In this crime-comedy, suave 1929 gangster **Cesar Romero** is loved by Virginia Gilmore, even though she tries to resist him. It's OK, he turns out to be the good-bad man with Sheldon Leonard, the bad-bad man.

MORROW, FRED
KEY WITNESS (1960, MGM)—A street gang pressures **Jeffrey Hunter's** family into preventing his wife from testifying in a criminal case.

MORROW, KAY
GOLD DIGGERS IN PARIS (1938, Warner Brothers)—**Rosemary Lane** is one of the stars of this film but the big hits are the Busby Berkeley musical numbers.

MORTLAKE, DAVID

DAVID AND JONATHAN (1920, Silent, GB, General)—**Geoffrey Webb**, Richard Ryan and Madge Titheradge are shipwrecked together on an island off the coast of Africa.

MORTON, EMMA

THE VAMPIRE LOVERS (1970, GB, Hammer)—**Madeleine Smith** is one of the female victims of lesbian-vampire Ingrid Pitt in Hammer's first horror film featuring nudity.

MORTON, KEN

WHIRLWIND HORSEMAN (1938, Grand National)—**Ken Maynard** is looking for his gold prospecting pal. What he finds is a good-looking gal and some varmints he defeats with his fists.

MORTON, MARIA

MADONNA OF AVENUE A (1929, Warner Brothers)—**Dolores Costello** goes to pieces when she discovers that her mother, whom she thought a respectable woman, is actually a dance-hall hostess in a sleazy joint. For some reason this causes Costello to act as if she was no good, and she marries a bootlegger.

MORTON, MARY

A GIRL WITH IDEAS (1937, Universal)—**Wendy Barrie**, the wacky daughter of a banker, takes over the running of a crusading newspaper.

MORTON, REGGIE

REGGIE MIXES IN (1916, Silent, Triangle)—Millionaire **Douglas Fairbanks** really likes to slug it out, especially with guys bigger than he. He also loves slum girl Bessie Love. If you're rich this behavior is called eccentric, if poor, you're a nut.

"MOSCA DEL FUEGO See NINA MARIA AZARS

MOSCA, GITTEL

TWO FOR THE SEESAW (1962, UA)—**Shirley MacLaine** is something of a kooky Greenwich Village girl who has a brief (talky) affair with lonely businessman Robert Mitchum, who is planning to divorce his wife. It's a very stagy movie.

MOSELEY, EDIE

GIRL OF THE OZARKS (1936, Paramount)—**Virginia Weidler** needs the help of newspaper editor Leif Erickson to get out of a series of childish scrapes.

MOSELY, SLIM JR.

PARDNERS (1956, Paramount)—**Dean Martin** and Jerry Lewis split the role of Bing Crosby in this decent remake of RHYTHM ON THE RANGE (1936).

MOSER, IVAN

DESTROYER (1988, Moviestore)—Ex-NFL football madman **Lyle Alzado** is a dead serial killer, haunting a recently reopened prison.

MOSES

MOSES (1976, GB/Italy, Avco Embassy)—**Burt Lancaster's** interpretation of the Hebrew raised by Egyptians who leads his people out of bondage is different than that of Charlton Heston in *The Ten Commandments*, but not necessarily better.

MOSES, JOE

MISTER MOSES (1965, UA)—Diamond smuggler **Robert Mitchum** leads the people of an African village to a new location away from their home, which is about to be flooded by the creation of a dam.

MOSKOWITZ, SEYMOUR

MINNIE AND MOSKOWITZ (1971, Universal)—**Seymour Cassel**, a loony parking lot attendant, has a romance with Gena Rowlands, a lonely museum curator.

MOSS, JACK

THE THING WITH TWO HEADS (1972, American International)—**Rosey Grier** portrays a volunteer death row convict onto whose body is transplanted the head of dying racist scientist Ray Milland. We offer our condolences to both gentlemen.

MOSS, JOANNA

GIVE A GIRL A BREAK (1953, MGM)—**Helen Wood** is one of three show girls hoping to move into the lead in a Broadway show when the star quits. As the other two are Marge Champion and Debbie Reynolds, you may not care for Wood's chances.

MOTEL

MOTEL, THE OPERATOR (1940, Cinema Film)—In this Yiddish feature, **Chaim Tauber**, the organizer of a clothing worker's strike loses his wife in childbirth and then the child, whom he does not find until the baby is grown.

MOTHER

MOTHER AND SON (1931, Monogram)—**Clara Kimball Young** keeps the fact that she runs a gambling den from her son until he's grown. The news of how she earns a living alienates the son, but there is a tearful reunion.

MOTHER

MOTHER, JUGS & SPEED (1976, 20th Century Fox)—**Bill Cosby** is one of three L.A. drivers of private commercial ambulances in a story containing both comedy and tragedy.

MOTO, MR.

THANK YOU MR. MOTO (1937, 20th Century Fox); THINK FAST MR. MOTO (1937, 20th Century Fox); MR. MOTO TAKES A CHANCE (1938, 20th Century Fox); MR. MOTO TAKES A VACATION (1938, 20th Century Fox); MR. MOTO'S GAMBLE (1938, 20th Century Fox); MYSTERIOUS MR. MOTO (1938, 20th Century Fox); MR. MOTO IN DANGER ISLAND (1939, 20th Century Fox); MR. MOTO'S LAST WARNING (1939, 20th Century Fox)—**Peter Lorre**; THE RETURN OF MR. MOTO (1965, GB, 20th Century Fox)—**Henry Silva**;—The Japanese detective created by John P. Marquand was portrayed by Peter Lorre in better than average second features which still can be caught on TV late at night. Henry Silva in 1965 is not likely to make us forget Lorre or hope for a continuation of the series.

MOULSWORTH, JULIET

ROMANOFF AND JULIET (1961, Universal)—In this Romeo-and-Juliet-like story written and directed by Peter Ustinov, **Sandra Dee** is an American girl falling for Russian diplomat John Gavin while both are in the nation of Concordia where, who else?, Peter Ustinov is its general.

MOURA

THE FOOL AND THE PRINCESS (1948, GB, GFD)—In Germany after WWII, married officer Bruce Lester falls in love with displaced person **Adina Mandlove**, believing her to be a Russian princess.

MOUSEKEWITZ, FIEVEL

AN AMERICAN TAIL: FIEVEL GOES WEST (1991, Animated, Universal)—In this sequel to 1986's *An American Tale*, **Phillip Glasser** is the voice of the Russian immigrant mouse, who lives with his family in the mean streets of the turn-of-the-century Bronx.

Seeking the real promise of America, they move to the open spaces of the western frontier.

MOUTH
THE GOONIES (1985, Warner Brothers)—**Corey Feldman** and a group of other housing development kids have some swashbuckling adventures one Saturday afternoon.

MOZART, WOLFGANG AMADEUS
MOZART (1940, GB, ABF/Lopert); AMADEUS (1984, Orion)—**Stephen Haggard** is cast in a poor presentation of episodes in the life of the great composer. On the other hand, **Tom Hulce** was brilliant as the young musical genius who had too little life to waste any time by flattering the various people who could have saved him from a pauper's grave.

MUDD, DR. SAMUEL A.
THE PRISONER OF SHARK ISLAND (1936, 20th Century Fox)—**Warner Baxter** portrays the physician who was imprisoned as a conspirator in the Lincoln assassination because of giving medical treatment to John Wilkes Booth.

MUELLER, JOE
FATHER (1990, Australia, Barron)—Unfortunately for this interesting production, the story is almost identical to that of Costa-Gavras' MUSIC BOX, released in 1989. German-born **Max Von Sydow** lives in comfort in Melbourne with his daughter Carol Drinkwater, son-in-law Steve Jacobs and two granddaughters. His peaceful lifestyle is disrupted when an old woman, Julia Blake, accuses him of having committed war crimes. His trial and downfall are much the same as that of Armin Mueller-Stahl in the Costa-Gavras production.

MUFFITT, GEORGE
HERE'S GEORGE (1932, GB, Producers Distributing)—**George Clarke** borrows a friend's classy digs to impress his girl's parents.

MUIR, KATE & RICHARD
WEEKEND WITH KATE (1990, Australia, Emmanuel)—In a modest screwball comedy, **Catherine McClements** and her husband **Colin Friels** have different reasons for spending a weekend alone together at her family's beach house. She wants to get pregnant. He wants to tell her he's leaving her for his mistress Helen Mutkins.

MUIR, LUCY
THE GHOST AND MRS. MUIR (1942, 20th Century Fox)—**Gene Tierney** moves into a seaside house and is not frightened when she discovers that the ghost of the former sea captain owner, Rex Harrison, still lives there. He dictates his memoirs to her, which she publishes, and the two fall in love, finally to be united with her death.

MUIR, VENICE
LADY WITH A PAST (1932, RKO)—Wealthy but shy **Constance Bennett** accidentally finds herself with a reputation of being a shady lady.

MULAY EL RAISULI
THE WIND AND THE LION (1975, MGM/UA)—In 1904 Tangier, Riffian chief **Sean Connery** kidnaps Candace Bergen, an American widow and her two children. President Teddy Roosevelt (Brian Keith) swears they will be rescued.

MULDOON, DANNY
ONLY THE LONELY (1991, 20th Century Fox)—Good-natured Chicago cop **John Candy** would like to marry shy mortician's daughter Ally Sheedy, but his harridan mother Maureen O'Hara (looking as beautiful as ever in her first film in 20 years) has him under her thumb. Even though he harbors a long-submerged anger towards her, he's afraid to leave her and find his own life.

MULDOWNEY, SHIRLEY "CHA-CHA"
HEART LIKE A WHEEL (1983, Aurora/20th Century Fox)—**Bonnie Bedelia** stars as the wife of a gas station owner. She develops an obsession for becoming a race car driver. It's a true story and rather interesting, considering the subject matter.

MULDOWNEY, TUCKER
LISTEN TO ME (1989, Columbia)—Few wanted to listen to **Kirk Cameron** in this weary yarn of three college debaters.

MULLANEY, MARY & BILL
HIS BUDDY'S WIFE (1925, Silent, Associated Exhibitors)—**Edna Murphy** and **Douglas Gilmore** are husband and wife. When he is listed as presumed dead in WWI, his buddy Glenn Hunter comes to Murphy's farm to care for him as he had promised Gilmore. Murphy and Hunter are about to marry when Gilmore arrives home.

MULLER, GRETA
ONE IN A MILLION (1936, 20th Century Fox)—**Sonja Henie**, the daughter of a Swiss innkeeper, becomes an Olympian champion ice skater. Talk about type-casting.

MULLER, KARL
ALIAS THE DOCTOR (1932, First National)—Orphan **Richard Barthelmess** is raised by a family who sends both him and their own son to medical school. Barthelmess succeeds where the other lad does not. However, our hero takes the blame for a mistake that his "brother" made and is sentenced to three years in jail.

MULLER, SCOTT
THIEF OF HEARTS (1985, Paramount)—**Steven Bauer** steals the diary of Barbara Williams, discovers her fantasies and delivers them for her.

MULLER, WOLFGANG
EXPLORERS (1985, Paramount)—**River Phoenix** is one of three kids who experience their dream of travelling in space and meeting some very interesting aliens.

MULLIGAN
TOP SERGEANT MULLIGAN (1941, Monogram)—When two salesmen join the army to escape the tax collector, they find he's their sergeant, **Nat Pendleton**.

MULLIGAN, JERRY
AN AMERICAN IN PARIS (1951, MGM)—In one of the super MGM musicals, **Gene Kelly** is a carefree American artist in Paris after WWII where he must decide between the sponsorship of wealthy Nina Foch or the innocence of French gamin Leslie Caron. Everything about the film is first rate but especially the music by the Gershwins and the dancing choreographed by Gene Kelly.

MULLIGAN, JIMMY
DANCE TEAM (1932, Fox)—**James Dunn** and Sally Eilers form a dance team which is a success but is split apart by his jealously over the attention paid to her by a rich man.

MULLINS, JEFF & BILL
THREE MARRIED MEN (1936, Paramount)—**Lynne Overman** and **William Frawley** are married brothers who make life difficult for their sister and her new husband.

MULVAIN, ATHENA

ATHENA (1954, MGM)—In a dumb musical, young lawyer Edmund Purdom falls in love with **Jane Powell**, the eldest of seven daughters brought up with the highest standards of moral and physical fitness by their grandparents. If exercise is so good for you, what happened to the parents of these healthy young things?

MULVANEY, MARY

HOLD THAT WOMAN (1940, PRC)—**Frances Gifford** and her real-life husband James Dunn played reel-life husband and wife partners in the "skip-chasing" business. That is they sought dead beats who hadn't paid their installment payments.

MULVANY

A YANK IN INDO-CHINA (1952, Columbia)—**John Archer** is one of the American pilots involved in guerrilla warfare in Indochina while it was still the French's headache.

MUMMY, THE

THE MUMMY'S SHROUD (1967, GB, Hammer)—**Eddie Powell** plays the mummy of an Egyptian slave who is revived when a 20th century expedition breaks into a tomb. The results of this desecration are about what one would expect.

MUMSIE

MUMSIE (1927, Silent, GB, Wilcox/W&F)—**Pauline Frederick** doesn't know what to make of pacifist gambler Nelson Keys, who becomes a spy for the enemy and gives his new employers the plans to his father's gas factory.

MUNCHAUSEN, BARON

THE ADVENTURES OF BARON MUNCHAUSEN (1989, Columbia-Tri-Star)—**John Neville** is the German soldier and nobleman, who with the help of his three talented servants, takes on the troops of the Ottoman Empire who are laying siege to his walled-city.

MUNCHIE

MUNCHIE (1992, Concorde Pictures)—In the sequel to the 1987 film *Munchies*, **Dom De Luise** is the voice of an oversized wisecracking puppet who helps young Jaime McEnnan deal with bullies at school by magically granting his wishes.

MUNDSON, GILDA

GILDA (1946, Columbia)—**Rita Hayworth** has been quoted that men married Gilda and woke up in bed with her. It's understandable; Gilda was one of the most desirable women ever to appear on the silver screen, and males in the audiences will never forgive Glenn Ford for stopping her from completing her striptease. Oh, the story? She's married to South American gambler George Macready but renews a romance with her husband's manager Glenn Ford.

MUNSTER, HERMAN

MUNSTER, GO HOME (1966, Universal)—**Fred Gwynne** repeats his TV role as a Frankenstein-monster-like dummy, married to a vampire wife Yvonne De Carlo. The Munsters go to England where they have inherited an estate being used as the headquarters of a gang of counterfeiters.

MURDOCK, ANNE

THE OFFICE WIFE (1930, Warner Brothers)—**Dorothy Mackaill** sets her cap for her older married employer Lewis Stone, and takes him away from his independent wife.

MURDOCK, CHUCK

AMAZING GRACE AND CHUCK (1987, Tri-Star)—Twelve-year-old baseball whiz **Joshua Zuehlke** announces he's giving up playing baseball until the world agrees to nuclear disarmament. Soon other athletes around the world join the protest, by making similar announcements.

MURDOCK, DR.

THE MAN WHO TURNED TO STONE (1957, Columbia)—**Victor Jory** is the leader of a group of 200-year-old men who stay alive by putting live women in a tub of chemicals and sapping their energy. Did you every hear of anything so silly?

MURDOCK, MRS.

PART TIME WIFE (1930, Fox)—Golf brings **Lelia Hyams** and her ex-husband Edmund Lowe back together again after she divorces him because he has so little time for her.

MURFREE, CHARLES

HIS FAMILY TREE (1936, RKO)—At one time, signs were posted in this country when announcing jobs, "Irish need not apply." This may explain why **William Harrigan** changed his name from Murphy to Murfree when he decided to run for mayor in an Iowa town, but the arrival of his father from Ireland blows his cover.

MURIETA, JOAQUIN

THE FIREBRAND (1962, 20th Century Fox)—**Valentin De Vargas** is a Mexican bandit at the time of the California gold rush. He acts like Robin Hood as he steals from the gold-crazy prospectors.

MURKILL, STEVE

KING OF ALCATRAZ (1938, Paramount)—**J. Carroll Naish** leads a group of escaped convicts in the takeover of a ship.

MURPHY

MURPHY'S WAR (1971, GB, Paramount)—Merchant seaman **Peter O'Toole** repairs a plane and teaches himself to fly it so he can attack the U-boat that sank his ship.

MURPHY, ALEX J.

ROBOCOP (1987, Orion); ROBOCOP 2 (1990, Orion)—Mortally wounded cop **Peter Weller** is put together with machinery and computers that make the Six Million Dollar Man look like a pauper. He becomes a violent defender of justice. By the sequel, he's lost all claim to his former human identity, and has become a futuristic crime-fighting machine.

MURPHY, BRIDEY

THE SEARCH FOR BRIDEY MURPHY (1956, Paramount)—**Eilene Janssen**, 15; **Hallene Hill**, 66; **Denise Freeborn**, 8; **Ruth Robinson**, 4 each appear as the Irish peasant who is reincarnated into American housewife Teresa Wright when she is put under by amateur hypnotist Louis Hayward. Later he finds he can't bring Wright back.

MURPHY, IZZY

PRIVATE IZZY MURPHY (1926, Silent, Warner Brothers); SAILOR IZZY MURPHY (1927, Silent, Warner Brothers)—**George Jessel** is a Jewish boy who falls for a Catholic girl, but until the end of the 1916 picture she doesn't know he's Jewish because he calls himself Murphy. By the second film he's on the scent of another girl whose perfume he likes. Fickle, Fickle, Fickle!

MURPHY, JACK

MURPH THE SURF (1974, Caruth C. Byrd)—In this film based on a real event, **Don Stroud** and his beatnik buddy decide to steal the 564-carat Star of India diamond from New York's American Museum of Natural History.

MURPHY, JACK
MURPHY'S LAW (1986, Cannon)—**Charles Bronson** is a cop framed for the murder of his ex-wife. Now they did it. They made him mad and when he's mad, he's mean. He does develop a soft spot for the teenage girl who's hand-cuffed to him when he escapes to clear himself, even if she did steal his car.

MURPHY, ROSEMARY
ABIE'S IRISH ROSE (1928, Part-Talkie, Paramount); (1946, UA)—**Nancy Carroll** and **Joanne Dru** each portray the Irish Catholic girl who marries a Jewish boy in three different ceremonies, a secular one, a Jewish one and a Catholic one. It still doesn't satisfy their bigoted parents.

MURRAY, ELLEN & ANN
YES, MY DARLING DAUGHTER (1939, Warner Brothers)—This innocent comedy ran into a lot of trouble with the censors because it has **Priscilla Lane** telling her mother **Fay Bainter** that she plans to spend a weekend with her fiance'.

MURRAY, MIDGE
YOUNG DONOVAN'S KID (1931, RKO)—Six-year-old orphan **Jackie Cooper** reforms a violent gunman who adopts Cooper after his brother is sent to prison.

MURRAY, PATRICIA
JAZZ CINDERELLA (1930, Chesterfield)—**Nancy Welford**, a model in a dress shop, is not the girl that the wealthy mother of Jason Robards Sr. has in mind as a wife for her son. But mother doesn't always know best.

MURRAY, ST. ELMO
ST. ELMO (1923, Silent, Capital)—**Shayle Gardner** becomes a minister after killing a rival in a duel.

MURRIETA, JOAQUIN
ROBIN HOOD OF DORADO (1936, MGM)—**Warner Baxter** becomes a bandit to avenge himself on those who killed his wife. The story has little to do with the life of the real western bandit, but such films seldom did.

MYER, LANE
BETTER OFF DEAD (1985, Warner Brothers)—Teenager **John Cusack** feels his life is over when the girl of his dreams falls for a creep. Of the teenage exploitation films, this one isn't quite as gross as usual.

MYERS, MICHAEL
HALLOWEEN IV: THE RETURN OF MICHAEL MYERS (1988, Galaxy); HALLOWEEN 5: THE REVENGE OF MICHAEL MYERS (1989, Galaxy)—**George P. Wilbur** as Michael has survived the fiery blast that appeared to kill him in Halloween III, and he's back happily killing young people. **Donald Shanks** does the honors in the 1989 production.

MYERS, EMMETT
THE HITCHHIKER (1953, RKO)—**William Talman** has the film role of his life in this Ida Lupino directed suspense story. He's a vicious kill-crazy hitchhiker who holds two vacationing fishermen hostage as he makes his way towards the Mexican border.

MYNORS, VIRGINIA
THE DAUGHTER PAYS (1920, Silent, Selznick)—**Elaine Hammerstein** is threatened by the man her mother jilted years earlier. He intends to ruin her to take his revenge.

MYNTER, MYRT
MYRT AND MARGE (1934, Universal)—**Myrtle Vail** and her real-life daughter Donna Damerel bring their zany radio antics to the screen, with about the expected success in these kinds of endeavors.

MYRA
THREE LITTLE GIRLS IN BLUE (1946, 20th Century Fox)—In a musical remake of THREE BLIND MICE, cute **Vera-Ellen** is one of three midwestern girls who have come to the big city to find rich husbands.

N

NADASKY, COUNTESSS ELIZABETH
COUNTESS DRACULA (1972, GB, Hammer)—**Ingrid Pitt** remains ever youthful and beautiful by bathing in the blood of virgins.

NADIA
THE SOLDIER AND THE LADY (1937, GB, RKO)—**Elizabeth Allen** is the good woman loved by Anton Walbrook, the loyal courier of the Russian Czar, who is entrusted with taking new military strategy to the Russian armies in Siberia for their battle with the Tartars.

NADINA, QUEEN
THE RUNAWAY QUEEN (1935, GB, UA)—Exiled Queen **Anna Neagle** and revolutionary leader Fernand Gravey who deposed her are both staying incognito at the same ski resort. When they fall in love, their country becomes a joint monarchy-dictatorship. Silliee!

NADINE
DANCERS (1987, Cannon)—**Leslie Browne** who co-starred with Mikhail Baryshnikov in THE TURNING POINT is now just one of several dancers whom the ballet star beds, even though she's a man-hater, ever since he broke her heart as a young dancer.

NADJA
STRANGE WIVES (1935, Universal)—Russian **June Clayworth** marries American Roger Pryor, even though she is already encumbered with both a husband and an unwanted lover.

NADJA, PRINCESS
PRISONERS OF THE CASBAH (1953, Columbia)—Princess **Gloria Grahame** and her lover must flee killers out to get them in the Casbah.

NAJA
COBRA WOMAN (1944, Universal)—**Maria Montez** plays both a good native girl and her evil sister. They battle for control of their island where snakes are worshiped, and now and then some maiden is thrown into an active volcano to appease the gods.

NAJA
THE WARRIOR AND THE SORCERESS (1984, New World)—Sorceress **Maria Socas** appears topless throughout this film about a stranger who sells his services to both sides in a dispute over a well.

NAN

THE DOUGHGIRLS (1944, Warner Brothers)—**Alexis Smith** is one of several Washington working girls, looking for husbands during WWII. While the play on which it was based reportedly was quite funny, the movie has far too few laughs.

NAN

THE LITTLE SCHOOL MA'AM (1916, Silent, Triangle)—**Dorothy Gish** a country schoolteacher, puts an end to the gossip about her conduct with men when she marries a successful writer.

NANA

NANA (1934, UA)—Samuel Goldwyn had great plans for European actress **Anna Sten**, claiming she was all the great actresses—Greta Garbo, Marlene Dietrich and others—rolled into one. "Goldwyn's Folly" as this movie came to be known showed otherwise. Sten portrays Emile Zola's guttersnipe, who becomes the toast of Paris. She also comes between two brothers and commits suicide.

NANCY

MY MAN AND I (1952, MGM)—**Shelley Winters** is a suicidal taxi-dancer, whom Ricardo Montalban seems to prefer to Claire Trevor.

NANCY

NANCY FROM NOWHERE (1922, Silent, Paramount)—**Bebe Daniels** is adopted by a poor family that treats her cruelly, working her as a drudge. She meets a society man, Edward Sutherland, on a fishing trip, and when her foster father attacks her, she escapes by hiding herself in the back of Sutherland's car. When he discovers her, he buys her new clothes, which doesn't set well with his fiancee. Although she reluctantly returns to her foster parents, he follows and asks her to marry him.

NANCY, COUSIN

THE COUNTRY COUSIN (1919, Silent, Selznick)—**Elaine Hammerstein**, a Booth Tarkington heroine, must decide between an English dude and a gentlemanly villain.

NANETA

THE CRIMINAL (1916, Silent, Triangle)—Not really a criminal, **Clara Williams** is just unfortunate enough to be born out of wedlock, and spends her life as an outcast. When she finds an abandoned baby, she seeks to give it a better life than she's had, but the child had been kidnapped and she's suspected of the crime.

NANETTE

THE CARNIVAL GIRL (1926, Silent, Associated Exhibitors)—**Marian Mack** and her brother are left with a cruel guardian when their mother dies. She falls in love with Allan Forrest, whom she sees secretly. When her guardian discovers her meetings with Forrest, he beats her severely. The blackguard is a rumrunner, who eventually runs afoul of Mack's young man, the commander of a Coast Guard cutter.

NANETTE

NO, NO NANETTE (1930, First National); (1940, RKO)—In this happy musical comedy **Bernice Claire** and **Anna Neagle** each star as the girl for whom a Broadway show has been written. The backer's wife suspects her husband of having more than a cultural interest in Nanette.

NANNI, MARIO

MY COUSIN (1918, Silent, Artcraft)—It's a crime to have **Enrico Caruso** in a medium in which his great voice can't be heard. In this film, he showed a talent for comedy but the public didn't buy it.

NANNIE

A KENTUCKY CINDERELLA (1917, Silent, Bluebird)—When her father dies, **Ruth Clifford** goes to live with her uncle in Kentucky. Her uncle has married a widow with a spoiled daughter. The two make life very hard for Clifford until she meets a handsome young man and has her Cinderella ending.

NANNY

THE NANNY (1965, GB, 20th Century Fox)—**Bette Davis** is a veteran nursemaid for children. Her mind has gone and now she is a murderous threat to her young charges.

NANON

THE VEILED WOMAN (1929, Fox)—When **Lia Tora** rescues a young girl from a masher, she relates the story of her loves. When she is finished she hails a cab for the girl and finds the driver to be her long lost love whom she has just been describing.

NANU

THE WORLD'S GREATEST ATHLETE (1973, Buena Vista)—**Jan-Michael Vincent**, the world's greatest natural athlete, is discovered in Africa by college coach John Amos and his assistant Tim Conway. They trick him into coming to the U.S. and enrolling at their school. Vincent single-handedly takes on all the other teams at the NCAA track and field championships.

NAPOLEON (BONAPARTE)

A ROYAL DIVORCE (1938, GB, Paramount); EAGLE IN A CAGE (1971, National General)-When Josephine, played by Ruth Chatterton can't give him an heir **Pierre Blanchar**, as Napoleon, divorces her. The second film stars **Kenneth Haigh** as Napoleon during his early days in exile on St. Helena.

NAPOLEON, LOUIS III

SPY OF NAPOLEON (1939, GB, Syndicate)—**Frank Vosper** appears as the Emperor in this story of intrigue and spying by his perhaps illegitimate daughter.

NASA

CALL HER SAVAGE (1932, Fox)—Half-breed **Clara Bow** tries unsuccessfully to find happiness in the so-called civilized world. It's another insult to Indians.

NASH, BILLIE

WICKED WOMAN (1953, UA)—Sexy blonde **Beverly Michaels** separates Richard Egan, a California bar owner, from his alcoholic wife. Not much of an accomplishment if you think about it.

NASH, DAVE

RAMROD (1947, UA)—**Joel McCrea** helps Veronica Lake take revenge on Preston Foster. The latter drove her fiance away in this Luke Short western.

NATASHA

A COUNTESS FROM HONG KONG (1967, GB, Rank)—In a movie which demonstrates that Charles Chaplin had lost his comical touch, **Sophia Loren** is a Russian emigre hidden in his ocean liner cabin by American ambassador Marlon Brando.

NATASHA

THREE RUSSIAN GIRLS (1943, UA)—**Anna Sten** tries once more to make it in Hollywood, but this film meant to demonstrate the friendship between the United States and the Soviet Union didn't help. She's a Russian nurse who cares for a downed American pilot.

NATHAN

PARENTHOOD (1989, Universal)—**Rick Moranis** is obsessed about his children. He has his toddler studying Karate, Spanish and Kafka, but doesn't have time to offer his wife any romance.

NAUGHTON, BOB

BROTHERS (1930, Columbia)—**Bert Lytell** plays twin brothers separated at birth. Naughton becomes a successful lawyer but kills the husband of one of his clients. His brother is accused of the crime, but Naughton clears him, and then is sent to a mental institution, where he dies. His brother ends up with Naughton's fiancee.

NAUGHTON, CLAUDIA & DAVID

CLAUDIA (1943, 20th Century Fox); CLAUDIA AND DAVID (1946, 20th Century Fox)—**Dorothy McGuire** made her film debut as the delightful child-like bride of **Robert Young**, who wisely allows her to mature at her own pace. In the sequel, McGuire is now a mother living with Young and the baby in Connecticut. It's not as appealing as the original, but McGuire is still charming.

NAVAJO KID

THE NAVAJO KID (1946, PRC)—**Bob Steele**, who appeared in over 400 movies, is a white raised by Indians. He's searching for the murderer of his adoptive father.

NAZERMAN, SOL

THE PAWNBROKER (1965, Allied Artists)—A survivor of the Holocaust, **Rod Steiger** has lost his spirit, and his bleak life is reflected by the pawnshop he operates in Harlem.

NED

A KILLER WALKS (1952, GB, Grand National)—**Lawrence Harvey** murders his grandmother to get money to keep his city girlfriend in style. He tries to blame the crime on his half-witted brother.

NED/FR. REILLY

WE'RE NO ANGELS (1989, Paramount)—During the Depression, prisoners **Robert De Niro** and Sean Penn become reluctant escapees when a condemned prisoner takes them along when he makes his break. Separated from the brains, the two disguise themselves as priests attending an annual rite honoring a shrine of a weeping Virgin Mary.

NEDERLANDER, NED

THREE AMIGOS (1986, Orion)—**Martin Short** is one of three movie cowboys invited to a Mexican town plagued by bandits. The villagers believe they are real heroes, while the actors believe the people are going to pay them a large sum of money to appear in a movie. It's a stinker.

NEEDHAM, JOHN & NORBURY, JOSEPH

JOHN NEEDHAM'S DOUBLE (1916, Silent, Bluebird)—**Tyrone Power, Sr.** stars both as a nobleman, who has wasted his ward's fortune and committed a murder, and his exact double, whom he hopes will shoulder the blame.

NEILL, JANE

JANE GOES A'WOOING (1919, Silent, Paramount)—**Vivian Martin** raises her twin sisters and runs the family lunch wagon after her parents die. She employs a young man who adores her to run the lunch wagon while she takes a job as secretary to a millionaire. When the latter dies he leaves everything to Martin. But she tears up the will and returns to the man who loves her. Her sacrifice does not go unrewarded.

NEILSON, DONALD

THE BLACK PANTHER (1977, GB, Impico)—**Donald Sumpter** is a murderous kidnapper, circa 1972, in this film based on actual crimes.

NELL, MISTRESS

MISTRESS NELL (1915, Silent, Famous Players)—**Mary Pickford** is orange and flower seller Nell Gwyn. She captures the heart of England's King Charles II.

NELLIE

NELLIE, THE BEAUTIFUL CLOAK MODEL (1924, Silent, Cosmopolitan)—Unaware that she is the heir to a large fortune, **Claire Windsor** takes a job as a model. Her mother's unscrupulous nephew tries to insure she's not around to inherit her money by tying her to the tracks of a train, but her lover rescues her in the nick of time.

NELLO

A BOY OF FLANDERS (1924, Silent, MGM)—**Jackie Coogan** befriends a little dog, but back home he finds his last surviving relative, his grandfather, has died. Now on his own, Coogan and the dog are ultimately adopted by an artist.

NELLY

NELLY'S VERSION (1983, GB, Mithros)—Amnesiac **Eileen Atkins** may be involved in a series of crimes. When she recovers her memory, she goes back to her boring life as a housewife.

NELSON

FLATLINERS (1990, Columbia)—**Kiefer Sutherland** is the leader of a group of young interns experimenting with the brink of death to learn about the afterlife. He finds himself haunted by Billy Mahoney, an aggressive demon child from his past.

NELSON, BABY FACE

BABY FACE NELSON (1957, UA)—Would you believe it? That nice Andy Hardy boy, **Mickey Rooney**, appears as one of the criminals who made it to the top of the Most Wanted List.

NELSON, HORATIO

NELSON (1918, GB, Silent, Apex); (1926, GB, Silent, British International); THE NELSON AFFAIR (1973, GB, Universal)—**Donald Calthrop**, **Cedric Hardwicke** and **Peter Finch** each appeared as England's great naval hero who has a scandalous affair with Lady Hamilton.

NELSON, NELLIE *See* SAM BRADSHAW

NELSON, OZZIE, HARRIET, RICKY & DAVID

HERE COME THE NELSONS (1952, Universal)—**Ozzie, Harriet, Ricky** and **David Nelson** appear as themselves in the dull but wholesome story of radio and television's number one family.

NELSON, SCOTT

4D MAN (1959, Universal)—Scientist **Robert Lansing** finds too late that the formula which allows him to pass through any substance is also changing him into a monster.

NELSON, STEVE

KID NIGHTINGALE (1939, Warner Brothers)—In this boxing comedy, **John Payne** is a pugilist who gets involved with a crooked promoter, but is rescued by Jane Wyman.

NELSON, TOMMY

ABBOTT AND COSTELLO MEET THE INVISIBLE MAN (1951, Universal)—Abbott and Costello's scientist friend **Arthur Franz** discovers a serum which makes him invisible, but it also alters his personality.

NELVILLE, MR.
THE DRAUGHTSMAN'S CONTRACT (1983, GB, UA)—In 1694, draughtsman **Anthony Higgins** is given the assignment of designing a British aristocrat's house and gardens. His payment includes the Lord's wife.

NEMO, CAPTAIN
CAPTAIN NEMO AND THE UNDERWATER CITY (1969, GB, MGM)—Shipwreck survivors are taken to **Robert Ryan's** doomed underwater city.

NERD, NAT
THE GARBAGE PAILS KID (1987, Atlantic Entertainment)—**Larry Green** is another of the disgusting characters whose name describes his special shortcoming in this totally unnecessary movie.

NESILS, AHMED BEY
THE SHEIK STEPS OUT (1937, Republic)—When Lois Lane, an ill-mannered rich girl, mistakes sheik **Ramon Novarro** for a native guide in Arabia, he decides to teach her a lesson. He stages a fake kidnapping and then abandons her in the desert. Something happens on those desert nights as he later snatches her from the altar as she is about to wed her fiancee, taking her as his bride.

NESS, ELIOT
THE UNTOUCHABLES (1987, Paramount)—**Kevin Costner** is a U.S. Treasury agent assigned the job of bringing down the empire of Al Capone. An accountant on his team, who is killed, shows him how.

NETHERBY, MARCUS
THE MATING OF MARCUS (1924, Silent, Stoll)—**David Hawthorne** overcomes the taunts of his neighbors when he rescues two girls from a flood, and wins the heart of one of them.

NETTA
BLACK GIRL (1972, Cinerama)—**Leslie Uggams** is given a hard time by three sisters with whom she has been raised.

NEVADA
NEVADA (1927, Silent, Paramount)—**Gary Cooper** is a feared gunman who vacillates from being on the side of law and order or that of rustlers. He sees the light in the end.

NEVADA
NEVADA (1936, Paramount)—**Larry "Buster" Crabbe** is a cowboy in a Zane Grey western, who when accused of murder during a gold rush, finds the real killer.

NEVADA, WANDA
WANDA NEVADA (1979, UA)—Sexy 12-year-old **Brooke Shields** is won in a poker game by gambler Peter Fonda. Other than dirty old Humbert Humberts looking at Shields lustfully, there's nothing in the movie to recommend it.

NEVILLE, ROBERT
THE OMEGA MAN (1971, Warner Brothers)—After a germ-warfare attack gets out of hand, **Charlton Heston** is one of the few human survivors. He must protect the others from disease-carrying mutants.

NEVILLE, SHIRLEY
LORD CAMBER'S LADIES (1932, GB, British Int.)—Peer Nigel Bruce loves Benita Hume but allows himself to be lured into a

marriage to vaudeville star **Gertrude Lawrence**. She doesn't survive very long.

NEVINS, NOEL
RICH PEOPLE (1929, Pathe)—**Robert Ames** is the wealthy society man to whom Constance Bennett is engaged. She is not so sure about marriage, because her mother claims Bennett's father's wealth has always made her unhappy. Fortunately Constance finds a young man who doesn't have much money.

NEWBERG, MARY
MY SONG FOR YOU (1935, GB, Gaumont)—Opera singer **Aileen Marsen** makes use of the company star's infatuation for her to get her lover a job with the opera.

NEWBIGGIN, CELIA
THE MIDSHIPMAID (1932, GB, Gaumont)—**Jessie Matthews** is the pretty daughter of an economy expert, inspecting the British fleet at Malta to see what cuts can be made. Matthews has plenty of naval attention but becomes engaged to the son of the First Sea Lord. The pretty ones always go for the officers.

NEWBOLT, PETER
THE BOND BOY (1922, Silent, Associated First National)—In order to get money for his impoverished mother **Richard Barthelmess** bonds himself to cruel Charles Hill Mailes. Barthelmess tries to convince Mailes' wife not to run away from her brute of a husband with another man. Mailes shows up, misunderstands what's going on and is accidently killed. Barthelmess refuses to compromise Mailes' wife and is sentenced to hang. He escapes when the wife tells the truth.

NEWLANDER, TONY
I'LL GIVE A MILLION (1938, 20th Century Fox)—**Warner Baxter**, disillusioned with people who try to be his friend only because he's a millionaire, exchanges clothes with a hobo and hits the road, but not before letting it be known that he'll give a million to the first person who genuinely treats him kindly. Bums all over the country are given blue ribbon treatment.

NEWMAN, CAPT. JOSIAH
CAPTAIN NEWMAN M.D. (1963, Universal)—**Gregory Peck**, an idealistic military psychiatrist, has to battle both his patients and the military in trying to help fighting men who have developed mental illness.

NEWMAN, VINCE
NEWMAN'S LAW (1974, Universal)—Honest cop **George Peppard** is framed for a crime when he won't play ball with crooked politicians and the underworld.

NEWTON
THE NITWITS (1935, RKO)—**Robert Woolsey** and his partner Bert Wheeler are cigar salesmen who take the blame when the music publisher for whom Betty Grable works is shot and killed. Of course the real murderer is found in due time.

NEWTON, JEAN
LUCKY PARTNERS (1940, RKO)—**Ginger Rogers** and Ronald Colman, all but strangers, share a lottery ticket and win a trip to Niagara Falls which she talks her fiance Jack Carson into agreeing to. There she and Colman fall in love.

NEWTON, ORVIL
THOSE MAGNIFICENT MEN IN THEIR FLYING MACHINES (1965, GB, 20th Century Fox)—**Stuart Whitman** is an American pilot out

to win the $25,000 first prize put up by Sarah Miles' newspaper publisher father for a flight from London to Paris, during the early days of air travel. He wins Miles.

NEWTON, THOMAS JEROME

THE MAN WHO FELL TO EARTH (1976, GB, British Lion) -Space Alien **David Bowie** lands in New Mexico, and revolutionizes the communications industry with his inventions.

NICHOLAS

NICHOLAS AND ALEXANDRA (1971, GB, Columbia)—**Michael Jayston** is the last Czar of Russia. His wife is under the influence of the mad monk Rasputin. He and his entire family are executed by the Communists.

NICHOLS, BOB

NEW CHAMPION (1925, Silent, Columbia)—**William Fairbanks** replaces his boxing buddy in a match when the latter hurts his hand in an accident. Although at first he takes quite a beating, he comes through with a victory.

NICHOLS, STEVE

HERO AT LARGE (1980, MGM)—**John Ritter**, an out-of-work actor, takes a job impersonating a comic book super hero, Captain Avenger, and finds he really likes how kids relate to him.

NICHOLS, STEVE

I CAN'T ESCAPE (1934, Syndicate Releasing Corp.)—Having served a prison term for a crime he didn't commit makes it very hard for **Onslow Stevens** to get a job until he foils some phony stock swindlers and clears his name.

NICHOLS, SYD

THE TROJAN BROTHERS (1946, GB, Anglo-American)—**David Farrar** is the front half of a horse in a music-hall revue. He falls in love with a socialite sitting in the audience. He almost makes a horses' ass of himself.

NICHOLSON, MR.

THE MYSTERIOUS MR. NICHOLSON (1947, GB, Ambassador)—Gentleman thief **Anthony Hulme** helps a girl track down a murderer.

NICK

THE DEVIL'S PARTNER (1958, Huron)—**Ed Nelson** is an old man in Texas, who is possessed by the devil. When he dies he comes back to life as his younger self. He tries to steal a woman for his ritualistic practices, but the sheriff shoots and kills Nelson.

NICK

HE RAN ALL THE WAY HOME (1957, UA)—In his last film, always angry actor **John Garfield** is a killer hiding out in a home whose occupants he holds as hostages.

NICK

JAIL BIRDS (1939, GB, Butchers)—**Charles Hawtrey** and his mate escape from prison dressed as women, and take jobs in a bakery. Another escapee brings them some jewelry to hide which they bake into some bread. It ends up on the table of the detective fiance of Hawtrey's friend's daughter. Hawtrey and his buddy go back to prison acting as if they had never been away.

NICK

SPEED CRAZY (1959, Allied Artists)—**Brett Halsey** is a sports car racer in a story that features a lot of running around in circles and a murder.

NICKERSON, MIKE

THE VISITORS (1972, UA)—Vietnam vet **Steve Railsback** and his fellow sex criminal buddy Chico Martinez invade the home of another vet James Woods, who testified against them in the trial that sent them to prison.

NICKEY

MIKEY AND NICKEY (1976, Paramount)—**John Cassavetes** and Peter Falk, two small-time hoods, friends from childhood, have a falling-out.

NICKIE

PICKUP ON 101 (1972, American Int.)—**Lesley Ann Warren** teams up with old hobo Jack Albertson. With the help of singer Martin Sheen, she grants Albertson's dying request that his remains end up on a farm he once owned.

NICKLEBY, NICHOLAS

NICHOLAS NICKLEBY (1947, GB, Ealing)—Young teacher **Derek Bond** is hounded by his wicked uncle in this unexceptional adaptation of the Charles Dickens story.

NICOLAI, LT.

RED SCORPION (1989, Shapiro Glickenhaus)—Russian assassin **Dolph Lundgren** is sent to an unnamed African nation to kill a tribal leader who is making trouble for Cuban forces occupying his country. Instead, Lundgren makes a political conversion and joins the rebels.

NIFTY, NINA & NAT

FOUR JACKS AND A JILL (1941, RKO)—**Ray Bolger, Anne Shirley** and **Jack Briggs** are three-fifths of the title characters who make up a nightclub combo and its female singer. There's not much story and the music is as forgettable as is the movie.

NIGGER CHARLEY

THE LEGEND OF NIGGER CHARLEY (1972, Paramount); THE SOUL OF NIGGER CHARLEY (1973, Paramount)—In the first film, **Fred Williamson** is a violent black freedom fighter and former Virginia slave, who escapes after killing a cruel overseer. In the sequel he teams with a Mexican bandit to thwart a villain who captures runaway slaves, taking them to Mexico.

NIGHTINGALE, FLORENCE

THE WHITE ANGEL (1936, First National); THE LADY WITH A LAMP (1951, GB, British Lion) - **Kay Francis** is a poor choice for the gentlewoman who, with other angels of mercy, tends to the dying and wounded during the Crimean War, but she struggled valiantly with the role. **Anna Neagle** is a bit better in the 1951 picture as the champion of hospital reform.

NIJINSKY, VASLAV

NIJINSKY (1980, GB, Paramount)—When **George de la Pena** of the American Ballet theatre is dancing, the film is beautiful. Unfortunately, he's also expected to act as the brilliant dancer when off the stage as well.

NIKI

THE SMILING LIEUTENANT (1931, Paramount)—**Maurice Chevalier** smiles at violinist Claudette Colbert at a reception for plain princess Miriam Hopkins, but Hopkins intercepts the pass and thinks it's meant for her. Although, Colbert stays for breakfast with Chevalier, he's ordered to marry Hopkins. Seeing no future for her, Colbert takes pity on Hopkins and teaches her how to improve her looks and win Chevalier's love.

NILES, ADAM J.

BACHELOR IN PARADISE (1961, MGM)—In a time when wives stayed home and minded the house and children, while their husbands were off at work, writer **Bob Hope** moves into a middle-class development, where he's the only male resident during the day. This causes some concern for the husbands of the young wives, but Hope is more interested in mature Lana Turner.

NILLSON, CARLA

INTERNATIONAL LADY (1941, UA)—Lovely singer **Ilona Massey** was always at best a second string Jeanette MacDonald, as in this film in which she is a German spy who sings secrets in code over radio broadcasts. The film didn't do much to get Ilona a starting job.

NINA

NINA, THE FLOWER GIRL (1917, Silent, Triangle)—Blind flower girl **Bessie Love** loves hunchbacked newspaper peddler Elmer Clifton, whom she imagines as tall and handsome. When a wealthy man arranges for an operation that restores her sight, Clifton tries to kill himself rather than let her see him as he really is, but her benefactor intercedes once again and arranges for an operation which cures his problems.

NO, DR.

DR. NO (1962, GB, UA)—**Joseph Wiseman**, as a handless evil Oriental scientist intent on ruling the world, is the first film villain to cross swords with 007, James Bond.

NOAH

NOAH'S ARK (1928, Warner Brothers)—**Paul McAllister** appears as the Biblical ark builder who takes two of each animals aboard to save the breeds, when God purges the earth of sinners and idolaters.

NOBBIN, IDALENE

THE WALL FLOWER (1922, Silent, Goldwyn)—**Colleen Moore**, always ignored by boys, is pleased when the football captain pays attention to her at a dance. But it's all a cruel jest. She throws herself in front of a car of a society girl who takes Moore in and teaches her to be attractive. She succeeds so well, she attracts her benefactor's beau.

NOBLE, DR.

HOLD THAT HYPONIST (1957, Allied Artists)—**Robert Foulk** plays a crooked hypnotist in a Bowery Boys movie.

NOBODY, JOHNNY

JOHNNY NOBODY (1965, GB, Viceroy-Medallion)—A priest proves that explorer **Aldo Ray** was not divinely directed to shoot a drunken author.

NOBODY, MR.

MR. NOBODY (1927, GB, Silent, Fox)—**Frank Stanmore**, a student expelled from school for cheating, returns from abroad in time to collect his inheritance.

NOGGS, LADY

LADY NOGGS—PEERESS (1929, GB, Silent, Butchers)—**Joan Morgan** saves a member of Parliament's grandson from a foreign gold digger.

NOLAN, GYPO

THE INFORMER (1929, GB, British Int.); (1935, RKO)—Swedish **Lars Hansen** in 1929 and the lovely Irish mug **Victor McLaglen** in 1935 appear as the none too bright lout who betrays an IRA leader to the English for the price of a ticket out of the country. He learns that he is to be killed by the IRA on sight, but first he wants the forgiveness of the mother of the man he sent to his death. McLaglen won the Academy Award for Best Actor for his performance.

NOLAN, JIM

JIM, THE WORLD'S GREATEST (1976, Universal)—High school student **Gregory Harrison** lives unhappily with his alcoholic father and abused younger brother.

NOLAN, KENNETH

WOMAN CHASES MAN (1937, UA)—**Joel McCrea** is a cheap millionaire, whom attractive architect Miriam Hopkins corrals after some modest screwball comedy adventures.

NOLAN, RUBY

TRUE TO THE NAVY (1930, Paramount)—**Clara Bow** works at a soda fountain, and has dozens of boyfriends on every ship that sails into port. She also marries one on the floor of a dance contest to get a $100 prize.

NOLAN, SUSIE

A KISS FOR SUSIE (1917, Silent, Paramount) - **Vivian Martin** becomes the object of affection of the son of a millionaire, when the lad takes a job as a laborer to learn the business from the ground up.

NOOKEY, DR. JAMES

CARRY ON AGAIN, DOCTOR (1969, GB, Rank)—When the "Carry On" series had to recycle ideas, it had to rely on obvious sexual jokes such as **Jim Dale's** character's name.

NOON

A MAN CALLED NOON (1973, GB, National General)—Amnesiac **Richard Crenna** discovers he is a businessman turned gunslinger.

NORA

THE GIRL FROM SAN LORENZO (1950, UA)—**Jane Adams** is the title female in this Cisco Kid film with Duncan Renaldo as the Kid and Leo Carrillo as his sidekick.

NORA

HALF ANGEL (1951, 20th Century Fox)—Engaged nurse **Loretta Young** falls in love with former sweetheart Joseph Cotten and the conflict in her mind over the two men in her life causes her to become a sleepwalker.

NORCROSS, FRANCES

HER BIG NIGHT (1926, Silent, Universal)—**Laura La Plante** impersonates a movie star, whom she resembles, causing herself all kinds of trouble.

NORMA

LADIES MUST PLAY (1930, Columbia)—Bankrupt Newport social-ite Neil Hamilton arranges for his pretty stenographer **Dorothy Sebastian** to marry a millionaire on the condition that he receive 10% of any marriage settlement.

NORMA RAE

NORMA RAE (1979, 20th Century Fox)—**Sally Field** wins her first Oscar for her role as a southern factory girl who helps an out-of-town labor organizer form a union, despite the intimidating actions of management.

NORMAN

THE DRESSER (1983, Columbia)—**Tom Courtenay** is the homosexual dresser of Shakespearian actor Albert Finney on tour in England during WWII.

NORMAN

JUST MY LUCK (1957, GB, Rank)—In order to win enough money to marry his girl, **Norman Wisdom** bets one pound on a jockey to win all six races in one day. Guess what?

NORMAN

MAN OF THE MOMENT (1955, GB, Group)—**Norman Wisdom**, a junior filing clerk, accidentally is put in charge of the Tawaki Island, but when he visits it, a volcano erupts and Tawaki sinks into the ocean.

NORMAN, JACK

THE MILLIONAIRE (1921, Silent, Universal)—**Herbert Rawlinson** inherits 80 million dollars from a murdered financier who once loved his mother. His girl won't marry him until she sees what effect all that money will have on him.

NORMAN, VICTOR ALBEE

THE HUCKSTERS (1947, MGM)—Just back from the service **Clark Gable** resumes his job at an advertising agency, where his biggest client is disgusting Sydney Greenstreet, whose company makes soap. Although this puts him into contact with both Deborah Kerr and Ava Gardner, in the end Gable tells Greenstreet what he can do with his product.

NORMAND, SIR WILLIAM

THE MAN WHO WON (1933, GB, British Int.)—**Henry Kendell**, the heir to a farm, falls for his hostile neighbor's daughter.

NORRAY, YORKE

MAN FROM HEADQUARTERS (1928, Silent, Rayart)—**Cornelius Keefe** fights a gang of international criminals for the possession of secret documents and a gold shipment.

NORRIS, DRAKE

THE LAWYER'S SECRET (1931, Paramount)—**Clive Brook** can't disclose what he knows about a murder because of the client-attorney relation.

NORRIS, VICKI

PISTOL PACKIN' MAMA (1943, Republic)—In this minor musical **Ruth Terry** is the owner of a gambling den in Nevada. A cheat comes along and wins everything she has and goes back to New York to open his own gambling house. Terry assumes a new identity and gets a job singing in his club and then wins the club from him.

NORSON, DEWEY

THE YOUNG RUNAWAYS (1968, MGM)—**Kevin Coughlin** and other teens drift into anti-social behavior because they are bored. Get a job!

NORSON, DANIEL

TENNESSEE CHAMP (1954, MGM)—**Dewey Martin** is an honest boxer who reforms his crooked boss.

NORTH, JOE

ADVENTURES OF A TAXI DRIVER (1976, GB, Salon/Alpha)—This film is just a series of bedding down of assorted British beauties by cabdriver **Barry Evans**.

NORTH, PAMELA & GERALD P.

MR. & MRS. NORTH (1941, MGM)—**Gracie Allen** and **William Post, Jr.** portray the radio detectives who find the bodies piling up before they solve the mystery.

NORTH, TEDDY

THE COWBOY AND THE LADY (1922, Silent, Paramount)—**Tom Moore** is just the kind of man Mary Miles Minter is looking for after a marriage to a philanderer. He's a gentleman rancher who has eyes only for her.

NORTH, THEOPHILUS

MR. NORTH (1988, Goldwyn)—This movie, co-scripted by John Huston, just before his death, is based on an autobiographical story written by Thornton Wilder when he was 76. It is the story of artist, faith-healer, and all-around fixer **Anthony Edwards** who makes a major impact on Newport, R.I. high society in the 1920s.

NORTON, BETTY

THE BIG SISTER (1916, Silent, Paramount)—**Mae Murray** is a slum girl with no one to watch over her or her little brother, when her father is sent to prison. She and her brother attempt to run from a white slaver, and a rich man's auto runs over the little boy. After this anyone can fill in the rest of the screenplay.

NORTON, CRAIG

A MAN FOUR-SQUARE (1926, Silent, Fox)—**Buck Jones**, a gentleman rancher, returns from a holiday to clear his foreman and friend of a charge of cattle rustling.

NORTON, DAVE

TWO AGAINST THE WORLD (1932, Warner Brothers)—Young lawyer **Neil Hamilton** defends the young woman he loves against a murder charge when she takes the rap for her worthless brother.

NORTON, ELINOR

ELINOR NORTON (1935, Fox)—While her husband is away at war, **Claire Trevor** falls under the romantic sway of a suave South American coffee magnate. When her shell-shocked husband arrives home, Trevor takes him west to a ranch for a cure. The South American follows and the two men become friends.

NORTON, JANE

DAY-TIME WIFE (1939, 20th Century Fox)—When **Linda Darnell** wrongly concludes that executive husband Tyrone Power is having an affair with his secretary Wendy Barrie, she takes a job as secretary to playboy Warren William and now Power concludes she's having an affair with her boss.

NORTON, LOUISA

LOUISA (1950, Universal)—**Spring Byington** comes to live with her son Ronald Reagan, and attracts the romantic attention of both grocer Edmund Gwenn and Reagan's boss Charles Coburn. It's never too late for love.

NORTON, MADGE

THE PLAY GIRL (1928, Silent, Fox)—**Madge Bellamy**, who works for a florist, loses her job after an encounter with a man taking a bath when she delivers a flower arrangement to his apartment. She becomes a play girl, but the man she took by surprise asks her to marry him.

NOSTRADAMUS

THE MAN WITHOUT A BODY (1957, GB, Eros)—George Coulouris steals the head of 16th century astrologer Nostradamus. He grafts the head on his assistant **Michael Golden**, whom he maims when he discovers his wife plans to run away with the younger man. The creature throws Courlouris from the top of a bell-tower. Did Nostradamus predict it?

NOVAK, JOE
THE CHRISTMAS KID (1968, Producers Releasing Corp.)—**Jeffrey Hunter** is a cowpoke searching for his identity in this class "C" western.

NOVAK, JAN
THE MAN WHO DARED (1933, Fox)—**Preston Foster** appears as a fictional character based on Chicago's mayor Anton Cermak who was killed in an assassination attempt on the life of Franklin D. Roosevelt.

NOVAK, STEVE
SATURDAY'S HERO (1951, Columbia)—**John Derek** wins a football scholarship and discovers getting an education is not part of the deal. Sounds timely.

NOVIK, HUGO
DEVIL DOLL (1964, GB, Galsworthy)—**David Charlesworth** is a ventriloquist's dummy who gets ideas of his own after the soul of a girl is transferred to its body.

NUGENT, AMY
THE SPELL OF AMY NUGENT (1945, GB, Pyramid)—**Diana King** is the dead fiancee of a man who is almost driven mad when a spiritualist materializes her.

NUGENT, DICK
THE BACHELOR AND THE BOBBYSOXER (1947, RKO)—When teen Shirley Temple develops a crush on Cary Grant, her sister, Judge Myrna Loy, more his type, orders Grant to pay Temple court until she wises up. She does and so does Grant who notices how attractive is Her Honor.

NUGGET NELL
NUGGET NELL (1919, Silent, Paramount)—**Dorothy Gish**, a superb comedienne, is a gun-wearing saloon owner who falls in love with an easterner, but drops him to go back to her cowboy lover.

NUN, THE
THE NUN AND THE SERGEANT (1962, UA)—Now in a character role, **Anna Sten**, who found her career more suited to Europe, plays a nun who helps a platoon of Dirty Dozen-like marines become heroes in Korea.

NYAH
DEVIL GIRL FROM MARS (1954, GB, British Lion)—**Patricia Laffan** is the leader of a female-dominated Mars society. She comes to Earth, landing by mistake in the Scottish Highlands, and has her space ship blown up by an escaped convict.

NYLON
THE WOMAN FROM TANGIER (1948, Columbia)—Cafe entertainer **Adele Jergens** helps an insurance investigator solve the mystery of two murders and the theft of 50,000 pounds of sterling.

OAHN
CASUALTIES OF WAR (1989, Columbia)—When a squad of marines is sent on a dangerous mission in Vietnam, sergeant Sean Penn kidnaps native girl **Thuy Thu Le**, whom he and his men repeatedly rape. When her presence threatens to give their position away to the enemy, Penn kills her. The one member of the squad who didn't participate in her abuse reports the events to the higher command, who don't seem bothered or even interested.

OAKES, BOYSIE
THE LIQUIDATOR (1966, GB, MGM)—Reluctant secret agent **Rod Taylor** foils a plot to kill the Duke of Edinburgh.

OAKLEY, ANNIE
ANNIE OAKLEY (1935, RKO); ANNIE GET YOUR GUN (1950, MGM)—**Barbara Stanwyck** portrayed the famous female sharp-shooter in a highly fictionalized account of her life. It was even more make believe in the musical starring **Betty Hutton** who gave rousing renditions of songs that Ethel Merman did so well on Broadway. They included: "You Can't Get a Man with a Gun" and "There's No Business Like Show Business."

OAKROYD, JESS
THE GOOD COMPANIONS (1933, GB, Gaumont); (1957, GB, AB-Pathe)—**Edmund Gwenn** and **Eric Portman** appear as the Yorkshire joiner who teams with a middle-aged spinster and a disillusioned music teacher to finance a failing traveling music show which soon becomes a success.

OATFIELD, WINNIE & HENRY
WANTED (1937, GB, Sound City)—**Zasu Pitts** and **Claude Dampier**, mistaken for jewel thieves, are forced to pose as big-game hunters in order to steal some famous jewels.

OBERG, BERTHA
LUMMOX (1930, UA)—Swedish drudge **Winifred Westover** is seduced by a reprobate poet and becomes pregnant. When the baby is born, Westover gives the child up for adoption and watches from a distance as her son grows to be a great pianist.

OBIE
BIG SHOTS (1987, 20th Century Fox)—Shy white boy **Rickie Buster** and street-smart black Darius McCrary become involved with murder and mayhem.

O'BRIEN, BILL
OFFICER O'BRIEN (1930, Pathe)—**William Boyd** is promoted to lieutenant in the police department when he arrests a gang leader for murder. About that time Boyd's father is released from prison, not knowing that his son is a policeman. The two incidents merge with the father saving his son from disgrace.

O'BRIEN, BUDDY
BYE-BYE BUDDY (1929, Part-Talkie, Trinity)—**Bud Shaw** is kept in the dark about his mother's ownership of a notorious nightclub until she becomes involved in a murder.

O'BRIEN, CHINA
CHINA O'BRIEN (1991, Imperial Entertainment/Golden Harvest)—Produced in 1988, the film features big-city cop Cyntha Rothrock, who teaches martial arts after hours. She quits the force after accidently shooting a child. She heads home to Utah, where she helps her daddy, David Blackwell, contend with gangsters led by Steven Kerby.

O'BRIEN, DENNIS
T-MEN (1947, Eagle-Lion)—**Dennis O'Keefe** is one of two treasury agents who have gone undercover to get the goods on a counterfeiting ring. The other one is Alfred Ryder, whose cover is innocently blown

by his wife. O'Keefe must look on helplessly as his fellow agent is killed, but not before providing O'Keefe with the needed evidence to put the ring out of business. This is excellent "B" film noir.

O'BRIEN, GLENDA
WOMAN ACCUSED (1933, Paramount)—Ten well-known authors each wrote a chapter of the story of this movie without consultation. Poor **Nancy Carroll** got stuck with the job of trying to bring some sense to the crazy twisting plot line about an actress whose pleasure cruise is interrupted by an ex-lover. When he's killed, Carroll has to survive a ship-board mock trial.

O'BRIEN, HERRARA "HERO"
HERO AND THE TERROR (1988, Cannon)—By accident, police detective **Chuck Norris** captures hulking psycho Jack O'Halloran. The press names him a hero, but his adversary escapes and comes looking for the quaking Norris.

O'BRIEN, JIM
TODAY I HANG (1942, PRC)—**Walter Woolf King** is convicted of a murder he didn't commit. It's up to Mona Barrie to prove him innocent before his execution.

O'BRIEN, JIMMY
BROADWAY BIG SHOT (1942, PRC)—**Ralph Byrd** is a crime reporter and star quarterback for a college team. He arranges to go to prison so he can get a story on an imprisoned union official. He not only gets the story, he wins the warden's daughter, and is elected president of the union.

O'BRIEN, JOAN
WATERFRONT LADY (1935, Mascot-Republic)—Frank Albertson's boss, the owner of a gambling boat, is a suspect in a killing, and Albertson attempts to divert suspicion to himself by going on the run. While he is posing as a sailor on the houseboat of a gob and his daughter **Ann Rutherford**, a romance develops.

O'BRIEN, JOEY
CADILLAC MAN (1990, Orion)—Con-man **Robin Williams** can unload any lemon of his automobile dealership lot. He needs all of his hard-selling skills when Tim Robbins, the husband of his mistress, goes berserk and holds the dealership hostage.

O'BRIEN, KITTY
THE TELEPHONE GIRL (1927, Silent, Lasky)—Telephone operator **Madge Bellamy** refuses to become part of a plot to ruin a political candidate's reputation.

O'BRIEN, PATRICIA
THE CHORUS LADY (1924, Silent, Warner Brothers)—Chorus girl **Margaret Livingston** plans to marry horseman Alan Roscoe, but a fire in his stable blinds his prize filly and forces a postponement of the wedding. She moves in with her sister, and the girls find work in the Follies. When Roscoe comes to get his intended, he's shocked to find her in the apartment of a notorious philanderer. After some predictable confusion, the two are reconciled and marry.

O'CALLAGHAN, SEAN
SONG O' MY HEART (1930, Fox)—Famous tenor **John McCormack** portrays a talented singer who years earlier gave up his career when the woman he loved was forced to marry a wealthy man. He helps her raise her children when their father deserts them.

OCEAN, DANNY
OCEAN'S ELEVEN (1960, Warner Brothers)—In a film which seemed to be made up as it was filmed, **Frank Sinatra** leads his former squad of army rangers in a heist of millions from the five largest casinos in Las Vegas precisely at midnight on New Year's Eve. It's watchable.

O'CLOCK, JOHNNY
JOHNNY O'CLOCK (1947, Columbia)—**Dick Powell**, part-owner of a gambling casino, becomes involved in the murders of a dishonest policeman and the cop's girlfriend. He ultimately has a shootout with his senior partner in which he is wounded and the other man is killed. The deceased's wife, rejected by Powell, tells the police that Powell killed her husband in cold blood.

O'CONNELL, PEG
PEG O' MY HEART (1933, MGM)—Spunky Irish lass **Marion Davies** leaves her father, moving to an English manor, in order to meet the conditions of an inheritance.

O'CONNERS, MUSHY
OCEAN'S ELEVEN (1960, Warner Brothers)—**Joey Bishop** is one of eleven army buddies led by Frank Sinatra who "hit" five Las Vegas casinos at the same time.

O'CONNOR, BARRY
PRINCE OF AVENUE A (1920, Silent, Universal)—Boxer **James J. Corbett** didn't embarrass himself as a young fellow who climbs to the top of the political world without turning his back on those who knew him when.

O'CONNOR, DONOGH
IRISH AND PROUD OF IT (1938, Ireland, Crusade)—Food tablet manufacturer **Richard Hayward** foils gangster moonshiners from Chicago.

O'CONNOR, EVIE
A LETTER FOR EVIE (1945, MGM)—**Marsha Hunt** finds it difficult to choose between her pen-pal and his friend for her one true love.

O'CONNOR, JERRY
BURN 'EM UP O'CONNOR (1939, MGM)—**Dennis O'Keefe** loves to drive fast and hopes to be the first driver to survive the cars designed by a somewhat manic car builder.

O'CONNOR, JIMMY
JIMMY AND SALLY (1933, Fox)—Ambitious **James Dunn** confuses his priorities, and for a short time forgets his love for Claire Trevor.

O'CONNOR, KATHLEEN
SMILING IRISH EYES (1929, Warner Brothers)—**Colleen Moore**, in her first all-talking, all-singing, all-dancing picture, follows her song-writing violinist boyfriend from Ireland to Broadway.

OCTOPUSSY
OCTOPUSSY (1983, GB, MGM/UA)—**Maud Adams** is the latest in distractions for 007 as he fights the evil Louis Jourdan, who plots with a Russian general to bring the two super-powers down on each other. Adams is somewhat of a villain but James Bond's influence brings out the best in her.

O'DARE, IRENE
IRENE (1926, Silent, First National); (1940, RKO)—**Colleen Moore**, a pretty Irish girl, has a Cinderella -like romance with a millionaire whom she meets while working at a fashion salon. **Anna Neagle** brings meager musical talents to the 1940 version, whose songs include "Alice Blue Gown" and "Out on a Limb."

O'DARE, MABEL

CAIN AND MABEL (1936, Warner Brothers)—Waitress-turned musical comedy star **Marion Davies** falls in love with boxer Clark Gable, after a press agent sets up a phony romance between them.

O'DAWN, GLEAM

GLEAM O'DAWN (1922, Silent, Fox)—Artist **John Gilbert**, living in the Canadian woods, befriends a man and his daughter. Gilbert later discovers that the man may have been his father, whom Gilbert has cause to hate for deserting him at birth.

O'DAY, JIMMY

ONE PUNCH O'DAY (1926, Silent, Rayart)—Boxing champion **Billy Sullivan** wins enough money to pay for the oil leases on some land and foil crooked developers.

O'DAY, JOHNNY

JOHNNY GET YOUR HAIR CUT (1927, Silent, MGM)—Orphan **Jackie Coogan** saves the daughter of a horse breeder and rides the man's prize horse to victory in the big race.

O'DAY, KATHLEEN

KLONDIKE KATE (1944, Columbia)—**Ann Savage** portrays the real life queen of the Alaskan gold rush of the late 1890s.

O'DAY, KITTY

ADVENTURES OF KITTY O'DAY (1944, Monogram); DETECTIVE KITTY O'DAY (1944, Monogram)—Telephone operator **Jean Parker** overhears a plot that results in three murders and that she solves herself.

O'DAY, LARRY

THE HANDSOME BRUTE (1925, Silent, Columbia)—**William Fairbanks** loses his job on the police force. Nevertheless, he goes after a gang of thugs, and discovers that a world famous detective is the leader of the crooks.

O'DAY, MA & TOMMY

MOTHER'S BOY (1929, Pathe)—In a sort of Christian JAZZ SINGER, **Morton Downey** is thrown out by his father, unjustly accusing him of stealing the family's savings. Downey goes on to become a star singer. On the night of his Broadway debut word comes to him that his mother **Beryl Mercer**, whom he hasn't seen since he left home, is dying. Downey rushes to her side, sings for her and nurses her back to health, and then makes his delayed opening which is a great success.

O'DAY, PADDY

PADDY O'DAY (1935, Fox)—**Jane Withers**, an immigrant girl freshly arrived in the U.S., finds that her mother who had come across earlier has died. Jane escapes from Ellis Island and becomes an entertainer.

O'DAY, TEDDY

THE HEART OF A FOLLIES GIRL (1928, Silent, First National) - Male secretary Larry Kent commits forgery to be able to buy an engagement ring for Follies girl **Billie Dove**. He goes to prison but she waits for him.

O'DAY, TOM & BARRY

MY DAD (1922, Silent, R-C/FBO)—**Johnny Walker** loves the stepdaughter of a man who accuses his father **Wilbur Higby** of being a murderer. Walker clears his father's name and wins the girl.

O'DELL, MARGARET

THE CANARY MURDER CASE (1929, Paramount)—The canary in this revamped silent Philo Vance murder mystery is blackmailing Broadway singer **Louise Brooks**. Her refusal to return from Europe for the dialogue dubbing caused the studio to substitute the voice of Margaret Livingston. Brooks was dead in Hollywood ever after.

ODETTE

ODETTE (1951, GB, UA)—**Anna Neagle** stars in a gripping biopic of the famous French resistance fighter and spy.

ODONGO

ODONGO (1956, GB, Columbia)—A trapper for circuses in Africa suspects native lad **Juma** is releasing the animals he captures.

O'DONNELL, HUGH

THE FIGHTING PRINCE OF DONEGAL (1966, GB, Buena Vista)—Irish prince **Peter McEnery** escapes from the British to unite the clans, and save his love.

O'DONNELL, ROY

TWO BRIGHT BOYS (1939, Universal)—Young **Jackie Cooper** inherits some valuable Texas property, but almost loses it to an unscrupulous oil man. He's saved by his friend Freddie Bartholomew and Freddie's father Melville Cooper.

O'DOWD, MARIUS

DR. O'DOWD (1940, GB, Warner Brothers)—Drunken Irish doctor **Shaun Glenville** is reinstated to his hospital post after saving his engineer son from a diptheria epidemic.

OEDIPUS

OEDIPUS REX (1957, Canada, Motion Pictures); OEDIPUS THE KING (1968, GB, Universal)—**Douglas Campbell** and **Christopher Plummer** portray Sophocles' tragic king who has killed his father and married his own mother.

O'FALLON, KATHY

MRS. MIKE (1949, UA)—Boston society woman **Evelyn Keyes** gives up everything to follow her mountie husband Dick Powell to his outpost in the frozen North of 1907.

O'FARRELL, COLIN

KING OF THE CASTLE (1925, Silent, GB, Stoll)—**Brian Aherne** earns the love of Marjorie Hume who is forced to marry him after he saves her child from death.

O'FARRELL, MASTER SGT. DAN

THE PRIVATE NAVY OF SGT. O'FARRELL (1968, UA) -**Bob Hope** is too old for this kind of nonsense. An officer on a lonely South Seas island, he hopes to improve the morale of his troops by importing nurses. Big deal—he gets Gina Lollobrigida and sticks the men with Phyllis Diller.

O'FLYNN, THE

THE FIGHTING O'FLYNN (1949, Universal)—As dashing as his father, **Douglas Fairbanks, Jr.** is an Irish soldier of fortune, who leads the forces against troops of Napoleon when they invade Ireland.

O'FLYNN, FATHER

FATHER O'FLYNN (1938, Ireland, Butchers)—Irish priest **Tom Burke** adopts the daughter of an imprisoned member of his parish. She's loved by the son of the squire.

OGDEN, JOAN

UNASHAMED (1932, MGM)—Rebellious **Helen Twelvetrees** is in love with a scoundrel, who is only after her body and money. When her father won't give permission for her marriage, she elopes with the bum, but her brother follows and accidently kills her intended.

OGDEN, REGGIE

THE SHADOW (1936, GB, UA)—Novelist **Henry Kendall** helps police learn the identity of a murderous blackmailer.

O'GILL, DARBY

DARBY O'GILL AND THE LITTLE PEOPLE (1959, Buena Vista)—Irish caretaker **Albert Sharpe** briefly gets the best of Jimmy O'Dea, the King of the Leprechauns.

OGILVIE, OLIVER CROMWELL, "O.C."

O.C. AND STIGGS (1987, MGM/UA)—**Daniel H. Jenkins'** father cuts off the insurance policy of Neill Barry's father in this inconsequential teen exploitation film about the summer adventures of two youngsters.

O'GRADY, PATRICIA

THE DAUGHTER OF ROSIE O'GRADY (1950, Warner Brothers) - Irish entertainer **June Havoc** falls in love with impresario Tony Pastor (Gordon MacRae) despite the objections of her usually drunk father James Barton.

O'GRADY, ROSE

SECOND HAND ROSE (1922, Silent, Universal)—**Gladys Walton**, the adopted daughter of the Rosensteins, accepts the marriage proposal of an older admirer when he offers to pay the bail for her brother, who has been accused of embezzlement. When the young man proves his innocence, Walton's intended, seeing that she really loves another, releases her from her promise so she can marry her true love.

O'GRADY, ROSIE *See* MADELINE MARLOWE

O'GRADY, TOM

LUCKY LOSER (1934, GB, Paramount)—**Richard Dolman** sells an antique desk and then realizes that a winning sweeps-stake ticket is in it.

O'HALLORAN, MICHAEL

MICHAEL O'HALLORAN (1937, Republic); (1948, Monogram)—**Jackie Moran and Scotty Beckett** each appear as an orphan newsboy who takes in a crippled girl when her alcoholic mother is injured. He finds a doctor who discovers that the girl's illness is all in the mind, brought on by her mother's abuse.

O'HARA, BOB & HARRY

O'HARA'S WIFE (1983, Davis-Panzer)—**Ed Asner** is the only one who can see his deceased wife **Mariette Hartley**, and no one else really cares to in this poor rip-off of TOPPER.

O'HARA, BUNNY

BUNNY O'HARA (1971, American International)—Senior citizen **Bette Davis** and ex-con plumber Ernest Borgnine dress as hippies to rob a bank.

O'HARA, DAN

BIG DAN (1923, Silent, Fox)—Returning from WWI, **Charlie Jones** finds his wife has left him. He turns his home into a camp where he trains boys to become boxers. He takes in Marian Nixon when he rescues her from an unwanted suitor, and when his wife dies, marries Nixon.

O'HARA, DENNIS

THE RAWHIDE KID (1928, Silent, Universal)—Each year Irishman **Hoot Gibson** defeats his town's leading citizen, Frank Hagney, in the annual horse race, much to the latter's annoyance. Hagney acquires Gibson's horse in a gambling game, and when he won't sell the animal back, Gibson steals it, and in the big race beats Hagney's rider and horse and then gives Hagney a whipping, to the delight of the citizens because Hagney had been cheating all of them.

O'HARA, JOHN

I COVER THE UNDERWORLD (1955, Republic)—Clergyman **Sean McClory's** convict twin brother has just been released from prison. You just know there will be some mistaken identity problems.

O'HARA, JOHN

TOO TOUGH TO KILL (1935, Columbia)—Engineer **Victor Jory** is sent into the mountains to find out what's holding up the construction of a tunnel. He gets the job done and fires all the troublemakers.

O'HARA, JOHNNY

THE PEOPLE AGAINST O'HARA (1951, MGM)—**James Arness** is accused of gunning down a man in the streets. Not being able to afford a good lawyer, his parents hire the services of alcoholic ex-D.A. Spencer Tracy who gives his life to prove Arness innocent.

O'HARA, KATHLEEN

THE FIFTY-FIFTY GIRL (1928, Silent, Paramount)—**Bebe Daniels** bets her partner that she can run the ranch better than he can the house. The first one to ask for help gets full ownership of the ranch. She wins.

O'HARA, KITTY

MY BEST GAL (1944, Republic)—**Jane Withers** helps find a backer for the musical show written by her boyfriend Jimmy Lydon.

O'HARA, PRINCESS

PRINCESS O'HARA (1935, Universal)—In this Damon Runyan story a group of 42nd street hoods offer helpless and homeless **Jean Parker** their protection.

O'HARA, SALLY

THE MERRY WIDOW (1925, Silent, MGM)—While on a tour of Europe, follies girl **Mae Murray** meets prince John Gilbert and Roy D'Arcy, the Crown prince of the kingdom of Monteblanco. She favors Gilbert who announces he plans to marry her, but the king and queen of Monteblanco will not sanction the union. Feeling she has been jilted, Murray marries the richest man in Monteblanco who dies of excitement on their wedding night. Murray goes to Paris where she gains the reputation of being the "Merry Widow." After some further complications, including a duel between Gilbert and D'Arcy, the death of the king, the assassination of D'Arcy, and Gilbert made king, Murray and Gilbert marry.

O'HARA, SKIP

DIARY OF A BACHELOR (1964, American International)—When his fiancee reads **William Taylor's** diary she learns what a naughty boy he has been. By the time he reforms, she's discovered the fun of swinging.

O'KEEFE, DANNO

LAUGHING IRISH EYES (1936, Republic)—Irish blacksmith **Phil Regan** has ambitions to become a singer. He does.

O'KEEFE, CAPT. DAVID

HIS MAJESTY O'KEEFE (1953, Warner Brothers)—American trader **Burt Lancaster** journeys to the South Seas in the 1870s where he plans to make a fortune in copra. Lancaster is full of derring-do and grinning charm.

OKICHI

THE BARBARIAN AND THE GEISHA (1958, 20th Century Fox)—**Eiko Ando** portrays a beautiful geisha who is planted in the home of John Wayne, America's first consul to Japan in 1856, to distract him from his mission, but she falls in love with the Duke.

OKTYABRINA

THE GIRL FROM PETROVKA (1974, Universal)—Russian **Goldie Hawn** is tired of the restrictive nature of Soviet life. She has a ho-hum affair with American newsman Hal Holbrook before being sent to prison for having faulty citizenship papers.

OLAF, PRINCE

THE PRINCE AND THE BEGGERMAID (1921. GB, Silent, Stoll)—King Hildred of Ruritania (Harvey Braban) goes to war with a neighboring country to force its princess to wed his ugly hunchback brother **Henry Ainley**.

OLCOTT, CHAUNCEY

MY WILD IRISH ROSE (1947, Warner Brothers)—**Dennis Morgan** portrays singer-composer Chauncey Olcott who writes the title number to glorify the woman who would become his wife, portrayed in this biopic by Arlene Dahl.

OLD BILL

OLD BILL THROUGH THE AGES (1924, GB, Silent, Ideal)—**Syd Walker**, a British private, dreams in succession that he is William the Conqueror, present at Runnymede, with the Pilgrims at Plymouth Rock, and a participant at the Boston Tea Party.

OLD MAN, THE

THE OLD MAN AND THE SEA (1958, Warner Brothers)—Dignified old fisherman **Spencer Tracy** battles the forces of nature in this film based on an Ernest Hemingway novella.

OLDHAM, STEVE

THE CUB (1915, Silent, World)—Cub reporter **Johnny Hines** is sent to cover a feud between hillbilly families, much in the manner of a war correspondent, becoming involved with both factions.

OLE BILL

THE BETTER 'OLE (1926, Silent, Warner Brothers)—In a funny film, **Syd Chaplin** portrays a British WWI sergeant who discovers that his major is a German spy.

O'LEARY, LANCE

THE PATIENT IN ROOM 18 (1938, Warner Brothers)—Detective **Patric Knowles** is confined to a hospital where a patient is killed and $100,000 is stolen. Knowles gets to the bottom of the mystery.

OLER, WENDALL

THE WIZARD OF LONELINESS (1988, Skouras)—Twelve-year-old **Lukas Haas** comes to live with his grandparents after the death of his unloving mother and the departure of his alienated father for the war. At first all Haas wishes to do is steal enough money to run away, but he comes to love and be a part of his extended family and its community.

OLGA

HOUSEKEEPER'S DAUGHTER (1939, UA)—Housekeeper **Peggy Wood** and her daughter Joan Bennett help sappy John Hubbard solve the case of a murdered showgirl.

OLGA

THE MAN WHO LOVED REDHEADS (1955, GB, London Films)—Olga is the third redhead played by **Moira Shearer**, and one of the four great loves in the life of John Justin.

OLGA

THE THREE SISTERS (1970, GB, British Lion); (1977, Actor Studios Theatre)—**Jeanne Watts** and **Geraldine Page** appear as one of three orphaned sisters in these two adaptations of the Anton Chekhov play.

OLGA, PRINCESS

THE PRINCESS COMES ACROSS (1936, Paramount)—**Carole Lombard** travels to Europe third-class. On the return trip the Brooklyn showgirl travels first class posing as a Swedish princess. She falls for shipboard musician Fred MacMurray.

OLGA THE ROBOT

THE PERFECT WOMAN (1950, GB, Rank/Ealing)—**Pamela Devis** has the role of a robot invented by a scientist. The man's niece takes the place of the robot, but things get a bit confusing when Devis shows up also.

OLIVER

ONCE A GENTLEMAN (1926, Silent, Rayart)—**Edward Everett Horton** is rewarded for his excellent work as a valet when his employer gives him a month's paid vacation and a new wardrobe. Horton is mistaken for a nobleman just back from India by the members of the exclusive Gotham Club. After some interesting experiences, he is exposed, but returns to his employer with a new love.

OLIVER

OLIVER & COMPANY (1988, Animated, Buena Vista)—In this Disney adaptation of "Oliver Twist," **Joey Lawrence** is the voice of a scared little New York kitten, who falls in with a scrappy dog, named Dodger (voice of Billy Joel). Oliver has the usual experiences in this disappointing film.

OLIVER, DEKE & DELLA

TWO GALS AND A GUY (1951, UA)—**Robert Alda** and **Janis Paige** are a husband-and-wife television team. Paige leaves the show to adopt and raise twins. He has to find a replacement on their show.

OLLANTE

THE JUNGLE CHILD (1916, Silent, Triangle)—When her parents die in a South American jungle, a Spanish child is taken in and raised by Indians. She grows up to be a beautiful Amazon played by **Dorothy Dalton**.

OLLIE

THE FLYING DEUCES (1939, RKO); AIR RAID WARDENS (1943, MGM); THE SAPS AT SEA (1940, UA); DANCING MASTERS (1943, 20th Century Fox)—**Oliver Hardy** and Stan Laurel are beloved comedians whose work runs the gamut from the inspired to the inane. Of the two, Hardy's character was supposed to be a bit brighter than that of Laurel's, but he still was pretty much of a dimwit who suffered extensively because of Laurel's naive and innocent approach to everything. The films listed above are not among their best work but they give enough of a glimpse of the talent of the team to understand why they are legends.

OLSEN, KNUTE
OLSEN'S BIG MOMENT (1934, Fox)—Swedish janitor **El Brendel** has nothing but trouble each time he has a night off. "Yummin' Yimmity" who cares?

OLSEN, OLE
THE GHOST CATCHERS (1944, Universal)—Zany **Ole Olsen** and his partner Chic Johnson appear in perhaps their only movie with even a semblance of a plot. They help out a southern family who discover the city brownstone mansion they plan to turn into a nightclub is haunted.

OLSON, JOAN
POLICE NURSE (1963, 20th Century Fox)—Police nurse **Merry Anders** gets police sergeant Ken Scott to investigate her sister's suicide.

OLSSON, KELLY
THE SWINGER (1966, Paramount)—Innocent **Ann-Margret** writes a sexy autobiography to break into the writing game. Everyone believes she's as hot as she says she is in her book.

O'MALLEY
O'MALLEY OF THE MOUNTED (1921, Silent, Paramount); (1936, 20th Century Fox)—**William S. Hart** and **George O'Brien** each portray the mountie who pretends to be an outlaw, in order to join a gang that is terrorizing American border towns.

O'MALLEY, HATTIE
MRS. O'MALLEY AND MR. MALONE (1950, MGM)—Small-town woman **Marjorie Main** wins a contest. While traveling to New York to collect her prize, she encounters a murder.

O'MALLEY, JAMES ALOYSIUS
THE GREAT O'MALLEY (1937, Warner Brothers)—Tough cop **Pat O'Brien** has a running feud with long-suffering Humphrey Bogart.

O'MALLEY, ROSE
ROSE OF TRALEE (1938, Ireland, Butchers)—Irish singer Fred Conyngham returns to Ireland from America to seek his wife **Binkie Stuart**.

OMAR
THE DESERT HAWK (1950, Universal)—Persian blacksmith **Richard Greene** takes up the sword to fight cruel George Macready who is oppressing the people. In the process, Greene tricks Yvonne de Carlo into marrying him and then goes about winning her love.

O'MOORE, KATHLEEN
KATHLEEN (1938, Ireland, Hoffberg)—Irish waitress **Sally O'Neill** rejects a wealthy landowner in favor of a singing stevedore.

O'MOORE, NEAL
MEN OF IRELAND (1938, Ireland, First National)—Blasket Island girl Eileen Curran falls in love with a visiting medical student from Dublin, **Cecil Ford**.

O'MORE, DANNY & PATRICK
MY BROTHER, THE OUTLAW (1951, Eagle-Lion)—City slicker **Mickey Rooney** travels West to visit his brother **Robert Stack** who turns out to be an outlaw.

O'MOYNE, SALLY
SALLY AND SAINT ANNE (1952, Universal)—Devout Irish Catholic girl **Ann Blyth** prays to St. Anne, mother of the Virgin Mary and patron saint of young girls, to help her and her grandpop, Edmund Gwenn, save their home from a town alderman, with whom they have had a long standing feud.

O'NEALE, NORAH
NORAH O'NEALE (1934, GB, Du World)—In what is claimed to be the first all-talkie Irish film, **Nancy Byrne** is a nurse, who saves the life of a doctor fighting an outbreak of typhus in an Irish coastal village.

O'NEIL
WOMEN IN WAR (1940, Republic)—**Elsie Janis** is one of two volunteer nurses in London in love with the same pilot.

O'NEIL, JIMMY
DIRTY O'NEIL (1974, American International)—West Coast cop **Morgan Paull** doesn't get his men but he certainly beds his women.

O'NEIL, PATRICIA
CALENDAR GIRL (1947, Republic)—**Jane Frazee** lives in a boarding house whose other guests include artist James Ellison and composer William Marshall. Both love her, but Ellison featuring her as a calendar girl causes her all kinds of trouble.

O'NEIL, STEVE
DRIVING FORCE (1990, Australia, J&M)—In a contrived action piece, **Sam J. Jones** is a tow-truck driver who has problems with villain Don Swayze. The latter causes accidents for other drivers in order to drum up more business for himself.

O'NEILL, JIM
SATURDAY'S CHILDREN (1929, Warner Brothers)—In this film set at the beginning of the Depression, **Grant Withers** is an impractical inventor who marries an ambitious girl.

O'NEILL, KATIE
UNTAMED (1955, 20th Century Fox)—**Susan Hayward** is an Irish immigrant to South Africa's Boer country. Her husband is killed by the attacking Zulus. It's just as well; she's having a tempestuous love affair with Tyrone Power.

O'NEILL, MOLLY
DANCING SWEETIES (1930, Warner Brothers)—**Sue Carol** meets her husband-to-be at a dance contest which they win. They team up professionally as well as personally, but he dumps her when she can't perfect new intricate dance steps. Later they work things out and dance off together into the sunset.

O'NEILL, MOLLY
THEY DRIVE BY NIGHT (1938, GB, Warner Brothers)—**Anna Konstram** and a truck driver help a fugitive ex-con catch a silk-stocking strangler.

O'NEILL, TERRY ELLERTON
THE HOODLUM SAINT (1946, MGM)—When **William Powell** gets out of the service after WWI, he discovers his ideals won't get him anywhere, so he becomes a cynical con man.

ONE EYE
CORNBREAD, EARL AND ME (1975, American International)—**Antonio Fargas** narrates the story of Keith Wilkes, a young black basketball player who is the hope of his slum community until he is mistakenly slain by a policeman.

ONE-ROUND

THE LADYKILLERS (1956, GB, Ealing)—**Danny Green** is strong of back, but weak of mind, as one of a gang of robbers pretending to be a chamber ensemble. After the heist, the loot is discovered by their landlady. She ends up with the money.

ORALIE

THE KING AND FOUR QUEENS (1956, UA)—Naive **Sara Shane** is one of four women waiting with their mother-in-law Jo Van Fleet for the arrival of their outlaw husbands to a deserted western town. Clark Gable shows up instead and he looks pretty good to all the women.

ORDEYNE, SIR MARCUS

THE MORALS OF MARCUS (1936, GB, Realart)—**Ian Hunter**, a confirmed bachelor archeologist, helps half-caste stowaway Lupe Velez. He brings her to London where she becomes a darling of society. The unlikely duo eventually find that they are perfect for each other.

ORDWAY, DR. ROBERT

CRIME DOCTOR (1943, Columbia); THE CRIME DOCTOR'S STRANG-EST CASE (1943, Columbia); THE CRIME DOCTOR'S CHALLENGE (1945, Columbia); CRIME DOCTOR'S WARNING (1945, Columbia); CRIME DOCTOR'S MAN HUNT (1946, Columbia); CRIME DOC-TOR'S GAMBLE (1947, Columbia); THE CRIME DOCTOR'S DIARY (1949, Columbia)—**Warner Baxter** starred in this series about an amnesiac who doesn't remember that he was a gang leader until after he becomes one of the world's leading criminologists. This leads him to solve some ten standard but enjoyable whodunits.

ORIENT, HENRY

THE WORLD OF HENRY ORIENT (1964, UA)—Concert pianist **Peter Sellers'** plans for having an affair with married Paula Prentiss is constantly interrupted by two admiring 14-year-old girls, Tippy Walker and Merrie Spaeth.

O'REILLY

THE MAGNIFICENT SEVEN (1960, UA)—**Charles Bronson**, Irish on one side and Mexican on the other, is one of seven gunslingers who come to the rescue of Mexican villagers when the peons decide to stand up to the bandits who yearly take everything the farmers can grow. He's adopted by three boys who make good on their promise of putting flowers on his grave if he's killed.

O'REILLY, PADDO

HOME IS THE HERO (1959, Ireland, British Lion)—Crippled cobbler **Walter Macken** subdues his ex-con father.

O'REILLY, TIMOTHY

SEZ O'REILLY TO MACNAB (1938, GB, Gaumont)—Irish sharepusher **Will Mahoney** and Scots businessman Will Fyffe try to make their fortune selling reducing pills.

ORIN

STARCHASER: THE LEGEND OF ORIN (1985, Animated, Atlan-tic)—**Joe Corrigan** is the voice of a boy who saves a future world from malevolent forces.

ORLAC, STEPHEN

THE HANDS OF ORLAC (1964, GB, Riviera-Pendennuis)—Concert pianist **Mel Ferrer's** hands are destroyed in a plane crash. A surgeon grafts the hands of a condemned strangler onto Ferrer, who then believes he's a killer.

ORLOFF, CAPT.

THE GAY DIPLOMAT (1931, RKO)—When this film was made, "gay" meant lively, lighthearted, merry, joyous and happy—all words to describe dashing Russian officer **Ivan Lebedeff**, who is assigned to Bucharest to neutralize a woman spy who has been leaking Russian secrets. But first he has to identify her.

ORMSBY, MARIAN

A LOST LADY (1934, Warner Brothers)—Out of gratitude **Barbara Stanwyck** marries an elderly attorney, but finds what a mistake she's made when she falls in love with Ricardo Cortez.

ORNOFF, SUZANNE

HER GILDED CAGE (1922, Silent, Paramount)—**Gloria Swanson**, a French actress and daughter of an aristocratic family, goes along with a press agent's stunt of billing her as the lover of a king who she once briefly met. Her fiance is not very understanding but they are eventually reconciled.

O'ROURKE, KATHY

KATHY O' (1958, Universal)—**Patty McCormack** as a child film star is no Shirley Temple. She's a real brat and a handful for studio publicist Dan Duryea, who must convince the press and public that she's a sweet adorable child.

O'ROURKE, KITTY

KITTY AND THE BAGMAN (1983, Australia, Quartet)—**Liddy Clark** earns the title of queen of the Sydney underworld during the 20s.

O'ROURKE, PAT

IDEA GIRL (1946, Universal)—**Julie Bishop** is a song plugger, promoting an amateur song contest to enhance the reputation of the music publishing concern for which she works. She causes the company a lot of headaches in the process.

O'ROURKE, PRINCESS MARIA

PRINCESS O'ROURKE (1943, Warner Brothers)—**Olivia de Havilland**, a princess, falls for pilot Robert Cummings, which causes quite a diplomatic flap.

O'ROURKE, SALTY

SALTY O'ROURKE (1945, Paramount)—Gambler **Alan Ladd** is part of a scheme to fix a race. When things go wrong, Ladd follows Gail Russell's urging and seeks a quieter and more honest line of work.

OROWITZ, SAM & GENE

SAM'S SON (1984, Invictus)—**Eli Wallach** and **Timothy Patrick Murphy** are father and son. Wallach is a frustrated man who never achieved any of his goals, and Murphy is a champion javelin thrower.

ORPHEUS

SHREDDER ORPHEUS (1990, Image)—This version of the Greek legend of Orpheus and Eurydice is set in a post-apocalypse world, in which band leader **Robert McGinley** has become a TV star. In a very amateurish production, McGinley spends most of his time searching for his Eurydice, Megan Murphy.

ORSANI, BARONESS

WIDOW IN SCARLET (1932, Mayfair)—**Dorothy Revier** bets she can steal the jewels of a society friend right under the noses of the police. She does with the help of a thief posing as a policeman.

ORSINI, DIANE

DIANE OF STAR HOLLOW (1921, Silent, Producers Security)—**Evelyn Greeley**, daughter of a rich Italian suspected of being the head of the Black Hand, is loved by Bernard Durning, the local chief of state constabulary. Greeley ultimately chooses her man over her father.

O'RYAN, MARY

NINE GIRLS (1944, Columbia)—**Evelyn Keyes** is one of the suspects in the murder of sorority sister Anita Louise. The latter threatened to expose the legal troubles of Keyes' brother.

OSBORNE, FREDERIC, SR.

FATHER TAKES A WIFE (1941, RKO)—**Adolphe Menjou** is an aging widower who falls for a famous actress, Gloria Swanson (before the cameras for the first time in seven years). Their problem is Menjou's stuffy son John Howard.

OSCAR, CROWN PRINCE

THE CROWN PRINCE'S DOUBLE (1916, Silent, Blue Ribbon)—Crown Prince **Maurice Costello** is to marry a girl from a neighboring country, but before the ceremony he's deposed. He goes to America, falls in love and marries. Then his nation decides it wants him back to marry his intended. He finds a double to take his place back at his old job.

OSGOOD, JANE

IT HAPPENED TO JANE (1954, Columbia)—**Doris Day**, owner of a Maine lobstery, has a romance with Jack Lemmon and a feud with Ernie Kovacs.

O'SHAUGHNESSY, WINDY & STUBBY

O'SHAUGHNESSY'S BOY (1935, MGM)—**Wallace Beery** searches for his son **Jackie Cooper**, taken from him by his cruel wife.

OSTERMAN, BERNARD

THE OSTERMAN WEEKEND (1983, 20th Century Fox)—TV writer Rutger Hauer holds an annual weekend party for friend **Craig T. Nelson** and neighbors. The CIA has convinced Hauer that his friends are enemy agents. They aren't but the CIA agents are.

OTELLO (OTHELLO)

OTHELLO (1955, UA); (1965, Warner Brothers); (1987, Cannon)—**Orson Welles** and **Laurence Olivier** each bring their own distinctive genius to the role of Shakespeare's Moor whose love for his wife Desdemona is poisoned by the lies of Iago. **Placido Domingo** is in excellent voice in the beautiful production of the Verdi opera.

OTIS

DADDY'S BOYS (1988, Concorde)—Character actor **Christian Clemenson** gives a fine performance as a dimwitted son of a nasty father. These two and Clemenson's two brothers are looking for some woman to play mommy for them.

OTLEY, GERALD ARTHUR

OTLEY (1969, GB, Columbia)—Framed for murder, **Tom Courtenay** becomes involved with spies.

O'TOOLE, SHEILA

THE PRINCESS FROM HOBOKEN (1927, Silent, Tiffany)—**Blanche Mehaffey** poses as an expatriate Russian princess in order to help her father's restaurant. She attracts a lot of romantic attention and things get complicated when the real princess shows up.

O'TOOLE, TERRY

CONDUCTOR 1492 (1924, Silent, Regal)—Streetcar conductor **Johnny Hines** rescues the son of the company president, thwarts the attempts of crooks taking over the company, and marries the boss' daughter.

O'TOOLE, THOMAS PATRICK

THE FIGHTING CUB (1925, Silent, Truart)—Copy boy **Wesley Barry** wants to become a cub reporter. He is told the job is his if he can get an interview with a reclusive philanthropist. He does but discovers the man once headed a notorious gang of thieves, who don't care for his retirement. With Barry's help the man escapes his sordid past.

O'TOOLE, TOMMY

DEVIL DOGS OF THE AIR (1935, Warner Brothers)—**James Cagney** and Pat O'Brien appear in their usual friendly adversary roles as two Air Force pilots after the same girl. As usual Cagney pays no attention to the service regulations and this causes problems for O'Brien and others.

OTTO

DESPERATE CHARACTERS (1971, Paramount)—**Kenneth Mars** and his wife Shirley MacLaine's marriage is crumbling just as is the New York neighborhood they live in.

OUDRY, CLAIRE

SEVEN WOMEN FROM HELL (1961, 20th Century Fox)—French thief **Denise Darcel** is one of seven women who escape from a Japanese prison camp in New Guinea during WWII, and try to make it to safety.

OWEN, ELLIOTT

HER HUSBAND'S SECRET (1925, Silent, First National)—**Antonio Moreno** is secretly married to the daughter of a man who has been his mother's lover for over 25 years—ever since his father took him away from her when he discovered her infidelity.

OWEN, WILL

THE OUTRIDERS (1950, MGM)—**Joel McCrea** leads a wagon train across Indian territory, and must contend with rebel soldiers out to steal Union gold.

OWENS, DON

THE COUNTERFEIT KILLER (1969, Universal)—Cop **Jack Lord** goes undercover to get the goods on the syndicate.

OWENS, JIMMY

TWO IN A TAXI (1941, Columbia)—Cab driver **Russell Hayden** hopes to raise enough money to buy a gasoline station so he can marry his girlfriend, but reaching his goal is not easy.

OXFORD, JIM

TWO MEN AND A MAID (1929, Tiffany)—Suspecting his wife had a previous lover, **William Collier, Jr.** runs off and joins the French Foreign Legion where he becomes part of a triangle involving the cruel adjutant and a native girl. When the latter is killed, he makes it back to his blameless wife who still loves him.

OZZIE

ON THE TOWN (1949, MGM)—**Jules Munshin** is the comic relief for Gene Kelly and Frank Sinatra as three sailors find romance in New York City during a 24-hour leave. Munshin's sweetie is Ann Miller.

P

P.S. "BILL"

CAREFUL, HE MIGHT HEAR YOU (1984, Australia, 20th Century Fox)—**Nicholas Gledhill** is the center of a custody fight between wealthy Wendy Hughes and her working class sister Robyn Nevin when the boy's mother dies and his father deserts him.

P.K.

THE POWER OF ONE (1992, Warner Brothers)—In this story of a boy's struggle to find the courage to deal with the injustice that, in South Africa, surrounds him, **Guy Witcher** has the role at age seven. He's a white English orphan in an Afrikaaner boarding school in 1930s Zimbabwe, where he's brutally treated. By the age of 12, he's played by **Simon Fenton** and trained into a boxing champion by Morgan Freeman. At 18, played by **Stephen Dorff**, he defies the brutal racist regime and, with black boxer Alois Moyo, works to spread literacy in the African townships.

PABLITO

THE LITTLEST OUTLAW (1955, Buena Vista)—**Andres Velaquez'** cruel stepfather is a Mexican general's horse trainer who trains a prize horse to be a jumper by torturing it. The horse develops a deathly fear of jumps. When the general's daughter is thrown by the horse because it won't take a jump, the general orders the horse destroyed. Velaquez runs away with the horse, travelling all over Mexico. As is usual in Disney films, there is a happy ending.

PACKARD, GEORGE

HIS WIFE'S HUSBAND (1922, Silent, Pyramid)—Successful lawyer **Huntley Gordon** marries Betty Blythe, and soon after becomes mayor. A former husband shows up, threatening blackmail, but the couple are able to prove that this lout was already married when he wed Blythe.

PACKARD, CAPT. JEFF

I KILLED GERONIMO (1950, Eagle-Lion)—Army captain **James Ellison** poses as an outlaw in order to infiltrate a band of gun-runners and gets their best client Geronimo as well.

PACKETT, JULIA

JULIA MISBEHAVES (1948, MGM)—Showgirl **Greer Garson** returns to her prudish husband Walter Pidgeon when daughter Elizabeth Taylor is to be married.

PACO

BAD BOYS (1983, EMI/Universal)—**Esai Moralas** has sworn to kill his street enemy Sean Penn, while they are both in the lock-up. Penn has made a similar promise.

PACO

THE BOY WHO STOLE A MILLION (1960, GB, British-Lion)—**Maurice Reyna** is a 12 year old who "borrows" a million pesetas from a bank to help his widower father get his taxi out of hock.

PAGAN, LESLIE

THE SHIPBUILDERS (1957, GB, Anglo-American)—Ship-builder **Clive Brook** fights to maintain Great Britain as a major sea power.

PAGE, BEATRICE

FOREVER FEMALE (1953, Paramount)—Aging stage actress **Ginger Rogers** finally catches on to the fact that she's playing roles meant for younger actresses.

PAGE, MRS.

THE BATTLE AXE (1962, GB, Danzinger)—Francis Matthews sues Jill Ireland for breach of promise, proving in court that Ireland's dominating mother, **Joan Hawthorne**, queered the romance.

PAGE, NORMA & PATRICIA

FOUR GIRLS IN WHITE (1939, MGM)—**Florence Rice** and **Ann Rutherford** are two of four probationary student nurses, featured in this routine B movie. Rice marries doctor Alan Marshall, and Rutherford weds wealthy Kent Taylor. They're lucky, another of their number is murdered by a maniac.

PAGE, TAD

THE MAGNIFICENT DOPE (1942, 20th Century Fox)—Naive small town hick **Henry Fonda** is brought to the big city for publicity for a success school run by Don Ameche. Fonda is billed by Ameche as America's greatest failure, but he's smart enough to deal with the city slickers.

PAGE, TONY

MEET THE BOY FRIEND (1937, Republic)—**David Caryle (Robert Paige)** is billed as "America's Boy Friend," a title the crooner despises. An actress tries to trick him into marrying her, but he falls for the niece of an insurance executive who has issued a non-marriage policy on Caryle.

PAGURA, AL

BORN TO RACE (1988, MGM-United Artists)—Seems race car driver **Joseph Bottoms** has been chosen by beautiful Italian auto designer Marla Heasley to do more than drive her new car at the North Carolina Hickory Speedway.

PAIGE, NORA

BORN TO DANCE (1936, MGM)—High-spirited hoofer **Eleanor Powell** falls in love with sailor James Stewart while he is on leave in New York City. She gets to replace temperamental star Virginia Bruce in a Broadway show. The little technicality that Bruce is a singer isn't allowed to interfere with presenting Powell's superb tap dancing.

PAINTER, CHRISTINE

PERSONAL SERVICES (1987, GB, Zenith/ULP-Vestron)—Based on the real life experiences of Britain's Cynthia Payne, **Julie Walters** accidentally finds herself a madam, who discovers what a good business sex is.

PALAFFI, COUNT WILLIE

I MARRIED AN ANGEL (1942, MGM)—In their last film together **Nelson Eddy** dreams that he marries angel Jeannette MacDonald.

PALMER, BETTY

CINDERELLA SWINGS IT (1942, RKO)—When struggling singer **Gloria Warren** changes her style from classical to swing, she's a hit.

PALMER, CATHY

AMERICAN DREAMER (1984, Warners)—Housewife **Jo Beth Williams** wins a trip to Paris and imagines herself a daring heroine of adventure thrillers after a blow to the head.

PALMER, ENSIGN CHUCK

AN AMERICAN GUERRILLA IN PHILIPPINES (1950, 20th Century Fox)—When American forces in the Philippines surrender to the Japanese, PT boat captain **Tyrone Power** forms a guerrilla force on Leyte.

PALMER, DARRYL & DEBBY
THE SLUGGER'S WIFE (1985, Columbia)—**Michael O'Keefe** is an egotistical baseball player who forces himself on aspiring rock singer **Rebecca De Mornay**. Neither are very appealing people.

PALMER, HARRY
FOR ME AND MY GAL (1942, MGM)—Pre-WWI vaudeville team **Gene Kelly** and Judy Garland are working towards an appearance at the Palace.

PALMER, JANE
LADY IN A JAM (1942, Universal)—In this second-string screwball comedy, **Irene Dunne** convinces psychiatrist Patric Knowles to marry her, so he can cure her of all her phobias.

PALOOKA, JOE
PALOOKA (1934, United Artists); JOE PALOOKA, CHAMP (1946, Monogram); JOE PALOOKA IN WINNER TAKE ALL (1948, Monogram); JOE PALOOKA IN THE BIG FIGHT (1949, Monogram); JOE PALOOKA IN CONNECTICUT (1949, Monogram); JOE PALOOKA IN THE SQUARED CIRCLE (1950, Monogram); JOE PALOOKA MEETS HUMPHREY (1950, Monogram); JOE PALOOKA IN THE TRIPLE CROSS (1951, Monogram)—**Stuart Erwin** in the 1934 film and **Joe Kirkwood, Jr.** in the rest portray the bashful young cartoon strip boxer who becomes heavy-weight champion of the world with the help of his manager Knobby Walsh, played by Jimmy Durante in 1934, and with Leon Errol, William Frawley and James Gleason taking a swing at the role with Kirkwood.

PALUSO, SONNY
THE SURVIVORS (1983, Columbia)—**Walter Matthau** adopts Robin Williams, who has lost his job, and is in danger of being "hit" when he identifies a robber. They arm themselves to the teeth and are more dangerous to each other than the amicable hit man, Jerry Reed, out to get them.

PAM
THREE LITTLE GIRLS IN BLUE (1946, 20th Century Fox)—Set in turn-of-the-century Atlantic City, the movie tells the oft-told tale of three girls, including **June Haver**, looking to find rich husbands. The world is waiting for a sex-reversal version of the standard plot: three boys looking for rich wives.

PAMELA, LADY
THE WOMAN DECIDES (1932, GB, British International)—**Adrianne Allen** has a difficult time deciding between the Conservative party candidate and his Labor party rival. Oh, not for Parliament. She's the mistress of the former and has fallen in love with the latter.

PAN
SEVEN FACES OF DR. LAO (1964, MGM)—Pan is just one of seven appearances of elderly Chinese showman **Tony Randall** who sets up his magic circus in a small western town. He changes the lives of many of its inhabitants.

PAN, PETER
PETER PAN (1924, Silent, Paramount)—**Betty Bronson** is a delight as the boy who never grew up. While looking for his shadow in the home of the Darlings, he awakens the children—Wendy, John and Michael—and guides them to his home in never-never land, where they have adventures with jealous fairy Tinker Bell and a pirate, Captain Hook.

PANTHER, JOE
JOE PANTHER (1976, Artists Creation)—Modern-day Seminole Indian **Ray Tracey** tries to survive in the white man's world.

PAPAS, MICHAEL
SUMMER LOVERS (1982, Orion)—**Peter Gallagher** is part of a menage a trois on a Greek island.

PAPASANO, ROCKY
LOVE WITH THE PROPER STRANGER (1963, Paramount)—When trumpet player **Steve McQueen** gets New York working girl Natalie Wood pregnant, he doesn't want to get married. He arranges for her to have an abortion. When she can't go through with it, he changes his mind and proposes marriage.

PAPILLON See HENRI CHARRIERE

PARADINE, MADDALENA ANNA
THE PARADINE CASE (1947, United Artists)—**Alida Valli** is on trial for the murder of her elderly husband. Her barrister, Gregory Peck, falls in love with her. He is certain that she is protecting the deceased's valet Louis Jourdan. When the latter commits suicide, Peck sees this as a confession, but Valli announces that he was her lover and she did kill her husband, and now has nothing to live for.

PARAGOT
THE BELOVED VAGABOND (1936, GB, Toeplitz/Columbia)—At the turn of the century jilted French artist **Maurice Chevalier** becomes a vagabond, and falls in love with an orphan girl.

PARCHMAN, EUNICE
THE HOUSEKEEPER (1987, Canada, Castlehill-Kodiak)—Homely, illiterate **Rita Tushingham** takes revenge on a world that has consistently mistreated her by murdering those who cross her.

PARDWAY, GENE, BERT & FREDDIE
THREE SONS (1939, RKO)—Chicago department store owner Edward Ellis has built up his business from the time of the Great Fire, but none of his three sons **Kent Taylor**, **Robert Stanton** and **Dick Hagan** show any interest in taking over the operation. Marshall Field had the same problem.

PAREIGA, EPIFANIA
THE MILLIONAIRESS (1960, GB, 20th Century Fox)—Millionaire **Sophia Loren** cannot marry her Indian doctor and lover Peter Sellers until she has earned a living for three months.

PARELLI, DR. TONY
THE NEW INTERNS (1964, Columbia)—In his debut, **George Segal** has been brought up in a ghetto and still has a chip on his shoulder. He's an intern out to bed Inger Stevens, who has been cold to the idea of sex since she was gang-raped.

PARFITT, MOPPY
DEVIL ON HORSEBACK (1954, GB, British Lion)—**Jeremy Spenser**, a natural jockey, develops a cruel streak, killing one of his mounts by beating it too much. After a suspension, alcoholic ex-jockey Liam Redmond puts Spenser's head on straight.

PARIS, WANDA
SUCH WOMEN ARE DANGEROUS (1934, Fox)—**Mona Barrie** is one of the women playboy Warner Baxter loves and leaves. As a result, his vindictive ex-lovers are pleased when he is charged with a murder he didn't commit.

PARKER, AL

THE AIR HAWK (1924, Silent, FBO)—Aviator **Al Wilson**, a secret service agent, foils a gang of bandits who have been robbing a platinum mine.

PARKER, BONNIE

THE BONNIE PARKER STORY (1958, American International); BONNIE AND CLYDE (1967, Warners)—**Dorothy Provine** is cute but unconvincing as a ruthless bank robber. Her portrayal pales in every way when compared to **Faye Dunaway's** in the violent but highly entertaining later film.

PARKER, CHARLIE

BIRD (1988, Warners)—**Forrest Whittaker**, so good in GOOD MORNING VIETNAM, is superb starring as the jazz genius, who changed the character of jazz in his short life. He died at 34 because of poor health, social inequities, and a monster appetite for drugs, alcohol and sex.

PARKER, CHRIS

ADVENTURES IN BABYSITTING (1987, Buena Vista)—**Elisabeth Shue**, babysitting in a Chicago suburb, is forced to take her charges with her to downtown Chicago to rescue a friend. She has an unbelievable series of dangerous but funny adventures.

PARKER, CHUCK

SITTING PRETTY (1933, Paramount)—Songwriting team **Jack Oakie** and Jack Haley (well, actually Mack Gordon and Harry Revel) write the ditty "Did You Ever See a Dream Walking"—the best thing in the musical comedy.

PARKER, GREG

HELLFIGHTERS (1968, Universal)—**Jim Hutton** is part of John Wayne's oil fighting crew. His wife isn't sure this is the best way to make a living.

PARKER, HENRY T.

FRAMED (1940, Universal)—Accused of murder, reporter **Frank Albertson** finds the real culprit.

PARKER, HOLLY *See* JACQUELINE (FLEURIOT) (MADAME X)

PARKER, SGT. JACKIE

SCORCHY (1976, American International)—Seattle undercover cop **Connie Stevens** is out to break up a drug ring.

PARKER, JANE

TARZAN AND HIS MATE (1934, MGM)—Looking more fetching than anyone has a right to, **Maureen O'Sullivan** becomes Tarzan's mate and appears in four other movies in the series. Bluenoses complained about O'Sullivan's costume, which they claimed revealed too much and so this was modified (rectified is more appropriate, we suppose). No one seemed too terribly concerned that Jane and Tarzan were living as man and wife apparently without benefit of clergy.

PARKER, JOEL

THE PINCH HITTER (1917, Silent, Triangle)—Country boob **Charles Ray** is sent to college by his father to satisfy a death bed promise to his mother. He is the butt of student jokes until he comes off the bench and hits a pinch home run to win a baseball game.

PARKER, LOLA

MAN AGAINST WOMAN (1932, Columbia)—Singer **Lillian Miles** goes to Bermuda with criminal Walter Connolly. Detective Jack Holt, who loves Miles is conned by members of Connolly's gang to bring him back to them. This accomplished, the gang members plan to kill both Holt and Connolly, but Holt survives and has an open field with Miles.

PARKER, MARILYN

GOOD SPORT (1931, Fox)—**Linda Watkins** discovers that her husband has had some affairs. She has one herself, and gets mixed up with some high class and costly ladies-of-the-evening.

PARKER, MOLLY

MOLLY AND LAWLESS JOHN (1972, Producers Distributing Corp.)—Outlaw Sam Elliott turns on his charm for sheriff's wife **Vera Miles**. She helps Elliott break out of jail. She accompanies him, but finds his treatment of her changes in direct proportion to how far away they are from the calaboose. Miles kills Elliott, returns to her husband claiming to have been kidnapped, and demands the reward money for eliminating Elliott. Now that's chutzpah.

PARKER, POLLY

GOLD DIGGERS OF 1933 (1933, Warners)—Wealthy Dick Powell doesn't tell showgirl **Ruby Keeler** about his fortune when he writes a Broadway show to star Keeler and her roommates Joan Blondell and Aline MacMahon. The cat's out of the bag, when Powell's older brother and the family lawyer come to save Powell from Keeler. Blondell and MacMahon take care of these two.

PARKER, RUSTY

COVER GIRL (1944, Columbia)—**Rita Hayworth** changes her name from Maribelle Hicks, and becomes a top magazine cover girl. But she can't decide which of her many admirers to marry.

PARKER, SUSAN

BLONDE FROM BROOKLYN (1945, Columbia)—**Lynn Merrick**, a singer in a southern bar, teams up with crooner Robert Stanton to appear as a hick couple, so they may get a job with a coffee manufacturer.

PARKER, SUSIE

IF YOU KNEW SUSIE (1948, RKO)—**Joan Davis** and Eddie Cantor are a show business couple in a routine musical comedy.

PARKINGTON, SUSIE

MRS. PARKINGTON (1944, MGM)—Audiences are able to watch **Greer Garson** age 53 years as she progresses from a maid in a boarding house to a woman of great distinction and wealth in her eighties. Garson was nominated for an Oscar but the Academy did that just about every year in the 1940s.

PARKY

THREE SAILORS AND A GIRL (1953, Warners)—Fat **Jack E. Leonard** is supposed to supply the comedy relief in a story of three sailors who invest their ship's surplus funds in a musical starring Jane Powell. Fat Jack is not funny.

PARNELL, CHARLES STEWART

PARNELL (1937, MGM)—In what many consider **Clark Gable's** worst performance, the King portrays the Irish politician whose fight for Irish Home Rule was destroyed by his affair with a married woman.

PARR, CATHERINE

HENRY VIII AND HIS SIX WIVES (1972, GB, EMI/MGM)—Parr, played by **Barbara Leigh-Hunt**, became Henry VIII's queen when her predecessor Catherine Howard went to the executioner's block. Parr championed Protestant causes. His sixth wife, Parr survived Henry.

PASCALI, BASIL
PASCALI'S ISLAND (1988, GB, Avenue)—For 20 years leading up to 1908, half-Turkish and half-European **Ben Kingsley** has been spying on the visitors and potentially rebellious Greek inhabitants of the sun-drenched island of Nisi. He's never been sure if his lengthy reports have even been read by anyone in the government of the Ottoman Empire.

PASCOE, DANIEL
DEALERS (1989, GB, Rank)—When one of the traders of the London branch of an American bank blows out his brains, the firm's young star **Paul McGann** is certain he will be promoted. Instead, the bank brings in hotshot American Rebecca De Mornay. Their adversarial relationship will lead to romance.

PATAKANGO
WHO SHOT PATAKANGO (1990, Patakango Ltd.)—When slow-witted teen **Brad Randall** shows up at his 1950s vocational school with a gunshot wound in the arm, he can't remember who shot him. The film is a nostalgic look at the coming of age of white youths in Brooklyn's Bedford-Stuyvesant district before drugs and the hatred between black and white gangs made it hell on earth.

PATCHETT, RUTH
SHE-DEVIL (1989, Orion)—As a stand-up comedian we found **Roseanne Barr** moderately amusing—in a somewhat gross way. Her success with her TV series only supports our conviction that situation comedies usually appeal to those who crave repetition, not originality. In this poor excuse for a comedy, Barr portrays the slovenly wife of Ed Begley, Jr. She loses him to glamorous romance novelist Meryl Streep. She takes revenge. Big, unfunny deal!

PATRIARCH, THE
THE MIRACLE MAN (1919, Silent, Paramount); (1932, Paramount)—A trio of con artists attempt to make a fortune running a faith-healing sting with **Joseph J. Dowling** and **Hobart Bosworth**, respectively, being the man who really believes he can perform miracles. Lon Chaney appeared as one of the con men in the silent film.

PATRICK
PATRICK (1979, Australia, Filmways)—Even though **Robert Thompson** is comatose after murdering his mother, his psychokinetic powers still cause havoc.

PATRICK, ST.
IN THE DAYS OF ST. PATRICK (1920, Silent, GB, Janus)—The fact that St. Patrick may be only a legendary figure doesn't diminish the appeal of this film starring **Ian Allen** as the bishop who brings Christianity to Ireland.

PATSY
BAD LITTLE ANGEL (1939, MGM)—**Virginia Weidler**, a waif on the run, is befriended by a shoe shine boy, who introduces her to a newspaper editor, who takes her home to his wife.

PATSY
PATSY (1921, Silent, Truart)—Orphaned tomboy **Zasu Pitts** runs away from the farm where she is expected to do most of the chores, and makes her way to California. There she meets a kindly scientist who, thinking her a boy, takes her into his home.

PATSY
THREE MEN ON A HORSE (1936, Warners)—**Sam Levene** and two other horse bettors kidnap greeting card writer Frank McHugh, who has a remarkable ability to handicap horse races. It's a funny farce.

PATTERSON, AUSTIN
THE MASKED AVENGER (1922, Silent, Doubleday)—**Lester Cueno** puts on a mask and rides out to take revenge against a band of outlaws who rustled his cattle.

PATTERSON. BARBARA
MONEY AND THE WOMAN (1940, Warners)—In a routine "B," **Brenda Marshall** embezzles money from a bank.

PATTERSON, CHARLIE
THE OLYMPIC HERO (1928, Silent, Zakaro-Supreme)—Olympian **Charles Paddock** portrays a fictionalized version of himself and repeats his exploits at the 1924 Olympic Games. You may remember his character in CHARIOTS OF FIRE, played by Dennis Christopher.

PATTERSON, CHARLEY, EDDIE & KENNETH
THREE SONS O' GUNS (1941, Warners)—Ne'er-do-wells, **Wayne Morris, Tom Brown** and **William T. Orr** dodge the draft, but are forced into the service anyway, where the Army makes men of them despite their resistance.

PATTERSON, DAN
THE COWBOY AND THE FLAPPER (1924, Silent, Truart)—Marshal **William Fairbanks** poses as an outlaw, so he can infiltrate a gang. Its captive, Dorothy Revier, doesn't trust him at first.

PATTERSON, SGT. JOHN
A YANK IN LONDON (1946, GB, 20th Century Fox)—**Dean Jagger**, a U.S. sergeant stationed in London, falls in love with Anna Neagle, a duke's daughter, engaged to British Major Rex Harrison. Although Neagle comes to feel similiar feelings for Jagger, the romance comes to nought, as Dean is killed in a plane crash.

PATTERSON, MARY JANE
ARIZONA WILDCAT (1938, 20th Century Fox)—**Jane Withers** clears her foster father's name when he is accused of stealing a gold shipment in 1870 Arizona territory.

PATTERSON, PATSY
LADY BY CHOICE (1934, Columbia)—Dancer Carole Lombard makes a lady out of down-and-out **May Robson**

PATTI
SATAN'S CHEERLEADER (1977, World Amusements)—**Kerry Sherman** is one of four high school cheerleaders who, along with a female teacher, are kidnapped by black-hooded satanists. She's no use to them for the virgin sacrificial part of their ceremony.

PATTIE
THE WILD GIRL (1925, Silent, Truart)—**Louise Lorraine**, a wild girl of the forest, lives in a cabin with her grandfather. She becomes the rope in a tug-of-war between a mountain man who frames her grandfather for murder in an attempt to own her, and photographer Art Acord, to whom she is attracted.

PATTIS, FOXY
AERIAL GUNNER (1943, Paramount)—**Chester Morris** gives up his life to enable Richard Arlen, his longtime rival and gunnery student, to escape in an airplane from a WWII Japanese controlled island.

PATTON, GABRIEL
I'LL TELL THE WORLD (1945, Universal)—**Lee Tracy**, with his rasping voice, saves a failing radio station by coming up with ingenious ideas for attracting listeners.

PATTON, GENERAL GEORGE S.

PATTON (1970, 20th Century Fox)—**George C. Scott** won a most deserved Oscar, which he refused, for his portrayal of the American tank general who was a brilliant military strategist, but often in trouble when he spoke his mind.

PATTON, PEGGY

PERSUASIVE PEGGY (1917, Silent, Mayfair)—**Peggy Hyland** marries gentleman farmer William B. Davidson, who announces that they will attend the state fair rather than go to Niagara Falls for their honeymoon as agreed to. The next morning he finds that Hyland has hightailed it for Buffalo as planned. Davidson follows, promising to be more attentive to her wishes.

PAUL

DETECTIVE SCHOOL DROPOUTS (1986, Cannon)—Private eye **Lorin Dreyfuss** gives lessons on how to be a sleuth to David Landsberg. The two accidentally solve a crime involving star-crossed lovers. If you're in a silly mood, it's a very funny movie.

PAUL

THE FOX (1967, Warners)—The lesbian relationship of Sandy Dennis and Anne Heywood is spoiled by the arrival of **Keir Dullea**.

PAUL

MEN'S CLUB (1986, Paramount)—In a ridiculous and disappointing film, **Craig Wasson** is one of seven males who start an encounter group where they explore their attitudes about women.

PAUL, PETER & DAVID

DOUBLE TROUBLE (1992, MPCA)—Detective **David Paul** gets a surprise when a wisecracking jewel thief turns out to be his long-lost twin **Peter Paul**. The two feuding brothers are teamed to crack a smuggling ring.

PAULA

THE LEOPARD LADY (1928, Silent, Pathe)—Leopard trainer **Jacqueline Logan** is hired by the police to join a circus to investigate a series of murders. The culprit is an ape trained by its owner to be a killer.

PAULA

PAULA (1915, GB, Silent, Holmuth/Initial)—British **Hettie Payne** follows Frank McClellan, the man she loves, to Italy where she dies giving him her blood to save his life.

PAULA

RED BLOODED AMERICAN GIRL (1990, Canada, SC Entertainment)—Scientist Andrew Stevens goes to work for Christopher Plummer, who runs a viral blood disorder laboratory. Stevens' job is to find a cure for a virus that engenders symptoms of vampirism and has infected Plummer and his staff. When Stevens' love interest **Heather Thomas** is infected, the scientist is in a race against time to save her.

PAULA THE APE WOMAN

JUNGLE CAPTIVE (1945, Universal)—**Vicky Lane** takes over from Aquanetta in the ape woman role. The film also features the unfortunate grotesque non-actor Rondo Hatton.

PAULIE

THE POPE OF GREENWICH VILLAGE (1984, MGM/United Artists)—**Eric Roberts** is a constant pain to his cousin Mickey Rourke, what with all his half-assed brainstorms. The film is set in New York's Little Italy.

PAULINE

THE PERILS OF PAULINE (1967, Universal)—Pat Boone searches all over the world for his childhood sweetheart **Pamela Austin**

PAULSON, HENRY

THE EMBEZZLER (1954, GB, GFD)—Dying bank clerk **Charles Victor** steals from his own bank, but is caught. He escapes and flees to the coast, where he saves a young bride from the blackmailing attempts of her former husband at the cost of his own life.

PAUREL, JEAN

THE GREAT LOVER (1931, MGM)—Aging opera star **Adolphe Menjou** pursues a new young member of his troupe, Irene Dunne. While attracted to his talent, she has no intention of being just one more of his conquests.

PAWLEY, MARTIN

THE SEARCHERS (1956, Warners)—**Jeffrey Hunter**, the half-breed adopted brother of Natalie Wood, helps John Wayne search for the girl. She was taken by a band of renegade Indians when they attacked her home, killing her father, mother and sister. The search takes five years. It's only when the end is in sight that Hunter realizes that Wayne means to kill his niece Wood, because she had been "spoiled."

PAYNNE, AMANDA CHASE

PRIVATE LIVES (1931, MGM)—**Norma Shearer** is on her honeymoon with new husband Reginald Denny. In the next suite is her ex-husband Robert Montgomery with his new wife Una Merkel. The predictable story isn't much but the Noel Coward lines are still bright.

PAYTON, DEAN

THE LAST OUTLAW (1936, RKO)—On release from jail, aging cowboy **Harry Carey** finds civilization sneaking up on him. He must contend with racketeers and a hoodlum after his daughter.

PEABODY, CAPT. ABE

THE CAPTAIN IS A LADY (1940, MGM)—Old sea captain **Charles Coburn** moves into an old ladies home with his wife where he is affectionately known as old lady 31.

PEABODY, MR.

MR. PEABODY AND THE MERMAID (1948, Universal)—**William Powell**, who delivers the wonderful line "Fifty, the old age of youth and the youth of old age," snags amorous mermaid Ann Blyth while fishing. He transfers her to his swimming pool with the expected comical results.

PEABODY, GEORGE

THERE WAS A YOUNG MAN (1937, GB, Fox British)—Shy small town man **Oliver Wakefield** finds himself in the middle of a crooked land development scheme, and the plans of an Oriental gang to recover an ancient relic.

PEACHE, CLIFFORD

MY BODYGUARD (1980, 20th Century Fox)—In a very good picture, shy youngster **Chris Makepeace** is new to a Chicago high school ruled by bully Matt Dillon. The latter makes Makepeace the target of his abuse and protection racket. Makepeace hires reclusive giant Adam Baldwin as his bodyguard, but he still must face up to Dillon.

PEACHES

ASSAULT OF THE KILLER BIMBOS (1988, Titan/Empire)—**Christine Whitaker** is the star dancer in a sleazy nightclub. When the sexist manager is murdered by the mob, Whitaker and two other "cheap broads" are believed responsible. It's up to them to find the hit-man and clear themselves.

PEACOCK, ABNER AUDUBON

THE LOVE GOD? (1969, Universal)—**Don Knotts**, the editor of a bird watching magazine, becomes a national sex symbol. Oh, Barney, why did you ever leave Mayberry?

PEALE, DOTTIE

TOP SECRET AFFAIR (1957, Warners)—Magazine publisher **Susan Hayward** tries to get the goods on Kirk Douglas, a general just appointed to the Joint Chiefs of Staff, but finds romance instead.

PEALE, NORMAN VINCENT

ONE MAN'S WAY (1964, UA)—**Don Murray**, who believes in such things, is quite good in this fictionalized biopic of the famous preacher.

PEAR, EMILY

DON'T TELL HER IT'S ME (1990, Hemdale)—In an extremely callous comedy, **Jami Gertz** is the object of the affections of Steve Guttenberg, who has a pathetic appearance as a result of his treatment for Hodgkin's disease. Gertz is shallow and has superficial standards. When Shelley Long turns her brother Guttenberg into a long-haired Mad Max-like New Zealander, Gertz's only prerequisites in deciding to date him is to be sure he's not gay and he's free of disease.

PEARCE, AL See ELMER BLURT

PEARCE, CHARLES

THE CASE OF CHARLES PEARCE (1943, GB, Argyle/Monarch)—**Michael Martin Harvey** portrays the notorious English burglar who invented most of the burglary tools now in use. He was also a murderer which earned him an appointment with the hangman.

PEARL

THE GIRL SAID NO (1937, Grand National)—**Irene Hervey** and Robert Armstrong are the nominal leads of a picture highlighted by Gilbert and Sullivan numbers.

PEARL, CHARLEY

THE MARRYING MAN (1991, Hollywood Pictures)—Engaged to marry Elizabeth Shue, **Alec Baldwin** falls in lust with Las Vegas lounge singer Kim Basinger. They are found in bed by her lover, Bugsy Siegel, played by Armand Assante. The latter, having grown tired of Basinger, decides not to kill them—but forces them to get married. From then on, the film is a series of divorces and repeat marriages for Baldwin and Basinger.

PEARL

THE SIN SISTER (1929, Silent, Fox)—Vaudeville dancer **Nancy Carroll** shows up in a Northern trading post. She falls for a wealthy young man who has fallen in with bad companions.

PEARL, JENNY

DANCE PRETTY LADY (1932, GB, British Lion)—Ballet dancer **Ann Casson** finds her life going down hill in the early 1900s. She refuses to become the mistress of the artist she loves and marries a farmer instead.

PEARSON, DR. JIM

WELCOME STRANGER (1947, Paramount)—Young doctor **Bing Crosby**, filling in for vacationing older doctor Barry Fitzgerald, finds their views on medicine don't jibe. The film is a secular GOING MY WAY.

PEARSON, KATHLEEN

NO MOTHER TO GUIDE HER (1923, Silent, Fox)—**Dolores Rousse** marries a man, and later discovers the ceremony was a fake. She goes abroad but returns with what would appear to be an illegitimate child.

PEARSON, NANETTE

NAUGHTY NANETTE (1927, Silent, R-C/FBO)—**Viola Dane** poses as a poor girl, whose parents were ruined by her wealthy but mean grandfather. Dane gets on the good side of the old grouch and when she is exposed, he agrees to take in his real granddaughter.

PECK, BILL & MR. (DAD)

PECK'S BAD BOY (1921, Silent, Associated First National); (1934, Fox); PECK'S BAD BOY WITH THE CIRCUS (1938, RKO)—**Jackie Coogan** and **James Corrigan**; **Jackie Cooper** and **Thomas Meighan**; **Tommy Kelly** and **Grant Mitchell** are the son and father Pecks in this naive story about a mischievous but basically decent youngster.

PECK, MINNIE

PECK'S BAD GIRL (1918, Silent, Fox)—**Mabel Normand's** pranks (including one that causes a run on the bank) have become more that her town can bear. Authorities decide to reserve some space for her at a reformatory, but she is spared this fate when a job modeling clothes changes her behavior.

PECKINPAUGH, LOU

THE CHEAP DETECTIVE (1979, Columbia)—**Peter Falk** plays a Humphrey Bogart like character in a parody of many of Bogie's most famous pictures, including THE MALTESE FALCON, CASABLANCA and THE BIG SLEEP.

PEDAK, EDDIE

ONCE A THIEF (1965, MGM)—Young ex-con **Alain Delon** tries to go straight but circumstances involve him in another crime.

PEG

PEG OF THE PIRATES (1918, Silent, Fox)—**Peggy Hyland** appears in either an adventure film or a comedy picture but no one is quite sure which it is.

PEG

SCALAWAG (1973, Paramount)—**Kirk Douglas** is a peg-legged pirate, who plays a Long John Silver type to young Mark Lester in Mexico in the 1840s.

PEGGY

APARTMENT FOR PEGGY (1948, 20th Century Fox)—**Jeanne Crain** and her new husband take an apartment with college professor Edmund Gwenn who is contemplating suicide. Crain is able to give Gwenn a reason for living.

PELHAM, HAROLD

THE MAN WHO HAUNTED HIMSELF (1970, GB, Associated British)—After an operation **Roger Moore** encounters his exact double who severely complicates his life.

PELL, BARBARA

SWEETIE (1929, Paramount)—**Nancy Carroll** inherits a college and institutes a program of testing to see if football players are learning anything before they are allowed in a game. Good thing for many universities that this strange notion never caught on.

PEMBERTON, PAT

PAT AND MIKE (1952, MGM)—College P.E. instructor **Katharine Hepburn** is a brilliant natural athlete, except when in the presence of her fiance. Spencer Tracy is a sports promoter with whom she falls in love.

PENBROOK, GLORY See MARTHA CARSTAIRS

PENDERGAST, BELINDA

GO WEST, YOUNG LADY (1941, Columbia)—While out west, eastern tomboy **Penny Singleton** battles a dance-hall girl for a marshal.

PENDLEBURY

THE LAVENDER HILL MOB (1951, GB, Ealing)—**Stanley Holloway** is precisely the partner that meek bank clerk Alec Guinness needs to pull off his long-planned heist of his bank's gold bullion. Holloway has the means to melt the gold down and recast it into miniature Eiffel Towers which can easily be transported out of the country.

PENDLETON, BILL

THE FIGHTING AMERICAN (1924, Silent, Universal)—**Pat O'Malley** accepts a wager to propose marriage to any girl selected by his fraternity brothers. Their choice is a girl who has long loved O'Malley. His deceit is discovered and she goes to China as a missionary, later to be rescued from revolutionaries by O'Malley.

PENDLETON, JERVIS

DADDY LONG LEGS (1919, Silent, First National); (1931, Fox); (1955, 20th Century Fox)—**Mahlon Hamilton, Warner Baxter** and **Fred Astaire** portray the benefactor of a young girl. In each case they marry their ward when she grows up. The girls are respectively, Mary Pickford, Janet Gaynor and Leslie Caron.

PENDLETON, PETE

SITTING PRETTY (1933, Paramount)—Hollywood songwriters **Jack Haley** and Jack Oakie become involved with wholesome Ginger Rogers and vampish Thelma Todd.

PENFIELD, JAMES

THE PLOUGHMAN'S LUNCH (1984, GB, Goldwyn)—Radio news editor **Jonathan Pryce** plans to use the book he's writing on Suez to fuel his affair with a television researcher.

PENN

PENN AND TELLER GET KILLED (1989, Warners)—Everyone seemed to hate this film in which the comedy-magic team of **Jillette Penn** and mute partner Teller combine their strange act with perhaps a plot to kill them. No one is really sure about anything in this movie.

PENN, WILLIAM

THE COURAGEOUS MR. PENN (1941, GB, British National)—In a fictional account of the life of the founder of the Quaker movement, **Clifford Evans** is adequate to the role of the crusader for religious freedom and founder of Pennsylvania.

PENNING, JUDSON, DR.

DOCTOR'S WIVES (1931, Fox)—Doctor **Warner Baxter's** wife Joan Bennett suspects he is having an affair with another woman. Then it appears to Baxter that Bennett is having an affair with his best friend. Both are wrong.

PENNINGTON, JACK

ALIAS BULLDOG DRUMMOND (1935, GB, Gaumont)—When Bulldog Drummond is injured in an accident, he asks passer-by **Jack Hulbert** to take over the case he is working on. Hulbert is up to the task.

PENNINGTON, ROBERT

PENNINGTON'S CHOICE (1915, Silent, Metro)—New York society lad **Francis X. Bushman** falls in love with Beverly Bayne, a girl from the far north in Canada. He goes to her home to win her father's approval of their marriage, and is subjected to Bayne's testing him by making a play for him as her twin sister. He also takes a beating from the locals, but with the help of heavyweight boxing champion Jim Jeffries he gives the bullies what for and wins the lovely Bayne.

PENNY, HENRY

MEET MR. PENNY (1938, GB, British National)—Henpecked drunk **Richard Golden** prevents a chain store from building on local allotments.

PENNY WILL

WILL PENNY (1968, Paramount)—Aging cowboy **Charlton Heston** falls in love with widow Joan Hackett, and has to protect her from some bad 'uns.

PENNYFEATHER, PAUL

DECLINE AND FALL . . . OF A BIRD WATCHER (1969, GB, Fox)—The film details expelled divinity student **Robin Phillips'** adventures as a teacher, tutor and white slaver. It's a natural threesome, we guess.

PENNYFEATHER, SAMUEL

WHAT A MAN! (1937, GB, British Lion)—**Sydney Howard** is entrusted with the council's state club funds. He hides them in an old bureau, which his wife promptly sells. Getting the funds back causes him to become a hero and to be elected mayor.

PENNYPACKER, PA

THE REMARKABLE MR. PENNYPACKER (1959, 20th Century Fox)-What makes **Clifton Webb** remarkable is that he is a bigamist in Pennsylvania in the 1890s with one family in Philadelphia and another in Harrisburg. Between his families he has seventeen children. He needs at least two wives! His wives need some relief.

PENNYWORTH, HUMPHREY

JOE PALOOKA MEETS HUMPHREY (1950, Monogram); HUMPHREY TAKES A CHANCE (1950, Monogram)—**Robert Coogan** is a boxer of immense physique and strength, but a weak mind. The gentle giant is not only Joe Palooka's opponent but his friend.

PENROSE, LEWIS & JOHN S.

MY BROTHER TALKS TO HORSES (1946, MGM)—**Butch Jenkins** has the special talent referred to in the title. He passes the information as to which horse will win a race to brother **Peter Lawford**. Naturally some nasty gamblers get into the act.

PEPE

PEPE (1960, Columbia)—**Cantinflas**, born Mario Moreno, was the most popular performer in the Spanish-speaking world, but this long film might make people from the rest of the world wonder what special talents he had that made him so popular. The film has an all-star cast but no apparent direction.

PEPITA

LADIES' DAY (1943, RKO)—For those who have never seen **Lupe Velez's** work, this baseball comedy with Eddie Albert will give audiences a fair notion of her acting talent, which consisted of shrieking, bouncing and generally insulting Mexican women with her stereotyped behavior.

PEPPER, CHRISTOPHER

SALT & PEPPER (1968, GB, UA)—London nightclub owners **Peter Lawford** and his partner Sammy Davis Jr. foil a plot to hijack a Polaris submarine. If you believe that's a credible story, we have a bridge we'd like to sell you.

PEPPER, POLLY, BEN, JOEY, DAVIE & PHRONSIE

FIVE LITTLE PEPPERS AND HOW THEY GREW (1939, Columbia) FIVE LITTLE PEPPERS AT HOME (1940, Columbia); FIVE LITTLE PEPPERS IN TROUBLE (1940, Columbia)—OUT WEST WITH THE PEPPERS (1940, Columbia)—**Edith Fellows, Charles Peck, Tommy Bond, Jimmy Leake/Bobby Larson** and **Dorothy Ann Seese** are the children in this wholesome but dull series about a working mother whose oldest daughter, Fellows, minds the other four children.

PEPPER, SGT.

SGT. PEPPER'S LONELY HEARTS CLUB BAND (1978, Universal)—The Beatle's Sgt. Pepper is played by **Billy Preston** in this film starring the Bee Gees, Peter Frampton and George Burns.

PEPPER, WALDO

THE GREAT WALDO PEPPER (1975, Universal)—Barnstorming pilot **Robert Redford** is hired as a stunt pilot for a movie. He gets to film a dogfight with a German ace he didn't have the opportunity to fly against in WWI.

PEPPERTREE, MARY

FOR THE LOVE OF MARY (1948, Universal)—White House switchboard operator **Deanna Durbin's** romances interfere with her work.

PEREZ, CONCHA

THE DEVIL IS A WOMAN (1935, Paramount)—**Marlene Dietrich**, a heartless Carmen-like Spanish beauty in Seville, ruins all men who love her.

PERKINS, GRACE

QUEEN OF HEARTS (1936, GB, Associated Talking Pictures)—Seamstress **Gracie Fields** works across the street from a theater where her idol John Loder is appearing. Fields is mistaken for the backer of the show, who has insisted she will provide the funds only if she is Loder's co-star. Fields goes on and is a smash, also winning the man she has long admired.

PERKINS, MARCO

THE SOCIAL LION (1930, Paramount)—**Jack Oakie** is reluctantly accepted by the country club set because he's a star polo player. He's loved by a hat check girl, but he's infatuated with a selfish society girl. Oakie wins the big match, but he also tells off his false friends.

PERKINS, TOMMY

THE CRACKERJACK (1925, Silent, East Coast Films)—**Johnny Hines** works his way through college flipping pancakes. After school he goes south of the border to manage his father's pickle factory, and gets involved with a customer planning to ship bullets to revolutionaries in pickles.

PERLMUTTER, MAWRUSS

IN HOLLYWOOD WITH POTASH AND PERLMUTTER (1924, Silent, Goldwyn); PARTNERS AGAIN (1926, Silent, UA)—**Alexander Carr** and his partner in the textile business take up a new line, producing motion pictures. A screen vamp nearly ruins both their marriages.

In the 1926 movie, the partners try their hands at selling automobiles. Carr bails out his old friend Abe Potash played by George Sidney when the latter gets in over his head in merchandizing a new engine which doesn't deliver.

PERRIN, VINCENT

MR. PERRIN AND MR. TRAILL (1948, GB, Ealing)—Cornish school master **Marius Goring** has a cool relation with new master David Farrar. Things go from bad to worse when Farrar wins the school nurse, whom Goring loves. His mind cracks and he attacks Farrar with a knife, but comes to his senses and, at the cost of his own life, rescues his rival, who has gone over a cliff.

PERRY

FUNNYMAN (1967, Korty)—Improvisational comic **Peter Bonerz** believes he should do something more important with his life. So do we.

PERRY, CASSANDRA

BLACK MAGIC WOMAN (1991, Trimark)—Voluptuous **Apollonia Kotero** seduces macho cad Mark Hamill. They spend a lot of time in bed, but when Hamill drops her for another woman, Kotero raises hell.

PERRY, CYNTHIA

SWEET SIXTEEN (1928, Silent, Rayart)—**Helen Foster** won't listen to her older sister's warnings about the intentions of a no-good suitor. Finally, the sister, played by Gertrude Olmstead, risks her own reputation and engagement to save her sister from the clutches of the cad.

PERRY, GABRIEL

THE CASE OF GABRIEL PERRY (1935, GB, British Lion)—Justice of the peace **Henry Oscar** commits a murder.

PERRY, HOLLAND

THE OTHER (1972, 20th Century Fox)—**Martin Udvarnoky**, the evil and probably dead twin of Chris Udvarnoky, encourages his sibling to cause the death of some neighbors.

PERRY, MEG AND NED

THREE FUGITIVES (1989, Buena Vista)—Desperate to find the money to send his little daughter **Sarah Rowland Doroff** to a special school, because she has not spoken since the death of her mother, **Martin Short** robs a bank. He takes just-paroled robber Nick Nolte as a hostage. Since the police believe that Nolte is the robber, he, Short and Doroff must go on the lam. The girl begins to open up to the big bear of a man, Nolte.

PESHKIN, ANDRIAN

THE RUNAWAY (1964, GB, Columbia)—Polish scientist **Alex Gallier** and his synthetic ballistic chemical are saved from Russian spies through the efforts of British agent Paul Williamson.

PETE

THE DEVIL'S PARTNER (1958, Huron)—**Ed Nelson**, an old man living in a remote part of Texas, is possessed by the devil. When he dies his demon is passed on to a younger self.

PETE

FOR PETE'S SAKE (1977, Columbia)—Barbra Streisand will do anything for her husband **Michael Sarrazin**, including stealing, selling her body, and perhaps even murder. It's a mildly funny black comedy with Sarrazin having little to do.

PETE

I'M FROM THE CITY (1938, RKO)—Comedian **Joe Penner** is a circus bare-back rider with a deathly fear of horses.

PETE

JACK, SAM AND PETE (1919, Silent, GB, Pollock-Daring)—**Ernest A. Trimingham** is one of three American cowboys who rescue a boy from kidnappers seeking a hidden fortune.

PETE

THE LEATHER BOYS (1965, GB, Allied Artists)—When motorcycle enthusiast Colin Campbell marries Rita Tushingham, he finds that she will not work around the house, but she is willing to sleep with all comers. Campbell turns to his gay friend **Dudley Sutton**. But the arrangement doesn't last, as Sutton enjoys himself too much with a group of sailors to share Campbell's interest in riding around on "hogs."

PETE

RIKKY AND PETE (1988, Australia, MGM/UA)—**Steve Kearney's** skill of inventing weird contraptions has gotten him in trouble with the police. However, when he comes up with a machine that streamlines the mining process, he and his sister strike it rich.

PETER

THE BOY WITH GREEN HAIR (1949, RKO)—In the anti-war film that introduced Nat King Cole's hit song "Nature Boy," **Dean Stockwell** learns that his parents have been killed in an air raid, and his hair turns green. He parades himself as an image of the futility and absurdity of war.

PETER

COME BACK PETER (1971, GB, Donwin)—Butcher's helper **Christopher Matthews** sets out to bed every "bird" he fancies in London and pretty much succeeds.

PETER

THE RAILWAY CHILDREN (1971, GB, Universal)—**Gary Warren** is one of a trio of children out to clear their father of charges of espionage. They play in the Yorkshire railway yards.

PETER, PIKE & MRS.

THEY HAD TO SEE PARIS (1929, Fox)—Garage owner **Will Rogers** strikes it rich in oil. His wife **Irene Rich** insists they must visit Paris, where she hopes to marry her daughter to an aristocrat. Rogers finally gets his wife to go home with him when he gives signs of having an affair with a French singer.

PETER, PRINCE

PRINCE OF ARCADIA (1933, GB, Woolf & Friedman)—**Carl Brisson** is forced to abdicate his throne. He spends his exile on the Riviera where he meets and falls in love with an actress, whom he plans to marry despite the objections of his aunt, the Queen.

PETERS, CHARLIE

THE PRINCESS AND THE PLUMBER (1930, Fox)—**Charles Farrell**, the son of a plumbing contractor, is working his way up from the bottom for his father. He is given some work in the castle of an impoverished prince and his daughter, Maureen O'Sullivan. She decides he's just the lad for her.

PETERS, JANE

NINE GIRLS (1944, Columbia)—**Jinx Falkenberg** is one of the sorority girls who has a reason to kill nasty Anita Louise.

PETERS, JENNIFER

STOP PRESS GIRL (1949, GB, GFD)—Teenager **Sally Ann Howes** has the unusual power to stop any piece of machinery, merely by being near it for fifteen minutes.

PETERS, PEACEFUL

PEACEFUL PETERS (1922, Silent, Arrow)—A dying prospector tells **William Fairbanks** the location of his mine. Fairbanks must deal with a crooked assayer and a claim-jumping dancehall-owner before discovering the dancer he has fallen in love with is the daughter of the deceased prospector.

PETERS, "PETROV" PETE

SHALL WE DANCE (1937, RKO)—Renowned ballet dancer **Fred Astaire** is reported to have married musical comedy star Ginger Rogers, and they can't convince anyone they haven't.

PETERSON, IRMA

MY FRIEND IRMA (1949, Paramount); MY FRIEND IRMA GOES WEST (1950, Paramount)—Sexy radio ding-a-ling **Marie Wilson** and her friend Diana Lynn are the nominal stars of these two films, but a young comedy team steals the show—Dean Martin and Jerry Lewis.

PETERSEN, TONY "JOCK"

PETERSEN (1974, Australia, Avco Embassy)—**Jack Thompson**, a married electrician, goes to college to better himself. He does well with the co-eds and female faculty.

PETHER, FLORRIE

SEVEN WOMEN (1966, MGM)—**Betty Field** is one of a group of American women staffing a mission in China in 1935 that is overrun by bandits.

PETRO

THE MAD MONSTER (1942, PRC)—George Zucco transforms farmhand **Glenn Strange** into a hairy monster who kidnaps a little girl.

PETROCELLI, TONY

THE LAWYER (1969, Paramount)—Earnest young attorney **Barry Newman** defends Robert Colbert, a physician accused of murdering his wife. The film is loosely based on the Sam Sheppard murder case.

PETROVA, NADIA

DRESSED TO THRILL (1935, Fox)—**Tutta Rolf** portrays a Russian singer and her look-alike dressmaker in a very predictable story with forgettable songs and singing by the star.

PETROVICH, PRINCESS

THE TIGER WOMAN (1917, Silent, Fox)—**Theda Bara** vamps her way through this picture as a wicked woman, who ruins a family by causing a son to kill his father. In the end she ends her life with a dagger.

PETRUCHIO *See* **FRED GRAHAM**

PETTIGREW, HELEN

I'LL NEVER FORGET YOU (1951, 20th Century Fox)—In a remake of BERKELEY SQUARE, American Tyrone Power, working in London, is transported back to the 18th century where he falls in love with **Ann Blyth**

505

PETTS, HAROLD
POSTMAN'S KNOCK (1962, GB, MGM)—When efficient village postman **Spike Milligan** is transferred to London, he thwarts thieves posing as mailmen.

PETTY, GEORGE
THE PETTY GIRL (1950, Columbia)—Calendar artist **Robert Cummings** thinks college professor Virginia Mayo is just perfect to be his new model. His persistence costs her her job. They straighten things out and marry.

PFEIFFER, KARL
FRIENDLY ENEMIES (1942, UA)—German-American **Charles Winninger** has a running feud with his friend Charlie Ruggles, a die-hard American patriot. Winninger is initially sympathetic to the Nazis but comes to realize their true nature.

PFINK, RAT
RAT PFINK AND BOO BOO (1966, Morgan/Craddock)—Rock singer **Vin Saxon** and his gardener friend Titus Moede become superheroes. They rescue Saxon's girlfriend from a villain.

PHAEDRA
PHAEDRA (1962, Lopert)—Tycoon Raf Vallone's wife **Melina Mercouri** has an affair with her stepson, Anthony Perkins.

PHALEN, COUNT
THE PATRIOT (1928, Paramount)—Sadly, **Lewis Stone** decides that he must kill his friend Emil Jannings, the Czar of Russia, because the man is in a murderous rage. Stone succeeds, but is killed himself, noting that he had been a better patriot than friend.

PHANTOM
PHANTOM FROM SPACE (1953, UA)—**Dick Sands** is an invisible alien trapped in an observatory. He becomes visible when he dies.

PHANTOM, THE
THE PHANTOM OF THE OPERA (1989, 21st Film)—There have been so many decent productions of Gaston Leroux's story, both on the stage and the screen, that it's difficult to understand the need for this boring version staring **Robert Englund.**

PHARO, PHILLIP
THE PARSON OF PANAMINT (1916, Silent, Pallas)—Fighting parson **Dustin Farnum** is brought into a western mining town where he builds his church, gets rid of the town's bad guys, and sacrifices his life in a fire to save an enemy.

PHIBES, DR. ANTON
THE ABOMINABLE DR. PHIBES (1971, American Int.) DOCTOR PHIBES RISES AGAIN (1972, GB, American International)—Horribly mutilated, lunatic doctor **Vincent Price** has sworn to murder the physicians who butchered his wife while operating on her. He dooms the quacks to death, paralleling the plagues brought down on Pharaoh by God through Moses. In the sequel, Price is in Egypt seeking an elixir which will restore his wife to life. These are comedy-horror movies but the gore isn't funny.

PHILBROOK, CLINTON
THE COWARD (1927, Silent, R-C Pictures)—In a story that reads like a Charles Atlas ad, **Warner Baxter** loses his girl when he takes a beating from a man who is annoying her. Baxter goes to a lumber camp in Canada, turns himself into a real man, returns and teaches both his ex-girlfriend and the ruffian a lesson.

PHILIP
MEN'S CLUB (1986, Paramount)—**David Dukes** is one of a group of men who get together to explore their disturbing attitudes towards women.

PHILIP
THE SUSPECT (1944, Universal)—**Charles Laughton** murders his shrewish wife, after meeting and falling in love with Ellen Drew. Everything looks good until neighbor Henry Daniell gets wise and tries some blackmail. Laughton eliminates him, and it looks like he may get away with it—but, then . . . .

PHILIP, KING
THE KING'S VACATION (1933, Warners)—When monarch **George Arliss** visits his ex-wife, he finds she's better off than he is.

PHILIP II, KING
IN THE PALACE OF THE KING (1923, Silent, Goldwyn)—Spanish king **Sam De Grasse**, jealous of the popularity of his brother Don John (Edmund Lowe), sends him off to do battle with the Moors, hoping that he'll be killed. Instead, Don John returns victorious. De Grasse stabs his brother, leaving him for dead, but a general's daughter, Blanche Sweet, knows the king is the guilty party. She settles everything with a little blackmail.

PHILLIP
ORPHANS (1987, Lorimar)—**Kevin Anderson** is a slow-witted youngster, completely dominated by his streetwise brother Matthew Modine. The latter kidnaps Albert Finney, who takes over their lives and brings Anderson out of the shell Modine has imposed on him out of fear of losing him as he lost his parents.

PHILLIPE *See* **LOUIS XIV (THE MAN IN THE IRON MASK)**

PHILLIPRO, BOBBY
WEDNESDAY'S CHILD (1934, RKO)—After **Frankie Thomas** is forced to testify in his parent's bitter divorce hearing, he finds himself shipped off to a military school, because neither his father nor mother wants him.

PHILLIPS, CLAIRE
I WAS AN AMERICAN SPY (1951, Monogram, Allied Artists) -At the beginning of WWII, **Ann Dvorak** gets to sing "Because of You" while fighting the Japanese in the Philippines.

PHILLIPS, EVA
QUEEN BEE (1955, Columbia)—Evil, depraved **Joan Crawford** dominates everyone around her, destroying anyone who dares cross her or challenge her right to control everyone's lives.

PHILLIPS, FRANNY
RICH KIDS (1979, UA)-Faced with the divorce of her parents, **Trini Alvardo** runs away with a young boy. They experience a bizarre weekend.

PHIPPS, RITA
A LETTER TO THREE WIVES (1948, 20th Century Fox)—**Ann Sothern** and two other women are about to leave on a boat trip on the Hudson when they each receive a letter from Addie Ross. She claims to be running away with one of their husbands. Sothern thinks of her marriage to school teacher Kirk Douglas, who has grown to resent the fact that she is the breadwinner because of the soap opera she writes.

PHOEBE

ZELLY AND ME (1988, Columbia)—Orphan **Alexandra Johnes** is being raised by her rich, possessive grandmother Glynis Johns on a magnificent Virginia Tidewater estate in 1958. Grandma alternately indulges Alexandra and humiliates her. Looking on helplessly is Mademoiselle (Isabelle Rossellini), the girl's nanny, who fills the child's head with stories of the martyrdom of Joan of Arc. The story would be better read than viewed.

PHOEBE, AUNT

THE PILGRIM LADY (1947, Republic)—School teacher **Helen Freeman** writes a sexy novel. When it becomes a huge hit, the identity of the author must be revealed. Freeman induces her niece Lynne Roberts to pose as the author.

PHRED

THE STUDENT NURSES (1970, New World)—**Karen Carlson** is one of four beautiful student nurses who, as the ads say, "are learning fast."

PHYLLIS

COUNTERFEIT LADY (1937, Columbia)—Diamond thief **Joan Parry** is pursued by private eye Ralph Bellamy.

PHYLLIS

THE RAILWAY CHILDREN (1971, GB, Universal)—Forced to move from lush surroundings when their father is falsely accused of treason and sent to prison, **Sally Thomsett** and her brother and sister are forced to play in the railway yard. One day they meet a man there who has evidence to clear their father's name.

PIATO, DUKE

THE SAINT'S DOUBLE TROUBLE (1940, RKO)—**George Sanders** plays both his Simon Templar role and that of The Boss, a notorious jewel thief. Impersonations abound in this humorous suspenseful picture.

PICKWICK, SAMUEL

THE ADVENTURES OF MR. PICKWICK (1921, Silent, GB, Bentley); THE PICKWICK PAPERS (1952, GB, Renown)—**Fred Volpe** and **James Hayter** appear as Dickens' club man whose jaunt with friends leads him to a breach of promise suit.

PIED PIPER

THE PIED PIPER (1972, GB, Paramount)—British folk balladeer **Donovan** portrays the minstrel who, in 1349, rids the town of Hamelin of its plague of rats. When he is not paid, he leads off the town's children as well.

PIERCE, MILDRED

MILDRED PIERCE (1945, Warners)—**Joan Crawford** leaves her husband Bruce Bennett after the death of her younger daughter. She works hard as a waitress, and eventually owns a chain of successful restaurants. Crawford provides her ungrateful daughter Ann Blyth with every luxury, but when Crawford marries penniless society man Zachary Scott, she finds herself competing with Blyth for his affection.

PIERRE

PIERRE OF THE PLAINS (1914, Silent, All Star); (1942, MGM)—**Edgar Selwyn** wrote and starred in the silent feature about a northwest Canadian trapper whose adventures threaten his romance with an innkeeper. Selwyn produced the 1942 film, his last, with **John Carroll** as the trapper.

PIERRE

WEEKEND MILLIONAIRE (1937, GB, Gaumont)—In Paris bank clerk **Buddy Rogers**, mistaken for a millionaire, falls in love with Mary Brian, a clothes model posing as a countess.

PIFFLE

THE CLOWN (1916, Silent, Paramount)—**Victor Moore**, a clown with a circus, marries a girl to give her expected child a name. Even though he loves her, he bows out when the real father, believed dead, comes to claim her and their child.

PIKE

A TENDERFOOT GOES WEST (1937, Hoffberg)—Western pulp writer **Russell Gleason** leaves the city for the West where he has adventures similar to the ones he writes about.

PIKE, ADAM

SAILOR'S HOLIDAY (1929, Pathe)—**Alan Hale** and his buddy are swindled by a streetwalker while on leave. They refuse to be fooled when another girl gives them the same story, only hers is true.

PIKE, CISCO

CISCO PIKE (1971, Columbia)—Former pop group performer and dope pusher **Kris Kristofferson** is blackmailed by a cop into selling heroin.

PIKE, DANIEL VORHEES

THE MAN FROM HOME (1914, Silent, Lasky)—**Charles Richman** travels to Sorrento to save his ward from marrying the wrong man. He prevents a Russian prisoner from being recaptured, and walks away with a beautiful woman for himself.

PILGRIM, THE

THE PILGRIM (1923, Silent, Associated First National)—Escaped convict **Charles Chaplin** steals a preacher's clothes. He takes a position as a minister with a Texas church, until his identity is revealed by another ex-con.

PILGRIM, CYNTHIA

THE SHOCKING MISS PILGRIM (1947, 20th Century Fox)—In Boston in 1894, stenographer **Betty Grable** fights for women's rights.

PILGRIM, JOE

THE MAYOR'S NEST (1932, GB, British & Dominions)—Out-of-work trombonist **Sydney Howard** is persuaded to run for the city council. He ultimately becomes mayor and helps a social worker clean up the slums.

PILGRIM, LARAMIE

MISS PILGRIM'S PROGRESS (1950, GB, Grand National)—**Yolande Donlan**, a factory worker from America, comes to England through an exchange program. She falls in love with the village where she stays and leads the fight against the planners who would drastically change it and its traditions.

PILKINGTON, JANE "PILKY"

SHE GETS HER MAN (1945, Universal)—In this comedy-mystery, country girl **Joan Davis** finds a killer in New York who uses a blowgun.

PILLETTI, MARTY

MARTY (1959, UA)—Brooklyn butcher **Ernest Borgnine** would like to marry as his brothers and sisters have, but with his looks he has almost despaired of ever finding a woman to love him. When he meets Betsy Blair, his mother doesn't approve of her. Borgnine, who has always honored his mother, decides that he's entitled to some happiness and aims to have it with Blair.

PINCELLI, ANGELO

THOSE DARING YOUNG MEN IN THEIR JAUNTY JALOPIES (1969, GB/France/Italy, Paramount)—**Walter Chiari** is the Italian entry in the 1920, five country, 1500 miles, Monte Carlo auto rally.

PINK, EDDIE

STRIKE ME PINK (1936, UA)-Timid tailor **Eddie Cantor** takes over the running of an amusement park and has trouble with gangsters who control slot machines.

PINKERTON, MISS

MISS PINKERTON (1932, First National)—**Joan Blondell** is a nurse in this mystery which keeps audiences guessing as to who killed the head of a household.

PINKEY, VERNON

THE DIRTY DOZEN (1967, GB, MGM)—G.I. convict **Donald Sutherland** is recruited with eleven others to go behind enemy lines on a dangerous mission. During the training, Sutherland poses as a general reviewing the troops of Colonel Robert Ryan.

PINNEY, WALLY

THE PUNCH AND JUDY MAN (1963, GB, Warner-Pathe)—Seaside entertainer **Tony Hancock**, married to a social climber, ruins the mayor's victory celebration.

PIP-EMMA

THE UNDER-PUP (1939, Universal)—Girl from the slums **Gloria Jean** wins a month's vacation at a resort filled with snobbish rich girls.

PIPER, AUBREY

THE SHOW OFF (1926, Silent, Paramount); (1934, MGM); (1946, MGM); MEN ARE LIKE THAT (1930, Paramount);—**Ford Sterling** was the first of several actors to portray this loud-mouthed, bragging railroad clerk, who almost ruins his wife's family with his harebrained schemes, until one actually works. **Hal Skelly, Spencer Tracy** and **Red Skelton** follow this well-worn path in essentially the same stories.

PIPER, PENNY

FORTY POUNDS OF TROUBLE (1962, Universal)—**Claire Wilcox** is a little girl who becomes the ward of casino manager Tony Curtis when her father is killed. It's a remake of LITTLE MISS MARKER and SORROWFUL JONES.

PIRANDELLO, NICK

REAL MEN (1987, MGM/UA)—Tough CIA agent **James Belushi's** assignment is to keep his eye on wimp John Ritter, who has been chosen to transport a secret map from California to Washington. Why they didn't just fax it and forget this dismal movie, we'll never know.

PIRATE KING, THE

THE PIRATES OF PENZANCE (1983, Universal)—**Kevin Kline** is dashing as the Pirate King in this enjoyable production of the Gilbert and Sullivan favorite.

PIRDY, AUGUSTUS "RED"

THE YELLOW CAB MAN (1950, MGM)—Taxi driver and inventor **Red Skelton** has one disaster after another in a film filled with funny sight gags.

PIRELLE, ANTOINE

MELODY FOR THREE (1941, RKO)—In this Dr. Christian movie, **Walter Woolf King** is an orchestra conductor separated from his music teacher wife and 12-year-old violinist prodigy son.

PIRIMBA, GIG "GIGGY"

MADE FOR EACH OTHER (1971, 20th Century Fox)—New York losers, **Joseph Bologna** and Renee Taylor married in real life and the authors of the script for this movie, meet at a group-therapy session and fall in love. It's poignant and funny.

PITKIN, NORMAN

THE SQUARE PEG (1958, GB, Rank); THE EARLY BIRD (1965, GB, Rank)—In the first named film, captured parachutist **Norman Wisdom** saves his friends by posing as his German double. In the second entry, he is a milkman who, together with a small dairy owner, fights a large milk combine trying to put them both out of business.

PITT, ROBERT

A GENTLEMAN OF LEISURE (1923, Silent, Paramount)—Playboy **Jack Holt** wagers that he will obtain a photograph with a fond inscription to him, from a girl he has never met, now seated across the room from him in a restaurant.

PITT, ROBERT

THEY CAN'T HANG ME (1955, GB, British Lion)—Yes, they can and do, even though **Andre Morell** tries to barter his life for information about atomic spies.

PITT, WILLIAM

THE YOUNG MR. PITT (1942, GB, 20th Century Fox)—**Robert Donat** is marvelous as the man who became British Prime Minister at 24. He sees his career in decline as well as his health, but is recalled to lead the nation in 1804, living long enough to see Napoleon beaten at Trafalgar. Pitt died at 46.

PITZPORTER, ADMIRAL

THE ADMIRAL'S SECRET (1934, GB, Realart/RKO)—When he retires from the navy, **Edmund Gwenn** absconds with some jewels, and is pursued by bungling Spanish cutthroats.

PLAFAIR, JUSTIN

THEY MIGHT BE GIANTS (1971, Universal)—**George C. Scott** has delusions that he is Sherlock Holmes. His relatives hire psychiatrist Joanne Woodward, who just happens to be named Watson, to get the goods on him, so he can be put away. The twosome have some interesting adventures, some real—some imagined.

PLIMPTON, GEORGE

PAPER LION (1968, UA)—**Robert Alda** portrays the author who likes to get involved in the sports stories he writes about. In this one he takes the role of a quarterback for the Detroit Lions with the plan to take one snap of the ball in a real game.

PLUM, LESTER

STAND IN (1937, UA)—Stand-in **Joan Blondell** rescues New York accountant Leslie Howard from a vamp while he's in Hollywood to balance the books of a studio. She also helps him stand up to the unscrupulous studio heads.

PLUMMER, JIM

THE LAST BANDIT (1949, Republic)—**Forest Tucker** and brother Wild Bill Elliott find themselves on opposite sides of the law when Tucker robs a train Elliott is guarding.

PLUNKETT, ASA
THE CAPTAIN'S KID (1937, First National/Warners)—**Guy Kibbee** is an eccentric, but entertaining town drunk, beloved by all the children for his tall tales. One day he discovers a buried treasure. He kills a man who attacks him to get the loot. The testimonies of the children save him.

PLUNKETT, MARY
HIGH SPIRITS (1988, Tri-Star)—Beautiful **Daryl Hannah** is a ghost in a castle owned by Peter O'Toole. Every night she again endures being murdered by her 300-year-dead husband, who killed her on their wedding night, believing her unfaithful. One fatal night, tourist Steve Guttenberg interrupts the reenactment. As a result, he and Hannah fall in love.

POCAHONTAS
CAPTAIN JOHN SMITH AND POCAHONTAS (1953, UA)—It's a straightforward account of the legendary Pocohontas (**Jody Lawrence**) saving Captain John Smith (Anthony Dexter) from being beheaded by angry Indians. The couple marry but he must return to England, freeing his bride to marry another.

POE, EDGAR ALLAN
THE LOVES OF EDGAR ALLAN POE (1942, 20th Century Fox)— THE MAN WITH THE CLOAK (1951, MGM); THE SPECTRE OF EDGAR ALLAN POE (1974, Cinerama)—**John Shepperd (Shepperd Strudwick)**, **Joseph Cotten** and **Robert Walker** Jr. each made appearances as the celebrated author of horror stories and poetry.

POE, JOSLYN
THE TAXI DANCER (1927, Silent, MGM)—**Joan Crawford** arrives in New York, hoping to become a Broadway star, but must take work in a dime-a-dance dump where she becomes involved with Douglas Gilmore, a cad whom she hides when he kills a man.

POICCARD, LEON
THE SECRET FOUR (1940, GB, Ealing)—**Francis L. Sullivan** is one of three men who avenge the death of their friend by killing a member of Parliament, who is behind a plot to block the Suez Canal.

POINTER, CARLEY
NEW YORK'S FINEST (1988, Platinum)—**Heidi Payne** is one of three hookers who lead double lives after learning to be "ladies" from a transvestite. They alternate turning tricks for a blackmailing madam and dating New York's elite.

POINTER, PERCY
MISTER TEN PERCENT (1967, GB, Associated British)—Builder **Charles Drake** writes a drama which becomes a hit as a comedy.

POLICE COMMISSIONER
REPORT TO THE COMMISSIONER (1975, UA)—**Stephen Elliott** has the small role of the commissioner in this story of the failed attempt by Michael Moriarty to be a new breed of cop in New York City.

POLIN, ABE
MEMORIES OF ME (1988, MGM/UA)—The movie has a lot in common with the 1986 film NOTHING IN COMMON, although **Alan King** and Billy Crystal as the father and son who don't know each other, how to know each other, or even if they want to know each other, aren't as real as Jackie Gleason and Tom Hanks.

POLLIFAX, MRS. EMILY
MRS. POLLIFAX, SPY (1971, UA)—In her last film, matronly **Rosalind Russell** offers her services to the CIA. Russell should have retired before this stinker.

POLLITT, MAGGIE
CAT ON A HOT TIN ROOF (1958, MGM)—**Elizabeth Taylor** is married to Paul Newman who can't seem to bring himself to have sex with his desirable wife. Her crude old father-in-law, Burl Ives, would be glad to oblige her, however.

POLO, MARCO
THE ADVENTURES OF MARCO POLO (1938, UA) MARCO (1973, Cinerama)—**Gary Cooper** and **Desi Arnaz**, Jr. portray the 13th century traveler to Cathay who becomes involved in the intrigues of the court of Kublai Khan, and falls for a princess. While Cooper seemed at home in the role, Arnaz is an unfunny joke.

POLLY
LADIES AT EASE (1927, Silent, First Division)—Lingerie models **Pauline Garon** and Gertrude Short steal the boyfriends of two song and dance sisters. Garon and Short somehow are forced to go on stage instead of the sisters, and their ineptitude is applauded by the audience.

POLLY
LADY FROM NOWHERE (1936, Columbia)—**Mary Astor** witnesses a murder. Now both the cops and the mob are out to find her. She hides out, but the gangsters have a better investigating team than do the police.

POLLY
POLLY OF THE CIRCUS (1917, Silent, Goldwyn)—Circus bareback rider **Mae Marsh's** romance with handsome young minister Vernon Steele is not blessed by the reverend's parishioners.

POLLY
THE POPPY GIRL'S HUSBAND (1919, Silent, Artcraft)—Before her marriage to William S. Hart, **Juanita Hansen** was named the Poppy Girl. When he is released from solitary confinement after ten years, Hart discovers that his wife has married the detective who had forged the evidence against him. Hansen learns that Hart is seeing their son, and fearful that he will hurt her, has the detective prepare to frame him again. Hart breaks in on Hansen and is about to brand her when his son's sobs prevent him from doing so.

POLLY, ALFRED
THE HISTORY OF MR. POLLY (1949, GB, Rank)—In 1900, draper **John Mills**, weary of his life and nagging wife, sets fire to his own store, hits the road and settles down to a fine life with the Plump Woman (Megs Jenkins) who runs an inn.

POLLYANNA
POLLYANNA (1920, Silent, UA); (1960, Buena Vista)—**Mary Pickford** and **Hayley Mills** both appear as the daughter of a missionary who has been taught to be "glad" because things could always be worse. When her father dies, Pollyanna goes to live with her aunt who believes things are worse than they really are. In this battle, Pollyanna comes out on top.

POMPADOR, MME.
MADAME POMPADOR (1927, Silent, GB, Paramount)—**Dorothy Gish** is the infamous courtesan, who here has a love affair with prisoner Antonio Moreno.

PONSONBY, JACK
JACK AHOY! (1935, GB, Gaumont)—Seaman **Jack Hulbert** serves on a battleship bound for Chinese waters. He falls for the admiral's daughter, rescuing both her and her father from revolutionaries.

PONTABEE, ADAM, BENJAMIN, CALEB, DANIEL, EPHRAIM, FRANK & GIDEON
SEVEN BRIDES FOR SEVEN BROTHERS (1954, MGM)—When mountain man **Howard Keel** brings home Jane Powell as his wife, his brothers, **Jeff Richards, Matt Mattox, Marc Platt, Jacques d'Amboise, Tommy Rall** and **Russ Tamblyn** all reckon they'd like brides too. Encouraged by Keel, they kidnap six comely young lasses from town. An avalanche prevents the pursuing parents and boyfriends from getting to the Pontabee's farm until spring time—plenty of time for romance to grow. The dancing in this exuberant musical is marvelous but there are no songs that would become standards.

PONTIAC, CHIEF
BATTLE OF CHIEF PONTIAC (1952, Real Art)—When the peace treaty between the Indians, led by **Lon Chaney Jr.**, and the white men doesn't work out, there's a lot of violence and bloodshed on both sides.

PONTICELLI, COUNT EMILIO
THOSE MAGNIFICENT MEN IN THEIR FLYING MACHINES (1965, GB, 20th Century Fox)—**Alberto Sordi** is an Italian count who travels with his wife and large brood of kids. He is an entrant in a 1910 air race from London to Paris. He is rescued by Stuart Whitman when his plane goes down in flames near the finish line, the result of sabotage by villain Terry-Thomas.

POOKIE
THE STERILE CUCKOO (1969, Paramount)—**Liza Minnelli** received an Academy Award nomination for her portrayal of an eccentric girl who forces her attentions on a reluctant college student.

POOLE, BIDDEFORD "POGO"
THE PLEASURE OF HIS COMPANY (1961, Paramount) Long absent **Fred Astaire** shows up in time to get in the way of preparations for his daughter Debbie Reynolds' wedding. Reynolds is delighted, but not so mother Lilli Palmer.

POOLE, INSPECTOR
AN INSPECTOR CALLS (1954, GB, British Lion)—Inspector **Alastair Sim** visits a provincial family in 1912, investigating the death of a girl who poisoned herself. Everyone is partially to blame. By the end of the film, Sim proves to be a bogus inspector—perhaps he never existed.

POOLE, LEON "FOGGY"
THE KILLER IS LOOSE (1956, UA)—Psychopath **Wendell Corey** has escaped from a mental institution where he was sent after being captured by detective Joseph Cotten. Corey blames Cotten for his wife's death and has promised to murder Cotten's wife, Rhonda Fleming.

POOLE, MISS
EVERY LITTLE CROOK AND NANNY (1972, MGM)—**Lynn Redgrave's** dancing school is taken over by Victor Mature's mob to be used as a betting parlor. Redgrave disguises herself as a nanny and kidnaps Mature's son. From then on nothing much happens.

POORE, JOHN
FLAME OF THE WEST (1945, Monogram)—**Johnny Mack Brown**, a doctor with pacifist views, is considered a coward by townspeople when he won't face up to the local outlaws. He finally gets angry enough to fight after the murder of the sheriff.

POP
THE PICTURE SHOW MAN (1980, Australia, Limelight)—In the 1920s **John Meillon** takes his movie equipment to the Australian outback where he shares its magic with the delighted citizens.

POPE, DANNY
RUNNING ON EMPTY (1988, Warners)—Extremely gifted pianist **River Phoenix** would like to go to Julliard as his music teacher encourages him to do, but since he is the son of sixties radicals Judd Hirsch and Christine Lahti, who have been on the run since planting a bomb in a university lab in 1971, he knows he can't do anything that would expose his parents to capture.

POPE, MILES
TRUE IDENTITY (1991, Buena Vista/Touchstone)—Unfortunately for New York black actor **Lenny Henry**, he accidently learns that a pillar of the community, Frank Langella, is actually a gangster. With a hit man on his trail, Henry disguises himself as a white man.

POPEYE
POPEYE (1980, Paramount)—**Robin Williams** is unmemorable as the cartoon sailor who gets his strength from spinach.

POPOLINO, PIPPO
CASANOVA'S BIG NIGHT (1954, Paramount)—**Bob Hope** must impersonate Casanova in a not so funny farce.

POPPEA *See* LILLIAN MARCHARD

POPPINS, MARY
MARY POPPINS (1964, Buena Vista)—Magical nanny **Julie Andrews** takes control of two unruly children and their parents as well. Andrews didn't get to repeat her Broadway success as Eliza Doolittle but she walked off with the Oscar for Best Actress for this effort.

PORGY
PORGY AND BESS (1959, Columbia)—**Sidney Poitier** is the cripple who loves Bess, but finds it's hard to keep her. Despite the Gershwin music, the production is just average.

PORKY
PORKY (1982, 20th Century Fox); PORKY'S REVENGE (1985, 20th Century Fox)—**Chuck Mitchell**, gross, obese proprietor of a Florida gambling den and whorehouse, isn't happy when some horny high school boys invade his den of iniquity. He treats them roughly and they seek revenge. The adolescent sex comedy was a surprise hit, spawning two sequels, only the second in which Mitchell reappeared as Porky.

POROK, JOHANN
THE BARONESS AND THE BUTLER (1938, 20th Century Fox)—Butler **William Powell** falls for Annabella, the daughter of the Hungarian prime minister. Powell joins the opposition party, becomes it's leader and as a full-time politician announces his love for the baroness.

PORTER, APPLETON

THE TROUBLE WITH SPIES (1987, Brigade/DEG)—**Donald Sutherland**, a bumbling British secret agent, is used as bait by his superiors to smoke out a soviet spy.

PORTER, CMDR. DAVID

YANKEE BUCCANEER (1952, Universal)—**Jeff Chandler** disguises his ship as a pirate vessel in order to destroy a real buccaneer fleet.

PORTER, EVE

EVE KNEW HER APPLES (1945, Columbia)—Weary radio singing star **Ann Miller** runs away, hiding in a car which belongs to a reporter. This is a poorly conceived knockdown of IT HAPPENED ONE NIGHT.

PORTER, PAUL

FUGITIVE LOVERS (1934, MGM)—Fugitive from justice **Robert Montgomery** pursues chorus girl Madge Evans while they are travelling on a bus. Yeah, we know it sounds like he's chasing her down the aisle, but we can't think of another way of describing it.

PORTER, WILLIAM

OH, MR. PORTER (1937, GB, GFD/Gainsborough)—Bungling railroad worker **Will Hay** is appointed stationmaster at a rundown station where he is driven to distraction by his nit-wit workers Moore Marriott and Graham Moffatt. The trio must also deal with a gang of gun-runners. It's a classic comedy for those who consider Hay, Marriott and Moffatt, classic comedians.

PORTERFIELD, ULYSSES

I AM NOT AFRAID (1939, Warners)—In a film also known as THE MAN WHO DARED, grandpa **Charley Grapewin** rescues his grandson who has been kidnapped and threatened with death by gangsters to insure his family won't talk about a murder they witnessed.

PORTHOS

THE THREE MUSKETEERS (1921, Silent, UA); (1935, RKO); (1939, 20th Century Fox); (1948, MGM), (1974, 20th Century Fox); THE FOUR MUSKETEERS (1975, 20th Century Fox)—**George Seigman, Moroni Olsen, Russell Hicks, Gig Young** and **Frank Finlay** each appeared as the musketeer Porthos.

PORTNOY, ALEXANDER

PORTNOY'S COMPLAINT (1972, Warners)—**Richard Benjamin**, a second generation New Jersey Jew, attempts to fulfill his sexual fantasies but he's not particularly successful. It was funnier reading Philip Roth's novel than watching the film.

POSEY, SAMSON

THE DIRTY DOZEN (1967, GB, MGM)—Gentle giant **Clint Walker** is nevertheless a condemned G.I., apparently pushed too far by someone. He joins with eleven other dishonorable and mentally deficient American soldiers to go behind enemy lines in France and kill a passel of high-ranking German officers who are doing a little Rest and Relaxation in a huge chateau. Walker doesn't make it back—but we figured that all along.

POSNER, SAM

THE LUCKIEST MAN IN THE WORLD (1989, Second Effort)—After missing a plane by ten minutes that crashed and left no survivors, **Philip Bosco** is inspired to reform and reassess his life.

POST, FRANK

WILD ROVERS (1971, MGM)—Naive youngster **Ryan O'Neal** teams with aging cowboy William Holden to rob a bank. It's a fun Western with both O'Neal and Holden in top form. Some critics saw a homosexual bond between the two men, but some critics always see a homosexual bond between two men appearing together in a movie.

POTASH, ABE

IN HOLLYWOOD WITH POTASH AND PERLMUTTER (1924, Silent, Goldwyn); PARTNERS AGAIN (1926, Silent, UA)—**George Sidney** and his partner Alexander Carr become movie producers and their picture starring vamp Betty Blythe is a huge success, but almost at the cost of both their marriages. In the second feature, an argument breaks up the partnership and Sidney is set up by a pair of swindlers but Carr comes to the rescue.

POTTER, BRIDGET

OBLIGING YOUNG LADY (1941, RKO)—Nine-year-old **Joan Carroll** is hidden by a secretary who hopes the action will reunite the child's divorcing parents.

POTTER, CALVIN

GOING STEADY (1958, Columbia)—**Alan Reed, Jr.** and Molly Bee are high school sweethearts who run away to get married, move in with her parents and soon discover that she's pregnant. It's the mother's family who always suffers.

POTTER, CYNTHIA

TOO YOUNG TO KISS (1951, MGM)—Nineteen-inch waist **June Allyson** just about can get away with posing as a child prodigy so she can get noticed as a pianist. Problem is she'd like Van Johnson to see her as an adult.

POTTER, GEORGE

I MET HIM IN PARIS (1937, Paramount)—Playwright **Melvyn Douglas** pursues workaholic fashion designer Claudette Colbert in Paris. His rival is married novelist Robert Young.

POTTER, JUNIOR

SON OF PALEFACE (1952, Paramount)—In the sequel to THE PALEFACE, **Bob Hope** is once again joined by Jane Russell in a western spoof. Hope is a tenderfoot who returns west to pick up a fortune supposedly left him by his father.

POTTER, PA & MA

THE POTTERS (1927, Silent, Paramount)—**W.C. Fields** absconds with the family fortune of $4,000, investing it in oil stock, giving a fifth of the stock to his daughter. His wife **Mary Alden** gets wind of what Fields has done and orders him to get back the money. In the mean time oil is discovered on the land and the entrepreneurs are happy to give Fields back his money with a $1,000 profit. Fields and Alden hearing of the oil strike are crestfallen until they discover that the oil was found on the land belonging to their daughter.

POTTER, "PAINLESS" PETER

THE PALEFACE (1948, Paramount)—Dentist **Bob Hope** becomes a stooge for Calamity Jane (Jane Russell) who needs a cover as she tracks down a gang selling guns to the Indians. In this delightful western comedy Hope and Russell sing the Academy Award winning "Buttons and Bows."

POTTER, PHIL

STARTING OVER (1979, Paramount)—**Burt Reynolds** plays a sensitive divorced man whose relationship with divorcee Jill Clayburgh is briefly jeopardized when his glamorous ex-wife Candice Bergen comes back into the picture.

POTTER, PVT.

PRIVATE POTTER (1963, MGM)—Young soldier **Tom Courtenay** claims to have had a vision of God while on a mission in which another soldier was killed. A decision must be made as to whether to court-martial him or not.

POTTS, GEORGE

MR. POTTS GOES TO MOSCOW (1953, GB, Stratford)—Soviet spies kidnap sanitary engineer **George Cole** whom they mistake for an atomic scientist.

POTTS, WILLIAM

THE GOOSE STEPS OUT (1942, GB, Ealing)—**Will Hay** is the double of an infamous Nazi spy. Hay is parachuted into Germany to steal a secret weapon.

POWELL, CHRISTINE

WOMAN OF THE NORTH COUNTRY (1952, Republic)—**Ruth Hussey** uses her charms on Rod Cameron to get him to dump his sweetheart, and give up his plans to start a Minnesota iron-ore mine which her parents oppose.

POWELL, ELLEN

PARTY GIRL (1930, Tiffany)—Former party girl **Jeanette Loft** is crestfallen when her fiance is tricked into marrying another party girl. Fortunately for Loft, the police discover the other girl's scheme and she is killed in a fall, allowing Loft to be reunited with her love.

POWELL, PREACHER HARRY

THE NIGHT OF THE HUNTER (1955, UA)—Psychotic, self-ordained preacher **Robert Mitchum** shows up to give comfort to the widow of his cell mate who was executed for a robbery and killing. Mitchum knows that the loot was never found. He marries the widow, Shelley Winters and when he deduces that her young son and daughter know the whereabouts of the money, he kills Winters and chases after the kids who are given refuge by Lillian Gish. This, the only film directed by Charles Laughton, is a classic thriller.

POWELL, LINDA

G.I. WAR BRIDES (1946, Republic)—Chinese **Anna Lee** is saved from deportation by reporter James Ellison, when the man she married overseas wants nothing to do with her.

POWERS, LILY, "BABY FACE"

BABY FACE (1933, Warners)—**Barbara Stanwyck**, an ambitious working girl, moves from man to man in an amorous ascent up her career ladder. Her response and expression when she answers the question "Do you have any experience?" are priceless. "Plenty" she delivers in a sly voice.

POWERS, TOM

THE PUBLIC ENEMY (1931, Warners)—This is the film that made a movie star out of **James Cagney** and a trivia question of Mae Clarke as the girl who gets a grapefruit shoved in her face by hoodlum Cagney. He went from a slum kid involved in petty thefts to a prohibition figure who gets too big for his britches and is delivered wrapped like a mummy to his mother's house by those who killed him. As Jimmy says at one point, "I'm not so tough."

POWIS-PORTER, MR.

HEAD OF THE FAMILY (1933, GB, First National/ Warners) - Industrialist **Arthur Maude** is all but forced out of business by his competition. He declares bankruptcy, becomes a night watchman for his rival, and is instrumental in preventing a robbery. The two firms merge and his rival marries Maude's daughter.

POYNTER, DARYL

CLEAN AND SOBER (1988, Warners)—In a movie that is doing great video business after quickly disappearing from the theaters, **Michael Keaton** is a real estate broker with a multiple substance abuse problem. In addition he has "borrowed" money from his company and brings a woman home for an all-nighter who doesn't survive till dawn. The man has problems. How will he come to deserve the description of the film's title? Better rent the video.

PRAISEWORTHY, VERNON

THE BILLION DOLLAR HOBO (1977, International Picture Show)—In order to collect an inheritance **Tim Conway** must adopt the hobo life style of his deceased relative.

PRATT, NORWOOD

NORWOOD (1970, Paramount)—Ex-G.I. **Glen Campbell** leaves his Texas home to become a singer.

PRAWN, MR.

THE AMOROUS MR. PRAWN (1964, GB, British Lion)—The wife of an English general converts his military headquarters in Scotland into a hotel for tourists with the general's loyal staff as chefs, maids and bellhops. Things look bad when the minister of war **Dennis Price** shows up, but he keeps his mouth closed because the blonde he's found in bed with isn't his wife.

PREACHER

BUCK AND THE PREACHER (1972, Columbia)—Con-man preacher **Harry Belafonte** teams with wagon master Sidney Poitier to outwit nightriders who are chasing runaway slaves.

"PREACHER, THE"

PEACE FOR A GUNFIGHTER (1967, Crown International)—Tired of his reputation as the fastest gun in the West, **Burt Berger** tries to settle down, but has to strap on his shootin' irons once more before being allowed a new life with a dance hall girl.

PREDATOR

PREDATOR (1987, 20th Century Fox); PREDATOR 2 (1990, 20th Century Fox)—**Kevin Peter Hall** plays an otherworld adversary for muscular Arnold Schwarzenegger and returns in the sequel to bedevil Danny Glover.

PRENTICE, JOHN

GUESS WHO'S COMING TO DINNER (1967, Columbia)—**Sidney Poitier** is a handsome young black doctor engaged to the daughter of ultra-liberals Spencer Tracy and Katharine Hepburn. It's a test of their convictions.

PRENTISS, ABIGAIL

THE CAPTAIN'S KID (1937, First National/Warners)—**Sybil Jason's** testimony helps free beloved old ex-sea captain Guy Kibbee, who has killed a man trying to steal the buried treasure Kibbee has found.

PRENTISS, AMY

GOLD DIGGERS OF 1935 (1935, Warners)—Pretty hotel guest **Gloria Stuart** meets medical student Dick Powell who is serving as a desk clerk. They both begin to operate.

PRENTISS, LINDA

LINDA BE GOOD (1947, PRC)—Novelist **Elyse Knox** takes in the nightclub scene to get material for her next book. She runs into her husband's boss who is with a show girl. Knox uses this leverage to get her husband a promotion. Blackmail is a kind of writing, isn't it?

PRENTISS, NORA
NORA PRENTISS (1947, Warners)—Nightclub singer **Ann Sheridan's** affair with married doctor Kent Smith ruins his career.

PRESCOTT, GEORGE
I'LL BE YOURS (1947, Universal)—Deanna Durbin picks attorney **Tom Drake's** name out of the telephone book, getting him a job representing a wealthy meat packer. Of course this good deed leads to romance in this remake of THE GOOD FAIRY.

PRESCOTT, MARION
CARNIVAL QUEEN (1937, Universal)—When her father dies, **Dorothea Kent** inherits controlling interest in a carnival. She decides to join it incognito to see if there is any way to save the floundering financial flop.

PRESCOTT, TRACEY
RECKLESS (1984, MGM/UA)—**Darryl Hannah**, a good girl from a good family becomes involved with Aidan Quinn, a boy with a bad reputation. Her reputation and behavior change drastically through the relationship.

PRESIDENT, THE
JOE AND ETHEL TURP CALL ON THE PRESIDENT (1939, MGM)—**Lewis Stone**, as the president of the United States, gets an earful from Brooklyn couple William Gargan and Ann Sothern when their mailman loses his job.

PRESTON, AMY
WOMAN IN A DRESSING GOWN (1957, GB, Warners)—Slovenly **Yvonne Mitchell** is losing her husband to another woman.

PRESTON, BILL S.
BILL & TED'S EXCELLENT ADVENTURE (1989, Orion)—Acting like he was brain-damaged, **Alex Winter**, whose sexy stepmother was a senior in high school when he was a freshman, is in danger of flunking history. He and his equally obtuse friend Keanu Reeves are spared that embarrassment by traveling to the past in a telephone booth time machine.

PRESTON, GAIL
WHO KILLED GAIL PRESTON? (1938, Columbia)—**Rita Hayworth** is murdered half-way through the movie. What a waste!

PRESTON, JACK
FIRE BIRDS (1990, Buena Vista)—The only thing worth seeing in this TOP GUN rip-off is Sean Young in tight overalls. As for the story, Apache helicopter pilots including **Nicholas Cage** take on a South American drug cartel.

PRESTON, JOHN
ALIAS JOHN PRESTON (1956, GB, British Lion)—**Christopher Lee** consults psychiatrist Alexander Knox about recurring nightmares in which he kills a girl and bludgeons Knox with a poker. The nightmares are true events in his previous life.

PRESTON, SAM & MARY JANE
MARY JANE'S PA (1935, First National)—**Guy Kibbee**, a middle-aged newspaperman, deserts his wife Aline MacMahon and daughter **Betty Jean Haney**. Years later he returns to find that they have done quite well without him.

PRESTON, STEVE
THE BAREFOOT MAILMAN (1951, Columbia)—One hundred years ago in Florida the mail is delivered by a bare foot mailman **Jerome Courtland**, who walks from Palm Beach to Miami with a New York con man and a young woman dressed as a child so she won't be molested.

PRICE, DONNA
REFORM SCHOOL GIRL (1957, American International)—**Gloria Costello** finds herself in the same cellblock as Luana Anders, both hooked on Edd "Kookie" Byrnes. He framed both of them, but lets them think that the girls set each other up.

PRICE, RUSSELL
UNDER FIRE (1983, Orion)—While covering the revolution in Nicaragua, photographer **Nick Nolte** maintains he doesn't take sides, but the lifestyle of the Supporters of President Somoza has him leaning towards the Sandinistas.

PRICE, TOMMY
YOUNG AND DANGEROUS (1952, 20th Century Fox)—**Mark Damon** straightens himself out in order to make it with a nice girl. It's a big nothing.

PRIDE, JONATHAN
DANCING PIRATE (1936, RKO)—**Charles Collins** is a dancing pirate. Isn't that interesting? No? Neither is this film.

PRIEST, CLINT
THE OUTRIDERS (1950, MGM)—Escaped Confederate prisoners **James Whitmore**, Joel McCrea and Barry Sullivan unwillingly hook up with Quantrill's raiders. They foil a plot by the irregulars to hijack a wagon train carrying silver bullion.

PRIEST, JUDGE WILLIAM "BILLY"
JUDGE PRIEST (1934, Fox)—**Will Rogers** is a small-town judge who applies horse sense in making his decisions.

PRIEST, YOUNGBLOOD
SUPERFLY (1972, Warners); SUPERFLY T.N.T. (1973, Paramount); THE RETURN OF SUPERFLY (1990, Triton)—**Ron O'Neal**, portraying what is perhaps a questionable role model for young black men, is a charismatic black cocaine pusher in New York. The title refers not only to O'Neal but also to what the drug is called in the ghetto. O'Neal plans one last score before retiring. In the 1973 sequel, he interrupts his life in Rome to help rid an African nation of a dictator. In the 1990 sequel, **Nathan Purdee** steps into the role and sets out to dismantle his old gang after they double-cross him.

PRINCE, THE
A REGULAR FELLOW (1925, Silent, Paramount)—**Raymond Griffith**, the prince of a mythical Balkan country, is appointed to oversee his country's public relations. He falls in love with a tourist, but his family insists he marry a princess. When he succeeds his father to the throne, he encourages a revolution. His country—now a republic—elects him as president and he is free to marry his sweetheart.

PRINCE, HOWARD
THE FRONT (1976, Columbia)—**Woody Allen** lends his name to blacklisted writers who can't sell their work. When he is finally exposed as a phony he goes to prison rather than reveal who he represented.

PRINCESS CHARMING
PRINCESS CHARMING (1935, GB, Gaumont)—Princess **Evelyn Laye** escapes from some revolutionaries, and marries a captain of the guards even though she is engaged to the ruler of a nearby

country. Her husband is placed in prison for failing to agree to an annulment. Laye must find a way to free him so the two can be together.

PRISCILLA

THE STUDENT NURSES (1970, New World)—**Barbara Leigh** is one of the aspiring angels of mercy who finds the medicine game to be a good place to find all the sexual activity one could want.

PRISONER, THE

THE PRISONER (1955, GB, Columbia)—Communist interrogator Jack Hawkins' methods eventually cause Cardinal **Alec Guinness** to confess to treason.

PRITCHETT, JOHN

JOHN AND JULIE (1957, GB, British Lion)—**Colin Gibson** is one of two six-year-old children who walk to London to see a coronation.

PRIZZI, DON CORRADO

PRIZZI'S HONOR (1985, 20th Century Fox)—**William Hickey**, the elderly head of a Mafia family, orders one of his top soldiers, Jack Nicholson, to kill his own wife, Kathleen Turner, a hit woman.

PROFESSOR TIM

PROFESSOR TIM (1957, Ireland, RKO)—After travelling the world for twenty years, **Seamus Kavanaugh** returns to his village home. He doesn't tell his greedy family that he has inherited a fortune.

PROFITT, ANNIE *See* **JOANNA STAYTON**

PROJECTIONIST

THE PROJECTIONIST (1970, Maglan/Maron)—Lovable loser **Chuck McCann** prefers to live in a fantasy world, thinking of himself as a super-hero known as "Captain Flash."

PROKOSZAY, COL.

ME AND THE COLONEL (1958, Columbia)—Anti-Semitic Polish colonel **Curt Jurgens** teams with Jewish refugee Danny Kaye in evading the Nazis who are marching into Paris.

PROPHET, PEARL

CYBORG (1989, Cannon)—Part computer, part human being, **Dayle Haddon** is trying to escape from the ruins of a bombed-out city with information about a serum that can combat a plague. Vincent Klyn, the brutal leader of the cannibalistic Flesh Pirates, is out to stop her. Haddon's cause will be championed by a pint-sized Arnold Schwarzenegger named Jean-Claude Van Damme.

PROTHERO, POKEY

THE GROUP (1966, UA)—**Mary-Robin Redd** is the most maternal of the eight friends who graduate from Smith in the middle of the Depression. She has two sets of twins.

PROTHERO, PRISCILLA

SHE WAS ONLY A VILLAGE MAIDEN (1933, GB, MGM)—Thirtyish **Anne Grey** is brought up by two elderly sisters, one who leaves her a fortune on the condition that she not leave the other sister for at least six months. She has her share of suitors and to keep some of them at bay, she claims to be engaged to a local doctor, whom she eventually marries.

PROUD, PETER

THE REINCARNATION OF PETER PROUD (1975, American International)—**Michael Sarrazin** begins to suspect that he is the reincarnation of a man who drowned many years earlier. To complicate things the dead man's daughter falls in love with him.

PROVO, ZACH

THE LAST HARD MAN (1976, 20th Century Fox)—**James Coburn** escapes from a chain gang in Arizona in 1906, taking six other cons with him. He seeks out the retired sheriff, whom he holds responsible for the death of his wife in the gun battle in which he was captured. Coburn plans to take his revenge through the sheriff's daughter. It seems to be a change of genre remake of THE KILLER IS LOOSE.

PROZOR, DANILO

FOUR FRIENDS (1981, Filmways)—**Craig Wasson**, one of four high school friends of the early 1960s, maintains his bond of friendship with the others through the difficult counter-culture years that follow.

PROHACK, ARTHUR

DEAR MR. PROHACK (1949, GB, GFD)—Treasury official **Cecil Parker** inherits a fortune, but finds he can't handle his own finances as well as he can those of the nation.

PRUETT, JIM

MAROONED (1969, Columbia)—**Richard Crenna** is one of three American astronauts trapped in a space ship. The best escape plans the experts can come up with will only save two of them.

PRUNELLA

PRUNELLA (1918, Silent, Paramount)—Romantic, young **Marguerite Clark** runs away to be with a strolling player. She has her heart broken, but eventually finds happiness.

PU YI, AISIN-GIRORO "HENRY"

THE LAST EMPEROR (1987, Columbia)—**John Lone** is the actor who played the last emperor of China as an adult. When his royal prerogatives are denied him, Lone becomes a puppet of the Japanese. After the war, the Communists imprison him. When he is released, he lives out his life in menial jobs. Other actors portraying the emperor are **Richard Vuu, Tijger Tsou** and **Wu Tao** at three, eight and 15, respectively.

PUJAL, ARISTIDE

THE JOYOUS ADVENTURES OF ARISTIDE PUJOL (1920, Silent, GB, Foss-Phillips)—**Kenelm Foss**, passing himself off as a nobleman in France, comes up with a cure for corns, adopts a child and marries a wealthy woman.

PULHAN, HARRY

H.M. PULHAM, ESQ. (1941, MGM)—Wealthy **Robert Young** falls in love with New York copywriter Hedy Lamarr, but is induced by his Boston family to give her up and marry Ruth Hussey, a more appropriate match. Twenty years later Young and Lamarr resume their affair, but deciding that one cannot turn back the clock, Young returns to the forgiving Hussey.

PULLING, HENRY

TRAVELS WITH MY AUNT (1972, GB, MGM)—English banker **Alec McCowen** first meets his eccentric aunt, Maggie Smith, at his mother's cremation. McGowan agrees to accompany her to Paris, where the two have many strange adventures and encounters.

PULVER, ENSIGN FRANK

ENSIGN PULVER (1964, Warners)—In the sequel to MR. ROBERTS, **Robert Walker Jr.** takes over from Jack Lemmon as the goldbricking ensign who feuds with the captain over his treatment of the men.

PUMA, EL *See* LIGHTNING BILL CARSON

PUMPKINHEAD
PUMPKINHEAD (1988, MGM-UA)—When his son is accidently killed because of the carelessness of some bikers, widower farmer **Lance Henriksen** seeks revenge. He goes to the cabin of an ancient witch and has her summon vicious demon **Tom Woodruff, Jr.**, who dispatches the bikers, male and female, one by one. Henriksen develops feelings of guilt for what he has wrought, and gives his own life to save the surviving pair of bikers.

PUPKIN, RUPERT
THE KING OF COMEDY (1983, 20th Century Fox)—**Robert De Niro** believes that with a little luck he can be a TV success like his idol, talk-show host Jerry Lewis. De Niro and his girlfriend kidnap Lewis with the ransom being an appearance on Lewis' show.

PURCELL, KIT
THE ROWDY (1921, Silent, Universal)—**Gladys Walton** was found in a storm as a baby, and raised by a New England seaman. She discovers that she is the long lost daughter of a wealthy family. She becomes a woman of society but longs for her former life. She is quite pleased when she discovers she was really only the daughter of the maid of the rich family and can return to the docks.

PURCELL, RICHARD
BROADWAY GONDOLIER (1935, Warners)—Singing New York cab driver **Dick Powell** is hired by a radio station to pose as a real Venetian gondolier.

PURPLE, ALVIN
ALVIN PURPLE (1974, Australia, Roadshow); ALVIN RIDES AGAIN (1974, Australia, Roadshow); MELVIN, SON OF ALVIN—**Graeme Blunell** stars in these Aussie adult comedies about a man whom women find irresistible.

PURVIS, VALERIE
SATAN MET A LADY (1936, Warners)—**Bette Davis** never wanted to make this version of THE MALTESE FALCON and her judgment was on the mark. The story is supposedly played for laughs but Davis never found any reference to this movie amusing.

PUSHER, THE
THE PUSHER (1960, UA)—Supplier **Felice Orlandi** is responsible for the death of a young narcotics addict. She is an addict herself.

PUSSER, BUFORD
WALKING TALL (1973, Cinerama); WALKING TALL, PART II (1975, American International)—**Joe Don Baker** and Bo Svenson portray an honest sheriff who endures brutal beatings, torture and gunshot wounds, but he won't give up his crusade to clean up his town.

PYE, LORD
OH DADDY! (1935, GB, Gaumont)—**Leslie Henson**, the leader of a Purity League, is put up at a London hotel, where he is attracted to a showgirl, who turns out to be the stepdaughter he has never seen.

PYM, MRS.
MRS. PYM OF SCOTLAND YARD (1939, GB, Grand National)—Detective **Mary Clare** joins a psychic club, two of whose members have been murdered. She prevents another murder just in the nick of time.

PYTHIAS
DAMON AND PHYTHIAS (1962, MGM)—**Don Burnett** is a proponent of a pre-Christ, love thy neighbor philosophy in this cardboard story based on the Damon and Phythias legend.

PYTHIAS, SIDNEY
THE DELICATE DELINQUENT (1957, Paramount)—Friendly policeman Darren McGavin replaces Dean Martin as the one who looks after simpleton **Jerry Lewis**, here a janitor arrested along with slum hoods.

Q

QUAID/HAUSER
TOTAL RECALL (1990, Triton)—In this summer sci-fi hit set in the year 2084, **Arnold Schwarzenegger** discovers that he is a victim of mind-tampering that replaced his memory. He must travel to Mars to find his real past. The visual effects are spectacular, but the violence is almost too much.

QUAID, AMANDA
THE DUCHESS AND THE DIRTWATER FOX (1976, 20th Century Fox) -Old West dance hall girl **Goldie Hawn** teams up with gambler George Segal. Their many adventures are shared with migrating Mormons, guests at a Jewish wedding and an outlaw gang. Goldie is a delight as a very cheap entertainer-prostitute looking for a life with a Mormon consisting of "one night on, six nights off."

QUAIL, MA
MOTHER KNOWS BEST (1928, Fox)—**Louise Dresser** takes money from the cash register in her husband's drugstore to pay for her eight-year-old daughter's singing and dancing lessons. As the years pass, Dresser pushes her daughter into a show business career, but drives away the man the girl loves. Finally Dresser sees what's she doing and reunites the sweethearts.

QUANTRILL, WILLIAM
QUANTRILL'S RAIDERS (1958, Allied Artists)—Civil War outlaw **Leo Gordon** plans an attack on a Kansas arsenal.

QUATERMAIN, ALLAN
ALLAN QUATERMAIN AND THE LOST CITY OF GOLD (1987, Cannon)—**Richard Chamberlain** is merely adequate as the greatest white hunter of all time. For more lively portrayals see Cedric Hardwicke and Stewart Granger in the 1937 and 1950 filming of KING SOLOMON'S MINES.

QUASIMODO
THE HUNCHBACK OF NOTRE DAME (1923, Silent, Universal); (1939, RKO)—Both **Lon Chaney, Sr.** and **Charles Laughton** give masterful performances as the hideously deformed bell ringer of the cathedral of Notre Dame. He gives sanctuary to gypsy girl Esmerelda, after she is condemned to death for witchcraft. She had given him something to drink while he was unjustly suffering public punishment. Quasimodo takes Esmerelda to the bell rafters as the thieves and beggars of Paris assault the cathedral to get the girl and saves her from the aristocrats who would carry out her sentence of death.

QUEED, MARTHA

THE SIN OF MARTHA QUEED (1921, Silent, Associated Exhibitors)—**Mary Thurman** fakes a sprained ankle to see the inside of Niles Welch's cabin. This is reported to her puritanical tyrant of a father who forces her to marry a man she does not love. When the father is found dead, suspicion falls on Welch, but all works out when a deformed boy admits the murder and commits suicide.

QUEEN

SHE-DEVILS ON WHEELS (1968, Mayflower)—**Betty Connell** is one of the leaders of the "Man-Eaters" motorcycle gang, who choose their lovers for the evening from "stud lines."

QUEEN, ELLERY

ELLERY QUEEN, MASTER DETECTIVE (1940, Columbia); ELLERY QUEEN AND THE MURDER RING (1941, Columbia); ELLERY QUEEN AND THE PERFECT CRIME (1941, Columbia); ELLERY QUEEN'S PENTHOUSE MYSTERY (1941, Columbia); ENEMY AGENTS MEET ELLERY QUEEN (1942, Columbia)—**Ralph Bellamy**; A CLOSE CALL FOR ELLERY QUEEN (1942, Columbia); A DESPERATE CHANCE FOR ELLERY QUEEN (1942, Columbia)—**William Gargan**; Good old dependable Ralph Bellamy appears as the debonair detective in the above named second features, which were well-received by audiences. When Bellamy was needed for secondary leads in A movies, William Gargan filled in.

QUEEN OF ARDENBERG

LADY IN DANGER (1934, GB, Gaumont)—**Yvonne Arnaud**, the exiled queen of a small European country, is brought to safety in England by businessman Tom Walls. His fiancee misconstrues his interest in the royal lady.

"QUEEN OF BLOOD"

QUEEN OF BLOOD (1966, American International)—Basil Rathbone leads an expedition to Mars where the only survivor of a crashed spaceship is green-skinned alien **Florence Morley** who drains the blood of several crewmen.

QUEEN OF SHEBA

THE QUEEN OF SHEBA (1921, Silent, Fox)—**Betty Blythe**, as the Queen of Sheba, visits Solomon. They fall in love, provoking the wrath of Solomon's wife and her father, the pharaoh. Ultimately, the lovers separate, with Blythe returning to Sheba with their son.

QUENTIN, SIR JAMES

THE HIGH COMMISSIONER (1968, US/GB, Rank/Cinerama)—Australian Diplomat **Christopher Plummer** is arrested for the murder of his first wife, some twenty years earlier, just when he's involved in some sensitive Cold War negotiations. The police sergeant who has been sent to London to bring him back home convinces his superiors to keep a lid on the arrest until the conference is over.

QUESNE, MARSHALL *See* DR. MAURICE XAVIER

QUEX, LORD

THE GAY LORD QUEX (1917, GB, Silent, Ideal)—Engaged Lord **Ben Webster** tries to compromise a maid who witnessed his affair with a Duchess. His affairs are strictly heterosexual, for any who may wonder.

"QUICO," ENRIQUE, THE LLANO KID

THE TEXAN (1930, Paramount)—Bandit **Gary Cooper** poses as a woman's long lost son, but his past catches up with him.

QUIGLEY

STRANGERS ON A HONEYMOON (1937, GB, Gaumont)—Titled **Hugh Sinclair**, posing as a tramp, marries a girl and saves her land from crooks.

QUIGLEY, DAN

LADY KILLER (1933, Warner Brothers)—When movie usher **James Cagney** is fired, he turns to crime. While hiding from the police, he accidentally finds himself appearing in a movie which makes him a star.

QUIGLEY, GRACE

THE ULTIMATE SOLUTION OF GRACE QUIGLEY (1984, MGM/UA)—Lonely, old **Katharine Hepburn** hires hit man Nick Nolte to kill those like her who would just as soon be dead.

QUIGLEY, MATTHEW

QUIGLEY DOWN UNDER (1990, MGM/UA)—In a dreary Australian Western, **Tom Selleck** is bored and boring as a sharpshooter seeking adventure. He should have sought a decent script instead.

QUILLER

THE QUILLER MEMORANDUM (1966, GB, 20th Century Fox)—American agent **George Segal** is in Berlin, trying to get the lowdown on a group of neo-Nazis headed by Max Von Sydow. They capture and torture him, but he gets away to spy another day.

QUILLIAM, PETE

THE MANXMAN (1929, GB, Silent, British International)—Isle of Man fisherman **Carl Brisson**, believed dead, returns to marry his sweetheart, not knowing she's carrying his best friend's baby.

QUILLIGAN, PATRICK

DON JUAN QUILLIGAN (1945, 20th Century Fox)—Hudson River barge captain **William Bendix** has overly romantic notions about the ladies because of his special feelings for his mother. The result is that he finds himself engaged to two women at the same time, and not to disappoint anyone he marries both.

QUILP, DANIEL

MR. QUILP (1975, GB, Avco Embassy)—Deformed pawnbroker **Anthony Newley** pursues a girl and her grandfather in this version of Charles Dickens' *The Old Curiosity Shop*.

QUILTY, BIRDIE

THE ADVENTURESS (I SEE A DARK STRANGER) (1946, GB, General Films)—Irish lass **Deborah Kerr** deeply hates the British. She wishes to join the IRA but becomes a pawn of Nazi agents until Trevor Howard changes her mind about England.

QUINCANNON, LINUS

QUINCANNON, FRONTIER SCOUT (1956, UA)—When **Tony Martin** appeared in a film in which he doesn't sing he checked his talents with his tux. In this minor western, Martin investigates the theft of repeating rifles by Indians.

QUINCEY, MR.

MR. QUINCEY OF MONTE CARLO (1933, GB, Warner Brothers)—Bank clerk **John Stuart** uses his inheritance to finance a movie company.

QUINLAN, JOHNNY

THE FALL GUY (1930, RKO)—When drugstore clerk **Jack Mulhall** loses his job during the Depression, he soon gets involved with the underworld, becoming what the title suggests when a cache of drugs is found in his possession.

QUINN, JIMMY

Q: QUETZALCOATL (1982, United Film Distributors)—**Michael Moriarty** knows the location of an ancient Aztec god which flies from its nest atop a New York skyscraper, and rips off the heads of assorted victims.

QUINN, XAVIER

THE MIGHTY QUINN (1989, MGM/UA)—Dedicated police chief **Denzel Washington** isn't particularly popular with either the rich whites who dominate the tourist industry of his Caribbean island nation or his black country men, who see him as a latter-day Uncle Tom. He's not afraid to offend anyone while investigating a brutal murder, even when the main murder suspect is his boyhood friend and island hero, Robert Townsend.

QUINELLE, DONALD

THE SURVIVORS (1983, Columbia)—When **Robin Williams** loses his job, he arms himself to the teeth and takes to the hills in a desperate attempt to survive.

QUINTARD, ANTHONY

THE CINDERELLA MAN (1917, Silent, Goldwyn)—**Tom Moore**, a poor poet, lives in a garret across a tin roof from the home of an old grouch and his daughter Mae Marsh. Hearing of the starving young man, she sneaks across the roof with three of her father's old friends, bringing everything necessary for a genuine Merry Christmas. This charity will lead to love.

QUINTERO, ESPERANZA

SALT OF THE EARTH (1954, International Prod.)—Mexican-American **Rosaura Revueltas**, the wife of a zinc-miner, is one of the leaders of a strike. When the mine owners get a Taft-Hartley injunction forbidding the men to picket the mines, the women led by Revueltas take up the picketing. At the time of the film, it was branded communistic propaganda as it showed American Capitalism in an unpleasant light.

QUINTON, WILLIE

FOOLS OF FORTUNE (1990, GB, Palace)—At the time of the Irish war of independence, when he was just a child, **Iain Glen** saw his family massacred by the British-employed soldiers known as the Black and Tans. Only he and his mother, Julie Christie, survived. Christie becomes a manic depressive alcoholic, who finally commits suicide. Tortured soul Glen is comforted by Mary Elizabeth Mastrantonio, but goes into self-imposed exile on an island off Wales without learning that Mastrantonio has given birth to their daughter. They will ultimately be reunited.

QUIXOTE *See* DON QUIXOTE

R

R.J.

TIME TRACKERS (1989, Concorde)—In 2033, scientists **Kathleen Beller** and Wil Shriner are experimenting with a time machine. Evil Lee Bergere steals the machine's computer chip and uses a prototype of the device to escape to the past. It's up to Beller, Shriner and weapons expert Bridget Hoffman to chase him through time.

RABBIT, ROGER

WHO FRAMED ROGER RABBIT (1988, partly animated, Buena Vista)—**Charlie Fleischer** is the voice of the "toon" character Robert Rabbit who hires detective Bob Hoskins to help him, when he's framed of murdering his producer. The blending of cartoon characters along side humans in this spoof of 1940s-style pictures is a remarkable achievement, underappreciated by the Academy of Motion Pictures Arts and Sciences.

RABBITTE, JIMMY

THE COMMITMENTS (1991, GB, 20th Century Fox)—Twenty-one-year-old entrepreneur **Robert Arkins** puts together a 10-piece band of poor Irish men and women to bring soul music to Dublin.

RACHEL

FLATLINERS (1990, Columbia)—**Julia Roberts** is one of a group of daring young medical students who experiment with experiencing death and returning to life. They stop their heart and brain from functioning, thus "flatlining"—i.e., producing a flat line on their EKG and EEG monitors.

RACHEL

RACHEL AND THE STRANGER (1948, RKO)—**Loretta Young** is an 1820s bonds woman, purchased by backwoodsman William Holden to care for his motherless son. Holden pays no mind to Young until stranger Robert Mitchum comes a courting. Then violent emotions erupt, put aside long enough for the three to fight off an Indian attack.

RACHEL, AUNT

AUNT RACHEL (1920, Silent, GB, Samuelson/Granger)—Jilted **Isobel Elsom** won't allow her niece to marry a violinist's nephew, because the uncle is the cad that left her at the altar.

RADCLIFFE, GEOFFREY

THE INVISIBLE MAN RETURNS (1940, Universal)—When scientist Cedric Hardwicke discovers the secret of invisibility, he tries it out on **Vincent Price**, convicted of murdering his brother. Price goes after the real murderer.

RADEK

THE MAN ON THE EIFFEL TOWER (1949, RKO)—French inspector Charles Laughton tries to get maniacal killer **Franchot Tone** to confess. The psychological pressure becomes too much for Tone, who escapes and is chased across the Eiffel Tower.

RADEK, CRYSTAL

THE MERRY WIDOW (1952, MGM)—**Lana Turner** looks lovely in widow weeds, particularly her black lingerie, in this familiar and perhaps dated Franz Lehar operetta about a mythical country and the widow who owns it all.

RADHOFF, VICTOR

VAMPIRE AT MIDNIGHT (1988, Skouras)—In a straight-to-video release, **Gustav Vintas** is a fiendish serial killer, who just may be a vampire.

RADLER, PIERRE

A MODERN HERO (1934, Warner Brothers)—In German director G.W. Pabst's only American film, **Richard Barthelmess** is a callous, ambitious circus performer, ruined in the stock market crash.

RADWAY, VIRGINIA

MARRY THE GIRL (1937, Warner Brothers)—News syndicate owners, brother and sister Hugh Herbert and Mary Boland, try to prevent their niece **Carol Hughes** from making an unsuitable marriage with Mischa Auer.

RAE, DEMPSEY
MAN WITHOUT A STAR (1955, Universal)—Cowboy **Kirk Douglas** fights for both sides in a range war, changing over when the wranglers working for ruthless rancher Claire Trevor give him a beating.

RAEBURN, CLAIRE
THE WOMEN MEN MARRY (1937, MGM)—Editor Sidney Blackmer stabs his star reporter in the back by having an affair with the latter's wife, **Claire Dodd**.

RAEBURN, JENNIE *See* LA SYRENA

RAFFERTY
RAFFERTY AND THE GOLD DUST TWINS (1975, Warner Brothers)—None-too-bright driving instructor **Alan Arkin** is kidnapped by Sally Kellerman and Michelle Phillips. At gunpoint, they demand he drive them from Los Angeles to Las Vegas. Three lonely people become friends before they reach their destination.

RAFFERTY, BILL
DERELICT (1930, Paramount)—Freighter officer **George Bancroft** competes both for a captaincy and Jessie Royce Landis while his ship is bound for Rio.

RAFFLES, A.J.
MR. JUSTICE RAFFLES (1921, GB, Silent, Hepworth); RAFFLES, THE AMATEUR CRACKSMAN (1925, Universal); RAFFLES (1930, UA); (1939, UA) THE RETURN OF RAFFLES (1932, GB, Markham)—**Gerald Ames, House Peters, Ronald Colman, David Niven** and **George Barraud** all appeared as the gentleman thief about whom even his major adversary, an always defeated Scotland Yard Inspector, admits: "You can't help liking him." Of the various performers who acted the role of man-about-town amateur cricketer and jewel thief, surely Ronald Colman will be found the most appealing.

RAFT, GEORGE
THE GEORGE RAFT STORY (1961, Allied Artists)—**Ray Danton** is quite good in this absorbing biopic of the career of the one-time dancer who became a film star playing gangsters. His realism in the roles comes from knowing so many real-life mobsters.

RAFTIS, FRANK
FALLING IN LOVE (1984, Paramount)—Married **Robert De Niro** and married Meryl Streep (but not to each other) feel a mutual attraction as they make the daily commute from the suburbs to Manhattan. The movie has some touches similiar to BRIEF EN-COUNTER with light comedy nuances added to a growing tender love affair, going nowhere.

RAGATZY, ANTON
THE OUTSIDER (1926, Silent, Fox); (1933, GB, MGM); (1940, GB, Associate British Films)—**Lou Tellegen, Harold Huth** and **George Sanders** each appear as the unlicensed osteopath who cures a surgeon's crippled daughter.

RAGGHIANTI, MARIE
MARIE (1985, MGM/UA)—In this true story, divorced mother of three **Sissy Spacek** gets a job with the state of Tennessee and blows the whistle on corruption in the parole system. This gets her into plenty of hot water.

RAGLAND, RICHARD
RAILROADED (1923, Silent, Universal)—**Herbert Rawlinson**, the son of England's most prominent jurist, is framed for a crime and sent to prison. He escapes and falls in love with a woman with whom he flees to Africa.

RAGNAR, KING
THE VIKINGS (1958, UA)—**Ernest Borgnine** goes to his death with a sword in his hand, given to him by his illegitimate son Tony Curtis, whom he doesn't know. Helping Borgnine have an honorable Viking battle death costs Curtis his good right arm.

RAINWOOD, JIMMIE
AN INNOCENT MAN (1989, Buena Vista)—Two narcotic agents get the address of a bust wrong and break in on Tom Selleck. Rather than admit their mistake, the two frame Selleck on a drug dealing charge. He's sent to prison, where he learns to hang tough from hardened con F. Murray Abraham, while on the outside his wife works for his release.

RALEIGH, DOROTHY
AN INNOCENT MAGDALENE (1916, Silent, Triangle)—Kentuckian **Lillian Gish** is disowned by her father when she marries a New York gambler. When her husband is sent to jail, she returns home but her father considers her dead, even though she is pregnant. She has the child and is about to kill herself, when her husband comes for her.

RALPH
THE HAPPY WARRIOR (1925, Silent, Vitagraph)—**Malcolm McGregor** discovers that he's the rightful heir to a title just as a friend who is a distant relative takes the title. McGregor considers making a claim but reasons he's happier being a boxer with the circus.

RALPH
KING RALPH (1991, Universal)—When Great Britain's entire royal family is wiped out in an unbelievable accident, Vegas lounge singer **John Goodman** becomes king. He's a well-meaning bull in a china shop.

RALPH
MY BEST FRIEND IS A VAMPIRE (1988, Kings Road)—The fate of **Evan Mirand's** best friend Robert Sean Leonard may be in store for Mirand as well.

RALPH, MICHAEL
STATE TROOPER (1933, Columbia)—Motorcycle cop **Regis Toomey** exchanges his badge for a job keeping an eye on an oil refinery threatened by saboteurs.

RALSTON, BOB
THE DUDE COWBOY (1926, Silent, Independent Pictures)—**Bob Custer**, on his way to take ownership of a dude ranch which he's inherited, saves a man and his daughter from bandits. He takes a job as chauffeur with the two, who are guess what?—on their way to the very same dude ranch.

RALSTON, CHRISTINE
TWILIGHT WOMEN (1953, GB, Lippert)—**Lois Maxwell** loses her baby when blackmailer and baby-farmer Freda Jackson won't call a doctor for the unwed mother.

RALSTON, DOROTHY
THE OUTSIDE WOMAN (1921, Silent, Fox)—**Wanda Hawley** mistakenly trades a priceless Aztec idol for a silk shawl. The rest of the film deals with her Lucille Ball-like efforts to get the idol back.

RALSTON, JAMES
JIM THE PENMAN (1921, Silent, Associated First National) -**Lionel Barrymore** turns to a life of crime in order to save the father of the woman he loves from financial ruin. He ultimately will play judge, jury and executioner for himself and his crooked associates.

RAM, GUNGA
THE HINDU (1953, GB, UA)—Young Indian animal trainer **Nino Marcel** is out to take revenge on the leader of a religious cult which accidentally killed Nino's parents in a forest fire it set.

RAMBLER, THE
THE WAGON MASTER (1929, Universal)—**Ken Maynard** prevents Tom Santschi from cheating a group of miners.

RAMBO
RAMBO: FIRST BLOOD, PART II (1985, Tri-Star); RAMBO III (1988, Tri-Star)—The initial film in this series was called FIRST BLOOD and featured muscular **Sylvester Stallone** as an angry Vietnam veteran who takes on everyone in a violent bloody clash in the American Northwest. In the sequel, his killing ability is put to better use as he attempts to free some MIA's in Cambodia. In the third film, he's off to Afghanistan where he can kill him some Russkies.

RAMIREZ, CHU CHU
MY MAN AND I (1952, MGM)—Mexican-born **Ricardo Montalban** is proud of having received American citizenship. He's a hard worker, but when a check given to him by Mexican-hater Wendell Corey bounces, Montalban confronts him and Corey is wounded in a struggle by his own gun. Montalban lands in jail when Corey and his wife concoct a story of how Montalban attacked Corey. His friends are able to get a confession from Corey and free Montalban.

RAMON
THE PENITENT (1988, Cineworld)—**Raul Julia** joins a two-century-old religious sect called "the penitente" that reenacts Christ's Crucifixion every year. The victim is chosen by lot, tied to a cross, and left for a day in the blistering sun. Will this year's sacrifice be Julia or his friend Armand Assante?

RAMONA
NEIGHBORS (1981, Columbia)—**Cathy Moriarty** and her equally loony husband Dan Aykroyd move next door to suburban couple John Belushi and Kathryn Walker, greatly disrupting their peaceful life.

RAMONA
RAMONA (1916, Silent, Clune); (1928, Silent, UA); (1936, 20th Century Fox)—**Adda Gleason, Dolores Del Rio** and **Loretta Young** each portray the half-Indian girl who defies her guardian and elopes with an Indian. Her baby dies because a white doctor refuses to treat a squaw. Her husband is murdered by white outlaws. After many hardships she is restored to her white foster parents.

RAMONA
THOSE LIPS, THOSE EYES (1980, UA)—**Glynnis O'Connor** is a chorus girl in summer stock. Its star Frank Langella is an actor only good enough to appear in small town productions. O'Connor is enough to distract him for the season.

RAMRODDER, THE
THE RAMRODDER (1969, Entertainment Ventures)—**Jim Gentry** is believed to have raped an Indian girl, so the Indians rape a settler's daughter. Gentry finds the white rapist, whom the Indians castrate.

RAMSBOTTOM, BILL
RAMSBOTTOM RIDES AGAIN (1956, GB, British Lion)—English publican **Arthur Askey** inherits a ranch in Canada and finds he has to mix it up with bad man Sid James—bad man Sid James?

RAMSEY, LAURA
THE WOMAN IN ROOM 13 (1932, Fox)—Ralph Bellamy, the ex-husband of composer **Elissa Landi**, tries to pin the murder of singer Gilbert Roland on her, but her current husband Neil Hamilton takes the blame.

RAMSEY, MRS.
STEPPING SISTERS (1932, Fox)—**Louise Dresser** and her two former burlesque buddies Minna Gombell and Jobyna Howland turn a society party on its ear as they drink and reminisce too much.

RAMSEY, MRS. MICHAEL
ADAM'S RIB (1923, Silent, Paramount)—**Anna Q. Nilsson's** daughter Pauline Garon hopes to prevent her mother from committing adultery by offering herself in her mother's stead. This doesn't set well with Garon's fiance Elliott Dexter. It takes Nilsson's neglected husband, Milton Sills, to put everything right.

RAND
A FACE IN THE RAIN (1963, Embassy)—During WWII, American spy **Rory Calhoun** is being hidden by Italian partisan Massimo Giulani, whose wife Marina Berti sides with the Germans.

RAND, ALBERT *See* CHICK GRAHAM

RAND, CAPT.
THE MAN WHO TURNED WHITE (1919, Silent, Superior)—**H.B. Warner** rejects the white man's world and poses as an Arab outlaw after suffering indignities in the British African Corps. Barbara Castleton saves his life and returns him to the "civilized world."

RAND, DAVID & MASON
HUNTER'S BLOOD (1987, Concorde)—**Sam Bottoms** and **Clu Gulager** are among a group of city men who have a hellish time with some rednecks when they go deer hunting in a remote part of Arkansas.

RAND, OLIVER
A MAN'S PREROGATIVE (1915, Silent, Mutual)—Married **Robert Edeson** has an affair with Billie West, known simply as "The Model."

RAND, SALLY
SALLY OF THE SCANDALS (1928, Silent, FBO)—**Bessie Love** becomes a chorus girl to support her crippled sister. She almost chooses the wrong man to become her husband, but such things were not often allowed in the movies of the time—at least not at the end.

RAND, STEVE
WHEN STRANGERS MARRY (1933, Columbia)—**Jack Holt**, a railroad man working in Malay, suddenly finds himself married to spoiled rich Lillian Bond.

RAND, TIM
THE TEXAS MARSHAL (1941, PRC)—**Tim McCoy** isn't fooled by the plans of a gang of gold thieves to pass themselves off as a group of upstanding, concerned citizens.

519

RAND, TRIGGER TIM

FRONTIER CRUSADER (1940, PRC)—**Tim McCoy** must deal with bad guys trying to prevent a mining company from uncovering a rich vein of gold.

RAND, WESLEY

I WALKED WITH A ZOMBIE (1943, Columbia)—**James Ellison's** half-brother is West Indies plantation owner Tom Conway, whose silent, sick wife got that way because of the family's voodoo ties.

RANDALL, BERNICE

THE SILVER SLAVE (1927, Silent, Warner Brothers)—Self-sacrificing mother **Irene Rich** is prepared to give herself to a cad to keep him from her daughter.

RANDALL, CLEM

MY SIX CONVICTS (1952, Columbia)—**Alf Kjellin** is one of six convicts who find prison more bearable when they join a therapy group run by the prison psychiatrist.

RANDALL, CONNIE

NO MAN OF HER OWN (1933, Paramount)—Smart big city girl, **Carole Lombard** plays opposite her husband of the future, Clark Gable, a crooked gambler who marries Lombard, thinking she's a shy small-town librarian.

RANDALL, DORIS & MR.

THE RAGMAN'S DAUGHTER (1974, GB, Penelope-Harpoors)—Young thief Simon Rouse falls in love with smashingly beautiful **Victoria Tennant** who, as the title says, is the daughter of ragman **Leslie Sands**.

RANDALL, EDDIE

FELLER NEEDS A FRIEND (1932, Cosmopolitan)—Crippled **Jackie Cooper** is not given the kind of attention he needs from his parents or other relatives. Won't someone love this boy?

RANDALL, PATRICIA

SMALL TOWN DEB (1941, 20th Century Fox)—**Jane Withers** stars in this family comedy intended to be her transition from young tomboy roles to a teenage girl interested in boys and clothes.

RANDALL, REBECCA

REBECCA OF SUNNYBROOK FARM (1917, Silent, Artcraft); (1932, Fox)—**Mary Pickford** and **Marian Nixon** each portray a child sent to live in a small New England town with her demanding aunt. She's something of a troublemaker, but grows up to be a fine-looking young lady, who snares the town's leading bachelor.

RANDALL, T.H. & VALERIE

HE MARRIED HIS WIFE (1940, 20th Century Fox)—**Joel McCrea's** work schedule leads to a divorce by his wife **Nancy Kelly**, whom he still loves. When his alimony payments become more than he can handle, he conspires with his lawyer to get her to marry again. Not pleased with her choice of Cesar Romero, he remarries her.

RANDOLPH, BILL

BROTHER RAT (1938, Warner Brothers); BROTHER RAT AND A BABY (1940, Warner Brothers)—**Wayne Morris** is the leading trouble maker at Virginia Military School. He laughs his way through school, wooing pretty Priscilla Lane on the side. The sequel is more of the same, but his post graduation antics seem more juvenile than funny.

RANDOLPH, JULIAN

HIS ROBE OF HONOR (1918, Silent, Paralta)—**Henry B. Walthall** makes it to the Supreme Court by playing ball with a political machine. When he falls in love with a proper young woman, he changes and takes a stand against a major corporation controlled by the machine.

RANDOLPH, STEPHEN

THE MAN WHO CAME BACK (1931, Fox)—**Charles Farrell**, a modern prodigal son, drinks away his money and ends up in an opium den with his lady love, Janet Gaynor. Somehow they pull themselves together, marry and patch things up with his father.

RANDOLPH, WHITNEY

THE EAGLE AND THE HAWK (1950, Paramount)—**Dennis O'Keefe** and John Payne are lawmen who discover a plot to overthrow Mexico's rule and invade Texas in 1863.

RANEVSKAYA, COUNTESS

QUEEN OF SPADES (1948, GB, ABF-Pathe/Monogram)—In this baroque chiller, **Edith Evans** is an aged countess who has sold her soul to the devil to learn the secret of winning at cards. In 1806, Russian officer Anton Walbrook is determined to get the secret from her, but scares Evans to death before she can share it with him.

RANGELOFF, MICHAEL

FINDERS KEEPERS (1984, CBS/Warner Brothers)—**Michael O'Keefe** is one of the passengers aboard a train bound from Nebraska for California, searching for five million dollars hidden aboard.

RANKIN, PROF. CHARLES

THE STRANGER (1946, RKO)—Nazi war-criminal **Orson Welles** has escaped the authorities. He takes up residence as a professor in a small Connecticut town. When Edward G. Robinson, an investigator, arrives in town, Welles is about to marry local belle, Loretta Young. It now becomes a psychological cat-and-mouse game with Young dangerously in the middle.

RANKIN, JAMES

THE HAUNTED STRANGLER (1958, GB, Anglo-Amalgamated)—Nineteenth-century criminologist **Boris Karloff** investigates a 20-year-old murder case. He discovers he's the guilty party.

RANNEY, JACK

JACK AND JILL (1917, Silent, Paramount)—Boxer **Jack Pickford** quits the ring after killing an opponent. He moves west and saves the ranch on which he works from Mexican bandits.

RANSOM, BASIL

THE BOSTONIANS (1984, Merchant/Ivory/Almi)—**Christopher Reeve**, a young southern lawyer in 19th-century Boston competes with militant suffragist Vanessa Redgrave for the love of a faith healer's daughter, Madeleine Potter.

RANSON, LT.

RANSON'S FOLLY (1915, Silent, Edison); (1926, Silent, First National)—**Marc MacDermott** and **Richard Barthelmess** appear in two versions of a novel by Richard Harding Davis, about an army officer accused of being a notorious outlaw. In the first version, the father of the girl MacDermott loves, kills himself, leaving a note saying he was the outlaw. In the second, Barthelmess confesses to being the outlaw to save his girl's father.

RAOUL

EATING RAOUL (1982, Bartel Film)—In this hilarious black comedy, married couple Paul Bartel and Mary Woronov come upon a scheme to make money. She advertises her services as a prostitute willing to act out any kink. When the johns come to their apartment, Bartel conks them with a very heavy skillet and collects any money the deceased was carrying. They have an accomplice in their scheme, **Robert Beltran**, who disposes of the bodies. When Bartel and Woronov discover that Beltram is making out better than they are, they kill him in the same good old-fashioned way and serve part of him for dinner to a business guest of Bartel.

RAPHAEL

TEENAGE MUTANT NINJA TURTLES (1990, New Line); TEENAGE MUTANT NINJA TURTLES II: THE SECRET OF OOZE (1991, New Line)—**Joch Pais** and his three teenage turtle comrades eat pizza, rock till they drop, play Trivial Pursuit and act like any group of charming, irrepressible adolescents. When their mentor, a large animatronic rat, is kidnapped, the turtles spring into action to use their martial arts to rescue him and save New York from baddies. In the sequel, **Kenn Troum** replaces Pais. The lean, green teens learn how they were transformed into superheroes by some green radio-active glop invented by eccentric scientist David Warner.

RASPUTIN

RASPUTIN AND THE EMPRESS (1932, MGM); RASPUTIN—THE MAD MONK (1966, GB, 20th Century Fox)—The 1932 movie was the only time the three Barrymore siblings appeared together in a movie. **Lionel Barrymore** is the mad, decadent monk whose influence on the Czarina, played by his sister Ethel, helped hasten the Russian Revolution of 1917. **Christopher Lee** portrays the gross monk as lusty, sexy and brutal. It takes quite an effort to kill him.

RASSMUSSON, BRITA

NAUGHTY CINDERELLA (1933, GB, Warner Brothers)—Danish girl **Winna Winfried** fools her guardian John Stuart by posing as a tomboy.

RATCLIFFE, JONATHAN

BLIND DATE (1984, New Line)—Blind **Joseph Bottoms** agrees to have a visual computer implanted in his brain so he can track down a psychopathic killer.

"THE RAT" See PIERRE BOUCHERON

RATBOY

RATBOY (1986, Warner Brothers)—**S.L. Baird** is Eugene, a boy with the face of a rat. He lives in a dump. Sondra Locke, who also directed the film, sets out to make Baird a media star. Locke should go back to appearing opposite one-time main squeeze Clint Eastwood in some nice violent movie.

RATH, TOM

THE MAN IN THE GREY FLANNEL SUIT (1956, 20th Century Fox)—**Gregory Peck**, a businessman who has neglected his family to become a success, looks at things a bit differently when he and his wife, Jennifer Jones, must deal with the fact that he has a child by his deceased war-time Italian mistress, Marisa Pavan.

RAVEN

THE DESERT RAVEN (1965, Allied Artists)—**Rachel Romen** falls in love with Rance Howard, the youngest member of a band of thieves and murderers, hiding out in her Indian mother's desert hovel.

RAVEN, EMMY LOU

THE THIRTY FOOT BRIDE OF CANDY ROCK (1959, Columbia)—In the only film he ever made without partner Bud Abbott, Lou Costello is a meek inventor who turns girlfriend **Dorothy Provine** into a thirty-foot tall woman. What a waste!

RAVEN, PHILIP

THIS GUN FOR HIRE (1942, Paramount)—**Alan Ladd**, who had appeared in dozens of bit and extra roles, became a star after his appearance as a killer-for-hire, set-up by his employer Laird Cregar to take the fall, and helped by sultry Veronica Lake. Let's hear it for short people.

RAVENNA, NATALIE

THE RAIN PEOPLE (1969, Warner Brothers)—Pregnant **Shirley Knight** abandons her suburban home and husband to head west. On the way she teams up with handsome brain damaged James Caan, whom she hopes to bed and widower cop Robert Duvall, travelling with his young daughter. Things go badly for the caravan.

RAVIER, MAISIE

MAISIE (1939, MGM); CONGO MAISIE (1940, MGM); GOLD RUSH MAISIE (1940, MGM); MAISIE WAS A LADY (1941, MGM); RINGSIDE MAISIE (1941, MGM); MAISIE GETS HER MAN (1942, MGM); SWING SHIFT MAISIE (1943, MGM); MAISIE GOES TO RENO (1944, MGM); UP GOES MAISIE (1946, MGM); UNDERCOVER MAISIE (1947, MGM)—**Ann Sothern** portrays the hard-boiled, but soft-hearted, gold-digging show girl in a series of moderately enjoyable films which depended almost totally upon the performance of the vivacious Sothern. In her own way, Maisie was a modern woman, fully independent and able to take care of herself.

RAWHEAD REX

RAWHEAD REX (1987, GB, Alpine-Paradise-Green Man)—**Heinrich von Schellendorf** portrays a huge, snarling, mythical monster, an ancient god in Ireland before the coming of Christianity. He's unleashed on the world when a farmer tries to dig up an ancient stone that has been standing in a field for centuries. How in the world shall we get rid of him?

RAWLEY, STEVE (SLICK) See JAMES BLAKE

RAWLINGS, GWEN

GOOD TIME GIRL (1950, GB, Rank)—When she is caught stealing, **Jean Kent** is fired by her boss and beaten by her father. She gets a job in a nightclub fencing stolen jewelry for the boss. She's sent to a reform school, breaks out, and becomes the mistress of a racketeer. She later teams up with two GI deserters. They shoot a man during a hold-up and she's sent to prison for 15 years.

RAWLINGS, RANDY

COACH (1978, Crown International)—**Cathy Lee Crosby** is hired to turn a losing boys' high school basketball team into a winner. Hope she has the horses.

RAWLINS, WADE

WHAT A MAN (1930, Sono-Art/WorldWide)—Decorated war hero **Reginald Denny** takes a job as a chauffeur and falls in love with one of the daughters of his employer.

RAWLINSON, SIR HENRY

SIR HENRY AT RAWLINSON END (1980, GB, Charisma)—Eccentric aristocrat **Trevor Howard** attempts to exorcise his brother's ghost during an annual dinner.

RAY

THE BIG SHOT (1931, RKO-Pathe)—Hotel clerk **Eddie Quillan** is conned into buying worthless swamp land, but later discovers that it contains a valuable sulphur spring. Pee-yew!

RAY

RUDE BOY (1980, GB, Atlantic)—**Ray Grange** plays himself in this movie of the life and crimes of the rock group, The Clash.

RAY, JANE

SOB SISTER (1931, Fox)—Reporters **Linda Watkins** and James Dunn, competitors for news stories, fall in love.

RAYE, MARTHA

FOUR JILLS IN A JEEP (1944, 20th Century Fox)—**Martha Raye** always had a big mouth, but at this point in her career, she was still presenting herself as a somewhat glamorous comedian, entertaining servicemen in England and North Africa, rather than the all-out screwball persona she would later adopt.

RAYMIE

RAYMIE (1960, Allied Artists)—Youngster **David Ladd's** greatest ambition is to catch a fish which always gets away from him. That's the same ambition quite a few anglers have, no matter what their age.

RAYMOND, BUGS

THE KID'S CLEVER (1929, Silent, Universal)—**Glenn Tryon**, the inventor of a fuel-less motor, wins a contract from an automobile manufacturer, despite having his invention sabotaged by a rival.

RAYMOND, FRANK

INVISIBLE AGENT (1942, Universal)—**Jon Hall** is injected with a chemical which makes him invisible. He uses this handy trick to outwit Japanese and German leaders while he steals their secrets.

RAYNOR, JIM

SUSPECTED PERSON (1943, GB, PRC)—Unwittingly, **Clifford Evans** ends up with the loot of American bank robbers. Reporter Evans almost makes a fool of himself over the money but is saved from doing so by his sister. Scotland Yard catch the robbers when they try to recover the loot from Evans.

RAYNOR, FATHER MICHAEL

TO THE DEVIL, A DAUGHTER (1976, GB, Hammer)—Ex-priest **Christopher Lee** arranges for 16-year-old Natassja Kinski to bear the devil's baby, with good Old Lee standing in for his demonic master.

RAYO, EL

THE GIRL AND THE GAMBLER (1939, RKO)—**Leo Carrillo** is a Mexican Robin Hood who comes between cabaret dancer Steffi Duna and her naive boyfriend, Tim Holt.

READ, JACK

THE OUTSIDER (1949, GB, Pilgrim/Variety)—Elementary school boy **Richard Attenborough** is accepted at a British public school as an experiment, and his life is made hellish. The film was released as THE GUINEA PIG in Great Britain.

REAGAN, HELEN

THE OFFICER AND THE LADY (1941, Columbia)—**Rochelle Hudson** is the hard-boiled girlfriend of cop Bruce Bennett. She won't set the date because her father, also a cop, was crippled in the line of duty.

REAGAN, SAL

PANAMA SAL (1957, Republic)—Playboy Edward Kemmer tries to transform Panamanian **Elena Verdugo** into a Beverly Hills socialite.

REANEY, PETER

THE MAN WHO HAD POWER OVER WOMEN (1970, GB, Avco Embassy) -London talent agent **Rod Taylor** grows disgusted with the amoral behavior of his associates.

REARDON

THE MACINTOSH MAN (1973, GB, Warner Brothers)—**Paul Newman** is a British secret service agent, posing as a diamond thief, so he can flush out a master spy.

REARDON, ARTHUR

THE YOUNG SAVAGES (1961, UA)—**John Davis Chandler** is one of three slum boys being prosecuted for the murder of a blind Puerto Rican boy. The D.A., Burt Lancaster, decides one of the boys is innocent.

REARDON, JEFF

ABROAD WITH TWO YANKS (1944, UA)—**Dennis O'Keefe** is a U.S. marine who falls for local girl Helen Walker when he arrives in Australia. But so does his marine buddy William Bendix. After about an hour of this farce, Walker turns them both down for a local lad.

REARDON, JIMMY

A NIGHT IN THE LIFE OF JIMMY REARDON (1988, Regal)—Rising star **River Phoenix**, Oscar nominated for RUNNING ON EMPTY, might like to forget this film in which he is a teenage sex fiend in 1962 Evanston, Illinois. He bed's his best friend's girl, sleeps with his mother's best friend, and treats his girl like dirt because she won't have sex with him.

REARDON, SALLY

THERE'S ALWAYS A WOMAN (1938, Columbia); THERE'S THAT WOMAN AGAIN (1938, Columbia)—Detective **Joan Blondell** and her district attorney husband Melvyn Douglas try to solve the same crime. The two films were Columbia's answer to Nick and Nora Charles. Not bad!

REARDON, TIM

TWO YANKS IN TRINIDAD (1942, Columbia)—**Pat O'Brien** and Brian Donlevy bond nicely in this comedy-adventure which was one of the first movies to take note of Pearl Harbor. The attack was grafted on after the fact through an announcement over the radio at the end of the film.

REAVIS, JAMES ADDISON

THE BARON OF ARIZONA (1950, Lippert)—**Vincent Price**, a clerk in a land office, systematically forges enough documents to show that Ellen Drew, an orphan he marries, is the heir to the land commonly called Arizona. He sets himself up as the Baron of Arizona. The film is loosely based on fact.

REBECCA

REBECCA THE JEWESS (1913, GB, Zenith/Big A)—**Edith Bracewell** appears in this version of IVANHOE, so called in Great Britain on its release. Scott's disowned knight saves Jewess Bracewell from being condemned as a sorceror, when she shows she has knowledge of means to heal wounds.

REBEL

REBEL (1986, Vestron)—**Matt Dillon**, a U.S. marine sergeant, goes AWOL in Australia during WWII, and falls for nightclub singer

Debbie Byrne. He is torn between staying with the lass, or making his way back to the States.

REBEL, JOHNNY
I KILLED WILD BILL HICKOK (1956, Wheeler)—**John Forbes (John Carpenter)** kills Hickok who, without any explanation, turns villain, and deserves what he gets. We always thought Wild Bill was shot by Jack McCall while playing poker.

RECKA, STEPHEN
DANGEROUS TO KNOW (1938, Paramount)—**Akim Tamiroff** is excellent as an organ-playing mob boss who torments his mistress Anna May Wong. She seeks revenge when Tamiroff attempts to dump her for Gail Patrick.

RED
HELL DRIVERS (1958, GB, Rank)—Sadistic champion driver **Patrick McGoohan** works for a company, whose rattletrap ancient trucks must be driven along dangerous cliff roads. He tries to force ex-con Stanley Baker's lorry over a cliff, but it is McGoohan who hurtles to his death.

RED SONJA
RED SONJA (1985, MGM/UA)—This sword and sorcery nonsense must have been produced only to show scantly dressed amazons like six-foot **Brigitte Nielsen**, exacting terrible violence on those who have slaughtered her sisters.

REDFERN DAN *See* **STEVE MALLOY**

REDFISH, TRAVIS W.
ROADIE (1980, UA)—**Meatloaf** has a non-musical role in this film which purports to show what happens as rock groups travel from one gig to the next. They don't get much more forgettable than this.

REE, ANGELE
LINGERIE (1928, Silent, Tiffany)—French girl **Alice White** nurses Malcolm McGregor back to health when he is seriously wounded in WWI. She follows him back home to the U.S. where he throws out his unfaithful wife and marries his little "Lingerie."

REED, ALICE
THE WOMAN IN THE WINDOW (1945, RKO)—Respected family man Professor Edward G. Robinson becomes romantically involved with **Joan Bennett**, a beautiful woman, whose portrait in a window has totally captivated him. In her apartment he commits an unplanned murder and then tries to cover up everything and save his career, family and reputation, but it's not to be—or is it? It's good film noir.

REED, BENJAMIN FRANKLIN
THE CRADLE BUSTER (1922, Silent, Patuwa Pictures)—Mama's boy **Glenn Hunter** breaks the apron strings and wins the love of the local belle.

REED, JIMMY
THE COURAGEOUS COWARD (1924, Silent, Sable)—**Jack Meehan** lacks courage, so his father ships him west to work on a dam project. He comes up short on several fistfights, but finally reaches down and finds some guts to prevent the wrecking of the project by a hired troublemaker.

REED, JOSH
WHEN I GROW UP (1951, Eagle Lion)—**Bobby Driscoll** and his grandfather, Charley Grapewin, bridge the generation gap when he can't seem to get any affection from his busy parents. Driscoll is his grandfather Grapewin when the movie flashes back to 1890.

REED, MIRANDA
SPELLBINDER (1988, MGM/UA)—Yuppie Timothy Daly hits on distressed **Kelly Preston**, which leads to his distress when he discovers she's a witch.

REED, TOM
MY PAL, THE KING (1932, Universal)—**Tom Mix** and his travelling Wild West Show come to the rescue of Mickey Rooney, the king of the mythical kingdom of Alvonia.

REEDER, J.G.
THE MYSTERIOUS MR. REEDER (1940, GB, Monogram)—Old detective **Will Fyffe** unmasks a chief forger as being the murderer of a club owner.

REEDY, MATT
FEDERAL AGENT AT LARGE (1950, Republic)—Treasury agent **Kent Taylor** is sent to smash a gold smuggling ring along the Mexican border.

REESE
A MAN, A WOMAN AND A BANK (1979, Canada, Bennett)—**Donald Sutherland** has his picture taken by an advertising agency woman Brooke Adams while in the process of robbing the bank. This leads to various complications for both, including romantic ones.

REEVES, JOHN
THE WORKING MAN (1933, Warner Brothers)—Shoe manufacturer **George Arliss** is told he must take a month's rest. In that time using an assumed name, he takes a job with the failing company of a competitor and reorganizes it into a successful operation.

REGAN
SEVEN WOMEN FROM HELL (1961, 20th Century Fox)—**Evadne Baker** is one of seven women who escape from a hellish Japanese prison in New Guinea, but doesn't survive the flight.

REGAN, CHUCK
THE WRECKER (1933, Columbia)—**Jack Holt**, who demolishes buildings, finds his marriage to Genevieve Tobin hit by a wrecking ball, namely Sidney Blackmer.

REGAN, JAMES
CRIMINAL LAWYER (1951, Columbia)—Alcoholic lawyer **Pat O'Brien** sobers up long enough to defend a friend facing a murder charge.

REGAN, KID
CELEBRITY (1928, Silent, Pathe Exchange)—Boxer **Robert Armstrong's** manager employs actors to pose as the pugilist's sweet mother and sister. He also hires a newspaperman to write poems to which Armstrong's name is penned. The plan works and the fighter becomes so well known that he gets a championship bout which he wins.

REGAN, SHELIA
ZIEGFELD GIRL (1941, MGM)—**Lana Turner** is one of three girls who find their lives greatly changed when they are recruited to be Ziegfeld girls for an all-star revue.

REGGIE
THE LEATHER BOYS (1965, GB, Allied Artists)—Rita Tushingham impulsively marries motorcycle mechanic **Colin Campbell** with

whom she is incompatible. Most people will not care one way or the other as to what happens to the people in this film.

REGGIE/REGINA
HE'S MY GIRL (1987, Scotti Brothers)—**T.K. Carter** dresses in drag so he can go with his buddy David Hallyday on a free trip to Hollywood. To enjoy this nonsense it helps if you have a severe case of the uncontrollable giggles.

REGINALD
THE BRIGHTON STRANGLER (1945, RKO)—Actor **John Loder** has been playing a brutal strangler on stage for over a year. When the theater is hit by a bomb during a WWII air raid, he becomes disoriented. When a passing stranger says his stage cue, he becomes the strangler. It's an interesting premise, well handled.

REID, ANN
THE CABARET GIRL (1919, Silent, Universal/Bluebird)—**Ruth Clifford's** ambitions to become an opera singer end with her accepting a job in a cabaret. The mother of a wealthy young man who loves her works to prevent her son from marrying below himself, but he does anyway.

REID, JOHN *See* **THE LONE RANGER**

REILEY, COLLEEN
COLLEEN (1936, Warner Brothers)—Once again **Ruby Keeler** is teamed with Dick Powell in a mindless story about an eccentric millionaire Hugh Herbert, his dress shop, gold-digging floozie Joan Blondell, the millionaire's nephew Dick Powell, and little Miss Innocence, Keeler. See the team's other entries.

REILLY, DUNDEE
KNOCKOUT REILLY (1927, Silent, Paramount)—Steel worker **Richard Dix** knocks out the champ in a cafe brawl. The pro frames Dix and he's sent to prison where hard labor on the rock pile builds up his muscles some more. Then he gets out and beats the champ in a ring.

REMBRANDT VAN RIJN
REMBRANDT (1936, GB, UA)—**Charles Laughton** gives a stunning performance as the complex Dutch painter, who struggles to exist while continuing to paint what interests him.

REMINGTON, ELISABETH AND VICTORIA
RABID GRANNIES (1989, Troma)—With the title of the year, this film tells the story of two, dotty and extremely wealthy, old ladies, **Danielle Daven** and **Anne Marie Fox**. Their beloved relatives are anxious for them to die. One disowned nephew magically transforms the old gals of the title, who proceed to practice cannibalism with their other kin.

REMSEN, DR.
DR. RHYTHM (1938, Paramount)—This film put a temporary damper on **Bing Crosby's** career. He's a physician who takes a job as bodyguard for Bea Lillie's ward Mary Carlisle, and falls in love with the girl. None of Bing's songs made it into his lifelong repertory.

RENALDO
RENALDO AND CLARA (1978, Lombard Street/Circuit)—**Bob Dylan** would have been well-advised to merely film his concerts and forget about trying to have some connecting story.

RENAULT, DR.
DR. RENAULT'S SECRET (1942, 20th Century Fox)—**George Zucco's** secret is that he's developed a serum which turns an ape into a humanoid. J. Carroll Naish, as the subject of Zucco's experiment, has enough sensitivity to resent what has been done to him so he kills several people including Zucco.

RENEE
HER SISTER'S SECRET (1944, PRC)—**Margaret Lindsay's** secret won't keep past nine months.

RENFREW
RENFREW OF THE ROYAL MOUNTED (1937, Grand National)—**James Newill**, a former singer with radio's Burns and Allen show, appears in the first of a series of films starring him as a mountie who always gets his men, in this case counterfeiters.

RENFREW, DOTTIE
THE GROUP (1966, UA)—After graduating from college in the 1930s with her seven female friends, proper Bostonian **Joan Hackett** has an affair with an artist but soon ends it to return home and marry the man her parents have chosen for her.

RENO, JOHNNY
JOHNNY RENO (1966, Paramount)—Marshal **Dana Andrews** arrives in a western town to visit saloon owner Jane Russell, and stays to wipe out the bad guys.

RENSSALLER, JOHANNA
JOHANNA ENLISTS (1918, Silent, Artcraft)—**Mary Pickford**, a Pennsylvania Dutch girl, longs for romance and a string of beaus. She gets both when a troop of hundreds of soldiers camp on her father's farm.

REUTER, JULIUS
A DISPATCH FROM REUTERS (1940, Warner Brothers)—**Edward G. Robinson** portrays the German founder of the celebrated news gathering agency which still bears his name.

REVEL, LAWRENCE "BEAU"
BEAU REVEL (1921, Silent, Paramount)—**Lewis R. Stone** and his son Lloyd Hughes vie for the love of dancer Florence Vidor. When things don't go well for him, Stone commits suicide by leaping from a window.

REVELL, JULIEN/PAULA
THE INFAMOUS MISS REVELL (1921, Silent, Metro)—**Alice Lake** portrays twins who try to support their many brothers and sisters by forming a singing act. A millionaire offers the money they need if one of the girls becomes his "companion" during his final years. Julien takes him up on the offer. When the millionaire dies, a tutor falls in love with Julien, but doesn't ask her to marry him because of her living conditions with the deceased. All ends well when it's revealed that Julien died soon after her benefactor and the survivor is Paula, still pure as the driven snow.

REVERE, PEGGY
STAGE STRUCK (1936, Warner Brothers)—**Joan Blondell** has no talent, but she does have money. She hires Dick Powell to direct a Broadway show starring her. The two don't get along in the beginning. Temperament! Temperament!

REVERE, VIVIAN
THREE ON A MATCH (1932, Warner Brothers)—Wealthy socialite **Ann Dvorak** defies the old superstition that the last of three to light a cigarette from the same match will die—and she dies. The notion behind it came from WWI when a sniper would have time to shoot at the light if three cigarettes were lit from the same match.

REVERS, CALEB & BILLY
MAN AND BOY (1972, Jemmin/Levitt/Pickman)—**Bill Cosby** has many talents. Making movies is not among them. He is a black Civil War veteran who together with his young son **George Spell** tries to homestead in Arizona, but encounters prejudice.

REYNAUD, JEAN
BETTINA LOVED A SOLDIER (1916, Silent, Bluebird)—**Rupert Julian** is a nice handsome young soldier whom Bettina, played by Louise Lovely (yes, that's right), decides on after turning down 35 marriage proposals from men who cared more for her money than for her. Julian's different, as he refuses to marry her because she has money and he has none. That convinces her.

REYNOLDS, ALLISON
THE BREAKFAST CLUB (1985, Universal)—**Ally Sheedy** is the most uncommunicative of the five high school students being punished with a Saturday detention at the school. She comes alive in the latter half of the movie when Molly Ringwald helps her apply some makeup and reveals a rather pretty face behind her mop of hair and asocial behavior.

REYNOLDS, BRENDA
SECRETS OF A CO-ED (1942, PRC)—**Tina Thayer** puts her father, criminal lawyer Otto Kruger, on the spot when she takes up with one of his slimy clients.

REYNOLDS, CHRISTOPHER
THE WIFE TAKES A FLYER (1942, Columbia)—During WWII American espionage agent **Franchot Tone** pretends to be Joan Bennett's husband in order to escape from Holland. It's supposed to be a comedy. We thought we should tell you.

REYNOLDS, HARRY
SWEET TALKER (1991, Australia, Seven Arts/New Line)—Ex-con **Bryan Brown** plans to swindle the citizens of a seaside village by pretending there's a wrecked 15th-century Portuguese galleon buried in the sand dunes near town. Brown is redeemed and turns the tables on a drug dealer and a greedy developer.

REYNOLDS, JOSEPH REVINGTON
I DOOD IT (1943, MGM)—Tailor **Red Skelton** falls in love with movie star Eleanor Powell. Everything else is Red clowning around as only he can do.

REYNOLDS, KERRY
HIS MYSTERY GIRL (1923, Silent, Universal)—**Herbert Rawlinson** is tricked by his friends into believing that he has found a girl in distress to rescue—he has!

REYNOLDS, MARIA
THE BEAUTIFUL MRS. REYNOLDS (1918, Silent, World)—**June Elvidge**, the mistress of Alexander Hamilton, is also admired by Aaron Burr, the man who will kill Hamilton in a duel.

REYNOLDS, NAN WILSON
HOUSEWIFE (1934, Warner Brothers)—**Claire Dodd** is the wife of copywriter George Brent, whom sexy home-wrecker Bette Davis tries unsuccessfully to steal.

REYNOLDS, PANDORA
PANDORA AND THE FLYING DUTCHMAN (1951, GB, MGM)—**Ava Gardner** is willing to die for James Mason, the Flying Dutchman, doomed to roam the seas for eternity. He is given six months every seven years to find a girl who loves him enough to give her life so he can end his eternal suffering.

REYNOLDS, PAT
SMART GIRL (1935, Paramount)—Orphans **Ida Lupino** and her sister Gail Patrick get each other's man in this minor comedy.

REYNOLDS, STEVE *See* THE DURANGO KID

RHAH
PLATOON (1987, Orion)—**Francesco Quinn** is one of the American soldiers in a platoon of infantrymen in Vietnam.

RHEIMER, PETER
OCEAN'S ELEVEN (1960, Warner Brothers)—**Norman Fell** is one of a group of ex-army buddies, led by Frank Sinatra, who successfully rob five Las Vegas casinos on New Year's Eve. They aren't caught but they don't get ill-gotten gains either.

RHODA
THE BAD SEED (1956, Warner Brothers)—**Patty McCormack's** bad habit is causing the death of anybody who crosses her. The child is pure evil and her mother, Nancy Kelly, finally realizes that her precocious monster must die.

RHODENBARR, BERNICE
BURGLAR (1987, Warner Brothers)—Cat burglar **Whoopi Goldberg** witnesses a murder, which she tries to solve herself. This talented comedian could use someone to find some good material for her to appear in.

RHODES, CECIL
RHODES OF AFRICA (1936, GB, Gaumont)—**Walter Huston** stars in this enjoyable historical epic about the visionary who united the southern African nation, and becomes the prime minister of the Cape Colony in 1890. He institutes reforms, but is forced to resign for his complicity in the infamous Jameson Raid. He dies at 49, and the country's problems continue to the present.

RHODES, LONESOME
A FACE IN THE CROWD (1957, Warner Brothers)—**Andy Griffith** makes an impressive screen debut as a down-home good ole boy country philosopher and entertainer. In reality, he is a power-hungry monster.

RHODES, ROCKY
ROCKY RHODES (1934, Universal)—**Charles "Buck" Jones** and his sidekick Stanley Fields leave Chicago, heading west to find the villains who killed Jones' father.

RIANO, JENNY
JENNY BE GOOD (1920, Silent, Realart)—The parents of orphan **Mary Miles Minter's** husband kidnap him and ship him out of the country while they try to annul the marriage. True love does prevail, but not before a series of silly soap opera twists.

RICARDO
THE KISSING BANDIT (1948, MGM)—Shy young **Frank Sinatra** is expected to fill his father's shoes as a masked highway man and ladies man in Old California. He's "reformed" by Kathryn Grayson.

RICARDO, LUIGI
ONE MORE AMERICAN (1918, Silent, Paramount); THE LOVES OF RICARDO (1926, Silent, Beban)—**George Beban**, who specialized

in Mediterranean types, is a new American citizen. A political wardheeler threatens Beban with deportation back to Italy. With the help of a crusading reporter, Beban exposes the corrupt politician. In the second film Beban loves his ward, Soliga Lee, but she plans to marry a city slicker. She comes to her senses in time.

RICARDO, VINCE
THE IN-LAWS (1979, Warner Brothers)—Crazy-acting CIA agent **Peter Falk** and dentist Alan Arkin's children are getting married. Falk and Arkin almost miss the ceremony as Falk involves unwilling Arkin in a covert operation in a South American dictatorship.

RICCO, JOE
MR. RICCO (1975, MGM/UA)—San Francisco lawyer **Dean Martin** gets client Thalmus Rasulala off on a murder charge and then is crushed that Rasulala goes on a cop-killing rampage. *Do* miss Martin's performance.

RICE, ARCHIE
THE ENTERTAINER (1960, GB, British Lion); (1975, Seven Keys)—**Laurence Olivier** and **Jack Lemmon** each star as a seedy comic who ruins everyone's life, and causes his father's death in staging a comeback. Olivier considered Archie Rice among his favorite roles. Lemmon can't match Olivier's performance.

RICH
THE WRONG GUYS (1988, New World)—Whining neurotic psychiatrist **Richard Lewis** is one of five former cub scouts staging a reunion. No badges for this one.

RICHARD
THE MAN WITH ONE RED SHOE (1985, 20th Century Fox)—**Tom Hanks** is innocently targeted for elimination by the CIA in a comedy which isn't very funny even with Hanks, Dabney Coleman, Jim Belushi and Charles Durning giving it their all.

RICHARD
RICHARD (1972, Aurora City Group)—**Richard M. Dixon** has the dubious distinction of looking somewhat like Richard Nixon. He has tried to make a living off the resemblance and the new name he chose for himself. This spoof is just about what one might expect—sophomoric smugness.

RICHARD, KING
KING RICHARD AND THE CRUSADERS (1954, Warner Brothers)—**George Sanders** leads a not-well-planned crusade against the clever Saladin, played by a brown-skinned Rex Harrison.

RICHARD OF GLOUCESTER
RICHARD III (1956, GB, Lopert)—**Laurence Olivier** is 15th-century Richard Crookback who murders those who stand in his way to the throne, including his brother and his two nephews. He marries the widow of one of his victims. He is made king but is killed by the forces of Henry Tudor at the Battle of Bosworth Field, where according to Shakespeare he shouted "My kingdom for a horse" as his life is taken. Olivier is magnificent as the wiley Gloucester.

RICHARD OF LAURENTIA, KING
KING'S RHAPSODY (1955, UA)—**Errol Flynn**, the exiled heir to the throne of the kingdom of Laurentia, is forced to give up his mistress Anna Neagle, return home to be king and marry princess Patrice Wymore (Flynn's wife at the time), whom he learns to love.

RICHARDS, BEN "BUTCHER OF BAKERSFIELD"
THE RUNNING MAN (1987, Tri-Star) -Convict **Arnold Schwarzenegger** appears on a TV game show whose gimmick is that used in the movie

THE MOST DANGEROUS GAME. He must run for his life and kill or be killed by heavily armed hunters, who are on his trail.

RICHARDS, BOB
THE SINGING SHERIFF (1944, Universal)—When **Bob Crosby** arrives in a western town, he's given a star and pointed in the direction of a gang of outlaws.

RICHARDS, JACK
THE SINGING COP (1938, GB, Warner Brothers)—Policeman **Keith Falkner** poses as an opera singer, so he can expose the prima donna as a spy.

RICHARDS, JANE
MY WIFE'S BEST FRIEND (1952, 20th Century Fox)—Anne Baxter's best friend **Catherine McLeod** is suspected of having an affair with Baxter's husband Macdonald Carey. It turns out only to have been an inconclusive flirtation.

RICHARDS, JOHN
SENTENCED FOR LIFE (1960, GB, UA)—His partner frames **Jack Gwillim** for selling blueprints to the enemy. Gwillim is sentenced to prison for life, but his lawyer soon clears his name.

RICHARDS, MARY
PICK-UP (1933, Paramount)—Sad-faced **Sylvia Sidney**, the jailed wife of convict William Harrigan, is paroled and falls in love with taxi driver George Raft. Her husband escapes and threatens them.

RICHARDS, MIKE
DISC JOCKEY (1951, Allied Artists)—Disc jockey **Michael O'Shea** claims he can make any unknown singer a star just through radio exposure. He proves his case with Ginny Simms, not a bad warbler.

RICHARDS, TOM
JOHNNY COME LATELY (1943, UA)—Unemployed reporter **James Cagney**, thrown into jail for vagrancy, is paroled into the custody of Marjorie Main, a publisher fighting crooked politicians.

RICHARDS, TOM
THE LARIAT KID (1929, Silent, Universal)—Deputy **Hoot Gibson** brings in the men who murdered his father.

RICHARDSON, MAJOR
THE BEST OF ENEMIES (1962, Columbia)—**David Niven** is the commander of a British unit in Northern Africa during WWII. He and Alberto Sordi, the commander of an Italian unit, discover the futility of war and the value of cooperation.

RICHELIEU, CARDINAL
UNDER THE RED ROBE (1923, Silent, Cosmopolitan); (1937, GB, 20th Century Fox); CARDINAL RICHELIEU (1935, Fox)—**Robert B. Mantell** and **Raymond Massey** appear as the villainous Cardinal and chief minister of French King Louis XIII. Richelieu spares the life of a convicted dentist under the condition that the latter capture the leader of the Huguenots. The dentist does but he also falls in love with the sister of his prey, and allows his captive to escape. **George Arliss** appears in another one of his historical roles as the grey eminence who controls the King in the 1935 production.

RICHMAN, JULIE
VALLEY GIRL (1983, Atlantic)—San Francisco "valley girl" **Deborah Freeman** freaks out her parents when she falls for leather-jacketed Nicolas Cage. It's a fine little movie directed by Martha Coolidge.

RICHMOND, ELIZABETH
LIZZIE (1957, MGM)—**Eleanor Parker** thought she might have an Oscar-winning role as a woman who has multiple-personalities, but she hadn't counted on the release of THREE FACES OF EVE with Joanne Woodward the same year.

RICK
PAPERBACK HERO (1973, Canada, Agincourt Int.)—Local hockey hero and ladies man **Keir Dullea** likes to imagine himself as a gunslinger.

RICKENBACHER, EDWARD
CAPTAIN EDDIE (1945, 20th Century Fox)—While drifting in a rubber raft after an air crash, **Fred MacMurray** reminisces about his career as America's leading flyer in WWI and pioneer in the development of aviation.

RICKEY, JIM
PRIVATE DETECTIVE (1939, Warner Brothers)—**Dick Foran** and Jane Wyman are friendly rivals working together for the first time on a murder case.

RICKS, CAPPY
CAPPY RICKS (1921, Silent, Paramount); CAPPY RICKS RETURNS (1935, Republic); AFFAIRS OF CAPPY RICKS (1937, Republic)—**Charles Abbe**, **Robert McWade** and **Walter Brennan** each play an old seaman who has various minor adventures, both on the sea and on land. There's not much to any of the three productions.

RICKSON, BUZZ
THE WAR LOVER (1962, Columbia)—Stationed in England during WWII, flying daredevil **Steve McQueen** vies with Robert Wagner for Shirley Anne Fields. McQueen takes himself out of competition in a most permanent way when he demonstrates that a plane and a cliff can't occupied the same space at the same time.

RICO *See* **CESARE ENRICO BANDELLO**

RICO, EDDIE GINO & JOHNNY
THE BROTHERS RICO (1957, Columbia)—**Richard Conte** goes to New York City to prevent the Syndicate from eliminating his two brothers **Paul Picerni** and **James Darren**.

RIDGEMONT, SUKIE
THE WITCHES OF EASTWICK (1987, Warner Brothers)—**Michelle Pfeiffer** and two other man-hungry New England women conjure up the ultimate male, the devil, played by Jack Nicholson. He satisfies their sexual needs and they each have his child. The film, which is fun at the beginning, moves towards a gross ending.

RIDGEWAY, CHRISTINE
ANGEL ON THE AMAZON (1948, Republic)—**Vera Ralston** is a woman who will never grow old, but no one said she wouldn't be a bore.

RIGA, TIZA
PRISONERS (1929, Warner Brothers)—Austrian cabaret dancer **Corinne Griffith** steals to attract the attention of lawyer Ian Keith. He can't keep her from going to jail, but he's waiting when she gets out.

RIGBY, BERT
BERT RIGBY, YOU'RE A FOOL (1989, Warner Brothers)—Tony Award-winning **Robert Linday** (for "Me and My Girl") flounders in this nothing musical comedy about a Cockney coal miner in Hollywood.

RIGGS, JOHNNY PARKSON
YOLANDA AND THE THIEF (1945, MGM)—Con man **Fred Astaire** convinces naive South American heiress Lucille Bremer that he's her guardian angel—but the real one is nearby.

RIGGS, MARTIN
LETHAL WEAPON (1987, Warner Brothers); LETHAL WEAPON 2 (1989, Warner Brothers); LETHAL WEAPON 3 (1992, Warner Brothers)—In the first feature, **Mel Gibson** is a loaded gun with a hair-trigger, always ready to go off as he and family man Danny Glover go undercover to bring a vicious drug ring to justice. In the first sequel, he's only slightly more subdued, as he and Glover, with the comical help of Joe Pesci, who's a witness in a drug-laundering racket, take on a group of crooked South African diplomats. In the second sequel, Gonzo cop Gibson finds a soul mate in internal affairs cop Rene Russo, who has as many wounds as Gibson and can inflict as much damage to the bad guys as Gibson can. In all three films, the body-count is high.

RIGOLETTO
RIGOLETTO (1949, Minerva/Superfilm)—**Tito Gobbi** gives a great performance in a film version of the Verdi opera. He's the clever hunchbacked jester in the court of the Duke of Mantua.

RIKKY
RIKKY AND PETE (1988, Australia, MGM/UA)—In this off-beat comedy, well-heeled, sometime street singer **Nina Landis** and her equally kooky brother Stephen Kearney grab their mother's car and head off for parts unknown.

RILEY
MOVING TARGETS (1987, Australia, Academy)—IRA killer **Michael Aitkens** is in Sydney looking up ex-love Carmen Duncan to get some money so he may flee his former colleagues who are after him for refusing to kill the family of one of his victims. Most of the movie takes place in flight, with Aitkens chasing Duncan and a hired killer after him.

RILEY, BUS
BUS RILEY'S BACK IN TOWN (1965, Universal)—**Michael Parks** returns home from the navy and looks up his former sweetheart, Ann-Margret.

RILEY, CHARLES
CHIVALROUS CHARLIE (1921, Silent, Selznick)—**Eugene O'Brien** can't resist an appeal from a woman in distress. This angers his father; but as O'Brien learns, there are worse faults.

RILEY, CHESTER A.
THE LIFE OF RILEY (1949, Universal)—**William Bendix** appears in his famous radio and TV role as a none-too-bright Irish working man who is perplexed when his daughter starts dating his boss' son.

RILEY, CONNIE
MY WOMAN (1933, Columbia)—**Helen Twelvetrees** puts up with a lot from her conceited song-and-dance husband Wallace Ford, while he's going up. She is very forgiving when he begins his slide downward.

RILEY, DEXTER
NOW YOU SEE HIM, NOW YOU DON'T (1972, Buena Vista); THE STRONGEST MAN IN THE WORLD (1975, Buena Vista—College student **Kurt Russell** has an invisibility formula that crooks wish to

use to rob a bank. In the sequel, Russell has come up with a formula which when mixed with breakfast cereal gives him super-strength. Now that's Snap, Crackle and Pop.

RILEY, HELEN
ME AND MY GAL (1932, Fox)—Waitress **Joan Bennett** is in love with cop Spencer Tracy who saves her brother and father when they get mixed up with a gangster.

RILEY, JAMES
RILEY THE COP (1928, Silent, Fox)—A cop loved by all, **J. Farrell MacDonald** finds real romance while in Europe to bring home a fugitive. Surprise, she's the sister of the cop on the next beat, a long time rival of MacDonald.

RILEY, OLD MOTHER
OLD MOTHER RILEY (1937, GB, Butchers); (1952, GB Renown); OLD MOTHER RILEY IN PARIS (1938, GB, Butchers); OLD MOTHER RILEY JOINS UP (1939, GB, Anglo-American); OLD MOTHER RILEY, MP (1939, GB, Butchers); OLD MOTHER RILEY IN BUSINESS (1940, GB, Anglo-American); OLD MOTHER RILEY IN SOCIETY (1940, GB, Anglo-American); OLD MOTHER RILEY'S CIRCUS (1941, GB, Anglo-American); OLD MOTHER RILEY'S GHOSTS (1941, GB, Anglo-American); OLD MOTHER RILEY, DETECTIVE (1943, GB, Anglo-American); OLD MOTHER RILEY OVERSEAS (1943, GB, Anglo-American); OLD MOTHER RILEY AT HOME (1945, GB, Anglo-American) OLD MOTHER RILEY, HEADMISTRESS (1950, GB, Renown); OLD MOTHER RILEY'S JUNGLE TREASURE (1951, GB, Renown); MY SON, THE VAMPIRE (1963, GB, Renown)—British music hall comedian **Arthur Lucan** is famous for his impersonation of Old Mother Riley, a comic Irish washerwoman who had more adventures than any ten men or women. His wife Kitty McShane usually played his daughter.

RILEY, RIP ROARING
RIP ROARING RILEY (1935, Puritan)—**Lloyd Hughes** foils the attempts of spies to get a formula for poison gas from a scientist stationed on an island.

RILEY, STEVE
PRIDE OF THE MARINES (1936, Columbia)—Kind-hearted marine **Charles Bickford** cares for little Billy Burrud, who wanders onto the base.

RILEY, TERENCE
KING OF THE UNDERWORLD (1952, GB, Bushey)—Genial but ruthless gang boss **Tod Slaughter** is versatile, having criminal adventures involving blackmail, jewel robbery and the theft of a secret formula.

RILEY, TOMMY
GLADIATOR (1992, Columbia)—The film's title should have remained "Gladiators," as it's as much about white boxer **James Marshall** as it is about black boxer **Cuba Gooding, Jr.**, who gets top billing. White businessman Brian Dennehy stages illegal boxing matches involving the boys.

RILLA
THE KIRLIAN WITNESS (1978, Sampson and Cranor)—**Nancy Snyder**, a woman with telepathic powers, tracks down the murderer of her sister.

RIMMER, MICHAEL
THE RISE AND RISE OF MICHAEL RIMMER (1970, GB, Warner Brothers)—Advertising man **Peter Cook** maneuvers his way up the corporate ladder to become president of his company. Cook is an opportunist who would make Robert Morse of HOW TO SUCCEED IN BUSINESS WITHOUT REALLY TRYING (1967) proud.

RINERO, PUNCH
MY SIX CONVICTS (1952, Columbia)—**Gilbert Roland** is the brightest of six cons, who form a therapy group run by prison psychiatrist John Beal.

"RINGER, THE" *See* **DR. LOMOND**

RINGO, JIMMY
THE GUNFIGHTER (1950, 20th Century Fox)—In a very adult realistic western, **Gregory Peck**, a tired gunslinger, weary of living up to his reputation, wants only the right to retire and start a new life with his wife and child. But when local fast-gun punk Skip Homeier shoots Peck in the back, the dying gunman insists that he lost to Homeier in a fair fight; that the kid was too fast for him. Thus Peck is condemning his killer to the life he had lived.

RINKER, DR. AMOS
THE COUNTRY DOCTOR (1927, Silent, Pathe Exchange)—**Rudolph Schildkraut**, prominent European actor and father of Joseph Schildkraut, is a kindly rural doctor who takes a "sinful" woman in his home and thus incurs the wrath of some of his neighbors.

RIORDAN, DENNIS
BELOVED ENEMY (1936, Goldwyn/UA)—**Brian Aherne**, an Irish rebel leader at the time of the 1921 rebellion, falls in love with Merle Oberon, the daughter of an English governor. He's killed by fanatics in his own party who believe he has betrayed the cause.

RIPLEY, SAILOR
WILD AT HEART (1990, Goldwyn)—One nice thing about appearing in a movie directed and written by David Lynch is that even **Nicholas Cage** can't be accused of overacting. He's a macho man who steps aside for no man. When not cracking open the heads of adversaries, he's making steamy love with his main squeeze Laura Dern. The two take to the road, where they encounter characters even more unsavory than the ones they leave behind. Most notable among these is Willem Dafoe, who literally loses his head.

RIPPER
JOCKS (1987, Crown)—**Don Gibb** is one of the members of an awful college tennis team entered in a Las Vegas tournament.

RITA
EDUCATING RITA (1983, Columbia)—**Julie Walters** is utterly charming, repeating her stage role as the married working class woman, who wants to better herself by studying literature. She chooses boozy failure Michael Caine as her tutor. She teaches him far more than he does her. Walters is a delight in her movie debut.

RITA
LADIES LOVE DANGER (1935, Fox)—**Mona Barrie** and playwright-detective Gilbert Roland solve the murders of several theatrical people.

RITA
RITA, SUE AND BOB TOO! (1987, GB, Orion)—**Siobhan Finneran** and her girlfriend are two somewhat heavy, ordinary-looking teen girls who babysit for George Costigan and his sexually unresponsive wife. Pretty soon Costigan and the two girls are bedmates.

RITCHER, MAXINE

FOUR FOR TEXAS (1963, Warner Brothers)—**Ursula Andress** should be called Ursula Undress for her general appearance in this western farce set in Galveston Texas of 1870. She, con-men Frank Sinatra and Dean Martin, and Anita Ekberg, another one who has trouble keeping her clothes on, divide up the illegal activities of the island town.

RITTER, PASTOR ARMIN

MESSENGER OF PEACE (1950, Astor)—Not too many people listened to the message of **John Beal** in this film, which traces his career from a young seminary student to an elderly pastor.

RIVARD, FATHER

THE RUNNER STUMBLES (1979, 20th Century Fox)—In 1927 priest **Dick Van Dyke** is accused of the brutal murder of a young nun, Kathleen Quinlan, whom he had come to love.

RIVERA, FILIPE

THE FIGHTER (1952, UA)—Mexican boxer **Richard Conte** takes on all comers to raise money to purchase big guns for the 1910 Mexican Revolution.

RIVERA, MOUNTAIN

REQUIEM FOR A HEAVYWEIGHT (1962, Columbia)—Illiterate, aging prizefighter **Anthony Quinn** is told if he continues to fight he risks getting killed. But what else he can do to make a living?

RIVERS, LENA

LENA RIVERS (1932, Tiffany)—When her fisherman grandfather dies, **Charlotte Henry** moves in with her rich aunt, not knowing her real father lives next door.

RIVERS, SENATOR

THE SENATOR (1915, Silent, Equitable)—**Charles J. Ross**, a freshman senator from the Midwest, wins compensation for an elderly man for the use of his ship during the Revolutionary War.

RIZZOLI, DET. RITA

FATAL BEAUTY (1987, MGM/UA)—**Whoopi Goldberg** is stuck once again in inferior material as an undercover narcotics cop. After showing so much promise in her top flight THE COLOR PURPLE performance, Goldberg seems to be spinning her wheels in garbage.

ROALVANG

THE BOSS'S WIFE (1986, Tri-Star)—**Christopher Plummer's** wife is out to seduce a young stock broker who works for her husband. In a movie era when people jump into bed the moment they lay eyes on each other, it's difficult to get worked up over a "will-he or won't-he" type comedy.

ROAMER, JOYCE

THE LADY LIES (1929, Paramount)—Salesgirl **Claudette Colbert** has an affair with widower Walter Huston, and wins over his kids from their snooty relatives.

ROBAIX, PAUL

MY GEISHA (1962, Paramount)—**Yves Montand** doesn't catch on that the beautiful unknown Japanese girl he plans to star in a movie version of "Madame Butterfly" is his actress wife Shirley MacLaine, whom he has directed many times.

ROBBIA, LISA DELLA

ENTER MADAME (1935, Paramount)—Adorable looking **Elissa Landi** has trouble being credible as a temperamental opera star who doesn't have time for her husband Cary Grant.

ROBBIN, DOC

WHO KILLED "DOC" ROBBIN? (1948, UA)—Mad scientist **George Zucco** works in a haunted house using an "atomic firing chamber"—whatever that is. This is the second film in Producer Hal Roach, Jr's attempt to come up with a new "Our Gang" series modeled on that of his more famous father Hal Roach, Sr.

ROBBINS, GERTIE

FOUR GIRLS IN WHITE (1936, MGM)—**Una Merkel**, one of the film's four probationary nurses, ends up with intern Buddy Ebsen. It could be worse. Mary Howard is killed by a maniac.

ROBBINS, LETTY

SO LONG LETTY (1929, Warner Brothers)—Because **Charlotte Greenwood** is too eccentric to make the right kind of impression on her husband's rich uncle, she agrees to allow Ruth Miller to act as her husband's wife during a visit by the uncle.

ROBBINS, MARTY

BALLAD OF A GUNFIGHTER (1964, Ward/Parade)—**Marty Robbins** had a great hit in "El Paso." Rather than make this routine western, he should have looked for another decent song to sing.

ROBBINS, MARY

THE GIRL OF THE GOLDEN WEST (1938, MGM)—The backdrops in this western-musical featuring **Jeannette MacDonald** and Nelson Eddy look so phony, one has trouble concentrating on what the two singers are doing up front. Come to think of it—that may be a blessing.

ROBBINS, MITCH

CITY SLICKERS (1991, Columbia)—**Billy Crystal** isn't having much success coming to grips with the doldrums of midlife as he turns 39. His wife, Patricia Wettig, sends him off to 'find your smile' with his two buddies Daniel Stern and Bruno Kirby. While participating in a modern cattle drive, he finds his smile and many other things as well.

ROBBINS, RUTH

THE IMPATIENT MAIDEN (1932, Universal)—Secretary **Mae Clarke's** dreams come true when her surgeon boyfriend, Lew Ayres, proves himself by performing an emergency appendectomy on her.

ROBBO

ROBIN AND THE SEVEN HOODS (1964, Warner Brothers)—In another of his rip-off romps with his Rat-pack, Clan or whatever his gang of hangers-on at the time were called, **Frank Sinatra** is a Chicago Prohibition mobster who steals from everybody and gives a bit to orphans.

ROBBY

LITTLE MEN (1940, RKO)—**Casey Johnson** is one of the boys in a school run by Jo March (Kay Francis) in a continuation of the "Little Women" story of Louisa May Alcott. Unfortunately, the production in no way compares favorably to the wonderful 1933 movie starring Katharine Hepburn as Jo.

ROBBY

ROBBY (1968, Bluewood)—Young white shipwrecked boy **Warren Raum** floats ashore to a tiny island, and is saved from drowning by young black boy, Ryp Siani. They have a number of adventures before they are taken from the island, Raun being returned to his wealthy parents, and Siani placed in an orphanage, despite their expressed desire to stay together.

ROBERT OF NOTTINGHAM
THE BANDIT OF SHERWOOD FOREST (1946, Columbia)—Robin Hood's son **Cornel Wilde** rallies the men of Sherwood Forest to deal with the same kind of no-goods who once crossed swords with his father.

ROBERTA
BELOVED BRAT (1938, Warner Brothers)—**Bonita Granville's** wealthy parents don't know how to deal with their mischievous daughter until an understanding teacher intervenes.

ROBERTA
ROBERTA (1935, RKO)—Randolph Scott, the nephew of famed Parisian dress designer **Helen Westley**, becomes romantically involved with White Russian princess, Irene Dunne, who makes a living as a prominent couturier. The real stars of the movie are, of course, Fred Astaire and Ginger Rogers, even though their names are farther down the list of credits.

ROBERTS, PROF. ARTEMIS
SWING IT, PROFESSOR (1937, Ambassador)—Music professor **Pinky Tomlin** loses his job because he won't recognize jazz as legitimate music. After taking a job in a nightclub he changes his mind. That's how it is with musicologists, wishy-washy.

ROBERTS, BOB
BOB ROBERTS (1992, Paramount/Miramax)—Highly successful singer **Tim Robbins** tries to ride his popularity into the U.S. Senate.

ROBERTS, BILL
BERLIN CORRESPONDENT (1942, 20th Century Fox)—American radio broadcaster **Dana Andrews** is stationed in Berlin prior to the U.S.'s entry into the war. He slips important strategic information into his daily broadcasts to America. The Gestapo assigns Virginia Gilmore to get the goods on Andrews. But she discovers her father is his source. After no little trouble, the three escape the country.

ROBERTS, DAVEY
PERSONALITY KID (1946, Columbia)—**Ted Donaldson** finds a donkey, which he persuades his parents to let him keep as a pet. It's harder to housebreak than a cat or a dog, you know.

ROBERTS. LT. (JG.) DOUG
MISTER ROBERTS (1955, Warner Brothers)—**Henry Fonda** recreates his Broadway role as the sensitive executive officer of a supply ship operating in the South Pacific during WWII. He wants to get into the shooting war, but his obnoxious captain, James Cagney, won't let him go. The film, basically a comedy, ends with the news of Fonda's death in combat after he achieves his goal.

ROBERTS, HELEN
NIGHT WAITRESS (1936, RKO)—**Margot Grahame** works in the title role in a shadowy waterfront dive, frequented by smugglers and other assorted good and bad guys.

ROBERTSON, BOBBY
THE RAINMAKER (1926, Silent, Paramount)—Because of a war wound, jockey **William Collier Jr.** is able to predict rain. He uses the knowledge in clever ways to earn money. But at the end, its his

prayers for rain, not his ability to anticipate precipitation which earns him the title, "rainmaker."

ROBERTSON, CHRIS
DAUGHTERS OF SATAN (1972, UA)—**Barra Grant** is the wife of American Tom Selleck, an art collector living in the Philippines. She is controlled by mysterious evil forces emanating from a painting, which require her to try to kill him.

ROBIN
AND GOD CREATED WOMAN (1988, Vestron) **Rebecca De Mornay**, an inmate of a woman's prison, is coveted by a middle-aged politician, but she weds a young carpenter instead to gain her parole. The bridegroom goes mad with jealousy when she shakes her fanny during a gig with a hard rock band. But the catharsis ensures a happy ending that's filled with martial bliss. Poor De Mornay. Every review (including this one) notes that her posterior is not as outstanding as that of Brigitte Bardot, who starred in the original production in 1956.

ROBIN HOOD
ROBIN HOOD (1922, Silent, UA); THE ADVENTURES OF ROBIN HOOD (1938, Warner Brothers); THE PRINCE OF THIEVES (1948, Columbia); TALES OF ROBIN HOOD (1951, Lippert); THE STORY OF ROBIN HOOD (1952, GB, Disney/RKO); MEN OF SHERWOOD FOREST (1957, GB, Hammer); A CHALLENGE FOR ROBIN HOOD (1968, GB, 20th Century Fox); ROBIN AND MARIAN (1976, GB, Columbia); ROBIN HOOD, PRINCE OF THIEVES (1991, Warner Brothers)—**Douglas Fairbanks, Errol Flynn, Jon Hall, Robert Clarke Richard Todd, Don Taylor, Barrie Ingham, Sean Connery** and **Kevin Costner** each appeared as Robert of Locksley, the Saxon nobleman-turned bandit, who steals from the rich and gives to the poor as he fights the attempts to usurp Richard the Lion-Hearted's throne by his scheming brother Prince John. (John would get the job later and lose much of his kingly powers when the English barons forced him to sign the Magna Carta at Runnymede, June 15, 1215, but that's another story.) While some who remember the silent days might make a strong case for Fairbanks as the best Robin Hood, most movie fans and critics will agree that Flynn's performance is definitive. The others are just also-rans. Miscast in the role that Flynn handled with such charm, Costner, after escaping from Jerusalem in 1194, returns to England to find his father has been slain by a delicious villain, Alan Rickman, as the Sheriff of Nottingham. Costner joins a band of not-so-merry men in Sherwood Forest, trains them and leads them to victory against those who would usurp Richard's throne. A bit of trivia: Alan Hale portrayed Little John in three different decades, in the 1920s with Fairbanks, in the 1930s with Flynn and in 1950 in ROGUES OF SHERWOOD FOREST with John Derek as Robin Hood's son.

ROBIN, JACK (JAKIE RABINOWITZ)
THE JAZZ SINGER (1927, Part-Talkie, Warner Brothers)—**Al Jolson** is given credit for being the first performer in a feature film to sing and talk, but that honor goes to Bobbie Gordon as Jakie at 13. The familiar story has cantor's son Jolson making it big in show business but in doing so is treated as dead by his father. The gulf between them is bridged when Jolson takes the place of his dying father to sing at the High Holy Day services.

ROBIN, JESS
THE JAZZ SINGER (1982, Associated Film/EMI)—**Neil Diamond** is not the greatest embarrassment in this disappointing and unnecessary remake of a movie, remembered more for its historical

significance than for its quality. That dubious distinction goes to Laurence Olivier, who played Diamond's cantor father as an embarrassing, whining Shylock.

ROBINSON, JACKIE
THE JACKIE ROBINSON STORY (1956, Eagle-Lion)—**Jackie Robinson** was a great baseball player, not just the first black major leaguer. Jackie Robinson was not a great actor as this film clearly shows. How can one not be convincing playing himself?

ROBINSON, WILLIAM, ELIZABETH & JACK
SWISS FAMILY ROBINSON (1940, RKO) (1960, Buena Vista)— **Thomas Mitchell, Edna Best** and **Freddie Bartholomew** are the main members of the shipwrecked family, who build a new life on an uninhabited island. Other members of the family created by Johann David Wyss are played by Tim Holt, Terry Kilburn and Baby Bobby Quillan. The 1960 Disney version starred **John Mills** as Father, **Dorothy McGuire** as Mother, and **James MacArthur** as Fritz.

ROBLES, DAVE
THE MAN FROM DEL RIO (1956, UA)—Mexican tramp **Anthony Quinn** takes the job seriously when asked to help a villainous saloon keeper take control of a western town. Quinn becomes sheriff and chases out all the bad guys including the saloon keeper.

"ROBOCOP" *See* ALEX J. MURPHY

ROBUR
MASTER OF THE WORLD (1961, American International)—Nineteenth century inventor **Vincent Price** plans to end all wars by destroying the earth's weapons from his space ship.

ROCCO, JOHNNY
JOHNNY ROCCO (1958, Allied Artists)—Gangster's son **Richard Eyer** is sought by just about everyone when he witnesses a murder.

ROCHARD, CAPT. HENRI
I WAS A MALE WAR BRIDE (1949, 20th Century Fox)—French Army Officer **Cary Grant** reluctantly falls in love with WAC officer Ann Sheridan, and then finds the red tape involved to gain permission to return with her to the U.S. is complicated because the bureaucracy only understands brides of GIs. Grant disguises himself as a woman and boards a ship bound for America with the other wives.

ROCK, DR. THOMAS
THE DOCTOR AND THE DEVILS (1985, GB, 20th Century Fox) - **Timothy Dalton** needs cadavers for his experiments and he's not going to ask the men who supply the bodies where they get them.

ROCKLIN
TALL IN THE SADDLE (1944, RKO)—Woman-hater **John Wayne** finds that the man who hired Wayne to be his foreman has been killed and the ranch is now being run by pretty Ella Raines. Well, Pilgrims, what do you think the Duke does?

ROCKLIN, MARSHALL MORG
HE RIDES TALL (1964, Universal)—New marshal **Tony Young** postpones his marriage after he's forced to kill the man who raised him.

ROCKNE, KNUTE
KNUTE ROCKNE-ALL AMERICAN (1940, Warner Brothers)—The inspirational University of Notre Dame football coach is played by

Pat O'Brien. His most famous player, George Gipp, portrayed by Ronald Reagan, tells Rockne, as he lays dying, to one day ask the team to "win one for the Gipper."

ROCKS, PATTI
PATTI ROCKS (1988, FilmDallas)—Married male chauvinist Chris Mulkey has been carrying on an affair with **Karen Langley**, who has informed him she's pregnant. She's a self-assured, no-nonsense woman who has no intentions of having an abortion; nor does she give a damn if she ever sees Mulkey again.

ROCKWELL, LEVI
ROCKET GIBRALTAR (1988, Columbia)—On his 77th birthday, **Burt Lancaster**, the patriarch of the Rockwell family, informs his grandchildren that he wants a Viking funeral. They give it to him.

ROCKY
THE ROCKY HORROR PICTURE SHOW (1975, GB, 20th Century Fox)—The plot of this midnight cult favorite isn't as important as the weird things members of the audiences do and say as they see it for the fortieth time. It's a spoof of old Hollywood horror stories. A young couple, Barry Bostwick and Susan Sarandon, take refuge in a dark old house. The inhabitants are aliens from the planet Transylvania, whose leader, Tim Curry, has his way with both Bostwick and Sarandon. The title character is Curry's swishy creation Peter Hinwood. See it with someone for whom you lust.

RODDY
TWO GENTLEMEN SHARING (1969, GB, American International)— Two Oxford graduates, white advertising executive **Robin Phillips** and black Jamaican born lawyer Hal Frederick, share Judy Geeson. The movie has very little of significance to say about race relations.

RODERIGO
BABES IN TOYLAND (1961, Buena Vista)—**Gene Sheldon** is one of the good guys in this lavish Disney production of the Victor Herbert operetta.

RODGER
ACE ELI AND RODGER OF THE SKY (1973, 20th Century Fox)— **Eric Shea** is the eleven-year-old son of WWI pilot Cliff Robertson. The two barnstorm around the Midwest in the 1920s, putting on air shows. The movie is so bad, the producer, writer and director don't give their real names, although everyone knows that the story is based on the work of a comer, Steven Spielberg.

RODOCK, JEREMY
TRIBUTE TO A BADMAN (1956, MGM)—In 1875, Wyoming rancher **James Cagney** takes the law into his own hands, hanging rustlers and treating everyone, including his wife Irene Papas, like dirt.

RODRIGUES DE SANTOS, GEN. MAXIMILIAN
VIVA MAX! (1969, Commonwealth United)—Modern day Mexican general **Peter Ustinov** and his troops emulate Santa Anna and take possession of the Alamo in downtown San Antonio.

RODRIGUEZ, ABRAHAM
POPI (1969, Allied Artists)—In this far-fetched story Hispanic **Alan Arkin** will do just about any-thing to see that his children escape the ghetto and have a better life.

RODRIGUEZ, ESTELITA
THE FABULOUS SENORITA (1952, Republic)—**Estelita**, daughter of a Cuban businessman, is engaged to a wealthy banker, but she falls in love with a professor, whom she snares by posing as identical twins.

RODRIGUEZ, RICKY

THE LAST OF THE FINEST (1990, Orion)—**Jeff Fahey** is one of the good suspended cops who rip off minor drug dealers to finance the purchase of heavy weapons to stage a war against corrupt feds and big-time drug traffickers.

RODRIGUEZ, TONY

THE VISITORS (1972, UA)—**Chico Martinez** and Steve Railsback are two Vietnam vets who come to the farmhouse occupied by ex-buddy James Woods, his girlfriend and her father. The two visitors are seeking revenge on Woods, whose testimony against them for raping a Vietnamese girl, got them sent to prison.

ROGAN, ALEX

THE LAST STARFIGHTER (1984, Universal)—**Lance Guest**, an expert at a video game, is recruited to fight intergalactic raiders.

ROGER

KILLERS THREE (1968, American International)—American Bandstand host **Dick Clark** is a demolition expert, who with fellow North Carolina backwoodsman Robert Walker, Jr., robs a bootlegger, kills several people and heads to California with Diane Varsi. Dick, we rate this as a flop.

ROGER THE LODGER

MY WIFE'S LODGER (1952, GB, Adelphi)—Dominic Roche unmasks his wife's favorite lodger, **Leslie Dwyer**, as a crook.

ROGERS

THREE BRAVE MEN (1957, 20th Century Fox)—Assistant Secretary of the Navy **Dean Jagger** agrees with the findings of lawyer Ray Milland that the firing of a veteran Naval Civil Service employee Ernest Borgnine because of some innocent flirtations with communism was wrong. He orders Borgnine reinstated.

ROGERS, BETTY *See* MRS. MURDOCK

ROGERS, BUCK

BUCK ROGERS IN THE 25TH CENTURY (1979, Universal)—**Gil Gerard** is no Buster Crabbe, but kids may have fun with the various adventures the galactic traveller encounters.

ROGERS, CAROL

SHE'S GOT EVERYTHING (1938, RKO)—Victor Moore and Helen Broderick attempt to play cupid by arranging a match between recently impoverished **Ann Sothern** and coffee magnate Gene Raymond.

ROGERS, CHARLIE

ROUSTABOUT (1964, Paramount)—**Elvis Presley** takes a job as a roustabout for a travelling carnival run by Barbara Stanwyck. He becomes a big hit when he starts singing on the midway.

ROGERS, CHEYENNE

THE DESPERADOES (1943, Columbia)—**Glenn Ford** stars in the studio's first color film as an outlaw persuaded by his girl Evelyn Keyes to go straight. Edgar Buchanan tries to frame Ford for a bank robbery and that riles Ford.

ROGERS, ELIZABETH

RICH, YOUNG AND PRETTY (1951, MGM)—**Jane Powell** is everything the title claims. She's also in Paris sightseeing, looking for and finding romance, while catching up with her long absent mother Danielle Darrieux.

ROGERS, GALE

PERSONAL SECRETARY (1938, Universal)—**Joy Hodges** and William Gargan are rival newspaper columnists. She becomes his secretary and eventually his wife. Together they prove Kay Linaker didn't kill her playboy husband.

ROGERS, KAY

CIRCUS GIRL (1937, Republic)—This tame romantic triangle story with a circus setting has Bob Livingston and Donald Cook competing for **June Travis**.

ROGERS, PAULA

PAULA (1952, Columbia)—Hit and run driver **Loretta Young** redeems herself by helping an injured child regain his speech.

ROGERS, PAULA

SMART WOMAN (1948, Monogram-Allied Artists)—Lawyer **Constance Bennett's** crusade against a crooked District Attorney threatens her romance.

ROGERS, PUFF (PAT)

LADY AND GENT (1932, Paramount); UNMARRIED (1939, Paramount)—**Wynne Gibson** and **Helen Twelvetrees** appear as a nightclub hostess who retires to a small town with her ex-boxer boyfriend to raise the son of the latter's deceased manager.

ROGERS, ROY

THE ARIZONA KID (1939, Republic); KING OF THE COWBOYS (1943, Republic); COWBOY AND THE SENORITA (1944, Eagle-Lion)—Singing cowboy **Roy Rogers** frequently appeared in western B movies playing himself, especially after he made the cover of Life magazine and was called "The King of the Cowboys," a title he used henceforth. The stories never amounted to much, just old fashioned good guys triumphing over out-and-out bad guys. In 1944, Rogers made his first film with Dale Evans, a former band singer who has ridden "happy trails" with Rogers ever since.

ROGERS. TED

THE STOOGE (1952, Paramount)—This film may tell the story of the split up of the team of Martin and Lewis. In the 1930s, song-and-dance man Martin finds the antics of his stooge **Jerry Lewis** getting all the attention, so they split.

ROGERS, TEX

KING COWBOY (1928, Silent, FBO)—**Tom Mix** and a group of rough and tumble cowboys arrive in a North African country looking for the boss of their ranch who has been kidnapped by Riffs. Mix not only defeats the evil Emir, he's named the successor to the deceased Riff leader.

ROGERS, WILL

THE STORY OF WILL ROGERS (1950, Warner Brothers)—**Will Rogers, Jr.** appears as his father in a fairly decent biopic of the beloved humorist.

ROGET, MARIE

THE MYSTERY OF MARIE ROGET (1942, Universal)—Detective Patric Knowles investigates the disappearance of beautiful actress **Maria Montez**.

ROGET, SUZANNE

FLAME OF CALCUTTA (1953, Columbia)—In 1750, Indian princess **Denise Darcel** champions the cause of her people against an evil caliph.

ROGUIN, NATALIE

THE LADY IN QUESTION (1940, Columbia)—Young Parisian **Rita Hayworth** is acquitted of murder. One of her jurors, Brian Aherne, takes her into his home without explaining her background. He becomes a tad concerned when his son Glenn Ford falls for her.

ROKETT, TEX

COWBOY FROM SUNDOWN (1940, Monogram)—Singing cowboy **Tex Ritter** saves a pretty miss from having her ranch stolen by crooks holding her mortgage.

ROLAND, JACQUELINE

JACQUELINE, OR BLAZING BARRIERS (1923, Silent, Arrow) - **Marguerite Courtot** lives in a timber camp in the North Woods. All the men want her, but she gives her heart to a newly arrived clean-cut Lew Cody who saves her from a forest fire.

ROLAND, PRINCE

PRINCE OF PIRATES (1953, Columbia)—Long before Bo, **John Derek** played handsomely in several minor swash-bucklers such as this one set at the time of the wars between France and Spain.

ROLFE, SUZANNE & JOHN

HIS FORGOTTEN WIFE (1924, Silent, FBO)—During WWI **Madge Bellamy** nurses amnesiac **Warner Baxter** back to health and gives him a new identity. They marry and in what is common Hollywood practice unwittingly take jobs as servants on his estate. He is soon recognized, and after an operation, regains his memory but doesn't know Bellamy. Just give him time.

ROLLINS, CHICK

MY WOMAN (1933, Columbia)—**Wallace Ford's** hat size increases in direct proportion to his show business success, but he's headed for a fall, and only his forgiving wife Helen Twelvetrees will be there to catch him.

ROLLINSON, HON. RICHARD

SALUTE THE TOFF (1952, GB, Butchers)—Novelist John Creasey's detective, played by **John Bentley**, saves a woman's boss from being kidnapped by an insurance swindler.

ROLLS, SIR DOUGLAS

THE GREAT DEFENDER (1934, GB, Wardour)—Ailing, famous counselor **Matheson Long** dies proving that his beloved's husband did not kill the latter's mistress.

RO-MAN

ROBOT MONSTER (1953, Three Dimensional Pictures)—**George Barrows** stars as the creature out to eliminate the last six humans in existence. The film took four days to shoot, the first three probably were spent forcing actors such as George Nader and Selena Royle to show up before the cameras.

ROMANIKOFF, ROSALIE

ROSALIE (1937, MGM)—**Eleanor Powell**, the princess of a mythical country, falls in love with West Point cadet Nelson Eddy. The plot is trash, Powell can't act (neither can Eddy, for that matter), but, oh, my can she dance and the production number of the title song is still worth the price of admission.

ROMANOFF, IGOR

ROMANOFF AND JULIET (1961, Universal)—Peter Ustinov, the general of a small but strategic mythical European country, encourages the romance of **John Gavin**, the son of the Russian ambassador, with Sandra Dee, the daughter of the U.S. ambassador.

ROME, TONY

TONY ROME (1967, 20th Century Fox)—**Frank Sinatra** plays a tough Miami private eye who runs into trouble when he takes home the drunken daughter of an underworld figure. Everybody seems out to get Sinatra, but with different, not all unpleasant notions of what to do with him.

ROMEO (MONTAGUE)

ROMEO AND JULIET (1916, Silent); (1936, MGM); (1954, GB, UA); (1966, GB, Embassy); (1968, GB, GB/Italy, Paramount)—**Harry Hilliard, Leslie Howard Laurence Harvey, Rudolf Nureyev and Leonard Whiting** each appeared as the teenage lover of the fair Juliet, despite the hatred which exits between their families. Only Whiting was the proper age to appear as one of Shakespeare's star-crossed lovers. Howard was particularly long in the tooth when he played opposite an equally ancient Norma Shearer in 1936. Nureyev danced the role and Harvey was satisfactory, which is high praise for him. As for Hilliard, he was forced to take a very far back seat to his co-star Theda Bara.

ROMEO *See* **SAM**

ROMERO, ARCHBISHOP OSCAR

ROMERO (1989, Four Seasons)—In a true story, **Raul Julia** portrays the martyred, liberal archbishop of El Salvador, murdered in 1980 by a member of a right wing death squad while performing mass in a hospital chapel. His killer has never been caught.

ROMMEL, ERWIN

THE DESERT FOX (1957, 20th Century Fox); RAID ON ROMMEL (1971, Universal)—Some veterans of WWII found it hard to like a movie in which the main figure was a German Field Marshall, responsible for so many Allied deaths. Still, **James Mason** is outstanding as the tough tank commander and favorite of Hitler, who at last became part of the plot to kill the fuhrer. Because of the latter's high regard for his country's hero, he was allowed to take poison rather than being slowly strangled to death through being hanged with piano wire on meat hooks—the fate of most of the other conspirators. In 1971, **Wolfgang Preiss** portrayed the Field Marshall, but the movie was carried by Richard Burton, as a British officer who leads the assault on Tobruk in North Africa.

ROMOLA

ROMOLA (1925, Silent, Metro-Goldwyn)—**Lillian Gish**, daughter of a blind intellectual of Florence, marries perfectly horrible scoundrel William Powell, who rises to the position of chief magistrate where he abuses his powers, and impregnates and deserts peasant girl Dorothy Gish. He executes a popular priest and champion of the people. He gets his comeuppance when his stepfather, who Powell had earlier abandoned to pirates, shows up and drowns him. Lillian Gish then marries artist Ronald Colman, who has always loved her, and together they raise Dorothy Gish's child.

RON

FRAMED (1975, Paramount)—After spending four years in prison, innocent **Joe Don Baker** takes the law in his own hands.

RONNIE

FIVE AGAINST THE HOUSE (1955, Columbia)—**Kerwin Mathews** is one of five college students who rob Las Vegas casinos to prove how easily it can be done and how bright they are, but watch out, not everyone sees it as a college prank.

ROONEY, ANNIE

LITTLE ANNIE ROONEY (1925, Silent, Triangle); MISS ANNIE ROONEY (1942, UA)—In the **Mary Pickford** film, Annie is the mischievous daughter of a policeman. With her brother, she seeks revenge when their father is killed. **Shirley Temple** is given her first screen kiss by Dickie Moore in a story of a poor girl falling for a rich man's son, with daddy not pleased, until her father comes up with a formula for synthetic rubber.

ROONEY, JAMES IGNATIUS

ROONEY (1958, GB, Rank)—Garbage man (called dustman in Great Britain) **John Gregson** falls in love with Cinderella like Muriel Pavlow, whose grandfather leaves his money to her. But at his funeral, she's accused of stealing a necklace. Irishman Gregson gets her released and proposes marriage.

ROOSEVELT, THEODORE

THE WIND AND THE LION (1975, MGM/UA)—In a film loosely based on a true incident, **Brian Keith**, as President Teddy Roosevelt, becomes involved when Moroccan sheik Sean Connery kidnaps American Candice Bergen and her two children.

ROSA

QUEEN OF HEARTS (1989, GB, Cinecom)—Against her will, **Anita Zagaria** is betrothed to Vittorio Amandola, the overbearing son of the village butcher. She loves oafish, but well-meaning Joseph Long. The two flee Italy and settle in London. With the help of a vision of a talking pig, Long prospers, and supports an ever-growing family. Years later, Amandola shows up, intent on revenge.

ROSALIE

THE CHILD (1977, Valiant, International)—Little **Rosalie Cole** has the power to command bodies of the dead to rise from their graves, and do quite a bit of damage to the living. Cole gets hers when her governess splits her head with an axe. Not for the kiddies.

ROSALIE

THE STRANGE VENGEANCE OF ROSALIE (1972, 20th Century Fox)—New Mexico Indian girl **Bonnie Bedelia** hitches a ride with salesman Ken Howard. She takes him to her cabin where she breaks his leg so she can care for him and he can't leave her. She kills a motorcycle punk who drops by to rape and rob her. It's a strange statement about something or other.

ROSALIND

VALET GIRLS (1987, Lexyn/Empire)—U.C.L.A. psychology student **April Stewart** works for a professional car parking service, but finds some of her clients believe that in hiring her they are getting a built-in playmate.

ROSALINDA

OH ROSALINDA!! (1956, GB, Pathe)—**Ludmilla Tcherina** stars in this adaptation of *Die Fledermaus*, with man-about-town Anton Walbrook planning revenge on French Colonel Michael Redgrave and his wife Tcherina for their part in a fiendish practical joke.

ROSANNA *See* MADDALEN LAMBARDI

ROSCOE

THE RAINMAKERS (1935, Radio Pictures)—**Robert Woolsey** and his comedy partner Bert Wheeler are inventors of a rainmaking machine which they claim will end a drought in the California bean fields. Rain isn't the only thing missing in this film. Where are the laughs?

ROSE

ALOHA, BOBBY AND ROSE (1975, Columbia)—Mechanic Paul LeMat and his girl **Dianne Hull** innocently become involved in an attempted robbery and murder.

ROSE

RAMBLING ROSE (1991, Seven Arts/New Line)—In what may have been the most appealing performance of the year, **Laura Dern** portrays a promiscuous innocent who moves in with Robert Duvall and Diane Ladd's family in 1935. Dern's raw sexuality and vulnerability is almost too unusual a combination for any man to deal with.

ROSE

THE ROSE (1979, 20th Century Fox)—Drink and drugs do in somewhat vulgar rock singer **Bette Midler** in a movie which surely was in part inspired by the life of Janis Joplin.

ROSE

TIGER ROSE (1930, Warner Brothers)—Half-caste **Lupe Velez** is desired by every man in Canada, including the local Mountie, Monte Blue, but she only has eyes for a railroadman Grant Withers. He kills a doctor before whisking her off to the big city. Blue has double reasons to track his man. Beside Velez, another star of the movie is that noble dog Rin-Tin-Tin.

ROSE

TRUCK STOP WOMEN (1974, LT Films)—Former Playboy Playmate of the Year **Claudia Jennings** is surprisingly good in this sleazy film about a ring of prostitutes who hijack trucks.

ROSE

TWO MEN AND A MAID (1929, Tiffany)—**Alma Bennett**, a camp follower of the French Foreign Legion, is loved by a brutal adjutant and an idealistic Englishman. She dies helping the latter escape from the former.

ROSE, BARBARA AND OLIVER

THE WAR OF THE ROSES (1989, 20th Century Fox)—In an uncompromising black comedy, directed by Danny De Vito, **Kathleen Turner** and husband **Michael Douglas** have prospered, but their once-happy marriage is over. They continue to live in the same house as they argue, fight, and then do battle to the death over their luxurious house and its tasteful furnishings.

ROSE, DANNY

BROADWAY DANNY ROSE (1984, Orion)—Second-rate booking agent **Woody Allen** has only one decent act, singer Nick Apollo Forte, a married man having an affair with Mia Farrow. Allen loses Forte but gets Farrow.

ROSE OF CIMARRON

BELLE STARR'S DAUGHTER (1947, 20th Century Fox)—**Ruth Roman** wants to kill Marshal George Montgomery, whom she believes has killed her infamous outlaw mother.

ROSE OF CIMARRON

ROSE OF CIMARRON (1952, 20th Century Fox)—White **Mala Powers** is brought up by Cherokees after her parents are killed by Comanches. When outlaws kill her Indian parents, she takes up with Marshal Jack Buetel, looking for the same group of bad men.

ROSE, PINKY

THREE WOMEN (1977, 20th Century Fox)—**Sissy Spacek**, a new member of the staff of a desert old folks home, develops a crush on attendant Shelley Duvall. Eventually Spacek believes she is Duvall.

ROSELLI, MR.

THE FRIGHTENED MAN (1952, GB, Tempean)—Junk dealer **Charles Victor**, the fence for jewel thieves, tries to prevent his son from taking part in a fool-hardy jewel heist, but is unsuccessful and the son is killed.

ROSENBERG

TEACHERS (1984, MGM/UA)—Teacher **Allen Garfield** is too scared of his superiors to buck their idiotic notions of education, but draws courage from fellow teacher Nick Nolte, who takes a stand for education and the students right to learn. It's a preachy movie with too many strawmen.

ROSENBLOOM, SKIPALONG

SKIPALONG ROSENBLOOM (1951, UA)—Ex-prizefighter **"Slapsie" Maxie Rosenbloom** spoofs TV westerns as he saves a ranch which is in danger of being taken by land-grabbers.

ROSENCRANTZ

ROSENCRANTZ AND GUILDENSTERN ARE DEAD (1990, Cinecom)— In Tom Stoppard's production of his award-winning play, **Gary Oldman** is a shrewd, awkward simpleton who is forever frustrating his comical partner Rosencrantz. In this story, Shakespeare's main characters—Hamlet, Ophelia, Claudius, Gertrude and Polonius— are forced to surrender center stage to this Danish Abbott and Costello.

ROSEPETTLE, MME., JONATHAN & DAD

OH DAD, POOR DAD, MAMA'S HUNG YOU IN THE CLOSET AND I'M FEELIN' SO SAD (1967, Paramount)—**Rosalind Russell**, **Robert Morse** and **Jonathan Winters** did nothing for their careers in this flat comedy about a smothering mother, a dimwit son and a nothing father, based on a New York play that wasn't exactly Tony material itself.

ROSETTI, MARIA

MANKILLERS (1987, Action)—**Christine Lunde** is one of a dozen young women recruited by the CIA to kill a renegade living south of the border.

ROSIE

EVERYTHING'S ROSIE (1931, Radio Pictures)—**Anita Louise** works in a fake medicine show with conman Robert Woolsey. He causes her embarrassment when he meets her fiance's parents.

ROSITA

BELLE OF OLD MEXICO (1950, Republic)—College president Robert Rockwell goes to Mexico to adopt the sister of a WWII buddy. Expecting a little tyke, he finds the kid is curvy, sexy **Estelita Rodriguez** whose adoption doesn't sit well back at the college or with Rockwell's fiancee.

ROSITA

ROSE OF THE RIO GRANDE (1938, Monogram)—**Movita** has little to do in this poorly produced story. Upper class Mexicans form a vigilante group to punish those who offend them.

ROSITA

ROSITA (1923, Silent, UA)—**Mary Pickford** called this Ernst Lubitsch directed film, the worst of her career. It's set in 18th Century Toledo where the King of Spain wishes to establish Pickford as his mistress, but she's in love with a nobleman who has been sentenced to death for treason. The queen intervenes and the lovers are reunited.

ROSS, BETSY

BETSY ROSS (1917, Silent, Peerless/World)—Philadelphia Quaker widow **Alice Brady** sews the first American flag at the request of George Washington.

ROSS, FRANK

EACH DAWN I DIE (1939, First National/Warner Brothers)— Reporter **James Cagney** is framed for manslaughter when his investigation of crooked politicians gets too hot. The prison experience almost makes him a real hardened criminal, but he's eventually cleared through the help of four-time loser George Raft.

ROSS, JERRY

THE LITTLE BROTHER (1917, Silent, Triangle)—**Enid Bennett** dresses in boy's clothes to make it easier for her to sell newspapers in the streets. She's adopted by a rich man who sends her away to school. She returns a beauty and he marries her.

ROSS, JULIA

MY NAME IS JULIA ROSS (1945, Columbia)—**Nina Foch** is outstanding in this B Film Noir of an unsuspecting woman, who, after answering an ad for a companion, is drugged. When she awakens she is told that she is the wife of the master of the house, George Macready. She doesn't know why but figures it's not for good purposes.

ROSS, KIT

ME AND MARLBOROUGH (1935, GB, Gaumont)—**Cicely Courtneidge** disguises herself as a man and joins Marlborough's army to locate her press-ganged husband. She ends up proving her spouse innocent of spying charges.

ROSS, MAJOR

FIRST YANK IN TOKYO (1945, RKO)—**Tom Neal's** face is transformed by plastic surgery so he can pass as Japanese when he is smuggled into the Land of the Rising Sun to rescue a scientist in a prison camp. With a little surgery to the film, the studio was able to turn a routine "B" adventure yarn into the first film to deal with the atomic bomb which was dropped on Hiroshima and Nagasaki as the film was being completed.

ROSS, ONE SHOT

ONE SHOT ROSS (1917, Silent, Triangle)—Great with shootin' irons, **Roy Stewart** is almost beaten to death on an occasion when he doesn't have them with him. It does give him a chance to fall in love with the rancher's daughter who nurses him back to health. He then straps on his guns and takes care of the gang who attacked him.

ROSSER, TOM

TOWN TAMER (1965, Paramount)—When his wife is killed by a bullet meant for him, westerner **Dana Andrews** becomes an earlier version of Charles Bronson and declares war on lawbreakers.

ROSSINI, ANGELA

HELLER IN PINK TIGHTS (1960, Paramount)—**Sophia Loren** is the star of a barn-storming 1880 theatrical troupe led by Anthony Quinn. Their excursion into the U.S. West gets them in trouble with sheriffs, gunslingers, creditors and Indians.

ROSSITER, PETER

THE ROSSITER CASE (1950, GB, Hammer)—**Clement McCallin** is having an affair with his sister-in-law which he'd like to end. His paralyzed wife is unaware of the arrangement, and tries to comfort her sister on losing the man in her life. A gun is produced and a struggle. The result is the sister is shot, the wife is cured and McCallin is suspected of the crime.

ROSSITER, SUSAN
MOON OVER HER SHOULDER (1941, 20th Century Fox)—**Lynn Bari's** husband John Sutton, a famed marital counselor, advises her to take up painting. This puts her into contact with yachtsman Dan Dailey, whom Sutton has to fight to keep his wife.

ROSSON, RIMES
SATURDAY'S CHILDREN (1940, Warner Brothers)—**John Garfield** takes a leave from his usual angry young man roles to appear as an inventor who dreams of moving to the Philippines. Instead he's tricked into marriage by Anne Shirley. Well, all right, he is a bit put out.

ROSY
KANSAS CITY PRINCESS (1934, Warner Brothers)—**Joan Blondell** played more gold diggers than anyone else in the history of movies. This time her partner in glitter is Glenda Farrell. The two have to escape two of their suckers, dressed like girl scouts.

ROTH, LILLIAN
I'LL CRY TOMORROW (1955, MGM)—**Susan Hayward** appears as singer Roth whose bouts with alcohol ruined her career. This is the kind of performance that Hayward did best.

ROTH, LEINEN
OLD EXPLORERS (1990, Taurus)—In a talky film that has seen only limited release, **James Whitmore** is an aging archaeologist who, together with ancient explorer Jose Ferrer, has vicarious thrills and chills in imagined expeditions.

ROTHSCHILD, FRANCIS
MISTER HOBO (1936, GB, Gaumont)—Tramp **George Arliss** is made director of a failing bank because he has the surname of the famous financier.

ROTHSCHILD, MAYER & NATHAN
THE HOUSE OF ROTHSCHILD (1934, Fox)—**George Arliss** portrays the founders of the great European banking house at the time of the Napoleonic Wars. It's an enjoyable biopic with Loretta Young extremely lovely as Arliss' daughter.

ROTHSTEIN, ARNOLD
KING OF THE ROARING TWENTIES (1961, Allied Artists)—**David Janssen** is adequate in his portrayal of the Jewish gambler and mobster, who reportedly was the brains behind paying White Sox baseball players to throw the 1919 World Series.

ROUND, MARION
THE MAN I WANT (1934, GB, British Lion)—**Wendy Barrie** is forbidden by her father to marry stuffy Henry Kendall, but dad relents when Kendall unwittingly recovers Barrie's family jewels.

ROWE, MICHAEL & MARY
MICHAEL AND MARY (1932, GB, Gainsborough)—**Herbert Marshall** and **Edna Best** marry after her husband deserts her during the Boer War. Never divorced, her husband returns many years later, and tries to blackmail Marshall and Best, but he is killed in a fall. Marshall and Best tell all to their son and his fiance and find the ordeal has only strengthened the bond between them.

ROXANNE, MLLE.
SEXTON BLAKE AND THE MADEMOISELLE (1935, GB, MGM)—**Lorraine Grey** has stolen bonds from a financier in order to take revenge for his having ruined her father. Sexton Blake, the detective employed to recover the bonds, discovers his employer is a crook.

ROY
FIVE AGAINST THE HOUSE (1955, Columbia)—**Alvy Moore** supplies the comic relief as one of five college students who plots to rob Las Vegas casinos to prove it can be done.

ROY/WENDY
I WANT WHAT I WANT (1972, GB, Cinerama)—Mayor's daughter **Anne Heywood**, loved by an instructor, has had a sex change operation.

ROYALE, MONTGOMERY
THE MAN WHO PLAYED GOD (1932, Warner Brothers)—**George Arliss** appeared in the silent version of this story of a concert pianist who is made deaf by a bomb explosion. He is befriended by Bette Davis, with whom he falls in love. However, his ability to read lips reveals that she loves another, but is willing to sacrifice her happiness to stay with Arliss, whom she deeply admires.

ROYCE, SIDNEY
THE LADY HAS PLANS (1942, Paramount)—**Paulette Goddard**, a news correspondent in Lisbon during WWII, is mistaken for a German spy. Only a mysterious tattoo (or lack of same) in some indelicate place will clear her.

ROYD, JANET
HAPPY IS THE BRIDE (1958, GB, Panthar/Kassler)—**Janette Scott** and her fiance Ian Carmichael almost call the whole thing off because of the antics of their families in preparing for their wedding.

ROYLE, JOAN DAISY
"THAT ROYLE GIRL" (1925, Silent, Paramount)—**Carol Dempster**, a crook's daughter, and band-leader Harrison Ford are accused of killing his wife.

ROZANNE
THE SINS OF ROZANNE (1920, Silent, Paramount)—**Ethel Clayton** grows up in South Africa with mysterious occult powers. Her mentor is a Malay nurse and witch. Clayton is unaware that she is being used to smuggle diamonds from the country until Jack Holt goes after the crooks.

ROZELLA, MIRIAM
MIRIAM ROZELLA (1924, GB, Silent, ASTRA-N)—**Moyna McGill**, the daughter of a suicide victim, becomes the mistress of a degenerate rich man, who reforms when he discovers his baby sister at one of his orgies.

RUBY
THE KING AND FOUR QUEENS (1956, UA)—**Jean Willes** is one of five women waiting in a ghost town for their men to come to them. Willes is sexy and unscrupulous, and makes a play for Clark Gable when he comes wandering into the town, but then so do three other of the women, the only exception being Jo Van Fleet who is the mother-in-law to the other four.

RUBY
RAMBLIN' GAL (1991, Aquarius)—Housewife and mother of four **Deborah Strang** leaves Kansas for New York and a songwriting career. Her feminist lyrics turn off male record label executives.

RUBY

RUBY (1971, Bartlett)—Raised in sin, **Ruth Hurd** has an affair with a supernatural being.

RUBY, JACK

RUBY (1992, Triumph)—It's a highly fictionalized biopic of the club owner and small-time hood who killed Lee Harvey Oswald on national television. With **Danny Aiello** in the title role, the film traces the events leading up to the murder. Like JFK, the film points the finger at the mob and CIA in the assassination of John F. Kennedy.

RUDABAUGH, ARKANSAS DAVE

YOUNG GUNS II (1990, 20th Century Fox)—A new young desperado is added for this sequel to the 1988 film. **Christian Slater** looks annoyed because he knows his character hasn't the reputation of his colleagues.

RUDDY, JOE

YOKEL BOY (1942, Republic)—**Eddie Foy Jr.** stars in a silly slapstick spoof of gangster movies.

RUDOLF, KING

THE PRISONER OF ZENDA (1922, Silent, Metro); (1937, UA); (1952, MGM); (1979, Universal)—**Lewis Stone, Ronald Colman, Stewart Granger** and **Peter Sellers** each appear in the dual roles as the kidnapped king-to-be of Ruritania and his look-alike English cousin who stands in for the missing monarch. The 1937 movie comes close to being a perfect film. It is so good that the 1952 film is a scene-for-scene, speech-for-speech duplicate. Sellers' spoof had his English character being a London cabbie who was too much of a buffoon to pass for any king-to-be, even the lisping one of this movie.

RUGGLES, MARMADUKE

RUGGLES OF RED GAP (1923, Silent, Paramount); (1935, Paramount)—**Edward Everett Horton** and **Charles Laughton** each portray the English butler won in a poker game by a westerner, who takes his winnings home. Because of the butler's way of speaking, it's believed he's a nobleman, a mistake his social climbing employer Mary Boland does not correct. But this gentleman's gentleman proves to be a real democrat.

RUMFORD, TOM

THE FIGHTING COWARD (1924, Silent, Paramount)—Raised in the North by Quakers, **Cullen Landis** returns to his southern home where "honor" is everything. He's disowned because of his ungentlemanly behavior, but wins their forgiveness when he finds something worth fighting for.

RUMPO KID

CARRY ON COWBOY (1966, GB, Warner Brothers/Pathe)—**Sid James** portrays the varmint who killed Calamity Jane's Pa which rankles her some. She teams up with sanitary engineer Jim Dale, sent to clean up Stodge City, to get the bad guy.

RUNYON, BRAD

THE FAT MAN (1951, Universal)—Obese but effective detective **J. Scott Smart** is hired by Julie London, when her boss, a dentist, is mysteriously killed.

RUPERT

RUPERT OF HENTZAU (1915, GB, Jury); (1923, Silent, Selznick)—**Gerald Ames** and **Lew Cody** portray one of the most endearing villains in literature in these two silent versions of THE PRISONER OF ZENDA. Hentzau merely wishes to steal the throne of Ruritania for himself. In sound versions of the Anthony Hope novel, first Douglas Fairbanks, Jr. and then James Mason made charming Ruperts, who knew when to fight and when to retreat.

RUPPERT, EVE

DANGER WOMAN (1946, Warner Brothers)—**Patricia Morison**, the wife of atomic scientist Don Porter, has been missing but not missed for three years. Porter has Brenda Joyce in his life now. That's OK by Morison. She only wants to steal the formulas he's been working on.

RUSSELL, BUCK

UNCLE BUCK (1989, Universal)—When their parents are called out of town to care for a sick relative, eight-year-old Macaulay Culkin, six-year-old Gaby Hoffman, and teenage Jean Kelly are left in the care of their uncle, John Candy. He's not exactly what they need or want, but things work out OK.

RUSSELL, DR.

DISTURBED (1990, Live)—Psychiatrist **Malcolm McDowell** preys on female patients at a secluded mental institution. He meets his match in put-upon Pamela Gidley.

RUSSELL, GEORGE

BRIGHT ANGEL (1990, Hemdale)—In a road picture, **Dermot Mulroney** is a naive and good-natured 18-year-old who offers to drive old-beyond-her-years Lili Taylor from Montana to Wyoming, where her brother is in prison.

RUSSELL, JOHN

HOMBRE (1967, 20th Century Fox)—White man **Paul Newman** has been brought up by the Apaches and is sympathetic to them. As a passenger on a stagecoach, he's required to ride on the coach rather than in it. But when the coach is attacked by outlaws, Newman shows his courage, losing his life, defending the other passengers.

RUSSELL, JOHN

A MAN OF SENTIMENT (1933, First Division)—Marian Marsh is engaged to marry wealthy Owen Moore, but after an auto accident she meets **William Bakewell** who appears to be penniless. She falls in love with him and rejects Moore. Guess what: Bakewell comes from a rich family that is anxious to take their prodigal son and his bride into their wallet—that is, home.

RUSSELL, KITTY

A VERY YOUNG LADY (1941, 20th Century Fox)—Tomboy **Jane Withers** resists attempts to have her act more lady-like, until she develops a crush on the head-master of the finishing school to which she is sent.

RUSSELL, LILLIAN

LILLIAN RUSSELL (1940, 20th Century Fox)—**Alice Faye** impersonates the famous musical star of the turn of the century, from the time she's discovered by bandleader Tony Pastor in 1880 until she retires in 1912 to marry a newspaperman. Faye is totally unbelievable as Russell. The production makes no serious attempt to capture the flavor of the period, either in song, costume or behavior.

RUSSELL, MRS.

SEVEN WOMEN (1966, MGM)—**Anna Lee** is one of seven women at a 1935 Chinese mission who are menaced by the troops of war lord Mike Mazurki.

RUSSELL, SUSIE

SUSIE STEPS OUT (1946, UA)—**Nita Hunter** poses as a nightclub singer, and becomes a TV star.

RUSSELL, SYLVIA
THIS WAS A WOMAN (1949, GB, 20th Century Fox)—**Sonia Dresdel** is a psychotic woman who takes out her anger on her family. She is particularly incensed when her daughter announces her engagement. When Dresdel finds a man she likes, she poisons her husband. She is convicted of murder, but is proven to be insane.

RUTFIELD, LADY KAY
OH, KAY (1928, Silent, First National)—Runaway bride-to-be **Colleen Moore** persuades Lawrence Gray to take her into his mansion, and pose as his wife to fool a detective who suspects her of being a bootlegger. The mansion is actually the bootleggers' hideout and their boss is Gray's butler. Moore gets her man and the bootleggers go straight.

RUTH
THE GIRL WHO COULDN'T QUITE (1949, GB, Monarch)—**Elizabeth Henson** hasn't smiled since she was a little girl, but her friendship with a hobo makes her laugh again.

RUTH
THE RAILWAY CHILDREN (1971, GB, Universal)—**Ann Lancaster** is one of three British children who play in a rail yard while their father is in prison. They meet a man who helps prove their father is innocent.

RUTH
SEVEN BRIDES FOR SEVEN BROTHERS (1954, MGM)—**Ruta Kilmonis (Lee)** is yet another of the kidnapped brides of six mountain men. By springtime she is more than happy to see her pappy, his shotgun and a preacher arrive at the farm which was snowed in all winter.

RUTH
THE STORY OF RUTH (1960, 20th Century Fox)—Moabite priestess **Elana Eden** renounces her graven gods for the God of Israel in order to marry Stuart Whitman. "Whither thou goest, I will go."

RUTH, GEORGE HERMAN "BABE"
THE BABE RUTH STORY (1948, Monogram/Allied Artists); THE BABE (1992, Universal)—**William Bendix** portrays the immortal "Sultan of Swat" in a reasonably good baseball story. It's all sentimentality and doesn't hue very close to the real life of "The Bambino," but such biopics seldom do. Bendix played him as what he no doubt was —the most dominating player in the history of the game. **John Goodman** looks more like Ruth and plays him as a man with large appetites, whereas Bendix was forced to play him as something of a buffoon. Although the 1948 movie was a little better, the newer film isn't interesting enough to get filmmakers busy on remakes of the Dizzy Dean, Grover Cleveland Alexander, or even Lou Gehrig stories.

RUTLEDGE, 1ST SGT. BRAXTON
SERGEANT RUTLEDGE (1960, Warner Brothers)—Black calvary sergeant **Woody Strode** is on trial for a double murder and the rape of a white woman—neither crime of which he's guilty. He's defended by white officer Jeffrey Hunter, but not believing he can get a fair trial, Strode deserts his unit, but returns when he learns his men are in danger.

RUTLEDGE, CAPT. CLARK
WHITE HUNTER (1936, 20th Century Fox)—African white hunter **Warner Baxter** is hired by the man responsible for the death of Baxter's father. All is forgiven when Baxter falls in love with his enemy's daughter June Lang.

RUTLEDGE, JOHNNY
FATHER IS A BACHELOR (1950, Columbia)—**William Holden** has been adopted by five kids, and finds that this makes him ideal husband material as far as Coleen Grey is concerned.

RUTLEDGE, JOHNNY
JOHNNY-ON-THE-SPOT (1919, Silent, Metro)—**Hale Hamilton** is an author living at a boardinghouse where writer Louise Lovely also resides. She is to come into a lot of money if she's married by a certain date. Without being told of the condition for her inheritance, Hamilton, who is leisurely writing a book called "Everything Comes to He Who Waits," asks for her hand in marriage in the nick of time.

RUTLEDGE, MONTE & ROY
HELL'S ANGELS (1930, UA)—**Ben Lyon** and **James Hall** are brothers and American WWI pilots, competing for the same girl, 19-year-old Jean Harlow (who replaced Norwegian Greta Nissen when Howard Hughes decided to make the movie a talkie). The most memorable line belongs to Harlow, the first to say: "Excuse me while I slip into something more comfortable."

RYAN, JERRY
TWO FOR THE SEESAW (1962, UA)—Lonely Omaha lawyer **Robert Mitchum**, on the verge of a divorce, has a tempestuous New York affair with dance instructor Shirley MacLaine. Both manage to look dumpy.

RYAN, JOE
CLAY PIDGEON (1971, Tracon/MGM)—After coming home from Vietnam, **Tom Stern** gets involved in the drug racket, but has a change of heart and goes after a big supplier.

RYAN, COL. JOSEPH L.
VON RYAN'S EXPRESS (1965, 20th Century Fox)—**Frank Sinatra** doesn't make it to the promised land as he leads a group of British and American POWs in an exciting railroad escape from pursuing Germans.

RYAN, LINDA
THE LADY ESCAPES (1937, 20th Century Fox)—**Gloria Stuart** and her husband Michael Whalen quarrel all the time. She goes to Paris, and becomes involved with a suave playboy, but Whalen arrives, realizing he'd rather fight than switch.

RYAN, MARY
MARY RYAN, DETECTIVE (1949, Columbia)—**Marsha Hunt** is on the trail of a fencer of stolen goods. She arranges to be arrested to have some credibility as she seeks her man.

RYAN, MICHAEL
SECRET ADMIRER (1985, Orion)—On the last day of summer vacation, 16-year-old **C. Thomas Howell** receives an anonymous letter from a girl claiming she loves him. Could the letter be from Kelly Preston, whom he has secretly dreamed about? We shall see.

RYAN, NORA
PERSONAL MAID (1931, Paramount)—**Nancy Carroll's** romance with her employer's son is interrupted by a charming rich man whom she meets on holiday.

RYAN, RAINBOW
THE RAINBOW MAN (1929, Paramount)—Song-and-dance man **Eddie Dowling** adopts a little boy and falls in love with the tyke's aunt.

RYAN, ROSALIE

BROADWAY LADY (1925, Silent, R-C Pictures)—Chorus girl **Evelyn Brent** sets her cap for Theodore von Eltz, the son of a wealthy family. She marries him, hoping to get revenge on his family which has snubbed her, but instead wins their affection when she takes the blame when her sister-in-law shoots a bounder. Both girls go free.

RYAN, ROSY & TOM

RYAN'S DAUGHTER (1970, GB, MGM)—Married to school teacher Robert Mitchum, **Sarah Miles** has an affair with shell-shocked English officer Christopher Jones. Miles is suspected of betraying IRA men during the 1916 Irish uprising. The real traitor is her father **Leo McKern**, who does nothing to spare her the shame of having her hair cut off for fraternizing with the enemy. She might have been killed on the spot if were not for the local priest, Trevor Howard. It's a beautifully photographed and captivating movie.

RYAN, STEVE

RAILROADED (1947, Eagle-Lion)—Innocent **Ed Kelly** is implicated in a robbery-murder, which was really pulled by sadistic psychopath John Ireland, who dips his bullets in perfume before using them.

RYDER, C.C.

C.C. AND COMPANY (1971, Avco Embassy)—As a football player, **Joe Namath** sometimes had the reputation of being a bad actor. They must of have been thinking of this motorcycle turkey. His leading lady, Ann-Margret, claimed she was always mindful of his bad knees in the love scenes.

RYDER, JOHN

THE HITCHER (1986, Tri-Star)—This movie is a good argument against picking up hitchhikers. Teen C. Thomas Howell picks up lunatic **Rutger Hauer**, and the latter makes the former's life hell.

RYDER, RED

THE COWBOY AND THE PRIZEFIGHTER (1950, Eagle-Lion); THE FIGHTING REDHEAD (1950, Eagle-Lion)—**Jim Bannon** had a brief run as Red Ryder in nothing stories which wouldn't appeal to the least demanding western fans.

RYKER, SGT. PAUL

SERGEANT RYKER (1968, Universal)—Convicted of treason, **Lee Marvin** wins the right to a new trial.

S

SAADIA

SAADIA (1953, MGM)—When French doctor Mel Ferrer saves **Rita Gam** from the spell of a witch-doctor in the Sahara, she repays him by saving his serum when the village is attacked by bandits.

SABICH, RUSTY

PRESUMED INNOCENT (1990 Warner Brothers)—Although a taut courtroom thriller, this otherwise enjoyable film disappoints in the ways it resolves the mystery. There are several lapses in logic in the plot, which are apparently contrivances to advance the story. Still, the picture proved to be enjoyable summer viewing, allowing one to watch former deputy prosecutor **Harrison Ford** squirm uncomfortably when he is brought to trial for murdering gorgeous lawyer Greta Scacchi, who had slept with Ford, and apparently every other man who could help advance her career.

SABINA

THE KING AND FOUR QUEENS (1956, UA)—**Eleanor Powell** is the queen who is wild in this story of four women waiting in a Western ghost town for their outlaw husbands to show up, when in rides Clark Gable. While all of the "ladies" make a play for the king, Powell is the most successful.

SABOURIN, CLEMENTI

DEATH OF A SCOUNDREL (1956, RKO)—Czech **George Sanders** makes a fortune in America through fraud and conning women into helping him get ahead.

SACH

NEWS HOUNDS (1947, Monogram)—**Huntz Hall** is a photographer for a newspaper where Leo Gorcey is a copyboy. Gorcey hopes to advance his chances of being a reporter by getting the goods on a mobster. The other Bowery Boys pitch in to help our heroes.

SACHS, SUSIE

BEAUTY AND THE BOSS (1937, GB, Twickenham/Wardour)—Down and out **Marian Marsh** gets a job as secretary to a banker. She gets him to the altar before he gets her into bed.

SADIE

QUEEN OF THE YUKON (1940, Monogram)—**Irene Rich** runs a boat in the Yukon to help pay to send her daughter to a fancy school in the States. She and her partner, Charles Bickford, come to the aid of the independent miners against the big mining concerns.

SADLER, SHERIFF BEN

MAN IN THE SHADOW (1954, Universal)—Sheriff **Jeff Chandler's** investigation of a murder in a small western town riles powerful rancher Orson Welles.

SADLER, DAVE & TOMMY

THE LITTLEST HORSE THIEVES (1977, Buena Vista)—Set in England at the turn of the century, this film deals with the efforts of children **Andrew Harrison** and **Benjee Bolger** to save ponies that work in the mines from abuse and death.

ST. CLAIR, AMBER

FOREVER AMBER (1947, 20th Century Fox)—**Linda Darnell** was raised a Puritan, but she easily shucks the teachings to become a courtesan in London during the reign of Charles II, eventually becoming the favorite of the king. She never regains the one man she really loved, soldier Cornel Wilde, the father of her child.

ST. CLAIR, MARIE

A WOMAN OF PARIS (1923, Silent, UA)—French country girl **Edna Purviance** loves a poor artist. Because of a misunderstanding, she believes he has abandoned her and she becomes the mistress of a wealthy Parisian. The artist reappears in her life, but commits suicide when she turns down his offer of marriage, believing herself not fit for him because of her affair. She also loses her rich protector and returns to the country to live.

ST. CLAIRE, ANNA MARIA

THE LUCKY STIFF (1949, UA)—Nightclub singer **Dorothy Lamour** is convicted of murdering her boss, but is reprieved just before her date with the electric chair. It is reported that she has been executed so she can appear as her own ghost to scare the real culprits into confessing. Farfetched? Why do you say that?

ST. GEORGE, NITA
MIDNIGHT LADY (1932, Chesterfield)—Speakeasy owner **Sarah Padden** fled her family years before to escape a tyrannical mother-in-law. When her daughter is accused of murder, Padden comes forward to take the blame. Both women are cleared of the crime and are happily reunited.

ST. GEORGE, ROY
LITTLE EVA ASCENDS (1922, Silent, Metro)—**Gareth Higbe** is forced by his actress mother to appear as Little Eva in her touring company's production of "Uncle Tom's Cabin." When he gets his chance he runs away to be with his father from whom he had been separated since his mother got the acting bug.

ST. GERMAIN, GEORGES
HIS PRIVATE LIFE (1928, Silent, Paramount)—Suave Parisian boulevardier **Adolph Menjou** is attracted to American Kathryn Carver, a close friend of his former fiancee, now married to a very jealous man. There are numerous comical complications before Menjou and Carver pledge their love for each other.

ST. IVES, RAYMOND
ST. IVES (1976, Warner Brothers)—When ex-L.A. crime reporter and would-be novelist **Charles Bronson** is hired to recover some stolen ledgers by a wealthy recluse, he finds himself a character in a murder story.

ST. JAMES, CAPT. HENRY
THE CAPTAIN'S PARADISE (1953, GB, London Films) **Alec Guinness**, the captain of a steamer making regular trips between Gibralter and Tangier, has a wife in each port, sedate Celia Johnson in Gibralter and wild Yvonne De Carlo in Tangier. Everything is fine until the two women yearn for different lifestyles.

ST. JAMES, JAMES
MEN AT WORK (1990, Triumph)—Oh the puns that could be made in reviewing this story of **Emilio Estevez** and his real-life brother Charlie Sheen as a pair garbage men up to their necks in some dirty business. Estevez has triple responsibility for this trash. He also wrote and directed it.

ST. MAURICE, MAYDA
THE COURTESAN (1916, Silent, Mutual)—**Eugenie Forde** works as a courtesan in order to support her son, who believes her dead, through law school. When the young man runs for the office of district attorney, his opponents expose his relationship with Forde, without knowing they are mother and son.

ST. NEOTS, MARK
THE MAN WHO LOVED REDHEADS (1955, London Films)—In this charming little comedy, **John Justin**, as a youngster, falls in love with redhead Moira Shearer, and although he marries a brunette, through the years he has a number of affairs, always with a redhead, each played by Shearer. It's only as a very old gent that he discovers how much his non-redhead wife means to him.

ST. QUINTON, JIMMY
JIMMY (1916, Silent, GB, Gaumont)—**John Astley**, the crooked son of a patriotic banker, enlists in the service during WWI, is wounded, decorated for bravery and comes home a changed man.

SAITO
SECRET AGENT OF JAPAN (1942, 20th Century Fox)—**Noel Madison** appears as a brutal Japanese agent, who underestimates the American will, at least that of Shanghai nightclub owner Preston Foster, who foils Madison's dastardly plans.

SAKNUSSEMM, WANDA
ALIENS FROM L.A. (1988, Cannon)—Mousy Valley girl **Kathy Ireland** heads to Africa to locate her missing explorer father.

SAL
SAL OF SINGAPORE (1929, Pathe)—When sea Captain Alan Hale finds an abandoned baby in a lifeboat on his ship, he abducts waterfront prostitute **Phyllis Haver** to care for the child. Trying to save the little tyke's life when it becomes sick with a fever brings Hale and Haver together. She abandons her old calling and the threesome become a family.

SALEM, SISSY
FORGOTTEN WOMEN (1932, Monogram)—Stage actress **Virginia Lee Corbin**, reduced to playing extra roles in films, is one of two women forgotten by newspaper reporter Rex Bell. He throws over Corbin for Marion Shilling, a publisher's daughter. But by the end of the film he's thrown over Shilling to take up with Corbin again.

SALINGER, MICKI & MAUDE
MICKI AND MAUDE (1984, Columbia)—**Ann Reinking** and **Amy Irving** each marry Dudley Moore and present him with a baby, born in the same hospital, at precisely the same time. When they become aware of each other, it is fair to say they are not pleased with Moore.

SALLY
AUNT SALLY (1933, GB, Gainsborough/Gaumont)—Stage-struck **Cicely Courtneidge** poses as a French star in order to save an American club owner from gangsters.

SALLY
THE CARDBOARD LOVER (1928, Silent, Universal)—**Marion Davies** is hired by tennis star Nils Asther to keep him away from gold-digger Jetta Goudal to whom he's attracted. Davies does such a good job, she scores love with Asther—or should that be an ace?

SALLY
DANCE, GIRL, DANCE (1933, Invincible)—**Evalyn Knapp** is deserted by her vaudeville partner and husband Edward Nugent. She is helped financially by a cabaret owner when she gives birth to a child. Nugent shows up and makes amends and we have a happy ending.

SALLY
FRISCO SAL (1945, Universal)—New Englander **Susanna Foster** goes to California to avenge the death of her brother.

SALLY
GALLANT LADY (1934, UA)—**Ann Harding** gives another one of her patented portrayals of a mother who will do anything for her children. In this one, she's an unmarried mother who must give up her son for adoption. Five years later she comes across her son again, and as coincidence would have it, the boy's adoptive dad is now a widower. A five-year-old child could write the ending to this one.

SALLY
I AM A GROUPIE (1970, GB, Eagle Films)—**Esme Johns** becomes the sexual plaything of a British rock group, hooked on drugs and passed around as casually as if she was a reefer being shared.

SALLY

SALLY (1925, Silent, First National); (1929, Warner Brothers)—**Colleen Moore** and **Marilyn Miller** appear as the orphaned waitress who finally sees her name in lights on Broadway. The 1929 movie featured Jerome Kern's music.

SALLY

SALLY OF THE SAWDUST (1925, Silent, UA)—**Carol Dempster** doesn't know that the circus juggler and conman W.C. Fields, whom she considers her father, adopted her when she was a baby.

SALLY

THE SECRET OF MADAME BLANCHE (1933, MGM)—**Irene Dunne** takes the blame for a murder committed by Douglas Walton, who doesn't realize she's the mother he never knew.

SALLY

SHE HAD TO CHOOSE (1934, Majestic)—Poor orphan **Isabel Jewell** marries Regis Toomey, even though she loves Buster Crabbe. Crabbe kills Toomey, and gets away with it to marry Jewell.

SALLY

SUMMER SCHOOL TEACHERS (1977, New World)—Art teacher **Pat Anderson** allows a student to take nude pictures of her. They are published in a magazine and result in her suspension.

SALLY

TOO MANY WIVES (1933, GB, Warner Brothers)—Maid **Viola Keats** is forced into service acting as businessman Jack Hobbs' wife when just prior to a dinner with an important client, his wife Nora Swinburne runs out on him. She comes back in time to muddy the water.

SALLY

THE VAGABOND QUEEN (1931, GB, Wardour)—In a female Prisoner of Zenda-like story, **Betty Balfour** portrays both a princess and her cockney double, who is crowned to thwart rebels.

SALLY

WHERE'S SALLY (1936, GB, Warner Brothers)—While on her honeymoon, **Renee Gadd** learns of her husband's past and runs away.

SALOME

SALOME (1922, Silent, Allied Productions & Distributors); (1953, Columbia)—**Nazimova** and **Rita Hayworth** both perform the dance of the seven veils for Herod, but Nazimova is delighted when John the Baptist's head is delivered on a silver platter as a reward, while Hayworth is shocked and sickened.

SALOME

SALOME, WHERE SHE DANCED (1945, Universal)—Beautiful Viennese dancer **Yvonne De Carlo** matches wits with a gang of outlaws in Drinkman's Wells, Arizona. It's not her logic that wins her points, however.

SALOME/ROSE

SALOME'S LAST DANCE (1988, Vestron)—**Imogen Millais-Scott**, a servant girl in a male brothel, portrays Salome in a special production of Oscar Wilde's work for the author and his lover "Bosie" in this salute to Wilde by director Ken Russell.

SALOMY JANE

SALOMY JANE (1914, Silent, California Motion Pictures); (1923, Silent, Paramount)—**Beatrix Michelena** and **Jacqueline Logan** appear as the western girl who helps a stranger escape being lynched by vigilantes when she gives him what is supposed to be a farewell kiss.

SALSBURY, JANICE

HATER OF MEN (1917, Silent, Triangle)—When reporter **Bessie Barriscale** covers the sensational divorce trial of a man who had numerous mistresses, she believes marriage is a mistake. She returns her fiance's engagement ring and begins living a bohemian life. She later sees the errors of her ways and marries.

SALT, CHARLES

SALT & PEPPER (1968, GB, UA)—**Sammy Davis, Jr.** and his partner in a nightclub, Peter Lawford, thwart a plot to take over Britain by hijacking a Polaris submarine.

SALVATION JANE

SALVATION JANE (1927, Silent, R-C Pictures)—Tenement girl **Viola Dana** becomes involved with a crook, when he offers to pay for her grandfather's medical bills if she will help him in his "work." Ultimately, the two decide to go straight and marry.

SALVATORE

A MAN ABOUT THE HOUSE (1947, GB, British Lion)—Butler **Kieron Moore** plans to kill his two rich spinster employers.

SAM

BORN TO KILL (1947, RKO)—Psychotic **Lawrence Tierney** involves his new wife Audrey Long in his criminal endeavors. He's encouraged by Long's sister Claire Trevor to kill his wife. He just about does, but shoots Trevor instead and then is gunned down by the police.

SAM

DOUBLING FOR ROMEO (1921, Silent, Goldwyn)—Arizona cowboy **Will Rogers's** love for Sylvia Breamer is going nowhere because she wants him to love her like Romeo loved Juliet. He has a dream in which he and his friends appear in the Romeo and Juliet story. When he awakens, he knows just what to do.

SAM

IMMEDIATE FAMILY (1989, Columbia)—When his girlfriend Mary Stuart Masterson gets pregnant, hoodish **Kevin Dillon** is more than willing to make childless couple Glenn Close and James Woods happy by letting them adopt the baby. By the time the child arrives, things are a little different.

SAM

JACK, SAM AND PETE (1919, Silent, GB, Pollock-Daring)—**Eddie Willey** is one of three cowpokes who rescue a kidnapped child.

SAM

THE LOST BOYS (1987, Warner Brothers)—**Corey Haim** is a member of a small California town teenage gang, all of whom are vampires.

SAM

THE OPTIMISTS (1973, GB, Paramount)—Street entertainer **Peter Sellers** takes two tough kids in hand in a minor and forgettable musical.

SAMANTHA

HEAVENLY BODIES (1985, Universal)—**Cynthia Dale** combines aerobics and songs, but neither will help audiences get through this loser.

SAMANTHA

NAPOLEON AND SAMANTHA (1972, Buena Vista)—**Jodie Foster** and Johnny Whittaker are two cute kids who run away from their farm community with an aging lion.

SAMIRA

PROGRAMMED TO KILL (1987, Trans World)—After PLO terrorist **Sandahl Bergman** is killed by the CIA, she is revived when computer chips are implanted in her brain, making her a killing machine for the "Company."

SAMMY

SAMMY AND ROSIE GET LAID (1987, GB, Cinecom)—When a powerful reactionary Indian government figure arrives in London to visit his son, **Ayub Khan Din**, the elder man cannot understand his son's life style, particularly his open sexual relationships.

SAMSON

BLACK SAMSON (1974, Warner Brothers)—**Rockne Tarkington** is a leader of a black neighborhood, fighting the efforts of a white gangster to exploit it as fresh territory for drugs.

SAMSON

SAMSON (1914, Silent, Universal); SAMSON AND DELILAH (1949, Paramount)—**J. Warren Kerrigan** and **Victor Mature** each played the Bible hero who lost his strength when given a haircut by Delilah, but gained it back long enough to pull down the temple of the Philistines on himself and his enemies.

SAMUEL

WITNESS (1985, Paramount)—Young Pennsylvannia Dutch boy **Lukas Haas** witnesses a murder committed by a cop. Police detective Harrison Ford hides out in the Amish community with Haas' family to protect the boy and his beautiful widow mother, Kelly McGillis. The film is rather violent at the end but you might find yourself cheering when the bad guys get theirs.

SAMUELS, FEET

A VERY HONORABLE GUY (1934, Warner Brothers)—**Joe E. Brown** finds himself in debt to very mean gamblers. Figuring he's a gone goose anyway, he sells his body to a mad scientist and pays off his debt. He still has one little problem.

SAND, LOU ANDREAS

PUZZLE OF A DOWNFALL CHILD (1970, Universal)—When a photographer interviews former model **Faye Dunaway**, she gives him the low-down on the seamier aspects of the profession.

SANDERS, INSPECTOR HARRY (R.G.)

SANDERS OF THE RIVER (1935, GB, UA); SANDERS (1969, GB, Hallam/ Planet)—In these tributes to the "white man's burden," civil servant commissioner Sanders, played by **Leslie Banks** and **Richard Todd**, keep the African natives in line with the help of tribal chiefs.

SANDERS, JIM

DATE WITH AN ANGEL (1987, De Laurentiis)—**Michael E. Knight**, an aspiring musician about to be married and employed in his future father-in-law's cosmetics factory, has his life changed when broken-winged angel Emmanuelle Beart crashes into his pool.

SANDERS, NELL

SALVATION NELL (1921, Silent, Associated First National)—Unmarried slum mother **Pauline Starke** joins the Salvation Army and distinguishes herself as a speaker. She has to choose between her superior and her former lover, now out of jail, for her husband. She chooses the father of her child, when he promises to become a good Christian.

SANDERS, PHEMIE

THE MAN HATER (1917, Silent, Triangle)—**Winifred Allen** comes to hate all men after growing up around her drunken father. She agrees to marry the village blacksmith in a union sans sex. He figures she'll come around if he's just patient. A year later, he's lost his patience and starts seeing a widow woman. This does the trick. Allen and her husband finally consummate their marriage.

SANDERSON, JIM

HER MAN O' WAR (1926, Silent, De Mille)—**William Boyd** poses as a deserter from the American troops in a German village during WWI, so he can gather strategic information about the enemy. He falls in love with a German girl, Jetta Goudal, who runs a farm at which he is staying. She is torn between her love for him and her country. Boyd and Goudal are ordered before a firing squad, but are saved by the arrival of the Americans.

SANDHAM, JOHNNY

OH JOHNNY, HOW YOU CAN LOVE (1940, Universal)—Handsome young **Tom Brown** has all the girls aflutter in this "B" musical.

SANDMAN, ALICE

THE LITTLEST HORSE THIEVES (1977, Buena Vista)—**Chloe Franks** and two young boys steal nine ponies to save them from abuse and death. It's a nice little story, set in England around the turn of the century.

SANDRA

NIGHT CALL NURSES (1974, New World)—**Mittie Lawrence** is one of the sexy nurses in this drive-in exploitation film, which is not to be taken seriously.

SANDRA

PROSTITUTE (1980, GB, Kestrel)—Birmingham prostitute **Eleanor Forsythe** joins an activist group, seeking to reform the laws dealing with her business. She moves on to become a London call girl.

SANDRIDGE, LORD RICHARD

LORD RICHARD IN THE PANTRY (1930, GB, Warner Brothers)—English lord **Richard Cooper** poses as a butler to prevent being framed for a theft.

SANDS, BRUCE

OCCASIONALLY YOURS (1920, Silent, R-C Pictures)—**Lew Cody**, trying to make a dying girl's last moments happy, promises to marry her, and then she survives.

SANDWICH MAN, THE

THE SANDWICH MAN (1966, GB, Rank)—The film traces one day's adventures of London sandwich man **John Le Mesurier**.

SANDY

LEAVE IT TO ME (1937, GB, British Lion); I'VE GOT A HORSE (1938, GB, British Lion)—In the first film, special constable **Sandy Powell** is dismissed from the Constabulary when he's drugged by Chinese crooks, but wins back his job when he recovers a famous stolen jewel. In the second film, newly married Powell takes a horse as payment on a bad debt, and decides to race it. However, the horse, trained in a circus to do tricks, has other ideas.

SANDY

SANDY GETS HER MAN (1940, Universal); SANDY IS A LADY (1940, Universal)—In the first movie, **Baby Sandy** gets to choose when both a policeman and a fireman ask her widow mother to marry them. In the second feature, the two-year old brings good luck to those around her.

SANFORD, BILL

SPEED MAD (1925, Silent, Columbia)—Motorcycle nut **William Fairbanks** enjoys outracing motorcycle cops. His antics get him thrown out of his father's home, but all is forgiven when he wins a big race, and foils the plot of a crook to steal his fiancee's land.

SANGER, TESS (TESSA)

THE CONSTANT NYMPH (1933, GB, Gaumont/Fox); (1943, Warner Brothers)—**Victoria Hopper** and **Joan Fontaine** each portray the sickly schoolgirl, in love with a composer, who doesn't realize how much she means to him until it's too late.

SANGSTER, BOB

HELL'S HEROES (1930, Universal)—**Charles Bickford** stars in this version of the frequently filmed "The Three Godfathers." He and two other outlaws on the run from the law come across a dying woman and her newborn baby in the desert. They promise to get the child to its father in New Jerusalem, the town where they just robbed the bank. All three die, but Bickford is able to get the child to the town just as church bells are tolling the Christmas services.

SANTA CLAUS

SANTA CLAUS CONQUERS THE MARTIANS (1964, Embassy); HERE COMES SANTA CLAUS (1984, New World); SANTA CLAUS THE MOVIE (1986, Tri-Star)-**John Call**, **Armand Meffre** and **David Huddleston** each had a go at the part of the jolly old elf, but children who believe in Santa Claus should not be exposed to these inane movies, and neither should their parents. That leaves teenagers and reindeer.

SANTANA

AMERICAN ME (1992, Universal)—As a 16-year-old (played by **Panchito Gomez**), **Edward James Olmos** formed a gang with his buddies. Later in Folsom prison, Olmos and his Mexican Mafia buddy William Forsythe are men of respect, but they must resort to acts of great brutality and murder to maintain their positions of power.

SANTE FE

THE KID FROM SANTE FE (1940, Monogram)—When the sheriff calls on **Jack Randall** for some help in capturing smugglers, our hero gets the job done in 57 minutes, and still has time to win the sheriff's daughter.

SANTE, JOE

I, MOBSTER (1959, 20th Century Fox)—**Steve Cochran** moves up the criminal ladder from modest beginnings as a collector for bookies, to a drug pusher, then a white collar criminal in a high syndicate position, and at long last, crime czar. As there's no retirement in his line of work, when he proves to be a liability, a contract is put out on him.

SANTEE

SANTEE (1973, Crown International)—Bounty hunter **Glenn Ford** befriends the son of a man he killed. It's Ford at his most violent.

SANTOS, LUIS

THE MAGNIFICENT MATADOR (1955, 20th Century Fox)—Veteran matador **Anthony Quinn** feels he has received a premonition of death, and so leaves Mexico City and the bullring. He's pursued by American Maureen O'Hara with whom he has a brief romance before returning to the bullring in glory with a young matador, whom he acknowledges to be his illegitimate son. A few years earlier, such an admission in a movie would be a death sentence.

SANTOS, ROBERTO

LATIN LOVERS (1953, MGM)—Heiress Lana Turner, on holiday in Brazil, is looking for a man who will love her for herself and not her money. **Ricardo Montalban** is able to convince her that she'd be just as attractive if she had only one mink coat.

SAP, THE

THE SAP (1929, Warner Brothers)—Daydreamer **Edward Everett Horton** takes the blame for an embezzlement scheme, and uses the money to make a killing in the stock market. He puts the misdirected funds back before anyone discovers the crime. No harm, no foul, we guess.

SAPPINGTON, CLAUDE

HIS DARKER SELF (1924, Silent, G and H Pictures)—Black-face entertainer and mystery writer **Lloyd Hamilton** infiltrates and captures a gang of black bootleggers. Racist? Oh, yes.

SARA/LAURA

SLEEPING WITH THE ENEMY (1991, 20th Century Fox) Abused physically and mentally by her husband Patrick Bergen, **Julia Roberts** fakes her own death and runs away to a small Iowa college town with a new identity. Her husband catches on and comes to look for her.

SARA, SISTER

TWO MULES FOR SISTER SARA (1970, Universal)—Wandering cowboy Clint Eastwood comes to the rescue of nun **Shirley MacLaine** who is in danger of being raped by three men. He feels responsible for her, but it turns out she's a prostitute, trying to get help for Mexican revolutionaries against the French troops of Maximilian.

SARAH

CHILDREN OF THE CORN (1984, New World)—**Annemarie McEvoy** is one of the murderous adolescents who have taken over a town. It's a nightmarish fantasy from a story by Stephen King.

SARAH

EVERY TIME WE SAY GOODBYE (1986, Tri-Star)—Sephardic Jew **Cristina Marsillach** falls in love with American pilot Tom Hanks in Jerusalem during WWII.

SARAH

THE FRENCH LIEUTENANT'S WOMAN (1981, UA)—**Meryl Streep** is the abandoned mistress of a French seaman. British gentleman Jeremy Irons forsakes his fiancee for Streep. The story set in 1867 Lyme Regis, has a modern counterpart in which Streep and Irons are actors, married to others, making the film of THE FRENCH LIEUTENANT'S WOMAN and having an affair on the side. Irons takes it more seriously than does Streep.

SARAH

SEVEN BRIDES FOR SEVEN BROTHERS (1954, MGM)—**Betty Carr** is one of the six kidnapped young women, meant to be brides for six wild mountain brothers.

SARDONICUS

MR. SARDONICUS (1961, Columbia)—**Guy Rolfe**'s face has been frozen in a perpetual grin ever since he opened his father's grave to get at a winning lottery ticket. His wife Audrey Dalton lures her former lover, Ronald Lewis, a famous surgeon, to their remote home to repair the damage.

SARGE

A MAN CALLED SARGE (1990, Cannon)—**Gary Kroeger** leads a company of American soldiers against the Germans in the North African campaign of WWII. It's meant to be a comedy, but the jokes are worse than the enemies.

SARGE

SARGE GOES TO COLLEGE (1947, Monogram)—Dumb, tough marine sergeant **Alan Hale, Jr.** goes to college, to allow the producers of this meager musical to put on some old college routines. The film features numerous musical stars and many songs including the novelty hit: "Open the Door, Richard."

SARGEANT, LAURA

A MOST IMMORAL LADY (1929, First National)—When her husband is wiped out in the stock market crash, **Leatrice Joy** helps her mate blackmail various men. She falls in love with one of the intended victims, but fails to save him from her husband's plots. She runs off to Paris, gets a divorce and becomes a cafe singer. She even takes a gigolo for a lover. After all of this, she gets back with the man she really loves, whoever that is.

SARGENT, ROSE

ROSE OF WASHINGTON SQUARE (1939, 20th Century Fox)—**Alice Faye** is clearly portraying a character very much like Fanny Brice. At least Brice thought so and sued. She settled out of court. In case there's any doubt, Faye's biggest song in the film is Brice's "My Man."

SARI

THE WHIP WOMAN (1928, Silent, First National)—Peasant **Estelle Taylor** has quite a way with a whip. She saves Hungarian nobleman Antonio Moreno from suicide. She marries him even though his mother doesn't approve of her.

SARI, COUNTESS THURZO

THE STOLEN BRIDE (1927, Silent, First National)—During WWI, Hungarian noblewoman **Billie Dove** falls in love with American-reared commoner Lloyd Hughes. They escape to the U.S. to start a new life as equals.

SARIA

PREHISTORIC WOMEN (1967, GB, 20th Century Fox)—**Edina Ronay** is one of a group of Amazon women in Africa, who enslave hunter Michael Latimer. The story is pure fantasy.

SARTO, LITTLE JOHN

BROTHER ORCHID (1940, First National/Warner Brothers) - Mobster **Edward G. Robinson** is taken for a ride by Humphrey Bogart and the boys. He survives and recovers at a monastery where he becomes a monk who raises orchids.

SATIN, BARNEY

THE DEVIL AND MAX DEVLIN (1981, Buena Vista)—Devil **Bill Cosby** offers unscrupulous apartment manager Elliott Gould a chance to escape hell after he's killed in a bus accident. He must deliver three young souls within two months.

SAUNDERS, BILL

KING OF HEARTS (1936, GB, Butchers)—Dock worker **Will Fyffe's** waitress daughter Gwenllian Gill loves rich Richard Dolman. The lad's mother causes Gill to lose her job, and tries to bribe Fyffe into helping break up the romance. Fyffe is too wily for her, and the wedding comes off as planned.

SAUNDERS, COLT, LORNA HUNTER & CINCH

THREE VIOLENT PEOPLE (1956, Paramount)—**Charlton Heston** brings his new bride, **Anne Baxter**, home after the Civil War to the family ranch, where she causes romantic stirrings in Heston's brother **Tom Tryon**.

SAUNDERS, DAISY

WOMEN IN PRISON (1938, Columbia)—**Mayo Methot** goes to prison after a robbery. She's the only member of the gang to know where the loot is hidden. One of her partners goes to great lengths to try to set her free, but nothing works.

SAUNDERS, JIMMY

ENEMY AGENT (1940, Universal)—After being framed as a spy, **Richard Cromwell** sets out to find the real enemy agents.

SAUNDERS, MARIE "OKLAHOMA"

THE OKLAHOMA WOMAN (1956, Sunset)—Dressed in a mud-splattered, low-cut gown, **Peggy Castle** faces Cathy Downs in a pistol showdown over Richard Denning. Castle is the villain who has framed Denning with murder.

SAUNDERS, MARILYN

MARILYN (1953, GB, Butchers)—**Sandra Dorne's** husband is killed by his employee, a garage mechanic in love with her.

SAUNDERS, "SKY-HIGH"

"SKY-HIGH" SAUNDERS (1927, Silent, Universal)—Stunt pilot **Al Wilson** plays twin brothers, one an ace flyer. He takes his smuggler brother's place after mistakenly shooting him down. Wilson bombs the smuggler's hideout with dynamite.

SAUNDERS, SUNDOWN

SUNDOWN SAUNDERS (1937, Supreme)—**Bob Steele** wins a ranch in a pony race, but keeping it is another matter.

SAUNDERS, WILD BILL

THE RETURN OF WILD BILL (1940, Columbia)—**Bill Elliott** is out to revenge his father's death. The only hitch is that the man responsible is the brother of the girl he loves.

SAVAARD, DR. HENRYK

THE MAN THEY COULD NOT HANG (1939, Columbia)—Convicted of murder, **Boris Karloff** is hanged, but brought back to life with a mechanical heart when it is discovered that he's innocent. Now Karloff's angry. He sets out to kill the jurors who sentenced him to death.

SAVAGE, DOC

DOC SAVAGE...THE MAN OF BRONZE (1975, Warner Brothers)—**Ron Ely** portrays the 1930s superman, who with his assistants, the Amazing Five, goes to South America to avenge his father's death.

SAVAGE, JOHN

WHO KILLED JOHN SAVAGE? (1937, GB, Warner Brothers)—**Nicholas Hannen**, the head of a chemical firm, fakes his death in order to collect his insurance.

SAVAGE, M/SGT. MURPHY

IMITATION GENERAL (1958, MGM)—In 1944 France, when an American general is killed, sergeant **Glenn Ford** takes his place to maintain the men's morale.

SAVELLI, PAUL

DADDY (1923, Silent, First National)—Violinist **Arthur Carewe** separates from his wife and loses all track of his son Jackie Coogan.

When Coogan's mother dies, the boy runs away and is befriended by a street musician, who had instructed Coogan's father, now a renowned musician, and reunites Coogan and Carewe.

SAVOY
BORN AMERICAN (1986, Cinema Group)—**Mike Norris** is one of three young Americans, vacationing in Finland, who accidentally stray into the Soviet Union. They must fight it out with Russian soldiers.

SAWYER, SALLY
TOO YOUNG TO KNOW (1945, Warner Brothers)—When her ex-husband Robert Hutton comes home from military service, **Joan Leslie** greets him with the news that she has literally given their child away.

SAWYER, SETH
THE DIRTY DOZEN (1967, GB, MGM)—Soldier-prisoner **Colin Maitland** and eleven others are given the chance to die gallantly in a behind-the-enemy-lines suicide mission, rather than rot in a military prison. Well, he dies.

SAWYER, TOM
TOM SAWYER (1930, Paramount); (1973, UA); THE ADVENTURES OF TOM SAWYER (1939, Selznick); HUCK AND TOM (1918, Silent, Paramount); TOM SAWYER, DETECTIVE—**Jackie Coogan, Johnny Whittaker, Tommy Kelly, Jack Pickford,** and **Billy Cook** appeared as that All-American boy, Tom Sawyer, perhaps Mark Twain's most endearing character. Each in their own way was good as the boy who is sweet on Becky Thacker and in trouble with Injun Joe. But our personal favorite is Tommy Kelly.

SAWYER, WALLY
I SPY (1933, GB, British International)—In this spoof, playboy **Ben Lyon** is mistaken for a spy by the secret service of a tiny mythical European country. He falls for Sally Eilers, who turns out to be the superspy everyone is looking for.

SCANLAN, JACK
PASSED AWAY (1992, Hollywood Pictures)—In a black comedy, **Jack Warden** brings his family of eccentrics together by dying.

SCANLON, MIKE
HERE COMES THE GROOM (1934, Paramount)—**Jack Haley** poses as a heiress's husband to help her out of a romantic jam. He finds himself blamed for the theft of her mother's jewels.

SCARAMANGA
THE MAN WITH THE GOLDEN GUN (1974, GB, UA)—Professional assassin **Christopher Lee**, working out of the Orient, has a solar-operated gun which could destroy the world. Not to worry, Bond is there.

SCARAMOUCHE
SCARAMOUCHE (1923, Silent, Metro); (1952, MGM)—**Ramon Novarro** and **Stewart Granger** each masquerade as a bumbling stage clown to avenge the death of a friend at the hands of a wicked marquis in France in the 18th century. The sword fight in the sound film between Granger and Mel Ferrer as the marquis lasted 6 1/2 film minutes, probably a record.

SCARLETT, CAPT.
CAPTAIN SCARLETT (1953, UA)—With the help of a runaway princess and a highwayman **Richard Greene** champions the cause of justice against tyranny in post-Napoleonic France.

SCARLETT, SYLVIA
SYLVIA SCARLETT (1936, RKO)—**Katharine Hepburn** poses as a boy in order to escape to France with her larcenous father. Films like this were enough to end careers of less talented actresses.

SCARLETT, WILL
MEN OF SHERWOOD FOREST (1957, GB, Hammer)—**John Van Eyssen** is Robin Hood's right-hand man, when Sir Robert of Locksley and his band rob from the rich to give to the poor.

SCHAEFER, DR. SIDNEY
THE PRESIDENT'S ANALYST (1967, Paramount)—Psychiatrist **James Coburn** treats the President of the United States. Agents of every country are out to find what he's learned from the chief executive.

SCHILLER, INA
FOUR GIRLS IN TOWN (1956, Universal)—German international beauty **Marianne Cook** is competing for the title role in a Hollywood movie.

SCHLAINE, TILLIE
PETE 'N' TILLIE (1972, Universal)—Lonely **Carol Burnett** meets and falls in love with loner Walter Matthau. They marry and have a son, who dies, setting up a real test for their marriage.

SCHLOCKTHROPUS, THE
SCHLOCK (1972, Gazotskie/Harris)—In this spoof of "B" horror movies, the missing link, **John Landis**, is loose in a small town.

SCHMID, AL
PRIDE OF THE MARINES (1948, Warner Brothers)—In this sudsy tear-jerker, **John Garfield** is a marine, blinded in combat, who must learn to adjust to his loss.

SCHMIDT, ADELINE
SWEET ADELINE (1926, Silent, Chadwick); (1935, Warner Brothers)—In the silent feature, **Gertrude Olmstead** is the prettiest girl in town and the object of affections of singer Charles Ray. He made a living in silent pictures playing country bumpkins. In the second feature, **Irene Dunne** is the main attraction of her father's beer garden, where she gets to sing several Jerome Kern and Oscar Hammerstein II songs.

SCHMIDT, ANDY
THE ONE AND ONLY (1978, Paramount)—Stage-struck egomaniac **Henry Winkler** finds success at the expense of his happiness with his wife, Kim Darby.

SCHMIDT, SUSIE
LADIES IN LOVE (1936, 20th Century Fox)—**Loretta Young** and two other young Budapest girls pool their resources hoping to attract rich suitors. Young falls for wealthy nobleman Tyrone Power, but he must marry someone of his own class. She considers taking poison, but consoles herself by opening a hat shop.

SCHNEIDER
CONFESSIONS OF A NAZI SPY (1939, Warner Brothers)—In this semi-documentary styled movie, German-American **Francis Lederer** offers to spy for the Nazis, but he's ferreted out by G-men, headed by Edward G. Robinson.

SCHOFIELD, CHESTER
THOSE DARING YOUNG MEN IN THEIR JAUNTY JALOPIES (1969, GB/France/Italy, Paramount)—**Tony Curtis** is the heroic American competing in a Monte Carlo road rally early in the century.

SCHOFIELD, LEON
OUR LEADING CITIZEN (1939, Paramount)—Lawyer **Bob Burns** and his daughter Susan Hayward are temporarily at odds with his junior partner Joseph Allen, Jr., who has taken ruthless industrialist Gene Lockhart as a client.

SCHOFIELD, PENROD
PENROD (1922, Silent, Associated First National); PENROD AND SAM (1923, Silent, Associated First National); (1931, First National); (1937, Warner Brothers) PENROD AND HIS TWIN BROTHER (1938, Warner Brothers); PENROD'S DOUBLE TROUBLE (1938, Warner Brothers)—**Wesley Barry, Ben Alexander, Leon Janney** and **Billy Mauch** each appeared as Booth Tarkington's mischievous All-American boy whose various pranks are supposed to set audiences laughing. Something must have got lost in the translation from the printed page to the silver screen.

SCHOTTLAND, GENERAL ALEX
THE TWO-HEADED SPY (1959, GB, Columbia)—In a true story, **Jack Hawkins** is a British spy, serving on the German general staff during the period 1939-1945.

SCHREBER, BIANCA
THE CRIMSON RUNNER (1925, Silent, PDC)—Daredevil Viennese thief **Priscilla Dean** heads a band of crooks to steal from the rich to feed the poor.

SCHRECK, DR. SANDOR
DR. TERROR'S HOUSE OF HORRORS (1965, GB, Amicus)—Death personified, **Peter Cushing**, predicts the demise of five fellow train passengers by voodoo, werewolf, creeping vine, vampire and a severed hand.

SCHULTZ, CHERIE
HER MAN O' WAR (1926, Silent, DeMille)—German **Jetta Goudal** falls in love with American deserter William Boyd during WWI. He is sending messages to his American comrades about German strength. Goudal and her lover are about to be executed by the Germans when American troops arrive and rescue them.

SCHULTZ, DUTCH
PORTRAIT OF A MOBSTER (1961, Warner Brothers)—**Vic Morrow** portrays violent twenties gangster Dutch Schultz. It's almost a parody of the subgenre.

SCHULTZ, LENA
A LADY TO LOVE (1930, MGM)—Waitress **Vilma Banky** receives a proposal of marriage by letter with a photograph of Robert Ames. The latter is the assistant of aging grape grower Edward G. Robinson, the one actually asking for her hand. She agrees but is shocked when she discovers Robinson's deception. She has a brief affair with Ames, but comes to love Robinson.

SCHULTZ, NORA
THE NEAR LADY (1923, Silent, Universal)—**Gladys Walton**, daughter of an inventor of a sausage-making machine, pretends to be having a romance with the son of a prominent local family to please her father, but soon the two find they no longer have to pretend.

SCHULTZ, PAULA
THE WICKED DREAMS OF PAULA SCHULTZ (1968, UA)—East German athlete **Elke Sommer** is helped to defect to the West by an American.

SCHULTZENBACH, HILDA
HIS FOREIGN WIFE (1927, Silent, Pathe Exchange)—German bride **Greta von Rue** is the victim of her father-in-law's bitterness over the death of one of his sons in WWI, when his other son brings her home after the war.

SCHUMAN, ANNA
DEALERS (1989, Rank)—When a leading trader for the London branch of an American bank kills himself, **Rebecca DeMornay** is sent from New York to compete for the job with hot-shot trader Paul McGann.

SCHUYLER, ANNE
PLATINUM BLONDE (1931, Columbia)—Snobbish society girl **Jean Harlow** loses her wisecracking reporter husband Robert Williams to fellow reporter Loretta Young.

SCHWECK
SCHWECK'S NEW ADVENTURES (1943, GB, Eden/Coronet)—Humorist **Lloyd Pearson** becomes the bodyguard of a Gestapo chief. He saves his friends from a concentration camp.

SCHWEITZER, ALBERT
SCHWEITZER (1990, Concorde)—**Malcom McDowell** impersonates the famous philosopher-musician-doctor in a fictional episode in his life set in 1947. The good doctor's ways of doing things don't satisfy his various sponsors, but no one is going to tell him how to run his French Congo hospital.

SCISSORHANDS, EDWARD
EDWARD SCISSORHANDS (1990, 20th Century Fox)—In a delightful fantasy directed by Tim Burton, **Johnny Depp** is the creation of inventor Vincent Price, who dies before he can replace Depp's five-fingered, foot-long blades with normal hands. Depp is rescued from his isolation in a gloomy mansion by Avon lady Dianne Wiest, who takes him to her suburban home and family. As everyone in the neighborhood is remarkably strange, Depp is initially accepted and even welcomed for his talents in trimming hedges and hair. But when he falls in love with Winona Ryder, one-time loveable nerd Anthony Michael Hall, the villain of the piece, ends the fairy tale.

SCOT, NANCE
THE GOODBYE PEOPLE (1984, Embassy)—**Pamela Reed** and Judd Hirsch help Martin Balsam realize his long-time dream of re-opening his Coney Island hot dog stand.

SCOTT, PRESIDENT ADAM
THE KIDNAPPING OF THE PRESIDENT (1980, Canada, Crown International)—President **Hal Holbrook** is kidnapped by terrorists and held captive in a remote location. It's a highly suspenseful film.

SCOTT, BABE
THE ANGEL OF BROADWAY (1927, Silent, Pathe Exchange)—**Leatrice Joy** upsets her boyfriend, when as part of her nightclub act, she performs in a Salvation Army uniform. Joy later will redeem herself and is reunited with her sweetheart.

SCOTT, BLIVENS
MY SIX CONVICTS (1952, Columbia)—**Marshall Thompson**, a hard-drinking baseball player, wrongly imprisoned when he takes the blame for a crime committed by his girlfriend, is one of six prison inmates who tell their troubles to the new prison psychologist John Beal.

SCOTT, CARNELLE

MISS FIRECRACKER (1989, Corsair)—Known locally as "Miss Hot Tamale," **Holly Hunter** desperately wishes to be selected "Miss Firecracker" at Yazoo City, Mississippi's annual Fourth of July pageant.

SCOTT, DIANA

DARLING (1965, GB, Embassy)—**Julie Christie** is an amoral (all right immoral) girl, who deserts her journalistic mentor Dirk Bogarde for company director Laurence Harvey, moves from him to a bisexual photographer and then marries an Italian prince. Christie was the ideal model for what many thought was the trendy Sixties girl, all wild hair and wild legs, ready to bed down with any male she fancied. Her performance won her an Oscar and the movie was highly praised, but even though Christie's portrayal and the movie are both strangely enjoyable, it's difficult to say that either are of much real significance.

SCOTT, JULIA

SHE MARRIED HER BOSS (1935, Columbia)—Secretary **Claudette Colbert** marries her boss Melvyn Douglas, but then feels she's taken for granted.

SCOTT, MALCOLM *See* JOHN EVANS

SCOTT, COL. MARION

THE MAN WHO WALKED ALONE (1945, PRC)—Returning soldier **David O'Brien** is mistaken for a deserter before it is shown that in fact he's a war hero.

SCOTT, MARY

NO SAD SONGS FOR ME (1950, Columbia)—When she discovers that she has only eight months to live, **Margaret Sullavan** uses her time to plan her husband's future. Sullavan may be dying, but her disease does not ravish her loveliness.

SCOTT, MICHAEL

CIRCUS BOY (1947, GB, GFD)—Schoolboy swimmer **James Kenney** loses his nervousness after becoming a circus clown.

SCOTT, CAPT. ROBERT FALCON

SCOTT OF THE ANTARCTIC (1949, GB, Ealing)—**John Mills** is most impressive in his portrayal of the tragic explorer whose 1912 expedition to the South Pole ends in his death and that of three other men. It's a beautifully photographed movie with moving performances from all the principals.

SCOTT, COL. ROBERT L.

GOD IS MY CO-PILOT (1945, Warner Brothers)—**Dennis Morgan** stars in this WWII flagwaver about the air adventures of pilots in the Pacific.

SCOTT, SUE, HALLIE & LILY

THREE LITTLE SISTERS (1944, Republic)—**Mary Lee** is confined to a wheelchair, but doesn't tell this to the GI with whom she's been corresponding. When he comes to visit, she and her two scrubwomen sisters **Ruth Terry** and **Cheryl Walker** pretend to be socialites. He falls in love with Lee and remains so even when he learns the truth.

SCOTT, TERRY

PERFECT STRANGERS (1950, Warner Brothers)—Single **Ginger Rogers** falls in love with married Dennis Morgan while they are serving on a jury. The case just happens to be about a love-nest murder.

SCOULAR, DANNY

THE BIG MAN (1990, Miramax)—Unemployed Scottish miner **Liam Neeson** agrees to fight in a bare-knuckles match with no rules. He's already troubled because his middle-class wife Joanne Whalley-Kilmer has taken up with a chap whom she considers closer to her social status. The fight is a grueling, bloody bit of violence.

SCRATCH, MR.

THE DEVIL AND DANIEL WEBSTER (1941, RKO)—**Walter Huston** is the most charming devil in this production of the story by Stephen Vincent Benet (also called ALL THAT MONEY CAN BUY). New Hampshire farmer James Craig is given seven years of prosperity by Huston for this little thing that can't be seen, his soul. When it's time to pay up, Craig gets Edward Arnold as Daniel Webster to intercede for him. Arnold wins back Craig's soul before a court of condemned Americans. This is a magical movie, worth seeing over and over again.

SCRAWDYKE, MALCOLM

LITTLE MALCOLM (1974, GB, Apple Films)—Expelled art student **John Hurt** starts the revolutionary Party of Dynamic Erection.

SCROOGE, AIMEE

A DAUGHTER IN REVOLT (1927, Silent, GB, Allied Artists)—**Mabel Poulton**, a lord's daughter, is suspected of burglary when she exchanges places with a friend.

SCROOGE, EBENEZER

SCROOGE (1935, GB, Paramount); (1951, GB, Renown); (1970, GB, National General)—**Seymour Hicks, Alastair Sim** and **Albert Finney** each have appeared as Dickens' miserly Scrooge, who is changed on Christmas Eve by the visit of the Spirits of Christmas Past, Present and Future. Others have portrayed Scrooge in movies entitled A CHRISTMAS CAROL, but whatever the title or media, for many Alastair Sim is Ebenezer Scrooge, and it wouldn't seem like Christmas if one was to miss another look at the 1951 classic during the Yuletide season.

SCURLOCK, DOC

YOUNG GUNS (1988, 20th Century Fox); YOUNG GUNS II (1990, 20th Century Fox)—**Keifer Sutherland** is one of the five young gunslingers who join Billy the Kid as part of the Regulator unit in the Johnson County Wars in Wyoming in the 1890s. The sequel is just a continuation of the romp of a likable gang of young desperadoes.

SEA WIFE

SEA WIFE (1957, GB, 20th Century Fox)—Young nun **Joan Collins**, RAF officer Richard Burton, business tycoon Basil Sydney and black purser Cy Grant, are adrift in the Indian Ocean in 1942 after the freighter they were traveling on is sunk. Collins doesn't reveal her calling and Burton falls in love with her, even though she gives him no encouragement.

SEABO

SEABO (1978, E.O. Corporation)—**Earl Owensby** directs and stars in this story of a half-breed who is willing to take on anyone who sees red when they see an Indian. He ends up on a chain gang run by a captain who hates the Indians. Owensby escapes when the sadistic warden plans a massacre of the prisoners.

SEABROOK, JULIA

THREE HEARTS FOR JULIA (1943, MGM)—Melvyn Douglas goes acourting once again when his wife **Ann Sothern** threatens to leave him for taking her for granted.

SEACROFT, RUTH

DEAR WIFE (1949, Paramount)—In the sequel to DEAR RUTH, **Joan Caulfield** and William Holden, now married, are forced to live with her family due to the housing shortage, never a good start to a healthy marriage. While audiences were amused, the young couple had all they could handle when Caulfield's bratty sister Mona Freeman tried to set up Holden as a rival candidate to father Edward Arnold in an election for state senator.

SEAN

LONGTIME COMPANION (1990, Goldwyn)—**Mark Lamos** portrays a gay television script writer who contracts AIDS and is cared for by his lover Bruce Davison until the end comes. This is not something that might have been a script for one of the many TV hospital series of the past. It is a compelling and chilling story of love, friendship and death.

SEBASTIAN

SEBASTIAN (1968, GB, Paramount)—**Dirk Bogarde** heads an office full of women cracking a Soviet cipher. He also has some direct contact with spies as he romances some lovely ladies.

SEBASTIAN, ARCHDUKE (JACK STRAW)

JACK STRAW (1926, Silent, Paramount)—Nobleman **Robert Warwick** doesn't take his impressive lineage too seriously, but when working as a waiter, just for the experience, he's approached to pose as a lord as part of a practical joke. He jumps at the chance, because the target of the gag is a girl he's interested in. He wins her and reveals he's a phony lord, but also a real one.

SEBASTIAN, DR. GEORGE

THE MAD DOCTOR (1941, Paramount)—Psychotic physician **Basil Rathbone** marries and murders his patients until he's stopped by the former fiance of his latest bride.

SECORD, CLIFF

THE ROCKETEER (1991, Buena Vista/Disney)—A portable rocket pack invented by Howard Hughes (Terry O'Quinn) falls into the hands of **Bill Cambell**. It allows him to become a high-flying superhero, who deals with the Nazis and mobsters who want the invention for themselves.

SEDLEY, JOHN

JOHNNY HANDSOME (1989, Tri-Star)—Severely-deformed down-and-outer **Mickey Rourke** is double-crossed by his colleagues in a robbery of a New Orleans coin store. He's sent to the pen where idealistic doctor Forest Whitaker performs plastic surgery miracles, making Rourke like—well, Rourke. The good doctor believes his physical change will also result in a character change. We shall see.

SEELEY, BLOSSOM

SOMEBODY LOVES ME (1952, Paramount)—**Betty Hutton** stars in this biopic of big-time vaudeville star Blossom Seeley and her romance with her partner Benny Fields, played by Ralph Meeker. This would be Hutton's last film appearance until 1957 as the temperamental star made too many demands and the studio decided they could do without her.

SELBY, ERNEST

THE DUDE RANGER (1934, Fox)—Easterner **George O'Brien** inherits a western ranch and finds rustlers are hitting his herd. He initially suspects the father of the girl he has come to love is the ringleader, but is relieved to find the culprit to be someone else.

SELLAR, MARIGOLD

MARIGOLD (1938, GB, Associate British Films)—In Scotland in 1824, **Sophie Stewart** runs away, so she won't have to marry her father's choice for her husband. She discovers her mother was an actress.

SELTZER, PETE

PETE 'N' TILLIE (1972, Universal)—The simple story of two lonely people who meet, fall in love, marry, have a child, and lose him when he dies at nine, is made special by the performances of **Walter Matthau** and co-star Carol Burnett.

SELWYN, MURRAY

THE HARASSED HERO (1954, GB, AB-Pathe)—Rich bachelor **Guy Middleton**, recuperating in a nursing home, foils a gang of thieves after a set of counterfeit plates.

SEMPLER, HANNAH

THE GREAT MAN'S LADY (1942, Paramount)—**Barbara Stanwyck** is a 109-year-old lady reminiscing about her life as the able partner to her husband Joel McCrea, whom she encouraged in his search for oil in the West.

SENDER, THE

THE SENDER (1982, GB, Paramount)—**Zeljko Ivanek** attempts suicide by drowning but is prevented from taking his life. At the psychiatric clinic to which he's taken, he "sends" or infects his doctor and others in the hospital with the terrors that are in his mind. It takes a lot of mental discipline on the part of his physician, Kathryn Harrold, to find a cure.

SENESH, HANNA

HANNA'S WAR (1988, Cannon)—**Maruschka Detmers** stars as the Israeli heroine who during WWII was parachuted into Yugoslavia, where she was to establish escape routes for downed Allied pilots. She was captured, taken to Hungary, tortured and executed even as Soviet tanks were entering Budapest.

SENNETT, THOMAS J.

MY GIRL (1991, Columbia)—Engaging and unaffected **Macaulay Culkin** gets to give 11-year-old Anna Chlumsky her first kiss before he's called to heaven.

SEQUIN

RIVER LADY (1948, Universal)—Mississippi gambling boat owner **Yvonne De Carlo** gets involved with crooked lumber operators in this adventure drama.

SERGE IV, KING OF MOLVANIA

THE KING ON MAIN STREET (1925, Silent, Paramount)—In order to save his country from financial ruin, **Adolphe Menjou** travels to the United States to negotiate a lease of his country's oil lands. He takes time away from the negotiations to visit Coney Island where he renews an acquaintance with a girl he met in Paris, but who doesn't know he is a king. He falls in love with her, but she's happily engaged to a nice guy, so Menjou returns home and marries the royal daughter from a nearby country, which provides Molvania with a large loan as a dowry.

SERGOYEV, ANTON "TONY"

DANCERS (1987, Cannon)—Don Juan-like ballet star **Mikhail Baryshnikov** becomes infatuated with an innocent young dancer while rehearsing a screen version of "Giselle."

SERPICO, FRANK

SERPICO (1973, Paramount)—**Al Pacino** gives an obsessive performance in his portrayal of the real life New York cop, obsessed with exposing the corruption in the police force. Pacino and Serpico are both intense individuals and the combination in this movie is powerful.

SETH-SMITH, RACHEL

THE RACHEL PAPERS (1989, UA)—Dexter Fletcher has turned swinging in London into a science. When he decides he wishes to bed a woman he pours all the information he can into a computer program, which supplies him with successful strategies. The New York model, **Ione Skye**, doesn't prove to be so programmable.

SEWARD, BOB

MEN MUST FIGHT (1933, MGM)—**Phillips Holmes** is one of the stars in this nearly forgotten film predicting war in New York City in 1940 unless America heeds pacifists' warnings.

SEYMOUR, GABY

ACCUSED (1936, GB, Criterion/UA)—In Paris when a dancer is stabbed to death, his wife **Dolores Del Rio** is believed to be the guilty party.

SEYMOUR, JANE

HENRY VIII AND HIS SIX WIVES (1972, GB, EMI/MGM)—**Jane Asher** is Henry's fourth wife and second to be sent to the chopping block.

SEYMOUR, MARSHALL & CHARLIE

VICE VERSA (1988, Columbia)—In one of the least interesting of the numerous recent movies dealing with body exchanges, ambitious young executive **Judge Reinhold** hardly has any time for his 11-year-old son **Fred Savage**, who lives with Reinhold's ex-wife. While the boy is visiting Reinhold, a mysterious skull prized by Buddhist monks causes father and son to switch places. The plot is further complicated by the fact that Reinhold has inadvertently become mixed up with ruthless smugglers.

SHADEY, OLIVER

SHADEY (1987, GB, Film Four/Skouras)—**Antony Sher** portrays a man who is able to "think pictures onto film." The Defense Department becomes greatly interested when his little movies turn out to predict the future.

SHADHOV, KING

A KING IN NEW YORK (1957, GB, Attica/Archway)—Penniless European king **Charles Chaplin** is at odds with the American way of life. As the U.S. had all but thrown Chaplin out of the country, he wasn't very pleased and he tried to show it in this supposed comedy.

"SHADOW, THE"

THE SHADOW STRIKES (1937, Grand National)—**Rod La Rocque** is Lamont Cranston, who as The Shadow, knows "what evil lurks in the hearts of men." He is able to cloud men's minds and become invisible, a trick he needs as he pursues a killer and a gangster chief, while the police are after La Rocque as a robbery suspect.

SHAFT, JOHN

SHAFT (1971, MGM); SHAFT IN AFRICA (1973, MGM); SHAFT'S BIG SCORE (1972, MGM)—Black private eye **Richard Roundtree** battles a racketeer in the highly successful first film, tracks down a gang of slavers in Ethiopia in the first sequel, and is up against murderers in the numbers racket in the final film.

SHAKESPEARE, WILLIAM

IMMORTAL GENTLEMAN (1935, GB, Equity)—In 1606 the Bard of Avon, portrayed by **Basil Gill**, discusses his work with friends. They each appear as one or more of his characters.

SHALAKO

SHALAKO (1968, GB, Cinerama)—In 1880 New Mexico, **Sean Connery** serves as a guide for European aristocratic big game hunters. The Indians resent the newcomers and attack.

SHALIMAR, PRINCESS

PRINCESS OF THE NILE (1954, 20th Century Fox)—Thirteenth century princess **Debra Paget** joins forces with the son of the Caliph of Baghdad, John Derek, to save Egypt from the ambitions of powerful Bedouin sheik Michael Rennie. That's the story, but it's only an excuse to have Paget and other lovely girls move around in scanty costumes while performing exotic dances.

SHAND, BOBO

WALK LIKE A MAN (1987, MGM/UA)—Lost in a woods as a boy, **Howie Mandel** is raised by wolves. He is discovered and returned to the home of his brother Christopher Lloyd, for whom Mandell causes a great deal of trouble.

SHANE

SHANE (1953, Paramount)—In perhaps his best performance, **Alan Ladd** is an aging gunfighter who rides onto the farm of Van Heflin. He puts away his guns and becomes Heflin's hired hand. Ladd is deeply admired by Heflin's young son, Brandon De Wilde, and apparently has an effect on the missus, Jean Arthur, as well. Ladd finds he can't retire when the fight between the farmers and the cattleman accelerates as hired gun Jack Palance is brought in.

SHANE, BILL

THE LAD (1935, GB, Twickenham)—Jailbird **Gordon Harker**, mistaken for a detective, saves a lord's jewelry from a thief.

SHANKS, MALCOLM

SHANKS (1974, Paramount)—Deaf-mute puppeteer **Marcel Marceau** gets his hands on a scientist's invention, a magic box that brings people back from the dead.

SHANNON

DOGS OF WAR (1980, GB, UA)—**Christopher Walken** is a battle-scarred mercenary paid to organize a coup to get rid of a corrupt president of a West African nation and install a new democratic leader. (Sure that's the democratic way to do it.)

SHANNON, JOE

UNCLE JOE SHANNON (1978, UA)—Musician **Burt Young** nearly loses his mind when his wife and child are killed in a fire, but he finds something to live for in a relationship with a young crippled boy abandoned by his no-good mother.

SHANNON, LAVERNE

THE TARNISHED ANGELS (1957, Universal)—**Dorothy Malone**, the wife of barnstorming ex-WWI ace pilot Robert Stack, is treated in a cavalier fashion by her husband, adored by mechanic Jack Carson, and ready to have an affair with New Orleans reporter Rock Hudson.

SHANNON, LUKE (BUSTER)

THE CAMERAMAN (1928, Silent, MGM)—In order to impress his girl, street photographer **Buster Keaton** becomes a newsreel cameraman. It's among the comedian's best works.

SHANNON, MARGE

SHE LOVED A FIREMAN (1937, Warners)—**Ann Sheridan** carries a torch for fireman Dick Foran—but the film failed to light many fans' fires.

SHANNON, MICKEY & EMMA

THE SHANNONS OF BROADWAY (1929, Universal)—In this film version of their Broadway play, **James Gleason** and **Lucille Webster Gleason** are a couple of vaudeville entertainers who, after being fired, buy a hotel, and discover that an airplane company wishes to purchase the adjoining land for an airport.

SHANNON, MOLLY

SISTERS (1930, Columbia)—Rural-born census taker Russell Gleason rightfully senses that dandy Morgan Wallace who is hanging around model Sally O'Neil is no good. When O'Neil's sister **Molly O'Day** has to come begging for money from her sister because her husband is out of work, Wallace moves in and tries to take advantage of O'Day, but Gleason saves the day and wins O'Neil.

SHAPIRO, JOSHUA & YOUNG JOSHUA

JOSHUA, THEN AND NOW (1985, Canada, 20th Century Fox)—**James Wood** is a Jewish writer having plenty of trouble making a go of things; **Eric Kimmel** is the resilient Joshua as a boy, whom we follow around in a series of flash-backs to his life with his criminal father, Alan Arkin, and his would-be entertainer mother, Linda Sorenson. If you enjoyed THE APPRENTICESHIP OF DUDDY KRAVITZ by the same screen-writer, Mordecai Richler, this one may be for you.

SHAREEN, PRINCESS

HAREM GIRL (1952, Columbia)—**Peggy Castle** is one member of the harem of an Arab prince, but the film is meant to feature comedian Joan Davis. It was to be her last movie.

SHARKY

SHARKY'S MACHINE (1982, Warners)—While he has her apartment under surveillance, vice cop **Burt Reynolds** falls for Rachel Ward, girlfriend of mobster Vittorio Gassman. When it appears she has been murdered, Burt goes on a violent rampage after her killers.

SHARON

SATAN'S CHEERLEADERS (1977, World Amusements)—**Sherry Marks** is one of the busload of cheerleaders captured by a Satanic cult. The film has no place to be shown, now that most drive-in theaters have closed.

SHARON

THE STUDENT NURSES (1970, New World)—Roger Corman made five movies about the sexy and violent life of nurses and this one featuring **Elaine Giftos** is the best, but that's a relative rating, of course.

SHARON, EVE

NINE GIRLS (1944, Columbia)—**Lynn Merrick** is one of nine college girls, members of a sorority house, where murder is a pledge.

SHARP, BECKY

BECKY SHARP (1935, Pioneer/RKO)--**Miriam Hopkins** stars in this film version of W.M. Thackeray's "Vanity Fair." She's an ambitious girl, making her way in Regency society. It is most notable for being the first movie to use three-color Technicolor. It's pretty but patchy.

SHARP, JACOB

THE PROFESSIONALS (1966, Columbia)—**Woody Strode** is handy with a bow and arrow, as he and three other mercenaries ride into Mexico to rescue Ralph Bellamy's young wife Claudia Cardinale from bandit and rebel leader Jack Palance.

SHARPE, JOAN & MAVIS

DAUGHTERS OF TODAY (1933, GB, UA)—Farm sisters **Betty Amman** and **Marguerite Allan** arrive in London looking for romance and adventure.

SHARRON, MARY

WOMAN OBSESSED (1959, 20th Century Fox)—Widow **Susan Hayward** and her eight-year-old son Dennis Holmes have a hard time running their Canadian Northwest farm. She hires Stephen Boyd to help out. They fall in love and marry, but he's mean to her and the boy. His temper gets him a month in the pokey. While he's away, Hayward loses her son in a violent storm and also suffers a miscarriage. Boyd searches for the boy but has to be saved by Holmes. The experience draws the three together as a family.

SHAW, LARRY

THE MUSIC BOX KID (1960, UA)—Gang leader **Ronald Fraser's** religious wife is persuaded by a priest to betray him.

SHAWN

THE CLOWN AND THE KID (1961, UA)—When his clown father dies, **Mike McGreevey** forms a circus act with an escaped convict.

SHAWN, MOLLY

MOLLY ENTANGLED (1917, Silent, Paramount)—**Vivian Martin** marries a man on his deathbed to save his fortune for the family who had taken care of her years before. Unfortunately, he recovers and it looks like she's out of luck with her true love, but it seems the priest who performed the wedding ceremony was a phony.

SHAY, JOHN

THE EXECUTIONER (1970, GB, Columbia)—British spy **George Peppard** suspects his colleague Keith Michell of being a double-agent.

SHAY, REV. JULIAN

RED-HEADED STRANGER (1987, Alive)—Preacher **Willie Nelson** takes on an evil family, headed by Royal Dano, which is terrorizing the citizens in his new parish.

SHAEFFER, ANDY

THE GIRL HE LEFT BEHIND (1956, Warners)—Spoiled youngster **Tab Hunter** finally becomes a man with the help of his saintly patient girlfriend Natalie Wood and the U.S. Army.

SHAYNE, MICHAEL

MICHAEL SHAYNE, PRIVATE DETECTIVE (1940, 20th Century Fox)—In the first of a series, **Lloyd Nolan** is a slick private eye hired to be the bodyguard for Marjorie Weaver, who has a weakness for gambling. When Weaver's boyfriend is murdered, Nolan finds himself a suspect. He solves the case and gets Weaver as well.

SHAYNE, TED

SATAN MET A LADY (1936, Warners)—**Warren William** plays the Sam Spade role in this ridiculous adaptation of Dashiell Hammett's **The Maltese Falcon**. Bette Davis considered it one of the low points in her career, but William and all the others in the cast could make the same claim.

SHE

SHE (1935, RKO); (1965, GB, MGM)—**Helen Gahagan**, wife of Melvyn Douglas, made only this one film appearance as "She Who Must Be Obeyed" in a failed production of the classic fantasy of eternal youth by H. Rider Haggard. Later she would be savagely attacked during a bitter congressional race by a young naval veteran Richard M. Nixon, who tried to tie red ribbons about her, and it won him the election. **Ursula Andress** made many movies other than the remake of the Haggard work, but aside from looking unbelievably voluptuous, she hasn't been a better actress than one-shot Gahagan.

SHEA, STELLA

A PERFECT COUPLE (1979, 20th Century Fox)—**Marta Heflin**, a junk-food devotee and manager of a rock group, is computer-matched with Paul Dooley, a gourmet cook and lover of classical music. Of course, they prove to be highly compatible.

SHEA, TOMMY

WORLD IN MY CORNER (1956, Universal)—Slum boy **Audie Murphy** becomes a successful prizefighter, falling in love with his mentor's daughter.

SHEBA

SHEBA BABY (1975, American International)—Black private eye **Pam Grier** tries to help her father save his loan business.

SHEENA

SHEENA (1984, Columbia)—As a female Tarzan, **Tanya Roberts** is lovely, but untalented. She is a white girl raised by an African tribe after her explorer parents are killed.

SHELA

SLAVE GIRLS FROM BEYOND INFINITY (1987, Titan/Urban Classics)—The film isn't as bad as it's title would suggest, but it's a close call. **Brinke Stevens** is one of three scantily-clad girls who crash land on a planet where they are hunted by evil Don Scribner and his android assistants.

SHELDON, LORD

TWO HEARTS IN HARMONY (1935, GB, British Lion)—In this musical, cabaret singer Bernice Clare marries the lord of the manor, **George Curzon**, after becoming his son's governess.

SHELDON, SUSANNAH

SUSANNAH OF THE MOUNTIES (1939, 20th Century Fox)—Orphan **Shirley Temple** is the only survivor of an Indian attack in the Canadian West. She is adopted by mountie Randolph Scott, who ultimately gets Temple a mother by marrying Margaret Lockwood. Before this happens, Shirley saves Scott from being burned at the stake, by putting the Indian chief wise to the corruption of his medicine man.

SHELLEY, JESSICA

PICTURE MOMMY DEAD (1966, Embassy)—**Zsa Zsa Gabor** dies in a fire, but her daughter is haunted by her spirit, directing her to watch out for her new stepmother who is trying to kill the youngster.

SHELLY, NORA

BRIDE FOR SALE (1949, RKO)—**Claudette Colbert** takes a job as office manager of an income tax firm in order to check its files to find a man who will meet her need for a wealthy husband. The owner of the company, George Brent, catches on to what she's up to and tries to teach her a lesson with the help of wealthy Robert Young. But as a Hollywood script would have it, both men fall in love with Colbert.

SHELTON, HOWARD

TEN GENTLEMEN FROM WEST POINT (1942, 20th Century Fox)—**John Sutton** is one of only ten cadets who survive the severe training of the first class at West Point. He's an aristocrat who fights a Kentucky hunter, George Montgomery, for the love of a local girl, Maureen O'Hara.

SHEPARD, STEVE

WHITE GHOST (1988, Gibraltar)—Dressed in Kabuki make-up, Rambo-like **William Katt** is still battling the Vietnamese.

SHEPHERD, MARA

SEVEN WOMEN FROM HELL (1961, 20th Century Fox)—**Margia Dean** is one of the good looking ladies who escape from a hellish Japanese prison camp in New Guinea in the early part of WWII. She doesn't make it to safety, however.

SHEPPARD, JACK

WHERE'S JACK (1969, GB, Paramount)—**Tommy Steele** stars as a highwayman in 18th century London who makes many stunning jailbreaks. He's always just one step ahead of Stanley Baker, who makes a living by setting up thieves for the reward money.

SHERIDAN, LEE

A YANK AT OXFORD (1938, MGM)—Cocky American **Robert Taylor** attends Oxford, but doesn't fit in until he proves he really is a regular guy. Good show, Robert!

SHERIDAN, PAUL

PUSHOVER (1954, Columbia)—Honest cop **Fred MacMurray** becomes involved with murder for profit, when Kim Novak, in her first featured role, turns her charms on him. He's the pushover, not her, although she is sort of easy.

SHERIDAN, TOM

MAN WANTED (1932, Warners)—**David Manners** is married to Kay Francis' secretary. He looks good to Francis when she and her husband tire of each other.

SHERLOCK, JR.

SHERLOCK, JUNIOR (1924, Silent, Metro)—Film projectionist **Buster Keaton** dreams of becoming a great detective.

SHERMAN, "HANK"

SWORN ENEMY (1936, MGM)—Young law student **Robert Young** is out to get enough evidence to put away Joseph Calleia, who is responsible for the murder of Young's boss, his brother's injury and any number of other crimes.

SHERMAN, JEFF

THE GUMSHOE KID (1990, Skouras)—Young **Jay Underwood** is obsessed with becoming a private eye. He gets his chance in this harmless little comedy, which finds him on the lam with heartthrob Tracy Scoggins.

SHERMAN, LLOYD

THE LITTLE COLONEL (1935, Fox)—**Shirley Temple** is a busy little Pollyanna as she helps put an end to a feud in her post-Civil War southern household, plays Cupid for her sister, routs some carpetbaggers, and improves the disposition of her cantankerous grandfather, Lionel Barrymore.

SHERRIN

FEDERAL MAN (1950, Eagle Lion)—Federal agent **William Henry** is sent to track down the drug dealers who have killed previous narcotics agents sent after them.

SHERRY

THE OTHER WOMAN (1954, 20th Century Fox)—Ambitious actress **Cleo Moore** lures director Hugo Haas to her apartment, drugs him, and then tries to blackmail him. Haas kills her. He tries to shift the blame onto a derelict, but doesn't get away with it. Moore, the real-life wife of Haas, was never much of an actress, usually playing the part of a floozy. But considering that she worked with Hollywood's absolute worst director, it's a wonder anyone ever saw her at all.

SHERWOOD, FANCY JIM

THE MAN FROM PAINTED POST (1917, Silent, Artcraft)—**Douglas Fairbanks** poses as a city dude in order to capture a gang of rustlers. His reward is pretty Eileen Percy.

SHERWOOD, PHYLLIS

PHYLLIS OF THE FOLLIES (1928, Silent, Universal)—**Alice Day** poses as her married friend to play a trick on a gentleman who only goes after married women. They fall in love and when he learns the truth, he makes an exception in Day's case and marries her.

SHERWOOD, RUTH & EILEEN

MY SISTER EILEEN (1942, Columbia); (1955, Columbia)—**Rosalind Russell** and **Janet Blair; Betty Garrett** and **Janet Leigh** each play the Sherwood sisters from Ohio, with Russell and Garrett being the practical one, trying to make it as a writer in New York, while watching out for naive but sexy younger sister Blair and Leigh.

SHEIK, THE

SON OF THE SHEIK (1926, Silent, UA)—The movie was released after **Rudolph Valentino's** death, and his faithful female fans went wild. In it, Rudi falls for nomadic dancer Vilma Banky, but all his screaming fans saw were his soulful hypnotic eyes. At any rate, Banky rides off with him to his desert sheikdom and, we assume, some wild nights under the stars. Valentino also played his father, who was featured in THE SHEIK (1921).

SHIMIZU, TAE

JAPANESE WAR BRIDE (1952, 20th Century Fox)—**Shirley Yamaguchi** nurses army officer Don Taylor, wounded in Korea. They marry, and when they get back to the states, his sister-in-law tries to break them up by writing an anonymous letter accusing Yamaguchi of an affair with a Japanese-American.

SHIPLEY, MISS

ONE OF OUR GIRLS (1914, Silent, Famous Players)—In her film debut, American musical comedy star **Hazel Dawn** is loved by a British officer, who fights a duel for her.

SHIRLEY

BABY, TAKE A BOW (1934, Fox)—Ex-con James Dunn is accused of theft but his little daughter, **Shirley Temple**, unmasks the real culprit. It was Temple's first starring vehicle and she was up to the task, personifying the word adorable.

SHIRLEY, ANNE

ANNE OF GREEN GABLES (1919, Silent, Realart); (1934, RKO); ANNE OF WINDY POPLARS (1940, RKO)—Orphan **Mary Miles Minter** goes to live in New England with her unaffectionate relatives. In 1934, Dawn O'Day repeats the role in the classic for little girls, taking the name of her character, **Anne Shirley**, as her

professional name. In the sequel, Shirley moves on to become a teacher and has a bit of trouble with the most prominent local family because of the misbehavior of their son.

SHOCKEY

HOOSIER SCHOOLBOY (1937, Monogram)—Indiana farmboy **Mickey Rooney** defends his drunken father, who has never recovered from being shell-shocked in WWI.

SHOESMITH, HENRY JR.

THE PAGAN (1929, MGM)—South Sea Islander **Ramon Novarro** falls in love with Renee Adoree, the daughter of a white trader.

SHOOTER

HOOSIERS (1986, Orion)—Former Indiana high school basketball star **Dennis Hopper**, who got his name for obvious reasons, is a bit of an alcoholic, living on past glories, until the new basketball coach, Gene Hackman, recruits Hopper to help coach the team. In small-town Indiana, basketball is king, believe us!

SHORE, JOEL & MARK

ALL THE BROTHERS WERE VALIANT (1923, Silent, Metro) (1953, MGM)—**Malcolm McGregor** and **Lon Chaney; Robert Taylor** and **Stewart Granger** are the sea-captain brothers, who compete not only for control of a whaling ship and a fortune in pearls, but also for the admiration of the wife of the younger. Chaney and Granger play the disreputable brother who redeems himself before the end, while McGregor and Taylor prove to be braver and more exciting than their wives believed.

SHORT, MADELINE

WHITE ZOMBIE (1932, UA)—**Madge Bellamy** is kidnapped by a zombie working for Bela Lugosi on the Island of Haiti. She is held in suspended animation, and is not freed from Lugosi's hypnotic powers until he is killed.

SHORTY

THE LAVENDER HILL MOB (1951, GB, Ealing)—**Alfie Bass** is one of the two lesser members of the gang put together by Alec Guinness to steal gold bullion from the bank for which he has worked as a meek clerk for many years.

SHORTY

SAILORS' HOLIDAY (1929, Pathe)—**George Cooper** and his buddy have a bit of trouble while on leave, listening to street women tell them sad tales of how they are looking for their long-lost brother, also a sailor.

SHUBUNKA

THE GANGSTER (1947, Allied Artists)—**Barry Sullivan** falls victim to his slum environment and becomes a crook, seeking revenge against another member of his gang.

SHU-JEN

CHINA DOLL (1958, UA)—In China in 1943, American officer Victor Mature marries his housekeeper, **Li Li Hua**. She is later killed by Japanese bombers when she follows him to the front with their child. Mature hides the child and then goes off on a mission from which he does not return. Years later, the now grown-up daughter is in the U.S., welcomed by members of her father's air crew.

SHUMANN, ROGER

THE TARNISHED ANGELS (1957, Universal)—Barnstorming, former WWII flying ace **Robert Stack** appears to hold everything in contempt, including his friend, his wife and even his own life.

SIDDONS, LEMUEL

FOLLOW ME BOYS! (1966, Buena Vista)—**Fred MacMurray** stars as a 1930s small town scoutmaster in one of the several wholesome but ordinary movies he made for Disney.

SIEGEL, BUGSY

MOBSTERS (1991, Universal); BUGSY (1991, Tri-Star)—It's no contest. **Richard Grieco**, as the young Bugsy, can't hold a gun to **Warren Beatty's** more mature version. Grieco seems to be included only to offer some male sex appeal for young girls in the audience. Beatty is a charmer, unless someone crosses him, insults Annette Bening or calls him Bugsy.

SIKORSKY, HENRY

THE DREAM TEAM (1989, Universal)—Former postal worker Christopher Lloyd works under the delusion that he's a doctor in the mental hospital to which he is committed. He's one of four non-dangerous patients who become stranded in New York City, when the doctor-chaperon who was taking them to a baseball game is sent to a hospital in a coma after being nearly killed by a pair of crooked cops.

SILK, JOHNNY

MEN OF CHANCE (1932, RKO)—**Ricardo Cortez** owns a race horse that a certain betting consortium would like to see lose the big race. They send in Mary Astor to seduce Cortez, so she can get close enough to the horse to drug it. Instead, she marries Cortez and cheers on his winning nag.

SILKWOOD, KAREN

SILKWOOD (1983, 20th Century Fox)—**Meryl Streep** portrays the courageous employee of a plutonium plant in Oklahoma. She collects evidence that her company's safety measures are not sufficient to protect the workers, and that records about faulty equipment have been falsified. She was on her way to talk to a New York reporter when she was killed in a car crash and the evidence she had gathered disappeared. Frighteningly, this is a true story.

SILVA, ANA & TONY

MY SON (1925, Silent, First National)—**Nazimova** and **Jack Pickford** are a Portuguese mother and son in a New England fishing town. He almost loses his mom's love and that of his local sweetheart when he comes under the spell of a visiting flapper.

SILVER, LONG JOHN

LONG JOHN SILVER (1954, Australia, DCA)—**Robert Newton** hams it up in this sequel to Treasure Island in which he and young Hawkins plan a return trip to the Island with new clues as to the location of the treasure.

SILVERMAN, ALAN

ALAN AND NAOMI (1992, Triton)—In 1944 Brooklyn, **Lukas Haas** is forced by his parents to befriend virtually catatonic neighbor girl Vanessa Zaouri. With the aid of his ventriloquist dummy, he gets through to the girl, who talks through her beloved doll.

SILVERMAN, MAX

THE GOODBYE PEOPLE (1984, Embassy)—**Martin Balsam** is among a group of middle-aged eccentrics who gather on a beach to talk, and talk, and talk . . . .

SILVERTHORN, CASE

THE GAMBLER WORE A GUN (1961, UA)—When gambler **Jim Davis** buys a ranch, he discovers that rustlers are using it as a cover for their illegal activities.

SILVERTON, KATHERINE

THE MARRIAGE OF KITTY (1915, Silent, Metro)—In Newport, an English lord marries impoverished **Fannie Ward** for a fee, to honor his pledge that he will never marry an actress, despite being infatuated with a music-hall entertainer back home. He learns to love his beautiful wife.

SIMMONS, JACK

THE DIRT BIKE KID (1985, Cinema Group)—**Peter Billingsley** buys an old dirt bike, only to discover it has an existence of its own.

SIMMS, EVIE & AD

THE PRIVATE LIVES OF ADAM AND EVE (1961, Universal)—**Mamie Van Doren** and **Martin Milner** are among a group of bus passengers from Reno who take refuge from a storm in a country church. After listening to the story of Adam and Eve, they and other passengers become characters in the Garden of Evil. Mickey Rooney gets the role of the devil.

SIMMS, MR.

THE BIG SHOT (1937, RKO)—**Guy Kibbee** is a small-town vet, and content to be one even when he inherits a fortune from an uncle who lived in the big city. Henpecked Kibbee is forced by his wife to move to the city, so their daughter can enter society. Kibbee finds that his uncle made his money illegally, and Kibbee has also inherited a gang of crooks who look to him for leadership.

SIMON

SIMON, KING OF THE WITCHES (1971, Fanfare)—Modern warlock **Andrew Prine** lives with his magic mirror in his home in a L.A. storm sewer. The ads read "The Evil Spirit Must Choose Evil! The Black Mass . . . The Spells . . . The Incantations . . . The Curses . . . The Ceremonial Sex." Sound interesting? You're right, it's not.

SIMON, GEORGE

COUNSELLOR-AT-LAW (1933, Universal)—**John Barrymore** is a shrewd, self-made Jewish lawyer, married to an uncaring gentile wife. She leaves him when he becomes in danger of being disbarred for some past professional misconduct. His secretary, Bebe Daniels, who has always loved him, comes to his rescue when he considers suicide.

SIMON PETER

THE BIG FISHERMAN (1959, Buena Vista)—The apostle Peter, played unconvincingly by **Howard Keel**, who looked like a man waiting for a song cue, dissuades an Arabian princess from killing her stepfather, Herod.

SIMON, PETER

RIVALS (1972, Avco Embassy)—When **Robert Klein** marries a widow, her young son plots his stepfather's death.

SIMONE

SOME GIRLS (1989, MGM-UA) **Ashley Greenfield** is one of two beautiful sisters of lovely Jennifer Connelly, who make things interesting for Patrick Dempsey when he visits Connelly and her family in Quebec City during the Christmas holidays.

SIMPKINS, AL

THE SKY SKIDDER (1929, Silent, Universal)—Stunt flyer **Al Wilson** portrays a pilot who invents a fuel which gets a thousand miles to a pint.

SIMPKINS, SUSIE

MRS. SLACKER (1918, Silent, Pathe)—Wealthy sissy Creighton Hale marries washerwoman **Gladys Hulette** to avoid being drafted.

When she learns his motives, she leaves him, but he wins her back when he enlists.

SIMPSON, KATIE

SHE'S OUT OF CONTROL (1989, Columbia)—Widower Tony Danza isn't equipped to deal with his teenage daughter **Ami Dolenz**, who almost overnight turns from an ugly duckling into a beautiful swan.

SIMPSON, MELVIN

MELVIN, SON OF ALVIN (1984, Australia, Roadshow)—**Gerry Sont** stars in this unfunny sequel to ALVIN PURPLE and ALVIN RIDES AGAIN. He's the 18-year-old son of Alvin, and has inherited his father's winning ways, but is frightened of women. For those who haven't seen the 1973 Australian hit, a lot of what happens in this movie will have no meaning. It won't have that much meaning for those who saw the previous two movies.

SIMPSON, SALLY

STRANDED (1927, Silent, Sterling)—Failed actress **Shirley Mason** is saved from having to give herself to a cad to get money for her mother's operation by the arrival of her sweetheart from back home.

SIMPSON, WINIFRED

SIX-DAY BIKE RIDER (1934, First National)—**Joe E. Brown** becomes a bike-racing champion in this comedy, funny only to fans who thought Big-mouthed Brown was the last word in humor.

SINBAD, CAPT.

SINBAD THE SAILOR (1947, RKO); SON OF SINBAD (1955, RKO) THE SEVENTH VOYAGE OF SINBAD (1958, Columbia); CAPTAIN SINBAD (1963, MGM); THE GOLDEN VOYAGE OF SINBAD (1974, GB, Columbia); SINBAD AND THE EYE OF THE TIGER (1977, Columbia)-**Douglas Fairbanks, Jr., Dale Robertson, Kerwin Mathews, Guy Williams, John Phillip Law** and **Patrick Wayne** were among the many actors who popped up in the role of the legendary sailor in one movie or another. Fairbanks proved he could grin and leap around just as did his father, but the story of Sinbad's eighth voyage in search of Deryabar, the island where Alexander the Great is supposed to have hidden his treasure, is not very exciting. Robertson had even less material to work with in the next feature. Kerwin Mathews was blessed with excellent special effects which made his ventures exciting. Williams and Law were adequate in their portrayals and poor Patrick Wayne should never have tried to follow his father into the acting profession.

SINCLAIR

ACES HIGH (1977, GB, Cine Artists)—**Christopher Plummer** is one of the older members of a 1917 RFC squadron stationed in France. He helps his younger companions when the pressure becomes too great.

SINCLAIR, DORA

THE GIRL ON THE STAIRS (1924, Silent, PDC)—**Patsy Ruth Miller** marries a rising young attorney, but can't get her letters back from a man with whom she had been carrying on a flirtation until she learned he was married. She enters the man's home in an unsuccessful attempt to retrieve the letters, and the next morning the man is found murdered. Now the manure smacks up against the oscillating cooling device.

SINCLAIR, HAROLD

A SOLDIER AND A MAN (1916, GB, Silent, British & Colonial)—**George Keene**, a general's son, is framed by a spy for being a cardsharp. The youngster enlists as a private and saves his father and his fiancee from capture by the enemy.

SINGER, JACOB

JACOB'S LADDER (1990, Tri-Star)—Vietnam veteran **Tim Robbins** is bedeviled by strange visions in a dull thriller, which is not only predictable, but always has the audience miles ahead of Robbins.

SINUHE

THE EGYPTIAN (1954, 20th Century Fox)—**Edmond Purdom** stepped in when Marlon Brando stepped out of this costume epic about a young physician in pre-Christian times who treats an epileptic Pharoah, Michael Wilding, and falls under the spell of a Babylonian courtesan, Bella Darvi, who nearly ruins him. He returns to his ever faithful love, Jean Simmons, who is slain for her religious convictions. Boy, did Brando know what he was doing!

SIRKI, PRINCE

DEATH TAKES A HOLIDAY (1934, Paramount)—**Fredric March** appears as the Angel of Death, who briefly takes on human form, so he may discover why humans fear him so. He gets Evelyn Venable to fall in love with him, and willingly accompany him into the unknown.

SIROCCO, CAPT.

THE PIRATES OF CAPRI (1949, Film Classics)—**Louis Hayward**, an unassuming member of the court of Naples, assumes the identity of swashbuckling Captain Sirocco (you know—a hot oppressive wind blowing across the Mediterranean into southern Europe), who champions the rebels who are trying to overthrow the Queen and her evil chief of police.

SITTING BULL, CHIEF

SITTING BULL (1954, UA)—**J. Carrol Naish** struggles valiantly to give a respectful performance as the great Sioux chief, but the story, including one more enactment of Custer's Last Stand, is more "bull" than history.

SKEFFINGTON, JOB

MR. SKEFFINGTON (1944, Warners)—Businessman **Claude Rains** and vain, irresponsible Bettye Davis marry when he forgives her adored brother who had embezzled $25,000 from Rains. Since she doesn't love him, she feels she is entitled to cheat on him whenever she feels like it. He finds comfort with several of his female employees. Years later, diptheria robs her of her once proud looks, and Rains returns from a Nazi concentration camp, blind. Finally, she realizes what a good man she has married, as they prepare to spend their declining years together.

SKELTON, LADY BARBARA

THE WICKED LADY (1946, GB, Gainsborough); (1983, GB, MGM/UA)—**Margaret Lockwood** and **Faye Dunaway** each portray a hot blooded and ambitious woman, who marries a man she does not love for his title and then, bored, becomes a highwaywoman and lover of a highwayman, whom she nearly has hanged. In the end the two fatally shoot each other.

SKINNER

THE MAGNIFICENT SEVEN RIDE (1972, UA)—**Luke Askew** is one of the convicts picked by Lee Van Cleef and Michael Callan to make up the magic number seven to ride to the rescue of some women captured by Mexican bandits in a second sequel to the magnificent THE MAGNIFICENT SEVEN. This one might be called THE PUTRID SEVEN.

SKINNER, CORNELIA OTIS

OUR HEARTS WERE YOUNG AND GAY (1944, Paramount) OUR HEARTS WERE GROWING UP (1946, Paramount)—**Gail Russell** who was menaced by Cornelia Otis Skinner in THE UNINVITED (1944) portrays the actress as a young girl in this filmed version of the recollection by Skinner and her friend Emily Kimbrough of how they kicked up their heels in Paris in 1923. In the sequel, the girls are now in college and have a time with boys and bootleggers.

SKINNER, SKIPPY
SKIPPY (1931, Paramount)—Nine-year-old **Jackie Cooper**, fresh from Hal Roach *Our Gang* comedies, was nominated for an Academy Award for best actor in this simple tale of two boys, Cooper and Robert Coogan (younger brother of Jackie Coogan), who become friends in the slums and try to raise enough money to get a dog back from the pound.

SKINNER, TESSIBEL
TESS OF THE STORM COUNTRY (1922, Silent, UA)—**Mary Pickford** first appeared in this role for Famous Players in 1914, and it made her America's Sweetheart. She is the daughter of a fisherman in love with the son of a mean land owner. The latter is out to deprive the fisherman of their livelihoods by buying land where people who smell of fish are excluded. Mary is able to soften the old skinflint's heart, making everyone happy.

SKINNER, WILLIAM HENRY
SKINNER'S DRESS SUIT (1917, Silent, Essnay); (1926, Silent, Universal); SKINNER'S BIG IDEAS (1928, Silent, FBO); SKINNER STEPS OUT (1929, Universal)—**Bryant Washburn, Reginald Denny** and **Glenn Tryon** each portray the henpecked man afraid to inform his wife that his request for a raise was turned down. Instead he tells her that he got a raise. She insists that he buy a dress suit to reflect his advanced standing. As for herself, she goes on a shopping spree and our hero loses his job. However, clothes do make the man and he impresses a millionaire and wins back his old job with a raise.

SKIPPER, THE
THE SKIPPER'S WOOING (1922, GB, Silent, Artistic)—**Gordon Hopkirk** and Cynthia Murtagh protest they can't stand each other, but a crafty schoolteacher sets them a task which has them returning as sweethearts.

SKIRDLOW, CLIFFORD
DOCTOR DETROIT (1983, Universal)—Nerdy professor **Dan Aykroyd** is blessed with a harem of high class call girls when their pimp feels the heat from mean and nasty Kate Murtagh, who plans to take over. To protect his "property," Aykroyd must become the iron-fisted mobster Dr. Detroit.

SKITCH, MR.
MISTER SKITCH (1933, Fox)—**Will Rogers** and his Missouri family move to California in this enjoyable star vehicle.

SKY PILOT, THE
THE SKY PILOT (1921, Silent, Associated First National) -**John Bowers**, a new minister in the Canadian Northwest, is not immediately appreciated by the cowboys until he handles himself in a fist fight with the ranch foreman, who becomes his friend.

SLADE
LADY SCARFACE (1941, RKO)—**Judith Anderson** stars as a gang leader responsible for a series of robberies and murders. The police don't know their adversary is a woman, one who has become a master criminal as a result of her bitterness over a scar which disfigures her face.

SLADE
MAN IN THE ATTIC (1953, 20th Century Fox)—In a remake of THE LODGER, **Jack Palance** is a psychotic murderer of London women in the late 1800s. He's depressed because his landlady's daughter, Constance Smith, doesn't share his love. Scotland Yard detective Byron Palmer closes in on knife-wielding Palance in time to save the poor girl.

SLADE, JACK
JACK SLADE (1953, Allied Artists); THE RETURN OF JACK SLADE (1955, Allied Artists)—**Mark Stevens** is impressive as a western gunman who becomes a psychopathic killer. His characteristic way of mowing down adversaries is to fan his six-iron. Since Slade was killed in the 1953 movie, **John Ericson** returns as his father's son. He's on the side of the law, infiltrating a gang of outlaws and proves to be as handy with a gun as was his father.

SLADE, JIM
THE MIDNIGHT MAN (1974, Universal)—After being paroled, ex-cop **Burt Lancaster** gets mixed up in a series of murders committed in a small town.

SLADE, SUSAN
SUSAN SLADE (1961, Warners)—In a typical soap opera, **Connie Stevens** attempts to commit suicide after the father of her illegitimate child is killed in a mountain climbing accident. She moves to California from Guatemala after the death of her father, and finally chooses shy veterinarian Troy Donahue over wealthy Bert Convy to be her husband. Some choice!

SLADEN, BINKIE
LITTLE MISS SOMEBODY (1937, GB, Butchers)—A wicked squire learns that a farmer's adopted daughter, **Binkie Stuart**, is an heiress. He sees a way he can turn this knowledge to his advantage.

SLAGLE, SUSIE
MISS SUSIE SLAGLE'S (1945, Paramount)—**Lillian Gish** runs a Baltimore boarding house for students attending Johns Hopkins medical school in 1910. This lovely lady helps her boarders with their problems and charms audiences. Lillian Gish is a national treasure.

SLATER, DAN
THE DOUBLE MAN (1967, Warners)—CIA agent **Yul Brynner's** son is pushed off an Alp in the Austrian Tyrol by Brynner's exact double, a Russian agent. The tepid thriller ends with another CIA agent faced with making the decision "which baldy is the phony."

SLATER, STEVEN
DEMONSTRATOR (1971, Australia, Columbia)—**Gerard Maguire** organizes a protest against militarism outside a meeting of the leaders of the Asian nations to ratify a military alliance proposed by Maguire's father, the Australian Minister for Defense.

SLATTERY, WILL
SLATTERY'S HURRICANE (1949, 20th Century Fox)—Former naval pilot **Richard Widmark** flies for a smuggling ring, until ex-sweetheart Linda Darnell gets him to reform. To show he's on the side of the right, he flies for the weather bureau during a Florida hurricane.

SLAUGHTER
SLAUGHTER (1972, American International); SLAUGHTER'S BIG RIP-OFF (1973, American International)—Black Vietnam veteran **Jim Brown** tracks down the underworld mobsters responsible for

the murders of his parents. The sequel is just more violence from Brown and the syndicate.

SLAUGHTER, M/SGT. MAXWELL

SOLDIER IN THE RAIN (1963, Allied Artists)—**Jackie Gleason** is a top kick in the service dreaming of what he'll do when his last hitch is up. His admiring buddy Steve McQueen tries to fix Gleason up with Tuesday Weld, but this doesn't work out and the Great One unexpectedly dies.

SLEDGE, LUTHER

A MAN CALLED SLEDGE (1971, Columbia)—**James Garner** plays against type, starring as a brutal outlaw who masterminds a robbery of gold stored in a prison.

SLIM

KING OF THE LUMBERJACKS (1940, Warners)—In this trite chestnut, **John Payne** is a lumberjack who unknowingly marries his best friend's sweetheart (perhaps she was aware), but that's only to provide a romantic basis for a film steeped in brawls, run-away trains and trouble in the forest.

SLIM

SAINTLY SINNERS (1962, UA)—**Stanley Clements** is one of a group of likeable felons reformed by a naive loveable old priest Don Beddoe.

SLIM

SLIM (1937, Warners)—**Henry Fonda** represents the brave workers who make their living repairing high tension cables at the top of electrical towers.

SLIM PRINCESS, THE

THE SLIM PRINCESS (1915, Silent, Essanay)—Francis X. Bushman, an American millionaire visiting Turkey, falls in love with slim princess **Ruth Stonehouse**, which delights her family because in Turkey only rotund women are valued as wives.

SLOAN, BERTHA

BERTHA THE SEWING MACHINE GIRL (1926, Silent, Fox)—**Madge Bellamy** loses her job as a sewing machine girl but is hired to be a lingerie model by the company's manager, who has this thing for her. He tries to abduct her for immoral purposes but she's rescued by shipping room clerk Allan Simpson who loves her. It turns out Simpson also owns the lingerie company.

SLOAN, LONNIE

OLD ENOUGH (1984, Orion Classics)—**Sarah Boyd** and Rainbow Harvest are two adolescent girls from different socioeconomic backgrounds who learn about life by learning about each others completely different life styles. Boyd is the wealthy one.

SLOAN, PATRICIA

BETWEEN TWO WOMEN (1937, MGM)—**Virginia Bruce** is a rich patient of earnest surgeon Franchot Tone. She's suffering from appendicitis but when she comes out of the operation, she's lassoed the doctor. They wed and she constantly complains of his hours. When the alcoholic husband of Maureen O'Sullivan, a nurse Tone once loved, goes to the hospital for emergency surgery, and dies because Tone is out entertaining Bruce rather than tending to his knitting, Tone dumps Bruce and goes back to O'Sullivan.

SLOANE, CHRISTY

A MILLIONAIRE FOR CHRISTY (1951, 20th Century Fox)—When **Eleanor Parker's** boss, Fred MacMurray, inherits a fortune, the little lady decides that she's going to marry him. The fact that he already has a fiancee is only a minor obstacle. Ah, love!

SLOANE, DULTITIA

HER REPUTATION (1931, GB, London Screenplay)—**Iris Hoey's** attempt to divorce her husband falls through due to the timidity of her accomplice.

SLOANE, KURT

KICKBOXER (1989, Kings Road/Pathe)—Here's one you can safely miss, unless you are intrigued by the sport of kickboxing. **Jean-Claude Van Damme** is a champ.

SLOANE, MR.

ENTERTAINING MR. SLOANE (1970, GB, Warners-Pathe)—Handsome young **Peter McErney** is invited into the home of grotesquely dressed Beryl Reid and her homosexual brother Edward Andrews, both who plan to seduce their young lodger. At the end of this offensive black comedy McErney is solemnly married to both Reid and Andrews.

SLOANE, WEB

PRISONER OF WAR (1954, MGM)—It was probably after appearing in this terrible movie about life in a POW camp in Korea that **Ronald Reagan** developed his hard line against communists.

SLOCUM, EDDIE

THE YOUNG LOVERS (1964, MGM)—**Peter Fonda** stars in this trashy film about how it wasn't on most college campuses in the early sixties.

SLOPER, KATHERINE

THE HEIRESS (1949, Paramount)—**Olivia De Havilland** gives one of the finest performances ever seen on screen as the plain and painfully shy daughter of prominent New York surgeon Ralph Richardson. Handsome young Montgomery Clift pays her court and she is ecstatic until her stern and cruel father proves the young man to be a fortune hunter. She becomes a hardened spinster and sheds no tears as her father dies. Years later, Clift returns pleading with her to marry him. She rejects him, observing: "Yes, I can be cruel; I have been taught by masters." The beautiful movie, based on Henry James's 1881 novel *Washington Square*, was nominated for eight Academy Awards and won four, including De Havilland's deserved Best Actress Oscar.

SMAGG, HANLICK (MIKE)

THE CAVEMAN (1915, Silent, Vitagraph); (1926, Silent, Warner Brothers)—**Robert Edeson** and **Matt Moore** each appear as a common laborer, whom a society girl passes off among her friends as an eccentric professor. She falls in love with him, but when she informs her friends of his true origins, they'll have nothing further to do with him. That's fine with the two lovers.

SMALL, BILL

MR. CHUMP (1938, Warner Brothers)—Trumpet playing dreamer **Johnnie Davis** convinces his friends to speculate in some business deals and everyone ends up in jail.

SMALL, SAM

SAM SMALL LEAVES TOWN (1937, GB, British Screen Service)—Actor Stanley Holloway bets a publisher that he can disappear, and not be found until he's ready. He swaps identities with holiday camp handyman **Johnnie Schofield**.

SMEDLEY, ETHEL

BEAUTY AND THE BARGE (1937, GB, Twickenham/Wardour)—**Judy Gunn**, the beautiful runaway daughter of a major, is adopted by a barge captain. She falls for a lieutenant, posing as a mate aboard the barge.

SMILEY, DUD

THE COWBOY KING (1922, Silent, Aywon)—**Guinn "Big Boy" Williams**, the two-fisted foreman on Patricia Palmer's ranch, fights it out with a neighbor, who has fenced off a water hole, depriving her cattle of water.

SMITH

LEAVE IT TO SMITH (1934, GB, Gaumont)—Thief **Tom Walls** gets into trouble after performing a good deed in this very British film, called JUST SMITH in the Empire.

SMITH

SMITH! (1969, Buena Vista)—Farmer **Glenn Ford** takes the unpopular position of defending an Indian accused of murder.

SMITH, ADAM

ADAM AND EVA (1923, Silent, Paramount)—Disappointed with his spoiled daughter Marion Davies' wild ways, Tom Lewis turns the running of his business over to employee **T. Roy Barnes** and disappears. Barnes tells extravagant Davies that the company is on the verge of bankruptcy and the family is broke. This news makes a remarkable change in her behavior. She goes to work to support her family, and when her father comes home she's ready to be a good practical wife for Barnes.

SMITH, ALLIE

YOUNG BRIDE (1932, RKO)—**Helen Twelvetrees** believes that she's found the man of her dreams when she marries Eric Linden, but finds he's an insufferable braggart with absolutely no sensitivity. Post-wedding blues are hell.

SMITH, ANDY

A YANK IN KOREA (1957, Columbia)—**Lon McCallister** doesn't look strong enough to be a soldier, but he works at it in this nothing actioneer.

SMITH, AMAZING GRACE

AMAZING GRACE AND CHUCK (1987, Tri-Star)—Pro basketball star **Alex English** joins 12-year-old Little League baseball star Joshua Zuehlke in boycotting all sports until the Great Powers get together on nuclear disarmament. Soon athletes all over the world have joined them.

SMITH, ANN & DAVID

MR. AND MRS. SMITH (1941, RKO)—**Carole Lombard** and **Robert Montgomery** appear in this screwball comedy directed by none other than Alfred Hitchcock. The couple discover that their marriage was illegal, and that they are "free." The rest of the film deals with whether they will reenlist in marital bliss.

SMITH, BILL

JAIL BIRDS (1939, GB, Butchers)—**Albert Bureton** and Charles Hawtrey escape from prison dressed in drag, and get jobs in a bakery. A third escapee joins them and gives them a piece of jewelry to hide. They bake it in a loaf of bread which ends up on the table of the detective fiance of Bureton's daughter. Albert and Hawtrey hurry back to jail, acting as they've never been away.

SMITH, BILLY

HURRICANE SMITH (1992, Australia, Warner Brothers/Greater Union)—American **Carl Weathers** searches for his missing sister in Australia's violent Gold Coast. The audience knows long before Weathers that Jurgen Prochow, hitman for a brothel owner, murdered Weathers' sister.

SMITH, DR. BRUCE

SHOULD A DOCTOR TELL? (1931, GB, British Lion)—The doctor's oath prevents **Basil Gill** from telling his son that he is engaged to an unmarried mother.

SMITH, CLARENCE

CLARENCE (1922, Silent, Paramount); (1937, Paramount)—**Wallace Reid** and **Roscoe Karns** each portray the ex-soldier, hired to work in a house filled with eccentrics. He survives all of their loony behavior, clears himself of charges of being a deserter, and wins the love of the governess.

SMITH, COLIN

THE LONELINESS OF THE LONG DISTANCE RUNNER (1962, GB, Woodfall-Seven Arts)—Rebellious teenager **Tom Courtenay** is sent to Borstal. He is encouraged by the governor to enter cross-country races, but Courtenay deliberately loses.

SMITH, DRUCILLA

PRETTY MRS. SMITH (1915, Silent, Paramount)—**Fritzi Scheff** faces a bit of trouble when all three of her husbands show up at the same time. She should be called a trigamist, we suppose.

SMITH, ERASTUS "DEAF"

DEAF SMITH AND JOHNNY EARS (1971, MGM)—**Anthony Quinn** and Franco Nero foil a plot by the Germans to establish a foothold in Texas in this spaghetti western.

SMITH, DR. FRANK

THE MAN WHO WOULDN'T TALK (1958, GB, British Lion)—**Anthony Quayle** and secret agent Zsa Zsa Gabor have been sworn to secrecy by a Hungarian scientist who tells them of germ warfare tests. When Gabor is killed, Quayle is charged with her murder. He is cleared by his counselor Anna Neagle, despite the fact that he refuses to talk because of his oath of secrecy.

SMITH, GEMMA

ESCAPE ME NEVER (1947, Warner Brothers)—Mother of an illegitimate baby, **Ida Lupino** marries composer Errol Flynn who loves another. This is not Flynn's cup of tea.

SMITH, HANK

THE HAIRY APE (1944, UA)—Boiler room stoker **William Bendix** becomes infatuated with rich Susan Hayward. She reviles him and uses him as a pawn. He almost kills her but it finally sinks into his thick head that she's no different and no better than the women he meets in waterfront saloons all over the world.

SMITH, HAP

JUMPING JACKS (1952, Paramount)—Song-and-dance man **Jerry Lewis** visits his old pal Dean Martin, now enrolled in paratrooper school. Jerry ends up having to make some jumps himself.

SMITH, HENRY

HENRY STEPS OUT (1940, GB, American International)—Henpecked **George Turner's** wife insists that he join the army. He fails, but somehow is assigned a job as a bathroom orderly in a female barracks. His wife shows up as a corporal and has him kicked out, lest he enjoy himself.

SMITH, PROF. HORATIO
PIMPERNEL SMITH (1942, GB, UA)—**Leslie Howard** updates his role as the Scarlet Pimpernel, playing an English professor who rescues prisoners held by the Nazis, helping them escape to England. Howard is excellent; and as a flag-waver, the film is effective.

SMITH, "HURRICANE"
HURRICANE SMITH (1942, Republic); (1952, Paramount)—**Ray Middleton** and **John Ireland** star as a charter boat skipper, who has trouble with a fortune hunter who hires him in the South Seas.

SMITH, JANET
DAUGHTER OF DR. JEKYLL (1957, Allied Artists)—**Gloria Talbot** is told by an evil doctor that she is the daughter of the infamous Dr. Jekyll, and as such, is responsible for a series of brutal murders.

SMITH, JEFFERSON
MR. SMITH GOES TO WASHINGTON (1939, Columbia)—Naive and extremely patriotic **James Stewart** is appointed to the United States Senate when the incumbent dies. The senior senator, Claude Rains, is in the pocket of political boss, Edward Arnold. When Stewart finally wakes up and sees all the corruption around him, he tries to blow the whistle, but the villains make him look like the crooked politician. It almost works, but his filibustering finally gets to Rains, a once honorable and honest politician.

SMITH, JENNIFER
LADY TAKES A SAILOR (1949, Warner Brothers)—**Jane Wyman**, a young woman dedicated to telling the truth, won't be silenced by government man Dennis Morgan, sent to prevent her from revealing that she was rescued by a mysterious experimental submarine when she had a sailing accident.

SMITH, JOBE
THE LAWNMOWER MAN (1992, New Line)—Mentally retarded gardener's assistant **Jeff Fahey** has his intelligence augmented by eccentric scientist Pierce Brosnan, who uses computer simulation. As Fahey becomes more aware of things, he begins to rebel against those who had abused him.

SMITH, JOE
JOE SMITH, AMERICAN (1942, MGM)—Aircraft factory worker **Robert Young** refuses to divulge secrets to Nazi agents who kidnap him. He escapes and is able to lead the FBI to the spies.

SMITH, CAPT. JOHN
CAPTAIN JOHN SMITH AND POCAHONTAS (1953, UA)—**Anthony Dexter** regales the court of James I in 1607 with tales of his adventures in the new world, and in particular how the beautiful Indian maid Pocahontas, played by Jody Lawrence, saved his head by throwing herself between Dexter and the poised tomahawk of a brave.

SMITH, JOHN
JOHN SMITH (1923, Silent, Selznick)—Wrongly convicted of a crime, **Eugene O'Brien** changes his name on release from prison, and takes a job with a wealthy family. His past catches up with him when his employer is robbed and killed. O'Brien is arrested, tried and is about to be sentenced when his parole officer saves the day by finding the real culprits.

SMITH, JOHN
THE MAN WHO FORGOT (1917, Silent, World)—When opium addict **Robert Warwick**, living in the Orient, decides to kick the habit, he returns to Cincinnati as a complete amnesiac. While in the slums, he falls in love with social worker Doris Kenyon, the daughter of a U.S. senator. The liquor trust tries to blackmail the senator by having a girl who shared the opium dens with Warwick back in China claim she is his wife. Warwick can't deny it, but the poor wretch recants in time and is helped to kick her own habit. The senator is then able to come out in support of Prohibition, while Warwick settles down soberly with the senator's daughter.

SMITH, JOHN
SMITHY (1933, GB, Warner Brothers)—Middle-aged clerk **Edmund Gwenn** dreams of wealth and adventure. When a course he's taken appears to change him, his fellow clerks believe he's inherited a fortune. When they discover that he has not, they turn against him. He learns that he has won 2,000 pounds in a competition, so he goes off to enjoy it, taking along a cabaret singer who had stood by him.

SMITH, JOSEPH
BACHELOR DADDY (1941, Universal)—**Edward Everett Horton** is a member of The Bachelors' Club. It is thrown in an uproar when someone leaves a baby on the club's door-step.

SMITH, LATIGO
SUPPORT YOUR LOCAL GUNFIGHTER (1971, UA)— Conman and compulsive gambler **James Garner** is mistaken for a famous gunslinger when he arrives in the town of Purgatory, divided into two warring mining camps. With the help of marvelous Jack Elam, he bungles his way through, even when he's forced to face the real gunman, Chuck Connors.

SMITH, LENA
THE CASE OF LENA SMITH (1929, Silent, Paramount)—**Esther Ralston**, a young peasant girl in 1890s Austria, is seduced by a young army officer. He commits suicide when his father takes their baby from them.

SMITH, LILI
DARLING LILI (1970, Paramount)—English music hall singer **Julie Andrews** is actually a German spy. The film received almost unanimous poor reviews, and was all but ignored by paying customers.

SMITH, LINDY
PENNY PRINCESS (1953, GB, Universal)—New Yorker **Yolande Donlan** goes to Europe to collect an inheritance, and is romanced by a British nobleman.

SMITH, LITTLE JOE
LITTLE JOE SMITH, THE WRANGLER (1942, Universal)—**Fuzzy Knight** gets to sing the title song, as does discredited sheriff Tex Ritter. They team up with falsely-accused Johnny Mack Brown to find the real murderers.

SMITH, LUKE "WHISPERING"
WHISPERING SMITH (1926, Silent, PDC); (1948, Paramount); WHISPERING SMITH SPEAKS (1935, Fox); WHISPERING SMITH VERSUS SCOTLAND YARD (1952, GB, RKO)—**H.B. Warner, Alan Ladd, George O'Brien** and **Richard Carlson** each took a crack at Frank Spearman's railroad detective, supposedly based on a real character. He investigates crimes against his railroad, including

train wreckers and looting. The 1948 picture was Ladd's first western and his first film in Technicolor. Carlson's portrayal is a modern Smith on vacation in England, but taking time out to show up Scotland Yard by showing that an apparent suicide case is really murder. Warner's version hues very close to Spearman's original story, while O'Brien's is a comedy.

SMITH, MADELEINE
MADELEINE (1958, GB, Rank)—**Ann Todd** appears in this true story of an engaged girl who, in 1857, may have fed arsenic to her blackmailing French lover.

SMITH, MARIE
TWO IN THE DARK (1936, RKO)—Unemployed actress **Margot Grahame** helps amnesiac Walter Abel, who fears he may have participated in a murder, resurrect his past.

SMITH, MARY
THE COWBOY AND THE LADY (1938, Goldwyn/UA)—**Merle Oberon**, the bored daughter of a presidential candidate, swaps places with her maid, falls in love with rodeo cowboy Gary Cooper, and elopes with him to Texas. When he discovers her real identity, he's angry. She rejoins her father, but he rescues her from the wealthy stiffs in Palm Springs, and she's gloriously happy. Sure, and Nancy Reagan wears hand-me-downs.

SMITH, MARY
THE GIRL ON THE CANAL (1947, GB, Ealing)—Canal girl **Jenny Laird** loves a barge worker, who joins the army unaware that she's pregnant. The film is called PAINTED BOATS in Great Britain.

SMITH, MAYBE
MAN OR GUN (1958, Republic)—**MacDonald Carey** cleans up a western town in this inconsequential oater.

SMITH, M'LISS
M'LISS (1918, Silent, Artcraft); (1936, RKO)—**Mary Pickford** and **Anne Shirley** portray a naive mountain girl who finds happiness with an earnest schoolteacher. These are pleasant, if not terribly exciting, homespun movies.

SMITH, MR.
MR. SMITH CARRIES ON (1937, GB, British & Dominions)—**Edward Rigby**, the secretary to a financier, accidentally shoots the boss during an argument. Rigby won't be a party to a fraud the magnate wishes to carry off. He hides the body and completes a pending big deal, which benefits small stock holders, before being found out. He gets off when the circumstances are understood.

SMITH, MRS.
LONELY WIVES (1931, RKO-Pathe)—**Esther Ralston's** unexpected arrival home upsets her husband Edward Everett Horton's plans to play with Laura La Plante.

SMITH, NEVADA
NEVADA SMITH (1966, Paramount)—When four outlaws rape and mutilate his mother, and then kill both his parents, **Steve McQueen** hunts them down, one by one, to take his revenge.

SMITH, PATTY
THE CASE OF PATTY SMITH (1962, Handel)—Pretty 21-year old **Dani Lynn** finds herself pregnant after being raped. She receives neither help nor sympathy from the medical community, nor her priest. She goes to an abortionist who butchers her and she dies. It's a pretty preachy story, with a lot of convenient straw men to knock down.

SMITH, PETE
THE COP (1928, Silent, Pathe Exchange)—Rookie cop **William Boyd** is assigned to bring in a notorious crook he had once befriended. Boyd is more determined to get his man, when the crook guns down Boyd's best friend. Boyd gets his revenge.

SMITH, ROXANNA
NOBODY'S WIDOW (1927, Silent, PDC)—**Leatrice Joy** hurriedly marries a flirtatious English duke. When she discovers him kissing another woman on their wedding night, she hurriedly returns to the U.S., where she announces her husband has died. The duke shows up, and after a time is able to convince Joy that he has truly repented and amended his ways.

SMITH, SAM
SMALL TOWN IDOL (1921, Silent, Associate Producers)—**Ben Turpin** has to flee his small town when he's accused of stealing. He turns up at a film studio where he stands in for an actor who unreasonably declines to jump from a high bridge. Turpin becomes a success in films and decides to return to his hometown. Rather than fans, he finds a lynch mob, and is saved only when his sweetheart's father confesses to the crime.

SMITH, SLICKER
BUCK PRIVATES (1941, Universal); BUCK PRIVATES COME HOME (1947, Universal)—**Bud Abbott** is only slightly brighter than his dimwitted buddy, Lou Costello in these two comedies. In the first, the pair find themselves accidentally in the army, adjusting to boot camp. They nearly destroy the service. In the sequel, WWII is over, and the boys come home, but Costello has smuggled an European orphan into the country. The boys also become involved in driving midget racing cars.

SMITH, SNUFFY
SNUFFY SMITH, YARD BIRD (1942, Monogram)—**Bud Duncan** stars as the comic-strip hillbilly drafted into the army. You can hardly imagine how bad this is.

SMITH, STEVIE
STEVIE (1978, GB, First Artists)—**Glenda Jackson** stars in this biopic of the eccentric poet who lived from 1902 to 1971.

SMITH, TONY
YOU'RE A LUCKY FELLOW, MR. SMITH (1943, Universal)—To get her inheritance Evelyn Ankers must marry before her 24th birthday. She chooses **Allan Jones** to fill her need for a husband in a hurry. She cuts him dead as soon as the ceremony is completed. Then she discovers she has to chase after him, because his signature is required on her checks.

SMITH, TUCSON
THE THREE MESQUITEERS (1936, Republic); PALS OF THE SADDLE (1938, Republic); THE TRAIL BLAZERS (1940, Republic); PALS OF THE PECOS (1941, Republic); SADDLEMATES (1941, Republic); THE PHANTOM PLAINSMEN (1942, Republic)—**Ray Corrigan** in the 1930s and **Bob Steele** in the 1940s contributed a lot of excitement for youngsters who enjoyed the adventures of the Three Mesquiteers, three modern cowboys who are always on the side of law and order and must deal with some rotten varmints with no redeeming characteristics. Steele was such a favorite of one of

your authors, that seeing him play a villain in OF MICE AND MEN almost was traumatic.

SMITH, VIC

DEPORTED (1950, Universal)—After being deported to Italy, American mobster **Jeff Chandler** tries his hand in the black market, and romances beautiful countess Marta Toren.

SMITH, WILL

THE STRANGE ADVENTURES OF MR. SMITH (1937, GB, RKO)—**Gus McNaughton** finds himself in the unusual position of being accused of murdering himself when he changes identities.

SMOKEY

GOVERNMENT GIRL (1943, RKO)—**Olivia De Havilland** didn't want to be in this dumb movie, and it showed. She portrays the secretary to Detroit automobile expert Sonny Tufts who's in Washington to speed up a bomber program, but needs Olivia to help him learn his way around the bureaucracy of the Capitol.

SNELL, WICKLAND

GENTLEMEN OF THE PRESS (1929, Paramount)—**Walter Huston** made his movie debut as a newspaperman who never has any time for his family. Too late, he discovers what he has lost.

SNYDER, CARRIE

VALIANT IS THE WORD FOR CARRIE (1936, Paramount)—**Gladys George** was Oscar nominated for her performance in this tearjerker about a small town's most fallen woman, redeemed by her love and care for two orphans. The film was a big hit with female fans.

SOAMES, JOHN

THE MIND OF MR. SOAMES (1970, GB, Columbia)—Thirty-year-old **Terence Stamp** is released from a lifetime in a synoptic coma after surgery.

SOFFEL, KATE

MRS. SOFFEL (1984, MGM/UA)—At the turn of the century, warden's wife **Diane Keaton** helps prisoners Mel Gibson and Matthew Modine escape from her husband's prison.

SOLANGE

THE MAIDS (1975, GB, Cine Films)—**Glenda Jackson** and her sister Susannah York plot to kill their Parisian employers.

SOLDIER, THE

THE SOLDIER (1982, Embassy)—**Ken Wahl** has a Mission Impossible-like assignment to sabotage the plot of Russian agents posing as terrorists with plans for setting off a nuclear explosion. Of course, if he's caught or killed, the Secretary will disavow any knowledge of . . . .

SOLOMON

SOLOMON AND SHEBA (1959, UA)—**Yul Brynner** replaced Tyrone Power who died of a heart attack while filming a sword fight with George Sanders. Brynner, wearing hair, gets to romance scantily clad Gina Lollobrigida as Sheba, and fight off the troops of his resentful brother Sanders. It's a spectacular, which means there's exciting action scenes but watch out when the actors have to talk to each other.

SOLOMON, ISADORE

WELCOME STRANGER (1924, Silent, PDC)—Jewish **Dore Davidson** is driven out of a New England town when he attempts to open a

store there. He is befriended by local handyman William V. Mong, as well as Florence Vidor, who are other unwelcome newcomers. They come up with the village's first electrical power and trolley car system, and now the townsfolk welcome the strangers.

SOLOMON, KING

KING SOLOMON OF BROADWAY (1935, Universal)—**Edmund Lowe** runs a Broadway nightspot he calls "Solomon's Place." He loses it to an underworld figure during a card game.

SOMMERS

THE NIGHT STALKER (1987, Chrystie-Striker/Almi)—**Robert Z'dar** is a serial killer who preys on L.A. prostitutes.

SON

MOTHER AND SON (1931, Monogram)—Clara Kimball Young keeps from her son **Bruce Warren** the fact that she earns their keep by running a gambling den. When he learns the truth, they are alienated, but they are reunited in a heart-tugging finale.

SONES, MARGARET

WOMEN WHO PLAY (1932, GB, Paramount British)—When his wife, **Benita Hume**, falls in with a group of parasites, author George Barraud hires actress Mary Newcomb to pose as a prostitute at a dinner party to teach her a lesson.

SONIA

THE MERRY WIDOW (1934, MGM)—**Jeanette MacDonald** and Maurice Chevalier are sparkling in Ernst Lubitsch's rousing version of the operetta in which a bankrupt king orders nobleman Chevalier to woo a wealthy widow, MacDonald. The principals handle the Franz Lehar music enchantingly.

SONNY

SONNY (1922, Silent, Associated First National)—**Richard Barthelmess** plays look-alikes: Sonny, a rich boy with a blind mother, and pool hall operator Joe, who impersonates his pal when Sonny is killed in a WWI battle. Barthelmess succeeds in convincing the mother that he's really her son, but he also falls in love with Sonny's sister. Fortunately, Mama has a dream which clears everything up.

SONNY BOY

SONNY BOY (1929, Warner Brothers)—Cute little **Davey Lee** portrays a tyke smuggled out of his home by his mother, Betty Bronson, prior to his parents' divorce. She fears his father might be given custody. She and Lee move into the home of bachelor lawyer Edward Everett Horton, who is away. Lee's mother is taken for Horton's wife, even by his parents. Through all this and more Lee just sits and smiles.

SONNY BOY

SONNY BOY (1990, Triumph)—**Michael Griffin** is the adult version of a kidnapped child who grows up in a family in which his "stepfather," Paul L. Smith, tortures him and even cuts out his tongue. His "stepmother" is David Carradine in drag. Smith uses Griffin to kill his enemies and drink their blood. Griffin finally rebels, but by this time surely no one is left in the theater to see it.

SOOKEY

SELF-MADE LADY (1932, GB, Paramount)—Slum girl **Heather Angel** becomes a fashion designer. She picks off a medical student, a lord and a boxer as sweethearts.

SOPHIA FREDERICA

THE SCARLET EMPRESS (1934, Paramount)—**Marlene Dietrich** is extremely glamorous in this strange, stylish movie, directed by her mentor Josef von Sternberg. She's a shy German princess, who is chosen as the bride of the idiot Grand Duke Peter of Russia, played by moronic-looking Sam Jaffe. When her dominating mother-in-law Louise Dresser dies, Dietrich beats Jaffe to the punch, has him killed before he can dispose of her, and becomes Catherine the Great of Russia.

SOPHIE
DESPERATE CHARACTERS (1971, Paramount)—The disintegration of **Shirley MacLaine's** neighborhood parallels the break-up of her marriage.

SOREL, CHARLIE
GOODBYE CHARLIE (1964, 20th Century Fox)—A playboy is murdered by a jealous husband. He is reincarnated in the form of cute little **Debbie Reynolds**, who finds out how it feels to be the prey of men, rather than the hunter. What might have been an interesting story line is so poorly handled that it falls on its face.

SOREL, DIANE
THE FORBIDDEN WOMAN (1920, Silent, Equity)—French actress **Clara Kimball Young** spurns a married suitor, who in despair kills himself. Despondent, she sails for the U.S. and takes up residence in a house next to that of a writer with whom she falls in love. When she learns that his sister is the wife of the man who killed himself over her, she tells the author about it. He believes she led his brother-in-law on and will have nothing further to do with her until his sister arrives and insists that Young was blameless in the matter.

SORRELL, CAPT. STEPHEN, KIT (child), KIT (man)
SORRELL AND SON (1934, GB, UA)—The fine actor **H.B. Warner** had played the same role seven years earlier in a silent version. Warner is a war hero reduced to scrubbing floors in a hotel, bullied by a hall porter. **Peter Penrose** and **Hugh Williams** portray his son as a child and an adult, respectively. Williams becomes a leading British surgeon, forced to make the decision to terminate his father's life, during a fatal illness.

SOUBIROUS, BERNADETTE
THE SONG OF BERNADETTE (1943, 20th Century Fox)—**Jennifer Jones** won an Academy Award for her thoughtful portrayal of a peasant girl who has a vision of the Virgin Mary at what becomes the shrine at Lourdes. Perhaps an indication of how convincing she was came when she divorced Robert Walker to marry David O. Selznick. She was roundly condemned from the pulpit of many Catholic Churches for having played a saint and then becoming a great sinner.

SOULTAKER
SOULTAKER (1990, Action)—**Joe Estevez** is sent by Angel of Death Robert Z'dar to pick up the souls of four teens who, as far as they can tell, have survived a car crash.

SOUSATZKA, MADAME
MADAME SOUSATZKA (1988, Cineplex Odeon)—In what many considered an Oscar-worthy performance, **Shirley Maclaine** is a piano teacher who demands nothing less than total commitment from her pupils. When a gifted Indian boy, Navin Chowdhry, becomes her student, she devotes all her energy to making him a true master. Her dedication is not appreciated by the boy's mother or by the prodigy himself.

SOUSE, EGBERT
THE BANK DICK (1940, Universal)—Lazy **W.C. Fields** accidentally prevents a bank robbery. He is rewarded by being given the job of bank guard. His troubles with the bank accelerate when he sells some phony stock. It's classic Fields, and a good example of his unique talent.

SPADE, JACK
I'M GONNA GET YOU SUCKA (1988, MGM-UA)—**Keenen Ivory Wayans** wrote and directed this hilarious parody of blaxploitation films, in which gold chains, not drugs, are ruining young black men.

SPANKY
GENERAL SPANKY (1937, MGM)—**Spanky McFarland** and his Our Gang buddies Alfalfa (Carl Switzer) and Buckwheat (Billie Thomas) fight for the Confederate cause in the Civil War, outsmarting stupid Union soldiers. This is the only full-length feature starring the "Our Gang" gang.

SPARROW, INSPECTOR
SOLO FOR SPARROW (1966, GB, Schoenfield)—When Scotland Yard interferes with his jurisdiction, local detective **Glyn Houston** takes a leave to prove a jeweller is responsible for a murder.

SPARROW, DR. SIMON
DOCTOR IN THE HOUSE (1954, GB, GFD); DOCTOR AT SEA (1955, GB, Rank); DOCTOR AT LARGE (1957, GB, Rank) DOCTOR IN DISTRESS (1963, GB, Rank)—**Dirk Bogarde** repeatedly came back to his role as the earnest young medical student and doctor who found himself in embarrassing situations, usually involving some young ladies and his senior colleague, Charles Robertson Justice. Audiences found the roles hilarious.

SPARTACUS
SPARTACUS (1960, Universal)—Roman slave **Kirk Douglas**, chosen to be a gladiator, leads a slave revolt. It is brutally put down by the troops of Laurence Olivier with all the revolting slaves being crucified along the Appian Way. It's a delightful epic with good performances from Charles Laughton, Tony Curtis, Jean Simmons and Peter Ustinov as well as by Douglas and Olivier.

SPAVINAW, DELMAR
THE HALF BREED (1922, Silent, Associated First National)—Unfortunately, educated half-breed **Wheeler Oakman** loves the daughter of a racist judge.

SPEAR, MARGE
MYRT AND MARGE (1934, Universal)—The zany radio comedy team of **Donna Damerel** and Myrtle Vail try their hands at the movies. Damerel is the real-life daughter of Vail.

SPECTOR, LINDA AND MICHAEL
IMMEDIATE FAMILY (1989, Columbia)—Unable to conceive a child, upper-middle class couple **Glenn Close** and **James Woods** arrange to adopt the baby of unmarried, working class kids Mary Stuart Masterson and Kevin Dillon. But watch out for maternal instincts.

SPEDDING, ANDREA
SHERLOCK HOLMES AND THE SPIDER WOMAN (1944, Universal)-**Gale Sondergaard** is marvelously wicked as the beautiful villain who uses spiders to commit her murders. She's a worthy adversary for Basil Rathbone and Nigel Bruce as Sherlock Holmes and Dr. Watson.

SPEED
MAN ALIVE (1945, RKO)—**Pat O'Brien** goes on a bender when he learns his wife has invited her old boyfriend for a visit. He has an

automobile accident, and is erroneously reported dead. The movie certainly is dead.

SPEED

MOTHER, JUGS AND SPEED (1976, 20th Century Fox)—Operator **Harvey Keitel** is the driver for a trio of hard-boiled paramedics who careen all over the city saving lives, and interacting with an assortment of weird characters.

SPEED, COP, THE

SPEED COP (1926, Silent, Rayart)—**Billy Sullivan** gives a judge's daughter a ticket for speeding. She falls for him on the spot. It takes a little doing but she lands her officer.

SPEED, DAVE

SUPER FUZZ (1981, Avco Embassy)—Exposed to radiation, Miami cop **Terence Hill** acquires super powers which he uses to collar a major criminal.

SPEED, JAKE

JAKE SPEED (1986, New World)—Paperback hero **Wayne Crawford** leaps off the pages to help a real-life woman whose life is in danger. A tough idea to present is handled about as badly as can be imagined.

SPELL, KARL

HEART OF A CHILD (1958, GB, Rank)—In 1918 Austria, youngster **Richard Williams** runs away when his father sells his St. Bernard.

SPENCE, JANET

A WOMAN'S VENGEANCE (1947, Universal)—**Jessica Tandy** loves Charles Boyer so much that she frames him for the murder of his wife when he shows an interest in young Ann Blyth, whom he plans to make his new spouse.

SPENCE, WILLIAM

ONE FOOT IN HEAVEN (1941, Warner Brothers)—**Fredric March** stars in this slow but pleasant story of the quiet life of a Methodist minister and his family.

SPENCER, ANATOL DE WITT

THE AFFAIRS OF ANATOL (1921, Silent, Paramount) -**Wallace Reid**, an amorous member of the upper class, always returns to his wife Gloria Swanson after tiring of his conquests.

SPENCER, CLAY

SPENCER'S MOUNTAIN (1963, Warner Brothers)—Wyoming dirt farmer **Henry Fonda** and his family struggle against poverty in this story by Earl Hammer Jr., which would ultimately see a more accurate depiction in the television series THE WALTONS.

SPENCER, HENRY

ERASERHEAD (1978, AFI/Libra)—Audiences have been known to walk out in groups at showings of this wildly experimental movie by director David Lynch. Of those who remained, especially at midnight showings, many were of a type whom other people wouldn't wish to meet either in or outside a theater. **John Nance** stars in this cult favorite as a zombie-like misfit who lives in some nauseating future where everyone is alienated, spastic, sexually retarded and half-human, existing in decayed industrial surroundings. Lynch went on to direct ELEPHANT MAN and BLUE VELVET, and thus hasn't lost his touch for the bizarre. Consider his 1990 film WILD AT HEART.

SPENGLER, DR. EGON

GHOSTBUSTERS (1984, Columbia); GHOSTBUSTERS II (1989, Columbia)—**Harold Ramis** is one of the nutty professors who go into the ghost disposal business. His is the least interesting character, probably because he seems most like a professor.

SPIDER WOMAN

KISS OF THE SPIDER WOMAN (1985, Island Alive)—**Sonia Braga** is the central character in the movie that homosexual William Hurt describes to political prisoner Raul Julia. She also portrays the woman that Julia dreams of being with again.

SPIELSDORF, LAURA

THE VAMPIRE LOVERS (1970, GB, Hammer)—**Pippa Steele** is one of the victims of lesbian vampire Ingrid Pitt, who really loses her head over her blood contributing lovers.

SPIKE *See* **FRANCIS ROTHSCHILD**

SPIKES, HARRY

THE SPIKES GANG (1974, UA)—Bank robber **Lee Marvin** is sheltered by three boys who join his gang. It's a violent western with the doomed ending of all concerned very predictable.

SPIRIT, THE

SATAN'S MISTRESS (1982, Motion Picture Marketing)—**Kabir Bedi** has his way with generally naked Lana Wood, a bored rich California housewife. Since he's invisible at these tender moments, we can't say if it's good for him too.

SPLUTTERS

SPARROWS (1926, Silent, UA)—**Monty O'Grady** is one of the youngsters whom Mary Pickford leads to safety across swamps from a baby farm where they are almost worked to death by cruel Gustav von Seyfferitz.

SPOCK, MR.

STAR TREK III: THE SEARCH FOR SPOCK (1984, Paramount)—Admiral Kirk (William Shatner) discovers that Mr. Spock (**Leonard Nimoy**) is not as dead as it seemed at the end of STAR TREK II: THE WRATH OF KHAN, but has been reborn as a Vulcan child.

SPOFFORD, HENRY

GENTLEMEN PREFER BLONDES (1928, Silent, Paramount) (1953, 20th Century Fox)—**Holmes Herbert** and **George "Foghorn" Winslow** play rich passengers on the ocean liner carrying gold-digging Lorelei Lee and her friend Dorothy to Europe. Lorelei makes a play for Spofford, but in the 1953 version Marilyn Monroe is disappointed to discover that Winslow is a ten-year-old boy. He's not unappreciative of Monroe's obvious charms.

SPOFFORD, JANE

THE WITCHES OF EASTWICK (1987, Warner Brothers)—In this disappointing black comedy, repressed **Susan Sarandon** and two other unconventional single women of a small hamlet unwittingly conjure up devil Jack Nicholson. He beds each and each woman presents him with a child.

SPOOFY

THREE LIVE GHOSTS (1922, Silent, Paramount); (1929, UA); (1935, MGM)—**Cyril Chadwick** in the silent and **Claude Allister** in the talkie plays one of three soldiers returning from WWI to find they are officially listed as dead. Their return causes comical complications.

SPRIGGINS, JOSEPHINE

VAGABOND LADY (1935, MGM)—Janitor's daughter **Evelyn Venable** is courted by the two very different sons of her boss. Robert Young is a bit of a nut, while Reginald Denny is quite serious. It goes down to the altar before she decides which one to marry.

SPRING

PRIVATE DUTY NURSES (1972, New World)—**Kathy Cannon**, one of three nurses who enter a program at a California hospital, is able to give a crazed Vietnam vet the understanding he needs—among other things.

SPRY, CONSTABLE ROBERT

IT'S A COP (1934, GB, British & Dominions)—Slow-witted constable **Sydney Howard** is lured from his post watching a house, which the police believe may be a burglary gang's next target, by a seductive member of the gang. He's fired but wins back his job by accidentally catching the crooks.

"SPUDS"

SPUDS (1927, Silent, Pathe Exchange)—Doughboy **Larry Semon** returns a payroll truck a friend has stolen by driving it across a battlefield under fire.

SPUNGEN, NANCY

SID & NANCY (1986, GB, Goldwyn)—**Chloe Webb**, a heroin addict, is killed by her lover, Gary Oldman, playing punk rocker Sid Vicious of the Sex Pistols. It's an unpleasantly violent film, loaded with sex and nudity.

SPUR

THE MAN FROM SNOWY RIVER (1983, Australia, 20th Century Fox)—**Kirk Douglas** portrays a pair of brothers, one a wealthy Australian rancher and the other, Spur, a hermit, who hasn't spoken to his brother for years because of their rivalry over a woman. The story is secondary to the photography and the exciting horse action sequences.

SPURLOCK, JACK

JACK SPURLOCK, PRODIGAL (1918, Silent, Fox)—After being thrown out of college for taking his pet bear to classes, **George Walsh** joins the union trying to organize his father's company and leads them to victory.

SQUIRE, TOM

THE AUDACIOUS MR. SQUIRE (1923, Silent, GB, British & Colonial)—An art collector mistakes thief **Jack Buchanan** for his daughter's secret husband.

STACEY

A MAN, A WOMAN AND A BANK (1979, Canada, Bennett)—**Brooke Adams** is appealing in this caper movie about the screwed up plans of Donald Sutherland and Paul Mazursky to rob a bank by computer.

STACEY, JANE

MY FRIEND IRMA (1949, Paramount): MY FRIEND IRMA GOES WEST (1950, Paramount)—**Diana Lynn** is meant to be the sane and sensible friend in these two films starring Marie Wilson as scatterbrained Irma, Dean Martin and Jerry Lewis in their first two films and other loonies including John Lund, Don De Fore and Hans Conreid.

STACY

STACY'S KNIGHTS (1983, Crown)—**Andia Millian** has the fever for blackjack gambling. She recruits a group of sharp gamblers to break the bank at the casino where goons killed her mentor Kevin Costner.

STAEBLER, JASON

THE KING OF MARVIN GARDENS (1972, Columbia)—**Bruce Dern** involves his late-night-radio-show-host brother, Jack Nicholson, in his nonsensical financial schemes.

STAHR, MONROE

THE LAST TYCOON (1976, Paramount)—**Robert De Niro** stars in F. Scott Fitzgerald's incomplete novel based on the life of "boy genius" Irving Thalberg. In his short life as head of production at MGM, Thalberg had a rare gift for hiring the right people and guiding their talents into making outstanding movies.

STALIN, JOSEPH

RED MONARCH (1983, GB, Enigma/Goldcrest)—**Colin Blakely** portrays the longtime communist leader as an eccentric buffoon. It's difficult to enjoy the incoherent and plotless film, particularly when it is known that Stalin was a purposeful mass murderer.

STAN

ACCUSED OF MURDER (1956, Republic)—**Warren Stevens** is accused of murdering crooked lawyer Sidney Blackmer. He didn't. The mouthpiece turned a gun on himself when Vera Ralston spurned his advances.

STAN

THE FLYING DEUCES (1939, RKO); A CHUMP AT OXFORD (1940, UA); SAPS AT SEA (1940, UA); AIR RAID WARDENS (1943, MGM); THE DANCING MASTERS (1943, 20th Century Fox)—**Stan Laurel** appeared in hundreds of shorts and many features with his longtime partner, Oliver Hardy. Although he played the bigger boob of the two, it was Laurel who wrote most of the stories on which their movies were based. Of course, it was the special magical blend of the two great comical talents that have endeared Mr. Laurel and Mr. Hardy to millions of fans all these years, with new generations discovering them all the time.

STANDISH, CLAIRE

THE BREAKFAST CLUB (1985, Universal)—**Molly Ringwald** gives an excellent performance as the high school girl who just seems to fit in well, even though she's stuck in a high school day-long detention with a nerd, a hood, a jock and a wacko.

STANDISH, DORIS

NOBODY'S BRIDE (1923, Silent, Universal)—**Edna Murphy** gets cold feet at her wedding. She runs into her ex-fiance Herbert Rawlinson, who is at her home with a gang of crooks to rob her. She begs him to run away with her. He does—in the getaway car. His colleagues give chase, capture Murphy and hold her for ransom. It's all down hill from there.

STANDISH, KATHERINE

KATIE DID IT (1951, Universal)—What small-town girl **Ann Blyth** did was pose semi-nude for artist Mark Stevens. She is furious when she finds her image appearing on billboards all over the country. She gets her revenge by marrying the soft pornographer.

STANDISH, MILES

THE COURTSHIP OF MILES STANDISH (1923, Silent, Associate Exhibitors)—Charles Ray, who had a special niche in movies playing country boys, got the bug to do something greater. The result is this overblown epic in which he plays John Alden, whom Miles Standish, played by **Alyn Warren**, sends to ask for the hand of

Priscilla Mullins. The film bombed and all but finished Ray. He quickly fell into supporting roles and before his death at 52, was reduced to appearing in movies as an extra.

STANDISH, PETER

I'LL NEVER FORGET YOU (1951, 20th Century Fox)—In this remake of BERKELEY SQUARE, **Tyrone Power** lives in the home of his ancestors in London, and dreams of the past. He's transported back in time a couple centuries, and falls in love with Ann Blyth who is the only one who understands that he is a visitor from the future. When he finally gets back to the 20th Century he meets a contemporary Blyth—and they lived happily ever after, we suppose.

STANHOPE, LAURA

THIRTEEN WOMEN (1932, RKO)—**Irene Dunne** gets top billing, but the star is Myrna Loy. She's a half-caste who works her way through the 12 women who snubbed her in college, killing them one by one.

STANHOPE, LINDA

WIFE VERSUS SECRETARY (1936, MGM)—When **Myrna Loy** begins to hear rumors about her husband Clark Gable and his secretary Jean Harlow, she decides action is called for.

STANHOPE, MARY

THE INNOCENT CHEAT (1921, Silent, Arrow)—**Kathleen Kirkham** listens quietly as the judge in her divorce suit rules for her husband and awards their child to the father. Then she tells such a sad and convincing story about the man's infidelity and mistreatment of her and the child that the jurist reverses his decision. Later, Kirkham encounters Roy Stewart who has been seeking the woman who spurned him, which led him to neglect his work and become a failure. But of course, Kirkham is the very same woman. She saves herself, her child and Stewart by pointing out that the child is his. That does the trick. All is forgiven and all is well with the world.

STANISLAV, RAOUL

THREE SINNERS (1928, Silent, Paramount)—When Pola Negri's husband takes her close friend as a lover, Negri heads to Vienna to visit relatives. On the way, she is seduced by famous musician **Tullo Carminati**. Ashamed, she leaves the train, which pulls out without her, crashes, killing all aboard. Negri chooses to allow her husband to believe her dead. They meet again but their reunion is not permanent.

STANLEY

THE BELLBOY (1960, Paramount)—**Jerry Lewis** has the audacity to star in a plotless movie in which he's a bellboy creating havoc in a luxury Miami hotel.

STANLEY

STANLEY AND IRIS (1990, MGM/UA)—Unfortunately, **Robert De Niro**, as an illiterate, and Jane Fonda, as a grieving widow, don't have the chemistry to make this film work. She teaches him to read. He helps her get over the loss of her husband. The romance that develops is flat.

STANLEY, "BRAINS"

I LOVE THAT MAN (1933, Paramount)—**Edmund Lowe** and Nancy Carroll, a pair of con artists touring the country, decide to go straight.

STANLEY, BULL

THREE ROGUES (1931, Fox)—Bank robber **Victor McLaglen** is one of three western no-goods who discover Fay Wray's attractiveness when they find she possesses a map indicating the location of a gold mine.

STANLEY, HENRY M.

STANLEY AND LIVINGSTONE (1939, 20th Century Fox)—Newspaperman **Spencer Tracy** is given the assignment of going to Africa to find lost Scottish missionary David Livingstone. He does, delivering the classic line: "Dr. Livingstone, I presume." He is not believed on his return, but the facts finally bear him out.

STANLEY, LUCY

ONLY 38 (1923, Silent, Paramount)—**May McAvoy** stars in this minor comedy drama about a clergyman's young widow, left to raise her teenage twins alone.

STANLEY, MARY & BILLY

MELODY FOR THREE (1941, RKO)—**Fay Wray** and **Schuyler Standish** are a music teacher and her 12-year-old violin virtuoso son. To supplement her income, she takes a job as a nurse with Dr. Christian (Jean Hersholt). The kindly old medic reunites mother and child with her ex-husband, an orchestral conductor, who was unaware of his son's talents.

STANNARD, BILL

THE INTERFERIN' GENT (1927, Silent, Pathe Exchange)—**Buffalo Bill, Jr.** witnesses a killing of a man by a hired assassin. Junior takes the identity of the deceased, believed to be the long-lost brother of Olive Hasbrouck, owner of a ranch the assassin's employer has designs on. The real brother is still alive, however, and Buffalo Bill, Jr. is arrested as an imposter. But he's able to identify the murderer and the man who hired him. In the end he finds happiness with Hasbrouck.

STANNARD, WILLIE

MY BROTHER'S KEEPER (1949, GB, Rank)—Innocent youth **George Cole** and hardened criminal Jack Warner are handcuffed together when they escape from prison. Warner kills a man who catches them sawing off the cuffs. Cole surrenders and is accused of the crime. Warner miscalculates as he attempts to escape the police across a mine field and is blown to bits.

STANTON, AGATHA

TWO WISE MAIDS (1937, Republic)—**Alison Skipworth** and Polly Moran are two tough schoolteachers who teach their students and colleagues more than the "three r's."

STANTON, JACK

ALADDIN FROM BROADWAY (1917, Silent, Vitagraph)—American **Antonio Moreno** poses as an Arab, in order to enter Mecca. While there he rescues the daughter of an Englishman, who had been abducted 18 years earlier.

STANTON, JIM

THE MAN WHO FOUND HIMSELF (1937, RKO)—Surgeon **John Beal** gives up the practice of medicine until he is forced to perform an operation high in the sky on a flying hospital.

STANTON, JOAN

HER SUMMER HERO (1928, Silent, FBO)—College co-ed **Duane Thompson** is rescued from drowning by lifeguard Hugh Trevor. They become summer sweethearts. Come the fall, a misunderstanding causes her to promise the lifeguard's chief rival, Harold Goodwin, that she'll wear his fraternity pin if he wins the big swimming race, but Trevor prevails in the water and on land with Thompson.

STANTON, LADDIE
LADDIE (1940, RKO)—Cute little Joan Carroll plays Cupid for her sister Virginia Gilmore and Indiana farmer **Tim Holt** in this version of the Gene Stratton Porter novel.

STANTON, LETTY & JANE
THE SAINTED SISTERS (1948, Paramount)—At the turn of the century, adventurers **Veronica Lake** and **Joan Caulfield** leave a small town for the city, where they learn to live on the right side of the law.

STANTON, PETER
THE CLOWN AND THE KID (1961, UA)—Ex-convict **John Lupton** forms a circus act with an orphan, and falls in love with the amusement park owner, Mary Webster.

STANTZ, DR. RAYMOND
GHOSTBUSTERS (1984, Columbia); GHOSTBUSTERS II (1989, Columbia)—Ex-professor **Dan Aykroyd** joins Bill Murray and Harold Ramis to form a concern which captures and stores ghosts and evil spirits. Their biggest job is a giant marshmallow like slime-man who lives atop an old apartment building. In the sequel, they must prevent Sigourney Weaver's baby from being the new home for the spirit of an ancient, evil Carpathian despot.

STARBUCK, BILL
THE RAINMAKER (1956, Paramount)— Western con man **Burt Lancaster** comes into a drought region, not only bringing the relief of rain, but also convincing plain old maid Katharine Hepburn that she is beautiful and desirable.

STARK, LT.
THE AMERICAN PRISONER (1929, GB, British International)—In 1815, American prisoner of war **Carl Bresson** escapes from Dartmoor and saves a squire's daughter.

STARK, NATHAN
THE TALL MEN (1955, 20th Century Fox)—Unscrupulous businessman **Robert Ryan** hires Texan brothers Clark Gable and Cameron Mitchell to drive a vast herd of cattle from Texas to Montana. Ryan competes with trail boss Gable for the affections of lusty Jane Russell, whom they rescued from an Indian attack along the way.

STARKEY, NICK
THE JANUARY MAN (1989, MGM-UA)—Mayor Rod Steiger insists that police commissioner Harvey Keitel assign Keitel's younger brother **Kevin Kline** to a serial murder case. Kline, once a cop, but now a fireman, and brother Keitel don't get along because Harvey is now married to Kevin's one-time lover, Susan Sarandon.

STARLING, JANICE
THE WASP WOMAN (1959, Allied Artists)—Looking for eternal youth and beauty, **Susan Cabot** uses a potion which is made from wasp enzymes. During the day, she's a beautiful woman; at night she flies around killing people. She splatters when she tries to fly at the wrong time.

STARMAN
STARMAN (1984, Columbia)—Stranded alien **Jeff Bridges** assumes the appearance of Karen Allen's late, beloved husband and enlists her aid in making a critical rendezvous with his space ship. As they run ahead of the scientists and officials who wish to capture him, Bridges' and Allen's relationship deepens, and he leaves her pregnant with the human child of its "father." Bridges is excellent in an Oscar-nominated performance.

STARR, ALVA
THIS PROPERTY IS CONDEMNED (1966, Paramount)—**Natalie Wood,** suffering from tuberculosis, escapes from her mother's broken-down Mississippi boarding house by marrying mom's lover Charles Bronson. Wood continues to meet her true love Robert Redford after the marriage, but after a showdown caused by her mother, Wood finds herself alone and fast becoming the town's number one slut.

STARR, ANNIE LAURIE
GUN CRAZY (1949, UA)—**Peggy Cummins** and John Dall star in an examination of the career of a Bonnie-and-Clyde-like pair of robbers and killers.

STARR, BELLE
BELLE STARR (1941, 20th Century Fox); MONTANA BELLE (1952, RKO)—**Gene Tierney** looks mighty fetching wearing a gun-belt slung low on her hip in a highly romanticized account of an infamous post-Civil-War Missouri bandit. She avenges the loss of her land to the Yankees by joining a Confederate guerilla band, which continues its raids after the defeat of the South. In the second film, **Jane Russell** is saved from lynching by the Dalton boys with whom she works. Her heart belongs to gambler George Brent, who ultimately sends her to prison, promising to wait for her release.

STARR, BLAZE
BLAZE (1989, Buena Vista)—Married three-term Louisiana governor Earl K. Long, portrayed by Paul Newman, falls hard for New Orleans' Bourbon Street stripper Blaze Starr, adequately played by **Lolita Davidovich.** It's a sanitized presentation of their affair.

STARR, DICK
FUGITIVES (1929, Silent, Fox)—Young D.A. **Don Terry** sends nightclub singer Madge Bellamy to prison. When he discovers she's innocent of murdering her boss, he helps her escape and prove her innocence. Apparently he hasn't much faith in the judicial system.

STARR, GALE
MELODY FOR TWO (1937, Warner Brothers)—**Patricia Ellis** patiently works on egotistical and constantly complaining band leader-singer James Melton, until he develops a more agreeable disposition. Audiences wondered why she bothered.

STARR, NINA
SHOULD A WIFE WORK? (1922, Silent, S.W. Film)—The title question seems ridiculous today, but once it was a hotly debated query. **Alice Lowe** chooses marriage, which means that, unlike her friend Edith Stockton, she will have no career.

STAVES, LT. CMDR. BEN
THE SHARKFIGHTERS (1956, UA)—Off the coast of Cuba during WWII, **Victor Mature** leads a group of scientists trying to develop a shark repellent which will save the lives of pilots forced down in the sea. It's not JAWS, but the sharks are plenty nasty.

STAYTON, JOANNA
OVERBOARD (1987, MGM/UA)—Insufferable, rich **Goldie Hawn** is travelling on a yacht with her loony husband. She falls overboard

and loses her memory. Workman **Kurt Russell**, whom she stiffed for a construction job he did for her aboard the yacht, claims she's his wife. He takes her home to his hovel and four unruly kids. As one might suspect, the initial cultural shock turns to love for all five of her men, even when her amnesia wears off.

STEAMBOAT BILL, JR.
STEAMBOAT BILL, JR. (1928, Silent, UA)—There are sight gags galore in this **Buster Keaton** movie. He's an effete young man who returns from college to help his father run his old tub of a ship up and down the Mississippi. The father is disappointed in his son, and to make matters worse, Keaton's girl is the daughter of a rival steamboat captain.

STECKERT, MARTIN
MARTIN'S DAY (1985, MGM/UA)—Escaped convict **Richard Harris** develops an unusual friendship with a young boy he kidnaps. Extremely ordinary.

STECKLE
FLATLINERS (1990, Columbia)—The last thing medical students like **Oliver Platt** hear before undergoing "flatlining" (the intentional stopping of heart and brain functions to induce a brief experience of death) is Julia Roberts' soft "See you soon."

STEELE, DOCTOR
CALLING DR. DEATH (1943, Universal)—When **Lon Chaney, Jr.'s** wife is murdered, the police arrest her lover, but we know he's not guilty , don't we?

STEELE, HELEN
THE MISLEADING LADY (1932, Paramount)—To prove she can handle a movie role she's seeking, **Claudette Colbert** vamps an unsuspecting bachelor, who abducts her, and the two fall in love.

STEELE, HENRY
ONE ON ONE (1977, Warner Brothers)—Local basketball star **Robby Benson** discovers that he's not as good as he believed when he leaves his Colorado home for a California university which recruited him.

STEELE, JANET
WOMEN IN THE WIND (1939, Warner Brothers)—**Kay Francis** must win the annual transcontinental race for women pilots to get the money for her brother's operation.

STEELE, NANCY
NANCY STEELE IS MISSING (1937, 20th Century Fox)—**June Lang** believes that Victor McLaglen, released from prison after serving seventeen years, is her father, but in fact she had been kidnapped when she was a baby. McLaglen returns Lang to her true father, a wealthy man who in gratitude offers McLaglen a reward and a job.

STEELE, RICHARD
EXPERT'S OPINION (1935, GB, Paramount)—Ballistics expert **Leslie Perrin** is the target of spies, after his formula for a new anti-aircraft gun. The secret is preserved due to the courage of his wife Lucille Lisle.

STEELE, SONNY
THE ELECTRIC HORSEMAN (1979, Columbia/Universal)—Former rodeo star **Robert Redford** has been reduced to unhappily appearing as the spokesman for a breakfast cereal. He rebels, and with the help of reporter Jane Fonda kidnaps his partner, a prize horse, with the intention of setting it free in the wilds.

STEELE, WES
A MAN ALONE (1955, Republic)—**Ray Milland** directed this film, in which he portrays a fugitive from a lynch mob who is hidden by a small-town sheriff's daughter, Mary Murphy.

STEFFENS, "CURLY"
OCEAN'S ELEVEN (1960, Warner Brothers)—**Richard Benedict** is another of Frank Sinatra's flunkies involved in the New Year's Eve robbery of five Las Vegas casinos.

STEIN
THE LONERS (1972, Fanfare)—**Dean Stockwell** is one of three bikers who drop out of society and take their motorcycles on a trip through the southwest.

STEIN, DR. VICTOR
THE REVENGE OF FRANKENSTEIN (1958, GB, Columbia)—**Peter Cushing** has found it advisable to alter his name. He runs a charity hospital for the poor, an ideal place to get body parts for his experiments. With the help of an assistant, he puts the brain of a cripple into a different body. The result has some of the usual failings, although the monster looks more normal.

STEINER, JOSEPH
SO ENDS OUR NIGHT (1941, UA)—Opposed to the Nazi regime, Aryan **Fredric March** is forced to flee from Germany. He meets Jewish Margaret Sullavan and Glenn Ford, who is the offspring of a Jewish-Ayran marriage in Austria. They are pursued from country to country as the Nazis take over new territories. March risks his life to return to Germany to visit his wife on her deathbed.

STEINER, PROF.
THE PROJECTED MAN (1967, GB, Universal)—**Bryant Halliday** uses lasers to transport matter. When he uses himself as a guinea pig, he develops a deadly electrical touch and the desire to use his power.

STELLA
STELLA (1950, 20th Century Fox)—**Ann Sheridan** is the only sane member of a family and is trying to locate the body of an uncle who died of a heart attack during an argument with his nephew. The latter promptly buried the body and then couldn't remember where. The reason the uncle is in such demand is he left a large insurance policy that cannot be collected upon unless he is proven dead.

STELLA
X, Y & ZEE (1972, GB, Columbia)—**Susannah York**, is the other woman in this tasteless story of perverted Elizabeth Taylor, and her equally sick husband Richard Burton, who develop a "count the possibilities" sexual relationship with York.

STEPANAWICZ, KING ZHARKO
KING OF THE GYPSIES (1978, Paramount)—**Sterling Hayden** stars in this saga of the violent life of three generations of a gypsy family.

STEPANEK, SUE ANN
PRETTY POISON (1968, 20th Century Fox)—**Tuesday Weld** is more deadly than her male counterpart, Anthony Perkins. A vicious,

coldly manipulative model high school student, Weld persuades former convict and psychotic Perkins to help her kill her mother and engage in other crimes. When caught, she reverts to being just a cute kid, while Perkins takes the blame for everything.

STEPHANIE
LOVELY TO LOOK AT (1952, MGM)—**Kathryn Grayson** is indeed lovely to look at in this remake of ROBERTA. The story about three Broadway producers, Howard Keel, Gower Champion and Red Skelton inheriting a Paris fashion house is almost incidental to the fashions and the Jerome Kern musical numbers. Grayson is especially effective singing "Yesterdays" and "Smoke Gets in Your Eyes," while Marge and Gower Champion dance enchantingly.

STEPHANIE
LOVING COUPLES (1980, 20th Century Fox)—Doctor Shirley Maclaine, believing her surgeon husband James Coburn is taking her for granted, begins an affair with young patient Stephen Collins. The latter's girlfriend, **Susan Sarandon**, springs the news of his wife's infidelity to Coburn. They play tit-for-tat by having an affair. The generation gap proves too strong for all concerned, and by the end of the film, everyone is back with his or her original partner.

STEPHENS, CHUCK
SAILORS ON LEAVE (1941, Republic)—**William Lundigan** stars in this breezy nautical comedy as a sailor trying to conquer gob-hating singer Shirley Ross. It's sort of a "B" ON THE TOWN.

STEPHENS, "DIRTY STEVE"
YOUNG GUNS (1988, 20th Century Fox)—**Dermot Mulroney** is one of five young gunslingers who ride with Billy the Kid, in this effort to revive interest in westerns by casting a number of the young Hollywood hunks in chaps and spurs. Mulroney's character takes his killings very seriously, sort of a rite of passage into manhood.

STEPHENS, JOSHUA
HINTON'S DOUBLE (1917, Silent, Thanhouser)—**Frederick Warde** portrays swindler John Evart Hinton and his exact double Stephens, who is persuaded by his dishonest look-alike to serve a prison sentence for Hinton in return for taking care of his family.

STEPHENSON, MAGNUS
THE PRODIGAL SON (1923, GB, Silent, Stoll)—In the longest British silent film ever made (17 reels, when norm was 5-7), **Stewart Rome** is a cad who steals his brother's sweetheart, deserts her at childbirth, sails for Nice where he seduces the woman's sister, and generally acts like a rotter. The film was released in two parts—the second half under the to be expected title of THE RETURN OF THE PRODIGAL.

STERLING, DR. TIMOTHY
DOCTOR TAKES A WIFE (1940, Columbia)—**Ray Milland** must pretend to be the husband of socialite Loretta Young in this diverting comedy.

STEVE
THE DEVIL THUMBS A RIDE (1947, RKO)—Mean and nasty **Lawrence Tierney** kills a theater manager in a hold-up. He escapes by hitching a ride with a naive motorist. When the latter picks up two girl passengers, the stage is set for more killings by Tierney.

STEVE
ESCORT FOR HIRE (1960, GB, MGM)—Unemployed actor **Noel Trevarthan** takes a job as a hired escort and is framed for the death of his rich client.

STEVE
HELL DIVERS (1932, MGM)—**Clark Gable** and Wallace Beery have a friendly rivalry as tough petty officers in the Naval Air Force. Beery saves Gable's life.

STEVE
IF I WERE BOSS (1933, GB, Columbia)—Conceited clerk **Bruce Seton** inherits a farm, and becomes the pawn of a gang of crooks.

STEVE
KING OF THE MOUNTAIN (1981, Universal)—**Harry Hamlin** stars in a routine car-racing drama.

STEVE
SUED FOR LIBEL (1940, RKO)—Radio broadcaster **Kent Taylor** teams with newspaper reporters Linda Hayes and Richard Lane to solve a triple murder and avert two libel suits.

STEVE
WIFE, DOCTOR AND NURSE (1937, 20th Century Fox)—**Virginia Bruce** is doctor Warner Baxter's efficient secretary. His wife Loretta Young decides that Bruce is just too attractive to keep around and forces her husband to fire Bruce. The result is that the doctor's practice suffers. Finally Young decides that Bruce best be brought back even though it's fairly clear that Bruce is in love with Baxter.

STEVEN
TWO (1975, Colmar)—Vietnam vet **Douglas Travis** escapes from a discharge hospital, kidnaps Sarah Venable, and hides away with her in a secluded mountain cabin, where they develop a rapport. Travis robs a bank while in town for supplies. Venable insists that he return the money. This leads to a tragic ending for Travis.

STEVENS, DIZZY
HENRY AND DIZZY (1942, Paramount)—**Charles Smith** plays Henry Aldrich's none-too-bright best friend.

STEVENS, DORIS
THE CROWN VS. STEVENS (1936, Warner Brothers)—Ex-dancer **Beatrix Thomson** kills a moneylender and her husband, and tries to frame his employee Patric Knowles for the crime.

STEVENS, FRANK
THE JACK RIDER (1921, Silent, Aywon)—Tenderfoot **Guinn "Big Boy" Williams** must prove himself a man to inherit his father's ranch. Of course he does.

STEVENS, LARRY
TWO IN A CROWD (1936, Universal)—Race-horse owner **Joel McCrea** and beautiful Joan Bennett each find half of a thousand dollar bill, torn in half and thrown out of a window on New Year's Eve by a drunk.

STEVENS, DR. MARY
MARY STEVENS, M.D. (1933, Warner Brothers)—Physician **Kay Francis** has an unhealthy yen for medical scoundrel Lyle Talbot, who thinks nothing of operating on children while he's drunk. Francis goes to Europe to have his illegitimate child, but the baby dies of infantile paralysis before she can return to the States.

STEVENS, MARY
SALLY, IRENE AND MARY (1938, 20th Century Fox)—**Marjorie Weaver** and her fellow manicurists, Alice Faye and Joan Davis, hope

to become Broadway stars. Weaver inherits a broken down ferry boat which the three turn into a successful supper club.

STEVENS, MAT

HIGH SCHOOL CAESAR (1960, Marathon Film Group)—Rich high school kid **John Ashley**, with an attitude problem, sets up a crime syndicate among his peers.

STEVENS, ROBERT

THIS WOMAN IS MINE (1941, Universal)—**Franchot Tone** is one of two crewmen and a captain who fall in love with beautiful stowaway Carol Bruce while they are on a dangerous fur-trading expedition.

STEVENS, JR., RUSSELL/JOHN Q. HULL

DEEP COVER (1992, New Line)—Tough, honest cop **Larry Fishburne** is recruited to infiltrate the cartel of drug dealer Arthur Medoza. Fishburne works so earnestly that he goes over the edge into addiction and money mania.

STEVENS, RUTH

SILK LEGS (1927, Silent, Fox)—**Madge Bellamy** appears as a hosiery sales clerk who finally forgets her competition with another clerk, James Hall, and marries him.

STEVENSON, CAPT. TERENCE

ADVENTURES OF TARTU (1943, GB, MGM)—British officer **Robert Donat** is in Czechoslovakia, posing as a Rumanian ex-diplomat in order to blow up a poison gas plant.

STEWART, BERT

CUSTOMS AGENT (1950, Columbia)—Undercover customs agent **William Eythe** infiltrates a gang which is importing drugs from China, and selling them on the U.S. black market.

STEWART, JAN

HER TWELVE MEN (1954, MGM)—Sugary **Greer Garson** is too well dressed to be living on a simple teacher's salary in this artificial tale of a school marm who reforms a difficult class in a boy's school. What a union she must have—only thirteen brats to contend with. Her class is a baker's dozen—or what use to be a baker's dozen.

STEWART, MARIE

CUPID BY PROXY (1918, Silent, Pathe)—**Baby Marie Osborne** toddles around looking adorable in this story in which the babe saves the romance of two young next door sweethearts.

STEWART, MARVIN

MARVIN AND TIGE (1983, Major)—Loser **John Cassavetes** takes in a homeless 11-year-old who had attempted to kill himself.

STEWART, MICHAEL & CANDACE GOODWIN

MEET THE STEWARTS (1942, Columbia)—When white-collar worker **William Holden** marries spoiled heiress **Frances Dee**, he insists that they live on his salary.

STEWART, MORGAN

MORGAN STEWART'S COMING HOME (1987, New Century-Vista)—Preppie **Jon Cryer** tries to reorder his family's priorities. Rotten know-it-all kid!

STEWART, STEVE

TALENT SCOUT (1937, Warner Brothers)—Hollywood heart-throb **Donald Woods** discovers a new talent, Jeanne Madden (Who?) and falls in love with her.

STICK

STICK (1985, Universal)—Fresh out of prison, **Burt Reynolds** is immediately mixed up in every kind of crime, murder, robbery, smuggling, drugs, etc. It's a strange mix of comedy and violence. Reynolds appears to be on the down-slide of his career.

STIGGS, MARK

O.C. AND STIGGS (1987, MGM/UA)—**Neill Barry** and his friend spend the summer making life miserable for an insurance agent who cut off Barry's grandfather's old age policy.

STILES, WILLARD

WILLARD (1971, Cinerama)—For some reason audiences made a hit of this story of shy withdrawn **Bruce Davison** and the rats which he breeds to kill his enemies.

STILLMAN, JUDGE

THE SPOILERS (1914, Silent, Selig); (1930, Paramount); (1947, Universal); (1955, Universal)—**N. MacGregory, Lloyd Ingraham, Samuel S. Hinds** and **Carl Benton Reid** each plays the crooked judge who enables claim jumpers in the Alaskan gold fields to operate quasi-legally.

STILLWATER, INDIANA

HER LORD AND MASTER (1921, Silent, Vitagraph)—**Alice Joyce**, spoiled daughter of a wealthy American railroad tycoon, marries nobleman Holmes Herbert and moves to England. Her behavior is not considered up to her husband's notions of social propriety, and he suggests a separation. She repents and they are reconciled.

STOCKLEY, BARBARA

SINNERS IN HEAVEN (1924, Silent, Paramount)—**Bebe Daniels** and pilot Richard Dix crash land on an island where the natives at first treat them as gods. When Dix cuts himself shaving, their divine status is downgraded, and their hosts—cannibals—are about to have them over for dinner. But then a rescue plane arrives.

STOCKMANN, DR. THOMAS

AN ENEMY OF THE PEOPLE (1978, Warner Brothers)—**Steve McQueen**, a heavily bearded doctor, costs himself his career by going public with the information that his small town's drinking water has been contaminated by tannery effluent. The film is from a play by Henrik Ibsen.

STOCKTON, CYNTHIA

THE NIGHT BRIDE (1927, Silent, PDC)—**Marie Prevost** is involved in an automobile accident with woman-hater Harrison Ford. Through a series of funny circumstances, Prevost spends the night in a spare bedroom of Ford's home. When Ford's father shows up and is shocked about the arrangement, Prevost claims they are married. Delighted, the father gives them tickets for an ocean cruise. By the time they have returned, Ford is no longer a woman-hater.

STOCKTON, JO

FUNNY FACE (1957, Paramount)—Book store clerk **Audrey Hepburn** is turned into a top model—the girl with the new look—by fashion photographer Fred Astaire. The two also fall in love after she gets a con man philosopher out of her system.

STODDARD, ADAM, JACK, DAVID, CHRIS & PHILIP

ADAM HAD FOUR SONS (1941, Columbia)—Governess Ingrid Bergman looks out for **Warner Baxter's** home and his four sons, **Richard Denning, Johnny Downs, Robert Shaw** and **Charles Lind**.

STOKES, MAURICE

MAURIE (1973, National General)—In this true story, black professional basketball star Stokes, played by **Bernie Casey**, develops a paralysis. His white teammate, Jack Twyman, played by Bo Svenson, has himself appointed Big Mo's guardian and dedicates himself to caring for his friend and directing his rehabilitation.

STONE

STONE (1974, Australia, BEF Australia)—Australian narcotics cop **Ken Shorter** infiltrates a biker gang to investigate a political assassination and a series of biker deaths.

STONE, BEN

DOC HOLLYWOOD (1991, Warner Brothers)—On the way to L.A. and a prospective fortune as a plastic surgeon, **Michael J. Fox** runs afoul of the law in Grady, South Carolina. He is sentenced to perform community service at the local clinic. The town leaders try to get him to stay. Feisty and sexy ambulance driver Julie Warner makes the offer tempting and the people are so gosh-darn nice—but this isn't a fairy tale.

STONE, BENJY

MY FAVORITE YEAR (1982, MGM/UA)—**Mark Linn-Baker** is delightful as the low man on the totem pole of the comedy writing team for a Sid Caesar-like TV comedy show of the Golden Age of Television. The film deals with the week that an Errol Flynn-like drunken movie star, played lovingly by Peter O'Toole, is to appear on the show. It's Linn-Baker's job to see that O'Toole shows up, mostly sober.

STONE, CLAYTON

MAROONED (1969, Columbia)—**James Franciscus** is one of three astronauts faced with the realization that there's no way to get their ship back to Earth.

STONE, DOROTHY (BECKY)

THE CASE OF BECKY (1921, Silent, Realart)—**Constance Binney's** mind is controlled by an evil traveling magician, Montagu Love. He had abducted Binney and her mother years earlier, using hypnotism as his control.

STONE, ERICA

TEACHER'S PET (1958, Paramount)—**Doris Day** teaches journalism. One of her new students is newspaper editor Clark Gable, who doesn't believe anything can be learned in a classroom. For him, "Who, What, When, Where, Why and How" are the only teachers a newspaperman needs. He does alter his opinion somewhat when the two fall in love.

STONE, GEORGE

THE UNTOUCHABLES (1987, Paramount)—**Andy Garcia** is one of three special lawmen who work with Kevin Costner's Elliott Ness to send Al Capone, played by Robert De Niro, to jail for income tax evasion.

STONE, KAREN

THE ROMAN SPRING OF MRS. STONE (1961, Warner Brothers)—Fading middle-aged actress **Vivien Leigh** retreats to Rome, where she purchases the attention of gigolo Warren Beatty. Leigh is stunning as the pitiful but proud woman.

STONE, ORVIE

LITTLE ORVIE (1940, RKO)—**John Sheffield** portrays Booth Tarkington's small hero, forbidden to own a dog. He adopts one for a day and then finds he can't get rid of it.

STONE, RACHEL

THE MODERNS (1988, Alive Films)—**Linda Fiorentino**, wife of artist John Lone, is in love with art forger and painter Keith Carradine. The film is moody and mostly an unentertaining slice of Parisian life in the twenties, peopled by some historical figures like Ernest Hemingway and Gertrude Stein, as well as some fictitious lesser lights.

STONE, T. WILLIAM

STONE OF SILVER CREEK (1939, Universal)—Straight-arrow owner of a dance-hall and gambling house, **Buck Jones** discovers and foils a plot to steal his gold.

STONE, THOMAS

GREEN FINGERS (1947, GB, Anglo-American)—Fisherman **Robert Beatty**, who has the gift of healing, becomes an unauthorized osteopath. He cures his landlady's crippled daughter and marries her. He has an affair with a socialite who shoots herself when he tries to end it. His lack of formal training for his profession comes out and he goes back to sea—temporarily.

STONER, HARRY

SAVE THE TIGER (1973, Paramount)—**Jack Lemmon** is in the garment business. To save his business, he hires a "torch" to burn down one of his warehouses, so he can collect the insurance money. One can only note that it was a bad year for male actors as Lemmon won an Oscar for his uninspired performance.

STORM, BOB

SIX GUN MAN (1946, PRC)—U.S. Marshal **Bob Steele** rounds up a gang of rustlers.

STORM BOY

STORM BOY (1976, Australia, South Australia Film)—**Greg Rowe**, a boy who lives along the Australian coast with his father, is encouraged to care for a nest of orphan pelicans by an old aborigine.

STORM, JOHN

THE CHRISTIAN (1923, Silent, Goldwyn)—Childhood sweethearts **Richard Dix** and Mae Busch leave the Isle of Man for London, where he plans to enter a monastery. Busch becomes a theater star and Dix, unable to forget her, leaves the monastery. Dix plans to kill Busch to save her soul from unsavory characters, such as a nobleman who makes a habit of seducing and dumping stage stars. Instead, she convinces him of her love for him. Confused, Dix wanders the streets and is mortally wounded by an angry crowd that has been told that Dix had predicted the end of the world, to correspond with the opening of the Epsom Downs Derby. Dix is able to marry Busch before expiring in her arms. The film was also made in 1914 with **Earle Williams** and Edith Storey in the leading parts.

STORM, KATHLEEN

LADIES OF THE BIG HOUSE (1932, Paramount)—**Sylvia Sidney** and her husband Gene Raymond are framed on a murder charge and sent to prison. Sidney looks like she's suffering even when she's happy. Come to think of it, she was never happy in any of her movies.

STORM, MASON

HARD TO KILL (1990, Warner Brothers)—**Steven Seagal** is a stitch. In this entry, he's a cop, and his wife is killed, his son disappears, and, after a corrupt politician's hirelings riddle his home with bullets, he plays Rip Van Winkle for seven years. Under the tender care of Kelly Le Brock, he finally comes out of his coma, only to discover that the politician is being considered for the presidency of the U.S. Now he's mad.

STORM, SARAH

SARAH AND SON (1930, Paramount)—Widow **Ruth Chatterton** seeks the baby her husband took from her years before. Once again Chatterton scores in a soapy mother love tale.

STORMCLOUD, TONITA

BEHOLD MY WIFE (1935, Paramount)—Gene Raymond marries and brings home Indian maiden **Sylvia Sidney** to spite his wealthy family who have been interfering with his romances. Everyone, including Raymond, comes to love her.

STORMY

STORMY (1935, Universal)—**Noah Beery, Jr.** searches for a thoroughbred lost after a train wreck.

STOUD, JOHN

THE MAN FROM THE ALAMO (1953, Universal)—**Glenn Ford**, the only survivor of the Battle of the Alamo, is branded a coward even though he left the fort to warn families of the Mexican invasion.

STOVALL, RED

HONKYTONK MAN (1982, Warner Brothers)—During the Depression, tubercular, alcoholic singer **Clint Eastwood** is headed for an appearance at the Grand Ole Opry. Strange, we figure Eastwood proved he was no singer in PAINT YOUR WAGON.

STOVER, MAMIE

THE REVOLT OF MAMIE STOVER (1956, 20th Century Fox)—Because of the times in which this film was made, Honolulu prostitute and madam **Jane Russell** is called a nightclub hostess. She loves author Richard Egan but he doesn't reciprocate her feelings. With the coming of WWII, and the flooding of the islands with horny servicemen, Russell makes a mint, buying up a lot of prime property before retiring to her Mississippi home.

STRAGER, MIKE

ROOKIES IN BURMA (1943, RKO)—**Alan Carney**, a scatter-brained army pirate, and his buddy Wally Brown double-talk themselves out of a Japanese prison camp.

STRAIVE, ERIC

THE BARBARIAN (1921, Silent, Pioneer)—Raised in the Canadian Northwest and educated by his erudite father, **Monroe Salisbury** is considered a barbarian after his father dies and swindlers try to steal his inheritance. He eventually gives his estate to found a conservatory where the poor will be taught to sing by the first white woman he ever set eyes on, Jane Novak.

STRANG, MARTIN

THE JUDGE (1949, Emerald)—Lawyer **Milburn Stone** discovers his wife is cheating on him. He gets a killer off on a murder charge, so the man may perform his noble work on Stone's unfaithful wife and her lover, but it's Stone who ends up dead.

STRANGE, PETER

THE STRANGE AFFAIR (1968, GB, Paramount)—Swinging Sixties London cop **Michael York** has an affair with Susan George. He finds himself facing blackmail when he becomes aware of the corruption of his superior officer.

STRANGER, THE

HIGH PLAINS DRIFTER (1973, Universal)—Stranger **Clint Eastwood** rides into a town where he is hired to protect the community from three gunslingers who have just been released from prison.

STRANGER, THE

THE STRANGER (1924, Silent, Paramount)—Poor London pub clean-up man **Tully Marshall** takes the blame when a man is killed attacking a barmaid. The real killer, Richard Dix, is just about to step forward and confess his crime, when Marshall dies of a heart attack, just before being hanged on the gallows. This story of strange morality is based on John Galsworthy's novel "The First and the Last."

STRANGER, THE

THE STRANGER FROM VENUS (1954, GB, Princess Pictures)—**Helmut Dantine**, a visitor from Venus, warns earthlings about the dangers to the universe from their continuing atomic experiments. It's another THE-DAY-THE-EARTH-STOOD-STILL clone.

STRANGER, THE

STRANGER ON THE THIRD FLOOR (1940, RKO)—Psychopathic killer **Peter Lorre's** crimes are blamed on reporter John McGuire. The film has been described as the first film noir.

STRANGELOVE, DR.

DR. STRANGELOVE OR: HOW I LEARNED TO STOP WORRYING AND LOVE THE BOMB (1964, Columbia)—**Peter Sellers** not only portrays a former Nazi scientist, now working for the United States, who advises the President on what actions to take when it appears that a doomsday bomb has been set in unstoppable motion, but he also plays the President and a British officer. It's a shudderingly funny black comedy, with Sellers in rare form.

STRANGLER, THE

STRANGLER OF THE SWAMP (1945, PRC)—**Charles Middleton** is the vengeful ghost of a man hanged for a crime he did not commit. Periodically, he returns to his village and strangles someone for revenge. He will only stop when someone will give up his life willingly. Rosemary La Planche makes the offer to save her lover, and Middleton is satisfied, sparing her.

STRATHPEFFER, LORD

THE MAN FROM BLANKLEY'S (1930, Warner Brothers); GUEST OF HONOR (1939, GB, Warner Brothers)—**John Barrymore** and **Henry Kendall** each portray a drunken peer who one evening wanders into the wrong house and is mistaken by the hostess as the man she has hired from Blankley's to make 14 at her dinner party, 13 of course being unlucky. The comic complications are quite entertaining.

STRATTON, DOROTHY

STAR 80 (1983, Warner Brothers)—**Mariel Hemingway** had silicone breast implants for this role of the former playmate-of-the-year and actress who was brutally murdered by Eric Roberts, her entrepreneur husband, who then took his own life.

STRATTON, MONTY

THE STRATTON STORY (1949, MGM)—**James Stewart** stars as a baseball pitcher with the Chicago White Sox who has an off-season hunting accident which costs him one of his legs. With the help of his loving wife, June Allyson, he makes a brief comeback.

STRATTON, SIDNEY

THE MAN IN THE WHITE SUIT (1952, GB, Rank)—**Alec Guinness** invents a fabric that never gets dirty. It almost ruins the British garment industry until it is discovered the fabric eventually falls apart.

STRAUSS, JOHANN "SHANI" JR.

STRAUSS' GREAT WALTZ (1934, GB, Gaumont)—**Esmond Knight** succeeds as a musician in 1840 Vienna with the help of a countess and despite his father, Johann Strauss, played by Edmund Gwenn. The film is entitled WALTZES FROM VIENNA in Great Britain.

STREET, JONATHAN

I DREAM TOO MUCH (1935, RKO)—American composer **Henry Fonda** falls in love with provincial French girl Lily Pons (in her screen debut). Her career as an opera star takes off while his compositions raise no interest. She transforms an opera he has written into a musical comedy which becomes a hit. It's another case of the little girl saying to the little boy: "I hate to rise above you—for you see, I love you."

STREET, ROBERT

THE AVIATOR (1929, Warner Brothers)—Successful author **Edward Everett Horton** lends his name to a book about airplanes. This leads to his being considered an expert on the subject. He's forced to enter an air race, despite his fear of flying and heights.

STRETCH

THE COWBOY AND THE LADY (1938, Goldwyn/UA)—Rodeo performer **Gary Cooper** falls in love with and marries Merle Oberon, without knowing her true identity as the daughter of a presidential candidate. He shows her the virtues of the simple life and she's delighted. Being a president's child is no fun—just ask the Reagans.

STRICKLAND, CHERRY & ALIX

SISTERS (1922, Silent, American Releasing)—When **Gladys Leslie**, the woman he loves, marries another man, Matt Moore marries Leslie's sister, **Seena Owen**. When Leslie's marriage breaks up, she moves in with Owen and Moore and soon the old feelings are disrupting Owen's marriage. When the two unfaithful lovers attempt to run away, Owen steps in, sends her sister back to her husband and puts Moore on a short leash after giving him the tongue-lashing of his life. Good for her!

STRINGFELLOW, JEREMY

MR. STRINGFELLOW SAYS NO (1937, GB, National Provincial)—Quiet Church Lads Brigade leader **Neil Hamilton** is told a secret by a dying spy, and finds agents and spies on his trail. His exploits cause him to be knighted and elected to Parliament. The film was rereleased in 1948 as ACCIDENTAL SPY.

STRIPPER, THE

STRIPPER (1986, 20th Century Fox)—**Janette Boyd** has the leading role in this documentary-like study of those who make their living by taking off exotic-styled clothes to suggestive music. The setting is an international stripper contest held in Las Vegas.

STRODE, LADY MARY

HER HERITAGE (1919, Silent, GB, Ward's)—**Phyllis Monkman**, a lady posing as a maid, is aided by an artist to steal her letters from a blackmailing cousin.

STROGOFF, MICHAEL

THE SOLDIER AND THE LADY (1937, RKO)—**Anton Walbrook**, a loyal courier of the Tzar, is entrusted to deliver a new military strategy to the troops in Siberia. Jules Verne's hero has many adventures, of which his favorite may be his encounter with seductive spy Margaret Grahame.

STRONG BOY

STRONG BOY (1929, Silent, Fox)—Railroad baggage handler **Victor McLaglen** is promoted a couple of times for saving a boy from being crushed by a trunk, and returning a pearl necklace to a movie star. However, he does have some trouble with his sweetheart along the way.

STRONG, CHRISTOPHER

CHRISTOPHER STRONG (1933, RKO)—Peer **Colin Clive** has a passionate affair with aviator Katharine Hepburn, resulting in a pregnancy. He finds he cannot desert his wife Billie Burke. Kate solves the problem by killing herself when she deliberately crashes her plane.

STRONG, KAY

THE GROUP (1966, UA)—**Joanna Pettet** marries playwright Larry Hagman after her graduation from college, but in his best J.R.-Ewing fashion, he proves to have a roving eye, which leads to the break-up of the marriage. While at a reunion with seven college chums, Pettet goes off the deep end. Believing the airplanes she hears in New York are Germans attacking the U.S., she falls out a window to her death.

STRONG, NORMAN

BORN TO BE BAD (1934, Fox/UA)—Unwed mother **Loretta Young** tricks wealthy married dairy farmer Cary Grant (hard to envision, isn't it?) into adopting her bratty son. At first, Young tries to get Grant for herself, but gives up the notion of further messing with his marriage and disappears. At least she is rid of the thoroughly unlikable little Jackie Kelk.

STROOD, SIR RODERICK

THE LAST MAN TO HANG (1956, GB, Columbia)—**Tom Conway** didn't really hang, but he almost is sentenced to the gallows for the murder of his neurotic wife. One jury member holds out for an innocent verdict and eventually is able to bring the others around to his way of thinking. Good thing—the wife is still alive.

STROUD, ROBERT

BIRDMAN OF ALCATRAZ (1962, UA)—**Burt Lancaster's** performance as the prison lifer who becomes an expert on the diseases of birds is riveting, but the film is somewhat claustrophobic, as most of it takes place in one prison cell or another.

STUARK, LIL

DON'T TELL MOM THE BABYSITTER'S DEAD (1991, Warner Brothers)—Left in a suburban L.A. home with five kids, **Eda Reiss Merin** turns out to be a babysitter from hell. When she dies from a heart attack, the kids, in order to keep their vacationing Mom away from home, drop Merin's body off at a local mortuary and act as if she's still watching them.

STUART, CHARLES

THE EXILE (1947, Universal)—Exiled British King Charles II, played by **Douglas Fairbanks, Jr.**, falls in love with a Dutch farm girl.

STUART, DON

THE FOREST RANGERS (1942, Paramount)—**Fred MacMurray** fights spectacular forest fires, and finds himself the center of attraction for two fiery females, Paulette Goddard and Susan Hayward. It's the film that introduced the hit song, "I've Got Spurs That Jingle Jangle Jingle," by Thomas Lilley.

STUART, MARION
FATAL LADY (1936, Paramount)—Her shady past threatens singer **Mary Ellis's** career and romance.

STUART, MARY
MARY OF SCOTLAND (1936, RKO); MARY, QUEEN OF SCOTS (1971, GB, Universal)—**Katharine Hepburn's** doomed Mary of Scotland did not win her much praise. It was beginning to appear that Hepburn was box-office poison. The film is a total bore with Kate appearing passionless in her life and death struggle with Elizabeth I, played by Florence Eldridge. **Vanessa Redgrave** didn't exactly cover herself with glory in the 1971 filming of basically the same inaccurate material, with Glenda Jackson as Queen Elizabeth. In real life the two women never met, but screenwriters couldn't allow that, so they included confrontations between the women in both films.

STUBBS, BRAD
WEEKEND WITH FATHER (1951, Universal)—Widower **Van Heflin** falls in love with widow Virginia Field, but their two pairs of kids have other partners picked out for their parents.

STURM, CMDR. CHARLES
DEVIL AND THE DEEP (1932, Paramount)—Submarine commander **Charles Laughton** gets his unfaithful wife Gloria Swanson and her lover Gary Cooper aboard his sub and sinks it. They survive, he doesn't.

STYLES, TRE
BOYZ 'N' THE HOOD (1991, Columbia/New Deal)—**Cuba Gooding, Jr.** is a bright-but-sullen teen who lives with his caring father Larry Fishburne. The movie is about what it takes to become a man in south central L.A. in 1984.

SUE
RITA, SUE AND BOB, TOO! (1987, GB, Orion Classics)—**Michelle Thomas** is one of two chubby baby sitters who enjoy some sexual romps with one of their clients, who has a sexually unresponsive wife. It's funny in a cheap way.

SUEDE, JOHNNY
JOHNNY SUEDE (1991, Vega/Balthazar Vista)—Dreamy, young **Brad Pitt** rejects reality, changes his name to Johnny Suede, sports a ridiculous pompadour and tries to emulate his hero, Ricky Nelson.

SUGARFOOT
SUGARFOOT (1951, Warner Brothers)—**Randolph Scott** and Raymond Massey are in deadly competition for dominance of the town of Prescott, Arizona.

SUGARMAN, JOY
NEW YORK'S FINEST (1988, Platinum)—New York hooker **Ruth Collins** gets no respect until she takes "lady" lessons from transvestite Scott Baker.

SULLIVAN, AL, FRANK, GEORGE, MATT AND JOE
THE SULLIVANS (1944, 20th Century Fox)—**Edward Ryan, John Campbell, James Caldwell, John Alvin** and **George Offerman, Jr.** appear as the adult Sullivan boys, all of whom died aboard the same ship during WWII. The heartbreaking story is presented with great sensitivity and is benefited by the strong performances of Thomas Mitchell and Selena Royle as the boys' parents. The brothers were played as boys respectively by Bobby Driscoll, Martin Davis, Buddy Swan, Billy Cummings and Johnny Calkins. It's a warm, nostalgic film about those who gave their lives in war and the families at home

who also suffered. Since it's release, the title has been changed to THE FIGHTING SULLIVANS.

SULLIVAN, AMY
WHAT EVERY GIRL SHOULD KNOW (1927, Silent, Warner Brothers)—Neither audiences nor **Patsy Ruth Miller** ever found the answer to the title question. Miller and her younger brothers are sent to separate institutions after their older brother, who was supporting them, is sent to jail.

SULLIVAN, ANNIE
THE MIRACLE WORKER (1962, UA)—**Anne Bancroft** won an Academy Award for her portrayal of the teacher of blind, deaf and dumb Helen Keller, played by Patty Duke, who also won an Oscar.

SULLIVAN, ARTHUR
THE GREAT GILBERT AND SULLIVAN (1953, GB, UA)—Composer **Maurice Evans** and librettist Robert Morley, as W.S. Gilbert, write a series of popular operettas despite clashing temperaments. When theatrical manager D'Orly Carte, played by Peter Finch, builds a theater for Sullivan's more serious work, they split, only to be reunited when Sullivan becomes seriously ill. The film is called THE STORY OF GILBERT AND SULLIVAN in Great Britain. The producers must have worried that Americans wouldn't know that Gilbert and Sullivan were great.

SULLIVAN, BURLEIGH
THE KID FROM BROOKLYN (1946, Goldwyn/RKO)—Mild-mannered milkman **Danny Kaye** accidentally wins a world's championship fight. Of greater value to the high-spirited comedian is Virginia Mayo.

SULLIVAN, DIANA
SHY PEOPLE (1988, Cannon)—New York writer **Jill Clayburgh** and her out-of-control daughter Martha Plimpton, travel to the Louisiana bayous to gather history of their family from Cajun relatives, headed by matriarch Barbara Hershey, who married Clayburgh's grandfather's brother when she was only 12. It's a moody, difficult-to-enjoy film, despite strong performances from the principals.

SULLIVAN, JOHN
VIOLENT STRANGER (1957, GB, Anglo-Amalgamated)—**Zachary Scott** is his usual suave no-gooder in this film called MAN IN THE SHADOW in Great Britain. A man is sentenced to death for a murder committed by Scott, and his wife Faith Domergue sets out to prove her husband's innocence.

SULLIVAN, JOHN J.
SULLIVAN'S EMPIRE (1967, Universal)—**Martin Milner** and his two brothers brave headhunters as they search for their powerful father who abandoned them in childhood.

SULLIVAN, JOHN L.
THE GREAT JOHN L (1945, UA)—**Greg McClure** portrays the last bare-knuckle heavyweight champion of the world.

SULLIVAN, JOHN L.
SULLIVAN'S TRAVELS (1941, Paramount)—Hollywood comedy director **Joel McCrea** yearns to create something the people really want. He goes on the bum across the country and finds they want to laugh.

SULLIVAN, RUTH, MARK, PAUL AND TOMMY
SHY PEOPLE (1988, Cannon)—New Yorker Jill Clayburgh and her coke-sniffing daughter Martha Plimpton go to the Louisiana bayous

to visit cousin **Barbara Hershey** and her three sons **Don Swayze, Pruitt Taylor Vance** and **John Philbin**. There's one more son, Merritt Buttrick, but since he left the family and moved to New Orleans, he's considered dead. Hershey is certain that she and her weird family are looked after by her husband, even though he is supposed to have drowned 15 years earlier.

SULLIVAN, SUNNY
SUNNY (1930, First National); (1941, RKO)—**Marilyn Miller's** stage success in this vehicle brought in the customers but didn't do much for her movie career. She and **Anna Neagle**, eleven years later, play a circus performer, disguised as a boy, who stows away on a ship on its way from England to the U.S. She has some problems with immigration officers, but everything is ultimately resolved and she's allowed to stay in the U.S.

SULLIVAN, TERENCE
THE GENTLE GUNMAN (1952, GB, Ealing)—In 1941, IRA agents **John Mills** and his brother Dirk Bogarde arrive in London with several cohorts to blow up underground stations. Appalled by the war damage, Mills changes his mind, but must rescue Bogarde, and be rescued himself from execution.

SULLIVAN, TOM
IF YOU COULD SEE WHAT I HEAR (1982, Cypress Grove)—**Marc Singer** appears as the blind singer-composer Tom Sullivan in a confused and not very enjoyable biopic.

SULLIVAN, WILLIE
THE LAMPLIGHTER (1921, Silent, Fox)—Old lamplighter **Raymond McKee** takes in an abandoned child in a teary film.

SULTAN
THE SULTAN'S DAUGHTER (1943, Monogram)—Underrated film comedian **Charles Butterworth** is a sultan and stripper Ann Corio is his daughter in this story of oil fields and WWII German agents.

SULTENFUSS, VADA
MY GIRL (1991, Columbia)—Exceedingly bright **Anna Chlumsky's** maturation is a painful process. The 11-year-old must deal with a crush on a poetry teacher, her widower father finding a new wife and the death of her chum, Macaulay Culkin, who gave her her first kiss.

SULTZMAN, GAY
A GIRL IN A MILLION (1946, GB, Oxford)—Scientist Hugh Williams divorces his nagging wife and marries dumb country girl **Joan Greenwood**. He makes the mistake of curing her and when she finds her voice, she's as much of a nag as his first wife.

SUMMERVILLE, GRANDAD
STAR WITNESS (1931, Warner Brothers)—Aging war veteran **Charles "Chic" Sale** refuses to be intimidated by a gang of crooks. His testimony puts their boss away for good.

SUMMERS, ALICE
MAMA RUNS WILD (1938, Republic)—**Mary Boland** stops a bank robber and decides to run for mayor. Her opponent is her husband. She loses.

SUMMERS, HENRY
THE CHIEF (1933, MGM)—Fireman's son **Ed Wynn** is a dummy candidate for alderman in the Bowery. Terrible!

SUMNER, DR. GERALD
THE LOVE DOCTOR (1929, Paramount)—**Richard Dix** is loved by his nurse and also by a patient. He fixes the latter up with another of his patients and marries his nurse.

SU-MURU
THE MILLION EYES OF SU-MURU (1967, GB, American International)—Beautiful and evil world-beater **Shirley Eaton** plans to conquer the world with an army of women. Frankie Avalon stands in her way, if you can believe that.

SUNDANCE KID, THE
RETURN OF THE BADMEN (1948, RKO); BUTCH CASSIDY AND THE SUNDANCE KID (1969, 20th Century Fox); BUTCH AND SUNDANCE, THE EARLY DAYS (1979, 20th Century Fox)—**John Ericson, Robert Redford** and **William Katt** each appeared as The Sundance Kid, a member of the "Hole-in-the-Wall" Gang. Redford, working with Paul Newman as Butch Cassidy, gives the most enjoyable performance. Ericson and Katt are merely mediocre.

SUNNY
TROOPERS THREE (1930, Tiffany)—Vaudevillian **Slim Summerville** and his two buddies Rex Lease and Roscoe Karns join the army. Pure cornball.

SUPER SPOOK
SUPER SPOOK (1975, Leavitt-Pickman)—Black private eye **Leonard Jackson** tries to get rid of Harlem baddies, but the task is too much for him.

SUPERCHICK
SUPERCHICK (1973, Crown)—**Joyce Jillson** is mousy brown-haired stewardess Tara B. True until criminals show up. Then she becomes erotic blonde Superchick, a karate expert. It's a complete waste of time and film.

SUPERGIRL
SUPERGIRL (1984, Tri-Star)—**Helen Slater** plays the comic strip superhero with about the same worried expression as she displayed in RUTHLESS PEOPLE. Her adversary, Faye Dunaway, acts like a drag queen.

SUPERMAN
SUPERMAN AND THE MOLE MEN (1951, Lippert); SUPERMAN (1978, Warner Brothers); SUPERMAN II (1981, Warner Brothers); SUPERMAN III (1983, Warner Brothers); SUPERMAN IV: THE QUEST FOR PEACE (1987, Warner Brothers) -**George Reeves** and **Christopher Reeve**, in no way related, divide up the chore of portraying the superhero from the planet Krypton who, when he's not saving the world from master criminals, poses as mild-mannered reporter Clark Kent, always tongue-tied around Lois Lane.

SURE THING, THE
THE SURE THING (1985, Embassy)—**Nicollette Sheridan's** role is minuscule. She's the "good time had by all," whom college student John Cusack travels across country to have a go at. Along the way, he teams up with Daphne Zuniga, who makes Sheridan superfluous.

SURSTER, SUSIE
THE OFFICE GIRL (1932, GB, RKO)—Stenographer **Renate Muller** takes a job with a Vienna bank and becomes romantically involved with the managing director, whom she believes is only a lowly clerk.

SURVIVOR
SURVIVOR (1988, Vestron)—In this Mad Max rip-off, NASA astronaut **Chip Mayer** returns to earth after WWIII to find it

destroyed. He wanders the desert wasteland, encountering a crazed despot who is hoarding a group of beautiful women.

SUSAN
DESPERATELY SEEKING SUSAN (1985, Orion)—Pop-singer **Madonna**, who wears her underwear on the outside and uses religious symbols as jewelry, isn't the star of this film. That honor goes to cutesy Rosanna Arquette, a bored housewife who follows the personal column love adventures of mysterious Madonna. Through a series of improbable plot devices the two end up trading places.

SUSAN
THEY CALL ME MACHO WOMAN (1990, Troma Team)—Young widow **Debra Sweaney** is looking for a home in the country. In the process, she witnesses a drug-smuggling operation. She's captured, but the gang has trouble with her. Just as they plan to rape or kill her, she escapes, arms herself with axes and steel spikes and takes on her adversaries with a vengeance.

SUSAN
SUSAN SLEPT HERE (1954, RKO)—A police detective drops seventeen-year-old runaway **Debbie Reynolds** in the lap of bachelor scriptwriter Dick Powell on Christmas Eve. Because of some weird circumstances, the engaged writer marries her, and then tries to avoid her so the marriage can't be consummated. It was the last movie in which Powell would appear.

SUSAN, LADY
SWEET SUZY (1973, Signal)—In the early 1800s, **Anouska Hempel** rules a Caribbean island with an iron fist until a young slave leads a revolt against her tyranny.

SUSIE
ONE NIGHT AT SUSIE'S (1930, Warner Brothers)—**Helen Ware** is a good soul who shares her boardinghouse with a gang of hoods and ministers to their every need.

SUTTER, JOHN
SUTTER'S GOLD (1936, Universal)—Gold is discovered on immigrant **Edward Arnold's** land in 1849 California but it doesn't make him rich.

SUTTON, JAIMIE
RIVALS (1972, Avco Embassy)—**Scott Jacoby** and his new stepmother don't get along. Murder may be the answer.

SUTTON, LOU
TAMING SUTTON'S GIRL (1957, Republic)—**Gloria Talbot** runs a boardinghouse in the California backwoods where hunter John Lupton is staying. He and Talbot get together, but not before they have to fight off the charges that Lupton killed the husband of May Wynn, who is wild for him.

SUTTON, SAM
THEY JUST HAD TO GET MARRIED (1933, Universal)—**Slim Summerville** stars with Zasu Pitts in another one of their zany farces. This time they are servants of a rich man who leaves them all his money. They marry because they now can afford to do so.

SUZANNA
SUZANNA (1922, Silent, Allied)—California peasant **Mabel Normand** is in love with an aristocrat, whom she is not allowed to marry until it's revealed that she was kidnapped as a child and is actually the daughter of a wealthy rancher.

SUZANNE
THE FABULOUS SUZANNE (1946, Republic)—Waitress **Barbara Britton** is able to pick racehorse winners by sticking a pin in the racing form. Seems as good a way as any.

SUZANNE
I AM SUZANNE (1934, Fox)—When dancer **Lillian Hervey** breaks her leg, she is cared for by a puppeteer with whom she falls in love. Nothing much here.

SUZANNE
THE SECOND COMING OF SUZANNE (1974, Barry)—**Sondra Locke** meets a Charlie Manson-like hypnotic movie director who plans to star her in a crucifixion.

SUZETTE
ABSOLUTE BEGINNERS (1986, GB, Orion)—**Patsy Kensit** is one of the young stars of this chronicle of the musical and social scene in the summer of 1958.

SVENGALI
SVENGALI (1931, Warner Brothers); (1955, GB, MGM)—**John Barrymore** and **Donald Wolfit** each star as the mysterious hypnotist who mesmerizes Trilby and turns her into a great opera star. But he can't hypnotize her into returning his love. Barrymore is awesome; Wolfit is average.

SWAGGER, CAPTAIN
CAPTAIN SWAGGER (1928, Silent, Pathe Exchange)—**Rod La Rocque** portrays Hugh Drummond who lives too high. He turns to crime as Captain Swagger, a hold-up man. He becomes dancing partners with a woman whose wealthy escort he was about to rob and finds a new way to pay for the fine things in life.

SWAMP THING
SWAMP THING (1987, Embassy); THE RETURN OF THE SWAMP THING (1989, Miramax)—**Dick Durock** is a part-human, part-plant monster-hero who takes on super-villain Louis Jourdan and saves busty Adrienne Barbeau from something or other. It should appeal to pre-teens and adults whose mental development has been delayed. The sequel is just more of the campy horror film, filled with cheap jokes and too many sub-plots.

SWANN, LYLE
TIMERIDER (1983, Jensen-Farley)—Biker **Fred Ward** and his motorcycle break the time barrier, ending up in the Old West where they are chased by cowboys. Dumb-De-Dumb-Dumb.

SWANSON, JENNY
THE LOTTERY BRIDE (1930, UA)—Norwegian **Jeanette MacDonald** marries a Yukon miner, only to find that she really loves his younger brother. No winner here, we're sorry to report.

SWATTLE, CHARLIE
FAST CHARLIE . . . THE MOONBEAM RIDER (1979, Universal) -Set in the 1920s. WWI vet **David Carradine** hopes to be the first winner of the transcontinental motorcycle race from St. Louis to San Francisco.

SWAZEY, MAE
THE MODEL AND THE MARRIAGE BROKER (1951, 20th Century Fox)—**Thelma Ritter** runs a dating service and is upset that lovely model Jeanne Crain is lonely. Ritter's answer is X-ray technician Scott Brady. Ritter steals the movie.

SWEENEY, SUSAN
ALL WOMAN (1918, Silent, Goldwyn)—**Mae Marsh** does it all as a city lass who inherits a country inn, cleans up a notorious saloon, brings a young couple together, and snatches an attorney for herself.

SWEENEY, PAT
MILLION DOLLAR BABY (1935, Monogram)—When his vaudevillian parents dress **Jimmy Fay** in a dress and curls to enter him in a Shirley Temple look-alike contest, he wins and soon is on his way to Hollywood. Not looking forward to life as a girl, he jumps off his train and is befriended by a tramp.

SWEET, JASON
THE SHEEPMAN (1958, MGM)—**Glenn Ford** moseys into a western town, asking who the meanest varmint around might be. When this worthy is pointed out, Ford punches the local champ out. Ford goes out of his way to prove how tough he is and how fast he is with a gun. The purpose for all this anti-social behavior is that he's a sheepman bringing a herd of sheep into cattle country.

SWEETLAND, SAMUEL & SIBLEY
THE FARMER'S WIFE (1941, GB, Pathe)—When widower **Basil Sydney** decides to remarry, he strikes out with three well-bred women and settles on his housekeeper, **Patricia Roc**.

SWENSON, GLORIA
GLORIA (1980, Columbia)—When his family is executed by the Mafia, eight-year-old Juan Adames is taken in by neighbor **Gena Rowlands**, a former mob boss' mistress. She goes on the lam with her charge. Rowlands gives a career performance in this spellbinding thriller.

SWENSON, KAREN
GIVE HER A RING (1936, GB, British International)—**Wendy Barrie** and her friend Zelma O'Neal get their dates mixed up, and she ends up with her boss rather than the singer she intended to go out with.

SWIFT, HAROLD "SPEEDY"
SPEEDY (1928, Silent, Paramount)—**Harold Lloyd**, in his last silent film, is a baseball nut who falls in love with the granddaughter of the owner of the last horse-drawn trolley line in New York City. He rallies old-timers to fight the goons hired by the other trolley lines to disrupt the company's service.

SWIFT, TOM
A HORSEMAN OF THE PLAINS (1928, Silent, Fox)—**Tom Mix**, the sheriff of a near-by town, is called in to catch swindlers who are fleecing their victims at a local fair.

SWIFTY
SWIFTY (1936, Division)—**Hoot Gibson** escapes hanging for the murder of a rancher and brings in the real culprit.

SWOPE, PUTNEY
PUTNEY SWOPE (1969, Cinema V Distributing)—**Arnold Johnson** and other blacks take over a Madison Avenue advertising agency, making many changes.

SYBIL
THE BLUFFER (1919, Silent, World)—**June Elridge** and her husband cheat at cards, and are always in a number of nasty scrapes. As a result of one of these, her husband is killed, leaving Elridge free to marry a man who's on the level.

SYKES, PVT. JOCK
SOLDIERS THREE (1951, MGM)—**Robert Newton**, Stewart Granger and David Niven play it for laughs in this unofficial remake of GUNGA DIN, without the water-bearing bheestie.

SYLVIA
JUST SYLVIA (1918, Silent, World)—**Barbara Castelton** and her husband John Hines discover millions of dollars worth of ore on their property. They must deal with all kinds of swindlers who would like to relieve them of their fortune.

SYLVIA, PRINCESS
THE ADORABLE DECEIVER (1926, Silent, FBO)—**Alberta Vaughn**, an European princess, and her father flee their country to settle in the U.S. After running out of money, impoverished Vaughn is hired to impersonate a princess as a joke. In this guise she exposes some jewel thieves and captures the heart of a wealthy young man.

SYMBOL, SAXIE
THREE NUTS IN SEARCH OF A BOLT (1964, Harlequin)—**Mamie Van Doren** and two other "nuts" can't afford a shrink so they hire actor Tommy Noonan to act out their problems before a psychiatrist so they can get advice for three for the price of one.

SYN, DR.
DOCTOR SYN (1937, GB, Gaumont); DR. SYN, ALIAS THE SCARECROW (1975, Disney/Buena Vista)—**George Arliss** and **Patrick McGoohan** each appear as the 1780 Vicar of Dymchurch who is really a pirate believed long dead.

SYRENA, LA
THE BALLET GIRL (1916, Silent, World)—Carnival dancer **Alice Brady** struggles with both her ambition and her love.

SZABO, JANOS
THE FACE BEHIND THE MASK (1941, Columbia)—When Hungarian watchmaker **Peter Lorre**, new to the U.S., is horribly burned in a tenement fire, he has an expressionless mask of his face made. He grows bitter and takes over the leadership of an underworld organization.

SZABO, VIOLETTE
CARVE HER NAME WITH PRIDE (1958, GB, Rank)—**Virginia McKenna** stars in the true story of a shop girl who worked with the French resistance and died in Ravensbruck.

SZALINSKI, WAYNE, DIANE, AMY AND NICK
HONEY, I SHRUNK THE KIDS (1989, Buena Vista)—Nutty inventor **Nick Moranis**, is trying to build a machine that will shrink things. His success results in the title confession to wife **Marcia Strassman** about their kids, **Amy O'Neill** and **Robert Oliveri**.

T

T.J.
MACKINTOSH & T.J. (1975, Penland)—Youngster **Clay O'Brien** is befriended by aging cowhand Roy Rogers in an old-fashioned western with a modern setting.

"T," MR.

TROUBLE MAN (1972, 20th Century Fox)—**Robert Hooks** is the first Mr. "T" in this violent story of an underworld troubleshooter caught in the middle of gang wars.

TABOR, ROSALYN

THE MISFITS (1961, UA)—Divorcee **Marilyn Monroe** teams up with three modern-day cowpokes when they set out to round up a herd of wild ponies, but tries to stop them when she learns that the animals are to be sold for dog food. It was Monroe's last appearance in a film that was released.

TACKETT, TYRONE

HIT MAN (1972, MGM)—Ex-pro football player **Bernie Casey** works hard trying to make a go of this violent crime melodrama, a black version of GET CARTER, but it just doesn't work.

TAFFIN, MARK

TAFFIN (1988, MGM-UA)—Ex-seminarian **Pierce Brosnan** now earns a living as a debt collector in a small Irish town. He's also a martial arts expert, a skill he has to use in his work. His major interest is preventing the local athletic field being destroyed in order to build a road to serve a chemical plant.

TAGER, JOSH

TAPEHEADS (1988, DEG-Avenue)—Video genius **Tim Robbins** is convinced by obnoxious con man John Cusack to make music videos. This inside look at the L.A. rock scene has some funny moments.

TAGGAR, "TAG"

GETTING EVEN (1986, American Distributing Group)—Government agent **Edward Albert** must deal with Joe Don Baker, who threatens to unleash a deadly poison gas in Dallas if he's not paid a $50 million ransom.

TAGGART, ARTIE

A STRANGER IS WATCHING (1982, MGM/UA)—Psychopath **Rip Torn** kidnaps a female TV newscaster and a youngster, and holds them hostage in the catacombs below New York's Grand Central Station.

TAGGART, KENT

TAGGART (1964, Universal)—**Tony Young**, out to avenge the murder of his parents, finds himself being stalked by a gunslinger in Indian territory.

TAI

THE WIFE OF GENERAL LING (1938, GB, Gaumont)—In China, **Adrianne Renn**, the caucasian wife of a Chinese merchant, helps a British agent unmask her husband as a bandit chief.

TAILSPIN TOMMY

STUNT PILOT (1939, Monogram)—When **John Trent** takes a job as a stunt pilot for a movie studio, he finds murder and mystery.

TALBOT, ANNE

THE LADY CONSENTS (1936, RKO)—**Ann Harding**, the wife of a prosperous physician, finds her husband, Herbert Marshall, is stepping out with younger and more vivacious Margaret Lindsay. Harding is understanding and does nothing, allowing the affair to play itself out. Marshall discovers he has made a mistake and comes back to Harding's waiting arms.

TALBOT, JUNE

THE LEECH WOMAN (1960, Universal)—When a middle-aged woman, married to a much younger man, makes use of the means discovered by an African tribe to be young again, she turns out looking like beautiful **Colleen Gray**. There's a catch, of course.

TALBOT, LAWRENCE

THE WOLF MAN (1941, Universal); FRANKENSTEIN MEETS THE WOLF MAN (1943, Universal)—In the first film, **Lon Chaney, Jr.** is bitten by a werewolf, and he learns from old gypsy woman Maria Ouspenskaya what's in store for him. Sure enough, with the coming of the full moon, Chaney experiences lycanthropy, that is, he becomes a wolf and rips apart anyone who crosses his path. In the sequel, Chaney seeks out the eminent Dr. Frankenstein to help him, but the Baron has died. His monster is still around and he doesn't care much for Chaney or werewolves.

TALBOT, CAPT. RICHMOND

MOON PILOT (1962, Buena Vista)—Astronaut **Tom Tryon** meets Dany Saval, a mysterious girl from another planet in this predictable Disney comedy.

TALLANT, CLAY

THE ARIZONIAN (1935, RKO)—**Richard Dix**, the Marshal of Silver City in the 1880s, is helped by reformed outlaw Preston Foster to bring law and order to the western town.

TALLEAH

QUEEN OF OUTER SPACE (1958, Allied Artists)—Rebel Venusian **Zsa Zsa Gabor** disagrees with Laurie Mitchell that four Earth astronauts should be destroyed. All the girls dress in skimpy, sexy attire and the dialogue is strictly from a high school boys' locker room.

TAMAHINE

TAMAHINE (1964, GB, MGM)—Polynesian half-caste **Nancy Kwan** stays with a public school headmaster and eventually marries his son.

TAMARA

ENEMIES, A LOVE STORY (1989, 20th Century Fox)—**Anjelica Huston** is superb as the Holocaust survivor, who surprises his husband Ron Silver and his new wife Margaret Sophie Stein, when she shows up in New York after the war. She also surprises Lena Olin, Silver's third wife.

TAMARA

THREE RUSSIAN GIRLS (1943, UA)—In 1944, the U.S. and Russia were allies. Hollywood, on occasion, came up with a little nothing like this story of three Russian nurses, **Mimy Forsaythe**, Anna Sten and Cathy Frye and their struggle to help their people. It was hoped that this would show how alike the people of the two countries were.

TAMARAH

LOTUS LADY (1930, Audible/Graves)—**Fern Andra**, a native of Indochina, marries American Ralph Emerson, who establishes himself in business in her country. She has to fight off the attempts of an old girlfriend to steal Emerson away.

TAMIKO

A GIRL NAMED TAMIKO (1962, Paramount)—Eurasian photographer Laurence Harvey uses both **France Nuyen** and Martha Hyer in an attempt to get American nationality.

TANCRED, LORD
SOUL MATES (1925, Silent, MGM)—**Edmund Lowe** is the man Aileen Pringle's nobleman uncle has in mind for her to marry in order to get the money to pay off the mortgage on their estate. She refuses to marry Lowe, whom she has never seen. As coincidence would have it, Pringle and Lowe meet and fall in love without being aware he was her uncle's choice for her husband all along.

TANGO, RAY
TANGO AND CASH (1989, Warner Brothers)—Sophisticated, wealthy star police detective **Sylvester Stallone** is teamed with scruffy Kurt Russell, also a well-respected detective, to end the activities of the area's biggest drug dealer. They are framed and thrown in jail. Then they get going.

TANGUAY, EVA
THE I DON'T CARE GIRL (1952, 20th Century Fox)—**Mitzi Gaynor** gives her usual vapid but appealing performance in the role of musical comedy star Tanguay, whose theme song is "I Don't Care!"

TANGUERAY, PAULA
THE SECOND MRS. TANGUERAY (1952, GB, Associate British)—**Pamela Brown**, the second wife of Hugh Sinclair, discovers his daughter by his first wife is in love with Brown's ex-lover. The ladies will have something spicy to talk about.

TANIA
THE MYSTERIOUS LADY (1928, Silent, MGM)—Russian spy **Greta Garbo** chooses love of her Austrian counterpart Conrad Nagel over duty to her country.

TANNERHILL, MARY
A DAUGHTER OF LOVE (1925, Silent, GB, Stoll)—The father of **Violet Hopson's** sweetheart won't let him marry her, because she was born out of wedlock. When it is discovered that her father is a prominent physician, this seems to make all the difference and the wedding is on with both daddies' blessings.

TANYA
TANYA'S ISLAND (1981, Canada, International Film Exchange)—Beauty **D.D. Winters** lives with beastly artist Richard Sargent. She has dreams of running naked on a beach and making friends with a blue-eyed ape. What's intended here? Don't ask us.

TANYA
TARZAN AND THE HUNTRESS (1947, RKO)—**Patricia Morison** leads an expedition into Tarzan's jungle to capture animals for zoos. Her cages remain empty, however.

TANZ, GENERAL
THE NIGHT OF THE GENERALS (1967, GB, Columbia)—**Peter O'Toole** is a crazy German general who enjoys brutally murdering prostitutes. German major Omar Sharif loses his life trying to arrest O'Toole for his crimes. But after the war and after O'Toole is released from prison for war crimes, a French policeman, Philippe Noiret, who had worked on the case with Sharif, is there to arrest O'Toole for the murder of the prostitutes. O'Toole takes his own life rather than surrender.

TARGETT, WILLIAM
THE SAILOR'S RETURN (1978, GB, Osprey)—During the Victorian era, sailor **Tom Bell** returns to England from Africa with a black wife. They haven't got a chance of finding a normal life.

TARJI
DREAM WIFE (1953, MGM)—American businessman Cary Grant believes a wife's place is in the home carrying for her husband. He dumps his career-woman fiancee Deborah Kerr for Middle Eastern princess **Betta St. John**, trained from childhood to please men. Unfortunately for Grant's way of thinking, she picks up some American notions before the wedding date and he returns to Kerr.

TARRY, FLAXEN
FLAME OF THE BARBARY COAST (1945, Republic)—Nightclub hostess **Ann Dvorak** falls in love with cowboy John Wayne. They survive the San Francisco earthquake together. Wayne picked up his nickname "Duke" from his character Duke Fergus in this movie.

TART, DR.
THE PRIVATE EYES (1980, New World)—**Tim Conway** and Don Knotts team up in a not very funny spoof of Dr. Watson and Sherlock Holmes movies.

TARZAN
TARZAN OF THE APES (1918, Silent, National Film Group); THE ROMANCES OF TARZAN (1918, Silent, First National) -**Elmo Lincoln**; JUNGLE TRAIL OF THE SON OF TARZAN (1923, Silent, National)—**Dempsey Tabler**; TARZAN, THE APE MAN (1932, MGM); TARZAN AND HIS MATE (1934, MGM); TARZAN ESCAPES (1936, MGM); TARZAN FINDS A SON (1939, MGM); TARZAN'S SECRET TREASURE (1941, MGM); TARZAN'S NEW YORK ADVENTURE (1942, MGM); TARZAN TRIUMPHS (1943, RKO); TARZAN'S DESERT MYSTERY (1943, RKO); TARZAN AND THE AMAZONS (1945, RKO); TARZAN AND THE LEOPARD WOMAN (1946, RKO); TARZAN AND THE HUNTRESS (1947, RKO); TARZAN AND THE MERMAIDS (1948, RKO)—**Johnny Weissmuller**; TARZAN THE FEARLESS (1933, Principal)—**Buster Crabbe**; NEW ADVENTURES OF TARZAN (1935, Republic); TARZAN AND THE GREEN GODDESS (1938, Principal)—**Herman Brix (Bruce Bennett)**; TARZAN'S REVENGE (1938, 20th Century Fox)—**Glenn Morris**; TARZAN'S MAGIC FOUNTAIN (1949, RKO); TARZAN AND THE SLAVE GIRL (1950, RKO); TARZAN'S PERIL (1949, RKO); TARZAN'S SAVAGE FURY (1952, RKO); TARZAN AND THE SHE-DEVIL (1953, RKO)—**Lex Barker**; TARZAN'S HIDDEN JUNGLE (1955, RKO); TARZAN AND THE LOST SAFARI (1957, GB, MGM); TARZAN'S FIGHT FOR LIFE (1958, MGM); TARZAN'S GREATEST ADVENTURE (1959, GB, Paramount); TARZAN THE MAGNIFICENT (1960, GB, Paramount)—**Gordon Scott**; TARZAN, THE APE MAN (1959, MGM)—**Denny Miller**; TARZAN GOES TO INDIA (1962, MGM); TARZAN'S THREE CHALLENGES (1963, MGM)—**Jock Mahoney**; TARZAN AND THE GREAT RIVER (1967, Paramount); TARZAN AND THE VALLEY OF GOLD (1966, American International); TARZAN AND THE JUNGLE BOY (1968, Paramount)—**Mike Henry**; TARZAN'S DEADLY SILENCE (1970, National General); TARZAN'S JUNGLE REBELLION (1970, National General)—**Ron Ely**; TARZAN, THE APE MAN (1981, MGM/UA)—**Miles O'Keefe**; GREYSTOKE: THE LEGEND OF TARZAN (1984, Warner Brothers)—**Christopher Lambert**—Very few years have gone by in the history of film in which someone didn't make, release or plan a movie based on the legend of Edgar Rice Burroughs' noble savage. In 1918, National Film Group offered the public a ten reeler that critics did not find a great picture but felt would appeal to the general public. And so it did. Gordon Griffith appeared as the ten-year-old Greystoke who would become Tarzan when his parents are killed in Africa and he is raised by apes. Elmo Lincoln is the adult Tarzan quite taken by Jane Porter, played by Enid Markey. Without a doubt, the most popular

Tarzan is Johnny Weissmuller and a great deal of his success is owed to the pains that MGM went to produce quality pictures. Maureen O'Sullivan as Jane helped as well, as later did Johnny Sheffield as Boy, Tarzan's adopted son. Weissmuller claimed the job was a piece of cake as long as he remembered to hold onto the vine when swinging from tree to tree. Other Tarzans have been successful in the role, in proportion to the studio efforts to make their films interesting. Perhaps the least enjoyable Tarzan film is the 1981 film in which the Ape Man looks to have the brain of a mentally defective ape and a physique that was developed by weight lifting not just swinging through trees. In the last film, till now, Christopher Lambert is adequate as a grunting savage, but when back in England and forced to share a scene with the likes of Sir Ralph Richardson, he makes one yearn for Cheetah the Chimp.

TASHI
AMAZONS (1987, MGM/UA)—**Penelope Reed** and Windsor Taylor Randolph are two Amazon warriors who must retrieve an ancient sword in order to defeat an evil villain, menacing their people. Catch ole Willie Nelson as the Amazons' wizard. This movie will definitely not "always be on his mind."

TASHMAN, MARTY S.
THE ERRAND BOY (1961, Paramount)—**Jerry Lewis** is a brainless paperhanger who nearly destroys a Hollywood studio, but becomes its new comedy sensation, acting very much like a Jerry Lewis.

TASHMAN, THELMA
WOMAN IN HIDING (1953, GB, Hammer)—**Lois Maxwell**, wife of guilty-but-insane killer Kieron Moore, changes her identity and marries Bill Travers. Moore escapes and with the help of detective Paul Henreid proves himself innocent, with the real murderer being Maxwell's former employer, Hugh Sinclair. The film is called MANTRAP in Great Britain.

TATE, ARTHUR
THE SECRET OF MY SUCCESS (1965, GB, MGM)—Policeman **James Booth** rises in his profession by proving that murderous women are innocent. The comedy could use some more laughs.

TATE
COHEN AND TATE (1989, Tri-Star)—Hit men **Adam Baldwin** and Roy Scheider kill nine-year-old Harley Cross' family, witnesses of a mob hit, and kidnap the boy, planning to deliver him to their bosses in Houston. On the trip from Oklahoma, Cross gradually works the antagonistic relationship of the two killers to his advantage.

TATE, JOHN
THE UNDERDOG (1943, PRC)—Dispossessed farmer **Barton Maclane** is ruined by drought, forcing him to move his family to a miserable urban setting. His son and his dog save Maclane from death at the hands of saboteurs.

TATIANA, GRAND DUCHESS
INTO HER KINGDOM (1923, Silent, First National)—Russian Grand Duchess **Corinne Griffith** escapes Bolshevik Russia to the U.S. with peasant Einar Hansen. They settle in New Jersey as man and wife. Later she disclaims her royal birth and they return with their child to the U.S.S.R.

TATLOCK, NAN
MISS TATLOCK'S MILLIONS (1948, Paramount)—Heiress **Wanda Hendrix** is assisted in her struggle to fight off predators by Hollywood stunt man John Lund who poses as her nutty relative.

The film was directed by funnyman Richard Haydn and is really quite amusing.

TATUM, JODIE
KISSIN' COUSINS (1964, MGM)—**Elvis Presley** helps his Tennessee uncle protect his still from the U.S. Air Force which wishes to build a missile installation on its site. Presley also plays a distant cousin, an Air Force officer sent into the hills to get the moonshiner's cooperation.

TAWES, SHERIFF HENRY
I WALK THE LINE (1970, Columbia)—Tennessee sheriff **Gregory Peck** protects moonshiners because he's in love with the daughter of the family, Tuesday Weld. When the revenuers investigate, it leads to bloodshed.

TAYLOR
THREE (1969, GB, UA)—**Sam Waterston**, his friend Robie Porter and English girl Charlotte Rampling, develop a cozy menage a trois as they travel around Europe in a beat-up old car.

TAYLOR, BILLY
THE WRESTLER (1974, Entertainment Ventures)—**Billy Robinson** stars in this inside story of the life of professional wrestlers. To add a little spice, he has to deal with some gangsters who want to cut themselves in on the profits. If this is your thing, you can see a lot of old time professional wrestlers.

TAYLOR, BUCK
RELENTLESS (1989, New Line)—Although trained from youth to be as tough as his dad, a super cop, **Judd Nelson** is rejected by the police department. His mind snaps and he begins a series of brutal, mindless killings. He first calls his victims to inform them that he's going to kill then and then follows through with his threats. It's up to police detectives Robert Loggia and Leo Rossi to bring in "The Sunset Killer," as Nelson is dubbed.

TAYLOR, CARL
MEN AT WORK (1990, Triumph)—This garbage about garbage men **Charlie Sheen** and real-life brother Emilio Estevez was intended to be a comedy, but jokes mostly based on excrement aren't very funny. The lads' main concern is what to do with the body of a corrupt political candidate that they find stashed in a can along their route.

TAYLOR, CHARLES
THE FRESHIE (1922, Silent, Herbst/Di Lorenzo)—**Guinn "Big Boy" Williams**, a poor cowboy, finds himself the butt of a series of practical jokes when he goes to college, but after catching a burglar, he's accepted as one of the boys and wins the campus queen.

TAYLOR, FRANK
THE CANADIAN (1926, Silent, Paramount)—Wheat farmer **Thomas Meighan** marries a English woman who has lost all of her money. Her initial distaste for her husband and Canada slowly changes to respect and love.

TAYLOR, JIMMY
HE WHO LAUGHS LAST (1925, Silent, Barsky Corp.)—**Kenneth McDonald**, a wild kid, is accused of being the notorious killer and robber of the area. He escapes prison to capture the real criminal.

TAYLOR, JOAN
LADIES CLUB (1986, New Line Cinema)—**Karen Austin** and Diana Scarwid form a support group for rape victims. It turns into a vigilante group that teaches some much-needed lessons to men who abuse women.

TAYLOR, LILLIE

GOOD DAME (1934, Paramount)—Penniless chorus girl, **Sylvia Sidney** falls for cardsharp Fredric March. My how this girl suffers.

TAYLOR, NAN

LADIES THEY TALK ABOUT (1933, Warner Brothers)—Tough wisecracking bank robber **Barbara Stanwyck** is sent to San Quentin where she takes control of the woman's division in no time. The film deals with the need for prison reform and how women manage without men. Bluenoses were aghast.

TAYLOR, NORA

LATIN LOVERS (1953, MGM)—**Lana Turner** is in South America seeking true love in this nothing romantic comedy.

TAYLOR, SQUIZZY

SQUIZZY TAYLOR (1984, Australia, Satori)—**David Atkins** stars as a notorious Melbourne gangster of the 1920s.

TAZA

TAZA, SON OF COCHISE (1954, Universal)—**Rock Hudson** looks and acts like a wooden Indian while playing the peace-loving eldest son of the great Apache chief. Hudson becomes chief with the death of his father. He clashes with his brother who rushes to join forces with Geronimo to fight the white man.

TECKMAN, MARTIN

THE TECKMAN MYSTERY (1955, GB, Associated Artists)—Test pilot **Michael Medwood** disappears but resurfaces when he changes his mind about giving air secrets to a foreign power.

TECUMSEH, CHIEF

BRAVE WARRIOR (1952, Columbia)—**Jay Silverheels** is the good Indian in this film in which government agent Jon Hall tries to discover who's stirring up the red man just prior to the War of 1812. Soon after this, Silverheels would start a long run as Tonto, who rides with the Lone Ranger.

TED

BOB AND CAROL AND TED AND ALICE (1969, Columbia)—**Elliott Gould** and his wife Dyan Cannon are a conservative married couple whose friends Robert Culp and Natalie Wood try to turn on to wife-swapping.

TED

THE LITTLE ONES (1965, GB, Columbia)—Police pursue **Kim Smith** and his half-caste friend Carl Gonzales to Liverpool when they run away from their cruel parents.

TEDDY

CROONER (1932, First National)—**David Manners** is a Rudy Valle-like college saxman who's overblown ego sends him down the ladder of success just as fast as he had climbed up it.

TEDDY

LITTLE MEN (1940, RKO)—**Richard Nichols** is one of several youngsters who attend Carl Esmond's school in this uninspired production of the follow-up to Louise May Alcott's "Little Women."

TEEN, HAROLD

HAROLD TEEN (1928, Silent, First National); (1934, Warner Brothers)—**Arthur Lake**, who would gain fame as another comic strip character, Dagwood Bumstead, and **Hal Le Roy** portray the dumb small-town journalist. The second film is a musical in which Le Roy shows he can dance.

TEENAGE MONSTER

I WAS A TEENAGE FRANKENSTEIN (1958, American International)—Teenager **Gary Conway**, making out in a parked car, becomes the unwilling donor of his head to a monster created by a latter-day Frankenstein, Whit Bissell.

TEGARTHEN, SYBIL

THE NOTORIOUS MRS. CARRICK (1924, Silent, GB, Stoll)—**Disa**, Cameron Carr's second wife, is blackmailed by her former husband over the murder of her lover. Busy gal isn't she?

TELLER

PENN AND TELLER GET KILLED (1989, Warner Brothers)—In the comedy-magic team of Penn and Teller, **Teller** never says anything, but he should have spoken up and objected to this confusing movie, which was released only in a single theater in Los Angeles, before disappearing.

TEMPERLEY, CAPT. JACK & SIR CHARLES

THE HOUSE OF TEMPERLEY (1913, Silent, GB, Jury)—**Charles Maude**, the adopted son of a blacksmith, is accused of murdering his cardsharp brother, **Ben Webster**. The film proved so popular it was rereleased in 1918.

TEMPLAR, SIMON

THE SAINT IN NEW YORK (1938, RKO); ; THE SAINT IN LONDON (1939, GB, RKO); THE SAINT STRIKES BACK (1939, RKO); THE SAINT TAKES OVER (1940, RKO); THE SAINT'S DOUBLE TROUBLE (1940, RKO); THE SAINT IN PALM SPRINGS (1941, RKO); THE SAINT'S VACATION (1941, GB, RKO); THE SAINT MEETS THE TIGER (1943, GB, RKO/Republic) THE SAINT'S GIRL FRIDAY (1954, GB, RKO) -**Louis Hayward** in the first and last pictures, **Hugh Sinclair** in THE SAINT'S VACATION and **George Sanders** in all the others appeared as Leslie Charteris' reformed gentleman criminal who becomes a Robin Hood of crime in a series of charming movies, whose titles say about all that is needed to get the gist of the story.

TEMPLE, BOB

MAN ABOUT TOWN (1939, Paramount)—**Jack Benny** portrays a Broadway producer in London flirting with two married women to make his singing star Dorothy Lamour jealous.

TEMPLE, GEORGE

FASTEST GUN ALIVE (1956, MGM)—While intoxicated, **Glenn Ford** brags that he's the fastest gun alive and then demonstrates his skill. The word gets to brutal gunslinger Broderick Crawford, who insists on testing Ford, or he will blow up the town. The only problem is that Ford has never faced a man with a gun before.

TEMPLE, PAUL

SEND FOR PAUL TEMPLE (1946, GB, Butchers); CALLING PAUL TEMPLE (1948, GB, Nettleford); PAUL TEMPLE'S TRIUMPH (1951, GB, Butchers); PAUL TEMPLE RETURNS (1952, GB, Butchers)—From time to time Scotland Yard calls novelist and amateur detective **John Bentley** in to help them with certain difficult cases. Paul Temple was a very popular radio detective in England during the 1940s.

TEMPLETON, CAROL

LOVER COME BACK (1961, Universal)—**Doris Day** is an advertising woman who doesn't approve of the means rival Rock Hudson uses to win accounts from her. He romances her without her knowing his real identity but the two merge by the finish.

TEMPLETON, IVY

AUDREY ROSE (1977, UA)—Anthony Hopkins is convinced that his 12-year-old daughter, who burned to death in a car accident 12 years earlier, has been reincarnated into **Susan Swift**, daughter of John Beck and Marsha Mason.

TEMPLETON, JOAN & DARBY

DARBY AND JOAN (1937, GB, MGM)—**Peggy Simpson** marries a rich nobleman for the sake of her blind sister **Pamela Bevan** and then her fiance returns.

TEMUJIN

THE CONQUEROR (1956, RKO); GENGHIS KHAN (1965, Columbia)—**John Wayne** and **Omar Sharif** each are ludicrous as the Mongol invader. Wayne was unusually disastrous in a costume piece that wasn't exactly a western. His reading of the lines sounded exactly like a reading, and the lines were trite to boot. The filming of Wayne's movie near the Yucca Flats Atomic Testing sight seems to have tragically taken the life of a large number of cast and crew who worked on the film by cancer. Besides Wayne himself, there is director Dick Powell, Susan Hayward, Pedro Armendariz (well, he committed suicide, but cancer was killing him), and Agnes Moorehead. As for the 1956 turkey, Sharif would have been better off entering a bridge tournament.

TENNESSEE

TENNESSEE'S PARTNER (1916, Silent, Lasky); (1955, RKO)—Forty years changed the sex of the title character. In the first, **Fannie Ward**, traveling west by stagecoach, is abducted by the man who killed her father and ran off with her mother. This skunk becomes the honored guest at a necktie party and Ward is reunited with her mother. In 1955, **John Payne**, a rough-and-tumble gambler, and his partner, Ronald Reagan, are wrongly accused of murdering an old prospector. Both stories are credited to Bret Harte, but he's only responsible for the earlier one, while four screen-writers labored to butcher the later version.

TEPPER, BILLY

TOY SOLDIERS (1991, Tri-Star)—**Sean Astin** heads up the opposition to a band of terrorists who invade a Virginia prep school.

TERESA

KISS ME A KILLER (1991, Califilm)—In a story reminiscent of *The Postman Always Rings Twice*, L.A. night club proprietor Guy Boyd pushes around his wife/employee **Julie Carmen**. She takes refuge in the arms of ex-con Robert Beltran, and they scheme to bump off Boyd.

TERESA

THE MAID OF THE MOUNTAINS (1932, GB, Wardour)—In this creaky adaptation of a stage musical, a Robin Hood-like bandit falls in love with the Governor's daughter, and is betrayed by his jealous sweetheart **Nancy Brown**.

TERESA

TERESA (1951, MGM)—Mama's boy, soldier John Ericson brings home an Italian war bride, **Pier Angeli**. Mama spank.

TERMINATOR

THE TERMINATOR (1984, Orion); TERMINATOR 2: JUDGMENT DAY (1991, Tri-Star)—**Arnold Schwarzenegger** is sent back in time on a mission of extermination. In the sequel, the cyborgs of the future dispatch **Robert Patrick** back to the past to slay Edward Furlong, who, if he lives, will lead the human resisters to cyborg domination in 2020. Arnie, reprogrammed by the revolutionaries, is sent back to protect Furlong.

TERRILL, THAD

GENTLEMAN FROM DIXIE (1941, Monogram)—Just out of prison, **Jack LaRue** saves his brother's family and takes revenge on the man responsible for his stint behind bars.

TERRIS, CATHERINE

SHE'S BACK ON BROADWAY (1953, Warner Brothers)—**Virginia Mayo** is a young movie star whose career has hit the skids. She figures a turn on Broadway will get her back on top again. Her director, Steve Cochran, is a former lover, whom she walked out on years before. They're back in each others arms before the film is ended.

TERRY

THE BACHELOR'S DAUGHTERS (1946, UA)—**Ann Dvorak** is one of four salesgirls, who with floorwalker Adolphe Menjou acting as their father, rent a Long Island house and pass themselves off as a wealthy family in the hopes of making good marriages for the girls.

TERRY

GET YOURSELF A COLLEGE GIRL (1964, MGM)—Former Miss America **Mary Ann Mobley** is a songwriting college student, who falls in love with a music publisher staying at a resort hotel.

TERRY

JUST ONE OF THE GUYS (1985, Columbia)—**Joyce Hyser** believes that she is being discriminated against in a competition for a journalism scholarship. She transfers to a new school and changes her sex for good measure. This becomes a bit of a pain when she develops a crush on a guy who considers her "just one of the guys." Her means of correcting his understanding is to rip off her shirt. We suppose she had bound herself to keep her not too little secret.

TERRY

MEN'S CLUB (1986, Paramount)—**Treat Williams** is one of a group of guys who turns a boys' night out into an exploration of their attitudes towards women.

TERRY

MY TUTOR (1983, Crown International)—Luscious college student **Caren Kaye** is hired by a wealthy family to tutor their hunky, lunky, virginal son Matt Lattanzi in French so he can graduate from high school. He understands her meaning quite well when she takes nude midnight swims in the lighted family pool just outside junior's room. Well, she has to go somewhere to dry off, doesn't she?

TERRY

THE SECRET FOUR (1940, GB, Ealing)—**Frank Lawton** is one of THE FOUR JUST MEN (the British title) opposed to all foreign plotters against the Empire. He is poisoned and shot, but before dying, he reveals his discovery of a plot to block the Suez Canal. The other Just Men avenge him and foil the plot.

TERRY

TEENAGE GANG DEBS (1966, Jode/Cid Ltd.)—**Diana Conti** promises gang member Joey Naudic that she will become his personal sex plaything if he becomes leader of his gang. He kills the current leader, making it appear an accident. Then, encouraged by Conti, he stages a gang war. A bit of Lady Macbeth here, perhaps? Well at least that Lady didn't have her faced slashed and the initials of the former gang leader carved on her chest.

TERRY, ANN

PHANTOM LADY (1944, Universal)—After having an argument with his wife, Franchot Tone goes to a bar where he meets beautiful but strange-acting **Fay Helm**. Without learning her name, he makes it a night out on the town with her. When he returns home, he finds his wife has been murdered and he's the prime suspect. Helm, the "phantom lady," must be found to establish Tone's alibi.

TERRY, ELSA

I'LL TAKE ROMANCE (1937, Columbia)—Opera diva **Grace Moore** reneges on her engagement in Buenos Aires when she gets a better offer to appear in Paris. Argentine impresario Melvyn Douglas follows her to France with the notion of kidnapping her. Through his charm, he's able to get her to return with him willingly.

TERRY, JINX

TWO LATINS FROM MANHATTAN (1941, Columbia)—**Jinx Falkenberg** and Joan Woodbury are rushed in to replace two Cuban show business sisters who are delayed in arriving for work in a Manhattan nightclub. The subs are a hit, but must ultimately deal with the two outraged Cuban sisters.

TERRY, JUNE

NO PLACE FOR A LADY (1943, Columbia)—**Margaret Lindsey** is private detective William Gargan's fiancee. Together they solve the murder of a wealthy widow in a manner suggestive of their work together in their Ellery Queen series.

TERRY, TOM

THE CIRCUS ACE (1927, Silent, Fox)—Fancy rider **Tom Mix** saves the circus for which he works from a small-town Arizona mayor who wishes to steal the show.

TERRYTON, MARTHA

THE BRIDE GOES WILD (1948, MGM)—**June Allyson** is hired as an illustrator for the writer of a children's book. She finds he's handsome young wild man Van Johnson, who must pretend to adopt an unruly orphan.

TERWILLIKER, DR.

THE 5,000 FINGERS OF DR. T (1953, Columbia)—A boy who despises his piano lessons dreams his teacher **Hans Conreid** is an evil genius who keeps 500 boys in a castle of musical instruments. The story, written by Dr. Seuss (Theodore Geisel), is not among his best works.

TESHA

TESHA (1929, GB, Wardour)—Russian ballerina **Maria Corda** marries a shell-shocked ex-serviceman, and has a child by his friend.

TESLA, ARMAND

THE RETURN OF THE VAMPIRE (1944, Columbia)—**Bela Lugosi** returns to his nightly searches for the blood of young female victims when the stake through his heart is inadvertently removed.

TESS

TESS OF THE STORM COUNTRY (1914, Silent, Famous Players)—**Mary Pickford** became a star of stars after her appearance as an innocent squatter who protects the baby of her lover's sister by claiming it to be hers. Also see TESSIBEL SKINNER.

TEVYA

TEVYA (1939, Jewish Historical Society)—**Maurice Schwartz** stars in this version of the Sholem Aleichem's stories of the Russian-Jewish milkman, which is better known by general audiences as the musical FIDDLER ON THE ROOF. Schwartz had long appeared in a stage version of the story. In the now familiar story, Tevya and his wife Golde have several daughters for whom they must seek the best marriages possible for a poor family. The main crisis of this production is that one of the daughters falls in love with a free-thinking goy.

THACKER, NED

A MODERN MUSKETEER (1917, Silent, Artcraft)—Born in Kansas to a mother who constantly reads "The Three Musketeers," **Douglas Fairbanks** attempts to be like these heroes in every way, but usually things go wrong. But when he moves West and saves the girl he will marry, he's a regular D'Artagnan.

THACKERY, MARK

TO SIR, WITH LOVE (1967, GB, Columbia)—**Sidney Poitier**, a teacher in a London East End high school, attended by students at the lower end of the socioeconomic scale, helps them develop a belief in themselves. It's a touching well-done film, with Poitier at his best.

THATCHER, CAROL

COOL IT, CAROL! (1970, GB, Miracle Films)—Country girl **Janet Lynn** and her lover get tangled up in the London vice scene.

THATCHER, EMMA

EMMA (1932, MGM)—**Marie Dressler** spends 20 years as nanny and housekeeper in the house of widower Jean Hersholt. She marries him, and when he dies, he leaves his fortune to her. His children attempt to break the will by claiming Dressler killed their father.

THAW, EVELYN NESBITT

GIRL IN THE RED VELVET SWING (1955, 20th Century Fox)—**Joan Collins's** unstable husband, played by Farley Granger, shoots and kills her wealthy lover, famous architect Stanford White, played by Ray Milland. Collins saves Granger from the death penalty by testifying as to what a cruel pervert her lover was. Among other things (although it seems innocent enough as explained in the film), Milland liked to push Collins in a red velvet swing that hung above their bed. The story is true. Only the facts have been sanitized here to make the piece an exceedingly long-winded bore, and, after her husband's trial, our tainted heroine entered show business, even making a series of movies.

THAYER, LT. HOWARD

MEN OF THE FIGHTING LADY (1954, MGM)—**Van Johnson** stars in this unexciting story of the adventures of aircraft carrier personnel during the Korean War.

THAYER, JOAN

RICH MAN, POOR GIRL (1938, MGM)—**Ruth Hussey**, the daughter of a poor family, is the choice of a millionaire for his wife. Both families are put into a tizzy by the news, but not a funny enough one to make the film memorable.

THELMA

THELMA AND LOUISE (1991, Pathe)—Hoping to escape her thoughtless husband, **Geena Davis** sets out on a weekend fishing trip with her good buddy, Susan Sarandon. Letting her hair down at a roadside bar, Davis gets into trouble with a redneck who won't take no for an answer. Davis is rescued by Sarandon, who shoots and kills the attacker. The two flee across the country, just a few miles ahead of assorted law enforcement officials. They have a grand old time, and, because the men in their lives are scum, they refuse to give themselves up to the law.

THEODOPOULIS, ALEX
A PERFECT COUPLE (1979, 20th Century Fox)—**Paul Dooley**, a middle-aged Greek, under the thumb of his father, meets musician Marta Heflin through a dating service. Even though they seem to have nothing in common, they fall in love.

THERESA
IDOL OF PARIS (1948, GB, Warner Brothers)—Paris ragman's daughter **Beryl Baxter** becomes queen of the demimondaines. She fights duels with other women, using a whip as the weapon. She's able to send Napoleon on his way, and inspires Offenbach to compose La Belle Helene.

THERESE
THERESE AND ISABELLE (1968, Audobon Films)—Unhappy school girl **Essy Persson** has disappointing sexual experiences with men and turns to fellow student Anna Gael for solace. This leads them into a lesbian relationship which ends badly.

THESEUS
THE WARRIOR'S HUSBAND (1933, Fox)—Greek Adonis **David Manners** leads an army of Greeks in an invasion of the land of the Amazons, where the women rule and the men are all effete. Elissa Landi, the Queen's sister, is the warrior who finds yielding to Manners to be enjoyable.

THIEF OF BAGDAD, THE
THE THIEF OF BAGDAD (1924, Silent, UA)—If you could only see one of **Douglas Fairbanks'** swashbuckling silents, this would be the one. The magical film has Fairbanks as a thief who outwits an evil Caliph, but it's how he gets the job done that makes this film still worth the price of admission.

THING, THE
THE THING (1951, RKO)—The shapeless, magnetic something that a military-scientific group at the North Pole haul from under an ice-block turns out to be **James Arness**, who would go on to a better role as TV's Matt Dillon on *Gunsmoke*. We don't see Arness as the "thing" until the end of the film, but he has quite an appetite for human food.

THISTLEWAITE, PAMELA
A WOMAN REBELS (1936, RKO)—Victorian feminist **Katharine Hepburn** fights for women's rights, but having an illegitimate baby doesn't help her cause.

THOMAS, BIGGER
NATIVE SON (1951, Classic); (1986, Cinecom)—**Richard Wright**, the author of the novel on which the two films are based, and **Victor Love** portray the poor frightened black chauffeur who unintentionally kills a white woman, which leads to more tragedy.

THOMAS, ELIZABETH
NURSE FROM BROOKLYN (1938, Universal)—When nurse **Sally Eilers'** brother is killed in a shootout, the detective who allegedly shot the boy is brought to her hospital for treatment.

THOMAS, JACK
GENTLEMAN'S FATE (1931, MGM)—**John Gilbert** tried a come-back of sorts with this underworld bootlegging story, but the public didn't buy it.

THOMAS, JANE
THESE GLAMOUR GIRLS (1939, MGM)—In her first leading role, **Lana Turner** is a dime-a-dance girl invited to a college for the annual party weekend by Lew Ayres. He forgets he issued the invitation but Turner shows up. The snobs gang up on her, but after doing a wild dance, at least the boys are happy to see her. By the end, Ayres has discovered that Turner is heads above all the phony debs he's been dating.

THOMAS, JIMMY
THE COWBOY AND THE KID (1936, Universal)—After his father is killed, young **Billy Burrud** is befriended by cowboy Buck Jones.

THOMAS, SAM
THE MAN I LOVE (1946, Warner Brothers)—In a dreary film noir (no, that's not redundant), nightclub singer **Ida Lupino** becomes involved with mobster Robert Alda.

THOMAS, ZACK
FOUR FOR TEXAS (1963, Warner Brothers)—**Frank Sinatra** and Dean Martin are competing Texas gamblers. They team up with voluptuous half-dressed Anita Ekberg and Ursula Andress to fight a crooked banker and a gang of outlaws.

THOMASINE
THOMASINE AND BUSHROD (1974, Columbia)—**Vonetta McKee** and Max Julien are a fictional black "Bonnie and Clyde," terrorizing New Mexico in 1912-1915.

THOMPSON, BILL "STOKER"
THE SET-UP (1949, RKO)—**Robert Ryan** is brilliant in this film noir story of an aging boxer who refuses to go into the tank in his last fight, thus double-crossing gamblers who give him the worst beating of his life.

THOMPSON, HAL
ME AND MY PAL (1939, GB, Pathe)—Truck driver **George Moon** and his buddy are conned into helping defraud an insurance company, believing they are actually helping the police.

THOMPSON, JEFF & MARI
THE LAST MARRIED COUPLE IN AMERICA (1980, Universal)—**George Segal** and **Natalie Wood** find all of their friends' marriages breaking up. The same thing almost happens to them, when Segal can't resist an offer of sex from Valerie Harper, a friend of Wood. She gives him a social disease which he passes on to Wood. The couple split and do a bit of recreational fooling around with people too young for them, but get back together at least for the time being by the end of the picture.

THOMPSON, JOEY BOY
JOEY BOY (1965, GB, British Lion)—In 1941, black marketeer **Harry H. Corbett**, forced to join the army, continues his illegal schemes while in uniform.

THOMPSON, MRS.
MRS. THOMPSON (1919, GB, Silent, Samuelson)—**Minna Grey**, a shopkeeper's daughter, marries a cad who ruins the family business.

THOMPSON, RON AND LITTLE RUSS
HONEY, I SHRUNK THE KIDS (1989, Buena Vista)—**Jared Rushton** and **Thomas Brown** are neighbor kids of nutty scientist Rick Moranis. They get shrunk along with Moranis' kids, when his shrinking invention proves a success. Now getting them back to their rightful size may be a problem.

THOMPSON, SADIE
SADIE THOMPSON (1928, Silent, UA); MISS SADIE THOMPSON (1953, Columbia)—**Gloria Swanson** and **Rita Hayworth** each portrayed the prostitute on the run from the police, stranded on a South Seas island. She falls in love with a marine, but runs afoul of a religious fanatic who threatens to expose her background to the local authorities unless she allows him to seek her redemption. When she reforms, the zealot rapes her, then in shame kills himself. Sadie reverts to type, and sets sail for Australia with her marine. Swanson was nominated for an Academy Award for her performance. Joan Crawford also played Sadie in a 1932 movie, using author W. Somerset Maugham's original title, RAIN.

THOMPSON, SHIRLEY
SHIRLEY THOMPSON VERSUS THE ALIENS (1968, Australia, Kolossal Films)—In this strange comedy **Jane Harders** can't get anyone to believe her encounter with outer space aliens posing as a motorcycle gang. We don't see why not.

THOMPSON, T.N. *See* **MR. DYNAMITE**

THOMPSON, WILLIAM ASBURY
I'D CLIMB THE HIGHEST MOUNTAIN (1951, 20th Century Fox)—Methodist preacher **William Lundigan** and his wife Susan Hayward face a difficult adjustment to his new parish in a remote part of Georgia.

THORKELL, DR.
DR. CYCLOPS (1940, Paramount)—Mad scientist **Albert Dekker** captures jungle explorers and miniaturizes them. The special effects just about make the picture work.

THORMONDE, SIR NICHOLAS
MAN AND MAID (1925, Silent, Metro-Goldwyn)—During WWI, British officer **Lew Cody's** life is saved by Red Cross nurse Harriet Hammond. After the war, she unwittingly becomes his secretary and later his wife.

THORN, DAMIEN
DAMIEN-OMEN II (1978, 20th Century Fox)—**Jonathan Scott-Taylor** is the teenage antichrist who wiped out his foster parents in THE OMEN and now is working on a second pair. The little devil!

THORN, MAJOR THOMAS
THEY CAME TO CORDURA (1959, Columbia)—Cryptic army major **Gary Cooper**, branded a coward, is transporting five army heroes of the American-Mexican conflict in 1916 and one woman, Rita Hayworth, across the northern part of Mexico to their home base at Cordura. The hardships of the journey show who's the real hero.

THORNE, ANGELA
A THOUSAND CONVICTS AND A WOMAN (1971, GB, American Int.) -For those who expected something salacious from the title—well, for once, you're right. **Alexandra Hay** is the daughter of a British prison governor. She sleeps with everyone in the prison—guards and prisoners.

THORNE, LT. REX
ACE OF ACES (1933, RKO)—Sculptor **Richard Arlen**, who resists enlistment with the outbreak of the war on moral grounds, is branded a coward by his fiancée. He joins the air corps and becomes one of the most successful and callous killers of the sky during the war. That'll show her.

THORNE, RICK
STRANGER ON HORSEBACK (1955, UA)—Traveling judge **Joel McCrea** makes certain his sentences are carried out by use of his six shooters.

THORNTON, SEAN
THE QUIET MAN (1952, Republic)—Boxer **John Wayne** leaves the ring when he kills a man. He returns to the Irish home of his youth, where his American ways cause him some problems when he goes acourting Maureen O'Hara. There's bad blood between the Duke and O'Hara's brutish brother Victor McLaglen over some land Wayne bought that McLaglen wanted. Wayne and O'Hara marry, but McLaglen refuses to part with her dowry. This is of no concern to Wayne, but O'Hara feels her man is a coward and won't sleep with him, because he won't fight her brother for what is rightly hers. The fight does come, of course, and it's a dandy donnybrook. The film is most charming, with the major performers being augmented perfectly by actors from The Abbey Players, most notably Jack MacGowran as McLaglen's weasely little toady.

THORNTON, ST. ELMO
ST. ELMO (1923, Silent, Fox)—After killing his sweetheart's lover, **John Gilbert** travels the world as a woman-hater, but returns home and is cured of his misogynist views by the blacksmith's daughter.

THORNTON, TOMMY N.
MR. DYNAMITE (1941, Universal)—Ballplayer **Lloyd Nolan** takes his girlfriend to a carnival, where he gets mixed up with a gang of saboteurs.

THORNWOOD, LEE
SHE MARRIED AN ARTIST (1938, Columbia)—When artist **John Boles** finds his work in demand by magazines, he marries Paris fashion designer Luli Deste, rather than his model Frances Drake, who has long loved him. The marriage fails and Boles returns to Drake.

THORPE
THE DECEIVER (1931, Columbia)—Shakespearean actor **Ian Keith** has ruined countless women in his career, and they all are suspects when he's murdered. The killer is the least suspected member of the cast. Mystery fans just hate that. But the same technique is used in 1990's PRESUMED INNOCENT.

THORPE, CAPT. GEOFFREY
THE SEA HAWK (1940, Warner Brothers)—English privateer **Errol Flynn**, secretly encouraged by Queen Elizabeth, adds to England's treasury by plundering Spanish ships. He has a marvelously long and exciting sword fight with villain Henry Daniell.

THORPE, JIM
JIM THORPE—ALL AMERICAN (1951, Warner Brothers)—**Burt Lancaster** stars as the Oklahoma Indian who becomes one of the greatest all-around athletes who ever lived. After being forced to return the medals he won as a track star in the 1912 Olympics, because he was declared a professional, he goes on to careers in both pro football and baseball.

THORPE, VICKI WALLACE
SMARTY (1934, Warner Brothers)—**Joan Blondell** and her husband Warren William are always squabbling, and acting irrational towards each other. By the end of the film, they have decided that despite their quarrels they love each other too much to divorce.

583

THORSON, PAPA
THE HUNTER (1980, Paramount)—In his last film before his death of cancer, **Steve McQueen** is an urban bounty hunter in a film with lots of action but lacking a logical screenplay.

THORVALD
THE NORSEMAN (1978, American International)—Eleventh century Norseman **Lee Majors** sails to the Americas to rescue his father-king, who has been abducted by Indians. Too bad Majors became a TV star before he learned to act.

THRONBERRY, BILL
OKAY BILL (1971, Four Star Excelsior)—**Bob Brady** is a young, successful stockbroker. He seems to have a perfect, sexy wife, but he has a yen to see what he's missing in the counterculture. Nothing it turns out.

THRUMM, OLI J.
THREE FOR BEDROOM C (1952, Warner Brothers)—Harvard professor **James Warren** has a romance aboard a train with movie actress Gloria Swanson. Things are complicated by the presence of Swanson's obnoxious little girl, Janine Perreau.

THUNDER, CAPT.
CAPTAIN THUNDER (1931, Warner Brothers)—**Victor Varconi** is supposed to be a Mexican bandit, who has a romance with senorita Fay Wray. As neither can be understood, because of the accents they adopted, we can't tell you much more of what happened between them.

THUNDERBIRD, C.J.
FIST FIGHTER (1989, Taurus)—This uninteresting story of the dangerous sport of bare-knuckle boxing stars **George Rivero** as a champion.

THUMB, TOM
TOM THUMB (1958, GB, MGM)—Two-inch-high forest boy **Russ Tamblyn** foils some thieves in this musical for children.

THURLOE, JIM
SPIES OF THE AIR (1940, GB, Associate British)—Test pilot **Barry K. Barnes** kills a blackmailer and betrays a designer's plans.

THURSDAY, MAX
GUILTY BYSTANDER (1950, Film Classics)—When policeman **Zachary Scott** is thrown off the force, he becomes an alcoholic house detective in a sleazy hotel. He sobers up when his ex-wife brings him the news that their son has been kidnapped. He finds his son and starts his life once again.

THX 1138
THX 1138 (1971, Warner Brothers)—In a future society, computerized automated human **Robert Duvall** breaks the rule of no emotion by falling in love. The object of his affection is killed for the offense, but Duvall escapes to fight the system. The film is the first movie directed by George Lucas.

TIBBETTS, PROF. BENJAMIN
OLD BONES OF THE RIVER (1938, GB, GFD)—**Will Hay**, a teacher acting as a commissioner, quells a native uprising in Africa.

TIBBS, CHARLEY
THE SADIST (1963, Fanway International)—Pyschopath **Arch Hall, Jr.** terrorizes three innocent people who make the mistake of stopping at a roadside filling station.

TIBBS, JONATHAN
THE SHERIFF OF FRACTURED JAW (1958, GB, 20th Century Fox)—British gunsmith **Kenneth More** visits the Old West to sell his wares. He is made the new sheriff of the town of Fractured Jaw and does a credible job despite himself.

TIBBS, VIRGIL
THEY CALL ME MISTER TIBBS (1970, UA)—Police lieutenant **Sidney Poitier** has reason to believe that a crusading local minister, Martin Landau, may be a murderer in this sequel to IN THE HEAT OF THE NIGHT

TICOORA
DAUGHTER OF THE JUNGLE (1947, Republic)—Female Tarzan **Lois Hall** lives in the jungle with her millionaire father, long missing from the outside world. When a plane crashes near by, Hall helps the survivors get back to their notion of civilization.

TIDD, TREM
CLOTHES MAKE THE PIRATE (1925, Silent, First National)—Eighteenth Century tailor **Leon Errol**, severely henpecked, dreams of the life of a pirate. Every now and then, he dresses up as a buccaneer. One night while so costumed, he's mistaken for their captain by a group of pirates. Taken back to their ship, he blunders his way through adventures flying the Jolly Roger, and even captures his wife traveling on one of the ships his lads attack. She doesn't recognize him, but he takes the opportunity to give her a bad time to get even for her years of nagging, before the two retreat back to a normal Boston life.

TIGER LADY, THE
HIS TIGER LADY (1928, Silent, Paramount)—Duchess **Evelyn Brent**, with an interest in tigers, falls in love with Adolphe Menjou, who poses as a rajah in a Folies revue.

TIGRI
PREHISTORIC WOMEN (1950, Eagle Lion)—**Laurette Luez** is one of a tribe of animal-skin dressed women, who hunt men, kill dragons, and travel with the help of a giant.

TILDA
TRUE TILDA (1920, Silent, GB, Jury)—Circus girl **Edna Flugarth** helps a boy escape from a cruel orphanage, and is richly rewarded when it's discovered that the lad is the son of a nobleman.

TILDEN, WILLIAM B.
KISS DADDY GOODNIGHT (1987, Beast of Eden)—**Paul Richards** becomes obsessed with the resemblance of the girl next door, Uma Thurman, to his missing daughter. Uma makes her way in life by donning sexy outfits, picking up strange men, drugging them, and taking their valuables. The film is billed as "a film noir in full color." Maybe.

TILL, MAX
THE KING OF PARIS (1934, GB, UA)—When his wife walks out on him, egotistical actor-producer **Cedric Hardwicke** picks up a friendless Russian girl, Marie Glory, makes her his new leading lady, and when she becomes a star, marries her. But she leaves him for his friend Ralph Richardson.

TILLEY, ERNEST
TIN MEN (1987, Buena Vista)—**Danny De Vito** is spectacular as a Baltimore aluminum siding salesman, circa 1963, who runs his big-finned Cadillac into the equally ostentatious new Caddie of another "tin man" (i.e. aluminum siding salesman) Richard Dreyfuss,

setting off a feud, which sees them wrecking each other's cars. Dreyfuss steals De Vito's wife, Barbara Hershey (which only pleases Danny). Both lose their licenses to sell aluminum siding because of dishonest practices. It's a funny, touching movie.

TIMBERLANE, CASS
CASS TIMBERLANE (1947, MGM)—Judge **Spencer Tracy** marries a much younger working girl, Lana Turner. They have difficulty adjusting to each other's way of life, but they eventually succeed. The same can't be said for the movie.

TIM
THE WRONG GUYS (1988, New World)—As a child, **Tim Thomerson** was an irresponsible airhead. As a grown-up, returning for a reunion of his Cub Scout pact, he's a surf bum.

TIMOTHY
TIMOTHY'S QUEST (1922, Silent, American Releasing)—Orphan **Joseph Depew** and the tot he protects flee their New York slum, ending up in a New England village where they are taken in by two spinsters. The two win the love of the women and then it's discovered that Depew is the long absent nephew of one of the ladies.

TINA
FALSE MADONNA (1932, Paramount)—**Kay Francis** claims to be the long-lost mother of a rich youth. She develops real affection for the boy and confesses her deception, but by this time he loves her also.

TINA
TRUCK STOP WOMEN (1974, LT Films)—**Jennifer Burton** is one of a gang of women who run a prostitution ring and truck hijacking racket.

TINDALL, DR.
GUILTY AS HELL (1932, Paramount)—**Henry Stephenson** commits what he imagines to be the perfect murder—but there is no such thing when the detective-reporter team of Victor McLaglen and Edmund Lowe are on the case.

TINKER
THE GIRL GETTERS (1966, GB, American International)—Beach photographer **Oliver Reed** beds a wealthy woman on holiday, and falls in love with her. In the olden days, things were done in the opposite order. Ah, progress. The film is called THE SYSTEM in Great Britain.

TINKLEPAW, TILLIE
TILLIE'S PUNCTURED ROMANCE (1914, Silent, Keystone) TILLIE'S TOMATO SURPRISE (1915, Silent, Lubin); TILLIE WAKES UP (1917, Silent, World); TILLIE'S PUNCTURED ROMANCE (1928, Silent, Paramount)—Country girl **Marie Dressler** is talked into stealing her father's money by smooth talking Charlie Chaplin. After they run away to the city together, Charlie dumps Dressler so he can continue a romance with another girl. He comes back to Dressler when he discovers she has inherited a fortune, but now the country girl is not so gullible. The 1914 film is the first feature-length comedy movie. In the 1928 film, **Louise Fazenda** leaves home to follow the lion tamer in a circus, whose ringmaster is W.C. Fields. The circus goes overseas to entertain the doughboys of WWI, but Fazenda, Fields, and circus owner Mack Swain end up in the German army.

TIRA
I'M NO ANGEL (1933, Paramount)—**Mae West** is also known as Sister Honky Tonk in what is probably her best picture. She's a carnival entertainer, with plans of climbing the social ladder, one man at a time. High on the ladder is wealthy Cary Grant, who balks at marriage so she slaps him with a breach-of-promise suit, but gets him in the good old-fashioned way, love based on sexual attraction.

TISA
SLAVE GIRL FROM BEYOND INFINITY (1987, Titan/Urban Classics)—Bikini clad bimbos **Cindy Beal** and Elizabeth Cyton escape from a space slave ship onto a planet where the only inhabitant hunts any visitors for the sport of it, ala THE MOST DANGEROUS GAME.

TOBIAS, SARAH
THE ACCUSED (1988, Paramount)—**Jodie Foster** is the victim of gang rape on a pin-ball machine in a cheap bar. Because Foster is not exactly virginal, arrived at the bar in a sexy outfit, got high on marijuana, drank a lot, and flirted with one of the men who would attack her, the assistant D.A., Kelly McGillis, allows the rapists to plea-bargain to lesser charges. McGillis has second thoughts and brings charges against those in the bar who witnessed and encouraged the rape, even though they did not actively participate. The point of the film is certainly that rape is rape, and the issue is not the victim's character. Foster is outstanding in a performance that won her a much-deserved Academy Award.

TODD, JESSIE & WILBUR
MAMA LOVES PAPA (1933, Paramount)—**Mary Boland** and **Charles Ruggles** star in a domestic comedy about an ambitious wife who must protect her furniture salesman husband from a temptress.

TODD, SKIPPER
THE TODD KILLINGS (1971, National General)—Ladies man **Robert F. Lyons** is actively involved in a series of murders.

TODD, SUSAN
AFFAIR OF SUSAN (1935, Universal)—**Zasu Pitts** travels to Coney Island, looking for romance, but ends up in jail.

TODD, SWEENEY
THE DEMON BARBER OF FLEET STREET (1939, GB, MGM)—Fiendish barber **Tod Slaughter** lures sailors and merchants to his dockside barbershop, where he shaves them, cuts their throats and disposes of their bodies in meat pies sold by his accomplice Stella Rho. Slaughter experiences a like fate.

TOKYO ROSE
TOKYO ROSE (1945, Paramount)—**Lotus Long** stars as the Japanese-American who made propaganda broadcasts to troops in the Pacific during WWII.

TOLINGER, CLINT
MAN WITH THE GUN (1955, UA)—**Robert Mitchum** is brought in to clean up a western town, but his brutal methods convince some that the cure is worse than the disease.

TOLLEA
COBRA WOMAN (1944, Universal)—Non-actress but exotic-looker **Maria Montez** gives her fans a double treat by portraying both a sarong-covered native girl and her evil, ornately-gowned high-priestess twin sister. It's all malarkey, but good Saturday afternoon escapism during WWII.

TOM
BAD MAN OF TOMBSTONE (1949, Monogram/Allied Artists)—**Barry Sullivan**, the gunman-lover of Marjorie Reynolds, follows badman Broderick Crawford to his death in the streets of Tombstone.

TOM
HIS BROTHER'S WIFE (1936, MGM)—**George Eldredge** helps his scientist brother Robert Taylor out of some difficulties with a gambler on the condition that Taylor disappear and leave the field to Barbara Stanwyck open to him. Eldredge marries Stanwyck, but she agrees to it only as part of her plot to take revenge for being used like a game token. She ruins Eldredge and then turns her attention to Taylor, but by the end of the film she shows redeeming qualities, helping Taylor during an epidemic.

TOM
THE PLAYBOYS (1992, US/Ireland, Goldwyn)—**Aidan Quinn**, the newest member of a traveling actors' troupe called "The Playboys," impresses unwed mother Robin Wright and promptly beds her. This doesn't sit well with local constable Albert Finney, who has a yen for Wright himself.

TOM
TOM, DICK AND HARRY (1941, RKO)—**George Murphy**, Burgess Meredith and Alan Marshal are the three men from among whom small-town girl Ginger Rogers must choose a husband in this light-as-air comedy.

TOM
THE TOMCAT (1968, GB, Tigon-Global)—**Anthony Trent** finds fantasizing about sexual encounters with the girls he sees in London's West End more satisfying than being with his conservative girlfriend.

TOMASIS, THEO
THE GREEK TYCOON (1978, Universal)—**Anthony Quinn** is too good-looking to portray the Onassis-like billionaire shipping magnate, who marries Jacqueline Bisset, the Jacqueline Kennedy-like widow of an American president. This should have been done as a made-for-TV movie. The story might have been more interesting if it broke for commercials now and then.

TOMMY
ORPHANS OF THE STREET (1939, Republic)—When his father dies there is no more money to keep **Tommy Ryan** in the military school he has been attending. Ryan hits the road, taking his police dog with him. The dog is accused of a killing and is sentenced to be destroyed, but Ryan clears everything up in time to save his friend's life.

TOMMY
TENTH AVENUE KID (1938, Republic)—12-year-old **Tommy Ryan** witnesses private eye Bruce Cabot gunning down his bank robber father. Cabot feels responsible for the boy, but also tries to get Ryan to lead him to the loot from a bank heist pulled off by his dad.

TOMMY
THAT'S MY BOY (1932, Columbia)—While working his way through college, football star **Richard Cromwell** gets involved with a phony stock-selling scheme. He wises up in time to save his good name and career.

TOMMY
THREE NUTS IN SEARCH OF A BOLT (1964, Harlequin)—**Tommy Noonan** is an actor hired by three "nuts" to portray their problems for an expensive shrink, so they can have all their phobias cured for the price of one. Noonan got to work with three of the biggest sex symbols of the post war period, Marilyn Monroe in GENTLEMEN PREFER BLONDES, Jayne Mansfield in PROMISES, PROMISES and here with Mamie Van Doren.

TOMMY JO
TOMBOY AND THE CHAMP (1961, Universal)—Farm girl **Candy Moore** loves her prize bull. No bull, that's about it.

TOMMY "T.S."
THREE FOR THE ROAD (1987, New Century/Vista)—**Alan Ruck** accompanies his friend, Charlie Sheen, a senator's aide, in driving the politician's troublesome daughter Kerri Green to a boarding school in a southern state which is little more than a reformatory. The girl gives them a lot of trouble, but learning that her father is a child abuser, they deliver the girl to her loving and understanding mother instead of to the school.

TOMPKINS, BOBBY
THE SECOND MATE (1950, GB, Associate British Films)—Thames barge worker **David Hannaford** poses as a crook to catch jewel thieves.

TOMPKINS, MARBLE HEAD
SAILOR'S HOLIDAY (1944, Columbia)—**Arthur Lake** and two of his merchant seaman friends find some romance on a tour through Columbia Studios. It's a cheap way to go on location.

TOMPKINS, TOMMY
MR. UNIVERSE (1951, Eagle-Lion)—**Vincent Edwards** is a wrestler promoted by Jack Carson in this quick, nothing comedy.

TOMPKINS, TOMMY
TOMMY THE TOREADOR (1960, GB, Warner Brothers-Pathe)—Poor seaman **Tommy Steele** replaces a bull fighter, framed for smuggling.

TONELLI
PUBLIC MENACE (1935, Columbia)—Mobster **Douglas Dumbrille** is the indirect cause of reporter George Murphy constantly being fired. Murphy keeps failing to get the story on the gangster, because he is distracted by his wife Jean Arthur.

TONI
HER SISTER'S SECRET (1946, PRC)—During WWII at New Orleans' Mardi Gras, **Nancy Coleman** falls in love with soldier Phillip Reed. When he is shipped overseas, she discovers that she is pregnant. Unsure whether Reed will ever return, Coleman allows her sister, Margaret Lindsay, to raise the baby. But daddy comes marching home and all are happy.

TONY
THE DANCERS (1930, Fox)—**Phillips Holmes** leaves England for the Canadian north woods to make his fortune. He meets Lois Moran in a dance hall and falls in love. They return to England when his relative dies and he becomes a new earl. The film gives one the rare chance to see and hear Mrs. Patrick Campbell, the original Liza Doolittle in Shaw's "Pygmalion."

TONY
I WAS A TEENAGE WEREWOLF (1957, American International)—**Michael Landon**, Little Joe of TV's Bonanza, is a troubled teenager

who can't control his temper. He goes to a psychiatrist Whit Bissell, who turns Landon into a snarling drooling prehistoric primate. The transformation takes place any time Landon is startled.

TONY

KISS ME A KILLER (1991, Califilm)—Ex-con **Robert Beltran** gets a job playing his guitar in an Anglo East L.A. night club, the clientele of which is Hispanic. He begins an affair with Julie Carmen, the abused wife of the club owner, Guy Boyd. Before long, Beltran and Carmen are making plans to kill Boyd.

TONY

MAN OF THE MOMENT (1935, GB, Warner Brothers)—**Douglas Fairbanks, Jr.** prevents Laura La Plante from drowning herself. He offers her a bed for the night, putting an end to his planned marriage to an heiress, whose money he could surely use. So he and La Plante head to Monte Carlo where they make a fortune.

TONY

THE SECOND MR. BUSH (1940, GB, Anglo-American)—Writer **Derrick de Marney** helps timid butterfly farmer Mr. Bush, who has inherited 500,000 pounds and is being pursued by reporters. De Marney poses as the heir, pretending to give his money away. The masquerade will cost de Marney in the romance area before everything is sorted out.

TONY

THEY KNEW WHAT THEY WANTED (1940, RKO)—**Charles Laughton**, an unattractive Italian grape grower in California's Napa Valley, proposes marriage by mail to waitress Carole Lombard, enclosing a picture of his handsome hired man William Gargan as himself. Lombard accepts his proposal, is seduced by Gargan, marries Laughton and comes to care for him. The film is a disaster on most counts, not the least being the miscasting of all three leading parts. The Pulitzer Prize-winning play had been filmed twice before as THE SECRET HOUR in 1928 and A LADY IN LOVE in 1930. It would in 1956 become the basis for Frank Loesser's "The Most Happy Fella," a delightful American operetta.

TOOMAI

ELEPHANT BOY (1937, GB, UA)—**Sabu** became an international star with his appearance as an elephant keeper, who helps government conservationists in India in this documentary drama.

TOOTLE, ARAMINTA

LOVE BIRDS (1934, Universal)—This teaming of **Zasu Pitts** and Slim Summerville as middle-aged people who survive a passel of misadventures is very routine.

TOPAZE, AUGUSTE

TOPAZE (1933, RKO); I LIKE MONEY (1962, GB, 20th Century Fox)—**John Barrymore** and **Peter Sellers** each star in the comedy about a French schoolteacher, who barely makes a living, until he allows crooked politicians to exploit him, and then he becomes prosperous.

TOPPER, COSMO

TOPPER (1937, MGM); TOPPER TAKES A TRIP (1939, UA); TOPPER RETURNS (1941, UA)—Stuffy banker **Roland Young** finds that he's the only one who can see or hear the ghosts of his sophisticated friends, Cary Grant and Constance Bennett. In the second feature, Bennett, minus Grant, helps Young save his wife Billie Burke from a Riviera philanderer. In the 1941 film, Young is aided by ghost Joan Blondell in solving her murder. Strangely, this last movie is the best of the funny lot.

TORNAI, COUNT PIERRE

THE SILENT LOVER (1926, Silent, First National) After squandering his fortune, French aristocrat **Milton Sills** joins the French Foreign Legion. He has romances both with an American girl and the daughter of a Bedouin chief, before saving his garrison from being slaughtered.

TOSCANI, NICO

ABOVE THE LAW (1988, Warner Brothers)—**Steven Seagal** stars in this strange action-adventure yarn about a small group of crazy CIA agents who have taken to drug trafficking. Martial expert Seagal, former member of "the Company" and a Vietnam vet, tries to save a U.S. senator marked for assassination by the CIA boys. The latter are accused of believing they are "above the law" by Seagal, but so does he, as he goes about wasting them.

TOTO

TOTO AND THE POACHERS (1958, GB, World Safari)—Native African boy **John Aloisi** helps game warden David Betts catch ivory poachers.

TOUHY, ROGER

ROGER TOUHY, GANGSTER (1944, 20th Century Fox)—**Preston Foster** portrays the Chicago bootlegging king who made a superior brew, corrupted local police and politicians with bribes, and is said to be the only mobster whom Al Capone feared. The son of a Chicago policeman, Roger Touhy was the leader of the Terrible Touhy's, a gang that included his five brothers. He was finally sent to prison for the kidnapping of international con man Jake "the Barber" Factor, in what was surely a put-up job masterminded by Factor and the Capone mob. Protesting his innocence, Touhy broke out of prison, was recaptured and had 199 additional years added to his initial sentence of 99 years. In 1959, after 25 years in prison, Touhy was released. Twenty-three days later, he was gunned down. He muttered as he lay dying: "I've been expecting it. The bastards never forget." Too bad someone hasn't come up with a new movie about Touhy. There's more drama in his life than in that of Capone's.

TOUZAC, MICHEL & KARIN

THIS LOVE OF OURS (1945, Universal)—Extremely jealous **Charles Korvin** mistakenly believes his wife **Merle Oberon** is having an affair. The film is based on the play "As Before, Better Than Before" by Luigi Pirandello.

TOWNEY, SARAH

THE GIRL FROM HIS TOWN (1915, Silent, American)—**Margarita Fischer**, while appearing in a London stage performance, saves her vulnerable young American sweetheart, C. Elliott Griffen, from the clutches of a British female opportunist.

TOWNLEY, RUTH

IF I WERE QUEEN (1922, Silent, R-C Pictures)—American heiress **Ethel Clayton** is mistaken for a princess by a prince of a mythical Balkan country.

TOWNSEND

PEACEMAKER (1990, Fries)—Two humanoid aliens, **Lance Edwards** and **Robert Forster**, crash land on Earth. One is an intergalactic serial killer and the other is a cop. Both claim to be the cop. It looks like medical examiner Hilary Shepard will have to sort out the identities.

TOWNSEND, MARGARET

THE LADY WHO DARED (1931, First National)—**Billie Dove** appears in some photographs that are being used in a blackmail plot against her consulate husband.

TOWNSLEY, MACE

TEXAS RANGERS RIDE AGAIN (1940, Paramount)—**Broderick Crawford** and his Texas Ranger partner John Howard arrive incognito at May Robson's ranch to investigate the mysterious disappearance of her cattle. They find ranch foreman Anthony Quinn is behind the thefts.

TOXIC AVENGER, THE

THE TOXIC AVENGER (1985, Troma); THE TOXIC AVENGER, PART II (1989, Troma); THE TOXIC AVENGER PART III: THE LAST TEMPTATION OF TOXIE (1989, Troma)—Nerd **Mitchel Cohen** is thrown into a tub of toxic waste and emerges a mutant super-hero. It's silly, but handled in a nice campy fashion. In the sequels, it took both **John Altamura** and **Ron Fazio** to handle the continuing role of a superhero who drinks Drano for lunch and disposes of adversaries in numerous violent ways.

TOY

WHARF ANGEL (1934, Paramount)—Working in the toughest dive along the San Francisco waterfront, **Dorothy Dell** gives love and friendship to Preston Foster, a man evading the police.

TRACE

DESERT WARRIOR (1985, Cinema Group)—**Gary Watkins** has a series of adventures, behaving like some kind of Mad Max. Cover this one with sand.

TRACEY, JOE

A YANK ON THE BURMA ROAD (1942, MGM)—Tough truck driver **Barry Nelson** turns from personal profit to patriotism when he learns of Pearl Harbor.

TRACY

MAHOGANY (1975, Paramount)—The love life of black model and fashion designer **Diana Ross** is explored in a throwback to the weepers of Joan Crawford and others who found it difficult to balance a career while trying to keep a man, in this case "the black Clark Gable," Billy Dee Williams.

TRACY, DICK

DICK TRACY (1945, RKO); DICK TRACY VS CUEBALL (1946, RKO) DICK TRACY MEETS GRUESOME (1947, RKO); DICK TRACY'S DILEMMA (1947, RKO); DICK TRACY (1990, Buena Vista)—**Morgan Conway**, as the jut-jawed police detective, bests a disfigured criminal named Splitface (Mike Mazurki) in the first film. In the second his nemesis is a baldheaded master criminal Dick Wessel. **Ralph Byrd** takes over in the two 1947 films and continues the fine work of knocking off the strange criminal creations of cartoonist Chester Gould, first Boris Karloff as Gruesome and then Jack Lambert as The Claw. In the 1990 film, even though he's dressed in a yellow overcoat and fedora, **Warren Beatty** doesn't convince us that he's the square-jawed hero of the comics. The villains, headed by Al Pacino and Dustin Hoffman, fare better. Madonna is sexy, but all in all, the film fails even to achieve high camp.

TRACY, HARRY

HARRY TRACY—DESPERADO (1982, Canada, Guardian)—**Bruce Dern**, the last of the gentleman western outlaws, always seems to be caught because his mind is on other things.

TRACY, JOAN

THE GIRL WHO WOULDN'T QUIT (1918, Silent, Universal)—Mine owner's daughter **Louise Lovely** works diligently to clear her father's name of being a robber.

TRACY, MIKE

THREE GUYS NAMED MIKE (1957, MGM)—Ad man **Barry Sullivan** is just one of three men named Mike who are after daffy trainee airline stewardess Jane Wyman.

TRACY, PAUL

THREE FOR THE ROAD (1987, New Century/Vista)—**Charlie Sheen** and his buddy are transporting Kerri Green, the daughter of Senator Raymond J. Barry to a psychiatric clinic in the South, which is little more than a reform school, so she won't be in her father's way as he tries for reelection. Sheen has his hands full with the girl, but comes to realize her father is the problem, and delivers Green to her mother, Sally Kellerman, instead of the clinic.

TRAILL, DAVID

MR. PERRIN AND MR. TRAILL (1948, GB, Ealing)—**David Farrar**, a new master at a Cornish coastal school, does not get along with fellow master, Marius Goring. When Farrar takes school nurse Greta Gynt from Goring, the latter's mental state deteriorates and he attacks Farrar with a knife; then saves Farrar's life at the expense of his own.

TRANT, MONICA

HIS OFFICIAL FIANCEE (1919, Silent, Paramount)—**Vivian Martin** is the daughter of a once wealthy family, but with the death of the father, they are almost destitute. She takes a position in an office and when her boss asks her to be his "official fiancee" for a while, she agrees. Naturally, they fall in love.

TRANTON, DR.

JACK THE RIPPER (1959, GB, Paramount)—Surgeon **John Le Mesurier** proves to be Jack the Ripper. He is finally able to kill the girl he was really after when he began brutally butchering London prostitutes, before being crushed to death himself in an elevator shaft. His end is the only color sequence in the film and may prove too graphic for many.

TRASK, ALICE

THE LOVE CAPTIVE (1934, Universal)—Hypnotist Nils Asther uses his powers to make **Gloria Stuart** fall in love with him. Maybe he can teach the trick to Svengali.

TRASK, BEN

THE TALL TEXAN (1953, Lippert)—Escaped murderer **Lloyd Bridges** joins a group seeking gold. They are set upon by Indians objecting to their mining in the red man's territory.

TRASK, DAVID

PHONE CALL FROM A STRANGER (1952, 20th Century Fox)—**Gary Merrill** flies to Los Angeles to escape what he believes is his failed marriage. While on the plane, he gets to know several passengers who pour out their troubles to him. The plane crashes and Merrill, the only survivor among these passengers, sees it as his duty to visit their families. One widow, Bette Davis, convinces him that he should call his own wife and try to save their marriage.

TRASK, TEMPLE

THE CLEVER MRS. CARFAX (1917, Silent, Paramount)—**Julian Eltinge** (the foremost female impersonator of his time) is a newspaper columnist who bets he can attend a luncheon dressed in drag without being detected. He has to keep his girdle on a bit longer when he's forced to go on an ocean cruise in order to save a young woman from a crook.

TRAVALIAN, IVAN
AUTHOR! AUTHOR! (1982, 20th Century Fox)—Successful playwright **Al Pacino's** fourth wife Tuesday Weld walks out on him, leaving behind her four children from three previous marriages. In addition, Pacino has a son living with him from another marriage. The idea here is how will this brood manage to live together and still leave Pacino time to write his play. It's not worth waiting for the answer.

TRAVELLER, THE
THE ARKANSAS TRAVELLER (1938, Paramount)—Itinerant printer **Bob Burns** helps widow Fay Bainter run her newspaper and fight corrupt politicians. Burns was just one of many humorists advanced unsuccessfully as candidates to fill Will Rogers' shoes.

TRAVERS, BROOK
THE DICTATOR (1922, Silent, Paramount)—**Wallace Reid** helps win the war for South American revolutionaries, siding against his father's company which all but owns the country.

TRAVERS, CORALIE
THE VEILED WOMAN (1917, Silent, GB, British Empire)—Gambler Cecil Humphreys' mistress **Gladys Mason** changes places with Marjorie Chard, the married woman he's attempting to blackmail into becoming his new mistress. Never heard of Humphreys, Mason and Chard? Movies like this may be the reason.

TRAVERS, JOAN
JOAN OF THE WOODS (1918, Silent, World)—In this unbelievably convoluted series of coincidences, **June Elvidge**, an abandoned girl, is secretly married to a sailor, whose baby she carries. It dies and she is charged with murder. She is brought before the judge who just happens to be her father. He has no pity for his daughter and is about to throw the book at her when her missing husband bursts into the courtroom and straightens things out.

TRAVERS, JOHN
THE STAR PACKER (1934, Monogram)—U.S. Marshal **John Wayne** is brought in to clean up a gang headed by "The Shadow," which has been terrorizing the area.

TRAVERS, RUTH
THE INNOCENCE OF RUTH (1916, Silent, Edison)—**Viola Dana** is taken in by a well-known womanizer Edward Earle after the death of her father. Her sweet innocence has a profound effect on him, and when another bounder tries to seduce Dana, Earle steps in and gives him what for, and looks ready to make Dana his wife.

TRAVIS
THE EXPERTS (1989, Paramount)—The KGB snatch nightclub owner **John Travolta** and his partner Ayre Gross to act as expert advisors on things American, in order to update things at a replicated U.S. town, where spies are trained.

TRAVIS, GEORGE
HELD BY THE LAW (1927, Silent, Universal)—**Ralph Lewis** is wrongly convicted and sentenced to death for the shooting death of the father of his daughter's fiancee at the couple's engagement party.

TRAVIS, JEFF
THE STRANGER WORE A GUN (1953, Columbia)—Former Quantrill raider **Randolph Scott** wishes to amend his ways but must face down George Macready before he can ride off into the sunset with Claire Trevor.

TRAVIS, MICK
O LUCKY MAN! (1973, GB, Warner Brothers)—In this comedy, the misadventures of coffee salesman **Malcolm McDowell** land him in jail.

TRAVIS, VIRGINIA
WOMAN CHASES MAN (1937, UA)—Promising architect **Miriam Hopkins** and young millionaire Joel McCrea's father, Charles Winninger, con his tightfisted son into investing in a building scheme.

TRAXX
TRAXX (1988, DEG)—In this funny film, mercenary **Shadoe Stevens** cares for two things: shooting people and making odd-flavored cookies.

TREADWAY, ROLLO
THE NAVIGATOR (1924, Silent, MGM)—Completely helpless millionaire **Buster Keaton** and his pampered socialite girlfriend Kathryn McGuire are the only people on a transatlantic ocean liner marooned in the middle of the ocean.

TREAT
ORPHANS (1987, Lorimar)—Homeless **Matthew Modine** and his helpless brother Keith Anderson kidnap gangster Albert Finney, but it is Finney who takes control of their lives. All three members of the cast are excellent in the adaptation of a play by Lyle Kessler.

TRELAWNEY, ROSE
THE ACTRESS (1928, Silent, MGM)—Well-known Victorian actress **Norma Shearer** is in love with Ralph Forbes, whose family does not approve of their marriage because of her profession.

TREMBOLT, ALEX
THE GUILTY (1947, Monogram)—**John Litel** murders the wrong twin girl (both played by Bonita Granville) and the blame falls on another man until Litel notices something missing when he kisses the surviving girl.

TREMAIN, JOHNNY
JOHNNY TREMAIN (1957, Buena Vista)—In 1773 Boston, apprentice silversmith **Hal Stalmaster** joins the Sons of Liberty and acts as the audience's eyes at a lot of Revolutionary history.

TREMAINE, JOHN JR.
BIG TREMAINE (1916, Silent, Metro)—**Harold Lockwood**, an innocent young man, is a social outcast after serving seven years in prison for a crime his brother committed. The latter finally clears Lockwood with a death bed confession.

TREMAYNE, DENISE
THE LAUGHING LADY (1946, GB, British National)—In 1790 France, artist Webster Booth must retrieve a valuable necklace, called The Pearls of Sorrow, from **Anne Ziegler**, living in England, so Robespierre will spare his mother from the guillotine. However, Booth falls in love with Ziegler, returns to France and is sentenced to death. Ziegler brings the necklace to Robespierre and wins her lover's freedom.

TREMAYNE, DIANE
ANGEL FACE (1953, RKO)—In this film noir, demented **Jean Simmons** kills anyone who crosses her, including her father and stepmother. When chauffeur Robert Mitchum refuses to marry her, she quickly throws the car they are sitting in into reverse, sending it and them over a cliff to their deaths.

TREMAYNE, MICHAEL & DAVID
THE JOKERS (1967, GB, Universal)—Two bored society brothers, **Michael Crawford** and **Oliver Reed** plan to steal and return the crown jewels for a lark.

TREMONT, JAKE
DAD (1989, Universal)—Old and increasingly feeble, **Jack Lemmon** is more and more dominated by his wife Olympia Dukakis. When she suffers a heart attack, their son Ted Danson decides he'd better become parent to his parents in their declining years.

TRENT, BILL
UNDERCOVER AGENT (1939, Monogram)—In one of many of this studio's second-rate crime features, **Russell Gleason** goes undercover to break up a gang of crooks. It's not only forgettable, it never registered.

TRENT, CAPTAIN
CAPTAIN'S ORDERS (1937, GB, Liberty)—Merchant ship captain **Henry Edwards** risks losing a race to New York from England when he stops to rescue actress Jane Carr from her iceberg-stricken yacht.

TRENT, DR. & JOHN
THE HOUSE OF TRENT (1933, GB, Ensign)—**John Stuart** plays both the doctor who saved the life of the daughter of a press baron, and also his medical student son, who later meets and falls in love with the very same girl.

TRENT, HOMES
RETURN OF A STRANGER (1962, GB, Danzinger)—Ex-convict **Cyril Shaps** plots to kill the husband of a schoolgirl he assaulted, which resulted in his being sent to prison.

TRENT, IRENE
THE NIGHT WALKER (1964, Universal)—Widow **Barbara Stanwyck** is haunted by a recurring nightmare about her husband, killed in an explosion.

TRENT, PHILIP
TRENT'S LAST CASE (1953, GB, British Lion)—Reporter-turned-detective **Michael Wilding** sets out to prove that the death of a wealthy man was not suicide, but murder, committed by the deceased's wife and lover. Wilding is wrong.

TRENT, SALLY
TORCH SINGER (1933, Paramount)—In this silly soap opera, nightclub queen **Claudette Colbert** abandons her baby and later has second thoughts about it, spending the rest of the film looking for the child.

TRENT, SUZY
SUZY (1936, MGM)—In London and Paris, during WWI, American show girl **Jean Harlow** has a League-of-Nations go at romances with an Irish inventor-pilot, A French air ace, and members of a German spy ring.

TREVELYAN, ADAM
ADAM AND EVIL (1927, Silent, MGM)—In this farce, **Lew Cody** plays identical twin brothers. Married Cody poses as his single brother so he may have a fling with gold digger Gwen Lee. He finds his wife Aileen Pringle can play games also.

"TREVOR, ANN," CARLOTTA
MY SIN (1931, Paramount)—Just as interior designer **Tallulah Bankhead** is about to marry a wealthy man, lawyer Fredric March, who defended her in her shady past as a cheap nightclub singer in Panama, comes forward to queer the deal.

TREVOR, JILL
CONFIDENTIAL LADY (1939, GB, Warner Brothers)—Jilted on her wedding day, when it is discovered that her father had met financial ruin, **Jane Baxter** swears to take revenge on all men. She settles for taking revenge on her ex-fiance who had been behind ruining her father.

TREVOR, MICHAEL
MAN OF THE WORLD (1931, Paramount)—Parisian gigolo **William Powell** blackmails the American women he services until he falls in love with Carole Lombard.

TREVOR, VIRGINIA
VIRGINIA'S HUSBAND (1928, GB, Silent, Butchers); (1934, GB, Fox)—**Lillian Oldland** and **Dorothy Boyd** portray a man-hater and feminist who is forced to take a "temporary" husband in order to satisfy her wealthy aunt, and then finds herself falling in love with the guy.

TREXEL, SUSAN
SUSAN AND GOD (1940, MGM)—Society woman **Joan Crawford** alienates her husband and family when she embraces a new religious movement, and preaches but does not practice its tenets.

TREY
THE DRIFTER (1988, Concorde)—When Kim Delaney picks up hunk hitchhiker **Miles O'Keefe**, she takes him to her bed, but on arriving at her destination, lets him know it was just a one night thing. Not according to his reckoning, it isn't.

TRICE, NAOMI
A WICKED WOMAN (1934, MGM)—**Mady Christians** kills her drunken husband to protect her children, but ultimately is exonerated.

TRIGGER BILL
BAD MAN OF BRIMSTONE (1938, MGM)—Aging bandit **Wallace Beery** discovers his long-lost son and reforms.

TRILBY
TRILBY (1915, Silent, World)—**Clara Kimball Young** is the young woman whom hypnotist Svengali (Wilton Lackaye) transforms into a great opera singer. But he can't force her to love him. The role was played by Marian Marsh and Hildegard Neff in the two productions, titled SVENGALI in 1931, and 1954.

TRINDALE, TERRY
HER CARDBOARD LOVER (1942, MGM)—**Robert Taylor** has the distinction of being Norma Shearer's co-star in her film swan song. Taylor is hired by Shearer to pretend to be her lover to make her fiance, George Sanders, jealous. Well, we guess we all know the outcome of such shenanigans.

TRIPP

HIS EXCITING NIGHT (1938, Universal)—Timid clerk **Charles Ruggles**, the butt of practical jokes, almost loses his bride on their wedding night, because his boss has hired a blonde to harass him. It's a cruel shivaree, but meant to be funny.

TRISH

TRUCK STOP WOMEN (1974, LT Films)—**Dolores Dorn** sells her body to truckers while others in her prostitution-hijacking ring empty out the trucks.

TROG

TROG (1970, GB, Warner Brothers)—Anthropologists capture primitive man **Joe Cornelius** who escapes and abducts a child.

TRON

TRON (1982, Buena Vista)—Computer game designer Jeff Bridges is zapped into one of his own creations. He must face **Bruce Boxleitner** in a sort of star wars gladiator video game. Look at it but don't bother to listen.

TROOP, JUBAL

JUBAL (1956, Columbia)—Drifter **Glenn Ford** is befriended by rancher Ernest Borgnine. He finds himself in the middle of a sexual hot house involving Borgnine's promiscuous wife Valerie French, who gives Ford an outrageous come-on, and the cold-blooded Rod Steiger, who wants French for himself.

TROTTA, JOEY

TOY SOLDIERS (1991, Tri-Star)—Andrew Divoff leads a band of terrorists who take over a rich kids' school, hoping to gain the release of Divoff's drug king father, who is on trial in Florida. **Wil Wheaton** is one of the lads who practice counter-terrorism.

TROTTER, GEORGE

I DIDN'T DO IT (1945, GB, Columbia)—When a murder is committed in a theatrical boarding house, the finger of suspicion points to **George Formby**. George is funny—isn't he?

TROUT, MRS.

HIS WIFE'S MOTHER (1932, GB, British International)—**Marian Dawson** spots her son-in-law Joy Verno in the company of a showgirl. He has to pose as his own double to fool the old dear.

TROUT, PARIS

PARIS TROUT (1991, Viacom Pictures)—Mean-spirited Southern storekeeper **Dennis Hopper** makes money by issuing high interest rate loans to poor blacks. When Eric Ware refuses to repay a note on a worthless car, Hopper and a hired gun go to Ware's house and kill his mother and 12-year-old sister. Racist Hopper is sure no jury will convict him for a crime against "nigras."

TROWER, CPL.

THE VICTORS (1963, Columbia)—**George Hamilton**, a member of an infantry squad making its way from Sicily into France and onto Germany during WWII, moves in with a girl in Berlin. When she leaves him for Russian soldier Albert Finney, he gets drunk and confronts Finney. As neither understands the other, they pull knives and kill each other.

TROY

KNIGHTS OF THE CITY (1986, New World)—**Leon Issac Kennedy** is a leader of a New York street gang, which is also a musical group. They take turns defending their turf and competing in a talent contest. Stupid!

TRUE, TARA B. *See* SUPERCHICK

TRUE, TROTTIE

THE GAY LADY (1949, GB, GFD)—In 1900, gaiety girl **Jean Kent** loves balloonist Andrew Crawford, but marries nobleman James Donald. It takes one last flight with Crawford for Kent to decide she has made the right choice.

TRUESDALE, MOLLIE

A LADY TAKES A CHANCE (1943, RKO)—While on holiday in Oregon, New York City office girl **Jean Arthur** falls in love with rodeo star John Wayne.

TRUEHEART, SUSIE MAY

TRUE HEART SUSIE (1919, Silent, Artcraft)—Country girl **Lillian Gish** loves Robert Harron, whose ambition is to become a minister. He takes no notice of Gish. She raises the tuition to send him to school by selling her prize cow. He returns to be a preacher in his hometown, but breaks Gish's heart when he marries another, a woman of many affairs, so to speak. The wife dies and the deceased's aunt straightens out the clergyman, who finally pledges his troth to Gish.

TRUESMITH, WOODROW LAFAYETTE PERSHING

HAIL THE CONQUERING HERO (1944, Paramount)—Army reject **Eddie Bracken** is mistakenly believed by people in his hometown to be a WWII hero. The error is encouraged by some real marine heroes. Even when Bracken confesses to the deception, the townsfolk still want him as their mayor. It's the best thing Bracken ever did, but he owes a lot of credit to director-writer Preston Sturges and fine performances from delightful character actors, William Demarest, Franklin Pangborn, Raymond Walburn and Alan Bridge.

TRUMBELL, SANDRA

SECOND HAND WIFE (1933, Fox)—Secretary **Sally Eilers** causes the break-up of her boss Ralph Bellamy's marriage to Helen Vinson.

TRUMBULL, BROCK

RICH MAN'S FOLLY (1931, Paramount)—In a modern day version of Charles Dickens' "Dombey and Son," **George Bancroft** is a money-mad shipbuilder.

TRUMBULL, HONORABLE JAMES

THREE WISE FOOLS (1923, Silent, Goldwyn); (1946, MGM)—**William H. Crane and Lewis Stone** appear as the jurist member of a trio of crotchety old men whose lives are changed when they are made responsible for a charming orphan girl.

TUBBS, HENRIETTA "MOM"

LADY TUBBS (1935, Universal)—Ex-cook **Alice Brady** crashes society and shows up pretenders.

TUCKER

PEEPER (1975, 20th Century Fox)—In 1947 Los Angeles, British private eye **Michael Caine** finds nothing but trouble as he seeks a man's lost daughter.

TUCKER, LIBBY

I OUGHT TO BE IN PICTURES (1982, Regal)—Young would-be actress **Dinah Manoff** hitchhikes to Hollywood hoping to break into pictures, with perhaps a bit of help from her estranged screenwriter father, Walter Matthau.

TUCKER, PRESTON

TUCKER, THE MAN AND HIS DREAMS (1988, Paramount)—**Jeff Bridges** is perfect as the charming American businessman, who stood the automobile world on its ears with his boundless energy, optimism and, oh yes, his automobile. According to this movie, the giants of the automobile industry ganged up on this challenger to their dominance of the market. The result was not only his ruination but placing a hold on much needed changes in automobile design and safety, which have slowly become standard in the forty-plus years since Tucker's dreams.

TUCKER, SAM

THE SOUTHERNER (1945, UA)—**Zachary Scott** gives one of his best and most atypical performances in this Jean Renoir-written and -directed story of penniless farmers in the deep South, trying desperately to scratch out a living and save their land.

TUCKER, VINCE

WEEKEND WARRIORS (1986, The Movie Store)—**Chris Lemmon** and some other incompetents join the National Guard to play soldier on weekends with expected comical results.

TUGBOAT ANNIE

CAPTAIN TUGBOAT ANNIE (1945, Republic)—**Jane Darwell** competes with her rival Edgar Kennedy for a big shipping contract. The two put aside their differences to combat a waterfront fire. Darwell and Kennedy are no Marie Dressler and Wallace Beery, but they try.

TUKKER, LITTLE JIM

LITTLE MISTER JIM (1946, MGM)—**Jackie "Butch" Jenkins** stars in this tearjerker about the trials of a youngster whose mother has died, and whose father has taken to drink.

TULIP, MILLICENT

MISS TULIP STAYS THE NIGHT (1955, GB, Adelphi)—**Cicely Courtneidge** portrays both the woman who interrupts a couple in their home late at night, demanding a bed, in which she is found dead in the morning, and her equally eccentric twin sister. It will be discovered that the latter nut killed the former.

TULLIVER, "TRUTHFUL"

TRUTHFUL TULLIVER (1917, Silent, Triangle)—**William S. Hart** arrives in Glory Hole to start a newspaper. When he sees two sisters being insulted by men hanging around a saloon, he rushes to their assistance, incurring the enmity of the owner of the saloon. Thus begins a feud which only ends when Hart runs the man and his goons out of town. After some doubt, Hart wins the sister of his choice.

TULLY, CHARLIE

GET CHARLIE TULLY (1976, GB, Quintain)—**Dick Emery** and his sidekick Derren Nesbitt are on the trail of four women who have the location of missing bonds tattooed on their bottoms. The Mafia becomes involved chasing Emery, chasing the girls from London to Rome. This may not be everyone's notion of humor, or perhaps anyone's.

TURA

HER JUNGLE LOVE (1938, Paramount)—**Dorothy Lamour** and Ray Milland scored so well with audiences in JUNGLE PRINCESS that the studio sent them back together to another jungle. Ray crash lands his plane and sarong-clad Lamour nurses him back to health. The lovers have the usual types of troubles with assorted villains, an earthquake, and an active volcano. The Technicolor helped but the best acting awards went to Lamour's pets, a chimp named Gaga and the lion cub, Meena.

TURGANEV, BORIS

MASTER SPY (1964, GB, Allied Artists)—**Stephen Murray's** assistant June Thoburn suspects the Russian scientist is a spy for the Soviets, but he's is double-agent working for British Intelligence.

TURNER, ARTHUR & MILDRED

OH MEN! OH, WOMEN! (1957, 20th Century Fox) **Dan Dailey** and **Ginger Rogers** are a married couple. He's an actor, with an image as a great lover. She knows better and is seeing analyst David Niven to see what can be done about Dailey's lack of passion at home.

TURNER, BRIAN

THE MISSOURI TRAVELLER (1958, Buena Vista)—Orphan **Brandon De Wilde** finds a home in a southern town in 1910.

TURNER, HENRY

REGARDING HENRY (1991, Paramount)—No-nonsense, no-mercy lawyer **Harrison Ford** is shot in the head during a robbery. The wound puts him in a hospital for a long period of rehabilitation, during which he must relearn even the most basic activities, like walking, reading and making love with his wife, Annette Bening. He returns to his law firm, but is now a caring, concerned individual. The movie suggests that these are not the qualities that are sought for in a corporate attorney.

TURNER, JANE

WANTED, JANE TURNER (1936, RKO)—**Judith Blake** is an innocent girl, whose name just happens to be the one used by crooks as the renter of a general delivery box in a mail fraud scam.

TURNER, JOE

A YANK IN ERMINE (1955, GB, Monarch)—In this broad comedy, American **Peter Thompson** moves to England when he inherits an earldom, and falls in love with English girl Noelle Middleton. An old flame almost ruins the love match, but she's taken out of the picture by a charming Englishman.

TURNER, JULIE ANN

GOING STEADY (1958, Columbia)—High school sweethearts **Molly Bee** and Alan Reed, Jr. elope. They move in with her parents and soon discover that babies are going to have a baby.

TURNER, LILY

LILY TURNER (1933, Warner Brothers)—**Ruth Chatterton** unwittingly marries a bigamist and then weds a drunk to give her child a name. She falls in love with yet a third man, but stays with the second because he breaks his back defending her from a killer. Films like this give mother love a bad name.

TURNER, LINDA

TED AND VENUS (1991, Double Helix)—Initially, **Kim Adams** is flattered that hippie poet Bud Cort feels she is his Venus rising out of the sea. Later, his attentions degenerate into obscene phone calls and molestations. When the authorities are unable to do anything, she buys a gun.

TURNER, MARJORIE

SIBLING RIVALRY (1990, Columbia)—Although totally unbelievable, this black farce is worth a look. Bored **Kirstie Alley** takes an adulterous fling with her brother-in-law, Sam Elliott, and the experience proves too strenuous for him. He has a heart attack and dies. Attempting to make his death appear a suicide leads to some amusing if morbid set pieces.

TURNER, ROD

YESTERDAY'S HERO (1979, GB, EMI)—Alcoholic ex-soccer player **Ian McShane** attempts a come-back with the help of rock star Suzanne Somers. A lot of help she'll be.

TURNER, ROY

THE NIGHT RUNNER (1957, Universal)—Although not fully recovered, **Ray Danton** is released from a mental hospital.

TURNER, SCOTT

TURNER & HOOCH (1989, Buena Vista)—Actors are warned against starring with children and dogs. **Tom Hanks** ignores the warning when this police detective adopts Beasley the Dog, the only eyewitness to a murder. The partners don't initially get along very well, partly because Beasley is such a slob.

TURNER, SUSAN

THE BACHELOR AND THE BOBBYSOXER (1947, RKO)—Teenager **Shirley Temple** develops a huge crush on playboy Cary Grant. Temple's judge sister Myrna Loy orders Grant to court the kid until Temple gets over her infatuation. She does, but it looks like she'll get Grant as a brother-in-law.

TURNER, TERRY

TWICE BLESSED (1945, MGM)—**Lee Wilde** conspires with her twin sister to get their parents back together.

TURNER, TOMMY

THE MALE ANIMAL (1942, Warner Brothers)—College professor **Henry Fonda** sheds his retiring image when his wife's old boyfriend shows up for a visit.

TURNER, TRUCK

TRUCK TURNER (1974, American International)—**Issac Hayes** is a skip-tracer (i.e. he is a bounty hunter for bail-jumpers) in this extremely violent black exploitation film.

TURP, ETHEL & JOE

JOE AND ETHEL TURP CALL ON THE PRESIDENT (1939, MGM)—**Ann Sothern** and **William Gargan** are a Brooklyn couple who come to the aid of their fired mailman, taking his case all the way to the White House where they are heard by the president played wisely by Lewis Stone in his Judge Hardy style.

TURPIN, DICK

DICK TURPIN (1925, Silent, Fox); (1933, GB, Gaumont); THE LADY AND THE BANDIT (1951, Columbia)—**Tom Mix, Victor McLaglen** and **Louis Hayward** each appeared as the infamous British highwayman in highly romanticized stories, with the leading character more a misunderstood hero than villain. McLaglen's appearance was enough to get him called to Hollywood.

TURRIN, JEFF

OLD BOYFRIENDS (1979, Avco Embassy)—**Richard Jordan** is one of a Talia Shire's former lovers, whom she seeks out to analyze her past. It's a dumb idea, poorly handled.

TUSTINE, KATE

CITY GIRL (1930, Fox)—City girl **Mary Duncan** finds the country has plenty to offer her.

TUTTLE, ELMER

PASSIONATE PLUMBER (1932, MGM)—Parisian Irene Purcell hires **Buster Keaton** to act as her lover to make Gilbert Roland jealous. This is not good Keaton material.

TUTTLE, JONAS, CHESTER & MAMA RUSU

TUTTLES OF TAHITI (1942, RKO)—**Charles Laughton, Jon Hall** and **Adeline de Walt Reynolds** live on a South Sea island paradise where they do nothing but eat, drink and make merry. Everything is OK until Hall falls in love with Peggy, the daughter of a family with quite different values. The Tuttles seem to have the right idea as far as we're concerned.

TUTTLE, PHOEBE

WOMAN IN DISTRESS (1937, Columbia)—**May Robson** owns a Rembrandt painting that is stolen by a gang of thieves, who then decide to kill her. Two reporters, Dean Jagger and Irene Hervey, come to her rescue.

TUTTLE, WILMA

ACCUSED (1949, Paramount)—In an interesting film noir, college professor **Loretta Young** accidentally kills one of her students when he tries to assault her. She attempts to make it appear that he accidentally died of drowning. Detective Wendell Corey, who is attracted to Young, doesn't buy it and gathers enough evidence to bring her to trial, where she is acquitted on the basis of self-defense.

TWAIN, MARK *See* **SAMUEL CLEMENS**

TWEEDHAM, LORD

TAKE THE HEIR (1930, Big 4)—Frequently drunk Englishman **Frank Elliott** inherits the estate of his wealthy American uncle. Because of his state, his valet Edward Everett Horton masquerades as the master and has several romantic encounters.

TWEEDLEDEE

THE UNHOLY THREE (1925, Silent, MGM)—**Harry Eccles** is the dwarf member of a circus gang who carry out a series of crimes. Eccles also played the role in the 1930 sound remake, where he is only called Midget.

TWEESDALE, NANCY

WIDOWS MIGHT (1934, GB, Warner Brothers)—**Laura La Plante** and Yvonne Arnaud are two widows out to get new husbands and will stop at nothing to succeed.

TWILLIE, CUTHBART, J.

MY LITTLE CHICKADEE (1940, Universal)—**W.C. Fields**, a medicine man, meets Mae West, a shady lady who's been run out of town, on a train. She promotes a fake marriage with Fields and sees him made sheriff of Greasewood City. The film isn't as funny as it should have been, because each star wrote his or her own part of the screenplay to ensure the other wasn't shown to an advantage.

TWINKLETOES

TWINKLETOES (1926, Silent, First National)—Brunette **Colleen Moore** appears as a blonde in this picture about a slum girl who makes the most of her talent for dancing and falls in love with a boxer, who saves her from suicide at a low point in her life.

TWIST, OLIVER

OLIVER TWIST (1916, Silent, Lasky); (1922, Silent, Associated First National); (1933, Monogram); (1951, GB, Rank); OLIVER! (1968, GB, Columbia)—**Marie Doro, Jackie Coogan, Dickie Moore, John Howard Davies** and **Mark Lester** each appear as Charles Dickens' orphan, who falls in with a gang of child pickpockets led by crafty teacher of thieves, Fagin, and the brutal Bill Sykes, before being restored to the home of his mother's wealthy uncle.

TWIST, OLIVER, JR.
OLIVER TWIST JR. (1921, Silent, Fox)—**Harold Goodwin** stars in this contemporary American version of Dickens' story. It's not great, but it's not terrible, either. We suppose that means it's mediocre.

TWITCH
THREE SAILORS AND A GIRL (1953, Warner Brothers)—**Gene Nelson**, Gordon MacRae and Jack E. Leonard are three sailors entrusted with investing a ship's funds in a musical show starring Jane Powell.

TWITCHELL, ANGELA
THE TRAVELING SALESLADY (1935, First National)—**Joan Blondell**, the daughter of a toothpaste manufacturer, proves the value of advertising to her father.

TYAN-HWA
CHINA GIRL (1987, Great American Vestron)—**Sari Chang** and Richard Panebianco are the star-crossed lovers in this Romeo and Juliet story of warring New York City Chinese and Italian gangs. Are there any combinations left unexplored?

TYLER, BILL
THE MOUNTAIN MEN (1980, Columbia)—**Charlton Heston's** son Frazer Clarke Heston wrote this primitive western about two 19th century trappers and their encounters with Indians. Perhaps Charlton has forgiven his son by now.

TYLER, CICELY & CHRISTOPHER
NEXT TIME WE LOVE (1936, Universal)—The marriage of Broadway actress **Margaret Sullavan** and reporter **James Stewart** is threatened by the demands of each other's careers. Family friend Ray Milland, long in love with Sullavan, doesn't help matters.

TYLER, GRACE & RUTH
NOT MY SISTER (1916, Silent, Triangle)—**Bessie Barriscale** protects her younger sister, **Alice Taaffe**, from the attentions of the caddish sculptor who had abandoned Barriscale after seducing her and leaving her pregnant. She has to kill the bounder. Her new husband is accused of the murder, but everything works out OK.

TYLER, JED
THE DESERT RIDER (1929, Silent, MGM)—Pony Express rider **Tim McCoy** tracks down the men who robbed him to get a land grant owned by a beautiful Mexican girl, Raquel Torres.

TYLER, JIM
THEY WANTED TO MARRY (1937, RKO)—**Gordon Jones** wishes to marry debutante Betty Furness, but her father doesn't think the news photographer is good enough husband material for his little girl.

TYLER, JOHN DEWITT III
MY MARRIAGE (1936, 20th Century Fox)—Pauline Frederick tries to prevent the marriage of her son **Kent Taylor** to Claire Trevor, whose father's murder revealed his connections with racketeers. It turns out that one of Taylor's brothers is involved in the murder.

TYLER, JUDE & SATAN
SATAN'S SISTER (1925, Silent, GB, Woodfall)—Man-hater **Betty Balfour** and her brother **Guy Phillips**, known as Satan, are in Jamaica seeking buried treasure. Instead, she finds romance with Phillip Stevens.

TYLER, RED
SHE LOVED A FIREMAN (1937, Warner Brothers)—**Dick Foran** stars in a most routine story about a fireman who becomes a hero.

TYLER, TOBY
TOBY TYLER (1960, Buena Vista)—**Kevin Corcoran** runs away from home to join the circus. If you think Corcoran is cute, there just might be enough here to hold your interest.

TYNAN, JOE
THE SEDUCTION OF JOE TYNAN (1979, Universal)—**Alan Alda** is a Kennedy-like liberal senator, seduced by power, although he does forget about wife Barbara Harris long enough to have an affair with married Meryl Streep.

TYREE, TAMMY
TAMMY AND THE BACHELOR (1957, Universal); TAMMY, TELL ME TRUE (1961, Universal); TAMMY AND THE DOCTOR (1963, Universal); TAMMY AND THE MILLIONAIRE (1967, Universal)—**Debbie Reynolds** originated the role of the backwoods tomboy who falls for a stranded flyer. She even had a million-dollar hit song, "Tammy." She was followed in the three lesser-quality sequels by **Sandra Dee** in the middle two and **Debbie Walton**, in the last.

TYROON, HENRY
THE WHEELER DEALERS (1963, MGM)—Harvard MBA **James Garner** adopts a Texas "good ole boy" persona, the better to use his flair for making money work for him to make new money without ever producing any products. This may explain the U.S.'s trade deficit and the growing supremacy of Japanese business and industry.

TZARAKOV, IVAN
THE MAD GENIUS (1931, Warner Brothers)—Crippled, raving mad puppeteer **John Barrymore** adopts Frankie Darro, and turns the boy into a great dancer by the time he grows into Donald Cook.

U

UDELL, MAIZIE
THE SHOW GIRL (1927, Silent, Rayart)—**Mildred Harris** owns the Honky-Tonk Cafe with Gaston Glass. A famous theatrical producer and a roue are both interested in Harris for different reasons. By the end, Harris is the star of a revue put on by the producer and marries her old partner Glass.

UFGOOD, WILLOA
WILLOW (1988, MGM)—In this entertaining fantasy, apprentice sorcerer, **Warwick Davis**, one of a race of little people, strives to save a magical child from the forces of evil, led by the sorceress queen Jean Marsh.

ULAH
THE JUNGLE PRINCESS (1936, Paramount)—**Dorothy Lamour**, looking marvelous in a sarong, is raised with her pet tiger by natives on a tropical isle. She falls in love with visiting Ray Milland but their romance is not approved by all.

ULYSSES

MAKING MR. RIGHT (1987, Orion)—Scientist **John Malkovich** has created an almost human android in his own image. It's not a film this very fine actor will wish long to remember.

ULZANA

ULZANA'S RAID (1972, Universal)—In a very violent film, **Joaquin Martinez** portrays the Apache leader of a pack of marauding Indians.

UNCAS

LAST OF THE REDMEN (1947, Columbia)—**Rick Vallin**—In this adaptation of *The Last of the Mohicans,* there is no Chingaghook, so it falls to Rick Vallin as Uncas to represent the last of the Mohican Indians.

UNDERSHAFT, MAJOR BARBARA

MAJOR BARBARA (1941, GB, Rank)—**Wendy Hiller,** the daughter of munitions manufacturer Robert Morley, is an officer in the Salvation Army, disillusioned when it appears that her superiors are being taken in by her father's charity.

UNGAR, FELIX

THE ODD COUPLE (1968, Paramount)—Fussy hypochondriac **Jack Lemmon** moves in with sloppy divorced Walter Matthau, when Jack's wife throws him out. The two nearly drive each other crazy.

UNKNOWN, THE

THE UNKNOWN (1921, Silent, Goldstone)—**Richard Talmadge** lives a double life. He is the wastrel son of a rich man with the controlling interest in the flour market, and unbeknownst to his father or others, he is a champion of the people out to beat down high prices.

UNMAN

UNMAN, WITTERING AND ZIGO (1971, GB, Paramount)—**Michael Howe** is the third from the last of the boys named on the roll call of an upper-class boys school. The behavior of the boys is certainly not upper-class. Zigo is always absent so no one portrays him.

UPPINGTON, LAURA & EDWARD

HIS WIFE'S MONEY (1920, Silent. Select)—When **Louise Prussing** and **Ned Hay** marry, he is unaware that she is wealthy. Determined that she will not pay all the bills, he works a mine that has never yielded any profits. It does now.

UPTON, STEPHEN

THE DESPERADOES (1943, Columbia)—**Randolph Scott** and Glenn Ford go straight, and clean up a western town.

URQUHART

LOCAL HERO (1983, GB, Warner Brothers)—When Burt Lancaster, the head of an American oil company, sends Peter Riegart to Scotland to buy an entire village so the company can drill its North Sea oil reserves, **Denis Lawson** is the local lad who represents all the villagers in the transactions, and he's quite a sharpie.

USHER, LORD RODERICK & MADELEINE

THE FALL OF THE HOUSE OF USHER (1952, GB, Vigilant)—**Kay Tendeter** and **Gwendoline Watford;** (1980, Sunn Classics) -**Martin Landau;** THE HOUSE OF USHER (1960, American International)—**Vincent Price** and **Myrna Fahey;** The 1952 version of the Edgar Allan Poe tale about a lord's sister who is revived after being buried alive is only modestly terrifying. The Martin Landau version in 1980 is pure bunk, but supersensitive recluse Vincent Price is perfect in the moody 1960 masterpiece brought to the screen by Roger Corman. Myrna Fahey as the buried-alive sister is merely an attractive decoration.

VACARRI, VINCENT

THE IDOLMAKER (1980, UA)—**Ray Sharkey's** character is loosely based on the career of Bob Marcucci, who groomed Frankie Avalon and Fabian for stardom.

VAL

SATURDAY'S HEROES (1937, RKO)—Even in 1937, Universities were having problems with the tale wagging the dog with their football teams. Star quarterback **Van Heflin,** burned by the system, proposes that colleges admit their athletic programs are professional and subsidize the players. Sound familiar?

VALANCE, LIBERTY

THE MAN WHO SHOT LIBERTY VALANCE (1962, Paramount)—**Lee Marvin** is a bad one. He not only robs stagecoaches and terrorizes the passengers, he brutally gun-whips one, James Stewart. The latter will later be credited with killing Marvin in a showdown, but John Wayne actually fires the fatal shot.

VALACHI, JOSEPH

THE VALACHI PAPERS (1972, Columbia)—Minor Mafia figure **Charles Bronson** tells what he knows. It's not a pretty picture, nor are the production values anything special.

VALDEK, MILO

THE DIRTY DOZEN (1967, GB, MGM)—**Tom Busby** is one of the twelve condemned American soldiers who are given a chance to win a pardon if they participate in a special mission against a chateau in France where high ranking German officers take R & R. Busby's death is early in the assault.

VALDEZ, BOB

VALDEZ IS COMING (1971, UA)—When the leader of a group of powerful men won't give $100 to **Burt Lancaster** for the widow of a man he was forced to kill in their defense, Lancaster kidnaps the man's wife and heads for the mountains.

VALDEZ, CHINO

CHINO (1976, de Laurentiis)—Half-breed **Charles Bronson** runs a New Mexico ranch with the help of a runaway boy.

VALE, CHARLOTTE

NOW, VOYAGER (1942, Warner Brothers)—Repressed spinster **Bette Davis** is helped out of her shell by psychiatrist Claude Rains. She takes a cruise on which she meets and falls in love with married Paul Henreid. Although he can not divorce his wife for her, Bette is thankful for what she has.

VALE, CHRISTINE HELM

WITNESS FOR THE PROSECUTION (1957, UA)—When her husband, Tyrone Power, is arrested for the murder of an older woman who leaves him her fortune, **Marlene Dietrich** appears as a witness for the prosecution, but Power's barrister, Charles Laughton, is able to show that she has perjured herself on the stand and Power is acquitted. Then for the surprise ending to this Agatha Christie gem . . . .

VALE, ULA

TARZAN AND THE GREEN GODDESS (1938, Principal)—**Ula Holt** isn't green and she's not a goddess, but Tarzan in the person of Herman Brix (Bruce Bennett) leads an expedition to find her.

VALENTIN, LIBBY
THE MODERNS (1958, Alive Films)—In this ironic look at the Paris art scene of the Twenties, **Genevieve Bujold** is the crafty agent for art-forger Keith Carradine.

VALENTIN, RALPH
SLAVE OF DESIRE (1923, Silent, Goldwyn)—Poet **George Walsh** is played with by a vampish countess, Carmel Myers. He is about to die "a slave of desire" when he is saved by a girl he once loved and deserted, Bessie Love.

VALENTINE, BILLY RAY
TRADING PLACES (1983, Paramount)—Street beggar **Eddie Murphy** gets the chance to trade places with wealthy young executive Dan Aykroyd to satisfy a bet of two old, crooked multi-millionaire stockbrokers, Don Ameche and Ralph Bellamy. Murphy and Aykroyd later band together to take revenge on their tormentors. Murphy is excellent.

VALENTINE, CHARITY HOPE
SWEET CHARITY (1969, Universal)—New York taxi dancer **Shirley MacLaine** has nothing but bad luck with men in this so-so musical based on Fellini's NIGHTS OF CABIRIA.

VALENTINE, HARRY
WISE GUYS (1986, MGM/UA)—**Danny DeVito** is a gofer for a New Jersey gangster. When he and his friend Joe Piscopo mis-bet $10,000 of the boss's money, they forfeit their lives. They're given a chance to survive, however: each is given a contract on his buddy's life. DeVito finds a way to get them both out of trouble.

VALENTINE, JIMMY
ALIAS JIMMY VALENTINE (1928, MGM)—Safecracker **William Haines** falls in love with Lelia Hyams and vows to go straight. He moves to the town where Hyams lives to settle down, but is trailed by a police detective who suspects his motives. When the latter sees that Haines is on the level, he allows Haines to marry his girl.

VALENTINE, RUDY
THE WORLD'S GREATEST LOVER (1977, 20th Century Fox)—**Gene Wilder** arrives in Hollywood in the twenties to appear in a Rudolph Valentino contest. He gets some tips from the real Rudy to please his wife Carol Kane, a great fan of the famous screen lover, but Wilder is too scared to go through with a screen test.

VALENTINO, RUDOLPH
VALENTINO (1951, Columbia);—(1977, GB, UA)—Pardon the observation but if Rudolph Valentino had the sex appeal of **Anthony Dexter**, who portrayed him in 1951, few woman would have swooned when he looked at them with smoldering eyes. Russian ballet dancer **Rudolf Nureyev** not only lacks the looks to be "The Sheik," he's also stuck with a script that seems to have but little to do with Valentino's life.

VALENTINE-BRADSHAW, SHIRLEY
SHIRLEY VALENTINE (1989, GB, Paramount)—Recreating her stage success, Academy Award nominated **Pauline Collins** portrays a dreamer and rebel, who only wanted to taste the fullness of life, but somehow got sidetracked. But it's never too late to pursue one's dreams.

VALERIE
VALERIE (1957, UA)—Swedish sex symbol **Anita Ekberg** is the wife of Civil War hero Sterling Hayden, on trial for allegedly having killed his in-laws and wounding Ekberg.

VALERY, VIOLETTA
LA TRAVIATA (1982, Accent Film)—**Teresa Stratas** appears as Verdi's heroine in this highly praised filmed version of the opera with Placido Domingo.

VALIANT, PRINCE
PRINCE VALIANT (1954, 20th Century Fox)—**Robert Wagner** looks as silly as he must feel with his page boy haircut for his role as the comic strip Viking prince who wishes to become a knight in King Arthur's court. He has a benefactor, Sterling Hayden; a love, Janet Leigh; and a powerful enemy, James Mason.

VALLANCE, TIM
THE TRAITOR (1936, Puritan)—Texas Ranger **Tim McCoy** pretends to have to give up his badge in disgrace, so he can go undercover to break up a gang of crooks.

VALLO
THE CRIMSON PIRATE (1952, Warner Brothers)—With his tongue firmly planted in his cheek, **Burt Lancaster**, an ex-acrobat, portrays an ex-acrobat of the 18th century who becomes a charming pirate and leads the oppressed citizens of a Caribbean island against a tyrant.

VALMI, BARON
THE BOUDOIR DIPLOMAT (1930, Universal)—**Ian Keith**, the attache to the ambassador of a mythical kingdom, uses the art of seduction to win a powerful post.

VALERIE
THREE BAD SISTERS (1956, UA)—Is **Kathleen Hughes** the sister plotting to kill her two sisters in order to inherit her father's millions? Try and catch the answer on TV sometime, probably very late at night.

VAMPIRE UNCLE
BILLY THE KID VS. DRACULA (1966, Circle/EM)—Billy the Kid tries to go straight and settle down on a ranch with the girl of his choice. He doesn't know that her uncle, **John Carradine**, is a vampire.

VAN ALSTYNE, BERTIE
THE SAPHEAD (1921, Silent, Metro)—**Buster Keaton**, the dumb son of a Wall Street big shot, is, nevertheless, able at the end to save his dad from financial ruin.

VAN BUREN, MYRNA
THE HEADLINE WOMAN (1935, Mascot)—Publisher's daughter **Heather Angel** is kidnapped by a reporter, so he can get her information on the murder of a gambler for a scoop.

VAN DERLIN, ANOUK
THE SURROGATE (1984, Cinepix)—Sex-therapist **Carole Laure** is consulted by a couple who are dissatisfied with their marriage. This is closely followed by sexually related murders. There seems to be more than a casual connection.

VAN DER MAL, GABRIELLE *See* **SISTER LUKE**

VAN DER ZEE, HENDRICK
PANDORA AND THE FLYING DUTCHMAN (1951, GB, MGM)—Rich, selfish, American girl Ava Gardner gives her life to free Dutch sea captain **James Mason** from a forced eternal life on his ghost ship.

VAN DORN, MRS.
ENEMY AGENT MEETS ELLERY QUEEN (1942, Columbia)—The title says it all. **Gale Sondergaard** is wasted as a spy who matches wits with the famous detective.

VAN DYKE, CAROL
SHE COULDN'T TAKE IT (1935, Columbia)—In this combination crime yarn and screwball comedy, **Joan Bennett** is the daughter of a man imprisoned for income tax evasion. Her father is so impressed with former bootlegger George Raft that he names him executor of his estate, and then promptly dies. Bennett and her mother are not pleased that they are now dependent upon an ex-crook.

VAN DYKE, COLONEL
NIGHT PEOPLE (1954, 20th Century Fox)—When an American soldier is kidnapped by the Russians in Berlin, it's up to intelligence officer **Gregory Peck** to get him back. The offer from the Russians is the boy for an elderly German couple, who had been anti-Nazis.

VAN GLOCK, DR.
THE CREEPER (1948, 20th Century Fox)—Two scientists discover a serum that changes humans into cats. The beneficiary of this discovery is **Eduardo Ciannelli**, who, when given the serum, becomes a murderer. We always wondered about the anti-social behavior of cats.

VAN GOGH, VINCENT AND THEO
VINCENT AND THEO (1990, GB/Fr., Hemdale)—In this splendid film, **Tim Roth** gives a deeply personal performance as the tormented Dutch painter, and **Paul Rhys** is superb as the supportive brother. Rhys is unable to win acceptance for his brother's work in the art world. It's sad commentary that Vincent van Gogh, whose paintings now sell for record-breaking millions, was forced to live in rags and squalor before finally succumbing to his growing madness.

VAN LAER, ANN
SEVEN WOMEN FROM HELL (1961, 20th Century Fox)—**Sylvia Daneel** is one of the women who escape from a hellish Japanese prison camp in New Guinea during WWII. She doesn't quite make it to safety.

VAN RYCKE, MARK
TWO LOVERS (1928, Silent, UA)—In the last teaming of **Ronald Colman** with Vilma Banky, he is a 1572 Flemish patriot who defends helpless Flemings from the brutal treatment of their conquerors, the Spaniards.

VAN RIJN, REMBRANDT See REMBRANDT

VAN SAYNT, BUBBLES
BUBBLES (1920, Silent, Pioneer)—The niece of an eccentric professor, **Mary Anderson** regrets her sex, wears male clothes, and acts a tomboy—until the right young man comes along.

VAN SUYDEN, AGNES
A MAN AND THE WOMAN (1917, Silent, Art Dramas)—When French country girl **Edith Hallor** learns that her lover is married, she is already pregnant. She is forced to marry a poor and struggling lawyer to avoid a scandal. The lawyer comes to love the child and his wife of convenience, and sets out to win her love.

VAN TASSEL, ST. CLAIR
THE UNTAMED LADY (1926, Silent, Paramount)—Hot-tempered society girl **Gloria Swanson** is taught a lesson or two by yachtsman Lawrence Gray during a storm. Sounds a bit like Lina Wertmuller's SWEPT AWAY.

VANCE
THE GREAT MAN VOTES (1939, RKO)—In his last decent performance, **John Barrymore** proves that one man's vote does make a difference.

VANCE, PHILO
CALLING PHILO VANCE (1940, Warner Brothers)—**James Stephenson** PHILO VANCE RETURNS (1947, Producers Releasing Corp.)—**William Wright**; PHILO VANCE'S GAMBLE (1947, Producers Releasing Corp.); PHILO VANCES' SECRET MISSION (1947, Producers Releasing Corp.)—**Alan Curtis**. The films featuring S.S. Van Dyke's smooth sleuth were popular in the 1930s under titles such as THE CANARY MURDER CASE, THE BENSON MURDER CASE, THE KENNEL MURDER CASE, starring **William Powell**, THE DRAGON MURDER CASE with **Warren William**, THE CASINO MURDER CASE with **Paul Lukas**, THE GARDEN MURDER CASE with **Edmund Lowe**, NIGHT OF MYSTERY with **Grant Richards**, and THE SCARAB MURDER CASE with **Wilfrid Hyde White**. By the forties, the films were running out of steam.

VANDAN, ELIZA
ELIZA COMES TO STAY (1936, GB, Twickenham)—Dowdy **Betty Balfour** falls in love with her aging guardian.

VANDELEUR, MISS (PRINCESS BRENDA)
TROUBLE FOR TRUE (1936, MGM)—Based on a Robert Louis Stevenson story, **Rosalind Russell** and Robert Montgomery join a suicide club.

VANDERHORN, GRETA
JUNGLE GODDESS (1948, Lippert)—Two explorers are sent into a jungle to locate a missing heiress, **Wanda McKay**. They do. She's now a leopard-skin-dressed chief-executioner for a local tribe.

VANDERSMA, POLLY
I'VE HEARD THE MERMAID SINGING (1987, Canada, Miramax) - Amateur photographer **Sheila McCarthy** is hired to be an assistant to lesbian curator Gabrielle St. Peres at an art gallery. The title is taken from T.S. Eliot's "The Love Song of J. Alfred Prufrock."

VANE, PEGGY
WORST WOMAN IN PARIS (1933, Lasky/Fox)—**Benita Hume** wins the title when she is linked with wealthy shipping magnate Adolphe Menjou. She later is acclaimed a heroine during a train wreck back in Kansas.

VANE, REX
CHATTERBOX (1943, Republic)—When broadcaster-turned-film-actor **Joe E. Brown** falls off a horse, and has to be rescued by Judy Canova, his career is in jeopardy. He saves it with a dangerous stunt.

VANE, SHEILA
SHE WAS A LADY (1934, Fox)—**Helen Twelvetrees'** father dies before she can establish that her family has an aristocratic past predating its arrival in the U.S. The wealthy father of the lad Twelvetrees fancies doesn't believe Helen is good enough for his son, but ultimately her rank as a lady is proven and a marriage is in the offing.

VANESSA
DRACULA'S WIDOW (1988, DEG)—**Sylvia Kristel** has just learned that her hubby was killed by Von Helsing, many years before. Is she steamed!

VANESSA
VANESSA, HER LOVE STORY (1935, MGM)—When **Helen Hayes'** husband, Otto Kruger, goes mad, she has an affair with gypsy Robert Montgomery.

VANESSI, LILLI (KATHERINE)
KISS ME KATE (1959, MGM)—**Kathryn Grayson** is a delight in the dual role of a musical comedy star appearing with her ex-husband, Howard Keel, in a musical version of Shakespeare's *The Taming of Shrew*, and in the play as Kate, the shrew.

VANUCCI, ALDO
AFTER THE FOX (1966, UA)—Italian mobster **Peter Sellers** and his gang steal gold bullion bars in Cairo. In order to unload them at an Italian coastal village, they pretend to be movie-makers with Sellers an eccentric director. The best thing about the movie is Victor Mature, good-naturedly kidding his own screen persona.

VARNEY, DOC PETER
THE PHANTOM PRESIDENT (1932, Paramount)—If you wish to enjoy **George M. Cohan**, see YANKEE DOODLE DANDY where he is impersonated by James Cagney. This talking picture debut of the star-songwriter-playwright-producer as a presidential candidate and his look-alike was hated by critics, audiences and the star himself.

VARRICK, CHARLEY
CHARLEY VARRICK (1973, Universal)—Small-time bank robber **Walter Matthau** and his partner knock over a small New Mexico bank and get away with $750,000 which turns out to be Mafia money and the boys in wing-tipped shoes want it back.

VASTO/LOLA
THE DANCER'S PERIL (1917, Silent, World)—**Alice Brady** is the daughter of the premier dancer of the Russian Imperial Ballet and the Grand Duke of Russia, whose family did not approve of the union and sent Brady's mother away. Brady, who plays both the mother and daughter, becomes a world renowned dancer, and when an impresario forces himself on her, the mother shoots and kills the would be rapist. The Grand Duke, who just happens to be in Paris at the time, takes the blame. The result is that the three are brought together again as a family.

VAUBERNIER, JEANETTE
DU BARRY, WOMAN OF PASSION (1930, UA)—Is silent screen star **Norma Talmadge** the inspiration for Jean Hagen's star with the horrible voice in SINGIN' IN THE RAIN? She certainly seems unsuited for speaking the lines of the French milliner who became Louis XV's mistress.

VAUGHN, DR. JOHN
THE FLYING DOCTOR (1936, Australia, GFD)—**James Raglan** makes house calls by helicopter to the Australian outback.

VEASEY, SIR JOHN
THE HANGING JUDGE (1918, Silent, GB, Hepworth)—**Hamilton Stewart**, the judge of the title, disowns his son Henry Edwards, who becomes a crusading reporter and marries the daughter of a man his father has unjustly convicted.

VECCHI, LORNA
BAD BLONDE (1953, GB, Lippert)—**Barbara Payton**, the wife of boxer Tony Wright's manager, has an affair with the pugilist. When she tells him she is pregnant, they drown her husband, but the boxer, unable to bear the pressure of his guilt, confesses. Payton promptly poisons him.

VECCHIO, RICHIE
LOVERS AND OTHER STRANGERS (1970, ABC/Cinerama)—**Joseph Hindy** and **Bonnie Bedelia** are getting married in this lovely comical and moving film, but everyone else in the wedding party is having difficulty staying together.

VEGA, DON DIEGO *See* ZORRO

VELEZ, LUPE
LUPE (1967, Film Maker Corp.)—Transvestite **Mario Montez** appears as fiery Mexican actress Lupe Velez in this trashy biopic.

VENARES, ANKH MUMMY
TIME WALKER (1982, New World)—**Jack Olson** plays a mummy brought back to life in this lame brain film, which ends abruptly with a "To Be Continued" message on the screen. Until this point, the producers haven't continued—which is the only blessing about the movie.

VENDEG, HORACE
RUTHLESS (1948, Eagle Lion)—Skunk **Zachary Scott** uses everyone as rungs on his ladder to success.

VENKMAN, DR. PETER
GHOSTBUSTERS (1984, Columbia); GHOSBUSTERS II (1989, Columbia)—When sardonic, college professor **Bill Murray** and two of his academic dilettante friends lose their university jobs, they go into the business of capturing ghosts. Their biggest job is in the old apartment building where Murray's new love Sigourney Weaver lives. By the time of the 1989 movie, audiences discover that Murray didn't get Weaver, but she did get a baby, who is in danger of becoming the new home of an ancient evil Carpathian despot, named Vigo.

VENUS
ONE TOUCH OF VENUS (1948, Universal)—Window dresser Robert Walker, in love with a statue of the goddess Venus, is astonished when the statue comes to life in the person of **Ava Gardner**.

VENUS
VAMPING VENUS (1928, Silent, First National)—Ice-cream blonde **Thelma Todd** is the goddess whom Irish-American politician Charles Murray encounters when, after a bump on the head, he awakens to find himself in ancient Greece.

VERA
ON YOUR TOES (1939, Warner Brothers)—Ballerina **Vera Zorina** should have danced all night. When the musical numbers end, she is expected to act as a ballerina off-stage would and she's clearly not equipped for the role. She has a romance with Eddie Albert, an American composer, whom a Russian ballet company mistakes for a traitor.

VERA
THEY WERE SISTERS (1945, GB, Universal)—In this story of three sisters and the problems they endure, **Anne Crawford** marries James Mason, who turns out to be a sadistic beast.

VERDOUX, HENRI
MONSIEUR VERDOUX (1947, UA)—**Charles Chaplin** chooses a strange vehicle to return to the screen after an absence of six years. He is the dapper and infamous Bluebeard who marries women for

their money and then kills them. The laughs aren't in abundance here, nor can one depend on pathos.

VERIN, PAUL
THE MAN WHO RECLAIMED HIS HEAD (1935, Universal)—Poor but brilliant writer **Claude Rains** sells his ideas to a publisher who prints them as his own, driving Rains to madness and the desire for revenge. Rains has a similar role in THE PHANTOM OF THE OPERA (1943).

VERITY, LAURA
THEY MET IN THE DARK (1945, GB, Excelsior/English Films)—Canadian **Joyce Howard** teams up with disgraced James Mason, dismissed from the Royal Navy after being framed by the Nazis. They uncover the spy ring that set up Mason and killed a girl who knew too much about the episode.

VERNEY, TOM
TAKE A LETTER, DARLING (1942, Paramount)—Hollywood's busiest movie career woman Rosalind Russell is an advertising executive with a male secretary, **Fred MacMurray**. There are few surprises in this gender-role-reversal comedy and there weren't any more when it was first released.

VERONICA, PRINCESS
HER HIGHNESS AND THE BELLBOY (1945, MGM)—In her last film for MGM, visiting royalty **Hedy Lamarr** has a brief romance with New York bellboy Robert Walker, at the hotel where she's staying.

VERONIKA
THE STUDENT'S ROMANCE (1936, GB, British Int.)—In 1825, Heidelberg student and songwriter Patric Knowles is being pressed to pay off his debts. Innkeeper **Carol Goodner**, who secretly loves him, bails him out without his knowledge. Before she get's her reward, namely Knowles, she has to put up with him falling for Grete Natzler, the daughter of the Grand Duke.

VERTER
WOMAN TO WOMAN (1929, Tiffany)—Shell-shocked WWI veteran George Barraud marries wealthy **Juliette Compton**, when he forgets his promise to pregnant ballerina Betty Compson. Years later Barraud and Compson meet again. As Compton can't have children, Compson unselfishly gives up her child to her lover's wife so he can have the luxuries she can't give him.

VIC
A BOY AND HIS DOG (1975, LQJ Films)—Scavenger **Don Johnson** and his telephatic dog roam earth in 2024 after a nuclear holocaust.

VIC
HARD GUY (1941, Producers Releasing Corp.)—Nightclub owner **Jack La Rue** marries off his showgirls to young playboys and then collects payoffs from their fathers to arrange annulments.

VIC
NEIGHBORS (1981, Columbia)—**Dan Aykroyd** and his wife are wackos who almost drive their neighbor John Belushi crazy.

THE VICAR OF BRAY
THE VICAR OF BRAY (1937, GB, Associate British)—Irish Vicar **Stanley Holloway** is called to the court of England's Charles I as a tutor for the king's careless son. He's so successful, that the future king offers to grant Holloway any request when the former ascends to the throne. Holloway uses the promise to save an unjustly imprisoned man.

VICIOUS, SID
SID & NANCY (1986, GB, Goldwyn)—**Garry Oldman** portrays British punk rocker Sid Vicious of The Sex Pistols, who murders groupie Chloe Webb, with whom he is involved. Both Oldman and Webb are excellent in unsympathetic character roles.

VICKERS, ANN
ANN VICKERS (1933, RKO)—A love affair with cad Bruce Cabot leaves **Irene Dunne** an unwed mother, but she finds love with judge Walter Huston.

VICKERS, LINDA
SMART GIRLS DON'T TALK (1948, Warner Brothers)—Society woman **Virginia Mayo** falsely reports the theft of her jewels when a nightclub she's attending is robbed.

VICKERY, KITTY
HER NIGHT OUT (1932, GB, First National/Warner Brothers) -In this mild comedy, **Dorothy Bartlam**, the jealous wife of a golfer, has a flirtation with a bank robber.

VICKI
THREE BAD SISTERS (1956, UA)—**Marla English** and her two sisters fight over their father's estate, with one planning to take the other two out of the picture permanently.

VICTOR/VICTORIA
VICTOR/VICTORIA (1982, MGM/UA)—Starving singer **Julie Andrews** meets gay Robert Preston in Paris in the 1930s. He sets her up as a female impersonator in a cabaret, where she's a smash. She falls for visiting Chicago gangster James Garner, who discovers that the he who's pretending to be a she is really a she, but to everyone else it seems his romance with Andrews means he's come out of the closet.

VICTOR, CPL.
UNDER TWO FLAGS (1936, 20th Century Fox)—Mysterious Englishman **Ronald Colman** joins the French Foreign Legion. Camp follower Claudette Colbert falls in love with Colman, but he falls in love with a society visitor to the camp, Rosalind Russell.

VICTOR, JOE
A BULLET FOR JOEY (1955, UA)—Racketeer **George Raft** is in Montreal to kidnap a nuclear scientist for a spy ring. Standing in the way of his assignment is plainclothes inspector Edward G. Robinson.

VICTOR, "JOHNNY"
BEAUTIFUL STRANGER (TWIST OF FATE)—(1954, GB, British Lion)—**Ginger Rogers** contemplates suicide when she discovers that her married lover is mixed up in the rackets, and has no intention of divorcing his wife. Instead, she becomes involved with Jacques Bergerac, and both are implicated in the murder of her former lover.

VICTORIA, QUEEN
VICTORIA THE GREAT (1937, GB, RKO)—**Anna Neagle** portrays the British monarch from the age of 18, when she ascended the throne, through her 64-year reign.

VIDA
I WANT MY MAN (1925, Silent, First National)—American soldier Milton Sills, blinded in WWI, marries his nurse **Doris Kenyon**. Surgeons restore Sills' sight, but he finds Kenyon has left him and

obtained a divorce. Later, the two meet in the U.S., and, after some complications, their love blooms again.

VIK, JOHNNY
JOHNNY VIK (1973, Nauman)—Indian half-breed **Warren Hammack** is arrested, and sent to 30 days in jail for urinating in public. He escapes and heads for the hills, meets a girl, has some brief happiness, is tracked down by a posse, and shot.

VILLA, PANCHO
VIVA VILLA! (1934, MGM); VILLA! (1958, 20th Century Fox) VILLA RIDES (1968, Paramount)—**Wallace Beery** is not totally likeable in this biopic of the Mexican bandit and revolutionary who treated his enemies and even some of his followers quite harshly. In the end he's assassinated and dies in the arms of reporter Stuart Erwin who made him a folk hero. In 1958, at least **Rodolfo Hoyas** is Mexican. In the 1968 film **Yul Brynner** dons some hair to recreate the campaign exploits of Villa.

VILLON, FRANCOIS
BELOVED ROGUE (1927, Silent, UA)—**John Barrymore**; IF I WERE KING (1938, Paramount)—**Ronald Colman**; THE VAGABOND KING (1930, Paramount)—**Dennis King**; (1956, Paramount)—**Oreste "Kirkop"**—The life of poet and ardent patriot Villon made for some enjoyable film viewing with John Barrymore and Ronald Colman in rare old form as the likeable rascal who becomes a favorite of King Louis XI and helps defeat the Duke of Burgundy. The 1930 film, starring Dennis King, was Paramount's first all-color, all-talkie film. The Rudolf Friml songs were better performed by Oreste in 1956 with considerable help from Kathryn Grayson.

VIN
THE MAGNIFICENT SEVEN (1960, UA)—Laconic gunman **Steve McQueen** joins with six others of his profession to defend a village of Mexican farmers against a band of bandits. He is one of the three survivors.

VINCENT, ROBERT JEROME
THE NO-GUN MAN (1924, Silent, FBO)—**Lefty Flynn**, a stranger in town, is in reality the president of a bank robbed by a gang that he infiltrates. Flynn rescues a girl, who will become his wife, from a handcar, which is heading down the line toward an on-coming train. Oh yes, he rounds up the robbers.

VINCENT, RUTH
THE SECRET BRIDE (1935, Warner Brothers)—**Barbara Stanwyck's** marriage to District Attorney Warren William has to be kept a secret while he's trying to clear Barbara's father of charges of political corruption.

VINCENTE, TONI
STRANGE BEDFELLOWS (1965, Universal)—Oil executive Rock Hudson is in deep trouble when he decides to divorce his volatile Italian wife **Gina Lollobrigida.**

VINCENZINI, FRANCESCO
THE TIGER AND THE PUSSYCAT (1967, Embassy)—Middle-aged Italian businessman **Vittorio Gassman** innocently becomes involved with promiscuous American Ann-Margret.

VINE, CHARLES
THE SECOND BEST SECRET AGENT IN THE WORLD (1965, GB, Embassy)—Secret agent **Tom Adams** thwarts spies out to steal an anti-gravity machine. The title refers to Adams status vis-a-vis James Bond, we suppose.

VINNIE
MY BLUE HEAVEN (1990, Warner Brothers)—Mobster **Steve Martin** has been exiled to the suburbs through the Federal Witness Protection Program. For him, it's a foreign country. FBI agent Rick Moranis is assigned to keep and eye on the restless gangster. Funny, it's not funny.

VINSON, CONNIE
TARNISHED ANGEL (1938, RKO)—Phony evangelist **Sally Eilers** uses fear of damnation to fleece her flock of their money and jewels. Her kind apparently are still around, flourishing on television.

VIOLET
PRETTY BABY (1978, Paramount)—Twelve-year-old child prostitute **Brooke Shields** lives in a 1917 New Orleans bordello with her prostitute mother Susan Sarandon. Shields is a particular favorite of photographer Keith Carradine, who finally takes her away.

VIRGINIAN, THE
THE VIRGINIAN (1914, Silent, Lasky); (1923, Silent, Premier); (1929, Paramount); (1946, Paramount)—**Dustin Farnum, Kenneth Harlan, Gary Cooper and Joel McCrea** each portrayed Cwen Wister's legendary western hero, known only as The Virginian. By the Code of the West, the Virginian is forced to hang his best friend when the latter becomes involved with rustling, but our hero knows the real villain is Trampas, whom he kills in a showdown. In the 1929 version, Gary Cooper speaks the often misquoted line to Walter Huston: "If you want to call me that, smile." In 1946, McCrea delivered it the way Wister wrote it, and most people remember: "When you call me that, smile."

VISITOR FROM VENUS
IT CONQUERED THE WORLD (1956, American International) - Venusian **Paul Blaisdell** is accompanied to earth by alien bats whose bites turn their victims into slaves.

VITELLI, NICCOLO "MAC"
MAC (1992, Tennenbaum/Goodman)—**John Turturro** is the oldest of three brothers who live in Queens. When his father dies, Turturro leaves his construction job to start his own business of building homes.

VIVIAN
THE DOUGHGIRLS (1944, Warner Brothers)—**Jane Wyman** is one of a group of husband-seeking girls living in a Washington hotel during World War II. The pickings are slim as are the jokes in the film.

VIVIAN
SWEETHEART OF SIGMA CHI (1933, Monogram)—Flirtatious co-ed **Mary Carlisle** is pursued by all the fraternity boys, but she plays hard-to-get until rowing star Buster Crabbe shows her his muscles.

VIVIENNE
LADY IN DISTRESS (1942, GB, GFD)—**Sally Gray** is killed by her illusionist husband, Paul Lukas, when she becomes involved with crane-driver Michael Redgrave.

VOICE, THE
THE THIRD VOICE (1960, 20th Century Fox)—**Edmond O'Brien** is hired by Laraine Day to kill her current lover, a wealthy businessman. The plan is for O'Brien to take the dead man's place and the two will share his money. O'Brien gets greedy and Day almost gets dead.

VOICE OF TERROR

SHERLOCK HOLMES AND THE VOICE OF TERROR (1942, Universal)—**Edgar Barrier** announces intended sabotage to the British war effort over the radio just before terrorists carry it out. Sherlock Holmes must put an end to the gang of saboteurs and silence the voice of terror.

VOINITSKY, IVAN PETROVICH

UNCLE VANYA (1958, Continental); (1977, GB, British Home Entertainment)—**George Voskovic** and **Michael Redgrave** star in the title role of Anton Chekhov's play about a frustrated old man dissatisfied with the life he's led.

VOLTAIRE, FRANCOIS MARIE ARONET

VOLTAIRE (1933, Warner Brothers)—**George Arliss** is a perfect choice to play the 18th century philosopher and wit.

VOMIT, VALERIE

THE GARBAGE PAIL KIDS (1987, Atlantic Entertainment)—The specialty of **Debbie Lee Carrington** in this disgusting movie based on sick bubble gum cards is indicated by her name.

VON BRAUN, WERNHER

I AIM AT THE STARS (1960, Columbia)—**Curt Jurgens** gives a polished performance as the German rocket scientist.

VON CARTIER, DELORIS

SISTER ACT (1992, Touchstone)—Having witnessed a murder by her mobster boyfriend, Harvey Keitel, Reno lounge singer **Whoopi Goldberg** is hidden by the law in a San Francisco convent, where the irreverent lapsed Catholic brings the nuns' dreadful choir into the rock generation.

VON CLAUDWIG, "Countess" (Martha Hicks)

MADAME RACKETEER (1932, Paramount)—Con woman **Alison Skipworth** has to sort out the problems of her family.

VON DUREN, ANYA

THEY MET IN BOMBAY (1941, MGM)—Pretending to be a friend of the Royal family, in reality **Rosalind Russell** is a jewel thief, looking for her chance to steal a diamond necklace. Clark Gable is in Bombay with the same goal in mind.

VON ELTZ, FELICITAS

FLESH AND THE DEVIL (1926, Silent, MGM)—**Greta Garbo** is the entrancing beauty who comes between the friendship of John Gilbert and Lars Hanson. As boys they swore eternal devotion to each other. Their desire for Garbo is so intense that they resort to a duel, but neither is able to fire the fatal shot. Garbo hurrying to the site of the duel falls through an ice floe and is lost, leaving the two old friends to console each other.

VON EYRICK, LT.

MADEMOISELLE FIFI (1944, RKO)—The title of this film is the nickname of **Kurt Krueger**, a brutal, savage Prussian, who seems to enjoy tormenting the inhabitants of a French village during the Franco-Prussian War. Retribution is taken by a laundress, Simone Simon.

VON HARDEN, LEO

FLESH AND THE DEVIL (1926, Silent, MGM)—**John Gilbert's** obsession with married Greta Garbo leads him to kill her husband in a duel. Forced to leave the country, he asks his life-long friend Lars Hansen to look in on the widow Garbo. Hansen does and even marries her. Three years later, when Gilbert returns, the state of affairs forces them to the dueling field, but it's Garbo who doesn't survive.

VON HARTMANN, HEDI

HOT MONEY GIRL (1962, GB, United Producers)—The daughter of a Nazi general, **Dawn Addams**, now a prostitute, joins with American O.S.S. man Eddie Constantine to find some jewels hidden by her father shortly after WWII.

VON HOLSTEIN, COL. MANFRED

THOSE MAGNIFICENT MEN IN THEIR FLYING MACHINES (1965, GB, 20th Century Fox)—In this campy film about a 1910 London to Paris air race, **Gert Forbe** is a comical but stereotyped German officer. He has been ordered by the Kaiser to win the race, even though he knows nothing about planes.

VON HOUSEN, BARON

MY SON, THE VAMPIRE (1963, GB, Renown)—Criminal **Bela Lugosi** believes he's a vampire. Few cared.

VON HULDA, BARONESS

MADAME SPY (1918, Silent, Butterfly)—German spy **Claire Du Brey** receives secrets from Jack Mulhall's father's butler. Mulhall captures Du Brey, impersonates her and smashes the spy ring.

VON KEMPER, EARL

MELODY MAN (1930, Columbia)—Viennese composer **John St. Polis** kills his unfaithful wife and her lover. He flees to the U.S. with his daughter. Eighteen years later, his musician daughter rearranges one of St. Polis' old compositions. When it becomes a hit, the Austrian authorities come after him.

VON RAGENSTEIN, BARON LEOPOLD (SIR EDWARD DOMINEY)

THE GREAT IMPERSONATION (1935, Universal); (1942, Universal)—**Edmond Lowe** and **Ralph Bellamy** portray a German spy posing as an English nobleman. The imposter is in the employ of a greedy munitions dealer.

VON RICHTHOFEN, BARON MANFRED

VON RICHTHOFEN AND BROWN (1970, UA)—**John Philip Law** appears as the German WWI ace known as the Red Baron.

VON ROTENBERG, PRINCE KURT

THEY DARE NOT LOVE (1941, Columbia)—**George Brent**, in love with Austrian Martha Scott, nobly offers his life in exchange for the release of Nazi prisoners, one of whom is Scott's fiance.

VON SEIDLITZ-GABLER, GENERAL

THE NIGHT OF THE GENERALS (1967, GB, Columbia)—**Charles Gray** is one of the German generals stationed in Paris at the time of the assassination plot on Hitler. Gray is a suspect in the case of brutal murders of prostitutes during the war.

VON SEPPER, BARON

BLUEBEARD (1972, Cinerama)—American dancer Raquel Welch, married to Australian aristocrat **Richard Burton**, discovers the frozen bodies of seven women in his refrigerated vault and correctly guesses he has a place there for her.

VON STOLBERG

THE ENEMY BELOW (1957, 20th Century Fox)—In this excellent WWII film, German U-boat commander **Curt Jurgens** has a battle of wits with Robert Mitchum, the captain of a U.S. destroyer. The tense struggle ends in a draw with both vessels being sunk, but the two officers have come to respect each other's naval skills.

VON STURM, MRS.
THE PSYCHOPATH (1966, GB, Paramount)—**Margaret Johnston** lives with her dolls and when several murders are committed in the area, a doll is always left behind.

VON ULLRICH, BARON
BEAUTY AND THE BOSS (1932, Warner Brothers)—Viennese businessman **Warren William** finds that pretty secretaries are distracting, so he hires plain Marian Marsh for the job. She blossoms into a beauty and William can think of only one obvious solution—marry her.

VON WERRA, FRANZ
THE ONE THAT GOT AWAY (1958, GB, Rank)—German pilot **Hardy Kruger**, captured by the British early in WWII, escapes twice and is recaptured. Sent to a prison camp, he escapes to the U.S. (at that time not in the war) and makes his way back to Germany, only to be killed on the Russian front.

VRONSKY, COUNTESS TANYA
I WAS AN ADVENTURESS (1940, 20th Century Fox)—Ballerina **Vera Zorina** appears as a phony countess, teamed with a pair of slick crooks using her as a decoy. She falls in love with their mark.

VROODER, JULIUS
THE CRAZY WORLD OF JULIUS VROODER (1974, 20th Century Fox)—His experiences in Vietnam has made **Timothy Bottoms** both deranged and incorrigible. He's a patient in a military hospital, and would like to escape and marry his nurse.

W

WACO
WACO (1966, Paramount)—Aging stars like **Howard Keel** often ended their careers in westerns. In this one, he's a gunfighter hired to clean up a town in which his ex-love Jane Russell is married to a preacher.

WADDINGTON, JEAN
CHILDREN OF DIVORCE (1927, Silent, Paramount)—Because she came from a broken home, **Esther Ralston** will not accept a marriage proposal from Gary Cooper until he proves himself. He does—sort of, with Clara Bow, but when the latter takes poison, Esther and Gary marry.

WADE
ONE MAN JURY (1978, Cal-Am Artists)—In a "Dirty Harry" rip off, **Jack Palance** is a tough cop who acts as judge, jury and executioner where felons are concerned.

WADE, BEN
THE MYSTERIOUS RIDER (1938, Paramount)—Also known as Pecos Bill, **Douglass Dumbrille**, wrongly accused of murder, comes to the aid of some homesteaders.

WADE, BILLY
NICE PEOPLE (1922, Silent, Paramount)—**Wallace Reid** is able to rescue Bebe Daniels from the unwanted advances of her date when the three take refuge from a storm in an abandoned farmhouse, but he can't prevent a scandal that sees her disowned by her father.

WADE, BOB
THE ARIZONA RANGER (1948, RKO)—**Tim Holt** returns home after service with Teddy Roosevelt's Rough Riders. Haunted by war, he becomes alienated from his father when he refuses to join the family ranching business, until he can find himself.

WADE, JACOB
THE LONELY MAN (1957, Paramount)—Gunfighter **Jack Palance** who deserted his family seventeen years earlier, tries to establish a relationship with his son, Anthony Perkins, but it's not easy.

WADE, JAKE
THE LAW AND JAKE WADE (1958, MGM)—Before settling down to the peaceful life of a lawman, **Robert Taylor** had been a member of Richard Widmark's gang of bank robbers, and run off with the loot. Taylor saves Widmark from a lynching, but the latter isn't thankful or forgiving.

WADE, JESS
CHARRO! (1969, National General)—Reformed outlaw **Elvis Presley** is framed for the theft of Mexico's gold and silver Victory gun, reportedly the weapon that fired the last shot in the battle for freedom against Emperor Maximilian.

WADE, MARA
MARA OF THE WILDERNESS (1966, Allied Artists)—Orphaned in Alaska when her parents are killed by a bear, **Linda Saunders** is raised in the wilderness by wolves. When grown, she's threatened by a man who wishes to put her in a circus, but is saved by Adam West who wishes to ease her back into civilization.

WAGNER, KARL
THE HUN WITHIN (1918, Silent, Paramount)—German immigrant George Fawcett comes to the U.S. and makes his fortune. Sometime before WWI, he sends his son **Charles Gerard** back to the fatherland as a student. When Gerard returns, to his father's horror, he's intent on sabotaging the American war effort.

WAGNER, RICHARD
WAGNER (1983, GB, London Trust)—Originally made as a British TV mini-series, this dull biography stars **Richard Burton** as the famed composer. In his last film appearance, Burton seems hardly to be trying.

WAINWRIGHT, HARRY
THE MAN OUTSIDE (1933, GB, RKO)—Blundering private detective **Henry Kendall** unmasks a murderer while seeking stolen jewels.

WAINWRIGHT, TIM
THE PERFECT MATCH (1987, Artcraft)—Nearing 30, **Marc McClure**, whose experiences with women have been disappointing and bizarre, advertises for a nice girl and finds one in Jennifer Edwards. It's a likable romantic-comedy.

WAKE, DAN
I WAS A TEENAGE ZOMBIE (!987, Horizon)—In this low-budget comedy-horror, **Michael Rubin** is a good-guy zombie who takes on a bad-guy zombie. Both "live" on toxic waste.

WAKEFIELD, WILLIAM
CARRY ON TEACHER (1962, GB, Anglo-Amalgamated)—**Ted Ray**, a British headmaster, wants a new post, but his students sabotage an inspection by the Ministry of Education so he'll be forced to stay.

WALDEN, LUCKY
BAD GUY (1937, MGM)—Power plant worker **Bruce Cabot** is sent to the pen for killing a gambler. He is fried while trying to escape by applying high-voltage electricity to the prison bars.

WALDEN, RED
A RACING ROMEO (1927, Silent, R-C Pictures)—Football's "Galloping Ghost," **Harold "Red" Grange** proves he's no actor. He's a garage owner who wins a big auto race, and his hometown girlfriend after a brief fling with a movie star.

WALDO, WILLIAM
RACKETEERS IN EXILE (1937, Columbia)—Big-city mobster **George Bancroft** and his gang hide out in his old hometown, where he becomes a phony evangelist. He pockets the money from the scam, but is eventually "born again."

WALES, JOSEY
THE OUTLAW JOSEY WALES (1983, Warner Brothers); THE RETURN OF JOSEY WALES (1987, Multi-Tacar)—**Clint Eastwood** creates the role of the ex-Confederate soldier who trails the renegade Union soldiers who have killed his wife and son. **Michael Parks** reprises the role, picking up the story of the farmer who became a murdering machine, a few years later in Mexico in another story of vengeance and violence.

WALKER, BOB
COWBOY MILLIONAIRE (1935, Fox)—Dude ranch owner **George O'Brien** falls in love with visiting Englishwoman Evalyn Bostock, but nearly loses her due to a misunderstanding.

WALKER, BUTCH
MY AMERICAN COUSIN (1986, Canada, Spectrafilms)—Seventeen-year-old **John Widman** from California visits his 12-year-old Canadian cousin, feisty Margaret Langrick. It's a charming character study, which seems meaningful in comparison with all the mindless teen exploitation films of the period.

WALKER, DOT
THE LITTLE IRISH GIRL (1926, Silent, Warner Brothers)—**Dolores Costello** works with a gang of crooked cardsharps, but is redeemed through the love of a good man and a grandma who isn't taken in by con artists.

WALKER, J.D.
J.D.'S REVENGE (1976, American International)—In this black exploitation film, **David McKnight** is murdered in 1942 on Bourbon Street in New Orleans. In 1976, the deceased's spirit takes possession of a law student.

WALKER, JIMMY
BEAU JAMES (1957, Paramount)—**Bob Hope** gives a breezy performance as the flamboyant and corrupt Roaring Twenties mayor of New York City.

WALKER, JOHNNY
HOMEBOY (1989, 20th Century Fox)—**Mickey Rourke's** character is an endearing movie cliche, a naive pug, taken in by the glamour of the boxing world, only to be destroyed by its corruption.

WALKER, JOHNNY
JOHNNY BE GOOD (1988, Orion)—It's hard to see **Anthony Michael Hall** as an All-American high school football star, whom college coaches all over the country are standing in line to corrupt—we mean recruit. The movie might have worked if it was a serious look at the pressure put upon youngsters who are treated as if they were athletic gods before they have lost their zits, or if it had taken an amusing look at the same question. But those responsible for the movie decided to be cute. In deciding whether to see this movie or not, we recommend that all football fans should "pass." We do admit that young model Uma Thurman, who makes her debut in the film, is something special with her pouty lips and sleepy eyes.

WALKER, DR. RICHARD
FRANTIC (1988, Warner Brothers)—Surgeon **Harrison Ford** and his wife Betty Buckley are in Paris, where he is to address a convention. While Ford is taking a shower, Buckley receives a telephone call and leaves the hotel room. She is not just out, she has disappeared. Ford frantically makes a desperate search for her, experiencing mostly frustration and anxiety. It's worth a look to find out if he finds her and why she's gone.

WALKER, TOMMY
TOMMY (1975, GB, Columbia)—**Roger Daltrey**, lead singer of "The Who," stars in the group's rock opera as a deaf, dumb and blind boy who first becomes a "Pinball Wizard" and then a new Messiah.

WALKER, VIRGIL
SING, BOY, SING (1958, 20th Century Fox)—Rock 'n' Roll star **Tommy Sands** portrays a Rock 'n' Roll star whose life is not all acclaim and groupies.

WALKER, WADE "CRY BABY"
CRY BABY (1990, Universal)—In John Waters' hit-and-miss spoof of teenage exploitation films, **Johnny Depp** portrays the leader of a gang of leather-jacket outcasts who is in a constant struggle with the squares. One square, Amy Locane, would rather switch than fight. The rag-tag Romeo-and-Juliet story isn't much, but some of the supporting cast, including Ricki Lake, Traci Lords and Kim McGuire, are briefly allowed to shine.

WALKER, WILLIAM
WALKER (1987, Universal)—**Ed Harris** is an adventurer who invades various Central American nations, intent on bringing his own warped version of democracy to "heathens." Based on a historical character, director Alex Cox works too hard to make the parallel with current U.S. foreign policy in the region.

WALL, DOLLY
SINGED (1927, Silent, Fox)—Dancehall girl **Blanche Sweet** is in love with irresponsible Warren Baxter, but through her efforts, he becomes a financial success. Then he looks elsewhere for romance. After accidently shooting Sweet, who threatens to splash acid in Baxter's face, the two get back together. Ah, love!

WALLACE, BUDDY
WALLOPING WALLACE (1924, Silent, Artclass)—Foreman of the Lazy B Ranch, **Buddy Roosevelt** is framed for kidnapping the owner, Violet La Plante, but succeeds in rescuing her, saving the ranch's cattle, squaring things with the bad guy, and winning Violet.

WALLACE, CORKY
THE HOLY TERROR (1937, 20th Century Fox)—In this showcase for the many talents of **Jane Withers**, she finds time to thwart spies between numbers.

WALLACE, DICK

HIS PRIVATE SECRETARY (1933, Screencraft)—Would you believe **John Wayne** as a woman-chasing playboy, who has a falling-out with his millionaire father? The Duke later falls for a preacher's granddaughter.

WALLACE, DUKE

THREE BLONDES IN HIS LIFE (1961, Cinema Associates)—While trying to solve the murder of a colleague, private eye **Jock Mahoney** finds himself involved with three blondes: Greta Thyssen, Valerie Porter and Elaine Edwards.

WALLACE, EVELYNE

ADAM AND EVELYNE (1950, GB, Rank/Two Cities)—Homeless **Jean Simmons** is taken in by Stewart Granger, a gambler friend of her deceased father. She falls in love with her benefactor.

WALLACE, JESSE

THE OUTRIDERS (1950, MGM)—Confederate soldier **Barry Sulli-van** and his companions, Joel McCrea and James Whitmore, join up with a gang of raiders after a wagon train carrying bullion. Eventually, they desert the gang and prevent the robbery.

WALLACE, JOANNA AND MARK

TWO FOR THE ROAD (1967, GB, 20th Century Fox) In a film that was better received when first released than today, **Audrey Hepburn** and **Albert Finney's** love and marriage is traced by jumping back and forth from four journeys they take together in Europe. Can this marriage be saved? In the hopeful 1960s, of course!

WALLACE, JOHN

MAN OF COURAGE (1943, Producers Releasing Corp.)—Although more often the villain in his movies, here **Barton Maclane** is an honest district attorney who brings a murderous mobster to justice.

WALLACE, MARY

TO MARY WITH LOVE (1936, 20th Century Fox)—The rocky marriage of **Myrna Loy** and Warner Baxter is presented between scenes of newsreel coverage of what's happening from 1925 to 1935, while he rises in business and both take lovers. As expected, they learn they still love each other.

WALLACE, OSCAR

THE UNTOUCHABLES (1987, Paramount)—**Charles Martin Smith** is a federal accountant assigned to work with Elliott Ness (Kevin Costner) and others in bringing Al Capone (Robert De Niro) to justice. He comes up with the scheme of getting "Scarface" on income tax evasion, but he is murdered before be can see the plan succeed.

WALLENTIN, BARONESS GERDA & COUNT DIETRICH

THREE SINNERS (1928, Silent, Paramount)—Deciding that her husband **Paul Lukas** no longer loves her, **Pola Negri** takes a lover, which causes her to miss a train that later crashes with all aboard reported dead. She does not reveal that she has survived. Years later, she meets her husband again. He is attracted to her because she "reminds him of his late wife." She reveals her true identity and returns to him, but discovers her first impression was correct. He does not love her.

WALLETT, CORKY

CORKY OF GASOLINE ALLEY (1951, Columbia)—**Scotty Beckett** appears as the comic-strip character. In this film, he must deal with a sponging relative of his wife who has moved in with them and is causing considerable trouble.

WALLINGFORD, J. RUFUS

THE NEW ADVENTURES OF GET-RICH-QUICK WALLINGFORD (1931, MGM)—In this comedy which introduced Jimmy Durante to movie fans, **William Haines** is a con man who goes straight when he meets the right girl, Leila Hyams.

WALLRAFF, GUNTHER

THE MAN INSIDE (1990, New Line)—In this political thriller, powerful West German political and business leaders try to "neutralize" investigative reporter **Jurgen Prochnow**.

WALLY

MY DINNER WITH ANDRE (1981, New Yorker)—**Wallace Shawn** has dinner with Andre Gregory, with the latter carrying most of the conversation.

WALLY

TWO SMART MEN (1940, GB, Anglo International)—**Wally Patch** and his partner Leslie Fuller, unsuccessful actor's agents, pose as a butler and cook at a society party where they save a duchess' jewels from a scoundrel.

WALSH, MONTE

MONTE WALSH (1970, National General)—**Lee Marvin** and Jack Palance are two aging cowboys who find it harder and harder to adjust to the changes taking place in their lives. When Palance is killed by another old buddy, Marvin repays the favor.

WALSH, ROSEMARY

PRISON GIRL (1942, Producers Releasing Corp.)—After escaping from prison where she had been sent for a mercy killing, **Rose Hobart** is sheltered by a doctor, Sidney Blackmer, who helps her clear her name.

WALSH, ROY

THE SLASHER (1953, GB, Lippert)—**James Kenney's** chosen line of work is slugging little old ladies in London, and snatching their purses. Before long he finds himself in jail on a charge of attempted murder.

WALTER

THE ADVENTURES OF THE ACTION HUNTERS (1987, Bonner/ Troma)—**Ronald Hunter** joins Sean Murphy in a dangerous quest for $500,000. They survive explosions and shootouts as they are chased by gangsters also after the booty.

WALTER

LOVING COUPLES (1980, 20th Century Fox)—Physician **James Coburn** becomes bored with his wife and colleague Shirley Maclaine, and has an affair with Susan Sarandon. Shirley had beat him to the punch, bedding down with young stud Stephen Collins.

WALTON, MARION

THE MOTH AND THE FLAME (1915, Silent, Paramount)—**Adele Ray**, seduced and scorned by a scoundrel, gains her revenge by breaking up his wedding.

WANDA

SEDUCTION: THE CRUEL WOMAN (1989, First Run Features)— Here's a film for the S&M set. **Mechthild Grossman** runs a sex gallery in which her friends and lovers entertain audiences with scenes of sadism and masochism.

WANDA

TWENTY-ONE DAYS TOGETHER (1937, GB, Columbia)—**Vivien Leigh's** husband is accidentally killed by her lover Laurence Olivier. When a mentally-deranged man is accused of the crime, Leigh and Olivier attempt to enjoy the 21 days they will have together before Lord Larry has to confess in court.

WANDA

WANDA (1971, Bardene International)—Passive **Barbara Loden** takes up with a small-time crook, Michael Higgins.

WANDA JUNE

HAPPY BIRTHDAY, WANDA JUNE (1971, Columbia)—In this black comedy, **Pamelyn Ferdin**, the daughter of strange Rod Steiger and Susannah York, is happy that she was hit and killed by an ice cream truck on her birthday.

THE WANDERING JEW

THE WANDERING JEW (1935, GB, Gaumont)—Having demanded the release of Barabbas and the death of Christ, **Conrad Veidt** is condemned to wander the earth through the centuries until Christ comes to him and grants him death.

WANER, BICKFORD

KID BLUE (1973, 20th Century Fox)—Turn of the century outlaw **Dennis Hopper** tries to go straight, but he doesn't have much talent for anything but train robbing.

WARBONNET(JIM AHERN)

THE SAVAGE (1953, Paramount)—White man **Charlton Heston** has been raised by a tribe of noble red men. The film tries to show things from the Indian's point of view when encroaching white men threaten their way of life.

WARBURTON, BOB

THE MAN ON THE BOX (1925, Silent, Warner Brothers)—Infatuated with Alice Calhoun, wealthy bachelor **Sydney Chaplin** takes a job as her gardener and thwarts an enemy agent before winning the girl.

WARD, CHARLES DEXTER/JOSEPH CURWEEN

THE RESURRECTED (1992, Scotti Brothers)—Investigator John Terry discovers that **Chris Sarandon** has a fixation with his 18th-century ancestor, a sorcerer, who experimented with bringing back the dead. Sarandon is accused of various crimes, including grave robbery.

WARD, DULCY

DULCY (1940, MGM)—Silly **Ann Sothern** spends a hectic weekend at a mountain cabin plotting ways to help her boyfriend find a backer for the new airplane carburetor he has invented.

WARD, (LT.) DANNY

LIEUT. DANNY, U.S.A. (1916, Silent, Triangle)—Fresh from West Point, **William Desmond** is sent to the Mexican border, where he falls in love with a comely senorita and survives a firing squad.

WARD, DON

THE MAN WORTH WHILE (1921, Silent, Hillfield)—**Romaine Fielding**, a ranger in Northern Canada, sets out to kill the rotter who deserted the woman Romaine loved, leaving her pregnant.

WARD, ELLEN

CITY GIRL (1938, 20th Century Fox)—Dumb waitress **Phyllis Brooks** dumps her district attorney boyfriend to take up with a gangster who uses her to get information from her ex-boyfriend.

WARD, JOHNNY AND CAROL

KILLERS THREE (1968, American International)—Backwoodsman **Robert Walker Jr.** and a friend kill **Diane Varsi's** bootlegging husband, after which the three hit the road for California.

WARD, SAM

BULLET FOR A BADMAN (1964, Universal)—It's bad enough that western outlaw **Darren McGavin** is captured by a posse led by old friend Audie Murphy, but the latter is now married to McGavin's ex-wife.

WARD, VIVIAN

PRETTY WOMAN (1990, Buena Vista)—If one doesn't examine the premise or logic of the story of this film, it's easy to enjoy this fairy tale about a handsome, wealthy corporate raider (Richard Gere) and gorgeous hooker **Julia Roberts**, who looks innocent and hot at the same time. They are a most unlikely couple looking to live happily ever after.

WARE, SIR HUBERT

THE WARE CASE (1917, GB, Silent, FBO); THE WARE CASE (1939, GB, Ealing)—Acquitted knight **Matheson Lang** confesses to drowning his wife's rich brother. He pays for his crime by taking poison. In 1939, **Clive Brook** achieves the same "end" by jumping from a window.

WARE, LORD MICHAEL

HER IMAGINARY LOVER (1933, GB, First National/ Warners)—Beset by fortune hunters, heiress Laura La Plante invents a fiance who turns up in the person of **Percy Marmont.**

WARE, VIVIENNE

THE TRIAL OF VIVIENNE WARE (1932, Fox)—**Joan Bennett** portrays a woman on trial for murder in this mystery which takes place almost entirely in a courtroom.

WARE-ARMITAGE, SIR CUTHBERT

THOSE DARING YOUNG MEN IN THEIR JAUNTY JALOPIES (1969, GB/France/Italy, Paramount)—Like his relative in THOSE MAGNIFICENT MEN IN THEIR FLYING MACHINES **Terry-Thomas** is a villain who will do anything to win a Monte Carlo Car Rally.

WARE-ARMITAGE, SIR PERCIVAL

THOSE MAGNIFICENT MEN IN THEIR FLYING MACHINES (1965, GB, 20th Century Fox)—**Terry-Thomas** is the hissable British villain in this campy tale of a 1910 London to Paris air race.

WARING, DR. ALEX

THE SURGEON'S KNIFE (1957, GB, Grand National)—Physician **Donald Houston** becomes a success in polite society and kills a blackmailer.

WARING, DRUE

I'VE BEEN AROUND (1935, Universal)—Society woman **Rochelle Hudson** marries Chester Morris, but within a week confesses she doesn't love him. Later, she decides she does and tries to commit suicide.

WARNER, SUE

SIOUX CITY SUE (1946, Republic)—Movie talent scout **Lynne Roberts** discovers Gene Autry and whisks him off to Hollywood to star in a movie—an animated feature in which he is the voice of a donkey.

WARREN, AGATHA, GENERAL, MRS. & ARTHUR

THE WARRENS OF VIRGINIA (1915, Silent, Lasky)—**Blanche Sweet, James Neill, Mabel Van Buren** and **Page Peters** are the daughter, son, mother and father of an aristocratic southern family at the time of the American Civil War. The sweetheart of heroine Sweet joins the Union forces and returns to Virginia as a spy. Despite torn loyalties, Sweet hides her lover from Confederate soldiers.

WARREN, DON

TOP MAN (1943, Universal)—While his father is off at war, **Donald O'Connor** heads the family in this minor musical comedy.

WARREN, ERIC

SPOILERS OF THE FOREST (1957, Republic)—Lumbermen **Ray Collins** and his partner Rod Cameron wish to gain control of thousands of acres of timberland owned by Vera Ralston in Montana.

WARREN, EVELYN

THE LADY PAYS OFF (1951, Universal)—When **Linda Darnell**, a schoolteacher with a gambling problem runs up a big debt, she agrees to become the tutor of the daughter of the casino owner who holds her marker.

WARREN, FRANK

THE UNDERCOVER MAN (1949, Columbia)—**Glenn Ford** is a secret service agent, something like an Elliott Ness, trying to nail an Al Capone-like mobster on income tax evasion.

WARREN, JOAN

SING, BABY, SING (1936, 20th Century Fox)—Drunken movie star Adolphe Menjou develops a fixation for nightclub singer **Alice Faye**, declaring his undying love, something he regrets the next morning—but Faye isn't so easy to get rid of.

WARREN, JIMMY

THE BOY AND THE PIRATES (1960, UA)—A genie transports young **Charles Herbert** to the pirate ship of Blackbeard.

WARREN, KAY

GIRLS OF THE ROAD (1940, Columbia)—During the Depression, a governor's daughter, **Ann Dvorak**, hits the road with some female hoboes to get the lowdown on their plight.

WARREN, LEE

DEAR MURDERER (1947, GB, Gainsborough)—**Eric Portman's** perfect crime, of blaming one of his wife's lovers for the murder of another, backfires when she outsmarts him.

WARREN, ROSIE

ROSIE THE RIVETER (1944, Republic)—**Jane Frazee** and four other girls represent the "Rosies" of WWII who went into factories to build planes, tanks and ships while their men were at war. After the war, they were told their services were no longer needed.

WARREN, SALLY

THE BRIDE WORE BOOTS (1946, Paramount)—In this screwy comedy, horse-lover **Barbara Stanwyck** separates from her husband Bob Cummings due to some misunderstandings, but the two are reunited when he wins a steeplechase race.

WARRENDER, JACK

THE TWO OF US (1938, GB, Gaumont)—In this British musical, unemployed **Jack Hulbert** talks his way into the world of high finance and catches a gang of arsonists.

WARRINGTON, DAVID

AN OLD FASHIONED BOY (1920, Silent, Paramount)—When **Charles Ray** buys and furnishes a house without consulting his fiancee, she breaks off their engagement, but Ray wins her hand once again.

WARROW, MARK

I MET A MURDERER (1939, GB, Grand National)—Farmer **James Mason** is pushed too far by his shrewish wife when she deliberately kills his dog. He retaliates and shoots her. While on the run, he meets a female writer with whom he spends a few happy days, but when he is wounded by pursuing police, he wades into the sea, taking his life.

WARSAW, CHUCK (TIGER)

TIGER WARSAW (1988, Sony)—**Patrick Swayze** returns home to his family which he had to leave 15 years earlier. He had wounded his father, shooting the older man when Swayze was caught spying on his sister, who at the time was in her undies. There are no lessons to be learned from this dull story, dully produced.

WARSHAWSKI, V.I.

V.I. WARSHAWSKI (1991, Hollywood Pictures)—Daughter of a cop and a habitue of Chicago's North Side sports bars, **Kathleen Turner** gets involved in the dirty business of three warring brothers and becomes responsible for the daughter of one when he's killed.

WASHBURN, MARIAN

A WOMAN'S SECRET (1949, RKO)—In flashback we learn why **Maureen O'Hara** kills Gloria Grahame, whom O'Hara was grooming for stardom as a singer.

WASHINGTON, GEORGE

WASHINGTON AT VALLEY FORGE (1914, Silent, Universal) - Director John Ford's older brother, **Francis Ford**, a matinee idol of the silent screen, wrote, directed and starred in this film about the historical origins of the U.S.

WASSELL, DR. CROYDON M.

THE STORY OF DR. WASSELL (1944, Paramount)—**Gary Cooper**, a Navy physician from Arkansas, saves a group of wounded marines on the island of Java, when the Japanese invade, by leading them through jungles to safety in Australia.

WATERBERRY, BLIX

THE ATOMIC KID (1954, Republic)—Prospector **Mickey Rooney** survives a nuclear blast in Nevada, giving him special powers which he uses in a comical way in Las Vegas casinos.

WATERBURY, OWEN

MY DEAR SECRETARY (1948, UA)—Playboy author **Kirk Douglas** marries his secretary, but the union suffers when his novel goes unpublished and his wife writes a best seller.

WATERS, ESTHER

ESTHER WATERS (1948, GB, Rank/GFD)—In 1873, servant-girl **Kathleen Ryan** is seduced by a groom, resulting in the birth of her child in a workhouse. She suffers greatly; but upon meeting the groom once again, they marry. For a while they prosper, but his health fails and when he dies, Ryan finds herself back as a servant in the home where she worked at the beginning.

WATERS, SGT.

A SOLDIER'S STORY (1984, Columbia)—**Adolphe Caesar** is a tough black top sergeant at Fort Neal, Louisiana, a holding area for black soldiers in WWII. One night he drunkenly returns to the base and someone shoots him dead. A black officer is sent in to investigate the case.

WATERS, WILLIAM

HIS OFFICIAL FIANCEE (1919, Silent, Paramount)—**Forrest Stanley** asks his secretary, a member of a family which has fallen on hard times, to become "his official fiancee" for a time to fend off other women who after him. She agrees, and, as one would expect, they fall in love.

WATSON, DENISE

SOLE SURVIVOR (1984, Grand National)—**Anita Skinner** is the only survivor of a plane crash in a remote area, but she's not alone. Flesh-eating zombies are on her trail.

WATNEY, WARNER

OLD EXPLORERS (1990, Taurus)—In a production that is better suited for the stage from which it derives, **Jose Ferrer** and his old friend James Whitmore play mind games as they plot expeditions to the lost city of Atlantis and similar fabled locations.

WATSON, JACK

18 AGAIN (1988, New World)—81-year-old **George Burns** makes a body switcheroo with his 18-year-old grandson. In his new body, he teaches his fraternity brothers, a thing or two about poker, hazing, pep rallies, bond fires and the Charleston. He gets the attention of a girl his grandson is sweet on, because she's writing a term paper on Harry S Truman, a personal friend of Burns. Possibly the best thing about the movie with the all-too-familiar plot is Anita Morris, once again doing her spoof of a super voluptuous mistress, much the same as her role in RUTHLESS PEOPLE.

WATSON, MARK

SOUL MAN (1986, New World)—In a silly film, **C. Thomas Howell**, desperate to get into Harvard, masquerades as black in order to be eligible for a minority scholarship.

WATSON, DR. MILDRED

THEY MIGHT BE GIANTS (1971, Universal)—**Joanne Woodward** is hired to help put away George C. Scott, who imagines himself to be Sherlock Holmes. But with a name like Dr. Watson, you just know the two will be on the look out for Professor Moriarty types.

WATSON, PENNY

THREE SAILORS AND A GIRL (1953, Warner Brothers)—**Jane Powell** and sailors Gordon MacRae, Gene Nelson and Jack E. Leonard attempt to transform a revue into a Broadway hit.

WATSON, PETER

THE MAN UPSTAIRS (1959, GB, British Lion)—When **Richard Attenborough** goes berserk and barricades himself in his room, the police and welfare authorities differ on how to get him out before he commits suicide. A young housewife is able to talk him into giving up.

WATT, DR. ELI

ONE MAN'S JOURNEY (1933, RKO)—**Lionel Barrymore**, a noble and self-sacrificing rural doctor, helps a young couple find the path of true love. The film was remade in 1938 (A MAN TO REMEMBER) with Edward Ellis.

WATTS

THE HEAD MAN (1928, Silent, First National)—Drunken ex-senator **Charlie Murray's** alcohol abuse indirectly leads to his election as mayor.

WAVE, MIKE R.

REVENGE OF THE RADIOACTIVE REPORTER (1990, Canada, Pryceless)—How about that name? It's the cleverest thing in this dumb sci-fi story about reporter **David Scrammell**, who, while investigating a radioactive leak, is pushed into a vat of radioactive waste. He emerges a disfigured but energized freak, whose mere touch brings flaming death.

WAYNE

W.W. AND THE DIXIE DANCEKINGS (1975, 20th Century Fox)—**Jerry Reed** is the leader of a third-rate country music act which teams up with Burt Reynolds, a charming Southern con man, who helps them get to the Grand Ole Opry in Nashville.

WAYNE, BRUCE *See* BATMAN

WAYNE, CRYSTAL

THE COWBOY AND THE BLONDE (1941, 20th Century Fox)—In a western "Taming of the Shrew" comedy, **Mary Beth Hughes** causes all kinds of trouble for rodeo cowboy George Montgomery.

WAYNE, DOROTHY

GO INTO YOUR DANCE (1935, Warner Brothers)—In the only film she ever made with husband Al Jolson, **Ruby Keeler** spends her time trying to straighten out Jolson. He has an attitude problem that almost ruins his career.

WAYNE, JULIA

TWO IN A CROWD (1936, Universal)—At a New Year's Eve party, a drunk throws two halves of a $1000 bill out the window. One half is found by beautiful **Joan Bennett**, and the other half by racehorse owner Joel McCrea. Tape, anyone?

WAYNE, LUCY CHASE

FIRST LADY (1937, Warner Brothers)—**Kay Francis**, the wife of the Secretary of State, has an on-going feud with Verree Teasdale, the wife of a Supreme Court Justice.

WAYNE, SHIRLEY

FBI GIRL (1951, Lippert)—**Audrey Totter** is a member of a team of federal agents tracking down an extortion gang.

WAYNE, SOOKY

SOOKY (1931, Paramount)—**Robert Coogan** is a friend of Jackie Cooper as Skippy in this sequel to SKIPPY. He helps Cooper's father election plans but loses his mother.

WEAVER

THE VICTORS (1963, Columbia)—In Carl Foreman's valiant attempt to capture the actual feel of WWII, **Peter Fonda** is one of the infantrymen, plodding their way across Europe, living if then can, dying if they must.

WEAVER, BUCK

EIGHT MEN OUT (1988, Orion)—Although he didn't take any money from gamblers and played all-out in the 1919 World Series, **John Cusack** is thrown out of baseball for life along with his seven guilty Chicago Black Sox team-mates, because he knew what was going on and didn't turn them in. Weaver spent the rest of his life trying to clear his name.

WEAVER, CATHERINE

BETRAYED (1988, MGM/UA)—G-woman **Debra Winger** infiltrates a group of violent white supremacists who wish to establish their own nation, and falls in love with the head bigot Tom Berenger.

WEAVER, TOD

MELODY FOR TWO (1937, Warner Brothers)—Irish tenor **James Melton** is an unsympathetic bandleader always bitching about his arrangements.

WEATHERBY, HARRY & MARY ELLEN

HIS WIFE'S GOOD NAME (1916, Silent, Vitagraph) - **Huntley Gordon's** parents object to the young man's marriage to **Lucille Lee Stewart**, with the father trying to poison his son's love for his new wife.

WEBB, MARY

CONFIDENCE GIRL (1952, UA)—**Hilary Brooke** and partner Tom Conway are con artists who baffle the police until she decides to go straight.

WEBB, PRUDENCE

TEXAS LADY (1955, RKO)—**Claudette Colbert** makes her first appearance in a Western as a newspaper woman in Fort Ralston, Texas who takes revenge on a man she blames for her father's death and goes to war against two dishonest cattle barons.

WEBSTER

THE THIEF WHO CAME TO DINNER (1973, Warner Brothers)—Dissatisfied computer analyst **Ryan O'Neal** becomes an accomplished jewel thief, falls in love with beautiful society girl Jacqueline Bisset, and is hounded by Warren Oates, a suspicious insurance investigator.

WEBSTER, ANNE

GIRL FROM GOD'S COUNTRY (1940, Republic)—Nurse **Jane Wyatt** joins selfless doctor Chester Morris, sought for mercy killing, in the frozen North, which she hates until she falls in love with Morris and his dedication.

WEBSTER, DANIEL

THE DEVIL AND DANIEL WEBSTER (1941, RKO)—**Edward Arnold**, as the famous New Hampshire congressman and orator, defends New England farmer James Craig, who has sold his soul to the devil, in a trial before a jury of the damned.

WEBSTER, JIMMY

THE WEBSTER BOY (1962, GB, Regal)—**Richard O'Sullivan** is persecuted by Geoffrey Bayldon, a sadistic school-teacher because he believes the boy is an ex-con's son.

WEBSTER, JOAN

I KNOW WHERE I'M GOING (1947, GB, Archers)—**Wendy Hiller** travels to wed a rich man but falls for a poor lord while stranded during a storm.

WEBSTER, JOHN

THE LABOUR LEADER (1917, Silent, GB, British Actors)—Socialist **Fred Groves** marries a pregnant laundress and becomes the first Labour Party member elected to Parliament. (Not because of whom he married.)

WEBSTER, LORNA

WOMAN WHO CAME BACK (1945, Republic)—**Nancy Kelly** is convinced an ancestor has made her a witch.

WEBSTER, MA

QUEEN OF THE MOB (1940, Paramount)—**Blanche Yurka** plays a Ma Barker-like character who raises her boys to be killers.

WEBSTER, MAXWELL

YOUNG MAN WITH IDEAS (1952, MGM)—**Glenn Ford** displays unexpected comedy skills as a small-town lawyer, who moves to Los Angeles to better himself.

WEBSTER, SCOTT & SUSAN

THE MONSTER AND THE GIRL (1941, Paramount)—**Phillip Terry** is wrongly executed for a crime and his brain is implanted into an ape. His sister **Ellen Drew** is forced into prostitution by those who framed him, but the ape takes care of them.

WEBSTER, TWIG

THE PARTY CRASHERS (1958, Paramount)—**Mark Damon** is a teenage punk, who gets his kicks ruining others' good times. Sounds like some people we know.

WELDON, LT. JOE

CALIFORNIA JOE (1944, Republic)—During the Civil War, Union Cavalry officer **Don "Red" Barry** must contend with Confederate sympathizers.

WELDON, MARGARET & WILLIAM

HER HUSBAND'S AFFAIRS (1947, Columbia)—Long before her TV series with Desi Arnaz, the late, beloved **Lucille Ball** was poking her nose in her husband **Franchot Tone's** business.

WELLING, MARY

DEATH OF AN ANGEL (1952, GB, Hammer)—Doctor's wife **Jane Baxter** is murdered, and both her husband and daughter are suspects.

WELLINGTON, DUKE OF

THE IRON DUKE (1935, GB, Gaumont)—**George Arliss** portrays the Duke of Wellington in this routine historical biopic.

WELLS, ALBERT

THE CLOWN (1927, Silent, Columbia)—Circus owner **William V. Mong** is sentenced to life-imprisonment for accidentally killing his faithless wife. Years later he escapes to rescue his daughter from his wife's lover.

WELLS, COURTNEY

RICH GIRL (1991, Studio Three/Film West)—Rich L.A. kid **Jill Schoelen** rebels against her Dad, Paul Gleason, and her yuppie fiance Sean Kanan. She takes a job as a cocktail waitress in a nightclub and falls for handsome hunk Don Michael Paul.

WELLS, DAMON

THE MAN WITH TWO FACES (1934, Warner Brothers)—Egotistical actor **Edward G. Robinson** gets away with murder when he does in his brother-in-law who is driving Robinson's sister crazy.

WELLS, DR. MALCOLM

THE BAT (1959, Allied Artists)—**Vincent Price** is searching for a million dollars of securities. He rips the throats of anyone who interferes with his plans. Now, Vincent, behave!

WELLS, TED

SINNERS IN LOVE (1928, Silent, FBO)—Gambler **Huntley Gordon** falls in love with Olive Borden, an innocent girl from a mill town, using her so he can cheat rich customers in his club. When she learns of this, she flees. Gordon catches up with her and pledges to change his ways.

WELWYN, TILLY
TILLY OF BLOOMSBURY (1931, GB, Sterling); (1940, GB, RKO) - **Phyllis Konstam** and **Jean Gillie** star as the daughter of a boarding-house keeper, whose love for a young society man is objected to by the boy's mother.

WENDELL
THE EXPERTS (1989, Paramount)—What will happen to silly films like this now that the U.S. is no longer into the sport of communism-bashing? **Ayre Gross** and John Travolta are nightclub owners whom the KGB mistakenly believe are experts on things American. They are whisked away to a replicated Hometown USA where future spies are trained, and put to work in updating the curriculum.

WENDELL, FLORENCE
SECOND WIFE (1930, RKO)—**Lila Lee** marries Conrad Nagel, a widower who soon leaves her to tend for his seriously ill seven-year-old son in Europe. Feeling deserted and now pregnant, Lee decides to run away with former suitor Hugh Huntley, but she changes her mind when he makes it clear he doesn't want the child.

WENDY/ROY
I WANT WHAT I WANT (1972, GB, Cinerama)—An instructor tries to rape a major's "daughter," **Anne Heywood**, who is really a man. We know what we don't want—this movie.

WENDY
WENDY CRACKED A WALNUT (1990, Australia, Classic Films)—It looks more like **Rosanna Arquette** laid an egg in this inept fantasy-comedy. She's a Sydney housewife, married to a dull husband. She drifts into a dream world in which she encounters an ideal lover, Hugo Weaving.

WENTWORTH, EGGHEAD
EGGHEAD'S ROBOT (1970, GB, Interfilm)—Inventor's son **Keith Chegwin** uses his father's robot as his double.

WENTWORTH, MARY
THE LAW IN HER HANDS (1936, Warner Brothers)—**Margaret Lindsay**, an attorney for underworld characters, marries the District Attorney, Warren Hull.

WERFORD, JOHN
JACK'S BACK (1988, Palisades)—Young physician **James Spader** is the prime suspect when L.A. prostitutes are killed in a grisly fashion 100 years to the day of similar killings by Jack the Ripper.

WERNER, MAX
THE BIG BRAIN (1933, RKO)—Barber **George E. Stone** comes up with a fake stock scheme which makes him rich, until the authorities catch up with him.

WERTHAN, MISS DAISY
DRIVING MISS DAISY (1989, Warner Brothers)—**Jessica Tandy's** Academy Award for her performance as an aging southern Jewish woman and her 25 year association with her chauffeur Morgan Freeman, was a popular choice. Well, there may have been four dissenters.

WESLEY, ANN
THE HIDDEN WOMAN (1922, Silent, American Releasing Corp.)—"Girl in the Red Velvet Swing" **Evelyn Nesbit**, a well-to-do society girl, is reproached for her frivolity by the man who loves her. When she loses her wealth in a stockmarket panic, she retires to live quietly at a settlement in the Adirondacks, where she provokes a great deal of emotional problems until her former lover rescues her.

WESLEY, JOHN
JOHN WESLEY (1954, GB, Commission of Methodist Church)—**Leonard Sachs** portrays the religious reformer in this modest biopic.

WESLEY, MARTIN
HIS PARISIAN WIFE (1919, Silent, Artcraft)—American lawyer **David Powell** marries a young Parisian writer, Elsie Ferguson. When they return to his staid home, his parents don't understand her, and Powell takes Mom and Dad's side.

WEST, BOB
ADVENTURES OF A PRIVATE EYE (1977, GB, Salon/Alpha)—In this sexual comedy, detective's assistant **Christopher Neil** investigates a blackmail racket involving pornographic photographs.

WEST, JOHNNY
THREE STRANGERS (1946, Warner Brothers)—Small-time criminals **Peter Lorre**, Sydney Greenstreet and Geraldine Fitzgerald share a winning sweepstake ticket—but there are a few complications.

WEST, KATHERINE
COUNSEL FOR THE DEFENSE (1925, Silent, Associated Exhibitors)—Recent law school graduate **Betty Compson** finds her first client to be her father, framed for accepting a bribe.

WEST, RODEO *See* MAMIE HUDLER

WEST, SYLVIA
SYLVIA (1965, Paramount)—**Carroll Baker** is just about to marry millionaire Peter Lawford, but he hires private investigator George Maharis to check out her past life and is it sleazy.

WESTCOTT, GEORGE
I'M A STRANGER (1952, GB, Corsair/Apex)—Window cleaner **Patric Doonan** helps Norwegian film star Greta Gynt (playing herself) find a missing will.

WESTCOTT, RUTH
THREE ON A MATCH (1932, Warner Brothers)—**Bette Davis** and two other ex-slum girls, Joan Blondell and Ann Dvorak, meet after twelve years to discuss old times and their present situations over a lunch. They ignore the WWI superstition that when three light cigarettes with one match, the last one lit will die imminently.

WESTCOURT, ETHEL
DANCING MOTHERS (1926, Silent, Paramount)—**Alice Joyce** discovers that her husband is having an affair, and her daughter is much too involved with Conway Tearle. She leaves her cheating hubby and wins Tearle from her child.

WESTEBY, JUDY
THERE GOES THE BRIDE (1980, GB, Vanguard)—Flapper's ghost **Toria Fuller** shows up on the eve of the wedding of Tom Smothers' daughter. Dickie was smart enough not to appear in this turkey.

WESTHANGER, KATE
KATE PLUS TEN (1938, GB, GFD)—Police inspector Jack Hulbert falls for **Genevieve Tobin** whose gang of ten steals a train load of gold bullion.

WESTON, FAY
SHE HAS WHAT IT TAKES (1943, Columbia)—**Jinx Falkenberg** pretends to be the daughter of a once prominent stage actress in order to be considered for a part in a show.

WESTON, JESSICA

THE COWBOY AND THE LADY (1922, Silent, Paramount)—When her philandering husband is killed on a Wyoming ranch, both **Mary Miles Minter** and her newest admirer Tom Moore are suspected of the crime.

WESTON, PAMELA

ALF'S BABY (1953, GB, Adelphi)—**Pauline Stroud** has been raised from childhood by three bachelor brothers. She gets involved with a "rotter" but the aging boys come to her rescue.

WETHERLY, BLANCHE

LEAVE IT TO BLANCHE (1934, GB, Warner Brothers)—When her husband pretends to murder her lover, **Olive Blakeney** convinces him he has succeeded.

WEYRE, LADY AVRIL

HER LAST AFFAIRE (1935, GB, Producers Dist.)—Secretary **Viola Keats** clears her father's name after compromising her employer's wife and causing her death.

WEYRINGER, HELEN & LOLA

HER SISTER FROM PARIS (1925, Silent, First National)—When her husband loses interest in her, **Constance Talmadge** pretends to be her sister, an international vamp, and renews his love for her.

WHA, LIEU

THE SON-DAUGHTER (1932, MGM)—Romance for San Francisco Chinese youngsters **Helen Hayes** and Ramon Novarro is put on hold because of wars between Tongs to which their two families belong.

WHALEN, LARRY

THE MAN FROM SUNDOWN (1939, Columbia)—**Charles Starrett** takes on a Texas outlaw who kills anybody who gets in his way.

WHALEN, CAPT. SAM

HIS WOMAN (1931, Paramount)—Skipper **Gary Cooper** rescues a baby adrift in a boat and hires Claudette Colbert, a girl involved in a blackmail case, to care for the child.

WHARTON, MAX

OVER 21 (1945, Columbia)—Middle-aged **Alexander Knox** attempts to become a "90-day wonder" lieutenant during WWII.

WHARTON, PAUL

THE YANKEE SENOR (1926, Silent, Fox)—**Tom Mix** arrives at the ranch of an aging Spanish rancher, claiming to be the man's long lost grandson. Not all of his relatives are pleased to see him.

WHARTON, WINNIE

BROADWAY HOSTESS (1935, Warner Brothers)—**Wini Shaw** is a top singer, unlucky in love.

WHEAT, SAM

GHOST (1990, Paramount)—When a hired mugger murders **Patrick Swayze** as he walks down the street with lover Demi Moore, he's not ready to go to his heavenly reward until he discovers who's behind his murder. With the help of a hilarious Whoopi Goldberg, a bogus psychic, he gets his revenge and one last snuggle with Moore. This fantasy captured the imagination of audiences. It was helped by some sultry love-making to the song "Unchained Melody," as performed by the Righteous Brothers.

WHEELER, LYLE

BOBBIE JO AND THE OUTLAW (1976, American International) Ex-child preacher **Marjoe Gortner** stars as the vicious leader of a gang of robbers and murderers, who has Lynda Carter hungry for excitement as his camp-follower.

WHEELER, THE MUDLARK

THE MUDLARK (1950, GB, 20th Century Fox)—Scruffy street urchin **Andrew Ray** breaks into Windsor castle to meet Queen Victoria (Irene Dunne). She has spent years in seclusion since the death of her beloved consort, Alfred. Ray helps the queen decide that it's time to come out, once more.

WHEELER, SENATOR ZACHARY

THE RESURRECTION OF ZACHARY WHEELER (1971, Gold Key)—Playboy US Senator **Bradford Dillman** is ressurrected from the dead using organ transplants from zombies.

WHIM, TILLIE

THEIR BIG MOMENT (1934, RKO)—**Zasu Pitts** and her comedy side-kick Slim Summerville deal with the discovery that she has psychic powers.

WHIMPERLY, EDWARD

I'M AN EXPLOSIVE (1933, GB, Fox)—Professor's son **Billy Hartnell** mistakes a liquid explosive for whiskey. It's got quite a kick.

WHIPPLE, ASH

HIS DIVORCED WIFE (1919, Silent, Universal)—**Monroe Salisbury** is a village blacksmith in the southern U.S. hills. He wins the town belle in marriage, but she divorces him when he is accused of a murder. When his innocence is proven, she returns to him. Love, honor and obey, in sickness and in health—but not murder.

WHIPPLE, HENRY

LOVE BIRDS (1934, Universal)—**Slim Summerville** and **Zasu Pitts** are a middle-aged couple who find romance while sharing numerous adventures.

WHIPPLE, JERRY

THE COWBOY AND THE COUNTESS (1926, Silent, Fox)—**Buck Jones**, a performer with a Wild West show touring Europe, saves Helen D'Algy from a state marriage to a duke, the secret leader of a gang of thieves.

WHIPPLE, SALLY

THE AVERAGE WOMAN (1924, Silent, C.C. Burr)—**Pauline Garon**, dubbed the average woman by a reporter, is forced to agree to marry a despicable man. The latter has a packet of letters written by Pauline's mother which he threatens to use against Garon's father, a judge.

WHISKERS (BRUTE HANSON)

SO YOU WON'T TALK (1940, Columbia)—Bookkeeper **Joe E. Brown** is mistaken for a notorious gangster.

WHISKEY, SAM

SAM WHISKEY (1969, UA)—Itinerant gambler **Burt Reynolds** is hired by Angie Dickinson to retrieve a cache of gold from a sunken ship in a Colorado river.

WHISTLER, NICHOLAS

AGENT 8 3/4 (1965, GB, Rank/Continental)—Writer **Dirk Bogarde** is an unwitting and untalented spy for the British in Prague.

WHITCOMB, KATY

THE LIEUTENANT WORE SKIRTS (1956, 20th Century Fox)—When her new husband Tom Ewell is called back to active duty with the

Air Force, **Sheree North** enlists to be near him and is sent to Hawaii. In the meantime, Ewell is rejected for medical reasons, and he must become her camp follower.

WHITCOMBE, DIANE

TO BE A LADY (1934, GB, British & Dominions)—Country girl **Dorothy Bouchier** becomes a London hairdresser, and is wrongly convicted of a crime.

WHITE, BRYDIE

GYPSY GIRL (1966, GB, Rank)—At seventeen, **Hayley Mills**, traumatized seven years earlier when she saw a playmate killed by a shotgun his father had carelessly left lying around, falls in love with Ian McShane, a boy travelling with a gypsy caravan. She joins him in his travels.

WHITE, BUCHANAN "SPEC"

THE BUSH LEAGUER (1927, Silent, Warner Brothers) -Idaho garage-owner **Monte Blue** becomes the star pitcher for a Los Angeles team, owned by the girl of his dreams, Lelia Hyams.

WHITE, CARRIE

CARRIE (1976, UA)—Misfit high school girl **Sissy Spacek**, humiliated by her classmates and stifled by her religious fanatic mother, gains revenge by unleashing her telekinetic powers, wiping out a gym full of students and teachers. Then she goes home to battle mama.

WHITE, CMDR.

SUBMARINE COMMAND (1951, Paramount)—Submarine officer **William Holden** is forced by an enemy attack to submerge and leave his captain topside.

WHITE, FRANK

THE KING OF NEW YORK (1990, Italy/U.S., Reteitalia/Scena)—Fresh out of prison, gangster **Christopher Walken** makes good on his pledge to take over New York's drug rackets. The crown isn't his to keep for very long.

WHITE, GLENDA

PARACHUTE NURSE (1942, Columbia)—Now get this, **Marguerite Chapman** is among the US nurses who learned to jump from planes in order to be more valuable to the war effort.

WHITE, KATHERINE

THE OFFSPRING (1987, Conquest/TMS)—As the film begins, **Martine Beswick** is given a lethal injection for committing a series of murders. In flashback we learn that she was doomed from birth.

WHITE, PEANUTS

MY FAVORITE SPY (1951, Paramount)—Burlesque comic **Bob Hope** is conned into posing as an international spy who is his exact double. As a result, he finds himself in Tangier in danger for different reasons from Hedy Lamarr and Francis L. Sullivan.

WHITE, PEARL

THE PERILS OF PAULINE (1947, Paramount)—**Betty Hutton** portrays silent screen star Pearl White in this fine musical biopic.

WHITE EAGLE

WHITE EAGLE (1932, Columbia)—**Buck Jones**, believing himself to be an Indian, reveals that white men are rustling government cattle and blaming it on Indians. In exposing them, he discovers he's a white man raised by Indians.

WHITEACRE, MICHAEL

THE YOUNG LIONS (1958, 20th Century Fox)—Entertainer **Dean Martin's** life becomes intertwined with Jewish Montgomery Clift when the two serve together in the army during WWII.

WHITECLIFFE, TONY

THE DUKE WORE JEANS (1958, GB, Anglo-Amalgamated)—**Tommy Steele** appears as a nobleman's son and his cockney double, who woos a princess as a favor for the former.

WHITEHEAD, ETHEL

THE DAMNED DON'T CRY (1950, Warner Brothers)—After the death of her child, housewife **Joan Crawford** walks out on her laborer husband and becomes the mistress of crime boss David Brian. He sets her up as a Texas heiress, Laura Hansen Forbes. Brian later guns down Crawford just before being shot to death by loyal Kent Smith. The picture ends without revealing whether she will survive or not.

WHITEMAN, PAUL

THE KING OF JAZZ (1930, Universal)—In a series of musical sketches, **Paul Whiteman** explains how he got the title "King of Jazz."

WHITERSPOON, JANE

THE COLLEGE WIDOW (1927, Silent, Warner Brothers)—To help save her father's job as president of Atwater College, beautiful **Dolores Costello** uses her charm to get top football players from neighboring schools to transfer to Atwater. What's the NCAA's policy on this type of recruitment?

WHITESIDE, SHERIDAN

THE MAN WHO CAME TO DINNER (1942, Warner Brothers)—When writer, critic, and radio columnist **Monty Woolley** falls on the steps of an Ohio household, he takes over the house, and runs the family like a caustic tyrant. His role is loosely based on Alexander Woollcott and many of the other characters are readily recognizable as Noel Coward, Harpo Marx and Gertrude Lawrence.

WHITLEY, TED

TED AND VENUS (1991, Double Helix)—Thirty-five-year-old hippie poet **Bud Cort** is obsessed with a vision of a gorgeous young lady coming from the sea. The girl is Kim Adams, a community service worker who is helping disabled Cort find an apartment. His romantic overtures quickly become harassment, and she's forced to deal with him in a violent way.

WHITLOCK, WARDEN

THE BIG GUY (1939, Universal)—When prisoners escape from a reformatory, captain of the guards **Victor McLaglen** helps apprehend them. In the process, he keeps some of the stolen money in their possession. As a reward he is made warden at the prison where one of the escapees, Jackie Cooper, wrongly tried and sentenced to death for a killing during the break, is on Death Row. Will Victor keep the money and let Cooper go to the chair? Don't be silly.

WHITNEY, ARLENE

THE PAINTED FLAPPER (1924, Silent, Associated First National)—**Pauline Garon** saves her sister from marrying a socialite, whom she is able to prove is an international crook.

WHITNEY, PAUL

THE INTERLOPER (1918, Silent, World)—**Irving Cummings**, the son of a New York railroad corporation president, goes south to convince Kitty Gordon to sell her estate. He falls in love with her.

WHITNEY, ROSE
SOME BLONDES ARE DANGEROUS (1937, Universal)—**Dorthea Kent** is a beauty who ruins prizefighters.

WHITTAKER, BILLY
BAREFOOT BOY (1938, Monogram)—Wholesome juvenile **Jackie Moran** pulls off a barrel of pranks before helping clear the father of a friend, falsely accused of a robbery.

WHITTAKER, CELIA
LADY OF SECRETS (1936, Columbia)—Because of one unfortunate love affair, **Ruth Chatterton** chooses a life of loneliness.

WHITTAKER, JACK
WEREWOLF OF WASHINGTON (1973, Milicol Diplomat)—White House press secretary **Dean Stockwell** becomes a werewolf.

WHITTAKER, KENNETH
THREE HUSBANDS (1950, UA)—In this role reversal film based on A LETTER TO THREE WIVES, **Robert Karnes** is one of three husbands, who receives a posthumous letter from a deceased bachelor friend, claiming to have had an affair with their wives.

WHO, DOCTOR
DR. WHO AND THE DALEKS (1965, GB, Aaru)—Eccentric old scientist **Peter Cushing** takes a trip through time and space to a planet, where he helps the peace-loving Daleks against an army of mutants.

WHYMAN, DIANA
THE LADYBIRD (1927, Silent, First Division)—Society girl **Betty Compson** leaves her guardian, and takes a dancing job in a New Orleans club. She unwittingly falls in with some crooks at Carnival time.

WICKS, GERALD BERESFORD
THE PERFECT SPECIMEN (1937, Warner Brothers)—**Errol Flynn** doesn't have the comic timing to pull off his role as an upper-class gentleman, who becomes a boxer and falls in love with newspaper reporter Joan Blondell.

THE WIFE
NEGLECTED WIVES (1920, Silent, Wisteria)—Neglected wife **Anne Luther** is almost compromised by a political boss.

THE WIFE
SUNRISE—A SONG OF TWO HUMANS (1927, Silent, Fox)—**Janet Gaynor** is the wife of George O'Brien, a young farmer who becomes infatuated with a woman from the city. The latter urges him to kill Gaynor. He almost does, but their love wins out in this hauntingly beautiful film.

WIGGLEWORTH, BUNNY *See* **ZORRO**

WIGGINS, JOHNNY
JOHNNY GET YOUR GUN (1919, Silent, Paramount)—Cowboy movie star **Fred Stone** goes east to save an old friend's sister from a fortune hunter.

WIGGS, ELDER
WAGONMASTER (1950, RKO)—**Ward Bond**, who would play a similar role on television, heads up a wagon train of Mormans sent to establish a new colony in the West. They encounter all the to be expected difficulties.

WIGGS, MRS. ELVIRA
MRS. WIGGS OF THE CABBAGE PATCH (1934, Paramount) (1942, Paramount)—**Pauline Lord** and **Fay Bainter** portray the poor mother of many children, who smiles through her tears while living in a shantytown.

WILBY
THE WILBY CONSPIRACY (1975, UA)—**Joseph De Graf** is the leader of a black liberation movement in South Africa. Sidney Poitier, Michael Caine and Prunella Gee are taking diamonds to De Graf to finance the movement, hotly pursued by fascist police officer Nicol Williamson.

WILCOX, CHARLIE
SUBURBAN COMMANDO (1991, New Line)—When intergalactic warrior Hulk Hogan comes to earth for a vacation, he stays in the suburban home of Casper Milquetoast-like **Christopher Lloyd** and his wife, Shelley Duvall. Lloyd briefly becomes the title character when he dons Hogan's muscle-enhancing power suit.

WILCOX, SANDY
MY AMERICAN COUSIN (1986, Canada, Spectrafilm)—In 1959, British Columbian **Margaret Langrick** is infatuated with her visiting American cousin. He's so cool, just like James Dean.

WILD, ADAM and KEVIN
BROTHERS (1984, Australia, Areflex)—Based on a true story, brute **Chard Hayward** and his brother **Ivar Kants** are journalists who survived a series of killings of reporters in 1975. Years later, Hayward shows up in New Zealand, upset that his brother has settled down. He's still an unpleasant hell-raiser with trouble just naturally following him.

WILD THING
WILD THING (1987, Atlantic)—Young hippie **Rob Knepper** sneaks around at night in the worst part of town, acting like a modern day Robin Hood or Spiderman.

WILDE, OSCAR
THE MAN WITH THE GREEN CARNATION (1960, GB, Warwick)—OSCAR WILDE (1960, GB, Vantage)—**Peter Finch** and **Robert Morley**, in the same year, appear as the playwright and wit. Both movies pay special attention to Wilde's trials for sodomy.

WILDELEY, HILARY
TOO MANY WIVES (1933, GB, Warner Brothers)—House maid **Nora Swinburne** agrees to pose as her employer's absent wife in order to entertain a client.

WILEY, BOB
THE PATRIOT (1916, Silent, Triangle)—When his mine is stolen by a swindler, Spanish American War hero **William S. Hart** goes crazy. When his son dies he joins a band of Mexican bandits and turns his hatred against the U.S. But during a battle, he comes to his senses, and rejoins his country.

WILKINS, HUBERT
HE HIRED THE BOSS (1943, 20th Century Fox)—Timid bookkeeper **Stuart Erwin**, prodded by his girl friend, acquires enough wealth to buy the company for which he has been working. He fires his boss Thurston Hall, but a few hours later hires him back.

WILKINS, MIRIAM
DEAR BRAT (1951, Paramount)—Teenage **Mona Freeman**, still up to her well-meaning but troublesome exploits, hires as the family

gardener a man whom her father, a judge and now a senator, had sentenced to prison.

WILKINS, RUTH

DEAR RUTH (1947, Paramount)—When the soldier her sister Mona Freeman had been corresponding with shows up on her doorstep ready for romance, **Joan Caulfield** doesn't know what he's talking about. Mona Freeman signed her sister's name to the letters and sent the young man, William Holden, Joan's photo. Things work out predictably but pleasantly so.

WILKINS, SGT.

CARRY ON CONSTABLE (1960, GB, Anglo-Amalgamated)—**Sid James** is faced with turning some very raw recruits into police officers in this bawdy comedy. It's a British POLICE ACADEMY, but funnier.

WILKINSON, LEW

THE VIOLENT MEN (1955, Columbia)—Unscrupulous crippled rancher **Edward G. Robinson** dreams of empire building, but he gets no help from his unfaithful wife Barbara Stanwyck. He's opposed by squatter Glenn Ford.

WILL

ROBIN AND THE SEVEN HOODS (1964, Warner Brothers)—**Sammy Davis Jr.** has the Will Scarlett role in this Prohibition period take-off on Robin Hood and his Merry Men as played by Frank Sinatra's Rat Pack.

WILLENS, LADY SUSAN

THE GAMBLER AND THE LADY (1952, GB, Hammer)—**Naomi Chance** is involved with American gambler Dane Clark, who tries to crash London society.

WILLENS, PETER

OUTCAST OF THE ISLANDS (1952, GB, British Lion)—When he is fired for embezzlement, **Trevor Howard** is taken by Ralph Richardson to a remote trading post he owns in the islands. There Howard betrays the trader's secret channel because of his love for a native princess.

WILLIAM

SWEET WILLIAM (1980, GB, World Northal)—**Sam Waterston** is a loose-living American playwright. He impregnates Jenny Agutter, a girl already engaged.

WILLIAM, LORD

MAN OF MAYFAIR (1931, GB, Paramount)—English lord **Jack Buchanan** poses as a workman to win dancer Joan Barry, temporarily working as a waitress.

WILLIAMS, ABBY

ABBY (1974, American International)—In another black exploitation film, **Carol Speed** is possessed by a devil. She changes from a nice church-going girl to a murderous slut.

WILLIAMS, BUD

KING FOR A NIGHT (1933, Universal)—Boxer **Chester Morris** is convicted of a murder committed by his sister Helen Twelvetrees.

WILLIAMS, CANDY

LUCKY ME (1954, Warner Brothers)—**Doris Day** is the star of a theatrical revue stranded in Miami. Dodo tries hard but not even this talented lady can make a silk purse out of this pig's ear.

WILLIAMS, DING DONG

DING DONG WILLIAMS (1946, RKO)—Clarinetist **Glenn Vernon** is hired to compose a blues score for a new film, but his mood changes make this a formidable task.

WILLIAMS, EDDIE

THE KID FROM SPAIN (1932, UA)—**Eddie Cantor** and his Mexican roommate are expelled from college when they are caught in the girl's dormitory in a sequence that is a voyeur's delight. They are implicated in a bank robbery, and when they flee to the roommate's home in Mexico, Cantor is mistaken for a famous Spanish matador.

WILLIAMS, HENRY

THE NERVOUS WRECK (1926, Silent, Producers Dist. Corp.) - Believing himself the victim of a fatal illness, **Harrison Ford** moves to an Arizona ranch, where his actions seem out of control until he discovers he's healthier than he'd believed.

WILLIAMS, KAY

LOVER COME BACK (1946, Universal)—**Lucille Ball** is faithful while her husband is away during WWII despite plenty of attention from men at work. Her husband, George Brent, on the other hand, chases every skirt in sight.

WILLIAMS, KENNY

AMAZING MR. WILLIAMS (1939, Columbia)—**Melvin Douglas** delays his marriage to solve a murder case in this enjoyable comedy-mystery.

WILLIAMS, MAGGIE & DALE

THE PERFECT MARRIAGE (1946, Paramount)—**Loretta Young** and **David Niven** are a rich and recently married couple who almost divorce. Despite interference from friends, relatives and new lovers, they get back together.

WILLIAMS, MAGGIE

THE PLEASURE SEEKERS (1964, 20th Century Fox)—**Carol Lynley**, an American working as a secretary in Madrid, along with Ann-Margret and Pamela Tiffin, is seeking a husband and finds one, as do her friends. It's a Spanish version of THREE COINS IN THE FOUNTAIN, without a good title song.

WILLIAMS, MARSH

CARBINE WILLIAMS (1952, MGM)—Moonshiner **James Stewart**, sentenced to thirty years in prison for second-degree murder, invents the M-1 carbine rifle and wins a pardon after serving eight years.

WILLIAMS, MARY K.

MOTHERS CRY (1930, First National)—A 30-year period is covered in the life of **Dorothy Peterson**, as she attempts to raise her four children to be respectable members of society.

WILLIAMS, PRISCILLA

WEE WILLIE WINKLE (1937, 20th Century Fox)—Kipling's boy hero becomes a girl to accommodate **Shirley Temple**. She charms her crusty old grandfather, the colonel of a British regiment based in India in the late 19th century. Captured by rebels, she is able to talk their leader out of attacking her grandfather's troops.

WILLIAMS, RENO

RENO WILLIAMS: THE ADVENTURE BEGINS (1985, Orion)—New York cop **Fred Ward** is recruited by a secret society out to avenge society's wrongs.

WILLIAMS, SALLY

SALLY IN OUR ALLEY (1927, Silent, Columbia)—**Shirley Mason**, a girl of the tenements, is adopted by three neighbors when her mother dies, but her wealthy aunt takes the girl away from her friends. When she reaches 18, she leaves the snobs she has come to abhor.

WILLIAMS, SAM

PENROD AND SAM (1923, Silent, Associated First National) PENROD AND SAM (1931, First National); (1937, Warner Brothers) **Joe Butterworth, Junior Coghlan** and **Harry Watson** each appeared as one of Booth Tarkington's boy heroes, who share adventures with Penrod. The films were meant to bring nostalgic tears to adults who saw them. The effect of viewing them today wouldn't be the same.

WILLIAMS, TOMMY

BABES ON BROADWAY (1941, MGM)—**Mickey Rooney** does just about everything in this delightful musical comedy about a bunch of youngsters seeking their Broadway break. Rooney and co-star Judy Garland are extremely talented and appealing.

WILLIAMS, WALLY

THERE'S SOMETHING ABOUT A SOLDIER (1943, Columbia)—**Tom Neal** stars in this B-movie training camp drama, with Evelyn Keyes as his love interest.

WILLIE BOY

TELL THEM WILLIE BOY IS HERE (1969, Universal)—In 1909, young American Indian **Robert Blake** is hunted by sheriff Robert Redford after Blake accidentally becomes involved in a killing.

WILLIS, JEFFREY

FLAMINGO KID (1984, 20th Century Fox)—Teenage **Matt Dillon** is impressed by wealthy car dealer Richard Crenna, who plays gin all the time at the country club where Dillon is employed for the summer. Matt under-appreciates the good sense of his father Hector Elizondo, until his new hero proves to have feet of clay, and is discovered to be a cheat.

"WILLIS, SAL See CHRISTINE MILLER

WILLOUGHBY, LONG JOHN

MEET JOHN DOE (1941, Warner Brothers)—Ex-ballplayer **Gary Cooper** is picked by newspaper columnist Barbara Stanwyck to be the John Doe she has created. This John Doe has promised to commit suicide if something isn't done for the poor of the country. Coop is used by fascist publisher Edward Arnold, but as is the case in Frank Capra movies, the little guy wins out over the corrupt big guy, although it's a close call. Cooper is almost forced to honor his pledge.

WILLS, FRANKLIN

MAN ON A SWING (1974, Paramount)—Clairvoyant **Joel Grey** helps the police find a sex-mad murderer.

WILMER, LORD BILL

HIS LORDSHIP GOES TO PRESS (1939, GB, Canterbury/ RKO) - Lord **Hugh Williams** poses as a farmer to fool an American girl reporter.

WILOZEK, KEN

THE MEN (1950, UA)—Paraplegic ex-GI **Marlon Brando** must face up not only to his physical limitations, but his psychological and sexual ones as well. In this he is helped by his understanding fiancee Teresa Wright and some sensitive doctors.

WILSON, BOB

REAL MAN (1987, MGM/UA)—**John Ritter** is a family man drafted by the CIA to take a secret map from California to Washington. He's aided by a tough CIA agent and some benevolent aliens from outer space.

WILSON, CANDY

WEEKEND WITH THE BABYSITTER (1970, Dundee)—**Susan Romen** is the regular babysitter for a writer. She stops by when his wife is away and he lets her read his new story about young people. She offers to show him how teenagers really act. It's all sex and drugs from then on.

WILSON, DANNY

MEET DANNY WILSON (1952, Universal)—Singer **Frank Sinatra's** career is almost ruined by his association with underworld figures. It didn't seem to hurt Frank in real life.

WILSON, EDDIE (JOE WEST)

EDDIE AND THE CRUISERS II: EDDIE LIVES (1989, Alliance-Aurora/Scotti)—Unable to handle the role of a rock 'n' roll superstar, **Michael Pare** disappeared in the early 1960s, apparently drowned after a car wreck. Not so, he went to Canada and changed his name, taking work as a construction worker, but he makes a comeback and is a big a star as ever—Sure!

WILSON, EDDIE JR.

KID MILLIONS (1934, UA)—**Eddie Cantor**, a kid from New York's lower East Side, inherits millions from his archeologist father who has hidden the money somewhere in Egypt. Various characters want to help him find it and then help themselves to the fortune.

WILSON, FENNIS

THURSDAY'S CHILD (1943, GB, Pathe)—Child star **Sally Ann Howes's** success causes trouble for her family.

WILSON, FRANCES

THE TWO OF US (1938, GB, Gaumont)—**Gino Malo** helps Jack of all trades Jack Hulbert bluff his way into big business and set up his own company.

WILSON, GEORGE

CHAMP FOR A DAY (1953, Republic)—Honest boxer **Alex Nicol** is trying to discover who killed his manager.

WILSON, HELEN "WHITEY"

WIFE VERSUS SECRETARY (1936, MGM)—**Jean Harlow** is almost indispensable as Clark Gable's sexy secretary, something which is not lost on Gable's attractive wife, Myrna Loy. She suspects Harlow of having an affair with her husband.

WILSON, JAMES, DAN & MRS.

I ACCUSE MY PARENTS (1945, Producers Releasing Corp.)—**Robert Lowell, John Miljan** and **Vivienne Osborne** appear as a juvenile delinquent and his parents, whom he blames for his becoming an anti-social punk. Seems Miljan and Osborne didn't understand Lowell. Even the judge believes they set a bad example for their son. It was typical of the period to attempt to find someone other than the kid to blame, when he goes wrong. Some kids are just no good. Sorry about that Father Flanagan.

WILSON, JEAN

LADY POSSESSED (1952, Republic)—Sick **June Havoc** believes that she is possessed by James Mason's first wife.

WILSON, JOCKO

THE MAN FROM DOWN UNDER (1943, MGM)—The role played by **Charles Laughton** screams for Wallace Beery. Laughton is a WWI veteran who smuggles two youngsters into Australia.

WILSON, JOHN

WHITE HUNTER, BLACK HEART (1990, Warner Brothers)—Can you visualize **Clint Eastwood** as director John Huston? Well, that's who his character is based on, and the story is the behind-the-scenes tale of the making of THE AFRICAN QUEEN.

WILSON, LARRY & KAY

I LOVE YOU AGAIN (1940, MGM)—It seems that the team of **William Powell** and **Myrna Loy** could have pleased audiences in just about any vehicle. Here they're a married couple who must deal with his recovery from an eight-year attack of amnesia, which changes him from a stodgy lawyer into a wild and crazy guy.

WILSON, LUCKY

I'LL WAIT FOR YOU (1941, MGM)—Big-city gangster **Robert Sterling** hides out in the country. He discovers he likes the bucolic settings, especially when they include farm girl Marsha Hunt.

WILSON, MOLLY & JIM

MOLLY AND ME (1929, Tiffany/Stahl)—**Belle Bennett** and **Joe E. Brown** have been waiting for 10 years for their chance on Broadway, but when it comes it's for Brown only. Later he falls for another girl and tries to break with Bennett, but comes to his senses and sends for her.

WILSON, NAPOLEON

NAPOLEON AND SAMANTHA (1972, Buena Vista)—**Johnny Whitaker** and Jodie Foster run away with a pet lion, taking refuge at a friend's mountain cabin.

WILSON, RITA

HIS BROTHER'S WIFE (1936, MGM)—Sometime after the completion of this movie, **Barbara Stanwyck** and her co-star Robert Taylor married. In it, she is a nightclub hostess who marries Taylor's brother because she is miffed that medical researcher Taylor left her to go to the tropics to investigate spotted fever. By the fade-out Barbara has spotted fever and Taylor. Brother John Elderidge gets nothing.

WILSON, RITA

SECRETS OF A MODEL (1940, Continental-Times)—Small-town girl **Sharon Lee** moves to the big city to become a model and guess what, the big city is different than a small town.

WILSON, RUTH

THE GIRL FROM JONES BEACH (1949, Warner Brothers)—Commercial artist Ronald Reagan in search of the perfect girl, finds **Virginia Mayo** fills the bill.

WILSON, STEVE

I COVER THE BIG TOWN (1947, Paramount)—**Philip Reed** is the editor of a big town newspaper in this film based on the radio series.

WILSON, TERRY

MEET THE GIRLS (1938, 20th Century Fox)—Entertainers **Lynn Bari** and June Lang, stranded in Honolulu, become stowaways to get back to San Francisco.

WILSON, THOMAS WOODROW

WILSON (1944, 20th Century Fox)—**Alexander Knox** gives a fine, believable performance as President Woodrow Wilson. The film is exceptional, but the time of its release did not offer it much chance to become a box-office hit.

WILTON, JANE

JANE STEPS OUT (1938, GB, Associated British)—Plain **Diana Churchill** is a cinderella in her family, but with the help of her old granny, snatches the husband meant for her sister.

WILTON, LAURA

THE DEPRAVED (1957, GB, UA)—**Anne Heywood** and her U.S. Army officer lover Robert Arden kill her abusive drunkard husband.

WILTSHIRE, HON. FREDDIE

THE MEDICINE MAN (1933, GB, Real Art)—**Claude Allister** switches identities with a doctor. A criminal gang want him to perform a leg amputation on one of their wounded members.

WINCH, SALLY

SALLY IN OUR ALLEY (1931, GB, RKO)—In this light musical comedy, **Gracie Fields** is a cafe singer in love with a wounded soldier. She must deal with a rival who wants to break up the romance.

WINDERMERE, LADY

LADY WINDERMERE'S FAN (1925, Warner Brothers)—**May McAvoy's** mother Irene Rich saves her daughter from a foolish indiscretion, which is almost revealed on account of a missing fan.

WINDERMERE, MAURICE

THE SILENT PASSENGER (1935, GB, Associate British Films)—Railway detective Donald Wolfit plans the perfect murder of blackmailer **Leslie Perrins**.

WINDOM, DR. ALEC

WINDOM'S WAY (1958, GB, Rank)—**Peter Finch**, the idealistic head of a small Malay hospital, is reconciled with his wife after a trial separation.

WINDRUCH, STANLEY

PRIVATE'S PROGRESS (1956, GB, British Lion)—Inept undergraduate **Ian Carmichael** is summoned for army service in WWII. He quickly learns to be an A-number 1 goldbrick.

WINDSOR, VANESSA

THE FEMALE ANIMAL (1958, Universal)—Beautiful movie star **Hedy Lamarr's** adoptive daughter becomes involved with an extra.

WINDWALKER

WINDWALKER (1980, Pacific International)—Aging Indian chief **Trevor Howard** tells the story of his life on his deathbed.

WINDY

HELL DIVERS (1932, MGM)—**Wallace Beery** is excellent as an experienced naval petty officer who has differences of opinion with Clark Gable on how things should be run.

WINFIELD, JOAN

THE BRIDE CAME C.O.D. (1941, Warner Brothers)—While trying to elope with a band leader, runaway heiress **Bette Davis** is kidnapped by charter pilot James Cagney. The two get to know each better when their plane goes down in a desert.

WING TOY

WING TOY (1921, Silent, Fox)—**Shirley Mason**, whose father was Chinese and mother American, is promised in marriage to a powerful underworld figure, but ends up with an American reporter who shows that she is really the daughter of the District Attorney.

WINGATE, "MOM"
MOTHERS-IN-LAW (1923, Silent, Preferred)—**Edith Yorke** comes to live with her son and his wife when her husband dies. She kidnaps her own grandchild to bring her daughter-in-law to her senses.

WINGO, TOM
THE PRINCE OF TIDES (1991, Columbia)—His marriage in danger, Southerner **Nick Nolte** is called to New York by Barbra Streisand, the psychiatrist of his sister, Melinda Dillon. Dillon has tried to commit suicide, and Streisand wants Nolte's help in reconstructing Dillon's troubled past, which Nolte has shared. Streisand, violating medical ethics, becomes Nolte's lover. When she helps him face the horrors of his childhood, he's able to leave her and return to his wife and children.

WINKLE, WILBERT GEORGE
MR. WINKLE GOES TO WAR (1944, Columbia)—Henpecked middle-aged **Edward G. Robinson** is accidentally drafted, and becomes a hero.

WINSBY, HORACE
MAKING A MAN (1922, Silent, Paramount)—Wealthy snob **Jack Holt** is refused by Eva Novak when he proposes marriage because of his selfish attitudes. He goes to New York where everything goes wrong, but he learns humility.

WINSHIP, CHARMION
THE DARLING OF THE RICH (1923, Silent, B.B. Prod.) Left penniless by her father, **Betty Blythe** goes to New York where she poses as a princess to help a gang of crooks get into the homes of the rich. One of her suitors puts her on the right track and wins her hand.

WINSHIP, INSPECTOR
THE PRIVATE EYES (1980, New World)—**Don Knotts** and Tim Conway are dimwitted Scotland Yard detectives, who go to a mansion to investigate a millionaire's murder.

WINSLOW, PATIENCE
HALF A BRIDE (1928, Paramount)—When the yacht of her middle-aged husband is sunk **Esther Ralston** is stranded on a desert island with the ship's handsome young captain, Gary Cooper.

WINSLOW, PIKE
THE PUBLIC DEFENDER (1931, Fox)—Lawyer **Richard Dix** believes a bank vice president, who has been sent to prison when a bank fails, is innocent. He works with the man's daughter to obtain his release.

WINSLOW, RITA
RIO RITA (1942, MGM)—**Kathryn Grayson** and John Carroll are the romantic leads in this pleasant musical set south of the border, but Abbott and Costello dominate the proceedings

WINSLOW, RONNIE
THE WINSLOW BOY (1950, GB, Eagle-Lion)—Young naval cadet **Neil North** is sent down from the school when he is accused of a theft. His father Cedric Hardwicke, convinced of his son's innocence, spends all of his funds and health to have the boy cleared. "Let justice be done!" Robert Donat, as the ill barrister who takes the case of the boy, is marvelous.

WINSLOW, SHARON
THE TIGER WOMAN (1945, Republic)—Tiger woman **Adele Mara** has a series of adventures trying to prevent the wrong people from finding hidden gold.

WINSLOW THE PHANTOM
PHANTOM OF THE PARADISE (1974, 20th Century Fox)—In this rock 'n' roll version of the PHANTOM OF THE OPERA, **William Finley** is a songwriter, cheated by rock producer Paul Williams, and framed for a crime. Finley takes his revenge as he tries to advance the career of a singer he loves from a distance.

WINSTANLEY
WINSTANLEY (1979, GB, British Film Institute)—Poor ex-soldier **Miles Halliwell** forms a cooperative settlement in Surrey, England.

WINSTEAD, REBECCA
REBECCA OF SUNNYBROOK FARM (1938, 20th Century Fox)—**Shirley Temple's** uncle dumps her on a farm to live with an aunt, who has no use for show business. She forbids Shirley from having anything to do with neighbor Randolph Scott, who is a talent scout. Nevertheless, Scott arranges for Temple to become a success on radio.

WINSTON
DAREDREAMER (1990, Lensman)—**Tim Nosh** portrays a latter-day Walter Mitty who zonks out into fantasy worlds at the slightest provocation. It looks as if his little problem may prevent him from graduating from high school.

WINSTON, DALLAS
THE OUTSIDERS (1983, Warner Brothers)—**Matt Dillon** is one of a group of troubled Oklahoma teenagers in the 1960s.

WINSTON, WINDY
THE GARBAGE PAIL KIDS (1987, Atlantic Entertainment)—In this tasteless film **Arturo Gil's** specialty is breaking wind.

WINTERBOTTOM, AUGUSTUS & TILLIE
TILLIE AND GUS (1933, Paramount)—Card shark **W.C. Fields** and his wife **Alison Skipworth** team up to outwit a crook out to swindle their niece.

WINTERHAWK, CHIEF
WINTERHAWK (1976, Howco)—When Blackhawk Indian brave **Michael Dante** seeks serum for smallpox from a white man, he is attacked instead.

WINTERS, ELOISE
MY FOOLISH HEART (1949, RKO)—**Susan Hayward**, a college girl from Idaho, falls for military wolf Dana Andrews, and becomes pregnant. She marries a man she doesn't love when Andrews is killed. She becomes a cynical alcoholic who almost loses the love of her child before she takes a good look at herself, and finally realizes what self-pity has done to her life.

WINTERS, GLORIA
SHE KNEW ALL THE ANSWERS (1941, Columbia)—**Joan Bennett** wants to marry a wealthy playboy, but her guardian, Franchot Tone, won't hear of it, because he loves her.

WINTERS, LIZ
PERFECT VICTIM (1988, Vertigo)—An AIDs-infected killer has already raped two fashion models, and **Deborah Shelton** is his next intended victim.

WINTERS, MARK JONAH
80 STEPS TO JONAH (1969, Warner Brothers)—Pop singer **Wayne Newton** plays a migrant worker, picked up by Sal Mineo who is driving a stolen car. The police chase the duo, the car goes over a

cliff, Mineo is killed, and Newton is thrown into the driver's seat which gets him charged with manslaughter.

WINTERS, VERGIE
THE LIFE OF VERGIE WINTERS (1934, RKO)—In this tearjerker, **Ann Harding** becomes John Boles' mistress. She stoically accepts her fate for 22 years, even to the point of giving up her daughter, so the girl can be raised in luxury while her mother is ostracized.

WINTERTON, SIR BASIL
BACHELOR FATHER (1931, MGM)—**C. Aubrey Smith** visits his children in a rather dull social comedy.

WINTHRAM, PERCY
RATTLE OF A SIMPLE MAN (1964, GB, Associated British Films)—**Harry H. Corbett**, a Manchester football fan, falls for a Soho prostitute.

WINTHROP, LOUIS III
TRADING PLACES (1983, Paramount)—**Dan Aykroyd**, a member of the privileged class, is framed by big-time crooked financiers Don Ameche and Ralph Bellamy. His job is given to a jive-talking poor black in order to settle a bet between the two old men as to which is more important, heredity or environment.

WINTHROP, KATHERINE
A WOMAN POSSESSED (1958, GB, UA)—When her son returns from America with a wife, **Margaretta Scott** insists that the young couple live with her. She gives them both a hard time, almost resulting in the death of her daughter-in-law when pills get switched.

WINTHROP, OFFICER
WOMAN UNAFRAID (1934, Goldsmith)—Lady cop **Lucille Gleason** puts away a criminal big shot no one else can touch.

WINTHROP, SHELIA
HER PRIMITIVE MAN (1944, Universal)—**Louise Allbritton** plans to prove that a writer's notions about savages is all wrong. She sets out to find a primitive man. She does—the author in disguise.

WISECARVER, ELLSWORTH "SONNY"
IN THE MOOD (1987, Lorimar)—**Patrick Dempsey** is the "Woo Woo Kid," a 14-year-old whom older women want to marry, and do. It gets him thrown in jail. Guess the statutory rape laws of the state applied only to men with underage girls.

WITHNAIL
WITHNAIL AND I (1987, GB, Cineplex Odeon)—Dissipated, gaunt actor **Richard E. Grant**, who pops amphetamines, hasn't slept for 60 hours. He is freezing in his apartment that he shares with another actor, the unnamed "I" of the title. They decide to take a holiday in the country.

WITTERING
UNMAN, WITTERING AND ZIGO (1971, GB, Paramount)—**Colin Barrie** is the second to last schoolboy named on the school's roster. The boys threaten to kill the new headmaster as they did his predecessor.

THE WIZ
THE WIZ (1978, Universal)—In this black musical version of THE WIZARD OF OZ, **Richard Pryor** portrays the Wizard, to whom Diana Ross' Dorothy appeals for help.

WIZARD OF MARS
WIZARD OF MARS (1964, American General)—When four astronauts crash land on Mars they find the last survivor of a lost civilization is **John Carradine**.

THE WIZARD OF OZ
THE WIZARD OF OZ (1922, Silent, Universal); (1939, MGM) - **Charles Murray** and **Frank Morgan** are the Wizards that Dorothy and her new friends, the Scarecrow, the Tin Man and The Cowardly Lion seek to grant their wishes.

WLADISLAW, JOSEPH
THE DIRTY DOZEN (1967, GB, MGM)—**Charles Bronson** is the only one of 12 condemned G.I.'s who survives an assault on a chateau filled with Nazi brass.

WOFFINGTON, PEG
PEG OF OLD DRURY (1936, GB, Paramount)—Dublin-born **Anna Neagle** goes to Drury Theatre, and under the sponsorship of David Garrick becomes a famous actress.

THE WOLF MAN *See* LAWRENCE TALBOT

WOLF, CHARLIE
THE HALF-BREED (1952, RKO)—Half-breed Apache **Jack Buetel** hopes to be the instrument for bringing peace between the two races of which he is a part. Not a chance!

WOLFE, GREGORY
HARLEQUIN (1980, Australia, Hemdale/New Image)—Faith healer **Robert Powell** helps a politician's son who has leukemia, and finds the boy's mother romantically interested in him.

WOLFE, NERO
MEET NERO WOLFE (1936, Columbia)—Beer drinking, orchid growing detective **Edward Arnold** solves crimes without ever leaving his home.

WOLFF
SPACEHUNTER: ADVENTURES IN THE FORBIDDEN ZONE (1983, Columbia)—In this 3-D film, **Peter Strauss** is a mercenary salvage ship captain. He teams up with a young Molly Ringwald and others to search for three stranded girls on planet Terra Eleven.

WOLFINGER, AMBROSE
THE MAN ON THE FLYING TRAPEZE (1935, Paramount)—Put upon by his shrewish wife and everyone else in his world, except a sympathetic daughter, **W.C. Fields** is, nevertheless, able to turn the tables on his tormentors.

WOMAN
STRANGER IN HOLLYWOOD (1968, Roda/Emerson)—When **Sue Bernard** discovers oil, she moves to Hollywood to have a good time, but doesn't find much.

WON, BRUCE
THEY CALL ME BRUCE (1982, Film Ventures); THEY STILL CALL ME BRUCE (1987, Ji Hee-Pandia/Shapiro)—Comedian **Johnny Yune** stars in these two amusing spoofs of the Bruce Lee-Kung Fu movies.

WONDER, AL
WONDER BAR (1934, Warner Brothers)—**Al Jolson** is the owner of a Paris nightclub. Both he and band-singer Dick Powell are in love with the club's main attraction Dolores Del Rio.

WONG, JAMES LEE

MR. WONG, DETECTIVE (1938, Monogram); MR. WONG IN CHINATOWN (1939, Monogram); THE MYSTERIOUS MR. WONG (1939, Monogram)—**Boris Karloff** portrays Monogram's answer to Charlie Chan in routine detective stories.

WONG LOW GET

THE HATCHET MAN (1932, First National/Warner Brothers)—**Edward G. Robinson**, a powerful member of San Francisco's Chinese community, finds himself in the middle of Tong Wars, and has trouble with an unfaithful wife.

WONG, MR., MANDARIN

MYSTERIOUS MR. WONG (1935, Monogram)—**Bela Lugosi** is an oriental madman after the "twelve coins of Confucius."

WONG, SUZIE

THE WORLD OF SUZIE WONG (1960, Paramount)—Hong Kong prostitute **Nancy Kwan** seems as unaffected by her occupation as if she were a nun instead. She readily accepts artist William Holden's offer of a job as his model. Despite differences in race and class, they fall in love.

WONKA, WILLIE

WILLIE WONKA AND THE CHOCOLATE FACTORY (1971, Paramount) Candy-making wizard **Gene Wilder** allows five "lucky" youngsters free reign in his factory.

WOOD, PENNY

HER FIRST BEAU (1941, Columbia)—**Jane Withers** and Jackie Cooper are childhood sweethearts. When he becomes to busy for her, Withers is attracted to an older man, but soon discovers his intentions are too mature for her and returns to Cooper.

WOODHOUSE, ROSEMARY

ROSEMARY'S BABY (1968, Paramount)—**Mia Farrow** and her husband John Cassavetes fall in with a cult of Satanists. Farrow is impregnated by the devil, whose son she delivers.

WOODLEY

YOUNG WOODLEY (1930, GB, British International)—Schoolboy **Frank Lawton** falls in love with the beautiful young wife of an elderly pompous schoolmaster.

WOODNER, RICKI

TWO SMART PEOPLE (1946, MGM)—**Lucille Ball** teams with John Hodiak in a lame comedy of crook-chasing.

WOODROFFE, JASSY

JASSY (1948, GB, Gainsborough)—Gypsy **Margaret Lockwood** marries the owner of a manor. When he is poisoned, she is suspected, but later cleared, of his murder.

WOODRUFF, CLAIRE

WHEN LADIES MEET (1933, MGM); (1941, MGM)—**Ann Harding** and **Greer Garson** portray the wife of a publisher, who clashes with his novelist mistress in two enjoyable comedies.

WOODS, AL

ONIONHEAD (1958, Warner Brothers)—Love-sick Oklahoman **Andy Griffith** leaves college when his romance breaks up, joining the Coast Guard as a cook. His troubles include losing his hair.

WOODS, DARREN

EXPLORERS (1985, Paramount)—**Jason Presson** and his young friends have their wish for space travel fulfilled.

WOODS, JIMMY

THE WIZARD (1989, Universal)—He doesn't have much to say, but deeply traumatized **Luke Edwards** certainly is a wiz at video games.

WOODSON, BEN *See* **FRANK JAMES**

WOODSTOCK, SIR HENRY

OLD IRON (1938, British Lion)—Tyrannical shipping magnate **Tom Walls** disinherits his daughter because he disapproves of her marriage.

WOODY

CONDORMAN (1981, Disney/Buena Vista)—**Michael Crawford**, the comic-book artist who draws Condorman, becomes his own super hero when he is called on to deliver papers to a beautiful Russian agent from the CIA, and falls in love with her.

WOOLEY, GILBERT

THE GEISHA BOY (1958, Paramount)—**Jerry Lewis**, a clumsy magician in Korea to entertain the troops, finds himself adopted by a little oriental boy.

WOOLEY, WALLACE

I MARRIED A WITCH (1942, Paramount/UA)—**Fredric March's** Puritan ancestor had witch Veronica Lake and her father burned. In the 1940s the tree which held their spirits is struck by lighting, freeing them. Lake decides to take revenge by making her tormentor's descendant fall in love with her, and ruin his political career.

WORMOLD, JIM

OUR MAN IN HAVANA (1960, GB, Columbia)—Vacuum cleaner salesman **Alec Guinness**, living in Havana, Cuba, is recruited to be a spy for the British government. He fabricates his reports but they are believed both by his superiors and the Cubans.

WORRELL, ERNEST P.

ERNEST GOES TO CAMP (1987, Buena Vista); ERNEST SAVES CHRISTMAS (1988, Touchstone); ERNEST GOES TO JAIL (1990, Buena Vista); ERNEST SCARED STUPID (1991, Touchstone)—Only a child or a very secure adult is going to admit that they enjoy the annoying **Jim Varney**, "knowwhirlmean Vern?" In the first picture, he's a know-it-all handy-man who wishes to become a camp counselor. He gets a job overseeing a group of kid misfits. In the sequel, Goofy incarnate helps Santa save Christmas. In the best (and that's not saying a lot) of the "Ernest" films, Varney finds himself in prison when he's mistaken for a look-alike criminal. In a sort of perverted *Prince and the Pauper*, audiences are treated to the slapstick antics of the innocent behind bars and a sinister villain on the outside planning a bank robbery. In the last film, ignoring the warning of witch Eartha Kitt, Varney accidently unleashes a hairy, grotesque troll, played by Jonas Moscartolo. The latter turns kids into wooden voodoo dolls and brings scores of ghouls to life.

WORSHIP, DR. LEW

THE NEW INTERNS (1964, Columbia)—In this follow-up to THE INTERNS, **Dean Jones** is one of the new young doctors who must deal with life and death, and then, of course, there are some patients with problems as well.

WORTH, BARBARA *See* **LADY BARBARA SKELTON**

WORTH, BARBARA

THE WINNING OF BARBARA WORTH (1926, Silent, UA)—An eastern engineer comes west where he meets **Vilma Banky**, adopted daughter of a banker. They fall in love, but must contend with crooks who wish to swindle the settlers.

WORTH, PRUDENCE
ANGEL AND THE BADMAN (1947, Republic)—Quaker **Gail Russell** reforms western outlaw John Wayne in this lovely but slowed paced action-romance.

WORTH, TAYLOR
WORTH WINNING (1989, 20th Century Fox)—This stupid film is worth losing. **Tom Harmon** bets that he can get three women to accept his proposal of marriage. He wins, but it seems like losing.

WORTHING, DR. JOHN
MAN AND HIS WOMAN (1920, Silent, Pathe)—**Herbert Rawlinson** is a doctor ruined by alcohol and drug addiction.

WORTHING, NANCY
NANCY COMES HOME (1918, Silent, Triangle)—Home from school, **Myrtle Lind** is ignored by her parents. She sells some of her mother's clothes, hires a limousine and a chauffeur, and goes out on the town, where she gets involved in a shooting.

WORTHINGTON, MAJOR HENRY
THE SINGLE MAN (1919, GB, Silent, Ideal)—Old author **Cecil Mannering** marries a secretary after having flings with a flapper and a spinster.

WORTHINGTON, ROBIN
A SINGLE MAN (1929, Silent, MGM)—In this comedy, **Lew Cody** gets over his infatuation with a girl too young for him, and marries his secretary.

WOTAN, CHRIS
THE YOUNG SINNER (1965, United Screens)—High school athlete **Tom Laughlin** tells a priest about his sins; how his home is in shambles because of his alcoholic father; and how he's been put on probation at school—and then, of course, there are the girls.

WOTTERS, DR. ANN
SHE WENT TO THE RACES (1945, MGM)—In a B picture, singer **Frances Gifford** becomes involved with some professors who try to come up with a scientific way of placing bets on horseraces.

WOVERMAN, ANITA
THE WIFE TAKES A FLYER (1942, Columbia)—**Joan Bennett**, a Dutch woman nearing a divorce, provides shelter for British-based pilot Franchot Tone, downed over Nazi-occupied Holland during WWII.

WREN, LADY
LES GIRLS (1957, MGM)—**Kay Kendall**, now married to an English peer, writes her autobiography, telling about her life as part of a popular act featuring Gene Kelly, Mitzi Gaynor and Tania Elg. The latter's husband believes the revelations are just too candid, and institutes a libel suit against Kendall. This brings the four comrades together again as each remembers things differently.

WRIGHT, COLLIE AND WILLIAM
THE WINTER PEOPLE (1989, Columbia)—When the brutal father of her baby is accidently killed, unwed mother **Kelly McGillis** is forced to turn her child over to its paternal godfather, Mitchell Ryan, in order to prevent bloodshed in the feud between his family and that of her own father, **Lloyd Bridges**.

WRIGHT, ERNEST
THE CRACKSMAN (1963, GB, Warner Brothers-Pathe)—In this comedy, rival gangs combine to force locksmith **Charlie Drake** to steal museum jewels.

WRIGHT, EUGENE
IF A MAN ANSWERS (1962, Universal)—Sandra Dee decides to make her husband **Bobby Darin** jealous.

WRIGHT, JOAN
SUMMER LOVE (1958, Universal)—**Judy Meredith** is part of a musical group whose first job is at a co-ed summer camp.

WRIGHT, KAREN
THESE THREE (1936, UA)—**Merle Oberon** and her friend Miriam Hopkins open a school for the daughters of the rich. Her plans for the school and her love for a doctor, Joel McCrea, are all but destroyed by the viciousness of a student, Bonita Granville.

WRIGHT, WILL
NOBODY'S FOOL (1936, Universal)—New to the city, country bumpkin **Edward Everett Horton** becomes involved with racketeers trying to swindle an old lady.

WU, MR.
MR. WU (1919, GB, Silent, Stoll); (1927, Silent, MGM)—**Matheson Lang** and **Lon Chaney** are both properly menacing as the Oriental who murders his daughter rather than see her marry a man of a different race.

WU SIN
SECRETS OF WU SIN (1932, Invincible/Chesterfield)—Villain **Tetsu Komai** smuggles Chinese workers into Chinatown.

WYATT
EASY RIDER (1969, Columbia)—**Peter Fonda** and Dennis Hopper sell drugs, and use the money to motorcycle across the country to New Orleans. Both are killed by rednecks.

WYATT, COL. ED
SKY COMMANDO (1953, Columbia)—During WWII, fighter pilot squadron leader **Dan Duryea**, disliked by his men, proves himself on a dangerous mission over Rumania.

WYATT, MICHAEL
FRONTIER MARSHAL (1934, Fox)—**George O'Brien**, essentially portraying Wyatt Earp, brings law and order to a frontier town.

WYCKHAM, CHARLIE
CHARLEY'S AUNT (1941, 20th Century Fox)—In the third filming of the Brandon Thomas comedy, the studio changed the spelling of the name of **Richard Haydn's** character, whose missing aunt must be replaced by an Oxford student when two young ladies visiting Haydn and James Ellison need a chaperon.

WYCKOFF, EVELYN
GOOD LUCK, MISS WYCKOFF (1979, Bel Air-Gradison)—**Anne Heywood** is a mid-30s white schoolteacher, who has her first sexual experience when she is raped by a black janitor. Various physicians try to help her deal with the trauma, but the drama is lacking.

WYE, 2nd Lt. MERLE
THE HORIZONTAL LIEUTENANT (1962, MGM)—For the censors sake, **Jim Hutton** is conveniently knocked out each time he seems about to make it with nurse Paula Prentiss on a Pacific island in 1944.

WYKEHAM, CHARLEY

CHARLEY'S AUNT (1925, Silent, Cristie); CHARLEY'S AUNT (1930, Columbia); WHERE'S CHARLEY (1952, GB, Warner Brothers) **Jimmy Harrison** in 1925 and **Hugh Williams** in 1930 portray the Oxford undergraduate whose aunt from Brazil is impersonated by a classmate so young ladies may be entertained at the school, properly chaperoned. In the 1952 musical, **Ray Bolger** handles the chore himself and sings "Once In Love With Amy."

WYLIE, MAGGIE

WHAT EVERY WOMAN KNOWS (1917, GB, Silent, Lucoque)— (1921, Silent, Paramount); (1934, MGM)-**Hilda Trevelyan Lois Wilson** and **Helen Hayes** all help their politician husband's career by smoothing off the rough edges of his incredibly bad judgement.

WYMAN, DIANA

THE MOTH (1934, Showmen's Pictures)—Ding-a-ling heiress **Sally O'Neill** lives beyond her means, then deserts her family after creating a scandal. Things begin to turn around for her in New Orleans during Mardi Gras.

WYNANT, CLYDE

THE THIN MAN (1934, MGM)—Although in all sequels the title "Thin Man" will refer to detective Nick Charles, in the first of the series it denotes the murder victim of the piece, a scientist played by **Edward Ellis**.

WYNDHAM, NINA

DOCTOR'S WIVES (1931, Fox)—In this dismal film, **Joan Bennett** demonstrates how dreary it can be to be the wife of a successful physician, Warner Baxter.

WYNGATE, CAPT. JAMES

THE SQUAW MAN (1914, Silent, Lasky); (1918, Silent, Paramount); (1931, MGM)—**Dustin Farnum** starred in this first feature-length film made in Hollywood. It's the creaky story of an English gentleman who marries an American Indian and earns the derisive name of the title. In the 1918 remake, Elliott Dexter had the title role, but his character's name was spelled Wynnegate and he also went by the name Jim Carsten. In 1931 (we hope) Warner Baxter put the character to rest.

WYNN, LILY

LILY IN LOVE (1985, New Line Cinema)—In this disguised version of THE GUARDSMAN, egotistical actor Christopher Plummer disguises himself as an Italian, and pays court to his wife **Maggie Smith**.

WYNN, MARIE

MY HUSBAND'S WIVES (1924, Silent, Fox)—**Evelyn Brent** is invited to visit Shirley Mason, not knowing that the latter was married to the former's husband.

suspects jewel thief Robert Montgomery of being the culprit, so to save himself. Montgomery tracks down Mudie.

X, MADAME *See* JACQUELINE (FLEURIOT)

X, MOLLY *See* MOLLY X

X-27

DISHONORED (1931, Paramount)—**Marlene Dietrich**, the widow of a WWI officer, has become a streetwalker. She is recruited to spy for the Austrians. She falls in love with a Russian agent, is tried for treason by the Austrians, and goes to her death in front of a firing squad.

XAVIER, D. JAMES

"X"—THE MAN WITH X-RAY EYES (1963, American International)—Scientist **Ray Milland** uses himself as his guinea pig, trying X-ray vision eyedrops with horrifying results. He sees through skin, making it a breeze to diagnose a patient's illness. As time passes his sight gets stronger and stronger, allowing him to see to "infinity" and this is torture.

XAVIER, DOCTOR

DOCTOR X (1932, Warner Brothers)—Police suspect scientific researcher **Lionel Atwill** of cannibalistic murders. Actually, it is his assistant, Preston Foster, the discoverer of the secret of eternal life, who is behind the murders. To prepare for work, he covers his body with synthetic flesh giving himself most unusual powers.

XAVIER, DR. MAURICE

THE RETURN OF DR. X (1939, Warner Brothers)—**Humphrey Bogart** is Marshall Quesne, alias Dr. Xavier, an executed murderer, brought back to life as a blood sucking vampire. Bogie's make-up is a scream.

XAVIER, VAL

THE FUGITIVE KIND (1960, UA)—Drifter **Marlon Brando** arrives in a small Mississippi town and raises sexual havoc with two women, middle-aged Italian born Anna Magnani, the wife of a dying man, and Joanne Woodward, the alcoholic, nymphomaniac daughter of a wealthy family.

XENOBIA, MS.

DR. ALIEN (1989, Phantom)—Nerdish teen Billy Jacoby is selected for some extra-credit research after school by lucious substitute biology teache **Judy Landers**. The sexy teacher is actually an alien who turns Jacoby into an irresitible stud.

X

X, MR.

THE MYSTERY OF MR. X (1934, MGM)—**Leonard Mudie** is a maniacal killer just released from prison after serving 15 years. He goes on a killing spree of London police officers. Scotland Yard

Y

YADWIGA

ENEMIES, A LOVE STORY (1989, 20th Century Fox)—Believing his wife Anjelica Huston is dead, holocaust survivor Ron Silver marries Polish servant girl **Margaret Sophie Stein** and moves to New York. She thinks she's seen a ghost when Silver's first wife Huston shows up. She's not very happy about his third wife, Lena Olin, either.

YAKUSHOVA, LENA See **NINOTCHKA**

YAMAMOTO
THOSE MAGNIFICENT MEN IN THEIR FLYING MACHINES (1965, GB, 20th Century Fox)—**Yujiro Ishihara** is the Japanese entry in the international air race from London to Paris for a $25,000 prize.

YANCEY, ROBERT
THE VANISHING VIRGINIAN (1941, MGM)—In this charming family movie **Frank Morgan** is the father of a nice respectable southern family to which nothing very exciting happens.

YANG, GENERAL
THE GENERAL DIED AT DAWN (1936, Paramount)—Brutal Chinese warlord **Akim Tamiroff's** attempt to conquer the peasants of the region is resisted by American soldier of fortune, Gary Cooper.

YARNO, KATYA
LADY BEWARE (1987, International Video Entertainment)—Window dresser **Diane Lane's** kinky arrangements attract the attention of a demented sex-maniac. Lane was the lovely youngster in A LITTLE ROMANCE. How sad that she has grown up to appear in such trash.

YATELY, TOM
HELL DRIVERS (1958, GB, Rank)—Fresh from prison, **Stanley Baker** takes a dangerous job driving decrepit trucks over equally bad roads. Since so many loads have to be carried each day, it's no place for the careful.

YATES
PEACEMAKER (1990, Fries)—**Robert Forster** claims to be an alien cop when he crash lands on Earth. With him is Lance Edwards, who Forster insists is an intergalactic serial killer he's taking in. Funny, Edwards tells the same story, with the roles reversed.

YATES, ANDREW
HANDY ANDY (1934, Fox)—Druggist **Will Rogers's** wife has social aspirations. She convinces him to sell his business to a chain. He tries to keep himself busy with hobbies while his wife is making a fool of herself in high society.

YATES, ELINOR
SISTERS UNDER THE SKIN (1934, Columbia)—This B picture is the not-too-interesting tale of a romantic triangle involving **Doris Lloyd**, her husband Frank Morgan and an actress, Elissa Landi.

YATES, JENNY
CHATTERBOX (1936, RKO)—Stagestruck **Anne Shirley** arrives in New York from Vermont ready to take show business by storm, but her Broadway debut is a bust. Luckily she finds romantic happiness to soften the blow.

YATES, OLIVER
GOOD LUCK, MR. YATES (1943, Columbia)—**Jess Barker**, a teacher at a military school, tries to enlist but is rejected because of a punctured eardrum. He is reluctant to return to his job and face his students. Instead, he takes a job in a defense plant. He corresponds with his students with the help of a soldier, pretending he's in the service. Before long his deception begins to unravel and he's even suspected of being a Nazi spy. All ends well, of course.

YELLOW HAIR
YELLOW HAIR AND THE FORTUNES OF GOLD (1984, Crown)—To find a hidden fortune, a princess must find a strange man, **Laurence Landon**, who lives in an elk's horn.

YELLOWBEARD
YELLOWBEARD (1983, Orion)—Monty Python's **Graham Chapman** is a villainous pirate looking for a treasure he buried years earlier. It's not good Monty Python nor is it good adventure material.

YELLOWLEG
THE DEADLY COMPANIONS (1961, Pathe-American)—When gunslinger **Brian Keith** accidentally kills Maureen O'Hara's son, he feels some obligation to guide her through hostile Indian territory.

YEN, GENERAL
THE BITTER TEA OF GENERAL YEN (1933, Columbia)—While his prisoner, American missionary Barbara Stanwyck falls in love with Chinese warlord **Nils Asther**. The pair are punished for even the possibility of miscegenation by having Asther die.

YENTL
YENTL (1983, MGM/UA)—Russian Jew **Barbra Streisand** is so eager for an education, she cuts her hair and poses as a male, so she may enter a school. Her thirst for knowledge is complicated when she secretly falls in love with Mandy Patinkin and finds herself forced to marry Amy Irving.

YOKUM, LI'L ABNER
LI'L ABNER (1940, RKO); (1959, Paramount)—**Granville Owens** had the dopey look one had come to expect of Al Capp's Dogpatch hero. He continues to elude Martha O'Driscoll as Daisy Mae, who has plans for their marriage. In 1959, ex-college football player **Peter Palmer** appeared in the musical production in which the U.S. plans to drop an atomic bomb on Dogpatch, the most useless place in the United States.

YOLANDA
YOLANDA AND THE THIEF (1945, MGM)—Having just enough plot to frame the dance numbers, the film sees Fred Astaire convince naive wealthy South American **Lucille Bremer** that he's her guardian angel. He plans to con her out of some money, but the real guardian angel whom she's been praying for shows up.

YORGA, COUNT
COUNT YORGA, VAMPIRE (1970, American International)—THE RETURN OF COUNT YORGA (1971, American International)—**Robert Quarry** is a modern vampire flying around Los Angeles. The film made so much money that a quick sequel was made and it looked it. In it Quarry stalks an orphanage for his favorite refreshment.

YORK, ALVIN C.
SERGEANT YORK (1941, Warner Brothers)—**Gary Cooper** won an Academy Award for his portrayal of a hell-raising mountain man, who gets religion. He is drafted into WWI even though he claims to be a conscientious objector. He decides that fighting the war is something that he should do, and goes on to become the most decorated American soldier of the war.

YORK, EDDIE
PARDON MY PAST (1945, Columbia)—Unsuspecting **Fred MacMurray** is taken for his exact double, a shady playboy. He is expected to pay the man's debts.

YORKE, ALEXANDER
SATAN'S SLAVE (1976, GB, Crown)—**Michael Gough**, the leader of a coven of witches, plans to use an accident victim in a ceremony to ressurrect a dead witch.

YORKE, DR. DAVID

THE MAN CALLED BACK (1932, Tiffany)—**Conrad Nagel**, who has a drinking problem, helps the wife of a suicide, who made it appear that she killed him.

YORKE, SHIRLEY

THE STORY OF SHIRLEY YORKE (1948, GB, Butchers)—Nurse **Dinah Sheridan** must provide medical treatment and company for the wife of a man who once jilted her. When the wife is found dead, Sheridan is arrested and tried for murder, but her boss, John Robinson, proves her innocent and unmasks the real killer to boot.

YORKE, SPENCER

THE COWBOY STAR (1936, Columbia)—Movie cowboy **Charles Starrett** is fed up with Hollywood. He flees to Arizona where he buys a ranch, courts a local beauty and rescues a kidnapped child.

YOUNG, BILLY

YOUNG BILLY YOUNG (1969, UA)—Hired killer **Robert Walker, Jr.** teams up with Robert Mitchum, when the latter is named marshal of Lordsburg. Later Walker is left in charge of the town as deputy marshal.

YOUNG, BRIGHAM

BRIGHAM YOUNG, FRONTIERSMAN (1940, 20th Century Fox)—**Dean Jagger** is superb as the follower of Joseph Smith, founder of the Mormans. When the Mormans are driven out of one settlement after another and Joseph Smith, played by Vincent Price, is killed, Jagger leads them across the country until they reach the Great Salt Lake where he announces "This is the place."

YOUNG, JERRY

THE EAGLE AND THE HAWK (1933, Paramount)—**Fredric March**, an ace pilot in the Royal Flying Squadron, has seen too many of his friends and comrades killed in the skies. Disillusioned, March kills a German ace in an engagement in the sky, but loses his observer, a green kid. When he returns, he goes to his room and kills himself.

YOUNG, LARRY

ALIAS MIKE MORAN (1919, Silent, Paramount)—Shirker **Wallace Reid** hires an ex-convict to take his place in the draft during WWI. After his stand-in dies a hero's death, Reid reforms, joins the Canadian Army, fights valiantly and loses a hand.

YOUNG, MISS

CHINA GIRL (1942, 20th Century Fox)—**Gene Tierney**, a Chinese beauty with an American education, resides in Mandalay just prior to the Japanese attack on Pearl Harbor. She helps a newsreel cameraman with military information escape the clutches of Japanese agents.

YOUNG, NORMAN

I ADORE YOU (1933, GB, Warner Brothers/First National)—In a musical comedy, **Harold French** falls in love with film star Margot Grahame, whom he wins when he buys up the failing production company for which she works.

YOUNG, PATRICIA

FORGOTTEN WOMEN (1932, Monogram)—**Marion Schilling**, a publisher's daughter, is a rival of stage star Virginia Lee Corbin for reporter Rex Bell. Although Shilling gets most of his attention throughout the film, he chooses Corbin in the end.

YOUNGBLOOD

YOUNGBLOOD (1978, American International)—**Bryan O'Dell**, a young black living in the Los Angeles ghetto, learns the gang life.

When a friend dies of a drug overdose, the gang goes after the pushers, who include O'Dell's older brother.

YOUNGBLOOD, DEAN

YOUNGBLOOD (1986, MGM/UA)—**Rob Lowe** is a troubled, sensitive teenager and a hockey star. Its a not very effective rip-off of ROCKY.

YOUNGER, COLE, BOB, JIM & JOHN

BAD MEN OF MISSOURI (1941, First National/Warner Brothers)—**Dennis Morgan, Wayne Morris** and **Arthur Kennedy**; COLE YOUNGER, GUNFIGHTER (1958, Allied Artists)—**Frank Lovejoy**; RETURN OF THE BADMEN (1948, RKO)—**Steve Brodie**; THE YOUNGER BROTHERS (1949, Warner Brothers)—**Wayne Morris, James Brown, Bruce Bennett** and **Robert Hutton**; THE LONG RIDERS (1980, UA)—**David, Keith** and **Robert Carradine** and **Kevin Brophy**;—Hollywood has shown a lot of interest in western badmen including the four Younger brothers. Not all four are featured in all of the films, but one could count on Cole and Bob to rob a bank and shoot it out with the law.

YUKI

A JAPANESE NIGHTINGALE (1918, Silent, Pathe)—Little Japanese girl **Fannie Ward's** heartless stepmother wishes Ward to marry a vicious wealthy, old man. Ward runs away, becomes a Geisha girl and meets a young American who falls in love with her. They marry but happiness must wait as the film sifts through a series of plots and subplots.

YVETTE

THE VIRGIN AND THE GYPSY (1970, GB, Chevron)—Rector's daughter **Joanna Shimkus** takes up with amoral gypsy Franco Nero.

YVONNE

LADIES OF THE MOB (1928, Silent, Paramount)—**Clara Bow**, the daughter of a man electrocuted when she was a child, has been raised by her mother to be a crook. Fearing that her lover and partner in crime will end up like her father, she shoots him in the shoulder when he tries to get involved in a bank robbery. They give themselves up, pay their debt to society and start a new life.

Z

ZACK

TWO OF A KIND (1983, 20th Century Fox)—God is fed up with the human race but four angels argue to spare them. But the two examples they use to make their argument aren't the best. **John Travolta** is an inventor turned bank robber and Olivia Newton-John is a less than innocent bank teller.

ZACHARIAH

ZACHARIAH (1971, ABC Pictures)—In the 1870s, **John Rubinstein** kills a man, decides he wishes to be the fastest gun in the West, kills a black outlaw, and takes up with the deceased's gang. He ultimately is put on the straight and narrow by an old man.

ZACHARY, RACHEL

THE UNFORGIVEN (1960, UA)—**Audrey Hepburn** is claimed as the daughter of the family of Lillian Gish, Burt Lancaster and Audie

Murphy, but Indians attack their homestead claiming she's one of theirs. Other whites would like to see her given up to the red men.

ZACK, SGT.

THE STEEL HELMET (1951, Lippert)—In his best role and one of the better war movies, **Gene Evans** is a cold tough non-com during the Korean War. He is helped by a small boy when everyone else in his platoon is wiped out by a sniper. The boy tags along with Evans, much to his annoyance. Later when a North Korean officer causes the boy's death, Evans' feelings for his young friend come to the surface.

ZADOR, ANNA (BRIGITTA)

I MARRIED AN ANGEL (1942, MGM)—**Jeanette MacDonald** is a shy employee of bored rich Budapest playboy Nelson Eddy. All of the eligible society ladies are mad to get him to marry them. During a dream, Eddy imagines MacDonald to be an angel who has come to marry him. When he awakens, Eddy knows what to do. This was the last film teaming Eddy and MacDonald.

ZAGON

THE BEAST OF BUDAPEST (1958, Bailene/Allied Artists)—**Gerald Milton** rules Hungary with an iron hand. He survives the Revolution of 1956, when Hungarians attempted to break free of Russian domination.

ZAIDA

SHE'S A SHEIK (1927, Silent, Paramount)—**Bebe Daniels**, born of a Spanish mother and an Arabian father, insists she will only have a Christian husband, which doesn't sit well with a desert sheik who insists he will have her.

ZAIRA

GUERILLA GIRL (1953, UA)—Gypsy girl **Marianna** has an affair with Greek officer Helmut Dantine. He has fled Athens when the Germans invaded the country. She is a member of the communist revolutionaries and tries to warn her lover that he's on a communist death list, but both are shot and killed.

ZALESKA, COUNTESS MARYA

DRACULA'S DAUGHTER (1936, Universal)—Dracula's daughter **Gloria Holden** wishes to resist the urge to follow her father's way of life but, you see it's in her blood.

ZAMIN, ALI *See* CAPT. RAND

ZANDER

ZANDER THE GREAT (1925, Silent, MGM)—When his mother dies in an orphanage, Marion Davies takes **Master Jack Huff** West to search for the boy's father.

ZANY, JOE

MILLIONAIRE PLAYBOY (1940, RKO)—Every time millionaire's son **Joe Penner** kisses a girl, he gets a bad case of the hiccups. His father hires a psychologist to cure Penner. The analyst takes Penner to a resort filled with beautiful girls to undertake his cure.

ZAPATA, EMILIANO

VIVA ZAPATA! (1952, 20th Century Fox)—**Marlon Brando** stars as the Mexican revolutionary and one time President, betrayed and gunned down in a hail of bullets.

ZARDOZ

ZARDOZ (1974, GB, 20th Century Fox)—Actually Zardoz is a giant head worshipped by a group of Earthlings in the year 2293 A.D., but

Niall Buggy resides in the head and uses it for his own ends until Sean Connery settles his hash.

ZAWISTOWSKA, SOPHIE

SOPHIE'S CHOICE (1982, Universal)—**Meryl Streep** won an Oscar for her performance as a Polish Christian who, when sent to a German concentration camp, had to choose which of her two children would live and which would die. She loses both of them. Years later she lives in Brooklyn, falls in love with Kevin Kline, but he has so many problems, the two commit suicide.

ZAZA

ZAZA (1939, Paramount)—French music hall performer **Claudette Colbert** falls in love with married Herbert Marshall. Colbert is endearing and does her own singing but the drama is ho-hum.

ZEDDMORE, WINSTON

GHOSTBUSTERS (1984, Columbia): GHOSTBUSTERS II (1989, Columbia)—**Ernie Hudson** joins three zany college professors to form a business which captures ghosts and keeps them trapped in specially designed vaults. In the sequel, he's required to play the stereotype of the scared black, usually associated with Step'n Fetchit and Mantand Moreland.

ZELIG, LEONARD

ZELIG (1983, Orion)—**Woody Allen** portrays a chamelon-like character, who becomes a celebrity in the crazy 1920s. Director Allen has cleverly used newsreel footage of famous occurrences in which his character appears.

ZELLY (MADEMOISELLE)

ZELLY AND ME (1988, Columbia)—Little orphan Alexandra Johnes is being raised by her rich, strange grandmother Glynis Johns. The latter sometimes lets Alexandra do whatever she pleases, but this is soon followed by the child being forced to her knees to beg forgiveness for minor infractions. The child's nanny, **Isabella Rossellini**, who befriends the child, is rather strange herself, having something of a fixation with Joan of Arc.

ZENDI

SIREN OF BAGDAD (1953, Columbia)—**Patricia Medina's** father is a deposed sultan in this comedy-adventure film. Paul Henreid and Hans Conreid help her regain her rightful place in Bagdad society.

ZENIA, GRAND DUCHESS

THE GRAND DUCHESS AND THE WAITER (1926, Silent, Paramount)—Millionaire Adolphe Menjou becomes infatuated with Grand Duchess **Florence Vidor**. Unable to meet her, he poses as a waiter, whom she hires him for her personal staff. In spite of herself, she falls in love with him.

ZENA

THE NEW YORK PEACOCK (1917, Silent, Fox)—Vamp **Valeika Suratt** lures businssmen into letting a munitions cartel obtain their factories.

ZERO, MR.

KILLER AT LARGE (1936, Columbia)—**Henry Brandon** is a detective chasing a murderer who turns out to be himself.

ZHIVAGO, YURI

DR. ZHIVAGO (1965, MGM)—Physician and poet **Omar Sharif** is a witness and reluctant participant in the Russian Revolution and the

Battle between the Red and White Russians that follows. He's married to Geraldine Chaplin, but his passion is Julie Christie.

ZIEGFELD, FLORENZ
THE GREAT ZIEGFELD (1936, MGM); THE ZIEGFELD FOLLIES (1945, MGM)—The 1936 movie is an elaborate and mostly fictitious account of the life and loves of the great showman. It is filled with memorable production numbers. **William Powell** is admirable in the role. In the 1945 film, Powell reprises his part, this time from heaven as he imagines whom among the "new" stars he would feature if he put on one last follies. Audiences see the results.

ZINA
ZINA (1985, Film Forum)—The obsessions of Leon Trotsky's daughter **Domiziana Giorodano** are explored while she is in psychoanalysis.

ZITO, FRANK
MANIAC (1980, Magnum)—Schizophrenic killer **Joe Spivak** murders women, scalps them and puts their bloody hair on manequins that grace his filthy apartment.

ZOLA, EMILE
THE LIFE OF EMILE ZOLA (1937, Warner Brothers); I ACCUSE (1958, GB, MGM)—**Paul Muni** and **Emlyn Williams** impersonate the great French writer who intervenes in the infamous Dreyfus case in which a Jewish officer is sentenced to Devil's Island for treason even though it's well known that another officer is the traitor.

ZORBA, ALEXIS
ZORBA THE GREEK (1964, 20th Century Fox)—Gregarious Greek **Anthony Quinn** befriends English writer Alan Bates on Crete. Years later, Quinn would take up the role again in a Broadway musical version of the story.

ZORRO (DON DIEGO VEGA)
MARK OF ZORRO (1920, Silent, UA)—**Douglas Fairbanks**; DON Q, SON OF ZORRO (1925, Silent, UA)—**Douglas Fairbanks**; BOLD CABALLERO (1936, Republic)—**Robert Livingston**; MARK OF ZORRO (1940, 20th Century Fox)—**Tyrone Power**; THE SIGN OF ZORRO (1960, Buena Vista)—**Guy Williams**; ZORRO THE GAY BLADE (1981, 20th Century Fox)—**George Hamilton**—The story of the son of a Spanish California aristocratic family who, upon his return from school in Spain, finds a tyrant oppressing the people, and becomes the masked avenger Zorro has been brought to the screen with considerable success starting with the acrobatic Douglas Fairbanks, followed by stalwart Robert Livingston, then with dashing Tyrone Power in the dual role of the ineffective dandy Don Diego Vega and the bold swordsman Zorro, to be followed by Guy Williams who found success in the role on TV and finally with George Hamilton just a bit effeminate.

THE
FILMS

A

AARON LOVES ANGELA (1975, Columbia)
Aaron—Kevin Hooks
Angela—Irene Cara
Director—Gordon Parks, Jr.
Leading Players—Robert Hooks, Emestine Jackson, Leon
Pinkney, Wanda Velez, Lou Quinones

AARON SLICK FROM PUNKIN CRICK (1952, Paramount)
Aaron Slick—Alan Young
Director—Claude Binyon
Leading Players—Dinah Shore, Robert Merrill, Adele Jergens,
Minerva Urecal, Martha Stewart

ABBOTT AND COSTELLO MEET CAPTAIN KIDD (1952, Warner
Brothers)
Captain Kidd—Charles Laughton
Director—Charles Lamont
Leading Players—Bud Abbott, Lou Costello, Hillary Brooke,
Fran Warren, Bill Shirley, Leif Erickson

ABBOTT AND COSTELLO MEET DR. JEKYLL AND MR. HYDE
(1954, Universal)
Dr. Henry Jekyll—Boris Karloff
Mr. Hyde—Eddie Parker
Director—Charles Lamont
Leading Players—Bud Abbott, Lou Costello, Craig Stevens,
Helen Wescott, Reginald Denny

ABBOTT AND COSTELLO MEET FRANKENSTEIN (1948,
Universal)
Frankenstein's Monster—Glenn Strange
Director—Charles T. Barton
Leading Players—Bud Abbott, Lou Costello, Lon Chaney, Jr.,
Bela Lugosi, Lenore Aubert, Jane Randolph

ABBOTT AND COSTELLO MEET THE INVISIBLE MAN (1951,
Universal)
Tommy Nelson—Arthur Franz
Director—Charles Lamont
Leading Players—Bud Abbott, Lou Costello, Nancy Guild, Adele
Jergens, Sheldon Leonard

**ABBOTT AND COSTELLO MEET THE KILLER, BORIS
KARLOFF** (1949, Universal)
Melton—Alan Mowbray
Director—Charles T. Barton
Leading Players—Bud Abbott, Lou Costello, Boris Karloff,
Lenore Aubert, Gar Moore, Donna Martell

ABBOTT AND COSTELLO MEET THE MUMMY—(1955,
Universal)
Kharis—Edwin Parker
Director—Charles Lamont
Leading Players—Bud Abbott, Lou Costello, Marie Windsor,
Michael Ansara, Dan Seymour, Kurt Katch

ABBY (1974, American International)
Abby Williams—Carol Speed
Director—William Girdler
Leading Players—William Marshall, Terry Carter, Austin Stoker,
Juanita Moore, Charles Kissinger

ABDUL THE DAMNED (1935, GB, British International)
Abdul Hamid II—Fritz Kortner
Director—Karl Grune
Leading Players—Nils Asther, Adrienne Ames, John Stuart,
Walter Rilla, Charles Carson

ABDULLA'S HAREM (1956, GB, Sonofilms)
Abdulla—Gregory Ratoff
Director—Gregory Ratoff
Leading Players—Kay Kendall, Sydney Chaplin, Marina Berti

ABE LINCOLN IN ILLINOIS (1940, RKO)
Abraham Lincoln—Raymond Massey
Director—John Cromwell
Leading Players—Gene Lockhart, Ruth Gordon, Mary Howard,
Dorothy Tree, Harvey Stephens, Minor Watson

ABIE'S IRISH ROSE (1928, Part-talkie, Paramount)
Abie Levy—Charles Rogers
Rosemary Murphy—Nancy Carroll
Director—Victor Fleming
Leading Players—Jean Hersholt, J. Farrell MacDonald, Bernard
Gorcey, Ida Kramer, Nick Cogley

ABIE'S IRISH ROSE (1946, UA)
Abie Levy—Richard Norris
Rosemary Murphy—Joanne Dru
Director—Edward Sutherland
Leading Players—Michael Chekhov, J.M. Kerrigan, George E.
Stone, Vera Gordon, Emory Parnell, Art Baker

THE ABLEMINDED LADY (1922, Silent, Pacific Film)
Widow McGee—Helen Raymond
Director—Ollie Sellers
Leading Players—Henry B. Walthall, Elinor Fair

THE ABOMINABLE DR. PHIBES (1971, American International)
Dr. Anton Phibes—Vincent Price
Director—Robert Fuest
Leading Players—Joseph Cotten, Hugh Griffith, Terry-Thomas,
Virginia North, Audrey Woods

ABOUT MRS. LESLIE (1954, Paramount)
Mrs. Vivien Leslie—Shirley Booth
Director—Daniel Mann
Leading Players—Robert Ryan, Marjie Millar, Alex Nicol

ABOVE THE LAW (1988, Warner Brothers)
Nico Toscani—Steven Seagal
Director—Andrew Davis
Leading Players—Henry Silva, Pam Grier, Sharon Stone

ABRAHAM LINCOLN (1930, UA)
Abraham Lincoln—Walter Huston
Director—D.W. Griffith
Leading Players—Una Merkel, Kay Hammond, E. Alyn Warren,
Hobart Bosworth, Henry B. Walthall

ABROAD WITH TWO YANKS (1944, UA)
Biff Koraski—William Bendix
Jeff Reardon—Dennis O'Keefe
Director—Allan Dwan
Leading Players—Helen Walker, John Loder, Janet Lambert

THE ABSENT-MINDED PROFESSOR (1961, Walt Disney)
Prof. Ned Brainard—Fred MacMurray

Director—Robert Stevenson
Leading Players—Nancy Olsen, Keenan Wynn, Tommy Kirk, Leon Ames, Elliott Reid, Edward Andrews

ABSOLUTE BEGINNERS (1986, GB, Orion)
Colin—Eddie O'Connell
Suzette—Patsy Kensit
Director—Julien Temple
Leading Players—David Bowie, James Fox, Ray Davies, Mandy Rice-Davies

THE ABYSMAL BRUTE (1923, Silent, Universal)
Pat Glendon, Jr.—Reginald Denny
Director—Hobart Henley
Leading Players—Mabel Julienne Scott, Charles French, Hayden Stevenson, David Torrence

THE ACCIDENTAL TOURIST (1988, Warner Brothers)
Macon Leary—William Hurt
Director—Lawrence Kasdan
Leading Players—Kathleen Turner, Geena Davis, Robert Gorman, Amy Wright, Bill Pullman

ACCOMPLICE (1946, Producers Releasing Corp.)
Joyce Bonniwell—Veda Ann Borg
Director—Walter Colmes
Leading Players—Richard Arlen, Tom Dugan, Michael Branden

ACCORDING TO MRS. HOYLE (1951, Monogram)
Mrs. Hoyle—Spring Byington
Director -Jean Yarborough
Leading Players—Anthony Caruso, Brett King, Tanis Chandler

ACCUSED (1936, GB, Criterion/UA)
Gaby Seymour—Dolores Del Rio
Director—Thornton Freeland
Leading Players—Douglas Fairbanks, Jr., Florence Desmond, Basil Sydney, Athole Stewart

ACCUSED (1949, Paramount)
Wilma Tuttle—Loretta Young
Director—William Dieterle
Leading Players—Robert Cummings, Wendell Corey, Sam Jaffe, Douglas Dick, Suzanne Dalbert

ACCUSED, THE (1988, Paramount)
Sarah Tobias—Jodie Foster
Director—Jonathan Kaplan
Leading Players—Kelly McGillis, Lee Rossi, Carmen Argenziano, Ann Hearn

ACCUSED OF MURDER (1974, Republic)
Stan—Warren Stevens
Director—Joseph Kane
Leading Players—David Brian, Vera Ralston, Sidney Blackmer

ACE ELI AND RODGER OF THE SKY (1973, 20th Century Fox)
Eli—Cliff Robertson
Rodger—Eric Shea
Director—Bill Sampson
Leading Players—Pamela Franklin, Rosemary Murphy, Bernadette Peters, Alice Ghostley

ACE OF ACES (1933, RKO)
Lt. Rex Thorne—Richard Arlen
Director—Walter Ruben

Leading Players—Elizabeth Allan, Ralph Bellamy, Bill Cagney

ACES HIGH (1977, GB, Cine Artists/EMI)
Gresham—Malcolm McDowell
Sinclair—Christopher Plummer
Crawford—Simon Ward
Croft—Peter Firth
Director—Jack Gold
Leading Players—John Gielgud, Trevor Howard, Ray Milland, Richard Johnson, David Wood

ACQUITTED (1929, Columbia)
Marian—Margaret Livingston
Director—Frank Strayer
Leading Players—Lloyd Hughes, Sam Hardy, Charles West

ACTION JACKSON (1988, Lorimar)
Action Jackson—Carl Weathers
Director—Craig R. Baxley
Leading Players—Craig T. Nelson, Vanity, Sharon Stone

THE ACTRESS (1928, Silent, MGM)
Rose Trelawney—Norma Shearer
Director—Sidney Franklin
Leading Players—Owen Moore, Ralph Forbes, O.P. Heggie

THE ACTRESS (1953, MGM)
Ruth Gordon Jones—Jean Simmons
Director—George Cukor
Leading Players—Spencer Tracy, Teresa Wright, Anthony Perkins, Ian Wolfe, Kay Williams

ADA (1961, MGM)
Ada Gillis—Susan Hayward
Director—Daniel Mann
Leading Players—Dean Martin, Wilfrid Hyde-White, Ralph Meeker, Martin Balsam

ADAM AND EVA (1923, Silent, Paramount)
Adam Smith—T. Roy Barnes
Eva King—Marion Davies
Director—Robert G. Vignola
Leading Players—Tom Lewis, William Norris, Percy Ames

ADAM AND EVELYNE (1950, GB, Rank/Two Cities)
Adam Black—Stewart Granger
Evelyne Wallace—Jean Simmons
Director—Harold French
Leading Players—Edwin Styles, Raymond Young, Helen Cherry

ADAM AND EVIL (1927, Silent, MGM)
Adam Trevelyan—Lew Cody
Director—Robert Z. Leonard
Leading Players—Aileen Pringle, Gwen Lee, Gertrude Short

ADAM AT 6 A.M. (1970, Solar/National General)
Adam Gaines—Michael Douglas
Director—Robert Scheerer
Leading Players—Lee Purcell, Joe Don Baker, Charles Aidman

ADAM BEDE (1918, Silent; GB, International Exclusives)
Adam Bede—Bransby Williams
Director—Maurice Elvey
Leading Players—Ivy Close, Malvina Longfellow, Gerald Ames

ADAM HAD FOUR SONS (1941, Columbia)
Adam Stoddard—Warner Baxter
Jack Stoddard—Richard Denning
David Stoddard—Johnny Downs
Chris Stoddard—Robert Shaw
Philip Stoddard—Charles Lind
Director—Gregory Ratoff
Leading Players—Ingrid Bergman, Susan Hayward, Fay Wray, Helen Westley

ADAM'S RIB (1923, Silent, Paramount)
Mrs. Michael Ramsay—Anna Q. Nilsson
Director—Cecil B. De Mille
Leading Players—Milton Sills, Elliott Dexter, Theodore Kosloff, Pauline Garon

ADAM'S RIB (1949, MGM)
Amanda Bonner—Katharine Hepburn
Adam Bonner—Spencer Tracy
Director—George Cukor
Leading Players—Judy Holliday, Tom Ewell, David Wayne, Jean Hagen

ADAM'S WOMAN (1972, Australia, Warner Brothers)
Bess—Jane Merrow
Adam—Beau Bridges
Director—Phillip Leacock
Leading Players—James Booth, Andrew Keir, Tracy Reed

THE ADDAMS FAMILY (1991, Paramount)
Morticia Addams—Anjelica Huston
Gomez Addams—Raul Julia
Uncle Fester Addams—Christopher Lloyd
Granny Addams—Judith Malina
Wednesday Addams—Christina Ricci
Pugsley Addams—Jimmy Workman
Director—Barry Sonnenfield
Leading Players—Dan Hedaya, Elizabeth Wilson, Carel Struycken, Dana Ivey

ADELE (1919, Silent, UA)
Adele Bleneau—Kitty Gordon
Director—Wallace Worsley
Leading Players—Mahlon Hamilton

THE ADMIRABLE CRICHTON (1918, Silent, GB, Samuelson/Jury)
Crichton—Basil Gill
Director—G.B. Samuelson
Leading Players—Mary Dibley, James Lindsay, Lennox Pawle

THE ADMIRABLE CRICHTON (1957, GB, Columbia)
Bill Crichton—Kenneth More
Director—Lewis Gilbert
Leading Players—Diane Cilento, Cecil Parker, Sally Ann Howes, Martita Hunt, Jack Watling

THE ADMIRAL WAS A LADY (1950, UA)
Jean Madison—Wanda Hendrix
Director—Albert G. Rogell
Leading Players—Edmond O'Brien, Rudy Vallee, Johnny Sands, Steve Brodie, Richard Erdman, Hillary Brooke

THE ADMIRAL'S SECRET (1934, GB, Realart/RKO)
Admiral Pitzporter—Edmund Gwenn

Director—Guy Newall
Leading Players—James Raglan, Hope Davy, Aubrey Mather

THE ADOPTED SON (1917, Silent, Metro)
Two-Gun Carter—Francis X. Bushman
Director—Charles Brabin
Leading Players—Beverly Bayne, Leslie Stone, J.W. Johnston

THE ADORABLE CHEAT (1928, Silent, Chesterfield)
Marian Dorsey—Lila Lee
Director—Burton King
Leading Players—Cornelius Keefe, Burr McIntosh

THE ADORABLE DECEIVER (1926, Silent, Film Booking Offices)
Princess Sylvia—Alberta Vaughn
Director—Phil Rosen
Leading Players—Dan Marenko, Harlan Tucker, Frank Leigh

THE ADVENTURE OF THE ACTION HUNTERS (1987, Bonner/Troma)
Walter—Ronald Hunter
Betty—Sean Murphy
Director—Lee Bonner
Leading Players—Joseph Cimino, Art Donovan, Steve Beauchamp

THE ADVENTURE OF SHERLOCK HOLMES' SMARTER BROTHER (1975, GB, 20th Cent.)
Sigerson Holmes—Gene Wilder
Sherlock Holmes—Douglas Wilmer
Director—Gene Wilder
Leading Players—Madeline Kahn, Marty Feldman, Dom Deluise, Leo McKern, Roy Kinnear

THE ADVENTURER (1928, Silent, MGM)
Jim McClellan—Tim McCoy
Director—Viachetslav Tourjansky
Leading Players—Dorothy Sebastian, Charles Delaney

ADVENTURES IN BABYSITTING (1987, Buena Vista)
Chris Parker—Elisabeth Shue
Director—Chris Columbus
Leading Players—Maia Brewton, Keith Coogan, Anthony Rapp

ADVENTURES OF A PRIVATE EYE (1977, GB, Salon/Alpha)
Bob West—Christopher Neil
Director—Stanley Long
Leading Players—Suzy Kendall, Harry H. Corbett, Liz Fraser

ADVENTURES OF A ROOKIE (1943, RKO)
Jerry Miles—Wally Brown
Director—Leslie Goodwins
Leading Players—Alan Carney, Richard Martin, Margaret Landry

ADVENTURES OF A TAXI DRIVER (1976, GB, Salon/Alpha)
Joe North—Barry Evans
Director—Stanley Long
Leading Players—Judy Geeson, Adrienne Posta, Diana Dors

ADVENTURES OF A YOUNG MAN (1962, 20th Century Fox)
Nick Adams—Richard Beymer
Director—Martin Ritt
Leading Players—Diane Baker, Corinne Calvert, Dan Dailey, James Dunn, Juano Hernandez, Arthur Kennedy, Susan Strasberg, Eli Wallach, Paul Newman

THE ADVENTURES OF BARON MUNCHAUSEN (1989, Columbia/ Tri-Star)

    Baron Munchausen—John Neville
    Director—Terry Gilliam
    Leading Players—Eric Idle, Sarah Polley, Oliver Reed, Charles McKeown, Winston Dennis

ADVENTURES OF BARRY MCKENZIE (1972, Australia, Longford)

    Barry McKenzie—Barry Crocker
    Director—Bruce Beresford
    Leading Players—Barry Humphries, Paul Bertram, Dennis Price

THE ADVENTURES OF BUCKAROO BANZAI: ACROSS THE 8TH DIMENSION (1984, 20th Century Fox)

    Buckaroo Banzai—Peter Weller
    Director—W.D. Ritcher
    Leading Players—John Lithgow, Ellen Barkin, Jeff Goldblum, Christopher Lloyd, Rosalind Cash

THE ADVENTURES OF BULLWHIP GRIFFIN (1967, Disney/ Buena Vista)

    Bullwhip Griffin—Roddy McDowall
    Director—James Neilson
    Leading Players—Suzanne Pleshette, Karl Malden, Harry Guardino, Mike Mazurki

ADVENTURES OF CAPTAIN FABIAN (1951, Republic)

    Capt. Fabian—Errol Flynn
    Director—William Marshall
    Leading Players—Micheline Presle, Vincent Price, Agnes Moorehead, Victor Francen

ADVENTURES OF CASANOVA (1948, Eagle-Lion)

    Casanova—Arturo De Cordova
    Director—Roberto Galvadon
    Leading Players—Lucille Bremer, Turhan Bey, John Sutton

ADVENTURES OF DICK DOLAN (1917, Silent, GB, Broadwest)

    Dick Dolan—Basil Gil
    Director—Frank Wilson
    Leading Players—Violet Hopson, Ivy Close, John McMahon

ADVENTURES OF DON COYOTE (1947, Comet/UA)

    Don Coyote—Richard Martin
    Director—Reginald Leborg
    Leading Players—Frances Rafferty, Marc Cramer, Val Carlo

ADVENTURES OF DON JUAN (1949, Warner Brothers)

    Don Juan—Errol Flynn
    Director—Vincent Sherman
    Leading Players—Viveca Lindfors, Robert Douglas, Alan Hale, Romney Brent, Ann Rutherford

THE ADVENTURES OF FORD FAIRLANE (1990, 20th Century Fox/Silver)

    Ford Fairlane—Andrew Dice Clay
    Director—Renny Harlin
    Leading Players—Wayne Newton, Priscilla Presley, Morris Day, Lauren Holly, Maddie Corman

THE ADVENTURES OF GERARD (1970, GB, Nigel Films/UA)

    Col. Etienne Gerard—Peter McEnery
    Director—Jerzy Skolimowski
    Leading Players—Claudia Cardinale, Eli Wallach, Jack Hawkins

ADVENTURES OF HAJJI BABA (1954, 20th Century Fox)

    Hajji Baba—John Derek
    Director—Don Weis
    Leading Players—Elaine Stewart, Thomas Gomez, Amanda Blake, Paul Picerni, Rosemarie Bowe

THE ADVENTURES OF HUCKLEBERRY FINN (1960, MGM)

    Huckleberry Finn—Eddie Hodges
    Director—Michael Curtiz
    Leading Players—Tony Randall, Archie Moore, Patty McCormack, Neville Brand, Mickey Shaughnessy

THE ADVENTURES OF JANE (1949, GB, New World/Keystone)

    Jane—Chrisabel Leighton-Porter
    Director—Edward G. Whiting
    Leading Players—Stanelli, Michael Hogarth, Wally Patch

ADVENTURES OF JANE ARDEN (1939, Warner Brothers)

    Jane Arden—Rosella Towne
    Director—Terry Morse
    Leading Players—William Gargan, James Stephenson, Benny Rubin, Dennie Moore, Peggy Shannon

ADVENTURES OF KITTY O'DAY (1944, Monogram)

    Kitty O'Day—Jean Parker
    Director—William Beaudine
    Leading Players—Peter Cookson, Tim Ryan, Ralph Sanford

THE ADVENTURES OF MARCO POLO (1938, UA)

    Marco Polo—Gary Cooper
    Director—Archie Mayo
    Leading Players—Sigrid Gurie, Basil Rathbone, Ernest Truex, George Barrier, Binnie Barnes, Alan Hale

THE ADVENTURES OF MARK TWAIN (1944, Warner Brothers)

    Samuel Clemens/Mark Twain—Fredric March
    Director—Irving Rapper
    Leading Players—Alexis Smith, Donald Crisp, Alan Hale, C. Aubrey Smith, John Carradine

THE ADVENTURES OF MARTIN EDEN (1942, Columbia)

    Martin Eden—Glenn Ford
    Director—Sidney Salkow
    Leading Players—Claire Trevor, Evelyn Keyes, Stuart Erwin, Dickie Moore, Ian MacDonald, Frank Conroy

THE ADVENTURES OF MR. PICKWICK (1921, Silent, GB, Bentley Pictures)

    Samuel Pickwick—Fred Volpe
    Director—Thomas Bentley
    Leading Players—Mary Brough, Bransby Williams, Ernest Thesiger, Kathleen Vaughn

THE ADVENTURES OF QUENTIN DURWARD (1956, GB, MGM British)

    Quentin Durward—Robert Taylor
    Director—Richard Thorpe
    Leading Players—Kay Kendall, Robert Morley, Duncan Lamont

THE ADVENTURES OF ROBIN HOOD (1938, Warner Brothers/ First National)

    Robin Hood—Errol Flynn
    Directors—Michael Curtiz & William Keighley
    Leading Players—Olivia de Havilland, Basil Rathbone, Claude Rains, Patric Knowles, Eugene Pallette, Alan Hale, Melville Cooper, Una O'Connor

THE ADVENTURES OF ROBINSON CRUSOE (1954, UA)
Robinson Crusoe—Dan O'Herlihy
Director—Luis Bunuel
Leading Players—Jaime Fernandez, Felipe De Alba

THE ADVENTURES OF SADIE (1955, GB, Renown/20th Century Fox)
Sadie Patch—Joan Collins
Director—Noel Langley
Leading Players—George Cole, Kenneth More, Robertson Hare

THE ADVENTURES OF SHERLOCK HOLMES (1939, 20th Century Fox)
Sherlock Holmes—Basil Rathbone
Director—Alfred Werker
Leading Players—Nigel Bruce, Ida Lupino, Alan Marshal, Terry Kilburn, George Zucco, Henry Stephenson

ADVENTURES OF TARTU (1943, GB, MGM)
Capt. Terence Stevenson—Robert Donat
Director—Harold S. Bucquet
Leading Players—Valerie Hobson, Walter Rilla, Glynis Johns

THE ADVENTURES OF TOM SAWYER (1939, Selznick International)
Tom Sawyer—Tommy Kelly
Director—Norman Taurog
Leading Players—Jackie Moran, Ann Gillis, May Robson, Walter Brennan, Victor Jory

THE ADVENTURESS (I SEE A DARK STRANGER) (1946, GB, General Films)
Bridie Quilty—Deborah Kerr
Director—Frank Launder
Leading Players—Trevor Howard, Raymond Huntley, Michael Howard, Norman Shelley, Liam Redford

ADVENTUROUS BLONDE (1937, Warner Brothers)
Torchy Blane—Glenda Farrell
Director—**Frank McDonald**
Leading Players—Barton MacLane, Anne Nagel, Tom Kennedy, George E. Stone, Natalie Moorhead

THE ADVENTUROUS SOUL (1927, Silent, Hi-Mark Productions)
Dick Barlow—Jimmy Fulton
Director—Harriet Virginia
Leading Players—Mildred Harris, Tom Santschi, Arthur Rankin

AERIAL GUNNER (1943, Paramount)
Foxy Pattis—Chester Morris
Director—William H. Pine
Leading Players—Richard Arlen, Lita Ward, Jimmy Lydon

AFFAIR OF SUSAN (1935, Universal)
Susan Todd—Zasu Pitts
Director—Kurt Neumann
Leading Players—Hugh O'Connell, Walter Catlett, Inez Courtney, James Burke, Thomas Dugan,

AFFAIR WITH A STRANGER (1953, RKO)
Janet Boothe—Monica Lewis
Director—Roy Rowland
Leading Players—Jean Simmons, Victor Mature, Jane Darwell

AFFAIRS OF A GENTLEMAN (1934, Universal)
Gresham—Paul Lukas
Director—Edward L. Marin
Leading Players—Leila Hyams, Patricia Ellis, Phillip Reed, Onslow Stevens, Dorothy Burgess

AFFAIRS OF ADELAIDE (1949, 20th Century Fox)
Adelaide Culver—Maureen O'Hara
Director—Jean Negulesco
Leading Players—June Allen, Dana Andrews, Sybil Thorndike

AFFAIRS OF ANNABEL (1938, RKO)
Annabel—Lucille Ball
Director—Ben Stoloff
Leading Players—Jack Oakie, Ruth Donnelly, Bradley Page

THE AFFAIRS OF ANATOL (1921, Silent, Paramount)
Anatol De Witt Spencer—Wallace Reid
Director—Cecil B. De Mille
Leading Players—Gloria Swanson, Elliott Dexter, Bebe Daniels

AFFAIRS OF CAPPY RICKS (1937, Republic)
Cappy Ricks—Walter Brennan
Director—Ralph Staub
Leading Players—Mary Brian, Lyle Talbot, Frank Shields

THE AFFAIRS OF CELLINI (1934, Fox/UA)
Benvenuto Cellini—Fredric March
Director—Gregory La Cava
Leading Players—Constance Bennett, Frank Morgan, Fay Wray, Vince Barnett, Jessie Ralph

THE AFFAIRS OF DOBIE GILLIS (1953, MGM)
Dobie Gillis—Bobby Van
Director—Don Weis
Leading Players—Debbie Reynolds, Barbara Ruick, Bob Fosse

AFFAIRS OF GERALDINE (1946, Republic)
Geraldine Cooper—Jane Withers
Director—George Blair
Leading Players—James Lydon, Raymond Walburn, Donald Meek

THE AFFAIRS OF MARTHA (1942, MGM)
Martha Lindstrom—Marsha Hunt
Director—Jules Dassin
Leading Players—Richard Carlson, Marjorie Main, Virginia Weidler, Spring Byington, Allyn Joslyn

AFFAIRS OF SUSAN (1945, Paramount)
Susan Darell—Joan Fontaine
Director—William A. Seiter
Leading Players—George Brent, Dennis O'Keefe, Don Defore, Rita Johnson, Walter Abel

AFTER MIDNIGHT WITH BOSTON BLACKIE (1943, Columbia)
Boston Blackie—Chester Morris
Director—Lew Landers
Leading Players—George E. Stone, Richard Lane, Cy Kendall, Ann Savage, George McKay, Al Hill

AFTER THE FOX (1966, UA)
Aldo Vanucci—Peter Sellers
Director—Vittorio De Sica
Leading Players—Victor Mature, Britt Ekland, Martin Balsam, Akim Tamiroff, Paolo Stoppa

AFTER THE THIN MAN (1936, MGM)
Nick Charles—William Powell
Director—W.S. Van Dyke
Leading Players—Myrna Loy, James Stewart, Joseph Calleia, Elissa Landi, Jessie Ralph, Alan Marshal

AGATHA (1979, GB, Sweetwal/Warner Brothers)
Agatha Christie—Vanessa Redgrave
Director—Michael Apted
Leading Players—Dustin Hoffman, Timothy Dalton, Helen Morse

AGENT 8 3/4 (1965, GB, Rank/Continental)
Nicholas Whistler—Dirk Bogarde
Director—Ralph Thomas
Leading Players—Sylvia Koscina, Robert Morley, Leo McKern

AGENT FOR H.A.R.M. (1966, Universal)
Adam Chance—Mark Richman
Director—Gerd Oswald
Leading Players—Wendell Corey, Carl Esmond, Barbara Bouchet

AGGIE APPLEBY, MAKER OF MEN (1933, RKO)
Aggie Appleby—Wynne Gibson
Director—Mark Sandrich
Leading Players—Charles Farrell, William Gargan, Zasu Pitts

AGNES OF GOD (1985, Columbia)
Sister Agnes—Meg Tilly
Director—Norman Jewison
Leading Players—Jane Fonda, Anne Bancroft

THE AIR HAWK (1924, Silent, Film Booking Offices)
Al Parker—Al Wilson
Director—Bruce Mitchell
Leading Players—Webster Cullinson, Virginia Brown Faire

AIR HOSTESS (1933, Columbia)
Kitty King—Evalyn Knapp
Director—Albert Rogell
Leading Players—James Murray, Arthur Pierson, Jane Darwell

THE AIR MAIL PILOT (1928, Silent, Hi-Mark Productions)
Jimmie Dean—James F. Fulton
Director—Gene Carroll
Leading Players—Earl Metcalffe, Blanche Mehaffey

AIR RAID WARDENS (1943, MGM)
Stan & Ollie—Stan Laurel & Oliver Hardy
Director—Edward Sedgwick
Leading Players—Edgar Kennedy, Jacqueline White, Stephen McNally, Russell Hicks, Nella Walker

AL CAPONE (1959, Allied Artists)
Al Capone—Rod Steiger
Director—Richard Wilson
Leading Players—Fay Spain, James Gregory, Martin Balsam, Nehemiah Persoff, Murvyn Vye, Joe De Santis

AL JENNINGS OF OKLAHOMA (1951, Columbia)
Al Jennings—Dan Duryea
Director—Ray Nazarro
Leading Players—Dick Foran, Gale Storm, Gloria Henry

ALADDIN (1917, Silent, Fox Film Corp.)
Aladdin—Francis Carpenter

Director—Harlan Thompson
Leading Players—Fred Turner, Virginia Corbin, Alfred Paget, Violet Radcliffe, Buddy Messenger

ALADDIN AND HIS LAMP (1952, Monogram)
Aladdin—John Sands
Director—Lew Landers
Leading Players—Patricia Medina, Richard Erdman, John Dehner, Billy House, Ned Young, Charles Horvath

ALADDIN FROM BROADWAY (1917, Silent, Vitagraph)
Jack Stanton—Antonio Moreno
Director—William Wolbert
Leading Players—Edith Storey, William Duncan, Otto Lederer

ALAN AND NAOMI (1992, Triton Pictures)
Alan Silverman—Lukas Haas
Naomi Kirschenbaum—Vanessa Zaoui
Director—Sterling Van Wagenen
Leading Players—Michael Gross, Amy Aquino, Kevin Connolly, Zohra Lampert, Victoria Christian

ALARM CLOCK ANDY (1920, Silent, Paramount)
Andrew Gray—Charles Ray
Director—Jerome Storm
Leading Players—George Webb, Millicent Fisher, Tom Guise

THE ALASKIAN (1924, Silent, Paramount)
Alan Holt—Thomas Meighan
Director—Herbert Brenon
Leading Players—Estelle Taylor, John Sainpolis, Frank Campeau

ALEX AND THE GYPSY (1976, 20th Century Fox)
Alexander Main—Jack Lemmon
Maritza—Genevieve Bujold
Director—John Korty
Leading Players—James Woods, Gino Ardito, Robert Emhardt

ALEX IN WONDERLAND (1970, MGM)
Alex—Donald Sutherland
Director—Paul Mazursky
Leading Players—Ellen Burstyn, Meg Mazursky, Glenna Sergent

ALEX THE GREAT (1928, Silent, FBO Pictures)
Alex—Richard "Skeets" Gallagher
Director—Dudley Murphy
Leading Players—Albert Conti, Patricia Avery, Ruth Dwyer

ALEXA (1989, Platinum-B Tru)
Alexa Avery—Christine Moore
Director—Sean Delgado
Leading Players—Kirk Baily, Ruth Collins, Joseph P. Giardina

ALEXANDER HAMILTON (1931, Warner Brothers)
Alexander Hamilton—George Arliss
Director—John G. Adolfi
Leading Players—Doris Kenyon, Dudley Digges, Alan Mowbray

ALEXANDER THE GREAT (1956, UA)
Alexander The Great—Richard Burton
Director—Robert Rossen
Leading Players—Fredric March, Claire Bloom, Danielle Darrieux, Harry Andrews, Stanley Baker

ALEXANDER'S RAGTIME BAND (1938, 20th Century Fox)
Roger Grant—Tyrone Power
Director—Henry King
Leading Players—Alice Faye, Don Ameche, Ethel Merman

ALFIE (1966, GB, Paramount)
Alfie Elkins—Michael Caine
Director—Lewis Gilbert
Leading Players—Shelley Winters, Millicent Martin, Julia
    Foster, Jane Asher, Shirley Ann Field

ALFIE DARLING (1975, GB, Signal/EMI)
Alfie Elkins—Alan Price
Director—Ken Hughes
Leading Players—Jill Townsend, Paul Copley, Joan Collins

ALFRED THE GREAT (1969, GB, MGM)
Alfred The Great—David Hemmings
Director—Clive Donner
Leading Players—Michael York, Prunella Ransome, Colin
    Blakely, Julian Glover

ALF'S BABY (1953, GB, Adelphi)
Alf Donkin—Jerry Desmonde
Pamela Weston—Pauline Stroud
Director—Maclean Rogers
Leading Players—Olive Sloane, Peter Hammond, Sandra Dome

ALF'S BUTTON (1930, GB, Gaumont)
Alf Higgins—Tubby Edlin
Director—W.P. Kellino
Leading Players—Alf Goddard, Nora Swinburne, Polly Ward

ALF'S BUTTON AFLOAT (1938, GB, Gainsborough)
Alf Higgins—Bud Flanagan
Director—Marcel Varnel
Leading Players—Chesney Allen, Jimmy Nervo, Teddy Knox

ALF'S CARPET (1929, GB, British International)
Alf Higgins—Pat Patachon
Director—W.P. Kellino
Leading Players—Janice Adair, Gerald Rawlinson, Gladys
    Hamer

ALI BABA AND THE FORTY THIEVES (1944, Universal)
Ali Baba—Jon Hall
Director—Arthur Lubin
Leading Players—Maria Montez, Turhan Bey, Andy Devine, Kurt
    Katch, Frank Puglia

ALI BABA GOES TO TOWN (1937, 20th Century Fox)
Ali Baba—Eddie Cantor
Director—David Butler
Leading Players—Tony Martin, Roland Young, June Lang

ALIAS A GENTLEMAN (1948, MGM)
Jim Breedin—Wallace Beery
Director—Harry Beaumont
Leading Players—Tom Drake, Dorothy Patrick, Gladys George

ALIAS BOSTON BLACKIE (1942, Columbia)
Boston Blackie—Chester Morris
Director—Lew Landers
Leading Players—Adele Mara, Richard Lane, George E. Stone

ALIAS BULLDOG DRUMMOND (1935, GB, Gaumont)
Jack Pennington—Jack Hulbert
Director—Walter Forde
Leading Players—Fay Wray, Claude Hulbert, Ralph Richardson

ALIAS FRENCH GERTIE (1930, RKO)
Marie—Bebe Daniels
Director—George Archainbaud
Leading Players—Ben Lyon, Robert Emmett O'Connor, John
    Ince

ALIAS JESSE JAMES (1959, UA)
Milford Farnsworth—Bob Hope
Director—Norman McLeod
Leading Players—Rhonda Fleming, Wendell Corey, Jim Davis

ALIAS JIMMY VALENTINE (1928, MGM)
Jimmy Valentine—William Haines
Director—Jack Conway
Leading Players—Karl Dane, Lionel Barrymore, Leila Hyams

ALIAS JOHN PRESTON (1956, GB, British Lion)
John Preston—Christopher Lee
Director—David MacDonald
Leading Players—Betta St. John, Alexander Knox, Sandra
    Dorne

ALIAS JULIUS CAESAR (1922, Silent, Associated First National)
Billy Barnes—Charles Ray
Director—Charles Ray
Leading Players—Barbara Bedford, William Scott, Robert
    Fernandez, Fred Miller

ALIAS LADYFINGERS (1921, Silent, Metro)
Robert Ashe (Ladyfingers)—Bert Lytell
Director—Bayard Veiller
Leading Players—Ora Carew, Frank Elliott, Edythe Chapman

ALIAS MARY BROWN (1918, Silent, Triangle)
Dick Browning—Casson Ferguson
Director—Charles J. Brabin
Leading Players—Pauline Starke, A.N. Millett, Eugene Burr

ALIAS MARY DOW (1935, Universal)
Sally Gates—Sally Eilers
Director—Kurt Neumann
Leading Players—Ray Milland, Henry O'Neill, Katherine
    Alexander, Chick Chandler

ALIAS MARY FLYNN (1925, Silent, Film Booking Offices)
Mary Flynn—Evelyn Brent
Director—Ralph Ince
Leading Players—Malcolm McGregor, William V. Mong, Gladden
    James, Lou Payne

ALIAS MIKE MORAN (1919, Silent, Paramount)
Larry Young—Wallace Reid
Director—James Cruze
Leading Players—Ann Little, Emory Johnson, Charles Ogle

ALIAS NICK BEAL (1949, Paramount)
Nick Beal—Ray Milland
Director—John Darrow
Leading Players—Thomas Mitchell, Audrey Totter, Geraldine
    Wall, George Macready

ALIAS THE DEACON (1928, Silent, Universal)
The Deacon—Jean Hersholt
Director—Edward Sloman
Leading Players—June Marlowe, Ralph Graves, Myrtle Sherman

ALIAS THE DEACON (1940, Universal)
Deke Caswell—Bob Burns
Director—Christy Cabanne
Leading Players—Mischa Auer, Peggy Moran, Dennis O'Keefe

ALIAS THE DOCTOR (1932, First National)
Karl Muller—Richard Barthelmess
Director—Lloyd Bacon
Leading Players—Marian Marsh, Lucille La Verne, Norman Foster, Adrienne Dore

ALIAS THE LONE WOLF (1927, Silent, Columbia)
Michael Lanyard—Bert Lytell
Director—Edward H. Griffith
Leading Players—Lois Wilson, William V. Mong, Ned Sparks

ALIAS THE NIGHT WIND (1923, Silent, Fox)
Bing Howard—William Russell
Director—Joseph Franz
Leading Players—Maude Wayne, Charles K. French, Wade Boteler

ALIBI IKE (1935, Warner Brothers)
Frank X. Farrell—Joe E. Brown
Director—Ray Enright
Leading Players—Olivia De Havilland, Roscoe Karns, William Frawley, Joseph King

ALICE (1990, Orion)
Alice—Mia Farrow
Director—Woody Allen
Leading Players—Joe Mantegna, Alec Baldwin, Blythe Danner, Judy Davis, William Hurt, Keye Luke, Bernadette Peters, Cybill Shepherd, Gwen Verdon, Julie Kavner

ALICE ADAMS (1923, Silent, Associated Exhibitors)
Alice Adams—Florence Vidor
Director—Rowland V. Lee
Leading Players—Claude Gillingwater, Harold Goodwin, Margaret McWade, Thomas Ricketts

ALICE ADAMS (1935, RKO)
Alice Adams—Katharine Hepburn
Director—George Stevens
Leading Players -Fred MacMurray, Fred Stone, Evelyn Venable, Frank Albertson, Anne Shoemaker

ALICE DOESN'T LIVE HERE ANYMORE (1975, Warner Brothers)
Alice Hyatt—Ellen Burstyn
Director—Martin Scorsese
Leading Players—Kris Kristofferson, Billy Green Bush, Diane Ladd, Leila Goldoni, Harvey Keitel

ALICE IN WONDERLAND (1933, Paramount)
Alice—Charlotte Henry
Director—Norman McLeod
Leading Players—Richard Arlen, Gary Cooper, Leon Errol, W.C. Fields, Cary Grant, Edward Everett Horton, Jack Oakie, Edna May Oliver, May Robson

ALICE, SWEET ALICE (1978, Allied Artists)
Alice—Paula Sheppard
Director—Alfred Sole
Leading Players—Brooke Shields, Linda Miller, Jane Lowry

ALICE'S ADVENTURES IN WONDERLAND (1972, GB, Am. National)
Alice—Fiona Fullerton
Director—William Sterling
Leading Players—Michael Crawford, Ralph Richardson, Flora Robson, Peter Sellers, Dudley Moore

ALICE'S RESTAURANT (1969, UA)
Alice—Pat Quinn
Director—Arthur Penn
Leading Players—Arlo Guthrie, James Broderick, Michael McClanathan, Geoff Outlaw, Tina Chen

ALIEN FROM L.A. (1988, Cannon)
Wanda Saknussemm—Kathy Ireland
Director—Albert Pyun
Leading Players—Thom Matthews, Don Michael Paul, Linda Kerridge

ALL ABOUT EVE (1950, 20th Century Fox)
Eve Harrington—Anne Baxter
Director—Joseph L. Mankiewicz
Leading Players—Bette Davis, George Sanders, Celeste Holm, Gary Merrill, Hugh Marlowe, Thelma Ritter, Gregory Ratoff, Marilyn Monroe

THE ALL-AMERICAN (1932, Universal)
Garry King—Richard Arlen
Director—Russell Mack
Leading Players—Andy Devine, Gloria Stuart, James Gleason

THE ALL-AMERICAN (1953, Universal)
Nick Bonelli—Tony Curtis
Director—Jesse Hibbs
Leading Players—Lori Nelson, Richard Long, Mamie Van Doren

THE ALL-AMERICAN BOY (1973, Warner Brothers)
Vic Bealer—Jon Voight
Director—Charles Eastman
Leading Players—Carol Androsky, Annie Archer, Gene Borkan

ALL-AMERICAN CHUMP (1936, MGM)
Elmer—Stuart Erwin
Director—Edwin L. Marin
Leading Players—Robert Armstrong, Betty Furness, Edmund Gwenn

ALL-AMERICAN SWEETHEART (1937, Columbia)
Connie Adams—Patricia Farr
Director—Lambert Hillyer
Leading Players—Scott Colton, Gene Morgan, Jimmy Eagles

ALL DOGS GO TO HEAVEN (1989, UA)
Charlie's voice—Burt Reynolds
Directors—Gary Goldman, Dan Kuenster & Don Bluth
Leading Players—Dom DeLuise, Vic Tayback, Melba Moore, Charles Nelson Reilly, Loni Anderson

ALL FOR MARY (1956, GB, Rank)
Mary—Jill Day
Director—Wendy Toye

Leading Players—Nigel Patrick, Kathleen Harrison, David Tomlinson, David Hurst

ALL MAN (1916, Silent, Peerless/World)
Jim Blake—Robert Warwick
Director—Emil Chautard
Leading Players—Louis Crisel, Charles Duncan, Alec B. Francis, Gerda Holmes

ALL MY SONS (1948, Universal)
Joe Keller—Edward G. Robinson
Chris Keller—Burt Lancaster
Director—Irving Reis
Leading Players—Mady Christians, Louisa Horton, Howard Duff

ALL OF ME (1934, Paramount)
Don Ellis—Fredric March
Director—James Flood
Leading Players—Miriam Hopkins, George Raft, Helen Mack

ALL OF ME (1984, Universal)
Roger Cobb—Steve Martin
Edwina Cutwater—Lily Tomlin
Director—Carl Reiner
Leading Players—Victoria Tennant, Madolyn Smith, Richard Libertini, Dana Elcar

ALL THE BROTHERS WERE VALIANT (1923, Silent, Metro)
Joel Shore—Malcolm McGregor
Mark Shore—Lon Chaney
Director—Irving V. Willat
Leading Players—Billie Dove, William H. Orlamond, Robert McKim, Robert Kortman

ALL THE BROTHERS WERE VALIANT (1953, MGM)
Joel Shore—Robert Taylor
Mark Shire—Stewart Granger
Director—Richard Thorpe
Leading Players—Ann Blyth, Betta St. John, Keenan Wynn, James Whitmore, Kurt Kasznar

ALL WOMAN (1918, Silent, Goldwyn)
Susan Sweeney—Mae Marsh
Director—Hobart Henley
Leading Players—Jere Austin, Arthur Housman, John Sainpolis

ALLAN QUATERMAIN AND THE LOST CITY OF GOLD (1987, Cannon)
Allan Quatermain—Richard Chamberlain
Director—Gary Nelson
Leading Players—Sharon Stone, James Earl Jones, Henry Silva

ALMOST A LADY (1926, Silent, Producers Distributing Corp.)
Marcia Blake—Marie Prevost
Director—E. Mason Hopper
Leading Players—Harrison Ford, George K. Arthur, Trixie Friganza, John Miljan

ALMOST AN ANGEL (1990, Paramount/Ironbark)
Terry Dean—Paul Hogan
Director—John Cornell
Leading Players—Elias Koteas, Linda Kozlowski, Charlton Heston, Doreen Lang, Joe Dallesandro

ALOHA, BOBBY AND ROSE (1975, Columbia)
Bobby—Paul LeMat

Rose—Dianne Hull
Director—Floyd Mutrux
Leading Players—Tim McIntire, Leigh French, Noble Willingham

ALOMA OF THE SOUTH SEAS (1926, Silent, Paramount)
Aloma—Gilda Gray
Director—Maurice Tourneur
Leading Players—Percy Marmont, Warner Baxter, Harry Morey

ALOMA OF THE SOUTH SEAS (1941, Paramount)
Aloma—Dorothy Lamour
Director—Alfred Santell
Leading Players—Jon Hall, Lynne Overman, Phillip Reed

ALONG CAME JONES (1945, RKO)
Melody Jones—Gary Cooper
Director—Stuart Heisler
Leading Players—Loretta Young, Dan Duryea, William Demarest

ALONG CAME RUTH (1924, Silent, MGM)
Ruth Ambrose—Viola Dana
Director—Edward Cline
Leading Players—Walter Hiers, Tully Marshall, Raymond McKee

ALONG CAME SALLY (1934, GB, Gaumont)
Sally Bird—Cicely Courtneidge
Director—Tim Whelan
Leading Players—Sam Hardy, Phyllis Clare, Billy Milton

ALVAREZ KELLY (1966, Columbia)
Alvarez Kelly—William Holden
Director—Edward Dmytryk
Leading Players—Richard Widmark, Janice Rule, Patrick O'Neal

ALVIN PURPLE (1974, Australia, Roadshow)
Alvin Purple—Graeme Blundell
Director—Tim Burstall
Leading Players—George Whaley, Penne Hackforth-Jones, Elli Maclure

ALVIN RIDES AGAIN (1974, Australia, Roadshow)
Alvin Purple—Graeme Blundell
Director—Tim Burstall
Leading Players—Alan Finney, Brionny Behets, Abigail, Frank Thring, Chantal Contouri

ALWAYS A BRIDE (1954, GB, General)
Clare Hemsley—Peggy Cummins
Director—Ralph Smart
Leading Players—Terence Morgan, Ronald Squire, James Hayter

AMADEUS (1984, Orion)
Wolfgang Amadeus Mozart—Tom Hulce
Director—Milos Forman
Leading Players—F. Murray Abraham, Elizabeth Berridge, Simon Callow, Roy Dotrice, Christine Ebersole, Jeffrey Jones

AMARILLY OF CLOTHESLINE ALLEY (1918, Silent, Artcraft)
Amarilly Jenkins—Mary Pickford
Director—Marshall Neilan
Leading Players—William Scott, Norman Kerry, Ida Waterman

THE AMATEUR (1982, 20th Century Fox)
Heller—John Savage

Director—Charles Jarrott
Leading Players—Christopher Plummer, Marthe Keller, Arthur Hill, Ed Lauter

AMATEUR DADDY (1932, 20th Century Fox)
Jim Gladden—Warner Baxter
Director—John Blystone
Leading Players—Marian Nixon, Rita Leroy, Lucille Powers

AN AMATEUR DEVIL (1921, Silent, Paramount)
Carver Endicott—Bryant Washburn
Director—Maurice Campbell
Leading Players—Charles Wingate, Ann May, Sidney Bracey

THE AMATEUR GENTLEMAN (1926, Silent, First National)
Barnabas Barty—Richard Barthelmess
Director—Sidney Olcott
Leading Players—Dorothy Dunbar, Gardner James, Nigel Barrie

AMATEUR GENTLEMAN (1936, GB, UA)
Barnabas Barty—Douglas Fairbanks, Jr.
Director—Thornton Freeland
Leading Players—Elissa Landi, Gordon Harker, Basil Sydney

THE AMAZING COLOSSAL MAN (1957, American International)
Lt. Col. Glenn Manning—Glenn Langan
Director—Bert I. Gordon
Leading Players—Cathy Downs, William Hudson, James Seary

THE AMAZING DR. CLITTERHOUSE (1938, Warner Brothers)
Dr. Clitterhouse—Edward G. Robinson
Director—Anatole Litvak
Leading Players—Claire Trevor, Humphrey Bogart, Gale Page

AMAZING GRACE (1974, Paramount)
Grace—Moms Mabley
Director—Stan Lathan
Leading Players—Slappy White, Moses Gunn, Rosalind Cash

AMAZING GRACE AND CHUCK (1987, Tri-Star)
Amazing Grace Smith—Alex English
Chuck Murdock—Joshua Zuehlke
Director—Mike Newell
Leading Players—Jamie Lee Curtis, Gregory Peck, William L. Petersen

THE AMAZING MR. BEECHAM (1949, GB, Two Cities)
Benjamin Beecham—Cecil Parker
Director—John Paddy Carstairs
Leading Players—A.E. Matthews, David Tomlinson, Lana Morris

THE AMAZING MR. BLUNDEN (1973, GB, Hemisphere)
Mr. Blunden—Laurence Naismith
Director—Lionel Jeffries
Leading Players—James Villiers, Diana Dors, David Lodge

THE AMAZING MR. FORREST (1943, GB, Producers Releasing)
John Forrest—Jack Buchanan
Director—Thornton Freeland
Leading Players—Edward Everett Horton, Otto Kruger, Jack Larue, Googie Withers

AMAZING MR. WILLIAMS (1939, Columbia)
Kenny Williams—Melvyn Douglas
Director—Alexander Hall
Leading Players—Joan Blondell, Clarence Kolb, John Wray

AMAZING MRS. HOLLIDAY (1943, Universal)
Ruth Kirke—Deanna Durbin
Director—Bruce Manning
Leading Players—Edmond O'Brien, Barry Fitzgerald, Arthur Treacher, Harry Davenport

THE AMAZING QUEST OF ERNEST BLISS (1936, GB, Klement)
Ernest Bliss—Cary Grant
Director—Alfred Zeisler
Leading Players—Mary Brian, Henry Kendall, Leon M. Lion

THE AMAZING VAGABOND (1929, RKO)
Jimmy Hobbs—Bob Steele
Director—Wallace W. Fox
Leading Players—Tom Lingham, Jay Morley, Perry Murdock

AMAZONS (1987, MGM/UA)
Dyala—Windsor Taylor Randolph
Tashi—Penelope Reed
Director—Alex Sessa
Leading Players—Joseph Whipp, Danitza Kingsley, Wolfram Hoechst

THE AMBASSADOR (1985, Cannon)
Ambassador Peter Hacker—Robert Mitchum
Director—J. Lee Thompson
Leading Players—Ellen Burstyn, Rock Hudson, Fabio Testi, Donald Pleasence

AMBASSADOR BILL (1931, 20th Century Fox)
Bill Harper—Will Rogers
Director—Sam Taylor
Leading Players—Marguerite Churchill, Greta Nissen, Tad Alexander, Ray Milland

THE AMBASSADOR'S DAUGHTER (1956, UA)
Joan Fiske—Olivia de Havilland
Director—Norman Krasna
Leading Players—John Forsythe, Myrna Loy, Adolphe Menjou

AMERICAN BEAUTY (1927, Silent, First National)
Millicent Howard—Billie Dove
Director—Richard Wallace
Leading Players—Lloyd Hughes, Walter McGrail, Margaret Livingston, Lucien Prival

AMERICAN DREAMER (1984, Warner Brothers)
Cathy Palmer—JoBeth Williams
Director—Rick Rosenthal
Leading Players—Tom Conti, Giancarlo Giannini, Coral Browne

AMERICAN FLYERS (1985, Warner Brothers)
Marcus—Kevin Costner
David—David Grant
Director—John Badham
Leading Players—Rae Dawn Chong, Alexandra Paul, Janice Rule

AMERICAN FRIENDS (1991, GB, MCEG/Virgin Vision)
Caroline Hartley—Connie Booth
Elinor Hartley—Trini Alvarado
Director—Tristram Powell
Leading Players—Michael Palin, Alfred Molina, David Calder, Simon James, Robert Eddison

AMERICAN GIGOLO (1980, Paramount)
Julian—Richard Gere
Director—Paul Schrader
Leading Players—Lauren Hutton, Hector Elizondo, Nina Van Pallandt, Bill Duke

AN AMERICAN GUERILLA IN THE PHILIPPINES (1950, 20th Century Fox)
Ensign Chuck Palmer—Tyrone Power
Director—Fritz Lang
Leading Players—Micheline Presle, Tom Ewell, Bob Patten

THE AMERICAN HEIRESS (1917, Silent, GB, Hepworth)
Bessie—Alma Taylor
Director—Cecil M. Hepworth
Leading Players—Violet Hopson, Stewart Rome, Lionelle Howard

AN AMERICAN IN PARIS (1951, MGM)
Jerry Mulligan—Gene Kelly
Director—Vincente Minnelli
Leading Players—Leslie Caron, Oscar Levant, Georges Guetay, Nina Foch

AMERICAN ME (1992, Universal)
Santana—Edward James Olmos
Director—Edward James Olmos
Leading Players—William Forsythe, Pepe Serna, Danny De La Paz, Evelina Fernandez, Panchito Gomez

THE AMERICAN PRISONER (1929, GB, British International)
Lt. Stark—Carl Brisson
Director—Thomas Bentley
Leading Players—Madeline Carroll, Cecil Barry, Carl Harbord

AN AMERICAN TAIL: FIEVEL GOES WEST (1991, Animated, Universal)
Fievel Mousekewitz—Voice of Phillip Glasser
Director—Phil Nibbelink
Leading Players—Voices of James Stewart, Erica Yohn, Cathy Cavadini, Nehemiah Persoff, Dom De Luise, Amy Irving, John Cleese, Jon Lovitz

THE AMERICAN VENUS (1926, Silent, Paramount)
Mary Gray—Esther Ralston
Director—Frank Tuttle
Leading Players—Lawrence Gray, Ford Sterling, Fay Lamphier

AN AMERICAN WEREWOLF IN LONDON (1981, Universal)
David Kessler—David Naughton
Director—John Landis
Leading Players—Jenny Agutter, Griffin Dunne, John Woodvine

THE AMERICANIZATION OF EMILY (1964, MGM)
Emily Barham—Julie Andrews
Director—Arthur Hiller
Leading Players—James Garner, Melvyn Douglas, James Coburn

THE AMERICANO (1955, RKO)
Sam Dent—Glenn Ford
Director—William Castle
Leading Players—Frank Lovejoy, Cesar Romero, Ursula Theiss

THE AMOROUS ADVENTURES OF MOLL FLANDERS (1965, Paramount)
Moll Flanders—Kim Novak

Director—Terence Young
Leading Players—Richard Johnson, Angela Lansbury, Vittorio De Sica, Leo McKern, George Sanders

THE AMOROUS MR. PRAWN (1964, GB, British Lion)
Mr. Prawn—Dennis Price
Director—Anthony Kimmins
Leading Players—Joan Greenwood, Cecil Parker, Ian Carmichael

AMOS 'N' ANDY (1930, Radio)
Amos Jones—Freeman Gosden
Andy Brown—Charles Correll
Director—Melville Brown
Leading Players—Sue Carol, Charles Morton, Ralf Harolde

AMY (1981, Buena Vista)
Amy—Jenny Agutter
Director—Vincent McEveety
Leading Players—Barry Newman, Kathleen Nolan, Chris Robinson

ANASTASIA (1956, 20th Century Fox)
Anastasia—Ingrid Bergman
Director—Anatole Litvak
Leading Players—Yul Brynner, Helen Hayes, Akim Tamiroff

THE ANCIENT MARINER (1925, Silent, 20th Century Fox)
The Mariner—Paul Panzer
Directors—Henry Otto & Chester Bennett
Leading Players—Clara Bow, Earle Williams, Leslie Fenton

AND GOD CREATED WOMAN (1988, Vestron)
Robin—Rebecca De Mornay
Director—Roger Vadim
Leading Players—Vincent Spano, Frank Langella, Donovan Leitch

AND NOW MIGUEL (1966, Universal)
Miguel—Pat Cardi
Director—James B. Clark
Leading Players—Michael Ansara, Guy Stockwell, Clu Gluager

THE ANDERSON TAPES (1971, Columbia)
Anderson—Sean Connery
Director—Sidney Lumet
Leading Players—Dyan Cannon, Martin Balsam, Ralph Meeker

ANDROCLES AND THE LION (1952, RKO)
Androcles—Alan Young
Director—Chester Erskine
Leading Players—Jean Simmons, Victor Mature, Robert Newton

ANDROID (1982, New World)
Max 404—Dan Opper
Director—Aaron Lipstadt
Leading Players—Klaus Kinski, Brie Howard, Norbert Weisser

ANDY (1965, Universal)
Andy—Norman Alden
Director—Richard S. Sarafian
Leading Players—Tamara Daykarhonova, Zvee Scooler, Ann Wedgeworth

ANDY HARDY COMES HOME (1958, MGM)
Andy Hardy—Mickey Rooney

Director—Howard W. Koch
Leading Players—Patricia Breslin, Fay Holden, Cecilia Parker

ANDY HARDY GETS SPRING FEVER (1939, MGM)
Andy Hardy—Mickey Rooney
Director—W.S. Van Dyke II
Leading Players—Lewis Stone, Cecilia Parker, Ann Rutherford

ANDY HARDY MEETS DEBUTANTE (1940, MGM)
Andy Hardy—Mickey Rooney
Director—George B. Seitz
Leading Players—Lewis Stone, Fay Holden, Judy Garland, Sara Haden, Ann Rutherford

ANDY HARDY'S BLONDE TROUBLE (1944, MGM)
Andy Hardy—Mickey Rooney
Director—George B. Seitz
Leading Players—Lewis Stone, Fay Holden, Sara Haden, Bonita Granville, Jean Porter

ANDY HARDY'S DOUBLE LIFE (1942, MGM)
Andy Hardy—Mickey Rooney
Director—George B. Seitz
Leading Players—Lewis Stone, Fay Holden, Cecilia Parker, Ann Rutherford, Esther Williams

ANDY HARDY'S PRIVATE SECRETARY (1941, MGM)
Andy Hardy—Mickey Rooney
Kathryn Land—Kathryn Grayson
Director—George B. Seitz
Leading Players—Lewis Stone, Fay Holden, Ian Hunter, Ann Rutherford

ANGEL (1937, Paramount)
Maria Barker—Marlene Dietrich
Director—Ernst Lubitsch
Leading Players—Herbert Marshall, Melvyn Douglas, Edward Everett Horton, Laura Hope Crews

ANGEL (1984, New World)
Angel/Molly—Donna Wilkes
Director—Robert Vincent O'Neil
Leading Players—Cliff Gorman, Susan Tyrrell, Dick Shawn, Rory Calhoun, John Diehl

ANGEL 3: THE FINAL CHAPTER (1988, New World)
Angel/Molly—Mitzi Kapture
Director—Tom DeSimone
Leading Players—Maud Adams, Mark Blankfield, Kin Shriner, Richard Roundtree, Tawny Fere

ANGEL AND THE BADMAN (1947, Republic)
Prudence Worth—Gail Russell
Quirt Evans—John Wayne
Director—James Edward Grant
Leading Players—Harry Carey, Bruce Cabot, Irene Rich

ANGEL BABY (1961, Allied Artists)
Angel Baby—Salome Jens
Director—Paul Wendkos
Leading Players—George Hamilton, Mercedes McCambridge, Henry Jones, Burt Reynolds, Joan Blondell

AN ANGEL COMES TO BROADWAY (1945, Republic)
Phineas Aloysius Higby—Charles Kemper
Director—Leslie Goodwins

Leading Players—Kaye Dowd, Robert Duke, David Street

ANGEL FACE (1953, RKO)
Diane Tremayne—Jean Simmons
Director—Otto Preminger
Leading Players—Robert Mitchum, Mona Freeman, Herbert Marshall, Leon Ames, Barbara O'Neil

AN ANGEL FROM TEXAS (1940, Warner Brothers)
Peter Coleman—Eddie Albert
Director—Ray Enright
Leading Players—Wayne Morris, Rosemary Lane, Jane Wyman, Ronald Reagan, Ruth Terry

ANGEL HEART (1987, Tri-Star)
Harry Angel—Mickey Rourke
Director—Alan Parker
Leading Players—Robert De Niro, Lisa Bonet, Charlotte Rampling, Stocker Fontelieu

THE ANGEL LEVINE (1970, UA)
Alexander Levine—Harry Belafonte
Director—Jan Kadar
Leading Players—Zero Mostel, Ida Kaminska, Milo O'Shea

THE ANGEL OF BROADWAY (1927, silent, Pathe Exchange)
Babe Scott—Leatrice Joy
Director—Lois Weber
Leading Players—Victor Varconi, May Robson, Alice Lake

THE ANGEL OF CROOKED STREET (1922, silent, Vitagraph)
Jennie Marsh—Alice Calhoun
Director—David Smith
Leading Players—Ralph McCullough, Scott McKee, Rex Hammel

ANGEL ON THE AMAZON (1948, Republic)
Christine Ridgeway—Vera Ralston
Director—John H. Auer
Leading Players—George Brent, Brian Aherne, Constance Bennett, Fortunio Bonanova

THE ANGEL WHO PAWNED HER HARP (1956, GB, British Lion)
The Angel—Diane Cilento
Director—Alan Bromly
Leading Players—Felix Aylmer, Jerry Desmonde, Robert Eddison

ANGELA (1977, Canada, Montreal Travel Co.)
Angela—Sophia Loren
Director—Boris Sagal
Leading Players—Steve Railsback, John Vernon, John Huston

ANN CARVER'S PROFESSION (1933, Columbia)
Ann Carver—Fay Wray
Director—Eddie Buzzell
Leading Players—Gene Raymond, Claire Dodd, Arthur Pierson

ANN VICKERS (1933, RKO)
Ann Vickers—Irene Dunne
Director—John Cromwell
Leading Players—Walter Huston, Conrad Nagel, Bruce Cabot

ANNA (1987, Magnus/Vestron)
Anna—Sally Kirkland
Director—Yurek Bogasyevicz
Leading Players—Robert Fields, Paulina Porizkova, Gibby Brand

ANNA AND THE KING OF SIAM (1946, 20th Century Fox)
Anna Leonowens—Irene Dunne
Director—John Cromwell
Leading Players—Rex Harrison, Linda Darnell, Lee J. Cobb, Gale Sondergaard

ANNA ASCENDS (1922, Silent, Paramount)
Anna Ayyob—Alice Brady
Director—Victor Fleming
Leading Players—Robert Willis, David Powell, Nita Naldi

ANNA CHRISTIE (1923, Silent, Associated First National)
Anna Christie—Blanche Sweet
Director—John Griffith
Leading Players—William Russell, George F. Marion, Eugenie Besserer

ANNA CHRISTIE (1930, MGM)
Anna Christie—Greta Garbo
Director—Clarence Brown
Leading Players—Charles Bickford, George F. Marion, Marie Dressler

ANNA KARENINA (1935, MGM)
Anna Karenina—Greta Garbo
Director—Clarence Brown
Leading Players—Fredric March, Freddie Bartholomew, Basil Rathbone, Maureen O'Sullivan, May Robson

ANNA KARENINA (1948, GB, Korda/British Lion)
Anna Karenina—Vivien Leigh
Director—Julien Duvivier
Leading Players—Ralph Richardson, Kieron Moore, Sally Ann Howes, Niall MacGinnis, Martita Hunt

ANNA LUCASTA (1949, Columbia)
Anna Lucasta—Paulette Goddard
Director—Irving Rapper
Leading Players—William Bishop, Oscar Homolka, John Ireland, Broderick Crawford, Will Geer

ANNA LUCASTA (1958, UA)
Anna Lucasta—Eartha Kitt
Director—Arnold Laven
Leading Players—Sammy Davis, Jr., Frederick O'Neal, Henry Scott, Rex Ingram, James Edwards

ANNABEL LEE (1921, Silent, Joam Film Sales)
Annabel Lee—Lorraine Harding
Director—William J. Scully
Leading Players—Jack O'Brien, Florida Kingsley, Louis Stearns, Ben Grauer, Arline Blackburn

ANNABEL TAKES A TOUR (1938, RKO)
Annabel—Lucille Ball
Director—Lew Landers
Leading Players—Jack Oakie, Ruth Donnelly, Bradley Page, Ralph Forbes

ANNABELLE'S AFFAIRS (1931, Fox Film Corp.)
Annabelle Leigh—Jeanette MacDonald
Director—Alfred Werker
Leading Players—Victor McLaglen, Roland Young, Sam Hardy

ANNE AGAINST THE WORLD (1929, Silent, Rayart Pictures)
Anne—Shirley Mason
Director—Duke Worne
Leading Players—Jack Mower, James Bradbury, Billy Franey

ANNE DEVLIN (1984, GB, Aeon Films)
Anne Devlin—Brid Brennan
Director—Pat Murphy
Leading Players—Bosco Hogan, Des McAleer, Gillian Hackett

ANNE OF GREEN GABLES (1919, Silent, Realart)
Anne Shirley—Mary Miles Minter
Director—William Desmond Taylor
Leading Players—George Stewart, Marcia Harris, Frederick Burton, Leila Romer, Lincoln Stedman

ANNE OF GREEN GABLES (1934, RKO)
Anne Shirley—Anne Shirley
Director—George Nichols, Jr.
Leading Players—Tom Brown, O.P. Heggie, Helen Westley, Sara Haden, Murray Kindell

ANNE OF LITTLE SMOKY (1921, Silent, Playgoers Pictures)
Anne Brockton—Winifred Westover
Director—Edward Connor
Leading Players—Dolores Cassinelli, Joe King, Frank Hagney

ANNE OF THE INDIES (1951, 20th Century Fox)
Anne—Jean Peters
Director—Jacques Tourneur
Leading Players—Louis Jordan, Debra Paget, Herbert Marshall, Thomas Gomez, James Robertson Justice

ANNE OF THE THOUSAND DAYS (1969, GB, Universal)
Anne Boleyn—Genevieve Bujold
Director—Charles Jarrott
Leading Players—Richard Burton, Irene Papas, Anthony Quayle, John Colicos, Michael Hordern

ANNE OF WINDY POPLARS (1940, RKO)
Anne Shirley—Anne Shirley
Director—Jack Hively
Leading Players—James Ellison, Henry Travers, Patric Knowles, Slim Summerville

ANNE ONE HUNDRED (1933, GB, British & Dominion/Paramount)
Anne Briston—Betty Stockfield
Director—Henry Edwards
Leading Players—Gyles Isham, Dennis Wyndham, Evelyn Roberts

ANNIE (1982, Columbia)
Annie—Aileen Quinn
Director—John Huston
Leading Players—Albert Finney, Carol Burnett, Bernadette Peters, Ann Reinking

ANNIE GET YOUR GUN (1950, MGM)
Annie Oakley—Betty Hutton
Director—George Sidney
Leading Players—Howard Keel, Louis Calhern, J. Carrol Naish, Edward Arnold, Keenan Wynn

ANNIE HALL (1977, UA)
Annie Hall—Diane Keaton
Director—Woody Allen

Leading Players—Woody Allen, Carol Kane, Tony Roberts, Paul Simon, Janet Margolin, Shelley Duvall

ANNIE LAURIE (1927, silent, MGM)
Annie Laurie—Polly Ward
Director—Walter Tennyson
Leading PLayers—Will Fyffe, Bruce Seaton, Vivienne Chatterton, Romily Lunge

ANNIE OAKLEY (1935, RKO)
Annie Oakley—Barbara Stanwyck
Director—George Stevens
Leading Players—Preston Foster, Melvyn Douglas, Moroni Olsen, Pert Kelton, Chief Thundercloud

ANOTHER THIN MAN (1939, MGM)
Nick Charles—William Powell
Director—W.S. Van Dyke
Leading Players—Myrna Loy, Virginia Grey, Otto Kruger, C. Aubrey Smith, Ruth Hussey, Nat Pendleton

ANOTHER WOMAN (1988, Orion)
Marion—Gena Rowlands
Director—Woody Allen
Leading Players—Gene Hackman, John Houseman, Martha Plimpton Mia Farrow, Sandy Dennis, Ian Holm, Blythe Danner,

ANOTHER YOU (1991, Tri-Star)
George/Abe Fielding—Gene Wilder
Director—Maurice Phillips
Leading Players—Richard Pryor, Mercedes Ruehl, Stephen Lang, Vanessa Williams, Phil Rubenstein

ANTHONY ADVERSE (1936, Warner Brothers)
Anthony Adverse—Fredric March
Director—Mervyn LeRoy
Leading Players—Olivia de Havilland, Edmund Gwenn, Claude Rains, Anita Louise, Louis Hayward, Gale Sondergaard, Steffi Duna

ANTONIA AND JANE (1991, GB, Miramax)
Antonia McGill—Saskia Reeves
Jane Hartman—Imelda Stauton
Director—Beeban Kidron
Leading Players—Bill Nighy, Allan Corduner, Brenda Bruce

ANTONY AND CLEOPATRA (1973, GB, Rank)
Antony—Charlton Heston
Cleopatra—Hildegard Neil
Director—Charlton Heston
Leading Players—Eric Porter, John Castle, Fernando Rey

ANYBODY HERE SEEN KELLY? (1928, Silent, Universal)
Pat Kelly—Tom Moore
Director—William Wyler
Leading Players—Bessie Love, Kate Price, Addie McPhail

ANYBODY'S BLONDE (1931, Action Pictures)
Janet—Dorothy Revier
Director—Frank Strayer
Leading Players—Reed Howes, Lloyd Whitlock, Edna Murphy

ANYBODY'S WOMAN (1930, Paramount)
Pansy Gray—Ruth Chatterton
Director—Dorothy Arzner

Leading Players—Clive Brook, Paul Lukas, Huntly Gordon

THE APACHE (1928, Silent, Columbia)
Gaston Laroux—Warner Richmond
Director—Philip Rosen
Leading Players—Margaret Livingston, Don Alvarado, Philo McCullough

APACHE (1954, UA)
Massai—Burt Lancaster
Director—Robert Aldrich
Leading Players—Jean Peters, John McIntire, John Dehner

THE APACHE RAIDER (1928, Silent, Pathe Exchange)
Apache Bob—Leo Maloney
Director—Leo D. Maloney
Leading Players—Eugenia Gilbert, Don Coleman, Tom London

APACHE WARRIOR (1957, 20th Century Fox)
Apache Kid—Keith Larsen
Director—Elmo Williams
Leading Players—Jim Davis, Rodolfo Acosta, John Miljan

APACHE WOMAN (1955, Golden State)
Anne Libeau—Joan Taylor
Director—Roger Corman
Leading Players—Lloyd Bridges, Lance Fuller, Morgan Jones

APARTMENT FOR PEGGY (1948, 20th Century Fox)
Peggy—Jeannie Crain
Director—George Seton
Leading Players—William Holden, Edmund Gwenn, Gene Lockhart

THE APE MAN (1943, Monogram)
Dr. James Brewster—Bela Lugosi
Director—William Beaudine
Leading Players—Louise Currie, Wallace Ford, Henry Hall

THE APPLEGATES—(1990, Australia, Roadshow/New World)
Dick Applegate—Ed Begley, Jr.
Jane Applegate—Stockard Channing
Sally Applegate—Cami Cooper
Johnny Applegate—Bobby Jacoby
Director—Michael Lehmann
Leading Players—Dabney Coleman, Glenn Shaddix, Adam Biesk

APPRENTICE TO MURDER (1988, New World)
Billy Kelly—Chad Lowe
Director—R.L. Thomas
Leading Players—Donald Sutherland, Mia Sara, Knut Husebo, Rutanya Alda

THE APPRENTICESHIP OF DUDDY KRAVITZ (1974, Canada, Astral/Paramount)
Duddy Kravitz—Richard Dreyfuss
Director—Ted Kotcheff
Leading Players—Micheline Lanctot, Jack Warden, Randy Quaid

APRIL FOOLS (1969, Jaelm/National General)
Howard Brubaker—Jack Lemmon
Catherine Gunther—Catherine Deneuve
Director—Stuart Rosenberg
Leading Players—Peter Lawford, Harvey Korman, Sally Kellerman, Melinda Dillon, Kenneth Mars

THE ARAB (1924, Silent, MGM)
Jamil Abdullah Azam—Ramon Novarro
Director—Rex Ingram
Leading Players—Alice Terry, Maxudian, Jean De Limur

AN ARABIAN KNIGHT (1920, Silent, Haworth)
Ahmed—Sessue Hawakawa
Director—Charles Swickard
Leading Players—Lillian Hall, Jean Acker, Marie Pavis, Elaine Innescourt, Harvey Clarke, Fred Jones

THE ARGYLE CASE (1917, Warwick Co.)
Bruce Argyle—Arthur Albertson
Director—Ralph Ince
Leading Players—Robert Warwick, Charles Hines, Gazelle Marche

THE ARGYLE CASE (1929, Warner Brothers)
Bruce Argyle—John Darrow
Director—Howard Bretherton
Leading Players—Thomas Meighan, H.B. Warner, Lila Lee, Zasu Pitts

THE ARIZONA COWBOY (1950, Republic)
Rex Allen—Rex Allen
Director—R.G. Springsteen
Leading Players—Teala Loring, Gordon Jones, Minerva Urecal

THE ARIZONA KID (1939, Republic)
Roy Rogers—Roy Rogers
Director—Joseph Kane
Leading Players—Gabby Hayes, Sally March, Stuart Hamblen

THE ARIZONA RANGER (1948, RKO)
Bob Wade—Tim Holt
Director—John Rawlins
Leading Players—Jack Holt, Nan Leslie, Richard Martin

THE ARIZONA ROMEO (1925, Silent, Fox Film Corp.)
Tom Long—Buck Jones
Director—Edmund Mortimer
Leading Players—Lucy Fox, Maine Geary, Thomas R. Mills

ARIZONA WILDCAT (1938, 20th Century Fox)
Mary Jane Patterson—Jane Withers
Director—Herbert I. Leeds
Leading Players—Leo Carillo, Pauline Moore, William Henry

THE ARIZONIAN (1935, RKO)
Clay Talbot—Richard Dix
Director—Charles Vidor
Leading Players—Margot Grahame, Preston Foster, Louis Calhern, James Bush

ARKANSAS JUDGE (1941, Republic)
Abner—Leon Weaver
Director—Frank McDonald
Leading Players—Frank Weaver, June Weaver, Roy Rogers

THE ARKANSAS TRAVELLER (1938, Paramount)
The Traveller—Bob Burns
Director—Alfred Santell
Leading Players—Fay Bainter, John Beal, Jean Parker, Lyle Talbot

ARMED AND DANGEROUS (1986, Columbia)
Frank Dooley—John Candy
Norman Kane—Eugene Levy
Director—Mark L. Lester
Leading Players—Robert Loggia, Kenneth McMillan, Meg Ryan

ARMY GIRL (1938, Republic)
Julie Armstrong—Madge Evans
Director—George Nicholls
Leading Players—Preston Foster, James Gleason, Ruth Donnelly, Heather Angel

ARMY SURGEON (1942, RKO)
Capt. James Mason—James Ellison
Director—A. Edward Sutherland
Leading Players—Jane Wyatt, Kent Taylor, Walter Reed, Jack Briggs, James Burke

THE ARNELO AFFAIR (1947, MGM)
Tony Arnelo—John Hodiak
Director—Arch Oboler
Leading Players—George Murphy, Frances Gifford, Dean Stockwell, Eve Arden

ARNOLD (1973, Cinerama)
Arnold—Norman Stuart
Director—George Fenady
Leading Players—Stella Stevens, Roddy McDowall, Elsa Lanchester, Shani Wallis, Farley Granger

ARREST BULLDOG DRUMMOND (1939, GB, Paramount)
Capt. Hugh C. Drummond—John Howard
Director—James Hogan
Leading Players—Heather Angel. H.B. Warner, Reginald Denny

ARROWSMITH (1931, UA)
Dr. Martin Arrowsmith—Ronald Colman
Director—John Ford
Leading Players—Helen Hayes, Myrna Loy, Beulah Bondi, A.C. Anson, Richard Bennett, Claude King

ARSENE LUPIN (1932, MGM)
Duke of Charmerace—John Barrymore
Director—Jack Conway
Leading Players—Lionel Barrymore, Karen Morley, John Miljan

ARSENE LUPIN RETURNS (1938, MGM)
Arsene Lupin/Rene Farrand—Melvyn Douglas
Director—George Fitzmaurice
Leading Players—Virginia Bruce, Warren William, John Halliday, Nat Pendleton

ARTHUR (1981, Orion/Warner Brothers)
Arthur Bach—Dudley Moore
Director—Steve Gordon
Leading Players—Liza Minnelli, John Gielgud, Geraldine Fitzgerald, Jill Eikenberry

ARTHUR ON THE ROCKS (1988, Warner Brothers)
Arthur Bach—Dudley Moore
Director—Bud Yorkin
Leading Players—Liza Minnelli, Cynthia Sykes, John Gielgud, Geraldine Fitzgerald, Stephen Elliott

ARTHUR TAKES OVER (1948, 20th Century Fox)
Arthur Bixby—Skip Homeier

Director—Malcolm St. Clair
Leading Players—Lois Collier, Richard Crane, Ann E. Todd

ARTHUR'S HALLOWED GROUND (1986, GB, Cinecom)
Arthur—Jimmy Jewel
Director—Freddie Young
Leading Players—Jean Boht, David Swift, Michael Elphick

ASK BECCLES (1933, GB, British and Dominion)
Eustace Beccles—Garry Marsh
Director—Redd Davis
Leading Players—Mary Newland, Abraham Sofaer, Allan Jeayes

ASSAULT OF THE KILLER BIMBOS (1988, Titan/Empire)
Peaches—Christina Whitaker
LuLu—Elizabeth Kaitan
Director—Anita Rosenberg
Leading Players—Tammara Souza, Nick Cassavetes, Griffin
    O'Neal, David Marsh

ATHENA (1954, MGM)
Athena Mulvain—Jane Powell
Director—Richard Thorpe
Leading Players—Debbie Reynolds, Virginia Gibson, Edmond
    Purdom, Vic Damone, Louis Calhern

ATLAS (1960, Filmgroup)
Atlas—Michael Forrest
Director—Roger Corman
Leading Players—Frank Wolff, Barboura Morris, Walter Maslow

THE ATOMIC KID (1954, Republic)
Blix Waterberry—Mickey Rooney
Director—Leslie H. Martinson
Leading Players—Robert Strauss, Elaine Davis, Bill Goodwin

THE ATOMIC MAN (1955, Allied Artists)
Maitland—Donald Gray
Director—Ken Hughes
Leading Players—Gene Nelson, Faith Domergue, Joseph
    Tomelty

ATTA BOY (1926, Silent, Pathe Exchange)
Monty Milde—Monty Banks
Director—Edward H. Griffith
Leading Players—Virginia Bradford, Ernie Wood, Fred Kelsey

ATTACK OF THE 50 FOOT WOMAN (1958, Allied Artists)
Nancy Archer—Allison Hayes
Director—Nathan Hertz
Leading Players—William Hudson, Yvette Vickers, Roy Gordon

ATTORNEY FOR THE DEFENCE (1932, Columbia)
Burton—Edmund Lowe
Director—Irving Cummings
Leading Players—Evelyn Brent, Constance Cummings, Donald
    Dilloway, Dorothy Peterson, Dwight Frye

THE AUCTIONEER (1927, Silent, Fox Film Corp.)
Simon Levi—George Sidney
Director—Alfred E. Green
Leading Players—Marion Nixon, Gareth Hughes, Doris Lloyd

THE AUDACIOUS MR. SQUIRE (1923, silent, GB, British and
Colonial)
Tom Squire—Jack Buchanan

Director—Edwin Greenwood
Leading Players—Valia, Russell Thorndike, Malcolm Tod

AUDREY (1916, Silent, Lasky/Paramount)
Audrey—Pauline Frederick
Director—Robert Vignola
Leading Players—Charles Waldron, Margarete Christians

AUDREY ROSE (1977, UA)
Ivy Templeton—Susan Swift
Director—Robert Wise
Leading Players—Marsha Mason, Anthony Hopkins, John Beck

AUNT CLARA (1954, GB, British Lion)
Clara Hilton—Margaret Rutherford
Director—Anthony Kimmins
Leading Players—Ronald Shiner, A.E. Matthews, Fay Compton

AUNT RACHEL (1920, Silent, GB, Samuelson/Granger)
Aunt Rachel—Haidee Wright
Director—Albert Ward
Leading Players—Isobel Elsom, James Lindsay, Lionelle Howard

AUNT SALLY (1933, GB, Gainsborough/Gaumont)
Sally—Cicely Courtneidge
Director—Tim Whelan
Leading Players—Sam Hardy, Phyllis Clare, Billy Milton

AUNTIE MAME (1958, Warner Brothers)
Mame Dennis—Rosalind Russell
Director—Morton Da Costa
Leading Players—Forrest Tucker, Coral Browne, Fred Clark,
    Roger Smith, Peggy Cass, Jan Handzlik

AUTHOR! AUTHOR! (1982, 20th Century Fox)
Ivan Travalian—Al Pacino
Director—Arthur Hiller
Leading Players—Dyan Cannon, Tuesday Weld, Alan King

THE AVENGER (1933, Monogram)
Norman Craig—Ralph Forbes
Director—Edwin L. Marin
Leading Players—Adrienne Ames, Arthur Vinton, Claude
    Gillingwater

AVENGING ANGEL (1985, New World)
Angel/Molly—Betsy Russell
Director—Robert Vincent O'Neil
Leading Players—Rory Calhoun, Susan Tyrrell, Ossie Davis

THE AVENGING RIDER (1928, Silent, FBO Pictures)
Tom Larkin—Tom Tyler
Director—Wallace Fox
Leading Players—Florence Allen, Frankie Darro, Al Ferguson

THE AVERAGE WOMAN (1924, Silent, C.C. Burr Pictures)
Sally Whipple—Pauline Garon
Director—Christy Cabanne
Leading Players—David Powell, Harrison Ford, Burr McIntosh

THE AVIATOR (1929, Warner Brothers)
Robert Street -Edward Everett Horton
Director—Roy Del Ruth
Leading Players—Patsy Ruth Miller, Johnny Arthur, Lee Moran

THE AVIATOR (1985, MGM/UA)
Edgar Anscombe—Christopher Reeve

Director—George Miller
Leading Players—Rosanna Arquette, Jack Warden, Scott Wilson

AWAKENING OF JIM BURKE (1935, Columbia)
Jim Burke—Jack Holt
Director—Lambert Hillyer
Leading Players—Florence Rice, Kathleen Burke, Jimmie Butler

AWAKENINGS (1990, Columbia)
Leonard Lowe—Robert De Niro
Director—Penny Marshall
Leading Players—Robin Williams, Julie Kavner, Ruth Nelson, John Heard, Penelope Ann Miller, Alice Drummond

AYLWIN (1920, Silent, GB, Hepworth)
Hal Aylwin—Henry Edwards
Director—Henry Edwards
Leading Players—Chrissie White, Gerald Ames, Mary Dibley

B

B.F.'S DAUGHTER (1948, MGM)
Polly Fulton—Barbara Stanwyck
B.F. Fulton—Charles Coburn
Director—Robert Z. Leonard
Leading Players—Van Heflin, Richard Hart, Keenan Wynn, Margaret Lindsay, Spring Byington

BABBITT (1924, Silent, Warner Brothers)
George F. Babbitt—Willard Louis
Director—Harry Beaumont
Leading Players—Mary Alden, Carmel Myers, Raymond McKee, Maxine Elliott Hicks

BABBITT (1934, First National/Warner Brothers)
George F. Babbitt—Guy Kibbee
Director—William Keighley
Leading Players—Aline MacMahon, Claire Dodd, Maxine Doyle, Glen Boles, Minna Gombell

THE BABE (1992, Universal)
George Herman "Babe" Ruth—John Goodman
Director—Arthur Hiller
Leading Players—Kelly McGillis, Trini Alvarado, Bruce Boxleitner, Peter Donat, James Cromwell, J.C. Quinn, Joe Ragno

BABE COMES HOME (1927, Silent, First National)
Babe Dugan—Babe Ruth
Director—Ted Wilde
Leading Players—Anna Q. Nilsson, Louise Fazenda, Ethel Shannon, Arthur Stone

THE BABE RUTH STORY (1948, Monogram/Allied Artists)
George Herman "Babe" Ruth—William Bendix
Director—Ted Wilde
Leading Players—Claire Trevor, Charles Bickford, Sam Levene William Frawley

BABES IN ARMS (1939, MGM)
Mickey Moran—Mickey Rooney
Patsy Barton—Judy Garland
Director—Busby Berkeley
Leading Players—Charles Winninger, Guy Kibee, June Preisser, Grace Hayes

BABES IN TOYLAND (1934, MGM)
Stanley Dum—Stan Laurel
Oliver Dee—Oliver Hardy
Director—Gus Meins, Charles Rogers
Leading Players—Charlotte Henry, Felix Knight, Henry Kleinbach, Florence Roberts

BABES IN TOYLAND (1961, Buena Vista)
Gonzorgo—Henry Calvin
Roderigo—Gene Sheldon
Director—Jack Donahue
Leading Players—Ray Bolger, Tommy Sands, Annette Funicello, Ed Wynn, Tommy Kirk

BABES ON BROADWAY (1941, MGM)
Tommy Williams—Mickey Rooney
Penny Morris—Judy Garland
Director—Busby Berkeley
Leading Players—Fay Bainter, Virginia Weidler, Ray McDonald, Richard Quine, Donald Meek, Luis Alberni

BAB'S DIARY (1917, Silent, Paramount)
Babs Archibald—Marguerite Clark
Director—J. Searle Dawley
Leading Players—Nigel Barrie, Leonora Morgan, Frank Losee, Isabel O'Madigan

THE BABY AND THE BATTLESHIP (1957, GB, British Lion)
The Baby—Martyn Garrett
Director—Jay Lewis
Leading Players—John Mills, Richard Attenborough, Bryan Forbes, Harold Siddens

BABY BLUE MARINE (1976, Columbia)
Marion Hedgepth—Jan-Michael Vincent
Director—John Hancock
Leading Players—Glynnis O'Connor, Katherine Helmond, Dana Elcar, Bert Remsen, Richard Gere, Art Lund

BABY DOLL (1956, Warner Brothers)
Baby Doll—Carroll Baker
Director—Elia Kazan
Leading Players—Karl Malden, Eli Wallach, Mildred Dunnock

BABY FACE (1933, Warner Brothers)
Lily "Baby Face" Powers—Barbara Stanwyck
Director—Alfred E. Green
Leading Players—George Brent, Donald Cook, John Wayne, Henry Kokler, Arthur Hohl

BABY FACE HARRINGTON (1935, MGM)
Willie Harrington—Charles Butterworth
Director—Raoul Walsh
Leading Players—Una Merkel, Harvey Stephens, Eugene Pallette, Nat Pendleton, Ruth Selwyn

BABY FACE MORGAN (1942, Producers Releasing Corporation)
Baby Face Morgan—Richard Cromwell
Director—Arthur Dreifuss

Leading Players—Mary Carlisle, Robert Armstrong, Chick Chandler, Charles Judels

BABY FACE NELSON (1957, UA)
Baby Face Nelson—Mickey Rooney
Director—Donald Seigel
Leading Players—Cedric Hardwicke, Carolyn Jones, Chris Dark, Ted De Corsia, Leo Gordon

BABY, IT'S YOU (1983, Double Play/Paramount)
Jill—Rosanna Arquette
Director—John Sayles
Leading Players—Vincent Spano, Joanna Merlin, Jack Davidson, Leora Dana

THE BABY MAKER (1970, National General)
Tish Gray—Barbara Hershey
Director—James Bridges
Leading Players—Collin Wilcox-Horne, Sam Groom, Scott Glenn, Jeannie Berlin, Lily Valenty

BABY, TAKE A BOW (1934, Fox Film Corporation)
Shirley—Shirley Temple
Director—Harry Lachman
Leading Players—James Dunn, Claire Trevor, Alan Dinehart, Ray Walker, Dorothy Libaire

THE BACHELOR (1991, Greycat Films)
Dr. Emil Grasler—Keith Carradine
Director—Roberto Faenza
Leading Players—Miranda Richardson, Kristin Scott-Thomas, Sarah-Jane Fenton, Max Von Sydow

THE BACHELOR AND THE BOBBYSOXER (1947, RKO)
Dick Nugent—Cary Grant
Susan Turner—Shirley Temple
Director—Irving Reis
Leading Players—Myrna Loy, Rudy Vallee, Ray Collins, Harry Davenport, Johnny Sands

THE BACHELOR DADDY (1922, Silent, Paramount)
Richard Chester—Thomas Meighan
Director—Alfred Green
Leading Players—Leatrice Joy, Maude Wayne, Adele Farrington, J. Farrell MacDonald

BACHELOR DADDY (1941, Universal)
Joseph Smith—Edward Everett Horton
Director—Harold Young
Leading Players—Baby Sandy, Donald Woods, Raymond Walburn, Franklin Pangborn, Evelyn Ankers

BACHELOR FATHER (1931, MGM)
Sir Basil Winterton—C. Aubrey Smith
Director—Robert Z. Leonard
Leading Players—Marion Davies, Ralph Forbes, Ray Milland, Guinn "Big Boy" Williams

THE BACHELOR GIRL (1929, Part-talkie, Columbia)
Joyce—Jacqueline Logan
Director—Richard Thorpe
Leading Players—William Collier, Jr., Thelma Todd, Edward Hearn

BACHELOR IN PARADISE (1961, MGM)
Adam J. Niles—Bob Hope

Director—Jack Arnold
Leading Players—Lana Turner, Janis Paige, Jim Hutton, Paula Prentiss, Don Porter

BACHELOR IN PARIS (1953, GB, Lippert)
Matthew Ibbetson—Dennis Price
Director—John Guillermin
Leading Players—Anne Vernon, Mischa Auer, Hermione Baddeley, Brian Worth, Joan Kenney

BACHELOR MOTHER (1939, RKO)
Polly Parrish—Ginger Rogers
Director—Garson Kanin
Leading Players—David Niven, Charles Coburn, Frank Albertson, E. E. Clive

BACHELOR OF HEARTS (1958, GB, Rank)
Wolf Hansen—Hardy Kruger
Director—Wolf Rilla
Leading Players—Sylvia Syms, Ronald Lewis, Jeremy Burnham, Peter Myers, Philip Gilbert

BACHELOR PARTY (1984, 20th Century Fox)
Rick Gassko—Tom Hanks
Director—Neal Israel
Leading Players—Tawny Kitaen, Adrian Zmed, George Grizzard

BACHELOR'S AFFAIRS (1932, Fox Film Corporation)
Andrew Hoyt—Adolphe Menjou
Director—Alfred Werker
Leading Players—Minna Gombell, Arthur Pierson, Joan Marsh, Alan Dinehart, Irene Purcell

THE BACHELOR'S DAUGHTERS (1946, UA)
Eileen—Gail Russell
Cynthia—Claire Trevor
Terry—Ann Dvorak
Marta—Jane Wyatt
Mr. Moody—Adolphe Menjou
Director—Andrew Stone
Leading Players—Billie Burke, Eugene List, Damian O'Flynn, John Whitney, Russell Hicks

BAD BASCOMB (1946, MGM)
Zeb Bascomb—Wallace Beery
Director—Sylvan Simon
Leading Players—Margaret O'Brien, Marjorie Main, J. Carrol Naish, Frances Rafferty, Marshall Thompson

BAD BLONDE (1953, GB, Lippert)
Lorna Vecchi—Barbara Payton
Director—Reginald Leborg
Leading Players—Frederick Valk, John Slater, Sidney James, Tony Wright, Marie Burke

BAD BOY (1938, GB, Radius)
Nick Bryan—John Warwick
Director—John Blystone
Leading Players—John Longden, Kathleen Kelly, Brian Buchel, Gabrille Brune

BAD BOY (1949, Allied Artists/Monogram)
Danny Leister—Audie Murphy
Director—Kurt Neumann
Leading Players—Lloyd Nolan, Jane Wyatt, James Gleason, Stanley Clements, Martha Vickers

BAD BOYS (1983, EMI/Universal
    Mick—Sean Penn
    Paco—Esai Morales
    Director—Richard Rosenthal
    Leading Players—Reni Santoni, Jim Moody, Eric Gurry, Clancy Brown, Ally Sheedy

BAD CHARLESTON CHARLIE (1973, International Cinema)
    Charlie Jacobs—Ross Hagen
    Director—Ivan Nagy
    Leading Players—Kelly Thordsen, Hoke Howell, Dal Jenkins, Carmen Zappa, Mel Berger

BAD GIRL (1931, Fox Film Corporation)
    Dorothy Haley—Sally Eilers
    Director—Frank Borzage
    Leading Players—James Dunn, Minna Gombell, William Pawley

BAD GUY (1937, MGM)
    Lucky Walden—Bruce Cabot
    Director—Edward Cahn
    Leading Players—Virginia Grey, Edward Norris, Jean Chatburn

BAD INFLUENCE (1990, Triumph/Epic)
    Alex—Rob Lowe
    Director—Curtis Hanson
    Leading Players—James Spader, Lisa Zane, Christian Clemenson, Kathleen Wilhoite, Tony Maggio

BAD LIEUTENANT (1992, Odyssey)
    LT—Harvey Keitel
    Director—Abel Ferrara
    Leading Players—Frankie Thorn, Zoe Lund, Anthony Ruggerio, Eddie Daniels, Blanca Bakja

BAD LITTLE ANGEL (1939, MGM)
    Patsy—Virginia Weidler
    Director—William Thiele
    Leading Players—Gene Reynolds, Guy Kibbee, Ian Hunter, Elizabeth Patterson, Reginald Owen

THE BAD LORD BYRON (1949, GB, Triton/GFD)
    Lord Byron—Dennis Price
    Director—David MacDonald
    Leading Players—Mai Zetterling, Joan Greenwood, Linden Travers, Sonia Holm, Raymond Lovell

THE BAD MAN (1923, Silent, Associated First National)
    Pancho Lopez—Holbrook Blinn
    Director—Edwin Carewe
    Leading Players—Jack Mulhall, Walter McGrail, Enid Bennett

THE BAD MAN (1930, First National/Warner Brothers)
    Pancho Lopez—Walter Huston
    Director—Clarence Badger
    Leading Players—Dorothy Revier, James Rennie, O.P. Heggie

THE BAD MAN (1941, MGM)
    Pancho Lopez—Wallace Beery
    Director—Richard Thorpe
    Leading Players—Lionel Barrymore, Laraine Day, Ronald Reagan, Henry Travers

BAD MAN OF BRIMSTONE (1938, MGM)
    Trigger Bill—Wallace Beery
    Director—Walter Reuben

Leading Players—Virginia Bruce, Dennis O'Keefe, Joseph Calleia, Lewis Stone, Guy Kibbee

BAD MEN OF MISSOURI (1941, First National/Warner Brothers)
    Cole Younger—Dennis Morgan
    Bob Younger—Wayne Morris
    Jim Younger—Arthur Kennedy
    Jesse James—Alan Baxter
    Director—Ray Enright
    Leading Players—Jane Wyman, Victor Jory, Walter Catlett

BAD MEN OF TOMBSTONE (1949, Monogram/Allied Artists)
    Tom—Barry Sullivan
    Morgan—Broderick Crawford
    Director—Kurt Neumann
    Leading Players—Marjorie Reynolds, Fortunio Bonanova, Guinn "Big Boy" Williams

THE BAD ONE (1930, UA)
    Lita—Dolores Del Rio
    Director—George Fitzmaurice
    Leading Players—Edmund Lowe, Don Alvarado, Blanche Frederici

THE BAD SEED (1956, Warner Brothers)
    Rhoda—Patty McCormack
    Director—Mervyn LeRoy
    Leading Players—Nancy Kelly, Henry Jones, Eileen Heckart, Evelyn Varden, William Hopper

BAD SISTER (1931, Universal)
    Marianne—Sidney Fox
    Director—Hobart Henley
    Leading Players—Conrad Nagel, Bette Davis, Humphrey Bogart, ZaSu Pitts, Slim Summerville

THE BADGE OF MARSHAL BRENNAN (1957, Allied Artists)
    Marshal Brennan—Douglas Fowley
    Director—Albert C. Gannaway
    Leading Players—Jim Davis, Arleen Whelan, Lee Van Cleef

BAIL JUMPER (1990, Angelika)
    Elaine—Eszter Balint
    Director—Christian Faber
    Leading Players—B.J. Spalding, Tony Askin, Bo Brinkman, Alexandra Auder, Joie Lee

BAKER'S HAWK (1976, Doty-Dayton)
    Dan Baker—Clint Walker
    Director—Lyman D. Dayton
    Leading Players—Burl Ives, Diane Baker, Lee H. Montgomery, Alan Young, Taylor Lacher

BALLAD OF A GUNFIGHTER (1964, Ward/Parade)
    Marty Robbins—Marty Robbins
    Director—Bill Ward
    Leading Players—Joyce Reed, Bob Barron, Nestor Pavia

THE BALLAD OF CABLE HOGUE (1970, Warner Brothers)
    Cable Hogue—Jason Robards
    Director—Sam Peckinpah
    Leading Players—Stella Stevens, David Warner, Strother Martin, Slim Pickens

THE BALLAD OF GREGORIO CORTEZ (1983, Embassy Pictures)
    Gregorio Cortez—Edward James Olmos

Director—Robert M. Young
Leading Players—Tom Bower, Bruce McGill, James Gammon

THE BALLAD OF JOSIE (1968, Universal)
Josie Minick—Doris Day
Director—Andrew V. McLaglen
Leading Players—Peter Graves, George Kennedy, Andy Devine,
William Talman, David Hartman

THE BALLET GIRL (1916, Silent, World Pictures)
La Syrena—Jennie Raeburn—Alice Brady
Director—William A. Brady
Leading Players—Holbrook Blinn, Robert Frazer, Julia Stuart

THE BAMBOO BLONDE (1946, RKO)
Louise Anderson—Frances Langford
Director—Anthony Mann
Leading Players—Ralph Edwards, Russell Wade, Iris Adrian

THE BANDIT BUSTER (1926, Silent, Action Pictures)
Buddy Miller—Buddy Roosevelt
Director—Richard Thorpe
Leading Players—Molly Malone, Lafe McKee, Winifred Lewis

THE BANDIT OF SHERWOOD FOREST (1946, Columbia)
Robert of Nottingham—Cornel Wilde
Director—George Sherman
Leading Players—Anita Louise, Jill Esmond, Edgar Buchanan,
Henry Daniell, George Macready

THE BANDIT OF ZHOBE (1959, Columbia)
Kasin Khan—Victor Mature
Director—John Gilling
Leading Players—Anne Aubrey, Anthony Newley, Norman
Wooland

BANDIT QUEEN (1950, GB, Lippert)
Lola—Barbara Britton
Director—William Berke
Leading Players—Willard Parker, Philip Reed, Barton MacLane

THE BANDITS OF CORSICA (1953, Global/UA)
Mario & Carlos Franchi—Richard Greene
Director—Ray Nazzaro
Leading Players—Paula Raymond, Raymond Burr, Dona Drake,
Raymond Greenleaf, Lee Van Cleef

THE BANDIT'S SON (1927, Silent, FBO Pictures)
Bob McCall—Bob Steele
Director—Wallace W. Fox
Leading Players—Tom Lingham, Hal Davis, Stanley Taylor

THE BANDOLERO (1924, Silent, MGM)
Dorando, The Bandolero—Pedro De Cordoba
Director—Tom Terriss
Leading Players—Gustav von Seyffertitz, Manuel Granado,
Gordon Begg, Arthur Donaldson

THE BANK DICK (1940, Universal)
Egbert Souse—W.C. Fields
Director—Edward Cline
Leading Players—Cora Witherspoon, Una Merkel, Evelyn Del
Rio, Jessie Ralph, Franklin Pangborn

BANNING (1967, Universal)
Banning—Robert Wagner

Director—Ron Winston
Leading Players—Anjanette Comer, Jill St. John, Guy Stockwell,
James Farentino, Susan Clark

THE BANTAM COWBOY (1928, Silent, FBO Pictures)
David "Red" Hepner—Buzz Barton
Director—Louis King
Leading Players—Frank Rice, Tom Lingham, Dorothy Kitchen

THE BARBARIAN (1921, Silent, Pioneer)
Eric Straive—Monroe Salisbury
Director—Donald Crisp
Leading Players—George Burrell, Barney Sherry, Elinor
Hancock

THE BARBARIAN (1933, MGM)
Jamil—Ramon Novarro
Director—Sam Wood
Leading Players—Myrna Loy, Reginald Denny, Louise Closser
Hale, C. Aubrey Smith, Edward Arnold

THE BARBARIAN AND THE GEISHA (1958, 20th Century Fox)
Townsend Harris—John Wayne
Okichi—Eiko Ando
Director—John Huston
Leading Players—Sam Jaffe, So Yamamura, Norman Thomson,
James Robbins, Morita

THE BARBARIAN QUEEN (1985, Concorde/Cinema Group)
Amathea—Lana Clarkston
Director—Alex Sessa
Leading Players—Latta Shea, Frank Zagarino, Dawn Dunlap

BARBAROSA (1982, Universal)
Barbarosa—Willie Nelson
Director—Fred Schepisi
Leading Players—Gary Busey, Isela Vega, Gilbert Roland

BARBARY COAST GENT (1944, MGM)
Honest Plush Brannon—Wallace Beery
Director—Roy Del Ruth
Leading Players—Binnie Barnes, John Carradine, Bruce
Kellogg, Frances Rafferty, Chill Wills

THE BARBER OF STAMFORD HILL (1963, GB, British Lion)
Mr. Figg—John Bennett
Director—Casper Wrede
Leading Players—Meg Jenkins, Maxwell Shaw, John Graham

BARDELYS THE MAGNIFICENT (1926, Silent, MGM)
Bardelys—John Gilbert
Director—King Vidor
Leading Players—Eleanor Boardman, Roy D'Arcy, Lionel
Belmore, Emily Fitzroy, Arthur Lubin

THE BAREFOOT BOY (1923, Silent, Mission Film Co.)
Dick Alden—John Bowers
Director—David Kirland
Leading Players—Marjorie Daw, Sylvia Breamer, George
McDaniel, Raymond Hatton

BAREFOOT BOY (1938, Monogram)
Billy Whittaker—Jackie Moran
Director—Karl Brown
Leading Players—Marcia Mae Jones, Claire Windsor, Ralph
Morgan, Charles D. Brown

THE BAREFOOT MAILMAN (1951, Columbia)
Steven Pierton—Jerome Courtland
Director—Earl McEvoy
Leading Players—Robert Cummings, Terry Moore, John Russell, Will Geer, Arthur Shields

BARFLY (1987, Cannon)
Henry Chinaski—Mickey Rourke
Director—Barbet Schroeder
Leading Players—Faye Dunaway, Alice Krige, Jack Nance

THE BARKER (1928, Part-Talkie, First National/Warner Brothers)
Nifty Miller—Milton Sills
Director—George Fitzmaurice
Leading Players—Dorothy MacKaill, Betty Compson, Douglas Fairbanks, Jr., Sylvia Ashton

THE BARKLEYS OF BROADWAY (1949, MGM)
Josh Barkley—Fred Astaire
Dinah Barkley—Ginger Rogers
Director—Charles Walters
Leading Players—Oscar Levant, Billie Burke, Gale Robbins, Jacques Francois, George Zucco

BARNABY (1919, Silent, Barker)
Barnaby—Dick Webb
Director—Jack Denton
Leading Players—Cyril Vaughn, Athalie Davis, Dorothy Fane

BARNACLE BILL (1935, GB, City/Butchers Film Service)
Bill Harris—Archie Pitt
Director—Harry Hughes
Leading Players—Joan Gardner, Gus McNaughton, Jean Adrienne, Sybil Jason, Denis O'Neil

BARNACLE BILL (1941, MGM)
Bill Johansen—Wallace Beery
Director—Richard Thorpe
Leading Players—Marjorie Main, Leo Carillo, Virginia Weidler, Donald Meek, Barton MacLane

THE BARON OF ARIZONA (1950, Lippert)
James Addison Reavis—Vincent Price
Director—Samuel Fuller
Leading Players—Ellen Drew, Vladimir Sokoloff, Reed Hadley, Robert Barrat, Robin Short

THE BARONESS AND THE BUTLER (1938, 20th Century Fox)
Johann Porok—William Powell;
Baroness Katrina—Annabella
Director—Walter Lang
Leading Players—Helen Westley, Henry Stephenson, Joseph Schildkraut, J. Edward Bromberg

THE BARRETTS OF WIMPOLE STREET (1934, MGM)
Elizabeth Barrett—Norma Shearer
Edward Moulton Barrett—Charles Laughton
Director—Sidney Franklin
Leading Players—Fredric March, Maureen O'Sullivan, Katherine Alexander, Una O'Connor

THE BARRETTS OF WIMPOLE STREET (1957, MGM)
Elizabeth Barrett—Jennifer Jones
Edward Moulton Barrett—John Gielgud
Director—Sidney Franklin

Leading Players—Bill Travers, Virginia McKenna, Vernon Gray, Susan Stephen

BARRY LYNDON (1975, GB, Hawk-Peregrine)
Barry Lyndon—Ryan O'Neal
Director—Stanley Kubrick
Leading Players—Marisa Berenson, Patrick Magee, Hardy Kruger, Steven Berkoff, Gay Hamilton

BARRY MCKENZIE HOLDS HIS OWN (1975, Australia, Roadshow)
Barry McKenzie—Barry Crocker
Director—Bruce Beresford
Leading Players—Barry Humphries, Donald Pleasence, Dick Bentley, Ed Deveraux

THE BARNSTORMER (1922, Silent, Associated First National)
Joel "Utility" Matthews—Charles Ray
Director—Charles Ray
Leading Players—Wilfrid Lucas, Florence Oberle, Lionel Belmore, Philip Dunham, Gus Leonard

BARTLEBY (1970, GB, Pantheon/British Lion)
Bartleby—John McEnery
Director—Anthony Friedman
Leading Players—Paul Scofield, Thorley Walters, Colin Jeavons, Raymond Mason

BARTON FINK—(1991, 20th Century Fox)
Barton Fink—John Turturro
Director—Joel Cohen
Leading Players—John Goodman, Judy Davis, Michael Lerner, John Mahoney, Tony Shalhoub, Jon Polito

THE BARTON MYSTERY (1932, GB, British & Dominions)
Gerald Barton—Franklyn Bellamy
Director- Henry Edwards
Leading Players—Ursula Jeans, Ellis Jeffreys, Lyn Harding, Ion Swinley, Wendy Barrie

BASHFUL BUCCANEER (1925, Silent, Rayart Pictures)
Jerry Logan—Reed Howes
Director—Harry J. Brown
Leading Players—Dorothy Dwan, Sheldon Lewis, Bull Montana

THE BAT (1959, Allied Artists)
Dr. Malcolm Wells—Vincent Price
Director—Crane Wilbur
Leading Players—Agnes Moorehead, Gavin Gordon, John Sutton

BAT 21 (1988, Tri-Star)
Lt. Col. Iceal Hambleton—Gene Hackman
Director—Peter Markle
Leading Players—Danny Glover, David Marshall Grant, Clayton Rohner

THE BAT WHISPERS (1930, UA)
Detective Anderson—Chester Morris
Director—Roland West
Leading Players—Una Merkel, Chancer Ward, Grace Hampton, Maude Eburne, Spencer Charters

BATHING BEAUTY (1944, MGM)
Caroline Brooks—Esther Williams
Director—George Sidney

Leading Players—Red Skelton, Basil Rathbone, Bill Goodwin, Ethel Smith, Jean Porter

BATMAN (1966, 20th Century Fox)
Batman (Bruce Wayne)—Adam West
Director—Leslie H. Martinson
Leading Players—Lee Meriwether, Cesar Romero, Burgess Meredith, Frank Gorshin, Burt Ward

BATMAN (1989, Warner Brothers)
Batman (Bruce Wayne)—Michael Keaton
Director—Tim Burton
Leading Players—Jack Nicholson, Kim Basinger, Robert Wuhl, Pat Hingle, Billy Dee Williams, Michael Gough, Jack Palance, Jerry Hall

BATMAN RETURNS (1992, Warner Brothers)
Batman—Michael Keaton
Director—Tim Burton
Leading Players—Danny De Vito, Michelle Pfeiffer, Christopher Walken, Michael Gough, Michael Murphy, Cristi Conaway, Andrew Bryniarski, Pat Hingle

THE BATTLEAXE (1962, GB, Danzinger)
Mrs. Page—Joan Hawthorne
Director—Godfrey Grayson
Leading Players—Jill Ireland, Francis Matthews, Michael Beint, Olaf Pooley

BATTLE OF CHIEF PONTIAC (1952, Real Art)
Chief Pontiac—Lon Chaney, Jr.
Director—Felix Feist
Leading Players—Lex Barker, Helen Wescott, Berry Krueger

BATTLING BUNYON (1925, Silent, Crown Productions)
Aiken "Battling" Bunyon—Wesley Barry
Director—Paul Hurst
Leading Players—Molly Malone, Frank Campeau, Harry Mann

BATTLING BUTLER (1926, Silent, MGM)
Alfred Butler—Buster Keaton
Director—Buster Keaton
Leading Players—Sally O'Neil, Snitz Edwards, Francis MacDonald, Mary O'Brien

THE BATTLING FOOL (1924, Silent, Perfection Pictures)
Mark Jenkins—William Fairbanks
Director—W.S. Van Dyke
Leading Players—Eva Novak, Fred J. Butler, Laura Winston

BATTLING JANE (1918, Silent, Paramount)
Battling Jane—Dorothy Gish
Director—D.W. Griffith
Leading Players—George Nicholls, Bertram Grasby, Adolphe Lestina

BATTLING MASON (1924, Silent, Hercules Film Production)
Mason—Frank Merrill
Director—Jack Nelson
Leading Players—Eva Novak, Billy Elmer, Dick Sutherland

BAWBS O' BLUE RIDGE (1916, Silent, Triangle-Key Bee)
Barbara "Bawbs" Colby—Bessie Barriscale
Director—Charles Miller
Leading Players—Arthur Shirley, Joe Dowling, J. Frank Burke

THE BAWDY ADVENTURES OF TOM JONES (1976, GB, Universal)
Tom Jones—Nicky Henson
Director—Cliff Owen
Leading Players—Trevor Howard, Terry-Thomas, Arthur Lowe, Georgia Brown, Joan Collins

BAXTER (1973, GB, National General)
Robert Baxter—Scott Jacoby
Director—Lionel Jeffries
Leading Players—Patricia Neal, Jean-Pierre Cassel, Britt Eklund, Lynn Carlin

THE BAY BOY (1985, Orion)
Donald Campbell—Keifer Sutherland
Director—Daniel Petrie
Leading Players—Liv Ullmann, Alan Scarfe, Joe MacPherson

THE BEACHCOMBER (1938, GB, Mayflower/Paramount)
Ginger Ted—Charles Laughton
Director—Erich Pommer
Leading Players—Elsa Lanchester, Tyrone Guthrie, Robert Newton, Dolly Mollinger

THE BEACHCOMBER (1955, GB, MacQuitty /UA)
Ginger Ted—Robert Newton
Director—Muriel Box
Leading Players—Glynis Johns, Donald Sinden, Paul Rogers, Donald Pleasance

THE BEAR (1984, Embassy)
Paul "Bear" Bryant—Gary Busey
Director—Richard Sarafian
Leading Players—Cynthia Leake, Carmen Thomas, Cary Guffey

THE BEAST OF BUDAPEST (1958, Barlene/Allied Artists)
Zagon—Gerald Milton
Director—Harmon C. Jones
Leading Players—John Hoyt, Greta Thyssen, Michael Mills

THE BEASTMASTER (1982, MGM/UA)
Dar—Marc Singer
Director—Don Coscarelli
Leading Players—Tanya Roberts, Rip Torn, John Amos, Josh Milrad, Rod Loomis

BEASTMASTER 2: THROUGH THE PORTAL OF TIME (1991, New Line)
Dar—Marc Singer
Director—Sylvo Tabet
Leading Players—Kari Wuhner, Wings Hauser, Sarah Douglas, Charles Young

BEAU BANDIT (1930, RKO)
Montero—Rod La Rocque
Director—Lambert Hillyer
Leading Players—Mitchell Lewis, Doris Kenyon, Charles B. Middleton, George Duryea

BEAU BROCADE (1916, GB, Artistic)
Sir Humphrey Challoner—Charles Rock
Director—Thomas Bentley
Leading Players—Mercy Hatton, Austin Leigh, Cecil Mannering, George Foley

BEAU BRUMMELL (1924, Silent, Warner Brothers)
  George Bryan Brummell—John Barrymore
  Director—Harry Beaumont
  Leading Players—Mary Astor, Willard Louis, Carmel Myers,
    Irene Rich, Alec B. Francis

BEAU BRUMMELL (1954, MGM)
  George Bryan "Beau" Brummell—Stewart Granger
  Director—Curtis Bernhardt
  Leading Players—Elizabeth Taylor, Peter Ustinov, Robert
    Morley, James Donald, James Hayter

BEAU GESTE (1926, Silent, Paramount)
  Michael "Beau" Geste—Ronald Colman
  Director—Herbert Brenon
  Leading Players—Neil Hamilton, Ralph Forbes, Alice Joyce,
    Noah Beery, Norman Trevor

BEAU GESTE (1939, Paramount)
  Beau Geste—Gary Cooper
  Director—William A. Wellman
  Leading Players—Ray Milland, Robert Preston, Brian Donlevy,
    Susan Hayward, J. Carrol Naish

BEAU GESTE (1966, Universal)
  Beau Geste—Guy Stockwell
  Director—Douglas Heyes
  Leading Players—Doug McClure, Leslie Nielsen, Telly Savalas,
    David Mauro, Robert Wolders

BEAU JAMES (1957, Paramount)
  Jimmy Walker—Bob Hope
  Director—Melville Shavelson
  Leading Players—Vera Miles, Paul Douglas, Alexis Smith,
    Darren McGavin, Joe Mantell

BEAU REVEL (1921, Silent, Paramount)
  Lawrence "Beau" Revel—Lewis R. Stone
  Director—John Griffith
  Leading Players—Florence Vidor, Lloyd Hughes, Kathleen
    Kirkham, Richard Ryan

BEAU SABREUR (1928, Silent, Paramount)
  Major Henri De Beaujolais—Gary Cooper
  Director—John Waters
  Leading Players—Evelyn Brent, Noah Beery, William Powell,
    Roscoe Karns, Mitchell Lewis

THE BEAUTIFUL BLONDE FROM BASHFUL (1949, 20th Century
Fox)
  Freddie—Betty Grable
  Director—Preston Sturges
  Leading Players—Cesar Romero, Rudy Vallee, Olga San Juan,
    Sterling Holloway, Hugh Herbert, El Brendel

BEAUTIFUL BUT DUMB (1928, Silent, Tiffany-Stahl)
  Janet Brady—Patsy Ruth Miller
  Director—Elmer Clifton
  Leading Players—Charles Byer, George E. Stone, Shirley
    Palmer, Greta Yoltz

THE BEAUTIFUL CHEAT (1926, Silent, Universal)
  Mary Callahan—Laura La Plante
  Director—Edward Sloman
  Leading Players—Harry Myers, Bertram Grassy, Alexander Carr

THE BEAUTIFUL GAMBLER (1921, Silent, Universal)
  Molly Hanlon—Grace Darmond
  Director—William Worthington
  Leading Players—Jack Mower, Harry Van Meter, Charles
    Brinley

THE BEAUTIFUL LIAR (1921, Silent, Preferred Pictures)
  Helen Haynes—Katherine MacDonald
  Director—Wallace Worsley
  Leading Players—Charles Meredith, Joseph J. Dowling, Kate
    Lester, Wilfred Lucas

THE BEAUTIFUL MRS. REYNOLDS (1918, Silent, World Films)
  Maria Reynolds—June Elvidge
  Director—Arthur Ashley
  Leading Players—Arthur Ashley, Carlyle Blackwell, Carl Girard,
    Hubert Wilke

BEAUTIFUL STRANGER (TWIST OF FATE) (1954, GB, British
Lion)
  "Johnny" Victor—Ginger Rogers
  Director—David Miller
  Leading Players—Stanley Baker, Herbert Lom, Jacques
    Bergerac

BEAUTY AND THE BAD MAN (1925, Silent, Peninsula Studios)
  Cassie—Mabel Ballin
  Madoc Bill—Forrest Stanley
  Director—William Worthington
  Leading Players—Russell Simpson, Andre De Beranger, Edna
    Mae Cooper

BEAUTY AND THE BARGE (1937, GB, Twickenham/Wardour)
  Ethel Smedley—Judy Gunn
  Director—Henry Edwards
  Leading Players—Gordon Harker, Jack Hawkins, George Carney,
    Margaret Rutherford

BEAUTY AND THE BEAST (1963, UA)
  Lady Althea—Joyce Taylor
  Duke Eduardo—Mark Damon
  Director—Edward L. Cahn
  Leading Players—Eduard Franz, Michael Pate, Merry Anders

BEAUTY AND THE BEAST (1991, Animated, Buena Vista/
Disney)
  Belle—Voice of Paige O'Hara
  Beast—Voice of Robby Benson
  Director—Gary Trousdale and Kirk Wise
  Leading Players—Voices of Jerry Orbach, Angela Lansbury,
    Richard White, David Ogden Stiers, Jesse Corti, Rex Everhart

BEAUTY AND THE BOSS (1932, Warner Brothers)
  Susie Sachs—Marian Marsh
  Baron von Ullrich—Warren William
  Director—Roy Del Ruth
  Leading Players—Charles Butterworth, Frederick Kerr, Mary
    Doran, Lillian Bond

BECKET (1964, GB, Paramount)
  Thomas Becket—Richard Burton
  Director—Peter Glenville
  Leading Players—Peter O'Toole, Donald Wolfit, John Gielgud,
    Martita Hunt, Pamela Brown, Sian Phillips

BECKY (1927, Silent, MGM)
Rebecca O'Brien McCloskey—Sally O'Neil
Director—John P. McCarthy
Leading Players—Owen Moore, Harry Crocker, Gertrude Olmstead

BECKY SHARP (1935, Pioneer/RKO)
Becky Sharp—Miriam Hopkins
Director—Rouben Mamoulian
Leading Players—Frances Dee, Cedric Hardwicke, Billie Burke, Alison Skipworth, Nigel Bruce

BEDELIA (1946, GB, General Films)
Bedelia—Margaret Lockwood
Director—Lance Comfort
Leading Players—Ian Hunter, Barry K. Barnes, Anne Crawford

BEETLEJUICE (1988, Warner Brothers)
Betlegeuse—Michael Keaton
Director—Tim Burton
Leading Players—Alec Baldwin, Geena Davis, Jeffrey Jones, Catherine O'Hara, Sylvia Sidney, Winona Ryder

THE BEGUILED (1971, Universal)
John McBurney—Clint Eastwood
Director—Don Siegel
Leading Players—Geraldine Page, Elizabeth Hartman, Jo Ann Harris, Darleen Carr, Mae Mercer

BEHOLD MY WIFE (1920, Silent, Paramount)
Lali Amour—Mabel Julienne Scott
Frank Armour—Milton Sills
Director—George Melford
Leading Players—Winter Hall, Elliot Dexter, Helen Dunbar, Ann Forrest, Maude Wayne

BEHOLD MY WIFE (1935, Paramount)
Tonita Stormcloud—Sylvia Sidney
Michael Carter—Gene Raymond
Director—Mitchell Leisen
Leading Players—Julie Compton, Laura Hope Crews, H.B. Warner, Monroe Owsley, Ann Sheridan

BEHOLD THIS WOMAN (1924, Silent, Vitagraph)
Louise Maurel—Irene Rich
Director—J. Stuart Blackton
Leading Players—Marguerite De La Motte, Charles A. Post, Harry Myers, Rosemary Theby

THE BELGIAN (1917, Silent, Olcott Productions)
Victor Morenne—Walker Whiteside
Director—Sidney Olcott
Leading Players—Valentine Grant, Sally Crute, Georgio Majeroni, Anders Randolf

BELIZAIRE THE CAJUN (1986, Skouras)
Belizaire Breaux—Armand Assante
Director—Glen Pitre
Leading Players—Gail Youngs, Michael Schoeffling, Robert Duvall, Stephen McHattie

BELL-BOTTOM GEORGE (1943, GB, Columbia British)
George—George Formby
Director—John Baxter
Leading Players—Anne Firth, Reginald Purdell, Peter Murray Hill, Charles Farrell

BELLA DONNA (1915, Silent, Paramount)
Bella Donna—Pauline Frederick
Director—Sidney Olcott
Leading Players—Thomas Holding, Julian L'Estrange, Eugene Ormande, George Majeroni

BELLA DONNA (1923, Silent, Paramount)
Bella Donna—Pola Negri
Director—George Fitzmaurice
Leading Players—Conway Tearle, Conrad Nagel, Adolphe Menjou, Claude King

BELLAMY TRIAL (1929, Part-Talkie, MGM)
Stephen Bellamy—Kenneth Thompson
Director—Monta Bell
Leading Players—Leatrice Joy, Betty Bronson, Edward Nugent

THE BELLBOY (1960, Paramount)
Stanley—Jerry Lewis
Director—Jerry Lewis
Leading Players—Alex Gerry, Bob Clayton, Sonnie Sands, Herkie Styles, Milton Berle

BELLE LE GRAND (1951, Republic)
Belle Le Grand—Vera Ralston
Director—Allan Dwan
Leading Players—John Carroll, Muriel Lawrence, William Ching, Hope Emerson, Grant Withers

THE BELLE OF BROADWAY (1926, Silent, Columbia)
Marie Duval—Betty Compson
Director—Harry O. Hoyt
Leading Players—Herbert Rawlinson, Edith Yorke, Armand Kaliz

THE BELLE OF NEW YORK (1952, MGM)
Angela Bonfils—Vera-Ellen
Director—Charles Walters
Leading Players—Fred Astaire, Marjorie Main, Keenan Wynn

BELLE OF OLD MEXICO (1950, Republic)
Rosita—Estelita Rodriguez
Director—R.G. Springsteen
Leading Players—Robert Rockwell, Dorothy Patrick, Thurston Hall, Florence Bates

BELLE OF THE NINTIES (1934, Paramount)
Ruby Carter—Mae West
Director—Leo McCarey
Leading Players—Roger Pryor, Johnny Mack Brown, John Miljan, Katherine DeMille, James Conlan

BELLE OF THE YUKON (1944, RKO)
Belle DeValle—Gypsy Rose Lee
Director—Willaim A. Seiter
Leading Players—Randolph Scott, Dinah Shore, Charles Winninger, Bob Burns, Florence Bates

BELLE STARR (1941, 20th Century Fox)
Belle Starr—Gene Tierney
Director—Irving Cummings
Leading Players—Randolph Scott, Dana Andrews, John Sheppard, Elizabeth Patterson, Chill Wills

BELLE STARR'S DAUGHTER (1947, Alson/20th Century Fox)
Rose of Cimarron—Ruth Roman

Director—Lesley Selander
Leading Players—George Montgomery, Rod Cameron, Wallace Ford

BELLY OF THE ARCHITECT (1987, GB, Hemdale)
Stourley Kracklite—Brian Dennehy
Director—Peter Greenaway
Leading Players—Chloe Webb, Lambert Wilson, Vanni Corbellini

THE BELOVED ADVENTURESS (1917, Silent, Peerless/World)
Juliette La Monde—Kitty Gordon
Director—William A. Brady
Leading Players—Jack Drumier, Inez Shannon, Madge Evans

THE BELOVED BACHELOR (1931, Paramount)
Michael Morda—Paul Lukas
Director—Lloyd Corrigan
Leading Players—Dorothy Jordan, Betty Van Allen, Charles Ruggles, Vivienne Osborne, Leni Stengel

BELOVED BRAT (1938, Warner Brothers)
Roberta—Bonita Granville
Director—Arthur Lubin
Leading Players—Dolores Costello, Donald Crisp, Donald Briggs, Natalie Moorhead, Lucille Gleason

THE BELOVED BRUTE (1924, Silent, Vitagraph)
Charles Hinges—Victor McLaglen
Director—J. Stuart Blackton
Leading Players—Marguerite de la Motte, William Russell, Stuart Holmes, Frank Brownlee

BELOVED ENEMY (1936, Goldwyn/UA)
Helen Drummond—Merle Oberon
Dennis Riordan—Brian Aherne
Director—H.C. Potter
Leading Players—Karen Morley, Theodore Von Eltz, Jerome Cowan, David Niven, John Burton

BELOVED IMPOSTER (1936, GB, Stafford/Radio)
George -Fred Conyngham
Director—Victor Hanbury
Leading Players—Rene Ray, Germaine Aussey, Penelope Parkes

BELOVED INFIDEL (1959, 20th Century Fox)
F. Scott Fitzgerald—Gregory Peck
Director—Henry King
Leading Players—Deborah Kerr, Eddie Albert, Philip Ober

BELOVED ROGUE (1927, Silent, UA)
Francois Villon—John Barrymore
Director—Alan Crosland
Leading Players—Conrad Veidt, Marceline Day, Henry Victor

THE BELOVED VAGABOND (1923, Silent, GB, Astra-National)
Gaston de Nerac—Caryle Blackwell
Director—Fred Leroy
Leading Players—Madge Stuart, Phyllis Titmus, Sydney Fairbrother, Albert Chase

THE BELOVED VAGABOND (1936, GB, Toeplitz/Columbia)
Paragot—Maurice Chevalier
Director—Curtis Bernhardt
Leading Players—Betty Stockfield, Margaret Lockwood, Desmond Tester, Austin Trevor

BELPHEGOR THE MOUNTEBANK (1921, Silent, GB, Ideal)
Belphegor—Milton Rosmer
Director—Bert Wynne
Leading Players—Kathleen Vaughan, Warwick Ward, Nancy Price

BEN BLAIR (1916, Silent, Paramount)
Ben Blair—Dustin Farnum
Director—William D. Taylor
Leading Players—Winifred Kinston, Herbert Standing, Lamar Johnstone, Virginia Foltz

BEN-HUR (1925, Silent, MGM)
Judah Ben-Hur—Ramon Novarro
Director—Fred Niblo
Leading Players—Francis X. Bushman, May McAvoy, Betty Bronson, Claire McDowell

BEN-HUR (1959, MGM)
Judah Ben-Hur—Charlton Heston
Director—William Wyler
Leading Players—Jack Hawkins, Stephen Boyd, Haya Harareet, Hugh Griffith, Martha Scott, Sam Jaffe

THE BENNY GOODMAN STORY (1956, Universal)
Benny Goodman—Steve Allen
Director—Valentine Davies
Leading players—Donna Reed, Berta Gersten, Herbert Anderson

THE BENSON MURDER CASE (1930, Paramount)
Anthony Benson—Richard Tucker
Director—Frank Tuttle
Leading Players—William Powell, Natalie Moorhead, Eugene Pallette, Paul Lukas, William Boyd

BERLIN CORRESPONDENT (1942, 20th Century Fox)
Bill Roberts—Dana Andrews
Director—Eugene Forde
Leading Players—Virginia Gilmore, Mona Maris, Martin Kosleck

THE BERMONDSEY KID (1933, Great Brtiain, Warner Brothers/First National)
Eddie Martin—Esmond Knight
Director—Ralph Dawson
Leading Players—Pat Paterson, Ellis Irving, Ernest Sefton

BERT RIGBY, YOU'RE A FOOL (1989, Warner Brothers)
Bert Rigby—Robert Lindsay
Director—Carl Reiner
Leading Players—Cathryn Bradshaw, Robbie Coltrane, Anne Bancroft, Corbin Bernsen

BERTHA THE SEWING MACHINE GIRL (1926, Silent, Fox Film Corp.)
Bertha Sloan—Madge Bellamy
Director—Irving Cummings
Leading Players—Allan Simpson, Sally Phipps, Paul Nicholson

BEST FRIENDS (1982, Warner Brothers)
Richard Babson—Burt Reynolds
Paula McCullen—Goldie Hawn
Director—Norman Jewison
Leading Players—Jessica Tandy, Barnard Hughes, Audra Lindley

THE BEST OF ENEMIES (1962, Columbia)
Major Richardson—David Niven
Captain Blasi—Alberto Sordi
Director—Guy Hamilton
Leading Players—Michael Wilding, Harry Andrews, Noel Harrison, Ronald Fraser, David Opatoshu

BEST OF THE BEST (1989, Taurus)
Alex Grady—Eric Roberts
Director—Bob Radler
Leading Players—James Earl Jones, Sally Kirkland, Phillip Rhee, Christopher Penn, John Dye

BETRAYED (1988, MGM/UA)
Catherine Weaver—Debra Winger
Director—Constantin Costa-Gavras
Leading Players—John Heard, Tom Berenger, John Mahoney

BETSY ROSS (1917, Silent, Peerless/World)
Betsy Ross—Alice Brady
Director—Travers Yale
Leading Players—John Bowers, Lillian Cook, Victor Kennard

BETSY'S WEDDING—(1990, Touchstone)
Betsy Hopper—Molly Ringwald
Director—Alan Alda
Leading Players—Alan Alda, Madeline Kahn, Ally Sheedy, Anthony LaPaglia, Joe Pesci, Joey Bishop

BETTER OFF DEAD (1985, Warner Brothers)
Lane Myer—John Cusack
Director—Savage Steve Holland
Leading Players—David Ogden Steirs, Diane Franklin, Kim Darby, Amanda Wyss

THE BETTER 'OLE (1926, Silent, Warner Brothers)
Ole Bill—Syd Chaplin
Director—Charles Reisner
Leading Players—Doris Hill, Harold Goodwin, Theodore Lynch, Tom McGuire

BETTINA LOVED A SOLDIER (1916, Silent, Bluebird)
Bettina—Louise Lovely
Jean Reynaud—The Soldier—Rupert Julian
Director—Rupert Julian
Leading Players—George Berrill, Frencella Billington, Zoe Durae, Douglas Gerard

BETTY CO-ED (1946, Columbia)
Joanne Leeds—Jean Porter
Director—Arthur Dreifuss
Leading Players—Shirley Mills, William Mason, Rosemary La Planche, Kay Morley

BETWEEN TWO WOMEN (1937, MGM)
Claire Donahue—Maureen O'Sullivan
Patricia Sloan—Virginia Bruce
Director—George B. Seitz
Leading Players—Franchot Tone, Leonard Penn, Cliff Edwards

BEVERLY HILLS COP (1984, Paramount)
Axel Foley—Eddie Murphy
Director—Martin Brest
Leading Players—Judge Reinhold, John Ashton, Lisa Eilbacher, Ronny Cox

BEVERLY HILLS COP II (1987, Paramount)
Axel Foley—Eddie Murphy
Director—Tony Scott
Leading Players—Judge Reinhold, Jurgen Prochnow, Ronny Cox, John Ashton, Brigitte Nielsen

BEVERLY OF GRAUSTARK (1926, Silent, MGM)
Beverly Calhoun—Marion Davies
Director—Sidney Franklin
Leading Players—Antonio Moreno, Creighton Hale, Roy D'Arcy

BEWARE MY LOVELY (1952, RKO)
Mrs. Gordon—Ida Lupino
Director—Harry Homer
Leading Players—Robert Ryan, Taylor Holmes, Barbara Whiting

BEWARE OF BLONDIE (1950, Columbia)
Blondie Bumstead—Penny Singleton
Director—Edward Bernds
Leading Players—Arthur Lake, Larry Simms, Marjorie Kent

BEWITCHED (1945, MGM)
Joan Arlis Ellis—Phyllis Thaxter
Director—Arch Obler
Leading Players—Edmund Gwenn, Henry H. Daniels, Addison Richards, Francis Pierlot

BIDDY (1983, GB, Sands Film Prod.)
Biddy—Celia Bannerman
Director—Christine Edzard
Leading Players—Patricia Napier, Sam Ghazoros, Luke Duckett

BIG (1988, 20th Century Fox)
Joshua Baskin—Tom Hanks
Director—Penny Marshall
Leading Players—David Moscow, Elizabeth Perkins, Robert Loggia, Jared Rushton, John Heard

BIG BAD MAMA (1974, Columbia)
Wilma McClatchie—Angie Dickinson
Director—Steve Carver
Leading Players—William Shatner, Tom Skerritt, Susan Sennett, Robbie Lee

BIG BAD MAMA II (1987, Concorde)
Wilma McClatchie—Angie Dickinson
Director—Jim Wynorski
Leading Players—Robert Culp, Danielle Brisebois, Julie McCullough, Bruce Glover

THE BIG BOSS (1941, Columbia)
Jim Maloney—Otto Kruger
Director—Charles Barton
Leading Players—Gloria Dickson, John Litel, Don Beddoe

THE BIG BRAIN (1933, RKO)
Max Werner—George E. Stone
Director—George Archainbaud
Leading Players—Phillip Holmes, Fay Wray, Minna Gombell

BIG BROTHERS (1923, Silent, Paramount)
Jimmy Donovan—Tom Moore
Director—Allan Dwan
Leading Players—Edith Roberts, Raymond Hutton, Joe King

BIG BROWN EYES, (1936, Paramount)
Eve Fallon—Joan Bennett
Director—Raoul Walsh
Leading Players—Cary Grant, Walter Pidgeon, Lloyd Nolan

BIG BUSINESS GIRL (1931, Warner Brothers/First National)
Claire McIntyre—Loretta Young
Director—William Seiter
Leading Players—Frank Albertson, Ricardo Cortez, Joan
Blondell

BIG DADDY (1969, Syzygy/United)
A. Lincoln Beauregard—Victor Buono
Director—Carl K. Hittleman
Leading Players—Joan Blondell, Chill Wills, Tisha Sterling

BIG DAN (1923, Silent, Fox Film Corp.)
Dan O'Hara—Charlie Jones
Director—William A. Wellman
Leading Players—Marian Nixon, Ben Hendricks, Trilby Clark

BIG EXECUTIVE (1933, Paramount)
Victor Conway—Ricardo Cortez
Director—Erle C. Kenton
Leading Players—Richard Bennett, Elizabeth Young, Sharon
Lynn, Dorothy Peterson

BIG FELLA (1937, GB, Lion-Beaconsfield)
Joe—Paul Robeson
Director—J. Elder Wills
Leading Players—Elizabeth Welch, Roy Emerton, James Hayter

THE BIG FISHERMAN (1959, Buena Vista)
Simon Peter—Howard Keel
Director—Frank Borzage
Leading Players—Susan Kohner, John Saxon, Martha Hyer,
Herbert Lom, Ray Stricklyn

BIG GIRLS DON'T CRY . . . THEY GET EVEN (1992, New Line)
Laura—Hilary Wolf
Director—Joan Micklin Silver
Leading Players—David Strathairn, Margaret Whitton, Griffin
Dunne, Patricia Kalember

THE BIG GUY (1939, Universal)
Warden Whitlock—Victor McLaglen
Director—Arthur Lubin
Leading Players—Jackie Cooper, Edward Brophy, Ona Munson

A BIG HAND FOR THE LITTLE LADY (1966, Warner Brothers)
Mary—Joanne Woodward
Director—Fielder Cook
Leading Players—Henry Fonda, Jason Robards, Charles
Bickford, Burgess Meredith, Kevin McCarthy, Robert
Middleton, Paul Ford, John Qualen

BIG HEARTED HERBERT (1934, Warner Brothers)
Herbert Kainess—Guy Kibbee
Director—William Keighley
Leading Players—Aline McMahon, Patricia Ellis, Helen Lowell

BIG JACK (1949, MGM)
Big Jack Horner—Wallace Beery
Director—Richard Thorpe
Leading Players—Richard Conte, Marjorie Main, Edward Arnold

BIG JAKE (1971, National General)
Jacob McCandles—John Wayne
Director—George Sherman
Leading Players—Richard Boone, Maureen O'Hara, Patrick
Wayne, Chris Mitchum, Bobby Vinton

THE BIG MAN (1990, GB, Miramax/Palace)
Daddy—Bert Remsen
Director—Jack Fisk
Leading Players—Beau Bridges, Beverly D'Angelo, Tess Harper,
Judge Reinhold, Amy Wright, Keith Carradine

BIG JIM MCLAIN (1952, Warner Brothers)
Big Jim McLain—John Wayne
Director—Edward Ludwig
Leading Players—Nancy Olson, James Arness, Alan Napier,
Veda Ann Borg, Gayne Whitman

THE BIG MOUTH (1967, Columbia)
Gerald Clamson—Jerry Lewis
Director—Jerry Lewis
Leading Players—Harold J. Stone, Susan Day, Buddy Lester

THE BIG OPERATOR (1959, MGM)
Little Joe Braun—Mickey Rooney
Director—Charles Haas
Leading Players—Steve Cochran, Mamie Van Doren, Ray
Danton

THE BIG SHOT (1931, RKO-Pathe)
Ray—Eddie Quillan
Director—Ralph Murphy
Leading Players—Maureen O'Sullivan, Mary Nolan, Roscoe Ates

THE BIG SHOT (1937, RKO)
Mr. Simms—Guy Kibbee
Director—Edward Killy
Leading Players—Cora Witherspoon, Dorothy Moore, Gordon
Jones, Frank M. Thomas

THE BIG SHOT (1942, Warner Brothers)
Duke Berne—Humphrey Bogart
Director—Lewis Seller
Leading Players—Irene Manning, Richard Travis, Susan Peters

BIG SHOTS (1987, 20th Century Fox)
Obie—Rickie Buster
Jeremy "Scam" Henderson—Darius McCrary
Director—Robert Mandel
Leading Players—Robert Joy, Robert Prosky, Jerzy Skolimowski

THE BIG SHOW-OFF (1945, Republic)
Sandy Elliott—Arthur Lake
Director—Howard Bretherton
Leading Players—Dale Evans, Lionel Stander, George Meeker

THE BIG SISTER (1916, Silent, Paramount)
Betty Norton—Mae Murray
Director—John B. O'Brien
Leading Players—Matty Roubert, Harry C. Browne, Ida Darling

THE BIG STRONG MAN (1922, Silent, GB, Quality Plays)
George Herrick—George Turner
Director—George A. Cooper
Leading Players—Wyn Richmond, Frank Stanmore

BIG TOP PEE WEE (1988, Paramount)
Pee Wee Herman—Pee Wee Herman
Director—Randall Kleiser
Leading Players—Kris Kristofferson, Penelope Ann Miller, Valeria Golino

BIG TOWN CZAR (1939, Universal)
Phil Dailey—Barton Maclane
Director—Arthur Lubin
Leading Players—Tom Brown, Eve Arden, Jack La Rue

BIG TOWN GIRL (1937, 20th Century Fox)
Fay Loring—Claire Trevor
Director—Frank R. Strayer
Leading Players—Donald Woods, Alan Dinehart, Alan Baxter

BIG TREMAINE (1916, Silent, Metro)
John Tremaine, Jr.—Harold Lockwood
Director—Henry Otto
Leading Players—May Allison, Lester Cuneo, Albert Ellis

THE BIG WHEEL (1949, UA)
Billy Coy—Mickey Rooney
Director—Edward Ludwig
Leading Players—Thomas Mitchell, Michael O'Shea, Mary Hatcher, Spring Byington

THE BIGAMIST (1953, Filmakers)
Harry Graham—Edmond O'Brien
Director—Ida Lupino
Leading Players—Joan Fontaine, Ida Lupino, Edmund Gwenn

BILL AND TED'S BOGUS JOURNEY (1991, Orion)
Theodore "Ted" Logan—Keanu Reeves
Bill S. Preston—Alex Winter
Director—Peter Hewitt
Leading Players—William Sadler, Pam Grier, Joss Ackland, George Carlin, Amy Stock-Poynton

BILL AND TED'S EXCELLENT ADVENTURE (1989, Orion)
Theodore "Ted" Logan—Keanu Reeves
Bill S. Preston—Alex Winter
Director—Stephen Herek
Leading Players—George Carlin, Terry Camilleri, Dan Shor, Tony Steedman, Rod Loomis

BILL HENRY (1919, Silent, Paramount)
Bill Henry Jenkins—Charles Ray
Director—Jerome Storm
Leading Players—Edith Roberts, William Carroll, Bert Woodruff, Jennie Lee Courtright

BILLIE (1965, UA)
Billie—Patty Duke
Director—Donald Weis
Leading Players—Jim Backus, Jane Greer, Warren Berlinger

THE BILLION DOLLAR HOBO (1977, International Picture Show)
Vernon Praiseworthy—Tim Conway
Director—Stuart E. McGowan
Leading Players—Will Geer, Eric Weston, Sydney Lassick

BILLY BATHGATE (1991, Buena Vista/Touchstone)
Billy Bathgate—Loren Dean
Director—Robert Benton

Leading Players—Dustin Hoffman, Nicole Kidman, Bruce Willis, Steven Hill, Steve Buscemi, Billy Jaye

BILLY BUDD (1962, UA)
Billy Budd—Terence Stamp
Director—Peter Ustinov
Leading Players—Robert Ryan, Peter Ustinov, Melvyn Douglas, John Nelvile, Ronald Lewis

BILLY GALVIN (1986, Vestron)
Billy Galvin—Lenny Von Dohlen
Director—John Gray
Leading Players—Karl Malden, Joyce Van Patten, Toni Kalem

BILLY JACK (1971, Warner Brothers)
Billy Jack—Tom Laughlin
Director—Tom Laughlin
Leading Players—Delores Taylor, Clark Howat, Bert Freed

BILLY JACK GOES TO WASHINGTON (1977, Taylor-Laughlin)
Billy Jack—Tom Laughlin
Director—Tom Laughlin
Leading Players—Delores Taylor, E.G. Marshall, Teresa Laughlin, Sam Wannamaker, Lucie Arnaz

BILLY LIAR (1963, GB, Vic Films/Warner Brothers-Pathe)
Billy Fisher—Tom Courtenay
Director—John Schlesinger
Leading Players—Julie Christie, Wilfrid Pickles, Mona Washbourne, Ethel Griffies

BILLY THE KID (1930, MGM)
Billy Bonney—John Mack Brown
Director—King Vidor
Leading Players—Wallace Beery, Kay Johnson, Karl Dane

BILLY THE KID (1941, MGM)
Billy Bonney—Robert Taylor
Director—David Miller
Leading Players—Brian Donlevy, Ian Hunter, Mary Howard

BILLY THE KID VS. DRACULA (1966, Circle/EM)
Billy The Kid—Chuck Courtney
Vampire Uncle—John Carradine
Director—William Beaudine
Leading Players—Melinda Plowman, Walter Janovitz, Harry Carey, Jr., Roy Barcroft

BILLY THE KID WANTED (1941, Producers Releasing Corp.)
Billy The Kid—Buster Crabbe
Director—Sherman Scott
Leading Players—Al St. John, Dave O'Brien, Glenn Strange

BILLY TWO HATS (1973, GB, UA)
Billy Two Hats—Desi Arnaz, Jr.
Director—Ted Kotcheff
Leading Players—Gregory Peck, Jack Warden, Sian Barbara Allen, David Huddleston

BINGO LONG TRAVELING ALL-STARS AND MOTOR KINGS (1976, Motown/Pan Arts)
Bingo Long—Billy Dee Williams
Director—John Badham
Leading Players—James Earl Jones, Richard Pryor, Rico Dawson, Sam Briston, Leon Wagner

BIOGRAPHY OF A BACHELOR GIRL (1934, MGM)
Marion—Ann Harding
Director—Edward H. Griffith
Leading Players—Robert Montgomery, Edward Everett Horton, Edward Arnold, Una Merkel

BIRD (1988, Warner Brothers)
Charlie Parker—Forrest Whitaker
Director—Clint Eastwood
Leading Players—Diane Verona, Michael Zeiniker, Samuel F. Wright, Keith David, Michael McGuire

BIRD OF PARADISE (1932, RKO)
Luana—Dolores Del Rio
Director—King Vidor
Leading Players—Joel McCrea, John Halliday, Richard "Skeets" Gallagher, Lon Chaney, Jr.

BIRD OF PARADISE (1951, 20th Century Fox)
Kalua—Debra Paget
Director—Delmer Davies
Leading Players—Louis Jourdan, Jeff Chandler, Everett Sloane

BIRD ON A WIRE (1990, Universal/Badham)
Rick Jarman—Mel Gibson
Director—John Badham
Leading Players—Goldie Hawn, David Carradine, Bill Duke, Stephen Tobolowsy, Joan Servance, Jeff Corey

BIRDMAN OF ALCATRAZ (1962, UA)
Robert Stroud—Burt Lancaster
Director—John Frankenheimer
Leading Players—Karl Malden, Thelma Ritter, Betty Field, Neville Brand, Edmond O'Brien

BIRDY (1984, Tri-Star Pictures)
Birdy—Matthew Bodine
Director—Alan Parker
Leading Players—Nicolas Cage, John Harkins, Sandy Baron, Karen Young

THE BISHOP MISBEHAVES (1933, MGM)
Bishop—Edmund Gwenn
Director—E.A. DuPont
Leading Players—Maureen O'Sullivan, Lucille Watson, Reginald Owen, Dudley Digges, Norman Foster

THE BISHOP OF THE OZARKS (1923, Silent, Cosmopolitan Films)
Roger Chapman—Milford W. Howard
Director—Finis Fox
Leading Players—Derelys Perdue, Cecil Holland, William Kenton

THE BISHOP'S WIFE (1947, RKO)
Bishop Henry Brougham—David Niven
Julia Brougham—Loretta Young
Director—Henry Koster
Leading Players—Cary Grant, Monty Woolley, James Gleason, Gladys Cooper, Elsa Lanchester

THE BITTER TEA OF GENERAL YEN (1933, Columbia)
General Yen—Nils Asther
Director—Frank Capra
Leading Players—Barbara Stanwyck, Gavin Gordon, Lucien Littlefield, Toshia Mori, Richard Loo

BLACK BART (1948, Universal)
Charles E. Boles—Dan Duryea
Director—George Sherman
Leading Players—Yvonne De Carlo, Jeffrey Lynn, Percy Kilbride, Lloyd Gough, Frank Lovejoy

BLACK BELT JONES (1974, Warner Brothers)
Black Belt Jones—Jim Kelly
Director—Robert Clouse
Leading Players—Gloria Henry, Scatman Crothers, Alan Weeks

BLACK CAESAR (1973, American International)
Tommy Gibbs—Fred Williamson
Director—Larry Cohen
Leading Players—Phillip Roye, Gloria Hendry, Julius W. Harris, Val Avery

BLACK GIRL (1972, Cinerama)
Netta—Leslie Uggams
Director—Ossie Davis
Leading Players—Brock Peters, Claudia McNeil, Louise Stubbs

BLACK GUNN (1972, Columbia)
Gunn—Jim Brown
Director—Robert Hartfod Davis
Leading Players—Martin Landau, Brenda Sykes, Luciana Paluzzi, Vida Blue, Stephen McNally

BLACK JACK (1979, GB, Kestrel/National Film Finance)
Black Jack—Jean Franval
Director—Kenneth Loach
Leading Players—Stephen Hirst, Andrew Bennet, Louise Cooper

BLACK KING (1932, Southland)
Charcoal Johnson—A.B. Comethiere
Director—Bud Pollard
Leading Players—Vivianne Baber, Knolly Mitchell, Dan Michaels, Mike Jackson

THE BLACK KLANSMAN (1966, US Films)
Jerry—Richard Gilden
Director—Ted V. Mikels
Leading Players—Rima Kutner, Harry Lovejoy, Max Julien

THE BLACK KNIGHT (1954, Columbia)
John, The Black Knight—Alan Ladd
Director—Tay Garnett
Leading Players—Patricia Medina, Andre Morell, Harry Andrews

BLACK LIKE ME (1964, Continental)
John Finley Horton—James Whitmore
Director—Carl Lerner
Leading Players—Dan Priest, Walter Mason, John Marriott

BLACK MAGIC WOMAN (1991, Trimark)
Cassandra Perry—Apollonia Kotero
Director—Deryn Warren
Leading Players—Mark Hamill, Amanda Wyss, Victor Rivers, Abiday Viera, Carmen More

THE BLACK PANTHER (1977, GB, Impics Prod.)
Donald Neilson—Donald Sumpter
Director—Ian Merrick
Leading Players—Debbie Farrington, Marjorie Yates, Sylvia O'Donnell, Andrew Brut

THE BLACK PIRATE (1926, Silent, UA)
  Michel—Douglas Fairbanks
  Director—Albert Parker
  Leading Players—Billie Dove, Anders Randolf, Donald Crisp

BLACK ROBE (1991, Canada/Australia, Goldwyn/Alliance/Hoyts)
  Father Laforgue—Lothaire Bluteau
  Director—Bruce Beresford
  Leading Players—Aden Young, Sandrine Hall, August
    Schellenberg, Tantoo Cardinal, Frank Wilson, Billy Two
    Rivers, Lawrence Bayne

BLACK SAMSON (1974, Warner Brothers)
  Samson—Rockne Tarkington
  Director—Charles Bail
  Leading Players—William Smith, Connie Strickland, Carol
    Speed, Michael Payne

BLACK WIDOW (1987, 20th Century Fox)
  Catharine—Theresa Russell
  Director—Bob Rafelson
  Leading Players—Debra Winger, Sami Frey, Dennis Hopper,
    Nicol Williamson, Terry O'Quinn

BLACKBEARD THE PIRATE (1952, RKO)
  Blackbeard—Robert Newton
  Director—Raoul Walsh
  Leading Players—Linda Darnell, William Bendix, Keith Andes,
    Torin Thatcher, Irene Ryan

BLACKBEARD'S GHOST (1968, Buena Vista/Disney)
  Capt. Blackbeard—Peter Ustinov
  Director—Robert Stevenson
  Leading Players—Dean Jones, Suzanne Pleshette, Elsa
    Lanchester, Joby Baker

BLACKJACK KETCHUM, DESPERADO (1956, Columbia)
  Blackjack Ketchum—Howard Duff
  Director—Earl Bellamy
  Leading Players—Victor Jory, Maggie Mahoney, Angela Stevens

BLACULA (1972, American International)
  Blacula—William Marshall
  Director—William Crain
  Leading Players—Vonetta McGee, Denise Nicholas, Thalmus
    Rasulala

BLADE (1973, Green/Pintoff)
  Blade—John Marley
  Director—Ernest Pintoff
  Leading Players—Jon Cypher, Kathryn Walker, William Prince

BLAME IT ON THE BELLBOY (1992, GB/US, Buena Vista)
  Bellboy—Bronson Pinchot
  Director—Mark Herman
  Leading Players—Dudley Moore, Bryan Brown, Richard
    Griffiths, Andreas Katsoulis, Patsy Kensit, Alison Steadman

BLANCHE FURY (1948, GB, Universal)
  Blanche Fury—Valerie Hobson
  Director—Marc Allegret
  Leading Players—Stewart Granger, Walter Fitzgerald, Michael
    Gough, Maurice Denham

BLAZE (1989, Buena Vista)
  Blaze Starr—Lolita Davidovich

  Director—Ron Shelton
  Leading Players—Paul Newman, Jerry Hardin, Gailard Sartain,
    Jeffrey DeMunn, Garland Bunting

BLIND DATE (1984, New Line)
  Jonathan Ratcliffe—Joseph Bottoms
  Director—Nico Matsorakis
  Leading Players—Kirstie Alley, James Daughton, Lana Clarkson

BLIND DATE (1987, Tri-Star)
  Nadia Gates—Kim Basinger
  Walter Davis—Bruce Willis
  Director—Blake Edwards
  Leading Players—John Larroquette, William Daniels, George
    Coe, Mark Blum

BLINKY (1923, Silent, Universal)
  Geoffrey Arbuthnot "Blinky" Islip—Hoot Gibson
  Director—Edward Sedgwick
  Leading Players—Esther Ralston, Mathilde Brundage, De Witt
    Jennings, Elinor Field

THE BLISS OF MRS. BLOSSOM (1968, GB, Paramount)
  Harriett Blossom—Shirley Maclaine
  Director—Joseph McGrath
  Leading Players—Richard Attenborough, James Booth, Freddie
    Jones, William Rushton

BLITHE SPIRIT (1945, GB, Cineguild/Two Cities)
  Elvira Condomine—Kay Hammond
  Director—David Lean
  Leading Players—Rex Harrison, Constance Cummings, Margaret
    Rutherford

BLONDE ALIBI (1946, Universal)
  Marian Gale—Martha Driscoll
  Director—Will Jason
  Leading Players—Tom Neal, Donald McBride, Robert Armstrong

BLONDE BAIT (1956, Associated Film Dist. Corp.)
  Angela Booth—Beverly Michaels
  Director—Elmo Williams
  Leading Players—Jim Davis, Joan Rice, Richard Travis

THE BLONDE BANDIT (1950, Republic)
  Gloria Dell—Dorothy Patrick
  Director—Harry Keller
  Leading Players—Gerald Mohr, Robert Rockwell, Larry J. Blake

BLONDE COMET (1941, Producers Releasing Corp.)
  Beverly Blake—Virginia Vale
  Director—William Beaudine
  Leading Players—Robert Kent, Barney Oldfield, Vince Barnett

BLONDE FOR A NIGHT (1928, Silent, Pathe Exchange)
  Marie—Marie Prevost
  Director—E. Mason Hopper
  Leading Players—Franklin Pangborn, Harrison Ford, T. Roy
    Barnes

BLONDE FROM BROOKLYN (1945, Columbia)
  Susan Parker—Lynn Merrick
  Director—Del Lord
  Leading Players—Robert Stanton, Thurston Hall, Mary Treen

THE BLONDE FROM SINGAPORE (1941, Columbia)
Mary Brooks—Florence Rice
Director—Edward Dmytryk
Leading Players—Leif Erickson, Gordon Jones, Don Beddoe

BLONDE ICE (1949, Film Classics)
Claire—Leslie Brooks
Director—Jack Bernhard
Leading Players—Robert Paige, Walter Sande, John Holland

THE BLONDE SAINT (1926, Silent, First National)
Ghirlaine Bellamy—Doris Kenyon
Director—Svend Gade
Leading Players—Lewis Stone, Ann Rork, Gilbert Roland

BLONDE SAVAGE (1947, Ensign/Eagle-Lion)
Meelah—Gale Sherwood
Director—S.K. Seeley
Leading Players—Leif Erickson, Veda Ann Borg, Douglass Dumbrille, Frank Jenks

BLONDE SINNER (1956, GB, Allied Artists)
Mary Hilton—Diana Dors
Director—J. Lee Thompson
Leading Players—Yvonne Mitchell, Michael Craig, Geoffrey Keen, Olga Lindo

BLONDE VENUS (1932, Paramount)
Helen Faraday—Marlene Dietrich
Director—Josef von Sternberg
Leading Players—Herbert Marshall, Cary Grant, Dickie Moore, Francis Sayles, Robert Emmett O'Connor

BLONDIE (1938, Columbia)
Blondie Bumstead—Penny Singleton
Director-Frank R. Strayer
Leading Players—Arthur Lake, Larry Simms, Gene Lockhart, Ann Doran, Jonathan Hale

BLONDIE BRINGS UP BABY (1939, Columbia)
Blondie—Penny Singleton
Director—Frank R. Strayer
Leading Players—Arthur Lake, Larry Simms, Danny Mummert

BLONDIE FOR VICTORY (1942, Columbia)
Blondie—Penny Singleton
Director—Frank R. Strayer
Leading Players—Arthur Lake, Larry Simms, Majelle White, Stuart Erwin

BLONDIE GOES LATIN (1941, Columbia)
Blondie—Penny Singleton
Director—Frank R. Strayer
Leading Players—Arthur Lake, Larry Simms, Ruth Terry, Tito Guizar

BLONDIE GOES TO COLLEGE (1941, Columbia)
Blondie—Penny Singleton
Director—Frank R. Strayer
Leading Players—Arthur Lake, Larry Simms, Janet Blair, Larry Parks, Adele Mara

BLONDIE HAS SERVANT TROUBLE (1940, Columbia)
Blondie—Penny Singleton
Director—Frank R. Strayer

Leading Players—Arthur Lake, Larry Simms, Arthur Hohl, Esther Dale

BLONDIE HITS THE JACKPOT (1949, Columbia)
Blondie—Penny Singleton
Director—Edward Bernds
Leading Players—Arthur Lake, Larry Simms, Marjorie Kent

BLONDIE IN SOCIETY (1941, Columbia)
Blondie—Penny Singleton
Director—Frank R. Strayer
Leading Players—Arthur Lake, Larry Simms, William Frawley

BLONDIE IN THE DOUGH (1947, Columbia)
Blondie—Penny Singleton
Director—Abby Berlin
Leading Players—Arthur Lake, Larry Simms, Marjorie Kent, Jerome Cowan, Hugh Herbert

BLONDIE JOHNSON (1933, Embassy)
Blondie Johnson—Joan Blondell
Director—Ray Enright
Leading Players—Chester Morris, Allen Jenkins, Claire Dodd

BLONDIE KNOWS BEST (1946, Columbia)
Blondie—Penny Singleton
Director—Abby Berlin
Leading Players—Arthur Lake, Larry Simms, Steven Geray, Shemp Howard

BLONDIE MEETS THE BOSS (1939, Columbia)
Blondie—Penny Singleton
Director—Frank R. Strayer
Leading Players—Arthur Lake, Larry Simms, Dorothy Moore

BLONDIE OF THE FOLLIES (1932, MGM)
Blondie McClune—Marion Davies
Director—Edmund Goulding
Leading Players—Robert Montgomery, Billie Dove, Jimmy Durante, James Gleason

BLONDIE ON A BUDGET (1940, Columbia)
Blondie—Penny Singleton
Director—Frank R. Strayer
Leading Players—Arthur Lake, Larry Simms, Rita Hayworth

BLONDIE PLAYS CUPID (1940, Columbia)
Blondie—Penny Singleton
Director—Frank R. Strayer
Leading Players—Arthur Lake, Larry Simms, Glenn Ford, Luana Waters

BLONDIE TAKES A VACATION (1939, Columbia)
Blondie—Penny Singleton
Director—Frank R. Strayer
Leading Players—Arthur Lake, Larry Simms, Donald Meek, Donald MacBride

BLONDIE'S ANNIVERSARY (1947, Columbia)
Blondie—Penny Singleton
Director—Abby Berlin
Leading Players—Arthur Lake, Larry Simms, Collette Lyons

BLONDIE'S BIG MOMENT (1947, Columbia)
Blondie—Penny Singleton
Director—Abby Berlin

Leading Players—Arthur Lake, Larry Simms, Marjorie Kent, Anita Louise, Jack Rice

BLONDIE'S BLESSED EVENT (1942, Columbia)
Blondie—Penny Singleton
Director—Frank R. Strayer
Leading Players—Arthur Lake, Larry Simms, Norma Jean Wayne, Hans Conreid, Stanley Brown

BLONDIE'S HERO (1950, Columbia)
Blondie—Penny Singleton
Dagwood Bumstead—Arthur Lake
Director—Edward Bernds
Leading Players—Larry Simms, Marjorie Kent, William Frawley Danny Mummert, Joe Sawyer

BLONDIE'S HOLIDAY (1947, Columbia)
Blondie—Penny Singleton
Director—Abby Berlin
Leading Players—Arthur Lake, Larry Simms, Marjorie Kent, Jerome Cowan, Grant Mitchell

BLONDIE'S LUCKY DAY (1946, Columbia)
Blondie—Penny Singleton
Director—Abby Berlin
Leading Players—Arthur Lake, Larry Simms, Marjorie Kent, Robert Stanton, Angelyn Orr, Paul Harvey

BLONDIE'S REWARD (1948, Columbia)
Blondie—Penny Singleton
Director—Abby Berlin
Leading Players—Arthur Lake, Larry Simms, Marjorie Kent, Jerome Cowan, Gay Nelson

BLONDIE'S SECRET (1948, Columbia)
Blondie—Penny Singleton
Director—Edward Bernds
Leading Players—Arthur Lake, Larry Simms, Marjorie Kent, Thurston Hall, Jerome Cowan

BLOOD OF FRANKENSTEIN (1970, Independent-International)
Frankenstein—J. Carroll Naish
Director—Al Adamson
Leading Players—Lon Chaney, Jr., Regina Carroll, John Bloom

THE BLOOD OF FU MANCHU (1968, GB, Udastex Films)
Fu Manchu—Christopher Lee
Director—Jess Franco
Leading Players—George Gotz, Richard Greene, Howard Marion, Tsai Chin, Maria Rohm

BLOODBROTHERS (1978, Kings Road/Warners)
Chubby DeCoco—Paul Sorvino
Tommy DeCoco—Tony Lo Bianco
Director—Robert Mulligan
Leading Players—Richard Gere, Lelia Goldoni, Yvonne Wilder

BLOODY MAMA (1970, American International)
Kate "Ma" Barker—Shelley Winters
Director—Roger Corman
Leading Players—Pat Hingle, Don Stroud, Diane Varsi, Bruce Dern, Robert De Niro, Alex Nicol

BLUE (1968, Paramount)
Blue—Terence Stamp
Director—Silvio Narizzano

Leading Players—Joanna Pettet, Karl Malden, Ricardo Montalban, Anthony Costello

BLUEBEARD (1944, Producers Releasing Corp.)
Gaston—John Carradine
Director—Edgar G. Ulmer
Leading Players—Jean Parker, Nils Asther, Ludwig Stossel

BLUEBEARD (1972, Cinerama/Vulcano)
Baron Von Sepper—Richard Burton
Director—Edward Dmytryk
Leading Players—Raquel Welch, Joey Heatherton, Virni Lisi

BLUEBEARD'S 8TH WIFE (1923, Silent, Paramount)
Mona de Briac—Gloria Swanson
John Brandon—Huntley Gordon
Director—Sam Wood
Leading Players—Charles Green, Lianne Salvor, Paul Weigel

BLUEBEARD'S EIGHTH WIFE (1938, Paramount)
Nicole de Loiselle—Claudette Colbert
Michael Brandon—Gary Cooper
Director—Ernst Lubitsch
Leading Players—Edward Everett Horton, David Niven, Elizabeth Patterson, Herman Bing

BLUEBEARD'S TEN HONEYMOONS (1960, Allied Artists)
Landru—George Sanders
Director—W. Lee Wilder
Leading Players—Corinne Calvert, Jean Kent, Patricia Roc

THE BLUES BROTHERS (1980, Universal)
Joliet Jake—John Belushi
Elwood—Dan Aykroyd
Director—John Landis
Leading Players—James Brown, Cab Calloway, Ray Charles, Carrie Fisher, Aretha Franklin, Henry Gibson

THE BLUFFER (1919, Silent, World)
Sybil—June Elvidge
Director—Travers Vale
Leading Players—Irving Cummings, Frank Mayo, George MacQuarrie, Muriel Ostriche

BLUME IN LOVE (1973, Samuel Bronston)
Blume—George Segal
Director—Paul Mazursky
Leading Players—Susan Anspach, Kris Kristofferson, Marsha Mason, Shelley Winters

BOB AND CAROL AND TED AND ALICE (1969, Columbia)
Carol—Natalie Wood
Bob—Robert Culp
Alice—Dyan Cannon
Ted—Elliott Gould
Director—Paul Mazursky
Leading Players—Horst Ebersberg, Lee Bergere, Donald Muhich

BOB HAMPTON OF PLACER (1921, Silent, Associated First National)
Bob Hampton—James Kirkwood
Director—Marshall Neilan
Leading Players—Wesley Barry, Marjorie Daw, Pat O'Malley

THE BOB MATHIAS STORY (1954, Allied Artists)
Bob Mathias—Bob Mathias

Director—Francis D. Lyon
Leading Players—Ward Bond, Melba Mathias, Howard Petrie

BOB ROBERTS (1992, Paramount/Miramax)
Bob Roberts—Tim Robbins
Director—Tim Robbins
Leading Players—Giancarlo Esposito, Roy Wise, Brian Murray, Gore Vidal, Rebecca Jankins

BOBBIE JO AND THE OUTLAW (1976, American International)
Lyle Wheeler—Marjoe Gortner
Bobbie Jo James—Lynda Carter
Director—Mark L. Lester
Leading Players—Jesse Vint, Merrie Lynn Ross, Belinda Balaski, Gene Drew

BOBBIKINS (1959, GB, 20th Century Fox)
Bobbikins—Steven Stacker
Director—Robert Day
Leading Players—Max Bygraves, Shirley Jones, Billie Whitelaw

BOBBY DEERFIELD (1977, Columbia)
Bobby Deerfield—Al Pacino
Director—Sidney Pollack
Leading Players—Marthe Keller, Anny Duperey, Walter McGinn

THE BOBO (1967, GB, Warners)
Juan Bautista—Peter Sellers
Director—Robert Parrish
Leading Players—Britt Ekland, Rossano Brazzi, Adolfo Celi

THE BODY SNATCHER (1945, RKO)
John Gray—Boris Karloff
Director—Robert Wise
Leading Players—Bela Lugosi, Henry Daniell, Edith Atwater

BODYGUARD (1948, RKO)
Mike Carter—Lawrence Tierney
Director—Richard O. Fleischer
Leading Players—Priscilla Lane, Phillip Reed, June Clayworth

THE BOHEMIAN GIRL (1936, MGM)
Arline—Jacqueline Wells (Julie Bishop)
Director—James W. Horne
Leading Players—Stan Laurel, Oliver Hardy, Antonio Moreno

BOLD CABALLERO (1936, Republic)
Zorro—Robert Livingston
Director—Wells Root
Leading Players—Heather Angel, Sig Rumann, Ian Wolfe, Robert Warwick

BOMBA AND THE HIDDEN CITY (1950, Monogram)
Bomba—Johnny Sheffield
Director—Ford Beebe
Leading Players—Sue England, Paul Guilfoyle, Smoki Whitfield

BOMBA AND THE JUNGLE GIRL (1952, Monogram)
Bomba—Johnny Sheffield
The Jungle Girl, Boru—Suzette Harbin
Director—Ford Beebe
Leading Players—Walter Sande, Karen Sharpe, Martin Wilkins

BOMBA ON PANTHER ISLAND (1949, Monogram)
Bomba—Johnny Sheffield
Director—Ford Beebe

Leading Players—Allene Roberts, Lita Baron, Charles Irwin

BOMBA THE JUNGLE BOY (1949, Monogram)
Bomba—Johnny Sheffield
Director—Ford Beebe
Leading Players—Peggy Ann Garner, Onslow Stevens, Charles Irwin, Smoki Whitfield

BOMBSHELL (1933, MGM)
Lola—Jean Harlow
Director—Victor Fleming
Leading Players—Lee Tracy, Frank Morgan, Franchot Tone, Pat O'Brien, Una Merkel

THE BOND BOY (1922, Silent, Associated First National)
Peter Newbolt—Richard Barthelmess
Director—Henry King
Leading Players—Charles Hill Mailes, Ned Sparks, Lawrence D'Orsay, Mary Thurman

BONNIE AND CLYDE (1967, Warners)
Clyde Barrow—Warren Beatty
Bonnie Parker—Faye Dunaway
Director—Arthur Penn
Leading Players—Michael J. Pollard, Gene Hackman, Estelle Parsons, Denver Pyle, Dub Taylor

THE BONNIE PARKER STORY (1958, American International)
Bonnie Parker—Dorothy Provine
Director—William Witney
Leading Players—Jack Hogan, Richard Bakalyan, Joseph Turkel

BONNIE PRINCE CHARLIE (1948, GB, British Lion)
Prince Charles—David Niven
Director—Anthony Kimmons
Leading Players—Margaret Leighton, Judy Campbell, Jack Hawkins, Finlay Currie

BOOMERANG BILL (1922, Silent, Paramount)
Boomerang Bill—Lionel Barrymore
Director—Tom Terriss
Leading Players—Marguerite Marsh, Margaret Seddon, Frank Shannon, Matthew Betts

BOOTS MALONE (1952, Columbia)
Boots Malone—William Holden
Director—William Dieterle
Leading Players—Johnny Stewart, Stanley Clements, Basil Ruysdael, Carl Benton Reid, Ed Begley

BORN AMERICAN (1986, Cinema Group)
Savoy—Mike Norris
Mitch- Steve Durham
K.C.—David Coburn
Director—Renny Harlin
Leading Players—Thalmus Rasulala, Albert Salmi

BORN ON THE FOURTH OF JULY (1989, Universal)
Ron Kovic—Tom Cruise
Director—Oliver Stone
Leading Players—Bryan Larkin, Raymond J. Barry, Caroline Kava, Kyra Sedgwick, Willem Dafoe

BORN RECKLESS (1930, Fox Film Corp.)
Louis Beretti—Edmund Lowe
Director—John Ford

Leading Players—Catherine Dale Owen, Lee Tracy, Marguerite Churchill, Warren Hymer

BORN RECKLESS (1937, 20th Century Fox)
Bob "Hurry" Kane—Brian Donlevy
Director—Mal St. Clair
Leading Players—Rochelle Hudson, Barton MacLane, Robert Kent

BORN TO BE BAD (1934, Fox/United Artists)
Letty Strong—Loretta Young
Director—Lowell Sherman
Leading Players—Jackie Kelk, Cary Grant, Henry Travers

BORN TO BE BAD (1950, RKO)
Christabel—Joan Fontaine
Director—Nicholas Ray
Leading Players—Robert Ryan, Zachary Scott, Joan Leslie, Mel Ferrer

BORN TO BE LOVED (1959, Universal)
Dorothy—Carol Morris
Director—Hugo Haas
Leading Players—Vera Vague, Hugo Haas, Dick Kallman

BORN TO DANCE (1936, MGM)
Nora Paige—Eleanor Powell
Director—Roy Del Ruth
Leading Players—James Stewart, Virginia Bruce, Una Merkel, Sid Silvers, Francis Langford, Buddy Ebsen

BORN TO FIGHT (1938, Commodore Pictures)
Baby Face—Frankie Darro
Director—Charles Hutchinson
Leading Players—Kane Richmond, Jack LaRue, Frances Grant

BORN TO KILL (1947, RKO)
Sam—Lawrence Tierney
Director—Robert Wise
Leading Players—Claire Trevor, Walter Slezak, Philip Terry

BORN TO LOVE (1931, RKO)
Doris Kendall—Constance Bennett
Director—Paul L. Stein
Leading Players—Joel McCrea, Paul Cavanaugh, Frederick Kerr

BORN TO RACE (1988, MGM-United Artists)
Al Pagura—Joseph Bottoms
Director—James Fargo
Leading Players—Marc Singer, George Kennedy, Marla Heasley

BORN YESTERDAY (1951, Columbia)
Billie Dawn—Judy Holliday
Director—George Cukor
Leading Players—William Holden, Broderick Crawford, Howard St. John, Frank Otto

THE BOSS (1956, United Artists)
Matt Brady—John Payne
Director—Bryon Haskin
Leading Players—William Bishop, Gloria McGhee, Doe Avedon

BOSS NIGGER (1974, Boss/Dimension)
Boss Nigger—Fred Williamson
Director—Jack Arnold

Leading Players -D'Urville Martin, R.G. Armstrong, William Smith, Carmen Hayworth

THE BOSS'S SON (1978, New American Cinema)
Bobby—Asher Brauner
Joseph—Rudy Solari
Director—Bobby Roth
Leading Players—Rita Moreno, Henry G. Sanders, James Darren

THE BOSS' WIFE (1986, Tri-Star)
Louise—Arielle Dombasle
Roalvang—Christopher Plummer
Director—Ziggy Steinberg
Leading Players—Martin Mull, Daniel Stern, Fisher Stevens

BOSTON BLACKIE AND THE LAW (1946, Columbia)
Boston Blackie—Chester Morris
Director—D. Ross Lederman
Leading Players—Trudy Marshall, Constance Dowling, Richard Lane, George E. Stone

BOSTON BLACKIE BOOKED ON SUSPICION (1945, Columbia)
Boston Blackie—Chester Morris
Director—Arthur Dreifuss
Leading Players—Lynn Merrick, Richard Lane, Frank Sully Steve Cochran, George E. Stone

BOSTON BLACKIE GOES TO HOLLYWOOD (1942, Columbia)
Boston Blackie—Chester Morris
Director—Michael Gordon
Leading Players—George E. Stone, Richard Lane, Forrest Tucker, William Wright, Lloyd Corrigan

BOSTON BLACKIE'S CHINESE VENTURE (1949, Columbia)
Boston Blackie—Chester Morris
Director—Seymour Friedman
Leading Players—Maylia, Richard Lane, Don McGuire, Joan Woodbury, Sid Tomack

BOSTON BLACKIE'S RENDEZVOUS (1945, Columbia)
Boston Blackie—Chester Morris
Director—Arthur Dreifuss
Leading Players—Nina Foch, Steve Cochran, Richard Lane

THE BOSTON STRANGLER (1968, 20th Century Fox)
Albert DeSalvo—Tony Curtis
Director—Richard Fleischer
Leading Players—Henry Fonda, George Kennedy, Mike Kellin, Hurd Hatfield, Murray Hamilton

THE BOSTONIANS (1984, Merchant Ivory/Almi)
Basil Ransom—Christopher Reeve
Olive Chancellor—Vanessa Redgrave
Director—James Ivory
Leading Players—Madeleine Potter, Jessica Tandy, Nancy Marchand, Wesley Addy

BOUDOIR DIPLOMAT (1930, Universal)
Baron Valmi—Ian Keith
Director—Malcolm St. Clair
Leading Players—Betty Compson, Mary Duncan, Jeanette Loff

BOUGHT (1931, Warners)
Stephany Dale—Constance Bennett
Director—Archie Mayo

Leading Players—Ben Lyon, Richard Bennett, Dorothy Peterson Ray Milland

BOUND FOR GLORY (1976, United Artists)
Woody Guthrie—David Carradine
Director—Hal Ashby
Leading Players—Ronny Cox, Melinda Dillon, Gail Strickland

THE BOUNTY HUNTER (1954, Warners)
Jim Kipp—Randolph Scott
Director—Andre De Toth
Leading Players—Dolores Dorn, Marie Windsor, Howard Petrie

THE BOWERY BISHOP (1924, Silent, Selznick)
Norman Strong—Henry B. Walthall
Director—Colin Campbell
Leading Players -Leota Lorraine, George Fisher, Lee Shumway

BOWERY BOY (1940, Republic)
Sock Dolan—Jimmy Lydon
Director—William Morgan
Leading Players—Dennis O'Keefe, Louise Campbell, Helen Vinson, Roger Pryor

A BOWERY CINDERELLA (1927, Silent, Excellent Pictures)
Nora Denahy—Gladys Hulette
Director—Burton King
Leading Players—Pat O'Malley, Kate Bruce, Ernest Hilliard

BOXCAR BERTHA (1972, American International)
Bertha—Barbara (Hershey) Seagull
Director—Martin Scorsese
Leading Players—David Carradine, Barry Primus, Bernie Casey

BOY...A GIRL (1969, Jack Hanson)
The Boy—Dino Martin, Jr.
The Girl—Airion Fromer
Director—John Derek
Leading Players—Karen Steele, Kerwin Matthews

A BOY AND HIS DOG (1975, LQJ Films)
Vic—Don Johnson
Director—L.Q. Jones
Leading Players—Susanne Benton, Tim McIntire, Charles McGraw

THE BOY AND THE BRIDGE (1959, GB, Xanadu/Columbia)
Tommy Doyle—Ian MacLaine
Director—Kevin McClory
Leading Players—Liam Redmond, James Hayter, Norman Macowan

THE BOY AND THE PIRATES (1960, United Artists)
Jimmy Warren—Charles Herbert
Director—Bert I. Gordon
Leading Players—Susan Gordon, Martin Vye, Paul Guilfoyle

BOY FROM INDIANA (1950, Ventura/Eagle-Lion)
Lon Decker—Lon McCallister
Director—John Rawlins
Leading Players—Lois Butler, Billie Burke, George Cleveland

THE BOY FROM OKLAHOMA (1954, Warners)
Tom Brewster—Will Rogers, Jr.
Director—Michael Curtiz

Leading Players—Nancy Olson, Lon Chaney, Jr., Anthony Caruso

THE BOY GIRL (1917, Silent, Bluebird)
"Jack" Channing—Violet Mersereau
Director—Edwin Stevens
Leading Players—Charles Mason, Maud Cooling, Florida Kingsley, Caroline Harris

THE BOY IN BLUE (1986, 20th Century Fox)
Ned Hanlan—Nicolas Cage
Director—Charles Jarrott
Leading Players—Christopher Plummer, Cynthia Dale, David Naughton

A BOY OF FLANDERS (1924, Silent, MGM)
Nello—Jackie Coogan
Director—Victor Schertzinger
Leading Players—Nigel de Brulier, Lionel Belmore, Nell Craig

BOY OF THE STREETS (1937, Monogram)
Chuck—Jackie Cooper
Director—William Nigh
Leading Players—Maureen O'Connor, Kathleen Burke, Robert Emmett O'Connor, Marjorie Main

A BOY TEN FEET TALL (1965, GB, Paramount)
Sammy Hartland—Fergus McClelland
Director—Alexander MacKendrick
Leading Players—Edward G. Robinson, Constance Cummings

BOY! WHAT A GIRL (1947, Herald)
Bumpsie, The Girl—Tim Moore
Director—Arthur Leonard
Leading Players—Elwood Smith, Duke Williams, Al Jackson, Sheila Guyse, Belli Mays

BOY WHO CAUGHT A CROOK (1961, United Artists)
The Kid—Roger Mobley
Director—Edward L. Cahn
Leading Players—Wanda Hendrix, Don Beddoe, Johnny Seven

THE BOY WHO COULD FLY (1986, Lorimar)
Eric—Jay Underwood
Director—Nick Castle
Leading Players—Lucy Deakins, Bonnie Bedelia, Fred Savage

THE BOY WHO CRIED WEREWOLF (1973, Universal)
Richie Bridgeston—Scott Sealey
Director—Nathan H. Juran
Leading Players—Kerwin Matthews, Elaine Devry, Robert J. Wilke, Susan Foster

THE BOY WHO STOLE A MILLION (1960, GB, British-Lion)
Paco—Maurice Reyna
Director—Charles Crichton
Leading Players—Virgilio Texera, Marianne Benet, Harold Kasket, George Coulouris

THE BOY WITH GREEN HAIR (1949, RKO)
Peter—Dean Stockwell
Director—Joseph Losey
Leading Players—Pat O'Brien, Robert Ryan, Barbara Hale

BOYS FROM SYRACUSE (1940, Mayfair/Universal)
Antipholus of Syracuse—Allan Jones

Dromio of Syracuse—Joe Penner
Director—Edward Sutherland
Leading Players—Martha Raye, Rosemary Lane, Charles
  Butterworth, Irene Hervey, Alan Mowbray

BOYZ N THE HOOD (1991, Columbia)
Tre Styles—Cuba Gooding, Jr.
Ricky Baker—Morris Chestnut
Doughboy—Ice Cube
Director—John Singleton
Leading Players—Larry Fishburne, Nia Long, Tyra Ferrell,
  Angela Bassett, Meta King

BRADDOCK: MISSING IN ACTION III (1988, Cannon)
Col. James Braddock—Chuck Norris
Director—Aaron Norris
Leading Players—Aki Aleong, Roland Harrah III, Miki Kim

BRAIN DEAD (1990, Concorde)
Jack Halsey—Bud Cort
Director—Adam Simon
Leading Players—Bill Pullman, Bill Paxton, Nicholas Pryor,
  Patricia Charbonneau, George Kennedy

BRANNIGAN (1975, GB, United Artists)
Jim Brannigan—John Wayne
Director—Douglas Hickox
Leading Players—Richard Attenborough, Judy Geeson, Mel
  Ferrer, Lesley Ann Down

THE BRAT (1931, Fox Film Corp.)
The Brat—Sally O'Neil
Director—John Ford
Leading Players—Alan Dinehart, Frank Albertson, Virginia
  Cherrill, June Collyer

BRAVE WARRIOR (1952, Columbia)
Chief Tecumseh—Jay Silverheels
Director—Spencer G. Bennett
Leading Players—Jon Hall, Steve Ruddell, Christine Larson

BREAKER MORANT (1980, Australia, New World)
Lt. Harry Morant—Edward Woodward
Director—Bruce Beresford
Leading Players—Jack Thompson, John Waters, Bryan Brown

THE BREAKFAST CLUB (1985, Universal)
Andrew Clark—Emilio Estevez
Claire Standish—Molly Ringwald
Brian Johnson—Anthony Michael Hall
John Bender—Judd Nelson
Allison Reynolds—Ally Sheedy
Director—John Hughes
Leading Players—Paul Gleason, John Kapelos, Perry Crawford

BREEZY (1973, Universal)
Breezy—Kay Lenz
Director—Clint Eastwood
Leading Players—William Holden, Roger C. Carmel, Mark Dusay

BREWSTER MCCLOUD (1970, Lion's Gate/MGM)
Brewster McCloud—Bud Cort
Director—Robert Altman
Leading Players—Sally Kellerman, Michael Murphy, William
  Windom, Shelly Duvall

BREWSTER'S MILLIONS (1921, Silent, Paramount)
Monte Brewster—Roscoe "Fatty" Arbuckle
Director—Joseph Henabery
Leading Players—Betty Ross Clark, Fred Huntley, Marian
  Skinner, James Corrigan

BREWSTER'S MILLIONS (1935, GB, British & Dominion)
Jack Brewster—Jack Buchanan
Director—Thornton Freeland
Leading Players—Lili Damita, Nancy O'Neil, Sydney Fairbrother,
  Ian McLean

BREWSTER'S MILLIONS (1945, United Artists)
Monty Brewster -Dennis O'Keefe
Director—Allan Dwan
Leading Players—Helen Walker, Eddie "Rochester" Anderson,
  June Havoc, Gail Patrick, Mischa Auer

BREWSTER'S MILLIONS (1985, Universal)
Montgomery Brewster—Richard Pryor
Director—Walter Hill
Leading Players—John Candy, Lonette McKee, Stephen Collins,
  Pat Hingle, Hume Cronyn

BRIGHT ANGEL (1990, Hemdale-Northwood)
George Russell—Dermot Mulroney
Director—Michael Fields
Leading Players—Lili Taylor, Sam Shepard, Valerie Perrine, Bill
  Pullman, Burt Young, Sheila McCarthy, Mary Kay Place,
  Kevin Tighe

THE BRIDE (1985, Columbia)
Eva—Jennifer Beals
Director—Franc Roddam
Leading Players—Sting, Geraldine Page, Anthony Higgins,
  Clancy Brown, David Rappaport

THE BRIDE CAME C.O.D. (1941, Warners)
Joan Winfield—Bette Davis
Director—William Keighley
Leading Players—James Cagney, Stuart Erwin, Jack Carson,
  George Tobias, Eugene Pallette

THE BRIDE COMES HOME (1935, Paramount)
Jeanette Desmereau—Claudette Colbert
Director—Wesley Ruggles
Leading Players—Fred MacMurray, Robert Young, William
Collier, Sr., Donald Meek

BRIDE FOR SALE (1949, RKO)
Nora Shelly—Claudette Colbert
Director—William D. Russell
Leading Players—Robert Young, George Brent, Max Baer

THE BRIDE GOES WILD (1948, MGM)
Martha Terryton—June Allyson
Director—Norman Taurog
Leading Players—Van Johnson, Butch Jenkins, Hume Cronyn,
  Una Merkel, Arlene Dahl

THE BRIDE OF FRANKENSTEIN (1935, Universal)
Elizabeth Frankenstein—Valerie Hobson
The Bride of the Monster—Elsa Lanchester
Director—James Whale
Leading Players—Boris Karloff, Colin Clive, Ernest Thesiger

BRIDE OF HATE (1916, Silent, Triangle/Kay-Bee)
Mercedes Mendoza—Margery Wilson
Director—Walter Edwards
Leading Players—Frank Keenan, Jerome Story, David M. Hartford, Elvira Weil

BRIDE OF RE-ANIMATOR (1991, Wildstreet Pictures)
The Bride—Kathleen Kinmont
Director—Brian Yunzer
Leading Players—Jeffrey Combs, Bruce Abbott, Claude Earl Jones, Fabiana Udenio

BRIDE OF THE REGIMENT (1930, First National)
Countess Anna-Marie—Vivienne Segal
Director—John Francis Dillon
Leading Players—Allan Prior, Walter Pidgeon, Louise Fazenda

BRIDE OF VENGEANCE (1949, Paramount)
Lucretia Borgia—Paulette Goddard
Director—Mitchell Leisen
Leading Players—John Lund, Macdonald Carey, Albert Dekker

THE BRIDE WALKS OUT (1936, RKO)
Carolyn Martin—Barbara Stanwyck
Director—Leigh Jason
Leading Players—Gene Raymond, Robert Young, Ned Sparks, Helen Broderick, Willie Best

THE BRIDE WORE BOOTS (1946, Paramount)
Sally Warren—Barbara Stanwyck
Director—Irving Pichel
Leading Players—Robert Cummings, Diana Lynn, Patric Knowles, Peggy Wood, Robert Benchley

THE BRIDE WORE RED (1937, MGM)
Anni—Joan Crawford
Director—Dorothy Arzner
Leading Players—Robert Young, Franchot Tone, Billie Burke, Reginald Owen, George Zucco

THE BRIGAND (1952, Columbia)
Carlos DeLargo—Anthony Dexter
Director—Phil Carlson
Leading Players—Jody Lawrence, Gale Robbins, Anthony Quinn

BRIGHAM YOUNG—FRONTIERSMAN (1940, 20th Century Fox)
Brigham Young—Dean Jagger
Director—Henry Hathaway
Leading Players—Tyrone Power, Linda Darnell, Brian Donlevy, Mary Astor, Vincent Price, John Carradine

THE BRIGHTON STRANGLER (1945, RKO)
Reginald—John Loder
Director—Max Nosseck
Leading Players—June Duprez, Michael St. Angel, Miles Mander, Rose Hobart, Gilbert Emery

BRINGING UP FATHER (1928, Silent, MGM)
Jiggs—J. Farrell MacDonald
Director—Jack Conway
Leading Players—Jules Cowles, Polly Moran, Marie Dressler

BRINGING UP FATHER (1946, Monogram)
Jiggs—Joe Yule
Director—Eddie Cline
Leading Players—Renie Riano, George McManus, Tim Ryan, June Harrison

BRITISH AGENT (1934, First National)
Stephen Locke—Leslie Howard
Director—Michael Curtiz
Leading Players—Kay Francis, William Gargan, Phillip Reed

BROADWAY BAD (1933, Fox Film Corp.)
Tony Landers—Joan Blondell
Director—Sidney Lamfield
Leading Players—Ricardo Cortez, Ginger Rogers, Adrienne Ames

BROADWAY BIG SHOT (1942, Producers Releasing Corporation)
Jimmy O'Brien—Ralph Byrd
Director—William Beaudine
Leading Players—Virginia Vale, William Halligan, Dick Rush

BROADWAY DANNY ROSE (1984, Orion)
Danny Rose—Woody Allen
Director—Woody Allen
Leading Players—Mia Farrow, Nick Apollo Forte, Craig Vanderbergh

BROADWAY GONDOLIER (1935, Warners)
Richard Purcell—Dick Powell
Director—Lloyd Bacon
Leading Players—Joan Blondell, Adolphe Menjou, Louise Fazenda, William Gargan

THE BROADWAY HOOFER (1929, Columbia)
Adele—Marie Saxon
Director—George Archainbaud
Leading Players—Jack Egan, Louise Fazenda, Howard Hickman

BROADWAY HOSTESS (1935, Warners)
Winnie Wharton—Wini Shaw
Director—Frank McDonald
Leading Players—Genevieve Tobin, Lyle Talbot, Allen Jenkins

BROADWAY LADY (1925, Silent, R-C Pictures)
Rosalie Ryan—Evelyn Brent
Director—Wesley Ruggles
Leading Players—Marjorie Bonner, Theodore von Eltz, Joyce Compton, Clarissa Selwyn

BROADWAY MADONNA (1922, Silent, Quality Film)
Vivian Collins—Dorothy Revier
Director—Harry Revier
Leading Players—Jack Connolly, Harry Van Meter, Eugene Burr

BROADWAY ROSE (1922, Silent, Tiffany)
Rosalie Lawrence—Mae Murray
Director—Robert Z. Leonard
Leading Players—Monte Blue, Raymond Bloomer, Ward Crane

BRONCO BILLY (1980, Warners)
Bronco Billy—Clint Eastwood
Director—Clint Eastwood
Leading Players—Sondra Locke, Geoffrey Lewis, Sam Bottoms, Scatman Crothers

BRONCO BUSTER (1952, Universal)
Tom Moody—John Lund
Director—Budd Boetticher

Leading Players—Scott Brady, Joyce Holden, Chill Wills, Don Haggerty

BROTH OF A BOY (1959, GB, British Lion)
Patrick Farrell—Barry Fitzgerald
Director—George Pollack
Leading Players—Harry Brogan, Tony Wright, June Thornburn

THE BROTHER FROM ANOTHER PLANET (1984, A-Train Films)
The Brother—Joe Morton
Director—John Sayles
Leading Players—Darryl Edwards, Steve James, Tom Wright, Caroline Aaron, Randy Sue Carter

BROTHER JOHN (1971, Columbia)
John Kane—Sidney Poitier
Director—James Goldstone
Leading Players—Will Geer, Bradford Dillman, Beverly Todd

BROTHER ORCHID (1940, First National/Warners)
Little John Sarto—Edward G. Robinson
Director—Lloyd Bacon
Leading Players—Ann Sothern, Humphrey Bogart, Donald Crisp, Ralph Bellamy, Allen Jenkins

BROTHER RAT (1938, Warners)
Billy Randolph—Wayne Morris
Bing Edwards—Eddie Albert
Dan Crawford—Ronald Reagan
Director—William Keighley
Leading Players—Priscilla Lane, Johnnie Davis, Jane Bryan, Jane Wyman

BROTHER RAT AND A BABY (1940, Warners)
Billy Randolph—Wayne Morris
Bing Edwards—Eddie Albert
"Commencement"—Peter B. Goode
Dan Crawford—Ronald Reagan
Director—Ray Enright
Leading Players—Priscilla Lane, Jame Bryan, Jane Wyman, Larry Williams

BROTHER SUN, SISTER MOON (1972, GB, Paramount/Vic Films)
Francesco—Graham Faulkner
Clare—Judi Bowker
Director—Franco Zeffirelli
Leading Players—Alec Guinness, Leigh Lawson, Kenneth Cranham

BROTHERS (1929, Silent, Rayart Pictures)
Tom Conroy—Cornelius Keefe
Bob Conroy—Arthur Rankin
Director—Scott Pembroke
Leading Players—Barbara Bedford, Richard Carle, George Chesebro, Paddy O'Flynn

BROTHERS (1930, Columbia)
Bob Naughton/Eddie Connolly—Bert Lytell
Director—Walter Lang
Leading Players—Dorothy Sebastian, William Morris, Richard Tucker

BROTHERS (1984, Australia, Areflex)
Adam Wild—Chard Hayward

Kevin Wild—Ivar Kants
Director—Terry Bourke
Leading Players—Margaret Lawrence, Jennifer Cluff, Alyson Best

THE BROTHERS KARAMAZOV (1958, MGM)
Dmitri Karamazov—Yul Brynner
Ivan Karamazov—Richard Basehart
Alexey Karamazov—William Shatner
Smerdyakov—Albert Salmi
Director—Richard Brooks
Leading Players—Maria Schell, Claire Bloom, Lee J. Cobb, Judith Evelyn, David Opatoshu

THE BROTHERS RICO (1957, Columbia)
Eddie Rico—Richard Conte
Gino Rico—Paul Picerni
Johnny Rico—James Darren
Director—Phil Karlson
Leading Players—Dianne Foster, Kathryn Grant, Larry Gates

BROWN OF HARVARD (1918, Silent, Selig)
Tom Brown -Tom Moore
Director—Harry Beaumont
Leading Players—Hazel Day, Sidney Ainsworth, Warner Richmond

BROWN OF HARVARD (1926, Silent, MGM)
Tom Brown—William Haines
Director—Jack Conway
Leading Players—Jack Pickford, Mary Brian, Francis X. Bushman, Jr., Mary Alden, David Torrence

BRUBAKER (1980, 20th Century Fox)
Brubaker—Robert Redford
Director—Stuart Rosenberg
Leading Players—Yaphet Kotto, Jane Alexander, Murray Hamilton, David Keith

THE BRUTE MASTER (1920, Silent, Hodkinson/Pathe)
Bucko McAllister—Hobart Bosworth
Director—J. Parker Reed
Leading Players—Anna Q. Nilsson, William Conklin, Margaret Livingston

BUBBLES (1920, Silent, Pioneer)
Bubbles Van Saynt—Mary Anderson
Director—Wayne Mack
Leading Players—Jack Connolly, Bert Woodruff, Gertrude Elliott, Jack Mowrer

THE BUCCANEER (1938, Paramount)
Jean Lafite—Frederic March
Director—Cecil B. De Mille
Leading Players—Franciska Gaal, Akim Tamiroff, Margot Grahame, Walter Brennan, Ian Keith

THE BUCCANEER (1958, Paramount)
Jean Lafite—Yul Brynner
Director—Anthony Quinn
Leading Players—Charlton Heston, Claire Bloom, Charles Boyer, Inger Stevens, Henry Hull

BUCCANEER'S GIRL (1950, Universal)
Deborah McCoy—Yvonne De Carlo
Frederic Baptiste—Phillip Friend

Director—Frederick De Cordova
Leading Players—Robert Douglas, Elsa Lanchester, Andrea
King, Norman Lloyd

BUCHANAN RIDES ALONE (1958, Columbia)
Buchanan—Randolph Scott
Director—Budd Boetticher
Leading Players—Craig Stevens, Barry Kelley, Tol Avery

BUCK AND THE PREACHER (1972, Columbia)
Buck—Sidney Poitier
Preacher—Harry Belafonte
Director—Sidney Poitier
Leading Players—Ruby Dee, Cameron Mitchell, Denny Miller

BUCK BENNY RIDES AGAIN (1940, Paramount)
Buck Benny—Jack Benny
Director—Mark Sandrich
Leading Players—Ellen Drew, Eddie Anderson, Andy Devine,
Phil Harris, Dennis Day, Virginia Dale

BUCK PRIVATES (1941, Universal)
Slicker Smith—Bud Abbott
Herbie Brown—Lou Costello
Director—Arthur Lubin
Leading Players—Lee Bowman, Alan Curtis, The Andrews
Sisters, Jane Frazee, Nat Pendleton

BUCK PRIVATES COME HOME (1947, Universal)
Slicker Smith—Bud Abbott
Herbie Brown—Lou Costello
Director—Charles Barton
Leading Players—Tom Brown, Joan Fulton, Nat Pendleton,
Beverly Simmons, Don Beddoe

BUCK ROGERS IN THE 25TH CENTURY (1979, Universal)
Buck Rogers—Gil Gerard
Director—Daniel Haller
Leading Players—Pamela Hensley, Erin Gray, Henry Silva, Tim
O'Connor, Joseph Wiseman

THE BUCKSKIN LADY (1957, United Artists)
Angela Medley—Patricia Medina
Director—Carl Hittleman
Leading Players—Richard Denning, Gerald Mohr, Henry Hull

THE BUDDY HOLLY STORY (1978, Columbia)
Buddy Holly—Gary Busey
Director—Steve Rash
Leading Players—Don Stroud, Charles Martin Smith, Bill
Jordan, Maria Richwine

BUDDY'S SONG (1991, GB, Castle Premier)
Buddy—Chesney Hawkes
Director—Claude Whatham
Leading Players—Roger Daltrey, Sharon Duce, Michael Elphick,
Douglas Hodge

BUFFALO BILL (1944, 20th Century Fox)
Buffalo Bill Cody—Joel McCrea
Director—William A. Wellman
Leading Players—Maureen O'Hara, Linda Darnell, Thomas
Mitchell, Edgar Buchanan, Anthony Quinn

BUFFALO BILL AND THE INDIANS (1976, United Artists)
Buffalo Bill Cody—Paul Newman

Director—Robert Altman
Leading Players—Joel Grey, Frank Kaquitts, Kevin McCarthy,
Burt Lancaster, Geraldine Chaplin

BUFFALO BILL IN TOMAHAWK TERRITORY (1952, United
Artists)
Buffalo Bill Cody—Clayton Moore
Director—Bernard B. Ray
Leading Players—Slim Andrews, Rod Redwing, Sharon Dexter

BUFFALO BILL ON THE U.P. TRAIL (1926, Silent, Sunset)
Buffalo Bill Cody—Roy Stewart
Director—Frank S. Mattison
Leading Players—Kathryn McGuire, Cullen Landis, Sheldon
Lewis, Earl Metcalfe

BUFFALO BILL RIDES AGAIN (1947, Screen Guild)
Buffalo Bill Cody—Richard Arlen
Director—Bernard B. Ray
Leading Players—Jennifer Holt, Lee Schumay, Gil Patrick

BUGSY (1991, Tri-Star)
Ben "Bugsy" Siegel—Warren Beatty
Director—Barry Levinson
Leading Players—Annette Bening, Harvey Keitel, Ben Kingsley,
Elliot Gould, Joe Mategna, Bebe Neuwirth, Wendy Phillips,
Richard Sarafian

BUGSY MALONE (1976, GB, Paramount)
Bugsy Malone—Scott Baio
Director—Alan Parker
Leading Players—Jodie Foster, Florrie Dugger, John Cassisi

BULLDOG DRUMMOND (1929, United Artists)
Bulldog Drummond—Ronald Colman
Director—F. Richard Jones
Leading Players—Joan Bennett, Lilyan Tashman, Montagu Love

BULLDOG DRUMMOND AT BAY (1937, GB, Wardour/Republic)
Hugh Drummond—John Howard
Director—Norman Lee
Leading Players—Dorothy MacKaill, Victor Jory, Claud Allister,
Hugh Miller

BULLDOG DRUMMOND COMES BACK (1937, Paramount)
Bulldog Drummond—John Lodge
Director—Louis King
Leading Players—John Barrymore, Louise Campbell, Reginald
Denny, E.E. Clive

BULLDOG DRUMMOND ESCAPES (1937, Paramount)
Captain Drummond—Ray Milland
Director—James Hogan
Leading Players—Guy Standing, Heather Angel, Porter Hall,
Reginald Denny, E.E. Clive

BULLDOG DRUMMOND STRIKES BACK (1934, United Artists)
Capt. Hugh Drummond—Ronald Colman
Director—Roy Del Ruth
Leading Players—Loretta Young, C. Aubrey Smith, Charles
Butterworth, Una Merkel, Warner Oland

BULLDOG DRUMMOND'S PERIL (1938, GB,Paramount)
Bulldog Drummond—John Howard
Director—James Hogan

Leading Players—John Barrymore, Louise Campbell, Reginald Denny, E.E. Clive, Porter Hall

BULLET FOR A BADMAN (1964, Universal)
Sam Ward—Darren McGavin
Director—R.G. Springsteen
Leading Players—Audie Murphy, Ruta Lee, Beverley Owen, Skip Homeier, George Tobias

A BULLET FOR JOEY (1955, United Artists)
Joe Victor—George Raft
Director—Lewis Allen
Leading Players—Edward G. Robinson, Audrey Totter, George Dolenz, Peter Van Eyck

A BULLET FOR PRETTY BOY (1970, American International)
Pretty Boy Floyd—Fabian Forte
Director—Larry Buchanan
Leading Players—Jocelyn Lane, Astrid Warner, Michael Haynes

BULLETPROOF (1988, Cinetel-Virgin)
Frank 'Bulletproof' McBain—Gary Busey
Director—Steve Carver
Leading Players—Darlanne Fluegel, Henry Silva, Juan Fernandez, Rene Enriquez

BULLITT (1968, Warners)
Bullitt—Steve McQueen
Director—Peter Yates
Leading Players—Robert Vaughn, Jacqueline Bisset, Don Gordon, Robert Duvall, Simon Oakland

BUNKER BEAN (1936, RKO)
Bunker Bean—Owen Davis, Jr.
Director—William Hamilton
Leading Players—Louise Latimer, Robert McWade, Jessie Ralph, Edward Nugent

BUNNY O'HARE (1971, American International)
Bunny O'Hare—Bette Davis
Director—Gerd Oswald
Leading Players—Ernest Borgnine, Jack Cassidy, Joan Delaney, Jay Robinson, Reva Rose

BUNTY PULLS THE STRINGS (1921, Silent, Goldwyn Pictures)
Bunty Biggar—Leatrice Joy
Director—Reginald Barker
Leading Players—Russell Simpson, Raymond Hatton, Cullen Landis, Casson Ferguson

BUONA SERA, MRS. CAMPBELL (1968, United Artists)
Mrs. Campbell- Gina Lollobrigida
Director—Melvin Frank
Leading Players—Telly Savalas, Phil Silvers, Peter Lawford, Lou Grant, Shelley Winters, Marian Moses

THE BURGLAR (1956, Columbia)
Nat Harbin—Dan Duryea
Director—Paul Wendkos
Leading Players—Jayne Mansfield, Martha Vickers, Peter Capell, Mickey Shaughnessy

BURGLAR (1987, Warners)
Bernice Rhodenbarr—Whoopi Goldberg
Director—Hugh Wilson

Leading Players—Bob Goldthwait, G.W. Bailey, Lesley Ann Warren, James Handy

BURN 'EM UP BARNES (1921, Silent, Mastodon Films)
Burn 'Em Up Barnes—Johnny Hines
Directors—Johnny Hines and George A. Beranger
Leading Players—Edmund Breese, George Fawcett, Betty Carpenter, J. Barney Sherry

BURN 'EM UP O'CONNOR (1939, MGM)
Jerry O'Connor—Dennis O'Keefe
Director—Edward Sedgwick
Leading Players—Cecilia Parker, Nat Pendleton, Harry Carey

BUS RILEY'S BACK IN TOWN (1965, Universal)
Bus Riley—Michael Parks
Director—Harvey Hart
Leading Players—Ann-Margret, Janet Margolin, Brad Dexter

THE BUSH LEAGUER (1927, Silent, Warners)
Buchanan "Spec" White—Monte Blue
Director—Howard Bretherton
Leading Players—Clyde Cook, Lelia Hyams, William Demarest

BUSTER (1988, Tri-Star)
Buster Edwards—Phil Collins
Director—David Green
Leading Players—Julie Walters, Larry Lamb, Stephanie Lawrence, Ellen Beaven

THE BUSTER KEATON STORY (1957, Paramount)
Buster Keaton—Donald O'Connor
Director—Sidney Sheldon
Leading Players—Ann Blyth, Rhonda Fleming, Peter Lorre, Larry Keating, Jackie Coogan

BUTCH AND SUNDANCE, THE EARLY DAYS (1979, 20th Century Fox)
Sundance Kid—William Katt
Butch Cassidy—Tom Berenger
Director—Richard Lester
Leading Players—Jill Eickenberry, Paul Plunkett, Wesley Burgess, Jeff Corey

BUTCH CASSIDY AND THE SUNDANCE KID (1969, 20th Century Fox)
Butch Cassidy—Paul Newman
Sundance Kid—Robert Redford
Director—George Roy Hill
Leading Players—Katharine Ross, Strother Martin, Henry Jones

BUTCH MINDS THE BABY (1942, Universal)
Aloysius Grogan Butch—Broderick Crawford
Director—Albert Rogell
Leading Players—Virginia Bruce, Dick Foran, Porter Hall

THE BUTCHER'S WIFE (1991, Paramount)
Marina—Demi Moore
Leo—George Dzundza
Director—Terry Hughes
Leading Players—Jeff Daniels, Mary Steenburgen, Frances McDormand, Margaret Colin, Max Perlich

BUTLEY (1974, GB, American Film Theatre)
Ben Butley—Alan Bates
Director—Harold Pinter

Leading Players—Jessica Tandy, Richard O'Callaghan, Susan Engel, Michael Byrne

THE BUTTER AND EGG MAN (1928, Silent, First National)
Peter Jones—Jack Mulhall
Director—Richard Wallace
Leading Players—Greta Nissen, Sam Hardy, William Demarest

BUTTERFLY (1924, Silent, Universal)
Dora Collier—Laura La Plante
Director—Clarence Brown
Leading Players—Ruth Clifford, Kenneth Harlan, Norman Kerry, Cesare Gravina

THE BUTTERFLY GIRL (1921, Silent, Playgoers Pictures)
Edith Folsom—Marjorie Daw
Director—John Gorman
Leading Players—Fritzi Brunette, King Baggot, Jean de Briac

BUTTONS (1927, Silent, MGM)
Buttons—Jackie Coogan
Director—George Hill
Leading Players—Lars Hanson, Gertrude Olmstead, Paul Hurst

BYE BYE BIRDIE (1963, Columbia)
Conrad Birdie—Jesse Pearson
Director—George Sidney
Leading Players—Janet Leigh, Dick Van Dyke, Ann-Margret, Maureen Stapleton, Bobby Rydell

BYE-BYE BUDDY (1929, Part-Talkie, Trinity Pictures)
Buddy O'Brien—Bud Shaw
Director—Frank S. Mattison
Leading Players—Agnes Ayres, Fred Shanley, Ben Wilson

C

C.C. AND COMPANY (1971, Avco Embassy)
C.C. Ryder—Joe Namath
Director—Seymour Robbie
Leading Players—Ann-Margret, William Smith, Jennifer Billingsley, Don Chastain

C-MAN (1949, Film Classics)
Cliff Holden—Dean Jagger
Director—Joseph Lerner
Leading Players—John Carradine, Lottie Elwen, Harry Landers

THE CABARET GIRL (1919, Silent, Universal/Bluebird)
Ann Reid—Ruth Clifford
Director—Douglas Gerrard
Leading Players—Carmen Phillips, Ashton Dearholt, Harry V. Meter

THE CABINET OF CALIGARI (1962, 20th Century Fox)
Caligari—Dan O'Herlihy
Director—Roger Kay
Leading Players—Glynis Johns, Dick Davalos, Lawrence Dobkin

CADILLAC MAN (1990, Orion)
Joey O'Brien—Robin Williams
Director—Roger Donaldson
Leading Players—Tim Robbins, Pamela Reed, Fran Drescher, Zack Norman, Annabella Sciorra

CADDIE (1976, Australia, Atlantic)
Caddie—Helen Morse
Director—Donald Crombie
Leading Players—Takis Emmanuel, Jack Thompson, Jacki Weaver

THE CADDY (1953, Paramount)
Joe Anthony—Jerry Lewis
Director—Norman Taurog
Leading Players—Dean Martin, Donna Reed, Barbara Bates, Joseph Calleia, Fred Clark

CAESAR AND CLEOPATRA (1946, GB, Two Cities)
Julius Caesar—Claude Rains
Cleopatra—Vivien Leigh
Director—Gabriel Pascal
Leading Players—Stewart Granger, Flora Robson, Francis L. Sullivan, Basil Sydney, Cecil Parker

CAFE HOSTESS (1940, Columbia)
Jo—Ann Dvorak
Director—Sidney Salkow
Leading Players—Preston Foster, Douglas Fowley, Wynne Gibson

CAGED (1950, Warner Brothers)
Marie Allen—Eleanor Parker
Director—John Cromwell
Leading Players—Lee Patrick, Ellen Corby, Hope Emerson, Betty Garde, Jan Sterling, Agnes Moorehead

CAHILL, UNITED STATES MARSHAL (1973, Warner Brothers)
J.D. Cahill—John Wayne
Director—Andrew V. McLaglen
Leading Players—George Kennedy, Gary Grimes, Neville Brand, Clay O'Brien, Marie Windsor

CAIN AND MABEL (1936, Warner Brothers)
Mabel O'Dare—Marion Davies
Larry Cain—Clark Gable
Director—Lloyd Bacon
Leading Players—Allen Jenkins, Roscoe Karns, Walter Catlett

CAIN'S WAY (1969, M.D.A. Associates)
Captain Cain—Scott Brady
Director—Kent Osborne
Leading Players—John Carradine, Adair Jamison, Robert Dix

CAL (1984, Ireland)
Cal—John Lynch
Director—Pat O'Connor
Leading Players—Helen Mirren, Donal McCann, Kitty Gibson

CALAMITY JANE (1953, Warner Brothers)
Calamity Jane Canary—Doris Day
Director—David Butler
Leading Players—Howard Keel, Allyn McLerie, Philip Carey

CALAMITY JANE AND SAM BASS (1949, Universal)
Calamity Jane—Yvonne De Carlo

Sam Bass—Howard Duff
Director—George Sherman
Leading Players—Dorothy Hart, Willard Parker, Norman Lloyd

CALENDAR GIRL (1947, Republic)
Patricia O'Neil—Jane Frazee
Director—Allan Dwan
Leading Players—William Marshall, Gail Patrick, Kenny Baker, James Ellison, Victor McLaglen

CALIFORNIA FIREBRAND (1948, Republic)
Monte Hale—Monte Hale
Director—Phillip Ford
Leading Players—Adrian Booth, Paul Hurst, Alice Tyrrell

CALIFORNIA JOE (1944, Republic)
Lt. Joe Weldon—Don "Red" Barry
Director—Spencer Bennet
Leading Players—Wally Vernon, Helen Talbot, Twinkel Watts

THE CALIFORNIAN (1937, 20th Century Fox)
Ramon Escobar—Ricardo Cortez
Director—Gus Meins
Leading Players—Marjorie Weaver, Katherine De Mille, Maurice Black, Morgan Wallace

CALL HER SAVAGE (1932, Fox Film Corp.)
Nasa—Clara Bow
Director—John Francis Dillon
Leading Players—Monroe Owsley, Gilbert Roland, Thelma Todd, Estelle Taylor, Willard Robertson

CALL ME (1988, Vestron)
Anna—Patricia Charbonneau
Director—Sollace Mitchell
Leading Players—Patti D'Abanville, Stephen McHattie, Sam Freed, Boyd Gaines

CALL ME BWANA (1963, GB, Rank/UA)
Matt Merriwether—Bob Hope
Director—Gordon Douglas
Leading Players—Anita Ekberg, Lionel Jeffries, Percy Herbert, Edie Adams

CALL ME GENIUS (1961, GB, Associated British Films)
Anthony Hancock—Tony Hancock
Director—Robert Day
Leading Players—George Sanders, Paul Massie, Margit Saad

CALL ME MADAM (1953, 20th Century Fox)
Mrs. Sally Adams—Ethel Merman
Director—Walter Lang
Leading Players—Donald O'Connor, George Sanders, Vera-Ellen

CALL ME MAME (1933, GB, Warner Brothers)
Mame—Ethel Irving
Director—John Daumery
Leading Players—John Batten, Dorothy Bartlam, Winifred Oughton, Julian Royce

CALL ME MISTER (1951, 20th Century Fox)
Shep Dooley—Dan Dailey
Director—Lloyd Bacon
Leading Players—Betty Grable, Danny Thomas, Dale Robertson

CALLAN (1975, GB, Cinema National)
Callan—Edward Woodward
Director—Don Sharpe
Leading Players—Eric Porter, Catherine Schell, Peter Egan

CALLAWAY WENT THATAWAY (1951, MGM)
Smoky Callaway—Howard Keel
Director—Norman Panama
Leading Players—Dorothy McGuire, Fred MacMurray, Jesse White

CALLING BULLDOG DRUMMOND (1951, GB, MGM)
Hugh Drummond—Walter Pidgeon
Director—Victor Saville
Leading Players—Margaret Leighton, Robert Beatty, David Tomlinson

CALLING DR. DEATH (1943, Universal)
Doctor Steele—Lon Chaney, Jr.
Director—Reginald LeBorg
Leading Players—Patricia Morison, J. Carroll Naish, David Bruce, Ramsay Ames

CALLING DR. GILLESPIE (1942, MGM)
Dr. Leonard Gillespie—Lionel Barrymore
Director—Harold S. Bucquet
Leading Players—Philip Dorn, Donna Reed, Phil Brown, Nat Pendleton, Alma Kruger

CALLING DR. KILDARE (1939, MGM)
Dr. James Kildare—Lew Ayres
Director—Harold S. Bucquet
Leading Players—Lionel Barrymore, Laraine Day, Nat Pendleton, Lana Turner, Samuel S. Hinds

CALLING PAUL TEMPLE (1948, GB, Nettleford)
Paul Temple—John Bentley
Director—MacLean Rogers
Leading Players—Dinah Sheridan, Margaretta Scott, Abraham Sofaer, Celia Lipton

CALLING PHILO VANCE (1940, Warner Brothers)
Philo Vance—James Stephenson
Director—William Clemens
Leading Players—Margot Stevenson, Henry O'Neill, Edward Brophy, Ralph Forbes

CALLING WILD BILL ELLIOTT (1943, Republic)
Wild Bill Elliott—Bill Elliott
Director—Spencer Bennet
Leading Players—George "Gabby" Hayes, Anne Jeffreys, Herbert Heyes, Roy Barcroft

CALYPSO JOE (1957, Allied Artists)
Calypso Joe—Herb Jeffries
Director—Edward Dein
Leading Players—Angie Dickinson, Edward Kemme, Stephan Bekassy

CAMEO KIRBY (1915, Silent, Paramount)
Cameo Kirby—Dustin Farnum
Director—None Given
Leading Players—Winifred Kingston, Dick La Reno

CAMEO KIRBY (1930, Fox Film Corp.)
Cameo Kirby—J. Harold Murray

Director—Irving Cummings
Leading Players—Norma Terris, Douglas Gilmore, Robert Edeson

THE CAMERAMAN (1928, Silent, MGM)
Luke Shannon (Buster)—Buster Keaton
Director—Edward Sedgwick
Leading Players—Marceline Day, Harry Gibbon, Harold Goodwin

CAMERON'S CLOSET (1989, SVS)
Cameron Lansing—Scott Curtis
Director—Armand Mastroianni
Leading Players—Cotter Smith, Mel Harris, Chuck McCann

CAMILLE (1916, Silent, World Film)
Camille—Clara Kimball Young
Director—Albert Capellani
Leading Players—Paul Capellani, Lillian Cook, Robert Cummings, Dan Baker, Frederick C. Truesdale

CAMILLE (1921, Silent, Metro)
Camille—Nazimova
Director—Ray C. Smallwood
Leading Players—Rudolph Valentino, Arthur Hoyt, Zeffie Tillbury, Rex Cherryman, Patsy Ruth Miller

CAMILLE (1927, Silent, First National)
Marguerite Gautier (Camille)—Norma Talmadge
Director—Fred Niblo
Leading Players—Gilbert Roland, Lilyan Tashman, Rose Dione, Oscar Beregi, Harvey Clark

CAMILLE (1937, MGM)
Marguerite Gautier (Camille)—Greta Garbo
Director—George Cukor
Leading Players—Robert Taylor, Lionel Barrymore, Elizabeth Allan, Jessie Ralph, Henry Daniell

CAMILLE OF THE BARBARY COAST (1925, Silent, Associated Exhibitors)
Camille Balishaw—Mae Busch
Director—Hugh Dierker
Leading Players—Owen Moore, Fritzi Brunette, Harry Morey

CAMPBELL'S KINGDOM (1957, GB, Rank)
Bruce Cambell—Dirk Bogarde
Director—Ralph Thomas
Leading Players—Stanley Baker, Michael Craig, Barbara Murray. James Robertson Justice

THE CAMPUS FLIRT (1926, Silent, Paramount)
Patricia Mansfield—Bebe Daniels
Director—Clarence Badger
Leading Players—James Hall, El Brendel, Charles Paddock

CAMPUS MAN (1987, RKO-Paramount)
Todd Barrett—John Dye
Director—Ron Casden
Leading Players—Steve Lyon, Kim Delaney, Kathleen Wilhoite

THE CANADIAN (1926, Silent, Paramount)
Frank Taylor—Thomas Meighan
Director—William Beaudine
Leading Players—Mona Palmer, Wyndham Standing, Dale Fuller

THE CANARY MURDER CASE (1929, Paramount)
Margaret O'Dell—Louise Brooks
Director—Malcolm St. Clair
Leading Players—William Powell, James Hall, Jean Arthur, Gustav von Seyffertitz

THE CANDIDATE (1972, Warner Brothers)
Bill McKay—Robert Redford
Director—Michael Ritchie
Leading Players—Peter Boyle, Don Porter, Allen Garfield, Melvyn Douglas

CANDIDATE FOR MURDER (1966, GB, Schoenfield Films)
Helene Edwards—Erika Remberg
Director—David Villiers
Leading Players—Michael Gough, Hans Borsody, John Justin

CANDY (1968, Italy/France, Cinerama)
Candy—Ewa Aulin
Director—Christian Marquand
Leading Players—Charles Aznavour, Marlon Brando, Richard Burton, James Coburn, John Huston

CANNONBALL (1976, New World)
Cannonball Buckman—David Carradine
Director—Paul Bartel
Leading Players—Bill McKinney, Veronica Hamel, Gerrit Graham

CAN'T BUY ME LOVE (1987, Buena Vista)
Cindy Mancini—Amanda Peterson
Director—Steve Rash
Leading Players—Patrick Dempsey, Courtney Gains, Tina Caspary, Seth Green

THE CANTERVILLE GHOST (1944, MGM)
The Canterville Ghost—Charles Laughton
Director—Jules Dassin
Leading Players—Robert Young, Margaret O'Brien, William Gargan, Reginald Owen

CAPONE (1975, 20th Century Fox)
Al Capone—Ben Gazzara
Director—Steve Carver
Leading Players—Susan Blakely, Harry Guardino, John Cassavetes, Sylvester Stallone

CAPPY RICKS (1921, Silent, Paramount)
Cappy Ricks—Charles Abbe
Director—Tom Forman
Leading Players—Thomas Meighan, Agnes Ayres, Hugh Cameron

CAPPY RICKS RETURNS (1935, Republic)
Cappy Ricks—Robert McWade
Director—Mack Wright
Leading Players—Ray Walker, Florine McKinney, Lucien Littlefield, Bradley Page

THE CAPRICES OF KITTY (1915, Silent, Bosworth)
Kitty Bradley—Elsie Janis
Director—William Desmond Taylor
Leading Players—Courtenay Foote, Herbert Standing, Vera Lewis, Martha Mattox

CAPTAIN APACHE (1971, GB, Scotia International)
Captain Apache—Lee Van Cleef

Director—Alexander Singer
Leading Players—Carroll Baker, Stuart Whitman, Percy Herbert

CAPTAIN APPLEJACK (1931, Warner Brothers)
Captain Applejack—John Halliday
Director—Hobart Henley
Leading Players—Mary Brian, Kay Strozzi, Louise Closser Hale

CAPTAIN BILL (1935, GB, Fuller Films)
Captain Bill—Leslie Fuller
Director—Ralph Ceder
Leading Players—Judy Kelly, Hal Gordon, O.B. Clarence

CAPTAIN BLOOD (1925, Silent, Vitagraph)
Peter Blood—J. Warren Kerrigan
Director—David Smith
Leading Players—Jean Paige, Charlotte Merriam, James Morrison, Allan Forrest

CAPTAIN BLOOD (1939, Warner Brothers)
Dr. Peter Blood—Errol Flynn
Director—Michael Curtiz
Leading Players—Olivia de Havilland, Lionel Atwill, Basil Rathbone, Ross Alexander, Guy Kibbee

CAPTAIN BOYCOTT (1947, GB, GFD)
Captain Boycott—Cecil Parker
Director—Frank Launder
Leading Players—Stewart Granger, Kathleen Ryan, Robert Donat

CAPTAIN CALAMITY (1936, Grand National)
Capt. Calamity—George Houston
Director—John Reinhardt
Leading Players—Marion Nixon, Vince Barnett, Juan Torena

CAPTAIN CARELESS (1928, Silent, FBO Pictures)
Bob Gordon—Bob Steele
Director—Jerome Storm
Leading Players—Mary Mabery, Jack Donovan, Barney Furey

CAPTAIN CAREY, U.S.A. (1950, Paramount)
Webster Carey—Alan Ladd
Director—Mitchell Leisen
Leading Players—Wanda Hendrix, Francis Lederer, Celia Lovsky

CAPTAIN CAUTION (1940, UA)
Dan Marvin—Victor Mature
Director—Richard Wallace
Leading Players—Louise Platt, Leo Carillo, Bruce Cabot

CAPTAIN CHINA (1949, Paramount)
Captain China—John Payne
Director—Lewis R. Foster
Leading Players—Gail Russell, Jeffrey Lynn, Lon Chaney, Jr.

CAPTAIN COURTESY (1915, Silent, Bosworth)
Captain Courtesy—Dustin Farnum
Director—Hobart Bosworth
Leading Players—Herbert Standing, Winifred Kingston, Courtney Foote

CAPTAIN EDDIE (1945, 20th Century Fox)
Edward Rickenbacker—Fred MacMurray
Director—Lloyd Bacon
Leading Players—Lynn Bari, Charles Bickford, Thomas Mitchell, Lloyd Nolan, James Gleason

CAPTAIN FLY-BY-NIGHT (1922, Silent, R-C Pictures)
Captain Fly-By-Night—Francis McDonald
Director—William K. Howard
Leading Players—Johnnie Walker, Shannon Day, Edward Gribbon

CAPTAIN FROM CASTILE (1947, 20th Century Fox)
Pedro de Vargas—Tyrone Power
Director—Henry King
Leading Players—Jean Peters, Cesar Romero, Lee J. Cobb, John Sutton, Antonio Moreno

CAPTAIN FURY (1939, UA)
Captain Fury—Brian Aherne
Director—Hal Roach
Leading Players—Victor McLaglen, Paul Lukas, June Lang, John Carradine, George Zucco, Douglas Dumbrille

THE CAPTAIN HATES THE SEA (1934, Columbia)
Capt. Helquist—Walter Connolly
Director—Lewis Milestone
Leading Players—Victor McLaglen, Helen Vinson, John Gilbert, Alison Skipworth, Wynne Gibson

CAPTAIN HORATIO HORNBLOWER (1951, GB, Warner Brothers)
Horatio Hornblower—Gregory Peck
Director—Raoul Walsh
Leading Players—Virginia Mayo, Robert Beatty, James Robinson Justice, Denis O'Dea, Terence Morgan

CAPTAIN HURRICANE (1935, RKO)
Zenas Henry—James Barton
Director—John Robertson
Leading Players—Helen Westley, Helen Mack, Gene Lockhart

THE CAPTAIN IS A LADY (1940, MGM)
Capt. Abe Peabody—Charles Coburn
Director—Robert H. Sinclair
Leading Players—Beulah Bondi, Virginia Grey, Helen Broderick, Billie Burke, Dan Dailey

CAPTAIN JANUARY (1924, Silent, Principal Pictures)
Captain January—Baby Peggy
Director—Edward F. Cline
Leading Players—Hobart Bosworth, Irene Rich, Lincoln Stedman

CAPTAIN JANUARY (1936, 20th Century Fox)
Capt. January—Guy Kibbee
Director—David Butler
Leading Players—Shirley Temple, Slim Summerville, June Lang, Buddy Ebsen

CAPTAIN JOHN SMITH AND POCAHONTAS (1953, UA)
Capt. John Smith—Anthony Dexter
Pocahontas—Jody Lawrence
Director—Lew Landers
Leading Players—Alan Hale, Jr., Robert Clarke, Stuart Randall

CAPTAIN KIDD (1945, UA)
Capt. William Kidd—Charles Laughton
Director—Rowland V. Lee

Leading Players—Randolph Scott, Barbara Britton, Reginald Owen, John Carradine

CAPTAIN KIDD AND THE SLAVE GIRL (1954, Reliance/UA)
Capt. William Kidd—Anthony Dexter
Director—Lew Landers
Leading Players—Eva Gabor, Alan Hale, Jr., James Seay

CAPTAIN KIDD, JR. (1919, Silent, Artcraft)
Jim Gleason—Douglas MacLean
Director—William Desmond Taylor
Leading Players—Mary Pickford, Spottiswoode Aitken, Robert Gordon

CAPTAIN KRONOS: VAMPIRE HUNTER (1974, GB, Hammer/ Paramount)
Captain Kronos—Horst Janson
Director—Brian Clemens
Leading Players—John Carson, Shane Briant, Caroline Munro

CAPTAIN LASH (1929, Silent with musical score, Fox Film Corp.)
Captain Lash—Victor McLaglen
Director—John Blystone
Leading Players—Claire Windsor, Jane Winton, Clyde Cook

CAPTAIN LIGHTFOOT (1955, Universal)
Michael Martin—Rock Hudson
Director—Douglas Sirk
Leading Players—Barbara Rush, Jeff Morrow, Finlay Currie

CAPTAIN MOONLIGHT (1940, GB, Olympia)
Capt. Moonlight—John Stuart
Director—Henry Edwards
Leading Players—John Garrick, Winifred Shotter, Stanley Holloway

CAPTAIN NEMO AND THE UNDERWATER CITY (1969, GB, MGM)
Captain Nemo—Robert Ryan
Director—James Hill
Leading Players—Chuck Connors, Nanette Newman, Luciana Paluzzi

CAPTAIN NEWMAN M.D. (1963, Universal)
Capt. Josiah Newman—Gregory Peck
Director—David Miller
Leading Players—Tony Curtis, Bobby Darin, Eddie Albert, Angie Dickinson

CAPTAIN OF THE GRAY HORSE TROOP (1917, Silent, Vitagraph)
Capt. George Curtis—Antonio Moreno
Director—William Wolbert
Leading Players—Mrs. Bradbury, Otto Lederer, Al Jennings

CAPTAIN OF THE GUARD (1930, Universal)
Robert de Lisle—John Boles
Director—John S. Robertson
Leading Players—Laura La Plante, Sam de Grasse, James Marcus

CAPTAIN PIRATE (1952, Columbia)
Peter Blood—Louis Hayward
Director—Ralph Murray
Leading Players—Patricia Medina, John Sutton, Charles Irwin

CAPTAIN SALVATION (1927, Silent, MGM)
Anson Campbell—Lars Hanson
Director—John S. Robertson
Leading Players—Marceline Ray, Pauline Stark, Ernest Torrence

CAPTAIN SCARLETT (1953, UA)
Capt. Scarlett—Richard Greene
Director—Thomas Carr
Leading Players—Leonora Amar, Nedrick Young, Manolo Fabregas

CAPTAIN SINBAD (1963, MGM)
Capt. Sinbad—Guy Williams
Director—Bryon Haskin
Leading Players—Heidi Bruhl, Pedro Armendariz, Abraham Sofaer

CAPTAIN SWAGGER (1928, Silent, Pathe Exchange)
Captain Swagger (Hugh Drummond)—Rod La Rocque
Director—Edward H. Griffith
Leading Players—Sue Carol, Richard Tucker, Victor Potel

CAPTAIN THUNDER (1931, Warner Brothers)
Capt. Thunder—Victor Varconi
Director—Alan Crosland
Leading Players—Fay Wray, Charles Judels, Robert Elliott

CAPTAIN TUGBOAT ANNIE (1945, Republic)
Tugboat Annie—Jane Darwell
Director—Phil Rosen
Leading Players—Edgar Kennedy, Charles Gordon, Mantan Moreland, Pamela Blake

CAPTAINS COURAGEOUS (1937, MGM)
Manuel—Spencer Tracy
Director—Victor Fleming
Leading Players—Freddie Bartholomew, Lionel Barrymore, Mickey Rooney, Melvyn Douglas

THE CAPTAIN'S CAPTAIN (1919, Silent, Vitagraph)
Cap'n Abe—Arthur Donaldson
Director—Tom Terriss
Leading Players—Alice Joyce, Percy Standing, Julia Swayne Gordon

THE CAPTAIN'S KID (1937, First National/Warner Brothers)
Abigail Prentiss—Sybil Jason
Asa Plunkett—Guy Kibbee
Director—Nick Grinde
Leading Players—May Robson, Jane Bryan, Fred Lawrence

CAPTAINS OF THE CLOUDS (1942, Warner Brothers)
Brian MacLean—James Cagney
Johnny Dutton—Dennis Morgan
Director—Michael Curtiz
Leading Players—Alan Hale, Brenda Marshall, George Tobias

CAPTAIN'S ORDERS (1937, GB, Liberty Films)
Captain Trent—Henry Edwards
Director—Ivar Campbell
Leading Players—Jane Carr, Marie Lavarre, Franklyn Dyall

THE CAPTAIN'S PARADISE (1953, GB, London Films)
Capt. Henry St. James—Alec Guinness
Director—Anthony Kimmins

Leading Players—Celia Johnson, Yvonne De Carlo, Charles Goldner

THE CAPTAIN'S TABLE (1960, GB, 20th Century Fox/Rank)
Captain Ebbs—John Gregson
Director—Jack Lee
Leading Players—Peggy Cummins, Donald Sinden, Nadia Gray

CAPTIVE GIRL (1950, Columbia)
Joan—Anita Lhoest
Director—William Berle
Leading Players—Johnny Weismuller, Buster Crabbe

THE CAPTIVE GOD (1916, Silent, Triangle)
Chiapa—William S. Hart
Director—Thomas Ince
Leading Players—Enid Markey, P.D. Tabler, Dorothy Dalton

CAPTIVE WILD WOMAN (1943, Universal)
Paula Dupree—Acquanetta
Director—Edward Dmytryk
Leading Players—Evelyn Ankers, John Carradine, Milburn Stone

CARBINE WILLIAMS (1952, MGM)
Marsh Williams—James Stewart
Director—Richard Thorpe
Leading Players—Jean Hagen, Wendell Corey, Carl Benton Reid

THE CARDBOARD CAVALIER (1949, GB, GFD)
Sidcup Buttermeadow—Sid Field
Director—Walter Forde
Leading Players—Margaret Lockwood, Mary Clare, Jerry Desmonde

THE CARDBOARD LOVER (1928, Silent, MGM)
Sally—Marion Davies
Director—Robert Z. Leonard
Leading Players—Jetta Goudal, Nils Asther, Andre Desegurola

CARDIGAN (1922, Silent, American Releasing Corp.)
Michael Cardigan—William Collier, Jr.
Director—John W. Noble
Leading Players—Betty Carpenter, Thomas Cummings, William Pike

THE CARDINAL (1936, GB, Pathe)
Cardinal De Medici—Matheson Lang
Director—Sinclair Hill
Leading Players—Eric Portman, Robert Atkins, O.E. Clarence

THE CARDINAL (1963, Columbia)
Stephen Fermoyle—Tom Tryon
Director—Otto Preminger
Leading Players—Carol Lynley, Dorothy Gish, John Saxon, John Huston, Burgess Meredith, Raf Vallone

CARDINAL RICHELIEU (1935, Fox Film Corp.)
Cardinal Richelieu—George Arliss
Director—Rowland V. Lee
Leading Players—Edward Arnold, Halliwell Hobbes, Maureen O'Sullivan, Cesar Romero

CAREER GIRL (1944, Producers Releasing Corp.)
Joan—Frances Langford
Director—Wallace W. Fox
Leading Players—Edward Norris, Iris Adrian, Craig Woods

THE CAREER OF KATHERINE BUSH (1919, Silent, Paramount)
Katherine Bush—Catherine Calvert
Director—Roy W. Neill
Leading Players—John Galsworthy, Crauford Kent, Mathilda Brundage

CAREER WOMAN (1936, 20th Century Fox)
Carroll Aiken—Claire Trevor
Director—Lewis Seiler
Leading Players—Michael Whalen, Isabel Jewell, Eric Linden

CAREFUL, HE MIGHT HEAR YOU (1984, Australia, 20th Century Fox)
P.S. "Bill"—Nicholas Gledhill
Director—Carl Schultz
Leading Players—Wendy Hughes, Robyn Nevin, Peter Whidford

CARELESS LADY (1932, Fox Film Corp.)
Sally Brown/Mrs. Illington—Joan Bennett
Director—Kenneth McKenna
Leading Players—John Boles, Minna Gombell, Weldon Heyburn

THE CAREY TREATMENT (1972, MGM)
Peter Carey—James Coburn
Director—Blake Edwards
Leading Players—Jennifer O'Neill, Pat Hingle, Syke Aubrey

CARMEN (1915, Silent, Paramount)
Carmen—Geraldine Farrar
Director—Cecil B. DeMille
Leading Players—Wallace Reid, Horace B. Carpenter, Pedro De Cordoba

CARMEN (1931, GB, BIP/Wardour)
Carmen—Marguerite Namara
Director—Cecil Lewis
Leading Players—Thomas Burke, Lance Fairfax, Lester Matthews

CARMEN JONES (1954, 20th Century Fox)
Carmen Jones—Dorothy Dandridge
Director—Otto Preminger
Leading Players—Harry Belafonte, Olga James, Pearl Bailey, Diahann Carroll, Roy Glenn, Brock Peters

CARNATION KID (1929, Paramount)
Carnation Kid—Francis McDonald
Director—E. Mason Hopper
Leading Players—Douglas Maclean, Francis Lee, William B. Davidson

THE CARNIVAL GIRL (1926, Silent, Asociated Exhibitors)
Nanette—Marion Mack
Director—Cullen Tate
Leading Players—Gladys Brockwell, Frankie Darro, George Siegmann

CARNIVAL QUEEN (1937, Universal)
Marion Prescott—Dorothea Kent
Director—Nate Watt
Leading Players—Robert Wilcox, Hobart Cavanaugh, G. Pat Collins

CARNY (1980, UA)
Frankie—Gary Busey
Director—Robert Kaylor

Leading Players—Jodie Foster, Robbie Robertson, Meg Foster

CAROLYN OF THE CORNERS (1919, Silent, Anderson-Brunton/Pathe)
Carolyn—Bessie Love
Director—Robert Thornby
Leading Players—Charles Elder, Charlotte Mineau, Eunice Moore

THE CARPENTER (1989, Canada, Cinepix/Capstone)
Ed—Wings Hauser
Director—David Wellington
Leading Players—Lynne Adams, Pierre Lenoir, Barbara Jones

CARRIE (1952, Paramount)
Carrie Meeber—Jennifer Jones
Director—William Wyler
Leading Players—Laurence Olivier, Eddie Albert, Miriam Hopkins, Basil Ruysdael

CARRIE (1976, UA)
Carrie White—Sissy Spacek
Director—Brian De Palma
Leading Players—Piper Laurie, Amy Irving, William Katt, John Travolta, Nancy Allen

CARRY ON ADMIRAL (1957, GB, Renown)
Admiral Godfrey—A. E. Matthews
Director—Val Guest
Leading Players—David Tomlinson, Peggy Cummins, Brian Reece, Eunice Gayson

CARRY ON AGAIN, DOCTOR (1969, GB, Rank)
Dr. James Nookey—Jim Dale
Director—Gerald Thomas
Leading Players—Kenneth Williams, Sidney James, Charles Hawtrey, Joan Sims, Hattie Jacques

CARRY ON CABBIE (1963, GB, Warner Brothers/Pathe)
Charlie—Sid James
Director—Gerald Thomas
Leading Players—Hattie Jacques, Kenneth Conner, Charles Hawtrey, Esma Cannon

CARRY ON CLEO (1964, GB, Warner Brothers/Pathe)
Cleo—Amanda Barrie
Director—Gerald Thomas
Leading Players—Sid James, Kenneth Williams, Kenneth Conner, Charles Hawtrey, Joan Sims

CARRY ON CONSTABLE (1960, GB, Anglo-Amalgamated)
Sgt. Wilkins—Sid James
Director—Gerald Thomas
Leading Players—Eric Barker, Kenneth Conner, Charles Hawtrey, Hattie Jacques, Joan Sims

CARRY ON COWBOY (1966, GB, Warner Brothers/Pathe)
Rumpo Kid—Sid James
Director—Gerald Thomas
Leading Players—Kenneth Williams, Jim Dale, Charles Hawtrey, Joan Sims, Angela Douglas, Percy Herbert

CARRY ON DOCTOR (1968, GB, Rank)
Francis Bigger—Frankie Howerd
Director—Gerald Thomas

Leading Players—Sid James, Kenneth Williams, Charles Hawtrey, Jim Dale, Barbara Windsor

CARRY ON EMMANNUELLE (1978, GB, Hemdale)
Emmannuelle—Suzanne Danielle
Director—Gerald Thomas
Leading Players—Kenneth Williams, Kenneth Conner, Jack Douglas, Joan Sims, Peter Butterworth

CARRY ON HENRY VIII (1970, GB, Rank/AIP)
Henry VIII—Sid James
Director—Gerald Thomas
Leading Players—Kenneth Williams, Joan Sims, Charles Hawtrey, Terry Scott, Barbara Windsor

CARRY ON NURSE (1959, GB, Anglo-Amalgamated)
Matron—Hattie Jacques
Director—Gerald Thomas
Leading Players—Kenneth Conner, Kenneth Williams, Charles Hawtrey, Joan Hickson, Shirley Eaton

CARRY ON SERGEANT (1959, GB, Anglo-Amalgamated)
Sgt. Grimshaw—William Hartnell
Director—Gerald Thomas
Leading Players—Bob Monkhouse, Shirley Eaton, Eric Barker, Dora Bryan, Bill Owen, Kenneth Conner

CARRY ON TEACHER (1962, GB, Anglo-Amalgamated)
William Wakefield—Ted Ray
Director—Gerald Thomas
Leading Players—Kenneth Conner, Leslie Phillips, Charles Hawtrey, Joan Sims

CARSON CITY KID (1940, Republic)
Carson City Kid—Roy Rogers
Director—Joseph Kane
Leading Players—George "Gabby' Hayes, Bob Steele, Noah Beery, Jr., Pauline Moore

THE CARTER CASE (1947, Republic)
Elliott Carter—Bradley Page
Director—Bernard Vorhaus
Leading Players—James Ellison, Virginia Gilmore, Franklin Pangborn

CARVE HER NAME WITH PRIDE (1958, GB, Rank)
Violette Szabo—Virginia McKenna
Director—Lewis Gilbert
Leading Players—Paul Scofield, Jack Warner, Denise Grey

CARYL OF THE MOUNTAINS (1936, Marcy/Reliable)
Caryl Foray—Lois Wild
Director—Bernard B. Ray
Leading Players—Francis X. Bushman, Earl Dwire, Robert Walker

CASANOVA BROWN (1944, RKO)
Casanova Brown—Gary Cooper
Director—Sam Wood
Leading Players—Teresa Wright, Frank Morgan, Anita Louise, Patricia Collinge

CASANOVA IN BURLESQUE (1944, Republic)
Joseph M. Kelly, Jr.—Joe E. Brown
Director—Leslie Goodwins
Leading Players—June Havoc, Dale Evans, Marjorie Gateson

CASANOVA'S BIG NIGHT (1954, Paramount)
Pippo Popolino—Bob Hope
Casanova—Vincent Price
Director—Norma Z. McLeod
Leading Players—Joan Fontaine, Audrey Dalton, Basil Rathbone, Hugh Marlowe

THE CASE AGAINST MRS. AMES (1936, Paramount)
Hope Ames—Madeleine Carroll
Director—William A. Seiter
Leading Players—George Brent, Arthur Treacher, Alan Baxter, Beulah Bondi, Alan Mowbray

THE CASE OF BECKY (1921, Silent, Realart)
Dorothy Stone (Becky)—Constance Binney
Director—Chester M. Franklin
Leading Players—Glenn Hunter, Frank McCormack, Montague Love, Margaret Seddon

THE CASE OF CHARLES PEACE (1949, GB, Argyle/Monarch)
Charles Peace—Michael Martin Harvey
Director—Norman Lee
Leading Players—Chili Boucher, Valentine Dyall, Bruce Belfrage, Ronald Adam

THE CASE OF CLARA DEANE (1932, Paramount)
Clara Deane—Wynne Gibson
Director—Louis Gasnier & Max Marcin
Leading Players—Pat O'Brien, Frances Dee, Dudley Digges

THE CASE OF GABRIEL PERRY (1935, GB, British Lion)
Gabriel Perry—Henry Oscar
Director—Albert De Courville
Leading Players—Olga Lindo, Margaret Lockwood, Franklyn Dyall, Raymond Lovell

THE CASE OF LENA SMITH (1929, Silent, Paramount)
Lena Smith—Esther Ralston
Director—Josef von Sternberg
Leading Players—James Hall, Gustav von Seyfferitz, Emily Fitzroy

THE CASE OF PATTY SMITH (1962, Handel)
Patty Smith—Dani Lynn
Director—Leo A. Handel
Leading Players—Merry Anders, J. Edward McKinley, Carleton Crane

THE CASE OF SERGEANT GRISCHA (1930, RKO)
Sgt. Grischa—Chester Morris
Director—Herbert Brenon
Leading Players—Betty Compson, Jean Hersholt, Alec B. Francis, Gustav von Seyfferitz

THE CASE OF THE FRIGHTENED LADY (1940, GB, British Lion)
Dowager Lady Lebanon—Helen Haye
Director—George King
Leading Players—Marius Goring, Penelope Dudley Ward, Felix Aylmer

THE CASE OF THE LUCKY LEGS (1935, First National/Warner Brothers)
Margie Clune—Patricia Ellis
Director—Archie Mayo

Leading Players—Warren William, Genevieve Tobin, Lyle Talbot, Allen Jenkins, Barton MacLane

THE CASE OF THE STUTTERING BISHOP (1937, First National/ Warner Brothers)
Bishop Mallory—Edward McWade
Director—William Clemens
Leading Players—Donald Woods, Ann Dvorak, Anne Nagel

CASEY AT THE BAT (1916, Silent, Triangle-Fine Arts)
Casey—DeWolf Hopper
Director—DeWolf Hopper
Leading Players—Kate Toncray, May Garcia, Carl Stockdale

CASEY AT THE BAT (1927, Silent, Paramount)
Casey—Wallace Beery
Director—Monte Brice
Leading Players—Ford Sterling, Zasu Pitts, Sterling Holloway

CASEY JONES (1927, Silent, Rayart)
Casey Jones—Ralph Lewis
Director—Charles J. Hunt
Leading Players—Kate Price, Al St. John, Jason Robards

CASH MCCALL (1960, Warner Brothers)
Cash McCall—James Garner
Director—Joseph Pevney
Leading Players—Natalie Wood, Nina Foch, Dean Jagger, E.G. Marshall, Henry Jones

CASS TIMBERLANE (1947, MGM)
Cass Timberlane—Spencer Tracy
Director—George Sidney
Leading Players—Lana Turner, Zachary Scott, Tom Drake, Mary Astor, Albert Dekker

CASSIDY OF BAR 20 (1938, Paramount)
Hopalong Cassidy—William Boyd
Director—Lesley Selander
Leading Players—Russell Hayden, Frank Darien, Nora Lane

THE CASTAWAY COWBOY (1974, Buena Vista/Disney)
Lincoln Costain—James Garner
Director—Vincent McEveety
Leading Players—Vera Miles, Robert Culp, Eric Shea, Elizabeth Smith

THE CASTLE OF FU MANCHU (1968, GB, International Cinema)
Fu Manchu—Christopher Lee
Director—Jess Franco
Leading Players—Richard Greene, Howard Marion Crawford, Tsai Chin, Gunther Stoll

CASUALTIES OF WAR (1989, Columbia)
Oahn—Thuy Thu Le
Director—Brian DePalma
Leading Players—Michael J. Fox, Sean Penn, Don Harvey

CAT BALLOU (1965, Columbia)
Katherine "Cat" Ballou—Jane Fonda
Director—Elliot Silverstein
Leading Players—Lee Marvin, Michael Callan, Dwayne Hickman, Tom Nardini, John Marley, Reginald Denny

THE CAT BURGLAR (1961, UA)
Jack Coley—Jack Hogan

Director—William Witney
Leading Players—June Kenney, Gregg Palmer, Will J. White

CAT GIRL (1957, American International)
Leonora—Barbara Shelley
Director—Alfred Shaughnessy
Leading Players—Robert Ayres, Kay Callard, Paddy Webster

CAT ON A HOT TIN ROOF (1958, MGM)
Maggie Pollitt—Elizabeth Taylor
Director—Richard Brooks
Leading Players—Paul Newman, Burl Ives, Jack Carson, Judith Anderson, Madeleine Sherwood

CAT PEOPLE (1942, RKO)
Irena Dubrovna—Simone Simon
Director—Jacques Tourneur
Leading Players—Kent Smith, Tom Conway, Jane Randolph

CAT PEOPLE (1982, Universal/RKO)
Irene Gallier—Nastassia Kinski
Director—Paul Schrader
Leading Players—Malcolm McDowell, John Heard, Annette O'Toole, Ruby Dee

CATHERINE THE GREAT (1934, Great Briatin, LMP/UA)
Catherine II—Elisabeth Bergner
Director—Paul Czinner
Leading Players—Douglas Fairbanks, Jr., Flora Robson, Gerald Du Maurier, Irene Vanbrugh

CATLOW (1971, MGM)
Catlow—Yul Brynner
Director—Sam Wannamaker
Leading Players—Richard Crenna, Leonard Nimoy, Daliah Lavi

THE CATMAN OF PARIS (1946, Republic)
Henry Borchard -Douglass Dumbrille
Director—Lesley Selander
Leading Players—Carl Esmond, Leonore Aubert, Adele Mara

CATTLE ANNIE AND LITTLE BRITCHES (1981, Universal)
Cattle Annie—Amanda Plummer
Jenny-Little Britches—Diane Lane
Director—Lamont Johnson
Leading Players—Burt Lancaster, John Savage, Rod Steiger

CATTLE KING (1963, MGM)
Sam Brassfield—Robert Taylor
Director—Tay Garnett
Leading Players—Joan Caulfield, Robert Loggia, Robert Middleton

CATTLE QUEEN (1951, UA)
Queenie Hart—Maria Hart
Director—Robert Tansey
Leading Players—Drake Smith, William Fawcett, Robert Gardette

CATTLE QUEEN OF MONTANA (1954, RKO)
Sierra Nevada Jones—Barbara Stanwyck
Director—Allan Dwan
Leading Players- Ronald Reagan, Gene Evans, Lance Fuller

CAUGHT IN THE DRAFT (1941, Paramount)
Don Gilbert—Bob Hope

Director—David Butler
Leading Players—Dorothy Lamour, Lynne Overman, Eddie Bracken

THE CAVALIER (1928, Tiffany/Stahl)
El Caballero—Richard Talmadge
Director—Irvin Willat
Leading Players—Barbara Bedford, Nora Cecil, David Torrence

THE CAVALIER OF THE STREETS (1937, GB, British & Dominions)
The Cavalier—Patrick Barr
Director—Harold French
Leading Players—Margaret Vyner, Carl Harbord, James Craven

CAVALRY SCOUT (1951, Monogram)
Kirby Frye—Rod Cameron
Director—Lesley Selander
Leading Players—Audrey Long, Jim Davis, James Millican

CAVANAUGH OF THE RANGERS (1918, Silent, Vitagraph)
Ross Cavanaugh—Alfred Whitman
Director—William Wolbert
Leading Players—Neil Shipman, Otto Lederer, Laura Winston

THE CAVE GIRL (1921, Silent, First National)
Margot—Teddie Gerard
Director—Joseph J. Franz
Leading Players—Charles Meredith, Wilton Taylor, Eleanor Hancock

CAVEGIRL (1986, Crown International)
Eba—Cindy Ann Thompson
Director—David Oliver
Leading Players—Daniel Roebuck, Sab Moor, Jeff Chayette

THE CAVEMAN (1915, Silent, Vitagraph)
Haulick Smagg—Robert Edeson
Director—Theodore Marston
Leading Players—Fay Wallace, Lillian Burns, George De Beck

THE CAVEMAN (1926, Silent, Warner Brothers)
Mike Smagg—Matt Moore
Director—Lewis Milestone
Leading Players—Marie Prevost, John Patrick, Myrna Loy

CAVEMAN (1981, UA)
Atouk—Ringo Starr
Director—Carl Gottlieb
Leading Players—Dennis Quaid, Shelley Long, Jack Gilford, John Matuszak, Barbara Bach

CECILIA OF THE PINK ROSES (1918, Silent, Select Pictures)
Cecilia Madden—Marion Davies
Director—Julius Steger
Leading Players—Edward O'Connor, Willete Kershaw, Charles Jackson

CELEBRITY (1928, Silent, Pathe Exchange)
Kid Regan—Robert Armstrong
Director—Tay Garnett
Leading Players—Clyde Cook, Lina Bacquette, Dot Farley

CELIA (1949, GB, Exclusive)
Celia—Hy Hazell
Director—Francis Searle

Leading Players—Bruce Lister, John Bailey, James Raglan

CELLAR DWELLER (1988, Dove/Empire
Cellar Dweller—Michael S. Deak
Director—John Carl Buechler
Leading Players—Pamela Bellwood, Deborah Mullowney, Brian Robbins

THE CENSUS TAKER (1984, Argentum/Borde)
Harvey McGraw—Garrett Morris
Director—Bruce Cook
Leading Players—Greg Mullavey, Meredith MacRae, Austen Taylor, Timothy Bottoms

A CERTAIN RICH MAN (1921, Silent, Great Authors Pictures)
John Barclay—Robert McKim
Director—Howard Hickman
Leading Players—Carl Gantvoort, Claire Adams, Jean Hersholt

A CERTAIN YOUNG MAN (1928, Silent. MGM)
Lord Gerald Brinsley—Ramon Novarro
Director—Hobart Henley
Leading Players—Marceline Day, Renee Adoree, Carmel Myers

CHAD HANNA (1940, 20th Century Fox)
Chad Hanna—Henry Fonda
Director—Henry King
Leading Players—Dorothy Lamour, Linda Darnell, Guy Kibbee, Jane Darwell, John Carradine

THE CHAIRMAN (1969, 20th Century Fox)
The Chairman—Conrad Yama
Director—J. Lee Thompson
Leading Players—Gregory Peck, Anne Heywood, Arthur Hill

A CHALLENGE FOR ROBIN HOOD (1968, GB, 20th Century Fox)
Robin Hood—Barrie Ingham
Director—C.M. Pennington-Richards
Leading Players—James Hayter, Leon Greene, Peter Blythe, Gay Hamilton, Jenny Till

THE CHAMP (1931, MGM)
Champ—Wallace Beery
Director—King Vidor
Leading Players—Jackie Cooper, Irene Rich, Roscoe Ates

THE CHAMP (1979, UA/MGM)
Billy—Jon Voight
Director—Franco Zeffirelli
Leading Players -Faye Dunaway, Ricky Schroder, Jack Warden

CHAMP FOR A DAY (1953, Republic)
George Wilson—Alex Nicol
Director—William A. Seiter
Leading Players—Audrey Totter, Charles Winninger, Hope Emerson, Joseph Wiseman

CHAMPAGNE CHARLIE (1936, 20th Century Fox)
Charlie Courtland—Paul Cavanaugh
Director—James Tinling
Leading Players—Helen Wood, Thomas Beck, Minna Gombell

CHAMPAGNE CHARLIE (1944, GB, Ealing)
George Leybourne—Tommy Trinder
Director—Alberto Cavalcanti
Leading Players—Stanley Holloway, Betty Warren, Austin Trevor

CHAMPION (1949, UA)
Midge Kelly—Kirk Douglas
Director—Mark Robson
Leading Players—Arthur Kennedy, Marilyn Maxwell, Paul Stewart, Ruth Roman, Lola Albright

CHAMPIONS (1984, GB, EMB)
Bob Champion—John Hurt
Director—John Irvin
Leading Players—Gregory Jones, Mick Dillon, Ann Bell

CHANDLER (1971, MGM)
Chandler—Warren Oates
Director—Paul Magwood
Leading Players—Leslie Caron, Alex Drier, Gloria Grahame

CHANDU THE MAGICIAN (1932, Fox Film Corp.)
Chandu—Edmund Lowe
Director—Marcel Varnel & William C. Menzies
Leading Players—Bela Lugosi, Irene Ware, Herbert Mundin

CHANNING OF THE NORTHWEST (1922, Silent, Selznick Pictures)
Channing—Eugene O'Brien
Director—Ralph Ince
Leading Players—Gladden James, Norma Shearer, James Seeley

THE CHANT OF JIMMIE BLACKSMITH (1980, Australia, Filmhouse Party Ltd.)
Jimmie Blacksmith—Tommy Lewis
Director—Fred Schepisi
Leading Players—Freddie Reynolds, Angela Punch, Ray Barrett

THE CHAPMAN REPORT (1962, Warner Brothers)
Dr. Chapman—Andrew Duggan
Director—George Cukor
Leading Players—Efrem Zimbalist Jr., Shelley Winters, Jane Fonda, Claire Bloom, Glynis Johns

THE CHARLATAN (1929, Universal)
Count Merlin/Peter Dwight—Holmes Herbert
Director—George Melford
Leading Players—Margaret Livingston, Rockliffe Fellowes, Philo McCullough

CHARLEY AND THE ANGEL (1973, Buena Vista/Disney)
Charley Appleby—Fred MacMurray
The Angel—Henry Morgan
Director—Vincent McEveety
Leading Players—Cloris Leachman, Kurt Russell, Kathleen Cody

CHARLEY VARRICK (1973, Universal)
Charley Varrick—Walter Matthau
Director—Don Siegel
Leading Players—Joe Don Baker, Felicia Farr, Andy Robinson

CHARLEY'S AUNT (1925, Silent, Cristie Film Co.)
Charley Wykeham—Jimmy Harrison
Sir Fancourt Babberley—Sydney Chaplin
Donna Lucia D'Alvadorez—Eulaie Jensen
Director—Scott Sidney
Leading Players—Ethel Shannon, James E. Page. Lucien Littlefield, Alec B. Francis

CHARLEY'S AUNT (1930, Columbia)
Donna D'Alvadoes—Doris Lloyd

Lord Babberly—Charlie Ruggles
Charlie Wykeham—Hugh Williams
Director—Al Christie
Leading Players—June Collyer, Halliwell Hobbes, Rodney McLennon, Flora Le Breton

CHARLEY'S AUNT (1941, 20th Century Fox)
Babbs (Lord Babberly)—Jack Benny
Donna Lucia D'Alvadores—Kay Francis
Charlie Wyckham—Richard Haydn
Director—Archie Mayo
Leading Players—James Ellison, Anne Baxter, Edmund Gwenn, Reginald Owen, Laird Cregar, Arleen Whelan

CHARLEY'S BIG-HEARTED AUNT (1940, GB, Gainsborough)
Arthur Linden-Jones—Arthur Askey
Aunt Lucy—Jeanne de Casalis
Director—Walter Forde
Leading Players—Richard Murdoch, Moore Marriott, Graham Moffatt, Phyllis Calvert

CHARLIE BUBBLES (1968, GB, Regency/Universal)
Charlie Bubbles—Albert Finney
Director—Albert Finney
Leading Players—Colin Blakely, Billie Whitelaw, Liza Minnelli

CHARLIE CHAN AND THE CURSE OF THE DRAGON QUEEN (1981, American Cinema)
Charlie Chan—Peter Ustinov
Dragon Lady—Angie Dickinson
Director—Clive Donner
Leading Players—Lee Grant, Richard Hatch, Brian Keith, Michelle Pfeiffer, Roddy McDowall

CHARLIE CHAN AT MONTE CARLO (1937, 20th Century Fox)
Charlie Chan—Warner Oland
Director—Eugene Forde
Leading Players—Keye Luke, Virginia Field, Sidney Blackmer

CHARLIE CHAN AT THE CIRCUS (1936, 20th Century Fox)
Charlie Chan—Warner Oland
Director—Harry Lachman
Leading Players—Keye Luke, George Brasno, Francis Ford

CHARLIE CHAN AT THE OLYMPICS (1937, 20th Century Fox)
Charlie Chan—Warner Oland
Director—H. Bruce Humberstone
Leading Players—Keye Luke, Katharine De Mille, Pauline Moore, Allan Lane

CHARLIE CHAN AT THE OPERA (1936, 20th Century Fox)
Charlie Chan—Warner Oland
Director—H. Bruce Humberstone
Leading Players—Boris Karloff, Keye Luke, Charlotte Henry

CHARLIE CHAN AT THE RACE TRACK (1936, 20th Century Fox)
Charlie Chan—Warner Oland
Director—H. Bruce Humberstone
Leading Players—Keye Luke, Helen Wood, Thomas Beck, Alan Dinehart

CHARLIE CHAN AT THE WAX MUSEUM (1940, 20th Century Fox)
Charlie Chan—Sidney Toler
Director—Lynn Shores

Leading Players—Sen Yung, C. Henry Gordon, Marc Lawrence

CHARLIE CHAN AT TREASURE ISLAND (1939, 20th Century Fox)
Charlie Chan—Sidney Toler
Director—Norman Foster
Leading Players—Cesar Romero, Pauline Moore, Sen Yung

CHARLIE CHAN CARRIES ON (1931, Fox Film Corp.)
Charlie Chan—Warner Oland
Director—Hamilton McFadden
Leading Players—John Garrick, Marguerite Churchill, Warren Hymer

CHARLIE CHAN IN BLACK MAGIC (1944, Monogram)
Charlie Chan—Sidney Toler
Director—Phil Rosen
Leading Players—Mantan Moreland, Frances Chan, Joe Crehan

CHARLIE CHAN IN EGYPT (1935, 20th Century Fox)
Charlie Chan—Warner Oland
Director—Louis King
Leading Players—Pat Paterson, Thomas Beck, Rita Casino

CHARLIE CHAN IN HONOLULU (1938, 20th Century Fox)
Charlie Chan—Sidney Toler
Director—H. Bruce Humberstone
Leading Players—Phyllis Brooks, Sen Yung, Eddie Collins

CHARLIE CHAN IN LONDON (1934, Fox Film Corp.)
Charlie Chan—Warner Oland
Director—Eugene Forde
Leading Players—Drue Leyton, Douglas Walton, Alan Mowbray

CHARLIE CHAN IN PANAMA (1940, 20th Century Fox)
Charlie Chan—Sidney Toler
Director—Norman Foster
Leading Players—Jean Rogers, Lionel Atwill, Mary Nash

CHARLIE CHAN IN PARIS (1935, 20th Century Fox)
Charlie Chan—Warner Oland
Director—Lewis Seiler
Leading Players—Mary Brian, Erik Rhodes, John Miljan

CHARLIE CHAN IN RENO (1939, 20th Century Fox)
Charlie Chan—Sidney Toler
Director—Norman Foster
Leading Players—Ricardo Cortez, Phyllis Brooks, Slim Summerville, Sen Yung

CHARLIE CHAN IN RIO (1941, 20th Century Fox)
Charlie Chan—Sidney Toler
Director—Harry Lachman
Leading Players—Mary Beth Hughes, Cobina Wright Jr., Ted North, Victor Jory

CHARLIE CHAN IN SHANGHAI (1935, 20th Century Fox)
Charlie Chan—Warner Oland
Director—James Tinling
Leading Players—Irene Hervey, Charles Locher, Keye Luke

CHARLIE CHAN IN THE CITY OF DARKNESS (1939, 20th Century Fox)
Charlie Chan—Sidney Toler
Director—Herbert I. Leeds
Leading Players—Lynn Bari, Richard Clarke, Harold Huber

CHARLIE CHAN IN THE SECRET SERVICE (1944, Monogram)
Charlie Chan—Sidney Toler
Director—Phil Rosen
Leading Players—Gwen Kenyon, Mantan Moreland, Arthur Loft

CHARLIE CHAN ON BROADWAY (1937, 20th Century Fox)
Charlie Chan—Warner Oland
Director—Eugene Forde
Leading Players—Keye Luke, Joan Marsh, J. Edward Bromberg

CHARLIE CHAN'S CHANCE (1932, Fox Film Corp.)
Charlie Chan—Warner Oland
Director—John Blystone
Leading Players—Ralph Morgan, H.B. Warner, Marion Nixon

CHARLIE CHAN'S COURAGE (1934, Fox Film Corp.)
Charlie Chan—Warner Oland
Director—Eugene Forde
Leading Players—Drue Leyton, Donald Woods, Murray Kinnell

CHARLIE CHAN'S GREATEST CASE (1933, Fox Film Corp.)
Charlie Chan—Warner Oland
Director—Hamilton MacFadden
Leading Players—Heather Angel, Roger Imhof, John Warburton

CHARLIE CHAN'S MURDER CRUISE (1940, 20th Century Fox)
Charlie Chan—Sidney Toler
Director—Eugene Forde
Leading Players—Marjorie Weaver, Lionel Atwill, Sen Yung

CHARLIE CHAN'S SECRET (1936, 20th Century Fox)
Charlie Chan—Warner Oland
Director—Gordon Wiles
Leading Players—Rosina Lawrence, Charles Quigley, Henrietta Crosman

CHARLIE MOON (1956, GB, British Lion)
Charlie Moon—Max Bygraves
Director—Guy Hamilton
Leading Players—Dennis Price, Michael Medwin, Florence Desmond, Shirley Eaton

CHARLOTTE CORDAY (1914, Silent, Kennedy Features)
Charlotte Corday—Constance Crawley
Director—Oscar Eagle
Leading Players—Arthur Maude, Harry Griffith, Felix Modjeska

CHARLOTTE'S WEB (1973, Animated, Paramount)
Charlotte—Voice of Debbie Reynolds
Director—Charles A. Nichols & Iwao Takamoto
Leading Players—Paul Lynde, Henry Gibson, Martha Scott

CHARLY (1968, Selmur)
Charly Gordon—Cliff Robertson
Director—Ralph Nelson
Leading Players—Claire Bloom, Lilia Skala, Leon Janney

THE CHARMER (1917, Silent, Bluebird)
Ambrosia Lee—Ella Hall
Director—Jack Conway
Leading Players—Belle Bennett, Martha Mattox, George Webb

THE CHARMER (1925, Silent, Paramount)
Mariposa—Pola Negri
Director—Sidney Olcott

Leading Players—Wallace MacDonald, Robert Frazer, Trixie Friganza, Cesare Gravina

THE CHARMING DECEIVER (1921, Silent, Vitagraph)
Edith Denton Marsden—Alice Calhoun
Director—George L. Sargent
Leading Players—Jack McLean, Charles Kent, Eugene Acker

CHARRO (1969, National General)
Jess Wade—Elvis Presley
Director—Charles Marquis Warren
Leading Players—Ina Balin, Victor French, Lynn Kellogg

CHARTER PILOT (1940, 20th Century Fox)
King Morgan—Lloyd Nolan
Director—Eugene Forde
Leading Players—Lynn Bari, Arleen Whelan, George Montgomery

THE CHASER (1938, MGM)
Thomas Z. Brandon—Dennis O'Keefe
Director—Edwin L. Marin
Leading Players—Ann Morriss, Lewis Stone, Nat Pendelton

CHASTITY (1969, American International)
Chastity—Cher
Director—Alessio de Paola
Leading Players—Barbara London, Stephen Whittaker, Tom Nolan

CHATO'S LAND (1972, UA)
Chato—Charles Bronson
Director—Michael Winner
Leading Players—Jack Palance, Richard Basehart, James Whitmore, Simon Oakland

CHATTERBOX (1936, RKO)
Jenny Yates—Anne Shirley
Director—George Nichols
Leading Players—Phillips Holmes, Edward Ellis, Erik Rhodes

CHATTERBOX (1943, Republic)
Rex Vane—Joe E. Brown
Director—Joseph Santley
Leading Players—Judy Canova, John Hubbard, Rosemary Lane

CHE! (1969, 20th Century Fox)
Che Guevara—Omar Sharif
Director—Richard Fleischer
Leading Players—Jack Palance, Cesare Danova, Robert Loggia

THE CHEAP DETECTIVE (1979, Columbia)
Lou Peckinpaugh—Peter Falk
Director—Robert Moore
Leading Players—Ann-Margret, Eileen Brennan, Sid Caesar, Stockard Channing, James Coco

THE CHEAT (1915, Silent, Paramount)
Edith Hardy—Fannie Ward
Director—Cecil B. DeMille
Leading Players—Jack Dean, Sessue Hayakawa, James Neill

THE CHEAT (1923, Silent, Paramount)
Carmelita De Cordoba—Pola Negri
Director—George Fitzmaurice

Leading Players—Jack Holt, Charles De Roche, Dorothy Cumming

THE CHEAT (1931, Paramount)
Elsa Carlyle—Tallulah Bankhead
Director—George Abbott
Leading Players—Irving Pichel, Harvey Stephens, Jay Fassett

CHEATING BLONDES (1933, Equitable)
Anne Merrick—Thelma Todd
Director—Joseph Levering
Leading Players—Ralf Harolde, Inez Courtney, Mae Busch

CHECKERS (1937, 20th Century Fox)
Checkers—Jane Withers
Director—H. Bruce Humberstone
Leading Players—Stuart Erwin, Una Merkel, Marvin Stephens

THE CHEER LEADER (1928, Silent, Gotham)
Jimmy Grant—Ralph Graves
Director—Alvin J. Neitz
Leading Players—Gertrude Olmstead, Shirley Palmer, Ralph Emerson

THE CHEERFUL FRAUD (1927, Silent, Universal)
Sir Michael Fairlie—Reginald Denny
Director—William A. Seiter
Leading Players—Gertrude Olmstead, Otis Harlan, Emily Fitzroy

CHEERS FOR MISS BISHOP (1941, UA)
Ella Bishop—Martha Scott
Director—Tay Garnett
Leading Players—William Gargan, Edmund Gwenn, Sterling Holloway

CHERRY 2000 (1988, Orion)
Cherry 2000—Pamela Gidley
Director—Steve De Jarnatt
Leading Players—Melanie Griffith, David Andrews, Ben Johnson

CHESTY ANDERSON, U.S. NAVY (1976, Atlas)
Chesty Anderson—Shari Eubank
Director—Ed Forsyth
Leading Players—Dorri Thomas, Rosanne Katon, Marcie Barkin

THE CHEYENNE KID (1933, RKO)
Cheyenne Kid—Tom Keene
Director—Robert Hill
Leading Players—Mary Mason, Roscoe Ates, Al Bridge

THE CHEYENNE KID (1940, Monogram)
The Cheyenne Kid—Jack Randall
Director—Raymond K. Johnson
Leading Players—Louise Stanley, Kenneth Duncan, Frank Yaconelli

CHEYENNE RIDES AGAIN (1937, Victory)
Cheyenne—Tom Tyler
Director—Robert Hill
Leading Players—Lucielle Brown, Jimmy Fox, Creighton Chaney

CHEYENNE TAKES OVER (1947, Eagle-Lion)
Cheyenne—Lash LaRue
Director—Ray Taylor

Leading Players—Al "Fuzzy" St. John, Nancy Gates, George Chesbro

CHICAGO JOE AND THE SHOWGIRL (1990, GB, Palace/New Line)
Rick Allen—Kiefer Sutherland
Georgina Grayson—Emily Lloyd
Director—Bernard Rose
Leading Players—Patsy Kensit, Keith Allen, Liz Fraser, Alexandra Pigg, Ralph Nossek

THE CHICAGO KID (1945, Republic)
Joe Ferrill—Donald Barry
Director—Frank McDonald
Leading Players—Otto Kruger, Tom Powers, Lynne Roberts

CHICK (1936, GB, UA)
Chick Beane—Sydney Howard
Director—Michael Hankinson
Leading Players—Betty Ann Davies, Fred Conyngham, Mai Bacon

CHICKIE (1925, Silent, First National)
Chickie—Dorothy Mackaill
Director—John Francis Dillon
Leading Players—John Bowers, Hobart Bosworth, Gladys Brockwell

THE CHIEF (1933, MGM)
Henry Summers—Ed Wynn
Director—Charles F. Reisner
Leading Players—Dorothy Mackaill, Charles "Chic" Sale, William Boyd

CHIEF CRAZY HORSE (1955, Universal)
Crazy Horse—Victor Mature
Director—George Sherman
Leading Players—Susan Ball, John Lund, Ray Danton, Keith Larsen, David Janssen

THE CHILD (1977, Valiant International)
Rosalie—Rosalie Cole
Director—Robert Voskanian
Leading Players—Laurel Barnett, Frank Janson, Ruth Ballen

THE CHILD AND THE KILLER (1959, GB, UA)
Capt. Joe Marsh—Robert Arden
Tommy Martin—Richard Williams
Director—Max Varnel
Leading Players—Patricia Driscoll, Ryck Rydon, Gordon Sterne

CHILD IN THE HOUSE (1956, GB, Eros)
Elizabeth Lorimer—Mandy Miller
Director—C. Raker Renfield
Leading Players—Phyllis Calvert, Eric Portman, Stanley Baker

CHILD OF DIVORCE (1946, RKO)
Bobby—Sharyn Moffett
Director—Richard O. Fleischer
Leading Players—Regis Toomey, Madge Meredith, Walter Reed

CHILD OF MANHATTAN (1933, Columbia)
Madeleine McGonegal—Nancy Carroll
Director—Eddie Buzzell
Leading Players—John Boles, Warburton Gamble, Clara Blandick

THE CHILDREN (1990, GB/West Germany, Isolde/Film Four/Arbo)
    Judith—Siri Neal
    Director—Tony Palmer
    Leading Players—Ben Kingsley, Kim Novak, Geraldine Chaplin, Joe Don Baker, Britt Ekland, Donald Sinden, Karen Black, Robert Stephens

CHILDREN OF DIVORCE (1927, Silent, Paramount)
    Jean Waddington—Esther Ralston
    Ted Larrabee—Gary Cooper
    Director—Frank Lloyd
    Leading Players—Clara Bow, Einar Hanson, Norman Trevor

CHILDREN OF THE CORN (1984, New World)
    Issac—John Franklin
    Malachai—Courtney Gains
    Job—Robby Kiger
    Sarah—Annemarie McEvoy
    Director—Fritz Klersch
    Leading Players—Peter Horton, Linda Hamilton, R.G. Armstrong

CHILD'S PLAY (1988, UA)
    Andy Barclay—Alex Vincent
    Director—Tom Holland
    Leading Players—Chris Sarandon, Catherine Hicks, Brad Dourif, Dinah Manoff

CHINA DOLL (1958, UA)
    Shu-Jen—Li Li Hua
    Director—Frank Borzage
    Leading Players—Victor Mature, Ward Bond, Bob Mathias

CHINA GIRL (1942, 20th Century Fox)
    Miss Young—Gene Tierney
    Director—Henry Hathaway
    Leading Players—George Montgomery, Lynn Bari, Victor McLaglen

CHINA GIRL (1987, Great American Vestron)
    Tyan-Hwa—Sari Chang
    Director—Abel Ferrara
    Leading Players—James Russo, Richard Panebianco, David Caruso

CHINA SLAVER (1929, Silent, Trinity Pictures)
    The Cobra—Sonjin
    Director—Frank S. Mattison
    Leading Players—Albert Valentino, Iris Yamoaka, Iris Shan

CHINA O'BRIEN (1991, Imperial Entertainment/Golden Harvest)
    China O'Brien—Cynthia Rothrock
    Director—Robert Clouse
    Leading Players—Richard Norton, Keith Cooke, Patrick Adamson, Steven Kerby, David Blackwell

CHINATOWN CHARLIE (1928, Silent, First National)
    Charlie—Johnny Hines
    Director—Charles Hines
    Leading Players—Louise Lorraine, Henry Gribbon, Sonjin

CHINO (1976, de Laurentiis
    Chino Valdez—Charles Bronson
    Director—John Sturges
    Leading Players—Jill Ireland, Vincent Van Patten, Marcel Bozzuffi

CHIP OF THE FLYING U (1926, Silent, Universal)
    Chip Bennett—Hoot Gibson
    Director—Lynn Reynolds
    Leading Players—Virginia Brown Faire, Philo McCullough, Nora Cecil

CHIP OF THE FLYING U (1940, Universal)
    Chip Bennett—Johnny Mack Brown
    Director—Ralph Staub
    Leading Players—Bob Baker, Fuzzy Knight, Doris Weston

CHISUM (1970, Warner Brothers)
    John Chisum—John Wayne
    Director—Andrew V. McLaglen
    Leading Players -Forrest Tucker, Christopher George, Ben Johnson, Glenn Corbett, Bruce Cabot

CHIVALROUS CHARLIE (1921, Silent, Selznick)
    Charles Riley—Eugene O'Brien
    Director—Robert Ellis
    Leading Players—George Fawcett, Nancy Deaver, D.J. Flanagan

THE CHOCOLATE SOLDIER (1941, MGM)
    Karl Lang—Nelson Eddy
    Director—Roy Del Ruth
    Leading Players—Rise Stevens, Nigel Bruce, Florence Bates

THE CHORUS KID (1928, Silent, Gotham)
    Beatrice Brown—Virginia Brown Faire
    Director—Howard Bretherton
    Leading Players—Bryant Washburn, Thelma Hill, Hedda Hopper

THE CHORUS LADY (1924, Silent, Regal)
    Patricia O'Brien—Margaret Livingston
    Director—Ralph Ince
    Leading Players—Alan Roscoe, Virginia Lee Corbin, Lillian Elliott

THE CHOSEN (1978, Great Britain/Italy, AIP)
    Angel Caine—Simon Ward
    Director—Alberto De Martino
    Leading Players—Kirk Douglas, Agostine Belli, Anthony Quayle, Virginia McKenna

THE CHRISTIAN (1923, Silent, Goldwyn)
    John Storm—Richard Dix
    Director—Maurice Tourneur
    Leading Players—Mae Busch, Gareth Hughes, Phyllis Haver

CHRISTINA (1929, Fox Film Corp.)
    Christina—Janet Gaynor
    Director—William K. Howard
    Leading Players—Charles Morton, Rudolph Schildkraut, Harry Cording

CHRISTINA (1974, Canada, New World)
    Christina—Barbara Parkins
    Director—Paul Krasny
    Leading Players—Peter Haskell, James McEachin, Marlyn Mason

THE CHRISTINE JORGENSON STORY (1970, UA)
    Christine Jorgenson—John Hansen
    Director—Irving Rapper
    Leading Players—Joan Tompkins, Quinn Redecker, John W. Himes

THE CHRISTINE KEELER AFFAIR (1964, GB, Topaz Film)
Christine Keeler—Yvonne Buckingham
Director—Robert Spafford
Leading Players—John Drew Barrymore, Alicia Brandet, Mel
Welles, Peter Prowse

CHRISTINE OF THE BIG TOP (1926, Silent, Banner Productions)
Christine—Pauline Garon
Director—Archie Mayo
Leading Players—Cullen Landis, Otto Matiesen, Robert Graves

CHRISTINE OF THE HUNGRY HEART (1924, Silent, First
National)
Christine Madison—Florence Vidor
Director—George Archainbaud
Leading Players—Clive Brook, Ian Keith, Warner Baxter

THE CHRISTMAS KID (1968, Producers Releasing Organization)
Joe Novak—Jeffrey Hunter
Director—Sidney W. Pink
Leading Players—Louis Hayward, Gustavo Rojo, Perla Cristal

CHRISTOPHER COLUMBUS (1949, GB, Rank/Universal)
Christopher Columbus—Frederic March
Director—David MacDonald
Leading Players—Florence Eldridge, Francis L. Sullivan,
Kathleen Ryan, Derek Bond

CHRISTOPHER STRONG (1933, RKO)
Christopher Strong—Colin Clive
Director—Dorothy Arzner
Leading Players—Katharine Hepburn, Billie Burke, Helen
Chandler, Ralph Forbes

CHU CHU AND THE PHILLY FLASH (1981, 20th Century Fox)
Flash—Alan Arkin
Emily—Carol Burnett
Director—David Lowell
Leading Players—Jack Warden, Danny Aiello, Adam Arkin

CHUBASCO (1968, Warner Brothers)
Chubasco—Christopher Jones
Director—Allen H. Miner
Leading Players—Richard Egan, Susan Strasberg, Ann Sothern

C.H.U.D. II: BUD THE C.H.U.D. (1989, Vestron)
Bud the Chud—Gerrit Graham
Director—David Irving
Leading Players—Brian Robbins, Bill Calvert, Tricia Leigh
Fisher, Robert Vaughn

CHUKA (1967, Paramount)
Chuka—Rod Taylor
Director—Gordon Douglas
Leading Players—Ernest Borgnine, John Mills, Luciana Paluzzi

A CHUMP AT OXFORD (1940, UA)
Stan—Stan Laurel
Director—Alfred Goulding
Leading Players—Oliver Hardy, Forrester Harvey, Wilfrid Lukas

THE CHURCH MOUSE (1934, GB, Warner Brothers)
Betty Miller—Laura La Plante
Director—Monty Banks
Leading Players—Ian Hunter, Edward Chapman, Jane Carr

THE CIMARRON KID (1951, Universal)
Cimarron Kid—Audie Murphy
Director—Budd Boetticher
Leading Players—Yvette Dugay, Beverly Tyler, John Hudson

THE CINCINNATI KID (1965, MGM)
Cincinnati Kid—Steve McQueen
Director—Norman Jewison
Leading Players—Edward G. Robinson, Ann-Margret, Karl
Malden, Tuesday Weld, Joan Blondell

CINDERELLA (1915, Silent, Famous Players)
Cinderella—Mary Pickford
Director—James Kirkwood
Leading Players—Owen Moore, Haywood Mack

CINDERELLA (1950, Animated, Disney/RKO)
Cinderella—Voice of Ilene Woods
Director—Wilfred Jackson, Hamilton Luske, Clyde Geronomi
Leading Players—Voices of William Phipps, Eleanor Audley,
Verna Felton

CINDERELLA (1985, Faerie Tale Theatre)
Cinderella—Jennifer Beals
Director—Mark Cullingham
Leading Players—Matthew Broderick, Jean Stapleton, Eve
Arden

CINDERELLA JONES (1946, Warner Brothers)
Judy Jones—Joan Leslie
Director—Busby Berkeley
Leading Players—Alan Alda, S.Z. Sakall, Edward Everett
Horton, Julie Bishop

THE CINDERELLA MAN (1917, Silent, Goldwyn)
Anthony Quintard—Tom Moore
Director—George L. Tucker
Leading Players—Mae Marsh, Alec B. Francis, George Fawcett

CINDERELLA OF THE HILLS (1921, Silent, Fox Film Corp.)
Norris Gradley—Barbara Bedford
Director—Howard M. Mitchell
Leading Players—Carl Miller, Cecil Van Auker, Wilson Hummel

CINDERELLA SWINGS IT (1942, RKO)
Betty Palmer—Gloria Warren
Director—Christy Cabanne
Leading Players—Guy Kibbee, Helen Parrish, Dick Hogan

CINDERFELLA (1960, Paramount)
Fella—Jerry Lewis
Director—Frank Tashlin
Leading Players—Ed Wynn, Judith Anderson, Anna Maria
Alberghetti, Henry Silva

CIRCE THE ENCHANTRESS (1924, Silent, MGM)
Circe-Cecilie Brunne—Mae Murray
Director—Robert Z. Leonard
Leading Players—James Kirkwood, Tom Ricketts, Charles
Gerard

THE CIRCUS ACE (1927, Silent, Fox Film Corp.)
Tom Terry—Tom Mix
Director—Ben Stoloff
Leading Players—Natalie Joyce, Jack Baston, Duke Lee

CIRCUS BOY (1947, GB, GFD)
Michael Scott—James Kenney
Director—Cecil Music
Leading Players—Florence Stephenson, George Stephenson, Denver Hall

CIRCUS CLOWN (1934, First National/Warner Brothers)
Happy Howard—Joe E. Brown
Director—Ray Enright
Leading Players—Patricia Ellis, Dorothy Burgess, Donald Dillaway

CIRCUS GIRL (1937, Republic)
Kay Rogers—June Travis
Director—John Auer
Leading Players—Bob Livingston, Donald Cook, Lucille Osborne

THE CIRCUS KID (1928, Film Booking Office)
Buddy—Frankie Darro
Director—George B. Seitz
Leading Players—Poodles Hanneford, Joe E. Brown, Helene Costello

THE CIRCUS MAN (1914, Silent, Lasky)
Thomas Braddock—Theodore Roberts
Director—Oscar Apfel
Leading Players—Mabel Van Buren, Florence Dagmar, Hubert Whitehead

CISCO KID (1931, Fox Film Corp.)
Cisco Kid—Warner Baxter
Director—Irving Cummings
Leading Players—Edmund Lowe, Conchita Montenegro, Nora Lane

THE CISCO KID AND THE LADY (1939, 20th Century Fox)
Cisco Kid—Cesar Romero
Julie Lawson—Marjorie Weaver
Director—Herbert I. Leeds
Leading Players—Chris-Pin Martin, George Montgomery, Robert Barrat, Virginia Field

THE CISCO KID RETURNS (1945, Monogram)
Cisco Kid—Duncan Renaldo
Director—John P. McCarthy
Leading Players—Martin Garralaga, Cecilia Callejo, Roger Pryor

CISCO PIKE (1971, Columbia)
Cisco Pike—Kris Kristofferson
Director—Bill L. Norton
Leading Players—Gene Hackman, Harry Dean Stanton, Joy Bang

CITIZEN KANE (1941, Mercury/RKO)
Charles Foster Kane—Orson Welles
Director—Orson Welles
Leading Players—Joseph Cotten, Dorothy Comingore, Everett Sloane, George Coulouris, Ray Collins, Ruth Warwick, Erskine Sanford, Agnes Moorehead, Paul Stewart

CITIZEN SAINT (1947, State-Rights)
Mother Frances Cabrini—Carla Dare
Director—Harold Young
Leading Players—Julie Haydon, June Harrison, Clark William

CITY GIRL (1930, Fox Film Corp.)
Kate Tustine—Mary Duncan
Director—F. W. Murnau
Leading Players—Charles Farrell, David Torrence, Edith Yorke

CITY GIRL (1938, 20th Century Fox)
Ellen Ward—Phyllis Brooks
Director—Alfred Werker
Leading Players—Ricardo Cortez, Robert Wilcox, Douglas Fowley

THE CITY GIRL (1984, Moon)
Anne—Laura Harrington
Director—Martha Coolidge
Leading Players—Joe Mastroianni, Carole McGill, Peter Riegert, Jim Carrington

CITY SLICKERS (1991, Columbia)
Mitch Robbins—Billy Crystal
Phil Berquist—Daniel Stern
Ed Furillo—Bruno Kirby
Director—Ron Underwood
Leading Players—Patricia Wettig, Helen Slater, Jack Palance, Noble Willingham, Tracey Walthers

CIVILIZATION'S CHILD (1916, Silent, Triangle)
Berna—Anna Lehr
Director—Charles Giblin
Leading Players—William H. Thompson, Jack Standing, Dorothy Dalton

THE CLAIRVOYANT (1935, GB, Gainsborough)
Maximus—Claude Rains
Director—Maurice Elvey
Leading Players—Fay Wray, Jane Baxter, Mary Clare, Ben Field

CLANCY IN WALL STREET (1930, Aristocrat)
Michael Clancy—Charles Murray
Director—Ted Wilde
Leading Players—Lucien Littlefield, Aggie Herring, Edward Nugent

CLANCY'S KOSHER WEDDING (1927, Silent, R-C Pictures)
Tom Clancy—Rex Lease
Director—Arvid E. Gillstrom
Leading Players—George Sidney, Will Armstrong, Ann Brody

CLARA'S HEART (1988, Warner Brothers)
Clara Mayfield—Whoopi Goldberg
Director—Robert Mulligan
Leading Players—Michael Ontkean, Kathleen Quinlan, Neil Patrick Harris

CLARENCE (1922, Silent, Paramount)
Clarence Smith—Wallace Reid
Director—William C. De Mille
Leading Players—Agnes Ayres, May McAvoy, Kathlyn Williams

CLARENCE (1937, Paramount)
Clarence Smith—Roscoe Karns
Director—George Archainbaud
Leading Players—Eleanore Whitney, Eugene Pallette, Johnny Downs, Inez Courtney

CLARENCE AND ANGEL (1978, Gardner)
Clarence—Darren Brown

Angel—Mark Cardova
Director—Robert Gardner
Leading Players—Cynthia McPherson, Louise Mike, Lolita Lewis

THE CLASS OF MISS MACMICHAEL (1978, GB, Brut)
Conor MacMichael—Glenda Jackson
Director—Silvio Narizzano
Leading Players—Oliver Reed, Michael Murphy, Rosalind Cash

CLAUDELLE INGLISH (1961, Warner Brothers)
Claudelle Inglish—Diane McBain
Director—Gordon Douglas
Leading Players—Arthur Kennedy, Will Hutchins, Constance Ford, Claude Akins

CLAUDIA (1943, 20th Century Fox)
Claudia Naughton—Dorothy McGuire
Director—Edmund Goulding
Leading Players—Robert Young, Ina Claire, Reginald Gardiner

CLAUDIA AND DAVID (1946, 20th Century Fox)
Claudia Naughton—Dorothy McGuire
David Naughton—Robert Young
Director—Walter Lang
Leading Players—Mary Astor, John Sutton, Gail Patrick

CLAUDINE (1974, 20th Century Fox)
Claudine—Diahann Carroll
Director—John Berry
Leading Players—James Earl Jones, Lawrence Hilton-Jacobs, Tamu, David Kruger

THE CLAY PIDGEON (1949, RKO)
Jim Fletcher—Bill Williams
Director—Richard O. Fleischer
Leading Players—Barbara Hale, Richard Quine, Richard Loo

CLAY PIDGEON (1971, Tracon/MGM)
Joe Ryan—Tom Stern
Director—Tom Stern
Leading Players—Telly Savalas, Robert Vaughn, John Marley, Burgess Meredith

CLEAN AND SOBER (1988, Warner Brothers)
Daryl Poynter—Michael Keaton
Director—Glenn Gordon Caron
Leading Players—M. Emmet Walsh, Morgan Freeman, Henry Judd Baker, Luca Bercovici

CLEGG (1969, GB, Tigon)
Harry Clegg—Gilbert Wynne
Director—Lindsay Shonteff
Leading Players—Garry Hope, Gilly Grant, Norman Claridge

CLEOPATRA (1934, Paramount)
Cleopatra—Claudette Colbert
Director—Cecil B. De Mille
Leading Players—Warren William, Henry Wilcoxon, Gertrude Michael, Joseph Schildkraut, Ian Keith, C. Aubrey Smith, Leonard Mudie

CLEOPATRA (1963, 20th Century Fox)
Cleopatra—Elizabeth Taylor
Director—Joseph L. Mankiewicz
Leading Players—Richard Burton, Rex Harrison, Pamela Brown, George Cole, Cesare Danova, Kenneth Haig, Hume Cronyn, Roddy McDowell

CLEOPATRA JONES (1973, Warner Brothers)
Cleopatra Jones—Tamara Dobson
Director—Jack Starrett
Leading Players—Bernie Casey, Brenda Sykes, Antonio Fargas

CLEOPATRA JONES AND THE CASINO OF GOLD (1975, Warner Brothers)
Cleopatra Jones—Tamara Dobson
Director—Chuck Bail
Leading Players—Stella Stevens, Tanny, Norman Fell, Albert Popwell

THE CLEVER MRS. CARFAX (1917, Silent, Paramount)
Temple Trask—Julian Eltinge
Director—Donald Crisp
Leading Players—Fred Church, Daisy Robinson, Jennie Lee

CLIVE OF INDIA (1935, Fox/UA)
Robert Clive—Ronald Colman
Director—Richard Boleslawski
Leading Players—Loretta Young, Colin Clive, Francis Lister

A CLOSE CALL FOR BOSTON BLACKIE (1946, Columbia)
Boston Blackie—Chester Morris
Director—Lew Landers
Leading Players—Lynn Merrick, Richard Lane, Frank Sully

A CLOSE CALL FOR ELLERY QUEEN (1942, Columbia)
Ellery Queen—William Gargan
Director—James Hogan
Leading Players—Margaret Lindsay, Charley Grapewin, Ralph Morgan

THE CLOSER (1991, Ion Pictures)
Chester Grant—Danny Aiello
Director—Dimitri Logothestis
Leading Players—Michael Pare, Joe Cortese, Justine Bateman, Tim Quill, Diane Baker

CLOTHES MAKE THE PIRATE (1925, Silent, First National)
Trem Tidd—Leon Errol
Director—Maurice Tourneur
Leading Players—Dorothy Gish, Nita Naldi, Tully Marshall

THE CLOWN (1916, Silent, Paramount)
Piffle—Victor Moore
Director—William C. De Mille
Leading Players—Thomas Meighan, Ernest Joy, Florence Dagmar

THE CLOWN (1927, Silent, Columbia)
Albert Wells—William V. Mong
Director—William James Craft
Leading Players—Dorothy Revier, Johnnie Walker, John Miljan

THE CLOWN (1953, MGM)
Dodo Delwyn—Red Skelton
Director—Robert Z. Leonard
Leading Players—Tim Considine, Jane Greer, Loring Smith

THE CLOWN AND THE KID (1961, UA)
Peter Stanton—John Lupton

Shawn—Mike McGreevey
Director—Edward L. Cahn
Leading Players—Donn Keefer, Mary Webster, Mary Adams

CLUNY BROWN (1946, 20th Century Fox)
Cluny Brown—Jennifer Jones
Director—Ernst Lubitsch
Leading Players—Charles Boyer, Richard Haydn, Una O'Connor, Peter Lawford, Helen Walker

COACH (1978, Crown International)
Randy Rawlings—Cathy Lee Crosby
Director—Bud Townsend
Leding Players—Michael Biehn, Keenan Wynn, Steve Nevil

COAL MINER'S DAUGHTER (1980, Universal)
Loretta Lynn—Sissy Spacek
Director—Michael Apted
Leading Players—Tommy Lee Jones, Levon Helm, Phyllis Boyens

COBRA (1986, Warner Brothers)
Marion Cobretti—Sylvester Stallone
Director—George P. Cosmatos
Leading Players—Brigitte Nielsen, Reni Santoni, Andrew Robinson

COBRA WOMAN (1944, Universal)
Tollea/Naja—Maria Montez
Director—Robert Siodmak
Leading Players—Jon Hall, Sabu, Edgar Barker, Mary Nash

THE COCA-COLA KID (1986, Cinecom)
Becker—Eric Roberts
Director—Dusan Makavejev
Leading Players—Greta Scacchi, Bill Kerr, Chris Hayward

COCK O' THE WALK (1930, Sono-Art-World-Wide)
Carlos—Joseph Schildkraut
Director—R. William Neill
Leading Players—Myrna Loy, Phillip Sleeman, Edward Peil

COCK OF THE AIR (1932, Hughes/UA)
Lt. Roger Craig—Chester Morris
Director—Tom Buckingham
Leding Players—Billie Dove, Matt Moore, Walter Catlett

COCKEYED CAVALIERS (1934, RKO)
Bert—Bert Wheeler
Bob—Robert Woolsey
Director—Mark Sandrich
Leading Players—Thelma Todd, Dorothy Lee, Noah Beery

THE CODE OF MARCIA GRAY (1916, Silent, Paramount)
Marcia Gray—Constance Collier
Director—Frank Lloyd
Leading Players—Henry Devere, Forrest Stanley, Herbert Standing, Helen Jerome Eddy

COFFY (1971, American International)
Coffy—Pam Grier
Director—Jack Hill
Leading Players—Booker Bradshaw, Robert DoQui, William Elliott

COHEN AND TATE (1989, Tri-Star)
Cohen—Roy Scheider
Tate—Adam Baldwin
Director—Eric Red
Leading Players—Harley Cross, Cooper Huckabee, Suzanne Savoy

THE COHENS AND THE KELLYS (1926, Silent, Universal)
Patrick Kelly—Charles Murray
Jacob Cohen—George Sidney
Mrs. Cohen—Vera Gordon
Mrs. Kelly—Kate Price
Director—Harry Pollard
Leading Players—Olive Hasbrouck, Nat Carr, Mickey Bennett

THE COHENS AND THE KELLYS IN ATLANTIC CITY (1929, Universal)
Jacob Cohen—George Sidney
Patrick Kelly—Mack Swain
Mrs. Kelly—Kate Price
Mrs. Cohen—Vera Gordon
Director—William J. Craft
Leading Players—Nora Lane, Tom Kennedy, Cornelius Keefe

COLE YOUNGER, GUNFIGHTER (1958, Allied Artists)
Cole Younger—Frank Lovejoy
Director—R.G. Springsteen
Leading Players—James Best, Abby Dalton, Jan Merlin

THE COLLECTOR (1965, Columbia)
Freddie Clegg—Terence Stamp
Director—William Wyler
Leading Players—Samantha Eggar, Mona Washbourne, Maurice Dallimore

COLLEEN (1936, Warner Brothers)
Colleen Reiley—Ruby Keeler
Director—Alfred E. Green
Leading Players—Dick Powell, Jack Oakie, Joan Blondell, Hugh Herbert

COLLEEN OF THE PINES (1922, Silent, Film Booking Offices)
Joan Cameron—Jane Novak
Director—Chester Bennett
Leading Players—Edward Hearn, Alfred Allen, J. Gordon Russell

THE COLLEGE BOOB (1926, Silent, Film Booking Offices)
Aloysius Appleby—Lefty Flynn
Director—Harry Garson
Leading Players—Jean Arthur, Jimmy Anderson, Bob Bradbury

COLLEGE COACH (1933, Warner Brothers)
Coach Gore—Pat O'Brien
Director—William Wellman
Leading Players—Dick Powell, Ann Dvorak, Arthur Bryon

THE COLLEGE COQUETTE (1929, Columbia)
Betty Forrester—Ruth Taylor
Director—George Archainbaud
Leading Players—William Collier, Jr., Jobyna Ralston, John Holland

THE COLLEGE HERO (1927, Silent, Columbia)
Bob Cantfield—Bobby Agnew
Director—Walter Lang

Leading Players—Pauline Garon, Ben Turpin, Rex Lease

THE COLLEGE ORPHAN (1915, Silent, Universal)
Jack Bennett, Jr.—Carter De Haven
Director—William Dowlin
Leading Players—Louis Morrison, Gloria Fonda, Val Paul

THE COLLEGE WIDOW (1927, Silent, Warner Brothers)
Jane Witherspoon—Dolores Costello
Director—Archie Mayo
Leading Players—William Collier, Jr., Douglas Gerrard, Anders Randolf

COLONEL BLIMP (THE LIFE AND DEATH OF COLONEL BLIMP) (1945, Great Britain, The Archers)
Clive Candy—Roger Livesey
Director—Michael Powell
Leading Players—Deborah Kerr, Anton Walbrook, Roland Culver

COLONEL BLOOD (1934, GB, MGM)
Colonel Blood—Frank Cellier
Director—W.P. Lipscomb
Leading Players—Anne Grey, Mary Lawson, Allan Jeayes

COLONEL BOGEY (1948, GB, GFD)
Voice of Uncle James (Col. Bogey)—Jack Train
Director—Terence Fisher
Leading Players—Mary Jerrold, Jane Barrett, John Stone

COLONEL EFFINGHAM'S RAID (1945, 20th Century Fox)
Col. Effingham—Charles Coburn
Director—Irving Pichel
Leading Players—Joan Bennett, William Ethye, Allyn Joslyn

COLONEL MARCH INVESTIGATES (1952, GB, Criterion)
Col. March—Boris Karloff
Director—Cyril Enfield
Leading Players—Ewan Roberts, Richard Wattis, Sheila Burrell

COLORADO KID (1938, Republic)
Colorado Kid—Bob Steele
Director—Sam Newfield
Leading Players—Marian Weldon, Karl Hackett, Ernie Adams

THE COLOSSUS OF NEW YORK (1970, Paramount)
The Colossus—Ed Wolff
The Colossus' Brain—Ross Martin
Director—Eugene Lourie
Leading Players—Mala Powers, Charles Herbert, John Baragrey

COLOSSUS: THE FORBIN PROJECT (1969, Universal)
Dr. Charles Forbin—Eric Brandon
Director—Joseph Sargent
Leading Players—Susan Clark, Gordon Pinsent, William Schallert, Stanford Brown

COLUMBUS (1923, Silent, Pathe Exchange)
Christopher Columbus—Fred Eric
Director—Edwin L. Hollywood
Leading Players—Paul McAllister, Howard Truesdell, Leslie Stowe

COME BACK PETER (1971, GB, Donwin)
Peter—Christopher Matthews
Director—Donovan Winter
Leading Players—Erika Bergmann, Penny Riley, Yolanda Turner

COME ON GEORGE (1939, GB, ATP/ABFD)
George—George Formby
Director—Anthony Kimmins
Leading Players—Pat Kirkwood, Joss Ambler, George Hayes

THE COMEDY MAN (1964, GB, British Lion)
Chick Byrd—Kenneth Moore
Director—Alvin Rakoff
Leading Players—Cecil Parker, Dennis Price, Billie Whitelaw

COMES A HORSEMAN (1978, UA)
Frank—James Caan
Director—Alan Pakula
Leading Players—Jane Fonda, Jason Robards, George Grizzard

THE COMIC (1969, Columbia)
Billy Bright—Dick Van Dyke
Director—Carl Reiner
Leading Players—Michelle Lee, Mickey Rooney, Cornel Wilde

THE COMING OF AMOS (1925, Silent, Cinema Corp. of America)
Amod Burden—Rod La Rocque
Director—Paul Sloane
Leading Players—Jetta Goudal, Noah Beery, Richard Carle

COMING TO AMERICA (1988, Paramount)
Prince Akeem—Eddie Murphy
Director—John Landis
Leading Players—Arsenio Hall, James Earl Jones, John Amos, Shari Hedley, Ralph Bellamy, Don Ameche

THE COMMANDING OFFICER (1915, Silent, Paramount)
Colonel Archer—Donald Crisp
Director—Allan Dwan
Leading Players—Alice Dovey, Marshall Neilan, Douglas Gerrard

COMMANDO (1985, 20th Century Fox)
John Matrix—Arnold Schwarzenegger
Director—Mark Lester
Leading Players—Rae Dawn Chong, Dan Hedaya, James Olson

THE COMMITMENTS (1991, GB, 20th Century Fox)
Jimmy Rabbitte—Robert Arkins
Joey "The Lips" Fagan—Johnny Murphy
Deco Cuffe—Andrew Strong
Director—Alan Parker
Leading Players—Michael Aherne, Angeline Ball, Maria Doyle, Dave Finnegan, Bronagh Gallagher, Felim Gormley

COMMON LAW WIFE (1963, Texas Film Producers)
Linda—Annabelle Lee
Director—Eric Sayers
Leading Players—Lacy Kelly, Shugfoot Rainey, Jody Works

THE COMPANY SHE KEEPS (1950, RKO)
Diane—Jane Greer
Director—John Cromwell
Leading Players—Lizabeth Scott, Dennis O'Keefe, Fay Baker

THE COMPULSORY HUSBAND (1930, GB, British International)
Monty—Monty Banks
Director—Harry Lachman
Leading Players—Lillian Manton, Clifford Heatherly, Gladys Frazin

THE COMPULSORY WIFE (1937, GB, Warner Brothers)
Bobby Carr—Joyce Kirby
Director—Arthur Woods
Leading Players—Henry Kendall, Margaret Yarde, Anthony Shaw

CONAN THE BARBARIAN (1982, Universal)
Conan—Arnold Schwarzenegger
Director—John Milius
Leading Players—James Earl Jones, Max Von Sydow, Sandahl Bergman, Ben Davidson, Mako

CONAN THE DESTROYER (1984, Universal)
Conan—Arnold Schwarzenegger
Director—Richard Fleischer
Leading Players—Grace Jones, Wilt Chamberlain, Mako, Tracy Walter, Olivia D'Abo

THE CONCENTRATIN' KID (1930, Universal)
Concentratin' Kid—Hoot Gibson
Director—Arthur Robson
Leading Players—Kathryn Crawford, Duke R. Lee, James Mason

CONCERNING MR. MARTIN (1937, GB, Fox British)
Leo Martin—Wilson Barrett
Director—Roy Kellino
Leading Players—William Devlin, Marjorie Peacock, Derek Williams

CONDEMNED TO DEATH (1932, GB, Twickenham)
Tobias Lantern—Bernard Brunel
Director—Walter Forde
Leading Players—Arthur Wontner, Edmund Gwenn, Gordon Harker

CONDORMAN (1981, Disney/Buena Vista)
Woody—Michael Crawford
Director—Charles Jarrot
Leading Players—Oliver Reed, Barbara Carrera, James Hampton

CONDUCTOR 1492 (1924, Silent, Warner Brothers)
Terry O'Toole—Johnny Hines
Director—Charles Hines & Frank Griffin
Leading Players—Doris May, Dan Mason, Ruth Renick

CONFESSIONS OF A NAZI SPY (1939, Warner Brothers)
Schneider—Francis Lederer
Director—Anatole Litvak
Leading Players—Edward G. Robinson, George Sanders, Paul Lukas, Henry O'Neill, Lya Lys, Sig Rumann

CONFESSIONS OF A POP PERFORMER (1975, GB, Columbia)
Timothy Lea—Robin Askwith
Director—Norman Cohen
Leading Players—Anthony Booth, Bill Maynard, Doris Hare

CONFESSIONS OF A QUEEN (1925, Silent, MGM)
Queen Frederika—Alice Terry
Director—Victor Seastrom
Leading Players—Lewis Stone, John Bowers, Eugenie Besserer, Helena D'Algy, Frankie Darro

CONFESSIONS OF A WIFE (1928, Silent, Excellent Pictures)
Marion Atwell—Helene Chadwick
Director—Albert Kelly
Leading Players—Arthur Clayton, Ethel Grey Terry, Walter McGrail

CONFESSIONS OF A WINDOW CLEANER (1974, GB, Columbia)
Timothy Lea—Robin Askwith
Director—Val Guest
Leading Players—Anthony Booth, Sheila White, Dandy Nichols

THE CONFESSIONS OF AMANS (1977, Bauer International)
Amans—William Bryan
Director—Gregory Nava
Leading Players—Michael St. John, Susannah MacMillan, Richard Gardener

CONFESSIONS OF AN OPIUM EATER (1962, Allied Artists)
DeQuincey—Vincent Price
Director—Albert Zugsmith
Leading Players—Linda Ho, Richard Loo, June Kim, Philip Ahn

CONFESSIONS OF BOSTON BLACKIE (1941, Columbia)
Boston Blackie—Chester Morris
Director—Edward Dmytryk
Leading Players—Harriet Hilliard, Richard Lane, George F. Stone

CONFIDENCE GIRL (1952, UA)
Mary Webb—Hilary Brooke
Director—Andrew L. Stone
Leading Players—Tom Conway, Eddie Marr, Dan Riss

THE CONFIDENCE MAN (1924, Silent, Paramount)
Dan Corvan—Thomas Meighan
Director—Victor Heerman
Leading Players—Virginia Valli, Laurence Wheat, Charles Dow Cook

CONFIDENTIAL AGENT (1945, Warner Brothers)
Denard—Charles Boyer
Director—Herman Shumlin
Leading Players—Lauren Bacall, Victor Francen, Wanda Hendrix, George Coulouris

CONFIDENTIAL CONNIE (1953, MGM)
Connie Bedloe—Janet Leigh
Director—Edward Buzzell
Leading Players—Van Johnson, Louis Calhern, Walter Slezak

CONFIDENTIAL LADY (1939, GB, Warner Brothers)
Jill Trevor—Jane Baxter
Director—Arthur Woods
Leading Players—Ben Lyon, Athole Stewart, Ronald Ward

CONGO MAISIE (1940, MGM)
Maisie Ravier—Ann Sothern
Director—Henry Potter
Leading Players—John Carroll, Rita Johnson, Shepperd Strudwick

A CONNECTICUT YANKEE (1931, Fox Film Corp.)
Hank Martin—Will Rogers
Director—David Butler
Leading Players—William Farnum, Myrna Loy, Maureen O'Sullivan

A CONNECTICUT YANKEE IN KING ARTHUR'S COURT (1921, Silent, Fox)
Martin Cavendish—Harry Myers
King Arthur—Charles Clary
Director—Emmett J. Flynn
Leading Players—Pauline Starke, Rosemary Theby, William V. Mong

A CONNECTICUT YANKEE IN KING ARTHUR'S COURT (1949, Paramount)
Hank Martin—Bing Crosby
King Arthur—Cedric Hardwicke
Director—Tay Garnett
Leading Players—William Bendix, Rhonda Fleming, Murvyn Vye, Virginia Field

THE CONQUEROR (1917, Silent, Standard Pictures)
Sam Houston—William Farnum
Director—R. A. Walsh
Leading Players—Jewel Carmen, Charles Clary, J.A. Marcus

THE CONQUEROR (1956, RKO)
Temujin—John Wayne
Director—Dick Powell
Leading Players—Susan Hayward, Pedro Armendariz, Agnes Moorehead, Thomas Gomez

CONQUEST OF COCHISE (1953, Columbia)
Cochise—John Hodiak
Director—William Castle
Leading Players—Robert Stack, Joy Page, Rico Alaniz

CONRACK (1974, 20th Century Fox)
Pat Conroy—Jon Voight
Director—Martin Ritt
Leading Players—Paul Winfield, Hume Cronyn, Madge Sinclair

CONSPIRATOR (1949, GB, MGM)
Major Michael Curragh—Robert Taylor
Director—Victor Saville
Leading Players—Elizabeth Taylor, Robert Flemyng, Harold Warrender

THE CONSTANT HUSBAND (1955, GB, British Lion)
Charles Hathaway—Rex Harrison
Director—Sidney Gilliat
Leading Players—Margaret Leighton, Kay Kendall, Cecil Parker, Nicole Maurey

THE CONSTANT NYMPH (1933, GB, Gaumont/Fox)
Tess Sanger—Victoria Hopper
Director—Basil Dean
Leading Players—Brian Aherne, Leonora Corbett, Lyn Harding

THE CONSTANT NYMPH (1943, Warner Brothers)
Tessa Sanger—Joan Fontaine
Director—Edmund Goulding
Leading Players—Charles Boyer, Alexis Smith, Charles Coburn

THE CONTENDER (1944, Producers Releasing Corp.)
Gary—Buster Crabbe
Director—Sam Newfield
Leading Players—Arline Judge, Julie Gibson, Donald Maye

CONVENTION GIRL (1935, Flacon/FD)
Babe Lavall—Rose Hobart
Director—Luther Reed
Leading Players—Weldon Heyburn, Sally O'Neill, Herbert Rawlinson

CONVICTED WOMAN (1940, Columbia)
Betty Andrews—Rochelle Hudson
Director—Nick Grinde
Leading Players—Frieda Inescort, June Lang, Lola Lane, Glenn Ford

COOGAN'S BLUFF (1968, Universal)
Coogan—Clint Eastwood
Director—Donald Siegel
Leading Players—Lee J. Cobb, Susan Clark, Tisha Sterling, Don Stroud

COOKIE (1989, Warner Brothers)
Carmella 'Cookie' Voltecki—Emily Lloyd
Director—Susan Seidelman
Leading Players—Peter Falk, Dianne Wiest, Brenda Vaccaro

COOL AS ICE (1991, Universal)
Johnny—Vanilla Ice
Director—David Kellogg
Leading Players—Kristin Minter, Michael Gross, Sydney Lassick, Dody Goodman, Naomi Campbell, Candy Clark

COOL HAND LUKE (1967, Warner Brothers)
Luke—Paul Newman
Director—Stuart Rosenberg
Leading Players—George Kennedy, J.D. Cannon, Strother Martin, Jo Van Fleet

COOL IT, CAROL! (1970, GB, Miracle Films)
Carol Thatcher—Janet Lynn
Director—Peter Walker
Leading Players—Robin Askwith, Peter Elliot, Jess Conrad

THE COOL MIKADO (1963, GB, UA)
Judge Mikado—Stubby Kaye
Director—Michael Winner
Leading Players—Frankie Howard, Tommy Cooper, Dennis Price

THE COP (1928, Silent, Pathe Exchange)
Pete Smith—William Boyd
Director—Donald Crisp
Leading Players—Alan Hale, Jacqueline Logan, Robert Armstrong

COP (1988, Atlantic)
Lloyd Hopkins—James Woods
Director—James B. Harris
Leading Players—Lesley Ann Warren, Charles Durning, Charles Haid, Raymond J. Barry

COQUETTE (1929, UA)
Norma Besant—Mary Pickford
Director—Sam Taylor
Leading Players—Johnny Mack Brown, Matt Moore, John Sainpolis

CORDELIA THE MAGNIFICIENT (1923, Silent, Metro)
Cordelia Marlowe—Clara Kimball Young
Director—George Archainbaud

Leading Players—Huntley Gordon, Carol Halloway, Lloyd Whitlock

CORKY (1972, MGM)
Corky—Robert Blake
Director—Leonard Horn
Leading Players—Charlotte Rampling, Patrick O'Neal, Christopher Connelly, Ben Johnson

CORKY OF GASOLINE ALLEY (1951, Columbia)
Corky Wallett—Scotty Beckett
Director—Edward Bernds
Leading Players—Jimmy Lydon, Don Beddoe, Gordon Jones

CORNBREAD, EARL AND ME (1975, American International)
Cornbread—Keith Wilkes
Earl—Tierre Turner
One Eye—Antonio Fargas
Director—Joe Manduke
Leading Players—Moses Gunn, Rosalind Cash, Bernie Casey

CORPORAL KATE (1926, Silent, Producers Distributing Corp.)
Kate—Vera Reynolds
Director—Paul Sloane
Leading Players—Julia Faye, Majel Coleman, Kenneth Thompson

THE CORSICAN BROTHERS (1941, UA)
Mario/Lucien—Douglas Fairbanks Jr.
Director—Gregory Ratoff
Leading Players—Ruth Warrick, Akim Tamiroff, J. Carrol Naish, H.B. Warner, John Emery

THE COSMIC MAN (1959, Allied Artists)
Cosmic Man—John Carradine
Director—Herbert Greene
Leading Players—Bruce Bennett, Angela Greene, Paul Langton

COUNSEL FOR CRIME (1937, Columbia)
William Mellon—Otto Kruger
Director—John Brahm
Leading Players—Douglass Montgomery, Jacqueline Wells, Thurston Hall, Nana Bryant

COUNSEL FOR THE DEFENSE (1925, Silent, Associated Exhibitors)
Katherine West—Betty Compson
Director—Burton King
Leading Players—Jay Hunt, House Peters, Rockliffe Fellowes

COUNSELLOR-AT-LAW (1933, Universal)
George Simon—John Barrymore
Director—William Wyler
Leading Players—Bebe Daniels, Doris Kenyon, Onslow Stevens, Isabell Jewell, Melvyn Douglas

COUNSEL'S OPINION (1933, GB, LFP/Paramount)
Logan—Henry Kendall
Director—Allan Dwan
Leading Players—Binnie Barnes, Cyril Maude, Lawrence Grossmith

COUNT DRACULA (1971, GB, Filmer/Phoenix/Korona)
Dracula—Christopher Lee
Director—Jesus Franco
Leading Players—Herbert Lom, Klaus Kinski, Soledad Miranda

COUNT DRACULA AND HIS VAMPIRE BRIDE (1978, GB, Hammer)
Dracula—Christopher Lee
Jessica—Joanna Lumley
Director—Alan Gibson
Leading Players—Peter Cushing, Michael Coles, William Franklyn, Freddie Jones

THE COUNT OF LUXEMBOURG (1926, Silent, Chadwick Pictures)
Rene Duval—George Walsh
Director—Arthur Gregor
Leading Players—Helen Lee Worthing, Michael Dark, Charles Requa

THE COUNT OF MONTE CRISTO (1934, UA)
Edmond Dantes—Robert Donat
Director—Rowland V. Lee
Leading Players—Elissa Landi, Louis Calhern, Sidney Blackmer, Raymond Walburn, O.P. Heggie

THE COUNT OF MONTE CRISTO (1976, GB, ITC)
Edmond Dantes—Richard Chamberlain
Director—David Greene
Leading Players—Tony Curtis, Trevor Howard, Louis Jourdan, Donald Pleasance, Kate Nelligan

COUNT YORGA, VAMPIRE (1970, American International)
Count Yorga—Robert Quarry
Director—Bob Kelljan
Leading Players—Roger Perry, Michael Murphy, Michael Macready, Donna Anders

THE COUNTERFEIT KILLER (1969, Universal)
Don Owens—Jack Lord
Director—Josef Leytes
Leading Players—Shirley Knight, Jack Weston, Charles Drake

COUNTERFEIT LADY (1937, Columbia)
Phyllis—Joan Perry
Director—D. Ross Lederman
Leading Players—Ralph Bellamy, Douglas Dumbrille, George McKay

THE COUNTERFEIT TRAITOR (1962, Paramount)
Eric Erickson—William Holden
Director—George Seaton
Leading Players—Lilli Palmer, Hugh Griffith, Ernst Schroder

COUNTERSPY MEETS SCOTLAND YARD (1950, Columbia)
David Harding—Howard St. John
Director—Seymour Friedman
Leading Players—Amanda Blake, Ron Randell, June Vincent

COUNTESS DRACULA (1972, GB, Hammer)
Countess Elizabeth Nadasdy—Ingrid Pitt
Director—Peter Sasdy
Leading Players—Nigel Green, Sandor Eles, Maurice Denham

A COUNTESS FROM HONG KONG (1967, GB, Rank)
Natasha—Sophia Loren
Director—Charles Chaplin
Leading Players—Marlon Brando, Sydney Chaplin, Margaret Rutherford, Patrick Cargill, Tippi Hedren, Charles Chaplin

THE COUNTESS OF MONTE CRISTO (1934, Universal)
Janet—Fay Wray
Director—Karl Freund
Leading Players—Paul Lukas, Reginald Owen, Patsy Kelly

THE COUNTESS OF MONTE CRISTO (1948, Universal)
Karen—Sonja Henie
Director—Frederick De Cordova
Leading Players—Olga San Juan, Dorothy Hart, Michael Kirby

COUNTRY BOY (1966, Ambassador Films)
Link Byrd, Jr.—Pat Boone
Director—Joe Kane
Leading Players—Sheb Wooley, Paul Brinegar, Majel Barrett

THE COUNTRY COUSIN (1919, Silent, Selznick)
Cousin Nancy—Elaine Hammerstein
Director—Alan Crosland
Leading Players—Lumsden Hare, Marguerite Siddon, Genevieve Tobin

THE COUNTRY DOCTOR (1927, Silent, Pathe Exchange)
Dr. Amos Rinker—Rudolph Schildkraut
Director—Rupert Julian
Leading Players—Junior Coughlan, Sam De Grasse, Virginia Bradford

THE COUNTRY DOCTOR (1936, 20th Century Fox)
Dr. John Luke—Jean Hersholt
Director—Henry King
Leading Players—June Lang, Slim Summerville, Michael Whalen, Dorothy Peterson, The Dionne Quintuplets

THE COUNTRY FLAPPER (1922, Silent, Producers Distributing Co.)
Jolanda—Dorothy Gish
Director—F. Richard Jones
Leading Players—Glenn Hunter, Mildred Marsh, Harlan Knight

THE COUNTRY GIRL (1954, Paramount)
Georgie Elgin—Grace Kelly
Director—George Seaton
Leading Players—Bing Crosby, William Holden, Anthony Ross

THE COUNTRY KID (1923, Silent, Warner Brothers)
Ben Applegate—Wesley Barry
Director—William Beaudine
Leading Players—Spec O'Donnell, Bruce Guerin, Kate Toncray

THE COUNTRY MOUSE (1914, Silent, Bosworth)
Addie Balderson—Adele Farrington
Director—Hobart Bosworth
Leading Players—Hobart Bosworth, Marshall Stedman, Rhea Haines

COUNTY CHAIRMAN (1914, Silent, Paramount)
The Honorable Jim Hackler—Macklyn Arbuckle
Director—Allan Dwan
Leading Players—Willis P. Sweatman, Harold Lockwood, Daisy Robinson

THE COUNTY CHAIRMAN (1935, Fox Film Corp.)
Jim Hackler—Will Rogers
Director—John Blystone
Leading Players—Evelyn Venable, Kent Taylor, Louise Dresser, Mickey Rooney

THE COURAGEOUS COWARD (1919, Silent, Haworth Pictures)
Suki Iota—Sessue Hayakawa
Director—William Worthington
Leading Players—Tsuru Aoki, George Henderson, Francis J. MacDonald

THE COURAGEOUS COWARD (1924, Silent, Sable Productions)
Jimmy Reed—Jack Meehan
Director—Paul Hurst
Leading Players—Jackie Saunders, Mary MacLaren, Earl Metcalf

THE COURAGEOUS DR. CHRISTIAN (1940, RKO)
Dr. Paul Christian—Jean Hersholt
Director—Bernard Vorhaus
Leading Players—Dorothy Lovett, Robert Baldwin, Tom Neal

THE COURAGEOUS MR. PENN (1941, GB, British National)
William Penn—Clifford Evans
Director—Lance Comfort
Leading Players—Deborah Kerr, Dennis Arundell, Aubrey Mallalieu, O.B. Lawrence

THE COURIER (1988, Vestron)
The Courier—Padrag O'Loingsigh
Director—Frank Deasy & Joe Lee
Leading Players—Cart O'Riordan, Ian Bannen, Patrick Bergen Andrew Connelly, Gabriel Byrne

THE COURT JESTER (1956, Paramount)
Hawkins—Danny Kaye
Director—Norman Panama
Leading Players—Glynis Johns, Basil Rathbone, Angela Lansbury, Cecil Parker, Mildred Natwick

THE COURT MARTIAL OF BILLY MITCHELL (1955, Warner Brothers)
Gen. Billy Mitchell—Gary Cooper
Director—Otto Preminger
Leading Players—Charles Bickford, Ralph Bellamy, Rod Steiger, Elizabeth Montgomery

THE COURT MARTIAL OF MAJOR KELLER (1961, GB, Danzinger)
Major Keller—Laurence Payne
Director—Ernest Morris
Leading Players—Susan Stephen, Ralph Michael, Richard Caldicott

THE COURTESAN (1916, Silent, Mutual Masterpieces)
Mayda St. Maurice—Eugenie Forde
Director—Arthur Maude
Leading Players- Hal Cooley, Al Fordyce, Charles Wheelock

THE COURTNEY AFFAIR (1947, GB, British Lion)
Sir Edward Courtney—Michael Wilding
Director—Herbert Wilcox
Leading Players—Anna Neagle, Gladys Young, Michael Medwin

THE COURTSHIP OF ANDY HARDY (1942, MGM)
Andy Hardy—Mickey Rooney
Director—George B. Seitz
Leading Players—Lewis Stone, Fay Holden, Cecilia Parker, Ann Rutherford, Donna Reed

THE COURTSHIP OF EDDIE'S FATHER (1963, MGM)
Tom Corbett—Glenn Ford
Eddie Corbett—Ronnie Howard
Director—Vincente Minnelli
Leading Players—Shirley Jones, Stella Stevens, Dina Merrill

THE COURTSHIP OF MILES STANDISH (1923, Silent, Associated Exhibitors)
Miles Standish—Alyn Warren
Director—Frederick Sullivan
Leading Players—Charles Ray, Enid Bennett, Joseph Dowling

COUSIN KATE (1921, Silent, Vitagraph)
Kate Curtis—Alice Joyce
Director—Mrs. Sidney Drew
Leading Players—Gilbert Emery, Beth Martin, Inez Shannon

COUSINS (1989, Paramount)
Larry Kozinski—Ted Danson
Maria Hardy—Isabella Rossellini
Director—Joel Schumacher
Leading Players—Sean Young, William Petersen, Lloyd Bridges, Norma Aleandro, Keith Coogan

COVER GIRL (1944, Columbia)
Rusty Parker/Maribelle Hicks—Rita Hayworth
Director—Charles Vidor
Leading Players—Gene Kelly, Lee Bowman, Phil Silvers, Jinx Falkenburg, Leslie Brooks, Eve Arden

COVER GIRL (1985, New World)
Kit—Irene Ferris
Director—Jean-Claude Lord
Leading Players—Jeff Conaway, Cathie Shirriff, Roberta Leighton

COVER GIRL KILLER (1960, GB, Eros)
The Man—Harry H. Corbett
Director—Terry Bishop
Leading Players—Felicity Young, Spencer Teakle, Victor Brooks

THE COWARD (1927, Silent, R-C Pictures)
Clinton Philbrook—Warner Baxter
Director—Alfred Raboch
Leading Players—Sharon Lynn, Freeman Wood, Raoul Paoli

COWBOY (1958, Columbia)
Frank Harris—Jack Lemmon
Director—Delmer Daves
Leading Players—Glenn Ford, Anna Kashfi, Brian Donlevy, Dick York, Richard Jaeckel

THE COWBOY AND THE BLONDE (1941, 20th Century Fox)
Crystal Wayne—Mary Beth Hughes
Lank Garrett—George Montgomery
Director—Ray McCarey
Leading Players—Alan Mowbray, Robert Conway, John Miljan

THE COWBOY AND THE COUNTESS (1926, Silent, Fox Film Corp.)
Jerry Whipple—Buck Jones
Countess Justina—Helen D'Algy
Director—R. William Neill
Leading Players—Diana Miller, Harvey Clark, Monte Collins

THE COWBOY AND THE FLAPPER (1924, Silent, Truart Film Corp.)
Dan Patterson—William Fairbanks
Alice Allison—Dorothy Revier
Director—Alvin J. Neitz
Leading Players—Jack Richardson, Milton Ross, Morgan Davis

THE COWBOY AND THE KID (1936, Universal)
Steve Davis—Buck Jones
Jimmy Thomas—Billy Burrud
Director—Ray Taylor
Leading Players—Dorothy Revier, Harry Worth, Charles Lemoyne

THE COWBOY AND THE LADY (1922, Silent, Paramount)
Jessica Weston—Mary Miles Minter
Teddy North—Tom Moore
Director—Charles Maigne
Leading Players—Viora Daniels, Patricia Palmer, Robert Schable

THE COWBOY AND THE LADY (1938, Goldwyn/UA)
Stretch—Gary Cooper
Mary Smith—Merle Oberon
Director—H.C. Potter
Leading Players—Patsy Kelly, Walter Brennan, Fuzzy Knight

THE COWBOY AND THE PRIZEFIGHTER (1950, Eagle Lion)
Red Ryder—Jim Bannon
Bull—Lou Nova
Director—Lewis D. Collins
Leading Players—Little Brown Jug, Emmett Lynn, Don Haggerty

COWBOY AND THE SENORITA (1944, Republic)
Roy Rogers—Roy Rogers
Ysobel Martinez—Dale Evans
Director—Joseph Kane
Leading Players—John Hubbard, Guinn "Big Boy" Williams, Fuzzy Knight

THE COWBOY COP (1926, Silent, R-C Pictures)
Jerry McGill—Tom Tyler
Director—Robert De Lacey
Leading Players—Jean Arthur, Irving Renard, Frankie Darro

COWBOY FROM BROOKLYN (1938, Warner Brothers)
Elly Jordan—Dick Powell
Director—Lloyd Bacon
Leading Players—Pat O'Brien, Priscilla Lane, Dick Foran, Ann Sheridan, Ronald Reagan

COWBOY FROM SUNDOWN (1940, Monogram)
Tex Rokett—Tex Ritter
Director—Spencer G. Bennett
Leading Players—Pauline Haddon, Rose Ates, Carleton Young

COWBOY IN MANHATTAN (1943, Universal)
Bob—Robert Paige
Director—Frank Woodruff
Leading Players—Frances Langford, Leon Errol, Walter Catlett

COWBOY IN THE CLOUDS (1943, Columbia)
Steve Kendall—Charles Starrett
Director—Benjamin Cline
Leading Players—Dub Taylor, Julie Duncan, Jimmy Wakely

THE COWBOY KID (1928, Silent, Fox Film Corp.)
Jim Barrett—Rex Bell
Director—Clyde Carruth
Leading Players—Mary Jane Temple, Brooks Benedict, Alice
Belcher

THE COWBOY KING (1922, Silent, Aywon Film Corp.)
Dud Smiley—Guinn "Big Boy" Williams
Director—Charles R. Seeling
Leading Players—Patricia Palmer, Elizabeth De Witt, William
Austin

COWBOY MILLIONAIRE (1935, Fox Film Corp.)
Bob Walker—George O'Brien
Director—Edward F. Cline
Leading Players—Evalyn Bostock, Edgar Kennedy, Alden Chase

THE COWBOY MUSKETEER (1925, Silent, R-C Pictures)
Tom Latigo—Tom Tyler
Director—Robert De Lacy
Leading Players—Jim London, Frances Dare, David Dunbar

THE COWBOY STAR (1936, Columbia)
Spencer Yorke—Charles Starrett
Director—David Selman
Leading Players—Iris Meredith, Si Jenks, Marc Lawrence

THE CRACKERJACK (1925, Silent, East Coast Films)
Tommy Perkins—Johnny Hines
Director—Charles Hines
Leading Players—Sigrid Holmquist, Henry West, Bradley Parker

THE CRACKSMAN (1963, GB, Warner Brothers-Pathe)
Ernest Wright—Charlie Drake
Director—Peter Graham Scott
Leading Players—George Sanders, Dennis Price, Nyree Dawn
Porter, Finlay Currie

THE CRADLE BUSTER (1922, Silent, Patuwa Pictures)
Benjamin Franklin Reed—Glenn Hunter
Director—Frank Tuttle
Leading Players—Marguerite Courtot, Mary Foy, William H.
Tooker

CRAIG'S WIFE (1928, Silent, Pathe Exchange)
Harriet Craig—Irene Rich
Walter Craig—Warner Baxter
Director—William C. De Mille
Leading Players—Virginia Bradford, Carroll Nye, Lilyan
Tashman, George Irving

CRAIG'S WIFE (1936, Columbia)
Harriet Craig—Rosalind Russell
Walter Craig—John Boles
Director—Dorothy Arzner
Leading Players—Billie Burke, Jane Darwell, Dorothy Wilson,
Alma Kruger, Thomas Mitchell

CRASH DONOVAN (1936, Universal)
Crash Donovan—Jack Holt
Director—William Nigh
Leading Players—John King, Nan Gray, Eddie Acuff

CRAZY JOE (1974, Columbia)
Joe Gallo—Peter Boyle
Director—Carlo Lizzani

Leading Players—Paula Prentiss, Fred Williamson, Charles
Cioffi, Rip Torn, Luther Adler

CRAZY MAMA (1975, New World)
Melba—Cloris Leachman
Director—Jonathan Demme
Leading Players—Stuart Whitman, Ann Sothern, Jim Backus

CRAZY PEOPLE (1990, Paramount)
Emory Lesson—Dudley Moore
Director—Tony Bill
Leading Players—Daryl Hannah, Paul Reiser, Mercedes Ruehl,
J.T. Walsh, Ben Hammer

THE CRAZY WORLD OF JULIUS VROODER (1974, 20th Century
Fox)
Julius Vrooder—Timothy Bottoms
Director—Arthur Hiller
Leading Players—Barbara Seagull (Hershey), Lawrence
Pressman, Albert Salmi

CRAZYLEGS, ALL AMERICAN (1953, Republic)
Crazylegs Hirsch—Elroy Hirsch
Director—Frances D. Lyon
Leading Players—Lloyd Nolan, Joan Vohs, James Millican

CREATOR (1985, Universal)
Harry—Peter O'Toole
Director—Ivan Passer
Leading Players—Mariel Hemingway, Vincent Spano, Virginia
Madsen, David Ogden Stiers

CREATURE FROM THE BLACK LAGOON (1954, Universal)
Gil Man—Ben Chapman (Ricou Browning in water sequences)
Director—Jack Arnold
Leading Players—Richard Carlson, Julia Adams, Richard
Denning, Antonio Moreno, Nesto Paiva

THE CREATURE WALKS AMONG US (1956, Universal)
The Creature—Don Megowan (Ricou Browning in water
sequences)
Director—John Sherwood
Leading Players—Jeff Morrow, Rex Reason, Leigh Snowden,
Gregg Palmer

THE CREATURE WASN'T NICE (1981, Creature Features)
Creature—Ron Kurowski
Director—Bruce Kimmel
Leading Players—Cindy Williams, Bruce Kimmel, Leslie Nielsen,
Patrick Macnee

THE CREEPER (1948, 20th Century Fox)
Dr. Van Glock—Eduardo Ciannelli
Director—Jean Yarborough
Leading Players—Onslow Stevens, June Vincent, Ralph Morgan

CRIME AGAINST JOE (1956, UA)
Joe Manning—John Bromfield
Director—Lee Sholem
Leading Players—Julie London, Henry Clavin, Patricia Blake

THE CRIME DOCTOR (1934, Radio Pictures)
Dan Gifford—Otto Kruger
Director—John Robertson
Leading Players—Karen Morley, Nils Asther, William Frawley,
Donald Crisp

CRIME DOCTOR (1943, Columbia)
Dr. Robert Ordway—Warner Baxter
Director—Michael Gordon
Leading Players—Margaret Lindsay, John Litel, Ray Collins

THE CRIME DOCTOR'S CHALLENGE (1945, Columbia)
Dr. Robert Ordway—Warner Baxter
Director—George Sherman
Leading Players—Hillary Brooke, Jerome Cowan, Robert Scott

THE CRIME DOCTOR'S DIARY (1949, Columbia)
Dr. Robert Ordway—Warner Baxter
Director—Seymour Friedman
Leading Players—Stephen Dunne, Lois Maxwell, Adele Jergens

CRIME DOCTOR'S GAMBLE (1947, Columbia)
Dr. Robert Ordway—Warner Baxter
Director—William Castle
Leading Players—Micheline Cheirel, Roger Dann, Steven Geray

CRIME DOCTOR'S MAN HUNT (1946, Columbia)
Dr. Robert Ordway—Warner Baxter
Director—William Castle
Leading Players—Ellen Drew, William Frawley, Frank Sully

CRIME DOCTOR'S STRANGEST CASE (1943, Columbia)
Dr. Robert Ordway—Warner Baxter
Director—Eugene J. Forde
Leading Players—Lynn Merrick, Lloyd Bridges, Rose Hobart, Barton Maclane

CRIME DOCTOR'S WARNING (1945, Columbia)
Dr. Robert Ordway—Warner Baxter
Director—William Castle
Leading Players—John Litel, Dusty Anderson, Coulter Irwin

THE CRIME OF DR. CRESPI (1936, Republic)
Dr. Crespi—Eric Von Stroheim
Director—John H. Auer
Leading Players—Dwight Frye, Paul Guilfoyle, Harriet Russell

CRIME OF DR. FORBES (1936, 20th Century Fox)
Dr. Michael Forbes—Robert Kent
Director—George Marshall
Leading Players—Gloria Stuart, Henry Armetta, J. Edward Bromberg

CRIME OF DR. HALLET (1938, Universal)
Dr. Paul Hallet—Ralph Bellamy
Director—S. Sylvan Simon
Leading Players—William Gargan, Josephine Hutchinson, Barbara Read, Nella Walker

THE CRIME OF PETER FRAME (1938, GB, Fox British)
Peter Frame—Frank Allenby
Director—Albert Parker
Leading Players—Frank Fox, Evelyn Ankers, A. Bromley Davenport

CRIMES OF STEPHEN HAWKE (1936, GB, MGM)
Stephen Hawke—Tod Slaughter
Director—George King
Leading Players—Marjorie Taylor, Eric Portman, Gerald Barry

THE CRIMINAL (1916, Silent, Triangle)
Naneta—Clara Williams

Director—Reginald Barker
Leading Players—William Desmond, Enid Dillis, Joseph J. Dowling

CRIMINAL LAWYER (1937, RKO)
Brandon—Lee Tracy
Director—Christy Cabanne
Leading Players—Margot Grahame, Eduardo Ciannelli, Erik Rhodes

CRIMINAL LAWYER (1951, Columbia)
James Regan—Pat O'Brien
Director—Seymour Friedman
Leading Players—Jane Wyatt, Carl Benton Reid, Mary Castle

THE CRIMSON DOVE (1917, Silent, World)
Adrienne Durant—June Elvidge
Director—Romine Fielding
Leading Players—Carlyle Blackwell, Marie La Varre, Henry West

THE CRIMSON PIRATE (1952, Warner Brothers)
Vallo—Burt Lancaster
Director—Robert Siodmak
Leading Players—Nick Cravat, Eva Bartok, Torin Thatcher

THE CRIMSON RUNNER (1925, Silent, Producers Distributing Corp.)
Bianca Schreber—Priscilla Dean
Director—Tom Forman
Leading Players—Bernard Siegal, Alan Hale, Ward Crane

CRITIC'S CHOICE (1963, Warner Brothers)
Parker Ballantine—Bob Hope
Director—Don Weis
Leading Players—Lucille Ball, Marilyn Maxwell, Rip Torn, Jessie Royce Landis

"CROCODILE" DUNDEE (1986, Australia, Paramount)
Mick "Crocodile" Dundee—Paul Hogan
Director—Peter Faiman
Leading Players—Linda Kozlowski, John Meillon, David Gulpilil, Ritchie Singer

"CROCODILE" DUNDEE II (1988, Australia, Paramount)
Mick "Crocodile" Dundee—Paul Hogan
Director—John Cornell
Leading Players—Linda Kozlowski, John Mellion, Ernie Dingo, Hector Ubarry

CROMWELL (1970, GB, Columbia)
Oliver Cromwell—Richard Harris
Director—Ken Hughes
Leading Players—Alec Guinness, Robert Morley, Dorothy Tutin

CROONER (1932, First National)
Teddy—David Manners
Director—Lloyd Bacon
Leading Players—Ann Dvorak, Ken Murray, Sheila Terry

THE CROSS BEARER (1918, Silent, Metro)
Cardinal Mercier—Montagu Love
Director—George Archainbaud
Leading Players—Jeanne Eagels, Anthony Merlo, George Moran

THE CROUCHING BEAST (1936, RKO)
Ahmed Bey—Fritz Kortner
Director—W. Victor Handbury
Leading Players—Wynne Gibson, Richard Bird, Andrews
Englemann

THE CROWN PRINCE'S DOUBLE (1916, Silent, Blue Ribbon)
Crown Prince Oscar—Maurice Costello
Barry Lawrence—Maurice Costello
Director—Van Dyke Brooke
Leading Players—Howard Hall, Norma Talmadge, Anders
Randolph

THE CROWN VS STEVENS (1936, Warner Brothers)
Doris Stevens—Beatrix Thomson
Director—Michael Powell
Leading Players—Patric Knowles, Reginald Purdell, Allan
Jeayes

THE CRUSADER (1932, Majestic)
Phillip Brandon—H.B. Warner
Director—Frank Strayer
Leading Players—Evelyn Brent, Lew Cody, Ned Sparks

CRUSOE (1989, Island)
Robinson Crusoe—Aidan Quinn
Director—Caleb Deschanel
Leading Players—Ade Spara, Elvis Payne, Richard Sharp

CRY-BABY (1990, Universal/Imagine)
Wade "Cry-Baby" Walker—Johnny Depp
Director—John Waters
Leading Players—Amy Locane, Susan Tyrrell, Polly Bergen, Iggy
Pop, Ricki Lake, Traci Lords

THE CRY BABY KILLER (1958, Allied Artists)
Jimmy—Jack Nicholson
Director—Jus Addiss
Leading Players—Harry Lauter, Carolyn Mitchell, Brett Halsey

A CRY IN THE WILD (1990, Concorde-New Horizons)
Brian—Jared Rushton
Director—Mark Griffiths
Leading Players—Pamela Sue Martin, Stephen Meadows, Ned
Beatty

THE CRYSTAL GAZER (1917, Silent, Paramount)
Norma Dugan—Fannie Ward
Director—George Melford
Leading Players—Jack Dean, Winifred Greenwood, Harrison
Ford

THE CUB (1915, Silent, World)
Steve Oldham—Johnny Hines
Director—Maurice Tourneur
Leading Players—Martha Hedman, Robert Cummings, Jessie
Lewis

THE CUB REPORTER (1922, Silent, Oldstone Productions)
Dick Harvey—Richard Talmadge
Director—Jack Dillon
Leading Players—Jean Calhoun, Edwin B. Tilton, Wilson
Hummel

CUPID BY PROXY (1918, Silent, Pathe)
Marie Stewart—Baby Marie Osborne

Director—William Bertram
Leading Players—Minnie Danvers, Mary Talbot, J.N. McDowell

CUPID'S FIREMAN (1923, Silent, Fox Film Corp.)
Andy McGee—Charles Jones
Director—William A. Wellman
Leading Players—Marian Nixon, Brooks Benedict, Eileen
O'Malley

CURLY SUE (1991, Warner Brothers)
Curly Sue Dancer—Alison Porter
Director—John Hughes
Leading Players—James Belushi, Kelly Lynch, John Getz, Fred
Dalton Thompson, Cameron Thor

CURLYTOP (1924, Silent, Fox Film Corp.)
Curlytop—Shirley Mason
Director—Maurice Elvey
Leading Players—Wallace MacDonald, Warner Oland, Diana
Miller

CURLY TOP (1935, Fox Film Corp.)
Elizabeth Blair—Shirley Temple
Director—Irving Cummings
Leading Players—John Boles, Rochelle Hudson, Jane Darwell

THE CURSE OF FRANKENSTEIN (1957, GB, Hammer)
Baron Victor Frankenstein—Peter Cushing
Director—Terence Fisher
Leading Players—Christopher Lee, Hazel Court, Robert
Urquhart

THE CURSE OF THE CAT PEOPLE (1944, RKO)
Irena—Simone Simon
Director—Robert Wise
Leading Players—Kent Smith, Jane Randolph, Ann Carter

CUSTER OF THE WEST (1968, Cinerama)
General George A. Custer—Robert Shaw
Director—Robert Siodmak
Leading Players—Mary Ure, Jeffrey Hunter, Ty Hardin, Robert
Ryan

CUSTOMS AGENT (1950, Columbia)
Bert Stewart—William Eythe
Director—Seymour Friedman
Leading Players—Marjorie Reynolds, Griff Barnett, Howard St.
John

CUTTER AND BONE (1981, UA)
Richard Bone—Jeff Bridges
Alex Cutter—John Heard
Director—Ivan Passer
Leading Players—Lisa Eichorn, Ann Dusenberry, Stephen Elliott

CYBORG (1989, Cannon)
Pearl Prophet—'Cyborg'—Dayle Haddon
Director—Albert Pyun
Leading Players—Jean-Claude Van Damme, Deborah Richter,
Vincent Klyn, Alex Daniels

CYCLONE BLISS (1921, Silent, Unity Photoplays)
Jack Bliss—Jack Hoxie
Director—Francis Ford
Leading Players—Frederick Moore, Evelyn Nelson, Fred Kohler

CYCLONE BUDDY (1924, Silent, Approved Pictures)
Buddy Blake—Buddy Roosevelt
Director—Alvin J. Neitz
Leading Players—Norman Conterno, Alfred Hewston, Bud
Osborne

CYCLONE JONES (1923, Silent, Aywon Film Corp.)
Cyclone Jones—Guinn "Big Boy" Williams
Director—Charles R. Seeling
Leading Players—Bill Patton, J.P. McKee, Kathleen Collins

THE CYCLONE RIDER (1924, Silent, Fox Film Corp.)
Richard Armstrong—Reed Howes
Director—Thomas Buckingham
Leading Players—Alma Bennett, William Bailey, Margaret
McWade

CYNTHIA (1947, MGM)
Cynthia Bishop—Elizabeth Taylor
Director—Robert Z. Leonard
Leading Players—George Murphy, S.Z. Sakall, Mary Astor, Gene
Lockhart

CYRANO DE BERGERAC (1950, UA)
Cyrano De Bergerac—Jose Ferrer
Director—Michael Gordon
Leading Players—Mala Powers, William Prince, Morris
Carnovsky, Ralph Clanton

THE CZAR OF BROADWAY (1930, Universal)
Mort Bradley—John Wray
Director—William James Craft
Leading Players—Betty Compson, John Harron, Claude Allister

D

D.A.R.Y.L. (1985, Paramount)
Daryl—Barret Oliver
Director—Simon Wincer
Leading Players—Mary Beth Hughes, Michael McKean, Daniel
Bryan Corkill

THE D.I. (1957, Warner Brothers)
T/Sgt. Jim Moore—Jack Webb
Director—Jack Webb
Leading Players—Don Dubbins, Jackie Loughery, Lin McCarthy

D.O.A. (1950, UA)
Frank Bigelow—Edmond O'Brien
Director—Rudolph Mate
Leading Players—Pamela Britton, Luther Adler, Beverly
Campbell

D.O.A. (1988, Touchstone)
Dexter Cornell—Dennis Quaid
Directors—Rocky Morton & Annabel Jankel
Leading Players—Meg Ryan, Daniel Stern, Charlotte Rampling,
Jane Kaczmarek

DA (1988, Filmdallas)
Da—Barnard Hughes
Director—Matt Clark
Leading Players—Martin Sheen, Karl Hayden, William Hickey,
Doreen Hepburn

DAD (1989, Universal)
Jake Tremont—Jack Lemmon
Director—Gary David Goldberg
Leading Players—Ted Danson, Olympia Dukakis, Kathy Baker,
Kevin Spacey, Ethan Hawke

DADDY (1923, Silent, First National)
Paul Savelli—Arthur Carewe
Director—E. Mason Hopper
Leading Players—Jackie Coogan, Josie Sedgwick, Cesare
Gravina

DADDY LONG LEGS (1919, Silent, First National)
Jervis Pendelton—Mahlon Hamilton
Director—Marshall Neilan
Leading Players—Mary Pickford, Milla Davenport, Wesley Barry

DADDY LONG LEGS (1931, Fox Film Corp.)
Jervis Pendelton—Warner Baxter
Director—Alfred Santell
Leading Players—Janet Gaynor, Una Merkel, John Arledge

DADDY LONG LEGS (1955, 20th Century Fox)
Jervis Pendelton—Fred Astaire
Director—Jean Negulesco
Leading Players—Leslie Caron, Terry Moore, Thelma Ritter

DADDY'S BOYS (1988, Concorde)
Daddy—Raymond J. Barry
Jimmy—Daryl Haney
Hawk—Dan Shor
Otis—Christian Clemenson
Director—Joe Minton
Leading Players—Laura Burkett, Ellen Gerstein, Robert V.
Barron

DAISY KENYON (1947, 20th Century Fox)
Daisy Kenyon—Joan Crawford
Director—Otto Preminger
Leading Players—Dana Andrews, Henry Fonda, Ruth Warrick,
Martha Stewart, Peggy Ann Garner

DAISY MILLER (1974, Paramount)
Annie P. "Daisy" Miller—Cybill Shepherd
Director—Peter Bogdanovich
Leading Players—Barry Brown, Cloris Leachman, Mildred
Natwick, Eileen Brennan

THE DAKOTA KID (1951, Republic)
Dakota Kid—Dean Morton
Director—Philip Ford
Leading Players—Michael Chapin, Eilene Janssen, James Bell

DAKOTA LIL (1950, 20th Century Fox)
Dakota Lil—Marie Windsor
Director—Lesley Selander
Leading Players—George Montgomery, Rod Cameron, John
Emery

THE DALTON GIRLS (1957, UA)
  Holly Dalton—Merry Anders
  Rose Dalton—Lisa Davis
  Columbine Dalton—Penny Edwards
  Marigold Dalton—Sue George
  Director—Reginald Le Borg
  Leading Players—John Russell, Ed Hinton, Glenn Dixon

THE DALTONS RIDE AGAIN (1945, Universal)
  Emmett Dalton—Alan Curtis
  Bob Dalton—Kent Taylor
  Grat Dalton—Lon Chaney, Jr.
  Ben Dalton—Noah Beery, Jr.
  Director—Ray Taylor
  Leading Players—Martha O'Driscoll, Jess Barker, Thomas Gomez

DAMES (1934, Warner Brothers)
  Mabel Anderson—Joan Blondell
  Barbara Hemingway—Ruby Keeler
  Director—Ray Enright
  Leading Players—Dick Powell, Zasu Pitts, Hugh Herbert, Guy Kibbee

DAMIEN-OMEN II (1978, 20th Century Fox)
  Damien Thorn—Jonathan Scott-Taylor
  Director—Don Taylor
  Leading Players—William Holden, Lee Grant, Robert Foxworth

DAMN CITIZEN (1958, Universal)
  Col. Francis C. Grevemberg—Keith Andes
  Director—Robert Gordon
  Leading Players—Maggie Hayes, Gene Evans, Lynn Bari

THE DAMNED DON'T CRY (1950, Warner Brothers)
  Ethel Whitehead (Lorna Hansen Forbes)—Joan Crawford
  Director—Vincent Sherman
  Leading Players—David Brian, Steve Cochran, Kent Smith

DAMON AND PYTHIAS (1962, MGM)
  Pythias—Don Burnett
  Damon—Guy Williams
  Director—Curtis Bernhardt
  Leading Players—Ilaria Occhini, Liana Orfei, Arnoldo Foa

A DAMSEL IN DISTRESS (1937, RKO)
  Lady Alice Marshmorton—Joan Fontaine
  Director—George Stevens
  Leading Players—Fred Astaire, George Burns, Gracie Allen

DAN (1914, Silent, All Star Feature)
  Dan—Lew Dockstader
  Director—Hal Reid
  Leading Players—Lois Meredith, Gil Kane, Beatrice Clevener

DAN MATTHEWS (1936, Columbia)
  Dan Matthews—Richard Arlen
  Director—Phil Rosen
  Leading Players—Charlotte Wynters, Douglass Dumbrille, Mary Kornman

DANCE, GIRL, DANCE (1933, Invincible)
  Sally—Evalyn Knapp
  Director—Frank Strayer
  Leading Players—Alan Dinehart, Edward Nugent, Gloria Shea

DANCE, GIRL, DANCE (1940, RKO)
  Judy—Maureen O'Hara
  Director—Dorothy Arzner
  Leading Players—Louis Hayward, Lucille Ball, Virginia Field

DANCE HALL HOSTESS (1933, Mayfair)
  Texas Guinan—Helen Chandler
  Director—Reeves Eason
  Leading Players—Jason Robards, Sr., Edward Nugent, Natalie Moorhead

DANCE LITTLE LADY (1954, GB, Renown)
  Jill Gordon—Mandy Miller
  Director—Val Guest
  Leading Players—Terence Morgan, Mai Zetterling, Guy Rolfe

DANCE PRETTY LADY (1932, GB, British Lion)
  Jenny Pearl—Ann Casson
  Director—Anthony Asquith
  Leading Players—Carl Harbord, Michael Hogan, Moore Marriott

DANCE TEAM (1932, Fox Film Corp.)
  Jimmy Mulligan—James Dunn
  Poppy Kirk—Sally Eilers
  Director—Sidney Lanfield
  Leading Players—Minna Gombell, Edward Crandall, Ralph Morgan

DANCE WITH A STRANGER (1985, GB, Goldwyn)
  Ruth Ellis—Miranda Richardson
  David Blakely—Rupert Everett
  Director—Mike Newell
  Leading Players—Ian Holm, Matthew Carroll, Tom Chadborn

DANCE WITH ME HENRY (1956, UA)
  Lou Henry—Lou Costello
  Director—Charles Barton
  Leading Players—Bud Abbott, Gigi Perreau, Rusty Hamer

THE DANCER'S PERIL (1917, Silent, World)
  Vasto/Lola—Alice Brady
  Director—Travers Vale
  Leading Players—Philip Hunt, Montagu Love, Alexis Kosloff

THE DANCERS (1930, Fox Film Corp.)
  Tony—Phillips Holmes
  Maxine—Mae Clarke
  Director—Chandler Sprague
  Leading Players—Lois Moran, Walter Bryon, Mrs. Patrick Campbell

DANCERS (1987, Cannon)
  Anton "Tony" Sergoyev—Mikhail Baryshnikov
  Francesca—Alessandra Ferri
  Nadine—Leslie Browne
  Director—Herbert Ross
  Leading Players—Thomas Rall, Lynn Seymour, Victor Barbee

DANCES WITH WOLVES (1990, Orion)
  Lt. John Dunbar—Kevin Costner
  Director—Kevin Costner
  Leading Players—Mary McDonnell, Graham Greene, Rodney A. Grant, Floyd Red Crow Westerman, Tantoo Cardinal

DANCING CO-ED (1939, MGM)
  Patty Marlow—Lana Turner

Director—S. Sylvan Simon
Leading Players—Richard Carlson, Artie Shaw, Ann Rutherford, Lee Bowman, Leon Errol

DANCING LADY (1933, MGM)
Janie Barlow—Joan Crawford
Director—Robert Z. Leonard
Leading Players—Clark Gable, Franchot Tone, Fred Astaire, Nelson Eddy, May Robson

DANCING MAN (1934, Pyramid)
Paul Drexell—Reginald Denny
Director—Albert Ray
Leading Players—Judith Allen, Edmund Breese, Natalie Moorhead

THE DANCING MASTERS (1943, 20th Century Fox)
Stanley—Stan Laurel
Ollie—Oliver Hardy
Director—Malcolm St. Clair
Leading Players—Trudy Marshall, Robert Bailey, Matt Briggs

DANCING MOTHERS (1926, Silent, Paramount)
Ethel Westcourt—Alice Joyce
Director—Herbert Brenon
Leading Players—Conway Tearle, Clara Bow, Donald Keith

DANCING PIRATE (1936, RKO)
Jonathan Pride—Charles Collins
Director—Lloyd Corrigan
Leading Players—Frank Morgan, Steffi Duna, Luis Alberni

DANCING SWEETIES (1930, Warner Brothers)
Bill Cleaver—Grant Withers
Molly O'Neill—Sue Carol
Director—Ray Enright
Leading Players—Edna Murphy, Eddie Phillips, Kate Price

DANDY, THE ALL AMERICAN GIRL (1976, MGM/UA)
Dandy—Stockard Channing
Director—Jerry Schatzberg
Leading Players—Sam Waterston, Richard Doughty, Norman Matlock

DANDY DICK (1935, GB, British International)
Rev. Richard Jedd—Will Hay
Director—William Beaudine
Leading Players—Nancy Burne, Esmond Knight, Davy Burnaby

A DANDY IN ASPIC (1968, GB, Columbia)
Alexander Eberlin—Laurence Harvey
Director—Anthony Mann
Leading Players—Tom Courtenay, Mia Farrow, Lionel Stander

DANGER WOMAN (1946, Universal)
Eve Ruppert—Patricia Morison
Director—Lewis D. Collins
Leading Players—Don Porter, Brenda Joyce, Milburn Stone

DANGEROUS (1936, Warner Brothers)
Joyce Heath—Bette Davis
Director—Alfred E. Green
Leading Players—Franchot Tone, Margaret Lindsay, Alison Skipworth

DANGEROUS DAVIES—THE LAST DETECTIVE (1981, GB, ITC)
Dangerous Davies—Bernard Cribbens
Director—Val Guest
Leading Players—Bill Maynard, Joss Ackland, Bernard Lee

DANGEOUS EXILE (1958, GB, Rank)
Louis XVII—Richard O'Sullivan
Director—Brian Desmond Hurst
Leading Players—Louis Jourdan, Belinda Lee, Keith Michell

DANGEROUS LIAISONS (1988, Warner Brothers)
Marquise de Merteuil—Glenn Close
Vicomte de Valmont—John Malkovich
Madame de Tourvel—Michelle Pfeiffer
Director—Stephen Frears
Leading Players—Swoosie Kurtz, Keanu Reeves, Uma Thurman, Mildred Natwick

DANGEROUS NAN MCGREW (1930, Paramount)
Nan McGrew—Helen Kane
Director—Malcolm St. Clair
Leading Players—Victor Moore, James Hall, Stuart Erwin

DANGEROUS PARTNERS (1945, MGM)
Jeff Caighn—James Craig
Carola Ballister—Signe Hasso
Director—Edward L. Cahn
Leading Players—Edmund Gwenn, Audrey Totter, Mabel Paige

DANGEROUS TO KNOW (1938, Paramount)
Stephen Recka—Akim Tamiroff
Director—Robert Florey
Leading Players—Anna May Wong, Gail Patrick, Lloyd Nolan

DANGEROUS TO MEN (1920, Silent, Metro)
Eliza—Viola Dana
Director—William C. Dowlan
Leading Players—Milton Sills, Edward Connelly, Josephine Crowell

DANGEROUS WHEN WET (1953, MGM)
Katy—Esther Williams
Director—Charles Walters
Leading Players—Fernando Lamas, Jack Carson, Charlotte Greenwood, Denise Darcel

DANGEROUS WOMAN (1929, Paramount)
Tania Gregory—Olga Baclanova
Director—Rowland V. Lee
Leading Players—Clive Brook, Neil Hamilton, Clyde Cook

DANIEL (1983, Paramount)
Daniel Isaccson—Timothy Hutton
Director—Sidney Lumet
Leading Players—Edward Asner, Mandy Patinkin, Lindsay Crouse

DANIEL BOONE (1936, RKO)
Daniel Boone—George O'Brien
Director—David Howard
Leading Players—Heather Angel, John Carradine, Ralph Forbes

DANIEL BOONE, TRAIL BLAZER (1957, Republic)
Daniel Boone—Bruce Bennett
Director—Albert C. Gannaway
Leading Players—Lon Chaney, Jr., Faron Young, Kem Dibbs

DANNY BOY (1934, GB, Panther)
Danny—Ronnie Hepworth
Director—Oswald Mitchell
Leading Players—Frank Forbes-Robinson, Dorothy Dickson, Archie Pitt

DANNY BOY (1941, GB, Butchers)
Danny—Grant Tyler
Director—Oswald Mitchell
Leading Players—David Farrar, Wilfred Lawson, Ann Todd

DANNY BOY (1984, Ireland, Triumph)
Danny—Stephen Rea
Director—Neil Jordan
Leading Players—Veronica Quilligan, Alan Devlin, Peter Caffrey

DANTE'S INFERNO (1924, Silent, Fox Film Corp.)
Dante Alighieri—Lawson Butt
Director—Henry Otto
Leading Players—Howard Gaye, Ralph Lewis, Pauline Starke

DAPHNE AND THE PIRATE (1916, Silent, Triangle)
Daphne La Tour—Lillian Gish
Director—Christy Cabanne
Leading Players—Elliot Dexter, Walter Long, Howard Gaye

DARBY AND JOAN (1937, GB, MGM)
Joan Templeton—Peggy Simpson
Darby Templeton—Pamela Bevan
Director—Syd Courtenay
Leading Players—Ian Fleming, Mickey Brantford, Tod Slaughter

DARBY O'GILL AND THE LITTLE PEOPLE (1959, Disney/Buena Vista)
Darby O'Gill—Albert Sharpe
King Brian—Jimmy O'Dea
Director—Robert Stevenson
Leading Players—Janet Munro, Sean Connery, Kieron Moore

DARBY'S RANGERS (1958, Warner Brothers)
Major William Darby—James Garner
Director—William Wellman
Leading Players—Etchika Choureau, Jack Warden, Edward Byrnes, Venetia Stevenson

DAREDREAMER (1990, Lensman)
Winston—Tim Noah
Director—Barry Cailler
Leading Players—Alyce LaTourelle, Adam Eastwood, Michael A. Jackson

THE DARING CABALLERO (1949, UA)
Cisco Kid—Duncan Renaldo
Director—Wallace Fox
Leading Players—Leo Carrillo, Kippee Valez, Charles Hallon

DARING DAUGHTERS (1933, Tower)
Terry Cummings—Marian Marsh
Betty Cummings—Joan Marsh
Director—Christy Cabanne
Leading Players—Kenneth Thomson, Bert Roach, Allen Vincent

THE DARING YOUNG MAN (1935, Fox Film Corp.)
Don McLane—James Dunn
Director—William A. Seiter
Leading Players—Mae Clarke, Neil Hamilton, Sidney Toler

DARKMAN (1990, Universal)
Darkman—Liam Neeson
Director—Dam Raimi
Leading Players—Frances McDormand, Colin Friels, Larry Drake, Nelson Mashita, Jesse Lawrence Ferguson

THE DARK MAN (1951, GB, GFD)
The Dark Man—Maxwell Reed
Director—Jeffrey Dell
Leading Players—Edward Underdown, Natasha Parry, William Hartnell

DARLING (1965, GB, Embassy)
Diana Scott—Julie Christie
Director—John Schlesinger
Leading Players—Laurence Harvey, Dirk Bogarde, Roland Curram

DARLING LILI (1970, Paramount)
Lili Smith—Julie Andrews
Director—Blake Edwards
Leading Players—Rock Hudson, Jeremy Kemp, Lance Percival

THE DARLING OF PARIS (1917, Silent, 20th Century Fox)
Esmeralda—Theda Bara
Director—J. Gordon Edwards
Leading Players—Glen White, Walter Law, Herbert Heyes

THE DARLING OF THE RICH (1923, Silent, B.B. Productions)
Charmion Winship—Betty Blythe
Director—John G. Adolfi
Leading Players—Gladys Leslie, Montagu Love, Charles Gerard

THE DARWIN ADVENTURE (1972, GB, 20th Century Fox)
Charles Darwin—Nicholas Clay
Director—Jack Couffer
Leading Players—Susan Macready, Ian Richardson, Robert Flemyng

DATE WITH AN ANGEL (1987, De Laurentiis)
Angel—Emmanuelle Beart
Jim Sanders—Michael E. Knight
Director—Tom McLoughlin
Leading Players—Phoebe Cates, David Dukes, Phil Brock

A DATE WITH JUDY (1948, MGM)
Judy Foster—Jane Powell
Director—Richard Thorpe
Leading Players—Wallace Beery, Elizabeth Taylor, Carmen Miranda, Xavier Cugat

A DATE WITH THE FALCON (1941, RKO)
Gay Lawrence, the Falcon—George Sanders
Director—Irving Reis
Leading Players—Wendy Barrie, James Gleason, Mona Maris

A DAUGHTER IN REVOLT (1927, Silent, GB, Allied Artists)
Aimee Scroope—Mabel Poulton
Director—Harry Hughes
Leading Players—Edward O'Neill, Patrick Susands, Lilian Oldland

DAUGHTER OF DARKNESS (1948, GB, Paramount)
Emily Beaudine—Siobhan McKenna
Director—Lance Comfort
Leading Players—Anne Crawford, Maxwell Reed, George Thorpe

DAUGHTER OF DR. JEKYLL (1957, Allied Artists)
Janet Smith—Gloria Talbot
Director—Edgar G. Ulmer
Leading Players—John Agar, Arthur Shields, John Dierkes

A DAUGHTER OF LOVE (1925, Silent, GB, Stoll)
Mary Tannerhill—Violet Hopson
Director—Walter West
Leading Players—John Stuart, Jameson Thomas, Fred Raynham

THE DAUGHTER OF ROSIE O'GRADY (1950, Warner Brothers)
Patricia O'Grady—June Haver
Director—David Butler
Leading Players—Gordon MacRae, James Barton, Debbie Reynolds

DAUGHTER OF SHANGHAI (1937, Paramount)
Lan Ying Lin—Anna May Wong
Director—Robert Florey
Leading Players—Phillip Ahn, Charles Bickford, Larry Crabbe

DAUGHTER OF THE DRAGON (1931, Paramount)
Ling Moy—Anna May Wong
Director—Lloyd Corrigan
Leading Players—Warner Oland, Sessue Hayakawa, Bramwell Fletcher

DAUGHTER OF THE JUNGLE (1949, Republic)
Ticoora—Lois Hall
Director—George Blair
Leading Players—James Cardwell, William Wright, Sheldon Leonard

A DAUGHTER OF THE SEA (1915, Silent, World)
The Girl—Muriel Ostriche
Director—Charles W. Seay
Leading Players—W.H. Tooker, Catherine Calhoun, Clara Whipple

DAUGHTER OF THE SUN GOD (1962, Condor)
Daughter of the Sun God—Juanita Llosa
Director—Kenneth Herts
Leading Players—William Holmes, Lisa Montell, Harry Knapp

DAUGHTER OF THE TONG (1939, Metropolitan)
The Illustrious One—Evelyn Brent
Director—Raymond K. Johnson
Leading Players—Grant Withers, Dorothy Short, Dave O'Brien

DAUGHTER OF THE WEST (1949, Film Classics)
Lolita Moreno—Martha Vickers
Director—Harold Daniels
Leading Players—Philip Reed, Donald Woods, Marion Carney

THE DAUGHTER PAYS (1920, Silent, Selznick)
Virginia Mynors—Elaine Hammerstein
Director—Robert Ellis
Leading Players—Norman Trevor, Robert Ellis, Theresa Maxwell

DAUGHTERS COURAGEOUS (1939, Warner Brothers)
Buff Masters—Priscilla Lane
Tinka Masters—Rosemary Lane
Linda Masters—Lola Lane
Cora Masters—Gale Page
Director—Michael Curtiz

Leading Players—John Garfield, Claude Rains, Jeffrey Lynn, Fay Bainter, Donald Crisp

DAUGHTERS OF SATAN (1972, UA)
Chris Robertson—Barra Grant
Director—Hollingsworth Morse
Leading Players—Tom Selleck, Tani Phelps Guthrie, Paraluman

DAUGHTERS OF TODAY (1933, GB, UA)
Joan Sharpe—Betty Amman
Mavis Sharpe—Marguerite Allan
Director—F.W. Kraemer
Leading Players—George Barraud, Gerald Rawlinson, Hay Petrie

DAVID AND BATHSHEBA (1951, 20th Century Fox)
David—Gregory Peck
Bathsheba—Susan Hayward
Director—Henry King
Leading Players—Raymond Massey, Kieron Moore, James Robertson Justice, Jayne Meadows

DAVID AND JONATHAN (1920, Silent, GB, General)
David Mortlake—Geoffrey Webb
Jonathan Hawksley—Richard Ryan
Director—Alexander Butler
Leading Players—Madge Titheradge, Sidney Wood, Jack Perks

DAVID AND LISA (1962, Continental)
David—Keir Dullea
Lisa—Janet Margolin
Director—Frank Perry
Leading Players—Howard Da Silva, Neva Patterson, Clifton James

DAVID COPPERFIELD (1935, MGM)
David as a man—Frank Lawton
David as a boy—Freddie Bartholomew
Director—George Cukor
Leading Players—W.C. Fields, Lionel Barrymore, Maureen O'Sullivan, Madge Evans, Edna May Oliver, Lewis Stone, Roland Young, Elizabeth Allan, Basil Rathbone, Lennox Pawle, Jean Cadell, Elsa Lanchester, Jessie Ralph

DAVID COPPERFIELD (1970, GB, 20th Century Fox)
David Copperfield—Robin Phillips
Little David—Alastair MacKenzie
Director—Delbert Mann
Leading Players—Richard Attenborough, Cyril Cusack, Edith Evans, Pamela Franklin, Susan Hampshire, Wendy Hiller, Ron Moody, Laurence Olivier, Ralph Richardson, Michael Redgrave

DAVID HARDING, COUNTERSPY (1950, Columbia)
David Harding—Howard St. John
Director—Ray Nazarro
Leading Players—Willard Parker, Audrey Long, Raymond Greenleaf

DAVID HARUM (1915, Silent, Famous Players)
David Harum—William H. Crane
Director—Allan Dwan
Leading Players—Kate Meeks, May Allison, Harold Lockwood

DAVID HARUM (1934, Fox Film Corp.)
David Harum—Will Rogers
Director—James Cruze

Leading Players—Louise Dresser, Evelyn Venable, Kent Taylor

DAVID LIVINGSTONE (1936, GB, MGM)
David Livingstone—Percy Marmont
Director—James A. Fitzpatrick
Leading Players—Marian Spencer, James Carew, Pamela Stanley

DAVY (1958, GB, Ealing)
Davy—Harry Secombe
Director—Michael Relph
Leading Players—Ron Randell, George Relph, Susan Shaw

DAVY CROCKETT AND THE RIVER PIRATES (1956, Disney)
Davy Crockett—Fess Parker
Director—Norman Foster
Leading Players—Buddy Ebsen, Jeff York, Kenneth Tobey

DAVY CROCKETT, INDIAN SCOUT (1950, UA)
Davy Crockett—George Montgomery
Director—Lew Landers
Leading Players—Ellen Drew, Philip Reed, Noah Beery, Jr.

DAVY CROCKETT, KING OF THE WILD FRONTIER (1955, Disney)
Davy Crockett—Fess Parker
Director—Norman Foster
Leading Players—Buddy Ebsen, Basil Ruysdael, Hans Conreid

DAWN (1979, Australia, Aquataurus)
Dawn—Bronwyn Mackay-Payne
Director—Ken Hannam
Leading Players—Tom Richards, John Dietrich, Bunney Brooke

DAWN RIDER (1935, Lone Star)
John Mason—John Wayne
Director—R.N. Bradbury
Leading Players—Marion Burns, Yakima Canutt, Reed Howes

A DAY IN THE DEATH OF JOE EGG (1972, GB, Columbia)
Jo—Elizabeth Robillard
Director—Peter Medak
Leading Players—Alan Bates, Janet Suzman, Peter Bowles

THE DAY OF THE JACKAL (1973, GB, Universal)
The Jackal—Edward Fox
Director—Fred Zinnemann
Leading Players—Michel Auclair, Alan Badel, Tony Britton, Donald Sinden, Timothy West

DAY OF THE OUTLAW (1959, UA)
Jack Bruhn—Burl Ives
Director—Andre De Toth
Leading Players—Robert Ryan, Tina Louise, Alan Marshal

DAY-TIME WIFE (1939, 20th Century Fox)
Jane Norton—Linda Darnell
Director—Gregory Ratoff
Leading Players—Tyrone Power, Warren William, Binnie Barnes, Wendy Barrie, Joan Davis

THE DAYDREAMER (1966, Embassy)
Hans Christian Anderson—Paul O'Keefe
Director—Jules Bass
Leading Players—Jack Gifford, Ray Bolger, Margaret Hamilton

DAYS OF JESSE JAMES (1939, Republic)
Jesse James—Donald Barry
Director—Joseph Kane
Leading Players—Roy Rogers, Gabby Hayes, Pauline Moore

DEAD AGAIN (1991, Paramount)
Grace—Emma Thompson
Director—Kenneth Branagh
Leading Players—Kenneth Branagh, Andy Garcia, Derek Jacobi, Robin Williams, Wayne Knight, Hanna Schygulla

DEAD MAN WALKING (1988, Metropolis)
John Luger—Wings Hauser
Director—Gregory Brown
Leading Players—Brion James, Pamela Ludwig, Leland Crooke

DEAD MEN DON'T DIE (1990, Trans Atlantic/Waymar)
Barry—Elliot Gould
Director—Malcolm Mormorstein
Leading Players—Melissa Anderson, Mark Moses, Mabel King, Philip Bruns, Jack Betts

DEAD RINGER (1964, Warner Brothers)
Margaret & Edith—Bette Davis
Director—Paul Henreid
Leading Players—Karl Malden, Peter Lawford, Philip Carey, Jean Hagen

DEAD RINGERS (1988, 20th Century Fox)
Beverly & Elliot Mantle—Jermey Irons
Director—David Cronenberg
Leading Players—Genevieve Bujold, Heidi von Palleske, Barbara Gordon, Shirley Douglas

DEADLIER THAN THE MALE (1967, GB, Universal)
Irma Eckman—Elke Sommer
Director—Ralph Thomas
Leading Players—Richard Johnson, Sylva Koscina, Nigel Green

THE DEADLY COMPANIONS (1961, Pathe-American)
Kit—Maureen O'Hara
Yellowleg—Brian Keith
Billy—Steve Cochran
Director—Sam Peckinpah
Leading Players—Chill Wills, Strother Martin, Will Wright

DEADLY DUO (1962, UA)
Sabena/Dara—Marcia Henderson
Director—Reginald LeBorg
Leading Players—Craig Hill, Dayton Lummis, Carlos Romero

DEADLY HERO (1976, Avco Embassy)
Ed Lacy—Don Murray
Director—Ivan Nagy
Leading Players—Diahn Williams, James Earl Jones, Lilia Skala

DEADLY TRACKERS (1973, Warner Brothers)
Kilpatrick—Richard Harris
Director—Barry Shear
Leading Players—Rod Taylor, Al Lettieri, Neville Brand

DEAF SMITH AND JOHNNY EARS (1971, MGM)
Erastus "Deaf" Smith—Anthony Quinn
Johnny Ears—Franco Nero
Director—Paolo Cavara

Leading Players—Pamela Tiffin, Franco Graziosi, Ira Furstenberg

DEALERS (1989, Rank, GB)
Daniel Pascoe—Paul McGann
Anna Schuman—Rebecca DeMornay
Director—Colin Bucksey
Leading Players—Derrick O'Connor, John Castle, Paul Guilfoyle

DEAR BRAT (1951, Paramount)
Miriam Wilkins—Mona Freeman
Director—William Seiter
Leading Players—Billy De Wolfe, Edward Arnold, Lyle Bettger

DEAR BRIGETTE (1965, 20th Century Fox)
Brigette Bardot—Brigette Bardot
Director—Henry Koster
Leading Players—James Stewart, Fabian, Glynis Johns, Cindy Carol, Billy Mumy

DEAR MR. PROHACK (1949, GB, GFD)
Arthur Prohack—Cecil Parker
Director—Thornton Freeland
Leading Players—Glynis Johns, Hermione Baddeley, Dirk Bogarde

DEAR MURDERER (1947, GB, Gainsborough)
Lee Warren—Eric Portman
Director—Arthur Crabtree
Leading Players—Greta Gynt, Dennis Price, Jack Warner

DEAR RUTH (1947, Paramount)
Ruth Wilkins—Joan Caulfield
Director—William D. Russell
Leading Players—William Holden, Edward Arnold, Mary Phillips, Mona Freeman

DEAR WIFE (1949, Paramount)
Ruth Seacroft—Joan Caulfield
Director—Richard Haydn
Leading Players—William Holden, Billy De Wolfe, Mona Freeman, Edward Arnold

DEATH OF A GUNFIGHTER (1969, Universal)
Marshal Frank Patch—Richard Widmark
Director—Allen Smithee
Leading Players—Lena Horne, Carroll O'Connor, David Opatoshu

DEATH OF A SALESMAN (1952, Columbia)
Willy Loman—Fredric March
Director—Laslo Benedek
Leading Players—Mildred Dunnock, Kevin McCarthy, Cameron Mitchell

DEATH OF A SCOUNDREL (1956, RKO)
Clementi Sabourin—George Sanders
Director—Charles Martin
Leading Players—Yvonne De Carlo, Zsa Zsa Gabor, Victor Jory

DEATH OF AN ANGEL (1952, GB, Hammer)
Mary Welling—Jane Baxter
Director—Charles Saunders
Leading Players—Patrick Barr, Julie Somers, Jean Lodge

DEATH OF AN ANGEL (1986, 20th Century Fox)
Father Angel—Nick Mancuso
Director—Petru Popescu
Leading Players—Bonnie Bedelia, Pamela Ludwig, Alex Colon

DEATH TAKES A HOLIDAY (1934, Paramount)
Prince Sirki—Fredric March
Director—Mitchell Leisen
Leading Players—Evelyn Venable, Sir Guy Standing, Katherine Alexander, Gail Patrick, Helen Westley

THE DEATHMASTER (1972, American International)
Khorda—Robert Quarry
Director—Ray Danton
Leading Players—Bill Ewing, Brenda Dickson, John Fiedler

THE DEATHSTALKER (1984, New World)
Deathstalker—Richard Hill
Director—John Watson
Leading Players—Barbi Benton, Lana Clarkson, Richard Brooker

DEATHSTALKER II (1988, Concorde)
Deathstalker—John Terlesky
Director—Jim Wynorski
Leading Players—Monique Gabrielle, John La Zar, Toni Naples

DEATHSTALKER AND THE WARRIORS FROM HELL (1989, Concorde)
Deathstalker—John Allen Nelson
Director—Alfonso Corona
Leading Players—Carla Herd, Terri Treas, Thom Christopher

DECEIVED (1991, Buena Vista/Touchstone)
Adrienne—Goldie Hawn
Director—Damian Harris
Leading Players—John Heard, Robin Bartlett, Ashley Peldon, Tom Irwin, Mora Filar, Jan Rubes

THE DECEIVER (1931, Columbia)
Thorpe—Ian Keith
Director—Louis King
Leading Players—Lloyd Hughes, Dorothy Sebastian, Natalie Moorhead

THE DECISION OF CHRISTOPHER BLAKE (1948, Warner Brothers)
Christopher Blake—Ted Donaldson
Director—Peter Godfrey
Leading Players—Alexis Smith, Robert Douglas, Cecil Kellaway

DECLINE AND FALL . . . OF A BIRD WATCHER (1969, GB, Fox)
Paul Pennyfeather—Robin Phillips
Director—John Krish
Leading Players—Michael Elwyn, Norman Scace, John Glynne Jones, Donald Sayne-Smith

DEEP COVER (1992, New Line)
Russell Stevens, Jr./John Q. Hull—Larry Fishburne
Director—Bill Duke
Leading Players—Jeff Goldblum, Victoria Dillard, Charles Martin Smith, Gregory Sierra, Clarence Williams III

THE DEER HUNTER (1978, Columbia/Warner Brothers)
Michael—Robert DeNiro
Director—Michael Cimino

Leading Players—John Cazale, John Savage, Christopher Walken, Meryl Streep

DEERSLAYER (1943, Republic)
Deerslayer—Bruce Kellogg
Director—Lew Landers
Leading Players—Jean Parker, Larry Parks, Warren Ashe

THE DEERSLAYER (1957, 20th Century Fox)
The Deerslayer—Lex Barker
Director—Kurt Neumann
Leading Players—Rita Moreno, Forrest Tucker, Cathy O'Donnell

THE DEFECTOR (1966, Warner Brothers)
Prof. James Bower—Montgomery Clift
Director—Raoul Levy
Leading Players—Hardy Kruger, Roddy McDowall, Macha Meril

THE DEFIANT ONES (1958, UA)
John "Joker" Jackson—Tony Curtis
Noah Cullen—Sidney Poitier
Director—Stanley Kramer
Leading Players—Theodore Bikel, Charles McGraw, Lon Chaney, Jr., King Donovan, Cara Williams

DEFENDING YOUR LIFE (1991, Warner Brothers)
Daniel Miller—Albert Brooks
Director—Albert Brooks
Leading Players—Meryl Streep, Rip Torn, Buck Henry, Lee Grant

THE DELICATE DELINQUENT (1957, Paramount)
Sidney Pythias—Jerry Lewis
Director—Don McGuire
Leading Players—Darren McGavin, Martha Hyer, Robert Ivers

DELIVERY BOYS (1984, New World)
Max—Joss Marcano
Joey—Tom Sierchio
Conrad—Jim Soriero
Director—Ken Handler
Leading Players—Nelson Vasquez, Victor Colicchio, Naylon Mitchell, Jody Oliver

DEMETRIUS AND THE GLADIATORS (1954, 20th Century Fox)
Demetrius—Victor Mature
Director—Delmer Daves
Leading Players—Susan Hayward, Michael Rennie, Debra Paget, Anne Bancroft, Jay Robinson

THE DEMON BARBER OF FLEET STREET (1939, GB, MGM)
Sweeney Todd—Tod Slaughter
Director—George King
Leading Players—Eva Lister, Bruce Seton, Davina Craig

DEMONSTRATOR (1971, Australia, Columbia)
Steven Slater—Gerard Maguire
Director—Warwick Freeman
Leading Players—Joe James, Irene Inescort, Wendy Lingham

DENTIST IN THE CHAIR (1960, GB, Renown)
David Cookson—Bob Monkhouse
Director—Don Chaffey
Leading Players—Peggy Cummins, Kenneth Connor, Eric Barker

DEPORTED (1950, Universal)
Vic Smith—Jeff Chandler
Director—Robert Siodmak
Leading Players—Marta Toren, Claude Dauphin, Marina Barti

THE DEPRAVED (1957, GB, UA)
Laura Wilton—Anne Heywood
Dave Dillon—Robert Arden
Director—Paul Dickson
Leading Players—Carroll Levis, Basil Dignam, Denis Shaw

THE DEPUTY DRUMMER (1935, GB, Columbia)
Adolphus Miggs—Lupino Lane
Director—Henry W. George
Leading Players—Jean Denis, Kathleen Kelly, Wallace Lupino

DEPUTY MARSHAL (1949, Lippert)
Ed Garry—Jon Hall
Director—William Berke
Leading Players—Frances Langford, Dick Foran, Julie Bishop

DERANGED (1974, Canada, American International)
Ezra Cobb—Roberts Blossom
Director—Jeff Gillen
Leading Players—Cosette Lee, Leslie Carlson, Robert Warner

DERELICT (1930, Paramount)
Bill Rafferty—George Bancroft
Director—Rowland V. Lee
Leading Players—Jessie Royce Landis, William Boyd, Donald Stuart

THE DERELICT (1937, GB, Independent Film Distributors)
Toby Merriman—Malcolm Morley
Director—Harold Simpson
Leading Players—Jane Griffiths, Charles Penrose, Frank Strickland

THE DESERT FLOWER (1925, Silent, First National)
Maggie Fortune—Colleen Moore
Director—Irving Cummings
Leading Players—Lloyd Hughes, Kate Price, Geno Corrado

THE DESERT FOX (1951, 20th Century Fox)
Erwin Rommel—James Mason
Director—Henry Hathaway
Leading Players—Cedric Hardwicke, Jessica Tandy, Luther Adler, Everett Sloane

THE DESERT HAWK (1950, Universal)
Omar—Richard Greene
Director—Frederick De Cordova
Leading Players—Yvonne De Carlo, Jackie Gleason, George Macready, Carl Esmond

THE DESERT PIRATE (1928, Silent, FBO)
Tom Corrigan—Tom Tyler
Director—James Dugan
Leading Players—Frankie Darro, Duane Thompson, Edward Hearne

THE DESERT RAVEN (1965, Allied Artists)
Raven—Rachel Romen
Director—Alan S. Lee
Leading Players—Rosalind C. Roberts, Robert Terry, Robert Ward

THE DESERT RIDER (1929, Silent, MGM)
Jed Tyler—Tim McCoy
Director—Nick Grinde
Leading Players—Raquel Torres, Bert Roach, Edward Connelly

DESERT WARRIOR (1985, Cinema Group)
Trace—Gary Watkins
Director—Cirio H. Santiago
Leading Players—Laura Banks, Lynda Wiesmeier, Linda Grovenor

DESERTED AT THE ALTAR (1922, Silent, Goldwyn)
Anna Moore—Bessie Love
Directors—William K. Howard and Al Kelley
Leading Players—William Scott, Tully Marshall, Barbara Tennant

DESIGNING WOMAN (1957, MGM)
Marilla Hagen—Lauren Bacall
Director—Vincente Minnelli
Leading Players—Gregory Peck, Dolores Gray, Sam Levene

DESIRABLE (1934, Warner Brothers)
Lois Johnson—Jean Muir
Director—Archie Mayo
Leading Players—George Brent, Veree Teasdale, John Halliday

DESIRE ME (1947, MGM)
Marise Aubert—Greer Garson
Director—Not Credited (George Cukor or Mervyn LeRoy probably)
Leading Players—Robert Mitchum, Richard Hart, Morris Ankrum

DESIREE (1954, 20th Century Fox)
Desiree Clary—Jean Simmons
Director—Henry Koster
Leading Players—Marlon Brando, Merle Oberon, Michael Rennie, Cameron Mitchell

THE DESPERADO (1954, Allied Artists)
Sam Garrett—Wayne Morris
Director—Thomas Carr
Leading Players—James J. Lydon, Beverly Garland, Rayford Baines

THE DESPERADOES (1943, Columbia)
Steve Upton—Randolph Scott
Cheyenne Rogers—Glenn Ford
Director—Charles Vidor
Leading Players—Claire Trevor, Evelyn Keyes, Edgar Buchanan

THE DESPERADOS (1969, Columbia)
Parson Josiah Galt—Jack Palance
Jacob Galt—George Maharis
Director—Henry Levin
Leading Players—Vince Edwards, Neville Brand, Sylvia Sims

A DESPERATE CHANCE FOR ELLERY QUEEN (1942, Columbia)
Ellery Queen—William Gargan
Director—James Hogan
Leading Players—Margaret Lindsay, Charley Grapewin, John Litel

DESPERATE CHARACTERS (1971, Paramount)
Sophie—Shirley Maclaine

Otto—Kenneth Mars
Director—Frank D. Gilroy
Leading Players—Gerald O'Loughlin, Sada Thompson, Jack Somack

THE DESPERATE MAN (1959, GB, Allied Artists)
Smith—William Hartnell
Director—Peter Maxwell
Leading Players—Jill Ireland, Conrad Phillips, Charles Gray

DESPERATELY SEEKING SUSAN (1985, Orion)
Susan—Madonna
Director—Susan Seidelman
Leading Players—Rosanna Arquette, Aidan Quinn, Mack Blum

THE DESPOILER (1915, Silent, Triangle)
Emir—Frank Keenan
Director—Thomas H. Ince
Leading Players—Charles K. French, Enid Markey, Roy Laidlaw

DESTROYER (1988, Moviestore)
Ivan Moser—Lyle Alzado
Director—Robert Kirk
Leading Players—Deborah Freeman, Clayton Rohner, Anthony Perkins

DESTRY (1954, Universal)
Tom Destry, Jr.—Audie Murphy
Director—George Marshall
Leading Players—Mari Blanchard, Lyle Bettger, Lori Nelson, Thomas Mitchell, Edgar Buchanan

DESTRY RIDES AGAIN (1932, Universal)
Tom Destry Jr.—Tom Mix
Director—Ben Stoloff
Leading Players—Claudia Dell, Zasu Pitts, Stanley Fields

DESTRY RIDES AGAIN (1939, Universal)
Tom Destry, Jr.—James Stewart
Director—George Marshall
Leading Players—Marlene Dietrich, Mischa Auer, Charles Winninger, Brian Donlevy, Una Merkel

THE DETECTIVE (1954, GB, Columbia)
Father Brown—Alec Guinness
Director—Robert Hamer
Leading Players—Joan Greenwood, Peter Finch, Cecil Parker, Bernard Lee

THE DETECTIVE (1968, 20th Century Fox)
Joe Leland—Frank Sinatra
Director—Gordon Douglas
Leading Players—Lee Remick, Ralph Meeker, Jack Klugman, Horace McMahon, Lloyd Bochner

DETECTIVE KITTY O'DAY (1944, Monogram)
Kitty O'Day—Jean Parker
Director—William Beaudine
Leading Players—Peter Cookson, Tim Ryan, Veda Ann Borg

DETECTIVE SCHOOL DROP OUTS (1986, Cannon)
Paul—Louis Dreyfuss
Donald—David Landsberg
Director—Philip Ottoni
Leading Players—George Eastman, Christian DeSica, Valeria Golino

DETECTIVE STORY (1951, Paramount)
Jim McLeod—Kirk Douglas
Director—William Wyler
Leading Players—Eleanor Parker, William Bendix, Cathy
O'Donnell, George Macready, Joseph Wiseman

THE DEVIL AND DANIEL WEBSTER (ALL THAT MONEY CAN
BUY) (1941, RKO)
Daniel Webster—Edward Arnold
Mr. Scratch—Walter Huston
Director—William Dieterle
Leading Players—Jane Darwell, James Craig, Simone Simon,
John Qualen, Anne Shirley

THE DEVIL AND MAX DEVLIN (1981, Buena Vista)
Max Devlin—Elliot Gould
Barney Satin—Bill Cosby
Director—Steven Hilliard Stern
Leading Players—Susan Anspach, Adam Rich, Julie Budd

THE DEVIL AND MISS JONES (1941, RKO)
Mary Jones—Jean Arthur
John P. Merrick—Charles Coburn
Director—Sam Wood
Leading Players—Robert Cummings, Edmund Gwenn, Spring
Byington, S.Z. Sakall

DEVIL AND THE DEEP (1932, Paramount)
Cmdr. Charles Sturm—Charles Laughton
Director—Marion Gering
Leading Players—Tallulah Bankhead, Gary Cooper, Cary Grant

DEVIL DOGS OF THE AIR (1935, Warner Brothers)
Tommy O'Toole—James Cagney
Lt. William Brannigan—Pat O'Brien
Director—Lloyd Bacon
Leading Players—Margaret Lindsay, Frank McHugh, Helen
Lowell

DEVIL DOLL (1964, GB, Galaworldfilm)
Hugo Novik—David Charlesworth
Director—Lindsay Shonteff
Leading Players—Bryant Halliday, William Sylvester, Yvonne
Romain

DEVIL GIRL FROM MARS (1954, GB, British Lion)
Nyah—Patricia Laffan
Director—David Macdonald
Leading Players—Hugh McDermott, Hazel Court, Peter
Reynolds

THE DEVIL IS A SISSY (1936, Metro)
Claude—Freddie Bartholomew
Director—W.S. Van Dyke
Leading Players—Jackie Cooper, Mickey Rooney, Ian Hunter,
Peggy Conklin, Katharine Alexander

THE DEVIL IS A WOMAN (1935, Paramount)
Concha Perez—Marlene Dietrich
Director—Josef von Sternberg
Leading Players—Lionel Atwill, Cesar Romero, Edward Everett
Horton, Alison Skipworth

THE DEVIL IS A WOMAN (1975, GB, Fox British)
Sister Geraldine—Glenda Jackson
Director—Damiano Damiani

Leading Players—Claudio Cassinelli, Lisa Harrow, Adolfo Celi

THE DEVIL MAKES THREE (1952, MGM)
Heisemann—Claus Clausen
Director—Andrew Marton
Leading Players—Gene Kelly, Pier Angeli, Richard Rober,
Richard Egan

DEVIL ON HORSEBACK (1954, GB, British Lion)
Moppy Parfitt—Jeremy Spenser
Director—Cyril Frankel
Leading Players—Googie Withers, John McCallum, Meredith
Edwards

THE DEVIL THUMBS A RIDE (1947, RKO)
Steve—Lawrence Tierney
Director—Felix Feist
Leading Players—Ted North, Nan Leslie, Betty Lawford

THE DEVIL WITH HITLER (1942, UA)
The Devil—Alan Mowbray
Adolf Hitler—Bobby Watson
Director—Gordon Douglas
Leading Players—George E. Stone, Joe Devlin, Marjorie
Woodworth

A DEVIL WITH WOMEN (1930, Fox Film Corp.)
Jerry Maxton—Victor McLaglen
Director—Irving Cummings
Leading Players—Mona Maris, Humphrey Bogart, Luana Alcaniz

THE DEVIL'S AGENT (1962, GB, British Lion)
George Droste—Peter Van Eyck
Director—John Paddy Carstairs
Leading Players—Macdonald Carey, Marianne Koch,
Christopher Lee, Billie Whitelaw

THE DEVIL'S BRIDE (1968, GB, Hammer)
Peggy de Richleau—Rosalyn Landor
Director—Terence Fisher
Leading Players—Christopher Lee, Charles Gray, Leon Greene

THE DEVIL'S BROTHER (1933, MGM)
Fra Diavolo/Marquis de San Marco—Dennis King
Director—Charles Rogers
Leading Players—Stan Laurel, Oliver Hardy, Thelma Todd,
James Finlayson

THE DEVIL'S DISCIPLE (1959, UA)
Richard Dudgeon—Kirk Douglas
Director—Guy Hamilton
Leading Players—Burt Lancaster, Laurence Olivier, Janette
Scott, Eva Le Gallienne, Harry Andrews

THE DEVIL'S IN LOVE (1933, Fox Film Corp.)
Lt. Andre Morand—Victor Jory
Director—William Dieterle
Leading Players—Loretta Young, Vivienne Osborne, David
Manners, C. Henry Gordon

THE DEVIL'S MISTRESS (1968, Holiday Films)
Liah—Joan Stapleton
Director—Orville Wanzer
Leading Players—Robert Gregory, Forrest Westmoreland,
Douglas Warren

THE DEVIL'S OWN (1967, GB, Hammer)
Stephanie Bax—Kay Walsh
Director—Cyril Frankel
Leading Players—Joan Fontaine, Alec McCowen, Ann Bell, Ingrid Brett

THE DEVIL'S PARTNER (1958, Huron)
Nick/Pete—Ed Nelson
Director—Charles R. Rondeau
Leading Players—Jean Allison, Edgar Buchanan, Richard Crane

THE DEVIL'S SISTERS (1966, Mustang Productions)
Carmen Alvarado—Velia Martinez
Rita Alvarado—Anita Crystal
Director—William Grefe
Leading Players—Sharon Saxon, Fred Pinero, Ramiro Gomez

THE DEVIL'S WIDOW (1972, GB, British International)
Michaela—Ava Gardner
Director—Roddy McDowall
Leading Players—Ian McShane, Stephanie Beacham, Cyril Cusack

THE DEVONSVILLE TERROR (1983, MPM/New West)
Jenny—Suzanna Love
Director—Ulli Lommel
Leading Players—Donald Pleasance, Deanna Haas, Mary Walden

DIAMOND JIM (1935, Universal)
Diamond Jim Brady—Edward Arnold
Director—Edward Sutherland
Leading Players—Jean Arthur, Binnie Barnes, Cesar Romero

THE DIAMOND QUEEN (1953, Warner Brothers)
Maya—Arlene Dahl
Director—John Brahm
Leading Players—Fernando Lamas, Gilbert Roland, Sheldon Leonard

DIANE (1955, MGM)
Diane de Poitiers—Lana Turner
Director—David Miller
Leading Players—Pedro Armendariz, Roger Moore, Marisa Pavan

DIANE OF STAR HOLLOW (1921, Silent, Producers Security)
Diane Orsini—Evelyn Greeley
Director—Oliver L. Sellers
Leading Players—Bernard Durning, George Majeroni, Fuller Mellish

DIARY OF A BACHELOR (1964, American International)
Skip O'Hara—William Taylor
Director—Sandy Howard
Leading Players—Dagne Crane, Joe Silver, Denise Lor

DIARY OF A CHAMBERMAID (1946, UA)
Celestine—Paulette Goddard
Director—Jean Renoir
Leading Players—Burgess Meredith, Hurd Hatfield, Francis Lederer, Judith Anderson

DIARY OF A HIGH SCHOOL BRIDE (1959, American International)
Judy—Anita Sands
Director—Burt Topper

Leading Players—Ronald Foster, Chris Robinson, Wendy Wilde

DIARY OF A MAD HOUSEWIFE (1970, Universal)
Tina Balser—Carrie Snodgress
Director—Frank Perry
Leading Players—Richard Benjamin, Frank Langella, Lorraine Cullen

DIARY OF A MADMAN (1963, UA)
Simon Cordier—Vincent Price
Director—Reginald Le Berg
Leading Players—Nancy Kovack, Chris Warfield, Elaine Devry

THE DIARY OF ANNE FRANK (1959, 20th Century Fox)
Anne Frank—Millie Perkins
Director—George Stevens
Leading Players—Joseph Schildkraut, Shelley Winters, Richard Beymer, Diane Baker, Lou Jacobi

DICK BARTON AT BAY (1950, GB, Hammer)
Dick Barton—Don Stannard
Director—Godfrey Grayson
Leading Players—Tamara Desni, George Ford, Meinhart Maur

DICK BARTON-SPECIAL AGENT (1948, GB, Hammer)
Dick Barton—Don Stannard
Director—Alfred Goulding
Leading Players—George Ford, Jack Shaw, Gillian Maude

DICK BARTON STRIKES BACK (1949, GB, Exclusive)
Dick Barton—Don Stannard
Director—Godfrey Grayson
Leading Players—Sebastian Cabot, Jean Lodge, James Raglan

DICK TRACY (1945, RKO)
Dick Tracy—Morgan Conway
Director—William Berke
Leading Players—Anne Jeffreys, Mike Mazurki, Jane Greer

DICK TRACY (1990, Buena Vista/Touchstone)
Dick Tracy—Warren Beatty
Director—Warren Beatty
Leading Players—Charlie Korsmo, Glenne Headley, Madonna, Al Pacino, Dustin Hoffman, William Forsythe, Charles Durning, Mandy Patinkin, Paul Sorvino

DICK TRACY MEETS GRUESOME (1947, RKO)
Dick Tracy—Ralph Byrd
Gruesome—Boris Karloff
Director—John Rawlins
Leading Players—Anne Gwynne, Edward Ashley, June Clayworth

DICK TRACY VS. CUEBALL (1946, RKO)
Dick Tracy—Morgan Conway
Cueball—Dick Wessel
Director—Gordon M. Douglas
Leading Players—Anne Jeffreys, Lyle Latell, Rita Corday

DICK TRACY'S DILEMMA (1947, RKO)
Dick Tracy—Ralph Byrd
Director—John Rawlins
Leading Players—Kay Christopher, Lyle Latell, Jack Lambert

DICK TURPIN (1925, Silent, Fox Film Corp.)
Dick Turpin—Tom Mix

Director—John G. Blystone
Leading Players—Kathleen Myers, Philo McCullough, James Marcus

DICK TURPIN (1933, GB, Gaumont)
Dick Turpin—Victor McLaglen
Director—John Stafford
Leading Players—Jane Carr, Frank Vosper, James Finlayson

THE DICTATOR (1922, Silent, Paramount)
Brook Travers—Wallace Reid
Director—James Cruze
Leading Players—Theodore Kosloff, Lila Lee, Kalla Pasha

DID YOU HEAR THE ONE ABOUT THE TRAVELING SALESLADY? (1968, Universal)
Agatha Knabehshu—Phyllis Diller
Director—Don Weis
Leading Players—Bob Denver, Joe Flynn, Eileen Wesson

DIE, DIE, MY DARLING (1965, GB, Hammer)
Pat Carroll—Stefanie Powers
Director—Silvio Narizzano
Leading Players—Tallulah Bankhead, Peter Vaughan, Maurice Kaufmann

DIE HARD (1988, 20th Century Fox)
John McClane—Bruce Willis
Director—John McTiernan
Leading Players—Bonnie Bedelia, Alexander Godunov, Alan Rickman

DIE HARD 2 (1990, 20th Century Fox/Gordon Co./Silver)
John McClane—Bruce Willis
Director—Renny Harlin
Leading Players—Bonnie Bedelia, William Atherton, Reginald VelJohnson, Franco Nero, William Sadler, John Amos

DIE SCREAMING, MARIANNE (1970, GB, London Screen)
Marianne—Susan George
Director—Pete Walker
Leading Players—Barry Evans, Christopher Sandford, Judy Huxtable

DILLINGER (1945, Monogram)
John Dillinger—Lawrence Tierney
Director—Max Nosseck
Leading Players—Edmund Lowe, Anne Jeffreys, Eduardo Ciannelli, Elisha Cook, Jr.

DILLINGER (1973, American International)
John Dillinger—Warren Oates
Director—John Milius
Leading Players—Ben Johnson, Michelle Phillips, Cloris Leachman, Harry Dean Stanton

DIMPLES (1916, Silent, Metro)
Dimples—Mary Miles Minter
Director—Edgar Jones
Leading Players—William Cowper, John J. Donough, Thomas J. Carrigan

DIMPLES (1936, 20th Century Fox)
Sylvia Dolores Appleby (Dimples)—Shirley Temple
Director—William A. Seiter
Leading Players—Frank Morgan, Helen West, Robert Kent

DING DONG WILLIAMS (1946, RKO)
Ding Dong Williams—Glenn Vernon
Director—William Berke
Leading Players—Marcy McGuire, Felix Bressart, Anne Jeffreys

DINKY (1935, Warner Brothers)
Dinky Daniels—Jackie Cooper
Directors—D. Ross Lederman and Howard Bretherton
Leading Players—Mary Astor, Roger Pryor, Henry Armetta

DINO (1957, Allied Artists)
Dino—Sal Mineo
Director—Thomas Carr
Leading Players—Brian Keith, Susan Kohner, Frank Faylen

DINTY (1920, Silent, First National)
Dinty—Wesley Barry
Director—Marshall Neilan
Leading Players—Colleen Moore, Tom Gallery, J. Barney Sherry

DIPLOMATIC COURIER (1952, 20th Century Fox)
Mike Kells—Tyrone Power
Director—Henry Hathaway
Leading Players—Patricia Neal, Stephen McNally, Hildegarde Neff, Karl Malden

THE DIRT BIKE KID (1985, Cinema Group)
Jack Simmons—Peter Billingsley
Director—Hoite C. Caston
Leading Players—Stuart Pankin, Anne Bloom, Patrick Collins

DIRTY DINGUS MAGEE (1970, MGM)
Dingus Magee—Frank Sinatra
Director—Burt Kennedy
Leading Players—George Kennedy, Anne Jackson, Lois Nettleton

THE DIRTY DOZEN (1967, GB, MGM)
Joseph Wladislaw—Charles Bronson
Robert Jefferson—Jim Brown
Victor Franko—John Cassavetes
Pedro Jiminez—Trini Lopez
Archer Maggott—Telly Savalas
Vernon Pinkey—Donald Sutherland
Samson Posey—Clint Walker
Milo Vladek—Tom Busby
Glenn Gilpin—Ben Carruthers
Roscoe Lever—Stuart Cooper
Seth Sawyer—Colin Maitland
Tassos Bravos—Al Mancini
Director—Robert Aldrich
Leading Players—Lee Marvin, Ernest Borgnine, Robert Ryan

DIRTY HARRY (1971, Warner Brothers)
Harry Callahan—Clint Eastwood
Director—Don Siegel
Leading Players—Reni Santoni, Harry Guardino, Andy Robinson

DIRTY LITTLE BILLY (1972, Columbia)
Billy Bonney—Michael J. Pollard
Director—Stan Dragoti
Leading Players—Lee Purcell, Richard Evans, Charles Aidman

DIRTY MARY, CRAZY LARRY (1974, 20th Century Fox)
Larry—Peter Fonda
Mary—Susan George

Director—John Hough
Leading Players—Adam Roarke, Vic Morrow, Fred Daniels

DIRTY O'NEIL (1974, American International)
Jimmy O'Neil—Morgan Paull
Director—Howard Freen
Leading Players—Art Metrano, Pat Anderson, Jean Manson

DIRTY ROTTEN SCOUNDRELS (1988, Orion)
Lawrence Jamison—Michael Caine
Freddy Benson—Steve Martin
Director—Frank Oz
Leading Players—Glenne Headly, Anton Rodgers, Barbara Harris

DIRTYMOUTH (1970, Superior)
Lenny Bruce—Bernie Travers
Director—Herbert S. Altman
Leading Players—Courtney Sherman, Wynn Irwin, Harry Spilman

DISBARRED (1939, Paramount)
Tyler Cradon—Otto Kruger
Director—Robert Florey
Leading Players—Gil Patrick, Robert Preston, Sidney Toler

DISC JOCKEY (1951, Allied Artists)
Mike Richards—Michael O'Shea
Director—Will Jason
Leading Players—Ginny Simms, Tom Drake, Jane Nigh

DISHONORED (1931, Paramount)
X-27—Marlene Dietrich
Director—Josef von Sternberg
Leading Players—Victor McLaglen, Lew Cody, Gutav von Seyffertitz, Warner Oland

DISHONORED LADY (1947, UA)
Madeleine Damien—Hedy Lamarr
Director—Robert Stevenson
Leading Players—Dennis O'Keefe, John Loder, William Lundigan

DISORDERLIES (1987, Warner Brothers)
Kool Rock—Damon Wimbley
Buffy—Darren Robinson
Markie—Mark Morales
Director—Michael Schultz
Leading Players—Ralph Bellamy, Tony Plana, Anthony Geary

THE DISORDERLY ORDERLY (1964, Paramount)
Jerome Littlefield—Jerry Lewis
Director—Frank Tashlin
Leading Players—Glenda Farrell, Everett Sloane, Karen Sharpe

A DISPATCH FROM REUTERS (1940, Warner Brothers)
Julius Reuter—Edward G. Robinson
Director—William Dieterle
Leading Players—Edna Best, Eddie Albert, Albert Basserman

DISRAELI (1929, Warner Brothers)
Benjamin Disraeli—George Arliss
Director—Alfred E. Green
Leading Players—Joan Bennett, Florence Arliss, Anthony Bushnell, David Torrence

DISTURBED (1990, Live/Odyssey)
Dr. Russell—Malcolm McDowell
Director—Charles Winkler
Leading Players—Geoffrey Lewis, Priscilla Pointer, Pamela Gidley

THE DIVINE WOMAN (1928, Silent, MGM)
Marianne—Greta Garbo
Director—Victor Seastrom
Leading Players—Lars Hansen, Lowell Sherman, Polly Moran

THE DIVORCE OF LADY X (1938, GB, London Films)
Lady Mere—Binie Barnes
Director—Tim Whelan
Leading Players—Merle Oberon, Laurence Olivier, Ralph Richardson

THE DIVORCEE (1930, MGM)
Jerry—Norma Shearer
Director—Robert Z. Leonard
Leading Players—Chester Morris, Conrad Nagel, Robert Montgomery, Florence Eldridge

DIXIANA (1930, RKO)
Dixiana—Bebe Daniels
Director—Luther Reed
Leading Players—Everett Marshall, Bert Wheeler, Robert Woolsey

DIXIE DUGAN (1943, 20th Century Fox)
Dixie Dugan—Lois Andrews
Director—Otto Brower
Leading Players—James Ellison, Charlotte Greenwood, Charlie Ruggles

D.O.A. (1988, Buena Vista)
Dexter Cornell—Dennis Quaid
Directors—Rocky Morton & Annabel Jankel
Leading Players—Meg Ryan, Charlotte Rampling, Daniel Stern

DOC (1971, UA)
Doc Holliday—Stacy Keach
Director—Frank Perry
Leading Players—Faye Dunaway, Harris Yulin, Mike Witney

DOC HOLLYWOOD (1991, Warner Brothers)
Ben Stone—Michael J. Fox
Director—Michael Caton-Jones
Leading Players—Julie Warner, Barnard Hughes, Woody Harrelson, David Ogden Stiers, Frances Sternhagen, George Hamilton, Bridget Fonda

DOC SAVAGE . . . THE MAN OF BRONZE (1975, Warner Brothers)
Doc Savage—Ron Ely
Director—Michael Anderson
Leading Players—Paul Gleason, Michael Miller, Eldon Quick

THE DOCTOR (1991, Buena Vista/Touchstone)
Dr. Jack McKee—William Hurt
Director—Randa Haines
Leading Players—Christine Lahti, Elizabeth Perkins, Wendy Crewson, Mandy Patinkin, Adam Arkin, Charley Korsmo

DOCTOR ALIEN (1989, Phantom)
Ms. Xenobia—Judy Landers

Director—David DeCoteau
Leading Players—Billy Jacoby, Olivia Barash, Stuart Fratkin

THE DOCTOR AND THE DEVILS (1985, GB, 20th Century Fox)
Dr. Thomas Rock—Timothy Dalton
Director—Freddie Francis
Leading Players—Jonathan Pryce, Twiggy, Julian Sands

THE DOCTOR AND THE GIRL (1949, MGM)
Dr. Michael Corday—Glenn Ford
Evelyn Heldon—Janet Leigh
Director—Curtis Bernhardt
Leading Players—Charles Coburn, Gloria De Haven, Bruce
Bennett

DOCTOR AT LARGE (1957, GB, Rank)
Simon Sparrow—Dirk Bogarde
Director—Ralph Thomas
Leading Players—Muriel Pavlow, Donald Sinden, James
Robertson Justice, Shirley Eaton

DOCTOR AT SEA (1955, GB, Rank)
Simon Sparrow—Dirk Bogarde
Director—Ralph Thomas
Leading Players—Brigitte Bardot, Brenda De Banzie, James
Robertson Justice, Maurice Denham

DR. BLACK AND MR. HYDE (1976, Dimension)
Dr. Black/Mr. Hyde—Bernie Casey
Director—William Crain
Leading Players—Rosalind Cash, Marie O'Henry, Ji-Tu
Cumbuka

DR. BLOOD'S COFFIN (1961, UA)
Dr. Peter Blood—Kieron Moore
Director—Sidney J. Furie
Leading Players—Hazel Court, Ian Hunter, Fred Johnson

DR. BROADWAY (1942, Paramount)
Dr. Timothy Kane—Macdonald Carey
Director—Anthony Mann
Leading Players—Jean Phillips, J. Carroll Naish, Eduardo
Ciannelli

DR. BULL (1933, Fox Film Corp.)
Dr. Bull—Will Rogers
Director—John Ford
Leading Players—Vera Allen, Marian Nixon, Howard Lally

DR. CHRISTIAN MEETS THE WOMEN (1940, RKO)
Dr. Paul Christian—Jean Hersholt
Director—William McGann
Leading Players—Dorothy Lovett, Edgar Kennedy, Rod
LaRocque

DR. COPPELIUS (1968, Gala)
Dr. Coppelius—Walter Slezak
Director—Ted Kneeland
Leading Players—Claudia Corday, Caj Selling, Eileen Elliott

DR. CRIPPEN (1963, GB, Pathe)
Dr. Hawley Harvey Crippen—Donald Pleasance
Director—Robert Lynn
Leading Players—Coral Browne, Samantha Eggar, James
Robertson Justice

DR. CYCLOPS (1940, Paramount)
Dr. Thorkell—Albert Dekker
Director—Ernest B. Schoedsack
Leading Players—Janice Logan, Thomas Coley, Charles Halton

DOCTOR DEATH: SEEKER OF SOULS (1973, Cinerama)
Dr. Death—John Considine
Director—Eddie Saeta
Leading Players—Barry Coe, Cheryll Miller, Stewart Moss

DOCTOR DETROIT (1983, Universal)
Clifford Skirdlow—Dan Aykroyd
Director—Michael Pressman
Leading Players—Howard Hesseman, Donna Dixon, Kate
Murtagh

DOCTOR DOOLITTLE (1967, 20th Century Fox)
Dr. John Doolittle—Rex Harrison
Director—Richard Fleischer
Leading Players—Anthony Newley, Peter Bull, William Dix

DR. EHRLICH'S MAGIC BULLET (1940, Warner Brothers)
Dr. Paul Ehrlich—Edward G. Robinson
Director—William Dieterle
Leading Players—Ruth Gordon, Otto Kruger, Donald Crisp

DOCTOR FAUSTUS (1967, GB, Columbia)
Dr. Faustus—Richard Burton
Directors—Richard Burton & Nevill Coghill
Leading Players—Elizabeth Taylor, Andreas Teuber, Ian Marter

DR. FRANKENSTEIN ON CAMPUS (1970, Canada, Agincourt-
Glen Warren)
Viktor Frankenstein—Robin Ward
Director—Gilbert W. Taylor
Leading Players—Kathleen Sawyer, Austin Willis, Sean Sullivan

DR. GILLESPIE'S CRIMINAL CASE (1943, MGM)
Dr. Leonard Gillespie—Lionel Barrymore
Director—Willis Goldbeck
Leading Players—Van Johnson, Donna Reed, Keye Luke, John
Craven

DR. GILLESPIE'S NEW ASSISTANT (1942, MGM)
Dr. Leonard Gillespie—Lionel Barrymore
Dr. Randall Adams—Van Johnson
Director—Willis Goldbeck
Leading Players—Susan Peters, Richard Quine, Keye Luke

DR. GOLDFOOT AND THE BIKINI MACHINE (1965, American
International)
Dr. Goldfoot—Vincent Price
Director—Norman Taurog
Leading Players—Frankie Avalon, Dwayne Hickman, Susan Hart

DR. GOLDFOOT AND THE GIRL BOMBS (1966, American
International)
Dr. Goldfoot—Vincent Price
Director—Mario Bava
Leading Players—Fabian, Franco Franchi, Ciccio Ingrassia

DR. HACKENSTEIN (1988, Vista Street)
Dr. Elliott Hackenstein—David Muir
Director—Richard Clark
Leading Players—Stacey Travis, Catherine Davis Cox, Dyanne
Di Rosario

DR. HECKYL AND MR. HYPE (1980, Cannon)
Dr. Heckyl/Mr. Hype—Oliver Reed
Director—Charles B. Griffith
Leading Players—Sunny Johnson, Maia Danzinger, Mel Welles

DOCTOR IN DISTRESS (1963, GB, Rank)
Simon Sparrow—Dirk Bogarde
Director—Ralph Thomas
Leading Players—Samantha Eggar, James Robertson Justice, Mylene Demongeot, Donald Houston

DOCTOR IN LOVE (1960, GB, Rank)
Dr. Richard Hare—Michael Craig
Director—Ralph Thomas
Leading Players—James Robertson Justice, Virginia Maskell, Carole Lesley

DOCTOR IN THE HOUSE (1954, GB, GFD)
Simon Sparrow—Dirk Bogarde
Director—Ralph Thomas
Leading Players—Muriel Pavlow, Kenneth More, Donald Sinden, James Robertson Justice, Donald Houston

DOCTOR IN TROUBLE (1970, GB, Rank)
Dr. Burke—Leslie Phillips
Director—Ralph Thomas
Leading Players—Harry Secombe, James Robertson Justice, Angela Scoular, Irene Handl

DOCTOR JACK (1922, Silent, Hal Roach)
Dr. Jack—Harold Lloyd
Director—Fred Newmeyer
Leading Players—Mildred Davis, John T. Prince, Eric Mayne

DR. JEKYLL AND MR. HYDE (1920, Silent, Paramount)
Dr. Jekyll/Mr. Hyde—John Barrymore
Director—John S. Robertson
Leading Players—Martha Mansfield, Brandon Hurst, Charles Lane

DR. JEKYLL AND MR. HYDE (1932, Paramount)
Dr. Henry Jekyll/Mr. Hyde—Fredric March
Director—Rouben Mamoulian
Leading Players—Miriam Hopkins, Rose Hobart, Holmes Herbert

DR. JEKYLL AND MR. HYDE (1941, MGM)
Dr. Harry Jekyl/Mr. Hyde—Spencer Tracy
Director—Victor Fleming
Leading Players—Ingrid Bergman, Lana Turner, Donald Crisp

DR. JEKYLL AND SISTER HYDE (1971, GB, Hammer)
Dr. Jekyll—Ralph Bates
Sister Hyde—Martine Beswick
Director—Roy Ward Baker
Leading Players—Gerald Sim, Lewis Flander, Dorothy Alison

DR. JEKYLL'S DUNGEON OF DEATH (1982, New American)
Dr. Jekyll—James Mathers
Director—James Wood
Leading Players—John Kearney, Tom Nicholson, Dawn Carver

DR. JIM (1921, Silent, Universal)
Dr. Jim Keene—Frank Mayo
Director—William Worthington

Leading Players—Claire Windsor, Oliver Cross, Stanhope Wheatcroft

DR. JOSSER KC (1931, GB, Pathe)
Jimmy Josser—Ernie Lotinga
Director—Norman Lee
Leading Players—Jack Hobbs, Molly Lamont, Joan Wyndham

DR. KILDARE GOES HOME (1940, MGM)
Dr. James Kildare—Lew Ayres
Director—Harold S. Bucquet
Leading Players—Lionel Barrymore, Laraine Day, Samuel S. Hinds, Gene Lockhart

DR. KILDARE'S CRISIS (1940, MGM)
Dr. James Kildare—Lew Ayres
Director—Harold S. Bucquet
Leading Players—Robert Young, Lionel Barrymore, Laraine Day, Emma Dunn, Nat Pendleton

DR. KILDARE'S STRANGEST CASE (1940, MGM)
Dr. James Kildare—Lew Ayres
Director—Harold S. Bucquet
Leading Players—Lionel Barrymore, Laraine Day, Shepperd Strudwick, Samuel S. Hinds

DR. KILDARE'S VICTORY (1941, MGM)
Dr. James Kildare—Lew Ayres
Director—W.S. Van Dyke II
Leading Players—Lionel Barrymore, Robert Sterling, Ann Ayars

DR. KILDARE'S WEDDING DAY (1941, MGM)
Dr. James Kildare—Lew Ayres
Director—Harold S. Bucquet
Leading Players—Lionel Barrymore, Laraine Day, Red Skelton, Fay Holden

DOCTOR MONICA (1934, Warner Brothers)
Dr. Monica Braden—Kay Francis
Director—William Keighley
Leading Players—Warren William, Jean Muir, Verree Teasdale

DR. MORELLE—THE CASE OF THE MISSING HEIRESS (1949, Great Britain Exclusive)
Dr. Morelle—Valentine Dyall
Director—Godfrey Grayson
Leading Players—Julia Lang, Philip Leaver, Jean Lodge

DR. NO (1962, GB, UA)
Dr. No—Joseph Wiseman
Director—Terence Young
Leading Players—Sean Connery, Jack Lord, Ursula Andress, Zena Marshall, John Kitzmiller

DR. O'DOWD (1940, GB, Warner Brothers)
Marius O'Dowd—Shaun Glenville
Director—Herbert Mason
Leading Players—Peggy Cummins, Mary Merrall, Liam Gaffney

DOCTOR PHIBES RISES AGAIN (1972, GB, American Internat.)
Dr. Anton Phibes—Vincent Price
Director—Robert Fuest
Leading Players—Robert Quarry, Valli Kemp, Hugh Griffith

DR. RENAULT'S SECRET (1942, 20th Century Fox)
Dr. Renault—George Zucco

Director—Harry Lachman
Leading Players—J. Carroll Naish, John Shepperd, Lynne Roberts

DR. RHYTHM (1938, Paramount)
Dr. Remsen—Bing Crosby
Director—Frank Tuttle
Leading Players—Mary Carlisle, Beatrice Lillie, Andy Devine

DR. SIN FANG (1937, GB, MGM)
Dr. Sin Fang—H. Agar Lyons
Director—Tony Frenguelli
Leading Players—Anne Grey, Robert Hobbs, George Mozart

DR. SOCRATES (1935, Warner Brothers)
Dr. Caldwell—Paul Muni
Director—William Dieterle
Leading Players—Ann Dvorak, Barton MacLane, Raymond Brown

DR. STRANGELOVE: OR HOW I LEARNED TO STOP WORRYING AND LOVE THE BOMB
(1964, Columbia)
Dr. Strangelove—Peter Sellers
Director—Stanley Kubrick
Leading Players—George C. Scott, Sterling Hayden, Keenan Wynn, Slim Pickens, Peter Bull

DOCTOR SYN (1937, GB, Gaumont)
Dr. Syn—George Arliss
Director—Roy William Neill
Leading Players—John Loder, Margaret Lockwood, Roy Emerton

DR. SYN, ALIAS THE SCARECROW (1975, Disney)
Dr. Syn—Patrick McGoohan
Director—James Neilson
Leading Players—Tony Britton, George Cole, Michael Hordern

DOCTOR TAKES A WIFE (1940, Columbia)
Dr. Timothy Sterling—Ray Milland
June Cameron—Loretta Young
Director—Alexander Hall
Leading Players—Reginald Gardiner, Gail Patrick, Edmund Gwenn

DR. TERROR'S HOUSE OF HORRORS (1965, GB, Amicus)
Dr. Schreck—Peter Cushing
Director—Freddie Francis
Leading Players—Christopher Lee, Roy Castle, Donald Sutherland, Neil McCallum

DR. WHO AND THE DALEKS (1965, GB, Aaru)
Dr. Who—Peter Cushing
Director—Gordon Flemyng
Leading Players—Roy Castle, Jennie Linden, Roberta Tovey

DOCTOR X (1932, Warner Brothers)
Doctor Xavier—Lionel Atwill
Director—Michael Curtiz
Leading Players—Lee Tracy, Fay Wray, Preston Foster

DOCTOR ZHIVAGO (1965, MGM)
Yuri Zhivago—Omar Shariff
Director—David Lean
Leading Players—Geraldine Chaplin, Julie Christie, Tom Courtenay, Alec Guinness, Ralph Richardson, Rod Steiger

A DOCTOR'S DIARY (1937, Paramount)
Dr. Clem Driscoll—George Bancroft
Director—Charles Vidor
Leading Players—Helen Burgess, John Trent, Ruth Coleman

THE DOCTOR'S DILEMMA (1958, GB, MGM)
Dr. Blenkenson—Michael Gwynn
Director—Anthony Asquith
Leading Players—Leslie Caron, Dirk Bogarde, Alastair Sim, Robert Morley, John Robinson

DOCTOR'S SECRET (1929, Paramount)
Dr. Brodie—Robert Edeson
Director—William C. De Mille
Leading Players—Ruth Chatterton, H.B. Warner, John Loder

DOCTORS' WIVES (1931, Fox Film Corp.)
Dr. Judson Penning—Warner Baxter
Nina Wyndham—Joan Bennett
Director—Frank Borzage
Leading Players—Victor Varconi, Helene Millard, Paul Porcasi

DOCTORS' WIVES (1971, Columbia)
Lorrie Dellman—Dyan Cannon
Mort Dellman—John Colicos
Note: There are any number of other doctors and wives in this film. Cannon and Colicos are chosen as repesentative because she gets top billing, and he's her medical spouse.
Director—George Schaefer
Leading Players—Richard Crenna, Gene Hackman, Carroll O'Connor, Rachel Roberts, Janice Rule, Diana Sands, Cara Williams

DODSWORTH (1936, UA)
Sam Dodsworth—Walter Huston
Director—William Wyler
Leading Players—Ruth Chatterton, Paul Lukas, Mary Astor, David Niven

DOGS OF WAR (1980, GB, UA)
Shannon—Christopher Walken
Drew—Tom Berenger
Director—John Irvin
Leading Players—Colin Blakely, Hugh Millais, Paul Freeman

DOIN' TIME ON PLANET EARTH (1989, Cannon)
Ryan Richmond—Nicholas Strouse
Director—Charles Matthau
Leading Players—Hugh Gillin, Gloria Henry, Hugh O'Brien, Adam West, Candice Azzara

DOLL FACE (1945, 20th Century Fox)
Doll Face—Vivian Blaine
Director—Lewis Seller
Leading Players—Dennis O'Keefe, Perry Como, Carmen Miranda

THE DOLLY SISTERS (1945, 20th Century Fox)
Jenny Dolly—Betty Grable
Rosie Dolly—June Haver
Director—Irving Cummings
Leading Players—John Payne, S.Z. Sakall, Reginald Gardiner

DOLLY'S VACATION (1918, Silent, Pathe)
Dolly McKenzie—Baby Marie Osborne
Director—William Bertram
Leading Players—Jack Connolly, Bob Gray, Little Sambo

DOMENICK AND EUGENE (1988, Orion)
Domenick Luciano—Tom Hulce
Eugene Luciano—Ray Liotta
Director—Robert M. Young
Leading Players—Jamie Lee Curtis, Todd Graff, Bill Cobbs, Mimi Cecchini

DOMINIQUE (1978, GB, Subotsky)
Dominique Ballard—Jean Simmons
Director—Michael Anderson
Leading Players—Cliff Robertson, Ron Moody, Jenny Agutter

DOMINO KID (1957, Columbia)
Domino—Rory Calhoun
Director—Ray Nazarro
Leading Players—Kristine Miller, Andrew Duggan, Yvette Dugay

DON CHICAGO (1945, GB, British National)
Don Chicago—Jackie Hunter
Director—MacLean Rogers
Leading Players—Eddie Gray, Joyce Heron, Claud Allister

THE DON IS DEAD (1973, Universal)
Don Aggimio Bernardo—J. Duke Russo
Director—Richard Fleischer
Leading Players—Anthony Quinn, Frederic Forrest, Robert Forster, Al Lettieri, Charles Cioffi

DON JUAN (1926, Silent, Warner Brothers)
Don Juan—John Barrymore
Director—Alan Crosland
Leading Players—Mary Astor, Willard Louis, Estelle Taylor, Helene Costello, Myrna Loy

DON JUAN QUILLIGAN (1945, 20th Century Fox)
Patrick Quilligan—William Bendix
Director—Frank Tuttle
Leading Players—Joan Blondell, Phil Silvers, Anne Revere

DON MIKE (1927, Silent, FBO)
Don Miguel Arguello—Fred Thompson
Director—Lloyd Ingraham
Leading Players—Ruth Cliffoer, Noah Young, Albert Prisco

DON Q, SON OF ZORRO (1925, Silent, UA)
Don Cesar de Vega/Zorro—Douglas Fairbanks
Director—Donald Crisp
Leading Players—Mary Astor, Donald Crisp, Stella de Lanti, Warner Oland

DON QUIXOTE (1923, GB, Silent, Stoll)
Don Quixote—Jerrold Robertshaw
Director—Maurice Elvey
Leading Players—George Robey, Bertram Burleigh, Sydney Fairbrother

DON X (1925, Silent, Steen/Goodman)
Don X/Frank Blair—Bruce Gordon
Director—Forrest Sheldon
Leading Players—Josephine Hill, Boris Bullock, Victor Allen

DONDI (1961, Allied Artists)
Dondi—David Kory
Director—Albert Zugsmith

Leading Players—David Janssen, Patti Page, Walter Winchell

THE DONOVAN AFFAIR (1929, Columbia)
Jack Donovan—John Roche
Director—Frank Capra
Leading Players—Jack Holt, Dorothy Revier, William Collier

DONOVAN'S BRAIN (1953, UA)
Tom Donovan—Michael Colgan
Director—Felix Feist
Leading Players—Lew Ayres, Gene Evans, Nancy Davis, Steve Brodie

DONOVAN'S REEF (1963, Paramount)
Guns Donovan—John Wayne
Director—John Ford
Leading Players—Lee Marvin, Elizabeth Allen, Jack Warden, Dorothy Lamour, Cesar Romero

DON'S PARTY (1976, Australia, Double Head Productions)
Don—John Hargreaves
Director—Bruce Beresford
Leading Players—Ray Barrett, Claire Binney, Pat Bishop

DON'T CALL ME LITTLE GIRL (1921, Silent, Realart)
Jerry—Mary Miles Minter
Director—Joseph Henabery
Leading Players—Winifred Greenwood, Ruth Stonehouse, Jerome Patrick

DON'T TELL HER IT'S ME (1990, Hemdale)
Gus Kubiek—Steve Guttenberg
Emily Pear—Jami Gertz
Director—Malcolm Mowbray
Leading Players—Shelley Long, Kyle MacLachlan, Kevin Scannell

DON'T TELL MOM THE BABYSITTER'S DEAD (1991, Warner Brothers)
Mrs. Crandall—Concetta Tomei
Lil Stuark—Eda Reiss Merin
Director—Stephen Herek
Leading Players—Christina Applegate, Joanna Cassidy, John Getz, Josh Charles, David Duchovny, Kimmy Robertson, Keith Coogan, Robert Hy Corman

DON'T TELL THE WIFE (1937, RKO)
Nancy Dorset—Una Merkel
Director—Christy Cabanne
Leading Players—Guy Kibbee, Lynne Overman, Thurston Hall

THE DOOLINS OF OKLAHOMA (1949, Columbia)
Bill Doolin—Randolph Scott
Director—Gordon Douglas
Leading Players—George Macready, Louise Allbritton, John Ireland, Virginia Huston

THE DOORS (1991, Tri-Star)
Jim Morrison—Val Kilmer
John Densmore—Kevin Dillon
Ray Manzarek—Kyle MacLachlan
Robby Krieger—Frank Whaley
Director—Oliver Stone
Leading Players—Meg Ryan, Mitchel Madsen, Kathleen Quinlan, Michael Wincott, Kristina Fulton, Crispin Glover

THE DOUBLE LIFE OF MR. ALFRED BURTON (1919, GB, Silent Ideal)
Alfred Burton—Kenelm Foss
Director—Arthur Rooke
Leading Players—Ivy Duke, Elaine Madison, Joe Peterman

THE DOUBLE MAN (1967, Warner Brothers)
Dan Slater/Kalmar—Yul Brynner
Director—Franklin J. Schaffner
Leading Players—Britt Ekland, Clive Revill, Anton Diffring

DOUBLE TROUBLE (1992, MPCA)
Peter—Peter Paul
David—David Paul
Director—John Paragon
Leading Players—Roddy McDowall, Steve Kanaly, James Doohan, A.J. Johnson, Bill Mumy, Troy Donahue

DOUBLE IMPACT (1991, Columbia)
Chad/Alex—Jean Claude Van Damme
Director—Sheldon Lettich
Leading Players—Geoffrey Lewis, Alan Scarfe, Alonna Shaw, Philip Chan Yan Lin, Corey Everson, Bolo Yeung

DOUBLING FOR ROMEO (1921, Silent, Goldwyn)
Sam/Romeo—Will Rogers
Director—Clarence Badger
Leading Players—Sylvia Breamer, Raymond Hatton, Sydney Ainsworth

DOUBTING THOMAS (1935, 20th Century Fox)
Thomas Brown—Will Rogers
Director—David Butler
Leading Players—Billie Burke, Alison Skipworth, Sterling Holloway

THE DOUGHGIRLS (1944, Warner Brothers)
Edna—Ann Sheridan
Nan—Alexis Smith
Vivian—Jane Wyman
Director—James V. Kern
Leading Players—Jack Carson, Irene Manning, Charles Ruggles, Eve Arden

DOWN AND OUT IN BEVERLY HILLS (1986, Touchstone)
Jerry Baskin—Nick Nolte
Director—Paul Mazursky
Leading Players—Richard Dreyfuss, Bette Midler, Little Richard, Tracy Nelson

DOWNHILL RACER (1969, Paramount)
Davis Chappellet—Robert Redford
Director—Michael Ritchie
Leading Players—Gene Hackman, Camilla Sparv, Karl Michael Volger, Jim McMullan

DRACULA (1931, Universal)
Count Dracula—Bela Lugosi
Director—Tod Browning
Leading Players—Helen Chandler, David Manners, Dwight Frye, Edward Van Sloan

DRACULA (1979, Universal)
Count Dracula—Frank Langella
Director—John Badham
Leading Players—Laurence Olivier, Donald Pleasence, Kate Nelligan, Trevor Eve, Jan Francis

DRACULA A.D. 1972 (1972, GB, Hammer)
Count Dracula—Christopher Lee
Director—Alan Gibson
Leading Players—Peter Cushing, Stephanie Beacham, Christopher Neame, Michael Coles

DRACULA HAS RISEN FROM HIS GRAVE (1968, GB, Hammer)
Count Dracula—Christopher Lee
Director—Freddie Francis
Leading Players—Rupert Davies, Veronica Carlson, Barbara Ewing

DRACULA—PRINCE OF DARKNESS (1966, GB, Hammer)
Count Dracula—Christopher Lee
Director—Terence Fisher
Leading Players—Barbara Shelley, Andrew Keir, Francis Matthews

DRACULA'S DAUGHTER (1936, Universal)
Countess Marya Zaleska—Gloria Holden
Director—Lambert Hillyer
Leading Players—Otto Kruger, Marguerite Churchill, Irving Pichel, Edward Van Sloan

DRACULA'S WIDOW (1988, DEG)
Vanessa—Sylvia Kristel
Director—Christopher Coppola
Leading Players—Josef Sommer, Lenny Von Dohlen, Marc Coppola

DRAGONSLAYER (1981, Disney/Paramount)
Galen—Peter McNichol
Director—Matthew Robbins
Leading Players—Caitlan Clarke, Ralph Richardson, Peter Eyre

DRAKE THE PIRATE (1935, GB, Wardour)
Francis Drake—Matheson Lang
Director—Arthur Woods
Leading Players—Athene Seyler, Jane Baxter, Harry Mollison

DRANGO (1957, UA)
Drango—Jeff Chandler
Director—Hall Bartlett
Leading Players—John Lupton, Joanne Dru, Morris Ankrum

THE DRAUGHTSMAN'S CONTRACT (1983, GB, UA)
Mr. Nelville—Anthony Higgins
Director—Peter Greenaway
Leading Players—Janet Suzman, Anne Louise Lambert, Hugh Fraser, Neil Cunningham

DREAM GIRL (1947, Paramount)
Georgina Allerton—Betty Hutton
Director—Mitchell Leisen
Leading Players—Macdonald Carey, Patric Knowles, Virginia Field, Walter Abel

DREAM LOVER (1986, MGM/UA)
Kathy Gardner—Kristy McNichol
Director—Alan J. Pakula
Leading Players—Ben Masters, Paul Shenar, Justin Deas

THE DREAM MAKER (1963, GB, British Lion)
Billy Bowles—Tommy Steele
Director—Don Sharp
Leading Players—Michael Medwin, Angela Douglas, Jean Harvey

THE DREAM TEAM (1989, Universal)
Billy Caulfield—Michael Keaton
Henry Sikorsky—Christopher Lloyd
Jack McDermott—Peter Boyle
Albert Ianuzzi—Stephen Furst
Director—Howard Zieff
Leading Players—Dennis Boutsikaris, Lorraine Bracco, Milo O'Shea

DREAM WIFE (1953, MGM)
Tarji—Betta St. John
Director—Sidney Sheldon
Leading Players—Cary Grant, Deborah Kerr, Walter Pidgeon, Eduard Franz

DREAMCHILD (1985, GB, Universal)
Alice Liddell Hargreaves—Coral Browne
Director—Gavin Miller
Leading Players—Ian Holm, Peter Gallagher, Nicola Cowper

DREAMER (1979, 20th Century Fox)
Dreamer—Tim Matheson
Director—Noel Nosseck
Leading Players—Susan Blakely, Jack Warden, Richard B. Shull

DRESSED TO KILL (1946, Universal)
Hilda Courtney—Patrica Morison
Director—Roy William Neill
Leading Players—Basil Rathbone, Nigel Bruce, Edmond Breon

DRESSED TO KILL (1980, Filmways)
Dr. Robert Elliott—Michael Caine
Director—Brian De Palma
Leading Players—Nancy Allen, Angie Dickinson, Keith Gordon

DRESSED TO THRILL (1935, Fox Film Corp.)
Colette Dubois/Nadia Petrova—Tutta Rolf
Director—Harry Lachman
Leading Players—Clive Brook, Nydia Westman, George Hassell

THE DRESSER (1983, Columbia)
Norman—Tom Courtenay
Director—Peter Yates
Leading Players—Albert Finney, Edward Fox, Zena Walker

THE DREYFUS CASE (1931, GB, Columbia)
Alfred Dreyfus—Cedric Hardwicke
Director—F. W. Kraemer
Leading Players—Charles Carson, George Merritt, Sam Livesey, Beatrix Thomson, Garry Marsh

THE DRIFTER (1932, State Rights)
The Drifter—William Farnum
Director—William O'Connor
Leading Players—Noah Beery, Phyllis Barrington, Charles Sellon

THE DRIFTER (1944, Producers Releasing Corp.)
Billy Carson/Drifter Davis—Buster Crabbe
Director—Sam Newfield
Leading Players—Al "Fuzzy" St. John, Carol Parker, Kermit Maynard

THE DRIFTER (1966, Surfilms)
Alan—John Tracy
Director—Alex Matter
Leading Players—Sadja Marr, Michael Fair, Lew Skinner

THE DRIFTER (1988, Concorde)
Trey—Miles O'Keeffe
Director—Larry Brand
Leading Players—Kim Delaney, Timothy Bottoms, Al Shannon

THE DRIVER (1978, 20th Century Fox)
The Driver—Ryan O'Neal
Director—Walter Hill
Leading Players—Bruce Dern, Isabelle Adjani, Ronee Blakley

DRIVING FORCE (1990, Australia, J&M/Eastern)
Steve O'Neil—Sam J. Jones
Director—A.J. Prowse
Leading Players—Catherine Bach, Don Swayze, Ancel Cook, Stephanie Mason, Billy Blanks

DRIVING MISS DAISY (1989, Warner Brothers)
Miss Daisy Werthan—Jessica Tandy
Hoke Colburn—Morgan Freeman
Director—Bruce Beresford
Leading Players—Dan Aykroyd, Patti LuPone, Esther Rolle

DROP DEAD FRED (1991, New Line)
Drop Dead Fred—Rik Mayall
Director—Ate DeJong
Leading Players—Phoebe Cates, Marsha Mason, Tim Matheson, Carrie Fisher, Keith Charles

DRUGSTORE COWBOY (1989, Avenue)
Bob—Matt Dillon
Director—Gus Van Sant, Jr.
Leading Players—Kelly Lynch, James Le Gros, Heather Graham

DRUM (1976, UA)
Drum—Ken Norton
Director—Steve Carver
Leading Players—Warren Oates, Isela Vega, Pamela Grier, Yaphet Kotto

DRUMS OF FU MANCHU (1943, Republic)
Fu Manchu—Henry Brandon
Director—William Witney and John English
Leading Players—William Royle, Robert Kellard, Gloria Franklin

DU BARRY WAS A LADY (1943, MGM)
Mme. Du Barry—Lucille Ball
Director—Roy Del Ruth
Leading Players—Red Skelton, Gene Kelly, Douglas Dumbrille

DU BARRY, WOMAN OF PASSION (1930, UA)
Jeanette Vaubernier/Mme. Du Barry—Norma Talmadge
Director—Sam Taylor
Leading Players—William Farnum, Hobart Bosworth, Conrad Nagel

THE DUCHESS AND THE DIRTWATER FOX (1976, 20th Century Fox)
Charlie Malloy—George Segal

Amanda Quaid—Goldie Hawn
Director—Melvin Frank
Leading Players—Conrad Janis, Thayer David, Jennifer Lee

THE DUCHESS OF IDAHO (1950, MGM)
Christine Riverton Duncan—Esther Williams
Director—Robert Z. Leonard
Leading Players—Van Johnson, John Lund, Paula Raymond

THE DUDE COWBOY (1926, Silent, Independent Pictures)
Bob Ralston—Bob Custer
Director—Jack Nelson
Leading Players—Flora Bramley, Billy Bletcher, Howard Truesdell

THE DUDE GOES WEST (1948, Allied Artists)
Daniel Bone—Eddie Albert
Director—Kurt Neumann
Leading Players—Gale Storm, James Gleason, Binnie Barnes, Gilbert Roland

THE DUDE RANGER (1934, Fox Film Corp.)
Ernest Selby—George O'Brien
Director—Edward F. Cline
Leading Players—Irene Hervey, Leroy Mason, Henry Hall

THE DUDE WRANGLER (1930, Independent)
Tom Keene—George Duryea
Director—Richard Thorpe
Leading Players—Lina Basquette, Clyde Cook, Francis X. Bushman

DUDES (1987, New Century-Vista)
Grant—Jon Cryer
Biscuit—Daniel Roebuck
Milo—Flea (Michael Balzary)
Director—Penelope Spheeris
Leading Players—Lee Ving, Catherine Mary Stewart, Billy Ray Sharkey

THE DUELLISTS (1977, GB, Paramount)
D'Hubert—Keith Carradine
Feraud—Harvey Keitel
Director—Ridley Scott
Leading Players—Albert Finney, Edward Fox, Cristina Raines

DUFFY (1968, GB, Columbia)
Duffy—James Coburn
Director—Robert Parrish
Leading Players—James Mason, James Fox, Susannah York

DUFFY OF SAN QUENTIN (1954, Warner Brothers)
Warden Clinton T. Duffy—Paul Kelly
Director—Walter Doniger
Leading Players—Louis Hayward, Joanne Dru, Maureen O'Sullivan, George Macready

DUGAN OF THE BAD LANDS (1931, Monogram)
Bill Dugan—Bill Cody
Director—Robert N. Bradbury
Leading Players—Andy Shuford, Blanche Mehaffey, Ethan Laidlaw

THE DUKE COMES BACK (1937, Republic)
Duke—Allan Lane
Director—Irving Pichel

Leading Players—Heather Angel, Genevieve Tobin, Frederick Burton

THE DUKE IS TOPS (1938, Million Dollar)
Duke Davis—Ralph Cooper
Director—William Nolte
Leading Players—Lena Horne, Lawrence Criner, Monte Hawley

DUKE OF CHICAGO (1949, Republic)
Jimmy Brody—Tom Brown
Director—George Blair
Leading Players—Audrey Long, Grant Withers, Paul Harvey

DUKE OF THE NAVY (1942, Producers Releasing Corp.)
"Breeze" Duke—Ralph Byrd
Director—William Beaudine
Leading Players—Veda Ann Borg, Stubby Kruger, Herbert Corthell

THE DUKE OF WEST POINT (1938, UA)
Steven Early—Louis Hayward
Director—Alfred E. Green
Leading Players—Joan Fontaine, Tom Brown, Richard Carlson

THE DUKE STEPS OUT (1929, Silent, MGM)
Duke—William Haines
Director—James Cruze
Leading Players—Joan Crawford, Karl Dane, Tenen Holtz

THE DUKE WORE JEANS (1958, GB, Anglo Amalgamated)
Tony Whitecliffe/Tommy Hudson—Tommy Steele
Director—Gerald Thomas
Leading Players—June Laverick, Michael Medwin, Eric Pohlmann

DULCIMA (1971, GB, EMI)
Dulcima Gaskain—Carol White
Director—Frank Nesbitt
Leading Players—John Mills, Stuart Wilson, Bernard Lee

DULCY (1940, MGM)
Dulcy Ward—Ann Sothern
Director—S. Sylvan Simon
Leading Players—Ian Hunter, Roland Young, Reginald Gardiner

DUMB GIRL OF PORTICI (1916, Silent, Universal)
Fenella—Anna Pavlova
Directors—Lois Weber & Phillips Smalley
Leading Players—Rupert Julian, Wendworth Harris, Douglas Gerrard

THE DUMMY (1929, Paramount)
Barney—Mickey Bennett
Director—Robert Milton
Leading Players—Ruth Chatterton, Fredric March, John Cromwell, Jack Oakie, Zasu Pitts

THE DUPE (1916, Silent, Lasky)
Ethel Hale—Blanche Sweet
Director—Frank Reicher
Leading Players—Ernest Joy, Verda McEvers, Thomas Meighan

THE DURANGO KID (1940, Columbia)
Bill Lowery/Durango Kid—Charles Starrett
Director—Lambert Hillyer

Leading Players—Luana Walker, Kenneth MacDonald, Francis Walker

DUTCH (1991, 20th Century Fox)
Dutch—Ed O'Neill
Director—Peter Faiman
Leading Players—Ethan Randall, Jo Beth Williams, Christopher McDonald, Art Meyers

DYING YOUNG (1991, 20th Century Fox)
Victor Geddes—Campbell Scott
Director—Joel Schumacher
Leading Players—Julia Roberts, Vincent D'Onofrio, Colleen Dewhurst, David Shelby, Ellen Burstyn

DYNAMITE DAN (1924, Silent, Sunset)
Dan—Kenneth McDonald
Director—Bruce Mitchell
Leading Players—Frank Rice, Boris Karloff, Eddie Harris

E

EACH DAWN I DIE (1939, First National/Warner Brothers)
Frank Ross—James Cagney
Director—William Keighley
Leading Players—George Raft, Jane Bryan, George Bancroft, Maxie Rosenbloom, Stanley Ridges

EADIE WAS A LADY (1945, Columbia)
Eadie Allen/Edithea Alden—Ann Miller
Director—Arthur Dreifuss
Leading Players—Joe Besser, William Wright, Jeff Donnell

THE EAGLE AND THE HAWK (1933, Paramount)
Jerry Young—Frederic March
Henry Crocker—Cary Grant
Director—Stuart Walker
Leading Players—Jack Oakie, Carole Lombard, Guy Standing

THE EAGLE AND THE HAWK (1950, Paramount)
Todd Croyden—John Payne
Whitney Randolph—Dennis O'Keefe
Director—Lewis R. Foster
Leading Players—Rhonda Fleming, Thomas Gomez, Fred Clark

EAGLE IN A CAGE (1971, National General Pictures)
Napoleon Bonaparte—Kenneth Haigh
Director—Fiedler Cook
Leading Players—John Gielgud, Ralph Richardson, Billie Whitelaw, Moses Gunn

EARL CARROLL'S VANITIES (1945, Republic)
Earl Carroll—Otto Kruger
Director—Joseph Santley
Leading Players—Dennis O'Keefe, Constance Moore, Eve Arden, Alan Mowbray

THE EARL OF CHICAGO (1940, MGM)
Silky Kilmount—Robert Montgomery

Director—Richard Thorpe
Leading Players—Edward Arnold, Reginald Owen, Edmund Gwenn, E.E. Clive, Norma Varden

THE EARLY BIRD (1965, GB, Rank)
Norman Pitkin—Norman Wisdom
Director—Robert Asher
Leading Players—Edward Chapman, Jerry Desmonde, Paddie O'Neill

EARTH GIRLS ARE EASY (1989, Vestron)
Valerie Dale—Geena Davis
Director—Julien Temple
Leading Players—Jeff Goldblum, Julie Brown, Jim Carrey, Damon Wayans

THE EARTHLING (1980, Filmways-Roadshow)
Patrick Foley—William Holden
Director—Peter Collinson
Leading Players—Ricky Schroder, Jack Thompson, Olivia Hamnett

EASY RIDER (1969, Columbia)
Wyatt—Peter Fonda
Director—Dennis Hopper
Leading Players—Dennis Hopper, Antonio Mendoza, Jack Nicholson, Karen Black, Robert Walker, Jr.

EASY TO LOOK AT (1945, Universal)
Judy—Gloria Jean
Director—Ford Beebe
Leading Players—Kirby Grant, George Dolenz, J. Edward Bromberg

EASY TO LOVE (1934, Warner Brothers)
Carol—Genevieve Tobin
Director—William Keighley
Leading Players—Adolphe Menjou, Mary Astor, Guy Kibbee, Edward Everett Horton

EASY TO LOVE (1953, MGM)
Julie Hallerton—Esther Williams
Director—Charles Walters
Leading Players—Van Johnson, Tony Martin, John Bromfield

EATING RAOUL (1982, 20th Century Fox)
Raoul—Robert Beltran
Director—Paul Bartel
Leading Players—Mary Woronov, Paul Bartel, Buck Henry

EDDIE AND THE CRUISERS (1983, Aurora)
Eddie—Michael Pare
Director—Martin Davidson
Leading Players—Tom Berenger, Joe Pantoliano, Matthew Laurance, Helen Schneider

EDDIE AND THE CRUISERS II: EDDIE LIVES (1989, Scotti)
Eddie Wilson/Joe West—Michael Pare
Director—Jean-Claude Lord
Leading Players—Marina Orsini, Bernie Coulson, Matthew Laurance

THE EDDIE CANTOR STORY (1953, Warner Brothers)
Eddie Cantor—Keefe Brasselle
Director—Alfred E. Green

Leading Players—Marilyn Erskine, Aline MacMahon, Arthur Franz

EDDIE MACON'S RUN (1983, Universal)
Eddie Macon—John Schneider
Director—Jeff Kanew
Leading Players—Kirk Douglas, Lee Purcell, Leah Ayres

THE EDDY DUCHIN STORY (1956, Columbia)
Eddy Duchin—Tyrone Power
Director—George Sidney
Leading Players—Kim Novak, Victoria Shaw, James Whitmore

EDISON, THE MAN (1940, MGM)
Thomas Alva Edison—Spencer Tracy
Director—Clarence Brown
Leading Players—Rita Johnson, Lynne Overman, Charles Coburn, Gene Lockhart, Henry Travers

EDUCATED EVANS (1936, GB, Warner Brothers/First National)
Evans—Max Miller
Director—William Beaudine
Leading Players—Nancy O'Neil, Clarice Mayne, Albert Whelan

EDUCATING FATHER (1936, 20th Century Fox)
John Jones—Jed Prouty
Director—James Tinling
Leading Players—Shirley Deane, Dixie Dunbar, Spring Byington

EDUCATING RITA (1983, Columbia)
Rita—Julie Walters
Director—Lewis Gilbert
Leading Players—Michael Caine, Michael Williams, Maureen Lipman, Jeananne Crowley, Malcolm Douglas

THE EDUCATION OF SONNY CARSON (1974, Paramount)
Sonny Carson—Rony Clanton
Director—Michael Campus
Leading Players—Don Gordon, Joyce Walker, Paul Benjamin

EDWARD, MY SON (1949, MGM)
Arnold Boult—Spencer Tracy
Director—George Cukor
Leading Players—Deborah Kerr, Ian Hunter, James Donald, Leueen McGrath, Mervyn Johns

EDWARD SCISSORHANDS (1990, 20th Century Fox)
Edward Scissorhands—Johnny Depp
Director—Tim Burton
Leading Players—Winona Ryder, Dianne Wiest, Anthony Michael Hall, Alan Arkin, Kathy Baker, Robert Oliver, Conchata Ferrell, Vincent Price

THE EGG AND I (1947, Universal)
Betty MacDonald—Claudette Colbert
Director—Chester Erskine
Leading Players—Fred MacMurray, Marjorie Main, Louise Allbritton, Percy Kilbride

EGGHEAD'S ROBOT (1970, GB, Interfilm)
Egghead Wentworth—Keith Chegwin
Director—Milo Lewis
Leading Players—Jeffrey Chegwin, Kathryn Dawe, Roy Kinnear

THE EGYPTIAN (1954, 20th Century Fox)
Sinuhe—Edmond Purdom
Director—Michael Curtiz
Leading Players—Jean Simmons, Victor Mature, Gene Tierney, Michael Wilding, Bella Darvi

EIGHT MEN OUT (1988, Orion)
Buck Weaver—John Cusack
Hap Felsch—Charlie Sheen
Shoeless Joe Jackson—D.B. Sweeney
Ed Cicotte—David Strathairn
Chick Gandil—Michael Rooker
Note: The other three Black Sox players banned from baseball for life were Lefty Williams, Swede Risberg and Fred McMullin. They were not featured prominently in this film. They were portrayed by James Read, Don Harvey, and Perry Lang, respectively.
Director—John Sayles
Leading Players—Clifton James, Michael Lerner, John Mahoney, Studs Terkel, Christopher Lloyd

EIGHTEEN AGAIN (1988, New World)
Jack Watson—George Burns
Director—Paul Flaherty
Leading Players—Charles Schlatter, Tony Roberts, Anita Morris, Red Buttons

EIGHTEEN AND ANXIOUS (1957, Republic)
Judy—Mary Webster
Director—Joe Parker
Leading Players—William Campbell, Martha Scott, Jackie Loughery, Jim Backus

80 STEPS TO JONAH (1969, Warner Brothers)
Mark Jonah Winters—Wayne Newton
Director—Gerd Oswald
Leading Players—Jo Van Fleet, Keenan Wynn, Diana Ewing

EL CID (1961, Allied Artists)
Rodrigo Diaz de Bivar (El Cid)—Charlton Heston
Director—Anthony Mann
Leading Players—Sophia Loren, John Fraser, Raf Vallone, Genevieve Page

EL GRECO (1966, 20th Century Fox)
El Greco—Mel Ferrer
Director—Luciano Salce
Leading Players—Rosanna Schiaffino, Franco Giacobini, Adolfo Celi, Angel Aranda

THE ELDER BROTHER (1937, GB, Paramount)
Ronald Bellairs—John Stuart
Director—Frederick Hayward
Leading Players—Marjorie Taylor, Basil Langton, Stella Bonheur

THE ELECTIC HORSEMAN (1979, Columbia/Universal)
Sonny Steele—Robert Redford
Director—Sidney Pollack
Leading Players—Jane Fonda, Valerie Perrine, Willie Nelson

ELENI (1985, Warner Brothers)
Eleni—Kate Nelligan
Director—Peter Yates
Leading Players—John Malkovich, Linda Hunt, Oliver Cotton

ELEPHANT BOY (1937, GB, UA)
Toomai—Sabu

Directors—Robert Flaherty & Zoltan Korda
Leading Players—Walter Hudd, Allan Jeayes, W.E. Holloway

THE ELEPHANT MAN (1980, GB, Paramount)
John Merrick—John Hurt
Director—David Lynch
Leading Players—Anthony Hopkins, Anne Bancroft, John Gielgud, Wendy Hiller

ELINOR NORTON (1935, Fox Film Corp.)
Elinor Norton—Claire Trevor
Director—Hamilton MacFadden
Leading Players—Gilbert Roland, Henrietta Crosman, Hugh Williams

ELIZA COMES TO STAY (1936, GB, Twickenham)
Eliza Vandan—Betty Balfour
Director—Henry Edwards
Leading Players—Seymour Hicks, Oscar Asche, Ellis Jeffreys

ELIZA FRASER (1976, Australia, Hexagon)
Eliza Fraser—Susannah York
Director—Tim Burstall
Leading Players—John Castle, Gerard Kennedy, Vicki Bray

ELIZABETH OF LADYMEAD (1949, GB, British Lion)
Beth/Elizabeth/Betty/Liz—Anna Neagle
Director—Herbert Wilcox
Leading Players—Hugh Williams, Bernard Lee, Isabel Jeans

ELIZA'S HOROSCOPE (1975, Canada, O-Zali)
Eliza—Elizabeth Moorman
Director—Gordon Sheppard
Leading Players—Tommy Lee Jones, Lila Kedrova, Rose Quong

ELLERY QUEEN AND THE MURDER RING (1941, Columbia)
Ellery Queen—Ralph Bellamy
Director—James Hogan
Leading Players—Margaret Lindsay, Charley Grapewin, Mona Barrie, Paul Hurst

ELLERY QUEEN AND THE PERFECT CRIME (1941, Columbia)
Ellery Queen—Ralph Bellamy
Director—James Hogan
Leading Players—Margaret Lindsay, Charley Grapewin, Spring Byington, H.B. Warner

ELLERY QUEEN, MASTER DETECTIVE (1940, Columbia)
Ellery Queen—Ralph Bellamy
Director—Kurt Neumann
Leading Players—Margaret Lindsay, Charley Grapewin, James Burke, Michael Whalen

ELLERY QUEEN'S PENTHOUSE MYSTERY (1941, Columbia)
Ellery Queen—Ralph Bellamy
Director—James Hogan
Leading Players—Margaret Lindsay, Charley Grapewin, Anna May Wong, Eduardo Ciannelli

ELLIE (1984, Film Ventures)
Ellie—Sheila Kennedy
Director—Peter Wittman
Leading Players—Shelley Winters, Edward Albert, Pat Paulsen

ELLIOTT FAUMAN PH.D. (1990, Taurus)
Elliott Fauman—Randy Dreyfuss

Director—Ric Klass
Leading Players—Jean Kasem, Tamara Williams, Shelley Berman

ELMER AND ELSIE (1934, Paramount)
Elmer Beebe—George Bancroft
Elsie Beebe—Frances Fuller
Director—Gilbert Pratt
Leading Players—Roscoe Karns, George Barbier, Nella Walker

ELMER GANTRY (1960, UA)
Elmer Gantry—Burt Lancaster
Director—Richard Brooks
Leading Players—Jean Simmons, Arthur Kennedy, Shirley Jones, Dean Jagger, Patti Page, Edward Andrews

ELMER THE GREAT (1933, Warner Brothers/First National)
Elmer—Joe E. Brown
Director—Mervyn LeRoy
Leading Players—Patricia Ellis, Frank McHugh, Claire Dodd

ELVIRA: MISTRESS OF DARKNESS (1988, New World)
Elvira—Cassandra Peterson
Director—James Signorelli
Leading Players—Edie McClurg, Pat Crawford Brown, William Duell

EMANON (1987, Paul Ent.)
Emanon—Stuart Paul
Director—Stuart Paul
Leading Players—Cheryl M. Lynn, Patrick Wright, Jeremy Miller

THE EMBEZZLER (1954, GB, GFD)
Henry Paulson—Charles Victor
Director—John Gilling
Leading Players—Zena Marshall, Cyril Chamberlain, Leslie Weston

EMIL (1938, GB, Gaumont)
Emil Blake—John Williams
Director—Milton Rosner
Leading Players—George Hayes, Mary Glynne, Clare Greet

EMIL AND THE DETECTIVES (1964, Buena Vista)
Emil—Bryan Russell
Director—Peter Tewksbury
Leading Players—Walter Slezak, Heinz Schubert, Cindy Cassel

EMILY (1976, GB, Emily)
Emily—Koo Stark
Director—Henry Herbert
Leading Players—Sarah Brackett, Victor Spinetti, Jane Hayden

EMMA (1932, MGM)
Emma Thatcher—Marie Dressler
Director—Clarence Brown
Leading Players—Richard Cromwell, Jean Hersholt, Myrna Loy

EMMA MAE (1976, Pro-International)
Emma Mae—Jerri Hayes
Director—James Fanaka
Leading Players—Ernest Williams II, Charles David Brooks, Eddie Allen

THE EMPEROR JONES (1933, UA)
Brutus Jones—Paul Robeson

Director—Dudley Murphy
Leading Players—Dudley Digges, Frank Wilson, Fred Washington, Ruby Elzy

EMPEROR OF THE NORTH POLE (1973, 20th Century Fox)
A No. 1—Lee Marvin
Director—Robert Aldrich
Leading Players—Ernest Borgnine, Keith Carradine, Charles Tyner

THE EMPEROR WALTZ (1948, Paramount)
Emperor Franz Josef—Richard Haydn
Director—Billy Wilder
Leading Players—Bing Crosby, Joan Fontaine, Roland Culver

ENCINO MAN (1992, Hollywood Pictures)
Link—Brendan Fraser
Director—Les Mayfield
Leading Players—Sean Astin, Pauly Short, Megan Ward, Robert Tunney

ENEMIES, A LOVE STORY (1989, 20th Century Fox)
Herman—Ron Silver
Tamara—Anjelica Huston
Yadwiga—Margaret Sophie Stein
Masha—Lena Olin
Director—Paul Mazursky
Leading Players—Alan King, Judith Malina, Rita Karin

ENEMY AGENT (1940, Universal)
Jimmy Saunders—Richard Cromwell
Director—Lew Landers
Leading Players—Helen Vinson, Robert Armstrong, Marjorie Reynolds, Jack Arnold

ENEMY AGENT MEETS ELLERY QUEEN (1942, Columbia)
Ellery Queen—William Gargan
Mrs. Van Dorn—Gale Sondergaard
Director—James Hogan
Leading Players—Margaret Lindsay, Charley Grapewin, Sig Ruman, Gilbert Roland

THE ENEMY BELOW (1957, 20th Century Fox)
Von Stolberg—Curt Jurgens
Director—Dick Powell
Leading Players—Robert Mitchum, Al Hedison, Theodore Bikel

THE ENEMY GENERAL (1960, Columbia)
General Burger—John Van Dreelen
Director—George Sherman
Leading Players—Van Johnson, Jean-Pierre Aumont, Dany Carrel

ENEMY MINE (1985, 20th Century Fox)
Davidge—Dennis Quaid
The Drac—Louis Gossett, Jr.
Director—Wolfgang Petersen
Leading Players—Brion James, Richard Marcus, Carolyn McCormick

AN ENEMY OF THE PEOPLE (1978, Warner Brothers)
Dr. Thomas Stockmann—Steve McQueen
Director—George Schaefer
Leading Players—Charles Durning, Bibi Andersson, Eric Christmas

ENEMY OF THE POLICE (1933, GB, Warner Brothers/First National)
John Meakin—John Stuart
Director—George King
Leading Players—Viola Keats, A. Bromley Davenport, Margaret Yarde

ENEMY OF WOMEN (1944, Monogram)
Paul Joseph Goebbels—Paul Andor
Director—Alfred Zeisler
Leading Players—Claudia Drake, Donald Woods, H.B. Warner

THE ENFORCER (1951, Warner Brothers)
Albert Mendoza—Everett Sloane
Director—Bretaigne Windust
Leading Players—Humphrey Bogart, Zero Mostel, Ted De Corsia, King Donovan

THE ENFORCER (1976, Malpaso/Warner Brothers)
Harry Callahan—Clint Eastwood
Director—James Fargo
Leading Players—Tyne Daly, Bradford Dillman, Harry Guardino, DeVeren Brookwalter

ENGLAND MADE ME (1973, GB, Cine Globe)
Anthony Farrant—Michael York
Director—Peter Duffell
Leading Players—Peter Finch, Hildegard Neil, Michael Hordern

ENID IS SLEEPING (1990, Vestron/Davis)
Enid—Maureen Mueller
Director—Maurice Phillips
Leading Players—Elizabeth Perkins, Judge Reinhold, Jeffrey Jones, Rhea Perlman

ENSIGN PULVER (1964, Warner Brothers)
Ensign Frank Pulver—Robert Walker, Jr.
Director—Joshua Logan
Leading Players—Burl Ives, Walter Matthau, Tommy Sands, Millie Perkins, Kay Medford

ENTER ARSENE LUPIN (1944, Universal)
Arsene Lupin—Charles Korvin
Director—Ford Beebe
Leading Players—Ella Raines, J. Carrol Naish, George Dolenz

ENTER INSPECTOR DUVAL (1961, GB, Columbia)
Inspector Duval—Anton Diffring
Director—Max Varnel
Leading Players—Diane Hart, Mark Singleton, Charles Mitchell

ENTER MADAME (1935, Paramount)
Lisa Della Robbia—Elissa Landi
Director—Elliott Nugent
Leading Players—Cary Grant, Lynne Overman, Sharon Lynne

ENTER THE NINJA (1982, Cannon)
Cole—Franco Nero
Director—Menahem Golan
Leading Players—Susan George, Sho Kosugi, Alex Courtney

THE ENTERTAINER (1960, GB, British Lion)
Archie Rice—Laurence Olivier
Director—Tony Richardson
Leading Players—Brenda de Banzie, Joan Plowright, Roger Livesey, Alan Bates, Daniel Massey

THE ENTERTAINER (1975, Seven Keys)
Archie Rice—Jack Lemmon
Director—Donald Wrye
Leading Players—Ray Bolger, Sada Thompson, Tyne Daly, Michael Cristofer

ENTERTAINING MR. SLOANE (1970, GB, Warner Brothers/Pathe)
Mr. Sloane—Peter McErney
Director—Douglas Hickox
Leading Players—Beryl Reid, Harry Andrews, Alan Webb

ERASERHEAD (1978, AFI/Libra)
Henry Spencer—John Nance
Director—David Lynch
Leading Players—Charlotte Stewart, Allen Joseph, Jeanne Bates

ERIK THE VIKING (1989, Orion, GB)
Erik—Tim Robbins
Director—Terry Jones
Leading Players—Gary Cady, Mickey Rooney, Eartha Kitt, Imogen Stubbs, John Cleese

ERNEST GOES TO CAMP (1987, Buena Vista)
Ernest P. Worrell—Jim Varney
Director—John R. Cherry III
Leading Players—Victoria Racimo, John Vernon, Iron Eyes Cody

ERNEST GOES TO JAIL (1990, Buena Vista/Touchstone)
Ernest P. Worrell—Jim Varney
Director—John Cherry
Leading Players—Gailard Sartain, Bill Byrge, Barbara Bush, Barry Scott, Randall (Tex) Cobb

ERNEST SAVES CHRISTMAS (1988, Touchstone)
Ernest P. Worrell—Jim Varney
Director—John R. Cherry III
Leading Players—Douglas Seale, Oliver Clark, Noelle Parker

ERNEST SCARED STUPID (1991, Touchstone)
Ernest P. Worrell—Jim Varney
Director—John Cherry
Leading Players—Eartha Kitt, Austin Nagler, Shay Astar, James Moscartolo, John Cadenhead, Bill Bryce

THE ERRAND BOY (1961, Paramount)
Morty S. Tashman—Jerry Lewis
Director—Jerry Lewis
Leading Players—Brian Donlevy, Dick Wesson, Howard McNear, Felicia Atkins

THE ESCAPE ARTIST (1982, Orion-Warner Brothers)
Danny Masters—Griffin O'Neal
Director—Caleb Deschanel
Leading Players—Raul Julia, Dezi Arnaz, Terri Garr, Joan Hackett

ESCAPE ME NEVER (1935, GB, UA)
Gemma Jones—Elisabeth Bergner
Director—Paul Czinner
Leading Players—Hugh Sinclair, Griffith Jones, Penelope Dudley-Ward

ESCAPE ME NEVER (1947, Warner Brothers)
Gemma Smith—Ida Lupino
Director—Peter Godfrey
Leading Players—Errol Flynn, Eleanor Parker, Gig Young

ESCORT FOR HIRE (1960, GB, MGM)
Steve—Noel Trevarthan
Director—Godfrey Grayson
Leading Players—June Thorburn, Peter Murray, Jan Holden

ESPIONAGE AGENT (1939, Warner Brothers)
Brenda Ballard—Brenda Marshall
Director—Lloyd Bacon
Leading Players—Joel McCrea, Jeffrey Lynn, George Bancroft

ESTHER AND THE KING (1960, 20th Century Fox)
Esther—Joan Collins
King Ahasuerus—Richard Egan
Director—Raoul Walsh
Leading Players—Dennis O'Dea, Sergio Fantoni, Rik Battaglia

ESTHER WATERS (1948, GB, Rank/GFD)
Esther Waters—Kathleen Ryan
Director—Peter Proud
Leading Players—Dirk Bogarde, Cyril Cusack, Ivor Barnard

THE ETERNAL FEMININE (1931, GB, Paramount)
Yvonne de la Roche—Doris March
Director—Arthur Varney
Leading Players—Guy Newall, Jill Esmond Moore, Garry Marsh

EVANGELINE (1929, UA)
Evangeline—Dolores Del Rio
Director—Edwin Carewe
Leading Players—Roland Drew, Alec B. Francis, Donald Reed

EVE (1968, GB, Commonwealth)
Eve—Celeste Yarnall
Director—Jeremy Summers
Leading Players—Robert Walker, Jr., Herbert Lom, Fred Clark

EVE KNEW HER APPLES (1945, Columbia)
Eve Porter—Ann Miller
Director—Will Jason
Leading Players—William Wright, Robert Williams, Ray Walker

EVEL KNIEVEL (1971, Fanfare)
Evel Knievel—George Hamilton
Director—Martin Chomsky
Leading Players—Sue Lyon, Bert Freed, Rod Cameron, Dub Taylor

EVELYN PRENTICE (1934, MGM)
Evelyn Prentice—Myrna Loy
Director—William K. Howard
Leading Players—William Powell, Una Merkel, Harvey Stephens

EVERY LITTLE CROOK AND NANNY (1972, MGM)
Miss Poole—Lynn Redgrave
Carmine Ganucci—Victor Mature
Director—Cy Howard
Leading Players—Paul Sand, Maggie Byle, Austin Pendleton

EVERY TIME WE SAY GOODBYE (1986, Tri-Star)
David—Tom Hanks
Sarah—Cristina Marsillach
Director—Moshe Mizrahi
Leading Players—Benedict Taylor, Anat Atzmon, Gila Almagor

EVERBODY'S ALL AMERICAN (1988, Warner Brothers)
Gavin "Grey Ghost" Grey—Dennis Quaid
Director—Taylor Hackford
Leading Players—Jessica Lange, Timothy Hutton, John
Goodman, Patricia Clarkson

EVERYBODY'S OLD MAN (1936, 20th Century Fox)
William Franklin—Irvin S. Cobb
Director—James Flood
Leading Players—Rochelle Hudson, Johnny Downs, Norman
Foster, Alan Dinehart

EVERYTHING'S ROSIE (1931, Radio Pictures)
Rosie—Anita Louise
Director—Clyde Bruckman
Leading Players—Robert Woolsey, John Darrow, Florence
Roberts

THE EVIL OF FRANKENSTEIN (1964, GB, Hammer/Universal)
Baron Frankenstein—Peter Cushing
Director—Freddie Francis
Leading Players—Peter Woodthorpe, Sandor Eles, Kiwi Kingston

EX-BAD BOY (1931, Universal)
Chester Binney—Robert Armstrong
Director—Vin Moore
Leading Players—Jean Arthur, Jason Robards, Spencer Charters

EX-CHAMP (1939, Universal)
Gunner Grey—Victor McLaglen
Director—Phil Rosen
Leading Players—Tom Brown, Nan Grey, William Frawley

EX-FLAME (1931, Tiffany)
Lady Catherine Austin—Marian Nixon
Director—Victor Halperin
Leading Players—Neil Hamilton, Norman Kerry, Judith Barrie

EX-LADY (1933, Warner Brothers)
Helen Bauer—Bette Davis
Director—Robert Florey
Leading Players—Gene Raymond, Frank McHugh, Monroe
Owsley

THE EX-MRS. BRADFORD (1936, RKO)
Paula Bradford—Jean Arthur
Director—Stephen Roberts
Leading Players—William Powell, James Gleason, Eric Blore,
Robert Armstrong

EXCUSE MY DUST (1951, MGM)
Joe Belden—Red Skelton
Director—Roy Rowland
Leading Players—Sally Forrest, Macdonald Carey, William
Demarest, Monica Lewis

EXCUSE MY GLOVE (1936, GB, ABF)
Don Carter—Len Harvey
Director—Redd Davis
Leading Players—Archie Pitt, Betty Ann Davies, Olive Blakeney

THE EXECUTIONER (1970, GB, Columbia)
John Shay—George Peppard
Director—Sam Wanamaker
Leading Players—Joan Collins, Judy Geeson, Oscar Homolka,
Charles Gray, Keith Michell

THE EXILE (1947, Universal)
Charles Stuart—Douglas Fairbanks, Jr.
Director—Max Ophuls
Leading Players—Maria Montez, Henry Daniell, Nigel Bruce,
Paula Corday, Robert Coote

THE EXORCIST (1973, Warner Brothers)
Father Merrin—Max Von Sydow
Director—William Friedkin
Leading Players—Ellyn Burstyn, Jason Miller, Lee J. Cobb,
Linda Blair, Jack McGowran

EXORCIST II: THE HERETIC (1977, Warner Brothers)
Father Lamont—Richard Burton
Director—John Boorman
Leading Players—Linda Blair, Louise Fletcher, Max Von Sydow,
Kitty Winn, Paul Henreid

THE EXORCIST III (1990, 20th Century Fox)
Father Morning—Nicol Williamson
Director—William Peter Blatty
Leading Players—George C. Scott, Ed Flanders, Brad Dourif,
Jason Miller, Scott Wilson, Nancy Fish

THE EXPERT (1932, Warner Brothers)
Grandpa Minick—Charles "Chic" Sale
Director—Archie Mayo
Leading Players—Dickie Moore, Lois Wilson, Earle Foxe

THE EXPERTS (1989, Paramount)
Travis—John Travolta
Wendell—Arye Gross
Director—Dave Thomas
Leading Players—Kelly Preston, Deborah Foreman, James
Keach, Charles Martin Smith

EXPERT'S OPINION (1935, GB, Paramount)
Richard Steele—Leslie Perrins
Director—Ivar Campbell
Leading Players—Lucille Lisle, Molly Fisher, Franklyn Bellamy

EXPLORERS (1985, Paramount)
Ben Crandall—Ethan Hawke
Wolfgang Muller—River Phoenix
Darren Woods—Jason Presson
Director—Joe Dante
Leading Players—Amanda Peterson, Dick Miller, Robert Picardo

THE EXTERMINATOR (1980, Interstar)
John Eastland—Robert Ginty
Director—James Glickenhaus
Leading Players—Christopher George, Samantha Eggar, Steve
James

EXTERMINATOR 2 (1984, Cannon)
Johnny Eastland—Robert Ginty
Directors—Mark Buntzman & William Sachs
Leading Players—Mario Van Peeples, Deborah Geffner, Frankie
Faison

THE EXTRAORDINARY SEAMAN (1969, MGM)
Lt. Commander Finchhaven—David Niven
Director—John Frankenheimer
Leading Players—Faye Dunaway, Alan Alda, Mickey Rooney

EYE WITNESS (1950, GB, Warner Brothers)
Mary Baxter—Jenny Laird
Director—Robert Montgomery
Leading Players—Robert Montgomery, Leslie Banks, Felix
  Aylmer, Patricia Wayne

EYES OF A STRANGER (1980, Warner Brothers)
Stanley Herbert—John DiSanti
Director—Ken Wiederhorn
Leading Players—Lauren Tewes, Jason Leigh, Peter DuPre

THE EYES OF ANNIE JONES (1963, GB, 20th Century Fox)
Annie Jones—Francesca Annis
Director—Reginald LeBorg
Leading Players—Richard Conte, Joyce Carey, Myrtle Reed

EYES OF LAURA MARS (1978, Columbia)
Laura Mars—Faye Dunaway
Director—Irvin Kershner
Leading Players—Tommy Lee Jones, Brad Dourif, Rene
  Auberjonois, Raul Julia

EYEWITNESS (1956, GB, Rank)
Lucy Church—Muriel Pavlow
Director—Muriel Box
Leading Players—Donald Sinden, Belinda Lee, Michael Craig

EYEWITNESS (1981, 20th Century Fox)
Daryll Deever—William Hurt
Director—Peter Yates
Leading Players—Sigourney Weaver, Christopher Plummer,
  James Woods, Irene Worth

F

F MAN (1936, Paramount)
Johnny Dime—Jack Haley
Director—Edward F. Cline
Leading Players—William Frawley, Grace Bradley, Adrienne
  Marden

FABIAN OF THE YARD (1954, GB, Beauchamp/Eros)
Superintendent Fabian—Bruce Seton
Director—Anthony Beauchamp
Leading Players—Richard Pearson, Gwen Cherrill, Viola Lyel

THE FABULOUS BAKER BOYS (1989, 20th Century Fox)
Jack Baker—Jeff Bridges
Frank Baker—Beau Bridges
Director—Steve Kloves
Leading Players—Michelle Pfeiffer, Ellie Raab, Xander
  Berkeley, Dakin Matthews

THE FABULOUS DORSEYS (1947, UA)
Tommy Dorsey—Tommy Dorsey
Jimmy Dorsey—Jimmy Dorsey
Director—Alfred E. Green
Leading Players—Janet Blair, Paul Whiteman, William Lundigan

THE FABULOUS SENORITA (1952, Republic)
Estelita Rodriguez—Estelita
Director—R.G. Springsteen
Leading Players—Robert Clarke, Nestor Paiva, Marvin Kaplan

THE FABULOUS SUZANNE (1946, Republic)
Suzanne—Barbara Britton
Director—Steve Sekely
Leading Players—Rudy Vallee, Otto Kruger, Richard Denning

THE FABULOUS TEXAN (1947, Republic)
Jim McWade—William Elliott
Director—Edward Ludwig
Leading Players—John Carroll, Catherine McLeod, Albert
  Dekker, Andy Devine

THE FACE AT THE WINDOW (1939, GB, British Lion)
The Face—Harry Terry
Director—George King
Leading Players—Tod Slaughter, Marjorie Taylor, John Warwick

THE FACE BEHIND THE MASK (1941, Columbia)
Janos Szabo—Peter Lorre
Director—Robert Florey
Leading Players—Evelyn Keyes, Don Beddoe, George E. Stone

FACE BEHIND THE SCAR (1940, GB, Premier-Stafford)
James Martin—Griffith Jones
Director—W. Victor Hanbury
Leading Players—Rosalyn Boulter, Ellis Jeffreys, Athole Stewart

A FACE IN THE CROWD (1957, Warner Brothers)
Lonesome Rhodes—Andy Griffith
Director—Elia Kazan
Leading Players—Patricia Neal, Anthony Franciosa, Walter
  Matthau, Lee Remick

A FACE IN THE FOG (1936, Victory)
Peter Fortune—Lawrence Gray
Director—Bob Hill
Leading Players—June Collyer, Lloyd Hughes, Al St. John

A FACE IN THE RAIN (1963, Embassy)
Rand—Rory Calhoun
Director—Irvin Kershner
Leading Players—Marina Berti, Niall McGinnis, Massimo
  Giuliani

FACE IN THE SKY (1933, Fox Film Corp.)
Madge—Marian Nixon
Director—Harry Lachman
Leading Players—Spencer Tracy, Stuart Erwin, Sam Hardy

FACE OF A FUGITIVE (1959, Columbia)
Jim Larson/Ray Kincaid—Fred MacMurray
Director—Paul Wendkos
Leading Players—Lin McCarthy, Dorothy Green, Alan Baxter,
  James Coburn

FACE OF A STRANGER (1964, GB, Allied Artists)
Vince Howard—Jeremy Kemp
Director—John Moxey
Leading Players—Bernard Archard, Rosemary Leach, Philip
  Locke

FACE OF FIRE (1959, Allied Artists)
Monk Johnson—James Whitmore
Director—Albert Band
Leading Players—Cameron Mitchell, Bettye Ackerman, Royal Dano, Miko Oscard

THE FACE OF FU MANCHU (1965, GB, Seven Arts)
Fu Manchu—Christopher Lee
Director—Don Sharp
Leading Players—Nigel Green, James Robertson Justice, Howard Marion Crawford, Tsai Chin

FAITHFUL IN MY FASHION (1946, MGM)
Jean Kendrick—Donna Reed
Director—Sidney Salkow
Leading Players—Tom Drake, Edward Everett Horton, Spring Byington

THE FALCON AND THE CO-EDS (1943, RKO)
Tom Lawrence—Tom Conway
Director—William Clemens
Leading Players—Jean Brooks, Rita Corday, Amelita Ward

THE FALCON AND THE SNOWMAN (1985, Orion)
Christopher Boyce—Timothy Hutton
Daulton Lee—Sean Penn
Director—John Schlesinger
Leading Players—Pat Hingle, Joyce Van Patten, Richard Dysart, Priscilla Pointer

THE FALCON IN HOLLYWOOD (1944, RKO)
Tom Lawrence—Tom Conway
Director—Gordon Douglas
Leading Players—Barbara Hale, Rita Corday, Jean Brooks

THE FALCON IN MEXICO (1944, RKO)
Tom Lawrence—Tom Conway
Director—William Berke
Leading Players—Mona Maris, Martha MacVicar, Nestor Paiva

THE FALCON IN SAN FRANCISCO (1945, RKO)
Tom Lawrence—Tom Conway
Director—Joseph H. Lewis
Leading Players—Rita Corday, Edward Brophy, Sharyn Moffett

THE FALCON OUT WEST (1944, RKO)
Tom Lawrence -Tom Conway
Director—William Clemens
Leading Players—Carole Gallagher, Barbara Hale, Joan Barclay

THE FALCON STRIKES BACK (1943, RKO)
Tom Lawrence—Tom Conway
Director—Edward Dmytryk
Leading Players—Harriett Hilliard, Jane Randolph, Edgar Kennedy

THE FALCON TAKES OVER (1942, RKO)
Gay Lawrence—George Sanders
Director—Irving Reis
Leading Players—Lynn Bari, James Gleason, Allen Jenkins, Helen Gilbert

THE FALCON'S ADVENTURE (1946, RKO)
Tom Lawrence—Tom Conway
Director—William Berke
Leading Players—Madge Meredith, Edward Brophy, Robert Warwick

THE FALCON'S ALIBI (1946, RKO)
Tom Lawrence—Tom Conway
Director—Ray McCarey
Leading Players—Rita Corday, Vince Barnett, Jane Greer

THE FALCON'S BROTHER (1942, RKO)
Gay Lawrence—George Sanders
Tom Lawrence—Tom Conway
Director—Stanley Logan
Leading Players—Jane Randolph, Don Barclay, Cliff Clark

THE FALL GUY (1930, RKO)
Johnny Quinlan—Jack Mulhall
Director—A. Leslie Pearce
Leading Players—Mae Clarke, Ned Sparks, Pat O'Malley

FALL GUY (1947, Monogram)
Tom Cochrane—Clifford Penn
Director—Reginald LeBorg
Leading Players—Teala Loring, Robert Armstrong, Virginia Dale

THE FALL OF EVE (1929, Columbia)
Eve Grant—Patsy Ruth Miller
Director—Frank Strayer
Leading Players—Ford Sterling, Gertrude Astor, Arthur Rankin

THE FALL OF THE HOUSE OF USHER (1952, GB, Vigilant)
Lord Roderick Usher—Kay Tendeter
Lady Usher—Gwendoline Watford
Director—Ivan Barnett
Leading Players—Irving Steen, Lucy Pavey, Vernon Charles

THE FALL OF THE HOUSE OF USHER (1980, Sunn Classic)
Roderick Usher—Martin Landau
Director—James L. Conway
Leading Players—Ray Walston, Charlene Tilton, Robert Hays

FALLEN ANGEL (1945, 20th Century Fox)
June Mills—Alice Faye
Director—Otto Preminger
Leading Players—Dana Andrews, Linda Darnell, Charles Bickford, Anne Revere, Bruce Cabot

THE FALLEN SPARROW (1943, RKO)
Kit—John Garfield
Director—Richard Wallace
Leading Players—Maureen O'Hara, Walter Slezak, Patricia Morison, Martha O'Driscoll

FALLGUY (1962, International Films)
Sonny Martin—Ed Dugan
Director—Donn Harling
Leading Players—George Andre, Lou Gartner, Don Alderette

FALLING IN LOVE (1984, Paramount)
Frank Raftis—Robert DeNiro
Molly Gilmore—Meryl Streep
Director—Ulu Grosbard
Leading Players—Harvey Keitel, Jane Kaczmarek, George Martin

FALSE IDENTITY (1990, RKO/Prism)
Ben—Stacy Keach

Director—James Keach
Leading Players—Geneveive Bujold, Tobin Bell, Mike Champion, Veronica Cartwright

FALSE MADONNA (1932, Paramount)
Tina—Kay Francis
Director—Stuart Walker
Leading Players—William "Stage" Boyd, Conway Tearle, John Breeden

FAMILY BUISNESS (1989, Tri-Star)
Jessie McMullen—Sean Connery
Vito McMullen—Dustin Hoffman
Adam McMullen—Matthew Broderick
Director—Sidney Lumet
Leading Players—Rosana DeSoto, Janet Carroll, Victoria Jackson, Bill McCutcheon

THE FAN (1981, Paramount)
Douglas Breen—Michael Biehn
Director—Edward Bianchi
Leading Players—Lauren Bacall, James Garner, Maureen Stapleton, Hector Elizondo

FANCY PANTS (1950, Paramount)
Humphrey—Bob Hope
Director—George Marshall
Leading Players—Lucille Ball, Bruce Cabot, Jack Kirkwood

FANNY (1961, Warner Brothers)
Fanny—Leslie Caron
Director—Joshua Logan
Leading Players—Maurice Chevalier, Charles Boyer, Horst Buchholz, Lionel Jeffries

FANNY FOLEY HERSELF (1931, RKO)
Fanny Foley—Edna May Oliver
Director—Melville Brown
Leading Players—Hobart Bosworth, Helen Chandler, John Darrow

FANNY HILL: MEMOIRS OF A WOMAN OF PLEASURE (1965, Favorite Films)
Fanny Hill—Letita Roman
Director—Russ Meyer
Leading Players—Miriam Hopkins, Walter Giller, Alex D'Arcy

FANTASY MAN (1984, Australia, Centaur)
Nick Bailey—Harold Hopkins
Director—John Meagher
Leading Players—Jeanie Drynan, Kerry Mack, Kate Fitzpatrick

FAREWELL, MY LOVELY (1975, Avco Embassy)
Mrs. Velma Grayle—Charlotte Rampling
Moose Malloy—Jack O'Halloran
Director—Dick Richards
Leading Players—Robert Mitchum, John Ireland, Sylvia Miles

FAREWELL TO CINDERELLA (1937, GB, RKO)
Margaret—Anne Pichon
Director—Maclean Rogers
Leading Players—John Robinson, Arthur Rees, Glennis Lorimer

FAREWELL TO THE KING (1989, Orion)
Learoyd—Nick Nolte
Director—John Milius

Leading Players—Nigel Havers, Frank McRae, Gerry Lopez

THE FARGO KID (1941, RKO)
Fargo Kid—Tim Holt
Director—Edward Killy
Leading Players—Ray Whitley, Emmett Lynn, Jane Drummond

THE FARMER (1977, Columbia)
Kyle Martin—Gary Conway
Director—David Berlatsky
Leading Players—Angel Tompkins, Michael Dante, George Memmoli

THE FARMER IN THE DELL (1936, RKO)
Pa Boyer—Fred Stone
Director—Ben Holmes
Leading Players—Jean Parker, Esther Dale, Moroni Olsen

THE FARMER TAKES A WIFE (1935, 20th Century Fox)
Molly Larkins—Janet Gaynor
Dan Harrow—Henry Fonda
Director—Victor Fleming
Leading Players—Charles Bickford, Slim Summerville, Andy Devine, Jane Withers

THE FARMER TAKES A WIFE (1953, 20th Century Fox)
Molly Larkins—Betty Grable
Dan Harrow—Dale Robertson
Director—Henry Levin
Leading Players—Thelma Ritter, John Carroll, Eddie Foy, Jr.

THE FARMER'S DAUGHTER (1940, Paramount)
Patience Bingham—Martha Raye
Tom Bingham—William Duncan
Director—James Hogan
Leading Players—Charlie Ruggles, Richard Denning, Gertrude Michael

THE FARMER'S DAUGHTER (1947, RKO)
Katrin Holstrom—Loretta Young
Mr. Holstrom—Harry Shannon
Director—H.C. Potter
Leading Players—Joseph Cotten, Ethel Barrymore, Charles Bickford, Rose Hobart

THE FARMER'S OTHER DAUGHTER (1965, United Producers)
June Brown—Judy Pennebaker
Horace Jefferson Brown—Harry Lovejoy
Director—John Hayes
Leading Players—Bill Michael, William Guhl, Jean Bennett

THE FARMER'S WIFE (1941, GB, Pathe)
Samuel Sweetland—Basil Sydney
Sibley Sweetland—Patricia Roc
Director—Norman Lee
Leading Players—Wilfrid Lawson, Nora Swinburne, Michael Wilding

FAR OUT MAN (1990, New Line/Cinetel)
Far Out Man—Tommy Chong
Director—Tommy Chong
Leading Players—Shelby Chong, Paris Chong, C. Thomas Howell, Martin Mull, Rae Dawn Chong

FAST CHARLIE . . . THE MOONBEAM RIDER (1979, Universal)
Charlie Swattle—David Carradine

Director—Steve Carver
Leading Players—Brenda Vaccaro, L.Q. Jones, R.G. Armstrong

THE FASTEST GUITAR ALIVE (1967, MGM)
Johnny—Roy Orbison
Director—Michael Moore
Leading Players—Sammy Jackson, Maggie Pierce, Joan Freeman

FASTEST GUN ALIVE (1956, MGM)
George Temple—Glenn Ford
Director—Russell Rouse
Leading Players—Jeanne Crain, Broderick Crawford, Russ Tamblyn

THE FAT MAN (1951, Universal)
Brad Runyon—J. Scott Smart
Director—William Castle
Leading Players—Julie London, Rock Hudson, Clinton Sundberg

FAT SPY (1966, Magna)
Irving/Herman—Jack E. Leonard
Director—Joseph Cates
Leading Players—Phyllis Diller, Brian Donlevy, Jayne Mansfield

FATAL ATTRACTION (1987, Paramount)
Dan Gallagher—Michael Douglas
Alex Forrest—Glenn Close
Director—Adrian Lyne
Leading Players—Anne Archer, Ellen Hamilton Latzen, Stuart Pankin, Fred Gwynne

FATAL BEAUTY (1987, MGM/UA)
Det. Rita Rizzoli—Whoopi Goldberg
Director—Tom Holland
Leading Players—Sam Elliott, Ruben Blades, Harris Yulin

FATAL LADY (1936, Paramount)
Marion Stuart/Maria Delasano/Malevo—Mary Ellis
Director—Edward Ludwig
Leading Players—Walter Pidgeon, Ruth Donnelly, Norman Foster

FATHER (1990, Australia, Barron Films/Latin Quarter)
Joe Mueller—Max Von Sydow
Director—John Power
Leading Players—Carol Drinkwater, Julia Blake, Steve Jacobs, Tim Robertson

FATHER AND SON (1929, Columbia)
Frank Fields—Jack Holt
Jimmy Fields—Mickey McBan
Director—Erle C. Kenton
Leading Players—Dorothy Reivier, Helene Chadwick, Wheeler Oakman

FATHER AND SON (1934, GB, Warner Brothers)
John Bolton—Edmund Gwenn
Michael Bolton—Esmond Knight
Director—Monty Banks
Leading Players—James Finlayson, Charles Carson, Daphne Courtney

FATHER BROWN, DETECTIVE (1935, Paramount)
Father Brown—Walter Connolly
Director—Edward Sedgwick

Leading Players—Paul Lukas, Gertrude Michael, Robert Loraine

FATHER CAME TOO (1964, GB, Rank)
Sir Beverly Grant—James Robertson Justice
Director—Peter Graham Scott
Leading Players—Leslie Phillips, Stanley Baxter, Sally Smith

FATHER GOOSE (1964, Universal)
Walter Eckland—Cary Grant
Director—Ralph Nelson
Leading Players—Leslie Caron, Trevor Howard, Jack Good

FATHER IS A BACHELOR (1950, Columbia)
Johnny Rutledge—William Holden
Director—Norman Foster
Leading Players—Coleen Gray, Mary Jane Saunders, Charles Winninger

FATHER IS A PRINCE (1940, Warner Brothers)
Herbert Bower—Grant Mitchell
Director—Noel Smith
Leading Players—Nana Bryant, John Litel, George Reeves

FATHER MAKES GOOD (1950, Monogram)
Henry Latham—Raymond Walburn
Director—Jean Yarborough
Leading Players—Walter Catlett, Barbara Brown, Gary Gray

FATHER O'FLYNN (1938, Ireland, Butchers)
Father O'Flynn—Tom Burke
Director—Wilfred Noy
Leading Players—Jean Adrienne, Robert Chishold, Henry Oscar

FATHER OF THE BRIDE (1950, MGM)
Stanley Banks—Spencer Tracy
Kay Banks—Elizabeth Taylor
Director—Vincente Minnelli
Leading Players—Joan Bennett, Don Taylor, Billie Burke, Moroni Olsen, Leo G. Carroll

FATHER OF THE BRIDE (1990, Buena Vista/Touchstone)
George Banks—Steve Martin
Annie Banks—Kimberly Williams
Director—Charles Shyer
Leading Players—Diane Keaton, Kieran Culkin, George Newburn, Martin Short, B.D. Wong, Peter Michael Goetz, Kate McGregor Stewart

FATHER STEPS OUT (1937, GB, RKO)
Joe Hardcastle—George Carney
Director—Maclean Rogers
Leading Players—Dinah Sheridan, Bruce Seton, Vivienne Chatterton

FATHER TAKES A WIFE (1941, RKO)
Frederic Osborne, Sr.—Adolphe Menjou
Leslie Collier—Gloria Swanson
Director—Jack Hively
Leading Players—John Howard, Desi Arnaz, Helen Broderick

FATHER TAKES THE AIR (1951, Monogram)
Henry Latham—Raymond Walburn
Director—Frank McDonald
Leading Players—Walter Catlett, Gary Gray, Florence Bates

FATHER WAS A FULLBACK (1949, 20th Century Fox)
George Cooper—Fred MacMurray
Director—John M. Stahl
Leading Players—Maureen O'Hara, Betty Lynn, Rudy Vallee

FATHER'S DOING FINE (1952, GB, Marble Arch)
Dougall—Richard Attenborough
Director—Henry Cass
Leading Players—Heather Thatcher, Noel Purcell, George
    Thorpe, Diane Hart

FATHER'S LITTLE DIVIDEND (1951, MGM)
Stanley Banks—Spencer Tracy
The Dividend—Donald Clark
Director—Vincente Minnelli
Leading Players—Joan Bennett, Elizabeth Taylor, Don Taylor

FATHER'S SON (1931, Warner Brothers)
Bill Emory—Leon Janney
William Emory—Lewis Stone
Director—William Beaudine
Leading Players—Irene Rich, John Halliday, Robert Dandridge

FATHER'S SON (1941, Warner Brothers)
Bill Emory—Billy Dawson
William Emory—John Litel
Director—D. Ross Lederman
Leading Players—Frieda Inescourt, Christian Rub, Bernice Pilot

FATHER'S WILD GAME (1950, Monogram)
Henry Latham—Raymond Walburn
Director—Herbert I. Leeds
Leading Players—Walter Catlett, Gary Gray, Barbara Brown

FATHOM (1967, 20th Century Fox)
Fathom Harvill—Raquel Welch
Director—Leslie H. Martinson
Leading Players—Tony Franciosa. Ronald Fraser, Greta Chi
    Clive Revill

FATSO (1980, 20th Century Fox)
Dominick DiNapoli—Dom DeLuise
Director—Anne Bancroft
Leading Players—Anne Bancroft, Ron Carey, Candice Azzara

FATTY FINN (1980, Australia, Children's Films)
Fatty Finn—Ben Oxenbould
Director—Maurice Murphy
Leading Players—Bert Newton, Noni Hazelhurst, Gerard
    Kennedy

FBI GIRL (1951, Lippert)
Shirley Wayne—Audrey Totter
Director—William Berke
Leading Players—Cesar Romero, George Brent, Tom Drake

FEARLESS FRANK (1967, American International)
Frank/False Frank—Jon Voight
Director—Phil Kaufman
Leading Players—Monique Van Vooren, Seven Darden, Joan
    Darling

THE FEARLESS LOVER (1925, Silent, Perfection)
Patrick Michael Casey—William Fairbanks
Director—Henry MacRae
Leading Players—Eva Novak, Tom Kennedy, Lydia Knott

FEDERAL AGENT (1936, Republic)
Bob—William Boyd
Director—Sam Newfield
Leading Players—Charles A. Browne, Irene Ware, George
    Cooper

FEDERAL AGENT AT LARGE (1950, Republic)
Matt Reedy—Kent Taylor
Director—George Blair
Leading Players—Dorothy Patrick, Robert Rockwell, Estelita
    Rodriguez

FEDERAL MAN (1950, Eagle Lion)
Sherrin—William Henry
Director—Robert Tansey
Leading Players—Pamela Blake, Robert Shayne, Lyle Talbot

FELLER NEEDS A FRIEND (1932, Cosmopolitan)
Eddie Randall—Jackie Cooper
Froggie—Andy Shuford
Director—Harry Pollard
Leading Players—Chic Sale, Ralph Graves, Dorothy Peterson

FEMALE (1933, Warner Brothers)
Alison Drake—Ruth Chatterton
Directors—Michael Curtiz & William Dieterle
Leading Players—George Brent, Philip Reed, Ruth Donnelly

THE FEMALE ANIMAL (1958, Universal)
Vanessa Windsor—Hedy Lamarr
Director—Harry Keller
Leading Players—Jane Powell, Jan Sterling, George Nader

FEMALE FUGITIVE (1938, Monogram)
Peggy Mallory—Evelyn Venable
Director—William Nigh
Leading Players—Craig Reynolds, Reed Hadley, John Kelly

FEMALE OF THE SPECIES (1917, Silent, Triangle)
Gloria Marley—Dorothy Dalton
Director—Raymond B. West
Leading Players—Enid Markey, Howard Hickman, Gertrude
    Claire

FEMALE ON THE BEACH (1955, Universal)
Lynn Markham—Joan Crawford
Director—Joseph Pevney
Leading Players—Jeff Chandler, Jan Sterling, Cecil Kellaway

FERRIS BUELLER'S DAY OFF (1986, Orion)
Ferris Bueller—Matthew Broderick
Director—John Hughes
Leading Players—Alan Ruck, Mia Sara, Jeffrey Jones, Jennifer
    Grey, Charlie Sheen

FFOLKES (NORTH SEA HIJACK) (1980, GB, Universal)
ffolkes—Roger Moore
Director—Andrew V. McLaglen
Leading Players—James Mason, Anthony Perkins, Michael
    Parks

FIDDLER ON THE ROOF (1971, UA)
Fiddler—Tutte Lemkow
Director—Norman Jewison
Leading Players—Chaim Topol, Norma Crane, Leonard Frey,
    Molly Picon, Paul Mann

FIEND OF DOPE ISLAND (1961, Essanay)
Charlie Davis—Bruce Bennett
Director—Nate Watt
Leading Players—Robert Bray, Tania Velia, Ralph Rodriguez

THE FIEND WHO WALKED THE WEST (1958, 20th Century Fox)
Felix Griffin—Robert Evans
Director—Gordon Douglas
Leading Players—Hugh O'Brian, Dolores Michaels, Linda Cristal, Stephen McNally

THE FIENDISH PLOT OF DR. FU MANCHU (1980, Orion)
Fu Manchu—Peter Sellers
Director—Piers Haggard
Leading Players—Helen Mirren, David Tomlinson, Sid Caesar

FIFTH AVENUE GIRL (1939, RKO)
Mary Grey—Ginger Rogers
Director—Gregory La Cava
Leading Players—Walter Connelly, Verree Teasdale, James Ellison, Tim Holt

THE FIFTY-FIFTY GIRL (1928, Silent, Paramount)
Kathleen O'Hara—Bebe Daniels
Director—Clarence Badger
Leading Players—James Hall, William Austin, George Kotsonaros

FIFTY-SHILLING BOXER (1937, GB, RKO)
Jack Foster—Bruce Seton
Director—Maclean Rogers
Leading Players—Nancy O'Neil, Moore Marriott, Eve Gray

52 PICK-UP (1986, Cannon)
Harry Mitchell—Roy Scheider
Director—John Frankenheimer
Leading Players—Ann-Margret, Vanity, John Glover, Robert Trebor, Kelly Preston, Clarence Williams III

THE FIGHTER (1921, Silent, Selznick Films)
Caleb Conover—Conway Tearle
Director—Henry Kolker
Leading Players—Winifred Westover, Arthur Housman, Ernest Lawford

THE FIGHTER (1952, UA)
Filipe Rivera—Richard Conte
Director—Herbert Kline
Leading Players—Vanessa Brown, Lee J. Cobb, Frank Silvera

THE FIGHTING AMERICAN (1924, Silent, Universal)
Bill Pendleton—Pat O'Malley
Director—Tom Forman
Leading Players—Mary Astor, Raymond Hatton, Warner Oland

FIGHTING BILL CARSON (1945, Producers Releasing Corp.)
Bill Carson—Buster Crabbe
Director—Sam Newfield
Leading Players—Al "Fuzzy" St. John, Lorraine Miller, Kay Hughes

FIGHTING BILL FARGO (1942, Universal)
Bill Fargo—Johnny Mack Brown
Director—Ray Taylor
Leading Players—Fuzzy Knight, Jeanne Kelly, Kenneth Harlan

THE FIGHTING BOOB (1926, Silent, R-C/FBO)
El Tigre—Bob Custer
Director—Jack Nelson
Leading Players—Frank Whitson, Sherry Tansey, Hugh Saxon

THE FIGHTING BUCKAROO (1943, Columbia)
Steve Harrison—Charles Starrett
Director—William Berke
Leading Players—Kay Harris, Arthur Hunnicutt, Stanley Brown

THE FIGHTING CHEAT (1926, Silent, Action/Artclass)
Wally Kenyon—Wally Wales
Director—Richard Thorpe
Leading Players—Jean Arthur, Ted Rackerby, Fanny Midgley

THE FIGHTING COWARD (1924, Silent, Paramount)
Tom Rumford—Cullen Landis
Director—James Cruze
Leading Players—Mary Astor, Noah Beery, Ernest Torrence, Phyllis Haver

THE FIGHTING CUB (1925, Silent, Truart)
Thomas Patrick O'Toole—Wesley Barry
Director—Paul Hurst
Leading Players—Mildred Harris, Pat O'Malley, Mary Carr

FIGHTING FATHER DUNNE (1948, RKO)
Father Dunne—Pat O'Brien
Director—Ted Tetzlaff
Leading Players—Darryl Hickman, Charles Kemper, Una O'Connor

THE FIGHTING FOOL (1932, Columbia)
Tim Collins—Tim McCoy
Director—Lambert Hillyer
Leading Players—Marceline Day, William V. Mong, Robert Ellis

THE FIGHTING GENTLEMAN (1932, Monarch)
Jack Duncan—William Collier, Jr.
Director—Fred Newymeyer
Leading Players—Josephine Dunn, Natalie Moorhead, Crauford Kent, Lee Moran

THE FIGHTING GRINGO (1939, RKO)
Wade Barton—George O'Brien
Director—David Howard
Leading Players—Lupita Tovar, Lucio Villegas, William Royle

THE FIGHTING KENTUCKIAN (1949, Republic)
John Breen—John Wayne
Director—George Waggner
Leading Players—Vera Ralston, Philip Dorn, Oliver Hardy, Marie Windsor

FIGHTING MAN OF THE PLAINS (1949, 20th Century Fox)
Jim Dancer—Randolph Scott
Director—Edwin L. Marin
Leading Players—Bill Williams, Victor Jory, Jane Nigh

THE FIGHTING O'FLYNN (1949, Universal)
The O'Flynn—Douglas Fairbanks, Jr.
Director—Arthur Pierson
Leading Players—Helena Carter, Richard Greene, Patricia Medina

THE FIGHTING PIMPERNEL (1950, GB, British Lion)
Sir Percy Blakeney—David Niven
Directors—Michael Powell & Emeric Pressburger
Leading Players—Margaret Leighton, Jack Hawkins, Cyril Cusack, Robert Coote

FIGHTING PLAYBOY (1937, Northern Films)
Don—Nick Stuart
Director—Robert F. Hill
Leading Players—Lucille Brown, James Magrath, Robert Webb

THE FIGHTING PRINCE OF DONEGAL (1966, GB, Buena Vista)
Hugh O'Donnell—Peter McEnery
Director—Michael O'Herlihy
Leading Players—Susan Hampshire, Tom Adams, Gordon Jackson

THE FIGHTING RANGER (1934, Columbia)
Jim—Buck Jones
Director—George B. Seitz
Leading Players—Dorothy Revier, Frank Rice, Bradley Page

THE FIGHTING REDHEAD (1950, Eagle-Lion)
Red Ryder—Jim Bannon
Director—Lewis D. Collins
Leading Players—Don Kay Reynolds, Emmett Lynn, Marin Sais

FIGHTING RENEGADE (1939, Victory)
Lighting Bill Carson/El Puma—Tim McCoy
Director—Sam Newfield
Leading Players—Joyce Bryant, Ben Corbett, Ted Adams

FIGHTING TEXAN (1937, Ambassador)
Glenn—Kermit Maynard
Director—Charles Abbott
Leading Players—Elaine Shepard, Frank LaRue, Budd Buster

THE FIGHTING TROOPER (1935, Ambassador)
Burke—Kermit Maynard
Director—Ray Taylor
Leading Players—Barbara Worth, Keroy Mason, Charlie Delaney

THE FILE ON THELMA JORDAN (1950, Paramount)
Thelma Jordan—Barbara Stanwyck
Director—Robert Sidomak
Leading Players—Wendell Corey, Paul Kelly, Joan Tetzel, Stanley Ridges

FINDERS KEEPERS (1984, CBS/Warner Brothers)
Michael Rangeloff—Michael O'Keefe
Director—Richard Lester
Leading Players—Beverly D'Angelo, Louis Gossett, Jr., Pamela Stephenson, Ed Lauter, David Wayne

FINGER MAN (1955, Allied Artists)
Casey Martin—Frank Lovejoy
Director—Harold Schuster
Leading Players—Forrest Tucker, Peggie Castle, Timothy Carey

FINIAN'S RAINBOW (1968, Warner Brothers)
Finian McLonergan—Fred Astaire
Director—Francis Ford Coppola
Leading Players—Petula Clark, Tommy Steele, Don Francks, Keenan Wynn, Al Freeman, Jr.

FINN AND HATTIE (1931, Paramount)
Finley P. Haddock—Leon Errol
Mildred Haddock—Mitzi Green
Directors—Norman Taurog & Norman McLeod
Leading Players—Zasu Pitts, Jackie Searl, Lilyan Tashman

FINNEGAN'S BALL (1927, Silent, First Division)
Danny Finnegan—Charles McHugh
Director—James P. Hogan
Leading Players—Blanche Mehaffey, Mack Swain, Cullen Landis, Aggie Herring

FINNEGAN'S WAKE (1965, Expanding Cinema)
Finnegan—Martin J. Kelly
Director—Mary Ellen Bute
Leading Players—Jane Reilly, Peter Haskell, Page Johnson

FINNEY (1969, Gold Coast)
Jim Finney—Robert Kilcullen
Director—Bill Hare
Leading Players—Bill Levinson, Joan Sundstrom, Anthony Mockus

FIRE BIRDS (1990, Buena Vista/Touchstone)
Jack Preston—Nicolas Cage
Director—David Green
Leading Players—Tommy Lee Jones, Sean Young, Bryan Kestner, Dale Dye, Mary Ellen Trainor

THE FIREBALL (1950, 20th Century Fox)
Johnny Casar—Mickey Rooney
Director—Tay Garnett
Leading Players—Pat O'Brien, Beverly Tyler, James Brown, Marilyn Monroe

THE FIREBRAND (1962, 20th Century Fox)
Joaquin Murieta—Valentin De Vargas
Director—Maury Dexter
Leading Players—Kent Taylor, Lisa Montell, Joe Raciti

FIREBRAND JORDAN (1930, National Players)
Firebrand Jordan—Lane Chandler
Director—Alvin J. Neitz
Leading Players—Yakima Canutt, Aline Goodwin, Tom London

FIRED WIFE (1943, Universal)
Tig Callahan—Louise Allbritton
Director—Charles Lamont
Leading Players—Diana Barrymore, Robert Paige, Walter Abel

THE FIREFLY (1937, MGM)
Nina Maria Azara ("Mosca del Fuego")—Jeanette MacDonald
Director—Robert Z. Leonard
Leading Players—Allan Jones, Warren William, Douglass Dumbrille, Billy Gilbert, Henry Daniell

FIREMAN, SAVE MY CHILD (1927, Silent, Paramount)
Elmer—Wallace Beery
Director—Edward Sutherland
Leading Players—Raymond Hatton, Josephine Dunn, Tom Kennedy

FIREMAN, SAVE MY CHILD (1932, Warner Brothers)
Joe Grant—Joe E. Brown
Director—Lloyd Bacon
Leading Players—Evalyn Knapp, Lilian Bond, George Meeker

FIRESTARTER (1984, Universal)
Charlie McGee—Drew Barrymore
Director—Mark L. Lester
Leading Players—David Keith, Freddie Jones, Heather Locklear

THE FIRM MAN (1975, Australia, Australian Film Institute)
Gerald Baxter—Peter Cummins
Director—John Dunigan
Leading Players—Eileen Chapman, Peter Carmody, Max Gilles

FIRST A GIRL (1935, GB, Gaumont British)
Elizabeth—Jessie Matthews
Director—Victor Saville
Leading Players—Sonnie Hale, Griffith Jones, Anna Lee

FIRST BORN (1984, Paramount)
Jake—Christopher Collet
Director—Michael Apted
Leading Players—Teri Garr, Peter Weller, Corey Haim

FIRST FAMILY (1980, Warner Brothers)
President Manfred Link—Bob Newhart
Gloria Link—Gilda Radner
Mrs. Link—Madeline Kahn
Director—Buck Henry
Leading Players—Fred Willard, Richard Benjamin, Bob Dishy

FIRST LADY (1937, Warner Brothers)
Lucy Chase Wayne—Kay Francis
Director—Stanley Logan
Leading Players—Anita Louise, Verree Teasdale, Preston Foster, Walter Connelly

THE FIRST MRS. FRASER (1932, GB, Sterling)
Janet Fraser—Dorothy Dix
Director—Sinclair Hill
Leading Players—Henry Ainley, Joan Barry, Harold Huth

THE FIRST TEXAN (1956, Allied Artists)
Sam Houston—Joel McCrea
Director—Bryon Haskin
Leading Players—Felicia Farr, Jeff Morrow, Wallace Ford

FIRST TO FIGHT (1967, Warner Brothers)
Shanghai Jack Connell—Chad Everett
Director—Christian Nyby
Leading Players—Marilyn Devin, Dean Jagger, Bobby Troup, Gene Hackman

THE FIRST TRAVELING SALESLADY (1956, RKO)
Rose Gillray—Ginger Rogers
Director—Arthur Lubin
Leading Players—Barry Nelson, Carol Channing, David Brian, James Arness, Clint Eastwood

FIRST YANK IN TOKYO (1945, RKO)
Major Ross—Tom Neal
Director—Gordon Douglas
Leading Players—Barbara Hale, Marc Cramer, Richard Loo, Keye Luke

A FISH CALLED WANDA (1988, MGM)
Wanda Gershwitz—Jamie Lee Curtis
Director—Charles Crichton
Leading Players—John Cleese, Kevin Kline, Michael Palin, Tom Georgeson

FISH HAWK (1981, Canada, Avco Embassy)
Fish Hawk—Will Sampson
Director—Donald Shebib
Leading Players—Charlie Fields, Geoffrey Bowes, Mary Pirie

THE FISHER KING (1991, Tri-Star)
Parry—Robin Williams
Director—Terry Gilliam
Leading Players—Jeff Bridges, Amanda Plummer, Mercedes Ruehl, Michael Jeter

FIST FIGHTER (1989, Taurus)
C.J. Thunderbird—George Rivero
Director—Frank Zuniga
Leading Players—Edward Albert, Mike Connors, Brenda Bakke

FITZCARRALDO (1982, New World Pictures)
Brian Sweeney Fitzgerald/Fitzcarraldo—Klaus Kinski
Director—Werner Herzog
Leading Players—Claudia Cardinale, Jose Lewgoy, Miguel Angel

FITZWILLY (1967, UA)
Fitzwilliam—Dick Van Dyke
Director—Delbert Mann
Leading Players—Barbara Feldon, Edith Evans, John McGiver

FIVE AGAINST THE HOUSE (1955, Columbia)
Al Mercer—Guy Madison
Kay Greylek—Kim Novak
Brick—Brian Keith
Roy—Alvy Moore
Ronnie—Kerwin Mathews
Director—Phil Karlson
Leading Players—William Conrad, Jack Dimond, Jean Willes

FIVE BOLD WOMEN (1960, Citation)
The Missouri Lady—Merry Anders
Big Pearl—Irish McCalla
Faro Kitty—Kathy Marlowe
Crazy Hannah—Dee Carroll
Maria The Knife—Lucita Blain
Director—Jorge Lopez-Portillo
Leading Players—Jeff Morrow, Jim Ross, Guinn "Big Boy" Williams

FIVE BRANDED WOMEN (1960, Paramount)
Marja—Barbara Bel Geddes
Jovanka—Silvano Mangano
Daniza—Vera Miles
Ljuba—Jeanne Moreau
Mira—Carla Gravina
Director—Martin Ritt
Leading Players—Richard Basehart, Harry Guardino, Steve Forrest, Alex Nicol

THE FIVE HEARTBEATS (1991, 20th Century Fox)
Duck—Robert Townsend
Eddie—Michael Wright
J.T.—Leon
Dresser—Harry J. Lennix
Choirboy—Tico Wells
Director—Robert Townsend
Leading Players—Chuck Patterson, Diahann Carroll, Hawthorne James, Harold Nicholas

FIVE LITTLE PEPPERS AND HOW THEY GREW (1939, Columbia)
Polly Pepper—Edith Fellows
Ben Pepper—Charles Peck
Joey Pepper—Tommy Bond
Davie Pepper—Jimmy Leake
Phronsie Pepper—Dorothy Ann Seese
Director—Charles Barton
Leading Players—Clarence Kolb, Dorothy Peterson, Ronald Sinclair

FIVE LITTLE PEPPERS AT HOME (1940, Columbia)
Polly Pepper—Edith Fellows
Ben Pepper—Charles Peck
Joey Pepper—Tommy Bond
Davie Pepper—Bobby Larson
Phronsie Pepper—Dorothy Ann Seese
Director—Charles Barton
Leading Players—Clarence Kolb, Dorothy Peterson, Ronald Sinclair

FIVE LITTLE PEPPERS IN TROUBLE (1940, Columbia)
Polly Pepper—Edith Fellows
Ben Pepper—Charles Peck
Joey Pepper—Tommy Bond
Davie Pepper—Bobby Larson
Phronsie Pepper—Dorothy Ann Seese
Director—Charles Barton
Leading Players—Dorothy Peterson, Pierre Watkin, Ronald Sinclair

THE FIVE POUND MAN (1937, GB, Fox British)
Richard Fordyce—Edwin Styles
Director—Albert Parker
Leading Players—Judy Gunn, Frank Allenby, Charles Bannister

THE 5,000 FINGERS OF DR. T. (1953, Columbia)
Dr. Terwilliker—Hans Conreid
Director—Roy Rowland
Leading Players—Peter Lind Hayes, Mary Healy, Tommy Rettig

THE FIXER (1968, MGM)
Yakov Bok—Alan Bates
Director—John Frankenheimer
Leading Players—Dirk Bogarde, Georgia Brown, Hugh Griffith

FIXER DUGAN (1939, RKO)
Charlie Dugan—Lee Tracy
Director—Lew Landers
Leading Players—Virginia Weidler, Peggy Shannon, Bradley Page

THE FLAG LIEUTENANT (1919, GB, Silent, Jury)
Lt. Dicky Lascelles—George Wynn
Director—Percy Nash
Leading Players—Ivy Close, Dorothy Fane, Ernest Wallace

THE FLAG LIEUTENANT (1926, GB, Silent, Astra)
Lt. Dicky Lascelles—Henry Edwards
Director—Maurice Elvey
Leading Players—Lillian Oldland, Dorothy Seacombe, Fred Raynham

THE FLAG LIEUTENANT (1932, GB, Gaumont)
Lt. Dicky Lascelles—Henry Edwards
Director—Henry Edwards
Leading Players—Anna Neagle, Joyce Bland, Peter Gawthorne

FLAME OF CALCUTTA (1953, Columbia)
Suzanne Roget—Denise Darcel
Director—Seymour Friedman
Leading Players—Patric Knowles, Paul Cavanaugh, George Keymas

THE FLAME OF NEW ORLEANS (1941, Universal)
Claire Ledeux—Marlene Dietrich
Director—Rene Clair
Leading Players—Bruce Cabot, Roland Young, Mischa Auer

FLAME OF STAMBOUL (1957, Columbia)
Lynette Garay—Lisa Ferraday
Director—Ray Nazarro
Leading Players—Richard Denning, Norman Lloyd, George Zucco

FLAME OF THE BARBARY COAST (1945, Republic)
Flaxen Tarry—Ann Dvorak
Director—Joseph Kane
Leading Players—John Wayne, Joseph Schildkraut, William Frawley, Virginia Grey

FLAME OF THE ISLANDS (1955, Republic)
Rosalind Dee—Yvonne De Carlo
Director—Edward Ludwig
Leading Players—Howard Duff, Zachary Scott, Kurt Kasznar

FLAME OF THE WEST (1945, Monogram)
John Poore—Johnny Mack Brown
Director—Lambert Hillyer
Leading Players—Raymond Hatton, Joan Woodbury, Douglas Dumbrille

FLAMINGO KID (1984, 20th Century Fox)
Jeffrey Willis—Matt Dillon
Director—Garry Marshall
Leading Players—Hector Elizondo, Molly McCarthy, Martha Gehman, Richard Crenna, Jessica Walter

FLANAGAN (1985, United Films)
James Flanagan—Philip Bosco
Director—Scott Goldstein
Leading Players—Geraldine Page, Linda Thorson, William Hickey

THE FLAPPER (1920, Silent, Selznick Films)
Ginger King—Olive Thomas
Director—Alan Crosland
Leading Players—Warren Cook, Louise Lindroth, Theodore Westman, Jr.

FLASH AND THE FIRECAT (1976, Sebastian)
Firecat—Roger Davis
Flash—Tricia Sembera
Director—Ferd & Beverley Sebastian
Leading Players—Dub Taylor, Richard Kiel, Joan Shawlee

FLASH GORDON (1936, Universal)
Flash Gordon—Larry "Buster" Crabbe
Director—Frederick Stephani
Leading Players—Jean Rogers, Charles Middleton, Priscilla Lawson, John Lipson, Frank Shannon

FLASH GORDON (1980, Universal)
Flash Gordon—Sam J. Jones
Director—Mike Hodges
Leading Players—Melody Anderson, Topol, Max Von Sydow, Brian Blessed, Timothy Dalton

FLATLINERS (1990, Columbia/Stonebridge)
Nelson—Keifer Sutherland
Rachel—Julia Roberts
Labraccio—Kevin Bacon
Joe—William Baldwin
Steckle—Oliver Platt
Director—Joel Schumacher
Leading Players—Kimberly Scott, Joshua Rudoy

FLAXY MARTIN (1949, Warner Brothers)
Flaxy Martin—Virginia Mayo
Director—Richard Bare
Leading Players—Zachary Scott, Dorothy Malone, Tom D'Andrea

FLESH AND THE DEVIL (1926, Silent, MGM)
Felicitas von Eltz—Greta Garbo
Leo von Harden—John Gilbert
Director—Clarence Brown
Leading Players—Lars Hanson, Barbara Kent, William Orlamond

FLETCH (1985, Universal)
Fletch—Chevy Chase
Director—Michael Ritchie
Leading Players—Joe Don Baker, Dana Wheeler-Nicholson, Tim Matheson, Geena Davis

FLETCH LIVES (1989, Universal)
Irwin Maurice 'Fletch' Fletcher—Chevy Chase
Director—Michael Ritchie
Leading Players—Hal Holbrook, Julianne Phillips, Cleavon Little, R. Lee Ermey

FLIGHT LIEUTENANT (1942, Columbia)
Danny Doyle—Glenn Ford
Director—Sidney Salkow
Leading Players—Pat O'Brien, Evelyn Keyes, Jonathan Hale

FLIGHT NURSE (1953, Republic)
Lt. Polly Davis—Joan Leslie
Director—Allan Dwan
Leading Players—Forrest Tucker, Arthur Franz, Jeff Donnell

THE FLIM-FLAM MAN (1967, 20th Century Fox)
Mordecai Jones—George C. Scott
Director—Irvin Kershner
Leading Players—Sue Lyon, Michael Sarrazin, Harry Morgan

THE FLIRT (1922, Silent, Universal)
Cora Madison—Eileen Percy
Director—Hobart Henley
Leading Players—George Nichols, Lydia Knott, Helen Jerome Eddy

THE FLIRTING WIDOW (1930, Warner Brothers)
Celia—Dorothy Mackaill
Director—William A. Seiter
Leading Players—Basil Rathbone, Leila Hyams, William Austin

THE FLORODORA GIRL (1930, MGM)
Daisy—Marion Davies
Director—Harry Beaumont
Leading Players—Lawrence Gray, Walter Catlett, Louis John Bartels

THE FLYING DEUCES (1939, RKO)
Stan—Stan Laurel
Ollie—Oliver Hardy
Director—A. Edward Sutherland
Leading Players—Jean Parker, Reginald Gardiner, Charles Middleton

THE FLYING DOCTOR (1936, Australia, GFD)
Dr. John Vaughn—James Raglan
Director—Miles Mander
Leading Players—Charles Farrell, Mary Maguire, Joe Valli

FLYING HOSTESS (1936, Universal)
Helen Brooks—Judith Barrett
Director—Murray Roth
Leading Players—William Gargan, William Hall, Astrid Allwyn

THE FLYING IRISHMAN (1939, RKO)
"Wrong Way" Corrigan—Douglas Corrigan
Director—Leigh Jason
Leading Players—Paul Kelly, Robert Armstrong, Gene Reynolds

FLYING ROMEOS (1928, Silent, First National)
Cohan—Charlie Murray
Cohen—George Sidney
Director—Mervyn LeRoy
Leading Players—Fritzi Ridgeway, Lester Bernard, Duke Martin

FOLKS (1992, 20th Century Fox)
Harry Aldrich—Don Ameche
Mildred Aldrich—Anne Jackson
Director—Ted Kotcheff
Leading Players—Tom Selleck, Christine Ebersole, Wendy Crewson, Robert Pastorelli, Michael Murphy

FOLLIES GIRL (1943, Producers Releasing Corp.)
Anne Merriday—Wendy Barrie
Director—William Rowland
Leading Players—Doris Nolan, Gordon Oliver, Anne Barrett

FOLLOW ME, BOYS! (1966, Buena Vista)
Lemuel Siddons—Fred MacMurray
Director—Norman Tokar
Leading Players—Vera Miles, Lillian Gish, Charlie Ruggles

THE FOOL (1990, GB, Sands/Film Four)
Sir John/Mr. Frederick—Derek Jacobi
Director—Christine Edzard
Leading Players—Cyril Cusack, Ruth Mitchell, Paul Brooke, Corin Redgrave, Alec Wallis

THE FOOL AND THE PRINCESS (1948, GB, GFD)
Harry Granville—Bruce Lester
Moura—Adina Mandlova
Director—William C. Hammond
Leading Players—Lesley Brook, Irene Handl, Murray Matheson

FOOL FOR LOVE (1985, Cannon)
Eddie—Sam Shepard
Director—Robert Altman

Leading Players—Kim Basinger, Harry Dean Stanton, Randy Quaid

THE FOOL KILLER (1965, Allied Artists)
Milo Bogardus—Anthony Perkins
Director—Servando Gonzalez
Leading Players—Edward Albert, Dana Elcar, Henry Hull

FOOLS OF FORTUNE (1990, GB, Palace/New Line)
Willie Quinton—Iain Glen
Marianne—Mary Elizabeth Mastrantonio
Director—Pat O'Connor
Leading Players—Julie Christie, Michael Kitchen, Sean T. McClory, Frankie McCafferty, Niamii Cusack

THE FOOTLOOSE HEIRESS (1937, Warner Brothers)
Kay Allyn—Ann Sheridan
Director—William Clemens
Leading Players—Craig Reynolds, Anne Nagel, William Hopper

FOR LOVE OF IVY (1968, Palomar/Cinerama)
Ivy Moore—Abbey Lincoln
Director—Daniel Mann
Leading Players—Sidney Poitier, Beau Bridges, Nan Martin

FOR ME AND MY GAL (1942, MGM)
Jo Hayden—Judy Garland
Harry Palmer—Gene Kelly
Director—Busby Berkeley
Leading Players—George Murphy, Marta Eggerth, Ben Blue

FOR PETE'S SAKE (1977, Columbia)
Pete—Michael Sarrazin
Director—Peter Yates
Leading Players—Barbra Streisand, Estelle Parsons, Molly Picon

FOR THE DEFENSE (1930, Paramount)
William Foster—William Powell
Director—John Cromwell
Leading Players—Kay Francis, Scott Kolk, William B. Davidson

FOR THE LOVE O'LIL (1930, Columbia)
Lil—Sally Starr
Director—James Tinling
Leading Players—Jack Mulhall, Elliot Nugent, Margaret Livingston

FOR THE LOVE OF MARY (1948, Universal)
Mary Peppertree—Deanna Durbin
Director—Frederick De Cordova
Leading Players—Edmond O'Brien, Don Taylor, Jeffrey Lynn

FOR THE LOVE OF MIKE (1933, GB, BIP/Wardour)
Mike—Constance Shotter
Director—Monty Banks
Leading Players—Bobby Howes, Arthur Riscoe, Renee Macready

THE FORBIDDEN WOMAN (1920, Silent, Equity Pictures)
Diane Sorel—Clara Kimball Young
Director—Harry Garson
Leading Players—Conway Tearle, Jiquel Fanol, Kathryn Adams

FOREIGN BODY (1986, GB, Orion)
Jo Masters—Jane Laurie
Director—Ronald Neame

Leading Players—Victor Banerjee, Warren Mitchell, Geraldine McEwan, Denis Quilley

FOREIGN CORRESPONDENT (1940, UA)
Johnny Jones/Huntley Haverstock—Joel McCrea
Director—Alfred Hitchcock
Leading Players—Laraine Day, Herbert Marshall, George Sanders, Albert Basserman, Edmund Gwenn

THE FOREST RANGERS (1942, Paramount)
Don Stuart—Fred MacMurray
Director—George Marshall
Leading Players—Paulette Goddard, Susan Hayward, Lynne Overmann, Albert Dekker

FOREVER AMBER (1947, 20th Century Fox)
Amber St. Clair—Linda Darnell
Director—Otto Preminger
Leading Players—Cornel Wilde, Richard Greene, George Sanders, Richard Haydn, Jessica Tandy

FOREVER FEMALE (1953, Paramount)
Beatrice Page—Ginger Rogers
Director—Irving Rapper
Leading Players—William Holden, Paul Douglas, James Gleason, Pat Crowley, Jesse White

FOREVER, LULU (1987, Tri-Star)
Lulu—Deborah Harry
Director—Amos Kollek
Leading Players—Hanna Schygulla, Alec Baldwin, Annie Golden

THE FORGOTTEN WOMAN (1939, Universal)
Anne Kennedy—Sigrid Gurie
Director—Harold Young
Leading Players—Eve Arden, William Lundigan, Donald Briggs

FORGOTTEN WOMEN (1932, Monogram)
Patricia Young—Marion Shilling
Sissy Salem—Virginia Lee Corbin
Director—Richard Thorpe
Leading Players—Rex Bell, Beryl Mercer, Carmelita Geraghty

THE FORTUNATE FOOL (1933, GB, Associated British)
Jim Falconer—Hugh Wakefield
Director—Norman Walker
Leading Players—Joan Wyndham, Jack Raine, Elizabeth Jenns

THE FORTUNE HUNTER (1927, Silent, Warner Brothers)
Nat Duncan—Sydney Chaplin
Director—Charles F. Reisner
Leading Players—Helene Costello, Clara Horton, Duke Martin

FORTUNES OF CAPTAIN BLOOD (1950, Columbia)
Capt. Peter Blood—Louis Hayward
Director—Gordon Douglas
Leading Players—Patricia Medina, George Macready, Alfonso Bedoya, Dona Drake

FORTY POUNDS OF TROUBLE (1962, Universal)
Penny Piper—Claire Wilcox
Director—Norman Jewison
Leading Players—Tony Curtis, Phil Silvers, Suzanne Pleshette

4D MAN (1959, Universal)
Scott Nelson—Robert Lansing

Director—Irvin Shortess Yeaworth, Jr.
Leading Players—Lee Meriwether, James Congdon, Jasper Deeter

FOUR DAUGHTERS (1938, Warner Brothers)
Ann Lemp—Priscilla Lane
Thea Lemp—Lola Lane
Kay Lemp—Rosemary Lane
Emma Lemp—Gale Page
Director—Michael Curtiz
Leading Players—Claude Rains, May Robson, John Garfield, Jeffrey Lynn, Dick Foran

FOUR FOR TEXAS (1963, Warner Brothers)
Zack Thomas—Frank Sinatra
Joe Jarrett—Dean Martin
Elya Carlson—Anita Ekberg
Maxine Ritcher—Ursula Andress
Director—Robert Aldrich
Leading Players—Charles Bronson, Victor Buono, Edric Connor, the Three Stooges

FOUR FRIENDS (1981, Filmways Pictures)
Danilo Prozor—Craig Wasson
Georgia Miles—Jodi Thelen
Tom Donaldson—Jim Metzler
David Levene—Michael Huddleston
Director—Arthur Penn
Leading Players—Reed Birney, Julia Murray, David Graf

FOUR FRIGHTENED PEOPLE (1934, Paramount)
Judy Cavendish—Claudette Colbert
Arnold Ainger—Herbert Marshall
Mrs. Mardick—Mary Boland
Stewart Corder—William Gargan
Director—Cecil B. De Mille
Leading Players—Leo Carrillo, Nella Walker, Tetsu Komai

FOUR GIRLS IN TOWN (1956, Universal)
Kathy Conway—Julie Adams
Ina Schiller—Marianne Cook
Maria Antonelli—Elsa Martinelli
Vicki Dauray—Gia Scala
Director—Jack Sher
Leading Players—George Nader, Sydney Chaplin, Helene Stanton

FOUR GIRLS IN WHITE (1939, MGM)
Norma Page—Florence Rice
Gertie Robbins—Una Merkel
Patricia Page—Ann Rutherford
Mary Forbes—Mary Howard
Director—S. Sylvan Simon
Leading Players—Alan Marshal, Kent Taylor, Buddy Ebsen

FOUR JACKS AND A JILL (1941, RKO)
Nifty—Ray Bolger
Nina—Anne Shirley
Happy—Eddie Foy, Jr.
Nat—Jack Briggs
Eddie—William Blees
Director—Jack Hively
Leading Players—June Havoc, Desi Arnaz, Jack Durant

FOUR JILLS IN A JEEP (1944, 20th Century Fox)
Kay Francis—Kay Francis
Carole Landis—Carole Landis
Martha Raye—Martha Raye
Mitzi Mayfair—Mitzi Mayfair
Director—William A. Seiter
Leading Players—John Harvey, Phil Silvers, Dick Haymes

FOUR MEN AND A PRAYER (1938, 20th Century Fox)
Geoff Leigh—Richard Greene
Wyatt Leigh—George Sanders
Christopher Leigh—David Niven
Rodney Leigh—William Henry
Director—John Ford
Leading Players—Loretta Young, C. Aubrey Smith, J. Edward Bromberg, Alan Hale, John Carradine

FOUR MOTHERS (1941, Warner Brothers)
Ann Lemp Dietz—Priscilla Lane
Kay Lemp Forrest—Rosemary Lane
Thea Lemp Crowley—Lola Lane
Emma Lemp Talbot—Gale Page
Director—William Keighley
Leading Players—Claude Rains, Jeffrey Lynn, Eddie Albert, May Robson, Frank McHugh, Dick Foran

THE FOUR MUSKETEERS (1975, 20th Century Fox)
D'Artagnan—Michael York
Athos—Oliver Reed
Aramis—Richard Chamberlain
Porthos—Frank Finlay
Director—Richard Lester
Leading Players—Raquel Welch, Christopher Lee, Faye Dunaway, Charlton Heston, Simon Ward

THE FOUR SKULLS OF JONATHAN DRAKE (1959, UA)
Jonathan Drake—Eduard Franz
Director—Edward L. Cahn
Leading Players—Valerie French, Henry Daniell, Grant Richards

FOUR SONS (1928, Silent, Fox Film Corp.)
Joseph Bernie—James Hall
Johann Bernie—Charles Morton
Franz Bernie—Francis X. Bushman
Andres Bernie—George Meeker
Director—John Ford
Leading Players—Margaret Mann, Earle Foxe, Albert Gran

FOUR SONS (1940, 20th Century Fox)
Chris Bernie—Don Ameche
Karl Bernie—Alan Curtis
Fritz Bernie—George Ernest
Joseph Bernie—Robert Lowery
Director—Archie Mayo
Leading Players—Eugenie Leontovich, Mary Beth Hughes, Lionel Royce

FOUR WIVES (1939, Warner Brothers)
Emma Lemp—Gale Page
Ann Lemp—Priscilla Lane
Kay Lemp—Rosemary Lane
Thea Lemp—Lola Lane
Director—Michael Curtiz

Leading Players—Claude Rains, Jeffrey Lynn, May Robson, Eddie Albert, John Garfield

THE FOX (1967, Warner Brothers)
Paul—Keir Dullea
Director—Mark Rydell
Leading Players—Sandy Dennis, Anne Heywood

THE FOXES OF HARROW (1947, 20th Century Fox)
Stephen Fox—Rex Harrison
Odalie D'Arceneaux Fox—Maureen O'Hara
Director—John M. Stahl
Leading Players—Richard Haydn, Victor McLaglen, Vanessa Brown, Patricia Medina

FOXY BROWN (1974, American International)
Foxy Brown—Pam Grier
Director—Jack Hill
Leading Players—Antonio Fargas, Peter Brown, Terry Carter

FRAMED (1940, Universal)
Henry T. Parker—Frank Albertson
Director—Harold Schuster
Leading Players—Constance Moore, Jerome Cowan, Robert Armstrong

FRAMED (1947, Columbia)
Mike Lambert—Glenn Ford
Director—Richard Wallace
Leading Players—Janis Carter, Barry Sullivan, Edgar Buchanan

FRAMED (1975, Paramount)
Ron—Joe Don Baker
Director—Phil Karlson
Leading Players—Conny Van Dyke, Gabriel Dell, John Marley

FRANCES (1982, Universal)
Frances Farmer—Jessica Lange
Director—Graeme Clifford
Leading Players—Sam Shepard, Kim Stanley, Bart Burns

FRANCIS OF ASSISI (1961, 20th Century Fox)
Francis Bernardone—Bradford Dillman
Director—Michael Curtiz
Leading Players—Dolores Hart, Stuart Whitman, Pedro Armendariz, Cecil Kellaway

FRANKENHOOKER (1990, Glickenhaus)
Elizabeth—Patty Mullen
Director—Frank Henenlotter
Leading Players—James Lorinz, Charlotte Helmkamp, Shirley Stoler, Louise Lasser, Joseph Gonzalez

FRANKENSTEIN (1931, Universal)
Dr. Henry Frankenstein—Colin Clive
Director—James Whale
Leading Players—Mae Clarke, John Boles, Boris Karloff, Edward Van Sloan, Dwight Frye

FRANKENSTEIN AND THE MONSTER FROM HELL (1974, GB, Hammer)
Baron Frankenstein—Peter Cushing
The Monster—Dave Prowse
Director—Terence Fisher

Leading Players—Shane Briant, Madeline Smith, John Stratton

FRANKENSTEIN CREATED WOMAN (1965, GB, Hammer)
Baron Frankenstein—Peter Cushing
Christina—Susan Denberg
Director—Terence Fisher
Leading Players—Thorley Walters, Robert Morris, Peter Blythe

FRANKENSTEIN GENERAL HOSPITAL (1988, New Star)
Dr. Bob Frankenstein—Mark Blankfield
Director—Deborah Roberts
Leading Players—Leslie Jordan, Jonathan Farwell, Kathy Shower, Irwin Keyes

FRANKENSTEIN MEETS THE WOLF MAN (1943, Universal)
Lawrence Talbot/The Wolf Man—Lon Chaney, Jr.
Baroness Elsa Frankenstein—Ilona Massey
The Monster—Bela Lugosi
Director—Roy William Neill
Leading Players—Patric Knowles, Lionel Atwill, Maria Ouspenskaya, Dennis Hoey

FRANKENSTEIN MUST BE DESTROYED (1969, GB, Hammer)
Baron Frankenstein—Peter Cushing
Director—Terence Fisher
Leading Players—Veronica Carlson, Freddie Jones, Simon Ward

FRANKENSTEIN 1970 (1958, Allied Artists)
Baron Victor von Frankenstein—Boris Karloff
Director—Howard W. Koch
Leading Players—Tom Duggan, Jana Lund, Donald Barry

FRANKENSTEIN UNBOUND (1990, 20th Century Fox)
Dr. Frankenstein—Raul Julia
The Monster—Nick Brimble
Director—Roger Corman
Leading Players—John Hurt, Bridget Fonda, Catherine Rabett, Jason Patric, Michael Hutchence

FRANKIE AND JOHNNY (1936, Republic)
Frankie—Helen Morgan
Johnny—Chester Morris
Directors—Chester Erskine & John H. Auer
Leading Players—Florence Reed, Walter Kingsford, William Harrigan, Lilyan Tashman

FRANKIE AND JOHNNY (1966, UA)
Johnny—Elvis Presley
Frankie—Donna Douglas
Director—Frederick De Cordova
Leading Players—Harry Morgan, Sue Anne Langdon, Nancy Kovack

FRANKIE AND JOHNNY (1991, Paramount)
Frankie—Michelle Pfeiffer
Johnny—Al Pacino
Director—Garry Marshall
Leading Players—Hector Elizondo, Nathan Lane, Kate Nelligan, Jane Morris, Greg Lewis

FRANTIC (1988, Warner Brothers)
Dr. Richard Walker—Harrison Ford
Director—Roman Polanski
Leading Players—Betty Buckley, John Mahoney, Emmanuelle Seigner, Gerald Klein

FRAULEIN (1958, 20th Century Fox)
Erika Angermann—Dana Wynter
Director—Henry Koster
Leading Players—Mel Ferrer, Dolores Michaels, Maggie Hayes

THE FRECKLED RASCAL (1929, Silent, FBO/RKO)
Red Hepner—Buzz Barton
Director—Louis King
Leading Players—Milburn Morante, Tom Lingham, Lotus Thompson

FRECKLES (1935, RKO)
Freckles—Tom Brown
Director—Edward Killy
Leading Players—Virginia Weidler, Carol Stone, Lumsden Hare

FRECKLES (1960, 20th Century Fox)
Freckles—Martin West
Director—Andrew V. McLaglen
Leading Players—Carol Christensen, Jack Lambert, Steven Peck

FRECKLES COMES HOME (1942, Monogram)
Freckles—Johnny Downs
Director—Jean Yarborough
Leading Players—Gale Storm, Mantan Moreland, Bradley Page

FREDDY'S DEAD: THE FINAL NIGHTMARE (1991, New Line)
Freddy Krueger—Robert Englund
Director—Rachel Talalay
Leading Players—Lisa Zane, Shon Greenblatt, Lezlie Deane, Ricky Dean Logan, Breckin Meyer, Yaphet Kotto

FREE, BLONDE AND 21 (1940, 20th Century Fox)
Carol—Lynn Bari
Director—Ricardo Cortez
Leading Players—Mary Beth Hughes, Joan Davis, Henry Wilcoxon

A FREE SOUL (1931, MGM)
Jan Ashe—Norma Shearer
Director—Clarence Brown
Leading Players—Leslie Howard, Lionel Barrymore, Clark Gable

FREE, WHITE AND 21 (1963, American International)
Greta Mae Hansen—Annalena Lund
Director—Larry Buchanan
Leading Players—Frederick O'Neal, George Edgely, George Russell

FREEBIE AND THE BEAN (1974, Warner Brothers)
Bean—Alan Arkin
Freebie—James Caan
Director—Richard Rush
Leading Players—Loretta Swit, Jack Kruschen, Mike Kellin

THE FREEWAY MANIAC (1989, Cannon Group)
Arthur—James Courtney
Director—Paul Winters
Leading Players—Loren Winters, Shepard Sanders, Donald Hotton

THE FRENCH DOLL (1923, Silent, Tiffany/Metro)
Georgine Mazulier—Mae Murray
Director—Robert Z. Leonard

Leading Players—Orville Caldwell, Rod La Rocque, Rose Dione

THE FRENCH LIEUTENANT'S WOMAN (1981, UA)
Sarah—Meryl Streep
Director—Karel Reisz
Leading Players—Jeremy Irons, Hilton McRae, Emily Morgan, Leo McKern

FRENCH MISTRESS (1960, GB, British Lion)
Madeleine Lafarge—Agnes Laurent
Director—Roy Boulting
Leading Players—Cecil Parker, James Robertson Justice, Ian Bannen, Raymond Huntley

FRENCHIE (1950, Universal)
Frenchie Fontaine—Shelley Winters
Director—Louis King
Leading Players—Joel McCrea, Paul Kelly, Elsa Lanchester

THE FRESHIE (1922, Silent, Herbst/Di Lorenzo)
Charles Taylor—Guinn "Big Boy" Williams
Director—W. Hughes Curran
Leading Players—Molly Malone, Lincoln Stedman, James McElhern

THE FRESHMAN (1925, Silent, Pathe Exchange)
Harold "Speedy" Lamb—Harold Lloyd
Directors—Sam Taylor & Fred Newmeyer
Leading Players—Jobyna Ralston, Brooks Benedict, James Anderson

THE FRESHMAN (1990, Tri-Star/Lobell/Bergman)
Clark Kellogg—Matthew Broderick
Director—Andrew Bergman
Leading Players—Marlon Brando, Bruno Kirby, Penelope Ann Miller, Frank Whaley, Joe Polito

FREUD (1962, Universal)
Sigmund Freud—Montgomery Clift
Director—John Huston
Leading Players—Susannah York, Larry Parks, Susan Kohner

FRIDAY FOSTER (1975, American International)
Friday Foster—Pam Grier
Director—Arthur Marks
Leading Players—Yaphet Kotto, Godfrey Cambridge, Thalmus Rasulala

FRIDAY THE 13TH PART VIII—JASON TAKES MANHATTAN (1989, Paramount)
Jason—Kane Hodder
Director—Bob Hedden
Leading Players—Jensen Daggett, Scott Reeves, Peter Mark Richman, Barbara Bingham

FRIENDLY ENEMIES (1942, UA)
Karl Pfeiffer—Charles Winniger
Henry Block—Charlie Ruggles
Director—Allan Dwan
Leading Players—James Craig, Nancy Kelly, Otto Kruger

A FRIENDLY HUSBAND (1923, Silent, Fox Film Corp.)
Friend Husband—Lupino Lane
Director—John Blystone

Leading Players—Alberta Vaughn, Eva Thatcher

FRIENDS (1971, GB, Paramount)
Paul Harrison—Sean Bury
Michelle LaTour—Anicee Alvina
Director—Lewis Gilbert
Leading Players—Pascale Roberts, Sady Rebbot, Ronald Lewis

THE FRIGHTENED MAN (1952, GB, Tempean)
Mr. Roselli—Charles Victor
Director—John Gilling
Leading Players—Dermot Walsh, Barbara Murray, John Blythe

FRISCO JENNY (1933, Warner Brothers)
Frisco Jenny—Ruth Chatterton
Director—William A. Wellman
Leading Players—Donald Cook, James Murray, Louis Calhern

FRISCO KID (1935, Warner Brothers)
Bat Morgan—James Cagney
Director—Lloyd Bacon
Leading Players—Margaret Lindsay, Ricardo Cortez, Lily
Damita, Donald Woods

THE FRISCO KID (1979, Warner Brothers)
Avram Belinsky—Gene Wilder
Director—Robert Aldrich
Leading Players—Harrison Ford, Ramon Bieri, Penny Peyser

FRISCO LIL (1942, Universal)
Lillian Grayson—Irene Hervey
Director—Erle C. Kenton
Leading Players—Kent Taylor, Minor Watson, Jerome Cowan

FRISCO SAL (1945, Universal)
Sally—Susanna Foster
Director—George Waggner
Leading Players—Turhan Bey, Alan Curtis, Andy Devine

THE FROGMEN (1951, 20th Century Fox)
Lt. Cmdr. John Lawrence—Richard Widmark
Director—Lloyd Bacon
Leading Players—Dana Andrews, Gary Merrill, Jeffrey Hunter

**FROM THE MIXED-UP FILES OF MRS. BASIL E.
FRANKWEILER** (1973, Cinema 5)
Mrs. Frankweiler—Ingrid Bergman
Director—Fiedler Cook
Leading Players—Sally Prager, Johnny Doran, George Rose

THE FRONT (1976, Columbia)
Howard Prince—Woody Allen
Director—Martin Ritt
Leading Players—Zero Mostel, Herschel Bernardi, Michael
Murphy, Andrea Marcovicci

FRONT PAGE WOMAN (1935, Warner Brothers)
Ellen Garfield—Bette Davis
Director—Michael Curtiz
Leading Players—George Brent, Roscoe Karns, Winifred Shaw

FRONTIER AGENT (1948, Monogram)
"Nevada" Jack McKensie—Johnny Mack Brown
Director—Lambert Hillyer

Leading Players—Raymond Hatton, Reno Blair, Kenneth
MacDonald

FRONTIER CRUSADER (1940, Producers Releasing Corp.)
Trigger Tim Rand—Tim McCoy
Director—Pete Stewart
Leading Players—Dorothy Short, Lou Fulton, Karl Hackett

FRONTIER GAL (1945, Universal)
Lorena Dumont—Yvonne De Carlo
Director—Charles Lamont
Leading Players—Rod Cameron, Andy Devine, Fuzzy Knight

FRONTIER MARSHAL (1934, Fox Film Corp.)
Michael Wyatt—George O'Brien
Director—Lew Seiler
Leading Players—Irene Bentley, George E. Stone, Alan Edwards

FRONTIER MARSHAL (1939, 20th Century Fox)
Wyatt Earp—Randolph Scott
Director—Allan Dwan
Leading Players—Nancy Kelly, Cesar Romero, Binnie Barnes,
John Carradine

FRONTIER SCOUT (1939, Fine Arts)
Wild Bill Hickok—George Houston
Director—Sam Newfield
Leading Players—Al St. John, Beth Marion, Dave O'Brien

THE FUGITIVE (1940, GB, Universal)
Will Kobling—Ralph Richardson
Director—Brian Desmond Hurst
Leading Players—Diana Wynyard, Romney Brent, Mary Clare

THE FUGITIVE (1947, RKO)
The Fugitive—Henry Fonda
Director—John Ford
Leading Players—Dolores Del Rio, Pedro Armendariz, Ward
Bond, Leo Carrillo, J. Carroll Naish

THE FUGITIVE KIND (1960, UA)
Val Xavier—Marlon Brando
Director—Sidney Lumet
Leading Players—Anna Magnani, Joanne Woodward, Maureen
Stapleton, Victor Jory

FUGITIVE LADY (1934, Columbia)
Ann Duncan—Florence Rice
Director—Al Rogell
Leading Players—Neil Hamilton, Donald Cook, Clara Blandick

FUGITIVE LADY (1951, Republic)
Barbara Clementi—Janis Paige
Director—Sidney Salkow
Leading Players—Binnie Barnes, Massimo Serato, Eduardo
Ciannelli, Tony Centa

FUGITIVE LOVERS (1934, MGM)
Paul Porter—Robert Montgomery
Letty Morris—Madge Evans
Director—Richard Boleslawski
Leading Players—Ted Healy, Nat Pendleton, C. Henry Gordon

THE FUGITIVE SHERIFF (1936, Columbia)
Ken Marshall—Ken Maynard

Director—Spencer G. Bennett
Leading Players—Beth Marion, Walter Miller, Hal Price

FUGITIVES (1929, Silent, Fox Film Corp.)
Alice Carroll—Madge Bellamy
Dick Starr—Don Terry
Director—William Beaudine
Leading Players—Arthur Stone, Earle Foxe, Matthew Betz

FULL OF LIFE (1956, Columbia)
Emily Rocco—Judy Holliday
Director—Richard Quine
Leading Players—Richard Conte, Salvatore Bacaloni, Esther Minicotti

THE FULLER BRUSH GIRL (1950, Columbia)
Sally Elliot—Lucille Ball
Director—Lloyd Bacon
Leading Players—Eddie Albert, Carl Benton Reid, Gale Robbins

FULLER BRUSH MAN (1948, Columbia)
Red Jones—Red Skelton
Director—S. Sylvan Simon
Leading Players—Janet Blair, Don McGuire, Hilary Brooke

FUN WITH DICK AND JANE (1977, Columbia)
Dick Harper—George Segal
Jane Harper—Jane Fonda
Director—Ted Kotcheff
Leading Players—Ed McMahon, Dick Gautier, Allan Miller

FUNNY FACE (1957, Paramount)
Jo Stockton—Audrey Hepburn
Director—Stanley Donen
Leading Players—Fred Astaire, Kay Thompson, Michel Auclair

FUNNY GIRL (1968, Columbia)
Fanny Brice—Barbra Streisand
Director—William Wyler
Leading Players—Omar Sharif, Kay Medford, Anne Francis, Walter Pidgeon

FUNNY LADY (1975, Columbia)
Fanny Brice—Barbra Streisand
Director—Herbert Ross
Leading Players—James Caan, Omar Sharif, Roddy McDowall, Larry Gates, Ben Vereen

FUNNYMAN (1967, Korty)
Perry—Peter Bonerz
Director—John Korty
Leading Players—Sandra Archer, Carol Androsky, Larry Hankin

FURTHER ADVENTURES OF THE FLAG LIEUTENANT (1927, GB, Silent, Neo-Art)
Lt. Dicky Lascelles—Henry Edwards
Director—W.P. Kellino
Leading Players—Isabel Jeans, Lillian Oldland, Lyn Harding

THE FURTHER ADVENTURES OF TENNESSEE BUCK (1988, Trans World)
Buck Malone—David Keith
Director—David Keith
Leading Players—Kathy Shower, Brant Van Hoffman, Sillaiyoor Selvarajan

G

G.I. JANE (1951, Lippert)
Jan—Jean Porter
Director—Reginald Le Borg
Leading Players—Tom Neal, Iris Adrian, Jimmy Dodd, Jean Mahoney

G.I. WAR BRIDES (1946, Republic)
Linda Powell—Anna Lee
Director—George Blair
Leading Players—James Ellison, Harry Davenport, William Henry

G-MEN (1935, Warner Brothers)
James "Brick" Davis—James Cagney
Director—William Keighley
Leading Players—Ann Dvorak, Margaret Lindsay, Robert Armstrong, Barton MacLane

GABLE AND LOMBARD (1976, Universal)
Clark Gable—James Brolin
Carole Lombard—Jill Clayburgh
Director—Sidney J. Furie
Leading Players—Allen Garfield, Red Buttons, Joanne Linville

GABY (1956, MGM)
Gaby—Leslie Caron
Director—Curtis Bernhardt
Leading Players—John Kerr, Cedric Hardwicke, Tania Elg

GABY—A TRUE STORY (1987, Tri-Star)
Gabriella "Gaby" Brimmer—Rachel Levin
Director—Luis Mandoki
Leading Players—Liv Ullmann, Norma Aleandro, Robert Loggia

THE GAIETY GIRLS (1938, GB, UA)
Jeannette—Patricia Ellis
Director—Thornton Freeland
Leading Players—Jack Hulbert, Arthur Riscoe, Googie Withers

THE GAL WHO TOOK THE WEST (1949, Universal)
Lillian Marlowe—Yvonne De Carlo
Director—Frederick De Cordova
Leading Players—Charles Coburn, Scott Brady, John Russell

GALACTIC GIGOLO (1988, Urban Classics)
Eoj—Carmine Capobianco
Director—Gorman Bechard
Leading Players—Debi Thibeault, Ruth Collins, Angela Nichols

GALAXINA (1980, Crown International)
Galaxina—Dorothy R. Stratton
Director—William Sachs
Leading Players—Stephen Macht, James David, Avery Schreiber

THE GALAXY INVADER (1985, Moviecraft Entertainment)
Alien—Glenn Barnes
Director—Don Dohler
Leading Players—Richard Ruxton, Faye Tilles, George Stover

GALILEO (1975, GB, American Film Theatre)
Galileo Galilei—Topol
Director—Joseph Losey

Leading Players—Edward Fox, Colin Blakely, Georgia Brown

GALLANT DEFENDER (1935, Columbia)
Johnny Flagg—Charles Starrett
Director—David Selman
Leading Players—Joan Perry, Harry Woods, Edward J. Le Saint

THE GALLANT FOOL (1926, Silent, Rayart)
Billy Banner—Billy Sullivan
Director—Duke Worne
Leading Players—Hazel Deane, Ruth Boyd, Frank Baker

GALLANT LADY (1934, UA)
Sally—Ann Harding
Director—Gregory La Cava
Leading Players—Clive Brook, Otto Kruger, Tullio Carminati

THE GALLOPING ACE (1924, Silent, Universal)
Jim Jordon—Jack Hoxie
Director—Robert North Bradbury
Leading Players—Margaret Morris, Robert McKim, Frank Rice

GALLOPING GALLAGHER (1924, Silent, Monogram)
Bill Gallagher—Fred Thompson
Director—Albert Rogell
Leading Players—Hazel Keener, Frank Hagney, Nelson McDowell

THE GALLOPING MAJOR (1951, Great Britain, Independent Film Dist.)
Major Arthur Hill—Basil Radford
Director—Henry Cornelius
Leading Players—Jimmy Hanley, Janette Scott, A.E. Matthews

THE GAMBLER (1974, Paramount)
Axel—James Caan
Director—Karel Reisz
Leading Players—Paul Sorvino, Lauren Hutton, Morris Carnovsky, Jacqueline Brooks

THE GAMBLER AND THE LADY (1952, GB, Hammer)
Jim Forster—Dane Clark
Lady Susan Willens—Naomi Chance
Director—Pat Jenkins
Leading Players—Kathleen Bryon, Anthony Forwood, Meredith Edwards

THE GAMBLER FROM NATCHEZ (1954, 20th Century Fox)
Vance Colby—Dale Robertson
Director—Henry Levin
Leading Players—Debra Paget, Thomas Gomez, Lisa Daniels

THE GAMBLER WORE A GUN (1961, UA)
Case Silverthorn—Jim Davis
Director—Edward L. Cahn
Leading Players—Mark Allen, Addison Richards, Merry Anders

GAMBLER'S CHOICE (1944, Paramount)
Ross Hadley—Chester Morris
Director—Frank McDonald
Leading Players—Nancy Kelly, Russell Hayden, Sheldon Leonard

GAMBLING DAUGHTERS (1941, Producers Releasing Corp.)
Diana Cameron—Cecilia Parker
Lillian—Gale Storm

Director—Max Nosseck
Leading Players—Roger Pryor, Robert Baldwin, Sig Arno

GAMBLING LADY (1934, First National)
Lady Lee—Barbara Stanwyck
Director—Archie Mayo
Leading Players—Joel McCrea, Pat O'Brien, C. Aubrey Smith

GANDHI (1982, GB, Columbia)
Mahatma Gandhi—Ben Kingsley
Director—Richard Attenborough
Leading Players—Candice Bergen, Edward Fox, John Gielgud, Trevor Howard, John Mills, Martin Sheen

THE GANG BUSTER (1931, Paramount)
Charlie "Cyclone" Case—Jack Oakie
Director—A. Edward Sutherland
Leading Players—Jean Arthur, William "Stage" Boyd, Wynne Gibson

THE GANGSTER (1947, Allied Artists)
Shubunka—Barry Sullivan
Director—Gordon Wiles
Leading Players—Belita, Joan Lorring, Akim Tamiroff, Henry Morgan, John Ireland

GANGSTER STORY (1959, States Rights)
Jack Martin—Walter Matthau
Director—Walter Matthau
Leading Players—Carol Grace, Bruce McFarlan, Garrett Walberg

GANGSTER'S BOY (1938, Monogram)
Larry Kelly—Jackie Cooper
Tim "Knuckles" Kelly—Robert Warwick
Director—William Nigh
Leading Players—Lucy Gilman, Louise Lorimer, Tommy Wonder

GANJA AND HESS (1973, Kelly-Jordan)
Dr. Hess Green—Duane Jones
Ganja—Marlene Clark
Director—Bill Gunn
Leading Players—Sam Waymon, Leonard Jackson, Candece Tarpley

THE GARBAGE MAN (1963, Cinema Distributors of America)
Garbage Man—Toney Naylor
Director—Eric Sayers
Leading Players—Venita Beatrice, Joseph Lincoln, "Miss" Baby Bailey

THE GARBAGE PAIL KIDS (1987, Atlantic Entertainment)
Greaser Greg—Phil Fondacaro
Ali Gator—Kevin Thompson
Foul Phil—Robert Bell
Nat Nerd—Larry Green
Windy Winston—Arturo Gil
Messy Tessie—Sue Rossitto
Valerie Vomit—Debbie Lee Carrington
Director—Rod Amateau
Leading Players—Anthony Newley, Mackenzie Astin, Katie Barberi, Ron MacLachlan

GARBO TALKS (1984, MGM/UA)
Greta Garbo—Nina Zoe
Director—Sidney Lumet

Leading Players—Anne Bancroft, Ron Silver, Carrie Fisher

GARRISON'S FINISH (1923, Silent, Allied Producers)
Billy Garrison—Jack Pickford
Director—Arthur Rosson
Leading Players—Madge Bellamy, Charles A. Stevenson, Tom Guise

GASOLINE GUS (1921, Silent, Paramount)
Gasoline Gus—Roscoe Arbuckle
Director—James Cruze
Leading Players—Lila Lee, Charles Ogle, Theodore Lorch

THE GATE CRASHER (1928, Silent, Universal)
Dick Henshaw—Glenn Tryon
Director—William James Craft
Leading Players—Patsy Ruth Miller, T. Roy Barnes, Beth Laemmle

GATOR (1976, UA)
Gator McKlusky—Burt Reynolds
Director—Burt Reynolds
Leading Players—Jack Weston, Lauren Hutton, Jerry Reed

THE GAUCHO (1928, Silent, UA)
The Gaucho—Douglas Fairbanks
Director—F. Richard Jones
Leading Players—Lupe Velez, Gervaine Greear, Eve Southern

GAWAIN AND THE GREEN KNIGHT (1973, GB, UA)
Gawain—Murray Head
Green Knight—Nigel Green
Director—Stephen Weeks
Leading Players—Ciaran Madden, Robert Hardy, Davil Leland

THE GAY AMIGO (1949, UA)
Cisco Kid—Duncan Renaldo
Director—Wallace Fox
Leading Players—Leo Carrillo, Joe Sawyer, Walter Baldwin

GAY AND DEVILISH (1922, Silent, Robertson-Cole)
Franchon Browne—Doris May
Director—William A. Seiter
Leading Players—Cullen Landis, Otis Harlan, Jacqueline Logan

THE GAY BRIDE (1934, MGM)
Mary Magiz—Carole Lombard
Director—Jack Conway
Leading Players—Chester Morris, Zasu Pitts, Leo Carrillo, Nat Pendleton

THE GAY BUCKAROO (1932, Allied)
Clint Hale—Hoot Gibson
Director—Phil Rosen
Leading Players—Merna Kennedy, Roy D'Arcy, Edward Pell

THE GAY CABALLERO (1932, Fox Film Corp.)
Don Bob Harkness—Victor McLaglen
Director—Alfred Werker
Leading Players—George O'Brien, Conchita Montenegro, Linda Watkins, C. Henry Gordon

THE GAY CABALLERO (1940, 20th Century Fox)
Cisco Kid—Cesar Romero
Director—Otto Brower
Leading Players—Sheila Ryan, Robert Sterling, Chris-Pin Martin

THE GAY CORINTHIAN (1924, GB, Silent, Butchers)
Squire Hardcastle—Victor McLaglen
Director—Arthur Rooke
Leading Players—Betty Faire, Cameron Carr, Humberston Wright

THE GAY DECEIVERS (1969, Fanfare)
Danny Devlin—Kevin Coughlin
Elliot Crane—Larry Casey
Director—Bruce Kessler
Leading Players—Brooke Bundy, Jo Ann Harris, Michael Greer

THE GAY DESPERADO (1936, UA)
Pablo Braganza—Leo Carrillo
Director—Rouben Mamoulian
Leading Players—Nino Martini, Ida Lupino, Harold Huber

THE GAY DIPLOMAT (1931, RKO)
Capt. Orloff—Ivan Lebedeff
Director—Richard Boleslavsky
Leading Players—Genevieve Tobin, Betty Compson, Ilka Chase

THE GAY DIVORCEE (1934, RKO)
Mimi Glossop—Ginger Rogers
Director—Mark Sandrich
Leading Players—Fred Astaire, Alice Brady, Edward Everett Horton, Erik Rhodes

THE GAY FALCON (1941, RKO)
Gay Lawrence, The Falcon—George Sanders
Director—Irving Reis
Leading Players—Wendy Barrie, Allen Jenkins, Anne Hunter

THE GAY LADY (1949, GB, GFD)
Trottie True—Jean Kent
Director—Brian Desmond Hurst
Leading Players—James Donald, Hugh Sinclair, Lana Morris

THE GAY LORD QUEX (1917, GB, Silent, Ideal)
Lord Quex—Ben Webster
Director—Maurice Elvey
Leading Players—Irene Vanbrugh, Lilian Braithwaite, Hayford Hobbs

THE GAY SISTERS (1942, First National)
Fiona Gaylord—Barbara Stanwyck
Evelyn Gaylord—Geraldine Fitzgerald
Susanna Gaylord—Nancy Coleman
Director—Irving Rapper
Leading Players—George Brent, Donald Crisp, Gig Young

THE GEISHA BOY (1958, Paramount)
Gilbert Wooley—Jerry Lewis
Director—Frank Tashlin
Leading Players—Marie McDonald, Sessue Hayakawa, Barton MacLane, Suzanne Pleshette

THE GENE KRUPA STORY (1959, Columbia)
Gene Krupa—Sal Mineo
Director—Don Weis
Leading Players—Susan Kohner, James Darren, Susan Oliver, Yvonne Craig

GENERAL CRACK (1929, Warner Brothers)
General Crack—John Barrymore
Director—Alan Crosland
Leading Players—Lowell Sherman, Marian Nixon, Armida, Hobart Bosworth

THE GENERAL DIED AT DAWN (1936, Paramount)
Gen. Yang—Akim Tamiroff
Director—Lewis Milestone
Leading Players—Gary Cooper, Madeleine Carroll, Dudley Digges, Porter Hall

GENERAL MASSACRE (1973, Burr Jerger)
Gen. Massacre—Burr Jerger
Director—Burr Jerger
Leading Players—Christine Gish, Tiffany Tate, Tsai, Guy Williams

GENERAL SPANKY (1937, MGM)
Spanky—Spanky McFarland
Director—Fred Newmeyer
Leading Players—Phillips Holmes, Ralph Morgan, Irving Pichel

GENGHIS KHAN (1965, Columbia)
Temujin-Genghis Khan—Omar Sharif
Director—Henry Levin
Leading Players—Stephen Boyd, James Mason, Eli Wallach

GENTLE ANNIE (1944, MGM)
Annie Goss—Marjorie Main
Director—Andrew Marton
Leading Players—James Craig, Donna Reed, Henry Morgan

A GENTLE GANGSTER (1943, Republic)
Mike Hallit—Barton MacLane
Director—Phil Rosen
Leading Players—Molly Lamont, Dick Wessel, Joyce Compton

THE GENTLE GUNMAN (1952, GB, Ealing)
Terence Sullivan—John Mills
Director—Basil Dearden
Leading Players—Dirk Bogarde, Robert Beatty, Elizabeth Sellars

GENTLE JULIA (1923, Silent, Fox Film Corp.)
Julia Atwater—Bessie Love
Director—Rowland V. Lee
Leading Players—Harold Goodwin, Frank Elliott, Charles K. French

GENTLE JULIA (1936, 20th Century Fox)
Julia Atwater—Marsha Hunt
Director—John Blystone
Leading Players—Jane Withers, Tom Brown, Jackie Searl

A GENTLEMAN AFTER DARK (1942, UA)
Harry Melton—Brian Donlevy
Director—Edwin L. Martin
Leading Players—Miriam Hopkins, Preston Foster, Harold Huber, Philip Reed, Gloria Holden

A GENTLEMAN AT HEART (1942, 20th Century Fox)
Tony Miller—Cesar Romero
Director—Ray McCarey
Leading Players—Carole Landis, Milton Berle, J. Carroll Naish, Rose Hobart

GENTLEMAN FROM DIXIE (1941, Monogram)
Thad Terrill—Jack La Rue
Director—Al Herman
Leading Players—Marian Marsh, Clarence Muse, Mary Ruth

GENTLEMAN FROM LOUISIANA (1936, Republic)
Tod Mason—Eddie Quillan
Director—Irving Pichel
Leading Players—Charles "Chic" Sale, Charlotte Henry, Marjorie Gateson

THE GENTLEMAN FROM NOWHERE (1948, Columbia)
Earl Donovan—Warner Baxter
Director—William Castle
Leading Players—Fay Baker, Luis Van Rooten, Charles Lane

GENTLEMAN JIM (1942, Warner Brothers)
James J. Corbett—Errol Flynn
Director—Raoul Walsh
Leading Players—Alexis Smith, Jack Carson, Alan Hale, John Loder, Ward Bond

A GENTLEMAN OF LEISURE (1923, Silent, Paramount)
Robert Pitt—Jack Holt
Director—Joseph Henabery
Leading Players—Casson Ferguson, Sigrid Holmquist, Alec Francis

A GENTLEMAN OF PARIS (1931, GB, Gaumont)
Judge Le Fevre—Arthur Wontner
Director—Sinclair Hill
Leading Players—Vanda Greville, Hugh Williams, Phyllis Konstam

GENTLEMAN'S FATE (1931, MGM)
Jack Thomas—John Gilbert
Director—Mervyn LeRoy
Leading Players—Louis Wolheim, Leila Hyams, Anita Page

A GENTLEMAN'S GENTLEMAN (1939, GB, First National)
Hepelwhite—Eric Blore
Director—Roy William Neill
Leading Players—Marie Lohr, Peter Coke, Patricia Hilliard

GENTLEMEN ARE BORN (1934, First National)
Bob Bailey—Franchot Tone
Director—Alfred E. Green
Leading Players—Jean Muir, Margaret Lindsay, Ann Dvorak, Ross Alexander, Dick Foran, Charles Starrett

GENTLEMEN MARRY BRUNETTES (1955, UA)
Bonnie—Jane Russell
Connie—Jeanne Crain
Charles Biddle—Alan Young
David Action—Scott Brady
Director—Richard Sale
Leading Players—Rudy Vallee, Guy Middleton, Eric Pohlmann

GENTLEMEN OF THE PRESS (1929, Paramount)
Wickland Snell—Walter Huston
Director—Millard Webb
Leading Players—Kay Francis, Charles Ruggles, Betty Lawford

GENTLEMEN PREFER BLONDES (1928, Silent, Paramount)
Lorelei Lee—Ruth Taylor
Gus Eisman—Ford Sterling

Francis Beekman—Mack Swain
Henry Spofford—Holmes Herbert
Director—Malcolm St. Clair
Leading Players—Alice White, Emily Fitzroy, Trixie Friganza

GENTLEMEN PREFER BLONDES (1953, 20th Century Fox)
Lorelei Lee—Marilyn Monroe
Gus Esmond—Tommy Noonan
Sir Francis Beekman—Charles Coburn
Henry Spofford III—George "Foghorn" Winslow
Director—Howard Hawks
Leading Players—Jane Russell, Elliott Reid, Marcel Dalio

GEORGE IN CIVVY STREET (1946, GB, Columbia)
George Harper—George Formby
Director—Marcel Varnel
Leading Players—Rosalyn Boulter, Ronald Shiner, Ian Fleming

THE GEORGE RAFT STORY (1961, Allied Artists)
George Raft—Ray Danton
Director—Joseph M. Newman
Leading Players—Jayne Mansfield, Julie London, Barrie Chase, Frank Gorshin, Barbara Nichols

GEORGY GIRL (1966, GB, Columbia)
Georgy—Lynn Redgrave
Director—Silvio Narizzano
Leading Players—James Mason, Alan Bates, Charlotte Rampling, Bill Owen

GERONIMO (1939, Paramount)
Geronimo—Chief Thundercloud
Director—Paul H. Sloane
Leading Players—Preston Foster, Ellen Drew, Andy Devine

GERONIMO (1962, UA)
Geronimo—Chuck Connors
Director—Arnold Laven
Leading Players—Kamala Devi, Ross Martin, Pat Conway

GERT AND DAISY CLEAN UP (1942, GB, Butchers)
Gert—Elsie Waters
Daisy—Doris Waters
Director—MacLean Rogers
Leading Players—Iris Vandeleur, Elizabeth Hunt, Joss Ambler

GERT AND DAISY'S WEEKEND (1941, GB, Butchers)
Gert—Elsie Waters
Daisy—Doris Waters
Director—MacLean Rogers
Leading Players—Iris Vandeleur, John Slater, Elizabeth Hunt

GET CARTER (1971, MGM)
Jack Carter—Michael Caine
Director—Mike Hodges
Leading Players—Ian Hendry, Britt Ekland, John Osborne

GET CHARLIE TULLY (1976, GB, Quintain)
Charlie Tully—Dick Emery
Director—Cliff Owen
Leading Players—Derren Nesbitt, Ronald Fraser, Pat Coombs

GET YOURSELF A COLLEGE GIRL (1964, MGM)
Terry—Mary Ann Mobley
Director—Sidney Miller
Leading Players—Joan O'Brien, Nancy Sinatra, Chad Everett

GETTING EVEN (1986, American Distributing Group)
"Tag" Taggar—Edward Albert
Director—Dwight H. Little
Leading Players—Audrey Landers, Joe Don Baker, Rod Pilloud

GETTING GERTIE'S GARTER (1945, UA)
Gertie—Marie McDonald
Director—Allan Dwan
Leading Players—Dennis O'Keefe, Barry Sullivan, Sheila Ryan

GETTING MARY MARRIED (1919, Silent, Selznick)
Mary—Marion Davies
Director—Allan Dwan
Leading Players—Norman Kerry, Matt Moore, Frederick Burton

GHOST (1990, Paramount)
Sam Wheat—Patrick Swayze
Director—Jerry Zucker
Leading Players—Demi Moore, Whoopi Goldberg, Tony Goldwyn, Rick Aviles, Gail Boggs, Ameila McQueen

THE GHOST AND MR. CHICKEN (1966, Universal)
Luther Heggs—Don Knotts
Director—Alan Rafkin
Leading Players—Joan Staley, Liam Redmond, Dick Sargent

THE GHOST AND MRS. MUIR (1942, 20th Century Fox)
Lucy Muir—Gene Tierney
Ghost of Capt. Daniel Gregg—Rex Harrison
Director—Joseph L. Mankiewicz
Leading Players—George Sanders, Edna Best, Vanessa Brown

THE GHOST BREAKERS (1940, Paramount)
Larry Lawrence—Bob Hope
Mary Carter—Paulette Goddard
Director—George Marshall
Leading Players—Richard Carlson, Paul Lukas, Willie Best, Pedro De Cordoba, Anthony Quinn

THE GHOST CATCHERS (1944, Universal)
Ole—Ole Olsen
Chic—Chic Johnson
Director—Edward F. Cline
Leading Players—Gloria Jean, Martha O'Driscoll, Leo Carrillo

THE GHOST COMES HOME (1940, MGM)
Vern Adams—Frank Morgan
Director—William Thiele
Leading Players—Billie Burke, Ann Rutherford, John Shelton

GHOST DAD (1990, Universal/S&H Enterprises)
Elliot—Bill Cosby
Director—Sidney Poitier
Leading Players—Kimberly Russell, Denise Nicholas, Ian Bannen, Salim Grant, Brooke Fontaine

THE GHOST GOES WEST (1936, UA)
Donald Glourie—Robert Donat
Director—Rene Clair
Leading Players—Jean Parker, Eugene Pallette, Elsa Lanchester, Ralph Bunker

GHOST IN THE INVISIBLE BIKINI (1966, American International)
Ghost—Susan Hart
Director—Don Weis

Leading Players—Tommy Kirk, Deborah Walley, Boris Karloff, Basil Rathbone

GHOSTBUSTERS (1984, Columbia)
Dr. Peter Venkman—Bill Murray
Dr. Raymond Stantz—Dan Aykroyd
Dr. Egon Spenler—Harold Ramis
Winston Zeddmore—Ernie Hudson
Director—Ivan Reitman
Leading Players—Sigourney Weaver, Rick Moranis, Annie Potts

GHOSTBUSTERS II (1989, Columbia)
Dr. Peter Venkman—Bill Murray
Dr. Raymond Stantz—Dan Aykroyd
Dr. Egon Spenler—Harold Ramis
Winston Zeddemore—Ernie Hudson
Director—Ivan Reitman
Leading Players—Sigourney Weaver, Rick Moranis, Annie Potts, Peter MacNicol

GHOSTS OF BERKELEY SQUARE (1947, GB, Pathe)
Gen. Burlap—Robert Morley
Col. Kelsoe—Felix Aylmer
Director—Vernon Sewell
Leading Players—Yvonne Arnaud, Robert Beaumont, Madge Brindley, Marie Lohr

THE GHOUL (1934, Gaumont)
Prof. Morlant—Boris Karloff
Director—T. Hayes Hunter
Leading Players—Cedric Hardwicke, Ernest Thesiger, Dorothy Hyson, Ralph Richardson, Kathleen Harrison

GIDEON OF SCOTLAND YARD (1959, GB, Columbia)
Insp. George Gideon—Jack Hawkins
Director—John Ford
Leading Players—Dianne Foster, Anna Lee, Anna Massey, Andrew Ray, Cyril Cusack

GIDGET (1959, Columbia)
Francie Lawrence—Sandra Dee
Director—Paul Wendkos
Leading Players—James Darren, Cliff Robertson, Arthur O'Connell

GIDGET GOES HAWAIIAN (1961, Columbia)
Gidget (Francie Lawrence)—Deborah Walley
Director—Paul Wendkos
Leading Players—James Darren, Michael Callan, Carl Reiner

GIDGET GOES TO ROME (1963, Columbia)
Gidget (Francie Lawrence)—Cindy Carol
Director—Paul Wendkos
Leading Players—James Darren, Jessie Royce Landis, Cesare Danova

GIGI (1958, MGM)
Gigi—Leslie Caron
Director—Vicente Minnelli
Leading Players—Maurice Chevalier, Louis Jourdan, Hermione Gingold, Eva Gabor, Isabel Jeans

GIGOLETTE (1935, RKO)
Kay Parrish—Adrienne Ames
Director—Charles Lamont

Leading Players—Ralph Bellamy, Donald Cook, Robert Armstrong

GIGOT (1962, 20th Century Fox)
Gigot—Jackie Gleason
Director—Gene Kelly
Leading Players—Katherine Kath, Gabrielle Dorziat, Jean Lefebvre

GILDA (1946, Columbia)
Gilda Mundson—Rita Hayworth
Director—Charles Vidor
Leading Players—Glenn Ford, George Macready, Joseph Calleia, Steven Geray

THE GILDED BUTTERFLY (1926, Silent, Fox Film Corp.)
Linda Haverhill—Alma Rubens
Director—John Griffith Wray
Leading Players—Bert Lytell, Huntley Gordon, Frank Keenan

THE GILDED LILY (1921, Silent, Paramount)
Lillian Drake—Mae Murray
Director—Robert Z. Leonard
Leading Players—Lowell Sherman, Jason Robards, Charles Gerard

THE GILDED LILY (1935, Paramount)
Lillian David—Claudette Colbert
Director—Wesley Ruggles
Leading Players—Fred MacMurray, Ray Milland, C. Aubrey Smith

GILDERSLEEVE ON BROADWAY (1943, RKO)
Throckmorton P. Gildersleeve—Harold Peary
Director—Gordon Douglas
Leading Players—Billie Burke, Claire Carleton, Richard LeGrand

GILDERSLEEVE'S BAD DAY (1943, RKO)
Throckmorton P. Gildersleeve—Harold Peary
Director—Gordon Douglas
Leading Players—Jane Darwell, Nancy Gates, Charles Arnt

GILDERSLEEVE'S GHOST (1944, RKO)
Throckmorton P. Gildersleeve—Harold Peary
Director—Gordon Douglas
Leading Players—Marion Martin, Richard LeGrand, Amelita Ward

GINGER (1935, Fox Film Corp.)
Ginger—Jane Withers
Director—Lewis Seiler
Leading Players—O.P. Heggie, Jackie Searl, Katharine Alexander

GINSBERG THE GREAT (1927, Silent, Warner Brothers)
Johnny Ginsberg—George Jessel
Director—Bryon Haskin
Leading Players—Audrey Ferris, Gertrude Astor, Douglas Gerard

THE GIRL (1987, GB, Lux/Shapiro)
Pat Carlson—Clare Powney
Director—Arne Mattson
Leading Players—Franco Nero, Bernice Stegers, Frank Brennan

A GIRL, A GUY AND A GOB (1941, RKO)
Coffee Cup—George Murphy
Dot Duncan—Lucille Ball
Stephen Herrick—Edmond O'Brien
Director—Richard Wallace
Leading Players—Henry Travers, Franklin Pangborn, George Cleveland

THE GIRL AND THE GAMBLER (1939, RKO)
El Rayo—Leo Carrillo
Dolores—Steffi Duna
Director—Lew Landers
Leading Players—Tim Holt, Donald MacBride, Chris-Pin Martin

THE GIRL CAN'T HELP IT (1956, 20th Century Fox)
Jerri Jordan—Jayne Mansfield
Director—Frank Tashlin
Leading Players—Tom Ewell, Edmond O'Brien, Henry Jones

GIRL-CRAZY (1943, MGM)
Danny Churchill, Jr.—Mickey Rooney
Director—Norman Taurog
Leading Players—Judy Garland, Gil Stratton, Robert E. Strickland, Rags Ragland

THE GIRL DOWNSTAIRS (1938, MGM)
Katerina Linz—Franciska Gaal
Director—Norman Taurog
Leading Players—Franchot Tone, Walter Connolly, Reginald Gardiner

GIRL FROM ALASKA (1942, Republic)
Mary "Pete" McCoy—Jean Parker
Director—Nick Grinde
Leading Players—Ray Middleton, Jerome Cowan, Robert Barrat

GIRL FROM AVENUE A (1940, 20th Century Fox)
Jane—Jane Withers
Director—Otto Brower
Leading Players—Kent Taylor, Katharine Aldridge, Elyse Knox

THE GIRL FROM CHICAGO (1927, Silent, Warner Brothers)
Mary Carlton—Myrna Loy
Director—Ray Enright
Leading Players—Conrad Nagel, William Russell, Carroll Nye

THE GIRL FROM DOWNING STREET (1918, GB, Silent, Butchers)
Peggy Marsden—Ena Beaumont
Director—Geoffrey H. Malins
Leading Players—Sidney Paxton, William Stack

GIRL FROM GOD'S COUNTRY (1940, Republic)
Anne Webster—Jane Wyatt
Director—Sidney Salkow
Leading Players—Chester Morris, Charles Bickford, Mala, Kate Lawson

THE GIRL FROM HIS TOWN (1915, Silent, American)
Sarah Towney—Margarita Fischer
Don Blair—C. Elliott Griffen
Director—Harry Pollard
Leading Players—Beatrice Van, Joseph Harris, Joseph Singleton

THE GIRL FROM HAVANA (1929, Fox Film Corp.)
Joan Anders—Lola Lane
Director—Benjamin Stoloff
Leading Players—Paul Page, Kenneth Thomson, Natalie Moorhead

GIRL FROM HAVANA (1940, Republic)
Havana—Claire Carlton
Director—Lew Landers
Leading Players—Dennis O'Keefe, Victor Jory, Steffi Duna

THE GIRL FROM JONES BEACH (1949, Warner Brothers)
Ruth Wilson—Virginia Mayo
Director—Peter Godfrey
Leading Players—Ronald Reagan, Eddie Bracken, Dona Drake

GIRL FROM MANDALAY (1936, Republic)
Jeannie—Kay Linaker
Director—Howard Bretherton
Leading Players—Conrad Nagel, Donald Cook, Esther Ralston

GIRL FROM MANHATTAN (1948, UA)
Carol Maynard—Dorothy Lamour
Director—Alfred E. Green
Leading Players—George Montgomery, Charles Laughton, Ernest Truex, Hugh Herbert

THE GIRL FROM MAXIM'S (1936, GB, London Films)
"La Mome"—Frances Day
Director—Alexander Korda
Leading Players—Lady Tree, Leslie Henson, George Grossmith

THE GIRL FROM MEXICO (1939, RKO)
Carmelita—Lupe Velez
Director—Leslie Goodwins
Leading Players—Donald Woods, Leon Errol, Linda Hayes

THE GIRL FROM MISSOURI (1934, MGM)
Eadie—Jean Harlow
Director—Jack Conway
Leading Players—Lionel Barrymore, Franchot Tone, Lewis Stone

THE GIRL FROM MONTEREY (1943, Producers Releasing Corp.)
Lita—Armida
Director—Wallace Fox
Leading Players—Edgar Kennedy, Veda Ann Borg, Jack La Rue, Anthony Caruso

THE GIRL FROM PETROVKA (1974, Universal)
Oktyabrina—Goldie Hawn
Director—Robert Ellis Miller
Leading Players—Hal Holbrook, Anthony Hopkins, Gregoire Aslan

THE GIRL FROM RIO (1927, Silent, Gotham)
Lola—Carmel Myers
Director—Tom Terris
Leading Players—Walter Pidgeon, Richard Tucker, Henry Herbert

THE GIRL FROM RIO (1939, Monogram)
Marquita—Movita
Director—Lambert Hillyer
Leading Players—Warren Hull, Alan Baldwin, Kay Linaker

THE GIRL FROM SAN LORENZO (1950, UA)
Nora—Jane Adams

741

Director—Derwin Abrahams
Leading Players—Duncan Renaldo, Leo Carrillo, Bill Lester

THE GIRL FROM SCOTLAND YARD (1937, Paramount)
Viola Beech—Karen Morley
Director—Robert Vignola
Leading Players—Robert Baldwin, Katherine Alexander,
Eduardo Ciannelli

THE GIRL FROM TENTH AVENUE (1935, First National)
Miriam Brady—Bette Davis
Director—Alfred E. Green
Leading Players—Ian Hunter, Colin Clive, Alison Skipworth,
John Eldredge

THE GIRL FROM WOOLWORTH'S (1929, First National)
Pat King—Alice White
Director—William Beaudine
Leading Players—Charles Delaney, Wheeler Oakman, Rita Flynn

THE GIRL GETTERS (1966, GB, American International)
Tinker—Oliver Reed
Director—Michael Winner
Leading Players—Jane Merrow, Barbara Ferris, Julia Foster

THE GIRL HE LEFT BEHIND (1956, Warner Brothers)
Susan Daniels—Natalie Wood
Andy Sheaffer—Tab Hunter
Director—David Butler
Leading Players—Jessie Royce Landis, Jim Backus, Henry Jones

THE GIRL IN A SWING (1989, GB/USA, Panorama/J&M)
Karin Foster—Meg Tilly
Director—Gordon Hessler
Leading Players—Rupert Frazer, Nicholas Le Prevost, Elspet
Gray, Lorna Heilbron

A GIRL IN EVERY PORT (1928, Silent, Fox Film Corp.)
Spike Madden—Victor McLaglen
Director—Howard Hawks
Leading Players—Maria Casjuana, Natalie Joyce, Louise Brooks,
Robert Armstrong

A GIRL IN A MILLION (1946, GB, Oxford)
Gay Sultzman—Joan Greenwood
Director—Francis Searle
Leading Players—Hugh Williams, Basil Redford, Naunton Wayne

GIRL IN BLACK STOCKINGS (1957, UA)
Beth Dixon—Anne Bancroft
Director—Howard W. Koch
Leading Players—Lex Barker, Mamie Van Doren, Ron Randell,
Marie Windsor

GIRL IN DANGER (1934, Columbia)
Gloria Gale—Shirley Grey
Director—D. Ross Lederman
Leading Players—Ralph Bellamy, J. Carroll Naish, Charles
Sabin

GIRL IN DISTRESS (1941, GB, GFD)
Jeannie McLean—Barbara Mullen
Director—Harold French
Leading Players—Wilfrid Lawson, Gus McNaughton, Michael
Redgrave, Phyllis Stanley

GIRL IN 419 (1933, Paramount)
Mary Dolan—Gloria Stuart
Director—George Sommes
Leading Players—James Dunn, David Manners, William
Harrigan

THE GIRL IN LOVER'S LANE (1960, Filmgroup)
Carrie—Joyce Meadows
Director—Charles R. Rondeau
Leading Players—Brett Halsey, Lowell Brown, Jack Elam

GIRL IN POSSESSION (1934, GB, First National)
Eve Chandler—Laura La Plante
Director—Monty Banks
Leading Players—Henry Kendall, Claude Hulbert, Monty Banks

THE GIRL IN THE DARK (1918, Silent, Bluebird)
Lois Fox—Carmel Myers
Director—Stuart Paton
Leading Players—Ashton Dearholt, Frank Tokanaga, Frank
Deschon

THE GIRL IN THE GLASS CAGE (1929, First National)
Gladys Cosgrove—Loretta Young
Director—Ralph Dawson
Leading Players—Carroll Nye, Matthew Betz, Lucien Littlefield

THE GIRL IN THE KREMLIN (1957, Universal)
Greta Grisenko—Zsa Zsa Gabor
Director—Russell Birdwell
Leading Players—Lex Barker, Jeffrey Stone, Maurice Manson,
William Schallert

THE GIRL IN THE NEWS (1941, GB, Fox British)
Anne Graham—Margaret Lockwood
Director—Carol Reed
Leading Players—Barry K. Barnes, Emlyn Williams, Roger
Livesey, Margaretta Scott

THE GIRL IN THE NIGHT (1931, GB, Wardour)
Cecile—Dorothy Boyd
Director—Henry Edwards
Leading Players—Henry Edwards, Sam Livesey, Reginald Bach

THE GIRL IN THE PAINTING (1948, GB, Gainsborough)
Hildegarde—Mai Zettering
Director—Terence Fisher
Leading Players—Robert Beatty, Guy Rolfe, Herbert Lom

THE GIRL IN THE PICTURE (1956, GB, Eros)
Pat Dryden—Junia Crawford
Director—Don Chaffey
Leading Players—Donald Houston, Patrick Holt, Maurice
Kaufmann

THE GIRL IN THE PICTURE (1986, Goldwyn)
Mary—Irina Brook
Director—Cary Parker
Leading Players—John Gordon-Sinclair, David McKay, Gregor
Fisher, Caroline Guthrie

GIRL IN THE RED VELVET SWING (1955, 20th Century Fox)
Evelyn Nesbitt Thaw—Joan Collins
Director—Richard Fleischer
Leading Players—Ray Milland, Farley Granger, Luther Adler

GIRL IN THE STREET (1938, GB, Gaumont)
Jacqueline—Anna Neagle
Director—Herbert Wilcox
Leading Players—Tullio Carminati, Robert Douglas, Horace Hodges

GIRL IN THE WOODS (1958, Republic)
Belle Cory—Maggie Hayes
Director—Tom Gries
Leading Players—Forrest Tucker, Barton MacLane, Diana Francis, Murvyn Vye

GIRL IN TROUBLE (1963, Vanguard)
Judy Collins—Tammy Clark
Director—Lee Beale
Leading Players—Ray Menard, Neomie Salatich, Larry Johnson

THE GIRL IN WHITE (1952, MGM)
Dr. Emily Barringer—June Allyson
Director—John Sturges
Leading Players—Arthur Kennedy, Gary Merrill, Mildred Dunnock, Jesse White

GIRL LOVES BOY (1937, Grand National)
Robert Conrad—Eric Linden
Dorothy McCarthy—Cecilia Parker
Director—Duncan Mansfield
Leading Players—Roger Imhof, Dorothy Peterson, Pedro de Cordoba

THE GIRL MOST LIKELY (1957, RKO/Universal)
Dodie—Jane Powell
Director—Mitchell Leisen
Leading Players—Cliff Robertson, Keith Andres, Kaye Ballard

A GIRL MUST LIVE (1941, GB, Gainsborough)
Leslie James—Margaret Lockwood
Director—Carol Reed
Leading Players—Renee Houston, Lilli Palmer, George Robey

A GIRL NAMED TAMIKO (1962, Paramount)
Tamiko—France Nuyen
Director—John Sturges
Leading Players—Laurence Harvey, Martha Hyer, Gary Merrill

THE GIRL NEXT DOOR (1953, 20th Century Fox)
Jeannie—June Haver
Director—Richard Sale
Leading Players—Dan Dailey, Dennis Day, Billy Gray

A GIRL OF LONDON (1925, GB, Silent, Stoll)
Lil—Genevieve Townsend
Director—Henry Edwards
Leading Players—Ian Hunter, Harvey Braban, G.H. Mulcaster

GIRL O' MY DREAMS (1935, Monogram)
Gwen—Mary Carlisle
Director—Raymond McCarey
Leading Players—Sterling Holloway, Eddie Nugent, Arthur Lake, Creighton (Lon Jr.) Chaney

THE GIRL OF THE GOLDEN WEST (1915, Silent, Lasky)
The Girl—Mabel Van Buren
Director—Cecil B. De Mille
Leading Players—House Peters, Theodore Roberts, Sidney Deane

THE GIRL OF THE GOLDEN WEST (1923, Silent, Associated First National)
The Girl—Sylvia Breamer
Director—Edwin Carewe
Leading Players—J. Warren Kerrigan, Russell Simpson, Rosemary Theby

GIRL OF THE GOLDEN WEST (1930, First National)
Minnie—Ann Harding
Director—John Francis Dillon
Leading Players—James Rennie, Harry Bannister, Ben Hendricks

THE GIRL OF THE GOLDEN WEST (1938, MGM)
Mary Robbins—Jeanette MacDonald
Director—Robert Z. Leonard
Leading Players—Nelson Eddy, Walter Pidgeon, Leo Carrillo

GIRL OF THE LIMBERLOST (1934, Monogram)
Elnora Comstock—Marian Marsh
Director—Christy Cabanne
Leading Players—Louise Dresser, Ralph Morgan, H.B. Walthall

THE GIRL OF THE LIMBERLOST (1945, Columbia)
Elnora Comstock—Dorinda Clifton
Director—Melchor G. Ferrer
Leading Players—Ruth Nelson, Loren Tindall, Gloria Holden

GIRL OF THE NIGHT (1960, Warner Brothers)
Bobbie—Anne Francis
Director—Joseph Cates
Leading Players—Lloyd Nolan, Kay Medford, John Kerr

GIRL OF THE OZARKS (1936, Paramount)
Edie Moseley—Virginia Weidler
Director—William Shea
Leading Players—Leif Erikson, Elizabeth Russell, Henrietta Crosman

GIRL OF THE RIO (1932, RKO)
Dolores—Dolores Del Rio
Director—Herbert Brenon
Leading Players—Leo Carrillo, Norman Foster, Lucille Gleason

THE GIRL ON THE BRIDGE (1951, 20th Century Fox)
Clara—Beverly Michaels
Director—Hugo Haas
Leading Players—Hugo Haas, Robert Dane, Tony Jochim

THE GIRL ON THE CANAL (1947, GB, Ealing)
Mary Smith—Jenny Laird
Director—Charles Crichton
Leading Players—Robert Griffith, Bill Blewett, Mary Hallatt

THE GIRL ON THE FRONT PAGE (1936, Universal)
Joan Langford—Gloria Stuart
Director—Harry Beaumont
Leading Players—Edmund Lowe, Reginald Owen, David Oliver

GIRL ON THE SPOT (1946, Universal)
Kathy Lorenz—Lois Collier
Director—William Beaudine
Leading Players—Jess Barker, George Dolenz, Fuzzy Knight

THE GIRL ON THE STAIRS (1924, Silent, Producers Distributing Corp.)
Dora Sinclair—Patsy Ruth Miller
Director—William Worthington
Leading Players—Frances Raymond, Arline Pretty, Shannon Day

GIRL OVERBOARD (1937, Universal)
Mary Chesbrooke—Gloria Stuart
Director—Sidney Salkow
Leading Players—Walter Pidgeon, Billy Burrud, Hobart Cavanaugh

THE GIRL SAID NO (1930, MGM)
Mary Howe—Leila Hyams
Director—Sam Wood
Leading Players—William Haines, Polly Moran, Francis X. Bushman, Marie Dressler

THE GIRL SAID NO (1937, Grand National)
Pearl—Irene Hervey
Director—Andrew L. Stone
Leading Players—Robert Armstrong, Paula Stone, Edward J. Brophy

GIRL SHY (1924, Silent, Pathe)
Harold Meadows—Harold Lloyd
Directors—Fred Newymeyer & Sam Taylor
Leading Players—Jobyna Ralston, Richard Daniels, Carlton Griffin

THE GIRL WHO CAME BACK (1935, First Division)
Gilda—Shirley Grey
Director—Charles Lamont
Leading Players—Sidney Blackmer, Noel Madison, Mathew Betz

THE GIRL WHO COULDN'T QUITE (1949, GB, Monarch)
Ruth—Elizabeth Henson
Director—Norman Lee
Leading Players—Bill Owen, Iris Hoey, Betty Stockfeld

THE GIRL WHO DARED (1920, Silent, Republic)
Barbara Hampton—Edythe Sterling
Director—Cliff Smith
Leading Players—Jack Carlyle, Steve Clements, Yakima Canutt

THE GIRL WHO FORGOT (1939, GB, Butchers)
Leonora Barradine—Elizabeth Allan
Director—Adrian Brunel
Leading Players—Ralph Michael, Enid Stamp-Taylor, Basil Radford, Jeanne de Casalis

THE GIRL WHO HAD EVERYTHING (1953, MGM)
Jean Latimer—Elizabeth Taylor
Director—Richard Thorpe
Leading Players—Fernando Lamas, William Powell, Gig Young, James Whitmore

THE GIRL WHO LOVES A SOLDIER (1916, GB, Silent, Moss)
Vesta Beaumont—Vesta Tilley
Director—Alexander Butler
Leading Players—Sydney Folker, James Lindsay, Norman Cheyne

THE GIRL WHO STAYED AT HOME (1919, Silent, Paramount)
Atoline France—Carol Dempster
Director—D. W. Griffith
Leading Players—Adolphe Lestina, Frances Parkes, Richard Barthelmess

THE GIRL WHO TOOK THE WRONG TURN (1915, GB, Silent, British Empire)
Sophie Coventry—Alice Belmore
Director—Leedham Bantock
Leading Players—Henry Lonsdale, Nina Lynn, Ronald Adair

THE GIRL WHO WOULDN'T QUIT (1918, Silent, Universal)
Joan Tracy—Louise Lovely
Director—Edgar Jones
Leading Players—Henry A. Barrows, Mark Fenton, Charles H. Mailes

THE GIRL WHO WOULDN'T WORK (1925, Silent, Schulberg)
Mary Hale—Marguerite De La Motte
Director—Marcel De Sano
Leading Players—Lionel Barrymore, Henry B. Walthall, Lilyan Tashman, Forrest Stanley

GIRL WITH GREEN EYES (1964, GB, Lopert)
Kate Brady—Rita Tushingham
Director—Desmond Davis
Leading Players—Peter Finch, Lynn Redgrave, Marie Kean

A GIRL WITH IDEAS (1937, Universal)
Mary Morton—Wendy Barrie
Director—S. Sylvan Simon
Leading Players—Walter Pidgeon, Kent Taylor, Dorothea Kent

THE GIRL WITHOUT A SOUL (1917, Silent, Metro)
Priscilla Beaumont—Viola Dana
Director—John H. Collins
Leading Players—Robert Walker, Fred Jones, Henry Hallam

GIRLS ABOUT TOWN (1931, Paramount)
Wanda Howard—Kay Francis
Marie Bailey—Lilyan Tashman
Director—George Cukor
Leading Players—Joel McCrea, Eugene Pallette, Alan Dinehart

GIRLS AT SEA (1958, GB, Seven Arts)
Mary—Anne Kimbell
Antoinette—Nadine Tallier
Jill—Mary Steele
Director—Gilbert Gunn
Leading Players—Guy Rolfe, Ronald Shiner, Alan White

GIRLS DEMAND EXCITEMENT (1931, Fox Film Corp.)
Joan Madison—Virginia Cherrill
Director—Seymour Felix
Leading Players—John Wayne, Marguerite Churchill, Helen Jerome Eddy

GIRLS GONE WILD (1929, Silent, Fox Film Corp.)
Babs Holworthy—Sue Carol
Director—Lewis Seiler
Leading Players—Nick Stuart, William Russell, Roy D'Arcy

GIRLS IN PRISON (1956, American International)
Anne Carson—Joan Taylor
Director—Edward L. Cahn
Leading Players—Richard Denning, Adele Jergens, Helen Gilbert

GIRLS JUST WANT TO HAVE FUN (1985, New World)
Janey Glenn—Sarah Jessica Parker
Director—Alan Metter
Leading Players—Lee Montgomery, Morgan Woodward, Jonathan Silverman, Helen Hunt

GIRLS OF PLEASURE ISLAND (1953, Paramount)
Violet Halyard—Joan Elan
Hester Halyard—Audrey Dalton
Gloria Halyard—Dorothy Bromiley
Director—F. Hugh Herbert
Leading Players—Don Taylor, Leo Genn, Elsa Lanchester

GIRLS OF THE BIG HOUSE (1945, Republic)
Jeanne Crail—Lynne Roberts
Director—George Archainbaud
Leading Players—Virginia Christine, Marian Martin, Adele Mara, Richard Powers

GIRLS OF LATIN QUARTER (1960, GB, New Realm)
Jill—Jill Ireland
Director—Alfred Travers
Leading Players—Bernard Hunter, Sheldon Lawrence, Danny Green

GIRLS OF THE ROAD (1940, Columbia)
Kay Warren—Ann Dvorak
Director—Nick Grinde
Leading Players—Helen Mack, Lola Lane, Ann Doran

GIRLS ON PROBATION (1938, Warner Brothers)
Connie Heath—Jane Bryan
Directors—William McGann & Harry Seymour
Leading Players—Ronald Reagan, Sheila Bromley, Anthony Averill, Sig Rumann, Susan Hayward

GIRLS WHO DARE (1929, Silent, Trinity)
Sally Casey—Priscilla Bonner
Director—Frank S. Mattison
Leading Players—Rex Lease, Rosemary Theby, Ben Wilson

GIRLS WILL BE BOYS (1934, GB, Associated British)
Pat Caverley—Dolly Haas
Director—Marcel Varnel
Leading Players—Cyril Maude, Esmond Knight, Irene Vanbrugh

GIVE A GIRL A BREAK (1953, MGM)
Madelyn Corlane—Marge Champion
Suzy Doolittle—Debbie Reynolds
Joanna Moss—Helen Wood
Director—Stanley Donen
Leading Players—Gower Champion, Bob Fosse, Kurt Kasznar

GIVE HER A RING (1936, GB, British Internaional)
Karen Swenson—Wendy Barrie
Director—Arthur Woods
Leading Players—Clifford Mollison, Zelma O'Neal, Erik Rhodes

THE GLAD RAG DOLL (1929, Warner Brothers)
Annabel Lea—Dolores Costello
Director—Michael Curtiz
Leading Players—Ralph Graves, Audrey Ferris, Albert Grant

GLADIATOR (1992, Columbia)
Lincoln—Cuba Gooding, Jr.
Tommy Riley—James Marshall
Director—Rowdy Harrington
Leading Players—Robert Loggia, Ossie Davis, Brian Dennehy, Cara Buono, John Heard, John Sada

THE GLADIATOR (1938, Columbia)
Hugo Kipp—Joe E. Brown
Director—Edward Sedgwick
Leading Players—Man Mountain Dean, June Travis, Dickie Moore

GLAMOUR GIRL (1947, Columbia)
Jennia Higgins—Susan Reed
Director—Arthur Dreifuss
Leading Players—Gene Krupa, Virginia Grey, Michael Duane

GLEAM O'DAWN (1922, Silent, Fox Film Corp.)
Gleam O'Dawn—John Gilbert
Director—Jack Dillon
Leading Players—Barbara Bedford, James Farley, John Gough

GLEN OR GLENDA (1953, Paramount)
Glen/Glenda—Daniel Davis (Edward D. Wood, Jr.)
Director—Edward D. Wood, Jr.
Leading Players—Bela Lugosi, Lyle Talbot, Dolores Fuller

THE GLENN MILLER STORY (1953, Universal)
Glenn Miller—James Stewart
Director—Anthony Mann
Leading Players—June Allyson, Charles Drake, George Tobias, Harry Morgan

GLORIA (1980, Columbia)
Gloria Swenson—Gena Rowlands
Director—John Cassavetes
Leading Players—Juan Adames, Buck Henry, Julie Carmen

GLORIFYING THE AMERICAN GIRL (1930, Paramount)
Gloria Hughes—Mary Eaton
Director—Millard Webb
Leading Players—Edward Crandall, Olive Shen, Dan Healey

GLORY BOY (1971, Cinerama)
Sgt. Martin Flood—Mitchell Ryan
Director—Edwin Sherin
Leading Players—Arthur Kennedy, William Devane, Michael Moriarity, Topo Swope

THE GO-BETWEEN (1971, GB, MGM-EMI/Columbia)
Leo Colston—Dominic Guard
Director—Joseph Losey
Leading Players—Julie Christie, Alan Bates, Margaret Leighton, Michael Redgrave

THE GO-GETTER (1937, Warner Brothers)
Bill Austin—George Brent
Director—Busby Berkeley
Leading Players—Anita Louise, Charles Winninger, John Eldridge

GO INTO YOUR DANCE (1935, Warner Brothers)
Dorothy Wayne—Ruby Keeler
Director—Archie Mayo
Leading Players—Al Jolson, Glenda Farrell, Helen Morgan, Barton MacLane

745

GO, JOHNNY, GO (1959, Hal Roach)
Johnny—Jimmy Clanton
Director—Paul Landres
Leading Players—Alan Freed, Sandy Stewart, Chuck Berry

GO WEST, YOUNG LADY (1941, Columbia)
Belinda Pendergast—Penny Singleton
Director—Frank R. Strayer
Leading Players—Glenn Ford, Ann Miller, Charlie Ruggles

GO WEST, YOUNG MAN (1919, Silent, Goldwyn)
Dick Latham—Tom Moore
Director—Harry Beaumont
Leading Players—Ora Carew, Melbourne MacDowell, Jack Richardson

GOD IS MY CO-PILOT (1945, Warner Brothers)
Col. Robert L. Scott—Dennis Morgan
Director—Robert Florey
Leading Players—Dane Clark, Raymond Massey, Alan Hale

GOD IS MY PARTNER (1957, 20th Century Fox)
Dr. Charles Grayson—Walter Brennan
Director—William F. Claxton
Leading Players—John Hoyt, Marion Ross, Jesse White

GOD IS MY WITNESS (1931, Astor)
God—George Grossmith
Director—Berthold Viertel
Leading Players—Bob McKenzie, John Aldredge, Alice White

THE GODDESS (1958, Columbia)
Emily Ann Faulkner—Kim Stanley
Director—John Cromwell
Leading Players—Betty Lou Holland, Joan Copeland, Lloyd Bridges, Bert Freed

THE GODFATHER (1972, Paramount)
Don Vito Corleone—Marlon Brando
Director—Francis Ford Coppola
Leading Players—Al Pacino, James Caan, Richard Castellano, Robert Duvall, Sterling Hayden, Richard Conte, Diane Keaton, Abe Vigoda, Talia Shire

THE GODFATHER, PART II (1974, Paramount)
Michael Corleone—Al Pacino
Vito Corleone—Robert De Niro
Director—Francis Ford Coppola
Leading Players—Robert Duvall, Diane Keaton, Talia Shire, John Cazale, Lee Strasberg, Michael V. Gazzo, Troy Donahue

THE GODFATHER PART III (1990, Paramount/Zoetrope)
Michael Corleone—Al Pacino
Director—Francis Ford Coppola
Leading Players—Diane Keaton, Talia Shire, Andy Garcia, Eli Wallach, Joe Mantegna, George Hamilton, Bridget Fonda, Sofia Coppola, Raf Vallone

THE GODLESS GIRL (1929, Pathe)
Judith Craig—Lina Basquette
Director—Cecil B. De Mille
Leading Players—Marie Prevost, George Duryea, Noah Beery

GOD'S COUNTRY AND THE WOMAN (1937, Warner Brothers)
Jo Barton—Beverly Roberts
Director—William Keighley
Leading Players—George Brent, Barton MacLane, Robert Barrat

GOD'S GIFT TO WOMEN (1931, Warner Brothers)
Jacques Duryea—Frank Fay
Director—Michel Curtiz
Leading Players—Laura La Plante, Joan Blondell, Charles Winninger

GOING STEADY (1958, Columbia)
Julie Ann Turner—Molly Bee
Calvin Potter—Alan Reed, Jr.
Director—Fred F. Sears
Leading Players—Bill Goodwin, Irene Hervey, Ken Miller

GOLD AND THE GIRL (1925, Silent, Fox Film Corp.)
Ann Donald—Elinor Fair
Director—Edmund Mortimer
Leading Players—Buck Jones, Bruce Gordon, Claude Peyton

THE GOLD DIGGERS (1923, Silent, Warner Brothers)
Jerry La Mar—Hope Hampton
Violet Dayne—Anne Cornwall
Director—Harry Beaumont
Leading Players—Wyndham Standing, Louise Fazenda, Gertrude Short, Alec Francis

GOLD DIGGERS IN PARIS (1938, Warner Brothers)
Kay Morrow—Rosemary Lane
Mona—Gloria Dickson
Director—Ray Enright
Leading Players—Rudy Vallee, Hugh Herbert, Allen Jenkins

GOLD DIGGERS ON BROADWAY (1929, Warner Brothers)
Jerry—Nancy Welford
Mabel—Winnie Lightner
Ann Collins—Ann Pennington
Director—Roy Del Ruth
Leading Players—Conway Tearle, Lilyan Tashman, William Bakewell

GOLD DIGGERS OF 1933 (1933, Warner Brothers)
Carol King—Joan Blondell
Trixie Lorraine—Aline MacMahon
Polly Parker—Ruby Keeler
Director—Mervyn LeRoy
Leading Players—Warren William, Dick Powell, Guy Kibbee

GOLD DIGGERS OF 1935 (1935, Warner Brothers)
Amy Prentiss—Gloria Stuart
Arline Davis—Dorothy Dare
Director—Busby Berkeley
Leading Players—Dick Powell, Adolphe Menjou, Grant Mitchell

GOLD DIGGERS OF 1937 (1936, Warner Brothers)
Norma Parry—Joan Blondell
Genevieve Larkin—Glenda Farrell
Director—Lloyd Bacon
Leading Players—Dick Powell, Victor Moore, Lee Dixon

GOLD DUST GERTIE (1931, Warner Brothers)
Gertie—Winnie Lightner
Director—Lloyd Bacon
Leading Players—Chic Johnson, Ole Olsen, Dorothy Christie

GOLD RUSH MAISIE (1940, MGM)
Maisie Ravier—Ann Sothern

Director—Edwin L. Marin
Leading Players—Lee Bowman, Virginia Weidler, Mary Nash

THE GOLDBERGS (1950, Paramount)
Molly Goldberg—Gertrude Berg
Jake Goldberg—Philip Loeb
Director—Walter Hart
Leading Players—Eli Mintz, Eduard Franz, Larry Robinson, Arline McQuade

GOLDEN BOY (1939, Columbia)
Joe Bonaparte—William Holden
Director—Rouben Mamoulian
Leading Players—Barbara Stanwyck, Adolphe Menjou, Lee J. Cobb, Joseph Calleia, Sam Levene

THE GOLDEN CHILD (1986, Paramount)
The Golden Child—J.L. Reate
Director—Michael Ritchie
Leading Players—Edward Murphy, Charlotte Lewis, Victor Wong

GOLDEN GIRL (1951, 20th Century Fox)
Lotta Crabtree—Mitzi Gaynor
Director—Lloyd Bacon
Leading Players—Dale Robertson, Dennis Day, James Barton

THE GOLDEN VOYAGE OF SINBAD (1974, GB, Columbia)
Sinbad—John Phillip Law
Director—Gordon Hessler
Leading Players—Caroline Munro, Tom Baker, Douglas Wilmer

GOLDENGIRL (1979, Avco Embassy)
Goldengirl—Susan Anton
Director—Joseph Sargent
Leading Players—James Coburn, Curt Jurgens, Lelsie Caron

GOLDFINGER (1964, GB, UA)
Goldfinger—Gert Frobe
Director—Guy Hamilton
Leading Players—Sean Connery, Honor Blackman, Shirley Eaton, Tania Mallett, Harold Sakata

GOLDIE (1931, Fox Film Corp.)
Goldie—Jean Harlow
Director—Benjamin Stoloff
Leading Players—Spencer Tracy, Warren Hymer, Lina Basquette

GOLDIE GETS ALONG (1933, RKO)
Goldie LaFarge—Lili Damita
Director—Malcolm St. Clair
Leading Players—Charles Morton, Sam Hardy, Nat Pendleton

GOOD AND NAUGHTY (1926, Silent, Paramount)
Germaine Morris—Pola Negri
Director—Malcolm St. Clair
Leading Players—Tom Moore, Ford Sterling, Miss Du Pont

THE GOOD BAD GIRL (1931, Columbia)
Marcia—Mae Clarke
Director—Roy William Neill
Leading Players—James Hall, Marie Prevost, Robert Ellis

THE GOOD BAD MAN (1916, Silent, Triangle)
"Passin' Through"—Douglas Fairbanks
Director—Allan Dwan

Leading Players—Sam de Grasse, Pomeroy Doc Cannon, Joseph Singleton, Bessie Love

GOOD COMPANIONS (1933, Great Brtiain, Gaumont)
Susie Dean—Jessie Matthews
Jess Oakroyd—Edmund Gwenn
Inigo Jolifant—John Gielgud
Director—Victor Saville
Leading Players—Mary Glynne, Percy Parsons, Dennis Hoey

THE GOOD COMPANIONS (1957, GB, AB-Pathe)
Susie Dean—Janette Scott
Jess Oakroyd—Eric Portman
Inigo Jolifant—John Fraser
Director—J. Lee Thompson
Leading Players—Celia Johnson, Hugh Griffith, Bobby Howes

GOOD DAME (1934, Paramount)
Lillie Taylor—Sylvia Sidney
Director—Marion Gering
Leading Players—Fredric March, Jack La Rue, Noel Francis

THE GOOD FAIRY (1935, Universal)
Luisa "Lu" Ginglebusher—Margaret Sullavan
Director—William Wyler
Leading Players—Herbert Marshall, Frank Morgan, Reginald Owen, Alan Hale

THE GOOD FELLOWS (1943, Paramount)
Jim Hilton—Cecil Kellaway
Director—Jo Graham
Leading Players—Mabel Paige, Helen Walker, James Brown

GOOD GIRLS GO TO PARIS (1939, Columbia)
Jenny Swanson—Joan Blondell
Director—Alexander Hall
Leading Players—Melvyn Douglas, Walter Connolly, Alan Curtis, Joan Perry

THE GOOD GUYS AND THE BAD GUYS (1969, Warner Brothers)
Flagg—Robert Mitchum
McKay—George Kennedy
Director—Burt Kennedy
Leading Players—David Carradine, Tina Louise, Douglas V. Fowley, Lois Nettleton, Martin Balsam

GOOD GUYS WEAR BLACK (1978, Mar Vista)
John T. Booker—Chuck Norris
Director—Ted Post
Leading Players—Anne Archer, Lloyd Haynes, James Franciscus

THE GOOD HUMOR MAN (1950, Columbia)
Biff Jones—Jack Carson
Director—Lloyd Bacon
Leading Players—Lola Albright, George Reeves, Jean Wallace

GOOD LUCK, MISS WYCKOFF (1979, Bel Air-Gradison)
Evelyn Wyckoff—Anne Heywood
Director—Martin J. Chomsky
Leading Players—Donald Pleasence, Robert Vaughn, Carolyn Jones, Dorothy Malone

GOOD LUCK MR. YATES (1943, Columbia)
Oliver Yates—Jess Barker
Director—Ray Enright
Leading Players—Claire Trevor, Edgar Buchanan, Tom Neal

GOOD MORNING, MISS DOVE (1955, 20th Century Fox)
 Miss Dove—Jennifer Jones
 Director—Henry Koster
 Leading Players—Robert Stack, Kipp Hamilton, Robert Douglas

THE GOOD MOTHER (1988, Touchstone)
 Anna Dunlap—Diane Keaton
 Director—Leonard Nimoy
 Leading Players—Liam Neeson, Jason Robards, Ralph Bellamy
 Teresa Wright, Asia Vieira

GOOD NEIGHBOR SAM (1964, Columbia)
 Sam Bissel—Jack Lemmon
 Director—David Swift
 Leading Players—Edward G. Robinson, Romy Schneider,
 Dorothy Provine, Michael Connors

GOOD NIGHT, PAUL (1918, Silent, Selznick)
 Paul Boudeaux—Harrison Ford
 Director—Walter Edwards
 Leading Players—Constance Talmadge, Norman Kerry, John
 Steppling

THE GOOD OLD SOAK (1937, MGM)
 Clem Hawley—Wallace Beery
 Director—J. Walter Ruben
 Leading Players—Una Merkel, Eric Linden, Judith Barrett

GOOD SAM (1948, RKO)
 Sam Clayton—Gary Cooper
 Director—Leo McCarey
 Leading Players—Ann Sheridan, Ray Collins, Edmund Lowe

GOOD SPORT (1931, Fox Film Corp.)
 Marilyn Parker—Linda Watkins
 Director—Kenneth MacKenna
 Leading Players—John Boles, Greta Nissen, Minna Gombell

GOOD TIME GIRL (1950, GB, Rank)
 Gwen Rawlings—Jean Kent
 Director—David MacDonald
 Leading Players—Dennis Price, Herbert Lom, Bonar Colleano

THE GOOD WIFE (1987, Australia, Atlantic)
 Marge Hills—Rachel Ward
 Director—Ken Cameron
 Leading Players—Bryan Brown, Steven Vidler, Sam Neill

GOODBYE CHARLIE (1964, 20th Century Fox)
 Charlie Sorel—Debbie Reynolds
 Director—Vincente Minnelli
 Leading Players—Tony Curtis, Pat Boone, Joanna Barnes

GOODBYE GEMINI (1970, GB, Cinerama)
 Jacki—Judy Geeson
 Julian—Martin Potter
 Director—Alan Gibson
 Leading Players—Michael Redgrave, Alexis Kanner, Mike Pratt

THE GOODBYE GIRL (1977, MGM/Warner Brothers)
 Paula McFadden—Marsha Mason
 Director—Herbert Ross
 Leading Players—Richard Dreyfuss, Quinn Cummings, Paul
 Benedict

GOODBYE MR. CHIPS (1939, GB, MGM)
 Charles Chipping—Robert Donat
 Director—Sam Wood
 Leading Players—Greer Garson, Terry Kilburn, John Mills, Paul
 Henreid, Judith Furse

GOODBYE MR. CHIPS (1969, APJAC/MGM)
 Arthur Chipping—Peter O'Toole
 Director—Herbert Ross
 Leading Players—Petula Clark, Michael Redgrave, George
 Baker, Sian Phillips, Michael Bryant

GOODBYE NORMA JEAN (1976, Filmways)
 Norma Jean Baker—Misty Rowe
 Director—Larry Buchanan
 Leading Players—Terrence Locke, Patch Mackenzie, Preston
 Hanson

THE GOODBYE PEOPLE (1984, Embassy)
 Arthur Korman—Judd Hirsch
 Max Silverman—Martin Balsam
 Nancie Scot—Pamela Reed
 Director—Herb Gardner
 Leading Players—Ron Silver, Michael Tucker, Gene Saks

GOODFELLAS (1990, Warner Brothers)
 James Conway—Robert DeNiro
 Henry Hill—Ray Liotta
 Tommy DeVito—Joe Pesci
 Director—Martin Scorsese
 Leading Players—Lorraine Bracco, Paul Sorvino, Frank Sivero,
 Tony Darrow, Mike Starr, Frank Vincent, Chuck Low

THE GOONIES (1985, Warner Brothers)
 Mickey—Sean Astin
 Chunk—Jeff Cohen
 Mouth—Corey Feldman
 Data—Ke Huy Quan
 Director—Richard Donner
 Leading Players—Josh Brolin, Kerri Green, Martha Plimpton,
 Anne Ramsey, John Matuszak

THE GOOSE GIRL (1915, Silent, Lasky)
 Gretchen—Marguerite Clark
 Director—Fred Thompson
 Leading Players—Monroe Salisbury, Sidney Deane, Robert N.
 Dunbar

THE GOOSE STEPS OUT (1942, Ealing)
 William Potts—Will Hay
 Director—Will Hay
 Leading Players—Frank Pettingell, Julien Mitchell, Charles
 Hawtrey

THE GOOSE WOMAN (1925, Silent, Universal)
 Mary Holmes/Marie de Nardi—Louise Dresser
 Director—Clarence Brown
 Leading Players—Jack Pickford, Constance Bennett, James O.
 Barrows

GORDON'S WAR (1973, 20th Century Fox)
 Gordon—Paul Winfield
 Director—Ossie Davis
 Leading Players—Carl Lee, David Downing, Tony King

THE GORGEOUS HUSSY (1936, MGM)
Peggy O'Neal Eaton—Joan Crawford
Director—Clarence Brown
Leading Players—Robert Taylor, Lionel Barrymore, Melvyn Douglas, James Stewart, Franchot Tone

GOVERNMENT GIRL (1943, RKO)
Smokey—Olivia de Havilland
Director—Dudley Nichols
Leading Players—Sonny Tufts, Anne Shirley, Jess Barker

THE GRADUATE (1967, Embassy Pictures)
Ben Braddock—Dustin Hoffman
Director—Mike Nichols
Leading Players—Anne Bancroft, Katharine Ross, William Daniels, Murray Hamilton, Elizabeth Wilson

THE GRAND DUCHESS AND THE WAITER (1926, Paramount)
Albert Durant—Adolphe Menjou
Grand Duchess Zenia—Florence Vidor
Director—Malcolm St. Clair
Leading Players—Lawrence Grant, Andre Beranger, Dot Farley

GRAND OLD GIRL (1935, RKO)
Laura Bayles—May Robson
Director—John S. Robertson
Leading Players—Fred MacMurray, Alan Hale, Hale Hamilton

GRANDMA'S BOY (1922, Silent, Associated Exhibitors)
The Boy—Harold Lloyd
Grandma—Anna Townsend
Director—Fred Newmeyer
Leading Players—Mildred Davis, Charles Stevenson, Noah Young

GRANDMOTHER'S HOUSE (1989, Omega)
Grandmother—Ida Lee
Director—Peter Rader
Leading Players—Eric Fisher, Kim Valentine, Brinke Stevens

GRANDPA GOES TO TOWN (1940, Republic)
Grandpa Higgins—Harry Davenport
Director—Gus Meins
Leading Players—James Gleason, Lucile Gleason, Russell Gleason

GRANNY GET YOUR GUN (1940, First National)
Minerva Hatton—May Robson
Director—George Amy
Leading Players—Harry Davenport, Margot Stevenson, Hardie Albright

THE GRASSHOPPER (1970, National General Pictures)
Christine—Jacqueline Bisset
Director—Jerry Paris
Leading Players—Jim Brown, Joseph Cotten, Corbett Monica

GRAYEAGLE (1977, American International)
Grayeagle—Alex Cord
Director—Charles B. Pierce
Leading Players—Ben Johnson, Iron Eyes Cody, Lana Wood

THE GREAT CARUSO (1951, MGM)
Enrico Caruso—Mario Lanza
Director—Richard Thorpe
Leading Players—Ann Blyth, Dorothy Kirsten, Jarmila Novotna, Richard Hageman

GREAT CATHERINE (1968, GB, Warner Brothers)
Catherine The Great—Jeanne Moreau
Director—Gordon Flemyng
Leading Players—Peter O'Toole, Zero Mostel, Jack Hawkins, Akim Tamiroff

THE GREAT DEFENDER (1934, GB, Wardour)
Sir Douglas Rolls—Matheson Lang
Director—Thomas Bentley
Leading Players—Margaret Bannerman, Arthur Margetson, Richard Bird

THE GREAT DICTATOR (1940, UA)
Adenoid Hynkel—Charles Chaplin
Director—Charles Chaplin
Leading Players—Paulette Goddard, Jack Oakie, Reginald Gardiner, Henry Daniell, Billy Gilbert

THE GREAT GABBO (1929, Art World Wide)
Great Gabbo—Erich von Stroheim
Director—James Cruze
Leading Players—Betty Compson, Don Douglas, Marjorie King

THE GREAT GAMBINI (1937, Paramount)
Gambini—Akim Tamiroff
Director—Charles Vidor
Leading Players—John Trent, Marian Marsh, Genevieve Tobin, Reginald Denny

THE GREAT GARRICK (1937, Warner Brothers)
David Garrick—Brian Aherne
Director—James Whale
Leading Players—Olivia de Havilland, Edward Everett Horton, Melville Cooper, Luis Alberni

THE GREAT GATSBY (1926, Paramount)
Jay Gatsby—Warner Baxter
Director—Herbert Brenon
Leading Players—Lois Wilson, Neil Hamilton, Georgia Hale, William Powell, Hale Hamilton, Carmelita Geraghty

THE GREAT GATSBY (1949, Paramount)
Jay Gatsby—Alan Ladd
Director—Elliott Nugent
Leading Players—Betty Field, Macdonald Carey, Ruth Hussey, Barry Sullivan, Howard Da Silva, Shelley Winters

THE GREAT GATSBY (1974, Paramount)
Jay Gatsby—Robert Redford
Director—Jack Clayton
Leading Players—Mia Farrow, Bruce Dern, Karen Black, Scott Wilson, Sam Waterston, Lois Chiles, Howard Da Silva

THE GREAT GILBERT AND SULLIVAN (1953, GB, UA)
W.S. Gilbert—Robert Morley
Arthur Sullivan—Maurice Evans
Director—Sidney Gilliat
Leading Players—Eileen Herlie, Martyn Green, Peter Finch

THE GREAT GILDERSLEEVE (1942, RKO)
Throckmorton P. Gildersleeve—Harold Peary
Director—Gordon Douglas
Leading Players—Jane Darwell, Nancy Gates, Charles Arnt

GREAT GUY (1936, Grand National)
Johnny Cave—James Cagney
Director—John G. Blystone
Leading Players—Mae Clarke, James Burke, Edward Brophy

THE GREAT IMPERSONATION (1935, Universal)
Baron Leopold Von Ragenstein/Sir Everard Dominey—
Edmund Lowe
Director—Alan Crosland
Leading Players—Valerie Hobson, Wera Engels, Henry Mollison

THE GREAT IMPERSONATION (1942, Universal)
Baron von Ragenstein/Sir Edward Dominey—Ralph Bellamy
Director—John Rawlins
Leading Players—Evelyn Ankers, Aubrey Mather, Edward Norris

THE GREAT IMPOSTER (1960, Universal)
Ferdinand Waldo Demara, Jr.—Tony Curtis
Director—Robert Mulligan
Leading Players—Karl Malden, Edmond O'Brien, Arthur
O'Connell, Gary Merrill, Joan Blackman

THE GREAT JASPER (1933, RKO)
Jasper Horn—Richard Dix
Director—J. Walter Ruben
Leading Players—Wera Engels, Edna May Oliver, Florence
Eldredge

THE GREAT JESSE JAMES RAID (1953, Lippert)
Jesse James—Willard Parker
Director—Reginald Le Borg
Leading Players—Barbara Payton, Tom Neal, Wallace Ford

THE GREAT JOHN L (1945, UA)
John L. Sullivan—Greg McClure
Director—Frank Tuttle
Leading Players—Linda Darnell, Barbara Britton, Lee Sullivan,
Otto Kruger

THE GREAT LOVER (1931, MGM)
Jean Paurel—Adolphe Menjou
Director—Harry Beaumont
Leading Players—Irene Dunne, Ernest Torrence, Neil Hamilton

THE GREAT LOVER (1949, Paramount)
Freddie Hunter—Bob Hope
Director—Alexander Hall
Leading Players—Rhonda Fleming, Roland Young, Roland
Culver

THE GREAT MACARTHY (1975, Australia, Seven Keys)
MacArthy—John Jarratt
Director—David Baker
Leading Players—Judy Morris, Kate Fitzpatrick, Sandra
MacGregor

THE GREAT MAN VOTES (1939, RKO)
Vance—John Barrymore
Director—Garson Kanin
Leading Players—Peter Holden, Virginia Weidler, Katherine
Alexander, Donald MacBride

THE GREAT MANHUNT (1951, GB, Columbia)
Dr. John Marlowe—Douglas Fairbanks, Jr.
Director—Sidney Gilliat
Leading Players—Glynis Johns, Jack Hawkins, Herbert Lom

THE GREAT MAN'S LADY (1942, Paramount)
Ethan Hoyt—Joel McCrea
Hannah Sempler—Barbara Stanwyck
Director—William A. Wellman
Leading Players—Brian Donlevy, Katharine Stevens, Thurston
Hall, Lloyd Corrigan

THE GREAT MCGINTY (1940, Paramount)
Dan McGinty—Brian Donlevy
Director—Preston Sturges
Leading Players—Akim Tamiroff, Muriel Angelus, Allyn Joslyn

THE GREAT MCGONAGALL (1975, GB, Scotia American)
William McGonagall—Spike Milligan
Director—Joseph McGrath
Leading Players—Peter Sellers, Julia Foster, John Bluthal

THE GREAT MR. HANDEL (1942, GB, GHW/Midfilm)
George Frederick Handel—Wilfrid Lawson
Director—Norman Walker
Leading Players—Elizabeth Allan, Malcolm Keen, Michael
Shepley

THE GREAT MR. NOBODY (1941, Warner Brothers)
Dreamy—Eddie Albert
Director—Ben Stoloff
Leading Players—Joan Leslie, Alan Hale, William Lundigan

THE GREAT O'MALLEY (1937, Warner Brothers)
James Aloysius O'Malley—Pat O'Brien
Director—William Dieterle
Leading Players—Humphrey Bogart, Frieda Inescort, Henry
O'Neill

THE GREAT PROFILE (1940, 20th Century Fox)
Evans Garrick—John Barrymore
Director—Walter Lang
Leading Players—Mary Beth Hughes, Gregory Ratoff, John
Payne, Anne Baxter, Lionel Atwill

THE GREAT SANTINI (1979, Orion/Warner Brothers)
Bull Meechum—Robert Duvall
Director—Lewis John Carlino
Leading Players—Blythe Danner, Michael O'Keefe, Lisa Jane
Persky

THE GREAT SINNER (1949, MGM)
Feodor Dostoyevsky—Gregory Peck
Director—Robert Siodmak
Leading Players—Ava Gardner, Melvyn Douglas, Walter Huston,
Ethel Barrymore, Frank Morgan

THE GREAT VICTOR HERBERT (1939, Paramount)
Victor Herbert—Walter Connolly
Director—Andrew L. Stone
Leading Players—Allan Jones, Mary Martin, Lee Bowman

THE GREAT WALDO PEPPER (1975, Universal)
Waldo Pepper—Robert Redford
Director—George Roy Hill
Leading Players—Bo Svenson, Bo Brundin, Susan Sarandon

THE GREAT WHITE HOPE (1970, 20th Century Fox)
The Kid—Jim Beattie
Director—Martin Ritt

Leading Players—James Earl Jones, Jane Alexander, Lou Gilbert, Joel Fluellen, Chester Morris

THE GREAT ZIEGFELD (1936, MGM)
Florenz Ziegfeld—William Powell
Director—Robert Z. Leonard
Leading Players—Luise Rainer, Myrna Loy, Frank Morgan, Reginald Owen, Nat Pendleton, Virginia Bruce

THE GREATEST (1977, Columbia)
Muhammad Ali—Muhammad Ali
Director—Tom Gries
Leading Players—Ernest Borgnine, Lloyd Haynes, John Marley, Robert Duvall, James Earl Jones

THE GREED OF WILLIAM HART (1948, GB, Butchers)
William Hart—Tod Slaughter
Director—Oswald Mitchell
Leading Players—Henry Oscar, Jenny Lynn, Winifred Melville

THE GREEK TYCOON (1978, Universal)
Theo Tomasis—Anthony Quinn
Director—J. Lee Thompson
Leading Players—Jacqueline Bisset, Raf Vallone, Edward Albert, James Franciscus

GREEN FINGERS (1947, Anglo-American)
Thomas Stone—Robert Beatty
Director—John Harlow
Leading Players—Carol Raye, Nova Pilbeam, Felix Aylmer

THE GREEN-EYED BLONDE (1957, Warner Brothers)
Greeneyes—Susan Oliver
Director—Bernard Girard
Leading Players—Linda Plowman, Beverly Long, Norma Jean Nilsson

GREGORY'S GIRL (1982, GB, Goldwyn)
Gregory—Gordon John Sinclair
Dorothy—Dee Hepburn
Director—Bill Forsyth
Leading Players—Jake D'Arcy, Clare Grogan, Robert Buchanan

GRETCHEN, THE GREENHORN (1916, Silent, Triangle)
Gretchen—Dorothy Gish
Director—Sidney A. Franklin
Leading Players—Ralph Lewis, Frank Bennett, Eugene Pallette

THE GREY FOX (1983, Canada, UA)
Bill Miner—Richard Farnsworth
Director—Philip Borsos
Leading Players—Jackie Burroughs, Wayne Robson, Ken Pogue

GREYSTOKE: THE LEGEND OF TARZAN (1984, Warner Brothers)
John Clayton/Tarzan—Christopher Lambert
Director—Hugh Hudson
Leading Players—Ralph Richardson, Ian Holm, Andie MacDowell, James Fox, Ian Charleson

THE GRIFTERS (1990, Miramax/Cineplex Odeon)
Roy Dillon—John Cusack
Lilly Dillon—Anjelica Huston
Myra Langtry—Annette Bening
Director—Stephen Frears
Leading Players—Pat Hingle, J.T. Walsh

GRISSLY'S MILLIONS (1945, Republic)
Grissly Morgan—Robert H. Barrat
Director—John English
Leading Players—Paul Kelly, Virginia Grey, Don Douglas

THE GRISSOM GANG (1971, Cinerama)
Slim Grissom—Scott Wilson
Ma Grissom—Irene Dailey
Director—Robert Aldrich
Leading Players—Kim Darby, Tony Musante, Robert Lansing, Connie Stevens

THE GROOM WORE SPURS (1951, Universal)
Ben Castle—Jack Carson
Director—Richard Whorf
Leading Players—Ginger Rogers, Joan Davis, Stanley Ridges

THE GROUP (1966, UA)
Lakey Eastlake—Candice Bergen
Dottie Renfrew—Joan Hackett
Priss Hartshorn—Elizabeth Hartman
Polly Andrews—Shirley Knight
Kay Strong—Joanna Pettet
Pokey Prothero—Mary-Robin Redd
Libby MacAusland—Jessica Walter
Helena Davison—Kathleen Widdoes
Director—Sidney Lumet
Leading Players—James Broderick, James Congdon, Larry Hagman, Hal Holbrook, Richard Mulligan

GRUMPY (1930, Paramount)
Grumpy Bullivant—Cyril Maude
Director—George Cukor
Leading Players—Phillips Holmes, Paul Cavanaugh, Frances Dade

GUARD THAT GIRL (1935, Columbia)
Jeanne—Barbara Kent
Director—Lambert Hillyer
Leading Players—Robert Allen, Florence Rice, Ward Bond

THE GUARDIAN (1990, Universal/Wizan)
Camilla—Jenny Seagrove
Director—William Friedkin
Leading Players—Dwier Brown, Carey Lowell, Brad Hall, Miguel Ferrer, Natalia Nogulich

GUARDIAN OF THE WILDERNESS (1977, Sunn Classics)
Galen Clark—Denver Pyle
Director—David O'Malley
Leading Players—John Dehner, Ken Berry, Cheryl Miller

THE GUARDSMAN (1931, MGM)
The Actor—Alfred Lunt
Director—Sidney Franklin
Leading Players—Lynn Fontanne, Roland Young, Zasu Pitts

GUERRILLA GIRL (1953, UA)
Zaira—Marianna
Director—John Christian
Leading Players—Helmut Dantine, Irene Champlin, Ray Julian

GUESS WHAT HAPPENED TO COUNT DRACULA (1970, Merrick International)
Count Dracula—Des Roberts
Director—Laurence Merrick

Leading Players—Claudia Barron, John Landon, Robert Branche

GUESS WHO'S COMING TO DINNER (1967, Columbia)
John Prentice—Sidney Poitier
Director—Stanley Kramer
Leading Players—Spencer Tracy, Katharine Hepburn, Katharine Houghton

THE GUEST (THE CARETAKER) (1963, GB, Janus)
Davis—Donald Pleasence
Director—Clive Donner
Leading Players—Alan Bates, Robert Shaw

THE GUEST (1984, GB, RM Production)
Eugene Marais—Athol Fugard
Director—Ross Devenish
Leading Players—Marius Weyers, Gordon Vorster, Wilma Stockenstrom

GUEST IN THE HOUSE (1944, UA)
Evelyn Heath—Anne Baxter
Director—John Brahm
Leading Players—Ralph Bellamy, Aline MacMahon, Ruth Warrick

GUEST OF HONOR (1934, GB, Warner Brothers)
Lord Strathpeffer—Henry Kendall
Director—George King
Leading Players—Miki Hood, Edward Chapman, Margaret Yarde

GUEST WIFE (1945, UA)
Mary—Claudette Colbert
Director—Sam Wood
Leading Players—Don Ameche, Richard Foran, Charles Dingle

A GUIDE FOR THE MARRIED MAN (1967, 20th Century Fox)
Paul Manning—Walter Matthau
Director—Gene Kelly
Leading Players—Robert Morse, Inger Stevens, Sue Ann Langdon

THE GUILT OF JANET AMES (1947, Columbia)
Janet Ames—Rosalind Russell
Director—Henry Levin
Leading Players—Melvyn Douglas, Sid Caesar, Betsy Blair, Nina Foch

THE GUILTY (1947, Monogram)
Alex Tremholt—John Litel
Director—John Reinhardt
Leading Players—Bonita Granville, Don Castle, Wally Carsell

GUILTY AS HELL (1932, Paramount)
Dr. Tindall—Henry Stephenson
Director—Eric Kenton
Leading Players—Edmund Lowe, Victor McLaglen, Richard Arlen

GUILTY BYSTANDER (1950, Film Classics)
Max Thursday—Zachary Scott
Director—Joseph Lerner
Leading Players—Faye Emerson, Mary Boland, Sam Levene

GUILTY BY SUSPICION (1991, Warner Brothers)
David Merrill—Robert De Niro

Director—Tamra Davis
Leading Players—Annette Bening, George Wendt, Patricia Wettig, Sam Wanamaker, Luke Edwards, Chris Cooper

GUILTY HANDS (1931, MGM)
Richard Grant—Lionel Barrymore
Director—W.S. Van Dyke II
Leading Players—Kay Francis, Madge Evans, William Bakewell

GUILTY OF TREASON (1950, Eagle-Lion)
Cardinal Mindszenty—Charles Bickford
Director—Felix Feist
Leading Players—Paul Kelly, Bonita Granville, Richard Derr

GULLIVER'S TRAVELS (1977, GB, Sunn Classic)
Lemuel Gulliver—Richard Harris
Director—Peter Hunt
Leading Players—Catherine Schell, Norman Shelley, Meredith Edwards

GUMSHOE (1972, GB, Columbia)
Eddie Ginley—Albert Finney
Director—Stephen Frears
Leading Players—Billie Whitelaw, Frank Finlay, Janice Rule

THE GUMSHOE KID (1990, Skouras/Argus)
Jeff Sherman—Jay Underwood
Director—Joseph Manduke
Leading Players—Tracy Scroggins, Vince Edwards, Arlene Golonka, Pamela Springsteen, Amy Lynne

GUN BROTHERS (1956, UA)
Chad—Buster Crabbe
Jubal—Neville Brand
Director—Sidney Salkow
Leading Players—Ann Robinson, Michael Ansara, Walter Sande

GUN CRAZY (1949, UA)
Annie Laurie Starr—Peggy Cummins
Director—Joseph H. Lewis
Leading Players—John Dall, Berry Kroeger, Morris Carnovsky

GUNCRAZY (1992, Zeta Entertainment)
Anita Minteer—Drew Barrymore
Director—Tamra Davis
Leading Players—James LeGros, Billy Drago, Rodney Harvey, Joe Dallesandro, Michael Ironside, Ione Skye

GUN FOR A COWARD (1957, Universal)
Bless Keough—Jeffery Hunter
Director—Abner Biberman
Leading Players—Fred MacMurray, Janice Rule, Chill Wills

THE GUN HAWK (1963, Allied Artists)
Blaine Madden—Rory Calhoun
Director—Edward Ludwig
Leading Players—Rod Cameron, Ruta Lee, Rod Lauren

THE GUN RANGER (1937, Republic)
Don Larson—Bob Steele
Director—R.N. Bradbury
Leading Players—Eleanor Stewart, John Merton, Ernie Adams

THE GUNFIGHTER (1950, 20th Century Fox)
Jimmy Ringo—Gregory Peck
Director—Henry King

Leading Players—Helen Wescott, Milard Mitchell, Jean Parker, Karl Malden, Skip Homeier

THE GUNFIGHTERS (1947, Columbia)
Brazos Kane—Randolph Scott
Director—George Waggner
Leading Players—Barbara Britton, Dorothy Hart, Bruce Cabot

GUNGA DIN (1939, RKO)
Gunga Din—Sam Jaffe
Director—George Stevens
Leading Players—Cary Grant, Victor McLaglen, Douglas Fairbanks, Jr., Eduardo Cianelli

GUNMAN'S WALK (1958, Columbia)
Lee Hackett—Van Heflin
Director—Phil Karlson
Leading Players—Tab Hunter, Kathryn Grant, James Darren

GUNN (1967, Paramount)
Peter Gunn—Craig Stevens
Director—Blake Edwards
Leading Players—Laura Devon, Edward Asner, Albert Paulsen

THE GUNRUNNER (1989, Canada, New World)
Ted Beaubien—Kevin Costner
Director—Nardo Castillo
Leading Players—Sara Botsford, Paul Soles, Gerard Parkes

GUNSLINGER (1956, Associated Releasing Corp.)
Cane Miro—John Ireland
Director—Roger Corman
Leading Players—Beverly Garland, Allison Hayes, Martin Kingsley

THE GURU (1969, 20th Century Fox)
Ustad Zafar Khan—Utpal Dutt
Director—James Ivory
Leading Players—Michael York, Saeed Jaffrey, Rita Tushingham

A GUY, A GAL AND A PAL (1945, Columbia)
Jimmy Jones—Ross Hunter
Helen Carter—Lynn Merrick
Granville Breckenridge—George Meeker
Director—Oscar Boetticher
Leading Players—Ted Donaldson, Jack Norton, Will Stanton

THE GUY WHO CAME BACK (1951, 20th Century Fox)
Harry Joplin—Paul Douglas
Director—Joseph Newman
Leading Players—Joan Bennett, Linda Darnell, Don DeFore

GUYS AND DOLLS (1955, MGM)
Sky Masterson—Marlon Brando
Sarah Brown—Jean Simmons
Nathan Detroit—Frank Sinatra
Miss Adelaide—Vivian Blaine
Director—Joseph L. Mankiewicz
Leading Players—Robert Keith, Stubby Kaye, B.S. Pully, Sheldon Leonard, Regis Toomey

GYPSY (1937, First National)
Hassina—Chili Bouchier
Director—Roy William Neill
Leading Players—Roland Young, Hugh Williams, Frederick Burtwell

GYPSY (1962, Warner Brothers)
Louise Hovick—Natalie Wood
Director—Mervyn LeRoy
Leading Players—Rosalind Russell, Karl Malden, Paul Wallace Ann Jillian, Harry Shannon

THE GYPSY AND THE GENTLEMAN (1958, GB, Rank)
Belle—Melina Mercouri
Sir Paul Deverill—Keith Mitchell
Director—Joseph Losey
Leading Players—Patrick McGoohan, June Laverick, Lyndon Brook, Flora Robson

GYPSY GIRL (1966, GB, Rank)
Brydie White—Hayley Mills
Director—John Mills
Leading Players—Ian McShane, Laurence Naismith, Geoffrey Bayldon

GYPSY OF THE NORTH (1928, Silent, Rayart)
Alice Culhane—Georgia Hale
Director—Scott Pembroke
Leading Players—Huntley Gordon, Jack Dougherty, William Quinn

GYPSY WILDCAT (1944, Universal)
Carla—Maria Montez
Director—Roy William Neill
Leading Players—Jon Hall, Leo Carrillo, Gale Sondergaard

H

H.M. PULHAM, ESQ. (1941, MGM)
Harry Pulham—Robert Young
Director—King Vidor
Leading Players—Hedy Lamarr, Ruth Hussey, Charles Coburn, Van Heflin, Fay Holden

HADLEY'S REBELLION (1984, East India Company/ADI)
Hadley Hickman—Griffin O'Neal
Director—Fred Walton
Leading Players—William Devane, Charles Durning, Adam Baldwin, Lisa Lucas

HAIL, HERO (1969, Cinema Center)
Carl Dixon—Michael Douglas
Director—David Miller
Leading Players—Arthur Kennedy, Teresa Wright, John Larch

HAIL THE CONQUERING HERO (1944, Paramount)
Woodrow Lafayette Pershing Truesmith—Eddie Bracken
Director—Preston Sturges
Leading Players—Ella Raines, William Demarest, Raymond Walburn, Franklin Pangborn, Elizabeth Patterson, Alan Bridge

HAIL THE WOMAN (1921, Silent, Associated Producers)
Judith Beresford—Florence Vidor
Director—John Griffith Wray

Leading Players—Lloyd Hughes, Theodore Roberts, Gertrude Claire

HAIR TRIGGER BAXTER (1926, Silent, Independent Pictures)
Baxter Brant—Bob Custer
Director—Jack Nelson
Leading Players—Eugenia Gilbert, Lew Meehan, Murdock MacQuarrie

THE HAIRY APE (1944, UA)
Hank Smith—William Bendix
Director—Alfred Santell
Leading Players—Susan Hayword, John Loder, Dorothy Comingore

HALDANE OF THE SECRET SERVICE (1923, Silent, Houdini Pictures)
Heath Haldane—Harry Houdini
Director—Harry Houdini
Leading Players—Gladys Leslie, William Humphrey, Richard Carlyle

HALF A BRIDE (1928, Silent, Paramount)
Patience Winslow—Esther Ralston
Director—Gregory La Cava
Leading Players—Gary Cooper, William Worthington, Freeman Wood, Mary Doran

HALF A HERO (1953, MGM)
Ben Dobson—Red Skelton
Director—Don Weis
Leading Players—Jean Hagen, Charles Dingle, Mary Wickes, Willard Waterman, Polly Bergen

HALF A SINNER (1934, Universal)
Deacon—Berton Churchill
Director—Kurt Neumann
Leading Players—Joel McCrea, Sally Blane, Mickey Rooney

HALF A SINNER (1940, Universal)
Anne Gladden—Heather Angel
Director—Al Christie
Leading Players—John King, Constance Collier, Walter Catlett

HALF ANGEL (1936, 20th Century Fox)
Allison Lang—Frances Dee
Director—Sidney Lanfield
Leading Players—Brian Donlevy, Charles Butterworth, Helen Westley, Henry Stephenson

HALF ANGEL (1951, 20th Century Fox)
Nora—Loretta Young
Director—Richard Sale
Leading Players—Joseph Cotten, Cecil Kellaway, Basil Ruysdael, Jim Backus, Irene Ryan

THE HALF BREED (1922, Silent, Associated First National)
Delmar Spavinaw—Wheeler Oakman
Director—Charles A. Taylor
Leading Players—Ann May, Mary Anderson, Hugh Thompson

THE HALF-BREED (1952, RKO)
Charlie Wolf—Jack Buetel
Director—Stuart Gilmore
Leading Players—Robert Young, Janis Carter, Barton MacLane

THE HALF PINT (1960, Sterling)
The Half Pint—Tommy Blackman
Director—Erven Jourdan
Leading Players—Pat Goldin, Ray Cordell, Douglas Lockwood

THE HALF-WAY GIRL (1925, Silent, First National)
Poppy La Rue—Doris Kenyon
Director—John Francis Dillon
Leading Players—Lloyd Hughes, Hobart Bosworth, Tully Marshall

HALLELUJAH, I'M A BUM (1933, UA)
Bumper—Al Jolson
Director—Lewis Milestone
Leading Players—Madge Evans, Frank Morgan, Harry Langdon

THE HALLIDAY BRAND (1957, UA)
Big Dan Halliday—Ward Bond
Director—Joseph H. Lewis
Leading Players—Joseph Cotten, Viveca Lindfors, Betsy Blair

HALLOWEEN IV: THE RETURN OF MICHAEL MYERS (1988, Galaxy)
Michael Myers—George P. Wilbur
Director—Dwight H. Little
Leading Players—Donald Pleasence, Ellie Cornell, Danielle Harris

HALLOWEEN V: THE REVENGE OF MICHAEL MYERS (1989, Galaxy)
Michael Myers—Donald L. Shanks
Director—Dominique Othenin-Girard
Leading Players—Danielle Harris, Donald Pleasence

HAMBONE AND HILLIE (1984, New World)
Hillie—Lillian Gish
Director—Roy Watts
Leading Players—Timothy Bottoms, Candy Clark, O.J. Simpson

HAMLET (1913, Silent, GB, Gaumont)
Hamlet—Johnston Forbes-Robertson
Director—Hay Plumb
Leading Players—Gertrude Elliot, Walter Ringham, Adeleine Bourne, J.H. Barnes

HAMLET (1948, GB, Rank)
Hamlet—Laurence Olivier
Director—Laurence Olivier
Leading Players—Eileen Herlie, Basil Sydney, Jean Simmons, Norman Wooland, Felix Aylmer

HAMLET (1964, Electronovision/Warner Brothers)
Hamlet—Richard Burton
Director—Bill Colleran
Leading Players—Alfred Drake, Hume Cronyn, Eileen Herlie, John Gielgud, Frederick Young

HAMLET (1969, GB, Woodfall-Filmways)
Hamlet—Nicol Williamson
Director—Tony Richardson
Leading Players—Gordon Jackson, Anthony Hopkins, Judy Parfitt, Mark Dignam, Marianne Faithful

HAMLET (1990, Warner Brothers/Icon)
Hamlet—Mel Gibson
Director—Franco Zeffirelli

Leading Players—Glenn Close, Alan Bates, Paul Scofield, Ian Holm, Helena Bonham-Carter, Stephen Dillane, Nathaniel Parker

HAMMER (1972, UA)
B.J. Hammer—Fred Williamson
Director—Bruce Clark
Leading Players—Bernie Hamilton, Vonetta McKee, William Smith

HAMMERHEAD (1968, Columbia)
Hammerhead—Peter Vaughan
Director—David Miller
Leading Players—Vince Edwards, Judy Geeson, Diana Dors

HAMMERSMITH IS OUT (1972, Cinerama)
Hammersmith—Richard Burton
Director—Peter Ustinov
Leading Players—Elizabeth Taylor, Peter Ustinov, Beau Bridges, Leon Ames

HAMMETT (1982, Orion/Warner Brothers)
Dashiell Hammett—Frederic Forrest
Director—Wim Wenders
Leading Players—Peter Boyle, Marilu Henner, Lydia Lei

THE HAND THAT ROCKS THE CRADLE (1992, Hollywood Pictures)
Peyton Flanders—Rebecca DeMornay
Director—Curtis Hanson
Leading Players—Annabelle Sciorra, Matt McCoy, Ernie Hudson, Madeline Zima, John de Lancie, Kevin Skousen

THE HANDMAID'S TALE (1990, Cinecom)
Kate—Natasha Richardson
Director—Volker Schlondorff
Leading Players—Robert Duvall, Faye Dunaway, Aidan Quinn, Elizabeth McGovern, Victoria Tennant

THE HANDS OF NARA (1922, Silent, Metro)
Nara Alexieff—Clara Kimball Young
Director—Harry Garson
Leading Players—John Orloff, Elliott Dexter, Edwin Stevens

THE HANDS OF ORLAC (1964, GB, Rivieria-Pendennis)
Steven Orlac—Mel Ferrer
Director—Edmond T. Greville
Leading Players—Christopher Lee, Dany Carrel, Felix Aylmer

THE HANDSOME BRUTE (1925, Silent, Columbia)
Larry O'Day—William Fairbanks
Director—Robert Eddy
Leading Players—Virginia Lee Corbin, Lee Shumway, Robert Bolder

HANDY ANDY (1921, Silent, GB, Ideal)
Andy—Peter Coleman
Director—Bert Wynne
Leading Players—Kathleen Vaughn, Warwick Ward, John Wyndham

HANDY ANDY (1934, Fox Film Corp.)
Andrew Yates—Will Rogers
Director—David Butler
Leading Players—Peggy Wood, Conchita Montenegro, Mary Carlisle

THE HANGING JUDGE (1918, Silent, GB, Hepworth)
Sir John Veasey—Hamilton Stewart
Director—Henry Edwards
Leading Players—Henry Edwards, Chrissie White, Randle Ayrton

THE HANGMAN (1959, Paramount)
Mackenzie Bovard—Robert Taylor
Director—Michael Curtiz
Leading Players—Tina Louise, Fess Parker, Jack Lord

HANGMEN ALSO DIE (1943, UA)
Reinhard Heydrich—Hans von Twardowski
Director—Fritz Lang
Leading Players—Brian Donlevy, Walter Brennan, Anna Lee, Gene Lockhart, Dennis O'Keefe

HANNAH AND HER SISTERS (1986, Orion)
Hannah—Mia Farrow
Lee—Barbara Hershey
Holly—Dianne Wiest
Director—Woody Allen
Leading Players—Michael Caine, Carrie Fisher, Lloyd Nolan, Maureen O'Sullivan, Daniel Stern, Woody Allen

HANNA'S WAR (1988, Cannon)
Hanna Senesh—Maruschka Detmers
Director—Menahem Golan
Leading Players—Ellen Burstyn, Anthony Andrews, Donald Pleasence, David Warner

HANNIBAL (1960, Warner Brothers)
Hannibal—Victor Mature
Director—Edgar G. Ulmer
Leading Players—Rita Gam, Gabriele Ferzetti, Milly Vitale

HANNIBAL BROOKS (1969, GB, UA)
Hannibal Brooks—Oliver Reed
Director—Michael Winner
Leading Players—Michael J. Pollard, Wolfgang Preiss, Helmut Lohner, Karin Baal

HANNIE CALDER (1971, GB, Paramount)
Hannie Calder—Raquel Welch
Director—Burt Kennedy
Leading Players—Robert Culp, Ernest Borgnine, Strother Martin, Diana Dors, Jack Elam

HANS CHRISTIAN ANDERSON (1952, RKO)
Hans Christian Anderson—Danny Kaye
Director—Charles Vidor
Leading Players—Farley Granger, Jeanmarie, Joey Walsh

THE HAPPIEST MILLIONAIRE (1967, Disney/Buena Vista)
Anthony J. Drexel Biddle—Fred MacMurray
Director—Norman Tokar
Leading Players—Tommy Steele, Greer Garson, Geraldine Page, Gladys Cooper, Hermione Baddeley

HAPPY BIRTHDAY, GEMINI (1980, UA)
Nick Geminiani—Robert Viharo
Director—Richard Benner
Leading Players—Madeline Kahn, Rita Moreno, Alan Rosenberg

HAPPY BIRTHDAY, WANDA JUNE (1971, Columbia)
Wanda June—Pamelyn Ferdin

Director—Mark Robson
Leading Players—Rod Steiger, Susannah York, George Grizzard

THE HAPPY HOOKER (1976, Cannon)
Xaviera Hollander—Lynn Redgrave
Director—Nicholas Sgarro
Leading Players—Jean Pierre Aumont, Lovelady Powell, Nicholas Pryor

THE HAPPY HOOKER GOES TO HOLLYWOOD (1980, Cannon)
Xaviera Hollander—Martine Beswick
Director—Alan Roberts
Leading Players—Adam West, Phil Silvers, Edie Adams

THE HAPPY HOOKER GOES TO WASHINGTON (1977, Cannon)
Xaviera Hollander—Joey Heatherton
Director—William A. Levey
Leading Players—George Hamilton, Ray Walston, Jack Carter

HAPPY IS THE BRIDE (1958, GB, Panthar/Kassler)
Janet Royd—Janette Scott
Director—Roy Boulting
Leading Players—Ian Carmichael, Cecil Parker, Terry-Thomas

THE HAPPY WARRIOR (1925, Silent, Vitagraph)
Ralph—Malcolm McGregor
Director—J. Stuart Blackton
Leading Players—Alice Calhoun, Mary Alden, Anders Randolf

THE HARASSED HERO (1954, GB, AB-Pathe)
Murray Selwyn—Guy Middleton
Director—Maurice Elvey
Leading Players—Joan Winmill, Elwyn Brooks-Jones, Mary Mackenzie

HARD BOILED MAHONEY (1947, Monogram)
Slip Mahoney—Leo Gorcey
Director—William Beaudine
Leading Players—Huntz Hall, Bobby Jordan, Billy Benedict

HARD GUY (1941, Producers Releasing Corp.)
Vic—Jack La Rue
Director—Elmer Clifton
Leading Players—Mary Healey, Iris Adrian, Gayle Mellott

HARD HITTIN' HAMILTON (1924, Silent, Action Pictures)
Bill Hamilton—Buffalo Bill, Jr.
Director—Richard Thorpe
Leading Players—Hazel Keener, Gordon Russell, William Ryno

THE HARD MAN (1957, Columbia)
Steve Burden—Guy Madison
Director—George Sherman
Leading Players—Valerie French, Lorne Greene, Barry Atwater

HARD ROCK HARRIGAN (1935, Fox Film Corp.)
"Hard Rock" Harrigan—George O'Brien
Director—David Howard
Leading Players—Irene Hervey, Fred Kohler, Dean Benton

HARD TO KILL (1990, Warner/Lee Rich Production)
Mason Storm—Steven Seagal
Director—Bruce Malmuth
Leading Players—Kelly Le Brock, Bill Sadler, Frederick Coffin, Bonnie Burroughs, Zachary Rosencrantz

HARDBOILED (1929, Silent, FBO)
Teena Johnson—Sally O'Neill
Director—Ralph Ince
Leading Players—Donald Reed, Lilyan Tashman, Bob Sinclair

HARD-BOILED HAGGERTY (1927, Silent, First National)
Hard-Boiled Haggerty—Milton Sills
Director—Charles Brabin
Leading Players—Molly O'Day, Mitchell Lewis, Arthur Stone

HARDBOILED ROSE (1929, Warner Brothers)
Rose Duhamel—Myrna Loy
Director—F. Harmon Wright
Leading Players—William Collier, Jr., John Miljan, Gladys Brockwell

HAREM GIRL (1952, Columbia)
Princess Shareen—Peggy Castle
Director—Edward Bernds
Leading Players—Joan Davis, Arthur Blake, Paul Marion

HARLEQUIN (1980, Australia, Hemdale/New Image)
Gregory Wolfe—Robert Powell
Director—Simom Powell
Leading Players—David Hemmings, Carmen Duncan, Broderick Crawford

HARLEY DAVIDSON AND THE MARLBORO MAN (1991, MGM)
Harley Davidson—Mickey Rourke
Marlboro—Don Johnson
Director—Simon Wincer
Leading Players—Chelsea Field, Daniel Baldwin, Tom Sizemore, Vanessa Williams

HARLOW (1965, Electronovision/Magna)
Jean Harlow—Carol Lynley
Director—Alex Segal
Leding Players—Efrem Zimbalist, Jr., Ginger Rogers, Barry Sullivan, Hurd Hatfield, Lloyd Bochner

HARLOW (1965, Paramount)
Jean Harlow—Carroll Baker
Director—Gordon Douglas
Leading Players—Martin Balsam, Red Buttons, Michael Connors, Angela Lansbury, Peter Lawford

HARMON OF MICHIGAN (1941, Columbia)
Tom Harmon—Tom Harmon
Director—Charles Barton
Leading Players—Anita Louise, Forest Evashevski, Oscar O'Shea

HAROLD AND MAUDE (1971, Paramount)
Maude—Ruth Gordon
Harold Chasen—Bud Cort
Director—Hal Ashby
Leading Players—Vivian Pickles, Cyril Cusack, Charles Tyner

HAROLD TEEN (1928, Silent, First National)
Harold Teen—Arthur Lake
Director—Mervyn LeRoy
Leading Players—Mary Brian, Lucien Littlefield, Jack Duffy

HAROLD TEEN (1934, Warner Brothers)
Harold Teen—Hal LeRoy
Director—Murray Roth
Leading Players—Rochelle Hudson, Patricia Ellis, Guy Kibbee

HARPER (1966, Warner Brothers)
Lew Harper—Paul Newman
Director—Jack Smight
Leading Players—Lauren Bacall, Julie Harris, Arthur Hill, Janet Leigh, Pamela Tiffin, Robert Wagner

HARRIET CRAIG (1950, Columbia)
Harriett Craig—Joan Crawford
Director—Vincent Sherman
Leading Players—Wendell Corey, Lucille Watson, Allyn Joslyn

HARRIGAN'S KID (1943, MGM)
Benny McNeil—Bobby Readick
Tom Harrigan—William Gargan
Director—Charles F. Reisner
Leading Players—Frank Craven, Jay Ward, J. Carroll Naish

HARRY AND SON (1984, Orion)
Harry—Paul Newman
Howard—Robby Benson
Director—Paul Newman
Leading Players—Ellen Barkin, Wilfrid Brimley, Joanne Woodward

HARRY AND THE HENDERSONS (1987, Universal)
George Henderson—John Lithgow
Nancy Henderson—Melinda Dillon
Sarah Henderson—Margaret Langrick
Ernie Henderson—Joshua Rudoy
Harry—Kevin Peter Hall
Director—William Dear
Leading Players—David Suchet, Lainie Kazan, Don Ameche

HARRY AND TONTO (1974, 20th Century Fox)
Harry Coombs—Art Carney
Director—Paul Mazursky
Leading Players—Ellen Burstyn, Chief Dan George, Geraldine Fitzgerald, Larry Hagman, Arthur Hunnicut

HARRY AND WALTER GO TO NEW YORK (1976, Columbia)
Harry Dighby—James Caan
Walter Hill—Elliott Gould
Director—Mark Rydell
Leading Players—Michael Caine, Diane Keaton, Charles Durning, Leslie Ann Warren

HARRY BLACK AND THE TIGER (1958, GB, 20th Century Fox)
Harry Black—Stewart Granger
Director—Hugo Fregonese
Leading Players—Barbara Rush, Anthony Steel, I.S. Johar

HARRY IN YOUR POCKET (1973, UA)
Harry—James Coburn
Director—Bruce Geller
Leading Players—Michael Sarrazin, Trish Van Devere, Walter Pidgeon

HARRY TRACY—DESPERADO (1982, Canada, Guardian)
Harry Tracy—Bruce Dern
Director—William A. Graham
Leading Players—Helen Shaver, Michael C. Gwynne, Gordon Lightfoot

HARRY'S MACHINE (1986, Cannon)
Harry—Robert Forster
Director—Robert Forster
Leading Players—Joe Spinell, Shannon Wilcox, Katherine Forster

HARRY'S WAR (1981, Taft International)
Harry—Edward Herrmann
Director—Keith Merrill
Leading Players—Geraldine Page, Karen Grassle, David Ogden Stiers, Salome Jens

THE HARVESTER (1927, Silent, R-C Pictures)
David Langston—Orville Caldwell
Director—Leo Meehan
Leading Players—Natalie Kingston, Will R. Walling, Jay Hunt

THE HARVESTER (1936, Republic)
David Langston—Russell Hardie
Director—Joseph Santley
Leading Players—Alice Brady, Ann Rutherford, Frank Craven

THE HARVEY GIRLS (1946, MGM)
Susan Bradley—Judy Garland
Alma—Virginia O'Brien
Deborah—Cyd Charisse
Director—George Sidney
Leading Players—John Hodiak, Ray Bolger, Preston Foster, Angela Lansbury, Marjorie Main

HARVEY MIDDLEMAN, FIREMAN (1965, Columbia)
Harvey Middleman—Gene Troobnick
Director—Ernest Pintoff
Leading Players—Hermione Gingold, Patricia Harty, Arlene Golonka

HAT CHECK GIRL (1932, Fox Film Corp.)
Gerry Marsh—Sally Eilers
Director—Sidney Lanfield
Leading Players—Ben Lyon, Ginger Rogers, Monroe Owsley

HAT CHECK HONEY (1944, Universal)
Susan Brent—Grace McDonald
Director—Edward F. Cline
Leading Players—Richard Davis, Leon Errol, Walter Catlett

THE HATCHET MAN (1932, First National/Warner Brothers)
Wong Low Get—Edward G. Robinson
Director—William Wellman
Leading Players—Loretta Young, Dudley Digges, Leslie Fenton

HATER OF MEN (1917, Silent, Triangle)
Janice Salsbury—Bessie Barriscale
Director—Charles Miller
Leading Players—Charles K. French, Jack Gilbert

HATTER'S CASTLE (1948, GB, Paramount)
James Brodie—Robert Newton
Director—Lance Comfort
Leading Players—Deborah Kerr, Beatrice Varley, James Mason

HAUNTED HONEYMOON (1986, Orion)
Larry Abbot—Gene Wilder
Vickie Pearle Abbot—Gilda Radner
Director—Gene Wilder
Leading Players—Dom DeLuise, Jonathan Pryce, Paul L. Smith

THE HAUNTED STRANGLER (1958, GB, Anglo-Amalgamated)
James Rankin—Boris Karloff

Director—Robert Day
Leading Players—Jean Kent, Elizabeth Allan, Anthony Dawson

THE HAUNTING OF JULIA (1981, GB/Canada, Discovery)
Julia—Mia Farrow
Director—Richard Loncraine
Leading Players—Keir Dullea, Tom Conti, Jill Bennett

THE HAUNTING OF M (1979, Nu-Image)
Marianna- Sheelagh Gilbey
Director—Anna Thomas
Leading Players—Nini Pitt, Evie Garratt, Alan Hay

THE HAUNTING OF MORELLA (1990, Concorde)
Morella—Nicole Eggert
Director—Jim Wynorski
Leading Players—David McCallum, Christopher Halsted, Lana Clarkson, Maria Ford

HAVANA ROSE (1951, Republic)
Estelita DeMarco—Estelita Rodriguez
Director—William Beaudine
Leading Players—Bill Williams, Hugh Herbert, Florence Bates

HAWK OF THE HILLS (1929, Silent, Pathe Exchange)
The Hawk—Frank Lacteen
Director—Spencer Gordon Bennett
Leading Players—Allene Ray, Walter Miller, Robert Chandler

HAWK THE SLAYER (1980, GB, Chips/ITC)
Hawk—John Terry
Director—Terry Marcel
Leading Players—Jack Palance, Bernard Bresslaw, Ray Charleston, Peter O'Farrell

THE HAWK'S NEST (1928, Silent, First National)
The Hawk/John Finchley—Milton Sills
Director—Benjamin Christensen
Leading Players—Montagu Love, Mitchell Lewis, Doris Kenyon

HAWLEY'S OF HIGH STREET (1933, GB, British Interational)
Bill Hawley—Leslie Fuller
Director—Thomas Bentley
Leading Players—Judy Kelly, Francis Lister, Amy Veness

HAWTHORNE OF THE U.S.A. (1919, Silent, Paramount)
Anthony Hamilton Hawthorne—Wallace Reid
Director—James Cruze
Leading Players—Harrison Ford, Lila Lee, Tully Marshall

HAZEL'S PEOPLE (1978, A People's Place)
Hazel—Rachel Thomas
Director—Charles Davis
Leading Players—Geraldine Page, Pat Hingle, Graham Beckel

HE COULDN'T SAY NO (1938, Warner Brothers)
Lambert Hunkins—Frank McHugh
Director—Lew Seiler
Leading Players—Jane Wyman, Cora Witherspoon, Diana Lewis

HE HIRED THE BOSS (1943, 20th Century Fox)
Hubert Wilkins—Stuart Erwin
Mr. Bates—Thurston Hall
Director—Thomas Z. Loring
Leading Players—Evelyn Venable, Vivian Blaine, James Bush

HE KNEW WOMEN (1930, RKO)
Geoffrey Clarke—Lowell Sherman
Director—Hugh Herbert
Leading Players—Alice Joyce, David Manners, Frances Dade

HE KNOWS YOU'RE ALONE (1980, MGM-UA)
The Killer—Tom Rolfing
Director—Armand Mastroianni
Leading Players—Don Scardino, Caitlin O'Heaney, Elizabeth Kemp

HE MARRIED HIS WIFE (1940, 20th Century Fox)
T.H. Randall—Joel McCrea
Valerie Randall—Nancy Kelly
Director—Roy Del Ruth
Leading Players—Roland Young, Mary Boland, Cesar Romero

HE RAN ALL THE WAY (1951, UA)
Nick—John Garfield
Director—John Berry
Leading Players—Shelley Winters, Wallace Ford, Selena Royle, Gladys George, Norman Lloyd

HE RIDES TALL (1964, Universal)
Marshal Morg Rocklin—Tony Young
Director—R.G. Springsteen
Leading Players—Dan Duryea, Jo Morrow, Madlyn Rhue

HE STAYED FOR BREAKFAST (1940, Columbia)
Paul Beloit—Melvyn Douglas
Director—Alexander Hall
Leading Players—Loretta Young, Alan Marshal, Eugene Pallette, Una O'Connor, Curt Bois

HE SAID, SHE SAID (1991, Paramount)
Dan Hansen—Kevin Bacon
Lorie Bryer—Elizabeth Perkins
Directors—Ken Kwapis & Marisa Silver
Leading Players—Nathan Lane, Anthony La Paglia, Sharon Stone, Stanley Anderson

HE STOOPS TO CONQUER (1944, GB, Playgoers/Columbia)
George Gribble—George Formby
Director—Marcel Varnel
Leading Players—Robertson Hare, Elizabeth Allan, Claude Bailey

HE WALKED BY NIGHT (1948, Eagle-Lion)
Davis Morgan—Richard Basehart
Director—Alfred Werker
Leading Players—Scott Brady, Roy Roberts, Whit Bissell, Jack Webb

HE WAS HER MAN (1934, Warner Brothers)
Flicker Hayes—James Cagney
Rose Lawrence—Joan Blondell
Director—Lloyd Bacon
Leading Players—Victor Jory, Frank Craven, Harold Huber, Ralf Harolde, Bradley Page

HE WHO GETS SLAPPED (1924, Silent, MGM)
"He Who Gets Slapped"—Lon Chaney
Director—Victor Seastrom
Leading Players—Norma Shearer, John Gilbert, Tully Marshall

HE WHO LAUGHS LAST (1925, Silent, Barsky Corp.)
Jimmy Taylor—Kenneth McDonald
Director—Jack Nelson
Leading Players—Margaret Cloud, David Torrence, Gino Corrado

THE HEAD MAN (1928, Silent, First National)
Watts—Charlie Murray
Director—Eddie Cline
Leading Players—Loretta Young, Larry Kent, Lucien Littlefield

THE HEAD OF THE FAMILY (1928, Silent, Gotham)
Eddie, The Plumber—William Russell
Director—Joseph C. Boyle
Leading Players—Mickey Bennett, Virginia Lee Corbin, Richard Walling, Alma Bennett

HEAD OF THE FAMILY (1933, GB, First National/Warner Brothers)
Mr. Powis-Porter—Arthur Maude
Director—John Daumery
Leading Players- Irene Vanbrugh, John Stuart, Pat Paterson

THE HEADLESS HORSEMAN (1922, Silent, W.D. Hodkinson Corp.)
The Headless Horseman—Ben Hendricks, Jr.
Director—Edward Venturini
Leading Players—Will Rogers, Lois Meredith, Mary Foy

THE HEADLEY'S AT HOME (1939, Standard)
Pamela Headley—Evelyn Venable
Ernest Headley—Grant Mitchell
Director—Chris Beute
Leading Players—Robert Whitney, Betty Roadman, Vince Barnett

THE HEADLINE GIRL (1935, Mascot)
Myrna Van Buren—Heather Angel
Director—William Nigh
Leading Players—Roger Pryor, Jack LaRue, Ford Sterling

HEADLINE SHOOTER (1933, RKO)
Bill Allen—William Gargan
Director—Otto Brower
Leading Players—Frances Dee, Ralph Bellamy, Jack La Rue

THE HEALER (1935, Monogram)
The Doctor—Ralph Bellamy
Director—Reginald Barker
Leading Players—Karen Morley, Mickey Rooney, Judith Allen

HEAR MY SONG (1991, GB, Miramax)
Josef Locke—Ned Beatty
Director—Peter Chelson
Leading Players—Adrian Dunbar, David McCallum, Tara Fitzgerald, Shirley Anne Field, William Hootkins, James Nesbitt

HEART CONDITION (1990, New Line)
Jack Moony—Bob Hoskins
Director—James D. Parriott
Leading Players—Denzel Washington, Chloe Webb, Robert E. Mosley, Janet DuBois, Alan Rachins

HEART LIKE A WHEEL (1983, Aurora/20th Century Fox)
Shirley "Cha Cha" Muldowney—Bonnie Bedelia

Director—Jonathan Kaplan
Leading Players—Beau Bridges, Leo Rossi, Hoyt Axon

HEART OF A CHILD (1958, GB, Rank)
Karl Speil—Richard Williams
Director—Clive Donner
Leading Players—Jean Anderson, Donald Pleasance, Maureen Pryor, John Glynn Jones

THE HEART OF A FOLLIES GIRL (1928, Silent, First National)
Teddy O'Day—Billie Dove
Director—John Francis Dillon
Leading Players—Larry Kent, Lowell Sherman, Clarissa Selwynne

HEART OF A SIREN (1925, Silent, First National)
Isabella Echevaria—Barbara La Marr
Director—Phil Rosen
Leading Players—Conway Tearle, Harry Morey, Paul Doucet

THE HEART OF A TEXAN (1922, Silent, Steiner Productions)
King Calhoun—Neal Hart
Director—Paul Hurst
Leading Players—William Quinn, Sarah Bindley, Hazel Maye

THE HEART OF LINCOLN (1922, Silent, New Era Productions)
Abraham Lincoln—Francis Ford
Director—Francis Ford
Leading Players—Grace Cunard, Ella Hall, William Quinn

THE HEART OF SALOME (1927, Silent, Fox Film Corp.)
Helene—Alma Rubens
Director—Victor Schertzinger
Leading Players—Walter Pidgeon, Holmes Herbert, Robert Agnew

THE HEART RAIDER (1923, Silent, Paramount)
Muriel Gray—Agnes Ayres
Director—Wesley Ruggles
Leading Players—Mahlon Hamilton, Charles Ruggles, Frazer Coulter

THE HEART SPECIALIST (1922, Silent, Paramount)
Rosalie Beckwith—Mary Miles Minter
Director—Frank Urson
Leading Players—Allan Forrest, Roy Atwell, Jack Matheis

THE HEART THIEF (1927, Silent, Metropolitan Pictures)
Paul Kurt—Joseph Schildkraut
Director—Nils Olaf Chrisander
Leading Players—Lya De Putti, Robert Edeson, Charles Gerrard

THE HEARTBREAK KID (1972, 20th Century Fox)
Lenny Cantrow—Charles Grodin
Director—Elaine May
Leading Players—Jeannie Berlin, Cybill Shepherd, Eddie Albert, Audra Lindley

HEARTBREAKERS (1984, Orion)
Blue Arthur—Peter Coyote
Eli Khan—Nick Mancuso
Director—Bobby Roth
Leading Players—Max Gail, James Laurenson, Carol Wayne, Jamie Rose, Kathryn Harrold

HEATHERS (1989, New World)
Heather Duke—Shannen Doherty
Heather McNamara—Lisanne Falk
Heather Chandler—Kim Walker
Director—Michael Lehmann
Leading Players—Winona Ryder, Christian Slater, Penelope Milford

HEAVEN KNOWS, MR. ALLISON (1957, 20th Century Fox)
Mr. Allison—Robert Mitchum
Director—John Huston
Leading Player—Deborah Kerr

HEAVEN WITH A GUN (1969, MGM)
Jim Killian—Glenn Ford
Director—Lee H. Katzin
Leading Players—Carolyn Jones, Barbara Hershey, John Anderson, David Carradine, J.D. Cannon

HEAVENLY BODIES (1985, Universal)
Samantha—Cynthia Dale
Director—Lawrence Dane
Leading Players—Richard Rebiere, Walter George Alton, Laura Henry, Stuart Stone

THE HEAVENLY KID (1985, Orion)
Bobby—Lewis Smith
Director—Cary Medoway
Leading Players—Jason Gedrick, Jane Kaczmarek, Richard Mulligan

HEDDA (1975, GB, Bowden)
Hedda Gabler—Glenda Jackson
Director—Trevor Nunn
Leading Players—Timothy West, Peter Eyre, Jennie Linden, Patrick Stewart, Constance Chapman

HEIDI (1937, 20th Century Fox)
Heidi—Shirley Temple
Director—Allan Dwan
Leading Players—Jean Hersholt, Arthur Treacher, Helen Westley, Pauline Moore

HEIDI'S SONG (1982, Animated, Paramount)
Heidi—Voice of Margery Gray
Director—Robert Taylor
Leading Players—Voices of Lorne Greene, Sammy Davis, Jr., Peter Cullen, Robert DeWitt

HEIR TO TROUBLE (1936, Columbia)
Ken Armstrong—Ken Maynard
Director—Spencer Gordon Bennett
Leading Players—Joan Perry, Harry Woods, Martin Faust

THE HEIRESS (1949, Paramount)
Catherine Sloper—Olivia De Havilland
Director—William Wyler
Leading Players—Montgomery Cliff, Ralph Richardson, Miriam Hopkins, Vanessa Brown, Mona Freeman

HELD BY THE LAW (1927, Silent, Universal)
George Travis—Ralph Lewis
Director—Edward Laemmle
Leading Players—Johnnie Walker, Marguerite De La Motte, Robert Ober

HELD TO ANSWER (1923, Silent, Metro)
John Hampstead—House Peters
Director—Harold Shaw
Leading Players—Grace Carlyle, John Sainpolis, Lydia Knott

THE HELEN MORGAN STORY (1959, Warner Brothers)
Helen Morgan—Ann Blyth
Director—Michael Curtiz
Leading Players—Paul Newman, Richard Carlson, Gene Evans, Alan King, Cara Williams

THE HELL CAT (1934, Columbia)
Geraldine Graham—Ann Sothern
Director—Albert Rogell
Leading Players—Robert Armstrong, Benny Baker, Minna Gombell

HELL DIVERS (1932, MGM)
Windy—Wallace Beery
Steve—Clark Gable
Director—George Hill
Leading Players—Conrad Nagel, Dorothy Jordan, Marjorie Rambeau, Marie Prevost

HELL DRIVERS (1958, GB, Rank)
Tom Yately—Stanley Baker
Red—Patrick McGoohan
Director—C. Raker Endfield
Leading Players—Herbert Lom, Peggy Cummins, William Hartnell

HELL-SHIP MORGAN (1936, Columbia)
Morgan—George Bancroft
Director—D. Ross Lederman
Leading Players—Ann Sothern, Victory Jory, George Regas

HELL-TO-PAY AUSTIN (1916, Silent, Triangle)
Hell-to-Pay Austin—Wilfred Lucas
Director—Paul Powell
Leading Players—Bessie Love, Ralph Lewis, Mary Alden

HELLER IN PINK TIGHTS (1960, Paramount)
Angela Rossini—Sophia Loren
Director—George Cukor
Leading Players—Anthony Quinn, Margaret O'Brien, Steve Forrest, Eileen Heckart, Edmund Lowe

HELLFIGHTERS (1968, Universal)
Chance Buckman—John Wayne
Greg Parker—Jim Hutton
Director—Andrew V. McLaglen
Leading Players—Katherine Ross, Vera Miles, Jay C. Flippen, Bruce Cabot

HELLO AGAIN (1987, Buena Vista)
Lucy Chadman—Shelley Long
Director—Frank Perry
Leading Players—Judith Ivey, Gabriel Byrne, Corbin Bernsen, Sela Ward, Austin Pendleton

HELLO, DOLLY! (1969, 20th Century Fox)
Dolly Levi—Barbra Streisand
Director—Gene Kelly
Leading Players—Walther Matthau, Michael Crawford, Louis Armstrong, Marianne McAndrew, E.J. Peaker

HELLO MARY LOU, PROM NIGHT II (1987, Canada, Simcom/Norstar)
Mary Lou Maloney—Lisa Schrage
Director—Bruce Pittman
Leading Players—Wendy Lyon, Michael Ironside, Justin Louis

HELLRAISER (1987, GB, New World)
Frank Cotton—Sean Chapman
Director—Clive Barker
Leading Players—Andrew Robinson, Clare Higgins, Ashley Laurence, Oliver Smith

HELL'S ANGELS (1930, UA)
Monte Rutledge—Ben Lyon
Roy Rutledge—James Hall
Director—Howard Hughes
Leading Players -Jean Harlow, John Darrow, Lucien Prival, Frank Clarke, Roy Wilson

HELL'S HEROES (1930, Universal)
Bob Sangster—Charles Bickford
Barbwire Gibbons—Raymond Hatton
Wild Bill Kearney—Fred Kohler
Director—William Wyler
Leading Players—Fritzi Ridgeway, Maria Alba, Jose De LaCruz

HELLSHIP BRONSON (1928, Silent, Gotham Productions)
Capt. Ira Bronson—Noah Beery
Director—Joseph E. Henabery
Leading Players—Mrs. Wallace Reid, Reed Howes, Helen Foster

HENNESSY (1975, GB, American International)
Hennessy—Rod Steiger
Director—Don Sharp
Leading PLayers—Lee Remick, Richard Johnson, Trevor Howard

HENRY ALDRICH, BOY SCOUT (1944, Paramount)
Henry Aldrich—Jimmy Lydon
Director—Hugh Bennett
Leading Players—Charley Smith, John Litel, Olive Blakeney

HENRY ALDRICH, EDITOR (1942, Paramount)
Henry Aldrich—Jimmy Lydon
Director—Hugh Bennett
Leading Players—Charles Smith, Rita Quigley, John Litel

HENRY ALDRICH FOR PRESIDENT (1941, Paramount)
Henry Aldrich—James Lydon
Director—Hugh Bennett
Leading Players—Charles Smith, June Preisser, Mary Anderson

HENRY ALDRICH GETS GLAMOUR (1942, Paramount)
Henry Aldrich—Jimmy Lydon
Director—Hugh Bennett
Leading Players—Charlie Smith, John Litel, Diana Lynn

HENRY ALDRICH HAUNTS A HOUSE (1943, Paramount)
Henry Aldrich—Jimmy Lydon
Director—Hugh Bennett
Leading Players—Charles Smith, John Litel, Joan Mortimer

HENRY ALDRICH PLAYS CUPID (1944, Paramount)
Henry Aldrich—Jimmy Lydon
Director—Hugh Bennett
Leading Players—Charles Smith, Diana Lynn, John Litel

HENRY ALDRICH SWINGS IT (1943, Paramount)
Henry Aldrich—Jimmy Lydon
Director—Hugh Bennett
Leading Players—Charlie Smith, Mimi Chandler, Olive Blakeney

HENRY ALDRICH'S LITTLE SECRET (1944, Paramount)
Henry Aldrich—Jimmy Lydon
Director—Hugh Bennett
Leading Players—Charles Smith, Joan Mortimer, Ann Doran

HENRY AND DIZZY (1942, Paramount)
Henry Aldrich—Jimmy Lydon
Dizzy Stevens—Charles Smith
Director—Hugh Bennett
Leading Players—Mary Anderson, John Litel, Olive Blakeney

HENRY AND JUNE (1990, Universal/Walrus)
Henry Miller—Fred Ward
June Miller—Uma Thurman
Director—Philip Kaufman
Leading Players—Maria de Medeiros, Richard E. Grant, Kevin Spacey, Jean-Philippe Ecoffey, Bruce Myers

HENRY VIII AND HIS SIX WIVES (1972, GB, EMI/MGM)
Henry VIII—Keith Michell
Anne Boleyn—Charlotte Rampling
Jane Seymour—Jane Asher
Katharine Of Aragon—Frances Cuka
Catherine Howard—Lynne Frederick
Anne Of Cleves—Jenny Bos
Catherine Parr—Barbara Leigh-Hunt
Director—Waris Hussein
Leading PLayers—Donald Pleasence, Michael Gough, Brian Blessed, Michael Goodliffe

HENRY V (1946, GB, Two Cities/UA)
Henry V—Laurence Olivier
Directors—Laurence Olivier and Reginald Beck
Leading Players—Robert Newton, Leslie Banks, Renee Asherson, Esmond Knight, Leo Genn, Felix Aylmer

HENRY V (1989, GB, Goldwyn)
Henry V—Kenneth Branagh
Director—Kenneth Branagh
Leading Players—Derek Jacobi, Simon Shepherd, Brian Blessed, Ian Holm, Robert Stephens, Paul Scofield

HENRY GOES ARIZONA (1939, MGM)
Henry Conroy—Frank Morgan
Director—Edwin L. Marin
Leading Players—Virginia Weidler, Guy Kibbee, Slim Summerville

HENRY: PORTRAIT OF A SERIAL KILLER (1989, Maljack)
Henry—Michael Rooker
Director—John McNaughton
Leading Players—Tom Towles, Tracy Arnold

HENRY STEPS OUT (1940, GB, American International)
Henry Smith—George Turner
Director—Widgey R. Newman
Leading Players—Margaret Yarde, Wally Patch

HENRY THE RAINMAKER (1949, Monogram)
Henry Latham—Raymond Walburn
Director—Jean Yarborough

Leading Players—Walter Catlett, William Tracy, Mary Stuart

HER ACCIDENTAL HUSBAND (1923, Silent, Belasco Productions)
Rena Goring—Miriam Cooper
Gordon Gray—Forrest Stanley
Director—Dallas M. Fitzgerald
Leading Players—Mitchell Lewis, Richard Tucker, Kate Lester

HER ALIBI (1989, Warner Brothers)
Phil Blackwood—Tom Selleck
Nina Ionescu—Paulina Porizkova
Director—Bruce Beresford
Leading Players—William Daniels, James Farentino, Hurd Hatfield, Ronald Guttman

HER BIG ADVENTURE (1926, Silent, Kerman Films)
Betty Burton—Grace Diamond
Director—John Ince
Leading Players—Herbert Rawlinson, Vola Vale, Carlton Griffin

HER BIG NIGHT (1926, Silent, Universal)
Frances Norcross/Daphne Dix—Laura La Plante
Director—Melville W. Brown
Leading Players—Einar Hansen, Zasu Pitts, Tully Marshall

HER BODYGUARD (1933, Paramount)
Casey McCarthy—Edmund Lowe
Margot Brienne—Wynne Gibson
Director—William Beaudine
Leading Players—Edward Arnold, Johnny Hines, Marjorie White

HER CARDBOARD LOVER (1942, MGM)
Consuelo Croyden—Norma Shearer
Terry Trindale—Robert Taylor
Director—George Cukor
Leading Players—George Sanders, Frank McHugh, Elizabeth Patterson

HER FACE VALUE (1921, Silent, Paramount)
Peggy Malone—Wanda Hawley
Director—Thomas N. Heffron
Leading Players—Lincoln Plummer, Dick Rosson, T. Roy Barnes

HER FATAL MILLIONS (1923, Silent, Metro)
Mary Bishop—Viola Dana
Director—William Beaudine
Leading Players—Huntly Gordon, Allan Forrest, Peggy Browne

HER FATHER SAID NO (1927, Silent, R-C Pictures)
Charlotte Hamilton—Mary Brian
John Hamilton—John Steppling
Director—Jack McKeown
Leading Players—Danny O'Shea, Al Cooke, Kit Guard

HER FIGHTING CHANCE (1917, Silent, Jacobs/Hall)
Marie—Jane Grey
Director—Edwin Carewe
Leading Players—Thomas Holding, Percy G. Standing, Edward Porter

HER FIRST AFFAIRE (1932, GB, Sterling)
Anne—Ida Lupino
Director—Allan Dwan

Leading Players—George Cuzon, Diana Napier, Harry Tate

HER FIRST BEAU (1941, Columbia)
Chuck Harris—Jackie Cooper
Penny Wood—Jane Withers
Director—Theodore Reed
Leading Players—Edith Fellows, Josephine Hutchinson, William Tracy

HER FIRST MATE (1933, Universal)
John Horner—Slim Summerville
Mary Horner—Zasu Pitts
Director—William Wyler
Leading Players—Una Merkel, Warren Hymer, Berton Churchill

HER FIRST ROMANCE (1951, Columbia)
Betty Foster—Margaret O'Brien
Director—Seymour Friedman
Leading Players—Allen Martin, Jr., Jimmy Hunt, Sharyn Moffett

HER FIVE-FOOT HIGHNESS (1920, Silent, Universal)
Eileen—Edith Roberts
Director—Harry L. Franklin
Leading Players—Virginia Ware, Ogden Crane, Harold Miller

HER GILDED CAGE (1922, Silent, Paramount)
Suzanne Ornoff—Gloria Swanson
Director—Sam Wood
Leading Players—David Powell, Harrison Ford, Anne Cornwall

HER GREAT CHANCE (1918, Silent, Selznick)
Lola Gray—Alice Brady
Director—Charles Maigne
Leading Players—David Powell, Nellie Parker Spaulding, Gloria Goodwin

HER HERITAGE (1919, Silent, GB, Ward's)
Lady Mary Strode—Phyllis Monkman
Director—Bannister Merwin
Leading Players—Jack Buchanan, E. Holman Clark, Edward O'Neill

HER HIGHNESS AND THE BELLBOY (1945, MGM)
Princess Veronica—Hedy Lamarr
Jimmy Dobson—Robert Walker
Director—Richard Thorpe
Leading Players—June Allyson, Carl Esmond, Agnes Moorehead

HER HONOR THE GOVERNOR (1926, Silent, R-C Pictures)
Adele Fenway—Pauline Frederick
Director—Chet Withey
Leading Players—Carroll Nye, Greta von Rue, Tom Santschi

HER HUSBAND'S AFFAIRS (1947, Columbia)
Margaret Weldon—Lucille Ball
William Weldon—Franchot Tone
Director—S. Sylvan Simon
Leading Players—Edward Everett Horton, Mikhail Rasumny, Gene Lockhart

HER HUSBAND'S SECRET (1925, Silent, First National)
Judy Brewster—Patsy Ruth Miller
Elliott Owen—Antonio Moreno
Director—Frank Lloyd
Leading Players—Ruth Clifford, David Torrence, Walter McGrail

HER HUSBAND'S SECRETARY (1937, First National/Warner Brothers)
Carol—Jean Muir
Diane—Beverly Roberts
Bart—Warren Hull
Director—Frank McDonald
Leading Players—Joseph Crehan, Clara Blandick, Addison Richards

HER HUSBAND'S TRADEMARK (1922, Silent, Paramount)
Lois Miller—Gloria Swanson
James Berkeley—Stuart Holmes
Director—Sam Wood
Leading Players—Richard Wayne, Lucien Littlefield, Charles Ogle

HER IMAGINARY LOVER (1933, GB, First National/Warner Brothers)
Celia—Laura La Plante
Lord Michael Ware—Percy Marmont
Director—George King
Leading Players—Lady Tree, Bernard Nedell, Olive Blakeney

HER JUNGLE LOVE (1938, Paramount)
Tura—Dorothy Lamour
Bob Mitchell—Ray Milland
Director—George Archainbaud
Leading Players—Lynne Overman, J. Carroll Naish, Dorothy Howe

HER KIND OF MAN (1946, Warner Brothers)
Georgia King—Janis Paige
Don Corwin—Dane Clark
Director—Frederick de Cordova
Leading Players—Zachary Scott, Faye Emerson, George Tobias

HER LAST AFFAIRE (1935, GB, Producers Distributors)
Lady Avril Weyre—Viola Keats
Director—Michael Powell
Leading Players—Hugh Williams, Francis L. Sullivan, Sophie Stewart, Cecil Parker

HER LORD AND MASTER (1921, Silent, Vitagraph)
Indiana Stillwater—Alice Joyce
Viscount Canning—Holmes Herbert
Director—Edward Jose
Leading Players—Frank Sheridan, Walter McEwen, Marie Shotwell

HER LOVE STORY (1924, Silent, Paramount)
Princess Marie—Gloria Swanson
Director—Allan Dwan
Leading Players—Ian Keith, George Fawcett, Echlin Gayer

HER LUCKY NIGHT (1945, Universal)
Connie—Martha O'Driscoll
Director—Edward Lilley
Leading Players—The Andrews Sisters, Noah Beery, Jr., George Barbier

HER MAD BARGAIN (1921, Silent, Associated First National)
Alice Lambert—Anita Stewart
Director—Edwin Carewe
Leading Players—Arthur Edmund Carew, Helen Raymond, Adele Farrington

HER MAJESTY (1922, Silent, Playgoers Pictures)
Rosalie Bowers—Mollie King
Director—George Irving
Leading Players—Creighton Hale, Rose Tapley, Neville Percy

HER MAN (1930, Pathe)
Frankie—Helen Twelvetrees
Johnnie—Ricardo Cortez
Director—Tay Garnett
Leading Players—Marjorie Rambeau, Phillips Holmes, James Gleason, Franklin Pangborn

HER MAN GIBLEY (1949, GB, Two Cities/Universal)
Tom Gibley—Michael Wilding
Joan Heseltine—Penelope Ward
Director—Harold French
Leading Players—Lilli Palmer, Claude Dauphin, Roland Culver

HER MAN O' WAR (1926, Silent, De Mille Pictures)
Cherie Schultz—Jetta Goudal
Jim Sanderson—William Boyd
Director—Frank Urson
Leading Players—Jimmie Adams, Grace Darmond, Kay Deslys

HER MARKET VALUE (1925, Silent, Powell Productions)
Nancy Dumont—Agnes Ayres
Director—Paul Powell
Leading Players—George Irving, Anders Randolf, Hedda Hopper

HER MARRIAGE VOW (1924, Silent, Warner Brothers)
Carol Hilton—Beverly Bayne
Director—Millard Webb
Leading Players—Monte Blue, Willard Louis, Margaret Livingston

HER NIGHT OF NIGHTS (1922, Silent, Universal Film)
Molly May Mahone—Marie Prevost
Director—Hobart Henley
Leading Players—Edward Hearn, Hal Cooley, Betty Francisco

HER NIGHT OF ROMANCE (1924, Silent, First National)
Dorothy Adams—Constance Talmadge
Director—Sidney A. Franklin
Leading Players—Ronald Colman, Jean Hersholt, Albert Gran

HER NIGHT OUT (1932, GB, First National/Warner Brothers)
Kitty Vickery—Dorothy Bartlam
Director—William McGann
Leading Players—Lester Matthews, Joan Marin, Jack Raine

HER OWN FREE WILL (1924, Silent, Eastern Productions)
Nan Everard—Helene Chadwick
Director—Paul Scardon
Leading Players—Holmes Herbert, Allan Simpson, George Backus

HER OWN MONEY (1922, Silent, Paramount)
Mildred Carr—Ethel Clayton
Director—Joseph Henabery
Leading Players—Warner Baxter, Charles French, Clarence Burton

HER PRIMITIVE MAN (1944, Universal)
Sheila Winthrop—Louise Albritton
Pete Matthews—Robert Paige
Director—Charles Lamont

Leading Players—Robert Benchley, Edward Everett Horton, Helen Broderick

HER PRIVATE AFFAIR (1930, Pathe)
Vera Kessler—Ann Harding
Director—Paul Stein
Leading Players—Harry Bannister, John Loder, Kay Hammond

HER PRIVATE LIFE (1929, First National/Warner Brothers)
Lady Helen Haden—Billie Dove
Director—Alexander Korda
Leading Players—Walter Pidgeon, Holmes Herbert, Montagu Love, Thelma Todd

HER REPUTATION (1923, Silent, Associated First National)
Jacqueline Lanier—May McAvoy
Director—John Griffith Wray
Leading Players—Lloyd Hughes, James Corrigan, Casson Ferguson

HER REPUTATION (1931, GB, London Screenplays)
Sultitia Sloane—Iris Hoey
Director—Sidney Morgan
Leading Players—Frank Cellier, Malcolm Tearle, Lilian Hall-Davis, Maurice Braddell

HER SACRIFICE (1926, Silent, Sanford Productions)
Margarita Darlow—Ligia Golconda
Director—Wilfrid Lucas
Leading Players—Gaston Glass, Bryant Washburn, Herbert Rawlinson

HER SISTER FROM PARIS (1925, Silent, First National)
Helen Weyringer/Lola—Constance Talmadge
Director—Sidney Franklin
Leading Players—Ronald Colman, George K. Arthur, Margaret Mann

HER SISTER'S SECRET (1946, Producers Releasing Corp.)
Toni—Nancy Coleman
Renee—Margaret Lindsay
Director—Edgar G. Ulmer
Leading Players—Phillip Reed, Felix Bressart, Regis Toomey

HER SOCIAL VALUE (1921, Silent, Associated First National)
Marion Hoyte—Katharine MacDonald
Director—Jerome Storm
Leading Players—Roy Stewart, Bertram Grassby, Betty Ross Clarke

HER STRANGE DESIRE (1931, GB, British International)
Lady Diana Bromford—Nora Swinburne
Director—Maurice Elvey
Leading Players—Laurence Olivier, Norman McKinnel, Guy Newall, Donald Calthrop

HER SUMMER HERO (1928, Silent, FBO Pictures)
Kenneth Holmes—Hugh Trevor
Joan Stanton—Duane Thompson
Director—James Dugan
Leading Players—Harold Goodwin, James Pierce, Sally Blane

HER TEMPORARY HUSBAND (1923, Silent, Associated First National)
Thomas Burton—Owen Moore
Blanche Ingram—Sylvia Breamer

Director—John McDermott
Leading Players—Sydney Chaplin, Tully Marshall

HER TWELVE MEN (1954, MGM)
Jan Stewart—Greer Garson
Note—Actually teacher Garson has to oversee a class of 13 unruly boys. It doesn't seem fair to pick out one or two of these to be featured as none of their roles is very large.
Director—Robert Z. Leonard
Leading Players—Robert Ryan, Barry Sullivan, Richard Haydn

HER UNBORN CHILD (1930, Windsor Pictures Plays)
Dorothy Kennedy—Adele Ronson
Director—Albert Ray
Leading Players—Elisha Cook, Jr., Frances Underwood, Pauline Drake

HER WEDDING NIGHT (1930, Paramount)
Norma Martin—Clara Bow
Director—Frank Tuttle
Leading Players—Ralph Forbes, Charlie Ruggles, Skeets Gallagher

HER WILD OAT (1927, Silent, First National)
Mary Brown—Colleen Moore
Director—Marshall Neilan
Leading Players—Larry Kent, Hallam Cooke, Gwen Lee

HER WINNING WAY (1921, Silent, Paramount)
Ann Annington—Mary Miles Minter
Director—Joseph Henabery
Leading Players—Gaston Glass, Carrie Clark Ward, Fred Goodwins

HERCULES (1983, CANNON)
Hercules—Lou Ferrigno
Director—Lewis Coates
Leading Players—Mirella D'Angelo, Sybil Danning, Ingrid Anderson, William Berger

HERCULES IN NEW YORK (1970, RAF/UA)
Hercules—Arnold Strong (Arnold Schwarzenegger)
Director—Arthur A. Seideleman
Leading Players—Arnold Stang, Deborah Loomis, James Karen

HERCULES II (1985, Cannon)
Hercules—Lou Ferrigno
Director—Lewis Coates
Leading Players—Milly Carlucci, Sonia Viviani, William Berger, Carlotta Green

HERE COME THE HUGGETTS (1948, GB, Gainsborough)
Joe Huggett—Jack Warner
Ethel Huggett—Kathleen Harrison
Director—Ken Annakin
Leading Players—Jane Hylton, Susan Shaw, Petulia Clark

HERE COME THE NELSONS (1952, Universal)
Ozzie—Ozzie Nelson
Harriet—Harriet Nelson
Ricky—Ricky Nelson
David—David Nelson
Director—Frederick de Cordova
Leading Players—Rock Hudson, Barbara Lawrence, Sheldon Leonard, Jim Backus

HERE COMES CARTER (1936, First National/Warner Brothers)
Kent Carter—Ross Alexander
Director—William Clemens
Leading Players—Glenda Farrell, Anne Nagel, Craig Reynolds

HERE COMES ELMER (1943, Republic)
Elmer Blurt/Al Pearce—Al Pearce
Director—Joseph Stanley
Leading Players—Dale Evans, Frank Albertson, Gloria Stuart

HERE COMES KELLY (1943, Monogram)
Jimmy Kelly—Eddie Quillan
Director—William Beaudine
Leading Players—Joan Woodbury, Maxie Rosenbloom, Armida

HERE COMES MR. JORDAN (1941, Columbia)
Mr. Jordan—Claude Rains
Director—Alexander Hall
Leading Players—Robert Montgomery, Evelyn Keyes, Rita
    Johnson, Edward Everett Horton, James Gleason

HERE COMES SANTA CLAUS (1984, New World)
Santa Claus—Armand Meffre
Director—Christian Gion
Leading Players—Emeric Chapuis, Karen Cheryl, Alexia

HERE COMES THE GROOM (1934, Paramount)
Mike Scanlon—Jack Haley
Director—Edward Sedgwick
Leading Players—Mary Boland, Patricia Ellis, Neil Hamilton

HERE COMES THE GROOM (1951, Paramount)
Pete Garvey—Bing Crosby
Director—Frank Capra
Leading Players—Jane Wyman, Alexis Smith, Franchot Tone

HERE'S FLASH CASEY (1937, Grand National)
Flash Casey—Eric Linden
Director—Lynn Shores
Leading Players—Boots Malloy, Cully Richards, Holmes Herbert

HERE'S GEORGE (1932, GB, Producers Distributors)
George Muffitt—George Clarke
Director—Redd Davis
Leading Players—Pat Paterson, Ruth Taylor, Mariott Edgar

THE HERO (1923, Silent, Preferred Pictures)
Oswald Lane—Gaston Glass
Director—Louis J. Gasnier
Leading Players—Barbara La Marr, John Sainpolis, Martha
    Mattox

HERO (1982, GB, Maya)
Dermid—Derek McGuire
Director—Barney Platts Mills
Leading Players—Caroline Kenneil, Alastair Kenneil, Stewart
    Grant, Steven Hamilton

HERO AND THE TERROR (1988, Cannon)
Herrara "Hero" O'Brien—Chuck Norris
Director—William Tannen
Leading Players—Brynn Thayer, Steve James, Jack O'Halloran

HERO AT LARGE (1980, MGM)
Steve Nichols—John Ritter
Director—Martin Davidson

Leading Players—Anne Archer, Bert Convy, Kevin McCarthy

HERO FOR A DAY (1939, Universal)
Frank Higgins—Charley Grapewin
Director—Harold Young
Leading Players—Anita Louise, Dick Foran, Berton Churchill

A HERO FOR A NIGHT (1927, Silent, Universal)
Hiram Hastings—Glenn Tryon
Director—William James Craft
Leading Players—Patsy Ruth Miller, Lloyd Whitlock, Burr
    McIntosh

A HERO ON HORSEBACK (1927, Silent, Universal)
Billy Garford—Hoot Gibson
Director—Del Andrews
Leading Players—Ethlyne Clair, Edwards Davis, Edward Hearn

HE'S A COCKEYED WONDER (1950, Columbia)
Freddie Frisby—Mickey Rooney
Director—Peter Godfrey
Leading Players—Terry Moore, William Demarest, Charles Arnt

HE'S MY GIRL (1987, Scotti Brothers)
Reggie/Regina—T.K. Carter
Director—Gabrielle Beaumont
Leading Players—David Hallyday, Misha McK, Jennifer Tilly,
    Warwick Sims

HI BEAUTIFUL (1944, Universal)
Patty Callahan—Martha O'Driscoll
Director—Leslie Goodwins
Leading Players—Noah Beery, Jr., Hattie McDaniel, Walter
    Catlett, Tim Ryan

HI GAUCHO (1936, RKO)
Lucio—John Carroll
Director—Thomas Atkins
Leading Players—Steffi Duna, Rod La Rocque, Montagu Love

HI, GOOD-LOOKIN' (1944, Universal)
Kelly Clark—Harriet Hilliard
Director—Edward C. Lilley
Leading Players—Eddie Quillan, Kirby Grant, Betty Kean

HI, NELLIE! (1934, Warner Brothers)
Sam Bradshaw (Nellie Nelson)—Paul Muni
Director—Mervyn Le Roy
Leading Players—Glenda Farrell, Douglas Dumbrille, Robert
    Barrat, Ned Sparks

HIAWATHA (1952, Monogram)
Hiawatha—Vince Edwards
Director—Kurt Neumann
Leading Players—Yvette Dugay, Keith Larsen, Gene Iglesias

HICKEY AND BOGGS (1972, UA)
Al Hickey—Bill Cosby
Frank Boggs—Robert Culp
Director—Robert Culp
Leading Players—Rosalind Cash, Sheila Sullivan, Isabel
    Sanford, Ta-Ronce Allen

THE HIDDEN WOMAN (1922, Silent, American Releasing Corp.)
Ann Wesley—Evelyn Nesbit
Director—Allan Dwan

Leading Players—Crauford Kent, Murdock MacQuarrie, Ruth Darling, Russell Thaw

HIDEAWAY GIRL (1937, Paramount)
Helen Flint—Martha Raye
Director—George Archainbaud
Leading Players—Shirley Ross, Robert Cummings, Monroe Owsley

THE HIDEOUS SUN DEMON (1959, Pacific Internationl)
Dr. Gilbert McKenna—Robert Clarke
Director—Robert Clarke
Leading Players—Patricia Manning, Nan Peterson, Patrick Whyte

THE HIGGINS FAMILY (1938, Republic)
Joe Higgins—James Gleason
Lillian Higgins—Lucile Gleason
Stanley Higgins—Russell Gleason
Director—Gus Meins
Leading Players—Lynn Roberts, Harry Davenport, William Bakewell

HIGH AND HANDSOME (1925, Silent, R-C Pictures)
Joe Hanrahan—Maurice B. "Lefty" Flynn
Director—Harry Garson
Leading Players—Ethel Shannon, Tom Kennedy, Ralph McCullough

THE HIGH COMMISSIONER (1968, US/GB, Rank/Cinerama)
Sir James Quentin—Christopher Plummer
Director—Ralph Thomas
Leading Players—Rod Taylor, Lilli Palmer, Camilla Sparv, Daliah Lavi, Franchot Tone

HIGH GEAR JEFFREY (1921, Silent, American Film)
Jeffrey Claiborne—William Russell
Director—Edward Sloman
Leading Players—Francelia Billington, Clarence Burton, Al Ferguson

HIGH PLAINS DRIFTER (1973, Universal)
The Stranger—Clint Eastwood
Director—Clint Eastwood
Leading Players—Verna Bloom, Marianna Hill, Mitchell Ryan

HIGH ROYAL HIGHNESS (1918, Silent, World)
Jack Christie—Carlyle Blackwell
Director—Carlyle Blackwell
Leading Players—Evelyn Greeley, Kate Lester, Bert Honey

HIGH SCHOOL BIG SHOT (1959, Filmgroup-Sparta)
Marv—Tom Pittman
Director—Joel Rapp
Leading Players—Virginia Aldridge, Howard Viet, Malcolm Atterbury

HIGH SCHOOL CAESAR (1960, Marathon/Filmgroup)
Mat Stevens—John Ashley
Director—O'Dale Ireland
Leading Players—Gary Vinson, Lowell Brown, Steve Stevens

HIGH SCHOOL HERO (1927, Silent, Fox Film Corp.)
Pete Greer—Nick Stuart
Director—David Butler
Leading Players—Sally Phipps, William N. Bailey, John Darrow

HIGH SCHOOL HERO (1946, Monogram)
Freddie—Freddie Stewart
Director—Arthur Dreifuss
Leading Players—June Preisser, Noel Neill, Ann Rooney

HIGH SPIRITS (1988, Tri-Star)
Mary Plunkett—Darryl Hannah
Martin Brogan—Liam Neeson
Director—Neil Jordan
Leading Players—Peter O'Toole, Steve Guttenberg, Beverly D'Angelo, Peter Gallagher

HIGH YELLOW (1965, Dinero/Thunder)
Cindy—Cynthia Hall
Director—Larry Buchanan
Leading Players—Warren Hammack, Kay Taylor, Bill McGee

HIGHLANDER (1986, 20th Century Fox)
Connor MacLeod—Christopher Lambert
Director—Russell Mulcahy
Leading Players—Roxanne Hart, Clancy Brown, Sean Connery

THE HIGHWAYMAN (1951, Allied Artists/Monogram)
Jeremy—Philip Friend
Director—Lesley Selander
Leading Players—Charles Coburn, Wanda Hendrix, Cecil Kellaway, Victor Jory

HILDA CRANE (1956, 20th Century Fox)
Hilda Crane—Jean Simmons
Director—Phillip Dunne
Leading Players—Guy Madison, Jean Pierre Aumont, Judith Evelyn

HILDUR AND THE MAGICIAN (1969, Canyon Cinema Cooperative)
The Magician—John Graham
Hildur—Hildur Mahl
Director—Larry Jordan
Leading Players—Patricia Jordan, Jim Yensman, Jani Novak

THE HILL BILLY (1924, Silent, Allied Producers)
Jed McCoy—Jack Pickford
Director—George Hill
Leading Players—Lucille Rickson, Frank Leigh, Ralph Yearsley

THE HINDU (1953, GB, UA)
Gunga Ram—Nino Marcel
Director—Frank Ferrin
Leading Players—Boris Karloff, Lou Krugman, Reginald Denny

HINTON'S DOUBLE (1917, Silent, Thanhouser)
Joshua Stephens—Frederick Warde
John Evart Hinton—Frederick Warde
Director—Ernest Warde
Leading Players—Kathlyn Adams, Eldean Steuart, Wayne Arey

THE HIRED GUN (1957, MGM)
Gil McCord—Rory Calhoun
Director—Ray Nazarro
Leading Players—Anne Francis, Vince Edwards, John Litel

THE HIRED HAND (1918, Silent, Paramount)
Ezry Hollins—Charles Ray
Director—Charles Ray

Leading Players—Charles K. French, Gilbert Gordon, Lydia Knott

THE HIRED HAND (1971, Universal)
Harry Collings—Peter Fonda
Director—Peter Fonda
Leading Players—Warren Oates, Verna Bloom, Robert Pratt

HIRED WIFE (1934, Pinnacle)
Vivian Mathews—Greta Nissen
Director—George Melford
Leading Players—Weldon Heyburn, James Kirkwood, Molly O'Day

THE HIRELING (1973, GB, World/Columbia)
Leadbetter—Robert Shaw
Director—Alan Bridges
Leading Players—Sarah Miles, Peter Egan, Elizabeth Sellars

HIS AND HERS (1961, GB, Sabre/Eros)
Reggie Blake—Terry-Thomas
Fran Blake—Janette Scott
Director—Brian Desmond Hurst
Leading Players—Wilfrid Hyde-White, Nicole Maurey, Joan Sims

HIS BACK AGAINST THE WALL (1922, Silent, Goldwyn Pictures)
Jeremy Dice—Raymond Hatton
Director—Rowland V. Lee
Leading Players—Virginia Valli, Will Walling, Gordon Russell

HIS BROTHER'S KEEPER (1939, GB, Warner Brothers/First National)
Jack Cornell—Clifford Evans
Hicky Cornell—Peter Glenville
Director—Roy William Neill
Leading Players—Tamara Desni, Una O'Connor, Reginald Purdell

HIS BROTHER'S PLACE (1919, Silent, Metro)
Nelson Drake—Hale Hamilton
Barrington Drake—Hale Hamilton
Director—Harry L. Franklin
Leading Players—Marguerite Snow, Mary Melvor, Howard Crampton

HIS BROTHER'S WIFE (1916, Silent, World)
Howard Barton—Carlyle Blackwell
Helen Barton—Ethel Clayton
Richard Barton—Paul McAllister
Director—Harley Knoles
Leading Players—Charles Gerard, Bert Honey

HIS BROTHER'S WIFE (1936, MGM)
Chris—Robert Taylor
Rita Wilson—Barbara Stanwyck
Tom—George Eldredge
Director—W.S. Van Dyke
Leading Players—Jean Hersholt, Joseph Calleia, Samuel S. Hinds, Phyllis Clare

HIS BUDDY'S WIFE (1925, Silent, Associated Exhibitors)
Jimmy McMorrow—Glenn Hunter
Mary Mullaney—Edna Murphy
Bill Mullaney—Douglas Gilmore
Director—Tom Terriss

Leading Players—Gordon Begg, Harlan Knight, Cora Williams

HIS BUTLER'S SISTER (1943, Universal)
Ann Carter—Deanna Durbin
Martin Carter—Pat O'Brien
Charles Gerard—Franchot Tone
Director—Frank Borzage
Leading Players—Evelyn Ankers, Elsa Janssen, Akim Tamiroff, Walter Catlett, Alan Mowbray

HIS CAPTIVE WOMAN (1929, First National/Warner Brothers)
Officer McCarthy—Milton Sills
Anna Bergen—Dorothy MacKaill
Director—George Fitzmaurice
Leading Players—Gladden James, Gertrude Howard, Marion Bryon

HIS DARKER SELF (1924, Silent, G. and H. Pictures)
Claude Sappington—Lloyd Hamilton
Director—John W. Noble
Leading Players—Tom Wilson, Tom O'Malley, Lucille La Verne

HIS DIVORCED WIFE (1919, Silent, Universal)
Ash Whipple—Monroe Salisbury
Nancy Haws—Alice Elliot
Director—Douglas Gerrard
Leading Players—Charles West, Alfred Allen, Raymond Gallagher

HIS DOUBLE LIFE (1933, Paramount)
Priam Farrel—Roland Young
Director—Arthur Hopkins
Leading Players—Lillian Gish, Lumsden Hare, Lucy Beaumont

HIS EXCELLENCY (1952, Great Britain, Ealing)
George Harrison—Eric Portman
Director—Robert Hamer
Leading Players—Cecil Parker, Helen Cherry, Susan Stephen

HIS EXCITING NIGHT (1938, Universal)
Tripp—Charles Ruggles
Director—Gus Meins
Leading Players—Richard Lane, Stepin Fetchit, Maxie Rosenbloom, Marian Martin, Ona Munson

HIS FAMILY TREE (1936, RKO)
Charles Murfree—William Harrigan
Director—Charles Vidor
Leading Players—James Barton, Margaret Callahan, Addison Randall

HIS FATHER'S SON (1917, Silent, Metro)
J. Dabney Barron—Lionel Barrymore
Adam Barron—Charles Eldridge
Director—George D. Baker
Leading Players—Irene Howley, Frank Currier, Charles A. Wright

HIS FIRST COMMAND (1929, Pathe)
Terry Culver—William Boyd
Director—Gregory La Cava
Leading Players—Dorothy Sebastian, Gavin Gordon, Helen Parrish

HIS FIRST FLAME (1927, Silent, Sennett/Pathe Exchange)
Harry Howells—Harry Langdon

Ethel Morgan—Natalie Kingston
Director—Harry Edwards
Leading Players—Ruth Hiatt, Vernon Dent, Bud Jamieson

HIS FOREIGN WIFE (1927, Silent, Pathe Exchange)
Hilda Schultzenbach—Greta von Rue
Johnny Haines—Wallace MacDonald
Director—John P. McCarthy
Leading Players—Edna Murphy, Charles Clary, Elsie Bishop

HIS FORGOTTEN WIFE (1924, Silent, Film Booking Offices)
Suzanne Rolfe—Madge Bellamy
Donald Allen-John Rolfe—Warner Baxter
Director—William Seiter
Leading Players—Maude Wayne, Hazel Keener, Tom Guise

HIS GIRL FRIDAY (1940, Columbia)
Walter Burns—Cary Grant
Hildy Johnson—Rosalind Russell
Director—Howard Hawks
Leading Players—Ralph Bellamy, Gene Lockhart, Helen Mack, Porter Hall, Ernest Truex

HIS GLORIOUS NIGHT (1929, MGM)
Captain Kovacs—John Gilbert
Director—Lionel Barrymore
Leading Players—Catherine Dale Owen, Nancy O'Neill, Gustav von Seyffertitz, Hedda Hopper

HIS GRACE GIVES NOTICE (1933, GB, Real Art/RKO)
George Barwick—Arthur Margetson
Director—George A. Cooper
Leading Players—Viola Keats, S. Victor Stanley, Barrie Livesey

HIS GREAT TRIUMPH (1916, Silent, Metro)
"Buttsy" Gallagher—William Nigh
Director—William Nigh
Leading Players—Julius D. Cowles, Roy Applegate, R.A. Bresee

HIS GREATEST SACRIFICE (1921, Silent, Fox Film Corp.)
Richard Hall—William Farnum
Director—J. Gordon Edwards
Leading Players—Alice Fleming, Lorena Volare, Evelyn Greeley

HIS HOUR (1924, Silent, Metro-Goldwyn)
Prince Gritzko—John Gilbert
Director—King Vidor
Leading Players—Aileen Pringle, Emily Fitzroy, Lawrence Grant, Dale Fuller

HIS HOUSE IN ORDER (1928, GB, Silent, Ideal)
Hilary Jesson—Ian Hunter
Director—Randle Ayrton
Leading Players—Tallulah Bankhead, David Hawthorne, Eric Maturin

HIS JAZZ BRIDE (1926, Silent, Warner Brothers)
Gloria Gregory—Marie Prevost
Dick Gregory—Matt Moore
Director—Herman C. Raymaker
Leading Players—Gayne Whitman, John Patrick, Mabel Julienne Scott

HIS KIND OF WOMAN (1951, RKO)
Dan Milner—Robert Mitchum
Lenore Brent—Jane Russell

Director—John Farrow
Leading Players—Vincent Price, Tim Holt, Charles McGraw

HIS LAST DOLLAR (1914, Silent, Paramount)
Joe Braxton—David Higgins
Director—David Higgins
Leading Players—Betty Gray, Hal Clarendon, E.L. Davenport

HIS LAST HAUL (1928, Silent, FBO Pictures)
Joe Hammond—Tom Moore
Director—Marshall Neilan
Leading Players—Seena Owen, Charles Mason, Al Roscoe

HIS LAST RACE (1923, Silent, Goldstone Productions)
Dick Carleton—Rex (Snowy) Baker
Director—Reeves Eason
Leading Players—Gladys Brockwell, William Scott, Harry Dapp

HIS LORDSHIP (1932, Great Britain, Westminister/UA)
Bert Gibbs—Jerry Verno
Director—Michael Powell
Leading Players—Janet Megrew, Ben Welden, Polly Ward

HIS LORDSHIP GOES TO PRESS (1939, Great Britain, Canterbury/RKO)
Lord Bill Wilmer—Hugh Williams
Director—Maclean Rogers
Leading Players—June Clyde, Romeny Brent, Louise Hampton

HIS LORDSHIP REGRETS (1938, GB, Canterbury/RKO)
Lord Cavender—Claude Hulbert
Director—Maclean Rogers
Leading Players—Winifred Shotter, Gina Malo, Aubrey Mallalieu

HIS LUCKY DAY (1929, Part-talkie, Universal)
Charles Blaydon—Reginald Denny
Director—Edward Cline
Leading Players—LaRayne Du Val, Otis Harlan, Eddie Phillips

HIS MAJESTY AND CO. (1935, GB, Fox Film Corp.)
King of Poldavia—Morton Selten
Director—Anthony Kimmins
Leading Players—John Garrick, Barbara Waring, Wally Patch, Mary Grey

HIS MAJESTY, BUNKER BEAN (1918, Silent, Paramount)
Bunker Bean—Jack Pickford
Director—William Desmond Taylor
Leading Players—Louise Huff, Jack McDonald, Frances Clanton

HIS MAJESTY, BUNKER BEAN (1925, Silent, Warner Brothers)
Bunker Bean—Matt Moore
Director—Harry Beaumont
Leading Players—Dorothy Devore, David Butler, George Nichols

HIS MAJESTY O'KEEFE (1953, Warner Brothers)
Capt. David O'Keefe—Burt Lancaster
Director—Bryon Haskin
Leading Players—Joan Rice, Andre Morell, Abraham Sofaer

HIS MAJESTY, THE AMERICAN (1919, Silent, UA)
William Brooks—Douglas Fairbanks
Director—Joseph Henaberry
Leading Players—Marjorie Daw, Frank Campeau, Sam Sothern

HIS MOTHER'S BOY (1918, Silent, Ince)
Matthew Denton—Charles Ray

Mrs. Denton—Gertrude Claire
Director—Victor L. Schertzinger
Leading Players—Doris Lee, William Elmer, Joseph Swickard

HIS MYSTERY GIRL (1923, Silent, Universal)
Kerry Reynolds—Herbert Rawlinson
Gloria Bliss—Ruth Dwyer
Director—Robert F. Hill
Leading Players—Margaret Campbell, Jere Austin

HIS NIBS (1921, Silent, Exceptional Pictures)
Theodore Bender—Charles (Chic) Sale
Director—Gregory La Cava
Leading Players—Colleen Moore, Joseph Dowling, J.P. Lockney

HIS NIGHT OUT (1935, Universal)
Homer—Edward Everett Horton
Director—William Nigh
Leading Players—Irene Hervey, Robert McWade, Jack LaRue

HIS OFFICIAL FIANCEE (1919, Silent, Paramount)
Monica Trant—Vivian Martin
William Waters—Forrest Stanley
Director—Robert G. Vignola
Leading Players—Mollie McConnell, Vera Sisson, Hugh Huntley

HIS OWN HOME TOWN (1918, Silent, Ince)
Jimmy Duncan—Charles Ray
Director—Victor L. Schertzinger
Leading Players—Katherine MacDonald, Charles French, Otto Hoffman

HIS PARISIAN WIFE (1919, Silent, Artcraft)
Fauvette—Elsie Ferguson
Martin Wesley—David Powell
Director—Emile Chautard
Leading Players—Courtney Foote, Frank Losee, Cora Williams

HIS PRIVATE LIFE (1928, Silent, Paramount)
Georges St. Germain—Adolphe Menjou
Director—Frank Tuttle
Leading Players—Kathryn Carver, Margaret Livingston, Eugene Pallette

HIS PRIVATE SECRETARY (1933, Screencraft)
Dick Wallace—John Wayne
Marion Hall—Evalyn Knapp
Director—Philip H. Whitman
Leading Players—Alec B. Francis, Reginald Barlow, Natalie Kingston

HIS RISE TO FAME (1927, Silent, Excellent Pictures)
Jerry Drake—George Walsh
Director—Bernard McEveety
Leading Players—Peggy Shaw, Bradley Parker, Mildred Reardon

HIS ROBE OF HONOR (1918, Silent, Paralta Pictures)
Julian Randolph—Henry B. Walthall
Director—Rex Ingram
Leading Players—Mary Charleston, Lois Wilson, Noah Beery

HIS SECRETARY (1925, Silent, MGM)
Ruth Lawrence—Norma Shearer
David Colman—Lew Cody
Director—Hobart Henley
Leading Players—Willard Louis, Karl Dane, Gwen Lee

HIS SUPREME MOMENT (1925, Silent, First National)
John Douglas—Ronald Colman
Director—George Fitzmaurice
Leading Players—Blanche Sweet, Kathleen Myers, Belle Bennett, Cyril Chadwick

HIS TIGER LADY (1928, Silent, Paramount)
Henri—Adolphe Menjou
The Tiger Lady—Evelyn Brent
Director—Hobart Henley
Leading Players—Rose Dione, Emil Chautard, Maria Carillo

HIS WIFE'S GOOD NAME (1916, Silent, Vitagraph)
Mary Ellen Weatherby—Lucille Lee Stewart
Harry Weatherby—Huntley Gordon
Director—Ralph Ince
Leading Players—Jessie Miller, Frank Currier, John Robertson

HIS WIFE'S HUSBAND (1922, Silent, Pyramid Pictures)
Olympia Brewster—Betty Blythe
George Packard—Huntley Gordon
John Brainerd—Arthur Carewe
Director—Kenneth Webb
Leading Players—George Fawcett, Grace Goodall, Blanche Davenport

HIS WIFE'S MONEY (1920, Silent, Select)
Laura Uppington—Louise Prussing
Edward Uppington—Ned Hay
Director—Ralph Ince
Leading Players—Dorothy Kent, Cyril Chadwick, Zeena Keefe

HIS WIFE'S MOTHER (1932, GB, British International)
Henry—Jerry Verno
Cynthia—Molly Lamont
Mrs. Trout—Marion Dawson
Director—Harry Hughes
Leading Players—Gus Naughton, Jack Hobbs, Jimmy Godden

HIS WOMAN (1931, Paramount)
Capt. Sam Whalan—Gary Cooper
Sally Clark—Claudette Colbert
Director—Edward Sloman
Leading Players—Averill Harris, Richard Spiro, Douglas Dumbrille

THE HISTORY OF MR. POLLY (1949, GB, Rank)
Alfred Polly—John Mills
Director—Anthony Pelissier
Leading Players—Sally Ann Howes, Megs Jenkins, Finlay Currie, Diana Churchill

HIT MAN (1972, MGM)
Tyrone Tackett—Bernie Casey
Director—George Armitage
Leading Players—Pamela Grier, Lisa Moore, Bhetty Waldron, Sam Lewis

THE HITMAN (1991, Cannon)
Garret/Grogan—Chuck Norris
Director—Aaron Norris
Leading Players—Michael Parks, Al Waxman, Alberts Watson, Salim Grant, Ken Pogue, Marcel Sabourin

HITCH HIKE LADY (1936, Republic)
Mrs. Amelia Blake—Alison Skipworth

Director—Aubrey Scotto
Leading Players—Mae Clark, Arthur Treacher, Jimmy Ellison

THE HITCH-HIKER (1953, RKO)
Emmett Myers—William Talman
Director—Ida Lupino
Leading Players—Edmond O'Brien, Frank Lovejoy, Jose Torvay

THE HITCHER (1986, Tri-Star)
John Ryder—Rutger Hauer
Director—Robert Harmon
Leading Players—C. Thomas Howell, Jennifer Jason Leigh, Jeffrey DeMunn

HITLER (1962, Allied Artists)
Adolf Hitler—Richard Basehart
Director—Stuart Heisler
Leading Players—Cordula Trantow, Maria Emo, Martin Kosleck, John Banner, Martin Brandt

HITLER—DEAD OR ALIVE (1942, Charles House)
Adolf Hitler—Bobs Watson
Director—Nick Grinde
Leading Players—Ward Bond, Dorothy Tree, Warren Hymer

THE HITLER GANG (1944, Paramount)
Adolf Hitler—Bobs Watson
Director—John Farrow
Leading Players—Roman Bohnen, Martin Kosleck, Victor Varconi, Luis Van Rooten, Alexander Pope

HITLER: THE LAST TEN DAYS (1973, GB, Paramount)
Adolf Hitler—Alec Guinness
Director—Ennio De Concini
Leading Players—Simon Ward, Adolph Celi, Diane Cilento, Doris Kunstmann

HITLER'S MADMAN (1943, MGM)
Reinhard Heydrich—John Carradine
Director—Douglas Sirk
Leading Players—Patricia Morison, Alan Curtis, Ralph Morgan

HOBBS IN A HURRY (1918, Silent, Pathe)
J. Warren Hobbs, Jr.—William Russell
Director—Henry King
Leading Players—Henry Barrows, Winifred Westover, Hayward Mack

HOBSON'S CHOICE (1931, GB, British International)
Hobson—James Hartcourt
Director—Thomas Bentley
Leading Players—Viola Lyel, Frank Pettingell, Belle Chrystal

HOBSON'S CHOICE (1954, GB, British Lion)
Henry Horatio Hobson—Charles Laughton
Director—David Lean
Leading Players—John Mills, Brenda de Banzie, Daphne Anderson, Prunella Scales

HOFFMAN (1970, GB, Associated British Films)
Benjamin Hoffman—Peter Sellers
Director—Alvin Rakoff
Leading Players—Sinead Cusack, Jeremy Bulloch, Ruth Dunning

THE HOLCROFT COVENANT (1985, Universal)
Noel Holcroft—Michael Caine
Director—John Frankenheimer
Leading Players—Anthony Andrews, Victoria Tennant, Lilli Palmer, Mario Adorf

HOLD THAT BLONDE (1945, Paramount)
Sally Martin—Veronica Lake
Director—George Marshall
Leading Players—Eddie Bracken, Albert Dekker, Frank Fenton, George Zucco

HOLD THAT CO-ED (1938, 20th Century Fox)
Lizzie—Joan Davis
Director—George Marshall
Leading Players—John Barrymore, George Murphy, Marjorie Weaver, Jack Haley

HOLD THAT GIRL (1934, Fox Film Corp.)
Tony Bellamy—Claire Trevor
Director—Hamilton McFadden
Leading Players—James Dunn, Alan Edwards, Gertrude Michael

HOLD THAT HYPNOTIST (1957, Allied Artists)
Dr. Noble—Robert Foulk
Director—Austen Jewell
Leading Players—Huntz Hall, Stanley Clements, Jane Nigh

HOLD THAT WOMAN (1940, Producers Releasing Corp.)
Mary Mulvaney—Frances Gifford
Director—Sherman Scott
Leading Players—James Dunn, George Douglas, Martin Spellman

HOLD YOUR MAN (1933, MGM)
E. "Eddy" Huntington Hall—Clark Gable
Director—Sam Wood
Leading Players—Jean Harlow, Stuart Erwin, Dorothy Burgess

HOLLYWOOD COWBOY (1937, RKO)
Jeffrey Carson—George O'Brien
Director—Ewing Scott
Leading Players—Cecilia Parker, Maude Eburne, Joe Caits

HOLLYWOOD HOT TUBS 2: EDUCATING CRYSTAL (1990, Alimar)
Crystal—Jewel Shepard
Director—Ken Raich
Leading Players—Patrick Day, David Tiefen, Remy O'Neill, Rob Garrison, Bart Braverman

THE HOLLYWOOD REPORTER (1926, Silent, Hercules Film)
Billy Hudson—Frank Merrill
Director—Bruce Mitchell
Leading Players—Charles K. French, Peggy Montgomery, William Hayes, Jack Richardson

A HOLY TERROR (1931, Fox Film Corp.)
Tony Hard—George O'Brien
Director—Irving Cummings
Leading Players—Sally Eilers, Rita La Roy, Humphrey Bogart, James Kirkwood

THE HOLY TERROR (1937, 20th Century Fox)
Corky Wallace—Jane Withers
Director—James Tinling

Leading Players—Anthony Martin, Leah Ray, Joan Davis, El Brendel, Joe E. Lewis

HOMBRE (1967, 20th Century Fox)
John Russell—Paul Newman
Director—Martin Ritt
Leading Players—Fredric March, Richard Boone, Diane Cilento, Cameron Mitchell, Barbara Rush

HOME ALONE (1990, 20th Century Fox)
Kevin—Macaulay Culkin
Director—Chris Columbus
Leading Players—Joe Pesci, Daniel Stern, Catherine O'Hara, John Heard, Roberts Blossom, John Candy

HOME IS THE HERO (1959, Ireland, British Lion)
Paddo O'Reilly—Walter Macken
Director—J. Fielder Cook
Leading Players—Eileen Crowe, Arthur Kennedy, Joan O'Hara

HOME IS WHERE THE HART IS (1987, Canada, Atlantic)
Slim "Paddy" Hart—Joe Austin
Director—Rex Bromfield
Leading Players—Valri Bromfield, Stephen E. Miller, Deane Henry, Martin Mull, Eric Christmas, Ted Stidder

HOME JAMES (1928, Silent, Universal)
James Lacey—Charles Delaney
Director—William Beaudine
Leading Players—Laura La Plante, Aileen Manning, Joan Standing, George Pearce

THE HOME MAKER (1925, Silent, Universal)
Lester Knapp—Clive Brook
Director—King Baggot
Leading Players—Alice Joyce, Billy Kent Schaeffer, George Fawcett

THE HOME TOWN GIRL (1919, Silent, Paramount)
Nell Fanshawe—Vivian Martin
Director—Robert Vignola
Leading Players—Ralph Graves, Lee Phelps, Carmen Phillips

HOMEBOY (1989, 20th Century Fox)
Johnny Walker—Mickey Rourke
Director—Michael Seresin
Leading Players—Christopher Walken, Debra Feuer, Thomas Quinn

THE HOMEBREAKER (1919, Silent, Paramount)
Mary Marsden—Dorothy Dalton
Director—Victor Schertzinger
Leading Players—Douglas McLean, Beverly Travers, Frank Leigh

HOMER (1970, Palomar/National General)
Homer Edwards—Don Scardino
Director—John Trent
Leading Players—Alex Nicol, Tisa Farrow, Lenka Petersen

HOMER COMES HOME (1920, Silent, Triangle Pictures)
Homer Cavender—Charles Ray
Director—Jerome Storm
Leading Players—Otto Hoffman, Priscilla Bonner, Ralph McCullough

A HOMESPUN VAMP (1922, Silent, Paramount)
Meg Mackenzie—May McAvoy
Director—Frank O'Connor
Leading Players—Darrel Foss, Lincoln Stedman, Josephine Crowell

HONDO (1953, Warner Brothers)
Hondo Lane—John Wayne
Director—John Farrow
Leading Players—Geraldine Page, Ward Bond, Michael Pate, James Arness, Rodolfo Acosta

AN HONEST MAN (1918, Silent, Triangle Pictures)
Benny Boggs—William Desmond
Director—Frank Borzage
Leading Players—Mary Warren, Ann Kroman, Graham Pettie

HONEY, I SHRUNK THE KIDS (1989, Buena Vista)
Wayne Szalinski—Rick Moranis
Diane Szalinski—Marcia Strassman
Amy Szalinski—Amy O'Neill
Nick Szalinski—Robert Oliveri
Little Russ Thompson—Thomas Brown
Ron Thompson—Jared Rushton
Director—Joe Johnston
Leading Players—Matt Frewer, Kristine Sutherland, Carl Stevens

HONKY (1971, Getty-Fromkess-Stonehenge)
Wayne "Honky" Divine—John Nielson
Director—William A. Graham
Leading Players—Brenda Sykes, Maia Danzinger, John Lasell, William Marshall

HONKYTONK MAN (1982, Warner Brothers)
Red Stovall—Clint Eastwood
Director—Clint Eastwood
Leading Players—Kyle Eastwood, John McIntire, Alexa Kenin, Verna Bloom

HONOLULU LU (1941, Columbia)
Consuelo Cordoba—Lupe Velez
Director—Charles Barton
Leading Players—Bruce Bennett, Leo Carillo, Marjorie Gateson

THE HONOR OF MARY BLAKE (1916, Silent, Bluebird)
Mary Blake—Violet Mersereau
Director—Edwin Stevens
Leading Players—Tina Marshall, Caroline Harris, Sidney Mason

THE HONORABLE ALGY (1916, Silent, Triangle Pictures)
The Honorable Algy—Charles Ray
Director—Jerome Storm
Leading Players—Margaret Thompson, Howard Hickman, Margery Wilson

THE HOODLUM (1919, Silent, First National)
Amy Burke—Mary Pickford
Director—Sidney A. Franklin
Leading Players—Ralph Lewis, Kenneth Harlan, Melvin Messenger

THE HOODLUM PRIEST (1961, UA)
Rev. Charles Dismas Clark, S.J.—Don Murray
Director—Irvin Kershner

Leading Players—Larry Gates, Cindi Wood, Keir Dullea, Logan Ramsey

THE HOODLUM SAINT (1946, MGM)
Terry Ellerton O'Neill—William Powell
Director—Norman Taurog
Leading Players—Esther Williams, Angela Lansbury, James Gleason, Lewis Stone

HOOK (1991, Tri-Star)
Captain Hook—Dustin Hoffman
Director—Steven Spielberg
Leading Players—Robin Williams, Julia Roberts, Bob Hoskins, Maggie Smith, Caroline Goodall, Charlie Korsmo, Amber Scott, Laurel Cronin

HOOPER (1978, Warner Brothers)
Sonny Hooper—Burt Reynolds
Director—Hal Needham
Leading Players—Jan-Michael Vincent, Sally Field, Brian Keith, John Marley, Robert Klein

HOOSIER SCHOOLBOY (1937, Monogram)
Shockey—Mickey Rooney
Director—William Nigh
Leading Players—Anne Nagel, Frank Shields, Edward Pawley

THE HOOSIER SCHOOLMASTER (1914, Silent, Alliance)
Ralph Hartsook—Max Figman
Director—Max Figman
Leading Player—Lolita Robertson

THE HOOSIER SCHOOLMASTER (1924, Silent, W.W. Hodkinson Corp.)
Ralph Hartsook—Henry Hull
Director—Oliver L. Sellers
Leading Players—Jane Thomas, Frank Dane, Mary Foy

HOOSIER SCHOOLMASTER (1935, Monogram)
Ralph Hartsook—Norman Foster
Director—Lewis D. Collins
Leading Players—Charlotte Henry, Dorothy Libaire, Sarah Padden

HOOSIERS (1986, Orion)
Myrna Fleener—Barbara Hershey
Shooter—Dennis Hopper
Note—There were of course many Indiana residents, including the players on the basketball team, but Hershey and Hopper, in starring roles, represent them all.
Director—David Anspaugh
Leading Players—Gene Hackman, Shep Wooley, Fern Persons, Brad Boyle, Steve Hollar, Brad Long

HOPALONG CASSIDY (1935, Paramount)
Hopalong Cassidy—William Boyd
Director—Howard Bretherton
Leading Players—James Ellison, Paula Stone, Robert Warwick

HOPALONG CASSIDY RETURNS (1936, Paramount)
Hopalong Cassidy—William Boyd
Director—Nat Watt
Leading Players—George Hayes, Gail Sheridan, Evelyn Brent

HOPALONG RIDES AGAIN (1937, Parmount)
Hopalong Cassidy—William Boyd

Director—Les Selander
Leading Players—George Hayes, Russell Hayden, William Duncan

THE HOPPER (1918, Silent, Triangle Pictures)
The Hopper—William V. Mong
Director—Thomas N. Heffron
Leading Players—Thomas Kuribara, George Hernandez, Irene Hunt, Walt Whitman

HOPPY SERVES A WRIT (1943, UA)
Hopalong Cassidy—William Boyd
Director—George Archainbaud
Leading Players—Andy Clyde, Jay Kirby, Victor Jory, George Reeves, Jan Christy

HOPPY'S HOLIDAY (1947, UA)
Hopalong Cassidy—William Boyd
Director—George Archainbaud
Leading Players—Andy Clyde, Rand Brooks, Andrew Tombes

THE HORIZONTAL LIEUTENANT (1962, MGM)
2nd Lt. Merle Wye—Jim Hutton
Director—Richard Thorpe
Leading Players—Paula Prentiss, Jack Carter, Jim Backus

THE HORROR OF DRACULA (1958, GB, Hammer/Universal)
Count Dracula—Christopher Lee
Director—Terence Fisher
Leading Players—Peter Cushing, Michael Gough, Melissa Stribling, Carol Marsh

THE HORROR OF FRANKENSTEIN (1970, GB, Hammer/EMI)
Victor Frankenstein—Ralph Bates
Director—Jimmy Sangster
Leading Players—Kate O'Mara, Graham James, Veronica Carlson, Dennis Price

A HORSEMAN OF THE PLAINS (1928, Silent, Fox Film Corp.)
Tom Swift—Tom Mix
Director—Benjamin Stoloff
Leading Players—Sally Blane, Heine Conklin, Charles Byer

THE HORSEPLAYER (1990, Relentless)
Bud—Brad Dourif
Director—Kurt Voss
Leading Players—Sammi Davis, M.K. Harris, Vic Tayback, Max Perlich

THE HOSTAGE (1917, Silent, Paramount)
Lt. Ivo Kemper—Wallace Reid
Director—Robert Thornby
Leading Players—Dorothea Abril, Gertrude Short, C.H. Geldert

THE HOSTAGE (1956, GB, Fairbanks-Westridge/Eros)
Rosa Gonzuelo—Mary Parker
Director—Harold Huth
Leading Players—Ron Randell, John Bailey, Carl Jaffe

THE HOSTAGE (1966, Heartland/Crown)
Davey Cleaves—Danny Martins
Director—Russell S. Doughton
Leading Players—Don O'Kelly, Harry Dean Stanton, John Carradine, Ron Hagerthy

HOSTILE WITNESS (1968, GB, UA)
Simon Crawford—Ray Milland
Director—Ray Milland
Leading Players—Sylvia Sims, Felix Aylmer, Raymond Huntley, Geoffrey Lumsden

HOT HEIRESS (1931, First National/Warner Brothers)
Juliette Hunter—Ona Munson
Director—Clarence Badger
Leading Players—Ben Lyon, Walter Pidgeon, Tom Dugan

HOT MONEY GIRL (1962, GB, United Producers)
Hedi von Hartmann—Dawn Addams
Director—Alvin Rakoff
Leading Players—Willy Witte, Eddie Constantine, Gaylord Cavallaro, Marius Goring

HOT ROD GIRL (1956, American International)
Lisa—Lori Nelson
Director—Leslie H. Martinson
Leading Players—John Smith, Chuck Connors, Frank Gorshin

HOT SHOT (1987, Arista)
Jimmy Kristidis—Jim Youngs
Director—Rick King
Leading Players—Pele, Billy Warlock, Leon Russom

HOT SHOTS (1991, 20th Century Fox)
Topper Harley—Charlies Sheen
Kent Gregory—Cary Elwes
Director—Jim Abrahams
Leading Players—Valeria Golino, Lloyd Bridges, Kevin Dunn, Jon Cryer, William O'Leary, Kristy Swanson

THE HOTEL MOUSE (1923, Silent, GB, Jury)
Mauricette—Lilian Hall Davis
Director—Fred Paul
Leading Players—Campbell Gullan, Warwick Ward, Josephine Earle

HOUDINI (1953, Paramount)
Harry Houdini—Tony Curtis
Director—George Marshall
Leading Players—Janet Leigh, Torin Thatcher, Angela Clark

HOUND OF THE BASKERVILLES (1932, GB, Gainsborough)
Sir Hugo Baskerville—Sam Livesey
Sir Henry Baskerville—John Stuart
Director—V. Gareth Gundrey
Leading Players—Robert Rendel, Frederick Lloyd, Reginald Bach, Heather Angel

THE HOUND OF THE BASKERVILLES (1939, 20th Century Fox)
Sir Hugo Baskerville—Ralph Forbes
Sir Henry Baskerville—Richard Greene
Director—Sidney Lanfield
Leading Players—Basil Rathbone, Wendy Barrie, Nigel Bruce, Lionel Atwill, John Carradine

THE HOUND OF THE BASKERVILLES (1959, GB, Hammer)
Sir Hugo Baskerville—David Oxley
Sir Henry Baskerville—Christopher Lee
Director—Terence Fisher
Leading Players—Peter Cushing, Andre Morell, Marla Landi, Miles Malleson, Frances De Wolff

THE HOUND OF THE BASKERVILLES (1980, GB, Hemdale)
Sir Henry Baskerville—Kenneth Williams
Director—Paul Morrissey
Leading Players—Peter Cook, Dudley Moore, Denholm Elliott, Joan Greenwood, Terry-Thomas

THE HOUND OF THE BASKERVILLES (1983, GB, Mapelton)
Sir Henry Baskerville—Martin Shaw
Director—Douglas Hickox
Leading Players—Ian Richardson, Donald Churchill, Nicholas Clay, Denholm Elliott

THE HOUND-DOG MAN (1959, 20th Century Fox)
Clint—Fabian
Director—Don Siegel
Leading Players—Carol Lynley, Stuart Whitman, Arthur O'Connell, Dodie Stevens

HOUR OF THE ASSASSIN (1987, Concorde)
Martin Fierro—Erik Estrada
Director—Luis Llosa
Leading Players—Robert Vaughn, Alfred Calderon, Roland Sacha, Laura Burton

HOUSE OF DRACULA (1945, Universal)
Count Dracula—John Carradine
Director—Erle C. Kenton
Leading Players—Lon Chaney, Jr., Martha O'Driscoll, Lionel Atwill, Jane Adams, Glenn Strange

THE HOUSE OF ROTHSCHILD (1934, 20th Century)
Mayer Rothschild—George Arliss
Nathan Rothschild—George Arliss
Director—Alfred Werker
Leading Players—Boris Karloff, Loretta Young, Robert Young, C. Aubrey Smith, Helen Westley

THE HOUSE OF TEMPERLEY (1913, Silent, GB, Jury)
Capt. Jack Temperley—Charles Maude
Sir Charles Temperley—Ben Webster
Director—Harold M. Shaw
Leading Players—Lillian Logan, Charles Rock, Edward O'Neill

THE HOUSE OF TRENT (1933, GB, Ensign)
Dr. Trent—John Stuart
John Trent—John Stuart
Director—Norman Walker
Leading Players—Anne Grey, Wendy Barrie, Norah Baring, Peter Gawthorne

THE HOUSE OF USHER (1960, American International)
Roderick Usher—Vincent Price
Madeline Usher—Myrna Fahey
Director—Roger Corman
Leading Players—Mark Damon, Harry Ellerbe, Bill Borzage

THE HOUSEKEEPER (1987, Canada, Castlehill-Kodiak)
Eunice Parchman—Rita Tushingham
Director—Ousama Rawi
Leading Players—Ross Petty, Shelley Peterson, Jonathan Crombie, Jessica Stern

HOUSEKEEPER'S DAUGHTER (1939, UA)
Hilda—Joan Bennett
Olga—Peggy Wood
Director—Hal Roach

Leading Players—Adolphe Menjou, John Hubbard, William Gargan, George E. Stone

HOUSEMASTER (1938, GB, Associated British)
Charles Donkin—Otto Kruger
Director—Herbert Brenon
Leading Players—Diana Churchill, Phillips Holmes, Joyce Barbour

HOUSESITTER (1992, Universal)
Gwen—Goldie Hawn
Director—Frank Oz
Leading Players—Steve Martin, Dana Delany, Julie Harris, Donald Moffat, Peter MacNicol

HOUSEWIFE (1934, Warner Brothers)
Nan Wilson Reynolds—Ann Dvorak
Director—Alfred E. Green
Leading Players—George Brent, Bette Davis, John Halliday

HOW BAXTER BUTTED IN (1925, Silent, Warner Brothers)
Henry Baxter—Matt Moore
Director—William Beaudine
Leading Players—Dorothy Devore, Ward Crane, Wilfred Lucas

HOW COULD YOU CAROLINE? (1918, Silent, Pathe)
Caroline—Bessie Love
Director—Frederick Thompson
Leading Players—James Morrison, Dudley Hawley, Henry Hallam

HOW COULD YOU JEAN? (1918, Silent, Artcraft)
Jean Mackaye—Mary Pickford
Director—William Desmond Taylor
Leading Players—Casson Ferguson, Herbert Standing, Spottiswoode Aitken

HOW I GOT INTO COLLEGE (1989, 20th Century Fox)
Marlon Browne—Corey Parker
Director—Savage Steve Holland
Leading Players—Anthony Edwards, Lara Flynn Boyle, Finn Carter

HOW I WON THE WAR (1967, GB, UA)
Lt. Ernest Goodbody—Michael Crawford
Director—Richard Lester
Leading Players—John Lennon, Roy Kinnear, Lee Montague, Jack MacGowran, Michael Hordern

HOW MOLLY MADE GOOD (1915, Silent, Kulee Features)
Molly Malone—Marguerite Gale
Director—Lawrence B. McGill
Leading Players—William T. Hooker, Helen Hilton, W.A. Williams

HOW TO MURDER A RICH UNCLE (1957, GB, Columbia)
Uncle George—Charles Coburn
Director—Nigel Patrick
Leading Players—Nigel Patrick, Wendy Hiller, Anthony Newley

HOW TO SEDUCE A PLAYBOY (1968, Australia, Intercontinental)
Peter Keller—Peter Alexander
Director—Michael Pfleghar
Leading Players—Renato Salvatori, Antonella Lualdi, Scilla Gabel, Joachim Fuchsberger

THE HOWARD CASE (1936, GB, Universal)
Howard—Arthur Seaton
Director—Frank Richardson
Leading Players—Jack Livesey, Olive Sloane, David Keir

HOWARD THE DUCK (1986, Universal)
Howard T. Duck—Ed Gale/Chip Zien/Tim Rose/Steve Sleap/ Peter Baird/Mary Wells/Lisa Sturz/Jordan Prentice
Director—Willard Huyck
Leading Players—Lea Thompson, Jeffrey Jones, Tim Robbins

THE HOWARDS OF VIRGINIA (1940, Columbia)
Matt Howard—Cary Grant
Jane Peyton Howard—Martha Scott
Director—Frank Lloyd
Leading Players—Cedric Hardwicke, Alan Marshal, Richard Carlson, Paul Kelly

HOWZER (1973, Universal)
Howard "Howzer" Carsell—Peter Desiante
Director—Ken Laurence
Leading Players—Melissa Stocking, Royal Dano, William Gray

HUCK AND TOM (1918, Paramount)
Tom Sawyer—Jack Pickford
Huck Finn—Robert Gordon
Director—William Desmond Taylor
Leading Players—George Hackathorne, Alice Marvin, Edythe Chapman, Clara Horton

HUCKLEBERRY FINN (1920, Silent, Paramount)
Huckleberry Finn—Lewis Sargent
Director—William Desmond Taylor
Leading Players—Katherine Griffith, Martha Mattox, Frank Lanning, George Reed, Orral Humphrey

HUCKLEBERRY FINN (1931, Paramount)
Huckleberry Finn—James Durkin
Director—Norman Taurog
Leading Players—Jackie Coogan, Mitzi Green, Jackie Searl, Clarence Muse, Clara Blandick

HUCKLEBERRY FINN (1939, MGM)
Huckleberry Finn—Mickey Rooney
Director—Richard Thorpe
Leading Players—Walter Connolly, William Frawley, Rex Ingram, Lynn Carver, Victor Kilian

HUCKLEBERRY FINN (1974, UA)
Huckleberry Finn—Jeff East
Director—J. Lee Thompson
Leading Players—Paul Winfield, Harvey Korman, David Wayne, Arthur O'Connell, Gary Merrill

THE HUCKSTERS (1947, MGM)
Victor Albee Norman—Clark Gable
Mr. Kimberly—Adolphe Menjou
Director—Jack Conway
Leading Players—Deborah Kerr, Sydney Greenstreet, Ava Gardner

HUD (1963, Paramount)
Hud Bannon—Paul Newman
Director—Martin Ritt
Leading Players—Melvyn Douglas, Patricia Neal, Brandon De Wilde

HUDSON HAWKE (1991, Tri-Star)
Hudson Hawke—Bruce Willis
Director—Michael Lehmann
Leading Players—Danny Aiello, Andie MacDowell, James
Coburn, Richard E. Grant, Sandra Bernhard, Donald Burton

HULDA FROM HOLLAND (1916, Silent, Artcraft)
Hulda—Mary Pickford
Director—John B. O'Brien
Leading Players—Frank Losee, John Bowers, Russell Bassett

THE HUMAN SHIELD (1992, Cannon)
Ben Matthews—Tommy Hinkley
Director—Ted Post
Leading Players—Michael Dudikoff, Hana Azoulay-Hasfari,
Steve Inwood

THE HUMAN TORNADO (1925, Silent, R-C Pictures)
Jim Marlow—Yakima Canutt
Director—Ben Wilson
Leading Players—Bert Sprotte, Nancy Leeds, Lafe McKee

HUMDRUM BROWN (1918, Silent, Essanay)
Humdrum Brown—Henry B. Walthall
Director—Rex Ingram
Leading Players—Mary Charleson, Dorothy Love Clark, Howard
Crampton

HUMPHREY TAKES A CHANCE (1950, Monogram)
Humphrey Pennyworth—Robert Coogan
Director—Jean Yarbrough
Leading Players—Leon Errol, Joe Kirkwood, Lois Collier

THE HUN WITHIN (1918, Silent, Paramount)
Karl Wagner—Charles Gerard
Director—Chester Withey
Leading Players—George Fawcett, Dorothy Gish, Douglas
MacLean

THE HUNCHBACK OF NOTRE DAME (1923, Silent, Universal)
Quasimodo—Lon Chaney
Director—Wallace Worsley
Leading Players—Ernest Torrence, Patsy Ruth Miller, Norman
Kerry, Raymond Hatton, Brandon Hurst

THE HUNCHBACK OF NOTRE DAME (1939, RKO)
Quasimodo—Charles Laughton
Director—William S. Dieterle
Leading Players—Cedric Hardwicke, Thomas Mitchell, Maureen
O'Hara, Edmond O'Brien, Alan Marshal

HUNK (1987, Crown International)
Hunk Golden—John Allen Nelson
Director—Lawrence Bassoff
Leading Players—Steve Levitt, Deborah Shelton, Rebecca Bush,
James Coco, Robert Morse

HUNT THE MAN DOWN (1950, RKO)
Kincaid—James Anderson
Director—George Archainbaud
Leading Players—Gig Young, Lynne Robert, Mary Anderson

THE HUNTED WOMAN (1925, Silent, Fox Film Corp.)
Joanne Gray—Seena Owen
Director—Jack Conway
Leading Players—Earl Schneck, Diana Miller, Cyril Chadwick

THE HUNTER (1980, Paramount)
Papa Thorson—Steve McQueen
Director—Buzz Kulik
Leading Players—Eli Wallach, Kathryn Harrold, LeVar Burton

HUNTER'S BLOOD (1987, Concorde)
David Rand—Sam Bottoms
Mason Rand—Clu Gulager
Al Coleman—Ken Swofford
Marty Adler—Joey Travolta
Ralph Coleman—Mayf Nutter
Director—Robert C. Hughes
Leading Players—Kim Delaney, Lee DeBroux, Bruce Glover

THE HUNTRESS (1923, Silent, Associated First National)
Bela—Colleen Moore
Director—Lynn Reynolds
Leading Players—Lloyd Hughes, Russell Simpson, Walter Long

THE HURRICANE KID (1925, Silent, Universal)
The Hurricane Kid—Hoot Gibson
Director—Edward Sedgwick
Leading Players—Marion Nixon, William A. Steele, Arthur
Machley

HURRICANE SMITH (1942, Republic)
Hurricane Smith—Ray Middleton
Director—Bernard Vorhaus
Leading Players—Jane Wyatt, Harry Davenport, J. Edward
Bromberg

HURRICANE SMITH (1952, Paramount)
Hurricane Smith—John Ireland
Director—Jerry Hopper
Leading Players—Yvonne De Carlo, James Craig, Forrest Tucker

HURRICANE SMITH (1992, Australia, Warner Brothers/Greater
Union)
Billy Smith—Carl Weathers
Director—Jurgen Prochow, Cassandra Delaney, Tony Banner,
David Argue

HURRICANE'S GAL (1922, Silent, Associated First National)
Lola—Dorothy Phillips
Director—Allen Holubar
Leading Players—Robert Ellis, Wallace Beery, James O.
Barrows, Gertrude Astor

HUSBAND HUNTERS (1927, Silent, Tiffany)
Marie Devere—Mae Busch
Letty Crane—Jean Arthur
Helen Gray—Duane Thompson
Director—John G. Adolfi
Leading Players—Charles Delaney, Walter Hiers, Mildred
Harris, Robert Cain

HUSBANDS (1970, Columbia)
Harry—Ben Gazarra
Archie—Peter Falk
Gus—John Cassavetes
Director—John Cassavetes
Leading Players—Jenny Runacre, Jenny Lee Wright, Noelle Kao

HUSBAND'S HOLIDAY (1931, Paramount)
George Boyd—Clive Brook
Director—Ernest Pascal

Leading Players—Charles Ruggles, Vivienne Osborne, Juliette Compton

HUSH . . . HUSH SWEET CHARLOTTE (1964, 20th Century Fox)
Charlotte—Bette Davis
Director—Robert Aldrich
Leading Players—Olivia De Havilland, Joseph Cotten, Agnes Moorehead, Cecil Kellaway

THE HUSTLER (1961, 20th Century Fox)
"Fast" Eddie Felson—Paul Newman
Director—Robert Rossen
Leading Players—Jackie Gleason, Piper Laurie, George C. Scott, Myron McCormick

HUTCH STIRS 'EM UP (1923, Silent, GB, Ideal)
Hurricane Hutch—Charles Hutchinson
Director—Frank H. Crane
Leading Players—Joan Barry, Malcolm Tod, Gibson Gowland

I

I ACCUSE (1958, GB, MGM)
Emile Zola—Emlyn Williams
Director—Jose Ferrer
Leading Players—Jose Ferrer, Anton Walbrook, Viveca Lindfors, Leo Genn, Herbert Lom

I ACCUSE MY PARENTS (1945, Producers Releasing Corp.)
James Wilson—Robert Lowell
Dan Wilson—John Miljan
Mrs. Wilson—Vivienne Osborne
Director—Sam Newfield
Leading Players—Mary Beth Hughes, George Meeker, Edward Earle

I ADORE YOU (1933, GB, Warner Brothers/First National)
Norman Young—Harold French
Margot Grahame—Margot Grahame
Director—George King
Leading Players—Clifford Heatherley, O. B. Clarence, Peggy Novak

I AIM AT THE STARS (1960, Columbia)
Werner von Braun—Curt Jurgens
Director—J. Lee Thompson
Leading Players—Victoria Shaw, Herbert Lom, Gia Scala, James Daly

I AM A CAMERA (1955, GB, Romulus-Remus)
Christopher Isherwood—Laurence Harvey
Director—Henry Cornelius
Leading Players—Julie Harris, Shelley Winters, Ron Randell

I AM A CRIMINAL (1939, Monogram)
Brad McArthur—John Carroll
Director—William Nigh
Leading Players—Kay Linaker, Craig Reynolds, Martin Spellman

I AM A FUGITIVE FROM A CHAIN GANG (1932, Warner Brothers)
James Allen (Allen James)—Paul Muni
Director—Mervyn LeRoy
Leading Players—Glenda Farrell, Helen Vinson, Preston Foster, Allen Jenkins, Edward Ellis

I AM A GROUPIE (1970, GB, Eagle Films)
Sally—Esme Johns
Director—Derek Ford
Leading Players—Billy Boyle, Richard Shaw, Neil Hallett

I AM A THIEF (1935, Warner Brothers)
Odette Mauclair—Mary Astor
Director—Robert Florey
Leading Players—Ricardo Cortez, Dudley Digges, Robert Barrat, Irving Pichel

I AM GUILTY (1921, Silent, Associated Producers)
Connie MacNair—Louise Glaum
Director—Jack Nelson
Leading Players—Mahlon Hamilton, Claire Du Brey, Joseph Kilgour

I AM NOT AFRAID (1939, Warner Brothers)
Ulysses Porterfield—Charley Grapewin
Director—Crane Wilbur
Leading Players—Jane Bryan, Henry O'Neill, Elizabeth Risdon

I AM SUZANNE (1934, Fox Film Corp.)
Suzanne—Lillian Hervey
Director—Rowland V. Lee
Leading Players—Gene Raymond, Leslie Banks, Georgia Caine

I AM THE CHEESE (1983, Almi Productions)
Adam—Robert MacNaughton
Director—Robert Jiras
Leading Players—Hope Lange, Don Murray, Robert Wagner

I AM THE LAW (1922, Silent, Affiliated Distributors)
Robert Fitzgerald—Kenneth Harlan
Director—Edwin Carewe
Leading Players—Alice Lake, Rosemary Theby, Gaston Glass

I AM THE LAW (1938, Columbia)
John Lindsay—Edward G. Robinson
Director—Alexander Hall
Leading Players—Barbara O'Neill, John Beal, Wendy Barrie, Otto Kruger

I AM THE MAN (1924, Silent, Chadwick Pictures)
James McQuade—Lionel Barrymore
Director—Ivan Abramson
Leading Players—Seena Owen, Gaston Glass, Martin Faust

I BECAME A CRIMINAL (1947, Alliance/Warner Brothers)
Clem Morgan—Trevor Howard
Director—Alberto Cavalcanti
Leading Players—Sally Gray, Griffith Jones, Rene Ray

I BURY THE LIVING (1958, UA)
Robert Kraft—Richard Boone
Director—Albert Band
Leading Players—Theodore Bikel, Peggy Maurer, Herb Anderson

I CAN EXPLAIN (1922, Silent, Metro)
Jimmy Berry—Gareth Hughes
Director—George D. Baker
Leading Players—Bartine Burkett, Grace Darmond, Herbert Hayes

I CAN'T ESCAPE (1934, Syndicate Releasing Corp.)
Steve Nichols/Cummings—Onslow Stevens
Director—Otto Brower
Leading Players—Lila Lee, Russell Gleason, Otis Harlan

I CAN'T GIVE YOU ANYTHING BUT LOVE, BABY (1940, Universal)
Sonny McGann—Broderick Crawford
Linda Carroll—Peggy Moran
Director—Albert S. Rogell
Leading Players—Johnny Downs, Warner Hymer, John Sutton

I CHEATED THE LAW (1949, 20th Century Fox)
John Campbell—Tom Conway
Director—Edward L. Cahn
Leading Players—Steve Brodie, Robert Osterloh, Barbara Billingsley

I CONFESS (1953, Warner Brothers)
Otto Keller—O.E. Hasse
Director—Alfred Hitchcock
Leading Players—Montgomery Clift, Anne Baxter, Karl Malden, Brian Aherne

I COULD GO ON SINGING (1963, UA)
Jenny Bowman—Judy Garland
Director—Ronald Neame
Leading Players—Dirk Bogarde, Jack Klugman, Aline MacMahon

I COVER BIG TOWN (1947, Paramount)
Steve Wilson—Philip Reed
Director—William C. Thomas
Leading Players—Hilary Brooke, Robert Lowery, Robert Shayne

I COVER CHINATOWN (1938, Banner Films)
Barton—Norman Foster
Director—Norman Foster
Leading Players—Elaine Stewart, Theodore Von Eltz, Polly Ann Young, Arthur Lake

I COVER THE UNDERWORLD (1955, Republic)
John O'Hara—Sean McClory
Director—R.G. Springsteen
Leading Players—Joanne Jordan, Ray Middleton, Jaclynne Greene

I COVER THE WAR (1937, Universal)
Bob Adams—John Wayne
Director—Arthur Lubin
Leading Players—Gwen Gaze, Don Barclay, Pat Somerset

I COVER THE WATERFRONT (1933, UA)
Joseph Miller—Ben Lyon
Director—James Cruze
Leading Players—Claudette Colbert, Ernest Torrence, Hobart Cavanaugh

I DIDN'T DO IT (1945, GB, Columbia)
George Trotter—George Formby

Director—Marcel Varnel
Leading Players—Billy Caryll, Hilda Mundy, Gaston Palmer

I DIED A THOUSAND TIMES (1955, Warner Brothers)
Roy Earle—Jack Palance
Director—Stuart Heisler
Leading Players—Shelley Winters, Lori Nelson, Lee Marvin, Earl Holliman, Lon Chaney, Jr.

I DON'T BUY KISSES ANYMORE (1992, Skouras)
Bernie Fishbine—Jason Alexander
Director—Robert Marcarelli
Leading Players—Nia Peeples, Lainie Kazan, Lou Jacobi, Eileen Brennan, David Bowie

THE I DON'T CARE GIRL (1952, 20th Century Fox)
Eva Tanguay—Mitzi Gaynor
Director—Lloyd Bacon
Leading Players—David Wayne, Oscar Levant, Bob Graham, Craig Hill, Warren Stevens

I DOOD IT (1943, MGM)
Joseph Rivington Reynolds—Red Skelton
Director—Vincente Minnelli
Leading Players—Eleanor Powell, Richard Ainley, Patricia Dane

I DREAM TOO MUCH (1935, RKO)
Jonathan Street—Henry Fonda
Director—John Cromwell
Leading Players—Lily Pons, Eric Blore, Osgood Perkins

I ESCAPED FROM DEVIL'S ISLAND (1973, UA)
Le Bras—Jim Brown
Director—William Witney
Leading Players—Christopher George, Rick Ely, Richard Rust

I FOUND STELLA PARISH (1935, First National/Warner Brothers)
Stella Parish—Kay Francis
Director—Mervyn LeRoy
Leading Players—Ian Hunter, Paul Lukas, Sybil Jason

I GIVE MY LOVE (1934, Universal)
Judy Blair—Wynne Gibson
Director—Karl Freund
Leading Players—Paul Lukas, Eric Linden, Anita Louise

I JANE DOE (1948, Republic)
Annette Dubois, alias Jane Doe—Vera Ralston
Director—John H. Auer
Leading Players—Ruth Hussey, John Carroll, Gene Lockhart

I KILLED GERONIMO (1950, Eagle Lion)
Capt. Jeff Packard—James Ellison
Geronimo—Chief Thunder Cloud
Director—John Hoffman
Leading Players—Virginia Herrick, Smith Ballew, Ted Adams

I KILLED WILD BILL HICKOK (1956, Wheeler Pictures)
Johnny Rebel—John Forbes (John Carpenter)
Wild Bill Hickok—Tom Brown
Director—John Carpenter
Leading Players—Helen Wescott, Virginia Gibson, Denver Pyle

I KNOW WHERE I'M GOING (1947, GB, Archers)
Joan Webster—Wendy Hiller

Directors—Michael Powell & Emeric Pressburger
Leading Players—Roger Livesey, Pamela Brown, Nancy Price, Finlay Currie, John Laurie

I LIKE MONEY (MR. TOPAZE) (1962, GB, 20th Century Fox)
Mr. Topaze—Peter Sellers
Director—Peter Sellers
Leading Players—Nadia Gray, Herbert Lom, Leo McKern, Martita Hunt, John Neville

I LIVE FOR LOVE (1935, Warner Brothers)
Donna Alvares—Dolores Del Rio
Director—Busby Berkeley
Leading Players—Everett Marshall, Guy Kibbee, Allen Jenkins

I LIVE MY LIFE (1935, MGM)
Kay—Joan Crawford
Director—W.S. Van Dyke II
Leading Players—Brian Aherne, Frank Morgan, Aline MacMahon

I LIVE ON DANGER (1942, Paramount)
Jeff Morrell—Chester Morris
Director—Sam White
Leading Players—Jean Parker, Elizabeth Risdon, Edward Norris

I LOVE A SOLDIER (1944, Paramount)
Eva Morgan—Paulette Goddard
Dan Gilgore—Sonny Tufts
Director—Mark Sandrich
Leading Players—Mary Treen, Walter Sande, Ann Doran

I LOVE MELVIN (1953, MGM)
Melvin Hooper—Donald O'Connor
Judy LeRoy—Debbie Reynolds
Director—Don Weis
Leading Players—Una Merkel, Richard Anderson, Allyn Joslyn

I LOVE MY WIFE (1970, Universal)
Dr. Richard Burrows—Elliott Gould
Judy Burrows—Brenda Vacarro
Director—Mel Stuart
Leading Players—Angel Tompkins, Dabney Coleman, Joan Tompkins, Leonard Stone

I LOVE THAT MAN (1933, Paramount)
"Brains" Stanley—Edmund Lowe
Grace Clark—Nancy Carroll
Director—Harry Joe Brown
Leading Players—Lew Cody, Robert Armstrong, Warren Hymer

I LOVE TROUBLE (1947, Columbia)
Stuart Bailey—Franchot Tone
Director—S. Sylvan Simon
Leading Players—Janet Blair, Janis Carter, Adele Jergens, Glenda Farrell, Steven Geray

I LOVE YOU (1918, Silent, Triangle)
Felice—Alma Rubens
Jules Mardon—Francis McDonald
Director—Walter Edwards
Leading Players—John Lince, Wheeler Oakman, Frederick Vroom

I LOVE YOU AGAIN (1940, MGM)
Larry Wilson/George Carey—William Powell

Kay Wilson—Myrna Loy
Director—W.S. Van Dyke II
Leading Players—Frank McHugh, Edmund Lowe, Donald Douglas

I LOVE YOU TO DEATH (1990, Tri-Star)
Rosalie Boca—Tracey Ullman
Joey Boca—Kevin Kline
Director—Lawrence Kasdan
Leading Players—Joan Plowright, River Phoenix, William Hurt, Keanu Reeves, James Gammon, Victoria Jackson

I LOVED A WOMAN (1933, First National/Warner Brothers)
Laura McDonald—Kay Francis
John Hayden—Edward G. Robinson
Director—Alfred Green
Leading Players—Genevieve Tobin, J. Farrell MacDonald, Henry Kolker, Robert Barratt

I, MADMAN (1989, Trans World)
Malcolm Brand—Randall William Cook
Director—Tibor Takacs
Leading Players—Jenny Wright, Clayton Rohner, Steven Memel

I MARRIED A DOCTOR (1936, First National/Warner Brothers)
Dr. William P. Kennicott—Pat O'Brien
Carol Kennicott—Josephine Hutchinson
Director—Archie Mayo
Leading Players—Ross Alexander, Guy Kibbee, Louise Fazenda

I MARRIED A MONSTER FROM OUTER SPACE (1958, Paramount)
Bill Farrell—Tom Tryon
Marge Farrell—Gloria Talbott
Director—Gene Fowler
Leading Players—Peter Baldwin, Robert Ivers, Chuck Wassil

I MARRIED A WITCH (1942, Paramount/UA)
Wallace Wooley—Fredric March
Jennifer—Veronica Lake
Director—Rene Clair
Leading Players—Robert Benchley, Susan Hayward, Cecil Kellaway, Elizabeth Patterson

I MARRIED A WOMAN (1958, RKO/Universal)
Marshall "Mickey" Briggs—George Gobel
Janice Briggs—Diana Dors
Director—Hal Kanter
Leading Players—Adolphe Menjou, Jessie Royce Landis, Nita Talbot

I MARRIED AN ANGEL (1942, MGM)
Anna Zador/Brigitta—Jeanette MacDonald
Count Willie Palaffi—Nelson Eddy
Director—W.S. Van Dyke II
Leading Players—Binnie Barnes, Edward Everett Horton, Reginald Owen, Mona Maris

I, MAUREEN (1978, Canada, New Cinema)
Maureen—Colleen Collins
Director—Janine Manatis
Leading Players—Diane Bigelow, Donna Preece, Robert Crone

I MET A MURDERER (1939, GB, Grand National)
Mark Warrow—James Mason
Jo—Pamela Kellino

Director—Roy Kellino
Leading Players—Sylvia Coleridge, William Devlin, Peter Coke

I MET HIM IN PARIS (1937, Paramount)
Kay Denham—Claudette Colbert
George Potter—Melvyn Douglas
Director—Wesley Ruggles
Leading Players—Robert Young, Lee Bowman, Mona Barie

I MET MY LOVE AGAIN (1938, UA)
Julie—Joan Bennett
Ives—Henry Fonda
Director—Arthur Ripley
Leading Players—Dame May Whitty, Alan Marshal, Louise Platt

I, MOBSTER (1959, 20th Century Fox)
Joe Sante—Steve Cochran
Director—Roger Corman
Leading Players—Lita Milan, Robert Strauss, Celia Lovsky

I, MONSTER (1971, GB, Amicus/Cannon)
Dr. Marlowe/Mr. Blake—Christopher Lee
Director—Stephen Weeks
Leading Players—Peter Cushing, Mike Raven, Richard Hurndall

I NEVER SANG FOR MY FATHER (1970, Columbia)
Tom Garrison—Melvyn Douglas
Gene Garrison—Gene Hackman
Director—Gilbert Cates
Leading Players—Dorothy Stickney, Estelle Parsons, Elizabeth Hubbard

I OUGHT TO BE IN PICTURES (1982, 20th Century Fox)
Libby Tucker—Dinah Manoff
Director—Herbert Ross
Leading Players—Walter Matthau, Ann-Margret, Lance Guest, Lewis Smith

I PASSED FOR WHITE (1960, Allied Artists)
Bernice Lee/Lila Brownell—Sonya Wilde
Director—Fred Wilcox
Leading Players—James Franciscus, Pat Michon, Elizabeth Council

I PROMISE TO PAY (1937, Columbia)
Eddie Lang—Chester Morris
Director—J. Ross Lederman
Leading Players—Leo Carrillo, Helen Mack, Thomas Mitchell

I REMEMBER MAMA (1948, RKO)
Mama—Irene Dunne
Katrin—Barbara Bel Geddes
Director—George Stevens
Leading Players—Oscar Homolka, Philip Dorn, Cedric Hardwicke

I SAILED TO TAHITI WITH AN ALL GIRL CREW (1969, World)
Gardner—Gardner McKay
Director—Richard Bare
Leading Players—Fred Clark, Pat Buttram, Diane McBain, Richard Denning, Edy Williams

I SAW WHAT YOU DID (1965, Universal)
Steve Marak—John Ireland
Kit—Sarah Lane
Libby—Andi Garrett

Director—William Castle
Leading Players—Joan Crawford, Leif Erickson, Sharyl Locke

I SEE ICE (1938, GB, Associated British)
George Bright—George Formby
Director—Anthony Kimmins
Leading Players—Kay Walsh, Betty Stockfield, Cyril Ritchard

I SELL ANYTHING (1934, First National/Warner Brothers)
Spot Cash Cutler—Pat O'Brien
Director—Robert Florey
Leading Players—Ann Dvorak, Claire Dodd, Roscoe Karns

I SHOT BILLY THE KID (1950, Lippert)
Billy The Kid—Don Barry
Pat Garrett—Robert Lowery
Director—William Berke
Leading Players—Wally Vernon, Tom Neal, Wendy Lee

I SHOT JESSE JAMES (1949, Lippert)
Bob Ford—John Ireland
Jesse James—Reed Hadley
Director—Samuel Fuller
Leading Players—Preston Foster, Barbara Britton, J. Edward Bromberg

I SPIT ON YOUR GRAVE (1983, Cinemagic)
Jennifer—Camille Keaton
Director—Meir Zarchi
Leading Players—Eron Tabor, Richard Pace, Gunter Kleeman

I SPY (1933, GB, British International)
Wally Sawyer—Ben Lyon
Director—Allan Dwan
Leading Players—Sally Eilers, Harry Tate, H.F. Maltby

I STOLE A MILLION (1939, Universal)
Joe Laurik (Harris)—George Raft
Director—Frank Tuttle
Leading Players—Claire Trevor, Dick Foran, Henry Armetta

I TAKE THIS WOMAN (1931, Paramount)
Tom McNair—Gary Cooper
Kay Dowling—Carole Lombard
Director—Martin Gering
Leading Players—Helen Ware, Lester Vail, Charles Trowbridge

I TAKE THIS WOMAN (1940, MGM)
Karl Decker—Spencer Tracy
Georgi Gragore—Hedy Lamarr
Director—W.S. Van Dyke
Leading Players—Verree Teasdale, Kent Taylor, Mona Barrie

I, THE JURY (1953, UA)
Mike Hammer—Biff Elliot
Director—Harry Essex
Leading Players—Preston Foster, Peggy Castle, Margaret Sheridan

I, THE JURY (1982, 20th Century Fox)
Mike Hammer—Armand Assante
Director—Richard T. Heffron
Leading Players—Barbara Carrera, Laurence Landon, Alan King

I WALK ALONE (1948, Paramount)
Frankie Madison—Burt Lancaster

Director—Bryon Haskins
Leading Players—Kirk Douglas, Lizabeth Scott, Wendell Corey

I WALK THE LINE (1970, Columbia)
Sheriff Henry Tawes—Gregory Peck
Director—John Frankenheimer
Leading Players—Tuesday Weld, Estelle Parsons, Ralph Meeker

I WALKED WITH A ZOMBIE (1943, Columbia)
Wesley Rand—James Ellison
Jessica Holland—Christine Gordon
Director—Jacques Tourneur
Leading Players—Frances Dee, Tom Conway, Edith Barrett

I WANT MY MAN (1925, Silent, First National)
Vida—Doris Kenyon
Gulian Eyre—Milton Sills
Director—Lambert Hillyer
Leading Players—Phyllis Haver, May Allison, Kate Bruce

I WANT TO FORGET (1918, Silent, Fox Film Corp.)
Varda Deering—Evelyn Nesbit
Director—James Kirkwood
Leading Players—Russel Thaw, Henry Clive, Alphonz Ethier

I WANT TO LIVE! (1958, UA)
Barbara Graham—Susan Hayward
Director—Robert Wise
Leading Players—Simon Oakland, Virginia Vincent, Theodore Bikel

I WANT WHAT I WANT (1972, GB, Cinerama)
Roy/Wendy—Anne Heywood
Director—John Dexter
Leading Players—Harry Andrews, Jill Bennett, Paul Rogers

I WAS A COMMUNIST FOR THE F.B.I. (1951, Warner Brothers)
Matt Cvetic—Frank Lovejoy
Director—Gordon Douglas
Leading Players—Dorothy Hart, Philip Carey, Dick Webb

I WAS A MALE WAR BRIDE (1949, 20th Century Fox)
Capt. Henri Rochard—Cary Grant
Director—Howard Hawks
Leading Players—Ann Sheridan, William Neff, Marion Marshall

I WAS A PRISONER ON DEVIL'S ISLAND (1941, Columbia)
Joel Grant—Donald Woods
Director—Lew Landers
Leading Players—Sally Eilers, Eduardo Ciannelli, Victor Kilian

I WAS A SHOPLIFTER (1950, Universal)
Faye Burton—Mona Freeman
Director—Charles Lamont
Leading Players—Scott Brady, Andrea King, Tony Curtis

I WAS A SPY (1934, GB, Gaumont)
Martha Cnockhaert—Madeleine Carroll
Director—Victor Saville
Leading Players—Conrad Veidt, Herbert Marshall, Gerald du Maurier, Edmund Gwenn

I WAS A TEENAGE FRANKENSTEIN (1958, American International)
Teenage Monster—Gary Conway
Director—Herbert L. Strock

Leading Players—Whit Bissell, Phyllis Coates, Robert Burton

I WAS A TEENAGE WEREWOLF (1957, American International)
Tony—Michael Landon
Director—George Fowler, Jr.
Leading Players—Yvonne Lime, Whit Bissell, Tony Marshall

I WAS A TEENAGE ZOMBIE (1987, Horizon)
Dan Wake—Michael Ruben
Director—John Elias Michalakias
Leading Players—George Seminara, Steve McCoy, Peter Bush

I WAS AN ADVENTURESS (1940, 20th Century Fox)
Countess Tanya Vronsky—Vera Zorina
Director—Gregory Ratoff
Leading Players—Richard Greene, Erich von Stroheim, Peter Lorre

I WAS AN AMERICAN SPY (1951, Monogram-Allied Artists)
Claire Phillips—Ann Dvorak
Director—Lesley Selander
Leading Players—Gene Evans, Douglas Kennedy, Richard Loo

I WAS FRAMED (1942, Warner Brothers)
Ken Marshall—Michael Ames
Director—D. Ross Lederman
Leading Players—Julie Bishop, Regis Toomey, Patty Hale

I WILL...I WILL...FOR NOW (1976, 20th Century Fox)
Les Bingham—Elliott Gould
Director—Norman Panama
Leading Players—Diane Keaton, Paul Sorvino, Victoria Principal

I'D CLIMB THE HIGHEST MOUNTAIN (1951, 20th Century Fox)
William Asbury Thompson—William Lundigan
Director—Henry King
Leading Players—Susan Hayward, Rory Calhoun, Barbara Bates

I'D GIVE MY LIFE (1936, Parmount)
Nickie Elkins—Tom Brown
Director—Edwin L. Marin
Leading Players—Guy Standing, Frances Drake, Janet Beecher

I'LL BE SEEING YOU (1944, UA)
Mary Marshall—Ginger Rogers
Zachary Morgan—Joseph Cotten
Director—William Dieterle
Leading Players—Shirley Temple, Spring Byington, Tom Tully

I'LL BE YOURS (1947, Universal)
Louise Ginglebusher—Deanna Durbin
George Prescott—Tom Drake
Director—William A. Seiter
Leading Players—William Bendix, Adolphe Menjou, Walter Catlett

I'LL CRY TOMORROW (1955, MGM)
Lillian Roth—Susan Hayward
Director—Daniel Mann
Leading Players—Richard Conte, Eddie Albert, Jo Van Fleet, Don Taylor, Ray Danton

I'LL FIX IT (1934, Columbia)
Bill Grimes—Jack Holt
Director—Roy William Neill
Leading Players—Mona Barrie, Winnie Lighter, Jimmy Butler

I'LL GET HIM YET (1919, Silent, First National)
Suzy Faraday Jones (Skinflint Jones)—Dorothy Gish
Scoop McCreedy—Richard Barthelmess
Director—Elmer Clifton
Leading Players—George Fawcett, Ralph Graves, Edward Pell

I'LL GIVE A MILLION (1938, 20th Century Fox)
Tony Newlander—Warner Baxter
Director—Walter Lang
Leading Players—Marjorie Weaver, Peter Lorre, John Carradine, Jean Hersholt, Lynn Bari

I'LL LOVE YOU ALWAYS (1935, Columbia)
Nora Clegg—Nancy Carroll
Carl Brent—George Murphy
Director—Leo Bulgakov
Leading Players—Raymond Walburn, Jean Dixon, Arthur Hohl

I'LL NEVER FORGET YOU (1951, 20th Century Fox)
Peter Standish—Tyrone Power
Helen Pettigrew—Ann Blyth
Director—Roy Baker
Leading Players—Michael Rennie, Dennis Price, Beatrice Campbell

I'LL REMEMBER APRIL (1945, Universal)
April—Gloria Jean
Director—Harold Young
Leading Players—Kirby Grant, Milburn Stone, Samuel S. Hinds

I'LL SEE YOU IN MY DREAMS (1951, Warner Brothers)
Grace LeBoy Kahn—Doris Day
Gus Kahn—Danny Thomas
Director—Michael Curtiz
Leading Players—Frank Lovejoy, Patrice Wymore, James Gleason

I'LL TAKE ROMANCE (1937, Columbia)
Elsa Terry—Grace Moore
Director—Edward H. Griffith
Leading Players—Melvyn Douglas, Helen Westley, Stuart Erwin, Margaret Hamilton

I'LL TAKE SWEDEN (1965, UA)
Bob Holcomb—Bob Hope
Director—Frederick DeCordova
Leading Players—Tuesday Weld, Frankie Avalon, Dina Merrill, Jeremy Slate

I'LL TELL THE WORLD (1934, Universal)
Stanley Brown—Lee Tracy
Director—Edward Sedgwick
Leading Players—Gloria Stuart, Roger Pryor, Onslow Stevens

I'LL TELL THE WORLD (1945, Universal)
Gabriel Patton—Lee Tracy
Director—Leslie Goodwins
Leading Players—Brenda Joyce, Raymond Walburn, June Preisser, Thomas Gomez

I'LL WAIT FOR YOU (1941, MGM)
"Lucky" Wilson—Robert Sterling
Pauline Miller—Marsha Hunt
Director—Robert B. Sinclair
Leading Players—Virginia Weidler, Paul Kelly, Fay Holden, Henry Travers

I'M A STRANGER (1952, GB, Corsair/Apex)
George Westcott—Patric Doonan
Director—Brock Williams
Leading Players—Greta Gynt, James Hayter, Hector Ross

I'M AN EXPLOSIVE (1933, GB, Fox Film Corp.)
Edward Whimperly—Billy Hartnell
Director—Adrian Brunel
Leading Players—Gladys Jennings, Eliot Makeham, D.A. Clarke-Smith

I'M DANCING AS FAST AS I CAN (1982, Paramount)
Barbara Gordon—Jill Clayburgh
Director—Jack Hofsiss
Leading Players—Nicol Williamson, Dianne Wiest, Joe Pesci, Geraldine Page

I'M FROM MISSOURI (1939, Paramount)
Sweeney Bliss—Bob Burns
Director—Theodore Reed
Leading Players—Gladys George, Gene Lockhart, Judith Barrett

I'M FROM THE CITY (1938, RKO)
Pete—Joe Penner
Director—Ben Holmes
Leading Players—Richard Lane, Lorraine Kramer, Paul Guilfoyle

I'M GOING TO GET YOU...ELLIOT BOY (1971, Canada, Columbia)
Elliot Markson—Ross Stephenson
Director—Edward J. Forsyth
Leading Players—Maureen McGill, Richard Gishler, Jeremy Hart

I'M GONNA GET YOU SUCKA (1988, MGM-UA)
Jack Spade—Keenan Ivory Wayans
Mr. Big—John Vernon
Director—Keenan Ivory Wayans
Leading Players—Bernie Casey, Antonio Fargas, Steve James, Issac Hayes, Jim Brown, Ja'net DuBois

I'M NO ANGEL (1933, Paramount)
Tira—Mae West
Director—Wesley Ruggles
Leading Players—Cary Grant, Gregory Ratoff, Edward Arnold

I'M STILL ALIVE (1940, RKO)
Steve Bonnett—Kent Taylor
Director—Irving Reis
Leading Players—Linda Hayes, Howard da Silva, Ralph Morgan

I'VE BEEN AROUND (1935, Universal)
Drue Waring—Rochelle Hudson
Director—Philip Cahn
Leading Players—Chester Morris, Isabel Jewell, Gene Lockhart

I'VE GOT A HORSE (1938, GB, British Lion)
Sandy—Sandy Powell
Director—Herbert Smith
Leading Players—Norah Howard, Felix Aylmer, Evelyn Roberts

I'VE GOTTA HORSE (1965, GB, Warner Brothers-Pathe)
Billy—Billy Fury
Director—Kenneth Hume
Leading Players—Amanda Barrie, Michael Medwin, Marjorie Rhodes

I'VE HEARD THE MERMAIDS SINGING (1987, Canada, Miramax)
Polly Vandersma—Sheila McCarthy
Director—Patricia Rozema
Leading Players—Paule Baillargeon, Ann-Marie McDonald, John Evans, Brenda Kamino

I'VE LIVED BEFORE (1956, Universal)
John Bolan—Jock Mahoney
Director—Richard Bartlett
Leading Players—Leigh Snowden, Ann Harding, John McIntire

THE ICE PIRATES (1984, MGM/UA)
Jason—Robert Urich
Director—Stewart Raffill
Leading Players—Mary Crosby, Michael D. Roberts, Anjelica Huston, John Matuszak

ICEMAN (1984, Universal)
Charlie—John Lone
Director—Fred Schepsi
Leading Players—Timothy Hutton, Lindsay Crouse, Josef Sommer

THE IDAHO KID (1937, Republic)
Idaho—Rex Bell
Director—Robert Hill
Leading Players—Marian Schilling, Dave Sharpe, Earl Dwire

IDEA GIRL (1946, Universal)
Pat O'Rourke—Julie Bishop
Director—Will Jason
Leading Players—Jess Barker, George Dolenz, Alan Mowbray

AN IDEAL HUSBAND (1948, GB, British Lion)
Sir Robert Chiltern—Hugh Williams
Director—Alexander Korda
Leading Players—Paulette Goddard, Michael Wilding, Diana Wynyard

IDENTITY UNKNOWN (1945, Republic)
Johnny March—Richard Arlen
Director—Walter Colmes
Leading Players—Cheryl Walker, Roger Pryor, Bobby Driscoll

IDIOT'S DELIGHT (1939, MGM)
Irene Fellara—Norma Shearer
Director—Clarence Brown
Leading Players—Clark Gable, Edward Arnold, Charles Coburn, Joseph Schildkraut, Burgess Meredith

THE IDLER (1915, Silent, Box Office Attractions)
Mark Cross—Charles Richman
Director—Lloyd B. Corrigan
Leading Players—Catherine Countiss, Walter Hitchcock, Stuart Holmes

THE IDOL (1966, GB, Embassy Pictures)
Marco—Michael Douglas
Director—Daniel Petrie
Leading Players—Jennifer Jones, John Leyton, Jennifer Hilary

THE IDOL DANCER (1920, Silent, First National)
Mary—Clarine Seymour
Director—D.W. Griffith

Leading Players—Richard Barthelemess, George McQuarrie, Creighton Hale, Kate Bruce

IDOL OF THE CROWDS (1937, Universal)
Johnny Hanson—John Wayne
Director—Arthur Lubin
Leading Players—Sheila Bromley, Charles Brokaw, Billy Burrud

THE IDOL OF THE NORTH (1921, Silent, Paramount)
Colette Brissac—Dorothy Dalton
Director—R. William Neill
Leading Players—Edwin August, E.J. Ratcliffe, Riley Hatch

IDOL OF PARIS (1948, GB, Warner Brothers)
Theresa—Beryl Baxter
Director—Leslie Arliss
Leading Players—Michael Rennie, Christine Norden, Miles Malleson

IDOL ON PARADE (1959, GB, Columbia)
Jeep Jackson—Anthony Newley
Director—John Gilling
Leading Players—William Bendix, Anne Aubrey, Lionel Jeffries

THE IDOLMAKER (1980, UA)
Vincent Vacarri—Ray Sharkey
Director—Taylor Hackford
Leading Players—Tovah Feldshuh, Peter Gallagher, Paul Land

IF A MAN ANSWERS (1962, Universal)
Eugene Wright—Bobby Darin
Director—Henry Levin
Leading Players—Sandra Dee, Micheline Presle, John Lund, Cesar Romero

IF I MARRY AGAIN (1925, Silent, First National)
Jocelyn Margot—Doris Kenyon
Director—John Francis Dillon
Leading Players—Lloyd Hughes, Frank Mayo, Hobarth Bosworth

IF I WERE BOSS (1933, GB, Columbia)
Steve—Bruce Seton
Director—Maclean Rogers
Leading Players—Googie Withers, Ian Fleming, Zillah Bateman

IF I WERE FREE (1933, RKO)
Sarah Cazenove—Irene Dunne
Gordon Evers—Clive Brook
Director—Elliot Nugent
Leading Players—Nils Asther, Henry Stephenson, Vivian Tobin

IF I WERE KING (1938, Paramount)
Francois Villon—Ronald Colman
Director—Frank Lloyd
Leading Players—Basil Rathbone, Frances Dee, Ellen Drew, Henry Wilcoxon, Stanley Ridges

IF I WERE QUEEN (1922, Silent, R-C Pictures)
Ruth Townley—Ethel Clayton
Director—Wesley Ruggles
Leading Players—Andree Lejon, Warner Baxter, Victory Bateman

IF I WERE SINGLE (1927, Silent, Warner Brothers)
May Howard—May McAvoy
Director—Roy Del Ruth

Leading Players—Conrad Nagel, Myrna Loy, Andre Beranger

IF I'M LUCKY (1946, 20th Century Fox)
Allen Clark—Perry Como
Director—Lewis Seiler
Leading Players—Vivian Blaine, Harry James, Carmen Miranda, Phil Silvers

"IF ONLY" JIM (1921, Silent, Universal)
Jim Golden—Harry Carey
Director—Jacques Jaccard
Leading Players—Carol Halloway, Ruth Royce, Duke Lee

IF YOU COULD ONLY COOK (1936, Columbia)
Jim Buchanan—Herbert Marshall
Joan Hawthorne—Jean Arthur
Director—William Seiter
Leading Players—Leo Carrillo, Lionel Stander, Alan Edwards

IF YOU COULD SEE WHAT I HEAR (1982, Cypress Grove)
Tom Sullivan—Marc Singer
Director—Eric Till
Leading Players—R.H. Thompson, Sarah Torgov, Shari Belafonte Harper, Douglas Campbell

IF YOU KNEW SUSIE (1948, RKO)
Susie Parker—Joan Davis
Director—Gordon M. Douglas
Leading Players—Eddie Cantor, Allyn Joslyn, Charles Dingle

THE ILLUSTRATED MAN (1969, Warner Brothers)
Carl—Rod Steiger
Director—Jack Smight
Leading Players—Claire Bloom, Robert Drivas, Don Dubbins

THE IMAGEMAKER (1986, Castle Hill)
Roger Blackwell—Michael Nouri
Director—Hal Weiner
Leading Players—Jerry Orbach, Anne Twomey, Jessica Harper, Farley Granger

IMITATION GENERAL (1958, MGM)
M/Sgt. Murphy Savage—Glenn Ford
Director—George Marshall
Leading Players—Red Buttons, Taina Elg, Dean Jones, Kent Smith

IMMEDIATE FAMILY (1989, Columbia)
Linda Spector—Glenn Close
Michael Spector—James Woods
Lucy Moore—Mary Stuart Masterson
Sam—Kevin Dillon
Director—Jonathan Kaplan
Leading Players—Linda Darlow, Jane Greer, Jessica James

IMMEDIATE LEE (1916, Silent, Mutual)
Immediate Lee—Frank Borzage
Director—Frank Borzage
Leading Players—Anna Little, Jack Richardson, William Stowell

THE IMMIGRANT (1915, Silent, Lasky)
Masha—Valeska Suratt
Director—George Melford
Leading Players—Theodore Roberts, Thomas Meighan, Jane Wolf

IMMORTAL GENTLEMAN (1935, GB, Equity Pictures)
William Shakespeare—Basil Gill
Director—Widgey R. Newman
Leading Players—Rosalinde Fuller, Dennis Hoey, Anne Bolt

THE IMMORTAL SERGEANT (1943, 20th Century Fox)
Sgt. Kelly—Thomas Mitchell
Director—John Stahl
Leading Players—Henry Fonda, Maureen O'Hara, Allyn Joslyn, Reginald Gardiner, Melville Cooper

IMPATIENT MAIDEN (1932, Universal)
Ruth Robbins—Mae Clarke
Director—James Whale
Leading Players—Lew Ayres, Una Merkel, John Halliday, Andy Devine

THE IMPERFECT LADY (1947, Paramount)
Millicent Hopkins—Teresa Wright
Director—Lewis Allen
Leading Players—Ray Milland, Cedric Hardwicke, Virginia Field, Anthony Quinn, Reginald Owen

IMPOSSIBLE CATHERINE (1919, Silent, Pearson Photoplays)
Catherine Kimberly—Virginia Pearson
Director—John P. O'Brien
Leading Players—J.H. Gilmour, William B. Davidson, Ed Roseman

THE IMPOSSIBLE MRS. BELLEW (1922, Silent, Paramount)
Betty Bellew—Gloria Swanson
Director—Sam Wood
Leading Players—Robert Cain, Conrad Nagel, Richard Wayne

THE IMPOSSIBLE WOMAN (1919, Silent, GB, Ideal)
Mme. Kraska—Constance Collier
Director—Meyrick Milton
Leading Players—Langhorne Burton, Christine Rayner, Alan Byrne

THE IMPOSTER (1915, Silent, World)
"Blink" Gregson—Alex B. Collins
Director—Albert Capellani
Leading Players—Jose Collins

THE IMPOSTER (1926, Silent, Gothic Productions)
Judith Gilbert (Canada Nell)—Evelyn Brent
Director—Chet Withey
Leading Players—Carroll Nye, James Morrison, Frank Leigh

THE IMPOSTER (1944, Universal)
Clement—Jean Gabin
Director—Julien Duvivier
Leading Players—Richard Whorf, Allyn Joslyn, Ellen Drew

THE IMPROPER DUCHESS (1936, GB, GFD)
Duchess of Tann—Yvonne Arnaud
Director—Harry Hughes
Leading Players—Hugh Wakefield, Wilfred Caithness, Arthur Finn

IN HOLLYWOOD WITH POTASH AND PERLMUTTER (1924, Silent, Goldwyn)
Morris Perlmutter—Alexander Carr

Abe Potash—George Sidney
Director—Alfred Green
Leading Players—Vera Gordon, Betty Blythe, Belle Bennett

IN LIKE FLINT (1967, 20th Century Fox)
Derek Flint—James Coburn
Director—Gordon Douglas
Leading Players—Lee J. Cobb, Jean Hale, Andrew Duggan

IN PURSUIT OF POLLY (1918, Silent, Paramount)
Polly Marasen—Billie Burke
Director—Chester Withey
Leading Players—Thomas Meighan, Frank Losee, A.J. Herbert

IN SEARCH OF GREGORY (1970, GB/Italy, Universal)
Gregory—Michael Sarrazin
Director—Peter Wood
Leading Players—Julie Christie, John Hurt, Adolfo Celi

IN SEARCH OF HISTORIC JESUS (1980, Sunn Classics)
Jesus—John Rubenstein
Director—Henning Schellerup
Leading Players—John Anderson, Nehemiah Persoff, Brad Crandall, Morgan Brittany

IN THE DAYS OF ST. PATRICK (1920, Silent, GB, Janion)
St. Patrick—Ian Allen
Director—Norman Whitten
Leading Players—Vernon Whitten, Alice Cardinall, Dermot McCarthy

IN THE HOLLOW OF HER HAND (1919, Silent, Select)
Hetty Castelton—Alice Brady
Director—Charles Bagigne
Leading Players—Myrtle Stedman, Mrs. Louise Clark, A.J. Herbert

IN THE MOOD (1987, Lorimar)
Ellsworth "Sonny" Wisecarver—Patrick Dempsey
Director—Phil Alden Robinson
Leading Players—Talia Balsam, Beverly D'Angelo, Michael Constantine, Betty Jinnette

IN THE PALACE OF THE KING (1915, Silent, Essanay)
King Philip II—E.J. Ratcliffe
Director—Fred E. Wright
Leading Players—Richard C. Travers, Arleen Hackett, Lewis Edgard

IN THE PALACE OF THE KING (1923, Silent, Goldwyn)
King Philip II—Sam De Grasse
Director—Emmett Flynn
Leading Players—Blanche Sweet, Edmund Lowe, Hobart Bosworth

IN TROUBLE WITH EVE (1964, GB, Mancunian)
Eve—Sally Smith
Director—Francis Searle
Leading Players—Robert Urquhart, Hy Hazell, Garry Marsh

INCENDIARY BLONDE (1945, Paramount)
Texas Guinan—Betty Hutton
Director—George Marshall
Leading Players—Arturo De Cordova, Charles Ruggles, Albert Dekker, Barry Fitzgerald

THE INCORRIGIBLE DUKANE (1915, Silent, Paramount)
James A. Dukane, Jr.—John Barrymore
Director—James Durkin
Leading Players—W.T. Carleton, Stuart Baird, Helen Weir

THE INCREDIBLE MELTING MAN (1978, American International)
The Melting Man—Alex Rebar
Director—William Sachs
Leading Players—Burr DeBenning, Myron Healey, Michael Aldredge, Ann Sweeney

THE INCREDIBLE MR. LIMPET (1964, Warner Brothers)
Henry Limpet—Don Knotts
Director—Arthur Lubin
Leading Players—Carole Cook, Jack Weston, Andrew Duggan

THE INCREDIBLE SARAH (1976, GB, Readers Digest Prod.)
Sarah Bernhardt—Glenda Jackson
Director—Richard Fleischer
Leading Players—Daniel Massey, Yvonne Mitchell, Douglas Wilmer, David Langton

THE INCREDIBLE SHRINKING MAN (1957, Universal)
Scott Carey—Grant Williams
Director—Jack Arnold
Leading Players—Randy Stuart, April Kent, Paul Langton

THE INCREDIBLE SHRINKING WOMAN (1981, Universal)
Pat Kramer—Lily Tomlin
Director—Joel Schumacher
Leading Players—Charles Grodin, Ned Beatty, Henry Gibson

INCUBUS (1966, Daystar)
Incubus—Milos Milos
Director—Leslie Stevens
Leading Players—William Shatner, Allyson Ames, Eloise Hardt

THE INCUBUS (1982, Canada, Film Ventures)
Incubus—Dirk McLean
Director—John Hough
Leading Players—John Cassavetes, Kerrie Keane, Helen Hughes

THE INDESTRUCTIBLE MAN (1956, Allied Artists)
The Butcher—Lon Chaney, Jr.
Director—Jack Pollexfen
Leading Players—Marian Carr, Robert Shayne, Ross Elliott

INDIAN AGENT (1948, RKO)
Dave—Tim Holt
Director—Lesley Selander
Leading Players—Noah Beery, Jr., Richard Martin, Nan Leslie

THE INDIAN FIGHTER (1955, UA)
Johnny Hawks—Kirk Douglas
Director—Andre de Toth
Leading Players—Elsa Martinelli, Walter Abel, Walter Matthau, Diana Douglas

INDIANA JONES AND THE LAST CRUSADE (1989, Paramount)
Indiana Jones—Harrison Ford
Young Indy Jones—River Phoenix
Director—Steven Spielberg
Leading Players—Sean Connery, Denholm Elliott, Alison Doody, John Rhys-Davies, Julian Grover

INDIANA JONES AND THE TEMPLE OF DOOM (1984, Paramount)
Indiana Jones—Harrison Ford
Director—Steven Spielberg
Leading Players—Kate Capshaw, Ke Huy Quan, Amrish Puri

INDISCREET CORRINE (1917, Silent, Triangle)
Corrine Chilvere—Olive Thomas
Director—Jack Dillon
Leading Players—George Chesbro, Joseph Bennett, Josie Sedgwick

INDISCRETION OF AN AMERICAN WIFE (1954, Columbia)
Mary Forbes—Jennifer Jones
Director—Vittorio De Sica
Leading Players—Montgomery Clift, Gino Cervi, Richard Beymer

INDISCRETIONS OF EVE (1932, GB, British International)
Eve—Steffi Duna
Director—Cecil Lewis
Leading Players—Fred Conyngham, Lester Matthews, Tony Simpson

INEZ FROM HOLLYWOOD (1924, Silent, First National)
Inez Laranetta—Anna Q. Nilsson
Director—Alfred E. Green
Leading Players—Lewis S. Stone, Mary Astor, Laurence Wheat

THE INFAMOUS MISS REVELL (1921, Silent, Metro)
Julien Revell/Paula Revell—Alice Lake
Director—Dallas M. Fitzgerald
Leading Players—Cullen Landis, Jackie Saunders, Lydia Knott

THE INFIDEL (1922, Silent, Preferred Pictures)
Lola Daintry—Katherine MacDonald
Director—James Young
Leading Players—Robert Ellis, Joseph Dowling, Boris Karloff

THE INFORMER (1929, GB, British International)
Gypo Nolan—Lars Hansen
Director—Arthur Robison
Leading Players—Lya de Putti, Warwick Ward, Carl Harbord

THE INFORMER (1935, RKO)
Gypo Nolan—Victor McLaglen
Director—John Ford
Leading Players—Heather Angel, Preston Foster, Margot Grahame, Wallace Ford, Una O'Connor

THE IN-LAWS (1979, Warner Brothers)
Vince Ricardo—Peter Falk
Sheldon Kornpett—Alan Arkin
Director—Arthur Hiller
Leading Players—Richard Libertini, Nancy Dussault, Penny Peyser, Arlene Golonka

THE INNER MAN (1922, Silent, Playgoers)
Thurlow Michael Barclay, Jr.—Wyndham Standing
Director—Hamilton Smith
Leading Players—J. Barcaly Sherry, Louis Pierce, Leslie Hunt, Dorothy Mackaill

THE INNOCENCE OF RUTH (1916, Silent, Edison)
Ruth Travers—Viola Dana
Director—John H. Collins
Leading Players—Edward Earle, Augustus Phillips, L. Davril

THE INNOCENT CHEAT (1921, Silent, Arrow Film)
Mary Stanhope—Kathleen Kirkham
Director—Ben Wilson
Leading Players—Roy Stewart, Sidney De Gary, George Hernandez

AN INNOCENT MAGDALENE (1916, Silent, Triangle)
Dorothy Raleigh—Lillian Gish
Director—Allan Dwan
Leading Players—Spottiswoode Aitken, Sam De Grasse, Mary Alden

AN INNOCENT MAN (1989, Buena Vista)
Jimmie Rainwood—Tom Selleck
Director—Peter Yates
Leading Players—F. Murray Abraham, Laila Robbins, David Rasche, Richard Young

THE INNOCENT SINNER (1917, Silent, Fox Film Corp.)
Mary Ellen Ellis—Miriam Cooper
Director—R.A. Walsh
Leading Players—Charles Clary, Jack Standing, Jane Novak

THE INNOCENTS (1961, U.S./GB, 20th Century Fox)
Miles—Martin Stevens
Flora—Pamela Franklin
Director—Jack Clayton
Leading Players—Deborah Kerr, Michael Redgrave, Peter Wyngarde, Megs Jenkins

INNOCENT'S PROGRESS (1918, Silent, Mutual)
Tessa Fayne—Pauline Starke
Director—Frank Borzage
Leading Players—Lillian West, Alice Knowland, Jack Livingston

INSIDE DAISY CLOVER (1965, Warner Brothers)
Daisy Clover—Natalie Wood
Director—Robert Mulligan
Leading Players—Christopher Plummer, Robert Redford, Roddy McDowall, Ruth Gordon

AN INSPECTOR CALLS (1954, GB, British Lion)
Inspector Poole—Alastair Sim
Director—Guy Hamilton
Leading Players—Arthur Young, Olga Lindo, Eileen Moore

INSPECTOR CLOUSEAU (1968, GB, UA)
Inspector Jacques Clouseau—Alan Arkin
Director—Bud Yorkin
Leading Players—Delia Boccardo, Frank Finlay, Patrick Cargill, Beryl Reid

THE INSPECTOR GENERAL (1949, Warner Brothers)
Georgi—Danny Kaye
Director—Henry Koster
Leading Players—Walter Slezak, Barbara Bates, Elsa Lanchester, Gene Lockhart, Alan Hale

INSPECTOR HORNLEIGH (1939, GB, 20th Century Fox)
Inspector Hornleigh—Gordon Harker
Director—Eugene Forde

Leading Players—Alastair Sim, Miki Hood, Wally Patch

INSPECTOR HORNLEIGH ON VACATION (1939, GB, 20th Century Fox)
  Inspector Hornleigh—Gordon Harker
  Director—Walter Forde
  Leading Players—Alastair Sim, Linden Travers, Wally Patch

INSURANCE INVESTIGATOR (1951, Republic)
  Tom Davison—Richard Denning
  Director—George Blair
  Leading Players—Audrey Long, John Eldredge, Hillary Brooke

THE INTERFERIN' GENT (1927, Silent, Pathe Exchange)
  Bill Stannard—Buffalo Bill, Jr.
  Director—Richard Thorpe
  Leading Players—Olive Hasbrouck, Al Taylor, Harry Todd

THE INTERLOPER (1918, Silent, World)
  Paul Whitney—Irving Cummings
  Director—Oscar Apfel
  Leading Players—Kitty Gordon, Warren Cook, Isabelle Berwin

INTERNATIONAL LADY (1941, UA)
  Carla Nillson—Ilona Massey
  Director—Tim Whelan
  Leading Players—George Brent, Basil Rathbone, Gene Lockhart, George Zucco

INTERNES CAN'T TAKE MONEY (1937, Paramount)
  Jimmie Kildare—Joel McCrea
  Director—Alfred Santell
  Leading Players—Barbara Stanwyck, Lloyd Nolan, Stanley Ridges, Lee Bowman

INTO HER KINGDOM (1926, Silent, First National)
  Grand Duchess Tatiana—Corinne Griffith
  Director—Svend Gade
  Leading Players—Einar Hanson, Claud Gillingwater, Charles Crockett

INTRODUCE ME (1925, Silent, Associated Exhibitors)
  Jimmy Clark—Douglas MacLean
  Director—George J. Crone
  Leading Players—Robert Ober, E. J. Ratcliffe, Anne Cornwall

THE INTRUDER (1962, Pathe-America)
  Adam Cramer—William Shatner
  Director—Roger Corman
  Leading Players—Frank Maxwell, Beverly Lunsford, Robert Emhardt, Jeanne Cooper

INTRUDER IN THE DUST (1949, MGM)
  Lucas Beauchamp—Juano Hernandez
  Director—Clarence Brown
  Leading Players- David Brian, Claude Jarman, Jr., Porter Hall, Elizabeth Patterson, Will Geer

INVISIBLE AGENT (1942, Universal)
  Frank Raymond—Jon Hall
  Director—Edwin L. Marin
  Leading Players—Ilona Massey, Peter Lorre, Cedric Hardwicke, J. Edward Bromberg, Albert Basserman

THE INVISIBLE AVENGER (1958, Republic)
  Lamont Cranston- The Shadow—Richard Derr

Director—James Wong Howe
  Leading Players—Mark Daniels, Helen Wescott, Jeanne Neher

THE INVISIBLE BOY (1957, MGM)
  Timmie Merrinoe—Richard Eyer
  Director—Herman Hoffman
  Leading Players—Philip Abbott, Diane Brewster, Harold J. Stone, Robert H. Harris

THE INVISIBLE KID (1988, Columbia)
  Grover Dunn—Jay Underwood
  Director—Avery Crounse
  Leading Players—Wally Ward, Chynna Phillips, Karen Black, Nicholas De Toth

THE INVISIBLE MAN (1933, Universal)
  Jack Griffin—Claude Rains
  Director—James Whale
  Leading Players—Gloria Stuart, William Harrigan, Henry Travers, Una O'Connor

THE INVISIBLE MANIAC (1990, Tri-Star/Carolco)
  Jacob Singer—Tim Robbins
  Director—Rif Coogan
  Leading Players—Shannon Wilsey, Melissa Moore, Robert R. Ross, Jr.

THE INVISIBLE MAN RETURNS (1940, Universal)
  Geoffrey Radcliffe—Vincent Price
  Director—Joe May
  Leading Players—Cedric Hardwicke, Nan Grey, John Sutton, Cecil Kellaway

INVISIBLE MAN'S REVENGE (1944, Universal)
  Robert Griffin—Jon Hall
  Director—Ford Beebe
  Leading Players—Alan Curtis, Evelyn Ankers, Leon Errol, John Carradine

THE INVISIBLE WOMAN (1941, Universal)
  Kitty Carroll—Virginia Bruce
  Director—A. Edward Sutherland
  Leading Players—John Barrymore, John Howard, Charles Ruggles, Oscar Homolka

INVITATION TO A GUNFIGHTER (1964, UA)
  Jules Gaspard D'Estaing—Yul Brynner
  Director—Richard Wilson
  Leading Players—Janice Rule, Brad Dexter, Alfred Ryder, George Segal, Pat Hingle

IRENE (1926, Silent, First National)
  Irene O'Dare—Colleen Moore
  Director—Alfred E. Green
  Leading Players—Lloyd Hughes, George K. Arthur, Charles Murray

IRENE (1940, RKO)
  Irene O'Dare—Anna Neagle
  Director—Herbert Wilcox
  Leading Players—Ray Milland, Roland Young, Alan Marshal, May Robson, Billie Burke

IRIS (1915, Silent, GB, Ideal)
  Iris—Alma Taylor
  Director—Cecil P. Hepworth

Leading Players—Henry Ainley, Stewart Rome

IRISH AND PROUD OF IT (1938, Ireland, Crusade)
Donogh O'Connor—Richard Hayward
Director—Donovan Pedelty
Leading Players—Dinah Sheridan, Gwenillian Gill, George Pembroke

THE IRISHMAN (1978, Australia, Greater Union)
Paddy Doolan—Michael Craig
Director—Donald Crombie
Leading Players—Simon Burke, Robin Nevin, Lou Brown

IRMA LA DOUCE (1963, UA)
Irma La Douce—Shirley Maclaine
Director—Billy Wilder
Leading Players—Jack Lemmon, Lou Jacobi, Bruce Yarnell, Herschel Bernardi

THE IRON DUKE (1935, GB, Gaumont)
Duke of Wellington—George Arliss
Director—Victor Saville
Leading Players—Gladys Cooper, Emlyn Williams, Ellaline Terriss, A.E. Matthews

IRON EAGLE (1986, Tri-Star)
Doug—Jason Gedrick
Director—Sidney J. Furie
Leading Players—Lou Gossett, Jr., David Suchet, Tim Thompson

THE IRON MAJOR (1943, RKO)
Frank Cavanaugh—Pat O'Brien
Director—Ray Enright
Leading Players—Ruth Warrick, Robert Ryan, Leon Ames, Russell Wade, Bruce Edwards

THE IRON MAN (1925, Silent, Chadwick)
Philip Durban—Lionel Barrymore
Director—William Bennett
Leading Players—Mildred Harris, Winifred Barry, Dorothy Kingdon

THE IRON MAN (1931, Universal)
Kid Mason—Lew Ayres
Director—Tod Browning
Leading Players—Robert Armstrong, Jean Harlow, John Miljan

THE IRON MAN (1951, Universal)
Coke Mason—Jeff Chandler
Director—Joseph Pevney
Leading Players—Evelyn Keyes, Stephen McNally, Joyce Holden

THE IRON MASTER (1933, Allied Artists)
Steve Mason—Reginald Denny
Director—Chester M. Franklin
Leading Players—Lila Lee, J. Farrell McDonald, Esther Howard

THE IRON SHERIFF (1957, UA)
Sheriff Galt—Sterling Hayden
Director—Sidney Salkow
Leading Players—Constance Ford, John Dehner, Kent Taylor

THE IRON WOMAN (1916, Silent, Metro)
Sarah Maitland—Nance O'Neil

Director—Carl Harbaugh
Leading Players—Einar Linden, Alfred Hickman, Evelyn Brent

IRRECONCILABLE DIFFERENCES (1984, Warner Brothers)
Albert Brodsky—Ryan O'Neal
Lucy Van Patten Brodsky—Shelley Long
Casey Brodsky—Drew Barrymore
Director—Charles Shyer
Leading Players—Sam Wannamaker, Allen Garfield, Sharon Stone

THE IRRESISTABLE LOVER (1927, Silent, Universal)
J. Harrison Gray—Norman Kerry
Director—William Beaudine
Leading Players—Lois Moran, Gertrude Astor, Lee Moran

ISABEL (1968, Canada, Paramount)
Isabel—Genevieve Bujold
Director—Paul Almond
Leading Players—Mark Strange, Gerald Parkes, Therese Cadorette

ISADORA (1968, GB, Universal)
Isadora Duncan—Vanessa Redgrave
Director—Karel Reisz
Leading Players—James Fox, Jason Robards, Ivan Tchenko

THE ISLAND OF DR. MOREAU (1977, American International)
Dr. Moreau—Burt Lancaster
Director—Don Taylor
Leading Players—Michael York, Nigel Davenport, Barbara Carrera, Richard Basehart

ISOBEL (1920, Silent, Davis)
Isobel Deane—Jane Novak
Director—Edwin Carewe
Leading Players—House Peters, Edward J. Pell, Tom Wilson

ISSAC LITTLEFEATHERS (1984, Canada, Cinema Concepts/Lauron)
Issac Littlefeathers—William Korbut
Director—Les Rose
Leading Players—Lou Jacobi, Scott Hylands, Lorrain Behnan

IT! (1967, GB, Warner Brothers)
The Golem—Alan Sellers
Director—Herbert J. Leder
Leading Players—Roddy McDowall, Jill Haworth, Paul Maxwell

IT CONQUERED THE WORLD (1956, American International)
Visitor from Venus—Paul Blaisdell
Director—Roger Corman
Leading Players—Peter Graves, Beverly Garland, Lee Van Cleef

IT HAPPENED TO JANE (1959, Columbia)
Jane Osgood—Doris Day
Director—Richard Quine
Leading Players—Jack Lemmon, Ernie Kovacs, Steve Forrest

IT TAKES A THIEF (1960, GB, Alliance)
Billy Lacrosse—Jayne Mansfield
Director—John Gilling
Leading Players—Anthony Quayle, Carl Mohner, Peter Reynolds

IT! THE TERROR FROM BEYOND SPACE (1958, UA)
"It"—Ray "Crash" Corrigan

Director—Edward L. Cahn
Leading Players—Marshall Thompson, Shawn Smith, Kim Spalding

THE ITALIAN (1915, Silent, New York Motion Picture)
The Italian (Beppo Donnetti)—George Beban
Director—Reginald Barker
Leading Players—Clara Williams, Fanny Midgley, J. Frank Burke

IT'S A COP (1934, GB, Britain & Dominions)
Constable Robert Spry—Sydney Howard
Director—Maclean Rogers
Leading Players—Dorothy "Chili" Bouchier, Donald Calthrop, Garry Marsh

IT'S A WISE CHILD (1931, MGM)
Joyce—Marion Davies
Director—Robert Z. Leonard
Leading Players—Sidney Blackmer, James Gleason, Polly Moran

IT'S LOVE I'M AFTER (1937, Warner Brothers/First National)
Joyce Arden—Bette Davis
Director—Archie Mayo
Leading Players—Leslie Howard, Olivia de Havilland, Eric Blore, Patric Knowles

IT'S MY TURN (1980, Columbia)
Kate Gunzinger—Jill Clayburgh
Director—Claudia Weill
Leading Players—Michael Douglas, Charles Grodin, Beverly Garland, Steven Hill

IT'S THAT MAN AGAIN (1943, GB, Gainsborough)
Mayor Handley—Tommy Handley
Director—Walter Forde
Leading Players—Greta Gynt, Jack Train, Sidney Keith

IT'S TOUGH TO BE FAMOUS (1932, First National/Warner Brothers)
Scotty McClenahan—Douglas Fairbanks, Jr.
Director—Alfred E. Green
Leading Players—Mary Brian, Oscar Apfel, Emma Dunn

IVANHOE (1913, Silent, Imperator)
Ivanhoe—King Baggot
Director—Herbert Brenon
Leading Players—Leah Baird, Arthur Scott-Cravan, Wallace Bosco

IVANHOE (1952, GB, MGM)
Ivanhoe—Robert Taylor
Director—Richard Thorpe
Leading Players—Elizabeth Taylor, Joan Fontaine, George Sanders, Emlyn Williams, Robert Douglas

IVORY HUNTER (1952, GB, Ealing)
Mannering—Harold Warrender
Director—Harry Watt
Leading Players—Anthony Steel, Dinah Sheridan, Meredith Edwards

IVY (1947, Universal)
Ivy—Joan Fontaine

Director—Sam Wood
Leading Players—Patric Knowles, Herbert Marshall, Richard Ney, Cedric Hardwicke

J

J.D.'S REVENGE (1976, American International)
J.D. Walker—David McKnight
Director—Arthur Marks
Leading Players—Glynn Turman, Joan Pringle, Lou Gossett, Jr.

J.W. COOP (1971, Columbia)
J.W. Coop—Cliff Robertson
Director—Cliff Robertson
Leading Players—Geraldine Page, Christina Ferrare, R.G. Armstrong

JACK AHOY (1935, GB, Gaumont)
Jack Ponsonby—Jack Hulbert
Director—Walter Forde
Leading Players—Nancy O'Neill, Alfred Drayton, Tamara Desni

JACK AND JILL (1917, Silent, Paramount)
Jack Ranney—Jack Pickford
Mary Dwyer (Jill)—Louise Huff
Director—William Desmond Taylor
Leading Players—Leo Houck, Don Bailey, J.H. Holland

JACK AND THE BEANSTALK (1917, Silent, Fox Film Corp.)
Jack—Francis Carpenter
Directors—C.M. & S.A. Franklin
Leading Players—Virginia Lee Corbin, Violet Radcliffe, Vera Lewis

JACK AND THE BEANSTALK (1952, Warner Brothers)
Jack—Lou Costello
Director—Jean Yarborough
Leading Players—Bud Abbott, Buddy Baer, Dorothy Ford

THE JACK KNIFE MAN (1920, Silent, First National)
Peter Lane—Fred Turner
Director—King Vidor
Leading Players—Harry Todd, Bobby Kelso, Willis Marks

JACK LONDON (1943, UA)
Jack London—Michael O'Shea
Director—Alfred Santell
Leading Players—Susan Hayward, Osa Massen, Harry Davenport, Frank Craven

JACK MCCALL, DESPERADO (1953, Columbia)
Jack McCall—George Montgomery
Director—Sidney Salkow
Leading Players—Angela Stevens, Douglas Kennedy, James Seary

JACK O' CLUBS (1924, Silent, Universal)
John Francis Foley—Herbert Rawlinson
Director—Robert F. Hill

Leading Players—Ruth Dwyer, Eddie Gribbon, Esther Ralston

JACK OF DIAMONDS (1967, MGM)
Jeff Hill—George Hamilton
Director—Don Taylor
Leading Players—Joseph Cotten, Marie Laforet, Maurice Evans

JACK O'HEARTS (1926, Silent, Hartford Productions)
Jack Farber—Cullen Landis
Director—David Hartford
Leading Players—Gladys Hulette, Bert Cummings, Antrim Short

THE JACK RIDER (1921, Silent, Aywon)
Frank Stevens—Guinn "Big Boy" Williams
Director—Charles R. Seeling
Leading Players—Thelma Worth, S.D. Wilcox, J. Buckley Russell

JACK, SAM AND PETE (1919, Silent GB, Pollock-Daring)
Jack—Percy Moran
Sam—Eddie Willey
Pete—Ernest A. Trimingham
Director—Jack Daring (Percy Moran)
Leading Players—Manning Haynes, Enid Heather, Capt. Jack Kelly

JACK SLADE (1953, Allied Artists)
Jack Slade—Mark Stevens
Director—Harold Schuster
Leading Players—Dorothy Malone, Barton MacLane, John Litel

JACK SPURLOCK, PRODIGAL (1918, Silent, Fox Film Corp.)
Jack Spurlock—George Walsh
Director—Carl Harbaugh
Leading Players—Dan Mason, Ruth Taylor, Robert Vivian

JACK STRAW (1920, Silent, Paramount)
Archduke Sebastain (Jack Straw)—Robert Warwick
Director—William C. De Mille
Leading Players—Helene Sullivan, Charles Ogle, Sylvia Ashton

JACK TAR (1915, Silent, GB, Barker)
Lt. Jack Atherley—Jack Tessier
Director—Bert Haldane
Leading Players—Edith Yates, Eve Balfour, Thomas H. MacDonald

JACK THE GIANT KILLER (1962, UA)
Jack—Kerwin Mathews
Director—Nathan Juran
Leading Players—Judi Meredith, Torin Thatcher, Walter Burke

JACK THE RIPPER (1959, GB, Paramount)
Dr. Tranter—John Le Mesurier
Director—Robert S. Baker
Leading Players—Lee Patterson, Eddie Byrne, Betty McDowall

JACKIE (1921, Silent, Fox Film Corp.)
Jackie—Shirley Mason
Director—Jack Ford
Leading Players—William Scott, Harry Carter, George Stone

THE JACKIE ROBINSON STORY (1950, Eagle Lion)
Jackie Robinson—Jackie Robinson
Director—Alfred E. Green
Leading Players—Ruby Dee, Minor Watson, Louise Beavers, Richard Lane

JACKNIFE (1989, Cineplex Odeon)
Joseph 'Megs' Megessey—Robert De Niro
Director—David Jones
Leading Players—Ed Harris, Kathy Baker, Charles Dutton

JACK'S BACK (1988, Palisades)
John Wesford—James Spader
Director—Rowdy Herrington
Leading Players—Cynthia Gibb, Rod Loomis, Rex Ryon

JACOB'S LADDER (1990, Tri-Star/Carolco)
Jacob Singer—Tim Robbins
Director—Adrian Lyne
Leading Players—Elizabeth Pena, Danny Aiello, Matt Craven, Pruitt Taylor Vince, Jason Alexander

JACOB TWO-TWO MEETS THE HOODED FANG (1979, Canada, Gulkin)
Jacob Two-Two—Stephen Rosenberg
The Hooded Fang—Alex Karras
Director—Theodore J. Flicker
Leading Players—Guy L'Ecuyer, Joy Coghill, Earl Pennington

JACQUELINE (1956, GB, Rank)
Jacqueline McNeil—Jacqueline Ryan
Director—Roy Barker
Leading Players—John Gregson, Kathleen Ryan, Noel Purcell

JACQUELINE, OR BLAZING SADDLES (1923, Silent, Arrow)
Jacqueline Roland—Marguerite Courtot
Director—Dell Henderson
Leading Players—Helen Rowland, Gus Weinberg, Effie Shannon, Lew Cody

JACQUES BREL IS ALIVE AND WELL AND LIVING IN PARIS (1979, Am. Film)
Jacques Brel—Jacques Brel
Director—Denis Heroux
Leading Players—Elly Stone, Mort Shuman, Joe Masiell

JACQUES OF THE SILVER NORTH (1919, Silent, Select)
Jacques La Rouge—Mitchell Lewis
Director—Norval MacGregor
Leading Players—Fritzi Brunette, C.A. Van Auker, Murdock MacQuarrie

JAFFERY (1916, Silent, Frohman Amusement Corp.)
Jaffery—C. Aubrey Smith
Director—George Irving
Leading Players—Eleanor Woodruff, Florence Deehon, Doris Sawyer

JAGUAR LIVES (1979, American International)
Jaguar—Joe Lewis
Director—Ernest Pintoff
Leading Players—Christopher Lee, Donald Pleasance, Barbara Bach, Capucine, Joseph Wiseman

THE JAILBIRD (1920, Silent, Paramount)
Shakespeare Clancy—Douglas MacLean
Director—Lloyd Ingraham
Leading Players—Doris May, Lew Morrison, William Courtright

JAILBIRDS (1939, GB, Butchers Film Service)
Bill Smith—Albert Burdon
Nick—Charles Hawtrey

Director—Oswald Mitchell
Leading Players—Shaun Glenville, Charles Farrell, Lorraine Clewes

JAKE SPEED (1986, New World)
Jake Speed—Wayne Crawford
Director—Andrew Lane
Leading Players—Dennis Christopher, Karen Kopins, John Hurt

JAKE THE PLUMBER (1927, Silent, R-C Pictures)
Jake—Jess Devorska
Director—Edward I. Luddy
Leading Players—Sharon Lynn, Ross Rosanova, Ann Brody

JAN OF THE BIG SNOWS (1922, Silent, American Releasing Corp.)
Jan Allaire—Warner Richmond
Director—Charles M. Seay
Leading Players—Louise Prussing, William Peavy, Baby Eastman

JANE EYRE (1921, Silent, W.W. Hodkinson)
Jane Eyre—Mabel Ballin
Director—Hugo Ballin
Leading Players—Norman Trevor, Crauford Kent, Emily Fitzroy

JANE EYRE (1935, Monogram)
Jane Eyre—Virginia Bruce
Young Jane—Jean Darling
Director—Christy Cabanne
Leading Players—Colin Clive, Beryl Mercer, Jameson Thomas

JANE EYRE (1944, 20th Century Fox)
Jane Eyre—Joan Fontaine
Jane Eyre as a child—Peggy Ann Garner
Director—Robert Stevenson
Leading Players—Orson Welles, Margaret O'Brien, John Sutton, Sara Allgood, Henry Daniell, Agnes Moorehead

JANE EYRE (1971, GB, British Lion)
Jane Eyre—Susannah York
Young Jane—Sarah Gibson
Director—Delbert Mann
Leading Players—George C. Scott, Ian Bannen, Jack Hawkins, Nyree Dawn Porter, Rachel Kempson

JANE GOES A'WOOING (1919, Silent, Paramount)
Jane Neill—Vivian Martin
Director—George Melford
Leading Players—Niles Welch, Casson Ferguson, Spottiswoode Aitken

JANE STEPS OUT (1938, GB, Associated British)
Jane Wilton—Diana Churchill
Director—Paul L. Stein
Leading Players—Jean Muir, Peter Murray Hill, Fred Emery

JANICE MEREDITH (1924, Silent, Metro)
Janice Meredith—Marion Davies
Director—E. Mason Hopper
Leading Players—Holbrook Blinn, Harrison Ford, Maclyn Arbuckle

JANIE (1944, Warner Brothers)
Janie Conway—Joyce Reynolds
Director—Michael Curtiz

Leading Players—Robert Hutton, Edward Arnold, Ann Harding, Robert Benchley, Alan Hale

JANIE GETS MARRIED (1946, Warner Brothers)
Janie Conway—Joan Leslie
Director—Vincent Sherman
Leading Players—Robert Hutton, Edward Arnold, Ann Harding, Robert Benchley, Dorothy Malone

THE JANUARY MAN (1989, MGM-UA)
Nick Starkey—Kevin Kline
Director—Pat O'Connor
Leading Players—Susan Sarandon, Mary Elizabeth Mastrantonio, Harvey Keitel, Danny Aiello, Rod Steiger

A JAPANESE NIGHTINGALE (1918, Silent, Pathe)
Yuki—Fannie Ward
Director—George Fitzmaurice
Leading Players—W. E. Lawrence, Yukio Aoyama

JAPANESE WAR BRIDE (1952, 20th Century Fox)
Tae Shimizu—Shirley Yamaguchi
Director—King Vidor
Leading Players—Don Taylor, Cameron Mitchell, Marie Windsor

JASON AND THE ARGONAUTS (1963, Great Briatin, Columbia)
Jason—Todd Armstrong
Director—Don Chaffey
Leading Players—Nancy Kovack, Gary Raymond, Laurence Naismith, Niall MacGinnis

JASSY (1948, GB, Gainsborough)
Jassy Woodroffe—Margaret Lockwood
Director—Bernard Knowles
Leading Players—Patricia Roc, Dennis Price, Dermot Walsh

JAZZ BABIES (1932, Peerless)
Clarissa—Madge Evans
Babs—Elizabeth Patterson
Ellie—Marjorie Gateson
Director—Alexander Hall
Leading Players—Harvey Stephens, Hobart Bosworth, Lucien Littlefield

JAZZ CINDERELLA (1930, Chesterfield)
Patricia Murray—Nancy Welford
Director—Scott Pembroke
Leading Players—Myrna Loy, Jason Robards, Sr., Dorothy Phillips

THE JAZZ GIRL (1926, Silent, Motion Picture Guild)
Janet Marsh—Edith Roberts
Director—Howard Mitchell
Leading Players—Gaston Glass, Murdock MacQuarrie, Coit Albertson

THE JAZZ SINGER (1927, Part-Talkie, Warner Brothers)
Jack Robin (Jakie Rabinowitz)—Al Jolson
Director—Alan Crosland
Leading Players—May McAvoy, Warner Oland, Eugenie Besserer, Bobby Gordon, Otto Lederer

THE JAZZ SINGER (1953, Warner Brothers)
Jerry Golding—Danny Thomas
Director—Michael Curtiz

Leading Players—Peggy Lee, Mildred Dunnock, Eduard Franz, Tom Tully

THE JAZZ SINGER (1980, Associated Film/EMI)
Jess Robin—Neil Diamond
Director—Richard Fleischer
Leading Players—Laurence Olivier, Lucie Arnaz, Catlin Adams, Franklin Ajaye

JEANNE EAGELS (1957, Columbia)
Jeanne Eagels—Kim Novak
Director—George Sidney
Leading Players—Jeff Chandler, Agnes Moorehead, Charles Drake, Larry Gates, Virginia Grey

JEDDA, THE UNCIVILIZED (1956, Australia, Distributors Corp. of Am.)
Jedda—Narla Kunogh
Director—Charles Chauvel
Leading Players—Robert Tudewali, Betty Suttor, Paul Reynall

JEKYLL AND HYDE . . . TOGETHER AGAIN (1982, Paramount)
Dr. Jekyll—Mark Blankfield
Mr. Hyde—Mark Blankfield
Director—Jerry Belson
Leading Players—Bess Armstrong, Krista Erickson, Tim Thomerson

JENIFER HALE (1937, GB, 20th Century Fox)
Jenifer Hale—Rene Ray
Director—Bernard Mainwaring
Leading Players—Ballard Berkeley, John Longden, Paul Burke

JENNIE (1941, 20th Century Fox)
Jennie—Virginia Gilmore
Director—David Burton
Leading Players—William Henry, George Montgomery, Ludwig Stossel

JENNIE GERHARDT (1933, Paramount)
Jennie Gerhardt—Sylvia Sidney
Director—Marion Gering
Leading Players—Donald Cook, Mary Astor, Edward Arnold

JENNIFER (1978, American International)
Jennifer Baylor—Lisa Pelikan
Director—Brice Mack
Leading Players—Bert Convy, Nina Foch, Amy Johnson, John Gavin, Jeff Corey

JENNIFER ON MY MIND (1971, UA)
Jenny—Tippy Walker
Director—Noel Black
Leading Players—Michael Brandon, Lou Gilbert, Steve Vinovich

JENNY (1969, ABC-PAlomar)
Jenny Marsh—Marlo Thomas
Director—George Bloomfield
Leading Players—Alan Alda, Marian Hailey, Elizabeth Wilson

JENNY BE GOOD (1920, Silent, Realart)
Jenny Riano—Mary Miles Minter
Director—William Desmond Taylor
Leading Players—Jay Belasco, Margaret Shelby, Frederick Stanton

JEREMIAH JOHNSON (1972, Warner Brothers)
Jeremiah Johnson—Robert Redford
Director—Sydney Pollack
Leading Players—Will Geer, Stefan Gierasch, Allyn Ann McLerie

JEREMY (1973, UA)
Jeremy Jones—Robby Benson
Director—Arthur Barron
Leading Players—Glynnis O'Connor, Len Bari, Leonardo Cimino

THE JERK (1979, Universal)
Navin Johnson—Steve Martin
Director—Carl Reiner
Leading Players—Bernadette Peters, Catlin Adams, Mabel King

JESSE JAMES (1927, Silent, Paramount)
Jesse James—Fred Thomson
Director—Lloyd Ingraham
Leading Players—Nora Lane, Montagu Love, Mary Carr, James Pierce, Harry Woods

JESSE JAMES (1939, 20th Century Fox)
Jesse James—Tyrone Power
Director—Henry King
Leading Players—Henry Fonda, Nancy Kelly, Randolph Scott, Henry Hull, Brian Donlevy, John Carradine

JESSE JAMES AS THE OUTLAW (1921, Silent, Mesco Pictures)
Jesse James—Jesse James, Jr.
Director—Franklin B. Coates
Leading Players—Diana Reed, Marguerite Hungerford

JESSE JAMES AT BAY (1941, Republic)
Jesse James—Roy Rogers
Director—Joseph Kane
Leading Players- George "Gabby" Hayes, Sally Payne, Pierre Watkin

JESSE JAMES MEETS FRANKENSTEIN'S DAUGHTER (1966, Embassy)
Jesse James—John Lupton
Maria Frankenstein—Narda Onyx
Director—William Beaudine
Leding Players—Cal Bolder, Steven Geray, Felipe Turich

JESSE JAMES UNDER THE BLACK FLAG (1921, Silent, Mesco Pictures)
Jesse James—Jesse James, Jr.
Director—Franklin B. Coates
Leading Players—Diana Reed, Marguerite Hungerford, Franklin B. Coates

JESSCIA (1962, UA)
Jessica—Angie Dickinson
Director—Jean Negulesco
Leading Players—Maurice Chevalier, Noel Noel, Gabriele Ferzetti, Agnes Moorehead

JESUS (1979, Warner Brothers)
Jesus—Brian Deacon
Director—Peter Sykes
Leading Players—Rivka Noiman, Yossef Shiloah, Niko Nitai

JESUS CHRIST, SUPERSTAR (1973, Universal)
Jesus Christ—Ted Neeley

Director—Norman Jewison
Leading Players—Carl Anderson, Yvonne Elliman, Barry Dennen, Bob Bingham

JESUS OF NAZARETH (1928, Silent, Ideal Pictures)
Jesus Christ—Philip Van Loan
Director—Jean Conover
Leading Players—Anna Lehr, Charles McCaffrey

JET PILOT (1957, RKO/Universal)
Anna—Janet Leigh
Director—Josef von Sternberg
Leading Players—John Wayne, Jay C. Flippen, Paul Fix

THE JEWEL OF THE NILE (1985, 20th Century Fox)
Holy Man-"Joe"—Avner Eisenberg
Director—Lewis Teague
Leading Players—Michael Douglas, Kathleen Turner, Danny DeVito, Spiros Focas

JEZEBEL (1938, Warner Brothers)
Julie Morrison—Bette Davis
Director—William Wyler
Leading Players—Henry Fonda, George Brent, Margaret Lindsay, Fay Bainter, Richard Cromwell, Donald Crisp

JEZEBEL'S KISS (1990, Glickenhaus/Film Warriorrs)
Jezebel—Katherine Barrese
Director—Harvey Keith
Leading Players—Malcolm McDowell, Meredith Baxter-Birney, Meg Foster, Everett McGill

JIGGS AND MAGGIE IN SOCIETY (1948, Monogram)
Jiggs—Joe Yule
Maggie—Reno Riano
Director—Eddie Cline
Leading Players—Dale Carnegie, Arthur Murray, Sheliah Graham, Tim Ryan

JIGGS AND MAGGIE OUT WEST (1950, Monogram)
Jiggs—Joe Yule
Maggie—Reno Riano
Director—William Beaudine
Leading Players—George McManus, Tim Ryan, Jim Bannon

THE JIGSAW MAN (1984, GB, United Film)
Sir Philip Kimberly—Michael Caine
Director—Terence Young
Leading Players—Laurence Olivier, Susan George, Robert Powell

JIM BLUDSO (1917, Silent, Triangle)
Jim Bludso—Wilfred Lucas
Director—Tod Browning
Leading Players—Olga Grey, George Stone, Charles Lee

JIM GRIMSBY'S BOY (1916, Silent, Ince)
Jim Grimsby—Frank Keenan
"Bill" Grimsby—Enid Markey
Director—Reginald Barker
Leading Players—Robert McKim, Fanny Midgley, J.P. Lockney

JIM HANVEY, DETECTIVE (1937, Republic)
Jim Hanvey—Guy Kibbee
Director—Phil Rosen
Leading Players—Tom Brown, Lucie Kaye, Catherine Doucet

JIM THE CONQUEROR (1927, Silent, Metropolitan)
Jim Burgess—William Boyd
Director—George B. Seitz
Leading Players—Elinor Fair, Walter Long, Tully Marshall

JIM THE PENMAN (1921, Silent, Associated First National)
James Ralston—Lionel Barrymore
Director—Kenneth Webb
Leading Players—Doris Rankin, Anders Randolf, Douglas MacPherson

JIM, THE WORLD'S GREATEST ATHLETE (1976, Universal)
Jim Nolan—Gregory Harrison
Director—Don Coscarelli
Leading Players—Robbie Wolcott, Rory Guy, Marla Pennington

JIM THORPE—ALL AMERICAN (1951, Warner Brothers)
Jim Thorpe—Burt Lancaster
Director—Michael Curtiz
Leading Players—Charles Bickford, Steve Cochran, Phyllis Thaxter, Dick Wesson

JIMMIE'S MILLIONS (1925, Silent, Film Booking Offices)
Jimmie Wicherly—Richard Talmadge
Director—James P. Hogan
Leading Players—Betty Francisco, Charles Clary, Brinsley Shaw

JIMMY (1916, Silent, GB, Gaumont)
Jimmy St. Quinton—John Astley
Director—Elliot Stannard
Leading Players—George Tully, Letty Paxton, A.V. Bramble

JIMMY AND SALLY (1933, Fox Film Corp.)
Jimmy O'Connor—James Dunn
Sally Johnson—Claire Trevor
Director—James Tinling
Leading Players—Harvey Stephens, Lya Lys, Jed Prouty

JIMMY BOY (1935, GB, Universal)
Jimmy—Jimmy O'Dea
Director—John Baxter
Leading Players—Guy Middleton, Vera Sherburne, Enid Stamp-Taylor

JIMMY THE GENT (1934, Warner Brothers)
Jimmy Corrigan—James Cagney
Director—Michael Curtiz
Leading Players—Bette Davis, Alice White, Allen Jenkins

JIMMY THE KID (1982, New World)
Jimmy—Gary Coleman
Director—Gary Nelson
Leading Players—Paul LeMat, Dee Wallace, Don Adams

THE JINX (1919, Silent, Goldwyn)
Jinx—Mabel Normand
Director—George Loane Tucker
Leading Players—Florence Carpenter, Ogden Crane, Cullen Landis

JITTERBUGS (1943, 20th Century Fox)
Stan Laurel—Stan Laurel
Oliver Hardy—Oliver Hardy
Director—Malcolm St. Clair
Leading Players—Vivian Blaine, Bob Bailey, Douglas Fowley

JO JO DANCER, YOUR LIFE IS CALLING (1986, Columbia)
Jo Jo Dancer—Richard Pryor
Director—Richard Pryor
Leading Players—Debbie Allen, Art Evans, Fay Hauser

JO THE CROSSING SWEEPER (1918, Silent, GB, Barker)
Jo—Unity Moore
Director—Alexander Butler
Leading Players—Dora De Winton, Andre Beaulieu, Connie Lever

JOAN OF ARC (1948, RKO)
Joan of Arc—Ingrid Bergman
Director—Victor Fleming
Leading Players—Jose Ferrer, Francis L. Sullivan, J. Carroll Naish, Ward Bond, Shepperd Strudwick

JOAN OF OZARK (1942, Republic)
Judy Hull—Judy Canova
Director—Joseph Santley
Leading Players—Joe E. Brown, Eddie Foy Jr., Jerome Cowan

JOAN OF PARIS (1942, RKO)
Joan—Michellle Morgan
Director—Robert Stevenson
Leading Players—Paul Henreid, Thomas Mitchell, Laird Cregar, May Robson, Alan Ladd

JOAN OF PLATTSBURG (1918, Silent, Goldwyn)
Joan—Mabel Normand
Directors—George Loane Tucker & William Humphrey
Leading Players—Robert Elliott, William Fredericks, Joseph Smiley

JOAN OF THE WOODS (1918, Silent, World)
Joan Travers—June Elvidge
Director—Travers Vale
Leading Players—Walter Pratt Lewis, Albert Hart, George MacQuarrie

JOAN THE WOMAN (1916, Silent, Paramount)
Joan of Arc—Geraldine Farrar
Director—Cecil B. De Mille
Leading Players—Raymond Hatton, Hobart Bosworth, Theodore Roberts, Wallace Reid

JOANNA (1925, Silent, First National)
Joanna Manners—Dorothy Mackaill
Director—Edwin Carewe
Leading Players—Jack Mulhall, Paul Nicholson, George Fawcett

JOANNA (1968, GB, 20th Century Fox)
Joanna—Genevieve Waite
Director—Michael Sarne
Leading Players—Christian Doermer, Calvin Lockhart, Donald Sutherland

JOCKS (1987, Crown)
The Kid—Scott Strader
Jeff—Perry Lang
Chito—Trinidad Silva
Ripper—Don Gibb
Andy—Stoney Jackson
Director—Steve Carver
Leading Players—Mariska Hargitay, Richard Roundtree, R.G. Armstrong

JOE (1970, Cannon)
Joe Curran—Peter Boyle
Director—John G. Avildsen
Leading Players—Susan Sarandon, Patrick McDermott, Tim Lewis, Dennis Patrick

JOE AND ETHEL TURP CALL ON THE PRESIDENT (1939, MGM)
Ethel Turp—Ann Sothern
Joe Turp—William Gargan
The President—Lewis Stone
Director—Robert B. Sinclair
Leading Players—Walter Brennan, Marsha Hunt, Tom Neal

JOE BUTTERFLY (1957, Universal)
Joe Butterfly—Burgess Meredith
Director—Jesse Hibbs
Leading Players—Audie Murphy, George Nader, Keenan Wynn

JOE KIDD (1972, Universal)
Joe Kidd—Clint Eastwood
Director—John Sturges
Leading Players—Robert Duvall, John Saxon, Don Stroud, Stella Garcia

THE JOE LOUIS STORY (1953, UA)
Joe Louis—Coley Wallace
Director—Robert Gordon
Leading Players—Paul Stewart, Hilda Simms, James Edwards

JOE MACBETH (1955, Columbia)
Joe MacBeth—Paul Douglas
Director—Ken Hughes
Leading Players—Ruth Roman, Bonar Colleano, Gregorie Aslan

JOE PALOOKA, CHAMP (1946, Monogram)
Joe Palooka—Joe Kirkwood, Jr.
Director—Reginald Le Borg
Leading Players—Leon Errol, Elyse Knox, Eduardo Ciannelli

JOE PALOOKA IN CONNECTICUT (1949, Monogram)
Joe Palooka—Joe Kirkwood, Jr.
Director—Reginald Le Borg
Leading Players—Leon Errol, Elyse Knox, Marcel Journet

JOE PALOOKA IN THE BIG FIGHT (1949, Monogram)
Joe Palooka—Joe Kirkwood, Jr.
Director—Cyril Endfield
Leading Players—Leon Errol, Lina Romay, David Bruce

JOE PALOOKA IN THE SQUARED CIRCLE (1950, Monogram)
Joe Palooka—Joe Kirkwood, Jr.
Director—Reginld Le Borg
Leading Players—James Gleason, Lois Hall, Edgar Barrier

JOE PALOOKA IN THE TRIPLE CROSS (1951, Monogram)
Joe Palooka—Joe Kirkwood, Jr.
Director—Reginald Le Borg
Leading Players—James Gleason, Cathy Downs, John Emery

JOE PALOOKA IN WINNER TAKE ALL (1948, Monogram)
Joe Palooka—Joe Kirkwood, Jr.
Director—Reginald Le Borg
Leading Players—Elyse Knox, William Frawley, Stanley Clements

JOE PALOOKA MEETS HUMPHREY (1950, Monogram)
Joe Palooka—Joe Kirkwood, Jr.
Humphrey Pennyworth—Robert Coogan
Director—Jean Yarborough
Leading Players—Leon Errol, Jerome Cowan, Joe Besser

JOE PANTHER (1976, Artists Creation)
Joe Panther—Ray Tracey
Director—Paul Krasny
Leading Players—Brian Keith, Ricardo Montalban, Alan Feinstein

JOE SMITH, AMERICAN (1942, MGM)
Joe Smith—Robert Young
Director—Richard Thorpe
Leading Players—Marsha Hunt, Harvey Stephens, Darryl Hickman

JOEY (1985, GB, Satori)
Joey—Neill Barry
Director—Joseph Ellison
Leading Players—James Quinn, Elisa Heinsohn, Linda Thorson

JOEY BOY (1965, GB, British Lion)
Joey Boy Thompson—Harry H. Corbett
Director—Frank Launder
Leading Players—Stanley Baxter, Bill Fraser, Percy Herbert

JOHANNA ENLISTS (1918, Silent, Artcraft)
Johanna Renssaller—Mary Pickford
Director—William D. Taylor
Leading Players—Anne Schaefer, Fred Huntley, Monte Blue, Douglas MacLean, Wallace Beery

JOHN AND JULIE (1957, GB, British Lion)
John Pritchett—Colin Gibson
Julie—Lesley Dudley
Director—William Fairchild
Leading Players—Noelle Middleton, Moira Lister, Wilfrid Hyde-White

JOHN AND MARY (1969, 20th Century Fox)
John—Dustin Hoffman
Mary—Mia Farrow
Director—Peter Yates
Leading Players—Michael Tolan, Sunny Griffin, Stanley Beck

JOHN GLAYDE'S HONOR (1915, Silent, Gold Rooster)
John Glayde—C. Aubrey Smith
Director—Henry George Irving
Leading Players—Mary Lawton, Richard Hatteras, Ida Waterman

JOHN GOLDFARB, PLEASE COME HOME (1964, 20th Century Fox)
John Goldfarb—Richard Crenna
Director—J. Lee Thompson
Leading Players—Shirley MacLaine, Peter Ustinov, Jim Backus

JOHN HALIFAX—GENTLEMAN (1938, GB, MGM)
John Halifax—John Warwick
Director—George King
Leading Players—Nancy Burne, Ralph Michael, D.J. Williams

JOHN HERIOT'S WIFE (1920, Silent, GB, Anglo-Hollandia)
Camillia Heriot—Mary Odette

John Heriot—Henry Victor
Director—B.E. Doxat-Pratt
Leading Players—Adelqui Migliar, Anna Bosilova

JOHN LOVES MARY (1949, Warner Brothers)
John Lawrence—Ronald Reagan
Mary McKinley—Patricia Neal
Director—David Butler
Leading Players—Jack Carson, Wayne Morris, Edward Arnold

JOHN MEADE'S WOMAN (1937, Paramount)
John Meade—Edward Arnold
Teddy Connor—Francine Larrimore
Director—Richard Wallace
Leading Players—Gail Patrick, George Bancroft, John Trent

JOHN NEEDHAM'S DOUBLE (1916, Silent, Bluebird)
John Needham—Tyrone Power, Sr.
Joseph Norbury—Tyrone Power, Sr.
Directors—Lois Weber & Phillips Smalley
Leading Players—Marie Walcamp, Agnes Emerson, Frank Elliot

JOHN OF THE FAIR (1962, GB, Continental)
John Claydon—John Charlesworth
Director—Michael McCarthy
Leading Players—Arthur Young, Richard George, Michael Mulcaster

JOHN PAUL JONES (1959, Warner Brothers)
John Paul Jones—Robert Stack
Director—John Farrow
Leading Players—Bette Davis, Marisa Pavan, Charles Coburn

JOHN PETTICOATS (1919, Silent, Artcraft)
"Hardwood" John Haynes—William S. Hart
Director—Lambert Hillyer
Leading Players—Walt Whitman, George Webb, Winifred Westover

JOHN SMITH (1922, Silent, Selznick)
John Smith—Eugene O'Brien
Director—Victor Heerman
Leading Players—Viva Ogden, W.J. Ferguson, Tammany Young

JOHN WESLEY (1954, GB, Commission of Methodist Church)
John Wesley—Leonard Sachs
Director—Norman Walker
Leading Players—Gerald Lohman, Neil Heayes, Keith Pyott

JOHNNY ALLEGRO (1949, Columbia)
Johnny Allegro—George Raft
Director—Ted Tetzlaff
Leading Players—Nina Foch, George Macready, Will Geer, Gloria Henry

JOHNNY ANGEL (1945, RKO)
Johnny Angel—George Raft
Director—Edwin L. Marin
Leading Players—Claire Trevor, Signe Hasso, Lowell Gilmore, Hoagy Carmichael

JOHNNY APOLLO (1940, 20th Century Fox)
Bob Cain (Johnny Apollo)—Tyrone Power
Director—Henry Hathaway
Leading Players—Dorothy Lamour, Lloyd Nolan, Edward Arnold

JOHNNY BE GOOD (1988, Orion)
Johnny Walker—Anthony Michael Hall
Director—Bud Smith
Leading Players—Robert Downey, Jr., Paul Gleason, Uma
Thurman, Steve James

JOHNNY COME LATELY (1943, UA)
Tom Richards—James Cagney
Director—William K. Howard
Leading Players—Grace George, Marjorie Main, Marjorie Lord

JOHNNY COMES FLYING HOME (1946, 20th Century Fox)
Johnny Martin—Richard Crane
Director—Ben Stoloff
Leading Players—Faye Marlowe, Martha Stewart, Charles
Russell

JOHNNY CONCHO (1956, UA)
Johnny Concho—Frank Sinatra
Director—Don McGuire
Leading Players—Keenan Wynn, William Conrad, Phyllis Kirk

JOHNNY COOL (1963, UA)
Johnny Cool/Giordano—Henry Silva
Director—William Asher
Leading Players—Elizabeth Montgomery, Richard Anderson, Jim
Backus, Joey Bishop

JOHNNY DANGEROUSLY (1984, 20th Century Fox)
Johnny Dangerously—Michael Keaton
Director—Amy Heckerling
Leading Players—Joe Piscopo, Marilu Henner, Maureen
Stapleton, Peter Boyle

JOHNNY DARK (1954, Universal)
Johnny Dark—Tony Curtis
Director—George Sherman
Leading Players—Piper Laurie, Don Taylor, Paul Kelly

JOHNNY DOESN'T LIVE HERE ANYMORE (1944, Monogram)
Johnny Moore—William Terry
Director—Joe May
Leading Players—Simone Simon, James Ellison, Minna Gombell

JOHNNY EAGER (1942, MGM)
Johnny Eager—Robert Taylor
Director—Mervyn LeRoy
Leading Players—Lana Turner, Edward Arnold, Van Heflin

JOHNNY FRENCHMAN (1946, GB, Ealing)
Lanec Florrie—Francoise Rosay
Director—Charles Frend
Leading Players—Tom Walls, Patricia Roc, Ralph Michael

JOHNNY GET YOUR GUN (1919, Silent, Paramount)
Johnny Wiggins—Fred Stone
Director—Donald Crisp
Leading Players—Mary Anderson, Casson Ferguson, Dan
Crimmins

JOHNNY GET YOUR HAIR CUT (1927, Silent, MGM)
Johnny O'Day—Jackie Coogan
Director—B. Reeves Eason
Leading Players—Mattie Witting, Maurice Costello, Pat
Hartigan, James Corrigan

JOHNNY GOT HIS GUN (1971, Cinemation)
Joe Bonham—Timothy Bottoms
Director—Dalton Trumbo
Leading Players—Kathy Fields, Marsha Hunt, Jason Robards,
Donald Sutherland, Diane Varsi

JOHNNY GUITAR (1954, Republic)
Johnny Guitar—Sterling Hayden
Director—Nicholas Ray
Leading Players—Joan Crawford, Mercedes McCambridge, Scott
Brady, Ward Bond, Ben Cooper

JOHNNY HANDSOME (1989, Tri-Star)
John Sedley—Mickey Rourke
Director—Walter Hill
Leading Players—Ellen Barkin, Elizabeth McGovern, Morgan
Freeman, Forest Whitaker, Lance Henriksen

JOHNNY HOLIDAY (1949, UA)
Johnny Holiday—Allen Martin, Jr.
Director—Willis Goldbeck
Leading Players—William Bendix, Stanley Clements, Jack
Hagen

JOHNNY NOBODY (1965, GB, Viceroy-Medallion)
Johnny Nobody—Aldo Ray
Director—Nigel Patrick
Leading Players—Nigel Patrick, Yvonne Mitchell, William
Bendix, Cyril Cusack

JOHNNY O'CLOCK (1947, Columbia)
Johnny O'Clock—Dick Powell
Director—Robert Rossen
Leading Players—Evelyn Keyes, Lee J. Cobb, Ellen Drew, Nina
Foch, Thomas Gomez

JOHNNY ON THE RUN (1953, GB, International Realist)
Johnny—Eugeniusz Chylek
Director—Lewis Gilbert
Leading Players—Sydney Tafler, Michael Balfour, Jean
Anderson

JOHNNY ON THE SPOT (1919, Silent, Metro)
Johnny Rutledge—Hale Hamilton
Director—Harry L. Franklin
Leading Players—Louise Lovely, Philo McCullough, Ruth
Orlamond

JOHNNY ON THE SPOT (1954, GB, New Realm)
Johnny Breakes—Hugh McDermott
Director—MacLean Rogers
Leading Players—Elspet Gray, Paul Carpenter, Jean Lodge

JOHNNY RENO (1966, Paramount)
Johnny Reno—Dana Andrews
Director—R.G. Springsteen
Leading Players—Jane Russell, Lon Chaney, Jr., John Agar

JOHNNY ROCCO (1958, Allied Artists)
Johnny Rocco—Richard Eyer
Director—Paul Landres
Leading Players—Stephen McNally, Coleen Gray, Russ Conway

JOHNNY STOOL PIDGEON (1949, Universal)
Johnny Evans—Dan Duryea
Director—William Castle

Leading Players—Howard Duff, Shelley Winters, Tony Curtis

JOHNNY SUEDE (1991, Vega Films/Balthazar Pictures)
Johnny Suede—Brad Pitt
Director—Tom DiCillo
Leading Players—Calvin Levels, Alison Moir, Catherine Keeves, Tina Louise, Nick Cave

JOHNNY TIGER (1966, Universal)
Johnny Tiger—Chad Everett
Director—Paul Wendkos
Leading Players—Robert Taylor, Geraldine Brooks, Brenda Scott, Marc Lawrence

JOHNNY TREMAIN (1957, Buena Vista)
Johnny Tremain—Hal Stalmaster
Director—Rober Stevenson
Leading Players—Luana Patten, Jeff York, Sebastian Cabot

JOHNNY TROUBLE (1957, Warner Brothers)
Johnny—Stuart Whitman
Director—John H. Auer
Leading Players—Ethel Barrymore, Cecil Kellaway, Carolyn Jones, Jesse White

JOHNNY VIK (1973, Nauman)
Johnny Vik—Warren Hammack
Director—Charles Nauman
Leading Players—Kathy Amerman, Gina McCormick

JOHNNY, YOU'RE WANTED (1956, GB, Anglo-Amalgamted)
Johnny—John Slater
Director—Vernon Sewell
Leading Players—Alfred Marks, Garry Marsh, Chris Halward

THE JOKER IS WILD (1957, Paramount)
Joe E. Lewis—Frank Sinatra
Director—Charles Vidor
Leading Players—Mitzi Gaynor, Jeanne Crain, Eddie Albert, Beverly Garland, Jackie Coogan

THE JOKERS (1967, GB, Universal)
Michael Tremayne—Michael Crawford
David Tremayne—Oliver Reed
Director—Michael Winner
Leading Players—Harry Andrews, James Donald, Daniel Massey, Michael Hordern

A JOLLY BAD FELLOW (1964, GB, British Lion)
Prof. Bowles-Ottery—Leo McKern
Director—Don Chaffey
Leading Players—Janet Munro, Maxine Audley, Duncan Macrae

JOLSON SINGS AGAIN (1949, Columbia)
Al Jolson—Larry Parks
Director—Henry Levin
Leading Players—Barbara Hale, William Demarest, Ludwig Donath, Bill Goodwin, Myron McCormick

THE JOLSON STORY (1946, Columbia)
Al Jolson—Larry Parks
Director—Alfred E. Green
Leading Players—Evelyn Keyes, William Demarest, Bill Goodwin, Ludwig Donath, Tamara Shayne

JONI (1980, World Wide Pictures)
Joni Eareckson—Joni Eareckson
Director—James F. Collier
Leading Players—Bert Remsen, Katherine De Hetre, Cooper Huckabee

JORY (1972, Avco Embassy)
Jory—Robby Benson
Director—Jorge Fons
Leading Players—John Marley, B.J. Thomas, Brad Dexter

JOSEPH ANDREWS (1977, GB, Paramount)
Joseph Andrews—Peter Firth
Director—Tony Richardson
Leading Players—Ann-Margret, Michael Hordern, Beryl Reid

JOSEPHINE AND MEN (1955, GB, British Lion)
Josephine Luton—Glynis Johns
Director—Roy Boulting
Leading Players—Jack Buchanan, Donald Sinden, Peter Finch

JOSETTE (1938, 20th Century Fox)
Mlle. Josette—Tala Birell
Director—Allan Dwan
Leading Players—Don Ameche, Simone Simon, Robert Young, Bert Lahr, Joan Davis, William Collier, Sr.

JOSHUA (1976, Lone Star)
Joshua—Fred Williamson
Director—Larry Spangler
Leading Players—Isela Vega, Calvin Bartlett, Brenda Venus

JOSHUA, THEN AND NOW (1985, Canada, 20th Century Fox)
Joshua Shapiro—James Wood
Young Joshua Shapiro—Eric Kimmel
Director—Ted Kotcheff
Leading Players—Gabrielle Lazure, Alan Arkin, Michael Sarrazin

JOSSELYN'S WIFE (1926, Silent, Tiffany)
Lillian Josselyn—Pauline Frederick
Thomas Josselyn—Holmes Herbert
Director—Richard Thorpe
Leading Players—Josephine Kaliz, Josephine Hill, Carmelita Geraghty

JOSSER IN THE ARMY (1932, GB, British International)
Jimmy Josser—Ernie Lotinga
Director—Norman Lee
Leading Players—Betty Norton, Jack Hobbs, Hal Gordon

JOSSER JOINS THE NAVY (1932, GB, British International)
Jimmy Josser—Ernie Lotinga
Director—Norman Lee
Leading Players—Cyril McLaglen, Jack Hobbs, Lesley Wareing

JOSSER ON THE FARM (1934, GB, 20th Century Fox)
Jimmy Josser—Ernie Lotinga
Director—T. Hayes Hunter
Leading Players—Betty Astell, Garry Marsh, Muriel Aked

JOSSER ON THE RIVER (1932, GB, British International)
Jimmy Josser—Ernie Lotinga
Director—Norman Lee
Leading Players—Molly Lamont, Charles Hickman, Reginald Gardiner

JOURNEY FOR MARGARET (1942, MGM)
Margaret—Margaret O'Brien
Director—W.S. Van Dyke II
Leading Players—Robert Young, Laraine Day, Fay Bainter, Signe Hasso

THE JOURNEY OF NATTY GANN (1985, Buena Vista)
Natty Gann—Meredith Salenger
Director—Jeremy Kagan
Leading Players—John Cusack, Roy Wise, Lainie Kazan, Scatman Crothers

THE JOY GIRL (1927, Silent, Fox Film Corp.)
Jewel Courage—Olive Borden
Director—Allan Dwan
Leading Players—Neil Hamilton, Marie Dressler, Mary Alden

THE JOYOUS ADVENTURES OF ARISTIDE PUJOL (1920, Silent, GB, Foss-Phillips)
Aristide Pujol—Kenelm Foss
Director—Kenelm Foss
Leading Players—Pauline Peters, Barbara Everest, George Tawde

THE JOYOUS LIAR (1919, Silent, Hodkinson/Pathe)
Burge Harlan—J. Warren Kerrigan
Director—Ernest C. Warde
Leading Players—Lillian Walker, Joseph J. Dowling, Albert Cody

JUAREZ (1939, Warner Brothers)
Benito Juarez—Paul Muni
Director—William Dieterle
Leading Players—Bette Davis, Brian Aherne, Claude Rains, John Garfield, Donald Crisp

JUBAL (1956, Columbia)
Jubal Troop—Glenn Ford
Director—Delmer Daves
Leading Players—Ernest Borgnine, Rod Steiger, Valerie French, Felicia Farr

JUBILO (1919, Silent, Goldwyn)
Jubilo—Will Rogers
Director—Clarence D. Badger
Leading Players—Josie Sedgwick, Charles French, Willard Louis

JUD (1971, Duque Films)
Jud Carney—Joseph Kaufman
Director—Gunther Collins
Leading Players—Robert Deman, Alix Wyeth, Norman Burton

THE JUDGE (1949, Emerald)
Martin Strang—Milburn Stone
Director—Elmer Clifton
Leading Players—Katherine de Mille, Paul Guilfoyle, Stanley Waxman

JUDGE HARDY AND SON (1939, MGM)
Judge Hardy—Lewis Stone
Andy Hardy—Mickey Rooney
Director—George B. Seitz
Leading Players—Cecilia Parker, Ann Rutherford, Fay Holden, Sara Haden, Maria Ouspenskaya

JUDGE HARDY'S CHILDREN (1938, MGM)
Judge Hardy—Lewis Stone
Andy Hardy—Mickey Rooney
Marian Hardy—Cecilia Parker
Director—George B. Seitz
Leading Players—Fay Holden, Ann Rutherford, Betsy Ross Clarke, Ruth Hussey

JUDGE PRIEST (1934, Fox Film Corp.)
Judge William "Billy" Priest—Will Rogers
Director—John Ford
Leading Players—Henry B. Walthall, Tom Brown, Anita Louise, Rochelle Hudson

THE JUDGE STEPS OUT (1949, RKO)
Judge Bailey—Alexander Knox
Director—Boris Ingster
Leading Players—Ann Sothern, George Tobias, Sharyn Moffett

JUDITH (1965, Paramount)
Judith—Sophia Loren
Director—Daniel Mann
Leading Players—Peter Finch, Jack Hawkins, Hans Verner

JUDITH OF BETHULIA (1914, Silent, Biograph)
Judith of Bethulia—Blanche Sweet
Director—Larry Marsden
Leading Players—Henry Walthall, Lillian Gish, Dorothy Gish, Harry Carey

JUDITH OF THE CUMBERLANDS (1916, Silent, Signal)
Judith—Helen Holmes
Director—J.P. McGowan
Leading Players—Leo D. Maloney, Paul C. Hurst, Thomas G. Lingham

JUDY OF ROGUES' HARBOR (1920, Silent, Realart)
Judy—Mary Miles Minter
Director—William Desmond Taylor
Leading Players—Charles Meredith, Herbert Standing, Theodore Roberts

THE JUGGLER (1953, Columbia)
Hans Muller—Kirk Douglas
Director—Edward Dmytryk
Leading Players—Milly Vitale, Paul Stewart, Joey Walsh

JUKE GIRL (1942, Warner Brothers)
Lola Mears—Ann Sheridan
Director—Curtis Bernhardt
Leading Players—Ronald Reagan, Richard Whorf, George Tobias, Gene Lockhart, Alan Hale

JULES OF THE STRONG HEART (1918, Silent, Paramount)
Jules Lemaire—George Beban
Director—Donald Crisp
Leading Players—Helen Eddy, Charles Ogle, Raymond Hatton

JULIA (1977, 20th Century Fox)
Julia—Vanessa Redgrave
Director—Fred Zinnemann
Leading Players—Jane Fonda, Jason Robards, Maximilian Schell, Hal Holbrook, Rosemary Murphy

JULIA AND JULIA (1988, Cinecom)
Julia—Kathleen Turner

Director—Peter Del Monte
Leading Players—Gabriel Byrne, Sting, Gabriela Ferzetti, Angela Goodwin

JULIA HAS TWO LOVERS (1990, South Gate/Oneira)
Julia—Daphna Kastner
Daniel—David Duchovny
Jack—David Charles
Director—Bashar Shbib

JULIA MISBEHAVES (1948, MGM)
Julia Packett—Greer Garson
Director—Jack Conway
Leading Players—Walter Pidgeon, Peter Lawford, Cesar Romero, Elizabeth Taylor

JULIE (1956, MGM)
Julie Benton—Doris Day
Director—Andrew L. Stone
Leading Players—Louis Jourdan, Barry Sullivan, Frank Lovejoy

JULIUS CAESAR (1952, Avon/Brandon)
Julius Caesar—Harold Tasker
Director—David Bradley
Leading Players—Robert Holt, Charlton Heston, Theodore Cloak, David Bradley

JULIUS CAESAR (1953, MGM)
Julius Caesar—Louis Calhern
Director—Joseph L. Mankiewicz
Leading Players—James Mason, Marlon Brando, John Gielgud, Edmond O'Brien, Greer Garson, Deborah Kerr

JULIUS CAESAR (1970, GB, Commonwealth)
Julius Caesar—John Gielgud
Director—Stuart Burge
Leading Players—Charlton Heston, Jason Robards, Richard Johnson, Robert Vaughn, Richard Chamberlain

JUMPING JACKS (1952, Paramount)
Chick Allen—Dean Martin
Hap Smith—Jerry Lewis
Director—Norman Taurog
Leading Players—Mona Freeman, Don DeFore, Robert Strauss

JUNE BRIDE (1948, Warner Brothers)
Jeanne Brinker—Barbara Bates
Director—Bretaigne Windust
Leading Players—Bette Davis, Robert Montgomery, Fay Bainter, Betty Lynn, Tom Tully

JUNGLE BRIDE (1953, Monogram)
Doris Evans—Anita Page
Director—Harry O. Hoyt & Albert Kelly
Leading Players—Charles Starrett, Kenneth Thomson, Eddie Borden

JUNGLE CAPTIVE (1945, Universal)
Paula The Ape Woman—Vicky Lane
Director—Harold Young
Leading Players—Otto Kruger, Amelita Ward, Phil Brown

THE JUNGLE CHILD (1916, Silent, Triangle)
Ollante—Dorothy Dalton
Director—Walter Edwards

Leading Players—Howard Hickman, Gertrude Claire, Dorcas Matthews

JUNGLE GODDESS (1948, Lipert/Screen Guild)
Greta Vanderhorn—Wanda McKay
Director—Lewis D. Collins
Leading Players—George Reeves, Armida, Ralph Byrd

JUNGLE JIM (1948, Columbia)
Jungle Jim—Johnny Weissmuller
Director—William Berke
Leading Players—Virginia Grey, George Reeves, Lita Baron

JUNGLE JIM IN THE FORBIDDEN LAND (1952, Columbia)
Jungle Jim—Johnny Weissmuller
Director—Lew Landers
Leading Players—Angela Greene, Jean Willes, Lester Matthews

THE JUNGLE PRINCESS (1936, Paramount)
Ulah—Dorothy Lamour
Director—William Thiele
Leading Players—Ray Milland, Akim Tamiroff, Lynne Overman

JUNGLE TRAIL OF THE SON OF TARZAN (1923, Silent, National Films)
Jack, Son of Tarzan—Gordon Griffith
Tarzan—Dempsey Tabler
Director—Harry Revier
Leading Players—Karla Schramm, Kamuela Rubey, Manilla Martans

JUNGLE WOMAN (1944, Universal)
Paula Dupree—Acquanetta
Director—Reginald Le Borg
Leading Players—Evelyn Ankers, J, Carroll Naish, Samuel S. Hinds, Lois Collier

JUNIOR BONNER (1972, Cinerama)
Junior Bonner—Steve McQueen
Director—Sam Peckinpah
Leading Players—Robert Preston, Ida Lupino, Ben Johnson, Joe Don Baker, Barbara Leigh

JUNIOR MISS (1945, 20th Century Fox)
Judy Graves—Peggy Ann Garner
Director—George Seaton
Leading Players—Allyn Joslyn, Michael Dunne, Faye Marlowe

JUNO AND THE PAYCOCK (1930, GB, British International)
Juno Boyle—Sara Allgood
Capt. John "Paycock" Boyle—Edward Chapman
Director—Alfred Hitchcock
Leading Players—Sydney Morgan, John Longden, Kathleen O'Regan, John Laurie, Barry Fitzgerald

JUPITER'S DARLING (1955, MGM)
Amytis—Esther Williams
Director—George Sidney
Leading Players—Howard Keel, Marge Champion, Gower Champion, George Sanders, Richard Haydn

JUST A GIGOLO (1931, MGM)
Lord Robert Brummell—William Haines
Director—Jack Conway
Leading Players—Irene Purcell, C. Aubrey Smith, Charlotte Granville, Lilian Bond

JUST A GIRL (1916, Silent, GB, Samuelson)
Esmerelda—Daisy Burrell
Director—Alexander Butler
Leading Players—Owen Nares, J. Hastings Batson, Minna Grey

JUST A WOMAN (1925, Silent, First National)
June Holton—Claire Windsor
Director—Irving Cummings
Leading Players—Conway Tearle, Dorothy Brock, Percy Marmont

JUST ANOTHER BLONDE (1926, Silent, First National)
Jeanne Cavanaugh—Dorothy Mackaill
Director—Alfred Santell
Leading Players—Jack Mulhall, Louise Brooks, William Collier, Jr.

JUST BETWEEN FRIENDS (1986, Orion)
Holly Davis—Mary Tyler Moore
Sandy Dunlap—Christine Lahti
Director—Allan Burns
Leading Players—Ted Danson, Salome Jens, Julie Payne, Sam Waterston, Beverly Sanders

JUST LIKE A WOMAN (1923, Silent, W.W. Hodkinson)
Peggy Dean—Marguerite De La Motte
Director—Scott R. Beal
Leading Players—George Fawcett, Ralph Graves, Jane Keckley

JUST LIKE A WOMAN (1939, GB, Alliance)
Ann Heston—Gertrude Michael
Director—Paul Stein
Leading Players—John Lodge, David Burns, Jeanne de Casalis

JUST LIKE A WOMAN (1967, GB, Dormar/Monarch)
Scilla Alexander—Wendy Craig
Director—Robert Fuest
Leading Players—Francis Matthews, John Wood, Dennis Price

JUST MY LUCK (1933, GB, British & Dominions)
David Blake—Ralph Lynn
Director—Jack Raymond
Leading Players—Winifred Shotter, Davy Burnaby, Robertson Hare

JUST MY LUCK (1957, GB, Rank)
Norman—Norman Wisdom
Director—John Paddy Carstairs
Leading Players—Jill Dixon, Leslie Phillips, Delphi Lawrence

JUST ONE OF THE GUYS (1985, Columbia)
Terry—Joyce Hyser
Director—Lisa Gottlieb
Leading Players—Clayton Rohner, Billy Jacoby, Toni Hudson

JUST SYLVIA (1918, Silent, World)
Sylvia—Barbara Castelton
Director—Travers Vale
Leading Players—John Hines, Jack Drumier, Gertrude Berekley

JUST THE WAY YOU ARE (1984, MGM/UA)
Susan Berlanger—Kristy McNichol
Director—Edouard Molinaro
Leading Players—Michael Ontkean, Kaki Hunter, Andre Dussolier, Robert Carradine

JUST WILLIAM (1939, GB, Associated British)
William Brown—Dicky Lupino
Director—Graham Cutts
Leading Players—Fred Emney, Basil Radford, Amy Veness

JUST WILLIAM'S LUCK (1948, GB, UA)
William Brown—William Graham
Director—Val Guest
Leading Players—Garry Marsh, Jane Welsh, Hugh Cross

JUST YOU AND ME, KID (1979, Columbia)
Bill—George Burns
Kate—Brooke Shields
Director—Leonard Stern
Leading Players—Burl Ives, Lorraine Gary, Nicolas Coster

JUSTINE (1969, 20th Century Fox)
Justine—Anouk Aimee
Director—George Cukor
Leading Players—Dirk Bogarde, Robert Forster, Anna Karina

K

K-THE UNKNOWN (1924, Silent, Universal)
"K" Le Moyne—Percy Marmont
Director—Harry Pollard
Leading Players—Virginia Valli, Francis Feeney, Maurice Ryan

KAFKA (1991, Miramax)
Franz Kafka—Jeremy Irons
Director—Steven Soderbergh
Leading Players—Theresa Russell, Joel Grey, Ian Holm, Jeroen Krabbe, Armin Mueller-Stahl, Alec Guinness, Brian Glover

THE KAISER (BEAST OF BERLIN) (1918, Silent, Renowned Pictures)
The Kaiser—Rupert Julian
Director—Rupert Julian
Leading Players—Allan Sears, Lon Chaney, Mark Fenton, Jay Smith, Nigel de Brullier

THE KANGAROO KID (1950, Australia, Allied Australian)
Tex Kinnane—Jock O'Mahoney
Director—Lesley Selander
Leading Players—Veda Ann Borg, Douglas Dumbrille, Martha Hyer

THE KANSAN (1943, UA)
John Bonniwell—Richard Dix
Director—George Archainbaud
Leading Players—Jane Wyatt, Albert Dekker, Eugene Pallette, Victory Jory

KANSAS CITY BOMBER (1972, MGM)
Diane "K.C." Carr—Raquel Welch
Director—Jerrold Freedman
Leading Players—Kevin McCarthy, Helena Kallianiotes, Norman Alden

KANSAS CITY PRINCESS (1934, Warner Brothers)
Rosy—Joan Blondell
Director—William Keighley
Leading Players—Glenda Farrell, Robert Armstrong, Hugh Herbert

THE KARATE KID (1984, Columbia)
Daniel (La Russo)—Ralph Macchio
Director—John G. Avildsen
Leading Players—Noriyuki "Pat" Morita, Elisabeth Shue, Martin Kove

THE KARATE KID, PART 2 (1986, Columbia)
Daniel (La Russo)—Ralph Macchio
Director—John G. Avildsen
Leading Players—Noriyuki "Pat" Morita, Danny Kamekona, Nobu McCarthy, Tamlyn Yomita

THE KARATE KID PART III (1989, Columbia)
Daniel La Russo—Ralph Macchio
Director—John G. Avildsen
Leading Players—Noriyuki "Pat" Morita, Robyn Lively, Thomas Ian Griffith, Martin L. Kove

KATE PLUS TEN (1938, GB, GFD)
Kate Westhanger—Genevieve Tobin
Director—Reginald Denham
Leading Players—Jack Hulbert, Noel Madison, Francis L. Sullivan

KATHLEEN (1938, Ireland, Hoffberg)
Kathleen O'Moore—Sally O'Neil
Director—Norman Lee
Leading Players—Tom Burke, Jack Daly, Sara Allgood

KATHLEEN (1941, MGM)
Kathleen Davis—Shirley Temple
Director—Harold S. Bacquet
Leading Players—Herbert Marshall, Laraine Day, Gail Patrick

KATHLEEN MAVOURNEEN (1919, Silent, World)
Kathleen Mavoureen—Theda Bara
Director—Charles J. Brabin
Leading Players—Edward O'Connor, Jennie Dickerson, Raymond Mckee

KATHLEEN MAVOURNEEN (1930, Tiffany)
Kathleen Mavourneen—Sally O'Neil
Director—Albert Ray
Leading Players—Charles Delaney, Robert Elliott, Aggie Herring

KATHY O' (1958, Universal)
Kathy O'Rourke—Patty McCormack
Director—Jack Sher
Leading Players—Dan Duryea, Jan Sterling, Mary Fickett

KATIE DID IT (1951, Universal)
Katherine Standish—Ann Blyth
Director—Frederick de Cordova
Leading Players—Mark Stevens, Cecil Kellaway, Jesse White

KEATON'S COP (1990, Cannon)
Louie Keaton—Abe Vigoda
Mike Gable—Lee Majors
Director—Bob Burge

Leading Players—Tracy Brooks Swope, Don Rickles, June Wilkinson, Art LaFleur, Robert Hilliard

THE KEEPER (1976, Canada, Lions Gate)
The Keeper—Christopher Lee
Director—Tom Drake
Leading Players—Tell Schreiber, Sally Gray, Ross Vezarian

KEEPER OF THE BEES (1925, Silent, Film Booking Offices)
James Lewis MacFarlane—Robert Frazer
Director—James Leo Meehan
Leading Players—Josef Swickard, Martha Mattox, Clara Bow

KEEPER OF THE FLAME (1942, MGM)
Christine Forrest—Katharine Hepburn
Director—George Cukor
Leading Players—Spencer Tracy, Richard Whorf, Margaret Wycherly, Donald Meek

KEEPING UP WITH LIZZIE (1921, Silent, W. W. Hodkinson)
Lizzie Henshaw—Enid Bennett
Director—Lloyd Ingraham
Leading Players—Otis Harlan, Leo White, Victory Bateman

KEITH OF THE BORDER (1918, Silent, Triangle)
Jack Keith—Roy Stewart
Director—Clifford Smith
Leading Players—Josie Sedgwick, Norbert Cills, Pete Norrison

KELLY AND ME (1957, Universal)
Len Carmody—Van Johnson
Director—Robert Z. Leonard
Leading Players—Piper Laurie, Martha Hyer, Onslow Stevens

KELLY OF THE SECRET SERVICE (1936, Victory/Principal)
Ted Kelly—Lloyd Hughes
Director—Robert Hill
Leading Players—Sheila Manors, Fuzzy Knight, Syd Taylor

KELLY THE SECOND (1936, MGM)
Molly Kelly—Patsy Kelly
Director—Gus Meins
Leading Players—Guinn "Big Boy" Williams, Pert Kelton, Charley Chase

KELLY'S HEROES (1970, MGM)
Kelly—Clint Eastwood
Director—Brian G. Hutton
Leading Players—Telly Savalas, Donald Sutherland, Carroll O'Connor, Gavin McLeod, Don Rickles

KENNER (1969, MGM)
Kenner—Jim Brown
Director—Steve Sekely
Leading Players—Madlyn Rhue, Robert Coote, Ricky Cordell

KENNY AND CO. (1976, 20th Century Fox)
Kenny—Dan McCann
Director—Don Coscarelli
Leading Players—Mike Baldwin, Jeff Roth, Ralph Richmond

THE KENTUCKIAN (1955, UA)
Big Eli—Burt Lancaster
Director—Burt Lancaster
Leading Players—Dianne Foster, Diana Lynn, John McIntire, Walter Matthau, Una Merkel

A KENTUCKY CINDERELLA (1917, Silent, Bluebird)
Nannie—Ruth Clifford
Director—Rupert Julian
Leading Players—Harry Carter, Rupert Julian, Gretchen Lederer

KEPT HUSBANDS (1931, RKO)
Dick—Joel McCrea
Director—Lloyd Bacon
Leading Players—Dorothy Mackaill, Robert McWade, Florence Roberts

KEROUAC (1985, Daybreak)
Jack Kerouac—Jack Coulter
Director—John Antonelli
Leading Players—Peter Coyote, David Andrews, Jonah Pearson

THE KETTLES OF THE OZARKS (1956, Universal)
Ma Kettle—Marjorie Main
Sledge Kettle—Arthur Hunnicutt
Director—Charles Lamont
Leading Players—Ted De Corsia, Una Merkel, Richard Eyer

THE KETTLES ON MACDONALD'S FARM (1957, Universal)
Ma Kettle—Marjorie Main
Pa Kettle—Parker Fennelly
Director—Virgil Vogel
Leading Players—Gloria Talbot, John Smith, George Dunn

KEY WITNESS (1947, Columbia)
Milton Higby—John Beal
Director—D. Ross Lederman
Leading Players—Trudy Marshall, Jimmy Lloyd, Helen Mowery

KEY WITNESS (1960, MGM)
Fred Morrow—Jeffrey Hunter
Director—Phil Karlson
Leading Players—Pat Crowley, Dennis Hopper, Joby Baker

THE KIBITZER (1929, Paramount)
Ike Lazarus—Harry Green
Director—Edward Sloman
Leading Players—Mary Brian, Neil Hamilton, David Newell

KICKBOXER (1989, Kings Road/Pathe)
Kurt Sloane—Jean-Claude Van Damme
Directors—Mark DiSalle & David Worth
Leading Players—Dennis Alexio, Dennis Chan, Tong Po

THE KID (1916, Silent, Vitagraph)
The Kid—Lillian Walker
Director—Wilfred North
Leading Players—Ned Finley, Eulalie Jensen, Robert Gaillard

THE KID (1921, Silent, Associated First National)
The Kid—Jackie Coogan
Director—Charles Chaplin
Leading Players—Charles Chaplin, Edna Purviance, Carl Miller, Lita Grey

KID BLUE (1973, 20th Century Fox)
Bickford Waner—Dennis Hopper
Director—James Frawley
Leading Players—Warren Oates, Peter Boyle, Ben Johnson, Lee Purcell, Janice Rule

KID BOOTS (1926, Silent, Paramount)
Kid Boots—Eddie Cantor
Director—Frank Tuttle
Leading Players—Clara Bow, Billie Dove, Lawrence Gray

THE KID BROTHER (1927, Silent, Paramount)
Harold Hickory—Harold Lloyd
Director—Ted Wilde
Leading Players—Jobyna Ralston, Walter James, Leo Willis

THE KID COMES BACK (1937, Warner Brothers)
Rush Conway—Wayne Morris
Director—B. Reeves Eason
Leading Players—Barton MacLane, June Travis, Dickie Jones

THE KID FROM AMARILLO (1951, Columbia)
The Durango Kid—Charles Starrett
Director—Ray Nazarro
Leading Players—Smiley Burnette, Harry Lauter, Fred F. Sears

THE KID FROM BROKEN GUN (1952, Columbia)
The Durango Kid/Steve Reynolds—Charles Starrett
Director—Fred F. Sears
Leading Players—Smiley Burnette, Jock Mahoney, Angela Stevens

THE KID FROM BROOKLYN (1946, Goldwyn/RKO)
Burleigh Sullivan—Danny Kaye
Director—Norma Z. McLeod
Leading Players—Virginia Mayo, Vera-Ellen, Walter Abel, Eve Arden, Steve Cochran

THE KID FROM CANADA (1957, GB, British Lion)
Andy Cameron—Christopher Braden
Director—Kay Mander
Leading Players—Bernard Braden, Bobby Stevenson, Eleanor Laing

THE KID FROM CLEVELAND (1949, Republic)
Johnny Barrows—Russ Tamblyn
Director—Herbert Kline
Leading Players—George Brent, Lynn Bari, Tommy Cook

THE KID FROM KANSAS (1941, Universal)
Kansas—Dick Foran
Director—William Nigh
Leading Players—Leo Carrillo, Andy Devine, Ann Doran

THE KID FROM KOKOMO (1939, Warner Brothers)
Homer Baston—Wayne Morris
Director—Lewis Seiler
Leading Players—Pat O'Brien, Joan Blondell, Jane Wyman, May Robson

THE KID FROM LEFT FIELD (1953, 20th Century Fox)
Christy Cooper—Billy Chapin
Director—Harmon Jones
Leading Players—Dan Dailey, Anne Bancroft, Lloyd Bridges

THE KID FROM SANTE FE (1940, Monogram)
Sante Fe—Jack Randall
Director—Raymond K. Johnson
Leading Players—Clarene Curtis, Forrest Taylor, Claire Rochelle

THE KID FROM SPAIN (1932, UA)
Eddie Williams—Eddie Cantor

Director—Leo McCarey
Leading Players—Lyda Roberti, Robert Young, Ruth Hall, John Miljan, Noah Beery

THE KID FROM TEXAS (1939, MGM)
William Quincy Malone—Dennis O'Keefe
Director—S. Sylvan Simon
Leading Players—Florence Rice, Anthony Allan, Jessie Ralph

THE KID FROM TEXAS (1950, Universal)
Billy The Kid—Audie Murphy
Director—Kurt Neumann
LeadingPlayers—Gale Storm, Albert Dekker, Shepperd Strudwick

KID GALAHAD (1937, Warner Brothers)
Kid Galahad/Ward Guisenberry—Wayne Morris
Director—Michael Curtiz
Leading Players—Edward G. Robinson, Bette Davis, Humphrey Bogart, Jane Bryan

KID GALAHAD (1962, UA)
Kid Galahad/Walter Gulick—Elvis Presley
Director—Phil Karlson
Leading Players—Gig Young, Lola Albright, Joan Blackman, Charles Bronson

KID GLOVES (1929, Warner Brothers)
Kid Gloves—Conrad Nagel
Director—Ray Enright
Leading Players—Lois Wilson, Edward Earle, Edna Murphy

KID MILLIONS (1934, UA)
Eddie Wilson, Jr.—Eddie Cantor
Director—Roy Del Ruth
Leading Players—Ann Sothern, Ethel Merman, George Murphy

KID MONK BARONI (1952, Real Art)
Paul "Monk" Baroni—Leonard Nimoy
Director—Harold Schuster
Leading Players—Richard Rober, Bruce Cabot, Allene Roberts

KID NIGHTINGALE (1939, Warner Brothers)
Steve Nelson—John Payne
Director—George Amy
Leading Players—Jane Wyman, Walter Catlett, Ed Brophy

THE KID RIDES AGAIN (1943, Producers Releasing Corp.)
Billy The Kid—Buster Crabbe
Director—Sherman Scott
Leading Players—Al St. John, Iris Meredith, Glenn Strange

KID RODELO (1966, Paramount)
Kid Rodelo—Don Murray
Director—Richard Carlson
Leading Players—Janet Leigh, Broderick Crawford, Richard Carlson

THE KID SISTER (1927, Silent, Columbia)
Mary Hall—Ann Christy
Director—Ralph Graves
Leading Players—Marguerite De la Motte, Malcolm McGregor, Brooks Benedict

THE KID SISTER (1945, Producers Releasing Corp.)
Joan Hollingsworth—Judy Clark

Director—Sam Newfield
Leading Players—Roger Pryor, Constance Worth, Frank Jenks

KIDNAPPED (1938, 20th Century Fox)
David Balfour—Freddie Bartholomew
Director—Alfred Werker
Leading Players—Warner Baxter, Arleen Whelan, C. Aubrey Smith, Reginald Owen, John Carradine

KIDNAPPED (1948, Monogram)
David Balfour—Roddy McDowall
Director—William Beaudine
Leading Players—Sue England, Dan O'Herlihy, Roland Winters, Jeff Corey

KIDNAPPED (1960, Buena Vista)
David Balfour—James MacArthur
Director—Robert Stevenson
Leading Players—Peter Finch, Bernard Lee, Niall MacGinnis

KIDNAPPED (1971, GB, Omnibus/American International)
David Balfour—Lawrence Douglas
Director—Delbert Mann
Leading Players—Michael Caine, Trevor Howard, Jack Hawkins, Donald Pleasance, Gordon Jackson

THE KIDNAPPING OF THE PRESIDENT (1980, Canada, Crown International)
President Adam Scott—Hal Holbrook
Director—George Mendeluk
Leading Players—William Shatner, Van Johnson, Ava Gardner

THE KID'S CLEVER (1929, Universal)
Bugs Raymond—Glenn Tyron
Director—William James
Leading Players—Kathryn Crawford, Russell Simpson, Lloyd Whitlock

KIKI (1926, Silent, First National)
Kiki—Norma Talmadge
Director—Clarence Brown
Leading Players—Ronald Colman, Gertrude Astor, Marc MacDermott

KIKI (1931, UA)
Kiki—Mary Pickford
Director—Sam Taylor
Leading Players—Reginald Denny, Joseph Cawthorn, Margaret Livingston

KILDARE OF STORM (1918, Silent, Metro)
Mrs. Kildare—Emily Stevens
Director—Harry L. Franklin
Leading Players—King Baggot, Crauford Kent, Florence Short

KILL HER GENTLY (1958, GB, Columbia)
Kay Martin—Maureen Connell
Director—Charles Sanders
Leading Players—Marc Lawrence, George Mikell, Griffith Jones

KILL THE UMPIRE (1950, Columbia)
Bill Johnson—William Bendix
Director—Lloyd Bacon
Leading Players—Una Merkel, Ray Collins, Gloria Henry

KILLER AT LARGE (1936, Columbia)
Mr. Zero—Henry Brandon
Director—David Selman
Leading Players—Mary Brian, Russell Hardie, Betty Compson

KILLER DILL (1947, Screen Guild)
Johnny Dill—Stuart Erwin
Director—Leslie D. Collins
Leading Players—Anne Gwynne, Frank Albertson, Mike Mazurki

THE KILLER INSIDE ME (1976, Warner Brothers)
Lou Ford—Stacy Keach
Director—Burt Kennedy
Leading Players—Susan Tyrrell, Tisha Sterling, Keenan Wynn

THE KILLER IS LOOSE (1956, UA)
Leon "Foggy" Poole—Wendell Corey
Director—Budd Boetticher
Leading Players—Joseph Cotten, Rhonda Fleming, Alan Hale, Jr.

KILLER MCCOY (1947, MGM)
Tommy McCoy—Mickey Rooney
Director—Roy Rowland
Leading Players—Brian Donlevy, Ann Blyth, James Dunn

A KILLER WALKS (1952, GB, Grand National)
Ned—Laurence Harvey
Director—Ronald Drake
Leading Players—Trader Faulkner, Susan Shaw, Laurence Naismith

THE KILLERS (1946, Universal)
Al—Charles McGraw
Max—William Conrad
Director—Robert Siodmak
Leading Players—Edmond O'Brien, Ava Gardner, Albert Dekker, Sam Levine, Burt Lancaster

THE KILLERS (1964, Universal)
Charlie—Lee Marvin
Lee—Clu Gulager
Director—Donald Siegel
Leading Players—Angie Dickinson, John Cassavetes, Ronald Reagan, Claude Akins

THE KILLERS (1984, Roth Film)
Harry—Jack Kehoe
Bill—Raymond Mayo
Director—Patrick Roth
Leading Players—Allan Magicovsky, Suzanne Reed, Anne Ramsey

KILLERS THREE (1968, American International)
Johnny Ward—Robert Walker, Jr.
Carol Ward—Diane Varsi
Roger—Dick Clark
Director—Bruce Kessler
Leading Players—Norman Alden, Maureen Arthur, Tony York

THE KILLING OF A CHINESE BOOKIE (1976, Faces)
The Chinese Bookie—Soto Joe Hugh
Director—John Cassavetes
Leading Players—Ben Gazzara, Timothy Agoglia Carey, Zizi Johari, Meade Roberts

KILMENY (1915, Silent, Paramount)
Kilmeny—Lenore Ulrich
Director—Oscar Apfel
Leading Players—Herbert Standing, Howard Davies, Marshall Mackaye

KILROY WAS HERE (1947, Monogram)
John J. Kilroy—Jackie Cooper
Director—Phil Karlson
Leading Players—Jackie Coogan, Wanda MacKay, Frank Jenks

KIM (1950, MGM)
Kim—Dean Stockwell
Director—Victor Saville
Leading Players—Errol Flynn, Paul Lukas, Robert Douglas, Thomas Gomez, Cecil Kellaway

KIMBERLEY JIM (1965, South Africa, Embassy)
Jim Madison—Jim Reeves
Director—Emil Nofal
Leading Players—Madeleine Usher, Clive Parnell, Arthur Swemmer

KIND LADY (1935, MGM)
Mary Herries—Aline MacMahon
Director—George B. Seitz
Leading Players—Basil Rathbone, Mary Carlisle, Frank Albertson, Dudley Digges

KIND LADY (1951, MGM)
Mary Herries—Ethel Barrymore
Director—John Sturges
Leading Players—Maurice Evans, Angela Lansbury, Keenan Wynn, Betsy Blair

KINDERGARTEN COP (1990, Universal)
Kimble—Arnold Schwarzenegger
Director—Ivan Reitman
Leading Players—Penelope Ann Miller, Pamela Reed, Linda Hunt, Richard Tyson, Carroll Baker

THE KINDRED (1987, F-M Entertainment)
Anthony—Michael Shawn McCracken
Director—Jeffrey Obrow
Leading Players—David Allen Brooks, Rod Steiger, Amanda Pays, Talia Balsam, Kim Hunter

THE KING AND FOUR QUEENS (1956, UA)
Dan Kehoe—Clark Gable
Sabina—Eleanor Parker
Ruby—Jean Wilkes
Birdie—Barbara Nichols
Oralie—Sara Shane
Director—Raoul Walsh
Leading Players—Jo Van Fleet, Roy Roberts, Arthur Shields

THE KING AND I (1956, 20th Century Fox)
Anna Leonowens—Deborah Kerr
The King of Siam—Yul Brynner
Director—Walter Lang
Leading Players—Rita Moreno, Martin Benson, Terry Saunders, Rex Thompson, Carlos Rivas

THE KING AND THE CHORUS GIRL (1937, Warner Brothers)
Alfred—Fernand Gravet
Dorothy—Joan Blondell

Director—Mervyn LeRoy
Leading Players—Edward Everett Horton, Alan Mowbray, Jane Wyman

KING ARTHUR WAS A GENTLEMAN (1942, GB, Gainsborough)
Arthur King—Arthur Askey
Director—Marcel Varnel
Leading Players—Evelyn Dall, Anne Shelton, Max Bacon

KING BLANK (1983, Metafilms)
King Blank—Ron Vawter
Director—Michael Oblowitz
Leading Players—Rosemary Hochschild, Will Patton, Pete Richardson

KING COWBOY (1928, Silent, FBO Pictures)
Tex Rogers—Tom Mix
Director—Robert De Lacy
Leading Players—Sally Blane, Lew Meehan, Barney Furey

KING DAVID (1985, Paramount)
King David—Richard Gere
Director—Bruce Beresford
Leading Players—Ian Sears, Edward Woodward, Gina Bellman, Alice Krige, Cherie Lunghi, James Coombes

KING FOR A NIGHT (1933, Universal)
Bud Williams—Chester Morris
Director—Kurt Neumann
Leading Players—Helen Twelvetrees, Alice White, John Miljan, Grant Mitchell

A KING IN NEW YORK (1957, GB, Attica/Archway)
King Shadhov—Charles Chaplin
Director—Charles Chaplin
Leading Players—Dawn Addams, Oliver Johnston, Maxine Audley

KING KELLY OF THE U.S.A. (1934, Monogram)
Kelly—Guy Robertson
Director—Leonard Fields
Leading Players—Irene Ware, Edgar Kennedy, Frankin Pangborn

KING LEAR (1971, Great Britain/Denmark, Filmways)
King Lear—Paul Scofield
Director—Peter Brook
Leading Players—Irene Worth, Jack MacGowan, Alan Webb, Cyril Cusack, Patrick Magee

KING LEAR (1988, USA/France, Cannon)
Don Learo—Burgess Meredith
Director—Jean-Luc Godard
Leading Players—Peter Sellars, Molly Ringwald, Jean-Luc Godard, Woody Allen, Norman Mailer

KING, MURRAY (1969, Amran Nowak/EYR)
King, Murray—Murray Ramsey King
Directors—Jonathan Gordon and David Hoffman
Leading Players—Laura Kaye, Jackie Morris, Gloria Riegger

KING OF ALCATRAZ (1938, Paramount)
Steve Murkill—J. Carroll Naish
Director—Robert Florey
Leading Players—Gail Patrick, Lloyd Nolan, Harry Carey, Robert Preston, Anthony Quinn

KING OF BURLESQUE (1936, 20th Century Fox)
Kerry Bolton—Warner Baxter
Director—Sidney Lanfield
Leading Players—Alice Faye, Jack Oakie, Arline Judge

KING OF CHINATOWN (1939, Paramount)
Frank Baturin—Akim Tamiroff
Director—Nick Grinde
Leading Players—Anna May Wong, J. Carroll Naish, Sidney Toler, Phillip Ahn, Anthony Quinn

THE KING OF COMEDY (1983, 20th Century Fox)
Rupert Pupkin—Robert De Niro
Director—Martin Scorsese
Leading Players—Jerry Lewis, Diahnne Abbott, Sandra Bernhard

THE KING OF DIAMONDS (1918, Silent, Vitagraph)
Oliver Bennett—Harry Morey
Director—Paul Scardon
Leading Players—Betty Blythe, William Dennison, George Majeroni

KING OF DODGE CITY (1941, Columbia)
Wild Bill Hickok—Bill Elliott
Director—Lambert Hillyer
Leading Players—Tex Ritter, Judith Linden, Dub Taylor

KING OF GAMBLERS (1937, Paramount)
Steve Kalkas—Akim Tamiroff
Director—Robert Florey
Leading Players—Claire Trevor, Lloyd Nolan, Buster Crabbe, Helen Burgess

KING OF HEARTS (1967, Fr./Italy, UA)
Pvt. Charles Plumpnick—Alan Bates
Director—Philippe de Broca
Leading Players—Pierre Brasseur, Jean-Claude Brialy, Genevieve Bujold, Adolfo Celi, Micheline Presele

KING OF HEARTS (aka LITTLE GEL) (1936, GB, Butchers)
Bill Saunders—Will Fyffe
Director—Oswald Mitchell and Walter Tennyson
Leading Players—Gwenllian Gill, Richard Dolman, Amy Veness

KING OF HOCKEY (1936, Warner Brothers)
Gabby Dugan—Dick Purcell
Director—Noel Smith
Leading Players—Anna Nagel, Marie Wilson, Wayne Morris

THE KING OF JAZZ (1930, Universal)
Paul Whiteman—Paul Whiteman
Director—John Murray Anderson
Leading Players—John Boles, Bing Crosby, Laura La Plante, Glenn Tryon, Merna Kennedy

THE KING OF KINGS (1927, Silent, De Mille Pictures)
Jesus Christ—H.B. Warner
Director—Cecil B. De Mille
Leading Players—Dorothy Cummings, Ernest Torrence, Joseph Schildkraut, Jacqueline Logan, Victor Varconi, Montagu Love

KING OF KINGS (1961, MGM)
Jesus Christ—Jeffrey Hunter
Director—Nicholas Ray

Leading Players—Siobhan McKenna, Hurd Hatfield, Ron Randell, Viveca Lindfors, Rita Gam, Rip Torn

THE KING OF MARVIN GARDENS (1972, Columbia)
Jason Staebler—Bruce Dern
Director—Bob Rafelson
Leading Players—Jack Nicholson, Ellen Burstyn, Julia Anne Robinson, Scatman Crothers

KING OF NEW YORK (1990, Italy/U.S., Reteitalia/Scena)
Frank White—Christopher Walken
Director—Abel Ferrara
Leading Players—David Caruso, Larry Fishburne, Victor Argo, Wesley Snipes, Janet Julian

THE KING OF PARIS (1934, GB, UA)
Max Till—Cedric Hardwicke
Director—Jack Raymond
Leading Players—Marie Glory, Ralph Richardson, Phyllis Monkman

KING OF THE ARENA (1933, Universal)
Firebrand Kenton—Ken Maynard
Director—Alan James
Leading Players—Lucille Browne, John St. Polis, Bob Kortman

KING OF THE BANDITS (1948, Monogram)
Cisco Kid—Gilbert Roland
Director—Christy Cabanne
Leading Players—Angela Greene, Chris-Pin Martin, Anthony Warde

KING OF THE BULLWHIP (1950, Real Art)
Lash LaRue—Lash LaRue
Director—Ron Ormand
Leading Players—Al St. John, Jack Holt, Tom Neal, Anne Gwynne

KING OF THE CASTLE (1925, Silent, GB, Stoll)
Colin O'Farrell—Brian Aherne
Director—Henry Edwards
Leading Players—Marjorie Hunt, Dawson Millward, Prudence Vanbrugh

KING OF THE CASTLE (1936, GB, GFD)
Monty King—Billy Milton
Director—Redd Davis
Leading Players—June Clyde, Claude Dampier, Cynthia Stock

KING OF THE CORAL SEAS (1956, Australia, Allied Artists)
Ted King—Chips Rafferty
Directors—Lee Robinson and Noel Monkman
Leading Players—Charles Tingwell, Ilma Adey, Rod Taylor

KING OF THE COWBOYS (1943, Republic)
Roy Rogers—Roy Rogers
Director—Joseph Kane
Leading Players—Smiley Burnette, Peggy Moran, Bob Nolan and The Sons of the Pioneers

KING OF THE DAMNED (1936, GB, Gaumont)
Convict 83—Conrad Veidt
Director—Walter Forde
Leading Players—Helen Vinson, Noah Beery, Cecil Ramage

KING OF THE GYPSIES (1978, Paramount)
King Zharko Stepanowicz—Sterling Hayden
Director—Frank Pierson
Leading Players—Shelley Winters, Susan Sarandon, Brooke Shields, Annette O'Toole, Eric Roberts

KING OF THE JUNGLE (1933, Paramount)
Kaspa, the Lion Man—Buster Crabbe
Directors—H. Bruce Humberstone and Max Marcin
Leading Players—Frances Dee, Douglas Dumbrille, Robert Adair

KING OF THE KHYBER RIFLES (1953, 20th Century Fox)
Capt. Alan King—Tyrone Power
Director—Henry King
Leading Players—Terry Moore, Michael Rennie, John Justin

KING OF THE LUMBERJACKS (1940, Warner Brothers)
Slim—John Payne
Director—William Clemens
Leading Players—Gloria Dickson, Stanley Fields, Joe Sawyer

KING OF THE MOUNTAIN (1981, Universal)
Steve—Harry Hamlin
Director—Noel Nosseck
Leading Players—Joseph Bottoms, Deborah Van Valkenburgh, Richard Cox, Dennis Hopper

KING OF THE NEWSBOYS (1938, Republic)
Jerry Flynn—Lew Ayres
Director—Bernard Vorhaus
Leading Players—Helen Mack, Alison Skipworth, Victor Varconi

KING OF THE PECOS (1936, Republic)
John Clayburn—John Wayne
Director—Joseph Kane
Leading Players—Muriel Evans, Cy Kendall, Jack Clifford

KING OF THE RITZ (1933, GB, British Lion)
Claude King—Stanley Lupino
Director—Carmine Gallone
Leading Players—Betty Stockfield, Hugh Wakefield, Henry Kendall

KING OF THE ROARING TWENTIES (1961, Allied Artists)
Arnold Rothstein—David Janssen
Director—Joseph M. Newman
Leading Players—Dianne Foster, Mickey Rooney, Jack Carson, Diana Dors, Dan O'Herlihy

KING OF THE RODEO (1929, Silent, Universal)
Montana Kid—Hoot Gibson
Director—Henry MacRae
Leading Players—Kathryn Crawford, Slim Summerville, Charles K. French

KING OF THE ROYAL MOUNTED (1936, 20th Century Fox)
Sgt. King—Robert Kent
Director—Howard Bretherton
Leading Players—Rosalind Keith, Alan Dinehart, Frank McGlynn

KING OF THE TURF (1926, Silent, Film Booking Offices)
Colonel Fairfax—George Irving
Director—James P. Hogan
Leading Players—Patsy Ruth Miller, Kenneth Harlan, Al Roscoe

KING OF THE TURF (1939, UA)
Jim Mason—Adolphe Menjou
Director—Alfred E. Green
Leading Players—Roger Daniel, Dolores Costello, Walter Abel

KING OF THE UNDERWORLD (1939, Warner Brothers)
Joe Gurney—Humphrey Bogart
Director—Lewis Seiler
Leading Players—Kay Francis, James Stephenson, John Eldredge

KING OF THE UNDERWORLD (1952, GB, Bushey)
Terence Riley—Tod Slaughter
Director—Victor M. Grover
Leading Players—Patrick Barr, Tucker McGuire, Ingeborg Wells

THE KING ON MAIN STREET (1925, Silent, Paramount)
Serge IV, King of Molvania—Adolphe Menjou
Director—Monta Bell
Leading Players—Bessie Love, Greta Nissen, Oscar Shaw

KING RALPH (1991, Universal)
Ralph—John Goodman
Director—David S. Ward
Leading Players—Peter O'Toole, John Hurt, Camille Coduri, Richard Griffiths, Joely Richardson

KING RAT (1965, Columbia)
Cpl. King—George Segal
Director—Bryan Forbes
Leading Players—Patrick O'Neal, Todd Armstrong, James Fox, Tom Courtenay, John Mills, James Donald

KING RICHARD AND THE CRUSADERS (1954, Warner Brothers)
King Richard III—George Sanders
Director—David Butler
Leading Players—Rex Harrison, Virginia Mayo, Laurence Harvey

KING SOLOMON OF BROADWAY (1935, Universal)
King Solomon—Edmund Lowe
Director—Alan Crosland
Leading Players—Dorothy Page, Pinky Tomlin, Louise Henry

THE KING STEPS OUT (1936, Columbia)
Emperor Franz Josef—Franchot Tone
Director—Josef von Sternberg
Leading Players—Grace Moore, Walter Connolly, Raymond Walburn, Victory Jory

THE KING'S DAUGHTER (1916, Silent, GB, Jury)
Helene—Janet Ross
The King—Edward O'Neill
Director—Maurice Elvey
Leading Players—Gerald Ames, Hayford Hobbs, Hubert Willis

KINGS AND DESPERATE MEN (1984, GB, Blue Dolphin)
John Kingsley—Patrick McGoohan
Lucas Miller—Alexis Kanner
Director—Alexis Kanner
Leading Players—Andrea Marcovicci, Margaret Trudeau, John-Pierre Brown

KINGS OF THE SUN (1963, UA)
Black Eagle—Yul Brynner
Balam—George Chakiris
Director—J. Lee Thompson

Leading Players—Shirley Anne Field, Richard Basehart, Brad Dexter, Barry Morse, Leo Gordon

KING'S PIRATE (1967, Universal)
Lt. Brian Fleming—Doug McClure
Director—Don Weis
Leading Players—Jill St. John, Guy Stockwell, Mary Ann Moberly, Kurt Kasznar

KING'S RHAPSODY (1955, GB, UA)
King Richard of Laurentia—Errol Flynn
Director—Herbert Wilcox
Leading Players—Anna Neagle, Patrice Wymore, Martita Hunt, Finlay Currie

THE KING'S THIEF (1955, MGM)
Michael Dermott—Edmund Purdom
Director—Robert Z. Leonard
Leading Players—Ann Blyth, David Niven, George Sanders, Roger Moore

THE KING'S VACATION (1933, Warner Brothers)
King Philip—George Arliss
Director—John Adolfi
Leading Players—Florence Arliss, Marjorie Gateson, Dudley Digges, Dick Powell

THE KING'S WHORE (1990, France/Austria/GB/Italy, J&M Entertainment)
King Vittorio Amadeo—Timothy Dalton
Jeanne de Luynes—Valeria Golino
Director—Axel Corti
Leading Players—Stephane Freiss, Feodor Chaliapin, Eleanor David, Margaret Tyzack, Paul Crauchet

KINKAID, GAMBLER (1916, Silent, Universal)
Jim Kinkaid—R.A. Cavin
Director—Raymond Wells
Leading Players—Ruth Stonehouse, Raymond Whittaker, Noble Johnson

THE KINSMAN (1919, Silent, Hepworth)
Bert Gammage—Henry Edwards
Director—Henry Edwards
Leading Players—Chrissie White, Gwynne Herbert, James Carew

KIPPS (1921, Silent, GB, Stoll)
Arthur Kipps—George K. Arthur
Director—Harold Shaw
Leading Players—Edna Flugrath, Christine Rayner, Teddy Arundell

KIPPS (THE REMARKABLE MR. KIPPS) (1941, GB, 20th Century Fox)
Arthur Kipps—Michael Redgrave
Director—Carol Reed
Leading Players—Phyllis Calvert, Diana Wynyard, Arthur Riscoe

THE KIRLIAN WITNESS (1978, Sampson and Cranor)
Rilla—Nancy Snyder
Director—Jonathan Sarno
Leading Players—Ted Laplat, Joel Colodner, Nancy Boykin, Lawrence Tierney

KISENGA, MAN OF AFRICA (1952, GB, Two Cities)
Kisenga—Robert Adams
Director—Thorold Dickinson
Leading Players—Eric Portman, Orlando Martins, Phyllis Calvert

A KISS BEFORE DYING (1991, Universal)
Jonathan Corliss—Matt Dillon
Dory Carlsson—Sean Young
Director—James Dearden
Leading Players—Max Von Sydow, James Russo, Diane Ladd

KISS DADDY GOOD NIGHT (1987, Beast of Eden)
Laura—Uma Thurman
William B. Tilden—Paul Richards
Director—Peter Ily Huemer
Leading Players—Paul Dillon, Steve Buscemi, Annabelle Gurwitch

A KISS FOR CINDERELLA (1926, Silent, Paramount)
Cinderella—Betty Bronson
Director—Herbert Brenon
Leading Players—Tom Moore, Esther Ralston, Henry Vibart

A KISS FOR CORLISS (1949, UA)
Corliss Archer—Shirley Temple
Director—Richard Wallace
Leading Players—David Niven, Tom Tully, Daryl Hickman

A KISS FOR SUSIE (1917, Silent, Paramount)
Susie Nolan—Vivian Martin
Director—Robert Thornby
Leading Players—Tom Forman, John Burton, Jack Nelson

KISS ME KATE (1953, MGM)
Lilli Vanessi/Katherine—Kathryn Grayson
Fred Graham/Petruchio—Howard Keel
Director—George Sidney
Leading Players—Ann Miller, Tommy Rall, Bobby Van, Keenan Wynn, James Whitmore, Kurt Kasznar

KISS ME A KILLER (1991, Califilm)
Teresa—Julie Carmen
Tony—Robert Beltran
Director—Marcus De Leon
Leading Players—Guy Boyd, Ramon Franco, Charles Boswell, Sam Vlahos, Brad Blaisell

KISS OF THE SPIDER WOMAN (1985, Island Alive)
Spider Woman—Sonia Braga
Director—Hector Babenco
Leading Players—William Hurt, Raul Julia, Jose Lewgoy

KISS THE BRIDE GOODBYE (1944, GB, Butchers)
Joan Dodd—Patricia Medina
Director—Paul Stein
Leading Players—Jimmy Hanley, Frederick Leister, Marie Lohr

KISSES FOR MY PRESIDENT (1964, Warner Brothers)
Thad McCloud—Fred MacMurray
Leslie McCloud—Polly Bergen
Director—Curtis Bernhardt
Leading Players—Arlene Dahl, Edward Andrews, Eli Wallach

KISSIN' COUSINS (1964, MGM)
Josh Morgan and Jodie Tatum—Elvis Presley
Director—Gene Nelson
Leading Players—Arthur O'Connell, Glenda Farrell, Jack Albertson, Pam Austin, Cynthia Pepper

THE KISSING BANDIT (1948, MGM)
Ricardo—Frank Sinatra
Director—Laslo Benedek
Leding Players—Kathryn Grayson, J. Carroll Naish, Mildred Natwick

KIT CARSON (1928, Silent, Paramount)
Kit Carson—Fred Thomson
Director—Alfred L. Werker
Leding Players—Nora Lane, Dorothy Janis, Raoul Paoli

KIT CARSON (1940, UA)
Kit Carson—Jon Hall
Director—George B. Seitz
Leading Players—Lynn Bari, Dana Andrews, Harold Huber, Ward Bond, Renie Riano

KIT CARSON OVER THE GREAT DIVIDE (1925, Silent, Sunset)
Kit Carson—Jack Mower
Director—Frank S. Mattsion
Leading Players—Roy Stewart, Henry B. Walthall, Marguerite Snow

KITTEN WITH A WHIP (1964, Universal)
Jody Dvorak—Ann-Margret
Director—Douglas Heyes
Leading Players—John Forsythe, Peter Brown, Patricia Barry

KITTY (1929, GB, British International)
Kitty Greenwood—Estelle Brody
Director—Victor Saville
Leading Players—John Stuart, Dorothy Cumming, Marie Ault, Winter Hall

KITTY (1945, Paramount)
Kitty—Paulette Goddard
Director—Mitchell Leisen
Leading Players—Ray Milland, Patric Knowles, Reginald Owen, Cecil Kellaway, Constance Collier

KITTY AND THE BAGMAN (1983, Australia, Quartet)
Kitty O'Rourke—Liddy Clark
Bagman—John Stanton
Director—Donald Crombie
Leading Players—Val Lehman, Gerard McGuire, Collette Mann

KITTY FOYLE (1940, RKO)
Kitty Foyle—Ginger Rogers
Director—Sam Wood
Leading Players—Dennis Morgan, James Craig, Eduardo Ciannelli, Ernest Cossart

KIVALINA OF THE ICE LANDS (1925, Silent, B.C.R. Productions)
Kivalina—Kivalina
Director—Earl Rossman
Leading Players—Aguvaluk, Nashulik, Tokatoo, Nuwak

THE KLANSMAN (1974, Paramount)
Mayor Hardy—David Huddleston
Director—Terence Young
Leading Players—Lee Marvin, Richard Burton, Cameron Mitchell, Lola Falana, Linda Evans

KLONDIKE ANNIE (1936, Paramount)
Sister Annie Alden—Helen Jerome Eddy
Director—Raoul Walsh
Leading Players—Mae West, Victor McLaglen, Phillip Reed

KLONDIKE KATE (1944, Columbia)
Kathleen O'Day—Ann Savage
Director—William Castle
Leading Players—Tom Neal, Glenda Farrell, Constance Worth

KLUTE (1971, Warner Brothers)
John Klute—Donald Sutherland
Director—Alan J. Pakula
Leading Players—Jane Fonda, Charles Cioffi, Roy Scheider, Dorothy Tristan, Rita Gam

THE KNAVE OF HEARTS (1919, Silent, GB, Harma)
Lord Hillsdown—James Knight
Director—F. Martin Thornton
Leading Players—Evelyn Boucher, H. Agar Lyons, J. Edwards Barber

THE KNICKERBOCKER BUCKAROO (1919, Silent, Artcraft)
Teddy Drake—Douglas Fairbanks
Director—Albert Parker
Leading Players—Marjorie Daw, William Wellman, Edythe Chapman, Frank Campeau

A KNIGHT OF THE RANGE (1916, Silent, Universal)
Cheyenne Harry—Harry Carey
Director—Jacques Jaccard
Leading Players—Olive Golden, Hoot Gibson, William Canfield

A KNIGHT OF THE WEST (1921, Silent, W.B.M. Photoplays)
Jack "Zip" Garvin—Olin Francis
Director—Robert McKenzie
Leading Players—Estelle Harrison, Billy Franey, Otto Nelson

KNIGHT WITHOUT ARMOUR (ARMOR) (1937, GB, London Films)
Ainsley Fothergill—Robert Donat
Director—Jacques Feyder
Leading Players—Marlene Dietrich, Irene Vanbrugh, Herbert Lomas, Austin Trevor

KNIGHTS OF THE CITY (1986, New World)
Troy—Leon Issac Kennedy
Joey—Nicholas Campbell
Mookie—John Mengatti
Director—Dominic Orlando
Leading Players—Stoney Jackson, Dino Henderson, Curtis Lema

THE KNOCKOUT KID (1927, Silent, Paramount)
Jack Lanning—Jack Perrin
Director—Albert Rogell
Leading Players—Molly Malone, Eva Thatcher, Bud Osborne

KNOCKOUT REILLY (1927, Silent, Paramount)
Dundee Reilly—Richard Dix
Director—Malcolm St. Clair
Leading Players—Mary Brian, Jack Renault, Harry Gribbon

KNUTE ROCKNE—ALL AMERICAN (1940, Warner Brothers)
Knute Rockne—Pat O'Brien
Director—Lloyd Bacon
Leading Players—Gale Page, Ronald Reagan, Donald Crisp, Albert Basserman

KOSHER KITTY KELLY (1926, Silent, R-C Pictures)
Kitty Kelly—Viola Dane
Director—James W. Horne
Leading Players—Tom Forman, Vera Gordon, Kathleen Myers

KOTCH (1971, ABC-Cinerama)
Joseph P. Kotcher—Walther Matthau
Director—Jack Lemmon
Leading Players—Deborah Winters, Felicia Farr, Charles Aidman, Ellen Greer

KRAMER VS. KRAMER (1979, Columbia)
Ted Kramer—Dustin Hoffman
Joanna Kramer—Meryl Streep
Director—Robert Benton
Leading Players—Jane Alexander, Justin Henry, Howard Duff, George Coe, JoBeth Williams

THE KRAYS (1990, GB, Rank)
Violet Kray—Billie Whitelaw
Ronald Kray—Gary Kemp
Reginald Kray—Martin Kemp
Director—Peter Medak
Leading Players—Susan Fleetwood, Charlotte Cornwell, Jimmy Jewel, Avis Bunnage, Kate Hardie

KUFFS (1992, Universal)
George Kuffs—Christian Slater
Director—Bruce A. Evans
Leading Players—Tony Goldwyn, Mills Jovovich, Bruce Boxleitner, Troy Evans, George de la Pena, Leon Rippy

L

LA TRAVIATA (1982, Accent Films)
Violetta Valery—Teresa Stratas
Director—Franco Zeffirelli
Leading Players—Placido Domingo, Cornell MacNeil, Alan Monk

THE LABOUR LEADER (1917, Silent, GB, British Actors)
John Webster—Fred Groves
Director—Thomas Bentley
Leading Players—Fay Compton, Owen Nares, Christine Silver

THE LAD (1935, GB, Twickenham)
Bill Shane—Gordon Harker
Director—Henry Edwards
Leading Players—Betty Stockfield, Jane Carr, Gerald Barry, Geraldine Fitzgerald

LADDIE (1935, RKO)
Laddie Stanton—John Beal
Director—George Stevens
Leading Players—Gloria Stuart, Virginia Weidler, Charlotte Henry, Donald Crisp

LADDIE (1940, RKO)
Laddie—Tim Holt
Director—Jack Hively
Leading Players—Virginia Gilmore, Joan Carroll, Spring
Byington

LADIES AT EASE (1927, Silent, First Division)
Polly—Pauline Garon
Gert—Gertrude Short
Director—Jerome Storm
Leading Players—Gardner James, Raynond Glenn, Lillian
Hackett, Jean Van Vliet

LADIES AT PLAY (1926, Silent, First National)
Ann Harper—Doris Kenyon
Director—Alfred E. Green
Leading Players—Lloyd Hughes, Louise Fazenda, Ethel Wales

LADIES CLUB (1986, New Line Cinema)
Joan Taylor—Karen Austin
Lucy Bricker—Diana Scarwid
Director—A.K. Allen
Leading Players—Christine Belford, Bruce Davison, Shera
Danese, Beverly Todd

LADIES COURAGEOUS (1944, Universal)
Roberta Harper—Loretta Young
Virgie Alford—Geraldine Fitzgerald
Director—John Rawlins
Leading Players—Diana Barrymore, Anne Gwynne, Evelyn
Ankers

LADIES CRAVE EXCITEMENT (1935, Mascot)
Wilma Howell—Evalyn Knapp
Director—Nick Grinde
Leading Players—Norman Foster, Esther Ralston, Eric Linden

LADIES' DAY (1943, RKO)
Pepita—Lupe Velez
Director—Leslie Goodwins
Leading Players—Eddie Albert, Patsy Kelly, Max Baer

LADIES IN LOVE (1936, 20th Century Fox)
Martha Kerenye—Janet Gaynor
Susie Schmidt—Loretta Young
Yoli Haydn—Constance Bennett
Director—Edward H. Griffith
Leading Players—Simone Simon, Don Ameche, Paul Lukas,
Tyrone Power, Jr., Alan Mowbray

LADIES IN RETIREMENT (1941, Columbia)
Emily Creed—Elsa Lanchester
Louisa Creed—Edith Barrett
Director—Charles Vidor
Leading Players—Ida Lupino, Louis Hayward, Evelyn Keyes,
Isobel Elsom

LADIES LOVE BRUTES (1930, Paramount)
Joe Forziati—George Bancroft
Mimi Howell—Mary Astor
Director—Roland V. Lee
Leading Players—Fredric March, Margaret Quimby, Stanley
Fields

LADIES LOVE DANGER (1935, Fox Film Corp.)
Rita—Mona Barrie

Director—H. Bruce Humberstone
Leading Players—Gilbert Roland, Donald Cook, Adrienne Ames

LADIES' MAN (1931, Paramount)
Jamie Darricott—William Powell
Director—Lothar Mendes
Leading Players—Kay Francis, Carole Lombard, Gilbert Emery

LADIES' MAN (1947, Paramount)
Henry Haskell—Eddie Bracken
Director—William D. Russell
Leading Players—Cass Daley, Virginia Welles, Johnny Coy

THE LADIES' MAN (1961, Paramount)
Herbert H. Heebert—Jerry Lewis
Director—Jerry Lewis
Leading Players—Helen Traubel, Pat Stanley, Kathleen
Freeman

LADIES MUST DRESS (1927, Silent, Fox Film Corp.)
Eve—Virginia Valli
Director—Victor Herman
Leading Players—Lawrence Gray, Hallam Cooley, Nancy Carroll

LADIES MUST LOVE (1933, Universal)
Jeannie—June Knight
Director—E.A. du Pont
Leading Players—Neil Hamilton, Sally O'Neil, Dorothy Burgess

LADIES MUST PLAY (1930, Columbia)
Norma—Dorothy Sebastian
Director—Raymond Cannon
Leading Players—Neil Hamilton, Natalie Moorhead, John
Holland

LADIES OF LEISURE (1930, Columbia)
Kay Arnold—Barbara Stanwyck
Director—Frank Capra
Leading Players—Ralph Graves, Lowell Sherman, Marie Prevost

LADIES OF THE BIG HOUSE (1932, Paramount)
Kathleen Storm—Sylvia Sidney
Director—Marion Gering
Leading Players—Gene Raymond, Wynne Gibson, Rockliffe
Fellowes

LADIES OF THE CHORUS (1948, Columbia)
May Martin—Adele Jergens
Peggy Martin—Marilyn Monroe
Director—Phil Karlson
Leading Players—Rand Brooks, Nana Bryant, Eddie Carr

LADIES OF THE JURY (1932, RKO)
Mrs. Crane—Edna May Oliver
Director—Lowell Sherman
Leading Players—Ken Murray, Roscoe Ates, Kitty Kelly

LADIES OF THE MOB (1928, Silent, Paramount)
Yvonne—Clara Bow
Director—William Wellman
Leading Players—Richard Arlen, Helen Lynch, Mary Alden

LADIES OF WASHINGTON (1944, 20th Century Fox)
Carol—Trudy Marshall
Jerry—Sheila Ryan
Director—Louis King

Leading Players—Ronald Graham, Anthony Quinn, Robert Bailey

LADIES SHOULD LISTEN (1934, Paramount)
Anna Mirelle—Frances Drake
Director—Frank Tuttle
Leading Players—Cary Grant, Edward Everett Horton, Rosita Moreno

LADIES THEY TALK ABOUT (1933, Warner Brothers)
Nan Taylor—Barbara Stanwyck
Director—Howard Bretherton
Leading Players—Preston Foster, Lyle Talbot, Dorothy Burgess, Lillian Roth, Maude Eburne

LADIES WHO DO (1964, GB, Continental Distributing)
Mrs. Cragg—Peggy Mount
Director—C.M. Pennington-Richards
Leading Players—Robert Morley, Harry H. Corbett, Miriam Karlin

LADY AND GENT (1932, Paramount)
Slag Bailey—George Bancroft
Puff Rogers—Wynne Gibson
Director—Stephen Roberts
Leading Players—Charles Starrett, James Gleason, John Wayne

THE LADY AND THE BANDIT (1951, Columbia)
Dick Turpin—Louis Hayward
Joyce Greene—Patricia Medina
Director—Ralph Murphy
Leading Players—Suzanne Dalbert, Tom Tully, John Williams

THE LADY AND THE MOB (1939, Columbia)
Hattie Leonard—Fay Bainter
Director—Ben Stoloff
Leading Players—Ida Lupino, Lee Bowman, Henry Armetta

THE LADY AND THE MONSTER (1944, Republic)
Janice Farell—Vera Hruba Ralston
Patrick Cory—Richard Arlen
Director—George Sherman
Leading Players—Erich von Stroheim, Mary Nash, Sidney Blackmer, Helen Vinson

LADY BE GOOD (1941, MGM)
Marilyn Marsh—Eleanor Powell
Director—Norman Z. Leonard
Leading Players—Ann Sothern, Robert Young, Lionel Barrymore, John Carroll, Red Skelton

LADY BEHAVE (1937, Republic)
Clarice—Patricia Farr
Director—Lloyd Corrigan
Leading Players—Sally Eilers, Neil Hamilton, Joseph Schildkraut, Grant Mitchell

LADY BEWARE (1987, International Video Entertainment)
Katya Yarno—Diane Lane
Director—Karen Arthur
Leading Players—Michael Woods, Cotter Smith, Peter Nevargic

LADY BODYGUARD (1942, Paramount)
A.C. Baker—Anne Shirley
Director—William Clemens
Leading Players—Eddie Albert, Raymond Walburn, Ed Brophy

LADY BY CHOICE (1934, Columbia)
Patsy Patterson—May Robson
Director—David Burton
Leading Players—Carole Lombard, Roger Pryor, Walter Connolly

LADY CAROLINE LAMB (1972, GB, UA)
Lady Caroline Lamb—Sarah Miles
Director—Robert Bolt
Leading Players—Jon Finch, Richard Chamberlain, John Mills, Margaret Leighton

THE LADY CONSENTS (1936, RKO)
Anne Talbot—Ann Harding
Director—Stephen Roberts
Leading Players—Herbert Marshall, Margaret Lindsay, Walter Abel

THE LADY CRAVED EXCITEMENT (1950, GB, Hammer)
Pat—Hy Hazell
Director—Francis Searle
Leading Players—Michael Medwin, Sidney James, Thelma Grigg

THE LADY DRACULA (1974, Media Cinema)
Lemora—Lesley Gilb
Director—Richard Blackburn
Leading Players—Cheryl "Rainbeaux" Smith, William Whitton, Steve Johnson

THE LADY ESCAPES (1937, 20th Century Fox)
Linda Ryan—Gloria Stuart
Director—Eugene Forde
Leading Players—Michael Whalen, George Sanders, Cora Witherspoon

THE LADY EVE (1941, Paramount)
Jean Harrington/Eve—Barbara Stanwyck
Director—Preston Sturges
Leading Players—Henry Fonda, Charles Coburn, Eugene Pallette, William Demarest, Eric Blore

LADY FIGHTS BACK (1937, Universal)
Heather McHale—Irene Hervey
Director—Milton Carruth
Leading Players—Kent Taylor, William Lundigan, Willie Best

LADY FOR A DAY (1933, Columbia)
Apple Annie—May Robson
Director—Frank Capra
Leading Players—Warren William, Guy Kibbee, Glenda Farrell

LADY FOR A NIGHT (1941, Republic)
Jenny Blake—Joan Blondell
Director—Leigh Jason
Leading Players—John Wayne, Ray Middleton, Blanche Yurka

LADY FROM CHEYENNE (1941, Universal)
Annie—Loretta Young
Director—Frank Lloyd
Leading Players—Robert Preston, Edward Arnold, Frank Craven

LADY FROM CHUNGKING (1943, Producers Releasing Corp.)
Kwan Mei—Anna May Wong
Director—William Nigh
Leading Players—Harold Huber, Mae Clarke, Rick Vallin

LADY FROM LOUISIANA (1941, Republic)
Julie Mirbeau—Ona Munson
Director—Bernard Vorhaus
Leading Players—John Wayne, Ray Middleton, Henry Stephenson

LADY FROM NOWHERE (1936, Columbia)
Polly—Mary Astor
Director—Fred Niblo, Jr.
Leading Players—Charles Quigley, Thurston Hall, Victor Kilian

THE LADY FROM SHANGHAI (1948, Columbia)
Elsa Bannister—Rita Hayworth
Director—Orson Welles
Leading Players—Orson Welles, Everett Sloane, Glenn Anders

THE LADY FROM TEXAS (1951, Universal)
Miss Birdie—Josephine Hull
Director—Joseph Pevney
Leading Players—Howard Duff, Mona Freeman, Gene Lockhart, Craig Stevens

THE LADY FROM THE SEA (1929, GB, British International)
Claire le Grange—Mona Goya
Director—Castelton Knight
Leading Players—Moore Marriott, Raymond Milland, Bruce Gordon

THE LADY GAMBLES (1949, Universal)
Joan Boothe—Barbara Stanwyck
Director—Michael Gordon
Leading Players—Robert Preston, Stephen McNally, Edith Barrett, John Hoyt

LADY GODIVA (1955, Universal)
Lady Godiva—Maureen O'Hara
Director—Arthur Lubin
Leading Players—George Nader, Eduard Franz, Leslie Bradley

LADY GODIVA RIDES AGAIN (1955, GB, London/Carroll)
Marjorie Clark—Pauline Stroud
Director—Frank Launder
Leading Players—Dennis Price, John McCallum, Stanley Holloway

LADY GREY (1980, Maverick)
Lady Grey—Ginger Alden
Director—Worth Keeter
Leading Players—David Allen Coe, Paul Ott, Herman Bloodsworth

THE LADY HAS PLANS (1942, Paramount)
Sidney Royce—Paulette Goddard
Director—Sidney Lanfield
Leading Players—Ray Milland, Roland Young, Albert Dekker

LADY IN A CAGE (1964, Paramount)
Mrs. Hilyard—Olivia de Havilland
Director—Walter Grauman
Leading Players—Ann Sothern, Jeff Corey, James Caan

LADY IN A JAM (1942, Universal)
Jane Palmer—Irene Dunne
Director—Gregory La Cava
Leading Players—Patric Knowles, Ralph Bellamy, Eugene Pallette

LADY IN DANGER (1934, GB, Gaumont)
Queen of Ardenberg—Yvonne Arnaud
Director—Tom Walls
Leading Players—Tom Walls, Leon M. Lion, Anne Grey

LADY IN DISTRESS (A WINDOW IN LONDON) (1942, GB, GFD)
Vivienne—Sally Gray
Director—Herbert Mason
Leading Players—Michael Redgrave, Paul Lukas, Hartley Power

A LADY IN LOVE (1920, Silent, Paramount)
Barbara—Ethel Clayton
Director—Walter Edwards
Leading Players—Harrison Ford, Boyd Irwin, Ernest Joy

THE LADY IN QUESTION (1940, Columbia)
Natalie Roguin—Rita Hayworth
Director—Charles Vidor
Leading Players—Brian Aherne, Glenn Ford, Irene Rich

THE LADY IN RED (1979, New World)
Polly Franklin—Pamela Sue Martin
Director—Lewis Teague
Leading Players—Robert Conrad, Louise Fletcher, Robert Hogan

LADY IN THE DARK (1944, Paramount)
Liza Elliott—Ginger Rogers
Director—Mitchell Leisen
Leading Players—Ray Milland, Jon Hall, Warner Baxter, Barry Sullivan, Mischa Auer

LADY IN THE DEATH HOUSE (1944, Producers Releasing Corp.)
Mary—Jean Parker
Director—Steve Sekely
Leading Players—Lionel Atwill, Douglas Fowley, Marcia Mae Jones

LADY IN THE IRON MASK (1952, 20th Century Fox)
Princess Anne/Princess Louise—Patricia Medina
Director—Ralph Murphy
Leading Players—Louis Hayward, Alan Hale, Jr., Judd Holdren

LADY IN WHITE (1988, New Century/Vista)
Amanda—Katherine Helmond
Director—Frank La Loggia
Leading Players—Lukas Haas, Renata Vanni, Angele Bertolini, Len Cariou, Alex Rocco

THE LADY IS A SQUARE (1959, GB, Pathe ABF)
Frances Baring—Anna Neagle
Director—Herbert Wilcox
Leading Players—Frankie Vaughan, Janette Scott, Anthony Newley

THE LADY IS WILLING (1934, GB, Columbia)
Helene Dupont—Binnie Barnes
Director—Gilbert Miller
Leading Players—Leslie Howard, Cedric Hardwicke, Nigel Playfair

THE LADY IS WILLING (1942, Columbia)
Elizabeth Madden—Marlene Dietrich
Director—Mitchell Leisen
Leading Players—Fred MacMurray, Aline MacMahon, Stanley Ridges

LADY JANE (1986, GB, Paramount)
Lady Jane Grey—Helena Bonham Carter
Director—Trevor Nunn
Leading Players—Cary Elwes, John Wood, Michael Hordern, Jill Bennett, Jane Lapotaire

LADY JANE GREY (NINE DAYS A QUEEN) (1936, GB, Gaumont)
Lady Jane Grey—Nova Pilbeam
Director—Robert Stevenson
Leading Players—Cedric Hardwicke, John Mills, Felix Aylmer, Leslie Perrins

LADY KILLER (1933, Warner Brothers)
Dan Quigley—James Cagney
Director—Roy Del Ruth
Leading Players—Mae Clarke, Leslie Fenton, Margaret Lindsay

THE LADY LIES (1929, Paramount)
Joyce Roamer—Claudette Colbert
Director—Hobart Henley
Leading Players—Walter Huston, Charles Ruggles, Patricia Deering, Tom Brown

LADY NOGGS-PEERESS (1929, GB, Silent, Butchers)
Lady Noggs—Joan Morgan
Director—Sidney Morgan
Leading Players—George Bellamy, Yvonne Dulquette, Arthur Lennard

THE LADY OBJECTS (1938, Columbia)
Ann Adams—Gloria Stuart
Director—Erle C. Kenyon
Leading Players—Lanny Ross, Joan Marsh, Roy Benson

LADY OF BURLESQUE (1943, UA)
Dixie Daisy—Barbara Stanwyck
Director—William A. Wellman
Leading Players—Michael O'Shea, J. Edward Bromberg, Iris Adrian, Gloria Dickson

A LADY OF CHANCE (1928, MGM)
Dolly—Norma Shearer
Directors—Hobart Henley & Robert Z. Leonard
Leading Players—Lowell Sherman, Gwen Lee, John Mack Brown

THE LADY OF SCANDAL (1930, MGM)
Elsie—Ruth Chatterton
Director—Sidney Franklin
Leading Players—Basil Rathbone, Ralph Forbes, Nance O'Neil

LADY OF SECRETS (1936, Columbia)
Celia Whittaker—Ruth Chatterton
Director—Marion Gering
Leading Players—Otto Kruger, Lionel Atwill, Marian Marsh

THE LADY OF THE LAKE (1928, GB, Silent, Gainsborough)
Ellen Douglas—Benita Hume
Director—James A. Fitzpatrick
Leading Players—Percy Marmont, Haddon Mason, Lawson Butt

LADY OF THE NIGHT (1925, Silent, MGM)
Florence—Norma Shearer
Director—Monta Bell
Leading Players—Malcolm McGregor, George K. Arthur, Fred Esmellon

LADY OF THE PAVEMENTS (1929, UA)
Nanon del Rayon—Lupe Velez
Director—D.W. Griffith
Leading Players—William Boyd, Jetta Goudal, Albert Conti

LADY OF THE TROPICS (1939, MGM)
Manon De Vargnes—Hedy Lamarr
Director—Jack Conway
Leading Players—Robert Taylor, Joseph Schildkraut, Gloria Franklin

LADY ON A TRAIN (1945, Universal)
Nikki Collins—Deanna Durbin
Director—Charles David
Leading Players—Ralph Bellamy, Edward Everett Horton, George Coulouris

THE LADY PAYS OFF (1951, Universal)
Evelyn Warren—Linda Darnell
Director—Douglas Sirk
Leading Players—Stephen McNally, Gigi Perreau, Virginia Field

LADY POSSESSED (1952, Republic)
Jean Wilson—June Havoc
Directors—William Spier and Roy Kellino
Leading Players—James Mason, Stephen Dunne, Fay Compton

LADY ROBINHOOD (1925, Silent, R-C Pictures)
Senorita Catalina/La Ortiga—Evelyn Brent
Director—Ralph Ince
Leading Players—Robert Ellis, Boris Karloff, William Humphrey

THE LADY SAYS NO (1951, UA)
Dorinda—Joan Caulfield
Director—Frank Ross
Leading Players—David Niven, James Robertson Justice, Leonore Lonergan

LADY SCARFACE (1941, RKO)
Slade—Judith Anderson
Director—Frank Woodruff
Leading Players—Dennis O'Keefe, Frances Neal, Mildred Coles, Marc Lawrence

LADY SINGS THE BLUES (1972, Paramount)
Billie Holiday—Diana Ross
Director—Sidney J. Furie
Leading Players—Billy Dee Williams, Richard Pryor, James Callahan

A LADY SURRENDERS (1930, Universal)
Isabel Beauvel—Rose Hobart
Director—John Stahl
Leading Players—Conrad Nagel, Genevieve Tobin, Basil Rathbone, Carmel Myers

A LADY SURRENDERS (1947, GB, Gainsborough)
Lissa Cambell—Margaret Lockwood
Director—Leslie Arliss
Leading Players—Stewart Granger, Patricia Roc, Tom Walls

A LADY TAKES A CHANCE (1943, RKO)
Mollie Truesdale—Jean Arthur
Director—William A. Seiter
Leading Players—John Wayne, Charles Winninger, Phil Silvers

THE LADY TAKES A FLYER (1958, Universal)
Maggie Colby—Lana Turner
Director—Jack Arnold
Leading Players—Jeff Chandler, Richard Denning, Andra Martin

LADY TAKES A SAILOR (1949, Warner Brothers)
Jennifer Smith—Jane Wyman
Director—Michael Curtiz
Leading Players—Dennis Morgan, Eve Arden, Robert Douglas

A LADY TO LOVE (1930, MGM)
Lena Schultz—Vilma Banky
Director—Victor Seastrom
Leading Players—Edward G. Robinson, Robert Ames, Richard Carle

LADY TUBBS (1935, Universal)
Henrietta "Mom" Tubbs—Alice Brady
Director—Alan Crosland
Leading Players—Douglass Montgomery, Anita Louise, Alan Mowbray

THE LADY VANISHES (1938, GB, Gaumont)
Miss Froy—Dame May Whitty
Director—Alfred Hitchcock
Leading Players—Margaret Lockwood, Michael Redgrave, Paul Lukas, Cecil Parker, Linden Travers

THE LADY VANISHES (1980, GB, Rank)
Miss Froy—Angela Lansbury
Director—Anthony Page
Leading Players—Elliott Gould, Cybil Shepherd, Herbert Lom

THE LADY WANTS MINK (1953, Republic)
Nora Connors—Ruth Hussey
Director—William A. Seiter
Leading Players—Dennis O'Keefe, Eve Arden, William Demarest

THE LADY WHO DARED (1931, First National)
Margaret Townsend—Billie Dove
Director—William Beaudine
Leading Players—Sidney Blackmer, Conway Tearle, Judith Vosselli

LADY WINDERMERE'S FAN (1925, Silent, Warner Brothers)
Lady Windermere—May McAvoy
Director—Ernst Lubitsch
Leading Players—Ronald Colman, Irene Rich, Bert Lytell

THE LADY WITH A LAMP (1951, GB, British Lion)
Florence Nightingale—Anna Neagle
Director—Herbert Wilcox
Leading Players—Michael Wilding, Gladys Young, Felix Aylmer

LADY WITH A PAST (1932, RKO)
Venice Muir—Constance Bennett
Director—Edward H. Griffith
Leading Players—Ben Lyon, David Manners, Don Alvarado

LADY WITH RED HAIR (1940, Warner Brothers)
Mrs. Leslie Carter—Miriam Hopkins
Director—Kurt Bernhardt
Leading Players—Claude Rains, Richard Ainley, John Litel

A LADY WITHOUT A PASSPORT (1950, MGM)
Marianne Lorress—Hedy Lamarr
Director—Joseph H. Lewis
Leading Players—John Hodiak, James Craig, George Macready

THE LADYKILLERS (1956, GB, Ealing)
Professor Marcus—Alec Guinness
The Mayor—Cecil Parker
Louis—Herbert Lom
Harry—Peter Sellers
One-Round—Danny Green
Director—Alexander Mackendrick
Leading Players—Jack Warner, Katie Johnson, Philip Stainton

THE LADY'S FROM KENTUCKY (1939, Paramount)
Penelope "Penny" Hollis—Ellen Drew
Director—Alexander Hall
Leading Players—George Raft, Hugh Herbert, Zasu Pitts

A LADY'S MORALS (1930, MGM)
Jenny Lind—Grace Moore
Director—Sidney Franklin
Leading Players—Reginald Denny, Wallace Beery, Gus Shy

THE LADYBIRD (1927, Silent, First Division)
Diana Whyman—Betty Compson
Director—Walter Lang
Leading Players—Malcolm McGregor, Sheldon Lewis, Hank Mann

LADYHAWKE (1985, Warner Brothers/20th Century Fox)
Isabeau—Michelle Pfeiffer
Director—Richard Donner
Leading Players—Matthew Broderick, Rutger Hauer, Leo McKern

THE LAMPLIGHTER (1921, Silent, Fox Film Corp.)
Willie Sillivan—Raymond McKee
Director—Howard M. Mitchell
Leading Players—Shirley Mason, Albert Knott, Edwin Booth Tilton

LANCER SPY (1937, 20th Century Fox)
Lt. Michael Bruce—George Sanders
Director—Gregory Ratoff
Leading Players—Dolores Del Rio, Peter Lorre, Virginia Field

THE LANDLORD (1970, UA)
Elgar Enders—Beau Bridges
Director—Hal Ashby
Leading Players—Pearl Bailey, Diana Sands, Louis Gossett, Lee Grant

THE LARIAT KID (1929, Silent, Universal)
Tom Richards—Hoot Gibson
Director—Reaves Eason
Leading Players—Ann Christy, Cap Anderson, Mary Foy

LAS VEGAS LADY (1976, Crown International)
Lucky—Stella Stevens
Director—Noel Nosseck
Leading Players—Stuart Whitman, George DiCenzo, Lynne Moody

LASSITER (1984, Warner Brothers)
Lassiter—Tom Selleck

Director—Roger Young
Leading Players—Jane Seymour, Lauren Hutton, Bob Hoskins

THE LAST AMERICAN HERO (1973, 20th Century Fox)
Elroy Jackson, Jr.—Jeff Bridges
Director—Lamont Johnson
Leading Players—Valerie Perrine, Geraldine Fitzgerald, Ned Beatty

THE LAST AMERICAN VIRGIN (1982, Cannon)
Karen—Diana Franklin
Director—Boaz Davidson
Leading Players—Lawrence Monoson, Steve Antin, Joe Rubbo

THE LAST ANGRY MAN (1959, Columbia)
Dr. Sam Ableman—Paul Muni
Director—Daniel Mann
Leading Players—David Wayne, Betsy Palmer, Luther Adler

THE LAST BANDIT (1949, Republic)
Jim Plummer—Forrest Tucker
Director—Joseph Kane
Leading Players—William Elliott, Adrian Booth, Andy Devine

THE LAST BOY SCOUT (1991, Warner Brothers)
Joe Hallenbeck—Bruce Willis
Director—Tony Scott
Leading Players—Damon Wayans, Chelsea Field, Noble Willingham, Taylor Negron, Danielle Harris, Halle Berry, Bruce McGill

THE LAST EMPEROR (1987, Columbia)
Aisin-Gioro "Henry" Pu Yi as an adult—John Lone
Director—Bernardo Bertolucci
Leading Players—Joan Chen, Peter O'Toole, Ying Ruocheng, Victor Wong, Maggie Han, Richard Vuu, Tijger Tsou, Wu Tao, Ryuichi Sakamoto

THE LAST FLIGHT OF NOAH'S ARK (1980, Buena Vista)
Noah Dugan—Elliott Gould
Director—Charles Jarrott
Leading Players—Genevieve Bujold, Ricky Schroder, Tammy Lauren

THE LAST GANGSTER (1937, MGM)
Joe Krozac—Edward G. Robinson
Director—Edward Ludwig
Leading Players—James Stewart, Rose Stradner, Lionel Stander

THE LAST GENTLEMAN (1934, UA)
Cabot Barr—George Arliss
Director—Sidney Lanfield
Leading Players—Edna May Oliver, Janet Beecher, Charlotte Henry, Frank Albertson

THE LAST HARD MEN (1976, 20th Century Fox)
Sam Burgade—Charlton Heston
Zach Provo—James Coburn
Director—Andrew V. McLaglen
Leading Players—Barbara Hershey, Jorge Rivero, Michael Parks

THE LAST MAN ON EARTH (1964, American International)
Robert Morgan—Vincent Price
Directors—Ubaldo Ragona and Sidney Salkow
Leading Players—Franca Bettoia, Emma Danieli, Giacomo Rossi-Stuart

THE LAST MAN TO HANG (1956, GB, Columbia)
Sir Roderick Strood—Tom Conway
Director—Terence Fisher
Leading Players—Elizabeth Sellars, Eunice Grayson, Freda Jackson

THE LAST MARRIED COUPLE IN AMERICA (1980, Universal)
Jeff Thompson—George Segal
Mari Thompson—Natalie Wood
Director—Gilbert Cates
Leading Players—Richard Benjamin, Arlene Golonka, Valerie Harper, Dom DeLuise

THE LAST OF MRS. CHEYNEY (1929, MGM)
Mrs. Cheyney—Norma Shearer
Director—Sidney Franklin
Leading Players—Basil Rathbone, George Barraud, Herbert Bunston, Hedda Hopper

THE LAST OF MRS. CHEYNEY (1937, MGM)
Fay Cheyney—Joan Crawford
Director—Richard Boleslawski
Leading Players—Robert Montgomery, Frank Morgan, Nigel Bruce, William Powell

LAST OF THE BUCCANEERS (1950, Columbia)
Jean Lafite—Paul Henreid
Director—Lew Landers
Leading Players—Jack Oakie, Karin Booth, Mary Anderson

LAST OF THE DUANES (1930, Fox Film Corp.)
Buck Duane—George O'Brien
Director—Alfred Werker
Leading Players—Lucile Brown, Myrna Loy, Walter McGrail

LAST OF THE DUANES (1941, 20th Century Fox)
Buck Duane—George Montgomery
Director—James Tinling
Leading Players—Lynne Roberts, Eve Arden, Francis Ford

THE LAST OF THE FAST GUNS (1958, Universal)
Brad Ellison—Jock Mahoney
Director—George Sherman
Leading Players—Gilbert Roland, Linda Cristal, Eduard Franz

THE LAST OF THE FINEST (1990, Orion)
Frank Daly—Brian Dennehy
Wayne Gross—Joe Pantoliano
Ricky Rodriguez—Jeff Fahey
Howard (Hojo) Jones—Bill Paxton
Director—John Mackenzie
Leading Players—Deborra-Lee Furness, Guy Boyd, Henry Darrow, Lisa Jane Persky, Michael C. Gwynne

LAST OF THE INGRAHAMS (1917, Silent, Triangle)
Jules Ingraham—William Desmond
Director—Walter Edwards
Leading Players—Margery Wilson, Robert McKim, Walt Whitman

LAST OF THE LONE WOLF (1930, Columbia)
Michael Lanyard—Bert Lytell
Director—Richard Boleslawski
Leading Players—Patsy Ruth Miller, Lucien Prival, Otto Matieson

THE LAST OF THE MOHICANS (1920, Silent, Associated Producers)
Chingachgook—Theodore Lorch
Directors—Clarence Brown and Maurice Tourneur
Leading Players—Wallace Beery, Barbara Bedford, Lillian Hall, Henry Woodward, Harry Lorraine, Albert Roscoe

THE LAST OF THE MOHICANS (1936, UA)
Chingachgook—Robert Barret
Director—George B. Seitz
Leading Players—Randolph Scott, Binnie Barnes, Heather Angel, Henry Wilcoxon, Bruce Cabot, Phillip Reed

LAST OF THE PAGANS (1936, MGM)
Taro—Mala
Lilleo—Lotus Long
Director—Richard Thorpe
Leading Players—Telo A. Tematua, Ae A Faaturia, Rangapo A Taipoo

LAST OF THE RED HOT LOVERS (1972, Paramount)
Barney Cashman—Alan Arkin
Director—Gene Saks
Leading Players—Sally Kellerman, Paula Prentiss, Renee Taylor

LAST OF THE REDMEN (1947, Columbia)
Uncas—Rick Vallin
Director—George Sherman
Leading Players—Jon Hall, Michael O'Shea, Evelyn Ankers, Julie Bishop, Buster Crabbe

THE LAST OUTLAW (1936, RKO)
Dean Payton—Harry Carey
Director—Christy Cabanne
Leading Players—Hoot Gibson, Henry B. Walthall, Margaret Callahan

THE LAST REBEL (1971, Columbia)
Burnside Hollis—Joe Namath
Director—Denys McCoy
Leading Players—Jack Elam, Woody Strode, Ty Hardin, Victoria George

THE LAST REMAKE OF BEAU GESTE (1977, Universal)
Beau Geste—Michael York
Director—Marty Feldman
Leading Players—Ann-Margret, Marty Feldman, Peter Ustinov, James Earl Jones

THE LAST STARFIGHTER (1984, Universal)
Alex Rogan—Lance Guest
Director—Nick Castle
Leading Players—Dan O'Herlihy, Catherine Mary Stewart, Barbara Bosson, Robert Preston

THE LAST TEMPTATION OF CHRIST (1988, Universal)
Jesus Christ—Willem Dafoe
Director—Martin Scorsese
Leading Players—Barbara Hershey, Harvey Keitel, Harry Dean Stanton, David Bowie, Andre Gregory

THE LAST TIME I SAW ARCHIE (1961, UA)
Archie Hall—Robert Mitchum
Bill Bowers—Jack Webb
Director—Jack Webb
Leading Players—Martha Hyer, France Nuyen, Joe Flynn

THE LAST TYCOON (1976, Paramount)
Monroe Stahr—Robert De Niro
Director—Elia Kazan
Leading Players—Tony Curtis, Robert Mitchum, Jeanne Moreau, Jack Nicholson

THE LAST WARRIOR (1989, ITC-Label/SVS)
Jim Kemp—Gary Graham
Director—Martin Wragge
Leading Players—Maria Holvoe, Cary-Hiroyuki Tagawa, John Carson

THE LAST WITNESS (1925, GB, Silent, Stoll)
Letitia Brand—Isobel Elsom
Director—Fred Paul
Leading Players—Fred Paul, Stella Arbenina, Queenie Thomas

LATE FOR DINNER (1991, Columbia)
Willie Husband—Brian Wimmer
Director—W. D. Richter
Leading Players—Peter Berg, Marcia Gay Harden, Colleen Flynn, Kyle Secor, Michael Beach, Peter Gallagher

THE LATE GEORGE APLEY (1947, 20th Century Fox)
George Apley—Ronald Colman
Director—Joseph L. Mankiewicz
Leading Players—Peggy Cummins, Vanessa Brown, Richard Haydn

THE LATE LIZ (1971, Gateway)
Liz Adams Hatch—Anne Baxter
Director—Dick Ross
Leading Players—Steve Forrest, James Gregory, Coleen Gray

LATIN LOVERS (1953, MGM)
Nora Taylor—Lana Turner
Roberto Santos—Ricardo Montalban
Director—Mervyn LeRoy
Leading Players—John Lund, Louis Calhern, Jean Hagen

LATINO (1986, Cinecom International)
Eddie Guerrero—Robert Beltran
Director—Haskel Wexler
Leading Players—Annette Cardona, Tony Plana, Julio Medina

LAUGH, CLOWN, LAUGH (1928, Silent, MGM)
The Beppi—Lon Chaney
Director—Herbert Brenon
Leading Players—Bernard Siegel, Loretta Young, Cissy Fitzgerald

LAUGHING ANNIE (1954, GB, Republic)
Laughing Annie—Margaret Lockwood
Director—Herbert Wilcox
Leading Players—Wendell Corey, Forrest Tucker, Ronald Shiner

LAUGHING BOY (1934, MGM)
Laughing Boy—Ramon Novarro
Director—W. S. Van Dyke
Leading Players—Lupe Velez, William B. Davidson, Chief Thunderbird

LAUGHING IRISH EYES (1936, Republic)
Danno O'Keefe—Phil Regan
Director—Joseph Santley
Leading Players—Walter C. Kelly, Evelyn Knapp, Ray Walker

THE LAUGHING LADY (1930, Paramount)
Marjorie Lee—Ruth Chatterton
Director—Victor Schertzinger
Leading Players—Clive Brook, Dan Healey, Nat Pendleton

THE LAUGHING LADY (1946, GB, British National)
Denise Tremayne—Anne Ziegler
Director—Paul L. Stein
Leading Players—Webster Booth, Francis L. Sullivan, Peter Graves

THE LAUGHING POLICEMAN (1973, 20th Century Fox)
Jake Martin—Walter Matthau
Director—Stuart Rosenberg
Leading Players—Bruce Dern, Lou Gossett, Albert Paulsen

LAURA (1944, 20th Century Fox)
Laura Hunt—Gene Tierney
Director—Otto Preminger
Leading Players—Dana Andrews, Clifton Webb, Vincent Price, Judith Anderson

THE LAVENDER BATH LADY (1922, Silent, Universal)
Mamie Conroy—Gladys Walton
Director—King Baggot
Leading Players—Charlotte Pierce, Edward Burns, Tom Ricketts

THE LAVENDER HILL MOB (1951, GB, Ealing)
Henry Holland—Alec Guinness
Pendlebury—Stanley Holloway
Lackery—Sidney James
Shorty—Alfie Bass
Director—Charles Crichton
Leading Players—John Gregson, Edie Martin, Marjorie Fielding, Audrey Hepburn

THE LAW AND JAKE WADE (1958, MGM)
Jake Wade—Robert Taylor
Director—John Sturges
Leading Players—Richard Widmark, Patricia Owens, Robert Middleton

THE LAW AND THE LADY (1951, MGM)
Jane Hoskins—Greer Garson
Director—Edwin H. Knopf
Leading Players—Michael Wilding, Fernando Lamas, Marjorie Main

THE LAW IN HER HANDS (1936, First National)
Mary Wentworth—Margaret Lindsay
Director—William Clemens
Leading Players—Glenda Farrell, Warren Hull, Lyle Talbot

THE LAW VS. BILLY THE KID (1954, Columbia)
Billy The Kid—Scott Brady
Director—William Castle
Leading Players—Betta St. John, James Griffith, Alan Hale, Jr.

LAWMAN (1971, UA)
Marshal Jered Maddox—Burt Lancaster
Director—Michael Winner
Leading Players—Robert Ryan, Lee J. Cobb, Sheree North

A LAWMAN IS BORN (1937, Republic)
Tom Mitchell—Johnny Mack Brown
Director—Sam Newfield

Leading Players—Iris Meredith, Warner Richmond, Mary MacLaren

THE LAWNMOWER MAN (1992, New Line)
Jobe Smith—Jeff Fahey
Director—Brett Leonard
Leading Players—Pierce Brosnan, Jenny Wright, Mark Bringleson, Geoffrey Lewis, Jeremy Slate

LAWRENCE OF ARABIA (1962, GB, Columbia)
T.E. Lawrence—Peter O'Toole
Director—David Lean
Leading Players—Alec Guinness, Anthony Quinn, Jack Hawkins, Jose Ferrer, Anthony Quayle, Claude Rains, Arthur Kennedy, Omar Sharif

THE LAWYER (1969, Paramount)
Tony Petrocelli—Barry Newman
Director—Sidney J. Furie
Leading Players—Harold Gould, Diana Muldaur, Robert Colbert

LAWYER MAN (1933, Warner Brothers)
Anton Adam—William Powell
Director—William Dieterle
Leading Players—Joan Blondell, Helen Vinson, Alan Dinehart

THE LAWYER'S SECRET (1931, Paramount)
Drake Norris—Clive Brook
Directors—Louis Gasnier and Max Marcin
Leading Players—Charles "Buddy" Rogers, Richard Arlen

LAZYBONES (1925, Silent, Fox Film Corp.)
Lazybones—Charles Jones
Director—Frank Borzage
Leading Players—Madge Bellamy, Virginia Marshall, Edythe Chapman

LAZYBONES (1935, GB, RKO)
Sir Reginald Ford—Ian Hunter
Director—Michael Powell
Leading Players—Claire Luce, Sara Allgood, Bernard Nedell

LEADBELLY (1976, Paramount)
Huddie Ledbetter—Roger E. Mosley
Director—Gordon Parks
Leading Players—Paul Benjamin, Madge Sinclair, Alan Manson

LEAN ON ME (1989, Warner Brothers)
Joe Clark—Morgan Freeman
Director—John G. Avildsen
Leading Players—Robert Guillaume, Beverly Todd, Lynne Thigpen, Jermaine Hopkins

THE LEATHER BOYS (1965, GB, Allied Artists)
Reggie—Colin Campbell
Pete—Dudley Sutton
Director—Sidney J. Furie
Leading Players—Rita Tushingham, Gladys Henson, Avice London

THE LEATHER-PUSHERS (1940, Universal)
Dick—Richard Arlen
Director—John Rawlins
Leading Players—Andy Devine, Astrid Allwyn, Douglas Fowley

THE LEATHER SAINT (1956, Paramount)
Father Gil Allen—John Derek
Director—Alvin Ganzer
Leading Players—Paul Douglas, Jody Lawrence, Cesar Romero

THE LEATHERNECK (1929, Pathe)
Joseph Hanlon—William Boyd
Director—Howard Higgin
Leading Players—Alan Hale, Robert Armstrong, Fred Kohler

THE LEATHERNECKS HAVE LANDED (1936, Republic)
Woody Davis—Lew Ayres
Director—Howard Bretherton
Leading Players—Isabel Jewell, Jimmy Ellison, James Burke

LEAVE HER TO HEAVEN (1946, 20th Century Fox)
Ellen Berent—Gene Tierney
Director—John M. Stahl
Leading Players—Cornel Wilde, Jeanne Crain, Vincent Price

LEAVE IT TO BLANCHE (1934, GB, Warner Brothers)
Blanche Wetherby—Olive Blakeney
Director—Harold Young
Leading Players—Henry Kendall, Miki Hood, Griffith Jones

LEAVE IT TO BLONDIE (1945, Columbia)
Blondie—Penny Singleton
Director—Abby Berlin
Leading Players—Arthur Lake, Larry Simms, Marjorie Weaver

LEAVE IT TO HENRY (1949, Monogram)
Henry Latham—Raymond Walburn
Director—Jean Yarborough
Leading Players—Walter Catlett, Gary Gray, Mary Stuart

LEAVE IT TO ME (1933, GB, British International)
Sebastian Help—Gene Gerrard
Director—Monty Banks
Leading Players—Olive Borden, Molly Lamont, George Gee

LEAVE IT TO ME (1937, GB, British Lion)
Sandy—Sandy Powell
Director—Herbert Smith
Leading Players—Iris March, Franklin Dyall, Garry Marsh

LEAVE IT TO SMITH (1934, GB, Gaumont)
Smith—Tom Walls
Director—Tom Walls
Leading Players—Carol Goodner, Anne Grey, Allan Aynesworth

THE LEECH (1921, Silent, Pioneer)
Bill—Alex Hall
Director—Herbert Hancock
Leading Players—Ray Howard, Claire Whitney, Katherine Leon

THE LEECH WOMAN (1960, Universal)
June Talbot—Coleen Gray
Director—Edward Dein
Leading Players—Grant Williams, Phillip Terry, Gloria Talbot

THE LEFT-HANDED GUN (1958, Warner Brothers)
Biily Bonney—Paul Newman
Director—Arthur Penn
Leading Players—Lita Milan, John Dehner, Hurd Hatfield

LEGAL EAGLES (1986, Universal)
Tom Logan—Robert Redford

Laura Kelly—Debra Winger
Director—Ivan Reitman
Leading Players—Daryl Hannah, Brian Dennehy, Terence Stamp

LEGALLY DEAD (1923, Silent, Universal)
Will Campbell—Milton Sills
Director—William Parke
Leading Players—Margaret Campbell, Claire Adams, Edwin Sturgis

THE LEGEND OF BILLIE JEAN (1985, Tri-Star)
Billie Jean—Helen Slater
Director—Matthew Robbins
Leading Players—Keith Gordon, Christian Slater, Richard Bradford, Peter Coyote

THE LEGEND OF LYLAH CLARE (1968, MGM)
Lylah Clare/Elsa Brinkmann—Kim Novak
Director—Robert Aldrich
Leading Players—Peter Finch, Ernest Borgnine, Milton Selzer

THE LEGEND OF NIGGER CHARLEY (1972, Paramount)
Nigger Charley—Fred Williamson
Director—Martin Goldman
Leading Players—D'Urville Martin, Don Pedro Colley, Gertrude Jeanettte

THE LEGEND OF THE LONE RANGER (1981, Universal)
The Lone Ranger/John Reid—Klinton Spilsbury
Director—William A. Fraker
Leading Players—Michael Horse, Christopher Lloyd, Matt Clark

THE LEGEND OF TOM DOOLEY (1959, Columbia)
Tom Dooley—Michael Landon
Director—Ted Post
Leading Players—Jo Morrow, Jack Hogan, Richard Rust

THE LEMON DROP KID (1934, Paramount)
Wally Brooks—Lee Tracy
Director—Marshall Neilan
Leading Players—Helen Mack, William Frawley, Minna Gombell

THE LEMON DROP KID (1951, Paramount)
Lemon Drop Kid—Bob Hope
Director—Sidney Lanfield
Leading Players—Marilyn Maxwell, Lloyd Nolan, Jane Darwell

LENA RIVERS (1932, Tiffany)
Lena Rivers—Charlotte Henry
Director—Phil Rosen
Leading Players—Beryl Mercer, James Kirkwood, Morgan Galloway

LENA'S HOLIDAY (1991, Prism/Crown)
Lena Jung—Felicity Waterman
Director—Michael Kensch
Leading Players—Chris Lemmon, Nick Mancuso, Michael Sarrazin, Noriyuki "Pat" Morita, Bill Dana, Liz Torres

LENNY (1974, UA)
Lenny Bruce—Dustin Hoffman
Director—Bob Fosse
Leading Players—Valerie Perrine, Jan Miner, Stanley Beck

LEONARD PART 6 (1987, Columbia)
Leonard—Bill Cosby

Director—Paul Weiland
Leading Players—Tom Courtenay, Joe Don Baker, Moses Gunn

LEO THE LAST (1970, GB,UA)
Leo—Marcello Mastroianni
Director—John Boorman
Leading Players—Billie Whitelaw, Clavin Lockhart, Glenna Forster Jones

THE LEOPARD LADY (1928, Silent, Pathe)
Paula—Jacqueline Logan
Director—Rupert Julian
Leading Players—Alan Hale, Robert Armstrong, Hedwig Reicher

LEPKE (1975, Warner Brothers)
Louis "Lepke" Buchalter—Tony Curtis
Director—Menahem Golan
Leading Players—Anjanette Comer, Michael Callan, Warren Berlinger

LES GIRLS (1957, MGM)
Joy Henderson—Mitzi Gaynor
Lady Wren—Kay Kendall
Angele Ducros—Tania Elg
Director—George Cukor
Leading Players—Gene Kelly, Jacques Bergerac, Leslie Phillips

LET 'ER GO GALLEGHER (1928, Silent, Pathe)
Gallegher—Junior Coghlan
Director—Elmer Clifton
Leading Players—Harrison Ford, Elinor Fair, Wade Boteler

LET GEORGE DO IT (1940, GB, Ealing)
George—George Formby
Director—Marcel Varnel
Leading Players—Phyllis Calvert, Garry Marsh, Romeny Brent

LETHAL WEAPON (1987, Warner Brothers)
Martin Riggs—Mel Gibson
Director—Richard Donner
Leading Players—Danny Glover, Gary Busey, Mitchell Ryan, Tom Atkins, Darlene Love

LETHAL WEAPON 2 (1989, Warner Brothers)
Martin Riggs—Mel Gibson
Director—Richard Donner
Leading Players—Danny Glover, Joe Pesci, Joss Ackland, Derrick O'Connor, Patsy Kensit

LETHAL WEAPON 3 (1992, Warner Brothers)
Martin Riggs—Mel Gibson
Director—Richard Donner
Leading Players—Danny Glover, Joe Pesci, Rene Russo, Stuart Wilson, Steve Kahan, Darlene Love

LET'S GET HARRY (1986, Tri-Star)
Harry Burke, Jr.—Mark Harmon
Director—Alan Smithee
Leading Players—Michael Schoeffling, Tom Wilson, Rick Rossovitch, Ben Johnson, Gary Busey, Robert Duvall

LET'S KILL UNCLE (1966, Universal)
Major Harrison—Nigel Green
Director—William Castle
Leading Players—Mary Badham, Pat Cardi, Robert Pickering

LET'S SCARE JESSICA TO DEATH (1971, Paramount)
Jessica—Zohra Lampert
Director—John Hancock
Leading Players—Barton Heyman, Kevin O'Connor, Gretchen Corbett

A LETTER FOR EVIE (1945, MGM)
Evie O'Connor—Marsha Hunt
Director—Jules Dassin
Leading Players—John Carroll, Hume Cronyn, Spring Byington

LETTER FROM AN UNKNOWN WOMAN (1948, Universal)
Lisa Berndie—Joan Fontaine
Director—Max Ophuls
Leading Players—Louis Jourdan, Mady Christians, Marcel Journet

A LETTER TO THREE WIVES (1948, 20th Century Fox)
Deborah Bishop—Jeanne Crain
Lora May Hollingsway—Linda Darnell
Rita Phipps—Ann Sothern
Director—Joseph L. Mankiewicz
Leading Players—Kirk Douglas, Paul Douglas, Barbara Lawrence, Jeffrey Lynn

LETTY LYNTON (1932, MGM)
Letty Lynton—Joan Crawford
Director—Clarence Brown
Leading Players—Robert Montgomery, Nils Asther, Lewis Stone, May Robson

LIANNA (1983,UA)
Lianna—Linda Griffiths
Director—John Sayles
Leading Players—Jane Hallaren, Jon DeVries, Jo Henderson

LIBELED LADY (1936, MGM)
Connie Allenbury—Myrna Loy
Director—Jack Conway
Leading Players—William Powell, Jean Harlow, Spencer Tracy, Walter Connolly

THE LIBERATION OF L.B. JONES (1970, Columbia)
L.B. Jones—Roscoe Lee Browne
Director—William Wyler
Leading Players—Lee J. Cobb, Anthony Zerbe, Lola Falana

LICENSE TO DRIVE (1988, 20th Century Fox)
Les—Corey Haim
Director—Gregg Beeman
Leading Players—Corey Feldman, Carol Kane, Richard Masur, Heather Graham

LICENSE TO KILL (1989, MGM-United Artists)
James Bond—Timothy Dalton
Director—John Glen
Leading Players—Carey Lowell, Robert Davi, Talisa Soto, Anthony Zerbe, Frank McRae

LIEUT. DANNY, U.S.A. (1916, Silent, Triangle)
Lt. Danny Ward—William Desmond
Director—Walter Edwards
Leading Players—Enid Markey, Gertrude Claire, Thornton Edwards

LIEUTENANT DARING, RN (1935, GB, Butchers)
Lt. Bob Daring—Hugh Williams
Director—Reginald Denham
Leading Players—Geraldine Fitzgerald, Frederick Lloyd, Jerry Verno

LT. ROBIN CRUSOE, U.S.N. (1966, Buena Vista)
Lt. Robin Crusoe—Dick Van Dyke
Director—Bryon Paul
Leading Players—Nancy Kwan, Akim Tamiroff, Arthur Malet

THE LIEUTENANT WORE SKIRTS (1956, 20th Century Fox)
Katy Whitcomb—Sheree North
Director—Frank Tashlin
Leading Players—Tom Ewell, Rita Moreno, Rick Jason

THE LIFE AND TIMES OF GRIZZLY ADAMS (1974, Sunn Classic)
James Capen Adams—Dan Haggerty
Director—Richard Friendenberg
Leading Players—Don Shanks, Marjorie Harper, Lisa Jones

THE LIFE AND TIMES OF JUDGE ROY BEAN (1972, National General)
Judge Roy Bean—Paul Newman
Director—John Huston
Leading Players—Jacqueline Bisset, Ava Gardner, Ned Beatty, John Huston, Roddy McDowall, Anthony Perkins

LIFE BEGINS FOR ANDY HARDY (1941, MGM)
Andy Hardy—Mickey Rooney
Director—George B. Seitz
Leading Players—Lewis Stone, Judy Garland, Fay Holden

THE LIFE OF EMILE ZOLA (1937, Warner Brothers)
Emile Zola—Paul Muni
Director—William Dieterle
Leading Players—Gale Sondergaard, Joseph Schildkraut, Gloria Holden, Donald Crisp

A LIFE OF HER OWN (1950, MGM)
Lily Brannel James—Lana Turner
Director—George Cukor
Leading Players—Ray Milland, Tom Ewell, Louis Calhern, Ann Dvorak, Barry Sullivan

THE LIFE OF JIMMY DOLAN (1933, Warner Brothers)
Jimmy Dolan—Douglas Fairbanks, Jr.
Director—Archie Mayo
Leading Players—Loretta Young, Aline MacMahon, Guy Kibbee

THE LIFE OF RILEY (1949, Universal)
Chester A. Riley—William Bendix
Director—Irving Brecher
Leading Players—Rosemary Camp, James Gleason, Bill Goodwin

THE LIFE OF VERGIE WINTERS (1934, RKO)
Vergie Winters—Ann Harding
Director—Alfred Santell
Leading Players—John Boles, Helen Vinson, Betty Furness

LIFE WITH BLONDIE (1946, Columbia)
Blondie—Penny Singleton
Director—Abby Berlin
Leading Players—Arthur Lake, Larry Simms, Marjorie Kent

LIFE WITH FATHER (1947, Warner Brothers)
Clarence Day—William Powell
Director—Michael Curtiz
Leading Players—Irene Dunne, Elizabeth Taylor, Edmund Gwenn, Zasu Pitts, Jimmy Lydon

LIFE WITH HENRY (1941, Paramount)
Henry Aldrich—Jackie Cooper
Director—Jay Theodore Reed
Leading Players—Leila Ernst, Eddie Bracken, Fred Niblo

LIFEGUARD (1976, Paramount)
Rick Carlson—Sam Elliott
Director—Daniel Petrie
Leading Players—Anne Archer, Stephen Young, Parker Stevenson

LIGHT FINGERS (1929, Columbia))
Light Fingers—Ian Keith
Director—Joseph Henabery
Leading Players—Dorothy Revier, Carroll Nye, Ralph Theodore

LIGHT FINGERS (1957, GB, Archway)
Rose Levenham—Eunice Gayson
Director—Terry Bishop
Leading Players—Roland Culver, Guy Rolfe, Ronald Howard

LIGHT SLEEPER (1992, Seven Arts)
John Letour—Willem Dafoe
Director—Paul Schrader
Leading Players—Susan Sarandon, Dana Delany, David Clennon, Mary Beth Hurt, Victor Gruber, Jane Adams

LIGHTNIN' (1930, Fox Film Corp.)
"Lightnin'" Bill Jones—Will Rogers
Director—Henry King
Leading Players—Louise Dresser, Joel McCrea, Helen Cohan

LIGHTNIN' CRANDALL (1937, Republic)
Bob Crandall—Bob Steele
Director—Sam Newfield
Leading Players—Lois January, Charlie King, Frank LaRue

LIKE FATHER, LIKE SON (1987, Tri-Star)
Dr. Jack Hammond—Dudley Moore
Chris Hammond—Kirk Cameron
Director—Rod Daniel
Leading Players—Margaret Colin, Catherine Hicks, Patrick O'Neal, Sean Astin

LI'L ABNER (1940, RKO)
Li'l Abner Yokum—Granville Owen
Director—Albert S. Rogell
Leading Players—Martha O'Driscoll, Mona Ray, Johnny Morris, Buster Keaton

LI'L ABNER (1959, Paramount)
Li'l Abner Yokum—Peter Palmer
Director—Melvin Frank
Leading Players—Leslie Parrish, Stubby Kaye, Julie Newmar, Howard St. John, Stella Stevens

LILI (1953, MGM)
Lili Daurier—Leslie Caron
Director—Charles Walters

Leading Players—Mel Ferrer, Jean Pierre Aumont, Zsa Zsa Gabor, Kurt Kasznar

LILIOM (1930, Fox Film Corp.)
Liliom—Charles Farrell
Director—Frank Borzage
Leading Players—Rose Hobart, Estelle Taylor, Lee Tracy

LILITH (1964, Columbia)
Lilith Arthur—Jean Seberg
Director—Robert Rossen
Leading Players—Warren Beatty, Peter Fonda, Kim Hunter

LILLI MARLENE (1951, GB, RKO)
Lilli Marlene—Lisa Daniely
Director—Arthur Crabtree
Leading Players—Hugh McDermott, Richard Murdoch, Stanley Baker

LILLIAN RUSSELL (1940, 20th Century Fox)
Lillian Russell—Alice Faye
Director—Irving Cummings
Leading Players—Don Ameche, Henry Fonda, Edward Arnold, Warren William, Leo Carrillo

LILLY TURNER (1933, Warner Brothers)
Lilly Turner—Ruth Chatterton
Director—William A. Wellman
Leading Players—George Brent, Frank McHugh, Ruth Donnelly

LILY CHRISTINE (1932, GB, Paramount British)
Lily Christine—Corinne Griffith
Director—Paul Stein
Leading Players—Colin Clive, Margaret Bannerman, Miles Mander

LILY IN LOVE (1985, New Line Cinema)
Lily Wynn—Maggie Smith
Director—Karoly Malick
Leading Players—Christopher Plummer, Elke Sommer, Adolph Green

LILY OF THE ALLEY (1923, GB, Hepworth)
Lily—Chrissie White
Director—Henry Edwards
Leading Players—Henry Edwards, Campbell Gullan, Mary Brough

THE LINCOLN CONSPIRACY (1977, Sunn Classic)
Abraham Lincoln—John Anderson
Director—James L. Conway
Leading Players—Bradford Dillman, John Dehner, Robert Middleton, James Greene

LINDA (1929, Silent, Willis Kent)
Linda—Helen Foster
Director—Mrs. Wallace Reid
Leading Players—Warner Baxter, Noah Beery, Mitchell Lewis

LINDA (1960, GB, Independent Artists)
Linda—Carol White
Director—Don Sharp
Leading Players—Alan Rothwell, Cavan Malone, Edward Cast

LINDA BE GOOD (1947, Producers Releasing Corp.)
Linda Prentiss—Elyse Knox
Director—Frank McDonald
Leading Players—John Hubbard, Marie Wilson, Gordon Richards

LINGERIE (1928, Silent, Tiffany)
Angele Ree/"Lingerie"—Alice White
Director—George Melford
Leading Players—Malcolm McGregor, Milfred Harris, Armand Kaliz

THE LION IN WINTER (1968, GB, Avco Embassy)
King Henry II—Peter O'Toole
Director—Anthony Harvey
Leading Players—Katharine Hepburn, Jane Merrow, John Castle, Timothy Dalton, Anthony Hopkins

A LION IN THE STREETS (1953, Warner Brothers)
Hank Martin—James Cagney
Director—Raoul Walsh
Leading Players—Barbara Hale, Anne Francis, Warner Anderson

THE LIQUIDATOR (1966, GB, MGM)
Boysie Oakes—Rod Taylor
Director—Jack Cardiff
Leading Players—Trevor Howard, Jill St. John, Wilfrid Hyde-White

LISA (1962, GB, 20th Century Fox)
Lisa Held—Dolores Hart
Director—Philip Dunne
Leading Players—Stephen Boyd, Leo McKern, Hugh Griffith

LISA (1990, MGM/UA)
Lisa—Staci Keanan
Director—Gary Sherman
Leading Players—Cheryl Ladd, D.W. Moffett, Tanay Fenmore, Jeffrey Tambor, Edan Gross, Julie Cobb

LISETTE (1961, Medallion)
Lisette—Greta Chi
Director—John Agar
Leading Players—John Agar, Walter Klavun, John Cestare

THE LIST OF ADRIAN MESSENGER (1963, Universal)
Adrian Messenger—John Merivale
Director—John Huston
Leading Players—George C. Scott, Dana Wynter, Kirk Douglas, Clive Brook, Herbert Marshall

LISTEN TO ME (1989, Columbia)
Tucker Muldowney—Kirk Cameron
Director—Douglas Day Stewart
Leading Players—Jami Gertz, Roy Scheider, Amanda Peterson, Tim Quill, George Wyner

LISZTOMANIA (1975, GB, Warner Brothers)
Franz Liszt—Roger Daltrey
Director—Ken Russell
Leading Players—Sara Kestelman, Paul Nicholas, Fiona Lewis

THE LITTLE ADVENTURESS (1938, Columbia)
Pinky Horton—Edith Fellows
Director—D. Ross Lederman
Leading Players—Richard Fiske, Jacqueline Wells, Cliff Edwards

LITTLE ANNIE ROONEY (1925, Silent, UA)
Annie Rooney—Mary Pickford
Director—William Beaudine
Leading Players—William Haines, Walter James, Gordon Smith

THE LITTLE BALLERINA (1951, GB, Gaumont/British Lion)
Joan—Yvonne Marsh
Director—Lewis Gilbert
Leading Players—Marian Chapman, Doreen Richards, Kay Henderson

LITTLE BIG MAN (1970, National General)
Jack Crabb—Dustin Hoffman
Director—Arthur Penn
Leading Players—Faye Dunaway, Martin Balsam, Richard Mulligan, Chief Dan George, Jeff Corey

LITTLE BIG SHOT (1935, Warner Brothers)
Gloria Gibbs—Sybil Jason
Director—Michael Curtiz
Leading Players—Glenda Farrell, Robert Armstrong, Edward Everett Horton

LITTLE BOY LOST (1953, Paramount)
Jean—Christian Fourcade
Director—George Seaton
Leading Players—Bing Crosby, Claude Dauphin, Gabrielle Dorziat

THE LITTLE BROTHER (1917, Silent, Triangle)
Jerry Ross—Enid Bennett
Director—Charles Miller
Leading Players—William Garwood, Josephine Headley, Edmund Cobb

LITTLE CAESAR (1931, Warner Brothers)
Cesare Enrico Bandello/Rico-Little Caesar—Edward G. Robinson
Director—Mervyn LeRoy
Leading Players—Douglas Fairbanks, Jr., Glenda Farrell, William Collier, Jr., Ralph Ince

THE LITTLE CLOWN (1921, Realart)
Pat—Mary Miles Minter
Director—Thomas N. Heffron
Leading Players—Jack Mulhall, Winter Hall, Helen Dunbar

THE LITTLE COLONEL (1935, Fox Film Corp.)
Lloyd Sherman—Shirley Temple
Director—David Butler
Leading Players—Lionel Barrymore, Evelyn Venable, John Lodge

LITTLE COMRADE (1919, Silent, Paramount)
Genevieve Hubbard—Vivian Martin
Director—Chester Withey
Leading Players—Niles Welch, Gertrude Claire, Richard Cummings

THE LITTLE DAMOZEL (1933, GB, British & Dominions)
Julie Alardy—Anna Neagle
Director—Herbert Wilcox
Leading Players—James Rennie, Benita Hume, Athole Stewart

LITTLE DARLINGS (1980, Paramount)
Ferris—Tatum O'Neal
Angel—Kristy McNichol
Director—Ronald F. Maxwell
Leading Players—Armand Assante, Matt Dillon, Maggie Blye

LITTLE DOLLY DAYDREAM (1938, GB, Butchers)
Dolly—Binkie Stuart
Director—Oswald Mitchell
Leading Players—Talbot O'Farrell, Jane Welsh, Warren Jenkins

LITTLE DORRIT (1988, Cannon)
Little Dorrit—Sarah Pickering
Director—Christine Edzard
Leading Players—Alec Guinness, Derek Jacobi, Joan Greenwood, Max Wall, Cyril Cusack, Robert Morley

THE LITTLE DRUMMER GIRL (1984, Warner Brothers)
Charlie—Diane Keaton
Director—George Roy Hill
Leading Players—Yorgo Voyagis, Klaus Kinski, Sami Frey

LITTLE EGYPT (1951, Universal)
Izora—Rhonda Fleming
Director—Frederick de Cordova
Leading Players—Mark Stevens, Nancy Guild, Charles Drake

LITTLE EVA ASCENDS (1922, Silent, Metro)
Roy St. George/Little Eva—Gareth Hughes
Director—George D. Baker
Leading Players—Eleanor Fields, May Collins, Unice Vin Moore

LITTLE FAUSS AND BIG HALSY (1970, Paramount)
Big Halsy—Robert Redford
Little Fauss—Michael J. Pollard
Director—Sidney J. Furie
Leading Players—Lauren Hutton, Noah Beery, Jr., Lucille Benson

LITTLE 'FRAID LADY (1920, Silent, R-C Pictures)
Cecilia—Mae Marsh
Director—John G. Adolfi
Leading Players—Tully Marshall, Herbert Prior, Charles Meredith

LITTLE FRIEND (1934, GB, Gaumont)
Felicity Hughes—Nova Pilbeam
Director—Berthold Viertel
Leading Players—Matheson Lang, Lydia Sherwood, Arthur Margetson

THE LITTLE GIANT (1933, Warner Brothers)
James Francis "Bugs" Ahearn—Edward G. Robinson
Director—Roy Del Ruth
Leading Players—Helen Vinson, Mary Astor, Kenneth Thomson

THE LITTLE GIRL WHO LIVES DOWN THE LANE (1977, Canada, Rank)
Rynn Jacobs—Jodie Foster
Director—Nicholas Gessner
Leading Players—Martin Sheen, Alexis Smith, Mort Shuman

THE LITTLE GRAY LADY (1914, Silent, Famous Players)
Anna Grey—Jane Gray
Director—Francis Powers
Leading Players—James Cooley, Jane Fearnley, Hal Clarendon

LITTLE IODINE (1946,UA)
   Little Iodine—Jo Ann Marlowe
   Director—Reginald LeBorg
   Leading Players—Marc Cramer, Eve Whitney, Irene Ryan

THE LITTLE IRISH GIRL (1926, Silent, Warner Brothers)
   Dot Walker—Dolores Costello
   Director—Roy Del Ruth
   Leading Players—John Harron, Matthew Betz, Lee Moran

LITTLE JOE, THE WRANGLER (1942, Universal)
   Little Joe Smith—Fuzzy Knight
   Director—Lewis D. Collins
   Leading Players—Johnny Mack Brown, Tex Ritter, Jennifer Holt

LITTLE JOHNNY JONES (1930, Warner Brothers)
   Johnny Jones—Eddie Buzzell
   Director—Mervyn LeRoy
   Leading Players—Alice Day, Edna Murphy, Robert Edeson

THE LITTLE KIDNAPPERS (1954, GB,UA)
   Harry—Jon Whiteley
   Davy—Vincent Winter
   Director—Philip Leacock
   Leading Players—Duncan Macrae, Jean Anderson, Adrienne Corri

LITTLE LAURA AND BIG JOHN (1973, Crown International)
   Laura—Karen Black
   John—Fabian Forte
   Directors—Luke Moberly and Bob Woodburn
   Leading Players—Ivy Thayer, Kenny Miller, Cliff Frates

THE LITTLE LIAR (1916, Silent, Triangle)
   Maggie—Mae Marsh
   Director—Lloyd Ingraham
   Leading Players—Robert Harron, Olga Gray, Carl Stockdale

LITTLE LORD FAUNTLEROY (1914, GB, Silent, Kinematograph)
   Cedric Erroll—Gerald Royston
   Director—F. Martin Thornton
   Leading Players—Jene Wells, H. Agar Lyons, Bernard Vaughn

LITTLE LORD FAUNTLEROY (1921, Silent,UA)
   Cedric Erroll—Mary Pickford
   Directors—Alfred E. Green and Jack Pickford
   Leading Players—Claude Gillingwater, Joseph Dowling, James Marcus

LITTLE LORD FAUNTLEROY (1936,UA)
   Ceddie Erroll—Freddie Bartholomew
   Director—John Cromwell
   Leading Players—C. Aubrey Smith, Dolores Costello, Henry Stephenson, Guy Kibbee, Mickey Rooney

THE LITTLE MADEMOISELLE (1915, Silent, World)
   The French Girl—Vivian Martin
   Director—Oscar Eagle
   Leading Players—Arthur Ashley

LITTLE MALCOLM (1974, GB, Apple Films)
   Malcolm Scrawdyke—John Hurt
   Director—Stuart Cooper
   Leading Players—John McEnery, Raymond Platt, Rosalind Ayres

LITTLE MAN TATE (1991, Orion)
   Fred Tate—Adam Hann-Byrd
   Director—Jodie Foster
   Leading Players—Jodie Foster, Diane Wiest, Harry Connick, Jr., David Pierce, P. J. Ochlan, Debi Mazur

LITTLE MEN (1935, Mascot)
   Franz—Junior Durkin
   Dan—Frankie Darro
   Demi—Dickie Moore
   Director—Phil Rosen
   Leading Players—Ralph Morgan, Erin O'Brien-Moore, Cora Sue Collins, Phyllis Fraser

LITTLE MEN (1940, RKO)
   Dan—Jimmy Lydon
   Teddy—Richard Nichols
   Robby—Casey Johnson
   Director—Norman Z. McLeod
   Leading Players—Kay Francis, Jack Oakie, George Bancroft, Charles Esmond

THE LITTLE MERMAID (1989, Buena Vista)
   Ariel—Voice of Jodi Benson
   Directors—John Musker & Ron Clements
   Leading Players—Voices of Rene Auberjonois, Christopher Daniel Barnes, Pat Carroll, Paddi Edwards, Buddy Hackett

THE LITTLE MINISTER (1934, RKO)
   Gavin—John Beal
   Director—Richard Wallace
   Leading Players—Katharine Hepburn, Alan Hale, Donald Crisp

LITTLE MISS BIG (1946, Universal)
   Mary Jane Baxter—Fay Holden
   Director—Erle C. Kenton
   Leading Players—Beverly Simmons, Frank McHugh, Fred Brady

LITTLE MISS BROADWAY (1938, 20th Century Fox)
   Betsy Brown—Shirley Temple
   Director—Irving Cummings
   Leading Players—George Murphy, Jimmy Durante, Phyllis Brooks

LITTLE MISS BROWN (1915, Silent, World)
   Betty Brown—Vivian Martin
   Director—James Young
   Leading Players—Julia Stuart, Edward M. Kimball, Crauford Kent

LITTLE MISS HOOVER (1918, Paramount)
   Nancy Craddock—Marguerite Clark
   Director—John Stuart Robertson
   Leading Players—Eugene O'Brien, Alfred Hickman, Forrest Robinson

LITTLE MISS MARKER (1934, Paramount)
   Miss Marker—Shirley Temple
   Director—Alexander Hall
   Leading Players—Adolphe Menjou, Dorothy Dell, Charles Bickford, Lynn Overman

LITTLE MISS MARKER (1980, Universal)
   The Kid/Miss Marker—Sara Stimson
   Director—Walter Bernstein

Leading Players—Walter Matthau, Julie Andrews, Tony Curtis, Bob Newhart, Lee Grant

LITTLE MISS MOLLY (1940, Alliance)
Molly Martin—Binkie Stuart
Director—Alex Bryce
Leading Players—Maureen O'Hara, Tom Burke, Philip Reed

LITTLE MISS NOBODY (1933, GB, Warner Brothers)
Karen Bergen—Winna Winifried
Director—John Daumnery
Leading Players—Sebastian Shaw, Betty Huntley Wright, Alice O'Day

LITTLE MISS NOBODY (1936, 20th Century Fox)
Judy Devlin—Jane Withers
Director—John Blystone
Leading Players—Jane Darwell, Ralph Morgan, Sara Haden

LITLE MISS REBELLION (1920, Silent, Paramount)
Grand Duchess Marie—Dorothy Gish
Director—George Fawcett
Leading Players—Ralph Graves, George Siegmann, Riley Hatch

LITTLE MISS ROUGHNECK (1938, Columbia)
Foxine LaRue—Edith Fellows
Director—Aubrey Scotto
Leading Players—Leo Carrillo, Scott Colton, Jacqueline Wells

LITTLE MISS SMILES (1922, Silent, Fox Film Corp.)
Ruth Aaronson—Shirley Mason
Director—Jack Ford
Leading Players—Gaston Glass, George Williams, Martha Franklin

LITTLE MISS SOMEBODY (1937, GB, Butchers)
Binkie Sladen—Binkie Stuart
Director—Walter Tennyson
Leading Players—John Longden, Kathleen Kelly, Jane Carr

LITTLE MISS THOROUGHBRED (1938, Warner Brothers)
Mary Ann—Janet Chapman
Director—John Farrow
Leading Players—John Litel, Ann Sheridan, Frank McHugh

LITTLE MISTER JIM (1946, MGM)
Little Jim Tukker—Jackie "Butch" Jenkins
Director—Fred Zinnemann
Leading Players—James Craig, Frances Gifford, Luana Patten

LITTLE NELLIE KELLY (1940, MGM)
Nellie Kelly—Judy Garland
Director—Norman Taurog
Leading Players—George Murphy, Charles Winninger, Douglas McPhail

LITTLE NIKITA (1988, Columbia)
Jeff Grant—River Phoenix
Director—Richard Benjamin
Leading Players—Sidney Poitier, Richard Jenkins, Caroline Kava, Richard Bradford

THE LITTLE ONES (1965, GB, Columbia)
Jackie—Carl Gonzales
Ted—Kim Smith
Director—Jim O'Connolly

Leading Players—Dudley Foster, Derek Newark, Jean Marlow

LITTLE ORPHAN ANNIE (1932, RKO)
Little Orphan Annie—Mitzi Green
Director—John Robertson
Leading Players—Buster Phelps, May Robson, Kate Lawson, Edgar Kennedy

LITTLE ORPHAN ANNIE (1938, Paramount)
Little Orphan Annie—Ann Gillis
Director—Ben Holmes
Leading Players—Robert Kent, June Travis, J. Farrell MacDonald

LITTLE ORVIE 1940, RKO)
Orvie Stone—John Sheffield
Director—Ray McCarey
Leading Players—Ernest Truex, Dorothy Tree, Ann Todd

LITTLE PAL (1915, Famous Players)
"Little Pal"—Mary Pickford
Director—James Kirkwood
Leading Players—Russell Bassett, George Anderson, William Lloyd

A LITTLE PATRIOT (1917, Silent, Pathe)
The Little Patriot—Baby Marie Osborne
Director—William Bertram
Leading Players—Herbert Standing, Marian Warner, Jack Connolly

THE LITTLE PRINCE (1974, GB, Paramount)
The Little Prince—Steven Warner
Director—Stanley Donen
Leading Players—Richard Kiley, Bob Fosse, Gene Wilder

THE LITTLE PRINCESS (1939, 20th Century Fox)
Sara Crewe—Shirley Temple
Director—Walter Lang
Leading Players—Richard Greene, Anita Louise, Ian Hunter

THE LITTLE SCHOOL MA'AM (1916, Silent, Triangle)
Nan—Dorothy Gish
Directors—C.M. and S.A. Franklin
Leading Players—Elmer Clifton, George Pierce, Jack Brammall

LITTLE SHEPHERD OF KINGDOM COME (1961, 20th Century Fox)
Chad—Jimmie Rodgers
Director—Andrew V. McLaglen
Leading Players—Luana Patten, Chill Wills, Linda Hutchins

LITTLE TOUGH GUY (1938, Universal)
Johnny Boylan—Billy Halop
Director—Harold Young
Leading Players—Huntz Hall, Gabriel Dell, Bernard Punsley, David Gorcey, Hally Chester

THE LITTLE WILD GIRL (1928, Silent, Trinity)
Marie Celeste—Lila Lee
Director—Frank S. Mattison
Leading Players—Cullen Landis, Frank Merrill, Sheldon Lewis

LITTLE WILDCAT (1922, Vitagraph)
Mag O' the Alley—Alice Calhoun
Director—David Divad

Leading Players—Ramsey Wallace, Herbert Fortier, Oliver Hardy

LITTLE WOMEN (1933, RKO)
Jo March—Katharine Hepburn
Amy March—Joan Bennett
Beth March—Jean Parker
Meg March—Frances Dee
Director—George Cukor
Leading Players—Paul Lukas, Edna May Oliver, Henry Stephenson, Douglass Montgomery

LITTLE WOMEN (1949, MGM)
Jo March—June Allyson
Beth March—Margaret O'Brien
Amy March—Elizabeth Taylor
Meg March—Janet Leigh
Director—Mervyn LeRoy
Leading Players—Peter Lawford, Rosanno Brazzi, Mary Astor

THE LITTLEST HORSE THIEVES (1977, Buena Vista)
Dave Sadler—Andrew Harrison
Tommy Sadler—Benjie Bolgar
Alice Sandman—Chloe Franks
Director—Charles Jarrott
Leading Players—Alastair Sim, Peter Barkworth, Maurice Colbourne

THE LITTLEST OUTLAW (1955, Buena Vista)
Pablito—Andres Velasquez
Director—Roberto Gavaldon
Leading Players—Pedro Armendariz, Joseph Calleia, Rodolfo Acosta

THE LITTLEST REBEL (1935, Fox Film Corp.)
Virginia Houston Cary—Shirley Temple
Director—David Butler
Leading Players—John Boles, Jack Holt, Karen Morley, Bill Robinson

THE LIVE WIRE (1937, GB, British Lion)
James Cody—Bernard Nedell
Director—Herbert Brenon
Leading Players—Jean Gillie, Hugh Wakefield, Arthur Wontner

LIVES OF A BENGAL LANCER (1935, Paramount)
Lt. McGregor—Gary Cooper
Director—Henry Hathaway
Leading Players—Franchot Tone, Richard Cromwell, Guy Standing, C. Aubrey Smith, Monte Blue

LIVIN' LARGE (1991, Goldwyn)
Dexter Jackson—Terrence 'T.C.' Carson
Director—Michael Schultz
Leading Players—Lisa Arrindell, Blanche Baker, Nathaniel (Afrika) Hall, Julia Campbell

LIVING TO DIE (1990, PM Entertainment)
Maggie—Darcy DeMoss
Director—Wings Hauser
Leading Players—Wings Hauser, Asher Brauner, Arnold Vosloo, R.J. Walker, Minnie Madden, Wendy MacDonald

LIVINGSTONE (1925, GB, Silent, Butchers)
David Livingstone—M.A. Wetherell
Director—M.A. Wetherell

Leading Players—Molly Rogers, Henry Walton, Reginald Fox

LIZZIE (1957, MGM)
Elizabeth Richmond—Eleanor Parker
Director—Hugo Haas
Leading Players—Richard Boone, Joan Blondell, Hugo Haas

THE LLANO KID (1940, Paramount)
The Llano Kid—Tito Guizar
Director—Edward Venturini
Leading Players—Alan Mowbray, Gale Sondergaard, Jane Clayton

LOAN SHARK (1952, Lippert)
Joe Gargan—George Raft
Director—Seymour Friedman
Leading Players—Dorothy Hart, Paul Stewart, Helen Wescott

LOCAL BOY MAKES GOOD (1931, First National)
John Miller—Joe E. Brown
Director—Mervyn LeRoy
Leading Players—Dorothy Lee, Ruth Hall, Edward Woods

LOCAL HERO (1983, GB, Warner Brothers)
Urquhart—Denis Lawson
Director—Bill Forsyth
Leading Players—Burt Lancaster, Peter Riegert, Norman Chancer, Peter Capaldi, Rikki Fulton

THE LODGER (1926, Silent, GB, Gainsborough)
The Lodger/Jonathan Drew—Ivor Novello
Director—Alfred Hitchcock
Leading Players—Marie Ault, Arthur Chesney, Malcolm Keen

THE LODGER (1932, GB, Twickenham)
The Lodger—Ivor Novello
Director—Maurice Elvey
Leading Players—Elizabeth Allan, A.W. Baskomb, Jack Hawkins

THE LODGER (1944, 20th Century Fox)
The Lodger—Laird Cregar
Director—John Brahm
Leading Players—Merle Oberon, George Sanders, Cedric Hardwicke, Sara Allgood

LOGAN'S RUN (1976, MGM/UA)
Logan—Michael York
Director—Michael Anderson
Leading Players—Jenny Agutter, Richard Jordan, Roscoe Lee Browne, Farrah Fawcett-Majors, Peter Ustinov

LOLA (1914, Silent, World)
Lola—Clara Kimball Young
Director—James Young
Leading Players—Frank Holland, Alec B. Francis, James Young

LOLA (1971, GB, American International)
Lola "Twinky" Londonderry—Susan George
Director—Richard Donner
Leading Players—Charles Bronson, Michael Craig, Honor Blackman

LOLITA (1962, MGM)
Lolita Haze—Sue Lyon
Director—Stanley Kubrick
Leading Players—James Mason, Shelley Winters, Peter Sellers

LONE COWBOY (1934, Paramount)
Dobe Jones—Addison Richards
Director—Paul Sloane
Leading Players—Jackie Cooper, Lila Lee, John Wray

THE LONE EAGLE (1927, Silent, Universal)
Lt. William Holmes—Raymond Keane
Director—Emory Johnson
Leading Players—Barbara Kent, Nigel Barrie, Jack Pennick

THE LONE GUN (1954, UA)
Cruz—George Montgomery
Director—Ray Nazzaro
Leading Players—Dorothy Malone, Frank Faylen, Neville Brand

THE LONE HAND (1953, Universal)
Zachary Hallock—Joel McCrea
Director—George Sherman
Leading Players—Barbara Hale, Alex Nicol, Charles Drake

THE LONE RANGER (1955, Warner Brothers)
The Lone Ranger—Clayton Moore
Director—Stuart Heisler
Leading Players—Jay Silverheels, Lyle Bettger, Bonita Granville

THE LONE RANGER AND THE LOST CITY OF GOLD (1958, UA)
The Lone Ranger—Clayton Moore
Director—Lesley Selander
Leading Players—Jay Silverheels, Douglas Kennedy, Charles Watts

THE LONE RUNNER (1988, Trans World)
Garrett—Miles O'Keeffe
Director—Ruggero Deodato
Leading Players—Savina Gersak, Donal Hodson, Ronald Lacey

THE LONE STAR RANGER (1930, Fox Film Corp.)
Buck Duane—George O'Brien
Director—A. F. Erickson
Leading Players—Sue Carol, Walter McGrail, Warren Hymer

LONE STAR RANGER (1942, 20th Century Fox)
Buck Duane—John Kimbrough
Director—James Tinling
Leading Players—Sheila Ryan, Jonathan Hale, William Farnum

LONE TEXAN (1959, 20th Century Fox)
Clint Bannister—Willard Parker
Director—Paul Landres
Leading Players—Grant Williams, Audrey Dalton, Douglas Kennedy

THE LONE WOLF AND HIS LADY (1949, Columbia)
Michael Lanyard—Ron Randell
Grace Duffy—June Vincent
Director—John Hoffman
Leading Players—Alan Mowbray, William Frawley, Colette Lyons

LONE WOLF IN LONDON (1947, Columbia)
Michael Lanyard—Gerald Mohr
Director—Leslie Goodwins
Leading Players—Nancy Saunders, Eric Blore, Evelyn Ankers

THE LONE WOLF IN MEXICO (1947, Columbia)
Michael Lanyard—Gerald Mohr
Director—D. Ross Lederman
Leading Players—Sheila Ryan, Jacqueline de Wit, Eric Blore

THE LONE WOLF IN PARIS (1938, Columbia)
Michael Lanyard—Francis Lederer
Director—Albert S. Rogell
Leading Players—Frances Drake, Olaf Hytten, Walter Kingsford

THE LONE WOLF KEEPS A DATE (1940, Columbia)
Michael Lanyard—Warren William
Director—Sidney Salkow
Leading Players—Frances Robinson, Bruce Bennett, Eric Blore

LONE WOLF MCQUADE (1983, Orion)
J.J. McQuade—Chuck Norris
Director—Steve Carver
Leading Players—David Carradine, Barbara Carrera, Leon Issac Kennedy

THE LONE WOLF MEETS A LADY (1940, Columbia)
Michael Lanyard—Warren William
Director—Sidney Salkow
Leading Players—Jean Muir, Eric Blore, Victor Jory

THE LONE WOLF RETURNS (1936, Columbia)
Michael Lanyard—Melvyn Douglas
Director—Roy William Neill
Leading Players—Gail Patrick, Tala Birell, Henry Mollison

THE LONE WOLF SPY HUNT (1939, Columbia)
Michael Lanyard—Warren William
Director—Peter Godfrey
Leading Players—Ida Lupino, Rita Hayworth, Virginia Weidler, Ralph Morgan

THE LONE WOLF STRIKES (1940, Columbia)
Michael Lanyard—Warren William
Director—Sidney Salkow
Leading Players—Joan Perry, Eric Blore, Alan Baxter

THE LONE WOLF TAKES A CHANCE (1941, Columbia)
Michael Lanyard—Warren William
Director—Sidney Salkow
Leading Players—June Storey, Henry Wilcoxon, Eric Blore

THE LONE WOLF'S DAUGHTER (1929, Columbia)
Michael Lanyard—Bert Lytell
Helen Fairchild—Gertrude Olmstead
Director -Albert S. Rogell
Leading Players—Charles Gerrard, Lilyan Tashman, Donald Keith

THE LONELINESS OF THE LONG DISTANCE RUNNER (1962, GB, Woodfall-Seven Arts)
Colin Smith—Tom Courtenay
Director—Tony Richardson
Leading Players—Michael Redgrave, Avis Bunnage, Peter Madden

LONELY ARE THE BRAVE (1962, Universal)
Jack Burns—Kirk Douglas
Director—David Miller
Leading Players—Gena Rowlands, Walter Matthau, Michael Kane

THE LONELY GUY (1984, Universal)
Larry Hubbard—Steve Martin

Director—Arthur Hiller
Leading Players—Charles Grodin, Judith Ivey, Steve Lawrence

LONELY HEARTS (1991, Live Entertainment)
Alma—Beverly D'Angelo
Director—Andrew Lane
Leading Players—Eric Roberts, Joanna Cassidy, Herta Ware

THE LONELY LADY (1983, Universal)
Jerilee—Pia Zadora
Director—Peter Sasdy
Leading Players—Lloyd Bochner, Bibi Besch, Joseph Cali

THE LONELY MAN (1957, Paramount)
Jacob Wade—Jack Palance
Director—Henry Levin
Leading Players—Anthony Perkins, Neville Brand, Robert Middleton

THE LONELY PASSION OF JUDITH HEARNE (1987, GB, Island)
Judith Hearne—Maggie Smith
Director—Jack Clayton
Leading Players—Bob Hoskins, Wendy Hiller, Marie Kean

LONELY WIVES (1931, RKO-Pathe)
Mrs. Smith—Esther Ralston
Director—Russell Mack
Leading Players—Edward Everett Horton, Laura la Plante, Patsy Ruth Miller

THE LONERS (1972, Fanfare)
Stein—Dean Stockwell
Julio—Pat Stich
Director—Sutton Roley
Leading Players—Todd Susman, Scott Brady, Gloria Grahame

LONG JOHN SILVER (1954, Australia, Dist. Corp. of America)
Long John Silver—Robert Newton
Director—Bryon Haskin
Leading Players—Kit Taylor, Connie Gilchrist, Eric Reiman

LONG LOST FATHER (1934, RKO)
Carl Bellaire—John Barrymore
Director—Ernest B. Schoedsack
Leading Players—Helen Chandler, Donald Cook, Alan Mowbray

THE LONG RIDERS (1980, UA)
Cole Younger—David Carradine
Jim Younger—Keith Carradine
Bob Younger—Robert Carradine
Jesse James—James Keach
Frank James—Stacy Keach
Ed Miller—Dennis Quaid
Clell Miller—Randy Quaid
John Younger—Kevin Brophy
Director—Walter Hill
Leading Players—Harry Carey, Jr., Christopher Guest

LONGTIME COMPANION (1990, Goldwyn/American Playhouse)
David—Bruce Davison
Sean—Mark Lamos
Director—Norman Rene
Leading Players—Campbell Scott, Stephen Caffrey, Patrick Cassidy, Mary-Louise Parker, Dermot Mulroney

LONNIE (1963, Dolphin/Futuramic)
Lonnie—Scott Marlowe
Director—William Hale
Leading Players—Frank Silvera, Turina Hayes, Wilton Graff

LOOK WHO'S TALKING (1989, Tri-Star)
Voice of Mikey—Bruce Willis
Director—Amy Heckerling
Leading Players—John Travolta, Kirstie Alley, Olympia Dukakis, George Segal, Abe Vigoda

LOOK WHO'S TALKING TOO (1990, Tri-Star)
Julie—Voice of Roseanne Barr
Director—Amy Heckerling
Leading Players—John Travolta, Kirstie Alley, Olympia Dukakis, Elias Koteas, Twink Caplan, Voices of Bruce Willis and Damon Wayans

LOOKING FOR MR. GOODBAR (1977, Paramount)
Theresa Dunn—Diane Keaton
Director—Richard Brooks
Leading Players—Tuesday Weld, William Atherton, Richard Kiley, Richard Gere

LOOSE CANNONS (1990, Tri-Star)
Mac—Gene Hackman
Ellis—Dan Aykroyd
Director—Bob Clark
Leading Players—Dom DeLuise, Ronny Cox, Nancy Travis, Robert Prosky, Paul Koslo

LORD BABS (1932, GB, Gainsborough)
Lord Basil "Babs" Drayford—Bobby Howes
Director—Walter Forde
Leading Players—Jean Colin, Pat Paterson, Alfred Drayton

LORD CAMBER'S LADIES (1932, GB, British International)
Lord Camber—Nigel Bruce
Shirley Neville—Gertrude Lawrence
Janet King—Benita Hume
Director—Benn W. Levy
Leading Players—Gerald du Maurier, Clare Greeti, A. Bromley Davenport

LORD EDGEWARE DIES (1934, GB, Realart/RKO)
Lord Edgeware—C.V. France
Director—Henry Edwards
Leading Players—Austin Trevor, Jane Carr, Richard Cooper

LORD JEFF (1938, MGM)
Geoffrey Braemer—Freddie Bartholomew
Director—Sam Wood
Leading Players—Mickey Rooney, Charles Coburn, Herbert Mundin

LORD JIM (1925, Silent, Paramount)
Lord Jim—Percy Marmont
Director—Victor Fleming
Leading Players—Shirley Mason, Noah Beery, Raymond Hatton

LORD JIM (1965, GB, Columbia)
Lord Jim—Peter O'Toole
Director—Richard Brooks
Leading Players—James Mason, Curt Jurgens, Eli Wallach, Jack Hawkins, Paul Lukas, Akim Tamiroff, Dallah Lavi

LORD OF THE JUNGLE (1955, Allied Artists)
Bomba—Johnny Sheffield
Director—Ford Beebe
Leading Players—Wayne Morris, Nancy Hale, Paul Picerni

LORD RICHARD IN THE PANTRY (1930, GB, Warner Brothers)
Lord Richard Sandridge—Richard Cooper
Director—Walter Forde
Leading Players—Dorothy Seacombe, Marjorie Hume, Leo Sheffield

LORNA DOONE (1927, Silent, Associated First National)
Lorna Doone—Madge Bellamy
Director—Maurice Tourneur
Leading Players—John Bowers, Frank Keenan, Jack McDonald

LORNA DOONE (1935, GB, Associated British)
Lorna Doone—Victoria Hopper
Director—Basil Dean
Leading Players—John Loder, Margaret Lockwood, Roy Emerton

LORNA DOONE (1951, Columbia)
Lorna Doone—Barbara Hale
Director—Phil Karlson
Leading Players—Richard Greene, Carl Benton Reid, William Bishop

LOST ANGEL (1944, MGM)
Alpha—Margaret O'Brien
Director—Roy Rowland
Leading Players—James Craig, Marsha Hunt, Philip Merivale

LOST ANGELS (1989, Orion)
Tim Doolan—Adam Horovitz
Director—Hugh Hudson
Leading Players—Donald Sutherland, Amy Locane, Don Bloomfield, Celia Watson

THE LOST BOYS (1987, Warner Brothers)
Michael—Jason Patric
Sam—Corey Haim
Director—Joel Schumacher
Leading Players—Dianne Wiest, Barnard Hughes, Edward Herrmann, Kiefer Sutherland

LOST IN AMERICA (1985, Warner Brothers)
David Howard—Albert Brooks
Linda Howard—Julie Hagerty
Director—Albert Brooks
Leading Players—Maggie Roswell, Hans Wagner, Michael Greene

A LOST LADY (1924, Silent, Warner Brothers)
Marian Forrester—Irene Rich
Director—Harry Beaumont
Leading Players—Matt Moore, June Marlowe, John Roche

A LOST LADY (1934, Warner Brothers)
Marian Ormsby—Barbara Stanwyck
Director—Alfred E. Green
Leading Players—Frank Morgan, Ricardo Cortez, Lyle Talbot

THE LOST MAN (1969, Universal)
Jason Higgs—Sidney Poitier
Director—Robert Alan Arthur

Leading Players—Joanna Shimkus, Al Freeman, Jr., Michael Tolan

THE LOTTERY BRIDE (1930, UA)
Jenny Swanson—Jeanette MacDonald
Director—Paul Stein
Leading Players—John Garrick, Joe E. Brown, Zasu Pitts

LOTTERY LOVER (1935, Fox Film Corp.)
Gaby Aimee—Peggy Fears
Director—William Thiele
Leading Players—Lew Ayres, Pat Paterson, Sterling Holloway

LOTUS LADY (1930, Audible/Greiver)
Tamarah—Fern Andra
Director—Phil Rosen
Leading Players—Ralph Emerson, Betty Francisco, Lucien Prival

LOUISA (1950, Universal)
Louisa Norton—Spring Byington
Director—Alexander Hall
Leading Players—Ronald Reagan, Charles Coburn, Ruth Hussey, Edmund Gwenn, Piper Laurie

LOUISIANA HUSSY (1960, Bon Are/Howco)
Nina Duprez—Nan Peterson
Director—Lee Sholem
Leading Players—Robert Richards, Peter Coe, Betty Lynn

THE LOVEABLE CHEAT (1949, Film Classics)
Claude Mercadet—Charles Ruggles
Director—Richard Oswald
Leading Players—Peggy Ann Garner, Richard Ney, Alan Mowbray

LOVE BIRDS (1934, Universal)
Henry Whipple—Slim Summerville
Araminta Tootle—Zasu Pitts
Director—William A. Seiter
Leading Players—Mickey Rooney, Frederick Burton, Emmett Vogan

THE LOVE CAPTIVE (1934, Universal)
Alice Trask—Gloria Stuart
Director—Max Marcin
Leading Players—Nils Asther, Paul Kelly, Alan Dinehart

THE LOVE DOCTOR (1929, Paramount)
Dr. Gerald Sumner—Richard Dix
Director—Melville Brown
Leading Players—June Collyer, Morgan Farley, Miriam Seegar

LOVE FINDS ANDY HARDY (1938, MGM)
Andy Hardy—Mickey Rooney
Director—George B. Seitz
Leading Players—Lewis Stone, Judy Garland, Cecilia Parker

LOVE FROM A STRANGER (1937, GB, UA)
Gerald Lovell—Basil Rathbone
Director—Rowland V. Lee
Leading Players—Ann Harding, Binnie Hale, Bruce Seton

LOVE FROM A STRANGER (1947, Eagle-Lion)
Manuel Cortez—John Hodiak
Director—Richard Whorf

Leading Players—Sylvia Sidney, Ann Richards, John Howard

THE LOVE GAMBLER (1922, Silent, Fox Film Corp.)
Dick Manners—John Gilbert
Director—Joseph Franz
Leading Players—Carmel Myers, Bruce Gordon, Cap Anderson

THE LOVE GIRL (1916, Silent, Bluebird)
Ambrosia—Ella Hall
Director—Robert Z. Leonard
Leading Players—Adele Farrington, Betty Schade, Harry Depp

THE LOVE GOD? (1969, Universal)
Abner Audubon Peacock—Don Knotts
Director—Nat Hiken
Leading Players—Anne Francis, Edmund O'Brien, James Gregory

LOVE LAUGHS AT ANDY HARDY (1946, MGM)
Andy Hardy—Mickey Rooney
Director—Willis Goldbeck
Leading Players—Lewis Stone, Sara Haden, Bonita Granville

THE LOVE LIAR (1916, Silent, Centaur)
David McCare—Crane Wilbur
Director—Crane Wilbur
Leading Players—Fred Goodwins, Lucy Payton, Mae Gaston

LOVE SLAVES OF THE AMAZONS (1957, Universal)
Dr. Peter Masters—Don Taylor
Director—Curt Siodmak
Leading Players—Gianna Segale, Eduardo Ciannelli, Harvey Chalk

LOVE THAT BRUTE (1950, 20th Century Fox)
Big Ed Hanley—Paul Douglas
Director—Alexander Hall
Leading Players—Jean Peters, Cesar Romero, Keenan Wynn

LOVE WITH THE PROPER STRANGER (1963, Paramount)
Rocky Papasano—Steve McQueen
Director—Robert Mulligan
Leading Players—Natalie Wood, Edie Adams, Herschel Bernardi

THE LOVED ONE (1965, MGM)
Sir Francis Hinsley—John Gielgud
Director—Tony Richardson
Leading Players—Robert Morse, Jonathan Winters, Anjanette Comer, Rod Steiger

LOVELY TO LOOK AT (1952, MGM)
Stephanie—Kathryn Grayson
Director—Mervyn LeRoy
Leading Players—Howard Keel, Red Skelton, Marge Champion, Gower Champion, Ann Miller

LOVER COME BACK (1946, Universal)
Kay Williams—Lucille Ball
Director—William A. Seiter
Leading Players—George Brent, Vera Zorina, Charles Winninger

LOVER COME BACK (1961, Universal)
Carol Templeton—Doris Day
Director—Delbert Mann
Leading Players—Rock Hudson, Tony Randall, Edie Adams

LOVERBOY (1989, Tri-Star)
Randy Bodek—Patrick Dempsey
Director—Joan Micklin Silver
Leading Players—Kate Jackson, Robert Ginty, Nancy Valen, Charles Hunter Walsh, Barbara Carrera

LOVERS AND OTHER STRANGERS (1970, ABC/Cinerama)
Susan Henderson—Bonnie Bedelia
Richie Vecchio—Joseph Hindy
Director—Cy Howard
Leading Players—Gig Young, Bea Arthur, Anne Jackson, Harry Guardino, Richard Castellano, Michael Brandon, Diane Keaton, Bob Dishy, Marian Hailey, Cloris Leachman, Anne Meara

THE LOVES OF CARMEN (1948, Columbia)
Carmen Garcia—Rita Hayworth
Director—Charles Vidor
Leading Players—Glenn Ford, Ron Randell, Victor Jory

THE LOVES OF EDGAR ALLAN POE (1942, 20th Century Fox)
Edgar Allan Poe—John Shepperd (Shepperd Strudwick)
Director—Harry Lachman
Leading Players—Linda Darnell, Virginia Gilmore, Jane Darwell

THE LOVES OF JOANNA GODDEN (1947, GB, Ealing)
Joanna Godden—Googie Withers
Director—Charles Frend
Leading Players—Jean Kent, John McCallum, Derek Bond

THE LOVES OF MADAME DUBARRY (1938, GB, British Internat.)
Jeanne DuBarry—Gitta Alpar
Director—Marcel Varnel
Leading Players—Patrick Waddington, Owen Nares, Arthur Margetson

THE LOVES OF RICARDO (1926, Silent, George Beban)
Ricardo—George Beban
Director—George Beban
Leading Players—Soliga Lee, Amille Milane, Jack Singleton

THE LOVES OF ROBERT BURNS (1930, GB, British & Dominions)
Robert Burns—Joseph Hilsop
Director—Herbert Wilcox
Leading Players—Dorothy Seacombe, Eve Gray, Nancy Price

LOVESICK (1983, Warner Brothers)
Saul Benjamin—Dudley Moore
Director—Marshall Brickman
Leading Players—Elizabeth McGovern, Alec Guinness, Christine Baranski

LOVIN' MOLLY (1974, Columbia)
Molly—Blythe Danner
Director—Sidney Lumet
Leading Players—Anthony Perkins, Beau Bridges, Edward Binns

LOVING COUPLES (1980, 20th Century Fox)
Evelyn—Shirley MacLaine
Walter—James Coburn
Stephanie—Susan Sarandon
Gregg—Stephen Collins
Director—Jack Smight
Leading Players—Sally Kellerman, Nan Martin, Shelly Batt

LUCAS (1986, Warner Brothers)
Lucas—Corey Haim
Director—David Seltzer
Leading Players—Kerri Green, Charlie Sheen, Winona Ryder

THE LUCK OF A SAILOR (1934, GB, Wardour)
Capt. Colin—David Manners
Director—Robert Milton
Leading Players—Greta Nissen, Clifford Mollison, Camilla Horn

THE LUCK OF GINGER COFFEY (1964, Continental Distributing)
Ginger Coffey—Robert Shaw
Director—Irvin Kershner
Leading Players—Mary Ure, Liam Redmond, Tom Harvey

THE LUCKIEST GIRL IN THE WORLD (1936, Universal)
Pat Duncan—Jane Wyatt
Director—Eddie Buzzell
Leading Players—Louis Hayward, Nat Pendleton, Eugene Pallette

THE LUCKIEST MAN IN THE WORLD (1989, Second Effort)
Sam Posner—Philip Bosco
Director—Frank D. Gilroy
Leading Players—Doris Belack, Joanne Camp, Matthew Gottlieb

LUCKY BOY (1929, Tiffany)
Georgie Jessel—George Jessel
Directors—Norman Taurog (and others)
Leading Players—Rosa Rosanova, William K. Strauss, Margaret Quimby

LUCKY CISCO KID (1940, 20th Century Fox)
Cisco Kid—Cesar Romero
Director—H. Bruce Humberstone
Leading Players—Mary Beth Hughes, Dana Andrews, Evelyn Venable

LUCKY GIRL (1932, GB, Wardour)
Lady Moira Cavendish-Gascoyne—Molly Lamont
Directors—Gene Gerrard and Frank Miller
· Leading Players—Gene Gerrard, Gus McNaughton, Spencer Trevor

LUCKY JIM (1957, GB, Kinglsey International)
Jim Dixon—Ian Carmichael
Director—John Boulting
Leading Players—Terry-Thomas, Hugh Griffith, Sharon Acker

LUCKY JORDAN (1942, Paramount)
Lucky Jordan—Alan Ladd
Director—Frank Tuttle
Leading Players—Helen Walker, Sheldon Leonard, Mabel Paige

LUCKY LEGS (1942, Columbia)
Gloria Carroll—Jinx Falkenburg
Director—Stanley Rubin
Leading Players—Leslie Brooks, Kay Harris, Elizabeth Patterson

LUCKY LOSER (1934, GB, Paramount)
Tom O'Grady—Richard Dolman
Director—Reginald Denham
Leading Players—Aileen Marson, Anna Lee, Annie Esmond

LUCKY ME (1954, Warner Brothers)
Candy Williams—Doris Day
Director—Jack Donohue
Leading Players—Robert Cummings, Phil Silvers, Eddie Foy, Jr., Nancy Walker, Martha Hyer

LUCKY NICK CAIN (1951, 20th Century Fox)
Nick Cain—George Raft
Director—Joseph M. Newman
Leading Players—Coleen Gray, Enzo Staiola, Charles Goldner

LUCKY PARTNERS (1940, RKO)
David Grant—Ronald Colman
Jean Newton—Ginger Rogers
Director—Lewis Milestone
Leading Players—Jack Carson, Spring Byington, Cecilia Loftus

THE LUCKY STIFF (1949, UA)
Anna Marie St. Claire—Dorothy Lamour
Director—Lewis R. Foster
Leading Players—Brian Donlevy, Claire Trevor, Irene Hervey

THE LUCKY TEXAN (1934, Monogram)
Jerry Mason—John Wayne
Director—Robert N. Bradbury
Leading Players—Barbara Sheldon, George "Gabby" Hayes, Yakima Canutt

LUCY GALLANT (1955, Paramount)
Lucy Gallant—Jane Wyman
Director—Robert Parrish
Leading Players—Charlton Heston, Claire Trevor, Thelma Ritter, William Demarest

LULU (1962, Australia, Gloria)
Lulu—Nadja Tiller
Director—Rolf Thiele
Leading Players—O.E. Hasse, Hildegard Knef, Mario Adorf

LULU (1978, Chase)
Lulu—Elisa Leonelli
Director—Ronald Chase
Leading Players—Paul Shenar, John Roberdeau, Norma Leistiko

LULU BELLE (1948, Columbia)
Lulu Belle—Dorothy Lamour
Director—Leslie Fenton
Leading Players—George Montgomery, Albert Dekker, Otto Kruger, Glenda Farrell

LUM AND ABNER ABROAD (1956, Howco)
Lum—Chester Lauck
Abner—Morris Goff
Director—James Kern
Leading Players—Jill Alis, Lila Audres, Branko Spoylar

LUMMOX (1930, UA)
Bertha Oberg—Winifred Westover
Director—Herbert Brenon
Leading Players—Dorothy Janis, Lydia Yeamans Titus, Ida Darling

LUNATICS: A LOVE STORY (1991, Renaissance Pictures)
Hank—Theodore Raimi
Nancy—Deborah Foreman
Director—Josh Becker
Leading Players—Bruce Campbell, George Aguilar, Brian McCree

LUPE (1967, Film-Makers Cooperative)
Lupe Velez—Mario Montez
Director—Jose Rodriguez-Soltero
Leading Players—Medea Reid, Bill Vehr, Charles Frehse

LUST FOR A VAMPIRE (1971, GB, Hammer)
Mircalla/Carmilla—Yutte Stensgaard
Director—Jimmy Sangster
Leading Players—Ralph Bates, Barbara Jefford, Suzanna Leigh, Michael Johnson

THE LUSTY MEN (1952, RKO)
Jeff McCloud—Robert Mitchum
Wes Merritt—Arthur Kennedy
Director—Nicholas Ray
Leading Players—Susan Hayward, Arthur Hunnicutt, Frank Faylen

LUTHER (1974, American Film Theatre)
Martin Luther—Stacy Keach
Director—Guy Green
Leading Players—Patrick Magee, Hugh Griffith, Robert Stephens, Alan Badel, Judi Dench

LYDIA (1941, UA)
Lydia MacMillan—Merle Oberon
Director—Julien Duvivier
Leading Players—Edna May Oliver, Alan Marshall, Joseph Cotten, Hans Yaray, George Reeves

LYDIA (1964, Canada, Libra)
Lydia—Anna Hagen
Director—Cedric d'Ailly
Leading Players—Gordon Pinset, Berentino Costa, Malena Anousaki

LYDIA BAILEY (1952, 20th Century Fox)
Lydia Bailey—Anne Francis
Director—Jean Negulesco
Leading Players—Dale Robertson, Charles Korvin, William Marshall

M

M (1951, Columbia)
Martin Harrow—David Wayne
Director—Joseph Losey
Leading Players—Howard Da Silva, Luther Adler, Martin Gabel

MA AND PA KETTLE (1949, Universal)
Ma Kettle—Marjorie Main
Pa Kettle—Percy Kilbride
Director—Charles Lamont
Leading Players—Richard Long, Meg Randall, Patricia Alphin

MA AND PA KETTLE AT HOME (1954, Universal)
Ma Kettle—Marjorie Main
Pa Kettle—Percy Kilbride
Director—Charles Lamont

Leading Players—Alan Mowbray, Ross Elliott, Alice Kelley

MA AND PA KETTLE AT THE FAIR (1952, Universal)
Ma Kettle—Marjorie Main
Pa Kettle—Percy Kilbride
Director—Charles Barton
Leading Players—Lori Nelson, James Best, Esther Dale

MA AND PA KETTLE AT WAIKIKI (1955, Universal)
Ma Kettle—Marjorie Main
Pa Kettle—Percy Kilbride
Director—Lee Sholem
Leading Players—Lori Nelson, Bryon Palmer, Loring Smith

MA AND PA KETTLE BACK ON THE FARM (1951, Universal)
Ma Kettle—Marjorie Main
Pa Kettle—Percy Kilbride
Director—Edward Sedgwick
LeAding Players—Richard Long, Meg Randall, Ray Collins

MA AND PA KETTLE GO TO TOWN (1950, Universal)
Ma Kettle—Marjorie Main
Pa Kettle—Percy Kilbride
Director—Charles Lamont
Leading Players—Richard Long, Meg Randall, Barbara Brown

MA AND PA KETTLE ON VACATION (1953, Universal)
Ma Kettle—Marjorie Main
Pa Kettle—Percy Kilbride
Director—Charles Lamont
Leading Players—Ray Collins, Bodil Miller, Sig Ruman

MA BARKER'S KILLER BROOD (1960, Filmservice)
Ma Barker—Lurene Tuttle
Director—Bill Karn
Leading Players—Tris Coffin, Paul Dubov, Nelson Leigh

MAC (1992, Tennenbaum/Goodman)
Niccolo 'Mac' Vitelli—John Turturro
Director—John Turturro
Leading Players—Michael Badalucco, Carl Capotorto, Katherine Borowitz, Ellen Barkin, John Amos

MAC AND ME (1988, Orion)
Eric Cruise—Jade Calegory
Director—Stewart Raffill
Leading Players—Christine Ebersole, Jonathan Ward, Katrina Caspary, Lauren Stanley

MACARTHUR (1977, Universal)
Gen. Douglas MacArthur—Gregory Peck
Director—Joseph Sargent
Leading Players—Ed Flanders, Dan O'Herlihy, Ivan Bonar

MACBETH (1948, Republic)
Macbeth—Orson Welles
Director—Orson Welles
Leading Players—Jeanette Nolan, Dan O'Herlihy, Roddy McDowall, Edgar Barrier

MACBETH (1963, Prominent)
Macbeth—Maurice Evans
Director—George Schaefer
Leading Players—Judith Anderson, Michael Hordern, Ian Bannen

MACBETH (1971, GB, Columbia)
Macbeth—Jon Finch
Director—Roman Polanski
Leading Players—Francesca Annis, Martin Shaw, Nicholas Selby

MACHINE GUN KELLY (1958, American International)
Machine Gun Kelly—Charles Bronson
Director—Roger Corman
Leading Players—Susan Cabot, Morey Amsterdam, Jack Lambert

MACHO CALLAHAN (1970, Avco Embassy)
Diego "Macho" Callahan—David Janssen
Director—Bernard L. Kowalski
Leading Players—Jean Seberg, Lee J. Cobb, James Booth

MACKENNA'S GOLD (1969, Columbia)
MacKenna—Gregory Peck
Director—J. Lee Thompson
Leading Players—Omar Sharif, Telly Savalas, Camilla Sparv, Keenan Wynn, Julie Newmar

MACKINTOSH & T.J. (1975, Penland)
Mackintosh—Roy Rogers
T.J.—Clay O'Brien
Director—Marvin J. Chomsky
Leading Players—Billy Green Bush, Andrew Robinson, Joan Hackett

THE MACKINTOSH MAN (1973, GB, Warner Brothers)
Rearden—Paul Newman
Director—John Huston
Leading Players—Dominique Sanda, James Mason, Harry Andrews

THE MACOMBER AFFAIR (1947, UA)
Margaret Macomber—Joan Bennett
Director—Zoltan Korda
Director—Gregory Peck, Robert Preston, Reginald Denny

MAD ABOUT MEN (1954, GB, GFD)
Miranda—Glynis Johns
Director—Ralph Thomas
Leading Players—Anne Crawford, Donald Sinden, Margaret Rutherford

MAD ABOUT MUSIC (1938, Universal)
Gloria Harkinson—Deanna Durbin
Director—Norman Taurog
Leading Players—Herbert Marshall, Arthur Treacher, Gail Patrick

THE MAD BOMBER (1973, Cinemation)
William Dorn—Chuck Connors
Director—Bert I. Gordon
Leading Players—Vince Edwards, Neville Brand, Hank Brandt

MAD DANCER (1925, Silent, Janus)
Mimi—Ann Pennington
Director—Burton King
Leading Players—Johnny Walker, Coit Albertson, John Woodward

THE MAD DOCTOR (1941, Paramount)
Dr. George Sebastian—Basil Rathbone
Director—Tim Whelan

Leading Players—Ellen Drew, John Howard, Barbara Allen

THE MAD DOCTOR OF MARKET STREET (1942, Universal)
Dr. Benson—Lionel Atwill
Director—Joseph H. Lewis
Leading Players—Una Merkel, Nat Pendleton, Claire Dodd

MAD DOG COLL (1961, Columbia)
Vincent Coll—John Chandler
Director—Burt Balaban
Leading Players—Neil Nephew, Brooke Hayward, Joy Harmon

MAD DOG MORGAN (1976, Australia, Motion Picture Co/BEF)
Daniel Morgan—Dennis Hopper
Director—Philippe Mora
Leading Players—Jack Thompson, David Gulpilil, Frank Thring

THE MAD EMPRESS (1940, Warner Brothers)
Empress Carlotta—Medea Novara
Director—Miguel C. Torres
Leading Players—Lionel Atwill, Conrad Nagel, Guy Bates

THE MAD GENIUS (1931, Warner Brothers)
Ivan Tzarakov—John Barrymore
Director—Michael Curtiz
Leading Players—Marian Marsh, Donald Cook, Charles Butterworth, Luis Alberni

THE MAD GHOUL (1943, Universal)
Dr. Alfred Morris—George Zucco
Director—James Hogan
Leading Players—David Bruce, Evelyn Ankers, Robert Armstrong, Turhan Bey

THE MAD MAGICIAN (1954, Columbia)
Gallico—Vincent Price
Director—John Brahm
Leading Players—Mary Murphy, Eva Gabor, John Emery

THE MAD MARTINDALES (1942, 20th Century Fox)
Kathy Martindale—Jane Withers
Evelyn Martindale—Marjorie Weaver
Hugo Martindale—Alan Mowbray
Director—Alfred Werker
Leading Players—Jimmy Lydon, Bryon Barr, George Reeves

MAD MAX (1979, Australia, Filmways)
Max—Mel Gibson
Director—George Miller
Leading Players—Joanne Samuel, Hugh Keays-Byme, Steve Bisley, Roger Ward

MAD MAX BEYOND THUNDERDOME (1985, Australia, Warner Brothers)
Max—Mel Gibson
Director—George Miller
Leading Players—Bruce Spence, Adam Cockburn, Tina Turner

THE MAD MISS MANTON (1938, RKO)
Melsa Manton—Barbara Stanwyck
Director—Leigh Jason
Leading Players—Henry Fonda, Sam Levene, Frances Mercer

THE MAD MONSTER (1942, Producers Releasing Corp.)
Petro—Glenn Strange
Director—Sam Neufield

Leading Players—Johnny Downs, George Zucco. Anne Nagel

MADAME BOVARY (1949, MGM)
Emma Bovary—Jennifer Jones
Director—Vincente Minnelli
Leading Players—James Mason, Van Heflin, Louis Jourdan

MADAME BUTTERFLY (1915, Silent, Famous Players)
Choo-Choo-San—Mary Pickford
Director—Sidney Olcott
Leading Players—Olive West, Jane Hall, Lawrence Wood

MADAME BUTTERFLY (1932, Paramount)
Cho-Cho San—Sylvia Sidney
Director—Marion Gering
Leading Players—Cary Grant, Charles Ruggles, Sandor Kallay

MADAME CURIE (1943, MGM)
Marie Curie—Greer Garson
Director—Mervyn LeRoy
Leading Players—Walter Pidgeon, Robert Walker, Dame May Whitty, Henry Travers, C. Aubrey Smith

MADAME DU BARRY (1934, Warner Brothers)
Mme. Du Barry—Dolores Del Rio
Director—William Dieterle
Leading Players—Reginald Owen, Victor Jory, Osgood Perkins

MADAME LOUISE (1951, GB, Butchers)
Mme. Louise—Hilda Bayley
Director—Maclean Rogers
Leading Players—Richard Hearne, Petula Clark, Garry Marsh

MADAME POMPADOUR (1927, GB, Paramount)
Mme. Pompadour—Dorothy Gish
Director—Herbert Wilcox
Leading Players—Antonio Moreno, Nelson Keys, Henri Bosc

MADAME RACKETEER (1932, Paramount)
"Countess von Claudwig"/Martha Hicks—Alison Skipworth
Director—Alexander Hall
Leading Players—Richard Bennett, George Raft, Evalyn Knapp, Gertrude Messinger

MADAME SATAN (1930, MGM)
Angela Brooks—Kay Johnson
Director—Cecil B. DeMille
Leading Players—Reginald Denny, Lillian Roth, Roland Young

MADAME SOUSATZKA (1988, Cineplex Odeon)
Madame Irina Sousatzka—Shirley Maclaine
Director—John Schlesinger
Leading Players—Navin Chowdhry, Leigh Lawson, Shabana Azmi, Peggy Ashcroft

MADAME SPY (1918, Silent, Butterfly)
Baroness Von Hulda—Claire Du Brey
Director—Douglas Gerrard
Leading Players—Jack Mulhall, Wadsworth Harris, Jean Hersholt

MADAME SPY (1934, Universal)
Maria Franck/B-24—Fay Wray
Director—Karl Freund
Leading Players—Nils Asther, Edward Arnold, John Miljan

MADAME SPY (1942, Universal)
Joan Bannister—Constance Bennett
Director—Roy William Neill
Leading Players—Don Porter, John Litel, Edward Brophy

MADAME X (1929, MGM)
Jacqueline—Ruth Chatterton
Director—Lionel Barrymore
Leading Players—Lewis Stone, Raymond Hackett, Holmes Herbert

MADAME X (1937, MGM)
Jacqueline Fleuriot—Gladys George
Director—Sam Wood
Leading Players—John Beal, Warren William, Reginald Owen

MADAME X (1966, Universal)
Holly Parker—Lana Turner
Director—David Lowell Rich
Leading Players—John Forsythe, Ricardo Montalban, Burgess Meredith, Constance Bennett, Keir Dullea

MADCAP BETTY (1915, Silent, Bosworth)
Betty—Elsie Janis
Director—Phillip Smalley
Leading Players—Owen Moore, June Hastings, Herbert Standing

MADE FOR EACH OTHER (1939, UA)
Jane Mason—Carole Lombard
Johnny Mason—James Stewart
Director—John Cromwell
Leading Players—Charles Coburn, Lucille Watson, Harry Davenport

MADE FOR EACH OTHER (1971, 20th Century Fox)
Pandora "Panda" Gold—Renee Taylor
Gig "Giggy" Pinimba—Joseph Bologna
Director—Robert B. Bean
Leading Players—Paul Sorvino, Olympia Dukakis, Helen Verbit

MADELEINE (1950, GB, Rank)
Madeleine Smith—Ann Todd
Director—David Lean
Leading Players—Norman Wooland, Ivan Desny, Leslie Banks

MADELEINE IS (1971, Canada, Alliance)
Madeleine—Nicola Lipman
Director—Sylvia Spring
Leading Players—John Juliani, Wayne Specht, Gordon Robertson

MADEMOISELLE FIFI (1944, RKO)
Lt. von Eyrick—Kurt Kreuger
Director—Robert Wise
Leading Players—Simone Simon, John Emery, Alan Napier

MADIGAN (1968, Universal)
Det. Daniel Madigan—Richard Widmark
Director—Donald Siegel
Leading Players—Henry Fonda, Inger Stevens, Harry Guardino, James Whitmore, Susan Clark

MADONNA OF AVENUE A (1929, Warner Brothers)
Maria Morton—Dolores Costello
Director—Michael Curtiz

Leading Players—Grant Withers, Douglas Gerrard, Louise Dresser

MADONNA OF THE SEVEN MOONS (1945, GB, Gainsborough)
Maddalena Lambardi/Rosanna—Phyllis Calvert
Director—Arthur Crabtree
Leading Players—Stewart Granger, Patricia Roc, Peter Glenville

MADRON (1970, Four Star Excelsior)
Madron—Richard Boone
Director—Jerry Hopper
Leading Players—Leslie Caron, Gabi Amrani, Chaim Banai

THE MADWOMAN OF CHAILLOT (1969, Warner Brothers)
Countess Aurelia—Katharine Hepburn
Director—Bryan Forbes
Leading Players—Charles Boyer, Claude Dauphin, Edith Evans, John Gavin, Paul Henreid, Yul Brynner, Danny Kaye

THE MAGIC GARDEN OF STANLEY SWEETHART (1970, MGM)
Stanley Sweethart—Don Johnson
Director—Leonard Horn
Leading Players—Linda Gillin, Michael Greer, Dianne Hull

THE MAGNIFICENT AMBERSONS (1942, RKO)
Major Amberson—Richard Bennett
Isabel Amberson Minafer—Dolores Costello
George Amberson Minafer—Tim Holt
Director—Orson Welles
Leading Players—Joseph Cotten, Anne Baxter, Agnes Moorehead, Ray Collins

THE MAGNIFICENT BRUTE (1936, Universal)
Big Steve Andrews—Victor McLaglen
Director—John G. Blystone
Leading Players—Binnie Barnes, William Hall, Jean Dixon

MAGNIFICENT DOLL (1946, Universal)
Dolly Payne Madison—Ginger Rogers
Director—Frank Borzage
Leading Players—David Niven, Burgess Meredith, Stephen McNally, Peggy Wood

THE MAGNIFICENT DOPE (1942, 20th Century Fox)
Tad Page—Henry Fonda
Director—Walter Lang
Leading Players—Lynn Bari, Don Ameche, Edward Everett Horton

THE MAGNIFICENT FLIRT (1928, Silent, Paramount)
Mme. Florence Laverne—Florence Vidor
Director—Harry D'Abbadie D'Arrast
Leading Players—Albert Conti, Loretta Young, Matty Kemp

THE MAGNIFICENT FRAUD (1939, Paramount)
Jules LaCroix/President Alvarado—Akim Tamiroff
Director—Robert Florey
Leading Players—Lloyd Nolan, Mary Boland, Patricia Morison

THE MAGNIFICENT MATADOR (1955, 20th Century Fox)
Luis Santos—Anthony Quinn
Director—Budd Boetticher
Leading Players—Maureen O'Hara, Richard Denning, Thomas Gomez

THE MAGNIFICENT SEVEN (1960, UA)
Chris—Yul Brynner
Vin—Steve McQueen
Chico—Horst Buchholz
O'Reilly—Charles Bronson
Lee—Robert Vaughn
Harry Luck—Brad Dexter
Britt—James Coburn
Director—John Sturges
Leading Players—Eli Wallach, Vladimir Sokoloff, Rosenda Monteros

THE MAGNIFICENT SEVEN RIDE (1972, UA)
Chris—Lee Van Cleef
Noah Forbes—Michael Callan
Skinner—Luke Askew
Pepe Carral—Pedro Armendariz, Jr.
Walt Drummond—William Lucking
Hayes—James B. Sikking
Scott Elliott—Ed Lauter
Director—George McGowan
Leading Players—Stefanie Powers, Mariette Hartley, Melissa Murphy

THE MAGNIFICENT TWO (1967, Rank)
Eric—Eric Morecambe
Ernie—Ernie Wise
Director—Cliff Owen
Leading Players—Margit Saad, Virgilo Texeira, Cecil Parker

THE MAGNIFICENT YANKEE (1950, MGM)
Oliver Wendell Holmes—Louis Calhern
Director—John Sturges
Leading Players—Ann Harding, Eduard Franz, Philip Ober

MAHLER (1974, GB, Mayfair)
Gustav Mahler—Robert Powell
Director—Ken Russell
Leading Players—Georgina Hale, Richard Morant, Lee Montague

MAHOGANY (1975, Paramount)
Tracy/Mahogany—Diana Ross
Director—Berry Gordy
Leading Players—Billy Dee Williams, Anthony Perkins, Jean-Pierre Aumont, Nina Foch

MAID OF SALEM (1937, Paramount)
Barbara Clarke—Claudette Colbert
Director—Frank Lloyd
Leading Players—Fred MacMurray, Harvey Stephens, Gale Sondergaard, Louise Dresser

MAID OF THE MOUNTAINS (1932, GB, Wardour)
Teresa—Nancy Brown
Director—Lupino Lane
Leading Players—Harry Welchman, Betty Stockfeld, Albert Burdon

MAID OF THE WEST (1921, Silent, Universal)
Betty—Eileen Percy
Director—Philo McCullough
Leading Players—William Scott, Hattis Buskirk, Charles Meakin

MAID TO ORDER (1987, New Century-Vista)
Jessie Montgomery—Ally Sheedy
Director—Amy Jones
Leading Players—Beverly D'Angelo, Michael Ontkean, Valerie
    Perrine, Dick Shawn, Tom Skerritt

THE MAIDS (1975, GB, CineFilms)
Solange—Glenda Jackson
Claire—Susannah York
Director—Christopher Miles
Leading Players—Vivien Merchant, Mark Burns

MAID'S NIGHT OUT (1938, RKO)
Sheila Harrison—Joan Fontaine
Director—Ben Holmes
Leading Players—Allan Lane, Hedda Hopper, George Irving

MAIL ORDER BRIDE (1964, MGM)
Annie Boley—Lois Nettleton
Director—Burt Kennedy
Leading Players—Buddy Ebsen, Keir Dullea, Warren Oates

THE MAILMAN (1923, Silent, Film Booking Office of America)
Johnnie Morley—Johnnie Walker
Director—Emory Johnson
Leading Players—Ralph Lewis, Martha Sleeper, Virginia True
    Boardman

MAIN STREET LAWYER (1939, Republic)
Link—Edward Ellis
Director—Dudley Murphy
Leading Players—Anita Louise, Margaret Hamilton, Harold
    Huber

MAISIE (1939, MGM)
Maisie Ravier—Ann Sothern
Director—Edwin L. Marin
Leading Players—Robert Young, Ruth Hussey, Ian Hunter

MAISIE GETS HER MAN (1942, MGM)
Maisie Ravier—Ann Sothern
Director—Roy Del Ruth
Leading Players—Red Skelton, Allen Jenkins, Donald Meek

MAISIE GOES TO RENO (1944, MGM)
Maisie Ravier—Ann Sothern
Director—Harry Beaumont
Leading Players—John Hodiak, Tom Drake, Marta Linden

MAISIE WAS A LADY (1941, MGM)
Maisie Ravier—Ann Sothern
Director—Edwin L. Marin
Leading Players—Lew Ayres, Maureen O'Sullivan, C. Aubrey
    Smith

THE MAJOR AND THE MINOR (1942, Paramount)
Susan Applegate—Ginger Rogers
Major Kirby—Ray Milland
Director—Billy Wilder
Leading Players—Rita Johnson, Robert Benchley, Diana Lynn

MAJOR BARBARA (1941, GB, Rank)
Major Barbara Undershaft—Wendy Hiller
Director—Gabriel Pascal
Leading Players—Rex Harrison, Robert Morley, Emlyn Williams,
    Robert Newton, Marie Lohr

MAJOR DUNDEE (1965, Columbia)
Major Amos Charles Dundee—Charlton Heston
Director—Sam Peckinpah
Leading Players—Richard Harris, Jim Hutton, James Coburn,
    Senta Berger

A MAJORITY OF ONE (1961, Warner Brothers)
Mrs. Jacoby—Rosalind Russell
Director—Mervyn LeRoy
Leading Players—Alec Guinness, Ray Danton, Madlyn Rhue

MAKE WAY FOR A LADY (1936, RKO)
June Drew—Anne Shirley
Director—David Burton
Leading Players—Herbert Marshall, Gertrude Michael, Margot
    Grahame

MAKER OF MEN (1931, Columbia)
Dudley—Jack Holt
Director—Edward Sedgwick
Leading Players—Richard Cromwell, Joan Marsh, Robert Alden

MAKING A MAN (1922, Silent, Paramount)
Horace Winsby—Jack Holt
Director—Joseph Henabery
Leading Players—J.P. Lockney, Eva Novak, Bert Woodruff

MAKING MR. RIGHT (1987, Orion)
Ulysses—John Malkovich
Director—Susan Seidelman
Leading Players—Ann Magnuson, Glenne Headly, Ben Masters

MALE AND FEMALE (1919, Silent, Paramount)
Crichton—Thomas Meighan
Lady Mary Lasenby—Gloria Swanson
Director—Cecil B. DeMille
Leading Players—Lila Lee, Theodore Roberts, Raymond Hatton

THE MALE ANIMAL (1942, Warner Brothers)
Tommy Turner—Henry Fonda
Director—Elliott Nugent
Leading Players—Olivia de Havilland, Jack Carson, Joan Leslie,
    Eugene Pallette, Herbert Anderson

MALCOLM (1986, Australia, Vestron)
Malcolm—Colin Friels
Director—Nadia Tass
Leading Players—John Hargreaves, Lindy Davies, Chris
    Haywood

MALONE (1987, Orion)
Richard Malone—Burt Reynolds
Director—Harley Cokliss
Leading Players—Cliff Robertson, Kenneth McMillan, Cynthia
    Gibb, Scott Wilson

MAMA LOVES PAPA (1933, Paramount)
Jessie Todd—Mary Boland
Wilbur Todd—Charlie Ruggles
Director—Norman McLeod
Leading Players—Lilyan Tashman, George Barbier, Morgan
    Wallace

MAMA LOVES PAPA (1945, RKO)
Wilbur Todd—Leon Errol
Jessie Todd—Elisabeth Risdon

Director—Frank Strayer
Leading Players—Edwin Maxwell, Emory Parnell, Charles Halton

MAMA RUNS WILD (1938, Republic)
Alice Summers—Mary Boland
Director—Ralph Staub
Leading Players—Ernest Truex, William Henry, Lynn Roberts

MAMA STEPS OUT (1937, MGM)
Ada Cuppy—Alice Brady
Director—George B. Seitz
Leading Players—Guy Kibbee, Betty Furness, Stanley Morner

THE MAMBO KINGS (1992, Warner Brothers)
Cesar Castillo—Armanda Assante
Nestor Castillo—Antonio Banderas
Director—Arne Glimcher
Leading Players—Cathy Moriarty, Maruschka Detmers, Desi Arnaz, Jr., Celia Cruz, Roscoe Lee Browne

MAME (1974, Warner Brothers)
Mame Dennis—Lucille Ball
Director—Gene Saks
Leading Players—Robert Preston, Beatrice Arthur, Bruce Davison, Joyce Van Patten

THE MAN (1972, Paramount)
Douglas Dilman—James Earl Jones
Director—Joseph Sargent
Leading Players—Martin Balsam, Burgess Meredith, Lew Ayres, William Windom, Barbara Rush

A MAN, A WOMAN, AND A BANK (1979, Canada, Bennett Films)
Reese—Donald Sutherland
Stacey—Brooke Adams
Director—Noel Black
Leading Players—Paul Mazursky, Allan Magicovsky, Leigh Hamilton

A MAN ABOUT THE HOUSE (1947, GB, British Lion)
Salvatore—Kieron Moore
Director—Leslie Arliss
Leading Players—Margaret Johnston, Dulcie Gray, Guy Middleton

MAN ABOUT TOWN (1939, Paramount)
Bob Temple—Jack Benny
Director—Mark Sandrich
Leading Players—Dorothy Lamour, Edward Arnold, Binnie Barnes

MAN ABOVE THE LAW (1918, Silent, Triangle)
Duce Chalmers—Jack Richardson
Director—Raymond Wells
Leading Players—Josie Sedgwick, Claire McDowell, May Giraci

MAN ACCUSED (1959, UA)
Bob Jenson—Ronald Howard
Director—Montgomery Tully
Leading Players—Carol Marsh, Ian Fleming, Catherina Ferraz

MAN AFRAID (1957, Universal)
Rev. David Collins—George Nader
Director—Harry Keller
Leading Players—Phyllis Thaxter, Tim Hovey, Eduard Franz

MAN AGAINST WOMAN (1932, Columbia)
Johnny McCloud—Jack Holt
Lola Parker—Lillian Miles
Director—Irving Cummings
Leading Players—Walter Connolly, Gavin Gordon, Arthur Vinton

MAN ALIVE (1945, RKO)
Speed—Pat O'Brien
Director—Ray Enright
Leading Players—Adolphe Menjou, Ellen Drew, Rudy Vallee

A MAN ALONE (1955, Republic)
Wes Steele—Ray Milland
Director—Ray Milland
Leading Players—Mary Murphy, Ward Bond, Raymond Burr

MAN AND BOY (1972, Jemmin/Levitt/Pickman)
Caleb Revers—Bill Cosby
Billy Revers—George Spell
Director—E.W. Swackhamer
Leading Players—Gloria Foster, Leif Erickson, Yaphett Kotto

MAN AND HIS WOMAN (1920, Silent, Pathe)
Dr. John Worthing—Herbert Rawlinson
Clare Eaton—Eulalie Jensen
Director—J. Stuart Blackton
Leading Players—May McAvoy, Warren Chandler, Louis Dean

MAN AND MAID (1925, Silent, Metro-Goldwyn)
Sir Nicholas Thormonde—Lew Cody
Alathea Bulteel—Harriet Hammond
Director—Victor Schertzinger
Leading Players—Rene Adore, Paulette Duval, Alec Francis

A MAN AND THE WOMAN (1917, Silent, Art Dramas)
Agnes van Suyden—Edith Hallor
James Duncan—Leslie Austen
Director—Alice Guy
Leading Players—Kirke Browne, H. Bradley Barker, Yolande Doquette

MAN AT THE TOP (1973, GB, Anglo-EMI)
Joe Lampton—Kenneth Haigh
Director—Mike Vardy
Leading Players—Nanette Newman, Harry Andrews, William Lucas

MAN BAIT (1926, Silent, Producers Distributing Corp.)
Madge Dreyer—Marie Prevost
Director—Donald Crisp
Leading Players—Kenneth Thomson, Douglas Fairbanks, Jr., Louis Natheaux

THE MAN BEHIND THE GUN (1952, Warner Brothers)
Major Callicut—Randolph Scott
Director—Felix Feist
Leading Players—Patrice Wymore, Dick Wesson, Philip Carey

A MAN BETRAYED (1941, Republic)
Lynn Hollister—John Wayne
Director—John Auer
Leading Players—Frances Dee, Edward Ellis, Wallace Ford

THE MAN BETWEEN (1953, GB, UA)
Ivo Kern—James Mason
Director—Carol Reed

Leading Players—Claire Bloom, Hildegarde Neff, Geoffrey Toone

A MAN CALLED ADAM (1966, Embassy)
Adam Johnson—Sammy Davis, Jr.
Director—Leo Penn
Leading Players—Ossie Davis, Cicely Tyson, Louis Armstrong

THE MAN CALLED BACK (1932, Tiffany)
Dr. David Yorke—Conrad Nagel
Director—Robert Florey
Leading Players—Doris Kenyon, John Halliday, Juliette Compton

A MAN CALLED DAGGER (1967, MGM)
Dick Dagger—Paul Mantee
Director—Richard Rush
Leading Players—Terry Moore, Jan Murray, Sue Ane Langdon

A MAN CALLED GANNON (1969, Universal)
Gannon—Tony Franciosa
Director—James Goldstone
Leading Players—Michael Sarrazin, Judi West, Susan Oliver

A MAN CALLED HORSE (1970, National General Pictures)
Lord John Morgan—Richard Harris
Director—Elliot Silverstein
Leading Players—Judith Anderson, Jean Gascon, Manu Tupou

THE MAN CALLED NOON (1973, GB, National General)
Noon—Richard Crenna
Director—Peter Collinson
Leading Players—Stephen Boyd, Rosanna Schiaffino, Farley Granger

THE MAN CALLED PETER (1955, 20th Century Fox)
Peter Marshall—Richard Todd
Director—Henry Koster
Leading Players—Jean Peters, Marjorie Rambeau, Jill Esmond

A MAN CALLED SARGE (1990, Cannon)
Sarge—Gary Kroeger
Director—Stuart Gillard
Leading Players—Marc Singer, Jennifer Runyon, Gretchen German, Michael Mears, Andy Greenhalgh

A MAN CALLED SLEDGE (1971, Columbia)
Luther Sledge—James Garner
Director—Vic Morrow
Leading Players—Dennis Weaver, Claude Akins, John Marley

A MAN COULD GET KILLED (1966, Universal)
William Beddoes—James Garner
Director—Ronald Neame
Leading Players—Melina Mercouri, Sandra Dee, Tony Franciosa

MAN CRAZY (1927, Silent, First National)
Clarissa Janeway—Dorothy Mackaill
Director—John Francis Dillon
Leading Players—Jack Mulhall, Edythe Chapman, Phillips Smalley

A MAN FOR ALL SEASONS (1966, GB, Columbia)
Sir Thomas More—Paul Scofield
Director—Fred Zinneman
Leading Players—Wendy Hiller, Leo McKern, Robert Shaw, Orson Welles, Susannah York, John Hurt

A MAN FOUR-SQUARE (1926, Silent, Fox Film Corp.)
Craig Norton—Buck Jones
Director—R. William Neill
Leading Players—Marion Harlan, Harry Woods, William Lawrence

MAN FRIDAY (1975, GB, Avco Embassy)
Friday—Richard Roundtree
Director—Jack Gold
Leading Players—Peter O'Toole, Peter Cellier, Christopher Cabot

THE MAN FROM BEYOND (1922, Silent, Houdini)
The Man from Beyond—Harry Houdini
Director—Burton King
Leading Players—Arthur Maude, Albert Travernier, Erwin Connelly

THE MAN FROM BITTER RIDGE (1955, Universal)
Jeff Carr—Lex Barker
Director—Jack Arnold
Leading Players—Mara Corday, Stephen McNally, John Dehner

THE MAN FROM BLANKLEY'S (1930, Warner Brothers)
Lord Strathpeffer—John Barrymore
Director—Alfred E. Green
Leading Players—Loretta Young, William Austin, Albert Gran

THE MAN FROM CAIRO (1953, Lippert)
Mike Canelli—George Raft
Director—Ray H. Enright
Leading Players—Gianna Maria Canale, Massimo Serato, Irene Papas

THE MAN FROM CHICAGO (1931, GB, British International)
Nick Dugan—Bernard Nedell
Director—Walter Summers
Leading Players—Dodo Watts, Joyce Kennedy, Morris Harvey

THE MAN FROM COLORADO (1948, Columbia)
Col. Owen Devereaux—Glenn Ford
Director—Henry Levin
Leading Players—William Holden, Ellen Drew, Ray Collins

THE MAN FROM DAKOTA (1940, MGM)
Sgt. Barstow—Wallace Beery
Director—Leslie Fenton
Leading Players—John Howard, Dolores Del Rio, Donald Meek

MAN FROM DEL RIO (1956, UA)
Dave Robles—Anthony Quinn
Director—Harry Horner
Leading Players—Katy Juardo, Peter Whitney, Douglas Fowley

THE MAN FROM DOWN UNDER (1943, MGM)
Jocko Wilson—Charles Laughton
Director—Robert Z. Leonard
Leading Players—Binnie Barnes, Richard Carlson, Donna Reed

MAN FROM FRISCO (1944, Republic)
Matt Braddock—Michael O'Shea
Director—Robert Florey
Leading Players—Anne Shirley, Gene Lockhart, Dan Duryea

THE MAN FROM GALVESTON (1964, Warner Brothers)
Timothy Higgins—Jeffrey Hunter

Director—William Conrad
Leading Players—Preston Foster, James Coburn, Joanna Moore

MAN FROM GOD'S COUNTRY (1958, Allied Artists)
Dan Beattie—George Montgomery
Director—Paul Landres
Leading Players—Randy Stuart, Gregg Barton, Kim Charney

THE MAN FROM GUN TOWN (1936, Puritan)
Tim Hanlon—Tim McCoy
Director—Ford Beebe
Leading Players—Billie Seward, Rex Lease, Jack Clifford

MAN FROM HEADQUARTERS (1928, Silent, Rayart)
Yorke Norray—Cornelius Keefe
Director—Duke Worne
Leading Players—Edith Roberts, Charles West, Lloyd Whitlock

THE MAN FROM HOME (1914, Silent, Lasky)
Daniel Vorhees Pike—Charles Richman
Director—Cecil B. De Mille
Leading Players—Theodore Roberts, Fred Montague, Monroe Salisbury

THE MAN FROM LARAMIE (1955, Columbia)
Will Lockhart—James Stewart
Director—Anthony Mann
Leading Players—Arthur Kennedy, Donald Crisp, Cathy O'Donnell, Alex Nicol

THE MAN FROM MONTANA (1917, Silent, Universal)
Duke Farley—Neal Hart
Director—George Marshall
Leading Players—George Berrell, E.J. Peil, Betty Lamb

MAN FROM MONTANA (1941, Universal)
Bob Dawson—Johnny Mack Brown
Director—Ray Taylor
Leading Players—Fuzzy Knight, Billy Lenhart, Kenneth Brown

THE MAN FROM MONTEREY (1933, Warner Brothers)
Capt. John Holmes—John Wayne
Director—Mack V. Wright
Leading Players—Ruth Hall, Luis Alberni, Francis Ford

THE MAN FROM MONTREAL (1940, Universal)
Clark Manning—Richard Arlen
Director—Christy Cabanne
Leading Players—Andy Devine, Kay Sutton, Anne Gwynne

THE MAN FROM PAINTED POST (1917, Silent, Artcraft)
Fancy Jim Sherwood—Douglas Fairbanks
Director—Joseph Henabery
Leading Players—Eileen Percy, Frank Cambeau, Frank Clark

THE MAN FROM SNOWY RIVER (1983, Australia, 20th Century Fox)
Spur—Kirk Douglas
Director—George Miller
Leading Players—Jack Thompson, Tom Burlinson, Terence Donovan

THE MAN FROM SUNDOWN (1939, Columbia)
Larry Whalen—Charles Starrett
Director—Sam Nelson
Leading Players—Iris Meredith, Richard Fiske, Jack Rockwell

THE MAN FROM TEXAS (1948, Eagle-Lion)
El Paso Kid—James Craig
Director—Leigh Jason
Leading Players—Lynn Bari, Johnnie Johnston, Una Merkel

THE MAN FROM THE ALAMO (1953, Universal)
John Stoud—Glenn Ford
Director—Budd Boetticher
Leading Players—Julia Adams, Chill Wills, Victor Jory

THE MAN FROM THE DINER'S CLUB (1963, Columbia)
Ernie Klenk—Danny Kaye
Director—Frank Tashlin
Leading Players—Cara Williams, Martha Hyer, Telly Savalas

THE MAN FROM THE RIO GRANDE (1943, Republic)
Lee Grant—Don "Red" Barry
Director—Howard Bretherton
Leading Players—Wally Vernon, Twinkle Watts, Harry Cording

THE MAN FROM WYOMING (1924, Silent, Universal)
Ned Bannister—Jack Hoxie
Director—Robert North Bradbury
Leading Players—Lillian Rich, William Welsh, Claude Payton

A MAN FROM WYOMING (1930, Paramount)
Jim Baker—Gary Cooper
Director—Rowland V. Lee
Leading Players—June Collyer, Regis Toomey, Morgan Farley

THE MAN FROM YESTERDAY (1932, Paramount)
Capt. Tony Clyde—Clive Brook
Director—Berthold Viertel
Leading Players—Claudette Colbert, Charles Boyer, Andy Devine, Alan Mowbray

THE MAN HATER (1917, Silent, Triangle)
Phemie Sanders—Winifred Allen
Director—Albert Parker
Leading Players—Jack Meredith, Harry Neville, Jessie Shirley

THE MAN I LOVE (1929, Paramount)
Dum-Dum Brooks—Richard Arlen
Celia Fields—Mary Brian
Director—William A. Wellman
Leading Players—Olga Baclanova, Harry Green, Jack Oakie

THE MAN I LOVE (1946, Warner Brothers)
Petey Brown—Ida Lupino
Sam Thomas—Bruce Bennett
Director—Raoul Walsh
Leading Players—Robert Alda, Andrea King, Martha Vickers

THE MAN I MARRIED (1940, 20th Century Fox)
Carol Hoffman—Joan Bennett
Eric Hoffman—Francis Lederer
Director—Irving Pichel
Leading Players—Lloyd Nolan, Anna Sten, Otto Kruger

THE MAN I MARRY (1936, Universal)
Rena Allen—Doris Nolan
Ken Durkin—Michael Whalen
Director—Ralph Murphy
Leading Players—Marjorie Gateson, Gerald Oliver Smith, Nigel Bruce

THE MAN I WANT (1934, GB, British Lion)
Peter Mason—Henry Kendall
Marion Round—Wendy Barrie
Director—Leslie Hiscott
Leading Players—Betty Astell, Davy Burnaby, Hal Walters

MAN IN A COCKED HAT (1960, GB, Boulting Bros.)
Cardogen de Vere Carlton-Browne—Terry-Thomas
Directors—Jeffrey Dell and Roy Boulting
Leading Players—Peter Sellers, Luciana Paoluzzi, Thorley Walters

THE MAN IN BLACK (1950, GB, Hammer)
Henry Clavering—Sidney James
Director—Francis Searle
Leading Players—Betty Ann Davies, Anthony Forwood, Sheila Burrell

THE MAN IN BLUE (1937, Universal)
Martin Dunne—Edward Ellis
Director—Milton Carruth
Leading Players—Robert Wilcox, Nan Grey, Richard Carle

THE MAN IN GREY (1943, GB, Gaumont)
Marquis of Rohan—James Mason
Director—Leslie Arliss
Leading Players—Margaret Lockwood, Phyllis Calvert, Stewart Granger, Helen Haye

THE MAN IN HALF-MOON STREET (1944, Paramount)
Julian Karell—Nils Asther
Director—Ralph M. Murphy
Leading Players—Helen Walker, Reinhold Schunzel, Paul Cavanaugh

THE MAN IN POSSESSION (1931, MGM)
Raymond Dabney—Robert Montgomery
Director—Sam Wood
Leading Players—Charlotte Greenwood, Irene Purcell, C. Aubrey Smith

MAN IN THE ATTIC (1953, 20th Century Fox)
Slade—Jack Palance
Director—Hugo Fregonese
Leading Players—Constance Smith, Bryon Palmer, Frances Bavier

MAN IN THE DARK (1953, Columbia)
James Blake/Steve Rawley—Edmond O'Brien
Director—Lew Landers
Leading Players—Audrey Totter, Ted De Corsia, Horace McMahon

THE MAN IN THE DINGHY (1951, GB, Snader)
Nicholas Foster—Michael Wilding
Director—Herbert Wilcox
Leading Players—Odile Versois, Jack Hulbert, Constance Cummings

THE MAN IN THE GLASS BOOTH (1975, American Film Theatre)
Arthur Goldman—Maximilian Schell
Director—Arthur Hiller
Leading Players—Lois Nettleton, Luther Adler, Lawrence Pressman

THE MAN IN THE GREY FLANNEL SUIT (1956, 20th Century Fox)
Tom Rath—Gregory Peck
Director—Nunnally Johnson
Leading Players—Jennifer Jones, Fredric March, Marisa Pavan, Ann Harding, Lee J. Cobb

THE MAN IN THE IRON MASK (1939, UA)
Louis XIV/Philippe—Louis Hayward
Director—James Whale
Leading Players—Joan Bennett, Warren William, Joseph Schildkraut, Alan Hale, Miles Mander

MAN IN THE MIDDLE (1964, 20th Century Fox)
Lt. Col. Barney Adams—Robert Mitchum
Director—Guy Hamilton
Leading Players—France Nuyen, Barry Sullivan, Trevor Howard, Keenan Wynn, Sam Wanamaker, Alexander Knox

THE MAN IN THE MIRROR (1936, GB, Wardour)
Jeremy Dike—Edward Everett Horton
Director—Maurice Elvey
Leading Players—Genevieve Tobin, Garry Marsh, Ursula Jeans

MAN IN THE MOON (1961, GB, TransLux)
William Blood—Kenneth More
Director—Basil Dearden
Leading Players—Shirley Ann Field, Norman Bird, Michael Hordern

THE MAN IN THE NET (1959, UA)
John Hamilton—Alan Ladd
Director—Michael Curtiz
Leading Players—Carolyn Jones, Diane Brewster, John Lupton

A MAN IN THE OPEN (1919, Silent, United Pictures Theatres)
Sailor Jesse—Dustin Farnum
Director—Ernest C. Warde
Leading Players—Hershall Mayall, Lamar Johnstone, Joseph Dowling

THE MAN IN THE ROAD (1957, GB, Republic)
Ivan Mason—Derek Farr
Director—Lance Comfort
Leading Players—Ella Raines, Donald Wolfit, Lisa Daniely

MAN IN THE ROUGH (1928, Silent, FBO)
Bruce Sherwood—Bob Steele
Director—Wallace Fox
Leading Players—Marjorie King, Tom Lingham, William Norton Bailey

MAN IN THE SADDLE (1951, Columbia)
Owen Merritt—Randolph Scott
Director—Andre De Toth
Leading Players—Joan Leslie, Ellen Drew, Alexander Knox

MAN IN THE SHADOW (1957, Universal)
Sheriff Ben Sadler—Jeff Chandler
Director—Jack Arnold
Leading Players—Orson Welles, Colleen Miller, Ben Alexander

MAN IN THE VAULT (1956, RKO)
Tommy Dancer—William Campbell
Director—Andrew V. McLaglen
Leading Players—Karen Sharpe, Anita Ekberg, Berry Kroeger

THE MAN IN THE WATER (1963, Crown International)
Capt. James—Mark Stevens
Director—Mark Stevens
Leading Players—Jack Donner, Linda Scott, David Aldrich

THE MAN IN THE WHITE SUIT (1952, GB, Rank)
Sidney Stratton—Alec Guinness
Director—Alexander Mackendrick
Leading Players—Joan Greenwood, Cecil Parker, Michael Gough

MAN IN THE WILDERNESS (1971, Warner Brothers)
Zachary Bass—Richard Harris
Director—Richard C. Sarafin
Leading Players—John Huston, Henry Wilcoxon, Percy Herbert

THE MAN INSIDE (1958, GB, Columbia)
Sam Carter—Nigel Patrick
Director—John Gilling
Leading Players—Jack Palance, Anita Ekberg, Anthony Newley

THE MAN INSIDE (1990, New Line)
Gunther Wallraff—Jurgen Prochnow
Director—Bobby Roth
Leading Players—Peter Coyote, Nathalie Baye

MAN MADE MONSTER (1941, Universal)
Dan McCormick—Lon Chaney, Jr.
Director—George Waggner
Leading Players—Lionel Atwill, Anne Nagel, Frank Albertson

MAN OF A THOUSAND FACES (1957, Universal)
Lon Chaney—James Cagney
Director—Joseph Pevney
Leading Players—Dorothy Malone, Jane Greer, Robert Evans

MAN OF AFFAIRS (1937, GB, Gaumont)
Lord Dunchester—George Arliss
Director—Herbert Mason
Leading Players—Romilly Lunge, Jessie Winter, John Ford

MAN OF AFRICA (1956, GB, Eden)
Jonathan—Frederick Bijuerenda
Director—Cyril Frankel
Leading Players—Violet Mukabuerza, Members of the Bakiga and Batwa Tribes

MAN OF CONFLICT (1953, Atlas)
J.R. Compton—Edward Arnold
Director—Hal R. Makelim
Leading Players—John Agar, Susan Morrow, Fay Roope

MAN OF CONQUEST (1939, Republic)
Sam Houston—Richard Dix
Director—George Nichols, Jr.
Leading Players—Gail Patrick, Edward Ellis, Joan Fontaine, Victor Jory

MAN OF COURAGE (1943, Producers Releasing Corp.)
John Wallace—Barton MacLane
Director—Alexis Thurn-Taxis
Leading Players—Charlotte Wynters, Lyle Talbot, Dorothy Burgess

MAN OF EVIL (1948, GB, Gainsborough)
Lord Manderstoke—James Mason
Director—Anthony Asquith

Leading Players—Phyllis Calvert, Wilfrid Lawson, Stewart Granger, Margaretta Scott

MAN OF FLOWERS (1984, Australia, International Spectrafilm)
Charles Bremer—Norman Kaye
Director—Paul Cox
Leading Players—Alyson Best, Chris Haywood, Sarah Walker

MAN OF IRON (1935, Warner Brothers)
Chris Bennett—Barton MacLane
Director—William McGann
Leading Players—Mary Astor, John Eldredge, Dorothy Peterson

MAN OF LA MANCHA (1972, UA)
Don Quixote—Peter O'Toole
Director—Arthur Hiller
Leading Players—Sophia Loren, James Coco, Harry Andrews

MAN OF MAYFAIR (1931, GB, Paramount)
Lord William—Jack Buchanan
Director—Louis Mercanton
Leading Players—Joan Barry, Warwick Ward, Nora Swinburne

A MAN OF NERVE (1925, Silent, FBO)
Hackamore Henderson—Bob Custer
Director—Louis Chaudet
Leading Players—Jean Arthur, Leon Holmes, David Dunbar

A MAN OF SENTIMENT (1933, First Division)
John Russell—William Bakewell
Director—Richard Thorpe
Leading Players—Marian Marsh, Owen Moore, Christian Rub

MAN OF THE FOREST (1933, Paramount)
Brett Dale—Randolph Scott
Director—Henry Hathaway
Leading Players—Verna Hillie, Harry Carey, Noah Beery, Sr.

MAN OF THE MOMENT (1935, GB, Warner Brothers)
Tony—Douglas Fairbanks, Jr.
Director—Monty Banks
Leading Players—Laura la Plante, Claude Hulbert, Margaret Lockwood

MAN OF THE MOMENT (1955, GB, Group)
Norman—Norman Wisdom
Director—John Paddy Carstairs
Leading Players—Lana Morris, Belinda Lee, Jerry Desmonde

MAN OF THE PEOPLE (1937, MGM)
Jack Moreno—Joseph Calleia
Director—Edwin L. Marin
Leading Players—Florence Rice, Thomas Mitchell, Ted Healy

MAN OF THE WEST (1958, UA)
Link Jones—Gary Cooper
Director—Anthony Mann
Leading Players—Julie London, Lee J. Cobb, Arthur O'Connell, Jack Lord

MAN OF THE WORLD (1931, Paramount)
Michael Trevor—William Powell
Directors—Richard Wallace and Edward Goodman
Leading Players—Carole Lombard, Wynne Gibson, Guy Kibbee

MAN ON A STRING (1960, Columbia)
Boris Mitrov—Ernest Borgnine

Director—Andre de Toth
Leading Players—Kerwin Mathews, Colleen Dewhurst, Alexander Scourby

MAN ON A SWING (1974, Paramount)
Franklin Wills—Joel Grey
Director—Frank Perry
Leading Players—Cliff Robertson, Dorothy Tristan, Peter Masterson

MAN ON A TIGHTROPE (1953, 20th Century Fox)
Karel Cernik—Fredric March
Director—Elia Kazan
Leading Players—Terry Moore, Gloria Grahame, Cameron Mitchell, Adolphe Menjou

MAN ON FIRE (1957, MGM)
Earl Carleton—Bing Crosby
Director—Ranald MacDougall
Leading Players—Inger Stevens, Mary Pickett, E.G. Marshall

THE MAN ON THE BOX (1925, Silent, Warner Brothers)
Bob Warburton—Sydney Chaplin
Director—Charles Reisner
Leading Players—David Butler, Alice Calhoun, Kathleen Calhoun

THE MAN ON THE EIFFEL TOWER (1949, RKO)
Radek—Franchot Tone
Director—Burgess Meredith
Leading Players—Charles Laughton, Burgess Meredith, Robert Hutton, Jean Wallace, Patricia Roc

THE MAN ON THE FLYING TRAPEZE (1935, Paramount)
Ambrose Wolfinger—W.C. Fields
Director—Clyde Bruckman
Leading Players—Mary Brian, Kathleen Howard, Grady Sutton

MAN ON THE PROWL (1957, UA)
Doug Gerhardt—James Best
Director—Art Napoleon
Leading Players—Mala Powers, Ted De Corsia, Jerry Paris

MAN ON THE RUN (1949, GB, Pathe)
Peter Burdon—Derek Farr
Director—Lawrence Huntington
Leading Players—Joan Hopkins, Edward Chapman, Laurence Harvey

MAN OR GUN (1958, Republic)
Maybe Smith—MacDonald Carey
Director—Albert C. Gannaway
Leading Players—Audrey Totter, James Craig, James Gleason

THE MAN OUTSIDE (1933, GB, RKO)
Harry Wainwright—Henry Kendall
Director—George A. Cooper
Leading Players—Gillian Lind, Joan Gardner, Michael Hogan

THE MAN OUTSIDE (1968, GB, Allied Artists)
Bill MacLean—Van Heflin
Director—Samuel Gallu
Leading Players—Heidelinde Weis, Pinkas Braun, Peter Vaughan

MAN OUTSIDE (1988, Virgin Vision)
Jack Avery—Robert Logan
Director—Mark Stouffer
Leading Players—Kathleen Quinlan, Bradford Dillman, Levon Helm, Andrew Barach

THE MAN THEY COULD NOT HANG (1939, Columbia)
Dr. Henryk Savaard—Boris Karloff
Director—Nick Grinde
Leading Players—Lorna Gray, Robert Wilcox, Roger Pryor

MAN TO MAN (1931, Warner Brothers)
Barber John Bolton—Grant Mitchell
Michael Bolton—Phillips Holmes
Director—Allan Dwan
Leading Players—Lucille Powers, George Marion, Otis Harlan

A MAN TO REMEMBER (1938, RKO)
Dr. John Abbott—Edward Ellis
Director—Garson Kanin
Leading Players—Anne Shirley, Lee Bowman, William Henry

THE MAN UPSTAIRS (1959, GB, British Lion)
Peter Watson—Richard Attenborough
Director—Don Chaffey
Leading Players—Bernard Lee, Donald Houston, Dorothy Alison

MAN WANTED (1932, Warner Brothers)
Tom Sheridan—David Manners
Director—William Dieterle
Leading Players—Kay Francis, Andy Devine, Una Merkel

THE MAN WHO (1921, Silent, Metro)
Bedford Mills—Bert Lytell
Director—Maxwell Karger
Leading Players—Lucy Cotton, Virginia Valli, Frank Currier

THE MAN WHO BROKE THE BANK AT MONTE CARLO (1935, Fox Film Corp.)
Paul Gallard—Ronald Colman
Director—Stephen Roberts
Leading Players—Joan Bennett, Colin Clive, Nigel Bruce

THE MAN WHO CAME BACK (1931, Fox Film Corp.)
Stephen Randolph—Charles Farrell
Director—Raoul Walsh
Leading Players—Janet Gaynor, Kenneth MacKenna, William Holden

THE MAN WHO CAME TO DINNER (1942, Warner Brothers)
Sheridan Whiteside—Monty Woolley
Director—William Keighley
Leading Players—Bette Davis, Ann Sheridan, Jimmy Durante, Richard Travis, Reginald Gardiner, Mary Wickes

THE MAN WHO CHANGED HIS NAME (1928, Silent, British Lion)
Selby Clive—Stewart Rome
Director—A.V. Bramble
Leading Players—Betty Faire, James Raglan, Ben Field

THE MAN WHO CHANGED HIS NAME (1934, GB, DuWorld)
Selby Clive—Lyn Harding
Director—Henry Edwards
Leading Players—Betty Stockfeld, Leslie Perrins, Ben Welden

THE MAN WHO CHEATED HIMSELF (1951, 20th Century Fox)
Ed Cullen—Lee J. Cobb
Director—Felix E. Feist
Leading Players—John Dall, Jane Wyatt, Lisa Howard

THE MAN WHO COULD CHEAT DEATH (1959, GB, Hammer)
Dr. Georges Bonner—Anton Diffring
Director—Terence Fisher
Leading Players—Hazel Court, Christopher Lee, Arnold Marle

THE MAN WHO COULD NOT LOSE (1914, Silent, Favorite Players)
Champneys Carter—Carlyle Blackwell
Director—Robert A. Dillon
Leading Players—Hal Clements, Wiliam Branton, James J. Sheehan

THE MAN WHO COULD WORK MIRACLES (1937, GB, UA)
George McWhirter Fotheringay—Roland Young
Director—Lothar Mendes
Leading Players—Ralph Richardson, Edward Chapman, Ernest Thesiger, Joan Gardner

THE MAN WHO COULDN'T WALK (1964, GB, Falcon-Taurus)
The Consul—Eric Pohlmann
Director—Henry Cass
Leading Players—Peter Reynolds, Pat Clavin, Reed De Rouen

THE MAN WHO CRIED WOLF (1937, Universal)
Lawrence Fontaine—Lewis Stone
Director—Lewis R. Foster
Leading Players—Tom Brown, Barbara Reed, Marjorie Main

THE MAN WHO DARED (1933, Fox Film Corp.)
Jan Novak—Preston Foster
Director—Hamilton McFadden
Leading Players—Zita Johann, Joan Marsh, Irene Biller

THE MAN WHO DIED TWICE (1958, Republic)
Bill Brennon—Rod Cameron
Director—Joe Kane
Leading Players—Vera Ralston, Mike Mazurki, Gerald Milton

THE MAN WHO FELL TO EARTH (1976, GB, British Lion)
Thomas Jerome Newton—David Bowie
Director—Nicolas Roeg
Leading Players—Rip Torn, Candy Clark, Buck Henry

THE MAN WHO FORGOT (1917, Silent, World)
John Smith—Robert Warwick
Director—Emile Chautard
Leading Players—Gerda Holmes, Doris Kenyon, Alex Shannon

THE MAN WHO FOUND HIMSELF (1937, RKO)
Jim Stanton—John Beal
Director—Lew Landers
Leading Players—Joan Fontaine, Philip Huston, Jane Walsh

THE MAN WHO HAD POWER OVER WOMEN (1970, GB, Avco Embassy)
Peter Reaney—Rod Taylor
Director—John Krish
Leading Players—Carol White, James Booth, Penelope Horner

THE MAN WHO HAUNTED HIMSELF (1970, GB, Assoc. British)
Harold Pelham—Roger Moore
Director—Basil Dearden
Leading Players—Hildegard Neil, Alastair Mackenzie, Hugh Mackenzie

THE MAN WHO KNEW TOO MUCH (1935, GB, Gaumont)
Bob Lawrence—Leslie Banks
Director—Alfred Hitchcock
Leading Players—Edna Best, Peter Lorre, Frank Vosper

THE MAN WHO KNEW TOO MUCH (1956, Paramount)
Dr. Ben McKenna—James Stewart
Director—Alfred Hitchcock
Leading Players—Doris Day, Brenda de Banzie, Bernard Miles

THE MAN WHO LAUGHS (1927, Silent, Universal)
Gwynplaine—Conrad Veidt
Director—Paul Leni
Leading Players—Mary Philbin, Olga Baclanova, Josephine Crowell

THE MAN WHO LIKED FUNERALS (1959, GB, Rank)
Simon Hurd—Leslie Phillips
Director—David Eady
Leading Players—Susan Beaumont, Bill Fraser, Mary Mackenzie

THE MAN WHO LIVED AGAIN (1936, GB, Gaumont)
Dr. Laurience—Boris Karloff
Director—Robert Stevenson
Leading Players—Anna Lee, Donald Calthrop, John Loder

MAN WHO LIVED TWICE (1936, Columbia)
James Blake/Slick Rawley—Ralph Bellamy
Director—Harry Lachman
Leading Players—Marian Marsh, Thurston Hall, Isabel Jewell

THE MAN WHO LOST HIMSELF (1941, Universal)
John Evans/Malcolm Scott—Brian Aherne
Director—Edward Ludwig
Leading Players—Kay Francis, Henry Stephenson, S.Z. Sakall

THE MAN WHO LOVED CAT DANCING (1973, MGM)
Jay Grobart—Burt Reynolds
Catherine Crocker—Sarah Miles
Director—Richard G. Sarafian
Leading Players—Lee J. Cobb, Jack Warden, George Hamilton

THE MAN WHO LOVED REDHEADS (1955, London Films)
Mark St. Neots—John Justin
Sylvia/Daphne/Olga/Colette—Moira Shearer
Director—Harold French
Leading Players—Roland Culver, Gladys Cooper, Denholm Elliott

THE MAN WHO LOVED WOMEN (1983, Columbia)
David—Burt Reynolds
Director—Blake Edwards
Leading Players—Julie Andrews, Kim Basinger, Marilu Henner, Cynthia Sikes, Jennifer Edwards

THE MAN WHO MADE DIAMONDS (1937, GB, Warner Brothers)
Prof. Calthrop—J. Fisher White
Director—Ralph Ince
Leading Players—Noel Madison, James Stephenson, Lesley Brook

THE MAN WHO MADE GOOD (1917, Silent, Triangle)
Tom Burton—Jack Devereaux
Director—Arthur Rosson
Leading Players—Winifred Allen, Henry P. Dixon, Barney Gilmore

THE MAN WHO PLAYED GOD (1922, Silent, UA)
John Arden—George Arliss
Director—Harmon Weight
Leading Players—Ann Forrest, Ivan Simpson, Edward Earle

THE MAN WHO PLAYED GOD (1932, Warner Brothers)
Montgomery Royale—George Arliss
Director—John G. Adolfi
Leading Players—Violet Heming, Ivan Simpson, Louise Closser Hale

THE MAN WHO RECLAIMED HIS HEAD (1935, Universal)
Paul Verin—Claude Rains
Director—Edward Ludwig
Leading Players—Joan Bennett, Lionel Atwill, Baby Jane Quigley

THE MAN WHO RETURNED TO LIFE (1942, Columbia)
David Jameson—John Howard
Director—Lew Landers
Leading Players—Lucile Fairbanks, Ruth Ford, Marcelle Martin

THE MAN WHO SAW TOMORROW (1922, Silent, Paramount)
Burke Hammond—Thomas Meighan
Director—Alfred E. Green
Leading Players—Theodore Roberts, Leatrice Joy, Albert Roscoe

THE MAN WHO SHOT LIBERTY VALANCE (1962, Paramount)
Tom Doniphon—John Wayne
Liberty Valance—Lee Marvin
Director—John Ford
Leading Players—James Stewart, Vera Miles, Edmond O'Brien

THE MAN WHO TALKED TOO MUCH (1940, Warner Brothers)
Stephen Forbes—George Brent
Director—Vincent Sherman
Leading Players—Virginia Bruce, Brenda Marshall, Richard Barthelmess, William Lundigan

THE MAN WHO TURNED TO STONE (1957, Columbia)
Dr. Murdock—Victor Jory
Director—Leslie Kardos
Leading Players—Ann Doran, Charlotte Austin, William Hudson

THE MAN WHO TURNED WHITE (1919, Silent, Superior)
Capt. Rand/Ali Zaman—H.B. Warner
Director—Park Frame
Leading Players—Barbara Castleton, Wedgewood Nowell, Carmen Phillips

THE MAN WHO UNDERSTOOD WOMEN (1959, 20th Century Fox)
Willie Bauche—Henry Fonda
Director—Nunnally Johnson
Leading Players—Leslie Caron, Cesare Danova, Myron McCormick

THE MAN WHO WALKED ALONE (1945, Producers Releasing Corp.)
Cpl. Marion Scott—David O'Brien
Director—Christy Cabanne
Leading Players—Kay Aldridge, Walter Catlett, Guinn "Big Boy" Williams

THE MAN WHO WON (1933, GB, British International)
Sir William Normand—Henry Kendall
Director—Normal Walker
Leading Players—Heather Angel, Nora Swinburne, Sam Livesey

THE MAN WHO WOULD BE KING (1975, GB, Allied Artists)
Daniel Dravot—Sean Connery
Director—John Huston
Leading Players—Michael Caine, Christopher Plummer, Saeed Jaffrey, Shakira Caine

THE MAN WHO WOULDN'T TALK (1940, 20th Century Fox)
Joe Monday—Lloyd Nolan
Director—David Burton
Leading Players—Jean Rogers, Richard Clarke, Onslow Stevens

THE MAN WHO WOULDN'T TALK (1958, GB, British Lion)
Dr. Frank Smith—Anthony Quayle
Director—Herbert Wilcox
Leading Players—Anna Neagle, Zsa Zsa Gabor, Katherine Kath

THE MAN WITH A CLOAK (1951, MGM)
Dupin (Edgar Allan Poe)—Joseph Cotten
Director—Fletcher Markle
Leading Players—Barbara Stanwyck, Louis Calhern, Leslie Caron, Joe De Santis

MAN WITH A MILLION (1954, GB, UA)
Jerry Adams—Gregory Peck
Director—Ronald Neame
Leading Players—Jane Griffiths, Ronald Squire, A.E. Matthews, Wilfrid Hyde-White

THE MAN WITH BOGART'S FACE (1980, 20th Century Fox)
Sam Marlow—Robert Sacchi
Director—Robert Day
Leading Players—Franco Nero, Michelle Phillips, Olivia Hussey

THE MAN WITH MY FACE (1951, UA)
Chick Graham/Albert Rand—Barry Nelson
Director—Edward J. Montaigne
Leading Players—Lynn Ainley, John Harvey, Carole Mathews

THE MAN WITH NINE LIVES (1940, Columbia)
Dr. Leon Kravaal—Boris Karloff
Director—Nick Grinde
Leading Players—Roger Pryor, Jo Ann Sayers, Stanley Brown

THE MAN WITH ONE RED SHOE (1985, 20th Century Fox)
Richard—Tom Hanks
Director—Stan Dragoti
Leading Players—Dabney Coleman, Lori Singer, Charles Durning, Carrie Fisher, Jim Belushi

THE MAN WITH THE GOLDEN ARM (1955, UA)
Frankie Machine—Frank Sinatra
Director—Otto Preminger
Leading Players—Kim Novak, Eleanor Parker, Arnold Stang, Darren McGavin

THE MAN WITH THE GOLDEN GUN (1974, GB, UA)
Scaramanga—Christopher Lee

Director—Guy Hamilton
Leading Players—Roger Moore, Britt Ekland, Maud Adams

THE MAN WITH THE GREEN CARNATION (1960, GB, Warwick)
Oscar Wilde—Peter Finch
Director—Ken Hughes
Leading Players—John Fraser, Yvonne Mitchell, Lionel Jeffries, Nigel Patrick, James Mason

MAN WITH THE GUN (1955, UA)
Clint Tolinger—Robert Mitchum
Director—Richard Wilson
Leading Players—Jan Sterling, Karen Sharpe, Henry Hull

THE MAN WITH TWO BRAINS (1983, Warner Brothers)
Dr. Michael Hfuhruhurr—Steve Martin
Director—Carl Reiner
Leading Players—Kathleen Turner, Voice of Sissy Spacek, David Warner, Paul Benedict

THE MAN WITH TWO FACES (1934, Warner Brothers)
Damon Wells—Edward G. Robinson
Director—Archie Mayo
Leading Players—Mary Astor, Ricardo Cortez, Mae Clarke

THE MAN WITHOUT A BODY (1957, GB, Eros)
Nostradamus—Michael Golden
Director—W. Lee Wilder
Leading Players—Robert Hutton, George Coulouris, Julia Arnall

MAN WITHOUT A STAR (1955, Universal)
Dempsey Rae—Kirk Douglas
Director—King Vidor
Leading Players—Jeanne Crain, Claire Trevor, William Campbell, Richard Boone

THE MAN WITHOUT DESIRE (1923, GB, Silent, Atlas Biocraft)
Count Vittorio Donaldo—Ivor Novello
Director—Adrian Brunel
Leading Players—Nina Vanna, Sergio Mari, Chris Walker

MAN, WOMAN AND CHILD (1983, Paramount)
Bob Beckwith—Martin Sheen
Sheila Beckwith—Blythe Danner
Jean-Claude Guerin—Sebastian Dungan
Director—Dick Richards
Leading Players—Craig T. Nelson, David Hemmings, Nathalie Nell

THE MAN WORTH WHILE (1921, Silent, Hillfield)
Don Ward—Romaine Fielding
Director—Romaine Fielding
Leading Players—Joan Arliss, Lawrence Johnson, Eugene Acker

A MAN'S CASTLE (1933, Columbia)
Bill—Spencer Tracy
Director—Frank Borzage
Leading Players—Loretta Young, Glenda Farrell, Walter Connolly

THE MANCHESTER MAN (1920, GB, Silent, Ideal)
Jabez Clegg—Hayford Hobbs
Director—Bert Wynne
Leading Players—Aileen Bagot, Warwick Ward, A. Harding Steerman

THE MANCHURIAN CANDIDATE (1962, UA)
Senator John Iselin—James Gregory
Director—John Frankenheimer
Leading Players—Frank Sinatra, Laurence Harvey, Janet Leigh, Angela Lansbury, Henry Silva

MANDINGO (1975, Paramount)
Mede—Ken Norton
Director—Richard Fleischer
Leading Players—James Mason, Susan George, Perry King, Richard Ward, Brenda Sykes

MANHATTAN ANGEL (1948, Columbia)
Gloria Cole—Gloria Jean
Director—Arthur Dreifuss
Leading Players—Ross Ford, Patricia White, Thurston Hall

MANHUNTER (1986, De Laurentiis)
Will Graham—William Peterson
Director—Michael Mann
Leading Players—Kim Greist, Joan Allen, Brian Cox

MANIAC (1980, Magnum)
Frank Zito—Joe Spinell
Director—William Lustig
Leading Players—Caroline Munro, Gail Lawrence, Kelly Piper

MANIAC COP (1988, Shapiro Glickenhaus)
Matt Cordell—Robert Z'dar
Director—William Lustig
Leading Players—Tom Atkins, Bruce Campbell, Laurene Landon

MANIAC COP 2 (1990, Movie House Sales)
Matt Cordell—Robert Z'dar
Director—William Lustig
Leading Players—Robert Davi, Claudia Christian, Michael Lerner, Bruce Campbell, Laurene Landon

MANKILLERS (1987, Action)
Rachel McKenna—Lynda Aldon
Maria Rosetti—Christine Lunde
Director—David A. Prior
Leading Players—Edd Byrnes, Gail Fisher, Edy Williams, William Zipp

MANNEQUIN (1937, MGM)
Jessie Cassidy—Joan Crawford
Director—Frank Borzage
Leading Players—Spencer Tracy, Alan Curtis, Ralph Morgan

MANNEQUIN (1987, 20th Century Fox)
Emmy—Kim Cattrall
Director—Michael Gottlieb
Leading Players—Andrew McCarthy, Estelle Getty, James Spader

MANNEQUIN ON THE RUN (1991, 20th Century Fox)
Jessie—Kristy Swanson
Director—Stewart Raffill
Leading Players—Meshach Taylor, William Ragsdale, Terry Kiser, Stuart Pankin, Cynthia Harris

A MAN'S MAN (1929, Silent, MGM)
Mel—William Haines
Director—James Cruze
Leading Players—Josephine Dunn, Sam Hardy, Mae Busch

A MAN'S PEROGATIVE (1915, Silent, Mutual Masterpiece)
Oliver Rand—Robert Edeson
Director—George Nichols
Leading Players—Mary Alden, Charles Cleary, Billie West

A MAN'S SHADOW (1920, GB, Silent, Butchers)
Peter Beresford/Julian Grey—Langhorne Burton
Director—Sidney Morgan
Leading Players—Violet Graham, Gladys Mason, J. Denton-Thompson

THE MANXMAN (1929, GB, Silent, British International)
Pete Quilliam—Carl Brisson
Director—Alfred Hitchcock
Leading Players—Malcolm Keen, Anny Ondra, Randle Ayrton

MARA OF THE WILDERNESS (1966, Allied Artists)
Mara Wade—Linda Saunders
Director—Frank McDonald
Leading Players—Adam West, Theo Marcuse, Denver Pyle

MARATHON MAN (1976, Paramount)
Babe Levy—Dustin Hoffman
Director—John Schlesinger
Leading Players—Laurence Olivier, Roy Scheider, William Devane, Marthe Keller

MARCO (1973, Cinerama)
Marco Polo—Desi Arnaz, Jr.
Director—Seymour Robbie
Leading Players—Zero Mostel, Jack Weston, Cie Cie Win

MARGIE (1940, Universal)
Margie—Nan Grey
Director—Otis Garrett
Leading Players—Tom Brown, Mischua Auer, Edgar Kennedy

MARGIE (1946, 20th Century Fox)
Margie McDuff—Jeanne Crain
Director—Henry King
Leading Players—Glenn Langan, Lynn Bari, Alan Young

MARIA CHAPDELAINE (1986, Canada, The Movie Store)
Maria Chapdelaine—Carol Laure
Director—Gilles Carle
Leading Players—Nick Mancuso, Claude Rich, Amulette Garneau

MARIANNE (1929, MGM)
Marianne—Marion Davies
Director—Robert Z. Leonard
Leading Players—Cliff Edwards, Lawrence Gray, Benny Rubin

MARIA'S LOVERS (1985, Cannon)
Maria Bosic—Nastassia Kinski
Director—Andrei Konchalovsky
Leading Players—John Savage, Robert Mitchum, Keith Carradine

MARIE (1985, MGM/UA)
Marie Ragghianti—Sissy Spacek
Director—Roger Donaldson
Leading Players—Jeff Daniels, Keith Szarabajka, Morgan Freeman

MARIE-ANN (1978, Canada, Canadian Film Production)
Marie-Ann—Andrea Pelletier
Director—R. Martin Walters
Leading Players—John Juliani, Tantoo Martin, Gordon Tootoosie

MARIE ANTOINETTE (1938, MGM)
Marie Antoinette—Norma Shearer
Director—W.S. Van Dyke II
Leading Players—Tyrone Power, John Barrymore, Gladys George, Robert Morley, Anita Louise, Joseph Schildkraut

MARIE GALANTE (1934, Fox Film Corp.)
Marie Galante—Ketti Gallian
Director—Henry King
Leading Players—Spencer Tracy, Ned Sparks, Helen Morgan

MARIGOLD (1938, GB, Associated British Films)
Marigold Sellar—Sophie Stewart
Director—Thomas Bentley
Leading Players—Patrick Barr, Phyllis Dare, Edward Chapman

MARILYN (1953, GB, Butchers)
Marilyn Saunders—Sandra Dorne
Director—Wolf Rilla
Leading Players—Maxwell Reed, Leslie Dwyer, Vida Hope

MARJORIE MORNINGSTAR (1958, Warner Brothers)
Marjorie Morgenstern—Natalie Wood
Director—Irving Rapper
Leading Players—Gene Kelly, Claire Trevor, Everett Sloane, Martin Milner, Ed Wynn, Carolyn Jones

MARK OF ZORRO (1920, Silent, UA)
Don Diego Vega—Douglas Fairbanks
Director—Fred Niblo
Leading Players—Noah Beery, Marguerite de la Motte, Robert McKim, Charles Hill Mailes, Claire McDowell

THE MARK OF ZORRO (1940, 20th Century Fox)
Don Diego Vega—Tyrone Power
Director— Ruben Mamoulian
Leading Players—Linda Darnell, Basil Rathbone, Gale Sondergaard, Eugene Pallette, J. Edward Bromberg

MARKED FOR DEATH (1990, 20th Century Fox)
Hatcher—Steven Seagal
Director—Dwight H. Little
Leading Players—Basil Wallace, Keith David, Tom Wright, Joanna Pacula

MARKED WOMAN (1937, Warner Brothers)
Mary Dwight—Bette Davis
Director—Lloyd Bacon
Leading Players—Humphrey Bogart, Jane Bryan, Eduardo Ciannelli, Isabel Jewell

MARLOWE (1969, MGM)
Philip Marlowe—James Garner
Director—Paul Bogart
Leading Players—Gayle Hunnicutt, Carol O'Connor, Rita Moreno

MARNIE (1964, Universal)
Marnie Edgar—Tippi Hedren
Director—Alfred Hitchcock

Leading Players—Sean Connery, Diane Baker, Martin Gabel, Louise Latham

MAROONED (1969, Columbia)
Jim Pruett—Richard Crenna
Clayton Stone—James Franciscus
Buzz Lloyd—Gene Hackman
Director—John Sturges
Leading Players—Gregory Peck, David Janssen, Lee Grant, Nancy Kovack, Mariette Hartley

THE MARRIAGE OF A YOUNG STOCKBROKER (1971, 20th Century Fox)
William Arlen—Richard Benjamin
Director—Lawrence Turman
Leading Players—Joanna Shimkus, Elizabeth Ashley, Adam West

THE MARRIAGE OF KITTY (1915, Silent, Metro)
Katherine Silverton—Fannie Ward
Director—George Melford
Leading Players—Richard Morris, Jack Dean, Cleo Ridgely

THE MARRIAGE OF WILLIAM ASHE (1921, Silent, Metro)
William Ashe—Wyndham Standing
Director—Edward Sloman
Leading Players—May Allison, Zeffie Tilbury, Frank Elliot

MARRIED BACHELOR (1941, MGM)
Randolf Haven—Robert Young
Director—Edward Buzzell
Leading Players—Ruth Hussey, Felix Bressart, Lee Bowman

MARRIED TO THE MOB (1988, Orion)
Angela DeMarco—Michelle Pfeiffer
Director—Jonathan Demme
Leading Players—Matthew Modine, Dean Stockwell, Mercedes Ruehl, Alec Baldwin, Joan Cusack

MARRY THE BOSS' DAUGHTER (1941, 20th Century Fox)
Fredericka Barrett—Brenda Joyce
J.W. Barrett—George Barbier
Director—Thorton Freeland
Leading Players—Bruce Edwards, Hardie Albright, Ludwig Stossel

MARRY THE GIRL (1928, Silent, Sterling)
Elinor—Barbara Bedford
Director—Philip Rosen
Leading Players—Robert Ellis, De Witt Jennings, Freddie Frederick

MARRY THE GIRL (1935, GB, British Lion)
Doris Chattaway—Winifred Shotter
Director—P. Maclean Rogers
Leading Players—Sonnie Hale, Hugh Wakefield, Judy Kelly

MARRY THE GIRL (1937, Warner Brothers)
Virginia Radway—Carol Hughes
Director—William McGann
Leading Players—Mary Boland, Frank McHugh, Hugh Herbert, Allen Jenkins, Mischa Auer

THE MARRYING KIND (1952, Columbia)
Florence Keefer—Judy Holliday
Chet Keefer—Aldo Ray

Director—George Cukor
Leading Players—Madge Kennedy, Sheila Bond, John Alexander

THE MARRYING MAN (1991, Buena Vista)
Charley Pearl—Alec Baldwin
Director—James Rees
Leading Players—Kim Basinger, Robert Loggia, Elizabeth Shire, Armand Assante, Paul Reiser

THE MARSHAL OF MESA CITY (1939, RKO)
Mason—George O'Brien
Director—David Howard
Leading Players—Virginia Vale, Henry Brandon, Lloyd Ingraham

THE MARSHAL'S DAUGHTER (1953, UA)
Laurie Dawson—Laurie Anders
Ben Dawson—Hoot Gibson
Director—William Berke
Leading Players—Ken Murray, Harry Lauter, Bob Bray

MARTHA'S VINDICATION (1916, Silent, Triangle)
Martha—Norma Talmadge
Directors—Sidney and Chester Franklin
Leading Players—Seena Owen, Ralph Lewis, Tully Marshall

MARTIN (1979, Libra)
Martin—John Amplas
Director—George A. Romero
Leading Players—Lincoln Maazel, Christine Forrest, Elayne Nadeau

MARTIN LUTHER (1953, De Rochemont)
Martin Luther—Niall MacGinnis
Director—Irving Pichel
Leading Players—John Ruddock, Pierre Lefevre, Guy Verney

MARTIN'S DAY (1985, MGM/UA)
Martin Steckert—Richard Harris
Director—Alan Gibson
Leading Players—Lindsay Wagner, James Coburn, Justin Henry Karen Black, John Ireland

MARTY (1955, UA)
Marty Pilletti—Ernest Borgnine
Director—Delbert Mann
Leading Players—Betsy Blair, Esther Minciotti, Karen Steele, Joe Mantell

MARVIN AND TIGE (1983, Major)
Marvin Stewart—John Cassavetes
Tige Jackson—Gibran Brown
Director—Erick Weston
Leading Players—Billy Dee Wiliams, Denise Nicholas-Hill, Fay Hauser

MARY BURNS, FUGITIVE (1935, Paramount)
Mary Burns—Sylvia Sidney
Director—William K. Howard
Leading Players—Melvyn Douglas, Alan Baxter, Pert Kelton, Wallace Ford

MARY HAD A LITTLE (1961, GB, UA)
Mary Kirk—Agnes Laurent
Director—Edward Buzzell
Leading Players—John Bentley, Jack Watling, Hazel Court

MARY JANE'S PA (1935, First National)
Sam Preston—Guy Kibbee
Mary Jane Preston—Betty Jean Haney
Director—William Keighley
Leading Players—Aline MacMahon, Tom Brown, Robert McWade

MARY LATIMER, NUN (1920, Silent, GB, Famous Pictures)
Mary Latimer—Malvina Longfellow
Director—Bert Haldane
Leading Players—Warwick Ward, Ethel Fisher, George Foley

MARY LOU (1948, Columbia)
Mary Lou—Abigail Adams
Director—Arthur Dreifuss
Leading Players—Joan Barton, Glenda Farrell, Frank Jenks

MARY, MARY (1963, Warner Brothers)
Mary McKellaway—Debbie Reynolds
Director—Mervyn LeRoy
Leading Players—Barry Nelson, Diane McBain, Michael Rennie

MARY, MARY, BLOODY MARY (1975, Translor-Proa)
Mary—Cristina Ferrare
Director—Juan Lopez Moctezuma
Leading Players—David Young, Helena Rojo, John Carradine

MARY OF SCOTLAND (1936, RKO)
Mary Stuart—Katharine Hepburn
Director—John Ford
Leading Players—Fredric March, Florence Eldridge, Douglas Walton, John Carradine

MARY POPPINS (1964, Buena Vista)
Mary Poppins—Julie Andrews
Director—Robert Stevenson
Leading Players—Dick Van Dyke, David Tomlinson, Glynis Johns, Hermione Baddeley

MARY, QUEEN OF SCOTS (1971, GB, Universal)
Mary Stuart—Vanessa Redgrave
Director—Charles Jarrott
Leading Players—Glenda Jackson, Patrick McGoohan, Timothy Dalton, Nigel Davenport, Trevor Howard

MARY RYAN, DETECTIVE (1949, Columbia)
Mary Ryan—Marsha Hunt
Director—Abby Berlin
Leading Players—John Litel, June Vincent, Harry Shannon

MARY STEVENS, M.D. (1933, Warner Brothers)
Dr. Mary Stevens—Kay Francis
Director—Lloyd Bacon
Leading Players—Lyle Talbot, Glenda Farrell, Thelma Todd

MASK (1985, Universal)
Rocky Dennis—Eric Stoltz
Director—Peter Bogandovich
Leading Players—Cher, Sam Elliott, Estelle Getty

THE MASK OF DILJON (1946, Producers Releasing Corp.)
Diljon—Erich von Stroheim
Director—Lew Landers
Leading Players—Jeanne Bates, William Wright, Edward Van Sloan

THE MASK OF DIMITRIOS (1944, Warner Brothers)
Dimitrios—Zachary Scott
Director—Jean Negulesco
Leading Players—Sydney Greenstreet, Faye Emerson, Peter Lorre, George Tobias

THE MASK OF FU MANCHU (1932, MGM)
Dr. Fu Manchu—Boris Karloff
Directors—Charles Brabin & King Vidor
Leading Players—Lewis Stone, Karen Morley, Charles Starrett, Myrna Loy, Jean Hersholt

MASK OF THE AVENGER (1951, Columbia)
Capt. Renato Dimorna—John Derek
Director—Phil Karlson
Leading Players—Anthony Quinn, Jody Lawrance, Arnold Moss

MASKED ANGEL (1928, GB, Silent, Chadwick)
Betty Carlisle—Betty Compson
Director—Frank O'Connor
Leading Players—Erick Arnold, Wheeler Oakman, Jocelyn Lee

THE MASKED AVENGER (1922, Silent, Doubleday)
Austin Patterson—Lester Cuneo
Director—Frank Fanning
Leading Players—Mrs. Wallace Reid, Billy Reid, Claude Payton

THE MASQUERADER (1933, UA)
John Loder—Ronald Colman
Director—Richard Wallace
Leading Players—Elissa Landi, Juliette Compton, Halliwell Hobbes, David Torrence

THE MASTER CRACKSMAN (1914, Silent, Progressive Motion Picture)
Gentleman Joe—Harry Carey
Director—Harry Carey
Leading Players—E.A. Lock, Rexford Burnett, Fern Foster

THE MASTER GUN FIGHTER (1975, Taylor-Laughlin)
Finley—Tom Laughlin
Director—Tom Laughlin
Leading Players—Ron O'Neal, Lincoln Kilpatrick, GeoAnn Sosa, Barbara Carrera

THE MASTER MIND (1920, Silent, First National)
Henry Allen—Lionel Barrymore
Director—Kenneth Webb
Leading Players—Gypsy O'Brien, Ralph Kellard, Bradley Barker

THE MASTER OF BALLANTRAE (1953, Warner Brothers)
James Durrisdeer—Errol Flynn
Director—William Keighley
Leading Players—Roger Livesey, Anthony Steel, Beatrice Campbell

THE MASTER OF BANKDAM (1947, GB, GFD)
Simeon Crowther, Sr.—Tom Walls
Director—Walter Forde
Leading Players—Anne Crawford, Dennis Price, Stephen Murray, Linden Travers, Jimmy Hanley

MASTER OF DRAGONARD HILL (1990, Cannon)
Richard Abdee—Patrick Warburton
Director—Gerard Kikoine

Leading Players—Oliver Reed, Eartha Kitt, Herbert Lom, Kimberly Sissons, Claudia Udy

MASTER OF MEN (1933, Columbia)
Buck Garrett—Jack Holt
Director—Lambert Hillyer
Leading Players—Fay Wray, Theodore von Eltz, Walter Connolly

MASTER OF THE WORLD (1961, American International)
Robur—Vincent Price
Director—William Witney
Leading Players—Charles Bronson, Henry Hull, Mary Webster

MASTER SPY (1964, GB, Allied Artists)
Boris Turganev—Stephen Murray
Director—Montgomery Tully
Leading Players—June Thorburn, Alan Wheatley, John Carson

MASTERMIND (1977, Goldstone)
Inspector Hoku—Zero Mostel
Director—Alex March
Leading Players—Bradford Dillman, Gawn Grainger, Keiko Kishi

MASTERS OF MENACE (1990, New Line/Cinetel)
Buddy—David Rasche
Director—Daniel Raskov
Leading Players—Catherine Bach, Lance Kinsey, Teri Copley, Ray Baker, Malcolm Smith

MASTERSON OF KANSAS (1954, Columbia)
Bat Masterson—George Montgomery
Director—William Castle
Leading Players—Nancy Gates, James Griffith, Jean Willes

MATA HARI (1931, MGM)
Mata Hari—Greta Garbo
Director—George Fitzmaurice
Leading Players—Ramon Novarro, Lionel Barrymore, Lewis Stone, C. Henry Gordon

MATA HARI (1985, Cannon)
Mata Hari—Sylvia Kristel
Director—Curtis Harrington
Leading Players—Christopher Cazenove, Oliver Tobias, Gottried John

THE MATCH KING (1932, First National)
Paul Kroll—Warren William
Director—Howard Bretherton
Leading Players—Lili Damita, Glenda Farrell, Harold Huber

THE MATCHMAKER (1958, Paramount)
Dolly Levi—Shirley Booth
Director—Joseph Anthony
Leading Players—Anthony Perkins, Shirley MacLaine, Paul Ford, Robert Morse

THE MATING OF MARCUS (1924, Silent, Stoll)
Marcus Netherby—David Hawthorne
Director—W.P. Kellino
Leading Players—Vivi Chester, Naomi Chester, George Bellamy

THE MATING OF MILLIE (1948, Columbia)
Millie McGonigle—Evelyn Keyes
Director—Henry Levin
Leading Players—Glenn Ford, Ron Randell, Willard Parker

THE MATRIMANIAC (1916, Silent, Triangle)
Jimmy Conroy—Douglas Fairbanks
Director—Paul Powell
Leading Players—Constance Talmadge, Wilbur Higby, Clyde Hopkins

MAURICE (1987, GB, Cinecom)
Maurice Hall—James Wilby
Director—James Ivory
Leading Players—Hugh Grant, Rupert Graves, Denholm Elliott

MAURIE (1973, National General)
Maurice Stokes—Bernie Casey
Director—Daniel Mann
Leading Players—Bo Swenson, Janet MacLachlan, Stephanie Edwards

THE MAVERICK QUEEN (1956, Republic)
Kit Banion—Barbara Stanwyck
Director—Joe Kane
Leading Players—Barry Sullivan, Scott Brady, Mary Murphy

MAX DUGAN RETURNS (1983, 20th Century Fox)
Max Dugan—Jason Robards, Jr.
Director—Herbert Ross
Leading Players—Marsha Mason, Donald Sutherland, Matthew Broderick

MAXIE (1985, Orion)
Maxie—Glenn Close
Director—Paul Aaron
Leading Players—Mandy Patinkin, Ruth Gordon, Barnard Hughes, Valerie Curtin

MAXWELL ARCHER, MASTER DETECTIVE (1942, GB, Monogram)
Maxwell Archer—John Loder
Director—John Paddy Carstairs
Leading Players—Leueen MacGrath, Athole Stewart, Marta Labarr

MAYFAIR GIRL (1934, GB, Warner Brothers)
Brenda Maon—Sally Blane
Director—George King
Leading Players—John Stuart, D.A. Clarke-Smith, Glen Alyn

THE MAYOR OF 44TH STREET (1942, RKO)
Joe Jonathan—George Murphy
Director—Alfred E. Green
Leading Players—Anne Shirley, William Gargan, Richard Barthelmess

THE MAYOR OF HELL (1933, Warner Brothers)
Patsy Gargan—James Cagney
Director—Archie Mayo
Leading Players—Madge Evans, Allen Jenkins, Dudley Digges, Frankie Darro

THE MAYOR'S NEST (1932, GB, British & Dominions)
Joe Pilgrim—Sydney Howard
Director—Maclean Rogers
Leading Players—Claude Hulbert, Al Bowlly, Muriel Aked

MCBAIN (1991, Shapiro Glickenhaus Entertainment)
McBain—Christopher Walken
Director—James Glickenhaus

Leading Players—Maria Conchita Alonso, Michael Ironside, Steve James, Jay Patterson, Chuck Vennera

MCCABE AND MRS. MILLER (1971, Warner Brothers)
John McCabe—Warren Beatty
Constance Miller—Julie Christie
Director—Robert Altman
Leading Players—Rene Auberjonois, John Schuck, Bert Remsen

THE MCCONNELL STORY (1955, Warner Brothers)
Joseph C. "Mac" McConnell, Jr.—Alan Ladd
Director—Gordon Douglas
Leading Players—June Allyson, James Whitmore, Frank Faylen

MCFADDEN'S FLATS (1935, Paramount)
Dan McFadden—Walter C. Kelly
Director—Ralph Murphy
Leading Players—Andy Clyde, Richard Cromwell, Jane Darwell

MCGUIRE, GO HOME! (1966, GB, Rank)
Major McGuire—Dirk Bogarde
Director—Ralph Thomas
Leading Players—George Chakiris, Susan Strasberg, Denholm Elliott

MCHALE'S NAVY (1964, Universal)
Lt. Cmdr. Quinton McHale—Ernest Borgnine
Director—Edward J. Montagne
Leading Players—Tim Conway, Joe Flynn, Bob Hastings

MCLINTOCK! (1963, UA)
George Washington McLintock—John Wayne
Director—Andrew V. McLaglen
Leading Players—Maureen O'Hara, Stefanie Powers, Yvonne De Carlo, Patrick Wayne

THE MCMASTERS (1970, Chevron)
Neal McMasters—Burl Ives
Director—Alf Kjellin
Leading Players—Brock Peters, David Carradine, Nancy Kwan

MCQ (1974, Warner Brothers)
Detective Lt. Lon McQ—John Wayne
Director—John Sturges
Leading Players—Eddie Albert, Diana Muldaur, Collen Dewhurst, Clu Gulager

MCVICAR (1982, GB, Crown International)
McVicar—Roger Daltrey
Director—Tom Clegg
Leading Players—Adam Faith, Cheryl Campbell, Steven Berkoff

ME AND MARLBOROUGH (1935, GB, Gaumont)
Kit Ross—Cicely Courtneidge
Duke of Marlborough—Tom Walls
Director—Victor Saville
Leading Players—Barry Mackay, Alfred Drayton, Iris Ashley

ME AND MY GAL (1932, Fox Film Corp.)
Dan Dolan—Spencer Tracy
Helen Riley—Joan Bennett
Director—Raoul Walsh
Leading Players—Marion Burns, George Walsh, J. Farrell MacDonald

ME AND MY PAL (1939, GB, Pathe)
Dave Craig—Dave Willis
Hal Thomson—George Moon
Director—Thomas Bentley
Leading Players—Pat Kirkwood, A. Giovanni, John Warwick

ME AND THE COLONEL (1958, Columbia)
S.I. Jacobowsky—Danny Kaye
Col. Prokoszny—Curt Jurgens
Director—Peter Glenville
Leading Players—Nicole Maurey, Francoise Rosay, Akim Tamiroff

ME, NATALIE (1969, National General)
Natalie Miller—Patty Duke
Director—Fred Coe
Leading Players—James Farentino, Martin Balsam, Elsa Lanchester, Salome Jens

MEAN JOHNNY BARROWS (1976, Atlas)
Johnny Barrows—Fred Williamson
Director—Fred Williamson
Leading Players—Roddy McDowall, Stuart Whitman, Luther Adler

THE MEANEST MAN IN THE WORLD (1943, 20th Century Fox)
Richard Clark—Jack Benny
Director—Sidney Lanfield
Leading Players—Priscilla Lane, Eddie "Rochester" Anderson, Edmund Gwenn

THE MECHANIC (1972, UA)
Arthur Bishop—Charles Bronson
Director—Michael Winner
Leading Players—Jan-Michael Vincent, Keenan Wynn, Jill Ireland

THE MEDDLER (1925, Silent, Universal)
Richard Gilmore—William Desmond
Director—Arthur Rosson
Leading Players—Dolores Rousse, Claire Anderson, Albert J. Smith

THE MEDIATOR (1916, Silent, Fox Film Corp.)
Lish Henley—George Walsh
Director—Otis Turner
Leading Players—Juanita Hansen, James Marcus, Lee Willard

MEDICINE MAN (1992, Hollywood Pictures)
Dr. Robert Campbell—Sean Connery
Director—John McTiernan
Leading Players—Lorraine Bracco, Jose Wilkes, Rodolfo De Alexandre

THE MEDICINE MAN (1930, Tiffany)
Dr. John Harvey—Jack Benny
Director—Scott Pembroke
Leading Players—Betty Bronson, Eva Novak, E. Alyn Warren

THE MEDICINE MAN (1933, GB, Real Art)
Hon. Freddie Wiltshire—Claude Allister
Director—Redd Davis
Leading Players—Frank Pettingell, Pat Paterson, Ben Welden

THE MEDICO OF PAINTED SPRINGS (1941, Columbia)
Dr. Steven Monroe—Charles Starrett

Director—Lambert Hillyer
Leading Players—Terry Walker, Ben Taggart, Ray Bennett

THE MEDIUM (1951, Transfilm)
Mme. Flora—Marie Powers
Director—Gian-Carlo Menotti
Leading Players—Anna Maria Alberghetti, Leo Coleman, Belva Kibler

MEET BOSTON BLACKIE (1941, Columbia)
Boston Blackie—Chester Morris
Director—Robert Florey
Leading Players—Rochelle Hudson, Richard Lane, Charles Wagenheim

MEET DANNY WILSON (1952, Universal)
Danny Wilson—Frank Sinatra
Director—Joseph Pevney
Leading Players—Shelley Winters, Alex Nicol, Raymond Burr

MEET DR. CHRISTIAN (1939, RKO)
Dr. Paul Christian—Jean Hersholt
Director—Bernard Vorhaus
Leading Players—Dorothy Lovett, Robert Baldwin, Enid Bennett

MEET JOHN DOE (1941, Warner Brothers)
Long John Willoughby—Gary Cooper
Director—Frank Capra
Leading Players—Barbara Stanwyck, Edward Arnold, Walter Brennan, James Gleason

MEET MR. CALLAGHAN (1954, GB, Pinnacle)
Slim Callaghan—Derrick de Marney
Director—Charles Saunders
Leading Players—Harriette Johns, Peter Neil, Adrienne Corri

MEET MR. LUCIFER (1953, GB, Ealing)
Sam Hollingsworth/Mr. Lucifer—Stanley Holloway
Director—Anthony Pelissier
Leading Players—Peggy Cummins, Jack Watling, Barbara Murray

MEET MR. PENNY (1938, GB, British National)
Henry Penny—Richard Golden
Director—David Macdonald
Leading Players—Vic Oliver, Fabia Drake, Kay Walsh

MEET NERO WOLFE (1936, Columbia)
Nero Wolfe—Edward Arnold
Director—Herbert Biberman
Leading Players—Joan Perry, Lionel Stander, Victor Jory

MEET SEXTON BLAKE (1944, GB, British National)
Sexton Blake—David Farrar
Director—John Harlow
Leading Players—John Varley, Magda Kun, Gordon McLeod

MEET SIMON CHERRY (1949, GB, Hammer)
Rev. Simon Cherry—Hugh Moxey
Director—Godfrey Grayson
Leading Players—Zena Marshall, John Bailey, Anthony Forwood

MEET THE BARON (1933, MGM)
The Baron—Jack Pearl
Director—Walter Lang
Leading Players—Jimmy Durante, Zasu Pitts, Ted Healy

MEET THE BOY FRIEND (1937, Republic)
Tony Page—David Carlyle (Robert Paige)
Director—Ralph Staub
Leading Players—Carol Hughes, Warren Hymer, Pert Kelton

MEET THE CHUMP (1941, Universal)
Hugh Mansfield—Hugh Herbert
Director—Edward F. Cline
Leading Players—Lewis Howard, Jeanne Kelly, Anne Nagel

MEET THE DUKE (1949, GB, Associated British Films)
Duke Hogan—Farnham Baxter
Director—James Corbett
Leading Players—Heather Chasen, Gale Douglas

MEET THE GIRLS (1938, 20th Century Fox)
Judy Davis—June Lang
Terry Wilson—Lynn Bari
Director—Eugene Forde
Leading Players—Robert Allen, Ruth Donnelly, Gene Lockhart

MEET THE HOLLOWHEADS (1989, Moviestore)
Henry Hollowhead—John Glover
Miriam Hollowhead—Nancy Mette
Billy Hollowhead—Matt Shakman
Cindy Hollowhead—Juliette Lewis
Bud Hollowhead—Lightfield Lewis
Director—Tom Burman
Leading Players—Richard Portnow, Joshua Miller, Logan Ramsey

MEET THE MAYOR (1938, Times)
Spencer Brown—Frank Fay
Director—Ralph Cedar
Leading Players—Ruth Hall, Hale Hamilton, George Meeker

MEET THE MISSUS (1937, RKO)
Emma Foster—Helen Broderick
Director—Joseph Santley
Leading Players—Victor Moore, Anne Shirley, Alan Bruce

MEET THE STEWARTS (1942, Columbia)
Michael Stewart—William Holden
Candace Goodwin Stewart—Frances Dee
Director—Alfred E. Green
Leading Players—Grant Mitchell, Marjorie Gateson, Anne Revere

MEET THE WIFE (1931, Columbia)
Gertrude Lennox—Laura LaPlante
Director—A. Leslie Pearce
Leading Players—Lew Cody, Joan Marsh, Harry Myers

MEG (1926, GB, Silent, Wardour)
Meg—Mabel Armstrong
Director—Walter Shaw
Leading Players—Noel Greenwood, Ruth Kalinsky

MELANIE (1982, Canada, Embassy Pictures)
Melanie Daniel—Glynnis O'Connor
Director—Rex Bromfield
Leading Players—Burton Cummings, Paul Sorvino, Don Johnson

MELBA (1953, GB, UA)
Nellie Melba—Patrice Munsel
Director—Lewis Milestone

Leading Players—Robert Morley, John McCallum, John Justin

MELINDA (1972, MGM)
Melinda—Vonetta McGee
Director—Hugh A. Robertson
Leading Players—Calvin Lockhart, Rosalind Cash, Paul Stevens

MELODY FOR THREE (1941, RKO)
Mary Stanley—Fay Wray
Antoine Pirelle—Walter Woolf King
Billy Stanley—Schuyler Standish
Director—Erle C. Kenton
Leading Players—Jean Hersholt, Patsy Lee Parsons, Maude Eburne

MELODY FOR TWO (1937, Warner Brothers)
Tod Weaver—James Melton
Gale Starr—Patricia Ellis
Director—Louis King
Leading Players—Marie Wilson, Fred Keating, Winifred Shaw

THE MELODY MAKER (1933, GB, Warner Brothers)
Tony Borrodaile—Lester Matthews
Director—Leslie Hiscott
Leading Players—Joan Marion, Evelyn Roberts, Wallace Lupino

MELODY MAN (1930, Columbia)
Earl Von Kemper—John St. Polis
Director—R. William Neill
Leading Players—William Collier, Jr., Alice Day, Johnny Walker

MELVIN AND HOWARD (1980, Universal)
Howard Hughes—Jason Robards, Jr.
Melvin Dummar—Paul LeMat
Director—Jonathan Demme
Leading Players—Elizabeth Cheshire, Mary Steenburgen, Chip Taylor

MELVIN, SON OF ALVIN (1984, Australia, Roadshow)
Melvin Simpson—Gerry Sont
Alvin Purple—Graeme Blundell
Director—John Eastway
Leading Players—Lenita Psillakis, Jon Finlyson, Tina Bursill

MEMBER OF THE JURY (1937, GB, 20th Century Fox)
Walter Maitland—Ellis Irving
Director—Bernard Mainwaring
Leading Players—Marjorie Hume, Franklyn Bellamy, Arnold Lucy

THE MEMBER OF THE WEDDING (1952, Columbia)
Frankie Addams—Julie Harris
Director—Fred Zinnemann
Leading Players—Ethel Waters, Brandon De Wilde, Arthur Franz

MEMOIRS OF A SURVIVOR (1981, GB, EMI)
"D"—Julie Christie
Director—David Gladwell
Leading Players—Christopher Guard, Leonie Mellinger, Debbie Hutchings

MEMOIRS OF AN INVISIBLE MAN (1992, Warner Brothers)
Nick Halloway—Chevy Chase
Director—John Carpenter

Leading Players—Daryl Hannah, Sam Neill, Michael McKean, Stephen Tobolowsky, Jim Norton

MEMORIES OF ME (1988, MGM/UA)
Abe Polin—Alan King
Director—Henry Winkler
Leading Players—Billy Crystal, Jo Beth Williams, Janet Carroll

THE MEN (1950, UA)
Ken Wilozek—Marlon Brando
Director—Fred Zinnemann
Leading Players—Teresa Wright, Everett Sloane, Jack Webb

MEN AGAINST THE SKY (1940, RKO)
Phil Mercedes—Richard Dix
Director—Leslie Goodwins
Leading Players—Kent Taylor, Edmund Lowe, Wendy Barrie

MEN ARE LIKE THAT (1930, Paramount)
Aubrey Piper—Hal Skelly
Director—Frank Tuttle
Leading Players—Doris Hill, Charles Sellon, Clara Blandick

MEN ARE LIKE THAT (1931, Columbia)
Lt. Bob Benton—John Wayne
Director—George B. Seitz
Leading Players—Laura La Plante, June Clyde, Forrest Stanley

MEN ARE SUCH FOOLS (1933, RKO)
Tony Mello—Leo Carrillo
Director—William Nigh
Leading Players—Vivienne Osborne, Una Merkel, Joseph Cawthorn

MEN AT WORK (1990, Triumph/Epic)
Carl Taylor—Charlie Sheen
James St. James—Emilio Estevez
Director—Emilio Estevez
Leading Players—Leslie Hope, Keith David, Dean Cameron, John Getz, Hawk Wolinski, John Lavachielli

MEN DON'T LEAVE (1990, Warner Brothers/Brinkman-Avnet)
Chris Macauley—Chris O'Donnell
Matt Macauley—Charlie Korsmo
Director—Paul Brickman
Leading Players—Jessica Lange, Arliss Howard, Joan Cusack, Tom Mason, Kathy Bates

MEN IN WHITE (1934, MGM)
Dr. Ferguson—Clark Gable
Director—Richard Boleslawski
Leading Players—Myrna Loy, Jean Hersholt, Elizabeth Allan

MEN MUST FIGHT (1933, MGM)
Bob Seward—Phillips Holmes
Director—Edgar Selwyn
Leading Players—Diana Wynyard, Lewis Stone, Ruth Selwyn

MEN OF BOYS TOWN (1941, MGM)
Whitey Marsh—Mickey Rooney
Director—Norman Taurog
Leading Players—Spencer Tracy, Bobs Watson, Larry Nunn

MEN OF CHANCE (1932, RKO)
Johnny Silk—Ricardo Cortez
Director—George Archainbaud

Leading Players—Mary Astor, John Halliday, Ralph Ince

MEN OF IRELAND (1938, Ireland, Irish National)
Neal O'Moore—Cecil Ford
Liam—Brian O'Sullivan
Director—Dick Bird
Leading Players—Eileen Curran, Gabriel Fallon, Daisy Murphy

MEN OF RESPECT (1990, Central City/Goldblatt)
Mike Battaglia—John Turturro
Director—William Reilly
Leading Players—Katherine Borowitz, Dennis Farina, Peter Boyle, Rod Steiger, Steven Wright

MEN OF SHERWOOD FOREST (1957, GB, Hammer)
Robin Hood—Don Taylor
Friar Tuck—Reginald Beckwith
Will Scarlett—John Van Eyssen
Little John (Little)—Leslie Linder
Director—Val Guest
Leading Players—Eileen Moore, David King-Wood, Patrick Holt

MEN OF STEEL (1932, GB, UA)
James "Iron" Harg—John Stuart
Director—George King
Leading Players—Benita Hume, Franklyn Dyall, Heather Angel

MEN OF THE FIGHTING LADY (1954, MGM)
Lt. Howard Thayer—Van Johnson
Director—Andrew Marton
Leading Players—Walter Pidgeon, Louis Calhern, Dewey Martin, Keenan Wynn, Frank Lovejoy

MEN OF THE NORTH (1930, MGM)
Louis LeBey—Gilbert Roland
Director—Hal Roach
Leading Players—Barbara Leonard, Arnold Korff, Robert Elliott

MEN OF THE SEA (1951, GB, Astor)
Jack Easy—Hughie Green
Director—Carol Reed
Leading Players—Margaret Lockwood, Harry Tate, W. Robert Adams

MEN WITH WINGS (1938, Paramount)
Pat Falconer—Fred MacMurray
Scott Barnes—Ray Milland
Director—William A. Wellman
Leading Players—Louise Campbell, Andy Devine, Lynne Overman, Walter Abel

MEN'S CLUB (1986, Paramount)
Philip—David Dukes
Kramer—Richard Jordan
Solly Berliner—Harvey Keitel
Harold Canterbury—Frank Langella
Cavanaugh—Roy Scheider
Paul—Craig Wasson
Terry—Treat Williams
Director—Peter Medak
Leading Players—Stockard Channing, Gina Gallegos, Cindy Pickett, Gwen Welles, Penny Baker, Rebecca Bush, Claudia Cron, Jennifer Jason Leigh, Marilyn Jones, Ann Wedgewood

THE MERCHANT OF VENICE (1916, GB, Silent, Broadwest)
Antonio—George Skillan

Director—Walter West
Leading Players—Matheson Lang, Nellie Hutin Britton, J.R. Tozer

MERELY MARY ANN (1931, Fox Film Corp.)
Mary Ann—Janet Gaynor
Director—Henry King
Leading Players—Charles Farrell, Beryl Mercer, J.M. Kerrigan

MERELY MR. HAWKINS (1938, GB, RKO)
Alfred Hawkins—Eliot Makeham
Director—Maclean Rogers
Leading Players—Sybil Grove, Dinah Sheridan, George Pembroke

THE MERMAIDS OF TIBURON (1962, Aquarex-Pacifica)
Mermaid Queen—Diane Webber
Director—John Lamb
Leading Players—George Rowe, Timothy Carey, Jose Gonzalez-Gonzalez

MERRILL'S MARAUDERS (1962, Warner Brothers)
Brig. Gen. Merrill—Jeff Chandler
Director—Samuel Fuller
Leading Players—Ty Hardin, Peter Brown, Andrew Duggan

MERRY ANDREW (1958, MGM)
Andrew Larabee—Danny Kaye
Director—Michael Kidd
Leading Players—Pier Angeli, Baccaloni, Noel Purcell

MERRY CHRISTMAS MR. LAWRENCE (1983, GB, Universal)
Col. John Lawrence—Tom Conti
Director—Nagisa Oshima
Leading Players—David Bowie, Ryuichi Sakamoto, Jack Thompson

THE MERRY MONAHANS (1944, Universal)
Jimmy Monahan—Donald O'Connor
Patsy Monahan—Peggy Ryan
Pete Monahan—Jack Oakie
Director—Charles Lamont
Leading Players—Ann Blyth, Rosemary De Camp, John Miljan

THE MERRY WIDOW (1925, Silent, MGM)
Sally O'Hara—Mae Marsh
Director—Erich von Stroheim
Leading Players—John Gilbert, Roy D'Arcy, Tully Marshall, Josephine Crowell

THE MERRY WIDOW (1934, MGM)
Sonia—Jeanette MacDonald
Director—Ernst Lubitsch
Leading Players—Maurice Chevalier, Edward Everett Horton, Una Merkel, George Barbier

THE MERRY WIDOW (1952, MGM)
Crystal Radek—Lana Turner
Director—Curtis Bernhardt
Leading Players—Fernando Lamas, Una Merkel, Richard Haydn, Thomas Gomez

MERTON OF THE MOVIES (1924, Silent, Paramount)
Merton Gill—Glenn Hunter
Director—James Cruze
Leading Players—Viola Dana, Charles Sellon, Sadie Gordon

MERTON OF THE MOVIES (1947, MGM)
Merton Gill—Red Skelton
Director—Robert Alton
Leading Players—Virginia O'Brien, Gloria Grahame, Leon Ames

A MESSAGE TO GARCIA (1936, 20th Century Fox)
General Garcia—Enrique Acosta
Director—George Marshall
Leading Players—Wallace Beery, John Boles, Barbara Stanwyck

MESSENGER OF PEACE (1950, Astor)
Pastor Armin Ritter—John Beal
Director—Frank Strayer
Leading Players—Peggy Stewart, William Bakewell, Paul Guilfoyle

METALSTORM: THE DESTRUCTION OF JARED-SYN (1983, Universal)
Jared-Syn—Mike Preston
Director—Charles Band
Leading Players—Jeffrey Bryon, Tim Thomerson, Kelly Preston

MEXICALI ROSE (1929, Columbia)
Mexicali Rose—Barbara Stanwyck
Director—Erle C. Kenton
Leading Players—Sam Hardy, William Janney, Louis Natheaux

MEXICAN SPITFIRE (1939, RKO)
Carmelita Lindsay—Lupe Velez
Director—Leslie Goodwins
Leading Players—Leon Errol, Donald Woods, Linda Hayes

MEXICAN SPITFIRE AT SEA (1942, RKO)
Carmelita Lindsay—Lupe Velez
Director—Leslie Goodwins
Leading Players—Leon Errol, Charles "Buddy" Rogers, Zasu Pitts

MEXICAN SPITFIRE OUT WEST (1940, RKO)
Carmelita Lindsay—Lupe Velez
Director—Leslie Goodwins
Leading Players—Leon Errol, Donald Woods, Elizabeth Risdon

MEXICAN SPITFIRE SEES A GHOST (1942, RKO)
Carmelita Lindsay—Lupe Velez
Director—Leslie Goodwins
Leading Players—Leon Errol, Charles "Buddy" Rogers, Donald McBride

MEXICAN SPITFIRE'S BABY (1941, RKO)
Carmelita Lindsay—Lupe Velez
Director—Leslie Goodwins
Leading Players—Leon Errol, Charles "Buddy" Rogers, Elizabeth Risdon

MEXICAN SPITFIRE'S BLESSED EVENT (1943, RKO)
Carmelita Lindsay—Lupe Velez
Director—Leslie Goodwins
Leading Players—Leon Errol, Walter Reed, Elizabeth Risdon

MEXICAN SPITFIRE'S ELEPHANT (1942, RKO)
Carmelita Lindsay—Lupe Velez
Director—Leslie Goodwins
Leading Players—Leon Errol, Walter Reed, Lydia Bilbrook

MICHAEL AND MARY (1932, GB, Gainsborough)
Michael Rowe—Herbert Marshall
Mary Rowe—Edna Best
Director—Victor Saville
Leading Players—Frank Lawton, Elizabeth Allan, D.A. Clarke-Smith

MICHAEL O'HALLORAN (1937, Republic)
Michael O'Halloran—Jackie Moran
Director—Karl Brown
Leading Players—Wynne Gibson, Warren Hull, Charlene Wyatt

MICHAEL O'HALLORAN (1948, Monogram)
Michael O'Halloran—Scotty Beckett
Director—John Rawlins
Leading Players—Allene Roberts, Tommy Cook, Isabel Jewell

MICHAEL SHAYNE, PRIVATE DETECTIVE (1940, 20th Century Fox)
Michael Shayne—Lloyd Nolan
Director—Eugene Forde
Leading Players—Marjorie Weaver, Joan Valerie, Walter Abel

THE MICHIGAN KID (1928, Silent, Universal)
Jimmy Cowan—Conrad Nagel
Director—Irvin Willat
Leading Players—Renee Adoree, Fred Esmelton, Virginia Grey

THE MICHIGAN KID (1947, Universal)
Michigan Kid—Jon Hall
Director—Ray Taylor
Leading Players—Victor McLaglen, Rita Johnson, Andy Devine

MICKEY (1919, Silent, Sennett)
Mickey—Mabel Normand
Director—F. Richard Jones
Leading Players—Lew Cody, Minta Durfee, Wheeler Oakman

MICKEY (1948, Eagle Lion)
Mickey—Lois Butler
Director—Ralph Murphy
Leading Players—Bill Goodwin, Irene Hervey, John Sutton

MICKEY ONE (1965, Columbia)
Mickey One—Warren Beatty
Director—Arthur Penn
Leading Players—Alexandra Stewart, Hurd Hatfield, Franchot Tone

MICKEY, THE KID (1939, Republic)
Mickey—Tommy Ryan
Director—Arthur Lubin
Leading Players—Bruce Cabot, Ralph Byrd, Zasu Pitts

MICKI AND MAUDE (1984, Columbia)
Micki Salinger—Ann Reinking
Maude Salinger—Amy Irving
Director—Blake Edwards
Leading Players—Dudley Moore, Richard Mulligan, George Gaynes, Wallace Shawn

MIDNIGHT ANGEL (1941, Paramount)
Mary—Martha O'Driscoll
Director—Ralph Murphy
Leading Players—Robert Preston, Phillip Merivale, Eva Gabor

MIDNIGHT COWBOY (1969, UA)
Joe Buck—Jon Voight
Director—John Schlesinger
Leading Players—Dustin Hoffman, Sylvia Miles, John McGiver,
Brenda Vaccaro

MIDNIGHT LADY (1932, Chesterfield)
Nita St. George—Sarah Padden
Director—Richard Thorpe
Leading Players—John Darrow, Claudia Dell, Theodore Von Eltz

MIDNIGHT MADONNA (1937, Paramount)
Kay Barrie—Mady Correll
Director—James Flood
Leading PLayers—Warren William, Kitty Clancy, Edward Ellis

THE MIDNIGHT MAN (1974, Universal)
Jim Slade—Burt Lancaster
Directors—Roland Kibbee and Burt Lancaster
Leading Players—Susan Clark, Cameron Mitchell, Morgan
Woodward

MIDNIGHT MARY (1933, MGM)
Mary Martin—Loretta Young
Director—William A. Wellman
Leading Players—Ricardo Cortez, Franchot Tone, Andy Devine

THE MIDSHIPMAID (1932, GB, Gaumont)
Celia Newbiggin—Jessie Matthews
Director—Albert de Courville
Leading Players—Fred Kerr, Basil Sydney, A.W. Baskcomb

MIDSHIPMAN JACK (1933, RKO)
Jack Austin—Bruce Cabot
Director—Christy Cabanne
Leading Players—Betty Furness, Frank Albertson, Arthur Lake

THE MIGHTY (1929, Paramount)
Blake Greeson—George Bancroft
Director—John Cromwell
Leading Players—Esther Ralston, Warner Oland, Raymond
Hatton

THE MIGHTY BARNUM (1934, UA)
Phineas T. Barnum—Wallace Beery
Director—Walter Lang
Leading Players—Adolphe Menjou, Virginia Bruce, Rochelle
Hudson

THE MIGHTY MCGURK (1946, MGM)
Roy "Slag" McGurk—Wallace Beery
Director—John Waters
Leading Players—Dean Stockwell, Edward Arnold, Aline
MacMahon, Cameron Mitchell

THE MIGHTY QUINN (1989, MGM-UA)
Xavier Quinn—Denzel Washington
Director—Carl Schenkel
Leading Players—Robert Townsend, James Fox, Mimi Rogers,
M. Emmet Walsh, Sheryl Lee Ralph

THE MIKADO (1939, GB, Universal)
The Mikado—John Barclay
Director—Victor Schertzinger
Leading Players—Kenny Baker, Martyn Green, Sydney Granville

THE MIKADO (1967, GB, Warner Brothers)
The Mikado—Donald Adams
Director—Stuart Burge
Leading Players—Philip Potter, John Reed, Kenneth Sandford

MIKE (1926, Silent, MGM)
Mike—Sally O'Neil
Director—Marshall Neilan
Leading Players—William Haines, Charlie Murray, Ned Sparks

MIKE'S MURDER (1984, Warner Brothers)
Mike—Mark Keyloun
Director—James Bridges
Leading Players—Debra Winger, Paul Winfield, Darrell Larson

MIKEY AND NICKY (1976, Paramount)
Mikey—Peter Falk
Nicky—John Cassavetes
Director—Elaine May
Leading Players—Ned Beatty, Rose Arrick, Carol Grace

MILDRED PIERCE (1945, Warner Brothers)
Mildred Pierce—Joan Crawford
Director—Michael Curtiz
Leading Players—Jack Carson, Zachary Scott, Eve Arden, Ann
Blyth, Bruce Bennett

THE MILKMAN (1950, Universal)
Roger Bradley—Donald O'Connor
Director—Charles T. Barton
Leading Players—Jimmy Durante, Joyce Holden, William
Conrad

MILLIE (1931, RKO)
Millie—Helen Twelvetrees
Director—John Francis Dillon
Leading Players—Robert Ames, Lilyan Tashman, Joan Blondell

MILLION DOLLAR BABY (1935, Monogram)
Pat Sweeney—Jimmy Fay
Director—Joseph Santley
Leading Players—Arline Judge, Ray Walker, George E. Stone

MILLION DOLLAR BABY (1941, Warner Brothers)
Pamela McAllister—Priscilla Lane
Director—Curtis Bernhardt
Leading Players—Jeffrey Lynn, Ronald Reagan, May Robson

MILLION DOLLAR KID (1944, Monogram)
Roy Cortland—Johnny Duncan
Director—Wallace Fox
Leading Players—Leo Gorcey, Huntz Hall, Gabriel Dell, Billy
Benedict

MILLION DOLLAR MERMAID (1952, MGM)
Annette Kellerman—Esther Williams
Director—Mervyn LeRoy
Leading Players—Victor Mature, Walter Pidgeon, David Brian

THE MILLION EYES OF SU-MURU (1967, GB, Am.
International)
Su-Muru—Shirley Eaton
Director—Lindsay Shonteff
Leading Players—Frankie Avalon, George Nader, Wilfrid Hyde-
White, Klaus Kinski

THE MILLIONAIRE (1921, Silent, Universal)
Jack Norman—Herbert Rawlinson
Director—Jack Conway
Leading Players—Bert Roach, William Courtwright, Verne
Winter

THE MILLIONAIRE (1931, Warner Brothers)
James Alden—George Arliss
Director—John G. Adolfi
Leading Players—Evalyn Knapp, David Manners, James Cagney

A MILLIONAIRE FOR CHRISTY (1951, 20th Century Fox)
Peter Ulysses Lockwood—Fred MacMurray
Christy Sloane—Eleanor Parker
Director—George Marshall
Leading Players—Richard Carlson, Kay Buckley, Una Merkel,
Douglas Dumbrille

MILLIONAIRE PLAYBOY (1940, RKO)
Joe Zany—Joe Penner
Director—Leslie Goodwins
Leading Players—Linda Hayes, Russ Brown, Fritz Feld

MILLIONAIRES IN PRISON (1940, RKO)
James Brent—Morgan Conway
Sidney Keats—Chester Clute
Director—Ray McCarey
Leading Players—Lee Tracy, Linda Hayes, Raymond Walburn

THE MILLIONAIRESS (1960, GB, 20th Century Fox)
Epifania Parerga—Sophia Loren
Director—Anthony Asquith
Leading Players—Peter Sellers, Alastair Sim, Vittorio De Sica,
Dennis Price

MIMI (1935, GB, Alliance)
Mimi—Gertrude Lawrence
Director—Paul L. Stein
Leading Players—Douglas Fairbanks, Jr., Diana Napier, Harold
Warrender

MIN AND BILL (1930, MGM)
Min Divot—Marie Dressler
Bill—Wallace Beery
Director—George Hill
Leading Players—Dorothy Jordan, Marjorie Rambeau, Donald
Dillaway

THE MIND OF MR. SOAMES (1970, GB, Columbia)
John Soames—Terence Stamp
Director—Alan Cooke
Leading Players—Robert Vaughn, Nigel Davenport, Donal
Donnelly

THE MIND READER (1933, First National)
Chandra Chandler—Warren William
Director—Roy Del Ruth
Leading Players—Constance Cummings, Allen Jenkins, Donald
Dillaway

THE MINIVER STORY (1950, GB, MGM)
Kay Miniver—Greer Garson
Clem Miniver—Walter Pidgeon
Director—H.C. Potter
Leading Players—John Hodiak, Leo Genn, Cathy O'Donnell

MINNIE AND MOSKOWITZ (1971, Universal)
Minnie Moore—Gena Rowlands
Seymour Moskowitz—Seymour Cassel
Director—John Cassavetes
Leading Players—Val Avery, Tom Carey, Katherine Cassavetes

THE MINSTREL BOY (1937, GB, Butchers)
Mike—Fred Conyngham
Director—Sydney Morgan
Leading Players—Chili Bouchier, Lucille Lisle, Kenneth Buckley

MINSTREL MAN (1944, Producers Releasing Corp.)
Dixie Boy Johnson—Benny Fields
Director—Joseph H. Lewis
Leading Players—Gladys George, Alan Dinehart, Roscoe Karns

MIRACLE KID (1942, Producers Releasing Corp.)
Jimmy—Tom Neal
Director—William Beaudine
Leading Players—Carol Hughes, Vicki Lester, Betty Blythe

THE MIRACLE MAN (1919, Silent, Paramount)
The Patriarch—Joseph J. Dowling
Director—George Loane Tucker
Leading Players—Thomas Meighan, Betty Compson, Lon Chaney

THE MIRACLE MAN (1932, Paramount)
The Patriarch—Hobart Bosworth
Director—Norman Z. McLeod
Leading Players—Sylvia Sidney, Chester Morris, Robert Coogan,
John Wray, Ned Sparks

THE MIRACLE WOMAN (1931, Columbia)
Florence "Faith" Fallon—Barbara Stanwyck
Director—Frank Capra
Leading Players—David Manners, Sam Hardy, Beryl Mercer

THE MIRACLE WORKER (1962, UA)
Annie Sullivan—Anne Bancroft
Director—Arthur Penn
Leading Players—Patty Duke, Victor Jory, Inga Swenson

MIRIAM ROZELLA (1924, GB, Silent, ASTRA-N)
Miriam Rozella—Moyna McGill
Director—Sidney Morgan
Leading Players—Owen Nares, Gertrude McCoy, Ben Webster

MIRANDA (1949, GB, Ealing)
Miranda—Glynis Johns
Director—Ken Annakin
Leading Players—Googie Withers, Griffith Jones, John
McCallum, Margaret Rutherford

THE MISADVENTURES OF MERLIN JONES (1964, Buena Vista)
Merlin Jones—Tommy Kirk
Director—Robert Stevenson
Leading Players—Annette Funicello, Leon Ames, Stuart Erwin

THE MISFITS (1961, UA)
Gay Langland—Clark Gable
Roslyn Taber—Marilyn Monroe
Perce Howland—Montgomery Clift
Director—John Huston
Leading Players—Thelma Ritter, Eli Wallach, James Barton

THE MISLEADING LADY (1932, Paramount)
Helen Steele—Claudette Colbert
Director—Stuart Walker
Leading Players—Edmund Lowe, Stuart Erwin, Robert Strange

MISS ANNIE ROONEY (1942, UA)
Annie Rooney—Shirley Temple
Director—Edwin L. Marin
Leading Players—William Gargan, Guy Kibbee, Dickie Moore

MISS BLUEBEARD (1925, Silent, Paramount)
Colette Girard—Bebe Daniels
Director—Frank Tuttle
Leading Players—Robert Frazer, Kenneth MacKenna, Raymond Griffith

MISS BREWSTER'S MILLIONS (1926, Silent, Paramount)
Polly Brewster—Bebe Daniels
Director—Clarence Badger
Leading Players—Warner Baxter, Ford Sterling, Andre De Beranger

MISS CRUSOE (1919, Silent, World)
Dorothy Evans—Virginia Hammond
Director—Frank Crane
Leading Players—Rod La Rocque, Nora Cecil, Irving Brooks

MISS DULCIE FROM DIXIE (1919, Silent, Vitagraph)
Dulcie—Gladys Leslie
Director—Joseph Gleason
Leading Players—Charles Kent, Arthur Donaldson, Julia Swayne

MISS FANE'S BABY IS STOLEN (1934, Paramount)
Madeline Fane—Dorothea Wieck
Michael Fane—Baby LeRoy
Director—Alexander Hall
Leading Players—Alice Brady, William Frawley, George Barbier

MISS FIRECRACKER (1989, Corsair)
Carnelle Scott—Holly Hunter
Director—Thomas Schlamme
Leading Players—Mary Steenburgen, Tim Robbins, Alfre Woodard

MISS GRANT TAKES RICHMOND (1949, Columbia)
Ellen Grant—Lucille Ball
Director—Lloyd Bacon
Leading Players—William Holden, Janis Carter, James Gleason

MISS HOBBS (1920, Silent, Realart)
Miss Hobbs—Wanda Hawley
Director—Donald Crisp
Leading Players—Harrison Ford, Helen Jerome Eddy, Walter Hiers

MISS LONDON LTD. (1943, GB, GFD)
Terry Arden—Evelyn Dall
Director—Val Guest
Leading Players—Arthur Askey, Anne Shelton, Richard Hearne

MISS MINK OF 1949 (1949, 20th Century Fox)
Alice Forrester—Lois Collier
Director—Glenn Tryon
Leading Players—Jimmy Lydon, Richard Lane, Barbara Brown

MISS NOBODY (1926, Silent, First National)
Barbara Brown—Anna Q. Nilsson
Director—Lambert Hillyer
Leading Players—Walter Pidgeon, Louise Fazenda, Mitchell Lewis

MISS PACIFIC FLEET (1935, Warner Brothers)
Gloria Fay—Joan Blondell
Director—Ray Enright
Leading Players—Glenda Farrell, Warren Hull, Allen Jenkins

MISS PILGRIM'S PROGRESS (1950, GB, Grand National)
Laramie Pilgrim—Yolande Donlan
Director—Val Guest
Leading Players—Michael Rennie, Garry Marsh, Emrys Jones

MISS PINKERTON (1932, First National)
Miss Pinkerton—Joan Blondell
Director—Lloyd Bacon
Leading Players—George Brent, Mae Madison, John Wray

MISS ROBIN HOOD (1952, GB, Union)
Miss Honey—Margaret Rutherford
Director—John Guillermin
Leading Players—Richard Hearne, Michael Medwin, Peter Jones

MISS SADIE THOMPSON (1953, Columbia)
Sadie Thompson—Rita Hayworth
Director—Curtis Bernhardt
Leading Players—Jose Ferrer, Aldo Ray, Russell Collins

MISS SUSIE SLAGLE'S (1945, Paramount)
Susie Slagle—Lillian Gish
Director—John Berry
Leading Players—Veronica Lake, Sonny Tufts, Joan Caulfield

MISS TATLOCK'S MILLIONS (1948, Paramount)
Nan Tatlock—Wanda Hendrix
Director—Richard Haydn
Leading Players—John Lund, Barry Fitzgerald, Monty Woolley

MISS TULIP STAYS THE NIGHT (1955, GB, Adelphi)
Millicent Tulip—Cicely Courtneidge
Director—Leslie Arliss
Leading Players—Diana Dors, Patrick Holt, Jack Hulbert

MISS V FROM MOSCOW (1942, Producers Releasing Corp.)
Vera Marova—Lola Lane
Director—Albert Herman
Leading Players—Noel Madison, Howard Banks, Paul Weigel

MISSING (1982, Universal)
Charles Horman—John Shea
Director—Costa-Gavras
Leading Players—Jack Lemmon, Sissy Spacek, Melanie Mayron

MISSING, BELIEVED MARRIED (1937, GB, British & Dominions)
Hermione Blakiston—Hazel Terry
Director—John Paddy Carstairs
Leading Players—Wally Patch, Julien Vedey, Emilo Cargher

THE MISSIONARY (1982, Columbia)
Rev. Charles Fortescue—Michael Palin
Director—Richard Loncraine
Leading Players—Maggie Smith, Trevor Howard, Denholm Elliott, Michael Hordern

MISSISSIPPI GAMBLER (1929, Universal)
Jack Morgan—Joseph Schildkraut
Director—Reginald Barker
Leading Players—Joan Bennett, Carmelita Geraghty, Alec B. Francis

MISSISSIPPI GAMBLER (1942, Universal)
Johnny Forbes—Kent Taylor
Director—John Rawlins
Leading Players—Francis Langford, John Litel, Shemp Howard

THE MISSISSIPPI GAMBLER (1953, Universal)
Mark Fallon—Tyrone Power
Director—Rudolph Mate
Leading Players—Piper Laurie, Julia Adams, John McIntire

THE MISSOURI TRAVELLER (1958, Buena Vista)
Brian Turner—Brandon De Wilde
Director—Jerry Hopper
Leading Players—Lee Marvin, Gary Merrill, Paul Ford

MR. ACE (1946, UA)
Eddie Ace—George Raft
Director—Edwin L. Marin
Leading Players—Sylvia Sidney, Stanley Ridges, Sara Haden

MR. AND MRS. BRIDGE (1990, Miramax/Cineplex Odeon)
Walter Bridge—Paul Newman
India Bridge—Joanne Woodward
Director—James Ivory
Leading Players—Robert Sean Leonard, Margaret Welsh, Kyra Sedgwick, Blythe Danner, Simon Callow

MR. AND MRS. NORTH (1941, MGM)
Pamela North—Gracie Allen
Gerald P. North—William Post, Jr.
Director—Robert B. Sinclair
Leading Players—Paul Kelly, Rose Hobart, Virginia Grey

MR. AND MRS. SMITH (1941, RKO)
Ann Smith—Carole Lombard
David Smith—Robert Montgomery
Director—Alfred Hitchcock
Leading Players—Gene Raymond, Jack Carson, Philip Merivale

MISTER ANTONIO (1929, Tiffany)
Antonio Camaradino—Leo Carrillo
Directors—James Flood and Frank Reicher
Leading Players—Gareth Hughes, Frank Reicher, Eugenie Besserer

MR. ARKADIN (1962, GB, Talbot-Cari)
Gregory Arkadin—Orson Welles
Director—Orson Welles
Leading Players—Robert Arden, Paola Mori, Michael Redgrave, Patricia Medina

MR. BARNES OF NEW YORK (1914, Silent, Vitagraph)
Mr. Barnes—Maurice Costello
Directors—Maurice Costello and Robert Gaillord
Leading Players—Mary Charleson, Charles Kent, William Humphrey

MR. BELVEDERE GOES TO COLLEGE (1949, 20th Century Fox)
Lynn Belvedere—Clifton Webb
Director—Elliott Nugent

Leading Players—Shirley Temple, Tom Drake, Alan Young, Jesse Royce Landis

MR. BELVEDERE RINGS THE BELL (1951, 20th Century Fox)
Lynn Belvedere—Clifton Webb
Director—Henry Koster
Leading Players—Joanne Dru, Hugh Marlowe, Zero Mostel, William Lynn, Doro Merande

MR. BIG (1943, Universal)
Donald—Donald O'Connor
Director—Charles Lamont
Leading Players—Gloria Jean, Peggy Ryan, Elyse Knox

MR. BILLINGS SPENDS HIS DIME (1923, Silent, Paramount)
John Percival Billings—Walter Hiers
Director—Wesley Ruggles
Leading Players—Jacqueline Logan, George Fawcett, Robert McKim

MR. BILLION (1977, 20th Century Fox)
Guido Falcone—Terence Hill
Director—Jonathan Kaplan
Leading Players—Valerie Perrine, Jackie Gleason, Slim Pickens

MR. BLANDINGS BUILDS HIS DREAM HOUSE (1948, RKO)
Jim Blandings—Cary Grant
Director—H.C. Potter
Leading Players—Myrna Loy, Melvyn Douglas, Reginald Denny, Louise Beavers

MR. BOGGS STEPS OUT (1938, Grand National)
Oliver Boggs—Stuart Erwin
Director—Gordon Wiles
Leading Players—Helen Chandler, Toby Wing, Tully Marshall

MISTER BROWN (1972, Andrieux)
George Brown—Al Stevenson
Director—Roger Andrieux
Leading Players—Judith Elliotte, Tyrone Fulton, Nancy Goddard

MR. BROWN COMES DOWN THE HILL (1966, GB, Westminster)
Mr. Brown—Eric Flynn
Director—Henry Cass
Leading Players—Mark Heath, Lillas Walker, John Richmond

MISTER BUDDWING (1966, MGM)
Mister Buddwing—James Garner
Director—Delbert Mann
Leading Players—Jean Simmons, Suzanne Pleshette, Katharine Ross, Angela Lansbury

MR. CHUMP (1938, Warner Brothers)
Bill Small—Johnnie Davis
Director—William Clemens
Leading Players—Lola Lane, Penny Singleton, Donald Briggs

MISTER CINDERELLA (1936, MGM)
Joe Jenkins—Jack Haley
Director—Edward Sedgwick
Leading Players—Betty Furness, Arthur Treacher, Raymond Walburn

MISTER CINDERS (1934, GB, Wardour)
Jim Lancaster—Clifford Mollison
Director—Fred Zelnik

Leading Players—Zelma O'Neal, Kenneth Western, George Western

MR. COHEN TAKES A WALK (1936, GB, Warner Brothers)
Jake Cohen—Paul Graetz
Director—William Beaudine
Leading Players—Violet Farebrother, Chili Bouchier, Mickey Brantford

MISTER CORY (1957, Universal)
Cory—Tony Curtis
Director—Blake Edwards
Leading Players—Martha Hyer, Charles Bickford, Kathryn Grant

MR. DEEDS GOES TO TOWN (1936, Columbia)
Longfellow Deeds—Gary Cooper
Director—Frank Capra
Leading Players—Jean Arthur, George Bancroft, Lionel Stander, Douglas Dumbrille

MR. DENNING DRIVES NORTH (1953, GB, London Films)
Tom Denning—John Mills
Director—Anthony Kimmins
Leading Players—Phyllis Calvert, Sam Wannamaker, Herbert Lom

MR. DESTINY (1990, Buena Vista/Touchstone)
Larry Burrows—James Belushi
Director—James Orr
Leading Players—Linda Hamilton, Michael Caine, Jon Lovitz, Hart Bochner, Bill McCutcheon, Rene Russo

MR. DISTRICT ATTORNEY (1941, Republic)
P. Cadwallader Jones—Dennis O'Keefe
Director—William Morgan
Leading Players—Florence Rice, Peter Lorre, Stanley Ridges

MR. DISTRICT ATTORNEY (1946, Columbia)
Steve Bennett—Dennis O'Keefe
Director—Robert B. Sinclair
Leading Players—Adolphe Menjou, Marguerite Chapman, Michael O'Shea

MR. DODD TAKES THE AIR (1937, First National)
Claude Dodd—Kenny Baker
Director—Alfred E. Green
Leading Players—Alice Brady, Jane Wyman, Henry O'Neill

MR. DOODLE KICKS OFF (1938, RKO)
Doodle Bugs—Joe Penner
Director—Leslie Goodwins
Leading Players—June Travis, Richard Lane, Ben Alexander

MR. DRAKE'S DUCK (1951, GB, UA)
Don Drake—Douglas Fairbanks, Jr.
Director—Val Guest
Leading Players—Yolande Donlan, Howard Marion-Crawford, Reginald Beckwith

MR. DYNAMITE (1935, Universal)
"Mr. Dynamite" T.N. Thompson—Edmund Lowe
Director—Alan Crosland
Leading Players—Jean Dixon, Esther Ralston, Victor Varconi

MR. DYNAMITE (1941, Universal)
Tommy N. Thornton—Lloyd Nolan

Director—John Rawlins
Leading Players—Irene Hervey, J. Carroll Naish, Robert Armstrong

MISTER 880 (1950, 20th Century Fox)
Skipper Miller—Edmund Gwenn
Director—Edward Goulding
Leading Players—Burt Lancaster, Dorothy McGuire, Millard Mitchell

MR. EMMANUEL (1945, GB, Ealing)
Mr. Emmanuel—Felix Aylmer
Director—Harold French
Leading Players—Greta Gynt, Walter Rilla, Peter Mullins

MR. FIX-IT (1918, Silent, Artcraft)
Mr. Fix-It—Douglas Fairbanks
Director—Allan Dwan
Leading Players—Wanda Hawley, Marjorie Daw, Katherine MacDonald

MISTER FROST (1990, France/GB, Hugo/AAA/OMM/SVS)
Mr. Frost—Jeff Goldblum
Director—Philippe Setbon
Leading Players—Alan Bates, Kathy Baker, Roland Giraud, Jean-Pierre Cassel

MR. H.C. ANDERSON (1950, GB, British Foundation)
Hans Christian Anderson—Ashley Glynne
Director—Ronald Haines
Leading Players—Constance Lewis, Terence Noble, Stuart Sanders

MR. HOBBS TAKES A VACATION (1962, 20th Century Fox)
Roger Hobbs—James Stewart
Director—Henry Koster
Leading Players—Maureen O'Hara, Fabian, Lauri Peters, John Saxon, John McGiver

MISTER HOBO (1936, GB, Gaumont)
Francis Rothschild/Spike/The Guv'nor—George Arliss
Director—Milton Rosmer
Leading Players—Gene Gerrard, Frank Cellier, Patric Knowles

MR. IMPERIUM (1951, MGM)
Mr. Imperium—Ezio Pinza
Director—Don Hartman
Leading Players—Lana Turner, Marjorie Main, Barry Sullivan, Cedric Hardwicke, Debbie Reynolds

MR. JOHNSON (1990, Avenue)
Mister Johnson—Maynard Eziashi
Director—Bruce Beresford
Leading Players—Pierce Brosnan, Edward Woodward, Beatie Edney, Denis Quilley, Nick Reding

MR. JUSTICE RAFFLES (1921, GB, Silent, Hepworth)
A.J. Raffles—Gerald Ames
Director—Gerald Ames
Leading Players—Eileen Dennes, James Carew, Hugh Clifton

MR. LEMON OF ORANGE (1931, Fox Film Corp.)
Mr. Lemon—El Brendel
Director—John G. Blystone
Leading Players—Fifi Dorsay, William Collier, Ruth Warren

MR. LORD SAYS NO (1952, GB, London Independent)
Henry Lord—Stanley Holloway
Director—Muriel Box
Leading Players—Kathleen Harrison, Naunton Wayne, Dandy Nichols

MR. LOVE (1986, GB, Warner Brothers)
Donald Lovelace—Barry Jackson
Director—Roy Battersby
Leading Players—Maurice Denham, Margaret Tyzack, Linda Marlowe, Christina Collier

MR. LUCKY (1943, RKO)
Joe Adams—Cary Grant
Director—H.C. Potter
Leading Players—Laraine Day, Charles Bickford, Gladys Cooper

MR. MAJESTYK (1974, UA)
Vince Majestyk—Charles Bronson
Director—Richard Fleischer
Leading Players—Al Lettieri, Linda Cristal, Lee Purcell

MR. MOM (1983, 20th Century Fox)
Jack—Michael Keaton
Director—Stan Dragoti
Leading Players—Teri Garr, Martin Mull, Frederick Koehler

MISTER MOSES (1965, UA)
Joe Moses—Robert Mitchum
Director—Ronald Neame
Leading Players—Carroll Baker, Ian Bannen, Alexander Knox

MR. MOTO IN DANGER ISLAND (1939, 20th Century Fox)
Mr. Moto—Peter Lorre
Director—Herbert I. Leeds
Leading Players—Jean Hersholt, Amanda Duff, Warren Hymer

MR. MOTO TAKES A CHANCE (1938, 20th Century Fox)
Mr. Moto—Peter Lorre
Director—Norman Foster
Leading Players—Rochelle Hudson, Robert Kent, J. Edward Bromberg

MR. MOTO TAKES A VACATION (1938, 20th Century Fox)
Mr. Moto—Peter Lorre
Director—Norman Foster
Leading Players—Joseph Schildkraut, Lionel Atwill, Virginia Field

MR. MOTO'S GAMBLE (1938, 20th Century Fox)
Mr. Moto—Peter Lorre
Director—James Tinling
Leading Players—Keye Luke, Dick Baldwin, Lynn Bari

MR. MOTO'S LAST WARNING (1939, 20th Century Fox)
Mr. Moto—Peter Lorre
Director—Norman Foster
Leading Players—Richard Cortez, Virginia Field, John Carradine, George Sanders

MR. MUGGS RIDES AGAIN (1945, Monogram)
Ethelbert Aloysius "Muggs" McGinnis—Leo Gorcey
Director—Wallace Fox
Leading Players—Huntz Hall, Billy Benedict, Johnny Duncan

MR. MUGGS STEPS OUT (1943, Monogram)
Ethelbert Aloysius "Muggs" McGinnis—Leo Gorcey
Director—William Beaudine
Leading Players—Huntz Hall, Billy Benedict, Bobby Stone

MR. MUSIC (1950, Paramount)
Paul Merrick—Bing Crosby
Director—Richard Haydn
Leading Players—Nancy Olson, Charles Coburn, Robert Stack

MR. NOBODY (1927, GB, Silent, Fox Film Corp.)
Mr. Nobody—Frank Stanmore
Director—Frank Miller
Leading Players—Pauline Johnson, Pat Whitcombe, Cameron Carr

MR. NORTH (1988, Goldwyn)
Theophilus North—Anthony Edwards
Director—Danny Huston
Leading Players—Robert Mitchum, Harry Dean Stanton, Anjelica Huston, Mary Stuart Masterson, Lauren Bacall

MR. PATMAN (1980, Canada, Film Consortium of Canada)
Mr. Patman—James Coburn
Director—John Guillermin
Leading Players—Kate Nelligan, Fionnula Flanagan, Les Carlson

MR. PEABODY AND THE MERMAID (1948, Universal)
Mr.Peabody—William Powell
Mermaid—Ann Blyth
Director—Irving Pichel
Leading Players—Irene Hervey, Andrea King, Clinton Sundberg

MR. PERRIN AND MR. TRAILL (1948, GB, Ealing)
David Traill—David Farrar
Vincent Perrin—Marius Goring
Director—Lawrence Huntington
Leading Players—Greta Gynt, Raymond Huntley, Edward Chapman

MR. POTTS GOES TO MOSCOW (1953, GB, Stratford)
George Potts—George Cole
Director—Mario Zampi
Leading Players—Oscar Homolka, Nadia Gray, Frederick Valk

MR. QUILP (1975, GB, Avco Embassy)
Daniel Quilp—Anthony Newley
Director—Michael Tuchner
Leading Players—David Hemmings, David Warner, Michael Hordern, Jill Bennett

MR. QUINCEY OF MONTE CARLO (1933, GB, Warner Brothers)
Mr. Quincey—John Stuart
Director—John Daumery
Leading Players—Rosemary Ames, Ben Welden, George Merritt

MR. RECKLESS (1948, Paramount)
Jeff Lundy—William Eythe
Director—Frank McDonald
Leading Players—Barbara Britton, Walter Catlett, Minna Gombell

MR. RICCO (1975, MGM/UA)
Joe Ricco—Dean Martin
Director—Paul Bogart

Leading Players—Eugene Roche, Thalmus Rasulala, Denise Nichols

MISTER ROBERTS (1955, Warner Brothers)
Lt. (jg.) Doug Roberts—Henry Fonda
Directors—John Ford and Mervyn LeRoy
Leading Players—James Cagney, Jack Lemmon, William Powell, Ward Bond, Betsy Palmer

MR. ROBINSON CRUSOE (1932, UA)
Steve Drewel—Douglas Fairbanks, Sr.
Director—Edward Sutherland
Leading Players—William Farnum, Earle Browne, Maria Alba

MR. SARDONICUS (1961, Columbia)
Sardonicus—Guy Rolfe
Director—William Castle
Leading Players—Ronald Lewis, Audrey Dalton, Oscar Homolka

MR. SCOUTMASTER (1953, 20th Century Fox)
Robert Jordan—Clifton Webb
Director—Henry Levin
Leading Players—Edmund Gwenn, George "Foghorn" Winslow, Frances Dee

MR. SKEFFINGTON (1944, Warner Brothers)
Job Skeffington—Claude Rains
Director—Vincent Sherman
Leading Players—Bette Davis, Walter Abel, Richard Waring, George Coulouris

MISTER SKITCH (1933, Fox Film Corp.)
Mr. Skitch—Will Rogers
Director—James Cruze
Leading Players—Zasu Pitts, Rochelle Hudson, Florence Desmond

MR. SMITH CARRIES ON (1937, GB, British & Dominions)
Mr. Smith—Edward Rigby
Director—Lister Laurance
Leading Players—Julien Mitchell, H.F. Maltby, Dorothy Oldfield

MR. SMITH GOES TO WASHINGTON (1939, Columbia)
Jefferson Smith—James Stewart
Director—Frank Capra
Leading Players—Jean Arthur, Claude Rains, Edward Arnold, Guy Kibbee, Thomas Mitchell

MR. SOFT TOUCH (1949, Columbia)
Joe Miracle—Glenn Ford
Director—Henry Levin
Leading Players—Evelyn Keyes, John Ireland, Beulah Bondi

MR. STRINGFELLOW SAYS NO (1937, GB, National Provincial)
Jeremy Stringfellow—Neil Hamilton
Director—Randall Faye
Leading Players—Claude Dampier, Muriel Aked, Kathleen Gibson

MR. SYCAMORE (1975, Capricorn)
John Gwilt—Jason Robards, Jr.
Director—Pancho Kohner
Leading Players—Sandy Dennis, Jean Simmons, Robert Easton

MISTER TEN PERCENT (1967, GB, Associated British)
Percy Pointer—Charlie Drake

Director—Peter Graham Scott
Leading Players—Derek Nimmo, Wanda Ventham, John Le Mesurier

MR. UNIVERSE (1951, Eagle-Lion)
Tommy Tompkins—Vincent Edwards
Director—Joseph Lerner
Leading Players—Jack Carson, Janis Paige, Bert Lahr

MR. WALKIE TALKIE (1952, Lippert)
Sgt. Doubleday—William Tracy
Director—Fred L. Guiol
Leading Players—Joe Sawyer, Margia Dean, Russell Hicks

MR. WHAT'S HIS NAME (1935, GB, First National)
Alfred Henfield/Mons. Herbert Herbert—Seymour Hicks
Director—Ralph Ince
Leading Players—Olive Blakeney, Enid Stamp-Taylor, Garry Marsh

MR. WINKLE GOES TO WAR (1944, Columbia)
Wilbert George Winkle—Edward G. Robinson
Director—Alfred E. Green
Leading Players—Ruth Warrick, Ted Donaldson, Bob Haymes

MR. WISE GUY (1942, Monogram)
Ethelbert "Muggs" McGinnis—Leo Gorcey
Director—William Nigh
Leading Players—Bobby Jordan, Huntz Hall, Billy Gilbert

MR. WONG, DETECTIVE (1938, Monogram)
James Lee Wong—Boris Karloff
Director—William Nigh
Leading Players—Grant Withers, Maxine Jennings, Evelyn Brent

MR. WONG IN CHINATOWN (1939, Monogram)
James Lee Wong—Boris Karloff
Director—William Nigh
Leading Players—Grant Withers, Marjorie Reynolds, Peter Gordon Lynn

MR. WU (1919, GB, Silent, Stoll)
Mr. Wu—Matheson Lang
Director—Maurice Elvey
Leading Players—Lilah McCarthy, Meggie Albanesi, Roy Royston

MR. WU (1927, Silent, MGM)
Mr. Wu—Lon Chaney
Director—William Nigh
Leading Players—Louise Dresser, Renee Adoree, Holmes Herbert

MRS. BLACK IS BACK (1914, Silent, Famous Players)
Mrs. Black—May Irwin
Director—J. Searle Dawley
Leading Players—Charles Lane, Wellington A. Playter, Clara Blandick

MRS. BROWN, YOU'VE GOT A LOVELY DAUGHTER (1968, GB, MGM)
Mrs. Brown—Mona Washbourne
Judy Brown—Sarah Caldwell
Director—Saul Swimmer
Leading Players—Peter Noone, Stanley Holloway, Lance Percival

MRS. DANE'S DEFENCE (1933, GB, Paramount)
Mrs. Dane—Joan Barry
Director—A.V. Bramble
Leading Players—Basil Gill, Francis James, Ben Field

MRS. FITZHERBERT (1950, GB, British National)
Maria Fitzherbert—Joyce Howard
Director—Montgomery Tully
Leading Players—Peter Graves, Leslie Banks, Margaretta Scott

MRS. GIBBONS' BOYS (1962, GB, British Lion)
Mrs. Gibbons—Kathleen Harrison
Director—Max Varnel
Leading Players—Lionel Jeffries, Diana Dors, John Le Mesurier

MRS. MIKE (1949, UA)
Kathy O'Fallon—Evelyn Keyes
Sgt. Mike Flannigan—Dick Powell
Director—Louis King
Leading Players—J.M. Kerrigan, Angela Clarke, John Miljan

MRS. MINIVER (1942, MGM)
Kay Miniver—Greer Garson
Director—William Wyler
Leading Players—Walter Pidgeon, Teresa Wright, Dame May
    Whitty, Henry Travers

MRS. O'MALLEY AND MR. MALONE (1950, MGM)
Hattie O'Malley—Marjorie Main
John J. Malone—James Whitmore
Director—Norman Taurog
Leading Players—Ann Dvorak, Phyllis Kirk, Fred Clark

MRS. PARKINGTON (1944, MGM)
Susie Parkington—Greer Garson
Director—Tay Garnett
Leading Players—Walter Pidgeon, Edward Arnold, Frances
    Rafferty, Agnes Moorehead

MRS. POLLIFAX-SPY (1971, UA)
Mrs. Emily Pollifax—Rosalind Russell
Director—Leslie Martinson
Leading Players—Darren McGavin, Nehemiah Persoff, Harold
    Gould

MRS. PYM OF SCOTLAND YARD (1939, GB, Grand National)
Mrs. Pym—Mary Clare
Director—Fred Elles
Leading Players—Edward Lexy, Nigel Patrick, Janet Johnson

MRS. SLACKER (1918, Silent, Pathe)
Susie Simpkins—Gladys Hulette
Director—Hobart Henley
Leading Players—Creighton Hale, Paul Clerget

MRS. SOFFEL (1984, MGM/UA)
Kate Soffel—Diane Keaton
Director—Gillian Armstrong
Leading Players—Mel Gibson, Matthew Modine, Edward
    Herrmann

MRS. THOMPSON (1919, GB, Silent, Samuelson)
Mrs. Thompson—Minna Grey
Director—Rex Wilson
Leading Players—C.M. Hallard, Isobel Elsom, Bertram Burleigh

MRS. WIGGS OF THE CABBAGE PATCH (1934, Paramount)
Mrs. Elvira Wiggs—Pauline Lord
Director—Norman Taurog
Leading Players—W.C. Fields, Zasu Pitts, Evelyn Venable

MRS. WIGGS OF THE CABBAGE PATCH (1942, Paramount)
Mrs. Elvira Wiggs—Fay Bainter
Director—Ralph Murphy
Leading Players—Carolyn Lee, Hugh Herbert, Vera Vague

MISTRESS NELL (1915, Silent, Famous Players)
Mistress Nell—Mary Pickford
Director—James Kirkwood
Leading Players—Owen Moore, Arthur Hoops, Ruby Hoffman

THE MISTRESS OF SHENSTONE (1921, Silent, Robertson-Cole)
Lady Myra Ingleby—Pauline Frederick
Director—Henry King
Leading Players—Roy Stewart, Emmett C. King, Arthur Clayton

MITCHELL (1975, Allied Artists)
Mitchell—Joe Don Baker
Director—Andrew V. McLaglen
Leading Players—Martin Balsam, John Saxon, Linda Evans

M'LISS (1918, Silent, Artcraft)
M'liss Smith—Mary Pickford
Director—Marshall Neilan
Leading Players—Theodore Roberts, Thomas Meighan, Charles
    Ogle

M'LISS (1936, RKO)
M'liss Smith—Anne Shirley
Director—George Nichols, Jr.
Leading Players—John Beal, Guy Kibbee, Douglas Dumbrille

MOBSTERS (1991, Universal)
Lucky Luciano—Christian Slater
Meyer Lansky—Patrick Dempsey
Bugsy Siegel—Richard Grieco
Frank Costello—Costas Mandylor
Director—Michael Karbelnikoff
Leading Players—F. Murray Abraham, Lara Flynn Boyle,
    Michael Gambon, Christopher Penn, Anthony Quinn

THE MODEL AND THE MARRIAGE BROKER (1951, 20th
Century Fox)
Kitty Bennett—Jeanne Crain
Mae Swazey—Thelma Ritter
Director—George Cukor
Leading Players—Scott Brady, Zero Mostel, Michael O'Shea

MODEL FOR MURDER (1960, GB, Cinema Assocites)
Sally Meadows—Hazel Court
Director—Terry Bishop
Leading Players—Keith Andes, Jean Aubrey, Michael Gough

MODEL WIFE (1941, Universal)
Joan Keating Chambers—Joan Blondell
Director—Leigh Jason
Leading Players—Dick Powell, Ruth Donnelly, Charles Ruggles

A MODERN CINDERELLA (1917, Silent, Fox Film Corp.)
Joyce—June Caprice
Director—John G. Adolfi

Leading Players—Frank Morgan, Betty Prendergast, Stanhope Wheatcroft

MODERN GIRLS (1986, Atlantic)
Margo—Daphne Zuniga
Kelly—Virginia Madsen
Cece—Cynthia Gibb
Director—Jerry Kramer
Leading Players—Clayton Rohner, Chris Nash, Steve Shellen

A MODERN HERO (1934, Warner Brothers)
Pierre Radler—Richard Barthelmess
Director—G.W. Pabst
Leading Players—Jean Muir, Marjorie Rambeau, Verree Teasdale

A MODERN MONTE CRISTO (1917, Silent, Thanhouser)
Dr. Emerson—Vincent Serrano
Director—Eugene Moore
Leading Players—Thomas A. Curran, Helen Badgley, Boyd Marshall

A MODERN MUSKETEER (1917, Silent, Artcraft)
Ned Thacker—Douglas Fairbanks
Director—Allan Dwan
Leading Players—Marjorie Daw, Kathleen Kirkham, Tully Marshall

THE MODERNS (1988, Alive Films)
Nick Hart—Keith Carradine
Rachel Stone—Linda Fiorentino
Libby Valentin—Genevieve Bujold
Director—Alan Rudolph
Leading Players—Wallace Shawn, Geraldine Chaplin, Kevin O'Connor, John Lone

MODESTY BLAISE (1966, GB, 20th Century Fox)
Modesty Blaise—Monica Vitti
Director—Joseph Losey
Leading Players—Terence Stamp, Dirk Bogarde, Harry Andrews

MOKEY (1942, MGM)
Mokey Delano- Bobby Blake
Director—Wells Root
Leading Players—Dan Dailey, Donna Reed, Cordell Hickman

MOLLY AND LAWLESS JOHN (1972, Producers Distrbutors Corp.)
Molly Parker—Vera Miles
Johnny Lawler—Sam Elliott
Director—Gary Nelson
Leading Players—Clu Gulager, John Anderson, Cynthia Myers

MOLLY AND ME (1929, Tiffany/Stahl)
Molly Wilson—Belle Bennett
Jim Wilson—Joe E. Brown
Director—Albert Ray
Leading Players—Alberta Vaughn, Charles Byer

MOLLY AND ME (1945, 20th Century Fox)
Molly—Gracie Fields
Graham—Monty Woolley
Director- Lewis Seiler
Leading Players—Roddy McDowall, Reginald Gardiner, Natalie Schafer

MOLLY ENTANGLED (1917, Silent, Paramount)
Molly Shawn—Vivian Martin
Director—Robert Thornby
Leading Players—Harrison Ford, Noah Beery, G.S. Spaulding

MOLLY O' (1921, Silent, Associated First National)
Molly O'—Mabel Normand
Director—F. Richard Jones
Leading Players—George Nichols, Anna Hernandez, Albert Hackett

MOLLY OF THE FOLLIES (1919, Silent, American)
Molly Malone—Margarita Fischer
Director—Edward Sloman
Leading Players—Jack Mower, Lulu Warrenton, Millard L. Webb

THE MOLLYCODDLE (1920, Silent, UA)
Richard Marshall—Douglas Fairbanks
Director—Victor Fleming
Leading Players—Ruth Renick, Betty Boulton, Wallace Beery

MOMMIE DEAREST (1981, Paramount)
Joan Crawford—Faye Dunaway
Director—Frank Perry
Leading Players—Diana Scarwid, Steve Forrest, Howard Da Silva, Mara Hobel

MONEY AND THE WOMAN (1940, Warner Brothers)
Barbara Patterson—Brenda Marshall
Director—William K. Howard
Leading Players—Jeffrey Lynn, John Litel, Lee Patrick, Roger Pryor

THE MONKEY'S UNCLE (1965, Buena Vista)
Merlin Jones—Tommy Kirk
Director—Robert Stevenson
Leading Players—Annette Funicello, Leon Ames, Frank Faylen

MONSIEUR BEAUCAIRE (1924, Silent, Paramount)
Mons. Beaucaire—Rudolph Valentino
Director—Sidney Olcott
Leading Players—Bebe Daniels, Lois Wilson, Doris Kenyon

MONSIEUR BEAUCAIRE (1946, Paramount)
Mons. Beaucaire—Bob Hope
Director—George Marshall
Leading Players—Joan Caulfield, Patric Knowles, Marjorie Reynolds, Cecil Kellaway

MONSIEUR VERDOUX (1947, UA)
Henri Verdoux—Charles Chaplin
Director—Charles Chaplin
Leading Players—Mady Correll, Allison Roddan, Robert Lewis, Martha Raye

MONSIGNOR (1982, 20th Century Fox)
Monsignor Flaherty—Christopher Reeve
Director—Frank Perry
Leading Players—Genevieve Bujold, Fernando Rey, Jason Miller

THE MONSTER AND THE GIRL (1941, Paramount)
Scott Webster—Phillip Terry
The Ape—Charlie Gemora
Susan Webster—Ellen Drew
Director—Stuart Heisler
Leading Players—Robert Paige, Paul Lukas, Joseph Calleia

MONSTER IN THE CLOSET (1987, Troma)
The Monster—Kevin Peter Hall
Director—Bob Dahlin
Leading Players—Donald Grant, Denise DuBarry, Henry Gibson

THE MONSTER MAKER (1944, Producers Releasing Corp.)
Dr. Igor Markoff—J. Carrol Naish
Director—Sam Neufield
Leading Players—Ralph Morgan, Tala Birell, Wanda McKay

THE MONSTER OF HIGHGATE PONDS (1961, GB, Halas & Batchelor)
The Monster—Roy Vincente
Director—Alberto Cavalcanti
Leading Players—Ronald Howard, Rachel Clay, Michael Wade

THE MONSTER OF PIEDRAS BLANCAS (1959, Vanwick)
The Monster—Jack Kevan
Director—Irvin Berwick
Leading Players—Les Tremayne, Forrest Lewis, John Harmon

MONSTER ON THE CAMPUS (1958, Universal)
Dr. Donald Blake—Arthur Franz
Director—Jack Arnold
Leading Players—Joanna Moore, Judson Pratt, Nancy Walters

MONTANA BELLE (1952, RKO)
Belle Starr—Jane Russell
Director—Allan Dwan
Leading Players—George Brent, Scott Brady, Forrest Tucker

MONTE WALSH (1970, National General)
Monte Walsh—Lee Marvin
Director—William A. Fraker
Leading Players—Jeanne Moreau, Jack Palance, Mitch Ryan

MONTY PYTHON'S LIFE OF BRIAN (1979, GB, Warner Brothers)
Brian—Graham Chapman
Director—Terry Jones
Leading Players—Terry Jones, Michael Palin, John Cleese, Eric Idle, Terry Gilliam

MOON OVER HER SHOULDER (1941, 20th Century Fox)
Susan Rossiter—Lynn Bari
Director—Alfred Werker
Leading Players—John Sutton, Dan Dailey, Alan Mowbray

MOON PILOT (1962, Buena Vista)
Capt. Richmond Talbot—Tom Tryon
Director—James Neilson
Leading Players—Brian Keith, Edmond O'Brien, Dany Saval

THE MOONLIGHTER (1953, Warner Brothers)
Wes Anderson—Fred MacMurray
Director—Roy Rowland
Leading Players—Barbara Stanwyck, Ward Bond, William Ching

THE MOONRAKER (1958, GB, ABF-Pathe)
"The Moonraker", Earl Anthony of Dawlish—George Baker
Director—David MacDonald
Leading Players—Sylvia Syms, Peter Arne, Marius Goring

MOONSTRUCK (1987, MGM/UA)
Loretta Castorini—Cher
Ronny Cammareri—Nicolas Cage
Director—Norman Jewison

Leading Players—Vincent Gardenia, Olympia Dukakis, Danny Aiello, Julie Bovasso, John Mahoney

THE MORALS OF MARCUS (1936, GB, Real Art)
Sir Marcus Ordeyne—Ian Hunter
Director—Miles Mander
Leading Players—Lupe Velez, Adriannae Allen, Noel Madison

MORAN OF THE LADY LETTY (1922, Silent, Paramount)
Moran-Letty Sternersen—Dorothy Dalton
Director—George Melford
Leading Players—Rudolph Valentino, Charles Brinley, Walter Long

MORE DEAD THAN ALIVE (1968, UA)
"Killer" Cain—Clint Walker
Director—Robert Sparr
Leading Players—Vincent Price, Anne Francis, Paul Hampton, Mike Henry

MORE THAN A SECRETARY (1936, Columbia)
Carol Baldwin—Jean Arthur
Director—Alfred E. Green
Leading Players—George Brent, Lionel Stander, Ruth Donnelly

THE MORE THE MERRIER (1943, Columbia)
Connie Milligan—Jean Arthur
Joe Carter—Joel McCrea
Benjamin Dingle—Charles Coburn
Director—George Stevens
Leading Players—Richard Gaines, Bruce Bennett, Clyde Fillmore

MORGAN! (1966, GB, Cinema V)
Morgan Delt—David Warner
Director—Karel Reisz
Leading Players—Vanessa Redgrave, Robert Stephens, Irene Handl, Newton Blick

MORGAN STEWART'S COMING HOME (1987, New Century-Vista)
Morgan Stewart—Jon Cryer
Director—Alan Smithee (Terry Windsor, Paul Aaron)
Leading Players—Lynn Redgrave, Nicholas Pryor, Viveka Davis

MORGAN'S LAST RAID (1929, Silent, MGM)
Morgan—Allan Garcia
Director—Nick Grinde
Leading Players—Tim McCoy, Dorothy Sebastian, Wheeler Oakman

MORGAN'S MARAUDERS (1929, Distinctive)
Capt. Lucy Morgan—Margaret Livingston
Director—Fred Newmeyer
Leading Players—Vivienne Osborne, Dorothy Nolan, Ella Scott, Irene Dennis

MOSES (1976, Great Britain/Italy, Avco Embassy)
Moses—Burt Lancaster
Director—Giafranco de Bosio
Leading Players—Anthony Quayle, Ingrid Thulin, Irene Papas

THE MOST DANGEROUS MAN ALIVE (1961, Columbia)
Eddie Candell—Ron Randell
Director—Allan Dwan
Leading Players—Debra Paget, Elaine Stewart, Anthony Caruso

A MOST IMMORAL LADY (1929, First National)
Laura Sargeant—Leatrice Joy
Director—John Griffith Wray
Leading Players—Walter Pidgeon, Sydney Blackmer, Montagu Love

MOTEL, THE OPERATOR (1940, Cinema Film)
Motel—Chaim Tauber
Director—Joseph Seiden
Leading Players—Malvina Rappel, Joseph Schoengold, Gertrude Krause

THE MOTH (1934, Showmen's Pictures)
Diana Wyman—Sally O'Neil
Director—Fred Newmeyer, Jr.
Leading Players—Paul Page, Wilfred Lucas, Fred Kelsey

THE MOTH AND THE FLAME (1915, Silent, Paramount)
Marion Walton—Adele Ray
Edward Fletcher—Stewart Baird
Director—Sidney Olcott
Leading Players—Edwin Mordant, Bradley Barker, Arthur Donaldson

MOTHER AND SON (1931, Monogram)
Mother—Clara Kimbell Young
Son—Bruce Warren
Director—John P. McCarthy
Leading Players—Gordon Wood, Mildred Golden, John Elliott

MOTHER CAREY'S CHICKENS (1938, RKO)
Mrs. Carey—Fay Bainter
Nancy Carey—Anne Shirley
Kitty Carey—Ruby Keeler
Director—Rowland V. Lee
Leading Players—James Ellison, Walter Brennan, Frank Albertson, Alma Kruger

MOTHER IS A FRESHMAN (1949, 20th Century Fox)
Abigail "Abby" Fortitude Abbott—Loretta Young
Director—Lloyd Bacon
Leading Players—Van Johnson, Rudy Vallee, Barbara Lawrence

MOTHER, JUGS & SPEED (1976, 20th Century Fox)
Mother—Bill Cosby
Jugs—Raquel Welch
Speed—Harvey Keitel
Director—Walter Scott Herndon
Leading Players—Allen Garfield, Larry Hagman, L.Q. Jones

MOTHER KNOWS BEST (1928, Fox Film Corp.)
Ma Quail—Louise Dresser
Director—John Blystone
Leading Players—Madge Bellamy, Barry Norton, Albert Gran

MOTHER WORE TIGHTS (1947, 20th Century Fox)
Myrtle McKinley Burt—Betty Grable
Director—Walter Lang
Leading Players—Dan Dailey, Mona Freeman, Connie Marshall

MOTHER'S BOY (1929, Pathe)
Ma O'Day—Beryl Mercer
Tommy O'Day—Morton Downey
Director—Bradley Barker and James Semour
Leading Players—John T. Doyle, Brian Donlevy, Helen Chandler

MOTHERS CRY (1930, First National)
Mary K. Williams—Dorothy Peterson
Director—Hobart Henley
Leading Players—Helen Chandler, David Manners, Sidney Blackmer

MOTHERS-IN-LAW (1923, Silent, Preferred)
"Mom" Wingate—Edith Yorke
Director—Louis Gasnier
Leading Players—Ruth Clifford, Gaston Glass, Crauford Kent

THE MOUNTAIN MEN (1980, Columbia)
Bill Tyler—Charlton Heston
Director—Richard Lang
Leading Players—Brian Keith, Victoria Racimo, Stephen Macht

MOURNING BECOMES ELECTRA (1947, RKO)
Lavinia Mannon—Rosalind Russell
Director—Dudley Nichols
Leading Players—Michael Redgrave, Raymond Massey, Katina Paxinou, Leo Genn, Kirk Douglas

THE MOUTHPIECE (1932, Warner Brothers)
Vincent Day—Warren William
Director—James Flood and Elliot Nugent
Leading Players—Sidney Fox, Aline McMahon, William Janney

MOVING TARGETS (1987, Australia, Academy)
Eve—Carmen Duncan
Riley—Michael Aitkens
Director—Chris Langman
Leading Players—Shane Briant, Redmond Symons, Nicholas Eadie, Annie Jones

MOZART (1940, GB, ABF/Lopert)
Wolfgang Amadeus Mozart—Stephen Haggard
Director—Basil Dean
Leading Players—Victoria Hopper, John Loder, Liane Haid

THE MUDLARK (1950, GB, 20th Century Fox)
Wheeler, the Mudlark—Andrew Ray
Director—Jean Negulesco
Leading Players—Alec Guinness, Irene Dunne, Beatrice Campbell, Finlay Currie, Anthony Steel

MUMSIE (1927, Silent, GB, Wilcox/W&F)
Mumsie—Pauline Frederick
Director—Herbert Wilcox
Leading Players—Nelson Keys, Herbert Marshall, Frank Stanmore

THE MUMMY (1932, Universal)
Im-Ho-Tep—Boris Karloff
Director—Karl Freund
Leading Players—Zita Johann, David Manners, Edward Van Sloan

THE MUMMY (1959, GB, Hammer)
Kharis—Christopher Lee
Director—Terence Fisher
Leading Players—Peter Cushing, Yvonne Furneaux, Eddie Byrne

THE MUMMY'S CURSE (1944, Universal)
Kharis—Lon Chaney, Jr.
Director—Leslie Goodwins
Leading Players—Peter Coe, Virginia Christine, Kay Harding

THE MUMMY'S GHOST (1944, Universal)
Kharis—Lon Chaney, Jr.
Director—Reginald LeBerg
Leading Players—John Carradine, Ramsay Ames, Barton MacLane

THE MUMMY'S HAND (1940, Univeral)
Kharis—Tom Tyler
Director—Christy Cabanne
Leading Players—Dick Foran, Peggy Moran, Cecil Kellaway, Wallace Ford, George Zucco

THE MUMMY'S SHROUD (1967, GB, Hammer)
Mummy—Eddie Powell
Director—John Gilling
Leading Players—Andre Morell, John Phillips, David Buck

THE MUMMY'S TOMB (1942, Universal)
Kharis—Lon Chaney, Jr.
Director—Harold Young
Leading Players—Dick Foran, Elyse Knox, John Hubbard

MUNCHIE (1992, Concorde Pictures)
Munchie—Voice of Dom DeLuise
Director—Jim Wynorski
Leading Players—Loni Anderson, Andrew Stevens, Jaime McEnnan, Arte Johnson, Love Hewitt

A MUNITION GIRL'S ROMANCE (1917, Silent, GB, Broadwest)
Jenny Jones—Violet Hopson
Director—Frank Wilson
Leading Players—Gregory Scott, George Foley, Tom Beaumont

MUNSTER, GO HOME (1966, Universal)
Herman Munster—Fred Gwynne
Director—Earl Bellamy
Leading Players—Yvonne De Carlo, Al Lewis, Butch Patrick, Debbie Watson

MURDER MAN (1935, MGM)
Steve Gray—Spencer Tracy
Director—Tim Whelan
Leading Players—Virginia Bruce, Lionel Atwill, Harvey Stephens, Robert Barrat, James Stewart

THE MURDER OF DR. HARRIGAN (1936, First National)
Dr. Harrigan—John Eldredge
Director—Frank McDonald
Leading Players—Kay Linaker, Ricardo Cortez, Mary Astor

MURDER SHE SAID (1961, GB, MGM)
Miss Jane Marple—Margaret Rutherford
Director—George Pollock
Leading Players—Arthur Kennedy, Muriel Pavlow, James Robinson Justice

MURPH THE SURF (1974, Caruth C. Byrd)
Jack Murphy—Don Stroud
Director—Marvin Chomsky
Leading Players—Robert Conrad, Donna Mills, Robyn Mills

MURPHY'S LAW (1986, Cannon)
Jack Murphy—Charles Bronson
Director—J. Lee Thompson
Leading Players—Kathleen Wilhoite, Carrie Snodgress, Robert F. Lyons, Richard Romanus

MURPHY'S ROMANCE (1985, Columbia)
Murphy Jones—James Garner
Director—Martin Ritt
Leading Players—Sally Field, Brian Kerwin, Corey Haim

MURPHY'S WAR (1971, GB, Paramount)
Murphy—Peter O'Toole
Director—Peter Yates
Leading Players—Sian Philips, Philippe Noiret, Horst Janson

THE MUSIC BOX KID (1960, UA)
Larry Shaw—Ronald Fraser
Director—Edward L. Cahn
Leading Players—Luana Patten, Grant Richards, Johnny Seven

MUSIC FOR MADAME (1937, RKO)
Jean Clemens—Joan Fontaine
Director—John Blystone
Leading Players—Nino Martini, Alan Mowbray, Billy Gilbert

THE MUSIC MAN (1962, Warner Brothers)
Harold Hill—Robert Preston
Director—Morton DaCosta
Leading Players—Shirley Jones, Buddy Hackett, Hermione Gingold, Paul Ford

MUTANT ON THE BOUNTY (1989, Skouras)
Max—Kyle T. Heffner
Director—Robert Torrance
Leading Players—John Roarke, Deborah Benson, John Furey

MY AMERICAN COUSIN (1986, Canada, Spectrafilm)
Sandy Wilcox—Margaret Langrick
Butch Walker—John Widman
Director—Sandy Wilson
Leading Players—Richard Donat, Jane Mortifee, T.J. Scott

MY AMERICAN WIFE (1923, Silent, Paramount)
Natalie Chester—Gloria Swanson
Manuel La Tassa—Antonio Moreno
Director—Sam Wood
Leading Players—Josef Swickard, Eric Mayne, Gino Corrado

MY AMERICAN WIFE (1936, Paramount)
Count Ferdinand von und su Reidenach—Francis Lederer
Mary Cantillon- Ann Sothern
Director—Harold Young
Leading Players—Fred Stone, Billie Burke, Ernest Cossart

MY BEST FRIEND IS A VAMPIRE (1988, Kings Road)
Jeremy Capello—Robert Sean Leonard
Ralph—Evan Mirand
Director—Jimmy Huston
Leading Players—Cheryl Pollak, Rene Auberjonois, Cecilia Peck, David Warner

MY BEST GAL (1944, Republic)
Kitty O'Hara—Jane Withers
Johnny McCloud—Jimmy Lydon
Director—Anthony Mann
Leading Players—Frank Craven, Fortunio Bonanova, George Cleveland

MY BEST GIRL (1927, Silent, UA)
Maggie Johnson—Mary Pickford
Joe Grant—Charles Rogers

Director—Sam Taylor
Leading Players—Sunshine Hart, Lucien Littlefield, Carmelita Geraghty

MY BILL (1938, Warner Brothers)
Mary Colbrook—Kay Francis
Bill Colbrook—Dickie Moore
Director—John Farrow
Leading Players—Bonita Granville, Anita Louise, Bobby Jordan

MY BLUE HEAVEN (1950, 20th Century Fox)
Jack Moran—Dan Dailey
Director—Henry Koster
Leading Players—Betty Grable, David Wayne, Jane Wyatt, Mitzi Gaynor, Una Merkel

MY BLUE HEAVEN (1990, Warner Brothers/Hawn/Sylbert)
Vinnie—Steve Martin
Director—Herbert Ross
Leading Players—Rick Moranis, Joan Cusack, Melanie Mayron, Carol Kane, Bill Irwin

MY BOY (1922, Silent, Associated First National)
Jackie Blair—Jackie Coogan
Captain Bill—Claude Gillingwater
Director—Victor Heerman
Leading Players—Mathilde Brundage, Patsy Marks

MY BODYGUARD (1980, 20th Century Fox)
Clifford Peache—Chris Makepeace
Lindemann—Adam Baldwin
Director—Tony Bill
Leading Players—Matt Dillon, Paul Quandt, Joan Cusack

MY BRILLIANT CAREER (1980, Australia, New South Wales)
Sybylla Melvyn—Judy Davis
Director—Gillian Armstrong
Leading Players—Sam Neill, Wendy Hughes, Robert Grubb

MY BROTHER JONATHAN (1949, GB, Allied Artists)
Jonathan Dakers—Michael Denison
Harold Dakers—Ronald Howard
Director—Harold French
Leading Players—Dulcie Gray, Stephen Murray, Mary Clare

MY BROTHER TALKS TO HORSES (1946, MGM)
Lewis Penrose—"Butch" Jenkins
John S. Penrose—Peter Lawford
Director—Fred Zinnemann
Leading Players—Beverly Tyler, Edward Arnold, Charlie Ruggles

MY BROTHER, THE OUTLAW (1951, Eagle-Lion)
Denny O'More—Mickey Rooney
Patrick O'More—Robert Stack
Director—Elliott Nugent
Leading Players—Wanda Hendrix, Robert Preston, Carlos Muzquiz

MY BROTHER'S KEEPER (1949, GB, Rank)
George Martin—Jack Warner
Willie Stannard—George Cole
Directors—Alfred Roome and Roy Rich
Leading Players—Jane Hylton, David Tomlinson, Bill Owen

MY BROTHER'S WEDDING (1983, Burnett)
Pierce Monday—Everett Silas

Wendell Monday—Dennis Kemper
Director—Charles Burnett
Leading Players—Jessie Holmes, Gaye Shannon-Burnett, Ronnie Bell

MY BUDDY (1944, Republic)
Eddie Ballinger—Donald Barry
Jim Connelly—John Litel
Director—Steve Sekely
Leading Players—Ruth Terry, Lynne Roberts, Alexander Granach

MY CHAUFFEUR (1986, Crown)
Casey Meadows—Deborah Freeman
Director—David Beaird
Leading Players—Sam J. Jones, Sean McClory, Howard Hesseman, E.G. Marshall, Teller

MY COUSIN (1918, Silent, Artcraft)
Mario Nanni/Cesare Carulli—Enrico Caruso
Director—Edward Jose
Leading Players—Henry Leone, Caroline White, Joseph Riccardi

MY COUSIN RACHEL (1952, 20th Century Fox)
Rachel Ashley—Olivia de Havilland
Philip Ashley—Richard Burton
Director—Henry Koster
Leading Players—Audrey Dalton, Ronald Squire, George Dolenz

MY COUSIN VINNY (1992, 20th Century Fox)
Vinny Gambini—Joe Pesci
Director—Jonathan Lynn
Leading Players—Ralph Macchio, Marisa Tomei, Mitchell Whitfield, Fred Gwynne, Lane Smith, Austin Pendleton

MY DAD (1922, Silent, R-C/Film Booking Office)
Tom O'Day—Johnnie Walker
Barry O'Day—Wilbur Higby
Director—Cliff Smith
Leading Players—Mary Redmond, Ruth Clifford, Les Bates

MY DARK LADY (1987, Film Gallery)
Sam Booth—Fred A. Keller
Lorna Dahomey—Lorna Hill
Director—Frederick King Keller
Leading Players—Raymond Holder, John Buscaglia, Evan Perry

MY DARLING CLEMENTINE (1946, 20th Century Fox)
Wyatt Earp—Henry Fonda
Clementine—Cathy Downs
Director—John Ford
Leading Players—Linda Darnell, Victor Mature, Walter Brennan, Tim Holt, Ward Bond, Alan Mowbray

MY DEAR MISS ALDRICH (1937, MGM)
Martha Aldrich—Maureen O'Sullivan
Ken Morley—Walter Pidgeon
Director—George B. Seitz
Leading Players—Edna May Oliver, Rita Johnson, Janet Beecher

MY DEAR SECRETARY (1948, UA)
Stephanie Gaylord—Laraine Day
Owen Waterbury—Kirk Douglas
Director—Charles Martin
Leading Players—Keenan Wynn, Helen Walker, Rudy Vallee

MY DEMON LOVER (1987, New Line Cinema)
Kaz—Scott Valentine
Denny—Michelle Little
Director—Charles Loventhal
Leading Players—Arnold Johnson, Robert Trebor, Alan Fudge

MY DINNER WITH ANDRE (1981, New Yorker)
Wally—Wallace Shawn
Andre—Andre Gregory
Director—Louis Malle
Leading Players—Jean Lenauer, Roy Butler

MY FAIR LADY (1964, Warner Brothers)
Eliza Doolittle—Audrey Hepburn
Prof. Henry Higgins—Rex Harrison
Director—George Cukor
Leading Players—Stanley Holloway, Wilfrid Hyde-White, Gladys Cooper, Jeremy Brett, Theodore Bikel

MY FAVORITE BLONDE (1942, Paramount)
Larry Haines—Bob Hope
Karen Bentley—Madeline Carroll
Director—Sidney Lanfield
Leading Players—Gale Sondergaard, George Zucco, Lionel Royce

MY FAVORITE BRUNETTE (1947, Paramount)
Ronnie Jackson—Bob Hope
Carlotta Montay—Dorothy Lamour
Director—Elliott Nugent
Leading Players—Peter Lorre, Lon Chaney, Jr., Charles Dingle, Reginald Denny

MY FAVORITE SPY (1951, RKO)
Peanuts White—Bob Hope
Lily Dalbray—Hedy Lamarr
Director—Norman Z. McLeod
Leading Players—Francis L. Sullivan, Arnold Moss, John Archer, Luis Van Rooten

MY FAVORITE WIFE (1940, RKO)
Ellen Arden—Irene Dunne
Nick Arden—Cary Grant
Director—Garson Kanin
Leading Players—Randolph Scott, Gail Patrick, Ann Shoemaker

MY FAVORITE YEAR (1982, MGM-UA)
Benjy Stone—Mark Linn-Baker
Director—Richard Benjamin
Leading Players—Peter O'Toole, Jessica Harper, Joseph Bologna, Bill Macy, Lainie Kazan

MY FIRST WIFE (1985, Canada, Spectrafilm)
John—John Hargreaves
Helen—Wendy Hughes
Director—Paul Cox
Leading Players—Lucy Angwin, David Cameron, Julia Blake

MY FOOLISH HEART (1949, RKO)
Eloise Winters—Susan Hayward
Director—Mark Robson
Leading Players—Dana Andrews, Kent Smith, Lois Wheeler

MY FORBIDDEN PAST (1951, RKO)
Barbara Beaurevel—Ava Gardner
Director—Robert Stevenson

Leading Players—Robert Mitchum, Melvyn Douglas, Lucile Watson, Janis Carter

MY FRIEND FLICKA (1943, 20th Century Fox)
Ken McLaughlin—Roddy McDowall
Director—Harold Schuster
Leading Players—Preston Foster, Rita Johnson, James Bell

MY FRIEND IRMA (1949, Paramount)
Jane Stacey—Diana Lynn
Irma Peterson—Marie Wilson
Director—George Marshall
Leading Players—John Lund, Don DeFore, Dean Martin, Jerry Lewis

MY FRIEND IRMA GOES WEST (1950, Paramount)
Jane Stacey—Diana Lynn
Irma Peterson—Marie Wilson
Director—Hal Walker
Leading Players—John Lund, Dean Martin, Jerry Lewis

MY FRIEND THE KING (1931, GB, Fox Film Corp.)
Jim—Jerry Verno
King Ludwig—Eric Pavitt
Director—Michael Powell
Leading Players—Robert Holmes, Tracey Holmes, Phyllis Loring

MY GAL SAL (1942, 20th Century Fox)
Sally Elliott—Rita Hayworth
Paul Dreiser—Victor Mature
Director—Irving Cummings
Leading Players—John Sutton, Carole Landis, James Gleason

MY GEISHA (1962, Paramount)
Lucy Dell/Yoko Mori—Shirley MacLaine
Paul Robaix—Yves Montand
Director—Jack Cardiff
Leading Players—Edward G. Robinson, Bob Cummings, Yoko Tani

MY GIRL (1991, Columbia)
Thomas J. Sennett—Macaulay Culkin
Vada Sultenfuss—Anna Chlumsky
Director—Howard Zieff
Leading Players—Dan Aykroyd, Jamie Lee Curtis, Richard Mazur, Griffin Dunne, Ann Nelson

MY GIRL TISA (1948, Warner Brothers)
Tisa Kepes—Lilli Palmer
Mark Denek—Sam Wanamaker
Director—Elliot Nugent
Leading Players—Akim Tamiroff, Alan Hale, Hugo Haas

MY GUN IS QUICK (1957, UA)
Mike Hammer—Robert Bray
Directors—George White and Phil Victor
Leading Players—Whitney Blake, Pat Donahue, Donald Randolph

MY HUSBAND'S WIVES (1924, Silent, Fox Film Corp.)
Vale Harvey—Shirley Mason
William Harvey—Bryant Washburn
Marie Wynn—Evelyn Brent
Director—Maurice Elvey
Leading Players—Paulette Duval

MY KINGDOM FOR A COOK (1943, Columbia)
Rudyard Morley—Charles Coburn
Hattie—Almira Sessions
Director—Richard Wallace
Leading Players—Marguerite Chapman, Bill Carter, Isobel Elsom, Edward Gargan

MY LEARNED FRIEND (1943, GB, Ealing)
William Fitch—Will Hay
Claude Babbington—Claude Hulbert
Directors—Will Hay and Basil Dearden
Leading Players—Mervyn Johns, Laurence Hanray, Aubrey Mallalieu

MY LEFT FOOT (1989, Great Britain/Ireland, Miramax)
Christy Brown—Daniel Day-Lewis
Christy as a boy—Hugh O'Conor
Director—Jim Sheridan
Leading Players—Ray McAnally, Brenda Fricker, Ruth McCabe, Fiona Shaw, Adrian Dunbar

MY LIFE WITH CAROLINE (1941, RKO)
Anthony Mason—Ronald Colman
Caroline Mason—Anna Lee
Director—Lewis Milestone
Leading Players—Charles Winninger, Reginald Gardiner, Gilbert Roland

MY LITTLE CHICKADEE (1940, Universal)
Cuthbert J. Twillie—W. C. Fields
Flower Belle Lee—Mae West
Director—Edward Cline
Leading Players—Joseph Calleia, Dick Foran, Margaret Hamilton

MY LORD THE CHAUFFEUR (1927, GB, Silent, British Classics)
Philip Parr—Kim Peacock
Director—B. E. Doxat-Pratt
Leading Players—Pauline Johnson, Sydney Fairbrother, Jerold Robertshaw

MY LOVE CAME BACK (1940, Warner Brothers)
Amelia Cullen—Olivia de Havilland
Tony Baldwin—Jeffrey Lynn
Director—Curtis Bernhardt
Leading Players—Eddie Albert, Jane Wyman, Charles Winninger

MY LOVER, MY SON (1970, GB, MGM)
Francesca Anderson—Romy Schneider
James Anderson—Dennis Waterman
Director—John Newland
Leading Players—Donald Houston, Patricia Brake, Peter Sallis

MY MAN (1928, Warner Brothers)
Fannie Brand—Fannie Brice
Joe Halsey—Guinn "Big Boy" Williams
Director—Archie Mayo
Leading Players—Edna Murphy, Andre de Segurola, Richard Tucker

MY MAN AND I (1952, MGM)
Nancy—Shelley Winters
Chu Chu Ramirez—Ricardo Montalban
Director—William A. Wellman
Leading Players—Wendell Corey, Claire Trevor, Robert Burton

MY MAN GODFREY (1936, Universal)
Godfrey (Parke)—William Powell
Irene Bullock—Carole Lombard
Director—Gregory la Cava
Leading Players—Alice Brady, Eugene Pallette, Gail Patrick, Alan Mowbray, Jean Mischa Auer

MY MAN GODFREY (1957, Universal)
Irene Bullock—June Allyson
Godfrey—David Niven
Director—Henry Koster
Leading Players—Jessie Royce Landis, Robert Keith, Eva Gabor, Jay Robinson, Martha Hyer

MY MARRIAGE (1936, 20th Century Fox)
Carol Barton—Claire Trevor
John DeWitt Tyler III—Kent Taylor
Director—George Archainbaud
Leading Players—Pauline Frederick, Paul Kelly, Helen Wood

MY NAME IS JULIA ROSS (1945, Columbia)
Julia Ross—Nina Foch
Director—Joseph H. Lewis
Leading Players—Dame May Whitty, George Macready, Roland Varno

MY OWN TRUE LOVE (1948, Paramount)
Joan Clews—Phyllis Calvert
Clive Heath—Melvyn Douglas
Director—Compton Bennett
Leading Players—Wanda Hendrix, Philip Friend, Binnie Barnes

MY PAL GUS (1952, 20th Century Fox)
Dave Jennings—Richard Widmark
Gus Jennings—George Winslow
Director—Robert Parrish
Leading Players—Richard Widmark, Audrey Totter, Joan Banks

MY PAL, THE KING (1932, Universal)
Tom Reed—Tom Mix
King Charles V—Mickey Rooney
Director—Kurt Neumann
Leading Players—Paul Hurst, Noel Francis, Finis Barton

MY REPUTATION (1946, Warner Brothers)
Jessica Drummond—Barbara Stanwyck
Director—Curtis Bernhardt
Leading Players—George Brent, Warner Anderson, Lucile Watson

MY SCIENCE PROJECT (1985, Buena Vista)
Michael Harlan- John Stockwell
Director—Jonathan Beteul
Leading Players—Danielle Von Zerneck, Fisher Stevens, Raphael Sbarge

MY SIDE OF THE MOUNTAIN (1969, Paramount)
Sam Gribley—Teddy Eccles
Director—James B. Clark
Leading Players—Theodore Bikel, Tudi Wiggins, Frank Perry

MY SIN (1931, Paramount)
Carlotta ("Ann Trevor")—Tallulah Bankhead
Director—George Abbott
Leading Players—Fredric March, Harry Davenport, Scott Kolk

MY SISTER EILEEN (1942, Columbia)
Ruth Sherwood—Rosalind Russell
Eileen Sherwood—Janet Blair
Director—Alexander Hall
Leading Players—Brian Aherne, George Tobias, Allyn Joslyn

MY SISTER EILEEN (1955, Columbia)
Ruth Sherwood—Betty Garrett
Eileen Sherwood—Janet Leigh
Director—Richard Quine
Leading Players—Jack Lemmon, Bob Fosse, Kurt Kasznar

MY SIX CONVICTS (1952, Columbia)
Doc—John Beal
James Connie—Millard Mitchell
Punch Rinero—Gilbert Roland
Blivens Scott—Marshall Thompson
Clem Randall—Alf Kjellin
Dawson—Harry Morgan
Steve Kopac—Jay Adler
Director—Hugo Fregonese
Leading Players—Regis Toomey, Fay Roope, Carlton Young

MY SON (1925, Silent, First National)
Ana Silva—Nazimova
Tony Silva—Jack Pickford
Director—Edwin Carewe
Leading Players—Hobart Bosworth, Ian Keith, Mary Akin

MY SON IS A CRIMINAL (1939, Columbia)
Tim Halloran, Sr.—Willard Robertson
Tim Halloran, Jr.—Alan Baxter
Director—C.C. Coleman
Leading Players—Jacqueline Wells, Gordon Oliver, Joseph King

MY SON IS GUILTY (1940, Columbia)
Tim Kerry—Harry Carey
Ritzy Kerry—Bruce Cabot
Director—Charles Barton
Leading PLayers—Jacqueline Wells, Glenn Ford, Wynne Gibson

MY SON JOHN (1952, Paramount)
Lucille Jefferson—Helen Hayes
John Jefferson—Robert Walker
Director—Leo McCarey
Leading Players—Van Heflin, Dean Jagger, Minor Watson

MY SON, MY SON! (1940, UA)
William Essex—Brian Aherne
Oliver Essex—Louis Hayward
Director—Charles Vidor
Leading Players—Madeleine Carroll, Laraine Day, Henry Hull

MY SON, THE HERO (1943, Producers Releasing Corp.)
Big Time—Roscoe Karns
Michael—Joseph Allen, Jr.
Director—Edgar G. Ulmer
Leading Players—Patsy Kelly, Joan Blair, Carol Hughes

MY SON, THE VAMPIRE (1963, GB, Renown)
Baron Von Housen—Bela Lugosi
Old Mother Riley—Arthur Lucan
Director—John Gilling
Leading Players—Dora Bryan, Richard Wattis, Judith Furse

MY SONG FOR YOU (1935, GB, Gaumont)
Gatti—Jan Kiepura
Mary Newberg—Aileen Marson
Director—Maurice Elvey
Leading Players—Sonnie Hale, Emlyn Wiliams, Gina Malo

MY STEPMOTHER IS AN ALIEN (1988, Weintraub)
Celeste Mills—Kim Basinger
Jessie Mills—Alyson Hannigan
Director—Richard Benjamin
Leading Players—Dan Aykroyd, Jon Lovitz, Joseph Maher

MY TRUE STORY (1951, Columbia)
Ann Martin—Helen Walker
Director—Mickey Rooney
Leading Players—Willard Parker, Elisabeth Risdon, Emory Parnell

MY TUTOR (1983, Crown International)
Terry—Caren Kaye
Bobby Chrystal—Matt Lattanzi
Director—George Bowers
Leading Players—Kevin McCarthy, Clark Brandon, Bruce Bauer

MY WEAKNESS (1933, Fox Film Corp.)
Looloo Blake—Lillian Harvey
Director—David Butler
Leading Players—Lew Ayres, Charles Butterworth, Harry Langdon

MY WIFE'S BEST FRIEND (1952, 20th Century Fox)
Virginia Mason—Anne Baxter
George Mason—Macdonald Carey
Jane Richards—Catherine McLeod
Director—Richard Sale
Leading Players—Cecil Kellaway, Casey Adams, Leif Erickson

MY WIFE'S LODGER (1952, GB, Adelphi)
Willie Higginbotham—Dominic Roche
Maggie Higginbotham—Olive Sloane
Roger The Lodger—Leslie Dwyer
Director—Maurice Elvey
Leading Players—Diana Dors, Alan Sedgwick, Vincent Downing

MY WILD IRISH ROSE (1947, Warner Brothers)
Chauncey Olcott—Dennis Morgan
Rose Donovan—Arlene Dahl
Director—David Butler
Leading Players—Andrea King, Alan Hale, George Tobias

MY WOMAN (1933, Columbia)
Connie Riley—Helen Twelvetrees
Chick Rollins—Wallace Ford
Director—Victor Schertzinger
Leading Players—Victory Jory, Claire Dodd, Warren Hymer

MYRT AND MARGE (1934, Universal)
Myrt Minter—Myrtle Vail
Marge Spear—Donna Damerel
Director—Al Boasberg
Leading Players—Trixie Friganza, Eddie Foy, Jr., J. Farrell MacDonald

THE MYSTERIOUS DR. FU MANCHU (1929, Paramount)
Dr. Fu Manchu—Warner Oland
Director—Rowland V. Lee

Leading Players—Jean Arthur, Neil Hamilton, O.P. Heggie

THE MYSTERIOUS HOUSE OF DR. C (1976, Bronston)
Dr. Coppelius—Walter Slezak
Director—Ted Kneeland
Leading Players—Claudia Corday, Caj Selling, Eileen Elliott

THE MYSTERIOUS LADY (1928, Silent, MGM)
Tania—Greta Garbo
Director—Fred Niblo
Leading Players—Conrad Nagel, Gustav von Seyffertitz, Albert Pollet

MYSTERIOUS MR. MOTO (1938, 20th Century Fox)
Mr. Moto—Peter Lorre
Director—Norman Foster
Leading Players—Mary Maguire, Henry Wilcoxon, Erik Rhodes

THE MYSTERIOUS MR. NICHOLSON (1947, GB, Ambassador)
Mr. Nicholson—Anthony Hulme
Director—Oswald Mitchell
Leading Players—Lesley Osmond, Frank Hawkins, Andrew Laurence

THE MYSTERIOUS MR. REEDER (1940, GB, Monogram)
J.G. Reeder—Will Fyffe
Director—Jack Raymond
Leading Players—Kay Walsh, George Curzon, Chili Bouchier

MYSTERIOUS MR. WONG (1935, Monogram)
Mr. Wong, Mandarin—Bela Lugosi
Director—William Nigh
Leading Players—Wallace Ford, Arline Judge, Fred Warren

THE MYSTERIOUS RIDER (1933, Paramount)
Wade Benton—Kent Taylor
Director—Fred Allen
Leading Players—Lona Andre, Gail Patrick, Irving Pichel

THE MYSTERIOUS RIDER (1938, Paramount)
Ben Wade—Douglass Dumbrille
Director—Lesley Selander
Leading Players—Sidney Toler, Russell Hayden, Charlotte Field

THE MYSTERY MAN (1935, Monogram)
Larry—Robert Armstrong
Director—Ray McCarey
Leading Players—Maxine Doyle, Henry Kolker, LeRoy Mason

THE MYSTERY OF EDWIN DROOD (1935, Universal)
Edwin Drood—David Manners
Director—Stuart Walker
Leading Players—Claude Rains, Douglass Montgomery, Heather Angel, Valerie Hopson

THE MYSTERY OF MARIE ROGET (1942, Universal)
Marie Roget—Maria Montez
Director—Phil Rosen
Leading Players—Patric Knowles, Maria Ouspenskaya, Lloyd Corrigan

THE MYSTERY OF MR. BERNARD BROWN (1921, Silent, GB, Stoll)
Bernard Brown—Pardoe Woodman
Director—Sinclair Hill

Leading Players—Ruby Miller, Clifford Heatherley, Annie Esmond

THE MYSTERY OF MR. WONG (1939, Monogram)
James Lee Wong—Boris Karloff
Director—William Nigh
Leading Players—Grant Withers, Dorothy Tree, Craig Reynolds

THE MYSTERY OF MR. X (1934, MGM)
Mr. X—Leonard Mudie
Director—Edgar Selwyn
Leading Players—Elizabeth Allen, Lewis Stone, Ralph Forbes

MYSTERY WOMAN (1935, Fox Film Corp.)
Margaret Benoit—Mona Barrie
Director—Eugene Forde
Leading Players—Gilbert Roland, John Halliday, Rod LaRocque

N

NADINE (1987, Tri-Star)
Nadine Hightower—Kim Basinger
Director—Robert Benton
Leading Players—Jeff Bridges, Rip Torn, Gwen Verdon, Glenne Headly

THE NAKED MAJA (1959, United Artists)
Duchess of Alba—Ava Gardner
Director—Henry Koster
Leading Players—Anthony Franciosa, Amedeo Nazzari, Carlo Rizzo

THE NAKED PREY (1966, Paramount)
The Man—Cornel Wilde
Director—Cornel Wilde
Leading Players—Gert van den Berg, Ken Gampu, Patrick Mynhardt

THE NAKED RUNNER (1967, Great Britain, Warners)
Sam Laker—Frank Sinatra
Director—Sidney J. Furie
Leading Players—Peter Vaughn, Darren Nesbitt, Nadia Gray

THE NAKED WITCH (1964, Mishkin)
Beth—Beth Porter
Director—Andy Milligan
Leading Players—Robert Burgos, Lee Forbes, Maggie Rogers

NAME THE WOMAN (1928, Silent, Columbia)
Florence—Anita Stewart
Director—Erle C. Kenton
Leading Players—Huntly Gordon, Gaston Glass, Chappell Dossett

NAN OF MUSIC MOUNTAIN (1917, Silent, Paramount)
Nan Morgan—Ann Little
Director—George H. Melford
Leading Players—Wallace Reid, Theodore Roberts, James Cruze

NANA (1934, United Artists)
Nana—Anna Sten
Director—Dorothy Arzner
Leading Players—Phillip Holmes, Lionel Atwill, Richard Bennett

NANCY COMES HOME (1918, Silent, Triangle)
Nancy Worthing—Myrtle Lind
Director—Jack Dillon
Leading Players—Jack Gilbert, George Pearce, Myrtle Rishell

NANCY DREW AND THE HIDDEN STAIRCASE (1939, Warners)
Nancy Drew—Bonita Granville
Director—William Clemens
Leading Players—Frankie Thomas, John Litel, Frank Orth

NANCY DREW—DETECTIVE (1938, Warners)
Nancy Drew—Bonita Granville
Director—William Clemens
Leading Players—John Litel, James Stephenson, Frankie Thomas

NANCY DREW—REPORTER (1939, Warners)
Nancy Drew—Bonita Granville
Director—William Clemens
Leading Players—John Litel, Frank Thomas, Mary Lee

NANCY DREW, TROUBLE SHOOTER (1939, Warners)
Nancy Drew—Bonita Granville
Director—William Clemens
Leading Players—Frankie Thomas, John Litel, Aldrich Bowker

NANCY FROM NOWHERE (1922, Silent, Paramount)
Nancy—Bebe Daniels
Director—Chester M. Franklin
Leading Players—Edward Sutherland, Vera Lewis, James Gordon

NANCY GOES TO RIO (1950, MGM)
Nancy Barklay—Jane Powell
Director—Robert Z. Leonard
Leading Players—Ann Sothern, Barry Sullivan, Carmen Miranda

NANCY STEELE IS MISSING (1937, 20th Century Fox)
Nancy Steele—June Lang
Director—George Marshall
Leading Players—Victor McLaglen, Walter Connolly, Peter Lorre

NANCY'S BIRTHRIGHT (1916, Silent, Mutual)
Nancy Levine—Edythe Sterling
Director—Murdock MacQuarrie
Leading Players—Murdock MacQuarrie, Norbert A. Myles, Millard K. Wilson

THE NANNY (1965, Great Britain, 20th Century Fox)
Nanny—Bette Davis
Director—Seth Holt
Leading Players—Wendy Craig, Jill Bennett, James Villers

NAPOLEON AND SAMANTHA (1972, Buena Vista)
Napoleon Wilson—Johnny Whitaker
Samantha—Jodie Foster
Director—Bernard McEveety
Leading Players—Michael Douglas, Will Geer, Arch Johnson

NASHVILLE REBEL (1966, American International)
Arlin Grove—Waylon Jennings
Director—Jay Sheridan
Leading Players—Tex Ritter, Mary Frann, Gordon Oas-Heim

NATIVE SON (1951, Classic)
Bigger Thomas—Richard Wright
Director—Pierre Chenal
Leading Players—Jean Wallace, Nicholas Joy, Gloria Madison

NATIVE SON (1986, Cinecom)
Bigger Thomas—Victor Love
Director—Jerrold Freedman
Leading Players—Carroll Baker, Akousua Busia, Matt Dillon, Art Evans

THE NATURAL (1984, Tri-Star)
Roy Hobbs—Robert Redford
Director—Barry Levinson
Leading Players—Robert Duvall, Glenn Close, Kim Basinger, Wilford Brimley, Barbara Hershey

NAUGHTY ARLETTE (1951, Great Britain, United Artists)
Arlette—Mai Zetterling
Director—Edmond T. Greville
Leading Players—Hugh Williams, Margot Grahame, Petulia Clark

NAUGHTY BABY (1929, Silent, First National)
Rosie McGill—Alice White
Director—Mervyn LeRoy
Leading Players—Jack Mulhall, Thelma Todd, Doris Dawson

NAUGHTY CINDERELLA (1933, Great Britain, Warners)
Brita Rasmusson—Winna Winfried
Director—John Daumery
Leading Players—John Stuart, Betty Huntley, Marion Gerth

THE NAUGHTY FLIRT (1931, Warners)
Kay Elliott—Alice White
Director—Edward Cline
Leading Players—Paul Page, Myrna Loy, Robert Agnew

NAUGHTY MARIETTA (1935, MGM)
"Marietta Franini" (Princess Marie)—Jeanette MacDonald
Director—W.S. Van Dyke II
Leading Players—Nelson Eddy, Frank Morgan, Elsa Lanchester, Douglas Dumbrille

NAUGHTY NANETTE (1927, Silent, R-C/FBO)
Nanette Pearson—Viola Dana
Director—James Leo Meehan
Leading Players—Patricia Palmer, Edward Brownell, Helen Foster

THE NAVAJO KID (1946, Producers Releasing Corp.)
Navajo Kid—Bob Steele
Director—Harry Fraser
Leading Players—Syd Saylor, Edward Cassidy, Caren Marsh

THE NAVIGATOR (1924, Silent, MGM)
Rollo Treadway—Buster Keaton
Director—Donald Crisp
Leading Players—Kathryn McGuire, Frederick Vroom, Noble Johnson

THE NAVIGATOR (1989, Australia, Circle)
Griffin—Hamish McFarlane
Director—Vincent Ward
Leading Players—Bruce Lyons, Chris Haywood, Marshall Napier

NAVY SEALS (1990, Orion)
Hawkins—Charlie Sheen
Curran—Michael Biehn
Director—Lewis Teague
Leading Players—Joanne Whalley-Kilmer, Rick Rossovich, Cyril O'Reilly, Bill Paxton

NAVY WIFE (1936, 20th Century Fox)
Vicky Blake—Claire Trevor
Director—Allan Dwan
Leading Players—Ralph Bellamy, Jane Darwell, Ben Lyon

NAVY WIFE (1956, Allied Artists)
Peg Blain—Joan Bennett
Director—Edward L. Bernds
Leading Players—Gary Merrill, Judy Nugent, Maurice Manson

NAZI AGENT (1942, MGM)
Otto Becker—Conrad Veidt
Director—Jules Dassin
Leading Players—Ann Ayars, Frank Reicher, Dorothy Tree

THE NEANDERTHAL MAN (1953, UA)
Dr. Cliff Groves—Robert Shayne
Director—E.A. Dupont
Leading Players—Richard Crane, Doris Merrick, Joyce Terry

THE NEAR LADY (1923, Silent, Universal)
Nora Schultz—Gladys Walton
Director—Herbert Blache
Leading Players—Jerry Gendron, Hank Mann, Kate Price

NEARLY EIGHTEEN (1943, Monogram)
Jane—Gale Storm
Director—Arthur Dreifuss
Leading Players—Rick Vallin, Bill Henry, Luis Alberni

THE NEBRASKAN (1953, Columbia)
Wade Harper—Phil Carey
Director—Fred F. Sears
Leading Players—Roberta Haynes, Wallace Ford, Lee Van Cleef

NECROMANCER (1989, Bonaire/Spectrum)
Lisa, the Necromancer—Lois Masten
Director—Dusty Nelson
Leading Players—Elizabeth Kaitan, Russ Tamblyn, John Tyler, Rhonda Durton

NED KELLY (1970, GB, UA)
Ned Kelly—Mick Jagger
Director—Tony Richardson
Leading Players—Allen Bickford, Geoff Gilmour, Mark McManus

NED MCCOBB'S DAUGHTER (1929, Silent, Pathe)
Carrie McCobb—Irene Rich
Ned McCobb—Theodore Roberts
Director—William J. Cowen
Leading Players—Robert Armstrong, George Barraud, Edward Hearn

THE NE'ER-DO-WELL (1916, Silent, Selig)
Kirk Anthony—Wheeler Oakman
Director—Colin Campbell
Leading Players—Kathlyn Williams. Harry Lonsdale, Frank Clark

NEGLECTED WIVES (1920, Silent, Wisteria)
The Wife—Anne Luther
Director—Burton King
Leading Players—E.J. Radcliffe, Al Hart, Ivy Ward

NEIGHBORS (1981, Columbia)
Earl Keese—John Belushi
Enid Keese—Kathryn Walker
Vic—Dan Aykroyd
Ramona—Cathy Moriarty
Director—John G. Avildsen
Leading Players—Igors Gavon, Dru-Ann Chukron, Tim Kazurnisky

NELL GWYN (1935, GB, UA)
Nell Gwyn—Anna Neagle
Director—Herbert Wilcox
Leading Players—Cedric Hardwicke, Jeanne de Casalis, Muriel George, Miles Malleson

NELL GWYNNE (1926, GB, Silent, First National)
Nell Gwynne—Dorothy Gish
Director—Herbert Wilcox
Leading Players—Randle Ayrton, Juliette Compton, Sydney Fairbrother

NELLIE, THE BEAUTIFUL CLOAK MODEL (1924, Silent, Cosmopolitan)
Nellie—Claire Windsor
Director—Emmett Flynn
Leading Players—Ann Hisle, Edmund Lowe, Mae Busch

NELLY'S VERSION (1983, GB, Mithras)
Nelly—Eileen Atkins
Director—Maurice Hatton
Leading Players—Anthony Bate, Barbara Jefford, Nicholas Ball

NELSON (1918, GB, Silent, Apex)
Horatio Nelson—Donald Calthrop
Director—Maurice Elvey
Leading Players—Malvina Longfellow, Ivy Close, Ernest Thesiger

NELSON (1926, GB, Silent, British Instructional)
Horatio Nelson—Cedric Hardwicke
Director—Walter Summers
Leading Players—Gertrude McCoy, Frank Perfitt, Frank Arlton

THE NELSON AFFAIR (1973, GB, Universal)
Lord Horatio Nelson—Peter Finch
Director—James Cellan Jones
Leading Players—Glenda Jackson, Michael Jayston, Anthony Quayle, Margaret Leighton

NEPTUNE'S DAUGHTER (1949, MGM)
Eve Barrett—Esther Williams
Director—Edward Buzzell
Leading Players—Red Skelton, Ricardo Montalban, Betty Garrett

THE NERVOUS WRECK (1926, Silent, Producers Distributing Corp.)
Henry Williams—Harrison Ford
Director—Scott Sidney
Leading Players—Phyllis Haver, Chester Conklin, Mack Swain

NEVADA (1927, Silent, Paramount)
Nevada—Gary Cooper
Director—John Waters
Leading Players—Thelma Todd, William Powell, Philip Strange

NEVADA (1936, Paramount)
Nevada—Larry "Buster" Crabbe
Director—Charles Barton
Leading Players—Kathleen Burke, Syd Saylor, Monte Blue

NEVADA (1944, RKO)
Jim "Nevada" Lacy—Robert Mitchum
Director—Edward Killy
Leading Players—Anne Jeffreys, Nancy Gates, Craig Reynolds

NEVADA SMITH (1966, Paramount)
Nevada Smith-Max Brand—Steve McQueen
Director—Henry Hathaway
Leading Players—Karl Malden, Brian Keith, Arthur Kennedy, Suzanne Pleshette, Raf Vallone

THE NEVADAN (1950, Columbia)
Andrew Barkley—Randolph Scott
Director—Gordon Douglas
Leading Players—Dorothy Malone, Forrest Tucker, Frank Faylen

NEVER WAVE AT A WAC (1952, RKO)
Jo McBain—Rosalind Russell
Director—Norman Z. McLeod
Leading Players—Paul Douglas, Marie Wilson, William Ching

THE NEW ADVENTURES OF GET-RICH-QUICK WALLINGFORD (1931, MGM)
J. Rufus Wallingford—William Haines
Director—Sam Wood
Leading Players—Jimmy Durante, Ernest Torrence, Leila Hyams

THE NEW ADVENTURES OF PIPPI LONGSTOCKING (1988, Columbia)
Pippi Longstocking—Tami Erin
Director—Ken Annakin
Leading Players—Eileen Brennan, Dennis Dugan, Dianne Hull, Dick Van Patten

NEW ADVENTURES OF TARZAN (1935, Republic)
Tarzan—Herman Brix (Bruce Bennett)
Directors—Edward Kull and W.F. McGaugh
Leading Players—Ula Holt, Frank Baker, Dale Walsh

THE NEW CENTURIONS (1972, Columbia)
Sgt. Kilvinsky—George C. Scott
Roy Fehler—Stacy Keach
Director—Richard Fleischer
Leading Players—Jane Alexander, Scott Wilson, Rosalind Cash

NEW CHAMPION (1925, Silent, Columbia)
Bob Nichols—William Fairbanks
Director—Reeves Eason
Leading Players—Edith Roberts, Lotus Thompson, Lloyd Whitlock

THE NEW CLOWN (1916, GB, Silent, Ideal)
Lord Cyril Garston—James Welch
Director—Fred Paul
Leading Players—Manora Thew, Richard Lindsay, Tom Coventry

NEW GIRL IN TOWN (1977, New World)
Jamie—Monica Gayle
Director—Gus Trikonis
Leading Players—Glenn Corbett, Roger Davis, Johnny Rodriguez

THE NEW INTERNS (1964, Columbia)
Dr. Alec Considine—Michael Callan
Dr. Lew Worship—Dean Jones
Dr. Tony Parelli—George Segal
Director—John Rich
Leading Players—Barbara Eden, Stefanie Powers, Inger Stevens, Kay Stevens, Telly Savalas

A NEW LIFE (1988, Paramount)
Steve Giardino—Alan Alda
Director—Alan Alda
Leading PLayers—Ann-Margret, Veronica Hamel, Hal Linden, John Shea

THE NEW TEACHER (1922, Silent, Fox Film Corp.)
Constance Bailey—Shirley Mason
Director—Joseph Franz
Leading Players—Allan Forrest, Earl Metcalf, Otto Hoffman

THE NEW YORK PEACOCK (1917, Silent, Fox Film Corp.)
Zena—Valeska Suratt
Director—Kenean Buel
Leading Players—Harry Hilliard, Eric Mayne, Alice Gale

NEW YORK'S FINEST (1988, Platinum)
Loretta Michaels—Jennifer Delora
Joy Sugarman—Ruth Collins
Carley Pointer—Heidi Paine
Director—Chuck Vincent
Leading Players—Scott Baker, Jane Hamilton, Alan Naggar

NEWMAN'S LAW (1974, Universal)
Vince Newman—George Peppard
Director—Richard Heffron
Leading Players—Roger Robinson, Eugene Roche, Gordon Pinsent

NEWS HOUNDS (1947, Monogram)
Slip Mahoney—Leo Gorcey
Sach—Huntz Hall
Director—William Beaudine
Leading Players—Bobby Jordan, Gabriel Dell, Billy Benedict

NEWSIES (1992, Buena Vista/Disney)
Jack Kelly/Francis Sullivan—Christian Bale
Director—Kenny Ortega
Leading Players—David Moscow, Luke Edwards, Max Casella, Bill Pullman, Ann-Margret, Robert Duvall

THE NEXT MAN (1976, Allied Artists)
Khalif Abdul-Muhsen—Sean Connery
Director—Richard C. Sarafian
Leading Players—Cornelia Sharpe, Albert Paulsen, Adolfo Celi

NEXT OF KIN (1989, Warner Brothers)
Truman Gates—Patrick Swayze

Briar Gates—Liam Neeson
Director—John Irvin
Leading Players—Adam Baldwin, Helen Hunt, Andreas Katsulas, Bill Paxton, Ben Stiller

NEXT TIME I MARRY (1938, RKO)
Nancy Fleming—Lucille Ball
Director—Garson Kanin
Leading Players—James Ellison, Lee Bowman, Granville Bates

NEXT TIME WE LOVE (1936, Universal)
Cicely Tyler—Margaret Sullavan
Christopher Tyler—James Stewart
Director—Edward H. Griffith
Leading Players—Ray Milland, Grant Mitchell, Anna Demetrio

NICE GIRL? (1941, Universal)
Jane Dana—Deanna Durbin
Director—William A. Seiter
Leading Players—Franchot Tone, Walter Brennan, Robert Stack

A NICE GIRL LIKE ME (1969, Great Britain, Avco Embassy)
Candida—Barbara Ferris
Director—Desmond Davis
Leading Players—Harry Andrews, Gladys Cooper, Bill Hinnant

NICE GIRLS DON'T EXPLODE (1987, New World)
April—Michelle Meyrink
Director—Chuck Martinez
Leading Players—Barbara Harris, William O'Leary, Wallace Shawn

NICE PEOPLE (1922, Silent, Paramount)
Theodora "Teddy" Gloucester—Bebe Daniels
Billy Wade—Wallace Reid
Director—William De Mille
Leading Players—Conrad Nagel, Julie Faye, Claire McDowell

NICE WOMAN (1932, Universal)
Bess Girard—Sidney Fox
Director—Edwin H. Knopf
Leading Players—Frances Dee, Alan Mowbray, Lucille Webster

NICHOLAS AND ALEXANDRA (1971, Great Britain, Columbia)
Nicholas—Michael Jayston
Alexandra—Janet Suzman
Director—Franklin J. Schaffner
Leading Players—Roderic Noble, Ania Marson, Lynne Frederick, Irene Worth, Fiona Fullerton, Harry Andrews, Tom Baker

NICHOLAS NICKLEBY (1947, Great Britain, Ealing)
Nicholas Nickleby—Derek Bond
Director—Alberto Cavalcanti
Leading Players—Cedric Hardwicke, Stanley Holloway, Alfred Drayton

NICK CARTER, MASTER DETECTIVE (1939, MGM)
Nick Carter—Walter Pidgeon
Director—Jacques Tourneur
Leading Players—Rita Johnson, Henry Hull, Stanley C. Ridges

THE NICKEL QUEEN (1971, Australia, Woomera)
Meg Blake—Googie Withers
Director—John McCallum
Leading Players—John Laws, Alfred Sandor, Ed Devereaux

NIGHT ANGEL (1990, Fries/Paragon Arts)
Lilith—Isa Anderson
Director—Dominique Othenin-Girard
Leading Players—Karen Black, Linden Ashby, Debra Feuer, Helen Martin, Doug Jones, Garry Hudson

THE NIGHT ANGEL (1931, Paramount)
Yula Martini—Nancy Carroll
Director—Edmund Goulding
Leading Players—Fredric March, Alan Hale, Alison Skipworth

THE NIGHT BRIDE (1927, Silent, Producers Distributing Corp.)
Cynthia Stockton—Marie Prevost
Director—E. Mason Hopper
Leading Players—Harrison Ford, Franklin Pangborn, Robert Edeson

NIGHT CALL NURSES (1974, New World)
Barbara—Patricia T. Byrne
Janis—Alana Collins
Sandra—Mittie Lawrence
Director—Jonathan Kaplan
Leading Players—Clint Kimbrough, Felton Perry, Stack Pierce

NIGHT CLUB GIRL (1944, Universal)
Eleanor—Vivian Austin
Director—Eddie Cline
Leading Players—Edward Norris, Maxie Rosenbloom, Judy Clark

NIGHT CLUB LADY (1932, Columbia)
Lola Carewe—Mayo Methot
Director—Irving Cummings
Leading Players—Adolphe Menjou, Skeets Gallagher, Ruthelma Stevens

NIGHT CLUB QUEEN (1934, Great Britain, Universal)
Mary Brown—Mary Clare
Director—Bernard Vorhaus
Leading Players—Lewis Casson, Jane Carr, George Carney

A NIGHT IN THE LIFE OF JIMMY REARDON (1988, 20th Century Fox)
Jimmy Reardon—River Phoenix
Director—William Richert
Leading Players—Meredith Salenger, Ann Magnuson, Ione Syke, Matthew L. Perry

THE NIGHT INVADER (1943, Great Britain, Warners)
Dick Marlow—David Farrar
Director—Herbert Mason
Leading Players—Anne Crawford, Carl Jaffe, Sybilla Binder

THE NIGHT MAYOR (1932, Columbia)
Bobby Kingston—Lee Tracy
Director—Ben Stoloff
Leading Players—Evalyn Knapp, Eugene Pallette, Warren Hymer

NIGHT MONSTER (1942, Universal)
Kurt Ingston—Ralph Morgan
Director—Ford Beebe
Leading Players—Bela Lugosi, Lionel Atwill, Leif Erickson, Irene Hervey

'NIGHT, MOTHER (1986, Universal)
Thelma Cates—Anne Bancroft

Director—Tom Moore
Leading Players—Sissy Spacek, Ed Berke, Carol Robbins

NIGHT NURSE (1931, Warners)
Lora Hart—Barbara Stanwyck
Director—William A. Wellman
Leading Players—Ben Lyon, Joan Blondell, Charles Winninger

THE NIGHT OF THE GENERALS (1967, Great Britain, Columbia)
Gen. Tanz—Peter O'Toole
Gen. Kahlenberge—Donald Pleasence
Gen. von Seidlitz-Gabler—Charles Gray
Director—Anatole Litvak
Leading Players—Omar Sharif, Tom Courtenay, Joanna Pettet, Philippe Noiret

THE NIGHT OF THE HUNTER (1955, United Artists)
Preacher Harry Powell—Robert Mitchum
Director—Charles Laughton
Leading Players—Shelley Winters, Lillian Gish, Billy Chapin, Sally Jane Bruce

NIGHT OF THE WARRIOR (1991, Trimark)
Miles Keane—Lorenzo Lamas
Director—Rafal Zielinski
Leading Players—Anthony Geary, Kathleen Kinmont, Ken Foree, Felicity Waterman, Arlene Dahl

NIGHT PEOPLE (1954, 20th Century Fox)
Col. Van Dyke—Gregory Peck
Director—Nunnally Johnson
Leading Players—Broderick Crawford, Anita Bjork, Rita Gam, Buddy Ebsen, Jill Esmond

THE NIGHT PORTER (1974, Avco Embassy)
Max—Dirk Bogarde
Director—Liliana Cavani
Leading Players—Charlotte Rampling, Philippe Leroy, Gabriele Ferzetti

THE NIGHT RUNNER (1957, Universal)
Roy Turner—Ray Danton
Director—Abner Biberman
Leading Players—Colleen Miller, Willis Bouchey, Merry Anders

THE NIGHT STALKER (1987, Chrystie-Striker/Almi)
Sommers—Robert Z'dar
Director—Max Kleven
Leading Players—Charles Napier, Michelle Reese, Katherine Kelly Lang

THE NIGHT THEY ROBBED BIG BERTHA'S (1975, Scotia American)
Big Bertha—Hetty Galen
Director—Peter Kares
Leading Players—Robert Nichols, Doug Hale, Gray Allen

NIGHT WAITRESS (1936, RKO)
Helen Roberts—Margot Grahame
Director—Lew Landers
Leading Players—Gordon Jones, Vinton Haworth, Marc Lawrence

THE NIGHT WALKER (1964, Universal)
Irene Trent—Barbara Stanwyck
Director—William Castle

Leading Players—Robert Taylor, Lloyd Bochner, Hayden Rorke

A NIGHTMARE ON ELM STREET: THE DREAM MASTER (1988, New Line)
Freddy Krueger—Robert Englund
Director—Renny Harlin
Leading Players—Rodney Eastman, Danny Hassel, Andras Jones, Tuesday Knight, Toy Newkirk

NIJINSKY (1980, Great Britain, Paramount)
Vaslav Nijinsky—George De La Pena
Director—Herbert Ross
Leading Players—Alan Bates, Leslie Browne, Alan Badel

NINA, THE FLOWER GIRL (1917, Silent, Triangle)
Nina—Bessie Love
Director—Lloyd Ingraham
Leading Players—Elmer Clifton, Bert Hadley, Loyola O'Connor

NINE GIRLS (1944, Columbia)
Mary O'Ryan—Evelyn Keyes
Jane Peters—Jinx Falkenberg
Paula Canfield—Anita Louise
Roberta Holloway—Leslie Brooks
Eve Sharon—Lynn Merrick
"Butch" Hendricks—Jeff Donnell
Alice Blake—Nina Foch
"Tennessee" Collingwood—Shirley Mills
Shirley Berke—Marcia Mae Jones
Director—Leigh Jason
Leading Players—Ann Harding, Willard Robertson, William Demarest

NINETEEN AND PHYLLIS (1920, Silent, First National)
Phyllis Laurin—Clara Horton
Andrew Jackson Cavanaugh—Charles Ray
Director—Joseph De Grasse
Leading Players—George Nichols, Cora Drew, Frank Norcross

NINOTCHKA (1939, MGM)
Lena "Ninotchka" Yakushova—Greta Garbo
Director—Ernst Lubitsch
Leading Players—Melvyn Douglas, Ina Claire, Sig Rumann, Felix Bressart. Alexander Granach

THE NITWITS (1935, RKO)
Johnnie—Bert Wheeler
Newton—Robert Woolsey
Director—George Stevens
Leading Players—Fred Keating, Betty Grable, Evelyn Brent

NO LOVE FOR JOHNNIE (1961, GB, Rank)
Johnnie Byrne—Peter Finch
Director—Ralph Thomas
Leading Players—Stanley Holloway, Mary Peach, Donald Pleasence

NO MAN OF HER OWN (1933, Paramount)
Connie Randall—Carole Lombard
Director—Wesley Ruggles
Leading Players—Clark Gable, Dorothy Mackaill, Grant Mitchell

NO MAN OF HER OWN (1950, Paramount)
Helen Ferguson—Barbara Stanwyck
Director—Mitchell Leisen

Leading Players—John Lund, Jane Cowl, Phyllis Thaxter, Lyle Bettger

NO MOTHER TO GUIDE HER (1923, Silent, Fox Film Corp.)
Kathleen Pearson—Dolores Rousse
Director—Charles Horan
Leading Players—Genevieve Tobin, John Webb Dillon, Lolita Robertson

NO, NO NANETTE (1930, First National)
Nanette—Bernice Claire
Director—Clarence Badger
Leading Players—Alexander Gray, Lucien Littlefield, Louise Fazenda

NO, NO NANETTE (1940, RKO)
Nanette—Anna Neagle
Director—Herbert Wilcox
Leading Players—Richard Carlson, Victor Mature, Roland Young, Helen Broderick

NO ORCHIDS FOR MISS BLANDISH (1948, GB, Renown)
Miss Blandish—Linden Travers
Director—St. John Legh Clowes
Leading Players—Jack La Rue, Hugh McDermott, Walter Crisham

NO PLACE FOR A LADY (1943, Columbia)
June Terry—Margaret Lindsay
Director—James Hogan
Leading Players—William Gargan, Phyllis Brooks, Dick Purcell

NO PLACE FOR JENNIFER (1950, GB, Pathe)
Jennifer—Janette Scott
Director—Henry Cass
Leading Players—Leo Genn, Rosamund John , Beatrice Campbell

NO ROOM FOR THE GROOM (1952, Universal)
Alvah Morrell—Tony Curtis
Director—Douglas Sirk
Leading Players—Piper Laurie, Don DeFore, Spring Byingtom

NO SAD SONGS FOR ME (1950, Columbia)
Mary Scott—Margaret Sullavan
Director—Rudolph Mate
Leading Players—Wendell Corey, Viveca Lindfors, Natalie Wood

NOAH'S ARK (1928, Warner Brothers)
Noah—Paul McAllister
Director—Michael Curtiz
Leading Players—Dolores Costello, George O'Brien, Noah Beery

NOBODY'S BRIDE (1923, Silent, Universal)
Doris Standish—Edna Murphy
Director—Herbert Blache
Leading Players—Herbert Rawlinson, Alice Lake, Harry Van Meter

NOBODY'S FOOL (1921, Silent, Universal)
Polly Gordon—Marie Prevost
Director—King Baggot
Leading Players—Helen Harris, Vernon Snively, Harry Myers

NOBODY'S FOOL (1936, Universal)
Will Wright—Edward Everett Horton

Director—Arthur Greville Collins
Leading Players—Glenda Farrell, Cesar Romero, Frank Conroy

NOBODY'S FOOL (1986, Island Pictures)
Cassie—Rosanna Arquette
Director—Evelyn Purcell
Leading Players—Eric Roberts, Mare Winningham, Jim Youngs

NOBODY'S KID (1921, Silent, R-C Pictures)
Mary Cary—Mae Marsh
Director—Howard Hickman
Leading Players—Kathleen Kirkham, Anne Schaefer, Maxine Elliott Hicks

NOBODY'S WIDOW (1927, Silent, Producers Distributing Corp.)
Roxanna Smith—Leatrice Joy
Director—Donald Crisp
Leading Players—Charles Ray, Phyllis Haver, David Butler

NO-GUN MAN (1924, Silent, FBO)
Robert Jerome Vincent—Lefty Flynn
Director—Harry Garson
Leading Players—William Jack Quinn, Gloria Grey, Raymond Turner

NOOSE FOR A LADY (1953, GB, Anglo-Amalgamated)
Margaret Allan—Pamela Allan
Director—Wolf Rilla
Leading Players—Dennis Price, Rona Anderson, Ronald Howard

NORA PRENTISS (1947, Warner Brothers)
Nora Prentiss—Ann Sheridan
Director—Vincent Sherman
Leading Players—Kent Smith, Bruce Bennett, Robert Alda

NORAH O'NEALE (1934, GB, DuWorld)
Norah O'Neale—Nancy Burne
Director—Brian Desmond Hurst
Leading Players—Lester Matthews, Molly Lamont, Patric Knowles

NORMA RAE (1979, 20th Century Fox)
Norma Rae—Sally Field
Director—Martin Ritt
Leading Players—Beau Bridges, Ron Leibman, Pat Hingle, Barbara Baxley

NORMAN CONQUEST (1953, GB, Lippert)
Norman Conquest—Tom Conway
Director—Bernard Knowles
Leading Players—Eva Bartok, Joy Shelton, Sidney James

NORMAN...IS THAT YOU? (1976, MGM/UA)
Norman Chambers—Michael Warren
Director—George Schlatter
Leading Players—Redd Foxx, Pearl Bailey, Dennis Dugan

THE NORSEMAN (1978, American International)
Thorvald—Lee Majors
Director—Charles B. Pierce
Leading Players—Cornel Wilde, Mel Ferrer, Jack Elam

NORTHWEST MOUNTED POLICE (1940, Paramount)
Sgt. Jim Brett—Preston Foster
Constable McDuff—Robert Preston
Director—Cecil B. DeMille

Leading Players—Gary Cooper, Madeleine Carroll, Paulette Goddard, George Bancroft, Lynne Overman, Akim Tamiroff

NORWOOD (1970, Paramount)
Norwood Pratt—Glen Campbell
Director—Jack Haley, Jr.
Leading Players—Kim Darby, Joe Namath, Carol Lynley

NOT AS A STRANGER (1955, UA)
Lucas Marsh—Robert Mitchum
Director—Stanley Kramer
Leading Players—Olivia de Havilland, Frank Sinatra, Gloria Grahame, Broderick Crawford, Charles Bickford

NOT MY SISTER (1916, Silent, Triangle)
Grace Tyler—Bessie Barriscale
Ruth Tyler—Alice Taaffe
Director—Charles Giblyn
Leading Players—William Desmond, Franklin Ritchie, Louise Brownell

NOT OF THIS EARTH (1988, Concorde)
The Alien—Arthur Roberts
Director—Jim Wynorski
Leading Players—Traci Lords, Lenny Juliano, Ace Mask, Roger Lodge

NOT QUITE A LADY (1928, GB, Silent, Wardour)
Ethel Borridge—Mabel Poulton
Director—Thomas Bentley
Leading Players—Janet Alexander, Barbara Gott, Maurice Braddell

NOT SO DUMB (1930, MGM)
Dulcy—Marion Davies
Director—King Vidor
Leading Players—Elliott Nugent, Raymond Hackett, Franklin Pangborn

NOT SO DUSTY (1936, GB, RKO)
Dusty Gray—Wally Patch
Director—Maclean Rogers
Leading Players—Gus McNaughton, Muriel George, Phil Ray

NOT SO DUSTY (1956, GB, Eros)
Dusty—Bill Owen
Director—Maclean Rogers
Leading Players—Joy Nichols, Leslie Dwyer, Harold Berens

NOT WITH MY WIFE, YOU DON'T (1966, Warner Brothers)
Tom Ferris—Tony Curtis
Julie Ferris—Virna Lisi
Tank Martin—George C. Scott
Director—Norman Panama
Leading Players—Carroll O'Connor, Richard Eastham, Eddie Ryder

NOT WITHOUT MY DAUGHTER (1991, MGM/Pathe)
Betty Mahmoody—Sally Field
Mahtob Mahmoody—Sheila Rosenthal
Director—Brian Gilbert
Leading Players—Alfred Molina, Roshan Seth, Sarah Badel, Mony Rey

NOTHING BUT A MAN (1964, Cinema V)
Duff Anderson—Ivan Dixon
Director—Michael Roemer
Leading Players—Abby Lincoln, Gloria Foster, Julius Harris

NOTHING IN COMMON (1986, Tri-Star)
David Basner—Tom Hanks
Max Basner—Jackie Gleason
Director—Garry Marshall
Leading Players—Eva Marie Saint, Hector Elizondo, Barry Corbin, Bess Armstrong

NOTORIOUS (1946, RKO)
Alicia Huberman—Ingrid Bergman
Director—Alfred Hitchcock
Leading Players—Cary Grant, Claude Rains, Louis Calhern, Mme. Konstantin, Ivan Triesault

THE NOTORIOUS CLEOPATRA (1970, Boxoffice International)
Cleopatra—Sonora
Director—A.P. Stootsberry
Leading Players—Johnny Rocco, Jay Edwards, Dixie Donovan

A NOTORIOUS GENTLEMAN (1935, Universal)
Kirk Allen—Charles Bickford
Director—Edward Laemmle
Leading Players—Sidney Blackmer, Helen Vinson, Onslow Stevens

A NOTORIOUS GENTLEMAN (1945, GB, Rank)
Vivian Kenway—Rex Harrison
Director—Sidney Gilliat
Leading Players—Lili Palmer, Godfrey Tearle, Griffith Jones

THE NOTORIOUS LADY (1927, Silent, First National)
Mary Marlowe—Barbara Bedford
Director—King Baggot
Leading Players—Lewis Stone, Ann Rork, Earl Metcalfe

THE NOTORIOUS LANDLADY (1962, Columbia)
Carlye Hardwicke—Kim Novak
Director—Richard Quine
Leading Players—Jack Lemmon, Fred Astaire, Lionel Jeffries

THE NOTORIOUS LONE WOLF (1946, Columbia)
Michael Lanyard—Gerald Mohr
Director—D. Ross Lederman
Leading Players—Janis Carter, Eric Blore, John Abbott

THE NOTORIOUS LISLE (1920, Silent, First National)
Gaenor Lisle—Katherine MacDonald
Director—James Young
Leading Players—Nigel Barrie, Margaret Campbell, Ernest Joy

THE NOTORIOUS MR. MONKS (1958, Republic)
Benjamin Monks—Paul Fix
Director—Joe Kane
Leading Players—Vera Ralston, Don Kelly, Leo Gordon

THE NOTORIOUS MRS. CARRICK (1924, GB, Silent, Stoll)
Sybil Tegarthen—Disa
Director—George Ridgwell
Leading Players—Cameron Carr, A.B. Imeson, Sydney Folker

THE NOTORIOUS SOPHIE LANG (1934, Paramount)
Sophie Lang—Gertrude Michael
Director—Ralph Murphy

Leading Players—Paul Cavanaugh, Arthur Byron, Alison
Skipworth

NOW, VOYAGER (1942, Warner Brothers)
Charlotte Vale—Bette Davis
Director—Irving Rapper
Leading Players—Paul Henreid, Claude Rains, Gladys Cooper,
Bonita Granville

NOW YOU SEE HIM, NOW YOU DON'T (1972, Buena Vista)
Dexter Riley—Kurt Russell
Director—Robert Butler
Leading Players—Cesar Romero, Joe Flynn, Jim Backus

NUGGET NELL (1919, Silent, Paramount)
Nugget Nell—Dorothy Gish
Director—Frank Borzage
Leading PLayers—David Butler, Raymond Cannon, Regina Sarle

NUMBER ONE (1969, UA)
Ron "Cat" Catlan—Charlton Heston
Director—Tom Gries
Leading Players—Jessica Walter, Bruce Dern, John Randolph

NUMBER ONE (1984, GB, Stageforum)
Harry "Flash" Gordon— Bob Geldof
Director—Les Blair
Leading Players—Mel Smith, Alison Steadman, P. H. Moriarty

THE NUN AND THE SERGEANT (1962, UA)
Sgt. McGrath—Robert Webber
Nun—Anna Sten
Director—Frank Adreon
Leading Players—Leo Gordon, Hari Rhodes, Robert Easton

NUNS ON THE RUN (1990, GB, 20th Centruy Fox/Handmade)
Sister Euphemia (Brian Hope)—Eric Idle
Sister Inviolata (Charlie)—Robbie Coltrane
Director—Jonathan Lynn
Leading Players—Camille Coduri, Janet Suzman, Doris Hare,
Lila Kaye, Robert Patterson

THE NUN'S STORY (1959, Warner Brothers)
Sister Luke (Gabrielle Van Der Mal)—Audrey Hepburn
Director—Fred Zinnemann
Leading Players—Peter Finch, Edith Evans, Peggy Ashcroft,
Dean Jagger, Mildred Dunnock

NURSE EDITH CAVELL (1939, RKO)
Nurse Edith Cavell—Anna Neagle
Director—Herbert Wilcox
Leading Players—Edna May Oliver, George Sanders, May
Robson, Zasu Pitts, H.B. Warner

NURSE FROM BROOKLYN (1938, Universal)
Elizabeth Thomas—Sally Eilers
Director—S. Sylvan Simon
Leading Players—Paul Kelly, Larry Blake, Maurice Murphy

NURSE MARJORIE (1920, Silent, Realart)
Nurse Marjorie—Mary Miles Minter
Director—William Desmond Taylor
Leading Players—Clyde Fillmore, George Periolat, Mollie
McConnell

NURSE ON WHEELS (1964, GB, Anglo Amalgamated)
Joanna Jones—Juliet Mills
Director—Gerald Thomas
Leading Players—Ronald Lewis, Joan Sims, Athene Seyler

THE NURSE'S SECRET (1941, Warner Brothers)
Ruth Adams—Lee Patrick
Director—Noel M. Smith
Leading Players—Regis Toomey, Julie Bishop, Ann Edmonds

THE NUT (1921, Silent, UA)
Charlie Jackson—Douglas Fairbanks
Director—Theodore Reed
Leading Players—Marguerite De La Motte, William Lowery,
Gerald Pring

THE NUTTY PROFESSOR (1963, Paramount)
Prof. Julius Ferris Kelp—Jerry Lewis
Director—Jerry Lewis
Leading Players—Stella Stevens, Del Moore, Kathleen Freeman

O

O LUCKY MAN! (1973, GB, Warner Brothers)
Mick Travis—Malcolm McDowell
Director—Lindsay Anderson
Leading Players—Ralph Richardson, Rachel Roberts, Arthur
Lowe

O, MY DARLING CLEMENTINE (1943, Republic)
Clementine—Lorna Gray
Director—Frank McDonald
Leading Players—Roy Acuff, Harry "Pappy" Chesire, Isabel
Randolph

O.C. AND STIGGS (1987, MGM/UA)
Oliver Cromwell "O.C." Ogilvie—Daniel H. Jenkins
Mark Stiggs—Neill Barry
Director—Robert Altman
Leading Players—Paul Dooley, Jane Curtin, Jon Cryer, Ray
Walston

OBLIGING YOUNG LADY (1941, RKO)
Bridget Potter—Joan Carroll
Director—Richard Wallace
Leading Players—Edmond O'Brien, Ruth Warrick, Robert Smith,
Eve Arden

OCCASIONALLY YOURS (1920, Silent, R-C Pictures)
Bruce Sands—Lew Cody
Director—James W. Horne
Leading Players—Betty Blythe, Elinor Fair, J. Barney Sherry

OCEAN'S ELEVEN (1960, Warner Brothers)
Danny Ocean—Frank Sinatra
Sam Harmon—Dean Martin
Josh Howard—Sammy Davis, Jr.
Jimmy Foster—Peter Lawford
Anthony Bergdorf—Richard Conte

"Mushy" O'Conners—Joey Bishop
Roger Corneal—Henry Silva
Vincent Massler—Buddy Lester
"Curly" Steffens—Richard Benedict
Peter Rheimer—Norman Fell
Louis Jackson—Clem Harvey
Director—Lewis Milestone
Leading Players—Angie Dickinson, Cesar Romero, Patrice Wymore, Ilka Chase, George Raft, Shirley MacLaine

THE OCTOBER MAN (1948, GB, Eagle-Lion)
Jim Ackland—John Mills
Director—Roy Baker
Leading Players—Joan Greenwood, Edward Chapman, Kay Walsh

OCTOPUSSY (1983, GB, MGM/UA)
Octopussy—Maud Adams
Director—John Glen
Leading Players—Roger Moore, Louis Jourdan, Kristina Wayborn

THE ODD COUPLE (1968, Paramount)
Felix Ungar—Jack Lemmon
Oscar Madison—Walter Matthau
Director—Gene Saks
Leading Players—John Fiedler, Herb Edelman, David Sheiner, Larry Haines, Monica Evans, Carole Shelley

ODD MAN OUT (1947, GB, GFD)
Johnny McQueen—James Mason
Director—Carol Reed
Leading Players—Robert Newton, Kathleen Ryan, Robert Beatty, William Hartnell, Fay Compton

ODE TO BILLY JOE (1976, Warner Brothers)
Billy Joe McAllister—Robby Benson
Director—Max Baer
Leading Players—Glynnis O'Connor, Joan Hotchkis, Sandy McPeak

ODETTE (1951, GB, UA)
Odette—Anna Neagle
Director—Herbert Wilcox
Leading Players—Trevor Howard, Marius Goring, Peter Ustinov

ODONGO (1956, GB, Columbia)
Odongo—Juma
Director—John Gilling
Leading Players—Rhonda Fleming, Macdonald Carey, Eleanor Summerfield

OEDIPUS REX (1957, Canada, Motion Pictures)
Oedipus—Douglas Campbell
Director—Tyrone Guthrie
Leading Players—Douglas Rain, Eric House, Eleanor Stuart, Robert Goodier, Donald Davis

OEDIPUS THE KING (1968, GB, Universal)
Oedipus—Christopher Plummer
Director—Philip Saville
Leading Players—Lilli Palmer, Richard Johnson, Orson Welles, Cyril Cusack, Roger Livesey

OF MICE AND MEN (1939, UA)
Lennie—Lon Chaney, Jr.

George—Burgess Meredith
Director—Lewis Milestone
Leading Players—Betty Field, Charles Bickford, Roman Bohnen, Bob Steele, Noah Beery, Jr.

OF MICE AND MEN (1992, MGM)
Lennie—John Malkovich
George—Gary Sinise
Director—Gary Sinise
Leading Players—Ray Walston, Casey Siesmasko, Sherilyn Fenn, John Terry, Richard Riehle

THE OFFICE GIRL (1932, GB, RKO)
Susie Surster—Renate Muller
Director—Victor Saville
Leading Players—Jack Hulbert, Owen Nares, Morris Harvey

THE OFFICE WIFE (1930, Warner Brothers)
Anne Murdock—Dorothy Mackaill
Director—Lloyd Bacon
Leading Players—Lewis Stone, Hobart Bosworth, Blanche Frederici, Joan Blondell

AN OFFICER AND A GENTLEMAN (1982, Paramount)
Zack Mayo—Richard Gere
Director—Taylor Hackford
Leading Players—Debra Winger, David Keith, Louis Gossert, Jr., Robert Loggia, Lisa Blount

THE OFFICER AND THE LADY (1941, Columbia)
Helen Reagan—Rochelle Hudson
Bob Conlon—Bruce Bennett
Director—Sam White
Leading Players—Roger Pryor, Richard Fiske, Sidney Blackmer

OFFICER O'BRIEN (1930, Pathe)
Bill O'Brien—William Boyd
Director—Tay Garnett
Leading Players—Ernest Torrence, Dorothy Sebastian, Russell Gleason

THE OFFSPRING (1987, Conquest/TMS)
Katherine White—Martine Beswick
Director—Jeff Burr
Leading Players—Vincent Price, Clu Gulager, Terry Kiser, Harry Caesar, Rosalind Cash, Susan Tyrrell

OH BOY! (1938, GB, Associated British Films)
Percy Flower—Albert Burdon
Director—Albert de Courville
Leading Players—Mary Lawson, Bernard Nedell, Jay Laurier

OH DAD, POOR DAD, MAMA'S HUNG YOU IN THE CLOSET AND I'M FEELIN' SO SAD
(1967, Paramount)
Mme. Rosepettle—Rosalind Russell
Jonathan Rosepettle—Robert Morse
Dad Rosepettle—Jonathan Winters
Directors—Richard Quine & Alexander Mackendrick
Leading Players—Barbara Harris, Hugh Griffith, Lionel Jeffries

OH DADDY! (1935, GB, Gaumont)
Lord Pye—Leslie Henson
Director—Graham Cutts
Leading Players—Frances Day, Robertson Hare, Barry MacKay

OH, GOD! (1977, Warner Brothers)
God—George Burns
Director—Carl Reiner
Leading Players—John Denver, Teri Garr, Ralph Bellamy, Barry Sullivan

OH GOD! BOOK II (1980, Warner Brothers)
God—George Burns
Director—Gilbert Cates
Leading Players—Suzanne Pleshette, David Birney, John Louis

OH GOD! YOU DEVIL (1984, Warner Brothers)
God—George Burns
Director—Paul Bogart
Leading Players—John Doolittle, Julie Lloyd, Ian Giatti

OH, JOHNNY (1919, Silent, Goldwyn)
Johnny Burke—Louis Bennison
Director—Ira M. Lowry
Leading Players—Alphonse Ethier, Edward Roseman, John Daly Murphy

OH JOHNNY, HOW YOU CAN LOVE (1940, Universal)
Johnny Sandham- Tom Brown
Director—Charles Lamont
Leading Players—Peggy Moran, Allen Jenkins, Donald Meek

OH, KAY (1928, Silent, First National)
Lady Kay Rutfield—Colleen Moore
Director—Mervyn LeRoy
Leading Players—Lawrence Gray, Alan Hale, Ford Sterling

OH, LADY, LADY (1920, Silent, Realart)
May Barber—Bebe Daniels
Director—Maurice Campbell
Leading Players—Harrison Ford, Walter Hiers, Charlotte Woods

OH, MEN! OH, WOMEN! (1957, 20th Century Fox)
Arthur Turner—Dan Dailey
Mildred Turner—Ginger Rogers
Director—Nunnally Johnson
Leading Players—David Niven, Barbara Rush, Tony Randall

OH, MR. PORTER (1937, GB, GFD/Gainsborough)
William Porter—Will Hay
Director—Marcel Varnel
Leading Players—Moore Marriott, Graham Moffatt, Sebastian Smith

OH ROSALINDA (1956, GB, Pathe)
Rosalinda—Ludmilla Tcherina
Directors—Michael Powell & Emeric Pressburger
Leading Players—Michael Redgrave, Anton Walbrook, Mel Ferrer

OH, WHAT A NURSE! (1926, Silent, Warner Brothers)
June Harrison—Patsy Ruth Miller
Director—Charles Reisner
Leading Players—Sydney Chaplin, Gayne Whitman, Matthew Betz

OH, YOU BEAUTIFUL DOLL (1949, 20th Century Fox)
Doris Breitenbach—June Haver
Director—John M. Stahl
Leading Players—Mark Stevens, S.Z. "Cuddles" Sakall, Charlotte Greenwood, Gale Robbins

O'HARA'S WIFE (1983, Davis-Panzer)
Bob O'Hara—Ed Asner
Harry O'Hara—Mariette Hartley
Director—William S. Bartman
Leading Players—Jodie Foster, Perry Lang, Tom Bosley

OKAY BILL (1971, Four Star Excelsior)
Bill Thronberry—Bob Brady
Director—John Avildsen
Leading Players—Nancy Salmon, Gordon Felio, Roz Kelly

THE OKLAHOMA KID (1929, Silent, Syndicate Releasing Co.)
The Kid—Bob Custer
Director—J.P. McGowan
Leading Players—Henry Roquemore, Vivian Ray, Tommy Bay

THE OKLAHOMA KID (1939, Warner Brothers)
Jim Kincaid—James Cagney
Director—Lloyd Bacon
Leading Players—Humphrey Bogart, Rosemary Lane, Donald Crisp

THE OKLAHOMA WOMAN (1956, Sunset)
Marie "Oklahoma" Saunders—Peggie Castle
Director—Roger Corman
Leading Players—Richard Denning, Tudor Owen, Martin Kingsley

THE OKLAHOMAN (1957, Allied Artists)
Dr. John Brighton—Joel McCrea
Director—Francis D. Lyon
Leading Players—Barbara Hale, Brad Dexter, Gloria Talbott

OLD ACQUAINTANCE (1943, Warner Brothers)
Kitty Marlowe—Bette Davis
Millie Drake—Miriam Hopkins
Director—Vincent Sherman
Leading Players—Gig Young, John Loder, Dolores Moran, Philip Reed

OLD BILL AND SON (1940, GB, GFD)
Old Bill Busby—Morland Graham
Young Bill Busby—John Mills
Director—Ian Dalrymple
Leading Players—Mary Clare, Renee Houston, Rene Ray

OLD BILL THROUGHT THE AGES (1924, GB, Silent, Ideal)
Old Bill—Syd Walker
Director—Thomas Bentley
Leading Players—Arthur Cleave, Jack Denton, Gladys Folliott

OLD BONES OF THE RIVER (1938, GB, GFD)
Prof. Benjamin Tibbetts—Will Hay
Director—Marcel Varnel
Leading Players—Moore Marriott, Graham Moffatt, Robert Adams

OLD BOYFRIENDS (1979, Avco Embassy)
Jeff Turrin—Richard Jordan
Eric Katz—John Belushi
Director—Joan Tewkesbury
Leading Players—Talia Shire, Keith Carradine, John Houseman

OLD DRACULA (1975, GB, American International)
Count Dracula—David Niven
Director—Clive Donner

Leading Players—Teresa Graves, Peter Bayliss, Jennie Linden

OLD ENGLISH (1930, Warner Brothers)
Sylvanus Heythorp—George Arliss
Director—Alfred E. Green
Leading Players—Leon Janney, Doris Lloyd, Betty Lawford

OLD ENOUGH (1984, Orion Classics)
Lonnie Sloan—Sarah Boyd
Director—Marisa Silver
Leading Players—Rainbow Harvest, Neill Barry, Danny Aiello

OLD EXPLORERS (1990, Taurus/River Road)
Warner Watney—Jose Ferrer
Leinen Roth—James Whitmore
Director—William Pohland
Leading Players—Jeffrey Gadbois, Caroline Kaiser, William Warfield

AN OLD FASHIONED BOY (1920, Silent, Paramount)
David Warrington—Charles Ray
Director—Jerome Storm
Leading Players—Ethel Shannon, Alfred Allen, Wade Boteler

AN OLD-FASHIONED GIRL (1948, Eagle-Lion)
Polly Milton—Gloria Jean
Director—Arthur Dreifuss
Leading Players—Jimmy Lydon, John Hubbard, Frances Rafferty

OLD GRINGO (1989, Columbia)
Amboise Bierce—Gregory Peck
Director—Luis Puenzo
Leading Players—Jane Fonda, Jimmy Smits, Patricio Contreras, Jenny Gago, Jim Metzler

OLD HUTCH (1936, MGM)
Hutch—Wallace Beery
Director—J. Walter Ruben
Leading Players—Eric Linden, Cecilia Parker, Elizabeth Patterson

OLD IRON (1938, GB, British Lion)
Sir Henry Woodstock—Tom Walls
Director—Tom Walls
Leading Players—Eva Moore, Cecil Parker, Richard Ainley

THE OLD MAID (1939, Warner Brothers)
Charlotte Lovell—Bette Davis
Director—Edmund Goulding
Leading Players—Miriam Hopkins, George Brent, Jane Bryan, Donald Crisp, Louise Fazenda

THE OLD MAN AND THE SEA (1958, Warner Brothers)
The Old Man—Spencer Tracy
Director—John Sturges
Leading Players—Felipe Pazos, Harry Bellaver, Donald Diamond

OLD MOTHER RILEY (1937, GB, Butchers)
Mrs. Riley—Arthur Lucan
Director—Oswald Mitchell
Leading Players—Kitty McShane, Barbara Everest, Patrick Ludlow

OLD MOTHER RILEY (1952, GB, Renown)
Mrs. Riley—Arthur Lucan
Director—John Harlow

Leading Players—Kitty McShane, Chili Bouchier, Willer Neal

OLD MOTHER RILEY AT HOME (1945, GB, Anglo-American)
Mrs. Riley—Arthur Lucan
Director—Oswald Mitchell
Leading Players—Kitty McShane, Freddie Forbes, Richard George

OLD MOTHER RILEY, DETECTIVE (1943, GB, Anglo-American)
Mrs. Riley—Arthur Lucan
Director—Lance Comfort
Leading Players—Kitty McShane, Ivan Brandt, Owen Reynolds

OLD MOTHER RILEY, HEADMISTRESS (1950, GB, Renown)
Mrs. Riley—Arthur Lucan
Director—John Harlow
Leading Players—Kitty McShane, Enid Hewitt, Jenny Mathot

OLD MOTHER RILEY IN BUSINESS (1940, GB, Anglo-American)
Mrs. Riley—Arthur Lucan
Director—John Baxter
Leading Players—Kitty McShane, Cyril Chamberlain, Charles Victor

OLD MOTHER RILEY IN PARIS (1938, GB, Butchers)
Mrs. Riley—Arthur Lucan
Director—Oswald Mitchell
Leading Players—Kitty McShane, Jerry Verno, Magda Kun

OLD MOTHER RILEY IN SOCIETY (1940, GB, Anglo-American)
Mrs. Riley—Arthur Lucan
Director—John Baxter
Leading Players—Kitty McShane, John Stuart, Dennis Wyndham

OLD MOTHER RILEY JOINS UP (1939, GB, Anglo-American)
Mrs. Riley—Arthur Lucan
Director—Maclean Rogers
Leading Players—Kitty McShane, Bruce Seton, Martita Hunt

OLD MOTHER RILEY MP (1939, GB, Butchers)
Mrs. Riley—Arthur Lucan
Director—Oswald Mitchell
Leading Players—Kitty McShane, Torin Thatcher, Henry Longhurst

OLD MOTHER RILEY OVERSEAS (1943, GB, Anglo-American)
Mrs. Riley—Arthur Lucan
Director—Oswald Mitchell
Leading Players—Kitty McShane, Morris Harvey, Fred Kitchen, Jr.

OLD MOTHER RILEY'S CIRCUS (1941, GB, Anglo-Amalgamated)
Mrs. Riley—Arthur Lucan
Director—Thomas Bentley
Leading Players—Kitty McShane, John Longden, Roy Emerton

OLD MOTHER RILEY'S GHOSTS (1941, GB, Anglo-American)
Mrs. Riley—Arthur Lucan
Director—John Baxter
Leading Players—Kitty McShane, John Stuart, A. Bromley Davenport

OLD MOTHER RILEY'S JUNGLE TREASURE (1951, GB, Renown)
Mrs. Riley—Arthur Lucan
Director—Maclean Rogers

Leading Players—Kitty McShane, Garry Marsh, Roddy Hughes

THE OLD SOAK (1926, Silent, Universal)
Clement Hawley, Sr.—Jean Hersholt
Director—Edward Sloman
Leading Players—George Lewis, June Marlowe, William V. Mong

OLIVER! (1968, GB, Columbia)
Oliver Twist—Mark Lester
Director—Carol Reed
Leading Players—Ron Moody, Shani Wallis, Oliver Reed, Harry Secombe, Jack Wild

OLIVER & COMPANY (1988, Buena Vista)
Voice of Oliver—Joey Lawrence
Director—George Scribner
Leading Players—Voices of Billy Joel, Cheech Marin, Bette Midler, Dom Deluise

OLIVER TWIST (1916, Silent, Lasky)
Oliver Twist—Marie Doro
Director—James Young
Leading Players—Hobart Bosworth, Tully Marshall, Raymond Hatton

OLIVER TWIST (1922, Silent, Associate First National)
Oliver Twist—Jackie Coogan
Director—Frank Lloyd
Leading Players—Lon Chaney, Gladys Brockwell, George Siegmann

OLIVER TWIST (1933, Monogram)
Oliver Twist—Dickie Moore
Director—William Cowen
Leading Players—Irving Pichel, William "Stage" Boyd, Doris Lloyd, Barbara Kent

OLIVER TWIST (1951, GB, Rank)
Oliver Twist—John Howard Davies
Director—David Lean
Leading Players—Robert Newton, Alec Guinness, Kay Walsh, Francis L. Sullivan, Henry Stephenson

OLIVER TWIST, JR. (1921, Silent, Fox Film Corp.)
Oliver Twist, Jr.—Harold Goodwin
Director—Millard Webb
Leading Players—Lillian Hall, George Nichols, Harold Esboldt

OLIVER'S STORY (1978, Paramount)
Oliver Barrett IV—Ryan O'Neal
Director—John Korty
Leading Players—Candice Bergen, Nicola Pagett, Edward Binns

OLSEN'S BIG MOMENT (1934, Fox Film Corp.)
Knute Olsen—El Brendel
Director—Malcolm St. Clair
Leading Players—Walter Catlett, Barbara Weeks, Susan Fleming

THE OLYMPIC HERO (1928, Silent, Zakaro-Supreme)
Charlie Patterson—Charles Paddock
Director—R. William Neill
Leading Players—Julanne Johnston, Donald Stuart, Harvey Clark

O'MALLEY OF THE MOUNTED (1921, Silent, Paramount)
O'Malley—William S. Hart

Director—Lambert Hillyer
Leading Players—Eva Novak, Leo Willis, Alfred Allen

O'MALLEY OF THE MOUNTED (1936, 20th Century Fox)
O'Malley—George O'Brien
Director—David Howard
Leading Players—Irene Ware, Stanley Fields, James Bush

OMAR KHAYYAM (1957, Paramount)
Omar Khayyam—Cornel Wilde
Director—William Dieterle
Leading Players—Michael Rennie, Debra Paget, Raymond Massey

THE OMEGA MAN (1971, Warner Brothers)
Robert Neville—Charlton Heston
Director—Boris Segal
Leading Players—Anthony Zerbe, Rosalind Cash, Paul Koslo

ON HER WEDDING NIGHT (1915, Silent, Vitagraph)
Helen Carter—Edith Storey
Director—William Humphrey
Leading Players—Antonio Moreno, Carolyn Birch, Charles Kent

ON PROBATION (1924, Silent, Steiner)
Mary Forrest—Edith Thornton
Director—Charles Hutchinson
Leading Players—Robert Ellis, Joseph Kilgour, Wilfred Lucas

ON THE TOWN (1949, MGM)
Gabey—Gene Kelly
Chip—Frank Sinatra
Ozzie—Jules Munshin
Directors—Gene Kelly & Stanley Donen
Leading Players—Betty Garrett, Ann Miller, Vera-Ellen

ON YOUR TOES (1939, Warner Brothers)
Vera—Zorina
Director—Ray Enright
Leading Players—Eddie Albert, Alan Hale, Frank McHugh, James Gleason

ONCE A CROOK (1941, GB, 20th Century Fox)
Charlie Hopkins—Gordon Harker
Director—Herbert Mason
Leading Players—Sydney Howard, Kathleen Harrison, Carla Lehmann

ONCE A DOCTOR (1937, Warner Brothers)
Steven Brace—Donald Woods
Director—William Clemens
Leading Players—Jean Muir, Gordon Oliver, Joseph King

ONCE A GENTLEMAN (1930, Art-World)
Oliver—Edward Everett Horton
Director—James Cruze
Leading Players—Lois Wilson, Francis X. Bushman, King Baggot

ONCE A LADY (1931, Paramount)
Anna Keremazoff—Ruth Chatterton
Director—Guthrie McClintic
Leading Players—Ivor Novello, Jill Esmond, Suzanne Ransom

ONCE A SINNER (1931, Fox Film Corp.)
Diana Barry—Dorothy Mackaill
Director—Guthrie McClintic

Leading Players—Joel McCrea, John Halliday, C. Henry Gordon

ONCE A SINNER (1952, GB, Argyle/Hoffberg)
Irene James—Pat Kirkwood
Director—Lewis Gilbert
Leading Players—Jack Watling, Joy Shelton, Sydney Tafler

ONCE A THIEF (1935, GB, Paramount British)
Roger Drummond—John Stuart
Director—George Pearson
Leading Players—Nancy Burne, Lewis Shaw, Derek Gorst

ONCE A THIEF (1950, UA)
Mitch—Cesar Romero
Director—W. Lee Wilder
Leading Players—June Havoc, Marie McDonald, Lon Chaney, Jr.

ONCE A THIEF (1965, MGM)
Eddie Pedak—Alain Delon
Director—Ralph Nelson
Leading Players—Ann-Margret, Van Heflin, Jack Palance

ONCE MORE, MY DARLING (1949, Universal)
Marita Connell—Ann Blyth
Director—Robert Montgomery
Leading Players—Robert Montgomery, Jane Cowl, John Ridgely

ONCE UPON A SCOUNDREL (1973, Carlyle)
Carlos del Refugio—Zero Mostel
Director—George Schaefer
Leading Players—Katy Juardo, Titos Vandis, Priscilla Garcia

ONCE YOU KISS A STRANGER (1969, Warner Brothers)
Jerry—Paul Burke
Diana—Carol Lynley
Director—Robert Sparr
Leading Players—Martha Hyer, Peter Lind Hayes, Philip Carey

THE ONE AND ONLY (1978, Paramount)
Andy Schmidt—Henry Winkler
Director—Carl Reiner
Leading Players—Kim Darby, Gene Saks, William Daniels

ONE DAY IN THE LIFE OF IVAN DENISOVICH (1971, US/GB Cinerama)
Ivan Denisovich—Tom Courtenay
Director—Casper Wrede
Leading Players—Espen Skjonberg, James Maxwell, Alfred Burke

ONE FLEW OVER THE CUCKOO'S NEST (1975, UA)
Randle Patrick McMurphy—Jack Nicholson
Director—Milos Forman
Leading Players—Louise Fletcher, William Redfield, Brad Dourif, Will Samson, Scatman Crothers, Michael Berryman

ONE FOOT IN HEAVEN (1941, Warner Brothers)
William Spence—Fredric March
Director—Irving Rapper
Leading Players—Martha Scott, Beulah Bondi, Gene Lockhart, Grant Mitchell

ONE FOOT IN HELL (1960, 20th Century Fox)
Mitch Barrett—Alan Ladd
Director—James B. Clark
Leading Players—Don Murray, Dan O'Herlihy, Dolores Michaels

ONE GIRL'S CONFESSION (1953, Columbia)
Mary Adams—Cleo Moore
Director—Hugo Haas
Leading Players—Hugo Haas, Glenn Langan, Ellen Stanbury

ONE GOOD COP (1991, Hollywood Pictures)
Artie Lewis—Michael Keaton
Director—Heywood Gould
Leading Players—Rene Russo, Anthony La Paglia, Kevin Conway, Rachel Ticotin, Tony Plana

ONE HOUR WITH YOU (1932, Paramount)
Dr. Andre Bertier—Maurice Chevalier
Colette Bertier—Jeanette MacDonald
Director—Ernst Lubitsch
Leading Players—Genevieve Tobin, Charles Ruggles, Roland Young

100 MEN AND A GIRL (1937, Universal)
Patricia Cardwell—Deanna Durbin
Director—Henry Koster
Leading Players—Leopold Stokowski, Adolphe Menjou, Alice Brady

ONE IN A MILLION (1936, 20th Century Fox)
Greta Muller—Sonja Henie
Director—Sidney Lanfield
Leading Players—Adolphe Menjou, Jean Hersholt, The Ritz Brothers

ONE JUST MAN (1955, GB, Pathe)
Judge Craig—Alexander Knox
Director—David Macdonald
Leading Players—Peter Reynolds, Ron Randell, Joan Hawthorne

ONE LITTLE INDIAN (1973, Buena Vista)
Mark—Clay O'Brien
Director—Bernard McEveety
Leading Players—James Garner, Vera Miles, Pat Hingle, Morgan Woodward

ONE MAN (1979, Canada, National Film Board of Canada)
Jason Brady—Len Cariou
Director—Robin Spry
Leading Players—Jayne Eastwood, Carol Lazare, Barry Morse

ONE MAN JURY (1978, Cal-Am Artists)
Wade—Jack Palance
Director—Charles Martin
Leading Players—Christopher Mitchum, Pamela Shoop, Cara Williams

ONE MAN JUSTICE (1937, Columbia)
Larry Clarke—Charles Starrett
Director—Leon Barsha
Leading Players—Barbara Weeks, Hal Taliaferro, Jack Clifford

ONE MAN'S JOURNEY (1933, RKO)
Dr. Eli Watt—Lionel Barrymore
Director—John Robertson
Leading Players—May Robson, Dorothy Jordan, Joel McCrea

ONE MAN'S WAY (1964, UA)
Norman Vincent Peale—Don Murray
Director—Denis Sanders

Leading Players—Diana Hyland, William Windom, Virginia Christine

ONE MORE AMERICAN (1918, Silent, Paramount)
Luigi Ricardo—George Beban
Director—William C. De Mille
Leading Players—Camille Ankewitch, May Giraci, Helen Jerome Eddy

ONE NIGHT AT SUSIE'S (1930, Warner Brothers)
Susie—Helen Ware
Director—John Francis Dillon
Leading Players—Billie Dove, Douglas Fairbanks, Jr., Tully Marshall

ONE OF MANY (1917, Silent, Metro)
Shirley Bryson—Frances Nelson
Director—Christy Cabanne
Leading Players—Niles Welch, Mary Mersch, Caroline Harris

ONE OF OUR GIRLS (1914, Silent, Famous Players)
Miss Shipley—Hazel Dawn
Director—Thomas N. Heffron
Leading Players—William Roselle, Hal Clarendon, Lionel Adams

ONE OF THE BRAVEST (1925, Silent, Gotham/Lumis)
Dan Kelly—Edward Hearn
Director—Frank O'Connor
Leading Players—Ralph Lewis, Sidney Franklin, Marion Mack

ONE ON ONE (1977, Warner Brothers)
Henry Steele—Robby Benson
Janet Hays—Annette O'Toole
Director—Lamont Johnson
Leading Players—G.D. Spradlin, Gail Strickland, Melanie Griffith

ONE PUNCH O'DAY (1926, Silent, Rayart)
Jimmy O'Day—Billy Sullivan
Director—Harry J. Brown
Leading Players—Charlotte Merriam, Jack Herrick, William Malan

ONE-ROUND HOGAN (1927, Silent, Warner Brothers)
Robert Emmett Hogan—Monte Blue
Director—Howard Bretherton
Leading Players—Leila Hyams, James J. Jeffries, Frank Hagney

ONE SHOT ROSS (1917, Silent, Triangle)
One Shot Ross—Roy Stewart
Director—Cliff Smith
Leading Players—Josie Sedgwick, Jack Richardson, Louis Durham

1,000 CONVICTS AND A WOMAN (1971, GB, American International)
Angela Thorne—Alexandra Hay
Director—Ray Austin
Leading Players—Sandor Eles, Harry Baird, Neil Hallett

ONE TOUCH OF VENUS (1948, Universal)
Venus—Ava Gardner
Director—William A. Seiter
Leading Players—Robert Walker, Dick Haymes, Eve Arden, Olga San Juan

THE ONE WHO GOT AWAY (1958, GB, Rank)
Franz von Werra—Hardy Kruger
Director—Roy Baker
Leading Players—Colin Gordon, Michael Goodliffe, Terence Alexander

ONE WOMAN'S STORY (1949, GB, GFD/Universal)
Mary Justin—Ann Todd
Director—David Lean
Leading Players—Claude Rains, Trevor Howard, Isabel Dean

ONE WOMAN TO ANOTHER (1927, Silent, Paramount)
Rita Farrell—Florence Vidor
Miss Chapin—Marie Shotwell
Director—Frank Tuttle
Leading Players—Theodore Von Eltz, Hedda Hopper, Roy Stewart

ONE YEAR TO LIVE (1925, Silent, First National)
Elsie Duchanier—Aileen Pringle
Director—Irving Cummings
Leading Players—Dorothy Mackaill, Sam De Grasse, Rosemary Theby

ONIONHEAD (1958, Warner Brothers)
Al Woods—Andy Griffith
Director—Norman Taurog
Leading Players—Felicia Farr, Walter Matthau, Erin O'Brien

ONLY A SHOP GIRL (1922, Silent, C.B.C. Film Sales)
Josie Jerome—Mae Busch
Director—Edward J. Le Saint
Leading Players—Estelle Taylor, Wallace Beery, William Scott

ONLY THE BRAVE (1930, Paramount)
Capt. James Braydon—Gary Cooper
Director—Frank Tuttle
Leading Players—Mary Brian, Phillips Holmes, James Neill

ONLY THE LONELY (1991, 20th Century Fox)
Danny Muldoon—John Candy
Theresa Luna—Ally Sheedy
Director—Chris Columbus
Leading Players—Maureen O'Hara, Kevin Dunn, Milo O'Shea, Bert Ramsen, Anthony Quinn, James Belushi, Joe V. Greco

ONLY 38 (1923, Silent, Paramount)
Lucy Stanley—May McAvoy
Director—William C. De Mille
Leading Players—Lois Wilson, Elliott Dexter, George Fawcett

ONLY WHEN I LAUGH (1981, Columbia)
Georgia—Martha Mason
Director—Glenn Jordan
Leading Players—Kristy McNichol, James Coco, Joan Hackett

THE ONLY WOMAN (1924, Silent, First National)
Helen Brinsley—Norma Talmadge
Director—Sidney Olcott
Leading Players—Eugene O'Brien, Edwards Davis, Winter Hall

OPERATION EICHMANN (1961, Allied Artists)
Adolf Eichmann—Werner Klemperer
Director—R.G. Springsteen
Leading Players—Ruta Lee, Donald Buka, Barbara Turner, John Banner

OPERATOR 13 (1934, MGM)
Gail Loveless/"Ann Clairbourne"—Marion Davies
Director—Richard Boleslavsky (Boleslawski)
Leading Players—Gary Cooper, Jean Parker, Katharine Alexander

THE OPTIMISTS (1973, GB, Paramount)
Sam—Peter Sellers
Liz—Donna Mullane
Mark—John Chaffey
Director—Anthony Simmons
Leading Players—David Daker, Marjorie Yates, Katyana Kass

ORCHESTRA WIVES (1942, 20th Century Fox)
Connie Abbott—Ann Rutherford
Director—Archie Mayo
Leading Players—George Montgomery, Glenn Miller, Cesar Romero, Lynn Bari

ORDINARY PEOPLE (1980, Paramount)
Calvin—Donald Sutherland
Beth—Mary Tyler Moore
Conrad—Timothy Hutton
Director—Robert Redford
Leading Players—Judd Hirsch, M. Emmet Walsh, Elizabeth McGovern

ORPHANS (1987, Lorimar)
Treat—Matthew Modine
Phillip—Kevin Anderson
Director—Alan J. Pakula
Leading Players—Albert Finney, John Kellogg, Anthony Heald

ORPHANS OF THE STORM (1922, Silent, UA)
Henriette Girard—Lillian Gish
Louise Girard—Dorothy Gish
Director—D.W. Griffith
Leading Players—Joseph Schildkraut, Frank Losee, Katherine Emmett, Morgan Wallace, Frank Puglia, Creighton Hale

ORPHANS OF THE STREET (1939, Republic)
Tommy—Tommy Ryan
Director—John H. Auer
Leading Players—Robert Livingston, June Storey, Ralph Morgan

OSCAR WILDE (1960, GB, Vantage/Four City)
Oscar Wilde—Robert Morley
Director—Gregory Ratoff
Leading Players—Phyllis Calvert, John Neville, Ralph Richardson, Dennis Price, Alexander Knox

O'SHAUGHNESSY'S BOY (1935, MGM)
Windy O'Shaughnessy—Wallace Beery
Stubby O'Shaughnessy—Jackie Cooper
Director—Richard Boleslawski
Leading Players—George "Spanky" McFarland, Henry Stephenson, Sara Haden

THE OSTERMAN WEEKEND (1983, 20th Century Fox)
Bernard Osterman—Craig T. Nelson
Director—Sam Peckinpah
Leading Players—Rutger Hauer, John Hurt, Dennis Hopper, Burt Lancaster

OTELLO (1987, Cannon)
Otello—Placido Domingo
Director—Franco Zeffirelli
Leading Players—Katia Ricciarelli, Justino Diaz, Petra Malakova, Urbano Barberini

OTHELLO (1955, UA)
Othello—Orson Welles
Director—Orson Welles
Leading Players—Michael MacLiammoir, Suzanne Cloutier, Robert Coote, Hilton Edwards

OTHELLO (1965, Warner Brothers)
Othello—Laurence Olivier
Director—Stuart Burge
Leading Players—Frank Finlay, Maggie Smith, Robert Lang, Anthony Nichols, Derek Jacobi

THE OTHER (1972, 20th Century Fox)
Holland Perry—Martin Udvarnoky
Director—Robert Mulligan
Leading Players—Uta Hagen, Chris Udvarnoky, Diana Muldaur

THE OTHER WOMAN (1954, 20th Century Fox)
Sherry—Cleo Moore
Director—Hugo Haas
Leading Players—Hugo Haas, Lance Fuller, Lucille Barkley

OTLEY (1969, Columbia)
Gerald Arthur Otley—Tom Courtenay
Director—Dick Clement
Leading Players—Romy Schneider, Alan Badel, James Villiers

OUR BLUSHING BRIDES (1930, MGM)
Jerry Marsh—Joan Crawford
Connie—Anita Page
Franky—Dorothy Sebastian
Director—Harry Beaumont
Leading Players—Robert Montgomery, Raymond Hackett, John Miljan

OUR DANCING DAUGHTERS (1928, Silent, MGM)
Diana Medford—Joan Crawford
Ann—Anita Page
Director—Harry Beaumont
Leading Players—Johnny Mack Brown, Nils Asther, Dorothy Sebastian

OUR HEARTS WERE GROWING UP (1946, Paramount)
Cornelia Otis Skinner—Gail Russell
Emily Kimbrough—Diana Lynn
Director—William D. Russell
Leading Players—Brian Donlevy, James Brown, Bill Edwards

OUR HEARTS WERE YOUNG AND GAY (1944, Paramount)
Cornelia Otis Skinner—Gail Russell
Emily Kimbrough—Diana Lynn
Director—Lewis Allen
Leading Players—Charles Ruggles, Dorothy Gish, Beulah Bondi

OUR LEADING CITIZEN (1922, Silent, Paramount)
Thomas Bentley—Thomas Meighan
Director—Alfred E. Green
Leading Players—Lois Wilson, William P. Carleton, Theodore Roberts

OUR LEADING CITIZEN (1939, Paramount)
Lem Schofield—Bob Burns

Director—Alfred Santell
Leading Players—Gene Lockhart, Susan Hayward, Joseph Allen, Jr.

OUR LITTLE GIRL (1935, Fox Film Corp.)
Molly Middleton—Shirley Temple
Director—John Robertson
Leading Players—Rosemary Ames, Joel McCrea, Lyle Talbot

OUR LITTLE WIFE (1918, Silent, Goldwyn)
Dodo—Madge Kennedy
Director—Edward Dillon
Leading Players—George Forth, William Davidson, Wray Page

OUR MAN FLINT (1966, 20th Century Fox)
Derek Flint—James Coburn
Director—Daniel Mann
Leading Players—Lee J. Cobb, Gila Golan, Edward Mulhare

OUR MAN IN HAVANA (1960, GB, Columbia)
Jim Wormold—Alec Guinness
Director—Carol Reed
Leading Players—Burl Ives, Maureen O'Hara, Ernie Kovacs, Noel Coward, Ralph Richardson, Jo Morrow

OUR MISS BROOKS (1956, Warner Brothers)
Constance Brooks—Eve Arden
Director—Al Lewis
Leading Players—Gale Gordon, Don Porter, Robert Rockwell, Richard Crenna, Jane Morgan

OUR MRS. MCCHESNEY (1918, Silent, Metro)
Emma McChesney—Ethel Barrymore
Director—Ralph Ince
Leading Players—Huntley Gordon, Wilfred Lytell, Lucille Lee Stewart

OUR MODERN MAIDENS (1929, MGM)
Billie Brown—Joan Crawford
Kentucky—Anita Page
Director—Jack Conway
Leading Players—Rod LaRocque, Douglas Fairbanks, Jr., Albert Gran

OUR NEIGHBORS-THE CARTERS (1939, Paramount)
Ellen Carter—Fay Bainter
Doc Carter—Frank Craven
Director—Ralph Murphy
Leading Players—Edmund Lowe, Genevieve Tobin, Mary Thomas

OUR RELATIONS (1936, MGM)
Stan & Alfie Laurel—Stan Laurel
Oliver & Bert Hardy—Oliver Hardy
Director—Harry Lachman
Leading Players—Sidney Toler, Alan Hale, Sr., Daphne Pollard

OUR WIFE (1941, Columbia)
Babe Marvin—Ellen Drew
Director—John M. Stahl
Leading Players—Melvyn Douglas, Ruth Hussey, Charles Coburn

OUT COLD (1989, Hemdale)
Ernie Cannald—Bruce McGill
Director—Malcolm Mowbray
Leading Players—John Lithgow, Teri Garr, Randy Quaid, Lisa Blount

OUT FOR JUSTICE (1991, Warner Brothers)
Gino Felino—Steven Seagal
Director—John FLynn
Leading Players—William Forsythe, Jerry Orbach, Jo Champa, Shareen Mitchell, Sal Richards

THE OUT-OF-TOWNERS (1970, Paramount)
George Kellerman—Jack Lemmon
Gwen Kellerman—Sandy Dennis
Director—Arthur Hiller
Leading Players—Milt Kamen, Anna Meara, Ron Carey, Phil Burns

OUT WEST WITH THE HARDY'S (1938, MGM)
Judge Hardy—Lewis Stone
Andy Hardy—Mickey Rooney
Marian Hardy—Cecilia Parker
Mrs. Hardy—Fay Holden
Director—George B. Seitz
Leading Players—Ann Rutherford, Sara Haden, Don Castle

OUT WEST WITH THE PEPPERS (1940, Columbia)
Polly Pepper—Edith Fellows
Phronsie Pepper—Dorothy Ann Seese
Ben Pepper—Charles Peck
Joey Pepper—Tommy Bond
David Pepper—Bobby Larson
Director—Charles Barton
Leading Players—Dorothy Peterson, Victor Kilian, Emory Parnell

THE OUTCAST (1954, Republic)
Jet Cosgrave—John Derek
Director—William Witney
Leading Players—Joan Evans, Jim Davis, Catherine McLeod

OUTCAST (1928, Silent, First National)
Miriam—Corinne Griffith
Director—William A. Seiter
Leading Players—James Ford, Edmund Lowe, Huntley Gordon

OUTCAST LADY (1934, MGM)
Iris March—Constance Bennett
Director—Robert Z. Leonard
Leading Players—Herbert Marshall, Mrs. Patrick Campbell, Hugh Williams

OUTCAST OF THE ISLANDS (1952, GB, British Lion)
Peter Willens—Trevor Howard
Director—Carol Reed
Leading Players—Ralph Richardson, Robert Morley, Kerima

THE OUTLAW (1943, RKO)
Billy the Kid—Jack Beutel
Directors—Howard Hughes & Howard Hawks
Leading Players—Jane Russell, Thomas Mitchell, Walter Huston

THE OUTLAW JOSEY WALES (1976, Warner Brothers)
Josey Wales—Clint Eastwood
Director—Clint Eastwood
Leading Players—Chief Dan George, Sondra Locke, Bill McKinney

THE OUTLAW'S DAUGHTER (1925, Silent, Universal)
Flora Dale—Josie Sedgwick
Director—John B. O'Brien
Leading Players—Edward Hearne, Robert Walker, Jack Gavin

THE OUTLAW'S DAUGHTER (1954, 20th Century Fox)
Kate—Kelly Ryan
Director—Wesley Barry
Leading Players—Bill Williams, Jim Davis, Elisha Cook, Jr.

OUTLAW'S SON (1957, UA)
Nate Blaine—Dane Clark
Jeff Blaine—Ben Cooper
Director—Lesley Selander
Leading Players—Lori Nelson, Ellen Drew, Charles Watts

THE OUTRIDERS (1950, MGM)
Will Owen—Joel McCrea
Jesse Wallace—Barry Sullivan
Clint Priest—James Whitmore
Director—Roy Rowland
Leading Players—Arlene Dahl, Claude Jarman, Jr., Ramon
Novarro

THE OUTSIDE WOMAN (1921, Silent, Realart)
Dorothy Ralston—Wanda Hawley
Director—Douglas Bronston
Leading Players—Clyde Fillmore, Sidney Bracey, Rosita
Marstini

THE OUTSIDER (1926, Silent, Fox Film Corp.)
Anton Ragatzy—Lou Tellegen
Director—Rowland V. Lee
Leading Players—Jacqueline Logan, Walter Pidgeon, Roy Atwell

THE OUTSIDER (1933, GB, MGM)
Anton Ragatzy—Harold Huth
Director—Harry Lachman
Leading Players—Joan Barry, Norman McKinnel, Frank Lawton

THE OUTSIDER (1940, GB, Associated British Films)
Anton Ragatzy—George Sanders
Director—Paul L. Stein
Leading Players—Mary Maguire, Barbara Blair, Peter Murray
Hill

THE OUTSIDER (1949, GB, Pilgrim/Variety)
Jack Read—Richard Attenborough
Director—Roy Boulting
Leading Players—Sheila Sim, Bernard Miles, Cecil Trouncer

THE OUTSIDER (1962, Universal)
Ira Hamilton Hayes—Tony Curtis
Director—Delbert Mann
Leading Players—James Franciscus, Gregory Walcott, Bruce
Bennett

THE OUTSIDER (1980, Paramount)
Michael Flaherty—Craig Wasson
Director—Tony Luraschi
Leading Players—Patricia Quinn, Sterling Hayden, Niall Toibin

THE OUTSIDERS (1983, Warner Brothers)
Dallas Winston—Matt Dillon
Johnny Cade—Ralph Macchio
Ponyboy Curtis—C. Thomas Howell

Director—Francis Ford Coppola
Leading Players—Patrick Swayze, Rob Lowe, Emilio Estevez,
Tom Cruise, Diana Lane

OVER THE HILL (1992, Australia, Greater Union)
Alma Harris—Olympia Dukakis
Director—George Miller
Leading Players—Sigrid Thornton, Derek Fowlds, Bill Kerr,
Steve Bisley, Andrea Moor

OVER 21 (1945, Columbia)
Max Wharton—Alexander Knox
Director—Charles Vidor
Leading Players—Irene Dunne, Charles Coburn, Jeff Donnell

OVERBOARD (1987, MGM-UA)
Joanna Stayton ("Annie Proffitt")—Goldie Hawn
Director—Garry Marshall
Leading Players—Kurt Russell, Edward Herrmann, Katherine
Helmond, Michael Hagerty

THE OVERLANDERS (1946, Great Britain/Australia, Ealing)
Dan McAlpine—Chips Rafferty
Director—Harry Watt
Leading Players—John Nugent, Daphne Campbell, Jean Blue

THE OWL AND THE PUSSYCAT (1970, Columbia)
Doris—Barbra Streisand
Felix—George Segal
Director—Herbert Ross
Leading Players—Robert Klein, Allen Garfield, Roz Kelly

P

P.C. JOSSER (1931, GB, Gainsborough)
Jimmy Josser—Ernie Lotinga
Director—Milton Rosner
Leading Players—Jack Frost, Maisie Darrell, Robert Douglas

P.J. (1968, Universal)
P.J. Detweiler—George Peppard
Director—John Guillermin
Leading Players—Raymond Burr, Gayle Hunnicutt, Brock Peters

P.K. & THE KID (1987, Sunn Classics/Lorimar)
William "Kid" Kane—Paul LeMat
Paula Kathleen "P.K." Bayette—Molly Ringwald
Director—Lou Lombardo
Leading Players—Alex Rocco, Charles Hallahan, John Disanti

THE PACKAGE (1989, Orion)
Thomas Boyette—Tommy Lee Jones
Director—Andrew Davis
Leading Players—Gene Hackman, Joanna Cassidy, John Heard,
Kevin Crowley, Anatoly Davydov

PADDY (1970, Ireland, Allied Artists)
Paddy Maguire—Des Cave
Director—Daniel Haller

Leading Players—Milo O'Shea, Dearbhla Molloy, Maureen Toal

PADDY O'DAY (1935, Fox Film Corp.)
Paddy O'Day—Jane Withers
Director—Lewis Seiler
Leading Players—Rita Hayworth, Pinky Tomlin, Jane Darwell

PADDY, THE NEXT BEST THING (1923, GB, Graham/Wilcox)
Paddy Adair—Mae Marsh
Director—Graham Cutts
Leading Players—Darby Foster, Lilian Douglas, George K. Arthur

PADDY, THE NEXT BEST THING (1933, Fox Film Corp.)
Paddy Adair—Janet Gaynor
Director—Harry Lachman
Leading Players—Warner Baxter, Walter Connolly, Harvey Stephens

THE PAGAN (1929, MGM)
Henry Shoesmith, Jr.—Ramon Novarro
Director—W.S. Van Dyke
Leading Players—Renee Adoree, Donald Crisp, Dorothy Janis

PAGAN LADY (1931, Columbia)
Dot Hunter—Evelyn Brent
Director—John Francis Dillon
Leading Players—Conrad Nagel, Charles Bickford, Roland Young

PAGE MISS GLORY (1935, Warner Brothers)
"Dawn" Glory-Loretta Dalrymople—Marion Davies
Director—Mervyn LeRoy
Leading Players—Pat O'Brien, Dick Powell, Mary Astor, Frank McHugh

PAID TO DANCE (1937, Columbia)
Joan Bradley—Jacqueline Wells (Julie Bishop)
Director—Charles Coleman, Jr.
Leading Players—Don Terry, Rita Hayworth, Arthur Loft

PAID TO KILL (1954, GB, Hammer)
Paul Kirby—Paul Carpenter
Director—Montgomery Tully
Leading Players—Dane Clark, Thea Gregory, Cecile Chevreau

THE PAINTED ANGEL (1929, Warner Brothers)
Mamie Hudler-Rodeo West—Billie Dove
Director—Millard Webb
Leading Players—Edmund Lowe, J. Farrell MacDonald, George MacFarlane

THE PAINTED FLAPPER (1924, Silent, Associated First National)
Arline Whitney—Pauline Garon
Director—John Gorman
Leading Players—James Kirkwood, Claire Adams, Hal Cooley

PAINTED PEOPLE (1924, Silent, Associated First National)
Ellie Byrne—Colleen Moore
Don Lane—Ben Lyon
Director—Clarence Badger
Leading Players—Charlotte Merriam, Joseph Striker, Charles Murray

PAINTED WOMAN (1932, Fox Film Corp.)
Kiddo—Peggy Shannon
Director—John Blystone
Leading Players—Spencer Tracy, William "Stage" Boyd, Irving Pichel

PAL JOEY (1957, Columbia)
Joey Evans—Frank Sinatra
Director—George Sidney
Leading Players—Rita Hayworth, Kim Novak, Barbara Nichols, Bobby Sherwood

THE PALEFACE (1948, Paramount)
"Painless" Peter Potter—Bob Hope
Director—Norman Z. McLeod
Leading Players—Jane Russell, Robert Armstrong, Iris Adrian

PALOOKA (1934, UA)
Joe Palooka—Stuart Erwin
Director—Benjamin Stoloff
Leading Players—Jimmy Durante, Lupe Velez, Marjorie Rambeau

PALS OF THE PECOS (1941, Republic)
Stony Brooke—Robert Livingston
Tucson Smith—Bob Steele
Lullaby Joslin—Rufe Davis
Director—Les Orlebeck
Leading Players—Robert Winkler, June Johnson, Pat O'Malley

PALS OF THE SADDLE (1938, Republic)
Stony Brooke—John Wayne
Tucson Smith—Ray Corrigan
Lullaby Joslin—Max Terhune
Director—George Sherman
Leading Players—Doreen McKay, Josef Forte, George Douglas

PANAMA FLO (1932, RKO)
Flo Bennett—Helen Twelvetrees
Director—Ralph Murphy
Leading Players—Robert Armstrong, Charles Bickford, Marjorie Peterson

PANAMA HATTIE (1942, MGM)
Hattie Maloney—Ann Sothern
Director—Norman Z. McLeod
Leading Players—Dan Dailey, Red Skelton, Marsha Hunt, Virginia O'Brien

PANAMA LADY (1939, RKO)
Lucy—Lucille Ball
Director—Jack Hively
Leading Players—Allan Lane, Steffi Duna, Evelyn Brent

PANAMA SAL (1957, Republic)
Sal Reagan—Elena Verdugo
Director—William Witney
Leading Players—Edward Kemmer, Carlos Rivas, Harry Jackson

PANAMINT'S BAD MAN (1938, 20th Century Fox)
Gorman—Noah Beery, Sr.
Director—Ray Taylor
Leading Players—Smith Ballew, Evelyn Daw, Stanley Fields

PANDORA AND THE FLYING DUTCHMAN (1951, GB, MGM)
Hendrick van der Zee—James Mason

Pandora Reynolds—Ava Gardner
Director—Albert Lewin
Leading Players—Nigel Patrick, Sheila Sim, Harold Warrender

PAPA'S DELICATE CONDITION (1963, Paramount)
Jack "Papa" Griffith—Jackie Gleason
Director—George Marshall
Leading Players—Glynis Johns, Laurel Goodwin, Linda Bruhl, Charlie Ruggles

PAPER LION (1968, UA)
George Plimpton—Alan Alda
Director—Alex March
Leading Players—Lauren Hutton, David Doyle, Ann Turkel, Alex Karras

PAPER TIGER (1975, GB, MacLean)
Walter Bradbury—David Niven
Director—Ken Annakin
Leading Players—Toshiro Mifune, Hardy Kruger, Ando, Ivan Desny

PAPERBACK HERO (1973, Canada, Agincourt International)
Rick—Keir Dullea
Director—Peter Pearson
Leading Players—Elizabeth Ashley, John Beck, Dayle Haddon

PAPILLON (1973, Allied Artists)
Henri Charriere, Papillon—Steve McQueen
Director—Franklin J. Schaffner
Leading Players—Dustin Hoffman, Victor Jory, Don Gordon, Anthony Zerbe

PARACHUTE JUMPER (1933, Warner Brothers)
Bill Keller—Douglas Fairbanks, Jr.
Director—Alfred E. Green
Leading Players—Leo Carillo, Bette Davis, Frank McHugh, Claire Dodd

PARACHUTE NURSE (1942, Columbia)
Glenda White—Marguerite Chapman
Director—Charles Barton
Leading Players—William Wright, Kay Harris, Lauretta M. Schimmoler

THE PARADINE CASE (1947, UA)
Maddalena, Anna Paradine—Alida Valli
Director—Alfred Hitchcock
Leading Players—Gregory Peck, Charles Laughton, Charles Coburn, Ann Todd, Ethel Barrymore, Louis Jourdan

PARANOIAC (1963, GB, Universal)
Eleanor Ashby—Janette Scott
Director—Freddie Francis
Leading Players—Oliver Reed, Liliane Brousse, Alexander Davion

PARATROOPER (1954, GB, Columbia)
Canada MacKendrick—Alan Ladd
Director—Terence Young
Leading Players—Leo Genn, Susan Stephen, Harry Andrews, Donald Houston

PARDNERS (1956, Paramount)
Slim Mosely, Jr.—Dean Martin
Wade Kingsley, Jr.—Jerry Lewis

Director—Norman Taurog
Leading Players—Lori Nelson, Jeff Morrow, Jackie Loughery

PARDON MY PAST (1945, Columbia)
Eddie York—Fred MacMurray
Director—Leslie Fenton
Leading Players—Marguerite Chapman, Akim Tamiroff, William Demarest

PARENTHOOD (1989, Universal)
Gil Buckman—Steve Martin
Larry Buckman—Tom Hulce
Nathan—Rick Moranis
Frank Buckman—Jason Robards
Karen Buckman—Mary Steenburgen
Helen—Diane Wiest
Director—Ron Howard
Leading Players—Martha Plimpton, Keanu Reeves, Harley Kozak, Leaf Phoenix, Dennis Dugan, Ellen Ryan, Helen Shaw

PARENTS (1988, Vestron)
Dad (Nick Laemle)—Randy Quaid
Mom (Lily Laemle)—Mary Beth Hurt
Director—Bob Balaban
Leading Players—Sandy Dennis, Bryan Madorsky, Katherine Grody

PARIS TROUT (1991, Viacom)
Paris Trout—Dennis Hopper
Director—Stephen Gyllenhaal
Leading Players—Barbara Hershey, Ed Harris, Ray McKinnin, Tina Liffor, Darnita Henry, Eric Ware

PARK AVENUE LOGGER (1937, RKO)
Grant Curran—George O'Brien
Director—David Howard
Leading Players—Beatrice Roberts, Willard Robertson, Ward Bond

PARNELL (1937, MGM)
Charles Stewart Parnell—Clark Gable
Director—John M. Stahl
Leading Players—Myrna Loy, Edna May Oliver, Edmund Gwenn

PAROLE GIRL (1933, Columbia)
Sylvia Day—Mae Clarke
Director—Eddie Cline
Leading Players—Ralph Bellamy, Marie Prevost, Hale Hamilton

PARRISH (1961, Warner Brothers)
Parrish McLean—Troy Donahue
Director—Delmer Daves
Leading Players—Claudette Colbert, Karl Malden, Dean Jagger, Diane McBain, Connie Stevens

THE PARSON AND THE OUTLAW (1957, Columbia)
Billy the Kid—Anthony Dexter
Rev. Jericho Jones—Charles "Buddy" Rogers
Director—Oliver Drake
Leading Players—Jean Parker, Sonny Tufts, Robert Lowery, Marie Windsor

THE PARSON OF PANAMINT (1916, Pallas)
Phillip Pharo—Dustin Farnum
Director—William Desmond Taylor

Leading Players—Winifred Kingston, "Doc" Pomeroy Cannon, Howard Davies

PART TIME WIFE (1930, Fox Film Corp.)
Mrs. Murdock -Betty Rogers—Lelia Hyams
Director—Leo McCarey
Leading Players—Edmund Lowe, Tom Clifford, Walter McGrail

PARTNERS (1982, Paramount)
Benson—Ryan O'Neal
Kerwin—John Hurt
Director—James Burrows
Leading Players—Kenneth McMillan, Robyn Douglass, Jay Robinson

PARTNERS AGAIN (1926, Silent, UA)
Abe Potash—George Sidney
Morris Perlmutter—Alexander Carr
Director—Henry King
Leading Players—Betty Jewel, Allan Forrest, Robert Schable

PARTNERS IN CRIME (1928, Silent, Paramount)
Mike Doolin, the Detective—Wallace Beery
"Scoop" McGee, the Reporter—Raymond Hatton
Director—Frank Strayer
Leading Players—Mary Brian, William Powell, Jack Luden

PARTNERS IN TIME (1946, RKO)
Lum—Chester Lauck
Abner—Norris Goff
Director—William Nigh
Leading Players—Pamela Blake, John James, Teala Loring

THE PARTY CRASHERS (1958, Paramount)
Twig Webster—Mark Damon
Director—Bernard Girard
Leading Players—Bobby Driscoll, Connie Stevens, Frances Farmer

PARTY GIRL (1930, Tiffany)
Ellen Powell—Jeanette Loff
Director—Victor Halperin
Leading Players—Douglas Fairbanks, Jr., Judith Barrie, Marie Prevost

PARTY GIRL (1958, MGM)
Vicki Gaye—Cyd Charisse
Director—Nicholas Ray
Leading Players—Robert Taylor, Lee J. Cobb, John Ireland, Kent Smith

PARTY HUSBAND (1931, Warner Brothers)
Jay Hogarth—James Rennie
Director—Clarence Badger
Leading Players—Dorothy Mackaill, Dorothy Peterson, Donald Cook

PASCALI'S ISLAND (1988, Film Four)
Basil Pascali—Ben Kingsley
Director—James Dearden
Leading Players—Charles Dance, Helen Mirren, George Murcell

PASSED AWAY (1992, Hollywood Pictures)
Jack Scanlan—Jack Warden
Director—Charlie Peters

Leading Players—Bob Hoskins, William Petersen, Helen Lloyd Breed, Maureen Stapleton, Pamela Reed, Tim Curry, Peter Riegert, Blair Brown, Frances McDormand

PASSENGER TO LONDON (1937, GB, Fox British)
Frank Drayton—John Warwick
Director—Lawrence Huntington
Leading Players—Jenny Laird, Paul Neville, Ivan Wilmot

PASSIONATE PLUMBER (1932, MGM)
Elmer Tuttle—Buster Keaton
Director—Edgar Sedgwick
Leading Players—Jimmy Durante, Irene Purcell, Polly Moran

THE PASSIONATE SENTRY (1952, GB, Fine Arts)
Miles Cornwell—Nigel Patrick
Director—Anthony Kimmins
Leading Players—Peggy Cummins, Valerie Hobson, George Cole

PASSPORT HUSBAND (1938, 20th Century Fox)
Henry Cabot—Stuart Erwin
Director—James Tinling
Leading Players—Pauline Moore, Douglas Fowley, Joan Woodbury

THE PAST OF MARY HOLMES (1933, RKO)
Mary Holmes—Helen MacKellar
Directors—Harlan Thompson & Slavko Vorkapich
Leading Players—Eric Linden, Jean Arthur, Skeets Gallagher

PASTOR HALL (1940, GB, UA)
Pastor Frederick Hall—Wilfred Lawson
Director—Roy Boulting
Leading Players—Nova Pilbeam, Seymour Hicks, Marius Goring

PAT AND MIKE (1952, MGM)
Mike Conovan—Spencer Tracy
Pat Pemberton—Katharine Hepburn
Director—George Cukor
Leading Players—Aldo Ray, William Ching, Sammy White, George Mathews

PAT GARRETT AND BILLY THE KID (1973, MGM)
Pat Garrett—James Coburn
Billy the Kid—Kris Kristofferson
Director—Sam Peckinpah
Leading Players—Bob Dylan, Jason Robards, Jr., Richard Jaeckel, Katy Juardo, Slim Pickens

THE PATCHWORK GIRL OF OZ (1914, Oz)
The Patchwork Girl—Pierre Couderc
Director—J. Farrell MacDonald
Leading Players—Violet MacMillan, Frank Moore, Fred Woodward

THE PATHFINDER (1952, Columbia)
Pathfinder—George Montgomery
Director—Sidney Salkow
Leading Players—Helena Carter, Jay Silverheels, Walter Kingsford

THE PATIENT IN ROOM 18 (1938, Warner Brothers)
Lance O'Leary—Patric Knowles
Director—Bobby Connolly
Leading Players—Ann Sheridan, Eric Stanley, John Ridgely

PATRICIA BRENT, SPINSTER (1919, GB, Garrick)
Patricia Brent—Ena Beaumont
Director—Geoffrey H. Malins
Leading Players—Laurence Leyton, Victor Robson, Nessie Blackford

PATRICIA GETS HER MAN (1937, GB, First National)
Count Stephan D'Orlet—Hans Sonker
Patricia Fitzroy—Lesley Brook
Director—Reginald Purdell
Leading Players—Edwin Styles, Aubrey Mallalieu, Cissy Fitzgerald

PATRICK (1979, Australia, Filmways)
Patrick—Robert Thompson
Director—Richard Franklin
Leading Players—Susan Penhaligon, Robert Helpmann, Rod Mullinar

PATRICK THE GREAT (1945, Universal)
Pat Donahue, Jr.—Donald O'Connor
Director—Frank Ryan
Leading Players—Peggy Ryan, Frances Dee, Donald Cook, Eve Arden

THE PATRIOT (1916, Silent, Triangle)
Bob Wiley—William S. Hart
Director—William S. Hart
Leading Players—George Stone, Joe Goodboy, Roy Laidlaw

THE PATRIOT (1928, Paramount)
Count Pahlen—Lewis Stone
Director—Ernst Lubitsch
Leading Players—Emil Jannings, Florence Vidor, Neil Hamilton

PATSY (1921, Silent, Truart)
Patsy—Zasu Pitts
Director—John McDermott
Leading Players—John MacFarlane, Tom Gallery, Marjorie Daw

THE PATSY (1964, Paramount)
Stanley Belt—Jerry Lewis
Director—Jerry Lewis
Leading Players—Ina Balin, Everett Sloane, Phil Harris, Keenan Wynn

PATTI ROCKS (1988, Film Dallas)
Patti Rocks—Karen Landry
Director—David Burton Morris
Leading Players—Chris Mulkey, John Jenkins, Buffy Sedlachek

PATTON (1970, 20th Century Fox)
Gen. George S. Patton—George C. Scott
Director—Franklin J. Schaffner
Leading Players—Karl Malden, Michael Bates, Edward Binns, Lawrence Dobkin, John Doucette, James Edwards

PATTY HEARST (1988, Atlantic)
Patty Hearst—Natasha Richardson
Director—Paul Schrader
Leading Players—William Forsythe, Ving Rhames, Frances Fisher

PAUL TEMPLE RETURNS (1952, GB, Butchers)
Paul Temple—John Bentley
Director—Maclean Rogers
Leading Players—Patricia Dainton, Valentine Dyall, Christopher Lee

PAUL TEMPLE'S TRIUMPH (1951, GB, Butchers)
Paul Temple—John Bentley
Director—Maclean Rogers
Leading Players—Dinah Sheridan, Jack Livesey, Beatrice Varley

PAULA (1915, GB, Silent, Holmfirth/Initial)
Paula—Hettie Payne
Director—Cecil Birch
Leading Players—Frank McClellan

PAULA (1952, Columbia)
Paula Rogers—Loretta Young
Director—Rudolph Mate
Leading Players—Kent Smith, Alexander Knox, Tommy Rettig

THE PAWNBROKER (1965, Allied Artists)
Sol Nazerman—Rod Steiger
Director—Sidney Lumet
Leading Players—Geraldine Fitzgerald, Brock Peters, Jaime Sanchez, Thelma Oliver

PEACE FOR A GUNFIGHTER (1967, Crown International)
"The Preacher"—Burt Berger
Director—Raymond Boley
Leading Players—JoAnne Meredith, Everett King, Stirling Welker

PEACEFUL PETERS (1922, Silent, Arrow)
"Peaceful Peters"—William Fairbanks
Director—Lewis King
Leading Players—Henry La Mont, W.L. Lynch, Evelyn Nelson

PEACEMAKER (1990, Fries)
Yates—Robert Forster
Townsend—Lance Edwards
Director—Kevin S. Tenney
Leading Players—Hilary Shepard, Robert Davi, Bert Remsen

THE PEACEMAKER (1956, UA)
Terrall Butler—James Mitchell
Director—Ted Post
Leading Players—Rosemarie Bowe, Jan Merlin, Jess Barker

PEARL OF THE SOUTH PACIFIC (1955, RKO)
Rita Delaine—Virginia Mayo
Director—Allan Dwan
Leading Players—Dennis Morgan, David Farrar, Murvyn Vye

PECK'S BAD BOY (1921, Silent, Associate First National)
Bill Peck—Jackie Coogan
Mr. Peck—James Corrigan
Director—Sam Wood
Leading Players—Wheeler Oakman, Doris May, Raymond Hatton

PECK'S BAD BOY (1934, Fox Film Corp.)
Dad Peck—Thomas Meighan
Bill Peck—Jackie Cooper
Director—Edward F. Cline
Leading Players—Dorothy Peterson, Jackie Searl, O.P. Heggie

PECK'S BAD BOY WITH THE CIRCUS (1938, RKO)
Bill Peck—Tommy Kelly
Mr. Peck—Grant Mitchell

Director—Edward F. Cline
Leading Players—Ann Gillis, Edgar Kennedy, Benita Hume

PECK'S BAD GIRL (1918, Silent, Goldwyn)
Minnie Peck—Mabel Normand
Director—Charles Giblyn
Leading Players—Earle Foxe, Corinne Barker, Blanche Davenport

PEEPER (1975, 20th Century Fox)
Tucker—Michael Caine
Director—Peter Hyams
Leading Players—Natalie Wood, Kitty Winn, Thayer David, Liam Dunn

PEEPING TOM (1960, GB, Anglo-Amalgamated)
Mark Lewis—Karl Boehm
Director—Michael Powell
Leading Players—Moira Shearer, Anna Massey, Maxine Audley

PEER GYNT (1965, Willow/Brandon)
Peer Gynt—Charlton Heston
Director—David Bradley
Leading Players—Betty Hanisee, Mrs. Herbert Hyde, Lucielle Powell

PEG O' MY HEART (1933, MGM)
Peg O'Connell—Marion Davies
Director—Robert Z. Leonard
Leading Players—Onslow Stevens, J. Farrell MacDonald, Juliette Compton

PEG OF OLD DRURY (1936, GB, Paramount)
Peg Woffington—Anna Neagle
Director—Herbert Wilcox
Leading Players—Cedric Hardwicke, Margetta Scott, Jack Hawkins

PEG OF THE PIRATES (1918, Silent, Fox Film Corp.)
Peg—Peggy Hyland
Director—O.A.C. Lund
Leading Players—Sidney Mason, Carleton Macy, Frank Evans

PEGGY (1916, Silent, Triangle)
Peggy Cameron—Billie Burke
Director—Charles Giblyn
Leading Players—William H. Thompson, William Desmond, Charles Ray

PEGGY (1950, Universal)
Peggy Brookfield—Diana Lynn
Director—Frederick de Cordova
Leading Players—Charles Coburn, Charlotte Greenwood, Barbara Lawrence, Charles Drake

PEGGY SUE GOT MARRIED (1986, Tri-Star)
Peggy Sue Kelcher Bodell—Kathleen Turner
Director—Francis Coppola
Leading Players—Nicolas Cage, Barry Miller, Catherine Hicks, Barbara Harris, Don Murray, Maureen O'Sullivan

PENELOPE (1966, MGM)
Penelope Elcott—Natalie Wood
Director—Arthur Hiller
Leading Players—Ian Bannen, Dick Shawn, Peter Falk, Jonathan Winters

THE PENITENT (1988, New Century/Vista)
Ramon—Raul Julia
Director—Cliff Osmond
Leading Players—Armand Assante, Rona Freed, Julie Carmen, Lucy Rejna

PENN & TELLER GET KILLED (1989, Warner Brothers)
Penn—Penn Jillette
Teller—Teller
Director—Arthur Penn
Leading Players—Caitlan Clarke, David Patrick Kelly, Leonardo Cimino

PENNINGTON'S CHOICE (1915, Silent, Metro)
Robert Pennington—Francis X. Bushman
Director—William J. Bowman
Leading Players—Beverly Bayne, Wellington Playter, H. O'Dell

PENNY PRINCESS (1953, GB, Universal)
Lindy Smith—Yolande Donlan
Director—Val Guest
Leading Players—Dirk Bogarde, Edwin Styles, Reginald Beckwith

PENROD (1922, Silent, Associated First National)
Penrod Schofield—Wesley Barry
Director—Marshall Neilan
Leading Players—Tully Marshall, Claire McDowell, John Harron

PENROD AND HIS TWIN BROTHER (1938, Warner Brothers)
Penrod Schofield—Billy Mauch
Danny—Bobby Mauch
Director—William McGann
Leading Players—Frank Craven, Spring Byington, Charles Halton

PENROD AND SAM (1923, Silent, Associated First National)
Penrod Schofield—Ben Alexander
Sam Williams—Joe Butterworth
Director—William Beaudine
Leading Players—Buddy Messinger, Joe McGray, Eugene Jackson

PENROD AND SAM (1931, First National)
Penrod Schofield—Leon Janney
Sam Williams—Junior Coghlan
Director—William Beaudine
Leading Players—Matt Moore, Dorothy Peterson, Johnny Arthur

PENROD AND SAM (1937, Warner Brothers)
Penrod Schofield—Billy Mauch
Sam Williams—Harry Watson
Director—William McGann
Leading Players—Frank Craven, Spring Byington, Craig Reynolds

PENROD'S DOUBLE TROUBLE (1938, Warner Brothers)
Penrod Schofield—Billy Mauch
Danny—Bobby Mauch
Director—Lewis Seiler
Leading Players—Dick Purcell, Gene Lockhart, Kathleen Lockhart

THE PEOPLE AGAINST O'HARA (1951, MGM)
Johnny O'Hara—James Arness
Director—John Sturges

Leading Players—Spencer Tracy, Pat O'Brien, Diana Lynn, John Hodiak, Eduardo Cianelli

THE PEOPLE VS. DR. KILDARE (1941, MGM)
Dr. James Kildare—Lew Ayres
Director—Harold S. Bucquet
Leading Players—Lionel Barrymore, Laraine Day, Bonita Granville, Alma Kruger, Red Skelton

PEPE (1960, Columbia)
Pepe—Cantinflas
Director—George Sidney
Leading Players—Dan Dailey, Shirley Jones, Carlos Montalban

PEPPER (1936, 20th Century Fox)
Pepper Jolly—Jane Withers
Director—James Tinling
Leading Players—Irvin S. Cobb, Slim Summerville, Dean Jagger

A PERFECT COUPLE (1979, 20th Century Fox)
Alex Theodopoulos—Paul Dooley
Shella Shea—Marta Heflin
Director—Robert Altman
Leading Players—Titos Vandis, Belita Moreno, Henry Gibson

THE PERFECT GENTLEMAN (1935, MGM)
Major Chatteris—Frank Morgan
Director—Tim Whelan
Leading Players—Cicely Courtneidge, Heather Angel, Herbert Mundin

A PERFECT LADY (1918, Silent, Goldwyn)
Lucille Le Jambon-Lucy Higgins—Madge Kennedy
Director—Clarence Badger
Leading Players—Jere Austin, Walter Law, Rod La Rocque

THE PERFECT LADY (1931, GB, Wardour)
Anne Burnett—Moira Lynd
Director—Milton Rosmer
Leading Players—Henry Wilcoxon, Reginald Gardiner, Betty Amann

THE PERFECT LOVER (1919, Silent, Selznick)
Brian Lazar—Eugene O'Brien
Director—Ralph Ince
Leading Players—Lucille Lee Stewart, Marguerite Courtot, Mary Boland

THE PERFECT MARRIAGE (1946, Paramount)
Maggie Williams—Loretta Young
Dale Williams—David Niven
Director—Lewis Allen
Leading Players—Eddie Albert, Charlie Ruggles, Virginia Field

THE PERFECT MATCH (1987, Airtight)
Tim Wainwright—Marc McClure
Nancy Bryant—Jennifer Edwards
Director—Mark Deimel
Leading Players—Diane Stilwell, Rob Paulsen

THE PERFECT SNOB (1941, 20th Century Fox)
Martha Mason—Charlotte Greenwood
Director—Ray McCarey
Leading Players—Charlie Ruggles, Lynn Bari, Cornel Wilde, Anthony Quinn

THE PERFECT SPECIMEN (1937, Warner Brothers)
Gerald Beresford Wicks—Errol Flynn
Director—Michael Curtiz
Leading Players—Joan Blondell, Hugh Herbert, Edward Everett Horton

PERFECT STRANGERS (1950, Warner Brothers)
Terry Scott—Ginger Rogers
David Campbell—Dennis Morgan
Director—Bretaigne Windust
Leading Players—Thelma Ritter, Margalo Gillmore, Anthony Ross

THE PERFECT VICTIM (1988, Vertigo)
Liz Winters—Deborah Shelton
Director—Shuki Levy
Leading Players—Lyman Ward, Tom Dugan, Clarence Williams III

THE PERFECT WOMAN (1950, GB, Rank/Ealing)
Penelope Belmond—Patricia Roc
Olga the Robot—Pamela Devis
Director—Bernard Knowles
Leading Players—Stanley Holloway, Nigel Patrick, Miles Malleson

THE PERILS OF PAULINE (1947, Paramount)
Pearl White "Pauline"—Betty Hutton
Director—George Marshall
Leading Players—John Lund, Billy de Wolfe, William Demarest

THE PERILS OF PAULINE (1967, Universal)
Pauline—Pamela Austin
Director—Herbert B. Leonard
Leading Players—Pat Boone, Terry-Thomas, Edward Everett Horton

THE PERSECUTION AND ASSASSINATION OF JEAN-PAUL MARAT AS PERFORMED BY THE INMATES OF THE ASYLUM OF CHARENTON UNDER THE DIRECTION OF THE MARQUIS DE SADE—(1967, GB, UA)
Jean-Paul Marat—Ian Richardson
Marquis De Sade—Patrick Magee
Director—Peter Brook
Leading Players—Glenda Jackson, Robert Lloyd, Michael Williams, Clifford Rose, Freddie Jones

PERSONAL BEST (1982, Warner Brothers)
Chris Cahill—Mariel Hemingway
Director—Robert Towne
Leading Players—Scott Glenn, Patrice Donnelly, Kenny Moore

PERSONAL MAID (1931, Paramount)
Nora Ryan—Nancy Carroll
Director—Monta Bell
Leading Players—Pat O'Brien, Gene Raymond, Hugh O'Connell

PERSONAL MAID'S SECRET (1935, Warner Brothers)
Lizzie—Ruth Donnelly
Director—Arthur Greville Collins
Leading Players—Anita Louise, Warren Hull, Margaret Lindsay

PERSONAL SECRETARY (1938, Universal)
Gale Rogers—Joy Hodges
Director—Otis Garrett
Leading Players—William Gargan, Andy Devine, Ruth Donnelly

PERSONAL SERVICES (1987, GB, Zenith/UIP-Vestron)
Christine Painter—Julie Walters
Director—Terry Jones
Leading Players—Alec McCowen, Shirley Stelfox, Danny
Schiller, Victoria Hardcastle

THE PERSONALITY KID (1934, Warner Brothers)
Ritzy McCarthy—Pat O'Brien
Director—Alan Crosland
Leading Players—Glenda Farrell, Claire Dodd, Henry O'Neill

PERSONALITY KID (1946, Columbia)
Davey Roberts—Ted Donaldson
Director—George Sherman
Leading Players—Anita Louise, Michael Dunne, Barbara Brown

PERSUASIVE PEGGY (1917, Silent, Mayfair)
Peggy Patton—Peggy Hyland
Director—Charles J. Brabin
Leading Players—William B. Davidson, Mary Cecil Parker,
Gertrude Norman

THE PEST (1919, Silent, Goldwyn)
Jiggs—Mabel Normand
Director—Tod Browning
Leading Players—John Bowers, Charles Gerard, Alec B. Francis

PETE KELLY'S BLUES (1955, Warner Brothers)
Pete Kelly—Jack Webb
Director—Jack Webb
Leading Players—Janet Leigh, Edmond O'Brien, Peggy Lee, Lee
Marvin, Ella Fitzgerald

PETE 'N' TILLIE (1972, Universal)
Pete Seltzer—Walter Matthau
Tillie Schlaine—Carol Burnett
Director—Martin Ritt
Leading Players—Geraldine Page, Barry Nelson, Rene
Auberjonois

PETER IBBETSON (1935, Paramount)
Peter Ibbetson—Gary Cooper
Director—Henry Hathaway
Leading Players—Ann Harding, John Halliday, Ida Lupino

PETER PAN (1924, Silent, Paramount)
Peter Pan—Betty Bronson
Director—Herbert Brenon
Leading Players—Ernest Torrence, Cyril Chadwick, Virginia
Brown Faire

PETERSEN (1974, Australia, Avco Embassy
Tony "Jock" Petersen—Jack Thompson
Director—Tim Burstall
Leading Players—Jacki Weaver, Joey Hohenfels, Amanda Hunt

THE PETTY GIRL (1950, Columbia)
George Petty—Robert Cummings
Victoria Braymore—Joan Caulfield
Director—Henry Levin
Leading Players—Elsa Lanchester, Melville Cooper, Audrey
Long

PETULIA (1968, Warner Brothers)
Petulia Danner—Julie Christie
Director—Richard Lester

Leading Players—George C. Scott, Richard Chamberlain, Arthur
Hill

PHAEDRA (1962, Lopert)
Phaedra—Melina Mercouri
Director—Jules Dassin
Leading Players—Anthony Perkins, Raf Vallone, Elizabeth Ercy

PHANTOM FROM SPACE (1953, UA)
Phantom—Dick Sands
Director—W. Lee Wilder
Leading Players—Ted Cooper, Rudolph Anders, Noreen Nash

PHANTOM KILLER (1942, Monogram)
John G. Harrison—John Hamilton
Director—William Beaudine
Leading Players—Dick Purcell, Joan Woodbury, Warren Hymer

PHANTOM LADY (1944, Universal)
Ann Terry—Fay Helm
Director—Robert Siodmak
Leading Players—Franchot Tone, Ella Raines, Alan Curtis,
Aurora Miranda, Thomas Gomez

THE PHANTOM OF PARIS (1931, MGM)
Marquis du Touchais—Ian Keith
Director—John S. Robertson
Leading Players—John Gilbert, Leila Hyams, Lewis Stone, Jean
Hersholt, C. Aubrey Smith

PHANTOM OF THE OPERA (1925, Silent, Universal)
Erik, The Phantom—Lon Chaney
Director—Rupert Julian
Leading Players—Mary Philbin, Norman Kerry, Snitz Edwards

PHANTOM OF THE OPERA (1943, Universal)
Enrique Claudin—Claude Rains
Director—Arthur Lubin
Leading Players—Nelson Eddy, Susanna Foster, Edgar Barrier,
Leo Carrillo, Jane Farrar

THE PHANTOM OF THE OPERA (1962, GB, Universal)
Erik, The Phantom—Herbert Lom
Director—Terence Fisher
Leading Players—Heather Sears, Thorley Walters, Edward De
Souza

PHANTOM OF THE OPERA (1989, 21st Film)
The Phantom—Robert Englund
Director—Dwight H. Little
Leading Players—Jill Schoelen, Alex Hyde-White, Bill Nighy

PHANTOM OF THE PARADISE (1974, 20th Century Fox)
Winslow the Phantom—William Finley
Director—Brian De Palma
Leading Players—Paul Williams, Jessica Harper, George
Memmoli

THE PHANTOM PLAINSMEN (1942, Republic)
Stony Brooke—Tom Tyler
Tucson Smith—Bob Steele
Lullaby Joslin—Rufe Davis
Director—John English
Leading Players—Robert O. Davis, Lois Collier, Charles Miller

THE PHANTOM PRESIDENT (1932, Paramount)
Doc Peter Varney—George M. Cohan
Director—Norman Taurog
Leading Players—Claudette Colbert, Jimmy Durante, George Barbier

PHANTOM RANCHER (1940, Colony)
Mitchell—Ken Maynard
Director—Sam Newfield
Leading Players—Dorothy Short, Harry Harvey, Ted Adams

THE PHANTOM SPEAKS (1945, Republic)
Harvey Bogardus—Tom Powers
Director—John English
Leading Players—Richard Arlen, Stanley Ridges, Lynne Roberts

THE PHANTOM STRIKES (1939, GB, Monogram)
Dr. Lomond-"The Ringer"—Alexander Knox
Director—Walter Forde
Leading Players—Wilfrid Lawson, Sonnie Hale, Louise Henry, Patrick Barr

PHILO VANCE RETURNS (1947, Producers Releasing Corp.)
Philo Vance—William Wright
Director—William Beaudine
Leading Players—Terry Austin, Leon Belasco, Clara Blandick

PHILO VANCE'S GAMBLE (1947, Producers Releasing Corp.)
Philo Vance—Alan Curtis
Director—Basil Wrangell
Leading Players—Terry Austin, Frank Jenks, Tala Birell

PHILO VANCE'S SECRET MISSION (1947, Producers Releasing Corp.)
Philo Vance—Alan Curtis
Director—Reginald Le Borg
Leading Players—Sheila Ryan, Tala Birell, Frank Jenks

PHONE CALL FROM A STRANGER (1952, 20th Century Fox)
David Trask—Gary Merrill
Director—Jean Negulesco
Leading Players—Shelley Winters, Michael Rennie, Keenan Wynn, Bette Davis, Evelyn Varden

PHYLLIS OF THE FOLLIES (1928, Silent, Universal)
Phyllis Sherwood—Alice Day
Director—Ernst Laemmle
Leading Players—Matt Moore, Edmund Burns, Lilyan Tashman

THE PHYSICIAN (1928, GB, Silent, Gaumont)
Dr. Carey—Ian Hunter
Director—George Jacoby
Leading Players—Miles Mander, Elga Brink, Lissi Arna

PICADILLY JIM (1936, MGM)
Jim Crocker—Robert Montgomery
Director—Robert Z. Leonard
Leading Players—Frank Morgan, Madge Evans, Eric Blore, Billie Burke

PICK-UP (1933, Paramount)
Mary Richards—Sylvia Sidney
Director—Marion Gering
Leading Players—George Raft, William Harrigan, Lillian Bond

PICKUP (1951, Columbia)
Betty—Beverly Michaels
Director—Hugo Haas
Leading Players—Hugo Haas, Allan Nixon, Howland Chamberlain

THE PICKUP ARTIST (1987, 20th Century Fox)
Jack Jericho—Robert Downey
Director—James Toback
Leading Players—Molly Ringwald, Dennis Hopper, Danny Aiello, Mildred Dunnock, Harvey Keitel

PICKUP ON 101 (1972, American International)
Obediah Bradley—Jack Albertson
Nickie—Lesley Ann Warren
Director—John Florea
Leading Players—Martin Sheen, Michael Ontkean, Hal Baylor

THE PICKWICK PAPERS (1952, GB, Renown)
Samuel Pickwick—James Hayter
Director—Noel Langley
Leading Players—James Donald, Alexander Gauge, Lionel Murton, Nigel Patrick, Kathleen Harrison, Joyce Grenfell

PICTURE BRIDES (1934, Allied Pictures)
Mame—Dorothy Mackaill
Mary Lee—Dorothy Libaire
Director—Phil Rosen
Leading Players—Regis Toomey, Alan Hale, Will Ahern

PICTURE MOMMY DEAD (1966, Embassy)
Jessica Shelley—Zsa Zsa Gabor
Director—Bert I. Gordon
Leading Players—Don Ameche, Martha Hyer, Susan Gordon, Maxwell Reed

THE PICTURE OF DORIAN GRAY (1916, GB, Silent, Neptune)
Dorian Gray—Henry Victor
Director—Fred W. Durrant
Leading Players—Pat O'Malley, Jack Jordan, Sydney Bland

THE PICTURE OF DORIAN GRAY (1945, MGM)
Dorian Gray—Hurd Hatfield
Director—Albert Lewin
Leading Players—George Sanders, Donna Reed, Angela Lansbury, Lowell Gilmore, Peter Lawford, Reginald Owen

THE PICTURE SHOW MAN (1980, Australia, Limelight)
Pop—John Meillon
Director—John Power
Leading Players—Rod Taylor, John Ewart, Harold Hopkins

PICTURE SNATCHER (1933, Warner Brothers)
Danny Kean—James Cagney
Director—Lloyd Bacon
Leading Players—Ralph Bellamy, Patricia Ellis, Alice White

THE PIED PIPER (1942, 20th Century Fox)
Howard—Monty Woolley
Director—Irving Pichel
Leading Players—Roddy McDowall, Anne Baxter, Otto Preminger, J. Carrol Naish

THE PIED PIPER (1972, GB, Paramount)
Pied Piper—Donovan
Director—Jacques Denny

Leading Players—Jack Wild, Donald Pleasence, John Hurt, Michael Hordern

PIERRE OF THE PLAINS (1914, Silent, All Star)
Pierre—Edgar Selwyn
Director—Edgar Selwyn
Leading Players—William Conklin, Joseph Rieder, William Riley Hatch

PIERRE OF THE PLAINS (1942, MGM)
Pierre—John Carroll
Director—George B. Seitz
Leading Players—Ruth Hussey, Bruce Cabot, Phil Brown, Reginald Owen

THE PILGRIM (1923, Silent, Associate First National)
The Pilgrim—Charles Chaplin
Director—Charles Chaplin
Leading Players—Edna Purviance, Kitty Bradbury, Mack Swain

THE PILGRIM LADY (1947, Republic)
Aunt Pheobe—Helen Freeman
Director—Lesley Selander
Leading Players—Lynne Roberts, Warren Douglas, Alan Mowbray

PILOT NO. 5 (1943, MGM)
George Braynor Collins—Franchot Tone
Director—George Sidney
Leading Players—Marsha Hunt, Gene Kelly, Van Johnson, Alan Baxter

PIMPERNEL SMITH (1942, GB, UA)
Prof. Horatio Smith—Leslie Howard
Director—Leslie Howard
Leading Players—Francis L. Sullivan, Mary Morris, Hugh McDermott

PIN UP GIRL (1944, 20th Century Fox)
Lorry Jones—Betty Grable
Director—H. Bruce Humberstone
Leading Players—John Harvey, Martha Raye, Joe E. Brown

THE PINCH HITTER (1917, Silent, Triangle)
Joel Parker—Charles Ray
Director—Victor Schertzinger
Leading Players—Sylvia Breamer, Joseph J. Dowling, Jerome Storm

PINKY (1949, 20th Century Fox)
Pinky, Patricia Johnson—Jeanne Crain
Director—Elia Kazan
Leading Players—Ethel Barrymore, Ethel Waters, William Lundigan

THE PIRATE (1948, MGM)
Macoco, "Mack the Black"—Walter Slezak
Director—Vincente Minnelli
Leading Players—Judy Garland, Gene Kelly, Gladys Cooper, Reginald Owen, George Zucco, The Nicholas Brothers

THE PIRATES OF BLOOD RIVER (1962, GB, Hammer)
LaRoche—Christopher Lee
Director—John Gilling
Leading Players—Kerwin Mathews, Glenn Corbett, Marla Landi, Oliver Reed

THE PIRATES OF CAPRI (1949, Film Classics)
Capt. Sirocco—Louis Hayward
Director—Edgar G. Ulmer
Leading Players—Binnie Barnes, Alan Curtis, Rudolph Serato

THE PIRATES OF PENZANCE (1983, Universal)
Pirate King—Kevin Kline
Frederic—Rex Smith
Director—Wilford Leach
Leading Players—Angela Lansbury, Linda Ronstadt, George Rose

PIRATES OF TRIPOLI (1955, Columbia)
Edri-Al-Gadrin—Paul Henreid
Director—Felix Feist
Leading Players—Patricia Medina, Paul Newland, John Miljan

PISTOL PACKIN' MAMA (1943, Republic)
Vicki Norris-Sally Benson—Ruth Terry
Director—Frank Woodruff
Leading Players—Robert Livingston, Wally Vernon, Jack LaRue

PIZZA MAN (1991, Megalomania)
Elmo Bunn—Bill Maher
Director—'J.D. Athens' (Jonathan Lawton)
Leading Players—Annabelle Gurwitch, David McKnight, Bob Delegell, Bryan Clark

PLAIN CLOTHES (1988, Paramount)
Nick Dunbar/"Nick Springsteen"—Arliss Howard
Director—Martha Coolidge
Leading Players—Suzy Amis, George Wendt, Diane Ladd, Seymour Cassel

THE PLAINSMAN (1937, Paramount)
Wild Bill Hickok—Gary Cooper
Director—Cecil B. DeMille
Leading Players—Jean Arthur, James Ellison, Charles Bickford, Porter Hall, Helen Burgess, John Miljan

THE PLAINSMAN (1966, Universal)
Wild Bill Hickok—Don Murray
Director—David Lowell Rich
Leading Players—Guy Stockwell, Abby Dalton, Bradford Dillman

PLAINSMAN AND THE LADY (1946, Republic)
Sam Cotten—William Elliott
Ann Arnesen—Vera Ralston
Director—Joseph Kane
Leading Players—Gail Patrick, Joseph Schildkraut, Donald Barry

PLATINUM BLONDE (1931, Columbia)
Anne Schuyler—Jean Harlow
Director—Frank Capra
Leading Players—Loretta Young, Robert Williams, Louise Closser Hale

PLATOON (1987, Orion)
Sgt. Barnes—Tom Berenger
Sgt. Elias—Willem Dafoe
Chris—Charlie Sheen
Big Harold—Forest Whitaker
Rhah—Francesco Quinn
King—Keith David
Director—Oliver Stone

Leading Players—John C. McGinley, Richard Edson, Kevin Dillon, Reggie Johnson, John Depp

PLATOON LEADER (1988, Cannon)
Lt. Jeff Knight—Michael Dudikoff
Director—Aaron Norris
Leading Players—Robert F. Lyons, Michael De Lorenzo, Rich Fitts

PLAY GIRL (1932, Warner Brothers)
Buster—Loretta Young
Director—Ray Enright
Leading Players—Winnie Lightner, Norman Foster, Guy Kibbee

PLAY GIRL (1940, RKO)
Grace Herbert—Kay Francis
Director—Frank Woodruff
Leading Players—James Ellison, Mildred Coles, Nigel Bruce

THE PLAY GIRL (1928, Silent, Fox Film Corp.)
Madge Norton—Madge Bellamy
Director—Arthur Rosson
Leading Players—Johnny Mack Brown, Walter McGrail, Lionel Belmore

PLAYBOY OF PARIS (1930, Paramount)
Albert Loriflan—Maurice Chevalier
Director—Ludwig Berger
Leading Players—Frances Dee, Dorothy Cristy, Eugene Pallette

THE PLAYBOY OF THE WESTERN WORLD (1963, Ireland, Janus-Lion)
Christy Mahon—Gary Raymond
Director—Brian Desmond Hurst
Leading Players—Siobhan McKenna, Elspeth March, Michael O'Brian

THE PLAYBOYS (1992, US/Ireland, Goldwyn)
Tom—Aidan Quinn
Freddie—Milo O'Shea
Director—Gillis Mackinnon
Leading Players—Albert Finney, Robin Wright, Alan Devlin, Niamh Cusack, Ian McElhinney, Niall Buggy, Adrian Dunbar

PLAYGIRL (1954, Universal)
Phyllis Matthews—Colleen Miller
Director—Joseph Pevney
Leading Players—Shelley Winters, Barry Sullivan, Richard Long

THE PLAYER (1992, First Line/Avenue Pictures)
Griffin Mill—Tim Robbins
Director—Robert Altman
Leading Players—Greta Scacchi, Fred Ward, Whoopi Goldberg, Peter Gallagher, Brion James, Cynthia Stevenson, Vincent D'Onofrio, Dean Stockwell, Richard E. Grant

THE PLAYTHING (1929, GB, Wardour)
Joyce Bennett—Estelle Brody
Director—Castleton Knight
Leading Players—Heather Thatcher, Nigel Barrie, Marguerite Allan

PLEASE MURDER ME (1956, Distributors Corp. of America)
Craig Carlson—Raymond Burr
Director—Peter Godfrey
Leading Players—Angela Lansbury, Dick Foran, John Dehner

THE PLEASURE GIRLS (1966, GB, Times Film)
Sally Feathers—Francesca Annis
Marion—Rosemary Nicols
Dee—Suzanna Leigh
Angela—Anneke Wills
Director—Gerry O'Hara
Leading Players—Ian McShane, Klaus Kinski, Mark Eden, Tony Tanner

THE PLEASURE LOVERS (1964, GB, Butchers)
Carol—Leigh Madison
Eddie—Reed De Rouen
Director—Charles Saunders
Leading Players—Kenneth Cope, Arthur Lovegrove, Thomas Eytle

THE PLEASURE OF HIS COMPANY (1961, Paramount)
Biddeford "Pogo" Poole—Fred Astaire
Director—George Seaton
Leading Players—Debbie Reynolds, Lilli Palmer, Tab Hunter, Gary Merrill, Charles Ruggles

THE PLEASURE SEEKERS (1964, 20th Century Fox)
Fran Hobson—Ann-Margret
Maggie Williams—Carol Lynley
Susie Higgins—Pamela Tiffin
Director—Jean Negulesco
Leading Players—Tony Franciosa, Gardner McKay, Andre Lawrence, Gene Tierney, Brian Keith

THE PLOUGHMAN'S LUNCH (1984, GB, Goldwyn)
James Penfield—Jonathan Pryce
Director—Richard Eyre
Leading Players—Tim Curry, Rosemary Harris, Frank Finlay

THE PLOW GIRL (1916, Silent, Lasky)
Margot—Mae Murray
Director—Robert Z. Leonard
Leading Players—Elliott Dexter, Charles Gerard, Edythe Chapman

THE POACHER'S DAUGHTER (1960, GB, Show Corp. of America)
Sally Hamil—Julie Harris
Rabbit Hamil—Harry Brogan
Director—George Pollock
Leading Players—Tim Seely, Marie Kean, Brid Lynch

POET'S PUB (1949, GB, GFD)
Saturday Keith—Derek Bond
Director—Frederick Wilson
Leading Players—Rona Anderson, James Robertson Justice, John McLaren

POISON IVY (1992, New Line)
Ivy—Drew Barrymore
Director—Katt Shea Ruben
Leading Players—Sara Gilbert, Tom Skerritt, Cheryl Ladd

POLICE NURSE (1963, 20th Century Fox)
Joan Olson—Merry Anders
Director—Maury Dexter
Leading Players—Ken Scott, Oscar Beregi, Barbara Mansell

POLLY OF THE CIRCUS (1917, Silent, Goldwyn)
Polly—Mae Marsh
Directors—Charles Thomas Horan & Edwin L. Hollywood

Leading Players—Vernon Steele, Charles Eldridge, Wellington Playter

POLLY OF THE CIRCUS (1932, MGM)
Polly Fisher—Marion Davies
Director—Alfred Santell
Leading Players—Clark Gable, C. Aubrey Smith, Raymond Hatton

POLLY OF THE STORM COUNTRY (1920, Silent, First National)
Polly Hopkins—Mildred Harris Chaplin
Director—Arthur H. Rosson
Leading Players—Emory Johnson, Charlotte Burton, Harry Northrup

POLLYANNA (1920, Silent, UA)
Pollyanna—Mary Pickford
Director—Paul Powell
Leading Players—J. Wharton James, Katherine Griffith, Herbert Prior

POLLYANNA (1960, Buena Vista)
Pollyanna—Hayley Mills
Director—David Swift
Leading Players—Jane Wyman, Richard Egan, Karl Malden, Nancy Olson, Adolphe Menjou

POLO JOE (1936, Warner Brothers)
Joe Bolton—Joe E. Brown
Director—William McGann
Leading Players—Carol Hughes, Richard "Skeets" Gallagher, Joseph King

POLTERGEIST III (1988, MGM-UA)
Rev. Kane—Nathan Davis
Director—Gary Sherman
Leading PLayers—Tom Skerritt, Nancy Allen, Heather O'Rourke, Zelda Rubinstein, Lara Flynn Boyle

PONY EXPRESS RIDER (1976, Doty-Drayton)
Jimmy—Stewart Petersen
Director—Hal Harrison, Jr.
Leading Players—Henry Wilcoxon, Buck Taylor, Maureen McCormick

PONY SOLDIER (1952, 20th Century Fox)
Duncan MacDonald—Tyrone Power
Director—Joseph M. Newman
Leading Players—Cameron Mitchell, Thomas Gomez, Penny Edwards

POOR COW (1968, GB, National General Pictures)
Joy—Carol White
Director—Kenneth Loach
Leading Players—Terence Stamp, John Bindon, Kate Williams

POOR LITTLE RICH GIRL (1917, Silent, Artcraft)
Gwendolyn—Mary Pickford
Director—Maurice Tourneur
Leading Players—Madeline Traverse, Charles Wellesley, Gladys Fairbanks

POOR LITTLE RICH GIRL (1936, 20th Century Fox)
Barbara Barry—Shirley Temple
Director—Irving Cummings

Leading Players—Alice Faye, Gloria Stuart, Jack Haley, Michael Whalen

POOR OLD BILL (1931, GB, Wardour)
Bill—Leslie Fuller
Director—Monty Banks
Leading Players—Iris Ashley, Syd Courtenay, Peter Lawford

POPE JOAN (1972, GB, Columbia)
Joan—Liv Ullmann
Director—Michael Anderson
Leading Players—Olivia de Havilland, Lesley-Anne Down, Keir Dullea, Trevor Howard, Jeremy Kemp

THE POPE MUST DIET (1991, GB, Palace/Miramax)
Father David Albinizi—Robbie Coltrane
Director—Peter Richardson
Leading Players—Beverly D'Angelo, Herbert Lom, Paul Bartel, Salvatore Cascio, Balthazr Getty, Alex Rocco

THE POPE OF GREENWICH VILLAGE (1984, MGM-UA)
Paulie—Eric Roberts
Director—Stuart Rosenberg
Leading Players—Mickey Rourke, Daryl Hannah, Geraldine Page, Kenneth McMillan, Tony Musante, Burt Young

POPEYE (1980, Paramount)
Popeye—Robin Williams
Director—Robert Altman
Leading Players—Shelley Duvall, Ray Walston, Paul L. Smith

POPI (1969, UA)
Abraham Rodriguez—Alan Arkin
Director—Arthur Hiller
Leading Players—Rita Moreno, Miguel Alejandro, Ruben Figueroa

POPPY (1936, Paramount)
Poppy McGargle—Rochelle Hudson
Director—A. Edward Sutherland
Leading Players—W.C. Fields, Richard Cromwell, Granville Bates

THE POPPY GIRL'S HUSBAND (1919, Silent, Artcraft)
Polly—Juanita Hansen
Hairpin Harry Dutton—William S. Hart
Directors—William S. Hart & Lambert Hillyer
Leading Players—Fred Starr, David Kirby, Georgie Stone

PORGY AND BESS (1959, Columbia)
Porgy—Sidney Poitier
Bess—Dorothy Dandridge
Director—Otto Preminger
Leading Players—Sammy Davis, Jr., Pearl Bailey, Brock Peters, Diahann Carroll, Clarence Muse

PORKY'S (1982, 20th Century Fox)
Porky—Chuck Mitchell
Director—Bob Clark
Leading Players—Dan Monahan, Mark Herrier, Wyatt Knight, Roger Wilson, Nancy Parsons, Kaki Hunter

PORKY'S REVENGE (1985, 20th Century Fox)
Porky—Chuck Mitchell
Director—James Komack

Leading Players—Dan Monahan, Wyatt Knight, Tony Ganios, Mark Herrier, Kaki Hunter, Nancy Parsons

PORTNOY'S COMPLAINT (1972, Warner Brothers)
Alexander Portnoy—Richard Benjamin
Director—Ernest Lehman
Leading Players—Karen Black, Lee Grant, Jack Somack, Jeannie Berlin

PORTRAIT OF A MOBSTER (1961, Warner Brothers)
"Dutch Schultz" (Arthur Flegenheimer)—Vic Morrow
Director—Joseph Pevney
Leading Players—Leslie Parrish, Peter Breck, Ray Danton

PORTRAIT OF A SINNER (1961, GB, Renown)
Ila Hansen—Nadja Tiller
Director—Robert Siodmak
Leading Players—Tony Britton, William Bendix, Natasha Parry

PORTRAIT OF CLARE (1951, GB, Pathe)
Clare Hingston—Margaret Johnston
Director—Lance Comfort
Leading Players—Richard Todd, Robin Bailey, Ronald Howard

PORTRAIT OF JENNIE (1949, Selznick)
Jennie Appleton—Jennifer Jones
Director—William Dieterle
Leading Players—Joseph Cotten, Ethel Barrymore, Cecil Kellaway, David Wayne, Lillian Gish

A PORTRAIT OF THE ARTIST AS A YOUNG MAN (1979, Ireland, Mahler)
Stephen Dedalus—Bosco Hogan
Director—Joseph Strick
Leading Players—T.P. McKenna, John Gielgud, Rosaleen Linhan

POSSESSED (1931, MGM)
Marian Martin—Joan Crawford
Director—Clarence Brown
Leading Players—Clark Gable, Wallace Ford, Skeets Gallagher

POSSESSED (1947, Warner Brothers)
Louise Howell Graham—Joan Crawford
Director—Curtis Bernhardt
Leading Players—Van Heflin, Raymond Massey, Geraldine Brooks

THE POSSESION OF JOEL DELANEY (1972, Paramount)
Joel Delaney—Perry King
Director—Waris Hussein
Leading Players—Shirley MacLaine, Michael Hordern, David Elliott

POSTAL INSPECTOR (1936, Universal)
Bill Davis—Ricardo Cortez
Director—Otto Brower
Leading Players—Patricia Ellis, Bela Lugosi, Michael Loring

POSTMAN'S KNOCK (1962, GB, MGM)
Harold Petts—Spike Milligan
Director—Robert Lynn
Leading Players—Barbara Shelley, John Wood, Archie Duncan

THE POTTERS (1927, Silent, Paramount)
Pa Potter—W.C. Fields
Ma Potter—Mary Alden

Director—Fred Newymeyer
Leading Players—Ivy Harris, Jack Egan, "Skeets" Gallagher

THE POWER OF ONE (1992, Warner Brothers)
P.K. at 18—Stephen Dorff
P.K. at 12—Simon Fenton
P.K. at 7—Guy Witcher
Director—John G. Avildsen
Leading Players—Armin Mueller-Stahl, Morgan Freeman, John Gielgud, Marie Marais, Daniel Craig, Alois Moyo

THE POWERS GIRL (1942, UA)
Kay Evans—Carole Landis
Director—Norman Z. McLeod
Leading Players—George Murphy, Anne Shirley, Dennis Day

THE PRAIRIE WIFE (1925, Silent, Metro-Goldwyn)
Chaddie Green—Dorothy Devore
Director—Hugo Ballin
Leading Players—Herbert Rawlinson, Gibson Gowland, Leslie Stuart

THE PRAISE AGENT (1919, Silent, World)
Jack Bartling—Arthur Ashley
Director—Frank Crane
Leading Players—Dorothy Green, Jack Drumier, Lucille La Verne

PREDATOR (1987, 20th Century Fox)
Predator—Kevin Peter Hall
Director—John McTiernan
Leading Players—Arnold Schwarzenegger, Carl Weathers, Elpidia Carrillo

PREDATOR 2 (1990, 20th Century Fox)
The Predator—Kevin Peter Hall
Director—Stephen Hopkins
Leading Players—Danny Glover, Gary Busey, Ruben Blades, Maria Conchita Alonso, Bill Paxton

THE PREHISTORIC MAN (1924, GB, Silent, Stoll)
He-of-the-Beetle-Brow—George Robey
Director—A.E. Coleby
Leading Players—Marie Blanche, H. Agar Lyons, W.G. Saunders

PREHISTORIC WOMEN (1950, Eagle Lion)
Tigri—Laurette Luez
Lotee—Joan Shawlee
Eras—Judy Landon
Director—Gregg Tallas
Leading Players—Allan Nixon, Mara Lynn, Jo Carroll Summers

PREHISTORIC WOMEN (1967, GB, 20th Century Fox)
Queen Kari—Martine Beswick
Saria—Edina Ronay
Amyak—Stephanie Randall
Director—Michael Carreras
Leading Players—Michael Latimer, Carol White, Alexandra Stevenson

PRESENTING LILY MARS (1943, MGM)
Lily Mars—Judy Garland
Director—Norman Taurog
Leading Players—Van Heflin, Fay Bainter, Richard Carlson

THE PRESIDENT VANISHES (1934, Paramount)
President Stanley Craig—Arthur Byron
Director—William A. Wellman
Leading Players—Janet Beecher, Paul Kelly, Peggy Conklin

THE PRESIDENT'S ANALYST (1967, Paramount)
Dr. Sidney Schaefer—James Coburn
Director—Theodore J. Flicker
Leading Players—Godfrey Cambridge, Severn Darden, Joan
Delaney

THE PRESIDENT'S LADY (1953, 20th Century Fox)
Rachel Donelson Robards Jackson—Susan Hayward
Andrew Jackson—Charlton Heston
Director—Henry Levin
Leading Players—John McIntire, Fay Bainter, Whitfield Connor

PRESUMED INNOCENT (1990, Warner Brothers/Mirage)
Rusty Sabich—Harrison Ford
Director—Alan J. Pakula
Leading Players—Brian Dennehy, Raul Julia, Bonnie Bedelia,
Paul Winfield, Greta Scacchi, John Spencer, Joe Grifasi

THE PRESUMPTION OF STANLEY HAY, MP (1925, GB, Silent,
Stoll)
Stanley Hay—David Hawthorne
Director—Sinclair Hill
Leading Players—Betty Faire, Fred Raynham, Eric Bransby
Williams

THE PRETENDER (1947, Republic)
Kenneth Holden—Albert Dekker
Director—W. Lee Wilder
Leading Players—Catherine Craig, Charles Drake, Alan Carney

PRETTY BABY (1978, Paramount)
Violet—Brooke Shields
Director—Louis Malle
Leading Players—Keith Carradine, Susan Sarandon, Frances
Faye

PRETTY BOY FLOYD (1960, Continental)
Pretty Boy Floyd—John Ericson
Director—Herbert J. Leder
Leading Players—Barry Newman, Joan Harvey, Herbert Evers

PRETTY IN PINK (1986, Paramount)
Andie—Molly Ringwald
Director—Howard Deutch
Leading Players—Harry Dean Stanton, Jon Cryer, Anne Potts,
James Spader, Andrew McCarthy

PRETTY MRS. SMITH (1915, Silent, Paramount)
Drucilla Smith—Fritzi Scheff
Director—Hobart Bosworth
Leading Players—Owen Moore, Forrest Stanley, Louis Bennison

PRETTY POISON (1968, 20th Century Fox)
Sue Ann Stepanek—Tuesday Weld
Director—Noel Black
Leading Players—Anthony Perkins, Beverly Garland, John
Randolph

PRETTY WOMAN (1990, Buena Vista/Touchstone)
Vivian Ward—Julia Roberts
Director—Garry Marshall

Leading Players—Richard Gere, Ralph Bellamy, Jason
Alexander, Laura San Giacomo, Hector Elizondo

PRETTYKILL (1987, Dax Avant/Spectrafilm)
Francie—Suzanne Snyder
Director—George Kaczender
Leading Players—David Birney, Season Hubley, Susannah York,
Yaphet Kotto

THE PRIDE OF ST. LOUIS (1952, 20th Century Fox)
Dizzy Dean—Dan Dailey
Director—Harmon Jones
Leading Players—Joanne Dru, Richard Hylton, Richard Crenna

PRIDE OF THE FORCE (1925, Silent, Rayart)
Officer Moore—Tom Santschi
Director—Duke Worne
Leading Players—Edythe Chapman, Gladys Hulette, James
Morrison

PRIDE OF THE MARINES (1936, Columbia)
Steve Riley—Charles Bickford
Director—D. Ross Lederman
Leading Players—Florence Rice, Billy Burrud, Robert Allen

PRIDE OF THE MARINES (1945, Warner Brothers)
Al Schmid—John Garfield
Director—Delmer Daves
Leading Players—Eleanor Parker, Dane Clark, John Ridgely,
Rosemary De Camp, Ann Doran

PRIDE OF THE NAVY (1939, Republic)
Speed Brennan—James Dunn
Director—Charles Lamont
Leading Players—Rochelle Hudson, Gordon Oliver, Horace
MacMahon

THE PRIDE OF THE YANKEES (1942, RKO)
Lou Gehrig—Gary Cooper
Director—Sam Wood
Leading Players—Teresa Wright, Walter Brennan, Dan Duryea,
Babe Ruth, Elsa Janssen, Ludwig Stossel

PRIEST OF LOVE (1981, GB, Filmways)
D.H. Lawrence—Ian McKellen
Director—Christopher Miles
Leading Players—Janet Suzman, Ava Gardner, Penelope Keith

THE PRIME MINISTER (1941, GB, Warner Brothers)
Benjamin Disraeli—John Gielgud
Director—Thorold Dickinson
Leading Players—Diana Wynyard, Will Fyffe, Stephen Murray

THE PRIME OF MISS JEAN BRODIE (1969, GB, 20th Century
Fox)
Jean Brodie—Maggie Smith
Director—Ronald Neame
Leading Players—Robert Stephens, Pamela Franklin, Gordon
Jackson, Celia Johnson, Diane Grayson, Jane Carr

THE PRINCE AND THE BEGGARMAID (1921, GB, Silent, Ideal)
Prince Olaf—Henry Ainley
Princess Monika—Kathleen Vaughn
Director—A.V. Bramble
Leading Players—Harvey Braban, Sam Wilkinson, Sydney
Paxton

THE PRINCE AND THE PAUPER (1915, Silent, Famous Players)
Edward, Prince Of Wales—Marguerite Clark
Tom Canty—Marguerite Clark
Director—Edwin S. Porter
Leading Players—William Burrows, William Sorelle, William Frederick

THE PRINCE AND THE PAUPER (1937, Warner Brothers)
Tom Canty—Billy Mauch
Prince Edward—Bobby Mauch
Director—William Keighley
Leading Players—Errol Flynn, Claude Rains, Henry Stephenson, Barton MacLane, Alan Hale

THE PRINCE AND THE SHOWGIRL (1957, GB, Warner Brothers)
Elsie Marina—Marilyn Monroe
Charles, Prince Regent—Laurence Olivier
Director—Laurence Olivier
Leading Players—Sybil Thorndyke, Richard Wattis, Jeremy Spenser

PRINCE OF ARCADIA (1933, GB, Woolf & Freedman)
Prince Peter—Carl Brisson
Director—Hans Schwartz
Leading Players—Margot Grahame, Ida Lupino, Annie Esmond

PRINCE OF AVENUE A (1920, Silent, Universal)
Barry O'Conner—James J. Corbett
Director—Jack Ford
Leading Players—Mary Warren, Harry Northrup, Cora Drew

PRINCE OF DIAMONDS (1930, Columbia)
Rupert Endon—Ian Keith
Director—Karl Brown
Leading Players—Aileen Pringle, Fritzi Ridgeway, Tyrell Davis

PRINCE OF FOXES (1949, 20th Century Fox)
Andrea Corsini—Tyrone Power
Director—Henry King
Leading Players—Orson Welles, Wanda Hendrix, Everett Sloane, Marina Berti, Felix Aylmer

PRINCE OF PENNSYLVANIA (1988, New Line)
Rupert Marshetta—Keanu Reeves
Director—Ron Nyswaner
Leading Players—Fred Ward, Bonnie Bedelia, Amy Madigan

PRINCE OF PILSEN (1926, Silent, Producers Distributing Corp.)
Frederick, Prince of Pilsen—Allan Forrest
Director—Paul Powell
Leading Players—George Sidney, Anita Stewart, Myrtle Stedman

PRINCE OF PIRATES (1953, Columbia)
Prince Roland—John Derek
Director—Sidney Salkow
Leading Players—Barbara Rush, Carla Balenda, Whitfield Connor

PRINCE OF PLAYERS (1955, 20th Century Fox)
Edwin Booth—Richard Burton
Director—Philip Dunne
Leading Players—Maggie McNamara, John Derek, Raymond Massey, Charles Bickford

PRINCE OF THE CITY (1981, Warner Brothers)
Daniel Ciello—Treat Williams
Director—Sidney Lumet
Leading Players—Jerry Orbach, Richard Foronjy, Don Billett

THE PRINCE OF THIEVES (1948, Columbia)
Robin Hood—Jon Hall
Director—Howard Bretherton
Leading Players—Patricia Morison, Adele Jergens, Alan Mowbray

THE PRINCE OF TIDES (1991, Columbia)
Tom Wingo—Nick Nolte
Director—Barbra Streisand
Leading Players—Barbra Streisand, Blythe Danner, Kate Nelligan, Jeroen Krabbe, Melinda Dillon, George Carlin, Jason Gould, Brad Sullivan

A PRINCE THERE WAS (1921, Silent, Paramount)
Charles Edward Martin—Thomas Meighan
Director—Tom Forman
Leading Players—Mildred Harris, Charlotte Jackson, Nigel Barrie

PRINCE VALIANT (1954, 20th Century Fox)
Prince Valiant—Robert Wagner
Director—Henry Hathaway
Leading Players—James Mason, Janet Leigh, Debra Paget, Sterling Hayden, Victor McLaglen

THE PRINCE WHO WAS A THIEF (1951, Universal)
Julna—Tony Curtis
Director—Rudolph Mate
Leading Players—Piper Laurie, Everett Sloane, Betty Garde, Jeff Corey, Peggie Castle

THE PRINCESS AND THE PIRATE (1944, RKO)
"Sylvester The Great" Crosby—Bob Hope
Princess Margaret—Virginia Mayo
Director—David Butler
Leading Players—Water Brennan, Walter Slezak, Victor McLaglen

THE PRINCESS AND THE PLUMBER (1930, Fox Film Corp.)
Charlie Peters—Charles Farrell
Princess Louise—Maureen O'Sullivan
Director—Alexander Korda
Leading Players—H.B. Warner, Joseph Cawthorn, Bert Roach

THE PRINCESS BRIDE (1987, 20th Century Fox)
Buttercup—Robin Wright
Director—Rob Reiner
Leading Players—Cary Elwes, Mandy Patinkin, Chris Sarandon, Wallace Shawn, Andre The Giant

PRINCESS CHARMING (1935, GB, Gaumont)
Princess Charming—Evelyn Laye
Director—Maurice Elvey
Leading Players—Henry Wilcoxon, Yvonne Arnaud, George Grossmith

THE PRINCESS COMES ACROSS (1936, Paramount)
Princess Olga—Carole Lombard
Director—William K. Howard
Leading Players—Fred MacMurray, Douglas Dumbrille, Alison Skipworth

THE PRINCESS FROM HOBOKEN (1927, Silent, Tiffany)
Sheila O'Toole—Blanche Mehaffey
Director—Allan Dale
Leading Players—Edmund Burns, Ethel Clayton, Lou Tellegen

THE PRINCESS OF HAPPY CHANCE (1916, GB, Silent, Jury)
Princess Felicia—Elizabeth Risdon
Director—Maurice Elvey
Leading Players—Gerald Ames, Hayford Hobbs, Dallas Cairns

PRINCESS OF THE NILE (1954, 20th Century Fox)
Princess Shalimar—Debra Paget
Director—Harmon Jones
Leading Players—Jeffrey Hunter, Michael Rennie, Dona Drake

PRINCESS O'HARA (1935, Universal)
Princess O'Hara—Jean Parker
Director—David Burton
Leading Players—Chester Morris, Leon Errol, Vince Barnett

PRINCESS O'ROURKE (1943, Warner Brothers)
Princess Maria O'Rourke—Olivia de Havilland
Director—Norman Krasna
Leading Players—Robert Cummings, Charles Coburn, Jack
Carson, Jane Wyman, Harry Davenport

THE PRINCIPAL (1987, Tri-Star)
Rick Latimer—James Belushi
Director—Christopher Cain
Leading Players—Louis Gossett, Jr., Rae Dawn Chong, Michael
Wright

PRISON BREAKER (1936, GB, Columbia)
Bunny Barnes—James Mason
Director—Adrian Brunel
Leading Players—Andrews Englemann, Marguerite Allan, Ian
Fleming

PRISON GIRL (1942, Producers Releasing Corp.)
Rosemary Walsh—Rose Hobart
Director—William Beaudine
Leading Players—Sidney Blackmer, Claire Rochelle, Lynn Starr

PRISON NURSE (1938, Republic)
Judy—Marian Marsh
Director—James Cruze
Leading Players—Henry Wilcoxon, Bernadene Hayes, Ben
Welden

PRISON WARDEN (1949, Columbia)
Victor Burnell—Warner Baxter
Director—Seymour Friedman
Leading Players—Anna Lee, James Flavin, Harlan Warde

THE PRISONER (1955, GB, Columbia)
The Prisoner—Alec Guinness
Director—Peter Glenville
Leading Players—Jack Hawkins, Raymond Huntley, Jeannette
Sterke

THE PRISONER OF SECOND AVENUE (1975, Warner Brothers)
Mel—Jack Lemmon
Director—Melvin Frank
Leading Players—Anne Bancroft, Gene Saks, Elizabeth Wilson

THE PRISONER OF SHARK ISLAND (1936, 20th Century Fox)
Dr. Samuel A. Mudd—Warner Baxter
Director—John Ford
Leading Players—Gloria Stuart, Joyce Kay, Claude Gillingwater

THE PRISONER OF THE PINES (1918, Silent, Paralta)
Hillaire Latour—J. Warren Kerrigan
Director—Ernest C. Warde
Leading Players—Lois Wilson, Walter Perry, Claire Du Brey

PRISONER OF WAR (1954, MGM)
Web Sloane—Ronald Reagan
Director—Andrew Marton
Leading Players—Steve Forrest, Dewey Martin, Oscar Homolka

THE PRISONER OF ZENDA (1922, Silent, Metro)
King Rudolf—Lewis Stone
Director—Rex Ingram
Leading Players—Alice Terry, Robert Edeson, Stuart Holmes

THE PRISONER OF ZENDA (1937, UA)
King Rudolf V—Ronald Colman
Director—John Cromwell
Leading Players—Madeleine Carroll, Douglas Fairbanks, Jr.,
Mary Astor, C. Aubrey Smith, Raymond Massey, David Niven

THE PRISONER OF ZENDA (1952, MGM)
King Rudolf V—Stewart Granger
Director—Richard Thorpe
Leading Players—Deborah Kerr, James Mason, Louis Calhern,
Jane Greer, Lewis Stone, Robert Douglas

THE PRISONER OF ZENDA (1979, Universal)
Rudolph—Peter Sellers
Director—Richard Quine
Leading Players—Lynne Frederick, Lionel Jeffries, Elke
Sommer, Gregory Sierra, Jeremy Kemp

PRISONERS (1929, Warner Brothers)
Tiza Riga—Corinne Griffith
Director— William A. Seiter
Leading Players—James Ford, Bela Lugosi, Ian Keith

PRISONERS IN PETTICOATS (1950, Republic)
Joan Grey—Valentine Perkins
Director—Philip Ford
Leading Players—Robert Rockwell, Danni Sue Nolan, Anthony
Caruso

PRISONERS OF THE CASBAH (1953, Columbia)
Princess Nadja—Gloria Grahame
Ahmed—Turhan Bey
Director—Richard Bare
Leading Players—Cesar Romero, Nestor Paiva, Paul E. Newlan

PRIVATE ANGELO (1949, GB, ABF-Pathe)
Pvt. Angelo—Peter Ustinov
Director—Peter Ustinov
Leading Players—Godfrey Tearle, Maria Denis, Marjorie Rhodes

PRIVATE BENJAMIN (1980, Warner Brothers)
Judy Benjamin—Goldie Hawn
Director—Howard Zieff
Leading Players—Eileen Brennan, Armand Assante, Robert
Webber, Sam Wannamaker, Barbara Barrie

PRIVATE DETECTIVE (1939, Warner Brothers)
Jim Rickey—Dick Foran
Director—Noel Smith
Leading Players—Jane Wyman, Gloria Dickson, Maxie Rosenbloom

PRIVATE DETECTIVE 62 (1933, Warner Brothers)
Donald Free—William Powell
Director—Michael Curtiz
Leading Players—Margaret Lindsay, Ruth Donnelly, Gordon Westcott

PRIVATE DUTY NURSES (1972, New World)
Spring—Kathy Cannon
Lola—Joyce Williams
Lynn—Pegi Boucher
Director—George Armitage
Leading Players—Joseph Kaufmann, Dennis Redfield, Herbert Jefferson

THE PRIVATE EYES (1980, New World)
Dr. Tart—Tim Conway
Inspector Winship—Don Knotts
Director—Lang Elliott
Leading Players—Trisha Noble, Bernard Fox, Grace Zabriske

THE PRIVATE FILES OF J. EDGAR HOOVER (1978, American International)
J. Edgar Hoover—Broderick Crawford
Director—Larry Cohen
Leading Players—Jose Ferrer, Michael Parks, Ronee Blakeley, Rip Torn

PRIVATE IZZY MURPHY (1926, Silent, Warner Brothers)
Izzy Murphy—George Jessel
Director—Lloyd Bacon
Leading Players—Patsy Ruth Miller, Vera Gordon, Nat Carr

PRIVATE JONES (1933, Universal)
Bill Jones—Lee Tracy
Director—Russell Mack
Leading Players—Donald Cook, Gloria Stuart, Shirley Grey

THE PRIVATE LIFE OF BEL AMI (1947, UA)
Georges Duroy—George Sanders
Director—Albert Lewin
Leading Players—Angela Lansbury, Ann Dvorak, Frances Dee, John Carradine

THE PRIVATE LIFE OF DON JUAN (1934, UA)
Don Juan—Douglas Fairbanks, Jr.
Director—Alexander Korda
Leading Players—Merle Oberon, Binnie Barnes, Joan Gardner, Benita Hume

THE PRIVATE LIFE OF HENRY VIII (1933, UA)
Henry VIII—Charles Laughton
Director—Alexander Korda
Leading Players—Robert Donat, Lady Tree, Binnie Barnes, Elsa Lanchester, Merle Oberon, Wendy Barrie

THE PRIVATE LIFE OF SHERLOCK HOLMES (1970, GB, United Artists)
Sherlock Holmes—Robert Stephens
Director—Billy Wilder

Leading Players—Colin Blakely, Irene Handl, Stanley Holloway, Christopher Lee, Geraldine Page

PRIVATE LIVES (1931, MGM)
Amanda Chase Paynne—Norma Shearer
Elyot Chase—Robert Montgomery
Director—Sidney Franklin
Leading Players—Reginald Denny, Una Merkel, Jean Hersholt

THE PRIVATE LIVES OF ADAM AND EVE (1961, Universal)
Evie Simms/Eve—Mamie Van Doren
Ad Simms/Adam—Martin Milner
Directors—Albert Zugsmith & Mickey Rooney
Leading Players—Mickey Rooney, Fay Spain, Mel Torme

THE PRIVATE LIVES OF ELIZABETH AND ESSEX (1939, Warner Brothers)
Queen Elizabeth—Bette Davis
Robert Devereaux, Earl Of Essex—Errol Flynn
Director—Michael Curtiz
Leading Players—Olivia de Havilland, Donald Crisp, Alan Hale, Vincent Price, Henry Stephenson, Henry Daniell

THE PRIVATE NAVY OF SGT. O'FARRELL (1968, UA)
Master Sgt. Dan O'Farrell—Bob Hope
Director—Frank Tashlin
Leading Players—Phyllis Diller, Jeffrey Hunter, Gina Lollobrigida

PRIVATE NURSE (1941, 20th Century Fox)
Miss Adams—Jane Darwell
Mary Malloy—Brenda Joyce
Director—David Burton
Leading Players—Sheldon Leonard, Robert Lowery, Ann Todd

PRIVATE POTTER (1963, MGM)
Pvt. Potter—Tom Courtenay
Director—Casper Wrede
Leading Players—Mogens Wieth, Ronald Fraser, James Maxwell

THE PRIVATE WAR OF MAJOR BENSON (1955, Universal)
Major Bernard Benson—Charlton Heston
Director—Jerry Hopper
Leading Players—Julie Adams, William Demarest, Tim Considine

PRIVATE'S PROGRESS (1956, GB, British Lion)
Stanley Windrush—Ian Carmichael
Director—John Boulting
Leading Players—Richard Attenborough, Dennis Price, Terry-Thomas

THE PRIZE FIGHTER (1979, New World)
Bags—Tim Conway
Director—Michael Preece
Leading Players—Don Knotts, David Wayne, Robin Clark

THE PRIZEFIGHTER AND THE LADY (1933, MGM)
Belle Morgan—Myrna Loy
Steve Morgan—Max Baer
Director—W.S. Van Dyke
Leading Players—Primo Carnera, Jack Dempsey, Walter Huston

PRIZZI'S HONOR (1985, 20th Century Fox)
Don Corrado Prizzi—William Hickey
Director—John Huston

Leading Players—Jack Nicholson, Kathleen Turner, Robert Loggia, John Randolph, Lee Richardson, Anjelica Huston

PROBLEM CHILD (1990, Universal/Imagine)
Junior—Michael Oliver
Director—Dennis Dugan
Leading Players—John Ritter, Jack Warden, Gilbert Gottried, Amy Yasbeck, Michael Richards

PROBLEM CHILD 2 (1991, Universal)
Junior Healy—Michael Oliver
Director—Brian Levant
Leading Players—John Ritter, Jack Warden, Laraine Newman, Amy Yasbeck, Ivyann Schwan

THE PRODIGAL (1931, MGM)
Jeffrey Farraday—Lawrence Tibbett
Director—Harry Pollard
Leading Players—Esther Ralston, Roland Young, Cliff Edwards

THE PRODIGAL (1955, MGM)
Micah—Edmund Purdom
Director—Richard Thorpe
Leading Players—Lana Turner, Louis Calhern, Audrey Dalton, James Mitchell, Neville Brand

THE PRODIGAL SON (1923, GB, Silent, Stoll)
Magnus Stephenson—Stewart Rome
Director—A.E. Coleby
Leading Players—Henry Victor, Edith Bishop, Colette Brettelle

THE PRODIGAL WIFE (1918, Silent, Screencraft)
Marion Farnham—Mary Boland
Director—Frank Reicher
Leading Players—Lucy Cotton, Raymond Bloomer, Alfred Keppier

THE PRODUCERS (1967, Embassy)
Max Bialystock—Zero Mostel
Leo Bloom—Gene Wilder
Director—Mel Brooks
Leading Players—Dick Shawn, Kenny Mars, Estelle Winwood, Christopher Hewett, Lee Meredith

PROFESSIONAL SOLDIER (1936, 20th Century Fox)
Michael Donovan—Victor McLaglen
Director—Tay Garnett
Leading Players—Freddie Bartholomew, Gloria Stuart, Constance Collier, Michael Whalen

PROFESSIONAL SWEETHEART (1933, RKO)
Jim Davey—Norman Foster
Director—William Seiter
Leading Players—Ginger Rogers, Zasu Pitts, Frank McHugh, Allen Jenkins, Gregory Ratoff

THE PROFESSIONALS (1966, Columbia)
Bill Dolworth—Burt Lancaster
Henry Rico Farden—Lee Marvin
Hans Ehrengard—Robert Ryan
Jacob Sharp—Woody Strode
Director—Richard Brooks
Leading Players—Jack Palance, Claudia Cardinale, Ralph Bellamy

PROFESSOR BEWARE (1938, Paramount)
Prof. Dean Lambert—Harold Lloyd
Director—Elliott Nugent
Leading Players—Phyllis Welch, Raymond Walburn, Lionel Stander

PROFESSOR TIM (1957, Ireland, RKO)
Professor Tim—Seamus Kavanagh
Director—Henry Cass
Leading Players—Ray MacAnally, Marie Keane, Philip O'Flynn

PROGRAMMED TO KILL (1987, Trans World)
Samira—Sandahl Bergman
Directors—Allan Holzman & Robert Short
Leading Players—Robert Ginty, James Booth, Alex Courtney

THE PROJECTED MAN (1967, GB, Universal)
Prof. Steiner—Bryant Halliday
Director—Ian Curteis
Leading Players—Mary Peach, Norman Wooland, Ronald Allen

THE PROJECTIONIST (1970, Maglan/Maron)
Projectionist—Chuck McCann
Director—Harry Hurwitz
Leading Players—Ina Balin, Rodney Dangerfield, Jara Kohout

THE PROMOTER (1952, GB, Universal)
Edward Henry "Denry" Machin—Alec Guinness
Director—Ronald Neame
Leading Players—Glynis Johns, Valerie Hobson, Petula Clark

PROSPERO'S BOOKS (1991, GB/Fr., Miramax)
Prospero—John Gielgud
Director—Peter Greenaway
Leading Players—Michael Clark, Michel Blanc, Roland Josephson, Isabelle Fasco, Tom Bell, Kenneth Cranham

PROSTITUTE (1980, GB, Kestrel)
Sandra—Eleanor Forsythe
Director—Tony Garnett
Leading Players—Kate Crutchley, Kim Lockett, Nancy Samuels

THE PROUD REBEL (1958, Buena Vista)
John Chandler—Alan Ladd
Director—Michael Curtiz
Leading Players—Olivia de Havilland, Dean Jagger, David Ladd, Cecil Kellaway

PRUDENCE AND THE PILL (1968, GB, 20th Century Fox)
Prudence Hardcastle—Deborah Kerr
Director—Fielder Cook
Leading Players—David Niven, Robert Coote, Irina Demick, Joyce Redman, Judy Geeson

PRUNELLA (1918, Silent, Paramount)
Prunella—Marguerite Clark
Director—Maurice Tourneur
Leading Players—Jules Raycourt, Harry Leone, Marcia Harris

PSYCHIC KILLER (1975, Avco Embassy)
Arnold—Jim Hutton
Director—Raymond Danton
Leading Players—Julie Adams, Paul Burke, Nehemiah Persoff, Aldo Ray

PSYCHO (1960, Paramount)
Norman Bates—Anthony Perkins
Director—Alfred Hitchcock
Leading Players—Janet Leigh, Vera Miles, John Gavin, Martin Balsam

PYSCHO II (1983, Universal)
Norman Bates—Anthony Perkins
Director—Richard Franklin
Leading Players—Vera Miles, Meg Tilly, Robert Loggia, Dennis Franz

PSYCHO III (1986, Universal)
Norman Bates—Anthony Perkins
Director—Anthony Perkins
Leading Players—Diana Scarwid, Jeff Fahey, Roberta Maxwell

THE PSYCHOPATH (1966, GB, Paramount)
Mrs. Von Sturm—Margaret Johnston
Director—Freddie Francis
Leading Players—Patrick Wymark, John Standing, Alexander Knox, Judy Huxtable

THE PSYCHOTRONIC MAN (1980, International Harmony)
Rocky Foscoe—Peter Spelson
Director—Jack M. Sell
Leading Players—Christopher Carbis, Curt Colbert, Robin Newton

PSYCHOS IN LOVE (1987, ICN Bleecker Infinity)
Joe—Carmine Capobianco
Kate—Debi Thibeault
Director—Gorman Bechard
Leading Players—Frank Stewart, Cecilia Wilde, Donna Davidge

PUBLIC DEB. NO. 1 (1940, 20th Century Fox)
Penny Cooper—Brenda Joyce
Director—Gregory Ratoff
Leading Players—George Murphy, Elsa Maxwell, Mischa Auer, Charlie Ruggles, Ralph Bellamy

THE PUBLIC DEFENDER (1931, Fox Film Corp.)
Pike Winslow—Richard Dix
Director—J. Walter Ruben
Leading Players—Shirley Grey, Edmund Breese, Paul Hurst

THE PUBLIC ENEMY (1931, Warner Brothers)
Tom Powers—James Cagney
Director—William A. Wellman
Leading Players—Jean Harlow, Edward Woods, Joan Blondell, Beryl Mercer, Mae Clarke, Leslie Fenton

PUBLIC ENEMY'S WIFE (1936, Warner Brothers)
Judith Maroc—Margaret Lindsay
Gene Maroc—Cesar Romero
Director—Nick Grinde
Leading Players—Pat O'Brien, Robert Armstrong, Dick Foran

PUBLIC HERO NO. 1 (1935, MGM)
Jeff Crane—Chester Morris
Director—J. Walter Ruben
Leading Players—Jean Arthur, Lionel Barrymore, Paul Kelly, Lewis Stone, Joesph Calleia

THE PUBLIC LIFE OF HENRY THE NINTH (1934, GB, MGM)
Henry—Leonard Henry
Director—Bernard Mainwaring
Leading Players—Betty Frankiss, George Mozart, Wally Patch

PUBLIC MENACE (1935, Columbia)
Tonelli—Douglas Dumbrille
Director—Erle C. Kenton
Leading Players—Jean Arthur, George Murphy, George McKay

PUBLIC PIDGEON NO. 1 (1957, RKO/Universal)
Rusty Morgan—Red Skelton
Director—Norman Z. McLeod
Leading Players—Vivian Blaine, Janet Blair, Jay C. Flippen

PUBLIC STENOGRAPHER (1935, Screencraft/Marcy)
Ann McNair—Lola Lane
Director—Lew Collins
Leading Players—William Collier, Jr., Esther Muir, Duncan Renaldo

THE PUMPKIN EATER (1964, GB, Columbia)
Jake Armitage—Peter Finch
Director—Jack Clayton
Leading Players—Anne Bancroft, James Mason, Janie Gray, Cedric Hardwicke, Richard Johnson

PUMPKINHEAD (1988, MGM-UA)
Pumpkinhead—Tom Woodruff Jr.
Director—Stan Winston
Leading Players—Lance Henriksen, Matthew Hurley, Jeff East, John DiAquino, Kimberly Ross

THE PUNCH AND JUDY MAN (1963, GB, Warner-Pathe)
Wally Pinner—Tony Hancock
Director—Jeremy Summers
Leading Players—Sylvia Syms, Ronald Fraser, Barbara Murray

THE PUNISHER (1990, Castle Premier/New World)
Frank Castle—Dolph Lundgren
Director—Mark Goldblatt
Leading Players—Louis Gossett, Jr., Jeroen Krabbe, Bryan Marshall, Nancy Everhard, Barry Otto

THE PUPPET MAN (1921, GB, FBO)
Alcide le Beau—Hugh Miller
Director—Frank H. Crane
Leading Players—Molly Adair, Hilda Anthony, Marie Belocci

PUPPET ON A CHAIN (1971, GB, Cinerama)
Maggie—Barbara Parkins
Director—Geoffrey Reeve
Leading Players—Sven-Bertil Taube, Alexander Knox, Patrick Allen

THE PURSUIT OF D.B. COOPER (1981, Universal)
Meade (D.B. Cooper)—Treat Williams
Director—Roger Spottiswoode
Leading Players—Robert Duvall, Kathryn Harrold, Ed Flanders

THE PURSUIT OF PAMELA (1920, GB, Silent, Jury)
Pamela Dodder—Edna Flugrath
Director—Harold Shaw
Leading Players—Templar Powell, Douglas Munro, Ada Palmer

THE PUSHER (1960, UA)
The Pusher—Felice Orlandi
Director—Gene Milford

Leading Players—Kathy Carlyle, Douglas F. Rodgers, Sloan
Simpson

PUSHOVER (1954, Columbia)
Paul Sheridan—Fred MacMurray
Director—Richard Quine
Leading Players—Kim Novak, Phil Carey, Dorothy Malone, E.G.
Marshall

PUTNEY SWOPE (1969, Cinema V Distributing)
Putney Swope—Arnold Johnson
Director—Robert Downey
Leading Players—Stan Gottlieb, Allen Garfield, Archie Russell

PUZZLE OF A DOWNFALL CHILD (1970, Universal)
Lou Andreas Sand—Faye Dunaway
Director—Jerry Schatzberg
Leading Players—Barry Primus, Viveca Lindfors, Barry Morse,
Roy Scheider, Ruth Jackson

PYGMALION (1938, GB, MGM)
Prof. Henry Higgins—Leslie Howard
Directors—Anthony Asquith & Leslie Howard
Leading Players—Wendy Hiller, Wilfrid Lawson, Marie Lohr,
Scott Sunderland, Jean Cadell, David Tree

Q (aka: **THE WINGED SERPENT**) (1982, United Film
Distribution)
Jimmy Quinn—Michael Moriarty
Director—Larry Cohen
Leading Players—Candy Clark, David Carradine, Richard
Roundtree

QUACKSER FORTUNE HAS A COUSIN IN THE BRONX (1970,
UMC)
Quackser Fortune—Gene Wilder
Director—Waris Hussein
Leading Players—Margot Kidder, Eileen Colgan, Seamus Ford

QUADROON (1972, Presidio)
Coral—Kathrine McKee
Director—Jack Weis
Leading Players—Tim Kincaid, Robert Priest, Madelyn Sanders

THE QUALIFIED ADVENTURER (1925, GB, Silent, Stoll)
Peter Duff—Matheson Lang
Director—Sinclair Hill
Leading Players—Genevieve Townsend, Fred Raynham, Kyoshi
Tekase

QUANTRILL'S RAIDERS (1958, Allied Artists)
William Quantrill—Leo Gordon
Director—Edward Bernds
Leading Players—Steve Cochran, Diane Brewster, Gale Robbins

THE QUARTERBACK (1926, Silent, Paramount)
Jack Stone—Richard Dix

Director—Fred Newmeyer
Leading Players—Esther Ralston, Harry Beresford, David Butler

THE QUARTERBACK (1940, Paramount)
Bill Jones—Wayne Morris
Director—H. Bruce Humberstone
leading Players—Virginia Dale, Lilian Cornell, Edgar Kennedy

QUEEN BEE (1955, Columbia)
Eva Phillips—Joan Crawford
Director—Randal MacDougall
Leading Players—Barry Sullivan, Betsy Palmer, John Ireland

QUEEN CHRISTINA (1933, MGM)
Queen Christina—Greta Garbo
Director—Rouben Mamoulian
Leading Players—John Gilbert, Ian Keith, Lewis Stone,
Elizabeth Young, C. Aubrey Smith

QUEEN ELIZABETH (1912, Silent, Famous Players)
Elizabeth I—Sarah Bernhardt
Director—Louis Mercanton
Leading Players—Lou Tellegen, Members of the Comedie
Francaise

QUEEN KELLY (1929, Silent, UA)
Queen Kelly—Gloria Swanson
Director—Erich von Stroheim
Leading Players—Walter Bryon, Seena Owen, Wilhelm von
Brincken

QUEEN O' DIAMONDS (1926, R-C Pictures)
Jeanette Durant—Evelyn Brent
Director—Chet Withey
Leading Players—Elsa Lorimer, Phillips Smalley, William N.
Bailey

QUEEN OF BLOOD (1966, American International)
"Queen of Blood"—Florence Marly
Director—Curtis Harrington
Leading Players—John Saxon, Basil Rathbone, Judi Meredith

QUEEN OF BURLESQUE (1946, Producers Releasing Corp.)
Crystal McCoy—Evelyn Ankers
Director—Sam Newfield
Leading Players—Carleton Young, Marion Martin, Craig
Reynolds

QUEEN OF HEARTS (1936, GB, Associated Talking Pictures)
Grace Perkins—Gracie Fields
Director—Monty Banks
Leading Players—John Loder, Enid Stamp-Taylor, Fred Duprez

QUEEN OF HEARTS (1989, GB, Cinecom)
Rosa—Anita Zagaria
Director—Jon Amiel
Leading Players—Vittorio Duse, Joseph Long, Eileen Way,
Vittorio Amandola, Roberto Scateni, Ian Hawkes

QUEEN OF OUTER SPACE (1958, Allied Artists)
Talleah—Zsa Zsa Gabor
Director—Edward Bernds
Leading Players—Eric Fleming, Laurie Mitchell, Paul Birch

QUEEN OF SHEBA (1921, Silent, Fox Film Corp.)
Queen of Sheba—Betty Blythe

Director—J. Gordon Edwards
Leading Players—Fritz Leiber, Claire De Lorez, George Siegmann

QUEEN OF SPADES (1948, GB, Pathe)
Countess Ranevskaya—Edith Evans
Director—Thorold Dickinson
Leading Players—Anton Walbrook, Yvonne Mitchell, Ronald Howard

QUEEN OF THE MOB (1940, Paramount)
Ma Webster—Blanche Yurka
Director—James Hogan
Leading Players—Ralph Bellamy, Jack Carson, Richard Denning

QUEEN OF THE NIGHTCLUBS (1929, Warner Brothers)
Tex Malone—Texas Guinan
Director—Bryan Foy
Leading Players—John Davidson, Lila Lee, Arthur Housman

QUEEN OF THE WICKED (1916, GB, Silent, British Empire)
Ligeah Dupont—Nina Lynn
Director—Albert Wood
Leading Players—Henry Lonsdale, Janet Alexander

QUEEN OF THE YUKON (1940, Monogram)
Sadie—Irene Rich
Director—Phil Rosen
Leading Players—Charles Bickford, Melvin Lang, George Cleveland

QUEENIE (1921, Silent, 20th Century Fox)
Queenie Gurkin—Shirley Mason
Director—Howard M. Mitchell
Leading Players—George O'Hara, Wilson Hammond, Aggie Herring

QUENTIN DURWARD (1955, MGM)
Quentin Durward—Robert Taylor
Director—Richard Thorpe
Leading Players—Kay Kendall, Robert Morley, George Cole

THE QUICK GUN (1964, Columbia)
Clint Cooper—Audie Murphy
Director—Sidney Salkow
Leading Players—Merry Anders, James Best, Ted de Corsia

THE QUIET AMERICAN (1958, UA)
The American—Audie Murphy
Director—Joseph L. Mankiewicz
Leading Players—Michael Redgrave, Claude Dauphin, Giorgia Moll

THE QUIET GUN (1957, 20th Century Fox)
Carl—Forrest Tucker
Director—William Claxton
Leading Players—Mara Corday, Jim Davis, Kathleen Crowley, Lee Van Cleef

THE QUIET MAN (1952, Republic)
Sean Thornton—John Wayne
Director—John Ford
Leading Players—Maureen O'Hara, Victor McLaglen, Barry Fitzgerald, Ward Bond, Mildred Natwick, Arthur Shields

QUIGLEY DOWN UNDER (1990, MGM/UA/Pathe)
Matthew Quigley—Tom Selleck
Director—Simon Wincer
Leading Players—Laura San Giacomo, Alan Rickman, Chris Haywood

THE QUILLER MEMORANDUM (1966, GB, 20th Century Fox)
Quiller—George Segal
Director—Michael Anderson
Leading Players—Alec Guinness, Max Von Sydow, Senta Berger, George Sanders

QUINCANNON, FRONTIER SCOUT (1956, UA)
Linus Quincannon—Tony Martin
Director—Lesley Selander
Leading Players—Peggy Castle, John Bromfield, John Smith

R

RABBIT, RUN (1970, Warner Brothers)
Rabbit Angstrom—James Caan
Director—Jack Smight
Leading Players—Anjanette Comer, Jack Albertson, Melodie Johnson

RABID GRANNIES (1989, Troma)
Elizabeth Remington—Danielle Daven
Victoria Remington—Anne Marie Fox
Director—Emmanuel Kervyn
Leading Players—Catherine Aymerie, Caroline Braekman, Richard Cotica, Patricia Davia

THE RACERS (1955, 20th Century Fox)
Gino—Kirk Douglas
Director—Henry Hathaway
Leading Players—Bella Darvi, Gilbert Roland, Cesar Romero, Lee J. Cobb, Katy Jurado

RACHEL AND THE STRANGER (1948, RKO)
Rachel—Loretta Young
Jim Fairways—Robert Mitchum
Director—Norman Foster
Leading Players—William Holden, Gary Gray, Tom Tully, Sara Haden

THE RACHEL PAPERS (1989, UA)
Rachel Seth-Smith—Ione Skye
Director—Damian Harris
Leading Players—Dexter Fletcher, Jonathan Pryce, James Spader, Bill Paterson, Shirley Anne Field

RACHEL, RACHEL (1968, Warner Brothers)
Rachel Cameron—Joanne Woodward
Director—Paul Newman
Leading Players—James Olson, Kate Harrington, Estelle Parsons

RACING LADY (1937, RKO)
Ruth Martin—Ann Dvorak

Director—Wallace Fox
Leading Players—Smith Ballew, Harry Carey, Berton Churchill

RACING ROMEO (1927, Silent, R-C Pictures)
Red Walden—Harold "Red" Grange
Director—Sam Wood
Leading Players—Jobyna Ralston, Trixie Friganza, Walter Hiers

RACKET BUSTERS (1938, Warner Brothers)
Denny Jordan—George Brent
Hugh Allison—Walter Abel
Director—Lloyd Bacon
Leading Players—Humphrey Bogart, Gloria Dickson, Allen Jenkins, Penny Singelton, Oscar O'Shea

THE RACKETEER (1929, Pathe)
Mahlon Keane—Robert Armstrong
Director—Howard Higgins
Leading Players—Carole Lombard, Roland Drew, Jeanette Loff

RACKETEERS IN EXILE (1937, Columbia)
William Waldo—George Bancroft
Director—Erle C. Kenton
Leading Players—Evelyn Venable, Wynne Gibson, Marc Lawrence

RAFFERTY AND THE GOLD DUST TWINS (1975, Warner Brothers)
Rafferty—Alan Arkin
Mac Beachwood—Sally Kellerman
Frisbee—MacKenzie Phillips
Director—Dick Richards
Leading Players—Alex Rocco, Charles Martin Smith, Harry Dean Stanton

RAFFLES (1930, UA)
A.J. Raffles—Ronald Colman
Director—Harry D'Abbadie D'Arrast
Leading Players—Kay Francis, Bramwell Fletcher, Frances Dade

RAFFLES (1939, UA)
A.J. Raffles—David Niven
Directors—Sam Wood & William Wyler
Leading Players—Olivia de Havilland, Dame May Whitty, Dudley Digges

RAFFLES, THE AMATEUR CRACKSMAN (1925, Universal)
A.J. Raffles—House Peters
Director—King Baggot
Leading Players—Miss Du Pont, Hedda Hopper, Frederick Esmelton

THE RAG MAN (1925, Silent, Metro-Goldwyn)
Max Ginsberg—Max Davidson
Director—Eddie Cline
Leading Players—Jackie Coogan, Lydia Yeamans, Robert Edeson

THE RAGE OF PARIS (1921, Silent, Universal)
Joan Coolidge—Miss (Patricia) Du Pont
Director—Jack Conway
Leading Players—Elinor Hancock, Jack Perrin, Leo White

THE RAGE OF PARIS (1938, Universal)
Nicole de Cortillon—Danielle Darrieux

Director—Henry Koster
Leading Players—Douglas Fairbanks, Jr., Mischa Auer, Louis Hayward

THE RAGGED HEIRESS (1922, Silent, Fox Film Corp.)
Lucia Moreton—Shirley Mason
Director—Harry Beaumont
Leading Players—John Harron, Edwin Stevens, Cecil Van Auker

RAGGEDY MAN (1981, Universal)
Bailey—Sam Shepard
Director—Jack Fisk
Leading Players—Sissy Spacek, Eric Roberts, William Sanderson

RAGING BULL (1980, UA)
Jake LaMotta—Robert DeNiro
Director—Martin Scorsese
Leading Players—Cathy Moriarty, Joe Pesci, Frank Vincent, Nicholas Colasanto

THE RAGMAN'S DAUGHTER (1974, GB, Penelope-Harpoon)
Doris Randall—Victoria Tennant
Mr. Randall, the Ragman—Leslie Sands
Director—Harold Becker
Leading Players—Simon Rouse, Patrick O'Connell, Rita Howard

RAGS (1915, Silent, Famous Players)
"Rags"/Alice McCloud—Mary Pickford
Director—James Kirkwood
Leading Players—Marshall Neilan, Joseph Manning, J. Farrell MacDonald

RAID ON ROMMEL (1971, Universal)
General Erwin Rommel—Wolfgang Preiss
Director—Henry Hathaway
Leading Players—Richard Burton, John Colicos, Clinton Greyn

RAILROADED (1923, Silent, Universal)
Richard Ragland—Herbert Rawlinson
Director—Edmund Mortimer
Leading Players—Esther Ralston, Alfred Fisher, David Torrence

RAILROADED (1947, Eagle Lion)
Steve Ryan—Ed Kelly
Director—Anthony Mann
Leading Players—John Ireland, Sheila Ryan, Hugh Beaumont, Jane Randolph

THE RAILWAY CHILDREN (1971, GB, Universal)
Bobbie—Jenny Agutter
Phyllis—Sally Thomsett
Ruth—Ann Lancaster
Peter—Gary Warren
Director—Lionel Jeffries
Leading Players—Dinah Sheridan, Bernard Cribs, William Mervyn

RAIN MAN (1988, UA)
Raymond Babbitt—Dustin Hoffman
Director—Barry Levinson
Leading Players—Tom Cruise, Valeria Golino, Jerry Molden, Jack Murdock

THE RAIN KILLER (1990, Concorde/Calfilm)
Dalton—David Beecroft
Director—Ken Stein

Leading Players—Ray Sharkey, Tania Coleridge, Michael Chiklis

THE RAIN PEOPLE (1969, Warner Brothers)
Jimmie "Killer" Kilgannon—James Caan
Natalie Ravenna—Shirley Knight
Director—Francis Ford Coppola
Leading Players—Robert Duvall, Marya Zimmet, Tom Aldredge

THE RAINBOW THIEF (1990, Burrill/Europer)
Dima—Omar Sharif
Director—Alexandro Jodorowsky
Leading Players—Peter O'Toole, Christopher Lee, Berta Dominguez, Jane Chaplin

THE RAINBOW PRINCESS (1916, Silent, Famous Players)
Hope Daingerfield—Ann Pennington
Director—J. Searle Dawley
Leading Players—William Courtleigh, Jr., Augusta Anderson, Grant Stewart

RAINBOW MAN (1929, Paramount)
Rainbow Ryan—Eddie Dowling
Director—Fred Newmeyer
Leading Players—Marian Nixon, Frankie Darro, Sam Hardy

THE RAINMAKER (1926, Silent, Paramount)
Bobby Robertson—William Collier, Jr.
Director—Clarence Badger
Leading Players—Georgia Hale, Ernest Torrence, Brandon Hurst

THE RAINMAKER (1956, Paramount)
Bill Starbuck—Burt Lancaster
Director—Joseph Anthony
Leading Players—Katharine Hepburn, Wendell Corey, Lloyd Bridges, Earl Holliman, Cameron Prud'Homme

THE RAINMAKERS (1935, Radio Pictures)
Billy—Bert Wheeler
Roscoe—Robert Woolsey
Director—Fred Guiol
Leading Players—Dorothy Lee, Berton Churchill, George Meeker

RAISING ARIZONA (1987, 20th Century Fox)
Nathan Arizona, Jr.—T.J. Kuhn
Director—Joel Coen
Leading Players—Nicolas Cage, Holly Hunter, Trey Wilson, John Goodman, William Forsythe

RAMBLIN' GAL (1991, Aquarius)
Ruby—Deborah Strang
Director—Roberto Monticello
Leading Players—Andrew Krawetz, Kirk Condyles, Douglas Cole

RAMBLING ROSE (1991, Seven Arts/New Line)
Rose—Laura Dern
Director—Martha Coolidge
Leading Players—Robert Duvall, Diane Ladd, Lukas Haas, John Heard, Kevin Conway, Robert Burke, Lisa Jakub

RAMBO: FIRST BLOOD PART II (1985, Tri-Star)
John Rambo—Sylvester Stallone
Director—George P. Cosmatos
Leading Players—Richard Crenna, Charles Napier, Steven Berkoff, Julia Nickson

RAMBO III (1988, Tri-Star)
John Rambo—Sylvester Stallone
Director—Peter MacDonald
Leading Players—Richard Crenna, Marc de Jonge, Kurtwood Smith, Spiros Focas

RAMONA (1916, Silent, Clune)
Ramona—Adda Gleason
Director—Donald Crisp
Leading Players—Monroe Salisbury, Richard Sterling, Mabel Van Buren

RAMONA (1928, Silent, UA)
Ramona—Dolores Del Rio
Director—Edwin Carewe
Leading Players—Warner Baxter, Roland Drew, Vera Lewis, Michael Visaroff

RAMONA (1936, 20th Century Fox)
Ramona—Loretta Young
Director—Henry King
Leading Players—Don Ameche, Kent Taylor, Pauline Frederick, Jane Darwell, Katherine DeMille

RAMROD (1947, UA)
Dave Nash—Joel McCrea
Director—Andre De Toth
Leading Players—Veronica Lake, Ian McDonald, Charles Ruggles, Preston Foster

THE RAMRODDER (1969, Entertainment Ventures)
The Ramrodder—Jim Gentry
Director—Van Guylder
Leading Players—Julia Blackburn, Brave Eagle, Kathy Williams

RAMSBOTTOM RIDES AGAIN (1956, GB, British Lion)
Bill Ramsbottom—Arthur Askey
Director—John Baxter
Leading Players—Glenn Melvyn, Sidney James, Shani Wallis

RANDY RIDES ALONE (1934, Monogram)
Randy Bowers—John Wayne
Director—Harry Fraser
Leading Players—Alberta Vaughn, George 'Gabby' Hayes, Yakima Canutt

THE RANGER AND THE LADY (1940, Republic)
Capt. Colt—Roy Rogers
Jane—Jacqueline Wells (Julie Bishop)
Director—Joseph Kane
Leading Players—Gabby Hayes, Harry Woods, Henry Brandon

RANGER OF THE BIG PINES (1925, Silent, Vitagraph)
Ross Cavanaugh—Kenneth Harlan
Director—William S. Van Dyke
Leading Players—Helene Costello, Eulalie Jensen, Will Walling

RANGER OF THE CHEROKEE STRIP (1949, Republic)
Steve Howard—Monte Hale
Director—Philip Ford
Leading Players—Paul Hurst, Alice Talton, Roy Barcroft

RANSON'S FOLLY (1915, Silent, Edison)
Lt. Ranson—Marc MacDermott
Director—Richard Ridgely

Leading Players—Mabel Trunnelle, Marjorie Ellison, Edward Earle

RANSON'S FOLLY (1926, Silent, First National)
Lt. Ranson—Richard Barthelmess
Director—Sidney Olcott
Leading Players—Dorothy Mackaill, Anders Randolf, Pat Hartigan

RASPUTIN AND THE EMPRESS (1932, MGM)
Empress Alexandra—Ethel Barrymore
Rasputin—Lionel Barrymore
Director—Richard Boleslawsky (Charles Brabin-uncredited)
Leading Players—John Barrymore, Ralph Morgan, Diana Wynyard, Tad Alexander, C. Henry Gordon

RASPUTIN-THE MAD MONK (1966, GB, 20th Century Fox)
Rasputin—Christopher Lee
Director—Don Sharp
Leading Players—Barbara Shelley, Richard Pasco, Francis Matthews

THE RAT (1925, GB, Silent, Gainsborough)
"The Rat" Pierre Boucheron—Ivor Novello
Director—Graham Cutts
Leading Players—Mae Marsh, Isobel Jeans, Robert Scholtz

THE RAT (1938, GB, RKO)
"The Rat" Jean Boucheron—Anton Walbrook
Director—Jack Raymond
Leading Players—Ruth Chatterton, Rene Ray, Beatrix Lehman

RAT PFINK AND BOO BOO (1966, Morgan/Craddock)
Rat Pfink—Vin Saxon
Boo Boo—Titus Moede
Director—Ray Dennis Steckler
Leading Players—Carolyn Brandt, George Caldwell, Mike Kannon

RATBOY (1986, Warner Brothers)
Ratboy—S.L. Baird
Director—Sondra Locke
Leading Players—Sondra Locke, Robert Townsend, Christopher Hewett

RATTLE OF A SIMPLE MAN (1964, GB, Associate British Films)
Percy Winthram—Harry H. Corbett
Director—Muriel Box
Leading Players—Diane Cilento, Thora Hird, Michael Medwin, Charles Dyer, Brian Wilde, Hugh Futcher

RAWHEAD REX (1987, GB, Alpine-Paradise-Green Man)
Rawhead Rex—Heinrich Von Schellendorf
Director—George Pavlou
Leading Players—David Dukes, Kelly Piper, Hugh O'Conor, Cora Lunny

THE RAWHIDE KID (1928, Silent, Universal)
Dennis O'Hara—Hoot Gibson
Director—Del Andrews
Leading Players—Georgia Hale, William H. Strauss, Frank Hagney

RAYMIE (1960, Allied Artists)
Raymie—David Ladd
Director—Frank McDonald

Leading Players—Julie Adams, John Agar, Charles Winninger

READY, WILLING AND ABLE (1937, Warner Brothers)
Jane Clarke—Ruby Keeler
Director—Ray Enright
Leading Players—Lee Dixon, Allen Jenkins, Louise Fazenda, Ross Alexander

A REAL BLOKE (1935, GB, Universal)
Bill—George Carney
Director—John Baxter
Leading Players—Mary Clare, Diana Beaumont, Peggy Novak

REAL GENIUS (1985, Tri-Star)
Chris—Val Kilmer
Director—Martha Coolidge
Leading Players—Gabe Jarret, Robert Prescott, William Atherton

REAL MEN (1987, MGM/UA)
Nick Pirandello—James Belushi
Bob Wilson—John Ritter
Director—Dennis Feldman
Leading Players—Barbara Barrie, Bill Morey, Iva Anderson

REBECCA OF SUNNYBROOK FARM (1917, Silent, Artcraft)
Rebecca Randall—Mary Pickford
Director—Marshall Neilan
Leading Players—Eugene O'Brien, Helen Jerome Eddy, Charles Ogle

REBECCA OF SUNNYBROOK FARM (1932, Fox Film Corp.)
Rebecca—Marian Nixon
Director—Alfred Santell
Leading Players—Ralph Bellamy, Mae Marsh, Louise Closser Hale

REBECCA OF SUNNYBROOK FARM (1938, 20th Century Fox)
Rebecca Winstead—Shirley Temple
Director—Allan Dwan
Leading Players—Randolph Scott, Jack Haley, Gloria Stuart, Phyllis Brooks, Helen Westley

REBECCA THE JEWESS (1913, GB, Zenith/Big A)
Rebecca—Edith Bracewell
Director—Leedham Bantock
Leading Players—Lauderdale Maitland, Nancy Bevington, Hubert Carter

REBEL (1986, Vestron Pictures)
Rebel—Matt Dillon
Director—Michael Jenkins
Leading Players—Debbie Byrne, Bryan Brown, Bill Hunter

THE REBEL SON (1939, GB, UA)
Andrew Boulba—Anthony Bushell
Director—Alexis Granowsky
Leading Players—Harry Baur, Roger Livesey, Patricia Roc

REBEL WITHOUT A CAUSE (1955, Warner Brothers)
Jim—James Dean
Director—Nicholas Ray
Leading Players—Natalie Wood, Sal Mineo, Jim Backus, Ann Doran

REBELLIOUS DAUGHTERS (1938, Times)
Claire—Marjorie Reynolds
Babe—Verna Hillie
Flo—Sheila Bromley
Director—Jean Yarborough
Leading Players—George Douglas, Dennis Moore, Oscar O'Shea

RECKLESS (1935, MGM)
Mona Leslie—Jean Harlow
Director—Victor Fleming
Leading Players—William Powell, Franchot Tone, May Robson, Rosalind Russell

RECKLESS (1984, MGM-UA)
Tracey Prescott—Daryl Hannah
Director—James Foley
Leading Players—Aidan Quinn, Kenneth McMillan, Cliff De Young

RECKLESS LADY (1926, Silent, First National)
Mrs. Fleming—Belle Bennett
Director—Howard Higgin
Leading Players—Lois Moran, James Kirkwood, Lowell Sherman

RED BLOODED AMERICAN GIRL (1990, Canada, SC Entertainment)
Paula—Heather Thomas
Director—David Blyth
Leading Players—Andrew Stevens, Chirstopher Plummer, Kim Coates

RED HAIR (1928, Silent, Paramount)
"Bubbles" McCoy—Clara Bow
Director—Clarence Badger
Leading Players—Lane Chandler, William Austin, Jacqueline Gadsdon

THE RED-HAIRED ALIBI (1932, Tower)
Gloria—Shirley Temple
Director—Christy Cabanne
Leading Players—Merna Kennedy, Theodore Von Eltz, Grant Withers

RED HEAD (1934, Monogram)
Dale Carter—Grace Bradley
Director—Melville Brown
Leading Players—Bruce Cabot, Regis Toomey, Berton Churchill

RED HEADED STRANGER (1987, Alive)
Rev. Julian Shay—Willie Nelson
Director—William Wittliff
Leading Players—Morgan Fairchild, Katharine Ross, Royal Dano

RED HEADED WOMAN (1932, MGM)
Lil Andrews—Jean Harlow
Director—Jack Conway
Leading Players—Chester Morris, Lewis Stone, Leila Hyams

RED MONARCH (1983, GB, Engima/Goldcrest)
Joseph Stalin—Colin Blakely
Director—Jack Gold
Leading Players—David Suchet, Carroll Baker, Ian Hogg

RED SCORPION (1989, Shapiro Glickenhaus)
Lt. Nikolai—Dolph Lundgren
Director—Joseph Zito
Leading Players—M. Emmet Walsh, Al White, T.P. McKenna, Ruben Nthodi

RED SONJA (1985, MGM/UA)
Red Sonja—Brigitte Nielsen
Director—Richard Fleischer
Leading Players—Arnold Schwarzenegger, Sandahl Bergman, Paul Smith

REDHEAD (1941, Monogram)
Dale Carter—June Lang
Director—Edward Cahn
Leading Players—Johnny Downs, Eric Blore, Frank Jacquet

THE REDHEAD AND THE COWBOY (1950, Paramount)
Gil Kyle—Glenn Ford
Candace Bronson—Rhonda Fleming
Director—Leslie Fenton
Leading Players—Edmund O'Brien, Alan Reed, Morris Ankrum

REDHEAD FROM MANHATTAN (1954, Columbia)
Rita Manners—Lupe Velez
Director—Lew Landers
Leading Players—Michael Duane, Tim Ryan, Gerald Mohr, Lillian Yarbo

THE REDHEAD FROM WYOMING (1953, Universal)
Kate Maxwell—Maureen O'Hara
Director—Lee Sholem
Leading Players—Alex Nicol, Robert Strauss, William Bishop

THE REFEREE (1922, Silent, Selznick)
John McArdle—Conway Tearle
Director—Ralph Ince
Leading Players—Gladys Hulette, Anders Randolf, Gus Platz

REFORM GIRL (1933, Tower)
Lydia Johnson—Noel Johnson
Director—Sam Neufeld
Leading Players—Skeets Gallagher, Hale Hamilton, Robert Ellis

REFORM SCHOOL GIRL (1957, American International)
Donna Price—Gloria Castillo
Director—Edward Bernds
Leading Players—Ross Ford, Edward Byrnes, Ralph Reed, Jan England

THE REFORMER AND THE REDHEAD (1950, MGM)
Kathleen Maguire—June Allyson
Andrew Rockton Hale—Dick Powell
Directors—Norman Panama & Melvin Frank
Leading Players—David Wayne, Cecil Kellaway, Ray Collins

REGARDING HENRY (1991, Paramount)
Henry Turner—Harrison Ford
Director—Mike Nichols
Leading Players—Annette Bening, Bill Nunn, Mikki Allen, Donald Moffat, Nancy Marchand

REGGIE MIXES IN (1916, Triangle)
Reggie Morton—Douglas Fairbanks
Director—Christy Cabanne
Leading Players—Bessie Love, Joseph Singleton, W.E. Lowery

REGISTERED NURSE (1934, Warner Brothers)
Sylvia Benton—Bebe Daniels

Director—Robert Florey
Leading Players—Lyle Talbot, John Halliday, Irene Franklin

A REGULAR FELLOW (1925, Silent, Paramount)
The Prince—Raymond Griffith
Director—Edward Sutherland
Leading Players—Mary Brian, Tyrone Power, Sr., Edgar Norton

THE REINCARNATE (1971, Canada, Meridian)
Everett Julian—Jack Creley
Director—Don Haldane
Leading Players—Jay Reynolds, Trudy Young, Terry Tweed

THE REINCARNATION OF PETER PROUD (1975, American International)
Peter Proud—Michael Sarrazin
Director—J. Lee Thompson
Leading Players—Jennifer O'Neill, Margot Kidder, Cornelia Sharpe

THE REIVERS (1969, National General)
Boon Hoggenbeck—Steve McQueen
Lucius McCaslin—Mitch Vogel
Ned McCaslin—Rupert Crosse
Director—Mark Rydell
Leading Players—Sharon Farrell, Will Geer, Michael Constantine

THE REJECTED WOMAN (1924, Silent, Cosmopolitan)
Diane Du Prez—Alma Rubens
Director—Albert Parker
Leading Players—Bela Lugosi, George MacQuarrie, Conrad Nagel

THE REJUVENATOR (1988, SVS)
Dr. Gregory Ashton—John McKay
Director—Brian Thomas Jones
Leading Players—Vivian Lanko, James Hogue, Katell Pleven, Jessica Dublin

RELENTLESS (1989, New Line)
Buck Taylor—Judd Nelson
Director—William Lustig
Leading Players—Robert Loggia, Leo Rossi, Meg Foster, Patrick O'Bryan, Mindy Seger

THE RELUCTANT ASTRONAUT (1967, Universal)
Roy Fleming—Don Knotts
Director—Edward J. Montagne
Leading Players—Leslie Nielsen, Joan Freeman, Jesse White, Arthur O'Connell

THE RELUCTANT DEBUTANTE (1958, MGM)
Jane Broadbent—Sandra Dee
Director—Vincente Minnelli
Leading Players—Rex Harrison, Kay Kendall, John Saxon

THE RELUCTANT WIDOW (1951, GB, Fine Arts)
Elinor—Jean Kent
Director—Bernard Knowles
Leading Players—Guy Rolfe, Paul Dupuis, Lana Morris, Kathleen Byron

THE REMARKABLE ANDREW (1942, Paramount)
Andrew Long—William Holden
Director—Stuart Heisler

Leading Players—Ellen Drew, Brian Donlevy, Rod Cameron, Richard Webb

THE REMARKABLE MR. PENNYPACKER (1959, 20th Century Fox)
Pa Pennypacker—Clifton Webb
Director—Henry Levin
Leading Players—Dorothy McGuire, Charles Coburn, Jill St. John

REMBRANDT (1936, GB, UA)
Rembrandt van Rijn—Charles Laughton
Director—Alexander Korda
Leading Players—Gertrude Lawrence, Elsa Lanchester, Edward Chapman

REMEMBER MY NAME (1978, Columbia)
Emily—Geraldine Chaplin
Director—Alan Rudolph
Leading Players—Anthony Perkins, Berry Berenson, Moses Gunn

REMO WILLIAMS: THE ADVENTURE BEGINS... (1985, Orion)
Remo Williams—Fred Ward
Director—Guy Hamilton
Leading Players—Joel Grey, Wilfrid Brimley, George Cole

RENALDO AND CLARA (1978, Lombard Street/Circuit)
Renaldo—Bob Dylan
Clara—Sara Dylan
Director—Bob Dylan
Leading Players—Joan Baez, Ronnie Hawkins, Ronee Blakely

RENEGADES (1989, Universal)
Buster McHenry—Keifer Sutherland
Hank—Lou Diamond Phillips
Director—Jack Sholder
Leading Players—Jami Gertz, Rob Knepper, Bill Smitrovich

RENFREW OF THE ROYAL MOUNTED (1937, Grand National)
Renfrew—James Newill
Director—Al Herman
Leading Players—Carol Hughes, William Royle, Donald Reed

RENO AND THE DOC (1984, Canada, New World)
Reginald "Reno" Coltchinsky—Ken Welsh
Hugo "Doc" Billings—Henry Ramer
Director—Charles Dennis
Leading Players—Linda Griffiths, Gene Mack, Brian Grandbois

RENT-A-COP (1988, Kings Road)
Church—Burt Reynolds
Director—Jerry London
Leading Players—Liza Minnelli, James Remar, Richard Masur, Dionne Warwick

REPO MAN (1984, Universal)
Bud—Harry Dean Stanton
Director—Alex Cox
Leading PLayers—Emilio Estevez, Tracey Walter, Olivia Barash

REPORT TO THE COMMISSIONER (1975, UA)
Police Commissioner—Stephen Elliott
Director—Milton Katselas
Leading Players—Michael Moriarty, Yaphet Kotto, Susan Blakely, Hector Elizondo

REQUIEM FOR A GUNFIGHTER (1965, Embassy)
Dave McCloud—Rod Cameron
Director—Spencer G. Bennett
Leading Players—Stephen McNally, Chet Douglas, Mike Mazurki, Tim McCoy, Johnny Mack Brown, Bob Steele

REQUIEM FOR A HEAVYWEIGHT (1962, Columbia)
Mountain Rivera—Anthony Quinn
Director—Ralph Nelson
Leading Players—Jackie Gleason, Mickey Rooney, Julie Harris

THE RESURRECTED (1992, Scott Brothers Pictures)
Charles Dexter Ward/Joseph Curween—Chris Sarandon
Director—Dan O'Bannon
Leading Players—John Terry, Jane Sibbett, Richard Romanus, Laurie Briscoe, Ken Cameroux

THE RESURRECTION OF ZACHARY WHEELER (1971, Gold Key/Vidtronics)
Senator Zachary Wheeler—Bradford Dillman
Director—Robert Wynn
Leading Players—Leslie Nielsen, James Daly, Angie Dickinson

THE RETURN OF A MAN CALLED HORSE (1976, UA)
John Morgan—Richard Harris
Director—Irvin Kershner
Leading Players—Gale Sondergaard, Geoffrey Lewis, Bill Lucking

RETURN OF A STRANGER (1962, GB, Danzinger)
Homer Trent—Cyril Shaps
Director—Max Varnel
Leading Players—John Ireland, Susan Stephen, Timothy Beaton

THE RETURN OF BULLDOG DRUMMOND (1934, GB, British Int.)
Hugh Drummond—Ralph Richardson
Director—Walter Summers
Leading Players—Ann Todd, Joyce Kennedy, Francis L. Sullivan

THE RETURN OF CAPTAIN INVINCIBLE (1983, Australia, Keys)
Captain Invincible—Alan Arkin
Director—Philippe Mora
Leading Players—Christopher Lee, Kate Fitzpatrick, Bill Hunter

THE RETURN OF CAROL DEANE (1938, GB, Warner Brothers)
Carol Deane—Bebe Daniels
Director—Arthur Woods
Leading Players—Arthur Margetson, Zena Dare, Chili Bouchier

THE RETURN OF COUNT YORGA (1971, American International)
Count Yorga—Robert Quarry
Director—Bob Kelljan
Leading Players—Mariette Hartley, Roger Perry, Yvonne Wilder

THE RETURN OF DANIEL BOONE (1941, Columbia)
Dan Boone—Bill Elliott
Director—Lambert Hillyer
Leading Players—Betty Miles, Dub Taylor, Ray Bennett

THE RETURN OF DR. FU MANCHU (1930, Paramount)
Dr. Fu Manchu—Warner Oland
Director—Rowland V. Lee
Leading Players—Neil Hamilton, Jean Arthur, O.P. Heggie

THE RETURN OF DR. X (1939, Warner Brothers)
Marshall Quesne-Dr. Maurice Xavier—Humphrey Bogart
Director—Vincent Sherman
Leading Players—Rosemary Lane, Wayne Morris, Dennis Morgan, John Litel, Lya Lys

THE RETURN OF DRACULA (1958, UA)
Bellac—Francis Lederer
Director—Paul Landres
Leading Players—Norma Eberhardt, Ray Stricklyn, Greta Granstedt

THE RETURN OF FRANK JAMES (1940, 20th Century Fox)
Frank James (Ben Woodson)—Henry Fonda
Director—Fritz Lang
Leading Players—Gene Tierney, Jackie Cooper, Henry Hull, John Carradine

THE RETURN OF JACK SLADE (1955, Allied Artists)
Jack Slade—John Ericson
Director—Harold Schuster
Leading Players—Mari Blanchard, Neville Brand, Casey Adams

THE RETURN OF JESSE JAMES (1950, Lippert)
Johnny—John Ireland
Director—Arthur David Hilton
Leading Players—Ann Dvorak, Henry Hull, Hugh O'Brien, Reed Hadley

THE RETURN OF JIMMY VALENTINE (1936, Republic)
"Jimmy Valentine" Davis—Robert Warwick
Director—Lewis D. Collins
Leading Players—Roger Pyror, Charlotte Henry, James Burtis

THE RETURN OF JOSEY WALES (1987, Multi-Tacar)
Josey Wales—Michael Parks
Director—Michael Parks
Leading Players—Raphael Campos, Charlie McCoy, Everett Sifuentes

THE RETURN OF MR. MOTO (1965, GB, 20th Century Fox)
Mr. Moto—Henry Silva
Director—Ernest Morris
Leading Players—Martin Wyldeck, Terence Longdon, Suzanne Lloyd

THE RETURN OF MONTE CRISTO (1946, Columbia)
Edmund Dantes—Louis Hayward
Director—Henry Levin
Leading Players—Barbara Britton, George Macready, Una O'Connor

THE RETURN OF PETER GRIMM (1926, Silent, Fox Film Corp.)
Peter Grimm—Alec B. Francis
Director—Victor Schertzinger
Leading Players—John Roche, Janet Gaynor, Richard Walling

THE RETURN OF PETER GRIMM (1935, RKO)
Peter Grimm—Lionel Barrymore
Director—George Nicholls, Jr.
Leading Players—Helen Mack, Edward Ellis, Donald Meek, George Breakston

THE RETURN OF RAFFLES (1932, GB, Markham)
A.J. Raffles—George Barraud
Director—Mansfield Markham

Leading Players—Camilla Horn, Claude Allister, A. Bromley Davenport

THE RETURN OF SHERLOCK HOLMES (1929, Paramount)
Sherlock Holmes—Clive Brook
Director—Basil Dean
Leading Players—H. Reeves-Smith, Betty Lawford, Charles Hay

THE RETURN OF SOPHIE LANG (1936, Paramount)
Sophie Lang—Gertrude Michael
Director—George Archainbaud
Leading Players—Guy Standing, Ray Milland, Elizabeth Patterson

THE RETURN OF SUPERFLY (1990, Triton/Crash)
Youngblood Priest—Nathan Purdee
Director—Sig Shore
Leading Players—Margaret Avery, Leonard Thomas, Christopher Curry

THE RETURN OF THE APE MAN (1944, Monogram)
Ape Monster—Frank Moran
Director—Phil Rosen
Leading Players—Bela Lugosi, John Carradine, Judith Gibson

RETURN OF THE BADMEN (1948, RKO)
Sundance Kid—Robert Ryan
Cole Younger—Steve Brodie
Emmett Dalton—Lex Barker
Billy the Kid—Dean White
Director—Ray Enright
Leading Players—Randolph Scott, Anne Jeffreys, Gabby Hayes

RETURN OF THE CISCO KID (1939, 20th Century Fox)
Cisco Kid—Warner Baxter
Director—Herbert I. Leeds
Leading Players—Lynn Bari, Cesar Romero, Henry Hull

RETURN OF THE FLY (1959, 20th Century Fox)
Philippe Delambre—Brett Halsey
Director—Edward Bernds
Leading Players—Vincent Price, David Frankham, John Sutton

RETURN OF THE FRONTIERSMAN (1950, Warner Brothers)
Logan Barrett—Gordon MacRae
Director—Richard Bare
Leading Players—Julie London, Rory Calhoun, Jack Holt

THE RETURN OF THE RAT (1929, GB, Gainsborough)
Pierre "The Rat" Boucheron—Ivor Novello
Director—Graham Cutts
Leading Players—Isabel Jeans, Mabel Poulton, Bernard Nedell

RETURN OF THE SCARLET PIMPERNEL (1938, Great Brtiain, UA)
Sir Percy Blakeney—Barry K. Barnes
Director—Hans Schwartz
Leading Players—Sophie Stewart, Margaretta Scott, James Mason

RETURN OF THE SOLDIER (1983, GB, 20th Century Fox)
Chris—Alan Bates
Director—Alan Bridges
Leading Players—Julie Christie, Glenda Jackson, Ann-Margret, Ian Holm, Frank Finlay

THE RETURN OF THE SWAMP THING (1989, Miramax)
Swamp Thing—Dick Durock
Director—Jim Wynorski
Leading Players—Louis Jourdan, Heather Locklear, Sarah Douglas

RETURN OF THE TEXAN (1952, 20th Century Fox)
Sam Crockett—Dale Robertson
Director—Delmer Daves
Leading Players—Joanne Dru, Walter Brennan, Richard Boone, Tom Tully

THE RETURN OF THE VAMPIRE (1944, Columbia)
Armand Tesla—Bela Lugosi
Director—Lew Landers
Leading Players—Frieda Inescort, Nina Foch, Roland Varno

THE RETURN OF WILD BILL (1940, Columbia)
Wild Bill Saunders—Bill Elliott
Director—Joseph H. Lewis
Leading Players—Iris Meredith, George Lloyd, Luana Walters

REVEILLE WITH BEVERLY (1943, Columbia)
Beverly Ross—Ann Miller
Director—Charles Barton
Leading Players—William Wright, Dick Purcell, Franklin Pangborn

REVENGE OF BILLY THE KID (1992, GB, Montage Films)
Billy T. Kid—Julian Shaw
Director—Jim Groom
Leading Players—Michael Balfour, Samantha Perkins, Jackie D. Broad

THE REVENGE OF FRANKENSTEIN (1958, GB, Columbia)
Dr. Victor Stein—Peter Cushing
Director—Terence Fisher
Leading Players—Francis Matthews, Eunice Grayson, Michael Gwynn

REVENGE OF THE NERDS (1984, 20th Century Fox)
Lewis—Robert Carradine
Director—Jeff Kanew
Leading Players—Anthony Edwards, Tim Busfield, Andrew Cassese, Curtis Armstrong, Julie Montgomery

REVENGE OF THE NERDS II: NERDS IN PARADISE (1987, 20th Century Fox)
Lewis—Robert Carradine
Director—Joe Roth
Leading Players—Curtis Armstrong, Larry B. Scott, Timothy Busfield, Courtney Thorne-Smith, Andrew Cassese

REVENGE OF THE RADIOACTIVE REPORTER (1990, Canada, Pryceless)
Mike R. Wave—David Scammell
Director—Craig Pryce
Leading Players—Kathryn Boese, Derrick Strange, Randy Pearlstein

REVENUE AGENT (1950, Columbia)
Steve Adams—Douglas Kennedy
Director—Lew Landers
Leading Players—Jean Wiles, Onslow Stevens, William "Bill" Phillips

THE REVOLT OF MAMIE STOVER (1956, 20th Century Fox)
Mamie Stover—Jane Russell
Director—Raoul Walsh
Leading Players—Richard Egan, Joan Leslie, Agnes Moorehead

RHODES OF AFRICA (1936, GB, Gaumont)
Cecil Rhodes—Walter Huston
Director—Berthold Viertel
Leading Players—Oscar Homolka, Basil Sydney, Peggy Ashcroft,
Frank Cellier

RHYTHM RACKETEER (1937, GB, British International)
Harry Grand/Nap Connors—Harry Roy
Director—James Seymour
Leading Players—Princes Pearl, James Carew, Norma Varden

RICH AND FAMOUS (1981, MGM-UA)
Liz Hamilton—Jacqueline Bisset
Merry Noel Blake—Candice Bergen
Director—George Cukor
Leading Players—David Selby, Hart Bochner, Steven Hill

RICH AND STRANGE (1932, GB, British International)
Fred Hill—Henry Kendall
Emily Hill—Joan Barry
Director—Alfred Hitchcock
Leading Players—Percy Marmont, Betty Amann, Elsie Randolph

RICH GIRL (1991, Studio Three/Film West)
Courtney Wells—Jill Schoelen
Director—Joel Bender
Leading Players—Don Michael Paul, Ron Karabatsos, Sean
Kanan, Paul Gleason, Melanie Tomlin

RICH KIDS (1979, UA)
Franny Phillips—Trini Alvarado
Jamie Harris—Jeremy Levy
Director—Robert M. Young
Leading Players—Kathryn Walker, John Lithgow, Terry Kiser,
David Selby

RICH MAN, POOR GIRL (1938, MGM)
Bill Harrison—Robert Young
Joan Thayer—Ruth Hussey
Director—Reinhold Schunzel
Leading Players—Lew Ayres, Guy Kibbee, Lana Turner, Rita
Johnson

RICH MAN'S FOLLY (1931, Paramount)
Brock Trumbull—George Bancroft
Director—John Cromwell
Leading Players—Frances Dee, Robert Ames, Juliette Compton

RICH PEOPLE (1929, Pathe)
Connie Hayden—Constance Bennett
Noel Nevins—Robert Ames
Director—Edward H. Griffith
Leading Players—Regis Toomey, Mahlon Hamilton, Ilka Chase

RICH, YOUNG AND PRETTY (1951, MGM)
Elizabeth Rogers—Jane Powell
Director—Norman Taurog
Leading Players—Danielle Darrieux, Wendell Corey, Vic
Damone, Fernando Lamas

RICHARD (1972, Aurora City Group)
Richard—Richard M. Dixon
Director—Lorees Yerby
Leading Players—Dan Resin, Lynn Lipton, Hazen Glifford

RICHARD III (1956, GB, Lopert)
Richard of Gloucester—Laurence Olivier
Director—Laurence Olivier
Leading Players—Ralph Richardson, Claire Bloom, John
Gielgud, Cedric Hardwicke, Mary Kerridge, Pamela Brown

THE RICHEST GIRL IN THE WORLD (1934, RKO)
Dorothy Hunter—Miriam Hopkins
Director—William A. Seiter
Leading Players—Joel McCrea, Fay Wray, Henry Stephenson,
Reginald Denny

THE RICHEST MAN IN TOWN (1941, Columbia)
Abb Crothers—Frank Craven
Director—Charles Barton
Leading Players—Edgar Buchanan, Eileen O'Hearn, Roger Pryor

RIDDLE: THE WOMAN (1920, Silent, Pathe)
Lilla—Geraldine Farrar
Director—Edward Jose
Leading Players—Montagu Love, Adele Blood, William T.
Carleton

RIDE, KELLY, RIDE (1941, 20th Century Fox)
Corn Cob Kelly—Marvin Stephens
Director—Norman Foster
Leading Players—Eugene Pallette, Rita Quigley, Mary Healy

RIDE, RYDER, RIDE (1949, Eagle Lion)
Red Ryder—Jim Bannon
Director—Lewis D. Collins
Leading Players—Don Kay Reynolds, Emmett Lynn, Peggy
Stewart

RIDE THE MAN DOWN (1952, Republic)
Will Ballard—Rod Cameron
Director—Joseph Kane
Leading Players—Brian Donlevy, Ella Raines, Forrest Tucker

RIDERS OF THE STORM (1988, Miramax)
Captain—Dennis Hopper
Director—Maurice Phillips
Leading Players—Michael J. Pollard, Eugene Lipinski, James
Aubrey

RIDING SHOTGUN (1954, Warner Brothers)
Larry Delong—Randolph Scott
Director—Andre de Toth
Leading Players—Wayne Morris, Joan Weldon, Joe Sawyer

THE RIGHT HAND MAN (1987, Australia, New World)
Ned Devine—Hugo Weaving
Director—Di Drew
Leading Players—Rupert Everett, Arthur Dignam, Jennifer
Claire

RIGOLETTO (1949, Minerva/Superfilm)
Rigoletto—Tito Gobbi
Director—Carmine Gallone
Leading Players—Mario Filippeschi, Lina Pagliughi, Marcella
Govoni

RIKKY AND PETE (1988, Australia, MGM/UA)
Pete—Steve Kearney
Rikky—Nina Landis
Director—Nadia Tass
Leading Players—Bruno Lawrence, Tetchie Agboyoui, Bill Hunter

RILEY THE COP (1928, Silent, Fox Film Corp.)
James Riley—J. Farrell MacDonald
Director—John Ford
Leading Players—Louise Fazenda, Nancy Drexel, David Rollins

THE RINGER (1928, GB, Silent, Ideal)
Dr. Lomond—Leslie Faber
Director—Arthur Maude
Leading Players—Annette Benson, Lawson Butt, Nigel Barrie

THE RINGER (1932, GB, British Lion)
Dr. Lomond—Patrick Curwen
Director—Walter Forde
Leading Players—Franklyn Dyall, Carol Goodner, Gordon Harker

THE RINGER (1953, GB, London/Regent)
Dr. Lomond—Donald Wolfit
Director—Guy Hamilton
Leading Players—Herbert Lom, Mai Zetterling, Greta Gynt

RINGSIDE MAISIE (1941, MGM)
Maisie Ravier—Ann Sothern
Director—Edwin L. Marin
Leading Players—George Murphy, Robert Sterling, Natalie Thompson

RIO RITA (1929, RKO)
Rita Ferguson—Bebe Daniels
Director—Luther Reed
Leading Players—Bert Wheeler, Robert Woolsey, John Boles

RIO RITA (1942, MGM)
Rita Winslow—Kathryn Grayson
Director—S. Sylvan Simon
Leading Players—Bud Abbott, Lou Costello, John Carroll, Patricia Dane

RIP ROARING RILEY (1935, Puritan)
Rip Roaring Riley—Lloyd Hughes
Director—Elmer Clifton
Leading Players—Grant Withers, John Cowell, Marion Burns

RIP VAN WINKLE (1914, Silent, Rolfe/Alco)
Rip Van Winkle—Thomas Jefferson
Director—Edwin Middleton
Leading Players—Clariet Claire, H.B. Blackmore

RIP VAN WINKLE (1921, Silent, Lascelle/Hodkinson)
Rip Van Winkle—Thomas Jefferson
Director—Ward Lascelle
Leading Players—Mila Davenport, Daisy Robinson, Gertrude Messinger

THE RISE AND FALL OF LEGS DIAMOND (1960, Warner Brothers)
Jack "Legs" Diamond—Ray Danton
Director—Budd Boetticher
Leading Players—Karen Steele, Elaine Stewart, Jesse White

THE RISE AND RISE OF MICHAEL RIMMER (1970, GB, Warner Brothers)
Michael Rimmer—Peter Cook
Director—Kevin Billington
Leading Players—Denholm Elliott, Ronald Fraser, Arthur Lowe

THE RISE OF JENNIE CUSHING (1917, Silent, Artcraft)
Jennie Cushing—Elsie Ferguson
Director—Maurice Tourneur
Leading Players—Elliott Dexter, Fania Marinoff, Frank Goldsmith

RITA, SUE AND BOB TOO! (1987, GB, Orion Classics)
Sue—Michelle Holmes
Rita—Siobhan Finneran
Bob—George Costigan
Director—Alan Clarke
Leading Players—Lesley Sharp, Willie Ross, Patti Nichols

RIVALS (1972, Avco Embassy)
Peter Simon—Robert Klein
Jaimie Sutton—Scott Jacoby
Director—Krishna Shah
Leading Players—Joan Hackett, Jeanne Tanzy, Gene Hayes

RIVER LADY (1948, Universal)
Sequin—Yvonne De Carlo
Director—George Sherman
Leading Players—Dan Duryea, Rod Cameron, Helena Carter

THE RIVER RAT (1984, Paramount)
Billy—Tommy Lee Jones
Director—Tom Rickman
Leading Players—Martha Plimpton, Brian Dennehy, Shawn Smith

THE RIVER WOMAN (1928, Gotham/Lumas)
The Duchess—Jacqueline Logan
Director—Joseph E. Henabery
Leading Players—Lionel Barrymore, Charles Delaney, Sheldon Lewis

ROAD DEMON (1938, 20th Century Fox)
Blake—Henry Arthur
Director—Otto Brower
Leading Players—Joan Valerie, Henry Armetta, Thomas Beck

THE ROAD WARRIOR (1982, Australia, Warner Brothers)
Max—Mel Gibson
Director—George Miller
Leading Players—Bruce Spence, Vernon Wells, Emil Minty, Mike Preston

ROADIE (1980, UA)
Travis W. Redfish—Meatloaf
Director—Alan Rudolph
Leading Players—Kaki Hunter, Art Carney, Gailiard Sartain

ROAMING LADY (1936, Columbia)
Joyce—Fay Wray
Director—Albert S. Rogell
Leading Players—Ralph Bellamy, Thurston Hall, Edward Gargan

ROB ROY (1922, GB, Silent, Gaumont)
Rob Roy MacGregor—David Hawthorne
Director—W.P. Kellino

Leading Players—Gladys Jennings, Simeon Stuart, Wallace Bosco

ROB ROY, THE HIGHLAND ROGUE (1954, GB, Disney/RKO)
Rob Roy MacGregor—Richard Todd
Director—Harold French
Leading Players—Glynis Johns, James Robertson Justice, Michael Gough

ROBBY (1968, Bluewood)
Robby—Warren Raum
Director—Ralph C. Bluemke
Leading Players—Ryp Siani, John Garces, Rita Elliot

ROBERTA (1935, RKO)
Roberta—Helen Westley
Director—William A. Seiter
Leading Players—Irene Dunne, Fred Astaire, Ginger Rogers, Randolph Scott

ROBIN AND MARIAN (1976, GB, Columbia)
Robin Hood—Sean Connery
Maid Marian—Audrey Hepburn
Director—Richard Lester
Leading Players—Robert Shaw, Richard Harris, Nicol Williamson

ROBIN AND THE SEVEN HOODS (1964, Warner Brothers)
Robbo—Frank Sinatra
Little John—Dean Martin
Will—Sammy Davis, Jr.
Allen A. Dale—Bing Crosby
Director—Gordon Douglas
Leading Players—Peter Falk, Barbara Rush, Edward G. Robinson, Victor Buono

ROBIN HOOD (1922, Silent, UA)
Robin Hood—Douglas Fairbanks
Director—Allan Dwan
Leading Players—Wallace Beery, Sam De Grasse, Enid Bennett, Paul Dickey, William Lowery

ROBIN HOOD OF EL DORADO (1936, MGM)
Joaquin Murrieta—Warner Baxter
Director—William A. Wellman
Leading Players—Ann Loring, Bruce Cabot, Margo

ROBIN HOOD: PRINCE OF THIEVES (1991, Warner Brothers)
Robin of Locksley—Kevin Costner
Director—Kevin Reynolds
Leading Players—Morgan Freeman, Mary Elizabeth Mastrantonio, Christian Slater, Alan Rickman, Geraldine McEwan, Michael McShane, Michael Wincott, Nick Brimble, Brian Blessed

ROBINSON CRUSOE (1927, GB, Silent, Epic)
Robinson Crusoe—M.A. Wetherell
Director—M.A. Wetherell
Leading Players—Fay Compton, Herbert Waithe, Reginald Fox

ROBINSON CRUSOE OF MARS (1964, Paramount)
Cmdr. Christopher "Kit" Draper—Paul Mantee
Director—Byron Haskin
Leading Players—Vic Lundin, Adam West

ROBOCOP (1987, Orion)
Alex J. Murphy, "Robocop"—Peter Weller
Director—Paul Verhoeven
Leading Players—Nancy Allen, Ronny Cox, Kurtwood Smith, Miguel Ferrer

ROBOCOP 2 (1990, Orion)
Robocop—Peter Weller
Director—Irvin Kershner
Leading Players—Nancy Allen, Daniel O'Herlihy, Belinda Bauer, Tom Noonan, Gabriel Damon

ROBOT MONSTER (1953, Three Dimensional Pictures)
Ro-Man—George Barrows
Director—Phil Tucker
Leading Players—George Nader, Claudia Barrett, Selena Royle

THE ROCKETEER (1991, Buena Vista/Disney)
Cliff Secord—Bill Campbell
Director—Joe Johnston
Leading Players—Jennifer Connelly, Alan Arkin, Timothy Dalton, Paul Sorvino, Terry O'Quinn, Ed Lauter

ROCKY (1976, UA)
Rocky Balboa—Sylvester Stallone
Director—John G. Avildsen
Leading Players—Talia Shire, Burt Young, Carl Weathers, Burgess Meredith

ROCKY II (1979, UA)
Rocky Balboa—Sylvester Stallone
Director—Sylvester Stallone
Leading Players—Talia Shire, Burt Young, Carl Weathers, Burgess Meredith

ROCKY III (1982, MGM-UA)
Rocky Balboa—Sylvester Stallone
Director—Sylvester Stallone
Leading Players—Carl Weathers, Mr. T, Talia Shire, Burt Young, Burgess Meredith

ROCKY IV (1985, MGM/UA)
Rocky Balboa—Sylvester Stallone
Director—Sylvester Stallone
Leading Players—Talia Shire, Burt Young, Carl Weathers, Brigitte Nielsen, Dolph Lungden

ROCKY V (1990, MGM/UA)
Rocky Balboa—Sylvester Stallone
Director—John G. Avildsen
Leading Players—Talia Shire, Burt Young, Sage Stallone, Burgess Meredith, Tommy Morrison, Richard Gant

ROCKY GIBRALTAR (1988, Columbia)
Levi Rockwell—Burt Lancaster
Director—Daniel Petrie
Leading Players—Suzy Amis, Patricia Clarkson, Francis Conroy, Sinead Cusack, Macaulay Calkin, John Glover

THE ROCKY HORROR SHOW (1975, GB, 20th Century Fox)
Rocky Horror—Peter Hinwood
Director—Jim Sharman
Leading Players—Tim Curry, Susan Sarandon, Barry Bostwick, Richard O'Brien, Jonathan Adams

ROCKY RHODES (1934, Universal)
Rocky Rhodes—Charles "Buck" Jones
Director—Al Raboch
Leading Players—Sheila Terry, Stanley Fields, Walter Miller

ROGER TOUHY, GANGSTER (1944, 20th Century Fox)
Roger Touhy—Preston Foster
Director—Robert Florey
Leading Players—Victor McLaglen, Lois Andrews, Kent Taylor

ROGUE COP (1954, MGM)
Christopher Kelvaney—Robert Taylor
Director—Roy Rowland
Leading Players—Janet Leigh, George Raft, Steve Forrest, Anne Francis

ROGUE OF THE RIO GRANDE (1930, World-Wide)
El Malo—Jose Bohr
Director—Spencer Gordon Bennett
Leading Players—Raymond Hatton, Myrna Loy, Carmelita Geraghty

THE ROMAN SPRING OF MRS. STONE (1961, Warner Brothers)
Karen Stone—Vivien Leigh
Director—Jose Quintero
Leading Players—Warren Beatty, Coral Browne, Jill St. John

ROMANCE AND ARABELLA (1919, Silent, Selznick)
Arabella Cadenhouse—Constance Talmadge
Director—Walter Edwards
Leading Players—Harrison Ford, Gertrude Claire, Monte Blue

THE ROMANCE OF TARZAN (1918, Silent, First National)
Tarzan—Elmo Lincoln
Director—Wilfrid Lucas
Leading Players—Enid Markey, Cleo Madison, Thomas Jefferson

ROMANOFF AND JULIET (1961, Universal)
Juliet Moulsworth—Sandra Dee
Igor Romanoff—John Gavin
Director—Peter Ustinov
Leading Players—Peter Ustinov, Akim Tamiroff, Alix Talton

THE ROMANTIC ENGLISHWOMAN (1975, GB, New World)
Elizabeth Fielding—Glenda Jackson
Director—Joseph Losey
Leading Players—Michael Caine, Helmut Berger, Marcus Richardson

ROMEO AND JULIET (1916, Silent, Fox Film Corp.)
Juliet—Theda Bara
Romeo—Harry Hillard
Director—J. Gordon Edwards
Leading Players—Glen White, Walter Law, John Webb Dillon, Einar Linden, Elwin Eaton

ROMEO AND JULIET (1936, MGM)
Juliet—Norma Shearer
Romeo—Leslie Howard
Director—George Cukor
Leading Players—Edna May Oliver, John Barrymore, C. Aubrey Smith, Basil Rathbone, Henry Kolker, Reginald Denny

ROMEO AND JULIET (1954, GB, UA)
Romeo—Laurence Harvey
Juliet—Susan Shentall

Director—Renato Castellani
Leading Players—Flora Robson, Mervyn Johns, Bill Travers, Enzo Fiermonte, Aldo Zollo, Sebastian Cabot

ROMEO AND JULIET (1966, GB, Embassy)
Juliet—Margot Fonteyn
Romeo—Rudolf Nureyev
Director—Paul Czinner
Leading Players—David Blair, Desmond Doyle, Julia Farron, Michael Soames, Anthony Dowell

ROMEO AND JULIET (1968, Great Britain/Italy, Paramount)
Juliet—Olivia Hussey
Romeo—Leonard Whiting
Director—Franco Zeffirelli
Leading Players—Milo O'Shea, Murray Head, Micheal York, Jon McEnery, Pat Heywood, Natasha Parry

ROMERO (1989, Four Seasons)
Archbishop Oscar Romero—Raul Julia
Director—John Duigan
Leading Players—Richard Jordan, Ana Alicia, Tony Plana, Harold Gould

ROMOLA (1925, Silent, Metro-Goldwyn)
Romola—Lillian Gish
Director—Henry King
Leading Players—Dorothy Gish, William Powell, Ronald Colman

THE ROOKIE (1990, Warner Brothers/Malpaso)
David Ackerman—Charlie Sheen
Director—Clint Eastwood
Leading Players—Clint Eastwood, Raul Julia, Sonia Braga, Tom Skerritt, Lara Flynn Boyle, Pepe Serna

ROOKIE FIREMAN (1950, Columbia)
Joe Blake—Bill Williams
Director—Seymour Friedman
Leading Players—Barton MacLane, Marjorie Reynolds, Gloria Henry

ROOKIES IN BURMA (1943, RKO)
Jerry Miles—Wally Brown
Mike Strager—Alan Carney
Director—Leslie Goodwins
Leading Players—Erford Gage, Claire Carleton, Joan Barclay

ROONEY (1958, GB, Rank)
James Ignatius Rooney—John Gregson
Director—George Pollock
Leading Players—Muriel Pavlow, Barry Fitzgerald, June Thornburn

ROOSTER COGBURN (1975, Universal)
Rooster Cogburn—John Wayne
Director—Stuart Millar
Leading Players—Katharine Hepburn, Anthony Zerbe, Richard Jordan

ROSALIE (1937, MGM)
Rosalie Romanikoff—Eleanor Powell
Director—W.S. Van Dyke
Leading Players—Nelson Eddy, Ray Bolger, Frank Morgan, Ilona Massey, Edna May Oliver

THE ROSE (1979, 20th Century Fox)
Rose—Bette Midler
Director—Mark Rydell
Leading Players—Alan Bates, Frederic Forrest, Harry Dean Stanton

ROSE MARIE (1936, MGM)
Marie de Flor—Jeanette MacDonald
Director—W.S. Van Dyke II
Leading Players—Nelson Eddy, James Stewart, Reginald Owen

ROSE MARIE (1954, MGM)
Rose Marie Lemaitre—Ann Blyth
Director—Mervyn LeRoy
Leading Players—Howard Keel, Fernando Lamas, Bert Lahr, Marjorie Main

ROSE OF CIMARRON (1952, 20th Century Fox)
Rose Of Cimarron—Mala Powers
Director—Harry Keller
Leading Players—Jack Buetel, Bill Williams, Jim Davis

ROSE OF PARIS (1924, Silent, Universal)
Mitsi—Mary Philbin
Director—Irving Cummings
Leading Players—Robert Cain, John Sainpolis, Rose Dione

ROSE OF THE RANCHO (1936, Paramount)
Rosita Castro—Gladys Swarthout
Director—Marion Gering
Leading Players—John Boles, Charles Bickford, Willie Howard

ROSE OF THE RIO GRANDE (1938, Monogram)
Rosita—Movita
Director—William Nigh
Leading Players—John Carroll, Antonio Moreno, Lina Basquette

ROSE OF THE WORLD (1918, Silent, Artcraft)
Rosamund English—Elsie Ferguson
Director—Maurice Tourneur
Leading Players—Wyndham Standing, Percy Marmont, Ethel Martin

ROSE OF THE WORLD (1925, Silent, Warner Brothers)
Rose Kirby—Patsy Ruth Miller
Director—Harry Beaumont
Leading Players—Allan Forrest, Pauline Garon, Rockliffe Fellowes

ROSE OF THE YUKON (1949, Republic)
Rose Flambeau—Myrna Dell
Director—George Blair
Leading Players—Steve Brodie, William Wright, Emory Parnell

ROSE OF TRALEE (1938, Ireland, Butchers)
Rose O'Malley—Binkie Stuart
Director—Oswald Mitchell
Leading Players—Kathleen O'Regan, Fred Conyngham, Danny Malone

ROSE OF WASHINGTON SQUARE (1939, 20th Century Fox)
Rose Sargent—Alice Faye
Director—Gregory Ratoff
Leading Players—Tyrone Power, Al Jolson, William Frawley

ROSEANNA MCCOY (1949, RKO)
Roseanna McCoy—Joan Evans
Director—Irving Reis
Leading Players—Farley Granger, Charles Bickford, Raymond Massey

ROSEMARY'S BABY (1968, Paramount)
Rosemary Woodhouse—Mia Farrow
Director—Roman Polanski
Leading Players—John Cassavetes, Ruth Gordon, Sidney Blackmer, Maurice Evans, Ralph Bellamy

ROSENCRANTZ AND GUILDENSTERN ARE DEAD (1990, Cinecom/Brandenberg)
Rosencrantz—Gary Oldman
Guildenstern—Tim Roth
Director—Tom Stoppard
Leading Players—Richard Dreyfuss, Ian Glen, Joanna Roth, Donald Sumpter, Joanna Miles, Ljubo Zecevic, Ian Richardson

ROSIE! (1967, Universal)
Rosie Lord—Rosalind Russell
Director—David Lowell Rich
Leading Players—Sandra Dee, Brian Aherne, Audrey Meadows

ROSIE THE RIVETER (1944, Republic)
Rosie Warren—Jane Frazee
Director—Joseph Santley
Leading Players—Frank Albertson, Vera Vague, Frank Jenks

ROSITA (1923, Silent, UA)
Rosita—Mary Pickford
Director—Ernst Lubitsch
Leading Players—Holbrook Blinn, Irene Rich, George Walsh

THE ROSSITER CASE (1950, GB, Hammer)
Peter Rossiter—Clement McCallin
Director—Francis Searle
Leading Players—Helen Shingler, Sheila Burrell, Frederick Leister

THE ROUGHNECK (1924, Silent, Fox Film Corp.)
Jerry Delaney—George O'Brien
Director—Jack Conway
Leading Players—Billie Dove, Harry T. Morey, Cleo Madison

THE ROUNDERS (1965, MGM)
Ben Jones—Glenn Ford
Howdy Lewis—Henry Fonda
Director—Burt Kennedy
Leading Players—Sue Ane Langdon, Hope Holiday, Chill Wills

ROUSTABOUT (1964, Paramount)
Charlie Rogers—Elvis Presley
Director—John Rich
Leading Players—Barbara Stanwyck, Joan Freeman, Leif Erickson

THE ROWDY (1921, Silent, Universal)
Kit Purcell—Gladys Walton
Director—David Kirkland
Leading Players—Rex Roselli, Anna Hernandez, C. B. Murphy

THE ROWDYMAN (1973, Canada, Crowley)
Will Cole—Gordon Pinsent

Director—Peter Carter
Leading Players—Frank Converse, Will Geer, Linda Gorenson

ROXANNE (1987, Columbia)
Roxanne Kowalski—Daryl Hannah
Director—Fred Schepisi
Leading Players—Steve Martin, Rick Rossovitch, Shelley Duvall

ROXIE HART (1942, 20th Century Fox)
Roxie Hart—Ginger Rogers
Director—William A. Wellman
Leading Players—Adolphe Menjou, George Montgomery, Lynne Overman, Nigel Bruce, Phil Silvers

A ROYAL DIVORCE (1938, GB, Paramount)
Josephine—Ruth Chatterton
Napoleon Bonaparte—Pierre Blanchar
Director—Jack Raymond
Leading Players—Frank Cellier, Carol Goodner, Auriol Lee

THE ROYAL FAMILY OF BROADWAY (1930, Paramount)
Julia Cavendish—Ina Claire
Tony Cavendish—Fredric March
Gwen Cavendish—Mary Brian
Fanny Cavendish—Henriette Crosman
Directors—George Cukor & Cyril Gardner
Leading Players—Charles Starrett, Arnold Korff, Frank Conroy

ROYAL FLASH (1975, GB, 20th Century Fox)
Harry Flashman—Malcolm McDowell
Director—Richard Lester
Leading Players—Alan Bates, Florinda Bolkan, Oliver Reed, Britt Ekland

THE ROYAL RIDER (1929, Silent, First National)
King Michael XI—Phillippe De Lacey
Director—Harry J. Brown
Leading Players—Ken Maynard, Olive Hasbrouck, Theodore Lorch

RUBY (1971, Bartlett)
Ruby—Ruth Hurd
Director—Dick Bartlett
Leading Players—Phillip Weber, Joanie Andrews, George Bartlett

RUBY (1977, Dimension)
Ruby Claire—Piper Laurie
Directors—Curtis Harrington & Stephanie Rothman
Leading Players—Stuart Whitman, Roger Davis, Janit Baldwin

RUBY (1992, Triumph)
Jack Ruby—Danny Aiello
Director—John Mackenzie
Leading Players—Sherilyn Fenn, Arliss Howard, Tobin Bell, David Duchovny, Richard Sarafian, Joe Cortese

RUBY GENTRY (1952, 20th Century Fox)
Ruby Gentry—Jennifer Jones
Director—King Vidor
Leading Players—Charlton Heston, Karl Malden, Tom Tully

RUDE AWAKENING (1989, Orion)
Fred—Eric Roberts
Hesus—Cheech Marin
Directors—Aaron Russo & David Greenwalt

Leading Players—Julie Hagerty, Robert Carradine, Louise Lasser, Cliff DeYoung

RUDE BOY (1980, GB, Atlantic)
Ray—Ray Grange
Director—Jack Hazan
Leading Players—The Clash, John Green, Barry Baker

RUGGLES OF RED GAP (1923, Silent, Paramount)
Ruggles—Edward Everett Horton
Director—James Cruze
Leading Players—Ernest Torrence, Lois Wilson, Fritzi Ridgeway

RUGGLES OF RED GAP (1935, Paramount)
Marmaduke Ruggles—Charles Laughton
Director—Leo McCarey
Leading Players—Mary Boland, Charlie Ruggles, Zasu Pitts, Roland Young, Leila Hyams

THE RULING CLASS (1972, GB, Avco Embassy)
Jack, 14th Earl of Gurney—Peter O'Toole
Director—Peter Medak
Leading Players—Alastair Sim, Arthur Lowe, Harry Andrews, Coral Browne, Michael Bryant

THE RULING VOICE (1931, Warner Brothers)
Jack Bannister—Walter Huston
Director—Byron Morgan
Leading Players—Loretta Young, Doris Kenyon, David Manners

RUN, ANGEL, RUN (1969, Fanfare)
Angel—William Smith
Director—Jack Starrett
Leading Players—Valerie Starrett, Gene Shane, Lee De Broux

THE RUNAWAY (1964, GB, Columbia)
Andrian Peshkin—Alex Gallier
Director—Tony Young
Leading Players—Greta Gynt, Paul Williamson, Michael Trubshawe

RUNAWAY BRIDE (1930, RKO)
Mary—Mary Astor
Director—Donald Crisp
Leading Players—Lloyd Hughes, David Newall, Natalie Moorehead

THE RUNAWAY QUEEN (1935, GB, UA)
Queen Nadina—Anna Neagle
Director—Herbert Wilcox
Leading Players—Fernand Graavey, Muriel Aked, Michael Hogan

THE RUNNER STUMBLES (1979, 20th Century Fox)
Father Rivard—Dick Van Dyke
Director—Stanley Kramer
Leading Players—Kathleen Quinlan, Maureen Stapleton, Ray Bolger

RUNNING BRAVE (1983, Canada, Buena Vista)
Billy Mills—Robby Benson
Director—D.S. Everett
Leading Players—Pat Hingle, Claudia Cron, Jeff McCraken

THE RUNNING MAN (1963, GB, Columbia)
Rex Black—Laurence Harvey

Director—Carol Reed
Leading Players—Lee Remick, Alan Bates, Felix Aylmer

THE RUNNING MAN (1987, Tri-Star)
Ben "Butcher of Bakersfield" Richards—Arnold
  Schwarzenegger
Director—Paul Michael Glaser
Leading Players—Maria Cochita Alonso, Yaphet Kotto, Jim
  Brown, Jesse Ventura, Richard Dawson

RUNNING ON EMPTY (1988, Warner Brothers)
Danny Pope—River Phoenix
Director—Sidney Lumet
Leading PLayers—Christine Lahti, Judd Hirsch, Martha
  Plimpton, Jonas Arby

RUPERT OF HENTZAU (1915, GB, Jury)
Rupert—Gerald Ames
Director—George Loane Tucker
Leading Players—Henry Ainley, Jane Gail, Charles Rock

RUPERT OF HENTZAU (1923, Silent, Selznick)
Rupert—Lew Cody
Director—Victor Herman
Leading Players—Elaine Hammerstein, Bert Lytell, Claire
  Windsor

RUTHLESS (1948, Eagle Lion)
Horace Vendig—Zachary Scott
Director—Edgar G. Ulmer
Leading Players—Louis Hayward, Diana Lynn, Martha Vickers

RUTHLESS PEOPLE (1986, Buena Vista)
Ken Kessler—Judge Reinhold
Sandy Kessler—Helen Slater
Directors—Jim Abrahams, David & Jerry Zucker
Leading Players—Danny DeVito, Bette Midler, Anita Morris, Bill
  Pullman

RYAN'S DAUGHTER (1970, GB, MGM)
Rosy Ryan—Sarah Miles
Tom Ryan—Leo McKern
Director—David Lean
Leading Players—Robert Mitchum, Trevor Howard, Christopher
  Jones, John Mills, Barry Foster

S

S.O.B. (1981, Paramount)
Felix Farmer—Richard Mulligan
Director—Blake Edwards
Leading Players—Julie Andrews, William Holden, Marisa
  Berenson, Robert Preston, Robert Loggia, Shelley Winters

S*P*Y*S (1974, 20th Century Fox)
Griff—Elliott Gould
Brulard—Donald Sutherland
Director—Irvin Kershner
Leading Players—Zouzou, Joss Ackland, Kenneth Griffith

SAADIA (1953, MGM)
Saadia—Rita Gam
Director—Albert Lewin
Leading Players—Cornel Wilde, Mel Ferrer, Michel Simon

SABOTEUR (1942, Universal)
Frank Fry—Norman Lloyd
Director—Alfred Hitchcock
Leading Players—Priscilla Lane, Robert Cummings, Otto
  Kruger, Alan Baxter, Alma Kruger

SABRINA (1954, Paramount)
Sabrina Fairchild—Audrey Hepburn
Director—Billy Wilder
Leading Players—Humphrey Bogart, William Holden, John
  Williams

THE SAD SACK (1957, Paramount)
Bixby—Jerry Lewis
Director—George Marshall
Leading Players—David Wayne, Phyllis Kirk, Peter Lorre

SADDLE TRAMP (1950, Universal)
Chuck Connor—Joel McCrea
Director—Hugo Fregonese
Leading Players—Wanda Hendrix, John Russell, John McIntire

SADDLEMATES (1941, Republic)
Stony Brooke—Robert Livingston
Tucson Smith—Bob Steele
Lullaby Joslin—Rufe Davis
Director—Lester Orlebeck
Leading Players—Gale Storm, Forbes Murray, Cornelius Keefe

SADIE MCKEE (1934, MGM)
Sadie McKee—Joan Crawford
Director—Clarence Brown
Leading Players—Gene Raymond, Franchot Tone, Esther
  Ralston, Edward Arnold

SADIE THOMPSON (1928, Silent, UA)
Sadie Thompson—Gloria Swanson
Director—Raoul Walsh
Leading Players—Lionel Barrymore, Raoul Walsh, Blanche
  Frederici, Charles Lane

THE SADIST (1963, Fairway-International)
Charley Tibbs—Arch Hall, Jr.
Director—James Landis
Leading Players—Helen Hovey, Richard Alden, Marilyn
  Manning, Don Russell

SAFE IN HELL (1931, Warner Brothers)
Gilda Carlson—Dorothy MacKaill
Director—William A. Wellman
Leading Players—Donald Cook, Ralf Harolde, Morgan Wallace

THE SAFECRACKER (1958, GB, MGM)
Colley Dawson—Ray Milland
Director—Ray Milland
Leading Players—Barry Jones, Jeannette Sterke, Victor
  Maddern

SAILOR BE GOOD (1933, RKO)
Kelsey Jones—Jack Oakie
Director—James Cruze

Leading Players—Vivienne Osborne, George E. Stone, Lincoln Stedman

SAILOR BEWARE (1951, Paramount)
Melvin Jones—Jerry Lewis
Director—Hal Walker
Leading Players—Dean Martin, Corinne Calvet, Marion Marshall

THE SAILOR FROM GIBRALTER (1967, GB, Lopert)
Alan—Ian Bannen
Director—Tony Richardson
Leading Players—Jeanne Moreau, Vanessa Redgrave, Zia Mohyeddin

SAILOR IZZY MURPHY (1927, Silent, Warner Brothers)
Izzy Murphy—George Jessel
Director—Henry Lehman
Leading Players—Audrey Ferris, Warner Oland, John Miljan

A SAILOR-MADE MAN (1921, Silent, Pathe)
The Boy—Harold Lloyd
Director—Fred Newmeyer
Leading Players—Mildred Davis, Noah Young, Dick Sutherland

SAILOR OF THE KING (1953, GB, 20th Century Fox)
Andrew Brown—Jeffrey Hunter
Director—Roy Boulting
Leading Players—Michael Rennie, Wendy Hiller, Bernard Lee

THE SAILOR TAKES A WIFE (1946, MGM)
John—Robert Walker
Mary—June Allyson
Director—Richard Whorf
Leading Players—Hume Cronyn, Audrey Totter, Eddie "Rochester" Anderson

THE SAILOR WHO FELL FROM GRACE WITH THE SEA (1976, GB, Avco Embassy)
Jim Cameron—Kris Kristofferson
Director—Lewis John Carlino
Leading Players—Sarah Miles, Jonathan Kahn, Margo Cunningham

SAILORS' HOLIDAY (1929, Pathe)
Adam Pike—Alan Hale
Shorty—George Cooper
Director—Fred Newmeyer
Leading Players—Sally Eilers, Paul Hurst, Mary Carr

SAILORS' HOLIDAY (1944, Columbia)
Marble Head Tomkins—Arthur Lake
Bill Hayes—Bob Haymes
Iron Man Collins—Lewis Wilson
Director—William Berke
Leading Players—Jane Lawrence, Shelley Winters, Edmund MacDonald

SAILOR'S LADY (1940, 20th Century Fox)
Sally Gilroy—Nancy Kelly
Danny Malone—Jon Hall
Director—Allan Dwan
Leading Players—Joan Davis, Dana Andrews, Mary Nash, Buster Crabbe

SAILOR'S LUCK (1933, Fox Film Corp.)
Jimmy Harrigan—James Dunn

Director—Raoul Walsh
Leading Players—Sally Eilers, Sammy Cohen, Frank Moran, Victor Jory

SAILORS ON LEAVE (1941, Republic)
Chuck Stephens—William Lundigan
Director—Albert S. Rogell
Leading Players—Shirley Ross, Chick Chandler, Ruth Donnelly

THE SAILOR'S RETURN (1978, GB, NFFC/Osprey)
William Targett—Tom Bell
Director—Jack Gold
Leading Players—Shope Shodeinde, Mick Ford, Paola Dionisotti

A SAILOR'S SWEETHEART (1927, Silent, Warner Brothers)
Cynthia Botts—Louise Fazenda
Sandy MacTavish—Clyde Cook
Director—Lloyd Bacon
Leading Players—Myrna Loy, William Demarest, John Miljan

ST. BENNY THE DIP (1951, UA)
Benny—Dick Haymes
Director—Edgar G. Ulmer
Leading Players—Nina Foch, Roland Young, Lionel Stander, Freddie Bartholomew

ST. ELMO (1923, GB, Silent, Capital)
St. Elmo Murray—Shayle Gardner
Director—Rex Wilson
Leading Players—Gabrielle Gilroy, Madge Tree, Harding Thomas

ST. ELMO (1923, Silent, Fox Film Corp.)
St. Elmo Thornton—John Gilbert
Director—Jerome Storm
Leading Players—Barbara La Marr, Bessie Love, Warner Baxter, Nigel De Brulier

THE SAINT IN LONDON (1939, GB, RKO)
Simon Templar—George Sanders
Director—John Paddy Carstairs
Leading Players—Sally Gray, David Burns, Gordon McLeod

THE SAINT IN NEW YORK (1938, RKO)
Simon Templar—Louis Hayward
Director—Ben Holmes
Leading Players—Kay Sutton, Sig Rumann, Jonathan Hale

THE SAINT IN PALM SPRINGS (1941, RKO)
Simon Templar—George Sanders
Director—Jack Hively
Leading Players—Wendy Barrie, Paul Guilfoyle, Jonathan Hale

ST. IVES (1976, Warner Brothers)
Raymond St. Ives—Charles Bronson
Director—J. Lee Thompson
Leading Players—John Houseman, Jacqueline Bisset, Maxmillian Schell, Harry Guardino

SAINT JACK (1979, New World)
Jack Flowers—Ben Gazzara
Director—Peter Bogdanovich
Leading Players—Denholm Elliott, James Villiers, Joss Ackland

SAINT JOAN (1957, UA)
Joan of Arc—Jean Seberg
Director—Otto Preminger

Leading Players—Richard Widmark, Richard Todd, Anton Walbrook, John Gielgud, Felix Aylmer, Harry Andrews

THE ST. LOUIS KID (1934, Warner Brothers)
Eddie Kennedy—James Cagney
Director—Ray Enright
Leading Players—Patricia Ellis, Allen Jenkins, Robert Barrat

THE SAINT MEETS THE TIGER (1943, GB, RKO/Republic)
Simon Templar—Hugh Sinclair
Director—Paul Stein
Leading Players—Jean Gillie, Gordon Mcleod, Clifford Evans

THE SAINT STRIKES BACK (1939, RKO)
Simon Templar—George Sanders
Director—John Farrow
Leading Players—Wendy Barrie, Jonathan Hale, Jerome Cowan

THE SAINT TAKES OVER (1940, RKO)
Simon Templar—George Sanders
Director—Jack Hively
Leading Players—Wendy Barrie, Jonathan Hale, Paul Guilfoyle

A SAINTED DEVIL (1924, Silent, Paramount)
Don Alonzo Castro—Rudolph Valentino
Director—Joseph Henabery
Leading Players—Nita Naldi, Helen D'Algy, George Siegmann

THE SAINTED SISTERS (1948, Paramount)
Letty Stanton—Veronica Lake
Jane Stanton—Joan Caulfield
Director—William D. Russell
Leading Players—Barry Fitzgerald, William Demarest, George Reeves, Beulah Bondi

SAINTLY SINNERS (1962, UA)
Duke—Paul Bryar
Slim—Stanley Clements
Director—Jean Yarborough
Leading Players—Don Beddoe, Ellen Corby, Ron Hagerthy

THE SAINT'S DOUBLE TROUBLE (1940, RKO)
Simon Templar—George Sanders
Duke Piato—George Sanders
Director—Jack Hively
Leading Players—Helene Whitney, Jonathan Hale, Bela Lugosi

THE SAINT'S GIRL FRIDAY (1954, GB, RKO)
Simon Templar—Louis Hayward
Lady Carol Denby—Naomi Chance
Director—Seymour Friedman
Leading Players—Sydney Tafler, Charles Victor, Harold Lang

THE SAINT'S VACATION (1941, GB, RKO)
Simon Templar—Hugh Sinclair
Director—Leslie Fenton
Leading Players—Sally Gray, Arthur Macrae, Cecil Parker

SAL OF SINGAPORE (1929, Pathe)
Sal—Phyllis Haver
Director—Howard Higgin
Leading Players—Alan Hale, Fred Kohler, Sr., Noble Johnson

SALLY (1925, Silent, First National)
Sally—Colleen Moore
Director—Alfred E. Green

Leading Players—Lloyd Hughes, Leon Errol, Dan Mason

SALLY (1929, Warner Brothers)
Sally—Marilyn Miller
Director—John Frances Dillon
Leading Players—Alexander Gray, Joe E. Brown, T. Roy Barnes

SALLY AND SAINT ANNE (1952, Universal)
Sally O'Moyne—Ann Blyth
Director—Rudolph Mate
Leading Players—Edmund Gwenn, John McIntire, Palmer Lee, Hugh O'Brian

SALLY BISHOP (1932, Great Briatin, British Lion)
Sally Bishop—Joan Barry
Director—T. Haynes Hunter
Leading Players—Harold Huth, Isabel Jeans, Benita Hume

SALLY IN OUR ALLEY (1927, Silent, Columbia)
Sally Williams—Shirley Mason
Director—Walter Lang
Leading Players—Richard Arlen, Alice B. Francis, Paul Panzer

SALLY IN OUR ALLEY (1931, GB, RKO)
Sally Winch—Gracie Fields
Director—Maurice Elvey
Leading Players—Ian Hunter, Florence Desmond, Ivor Barnard

SALLY, IRENE AND MARY (1938, 20th Century Fox)
Sally Day—Alice Faye
Irene Keene—Joan Davis
Mary Stevens—Marjorie Weaver
Director—William S. Seiter
Leading Players—Tony Martin, Fred Allen, Jimmy Durante, Gregory Ratoff

SALLY OF THE SAWDUST (1925, Silent, UA)
Sally—Carol Dempster
Director—D.W. Griffith
Leading Players—W.C. Fields, Alfred Lunt, Erville Alderson

SALLY OF THE SCANDALS (1928, Silent, FBO)
Sally Rand—Bessie Love
Director—Lynn Shores
Leading Players—Irene Lambert, Allan Forrest, Margaret Quimby

SALOME (1922, Silent, Allied Productions & Distributors)
Salome—Nazimova
Director—Charles Bryant
Leading Players—Rose Dione, Mitchell Lewis, Nigel De Brulier

SALOME (1953, Columbia)
Princess Salome—Rita Hayworth
Director—William Dieterle
Leading Players—Charles Laughton, Stewart Granger, Judith Anderson, Cedric Hardwicke, Alan Badel

SALOME, WHERE SHE DANCED (1945, Universal)
Salome—Yvonne De Carlo
Director—Charles Lamont
Leading Players—Rod Cameron, David Bruce, Walter Slezak, Albert Dekker

SALOME'S LAST DANCE (1988, Vestron)
Salome/Rose—Imogen Millais-Scott

Director—Ken Russell
Leading Players—Nickolas Grace, Douglas Hodge, Glenda Jackson

SALOMY JANE (1914, Silent, California Motion Picture)
Salomy Jane—Beatrix Michelena
Director—J. Searle Dowley
Leading Players—House Peters, Andrew Robson, William Nigh

SALOMY JANE (1923, Silent, Paramount)
Salomy Jane—Jacqueline Logan
Director—George Melford
Leading Players—George Fawcett, Maurice B. Flynn, William Davidson

SALT & PEPPER (1968, GB, UA)
Charles Salt—Sammy Davis, Jr.
Christopher Pepper—Peter Lawford
Director—Richard D. Donner
Leading Players—Michael Bates, Ilona Rodgers, John Le Mesurier

SALT OF THE EARTH (1954, Independent Productions)
Esperanza Quintero—Rosaura Revueltas
Director—Herbert J. Biberman
Leading Players—Will Geer, David Wolfe, Melvin Williams, Juan Chacon

SALTY O'ROURKE (1945, Paramount)
Salty O'Rourke—Alan Ladd
Director—Raoul Walsh
Leading Players—Gail Russell, William Demarest, Stanley Clements, Bruce Cabot

SALUTE JOHN CITIZEN (1942, GB, British National)
Mr. Bunting—Edward Rigby
Director—Maurice Elvey
Leading Players—Mabel Constanduros, Stanley Holloway, George Robey, Jimmy Hanley

SALUTE THE TOFF (1952, GB, Butchers)
Hon. Richard Rollison—John Bentley
Director—Maclean Rogers
Leading Players—Carol Marsh, Valentine Dyall, Shelagh Fraser

SALVATION JANE (1927, Silent, R-C Pictures)
Salvation Jane—Viola Dana
Director—Phil Rosen
Leading Players—J. Parkes Jones, Fay Holderness, Erville Alderson

SALVATION NELL (1921, Silent, Associated First National)
Nell Sanders—Pauline Starke
Director—Kenneth Webb
Leading Players—Joseph King, Gypsy O'Brien, Edward Langford

SALVATION NELL (1931, Tiffany)
Nell Saunders—Helen Chandler
Director—James Cruze
Leading Players—Ralph Graves, Sally O'Neil, Jason Robards, Jr.

SAM SMALL LEAVES TOWN (1937, GB, British Screen Service)
Sam Small—Johnnie Schofield
Director—Alfred Goulding
Leading Players—Stanley Holloway, June Clyde, Fred Conyngham

SAM WHISKEY (1969, UA)
Sam Whiskey—Burt Reynolds
Director—Arnold Laven
Leading Players—Clint Walker, Ossie Davis, Angie Dickinson

SAMANTHA (1991, Planet Productions)
Samantha—Martha Plimpton
Director—Stephen La Rocque
Leading Players—Dermot Mulroney, Hector Elizondo, Mary Kay Place, Ione Skye, Marvin Silbersher

SAMMY AND ROSIE GET LAID (1987, GB, Cinecom)
Sammy—Ayub Khan Din
Rosie Hobbs—Frances Barber
Director—Stephen Frears
Leading Players—Shashi Kapoor, Claire Bloom, Roland Gift

SAM'S SON (1984, Invictus)
Sam Orowitz—Eli Wallach
Gene Orowitz—Timothy Patrick Murphy
Director—Michael Landon
Leading Players—Anne Jackson, Hallie Todd, Alan Hayes

SAMSON (1914, Silent, Universal)
Samson—J. Warren Kerrigan
Director—Lorimer Johnston
Leading Players—Kathleen Kerrigan, Mayme Kelso, Harold Lloyd

SAMSON AND DELILAH (1949, Paramount)
Delilah—Hedy Lamarr
Samson—Victor Mature
Director—Cecil B. DeMille
Leading Players—George Sanders, Angela Lansbury, Henry Wilcoxon

SANDERS (1963, GB, Hallam/Planet)
Inspector Harry Sanders—Richard Todd
Director—Lawrence Huntington
Leading Players—Marianne Koch, Vivi Bach, Walter Rilla

SANDERS OF THE RIVER (1935, GB, UA)
R. G. Sanders—Leslie Banks
DIrector—Zoltan Korda
Leading Players—Paul Robeson, Nina Mae McKinney, Robert Cochran

THE SANDWICH MAN (1966, GB, Rank)
The Sandwich Man—John le Mesurier
Director—Robert Hartford-Davis
Leading Players—Michael Bentine, Dora Bryan, Harry H. Corbett, Diana Dors, Stanley Holloway

SANDY (1926, Silent, Fox Film Corp.)
Sandy McNeil—Madge Bellamy
Director—Harry Beaumont
Leading Players—Leslie Fenton, Harrison Ford, Gloria Hope

SANDY GETS HER MAN (1940, Universal)
Sandy—Baby Sandy
Director—Otis Garrett
Leading Players—Stuart Erwin, Una Merkel, William Frawley

SANDY IS A LADY (1940, Universal)
Sandy—Baby Sandy
Director—Charles Lamont

Leading Players—Eugene Pallette, Nan Grey, Tom Brown

SANTA CLAUS CONQUERS THE MARTIANS (1964, Embassy)
Santa Claus—John Call
Director—Nicholas Webster
Leading Players—Leonard Hicks, Vincent Beck, Victor Stiles

SANTA CLAUS: THE MOVIE (1986, Tri-Star)
Santa Claus—David Huddleston
Director—Jeannot Szwarc
Leading Players—Dudley Moore, John Lithgow, Burgess Meredith

SANTE FE MARSHALL (1940, Paramount)
Hopalong Cassidy—William Boyd
Director—Lesley Selander
Leading Players—Russell Hayden, Marjorie Rambeau, Bernadene Hayes

SANTEE (1973, Crown International)
Santee—Glenn Ford
Director—Gary Nelson
Leading Players—Michael Burns, Dana Wynter, Jay Silverheels

THE SAP (1929, Warner Brothers)
The Sap—Edward Everett Horton
Director—Archie Mayo
Leading Players—Alan Hale, Patsy Ruth Miller, Russell Simpson

THE SAP FROM SYRACUSE (1930, Paramount)
Littleton Looney—Jack Oakie
Director—A. Edward Sutherland
Leading Players—Ginger Rogers, Granville Bates, George Barbier

THE SAPHEAD (1921, Silent, Metro)
Bertie Van Alstyne—Buster Keaton
Director—Herbert Blache
Leading Players—William H. Crane, Carol Holloway, Edward Connelly

SAPS AT SEA (1940, UA)
Ollie—Oliver Hardy
Stanley—Stan Laurel
Director—Gordon Douglas
Leading Players—James Finlayson, Ben Turpin, Dick Cramer

SARAH AND SON (1930, Paramount)
Sarah Storm—Ruth Chatterton
Bobby Storm Ashmore—Philippe de Lacey
Director—Dorothy Arzner
Leading Players—Fredric March, Fuller Melish, Jr., Gilbert Emery, Doris Lloyd

SARGE GOES TO COLLEGE (1947, Monogram)
Sarge—Alan Hale, Jr.
Director—Will Jason
Leading Players—Freddie Stewart, June Preisser, Frankie Darro

SARONG GIRL (1943, Monogram)
Dixie Barlow—Ann Corio
Director—Arthur Dreifuss
Leading Players—Tim Ryan, Irene Ryan, Mantan Moreland

SATAN IN HIGH HEELS (1962, Vega/Cosmic)
Stacey Kane—Meg Myles
Director—Jerald Intrator
Leading Players—Grayson Hall, Mike Keene, Robert Yuro

SATAN MET A LADY (1936, Warner Brothers)
Valerie Purvis—Bette Davis
Ted Shayne—Warren William
Director—William Dieterle
Leading Players—Alison Skipworth, Arthur Treacher, Winifred Shaw, Marie Wilson

SATAN'S CHEERLEADERS (1977, World Amusements)
Sharon—Sherry Marks
Chris—Hillary Horan
Patti—Kerry Sherman
Debbie—Alisa Powell
Director—Greydon Clark
Leading Players—John Ireland, Yvonne De Carlo, Jack Kruschen

SATAN'S MISTRESS (1982, Motion Picture Marketing)
Lisa—Lana Wood
The Spirit—Kabir Bedi
Director—James Polakof
Leading Players—Britt Ekland, Don Galloway, John Carradine

SATAN'S SADIST (1969, Independent-International)
Anchor—Russ Tamblyn
Director—Al Adamson
Leading Players—Scott Brady, Kent Taylor, John Cardos

SATAN'S SISTER (1925, Silent, GB, Woodfall)
Jude Tyler—Betty Balfour
Satan Tyler—Guy Phillips
Director—George Pearson
Leading Players—Phillips Stevens, James Carew, Frank Stanmore

SATAN'S SLAVE (1976, GB, Crown)
Alexander Yorke—Michael Gough
Director—Norman J. Warren
Leading Players—Candace Glendenning, Martin Potter, Barbara Kellerman

THE SATURDAY NIGHT KID (1929, Paramount)
Mayme—Clara Bow
Director—Lloyd Corrigan
Leading Players—James Hall, Jean Arthur, Charles Sellon

SATURDAY'S CHILDREN (1929, Warner Brothers)
Bobby Halvey—Corinne Griffith
Jim O'Neill—Grant Withers
Director—Gregory La Cava
Leading Players—Albert Conti, Alma Tell, Lucien Littlefield

SATURDAY'S CHILDREN (1940, Warner Brothers)
Rimes Rosson—John Garfield
Bobby Halvey—Anne Shirley
Director—Vincent Sherman
Leading Players—Claude Rains, Lee Patrick, George Tobias

SATURDAY'S HERO (1951, Columbia)
Steve Novak—John Derek
Director—David Miller
Leading Players—Donna Reed, Sidney Blackmer, Alexander Knox

SATURDAY'S HEROES (1937, RKO)
Val—Van Heflin
Director—Edward Killy
Leading Players—Marian Marsh, Richard Lane, Alan Bruce

THE SAVAGE (1953, Paramount)
Warbonnet-Jim Ahern—Charlton Heston
Director—George Marshall
Leading Players—Susan Morrow, Peter Hanson, Joan Taylor

THE SAVAGE GIRL (1932, Monarch)
The Goddess—Rochelle Hudson
Director—Harry S. Frazer
Leading Players—Walter Byron, Harry F. Myers, Theodore Adams

THE SAVAGE INNOCENTS (1960, GB, Paramount)
Inuk—Anthony Quinn
Asiak—Yoko Tani
Director—Nicholas Ray
Leading Players—Carlo Giustini, Marie Yang, Peter O'Toole

SAVAGE MESSIAH (1972, GB, MGM)
Henri Gaudier-Brzeska—Scott Antony
Director—Ken Russell
Leading Players—Dorothy Tutin, Helen Mirren, Lindsay Kemp

SAVANNAH SMILES (1983, Gold Coast)
Savannah Driscoll—Bridgette Anderson
Director—Pierre DeMoro
Leading Players—Mark Miller, Donovan Scott, Peter Graves

SAVE THE TIGER (1973, Paramount)
Harry Stoner—Jack Lemmon
Director—John G. Avildsen
Leading Players—Jack Gilford, Laurie Heineman, Norman Burton

SCALAWAG (1973, Paramount)
Peg—Kirk Douglas
Director—Kirk Douglas
Leading Players—Mark Lester, Neville Brand, George Eastman

SCANDALOUS JOHN (1971, Buena Vista)
John McCandless—Brian Keith
Director—Robert Butler
Leading Players—Alfonso Arau, Michele Carey, Rick Lenz

THE SCAPEGOAT (1959, GB, MGM)
John Barrett—Alec Guinness
Director—Robert Hamer
Leading Players—Bette Davis, Nicole Maurey, Irene Worth, Pamela Brown

SCARAMOUCHE (1923, Silent, Metro)
Scaramouche (Andre-Louis Moreau)—Ramon Novarro
Director—Rex Ingram
Leading Players—Alice Terry, Lewis Stone, Lloyd Ingraham, Julia Swayne Gordon, William Humphrey

SCARAMOUCHE (1952, MGM)
Scaramouche (Andre Moreau)—Stewart Granger
Director—George Sidney
Leading Players—Eleanor Parker, Janet Leigh, Mel Ferrer, Henry Wilcoxon, Nina Foch

SCARED TO DEATH (1947, Screen Guild)
Jane—Joyce Compton
Director—Christy Cabanne
Leading Players—Bela Lugosi, Douglas Fowley, George Zucco

SCARFACE (1932, UA)
Tony Camonte—Paul Muni
Director—Howard Hawks
Leading Players—Ann Dvorak, Karen Morley, Osgood Perkins, Boris Karloff, George Raft

SCARFACE (1983, Universal)
Tony Montana—Al Pacino
Director—Brian De Palma
Leading Players—Steven Bauer, Michelle Pfeiffer, Mary Elizabeth Mastrantonio, Robert Logia, F. Murray Abraham

SCARLET ANGEL (1952, Universal)
Roxy McClanahan—Yvonne De Carlo
Director—Sidney Salkow
Leading Players—Rock Hudson, Richard Denning, Bodil Miller, Amanda Blake

THE SCARLET EMPRESS (1934, Paramount)
Sophia Frederica, Catherine II—Marlene Dietrich
Director—Josef von Sternberg
Leading Players—John Lodge, Sam Jaffe, Louise Dresser, C. Aubrey Smith, Olive Tell

THE SCARLET LADY (1928, Silent, Columbia)
Lya—Lya De Putti
Director—Alan Crosland
Leading Players—Don Alvarado, Warner Oland, Otto Matiesen

THE SCARLET LILY (1923, Silent, Associate First National)
Dora Mason—Katherine MacDonald
Director—Victor Schertzinger
Leading Players—Orville Caldwell, Stuart Holmes, Edith Lyle

THE SCARLET PIMPERNEL (1935, GB, UA)
Sir Percy Blakeney—Leslie Howard
Director—Harold Young (Rowland Brown, Alexander Korda-uncred.)
Leading Players—Merle Oberon, Raymond Massey, Nigel Bruce, Bramwell Fletcher, Joan Gardner

THE SCARS OF DRACULA (1970, GB, Hammer-EMI)
Count Dracula—Christopher Lee
Director—Roy Ward Baker
Leading Players—Dennis Waterman, Jenny Hanley, Christopher Matthews

SCATTERBRAIN (1940, Republic)
Judy Hull—Judy Canova
Director—Gus Meins
Leading Players—Alan Mowbray, Ruth Donnelly, Eddie Foy, Jr.

SCATTERGOOD BAINES (1941, RKO)
Scattergood Baines—Guy Kibbee
Director—Christy Cabanne
Leading Players—Carol Hughes, John Archer, Francis "Dink" Trout

SCATTERGOOD MEETS BROADWAY (1941, RKO)
Scattergood Baines—Guy Kibbee
Director—Christy Cabanne

Leading Players—Emma Dunn, Joyce Compton, Bradley Page

SCATTERGOOD PULLS THE STRINGS (1941, RKO)
Scattergood Baines—Guy Kibbee
Director—Christy Cabanne
Leading Players—Bobs Watson, Susan Peters, James Corner

SCATTERGOOD RIDES HIGH (1942, RKO)
Scattergood Baines—Guy Kibbee
Director—Christy Cabanne
Leading Players—Jed Prouty, Dorothy Moore, Charles Lind

SCATTERGOOD SURVIVES A MURDER (1942, RKO)
Scattergood Baines—Guy Kibbee
Director—Christy Cabanne
Leading Players—John Archer, Margaret Hayes, Wallace Ford

SCHLOCK (1973, Gazotskie/Harris)
The Schlockthropus—John Landis
Director—John Landis
Leading Players—Saul Kahan, Joseph Piantadosi, Eliza Garrett

SCHWEIK'S NEW ADVENTURES (1943, GB, Eden/Coronet)
Schweik—Lloyd Pearson
Director—Karel Lamac
Leading Players—Margaret McGrath, Julian Mitchell, Richard Attenborough

SCHWEITZER (1990, Concorde)
Albert Schweitzer—Malcolm McDowell
Director—Grey Hofmyer
Leading Players—Susan Strasberg, Helen Jessop, Andrew Davis, John Carson

SCOBIE MALONE (1975, Australia, Kingcroft/Cemp-Regent)
Scobie Malone—Jack Thompson
Director—Terry Ohlsson
Leading Players—Judy Morris, Shane Porteous, Jacqueline Kott

SCORCHY (1976, American International)
Sgt. Jackie Parker—Connie Stevens
Director—Hikmet Avedis
Leading Players—Cesare Danova, William Smith, Normann Burton

SCORPIO (1973, UA)
Laurier—Alain Delon
Director—Michael Winner
Leading Players—Burt Lancaster, Paul Scofield, John Colicos, Gayle Hunnicutt, Joannne Linville

SCOTT JOPLIN (1977, Universal)
Scott Joplin—Billy Dee Williams
Director—Jeremy Paul Kagan
Leading Players—Art Carney, Clifton Davis, Margaret Avery

SCOTT OF THE ANTARTIC (1949, GB, Ealing)
Capt. Robert Falcon Scott—John Mills
Director—Charles Frend
Leading Players—Derek Bond, Harold Warrender, James Robertson Justice, Reginald Beckwith

THE SCOUNDREL (1935, Paramount)
Anthony Mallare—Noel Coward
Directors—Ben Hecht and Charles MacArthur
Leading Players—Julie Haydon, Stanley Ridges, Rosita Moreno

THE SCRAPPER (1922, Silent, Universal)
Malloy—Herbert Rawlinson
Director—Hobart Henley
Leading Players—Gertrude Olmstead, William Welsh, Frankie Lee

SCRATCH HARRY (1969, Cannon)
Harry—Harry Walker Staff
Director—Alex Matter
Leading Players—Victoria Wilde, Christine Kelly

SCREAM BLACULA SCREAM (1973, American International)
Manuwalde—William Marshall
Director—Bob Kelljan
Leading Players—Don Mitchell, Pam Grier, Michael Conrad

SCROOGE (1935, GB, Paramount)
Ebenezer Scrooge—Sir Seymour Hicks
Director—Henry Edwards
Leading Players—Donald Calthrop, Robert Cochran, Mary Glynne

SCROOGE (1951, GB, Renown)
Ebenezer Scrooge—Alastair Sim
Director—Brian Desmond Hurst
Leading Players—Mervyn Johns, Kathleen Harrison, Jack Warner, Michael Hordern, Hermione Baddeley

SCROOGE (1970, GB, National General)
Ebenezer Scrooge—Albert Finney
Director—Ronald Neame
Leading Players—Alec Guinness, Edith Evans, Kenneth More, Laurence Naismith, David Collings

SCROOGED (1988, Paramount)
Frank Cross—Bill Murray
Director—Richard Donner
Leading Players—Carol Kane, Bob Goldthwait, David Johansen, Karen Allen, John Glover, John Forsythe, Mary Lou Retton

THE SEA GOD (1930, Paramount)
Phillip "Pink" Barker—Richard Arlen
Director—George Abbott
Leading Players—Fay Wray, Eugene Pallette, Robert Glecker

THE SEA HAWK (1940, Warner Brothers)
Capt. Geoffrey Thorpe—Errol Flynn
Director—Michael Curtiz
Leading Players—Brenda Marshall, Claude Rains, Flora Robson, Donald Crisp, Henry Daniell, Alan Hale

SEA WIFE (1957, GB, 20th Century Fox)
Sea Wife—Joan Collins
Director—Bob McNaught
Leading Players—Richard Burton, Basil Sydney, Ronald Squire, Cy Grant

THE SEA-WOLF (1913, Silent, Bosworth)
Wolf Larsen—Hobart Bosworth
Director—Hobart Bosworth
Leading Players—Viola Barry, Herbert Rawlinson, J. Charles Hayden

THE SEA WOLF (1930, Fox Film Corp.)
Wolf Larsen—Milton Sills
Director—Alfred Santell

Leading Players—Jane Keith, Raymond Hackett, Mitchell Harris

THE SEA WOLF (1941, Warner Brothers)
Wolf Larsen—Edward G. Robinson
Director—Michael Curtiz
Leading Players—John Garfield, Ida Lupino, Alexander Knox, Gene Lockhart, Barry Fitzgerald

SEABO (1978, E.O. Corp.)
Seabo—Earl Owensby
Director—Jimmy Huston
Leading Players—David Allan Coe, Don Barry, Ed Parker

THE SEARCH FOR BRIDEY MURPHY (1956, Paramount)
Bridey Murphy at 15—Eilene Janssen
Bridey Murphy at 66—Hallene Hill
Bridey Murphy at 8—Denise Freeborn
Bridey Murphy at 4—Ruth Robinson
Director—Noel Langley
Leading Players—Teresa Wright, Louis Hayward, Nancy Gates

THE SEARCHERS (1956, Warner Brothers)
Ethan Edwards—John Wayne
Martin Pawley—Jeffrey Hunter
Director—John Ford
Leading Players—Vera Miles, Ward Bond, Natalie Wood, Henry Brandon, John Qualen, Olive Carey

SEBASTIAN (1968, GB, Paramount)
Sebastian—Dirk Bogarde
Director—David Greene
Leading Players—Susannah York, Lili Palmer, John Gielgud

THE SECOND BEST SECRET AGENT IN THE WORLD (1965, GB, Embassy)
Charles Vine—Tom Adams
Director—Lindsay Shonteff
Leading Players—Karel Stepanek, Veronica Hurst, Peter Bull

THE SECOND COMING OF SUZANNE (1974, Barry)
Suzanne—Sondra Locke
Director—Michael Barry
Leading Players—Paul Sand, Jared Martin, Richard Dreyfuss, Gene Barry

THE SECOND FACE (1950, Eagle Lion)
Phyllis Holmes—Ella Raines
Director—Jack Bernhard
Leading Players—Bruce Bennett, Rita Johnson, John Sutton

SECOND FIDDLE (1923, Silent, Hodkinson)
Jim Bradley—Glenn Hunter
Director—Frank Tuttle
Leading Players—Mary Astor, Townsend Martin, Mary Foy

SECOND HAND ROSE (1922, Silent, Universal)
Rose O'Grady—Gladys Walton
Director—Lloyd Ingraham
Leading Players—George B. Williams, Eddie Sutherland, Wade Boteler

SECOND HAND WIFE (1933, Fox Film Corp.)
Sandra Trumbell—Sally Eilers
Director—Hamilton McFadden
Leading Players—Ralph Bellamy, Helen Vinson, Clay Clement

THE SECOND IN COMMAND (1915, Silent, Metro)
Major Bingham—William Clifford
Director—William J. Bowman
Leading Players—Francis X. Bushman, Marguerite Snow, Lester Cuneo

THE SECOND MATE (1950, GB, Associate British Films)
Bobby Tomkins—David Hannaford
Director—John Baxter
Leading Players—Gordon Harker, Graham Moffatt, Beryl Walkley

THE SECOND MR. BUSH (1940, GB, Anglo-American)
Tony—Derrick de Marney
Director—John Paddy Carstairs
Leading Players—Wallace Evennett, Evelyn Roberts, Kay Walsh

THE SECOND MRS. TANQUERAY (1952, GB, Associate British)
Paula Tanqueray—Pamela Brown
Director—Dallas Bower
Leading Players—Hugh Sinclair, Ronald Ward, Virginia McKenna

SECOND WIFE (1930, RKO)
Florence Wendell—Lila Lee
Director—Russell Mack
Leading Players—Conrad Nagel, Hugh Huntley, Mary Carr

SECOND WIFE (1936, RKO)
Virginia Howard—Gertrude Michael
Director—Edward Killy
Leading Players—Walter Abel, Erik Rhodes, Emma Dunn

THE SECOND WOMAN (1951, UA)
Ellen Foster—Betsy Drake
Director—James V. Kern
Leading Players—Robert Young, John Sutton, Florence Bates

SECRET ADMIRER (1985, Orion)
Michael Ryan—C. Thomas Howell
Director—David Greenwalt
Leading Players—Lori Loughlin, Kelly Preston, Dee Wallace Stone

SECRET AGENT (1933, GB, British International Pictures)
Marchesa Marcella—Greta Nissen
Director—Arthur Woods
Leading Players—Carl Ludwig Diehl, Don Alvarado, Lester Matthews

THE SECRET AGENT (1936, GB, Gaumont)
Edgar Brodie (Richard Ashenden)—John Gielgud
Director—Alfred Hitchcock
Leading Players—Madeleine Carroll, Peter Lorre, Robert Young

SECRET AGENT OF JAPAN (1942, 20th Century Fox)
Saito—Noel Madison
Director—Irving Pichel
Leading Players—Preston Foster, Lynn Bari, Victor Sen Yung

THE SECRET BRIDE (1935, Warner Brothers)
Ruth Vincent—Barbara Stanwyck
Director—William Dieterle
Leading Players—Warren William, Glenda Farrell, Grant Mitchell

THE SECRET DIARY OF SIGMUND FREUD (1984, 20th Century Fox)
>**Sigmund Freud**—Bud Cort
>Director—Danford B. Greene
>Leading Players—Carol Kane, Klaus Kinski, Marisa Berenson, Carroll Baker

THE SECRET FOUR (1940, GB, Ealing)
>**Humphrey Mansfield**—Hugh Sinclair
>**James Brodie**—Griffith Jones
>**Leon Poiccard**—Francis L. Sullivan
>**Terry**—Frank Lawton
>Director—Walter Forde
>Leading Players—Anna Lee, Basil Sydney, Alan Napier

THE SECRET LIFE OF AN AMERICAN WIFE (1968, 20th Century Fox)
>**Victoria Layton**—Anne Jackson
>Director—George Axelrod
>Leading Players—Walter Matthau, Patrick O'Neal, Edy Williams

THE SECRET LIFE OF WALTER MITTY (1947, RKO)
>**Walter Mitty**—Danny Kaye
>Director—Norman Z. McLeod
>Leading Players—Virginia Mayo, Boris Karloff, Fay Bainter, Ann Rutherford, Thurston Hall, Florence Bates

THE SECRET OF DR. KILDARE (1939, MGM)
>**Dr. James Kildare**—Lew Ayres
>Director—Harold S. Bucquet
>Leading Players—Lionel Barrymore, Lionel Atwill, Laraine Day

THE SECRET OF MADAME BLANCHE (1933, MGM)
>**Sally**—Irene Dunne
>Director—Charles Brabin
>Leading Players—Lionel Atwill, Phillips Holmes, Una Merkel

THE SECRET OF MY SUCCESS (1965, GB, MGM)
>**Arthur Tate**—James Booth
>Director—Andrew L. Stone
>Leading Players—Shirley Jones, Stella Stevens, Honor Blackman, Lionel Jeffries

THE SECRET OF MY SUCCESS (1987, Universal)
>**Brantley Foster**—Michael J. Fox
>Director—Herbert Ross
>Leading Players—Helen Slater, Richard Jordan, Margaret Whitton

THE SECRET PARTNER (1961, GB, MGM)
>**Ralph Beldon**—Norman Bird
>Director—Basil Dearden
>Leading Players—Stewart Granger, Haya Harareet, Bernard Lee

SECRET PEOPLE (1952, GB, Ealing)
>**Maria Brentano**—Valentina Cortesa
>**Louis**—Serge Reggiani
>Director—Thorold Dickinson
>Leading Players—Charles Goldner, Audrey Hepburn, Megs Jenkins

SECRET SERVICE INVESTIGATOR (1948, Republic)
>**Steve Mallory** (Dan Redfern)—Lloyd Bridges
>Director—R.G. Springsteen
>Leading Players—Lynne Roberts, George Zucco, June Storey

THE SECRET WAR OF HARRY FRIGG (1968, Universal)
>**Harry Frigg**—Paul Newman
>Director—Jack Smight
>Leading Players—Sylva Koscina, Andrew Duggan, Tom Bosley, John Williams, Charles Gray, James Gregory

SECRETS OF A CO-ED (1942, Producers Releasing Corp.)
>**Brenda Reynolds**—Tina Thayer
>Director—Joseph H. Lewis
>Leading Players—Otto Kruger, Rick Vallin, Russell Hoyt

SECRETS OF A MODEL (1940, Continental-Times)
>**Rita Wilson**—Sharon Lee
>Director—Sam Newfield
>Leading Players—Harold Daniels, Julien Madison, Phyllis Barry

SECRETS OF A NURSE (1938, Universal)
>**Katherine MacDonald**—Helen Mack
>Director—Arthur Lubin
>Leading Players—Edmund Lowe, Dick Foran, Samuel S. Hinds

SECRETS OF A SECRETARY (1931, Paramount)
>**Helen Blake**—Claudette Colbert
>Director—George Abbott
>Leading Players—Herbert Marshall, George Metaxa, Betty Lawford

SECRETS OF AN ACTRESS (1938, Warner Brothers)
>**Ray Carter**—Kay Francis
>Director—William Keighley
>Leading Players—George Brent, Ian Hunter, Gloria Dickson

SECRETS OF THE LONE WOLF (1941, Columbia)
>**Michael Lanyard**—Warren William
>Director—Edward Dmytryk
>Leading Players—Ruth Ford, Roger Clark, Victor Jory

SECRETS OF WU SIN (1932, Invincible/Chesterfield)
>**Wu Sin**—Tetsui Komai
>Director—Richard Thorpe
>Leading Players—Lois Nelson, Grant Withers, Dorothy Revier

THE SEDUCTION OF JOE TYNAN (1979, Universal)
>**Joe Tynan**—Alan Alda
>Director—Jerry Schatzberg
>Leading Players—Barbara Harris, Meryl Streep, Rip Torn, Melvyn Douglas

SEDUCTION: THE CRUEL WOMAN (1989, First Run)
>**Wanda**—Mechthild Grossmann
>Director—Elfi Mikesch
>Leading Players—Carola Regnier, Udo Kier, Sheila McLaughlin

SEE HERE, PRIVATE HARGROVE (1944, MGM)
>**Pvt. Marion Hargrove**—Robert Walker
>Director—Wesley Ruggles
>Leading Players—Donna Reed, Robert Benchley, Keenan Wynn

SEE NO EVIL, HEAR NO EVIL (1989, Tri-Star)
>**Dave Lyons**—Gene Wilder
>**Wally Kanew**—Richard Pryor
>Director—Arthur Hiller
>Leading Players—Joan Severance, Kevin Spacey, Alan North

SEE YOU IN THE MORNING (1989, Warner Brothers)
>**Larry Livingston**—Jeff Bridges

Beth Goodwin—Alice Krige
Director—Alan J. Pakula
Leading Players—Farrah Fawcett, Drew Barrymore, Lukas Haas

SELF-MADE LADY (1932, GB, UA)
Sookey—Heather Angel
Director—George Brown
Leading Players—Henry Wilcoxon, Amy Veness, A. Bromley Davenport

THE SENATOR (1915, Silent, Equitable)
Senator Rivers—Charles J. Ross
Director—Joseph Golden
Leading Players—Joseph Burke, Ben Graham, Thomas Tracy

THE SENATOR WAS INDISCREET (1947, Universal)
Senator Melvin G. Ashton—William Powell
Director—George S. Kaufman
Leading Players—Ella Raines, Peter Lind Hayes, Arleen Whelan

SEND FOR PAUL TEMPLE (1946, GB, Butchers)
Paul Temple—Anthony Hulme
Director—John Argyle
Leading Players—Joy Shelton, Tamara Desni, Jack Raine

SEND ME NO FLOWERS (1964, Universal)
George Kimball—Rock Hudson
Director—Norman Jewison
Leading Players—Doris Day, Tony Randall, Paul Lynde, Hal March

THE SENDER (1982, GB, Paramount)
The Sender—Zeljko Ivanek
Director—Roger Christian
Leading Players—Kathryn Harrold, Shirley Knight, Paul Freeman

SENOR AMERICANO (1929, Universal)
Michael Banning—Ken Maynard
Director—Harry Joe Brown
Leading Players—Kathryn Crawford, Gino Corrado, J.P. McGowan

SENORITA FROM THE WEST (1945, Universal)
Jeannie Blake—Bonita Granville
Director—Frank Strayer
Leading Players—Allan Jones, Jess Barker, Olin Howlin

SENTENCED FOR LIFE (1960, GB, UA)
John Richards—Jack Gwillim
Director—Max Varnel
Leading Players—Francis Matthews, Jill Williams, Basil Dignam

THE SENTIMENTAL LADY (1915, Silent, Kleine)
Amy Cary—Irene Fenwick
Director—Sidney Olcott
Leading Players—Frank Belcher, John Davidson, Thomas McGrath

THE SENTINEL (1977, Universal)
Michael Lerman—Chris Sarandon
Director—Michael Winner
Leading Players—Cristina Raines, Martin Balsam, John Carradine, Jose Ferrer, Ava Gardner, Arthur Kennedy

SEPARATE VACATIONS (1986, RSK Entertainment)
Richard Moore—David Naughton
Sarah Moore—Jennifer Dale
Director—Michael Anderson
Leading Players—Mark Keyloun, Laurie Holden, Blanca Cuerra

SEPIA CINDERELLA (1947, Herald)
Barbara—Sheila Guyse
Director—Arthur Leonard
Leading Players—Billy Daniels, Tondeleyo, Ruble Blakey, Jack Carter, Dusty Freeman

THE SERGEANT (1968, Warner Brothers)
Master Sgt. Albert Callan—Rod Steiger
Director—John Flynn
Leading Players—John Phillip Law, Ludmila Mikael, Frank Latimore

SERGEANT DEADHEAD (1965, American International)
Sgt. O.K. Deadhead (Sgt. Donovan)—Frankie Avalon
Director—Norman Taurog
Leading Players—Deborah Walley, Cesar Romero, Fred Clark, Gale Gordon

SERGEANT MADDEN (1939, MGM)
Shaun Madden—Wallace Beery
Director—Josef von Sternberg
Leading Players—Tom Brown, Alan Curtis, Laraine Day, Fay Holden

SGT. PEPPER'S LONELY HEARTS CLUB BAND (1978, Universal)
Sgt. Pepper—Billy Preston
Director—Michael Schultz
Leading Players—Peter Frampton, The Bee Gees, George Burns

SERGEANT RUTLEDGE (1960, Warner Brothers)
1st Sgt. Braxton Rutledge—Woody Strode
Director—John Ford
Leading Players—Jeffrey Hunter, Constance Towers, Billie Burke, Juano Hernandez

SERGEANT RYKER (1968, Universal)
Sgt. Paul Ryker—Lee Marvin
Director—Buzz Kulik
Leading Players—Bradford Dillman, Vera Miles, Peter Graves

THE SERGEANT WAS A LADY (1961, Universal)
Sgt. Judy Fraser—Venetia Stevenson
Director—Bernard Glasser
Leading Players—Martin West, Bill Williams, Catherine McLeod

SERGEANT YORK (1941, Warner Brothers)
Alvin C. York—Gary Cooper
Director—Howard Hawks
Leading Players—Walter Brennan, Joan Leslie, George Tobias, Stanley Ridges, Margaret Wycherly

SERGEANTS 3 (1962, UA)
1st Sgt. Mike Merry—Frank Sinatra
Sgt. Chip Deal—Dean Martin
Sgt. Larry Barrett—Peter Lawford
Director—John Sturges
Leading Players—Sammy Davis, Jr., Joey Bishop, Henry Silva

SERPENT OF THE NILE (1953, Columbia)
Cleopatra—Rhonda Fleming
Director—William Castle
Leading Players—William Lundigan, Raymond Burr, Jean Byron

SERPICO (1973, Paramount)
Frank Serpico—Al Pacino
Director—Sidney Lumet
Leading Players—Tony Roberts, John Randolph, Jack Kehoe, Biff McGuire, Barbara Eda-Young

THE SERVANT (1964, GB, Springbok/Landau)
Hugo Barrett—Dirk Bogarde
Director—Joseph Losey
Leading Players—Sarah Miles, Wendy Craig, James Fox

THE SET-UP (1949, RKO)
Bill "Stoker" Thompson—Robert Ryan
Director—Robert Wise
Leading Players—Audrey Totter, George Tobias, Alan Baxter, Wallace Ford, James Edwards

SEVEN ANGRY MEN (1955, Allied Artists)
John Brown—Raymond Massey
Owen Brown—Jeffrey Hunter
Oliver Brown—Larry Pennell
Frederick Brown—John Smith
Jason Brown—James Best
John Brown, Jr.—Dennis Weaver
Salmon Brown—Guy Williams
Director—Charles Marquis Warren
Leading Players—Debra Paget, Leo Gordon, Tom Irish

SEVEN BRIDES FOR SEVEN BROTHERS (1954, MGM)
Adam Pontipee—Howard Keel
Milly—Jane Powell
Benjamin Pontipee—Jeff Richards
Dorcas—Julie Newmar
Caleb Pontipee—Matt Mattox
Ruth—Ruta Kilmonis (Lee)
Daniel Pontipee—Marc Platt
Martha—Norma Doggett
Ephraim Pontipee—Jacques d'Amboise
Liza—Virginia Gibson
Frank Pontipee—Tommy Rall
Alice—Nancy Kilgas
Gideon Pontipee—Russ Tamblyn
Sarah—Betty Carr
Director—Stanley Donen
Leading Players—Howard Petrie, Ian Wolfe, Matt Moore

SEVEN FACES OF DR. LAO (1964, MGM)
Dr. Lao—Tony Randall
Merlin the Magician—Tony Randall
Pan—Tony Randall
The Abominable Snowman—Tony Randall
Medusa—Tony Randall
The Great Serpent—Tony Randall
Appollonius of Tyana—Tony Randall
Director—George Pal
Leading Players—Barbara Eden, Arthur O'Connell, John Ericson

THE SEVEN LITTLE FOYS (1955, Paramount)
Brynie Foy—Billy Gray

Charley Foy—Lee Erickson
Richard Foy—Paul De Rolf
Mary Foy—Lydia Reed
Madeleine Foy—Linda Bennett
Eddie Foy, Jr.—Jimmy Baird
Irving Foy—Tommy Duran
Director—Melville Shavelson
Leading Players—Bob Hope, Milly Vitale, George Tobias, Angela Clarke, James Cagney

SEVEN WOMEN (1966, MGM)
Dr. D.R. Cartwright—Anne Bancroft
Emma Clark—Sue Lyon
Agatha Andrews—Margaret Leighton
Miss Binns—Flora Robson
Jane Argent—Mildred Dunnock
Florrie Pether—Betty Field
Mrs. Russell—Anna Lee
Director—John Ford
Leading Players—Eddie Albert, Mike Mazurki, Woody Strode

SEVEN WOMEN FROM HELL (1961, 20th Century Fox)
Grace Ingram—Patricia Owens
Claire Oudry—Denise Darcel
Mara Shepherd—Margia Dean
Janet Cook—Yvonne Craig
Mai-Lu Ferguson—Pilar Seurat
Ann Van Laer—Sylvia Daneel
Regan—Evadne Baker
Director—Billy Wilder
Leading Players—Cesar Romero, John Kerr, Richard Loo

SEVENTEEN (1940, Paramount)
William Sylvanus Baxter—Jackie Cooper
Director—Louis King
Leading Players—Betty Field, Otto Kruger, Ann Shoemaker

THE SEVENTH VOYAGE OF SINBAD (1958, Columbia)
Captain Sinbad—Kerwin Mathews
Director—Nathan Juran
Leading Players—Kathryn Grant, Richard Eyer, Torin Thatcher

SEX AND THE SINGLE GIRL (1964, Warner Brothers)
Dr. Helen Brown—Natalie Wood
Director—Richard Quine
Leading Players—Tony Curtis, Henry Fonda, Lauren Bacall, Mel Ferrer, Fran Jeffries

SEXTON BLAKE AND THE BEARDED DOCTOR (1935, GB, MGM)
Sexton Blake—George Curzon
Dr. Gibbs—Henry Oscar
Director—George A. Cooper
Leading Players—Tony Sympson, Gillian Maude, Phil Ray

SEXTON BLAKE AND THE HOODED TERROR (1938, GB, MGM)
Sexton Blake—George Curzon
Director—George King
Leading Players—Tod Slaughter, Greta Gynt, Charles Oliver

SEXTON BLAKE AND THE MADEMOISELLE (1935, GB, MGM)
Sexton Blake—George Curzon
Mlle. Roxanne—Lorraine Grey
Director—Alex Bryce
Leading Players—Tony Sympson, Edgar Norfolk, Rymond Lovell

SEZ O'REILLY TO MACNAB (1938, GB, Gaumont/GFD)
Timothy O'Reilly—Will Mahoney
Malcolm MacNab—Will Fyffe
Director—William Beaudine
Leading Players—Ellis Drake, Sandy McDougal, Jean Winstanley

SHADEY (1987, GB, Film Four/Skouras)
Oliver Shadey—Antony Sher
Director—Philip Saville
Leading Players—Billie Whitelaw, Patrick Macnee, Leslie Ash

THE SHADOW (1936, GB, UA)
Reggie Ogden, The Shadow—Henry Kendall
Director—George A. Cooper
Leading Players—Elizabeth Allan, Jeanne Stuart, Felix Aylmer

THE SHADOW OF MIKE EMERALD (1935, GB, Radio Pictures)
Mike Emerald—Leslie Perrins
Director—Maclean Rogers
Leading Players—Marjorie Mars, Martin Lewis, Vincent Holman

SHADOW OF THE THIN MAN (1941, MGM)
Nick Charles—William Powell
Director—W.S. Van Dyke II
Leading Players—Myrna Loy, Barry Nelson, Donna Reed, Sam Levene

THE SHADOW RETURNS (1946, Monogram)
Lamont Cranston (The Shadow)—Kane Richmond
Director—Phil Rosen
Leading Players—Barbara Reed, Tom Dugan, Joseph Crehan

THE SHADOW STRIKES (1937, Grand National)
"The Shadow"—Rod La Rocque
Director—Lynn Shores
Leading Players—Lynn Anders, Walter McGrail, James Blakely

THE SHADY LADY (1929, Pathe)
Lola Mantell—Phyllis Haver
Director—Edward H. Griffith
Leading Players—Robert Armstrong, Louis Wolheim, Russell Gleason

SHADY LADY (1945, Universal)
Lee Appleby—Ginny Simms
Director—George Waggner
Leading Players—Charles Coburn, Robert Paige, Alan Curtis

SHAFT (1971, MGM)
John Shaft—Richard Roundtree
Director—Gordon Parks, Jr.
Leading Players—Moses Gunn, Charles Cioffi, Christopher St. John, Gwenn Mitchell

SHAFT IN AFRICA (1973, MGM)
John Shaft—Richard Roundtree
Director—John Guillermin
Leading Players—Frank Finlay, Vonetta McGee, Neda Arneric

SHAFT'S BIG SCORE (1972, MGM)
John Shaft—Richard Roundtree
Director—Gordon Parks, Jr.
Leading Players—Moses Gunn, Drew Bundi, Joseph Mascolo, Kathy Imrie

THE SHAGGY D.A. (1976, Buena Vista)
Wilby Daniels—Dean Jones
Director—Robert Stevenson
Leading Players—Suzanne Pleshette, Tim Conway, Keenan Wynn

THE SHAGGY DOG (1959, Buena Vista)
Wilby Daniels—Tommy Kirk
Director—Charles Barton
Leading Players—Fred MacMurray, Jean Hagen, Annette Funicello

SHAKES THE CLOWN (1991, IRS Releasing)
Shakes the Clown—Bobcat Goldthwait
Director—Bobcat Goldthwait
Leading Players—Julie Brown, Tom Kenny, Blake Clark, Adam Sandler, Kathy Griffin, Paul Dooley, Robin Williams

SHALAKO (1968, GB, Cinerama)
Shalako—Sean Connery
Director—Edward Dmytryk
Leading Players—Brigitte Bardot, Stephen Boyd, Jack Hawkins

SHALL WE DANCE (1937, RKO)
"Petrov" Pete Peters—Fred Astaire
Linda Keene—Ginger Rogers
Director—Mark Sandrich
Leading Players—Edward Everett Horton, Eric Blore, Jerome Cowan

SHAME, SHAME, EVERYBODY KNOWS HER NAME (1969, J.E.R. Pictures)
Susan Barton—Karen Carlson
Director—Joseph Jacoby
Leading Players—Getti Miller, Augustus Sultatos, Tony Seville

SHAMUS (1973, Columbia)
Shamus McCoy—Burt Reynolds
Director—Buzz Kulik
Leading Players—Dyan Cannon, John Ryan, Joe Santos, Georgio Tozzi

SHANE (1953, Paramount)
Shane—Alan Ladd
Director—George Stevens
Leading Players—Jean Arthur, Van Heflin, Brandon De Wilde, Jack Palance, Ben Johnson, Emile Meyer

SHANGHAI LADY (1929, Universal)
Cassie Cook—Mary Nolan
Director—John S. Robertson
Leading Players—James Murray, Lydia Yeamans, Wheeler Oakman

SHANKS (1974, Paramount)
Malcolm Shanks—Marcel Marceau
Director—William Castle
Leading Players—Tsilla Chelton, Philippe Clay, Cindy Eilbacher

THE SHANNONS OF BROADWAY (1929, Universal)
Mickey Shannon—James Gleason
Emma Shannon—Lucille Webster Gleason
Director—Emmett J. Flynn
Leading Players—Charles Grapewin, Mary Philbin, John Breeden

THE SHARKFIGHTERS (1956, UA)
Lt. Cmdr. Ben Staves—Victor Mature
Director—Jerry Hopper
Leading Players—Karen Steele, James Olson, Philip Coolidge

SHARKY'S MACHINE (1982, Warner Brothers)
Sharky—Burt Reynolds
Director—Burt Reynolds
Leading Players—Vittorio Gassman, Brian Keith, Charles Durning, Rachel Ward, Henry Silva

SHARPSHOOTERS (1938, 20th Century Fox)
Steve Mitchell—Brian Donlevy
Director—James Tinling
Leading Players—Lynn Bari, Wally Vernon, John King

SHATTERED (1991, MGM/Pathe)
Dan Merrick—Tom Berenger
Director—Wolfgang Peterson
Leading Players—Bob Hoskins, Greta Scacchi, Joanne Whalley-Kilmer, Corbin Bernsen, Theodore Bikel, Debi A. Monahan

SHE (1935, RKO)
She—Helen Gahagan
Director—Irving Pichel
Leading Players—Randolph Scott, Helen Mack, Nigel Bruce

SHE (1965, GB, MGM)
Ayesha—Ursula Andress
Director—Robert Day
Leading Players—John Richardson, Peter Cushing, Bernard Cribbins

SHE COULDN'T SAY NO (1930, Warner Brothers)
Winnie Harper—Winnie Lightner
Director—Lloyd Bacon
Leading Players—Chester Morris, Sally Eilers, Johnny Arthur

SHE COULDN'T SAY NO (1941, Warner Brothers)
Alice Hinsdale—Eve Arden
Director—William Clemens
Leading Players—Roger Pryor, Cliff Edwards, Clem Bevans, Vera Lewis

SHE COULDN'T SAY NO (1954, RKO)
Corby Lane—Jean Simmons
Director—Lloyd Bacon
Leading Players—Robert Mitchum, Arthur Hunnicut, Edgar Buchanan

SHE COULDN'T TAKE IT (1935, Columbia)
Carol Van Dyke—Joan Bennett
Director—Tay Garnett
Leading Players—George Raft, Walter Connolly, Billie Burke, Lloyd Nolan

THE SHE-CREATURE (1956, American International)
Andrea—Marla English
Director—Edward L. Cahn
Leading Players—Chester Morris, Tom Conway, Cathy Downs

SHE DEVIL (1957, 20th Century Fox)
Kyra—Mari Blanchard
Director—Kurt Neumann
Leading Players—Albert Dekker, Jack Kelly, Blossom Rock

SHE-DEVIL (1989, Orion)
Ruth Patchett—Roseanne Barr
Director—Susan Seidleman
Leading Players—Meryl Streep, Ed Begley, Jr., Linda Hunt

SHE-DEVILS ON WHEELS (1968, Mayflower)
Queen—Betty Connell
Karen—Christie Wagner
Director—Herschell Gordon Lewis
Leading Players—Pat Poston, Nancy Lee Noble, Rodney Bedell

SHE DIDN'T SAY NO! (1962, GB, Warner Brothers)
Bridget Monahan—Eileen Herlie
Director—Cyril Frankel
Leading Players—Perlita Nielson, Wilfred Downing, Ann Dickins

SHE DONE HIM WRONG (1933, Paramount)
Lady Lou—Mae West
Capt. Cummings ("The Hawk")—Cary Grant
Director—Lowell Sherman
Leading Players—Owen Moore, Gilbert Roland, Noah Beery, Sr.

SHE FREAK (1967, Sonney)
Jade Cochran—Claire Brennan
Director—Byron Mabe
Leading Players—Lee Raymond, Lynn Courtney, Bill McKinney

SHE GETS HER MAN (1935, Universal)
Esmerelda—Zasu Pitts
Director—William Nigh
Leading Players—Hugh O'Connell, Helen Twelvetrees, Edward Brophy

SHE GETS HER MAN (1945, Universal)
Jane "Pilky" Pilkington—Joan Davis
Director—Erle C. Kenton
Leading Players—Leon Errol, William Gargan, Vivian Austin

SHE GOES TO WAR (1929, UA)
Joan Morant—Eleanor Boardman
Director—Henry King
Leading Players—John Holland, Edmund Burns, Al St. John

SHE GOT WHAT SHE WANTED (1930, Tiffany)
Mahyna—Betty Compson
Director—James Cruze
Leading Players—Lee Tracy, Alan Hale, Gaston Glass

SHE HAD TO CHOOSE (1934, Majestic)
Sally—Isabel Jewell
Director—Ralph Cedar
Leading Players—Buster Crabbe, Sally Blane, Regis Toomey

SHE HAD TO SAY YES (1933, Warner Brothers)
Florence Denny—Loretta Young
Director—Busby Berkeley
Leading Players—Lyle Talbot, Regis Toomey, Suzanne Kilborn

SHE HAS WHAT IT TAKES (1943, Columbia)
Fay Weston—Jinx Falkenburg
Director—Charles Barton
Leading Players—Tom Neal, Constance Worth, Douglas Leavitt

SHE KNEW ALL THE ANSWERS (1941, Columbia)
Gloria Winters—Joan Bennett
Director—Richard Wallace

Leading Players—Franchot Tone, John Hubbard, Eve Arden

SHE KNEW WHAT SHE WANTED (1936, GB, Wardour)
Frankie—Betty Ann Davies
Director—Thomas Bentley
Leading Players—Albert Burdon, Claude Dampier, W.H. Berry

SHE LEARNED ABOUT SAILORS (1934, 20th Century Fox)
Jean Legoi—Alice Faye
Director—George Marshall
Leading Players—Lew Ayres, Harry Green, Frank Mitchell

SHE LOVED A FIREMAN (1937, Warner Brothers)
Red Tyler—Dick Foran
Margie Shannon—Ann Sheridan
Director—John Farrow
Leading Players—Robert Armstrong, Eddie Acuff, Veda Ann Borg

SHE MADE HER BED (1934, Paramount)
Lura Gordon—Sally Eilers
Director—Ralph Murphy
Leading Players—Richard Arlen, Robert Armstrong, Grace Bradley

SHE MARRIED A COP (1939, Republic)
Jimmy—Phil Regan
Linda—Jean Parker
Director—Sidney Salkow
Leading Players—Jerome Cowan, Dorothea Kent, Benny Baker

SHE MARRIED AN ARTIST (1938, Columbia)
Lee Thornwood—John Boles
Toni Bonnet—Luli Deste
Director—Marion Gering
Leading Players—Frances Drake, Helen Westley, Alexander D'Arcy

SHE MARRIED HER BOSS (1935, Columbia)
Julia Scott—Claudette Colbert
Richard Barclay—Melvyn Douglas
Director—Gregory La Cava
Leading Players—Michael Bartlett, Raymond Walburn, Jean Dixon

SHE PLAYED WITH A FIRE (1957, GB, Columbia)
Sarah Moreton—Arlene Dahl
Director—Sidney Gilliat
Leading Players—Jack Hawkins, Dennis Price, Violet Farebrother

SHE SHALL HAVE MURDER (1950, GB, Independent Film)
Jane Hamish—Rosamund John
Director—Daniel Birt
Leading Players—Derrick de Marney, Mary Jerrold, Felix Aylmer

SHE WANTED A MILLIONAIRE (1932, Fox Film Corp.)
Jane Miller—Joan Bennett
Director—John Blystone
Leading Players—Spencer Tracy, Una Merkel, James Kirkwood

SHE WAS A LADY (1934, Fox Film Corp.)
Sheila Vane—Helen Twelvetrees
Director—Hamilton MacFadden
Leading Players—Donald Woods, Ralph Morgan, Monroe Owsley

SHE WAS ONLY A VILLAGE MAIDEN (1933, GB, MGM)
Priscilla Protheroe—Anne Grey
Director—Arthur Maude
Leading Players—Lester Matthews, Carl Harbord, Barbara Everest

SHE WENT TO THE RACES (1945, MGM)
Dr. Ann Wotters—Frances Gifford
Director—Willis Goldbeck
Leading Players—James Craig, Ava Gardner, Edmund Gwenn

THE SHE-WOLF (1931, Universal)
Harriet Breen—May Robson
Director—James Flood
Leading Players—James Hall, Lawrence Gray, Frances Dade

SHE-WOLF OF LONDON (1946, Universal)
Phyllis Allenby—June Lockhart
Director—Jean Yarborough
Leading Players—Don Porter, Sara Haden, Jan Wiley

SHE WORE A YELLOW RIBBON (1949, RKO)
Olivia Dandridge—Joanne Dru
Director—John Ford
Leading Players—John Wayne, John Agar, Ben Johnson, Harry Carey, Jr., Victor McLaglen, Mildred Natwick

SHE WOULDN'T SAY YES (1945, Columbia)
Susan Lane—Rosalind Russell
Director—Alexander Hall
Leading Players—Lee Bowman, Adele Jergens, Charles Winninger

SHE WROTE THE BOOK (1946, Universal)
Jane Featherstone—Joan Davis
Director—Charles Lamont
Leading Players—Jack Oakie, Mischa Auer, Kirby Grant

SHEBA BABY (1975, American International)
Sheba—Pam Grier
Director—William Girdler
Leading Players—Austin Stoker, D'Urville Martin, Rudy Challenger

SHEENA (1984, Columbia)
Sheena—Tanya Roberts
Director—John Guillermin
Leading Players—Ted Wass, Donovan Scott, Elizabeth of Toro

THE SHEEPMAN (1958, MGM)
Jason Sweet—Glenn Ford
Director—George Marshall
Leading Players—Shirley MacLaine, Leslie Nielsen, Mickey Shaughnessy, Edgar Buchanan

THE SHEIK (1921, Silent, Paramount)
Sheik Ahmed Ben Hassan—Rudolph Valentino
Director—George Melford
Leading Players—Agnes Ayres, Adolphe Menjou, Walter Long, Lucien Littlefield, Patsy Ruth Miller

THE SHEIK STEPS OUT (1937, Republic)
Ahmed Ben Nesib—Ramon Novarro
Director—Irving Pichel
Leading Players—Lola Lane, Gene Lockhart, Kathleen Burke

SHEILA LEVINE IS DEAD AND LIVING IN NEW YORK (1975, Paramount)
  Sheila Levine—Jeannie Berlin
  Director—Sidney J. Furie
  Leading Players—Roy Scheider, Rebecca Diana Smith, Janet Brandt

SHE'LL BE WEARING PINK PAJAMAS (1986, GB, Film Forum)
  Fran—Julie Walters
  Director—John Goldschmidt
  Leading Players—Anthony Higgins, Jane Evers, Janet Henfrey

THE SHEPHERD OF THE HILLS (1941, Paramount)
  Daniel Howitt—Harry Carey
  Director—Henry Hathaway
  Leading Players—John Wayne, Betty Field, James Barton, Beulah Bondi

THE SHEPHERD OF THE HILLS (1964, Macco/Howco)
  Daniel Howitt—James W. Middleton
  Director—Ben Parker
  Leading Players—Richard Arlen, Sherry Lynn, James Collie

THE SHERIFF OF FRACTURED JAW (1958, GB, 20th Century Fox)
  Jonathan Tibbs—Kenneth More
  Director—Raoul Walsh
  Leading Players—Jayne Mansfield, Henry Hull, William Campbell

SHERLOCK BROWN (1921, Silent, Metro)
  William Brown—Bert Lytell
  Director—Baynard Veiller
  Leading Players—Ora Carew, Sylvia Breamer, De Witt Jennings

SHERLOCK HOLMES (1922, Silent, Goldwyn)
  Sherlock Holmes—John Barrymore
  Director—Albert Parker
  Leading Players—Roland Young, Carol Dempster, Gustav von Seyffertitz, Louis Wolheim

SHERLOCK HOLMES (1932, Fox Film Corp)
  Sherlock Holmes—Clive Brook
  Director—William K. Howard
  Leading Players—Ernest Torrence, Reginald Owen, Miriam Jordan

SHERLOCK HOLMES AND THE SECRET WEAPON (1942, Universal)
  Sherlock Holmes—Basil Rathbone
  Director—Roy William Neill
  Leading Players—Nigel Bruce, Karen Verne, Lionel Atwill

SHERLOCK HOLMES AND THE SPIDER WOMAN (1944, Universal)
  Sherlock Holmes—Basil Rathbone
  Andrea Spedding—Gale Sondergaard
  Director—Roy William Neill
  Leading Players—Nigel Bruce, Dennis Hoey, Vernon Downing

SHERLOCK HOLMES AND THE VOICE OF TERROR (1942, Universal)
  Sherlock Holmes—Basil Rathbone
  Voice of Terror—Edgar Barrier
  Director—John Rawlins

  Leading Players—Nigel Bruce, Evelyn Ankers, Reginald Denny, Montagu Love, Henry Daniell

SHERLOCK HOLMES FACES DEATH (1943, Universal)
  Sherlock Holmes—Basil Rathbone
  Director—Roy William Neill
  Leading Players—Nigel Bruce, Dennis Hoey, Arthur Margetson, Hillary Brooke

SHERLOCK HOLMES' FATAL HOUR (1931, GB, First Division)
  Sherlock Holmes—Arthur Wontner
  Director—Leslie S. Hiscott
  Leading Players—Ian Fleming, Minnie Rayner, Leslie Perrins

SHERLOCK HOLMES IN WASHINGTON (1943, Universal)
  Sherlock Holmes—Basil Rathbone
  Director—Roy William Neill
  Leading Players—Nigel Bruce, Marjorie Lord, Henry Daniell, George Zucco

SHERLOCK, JR. (1924, Silent, Metro)
  Sherlock, Jr.—Buster Keaton
  Director—Buster Keaton
  Leading Players—Kathryn McGuire, Ward Crane, Joseph Keaton

SHE'S A SHEIK (1927, Silent, Paramount)
  Zaida—Bebe Daniels
  Director—Clarence Badger
  Leading Players—Richard Arlen, William Powell, Josephine Dunn

SHE'S A SWEETHEART (1944, Columbia)
  Maxine Lecour—Jane Frazee
  Director—Del Lord
  Leading Players—Larry Parks, Jane Darwell, Nina Foch, Ross Hunter

SHE'S BACK ON BROADWAY (1953, Warner Brothers)
  Catherine Terris—Virginia Mayo
  Director—Gordon Douglas
  Leading Players—Gene Nelson, Frank Lovejoy, Steve Cochran

SHE'S DANGEROUS (1937, Universal)
  Stephanie Duval—Tala Birell
  Director—Lewis R. Foster
  Leading Players—Cesar Romero, Walter Pidgeon, Walter Brennan

SHE'S GOT EVERYTHING (1938, RKO)
  Carol Rogers—Ann Sothern
  Director—Joseph Santley
  Leading Players—Gene Raymond, Victor Moore, Helen Broderick

SHE'S HAVING A BABY (1988, Paramount)
  Kristy Briggs—Elizabeth McGovern
  Director—John Hughes
  Leading Players—Kevin Bacon, Alec Baldwin, Isabel Lorca, William Windom

SHE'S IN THE ARMY (1942, Monogram)
  Diane—Veda Ann Borg
  Director—Jean Yarborough
  Leading Players—Lucille Gleason, Marie Wilson, Lyle Talbot

SHE'S OUT OF CONTROL (1989, Columbia)
Katie Simpson—Ami Dolenz
Director—Stan Dragoti
Leading Players—Tony Danza, Catherine Hicks, Wallace Shawn

SHE'S WORKING HER WAY THROUGH COLLEGE (1952, Warner Brothers)
Angela Gardner ("Hot Garters Gertie")—Virginia Mayo
Director—H. Bruce Humberstone
Leading Players—Ronald Reagan, Gene Nelson, Don DeFore

THE SHIPBUILDERS (1957, GB, Anglo-American)
Leslie Pagan—Clive Brook
Director—John Baxter
Leading Players—Morland Graham, Nell Ballantyne, Finlay Currie

SHIPMATES (1931, MGM)
Jonesy—Robert Montgomery
Kit Corbin—Dorothy Jordan
Director—Harry Pollard
Leading Players—Ernest Torrence, Hobart Bosworth, Gavin Gordon

SHIPMATES FOREVER (1935, Warner Brothers)
Richard John Melville III—Dick Powell
June Blackburn—Ruby Keeler
Director—Frank Borzage
Leading Players—Lewis Stone, Ross Alexander, Eddie Acuff, Dick Foran

SHIPYARD SALLY (1940, GB, 20th Century Fox)
Sally Fitzgerald—Gracie Fields
Director—Monty Banks
Leading Players—Sydney Howard, Morton Selten, Norma Varden

SHIRLEY THOMPSON VERSUS THE ALIENS (1968, Australia, Kolossal Films)
Shirley Thompson—Jane Harders
Director—Jim Sharman
Leading Players—John Likoxitch, Helmut Bakaitis, Tim Eliott

SHIRLEY VALENTINE (1989, Paramount)
Shirley Valentine-Bradshaw—Pauline Collins
Director—Lewis Gilbert
Leading Players—Tom Conti, Alison Steadman, Julia McKenzie

THE SHOCKING MISS PILGRIM (1947, 20th Century Fox)
Cynthia Pilgrim—Betty Grable
Director—George Seaton
Leading Players—Dick Haymes, Anne Revere, Allyn Joslyn

THE SHOOTING OF DAN MCGREW (1915, Silent, Metro)
Dan McGrew—William A. Morse
Director—Herbert Blache
Leading Players—Edmund Breese, Katheryn Adams, Audrine Stark

THE SHOOTIST (1976, Paramount)
John Bernard Books—John Wayne
Director—Don Siegel
Leading Players—Lauren Bacall, Ron Howard, James Stewart, Richard Boone, Hugh O'Brian

THE SHOPWORN ANGEL (1928, Paramount)
Daisy Heath—Nancy Carroll

Director—Richard Wallace
Leading Players—Gary Cooper, Paul Lukas, Emmett King

SHOPWORN ANGEL (1938, MGM)
Daisy Heath—Margaret Sullavan
Director—H.C. Potter
Leading Players—James Stewart, Walter Pidgeon, Nat Pendleton

SHOULD A DOCTOR TELL? (1931, GB, British Lion)
Dr. Bruce Smith—Basil Gill
Director—Manning Haynes
Leading Players—Norah Baring, Maurice Evans, Gladys Jennings

SHOULD A GIRL MARRY? (1929, Rayart)
Alice Dunn—Helen Foster
Director—Scott Pembroke
Leading Players—Donald Keith, William V. Mong, Andy Clyde

SHOULD A GIRL MARRY? (1939, Monogram)
Margaret—Anna Nagel
Director—Lambert Hillyer
Leading Players—Warren Hull, Mayo Methot, Weldon Heyburn

SHOULD A WIFE FORGIVE? (1915, Silent, World)
Mary Holmes—Mabel Van Buren
Director—Joseph E. Howard
Leading Players—Lillian Lorraine, Henry King, Lewis Cody

SHOULD A WIFE WORK? (1922, J.W. Film)
Nina Starr—Alice Lowe
Director—Horace G. Plympton
Leading Players—Edith Stockton, Stuart Robson, Louis Kimball

SHOULD A WOMAN TELL? (1920, Silent, Metro)
Meta Maxon—Alice Lake
Director—John E. Ince
Leading Players—Jack Mulhall, Frank Currier, Relyea Anderson

SHOULD HUSBANDS WORK? (1939, Republic)
Joe Higgins—James Gleason
Director—Gus Meins
Leading Players—Lucille Gleason, Russell Gleason, Harry Davenport

SHOULD LADIES BEHAVE? (1933, MGM)
Laura Merrick—Alice Brady
Director—Harry Beaumont
Leading Players—Lionel Barrymore, Conway Tearle, Katharine Alexander

THE SHOW GIRL (1927, Silent, Rayart)
Maizie Udell—Mildred Harris
Director—Charles J. Hunt
Leading Players—Gaston Glass, Mary Carr, Robert McKim

SHOW GIRL (1928, Warner Brothers)
Dixie Dugan—Alice White
Director—Alfred Santell
Leading Players—Donald Reed, Lee Moran, Charles Delaney

SHOW GIRL IN HOLLYWOOD (1930, Warner Brothers)
Dixie Dugan—Alice White
Director—Mervyn LeRoy
Leading Players—Jack Mulhall, Blanche Sweet, Ford Sterling

THE SHOW-OFF (1934, MGM)
Aubrey Piper—Spencer Tracy
Director—Charles F. Riesner
Leading Players—Madge Evans, Lois Wilson, Grant Mitchell

THE SHOW-OFF (1946, MGM)
Aubrey Piper—Red Skelton
Director—Harry Beaumont
Leading Players—Marilyn Maxwell, Marjorie Main, Virginia O'Brien

SHREDDER ORPHEUS (1990, Image Network)
Orpheus—Robert McGinley
Director—Robert McGinley
Leading Players—Stephen J. Bernstein, Megan Murphy, Gian-Carlo Scandiuzzi, Vera McCaughan

THE SHRIKE (1955, Universal)
Ann Downs—June Allyson
Director—Jose Ferrer
Leading Players—Jose Ferrer, Joy Page, Kendall Clark

SHUT MY BIG MOUTH (1942, Columbia)
Wellington Holmes—Joe E. Brown
Director—Charles Barton
Leading Players—Adele Mara, Victor Jory, Fritz Feld

SHY PEOPLE (1988, Cannon)
Ruth Sullivan—Barbara Hershey
Mike Sullivan—Merritt Butrick
Tommy Sullivan—John Philbin
Mark Sullivan—Don Swayze
Paul Sullivan—Pruitt Taylor Vince
Director—Andrei Konchalovsky
Leading Players—Jill Clayburgh, Martha Plimpton, Mare Winningham, Michael Audley

SIBLING RIVALRY (1990, Columbia/Castle Rock)
Marjorie Turner—Kirstie Alley
Jeannine—Jami Gertz
Director—Carl Reiner
Leading Players—Bill Pullman, Carrie Fisher, Scott Bakula, Sam Elliott, Ed O'Neill

THE SICILIAN (1987, 20th Century Fox)
Salvatore Giuliano—Christopher Lambert
Director—Michael Cimino
Leading Players—Terence Stamp, Joss Ackland, John Turturro, Richard Bauer

SID & NANCY (1986, GB, Goldwyn)
Sid Vicious—Gary Oldman
Nancy Spungen—Chloe Webb
Director—Alex Cox
Leading Players—Drew Schofield, David Hayman, Debby Bishop

SIDE STREET ANGEL (1937, GB, Warner Brothers)
Annie—Lesley Brook
Director—Ralph Ince
Leading Players—Hugh Williams, Henry Kendall, Reginald Purdell

THE SIDELONG GLANCES OF A PIDGEON KICKER (1970, MGM)
Jonathan—Jordan Christopher
Director—John Dexter
Leading Players—Jill O'Hara, Robert Walden, Kate Reid

SIERRA BARON (1958, 20th Century Fox)
Miguel Delmonte—Rick Jason
Director—James B. Clark
Leading Players—Brian Keith, Rita Gam, Mala Powers, Steve Brodie

SIERRA SUE (1941, Republic)
Sue Larrabee—Fay McKenzie
Director—William Morgan
Leading Players—Gene Autry, Smiley Burnette, Frank M. Thomas

THE SIGN OF ZORRO (1960, Buena Vista)
Zorro (Don Diego)—Guy Williams
Director—Norman Foster
Leading Players—George J. Lewis, Gene Sheldon, Britt Lomond, Henry Calvin

THE SILENCE OF DEAN MAITLAND (1934, Australia, Cinesound)
Dean Maitland—John Longden
Director—Ken G. Hall
Leading Players—George Lloyd, John Warwick, Charlotte Francis

THE SILENT LOVER (1926, Silent, First National)
Count Pierre Tornai—Milton Sills
Director—George Archainbaud
Leading Players—Natalie Kingston, William Humphrey, William V. Mong, Viola Dana

THE SILENT PARTNER (1923, Paramount)
Lisa Coburn—Leatrice Joy
Director—Charles Maigne
Leading Players—Owen Moore, Robert Edeson, Robert Schable

THE SILENT PARTNER (1979, Canada, EMC Film Corp.)
Miles Cullen—Elliott Gould
Director—Daryl Duke
Leading Players—Susannah York, Christopher Plummer, Celine Lomez, Michael Kirby

THE SILENT PASSENGER (1935, GB, Associate British Films)
Maurice Windermere—Leslie Perrins
Director—Reginald Denham
Leading Players—John Loder, Peter Haddon, Mary Newland, Austin Trevor, Donald Wolfit

THE SILENT WITNESS (1962, Emerson)
Danny—Billy Shanley
Director—Ken Kennedy
Leading Players—Tris Coffin, Marjorie Reynolds, George Kennedy

SILK HAT KID (1935, Fox Film Corp.)
Eddie Howard—Lew Ayres
Director—H. Bruce Humberstone
Leading Players—Mae Clarke, Paul Kelly, Ralf Harolde

SILK LEGS (1927, Silent, Fox Film Corp.)
Ruth Stevens—Madge Bellamy
Director—Arthur Rosson
Leading Players—James Hall, Joseph Cawthorn, Maude Fulton

SILKWOOD (1983, 20th Century Fox)
Karen Silkwood—Meryl Streep
Director—Mike Nichols
Leading Players—Kurt Russell, Cher, Craig T. Nelson, Diana Scarwid, Ron Silver

SILVER DOLLAR (1932, First National)
Yates "Silver Dollar" Martin—Edward G. Robinson
Director—Alfred E. Green
Leading Players—Bebe Daniels, Aline MacMahon, Jobyna Howland

THE SILVER SLAVE (1927, Silent, Warner Brothers)
Bernice Randall—Irene Rich
Director—Howard Bretherton
Leading Players—Audrey Ferris, Holmes Herbert, John Miljan

SILVER TOP (1938, GB, Paramount)
Mrs. Deeping—Marie Wright
Director—George King
Leading Players—Betty Ann Davies, Marjorie Taylor, David Farrar

SIMON (1980, Warner Brothers)
Simon Mendelssohn—Alan Arkin
Director—Marshall Brinkman
Leading Players—Madeline Kahn, Austin Pendleton, Judy Graubart

SIMON AND LAURA (1956, GB, Universal)
Simon Foster—Peter Finch
Laura Foster—Kay Kendall
Director—Muriel Box
Leading Players—Muriel Pavlow, Hubert Gregg, Maurice Denham

SIMON, KING OF THE WITCHES (1971, Fanfare)
Simon—Andrew Prine
Director—Bruce Kessler
Leading Players—Brenda Scott, George Paulsin, Norman Burton

SIMON THE JESTER (1915, Silent, Gold Rooster)
Simon de Gex—Edwin Arden
Director—Edward Jose
Leading Players—Edgar L. Davenport, Irene Warfield, Alma Tell

THE SIN OF MADELON CLAUDET (1931, MGM)
Madelon Claudet—Helen Hayes
Director—Edgar Selwyn
Leading Players—Lewis Stone, Neil Hamilton, Robert Young

THE SIN OF MARTHA QUEED (1921, Silent, Associated Exhibitors)
Martha Queed—Mary Thurman
Director—Allan Dwan
Leading Players—Joseph J. Dowling, Eugenie Besserer, Frankie Lee, Niles Welch

THE SIN OF MONA KENT (1961, Mermaid/Astor)
Mona Kent—Sandra Donat
Director—Charles J. Hundt
Leading Players—Johnny Olsen, Vic Ramos, Gil Brandsen

SIN OF NORA MORAN (1933, Majestic)
Nora Moran—Zita Johann
Director—Phil Goldstone
Leading Players—Alan Dinehart, Paul Cavanaugh, John Miljan

THE SIN SISTER (1929, Silent, Fox Film Corp.)
Pearl—Nancy Carroll
Director—Charles Klein
Leading Players—Lawrence Gray, Josephine Dunn, Myrtle Stedman

THE SIN THAT WAS HIS (1920, Silent, Selznick Films)
Raymond Chapelle—William Faversham
Director—Hobart Henley
Leading Players—Lucy Cotton, Pedro de Cordoba, Lulu Warrenton

SINBAD AND THE EYE OF THE TIGER (1977, Columbia)
Sinbad—Patrick Wayne
Director—Sam Wanamaker
Leading Players—Taryn Power, Margaret Whiting, Jane Seymour

SINBAD THE SAILOR (1947, RKO)
Sinbad—Douglas Fairbanks, Jr.
Director—Richard Wallace
Leading Players—Maureen O'Hara, Walter Slezak, Anthony Quinn

SINFUL DAVEY (1969, GB, UA)
Davey Haggart—John Hurt
Director—John Huston
Leading Players—Pamela Franklin, Nigel Davenport, Ronald Fraser

SING, BABY, SING (1936, 20th Century Fox)
Joan Warren—Alice Faye
Director—Sidney Lanfield
Leading Players—Adolphe Menjou, Gregory Ratoff, Patsy Kelly

SING, BOY, SING (1958, 20th Century Fox)
Virgil Walker—Tommy Sands
Director—Henry Ephron
Leading Players—Lili Gentile, Edmond O'Brien, John McIntire

SING, COWBOY, SING (1937, Grand National)
Tex Archer—Tex Ritter
Director—Robert N. Bradbury
Leading Players—Louise Stanley, Al St. John, Karl Hackett

SING SINNER, SING (1933, Majestic)
Lela Larson—Leila Hyams
Director—Howard Christy
Leading Players—Paul Lucas, Donald Dillaway, Ruth Donnelly

SINGAPORE WOMAN (1941, Warner Brothers)
Vicki Moore—Brenda Marshall
Director—Jean Negulesco
Leading Players—David Bruce, Virginia Field, Jerome Cowan

SINGED (1927, Silent, Fox Film Corp.)
Dolly Wall—Blanche Sweet
Director—John Griffith Wray
Leading Players—Warner Baxter, James Wang, Alfred Allen

SINGED WINGS (1922, Silent, Paramount)
Bonita Della Guerda—Bebe Daniels
Director—Penrhyn Stanlaws
Leading Players—Conrad Nagel, Adolphe Menjou, Robert Brower, Ernest Torrence, Mabel Trunnele

SINGER JIM McKEE (1924, Silent, Paramount)
"Singer" Jim McKee—William S. Hart
Director—Clifford S. Smith
Leading Players—Phyllis Haver, Gordon Russell, Bert Sprotte

THE SINGER NOT THE SONG (1961, GB, Rank/Warner Brothers)
Father Keogh—John Mills
Director—Roy Ward Baker
Leading Players—Dirk Bogarde, Mylene Demongeot, Laurence Naismith

SINGIN' IN THE RAIN (1952, MGM)
Don Lockwood—Gene Kelly
Directors—Gene Kelly and Stanley Donen
Leading Players—Donald O'Connor, Debbie Reynolds, Jean Hagen, Millard Mitchell, Cyd Charisse

THE SINGING COP (1938, GB, Warner Brothers)
Jack Richards—Keith Falkner
Director—Arthur Woods
Leading Players—Marta Labarr, Chili Bouchier, Ivy St. Heiler

THE SINGING COWGIRL (1939, Grand National)
Dorothy Hendrick—Dorothy Page
Director—Samuel Diege
Leading Players—Dorothy Page, David O'Brien, Vince Barnett

THE SINGING FOOL (1928, Warner Brothers)
Al—Al Jolson
Director—Lloyd Bacon
Leading Players—Betty Bronson, Josephine Dunn, Reed Howes

THE SINGING KID (1936, Warner Brothers)
Al Jackson—Al Jolson
Director—William Keighley
Leading Players—Allen Jenkins, Lyle Talbot, William Davidson

THE SINGING MARINE (1937, Warner Brothers)
Robert Brent—Dick Powell
Director—Ray Enright
Leading Players—Doris Weston, Lee Dixon, Hugh Herbert

THE SINGING NUN (1966, MGM)
Sister Ann—Debbie Reynolds
Director—Henry Koster
Leading Players—Ricardo Montalban, Greer Garson, Agnes Moorehead

THE SINGING SHERIFF (1944, Universal)
Bob Richards—Bob Crosby
Director—Leslie Goodwins
Leading Players—Fay McKenzie, Fuzzy Knight, Iris Adrian

THE SINGLE MAN (1919, GB, Silent, Ideal)
Major Henry Worthington—Cecil Mannering
Director—A.V. Bramble
Leading Players—Doris Lytton, George Mallett, Alice de Winton

A SINGLE MAN (1929, Silent, MGM)
Robin Worthington—Lew Cody
Director—Harry Beaumont
Leading Players—Aileen Pringle, Marceline Day, Edward Nugent

SINNERS IN HEAVEN (1924, Silent, Paramount)
Barbara Stockley—Bebe Daniels
Alan Croft—Richard Dix
Director—Alan Crosland
Leading Players—Holmes Herbert, Florence Billings, Betty Hilburn, Montagu Love

SINNERS IN LOVE (1928, Silent, FBO)
Ann Hardy—Olive Borden
Ted Wells—Huntley Gordon
Director—George Melford
Leading Players—Seena Owen, Ernest Hilliard, Daphne Pollard

SINNERS IN THE SUN (1932, Paramount)
Doris Blake—Carole Lombard
Jimmie Martin—Chester Morris
Director—Alexander Hall
Leading Players—Adrienne Ames, Alison Skipworth, Walter Byron

SINS OF JEZEBEL (1953, Lippert)
Jezebel—Paulette Goddard
Director—Reginald Le Borg
Leading Players—George Nader, John Hoyt, Eduard Franz

THE SINS OF RACHEL CADE (1960, Warner Brothers)
Rachel Cade—Angie Dickinson
Director—Gordon Douglas
Leading Players—Peter Finch, Roger Moore, Errol John, Woody Strode

THE SINS OF ROZANNE (1920, Silent, Paramount)
Rozanne—Ethel Clayton
Director—Tom Forman
Leading Players—Jack Holt, Fontaine La Rue, Mabel Van Buren

SIOUX CITY SUE (1946, Republic)
Sue Warner—Lynne Roberts
Director—Frank McDonald
Leading Players—Gene Autry, Sterling Holloway, Richard Lane

SIR HENRY AT RAWLINSON END (1980, GB, Charisma)
Sir Henry Rawlinson—Trevor Howard
Director—Steve Roberts
Leading Players—Patrick Magee, Denies Coffey, J.G. Devlin

SIREN OF ATLANTIS (1948, UA)
Queen Antinea—Maria Montez
Director—Gregg G. Tallas
Leading Players—Jean-Pierre Aumont, Dennis O'Keefe, Henry Daniell

SIREN OF BAGDAD (1953, Columbia)
Zendi—Patricia Medina
Director—Richard Quine
Leading Players—Paul Henreid, Hans Conreid, Charlie Lung

SIS HOPKINS (1941, Republic)
Sis Hopkins—Judy Canova
Director—Joseph Santley
Leading Players—Bob Crosby, Charles Butterworth, Susan Hayward

SISTER ACT (1992, Touchstone)
Delores Von Cartier—Whoopi Goldberg
Director—Emile Andolino

Leading Players—Maggie Smith, Kathy Najimy, Wendy Makkena, Mary Wickes, Harvey Keitel, Bill Nunn

SISTER KENNY (1946, RKO)
Elizabeth Kenny—Rosalind Russell
Director—Dudley Nichols
Leading Players—Alexander Knox, Dean Jagger, Philip Merivale

SISTER SISTER (1988, New World)
Lucy Bonnard—Jennifer Jason Leigh
Charlotte Bonnard—Judith Ivey
Director—Bill Condon
Leading Players—Eric Stoltz, Dennis Liscomb, Anne Pitoniak

A SISTER TO ASSIST'ER (1922, GB, Gaumont)
Mrs. Millie May—Mary Brough
Director—George Dewhurst
Leading Players—Pollie Emery, Muriel Aked, Cecil Morton York

A SISTER TO ASSIST'ER (1927, GB, Gaumont)
Mrs. Millie May—Mary Brough
Director—George Dewhurst
Leading Players—Pollie Emery, Humbertson Wright, A. Bromley Davenport

A SISTER TO ASSIST'ER (1930, GB, Gaumont)
Mrs. May—Barbara Gott
Director—George Dewhurst
Leading Players—Pollie Emery, Donald Stuart, Alec Hunter

A SISTER TO ASSIST'ER (1938, GB, Columbia)
Mrs. May—Muriel George
Directors—Widgey Newman and George Dewhurst
Leading Players—Pollie Emery, Charles Paton, Billy Percy

A SISTER TO ASSIST'ER (1948, GB, Premier)
Gladys May—Muriel George
Director—George Dewhurst
Leading Players—Muriel Aked, Michael Howard

SISTERS (1922, Silent, American Releasing)
Alix Strickland—Seena Owen
Cherry Strickland—Gladys Leslie
Director—Albert Capellani
Leading Players—Mildred Arden, Matt Moore, Joe King, Tom Guise

SISTERS (1930, Columbia)
Sally Malone—Sally O'Neil
Molly Shannon—Molly O'Day
Director—James Flood
Leading Players—Russell Gleason, Jason Robards, Sr., Morgan Wallace

THE SISTERS (1938, Warner Brothers)
Louise Elliott—Bette Davis
Helen Elliott—Anita Louise
Grace Elliott—Jane Bryan
Director—Anatole Litvak
Leading Players—Errol Flynn, Ian Hunter, Henry Travers, Beulah Bondi, Donald Crisp

SISTERS (1973, American International)
Danielle Breton—Margot Kidder
Director—Brian De Palma
Leading Players—Jennifer Salt, Charles Durning, Bill Finley

SISTERS UNDER THE SKIN (1934, Columbia)
Blossom Bailey—Elissa Landi
Elinor Yates—Doris Lloyd
Director—David Burton
Leading Players—Frank Morgan, Joseph Schildkraut, Clara Blandick

SITTING BULL (1954, UA)
Chief Sitting Bull—J. Carrol Naish
Director—Sidney Salkow
Leading Players—Dale Robertson, Mary Murphy, Iron Eyes Cody

SITTING PRETTY (1933, Paramount)
Chick Parker—Jack Oakie
Pete Pendleton—Jack Haley
Director—Harry Joe Brown
Leading Players—Ginger Rogers, Thelma Todd, Gregory Ratoff

SITTING PRETTY (1948, 20th Century Fox)
Lynn Belvedere—Clifton Webb
Director—Walter Lang
Leading Players—Robert Young, Maureen O'Hara, Richard Haydn, Louise Allbritton

SIX-DAY BIKE RIDER (1934, First National)
Wilfred Simpson—Joe E. Brown
Director—Lloyd Bacon
Leading Players—Maxine Doyle, Frank McHugh, Gordon Westcott

SIX GUN MAN (1946, Producers Releasing Corp.)
Bob Storm—Bob Steele
Director—Harry Fraser
Leading Players—Syd Saylor, Jimmie Martin, Jean Carlin

SIX HOURS TO LIVE (1932, Fox Film Corp.)
Capt. Paul Onslow—Warner Baxter
Director—William Dieterle
Leading Players—Miriam Johnson, John Boles, George Marion

SIX LESSONS FROM MADAME LA ZONGA (1941, Universal)
Madame La Zonga—Lupe Velez
Director—John Rawlins
Leading Players—Leon Errol, Helen Parrish, Charles Lang

SIX PACK ANNIE (1975, American International)
Annie—Lindsay Bloom
Director—Graydon F. David
Leading Players—Jana Bellan, Joe Higgins, Larry Mahan

SIXTEEN CANDLES (1984, Universal)
Samantha "Sam" Baker—Molly Ringwald
Director—John Hughes
Leading Players—Justin Henry, Michael Schoelfling, Haviland Morriss, Gedde Watanabe, Anthony Michael Hall

SKI BUM (1971, Avco Embassy)
Johnny—Zalman King
Director—Bruce Clark
Leading Players—Charlotte Rampling, Joseph Mell, Lori Shelle

SKIMPY IN THE NAVY (1949, GB, Advance/Adelphi)
Skimpy Carter—Hal Monty
Director—Stafford Dickens
Leading Players—Max Bygraves, Avril Angers, Les Ritchie

SKINNER STEPS OUT (1929, Universal)
William Henry Skinner—Glenn Tryon
Director—William James Craft
Leading Players—Merna Kennedy, E.J. Ratcliffe, Burr McIntosh

SKINNER'S BIG IDEA (1928, Silent, FBO)
William Henry Skinner—Bryant Washburn
Director—Lynn Shores
Leading Players—William Orlamond, James Bradbury, Sr., Robert Dudley, Martha Sleeper

SKINNER'S DRESS SUIT (1917, Silent, Essanay)
William Henry Skinner—Bryant Washburn
Director—Harry Beaumont
Leading Players—Hazel Day, Harry Dunkinson, James C. Carroll

SKINNER'S DRESS SUIT (1926, Silent, Universal)
Skinner—Reginald Denny
Director—William A. Seiter
Leading Players—Laura La Plante, Ben Hendricks, Jr., E.J. Ratcliffe

SKIPALONG ROSENBLOOM (1951, UA)
Skipalong Rosenbloom—"Slapsie" Maxie Rosenbloom
Director—Sam Newfield
Leading Players—Max Baer, Jackie Coogan, Fuzzy Knight

THE SKIPPER SURPRISED HIS WIFE (1950, MGM)
Cmdr. William Lattimer—Robert Walker
Daphne Lattimer—Joan Leslie
Director—Elliott Nugent
Leading Players—Edward Arnold, Spring Byington, Leon Ames

THE SKIPPER'S WOOING (1922, GB, Silent, Artistic)
The Skipper—Gordon Hopkirk
Director—Manning Haynes
Leading Players—Cynthia Murtagh, Johnny Butt, Thomas Marriott

SKIPPY (1931, Paramount)
Skippy Skinner—Jackie Cooper
Director—Norman Taurog
Leading Players—Robert Coogan, Mitzie Green, Jackie Searl

SKY BRIDE (1932, Paramount)
Ruth Dunning—Virginia Bruce
Director—Stephen Roberts
Leading Players—Richard Arlen, Jack Oakie, Robert Coogan

SKY COMMAND (1953, Columbia)
Col. Ed Wyatt—Dan Duryea
Director—Fred F. Sears
Leading Players—Francis Gifford, Mike Connors, Michael Fox

SKY HAWK (1929, Fox Film Corp.)
Jack Bardell—John Garrick
Director—John Blystone
Leading Players—Helen Chandler, Gilbert Emery, Lennox Pawle

"SKY-HIGH" SAUNDERS (1927, Silent, Universal)
"Sky-High" Saunders—Al Wilson
Director—Bruce Mitchell
Leading Players—Elsie Tarron, Frank Rice, Bud Osborne

THE SKY PILOT (1921, Silent, Associated First National)
The Sky Pilot—John Bowers
Director—King Vidor
Leading Players—Colleen Moore, David Butler, Harry Todd

THE SKY PIRATE (1970, Filmmakers Dist. Center)
Joe—Michael McClanathan
Director—Andrew Meyer
Leading Players—Claudia Leacock, Frank Meyer, Margaret Kramer

THE SKY SKIDDER (1929, Silent, Universal)
Al Simpkins—Al Wilson
Director—Bruce Mitchell
Leading Players—Helen Foster, Wilbur McGaugh, Pee Wee Holmes

SLANDER THE WOMAN (1923, Silent, Associate First National)
Yvonne Desmarest—Dorothy Phillips
Director—Allen Holubar
Leading Players—Lewis Dayton, Robert Anderson, Mayme Kelso

THE SLASHER (1953, GB, Lippert)
Roy Walsh—James Kenney
Director—Lewis Gilbert
Leading Players—Joan Collins, Betty Ann Davies, Robert Ayres, Hermione Baddeley

SLATE, WYN & ME (1987, Australia, Ukiyo/Hemdale)
Blanche McBride—Sigrid Thornton
Wyn Jackson—Simon Burke
Slate Jackson—Martin Sacks
Director—Don McLennan
Leading Players—Tommy Lewis, Lesley Baker, Harold Balgent

SLATTERY'S HURRICANE (1949, 20th Century Fox)
Will Slattery—Richard Widmark
Director—Andre De Toth
Leading Players—Linda Darnell, Veronica Lake, John Russell, Gary Merrill

SLAUGHTER (1972, American International)
Slaughter—Jim Brown
Director—Jack Starrett
Leading Players—Stella Stevens, Rip Torn, Don Gordon

SLAUGHTER'S BIG RIP-OFF (1973, American International)
Slaughter—Jim Brown
Director—Gordon Douglas
Leading Players—Ed McMahon, Brock Peters, Don Stroud

SLAVE GIRL (1947, Universal)
Francesca—Yvonne De Carlo
Director—Charles Lamont
Leading Players—George Brent, Broderick Crawford, Albert Dekker

SLAVE GIRLS FROM BEYOND INFINITY (1987, Titan/Urban Classics)
Daria—Elizabeth Cayton
Tisa—Cindy Beal
Shela—Brinke Stevens
Director—Ken Dixon
Leading Players—Don Scribner, Carl Horner, Kirk Graves

SLAVE OF DESIRE (1923, Silent, Goldwyn)
Ralph Valentin—George Walsh
Director—George D. Baker

Leading Players—Bessie Love, Carmel Myers, Wally Van

SLAVES (1969, Continental)
Cassy—Dionne Warwick
Luke—Ossie Davis
Director—Herbert J. Biberman
Leading Players—Stephen Boyd, Robert Kya-Hill, Barbara Ann Teer

SLAVES OF DESTINY (1924, GB, Silent, Stoll)
Luke Charnock—Matheson Lang
Director—Maurice Elvey
Leading Players—Valia, Henry Victor, Humbertson Wright

SLEEPER (1973, UA)
Miles Monroe—Woody Allen
Director—Woody Allen
Leading Players—Diane Keaton, John Beck, Marya Small

SLEEPING WITH THE ENEMY (1991, 20th Century Fox)
Sara/Laura—Julia Roberts
Martin—Patrick Bergin
Director—Joseph Ruben
Leading Players—Kevin Anderson, Elizabeth Lawrence, Kyle Secor, Claudette Nevins

SLEEPWALKER (1992, Columbia)
Charles Brady—Brian Krause
Mary Brady—Alice Krige
Director—Mick Carris
Leading Players—Madchen Amick, Jim Haynie, Cindy Pickett, Ron Perlman, Lyman Ward, Dan Martin

THE SLEEPWALKER (1922, Silent, Paramount)
Doris Dumond—Constance Binney
Director—Edward Le Saint
Leading Players—Jack Mulhall, Edythe Chapman, Florence Roberts

SLEEPYTIME GAL (1942, Republic)
Bessie Cobb—Judy Canova
Director—Albert S. Rogell
Leading Players—Tom Brown, Ruth Terry, Mildred Coles

SLIDE, KELLY, SLIDE (1927, Silent, MGM)
Jim Kelly—William Haines
Director—Edward Sedgwick
Leading Players—Sally O'Neil, Harry Carey, Junior Coughlin

SLIGHTLY USED (1927, Silent, Warner Brothers)
Cynthia Martin—May McAvoy
Director—Archie Mayo
Leading Players—Conrad Nagel, Robert Agnew, Audrey Ferris

SLIM (1937, Warner Brothers)
Slim—Henry Fonda
Director—Ray Enright
Leading Players—Pat O'Brien, Margaret Lindsay, Stuart Erwin

SLIM CARTER (1957, Universal)
Slim Carter—Jock Mahoney
Director—Richard H. Bartlett
Leading Players—Julie Adams, Tim Hovey, William Hopper

THE SLIM PRINCESS (1915, Silent, Essanay)
The Slim Princess—Ruth Stonehouse

Director—E.H. Calvert
Leading Players—Francis X. Bushman, Harry Dunkinson, Wallace Beery, Bryant Washburn

SLIPPY MCGEE (1923, Silent, Associate First National)
Slippy McGee—Wheeler Oakman
Director—Wesley Ruggles
Leading Players—Colleen Moore, Sam De Grasse, Edmund Stevens

SLIPPY MCGEE (1948, Republic)
Slippy McGee—Donald Barry
Director—Albert Kelley
Leading Players—Dale Evans, Tom Brown, Harry V. Cheshire

THE SLUGGER'S WIFE (1985, Columbia)
Darryl Palmer—Michael O'Keefe
Debby Palmer—Rebecca DeMornay
Director—Hal Ashby
Leading Players—Martin Ritt, Randy Quaid, Lisa Langlois

A SMALL CIRCLE OF FRIENDS (1980, UA)
Leo DaVinci—Brad Davis
Jessica—Karen Allen
Nick Baxter—Jameson Parker
Director—Rob Cohen
Leading Players—Shelley Long, John Friedrich, Gary Springer

SMALL TOWN BOY (1937, Grand National)
Henry—Stuart Erwin
Director—Glenn Tryon
Leading Players—Joyce Compton, Jed Prouty, Clara Blandick

SMALL TOWN DEB (1941, 20th Century Fox)
Patricia Randell—Jane Withers
Director—Harold Schuster
Leading Players—Jane Darwell, Bruce Edwards, Cobina Wright, Jr.

SMALL TOWN GIRL (1936, MGM)
Kay Brannan—Janet Gaynor
Director—William Wellman
Leading Players—Robert Taylor, Binnie Barnes, James Stewart, Lewis Stone

SMALL TOWN GIRL (1953, MGM)
Cindy Kimbell—Jane Powell
Director—Leslie Kardos
Leading Players—Farley Granger, Ann Miller, S.Z. Sakall, Robert Keith

SMALL TOWN IDOL (1921, Silent, Associate Producers)
Sam Smith—Ben Turpin
Director—Erle Kenton
Leading Players—James Finlayson, Phyllis Haver, Bert Roach

THE SMALL WORLD OF SAMMY LEE (1963, GB, British Lion)
Sammy Lee—Anthony Newley
Director—Ken Hughes
Leading Players—Julia Foster, Robert Stephens, Wilfrid Brambell

SMART ALEC (1951, GB, Grand National)
Alec Albion—Peter Reynolds
Director—John Guillermin
Leading Players—Mercy Haystead, Leslie Dwyer, Edward Lexy

SMART BLONDE (1937, Warner Brothers)
Torchy Blane—Glenda Farrell
Director—Frank McDonald
Leading Players—Barton MacLane, Winifred Shaw, Craig
Reynolds

SMART GIRL (1935, Paramount)
Pat Reynolds—Ida Lupino
Director—Aubrey Scotto
Leading Players—Kent Taylor, Gail Patrick, Joseph Cawthorn

SMART GIRLS DON'T TALK (1948, Warner Brothers)
Linda Vickers—Virginia Mayo
Director—Richard Bare
Leading Players—Bruce Bennett, Robert Hutton, Tom D'Andrea

SMART GUY (1943, Monogram)
Johnny—Rick Vallin
Director—Lambert Hillyer
Leading Players—Bobby Larson, Veda Ann Borg, Wanda McKay

SMART WOMAN (1931, RKO)
Nancy Gibson—Mary Astor
Director—Gregory La Cava
Leading Players—Robert Ames, Edward Everett Horton, Noel
Francis

SMART WOMAN (1948, Monogram-Allied Artists)
Paula Rogers—Constance Bennett
Director—Edward A. Blatt
Leading Players—Brian Aherne, Barry Sullivan, Michael O'Shea

SMARTEST GIRL IN TOWN (1936, RKO)
Francis Cooke—Ann Sothern
Director—Joseph Santley
Leading Players—Gene Raymond, Helen Broderick, Eric Blore

SMARTY (1934, Warner Brothers)
Vicki Wallace Thorpe—Joan Blondell
Director—Robert Florey
Leading Players—Warren William, Edward Everett Horton,
Frank McHugh, Claire Dodd

SMASH UP, THE STORY OF A WOMAN (1947, Universal)
Angie Evans—Susan Hayward
Director—Stuart Heisler
Leading Players—Lee Bowman, Marsha Hunt, Eddie Albert

SMILEY (1957, GB, 20th Century Fox)
Smiley Greevins—Colin Petersen
Director—Anthony Kimmins
Leading Players—Ralph Richardson, John McCallum, Chips
Rafferty

SMILEY GETS A GUN (1959, GB, 20th Century Fox)
Smiley Greevins—Keith Calvert
Director—Anthony Kimmins
Leading Players—Sybil Thorndike, Chips Rafferty, Bruce Archer

SMILING IRISH EYES (1929, Warner Brothers)
Kathleen O'Connor—Colleen Moore
Director—William A. Seiter
Leading Players—James Hall, Claude Gillingwater, Robert E.
Homans

THE SMILING LIEUTENANT (1931, Paramount)
Niki—Maurice Chevalier
Director—Ernst Lubitsch
Leading Players—Claudette Colbert, Miriam Hopkins, George
Barbier, Charles Ruggles

SMITH (1969, Buena Vista)
Smith—Glenn Ford
Director—Michael O'Herlihy
Leading Players—Nancy Olsen, Dean Jagger, Keenan Wynn,
Warren Oates

SMITHY (1933, GB, Warner Brothers)
John Smith—Edmund Gwenn
Director—George King
Leading Players—Peggy Novak, D.A. Clarke-Smith, Eve Gray

SMITHY (1946, Australia, Columbia)
Sir Charles Kingsford-Smith—Ron Randell
Director—Ken G. Hall
Leading Players—Muriel Steinbeck, John Tate, Joy Nicholls

SMOKE BELLEW (1929, Silent, First Division)
Kit "Smoke" Bellew—Conway Tearle
Director—Scott Dunlap
Leading Players—Barbara Bedford, Mark Hamilton, Alphonse
Ethier

SMOKEY AND THE BANDIT (1977, Universal)
Bandit—Burt Reynolds
Sheriff Buford T. Justice—Jackie Gleason
Director—Hal Needham
Leading Players—Sally Field, Jerry Reed, Mike Henry, Paul
Williams, Pat McCormick

SMOKEY AND THE BANDIT II (1980, Universal)
Bandit—Burt Reynolds
Sheriff Buford T. Justice—Jackie Gleason
Director—Hal Needham
Leading Players—Jerry Reed, Dom DeLuise, Sally Field, Paul
Williams, Pat McCormick

SMOKEY AND THE BANDIT-PART 3 (1983, Universal)
Bandit—Jerry Reed
The Real Bandit—Burt Reynolds
Sheriff Buford T. Justice—Jackie Gleason
Director—Dick Lowry
Leading Players—Paul Williams, Pat McCormick, Mike Henry,
Colleen Camp, Faith Minton

THE SMUGGLERS (1948, GB, Eagle-Lion)
Richard Carlyon—Michael Redgrave
Director—Bernard Knowles
Leading Players—Jean Kent, Joan Greenwood, Richard
Attenborough

THE SNAKE WOMAN (1961, GB, UA)
Atheris Adderson—Susan Travers
Director—Sidney J. Furie
Leading Players—John McCarthy, Geoffrey Danton, Arnold
Marle

THE SNIPER (1952, Columbia)
Eddie Miller—Arthur Franz
Director—Edward Dmytryk
Leading Players—Adolphe Menjou, Gerald Mohr, Marie Windsor

THE SNOB (1924, Silent, MGM)
Eugene Curry—John Gilbert
Director—Monta Bell
Leading Players—Norma Shearer, Conrad Nagel, Phyllis Haver

SNUFFY SMITH, YARD BIRD (1942, Monogram)
Snuffy Smith—Bud Duncan
Director—Edward F. Cline
Leading Players—Edgar Kennedy, Sarah Padden, Doris Linden

SO BIG (1924, Silent, First National)
Dirk Dejong as a boy—Frankie Darro
Director—Charles Brabin
Leading Players—Colleen Moore, Joseph De Grasse, John Bowers, Ben Lyon, Wallace Beery, Gladys Brockwell

SO BIG (1932, Warner Brothers)
Dirk Dejong—Dickie Moore
Director—William A. Wellman
Leading Players—Barbara Stanwyck, George Brent, Bette Davis, Guy Kibbee, Hardie Albright

SO BIG (1953, Warner Brothers)
Dirk DeJong—Tommy Rettig
Director—Robert Wise
Leading Players—Jane Wyman, Sterling Hayden, Nancy Olson, Steve Forrest, Elizabeth Fraser

SO ENDS OUR NIGHT (1941, UA)
Joseph Steiner—Fredric March
Ruth Holland—Margaret Sullavan
Ludwig Kern—Glenn Ford
Director—John Cromwell
Leading Players—Frances Dee, Anna Sten, Erich von Stroheim

SO EVIL MY LOVE (1948, GB, Paramount)
Mark Bellis—Ray Milland
Olivia Harwood—Ann Todd
Director—Lewis Allen
Leading Players—Geraldine Fitzgerald, Moira Lister, Raymond Lovell

SO EVIL SO YOUNG (1961, GB, UA)
Ann—Jill Ireland
Director—Godfrey Grayson
Leading Players—Ellen Pollock, John Charlesworth, Jocelyn Britton

SO LONG AT THE FAIR (1951, GB, Rank)
Johnny Barton—David Tomlinson
Director—Terence Fisher
Leading Players—Jean Simmons, Dirk Bogarde, Marcel Poncin, Cathleen Nesbitt, Honor Blackman

SO LONG, BLUE BOY (1973, Maryon/Dakota)
Isaiah Jenkinson—Rick Gates
Director—Gerald Gordon
Leading Players—Arthur Franz, Neile Adams McQueen, Richard Rowley

SO LONG LETTY (1929, Warner Brothers)
Letty Robbins—Charlotte Greenwood
Director—Lloyd Bacon
Leading Players—Grant Withers, Bert Roach, Claude Gillingwater

SO YOU WON'T TALK (1935, GB, Warner Brothers)
Tony Cazari—Monty Banks
Director—Monty Banks
Leading Players—Vera Pearce, Bertha Belmore, Enid Stamp-Taylor

SO YOU WON'T TALK (1940, Columbia)
Whiskers/Brute Hanson—Joe E. Brown
Director—Edward Sedgwick
Leading Players—Frances Robinson, Vivienne Osborne, Bernard Nedell

SO YOUNG, SO BAD (1950, UA)
Jackie—Anne Jackson
Loretta—Anne Francis
Dolores—Rita Moreno
Director—Bernard Vorhaus
Leading Players—Paul Henreid, Catherine McLeod, Grace Coppin

SOB SISTER (1931, Fox Film Corp.)
Jane Ray—Linda Watkins
Director—Alfred Santell
Leading Players—James Dunn, Minna Gombell, Howard Phillips

A SOCIAL CELEBRITY (1926, Silent, Paramount)
Max Haber—Adolphe Menjou
Director—Malcolm St. Clair
Leading Players—Louise Brooks, Elsie Lawson, Roger Davis

THE SOCIAL LION (1930, Paramount)
Marco Perkins—Jack Oakie
Director—A. Edward Sutherland
Leading Players—Mary Brian, Skeets Gallagher, Olive Borden

THE SOCIAL SECRETARY (1916, Silent, Triangle)
Mayme—Norma Talmadge
Director—John Emerson
Leading Players—Kate Lester, Helen Weir, Gladden James

SOCIETY DOCTOR (1935, MGM)
Dr. Morgan—Chester Morris
Director—George B. Seitz
Leading Players—Virginia Bruce, Robert Taylor, Billie Burke

SOCIETY GIRL (1932, Fox Film Corp.)
Judy Gelett—Peggy Shannon
Director—Sidney Lanfield
Leading Players—James Dunn, Spencer Tracy, Walter Byron

SOCIETY LAWYER (1939, MGM)
Christopher Durant—Walter Pidgeon
Director—Edwin L. Marin
Leading Players—Virginia Bruce, Leo Carrillo, Eduardo Ciannelli

SOL MADRID (1968, MGM)
Sol Madrid—David McCallum
Director—Brian G. Hutton
Leading Players—Stella Stevens, Telly Savalas, Ricardo Montalban, Rip Torn

THE SOLDIER (1982, Embassy)
The Soldier—Ken Wahl
Director—James Glickenhaus
Leading Players—Klaus Kinski, William Prince, Alberta Watson

943

A SOLDIER AND A MAN (1916, GB, Silent, British & Colonial)
Harold Sinclair—George Keene
Director—Dave Aylott
Leading Players—Minna Grey, A.V. Bramble, Charles Vane

THE SOLDIER AND THE LADY (1937, GB, RKO)
Michael Strogoff—Anton Walbrook
Nadia—Elizabeth Allan
Director—George Nicholls
Leading Players—Margot Grahame, Akim Tamiroff, Fay Bainter

SOLDIER BLUE (1970, Avco Embassy)
Pvt. Honus Gant—Peter Strauss
Director—Ralph Nelson
Leading Players—Candice Bergen, Donald Pleasence, Bob Carraway

SOLDIER IN THE RAIN (1963, Allied Artists)
M/Sgt. Maxwell Slaughter—Jackie Gleason
Director—Ralph Nelson
Leading Players—Steve McQueen, Tuesday Weld, Tony Bill, Tom Poston, Ed Nelson

SOLDIER OF FORTUNE (1955, 20th Century Fox)
Hank Lee—Clark Gable
Director—Edward Dmytryk
Leading Players—Susan Hayward, Michael Rennie, Gene Barry, Tom Tully, Alex D'Arcy

A SOLDIER'S STORY (1984, Columbia)
Sgt. Waters—Adolphe Caesar
Director—Norman Jewison
Leading Players—Howard E. Rollins, Jr., Art Evans, David Allen Grier, David Harris, Larry Riley

SOLDIERS THREE (1951, MGM)
Pvt. Archibald Ackroyd—Stewart Granger
Pvt. Jock Sykes—Robert Newton
Pvt. Dennis Malloy—Cyril Cusack
Director—Tay Garnett
Leading Players—Walter Pidgeon, David Niven, Greta Gynt

SOLE SURVIVOR (1984, Grand National)
Denise Watson—Anita Skinner
Director—Thom Eberhardt
Leading Players—Caren Larae Larkey, Robin Davidson, Kurt Johnson

THE SOLITARE MAN (1933, MGM)
Oliver Lane—Herbert Marshall
Director—Jack Conway
Leading Players—May Robson, Elizabeth Allan, Ralph Forbes

SOLO FOR SPARROW (1966, GB, Schoenfield)
Inspector Sparrow—Glyn Houston
Director—Gordon Flemyng
Leading Players—Anthony Newlands, Nadja Regin, Michael Coles

SOLOMON AND SHEBA (1959, UA)
Solomon—Yul Brynner
Magda, Queen of Sheba—Gina Lollobrigida
Director—King Vidor
Leading Players—George Sanders, David Farrar, Marisa Pavan, John Crawford, Laurence Naismith

SOLOMON KING (1974, Sal-Wa-Stage Struck)
Solomon King—Sal Watts
Director—Sal Watts
Leading Players—"Little Jaimie" Watts, Claudia Russo, Felice Kinchelow

SOME BLONDES ARE DANGEROUS (1937, Universal)
Rose Whitney—Dorothea Kent
Director—Milton Carruth
Leading Players—Noah Beery, Jr., William Gargan, Nan Grey

SOME GIRLS (1989, MGM-UA)
Gabby—Jennifer Connelly
Irenka—Sheila Kelley
Simone—Ashley Greenfield
Director—Michael Hoffman
Leading Players—Patrick Dempsey, Florinda Bolkan, Lila Kedrova

SOME KIND OF HERO (1982, Paramount)
Eddie Keller—Richard Pryor
Director—Michael Pressman
Leading Players—Margot Kidder, Ray Sharkey, Ronny Cox, Lynne Moody, Olivia Cole

SOME KIND OF NUT (1969, UA)
Fred Amidon—Dick Van Dyke
Director—Garson Kanin
Leading Players—Angie Dickinson, Rosemary Forsyth, Zohra Lampert

SOMEBODY KILLED HER HUSBAND (1978, Columbia)
Jenny Moore—Farrah Fawcett-Majors
Preston Moore—Laurence Guittard
Director—Lamont Johnson
Leading Players—Jeff Bridges, John Wood, Tammy Grimes

SOMEBODY LOVES ME (1952, Paramount)
Blossom Seeley—Betty Hutton
Director—Irving Brecher
Leading Players—Ralph Meeker, Robert Keith, Adele Jergens

SOMEBODY UP THEIR LIKES ME (1956, MGM)
Rocky Graziano (Barbella)—Paul Newman
Director—Robert Wise
Leading Players—Pier Angeli, Everett Sloane, Eileen Heckart, Sal Mineo, Harold J. Stone

SOMEONE TO REMEMBER (1943, Republic)
Dan Freeman—John Craven
Director—Robert Siodmak
Leading Players—Mabel Paige, Harry Shannon, Dorothy Morris

SOMEONE TO WATCH OVER ME (1987, Columbia)
Mike Keegan—Tom Berenger
Claire Gregory—Mimi Rogers
Director—Ridley Scott
Leading Players—Lorraine Bracco, Jerry Orbach, Andreas Katsulas

SOMEWHERE I'LL FIND YOU (1942, MGM)
Jonathan Davis—Clark Gable
Paula Lane—Lana Turner
Director—Wesley Ruggles
Leading Players—Robert Sterling, Reginald Owen, Lee Patrick

A SON COMES HOME (1936, Paramount)
Brennan Grady—Anthony Nace
Director—E.A. Dupont
Leading Players—Mary Boland, Julie Haydon, Donald Woods, Wallace Ford

THE SON-DAUGHTER (1932, MGM)
Lien Wha—Helen Hayes
Director—Clarence Brown
Leading Players—Ramon Novarro, Lewis Stone, Warner Oland

SON OF A SAILOR (1933, First National)
Handsome Callahan—Joe E. Brown
Director—Lloyd Bacon
Leading Players—Jean Muir, Thelma Todd, Johnny Mack Brown

SON OF A STRANGER (1957, GB, UA)
Tom Adams—James Kenney
Dr. Delaney—Basil Dignam
Director—Ernest Morris
Leading Players—Ann Stephens, Victor Maddern, Catharine Finn

SON OF ALI BABA (1952, Universal)
Kashma Baba—Tony Curtis
Ali Baba—Morris Ankrum
Director—Kurt Neumann
Leading Players—Piper Laurie, Susan Cabot, William Reynolds, Hugh O'Brien

SON OF BELLE STARR (1953, Allied Artists)
The Kid—Keith Larsen
Director—Frank McDonald
Leading Players—Dona Drake, Peggy Castle, Regis Toomey

SON OF BILLY THE KID (1949, Screen Guild)
Colt—John James
Billy the Kid—William Perrott
Director—Ray Taylor
Leading Players—Lash LaRue, Al St.John, June Carr

THE SON OF DAVY CROCKETT (1941, Columbia)
Dave Crockett—Bill Elliott
Director—Lambert Hillyer
Leading Players—Iris Meredith, Dub Taylor, Kenneth MacDonald

THE SON OF DR. JEKYLL (1951, Columbia)
Edward Jekyll—Louis Hayward
Director—Seymour Friedman
Leading Players—Jody Lawrence, Alexander Knox, Lester Matthews

SON OF DRACULA (1943, Universal)
Count Alucard—Lon Chaney, Jr.
Director—Robert Siodmak
Leading Players—Robert Paige, Louise Allbritton, Evelyn Ankers

SON OF DRACULA (1974, GB, Cinemation/Apple)
Count Down—Harry Nilsson
Director—Freddie Francis
Leading Players—Ringo Starr, Dennis Price, Freddie Jones

SON OF FRANKENSTEIN (1939, Universal)
Baron Wolf von Frankenstein—Basil Rathbone
Director—Rowland V. Lee
Leading Players—Boris Karloff, Bela Lugosi, Lionel Atwill, Josephine Hutchinson

SON OF FURY (1942, 20th Century Fox)
Benjamin Blake as a Boy—Roddy McDowall
Benjamin Blake as a Man—Tyrone Power
Director—John Cromwell
Leading Players—Gene Tierney, George Sanders, Frances Farmer, John Carradine, Elsa Lanchester

SON OF INDIA (1931, MGM)
Karim—Ramon Novarro
Director—Jacques Feyder
Leading Players—Conrad Nagel, Marjorie Rambeau, Madge Evans

SON OF MONTE CRISTO (1940, UA)
Count of Monte Cristo—Louis Hayward
Director—Rowland V. Lee
Leading Players—Joan Bennett, George Sanders, Florence Bates

SON OF OKLAHOMA (1932, World Wide)
Dan Clayton—Bob Steele
Director—Robert N. Bradbury
Leading Players—Josie Sedgwick, Robert E. Homans, Julian Rivero

SON OF PALEFACE (1952, Paramount)
Junior Potter—Bob Hope
Director—Frank Tashlin
Leading Players—Jane Russell, Roy Rogers, Bill Williams, Lloyd Corrigan, Douglas Dumbrille

SON OF ROBIN HOOD (1959, GB, 20th Century Fox)
Jamie—Al Hedison
Director—George Sherman
Leading Players—June Laverick, David Farrar, Marius Goring

SON OF SINBAD (1955, RKO)
Sinbad—Dale Robertson
Director—Ted Tetzlaff
Leading Players—Sally Forrest, Lili St. Cyr, Vincent Price, Mari Blanchard

SON OF THE GODS (1930, Warner Brothers)
Sam Lee—Richard Barthelmess
Director—Frank Lloyd
Leading Players—Constance Bennett, Dorothy Mathews, Barbara Leonard, Frank Albertson

SON OF THE NAVY (1940, Monogram)
Malone—James Dunn
Director—William Nigh
Leading Players—Jean Parker, Martin Spellman, William Royle

SON OF THE SHEIK (1926, Silent, UA)
Ahmed—Rudolph Valentino
The Sheik—Rudolph Valentino
Director—George Fitzmaurice
Leading Players—Vilma Banky, George Fawcett, Montagu Love

THE SONG AND DANCE MAN (1936, 20th Century Fox)
Hap Farrell—Paul Kelly
Director—Allan Dwan

Leading Players—Claire Trevor, Michael Whalen, Ruth Donnelly

A SONG FOR MISS JULIE (1945, Republic)
Julie—Jane Farrar
Director—William Rowland
Leading Players—Shirley Ross, Barton Hepburn, Roger Clark

SONG O' MY HEART (1930, Fox Film Corp.)
Sean O'Callaghan—John McCormack
Director—Frank Borzage
Leading Players—Maureen O'Sullivan, John Garrick, J.M. Kerrigan

THE SONG OF BERNADETTE (1943, 20th Century Fox)
Bernadette Soubirous—Jennifer Jones
Director—Henry King
Leading Players—William Eythe, Charles Bickford, Vincent Price, Lee J. Cobb, Gladys Cooper, Anne Revere

SONG OF SCHEHERAZADE (1947, Universal)
Cara de Talavera—Yvonne De Carlo
Director—Walter Reisch
Leading Players—Brian Donlevy, Jean Pierre Aumont, Eve Arden

SONG OF THE THIN MAN (1947, MGM)
Nick Charles—William Powell
Director—Eddie Buzzell
Leading Players—Myrna Loy, Keenan Wynn, Dean Stockwell, Phillip Reed, Patricia Morison

THE SONG OF THE WAGE SLAVE (1915, Silent, Metro)
Ned Lane—Edmund Breese
Director—Herbert Clache
Leading Players—Helen Martin, J. Byrnes, Fraunie Fraunholz

SONGWRITER (1984, Tri-Star)
Doc Jenkins—Willie Nelson
Director—Alan Rudolph
Leading Players—Kris Kristofferson, Melinda Dillon, Rip Torn

SONNY (1922, Silent, Associated First National)
Sonny—Richard Barthelmess
Director—Henry King
Leading Players—Margaret Seddon, Pauline Garon, Lucy Fox

SONNY BOY (1929, Warner Brothers)
Sonny Boy—Davey Lee
Director—Archie Mayo
Leading Players—Betty Bronson, Edward Everett Horton, Gertrude Olmstead

SONNY BOY (1990, Triumph/Trans World)
Sonny Boy—Michael Griffin
Director—Robert Martin Carroll
Leading Players—David Carradine, Paul L. Smith, Brad Dourif, Conrad Janis, Sydney Lassick

THE SONORA KID (1927, Silent, FBO)
Tom MacReady—Tom Tyler
Director—Robert De Lacy
Leading Players—Peggy Montgomery, Billie Bennett, Mark Hamilton

SONS AND LOVERS (1960, GB, 20th Century Fox)
Paul Morel—Dean Stockwell

Mrs. Morel—Wendy Hiller
Director—Jack Cardiff
Leading Players—Trevor Howard, Mary Ure, Heather Sears, William Lucas, Conrad Phillips

THE SONS OF KATIE ELDER (1965, Paramount)
John Elder—John Wayne
Tom Elder—Dean Martin
Bud Elder—Michael Anderson, Jr.
Matt Elder—Earl Holliman
Director—Henry Hathaway
Leading Players—Martha Hyer, Jeremy Slate, James Gregory

SOOKY (1931, Paramount)
Sooky Wayne—Robert Coogan
Director—Norman Taurog
Leading Players—Jackie Searl, Willard Robertson, Enid Bennett, Helen Jerome Eddy, Jackie Cooper

SOPHIE LANG GOES WEST (1937, Paramount)
Sophie Lang—Gertrude Michael
Director—Charles Reisner
Leading Players—Lee Bowman, Sandra Storme, Buster Crabbe

SOPHIE'S CHOICE (1982, Universal)
Sophie Zawistowska—Meryl Streep
Director—Alan J. Pakula
Leading Players—Kevin Kline, Peter MacNicol, Rita Karin, Stephen D. Newman, Greta Turken

SOPHIE'S PLACE (1970, Warner Brothers)
Lady Sophie Fitzmore—Edith Evans
Director—Jim O'Connolly
Leading Players—Telly Savalas, Warren Oates, Cesar Romero

THE SOPHOMORE (1929, Pathe)
Joe Collins—Eddie Quillan
Director—Leo McCarey
Leading Players—Sally O'Neil, Stanley Smith, Jeanette Loff

SORRELL AND SON (1934, GB, UA)
Capt. Stephen Sorrell—H.B. Warner
Kit Sorrell as a child—Peter Penrose
Kit Sorrell as a man—Hugh Williams
Director—Jack Raymond
Leading Players—Winifred Shotter, Margot Grahame, Donald Calthrop, Wally Patch

SORROWFUL JONES (1949, Paramount)
Sorrowful Jones—Bob Hope
Director—Sidney Lanfield
Leading Players—Lucille Ball, William Demarest, Bruce Cabot

SORROWS OF SATAN (1926, Silent, Paramount)
Prince Lucio de Rimanez—Adolphe Menjou
Director—D.W. Griffith
Leading Players—Ricardo Cortez, Lya De Putti, Carol Dempster, Ivan Lebedeff, Marcia Harris

SO'S YOUR OLD MAN (1926, Silent, Paramount)
Samuel Bisbee—W.C. Fields
Alice Bisbee—Kittens Reichert
Director—Gregory La Cava
Leading Players—Alice Joyce, Charles Rogers, Marcia Harris

SO'S YOUR UNCLE (1943, Universal)
Steve Curtis—Donald Woods
John L. Curtis—Paul Stanton
Director—Jean Yarborough
Leading Players—Billie Burke, Elyse Knox, Frank Jenks

SOUL MAN (1986, New World)
Mark Watson—C. Thomas Howell
Director—Steve Miner
Leading Players—Ayre Gross, Rae Dawn Chong, James Earl Jones

SOUL MATES (1925, Silent, MGM)
Velma Markrute—Aileen Pringle
Lord Tancred—Edmund Lowe
Director—Jack Conway
Leading Players—Phillips Smalley, Antonio D'Algy, Edythe Chapman

THE SOUL OF NIGGER CHARLEY (1973, Paramount)
Nigger Charley—Fred Williamson
Director—Larry Spangler
Leading Players—D'Urville Martin, Denise Nichols, Pedro Armendariz, Jr.

SOULTAKER (1990, Action/Pacific West)
Soultaker—Joe Estevez
Director—Michael Rissi
Leading Players—Vivian Schilling, Gregg Thomsen, Robert Z'dar

SOUTH AMERICAN GEORGE (1941, GB, Columbia)
George Butters—George Formby
Director—Marcel Varnel
Leading Players—Linden Travers, Enid Stamp-Taylor, Jacques Brown

SOUTH SEA ROSE (1929, Fox Film Corp.)
Rosalie Dumay—Leonore Ulric
Director—Allan Dwan
Leading Players—Charles Bickford, Kenneth MacKenna, J. Farrell MacDonald, Elizabeth Patterson

SOUTH SEA SINNER (1950, Universal)
Coral—Shelley Winters
Director—Bruce Humberstone
Leading Players—Macdonald Carey, Helena Carter, Luther Adler

SOUTH SEA WOMAN (1953, Warner Brothers)
Ginger Martin—Virginia Mayo
Director—Arthur Lubin
Leading Players—Burt Lancaster, Chuck Connors, Barry Kelley

A SOUTHERN MAID (1933, GB, Wardour)
Dolores/Juanita—Bebe Daniels
Director—Harry Hughes
Leading Players—Clifford Mollison, Harry Welchman, Lupino Lane

A SOUTHERN YANKEE (1948, MGM)
Aubrey Filmore—Red Skelton
Director—Edward Sedgwick
Leading Players—Brian Donlevy, Arlene Dahl, George Coulouris

THE SOUTHERNER (1945, UA)
Sam Tucker—Zachary Scott
Director—Jean Renoir
Leading Players—Betty Field, Beulah Bondi, Jean Vandervilt

SPACED INVADERS (1990, Buena Vista/Touchstone)
Blaznee—Kevin Thompson
Director—Patrick Reed Johnson
Leading Players—Douglas Barr, Royal Dano, Ariana Richards, J.J. Anderson, Gregg Berger

SPACEHUNTER: ADVENTURES IN THE FORBIDDEN ZONE
(1983, Columbia)
Wolff—Peter Strauss
Director—Lamont Johnson
Leading Players—Molly Ringwald, Ernie Hudson, Andrea Marcovicci

THE SPANISH GARDENER (1957, GB, Rank)
Jose—Dirk Bogarde
Director—Philip Leacock
Leading Players—Jon Whiteley, Michael Hordern, Cyril Cusack

SPARROWS (1926, Silent, UA)
Mama Mollie—Mary Pickford
Splutters—Monty O'Grady
Director—William Beaudine
Leading Players—Gustav von Seyfferitz, Roy Stewart, Mary Louise Miller, Charlotte Mineau, Spec O'Donnell

SPARTACUS (1960, Universal)
Spartacus—Kirk Douglas
Director—Stanley Kubrick
Leading Players—Laurence Olivier, Tony Curtis, Jean Simmons, Charles Laughton, Peter Ustinov, John Gavin

SPECIAL AGENT (1935, Warner Brothers)
Bill Bradford—George Brent
Director—William Keighley
Leading Players—Bette Davis, Ricardo Cortez, Joseph Sawyer

SPECIAL AGENT (1949, Paramount)
Johnny Douglas—William Eythe
Director—William C. Thomas
Leading Players—George Reeves, Laura Elliot, Paul Valentine

SPECIAL AGENT K-7 (1937, Syndicate Releasing Co.)
Lanny—Walter McGrail
Director—Raymond K. Johnson
Leading Players—Queenie Smith, Irving Pichel, Donald Reed

SPECIAL INSPECTOR (1939, Syndicate Releasing Co.)
Tom Evans—Charles Quigley
Director—Leon Barsha
Leading Players—Rita Hayworth, George McKay, Edgar Edwards

SPECIAL INVESTIGATOR (1936, RKO)
Bill Fenwick—Richard Dix
Director—Louis King
Leading Players—Margaret Callahan, Erik Rhodes, Owen Davis, Jr.

THE SPECIALIST (1975, Crown)
Londa—Ahna Capri
Director—Hikmet Avedis
Leading Players—Adam West, John Anderson, Alvy Moore

THE SPECTRE OF EDGAR ALLAN POE (1974, Cinerama)
Edgar Allan Poe—Robert Walker, Jr.
Director—Mohy Quandour
Leading Players—Cesar Romero, Tom Drake, Carol Ohmart

SPEED COP (1926, Silent, Rayart)
The Speed Cop—Billy Sullivan
Director—Duke Worne
Leading Players—Rose Blossom, Francis Ford

SPEED CRAZED (1926, Silent, Rayart)
Billy Meeks—Billy Sullivan
Director—Duke Worne
Leading Players—Andree Tourneur, Joseph W. Girard

SPEED CRAZY (1959, Allied Artists)
Nick—Brett Halsey
Director—William Hole, Jr.
Leading Players—Yvonne Lime, Charles Wilcox, Slick Slavin

THE SPEED GIRL (1921, Silent, Paramount)
Betty Lee—Bebe Daniels
Director—Maurice Campbell
Leading Players—Theodore von Eltz, Frank Elliott, Walter Hiers

SPEED KING (1923, Silent, Goldstone)
Jimmy Martin—Richard Talmadge
Director—Grover Jones
Leading Players—Virginia Warwick, Mark Fenton, Harry Van Meter

SPEED MAD (1925, Silent, Columbia)
Bill Sanford—William Fairbanks
Director—Jay Marchant
Leading Players—Edith Roberts, Lloyd Whitlock, Melbourne MacDowell

SPEEDY (1928, Silent, Paramount)
Harold "Speedy" Swift—Harold Lloyd
Director—Ted Wilde
Leading Players—Ann Christy, Bert Woodruff, Brooks Benedict

THE SPELL OF AMY NUGENT (1945, GB, Pyramid)
Amy Nugent—Diana King
Director—John Harlow
Leading Players—Derek Farr, Vera Lindsay, Frederick Leister

SPELL OF THE HYPNOTIST (1956, Exploitation)
Dr. Hamilton—Eric Fleming
Director—W. Lee Wilder
Leading Players—Nancy Malone, Frank Marth, Humphrey Davis

THE SPELLBINDER (1939, RKO)
Jed Marlowe—Lee Tracy
Director—Jack Hively
Leading Players—Barbara Reed, Patric Knowles, Allan Lane

SPELLBOUND (1945, UA)
John "J.B." Ballantine—Gregory Peck
Director—Alfred Hitchcock
Leading Players—Ingrid Bergman, Jean Acker, Michael Chekhov, John Emery, Leo G. Carroll

SPENCER'S MOUNTAIN (1963, Warner Brothers)
Clay Spencer—Henry Fonda
Director—Delmer Daves
Leading Players—Maureen O'Hara, James MacArthur, Donald Crisp, Wally Cox, Mimsy Farmer

SPENDTHRIFT (1936, Paramount)
Townsend Middleton—Henry Fonda
Director—Raoul Walsh
Leading Players—Pat Paterson, Mary Brian, George Barbier

THE SPIDER AND THE FLY (1952, GB, GFD)
Philippe de Ledocq—Guy Rolfe
Fernand Maubert—Eric Portman
Director—Robert Hamer
Leading Players—Nadia Gray, Edward Chapman, Maurice Denham

THE SPIDER WOMAN STRIKES BACK (1946, Universal)
Zenobia Dollard—Gale Sondergaard
Director—Arthur Lubin
Leading Players—Brenda Joyce, Kirby Grant, Rondo Hatton

SPIES OF THE AIR (1940, GB, Associate British Films)
Jim Thurloe—Barry K. Barnes
Director—David Macdonald
Leading Players—Roger Livesey, Joan Marion, Basil Radford

SPIKE OF BENSONHURST (1988, Filmdallas)
Spike Fumo—Sasha Mitchell
Director—Paul Morrissey
Leading Players—Ernest Borgnine, Anne DeSalvo, Sylvia Miles

THE SPIKES GANG (1974, UA)
Harry Spikes—Lee Marvin
Director—Richard Fleischer
Leading Players—Gary Grimes, Ron Howard, Charlie Martin Smith

SPIN A DARK WEB (1956, GB, Columbia)
Bella Francesi—Faith Domergue
Director—Vernon Sewell
Leading Players—Lee Patterson, Rona Anderson, Martin Benson

THE SPIRITUALIST (1948, Eagle Lion)
Alexis—Turhan Bey
Director—Bernard Vorhaus
Leading Players—Lynn Bari, Cathy O'Donnell, Richard Carlson

SPITE MARRIAGE (1929, MGM)
Elmer—Buster Keaton
Trilby Drew—Dorothy Sebastian
Director—Edward Sedgwick
Leading Players—Edward Earle, Leila Hyams, William Bechtel

THE SPITFIRE (1924, Silent, Associated Exhibitors)
Jean Bronson—Betty Blythe
Director—Christy Cabanne
Leading Players—Lowell Sherman, Elliott Dexter, Robert Warwick

SPITFIRE (1934, RKO)
Trigger Hicks—Katharine Hepburn
Director—John Cromwell
Leading Players—Robert Young, Ralph Bellamy, Martha Sleeper

THE SPITFIRE OF SEVILLE (1919, Silent, Universal)
Carmelita—Hedda Nova
Director—George Siegmann

Leading Players—Thurston Hall, Claire Anderson, Marion Skinner

THE SPOILERS (1914, Silent, Selig)
Helen Chester—Bessie Eyton
Alec McNamara—Thomas Santschi
Judge Stillman—N. MacGregory
Director—Colin Campbell
Leading Players—William Farnum, Kathlyn Williams, Frank Clark, Wheeler Oakman, Jack McDonald

THE SPOILERS (1930, Paramount)
Helen Chester—Kay Johnson
Alec McNamara—William "Stage" Boyd
Judge Stillman—Lloyd Ingraham
Director—Edwin Carewe
Leading Players—Gary Cooper, Betty Compson, Harry Green, Slim Summerville

THE SPOILERS (1942, Universal)
Helen Chester—Margaret Lindsay
Alexander McNamara—Randolph Scott
Judge Stillman—Samuel S. Hinds
Director—Ray Enright
Leading Players—Marlene Dietrich, John Wayne, Harry Carey, Sr., Richard Barthelmess, George Cleveland

THE SPOILERS (1955, Universal)
Helen Chester—Barbara Britton
Alex McNamara—Rory Calhoun
Judge Stillman—Carl Benton Reid
Director—Jesse Hibbs
Leading Players—Anne Baxter, Jeff Chandler, Ray Danton, John McIntire, Wallace Ford

SPOILERS OF THE FOREST (1957, Republic)
Boyd Caldwell—Rod Cameron
Eric Warren—Ray Collins
Director—Joe Kane
Leading Players—Vera Ralston, Hillary Brooke, Edgar Buchanan

SPOILERS OF THE NORTH (1947, Republic)
Matt Garraway—Paul Kelly
Director—Richard Sale
Leading Players—Adrian Booth, Evelyn Ankers, James A. Millican

SPOOK BUSTERS (1946, Monogram)
Terence "Slip" Mahoney—Leo Gorcey
Sach—Huntz Hall
Director—William Beaudine
Leading Players—Douglas Dumbrille, Bobby Jordan, Gabriel Dell

SPOOK CHASERS (1957, Allied Artists)
Horace Debussy "Sach" Jones—Huntz Hall
Stanislaus "Duke" Coreleski—Stanley Clements
Director—George Blair
Leading Players—David Gorcey, Jimmy Murphy, Percy Helton

THE SPOOK WHO SAT BY THE DOOR (1973, UA)
Dan Freeman—Lawrence Cook
Director—Ivan Dixon
Leading Players—Paula Kelly, Janet League, Paul Butler

SPUDS (1927, Silent, Pathe Exchange)
"Spuds"—Larry Semon
Director—Larry Semon
Leading Players—Dorothy Dwan, Edward Hearn, Kewpie Morgan

SPRINGTIME FOR HENRY (1934, Fox Film Corp.)
Henry Dewlip—Otto Kruger
Director—Frank Tuttle
Leading Players—Nancy Carroll, Nigel Bruce, Heather Angel

SPY CHASERS (1956, Allied Artists)
Terence Aloysius "Slip" Mahoney—Leo Gorcey
Horace Debussy "Sach" Jones—Huntz Hall
Director—Edward Bernds
Leading Players—Bernard Gorcey, David Gorcey, Bennie Bartlett

SPY FOR A DAY (1939, GB, Paramount)
Sam Gates—Duggie Wakefield
Director—Mario Zampi
Leading Players—Paddy Browne, Jack Allen, Albert Lieven

SPY OF NAPOLEON (1939, GB, Syndicate)
Gerard de Lancy—Richard Barthelmess
Louis Napoleon III—Frank Vosper
Director—Maurice Elvey
Leading Players—Dolly Haas, Francis L. Sullivan, Joyce Bland

THE SPY WHO CAME IN FROM THE COLD (1965, GB, Paramount)
Alec Leamas—Richard Burton
Director—Martin Ritt
Leading Players—Claire Bloom, Oskar Werner, Peter Van Eyck, Sam Wanamaker, George Voskovec

THE SPY WHO LOVED ME (1977, GB, UA)
James Bond—Roger Moore
Major Anya Amasova—Barbara Bach
Director—Lewis Gilbert
Leading Players—Curt Jurgens, Richard Kiel, Caroline Munro

SQUADRON LEADER X (1943, RKO)
Erich Kohler—Eric Portman
Director—Lance Comfort
Leading Players—Ann Dvorak, Walter Fitzgerald, Martin Miller

THE SQUARE PEG (1958, GB, Rank)
Norman Pitkin—Norman Wisdom
Director—John Paddy Carstairs
Leading Players—Honor Blackman, Edward Chapman, Campbell Singer

THE SQUAW MAN (1914, Silent, Lasky)
Capt. James Wyngate—Dustin Farnum
Directors—Cecil B. De Mille and Oscar Apfel
Leading Players—Winifred Kingston, Redwing, Monroe Salisbury

THE SQUAW MAN (1918, Silent, Paramount)
Capt. James Wyngate—Elliott Dexter
Director—Cecil B. De Mille
Leading Players—Ann Little, Katherine MacDonald, Theodore Roberts

THE SQUAW MAN (1931, MGM)
Capt. James Wynnegate (Jim Carsten)—Warner Baxter

Director—Cecil B. De Mille
Leading Players—Lupe Velez, Eleanor Boardman, Charles Bickford, Roland Young, Paul Cavanaugh

THE SQUEALER (1930, Columbia)
Margaret Hart—Dorothy Revier
Director—Harry Joe Brown
Leading Players—Jack Holt, Davey Lee, Matt Moore

SQUIBS (1921, Silent, GB, Jury)
Squibs Hopkins—Betty Balfour
Director—George Pearson
Leading Players—Hugh E. Wright, Fred Groves, Mary Brough

SQUIBS (1935, GB, Gaumont)
Squibs Hopkins—Betty Balfour
Director—Henry Edwards
Leading Players—Gordon Harker, Stanley Holloway, Margaret Yarde

SQUIBS' HONEYMOON (1926, GB, Silent, Gaumont)
Squibs Hopkins (Lee)—Betty Balfour
Director—George Pearson
Leading Players—Hugh E. Wright, Fred Groves, Frank Stanmore

SQUIBS MP (1923, GB, Silent, Gaumont)
Sqiubs Hopkins—Betty Balfour
Director—George Pearson
Leading Players—Hugh E. Wright, Fred Groves, Irene Tripod

SQUIBS WINS THE CALCUTTA SWEEP (1922, GB, Silent, Jury)
Squibs Hopkins—Betty Balfour
Director—George Pearson
Leading Players—Fred Groves, Hugh E. Wright, Bertram Burleigh

SQUIZZY TAYLOR (1984, Australia, Satori)
Squizzy Taylor—David Atkins
Director—Kevin Dobson
Leading Players—Jacki Weaver, Kim Lewis, Michael Long

STACEY (1973, New World)
Stacey Hansen—Anne Randall
Director—Andy Sidaris
Leading Players—Marjorie Bennett, Anitra Ford, Alan Landers

STACY'S KNIGHTS (1983, Crown)
Stacy—Andra Millian
Director—Jim Wilson
Leading Players—Kevin Costner, Eve Lilith, Mike Reynolds

STAGE MOTHER (1933, MGM)
Kitty Lorraine—Alice Brady
Director—Charles Brabin
Leading Players—Maureen O'Sullivan, Franchot Tone, Phillips Holmes, Ted Healy

STAGE STRUCK (1936, Warner Brothers)
Peggy Revere—Joan Blondell
Director—Busby Berkeley
Leading Players—Dick Powell, Warren William, Jean Madden

STAGE STRUCK (1958, RKO/Buena Vista)
Eva Lovelace—Susan Strasberg
Director—Sidney Lumet

Leading Players—Henry Fonda, Joan Greenwood, Herbert Marshall

STAND-IN (1937, UA)
Lester Plum—Joan Blondell
Director—Tay Garnett
Leading Players—Leslie Howard, Humphrey Bogart, Alan Mowbray, Maria Sheldon

STAND UP VIRGIN SOLDIERS (1977, GB, Warner Brothers)
Brigg—Robin Askwith
Sgt. Driscoll—Nigel Davenport
Director—Norman Cohen
Leading Players—George Layton, John Le Mesurier, Warren Mitchell, Pamela Stephenson, Lynda Bellingham

STANLEY AND IRIS (1990, MGM/UA)
Stanley—Robert De Niro
Iris—Jane Fonda
Director—Martin Ritt
Leading Players—Swoosie Kurtz, Martha Plimpton, Harley Cross, Jamey Sheridan, Feodor Chaliapin

STANLEY AND LIVINGSTONE (1939, 20th Century Fox)
Henry M. Stanley—Spencer Tracy
Dr. David Livingstone—Cedric Hardwicke
Director—Henry King
Leading Players—Nancy Kelly, Richard Greene, Walter Brennan, Charles Coburn, Henry Hull

THE STAR (1953, 20th Century Fox)
Margaret Elliot—Betty Davis
Director—Stuart Heisler
Leading Players—Sterling Hayden, Natalie Wood, Warner Anderson

STAR! (1968, 20th Century Fox)
Gertrude Lawrence—Julie Andrews
Director—Robert Wise
Leading Players—Richard Crenna, Michael Craig, Daniel Massey

STAR 80 (1983, Warner Brothers)
Dorothy Stratton—Mariel Hemingway
Director—Bob Fosse
Leading Players—Eric Roberts, Cliff Robertson, Carroll Baker

A STAR FELL FROM HEAVEN (1936, GB, Wardour)
Josef—Joseph Schmidt
Director—Paul Merzbach
Leading Players—Florine McKinney, Billy Milton, W.H. Berry

A STAR IS BORN (1937, UA)
Esther Blodgett/Vicki Lester—Janet Gaynor
Director—William A. Wellman
Leading Players—Fredric March, Adolphe Menjou, Andy Devine, May Robson, Lionel Stander

A STAR IS BORN (1954, Warner Brothers)
Esther Blodgett/Vicki Lester—Judy Garland
Director—George Cukor
Leading Players—James Mason, Jack Carson, Charles Bickford, Tommy Noonan, Lucy Marlow

A STAR IS BORN (1976, Warner Brothers)
Esther Hoffman—Barbra Streisand
Director—Frank Pierson

Leading Players—Kris Kristofferson, Gary Busey, Oliver Clark

THE STAR MAKER (1939, Paramount)
Larry Earl—Bing Crosby
Director—Roy Del Ruth
Leading Players—Linda Ware, Louise Campbell, Ned Sparks

THE STAR PACKER (1934, Monogram)
John Travers—John Wayne
Director—Robert N. Bradbury
Leading Players—Verna Hillie, Gabby Hayes, Yakima Canutt

STAR REPORTER (1939, Monogram)
John—Warren Hull
Director—Howard Bretherton
Leading Players—Marsha Hunt, Morgan Wallace, Clay Clement

STAR SPANGLED GIRL (1971, Paramount)
Amy Cooper—Sandy Duncan
Director—Jerry Paris
Leading Players—Tony Roberts, Todd Susman, Elizabeth Allen

STAR TREK II: THE WRATH OF KHAN (1982, Paramount)
Khan—Ricardo Montalban
Director—Nicholas Meyer
Leading Players—William Shatner, Leonard Nimoy, DeForest Kelley, James Doohan, Walter Koenig, George Takei, Nichelle Nichols

STAR TREK III: THE SEARCH FOR SPOCK (1984, Paramount)
Mr. Spock—Leonard Nimoy
Director—Leonard Nimoy
Leading Players—William Shatner, DeForrest Kelley, James Doohan, Walter Koenig, George Takei, Nichelle Nichols

STAR WITNESS (1931, Warner Brothers)
Grandad Summerville—Charles "Chic" Sale
Director—William Wellman
Leading Players—Walter Huston, Frances Starr, Grant Mitchell

STARCHASER: THE LEGEND OF ORIN (1985, Atlantic)
Orin—Joe Corrigan
Director—Stephen Hahn
Leading Players—Carmen Arzenziano, Noelle North, Anthony Delongis

STARMAN (1984, Columbia)
Starman—Jeff Bridges
Director—John Carpenter
Leading Players—Karen Allen, Charles Martin Smith, Richard Jaeckel

STARTING OVER (1979, Paramount)
Phil Potter—Burt Reynolds
Marilyn Homberg—Jill Clayburgh
Director—Alan J. Pakula
Leading Players—Candice Bergen, Charles Durning, Frances Sternhagen, Austin Pendleton

STATE TROOPER (1933, Columbia)
Michael Ralph—Regis Toomey
Director—D. Ross Lederman
Leading Players—Evalyn Knapp, Raymond Hatton, Matthew Betz

STATE OF GRACE (1990, Orion/Cinehaus)
Terry—Sean Penn
Director—Phil Joanou
Leading Players—Ed Harris, Gary Oldman, Robin Wright, John Turturro, John C. Reilly

STATE'S ATTORNEY (1932, RKO)
Tom Cardigan—John Barrymore
Director—George Archainbaud
Leading Players—Helen Twelvetrees, William "Stage" Boyd, Jill Esmond

STAY AWAY, JOE (1968, MGM)
Joe Lightcloud—Elvis Presley
Director—Peter Tewksbury
Leading Players—Burgess Meredith, Joan Blondell, Katy Juardo

STAYING TOGETHER (1989, Hemdale)
Duncan McDermott—Sean Astin
Kit McDermott—Dermot Mulroney
Brian McDermott—Tim Quill
Director—Lee Grant
Leading Players—Stockard Channing, Melinda Dillon, Jim Haynie, Leon Helm, Dinah Manoff

STEAMBOAT BILL, JR. (1928, Silent, UA)
Steamboat Bill, Jr.—Buster Keaton
Director—Charles E. Reisner
Leading Players—Ernest Torrence, Tom Lewis, Tom McGuire

THE STEEL HELMET (1951, Lippert)
Sgt. Zack—Gene Evans
Director—Samuel Fuller
Leading Players—Robert Hutton, Richard Loo, Steve Brodie, James Edwards, Sid Melton

STEEL MAGNOLIAS (1989, Tri-Star)
M'Lynn Eatenton—Sally Field
Truvy Jones—Dolly Parton
Ouiser Boudreaux—Shirley MacLaine
Annelle Dupuy Desoto—Daryl Hannah
Clairee Belcher—Olympia Dukakis
Shelby Eatenton Latcherie—Julia Roberts
Director—Herbert Ross
Leading Players—Tom Skerritt, Dylan McDermott, Kevin J. O'Connor, Sam Shepard

STELLA (1950, 20th Century Fox)
Stella—Ann Sheridan
Director—Claude Binyon
Leading Players—Victor Mature, David Wayne, Randy Stuart

STELLA (1990, Buena Vista/Touchstone)
Stella Claire Dallas—Bette Midler
Director—John Ernman
Leading Players—John Goodman, Trini Alvarado, Stephen Collins, Marsha Mason, Eileen Brennan, Linda Hart

STELLA DALLAS (1925, Silent, UA)
Stella Dallas—Belle Bennett
Director—Henry King
Leading Players—Ronald Colman, Alice Joyce, Jean Hersholt, Beatrix Pryor, Lois Moran

STELLA DALLAS (1937, UA)
Stella Martin Dallas—Barbara Stanwyck

Director—King Vidor
Leading Players—John Boles, Anne Shirley, Barbara O'Neil, Alan Hale, Marjorie Main

STELLA MARIS (1918, Silent, Artcraft)
Stella Maris—Mary Pickford
Director—Marshall Neilan
Leading Players—Conway Tearle, Camille Ankewich, Ida Waterman

STELLA MARIS (1925, Silent, Universal)
Stella Maris—Mary Philbin
Director—Charles Brabin
Leading Players—Elliott Dexter, Gladys Brockwell, Jason Robards

STEP LIVELY, JEEVES (1937, 20th Century Fox)
Jeeves—Arthur Treacher
Director—Eugene Forde
Leading Players—Patricia Ellis, Robert Kent, Alan Dinehart

STEPCHILD (1947, Producers Releasing Corp.)
Jim Bullock—Tommy Ivo
Tommy Bullock—Gregory Marshall
Director—James Flood
Leading Players—Brenda Joyce, Donald Woods, Terry Austin

THE STEPFATHER (1987, New Century-Vista)
Jerry Blake—Terry O'Quinn
Director—Joseph Ruben
Leading Players—Jill Schoelen, Shelley Hack, Charles Lanyer

STEPFATHER 2: MAKE ROOM FOR DADDY (1989, Millimeter)
Dr. Gene Clifford—Terry O'Quinn
Director—Jeff Burr
Leading Players—Meg Foster, Caroline Williams, Jonathan Brandis

THE STEPFORD WIVES (1975, Columbia)
Joanna—Katharine Ross
Bobby—Paula Prentiss
Carol—Nanette Newman
Charmaine—Tina Louise
Director—Bryan Forbes
Leading Players—Peter Masterson, Patrick O'Neal, Carol Rosson

STEPHEN STEPS OUT (1923, Silent, Paramount)
Stephen Harlow, Jr.—Douglas Fairbanks, Sr.
Director—Joseph Henabery
Leading Players—Theodore Roberts, Noah Beery, Harry Myers

STEPPING SISTERS (1932, Fox Film Corp.)
Mrs. Ramsey—Louise Dresser
Rosie La Marr—Minna Gombell
Lady Chetworth-Lynde—Jobyna Howland
Director—Seymour Felix
Leading Players—William Collier, Sr., Howard Phillip, Stanley Smith, Mary Forbes

THE STERILE CUCKOO (1969, Paramount)
Pookie—Liza Minnelli
Director—Alan J. Pakula
Leading Players—Wendell Burton, Tim McIntire, Elizabeth Harrower

STEVIE (1978, GB, First Artists)
Stevie Smith—Glenda Jackson
Director—Robert Enders
Leading Players—Mona Washbourne, Alec McCowen, Trevor Howard

STICK (1985, Universal)
Stick—Burt Reynolds
Director—Burt Reynolds
Leading Players—Candice Bergen, George Segal, Charles Durning, Jose Perez

STICKY FINGERS (1988, Spectrafilm)
Hattie—Helen Slater
Lolly—Melanie Mayron
Director—Catlin Adams
Leading Players—Danitra Vance, Eileen Brennan, Carol Kane, Stephen McHattie, Christopher Guest

STIR CRAZY (1980, Columbia)
Skip Donahue—Gene Wilder
Harry Monroe—Richard Pryor
Director—Sidney Poitier
Leading Players—Georg Stanford Brown, Jo Beth Williams, Miguelangel Suarez, Craig T. Nelson

THE STOKER (1932, Hoffman-Allied)
Dick—Monte Blue
Director—Chester M. Franklin
Leading Players—Dorothy Burgess, Noah Beery, Sr., Natalie Moorhead

THE STOKER (1935, GB, Gaumont)
Bill—Leslie Fuller
Director—Leslie Pearce
Leading Players—George Harris, Phyllis Clare, Leslie Bradley

THE STOLEN BRIDE (1927, Silent, First National)
Sari, Countess Thurzo—Billie Dove
Director—Alexander Korda
Leading Players—Lloyd Hughes, Armand Kaliz, Frank Beal

STOLEN FACE (1952, GB, Hammer/Lippert)
Alice Brent/Lilly—Lizabeth Scott
Director—Terence Fisher
Leading Players—Paul Henreid, Andre Morell, Mary MacKenzie

STOLEN LIFE (1939, Paramount)
Sylvina & Martina Lawrence—Elisabeth Bergner
Director—Paul Czinner
Leading Players—Wilfrid Lawson, Mabel Terry-Lewis, Michael Redgrave

A STOLEN LIFE (1946, Warner Brothers)
Kate & Pat Bosworth—Bette Davis
Director—Curtis Bernhardt
Leading Players—Glenn Ford, Dane Clark, Walter Brennan

STONE (1974, Australia, BEF Australia)
Stone—Ken Shorter
Director—Sandy Harbutt
Leading Players—Sandy Harbutt, Keryck Barnes, Roger Ward

THE STONE BOY (1984, 20th Century Fox)
Arnold Hillerman—Jason Presson
Director—Chris Cain

Leading Players—Robert Duvall, Frederic Forrest, Glenn Close

STONE OF SILVER CREEK (1935, Universal)
T. William Stone—Buck Jones
Director—Nick Grinde
Leading Players—Niles Welch, Murdock MacQuarrie, Noel Francis

THE STOOGE (1952, Paramount)
Ted Rogers—Jerry Lewis
Director—Norman Taurog
Leading Players—Dean Martin, Polly Bergen, Eddie Mayehoff

STOP ME BEFORE I KILL (1961, GB, Columbia)
Alan Colby—Ronald Lewis
Director—Val Guest
Leading Players—Claude Dauphin, Diane Cilento, Francoise Rosay

STOP OR MY MOTHER WILL SHOOT (1992, Universal)
Joe Bomowski—Sylvester Stallone
Tutti Bomowski—Estelle Getty
Director—Roger Spottiswoode
Leading Players—Jo Beth Williams, Roger Rees, Martin Ferrero, Gailard Sartain, Dennis Buckley

STOP PRESS GIRL (1949, GB, GFD)
Jennifer Peters—Sally Ann Howes
Director—Michael Barry
Leading Players—Gordon Jackson, Basil Radford, Naunton Wayne

STOP THE WORLD—I WANT TO GET OFF (1966, GB, Warner Brothers)
Littlechap—Tony Tanner
Director—Philip Saville
Leading Players—Millicent Martin, Valerie Croft, Neil Hawley

STORM BOY (1976, Australia, South Australia Film)
Storm Boy—Greg Rowe
Director—Henri Safran
Leading Players—Peter Cummins, David Gulpilil, Judy Dick

THE STORM DAUGHTER (1924, Silent, Universal)
Kate Masterson—Priscilla Dean
Director—George Archainbaud
Leading Players—Tom Santschi, William B. Davidson, J. Farrell MacDonald, Cyril Chadwick

THE STORM RIDER (1957, 20th Century Fox)
Jones—Scott Brady
Director- Edward Bernds
Leading Players—Mala Powers, Bill Williams, Olin Howlin

STORMY (1935, Universal)
Stormy—Noah Beery, Jr.
Director—Lew Landers
Leading Players—Jean Rogers, J. Farrell MacDonald, Fred Kohler

THE STORY OF ALEXANDER GRAHAM BELL (1939, 20th Century Fox)
Alexander Graham Bell—Don Ameche
Director—Irving Cummings
Leading Players—Loretta Young, Henry Fonda, Charles Coburn, Spring Byington, Gene Lockhart

A STORY OF DAVID (1960, GB, British Lion)
David—Jeff Chandler
Director—Bob McNaught
Leading Players—Basil Sydney, Peter Arne, David Knight

THE STORY OF DR. WASSELL (1944, Paramount)
Dr. Croydon M. Wassell—Gary Cooper
Director—Cecil B. DeMille
Leading Players—Laraine Day, Signe Hasso, Dennis O'Keefe, Carol Thurston, Carl Esmond

THE STORY OF ESTHER COSTELLO (1957, GB, Columbia)
Esther Costello—Heather Sears
Director—David Miller
Leading Players—Joan Crawford, Rossano Brazzi, Lee Patterson

THE STORY OF LOUIS PASTEUR (1936, Warner Brothers)
Louis Pasteur—Paul Muni
Director—William Dieterle
Leading Players—Josephine Hutchinson, Anita Louise, Donald Woods, Fritz Leiber

THE STORY OF MOLLY X (1949, Universal)
Molly X—June Havoc
Director—Crane Wilbur
Leading Players—John Russell, Dorothy Hart, Connie Gilchrist

THE STORY OF ROBIN HOOD (1952, GB, Disney/RKO)
Robin Hood—Richard Todd
Director—Ken Annakin
Leading Players—Joan Rice, Peter Finch, James Hayter, James Robertson Justice, Marita Hunt

THE STORY OF RUTH (1960, 20th Century Fox)
Ruth—Elana Eden
Director—Henry Koster
Leading Players—Stuart Whitman, Peggy Wood, Viveca Lindfors, Jeff Morrow, Thayer David

THE STORY OF SHIRLEY YORKE (1948, GB, Butchers)
Shirley Yorke—Dinah Sheridan
Director—Maclean Rogers
Leading Players—Derek Farr, Margaretta Scott, John Robinson

THE STORY OF TEMPLE DRAKE (1933, Paramount)
Temple Drake—Miriam Hopkins
Director—Stephen Roberts
Leading Players—Jack LaRue, William Gargan, Irving Pichel

THE STORY OF VERNON AND IRENE CASTLE (1939, RKO)
Vernon Castle—Fred Astaire
Irene Castle—Ginger Rogers
Director—H.C. Potter
Leading Players—Edna May Oliver, Walter Brennan, Lew Fields

THE STORY OF WILL ROGERS (1952, Warner Brothers)
Will Rogers—Will Rogers, Jr.
Director—Michael Curtiz
Leading Players—Jane Wyman, Carl Benton Reid, Eve Miller

STOWAWAY (1936, 20th Century Fox)
Ching-Ching—Shirley Temple
Director—William A. Seiter
Leading Players—Robert Young, Alice Faye, Eugene Pallette

STOWAWAY GIRL (1957, GB, Paramount)
Manuela Hunt—Elsa Martinelli
Director—Guy Hamilton
Leading Players—Trevor Howard, Leslie Weston, Donald
    Pleasence, Pedro Armendariz

STRANDED (1927, Silent, Sterling)
Sally Simpson—Shirley Mason
Director—Phil Rosen
Leading Players—William Collier, Jr., John Miljan, Florence
    Turner, Gale Henry

THE STRANGE ADVENTURES OF MR. SMITH (1937, GB, RKO)
Will Smith—Gus McNaughton
Director—Maclean Rogers
Leading Players—Norma Varden, Eve Gray, Aubrey Mallalieu

THE STRANGE AFFAIR (1968, GB, Paramount)
Peter Strange—Michael York
Director—David Greene
Leading Players—Jeremy Kemp, Susan George, Jack Watson

STRANGE BEDFELLOWS (1965, Universal)
Carter Harrison—Rock Hudson
Toni Vincente—Gina Lollobrigida
Director—Melvin Frank
Leading Players—Gig Young, Edward Judd, Terry-Thomas

THE STRANGE CASE OF CLARA DEANE (1932, Paramount)
Clara Deane—Wynne Gibson
Directors—Louis Gasnier and Max Marcin
Leading Players—Pat O'Brien, Frances Dee, Dudley Digges

THE STRANGE CASE OF DR. MANNING (1958, GB, Republic)
Dr. Manning—David Lander
Director—Arthur Crabtree
Leading Players—Ron Randell, Greta Gynt, Bruce Seton

STRANGE CASE OF DR. MEADE (1939, Columbia)
Dr. Meade—Jack Holt
Director—Lewis D. Collins
Leading Players—Beverly Roberts, Paul Everton, Noah Beery,
    Jr.

THE STRANGE CASE OF DR. RX (1942, Universal)
Dr. Fish—Lionel Atwill
Director—William Nigh
Leading Players—Patric Knowles, Anne Gwynne, Samuel S.
    Hinds

THE STRANGE DEATH OF ADOLF HITLER (1943, Universal)
Adolf Hitler—Ludwig Donath
Director—James Hogan
Leading Players—Gale Sondergaard, George Dolenz, Fritz
    Kortner

STRANGE LADY IN TOWN (1955, Warner Brothers)
Dr. Julia Winslow Garth—Greer Garson
Director—Mervyn LeRoy
Leading Players—Dana Andrews, Cameron Mitchell, Lois Smith

THE STRANGE LOVE OF MARTHA IVERS (1946, Paramount)
Martha Ivers—Barbara Stanwyck
Director—Lewis Milestone
Leading Players—Van Heflin, Lizabeth Scott, Kirk Douglas,
    Judith Anderson

THE STRANGE LOVE OF MOLLY LOUVAIN (1932, Warner
Brothers)
Molly Louvain—Ann Dvorak
Director—Michael Curtiz
Leading Players—Lee Tracy, Richard Cromwell, Guy Kibbee

THE STRANGE MR. GREGORY (1945, Monogram)
Mr. Gregory—Edmund Lowe
Director—Phil Rosen
Leading Players—Jean Rogers, Don Douglas, Frank Reicher

THE STRANGE MRS. CRANE (1948, Eagle Lion)
Gina Crane—Marjorie Lord
Director—Sherman Scott
Leading Players—Robert Shayne, Pierre Watkin, James Seay

THE STRANGE ONE (1957, Columbia)
Jocko De Paris—Ben Gazzara
Director—Jack Garfein
Leading Players—Pat Hingle, Mark Richman, Arthur Storch,
    George Peppard, Larry Gates

STRANGE TRIANGLE (1946, 20th Century Fox)
Francine Huber—Signe Hasso
Sam Crane—Preston Foster
Earl Huber—John Shepperd (Shepperd Strudwick)
Director—Ray McCarey
Leading Players—Anabel Shaw, Roy Roberts, Emory Parnell

THE STRANGE VENGEANCE OF ROSALIE (1972, 20th Century
Fox)
Rosalie—Bonnie Bedelia
Director—Jack Starrett
Leading Players—Ken Howard, Anthony Zerbe

STRANGE WIVES (1935, Universal)
Nadja—June Clayworth
Director—Richard Thorpe
Leading Players—Roger Pryor, Esther Ralston, Hugh O'Connell

THE STRANGE WOMAN (1946, UA)
Jenny Hager—Hedy Lamarr
Director—Edgar Ulmer
Leading Players—George Sanders, Louis Hayward, Gene
    Lockhart

THE STRANGER (1924, Silent, Paramount)
The Stranger—Tully Marshall
Director—Joseph Henabery
Leading Players—Betty Compson, Richard Dix, Lewis Stone,
    Mary Jane Irving, Robert Schable

THE STRANGER (1946, RKO)
Professor Charles Rankin/Franz Kindler—Orson Welles
Director—Orson Welles
Leading Players—Edward G. Robinson, Loretta Young, Philip
    Merivale, Richard Long

THE STRANGER (1987, Columbia)
Alice Kildee—Bonnie Bedelia
Director—Adolfo Aristarain
Leading Players—Peter Riegert, Barry Primus, David Spielberg

A STRANGER AMONG US (1992, Hollywood Pictures)
Emily Eden—Melanie Griffith
Director—Sidney Lumet

Leading Players—Erin Thal, John Pankow, Tracy Pollan, Lee Richardson, Mia Sara

STRANGER AT MY DOOR (1956, Republic)
Hollis Jarret—Macdonald Carey
Clay Anderson—Skip Homeier
Director—William Witney
Leading Players—Patricia Medina, Stephen Wootton, Louis Jean Heydt

THE STRANGER FROM VENUS (1954, GB, Princess Pictures)
Stranger—Helmut Dantine
Director—Burt Balaban
Leading Players—Patricia Neal, Derek Bond, Cyril Luckham

THE STRANGER IN BETWEEN (1952, GB, Universal)
Chris Lloyd—Dirk Bogarde
Director—Charles Crichton
Leading Players—Jon Whitely, Elizabeth Sellars, Kay Walsh

STRANGER IN HOLLYWOOD (1968, Roda/Emerson)
Woman—Sue Bernard
Director—Roidon Slipyj
Leading Players—Scott Every, Guy Mecoli, Mario Arezney

A STRANGER IN TOWN (1943, MGM)
John Josephus Grant—Frank Morgan
Director—Roy Rowland
Leading Players—Richard Carlson, Jean Rogers, Porter Hall

STRANGER IN TOWN (1957, GB, Eros)
John Madison—Alex Nicol
Director—George Pollock
Leading Players—Anne Page, Mary Laura Wood, Mona Washbourne

A STRANGER IS WATCHING (1982, MGM/UA)
Artie Taggart—Rip Torn
Director—Sean S. Cunningham
Leading Players—Kate Mulgrew, James Naughton, Shawn von Schreiber

STRANGER ON HORSEBACK (1955, UA)
Rick Thorne—Joel McCrea
Director—Jacques Tourneur
Leading Players—Miroslava, Kevin McCarthy, John McIntire

STRANGER ON THE THIRD FLOOR (1940, RKO)
Stranger—Peter Lorre
Director—Boris Ingster
Leading Players—John McGuire, Margaret Tallichet, Charles Waldron, Elisha Cook, Jr.

THE STRANGER WORE A GUN (1953, Columbia)
Jeff Travis—Randolph Scott
Director—Andre De Toth
Leading Players—Claire Trevor, Joan Weldon, George Macready

STRANGERS (1990, Australia, Genesis)
Anna—Anne Looby
Gary—James Healey
Director—Craig Lahiff
Leading Players—Melissa Docker, Tim Robertson, Paul Mason

STRANGERS IN LOVE (1932, Paramount)
Buddy Drake—Fredric March

Diana Merrow—Kay Francis
Director—Lothar Mendes
Leading Players—Stuart Erwin, Juliette Compton, George Barbier

STRANGERS MAY KISS (1931, MGM)
Lisbeth Corbin—Norma Shearer
Alan—Neil Hamilton
Director—George Fitzmaurice
Leading Players—Robert Montgomery, Marjorie Rambeau, Irene Rich

STRANGERS ON A HONEYMOON (1937, GB, Gaumont)
October Jones—Constance Cummings
Quigley—Hugh Sinclair
Director—Albert de Courville
Leading Players—Noah Beery, Sr., Beatrix Lehmann, David Burns

STRANGERS ON A TRAIN (1951, Warner Brothers)
Guy Haines—Farley Granger
Bruno Antony—Robert Walker
Director—Alfred Hitchcock
Leading Players—Ruth Roman, Leo G. Carroll, Patricia Hitchcock, Laura Elliott, Marion Lorne

STRANGERS WHEN WE MEET (1960, Columbia)
Larry Coe—Kirk Douglas
Maggie Gault—Kim Novak
Director—Richard Quine
Leading Players—Ernie Kovacs, Barbara Rush, Walter Matthau, Virginia Bruce, Kent Smith

THE STRANGLER (1964, Allied Artists)
Leo Kroll—Victor Buono
Director—Burt Topper
Leading Players—David McLean, Diane Sayer, Davey Davison, Ellen Corby

STRANGLER OF THE SWAMP (1945, Producers Releasing Corp.)
The Strangler—Charles Middleton
Director—Frank Wisbar
Leading Players—Rosemary La Planche, Robert Barrat, Blake Edwards

THE STRATTON STORY (1949, MGM)
Monty Stratton—James Stewart
Director—Sam Wood
Leading Players—June Allyson, Frank Morgan, Agnes Moorehead

STRAUSS' GREAT WALTZ (1934, GB, Gaumont)
Johann "Shani" Strauss, Jr—Esmond Knight
Director—Alfred Hitchcock
Leading Players—Jessie Matthews, Frank Vosper, Fay Compton

THE STRAW MAN (1953, GB, UA)
Mal Farris—Dermot Walsh
Director—Donald Taylor
Leading Players—Clifford Evans, Lana Morris, Amy Dalby

THE STRAWBERRY BLONDE (1941, Warner Brothers)
Virginia Brush—Rita Hayworth
Director—Raoul Walsh
Leading Players—James Cagney, Olivia de Havilland, Alan Hale

STREET ANGEL (1928, Fox Film Corp.)
Angela—Janet Gaynor
Director—Frank Borzage
Leading Players—Charles Farrell, Alberto Rabagliati, Gino Conti, Guido Trento

STREET GIRL (1929, RKO)
Frederika "Freddie" Joyzelle—Betty Compson
Director—Wesley Ruggles
Leading Players—John Harron, Ned Sparks, Jack Oakie

STREET HUNTER (1991, 21st Century)
Logan Blade—Steve James
Director—John A. Gallagher
Leading Players—Reb Brown, John Leguizamo, Valarie Pettiford, Frank Vincent, Tom Wright

THE STREET IS MY BEAT (1966, Harann/Emerson)
Della Martinson—Sharry Marshall
Director—Irvin Berwick
Leading Players—Todd Lasswell, John Harmon, Anne MacAdams

THE STREET SINGER (1937, GB, Wardour)
Richard King—Arthur Tracy
Director—Jean de Marguenat
Leading Players—Arthur Riscoe, Margaret Lockwood, Hugh Wakefield

STRICTLY DISHONORABLE (1931, Universal)
Count "Gus" Di Ruva—Paul Lukas
Director—John M. Stahl
Leading Players—Sidney Fox, Lewis Stone, George Meeker

STRICTLY DISHONORABLE (1951, MGM)
Augustino Caraffa—Ezio Pinza
Directors—Melvin Frank and Norman Panama
Leading Players—Janet Leigh, Millard Mitchell, Gale Robbins

STRIKE ME PINK (1936, UA)
Eddie Pink—Eddie Cantor
Director—Norman Taurog
Leading Players—Ethel Merman, Sally Eilers, William Frawley

STRIPPED TO KILL (1987, Concorde)
Eric—Pia Kamakahi
Director—Katt Shea Ruben
Leading Players—Kay Lenz, Greg Evigan, Norman Fell, Tracy Crowder, Athena Worthey

THE STRIPPER (1963, 20th Century Fox)
Lila Green—Joanne Woodward
Director—Franklin J. Schaffner
Leading Players—Richard Beymer, Claire Trevor, Carol Lynley

STRIPPER (1986, 20th Century Fox)
The Stripper—Janette Boyd
Director—Jerome Gary
Leading Players—Sara Costa, Kimberly Holcomb, Loree Menton

STROKER ACE (1983, Universal/Warner Brothers)
Stroker Ace—Burt Reynolds
Director—Hal Needham
Leading Players—Ned Beatty, Jim Nabors, Parker Stevenson, Loni Anderson, John Byner

STRONG BOY (1929, Silent, Fox Film Corp.)
Strong Boy—Victor McLaglen
Director—John Ford
Leading Players—Leatrice Joy, J. Farrell MacDonald, Clyde Cook

THE STRONG MAN (1926, Silent, First National)
Paul Bergot—Harry Langdon
Director—Frank Capra
Leading Players—Priscilla Bonner, Gertrude Astor, William V. Mong, Robert McKim, Arthur Thalasso

THE STRONGEST MAN IN THE WORLD (1975, Buena Vista)
Dexter Riley—Kurt Russell
Director—Vincent McEveety
Leading Players—Joe Flynn, Eve Arden, Cesar Romero

THE STUD (1979, GB, Trans-American)
Tony Blake—Oliver Tobias
Director—Quentin Masters
Leading Players—Joan Collins, Emma Jacobs, Sue Lloyd

THE STUDENT NURSES (1970, New World)
Sharon—Elaine Giftos
Phred—Karen Carlson
Lynn—Brioni Farrell
Priscilla—Barbara Leigh
Director—Stephanie Rothman
Leading Players—Reni Santoni, Richard Rust, Lawrence Casey

THE STUDENT PRINCE (1954, MGM)
Prince Karl—Edmund Purdom (sung by Mario Lanza)
Director—Richard Thorpe
Leading Players—Ann Blyth, John Ericson, Louis Calhern, Edmund Gwenn, S.Z. "Cuddles" Sakall

THE STUDENT'S ROMANCE (1936, GB, British International)
Max Brandt—Patric Knowles
Veronika—Carol Goodner
Director—Otto Kanturek
Leading Players—Grete Natzler, W.H. Berry, MacKenzie Ward

STUDS LONIGAN (1960, UA)
Studs Lonigan—Christopher Knight
Director—Irving Lerner
Leading Players—Frank Gorshin, Venetia Stevenson, Carolyn Craig

THE STUNT MAN (1980, 20th Century Fox)
Cameron—Steve Railsback
Director—Richard Rush
Leading Players—Peter O'Toole, Barbara Hershey, Allen Goorwitz

STUNT PILOT (1939, Monogram)
Tailspin Tommy—John Trent
Director—George Waggner
Leading Players—Marjorie Reynolds, Milburn Stone, Jason Robards, Sr.

SUBMARINE COMMAND (1951, Paramount)
Cmdr. White—William Holden
Director—John Farrow
Leading Players—Nancy Olson, William Bendix, Don Taylor

SUBURBAN COMMANDO (1991, New Line)
Charlie Wilcox—Christopher Lloyd
Director—Burt Kennedy
Leading Players—Hulk Hogan, Shelley Duvall, Larry Miller, William Ball, Jo Ann Dearing, Jack Elam, Roy Dotrice

SUCH A LITTLE QUEEN (1914, Silent, Famous Players)
Queen Anna Victoria—Mary Pickford
Director—Edwins S. Porter
Leading Players—Carlyle Blackwell, Harold Lockwood, Russell Bassett

SUCH A LITTLE QUEEN (1921, Silent, Realart)
Anne Victoria of Gzbfernigambia—Constance Binney
Director—George Fawcett
Leading Players—Vincent Coleman, J.H. Gilmour, Roy Fernandez

SUCH MEN ARE DANGEOUS (1930, Fox Film Corp.)
Ludwig Kranz—Warner Baxter
Director—Kenneth Hawks
Leading Players—Catherine Dale Owen, Albert Conti, Hedda Hopper

SUCH WOMEN ARE DANGEROUS (1934, Fox Film Corp.)
Vernie Little—Rochelle Hudson
Wanda Paris—Mona Barrie
Director—James Flood
Leading Players—Warner Baxter, Rosemary Ames, Herbert Mundin

SUDDEN BILL DORN (1938, Universal)
Sudden Bill Dorn—Buck Jones
Director—Ray Taylor
Leading Players—Noel Francis, Evelyn Brent, Frank McGlynn

SUED FOR LIBEL (1940, RKO)
Steve—Kent Taylor
Director—Leslie Goodwins
Leading Players—Linda Hayes, Lillian Bond, Morgan Conway

SUGARFOOT (1951, Warner Brothers)
Sugarfoot—Randolph Scott
Director—Edwin L. Marin
Leading Players—Adele Jergens, Raymond Massey, S.Z. Sakall

THE SULLIVANS (1944, 20th Century Fox)
Al Sullivan—Edward Ryan
Frank Sullivan—John Campbell
George Sullivan—James Cardwell
Matt Sullivan—John Alvin
Joe Sullivan—George Offerman, Jr
Director—Lloyd Bacon
Leading Players—Anne Baxter, Thomas Mitchell, Selena Royle, Trudy Marshall

SULLIVAN'S EMPIRE (1967, Universal)
John Sullivan, Jr.—Martin Milner
Director—Harvey Hart Carr
Leading Players—Linden Chiles, Don Quine, Clu Gulager

SULLIVAN'S TRAVELS (1941, Paramount)
John L. Sullivan—Joel McCrea
Director—Preston Sturges
Leading Players—Veronica Lake, Robert Warwick, William Demarest

THE SULTAN'S DAUGHTER (1943, Monogram)
Patra—Ann Corio
Sultan—Charles Butterworth
Director—Arthur Dreifuss
Leading Players—Tim Ryan, Irene Ryan, Eddie Norris

SUMMER LOVE (1958, Universal)
Jim Daley—John Saxon
Joan Wright—Judy Meredith
Erica Landis—Jill St. John
Director—Charles Haas
Leading Players—Molly Bee, Rod McKuen, John Wilder

SUMMER LOVERS (1982, Orion)
Michael Papas—Peter Gallagher
Cathy Feathererst—Daryl Hannah
Director—Randal Kleiser
Leading Players—Valerie Quennessen, Barbara Rush, Carole Cook

SUMMER SCHOOL TEACHERS (1977, New World)
Conklin T—Candice Rialson
Sally—Pat Anderson
Denise—Rhonda Leigh Hopkins
Director—Barbara Peters
Leading Players—Will Carney, Grainger Hines, Christopher Barrett, Dick Miller

SUNBONNET SUE (1945, Monogram)
Sue Casey—Gale Storm
Director—Ralph Murphy
Leading Players—Phil Regan, George Cleveland, Minna Gombell

SUNBURN (1979, Paramount)
Ellie—Farah Fawcett-Majors
Director—Richard C. Sarafian
Leading Players—Charles Grodin, Art Carney, Joan Collins

SUNDAY DINNER FOR A SOLDIER (1944, 20th Century Fox)
Eric Moore—John Hodiak
Director—Lloyd Bacon
Leading Players—Anne Baxter, Charles Winninger, Anne Revere

SUNDOWN JIM (1942, 20th Century Fox)
Jim Majors—John Kimbrough
Director—James Tinling
Leading Players—Virginia Gilmore, Arleen Whelan, Joseph Sawyer

SUNDOWN SAUNDERS (1937, Supreme)
Sundown Saunders—Bob Steele
Director—Robert N. Bradbury
Leading Players—Catherine Cotter, Earl Dwire, Ed Cassidy

SUNDOWN: THE VAMPIRE RETREAT (1990, Vestron)
Count Mardulak—David Carradine
Director—Anthony Hickox
Leading Players—Jim Metzler, Morgan Brittany, Maxwell Caulfield, M. Emmet Walsh, Deborah Foreman, Bruce Campbell, Dana Ashbrook, John Ireland

THE SUNDOWNERS (1950, Eagle Lion)
"Kid Wichita" Cloud—Robert Preston
Tom Cloud—Robert Sterling
Jeff Cloud—John Barrymore, Jr.
Director—George Templeton

Leading Players—Chill Wills, John Litel, Cathy Downs, Jack Elam

THE SUNDOWNERS (1960, Warner Brothers)
Ida Carmody—Deborah Kerr
Paddy Carmody—Robert Mitchum
Sean Carmody—Michael Anderson, Jr.
Director—Fred Zinnemann
Leading Players—Peter Ustinov, Glynis Johns, Dina Merrill, Chips Rafferty

SUNNY (1930, First National)
Sunny—Marilyn Miller
Director—William A. Seiter
Leading Players—Lawrence Gray, Joe Donahue, MacKenzie Ward

SUNNY (1941, RKO)
Sunny Sullivan—Anna Neagle
Director—Herbert Wilcox
Leading Players—Ray Bolger, John Carroll, Edward Everett Horton

SUNRISE—A SONG OF TWO HUMANS (1927, Silent, Fox Film Corp.)
The Man—George O'Brien
The Wife—Janet Gaynor
Director—F.W. Murnau
Leading Players—Bodil Rosing, Margaret Livingston, J. Farrell MacDonald

THE SUNSHINE BOYS (1975, UA)
Willy Clark—Walter Matthau
Al Lewis—George Burns
Director—Herbert Ross
Leading Players—Richard Benjamin, Lee Meredith, Carol Arthur

THE SUPER (1991, 20th Centruy Fox)
Louie Kritski—Joe Pesci
Director—Ron Daniel
Leading Players—Vincent Gardenia, Madolyn Smith Osbourne, Ruben Blades, Stacey Travis, Carole Shelley

THE SUPER COPS (1974, MGM/UA)
Dave Greenberg—Ron Leibman
Bob Hantz—David Selby
Director—Gordon Parks
Leading Players—Sheila E. Frazier, Pat Hingle, Dan Frazer

SUPER FUZZ (1981, Avco Embassy)
Dave Speed—Terence Hill
Director—Sergio Corbucci
Leading Players—Ernest Borgnine, Joanne Dru, Marc Lawrence

SUPER SLEUTH (1937, RKO)
Willard "Bill" Martin—Jack Oakie
Director—Ben Stoloff
Leading Players—Ann Sothern, Eduardo Ciannelli, Alan Bruce

SUPER SPOOK (1975, Leavitt-Pickman)
Super Spook—Leonard Jackson
Director—Anthony Major
Leading Players—Bill Jay, Tony King, Bob Reed, Virginia Fields

SUPERCHICK (1973, Crown)
Tara B. True (Superchick)—Joyce Jillson
Director—John Forsyth
Leading Players—Louis Quinn, Thomas Reardon, Tony Young

SUPERDAD (1974, Buena Vista)
Charlie McCready—Bob Crane
Director—Vincent McEveety
Leading Players—Barbara Rush, Kurt Russell, Joe Flynn, Kathleen Cody, Dick Van Patten

SUPERFLY (1972, Warner Brothers)
Youngblood Priest—Ron O'Neal
Director—Gordon Parks, Jr.
Leading Players—Carl Lee, Sheila Frazier, Julius W. Harris

SUPERFLY T.N.T. (1973, Paramount)
Youngblood Priest—Ron O'Neal
Director—Ron O'Neal
Leading Players—Roscoe Lee Browne, Sheila Frazier, Robert Guillaume, Jacques Sernas

SUPERGIRL (1984, Tri-Star)
Supergirl-Linda Lee—Helen Slater
Director—Jeannot Szwarc
Leading players—Faye Dunaway, Peter O'Toole, Mia Farrow

SUPERMAN (1978, Warner Brothers)
Superman-Clark Kent—Christopher Reeve
Director—Richard Donner
Leading Players—Marlon Brando, Gene Hackman, Ned Beatty, Jackie Cooper, Glen Ford, Margot Kidder, Valerie Perrine, Susannah York, Trevor Howard

SUPERMAN AND THE MOLE MEN (1951, Lippert)
Superman-Clark Kent—George Reeves
Director—Lee Sholem
Leading Players—Phyllis Coates, Jeff Corey, Walter Reed

SUPERMAN II (1980, Warner Brothers)
Superman-Clark Kent—Christopher Reeve
Director—Richard Lester
Leading Players—Gene Hackman, Ned Beatty, Jackie Cooper, Margot Kidder, Sarah Douglas, Terence Stamp, Jack O'Halloran

SUPERMAN III (1983, Warner Brothers)
Superman-Clark Kent—Christopher Reeve
Director—Richard Lester
Leading Players—Richard Pryor, Jackie Cooper, Margot Kidder, Annette O'Toole, Annie Ross, Robert Vaughn, Pamela Stephenson

SUPERMAN IV: THE QUEST FOR PEACE (1987, Warner Brothers)
Superman-Clark Kent—Christopher Reeve
Director—Sidney J. Furie
Leading Players—Gene Hackman, Jackie Cooper, Marc McClure, Jon Cryer, Sam Wannamaker, Margot Kidder

SUPPORT YOUR LOCAL GUNFIGHTER (1971, UA)
Latigo Smith—James Garner
Director—Burt Kennedy
Leading Players—Suzanne Pleshette, Jack Elam, Joan Blondell, Harry Morgan, Marie Windsor, John Dehner

SUPPORT YOUR LOCAL SHERIFF (1969, United Artsits)
Jason McCullough—James Garner
Director—Burt Kennedy
Leading Players—Joan Hackett, Walter Brennan, Harry Morgan, Jack Elam, Bruce Dern, Henry Jones

SURE FIRE FLINT (1922, Silent, Mastadon)
Sure Fire Flint—Johnny Hines
Director—Del Henderson
Leading Players—Edmund Breese, Robert Edeson, Effie Shannon

THE SURE THING (1985, Embassy)
The Sure Thing—Nicollette Sheridan
Director—Rob Reiner
Leading Players—John Cusack, Daphne Zuniga, Anthony Edwards

THE SURGEON'S KNIFE (1957, GB, Grand National)
Dr. Alex Waring—Donald Houston
Director—Gordon Parry
Leading Players—Adrienne Corri, Lyndon Brook, Jean Cadell

THE SURROGATE (1984, Cinepix)
Anouk Van Derlin—Carol Laure
Director—Don Carmody
Leading Players—Art Hindle, Shannon Tweed, Michael Ironside

THE SURVIVORS (1983, Columbia)
Sonny Paluso—Walter Matthau
Donald Quinelle—Robin Williams
Director—Michael Ritchie
Leading Players—Jerry Reed, James Wainwright, Kristen Vigard

SUSAN AND GOD (1940, MGM)
Susan Trexel—Joan Crawford
Director—George Cukor
Leading Players—Fredric March, Ruth Hussey, John Carroll, Rita Hayworth, Nigel Bruce

SUSAN LENOX-HER FALL AND RISE (1931, MGM)
Susan Lenox—Greta Garbo
Director—Robert Z. Leonard
Leading Players—Clark Gable, Jean Hersholt, John Miljan

SUSAN SLADE (1961, Warner Brothers)
Susan Slade—Connie Stevens
Director—Delmer Daves
Leading Players—Troy Donahue, Dorothy McGuire, Lloyd Nolan, Brian Aherne, Grant Williams

SUSAN SLEPT HERE (1954, RKO)
Susan—Debbie Reynolds
Director—Frank Tashlin
Leading Players—Dick Powell, Anne Francis, Alvy Moore, Glenda Farrell, Horace McMahon

SUSANNAH OF THE MOUNTIES (1939, 20th Century Fox)
Susannah Sheldon—Shirley Temple
Director—William A. Seiter
Leading Players—Randolph Scott, Margaret Lockwood, Martin Good Rider, J. Farrell MacDonald

SUSIE STEPS OUT (1946, UA)
Susie Russell—Nita Hunter
Director—Reginald Le Borg

Leading Players—David Bruce, Cleatus Caldwell, Howard Freeman

SUSPECT (1987, Tri-Star)
Carl Wayne Anderson—Liam Neeson
Director—Peter Yates
Leading Players—Cher, Dennis Quaid, Philip Bosco, John Mahoney

THE SUSPECT (1944, Universal)
Philip—Charles Laughton
Director—Robert Siodmak
Leading Players—Ella Raines, Dean Harens, Stanley C. Ridges, Henry Danieli, Rosalind Ivan

SUSPECTED PERSON (1943, GB, Producers Releasing Corp.)
Jim Raynor—Clifford Evans
Director—Lawrence Huntington
Leading Players—Patricia Roc, David Farrar, Anne Firth

SUTTER'S GOLD (1936, Universal)
John Sutter—Edward Arnold
Director—James Cruze
Leading Players—Lee Tracy, Binnie Barnes, Katherine Alexander

SUZANNA (1922, Silent, Allied)
Suzanna—Mabel Normand
Director—F. Richard Jones
Leading Players—George Nichols, Walter McGrail, Evelyn Sherman

SUZANNE (1980, Canada, Ambassador)
Suzanne McDonald—Jennifer Dale
Director—Robin Spry
Leading Players—Winston Rekert, Gabriel Arcand, Ken Pogue

SUZY (1936, MGM)
Suzy Trent—Jean Harlow
Director—George Fitzmaurice
Leading Players—Franchot Tone, Cary Grant, Benita Hume, Lewis Stone, Reginald Mason

SVENGALI (1931, Warner Brothers)
Svengali—John Barrymore
Director—Archie Mayo
Leading Players—Marian Marsh, Bramwell Fletcher, Donald Crisp

SVENGALI (1955, GB, MGM)
Svengali—Donald Wolfit
Director—Noel Langley
Leading Players—Hildegarde Neff, Terence Morgan, Derek Bond

SWAMP THING (1982, Embassy)
Swamp Thing—Dick Durock
Director—Wes Craven
Leading Players—Louis Jourdan, Adrienne Barbeau, Ray Wise

SWAMP WOMAN (1941, Producers Releasing Corp.)
Annabelle—Ann Corio
Director—Elmer Clifton
Leading Players—Jack LaRue, Jay Novello, Richard Deane

THE SWAN (1956, MGM)
Princess Alexandra—Grace Kelly

Director—Charles Vidor
Leading Players—Alec Guinness, Louis Jourdan, Agnes Moorehead, Jessie Royce Landis, Brian Aherne

SWEATER GIRL (1942, Paramount)
Susan Lawrence—June Preisser
Director—William Clemens
Leading Players—Eddie Bracken, Phillip Terry, Nils Asther

SWEEPSTAKES WINNER (1939, Warner Brothers)
Jenny Jones—Marie Wilson
Director—William McGann
Leading Players—Johnnie Davis, Allen Jenkins, Charley Foy

SWEET ADELINE (1926, Silent, Chadwick)
Adeline—Gertrude Olmstead
Director—Jerome Storm
Leading Players—Charles Ray, Jack Clifford, John P. Lockney

SWEET ADELINE (1935, Warner Brothers)
Adeline Schmidt—Irene Dunne
Director—Mervyn LeRoy
Leading Players—Donald Woods, Hugh Herbert, Ned Sparks

SWEET CHARITY (1969, Universal)
Charity Hope Valentine—Shirley MacLaine
Director—Bob Fosse
Leading Players—Sammy Davis, Jr., Ricardo Montalban, John McMartin, Chita Rivera, Paula Kelly

SWEET KITTY BELLAIRS (1930, Warner Brothers)
Sweet Kitty Bellairs—Claudia Dell
Director—Alfred E. Green
Leading Players—Ernest Torrence, Walter Pidgeon, June Collyer

SWEET MAMA (1930, First National)
Goldie—Alice White
Director—Edward Cline
Leading Players—David Manners, Kenneth Thompson, Rita Flynn

SWEET ROSIE O'GRADY (1943, 20th Century Fox)
Madeline Marlowe/Rosie O'Grady—Betty Grable
Director—Irving Cummings
Leading Players—Robert Young, Adolphe Menjou, Reginald Gardiner, Virginia Grey

SWEET SIXTEEN (1928, Silent, Rayart)
Cynthia Perry—Helen Foster
Director—Scott Pembroke
Leading Players—Gertrude Olmstead, Gladden James, Lydia Yeamans

SWEET SIXTEEN (1983, Century Intenational)
Melissa—Aleisa Shirley
Director—Jim Sotos
Leading Players—Bo Hopkins, Susan Strasberg, Don Stroud

SWEET SUZY (1973, Signal)
Lady Susan—Anouska Hempel
Director—Russ Meyer
Leading Players—David Warbeck, Percy Herbert, Milton McCollin

SWEET TALKER (1991, Australia, Seven Arts/New Line)
Harry Reynolds—Bryan Brown

Director—Michael Jenkins
Leading Players—Karen Allen, Justin Rosniak, Chris Haywood, Bill Kerr, Bruce Spence

SWEET WILLIAM (1980, GB, World Northal)
William—Sam Waterston
Director—Claude Whatham
Leading Players—Jenny Agutter, Anna Massey, Geraldine James

SWEETHEART OF SIGMA CHI (1933, Monogram)
Vivian—Mary Carlisle
Director—Edward L. Marin
Leading Players—Buster Crabbe, Charles Starrett, Florence Lake

SWEETHEART OF SIGMA CHI (1946, Monogram)
Betty Allen—Elyse Knox
Director—Jack Bernhard
Leading Players—Phil Regan, Phil Brito, Ross Hunter

SWEETHEART OF THE CAMPUS (1941, Columbia)
Betty Blake—Ruby Keeler
Director—Edward Dmytryk
Leading Players—Ozzie Nelson, Harriet Hilliard, Gordon Oliver

SWEETHEART OF THE NAVY (1937, Grand National)
Joan—Cecilia Parker
Director—Duncan Mansfield
Leading Players—Eric Linden, Roger Imhof, Bernadene Hayes

SWEETHEARTS (1938, MGM)
Gwen Marlowe—Jeanette MacDonald
Ernest Lane—Nelson Eddy
Director—W.S. Van Dyke II
Leading Players—Frank Morgan, Ray Bolger, Florence Rice, Mischa Auer, Fay Holden

SWEETIE (1929, Paramount)
Barbara Pell—Nancy Carroll
Director—Frank Tuttle
Leading Players—Helen Kane, Stanley Smith, Jack Oakie

SWEETIE (1989, Australia, Island)
Dawn (Sweetie)—Genevieve Lemon
Director—Jane Campion
Leading Players—Karen Colson, Tom Lycos, Jon Darling

SWELL GUY (1946, Universal)
Jim Duncan—Sonny Tufts
Director—Frank Tuttle
Leading Players—Ann Blyth, Ruth Warrick, William Gargan

THE SWELL-HEAD (1927, Silent, Columbia)
Lefty Malone—Ralph Graves
Director—Ralph Graves
Leading Players—Johnnie Walker, Eugenia Gilbert, Mildred Harris

THE SWELLHEAD (1930, Tiffany)
Bill "Cyclone" Hickey—Johnny Walker
Director—James Flood
Leading Players—James Gleason, Marion Schilling, Natalie Kingston

SWELL-HEAD (1935, Columbia)
Terry McCall—Wallace Ford

Director—Ben Stoloff
Leading Players—Dickie Moore, Barbara Kent, J. Farrell MacDonald

SWIFTY (1936, Diversion)
Swifty—Hoot Gibson
Director—Alan James
Leading Players—June Gale, George F. Hayes, Ralph Lewis

THE SWIMMER (1968, Columbia)
Ned Merrill—Burt Lancaster
Director—Frank Perry
Leading Players—Janet Landgard, Janice Rule, Marge Champion

SWING IT PROFESSOR (1937, Ambassador)
Prof. Artemis Roberts—Pinky Tomlin
Director—Marshall Neilan
Leading Players—Paula Stone, Mary Kornman, Milburn Stone

SWING OUT, SISTER (1945, Universal)
Donna—Frances Raeburn
Director—Edward Lilley
Leading Players—Rod Cameron, Billie Burke, Arthur Treacher

SWING SHIFT MAISIE (1943, MGM)
Maisie Ravier—Ann Sothern
Director—Norman Z. McLeod
Leading Players—James Craig, Jean Rogers, Connie Gilchrist

THE SWINGER (1966, Paramount)
Kelly Olsson—Ann-Margret
Director—George Sidney
Leading Players—Tony Franciosa, Robert Coote, Yvonne Romain

SWINGTIME JOHNNY (1944, Universal)
Jonathan—Peter Cookson
Director—Edward F. Cline
Leading Players—The Andrews Sisters, Harriet Hilliard, Tim Ryan

SWISS FAMILY ROBINSON (1940, RKO)
William Robinson—Thomas Mitchell
Elizabeth Robinson—Edna Best
Jack Robinson—Freddie Bartholmew
Director—Edward Ludwig
Leading Players—Terry Kilburn, Tim Holt, Baby Bobby Quillan

SWISS FAMILY ROBINSON (1960, Buena Vista)
Father Robinson—John Mills
Mother Robinson—Dorothy McGuire
Fritz Robinson—James MacArthur
Director—Ken Annakin
Leading Players—Janet Munro, Sessue Hayakawa, Tommy Kirk

SWITCH (1991, Warner Brothers)
Amanda Brooks—Ellen Barkin
Steve Brooks—Perry King
Director—Blake Edwards
Leading Players—Jimmy Smits, Jo Beth Williams, Lorraine Bracco, Tony Roberts, Lysette Anthony, Victoria Mahoney

THE SWORD OF ALI BABA (1965, Universal)
Ali Baba—Peter Mann
Director—Virgil W. Vogel
Leading Players—Jocelyn Lane, Peter Whitney, Gavin MacLeod

SWORD OF LANCELOT (1963, GB, Universal)
Lancelot—Cornel Wilde
Director—Cornel Wilde
Leading Players—Jean Wallace, Brian Aherne, George Baker

SWORD OF THE AVENGER (1948, Eagle Lion)
Roberto Bolagtas—Ramon Del Gado
Director—Sidney Salkow
Leading Players—Sigrid Gurie, Ralph Morgan, Duncan Renaldo

THE SWORDSMAN (1947, Columbia)
Alexander MacArden—Larry Parks
Director—Joseph H. Lewis
Leading Players—Ellen Drew, George Macready, Edgar Buchanan

SWORN ENEMY (1936, MGM)
"Hank" Sherman—Robert Young
Director—Edwin L. Marin
Leading Players—Florence Rice, Joseph Calleia, Lewis Stone

SYLVIA (1965, Paramount)
Sylvia West—Carroll Baker
Director—Gordon Douglas
Leading Players—George Maharis, Joanne Dru, Peter Lawford, Viveca Lindfors, Edmond O'Brien, Ann Sothern

SYLVIA (1985, MGM/UA)
Sylvia Henderson—Eleanor David
Director—Michael Firth
Leading Players—Nigel Terry, Tom Wilkinson, Mary Regan

SYLVIA SCARLETT (1936, RKO)
Sylvia Scarlett—Katharine Hepburn
Director—George Cukor
Leading Players—Cary Grant, Brian Aherne, Edmund Gwenn

SYNCOPATING SUE (1926, Silent, First National)
Susan Adams—Corinne Griffith
Director—Richard Wallace
Leading Players—Tom Moore, Rockliffe Fellowes, Lee Moran

T

T-MEN (1947, Eagle-Lion)
Dennis O'Brien—Dennis O'Keefe
Tony Genaro—Alfred Ryder
Director—Anthony Mann
Leading Players—Mary Meade, Wallace Ford, June Lockhart, Charles McGraw

THX 1138 (1971, Warner Brothers)
THX 1138—Robert Duvall
Director—George Lucas
Leading Players—Donald Pleasence, Don Pedro Colley, Maggie McOmie

TNT JACKSON (1975, New World)
TNT Jackson—Jeanne Bell
Director—Cirio Santiago
Leading Players—Stan Shaw, Pat Anderson, Ken Metcalf

T.R. BASKIN (1971, Paramount)
T.R. Baskin—Candice Bergen
Director—Herbert Ross
Leading Players—Peter Boyle, James Caan, Marcia Rodd

TAFFIN (1988, US/GB, MGM-UA)
Mark Taffin—Pierce Brosnan
Director—Francis Megahy
Leading Players—Ray McAnally, Alison Doody, Jeremy Child

TAGGART (1964, Universal)
Kent Taggart—Tony Young
Director—R.G. Springsteen
Leading Players—Dan Duryea, Dick Foran, Elsa Cardenas

A TAILOR MADE MAN (1922, Silent, UA)
John Paul Bart—Charles Ray
Director—Joseph De Grasse
Leading Players—Thomas Ricketts, Ethel Grandin, Victor Potel

A TAILOR MADE MAN (1931, MGM)
John Paul Bart—William Haines
Director—Sam Wood
Leading Players—Dorothy Jordan, Joseph Cawthorn, Marjorie Rambeau

THE TAILOR OF BOND STREET (1916, GB, Silent, Gerrard)
Marcovitch Einstein—Augustus Yorke
Director—J. Gerrard
Leading Players—Robert Leonard, Peggy Richards, Kenneth Barker

TAKE A GIRL LIKE YOU (1970, GB, Columbia)
Jenny Bunn—Hayley Mills
Director—Jonathan Miller
Leading Players—Oliver Reed, Noel Harrison, John Bird

TAKE A LETTER, DARLING (1942, Paramount)
Tom Verney—Fred MacMurray
Director—Mitchell Leisen
Leading Players—Rosalind Russell, Macdonald Carey, Constance Moore, Robert Benchley

TAKE CARE OF MY LITTLE GIRL (1951, 20th Century Fox)
Liz Erickson—Jeanne Crain
Director—Jean Negulesco
Leading Players—Dale Robertson, Mitzi Gaynor, Jean Peters, Jeffrey Hunter

TAKE HER, SHE'S MINE (1963, 20th Century Fox)
Mollie Michaelson—Sandra Dee
Director—Henry Koster
Leading Players—James Stewart, Audrey Meadows, Robert Morley

TAKE THE HEIR (1930, Big 4)
Lord Tweedham—Frank Elliott
Director—Lloyd Ingraham
Leading Players—Edward Everett Horton, Dorothy Devore, Edythe Chapman

TAKING CARE OF BUSINESS (1990, Buena Vista/Hollywood Pictures)
Jimmy—James Belushi
Director—Arthur Hiller
Leading Players—Charles Grodin, Anne DeSalvo, Loryn Locklin, Stephen Elliott, Hector Elizondo, Veronica Hamel, Mako, Gates McFadden

TALENT FOR THE GAME (1991, Paramount)
Sammy Bodeen—Jeff Corbett
Director—Robert M. Young
Leading Players—Edward James Olmos, Lorraine Bracco, Jamey Sheridan, Terry Kinney, Tom Bower

TALENT SCOUT (1937, Warner Brothers)
Steve Stewart—Donald Woods
Director—William Clemens
Leading Players—Jeanne Madden, Fred Lawrence, Rosalind Marquis

TALES OF A SALESMAN (1965, Rossmore)
Herman—David Reed
Director—Don Russell
Leading Players—Pope Hook, Terri Collins, Terri Dean

THE TALES OF HOFFMANN (1951, GB, Lopert)
Hoffmann—Robert Rounseville
Directors—Michael Powell and Emeric Pressburger
Leading Players—Moira Shearer, Robert Helpmann, Pamela Brown

TALES OF ROBIN HOOD (1951, Lippert)
Robin Hood—Robert Clarke
Director—James Tinling
Leading Players—Mary Hatcher, Paul Cavanaugh, Wade Crosby

THE TALISMAN (1966, Gillman)
The Indian—Ned Romero
Director—John Carr
Leading Players—Linda Hawkins, Richard Thies, Jerald Cormier

TALK ABOUT A LADY (1946, Columbia)
Janie Clark—Jinx Falkenberg
Director—George Sherman
Leading Players—Forrest Tucker, Joe Besser, Trudy Marshall

TALK ABOUT JACQUELINE (1942, GB, MGM)
Jacqueline Marlow—Carla Lehmann
Director—Harold French
Leading Players—Hugh Williams, Joyce Howard, Roland Culver

TALK OF THE DEVIL (1937, GB, Gaumont)
Ray Allen—Ricardo Cortez
Director—Carol Reed
Leading Players—Sally Eilers, Basil Sydney, Randle Ayrton

TALL, DARK AND HANDSOME (1941, 20th Century Fox)
Shep Morrison—Cesar Romero
Director—H. Bruce Humberstone
Leading Players—Virginia Gilmore, Charlotte Greenwood, Milton Berle

TALL IN THE SADDLE (1944, RKO)
Rocklin—John Wayne
Director—Edwin L. Marin
Leading Players—Ella Raines, Audrey Long, Gabby Hayes

TALL MAN RIDING (1955, Warner Brothers)
Larry Madden—Randolph Scott
Director—Lesley Selander
Leading Players—Dorothy Malone, Peggie Castle, Bill Ching

THE TALL MEN (1955, 20th Century Fox)
Ben Allison—Clark Gable
Nathan Stark—Robert Ryan
Clint Allison—Cameron Mitchell
Director—Raoul Walsh
Leading Players—Jane Russell, Juan Garcia, Harry Shannon

THE TALL STRANGER (1957, Allied Artists)
Ned Bannon—Joel McCrea
Director—Thomas Carr
Leading Players—Virginia Mayo, Barry Kelley, Michael Ansara

THE TALL T (1957, Columbia)
Pat Brennan—Randolph Scott
Director—Budd Boetticher
Leading Players—Richard Boone, Maureen O'Sullivan, Arthur Hunnicutt, Skip Homeier

THE TALL TARGET (1951, MGM)
Abraham Lincoln—Leslie Kimmell
Director—Anthony Mann
Leading Players—Dick Powell, Paula Raymond, Adolphe Menjou

THE TALL TEXAN (1953, Lippert)
Ben Trask—Lloyd Bridges
Director—Elmo Williams
Leading Players—Lee J. Cobb, Marie Windsor, Luther Adler

TAMAHINE (1964, GB, MGM)
Tamahine—Nancy Kwan
Director—Philip Leacock
Leading Players—John Fraser, Dennis Price, Coral Browne

THE TAMING OF DOROTHY (1950, GB, Eagle-Lion)
Dorothy—Jean Kent
Director—Mario Soldati
Leading Players—Robert Beatty, Margaret Rutherford, Rona Anderson

THE TAMING OF THE SHREW (1929, UA)
Katherine—Mary Pickford
Director—Samuel Taylor
Leading Players—Douglas Fairbanks, Edwin Maxwell, Joseph Cawthorn

THE TAMING OF THE SHREW (1967, Columbia)
Katharina—Elizabeth Taylor
Director—Franco Zeffirelli
Leading Players—Richard Burton, Cyril Cusack, Michael Hordern

TAMING SUTTON'S GAL (1957, Republic)
Lou Sutton—Gloria Talbot
Director—Lesley Selander
Leading Players—John Lupton, Jack Kelly, May Wynn

TAMMY AND THE BACHELOR (1957, Universal)
Tammy Tyree—Debbie Reynolds
Peter Brent—Leslie Nielsen
Director—Joseph Pevney

Leading Players—Walter Brennan, Mala Powers, Sidney Blackmer, Fay Wray

TAMMY AND THE DOCTOR (1963, Universal)
Tammy Tyree—Sandra Dee
Dr. Mark Cheswick—Peter Fonda
Director—Harry Keller
Leading Players—Macdonald Carey, Beulah Bondi, Margaret Lindsay, Reginald Owen

TAMMY AND THE MILLIONAIRE (1967, Universal)
Tammy Tyree—Debbie Watson
John Brent—Donald Woods
Director—Leslie Goodwins
Leading Players—Frank McGrath, Denver Pyle, George Furth

TAMMY, TELL ME TRUE (1961, Universal)
Tammy Tyree—Sandra Dee
Director—Harry Keller
Leading Players—John Gavin, Charles Drake, Virginia Grey

TANGO AND CASH (1989, Warner Brothers)
Ray Tango—Sylvester Stallone
Gabe Cash—Kurt Russell
Director—Andrei Konchalovsky
Leading Players—Teri Hatcher, Jack Palance, Brion James

TANYA'S ISLAND (1981, Canada, International Film Exchange)
Tanya—D.D. Winters
Director—Alfred Sole
Leading Players—Richard Sargent, Mariette Levesque, Don McCleod

TAPEHEADS (1988, DEG-Avenue)
Ivan Alexcov—John Cusack
Josh Tager—Tim Robbins
Director—Bill Fishman
Leading Players—Doug McClure, Connie Stevens, Clu Gulager, Mary Crosby, Katy Boyer

THE TAR HEEL WARRIOR (1917, Silent, Triangle)
Col. Dabney Mills—Walt Whitman
Director—E. Mason Hopper
Leading Players—Ann Kroman, William Shaw, James W. McLaughlin

TARGET: HARRY (1980, Corman/ABC)
Harry Black—Vic Morrow
Director—Harry Neill (Roger Corman)
Leading Players—Suzanne Pleshette, Victor Buono, Cesar Romero

TARNISHED ANGEL (1938, RKO)
Connie Vinson—Sally Eilers
Director—Leslie Goodwins
Leading Players—Lee Bowman, Ann Miller, Alma Kruger

THE TARNISHED ANGELS (1957, Universal)
Roger Shumann—Robert Stack
LaVerne Shannon—Dorothy Malone
Director—Douglas Sirk
Leading Players—Rock Hudson, Jack Carson, Robert Middleton

TARNISHED LADY (1931, Paramount)
Nancy Courtney—Tallulah Bankhead
Director—George Cukor

Leading Players—Clive Brook, Phoebe Foster, Alexander Kirkland

TARZAN AND HIS MATE (1934, MGM)
Tarzan—Johnny Weissmuller
Jane Parker—Maureen O'Sullivan
Director—Cedric Gibbons (Jack Conway, uncredited)
Leading Players—Neil Hamilton, Paul Cavanaugh, Forrester Harvey

TARZAN AND THE AMAZONS (1945, RKO)
Tarzan—Johnny Weissmuller
Amazon Queen—Maria Ouspenskaya
Director—Kurt Neumann
Leading Players—Brenda Joyce, Johnny Sheffield, Henry Stephenson, Barton Maclane

TARZAN AND THE GREAT RIVER (1967, Paramount)
Tarzan—Mike Henry
Director—Robert Day
Leading Players—Jan Murray, Manuel Padilla, Jr., Diana Millay

TARZAN AND THE GREEN GODDESS (1938, Principal)
Tarzan—Herman Brix (Bruce Bennett)
Ula Vale—Ula Holt
Director—Edward Kull
Leading Players—Frank Baker, Dale Walsh, Harry Ernest

TARZAN AND THE HUNTRESS (1947, RKO)
Tarzan—Johnny Weissmuller
Tanya—Patricia Morison
Director—Kurt Neumann
Leading Players—Brenda Joyce, Johnny Sheffield, Barton MacLane

TARZAN AND THE JUNGLE BOY (1968, Paramount)
Tarzan—Mike Henry
Buhara—Edward Johnson
Director—Robert Day
Leading Players—Rafer Johnson, Alizia Gur, Steven Bond

TARZAN AND THE LEOPARD WOMAN (1946, RKO)
Tarzan—Johnny Weissmuller
Lea—Acquanetta
Director—Kurt Neumann
Leading Players—Brenda Joyce, Johnny Sheffield, Edgar Barrier

TARZAN AND THE LOST SAFARI (1957, GB, MGM)
Tarzan—Gordon Scott
Director—Bruce Humberstone
Leading Players—Robert Beatty, Yolande Donlan, Betta St. John

TARZAN AND THE MERMAIDS (1948, RKO)
Tarzan—Johnny Weissmuller
Mara—Linda Christian
Director—Robert Florey
Leading Players—Brenda Joyce, John Lanenz, Fernando Wagner

TARZAN AND THE SHE-DEVIL (1953, RKO)
Tarzan—Lex Barker
Lyra—Monique Van Vooren
Director—Kurt Neumann
Leading Players—Joyce MacKenzie, Raymond Burr, Tom Conway

TARZAN AND THE SLAVE GIRL (1950, RKO)
Tarzan—Lex Barker
Lola—Denise Darcel
Director—Lee Sholem
Leading Players—Vanessa Brown, Robert Alda, Hurd Hatfield

TARZAN AND THE VALLEY OF GOLD (1966, American International)
Tarzan—Mike Henry
Director—Robert Day
Leading Players—Nancy Kovack, David Opatoshu, Manuel Padilla

TARZAN ESCAPES (1936, MGM)
Tarzan—Johnny Weissmuller
Director—Richard Thorpe
Leading Players—Maureen O'Sullivan, John Buckler, Benita Hume

TARZAN FINDS A SON (1939, MGM)
Tarzan—Johnny Weissmuller
Boy—Johnny Sheffield
Director—Richard Thorpe
Leading Players—Maureen O'Sullivan, Ian Hunter, Henry Stephenson, Laraine Day

TARZAN GOES TO INDIA (1962, MGM)
Tarzan—Jock Mahoney
Director—John Guillermin
Leading Players—Jai, Leo Gordon, Mark Dana, Feroz Khan

TARZAN OF THE APES (1918, Silent, National Film Corp.)
Tarzan—Elmo Lincoln
Director—Scott Sidney
Leading Players—Enid Markey, Gordon Griffith, True Boardman, Kathleen Kirkham

TARZAN, THE APE MAN (1932, MGM)
Tarzan—Johnny Weissmuller
Director—W.S. Van Dyke
Leading Players—Neil Hamilton, Maureen O'Sullivan, C. Aubrey Smith, Doris Lloyd, Forrester Harvey

TARZAN, THE APE MAN (1959, MGM)
Tarzan—Denny Miller
Director—Joseph Newman
Leading Players—Joanna Barnes, Cesare Danova, Robert Douglas

TARZAN, THE APE MAN (1981, MGM/UA)
Tarzan—Miles O'Keefe
Director—John Derek
Leading Players—Bo Derek, Richard Harris, John Philip Law

TARZAN THE FEARLESS (1933, Principal)
Tarzan—Buster Crabbe
Director—Robert Hill
Leading Players—Jacqueline Wells, E. Alyn Warren, Edward Woods

TARZAN THE MAGNIFICENT (1960, GB, Paramount)
Tarzan—Gordon Scott
Director—Robert Day
Leading Players—Jock Mahoney, Betta St. John, John Carradine

TARZAN TRIUMPHS (1943, RKO)
Tarzan—Johnny Weissmuller
Director—William Thiele
Leading Players—Johnny Sheffield, Frances Gifford, Stanley
  Ridges, Sig Rumann

TARZAN'S DEADLY SILENCE (1970, National General Pictures)
Tarzan—Ron Ely
Director—Robert L. Friend
Leading Players—Manuel Padilla, Jr., Jock Mahoney, Woody
  Strode

TARZAN'S DESERT MYSTERY (1943, RKO)
Tarzan—Johnny Weissmuller
Director—William Thiele
Leading Players—Johnny Sheffield, Nancy Kelly, Otto Kruger

TARZAN'S FIGHT FOR LIFE (1958, MGM)
Tarzan—Gordon Scott
Director—Bruce Humberstone
Leading Players—Eva Brent, Rickie Sorenson, Jill Jarmyn

TARZAN'S GREATEST ADVENTURE (1959, GB, Paramount)
Tarzan—Gordon Scott
Director—John Guillermin
Leading Players—Anthony Quayle, Sara Shane, Niall MacGinnis

TARZAN'S HIDDEN JUNGLE (1955, RKO)
Tarzan—Gordon Scott
Director—Harold Schuster
Leading Players—Vera Miles, Peter Van Eyck, Don Beddoe

TARZAN'S JUNGLE REBELLION (1970, National General)
Tarzan—Ron Ely
Director—William Witney
Leading Players—Manuel Padilla, Jr., Ulla Stromstedt, Sam
  Jaffe, William Marshall

TARZAN'S MAGIC FOUNTAIN (1949, RKO)
Tarzan—Lex Barker
Director—Lee Sholem
Leading Players—Brenda Joyce, Evelyn Ankers, Albert Dekker

TARZAN'S NEW YORK ADVENTURE (1942, MGM)
Tarzan—Johnny Weissmuller
Director—Richard Thorpe
Leading Players—Maureen O'Sullivan, John Sheffield, Virginia
  Grey, Charles Bickford, Paul Kelly

TARZAN'S PERIL (1951, RKO)
Tarzan—Lex Barker
Director—Bryon Haskin
Leading Players—Virginia Huston, George Macready, Douglas
  Fowley

TARZAN'S REVENGE (1938, 20th Century Fox)
Tarzan—Glenn Morris
Director—D. Ross Lederman
Leading Players—Eleanor Holm, C. Henry Gordon, Hedda
  Hopper

TARZAN'S SAVAGE FURY (1952, RKO)
Tarzan—Lex Barker
Director—Cy Endfield
Leading Players—Dorothy Hart, Patric Knowles, Charles Korvin

TARZAN'S SECRET TREASURE (1941, MGM)
Tarzan—Johnny Weissmuller
Director—Richard Thorpe
Leading Players—Maureen O'Sullivan, John Sheffield, Reginald
  Owen, Barry Fitzgerald, Tom Conway

TARZAN'S THREE CHALLENGES (1963, MGM)
Tarzan—Jock Mahoney
Director—Robert Day
Leading Players—Woody Strode, Tsuruko Kobayashi, Earl
  Cameron

TASTE THE BLOOD OF DRACULA (1970, GB, Hammer)
Dracula—Christopher Lee
Director—Peter Sasdy
Leading Players—Geoffrey Keen, Gwen Watford, Linda Hayden

THE TAXI DANCER (1927, Silent, MGM)
Joslyn Poe—Joan Crawford
Director—Harry Millarde
Leading Players—Owen Moore, Marc MacDermott, Gertrude
  Astor

TAXI DRIVER (1976, Columbia)
Travis Bickle—Robert De Niro
Director—Martin Scorsese
Leading Players—Cybill Shepherd, Jodie Foster, Peter Boyle,
  Harvey Keitel, Albert Brooks

TAZA, SON OF COCHISE (1954, Universal)
Taza—Rock Hudson
Cochise—Jeff Chandler
Director—Douglas Sirk
Leading Players—Barbara Rush, Gregg Palmer, Bart Roberts

TEACHERS (1984, MGM/UA)
Alex—Nick Nolte
Rosenberg—Allen Garfield
Ditto—Royal Dano
Herbert—Richard Mulligan
Director—Arthur Hiller
Leading Players—JoBeth Williams, Judd Hirsch, Lee Grant,
  Ralph Macchio

TEACHER'S PET (1958, Paramount)
Jim Gannon—Clark Gable
Erica Stone—Doris Day
Director—George Seaton
Leading Players—Gig Young, Mamie Van Doren, Nick Adams

THE TECKMAN MYSTERY (1955, GB, Associated Artists)
Martin Teckman—Michael Medwin
Director—Wendy Toye
Leading Players—Margaret Leighton, John Justin, Roland
  Culver

TED AND VENUS (1991, Double Helix)
Ted Whitley—Bud Cort
Linda Turner—Kim Adams
Director—Bud Cort
Leading Players—Jim Brolin, Carol Kane, Pamella D'Pella,
  Brian Thompson, Bettye Ackerman

TEEN WITCH (1989, Trans World)
Louise—Robyn Lively
Director—Dorian Walker

Leading Players—Dan Gauthier, Joshua Miller, Caren Kaye

TEEN WOLF (1985, Atlantic)
Scott Howard—Michael J. Fox
Director—Rod Daniel
Leading Players—James Hampton, Susan Ursetti, Jerry Levine

TEEN WOLF TOO (1987, Atlantic)
Todd Howard—Jason Bateman
Director—Christopher Leitch
Leading Players—Kim Darby, John Astin, Paul Sand, James Hampton

TEENAGE BAD GIRL (1959, GB, Everest/DCA)
Janet Carr—Sylvia Syms
Director—Herbert Wilcox
Leading Players—Anna Neagle, Norman Wooland, Wilfrid Hyde-White

TEENAGE CAVEMAN (1958, American International)
The Boy—Robert Vaughn
Director—Roger Corman
Leading Players—Darrah Marshall, Leslie Bradley, Frank De Kova

TEENAGE DOLL (1957, Allied Artists)
Barbara—June Kenney
Director—Roger Corman
Leading Players—Fay Spain, John Brinkley, Collette Jackson

TEENAGE GANG DEBS (1966, Jode/CID Ltd.)
Terry—Diana Conti
Director—Sande Johnsen
Leading Players—Linda Gale, Eileen Scott, Sandra Kane, Joey Naudic

TEENAGE MILLIONAIRE (1961, UA)
Bobby Chalmers—Jimmy Clanton
Director—Lawrence F. Doheny
Leading Players—Rocky Graziano, Zasu Pitts, Diane Jergens

TEENAGE MONSTER (1958, Marquette-Howco)
Charles Cannon—Gilbert Perkins
Director—Jacques Marquette
Leading Players—Anne Gwynne, Gloria Castillo, Stuart Wade

TEENAGE MUTANT NINJA TURTLES (1990, New Line)
Raphael—Joch Pais
Michelangelo—Michelan Sisti
Donatello—Leif Tilden
Leonardo—David Forman
Director—Steve Barron
Leading Players—Judith Hoag, Elias Koteas, Michael Turney, Jay Patterson, Raymond Gerra

TEENAGE MUTANT NINJA TURTLES II: THE SECRET OF OOZE (1991, New Line)
Raphael—Kenn Troum
Michelangelo—Michelan Sisti
Donatello—Leif Tilden
Leonardo—Mark Caso
Director—Michael Pressman
Leading Players—Paige Turco, David Warner, Kevin Clark, Ernie Reyes, Jr., Francois Chan

THE TELEPHONE GIRL (1927, Silent, Lasky)
Kitty O'Brien—Madge Bellamy
Director—Herbert Brenon
Leading Players—Holbrook Blinn, Warner Baxter, May Allison

TELL ME THAT YOU LOVE ME, JUNIE MOON (1970, Paramount)
Junie Moon—Liza Minnelli
Director—Otto Preminger
Leading Players—Ken Howard, Robert Moore, James Coco

TELL THEM WILLIE BOY IS HERE (1969, Universal)
Willie Boy—Robert Blake
Director—Abraham Polonsky
Leading Players—Robert Redford, Katharine Ross, Susan Clark

A TEMPORARY VAGABOND (1920, GB, Silent, Butchers)
Dick Derelict—Henry Edwards
Director—Henry Edwards
Leading Players—Chrissie White, Stephen Ewart, Gwynne Herbert

THE TEMPTRESS (1926, Silent, MGM)
Elena—Greta Garbo
Director—Fred Niblo
Leading Players—Antonio Moreno, Roy D'Arcy, Marc MacDermott

THE TEMPTRESS (1949, GB, Ambassador)
Lady Clifford—Joan Maude
Director—Oswald Mitchell
Leading Players—Arnold Bell, Don Stannard, Shirley Quentin

TEN GENTLEMEN FROM WEST POINT (1942, 20th Century Fox)
Dawson—George Montgomery
Howard Shelton—John Sutton
Director—Henry Hathaway
Leading Players—Maureen O'Hara, Laird Cregar, John Shepperd

TEN TALL MEN (1951, Columbia)
Sgt. Mike Kincaid—Burt Lancaster
Cpl. Luis Delgado—Gilbert Roland
Cpl. Pierre Molier—Kieron Moore
Director—Willis Goldbeck
Leading Players—Jody Lawrence, George Tobias, John Dehner

THE TENDERFOOT (1932, Warner Brothers)
Peter Jones—Joe E. Brown
Director—Ray Enright
Leading Players—Ginger Rogers, Lew Cody, Vivien Oakland

A TENDERFOOT GOES WEST (1937, Hoffberg)
Pike—Russell Gleason
Director—Maurice G. O'Neil
Leading Players—Jack LaRue, Virginia Carroll, Joseph Girard

TENNESSEE CHAMP (1954, MGM)
Daniel Norson—Dewey Martin
Director—Fred M. Wilcox
Leading Players—Shelley Winters, Keenan Wynn, Earl Holliman

TENNESSEE JOHNSON (1942, MGM)
Andrew Johnson—Van Heflin
Director—William Dieterle

Leading Players—Ruth Hussey, Lionel Barrymore, Marjorie Main

TENNESSEE'S PARTNER (1916, Silent, Lasky)
Tennessee—Fannie Ward
Jack Hunter—Jack Dean
Director—George Melford
Leading Players—Charles Clary, Jessie Mae Arnold, William Bradley

TENNESSEE'S PARTNER (1955, RKO)
Tennessee—John Payne
Cowpoke—Ronald Reagan
Director—Allan Dwan
Leading Players—Rhonda Fleming, Coleen Gray, Anthony Caruso

TENTH AVENUE ANGEL (1948, MGM)
Flavia Mills—Margaret O'Brien
Director—Roy Rowland
Leading Players—Angela Lansbury, George Murphy, Phyllis Thaxter

TENTH AVENUE KID (1938, Republic)
Tommy—Tommy Ryan
Director—Bernard Vorhaus
Leading Players—Bruce Cabot, Beverly Roberts, Ben Welden

TERESA (1951, MGM)
Teresa—Pier Angeli
Director—Fred Zinnemann
Leading Players—John Ericson, Patricia Collinge, Richard Bishop

THE TERMINAL MAN (1974, Warner Brothers)
Harry Benson—George Segal
Director—Mike Hodges
Leading Players—Joan Hackett, Richard A. Dysart, Jill Clayburgh

THE TERMINATOR (1984, Orion)
Terminator—Arnold Schwarzenegger
Director—James Cameron
Leading Players—Michael Biehn, Linda Hamilton, Paul Winfield

TERMINATOR 2: JUDGMENT DAY (1991, Tri-Star)
Terminator—Arnold Schwarzenegger
Director—James Cameron
Leading Players—Linda Hamilton, Edward Furlong, Robert Patrick, Earl Boen, Joe Morton, S. Epatha Merkerson

THE TERROR (1928, Warner Brothers)
Goodman—Holmes Herbert
Director—Roy Del Ruth
Leading Players—May McAvoy, Louise Fazenda, Edward Everett Horton, Alec B. Francis

THE TERROR (1941, GB, Alliance)
Goodman—Wilfrid Lawson
Director—Richard Bird
Leading Players—Bernard Lee, Arthur Wonter, Linden Travers, Henry Oscar

TERROR FROM THE YEAR 5,000 (1958, American International)
5,000 A.D. Woman—Salome Jens
Director—Robert J. Gurney, Jr.

Leading Players—Ward Costello, Joyce Holden, John Stratton

THE TERROR OF TINY TOWN (1938, Columbia)
Haines—Little Billy
Director—Sam Newfield
Leading Players—Billy Curtis, Yvonne Moray, Billy Platt

TESHA (1929, GB, Wardour)
Tesha—Maria Corda
Director—Victor Saville
Leading Players—Jameson Thomas, Paul Cavanaugh, Mickey Brantford

TESS (1980, Great Britain/France, Columbia)
Tess Durbeyfield—Nastassja Kinski
Director—Roman Polanski
Leading Players—Leigh Lawson, Peter Firth, John Collin

TESS OF THE D'UBERVILLES (1924, Silent, Metro-Goldwyn)
Tess—Blanche Sweet
Director—Marshall Neilan
Leading Players—Conrad Nagel, Stuart Holmes, George Fawcett

TESS OF THE STORM COUNTRY (1914, Silent, Famous Players)
Tess—Mary Pickford
Director—Edwin S. Porter
Leading Players—W.R. Walters, Olive Fuller Golden, David Hartford

TESS OF THE STORM COUNTRY (1922, Silent, UA)
Tessibel Skinner—Mary Pickford
Director—James S. Robertson
Leading Players—Lloyd Hughes, Gloria Hope, David Torrence

TESS OF THE STORM COUNTRY (1932, Fox Film Corp.)
Tess Howland—Janet Gaynor
Director—Alfred Santell
Leading Players—Charles Farrell, Dudley Digges, June Clyde

TESS OF THE STORM COUNTRY (1961, 20th Century Fox)
Tess MacLean—Diane Baker
Director—Paul Guilfoyle
Leading Players—Jack Ging, Lee Philips, Archie Duncan

TEST PILOT (1938, MGM)
Jim Lane—Clark Gable
Director—Victor Fleming
Leading Players—Myrna Loy, Spencer Tracy, Lionel Barrymore, Samuel S. Hinds

TEVYA (1939, Jewish Historical Society)
Tevya—Maurice Schwartz
Director—Maurice Schwartz
Leading Players—Miriam Riselle, Rebecca Weintraub, Paula Lubelska

TEX (1982, Buena Vista)
Tex McCormick—Matt Dillon
Director—Tim Hunter
Leading Players—Jim Meltzer, Meg Tilly, Bill McKinney

THE TEXAN (1930, Paramount)
Enrique "Quico", The Llano Kid—Gary Cooper
Director—John Cromwell
Leading Players—Fay Wray, Emma Dunn, Oscar Apfel

TEXAN MEETS CALAMITY JANE (1950, Columbia)
Calamity Jane—Evelyn Ankers
Gordon Hastings—James Ellison
Director—Andre Lamb
Leading Players—Lee "Lasses" White, Ruth Whitney, Jack
Ingram

THE TEXANS (1938, Paramount)
Kirk Jordan—Randolph Scott
Director—James Hogan
Leading Players—Joan Bennett, May Robson, Walter Brennan,
Robert Cummings

TEXAS BAD MAN (1953, Allied Artists)
Gil—Frank Ferguson
Director—Lewis D. Collins
Leading Players—Wayne Morris, Elaine Riley, Sheb Wooley

TEXAS LADY (1955, RKO)
Prudence Webb—Claudette Colbert
Director—Tim Whelan
Leading Players—Barry Sullivan, Greg Walcott, James Bell

THE TEXAS MARSHAL (1941, Producers Releasing Corp.)
Tim Rand—Tim McCoy
Director—Peter Stewart
Leading Players—Kay Leslie, Karl Hackett, Edward Piel, Sr.

THE TEXAS RANGERS (1936, Paramount)
Jim Hawkins—Fred MacMurray
Wahoo Jones—Jack Oakie
Director—King Vidor
Leading Players—Jean Parker, Lloyd Nolan, Edward Ellis

THE TEXAS RANGERS (1951, Columbia)
Johnny Carver—George Montgomery
Director—Phil Karlson
Leading Players—Gale Storm, Jerome Courtland, Noah Beery,
Jr.

TEXAS RANGERS RIDE AGAIN (1940, Paramount)
Jim Kingston—John Howard
Mace Townsley—Broderick Crawford
Director—James Hogan
Leading Players—Ellen Drew, Akim Tamiroff, May Robson,
Anthony Quinn

THE TEXICAN (1966, Columbia)
Jess Carlin—Audie Murphy
Director—Lesley Selander
Leading Players—Broderick Crawford, Diana Lorys, Aldo
Sambrell

THANK EVANS (1938, GB, Warner Brothers)
Evans—Max Miller
Director—Roy William Neill
Leading Players—Hal Walters, Polly Ward, Albert Whelan

THANK YOU, JEEVES (1936, 20th Century Fox)
Jeeves—Arthur Treacher
Director—Arthur Greville Collins
Leading Players—Virginia Field, David Niven, Lester Matthews

THANK YOU MR. MOTO (1937, 20th Century Fox)
Mr. Moto—Peter Lorre
Director—Norman Foster

Leading Players—Thomas Beck, Pauline Frederick, Jayne Regan

THAT BRENNAN GIRL (1946, Republic)
Ziggy Brennan—Mona Freeman
Director—Alfred Santell
Leading Players—James Dunn, William Marshall, June Duprez

THAT CERTAIN WOMAN (1937, Warner Brothers)
Mary Donnell—Bette Davis
Director—Edmund Goulding
Leading Players—Henry Fonda, Ian Hunter, Anita Louise

THAT FORSYTE WOMAN (1949, MGM)
Irene Forsyte—Greer Garson
Director—Compton Bennett
Leading Players—Errol Flynn, Walter Pidgeon, Robert Young,
Janet Leigh

THAT GIRL FROM PARIS (1937, RKO)
Nikki Martin—Lily Pons
Director—Leigh Jason
Leading Players—Gene Raymond, Jack Oakie, Herman Bing

THAT HAGEN GIRL (1947, Warner Brothers)
Mary Hagen—Shirley Temple
Director—Peter Godfrey
Leading Players—Ronald Reagan, Rory Calhoun, Lois Maxwell

THAT HAMILTON WOMAN (1941, UA)
Emma Hart Hamilton—Vivien Leigh
Director—Alexander Korda
Leading Players—Laurence Olivier, Alan Mowbray, Sara Allgood,
Gladys Cooper

THAT KIND OF GIRL (1963, GB, Topaz-IA)
Eva—Margaret-Rose Keil
Director—Gerry O'Hara
Leading Players—David Weston, Linda Marlowe, Peter Burton

THAT KIND OF WOMAN (1959, Paramount)
Kay—Sophia Loren
Director—Sidney Lumet
Leading Players—Tab Hunter, George Sanders, Jack Warden

THAT LADY (1955, 20th Century Fox)
Ana de Mendoza—Olivia de Havilland
Director—Terence Young
Leading Players—Gilbert Roland, Paul Scofield, Francoise Rosay

THAT LADY IN ERMINE (1948, 20th Century Fox)
Francesca—Betty Grable
Director—Ernest Lubitsch (Otto Preminger, uncredited)
Leading Players—Douglas Fairbanks, Jr., Cesar Romero, Walter
Abel, Reginald Gardiner

THAT MAN BOLT (1973, Universal)
Jefferson Bolt—Fred Williamson
Director—Henry Levin
Leading Players—Byron Webster, Miko Mayama, Teresa Graves

THAT MAN FROM TANGIER (1953, UA)
Henri—Nils Asther
Director—Robert Elwyn
Leading Players—Roland Young, Nancy Coleman, Margaret
Wycherly

THAT MAN'S HERE AGAIN (1937, Warner Brothers)
Thomas J. Jesse—Hugh Herbert
Director—Louis King
Leading Players—Mary Maguire, Tom Brown, Joseph King

THAT NAZTY NUISANCE (1943, UA)
Adolf Hitler—Bobby Watson
Director—Glenn Tryon
Leading Players—Joe Devlin, Johnny Arthur, Jean Porter

THAT OTHER WOMAN (1942, 20th Century Fox)
Emily—Virginia Gilmore
Director—Ray McCarey
Leading Players—James Ellison, Dan Duryea, Janice Carter

"THAT ROYLE GIRL" (1925, Silent, Paramount)
Joan Daisy Royle—Carol Dempster
Director—D.W. Griffith
Leading Players—W.C. Fields, James Kirkwood, Harrison Ford

THAT'S MY BABY (1926, Silent, Paramount)
Alan Boyd—Douglas MacLean
The Baby—Harry Earles
Director—William Beaudine
Leading Players—Margaret Morris, Claude Gillingwater, Eugenie Forde

THAT'S MY BOY (1932, Columbia)
Tommy—Richard Cromwell
Director—Roy William Neill
Leading Players—Dorothy Jordan, Mae Marsh, Arthur Stone

THAT'S MY BOY (1951, Paramount)
"Junior" Jackson—Jerry Lewis
"Jarring Jack" Jackson—Eddie Mayehoff
Director—Hal Walker
Leading Players—Dean Martin, Ruth Hussey, Marion Marshall

THAT'S MY GAL (1947, Republic)
Natalie Adams—Lynne Roberts
Director—George Blair
Leading Players—Donald Barry, Pinky Lee, Frank Jenks

THAT'S MY MAN (1947, Republic)
Joe Grange—Don Ameche
Ronnie Grange—Catherine McLeod
Director—Frank Borzage
Leading Players—Roscoe Karns, John Ridgely, Kitty Irish

THEIR BIG MOMENT (1934, RKO)
Tillie Whim—Zasu Pitts
Bill—Slim Summerville
Director—James Cruze
Leading Players—Julie Haydon, Ralph Morgan, William Gaxton

THEIR OWN DESIRE (1929, MGM)
Lally Marlett—Norma Shearer
Jack—Robert Montgomery
Director—E. Mason Hopper
Leading Players—Belle Bennett, Lewis Stone, Helen Millard

THELMA (1922, Silent, Film Booking Office of America)
Thelma Guildmar—Jane Novak
Director—Chester Bennett
Leading Players—Barbara Tennant, Gordon Mullen, Bert Sprotte

THELMA AND LOUISE (1991, Pathe Entertainment)
Thelma—Geena Davis
Louise—Susan Sarandon
Director—Ridley Scott
Leading Players—Harvey Keitel, Michael Madsen, Christopher McDonald, Brad Pitt

THEODORA GOES WILD (1936, Columbia)
Theodora Lynn—Irene Dunne
Director—Richard Boleslawski
Leading Players—Melvyn Douglas, Thomas Mitchell, Thurston Hall

THERE GOES THE BRIDE (1933, GB, Gaumont)
Annette Marquand—Jessie Matthews
Director—Albert de Courville
Leading Players—Owen Nares, Carol Goodner, Charles Carson

THERE GOES THE BRIDE (1980, GB, Vanguard)
Judy Westeby—Toria Fuller
Director—Terence Marcel
Leading Players—Tom Smothers, Twiggy, Martin Balsam

THERE GOES THE GROOM (1937, RKO)
Dick Mathews—Burgess Meredith
Director—Joseph Santley
Leading Players—Ann Sothern, Mary Boland, Onslow Stevens

THERE WAS A CROOKED MAN (1962, GB, UA)
McKillup—Andrew Cruickshank
Director—Stuart Burge
Leading Players—Norman Wisdom, Alfred Marks, Reginald Beckwith

THERE WAS A CROOKED MAN (1970, Warner Brothers)
Woodward Lopeman—Henry Fonda
Director—Joseph L. Mankiewicz
Leading Players—Kirk Douglas, Hume Cronyn, Warren Oates, Burgess Meredith, Arthur O'Connell

THERE WAS A YOUNG LADY (1953, GB, Butchers)
Elizabeth Foster—Dulcie Gray
Director—Lawrence Huntington
Leading Players—Michael Denison, Sydney Tafler, Geraldine McEwen

THERE WAS A YOUNG MAN (1937, GB, Fox British)
George Peabody—Oliver Wakefield
Director—Albert Parker
Leading Players—Nancy O'Neil, Clifford Heatherley, Robert Nainby

THERE'S A GIRL IN MY HEART (1949, Allied Artists)
Claire Adamson—Elyse Knox
Director—Arthur Dreifuss
Leading Players—Lee Bowman, Gloria Jean, Peggy Ryan

THERE'S A GIRL IN MY SOUP (1970, GB, Columbia)
Marion—Goldie Hawn
Director—Roy Boulting
Leading Players—Peter Sellers, Tony Britton, Nicky Henson

THERE'S ALWAYS A WOMAN (1938, Columbia)
Sally Reardon—Joan Blondell
Director—Alexander Hall
Leading Players—Melvyn Douglas, Mary Astor, Frances Drake

THERE'S SOMETHING ABOUT A SOLDIER (1943, Columbia)
Wally Williams—Tom Neal
Director—Alfred E. Green
Leading Players—Evelyn Keyes, Bruce Bennett, John Hubbard

THERE'S THAT WOMAN AGAIN (1938, Columbia)
Sally Reardon—Virginia Bruce
Director—Alexander Hall
Leading Players—Melvyn Douglas, Margaret Lindsay, Stanley Ridges

THERESE AND ISABELLE (1968, Audobon Films)
Therese—Essy Persson
Isabelle—Anna Gael
Director—Radley H. Metzger
Leading Players—Barbara Laage, Anne Vernon, Maurice Teynac

THESE GLAMOUR GIRLS (1939, MGM)
Jane Thomas—Lana Turner
Director—S. Sylvan Simon
Leading Players—Lew Ayres, Tom Brown, Richard Carlson, Jane Bryan, Anita Louise, Ann Rutherford

THESE THREE (1936, UA)
Martha Dobie—Miriam Hopkins
Karen Wright—Merle Oberon
Dr. Joseph Cardin—Joel McCrea
Director—William Wyler
Leading Players—Catherine Doucet, Alma Kruger, Bonita Granville, Marcia Mae Jones

THEY ALL KISSED THE BRIDE (1942, Columbia)
Margaret J. Drew—Joan Crawford
Director—Alexander Hall
Leading Players—Melvyn Douglas, Roland Young, Billie Burke, Allen Jenkins

THEY CALL ME BRUCE (1982, Film Ventures)
Bruce Won—Johnny Yune
Director—Elliott Hong
Leading Players—Ralph Mauro, Pam Huntington, Margaux Hemingway

THEY CALL ME MACHO WOMAN (1990, Troma Team)
Susan—Debra Sweaney
Director—Patrick G. Donahue
Leading Players—Brian Oldfield, Sean P. Donahue, Mike Donahue

THEY CALL ME MR. TIBBS (1970, UA)
Virgil Tibbs—Sidney Poitier
Director—Gordon Douglas
Leading Players—Martin Landau, Barbara McNair, Anthony Zerbe

THEY CAME TO CONDURA (1959, Columbia)
Major Thomas Thorn—Gary Cooper
Adelaide Geary—Rita Hayworth
Director—Robert Rossen
Leading Players—Van Heflin, Tab Hunter, Richard Conte, Michael Callan, Dick York, Robert Keith

THEY CAN'T HANG ME (1955, GB, British Lion)
Robert Pitt—Andre Morell
Director—Val Guest

Leading Players—Terence Morgan, Yolande Donlan, Ursula Howells

THEY DARE NOT LOVE (1941, Columbia)
Prince Kurt von Rotenberg—George Brent
Marta Keller—Martha Scott
Director—James Whale
Leading Players—Paul Lukas, Egon Brecher, Roman Bohnen

THEY DIED WITH THEIR BOOTS ON (1942, Warner Brothers)
George Armstrong Custer—Errol Flynn
Director—Raoul Walsh
Leading Players—Olivia de Havilland, Arthur Kennedy, Charles Grapewin, Gene Lockhart, Stanley Ridges

THEY DRIVE BY NIGHT (1938, GB, Warner Brothers)
Shorty Matthews—Emlyn Williams
Molly O'Neill—Anna Konstam
Director—Arthur Woods
Leading Players—Ernest Thesiger, Allan Jeayes, Anthony Holles

THEY DRIVE BY NIGHT (1940, Warner Brothers)
Joe Fabrini—George Raft
Paul Fabrini—Humphrey Bogart
Director—Raoul Walsh
Leading Players—Ann Sheridan, Ida Lupino, Gale Page, Alan Hale

THEY GAVE HIM A GUN (1937, MGM)
Jimmy David—Franchot Tone
Director—W. S. Van Dyke II
Leading Players—Spencer Tracy, Gladys George, Edgar Dearing

THEY GOT ME COVERED (1943, RKO)
Robert Kittredge—Bob Hope
Director—David Butler
Leading Players—Dorothy Lamour, Lenore Aubert, Otto Preminger, Eduardo Ciannelli

THEY HAD TO SEE PARIS (1929, Fox Film Corp.)
Pike Peters—Will Rogers
Mrs. Peters—Irene Rich
Director—Frank Borzage
Leading Players—Marguerite Churchill, Owen Davis, Jr., Fifi D'Orsay

THEY JUST HAD TO GET MARRIED (1933, Universal)
Sam Sutton—Slim Summerville
Molly Hull—Zasu Pitts
Director—Edward Ludwig
Leading Players—Roland Young, Verree Teasdale, Fifi D'Orsay

THEY KNEW WHAT THEY WANTED (1940, RKO)
Amy—Carole Lombard
Tony—Charles Laughton
Director—Garson Kanin
Leading Players—William Gargan, Harry Carey, Frank Fay

THEY LEARNED ABOUT WOMEN (1930, MGM)
Jack—Joseph T. Schenck
Jerry—Gus Van
Directors—Jack Conway and Sam Wood
Leading Players—Bessie Love, Mary Doran, J.C. Nugent

THEY LIVE BY NIGHT (1949, RKO)
Keechie—Cathy O'Donnell

Bowie—Farley Granger
Director—Nicholas Ray
Leading Players—Howard Da Silva, Jay C. Flippen, Helen Craig

THEY MADE HER A SPY (1939, RKO)
Irene Eaton—Sally Eilers
Director—Jack Hively
Leading Players—Allen Lane, Frank M. Thomas, Fritz Leiber

THEY MADE ME A CRIMINAL (1939, Warner Brothers)
Johnny Bradfield "Jack Dorney"—John Garfield
Director—Busby Berkeley
Leading Players—Gloria Dickson, Claude Rains, Ann Sheridan, May Robson, Billy Halop

THEY MADE ME A KILLER (1946, Paramount)
Tom Durling—Robert Lowery
Director—William C. Thomas
Leading Players—Barbara Britton, Frank Albertson, Lola Lane

THEY MET IN A TAXI (1936, Columbia)
Jimmy—Chester Morris
Mary—Fay Wray
Director—Alfred E. Green
Leading Players—Lionel Stander, Raymond Walburn, Henry Mollison

THEY MET IN ARGENTINA (1941, RKO)
Lolita—Maureen O'Hara
Tim Kelly—James Ellison
Directors—Leslie Goodwins and Jack Hively
Leading Players—Alberto Vila, Buddy Ebsen, Robert Barrat

THEY MET IN BOMBAY (1941, MGM)
Gerald Meldrick—Clark Gable
Anya Von Duren—Rosalind Russell
Director—Clarence Brown
Leading Players—Peter Lorre, Jesse Ralph, Reginald Owen

THEY MET IN THE DARK (1945, GB, Excelsior/English Films)
Cmdr. Richard Heritage—James Mason
Laura Verity—Joyce Howard
Director—Karel Lamac
Leading Players—Tom Walls, Phyllis Stanley, Edward Rigby

THEY MIGHT BE GIANTS (1971, Universal)
Dr. Mildred Watson—Joanne Woodward
Justin Playfair "Sherlock Holmes"—George C. Scott
Director—Anthony Harvey
Leading Players—Jack Gilford, Lester Rawlins, Rue McClanahan

THEY STILL CALL ME BRUCE (1987, Ji Hee-Pandra/Shapiro)
Bruce Won—Johnny Yune
Directors—Johnny Yune and James Orr
Leading Players—Robert Guillaume, Pat Paulsen, David Mendenhall

THEY WANTED TO MARRY (1937, RKO)
Sheila Hunter—Betty Furness
Jim Tyler—Gordon Jones
Director—Lew Landers
Leading Players—E.E. Clive, Patsy Lee Parsons, Henry Kolker

THEY WERE SISTERS (1945, GB, Universal)
Lucy—Phyllis Calvert
Vera—Anne Crawford

Charlotte—Dulcie Gray
Director—Arthur Crabtree
Leading Players—James Mason, Hugh Sinclair, Peter Murray Hill

THEY WON'T BELIEVE ME (1947, RKO)
Larry Ballentine—Robert Young
Director—Irving Pichel
Leading Players—Susan Hayward, Jane Greer, Rita Johnson

THEY'RE PLAYING WITH FIRE (1984, New World)
Diane—Sybil Danning
Jay—Eric Brown
Director—Howard Avedis
Leading Players—Andrew Prine, Paul Clemens, K.T. Stevens

THE THIEF (1952, UA)
Allan Fields—Ray Milland
Director—Russell Rouse
Leading Players—Martin Gabel, Rita Gam, Harry Bronson

THIEF (1981, UA)
Frank—James Caan
Director—Michael Mann
Leading Players—Tuesday Weld, Willie Nelson, James Belushi

THE THIEF OF BAGDAD (1924, Silent, UA)
The Thief of Bagdad—Douglas Fairbanks
Director—Raoul Walsh
Leading Players—Snitz Edwards, Charles Belcher, Julianne Johnston, Anna May Wong

THE THIEF OF BAGHDAD (1940, GB, London Films)
Abu—Sabu
Directors—Ludwig Berger, Michael Powell, Tim Whelan, Zoltan Korda and William Cameron Menzies
Leading Players—Conrad Veidt, June Duprez, John Justin, Rex Ingram, Miles Malleson

THIEF OF DAMASCUS (1952, Columbia)
Abu Andar—Paul Henreid
Director—Will Jason
Leading Players—John Sutton, Jeff Donnell, Lon Chaney, Jr.

THIEF OF HEARTS (1985, Paramount)
Scott Muller—Steven Bauer
Director—Douglas Day Stewart
Leading Players—Barbara Williams, John Gatz, David Caruso

THE THIEF OF VENICE (1952, 20th Century Fox)
Alfiere Lorenzo Contarini—Paul Christian
Director—John Brahm
Leading Players—Maria Montez, Massimo Serato, Faye Marlowe

THE THIEF WHO CAME TO DINNER (1973, Warner Brothers)
Webster—Ryan O'Neal
Director—Bud Yorkin
Leading Players—Jacqueline Bisset, Warren Oates, Jill Clayburgh

THIEVES LIKE US (1974, UA)
Bowie—David Carradine
Keechie—Shelley Duvall
Director—Robert Altman
Leading Players—John Schuck, Bert Remsen, Louise Fletcher

THE THIN MAN (1934, MGM)
Clyde Wynant—Edward Ellis
Director—W.S. Van Dyke
Leading Players—William Powell, Myrna Loy, Maureen O'Sullivan, Nat Pendleton, Porter Hall, Edward Brophy

THE THIN MAN GOES HOME (1944, MGM)
Nick Charles—William Powell
Director—Richard Thorpe
Leading Players—Myrna Loy, Lucile Watson, Gloria De Haven, Anne Revere

THE THING (1951, RKO)
The Thing—James Arness
Director—Christian Nyby (Howard Hawks, uncredited)
Leading Players—Kenneth Tobey, Margaret Sheridan, Robert Cornthwaite

THE THING WITH TWO HEADS (1972, American International)
Dr. Maxwell Kirshner—Ray Milland
Jack Moss—Rosey Grier
Director—Lee Frost
Leading Players—Don Marshall, Roger Perry, Kathy Baumann

THINK FAST MR. MOTO (1937, 20th Century Fox)
Mr. Moto—Peter Lorre
Director—Norman Foster
Leading Players—Virginia Field, Thomas Beck, Sig Rumann

THE THIRD MAN (1950, GB, London Films)
Harry Lime—Orson Welles
Director—Carol Reed
Leading Players—Joseph Cotten, Alida Valli, Trevor Howard

THIRD MAN ON THE MOUNTAIN (1959, Buena Vista)
Rudi Matt—James MacArthur
Director—Ken Annakin
Leading Players—Michael Rennie, Janet Munro, James Donald

THE THIRD VOICE (1960, 20th Century Fox)
The Voice—Edmond O'Brien
Director—Hubert Cornfield
Leading Players—Julie London, Laraine Day, Olga San Juan

THIRTEEN WOMEN (1932, RKO)
Laura Stanhope—Irene Dunne
Ursula Georgi—Myrna Loy
Director—George Archainbaud
Leading Players—Ricardo Cortez, Jill Esmond, Florence Eldredge, Kay Johnson, Julie Haydon, Harriett Hagman, Mary Duncan, Peg Entwistle, Elsie Prescott, Phyllis Fraser, Betty Furness
Note: There are thirteen women, but we have chosen only to concentrate on Dunne and Loy, the major female stars of the film. Note Peg Entwhistle was the starlet who leaped to her death from the HOLLYWOODLAND sign.

THIRTY-DAY PRINCESS (1934, Parmaount)
Nancy Lane—Sylvia Sidney
Director—Marion Gering
Leading Players—Cary Grant, Edward Arnold, Henry Stephenson

THE THIRTY FOOT BRIDE OF CANDY ROCK (1959, Columbia)
Emmy Lou Raven—Dorothy Provine
Director—Sidney Miller
Leading Players—Lou Costello, Gale Gordan, Jimmy Conlin

THIS GUN FOR HIRE (1942, Paramount)
Philip Raven—Alan Ladd
Director—Frank Tuttle
Leading Players—Veronica Lake, Robert Preston, Laird Cregar

THIS LAND IS MINE (1943, RKO)
Arthur Lory—Charles Laughton
Director—Jean Renoir
Leading Players—Maureen O'Hara, George Sanders, Walter Slezak, Kent Smith, Una O'Connor

THIS LOVE OF OURS (1945, Universal)
Karin Touzac—Merle Oberon
Michel Touzac—Charles Korvin
Director—William Dieterle
Leading Players—Claude Rains, Carl Esmond, Sue England

THIS MAN IN PARIS (1939, GB, Paramount)
Simon Drake—Barry K. Barnes
Director—David MacDonald
Leading Players—Valerie Hobson, Alastair Sim, Jacques Max Michel

THIS MAN IS MINE (1934, RKO)
Toni Dunlap—Irene Dunne
Jim Dunlap—Ralph Bellamy
Director—John Cromwell
Leading Players—Constance Cummings, Kay Johnson, Charles Starrett

THIS MAN IS MINE (1946, GB, Columbia British)
Millie—Glynis Johns
Bill McKenzie—Hugh McDermott
Director—Marcel Varnel
Leading Players—Tom Walls, Jeanne de Casalis, Nova Pilbeam

THIS MAN IS NEWS (1939, GB, Paramount)
Simon Drake—Barry K. Barnes
Director—David MacDonald
Leading Players—Valerie Hobson, Alastair Sim, John Warwick

THIS PROPERTY IS CONDEMNED (1966, Paramount)
Alva Starr—Natalie Wood
Director—Sydney Pollack
Leading Players—Robert Redford, Charles Bronson, Kate Reid, Mary Badham, Alan Baxter

THIS WAS A WOMAN (1949, GB, 20th Century Fox)
Sylvia Russell—Sonia Dresdel
Director—Tim Whelan
Leading Players—Walter Fitzgerald, Emrys Jones, Barbara White

THIS WOMAN IS DANGEROUS (1952, Warner Brothers)
Beth Austin—Joan Crawford
Director—Felix Feist
Leading Players—Dennis Morgan, David Brian, Richard Webb

THIS WOMAN IS MINE (1941, Universal)
Robert Stevens—Franchot Tone
Julie Morgan—Carol Bruce
Director—Frank Lloyd
Leading Players—John Carroll, Walter Brennan, Nigel Bruce

THE THOMAS CROWN AFFAIR (1968, UA)
Thomas Crown—Steve McQueen
Director—Norman Jewison
Leading Players—Faye Dunaway, Paul Burke, Jack Weston, Biff McGuire, Yaphet Kotto

THOMASINE AND BUSHROD (1974, Columbia)
Bushrod—Max Julien
Thomasine—Vonetta McGee
Director—Gordon Parks, Jr.
Leading Players—George Murdock, Glynn Turman, Juanita Moore

THOROUGHLY MODERN MILLIE (1967, Universal)
Millie Dillmount—Julie Andrews
Director—George Roy Hill
Leading Players—Mary Tyler Moore, Carol Channing, James Fox

THOSE CALLOWAYS (1964, Buena Vista)
Cam Calloway—Brian Keith
Liddy Calloway—Vera Miles
Bucky Calloway—Brandon De Wilde
Director—Norman Tokar
Leading Players—Walter Brennan, Ed Wynn, Linda Evans

THOSE DARING YOUNG MEN IN THEIR JAUNTY JALOPIES
(1969, Great Britain/ France/Italy, Paramount)
Chester Schofield—Tony Curtis
Sir Cuthbert Ware-Armitage—Terry-Thomas
Major Digby Dawlish—Peter Cook
Angelo Pincelli—Walter Chiari
Director—Ken Annakin
Leading Players—Susan Hampshire, Eric Sykes, Gert Frobe, Dudley Moore, Jack Hawkins, Bourvil

THOSE LIPS, THOSE EYES (1980, UA)
Ramona—Glynnis O'Connor
Director—Michael Pressman
Leading Players—Frank Langella, Tom Hulce, Kevin McCarthy

THOSE MAGNIFICENT MEN IN THEIR FLYING MACHINES
(1965, GB, 20th Century Fox)
Orvil Newton—Stuart Whitman
Richard Mays—James Fox
Count Emilio Ponticelli—Alberto Sordi
Pierre Dubois—Jean-Pierre Cassel
Col. Manfred von Holstein—Gert Frobe
Sir Percival Ware-Armitage—Terry-Thomas
Yamamoto—Yujiro Ishihara
Director—Ken Annakin
Leading Players—Sarah Miles, Robert Morley, Eric Sykes, Irina Demick, Tony Hancock

THOSE REDHEADS FROM SEATTLE (1953, Paramount)
Kathie Edmonds—Rhonda Fleming
Pat Edmonds—Teresa Brewer
Neil Edmonds—Kay Bell
Connie Edmonds—Cynthia Bell
Director—Lewis W. Foster
Leading Players—Gene Barry, Agnes Moorehead, Guy Mitchell

THOSE THREE FRENCH GIRLS (1930, MGM)
Charmaine—Fifi D'Orsay
Diane—Yola d'Avril
Madelon—Sandra Ravel

Director—Harry Beaumont
Leading Players—Reginald Denny, Cliff Edwards, George Grossmith

THREE (1969, GB, UA)
Marty—Charlotte Rampling
Bert—Robie Porter
Taylor—Sam Waterston
Director—James Salter
Leading players—Pascale Roberts, Edina Ronay, Gillian Hills

THREE AMIGOS (1986, Orion)
Dusty Bottoms—Chevy Chase
Lucky Day—Steve Martin
Ned Nederlander—Martin Short
Director—John Landis
Leading Players—Patrice Martinez, Alfonso Arau, Tony Plana

THREE BAD SISTERS (1956, UA)
Vicki—Marla English
Valerie—Kathleen Hughes
Lorna—Sara Shane
Director—Gilbert L. Kay
Leading Players—John Bromfield, Jess Barker, Madge Kennedy

THREE BLIND MICE (1938, 20th Century Fox)
Pamela Charters—Loretta Young
Moira Charters—Marjorie Weaver
Elizabeth Charters—Pauline Moore
Director—William A. Seiter
Leading Players—Joel McCrea, David Niven, Stuart Erwin, Binnie Barnes

THREE BLONDES IN HIS LIFE (1961, Cinema Associates)
Duke Wallace—Jock Mahoney
Helen Fortner—Greta Thyssen
Martha Carr—Valerie Porter
Lois Collins—Elaine Edwards
Director—Leon Chooluck
Leading Players—Anthony Dexter, Jesse White

THREE BRAVE MEN (1957, 20th Century Fox)
Joe Di Marco—Ray Milland
Bernie Goldsmith—Ernest Borgnine
Rogers—Dean Jagger
Director—Philip Dunne
Leading Players—Frank Lovejoy, Nina Foch, Virginia Christine

THREE COMRADES (1938, MGM)
Erich Lohkamp—Robert Taylor
Otto Koster—Franchot Tone
Gottfried Lenz—Robert Young
Director—Frank Borzage
Leading Players—Margaret Sullavan, Guy Kibbee, Lionel Atwill

THREE DARING DAUGHTERS (1948, MGM)
Tess Morgan—Jane Powell
Alix Morgan—Mary Eleanor Donahue
Ilka Morgan—Ann E. Todd
Director—Fred M. Wilcox
Leading Players—Jeanette MacDonald, Jose Iturbi, Edward Arnold

THREE DESPERATE MEN (1951, Lippert)
Tom Denton—Preston Foster

Fred Denton—Jim Davis
Matt Denton—Ross Latimer
Director—Sam Newfield
Leading Players—Virginia Grey, William Haade, Monte Blue

THE THREE FACES OF EVE (1957, 20th Century Fox)
Eve—Joanne Woodward
Director—Nunnally Johnson
Leading Players—David Wayne, Lee J. Cobb, Edwin Jerome

THREE FOR BEDROOM C (1952, Warner Brothers)
Ann Haven—Gloria Swanson
Oli J. Thrumm—James Warren
Barbara Haven—Janine Perreau
Director—Milton H. Bren
Leading Players—Fred Clark, Hans Conreid, Steve Brodie

THREE FOR THE ROAD (1987, New Century-Vista)
Paul Tracy—Charlie Sheen
Robin Kitteridge—Kerri Green
Tommy "T.S."—Alan Ruck
Director—B.W.L. Norton
Leading Players—Sally Kellerman, Blair Tefkin, Raymond J. Barry

THREE FUGITIVES (1989, Buena Vista)
Daniel Lucas—Nick Nolte
Ned Perry—Martin Short
Meg Perry—Sarah Rowland Doroff
Director—Francis Veber
Leading Players—James Earl Jones, Alan Ruck, Kenneth McMillan

THREE GIRLS ABOUT TOWN (1941, Columbia)
Hope Banner—Joan Blondell
Faith Banner—Binnie Barnes
Charity Banner—Janet Blair
Director—Leigh Jason
Leading Players—Robert Benchley, John Howard, Hugh O'Connell

THREE GODFATHERS (1936, MGM)
Bob—Chester Morris
Doc—Lewis Stone
Gus—Walter Brennan
Director—Richard Boleslawski
Leading Players—Irene Hervey, Sidney Toler, Dorothy Tree

THE THREE GODFATHERS (1948, MGM)
Robert Marmaduke Hightower—John Wayne
Pedro "Pete" Fuerte—Pedro Armendariz
William Kearney "The Abilene Kid"—Harry Carey, Jr.
Director—John Ford
Leading Players—Ward Bond, Mildred Natwick, Charles Halton

THREE GUYS NAMED MIKE (1951, MGM)
Michael Lawrence—Van Johnson
Mike Jamison—Howard Keel
Mike Tracy—Barry Sullivan
Director—Charles Walters
Leading Players—Jane Wyman, Phyllis Kirk, Anne Sargent

THREE HATS FOR LISA (1965, GB, Warner Brothers-Pathe)
Lisa Milan—Sophie Hardy
Director—Sidney Hayers

Leading Players—Joe Brown, Sophie Hardy, Sidney James

THREE HEARTS FOR JULIA (1943, MGM)
Julia Seabrook—Ann Sothern
Director—Richard Thorpe
Leading Players—Melvyn Douglas, Lee Bowman, Felix Bressart

THREE HUSBANDS (1950, UA)
Dan McCabe—Howard Da Silva
Arthur Evans—Shepperd Strudwick
Kenneth Whittaker—Robert Karnes
Director—Irving Reis
Leading Players—Eve Arden, Ruth Warrick, Vanessa Brown, Emlyn Williams

THREE IN THE ATTIC (1968, American International)
Tobey Clinton—Yvette Mimieux
Eulice—Judy Pace
Jan—Maggie Thrett
Director—Richard Wilson
Leading Players—Christopher Jones, Nan Martin, Reva Rose

THREE KIDS AND A QUEEN (1935, Universal)
Mary Jane Baxter—May Robson
Blackie—Frankie Darro
Flash—Billy Benedict
Doc—Billy Burrud
Director—Edward Ludwig
Leading Players—Charlotte Henry, Henry Armetta, Herman Bing

THREE LEGIONNAIRES (1937, General)
Chuck—Robert Armstrong
Jimmy—Lyle Talbot
U.S. Grant—Donald Meek
Director—Hamilton McFadden
Leading Players—Fifi D'Orsay, Anne Nagel, Stanley Fields

THREE LITTLE GIRLS IN BLUE (1946, 20th Century Fox)
Pam—June Haver
Liz—Vivian Blaine
Myra—Vera Ellen
Director—H. Bruce Humberstone
Leading Players—George Montgomery, Celeste Holm, Frank Latimore

THREE LITTLE SISTERS (1944, Republic)
Sue Scott—Mary Lee
Hallie Scott—Ruth Terry
Lily Scott—Cheryl Walker
Director—Joseph Santley
Leading Players—William Terry, Jackie Moran, Charles Arnt

THREE LIVE GHOSTS (1922, Silent, Paramount)
Billy Foster—Norman Kelly
Jimmy Grubbins—Edmund Goulding
Spoofy—Cyril Chadwick
Director—George Fitzmaurice
Leading Players—Anna Q. Nilsson, Claire Greet, John Miltern

THREE LIVE GHOSTS (1929, UA)
Jimmie Grubbins—Charles McNaughton
William Foster—Robert Montgomery
Spoofy—Claud Allister
Director—Thornton Freeland

Leading Players—Beryl Mercer, Hilda Vaughn, Harry Stubbs

THREE LIVE GHOSTS (1935, MGM)
Billy Foster—Richard Arlen
Spoofy—Claude Allister
Jimmie Grubbins—Charles McNaughton
Director—H. Bruce Humberstone
Leading Players—Beryl Mercer, Cecila Parker, Dudley Digges

THREE LOVES HAS NANCY (1938, MGM)
Nancy Briggs—Janet Gaynor
Director—Richard Thorpe
Leading Players—Robert Montgomery, Franchot Tone, Guy Kibbee

THREE MARRIED MEN (1936, Paramount)
Jeff Mullins—Lynne Overman
Bill Mullins—William Frawley
Peter Cary—Roscoe Karns
Director—Eddie Buzzell
Leading Players—Mary Brian, George Barbier, Marjorie Gateson

THREE MEN AND A BABY (1987, Buena Vista)
Peter Mitchell—Tom Selleck
Michael Kellam—Steve Guttenberg
Jack Holden—Ted Danson
Mary, the Baby—Lisa and Michelle Blair
Director—Leonard Nimoy
Leading Players—Nancy Travis, Margaret Colin, Celeste Holm

THREE MEN AND A LITTLE LADY (1990, Buena Vista/Touchstone)
Peter Mitchell—Tom Selleck
Michael Kellam—Steve Guttenberg
Jack Holden—Ted Danson
Mary—Robin Weisman
Director—Emile Ardolino
Leading Players—Nancy Travis, Christopher Cazenove, Sheila Hancock, Fiona Shaw

THREE MEN IN A BOAT (1933, GB, Associate British Films)
Harris—William Austin
George—Edmond Breon
Jimmy—Billy Milton
Director—Graham Cutts
Leading Players—Davy Burnaby, Iris March, Griffith Humphreys

THREE MEN IN A BOAT (1958, GB, Romulus/Valiant)
George—Laurence Harvey
Harris—Jimmy Edwards
J—David Tomlinson
Director—Ken Annakin
Leading Players—Shirley Eaton, Jill Ireland, Lisa Gaston

THREE MEN IN WHITE (1944, MGM)
Dr. Leonard Gillespie—Lionel Barrymore
Dr. Randall Adams—Van Johnson
Dr. Lee Wong How—Keye Luke
Director—Willis Goldbeck
Leading Players—Marilyn Maxwell, Ava Gardner, Alma Kruger

THREE MEN ON A HORSE (1936, Warner Brothers)
Patsy—Sam Levene
Frankie—Teddy Hart
Harry—Edgar Kennedy

Director—Mervyn LeRoy
Leading Players—Frank McHugh, Joan Blondell, Carol Hughes

THE THREE MESQUITEERS (1936, Republic)
Stony Brooke—Robert Livingston
Tuscon Smith—Ray Corrigan
Lullaby Joslin—Syd Saylor
Director—Ray Taylor
Leading Players—Kay Hughes, J.P. McGowan, Al Bridge

THE THREE MUSKETEERS (1921, Silent, UA)
Athos—Leon Barry
Porthos—George Siegmann
Aramis—Eugene Pallette
Director—Fred Niblo
Leading Players—Douglas Fairbanks, Boyd Irwin, Thomas Holding, Sidney Franklin, Nigel De Brulier, Barbara LaMarr, Marguerite De La Motte, Mary MacLaren

THE THREE MUSKETEERS (1935, RKO)
Athos—Paul Lukas
Porthos—Moroni Olsen
Aramis—Onslow Stevens
Director—Rowland V. Lee
Leading Players—Walter Abel, Margot Grahame, Heather Angel, Ian Keith, Rosamond Pinchot, Nigel de Brulier

THE THREE MUSKETEERS (1939, 20th Century Fox)
Three Lackeys—The Ritz Brothers
Athos—Douglass Dumbrille
Porthos—Russell Hicks
Aramis—John King
Director—Allan Dwan
Leading Players—Don Ameche, Binnie Barnes, Lionel Atwill, Gloria Stuart, Pauline Moore, Miles Mander

THE THREE MUSKETEERS (1948, MGM)
Athos—Van Heflin
Porthos—Gig Young
Aramis—Robert Coote
Director—George Sidney
Leading Players—Gene Kelly, Lana Turner, June Allyson, Angela Lansbury, Vincent Price, John Sutton

THE THREE MUSKETEERS (1974, 20th Century Fox)
Athos—Oliver Reed
Porthos—Frank Finlay
Aramis—Richard Chamberlain
Director—Richard Lester
Leading Players—Raquel Welch, Michael York, Christopher Lee, Faye Dunaway, Geraldine Chaplin, Charlton Heston, Simon Ward

THREE NUTS IN SEARCH OF A BOLT (1964, Harlequin International)
Saxie Symbol—Mamie Van Doren
Tommy—Tommy Noonan
Joe Lynch—Paul Gilbert
Bruce Bernard—John Cronin
Director—Tommy Noonan
Leading Players—Ziva Rodann, Peter Howard, T.C. Jones

THREE ON A COUCH (1966, Columbia)
Susan Manning—Mary Ann Mobley
Anna Jacque—Gila Golan

Mary Lou Mauve—Leslie Parrish
Director—Jerry Lewis
Leading Players—Jerry Lewis, Janet Leigh, James Best

THREE ON A MATCH (1932, Warner Brothers)
Mary Keaton—Joan Blondell
Vivian Revere—Ann Dvorak
Ruth Westcott—Bette Davis
Director—Mervyn LeRoy
Leading Players—Warren William, Lyle Talbot, Humphrey Bogart

THREE ROGUES (1931, Fox Film Corp.)
Bull Stanley—Victor McLaglen
Ace Beaudry—Lew Cody
Bronco Dawson—Eddie Gribbon
Director—Benjamin Stoloff
Leading Players—Fay Wray, Robert Warwick, Franklyn Farnum

THREE RUSSIAN GIRLS (1943, UA)
Natasha—Anna Sten
Tamara—Mimi Forsaythe
Chijik—Kathy Frye
Directors—Fedor Ozep and Henry Kesler
Leading Players—Kent Smith, Alexander Granach, Paul Guilfoyle

THREE SAILORS AND A GIRL (1953, Warner Brothers)
Penny Watson—Jane Powell
Choir Boy Jones—Gordon MacRae
Twitch—Gene Nelson
Parky—Jack E. Leonard
Director—Roy Del Ruth
Leading Players—Sam Levene, George Givot, Veda Ann Borg

THREE SINNERS (1928, Silent, Paramount)
Baroness Gerda Wallentin—Pola Negri
Count Dietrich Wallentin—Paul Lukas
Raoul Stanislav—Tullo Carminati
Director—Rowland V. Lee
Leading Players—Warner Baxter, Anders Randolph, Ivy Harris

THE THREE SISTERS (1930, Fox Film Corp.)
Carlotta—Joyce Compton
Elena—June Collyer
Antonia—Addie McPhail
Director—Paul Sloane
Leading Players—Louise Dresser, Tom Patricola, Kenneth McKenna

THREE SISTERS (1974, GB, British Lion)
Olga—Jeanne Watts
Masha—Joan Plowright
Irina—Louise Purnell
Director—Derek Jacobi, Sheila Reid, Kenneth Mackintosh

THE THREE SISTERS (1977, Actor Studios Theatre)
Olga—Geraldine Page
Masha—Kim Stanley
Irina—Sandy Dennis
Director—Paul Bogart
Leading Players—Gerald Hiken, Shelley Winters, Albert Paulsen

THREE SMART GIRLS (1937, Universal)
Penny Craig—Deanna Durbin

Joan Craig—Nan Grey
Kay Craig—Barbara Read
Director—Henry Koster
Leading Players—Binnie Barnes, Alice Brady, Ray Milland, Charles Winninger, Mischa Auer

THREE SMART GIRLS GROW UP (1939, Universal)
Penny Craig—Deanna Durbin
Joan Craig—Nan Grey
Kay Craig—Helen Parrish
Director—Henry Koster
Leading Players—Charles Winninger, Robert Cummings, William Lundigan

THREE SONS (1939, RKO)
Gene Pardway—Kent Taylor
Bert Pardway—Robert Stanton
Freddie Pardway—Dick Hogan
Director—Jack Hively
Leading Players—Edward Ellis, William Gargan, J. Edward Bromberg

THREE SONS O'GUNS (1941, Warner Brothers)
Charley Patterson—Wayne Morris
Eddie Patterson—Tom Brown
Kenneth Patterson—William T. Orr
Director—Ben Stoloff
Leading Players—Marjorie Rambeau, Irene Rich, Susan Peters

THREE STRANGERS (1946, Warner Brothers)
Arbutney—Sidney Greenstreet
Crystal—Geraldine Fitzgerald
Johnny West—Peter Lorre
Director—Jean Negulesco
Leading Players—Joan Lorring, Robert Shayne, Marjorie Riordan

THREE VIOLENT PEOPLE (1956, Paramount)
Colt Saunders—Charlton Heston
Lorna Hunter Saunders—Anne Baxter
Cinch Saunders—Tom Tryon
Director—Rudolph Mate
Leading Players—Gilbert Roland, Forrest Tucker, Bruce Bennett

THE THREE WEIRD SISTERS (1948, GB, Pathe)
Gertrude Morgan-Vaughn—Nancy Price
Maude Morgan-Vaughn—Mary Clare
Isobel Morgan-Vaughn—Mary Merrall
Director—Dan Birt
Leading Players—Nova Pilbeam, Anthony Hulme, Raymond Lovell

THREE WISE FOOLS (1923, Silent, Goldwyn)
Theodore Findley—Claude Gillingwater
Honorable James Trumbull—William H. Crane
Dr. Richard Gaunt—Alec B. Francis
Director—King Vidor
Leading Players—Eleanor Boardman, John Sainpolis, Brinsley Shaw

THREE WISE FOOLS (1946, MGM)
Dr. Richard Gaunght—Lionel Barrymore
Judge Thomas Trumbull—Lewis Stone
Theodore Findley—Edward Arnold

Director—Edward Buzell
Leading Players—Margaret O'Brien, Thomas Mitchell, Ray Collins

THREE WISE GIRLS (1932, Columbia)
Cassie Barnes—Jean Harlow
Gladys Kane—Mae Clarke
Dot—Marie Prevost
Director—William Beaudine
Leading Players—Walter Bryon, Andy Devine, Natalie Moorhead

THREE WOMEN (1977, 20th Century Fox)
Millie Lammoreaux—Shelley Duvall
Pinky Rose—Sissy Spacek
Willie Hart—Janice Rule
Director—Robert Altman
Leading Players—Robert Fortier, Ruth Nelson, John Cromwell

THE THREE WORLDS OF GULLIVER (1960, GB, Columbia)
Dr. Lemuel Gulliver—Kerwin Mathews
Director—Jack Sher
Leading Players—Jo Morrow, June Thornburn, Lee Patterson

THREE YOUNG TEXANS (1954, 20th Century Fox)
Rusty Blair—Mitzi Gaynor
Tony Ballew—Keefe Brasselle
Johnny Colt—Jeffrey Hunter
Director—Henry Levin
Leading Players—Harvey Stephens, Dan Riss, Michael Ansara

THROW MOMMA FROM THE TRAIN (1987, Orion)
Momma Lift—Anne Ramsey
Director—Danny DeVito
Leading Players—Danny DeVito, Billy Crystal, Kim Geist, Kate Mulgrew

THUNDERBOLT (1929, Parmaount)
"Thundebolt" Jim Lang—George Bancroft
Director—Josef von Sternberg
Leading Players—Fay Wray, Richard Arlen, Tully Marshall

THUNDERBOLT AND LIGHTFOOT (1974, UA)
John "Thunderbolt" Doherty—Clint Eastwood
Lightfoot—Jeff Bridges
Director—Michael Cimino
Leading Players—Geoffrey Lewis, Catherine Bach, Gary Busey

THURSDAY'S CHILD (1943, GB, Pathe)
Fennis Wilson—Sally Ann Howes
Director—Rodney Ackland
Leading Players—Wilfrid Lawson, Kathleen O'Regan, Eileen Bennett

THE TICKET OF LEAVE MAN (1937, GB, MGM)
Tiger Dalton—Tod Slaughter
Director—George King
Leading Players—Marjorie Taylor, John Warwick, Robert Adair

TIFFANY JONES (1976, Cineworld)
Tiffany Jones—Anouska Hempel
Director—Pete Walker
Leading Players—Ray Brooks, Eric Pohlmann, Martin Benson

THE TIGER AND THE PUSSYCAT (1967, Embassy)
Francesco Vincenzini—Vittorio Gassman
Carolina—Ann-Margret

Director—Dino Risi
Leading Players—Eleanor Parker, Caterina Boratto, Eleanora Brown

THE TIGER MAKES OUT (1967, Columbia)
Ben Harris—Eli Wallach
Director—Arthur Hiller
Leading Players—Anne Jackson, Bob Dishy, John Harkins

TIGER ROSE (1930, Warner Brothers)
Rose—Lupe Velez
Director—George Fitzmaurice
Leading Players—Monte Blue, H.B. Warner, Tully Marshall

TIGER WARSAW (1988, Sony)
Chuck "Tiger" Warsaw—Patrick Swayze
Director—Amin Q. Chaudhri
Leading Players—Barbara Williams, Lee Richardson, Mary McDonnell, Piper Laurie

THE TIGER WOMAN (1917, Silent, Fox Film Corp.)
Princess Petrovitch—Theda Bara
Director—J. Gordon Edwards
Leading Players—E.F. Roseman, Louis Dean, Emil De Varay

THE TIGER WOMAN (1945, Republic)
Sharon Winslow—Adele Mara
Director—Phillip Ford
Leading Players—Kane Richmond, Richard Fraser, Peggy Stewart

A TIGER'S TALE (1988, Atlantic)
Bubber Drumm—C. Thomas Howell
Director—Peter Douglas
Leading Players—Ann-Margret, Charles Durning, Kelly Preston

'TIL WE MEET AGAIN (1940, Warner Brothers)
Joan Ames—Merle Oberon
Dan Hardesty—George Brent
Director—Edmund Goulding
Leading Players—Pat O'Brien, Geraldine Fitzgerald, Binnie Barnes, Frank McHugh

TILL WE MEET AGAIN (1936, Paramount)
Alan Barclay—Herbert Marshall
Elsa Durnay—Gertrude Michael
Director—Robert Florey
Leading Players—Lionel Atwill, Rod LaRocque, Guy Bates

TILL WE MEET AGAIN (1944, Paramount)
John—Ray Milland
Sister Clothide—Barbara Britton
Director—Frank Borzage
Leading Players—Walter Slezak, Lucille Watson, Konstantin Shayne, Vladimir Sokoloff

TILLIE (1922, Silent, Paramount)
Tillie Getz—Mary Miles Minter
Director—Frank Urson
Leading Players—Noah Beery, Allan Forrest, Lucien Littlefield

TILLIE AND GUS (1933, Paramount)
Augustus Q. Winterbottom—W. C. Fields
Tillie Winterbottom—Alison Skipworth

Director—Francis Martin
Leading Players—Baby LeRoy, Jacqueline Wells, Clifford Jones

TILLIE THE TOILER (1927, Silent, MGM)
Tillie Jones—Marion Davies
Director—Hobart Henley
Leading Players—Matt Moore, Harry Crocker, George Fawcett

TILLIE THE TOILER (1941, Columbia)
Tillie Jones—Kay Harris
Director—Sidney Salkow
Leading Players—William Tracy, George Watts, Daphne Pollard

TILLIE WAKES UP (1917, Silent, World)
Tillie Tinklepaw—Marie Dressler
Director—Harry Davenport
Leading Players—Johnny Hines, Frank Beamish, Rubye de Remer

TILLIE'S PUNCTURED ROMANCE (1914, Silent, Keystone)
Tillie—Marie Dressler
Director—Mack Sennett
Leading Players—Charles Chaplin, Mabel Normand, Charles Bennett, Mack Swain

TILLIE'S PUNCTURED ROMANCE (1928, Silent, Paramount)
Tillie—Louise Fazenda
Director—Edward Sutherland
Leading Players—W.C. Fields, Chester Conklin, Mack Swain

TILLIE'S TOMATO SURPRISE (1915, Silent, Lubin)
Tillie—Marie Dressler
Director—Howell Hansel
Leading Players—Tom McNaughton, Colin Campbell, Sarah McVickar

TILLY OF BLOOMSBURY (1931, GB, Sterling)
Tilly Welwyn—Phyllis Konstam
Director—Jack Raymond
Leading Players—Sydney Howard, Richard Byrd, Edward Chapman

TILLY OF BLOOMSBURY (1940, GB, RKO)
Tilly Welwyn—Jean Gillie
Director—Leslie Hiscott
Leading Players—Sydney Howard, Henry Oscar, Athene Seyler

TIM (1981, Australia, Pisces/Satori)
Tim Melville—Mel Gibson
Director—Michael Pate
Leading Players—Piper Laurie, Alwyn Kurts, Pat Evison

TIM DRISCOLL'S DONKEY (1955, GB, British Lion)
Tim Driscoll—David Coote
Director—Terry Bishop
Leading Players—John Kelly, Hugh Latimer, Peggy Marshall

TIMBER QUEEN (1944, Paramount)
Elaine—Mary Beth Hughes
Director—Frank McDonald
Leading Players—Richard Arlen, June Havoc, Sheldon Leonard

THE TIME OF HIS LIFE (1955, GB, Renown)
Charles Pastry—Richard Hearne
Director—Leslie Hiscott
Leading Players—Ellen Pollock, Richard Wattis, Robert Moreton

THE TIME, THE PLACE AND THE GIRL (1929, Warner Brothers)
Mae Ellis—Gertrude Olmstead
Director—Howard Bretherton
Leading Players—Grant Withers, Betty Compson, James R. Kirkwood

THE TIME, THE PLACE AND THE GIRL (1946, Warner Brothers)
Victoria Cassel—Martha Vickers
Director—David Butler
Leading Players—Dennis Morgan, Jack Carson, Janis Paige

TIME TRACKERS (1989, Concorde)
Charles—Wil Shriner
R.J.—Kathleen Beller
Madeline—Brigit Hoffman
Director—Howard R. Cohen
Leading Players—Ned Beatty, Alex Hyde-White, Lee Bergere

TIME WALKER (1982, New World)
Ankh Venaris, Mummy—Jack Olson
Director—Tom Kennedy
Leading Players—Ben Murphy, Nina Axelrod, Kevin Brophy

TIMERIDER (1983, Jensen-Farley)
Lyle Swann—Fred Ward
Director—William Dear
Leading Players—Belinda Bauer, Peter Coyote, Ed Lauter

TIMES SQUARE LADY (1935, MGM)
Toni Bradley—Virginia Bruce
Director—George B. Seitz
Leading Players—Robert Taylor, Helen Twelvetrees, Isabel Jewell

TIMES SQUARE PLAYBOY (1936, Warner Brothers)
Vic Arnold—Warren William
Director—William McGann
Leading Players—June Travis, Barton MacLane, Gene Lockhart

TIMOTHY'S QUEST (1922, Silent, American Releasing)
Timothy—Joseph Depew
Director—Sidney Olcott
Leading Players—Baby Helen Rowland, Marie Day, Margaret Seddon

TIMOTHY'S QUEST (1936, Paramount)
Timothy—Dickie Moore
Director—Charles Barton
Leading Players—Virginia Weidler, Eleanore Whitney, Tom Keene

TIN MEN (1987, Buena Vista)
Bill "BB" Babowsky—Richard Dreyfuss
Ernest Tilley—Danny DeVito
Director—Barry Levinson
Leading Players—Barbara Hershey, John Mahoney, Jackie Gayle, Stanley Brock, Seymour Cassel, Bruno Kirby

TISH (1942, MGM)
Letitia Carberry—Marjorie Main
Director—S. Sylvan Simon
Leading Players—Zasu Pitts, Aline MacMahon, Lee Bowman, Susan Peters, Virginia Grey

TO BE A LADY (1934, GB, British and Dominions)
Diane Whitcombe—Dorothy Bouchier
Director—George King
Leading Players—Bruce Lister, Vera Boggetti, Charles Cullum

TO CATCH A THIEF (1955, Paramount)
Danielle Foussard—Brigitte Auber
Director—Alfred Hitchcock
Leading Players—Cary Grant, Grace Kelly, Jesse Royce Landis, John Williams

TO MARY WITH LOVE (1936, 20th Century Fox)
Mary Wallace—Myrna Loy
Director—John Cromwell
Leading Players—Warner Baxter, Ian Hunter, Jean Dixon

TO PLEASE A LADY (1950, MGM)
Regina Forbes—Barbara Stanwyck
Director—Clarence Brown
Leading Players—Clark Gable, Adolphe Menjou, Will Geer

TO SIR, WITH LOVE (1967, GB, Columbia)
Mark Thackeray—Sidney Poitier
Director—James Clavell
Leading Players—Christian Roberts, Judy Geeson, Suzy Kendall, Lulu, Faith Brook

TO THE DEVIL, A DAUGHTER (1976, GB, Hammer)
Father Michael Raynor—Christopher Lee
Catherine Beddows—Nastassia Kinski
Director—Peter Sykes
Leading Players—Richard Widmark, Honor Blackman, Denholm Elliott

TO THE LAST MAN (1923, Silent, Paramount)
Jean Isbell—Richard Dix
Director—Victor Fleming
Leading Players—Lois Wilson, Noah Beery, Robert Edeson

THE TOAST OF NEW ORLEANS (1950, MGM)
Pepe Abellard Duvalle—Mario Lanza
Director—Norman Taurog
Leading Players—Kathryn Grayson, David Niven, J. Carroll Naish

THE TOAST OF NEW YORK (1937, RKO)
Jim Fisk—Edward Arnold
Director—Rowland V. Lee
Leading Players—Cary Grant, Frances Farmer, Jack Oakie, Donald Meek

TOBY MCTEAGUE (1986, Canada, Spectrafilm)
Toby McTeague—Yannick Bisson
Director—Jean-Claude Lord
Leading Players—Winston Reckert, Timothy Webber, Stephanie Morgenstern

TOBY TYLER (1960, Buena Vista)
Toby Tyler—Kevin Corcoran
Director—Charles Barton
Leading Players—Henry Calvin, Gene Sheldon, Bob Sweeney

TODAY I HANG (1942, Producers Releasing Corp.)
Jim O'Brien—Walter Woolf King
Director—Oliver Drake
Leading Players—Mona Barrie, William Farnum, Harry Woods

THE TODD KILLINGS (1971, National General)
Skipper Todd—Robert F. Lyons
Director—Barry Shear
Leading Players—Richard Thomas, Belinda Montgomery, Barbara Bel Geddes

TOKYO JOE (1949, Columbia)
Joe Barrett—Humphrey Bogart
Director—Stuart Heisler
Leading Players—Alexander Knox, Florence Marly, Sessue Hayakawa

TOKYO ROSE (1945, Paramount)
Tokyo Rose—Lotus Long
Director—Lew Landers
Leading Players—Bryon Barr, Ona Massen, Don Douglas, Richard Loo, Keye Luke

TOL'ABLE DAVID (1921, Silent, Associated First National)
David Kinemon—Richard Barthelmess
Director—Henry King
Leading Players—Gladys Hulette, Walter C. Lewis, Ernest Torrence

TOL'ABLE DAVID (1930, Columbia)
David Kinemon—Richard Cromwell
Director—John Blystone
Leading Players—Noah Beery, Joan Peers, Henry B. Walthall

TOM AND HIS PALS (1926, Silent, R-C Pictures)
Tom Duffy—Tom Tyler
Director—Robert De Lacy
Leading Players—Doris Hill, Frankie Darro, Dicky Brandon, Helen Lynch

TOM BROWN OF CULVER (1932, Universal)
Tom Brown—Tom Brown
Director—William Wyler
Leading Players—H.B. Warner, Slim Summerville, Richard Cromwell, Ben Alexander

TOM BROWN'S SCHOOL DAYS (1940, RKO)
Tom Brown—Jimmy Lydon
Director—Robert Stevenson
Leading Players—Cedric Hardwicke, Freddie Bartholomew, Josephine Hutchinson, Billy Halop

TOM BROWN'S SCHOOL DAYS (1951, GB, UA)
Tom Brown—John Howard Davies
Director—Gordon Parry
Leading Players—Robert Newton, Diana Wynyard, Hermione Badderley, John Charlesworth, John Forrest

TOM, DICK AND HARRY (1941, RKO)
Tom—George Murphy
Dick Hamilton—Alan Marshal
Harry—Burgess Meredith
Director—Garson Kanin
Leading Players—Ginger Rogers, Joe Cunningham, Jane Seymour

TOM HORN (1980, Warner Brothers)
Tom Horn—Steve McQueen
Director—William Wiard
Leading Players—Linda Evans, Richard Farnsworth, Billy Green Bush, Slim Pickens

TOM JONES (1963, GB, Woodfall/Lopert)
Tom Jones—Albert Finney
Director—Tony Richardson
Leading Players—Susannah York, Hugh Griffith, Edith Evans,
Joan Greenwood, Diane Cilento, Joyce Redman

TOM SAWYER (1930, Paramount)
Tom Sawyer—Jackie Coogan
Director—John Cromwell
Leading Players—Junior Durkin, Mitzi Green, Lucien Littlefield,
Tully Marshall, Clara Blandick, Charles Stevens

TOM SAWYER (1973, UA)
Tom Sawyer—Johnny Whitaker
Director—Don Taylor
Leading Players—Celeste Holm, Warren Oates, Jeff East, Jodie
Foster

TOM SAWYER, DETECTIVE (1939, Paramount)
Tom Sawyer—Billy Cook
Director—Louis King
Leading Players—Donald O'Connor, Porter Hall, Phillip Warren

TOM THUMB (1958, GB, MGM)
Tom Thumb—Russ Tamblyn
Director—George Pal
Leading Players—Alan Young, Terry-Thomas, Peter Sellers,
Jessie Matthews

THE TOMB OF LIGEIA (1965, GB, American International)
Lady Ligeia Fell—Elizabeth Shepherd
Director—Roger Corman
Leading Players—Vincent Price, John Westbrook, Oliver
Johnston

TOMBOY (1940, Monogram)
Pat—Marcia Mae Jones
Director—Robert McGowan
Leading Players—Jackie Moran, Grant Withers, Charlotte
Wynters

TOMBOY (1985, Crown International)
Tommy Boyd—Betsy Russell
Director—Herb Freed
Leading Players—Jerry Dinome, Kristi Somers, Richard Erdman

TOMBOY AND THE CHAMP (1961, Universal)
Tommy Jo—Candy Moore
Director—Francis D. Lyon
Leading Players—Ben Johnson, Jesse White, Jess Kirkpatrick

THE TOMCAT (1968, GB, Tigon-Global)
Tom—Anthony Trent
Director—Georges Robin
Leading Players—Liza Rogers, Veronica Lang, Connie Frazer

TOMMY (1975, GB, Columbia)
Tommy Walker—Roger Daltrey
Director—Ken Russell
Leading Players—Ann-Margret, Oliver Reed, Elton John, Eric
Clapton, Keith Moon, Jack Nicholson, Tina Turner

TOMMY THE TOREADOR (1960, GB, Warner Brothers-Pathe)
Tommy Tomkins—Tommy Steele
Director—John Paddy Carstair
Leading Players—Janet Munro, Sidney James, Bernard Cribbins

TONY DRAWS A HORSE (1951, GB, Rank)
Tony Fleming—Anthony Lang
Director—John Paddy Carstsirs
Leading Players—Cecil Parker, Anne Crawford, Derek Bond

TONY ROME (1967, 20th Century Fox)
Tony Rome—Frank Sinatra
Director—Gordon Douglas
Leading Players—Jill St. John, Richard Conte, Sue Lyon, Gena
Rowlands, Simon Oakland

TOO LATE THE HERO (1970, Cinerama)
Lt. Lawson—Cliff Robertson
Director—Robert Aldrich
Leading Players—Michael Caine, Ian Bannen, Harry Andrews,
Denholm Elliott, Ronald Fraser

TOO MANY HUSBANDS (1940, Columbia)
Bill Cardew—Fred MacMurray
Henry Lowndes—Melvyn Douglas
Director—Wesley Ruggles
Leading Players—Jean Arthur, Harry Davenport, Dorothy
Peterson

TOO MANY WIVES (1933, GB, Warner Brothers)
Hilary Wildeley—Nora Swinburne
Sally—Viola Keats
Director—George King
Leading Players—Jack Hobbs, Claude Fleming, Alf Goddard

TOO TOUGH TO KILL (1935, Columbia)
John O'Hara—Victor Jory
Director—D. Ross Lederman
Leading Players—Sally O'Neil, Thurston Hall, Johnny Arthur

TOO YOUNG TO KISS (1951, MGM)
Cynthia Potter—June Allyson
Director—Robert Z. Leonard
Leading Players—Van Johnson, Gig Young, Paula Corday

TOO YOUNG TO KNOW (1945, Warner Brothers)
Sally Sawyer—Joan Leslie
Ira Enright—Robert Hutton
Director—Frederick de Cordova
Leading Players—Dolores Moran, Harry Davenport, Rosemary
De Camp

TOO YOUNG TO LOVE (1960, GB, Rank)
Elizabeth Collins—Pauline Hahn
Director—Muriel Box
Leading Players—Thomas Mitchell, Joan Miller, Austin Willis

TOO YOUNG TO MARRY (1931, Warner Brothers)
Elaine Bumpstead—Loretta Young
Director—Mervyn LeRoy
Leading Players—Grant Withers, O.P. Heggie, Emma Dunn

TOOTSIE (1982, Columbia)
Michael Dorsey/Dorothy Michaels—Dustin Hoffman
Director—Sydney Pollack
Leading Players—Jessica Lange, Teri Garr, Dabney Coleman,
Charles Durning, Bill Murray

TOP BANANA (1954, UA)
Jerry Biffle—Phil Silvers
Director—Alfred E. Green

Leading Players—Rose Marie, Danny Scholl, Judy Lynn, Jack Albertson

TOP FLOOR GIRL (1959, GB, Paramount)
Connie—Kay Callard
Director—Max Varnel
Leading Players—Neil Hallett, Robert Raikes, Maurice Kaufmann

TOP GUN (1955, UA)
Rick Martin—Sterling Hayden
Director—Ray Nazarro
Leading Players—William Bishop, Karen Booth, James Millican

TOP GUN (1986, Paramount)
Maverick—Tom Cruise
Director—Tony Scott
Leading Players—Kelly McGillis, Val Kilmer, Anthony Edwards, Tom Skerritt, Michael Ironside

TOP MAN (1943, Universal)
Don Warren—Donald O'Connor
Director—Charles Lamont
Leading Players—Susanna Foster, Lillian Gish, Richard Dix

TOP SECRET AFFAIR (1957, Warner Brothers)
Major General Melville Goodwin—Kirk Douglas
Dottie Peale—Susan Hayward
Director—H.C. Potter
Leading Players—Paul Stewart, Jim Backus, John Cromwell

TOP SERGEANT MULLIGAN (1941, Monogram)
Mulligan—Nat Pendleton
Director—Jean Yarbrough
Leading Players—Carol Hughes, Sterling Holloway, Marjorie Reynolds

TOPAZE (1933, RKO)
Auguste Topaze—John Barrymore
Director—Harry d'Abbadie d'Arrast
Leading Players—Myrna Loy, Albert Conti, Luis Alberni

TOPPER (1937, MGM)
Cosmo Topper—Roland Young
Director—Norman Z. McLeod
Leading Players—Constance Bennett, Cary Grant, Billie Burke, Alan Mowbray, Eugene Pallette

TOPPER RETURNS (1941, UA)
Cosmo Topper—Roland Young
Director—Roy Del Ruth
Leading Players—Joan Blondell, Carole Landis, Billie Burke, Dennis O'Keefe

TOPPER TAKES A TRIP (1939, UA)
Cosmo Topper—Roland Young
Director—Norman Z. McLeod
Leading Players—Constance Bennett, Billie Burke, Alan Mowbray

TORCH SINGER (1933, Paramount)
Sally Trent-Mimi Benton—Claudette Colbert
Director—Alexander Hall
Leading Players—Ricardo Cortez, David Manners, Lyda Roberti

TORCHY BLANE IN CHINATOWN (1938, Warner Brothers)
Torchy Blane—Glenda Farrell
Director—William Beaudine
Leading Players—Barton MacLane, Tom Kennedy, Patric Knowles

TORCHY BLANE IN PANAMA (1938, Warner Brothers)
Torchy Blane—Lola Lane
Director—William Clemens
Leading Players—Paul Kelly, Tom Kennedy, Anthony Averill

TORCHY GETS HER MAN (1938, Warner Brothers)
Torchy Blane—Glenda Farrell
Director—William Beaudine
Leading Players—Barton MacLane, Tom Kennedy, Willard Robertson

TORCHY PLAYS WITH DYNAMITE (1939, Warner Brothers)
Torchy Blane—Jane Wyman
Director—Noel Smith
Leading Players—Allen Jenkins, Tom Kennedy, Sheila Bromley

TORCHY RUNS FOR MAYOR (1939, Warner Brothers)
Torchy Blane—Glenda Farrell
Director—Ray McCarey
Leading Players—Barton MacLane, Tom Kennedy, John Miljan

TOTAL RECALL (1990, Tri-Star)
Quaid/Hauser—Arnold Schwarzenenegger
Director—Paul Verhoeven
Leading Players—Rachel Ticotin, Sharon Stone, Ronny Cox, Michael Ironside, Marshall Bell

TOTO AND THE POACHERS (1958, GB, World Safari)
Toto—John Aloisi
Director—Brian Salt
Leading Players—Mpigano, Shabani Hamisi, David Betts

TOUCHED BY LOVE (1980, Columbia)
Karen—Diane Lane
Director—Gus Trikonis
Leading Players—Deborah Raffin, Michael Learned, John Amos

TOUGH AS THEY COME (1942, Universal)
Tommy Clark—Billy Halop
Director—William Nigh
Leading Players—Huntz Hall, Bernard Punsley, Helen Parrish

TOUGH ENOUGH (1983, 20th Century Fox)
Art Long—Dennis Quaid
Director—Richard O. Fleischer
Leading Players—Carlene Watkins, Stan Shaw, Pam Grier

TOUGH GUY (1936, MGM)
Freddie—Jackie Cooper
Director—Chester M. Franklin
Leading Players—Joseph Calleia, Harvey Stephens, Jean Hersholt

TOUGH GUYS (1986, Touchstone)
Harry Doyle—Burt Lancaster
Archie Long—Kirk Douglas
Director—Jeff Kanew
Leading Players—Charles Durning, Alexis Smith, Dana Carvey, Darlanne Fluegel, Eli Wallach

TOUGH GUYS DON'T DANCE (1987, Cannon)
Tim Madden—Ryan O'Neal
Director—Norman Mailer
Leading Players—Isabella Rossellini, Debra Sandlund, Wings
Hauser

TOUGHEST MAN ALIVE (1955, Allied Artists)
Lee—Dane Clark
Director—Sidney Salkow
Leading Players—Lita Milan, Anthony Caruso, Ross Elliott

TOUGHEST MAN IN ARIZONA (1952, Republic)
Matt Landry—Vaughn Monroe
Director—R.G. Springsteen
Leading Players—Joan Leslie, Edgar Buchanan, Victor Jory

TOWN TAMER (1965, Paramount)
Tom Rosser—Dana Andrews
Director—Lesley Selander
Leading Players—Terry Moore, Pat O'Brien, Lon Chaney, Jr.,
Bruce Cabot, Lyle Bettger

THE TOXIC AVENGER (1985, Troma)
The Toxic Avenger—Mitchell Cohen
Directors—Michael Herz and Samuel Weil
Leading Players—Andree Marauder, Jennifer Baptist, Cindy
Manion

THE TOXIC AVENGER, PART II (1989, Troma)
The Toxic Avenger—Ron Fazio and John Altamura
Directors—Michael Herz and Lloyd Kaufman
Leading Players—Phoebe Legere, Rick Collins, Rikiya Yasuoka

**THE TOXIC AVENGER, PART III: THE LAST TEMPTATION OF
TOXIE** (1989, Troma)
The Toxic Avenger—Ron Fazio and John Altamura
Directors—Lloyd Kaufman and Michael Herz
Leading Players—Phoebe Legere, Rick Collins, Lisa Gaye

THE TOY (1982, Columbia)
Jack Brown—Richard Pryor
Director—Richard Donner
Leading Players—Jackie Gleason, Ned Beatty, Scott Schwartz

TOY SOLDIERS (1991, Tri-Star)
Billy Tepper—Sean Astin
Joey Trotta—Wil Wheaton
Snuffy Bradberry—Keith Coogan
Director—Daniel Petrie, Jr.
Leading Players—Andrew Divoff, Louis Gossett, Jr., Denholm
Elliott, T.E. Russell, Jerry Orbach

TOY TIGER (1956, Universal)
Timmie Harkinson—Tim Hovey
Director—Jerry Hopper
Leading Players—Jeff Chandler, Laraine Day, Cecil Kellaway

THE TOY WIFE (1938, MGM)
Gilberta Brigard—Luise Rainer
Director—Richard Thorpe
Leading Players—Melvyn Douglas, Robert Young, Barbara O'Neil

TRACK THE MAN DOWN (1956, GB, Republic)
Rick Lambert—George Rose
Director—R.G. Springsteen

Leading Players—Kent Taylor, Petula Clark, Renee Houston,
Walter Rilla

TRADER HORN (1931, MGM)
Trader Horn—Harry Carey
Director—W.S. Van Dyke II
Leading Players—Edwina Booth, Duncan Renaldo, Mutia
Omoolu

TRADER HORN (1973, MGM)
Trader Horn—Rod Taylor
Director—Reza S. Badiyi
Leading Players—Anne Heywood, Jean Sorel, Don Knight

TRADER HORNEE (1970, Entertainment Ventures)
Hamilton Hornee—Buddy Pantsari
Director—Tsanusdi
Leading Players—Elisabeth Monica, John Alderman, Christine
Murray

TRADING PLACES (1983, Paramount)
Louis Winthrop III—Dan Aykroyd
Billy Ray Valentine—Eddie Murphy
Director—John Landis
Leading Players—Ralph Bellamy, Don Ameche, Denholm Elliott,
Jamie Lee Curtis, Kristin Holby

THE TRAFFIC COP (1916, Silent, Thanhouser)
Casey of Traffic "C"—Howard M. Mitchell
Director—Howard M. Mitchell
Leading Players—Gladys Hulette, Ernest Howard, Theodore Von
Eltz

THE TRAIL BLAZERS (1940, Republic)
Stony Brooke—Robert Livingston
Tucson Smith—Bob Steele
Lullaby Joslin—Rufe Davis
Director—George Sherman
Leading Players—Pauline Moore, Weldon Heyburn, Carroll Nye

THE TRAITOR (1936, Puritan)
Tim Vallance—Tim McCoy
Director—Sam Newfield
Leading Players—Frances Grant, Karl Hackett, Jack Rockwell

TRAPPED BY BOSTON BLACKIE (1948, Columbia)
Boston Blackie—Chester Morris
Director—Seymour Friedman
Leading Players—June Vincent, Richard Lane, Patricia White

THE TRAVELING EXECUTIONER (1970, MGM)
Jonas Candide—Stacy Keach
Director—Jack Smight
Leading Players—Marianna Hill, Bud Cort, Graham Jarvis

TRAVELLING HUSBANDS (1931, RKO)
Barry—Frank Albertson
Ben—Carl Miller
Director—Paul Sloane
Leading Players—Evelyn Brent, Constance Cummings, Hugh
Herbert

TRAVELLING NORTH (1988, Australia, View)
Frank—Leo McKern
Director—Carl Schultz

Leading Players—Graham Kennedy, Henri Szeps, Michelle Fawdon

THE TRAVELLING SALESLADY (1935, First National)
Angela Twitchell—Joan Blondell
Director—Ray Enright
Leading Players—William Gargan, Glenda Farrell, Hugh Herbert

TRAVELLING SALESWOMAN (1950, Columbia)
Mabel King—Joan Davis
Director—Charles F. Reisner
Leading Players—Andy Devine, Adele Jergens, Joe Sawyer

TRAVELS WITH MY AUNT (1972, GB, MGM)
Aunt Augusta—Maggie Smith
Henry Pulling—Alec McCowen
Director—George Cukor
Leading Players—Lou Gossett, Robert Stephens, Cindy Williams

TRAXX (1988, DEG)
Traxx—Shadoe Stevens
Director—Jerome Gray
Leading Players—Priscilla Barnes, Willard E. Pugh, John Hancock

TRENT'S LAST CASE (1953, GB, British Lion)
Philip Trent—Michael Wilding
Director—Herbert Wilcox
Leading Players—Margaret Lockwood, Orson Welles, John McCallum

THE TRESPASSER (1929, UA)
Marion Donnell—Gloria Swanson
Director—Edmund Goulding
Leading Players—Robert Ames, Purnell Pratt, William Holden

THE TRIAL OF BILLY JACK (1974, Taylor-Laughlin)
Billy Jack—Tom Laughlin
Director—Frank Laughlin
Leading Players—Delores Taylor, Victor Izay, Teresa Laughlin

THE TRIAL OF MADAME X (1948, GB, EPC British)
Jacqueline—Mara Russell-Tavernan
Director—Paul England
Leading Players—Paul England, Edward Leslie, Frank Hawkins

THE TRIAL OF MARY DUGAN (1929, MGM)
Mary Dugan—Norma Shearer
Director—Bayard Veiller
Leading Players—Lewis Stone, H. B. Warner, Raymond Hackett

THE TRIAL OF MARY DUGAN (1941, MGM)
Mary Dugan—Laraine Day
Director—Norman Z. McLeod
Leading Players—Robert Young, Tom Conway, Frieda Inescort

THE TRIAL OF VIVIENNE WARE (1932, Fox Film Corp.)
Vivienne Ware—Joan Bennett
Director—William K. Howard
Leading Players—Donald Cook, Richard "Skeets" Gallagher, Zasu Pitts, Lillian Bond

TRIBUTE TO A BADMAN (1956, MGM)
Jeremy Rodock—James Cagney
Director—Robert Wise
Leading Players—Don Dubbins, Stephen McNally, Irene Papas

TRILBY (1915, Silent, World)
Trilby—Clara Kimball Young
Director—Maurice Tourneur
Leading Players—Wilton Lackaye, Paul McAllister, Chester Barnett

THE TRIUMPH OF SHERLOCK HOLMES (1935, GB, Real Art)
Sherlock Holmes—Arthur Wontner
Director—Leslie Hiscott
Leading Players—Ian Fleming, Lyn Harding, Leslie Perrins

TRIUMPHS OF A MAN CALLED HORSE (1983, Redwing-Transpacific)
Man Called Horse—Richard Harris
Director—John Hough
Leading Players—Michael Beck, Ana De Sade, Vaughn Armstrong

TROG (1970, GB, Warner Brothers)
Trog—Joe Cornelius
Director—Freddie Francis
Leading Players—Joan Crawford, Michael Gough, Bernard Kay

THE TROJAN BROTHERS (1946, GB, Anglo-American)
Sid Nichols—David Farrar
Benny Castelli—Bobby Howes
Director—Maclean Rogers
Leading Players—Patricia Burke, Barbara Mullen, Lesley Brook

THE TROJAN WOMEN (1971, Cinerama)
Hecuba—Katharine Hepburn
Cassandra—Genevieve Bujold
Andromache—Vanessa Redgrave
Helen—Irene Papas
Director—Michael Cacoyannis
Leading Players—Brian Blessed, Patrick Magee, Alberto Sanz

TRON (1982, Buena Vista)
Tron—Bruce Boxleitner
Director—Steven Lisberger
Leading Players—Jeff Bridges, David Warner, Cindy Morgan, Barnard Hughes

TROOPER HOOK (1957, UA)
Sgt. Hook—Joel McCrea
Director—Charles Marquis Warren
Leading Players—Barbara Stanwyck, Earl Holliman, Edward Andrews

TROOPERS THREE (1930, Tiffany)
Eddie Haskins—Rex Lease
Bugs—Roscoe Karns
Sunny—Slim Summerville
Director—Norman Taurog
Leading Players—Dorothy Gulliver, Tom London, Joseph Girard

TROUBLE FOR TRUE (1936, MGM)
Prince Florizel—Robert Montgomery
Miss Vandeleur (Princess Brenda)—Rosalind Russell
Director—J. Walter Ruben
Leading Players—Frank Morgan, Reginald Owen, Louis Hayward

TROUBLE MAN (1972, 20th Century Fox)
Mr. "T"—Robert Hooks
Director—Ivan Dixon

Leading Players—Paul Winfield, Ralph Waite, William Smithers, Paula Kelly

THE TROUBLE WITH ANGELS (1966, Columbia)
Mary Clancy—Hayley Mills
Rachel Devery—June Harding
Director—Ida Lupino
Leading Players—Rosalind Russell, Binnie Barnes, Camilla Sparv, Mary Wickes

THE TROUBLE WITH DICK (1987, Frolix)
Dick Kendred—Tom Villard
Director—Gary Walkow
Leading Players—Susan Dey, Elaine Giftos, Elizabeth Gorcey

THE TROUBLE WITH SPIES (1987, Brigade/DEG)
Appleton Porter—Donald Sutherland
Director—Burt Kennedy
Leading Players—Ned Beatty, Ruth Gordon, Lucy Gutteridge

THE TROUBLEMAKER (1964, Janus)
Jack Armstrong—Tom Aldredge
Director—Theodore J. Flicker
Leading Players—Joan Darling, Theodore J. Flicker, James Frawley, Buck Henry

TRUCK STOP WOMEN (1974, LT Films)
Anna—Lieux Dressler
Rose—Claudia Jennings
Trish—Dolores Dorn
Tina—Jennifer Burton
Director—Mark L. Lester
Leading Players—John Martino, Dennis Fimple, Gene Drew

TRUCK TURNER (1974, American International)
Truck Turner—Issac Hayes
Director—Jonathan Kaplan
Leading Players—Yaphet Kotto, Alan Weeks, Annazette Chase

TRUE BELIEVER (1989, Columbia)
Eddie Dodd—James Woods
Director—Joseph Ruben
Leading Players—Robert Downey, Jr., Margaret Colin, Yuki Okumoto

TRUE HEART SUSIE (1919, Silent, Artcraft)
Susie May Trueheart—Lillian Gish
Director—D.W. Griffith
Leading Players—Loyola O'Connor, Robert Harron, Walter Higby

TRUE IDENTITY (1991, Buena Vista/Touchstone)
Miles Pope—Lenny Henry
Director—Charles Lane
Leading Players—Frank Langella, Charles Lane, J.T. Walsh, Anne-Marie Johnson, Andreas Katsulas, Michael McKean

THE TRUE STORY OF ESKIMO NELL (1975, Australia, Quest/Filmways)
Eskimo Nell—Victoria Anoux
Director—Richard Franklin
Leading Players—Max Gillies, Serge Lazareff, Abigail, Grahame Bond

THE TRUE STORY OF JESSE JAMES (1957, 20th Century Fox)
Jesse James—Robert Wagner
Director—Nicholas Ray

Leading Players—Jeffrey Hunter, Hope Lange, Agnes Moorehead, Alan Hale, Jr., John Carradine

TRUE TILDA (1920, Silent, GB, Jury)
Tilda—Edna Flugrath
Director—Harold Shaw
Leading Players—Teddy Gordon Craig, Edward O'Neill, Sir Simeon Stuart

TRUE TO THE ARMY (1942, Paramount)
Daisy Hawkins—Judy Canova
Director—Albert S. Rogell
Leading Players—Allan Jones, Ann Miller, Jerry Colonna

TRUE TO THE NAVY (1930, Paramount)
Ruby Nolan—Clara Bow
Director—Frank Tuttle
Leading Players—Fredric March, Harry Green, Rex Bell

TRUTHFUL TULLIVER (1917, Silent, Triangle)
"Truthful" Tulliver—William S. Hart
Director—William S. Hart
Leading Players—Alma Rubens, Norbert A. Myles, Nina Byron

TUCKER, THE MAN AND HIS DREAM (1988, Paramount)
Preston Tucker—Jeff Bridges
Director—Francis Ford Coppola
Leading Players—Joan Allen, Martin Landau, Frederic Forrest, Mako, Dean Stockwell

TUGBOAT ANNIE (1933, MGM)
Annie Brennan—Marie Dressler
Director—Mervyn LeRoy
Leading Players—Wallace Beery, Robert Young, Maureen O'Sullivan

TUGBOAT ANNIE SAILS AGAIN (1940, Warner Brothers)
Tugboat Annie—Marjorie Rambeau
Director—Lewis Seiler
Leading Players—Jane Wyman, Ronald Reagan, Alan Hale

TURNER AND HOOCH (1989, Buena Vista)
Scott Turner—Tom Hanks
Director—Roger Spottiswoode
Leading Players—Beasley, Mare Winningham, Craig T. Nelson

TUTTLES OF TAHITI (1942, RKO)
Jonas Tuttle—Charles Laughton
Cheater Tuttle—Jon Hall
Mama Rusu Tuttle—Adeline de Walt Reynolds
Director—Charles Vidor
Leading Players—Peggy Drake, Victor Francen, Gene Reynolds

12 ANGRY MEN (1957, UA)
Juror No. 1—Martin Balsam
Juror No. 2—John Fiedler
Juror No. 3—Lee J. Cobb
Juror No. 4—E.G. Marshall
Juror No. 5—Jack Klugman
Juror No. 6—Edward Binns
Juror No. 7—Jack Warden
Juror No. 8—Henry Fonda
Juror No. 9—Joseph Sweeney
Juror No. 10—Ed Begley
Juror No. 11—George Voskovec
Juror No. 12—Robert Webber

Director—Sidney Lumet
Leading Players—Above

TWENTY-ONE DAYS TOGETHER (1937, GB, Columbia)
Wanda—Vivien Leigh
Larry Durrant—Laurence Olivier
Director—Basil Dean
Leading Players—Leslie Banks, Francis L. Sullivan, Hay Petrie

TWICE BLESSED (1945, MGM)
Terry Turner—Lee Wilde
Stephanie Hale—Lyn Wilde
Director—Harry Beaumont
Leading Players—Preston Foster, Gail Patrick, Richard Gaines

TWICE BRANDED (1936, GB, RKO)
Charles Hamilton—Robert Rendel
Director—Maclean Rogers
Leading Players—Lucille Lisle, James Mason, Eve Gray

TWILIGHT WOMEN (1953, GB, Lippert)
Vivianne Bruce—Rene Ray
Christine Ralston—Lois Maxwell
Director—Gordon Parry
Leading Players—Freda Jackson, Joan Dowling, Dora Bryan, Vida Hope, Mary Germaine

TWINKLETOES (1926, Silent, First National)
Twinkletoes—Colleen Moore
Director—Charles Brabin
Leading Players—Kenneth Harlan, Tully Marshall, Gladys Brockwell

TWINS (1988, Universal)
Julius Benedict—Arnold Schwarzenegger
Vincent Benedict—Danny DeVito
Director—Ivan Reitman
Leading Players—Kelly Preston, Chloe Webb, Bonnie Bartlett, Marshall Bell

TWINS OF EVIL (1971, GB, Universal)
Frieda Gellhorn—Madeleine Collinson
Maria Gellhorn—Mary Collinson
Director—John Hough
Leading Players—Peter Cushing, Kathleen Bryon, Dennis Price

TWO (1975, Colmar)
Ellen—Sarah Venable
Steven—Douglas Travis
Director—Charles Trieschmann
Leading Players—Clifford Villeneuve, Ray Houle, Florence Hadley

TWO AGAINST THE WORLD (1932, Warner Brothers)
Dell Hamilton—Constance Bennett
Dave Norton—Neil Hamilton
Director—Archie Mayo
Leading Players—Helen Vinson, Allen Vincent, Gavin Gordon

TWO AGAINST THE WORLD (1936, Warner Brothers)
Martha Carstairs (Glory Penbrook)—Helen MacKellar
Jim Carstairs—Henry O'Neill
Director—William McGann
Leading Players—Humphrey Bogart, Beverly Roberts, Linda Perry, Carlyle Moore, Jr.

TWO ALONE (1934, RKO)
Mazie—Jean Parker
Adam—Tom Brown
Director—Elliott Nugent
Leading Players—Zasu Pitts, Arthur Byron, Beulah Bondi

TWO BLONDES AND A REDHEAD (1947, Columbia)
Catherine Abbott—Jean Porter
Patti Calhoun—June Preisser
Vicki Adams—Judy Clark
Director—Arthur Dreifuss
Leading Players—Jimmy Lloyd, Rick Vallin, Douglas Wood

TWO BRIGHT BOYS (1939, Universal)
Roy O'Donnell—Jackie Cooper
David Harrington—Freddie Bartholomew
Director—Joseph Santley
Leading Players—Melville Cooper, Dorothy Peterson, Allan Dinehart

TWO DOLLAR BETTOR (1951, Real Art)
John Hewitt—John Litel
Director—Edward L. Cahn
Leading Players—Marie Windsor, Steve Brodie, Barbara Logan

TWO-FACED WOMAN (1941, MGM)
Karin Borg Blake-Katherine Borg—Greta Garbo
Directors—George Cukor and Andrew Marton
Leading Players—Melvyn Douglas, Constance Bennett, Roland Young

TWO-FISTED SHERIFF (1937, Columbia)
Dick Houston—Charles Starrett
Director—Leon Barsha
Leading Players—Barbara Weeks, Bruce Lane, Edward Pell, Sr.

TWO FOR THE ROAD (1967, GB, 20th Century Fox)
Joanna Wallace—Audrey Hepburn
Mark Wallace—Albert Finney
Director—Stanley Donen
Leading Players—Eleanor Bron, William Daniels, Claude Dauphin, Nadia Gray, Georges Descrieres

TWO FOR THE SEESAW (1962, UA)
Jerry Ryan—Robert Mitchum
Gittel Mosca—Shirley MacLaine
Director—Robert Wise
Leading Players—Edmond Ryan, Elisabeth Fraser, Eddie Firestone

TWO GALS AND A GUY (1951, UA)
Deke Oliver—Robert Alda
Della Oliver—Janis Paige
Sylvia Latour—Janis Paige
Director—Alfred E. Green
Leading Players—James Gleason, Lionel Stander, Arnold Stang

TWO GENTLEMEN SHARING (1969, GB, American International)
Roddy—Robin Phillips
Andrew—Hal Frederick
Director—Ted Kotcheff
Leading Players—Esther Anderson, Norman Rossington, Hilary Dwyer

TWO GIRLS AND A SAILOR (1944, MGM)
John Dyckman III—Van Johnson

Patsy Deyo—June Allyson
Jean Deyo—Gloria De Haven
Director—Richard Thorpe
Leading Players—Jimmy Durante, Tom Drake, Henry
    Stephenson

TWO GIRLS ON BROADWAY (1940, MGM)
Pat Mahoney—Lana Turner
Molly Mahoney—Joan Blondell
Director—S. Sylvan Simon
Leading Players—George Murphy, Kent Taylor, Richard Lane

TWO-GUN LADY (1956, Associated Releasing Co.)
Kate Masters—Peggie Castle
Director—Richard H. Bartlett
Leading Players—William Talman, Marie Windsor, Earle Lyon

TWO GUYS FROM TEXAS (1948, Warner Brothers)
Steve Carroll—Dennis Morgan
Danny Foster—Jack Carson
Director—David Butler
Leading Players—Dorothy Malone, Penny Edwards, Forrest
    Tucker

THE TWO-HEADED SPY (1959, GB, Columbia)
General Alex Schottland—Jack Hawkins
Director—Andre De Toth
Leading Players—Gia Scala, Erik Schumann, Alexander Knox,
    Felix Aylmer

TWO HEARTS IN HARMONY (1935, GB, British International)
Micky—Bernice Claire
Lord Sheldon—George Curzon
Director—William Beaudine
Leading Players—Enid Stamp-Taylor, Paul Hartley, Nora
    Williams

TWO HEARTS IN WALTZ TIME (1934, GB, Gaumont)
Carl Hoffman—Carl Brisson
Helene Barry—Frances Day
Director—Carmine Gallone
Leading Players—Bert Coote, Oscar Asche, C. Denier Warren

TWO IN A CROWD (1936, Universal)
Julia Wayne—Joan Bennett
Larry Stevens—Joel McCrea
Director—Alfred E. Green
Leading Players—Henry Armetta, Alison Skipworth, Nat
    Pendleton

TWO IN A TAXI (1941, Columbia)
Bonnie—Anita Louise
Jimmy Owens—Russell Hayden
Director—Robert Florey
Leading Players—Noah Beery, Jr., Dick Purcell, Chick Chandler

TWO IN THE DARK (1936, RKO)
The Man—Walter Abel
Marie Smith—Margot Grahame
Director—Benjamin Stoloff
Leading Players—Wallace Ford, Gail Patrick, Alan Hale

THE TWO JAKES (1990, Paramount)
Jake Gittes—Jack Nicholson
Jake Berman—Harvey Keitel
Director—Jack Nicholson

Leading Players—Meg Tilly, Madeleine Stowe, Eli Wallach,
    Frederic Forrest, David Keith, Richard Farnsworth

TWO LATINS FROM MANHATTAN (1941, Columbia)
Jinx Terry—Jinx Falkenburg
Lois Morgan—Joan Woodbury
Director—Charles Barton
Leading Players—Joan Davis, Fortunio Bonanova, Don Beddoe

THE TWO LITTLE BEARS (1961, 20th Century Fox)
Billy Davis—Butch Patrick
Timmy Davis—Donnie Carter
Director—Randall Hood
Leading Players—Eddie Albert, Jane Wyatt, Brenda Lee

TWO LIVING, ONE DEAD (1964, GB, Emerson)
Anderson—Bill Travers
Berger—Patrick McGoohan
John Kester—Peter Vaughan
Director—Anthony Asquith
Leading Players—Virginia McKenna, Dorothy Alison, Alf Kjellin

TWO LOVERS (1928, Silent, UA)
Mark Van Rycke—Ronald Colman
Donna Leonora de Vargas—Vilma Banky
Director—Fred Niblo
Leading Players—Noah Beery, Nigel De Brulier, Virginia
    Bradford

TWO MEN AND A MAID (1929, Tiffany)
Jim Oxford—William Collier, Jr.
Rose—Alma Bennett
Adjutant—Eddie Gribbon
Director—George E. Stone, Margaret Quimby

THE TWO MRS. CARROLLS (1947, Warner Brothers)
Sally Morton Carroll—Barbara Stanwyck
Christine Carroll—Anita Bolster
Director—Peter Godfrey
Leading Players—Humphrey Bogart, Alexis Smith, Nigel Bruce

TWO MULES FOR SISTER SARA (1970, Universal)
Sister Sara—Shirley MacLaine
Director—Don Siegel
Leading Players—Clint Eastwood, Manolo Fabregas, Alberto
    Morin

TWO OF A KIND (1951, Columbia)
Lefty Farrell—Edmond O'Brien
Brandy Kirby—Lizabeth Scott
Director—Henry Levin
Leading Players—Terry Moore, Alexander Knox, Griff Barnett

TWO OF A KIND (1983, 20th Century Fox)
Zack—John Travolta
Debbie—Olivia Newton-John
Director—John Herzfeld
Leading Players—Charles Durning, Beatrice Straight, Scatman
    Crothers

THE TWO OF US (1938, GB, Gaumont)
Jack Warrender—Jack Hulbert
Frances Wilson—Gina Malo
Director—Jack Hulbert

Leading Players—J. Robertson Hare, Athole Stewart, Felix Aylmer

TWO ON A GUILLOTINE (1965, Warner Brothers)
Melinda Duquense—Connie Stevens
Val Henderson—Dean Jones
Director—William Conrad
Leading Players—Cesar Romero, Parley Baer, Virginia Gregg

TWO PEOPLE (1973, Universal)
Evan Bonner—Peter Fonda
Deirdre McCluskey—Lindsay Wagner
Director—Robert Wise
Leading Players—Estelle Parsons, Alan Fudge, Philippe March

TWO RODE TOGETHER (1961, Columbia)
Guthrie McCabe—James Stewart
Lt. Jim Gary—Richard Widmark
Director—John Ford
Leading Players—Shirley Jones, Linda Cristal, Andy Devine

TWO SISTERS FROM BOSTON (1946, MGM)
Abigail Chandler—Kathryn Grayson
Martha Canford Chandler—June Allyson
Director—Henry Koster
Leading Players—Lauritz Melchior, Jimmy Durante, Peter Lawford

TWO SMART MEN (1940, GB, Anglo International)
Jimmy—Leslie Fuller
Wally—Wally Patch
Director—Widgey R. Newman
Leading Players—Margaret Yarde, Pamela Bevan, George Turner

TWO SMART PEOPLE (1946, MGM)
Ricki Woodner—Lucille Ball
Ace Connors—John Hodiak
Director—Jules Dassin
Leading Players—Lloyd Nolan, Hugo Haas, Lenore Ulric

TWO WEEKS TO LIVE (1943, RKO)
Abner—Norris Goff
Director—Malcolm St. Clair
Leading Players—Chester Lauck, Franklin Pangborn, Kay Linaker

TWO WISE MAIDS (1937, Republic)
Agatha Stanton—Alison Skipworth
Prudence Matthews—Polly Moran
Director—Phil Rosen
Leading Players—Hope Manning, Donald Cook, Jackie Searl

TWO WIVES AT ONE WEDDING (1961, GB, Paramount)
Janet—Christina Gregg
Annette—Lisa Daniely
Director—Montgomery Tully
Leading Players—Gordon Jackson, Andre Maranne, Humphrey Lestocq

TWO YANKS IN TRINIDAD (1942, Columbia)
Tim Reardon—Pat O'Brien
Vince Barrows—Brian Donlevy
Director—Gregory Ratoff

Leading Players—Janet Blair, Roger Clark, Donald MacBride

U

U-BOAT PRISONER (1944, Columbia)
Archie Gibbs—Bruce Bennett
Director—Lew Landers
Leading Players—Erik Rolf, John Abbott, John Wengraf

THE UGLY AMERICAN (1963, Universal)
Harrison Carter MacWhite—Marlon Brando
Director—George Englund
Leading Players—Eiji Okada, Sandra Church, Pat Hingle

THE UGLY DUCKLING (1959, GB, Columbia)
Henry Jekyll/Teddy Hyde—Bernard Bresslaw
Director—Lance Comfort
Leading Players—Reginald Beckwith, Jon Pertwee, Maudie Edwards

THE ULTIMATE SOLUTION OF GRACE QUIGLEY (1984, MGM-UA)
Grace Quigley—Katharine Hepburn
Director—Anthony Harvey
Leading Players—Nick Nolte, Elizabeth Wilson, Chip Zien

THE ULTIMATE WARRIOR (1975, Warner Brothers)
Carson—Yul Brynner
Director—Robert Clouse
Leading Players—Max von Sydow, Joanna Miles, William Smith

ULZANA'S RAID (1972, Universal)
Ulzana—Joaquin Martinez
Director—Robert Aldrich
Leading Players—Burt Lancaster, Bruce Davison, Jorge Luke

UNASHAMED (1932, MGM)
Joan Ogden—Helen Twelvetrees
Director—Harry Beaumont
Leading Players—Robert Young, Lewis Stone, Jean Hersholt

UNASHAMED (1938, Cine-Grand)
Rae Lane—Rae Kidd
Director—Allen Stuart
Leading Players—Robert Stanley, Lucille Shearer, Emily Todd

UNCERTAIN LADY (1934, Universal)
Doris—Genevieve Tobin
Director—Karl Freund
Leading Players—Edward Everett Horton, Renee Gadd, Paul Cavanaugh

UNCHAINED (1955, Warner Brothers)
Steve Davitt—Elroy Hirsch

Director—Hall Bartlett
Leading Players—Barbara Hale, Chester Morris, Todd Duncan

UNCHASTENED WOMAN (1925, Silent, Chadwick)
Caroline Knollys—Theda Bara
Director—James Young
Leading Players—Wyndham Standing, Dale Fuller, John Miljan

UNCIVILISED (1937, Australia, Box Office Attractions)
Mara—Dennis Hoey
Director—Charles Chauvel
Leading Players—Margot Rhys, Marcelle Marnay, Ashton Jarry

UNCLE BUCK (1989, Universal)
Uncle Buck Russell—John Candy
Director—John Hughes
Leading Players—Jean Kelly, Gaby Hoffman, Macaulay Culkin, Amy Madigan, Elaine Bromka

UNCLE JOE SHANNON (1978, UA)
Joe Shannon—Burt Young
Director—Joseph C. Hanwright
Leading Players—Doug McKeon, Madge Sinclair, Jason Bernard

UNCLE VANYA (1958, Continental Distributing)
Ivan Petrovich "Uncle Vanya" Voinitsky—George Voskovec
Director—John Goetz
Leading Players—Mary Perry, Franchot Tone, Clarence Derwent

UNCLE VANYA (1977, GB, British Home Entertainment)
Uncle Vanya—Michael Redgrave
Director—Stuart Burge
Leading Players—Sybil Thorndike, Laurence Olivier, Lewis Casson, Joan Plowright, Rosemary Harris

UNCONQUERED (1947, Paramount)
Abigail Martha "Abby" Hale—Paulette Goddard
Director—Cecil B. DeMille
Leading Players—Gary Cooper, Howard Da Silva, Boris Karloff, Cecil Kellaway, Ward Bond

UNDER AGE (1941, Columbia)
Jane Baird—Nan Grey
Director—Edward Dmytryk
Leading Players—Tom Neal, Mary Anderson, Alan Baxter

UNDER AGE (1964, American International)
Linda Jenkins—Judy Adler
Director—Larry Buchanan
Leading Players—Anne MacAdams, Roland Royter, George Russell

UNDER EIGHTEEN (1932, Warner Brothers)
Marge Evans—Marian Marsh
Director—Archie Mayo
Leading Players—Regis Toomey, Warren William, Anita Page

UNDER FIRE (1983, Orion)
Russell Price—Nick Nolte
Director—Roger Spottiswoode
Leading Players—Ed Harris, Gene Hackman, Joanna Cassidy

UNDER MY SKIN (1950, 20th Century Fox)
Dan Butler—John Garfield

Director—Jean Negulesco
Leading Players—Micheline Presle, Luther Adler, Orley Lindgren

UNDER THE GUN (1951, Universal)
Bert Galvin—Richard Conte
Director—Ted Tetzlaff
Leading Players—Audrey Totter, John McIntire, Sam Jaffe

UNDER THE RED ROBE (1923, Silent, Cosmopolitan)
Cardinal Richelieu—Robert B. Mantell
Director—Alan Crosland
Leading Players—John Charles Thomas, Alma Rubens, Otto Kruger

UNDER THE RED ROBE (1937, GB, 20th Century Fox)
Cardinal Richelieu—Raymond Massey
Director—Victor Seastrom
Leading Players—Conrad Veidt, Annabella, Romney Brent

UNDER SUSPICION (1991, GB, Columbia/Rank)
Tony Aaron—Liam Neeson
Director—Simon Moore
Leading Players—Laura San Giacomo, Alphonsia Emmanuel, Stephen Moore, Maggie O'Neill, Malcolm Storry

UNDER TWO FLAGS (1936, 20th Century Fox)
Cpl. Victor—Ronald Colman
Director—Frank Lloyd
Leading Players—Claudette Colbert, Victor McLaglen, Rosalind Russell, J. Edward Bromberg

UNDERCOVER AGENT (1939, Monogram)
Bill Trent—Russell Gleason
Director—Howard Bretherton
Leading Players—Shirley Deane, J. M. Kerrigan, Maude Eburne

UNDERCOVER AGENT (1935, GB, Lippert)
Manning—Dermot Walsh
Director—Vernon Sewell
Leading Players—Hazel Court, Hermione Baddeley, James Vivian

UNDERCOVER DOCTOR (1939, Paramount)
Dr. Bartley Morgan—J. Carroll Naish
Director—Louis King
Leading Players—Lloyd Nolan, Janice Logan, Heather Angel

UNDERCOVER GIRL (1950, Universal)
Christine Miller/"Sal Willis"—Alexis Smith
Director—Joseph Pevney
Leading Players—Scott Brady, Richard Egan, Gladys George

UNDERCOVER GIRL (1957, GB, Butchers)
Joan Foster—Kay Callard
Director—Francis Searle
Leading Players—Paul Carpenter, Monica Grey, Bruce Seton

UNDERCOVER MAISIE (1947, MGM)
Maisie Ravier—Ann Sothern
Director—Harry Beaumont
Leading Players—Barry Nelson, Mark Daniels, Leon Ames

UNDER-COVER MAN (1932, Paramount)
Nick Darrow—George Raft

Director—James Flood
Leading Players—Nancy Carroll, Lew Cody, Roscoe Karns

THE UNDERCOVER MAN (1949, Columbia)
Frank Warren—Glenn Ford
Director—Joseph H. Lewis
Leading Players—Nina Foch, James Whitmore, Barry Kelley

THE UNDERCOVER WOMAN (1946, Republic)
Marcia Conroy—Stephanie Bachelor
Director—Thomas Carr
Leading Players—Robert Livingston, Richard Fraser, Isabel Withers

THE UNDERDOG (1943, Producers Releasing Corp.)
John Tate—Barton MacLane
Director—William Nigh
Leading Players—Bobby Larson, Jan Wiley, Charlotte Wynters

UNDERGROUND AGENT (1942, Columbia)
Lee Graham—Bruce Bennett
Director—Michael Gordon
Leading Players—Leslie Brooks, Frank Albertson, Julian Rivero

THE UNDER-PUP (1939, Universal)
Pip-Emma—Gloria Jean
Director—Richard Wallace
Leading Players—Robert Cummings, Nan Grey, C. Aubrey Smith

UNDERSEA GIRL (1957, Allied Artists)
Val Hudson—Mara Corday
Director—John Peyser
Leading Players—Pat Conway, Florence Marley, Dan Seymour

UNDERWATER WARRIOR (1958, MGM)
Cmdr. David Forest—Dan Dailey
Director—Andrew Marton
Leading Players—Claire Kelly, James Gregory, Ross Martin

THE UNDYING MONSTER (1942, 20th Century Fox)
Oliver Hammond—John Howard
Director—John Brahm
Leading Players—James Ellison, Heather Angel, Bramwell Fletcher

THE UNEARTHLY STRANGER (1964, GB, American International)
Julie Davidson—Gabriella Licudi
Director—John Krish
Leading Players—John Neville, Philip Stone, Patrick Newell

UNEXPECTED FATHER (1932, Universal)
Jasper Jones—Slim Summerville
Director—Thornton Freeland
Leading Players—Zasu Pitts, Cora Sue Collins, Alison Skipworth, Dorothy Christy

UNEXPECTED FATHER (1939, Universal)
Jimmy Hanley—Dennis O'Keefe
Director—Charles Lamont
Leading Players—Baby Sandy, Shirley Ross, Mischa Auer

UNEXPECTED UNCLE (1941, RKO)
Seton Manley—Charles Coburn

Director—Peter Godfrey
Leading Players—Anne Shirley, James Craig, Ernest Truex

UNFAITHFUL (1931, Paramount)
Fay Kilkerry—Ruth Chatterton
Director—John Cromwell
Leading Players—Paul Lukas, Paul Cavanagh, Juliette Compton

THE UNFAITHFUL (1947, Warner Brothers)
Chris Hunter—Ann Sheridan
Director—Vincent Sherman
Leading Players—Lew Ayres, Zachary Scott, Eve Arden, Jerome Cowan

UNFAITHFULLY YOURS (1948, 20th Century Fox)
Sir Alfred de Carter—Rex Harrison
Daphne de Carter—Linda Darnell
Director—Preston Sturges
Leading Players—Barbara Lawrence, Rudy Vallee, Kurt Krueger

UNFAITHFULLY YOURS (1984, 20th Century Fox)
Claude Eastman—Dudley Moore
Daniella Eastman—Nastassia Kinski
Director—Howard Zieff
Leading Players—Armand Assante, Albert Brooks, Cassie Yates

THE UNFORGIVEN (1960, UA)
Rachel Zachary—Audrey Hepburn
Director—John Huston
Leading Players—Burt Lancaster, Audie Murphy, John Saxon, Charles Bickford, Lillian Gish

THE UNHOLY (1988, Vestron)
Demon—Nicole Fortier
Director—Camilio Vila
Leading Players—Ben Cross, Ned Beatty, Jill Carroll

UNHOLY PARTNERS (1941, MGM)
Bruce Corey—Edward G. Robinson
Merrill Lambert—Edward Arnold
Director—Mervyn LeRoy
Leading Players—Laraine Day, Marsha Hunt, Don Beddoe

UNHOLY ROLLERS (1972, American International)
Karen—Claudia Jennings
Director—Vernon Zimmerman
Leading Players—Louis Quinn, Betty Anne Rees, Roberta Collins

THE UNHOLY THREE (1925, Silent, MGM)
Professor Echo—Lon Chaney, Sr.
Tweedledee—Harry Eccles
Hercules—Victor McLaglen
Director—Tod Browning
Leading Players—Mae Busch, Matt Moore, Matthew Betz

THE UNHOLY THREE (1930, MGM)
Prof. Echo—Lon Chaney
Midget—Harry Eccles
Hercules—Ivan Linow
Director—Jack Conway
Leading Players—Lila Lee, Elliott Nugent, John Miljan

THE UNHOLY WIFE (1957, Universal)
Phyllis Hochen—Diana Dors

Director—John Farrow
Leading Players—Rod Steiger, Tom Tryon, Beulah Bondi

THE UNINVITED (1944, Paramount)
Ghost of Mary Meredith—Lynda Grey
Director—Lewis Allen
Leading Players—Ray Milland, Ruth Hussey, Donald Crisp, Gail Russell, Cornelia Otis Skinner

THE UNKNOWN (1921, Silent, Goldstone)
The Unknown—Richard Talmadge
Director—Grover Jones
Leading Players—Andree Tourneur, Mark Fenton, J.W. Early

THE UNKNOWN (1927, Silent, MGM)
Alonzo—Lon Chaney, Sr.
Director—Tod Browning
Leading Players—Norman Kerry, Joan Crawford, Nick De Ruiz

THE UNKNOWN MAN (1951, MGM)
Dwight Bradley Mason—Walter Pidgeon
Director—Richard Thorpe
Leading Players—Ann Harding, Barry Sullivan, Keefe Brasselle

UNKNOWN WOMAN (1935, Columbia)
Helen Griffith—Marian Marsh
Director—Albert Rogell
Leading Players—Richard Cromwell, Douglas Dumbrille, Henry Armetta

UNMAN, WITTERING AND ZIGO (1971, GB, Paramount)
Unman—Michael Howe
Wittering—Colin Barrie
Director—John Mackenzie
Leading Players—David Hemmings, Douglas Wilmer, Anthony Haygarth, Carolyn Seymour

UNMARRIED (1939, Paramount)
Pat Rogers—Helen Twelvetrees
Slag Bailey—Buck Jones
Director—Kurt Neumann
Leading Players—Donald O'Connor, John Hartley, Robert Armstrong

AN UNMARRIED WOMAN (1978, 20th Century Fox)
Erica—Jill Clayburgh
Director—Paul Mazursky
Leading Players—Alan Bates, Michael Murphy, Cliff Gorman, Pat Quinn

UNMASKED (1929, Artclass)
Prince Hamid—Milton Krims
Director—Edgar Lewis
Leading Players—Robert Warwick, Sam Ash, Susan Conroy

UNMASKED (1950, Republic)
Roger Lewis—Raymond Burr
Director—George Blair
Leading Players—Robert Rockwell, Barbara Fuller, Hillary Brooke

AN UNREMARKABLE LIFE (1989, SVS)
Frances McEllany—Patricia Neal
Director—Amin Q. Chaudhri

Leading Players—Shelley Winters, Mako, Rochelle Oliver

THE UNSINKABLE MOLLY BROWN (1964, MGM)
Molly Brown—Debbie Reynolds
Director—Charles Walters
Leading Players—Harve Presnell, Ed Begley, Jack Kruschen

THE UNSTOPPABLE MAN (1961, GB, Argo/Sutton)
James Kennedy—Cameron Mitchell
Director—Terry Bishop
Leading Players—Marius Goring, Harry H. Corbett, Lois Maxwell

THE UNSUSPECTED (1947, Warner Brothers)
Alexander Grandison—Claude Rains
Director—Michael Curtiz
Leading Players—Joan Caulfield, Audrey Totter, Constance Bennett, Hurd Hatfield

UNTAMED (1955, 20th Century Fox)
Katie O'Neill—Susan Hayward
Director—Henry King
Leading Players—Tyrone Power, Richard Egan, John Justin, Agnes Moorehead, Rita Moreno

UNTAMED (1929, MGM)
Bingo—Joan Crawford
Director—Jack Conway
Leading Players—Robert Montgomery, Ernest Torrence, Holmes Herbert

UNTAMED HEIRESS (1954, Republic)
Judy—Judy Canova
Director—Charles Lamont
Leading Players—Donald Barry, George Cleveland, Taylor Holmes

THE UNTAMED LADY (1926, Silent, Paramount)
St. Clair Van Tassel—Gloria Swanson
Director—Frank Tuttle
Leading Players—Lawrence Gray, Joseph Smiley, Charles Graham

THE UNTOUCHABLES (1987, Paramount)
Eliot Ness—Kevin Costner
James Malone—Sean Connery
Oscar Wallace—Charles Martin Smith
George Stone—Andy Garcia
Director—Brian De Palma
Leading Players—Robert De Niro, Richard Bradford, Jack Kehoe, Billy Drago, Patricia Clarkson

UNWED MOTHER (1958, Allied Artists)
Betty Miller—Norma Moore
Director—Walter A. Doniger
Leading Players—Robert Vaughn, Diana Darrin, Billie Bird

UP GOES MAISIE (1946, MGM)
Maisie Ravier—Ann Sothern
Director—Harry Beaumont
Leading Players—George Murphy, Hillary Brooke, Stephen McNally

UP IN MABEL'S ROOM (1944, UA)
Mabel Essington—Gail Patrick

Director—Allan Dwan
Leading Players—Dennis O'Keefe, Marjorie Reynolds, Mischa Auer

URBAN COWBOY (1980, Paramount)
Bud—John Travolta
Director—James Bridges
Leading Players—Debra Winger, Scott Glenn, Madolyn Smith

UTAH BLAINE (1957, Columbia)
Utah Blaine—Rory Calhoun
Director—Fred F. Sears
Leading Players—Susan Cummings, Angela Stevens, Max Baer

V

THE V.I.P.S (1963, GB, MGM)
Frances Andros—Elizabeth Taylor
Paul Andros—Richard Burton
Marc Champselle—Louis Jourdan
Duchess Of Brighton—Margaret Rutherford
Les Mangam—Rod Taylor
Max Buda—Orson Welles
Director—Anthony Asquith
Leading Players—Elsa Martinelli, Maggie Smith, Linda Christian, Dennis Price

V.I. WARSHAWSKI (1991, Hollywood Pictures)
V.I. Warshawski—Kathleen Turner
Director—Jeff Kanew
Leading Players—Jay O. Sanders, Charles Durning, Angela Goethals, Nancy Paul, Frederick Coffin, Charles McCaughan

THE VAGABOND KING (1956, Paramount)
Francois Villon—Oreste 'Kirkop'
Director—Michael Curtiz
Leading Players—Kathryn Grayson, Rita Moreno, Cedric Hardwicke, Walter Hampden, Leslie Nielsen

VAGABOND LADY (1935, MGM)
Josephine Spiggins—Evelyn Venable
Director—Sam Taylor
Leading Players—Robert Young, Berton Churchill, Reginald Denny

VAGABOND LOVER (1929, RKO)
Rudy Bronson—Rudy Vallee
Director—Marshall Neilan
Leading Players—Sally Blane, Marie Dressler, Charles Sellon

THE VAGABOND QUEEN (1931, GB, Wardour)
Sally—Betty Balfour
Director—Geza von Bolvary
Leading Players—Glen Byam Shaw, Ernest Thesiger, Harry Terry

THE VALACHI PAPERS (1972, Columbia)
Joseph Valachi—Charles Bronson
Director—Terence Young
Leading Players—Lino Ventura, Joseph Wiseman, Jill Ireland, Walter Chiari

VALDEZ IS COMING (1971, UA)
Bob Valdez—Burt Lancaster
Director—Edwin Sherwin
Leading Players—Susan Clark, Jon Cypher, Barton Heyman

VALENTINO (1951, Columbia)
Rudolph Valentino—Anthony Dexter
Director—Lewis Allen
Leading Players—Eleanor Parker, Richard Carlson, Patricia Medina, Joseph Calleia

VALENTINO (1977, GB, UA)
Rudolph Valentino—Rudolf Nureyev
Director—Ken Russell
Leading Players—Leslie Caron, Michelle Phillips, Carol Kane

VALENTINO RETURNS (1989, Skouras)
Wayne Gibbs—Barry Tubb
Director—Peter Hoffman
Leading Players—Frederic Forrest, Veronica Cartwright, Jenny Wright

VALERIE (1957, UA)
Valerie—Anita Ekberg
Director—Gerd Oswald
Leading Players—Sterling Hayden, Anthony Steel, Peter Walker

VALET GIRLS (1987, Lexyn/Empire)
Lucy—Meri D. Marshall
Rosalind—April Stewart
Director—Rafal Zielinski
Leading Players—Mary Kohnert, Christopher Weeks, Patricia Scott Michel

THE VALIANT (1929, Fox Film Corp.)
James Dyke—Paul Muni
Director—William K. Howard
Leading Players—Marguerite Churchill, DeWitt Jennings, Henry Kolker, Edith Yorke

THE VALIANT (1962, GB, UA)
Capt. Morgan—John Mills
Director—Roy Baker
Leading Players—Ettore Manni, Roberto Risso, Robert Shaw

VALIANT IS THE WORD FOR CARRIE (1936, Paramount)
Carrie Snyder—Gladys George
Director—Wesley Ruggles
Leading Players—Arline Judge, John Howard, Dudley Digges

VALLEY GIRL (1983, Atlantic)
Julie Richman—Deborah Foreman
Director—Martha Coolidge
Leading Players—Nicolas Cage, Elizabeth Daily, Michael Bowen

VALMONT (1989, Orion)
Vicomte de Valmont—Colin Firth
Director—Milos Forman
Leading Players—Annette Benning, Meg Tilly, Fairuza Balk, Sian Phillips, Jeffrey Jones, Henry Thomas

VAMPING VENUS (1928, Silent, First National)
Venus—Thelma Todd

Director—Eddie Cline
Leading Players—Charlie Murray, Louise Fazenda, Russ Powell

THE VAMPIRE (1957, UA)
Dr. Paul Beecher—John Beal
Director—Paul Landres
Leading Players—Coleen Gray, Kenneth Tobey, Lydia Reed

THE VAMPIRE LOVERS (1970, GB, Hammer)
Marcilla Karnstein—Ingrid Pitt
Laura Spielsdorf—Pippa Steele
Emma Morton—Madeleine Smith
Director—Roy Ward Baker
Leading Players—Peter Cushing, George Cole, Dawn Addams

THE VAMPIRE'S GHOST (1945, Republic)
Webb Fallon—John Abbott
Director—Lesley Selander
Leading Players—Charles Gordon, Peggy Stewart, Grant Withers

VAMPYRES, DAUGHTERS OF DRACULA (1977, GB, Cambist)
Fran—Marianne Morris
Miriam—Anulka
Director—Joseph Jose Larraz
Leading Players—Murray Brown, Brian Deacon, Sally Fulkner

VANESSA, HER LOVE STORY (1935, MGM)
Vanessa—Helen Hayes
Director—William K. Howard
Leading Players—Robert Montgomery, Otto Kruger, May Robson

THE VANISHING AMERICAN (1955, Republic)
Blandy—Scott Brady
Director—Joseph Kane
Leading Players—Audrey Totter, Forrest Tucker, Gene Lockhart

THE VANISHING VIRGINIAN (1941, MGM)
Robert Yancey—Frank Morgan
Director—Frank Borzage
Leading Players—Kathryn Grayson, Spring Byington, Natalie Thompson

THE VANISHING WESTERNER (1950, Republic)
John Fast—Arthur Space
Director—Philip Ford
Leading Players—Monte Hale, Paul Hurst, Aline Towne

VANITY (1935, Columbia)
Vanity Faire—Jane Cain
Director—Adrian Brunel
Leading Players—Percy Marmont, John Counsell, H.F. Maltby

THE VANQUISHED (1953, Paramount)
Rock Grayson—John Payne
Director—Edward Ludwig
Leading Players—Coleen Gray, Jan Sterling, Lyle Bettger

VARIETY GIRL (1947, Paramount)
Catherine Brown—Mary Hatcher
Director—George Marshall
Leading Players—Olga San Juan, De Forrest Kelley, William Demarest

THE VEILED WOMAN (1917, Silent, GB, British Empire)
Coralie Travers—Gladys Mason
Director—Leedham Bantock

Leading Players—Cecil Humphreys, Frank Randell, Marjorie Chard

THE VEILED WOMAN (1929, Fox Film Corp.)
Nanon—Lia Tora
Director—Emmett Flynn
Leading Players—Paul Vincenti, Walter McGrail, Josef Swickard

VENGEANCE IS MINE (1948, GB, Eros)
Charles Heywood—Valentine Dyall
Director—Alan Cullimore
Leading Players—Anne Firth, Richard Goolden, Sam Kydd

THE VENGEANCE OF FU MANCHU (1968, GB, Warner Brothers)
Fu Manchu—Christopher Lee
Director—Jeremy Summers
Leading Players—Tony Ferrer, Tsai Chin, Douglas Wilmer

THE VENGEANCE OF SHE (1968, GB, Hammer-Seven Arts)
Carol-"She"—Olinka Berova
Director—Cliff Owen
Leading Players—John Richardson, Edward Judd, Colin Blakely

VERNE MILLER (1988, Alive)
Verne Miller—Scott Glenn
Director—Rod Hewitt
Leading Players—Barbara Stock, Thomas G. Waites, Lucinda Jenney

A VERY HONORABLE GUY (1934, Warner Brothers)
Feet Samuels—Joe E. Brown
Director—Lloyd Bacon
Leading Players—Alice White, Robert Barrat, Alan Dinehart

A VERY YOUNG LADY (1941, 20th Century Fox)
Kitty Russell—Jane Withers
Director—Harold Schuster
Leading Players—Nancy Kelly, John Sutton, Janet Beecher

THE VICAR OF BRAY (1937, GB, Associate British Films)
The Vicar of Bray—Stanley Holloway
Director—Henry Edwards
Leading Players—Hugh Miller, K. Hamilton Price, Felix Aylmer

VICE VERSA (1988, Columbia)
Marshall Seymour—Judge Reinhold
Charlie Seymour—Fred Savage
Director—Brian Gilbert
Leading Players—Corinne Bohrer, Swoosie Kurtz, David Proval

VICKI (1953, 20th Century Fox)
Vicki Lynn—Jean Peters
Director—Harry Horner
Leading Players—Jeanne Crain, Elliot Reid, Richard Boone

VICTIM (1961, GB, Pathe)
Calloway—Dennis Price
Director—Basil Dearden
Leading Players—Dirk Bogarde, Sylvia Syms, Anthony Nicholls, Peter Copley, Peter McErney

VICTOR/VICTORIA (1982, MGM/UA)
Victor/Victoria—Julie Andrews
Director—Blake Edwards
Leading Players—James Garner, Robert Preston, Lesley Ann Warren, Alex Karras, John Rhys-Davies

VICTORIA THE GREAT (1937, GB, RKO)
Queen Victoria—Anna Neagle
Director—Herbert Wilcox
Leading Players—Anton Walbrook, Walter Rilla, Mary Morris,
H.B. Warner

THE VICTORS (1963, Columbia)
Baker—Vincent Edwards
Cpl. Trower—George Hamilton
Cpl. Chase—George Peppard
Sgt. Craig—Eli Wallach
Elridge—Michael Callan
Weaver—Peter Fonda
Grogan—Jim Mitchum
Director—Carl Foreman
Leading Players—Albert Finney, Melina Mercouri, Jeanne
Moreau, Maurice Ronet, Rosanno Schiaffino, Romy Schneider,
Elke Sommer

THE VIKINGS (1958, UA)
Einar—Kirk Douglas
King Ragnar—Ernest Borgnine
Director—Richard Fleischer
Leading Players—Tony Curtis, Janet Leigh, James Donald

VILLA! (1958, 20th Century Fox)
Pancho Villa—Rodolfo Hoyos
Director—James B. Clark
Leading Players—Brian Keith, Cesar Romero, Margia Dean

VILLA RIDES (1968, Paramount)
Pancho Villa—Yul Brynner
Director—Buzz Kulik
Leading Players—Robert Mitchum, Grazia Buccella, Charles
Bronson

THE VILLAGE SQUIRE (1935, GB, British & Dominions)
Squire Hollis—David Horne
Director—Reginald Denham
Leading Players—Leslie Perrins, Moira Lynd, Vivien Leigh

VILLAIN (1971, GB, EMI-MGM)
Vic Dakin—Richard Burton
Director—Michael Turchner
Leading Players—Ian McShane, Nigel Davenport, Donald Sinden

THE VILLAIN (1979, Columbia)
Cactus Jack—Kirk Douglas
Director—Hal Needham
Leading Players—Ann-Margret, Arnold Schwarzenegger, Paul
Lynde, Strother Martin

THE VILLAIN STILL PURSUED HER (1940, RKO)
Mary—Anita Louise
Cribbs—Alan Mowbray
Director—Edward F. Cline
Leading Players—Hugh Herbert, Buster Keaton, Joyce Compton

VINCENT AND THEO (1990, GB/France, Hemdale)
Vincent Van Gogh—Tim Roth
Theo Van Gogh—Paul Rhys
Director—Robert Altman
Leading Players—Jip Wijngaarden, Johanna Ter Steege,
Wladimir Yordanoff, Jean-Pierre Cassel

THE VIOLENT MEN (1955, Columbia)
John Parrish—Glenn Ford
Lew Wilkinson—Edward G. Robinson
Director—Rudolph Mate
Leading Players—Barbara Stanwyck, Dianne Foster, Brian Keith

VIOLENT STRANGER (1957, GB, Anglo Amalgamated)
John Sullivan—Zachary Scott
Director—Montgomery Tully
Leading Players—Faith Domergue, Peter Illing, Faith Brook

THE VIRGIN AND THE GYPSY (1970, GB, Chevron)
Yvette—Joanna Shimkus
Gypsy—Franco Nero
Director—Christopher Miles
Leading Players—Honor Blackman, Mark Burns, Maurice
Denham

THE VIRGIN QUEEN (1955, 20th Century Fox)
Queen Elizabeth—Bette Davis
Director—Henry Koster
Leading Players—Richard Todd, Joan Collins, Jay Robinson,
Herbert Marshall

THE VIRGIN QUEEN OF ST. FRANCIS HIGH (1987, Canada,
Crown Intl.)
Diane—Stacy Christensen
Director—Francesco Lucente
Leading Players—Joseph R. Straface, J. T. Wotton, Anna-Lisa
Iapaola

THE VIRGINIA JUDGE (1935, Paramount)
Judge Davis—Walter C. Kelly
Director—Edward Sedgwick
Leading Players—Marsha Hunt, Stepin Fetchit, Johnny Downs

THE VIRGINIAN (1914, Silent, Lasky)
The Virginian—Dustin Farnum
Director—Cecil B. DeMille
Leading Players—Winifred Kingston, J.W. Johnston, Billy Elmer

THE VIRGINIAN (1923, Silent, Premier)
The Virginian—Kenneth Harlan
Director—Tom Forman
Leading Players—Florence Vidor, Russell Simpson, Pat O'Malley

THE VIRGINIAN (1929, Paramount)
The Virginian—Gary Cooper
Director—Victor Fleming
Leading Players—Walter Huston, Mary Brian, Richard Arlen

THE VIRGINIAN (1946, Paramount)
The Virginian—Joel McCrea
Director—Stuart Gilmore
Leading Players—Brian Donlevy, Sonny Tufts, Barbara Britton

VIRGINIA'S HUSBAND (1928, GB, Silent, Butchers)
Virginia Trevor—Lillian Oldland
Bill Hemingway—Pat Aherne
Director—Harry Hughes
Leading Players—Mabel Poulton, Marie Ault, Fewlass Llewellyn

VIRGINIA'S HUSBAND (1934, GB, Fox Film Corp.)
Virginia Trevor—Dorothy Boyd
John Craddock—Reginald Gardiner
Director—Maclean Rogers

Leading Players—Enid Stamp-Taylor, Ena Grossmith, Annie Esmond

VIRTUOUS HUSBAND (1931, Universal)
Daniel Curtis—Elliott Nugent
Director—Vin Moore
Leading Players—Jean Arthur, Betty Compson, J.C. Nugent

THE VISITOR (1973, Canada, Highwood)
Becca—Pia Shandel
Director—John Wright
Leading Players—Eric Peterson, Hetty Clews, Alan Robertson

THE VISITOR (1980, International Picture Show)
Jersey Coloswitz—John Huston
Director—Michael J. Paradise
Leading Players—Mel Ferrer, Glenn Ford, Shelley Winters

THE VISITORS (1972, UA)
Tony Rodriguez—Chico Martinez
Mike Nickerson—Steve Railsback
Director—Elia Kazan
Leading Players—Patrick McVey, Patricia Joyce, James Woods

VIVA CISCO KID (1940, 20th Century Fox)
Cisco Kid—Cesar Romero
Director—Norman Foster
Leading Players—Jean Rogers, Chris-Pin Martin, Minor Watson

VIVA KNIEVEL! (1977, Warner Brothers)
Evel Knievel—Evel Knievel
Director—Gordon Douglas
Leading Players—Gene Kelly, Lauren Hutton, Red Buttons

VIVA MAX! (1969, Commonwealth United)
Gen. Maximilian Rodrigues de Santos—Peter Ustinov
Director—Jerry Paris
Leading Players—Pamela Tiffin, Jonathan Winters, John Astin

VIVA VILLA! (1934, MGM)
Pancho Villa—Wallace Beery
Director—Jack Conway (Howard Hawks, uncredited)
Leading Players—Fay Wray, Stuart Erwin, Leo Carrillo, Donald Cook, George E. Stone

VIVA ZAPATA! (1952, 20th Century Fox)
Emiliano Zapata—Marlon Brando
Director—George Stevens
Leading Players—Jean Peters, Anthony Quinn, Joseph Wiseman, Arnold Moss, Margo, Harold Gordon, Mildred Dunnock, Frank Silvera

VIVACIOUS LADY (1938, RKO)
Frances Brent—Ginger Rogers
Director—George Stevens
Leading Players—James Stewart, James Ellison, Charles Coburn

THE VOLGA BOATMAN (1926, Producers Distributing Corp.)
Feodor—William Boyd
Director—Cecil B. DeMille
Leading Players—Elinor Fair, Robert Edeson, Victor Varconi

VOLTAIRE (1933, Warner Brothers)
Francois Marie Arouet Voltaire—George Arliss
Director—John G. Adolfi

Leading Players—Doris Kenyon, Margaret Lindsay, Theodore Newton, Reginald Owen

VON RICHTHOFEN AND BROWN (1970, UA)
Baron Manfred von Richthofen—John Philip Law
Roy Brown—Don Stroud
Director—Roger Corman
Leading Players—Barry Primus, Peter Masterson, Robert Latourneaux

VON RYAN'S EXPRESS (1965, 20th Century Fox)
Col. Joseph L. Ryan—Frank Sinatra
Director—Mark Robson
Leading Players—Trevor Howard, Raffaela Carra, Brad Dexter, Sergio Fantoni, Edward Mulhare

VOODOO MAN (1944, Monogram)
Dr. Richard Marlowe—Bela Lugosi
Director—William Beaudine
Leading Players—John Carradine, George Zucco, Michael Ames

VOODOO WOMAN (1957, American International)
Marilyn Blanchard—Marla English
Director—Edward L. Cahn
Leading Players—Tom Conway, Mike Connors, Lance Fuller

W

W.C. FIELDS AND ME (1976, Universal)
W.C. Fields—Rod Steiger
Carlotta Monti—Valerie Perrine
Director—Arthur Hiller
Leading Players—John Marley, Jack Cassidy, Bernadette Peters

W.W. AND THE DIXIE DANCEKINGS (1975, 20th Century Fox)
W.W. Bright—Burt Reynolds
Dixie—Connie Van Dyke
Wayne—Jerry Reed
Director—John G. Avildsen
Leading Players—Ned Beatty, James Hampton, Don Williams, Art Carney

THE WAC FROM WALLA WALLA (1952, Republic)
Judy—Judy Canova
Director—William Witney
Leading Players—Stephen Dunne, George Cleveland, June Vincent

THE WACKY WORLD OF DR. MORGUS (1962, Calogne-Sevin)
Dr. Morgus—Sid Noel (Noel Rideau)
Director—Roul Haig
Leading Players—Dana Barton, Jeanne Teslof, David Kleinberger

WACO (1966, Paramount)
Waco—Howard Keel
Director—R.G. Springsteen
Leading Players—Jane Russell, Brian Donlevy, Wendell Corey

WAGNER (1983, GB, London Trust)
Richard Wagner—Richard Burton
Director—Tony Palmer
Leading Players—Vanessa Redgrave, Gemma Craven, Laszlo Galffi, John Gielgud, Ralph Richardson

THE WAGON MASTER (1929, Universal)
The Rambler—Ken Maynard
Director—Harry Joe Brown
Leading Players—Edith Roberts, Tom Santschi, Jack Hanlon

WAGONMASTER (1950, RKO)
Elder Wiggs—Ward Bond
Director—John Ford
Leading Players—Ben Johnson, Harry Carey, Jr., Joanne Dru

WAIT 'TIL THE SUN SHINES NELLIE (1952, 20th Century Fox)
Nellie Halper—Jean Peters
Director—Henry King
Leading Players—David Wayne, Hugh Marlowe, Albert Dekker

WAITING FOR CAROLINE (1969, Canada, National Film Board)
Caroline—Alexandra Stewart
Director—Ron Kelly
Leading Players—Francois Tasse, Robert Howay, Sharon Acker

WAITRESS (1982, Troma)
Andrea—Carol Drake
Jennifer—Carol Bevar
Lindsey—Renata Majer
Director—Samuel Weil
Leading Players—Jim Harris, David Hunt, Anthony Sarrero

WALK LIKE A MAN (1987, MGM/UA)
Bobo Shand—Howie Mandel
Director—Melvin Frank
Leading Players—Christopher Lloyd, Cloris Leachman, Colleen Camp, Amy Steel

WALK SOFTLY, STRANGER (1950, RKO)
Chris Hale—Joseph Cotten
Director—Robert Stevenson
Leading Players—Aida Valli, Spring Byington, Paul Stewart

WALKER (1987, Universal)
William Walker—Ed Harris
Director—Alex Cox
Leading Players—Richard Masur, Rene Auberjonois, Keith Szarabajka, Peter Boyle, Marlee Matlin

THE WALKING DEAD (1936, Warner Brothers)
John Ellman—Boris Karloff
Director—Michael Curtiz
Leading Players—Ricardo Cortez, Warren Hull, Robert Strange, Edmund Gwenn

WALKING TALL (1973, Cinerama)
Buford Pusser—Joe Don Baker
Director—Phil Karlson
Leading Players—Elizabeth Hartman, Gene Evans, Noah Beery, Jr., Brenda Benet

WALKING TALL, PART II (1975, American International)
Buford Pusser—Bo Svenson
Director—Earl Bellamy
Leading Players—Luke Askew, Noah Beery, Jr., John Chandler

THE WALKING TARGET (1960, UA)
Nick Harbin—Ronald Foster
Director—Edward L. Cahn
Leading Players—Joan Evans, Merry Anders, Robert Christopher

THE WALL FLOWER (1922, Silent, Goldwyn)
Idalene Nobbin—Colleen Moore
Director—Rupert Hughes
Leading Players—Richard Dix, Gertrude Astor, Laura La Plante

WALLFLOWER (1948, Warner Brothers)
Jackie Linnett—Joyce Reynolds
Director—Frederick de Cordova
Leading Players—Robert Hutton, Janis Paige, Barbara Brown

WALLOPING WALLACE (1924, Silent, Artclass)
Buddy Wallace—Buddy Roosevelt
Director—Richard Thorpe
Leading Players—Violet La Plante, Lew Meehan, N.E. Hendrix

WANDA (1971, Bardene International)
Wanda—Barbara Loden
Director—Barbara Loden
Leading Players—Michael Higgins, Charles Dosinan, Frank Jourdano

WANDA NEVADA (1979, UA)
Wanda Nevada—Brooke Shields
Director—Peter Fonda
Leading Players—Peter Fonda, Fiona Lewis, Luke Askew

WANDERER OF THE WASTELAND (1935, Paramount)
Adam Larey—Dean Jagger
Director—Otho Lovering
Leading Players—Gail Patrick, Edward Ellis, Benny Baker

WANDERER OF THE WASTELAND (1945, RKO)
Adam Larey—James Warren
Director—Edward Killy
Leading Players—Richard Martin, Audrey Long, Robert Clarke

WANDERING GIRLS (1927, Silent, Columbia)
Peggy Marston—Dorothy Revier
Director—Ralph Ince
Leading Players—Eugenie Besserer, Frances Raymond, Robert Agnew

THE WANDERING JEW (1935, GB, Gaumont)
The Wandering Jew—Conrad Veidt
Director—Maurice Elvey
Leading Players—Marie Ney, Anne Grey, Jack Livesey, Joan Maude, Peggy Ashcroft, Francis L. Sullivan

WANTED (1937, GB, Sound City)
Winnie Oatfield—Zasu Pitts
Henry Oatfield—Claude Dampier
Director—George King
Leading Players—Mark Daly, Norma Varden, Finlay Currie

WANTED—A COWARD (1927, Banne/Sterling)
Rupert Garland—Robert Frazer
Director—Roy Clements
Leading Players—Lillian Rich, Frank Brownlee, James Gordon

WANTED BY SCOTLAND YARD (1939, GB, Pathe/Monogram)
"Fingers"—James Stephenson
Director—Norman Lee
Leading Players—Betty Lynne, Leslie Perrins, Nadine March

WANTED BY THE POLICE (1938, Monogram)
Danny—Frankie Darro
Director—Howard Bretherton
Leading Players—Lillian Elliott, Robert Kent, Evalyn Knapp

WANTED: DEAD OR ALIVE (1987, New World)
Malak Al Rahim—Gene Simmons
Director—Gary Sherman
Leading Players—Rutger Hauer, Robert Guillaume, Mel Harris

WANTED FOR MURDER (1946, GB, 20th Century Fox)
Victor Colebrooke—Eric Portman
Director—Lawrence Huntington
Leading Players—Dulcie Gray, Derek Farr, Roland Culver,
Stanley Holloway

WANTED: JANE TURNER (1936, RKO)
Jane Turner—Judith Blake
Director—Edward Killy
Leading Players—Lee Tracy, Gloria Stuart, John McGuire

THE WAR AGAINST MRS. HADLEY (1942, MGM)
Stella Hadley—Fay Bainter
Director—Harold S. Bucquet
Leading Players—Edward Arnold, Richard Ney, Jean Rogers,
Sara Allgood

THE WAR LORD (1965, Universal)
Chrysagon—Charlton Heston
Director—Franklin J. Schaffner
Leading Players—Richard Boone, Rosemary Forsyth, Maurice
Evans, Guy Stockwell

THE WAR LOVER (1962, Columbia)
Buzz Rickson—Steve McQueen
Director—Phillip Leacock
Leading Players—Robert Wagner, Shirley Ann Field, Gary
Cockrell

WAR NURSE (1930, MGM)
Joy—Anita Page
Babs—June Walker
Director—Edward Selwyn
Leading Players—Robert Montgomery, Robert Ames, Zasu Pitts

THE WAR OF THE ROSES (1989, 20th Century Fox)
Oliver Rose—Michael Douglas
Barbara Rose—Kathleen Turner
Director—Danny DeVito
Leading Players—Danny DeVito, Marianne Sagebrecht, Sean
Astin, Heather Fairchild

WAR PARTY (1989, Tri-Star)
Sonny Crowkiller—Billy Wirth
Skitty Harris—Kevin Dillon
Warren Cutfoot—Tim Sampson
Director—Franc Roddman
Leading Players—Jimmie Ray Weeks, Kevin M. Howard, M.
Emmet Walsh, Cameron Thor

THE WARE CASE (1917, GB, Silent, FBO)
Sir Hubert Ware—Matheson Lang
Director—Walter West
Leading Players—Violet Hopson, Ivy Close, Gregory Scott

THE WARE CASE (1939, GB, Ealing)
Sir HUbert Ware—Clive Brook
Director—Robert Stevenson
Leading Players—Jane Baxter, Barry K. Barnes, C.V. France

THE WARRENS OF VIRGINIA (1915, Silent, Lasky)
Agatha Warren—Blanche Sweet
General Warren—James Neill
Mrs. Warren—Mabel van Buren
Arthur Warren—Page Peters
Director—Elmer Clifton
Leading Players—House Peters, Dick La Reno, Sidney Dean

THE WARRIOR AND THE SORCERESS (1984, New World)
Kain—David Carradine
Naja—Maria Socas
Director—John Broderick
Leading Players—Luke Askew, Anthony DeLongis, Harry Townes

WARRIOR QUEEN (1987, Seymour Borde)
Berenice—Sybil Danning
Director—Chuck Vincent
Leading Players—Donald Pleasence, Richard Hill, Josephine
Jacqueline Jones

THE WARRIOR'S HUSBAND (1933, Fox Film Corp.)
Antiope—Elissa Landi
Theseus—David Manners
Director—Walter Lang
Leading Players—Marjorie Rambeau, Ernest Truex, Helen Ware

WASHINGTON AT VALLEY FORGE (1914, Silent, Universal)
George Washington—Francis Ford
Director—Francis Ford
Leading Player—Grace Cunard

THE WASP WOMAN (1959, Allied Artists)
Janice Starling—Susan Cabot
Director—Roger Corman
Leading Players—Fred Eisley, Barboura Morris, Michael Marks

WATCH BEVERLY (1932, GB, Butchers)
Victor Beverly—Henry Kendall
Director—Arthur Maude
Leading Players—Dorothy Bartlam, Francis X. Bushman,
Frederic de Lara

WATCH IT SAILOR (1961, GB, Hammer)
Lt. Cmdr. Hardcastle—Dennis Price
Director—Wolf Rilla
Leading Players—Marjorie Rhodes, Irene Handl, Liz Fraser

THE WATER GYPSIES (1932, GB, RKO)
Jane Bell—Ann Todd
Director—Maurice Elvey
Leading Players—Sari Maritza, Ian Hunter, Peter Hannen

WATERFRONT LADY (1935, Mascot-Republic)
Joan O'Brien—Ann Rutherford
Director—Joseph Santley

Leading Players—Frank Albertson, J. Farrell MacDonald, Barbara Pepper

WATERMELON MAN (1970, Columbia)
Jeff Gerber—Godfrey Cambridge
Director—Melvin Van Peebles
Leading Players—Estelle Parsons, Howard Caine, D'Urville Martin

A WAVE, A WAC AND A MARINE (1944, Monogram)
Marian—Elyse Knox
Margaret Ames—Sally Eilers
Henny—Henny Youngman
Director—Phil Karlsen
Leading Players—Ramsey Ames, Ann Gillis, Alan Dinehart

WAY FOR A SAILOR (1930, MGM)
Jack Berley—John Gilbert
Director—Sam Wood
Leading Players—Wallace Beery, Leila Hyams, Jim Tully

WAY OF A GAUCHO (1952, 20th Century Fox)
Martin—Rory Calhoun
Director—Jacques Tourneur
Leading Players—Gene Tierney, Richard Boone, Hugh Marlowe

THE WAY OF A MAID (1921, Silent, Selznick)
Naida Castleton—Elaine Hammerstein
Director—William P.S. Earle
Leading Players—Niles Welch, Diana Allen, Charles D. Brown

WAY OF A WOMAN (1919, Silent, Selznick)
Nancy Lee—Norma Talmadge
Director—Robert Z. Leonard
Leading Players—Conway Tearle, Gertude Berkeley, May McAvoy

WAYNE'S WORLD (1992, Paramount)
Wayne Campbell—Mike Myers
Director—Penelope Spheeris
Leading Players—Dana Carvey, Rob Lowe, Tia Carrere, Brian Doyle-Murray, Lara Flynn Boyle, Kurt Fuller

THE VAGABOND KING (1930, Paramount)
Francois Villon—Dennis King
Director—Ludwig Berger
Leading Players—Jeanette MacDonald, O.P. Heggie, Lillian Roth, Warner Oland

THE WEBSTER BOY (1962, GB, Regal Films)
Jimmy Webster—Richard O'Sullivan
Director—Don Chaffey
Leading Players—John Cassavetes, Elizabeth Sellars, David Farrar

THE WEDDING OF LILLI MARLENE (1953, GB, Monarch)
Lilli Marlene—Lisa Daniely
Director—Arthur Crabtree
Leading Players—Hugh McDermott, Sidney James, Gabrielle Brune

WEDNESDAY'S CHILD (1934, RKO)
Bobby Phillips—Frankie Thomas
Director—John S. Robertson
Leading Players—Edward Arnold, Karen Morley, Shirley Grey

WEE GEORDIE (1956, GB, British & Dominions)
Geordie MacTaggart—Bill Travers
Director—Frank Launder
Leading Players—Alastair Sim, Norah Gorsen, Molly Urquhart

WEE WILLIE WINKLE (1937, 20th Century Fox)
Priscilla Williams—Shirley Temple
Director—John Ford
Leading Players—Victor McLaglen, C. Aubrey Smith, June Lang

WEEKEND AT BERNIE'S (1989, 20th Century Fox)
Bernie Lomax—Terry Kiser
Director—Ted Kotcheff
Leading Players—Andrew McCarthy, Jonathan Silverman, Catherine Mary Stuart, Don Calfa

WEEKEND FOR THREE (1941, RKO)
Jim Craig—Dennis O'Keefe
Ellen Craig—Jane Wyatt
Randy Bloodworth—Philip Reed
Director—Irving Reis
Leading Players—Edward Everett Horton, Zasu Pitts, Franklin Pangborn

WEEKEND MILLIONAIRE (1937, GB, Gaumont)
Pierre—Buddy Rogers
Director—Arthur Woods
Leading Players—Mary Brian, W.H. Berry, John Harwood

WEEKEND WARRIORS (1986, The Movie Store)
Vince Tucker—Chris Lemmon
Director—Bert Convy
Leading Players—Vic Tayback, Lloyd Bridges, Graham Jarvis

WEEKEND WITH FATHER (1951, Universal)
Brad Stubbs—Van Heflin
Director—Douglas Sirk
Leading Players—Patricia Neal, Gigi Perreau, Virginia Field

WEEKEND WITH KATE (1990, Australia, Emanuel)
Kate Muir—Catherine McClements
Richard Muir—Colin Friels
Director—Arch Nicholson
Leading Players—Jerome Ehlers, Helen Mutkins, Kate Sheil, Jack Mayers

WEEKEND WITH THE BABYSITTER (1970, Dundee/Crown)
Candy Wilson—Susan Romen
Director—Don Henderson
Leading Players—George E. Carey, James Almanzar, Luanne Roberts

WELCOME STRANGER (1924, Silent, Producers Distributors Corp.)
Isadore Solomon—Dore Davidson
Director—James Young
Leading Players—Florence Vidor, Virginia Brown Faire, Noah Beery, Lloyd Hughes

WELCOME STRANGER (1947, Paramount)
Dr. Jim Pearson—Bing Crosby
Director—Elliott Nugent
Leading Players—Joan Caulfield, Barry Fitzgerald, Frank Faylen, Elizabeth Patterson

WELL DONE, HENRY (1936, GB, Butchers)
Henry McNab—Will Fyffe
Director—Wilfred Noy
Leading Players—Cathleen Nesbitt, Charles Hawtrey, Iris March

THE WELL-GROOMED BRIDE (1946, Paramount)
Margie Dawson—Olivia de Havilland
Director—Sidney Lanfield
Leading Players—Ray Milland, Sonny Tufts, James Gleason

A WELSH SINGER (1915, GB, Silent, Butchers)
Mifanwy—Florence Turner
Director—Henry Edwards
Leading Players—Henry Edwards, Campbell Gullan, Malcolm Cherry

WENDY CRACKED A WALNUT (1990, Australia, Classic Films P/L)
Wendy—Rosanna Arquette
Director—Michael Pattinson
Leading Players—Bruce Spence, Hugo Weaving, Kerry Walker, Doreen Warburton, Desiree Smith

WE'RE NO ANGELS (1955, Paramount)
Joseph—Humphrey Bogart
Albert—Aldo Ray
Jules—Peter Ustinov
Director—Michael Curtiz
Leading Players—Joan Bennett, Basil Rathbone, Leo G. Carroll, Gloria Talbot

WE'RE NO ANGELS (1989, Paramount)
Ned/Fr. Reilly—Robert De Niro
Jim/Fr. Brown—Sean Penn
Director—Neil Jordan
Leading Players—Demi Moore, Hoyt Axton, Bruno Kirby, Ray McAnally, James Russo, Wallace Shawn

THE WEREWOLF (1956, Columbia)
Duncan March—Steven Ritch
Director—Fred F. Sears
Leading Players—Don Megowan, Joyce Holden, Eleanore Tanin

THE WEREWOLF OF LONDON (1935, Universal)
Dr. Glendon—Henry Hull
Director—Stuart Walker
Leading Players—Valerie Hobson, Warner Oland, Lester Matthews

WEREWOLF OF WASHINGTON (1973, Milico/Diplomat)
Jack Whittier—Dean Stockwell
Director—Milton Moses
Leading Players—Biff McGuire, Clifton James, Beeson Carroll

WEST POINT WIDOW (1941, Paramount)
Nancy Hull—Anne Shirley
Director—Robert Siodmak
Leading Players—Richard Carlson, Richard Denning, Frances Gifford

WEST SIDE KID (1943, Republic)
Johnny April—Donald "Red" Barry
Director—George Sherman
Leading Players—Henry Hull, Dale Evans, Chick Chandler

THE WESTERN ROVER (1927, Silent, Truart)
Art Hayes—Art Acord
Director—Albert Rogell
Leading Players—Ena Gregory, Charles Avery, William Welch

THE WESTERNER (1936, Columbia)
Tim Addison—Tim McCoy
Director—David Selman
Leading Players—Marion Shilling, Joseph Sauers, John H. Dilson

THE WESTERNER (1940, UA)
Cole Hardin—Gary Cooper
Director—William Wyler
Leading Players—Walter Brennan, Doris Davenport, Fred Stone, Paul Hurst

WHARF ANGEL (1934, Paramount)
Toy—Dorothy Dell
Director—William Cameron Menzies
Leading Players—Victor McLaglen, Preston Foster, Alison Skipworth

WHAT A MAN (1930, Sono-Art-Worldwide)
Wade Rawlins—Reginald Denny
Director—George J. Crone
Leading Players—Miriam Seegar, Harvey Clark, Lucile Ward

WHAT A MAN! (1937, GB, British Lion)
Samuel Pennyfeather—Sydney Howard
Director—Edmond T. Greville
Leading Players—Vera Pearce, Ivor Barnard, Jenny Laird

WHAT A MAN! (1944, Monogram)
Henry Burrows—Johnny Downs
Director—William Beaudine
Leading Players—Wanda McKay, Robert Kent, Etta McDaniel

WHAT A WIDOW (1930, UA)
Tamarind Brooks—Gloria Swanson
Director—Allan Dwan
Leading Players—Owen Moore, Lew Cody, Margaret Livingston

WHAT A WOMAN! (1943, Columbia)
Carol Ainsley—Rosalind Russell
Director—Irving Cummings
Leading Players—Brian Aherne, Willard Parker, Alan Dinehart

WHAT ABOUT BOB? (1991, Buena Vista/Tocuhstone)
Bob Wiley—Bill Murray
Director—Frank Oz
Leading Players—Richard Dreyfuss, Julie Hagerty, Charles Korsmo, Kathryn Erbe

WHAT BECAME OF JACK AND JILL? (1972, GB, 20th Cent. Fox)
Jill—Vanessa Howard
Johnny-Jack—Paul Nicholas
Director—Bill Bain
Leading Players—Peter Copley, Peter Jeffrey, Patricia Fuller

WHAT EVER HAPPENED TO AUNT ALICE? (1969, Palomar/Cinerama)
Mrs. Alice Dimmock—Ruth Gordon
Director—Lee H. Katzin

Leading Players—Geraldine Page, Rosemary Forsyth, Robert Fuller

WHAT EVER HAPPENED TO BABY JANE? (1962, Warner Brothers)
Jane Hudson—Bette Davis
Director—Robert Aldrich
Leading Players—Joan Crawford, Victor Buono, Anna Lee

WHAT EVERY GIRL SHOULD KNOW (1927, Silent, Warner Brothers)
Mary Sullivan—Patsy Ruth Miller
Director—Charles F. Reisner
Leading Players—Ian Keith, Carroll Nye, Mickey McBan

WHAT EVERY WOMAN KNOWS (1917, GB, Silent, Lucoque)
Maggie Wylie—Hilda Trevelyan
Director—Fred W. Durrant
Leading Players—Maud Yates, A.B. Imeson

WHAT EVERY WOMAN KNOWS (1921, Silent, Paramount)
Maggie Wylie—Lois Wilson
Director—William C. DeMille
Leading Players—Conrad Nagel, Charles Ogle, Fred Huntley

WHAT EVERY WOMAN KNOWS (1934, MGM)
Maggie Wylie—Helen Hayes
Director—Gregory La Cava
Leading Players—Brian Aherne, Madge Evans, Lucile Watson

WHAT HAPPENED TO FATHER (1927, Silent, Warner Brothers)
W. Bradberry—Warner Oland
Director—Joh G. Adolfi
Leading Players—Flobelle Fairbanks, William Demarest, Vera Lewis

WHAT HAPPENED TO HARKNESS (1934, GB, Warner Brothers)
Bernard Harkness—Brember Wills
Director—Milton Rosmer
Leading Players—Robert Hale, James Finlayson, John Turnbull

WHAT HAPPENED TO JONES (1926, Silent, Universal)
Tom Jones—Reginald Denny
Director—William A. Seiter
Leading Players—Marian Nixon, Melbourne MacDowell, Frances Raymond

WHAT HAPPENED TO ROSA? (1921, Silent, Goldwyn)
Mayme Ladd—Mabel Normand
Director—Victor Schertzinger
Leading Players—Hugh Thompson, Doris Pawn, Tully Marshall

WHAT NEXT, CORPORAL HARGROVE? (1945, MGM)
Cpl. Marion Hargrove—Robert Walker
Director—Richard Thorpe
Leading Players—Keenan Wynn, Jean Porter, Chill Wills

WHAT THE BUTLER SAW (1950, Hammer)
Bembridge—Henry Mollison
Director—Godfrey Grayson
Leading Players—Edward Rigby, Mercy Haystead, Michael Ward

WHAT'S THE MATTER WITH HELEN? (1971, UA)
Helen Hill—Shelley Winters
Director—Curtis Harrington

Leading Players—Debbie Reynolds, Dennis Weaver, Agnes Moorehead

WHAT'S UP, DOC? (1972, Warner Brothers)
Prof. Howard Bannister—Ryan O'Neal
Director—Peter Bogdanovich
Leading Players—Barbra Streisand, Madeline Kahn, Kenneth Mars, Austin Pendleton

THE WHEELER DEALERS (1963, MGM)
Henry Tyroon—James Garner
Director—Arthur Hiller
Leading Players—Lee Remick, Phil Harris, Chill Wills, Louis Nye, John Astin

WHEN A MAN'S A MAN (1935, Fox Film Corp.)
Larry Knight—George O'Brien
Director—Edward F. Cline
Leading Players—Dorothy Wilson, Paul Kelly, Harry Woods

WHEN A STRANGER CALLS (1979, Columbia)
Curt Duncan—Tony Beckley
Director—Fred Walton
Leading Players—Carol Kane, Rutanya Alda, Charles Durning, Rachel Roberts

WHEN A WOMAN SINS (1918, Silent, Fox Film Corp.)
Lillian Marchard/Poppea—Theda Bara
Director—J. Gordon Edwards
Leading Players—Joseph Swickard, Albert Roscoe, Alfred Fremont

WHEN HARRY MET SALLY... (1989, Columbia)
Harry Burns—Billy Crystal
Sally Albright—Meg Ryan
Director—Rob Reiner
Leading Players—Carrie Fisher, Bruno Kirby, Steven Ford, Lisa Jane Persky, Michelle Nicastro

WHEN I GROW UP (1951, Eagle Lion)
Josh Reed—Bobby Driscoll
Director—Michael Kanin
Leading Players—Robert Preston, Martha Scott, Sherry Jackson, Charley Grapewin

WHEN JOHNNY COMES MARCHING HOME (1943, Universal)
Johnny Kovacs—Allan Jones
Director—Charles Lamont
Leading Players—Gloria Jean, Donald O'Connor, Jane Frazee

WHEN LADIES MEET (1933, MGM)
Claire Woodruff—Ann Harding
Mary Howard—Myrna Loy
Director—Harry Beaumont
Leading Players—Robert Montgomery, Alice Brady, Frank Morgan

WHEN LADIES MEET (1941, MGM)
Mary Howard—Joan Crawford
Claire Woodruff—Greer Garson
Director—Robert Z. Leonard
Leading Players—Robert Taylor, Herbert Marshall, Spring Byington

WHEN STRANGERS MARRY (1933, Columbia)
Steve Rand—Jack Holt

Marian Drake—Lillian Bond
Director—Clarence Badger
Leading Players—Arthur Vinton, Barbara Barondess, Ward Bond

WHEN STRANGERS MARRY (1944, Monogram)
Paul Dean—Dean Jagger
Millie Dean—Kim Hunter
Director—William Castle
leading Players—Robert Mitchum, Neil Hamilton, Lon Lubin

WHEN THE DALTONS RODE (1940, Universal)
Grat Dalton—Brian Donlevy
Bob Dalton—Broderick Crawford
Ben Dalton—Stuart Erwin
Emmett Dalton—Frank Albertson
Director—George Marshall
Leading Players—Randolph Scott, Kay Francis, George Bancroft

WHEN THIEF MEETS THIEF (1937, Great Brtiain, UA-Anglo)
Ricky Morgan—Douglas Fairbanks, Jr.
Jim Dial/Col. Fane—Alan Hale
Director—Raoul Walsh
Leading Players—Valerie Hobson, Jack Melford, Anthony Ireland

WHEN WILLIE COMES MARCHING HOME (1950, 20th Century Fox)
Bill Kluggs—Dan Dailey
Director—John Ford
Leading Players—Corinne Calvert, Colleen Townsend, William Demarest, James Lydon

WHERE HAS POOR MICKEY GONE? (1964, GB, Ledeck-Indigo)
Mick—John Malcolm
Director—George Levy
Leading Players—Warren Mitchell, Raymond Armstrong, John Challis

WHERE IS PARSIFAL? (1984, GB, Young)
Parsifal Katzenellbogen—Tony Curtis
Director—Henri Helman
Leading Players—Cassandra Domencia, Erik Estrada, Peter Lawford, Ron Moody

WHERE'S CHARLEY (1952, GB, Warner Brothers)
Charley Wykeham—Ray Bolger
Director—David Butler
Leading Players—Allyn McLerie, Robert Shackleton, Horace Cooper, Margaretta Scott

WHERE'S JACK (1969, GB, Paramount)
Jack Sheppard—Tommy Steele
Director—James Clavell
Leading Players—Stanley Baker, Fiona Lewis, Alan Badel

WHERE'S SALLY (1936, GB, Warner Brothers)
Sally—Renee Gadd
Director—Arthur Woods
Leading Players—Gene Gerrard, Claude Hulbert, Reginald Purdell

THE WHIP WOMAN (1928, Silent, First National)
Sari—Estelle Taylor
Director—Allan Dwan
Leading Players—Antonio Moreno, Lowell Sherman, Hedda Hopper

WHIRLWIND HORSEMAN (1938, Grand National)
Ken Morton—Ken Maynard
Director—Bob Hill
Leading Players—Joan Barclay, Bill Griffith, Kenneth Harlan

WHISPERING SMITH (1926, Silent, Producers Distributing Corp.)
Whispering Smith—H.B. Warner
Director—George Melford
Leading Players—Lillian Rich, John Bowers, Lilyan Tashman

WHISPERING SMITH (1948, Paramount)
Luke "Whispering" Smith—Alan Ladd
Director—Leslie Fenton
Leading Players—Robert Preston, Brenda Marshall, Donald Crisp, William Demarest

WHISPERING SMITH SPEAKS (1935, Fox Film Corp.)
Whispering Smith—George O'Brien
Director—David Howard
Leading Players—Irene Ware, Kenneth Thomson, Maude Allen

WHISPERING SMITH VERSUS SCOTLAND YARD (1952, GB, RKO)
Whispering Smith—Richard Carlson
Director—Frances Searle
Leading Players—Greta Gynt, Herbert Lom, Rona Anderson

THE WHISTLE BLOWER (1987, GB, Hemdale)
Frank Jones—Michael Caine
Director—Simon Langton
Leading Players—James Fox, Nigel Havers, Felicity Dean, John Gielgud, Gordon Jackson

THE WHITE ANGEL (1936, First National)
Florence Nightingale—Kay Francis
Director—William Dieterle
Leading Players—Ian Hunter, Donald Woods, Nigel Bruce, Donald Crisp

THE WHITE BLACK SHEEP (1926, Silent, First National)
Robert Kincarin—Richard Barthelmess
Director—Sidney Olcott
Leading Players—Patsy Ruth Miller, Constance Howard, Erville Alderson

WHITE CARGO (1930, GB, Neo-Art)
Langford—Maurice Evans
Director—J.B. Williams
Leading Players—Leslie Faber, John Hamilton, Sebastian Smith, Gypsy Rhouma

WHITE CARGO (1942, MGM)
Langford—Richard Carlson
Director—Richard Thorpe
Leading Players—Walter Pidgeon, Hedy Lamarr, Frank Morgan, Reginald Owen

WHITE EAGLE (1932, Columbia)
White Eagle—Buck Jones
Director—Lambert Hillyer
Leading Players—Barbara Weeks, Robert Ellis, Jason Robards

WHITE GHOST (1988, Gibraltar)
Steve Shepard—William Katt
Director—B.J. Davis

Leading Players—Rosalind Chao, Martin Hewitt, Wayne Crawford

WHITE HUNTER (1936, 20th Century Fox)
Capt. Clark Rutledge—Warner Baxter
Director—Irving Cummings
Leading Players—June Lang, Gail Patrick, Alison Skipworth

WHITE HUNTER, BLACK HEART (1990, Warners/Malpaso)
John Wilson—Clint Eastwood
Director—Clint Eastwood
Leading Players—Jeff Fahey, George Dzundza, Alun Armstrong, Marisa Berenson, Timothy Spall, Richard Vanstone

WHITE HUNTRESS (1957, American International)
Ruth Meecham—Susan Stephen
Director—George Breakston
Leading Players—Robert Urquhart, John Bentley, Alan Tarlton

WHITE PANTS WILLIE (1927, Silent, First National)
Willie Bascom—Johnny Hines
Director—Charles Hines
Leading Players—Leila Hyams, Henry Barrows, Ruth Dwyer

WHITE SAVAGE (1943, Universal)
Kaloe—Jon Hall
Director—Arthur Lubin
Leading Players—Maria Montez, Sabu, Don Terry, Turhan Bey

THE WHITE SISTER (1923, Silent, Metro)
Angela Chiaromonte—Lillian Gish
Director—Henry King
Leading Players—Ronald Colman, Gail Kane, J. Barney Sherry

THE WHITE SISTER (1933, MGM)
Angela Chiaromonte—Helen Hayes
Director—Victor Fleming
Leading Players—Clark Gable, Lewis Stone, Louise Closser Hale, May Robson

THE WHITE SQUAW (1956, Columbia)
Ectay-O-Wahnee—May Wynn
Director—Ray Nazarro
Leading Players—David Brian, William Bishop, Nancy Hale

WHITE WITCH DOCTOR (1953, 20th Century Fox)
Ellen Burton—Susan Hayward
Director—Henry Hathaway
Leading Players—Robert Mitchum, Walter Slezak, Mashood Ajala

WHITE WOMAN (1933, Paramount)
Judith Denning—Carole Lombard
Director—Stuart Walker
Leading Players—Charles Laughton, Kent Taylor, Percy Kilbride, Charles B. Middleton

WHITE YOUTH (1920, Silent, Universal)
Aline Ann Belame—Edith Roberts
Director—Norman Dawn
Leading Players—Alfred Hollingsworth, Thomas Jefferson, Arnold Gregg

WHITE ZOMBIE (1932, UA)
Madeline Short—Madge Bellamy
Director—Victor Halperin

Leading Players—Bela Lugosi, John Harron, Joseph Cawthorn, Robert Frazer, Clarence Muse

WHO FRAMED ROGER RABBIT? (1988, Buena Vista)
Roger Rabbit—Voice of Charlie Fleischer
Director—Robert Zemeckis
Leading Players—Bob Hoskins, Christopher Lloyd, Joanna Cassidy, Kathleen Turner, Stubby Kaye

WHO KILLED AUNT MAGGIE? (1940, Republic)
Aunt Maggie Ambler—Elizabeth Patterson
Director—Arthur Lubin
Leading Players—John Hubbard, Wendy Barrie, Edgar Kennedy

WHO KILLED "DOC" ROBBIN? (1948, UA)
Doc Robbin—George Zucco
Director—Bernard Carr
Leading Players—Virginia Grey, Don Castle, Whitford Kane

WHO KILLED FEN MARKHAM? (1937, Great Brtian, Ambassador)
Fen Markham—Garry Marsh
Director—Thomas Bentley
Leading Players—Anthony Bushell, Nancy O'Neil, Eve Gray

WHO KILLED GAIL PRESTON? (1938, Columbia)
Gail Preston—Rita Hayworth
Director—Leon Barsha
Leading Players—Don Terry, Robert Paige, Wyn Cahoon

WHO KILLED JOHN SAVAGE? (1937, GB, Warner Brothers)
John Savage—Nicholas Hannen
Director—Maurice Elvey
Leading Players—Barry Mackay, Edward Chapman, Kathleen Kelly

WHO SHOT PATAKANGO? (1990, Patakango Ltd.)
Patakango—Brad Randall
Director—Robert Brooks
Leading Players—David Knight, Sandra Bullock, Kevin Otto, Aaron Ingram, Chris Cardona

WHO SLEW AUNTIE ROO? (1971, American International)
Rosie Forrest—Shelley Winters
Director—Curtis Harrington
Leading Players—Mark Lester, Ralph Richardson, Lionel Jeffries, Judy Cornwell

WHO WAS MADDOX? (1964, Anglo Amalgamated)
Maddox—Richard Gale
Director—Geoffrey Nethercott
Leading Players—Bernard Lee, Jack Watling, Suzanne Lloyd

WHORE (1991, Trimark)
Liz—Theresa Russell
Director—Ken Russell
Leading Players—Benjamin Mouton, Antonio Fargas, Sanjay, Elizabeth Morehead

THE WHOOPEE BOYS (1986, Paramount)
Jake—Michael O'Keefe
Barney—Paul Rodriguez
Director—John Byrum
Leading Players—Denholm Elliott, Carole Shelley, Andy Bumatai

WHO'S HARRY CRUMB? (1989, Tri-Star)
Harry Crumb—John Candy
Director—Paul Flaherty
Leading Players—Jeffrey Jones, Annie Potts, Tim Thomerson,
Barry Corbin, Shawnee Smith

WHO'S THAT GIRL? (1987, Warner Brothers)
Nikki Finn—Madonna
Director—James Foley
Leading Players—Griffin Dunne, Haviland Morris, John
McMartin

WHOSE LIFE IS IT ANYWAY? (1981, MGM/UA)
Ken Harrion—Richard Dreyfuss
Director—John Badham
Leading Players—John Cassavetes, Christine Lahti, Bob
Balaban

WHY ME? (1990, Triumph/Epic/Carolina)
Gus Cardinal—Christopher Lambert
Director—Gene Quintano
Leading Players—Christopher Lloyd, Kim Greist, J.T. Walsh,
Michael J. Pollard, Tony Plana

WHY SHOOT THE TEACHER (1977, Canada, Ambassador)
Max Brown—Bud Cort
Director—Silvio Narizzano
Leading Players—Samantha Eggar, Chris Wiggins, Gary Reineke

THE WICKED DREAMS OF PAULA SCHULTZ (1968, UA)
Paul Schultz—Elke Sommer
Director—George Marshall
Leading Players—Bob Crane, Werner Klemperer, Joey Forman

THE WICKED LADY (1946, GB, Gainsborough)
Barbara Worth;Lady Skelton—Margaret Lockwood
Director—Leslie Arliss
Leading Players—James Mason, Paticia Roc, Griffith Jones

THE WICKED LADY (1983, GB, MGM/UA)
Lady Barbara Skelton—Faye Dunaway
Director—Michael Winner
Leading Players—Alan Bates, John Gielgud, Denholm Elliott,
Prunella Scales

WICKED STEPMOTHER (1989, MGM-UA)
Miranda—Bette Davis
Director—Larry Cohen
Leading Players—Barbara Carrera, Colleen Camp, David Rasche

WICKED WIFE (1955, GB, Allied Artists)
Babs Coates—Moira Lister
Director—Bob McNaught
Leading Players—Nigel Patrick, Beatrice Campbell, Betty Ann
Davies, Michael Hordern

A WICKED WOMAN (1934, MGM)
Naomi Trice—Mady Christians
Director—Charles Brabin
Leading Players—Jean Parker, Charles Bickford, Betty Furness

WICKED WOMAN (1953, UA)
Billie Nash—Beverly Michaels
Director—Russell Rouse
Leading Players—Richard Egan, Percy Helton, Evelyn Scott

THE WICKER MAN (1974, GB, British Lion)
Sgt. Neil Howie—Edward Woodward
Director—Robin Hardy
Leading Players—Christopher Lee, Diane Cilento, Britt Ekland,
Ingrid Pitt, Lindsay Kemp

THE WIDOW FROM CHICAGO (1930, First National)
Polly Henderson—Alice White
Director—Edward Cline
Leading Players—Neil Hamilton, Edward G. Robinson, Frank
McHugh,

THE WIDOW FROM MONTE CARLO (1936, Warner Brothers)
Inez—Dolores Del Rio
Director—Arthur Greville Collins
Leading Players—Warren William, Louise Fazenda, Colin Clive

WIDOW IN SCARLET (1932, Mayfair)
Baroness Orsani—Dorothy Revier
Director—George B. Seitz
Leading Players—Kenneth Harlan, Lloyd Whitlock, Glenn Tryon

WIDOW'S MIGHT (1934, GB, Warner Brothers)
Nancy Tweesdale—Laura La Plante
Director—Cyril Gardner
Leading Players—Yvonne Arnaud, Garry Marsh, George Cuzon

WIFE, DOCTOR AND NURSE (1937, 20th Century Fox)
Ina Lewis—Loretta Young
Dr. Judd Lewis—Warner Baxter
Steve—Virginia Bruce
Director—Walter Lang
Leading Players—Jane Darwell, Sidney Blackmer, Minna
Gombell

WIFE, HUSBAND AND FRIEND (1939, 20th Century Fox)
Doris Blair Borland—Loretta Young
Leonard Borland—Warner Baxter
Cecil Carver—Binnie Barnes
Director—Gregory Ratoff
Leading Players—Cesar Romero, George Barbier, J. Edward
Bromberg

THE WIFE OF GENERAL LING (1938, GB, Gaumont)
Tai—Adrianne Renn
Director—Ladislas Vajda
Leading Players—Griffith Jones, Valery Inkijinoff, Alan Napier

THE WIFE OF MONTE CRISTO (1946, Producers Releasing
Corp.)
Haydee, Countess of Monte Cristo—Lenore Aubert
Director—Edgar G. Ulmer
Leading Players—John Loder, Charles Dingle, Fritz Kortner

THE WIFE TAKES A FLYER (1942, Columbia)
Anita Woverman—Joan Bennett
Christopher Reynolds—Franchot Tone
Director—Richard Wallace
Leading Players—Allyn Joslyn, Cecil Cunningham, Lloyd
Corrigan

WIFE VERSUS SECRETARY (1936, MGM)
Helen "Whitey" Wilson—Jean Harlow
Linda Stanhope—Myrna Loy
Director—Clarence Brown

Leading Players—May Robson, Hobart Cavanaugh, James Stewart

THE WILBY CONSPIRACY (1975, UA)
Wilby—Joseph De Graf
Director—Ralph Nelson
Leading Players—Sidney Poitier, Michael Caine, Nicol Williamson, Prunella Gee

WILD AT HEART (1990, Goldwyn/Polygram/Propaganda)
Sailor Ripley—Nicolas Cage
Lula Pace Fortune—Laura Dern
Director—David Lynch
Leading Players—Diane Ladd, Willem Dafoe, Isabella Rossellini, Harry Dean Stanton, Crispin Glover

WILD BILL HICKOK RIDES (1942, Warner Brothers)
Wild Bill Hickok—Bruce Cabot
Director—Ray Enright
Leading Players—Constance Bennett, Warren William, Betty Brewer, Walter Catlett

WILD BRIAN KENT (1936, 20th Century Fox)
Brian Kent—Ralph Bellamy
Director—Howard Bretherton
Leading Players—Mae Clarke, Helen Lowell, Stanley Andrews

THE WILD BUNCH (1969, Warner Brothers)
Pike Bishop—William Holden
Dutch Engstrom—Ernest Borgnine
Lyle Gorch—Warren Oates
Tector Gorch—Ben Johnson
Angel—Jaime Sanchez
Director—Sam Peckinpah
Leading Players—Robert Ryan, Edmond O'Brien, Emilio Fernandez, Strother Martin, Albert Dekker

THE WILD GIRL (1925, Silent, Truart)
Pattie—Louise Lorraine
Director—Henry MacRae
Leading Players—Art Acord, Andrew Waldron

WILD GIRL (1932, Fox Film Corp.)
Salomy Jane Clay—Joan Bennett
Director—Raoul Walsh
Leading Players—Charles Farrell, Ralph Bellamy, Eugene Pallette, Irving Pichel

WILD HORSE HANK (1979, Canada, Film Consortium of Canada)
Hank Bradford—Linda Blair
Director—Eric Till
Leading Players—Michael Wincott, Al Waxman, Richard Crenna

THE WILD ONE (1953, Columbia)
Johnny—Marlon Brando
Director—Laslo Benedek
Leading Players—Mary Murphy, Robert Keith, Lee Marvin

THE WILD PAIR (1987, Trans World Entertainment)
Joe Jennings—Beau Bridges
Benny Avalon—Bubba Smith
Director—Beau Bridges
Leading Players—Lloyd Bridges, Gary Lockwood, Raymond St. Jacques

WILD ROVERS (1971, MGM)
Ross Bodine—William Holden
Frank Post—Ryan O'Neal
Director—Blake Edwards
Leading Players—Karl Malden, Lynn Carlin, Tom Skerritt

WILD THING (1987, Atlantic)
Wild Thing—Rob Knepper
Director—Max Reid
Leading Players—Kathleen Quinlan, Robert Davi, Maury Chaykin

THE WILDERNESS WOMAN (1926, Silent, First National)
Juneau MacLean/Junie—Aileen Pringle
Director—Howard Higgin
Leading Players—Lowell Sherman, Chester Conklin, Henry Vibart

WILL PENNY (1968, Paramount)
Will Penny—Charlton Heston
Director—Tom Gries
Leading Players—Joan Hackett, Donald Pleasence, Lee Majors

WILL SUCCESS SPOIL ROCK HUNTER (1957, 20th Century Fox)
Rock Hunter—Tony Randall
Director—Frank Tashlin
Leading Players—Jayne Mansfield, Betsy Drake, Joan Blondell

WILLARD (1971, Cinerama)
Willard Stiles—Bruce Davison
Director—Daniel Mann
Leading Players—Elsa Lanchester, Ernest Borgnine, Sondra Locke

WILLIAM COMES TO TOWN (1948, GB, UA)
William Brown—William Graham
Director—Val Guest
Leading Players—Garry Marsh, Jane Welsh, A. E. Matthews

WILLIE AND PHIL (1980, 20th Century Fox)
Willie Kaufman—Michael Ontkean
Phil D'Amico—Ray Sharkey
Director—Paul Mazursky
Leading Players—Margot Kidder, Jan Miner, Tom Brennan

WILLIE DYNAMITE (1973, Universal)
Willie Dynamite—Roscoe Orman
Director—Gilbert Moses III
Leading Players—Diana Sands, Thalmus Rasulala, Joyce Walker

WILLIE WONKA AND THE CHOCOLATE FACTORY (1971, Paramount)
Willy Wonka—Gene Wilder
Director—Mel Stuart
Leading Players—Jack Albertson, Peter Ostrum, Michael Bollner

WILLOW (1988, MGM)
Willow Ufgood—Warwick Davis
Director—Ron Howard
Leading Players—Val Kilmer, Joanne Whalley, Billy Barty, Jean Marsh, Patricia Hayes

WILSON (1944, 20th Century Fox)
Thomas Woodrow Wilson—Alexander Knox
Director—Henry King

Leading Players—Charles Coburn, Geraldine Fitzgerald, Thomas Mitchell, Ruth Nelson, Cedric Hardwicke

THE WIND AND THE LION (1975, MGM/UA)
Theodore Roosevelt—Brian Keith
Mulay el Raisuli—Sean Connery
Director—John Milius
Leading Players—Candice Bergen, John Huston, Geoffrey Lewis

WINDBAG THE SAILOR (1937, GB, Gaumont)
Capt. Ben Cutlet—Will Hay
Director—William Beaudine
Leading Players—Moore Marriott, Graham Moffatt, Norma Varden

WINDOM'S WAY (1958, GB, Rank)
Dr. Alec Windom—Peter Finch
Director—Ronald Neame
Leading Players—Mary Ure, Natasha Parry, Robert Flemyng

WINDWALKER (1980, Pacific International)
Windwalker—Trevor Howard
Director—Keith Merrill
Leading Players—Nick Ramus, James Remar, Serene Hedin

WING TOY (1921, Silent, Fox Film Corp.)
Wing Toy—Shirley Mason
Director—Howard M. Mitchell
Leading Players—Raymond McKee, Edward McWade, Harry S. Northrup

WINGS AND THE WOMAN (1942, Great Brtiain, RKO)
Amy Johnson—Anna Neagle
Director—Herbert Wilcox
Leading Players—Robert Newton, Edward Chapman, Nora Swinburne

WINNER TAKE ALL (1932, Warner Brothers)
Jim Kane—James Cagney
Director—Roy Del Ruth
Leading Players—Marian Nixon, Virginia Bruce, Guy Kibbee

WINNER TAKE ALL (1939, 20th Century Fox)
Steve Bishop—Tony Martin
Director—Otto Brower
Leading Players—Gloria Stuart, Henry Armetta, Slim Summerville

THE WINNING OF BARBARA WORTH (1926, Silent, UA)
Barbara Worth—Vilma Banky
Director—Henry King
Leading Players—Ronald Colman, Charles Lane, Paul McAllister

THE WINSLOW BOY (1950, GB, Eagle-Lion)
Ronnie Winslow—Neil North
Director—Anthony Asquith
Leading Players—Robert Donat, Margaret Leighton, Cedric Hardwicke, Basil Radford, Kathleen Harrison

WINSTANLEY (1979, GB, British Film Institute)
Winstanley—Miles Halliwell
Director—Kevin Brownlow
Leading Players—Jerome Willis, Terry Higgins, David Bramley

THE WINTER PEOPLE (1989, Columbia)
Collie Wright—Kelly McGillis

William Wright—Lloyd Bridges
Drury Campbell—Mitchell Ryan
Director—Ted Kotcheff
Leading Players—Kurt Russell, Amelia Burnette, Landy Flaherty, Eileen Ryan

WINTERHAWK (1976, Howco International)
Chief Winterhawk—Michael Dante
Director—Charles B. Pierce
Leading Players—Woody Strode, Leif Erickson, Denver Pyle

WIRED (1989, Taurus)
John Belushi—Michael Chiklis
Director—Larry Peerce
Leading Players—Ray Sharkey, J.T. Walsh, Patti D'Arbanville

WISE GIRL (1937, RKO)
Susan Fletcher—Miriam Hopkins
Director—Leigh Jason
Leading Players—Ray Milland, Walter Abel, Henry Stephenson

WISE GIRLS (1930, MGM)
Kate Bence—Norma Lee
Ruth Bence—Marion Shilling
Director—E. Mason Hopper
Leading Players—Elliott Nugent, Roland Young, J.C. Nugent

WISE GUYS (1937, GB, 20th Century Fox)
Charlie—Charlie Naughton
Jimmy—Jimmy Gold
Director—Harry Langdon
Leading Players—Audrene Brier, Robert Nainby, Walter Roy

WISE GUYS (1986, MGM/UA)
Harry Valentini—Danny DeVito
Moe Dickstein—Joe Piscopo
Director—Brian DePalma
Leading Players—Harvey Keitel, Ray Sharkey, Dan Hedaya, Capt. Lou Albano, Julie Bovasso

THE WISTFUL WIDOW OF WAGON GAP (1947, Universal)
Widow Hawkins—Marjorie Main
Director—Charles T. Barton
Leading Players—Bud Abbott, Lou Costello, Audrey Young

WITCHCRAFT PART II: The Temptress (1990, Vista Street)
Dolores—Delia Sheppard
Director—Mark Woods
Leading Players—Charles Solomon, David L. Homb, Mia Ruiz, Jay Richardson, Cheryl Janecky

THE WITCHES (1990, Warners/Lorimar)
Grand High Witch—Anjelica Huston
Director—Nicolas Roeg
Leading Players—Mai Zetterling, Jasen Fisher, Rowan Atkinson, Bill Patterson, Brenda Blethyn, Jane Horrocks

THE WITCHES OF EASTWICK (1987, Warner Brothers)
Alexandra Medford—Cher
Jane Spofford—Susan Sarandon
Sukie Ridgemont—Michelle Pfeiffer
Director—George Miller
Leading Players—Jack Nicholson, Veronica Cartwright, Richard Jenkins

WITH A SONG IN MY HEART (1952, 20th Century Fox)
Jane Froman—Susan Hayward
Director—Walter Lang
Leading Players—Rory Calhoun, David Wayne, Thelma Ritter

WITHNAIL AND I (1987, GB, Cineplex Odeon)
Withnail—Richard E. Grant
Marwood "I"—Paul McGann
Director—Bruce Robinson
Leading Players—Richard Griffiths, Ralph Brown, Michael
    Elphick, Daragh O'Malley

WITHOUT A CLUE (1988, Orion)
Reginald Kincaid ('Sherlock Holmes')—Michael Caine
Director—Thom Eberhardt
Leading Players—Ben Kingsley, Jeffrey Jones, Lysette Anthony
    Matthew Sim, Paul Freeman

THE WITNESS (1959, GB, Anglo Amalgamated)
Peter Brindon—Martin Stephens
Director—Geoffrey Muller
Leading Players—Dermot Walsh, Greta Gynt, Russell Napier

WITNESS (1985, Paramount)
Samuel—Lukas Haas
Director—Peter Weir
Leading Players—Harrison Ford, Kelly McGillis, Josef Sommer

WITNESS FOR THE PROSECUTION (1957, UA)
Christine Helm Vole—Marlene Dietrich
Director—Billy Wilder
Leading Players—Tyrone Power, Charles Laughton, Elsa
    Lanchester, John Williams, Henry Daniell

WITNESS IN THE DARK (1959, GB, Rank)
Jane Pringle—Patricia Dainton
Director—Wolf Rilla
Leading Players—Conrad Phillips, Madge Ryan, Nigel Green

WITNESS TO MURDER (1954, UA)
Cheryl Draper—Barbara Stanwyck
Director—Roy Rowland
Leading Players—George Sanders, Gary Merrill, Jesse White

THE WITNESS VANISHES (1939, Universal)
Lucius Marplay—Barlow Borland
Director—Otis Garrett
Leading Players—Edmund Lowe, Wendy Barrie, Bruce Lester

THE WIZ (1978, Universal)
The Wiz—Richard Pryor
Director—Sidney Lumet
Leading Players—Diana Ross, Michael Jackson, Nipsey Russell,
    Ted Ross, Mabel King, Lena Horne

THE WIZARD (1989, Universal)
Jimmy Woods—Luke Edwards
Director—Todd Holland
Leading Players—Fred Savage, Christian Slater, Beau Bridges

THE WIZARD OF BAGHDAD (1960, 20th Century Fox)
Genii-Ali Mahmud—Dick Shawn
Director—George Sherman
Leading Players—Diane Baker, Barry Coe, John Van Dreelen

THE WIZARD OF GORE (1970, Mayflower)
Montag the Magnificent—Ray Sager
Director—Herschell Gordon Lewis
Leading Players—Judy Cler, Wayne Ratay, Phil Laurenson

THE WIZARD OF LONLINESS (1988, Skouras)
Wendall Oler—Lukas Haas
Director—Jenny Bowen
Leading Players—Lea Thompson, John Randolph, Anne Pitoniak

WIZARD OF MARS (1964, American General)
Wizard of Mars—John Carradine
Director—David L. Hewitt
Leading Players—Roger Gentry, Vic McGee, Jerry Rannow

THE WIZARD OF OZ (1922, Silent, Universal)
The Wizard of Oz—Charles Murray
Director—Larry Semon
Leading Players—Larry Semon, Bryant Washburn, Dorothy
    Dwan

THE WIZARD OF OZ (1939, MGM)
The Wizard of Oz—Frank Morgan
Director—Victor Fleming
Leading Players—Judy Garland, Ray Bolger, Bert Lahr, Jack
    Haley, Billie Burke, Margaret Hamilton, The Munchkins

WOLF LARSEN (1958, Allied Artists)
Wolf Larsen—Barry Sullivan
Director—Harmon Jones
Leading Players—Peter Graves, Gita Hall, Thayer David

THE WOLF MAN (1941, Universal)
Larry Talbot—Lon Chaney, Jr.
Director—George Waggner
Leading Players—Claude Rains, Evelyn Ankers, Ralph Bellamy,
    Warren William, Patric Knowles, Maria Ouspenskaya

WOLF OF NEW YORK (1940, Republic)
Chris Faulkner—Edmund Lowe
Director—William McGann
Leading Players—Rose Hobart, James Stephenson, Jerome
    Cowan

THE WOLF OF WALL STREET (1929, Paramount)
Jim Bradford—George Bancroft
Director—Rowland V. Lee
Leading Players—Olga Baclanova, Nancy Carroll, Paul Lukas

WOMAN ACCUSED (1933, Paramount)
Glenda O'Brien—Nancy Carroll
Director—Paul Sloane
Leading Players—Cary Grant, John Halliday, Irving Pichel,
    Louis Calhern

WOMAN AGAINST THE WORLD (1938, Columbia)
Anna Masters—Alice Moore
Director—David Selman
Leading Players—Ralph Forbes, Edgar Edwards, Collette Lyons

WOMAN AGAINST WOMAN (1938, MGM)
Maris Kent—Virginia Bruce
Cynthia Holland—Mary Astor
Director—Robert B. Sinclair
Leading Players—Herbert Marshall, Janet Beecher, Marjorie
    Rambeau

WOMAN BETWEEN (1931, RKO)
Mme. Julie—Lili Damita
Director—Victor Schertzinger
Leading Players—O.P. Heggie, Lester Vail, Miriam Seegar

WOMAN CHASES MAN (1937, UA)
Virginia Travis—Miriam Hopkins
Kenneth Nolan—Joel McCrea
Director—John Blystone
Leading Players—Charles Winninger, Erik Rhodes, Ella Logan

A WOMAN COMMANDS (1932, RKO)
Mme. Maria Draga—Pola Negri
Director—Paul L. Stein
Leading Players—Roland Young, Basil Rathbone, H.B. Warner

THE WOMAN DECIDES (1932, GB, British International)
Lady Pamela—Adrianne Allen
Director—Miles Mander
Leading Players—Owen Nares, C.M. Hallard, Barbara Hoffe

WOMAN DOCTOR (1939, Republic)
Judith—Frieda Inescourt
Director—Sidney Salkow
Leading Players—Henry Wilcoxon, Claire Dodd, Cora Witherspoon

A WOMAN FOR JOE (1955, GB, Rank)
Mary—Diane Cilento
Joe Harrao—George Baker
Director—George More O'Ferrall
Leading Players—Jimmy Karoubi, David Kossoff, Violet Farebrother

WOMAN FROM HEADQUARTERS (1950, Republic)
Joyce—Virginia Hutson
Director—George Blair
Leading Players—Robert Rockwell, Barbara Fuller, Norman Budd

THE WOMAN FROM MONTE CARLO (1932, First National)
Lottie Corlaix—Lil Dagover
Director—Michael Curtiz
Leading Players—Walter Huston, Warren William, John Wray

THE WOMAN FROM TANGIER (1948, Columbia)
Nylon—Adele Jergens
Director—Harold Daniels
Leading Players—Stephen Dunne, Michael Duane, Denis Green

THE WOMAN GOD CHANGED (1921, Silent, Paramount)
Anna Janssen—Seena Owen
Director—Robert G. Vignola
Leading Players—E.K. Lincoln, Henry Sedley, Lillian Walker

WOMAN HATER(1949, GB, Rank)
Lord Terence Datchett—Stewart Granger
Director—Terence Young
Leading Players—Edwige Feuillere, Ronald Squire, Jeanne de Casalis

THE WOMAN HE SCORNED (1930, GB, Warner Brothers)
Louise—Pola Negri
Director—Paul Czinner
Leading Players—Warwick Ward, Cameron Carr, Hans Rehmann

THE WOMAN I LOVE (1937, RKO)
Lt. Claude Maury—Paul Muni
Mme. Helene Maury—Miriam Hopkins
Director—Anatole Litvak
Leading Players—Louis Hayward, Colin Clive, Minor Watson

THE WOMAN I STOLE (1933, Columbia)
Jim Bradler—Jack Holt
Vida Corew—Fay Wray
Director—Irving Cummings
Leading Players—Noah Beery, Raquel Torres, Donald Cook

WOMAN IN A DRESSING GOWN (1957, GB, Warner Brothers)
Amy Preston—Yvonne Mitchell
Director—J. Lee Thompson
Leading Players—Anthony Quayle, Sylvia Syms, Andrew Ray

WOMAN IN CHAINS (1932, GB, RKO)
Grace Marwood—Betty Stockfield
Director—Basil Dean
Leading Players—Owen Nares, Allan Jeayes, George Curzon

THE WOMAN IN COMMAND (1934, GB, Gaumont)
Maisie Marvello—Cicely Courtneidge
Director—Maurice Elvey
Leading Players—Edward Everett Horton, Anthony Bushell, Dorothy Hyson

WOMAN IN DISTRESS (1937, Columbia)
Phoebe Tuttle—May Robson
Director—Lynn Shores
Leading Players—Irene Donovan, Dean Jagger, Douglas Dumbrille

THE WOMAN IN GREEN (1945, Universal)
Lydia Marlow—Hillary Brooke
Director—Roy William Neill
Leading Players—Basil Rathbone, Nigel Bruce, Henry Daniell

WOMAN IN HIDING (1949, Universal)
Deborah Chandler Clark—Ida Lupino
Director—Michael Gordon
Leading Players—Howard Duff, Stephen McNally, John Litel, Peggy Dow

WOMAN IN HIDING (1953, GB, Hammer)
Thelma Tasman—Lois Maxwell
Director—Terence Fisher
Leading Players—Paul Henreid, Kieron Moore, Hugh Sinclair

THE WOMAN IN RED (1935, Warner Brothers)
Shelby Barrett—Barbara Stanwyck
Director—Robert Florey
Leading Players—Gene Raymond, Genevieve Tobin, John Eldredge

THE WOMAN IN RED (1984, Orion)
Charlotte—Kelly Le Brock
Director—Gene Wilder
Leading Players—Gene Wilder, Charles Grodin, Joseph Bologna

THE WOMAN IN ROOM 13 (1932, Fox Film Corp.)
Laura Ramsey—Elissa Landi
Director—Henry King
Leading Players—Ralph Bellamy, Neil Hamilton, Myrna Loy, Gilbert Roland

WOMAN IN THE DARK (1934, RKO)
Louise Lorimer—Fay Wray
Director—Phil Rosen
Leading Players—Melvyn Douglas, Roscoe Ates, Reed Brown, Jr.

THE WOMAN IN THE HALL (1949, GB, Rank)
Lorna Blake—Ursula Jeans
Director—Jack Lee
Leading Players—Jean Simmons, Cecil Parker, Joan Miller

THE WOMAN IN THE WINDOW (1945, RKO)
Alice Reed—Joan Bennett
Director—Fritz Lang
Leading Players—Edward G. Robinson, Raymond Massey, Edmond Breon, Dan Duryea

THE WOMAN IN WHITE (1948, Warner Brothers)
Anne Catherick—Eleanor Parker
Director—Peter Godfrey
Leading Players—Alexis Smith, Sydney Greenstreet, Gig Young

THE WOMAN INSIDE (1981, 20th Century Fox)
Holly/Hollis—Gloria Manon
Director—Joseph Van Winkle
Leading Players—Dane Clark, Joan Blondell, Michael Champion

A WOMAN IS THE JUDGE (1939, Columbia)
Mary Cabot—Frieda Inescort
Director—Nick Grinde
Leading Players—Otto Kruger, Rochelle Hudson, Mayo Methot

WOMAN OBSESSED (1959, 20th Century Fox)
Mary Sharron—Susan Hayward
Director—Henry Hathaway
Leading Players—Stephen Boyd, Barbara Nichols, Dennis Holmes, Theodore Bikel

A WOMAN OBSESSED (1989, Platinum)
Arlene Bellings—Ruth Raymond
Director—Larry Vincent
Leading Players—Linda Blair, Gregory Patrick, Troy Donahue

A WOMAN OF AFFAIRS (1928, Silent, MGM)
Diana—Greta Garbo
Director—Clarence Brown
Leading Players—John Gilbert, Lewis Stone, John Mack Brown

A WOMAN OF DISTINCTION (1950, Columbia)
Susan Middlecott—Rosalind Russell
Director—Edward Buzzell
Leading Players—Ray Milland, Edmund Gwenn, Janis Carter

A WOMAN OF EXPERIENCE (1931, RKO)
Elsa—Helen Twelvetrees
Director—Harry Joe Brown
Leading Players—William Bakewell, Lew Cody, Zasu Pitts

WOMAN OF THE NORTH COUNTRY (1952, Republic)
Christine Powell—Ruth Hussey
Director—Joseph Kane
Leading Players—Rod Cameron, John Agar, Gale Storm

A WOMAN OF PARIS (1923, Silent, UA)
Marie St. Clair—Edna Purviance
Director—Charles Chaplin
Leading Players—Adolphe Menjou, Carl Miller, Lydia Knott

WOMAN OF STRAW (1964, GB, UA)
Maria—Gina Lollobrigida
Director—Basil Dearden
Leading Players—Sean Connery, Ralph Richardson, Alexander Knox, Johnny Sekka

THE WOMAN OF THE TOWN (1943, UA)
Dora Hand—Claire Trevor
Director—George Archainbaud
Leading Players—Albert Dekker, Barry Sullivan, Henry Hull

WOMAN OF THE YEAR (1942, MGM)
Tess Harding—Katharine Hepburn
Director—George Stevens
Leading Players—Spencer Tracy, Fay Bainter, Reginald Owen

THE WOMAN ON THE BEACH (1947, RKO)
Peggy Butler—Joan Crawford
Director—Jean Renoir
Leading Players—Robert Ryan, Charles Bickford, Nan Leslie

WOMAN ON THE RUN (1950, Universal)
Eleanor Johnson—Ann Sheridan
Director—Norman Foster
Leading Players—Dennis O'Keefe, Robert Keith, Frank Jenks

THE WOMAN ON TRIAL (1927, Silent, Paramount)
Julie—Pola Negri
Director—Mauritz Stiller
Leading Players—Einar Hanson, Arnold Kent, Andre Sarti

A WOMAN POSSESSED (1958, GB, UA)
Katherine Winthrop—Margaretta Scott
Director—Max Varnel
Leading Players—Francis Matthews, Kay Callard, Alison Leggatt

A WOMAN REBELS (1936, RKO)
Pamela Thistlewaite—Katharine Hepburn
Director—Mark Sandrich
Leading Players—Herbert Marshall, Elizabeth Allan, Donald Crisp

THE WOMAN THEY ALMOST LYNCHED (1953, Republic)
Sally Maris—Joan Leslie
Director—Allan Dwan
Leading Players—John Lund, Brian Donlvey, Audrey Totter

WOMAN TO WOMAN (1929, Tiffany)
Lola—Betty Compson
Vesta—Juliette Compton
Director—Victor Saville
Leading Players—George Barraud, Margaret Chambers, Reginald Sharland

WOMAN TO WOMAN (1946, GB, Anglo-American)
Nicolette Bonnet—Joyce Howard
Sylvia Anson—Adele Dixon
Director—Maclean Rogers
Leading Players—Douglas Montgomery, Yvonne Arnaud, Paul Collins

WOMAN UNAFRAID (1934, Goldsmith)
Officer Winthrop—Lucille Gleason
Director—William J. Cowen
Leading Players—Skeets Gallagher, Lona Andre, Warren Hymer

A WOMAN UNDER THE INFLUENCE (1974, International)
Mabel Longhetti—Gena Rowlands
Director—John Cassavetes
Leading Players—Peter Falk, Matthew Cassel, Matthew Laborteaux

WOMAN WANTED (1935, MGM)
Ann—Maureen O'Sullivan
Director—George B. Seitz
Leading Players—Joel McCrea, Lewis Stone, Louis Calhern

WOMAN WHO CAME BACK (1945, Republic)
Lorna Webster—Nancy Kelly
Director—Walter Colmes
Leading Players—John Loder, Otto Kruger, Ruth Ford

THE WOMAN WHO DID NOT CARE (1927, Silent, Lumis)
Iris Carroll—Lilyan Tashman
Director—Phil Rosen
Leading Players—Edward Martindel, Arthur Rankin, Philo McCullough

THE WOMAN WHO FOOLED HERSELF (1922, Silent, Associated Exhibitors)
Eva Lee—Mary Allison
Director—Charles A. Logue
Leading Players—Robert Ellis, Frank Currier, Bessie Wharton

THE WOMAN WHO WALKED ALONE (1922, Silent, Paramount)
Iris Champneys—Dorothy Dalton
Director—George Melford
Leading Players—Milton Sills, Wanda Hawley, Frederick J. Radcliffe

THE WOMAN WHO WOULDN'T DIE (1965, GB, Warner Brothers)
Ellen Garth—Georgina Cookson
Director—Gordon Hessler
Leading Players—Gary Merrill, Jane Merrow, Neil McCallum

A WOMAN'S FACE (1941, MGM)
Anna Holm—Joan Crawford
Director—George Cukor
Leading Players—Melvyn Douglas, Conrad Veidt, Reginald Owen, Albert Basserman

WOMAN'S PLACE (1921, Silent, Associated First National)
Josephine Gerson—Constance Talmadge
Director—Victor Fleming
Leading Players—Kenneth Harlan, Hassard Short, Florence Short

A WOMAN'S SECRET (1924, GB, Silent, Graham-Wilcox)
Dolores—Betty Blythe
Director—Herbert Wilcox
Leading Players—Herbert Langley, Randle Ayrton, Warwick Ward

A WOMAN'S SECRET (1949, RKO)
Marian Washburn—Maureen O'Hara
Director—Nicholas Ray
Leading Players—Melvyn Douglas, Gloria Grahame, Bill Williams, Victor Jory

A WOMAN'S TALE (1991, Australia, Beyond Films/Illumination Films)
Martha—Sheila Florance
Director—Paul Cox
Leading Players—Gosia Dobrowolska, Norman Kaye, Chris Haywood, Myrtle Woods, Ernest Gray

A WOMAN'S TEMPTATION (1959, GB, British Lion)
Betty—Patricia Driscoll
Director—Geoffrey Grayson
Leading Players—Robert Ayres, John Pike, Neil Hallett

A WOMAN'S VENGEANCE (1947, Universal)
Janet Spence—Jessica Tandy
Director—Zoltan Korda
Leading Players—Charles Boyer, Ann Blyth, Cedric Hardwicke

WOMAN'S WORLD (1954, 20th Century Fox)
Katie—June Allyson
Elizabeth—Lauren Bacall
Carol—Arlene Dahl
Director—Jean Negulesco
Leading Players—Clifton Webb, Van Heflin, Fred MacMurray, Cornel Wilde

THE WOMEN (1939, MGM)
Mary Haines—Norma Shearer
Chrystal Allen—Joan Crawford
Sylvia Fowler—Rosalind Russell
Director—George Cukor
Leading Players—Mary Boland, Paulette Goddard, Joan Fontaine, Lucille Watson, Phyllis Povah
Note: The film featured 135 women and no men. To make the number of title characters manageable, we have chosen the three leading women stars.

WOMEN ARE LIKE THAT (1938, First National)
Claire Landin—Kay Francis
Director—Stanley Logan
Leading Players—Pat O'Brien, Ralph Forbes, Melville Cooper

WOMEN IN BONDAGE (1943, Monogram)
Margot Bracken—Gail Patrick
Director—Steve Sekely
Leading Players—Nancy Kelly, Gertrude Michael, Anne Nagel

WOMEN IN LOVE (1969, GB, UA)
Gundrun Brangwen—Glenda Jackson
Ursula Brangwen—Jennie Linden
Director—Ken Russell
Leading Players—Alan Bates, Oliver Reed, Eleanor Bron

WOMEN IN PRISON (1938, Columbia)
Daisy Saunders—Mayo Methot
Director—Lambert Hillyer
Leading Players—Wyn Cahoon, Scott Colton, Arthur Loft

WOMEN IN THE WIND (1939, Warner Brothers)
Janet Steele—Kay Francis
Director—John Farrow
Leading Players—William Gargan, Victor Jory, Maxie Rosenbloom

WOMEN IN WAR (1940, Republic)
O'Neil—Elsie Janis
Director—John H. Auer
Leading Players—Wendy Barrie, Patric Knowles, Mae Clarke

WOMEN LOVE ONCE (1931, Paramount)
Helen Fields—Eleanor Boardman
Director—Edward Goodman
Leading Players—Paul Lukas, Juliette Compton, Geoffrey Kerr

THE WOMEN MEN MARRY (1937, MGM)
Claire Raeburn—Clarie Dodd
Director—Errol Taggart
Leading Players—George Murphy, Josephine Hutchinson, Sidney Blackmer

WOMEN MUST DRESS (1935, Monogram)
Linda—Minna Gombell
Director—Reginald Barker
Leading Players—Gavin Gordon, Hardie Albright, Suzanne Kaaren

WOMEN OF GLAMOUR (1937, Columbia)
Gloria Hudson—Virginia Bruce
Director—Gordon Wiles
Leading Players—Melvyn Douglas, Reginald Denny, Pert Kelton

WOMEN WHO PLAY (1932, GB, Paramount British)
Margaret Sones—Benita Hume
Director—Arthur Rosson
Leading Players—Mary Newcomb, George Barraud, Joan Barry

WOMEN WITHOUT NAMES (1940, Paramount)
Joyce King—Ellen Drew
Director—Robert Florey
Leading Players—Robert Paige, Judith Barrett, John Miljan

WONDER BAR (1934, Warner Brothers)
Al Wonder—Al Jolson
Director—Lloyd Bacon
Leading Players—Dolores Del Rio, Ricardo Cortez, Kay Francis, Dick Powell

WONDER MAN (1945, RKO)
Buzzy Ballew/Edwin Dingle—Danny Kaye
Director—Bruce Humberstone
Leading Players—Virginia Mayo, Vera-Ellen, Donald Woods, S.Z. Sakall, Steve Cochran

A WONDERFUL WIFE (1922, Silent, Universal)
Chum Lewin—Miss Du Pont
Director—Paul Scardon
Leading Players—Vernon Steele, Landers Stevens, Charles Arling

THE WONDERFUL WORLD OF THE BROTHERS GRIMM (1962, MGM)
Wilhelm Grimm—Laurence Harvey
Jacob Grimm—Karl Boehm
Director—Henry Levin
Leading Players—Claire Bloom, Walter Slezak, Barbara Eden, Oscar Homolka

WORKING GIRL (1988, 20th Century Fox)
Tess McGill—Melanie Griffith
Director—Mike Nichols
Leading Players—Harrison Ford, Sigourney Weaver, Joan Cusack, Alec Baldwin

THE WORKING MAN (1933, Warner Brothers)
John Reeves—George Arliss
Director—John G. Adolfi
Leading Players—Bette Davis, Hardie Albright, Theodore Newton

THE WORLD ACCORDING TO GARP (1982, Warner Brothers)
T.S. Garp—Robin Williams
Director—George Roy Hill
Leading Players—Mary Beth Hurt, Glenn Close, John Lithgow, Hume Cronyn, Jesscia Tandy

THE WORLD IN HIS ARMS (1952, Universal)
Jonathan Clark—Gregory Peck
Director—Raoul Walsh
Leading Players—Ann Blyth, Anthony Quinn, John McIntire

WORLD IN MY CORNER (1956, Universal)
Tommy Shea—Audie Murphy
Director—Jesse Hibbs
Leading Players—Barbara Rush, Jeff Morrow, John McIntire

THE WORLD OF HENRY ORIENT (1964, UA)
Henry Orient—Peter Sellers
Director—George Roy Hill
Leading Players—Paula Prentiss, Tippy Walker, Merrie Spaeth, Angela Lansbury, Tom Bosley

THE WORLD OF SUZIE WONG (1960, Paramount)
Suzie Wong—Nancy Kwan
Director—Richard Quine
Leading Players—William Holden, Sylvia Syms, Michael Wilding, Laurence Naismith

THE WORLD WAS HIS JURY (1958, Columbia)
Capt. Jerry Barrett—Robert McQueeney
Director—Fred F. Sears
Leading Players—Edmond O'Brien, Mona Freeman, Karin Booth

THE WORLD'S CHAMPION (1922, Paramount)
William Burroughs—Wallace Reid
Director—Phil Rosen
Leading Players—Lois Wilson, Lionel Belmore, Henry Miller

THE WORLD'S GREATEST ATHLETE (1973, Buena Vista)
Nanu—Jan-Michael Vincent
Director—Richard Scheerer
Leading Players—Tim Conway, John Amos, Roscoe Lee Browne

THE WORLD'S GREATEST LOVER (1977, 20th Century Fox)
Rudy Valentine—Gene Wilder
Director—Gene Wilder
Leading Players—Carol Kane, Dom DeLuise, Fritz Feld

THE WORLD'S GREATEST SINNER (1962, Frenzy)
Clarence Hilliard—Timothy Carey
Director—Timothy Carey
Leading Players—Gil Baretto, Betty Rowland, James Farley

WORST WOMAN IN PARIS (1933, Lasky/Fox)
Peggy Vane—Benita Hume
Director—Monta Bell
Leading Players—Adolphe Menjou, Harvey Stephens, Helen Chandler

WORTH WINNING (1989, 20th Century Fox)
Taylor Worth—Mark Harmon
Director—Will Mackenzie

Leading Players—Madeleine Stowe, Lesley Ann Warren, Maria Holvoe, Mark Blum, Andrea Martin

THE WRECKER (1933, Columbia)
Chuck Regan—Jack Holt
Director—Albert Rogell
Leading Players—Genevieve Tobin, George E. Stone, Sidney Blackmer, Ward Bond

THE WRESTLER (1974, Entertainment Ventures)
Billy Taylor—Billy Robinson
Director—Jim Westman
Leading Players—Verne Gagne, Edward Asner, Elaine Giftos

THE WRONG GUYS (1988, New World)
Louie—Louie Anderson
Richard—Richard Lewis
Belz—Richard Belzer
Franklyn—Franklyn Ajaye
Tim—Tim Thomerson
Director—Danny Bilson
Leading Players—Brion James, Biff Manard, John Goodman

THE WRONG MAN (1956, Warner Brothers)
Christopher "Manny" Balestrero^—Henry Fonda
Director—Alfred Hitchcock
Leading Players—Vera Miles, Anthony Quayle, Harold J. Stone

X

"X" THE MAN WITH X-RAY EYES (1963, American International)
D. James Xavier—Ray Milland
Director—Roger Corman
Leading Players—Diana Van Der Vils, Harold J. Stone, John Hoyt

X, Y & ZEE (1972, GB, Columbia)
Zee Blakeley—Elizabeth Taylor
Robert Blakely—Michael Caine
Stella—Susannah York
Director—Brian G. Hutton
Leading Players—Margaret Leighton, John Standing, Mary Larkin

Y

A YANK AT ETON (1942, MGM)
Timothy Dennis—Mickey Rooney
Director—Norman Taurog

Leading Players—Edmund Gwenn, Ian Hunter, Freddie Bartholomew, Marta Linden

A YANK AT OXFORD (1938, MGM)
Lee Sheridan—Robert Taylor
Director—Jack Conway
Leading Players—Lionel Barrymore, Maureen O'Sullivan, Vivien Leigh, Edmund Gwenn

A YANK IN ERMINE (1955, GB, Monarch)
Joe Turner—Peter Thompson
Director—Gordon Parry
Leading Players—Noelle Middleton, Harold Lloyd, Jr., Diana Decker

A YANK IN INDO-CHINA (1952, Columbia)
Mulvancy—John Archer
Clint Marshall—Douglas Dick
Director—Wallace A. Grissell
Leading Players—Jean Wiles, Maura Murphy, Hayward Soo Hoo

A YANK IN KOREA (1951, Columbia)
Andy Smith—Lon McCallister
Director—Lew Landers
Leading Players—William "Bill" Phillips, Brett King, Larry Stewart

A YANK IN LIBYA (1942, Producers Releasing Corp.)
Mike Malone—Walter Woolf King
Director—Albert Herman
Leading Players—H.B. Warner, Joan Woodbury, Duncan Renaldo

A YANK IN LONDON (1946, GB, 20th Century Fox)
Sgt. John Patterson—Dean Jagger
Director—Herbert Wilcox
Leading Players—Anna Neagle, Rex Harrison, Robert Morley

A YANK IN THE R.A.F. (1941, 20th Century Fox)
Tim Baker—Tyrone Power
Director—Henry King
Leading Players—Betty Grable, John Sutton, Reginald Gardiner

A YANK IN VIET-NAM (1964, Allied Artists)
Major Benson—Marshall Thompson
Director—Marshall Thompson
Leading Players—Enrique Magalona, Mario Barri, Kieu Chinh

A YANK ON THE BURMA ROAD (1942, MGM)
Joe Tracey—Barry Nelson
Director—George B. Seitz
Leading Players—Laraine Day, Stuart Crawford, Keye Luke

YANKEE BUCCANEER (1952, Universal)
Cmdr. David Porter—Jeff Chandler
Director—Frederick De Cordova
Leading Players—Scott Brady, Susan Ball, Joseph Calleia

YANKEE DOODLE DANDY (1942, Warner Brothers)
George M. Cohan—James Cagney
Director—Hugh MacMullan
Leading Players—Joan Leslie, Walter Huston, Richard Whorf, Irene Manning, Rosemary De Camp

YANKEE FAKIR (1947, Republic)
Yankee Davis—Douglas Fowley
Director—W. Lee Wilder

Leading Players—Joan Woodbury, Clem Bevans, Ransom Sherman

YANKEE PASHA (1954, Universal)
Jason—Jeff Chandler
Director—Joseph Pevney
Leading Players—Rhonda Fleming, Mamie Van Doren, Bart Roberts

THE YANKEE SENOR (1926, Silent, Fox Film Corp.)
Paul Wharton—Tom Mix
Director—Emmett Flynn
Leading Players—Olive Borden, Tom Kennedy, Francis McDonald

YANKS (1979, Universal)
Matt—Richard Gere
John—William Devane
Director—John Schlesinger
Leading Players—Lisa Eichhorn, Vanessa Redgrave, Chick Vennera

YANKS AHOY (1943, UA)
Sgt. Doubleday—William Tracy
Sgt. Ames—Joe Sawyer
Director—Kurt Neumann
Leading Players—Marjorie Woodworth, Minor Watson, Walter Woolf King

THE YEAR MY VOICE BROKE (1988, Australia, Avenue)
Danny—Noah Taylor
Director—John Duigan
Leading Players—Leone Carmen, Ben Mendelsohn, Graeme Blundell

THE YELLOW CAB MAN (1950, MGM)
Augustus "Red" Pirdy—Red Skelton
Director—Jack Donahue
Leading Players—Gloria De Haven, Walter Slezak, Edward Arnold

YELLOW HAIR AND THE FORTRESS OF GOLD (1984, Crown)
Yellow Hair—Laurence Landon
Director—Matt Cimber
Leading Players—Ken Roberson, John Ghaffari, Luis Lorenzo

YELLOWBEARD (1983, Orion)
Yellowbeard—Graham Chapman
Director—Mel Danski
Leading Players—Peter Boyle, Richard "Cheech" Marin, Tommy Chong, Peter Cook, Marty Feldman

YELLOWSTONE KELLY (1959, Warner Brothers)
Yellowstone Kelly—Clint Walker
Director—Gordon Douglas
Leading Players—Edward Byrnes, John Russell, Ray Danton

YENTL (1983, MGM/Untied Artists)
Yentl—Barbra Streisand
Director—Barbra Streisand
Leading Players- Mandy Patinkin, Amy Irving, Nehemiah Persoff

YES, GIORGIO (1982, MGM/UA)
Giorgio Fini—Luciano Pavarotti
Director—Franklin J. Schaffner

Leading Players—Kathryn Harrold, Eddie Albert, Paola Borboni

YES, MR. BROWN (1933, GB, British and Dominions)
Mr. Brown—Hartley Power
Director—Herbert Wilcox
Leading Players—Jack Buchanan, Elsie Randolph, Margot Grahame

YES, MY DARLING DAUGHTER (1939, Warner Brothers)
Ellen Murray—Priscilla Lane
Ann Murray—Fay Bainter
Director—William Keighley
Leading Players—Jeffrey Lynn, Roland Young, May Robson

YESTERDAY'S HERO (1979, GB, EMI)
Rod Turner—Ian McShane
Director—Neil Leifer
Leading Players—Suzanne Somers, Adam Faith, Paul Nicholas

YESTERDAY'S WIFE (1923, Silent, Columbia)
Megan Daye—Irene Rich
Director—Edward J. Le Saint
Leading Players—Eileen Percy, Lottie Williams, Josephine Crowell

YOKEL BOY (1942, Republic)
Joe Ruddy—Eddie Foy, Jr.
Director—Joseph Santley
Leading Players—Joan Davis, Albert Dekker, Alan Mowbray

YOLANDA AND THE THIEF (1945, MGM)
Johnny Parkson Riggs—Fred Astaire
Yolanda—Lucille Bremer
Director—Vincente Minnelli
Leading Players—Frank Morgan, Mildred Natwick, Mary Nash

YOU AND ME (1938, Paramount)
Helen Dennis—Sylvia Sidney
Joe Dennis—George Raft
Director—Fritz Lang
Leading Players—Harry Carey, Barton MacLane, Warren Hymer

YOU BELONG TO ME (1941, Columbia)
Helen Hunt—Barbara Stanwyck
Peter Kirk—Henry Fonda
Director—Wesley Ruggles
Leading Players—Edgar Buchanan, Roger Clark, Ruth Donnelly

YOU CAME ALONG (1945, Paramount)
Ivy Hotchkiss—Lizabeth Scott
Director—John Farrow
Leading Players—Robert Cummings, Don DeFore, Charles Drake

YOU FOR ME (1952, MGM)
Tony Brown—Peter Lawford
Katie McDermad—Jane Greer
Director—Don Weis
Leading Players—Gig Young, Paula Corday, Howard Wendell

YOU WERE MEANT FOR ME (1948, 20th Century Fox)
Peggy Mayhew—Jeanne Crain
Chuck Arnold—Dan Dailey
Director—Lloyd Bacon
Leading Players—Oscar Levant, Barbara Lawrence, Selena Royle

YOU WERE NEVER LOVELIER (1942, Columbia)
Maria Acuna—Rita Hayworth
Director—William A. Seiter
Leading Players—Fred Astaire, Adolphe Menjou, Leslie Brooks

YOU'LL LIKE MY MOTHER (1972, Universal)
Mrs. Kinsolving—Rosemary Murphy
Francesca Kinsolving—Patty Duke
Director—Lamont Johnson
Leading Players—Richard Thomas, Sian Barbara Allen, Dennis Rucker

YOUNG AND BEAUTIFUL (1934, Mascot)
June Dale—Judith Allen
Director—Joseph Santley
Leading Players—William Haines, Joseph M. Cawthorn, John Miljan

YOUNG AND DANGEROUS (1957, 20th Century Fox)
Tommy Price—Mark Damon
Director—Wiliam F. Claxton
Leading Players—Lili Gentile, Eddie Binns, Frances Mercer

YOUNG AND INNOCENT (1938, GB, Gaumont)
Erica Burgoyne—Nova Pilbeam
Director—Alfred Hitchcock
Leading Players—Derrick de Marney, Percy Marmont, Edward Rigby

THE YOUNG AND THE BRAVE (1963, MGM)
Han—Manuel Padilla
Director—Frances D. Lyon
Leading Players—Rory Calhoun, William Bendix, Richard Jaeckel

YOUNG BESS (1953, MGM)
Elizabeth I—Jean Simmons
Director—George Sidney
Leading Players—Stewart Granger, Deborah Kerr, Charles Laughton, Kay Walsh

YOUNG BILL HICKOK (1940, Republic)
Bill Hickok—Roy Rogers
Director—Joseph Kane
Leading Players—Gabby Hayes, Jacqueline Wells, John Miljan

YOUNG BILLY YOUNG (1969, UA)
Billy Young—Robert Walker, Jr.
Director—Burt Kennedy
Leading Players—Robert Mitchum, Angie Dickinson, David Carradine

YOUNG BRIDE (1932, RKO)
Allie Smith—Helen Twelvetrees
Director—William A. Seiter
Leading Players—Eric Linden, Arline Judge, Cliff Edwards

YOUNG BUFFALO BILL (1940, Republic)
Bill Cody—Roy Rogers
Director—Joseph Kane
Leading Players—Gabby Hayes, Pauline Moore, Hugh Sothern

YOUNG CASSIDY (1965, MGM)
John Cassidy—Rod Taylor
Director—Jack Cardiff

Leading Players—Flora Robson, Jack MacGowran, Maggie Smith, Michael Redgrave, Edith Evans, Julie Christie

YOUNG DANIEL BOONE (1950, Monogram)
Daniel Boone—David Bruce
Director—Reginald Le Borg
Leading Players—Kristine Miller, Damian O'Flynn, Don Beddoe

YOUNG DILLINGER (1965, Allied Artists)
John Dillinger—Nick Adams
Director—Terry O. Morse
Leading Players—Robert Conrad, John Ashley, Mary Ann Mobley

YOUNG DR. KILDARE (1938, MGM)
Dr. James Kildare—Lew Ayres
Director—Harold S. Bucquet
Leading Players—Lionel Barrymore, Lynne Carver, Nat Pendleton

THE YOUNG DOCTORS (1961, UA)
Dr. David Coleman—Ben Gazzara
Dr. Alexander—Dick Clark
Dr. Howard—George Segal
Director—Phil Karlson
Leading Players—Fredric March, Ina Balin, Eddie Albert

YOUNG DOCTORS IN LOVE (1982, 20th Century Fox)
Dr. Simon August—Michael McKean
Dr. Stephanie Brody—Sean Young
Director—Garry Marshall
Leading Players—Harry Dean Stanton, Patrick MacNee, Hector Elizondo, Dabney Coleman

YOUNG DONOVAN'S KID (1931, RKO)
Jim Donovan—Richard Dix
Midge Murray—Jackie Cooper
Director—Fred Niblo
Leading Playes—Marion Shilling, Frank Sheridan, Boris Karloff

YOUNG EINSTEIN (1989, Australia, Warner Brothers)
Albert Einstein—Yahoo Serious
Director—Yahoo Serious
Leading Players—Odile le Clezio, John Howard, Pee Wee Wilson

YOUNG FRANKENSTEIN (1974, 20th Century Fox)
Dr. Frederick Frankenstein—Gene Wilder
Director—Mel Brooks
Leading Players—Peter Boyle, Marty Feldman, Madeline Kahn, Cloris Leachman, Teri Garr

YOUNG GUNS (1988, 20th Century Fox)
Dick Brewer—Charlie Sheen
Billy the Kid Bonney—Emilio Estervez
Doc Scurlock—Keifer Sutherland
Chavez y Chavez—Lou Diamond Phillips
"Dirty Steve" Stephens—Dermot Mulroney
Charley Bowdre—Casey Siemaszko
Director—Chris Cain
Leading Players—Jack Palance, Terence Stamp, Alice Carter, Terry O'Quinn

YOUNG GUNS II (1990, 20th Centruy Fox/Morgan Creek)
William H. Bonney—Emilio Estevez
Doc Scurlock—Kiefer Sutherland
Chavez y Chavez—Lou Diamond Phillips

Arkansas Dave Rudabaugh—Christian Slater
Director—Geoff Murphy
Leading Players—William Petersen, Alan Ruck, R.D. Call, James Coburn, Balthazar Getty, Jack Kehoe

YOUNG JESSE JAMES (1960, 20th Century Fox)
Jesse James—Ray Stricklyn
Director—William F. Claxton
Leading Players—Willard Parker, Merry Anders, Robert Dix

THE YOUNG LIONS (1958, 20th Century Fox)
Christain Diestl—Marlon Brando
Noah Ackerman—Montgomery Clift
Michael Whiteacre—Dean Martin
Director—Edward Dmytryk
Leading Players—Hope Lange, Barbara Rush, May Britt, Maximilian Schell

THE YOUNG LOVERS (1964, MGM)
Eddie Slocum—Peter Fonda
Pam Burns—Sharon Hugueny
Director—Samuel Goldwyn, Jr.
Leading Players—Nick Adams, Deborah Walley, Beatrice Straight

YOUNG MAN OF MANHATTAN (1930, Paramount)
Toby McLean—Norman Foster
Director—Monta Bell
Leading Players—Claudette Colbert, Ginger Rogers, Charles Ruggles

YOUNG MAN WITH A HORN (1950, Warner Brothers)
Rick Martin—Kirk Douglas
Director—Michael Curtiz
Leading Players—Lauren Bacall, Doris Day, Hoagy Carmichael

YOUNG MAN WITH IDEAS (1952, MGM)
Maxwell Webster—Glenn Ford
Director—Mitchell Leisen
Leading Players—Ruth Roman, Denise Darcel, Nina Foch

YOUNG MR. LINCOLN (1939, 20th Century Fox)
Abraham Lincoln—Henry Fonda
Director—John Ford
Leading Players—Alice Brady, Marjorie Weaver, Arleen Whelan, Eddie Collins, Pauline Moore

THE YOUNG MR. PITT (1942, GB, 20th Century Fox)
William Pitt—Robert Donat
Director—Carol Reed
Leading Players—Robert Morley, Phyllis Calvert, Raymond Lovell

YOUNG NURSES IN LOVE (1989, Platinum)
Nurse Ellis—Jeanne Marie
Director—Chuck Vincent
Leading Players—Alan Fisler, Jane Hamilton, Jamie Gillis

THE YOUNG PHILADELPHIANS (1959, Warner Brothers)
Tony Lawrence—Paul Newman
Joan Dickinson—Barbara Rush
Director—Vincent Sherman
Leading Players—Alexis Smith, Brian Keith, Diane Brewster

THE YOUNG RUNAWAYS (1968, MGM)
Shelly Allen—Brooke Bundy

Dewey Norson—Kevin Coughlin
Deanie Donford—Patty McCormack
Director—Arthur Dreifuss
Leading Players—Lloyd Bochner, Lynn Bari, Norman Fell

THE YOUNG SAVAGES (1961, UA)
Arthur Reardon—John Davis Chandler
Anthony Aposto—Neil Nephew
Danny di Pace—Stanley Kristien
Director—John Frankenheimer
Leading Players—Burt Lancaster, Dina Merril, Edward Andrews

YOUNG SHERLOCK HOLMES (1985, GB, Paramount)
Sherlock Holmes—Nicholas Rowe
Director—Barry Levinson
Leading Players—Alan Cox, Sophie Ward, Anthony Higgins

THE YOUNG SINNER (1965, United Screens)
Chris Wotan—Tom Laughlin
Director—Tom Laughlin
Leading Players—Stefanie Powers, William Wellman, Jr., Robert Angelo

THE YOUNG STRANGER (1957, Universal)
Hal Ditmar—James MacArthur
Director—John Frankenheimer
Leading Players—Kim Hunter, James Daly, James Gregory

YOUNG TOM EDISON (1940, MGM)
Tom Edison—Mickey Rooney
Director—Norman Taurog
Leading Players—Fay Bainter, George Bancroft, Virginia Weidler

YOUNG WIDOW (1946, UA)
Joan Kenwood—Jane Russell
Director—Edwin L. Marin
Leading Players—Louis Hayward, Faith Domergue, Marie Wilson

YOUNG, WILLING AND EAGER (1962, GB, Brenner)
Carol Flynn—Christina Gregg
Director—Lance Comfort
Leading Players—Jess Conrad, Hermione Baddeley, Kenneth Griffith

YOUNG WINSTON (1972, GB, Columbia)
Winston Churchill—Simon Ward
Director—Richard Attenborough
Leading Players—John Mills, Anne Bancroft, Robert Shaw, Jack Hawkins, Jane Seymour

YOUNG WOODLEY (1930, GB, British International)
Woodley—Frank Lawton
Director—Thomas Bentley
Leading Players—Madeleine Carroll, Sam Livesey, Gerald Rawlinson

YOUNGBLOOD (1978, American International)
Youngblood—Bryan O'Dell
Director—Noel Nosseck
Leading Players—Lawrence-Hilton Jacobs, Ren Woods, Tony Allen

YOUNGBLOOD (1986, MGM/UA)
Dean Youngblood—Rob Lowe
Director—Peter Markle

Leading Players—Cynthia Gibb, Patrick Swayze, Ed Lauter, Jim Youngs, Eric Nesterenko

YOUNGBLOOD HAWKE (1964, Warner Brothers)
Youngblood Hawke—James Franciscus
Director—Delmer Daves
Leading Players—Suzanne Pleshette, Genevieve Page, Eva Gabor

THE YOUNGER BROTHERS (1949, Warner Brothers)
Cole Younger—Wayne Morris
Jim Younger—Bruce Bennett
Johnny Younger—Robert Hutton
Bob Younger—James Brown
Director—Edwin L. Marin
Leading Players—Janis Paige, Geraldine Brooks, Alan Hale

YOU'RE A LUCKY FELOW, MR. SMITH (1943, Universal)
Tony Smith—Allan Jones
Director—Felix Feist
Leading Players—Evelyn Ankers, Billie Burke, David Bruce

YOU'RE A SWEETHEART (1937, Universal)
Betty Bradley—Alice Faye
Director—David Butler
Leading Players—George Murphy, Ken Murray, William Gargan

YOUTH FOR SALE (1924, Silent, Burr)
Molly Malloy—Mary Allison
Director—William Christy Cabanne
Leading Players—Sigrid Holmquist, Richard Bennett, Charles Emmett Mack

YOUTH TO YOUTH (1922, Silent, Metro)
Eve Allinson—Billie Dove
Page Brookins—Cullen Landis
Director—Emile Chautard
Leading Players—Edythe Chapman, Hardee Kirkland, Sylvia Ashton, Noah Beery

Z

ZACHARIAH (1971, ABC Pictures)
Zachariah—John Rubenstein
Director—George Englund
Leading Players—Pat Quinn, Don Johnson, Elvin Jones

ZANDER THE GREAT (1925, Silent, MGM)
Zander—Master Jack Huff
Director—George Hill
Leading Players—Marion Davies, Holbrook Blinn, Harrison Ford

ZANDY'S BRIDE (1974, Warner Brothers)
Zandy Allan—Gene Hackman
Hannah Lund—Liv Ullmann
Director—Jan Troell

Leading Players—Eileen Heckart, Harry Dean Stanton, Joe Santos

ZARAK (1956, GB, Columbia)
Zarak Khan—Victor Mature
Director—Terence Young
Leading Players—Michael Wilding, Anita Ekberg, Bonar Colleano

ZARDOZ (1974, GB, 20th Century Fox)
Zardoz—Niall Buggy
Director—John Boorman
Leaing Players—Sean Connery, Charlotte Rampling, Sara Kestelman

ZAZA (1939, Paramount)
Zaza—Claudette Colbert
Director—George Cukor
Leading Players—Herbert Marshall, Bert Lahr, Helen Westley

ZELIG (1983, Orion)
Leonard Zelig—Woody Allen
Director—Woody Allen
Leading Players—Mia Farrow, John Buckwalter, Marvin Chatinover

ZELLY AND ME (1988, Columbia)
Joan 'Zelly' (Mademoiselle)—Isabella Rossellini
Phoebe—Alexandra Johnes
Director—Tina Rathbone
Leading Players—Glynis Johns, David Lynch, Kaiulani Lee, Joe Morton

ZIEGFELD FOLLIES (1945, MGM)
Florenz Ziegfeld—William Powell
Director—Vincente Minnelli
Leading Players—Fred Astaire, Lucille Ball, Lena Horne, Esther Williams, Judy Garland, Red Skelton, Gene Kelly, Kathryn Grayson

ZIEGFELD GIRL (1941, MGM)
Susan Gallagher—Judy Garland
Sandra Kolter—Hedy Lamarr
Shelia Regan—Lana Turner
Director—Robert Z. Leonard
Leading Players—James Stewart, Tony Martin, Jackie Cooper

ZINA (1985, Film Forum)
Zina—Domiziana Giordano
Director—Ken McMullen
Leading Players—Ian McKellen, Ron Anderson, Micha Bergese

ZORBA THE GREEK (1964, 20th Century Fox)
Alexis Zorba—Anthony Quinn
Director—Michael Cacoyannis
Leading Players—Alan Bates, Irene Papas, Lila Kedrova

ZORRO, THE GAY BLADE (1981, 20th Century Fox)
Don Diego Vega/Bunny Wigglesworth/Zorro—George Hamilton
Director—Peter Medak
Leading Players—Lauren Hutton, Brenda Vaccaro, Ron Leibman

Robert Anthony Nowlan, Jr., is a professor of mathematics and former Vice-President for Academic Affairs at Southern Connecticut State University in New Haven.

Gwendolyn Wright Nowlan is professor and former chairperson of the School of Library Science and Instructional Technology at Southern Connecticut State University.